R&A

The **R&A**

GOLFER'S HANDBOOK 2013

EDITOR RENTON LAIDLAW

The R&A is golf's world rules and development body and organiser of The Open Championship. It operates with the consent of more than 130 national and international, amateur and professional organisations, from over 120 countries and on behalf of an estimated 30 million golfers in Europe, Africa, Asia-Pacific and The Americas (outside the USA and Mexico). The United States Golf Association (USGA) is the game's governing body in the United States and Mexico.

hamlyn

An Hachette UK Company
www.hachette.co.uk

The R&A Golfer's Handbook first published 1899

This edition published 2013 by Hamlyn, a division of

Octopus Publishing Group Ltd
Endeavour House
189 Shaftesbury Avenue
London
WC2H 8JY
www.octopusbooks.co.uk

ISBN: 978-0-600-62585-8

A CIP catalogue record for this book is available from the British Library

Note

Whilst every care has been taken in compiling the information contained in this book, the Publishers, Editor and Sponsors accept no responsibility for any errors or ommissions.

10 9 8 7 6 5 4 3 2 1

Correspondence

Letters on editorial matters should be addressed to:
The Editor, The R&A Golfer's Handbook, Octopus Publishing Group, Endeavour House, Shaftesbury Avenue, London WC2H 8JY.

Designed and typeset by Penrose Typography, Maidstone, Kent
Printed and bound in Italy.

Contents

Pierre Bechmann takes over as Captain of The Royal and Ancient Golf Club

© GSR Photographic

Frenchman Pierre Bechmann is the first Captain of the Royal and Ancient Golf Club of St Andrews from Continental Europe. A lawyer and member of the Paris Bar, he will assume an ambassadorial role for The R&A supporting its work in developing the game around the world and attending all major golfing events.

"I am greatly looking forward to my year in office", said the new Captain, "and hope I can contribute to the important work The R&A does. I have been heavily involved in supporting the development of talented young players and look forward to continuing with this in my new role."

Born in Paris in 1957, M. Bechmann, who now lives at Chantilly, is a member of the Executive Committee of the French Golf Federation and of the European Golf Association's Championship Committee.

Since 2010 he has been President of his home club, Golf de Chantilly, where he plays off a handicap of 8. He is a former member of The R&A's General Committee and has served on the Championship Committee, the Rules of Golf Committee and The R&A Coaching Panel. He is also a former Captain of the Royal St George's Club.

From the Editor's Desk

We have new publishers this year. The 2013 edition of *The R&A's Golfer's Handbook* first produced in 1899, is now being handled by the Hamlyn branch of Octopus but you will see little change in the content of our "golfer's bible".

All the results, both amateur and professional, from around the world are included along with the usual statistical data and there are reports on all the majors and of course detailed coverage of the Ryder Cup which made 2012 so special.

Top writers from both Europe and America have been signed up to wax eloquently on a number of subjects included award winning James Lawton of the *Independent* who takes a more philosophical look at the Ryder Cup to complement Michael Aitken's blow-by-blow account of what was a magical week in Chicago.

Dan Jenkins, another award winning writer for America's *Golf Digest* – he also happened to write the script for the film *Caddyshack* – talks about his great friendship with the legendary Ben Hogan who 60 years ago won The Open at Carnoustie.

Derek Lawrenson, whose regular column and reporting of the game for the *Daily Mail* is so highly thought of, recalls last year's four majors, John Huggan of *Golf Digest* turns the spotlight on the Open champion Ernie Els and another of our regular contributers. Bill Elliott enjoyed writing about Roger Chapman, the English golfer who, in a fairytale but hugely creditable manner, won two Senior majors in America.

It is no surprise that Lewine Mair of *Global Golf Post*, our regular correspondent on women's golf, has chosen the world's amateur No 1 record breaker and history-maker Lydia Ko as her subject. On women's golf, Alistair Tait of *Golf Week* reminds us of the great fight-back that enabled the Great Britain and Ireland women to win the Curtis Cup at Nairn.

James Corrigan of the *Daily Telegraph* suggests the likely winners of majors over the next few years while there is an article, too, on the notable overseas personalities who have captained the Royal and Ancient Golf Club of St Andrews.

Fifty years ago, Sir Bob Charles became the first left-hander to win The Open and the New Zealander still plays well. Former Tour player and fellow Kiwi Greg Turner writes about the golfer who has done so much for the game not only in his own country but also around the world.

Another ex-Tour player, Ryder Cup golfer Ken Brown, tells us about his love affair with Augusta, annual venue of the Masters, and there are articles, too, on the venues for the other three majors of the year – Merion by Californian writer Art Spander, Oak Hill by Florida's Tim Rosaforte and Muirfield by Edinburgh-based Michael Aitken.

Without the sterling work put in by our typographer Mick Card (and his daughter Paula Taylor who looks after the clubs section) it is doubtful whether we would have ever got to press on time. Heather and Alan Elliott, who have a long association with the book, helped with the results and Vicky Lamb was the perfect secretary.

We wish Gill Sheldon, who has looked after her late husband's photographic library for the last few years, a happy retirement with grateful thanks for all her help over the years while David Cannon of Getty Images was invaluable in sourcing most of the pictures in this year's edition. To all involved, my grateful thanks.

Renton Laidlaw
Editor

Anchoring the putter threatens the future of the Game

Peter Dawson on the reasoning behind the proposed ban

R&A Chief Executive Peter Dawson explains why the ruling bodies in golf feel a rule change regarding anchoring putters is required

One of the questions we addressed at The R&A when considering what to do about the increase in the number of players who were anchoring their putters was is it too late to act on such a contentious issue?

Our view was it's never too late to do the right thing. That's why, at the end of 2012, we began a process through consultation which could prohibit the anchored stroke.

The truth of the matter is we didn't start down this road because there were examples of major winners who anchored the putter – Sherri Steinhauer, incidentally, was the first player to win using a long putter at the Ricoh Women's British Open in 2006. The real reason was the dramatic upsurge in the proliferation of long and belly putters.

On Tour, the number of professionals wielding these clubs has shot up from as little as two per cent to around 17 per cent. Among the 156 golfers who contested The Open Championship in 2012, we counted no fewer than seven long putters and 16 belly putters in the field.

And it wasn't just people having trouble with their putting who were switching, as a last resort, in search of redemption. There were also perfectly sound putters who changed because they believed it was a better method.

That was the defining reason the topic came back on the radar for The R&A and our colleagues at the United States Golf Association. Certainly, from our point of view, we fully appreciated this was a quarrelsome subject which required long and careful deliberation on our part. It was a substantial matter.

We came to the view that the future of the game was threatened by anchoring because we could see, if the use of the anchored stroke continued to increase, then it could endanger, or possibly eliminate, the traditional putting stroke.

The conventional putting stroke with all its frailties and pressures is an integral element of the game. So, here at The R&A, and in separate deliberations at the USGA, we both reached the same conclusion. Namely, that we should examine a proposal to prohibit the anchored stroke from the game in future.

Now, because this is a matter pertaining to the Rules of Golf, rather than an equipment issue, it would still be allowable, under our proposal, for players to use long and belly putters. What wouldn't be permitted is to anchor them to pivot points such as the belly or the chest.

So the recommended change (if approved) would fall under the four-year cycle of reviewing the Rules. The most recent rule book was issued in the January of 2012 and the next one will come out in January 2016. And it's from that date we suggest the prohibition of the anchored stroke should begin.

Effectively, those who had used this putting

method would have been put on three years' notice. Personally, I think that's very reasonable. Players, of course, could change sooner if they wished.

We made the first overture at the end of 2012, well in advance of when we would normally make these matters public, to give people as much advance warning of our intention as possible and asked for comments on the proposal by the end of February 2013 before a final decision is made.

As I've already noted, this is a contentious issue, but we believe there is widespread respect for the work of golf's governing bodies. We hoped players would see we would be acting in the best interest of the game and, while some may not agree with all our decisions, I hope they respect them. And I sincerely wish there are no litigious reactions to this proposition because the game of golf certainly doesn't need that.

Of course, I understand why some golfers changed to anchoring the putter and there was absolutely nothing wrong with what they did because it was allowed under the Rules of Golf.

Bobby Jones, for example, won a few events when the Rules of Golf were different – he played in the days of concave-faced iron clubs – but that doesn't detract from his success in any way.

I see the majors won by Keegan Bradley, Webb Simpson and Ernie Els in exactly the same way, because they obeyed the Rules at the time. There won't be any stigma attached to those victories, nor should there be any less respect for the players who won them.

Possible redundancy

Paul Runyan is thought to be the first golfer to anchor his putter at the Belmont Open in Boston in 1936 while Phil Rodgers, who lost a play-off to Sir Bob Charles at The Open in 1963, was the first to use a belly putter in 1967. So there's nothing new in this. What changed was the increase in numbers of those anchoring their strokes and the possibility of the traditional putting stroke becoming redundant.

Growing the game, of course, remains a challenge. At professional level, the sponsors are still there, by and large. True, the European Tour needs to travel further afield to find them, but they do find them. And in America, the PGA Tour is strong.

Looking at the number of people playing the game in established golfing territories such as Europe and the USA, however, there is a continuing drift away from club membership. Last November I attended a meeting of the Golf Forum and again heard how club membership is struggling in Great Britain and Ireland.

Too many courses

Whether the move is away from golf altogether, or into a more nomadic form of participation, is not clear. Many golf courses are busy. Here in St Andrews, as I look out from my office onto the Old Course, the first tee remains oversubscribed.

If you take Scotland as an example, we mustn't forget how, over the past 15 years, the number of courses has increased by around 20 per cent. Unsurprisingly, during that same period, club membership has declined. It's clear there's an oversupply of courses.

As far as the impact of technology, notably the ball, is having on the game, we remain true to our Joint Statement of Principles with the USGA issued in 2002 when we said that if hitting distances increased further than they were then we would do something about it. So far, that has not happened.

We've also become more interested in the issue of golf course sustainability and how courses are impacted by longer hitting distances. Courses are longer, wider, take up more acreage and cost more to run. That type of factor is now part of the debate and I'm sure we haven't heard the last on the subject.

One of the most momentous developments for golf last year was the success of Guan Tianlang, a teenager from China just turned 14, who won the Asia–Pacific Amateur Golf Championship and, as a result, qualified to play in the Masters Tournament as well as final qualifying for The Open.

I attended the tournament in Thailand, watched Guan assuredly hole a six foot putt for victory and thought it could be a very significant moment. In many ways, from my perspective, this was the golfing highlight of the year. The R&A have put such a lot of time, money and effort into assisting the development of golf in China.

For the game, China is the new frontier.

Further information on the proposed Rules change can be found on page 584

Men's Amateur Champions 2012

© The R&A

Alan Dunbar (NIR)
British Amateur Champion

© EGA

Rhys Pugh (WAL)
European Amateur Champion

â© The R&A

Guan Tianlang (CHN)
Asia–Pacific Amateur Champion

Courtesy and copyright of the USGA

Steven Fox (USA)
United States Amateur Champion

Women's Amateur Champions 2012

Stephanie Meadow (NIR)
British Amateur Champion

Celine Boutier (FRA)
European Amateur Champion

Lydia Ko (NZL)
United States Amateur Champion

GB&I win the Curtis Cup at Nairn

Nothing but smiles from the victorious 2012 GB&I Curtis Cup team and their captain Tegwen Perkins at Nairn. A tremendous last day fight back in the singles gave the team a first win since 1996.

Europe's Ryder Cup miracle at Medinah

Delighted Ryder Cup captain José Maria Olazábal is hoisted high by the members of his team after their dramatic last day comeback that shocked the Americans who had led 10–6 with 12 singles to come.

Many great golfing performances but nobody bettered McIlroy

Renton Laidlaw chooses his six of the best

Choosing the six golfers who made the most impact in 2012 seems on the face of it a simple enough exercise. Yet it is not that easy. It's not unlike being able to solve the first few crossword clues with ease then finding the remaining answers are far more difficult.

Three names in our golfing puzzle choose themselves for obvious reasons – the incredible Rory McIlroy who waltzed to a record-breaking eight shot victory in another major – the US PGA Championship – and played so well throughout the year except for one brief unexplained blip.

He was Europe and America's Player of the Year topping the money list on both sides of the Atlantic just as Luke Donald had done so famously a year earlier and ending the season with victory in the DP World Team Championship with a Tiger-like five closing birdies in a row to beat pace-setting Justin Rose. McIlroy's selection was a "given" as was that of the teenage New Zealand amateur Lydia Ko.

Not only did Lydia retain her No 1 spot on The R&A World Amateur Rankings, she proved her undoubted talent several times over during another outstanding year. She won the US Amateur Championship and then a few weeks later beat the LPGA professionals in the CN Canadian Open. Like McIlroy, history maker Lydia, the youngest ever winner on the LPGA Tour and the Australasian circuit, comes into the genuinely deserving category.

Although the four majors produced, as usual, memorable golf by the world's best players not even the game's four Blue Riband events could quite match the excitement, the drama, the quality of play on a breath-taking final day of the Ryder Cup at Medinah. Against all the bookmakers' odds the Europeans completed the comeback of the year to not only to retain the Cup but also, as a result of a uncharacteristically forgetful moment by Tiger Woods, win the match.

A word of praise for Germany's Martin Kaymer, who was off form pre-match but holed the putt on the treacherous final green that ensured the Cup was going to be travelling back with captain José Maria Olazábal to Europe and not ending on an American mantelpiece. Olazábal deserves praise and credit, too, for his captaincy of a team which gained inspiration throughout the week from another Spaniard there sadly in spirit only. The swashbuckling never-say-die performances of the late and great Severiano Ballesteros were on every European player's mind.

© Getty Images

Rory McIlroy ended his remarkable season with a double victory in Dubai, winning the Race to Dubai and scoring a fifth victory of the season in the DP World Tour Championship round Greg Norman's Earth course at Jumeirah. In an incredible finish he fired five birdies in a row to beat pace-setting Justin Rose by two.

Talking of the Cup, Ian Poulter is a well-merited No 3 on my list. He won all his games but more importantly on the second day when things looked decidedly bleak for his team Poulter caught fire. Suddenly he became, as McIlroy suggested later, "the Incredible Hulk", fearlessly single-putting the last five greens to post an unlikely point.

He gave the Europeans hope that Saturday afternoon with his magical performance. Quipped his caddie afterwards: "Why doesn't he play like that in normal events?" Well he can – and later did – to win a second World Golf Championship event, the HSBC Champions at Mission Hills in China.

Poulter is extrovert and outspoken and is a larger than life personality whose success in golf is the result of hard work. Few would have encouraged him to take up professional golf when he was playing off a handicap of 4 as a teenager but he believed he could make a go of it and has. The good news is that, like most of the 2012 European side, he should be around to play in many more Cup matches.

Tongue-in-cheek, there might have been a case for awarding a Top Six spot to Deputy Chief of Police Patrick Rollins who broke all the speed limits to get McIlroy to the course in time for his singles match against Keegan Bradley after the Ulsterman, whose teammates were unaware he had not arrived at the course, misread the time. Europe might not have won the Cup but for Mr Rollins getting Rory to the tee on time. Officer Rollins qualifies for sporting gesture of the year!

Now selection gets difficult. Let me throw a few names into the hat for urgent consideration. Likeable, dependable Ernie Els, a major winner again after ten years with his victory in The Open at Lytham (albeit with some help from Adam Scott); 42-year-old Paul Lawrie, a Ryder Cup player again 12 years after his previous appearance at Brookline; or the ever popular Miguel Angel Jiménez, 30 years a pro, whose 19th European Tour success and his third at Hong Kong meant that, at 48 years and 318 days, he is now the oldest winner on Tour. A hearty round of applause for the Spanish old-timer with the pony-tail who enjoys competing and plays consistently well on a generous sufficiency of Rioja and a supply of the best cigars.

Brilliant Brendan

Then there is proudly self-taught Bubba Watson, whose miracle winning shot at Augusta – a fearsome hook from out of the pines on to the green at the second extra hole – broke steady, reliable Louis Oosthuizen's heart at the Masters. Let us not forget, either, the big-time début of South African Branden Grace who earned his card for a second time at the European Tour's qualifying school in late 2011 and then won four times in 2012 including victory in the demanding Alfred Dunhill Links event in which he shot a record 60 round delightful Kingsbarns which hosts the event each year along with punishing Carnoustie and the immaculate Old Course at St Andrews.

On the US Champions Tour, England's Roger Chapman, to put it simply, re-discovered himself. A modest performer on the European Tour and European Senior Tour for over 25 years, he surprised everyone – not least himself – by winning two of the five US Senior major titles. His was perhaps an even greater fairy tale performance than that of Grace.

I have not forgotten the women challengers. Inbee Park of Korea topped the LPGA money list by a long way from Stacy Lewis who did, however, win the Player of the Year prize. Stacy's story is one of courage in adversity. Suffering from curvature of the spine caused by scoliosis, she spent seven and a half years in an uncomfortable back brace. She's a fighter and in 2012 won four times on the LPGA Tour and was named the Rolex US Player of the Year – the first American to win that accolade since Beth Daniel in 1994.

Worthy of serious consideration, too, is Shanshan Feng, the first Chinese golfer to win a major. She romped to victory the US Wegman's LPGA Championship – underlining just how much her country has embraced the game in recent years.

Even a 14-year-old Chinese player Guan Tianlang, coached albeit in America, had the audacity to beat a field of older and more experienced players in the re-named Asia–Pacific Championship in Thailand. What Guan lacked in length he made up with a razor sharp short game and earned a place in the 2013 Masters at Augusta where he will be the youngest ever contestant.

Talking of young talent, Matteo Manassero from Italy with victory in the Barclays Singapore Open, became the first golfer to win three times on the European Tour before celebrating his 20th birthday. Manassero had previously been the youngest golfer bidding to win a Green Jacket when he played at Augusta aged 16.

Back to the ladies. Often forgotten is the last day fightback of the Great Britain and Ireland side against America in the Curtis Cup at Nairn. The event produced as intense a final day, as the Ryder Cup did later in the year, with Stephanie Meadow stepping up to the plate to hole the winning putt and give GB and I a first win since 1996 and only the seventh in the history of the biennial match.

Cup winning putts

Modest Stephanie reminded us, too, that Northern Ireland does not just produce male players of high quality such as McIlroy, McDowell and Clarke when she went on to win the British title and, later in the year, reprised her pressured-packed last hole winning putt at Nairn to help the University of Alabama take the NCAA Championship for the first time.

All the above have a justification for being included on the list but when difficult decisions have to be made you have to grasp the metal as firmly as Stephanie did. So she is on the list as is China's history maker Shanshan while Chapman edges out teenager Manassero, Lawrie, Els and Jiménez for my sixth spot. With teenagers Guan Tianlang and Manassero on the short-list along with 48-year-old Jiménez there is a timely reminder that golf is a game for all ages. You might not agree with my half-dozen but you will surely accept that the short-list of candidates in 2012 was mightily impressive.

How the Olympics inspired Rory to a record major win

Derek Lawrenson on four intriguing 2012 majors

It was always going to require something special to divert attention from the compelling grip of the London Olympic Games. What sporting life had a chance when up against the feats of Mo Farah and Jessica Ennis, and the rest of an inspired group of young men and women who kept a nation in thrall?

As it turned out, one man was sufficiently inspired by what he was watching every day in his rented home on Kiawah Island to put in a record-breaking performance of his own.

What gave this story its own remarkable slant is that it was the same man who had confessed earlier in the year to taking his eye of the ball; who had missed four halfway cuts in five events at one point, including a miserable defence of his United States Open title.

Which just goes to show what happens when Rory McIlroy feels the love of competition again. When he wants to make his own contribution to a year that UK sport will never forget. When he turns up at a course and likes the feel of the parspalum grass; when he looks down the fairways and thinks to himself: this is a course that just fits my eye.

So it was that, just 14 months after blowing away the field to win his first major, McIlroy went and did it again to claim the season's final major, the US PGA Championship. Coming to the final hole, with a 20 foot putt to break the record for the largest margin of victory established by Jack Nicklaus in 1980, McIlroy rolled it in.

You better be able to walk the walk if you turn up dressed in Tiger-red when leading on the final day of the major, and trust Rory to sprint the sprint instead. Just over a year after becoming the youngest US Open Champion in almost 90 years, the 23 year old had become the youngest winner of this event since it adopted the stroke play format in 1958.

A year that had been given a B rating by the man himself had just been elevated to an A plus. It also left the rest of the golfing world to ask: if he can win a US Open in a year when he is recovering from throwing away the Masters, and a US PGA following a difficult summer juggling the demands of the personal and the professional, what on earth is he going to be like in years when everything is going smoothly?

McIlroy's stunning performance was the highlight of another captivating year in the majors, one that saw the gifted naturals of the game assume their allotted place on the pantheon.

Alongside a victory for the most wondrous talent the European game has seen since Seve Ballesteros, there were also triumphs for two more men whose innate skills have brought boundless pleasure.

© Getty Images

Rory McIlroy with the US PGA Championship trophy which he won with a stunning performance over the links at Kiawah

Who did not stand and applaud when Ernie Els ended some difficult years marked by agonising self-doubt to lift the Claret Jug at Royal Lytham? Only those who had placed a bet on the luckless Australian Adam Scott, perhaps.

Certainly this was a victory for perseverance and class, as the big South African won his fourth major at the age of 42 to move his tally a little closer to commensurate with his abilities.

Afterwards, Els admitted that he wondered whether his chances in the big ones had gone after throwing away a glorious opportunity to win the US Open at Pebble Beach in 2010. What followed was hard to bear for those of us who have enjoyed watching that textbook swing and rhythm over the years.

How cruel, it seemed, that a man who could still live with the best of them from tee to green was tormented by putting demons to such an extent it prevented him from finishing the job. In Florida in March, he missed short putts on each of the last two greens to lose the Transitions Championship and that, to all intents and purposes, appeared to be that.

But, when all is said and done, it is not the skills they were blessed with that distinguish the great ones. It is the heart and mind.

So it was, that Els picked himself up from the almighty indignity of not being considered good enough to make the field at the Masters and put together a back nine at Lytham for the ages. Play it like Seve, he told himself, standing on the 10th tee. Heck, he even missed the 16th green miles to the right with his drive, just as the great man did on his way to victory in 1979.

By the time he got to the 18th, Els stood over a birdie putt from 12ft to put real pressure on Scott, playing behind. When he drained the sort of putt that would have frightened him witless earlier in the year, we knew he was back. When poor Scott found, like so many before him, that the last four holes at Lytham can be a merciless stretch of acreage, Els had ended up with the ultimate reward for keeping the faith.

Bubba Watson's triumph at the Masters was another for a man who plays the game with feel and instinct. It's not an affectation to say Bubba has never had a lesson in his life. Believe it or not, it is a fact. Sometimes that lack of honed technique can let him down, but when he is on his game, as he was at Augusta, he is a sight to see.

Early in the final round he had a ringside seat as his playing partner Louis Oosthuizen became the first man in Masters history to get an albatross at the par five 2nd. It looked as if fate had decreed this would be Oosthuizen's day, just as it had his great friend Charl Schwartzel a year earlier.

Trust Watson to stand firm in the face of such argument. His wedge shot from the trees on the first play-off hole, the 10th, bent 40 yards around a couple of Augusta pines and finding the putting surface, will surely go down as one of the best in Masters history. A stroke worthy of winning any Green Jacket, as they say.

The challenge at the United States Open is invariably a different one, of course. A stringent test of patience and whether a player is up to the ultimate examination of attritional golf.

At the death, there were some familiar faces, men steeled in these arts; players like Graeme McDowell and Jim Furyk. But it was a fresh-faced American called Webb Simpson who would get his score in early and discover it was good enough to win. With its rolling fairways built on the side of a hill and small, tortuously fast greens, the Olympic Club in San Francisco has always had a reputation for being the graveyard of favourites. Here, it had added to its reputation.

Bubba Watson hit the shot of the year at the second extra hole to beat Louis Oosthuizen and win the Green Jacket at Augusta

Ten years on and Els is again Champion Golfer of the Year

Michael Aitken recalls a drama-packed Open at Lytham

At 6ft 3ins, Ernie Els is a big man. While his stature as a golfer is also sizeable – the South African's triumph at Royal Lytham matched the four major successes enjoyed by his compatriot, Bobby Locke – it was his generous standing as a human being which most impressed the huge galleries surrounding the 18th green as Els delivered a gracious victory speech at the conclusion of the 141st staging of The Open Championship full of respect for his beaten rival, Adam Scott.

Ten years after he last lifted the Claret Jug at Muirfield – only Henry Cotton in 1948 had to wait longer after his previous Open win in 1937 – Els had been through enough drama on and off the golf course to appreciate a career rarely runs smoothly. He enjoys a sense of perspective about life as well as the game.

Els' son, Ben, born in 2002, was diagnosed with autism and the South African moved his family to Florida to take advantage of the more advanced medical help available in the USA. And in 2005, when he was ranked third in the world, Els ruptured a cruciate knee ligament in a sailing accident. He was out of action for a year and for a long period of time thereafter struggled to match his past accomplishments. Little wonder the golfer known as the Big Easy in recognition of his genial temperament and flowing swing subsequently became so ill at ease.

In the circumstances, then, it was entirely fitting that Els, who was six shots shy of the lead after 54 holes, should reach out to Scott. The Australian, who remained four strokes clear with four holes to play – he was so close to winning his name had even been sketched on the gold medal – somehow contrived to run up successive bogeys at the 15th, 16th, 17th and 18th holes to hand the Jug to the South African.

This closing stretch of challenging holes at Lytham is known as "Murder Mile" and, thanks to an inexorable series of missed putts, pulled iron shots and poor club selections, Scott became its most famous victim to date. If Els was quick to sympathise with his friend's struggle – it was a collapse to compare with Jean Van de Velde's misfortune on the final hole at Carnoustie in 1999 and Greg Norman's closing round disintegration at the 1996 Masters – he could not sugar coat the outcome and described his win as "a gift".

Perhaps it was best illustrated, prior to this championship, how much Els had dropped down the batting order among the game's elite that he was not even the most favoured South African with the bookmakers to lift the title as Louis Oosthuizen and Charl Schwartzel stepped into the spotlight. After missing out on an invitation to the Masters in April, many now regarded the 42-year-old from Johannesburg in the twilight of his career and unlikely to add to his haul of major wins at the US Open in 1994 and 1997 and The Open in 2002.

Those examining the omens more closely, however, might have noted how Els had finished ninth at the US Open won by Webb Simpson in San Francisco. Moreover, he came to Lytham with fond memories of his past performances in Lancashire after finishing second in 1996 and third in 2001. A glorious bunker player and consummate ball striker, Els possessed all the gifts required to succeed on one of the most testing of all Open venues.

Help from a putting guru

In conversation with Ken Brown, the former Ryder Cup player and BBC commentator, on an Easyjet flight from London to Inverness prior to the Aberdeen Asset Scottish Open at Castle Stuart, Els confided to the Scot he felt something special was stirring. Now working on his swing with Claude Harmon, son of Butch, the golfer had also started to hole more putts thanks to the work he'd undertaken with Dr Sherylle Calder, the renowned South African "eye doctor" who was part of Sir Clive Woodward's team when England won the 2003 Rugby World Cup. Although reluctant to go into much detail, Calder likened the process to gym sessions for the eyes. "It's all about judging line and length with your eyes and then transferring that to your hands," she said.

Els had also turned to the belly putter in a bid to solve his problems on the greens. Though he felt the game's ruling bodies had missed a trick in failing to outlaw a stroke which is anchored to the body, Els admitted at the time when he first switched blades that "as long as it's legal, I'll keep cheating with the rest of them." It proved to be a shrewd move as he followed in the footsteps of Webb Simpson and Keegan Bradley by winning a major with the longer implement, the third golfer in four majors to do so.

It's a measure of the scale of Ernie's achievements in the game that his solid, unyielding performance at Lytham enabled him join Jack Nicklaus, Tiger Woods, Walter Hagen, Bobby Jones and Lee Trevino as only the sixth player in the game's history to win both The Open and The US Open twice. While much attention in the immediate aftermath of the championship focused, understandably, on Scott's collapse, it was a tournament in which Els was a model of consistency throughout, finding nearly 80 per cent of Lytham's greens in regulation figures. He signed for three rounds in the 60s, never returned a score above par and played with more assurance in the heat of battle than any other contender for the Claret Jug on Sunday afternoon. His winning total of 273, seven under par, was particularly notable for a brilliantly compiled closing inward half of 32 – seven shots fewer than Scott, who had looked all but unbeatable when he birdied the 14th.

Although he lay four strokes behind Scott after the opening 18 holes, Els was smartly positioned from the off, returning a first round score of 68 while managing the trick of both keeping himself in contention yet operating largely under the radar. This was because there were any number of intriguing storylines written by those ahead of the eventual winner on Thursday's leaderboard. The Masters' champion, Bubba Watson, was fancied by those who remembered the dazzling eye-catching performances produced by Seve Ballesteros at Lytham and the charismatic American didn't disappoint with 67. Paul Lawrie, the beneficiary of Van de Velde's collapse in 1999, had waited a long time to prove his mettle again in the oldest major as he carded a bewitching 65, a score which matched the lowest the Aberdonian had recorded in The Open. And Tiger Woods, as ever the bookmakers' favourite, reaped the reward from a conservative game plan of hitting irons from the tee by posting 66.

The performance of the first round, though, was Scott's impressive 64. Having celebrated his 32nd birthday a few days before the championship began, the Australian found himself on the 18th tee with a chance to make history. Another birdie and he would have set a new benchmark of 62 in the majors. A par and he could post 63, a feat which had never previously been accomplished in The Open at Lytham. Alas, needing a smooth swing, he seemed edgy for the first time and pulled his tee shot into the thick rough on the left, duly dropping a shot to par. Still, 64 was hardly a tale of what might have been since it matched the low score returned by champion Tom Lehman in 1996. The Australian's six under mark was just reward on a benign morning for a glorious display of ball striking which prised eight birdies from the old links.

Two rounds – no bunkers

On Friday, the championship's knack of delivering tales of the unexpected saw a young man from Nashville who had missed the cut in his three previous Opens match a formidable record. Twenty years after Nick Faldo had set the pace at the halfway mark on 130, Brandt Snedeker added a 64 to his opening 66 for the same low score as the three time champion. Relaxing by enjoying a few pints of the local ale, Snedeker's fondness for the ancient game played beside the sea saw him follow up an ace on the par 4 16th in practice by avoiding all of Lytham's 206 bunkers during two days of competition. Without so much as the blemish of a single bogey on his card, the amiable country and western fan talked about the secret of his success. "No bogeys around here is getting some good breaks as well as playing some pretty good golf," he acknowledged.

If Snedeker might have hoped to put some daylight between himself and the competition, Scott added a 67 to his first round of 64 to sit just one stroke off the lead and play with the American on Saturday in the final pairing at a major for the first time in his career. Again, Scott's play from tee to green was impressive. Adopting a more aggressive approach than Woods, who was hamstrung by concern over hitting wayward shots with the driver, Scott harnessed his power effectively – demolishing the par 5 seventh hole, for example, with a drive and 3 wood to set up a simple two putt birdie.

Woods, on the other hand, produced his most consistent start to a major since 2006 by returning another 67 which will live in the memory for the spectacular manner in which the round concluded. After finding a greenside bunker on the 18th, Woods ignited one of the biggest roars of the day when he took advantage of a lie on the upslope and aimed the wedge shot a cup outside the left of the hole and watched it drop into the hole. Interestingly, this marked the eighth time Woods had gone into the weekend action at the majors after compiling two rounds in the 60s. On all seven previous occasions, including his three victories in The Open, he went on to win each time. At Lytham, the run ended and Tiger came up a little short, partly because he doesn't hole out as well as he used to do and partly because he played too many of the long holes from too far back and didn't create enough birdie opportunities.

The other notable finish on Friday came from Tom Watson, the five time past champion, who holed a 30 foot putt to make the cut for the sixth time in eight years. After missing a three footer on the previous hole, Watson, 62, described the experience as shifting from the "ridiculous to the sublime".

On Saturday, Australia began to dream it might crown an Open champion for the first time since Greg Norman won at Royal St George's in 1993. Thanks to an unflustered 68, Scott opened up a four shot advantage over both Snedeker and Graeme McDowell, the Ulsterman who won the US Open at Pebble Beach in 2010. The good news for Scott was that in the previous 18 tournaments where he'd taken a lead into the final round he'd gone on to win 16 times. The bad news was he'd never attempted this challenge before in a major.

On another mild day when the breeze barely ruffled the flags, Snedeker's unfamiliarity with the hothouse of major championship golf was reflected in a nervy performance. He followed up his first bogey in 41 holes – a dropped shot on the fifth – by landing in his first bunker of the week on the sixth. Forced to emerge sideways, Snedeker duly gave another shot away and found his confidence dented.

The good news for Els, who followed up a level par 70 on Friday with 68 in the third round, was that the forecast for wind to finally blow during the denouement on Sunday proved more accurate than previous bulletins. Thanks to a rhythmic swing which usually gets slower in the kind of blustery conditions that tempt mere mortals to swing harder, Els had set himself apart during the bad weather which blew the rest of the field off course during the third round at Muirfield ten years earlier. Although overhead conditions were not half so demanding at Lytham, the wind speed made life tricky enough for the leaders to convince Els he still had a chance of overturning Scott's six stroke advantage.

Triple bogey for Tiger

Spared the stresses of those involved in the final groups who were weighed down by the pressures of expectation, Ernie was able to shrug off an indifferent start. He dropped a shot on the second hole and for a spell lay seven adrift of Scott. And by the time the South African reached the turn, with just nine holes remaining, the gap was still six shots.

Of the other challengers, McDowell, playing in the last group for the second successive major, enjoyed little luck over the opening holes and eventually made too many mistakes to give himself a realistic chance. Snedeker, on the front nine, was stricken by a brace of double bogeys. Woods, still attempting a safety first approach, came unstuck on the sixth hole when he was snared in one of Lytham's fiendish bunkers. Before the championship began, Padraig Harrington quipped that Lytham's bunkers should be surrounded by red stakes. Tiger got the message when he failed to get out of the

© Getty Images

Australian Adam Scott appeared to have The Open Championship won but a poor finish over Lytham's "Murder Mile" let Ernie Els in to take the title

sand with his first attempt and was fortunate the ball didn't strike him on the way back from the face of the trap. Now left with no stance to move the ball forward, Woods sat outside the bunker and somehow chiselled the ball out before carding his first triple bogey at a major in nine years.

Scott could have been forgiven for thinking he was all but out of sight as he reached the turn in level 4s before reeling off four consecutive pars between the 10th and 13th holes then making what seemed like a decisive move on the 14th courtesy of a birdie 3. Els, though, had not given up the fight and he, too, birdied the 14th. Keeping a cool head, Els avoided danger over the closing holes and finished off by holing a 12 foot putt for birdie on the last. Remarkably, Ernie's 68 was the 39th round of his career at The Open which bettered 70, more even than Sir Nick Faldo, Tom Watson and Jack Nicklaus have managed.

Mark you, the best the 42-year-old hoped for was a spot in a play-off as he strove to match the achievement of Darren Clarke, who was the same age as Els when he won at Sandwich in 2011. A black cloud, meanwhile, was forming over the Australian's head. He had begun to look shaky on the home straight, finding himself bunkered at the 15th, three-putting the 16th and pulling a mid-iron shot on the 17th. Suddenly, needing a par on the last just to join Els in a play-off, Scott chose a fairway wood which rolled out into a bunker when his caddie, Steve Williams, might have pressed a long iron into his hands which would have come up short of the danger. Faced with a putt of around eight feet on the 18th green to match Els, he tweaked it left before sinking to his knees, barely able to comprehend how the Claret Jug had slipped from his grasp.

Ernie Els lost in reverie after winning The Open for a second time ten years after his previous victory in golf's oldest major

Why success at the 2012 Open meant so much more to Ernie

John Huggan rejoices in the return of the "Big Easy"

It's the same anywhere and everywhere. Mention the words "Ernie" and "Els" to any golfer and the immediate reactions invariably involve a broad smile, a puffing of the cheeks followed by a softly whistling exhalation and maybe a knowing nod or two. All in unspoken admiration of first, the man's inherent decency, second, his almost universal popularity and third, one of the most graceful actions and smoothest rhythms ever to grace the game Scotland gave to the world.

Now 43, the big South African has always hit the kinds of shots that make mere mortals stop and look. And listen. It seems easy the way Ernie does it, the sound of club on ball distinctive, an elusive "whoosh" reserved for only the most skilful practitioners. But it is a vain hope for some of his obvious magic to somehow rub off.

The Open champion swings the club with an enviable and elusive economy of movement, the way the rest of us would like to ... but almost certainly never will. Pure ball striking, however, is but part of any winning golf equation. Putting – "the game within a game," according to Ben Hogan – has forever represented the most easily identifiable line between success and failure. And Els is living proof of that age-old maxim.

After years of ever-increasing frustration and ever-decreasing confidence on the greens, it was only when he rediscovered his touch – especially from close range – that he re-emerged as a threat to win at the highest level.

"I never got to the stage where I was 'yippy'," he says. "My problem was more technical than mental. The path of my stroke was off. So I felt uncomfortable over short putts. And that feeling eventually worked its way through the rest of my game and attitude. I just wasn't myself. I was grumpy and heading in a direction I didn't want to go. Throw all that into a pot, stir well and you get one unhappy person; me."

Indeed, many were those who chose to dismiss the notion of Els as a real contender for the game's biggest prizes. "I had been written off a lot, especially in South Africa," he says."That hurt. But I should be used to it, I guess. At the age of 14 I won the World Junior. I got a lot of attention for that. Rugby and cricket, our two biggest sports, weren't allowed to compete internationally. So the expectations placed on me have always been huge."

In contrast, when he arrived at Royal Lytham last July for what would be his twenty-first appearance in the world's oldest and most important championship, Els did so as though under cover of darkness. Despite finishing third and second (two of his 33 top-tens in majors) in two previous Opens played over the famous Lancashire links, few saw him as a potential winner, a full decade removed from his previous major victory.

It was an understandable oversight, however. In 2011, mired in the biggest slump of his career, Els failed to qualify for the weekend at each of the four Grand Slam events.

"The last decade has been very different for me," he reveals. "For the first 32 years of my life things went along pretty much the same. But so much has happened in the last ten years, all of which led to my game falling apart in 2011. I had doubts about my ability to win again. I missed the cut in all four majors. I had never done that before. It was worrying. I had no confidence on the greens. You can't win majors if you can't putt."

Still, the signs were at least promising. Only three weeks before, Els had finished a solid ninth in the US Open at The Olympic Club in San Francisco ... and, more importantly, enjoyed the feeling of being back in contention. All of which was in stark contrast to the desolate figure seen departing the same event at Pebble Beach two years earlier.

Third then behind eventual champion Graeme McDowell, Els had, in his own words, "putted like an idiot" in the final round. "The biggest difference between 2010 and 2012 was in my putting," he says with a characteristic smile. "I turned things round by focusing on things I worked on as a teenager. I went back to basics. It's weird; as you get older you try to play the way you did as a kid. And when you're a kid, you're always trying to play like you're older.

"My left eye is my dominant eye. But I had moved away from using it properly. I wasn't keeping my head steady. I wasn't accelerating the putter through the ball. Simple stuff like that. It wasn't complicated."

The vital decision

Even armed with such renewed confidence, Els sat six shots behind leader Adam Scott with 18 holes to play at Lytham. Good, but not yet great. And, halfway through the final round, things were looking much the same. "I made a very soft bogey on the 9th hole," recalls Els."It's the shortest and easiest of Lytham's par-3s. I wasn't best pleased. But that helped me make a decision. I had to play aggressively and apply myself 100 per cent to every shot. "At Lytham, that's so important. If you get careless, you get punished. The bunkers are so well placed.

"The only big risk I took was on the 16th. I saw on the replay how close my drive was to the fence on the right. But on every other hole, I hit driver because it felt right."

By the time he hunched over a missable birdie putt on the final green, Scott's lead was down to two strokes, the former Players champion having dropped shots at both the 15th and 16th. "I just had a feeling about that putt," says Els. "I wasn't in the best position at the time, so I could have a go. There was no thought of lagging, no pressure. Even if I missed, no one would criticise me. I had nothing to lose. And it went in like a train down a tunnel."

Throw in two more bogeys from Scott – an agonising ending for the likeable Aussie – and Els was "champion golfer of the year" for a second time. Typically, however, his first thoughts were for the hugely disappointed runner-up.

"When I knew I had won, it was an incredible feeling," he says. "But I've had it go the other way. I remember standing on the last green at Troon in 2004 having lost the Open to Todd Hamilton. I was devastated. So I knew how it would be for Adam.

"I wish I had said even more than I did. I cannot believe I actually forgot to mention Seve. I had thought about him a few times on the back nine – especially at the 16th. My Dad still cries when he talks of what Seve said to him after our great battle in the World Match Play Championship at Wentworth in 1994. 'I played very well today', Seve told my father, 'but your son – he is very special'. I wanted to thank him for that but in the moment I forgot.

"Winning meant more to me this time round. Don't get me wrong though. Every major win is special. But this one is in a different category. I took it all a little bit for granted when I was younger. I had been told all my life I was going to win majors. So when I did, I thought it was just what was meant to be. It was supposed to happen."

And, wouldn't you know, at Lytham it did happen again. To cheers all round.

Twice a winner of The Open at Lytham, Seve Ballesteros, seen here practising on the beach at Pedrena, was on 2012 winner Ernie Els' mind as he came home in 32 to win his fourth major title

Ernie's career highlights

Major championships: The Open (2002, 2012); US Open (1994, 1997).

European Tour: Twenty-seven victories; tour No 1: 2003, 2004; score average leader: 2003, 2004.

US PGA Tour: Nineteen victories.

Presidents Cup International side: 1996, 1998, 2000, 2003, 2007, 2009, 2011. He will be Captain in 2013.

Schoolgirl Lydia Ko takes her golfing success all in her stride

Lewine Mair only has praise New Zealand's record-breaker

Lydia Ko, who broke all records when she won the 2012 Canadian Women's Open at the age of 15 years and four months, does not go out of her way to look older than she is. The Korean-New Zealander is a regular 15-year-old … and an enchantingly unspoiled one at that.

No-one could argue that her win over the might of the LPGA Tour in Canada was a fluke. Not in a year when she additionally annexed the US Amateur title, the Smyth Salver at the Ricoh Women's British Open and the individual award at the World Amateur Team championships in Turkey. At the Turkish event, she finished a whopping eight shots clear of the field.

One striking aspect of Ko's game is that her focus is at the other end of the spectrum to that of most girls in her age-group. She chats with her playing companions as they leave the tee, while she and her mother, Tina, exchange the occasional glance. For the rest of the time, though, she finds much the same "cocoon of concentration" which used to be associated with the late and legendary Joyce Wethered.

Equally eye-catching is the manner in which her follow-through is the same every time, with none of those contortions employed by golfers willing the ball to head this way or that. The answer, here, is that Ko has no reason to suppose that her shots might be inclined to stray. She is unerringly consistent and, even when the wind was doing its best to throw her off course at the Ricoh, she carried on as if nothing were amiss.

No wonder that Tina was one of the less-agitated parents at Hoylake. Yes, she followed every shot but – and here is the key – she had no trouble in carrying on a conversation at the same time.

It was Tina who, ten or eleven years ago, wanted a change from their busy life in Korea. The family thought of heading for Australia before wondering if Canada might be a better bet. Then, prior finally to making up their minds, they visited New Zealand and fell in love with the landscape and the climate.

Golf, at that point, did not come into the equation and it was only when an aunt gave the then five-year-old Lydia a seven-iron and a putter that the child became the first in the family to give the game a try. She took lessons at the Pupike GC and showed promise from the start.

As applies with the Wies, the Kos are historically more academic than sporty. Lydia's father was in banking but is now retired, Tina is an English graduate, and Lydia's older sister has just qualified as an architect, though she is currently looking for something easier to do by way of making a living. "Too many exams," laughed her mother, by way of an explanation.

Lydia is clever and loves to read. At the start of the 2012 season, she was due to sit eight Cambridge Board "O" Grades at her New Zealand High School – a figure which seemed entirely in keeping with the 99% she achieved in a school maths exam. However, as her golf jumped a couple of levels, so it became clear that she was taking on too much.The Kos visited the school principal and cut those eight "O" Grades to four.

The Canadian Open victory – Lydia had rounds of 68, 68, 72 and 67 to defeat Inbee Park – came as a shock and, when the inevitable question arose as to when the new champion planned to turn professional, Lydia was caught unawares. Sensibly, Tina

When an aunt gave Lydia Ko a cut-down seven-iron and a putter as a present when she was just five years old it encouraged her to play golf

Laura Davies, still competing as she closes in on 50, is hugely impressed by Lydia Ko's achievements but feels that by the time the New Zealander is 30 she may have had enough of golf

made it clear that nothing was certain but, since that day, mother and daughter have started to explore the possibilities.

At Hoylake, Lydia spent time with Michelle Wie who made a very good case for going to college and playing professional golf at the same time. Meanwhile, Lydia herself has confirmed that when she turns professional, she would not want to be travelling the world for too long. With this scenario in mind, the Kos wonder how it would be if their younger daughter were to follow her golfing dream relatively soon and save college plans till later.

If this were their chosen path, it would tie in with what Laura Davies was saying during the Ricoh. Davies thinks the girl is brilliant but hazards a guess that she will not be playing beyond the age of 30. "By the time Lydia's that age," said Davies, "she will have had 23 years of beating balls on a daily basis. If she doesn't have injury problems by then – something which is pretty unlikely – she will simply have had enough."

For next year at least, Ko is unlikely to disappear from the amateur scene and will be back in the UK in a bid to defend her top amateur award at the Ricoh.

On being advised at Hoylake that the 2013 instalment is to be held over the Old Course, St Andrews, the teenager could not have been more taken aback. "Holy cow!" she exclaimed, in a manner which was entirely in keeping with her 15 years, "it's going to be tough again."

Lydia Ko's c/v includes youngest winner of pro event

Lydia Ko has been the top amateur, winning the Mark McCormack Medal for the past two years.

2009

Lydia reached the final of the New Zealand Amateur Championship losing out to another Korean teenager Cecilia Cho.

2010

As a 12-year-old she finished just five behind winner Laura Davies in New Zealand Women's Open She helped New Zealand finish runners-up in the Queen Sirikit Cup competition finishing fourth herself in the individual competition.

2011

She became the first golfer to win the Australian and New Zealand Stroke-play Championships in the same season.

*NSW Open – 2nd	*Handa Australian Open – 289th	*Pegasus NZ Open – 4th
†Riversdale Cup – 1st	†Queen Sirikit Cup – 13th	†Australian SP – 1st
†Australian Am. – quarter-finalist	†North Island SP – 1st	†New Zealand SP – 1st
†New Zealand Am. – winner	‡Muriwai Open – 1st	†North Shore Classic – 1st
†British Am.– lost 2nd round	†US Amateur – joint leading qualifier but lost 2nd round	

2012

Became the youngest amateur winner of a professional event when she landed the NSW Open title on the ALPG Tour. Later she won the US Amateur Championship and became the youngest winner on the LPGA Tour when she was successful in the Canadian Open. Later in the season she took individual honours in the World Amateur Team Championship (Espirito Santo Trophy).

†Australian Amateur – winner	*NSW Open –1st	*Australian Masters – 32nd
*Australian Open – 9th	*New Zealand Open – 17th	†Riversdale Cup – withdrew
†World Ladies C/ship – 2nd	†New Zealand SP – 2nd	†Queen Sirikit Cup – 1st
‡Muriwai Ladies – 1st	*CN Canadian Open – 1st	†British Amateur – 17th
†Espirito Santo – 1st	†US Amateur – leading qualifier and winner	

†Amateur event *Professional event ‡Amateur and Professional event

Last day heroics ensure that Europe keeps the Ryder Cup

Michael Aitken recalls the Miracle of Medinah

No event in world class sport is ever a foregone conclusion, even if the outcome often seems predictable. The bookmakers, though, make their living by knowing a likely upshot when they see one. Which is why, on home turf at Medinah in Illinois, going into Sunday's 12 singles matches leading by the clear margin of 10–6, the USA were an all but unbackable 50/1 on to win the 39th staging of golf's most exhilarating match play event. The Europeans, on the other hand, were offered to retain the Ryder Cup at a whopping 33/1. Perhaps not since Crisp led Red Rum by 20 lengths with only two fences remaining at the 1973 Grand National, had the outcome of a two horse race seemed quite so set in stone.

Yet, just as Red Rum tore up the record book and eventually outsprinted Crisp, someone forgot to tell Europe's golfers they couldn't grasp the destiny of the Cup in their own capable hands. And, amazingly, at the end of a tumultuous final day of singles, it was the golfing outsiders who made light of the previous four sessions in Chicago and delivered the most improbable comeback in Ryder Cup history.

For José Maria Olazábal's men, the foundations of what would become known in the aftermath of the event as the Miracle of Medinah were laid late on Saturday afternoon when the irrepressible Ian Poulter, winner of four points out of four, heeded the advice of the European team's inspiration, the late Seve Ballesteros, more passionately than anyone else.

Of course, no one was less likely to run up the white flag in Chicago than Poulter and it was the Englishman's resistance which proved critical in the third session. Europe were already trailing 10–4 and, at one stage, looked like falling 12–4 behind. To his great credit, Luke Donald, with three birdies in the last five holes, enabled Europe to salvage a point before his compatriot changed the entire complexion of the match.

Playing with Rory McIlroy, the British golfers were two down on the 12th to Jason Dufner and Zach Johnson. While the world number one holed a 15 foot putt to cut the deficit on the 13th, it was left to Poulter to finish the match with five consecutive birdies on his own ball to deliver a one hole victory which effectively turned the contest on its head.

Under the cosh for so much of the match, the European insurrection, which didn't get under way until Saturday afternoon, looked an improbable turn of events after the USA had dominated so much of the foursomes and fourballs. Friday's opening foursomes, for example, were notable in the main for the emergence of an energised American pairing of Phil Mickelson and Keegan Bradley. Feeding off the enthusiasm of the younger man, Mickelson produced one of his best ever Ryder Cup performances in the 4 and 3 win over the hitherto unbeaten duo of Donald and Sergio García, holing a testing 15 foot birdie putt on the 13th for a two hole advantage which paved the road to victory. As Dufner and Johnson took advantage of Lee Westwood's errant shot into the water on the 15th for a 3 and 2 win, it was left to the old firms of Poulter and Justin Rose and McIlroy and McDowell to earn the first points for Europe in a session which finished 2–2.

© Phil Sheldon Golf Picture Library

Passionate and patriotic Ian Poulter had another remarkable Ryder Cup

If the USA felt they'd played the better golf in the morning and were unfortunate not to establish a narrow lead, Love's men all but steamrollered Europe on Friday afternoon. But for a colossal performance, in partnership with a struggling Westwood, from debutant Nicolas Colsaerts who reeled off eight birdies and an eagle in a ten under par 62, to beat Tiger Woods and Steve

Stricker 1 up, the visitors could easily have been whitewashed.

In the opening fourball, Masters champion Bubba Watson and US Open winner Webb Simpson combined to stirring effect over the front nine in a collective seven under par to win six of the first eight holes against Paul Lawrie and Peter Hanson before closing out the match 5 and 4. Getting off to a fast start was also the brief for Mickelson and Bradley who rode the wave of their morning win by making birdies on four of the five opening holes against the European stalwarts, McIlroy and McDowell. The major winners from Northern Ireland never threw in the towel but were powerless to halt the American juggernaut as Mickelson hit his tee shot to inside two feet on the par 3 17th hole to clinch a 2 and 1 win.

America's third point from the afternoon's golf came from Dustin Johnson and Matt Kuchar, who also got off to a flier against Rose and Martin Kaymer. Three up after seven holes, the Americans were able to ham and egg it against a European pairing in which the German was a virtual non-contributor. In the circumstances, Rose did well to keep the margin of defeat down to 3 and 2 since Kaymer played so poorly he was not seen again until the singles.

Leading 5–3 as the second day's play got underway, the initiative lay with the home side. After being rested on Friday afternoon, Poulter was back in harness with Rose in Saturday's foursomes, helping to defeat Watson and Simpson by one hole. Both Englishmen holed decisive putts over the closing holes to add a sprinkling of cheer to an otherwise grim morning for Europe.

America buoyant

If anything, the effervescent pairing of Bradley and Mickelson was even more ebullient on Saturday, putting Westwood and Donald to the sword by the bruising margin of 7 and 6. This matched the heaviest defeat in Ryder Cup history and questioned the wisdom of sending out Westwood for a third session when he was so far below his best in the previous two. In the other ties, Colsaerts was unable to repeat his form from the day before in the company of García as the pair lost 2 and 1 to Dufner and Johnson. Avoiding mistakes is the key to winning points in foursomes and Europe cut their own throats with three bogeys in the closing six holes, including a tee shot from Colsaerts at the 17th which landed short in the water. As for the anchor match, McIlroy and McDowell lost their magic touch on the greens, failing to make a single birdie until the 14th, and lost by one hole to Furyk and Snedeker.

Now leading 8–4, America was buoyant going into the afternoon fourballs. If the decision to rest Mickelson and Bradley seemed perplexing even without the benefit of hindsight, the victories by Johnson and Kuchar by one hole over Colsaerts and Lawrie and Watson and Simpson by 5 and 4 over Rose and Molinari appeared to propel the USA ever closer to an impregnable advantage. At least that was how it looked until Donald, who lives in Chicago, partnered García to a one hole win over Stricker and Woods, notwithstanding a thrilling performance from Tiger on the back nine as he reeled off five birdies only to find himself on the losing end once more. All of which left centre stage in the final fourball tie to Poulter. He partnered McIlroy to a victory which produced any number of wild-eyed celebrations and restored a vestige of hope to Europe as they remembered what happened to a four point lead at Brookline in 1999.

Helped by the police!

Had it not been for the intervention of a quickwitted American policeman, local deputy chief Patrick Rollins, Sunday's denouement might have turned out very differently. McIlroy was still at the team hotel 25 minutes before his singles match against Bradley and it was only because Rollins broke every speed limit in a patrol car to the course that the Ulsterman didn't forfeit a point. As it was, with barely a practice swing, he defeated Bradley 2 and 1.

Out in the third match, McIlroy's success followed on from impressive wins for Donald over Watson, 2 and 1, in the opening tie and Poulter, 2 up, over Simpson. With no choice but to frontload his singles order with the most reliable performers, Olazábal could hardly have wished for a better outcome as all five of the men he sent out first came good. Inexplicably left out of foursomes, Lawrie served a timely reminder of his worth by demolishing Snedeker 5 and 3 while Rose delivered one of the most thrilling points of the match against Mickelson. One down with two to play, Rose holed a 35 foot birdie putt on the 17th to draw level after the American narrowly failed to chip in before making another 15 footer on the last for an astonishing success.

Dustin Johnson stopped the rot for the US, defeating Colsaerts 3 and 2 as the rookie played the last seven holes in three over par. Zach Johnson also revived captain Love's spirits with a 2 and 1 win over McDowell. Amazingly, though, only Dufner in the bottom five ties would add another full point for the home side as the phlegmatic American fought off a spirited fightback from Hanson. On the European side, García took advantage of a bogey-bogey finish from Furyk, Westwood played his best golf of the week in beating Kuchar 3 and 2 and Kaymer dug deep to take down the out-of-sorts Stricker.

The German had come to Medinah with his game in disarray. So, distraught at being left on the sidelines for much of the contest, he'd spoken at length to his mentor, Bernhard Langer. Ironically, the match would come down to Kaymer facing the same six foot putt which Langer had missed to tie the match at Kiawah in 1991. This time, however, the German holed out. Europe had retained the Cup and minutes later Molinari beat Woods to clinch overall victory by a point.

An unforgettable tribute to the memory of the great Seve

James Lawton on Europe's spectacular victory in Chicago

If you are very lucky you see a few things that you know right away you will always have and that from time to time they will come to you as fresh as when they first happened. They arrive in the mind's eye with a thoroughbred rush whenever you fall to recalling great deeds.

It is a habit that tends to keep pace with the lengthening shadows. Also, it is one that is in particular need of re-fuelling if a substantial part of your life has centred on the privilege of attending major sports events. This is because the years do not come without prejudice.

You see Rod Laver send a bullet backhand across the Centre Court and you suspect that the sensation of it will never be surpassed. Then, decades later, Roger Federer or Novak Djokovic or Rafael Nadal re-invent shots of their own and you know you were mistaken.

Muhammad Ali so many times announced himself the nonpareil but just a few years after he left the ring you saw Sugar Ray Leonard and Tommy Hearns produce what you had reason to believe may have been one of the greatest fights of them all.

Pele and Maradona and George Best in his maverick way crossed, you were sure, ultimate limits of football achievement but now, all these years on, it is mesmerising to see Lionel Messi and Cristiano Ronaldo.

There is also the extraordinary ability of the Ryder Cup to re-make itself every two years and if there was ever a time to make such a declaration it is surely this one when the memory of what happened at the Medinah Country Club near Chicago at the end of September is so vivid, and so clearly beyond any doubt, utterly durable.

It may be an odd to thing to say of an 85-year-old sports institution which has known so many tumultuous episodes since the winning captain in Medinah, José Maria Olazábal, performed his youthful dance of triumph at Jack Nicklaus' course at Dublin, Ohio, in 1987, but in the final moments of Europe's latest and most spectacular victory there was an inescapable conclusion. It was that the benevolent initiative of Sam Ryder, the St Albans corn merchant who wanted golf to have a new dimension of both competition and camaraderie, had finally come of age.

© Getty Images

The German golfer Martin Kaymer handled the pressure to hole the winning putt at Medinah

The message trailed in the Illinois sky had been "Do it for Seve" and indeed there could have been no greater tribute to the meaning of the great man than Europe's stunning and unprecedented comeback on the last day. But then the heroes of Europe, trailing 10–6 after the first two days, were surely making an even broader donation to the spirit of both their game and the competition which had drawn from them some of the most intense efforts of their lives.

The European golfers were relentless in their claim that they had come to honour the memory of Ballesteros. Along the way they also defined the genius of the Ryder Cup format. The *Chicago Sun-Times* declared that Europe's victory was a matter of Shock and Awwwe. More than anything, though, it was an astonishing vindication of Old Sam's dream that one of sport's most demanding of indi-

The European team at Medinah were determined to honour the memory of Severiano Ballesteros

vidual challenges could, every two years, produce a hugely heightened sense of team.

Before Martin Kaymer emerged from a year of dwindling horizons with the 6-foot putt that retained the trophy – and avenged the moment at Kiawah Island 21 years earlier when his compatriot Bernard Langer so narrowly missed sinking an equally vital putt – he had faced the same ordeal that his team-mate Graeme McDowell had overcome in a sodden Welsh valley two years before.

He had been required to separate the instincts – and the pressures – that attend the challenges of winning for yourself and that of delivering for a team, something which Tiger Woods once likened to the futility of canoe racing against a superior force.

McDowell, the hero of Celtic Manor, made a confession before the resumption of hostilities in Medinah. He said part of him relished the idea of a return to the heart of the most pivotal action. But there was also more than a touch of dread, a fear that he might discover the other side of the glory he found in Wales.

As it unfolded, McDowell struggled to re-impose his authority and it was Kaymer who was obliged to become the man of destiny. After beating the veteran Steve Stricker, he said, "There was no comparison with the feelings I had in winning my major title and those I had today. I won the major for myself and today I won it for my team and all the people. It was great pressure when José Maria told me we needed the point to win the Ryder Cup but when it came the feeling was so good I could hardly have imagined it."

Indeed, so much of Medinah stretched the imagination – the beauty of the American Fall, the great wings of Canadian geese heading south across a vast blue sky and the extraordinary, inexorable strength of the European recovery.

Lee Westwood defined the edge of the competition well enough when he resisted a moment of reproach for his singles opponent Matt Kuchar who declined to concede him the one-foot that gave him a crucial 3 and 1 victory. Westwood said that he had rarely known such fierce trepidation.

"Do it for Seve" was the message that had been towed across that vast sky and, in the end, a sporting crusade could hardly have been waged quite so ferociously.

Ian Poulter did it for Seve so brilliantly that his previous Ryder Cup heroics, formidable though they were, were dwarfed. Justin Rose unfurled a matador's finish worthy of the man he had come to honour and from the world's number one player, Rory McIlroy, there was the insouciant brilliance of his defeat of Keegan Bradley. He arrived in chaos at the first tee and then almost effortlessly outplayed the man who had threatened to be the hammer of the Europeans.

Yet this was more than an unforgettable tribute to one of golf's greatest figures and, surely, most enduring spirits. It was a supreme example of sport's ability to find new dimensions and new expression. And, no doubt, from the moment the American captain Davis Love III declared that it should not be mistaken for the outbreak of the Third World War, it was precisely what Sam Ryder always had in mind.

Gleneagles will host the next Ryder Cup in 2014

The match returns to Scotland for the first time since 1973 when the Centenary course at Gleneagles Hotel will be the venue. Several changes have been made by the designer Jack Nicklaus to ensure it provides a suitably demanding test for the Cup match including a redesigned 18th hole. When the last official match was played in Scotland the Americans were 19–13 winners.

Desire and determination the key to a majestic Cup victory

Alistair Tait on an outstanding team performance

While Europe's 2012 Ryder Cup victory will go down in history as one of the greatest comebacks of all time, 2012 produced another comeback that deserves recognition. The Great Britain & Ireland Curtis Cup team produced a final day's performance at Nairn Golf Club to rival the European men.

GB&I Captain Tegwen Matthews led a team to the glorious shores of the Moray Firth that were serious underdogs. No GB&I side had won the biennial match since 1996. Nothing over the first two days suggested the home side would eradicate 16 years of despair. Yet a united band of girls from England, Ireland, Scotland and Wales produced the goods when it mattered. Foreshadowing what would happen in the Ryder Cup three months later, Matthews' players came back from adversity to win 10½–9½ and pour contempt on the record books.

The omens were not good for the home team after the opening foursomes' session. The United States swept that session 3–0 and appeared to be heading for an eighth straight victory. No US team had lost the match the five previous times (1932, '54, '62, 2002 and '06) after sweeping the opening foursomes. Turn out the lights, the party seemed pretty much over.

That sense of doom never seemed to lift over the first two days. GB&I won the first day's four-balls 2–1, lost the second day's' foursomes 2–1 before rallying to win the final pairing session. A 2½–½ win in the second day's four-balls got them within a point of the US, trailing 5½–6½ heading into the singles. As far as history was concerned, it probably seemed more like a 10-point deficit. After all, only one US team, in 1956, had lost the match after taking a lead into the final singles session. US teams had won on 23 of 24 previous occasions they took the lead into the singles.

With only three and a half points needed to retain the cup, the US side seemed destined for an eighth successive win when Austin Ernst and Emily Tubert got the US team off to a fantastic start. Playing in the lead singles match against England's Kelly Tidy, Ernst raced to a three-hole lead after the first six holes. However, Tidy levelled the match by winning three straight holes from the seventh before going ahead with a birdie at the par-5, 12th hole. She did not falter, running out a 2 and 1 winner.

© Getty Images

A delighted Stephanie Meadow runs across the green after holing the winning putt in the 2012 Curtis Cup match at Nairn to give Great Britain and Ireland a first win since 1996

"That was vital," Matthews said. "Kelly's reputation in match play is second to none and was one of the factors in me putting her out number one. Her match was a turning point. I think it was vital for the rest of the team."

So it proved. Tubert was two up over Amy Boulden after eight holes but ended up losing 3 and 1. From a one-point deficit at the start of the final day, the home team had suddenly gone a point ahead. Suddenly they had that all-important intangible: momentum.

Holly Clyburn defeated Erica Popson 3 and 2, and 16-year-old Charley Hull trounced Lindy Duncan 5 and 3. The scene was left for Northern Ireland's Stephanie Meadow to deliver the telling point against Amy Anderson. She did just that, winning 4 and 2 to give GB&I a crucial 5–3 win in singles play.

"I just got it done," Meadow said. "I knew all along it would come down to my match. I was watching the boards. I knew how the first four matches had gone, so I knew what I had to do."

US captain Pat Cornett had to hobble around Nairn on crutches for two and a half days after breaking an ankle in a freak buggy accident on Friday. Curtis Cup legend and former US captain Carole Semple Thompson deputised for Cornett on the first afternoon and then spent the next two days driving Cornett around the course. The US captain pointed to the first two singles matches as crucial to her team's defeat.

"In the opening matches, I thought we started out hard and strong and saw that lead dissipate," Cornett said. "That was deflating. If we had come out and had been leading those it would have been deflating to GB&I."

Cornett also left Nairn wondering about her team's failure to perform in the four-balls. They lost that form of golf 4½–1½ over two sessions.

"I think that was huge," Cornett said. "If we had to analyse it, the four-balls were disappointing for us. Obviously, we are ecstatic about the foursomes, but it's hard to know what happened in the four-balls."

Matthews didn't have much soul searching to do when she left Nairn, just celebrating. "This is the best thing ever in my whole life," she said.

Despite much controversy over team selection in the run-up to the match, the eight GB&I players came together to do what no GB&I team had done since the 1996 team that included Karen Stupples and Janice Moodie.

"It is absolutely tantamount to their desire to win ... their determination," Matthews said. "Each character in this team is very, very strong. Very competitive, very strong and they wanted it more than anybody else. They were disappointed after Friday morning, so they are the ones who pulled it through.

"Having been with a number of the girls for the last two years in varying events, I was very confident that this team could win the Curtis Cup."

The victory might have been just the seventh for GB&I in Curtis Cup history against 27 defeats and three draws, but it completed a grand slam of biennial team competitions. For the first time ever the Curtis, Walker, Solheim and Ryder Cups all resided on the British and Irish side of the Atlantic Ocean. The last time a GB&I Curtis Cup side had a chance to do that was at Formby in 2004.

"We had joked about no pressure, no pressure with the three other cups being on this side of the pond," Matthews said. "I'm very competitive, probably more competitive than these girls. For me, that was a challenge I actually like. I really wanted it as badly as these girls did."

As if that wasn't enough motivation, the GB&I team also had the emotional incentive to win for former team manager Sue Turner, who died in February aged just 50. "Sue was always in the back of our minds," Matthews said. "It's absolutely majestic that we have done this for Sue."

Majestic, that pretty much sums up GB&I's victory at Nairn.

Two notable Curtis Cup players died in 2012

British Curtis Cup player Phyllis (Phyl) Wylie (*née* Wade) died last year at the grand old age of 101. Although Essex-born, Phyl Wylie spent most of her married life in Troon. She played in the fourth Curtis Cup match in 1938 at the Essex County Club in Massachusetts and had been the oldest surviving team member from either side of the Atlantic.

During the 2008 Curtis Cup match she fulfilled a life-long ambition when she was able to enter the Royal and Ancient clubhouse for the first time to attend the Past Curtis Cup Players' Dinner.

Shona Malcolm, the CEO of the Ladies Golf Union, took the Curtis Cup to Mrs. Wylie's 100th birthday party which was held in the clubhouse of the Troon Ladies. "It was an honour to take it there and hear first hand her stories of the 1938 match and of spending time with the Curtis Cup sisters Harriet and Margaret," said Ms Malcolm. "Phyl was as sharp as a tack, always took a keen interest in ladies golf and was convinced that the modern player doesn't have as much fun as she and her generation had. She had a great *joie de vivre* and always had a spring in her step."

Another Curtis Cup player Moira Milton (*née* Paterson), who won the Ladies British Open Amateur Championship at the 38th hole against Frances "Bunty" Stephens in a record seven hour final at Troon in 1952 and who was a member of the Curtis Cup team later that year which beat the Americans 5–4 at Muirfield died at the age of 88.

Talented Roger Chapman has the time of his life – at last

Bill Elliott on the English pro for whom life began at 50

There is a difference between winning and losing and it is big. The other fact is that the lines of definition here can be ludicrously small – a gust of wind at precisely the wrong time, an indiscriminate divot scrape or a putt that perversely chooses to lip out rather than drop in.

On such tiny and unpredictable things are reputations made, fortunes won and careers illuminated. For some this winning thing seems to come easy, for others it can take half a lifetime to figure it out. Some hapless, albeit talented, figures never do come up with the answer or maybe the good luck.

Jack Nicklaus, arguably – but not much – the greatest 'winner' of all time, reflected on this curious state of affairs and came up with the thought that "people don't seem to realise how often you have to come in second in order to finish first ... I've never met a winner who hadn't learned how to be a loser". For the record, Jack finished second in fifty-five of what one may describe as reasonably significant tournaments. No-one ever lost better than him.

By which tortuous route do we arrive at the name of Roger Chapman. If anyone in the modern game knows the fine detail where 'losing' is concerned then it is this tall, modest, instinctively quiet and eternally nice bloke.

During a long career on the main European Tour, Roger played 618 events – including 17 Open Championships – and won once. This victory came in Brazil at a tournament that it would be wrong to describe as the professional equivalent to the monthly medal but truth is it wouldn't be hugely wrong to attach such a description. I mean this, of course, with deep respect.

Quite why this talented golfer failed to secure other more meaningful victories during his European Tour odyssey is hard to fathom.

As an amateur he showed huge promise, winning the English Amateur title in 1979, making the Walker Cup side two years later and underlining the quality of his game and much else besides when beating Hal Sutton twice in one day.

© Getty Images

England's Roger Chapman won only once on the European Tour in his long career but in a fairy tale 2012 he picked up not one but two major trophies on America's Champions Tour

When he turned professional there was no trumpet blast but there was a muttered expectation amongst those of us who follow the old game closely that here was a player to watch. Yet despite a flurry of birdie charges and usually at least one big chance a year to win he, and we, remained frustrated at his inability to turn charge in to victory.

With hindsight what he lacked was real self-belief. Too often during his 25 years on the circuit he secretly suspected he didn't deserve to be there at all. Now, suddenly, thrillingly, at 53 years old he knows that he was there as of right. Self-belief is no longer a problem. Winning the Senior PGA Championship and then the Senior United States Open has solved that very swiftly indeed.

At the Senior PGA he blitzed the field with a third round 64 to build a reassuring lead that barricaded him against any rising doubts on the final Sunday. Not many weeks later he demonstrated a new-found versatility coming from four strokes behind on that final day to win the Senior US Open. The fact that he was four behind Bernhard Langer – almost everyone's idea of the best senior in the world – eloquently underlines the scale of Chapman's achievements in the high summer of 2012.

Ask him what he thinks of this win-double and the word he chooses to describe it is 'surreal'. "It's sinking in slowly what I've done but to have people like Tom Lehman, Joey Sindelar and John Cook greeting me with 'morning champ' still seems weird. Wonderfully weird. It's all a bit surreal."

What is real, however, is the £565,000 he banked from these victories. This money for a man who not so long ago had to sell one of the family cars to fund his playing in a few tournaments is a big and very important bonus. When he stepped away from the main tour after 25 years of endeavour he still had a couple of years to wait before hitting the senior trail.

He needed to earn during this waiting period and so he qualified as a rules official and was taken on by the senior tour. He enjoyed his eighteen month stint, enjoyed still being involved in a scene he knew well, even liked the long, often tedious, hours spent sitting on a buggy waiting to fight a fire somewhere. What he didn't enjoy was occasionally refusing relief to an old friend especially if this old friend was Sam Torrance putting on his scary face.

"No, it wasn't easy telling mates that they were five minutes behind the clock. But, yes, I enjoyed being a rules guy even if I was glad to get back to playing as soon as I turned fifty."

Now here he is a few years later, a man nudging the wrong end of mid-life but also a man avoiding any chance of a crisis. "Winning those two senior majors has changed everything for me, for my wife Cathy, for the family. When I won the second of them my old mate Tony Johnstone asked if I'd got a new brain, one with self-belief this time. I know what he means.

"But where this all came from I still don't really know. I'm just glad it did. I had been working really hard with my coach Gavin Christie for two years and I felt freed up to play more aggressively. Mind you, I was still asking the late George Will for some divine help towards the end of those majors. I hope George was looking down. He was a terrific professional in his day and mentored me from the age of thirteen until he died in 2010."

Oh, and the first of those 17 Open Championships was in 1977 at Turnberry. He says he remembers looking out over the Ailsa course and wondering "what on earth am I doing here?"

Well, now he knows ... he was preparing for the time of his life. This, it turned out, came 35 years later. Funny old game, golf. Don't you think?

© Getty Images

Spain's Miguel Angel Jiménez is not a senior golfer yet but when he does turn 50 in January 2014 he could be a force to be reckoned with on the European Senior Tour. Why? – because he is still playing so well on the main Tour. At the end of last year, Miguel Angel became the oldest winner on the European Tour at age 48 years and 318 days when he scored his 19th career triumph with a third victory at the UBS Hong Kong Open at Fanling.

For modest Sir Bob actions speak louder than words

Greg Turner praises New Zealand's incomparable left-hander

It is given to few to achieve beyond the ordinary. It is given to even fewer to change what is perceived to be possible. To do this one must create and walk a path that has not been walked before. Sometimes the breakthrough is achieved with dogged determination; a focus and desire that trembles on the brink of madness; sometimes by a relaxed and precocious skill; seemingly without effort. When golf and Spain are mentioned in the same sentence, the name of Severiano Ballesteros comes to mind. The same could be said of golf in South Africa and Gary Player. For New Zealand, Sir Bob Charles occupies the same rarified air.

In a country that lives and breathes its sport, to be synonymous with any one sport is no mean feat. In NZ it has been more the hard, rugged rural men, whose uncompromising physicality remains dominant in world rugby, that influenced the rest of the world's perception of the little country down under (not forgetting a certain Sir Edmund Hillary of course).

It's difficult to imagine a professional athlete cut from a more different cloth than Sir Bob. His slight physique has changed little in the 50 years since he became the first Kiwi to hoist the Open's Claret Jug. And nor has his even temperament, understated manner; his statesman like aplomb. His relaxed approach; the elegance of his swing; the apparent ease and longevity of his excellence suggest a prodigious talent that has been nurtured through the years. But the prolonged stay of Sir Bob on the world stage has not been achieved without commensurate effort: even today his unmistakable left-handed form will often be found in the early or late hours on the practice ground near his home at Clearwater in Christchurch.

To overlook his self-discipline is to misunderstand the man.

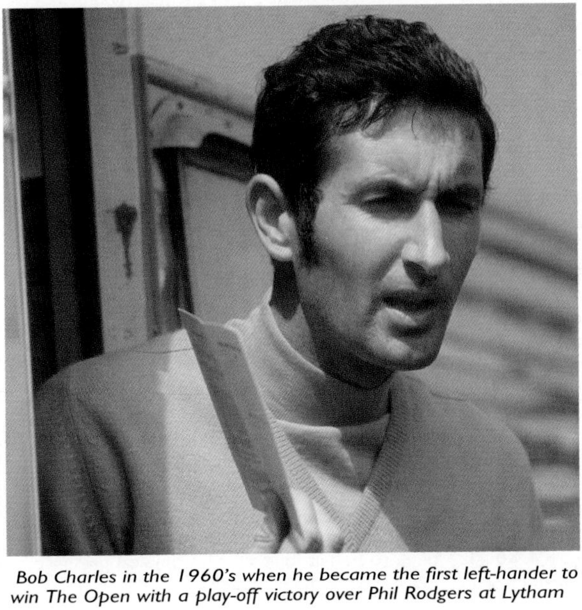

© Phil Sheldon Golf Picture Library

Bob Charles in the 1960's when he became the first left-hander to win The Open with a play-off victory over Phil Rodgers at Lytham

It would be fair to say that today's game bears little resemblance to that in which New Zealand's golfing knight plied his trade so admirably for so many years. The 1.62 inch diameter golf ball, persimmon headed woods and largely unirrigated fairways made for a game where guile and touch more often than not would trump raw power and athletic ability.

Sir Bob was quite rightly regarded as one of the finest putters of all time, in spite of playing through a period where the state of green surfaces rewarded a sharp tap as much as a smooth stroke. Goodness only knows how his smooth and metronomic stroke would have been regarded on today's billiard table like surfaces, but safe to say many a modern pro would move heaven and earth for such a nerveless technique.

Sir Robert James Charles today – still slim and fit, still one of the game's most talented approach putters and still enjoying his golf in New Zealand

I can well remember as a young pro being questioned by our greatest ever player as to the rationale behind my putting grip. I had been fortunate enough to have short-game guru Paul Runyon as a tutor and was employing a grip with hands opposed at 45 degrees rather than lightly on top of the shaft as was more normal at the time. I explained to Sir Bob that by having hands opposing meant that when nerves intervened over a short putt, any change in grip pressure wouldn't result in the putter face being affected. I can still recall his perplexed expression – the idea that one might feel nervous over a short putt was a concept he struggled to comprehend!

But it would be wrong to imply that his game was all about putting. His record really speaks for itself: six wins on the PGA Tour in America, four in Europe, eight in Australasia and over 20 on the Champion's Tour.

Clearly his victory in the Open Championship at Royal Lytham and St Annes (in 1963 in a play-off with, coincidentally, another short-game guru Phil Rodgers) stands out as the beacon, but a second playing in the US PGA (1968) and two thirds in the US Open (1964 and 1970) confirm he was a force to be reckoned with at the very top of the game).

And if for most mere mortals "breaking your age" is a feat rarely achieved, what would we say about Sir Bob doing so by a staggering 10 shots (66) at a recent event in Switzerland?

As for Sir Bob's impact on golf in NZ – it would be hard to overstate his influence. As the dominant Kiwi golfer for a fair portion of the 20th century, he won four national opens (including one as an amateur) and three NZ PGA titles.

He was also at the forefront of some of the country's first forays into the residential golf course market. The Millbrook Country Club (in New Zealand's tourist mecca of Queenstown) was the first resort/residential style development in the country and it has remained an outstanding success through the most trying of times economically. While the complex itself has since been extended to 27-holes and some modification has occurred, it is impossible not to recognize Sir Bob's influence (indeed he still owns a house alongside the course).

The Clearwater Golf Club, just outside Christchurch, is also influenced by Sir Bob and, perhaps fittingly, it currently plays host to both the NZ men's and women's Open Championships. The view from his current home is out over the links at Clearwater, across the wide and fertile Canterbury plains where he farms, to an horizon defined by the Southern Alps.

It would probably be fair to say his courses in some ways mirror his personality; solid and reliable rather than flashy or pretentious. And there is still a shirt style in NZ (in some ways aligned to what the rest of the world calls a polo shirt) which to many of the more senior generation will always be known as a Bob Charles shirt.

As the great knight approaches his eightieth year (he was born on the 14th of March, 1936), his playing career is winding down rather than coming to an end.

Some of us work hard at life because we want to be noticed, lauded and remembered. For professional athletes the baubles of fame are sometimes an essential motivation. Sir Bob goes about his business today as he has always done, his manner and demeanour largely unchanged from that of the quiet young bank teller who continued serving his customers for six years after sensationally winning his first New Zealand Open in 1954 at the age of 18.

A man of few words, Sir Bob has followed the maxim that actions speak louder. He has been a tireless worker for the game of golf, here in New Zealand and beyond. And fittingly he has provided support for many charitable causes, particularly underprivileged children.

For we New Zealanders, his influence will continue to be felt long after his physical presence no longer strolls the fairways.

The day I turned down Ben Hogan's offer of free lessons

Dan Jenkins remembers a golfing legend who won The Open 60 years ago

Since I wanted to become a golf writer anyhow, it was quite smart of me, don't you think, to get born and raised in Fort Worth, Texas, the same town as Ben Hogan? How else could I have done it? Grow up next door to Ky Laffoon in Zinc, Arkansas?

No, all in all, I think I went about it the right way. Take up the game at an early age. Learn to play it well enough not to get picked like a chicken by all the thieves that were around. Get a job right out of high school on the *Fort Worth Press*, one of the two daily newspapers in town. Go to college with a byline, which might make a youngster arrogant if he hadn't received proper training in the home. And get to know Ben Hogan.

I first met him at Colonial Country Club during his recovery from the bump in the road called a Greyhound bus, which had only given him a double-fractured pelvis, fractured collar bone, broken left ankle, three cracked ribs, a near-fatal blood clot, and a lifelong circulation problem in his legs. I'd watch him practice in that early fall of 1949, getting ready to make the greatest comeback in the history of sports in 1950.

I will admit I had an advantage over my golf writing competition, the guys on the other paper, who came and went. I could shoot almost the same thing as right around par, and none of them could break 110, or even 105, with a pencil and a loaded gun.

Over the entire decade of the 1950s, when Ben was at his peak, I played at least 40 recreational rounds with him. Sometimes nine holes, but more often 18. Sometimes just us, sometimes with two other club members he'd invite to join us.

Colonial was a tough old layout in those days, a real 280 golf course. It had hosted the 1941 U.S. Open. Confining, eaten up with rough, darkened by rows of overhanging trees, interwoven with the Trinity River.

The memory plays tricks on human being types, but I simply don't recall Ben ever shooting worse than a three-under 67 in all the rounds we played together.

One particular day back then has stayed with me like a haunting tune. It was a September day in 1956 when Ben insisted I be a member of his foursome at Colonial in an exhibition round for the benefit of the U.S. Olympic Fund. The Summer Olympics were coming up in November in Melbourne, Australia, and he'd been asked to help out the cause of the USA.

He had already lined up Ray Gafford, a terrific pro at another club in town, Royal Hogan, his brother, and a fine local amateur. When he called me at the paper to command my participation I asked if it was for comedy relief? He said no, I could hold my own, and I should have won the city championship a month earlier.

I agreed with that. I'd happened to have finished runnerup over the 72 holes to a player who didn't even live in the city. Which was why some wise guys at my paper crowned me Low Resident.

So I showed up for the exhibition after working half a day in the office. But little did I expect to find 4,000 paying customers lined up all the way down Colonial's first hole, a 565-yard par five.

Before the courses were roped off the fans walked shoulder to shoulder with Ben Hogan as he won his only Open at Carnoustie in 1953. Sadly, award winning writer Dan Jenkins missed the moment. The American press contingent comprised just one man and it wasn't him

I had nonchalantly arrived too late to hit any practice balls on the range, or even a putt.

Let me just say that seeing all those people and knowing I was going to be playing golf with Ben Hogan in front of them made me feel like I'd walked naked into church.

Prayer and muscle memory helped me hit a decent drive in the fairway on No. 1 without injuring myself or anyone around me. But next came the wretched part.

I cold-topped a 3-wood. I cold-stopped the 3-wood again. I cold-topped a 5-iron. What I wanted to do was dig a vast hole in the earth and disappear in it. I could only imagine the gallery remarks.

"Who's this jerk? ... Where'd they find this clown?"

It was when I was walking to my ball after the embarrassing, 50-yard, cold-topped 5-iron, that I realized Ben was walking beside me. And it was in that moment that he gave me the greatest golf tip I would ever receive in my whole life, under the conditions.

He said, "You can probably swing faster if you try hard enough."

I must have looked like I was swatting mosquitoes.

After the triple on the first hole I somehow managed to slow it down and get around in 77 while Ben shot his usual 67, and all ended well. There were even a few who shook my hand, as if I'd been a survivor of the *Titanic*.

Later that afternoon I sat in the Colonial grill room having a drink with Ben and his close friend Marvin Leonard, the man who built Colonial and had once loaned Hogan enough money to stay on the tour.

After some golf talk I heard Ben saying to Mr. Leonard, "He has length, you see, and he can putt."

I realized he was talking about me.

Then Ben turned to me.

He said, "Between the tee shot and the green, your golf game can use some help."

"I would be," I said, "the last person to argue with that."

He said, "If you will work with me three days a week for the next two or three months – and do everything I tell you to do – you could become good enough to compete in the National Amateur."

I was stunned. Ben Hogan was offering me free lessons. But I didn't want them.

I said, "Ben, that's very generous – and flattering. But, uh … I'm just a weekend golfer. I love the game, and I love a two-dollar Nassau as much as anybody, but … all I ever want to be is a good sportswriter."

He gave me the cold stare. I'd seen him give it to others. He looked like I'd run over his dog or dented his Cadillac. It seemed like a week passed before he spoke. Finally, he relaxed, leaned back, his expression lightening.

"Well," he said. "Keep working at it."

I can only say that is exactly what I've done – and still do.

Ben Hogan's Open victory at Carnoustie in 1953 was one of his greatest but his last major triumph

Ben Hogan, already the Masters champion in 1953 had decided – with the encouragement of wife Valerie and golfing friends – that he would travel to Britain to play for the first time in The Open whether or not he won the US Open that year.

In fact the 40-year-old, who had made a remarkable recovery from the near fatal crash he had when his car was hit in thick fog by a Greyhound bus, did win the US Championship for a fourth time. After all, he was playing some of the best golf of his illustrious career so there was added excitement in Scotland that Hogan might complete a hat-trick of major titles over Carnoustie one of the toughest – if not *the* toughest – of Open Championship venues.

With Hogan in the field that year's Open was extra special. Curt Samson in his book tells how the fans in Scotland loved him much more than he loved them because all the American's energy and intensity went into winning. Playing in very different conditions he felt the pressure more

He came to Scotland early, prepared meticulously, altered his swing to cope with the hard fairways and got to grips with greens much slower than those to which he was accustomed. Throughout his practice and during the Championship he was followed by thousands eager to catch a glimpse of the world's greatest golfer in action. Even Frank Sinatra, appearing in Dundee that week, went to the golf

The fairways were not roped off and The R&A ensured there was a bodyguard of policemen to protect him from the fans. The rest is history. He fired an opening 75, added a 71 and a 70 before finishing off with a 68 to win by four. His legendary status had been further enhanced and he returned home to a New York ticker-tape welcome down Broadway. What none of the cheering fans knew, however, was that Hogan, christened by the Scots "the wee ice mon" because of his temperament on course, would never win another major.

So many talented players still chasing a first major

James Corrigan on the potential challengers to Tiger

Another major Sunday, another major champion. It was possible to field a rugby union team – as well as a replacement – from the winners from the 2008 US PGA Championship to the 2012 US PGA.

From one (Padraig Harrington) to 16 (Ernie Els) there was a run of 16 different victors and, when the streak ended at the US PGA Championship at Kiawah Island, it did so because of a 23-year-old – Rory McIlroy. So much for experience being crucial. "Not been there, haven't done that", is rapidly becoming the buzz-phrase down golf's toughest stretches.

But surely the conveyor belt is running out of variety? By now, everyone who should have won a major has won a major, right? Wrong.

Consider that when the 2012 season ended, six of the world's top 10 had yet to break their major duck and you will appreciate that this trend could run and run. And the demographic of these should-be wannabes will make an extension to that major roll-of-honour board seem even more necessary.

Lee Westwood turns 40 after the Masters and is by far of the oldest of that sextet without the silverware which counts. He can be placed in a category along with his fellow Englishman Luke Donald. Let us generously call it the "Time Is Of The Essence" category. Donald is "only" 35 but he appears to be in his prime. His moment is now … this year.

Then there is Justin Rose and Adam Scott in the "Grab It While You Can" category. The pair are in their early 30's but have been around for so long that they will begin 2013 determined to end the waiting and delete that damned word "potential" from their respective CVs.

They are actually the same age as Brandt Snedeker, but the FedEx Cup champion from Nashville surely belongs in a separate category, along with Jason Dufner. How about the "Yes, We Can" category? They will have been inspired by the major-winning deeds of Lucas Glover and Stewart Cink. If the last half decade has told us anything it is that anyone up there in the rankings has a golden shot at immortality. And that is only the top 10.

In the top 50 there happen to be 35 players who have yet to win a major. They are populated by those who belong in each of the aforementioned categories, from Ian Poulter (with Donald and Westwood) to Sergio García (with Rose and Scott) to Nick Watney (with Snedeker and Dufner).

© Getty Images

US-based Justin Rose, seen here with the WGC Cadillac Trophy he won in 2012, is just one of number of European golfers with the ability and desire to win a major title

Yet we have yet to mention another very important category. It features youngsters such as Rickie Fowler and Matteo Manassero and forms "The Heirs of Tiger" category.

As ever, to golf's narrative, Mr Woods is all-important. The last time the game watched such a long procession of its first-time major-winners march down its most celebrated fairways was 1994–98.

The theories abound why this should be. The one constant in the debate was the barren run of Woods. For a period which took in the last major of 1999 and the first two of 2008, Woods won more than a third of the majors. Obviously his downfall was a big reason for the run of 16. But Paul Azinger believes the Woods factor is vital on another level.

"The generation which watched Tiger recognised they would have to beat him to be champions", says the 2008 Ryder Cup captain, "and it's like they've gone to another place mentally. If you were 14 years old watching Tiger, you're 28–29 now. And if you look at McIlroy winning twice, Keegan Bradley winning the 2011 US PGA, Charl Schwartzel winning the 2011 Masters and Webb Simpson winning at the 2012 US Open, these are young men. They were the generation who Tiger inspired."

Azinger's argument is essentially that because of Woods' example the newcomers are better prepared than they ever have been; not just between the ropes, but more so between the ears.

"You can tell that the concentration levels of a Rory, a Webb or a Keegan are a notch above where the players once were," says Azinger, who won the 1993 US PGA. "They embraced what Tiger did with the mind and because of it when they get into position themselves they are ready to stand the heat."

Nine of the last 11 major-winners have all been first-timers and, in many regards, that is more staggering than the statistic of different winners.

"Tiger's slip has opened the door for a lot of guys," says Azinger. "But there's more to it than that. This bunch would think they could win whatever Tiger is doing. There was the mindset a few years ago that it didn't matter how well you played Tiger was going to play better. He was so fit, he hit it so far and mentally they couldn't get in there, whatever 'there' was.

"This generation look at Tiger and think they are just as disciplined and work just as hard as Tiger. In this regard, Woods may be a victim of his own greatness. He set the bar so high and those coming along eventually rose to that standard."

These are wise words from Azinger and should help to bash down the misconception that golf is somehow weaker for its vast array of potential major champions. It is a strength, not a weakness.

While punters walk into bookmakers before Wimbledon knowing it will be one of three – or, with Andy Murray, four – they cannot be so nearly purposeful when it comes to The Open. One of 50 winners wouldn't be an exaggeration of the possibilities. The hows and whys can be debated all day but central to the argument is that in golf there are delicious invariables which not even Woods at his zenith could entirely conquer.

Weather conditions, the draw, sport's most uneven playing surfaces which makes luck such an influence on the result. Like it or lump it, that's golf. For those of us who will continue to love it this is such an intriguing major age in which we live. The majors have never seemed so attainable. Yet they have also never seemed so richly deserved.

Onward march the virgin golfers.

Tiger Woods raised the bar but the new breed of golfers raised their games and no longer fear him the way they once did

Francis Ouimet was first on the overseas list of R and A Captains

Renton Laidlaw on an exclusive club at the home of golf

When Frenchman Pierre Bechmann, as history demands, stepped on to the first tee at the Old course, St Andrews on a crisp autumn morning to drive himself into his year-long captaincy of the Royal and Ancient Golf Club of St Andrews he was writing another chapter in the long and impressive history of the club.

M. Bechmann, a member of the Paris Bar, is the first golfer from Continental Europe to hold the post and in doing so he joined a very exclusive club comprising just seven other notables – three Americans, an Irishman, a New Zealander, an Australian and a South African. The golfing eightsome are the only Captains in the 259 years history of the most famous golf club in the world who have not been British citizens.

The club was founded in 1754 but it was not until almost two centuries later in 1951 that a non-British Captain was elected by the committee of former Captains charged each year with finding the best man to act as the club's global golfing ambassador.

The man chosen to Captain the club in 1951 was American Francis Ouimet whose credentials were impeccable. Back in 1913 at The Country Club in Brookline Ouimet, a 20-year-old former caddie who lived across from the course, did what was considered the impossible, the unthinkable, the down-right amazing. In a play-off for the US Open title, the young American with his pint-sized 10-year-old caddie Eddie Lowery carrying his bag, saw off two giants of the game – four times Open champion Harry Vardon and the then reigning Open champion Ted Ray.

A year later, Ouimet won the US Amateur and might have won a few more had he not been banned from playing amateur golf by the USGA because he had opened a sports shop – a committee decision so unfair that it was later rescinded. He was eligable, therefore, to play in the first Walker Cup match in 1922 and in seven more. His ability as a golfer was further enhanced when 17 years after his first US Amateur success he won the title again in 1931.

The massive impact he had on the game in America which started with his unlikely but deserved victory at The Country Club earned Ouimet the sobriquet "The Father of American golf". It was a well deserved accolade because the game boomed between his magical year 1913 when it was estimated there were 350,000 players and 1923 when the total had grown to over two million.

Ouimet always loved the course on which he first made not just the sports but the main news headlines with the "David beats Goliath" win that captured everyone's imagination. When in 1963 the US Open returned to The Country Club for the 50th anniversary celebrations, Ouimet admitted that as far as he was concerned the sun shone always brighter on The Country Club than in any other place he had ever known.

Ouimet was an inspired choice as Captain of the Royal and Ancient Golf Club of St Andrews as was the second of the three Americans who have held the honour. Joseph C. (Joe) Dey, who has every claim to be considered the most influential adminis-

Pierre Bechmann gives the gold sovereign to the caddy who returned his ball after he drove into office last September

trator in the history of the game, was involved at the highest level in both the amateur and the professional codes. Not surprisingly he became known as "Mr Golf" at the United States Golf Association where he was executive director from 1934 to 1969 before taking on a new challenge as the first commissioner of the newly independent PGA Tour.

As a staunch guardian of the traditions of the game, he was responsible for the all-important unification of the rules of golf so that the USGA and The R&A were operating as one. Grant Spaeth, the president of the USGA at the time of Joe Dey's death in 1991, described him as "the overpowering force in golf over four decades." His appointment as the Captain of the Royal and Ancient Golf Club of St Andrews had given him particular pleasure.

When Stanley Melbourne Bruce, later Lord Melbourne, became the first Commonwealth Captain of the club in 1954 he, too, was delighted. The captaincy, along with his Rowing Blue at Cambridge and the honour of a Fellowship of the Royal Society, gave him the most pleasure in his exceptionally impressive life.

Born in Melbourne, he was always a keen sportsman. While attending Melbourne Grammar School he had captained the rowing, football, athletics and cricket teams but he would spend much of his adult life in London.

Lord Melbourne was a statesman in every sense of the word. He was the 9th Prime Minister of Australia and, at the age of 39, the second youngest. It was during his term of office that the Australian capital Canberra was completed and parliament was transferred from Melbourne to what is now known as the Australian Capital Territory. Later he served for 12 years as the Australian High Commissioner in London and was a member of the British War Cabinet.

A unique double

The third of the Americans to be honoured by being named Captain of the club was the distinguished West Virginian William C. (Bill) Campbell who never ever aspired to turning professional. He is a gentleman golfer who played the game happily as an amateur while running his insurance business. It was once said that he was a professional at being an amateur!

Campbell, who played in many Amateur Championships in Britain, competed in 33 consecutive US Amateurs between 1941 and 1977 and it was a surprise that he did not win it until 1964 when he was 41. His record in the Walker Cup was impressive too. A modest but always determined competitor he played in seven matches between 1951 and 1975 and never lost a single. Only Scotland's Ian Hutcheon from Monifieth managed to hold him to a halved game.

He remains the only golfer to have completed the unique double of having captained the Royal and Ancient and been President of the USGA. When he began his year in office at St Andrews Campbell, who like Ouimet and Dey has been elected to the World Golf Hall of Fame, stated his conception of the game in typically eloquent fashion:

"Golf is a game of relationships, dignity and self respect," he said. "It is an honourable game and an honourable institution – so that the people playing the game shouldn't need policemen to keep them straight. That goes with being a golfer."

Irrepressible Joe Carr

The only golfer from Southern Ireland to be honoured with the captaincy was another career amateur – the irrepressible Joe Carr. Winner of three Irish Amateur Championships and four British titles – he might have won more had Michael Bonallack not been around at the same time – Carr was a member of ten Walker Cup teams and memorably captained the Great Britain and Ireland side which won the Eisenhower Trophy at Olgiata in Rome in 1964. He twice led the GB and I side in the Walker Cup including the famous draw at Five Farms in 1965.

With his extrovert personality he was a perfect ambassador for golf. He was the first non American to win the Bob Jones award for distinguished sportsmanship, collected the Hagen Trophy for his contribution to Anglo-American goodwill and became the first Irishman to play in The Masters at Augusta.

The Championship victory that gave him most pleasure was his 1958 success in the final against Englishman Alan Thirlwell. He would have been devastated had he not been victorious because he had practised strenuously in the months leading up to the Championship – running early in the morning, practising sometimes under floodlights at night and putting on the bedroom carpet before retiring for the night.

When he died in 2004, Michael Bonallack summed up Carr's tremendous career by saying: "I have been fortunate to have played golf in the Joe Carr era. I still have to meet a finer sportsman."

More recently the late Harvey Douglas, who worked tirelessly in his own country for the game, became the first South African Captain of the club and Rt. Hon. Justice T. M. Gault DCNZM, a judge of the New Zealand Supreme Court became the second golfer from "Down Under" to be honoured. A member of Her Majesty's Privy Council, he was President of the New Zealand Golf Association from 1987 to 1996.

Now Pierre Bechmann, who lives in the delightful suburb of Chantilly just outside Paris, has joined the exclusive Captains' club. For 12 months he will be the club's global ambassador undertaking an enjoyable but demanding role. Being Captain of the Royal and Ancient Golf Club of St Andrews may be time-consuming and probably expensive but is hugely rewarding in every sense.

Augusta National – an honest test of golfing skill and nerve

Ken Brown and his love affair with the Masters Tournament

I turned off the Bobby Jones Freeway onto Washington Drive in Augusta and nothing seemed special or unusual. Surrounded by traffic lights, eating houses, the Outback Steakhouse, Hooters, Taco Bell and Famous Dave's, I could have been anywhere in the USA. A billboard outside saying "Plenty of room for all God's creatures right next to the mashed potatoes" made me smile. I kept my speed down as I knew I was approaching my destination and it was easy to miss Magnolia Lane. I managed not to drive by and turned my White Buick Impala rental car into the drive only to stop immediately as the uniformed guard stepped out of his white century box. "Can I see your credentials, please Sir?" I had a problem.

It was 1985 and at the time I was playing in America on the PGA Tour. We had just finished playing in Greensboro and Augusta National was set to host The Masters in a matter of days. I was not one of the lucky few to receive an invite that year and had the week off but a visit on my way to Hilton Head wasn't much of a detour so I thought I'd try my luck. My only problem was not having a entry pass to the Magic Kingdom.

Enticingly, I was looking straight down the lane so without saying a word and looking confident I lowered the car window and flashed my PGA Tour member's money clip in hope. "Straight on Sir", he said and like a child who had been promised a one on one with Mickey Mouse I set off into the grounds!

As I drove up Magnolia Lane the sunlight was dappled as it passed through the canopy of aged magnolias and at the end of this leafy tunnel was the shining light of the clubhouse. Making sure I kept my speed up so I wouldn't get stopped, I drove up next to the practice range and parked behind the grandstand. One of the many things Augusta do very well is security so I was anxious to see what I could do before getting a tap on the shoulder from a Pinkerton guard.

The white feather board clubhouse looked smart but not in any way flash; no bling to be seen. I slipped down the alley between the Pro shop and the players' bag room and there it was, the view I'd seen on TV many times. It always looked wonderful on TV but the reality was much, much better. In front of me was a sea of green, pine trees, a glimpse

Photo by Rob Brown

The par 3 12th hole at Augusta. The beauty of the National Club's course, a lasting memorial to club founder Bobby Jones, impresses everyone who goes there but it still provides a demanding challenge each year for the game's top players as they gather for the first major of the year – the Masters

of the yellow pin at the 9th and the whole scene smothered in patrons gliding across the turf.

I had arrived in the promised land and was standing outside the clubhouse looking down on golf's Shangri-La with no pass. It was the start of a long-standing and one-sided love affair.

Around Christmas two years later, the postman delivered a card with a green border – a ticket, not a patron's pass but one that cordially invited me to play in the Masters.

"Fore Please, Ken Brown now driving" was going to be heard on the first tee. I decided to prepare by playing a couple of practice rounds the week before the tournament as I had learned from watching on TV that it was going to take more time than most courses to get to know. I took one of the local caddies to get some help discovering how to play each hole and where the pins might be placed during the week.

The course was mesmerizing; it looked stunning in a way that no high definition television could ever capture. For me though, the true appeal of Augusta National was its unique challenge. The only other course I have played that gave me the same buzz was the Old Course at St Andrews.

Bobby Jones and Alister Mackenzie, the designers of Augusta, both admired St Andrews and tried to take its DNA over to Georgia. Both courses have wide fairways that give players options and with a variety of different shots available it becomes the player's responsibility to choose wisely. It engaged your mind and truly taxed your playing skills. Each hole can be tackled with a variety of strategies and the most effective can depend on the pin position, playing conditions and your personal strengths. It really captivated me, as Augusta National was a course that had heart and soul.

In 1988, I arrived to a slightly different course to the one I had seen before. Since my first visit the green staff had perfected the preparation of the relatively new bent grass greens in their relentless quest for quicker greens. They were firm and ultra fast and putting well on them required skill and nerve and I absolutely loved it!

On the Tuesday night, the club held the overseas invitees' dinner in the clubhouse with delicious food and wonderful company. That year there were 18 players from outside the United States and just six European players – two past champions, Seve Ballesteros and Bernhard Langer; the others being Nick Faldo, Ian Woosnam, Sandy Lyle and myself. It was very tough for international players to get a Masters invitation back then.

My only sadness was, although I played all four rounds, I finished outside the top 25 meaning I had no automatic place in the field the following year. I never made it back as a player, which was a huge disappointment. It would have been fabulous to put into practice all that had I had learnt from my rookie attempt. Of the six European players that played in 1988 five now have Green Jackets!

We can all dream … one of my dreams came true.

Augusta National Golf Club has the smartest venue of all sports and is run like a Swiss watch by its members. The Masters reigns supreme as the best event in the sporting calendar.

It looked bleak for Bubba until he produced his miracle winner

It was the shot of the year. From deep in the pines at the 10th – the second extra hole – at Augusta American left-hander Bubba Watson hooked a recovery shot with a wedge 40 yards on to the green and then two-putted to beat stunned South African Louis Oosthuizen who had earlier scored a first albatross 2 at the par 5 second on the final day. With his win Watson, who is virtually self-taught, became the third left hander to win the Masters. Canadian Mike Weir's win in 2003 and three victories by Phil Mickelson in 2004, 2006 and 2010 mean that five of the last ten winners of the Green Jacket have been left-handers.

Merion makes a wonderful comeback to US Open golf

Art Spander writes about the course they could not forget

Merion Golf Club, a course of history, and mystery, having been featured in a detective novel. It was where Bobby Jones attained his Slam, Ben Hogan made his marvellous comeback and Jack Nicklaus knew triumph as an amateur, and, relatively speaking, tragedy as a professional.

Miniscule by modern standards, Merion ranks large in accounts of the game. It has been the site of a record 18 USGA Championships and this summer is hosting an Open few believed could be held there again because of the property's size, or rather lack of it

Yet this is what Nicklaus said of a course laid out on just 125 acres: "Acre for acre it may be the best test of golf in the world."

Famous for the wicker baskets which top the pins in place of flags and for gleaming sand in upsweeping bunkers, Merion is located in Ardmore, Pennsylvania, the Main Line suburb of Philadelphia. It consists of two courses, the East, site of the US Open, and a mile away, the West, where the practice range and media centre will be for this year's Championship.

The first golf arrived at Merion in the early 1900s on a site where cricket and tennis were the primary forms of recreation and competition. Then Hugh Wilson, a Merion member who was born in Scotland and played golf for Princeton University in New Jersey, was chosen to create a new course. Never having designed one previously, Wilson, only 32, went about the task with considerable care and determination.

He returned across the Atlantic and spent seven months studying courses in England and Scotland, borrowing ideas and bringing back with him those wicker baskets, which came from Sunningdale outside London.

The East Course opened in 1912, and the layout that had been there originally was closed. The West, also built to a Wilson plan, opened in 1914.

A US Amateur held there a mere two years later was won by Chick Evans but is no less significant for the fact Bobby Jones, aged 14, was a tournament entrant for the first time. Indeed Jones would get his first Amateur victory when the event returned to Merion in 1924 – the year that Evans christened the bunkers "the white faces of Merion".

Yet Jones' and Merion's most memorable Amateur was the Championship staged in 1930. At the par-4 11th, "Baffling Brook", Eugene Homan's concession gave Jones an 8 and 7 win to complete the sweep of that year's four majors – The Open and the Amateur Championship in Britain and the US Open and US Amateur – a feat never to be equalled.

Courtesy and copyright of the USGA

Merion Golf Club was where Bobby Jones completed his Grand Slam in 1930 winning the Amateur and Open titles in both Britain and America. There is delight that it is back on the US Open Championship rota

Jack Nicklaus, seen here with his Congressional Medal of Honour which will be presented each year to the winner of the US Open, was in too many of Merion's bunkers and lost the title in 1971 to Lee Trevino

The Atlanta sports writer O. B. Keeler, borrowing from the card game bridge, called it a "Grand Slam". And so it is still known although using The Masters, The US PGA, the US Open and The Open today.

Olin Dutra, a pro from California, was the winner when the first US Open was played at Merion in 1934. The next Open, 1950, was the Open of Ben Hogan, the Open of the 1 iron that may have been a 2 iron, the Open of Lloyd Mangrum blowing away an insect and getting called.

Hogan had survived the near-fatal bus crash in the Texas fog in February 1949, incurring broken bones and needing veins to be tied to avoid blood clots reaching his heart. Eleven months later he tied Sam Snead for first in the Los Angeles Open but the format of the US Open, until 1965, was for a 36-hole finish on Saturday, and Hogan had had trouble walking 18 holes much less 36.

On that Saturday in 1950, Hogan was 200 yards from the green at the 72nd hole and the shot he played was recorded for immortality by the great photographer Hy Peskin, who had been allowed to stand behind Hogan. The record said it was a 1 iron but years later, in his book *Five Lessons: The Modern Fundamentals of Golf* with the great Herbert Warren Wind, Hogan claimed it was a 2 iron.

Whatever, he two-putted for a par and the next day faced Lloyd Mangrum and George Fazio in an 18-hole playoff, best remembered for Mangrum picking up his ball from the 16th green, puffing away a bug and, in a rule since changed, being nailed two shots. Hogan won by four.

Jack Nicklaus, a 20-year-old Ohio State University student at the time, won the 1960 World Amateur at Merion by 13 strokes with an amazing 11-under-par winning total of 269 but when the course held it's next Open, in 1971, Nicklaus was, in effect "snake-bitten" although not literally.

At the first tee of their 18-hole playoff for the title, Lee Trevino pulled a toy, rubber snake from his golf bag and tossed it at Jack, drawing laughter from the crowd but not from Jack.

Nicklaus proceeded to leave balls in those bunkers with white faces. He was simply unable to escape bunkers over the opening holes, and lost the Championship trophy to Trevino, who summed up Merion's challenge beautifully: "Merion might have 16 birdie holes, but it has 18 bogey holes too".

Merion also has a spot in Harlen Coben's novel *Back Spin* in which the son of the golfer leading a US Open at the course which Coben had visited, is kidnapped during the tournament.

Ian Fleming would have been proud. He used his club, Royal St George's in Kent, as the model for the fictional course in his James Bond adventure *Goldfinger*.

It wasn't Bobby Cruickshank's finger that was an issue in the 1934 Open – it was his head! Leading by two strokes on the final day after 10 holes, Cruickshank mis-hit his approach to the 11th, the hole where Jones had clinched the Grand Slam four years earlier.

Cruickshank's ball headed for the creek, but it hit a rock and bounced onto the green. Elated, Cruickshank hurled his club skyward, then staggered when it fell straight back down and conked him on the skull. He parred the hole but then made several bogies and lost by two shots.

The last US Open held at Merion in 1981 was won by the Australian David Graham who now lives in Montana. It was presumed that this would be the last time the course would play host to the national Championship because the game has become so much more commercial, and major tournaments these days require extra space for corporate and merchandise tents.

The 2013 US Open will have all those tents, on neighbouring front yards and the lawns of the adjacent Haverford College. Contrary to the golfing adage it will not be by how many but simply how the USGA solved a tricky problem of logistics and managed to keep Merion on the rota,

Happily they found a way.

Fifteen holes fine-tuned to stiffen Muirfield's challenge

Michael Aitken about a venue which is a test of driving precision

Even a cursory glance over the list of past winners at Muirfield since 1959 says much about the quality of golfers able to thrive on what is universally regarded as the fairest of all The Open Championship links. If you were looking for a collective noun to encompass the names of Gary Player, Jack Nicklaus, Lee Trevino, Tom Watson, Nick Faldo and Ernie Els, perhaps only a pride of champions may suffice.

Yet the consistent visage of the champions identified in East Lothian since the 19th century has been mirrored by the changing face of the links itself. When The Open was first held at Muirfield in 1892, only a matter of months after it was built by Old Tom Morris and David Plenderleith the previous year, the links was greeted with neither instant nor universal acclaim. Indeed, so severe was some of the early criticism, the course had been extended by 600 yards when Harry Vardon won the next Championship held there four years later.

More alterations followed in the 20th century after Muirfield was stretched to 6,425 yards for The Open of 1912. Even at this stage, the links was yet to acquire the classic status of one of the game's great seaside courses. So, in 1923, the Honourable Company of Edinburgh Golfers acquired 50 acres of additional land and Harry Colt was enlisted to lay out 14 new holes. Until now, there have been three versions of Muirfield: the original in 1891, the revised version of 1920 and Colt's re-working of 1928 which included a ninth hole that returns to the clubhouse.

In 2002 Muirfield, which has hosted 42 national and international tournaments with only St Andrews and Prestwick staging the oldest major more often – measured 7034 yards and played to a par of 71 but for its 16th Open in July – the course has been increased in length to 7,245 yards.

As for the challenge facing the world's best golfers in East Lothian this summer, no fewer than 15 holes have been tweaked or fine-tuned since Els lifted the Claret Jug 11 years ago. In the first significant overhaul of the links since Colt and Tom Simpson (whose name became attached to a famous bunker on the ninth) were involved nearly a century ago, The R&A brought in architect Martin Hawtree, designer of Donald Trump's course at Balmedie, to oversee changes designed to keep Muirfield relevant in the modern era.

As part of a £5 million programme to tighten and toughen all nine of the links which constitute the unofficial rota of courses that host The Open Championship – "the treatment" as it's become known – Muirfield underwent the subtlest of makeovers. Inevitably a balance had to be struck between preserving the integrity of such an historic layout and ensuring the test remains robust enough to challenge the game's élite.

© The R&A

The Muirfield course of he Honourable Company of Edinburgh Golfers is considered by most students of the game to be the fairest of all The Open Championship venues

Blessed with relatively flat fairways for a links and clear views of greens and hazards, Muirfield is always praised as the least quirky of all the courses used these days for The Open. Since you don't draw a moustache on the face of the Mona Lisa, the changes carried out for the return of this year's Championship are refined rather than obvious.

Alastair Brown, the secretary of the Honourable Company, explained how half-a-dozen holes, the second, fourth, ninth, 15th, 17th and 18th, all have new championship tees with the overall length of the links stretched by just over 200 yards. Moreover, on top of additional bunkering, there has been work undertaken around many of the greens to add fresh undulations and fringes. Some green areas originally designed by Colt were reclaimed and additional pin positions are now possible on the second, sixth, 10th and 11th holes. And the tenth, one of Nicklaus' favourites, has moved around 15 yards to the left. The overall impact of these nips and tucks has been to tighten up the drive areas as well as the approach shots into the greens.

Subtle changes

Ranked by *Golf Monthly* in 2012 as the No 1 course in Great Britain and Ireland – "a superbly crafted test of golf that asks you to hit every shot in the book" according to the magazine – Muirfield will, in all likelihood, set a more demanding exam paper in July than it did during 2002. Brown describes the work undertaken on the course during the intervening years as "very subtle". While the reviews undertaken in recent years by The R&A at Carnoustie and Birkdale, for example, involved significant re-modelling of certain holes, it was testimony to the enduring quality of Muirfield's lay-out that so many of the changes have been unobtrusive. Peter Dawson, Chief Executive of The R&A, agrees. "Apart from the ninth, you would never notice the changes had actually been done."

The story behind the new tee on the ninth, which adds 50 yards to one of Muirfield's legendary holes, is an intriguing one since it involved an exchange of land between the Honourable Company and their neighbours at the Renaissance Club. In exchange for a small parcel of land which allowed Muirfield to extend the ninth tee to the east, the Honourable Company gave away sufficient land in the dunes to enable the Renaissance, under the guidance of designer Tom Doak, to build three new eye-catching holes.

Brown confirmed the principle question asked by The R&A and the Honourable Company when it came to refreshing Muirfield for The Open was simple: will the links still challenge the best players? On the ninth, which played as a 508 yard par 5 in 2002, it was clear the hole had become something less of a puzzle for the world's finest. Notwithstanding the out-of-bounds wall on the left and Simpson's bunker, the ninth was the easiest hole on the course 11 years ago with a stroke average of 4.56. Now it measures 558 yards and features new bunkering. "Last time, the players could hit two iron shots and still reach the green," recalled Brown. "Now they will need a wood in their hands at some point."

As a test of golf, Muirfield always required players to remain vigilant. Set out in two loops of nine holes, the first running clockwise and the second largely anti-clockwise, golfers must tackle the sea breezes gusting in all directions. Whatever the cumulative effect of the changes overseen by Hawtree, one thing which will never alter here is the emphasis on shot-making. A framed cartoon once hung in the clubhouse that proclaimed 'Muirfield welcomes careful drivers'. The joke, which dates back to the 1966 Open, was accurate as well as wry. Just think of Sergio García at the 1998 Amateur Championship or Els, Watson, Nicklaus,Trevino, Player and Henry Cotton in the Opens held over Muirfield since 1948. All were shrewd off the tee. A test of precision rather than sledgehammer force, Muirfield also rewarded Nick Faldo with a brace of Claret Jugs in 1987 and 1992. "In terms of shot values, variety, intricacy and overall strength of the test, Muirfield is out there on its own," enthuses the six-time major winner.

Great champions

As always, though, with any outstanding seaside layout, the elements will play an influential role in dictating the scores of the game's élite. After all, who could forget the brutal weather which swept across the links from the Firth of Forth during the third round of The Open in 2002 when Tiger Woods' dream of winning the Grand Slam was swept away? Woods used 12 gloves that day, reaching for a 5-iron to hit the ball a meagre 135 yards on the third hole before eventually signing for an 8. Nevertheless, Tiger was impressed. "It's one of the fairest Open courses", he said. "There are no hidden agendas, no tricks."

In essence, Woods was echoing the view of the late American golf writer, Herbert Warren Wind, who argued Muirfield's outstanding characteristic was its frankness. Nicklaus, who first crossed swords with the links on May 16, 1959 at the Walker Cup, dismantling Dick Smith by 5 and 4, discovered there that major Championship golf is no blunt instrument. When Jack won The Open at Muirfield for the first time in 1966, he only used his driver 17 times in 72 holes and enjoyed a Damascene moment of revelation which informed the rest of his career. "I was struck," he recalled, "by how much more precision counts in golf than power."

A nail-biting Oak Hill finish but Jack Nicklaus was happy

Tim Rosaforte visits one of America's great major venues

The 1980 PGA Championship at Oak Hill CC was the first of 120 major championships I've covered, and as a 25-year-old golf writer for the *St. Petersburg Times* in Florida I thought I'd seen it all. Here was the legendary Jack Nicklaus, at the seemingly old age of 40, recording a seven-stroke victory over Andy Bean, in what was his 17th career major and his second that summer following the US Open at Baltusrol. While not an exciting conclusion, the win also made amends for a US Open loss to Lee Trevino at Oak Hill in 1968. "I guess it might have looked like a dull day to most people, but it wasn't to me," Nicklaus said. It certainly wasn't to me, either, nor have any of my visits to one of the great golfing datelines in the world, Pittsford, NY.

Oak Hill is one of those sweet spots where you take a small upstate New York market town like Rochester, give the town a major championship or a Ryder Cup, and "they come out of the woodwork," as head professional Craig Harmon likes to say. Harmon, the second oldest of four golfing brothers born to former Masters champion Claude Harmon, has been monitoring events at his club for 40 years, and speaks to the level of community support first hand, noting corporate hospitality was 95 percent sold out a year prior to this August's US PGA. "This is quite a golfing town so to speak," Harmon says. "Everybody is totally jacked up. The people are stimulated about golf. It's their pride and joy."

Harmon started at Oak Hill in 1972, four years after Trevino shot four rounds in the sixties and set an Open record (275) in beating Nicklaus by four strokes for his first professional win. By the time Harmon came up from Winged Foot, where he served as an apprentice to his father, the great Claude Harmon, the Oak Hill membership had already voted to bring in George and Tom Fazio for major renovations. The members wanted "intimidating holes that offered the threat of a double bogey."

What a virtual unknown like Trevino did in '68 was considered sacrilege – just as some consider it sacrilege that the original work of Donald Ross was recast by Robert Trent Jones prior to the club's first major, the 1956 US Open. Jones was a Rochester native who followed Ross around Oak Hill during its construction in the early 1920s and put his imprint on 17 holes. Dr. Cary Middlecoff won that Open by beating Ben Hogan and Julius Boros by a shot. Hogan, who missed a 28-inch putt on the 71st hole that would have forced a 36-hole playoff, certainly thought Jones' work was effective. "I would hate to have to go back out there tomorrow," he said.

Pittsford NY – an ordinary enough dateline for a famous golf club – Oak Hill where Rory McIlroy will defend the US PGA Championship title he won by eight shots last year

© Getty Images

Curtis Strange became only the fifth golfer to successfully defend the US Open title at Oak Hill in 1989 the year four players, all using a 7-iron, holed in one at the short sixth in the second round

What spawned from the Fazio's work before the 1980 US PGA Open was what Tom Weiskopf called "The Classic Golf Course Preservation Society", whereby "members get to carry loaded guns in case they see anybody touching a Donald Ross golf course," and was the theme leading up to the 1989 US Open. Nicklaus was the only player to break par in '80 and nobody finished under 280 during the 1984 US Senior Open won by Miller Barber at six over by two strokes over Arnold Palmer. But rains softened the course and Curtis Strange responded by tying Hogan's course record 64 during the second round for the 36-hole lead.

The ending of the tournament is best remembered for the collapse of third-round leader Tom Kite, who shot three straight rounds in the 60s and had a three-stroke lead playing the par-4 fifth hole, one of those redesigned by the Fazios. A watered tee ball led to a triple bogey and a final-round 78 that turned Kite into a saddened loser. "You don't forget something like this," Kite said in front of his locker. "I'll never forget it."

But what most won't forget were Strange's opening words upon entering the press tent after becoming the 16th man to win two Opens and only the fifth to win back-to-back. When Strange said, "Move over Ben," he was making reference to the back-to-back Open titles won by Hogan in 1950–1951. Some observers believe it led to a curse that hangs over Strange, who has not won since and who lost a pivotal singles match to Nick Faldo in the 1995 Ryder Cup at Oak Hill.

Eight years after Strange's triumph in 1989 the US PGA Championship returned to Oak Hill as part of a contract that included the Ryder Cup. This one lacked the star power of previous majors at the course but was not short on drama. Tiger Woods, going through a swing change, may have finished tied 39th and Phil Mickelson 23rd when trying to win his first major – he would win the 2004 Masters the following year – but less well known golfers Shaun Micheel and Chad Campbell made it memorable.

Tied for the lead on the 72nd hole, Micheel nearly holed a 7-iron from 175 yards to beat Campbell and win for the first and only time in his career. Oak Hill certainly handled the test of modern equipment, with only four players, including Tim Clark and Alex Cejka breaking par for the week. The only long hitter in the top-10 that included Loren Roberts, Fred Funk, Billy Andrade and Mike Weir was Ernie Els, who finished in a tie for fifth place.

There were no major revisions made by Tom Fazio prior to the 95th PGA. Based on the scores Oak Hill didn't need a re-do even though the game has changed so dramatically in the 45 years since Trevino beat Nicklaus. "I've got a stat here", Harmon said when I called last fall. "When we hosted the US Open in 1968, the average driving distance for the field was 248 yards. Lee Trevino averaged 242 yards. Jack Nicklaus was the longest at 271. That means Nicklaus would be the Corey Pavin of the world today."

The average driving distance this year will be in the 290-yard range. By that comparison, Harmon says, "Oak Hill would have to play 8,200 yards long." But since there's not enough real estate to accommodate the demands of technology and the modern golfer, Oak Hill's East course will be stretched to 7,150 yards and a par of 70. The closing two par-4s will be in the 500-yard range but for the most part driving accuracy will be a premium, with fairways narrowed to 18–24 yards and Oak Hill's trademark trees providing the greatest obstacles.

To defend, Rory McIlroy will have to hit more fairways (37) than he did at Kiawah Island. No doubt McIlroy will be picking the brain of Nicklaus at the Bears Club – or maybe Nicklaus should be picking McIlroy's brain, since Rory at Kiawah Island in 2012 did one better than Nicklaus at Oak Hill in 1980 – winning by eight strokes. It may have looked like a dull day to most people, but it certainly wasn't for Rory at Kiawah.

Championship dates

	The Masters	US Open	The Open	US PGA Championship
2013	**April 11–14** Augusta National, Augusta, GA	**June 13–16** Merion GC (East course), Ardmore, PA	**July 18–21** Muirfield, East Lothian	**August 15–18** Oak Hill CC (East Course), Pittsford, NY
2014	**April 10–13** Augusta National, Augusta, GA	**June 12–15** Pinehurst Resort (Course No 2), NC	**July 17–20** Royal Liverpool, Hoylake, Cheshire	**August 14–17** Valhalla GC, Louisville, KY
2015	**April 9–12** Augusta National, Augusta, GA	**June 18–21** Chambers Bay, University Place, WA	**July 16–19** St Andrews, Fife	**August 15–17** Whistling Straits GC (Straits Course), Kohler, WI
2016	**TBA** Augusta National, Augusta, GA	**June 16–19** Oakmont CC, PA		**TBA** Baltusrol GC (Lower Course), Springfield, NJ
2017	**April 6–9** Augusta National, Augusta, GA	**June 15–18** Erin Hills, Erin, WI		**August 17–20** Quail Hollow GC, Charlotte, NC

Ryder Cup

2014 Gleneagles Hotel, Perthshire, Scotland Sept 26–28
2016 Hazeltine National GC, Chaska, MN
2018 Le Golf National, Versailles, France
2020 Whistling Straits, Kohler, WI

Solheim Cup

2013 Colorado GC, Parker, CO August 16–18
2015 St Leon-Rot GC, Frankfurt, Germany

Presidents Cup

(USA *v* Rest of the World except Europe)
2013 Muirfield Village GC, Ohio – October 2–6
2015 South Korea – venue and date to be announced

Curtis Cup

2014 St Louis CC, Missouri – June 6–8
2016 Dun Laoghaire GC, Ireland

R&A Contacts

Peter Dawson, Chief Executive

Business Affairs

Michael Tate, Executive Director – Business Affairs
Robin Bell, Marketing Director   Malcolm Booth, Communications Director
Angus Farquhar, Commercial Director

Championships

Johnnie Cole-Hamilton, Executive Director – Championships.
Rhodri Price, Director – Championship Operations
Michael Wells, Director – Championship Staging
Euan Mordaunt, Director – Amateur Events

Finance

John Murray, Executive Director – Finance

Rules and Equipment Standards

David Rickman, Executive Director
Grant Moir, Director – Rules   Steve Otto, Director – Research and Testing

Working for Golf

Duncan Weir, Executive Director – Working for Golf
Angela Howe, Museum and Heritage Director   Steve Isaac, Director Golf Course Management
Peter Lewis, Director – Film Archive

Dominic Wall, Director – Asia/Pacific

Up-to-date news of The R&A and its activities can be found at www.RandA.org
The R&A can be contacted on: Tel 01334 460000 Fax 01334 460001

R&A championship dates, 2013–2015

	2013	2014	2015
The Open Championship	**July 18–21** Muirfield	**July 17–20** Royal Liverpool	**July 16–19** St Andrews
The Open Championship Final Qualifying (local)	**July 2** Dunbar Gullane No 1 Musselburgh North Berwick	**July 1** Glasgow – Gailes Links Hillside Royal Cinque Ports Woburn	TBA
The Senior Open Championship	**July 25–28** Royal Birkdale	**July 23–26** Venue TBA	TBA
The Amateur Championship	**June 17–22** Royal Cinque Ports Prince's	**June 16–21** Royal Portrush Portstewart	**June 15–20** Carnoustie Panmure
The Seniors Open Amateur Championship	**August 7–9** Royal Aberdeen	**August 6–8** Ganton	**August 5–7** Royal County Down
The Junior Open Championship	—	**July 14–16** West Lancashire	—
The Boys' Amateur Championship	**August 13–18** Royal Liverpool Wallasey	**August 12–17** Prestwick Dundonald Links	**August 11–16** Royal Birkdale Southport & Ainsdale
The Boys' Home Internationals	**August 6–8** Forest Pines	**August 5–7** Western Gailes	**August 4–6** Conwy (Caernarvonshire)
The Jacques Léglise Trophy	**August 30–31** Royal St Davids	**August 29–30** Sweden	**August 28–29** Royal Dornoch
The Walker Cup	**September 7–8** National Golf Links of America, Southampton, NY	—	**September 12–13** Royal Lytham & St Annes
The St Andrews Trophy	—	**August 29–30** Sweden	—
The World Amateur Team Championships (Espirito Santo Trophy)	—	**September 3–6** Karuizwa, Japan	—
The World Amateur Team Championships (Eisenhower Trophy)	—	**September 11–14** Karuizwa, Japan	—

Other fixtures and tour schedules can be found on pages 494–500

Abbreviations

AFG	Afghanistan	HON	Honduras	PAN	Panama
ALB	Albania	HKG	Hong Kong	PAR	Paraguay
ALG	Algeria	HUN	Hungary	PER	Peru
ARG	Argentina	INA	Indonesia	PHI	Philippines
AUS	Australia	IND	India	PNG	Papua New Guinea
AUT	Austria	IOM	Isle of Man	POL	Poland
BAH	Bahamas	IRI	Iran	POR	Portugal
BAN	Bangladesh	IRL	Ireland	PUR	Puerto Rico
BAR	Barbados	ISL	Iceland	QAT	Qatar
BDI	Burundi	ISR	Israel	ROM	Romania
BEL	Belgium	ITA	Italy	RSA	South Africa
BER	Bermuda	JAM	Jamaica	RUS	Russia
BHU	Bhutan	JOR	Jordan	SAM	Samoa
BOL	Bolivia	JPN	Japan	SCO	Scotland
BOT	Botswana	KAZ	Kazakhstan	SIN	Singapore
BRA	Brazil	KEN	Kenya	SKA	St Kitts & Nevis
BRN	Bahrain	KGZ	Kyrgyzstan	SLO	Slovenia
BUL	Bulgaria	KOR	Korea (South)	SOL	Solomonn Islands
CAM	Cambodia	KSA	Saudi Arabia	SRB	Serbia
CAN	Canada	KUW	Kuwait	SRI	Sri Lanka
CAY	Cayman Islands	LAO	Laos	SUI	Switzerland
CHI	Chile	LAT	Latvia	SVK	Slovakia
CHN	China	LBA	Libya	SWE	Sweden
CIV	Côte d'Ivoire	LBN	Lebanon	SWZ	Swaziland
COK	Cook Islands	LCA	Saint Lucia	TAN	Tanzania
COL	Colombia	LTU	Lithuania	TCI	Turks and Caicos Islands
CRC	Costa Rica	LUX	Luxembourg	THA	Thailand
CRO	Croatia	MAC	Macau	TPE	Taiwan (Chinese Taipei)
CYP	Cyprus	MAW	Malawi	TRI	Trinidad and Tobago
CZE	Czech Republic	MAR	Morocco	TUN	Tunisia
DEN	Denmark	MAS	Malaysia	TUR	Turkey
DOM	Dominican Rep.	MEX	Mexico	UAE	United Arab Emirates
ECU	Ecuador	MGL	Mongolia	UGA	Uganda
EGY	Egypt	MON	Monaco	UKR	Ukraine
ENG	England	MYA	Myanmar	URU	Uruguay
ESA	El Salvador	NAM	Namibia	USA	United States
ESP	Spain	NCA	Nicaragua	VAN	Vanuatu
EST	Estonia	NED	Netherlands	VEN	Venezuela
FIJ	Fiji	NEP	Nepal	VIE	Vietnam
FIN	Finland	NIG	Niger	WAL	Wales
FRA	France	NIR	Northern Ireland	ZAM	Zambia
GER	Germany	NGR	Nigeria	ZIM	Zimbabwe
GRE	Greece	NOR	Norway		
GUA	Guatemala	NZL	New Zealand		
GUM	Guam	PAK	Pakistan		

GB&I Great Britain and Ireland

(am)	Amateur	(M)	Match play	Jr	Junior
(D)	Defending champion	(S)	Stroke play	Sr	Senior

Where available, total course yardage and the par for a course are displayed in square brackets, i.e. [6686–70]

* indicates winner after play-off

PART 1

The Major Championships

The 141st Open at Royal Lytham

Ernie Els answers the doubters with a little help from Adam Scott

Followers of horse-racing form usually note how well some horses always run on certain courses. The aficionados who study the form of golfers would have been just as aware that Ernie Els enjoys playing The Open at Royal Lytham and St Annes. In the two previous Opens held there he had finished second and joint third.

Ernie Els

Those same aficionados would have noted, too, that after a period in the doldrums there were evident signs that the 42-year-old "Big Easy" was coming back to his best helped by the work he had been doing with his new putting guru Dr Sherylle Calder. He had done well at the US Open finishing ninth.

So his form coming into the 2012 Open was encouraging even if he was seldom mentioned as a possible winner in the papers, on radio and television not least perhaps because he had not won a major for 10 years. There was a distinct feeling that perhaps we had seen the best of Ernie ... but how wrong that would turn out to be.

Yet even up until the last hour of play on the famous and at times brutal Championship links it did not seem that the popular South African was going land a fourth major.

With four holes to play the stylish 32-year-old Australian Adam Scott held an apparently commanding four shot lead. Yet golf has never been predictable. To the surprise of many not least himself Scott faltered as he moved into the last four holes – one of the toughest finishes in major Championship golf. He bogeyed them all. Els, birdied the last and suddenly it was a South African clasping the Claret Jug and not an Australian.

Els on seven under par 273 had roared home in 32 for his second 68 of the weekend to win the 141st Open by a single shot. Scott, who had dominated the event and had looked so steady and reliable for so long, tumbled painfully and signed for a losing 75. It was devastating for the Australian and even Els was sorry for his young friend and adversary.

So Ernie Els became the second South African to win over the links first used in 1926 when legendary amateur Bobby Jones won. Back in 1952 another great South African had triumphed in the oldest of the majors when Bobby Locke shot 287 to score the third of his four title victories. I doubt whether Locke would have used the word when he won but for a relieved Ernie on that Sunday afternoon everything was "groovy".

Relieved because earlier in the year so many had been suggesting hurtfully that he was finished and that it was time for him to put the clubs back in he attic. "In the circumstances to come back and make that 15 foot birdie putt on the last to win is really satisfying," said the big fellow.

As ever, Els was gracious in victory taking the trouble to point out to Scott that he himself had been there. He had suffered the agonies of defeat in one of the four major golf events that mean so much in golf. Ernie told reporters: "Adam is only 32 years old. He has plenty of time to win majors. I have now won four but Adam may well win more than me."

It had been Scott who had moved out in front on the first day celebrating his birthday earlier in the week with a six under par record-equalling 64 – a shot clear of former Open winner Paul Lawrie from Scotland, 2007 Masters winner Zach Johnson from America and the big-hitting Belgian Nicolas Colsaerts.

Just in behind these three was fair-haired Brandt Snedeker on 66 giving him every hope that he would at last make the half-way cut in an Open having missed on his three previous appearances.

The impressive first day leaderboard included on 67 and tied sixth Tiger Woods, chasing his 15th major but his first since 2008, the 2011 US Open champion Rory McIlroy, the 2010 US Open champion Graeme McDowell, reigning Masters champion Bubba Watson, Steve Stricker, Peter Hanson, Toshinori Muto and Els.

Faring worse on the opening day was defending champion Darren Clarke who managed only one birdie in a round of 76 which he admitted left him "disgusted". Lee Westwood, still chasing a first major although he has had seven top three finishes in Grand Slam events, was on 73 with Phil Mickelson.

Tom Watson, a five-time Open champion and, at 62, the oldest man in the field began with a creditable 72 marred only by dropping shots at the last two holes.

Day two saw Snedeker move into pole position with a 64 which was so nearly an Open record-equalling 63. It helped the 31-year-old from Nashville not only into the lead but also with a share of the

36-hole Championship record aggregate of 130 set by Nick Faldo at Muirfield in 1992. In his first two rounds, the American had managed to avoid having to play out of any of the 206 bunkers which are such a feature of the Lancashire venue and had not dropped a shot to par.

Scott was still right there, however, making a birdie at the last to be only one behind Snedker on nine under par. Tiger Woods, playing conservatively, was third on six under just ahead of the talented young Dane Thorborn Olesen. Els was seven behind and attracting only limited attention as a possible winner although as always he was being followed by and encouraged by a sophisticated gallery of fans who just love watching him play.

There was a huge cheer at the last when Tom Watson ran in a long putt to make the half-way cut on the mark of 143 which also included Westwood but the defending champion Darren Clarke, adding a 71 to his opening 76 departed the scene as did a host of other big names including Mickelson, Duval, Justin Rose, Martin Kaymer, Sergio García, Davis Love III and Angel Cabrera.

> "No bogeys round here is getting some good breaks."
>
> *Brandt Snedeker after his 64*

For the first time since 2003 no silver medal was awarded because none of the amateurs in the field made it through to the weekend.

Scott may have lost his lead on Friday but he won it back impressively on Saturday when, using his long putter to good effect, he went round in 68 to open up a four shot gap on his closest rivals Snedeker and McDowell. With a round to go he was five in front of Woods.

So far it had been a good week for McDowell whose season had been comparitively quiet coming into Lytham. He impressed those in the 37,000 crowd who watched him by adding another 67 to earlier rounds of 67 and 69. Snedeker was unlikely to score as well on the third day as he had on the second – it seems always to be that way in golf! He dropped his first shot of the Championship at the fifth and was in his first bunker at the sixth. Although shooting 73 – nine more than on Day Two – the American still felt he had a chance of winning especially if, as predicted, it was going to be a little bit windier on Sunday. "If it's calm again then it looks good for Adam who did not show a lot of weaknesses out there today. It was as if he was giving a golfing clinic out there," said Snedeker

Tiger, five back and lying fourth, also felt that another calm day would favour Adam Scott becoming the 16th different major title winner in a row. Ernie Els, six back with Zach Johnson, was still operating under the radar.

It was much more blowy on the final day but Els was still six off the lead after the front nine. His fans were happy that he was playing as well as he was but could not have envisaged the drama that would unfold on the homeward stretch.

Scott, keen to emulate his countryman Greg Norman who won the title at Turnberry in 1986 and Royal St George's in 1992, had played so steadily for four days avoiding the rough which was much thicker this year after all the heavy rain of the previous weeks. When he moved to the 15th. tee he was till four in front. Snedeker, McDowell and Woods were no longer fancied to take the title, Els, too, was still an outsider.

Yet Scott would bogey the last four holes and lose five shots to Ernie. The two shot swing at the last where Els birdied and Scott, after using his driver off the tee, found a bunker and ended up with a bogey, only underlined how sweet and yet how cruel the game can be.

In the end, Woods and Snedeker finished joint third four behind Els, McDowell and Luke Donald, helped by an excellent final round 69 were joint fifth with Colsaerts and another South African Thomas Aitken, tied seventh on one under.

Only eight players had finished the Championship under par. Even if less bouncy than normal, Royal Lytham and St Annes had once again proved a worthy test and produced a winner of quality and class. While there was sadness for Scott there was delight that Ernie Els had proved the doubters he was far from finished.

Renton Laidlaw

First Round	**Second Round**	**Third Round**	**Fourth Round**
–6 Adam Scott	–10 Brandt Snedeker	–11 Adam Scott	–7 Ernie Els
–5 Paul Lawrie	–9 Adam Scott	–7 Graeme McDowell	–6 Adam Scott
–5 Zach Johnson	–6 Tiger Woods	–7 Brandt Snedeker	–3 Tiger Woods
–5 Nicolas Colsaerts	–5 Thorbjørn Olesen	–6 Tiger Woods	–3 Brandt Snedeker
–4 Brandt Snedeker	–4 Paul Lawrie	–5 Ernie Els	–2 Graeme McDowell
–3 Bubba Watson	–4 Graeme McDowell	–5 Zach Johnson	–2 Luke Donald
–3 Graeme McDowell	–4 Jason Dufner	–4 Thorbjørn Olesen	–1 Nicholas Colsaerts
–3 Tiger Woods	–4 Matt Kuchar	–3 Bill Haas	–1 Thomas Aiken
–3 Rory McIlroy	–4 Thomas Aiken	–3 Thomas Aiken	= Mark Calcavecchia
–3 Steve Stricker	–3 Ernie Els	–2 Mark Calcavecchia	= Ian Poulter

The Open Championship (141st) *Royal Lytham & St Annes* July 19–22 [7086–70]

Total Prize Money: £5 million. Entries: 2,012. 14 Regional Qualifying Courses: Abridge, Berwick-upon-Tweed (Goswick), Bruntsfield Links, Buckinghamshire, Clitheroe, Coventry, East Sussex National, Ferndown, Hankley Common, Lindrick, Mere, Moortown, Royal Dublin and The London.

International Final Qualifying:

Africa (Royal Johannesburg & Kensington) Jan 18–19

Grant Veenstra (RSA)	71-67—138
Andrew Georgiou (RSA)	71-68—139
Adilson Da Silva (BRA)	68-71—139

America (Gleneagles, Plano, TX) May 23

Harris English (USA)	60-63—123
Greg Owen (ENG)	66-61—127
Stephen Ames (CAN)	69-61—130
Andres Romero (ARG)	67-63—130
Justin Hicks (USA)	67-63—130
Bob Estes (USA)	66-65—131
Daniel Chopra (SWE)	64-67—131
James Driscoll (USA)	66-65—131

Asia (Amata Spring, Thailand) Mar 1–2

Anirban Lahiri (IND)	68-67—135
Prayad Marksaeng (THA)	73-64—137
Kodai Ichihara (JPN)	69-69—138
Mardan Mamat (SIN)	71-69—140

Australasia (Kingston Heath) Jan 17

Aaron Townsend (AUS)	70-70—140
Ashley Hall (AUS)	72-71—143
Nicholas Cullen (AUS)	70-73—143

Europe (Sunningdale, England) June 25

James Morrison (ENG)	63-68—131
Sam Walker (ENG)	68-65—133
Alejandro Canizares (ESP)	68-66—134
Richard Finch (ENG)	67-67—134
Matthew Baldwin (ENG)	69-65—134
Jamie Donaldson (WAL)	72-62—134
Ross Fisher (ENG)	64-70—134
Marcus Fraser (AUS)	66-68—134
Lee Slattery (ENG)	67-68—135
Thorbjørn Olesen (DEN)	67-68—135

Local Final Qualifying:

Hillside

Dale Whitnell (Five Lakes)	68-67—135
Warren Bennett (Prince's)	68-68—136
Steven Tiley (Royal Cinque Ports)	69-69—138

Southport & Ainsdale

Morten Orum Madsen (DEN)	65-71—136
Ian Keenan (Royal Liverpool)	70-68—138
Elliot Saltman (Archerfield Links)	68-70—138

St Annes Old Links

Paul Broadhurst (unattached)	70-67—137
Barry Lane (unattached)	68-70—138
Rafael Echenique (ARG)	67-71—138

West Lancashire

Steven Alker (NZL)	69-68—137
Scott Pinckney (USA)	75-64—139
Steven O'Hara (Al Ain)	70-69—139

Ernie Els, in his own words...

“I really feel for my buddy, Scottie, I really do. I've been there before. I've blown majors before and golf tournaments before, and I just hope he doesn't take it as hard as I did. Obviously I'm so happy that I've won. But I've been on the other end more times than I've actually been on the winning end, so to speak. And it's not a good feeling. I'm speaking for myself, but I think Adam is a little bit different than I am. I did see him afterwards in the scorer's hut and he seemed okay. I really said to him, I'm sorry how things turned out. I told him that I've been there many times and you've just got to bounce back quickly. Don't let this thing linger. So, yeah, I feel for him. But thankfully he's young enough. He's 32 years old. He's got the next 10 years that he can win more than I've won. I've won four now; I think he can win more than that.”

The final field of 156 players included two amateurs. 83 players (no amateurs) qualified for the last two rounds with scores of 143 or less.

1	Ernie Els (RSA)	67-70-68-68—273	£900,000
2	Adam Scott (AUS)	64-67-68-75—274	520,000
3	Tiger Woods (USA)	67-67-70-73—277	297,500
	Brandt Snedeker (USA)	66-64-73-74—277	297,500
5	Luke Donald (ENG)	70-68-71-69—278	195,000
	Graeme McDowell (NIR)	67-69-67-75—278	195,000
7	Nicolas Colsaerts (BEL)	65-77-72-65—279	142,500
	Thomas Aiken (RSA)	68-68-71-72—279	142,500
9	Geoff Ogilvy (AUS)	72-68-73-67—280	79,600
	Miguel Angel Jiménez (ESP)	71-69-73-67—280	79,600
	Ian Poulter (ENG)	71-69-73-67—280	79,600
	Alexander Noren (SWE)	71-71-69-69—280	79,600
	Vijay Singh (FIJ)	70-72-68-70—280	79,600
	Dustin Johnson (USA)	73-68-68-71—280	79,600
	Matt Kuchar (USA)	69-67-72-72—280	79,600
	Mark Calcavecchia (USA)	71-68-69-72—280	79,600
	Thorbjørn Olesen (DEN)	69-66-71-74—280	79,600
	Zach Johnson (USA)	65-74-66-75—280	79,600
19	Hunter Mahan (USA)	70-71-70-70—281	50,750
	Steven Alker (NZL)	69-69-72-71—281	50,750
	Louis Oosthuizen (RSA)	72-68-68-73—281	50,750
	Bill Haas (USA)	71-68-68-74—281	50,750
23	Carl Pettersson (SWE)	71-68-73-70—282	38,438
	Simon Dyson (ENG)	72-67-73-70—282	38,438
	Steve Stricker (USA)	67-71-73-71—282	38,438
	Peter Hanson (SWE)	67-72-72-71—282	38,438
	Matthew Baldwin (ENG)	69-73-69-71—282	38,438
	James Morrison (ENG)	68-70-72-72—282	38,438
	Nick Watney (USA)	71-70-69-72—282	38,438
	Bubba Watson (USA)	67-73-68-74—282	38,438
31	Rickie Fowler (USA)	71-72-70-70—283	30,167
	Anirban Lahiri (IND)	68-72-70-73—283	30,167
	Jason Dufner (USA)	70-66-73-74—283	30,167
34	John Senden (AUS)	70-71-75-68—284	26,000
	Jim Furyk (USA)	72-70-71-71—284	26,000
	Gary Woodland (USA)	73-70-70-71—284	26,000
	Paul Lawrie (SCO)	65-71-76-72—284	26,000
	Keegan Bradley (USA)	71-72-68-73—284	26,000
39	Richard Sterne (RSA)	69-73-73-70—285	20,500
	K J Choi (KOR)	70-73-71-71—285	20,500
	Troy Matteson (USA)	70-72-71-72—285	20,500
	Francesco Molinari (ITA)	69-72-71-73—285	20,500
	Padraig Harrington (IRL)	70-72-70-73—285	20,500
	Kyle Stanley (USA)	70-69-70-76—285	20,500
45	Ross Fisher (ENG)	72-71-74-69—286	14,839
	Bob Estes (USA)	69-72-74-71—286	14,839
	Pablo Larrazabal (ESP)	73-70-71-72—286	18,744
	Lee Westwood (ENG)	73-70-71-72—286	18,744
	Rafa Echenique (ARG)	73-69-71-73—286	18,744
	Joost Luiten (NED)	73-70-69-74—286	18,744
	Justin Hicks (USA)	68-74-69-75—286	18,744
	Greg Chalmers (AUS)	71-68-71-76—286	18,744
	Simon Khan (ENG)	70-69-71-76—286	18,744
54	Fredrik Jacobson (SWE)	69-73-73-72—287	12,850
	Yoshinori Fujomoto (JPN)	71-70-73-73—287	12,850
	Gonzalo Fernandez-Castaño (ESP)	71-71-72-73—287	12,850
	Greg Owen (ENG)	71-71-71-74—287	12,850
	Harris English (USA)	71-71-70-75—287	12,850
	Thomas Bjørn (DEN)	70-69-72-76—287	12,850

141st Open Championship *continued*

60	Rory McIlroy (NIR)	67-75-73-73—288	12,350
	Ted Potter Jr (USA)	69-71-74-74—288	12,350
	Jamie Donaldson (WAL)	68-72-72-76—288	12,350
	Dale Whitnell (ENG)	71-69-72-76—288	12,350
64	Charles Howell III (USA)	72-71-74-72—289	11,900
	Lee Slattery (ENG)	69-72-75-73—289	11,900
	Retief Goosen (RSA)	70-70-75-74—289	11,900
	S M Bae (KOR)	72-71-71-75—289	11,900
	Garth Mulroy (RSA)	71-69-72-77—289	11,900
69	Jeev Milkha Singh (IND)	70-71-76-73—290	11,500
	Aaron Baddeley (AUS)	71-71-74-74—290	11,500
	Adilson Da Silva (BRA)	69-74-71-76—290	11,500
72	Martin Laird (SCO)	70-69-82-70—291	11,100
	Chad Campbell (USA)	73-70-74-74—291	11,100
	Juvic Pagunsan (PHI)	71-72-73-75—291	11,100
	Brendan Jones (AUS)	69-74-72-76—291	11,100
	Toshinori Muro (JPN)	67-72-74-78—291	11,100
77	Tom Watson (USA)	71-72-76-73—292	10,650
	Warren Bennett (ENG)	71-70-75-76—292	10,650
	Jaidee Thongchai (THA)	69-71-74-78—292	10,650
	Branden Grace (RSA)	73-69-71-79—292	10,650
81	John Daly (USA)	72-71-77-74—294	10,350
	Rafael Cabrera-Bello (ESP)	70-71-76-77—294	10,350
83	Andres Romero (ARG)	70-69-77-82—298	10,200

The following players missed the cut:

84	Nicholas Cullen (AUS)	73-71—144	3,500
	Marcel Siem (GER)	74-70—144	3,500
	George Coetzee (RSA)	74-70—144	3,500
	Marcus Fraser (AUS)	71-73—144	3,500
	Mark Wilson (USA)	72-72—144	3,500
	Anders Hansen (DEN)	68-76—144	3,500
	Koumei Oda (JPN)	72-72—144	3,500
	Marc Leishman (AUS)	69-75—144	3,500
	Jbe Kruger (RSA)	68-76—144	3,500
	Richie Ramsay (SCO)	71-73—144	3,500
	Raphael Jacquelin (FRA)	72-72—144	3,500
	Y E Yang (KOR)	74-70—144	3,500
	Justin Rose (ENG)	74-70—144	3,500
	Sergio García (ESP)	72-72—144	3,500
	Charl Schwartzel (RSA)	69-75—144	3,500
	Steven Tiley (ENG)	72-72—144	3,500
	Aaron Townsend (AUS)	70-74—144	3,500
101	Scott Pinckney (USA)	68-77—145	2,600
	Tom Lehman (USA)	73-72—145	2,600
	Gregory Havret (FRA)	73-72—145	2,600
	K T Kim (KOR)	75-70—145	2,600
	Bo Van Pelt (USA)	71-74—145	2,600
	Morten Orum Madsen (DEN)	74-71—145	2,600
	David Duval (USA)	74-71—145	2,600
	Stewart Cink (USA)	72-73—145	2,600
109	Steven O'Hara (SCO)	74-72—146	2,600
	Jonathan Byrd (USA)	74-72—146	2,600
	Ashley Hall (AUS)	71-75—146	2,600
	Barry Lane (ENG)	73-73—146	2,600
	Sandy Lyle (SCO)	74-72—146	2,600
	Todd Hamilton (USA)	72-74—146	2,600
	Alejandro Canizares (ESP)	74-72—146	2,600
	Alan Dunbar (NIR) (am)	75-71—146	
	Ryo Ishikawa (JPN)	74-72—146	2,600
109T	Martin Kaymer (GER)	77-69—146	2,600
	Sam Walker (ENG)	76-70—146	2,600
120	Michael Thompson (USA)	74-73—147	2,600
	Toru Taniguchi (JPN)	72-75—147	2,600
	Robert Allenby (AUS)	75-72—147	2,600
	Stephen Ames (CAN)	74-73—147	2,600
	Darren Clarke (NIR)	76-71—147	2,600
	Daniel Chopra (SWE)	73-74—147	2,600
126	Lucas Glover (USA)	72-76—148	2,350
	Andrew Georgiou (RSA)	74-74—148	2,350
	Troy Kelly (USA)	72-76—148	2,350
	Tadahiro Takayama (JPN)	77-71—148	2,350
	John Huh (USA)	75-73—148	2,350
	Justin Leonard (USA)	75-73—148	2,350
	Hiroyuki Fujita (JPN)	76-72—148	2,350
	Brad Kennedy (AUS)	75-73—148	2,350
134	Chez Reavie (USA)	74-75—149	2,350
	Ben Curtis (USA)	75-74—149	2,350
	Trevor Immelman (RSA)	74-75—149	2,350
	Alvaro Quiros (ESP)	74-75—149	2,350
	Robert Rock (ENG)	78-71—149	2,350
	Johnson Wagner (USA)	73-76—149	2,350
140	Prayad Marksaeng (THA)	75-75—150	2,350
	Kodai Ichihara (JPN)	77-73—150	2,350
	Davis Love III (USA)	71-79—150	2,350
	Tim Clark (RSA)	76-74—150	2,350
	Kevin Na (USA)	73-77—150	2,350
145	Paul Casey (ENG)	72-79—151	2,350
	Phil Mickelson (USA)	73-78—151	2,350
	Elliot Saltman (SCO)	76-75—151	2,350
148	Angel Cabrera (ARG)	71-81—152	2,350
	James Driscoll (USA)	76-76—152	2,350
150	Paul Broadhurst (ENG)	75-78—153	2,350
	Richard Finch (ENG)	74-79—153	2,350
152	Michael Hoey (NIR)	79-75—154	2,350

153	Grant Veenstra (RSA)	77-79—156	2,350
154	Manuel Trappel (AUT) (am)	74-83—157	
155	Ian Keenan (ENG)	76-83—159	2,350
	Russ Cochran (USA)	WD	
	Mardan Mamat (SIN)	DQ	

2011 Open Championship *Royal St George's* July 14–17 [7204–70]

Total Prize Money: £5 million. Entries: 1,955. 16 Regional Qualifying Courses: Abridge, Berwick-upon-Tweed (Goswick), Bruntsfield Links, Buckinghamshire, Clitheroe, Coventry, East Sussex National, Enville, Ferndown, Gog Magog, Hankley Common, Lindrick, Mere, Pannal, Royal Dublin and The London. Final field: 156 (2 amateurs) of whom 71 (2 amateurs) made the half-way cut with scores of 146 or less.

1	Darren Clarke (NIR)	68-68-69-70—275	£900,000
2	Dustin Johnson (USA)	70-68-68-72—278	427,500
	Phil Mickelson (USA)	70-69-71-68—278	427,500
4	Thomas Bjørn (DEN)	65-72-71-71—279	260,000
5	Chad Campbell (USA)	69-68-74-69—280	181,666
	Rickie Fowler (USA)	70-70-68-72—280	181,666
	Anthony Kim (USA)	72-68-70-70—280	181,666
8	Raphaël Jacquelin (FRA)	74-67-71-69—281	130,000
9	Simon Dyson (ENG)	68-72-72-70—282	104,333
	Sergio García (ESP)	70-70-74-68—282	104,333
	Davis Love III (USA)	70-68-72-72—282	104,333
12	Lucas Glover (USA)	66-70-73-74—283	78,333
	Kaymer (GER)	68-69-73-73—283	78,333
	Steve Stricker (USA)	69-71-72-71—283	78,333
15	George Coetzee (RSA)	69-69-72-74—284	75,521
	Richard Green (AUS)	70-71-73-71—285	67,428
	Fredrik Jacobson (SWE)	70-70-73-72—285	67,428
	Zach Johnson (USA)	72-68-71-74—285	67,428
	Charl Schwartzel (RSA)	71-67-75-72—285	67,428
	Webb Simpson (USA)	66-74-72-73—285	67,428
15T	Y E Yang (KOR)	71-69-73-72—285	67,428
22	Anders Hansen (DEN)	69-69-72-76—286	44,666
	Tom Lehman (USA)	71-67-73-75—286	44,666
	Tom Watson (USA)	72-70-72-72—286	44,666
25	Miguel Angel Jiménez (ESP)	66-71-72-78—287	39,000
	Rory McIlroy (NIR)	71-69-74-73—287	39,000
	Adam Scott (AUS)	69-70-73-75—287	39,000
28	Charles Howell III (USA)	71-70-73-74—288	35,350
	Ryan Moore (USA)	69-74-76-69—288	35,350
30	Stewart Cink (USA)	70-71-77-71—289	28,642
	Jason Day (AUS)	71-70-76-72—289	28,642
	Pablo Larrazábal (ESP)	68-70-76-75—289	28,642
	Tom Lewis (ENG) (am)	65-74-76-74—289	Silver Medal
	Seung-yul Noh (KOR)	69-72-75-73—289	28,642
	Ryan Palmer (USA)	68-71-72-78—289	28,642
	Bubba Watson (USA)	69-72-74-74—289	28,642
	Gary Woodland (USA)	75-68-74-72—289	28,642

Other players who made the cut: Gary Boyd (ENG), Yuta Ikeda (JPN), Trevor Immelman (RSA), Simon Khan (ENG), Jeff Overton (USA), Robert Rock (ENG) 290; K J Choi (KOR), Spencer Levin (USA), Justin Rose (ENG), Kyle Stanley (USA) 291; Robert Allenby (AUS), Grégory Bourdy (FRA), Floris De Vries (NED), Jim Furyk (USA), Richard McEvoy (ENG), Peter Uihlein (USA) (am) 292; Paul Casey (ENG), Louis Oosthuizen (RSA), Rory Sabbatini (RSA) 293; Fredrik Andersson Hed (SWE), Ricky Barnes (USA), Stephen Gallacher (SCO), Bill Haas (USA), Grégory Havret (FRA), Bo Van Pelt (USA) 294; Joost Luiten (NED), Matthew Millar (AUS), Mark Wilson (USA) 296; Paul Lawrie (SCO), Edoardo Molinari (ITA) 297; Henrik Stenson (SWE) 298; Harrison Frazar (USA) 299; Kenneth Ferrie (ENG) 301; Jung-gon Hwang (KOR) 304

2010 Open Championship *Old Course, St Andrews* July 15–18 [7305–72]

Total Prize Money: £4.8 million. Entries: 2,500. 16 Regional Qualifying Courses: Abridge, Berwick upon Tweed (Goswick), Clitheroe, County Louth, Coventry, East Sussex National, Effingham, Enville, Ferndown, Gog Magog, Lindrick, Mere, Musselburgh, Old Fold Manor, Pannal, The London. Final field: 156 (7 amateurs) of whom 77 (1 amateur) made the half-way cut with scores of 146 or less.

1	Louis Oosthuizen (RSA)	65-67-69-71—272	£1,011,840
2	Lee Westwood (ENG)	67-71-71-70—279	595,200
3	Paul Casey (ENG)	69-69-67-75—280	305,536
	Rory McIlroy (NIR)	63-80-69-68—280	305,536
	Henrik Stenson (SWE)	68-74-67-71—280	305,536
6	Retief Goosen (RSA)	69-70-72-70—281	208,320
7	Martin Kaymer (GER)	69-71-68-74—282	144,336
	Sean O'Hair (USA)	67-72-72-71—282	144,336
	Robert Rock (ENG)	68-78-67-69—282	144,336
	Nick Watney (USA)	67-73-71-71—282	144,336
11	Luke Donald (ENG)	73-72-69-69—283	97,216
	Jeff Overton (USA)	73-69-72-69—283	97,216
	Alvaro Quiros (ESP)	72-70-74-67—283	97,216
14	Rickie Fowler (USA)	79-67-71-67—284	68,076
	Sergio García (ESP)	71-71-70-72—284	68,076
	Ignacio Garrido (ESP)	69-71-73-71—284	68,076
	J B Holmes (USA)	70-72-70-72—284	68,076
	Jin Jeong (KOR) (am)	68-70-74-72—284	Silver Medal
14T	Dustin Johnson (USA)	69-72-69-74—284	68,076
	Robert Karlsson (SWE)	69-71-72-72—284	68,076
	Tom Lehman (USA)	71-68-75-70—284	68,076
	Charl Schwartzel (RSA)	71-75-68-70—284	68,076
23	Stephen Gallacher (SCO)	71-73-70-71—285	49,996
	Trevor Immelman (RSA)	68-74-75-68—285	49,996
	Graeme McDowell (NIR)	71-68-76-70—285	49,996
	Tiger Woods (USA)	67-73-73-72—285	49,996
27	Robert Allenby (AUS)	69-75-71-71—286	37,200
	Alejandro Cañizares (ESP)	67-71-71-77—286	37,200
	Bradley Dredge (WAL)	66-76-74-70—286	37,200
	Ryo Ishikawa (JPN)	68-73-75-70—286	37,200
	Miguel Angel Jiménez (ESP)	72-67-74-73—286	37,200
	Matt Kuchar (USA)	72-74-71-69—286	37,200
	Edoardo Molinari (ITA)	69-76-73-68—286	37,200
	Kevin Na (USA)	70-74-70-72—286	37,200
	Adam Scott (AUS)	72-70-72-72—286	37,200
	Marcel Siem (GER)	67-75-74-70—286	37,200

2010 Open Championship *continued*

Other players who made the cut: Thomas Aiken (RSA), Woody Austin (USA), Grégory Bourdy (FRA), Bart Bryant (USA), Ariel Canete (ARG), David Duval (USA), Ross Fisher (ENG), Simon Khan (ENG), Graeme Storm (ENG), Camilo Villegas (COL), Mike Weir (CAN), Jay Williamson (USA) 296; Stuart Appleby (AUS), Michael Campbell (NZL), David Frost (RSA), Sergio García (ESP), Zach Johnson (USA), Doug Labelle II (USA), Anthony Wall (ENG) 297; Richard Finch (ENG), Tom Gillis (USA), Peter Hanson (SWE), Colin Montgomerie (SCO), Kevin Stadler (USA), Scott Verplank (USA) 298; Søren Hansen (DEN), Wen Chong Liang (CHN), Jonathan Lomas (ENG) 299; Jean-Baptiste Gonnet (FRA), David Horsey (ENG), Lee Westwood (ENG) 300; Brendan Jones (AUS), Pablo Larrazabal (ESP), Jose-Filipe Lima (POR), Jeff Overton (USA), Craig Parry (AUS), John Rollins (USA), Justin Rose (ENG), Martin Wiegele (AUT) 301; Nick Dougherty (ENG), Lucas Glover (USA) 302; Martin Kaymer (GER) 303; Philip Archer (ENG) 304; Sean O'Hair (USA) 306; Chih Bing Lam (SIN) 311

2009 Open Championship *Turnberry* July 16–19 [7173–70]

Total Prize Money: £4.26 million. Entries: 2,418. 16 Regional Qualifying Courses: Abridge, Alwoodley, Berwick-upon-Tweed (Goswick), Coventry, Effingham, Enville, Ferndown, Gog Magog, Lindrick, Mere, Musselburgh, Old Fold Manor, Pleasington, Rochester & Cobham Park, Royal Ashdown Forest, Royal Dublin. Final qualifying courses: Glasgow Gailes, Kilmarnock (Barassie), Western Gailes. Final field: 156 (2 amateurs) of whom 73 (1 amateur) made the half-way cut with scores of 144 or less.

1	Stewart Cink (USA)*	66-72-71-69—278	£750,000
2	Tom Watson (USA)	65-70-71-72—278	450,000
	**Cink won after a four-hole play-off*		
3	Lee Westwood (ENG)	68-70-70-71—279	255,000
	Chris Wood (ENG)	70-70-72-67—279	255,000
5	Luke Donald (ENG)	71-72-70-67—280	157,000
	Mathew Goggin (AUS)	66-72-69-73—280	157,000
	Retief Goosen (RSA)	67-70-71-72—280	157,000
8	Thomas Aiken (RSA)	71-72-69-69—281	90,400
	Ernie Els (RSA)	69-72-72-68—281	90,400
	Søren Hansen (DEN)	68-72-74-67—281	90,400
	Richard S Johnson (SWE)	70-72-69-70—281	90,400
	Justin Leonard (USA)	70-70-73-68—281	90,400
13	Ross Fisher (ENG)	69-68-70-75—282	50,900
	Thongchai Jaidee (THA)	69-72-69-72—282	50,900
	Miguel Angel Jiménez (ESP)	64-73-76-69—282	50,900
	Matteo Manassero (ITA) (am)	71-70-72-69—282	Silver Medal
	Francesco Molinari (ITA)	71-70-71-70—282	50,900
13T	Jeff Overton (USA)	70-69-76-67—282	50,900
	Andres Romero (ARG)	68-74-73-67—282	50,900
	Justin Rose (ENG)	69-72-71-70—282	50,900
	Henrik Stenson (SWE)	71-70-71-70—282	50,900
	Camilo Villegas (COL)	66-73-73-70—282	50,900
	Boo Weekley (USA)	67-72-72-71—282	50,900
24	Angel Cabrera (ARG)	69-70-72-72—283	36,333
	Peter Hanson (SWE)	70-71-72-70—283	36,333
	Oliver Wilson (ENG)	72-70-71-70—283	36,333
27	Mark Calcavecchia (USA)	67-69-77-71—284	29,357
	John Daly (USA)	68-72-72-72—284	29,357
	James Kingston (RSA)	67-71-74-72—284	29,357
	Søren Kjeldsen (DEN)	68-76-71-69—284	29,357
	Kenichi Kuboya (JPN)	65-72-75-72—284	29,357
	Davis Love III (USA)	69-73-73-69—284	29,357
	Nick Watney (USA)	71-72-71-70—284	29,357
34	Jim Furyk (USA)	67-72-70-76—285	23,500
	Martin Kaymer (GER)	69-70-74-72—285	23,500
	Graeme McDowell (NIR)	68-73-71-73—285	23,500
	Richard Sterne (RSA)	67-73-75-70—285	23,500

Other players who made the cut: Nick Dougherty (ENG), Sergio García (ESP), Thomas Levet (FRA), Steve Marino (USA), Vijay Singh (FIJ) 286; Branden Grace (RSA), Paul McGinley (IRL), Bryce Molder (USA), Anthony Wall (ENG) 287; Paul Casey (ENG), Gonzalo Fernandez-Castaño (ESP), Zach Johnson (USA), Paul Lawrie (SCO), Rory McIlroy (NIR) 288; Robert Allenby (AUS), Darren Clarke (NIR), Johan Edfors (SWE), David Howell (ENG), Billy Mayfair (USA), Kenny Perry (USA), Graeme Storm (ENG), Steve Stricker (USA) 289; Paul Broadhurst (ENG), David Drysdale (SCO), Tom Lehman (USA), Kevin Sutherland (USA) 290; Ryuji Imada (JPN) 291; Fredrik Andersson Hed (SWE), Stuart Appleby (AUS), Padraig Harrington (IRL), Sean O'Hair (USA) 292; J B Holmes (USA) 293; Fredrik Jacobson (SWE), Mark O'Meara (USA) 295; Paul Goydos (USA) 303; Daniel Gaunt (AUS) 304

Ernie Els, in his own words...

"I was really angry with myself at the ninth after making bogey and that almost set me in a different mindset. It really got me aggressive. I hit a lot of drivers on the back nine and I was just trying to make birdies. I felt good. I wasn't ahead, I wasn't behind, I was right in the moment, for once. I was really just playing the shot in the moment. When you've been around as long as I have, you've seen a lot of things happen. And I just felt that the golf course is such if you just doubt it a little bit, it was going to bite you. There's too many bunkers, too much trouble, and there was a bit of a breeze. So I felt I was going to hit the shots and I still felt I had a chance."

2008 Open Championship *Royal Birkdale* July 17–20 [7173–70]

Total Prize Money: £4.26 million. Entries: 2,418. 16 Regional Qualifying Courses: Abridge, Alwoodley, Berwick-upon-Tweed (Goswick), Coventry, Effingham, Enville, Ferndown, Gog Magog, Lindrick, Mere, Musselburgh, Old Fold Manor, Pleasington, Rochester & Cobham Park, Royal Ashdown Forest, Royal Dublin. Final qualifying courses: Hillside, Southport & Ainsdale, West Lancashire. Final field: 156 (5 amateurs) of whom 83 (2 amateurs) made the half-way cut with scores of 149 or less.

1	Padraig Harrington (IRL)	74-68-72-69—283	£750,000
2	Ian Poulter (ENG)	72-71-75-69—287	450,000
3	Greg Norman (AUS)	70-70-72-77—289	255,000
	Henrik Stenson (SWE)	76-72-70-71—289	255,000
5	Jim Furyk (USA)	71-71-77-71—290	180,000
	Chris Wood (ENG) (am)	75-70-73-72—290	Silver Medal
7	Robert Allenby (AUS)	69-73-76-74—292	96,944
	Stephen Ames (CAN)	73-70-78-71—292	96,944
	Paul Casey (ENG)	78-71-73-70—292	96,944
	Ben Curtis (USA)	78-69-70-75—292	96,944
	Ernie Els (RSA)	80-69-74-69—292	96,944
	David Howell (ENG)	76-71-78-67—292	96,944
	Robert Karlsson (SWE)	75-73-75-69—292	96,944
	Anthony Kim (USA)	72-74-71-75—292	96,944
	Steve Stricker (USA)	77-71-71-73—292	96,944
16	K J Choi (KOR)	72-67-75-79—293	53,166
	Justin Leonard (USA)	77-70-73-73—293	53,166
	Adam Scott (AUS)	70-74-77-72—293	53,166
19	Anders Hansen (DEN)	78-68-74-74—294	37,770
19T	Grégory Havret (FRA)	71-75-77-71—294	37,770
	Trevor Immelman (RSA)	74-74-73-73—294	37,770
	Fredrik Jacobson (SWE)	71-72-79-72—294	37,770
	Davis Love III (USA)	75-74-70-75—294	37,770
	Graeme McDowell (NIR)	69-73-80-72—294	37,770
	Rocco Mediate (USA)	69-73-76-76—294	37,770
	Phil Mickelson (USA)	79-68-76-71—294	37,770
	Alexander Noren (SWE)	72-70-75-77—294	37,770
	Thomas Sherreard (ENG) (am)	77-69-76-72—294	
	Jean Van de Velde (FRA)	73-71-80-70—294	37,770
	Simon Wakefield (ENG)	71-74-70-79—294	37,770
	Paul Waring (ENG)	73-74-76-71—294	37,770
32	Retief Goosen (RSA)	71-75-73-76—295	25,035
	Richard Green (AUS)	76-72-76-71—295	25,035
	Todd Hamilton (USA)	74-74-72-75—295	25,035
	Tom Lehman (USA)	74-73-73-75—295	25,035
	Nick O'Hern (AUS)	74-75-74-72—295	25,035
	Andres Romero (ARG)	77-72-74-72—295	25,035
	Heath Slocum (USA)	73-76-74-72—295	25,035

Other players who made the cut: Thomas Aiken (RSA), Woody Austin (USA), Grégory Bourdy (FRA), Bart Bryant (USA), Ariel Canete (ARG), David Duval (USA), Ross Fisher (ENG), Simon Khan (ENG), Graeme Storm (ENG), Camilo Villegas (COL), Mike Weir (CAN), Jay Williamson (USA) 296; Stuart Appleby (AUS), Michael Campbell (NZL), David Frost (RSA), Sergio García (ESP), Zach Johnson (USA), Doug Labelle II (USA), Anthony Wall (ENG) 297; Richard Finch (ENG), Tom Gillis (USA), Peter Hanson (SWE), Colin Montgomerie (SCO), Kevin Stadler (USA), Scott Verplank (USA) 298; Søren Hansen (DEN), Wen Chong Liang (CHN), Jonathan Lomas (ENG) 299; Jean-Baptiste Gonnet (FRA), David Horsey (ENG), Lee Westwood (ENG) 300; Brendan Jones (AUS), Pablo Larrazabal (ESP), Jose-Filipe Lima (POR), Jeff Overton (USA), Craig Parry (AUS), John Rollins (USA), Justin Rose (ENG), Martin Wiegele (AUT) 301; Nick Dougherty (ENG), Lucas Glover (USA) 302; Martin Kaymer (GER) 303; Philip Archer (ENG) 304; Sean O'Hair (USA) 306; Chih Bing Lam (SIN) 311

2012 Open Championship – rulings of the day – Thursday

Unplayable Ball

During the first round of the 141st Open Championship, Phil Mickelson had to employ one of the most frequently used Rules in the game of golf. Playing the 8th hole, Mickelson found the deep bunker on the left of the fairway with his tee shot. His ball came to rest near the edge of the bunker, leaving him with a difficult shot over the steep bunker face.

Due to the angle of the shot, the ball failed to clear the long grass at the top of the bunker. After a short ball search to locate the ball, it was found buried deep in the rough. Mickelson decided to proceed under the unplayable ball Rule – Rule 28.

Under this Rule, the player has three options for relief, each incurring a penalty of one stroke. The player can choose to proceed under the stroke and distance option by playing a ball as nearly as possible at the spot from which the original was last played from (Rule 28a). In Mickelson's case, this would have involved him dropping the ball back in the bunker and attempting the same shot again.

Alternatively, Mickelson could have dropped a ball within two club-lengths of where the ball lay but no nearer the hole (Rule 28c). For Mickelson, this option would have involved dropping the ball into further long grass, potentially leaving him with a similar difficult lie in the rough.

Instead, Mickelson decided to proceed under Rule 28b. This option permits the player to drop a ball behind the point where it lay, keeping that point between the hole and the spot on which the ball is dropped, with no limit to how far back the ball may be dropped. This decision afforded Mickelson the best outcome and allowed him to drop the ball behind the bunker and onto the fairway under penalty of one stroke

2007 Open Championship *Carnoustie* July 19–22 [7421–71]

Total Prize Money: £4.2 million. Entries: 2,443. 16 Regional Qualifying Courses: Ashridge, Effingham, Enville, Gog Magog, Minchinhampton, Musselburgh, Notts, Old Fold Manor, Pannal, Pleasington, Prestbury, Rochester & Cobham Park, Royal Ashdown Forest, Royal Dublin, Silloth-on-Solway, Trentham. Final qualifying courses: Downfield, Monifieth, Montrose, Panmure. Final field: 156 (6 amateurs) of whom 70 (1 amateur) made the half-way cut with scores of 146 or less.

1	Padraig Harrington (IRL)*	69-73-68-67—277	£750,000
2	Sergio García (ESP)	65-71-68-73—277	450,000
	**Four-hole play-off – Harrington 3-3-4-5; García 5-3-4-4*		
3	Andres Romero (ARG)	71-70-70-67—278	290,000
4	Ernie Els (RSA)	72-70-68-69—279	200,000
	Richard Green (AUS)	72-73-70-64—279	200,000
6	Stewart Cink (USA)	69-73-68-70—280	145,500
	Hunter Mahan (USA)	73-73-69-65—280	145,500
8	K J Choi (KOR)	69-69-72-71—281	94,750
	Ben Curtis (USA)	72-74-70-65—281	94,750
	Steve Stricker (USA)	71-72-64-74—281	94,750
	Mike Weir (CAN)	71-68-72-70—281	94,750
12	Markus Brier (AUT)	68-75-70-69—282	58,571
	Paul Broadhurst ENG)	71-71-68-72—282	58,571
	Telle Edberg (SWE)	72-73-67-70—282	58,571
	Jim Furyk (USA)	70-70-71-71—282	58,571
	Miguel Angel Jiménez (ESP)	69-70-72-71—282	58,571
	Justin Rose (ENG)	75-70-67-70—282	58,571
	Tiger Woods (USA)	69-74-69-70—282	58,571
19	Paul McGinley (IRL)	67-75-68-73—283	46,000
20	Rich Beem (USA)	70-73-69-72—284	42,000
20T	Zach Johnson (USA)	73-73-68-70—284	42,000
	Pat Perez (USA)	73-70-71-70—284	42,000
23	Jonathan Byrd (USA)	73-72-70-70—285	35,562
	Mark Calcavecchia (USA)	74-70-72-69—285	35,562
	Chris DiMarco (USA)	74-70-66-75—285	35,562
	Retief Goosen (RSA)	70-71-73-71—285	35,562
27	Paul Casey (ENG)	72-73-69-72—286	28,178
	Lucas Glover (USA)	71-72-70-73—286	28,178
	J J Henry (USA)	70-71-71-74—286	28,178
	Rodney Pampling (AUS)	70-72-72-72—286	28,178
	Ian Poulter (ENG)	73-73-70-70—286	28,178
	Adam Scott (AUS)	73-70-72-71—286	28,178
	Vijay Singh (FIJ)	72-71-68-75—286	28,178
34	Angel Cabrera (ARG)	68-73-72-74—287	24,000
35	Niclas Fasth (SWE)	75-69-73-71—288	20,107
	Mark Foster (ENG)	76-70-73-69—288	20,107
	Charley Hoffman (USA)	75-69-72-72—288	20,107
	Shaun Micheel (USA)	70-76-70-72—288	20,107
	Nick Watney (USA)	72-71-70-75—288	20,107
	Boo Weekley (USA)	68-72-75-73—288	20,107
	Lee Westwood (ENG)	71-70-73-74—288	20,107

Other players who made the cut: Nick Dougherty (ENG), Rory McIlroy (NIR) (am) (Silver Medal), Ryan Moore (USA) 289; Ross Bain (SCO), Arron Oberholser (USA), Carl Pettersson (SWE), John Senden (AUS) 290; Jerry Kelly (USA), Won Joon Lee (KOR) 291; Tom Lehman (USA), Kevin Stadler (USA) 293; Thomas Bjørn (DEN), Grégory Bourdy (FRA), Brian Davis (ENG), David Howell (ENG) 294; Michael Campbell (NZL), Anders Hansen (DEN), Scott Verplank (USA) 295; Trevor Immelman (RSA), Mark O'Meara (USA), Toru Taniguchi (JPN) 296; John Bevan (ENG), Luke Donald (ENG) 297; Raphaël Jacquelin (FRA), Sandy Lyle (SCO) 298; Alastair Forsyth (SCO), Sean O'Hair (USA) 299; Fredrik Andersson Hed (SWE), Peter Hanson (SWE) 300

2006 Open Championship *Royal Liverpool, Hoylake* July 20–23 [7528–72]

Total Prize Money: £3,898,000. Entries: 2,434. 16 Regional Qualifying Courses: Ashridge, County Louth, Effingham, Little Aston, Minchinhampton, Musselburgh, Notts, Old Fold Manor, Orsett, Pannal, Pleasington, Prestbury, Rochester & Cobham Park, Royal Ashdown Forest, Silloth-on-Solway, Trentham. Final qualifying courses: Conwy, Formby, Wallasey, West Lancashire. Final field: 156 (4 amateurs) of whom 71 (2 amateurs) made the half-way cut on 143 or less.

1	Tiger Woods (USA)	67-65-71-67—270	£720,000
2	Chris DiMarco (USA)	70-65-69-68—272	430,000
3	Ernie Els (RSA)	68-65-71-71—275	275,000
4	Jim Furyk (USA)	68-71-66-71—276	210,000
5	Sergio García (ESP)	68-71-65-73—277	159,500
	Hideto Tanihara (JPN)	72-68-66-71—277	159,500
7	Angel Cabrera (ARG)	71-68-66-73—278	128,000
8	Carl Pettersson (SWE)	68-72-70-69—279	95,333
	Andres Romero (ARG)	70-70-68-71—279	95,333
	Adam Scott (AUS)	68-69-70-72—279	95,333
11	Ben Crane (USA)	68-71-71-70—280	69,333
	S K Ho (KOR)	68-73-69-70—280	69,333
	Anthony Wall (ENG)	67-73-71-69—280	69,333
14	Retief Goosen (RSA)	70-66-72-73—281	56,500
	Sean O'Hair (USA)	69-73-72-67—281	56,500
16	Robert Allenby (AUS)	69-70-69-74—282	45,000
	Mikko Ilonen (FIN)	68-69-73-72—282	45,000
	Peter Lonard (AUS)	71-69-68-74—282	45,000
	Geoff Ogilvy (AUS)	71-69-70-72—282	45,000
	Robert Rock (ENG)	69-69-73-71—282	45,000
16T	Brett Rumford (AUS)	68-71-72-71—282	45,000
22	Mark Hensby (AUS)	68-72-74-69—283	35,375
	Phil Mickelson (USA)	69-71-73-70—283	35,375
	Greg Owen (ENG)	67-73-68-75—283	35,375
	Charl Schwartzel (RSA)	74-66-72-71—283	35,375
26	Paul Broadhurst (ENG)	71-71-73-69—284	29,100
	Jerry Kelly (USA)	72-67-69-76—284	29,100
	Hunter Mahan (USA)	73-70-68-73—284	29,100
	Rory Sabbatini (RSA)	69-70-73-72—284	29,100
	Lee Slattery (ENG)	69-72-71-72—284	29,100
31	Simon Khan (ENG)	70-72-68-75—285	24,500
	Scott Verplank (USA)	70-73-67-75—285	24,500
	Lee Westwood (ENG)	69-72-75-69—285	24,500
	Thaworn Wiratchant (THA)	71-68-74-72—285	35,591
35	Michael Campbell (NZL)	70-71-75-70—286	19,625
	Luke Donald (ENG)	74-68-73-71—286	19,625
	Marcus Fraser (AUS)	68-71-72-75—286	19,625
	Robert Karlsson (SWE)	70-71-71-74—286	19,625
	Rod Pampling (AUS)	69-71-74-72—286	19,625
	John Senden (AUS)	70-73-73-70—286	19,625

Other players who made the cut: Stephen Ames (CAN), Thomas Bjørn (DEN), Mark Calcavecchia (USA), Miguel Angel Jiménez (ESP), Brandt Jobe (USA), Søren Kjeldsen (DEN), Jeff Sluman (USA) 287; John Bickerton (ENG), Simon Dyson (ENG), Gonzalo Fernandez Castano (ESP), Andrew Marshall (ENG), Henrik Stenson (SWE), Marius Thorp (NOR) (am) (Silver Medal), Tom Watson (USA), Simon Wakefield (ENG) 288; Tim Clark (RSA), David Duval (USA), Keiichiro Fukabori (JPN), José-María Olazábal (ESP), Mike Weir (CAN) 289; Andrew Buckle (AUS), Graeme McDowell (NIR) 290; Mark O'Meara (USA), Marco Ruiz (PAR) 291; Chad Campbell (USA) 292; Fred Funk (USA), Vaughn Taylor (USA) 294; Todd Hamilton (USA), Edoardo Molinari (ITA) (am) 295; Bart Bryant (USA) 296; Paul Casey (ENG) 298

2005 Open Championship *St Andrews (Old Course)* June 14–17 [7279–72]

Total Prize Money: £3,854,900. Entries: 2,499 (record). 16 Regional Qualifying Courses: Alwoodley, Ashridge, Hadley Wood, Hindhead, The Island, Little Aston, Minchinhampton, Notts, Orsett, Pleasington, Prestbury, Renfrew, Rochester & Final qualifying courses: Ladybank, Leven, Lundin, Scotscraig. Cobham Park, Royal Ashdown Forest, Silloth-on-Solway, Trentham. Final Field: 156 (7 amateurs), of whom 80 (4 amateurs) made the half-way cut on 145 or less.

1	Tiger Woods (USA)	66-67-71-70—274	£720,000
2	Colin Montgomerie (SCO)	71-66-70-72—279	430,000
3	Fred Couples (USA)	68-71-73-68—280	242,500
	José-María Olazábal (ESP)	68-70-68-74—280	242,500
5	Michael Campbell (NZL)	69-72-68-72—281	122,167
	Sergio García (ESP)	70-69-69-73—281	122,167
	Retief Goosen (RSA)	68-73-66-74—281	122,167
	Bernhard Langer (GER)	71-69-70-71—281	122,167
	Geoff Ogilvy (AUS)	71-74-67-69—281	122,167
	Vijay Singh (FIJ)	69-69-71-72—281	122,167
11	Nick Faldo (ENG)	74-69-70-69—282	66,750
	Graeme McDowell (NIR)	69-72-74-67—282	66,750
	Kenny Perry (USA)	71-71-68-72—282	66,750
	Ian Poulter (ENG)	70-72-71-69—282	66,750
15	Darren Clarke (NIR)	73-70-67-73—283	46,286
	John Daly (USA)	71-69-70-73—283	46,286
	David Frost (RSA)	77-65-72-69—283	46,286
	Mark Hensby (AUS)	67-77-69-70—283	46,286
	Trevor Immelman (RSA)	68-70-73-72—283	46,286
	Sean O'Hair (USA)	73-67-70-73—283	46,286
	Nick O'Hern (AUS)	73-69-71-70—283	46,286
15T	Lloyd Saltman (SCO) (am)	73-71-68-71—283	Silver Medal
23	Bart Bryant (USA)	69-70-71-74—284	32,500
	Tim Clark (RSA)	71-69-70-74—284	32,500
	Scott Drummond (SCO)	74-71-69-70—284	32,500
	Brad Faxon (USA)	72-66-70-76—284	32,500
	Nicholas Flanagan (AUS)	73-71-69-71—284	32,500
	Tom Lehman (USA)	75-69-70-70—284	32,500
	Eric Ramsay (SCO) (am)	68-74-74-68—284	
	Tadahiro Takayama (JPN)	72-72-70-70—284	32,500
	Scott Verplank (USA)	68-70-72-74—284	32,500
32	Richard Green (AUS)	72-68-72-73—285	26,500
	Sandy Lyle (SCO)	74-67-69-75—285	26,500
34	Simon Dyson (ENG)	70-71-72-73—286	22,000
	Ernie Els (RSA)	74-67-75-70—286	22,000
	Peter Hanson (SWE)	72-72-71-71—286	22,000
	Thomas Levet (FRA)	69-71-75-71—286	22,000
	Joe Ogilvie (USA)	74-70-73-69—286	22,000
	Adam Scott (AUS)	70-71-70-75—286	22,000
	Henrik Stenson (SWE)	74-67-73-72—286	22,000

2012 Open Championship – rulings of the day – Friday

Casual Water in Bunker

The second day's play of the 141st Open Championship saw several players have difficulties with casual water in bunkers.

A player is entitled to free relief from casual water in a bunker if his ball lies in the casual water, his intended stance is in the casual water or his intended swing is interfered with by the casual water.

On Friday, both Keegan Bradley and Rory McIlroy had to consider their options for relief from casual water when they found the sand on the 15th and 17th holes respectively.

In taking free relief, the "nearest point of relief" must be in the bunker. If complete relief is impossible, a player is entitled to take "maximum available relief" in the bunker and drop the ball as near as possible to that point.

Alternatively, under penalty of one stroke, a player may drop out of the bunker keeping the point where the ball lay directly in line with the hole.

McIlroy was able to and chose to take free relief within the fairway bunker at the 17th and dropped the ball within a club-length of the nearest point of relief before but Bradley chose to play his ball at the 15th hole, despite the interference from the casual water.

Although a ball may lie in casual water, a player does not have to take relief from casual water in a bunker and may instead elect to play the ball as it lies.

Bradley may have decided to do this for a number of reasons. As the sand was damp, the ball may have plugged in the sand when dropped or the dropping area may have been close to the face or edge of the bunker leaving the player with a much more difficult stroke. Consequently, choosing not to take relief and play the ball from its original lie was, he felt, the best option.

2005 Open Championship *continued*

Other players who made the cut: Stuart Appleby (AUS), K J Choi (KOR), Hiroyuki Fujita (JPN), Søren Hansen (DEN), Tim Herron (USA), Simon Khan (ENG), Maarten Lafeber (NED), Paul McGinley (IRL), Bob Tway (USA), Tom Watson (USA), Steve Webster (ENG) 287; Robert Allenby (AUS), Luke Donald (ENG), Fredrik Jacobson (SWE), Thongchai Jaidee (THA), Miguel Angel Jiménez (ESP), Paul Lawrie (SCO), Justin Leonard (USA), Bo Van Pelt (USA) 288; John Bickerton (ENG), Mark Calcavecchia (USA), Phil Mickelson (USA), Edoardo Molinari (ITA) (am), Greg Norman (AUS), Tino Schuster (GER) 289; Peter Lonard (AUS) 290; Chris DiMarco (USA), Pat Perez (USA), Chris Riley (USA), Robert Rock (ENG), David Smail (NZL), Duffy Waldorf (USA) 291; Patrik Sjöland (SWE) 292; Scott Gutschewski (USA), S K Ho (KOR), Ted Purdy (USA) 293; Steve Flesch (USA), 294; Rodney Pampling (AUS), Graeme Storm (ENG) 296; Matthew Richardson (ENG) (am) 297

2004 Open Championship *Royal Troon* July 15–18 [7175–71]

Total Prize Money: £4,064,000. Entries: 2221 Regional Qualifying Courses: Alwoodley, Ashridge, Co.Louth, Hadley Wood, Hindhead, Little Aston, Minchinhampton, Notts, Orsett, Pleasington, Prestbury, Renfrew, Rochester & Cobham Park, Royal Ashdown Forest, Silloth-on-Solway, Trentham. Final qualifying courses: Glasgow (Gailes), Irvine, Turnberry Kintyre, Western Gailes. Final Field: 156 (5 amateurs), of whom 73 (1 amateur) made the half-way cut on 145 or less.

1	Todd Hamilton (USA)*	71-67-67-69—274	£720,000
2	Ernie Els (RSA)	69-69-68-68—274	430,000
Four-hole play-off: Hamilton 4-4-3-4; Els 4-4-4-4			
3	Phil Mickelson (USA)	73-66-68-68—275	275,000
4	Lee Westwood (ENG)	72-71-68-67—278	210,000
5	Thomas Levet (FRA)	66-70-71-72—279	159,500
	Davis Love III (USA)	72-69-71-67—279	159,500
7	Retief Goosen (RSA)	69-70-68-73—280	117,500
	Scott Verplank (USA)	69-70-70-71—280	117,500
9	Mike Weir (CAN)	71-68-71-71—281	89,500
	Tiger Woods (USA)	70-71-68-72—281	89,500
11	Mark Calcavecchia (USA)	72-73-69-68—282	69,333
	Darren Clarke (NIR)	69-72-73-68—282	69,333
	Skip Kendall (USA)	69-66-75-72—282	69,333
14	Stewart Fink (USA)	72-71-71-69—283	56,500
	Barry Lane (ENG)	69-68-71-75—283	56,500
16	K J Choi (KOR)	68-69-74-73—284	47,000
	Joakim Haeggman (SWE)	69-73-72-70—284	47,000
	Justin Leonard (USA)	70-72-71-71—284	47,000
	Kenny Perry (USA)	69-70-73-72—284	47,000
20	Michael Campbell (NZL)	67-71-74-73—285	38,100
20T	Paul Casey (ENG)	66-77-70-72—285	38,100
	Bob Estes (USA)	73-72-69-71—285	38,100
	Gary Evans (ENG)	68-73-73-71—285	38,100
	Vijay Singh (FIJ)	68-70-76-71—285	38,100
25	Colin Montgomerie (SCO)	69-69-72-76—286	32,250
	Ian Poulter (ENG)	71-72-71-72—286	32,250
27	Takashi Kamiyama (JPN)	70-73-71-73—287	29,000
	Rodney Pampling (AUS)	72-68-74-73—287	29,000
	Jyoti Randhawa (IND)	73-72-70-72—287	29,000
30	Kelichiro Fukabori (JPN)	73-71-70-74—288	24,500
	Shigeki Maruyama (JPN)	71-72-74-71—288	24,500
	Mark O'Meara (USA)	71-74-68-75—288	24,500
	Nick Price (ZIM)	71-71-69-77—288	24,500
	David Toms (USA)	71-71-74-72—288	24,500
	Bo Van Pelt (USA)	72-71-71-74—288	24,500
36	Stuart Appleby (AUS)	71-70-73-75—289	18,750
	Kim Felton (AUS)	73-67-72-77—289	18,750
	Tetsuji Hiratsuka (JPN)	70-74-70-75—289	18,750
	Steve Lowery (USA)	69-73-75-72—289	18,750
	Hunter Mahan (USA)	74-69-71-75—289	18,750
	Tjaart Van Der Walt (RSA)	70-73-72-74—289	18,750

Other players who made the cut: Kenneth Ferrie (ENG), Charles Howell III (USA), Trevor Immelman (RSA), Andrew Oldcorn (SCO), Adam Scott (AUS) 290; Paul Bradshaw (ENG), Alastair Forsyth (SCO), Mathias Grönberg (SWE), Migel Angel Jiménez (ESP), Jerry Kelly (USA), Shaun Micheel (USA), Sean Whiffin (ENG) 291; Steve Flesch (USA), Ignaçio Garrido (ESP), Rafaël Jacquelin (FRA) 292; James Kingston (RSA), Paul McGinley (IRL), Carl Pettersson (SWE) 293; Paul Broadhurst (ENG), Gary Emerson (ENG), Brad Faxon (USA) 294; Chris DiMarco (USA), Mark Foster (ENG), Stuart Wilson (SCO) (am) (Silver Medal) 296; Mårten Olander (SWE), Rory Sabbatini (RSA) 297; Martin Erlandsson (SWE), Paul Wesselingh (ENG) 298; Bob Tway (USA) 299; Rich Beem (USA), Christian Cévaër (FRA) 300; Sandy Lyle (SCO) 303

2012 Open Championship – rulings of the day – Saturday

Ball Unfit for Play

With sunny skies and a light breeze, there were fewer rulings on Saturday at the 141st Open Championship at Royal Lytham and St Annes. A ruling that did arise, however, on Saturday and during previous rounds, involved more than one player calling a referee to establish if his ball was unfit for play.

A ball is not unfit for play solely because mud or other materials stick to it. Equally, a ball is not unfit for play if its surface is scratched or scraped or its paint is damaged or discoloured. It must be visibly cut, cracked or out of shape to be considered unfit for play.

If you have reason to believe that your ball has become unfit for play you may lift it without penalty and mark it in order to determine whether it is or not. Under Rule 5-3 you must first announce your intention to do so to your opponent, marker, fellow-competitor. or referee. If you fail to comply with all or any part of this procedure you incur a penalty of one stroke.

If it is determined by the player and referee that the ball has become unfit for play, the player may substitute another ball without penalty, placing it on the spot where the original ball lay.

2003 Open Championship *Royal St George's* July 17–20 [7034–71]

Prize Money £3.9 million. Entries: 2152. Regional qualifying courses: Alwoodley, Ashridge, Blackmoor, Co.Louth, Hadley Wood, Hindhead, Little Aston, Minchinhampton, Notts, Ormskirk, Orsett, Renfrew, Silloth-on-Solway, Stockport, Trentham, Wildernesse. Final qualifying courses: Littlestone, North Foreland, Prince's, Royal Cinque Ports. Final Field: 156 (3 amateurs), of whom 75 (no amateurs) made the half-way cut on 150 or less.

1	Ben Curtis (USA)	72-72-70-69—283	£700,000
2	Thomas Bjørn (DEN)	73-70-69-72—284	345,000
	Vijay Singh (FIJ)	75-70-69-70—284	345,000
4	Davis Love III (USA)	69-72-72-72—285	185,000
	Tiger Woods (USA)	73-72-69-71—285	185,000
6	Brian Davis (ENG)	77-73-68-68—286	134,500
	Fredrik Jacobson (SWE)	70-76-70-70—286	134,500
8	Nick Faldo (ENG)	76-74-67-70—287	97,750
	Kenny Perry (USA)	74-70-70-73—287	97,750
10	Gary Evans (ENG)	71-75-70-72—288	68,000
	Sergio García (ESP)	73-71-70-74—288	68,000
	Retief Goosen (RSA)	73-75-71-69—288	68,000
	Hennie Otto (RSA)	68-76-75-69—288	68,000
	Phillip Price (WAL)	74-72-69-73—288	68,000
15	Stuart Appleby (AUS)	75-71-71-72—289	49,333
	Chad Campbell (USA)	74-71-72-72—289	49,333
	Pierre Fulke (SWE)	77-72-67-73—289	49,333
18	Ernie Els (RSA)	78-68-72-72—290	42,000
	Mathias Grönberg (SWE)	71-74-73-72—290	42,000
	Greg Norman (AUS)	69-79-74-68—290	42,000
	Tom Watson (USA)	71-77-73-69—290	42,000
22	Angel Cabrera (ARG)	75-73-70-73—291	32,917
	K J Choi (KOR)	77-72-72-70—291	32,917
22T	Peter Fowler (AUS)	77-73-70-71—291	32,917
	Padraig Harrington (IRL)	75-73-74-69—297	32,917
	Thomas Levet (FRA)	71-73-74-73—291	32,917
	JL Lewis (USA)	78-70-72-71—291	32,917
28	Mark Foster (ENG)	73-73-72-74—292	26,000
	SK Ho (KOR)	70-73-72-77—292	26,000
	Paul McGinley (IRL)	77-73-69-73—292	26,000
	Andrew Oldcorn (SCO)	72-74-73-73—292	26,000
	Nick Price (ZIM)	74-72-72-74—292	26,000
	Mike Weir (CAN)	74-76-71-71—292	26,000
34	Stewart Cink (USA)	75-75-75-68—293	18,778
	José Coceres (ARG)	77-70-72-74—293	18,778
	Bob Estes (USA)	77-71-76-69—293	18,778
	Shingo Katayama (JPN)	76-73-73-71—293	18,778
	Scott McCarron (USA)	71-74-73-75—293	18,778
	Adam Mednick (SWE)	76-72-76-69—293	18,778
	Gary Murphy (IRL)	73-74-73-73—293	18,778
	Marco Ruiz (PAR)	73-71-75-74—293	18,778
	Duffy Waldorf (USA)	76-73-71-73—293	18,778
43	Robert Allenby (AUS)	73-75-74-72—294	14,250
	Rich Beem (USA)	76-74-75-69—294	14,250
	Tom Byrum (USA)	77-72-71-74—294	14,250

Other players who made the cut: Markus Brier (AUT), Fred Couples (USA), Brad Faxon (USA), Mathew Goggin (AUS), Tom Lehman (USA), Ian Poulter (ENG), Anthony Wall (ENG) 295; Michael Campbell (NZL), Trevor Immelman (RSA), Raphaèl Jacquelin (FRA), David Lynn (ENG), Mark McNulty (ZIM), Rory Sabbatini (RSA) 296; Darren Clarke (NIR), Alastair Forsyth (SCO), Skip Kendall (USA), Peter Lonard (AUS), Phil Mickelson (USA), Craig Parry (AUS) 297; Charles Howell III (USA), Stephen Leaney (AUS), Len Mattiace (USA), Mark O'Meara (USA) 298; Katsuyoshi Tomori (JPN) 300; John Rollins (USA) 301; Chris Smith (USA) 302; John Daly (USA), Ian Woosnam (WAL) 303; Jesper Parnevik (SWE), Mark Roe (ENG) DQ

Ernie Els, in his own words…

"When I finished The R&A asked me what I wanted to do, did I want to watch or what? I said, no, I'll go to the putting green like I've done so many times. And I just thought I'll probably be disappointed again because so many times I've waited on a playoff. I mean, it even happened this year at New Orleans. You're not really hoping the other guy is going to make a mistake, but you're hoping you don't have to go to a playoff, you want to win outright. This one was different because I feel for Adam. I really didn't mind going to a playoff. At best I was hoping for a playoff."

2012 Open Championship – rulings of the day – Sunday

Lost Ball

During the final day's play of the 141st Open Championship, several players lost a ball in the stiff breeze

Brandt Snedeker, John Daly, Branden Grace and Jeev Milkha Singh all chose to play a provisional ball and decided that it would be to their advantage not to find the original ball.

Each did not search for the original ball but instead walked directly to his provisional ball and, as he is entitled to do, played it.

If in the meantime, howver, a spectator, a fellow-competitor or an opponent finds the original ball within the stipulated five minute search period the player must, having made sure it is his ball, continue to play with it or proceed under the unplayable ball Rule. The provisional ball in this case must then be abandoned.

Open Championship History

The Belt

Date		Winner	Score	Venue	Entrants	Prize money £
1860	Oct 17	W Park, Musselburgh	174	Prestwick	8	—
1861	Sept 26	T Morris Sr, Prestwick	163	Prestwick	12	—
1862	Sept 11	T Morris Sr, Prestwick	163	Prestwick	6	—
1863	Sept 18	W Park, Musselburgh	168	Prestwick	14	10
1864	Sept 16	T Morris Sr, Prestwick	167	Prestwick	6	15
1865	Sept 14	A Strath, St Andrews	162	Prestwick	10	20
1866	Sept 13	W Park, Musselburgh	169	Prestwick	12	11
1867	Sept 26	T Morris Sr, St Andrews	170	Prestwick	10	16
1868	Sept 23	T Morris Jr, St Andrews	154	Prestwick	12	12
1869	Sept 16	T Morris Jr, St Andrews	157	Prestwick	14	12
1870	Sept 15	T Morris Jr, St Andrews	149	Prestwick	17	12

Having won it three times in succession, the Belt became the property of Young Tom Morris and the Championship was held in abeyance for a year. In 1872 the Claret Jug was, and still is, offered for annual competition but it was not available to present at the time to Tom Morris Jr in 1872.

The Claret Jug

Date		Winner	Score	Venue	Entrants	Prize money £
1872	Sept 13	T Morris Jr, St Andrews	166	Prestwick	8	20
1873	Oct 4	T Kidd, St Andrews	179	St Andrews	26	20
1874	April 10	M Park, Musselburgh	159	Musselburgh	32	29
1875	Sept 10	W Park, Musselburgh	166	Prestwick	18	20
1876	Sept 30	B Martin, St Andrews	176	St Andrews	34	27
(D Strath tied but refused to play off)						
1877	April 6	J Anderson, St Andrews	160	Musselburgh	24	20
1878	Oct 4	J Anderson, St Andrews	157	Prestwick	26	20
1879	Sept 27	J Anderson, St Andrews	169	St Andrews	46	45
1880	April 9	B Ferguson, Musselburgh	162	Musselburgh	30	†
1881	Oct 14	B Ferguson, Musselburgh	170	Prestwick	22	21
1882	Sept 30	B Ferguson, Musselburgh	171	St Andrews	40	45
1883	Nov 16	W Fernie*, Dumfries	158	Musselburgh	41	20
**After a play-off with B Ferguson, Musselburgh: Fernie 158; Ferguson 159*						
1884	Oct 3	J Simpson, Carnoustie	160	Prestwick	30	23
1885	Oct 3	B Martin, St Andrews	171	St Andrews	51	34
1886	Nov 5	D Brown, Musselburgh	157	Musselburgh	46	20
1887	Sept 16	W Park Jr, Musselburgh	161	Prestwick	36	20
1888	Oct 6	J Burns, Warwick	171	St Andrews	53	24
1889	Nov 8	W Park Jr*, Musselburgh	155	Musselburgh	42	22
**After a play-off with A Kirkaldy: Park Jr 158; Kirkaldy 163*						
1890	Sept 11	J Ball, Royal Liverpool (am)	164	Prestwick	40	29.50
1891	Oct 6	H Kirkaldy, St Andrews	166	St Andrews	82	30.50
After 1891 the competition was extended to 72 holes and for the first time entry money was imposed						
1892	Sept 22–23	H Hilton, Royal Liverpool (am)	305	Muirfield	66	100
1893	Aug 31–Sept 1	W Auchterlonie, St Andrews	322	Prestwick	72	100
1894	June 11–12	J Taylor, Winchester	326	Royal St George's	94	100
1895	June 12–13	J Taylor, Winchester	322	St Andrews	73	100
1896	June 10–11	H Vardon*, Ganton	316	Muirfield	64	100
**After a 36-hole play-off with JH Taylor: Vardon 157; Taylor 161*						
1897	May 19–20	H Hilton, Royal Liverpool (am)	314	Royal Liverpool	86	100
1898	June 8–9	H Vardon, Ganton	307	Prestwick	78	100
1899	June 7–8	H Vardon, Ganton	310	Royal St George's	98	100
1900	June 6–7	J Taylor, Mid-Surrey	309	St Andrews	81	125
1901	June 5–6	J Braid, Romford	309	Muirfield	101	125
1902	June 4–5	A Herd, Huddersfield	307	Royal Liverpool	112	125
1903	June 10–11	H Vardon, Totteridge	300	Prestwick	127	125

† prize money not known

Date		Winner	Score	Venue	Entrants	Qualifiers	Prize-money £
1904	June 8–10	J White, Sunningdale	296	Royal St George's	144		125
1905	June 7–9	J Braid, Walton Heath	318	St Andrews	152		125
1906	June 13–15	J Braid, Walton Heath	300	Muirfield	183		125
1907	June 20–21	A Massy, La Boulie	312	Royal Liverpool	193		125
1908	June 18–19	J Braid, Walton Heath	291	Prestwick	180		125
1909	June 10–11	J Taylor, Mid-Surrey	295	Royal Cinque Ports	204		125
1910	June 22–24	J Braid, Walton Heath	299	St Andrews	210		135
1911	June 26–29	H Vardon*, Totteridge	303	Royal St George's	226		135
**After a play-off with A Massy. The play-off was over 36 holes, but Massy picked up at the 35th before holing out. He had taken 148 for 34 holes, and when Vardon holed out at the 35th hole his score was 143*							
1912	June 24–25	E Ray, Oxhey	295	Muirfield	215		135
1913	June 23–24	J Taylor, Mid-Surrey	304	Royal Liverpool	269		135
1914	June 18–19	H Vardon, Totteridge	306	Prestwick	194		135
1915–19	*No Championship*						
1920	June 30–July 1	G Duncan, Hanger Hill	303	Royal Cinque Ports	190	81	225
1921	June 23–25	J Hutchison*, Glenview, Chicago	296	St Andrews	158	85	225
**After a play-off with R Wethered (am): Hutchison 150; Wethered 159*							
1922	June 22–23	W Hagen, Detroit, USA	300	Royal St George's	225	80	225
1923	June 14–15	A Havers, Coombe Hill	295	Troon	222	88	225
1924	June 26–27	W Hagen, Detroit, USA	301	Royal Liverpool	277	86	225
1925	June 25–26	J Barnes, USA	300	Prestwick	200	83	225
1926	June 23–25	R Jones, USA (am)	291	Royal Lytham & St Annes	293	117	225
1927	July 13–15	R Jones, USA (am)	285	St Andrews	207	108	275
1928	May 9–11	W Hagen, USA	292	Royal St George's	271	113	275
1929	May 8–10	W Hagen, USA	292	Muirfield	242	109	275
1930	June 18–20	R Jones, USA (am)	291	Royal Liverpool	296	112	400
1931	June 3–5	T Armour, USA	296	Carnoustie	215	109	500
1932	June 8–10	G Sarazen, USA	283	Sandwich, Prince's	224	110	500
1933	July 5–7	D Shute*, USA	292	St Andrews	287	117	500
**After a play-off with C Wood, USA: Shute 149; Wood 154*							
1934	June 27–29	T Cotton, Waterloo, Belgium	283	Royal St George's	312	101	500
1935	June 26–28	A Perry, Leatherhead	283	Muirfield	264	109	500
1936	June 25–27	A Padgham, Sundridge Park	287	Royal Liverpool	286	107	500
1937	July 7–9	T Cotton, Ashridge	290	Carnoustie	258	141	500
1938	July 6–8	R Whitcombe, Parkstone	295	Royal St George's	268	120	500
1939	July 5–7	R Burton, Sale	290	St Andrews	254	129	500
1940–45	*No Championship*						
1946	July 3–5	S Snead, USA	290	St Andrews	225	100	1,000
1947	July 2–4	F Daly, Balmoral	293	Royal Liverpool	263	100	1,000
1948	June 30–July 2	T Cotton, Royal Mid-Surrey	284	Muirfield	272	97	1,000
1949	July 6–8	A Locke*, RSA	283	Royal St George's	224	96	1,500
**After a play-off with H Bradshaw: Locke 135; Bradshaw 147*							
1950	July 5–7	A Locke, RSA	279	Troon	262	93	1,500
1951	July 4–6	M Faulkner, England	285	Royal Portrush	180	98	1,700
1952	July 9–11	A Locke, RSA	287	Royal Lytham & St Annes	275	96	1,700
1953	July 8–10	B Hogan, USA	282	Carnoustie	196	91	2,500
1954	July 7–9	P Thomson, Australia	283	Royal Birkdale	349	97	3,500
1955	July 6–8	P Thomson, Australia	281	St Andrews	301	94	3,750
1956	July 4–6	P Thomson, Australia	286	Royal Liverpool	360	96	3,750
1957	July 3–5	A Locke, RSA	279	St Andrews	282	96	3,750
1958	July 2–4	P Thomson*, Australia	278	Royal Lytham & St Annes	362	96	4,850
**After a play-off with D Thomas: Thomson 139; Thomas 143*							
1959	July 1–3	G Player, RSA	284	Muirfield	285	90	5,000
1960	July 6–8	K Nagle, Australia	278	St Andrews	410	74	7,000
1961	July 12–14	A Palmer, USA	284	Royal Birkdale	364	101	8,500
1962	July 11–13	A Palmer, USA	276	Troon	379	119	8,500
1963	July 10–12	R Charles*, New Zealand	277	Royal Lytham & St Annes	261	119	8,500
**After a play-off with P Rodgers, USA: Charles 140; Rodgers 148*							
1964	July 8–10	T Lema, USA	279	St Andrews	327	119	8,500
1965	July 7–9	P Thomson, Australia	285	Royal Birkdale	372	130	10,000
1966	July 6–9	J Nicklaus, USA	282	Muirfield	310	130	15,000
1967	July 12–15	R De Vicenzo, Argentina	278	Royal Liverpool	326	130	15,000
1968	July 10–13	G Player, RSA	289	Carnoustie	309	130	20,000
1969	July 9–12	A Jacklin, England	280	Royal Lytham & St Annes	424	129	30,334
1970	July 8–11	J Nicklaus*, USA	283	St Andrews	468	134	40,000
**After a play-off with Doug Sanders, USA: Nicklaus 72; Sanders 73*							
1971	July 7–10	L Trevino, USA	278	Royal Birkdale	528	150	45,000
1972	July 12–15	L Trevino, USA	278	Muirfield	570	150	50,000
1973	July 11–14	T Weiskopf, USA	276	Troon	569	150	50,000

Open Championship Claret Jug winners history *continued*

Date	Winner	Score	Venue	Entrants	Qualifiers	Prize-money £
1974 July 10–13	G Player, RSA	282	Royal Lytham & St Annes	679	150	50,000
1975 July 9–12	T Watson*, USA	279	Carnoustie	629	150	50,000
**After a play-off with J Newton (AUS): Watson 71; Newton 72*						
1976 July 7–10	J Miller, USA	279	Royal Birkdale	719	150	75,000
1977 July 6–9	T Watson, USA	268	Turnberry	730	150	100,000
1978 July 12–15	J Nicklaus, USA	281	St Andrews	788	150	125,000
1979 July 18–21	S Ballesteros, Spain	283	Royal Lytham & St Annes	885	150	155,000
1980 July 17–20	T Watson, USA	271	Muirfield	994	151	200,000
1981 July 16–19	B Rogers, USA	276	Royal St George's	971	153	200,000
1982 July 15–18	T Watson, USA	284	Royal Troon	1,121	150	250,000
1983 July 14–17	T Watson, USA	275	Royal Birkdale	1,107	151	310,000
1984 July 19–22	S Ballesteros, Spain	276	St Andrews	1,413	156	445,000
1985 July 18–21	A Lyle, Scotland	282	Royal St George's	1,361	149	530,000
1986 July 17–20	G Norman, Australia	280	Turnberry	1,347	152	634,000
1987 July 16–19	N Faldo, England	279	Muirfield	1,407	153	650,000
1988 July 14–18	S Ballesteros, Spain	273	Royal Lytham & St Annes	1,393	153	700,000
1989 July 20–23	M Calcavecchia*, USA	275	Royal Troon	1,481	156	750,000
**Four-hole play-off (1st, 2nd, 17th and 18th): Calcavecchia 4-3-3-3, W Grady (AUS) 4-4-4-4, G Norman (AUS) 3-4-4-X*						
1990 July 19–22	N Faldo, England	270	St Andrews	1,707	152	825,000
1991 July 18–21	I Baker-Finch, Australia	272	Royal Birkdale	1,496	156	900,000
1992 July 16–19	N Faldo, England	272	Muirfield	1,666	156	950,000
1993 July 15–18	G Norman, Australia	267	Royal St George's	1,827	156	1,000,000
1994 July 14–17	N Price, Zimbabwe	268	Turnberry	1,701	156	1,100,000
1995 July 20–23	J Daly*, USA	282	St Andrews	1,836	159	1,250,000
**Four-hole play-off (1st, 2nd, 17th and 18th): Daly 4-3-4-4, C Rocca (ITA) 5-4-7-3*						
1996 July 18–21	T Lehman, USA	271	Royal Lytham & St Annes	1,918	156	1,400,000
1997 July 17–20	J Leonard, USA	272	Royal Troon	2,133	156	1,586,300
1998 July 16–19	M O'Meara*, USA	280	Royal Birkdale	2,336	152	1,800,000
**Four-hole play-off (15th–18th): O'Meara 4-4-5-4, B Watts (AUS) 5-4-5-5*						
1999 July 15–18	P Lawrie*, Scotland	290	Carnoustie	2,222	156	2,000,000
**Four-hole play-off: Lawrie 5-4-3-3, J Leonard (USA), J Van de Velde (FRA) 5-4-4-5*						
2000 July 20–23	T Woods, USA	269	St Andrews	2,477	156	2,750,000
2001 July 19–22	D Duval, USA	274	Royal Lytham & St Annes	2,255	156	3,300,000
2002 July 18–21	E Els*, RSA	278	Muirfield	2,260	156	3,800,000
**Four hole play-off: Els 4-3-5-4–16, T Levet (FRA) 4-2-5-5, S Appleby (AUS) 4-4-4-5, S Elkington (AUS) 5-3-4-5. Sudden death: Els 4, Levet 5*						
2003 July 17–20	B Curtis, USA	283	Royal St George's	2,152	156	3,898,000
2004 July 15–18	T Hamilton*, USA	274	Royal Troon	2,221	156	4,064,000
**Four-hole play-off: Hamilton 4-4-3-4, Els (RSA) 4-4-4-4*						
2005 July 14–17	T Woods, USA	274	St Andrews	2,499	156	4,000,000
2006 July 20–23	T Woods, USA	270	Royal Liverpool	2,434	156	4,000,000
2007 July 19–22	P Harrington, Ireland*	277	Carnoustie	2,443	156	4,200,000
**Four-hole play-off: Harrington 3-3-4-5, S Garcia (ESP) 5-3-4-4*						
2008 July 17–20	P Harrington, Ireland	283	Royal Birkdale	2,418	156	4,260,000
2009 July 16–19	S Cink*, USA	278	Turnberry	2,418	156	4,260,000
**Four-hole play-off: Cink 4-3-4-3, T Watson (USA) 5-3-7-5*						
2010 July 15–18	L Oosthuizen, RSA	272	St Andrews	2,500	156	4,800,000
2011 July 14–17	D Clarke, Northern Ireland	275	Royal St George's	1,995	156	5,000,000
2012 July 19–22	E Els, RSA	273	Royal Lytham & St Annes	2,012	156	5,000,000

Ernie Els, in his own words…

"This game is a tough game we play. It's a physical game. It's a mental game. You've got to have your wits with you, otherwise you have a missing link and it doesn't quite all come together. So to play the game as long as I have, for 23 years now as a professional, you're bound to go through every emotion out there and most of the things happen to you. As I said before, I've done what Adam has done. Just about everything that can happen in the game of golf, I've gone through. So to come through all that and sit here and speak to you guys with the Claret Jug is crazy. And it comes from a good attitude – being a bit more relaxed and believing in yourself."

The Open Silver Medal winners 1949–2011

The Open Championship's Silver Medal was first presented in 1949 to the leading amateur who plays all four rounds. In the early years, American Frank Stranahan was top amateur five out seven years from 1947 but won only four silver medals because he was leading amateur in 1947 before the medals were awarded.

Among those who had or still have silver medals in their trophy cabinets are Ireland's Joe Carr who was twice lowest amateur, England's Michael Bonallack, who took the medal on three occasions, Scotland's Ronnie Shade, England's Peter McEvoy, another double winner, Spain's José María Olazábal, Northern Ireland's Rory McIlroy, Jin Jeong, the only Asian winner of the medal and American Tiger Woods.

Today, in addition to the leading amateur receiving the silver medal, any amateur who makes all four rounds of the Championship earns a bronze medal. No medals have been awarded on 17 occasions since 1949 when no amateurs managed to complete 72 holes. Since 1946 the four leading amateurs who missed out on medals were:

1946 K Bell (ENG), St Andrews
1947 Frank Stranahan (USA), Royal Liverpool
1948 Mario Gonzalez (BRA), E Kingsley (USA), Muirfield

Year	Name	Venue	Final Position	Final Score
1949	Frank Stranahan (USA)	Royal St George's	13	290
1950	Frank Stranahan (USA)	Troon	9	286
1951	Frank Stranahan (USA)	Royal Portrush	12	295
1952	J W Jones (ENG)	Royal Lytham & St Annes	27	304
1953	Frank Stranahan (USA)	Carnoustie	2	286
1954	Peter Toogood (AUS)	Royal Birkdale	15	291
1955	Joe Conrad (USA)	St Andrews	22	293
1956	Joe Carr (IRL)	Hoylake	36	306
1957	W D Smith (SCO)	St Andrews	5	286
1958	Joe Carr (IRL)	Royal Lytham & St Annes	37	298
1959	Reid Jack (SCO)	Muirfield	5	288
1960	Guy Wolstenholme (ENG)	St Andrews	6	283
1961	Ronald White (ENG)	Royal Birkdale	38	306
1962	Charles Green (SCO)	Troon	37	308
1965	Michael Burgess (ENG)	Royal Birkdale	29	299
1966	Ronnie Shade (SCO)	Muirfield	16	293
1968	Michael Bonallack (ENG)	Carnoustie	21	300
1969	Peter Tupling (ENG)	Royal Lytham & St Annes	28	294
1970	Steve Melnyk (USA)	St Andrews	41	298
1971	Michael Bonallack (ENG)	Royal Birkdale	22	291
1973	Danny Edwards (USA)	Troon	39	296
1978	Peter McEvoy (ENG)	Carnoustie	39	293
1979	Peter McEvoy (ENG)	Royal Lytham & St Annes	17	294
1980	Jay Sigel (USA)	Muirfield	38	291
1981	Hal Sutton (USA)	Royal St George's	47	295
1982	Malcolm Lewis (ENG)	Royal Troon	42	300
1985	José-María Olazábal (ESP)	Royal St George's	24	289
1987	Paul Mayo (IRL)	Muirfield	57	297
1988	Paul Broadhurst (ENG)	Royal Lytham & St Annes	57	296
1989	Russell Claydon (ENG)	Royal Troon	69	293
1991	Jim Payne (ENG)	Royal Birkdale	38	284
1992	Daren Lee (ENG)	Muirfield	68	293
1993	Iain Pyman (ENG)	Royal St George's	27	281
1994	Warren Bennett (ENG)	Turnberry	70	286
1995	Steve Webster (ENG)	St Andrews	24	289
1996	Tiger Woods (USA)	Royal Lytham & St Annes	21	281
1997	Barclay Howard (SCO)	Royal Troon	59	293
1998	Justin Rose (ENG)	Royal Birkdale	4	282
2001	David Dixon (ENG)	Royal Lytham & St Annes	30	285
2004	Stuart Wilson (SCO)	Royal Troon	63	296
2005	Lloyd Saltman (SCO)	St Andrews	15	283
2006	Marius Thorp (NOR)	Hoylake	48	288
2007	Rory McIlroy (NIR)	Carnoustie	42	289
2008	Chris Wood (ENG)	Royal Birkdale	5	290
2009	Matteo Manassero (ITA)	Turnberry	13	282
2010	Jin Jeong (KOR)	St Andrews	14	284
2011	Tom Lewis (ENG)	Royal St George's	30	289

The 112th US Open at Olympic

Webb Simpson wins another Olympic tale of the unexpected

If the manner in which Webb Simpson emerged from the mist enveloping the Olympic Club in San Francisco to win America's national championship was, at only the second time of asking, as much of a surprise to the young American as everyone else, perhaps his background in the game should have signalled that here was a US Open champion in the making.

In common with Tiger Woods in 2008, Lucas Glover in 2009, Graeme McDowell in 2010 and Rory McIlroy in 2011, Simpson was the fifth consecutive winner of the US Open who had previously taken part in the Walker Cup match between the USA and Great Britain and Ireland as well as the second successive participant in the 2007 contest at Royal County Down to win a major championship.

© Getty Images

Webb Simpson

For the 15th major running, there was a fresh champion to celebrate. Moreover, it was the ninth time in a row a first time major winner had come out on top – evidence, surely, not only of the depth of talent in the game today but also confirmation that golfers in their 20s are better equipped to make a mark in the most prestigious events than ever before. "The prime age of a golfer ten or 15 years ago was a player in his mid 30s," observed Simpson. "Now it's moving closer to the mid 20s or late 20s. There's so many young guys. If I see Keegan Bradley win a major, I respect his game a ton. I feel like if Keegan Bradley won one, I want to go win one."

Perhaps one of the reasons Simpson, 26, was able to slip so effectively under the radar in California was because his form going into the second major of the year was largely indifferent. He'd missed the cut in both the events he'd entered prior to the US Open – the Players Championship and the Memorial – and was no one's idea of a likely winner as late in the game as Sunday afternoon in California when he ran up bogeys at two of the opening five holes and trailed the leader at that stage by six shots.

The Olympic Club is such a quirky and demanding test of golf, however, that no player in the field was safe from disaster. Just as Arnold Palmer once collapsed here on the back nine and Ben Hogan lost out to Jack Fleck, the San Francisco course once again produced a tale of the unexpected as McDowell and Jim Furyk – both past winners of the championship – came brutally unstuck. Padraig Harrington, Ernie Els and Lee Westwood were among the other notables who fell short through a combination of ill luck and misjudgement on a course set up in such a way that many of the fairways were tricky to hold.

Following in the footsteps of Bradley in the US PGA and Bubba Watson at the Masters, Simpson became the third consecutive golfer from the USA to win a major title on home turf thanks largely to a brilliant performance over the weekend when he compiled two rounds of 68 and signed for the winning total of 281, one over par.

Deliberately averting his gaze from the leaderboard and pursuing the old adage of concentrating on playing one shot at a time, Simpson admitted: "I never really wrapped my mind around winning. The place was so demanding, and all I was really concerned about was keeping the ball in front of me and making pars. You hear all the guys say it, but it's true, the course is so hard you don't know if you're going to make three or four bogeys in a row. I was two over par through five holes, but I didn't think anything of it because I knew I had hole seven coming up and a few other birdie [opportunities] on the back [nine]. I've been a leaderboard watcher my whole life but with the pressure a major brings, I just didn't think it would do me any good to see where I was."

Simpson's tunnel vision duly helped him make four birdies in five holes and, of even more significance at the major championship which places the highest premium on avoiding mistakes, eliminated any dropped shots between the sixth and 18th holes. It turned out to be good enough to edge one stroke clear of both McDowell and Michael Thompson, who had finished as the runner-up in the US Amateur championship held at Olympic five years previously.

It was Thompson, 27, who showed the rest the way in the first round, compiling a notable four under par mark of 66, one of the seven lowest scores ever recorded on the course at a US Open. Having come through sectional qualifying, the golfer was eager to put some disappointing performances on the PGA Tour behind him – he'd missed five cuts in 15 events – and take advantage of the local knowledge he gleaned from playing Olympic 11 times in ten days in 2007. The young American putted particularly well, enjoying eight single-putt greens and using his blade just 22 times.

Even though Thompson produced the outstanding performance of the opening round, most of the attention settled on Tiger Woods as the past champion started with 69, his best opening round in the event since shooting 67 at Bethpage in 2002. Paired with Phil Mickelson and Bubba Watson, who both struggled, Woods pieced together a judicious 70 for 139 and did not back down in Friday's second round. As Thompson fell back with 75, grabbed a share of the lead in the company of Jim Furyk and David Toms, two of the most steadfast professionals in American golf. Woods reckoned that patience was the key to performing well at Olympic. "This tournament, you just [keep] plodding along," he said. "This is a different tournament. You have to stay patient, got to stay in the present, and you're just playing for a lot of pars."

Few are more adept in those circumstances than Furyk, winner of the title in 2003, who made more birdies, three, than bogeys, two, but still didn't feel he was the master of his own fate. "It can snowball very quickly here," he said. "It's tough to kind of put a tourniquet on it and stop the bleeding and get the momentum changed back in the right direction on this golf course because there's not a lot of let up . . . there's a couple of disasters waiting."

> "I never wrapped my mind around winning. I was only concerned to make pars."
>
> *Webb Simpson on his US Open strategy*

One golfer who found calamity waiting at his door was the defending champion Rory McIlroy. Just 12 months after lapping the field at Congressional, the Ulsterman added 73 to his opening 77 and missed the cut for the fourth time in five tournaments. Meanwhile, those commanding centre stage in San Francisco were getting even younger as 17-year-old Beau Hossler reached the halfway mark on 143 and briefly led the US Open after completing the opening 11 holes of the second round in two under par.

While Woods was the bookmakers' favourite going into the weekend, his touch deserted him on Saturday as he struggled to card 75 after missing no fewer than seven fairways. Furyk, though, was still right there, making a tidy birdie on the 17th for 70 and a share of the lead with another past US Open winner, McDowell, who triumphed at Pebble Beach two years earlier. The Ulsterman's 68 was sufficient to spark dreams of a repeat performance. "What is it about Northern California?" he pondered. "I don't know. There's something about this kind of sea air coming off the Pacific that feels a little bit like home to me."

Apart from McDowell, there were sterling efforts from Westwood, who shot 67, the low round of the day, to force his way back into contention and Els, who jumped up the leaderboard courtesy of an eagle at 17th after holing a chip from the run-off area beside the green. Meanwhile, Simpson's 68 was sufficient to move him into the group on three over par, just four shots off the lead – the tipping point, according to McDowell, for those who had a chance of winning the championship on Sunday.

If he was barely mentioned in dispatches until the final round, Simpson, who was making only his fifth appearance at any of the majors, demonstrated over the weekend that his instinct for survival at Olympic was stronger than any other player. He set the mark of 281 for the rest to emulate or better and sat in the clubhouse with his wife, Dowd, and watched on TV as challenger after challenger came up short.

Westwood's hopes were undone by a double bogey on the fifth hole after his ball became lodged in a tree and was never seen again. It was a punishment which hardly fitted the crime since Westwood's tee shot was struck on pretty much the only line which might have retained the ball on a tilted fairway. McDowell, who missed eight fairways by narrow margins, showed plenty of resilience and gave himself a long putt on the closing hole to force a play-off. The deepest cut of all, though, was felt by Furyk. Having shouldered the pressure of leading for so long, he was flummoxed by the decision to move up the tee by 100 yards on the par 5 16th hole. "I was unprepared and didn't know exactly where to hit the ball off the tee," he admitted.

As for Simpson, he was just thrilled to emulate his namesake, Scott, who won the US Open at the same venue 25 years earlier. Webb's run of three consecutive birdies between the sixth and eighth holes produced the momentum required to maintain the Olympic club's reputation of identifying unexpected champions.

Michael Aitken

First Round	Second Round	Third Round	Fourth Round
–4 Michael Thompson	–1 Tiger Woods	–1 Graeme McDowell	+1 Webb Simpson
–1 Tiger Woods	–1 Jim Furyk	–1 Jim Furyk	+2 Graeme McDowell
–1 David Toms	–1 David Toms	+1 Freddie Jacobson	+2 Michael Thompson
–1 Nick Watney	+1 Nicolas Colsaerts	+2 Lee Westwood	+3 Jim Furyk
–1 Justin Rose	+1 Graeme McDowell	+2 Ernie Els	+3 David Toms
–1 Graeme McDowell	+1 Michael Thompson	+2 Nicolas Colsaerts	+3 Padraig Harrington
= Matt Kuchar	+1 John Peterson	+3 Webb Simpson	+3 Jason Dufner
= Jim Furyk	+2 Blake Adams	+3 Jason Dufner	+3 John Peterson
= Ian Poulter	+3 Raphael Jacquelin	+3 Beau Hossler	+4 Ernie Els
= Beau Hossler	+3 K J Choi	+3 John Peterson	+5 Lee Westwood

US Open Championship (112th) *Olympic Club, San Francisco, CA* [7170–70]

Prize Money: $8 million. Entries 9,006 June 14–17

Players are of American nationality unless stated

Final Qualifying

Walton Heath, Surrey, UK
Alexander Noren, (SWE) 67-68—135
Marc Warren (SCO) 70-65—135
Lee Slattery (ENG) 71-66—137
Grégory Bourdy (FRA) 67-70—137
Mikko Ilonen (FIN) 66-71—137
George Coetzee (RSA) 66-71—137
Søren Kjeldsen (DEN) 68-69—137
Matthew Baldwin (ENG) 67-71—138
Matteo Manessaro (ITA) 69-69—138
Peter Lawrie (IRL) 67-71—138
Raphael Jacquelin (FRA) 70-68—138

Shizuoka, Japan
Brendan Jones (AUS) 66-68—134
Toru Taniguchi (JPN) 69-68—137
J B Park (KOR) 67-71—138
Hiroyuki Fujita (JPN) 67-71—138
Dong-Hwan Lee (KOR) 70-68—138
Tadahiro Takayama (JPN) 66-72—138

Daly City, CA
James Hahn 66-70—136
Beau Hossler (am) 70-67—137
Alex Cejka (GER) 69-68—137
Scott Smith 68-69—137
Michael Allen 67-70—137
Matthew Bettencourt 69-69—138
Alberto Sanchez (am) 67-71—138

Glen Illyn, IL
Anthony Summers (AUS) 66-67—133
Tim Herron 68-66—134

Suwanee, GA
Jason Bohn 65-70—135
Casey Wittenberg 68-68—136
Tim Weinhart 69-68—137

Creswell, OR
Casey Martin 69-69—138
Nick Sherwood (am) 70-69—139

Memphis, TN
Tommy Biershenk 67-66—133
Aaron Watkins 68-66—134
Joe Ogilvie 68-66—134
Hunter Hamrick (am) 67-67—134
Joe Durant 67-67—134
Stephen Ames (CAN) 65-69—134
William Lunde 68-67—135
Hunter Haas 65-70—135
Roberto Castro 69-67—136

Lecanto, FL
Scott Langley 73-66—139
Samual Osborne (ENG) 71-70—141
Brookes Koepka 72-70—142

Rockville, MD
Shane Bertsch 69-71—140
Michael Thompson 74-68—142
Paul Claxton 75-68—143
Cole Howard 73-70—143
Darron Stiles 72-71—143
Nicholas Thompson 71-72—143
Jeff Curl 69-74—143

Houston, TX
Bob Estes 65-73—138
Alistair Presnell 71-69—140
Brian Rowell 69-71—140

Springfield, OH
Brice Garnett 66-65—131
John Peterson 64-68—132

Columbus, OH
Charlie Wi (KOR) 65-67—132
Blake Adams 67-68—135
Kevin Streelman 71-66—137
Brian Harman 67-70—137
D A Points 66-72—138
David Mathis 71-68—139
Steve Marino 69-70—139
Davis Love III 68-71—139
Steve Lebrun 71-69—140
Rod Pampling (AUS) 69-71—140
Martin Flores 69-71—140
Jesse Mueller 67-73—140
Edward Loar 65-75—140
Dennis Miller 71-70—141
Morgan Hoffmann 69-72—141
Scott Piercy 68-73—141

Summit, NJ
Cameron Wilson (am) 71-65—136
Jim Herman 68-69—137
Brian Gaffney 68-70—138
Mark McCormick 67-71—138

Final Field: 156 (8 amateurs), of whom 72 (including 3 amateurs) made the cut on 148 or less.

1	Webb Simpson	72-73-68-68—281	$1,440,000
2	Michael Thompson	66-75-74-67—282	695,216
	Graeme McDowell (NIR)	69-72-68-73—282	695,216
4	David Toms	69-70-76-68—283	276,841
	Padraig Harrington (IRL)	74-70-71-68—283	276,841
	John Peterson	71-70-72-70—283	276,841
	Jason Dufner	72-71-70-70—283	276,841
	Jim Furyk	70-69-70-74—283	276,841
9	Ernie Els (RSA)	75-69-68-72—284	200,280
10	Casey Wittenberg	71-77-67-70—285	163,594
	Retief Goosen (RSA)	75-70-69-71—285	163,594
	Kevin Chappell	74-71-68-72—285	163,594
	John Senden (AUS)	72-73-68-72—285	163,594
	Lee Westwood (ENG)	73-72-67-73—285	163,594
15	K J Choi (KOR)	73-70-74-69—286	118,969
	Steve Stricker	76-68-73-69—286	118,969
	Adam Scott (AUS)	76-70-70-70—286	118,969
	Aaron Watkins	72-71-72-71—286	118,969
	Martin Kaymer (GER)	74-71-69-72—286	118,969
	Fredrik Jacobson (SWE)	72-71-68-75—286	118,969
21	Nick Watney	69-75-73-70—287	86,348
	Jordan Spieth (am)	74-74-69-70—287	86,348
	Raphael Jacquelin (FRA)	72-71-73-71—287	86,348
	Justin Rose (ENG)	69-75-71-72—287	86,348
	Tiger Woods	69-70-75-73—287	86,348
	Blake Adams	72-70-70-75—287	86,348
27	Matt Kuchar	70-73-71-74—288	68,943
	Nicholas Colsaerts (BEL)	72-69-71-76—288	68,943
29	Davis Love III	73-74-73-69—289	53,168
	Alistair Presnell (AUS)	70-74-75-70—289	53,168
	Morgan Hoffmann	72-74-73-70—289	53,168
	Francesco Molinari (ITA)	71-76-72-70—289	53,168
	Robert Karlsson (SWE)	70-75-72-72—289	53,168
	Kevin Na	74-71-71-73—289	53,168
	Scott Langley	76-70-70-73—289	53,168
	Charlie Wi (KOR)	74-70-71-74—289	53,168
	Beau Hossler (am)	70-73-70-76—289	53,168
38	Charl Schwartzel (RSA)	73-70-74-73—290	44,144
	Hunter Mahan	72-71-73-74—290	44,144
	Sergio Garcia	73-71-71-75—290	44,144
41	Zach Johnson	77-70-73-71—291	38,816
	Patrick Cantlay (am)	76-72-71-72—291	38,816
	Rickie Fowler	72-76-71-72—291	38,816
	Ian Poulter (ENG)	70-75-73-73—291	38,816
	Alex Cejka (GER)	78-69-70-74—291	38,816
46	Matteo Manassero (ITA)	76-69-73-74—292	31,979
	Bob Estes	74-73-71-74—292	31,979
	Angel Cabrera (ARG)	72-76-69-75—292	31,979
	Steve LeBrun	73-75-69-75—292	31,979
	Hunter Hamrick	77-67-71-77—292	31,979
51	Simon Dyson (ENG)	74-74-74-71—293	24,912
	Jesse Mueller	75-73-74-71—293	24,912
	Nicholas Thompson	74-74-72-73—293	24,912
	Hiroyuki Fujita (JPN)	75-71-73-74—293	24,912
	Branden Grace (RSA)	71-74-73-75—293	24,912
56	J B Park (KOR)	70-74-77-73—294	21,995
	Michael Allen	71-73-77-73—294	21,995
	Jeff Curl	73-75-71-75—294	21,995
	Jonathan Byrd	71-75-71-77—294	21,995
60	Bo Van Pelt	78-70-76-71—295	19,995

US Open Championship *continued*

60T	Jason Day (AUS)	75-71-76-73—295	19,995
	Matthew Baldwin (ENG)	74-74-73-74—295	19,995
	Kevin Streelman	76-72-72-75—295	19,995
	Darron Stiles	75-71-73-76—295	19,995
65	Marc Warren (SCO)	73-72-74-77—296	18,593
	Phil Mickelson	76-71-71-78—296	18,593
	Kyung-Tae Kim (KOR)	74-72-74-77—297	18,113
68	Stephen Ames (CAN)	74-73-79-72—298	17,633
	Keegan Bradley	73-73-75-77—298	17,633
70	Rod Pampling (AUS)	74-73-74-78—299	17,153
71	Jason Bohn	70-75-78-78—301	16,833
72	Joe Ogilvie	73-75-76-79—303	16,512

The following players missed the half-way cut:

73	Thomas Björn (DEN)	78-71—149
	Grégory Bourdy (FRA)	74-75—149
	Roberto Castro	75-74—149
	Joe Durant	78-71—149
	Robert Garrigus	72-77—149
	Lucas Glover	76-73—149
	Bill Haas	76-73—149
	Brian Harman	77-72—149
	Justin Hicks	75-74—149
	Charles Howell III	72-77—149
	Mikko Ilonen (FIN)	75-74—149
	Ryo Ishikawa (JPN)	71-78—149
	Dustin Johnson	75-74—149
	Martin Laird (SCO)	77-72—149
	Casey Martin	74-75—149
	Louis Oosthuizen (RSA)	77-72—149
	Carl Pettersson (SWE)	75-74—149
	Alberto Sanchez (am)	72-77—149
	Lee Slattery (ENG)	79-70—149
	Bubba Watson	78-71—149
	Mark Wilson	76-73—149
	Y E Yang (KOR)	74-75—149
95	Sang-Moon Bae (KOR)	77-73—150
	Rafael Cabrera-Bello (ESP)	74-76—150
	Ben Crane	77-73—150
	Martin Flores	71-79—150
	Jim Herman	78-72—150
	Edward Loar	76-74—150
	Rory McIlroy (NIR)	77-73—150
	Alexander Noren (SWE)	75-75—150
95T	Geoff Ogilvy (AUS)	76-74—150
	Scott Piercy	75-75—150
	Alvaro Quiros (ESP)	75-75—150
	Chez Reavie	80-70—150
	Kyle Stanley	73-77—150
108	Olin Browne	77-74—151
	Tim Clark (RSA)	77-74—151
	Luke Donald (ENG)	79-72—151
	Anders Hansen (DEN)	72-79—151
	Tim Herron	74-77—151
	Brendan Jones (AUS)	76-75—151
	Peter Lawrie (IRL)	74-77—151
	Spencer Levin	74-77—151
	Toru Taniguchi (JPN)	78-73—151
	Gary Woodland	74-77—151
118	Stewart Cink	77-75—152
	Paul Claxton	75-77—152
	Samuel Osborne (ENG)	76-76—152
	D A Points	72-80—152
	Anthony Summers (AUS)	76-76—152
123	Shane Bertsch	78-75—153
	Matt Bettencourt	76-77—153
	Tommy Biershenk	74-79—153
	Michael Campbell (NZL)	79-74—153
	George Coetzee (RSA)	78-75—153
	James Hahn	73-80—153
	Peter Hanson (SWE)	78-75—153
	Colt Knost	75-78—153
	Bill Lunde	81-72—153
	David Mathis	78-75—153
	Robert Rock (ENG)	75-78—153
123T	Vijay Singh (FIJ)	75-78—153
	Tadahiro Takayama (JPN)	77-76—153
136	Aaron Baddeley (AUS)	75-79—154
	Brooks Koepka (am)	77-77—154
	Kyle Thompson	82-72—154
	Cameron Wilson (am)	77-77—154
140	Brian Gaffney	77-78—155
	Brice Garnett	78-77—155
	Hunter Haas	81-74—155
	Trevor Immelman (RSA)	80-75—155
144	Gonzalo Fernandez-Castaño (ESP)	80-76—156
	Dong-Hwan Lee (JPN)	77-79—156
146	Andy Zhang (CHN) (am)	79-77—156
	Tim Weinhart	78-79—157
148	Miguel Angel Jiménez (ESP)	81-77—158
	Nick Sherwood (am)	78-80—158
150	Mark McCormick	82-77—159
	Scott K Smith	78-81—159
152	Søren Kjeldsen (DEN)	85-75—160
153	Steve Marino	84-78—162
	Dennis Miller	80-82—162
155	Cole Howard	80-84—164
156	Brian Rowell	86-82—168

Four players are four time winners of the US Open

Only four players have managed to win the US Open Trophy four times – a Scot and three Americans. Willie Anderson was the first to do so in 1901, 1903, 1904 and 1905. Bobby Jones was successful in 1923, 1926, 1929 and in his Grand Slam year 1930, followed by Ben Hogan in 1948, 1950, 1951 and 1953. Last man to do it was Jack Nicklaus who was the winner in 1962, 1967, 1972 and 1980.

The youngest winner of the title is John McDermott who was only 19 when he won a play-off for the title at Wheaton, Illinois in 1911. The oldest winner is Hale Irwin. He had won the title in 1974 and 1979 and wrote himself into the history books when at the age of 45 and playing on a special exemption he took the title for a third time in 1990 at Medinah.

2011 US Open *Congressional CC, Bethesda, MD* June 16–19 [7574–71]

Prize money: $7.5 million. Entries: 8,300

1	Rory McIlroy (NIR)	65-66-68-69—268	$1,440,000
2	Jason Day (AUS)	71-72-65-68—276	865,000
3	Kevin Chappell	76-67-69-66—278	364,241
	Robert Garrigus	70-70-68-70—278	364,241
	Lee Westwood (ENG)	75-68-65-70—278	364,241
	Y E Yang (KOR)	68-69-70-71—278	364,241
7	Peter Hanson (SWE)	72-71-69-67—279	228,416
	Sergio García (ESP)	69-71-69-70—279	228,416
9	Charl Schwartzel (RSA)	68-74-72-66—280	192,962
	Louis Oosthuizen (RSA)	69-73-71-67—280	192,962
11	Brandt Snedeker	70-70-72-69—281	163,083
	Davis Love III	70-71-70-70—281	163,083
	Heath Slocum	71-70-70-70—281	163,083
14	Graeme McDowell (NIR)	70-74-69-69—282	129,517
	Webb Simpson	75-71-66-70—282	129,517
	Matt Kuchar	72-68-69-73—282	129,517
	Fredrik Jacobson (SWE)	74-69-66-73—282	129,517
	Bo Van Pelt	76-67-68-71—282	129,517
19	Johan Edfors (SWE)	70-72-74-67—283	105,905
19T	Steve Stricker	75-69-69-70—283	105,905
21	Ryan Palmer	69-72-73-70—284	97,242
	Patrick Cantlay (am)	75-67-70-72—284	
23	Robert Rock (ENG)	70-71-76-68—285	76,455
	Gary Woodland	73-71-73-68—285	76,455
	Retief Goosen (RSA)	73-73-71-68—285	76,455
	Dustin Johnson	75-71-69-70—285	76,455
	Bill Haas	73-73-68-71—285	76,455
	Brandt Jobe	71-70-70-74—285	76,455
	Henrik Stenson (SWE)	70-72-69-74—285	76,455
30	Ryo Ishikawa (JPN)	74-70-74-68—286	50,436
	Gregory Havret (FRA)	77-69-71-69—286	50,436
	Seung-yul Noh (KOR)	72-70-73-71—286	50,436
	Rory Sabbatini (RSA)	72-73-70-71—286	50,436
	John Senden (AUS)	70-72-72-72—286	50,436
	Do-Hoon Kim (KOR)	73-71-70-72—286	50,436
	Harrison Frazar	72-73-68-73—286	50,436
	Zach Johnson	71-69-72-74—286	50,436
	Kyung-tae Kim (KOR)	69-72-69-76—286	50,436

Other players who made the cut: Adam Hadwin (CAN), Martin Kaymer (GER), Sunghoon Kang (KOR) 287; Sang-Moon Bae (KOR), Lucas Glover, Russell Henley (am) 288; Charley Hoffman, Luke Donald (ENG), Michael Putnam, Chez Reavie, Robert Karlsson (SWE), Padraig Harrington (IRL) 289; Scott Piercy, Alexander Noren (SWE), Marc Leishman (AUS) 290; J J Henry, Anthony Kim (KOR), Phil Mickelson, Matteo Manassero (ITA), Edoardo Molinari (ITA), Alvaro Quiros (ESP) 291; Todd Hamilton, Justin Hicks, Marcel Siem (GER) 292; Bubba Watson, Brian Gay, Jeff Overton, William Cauley 293; Kevin Streelman 295; Alexandre Rocha (BRA), Christo Greyling (RSA), Kenichi Kuboya (JPN) 297; Wes Heffernan (CAN) 303; Brad Benjamin (am) 305

2010 US Open *Pebble Beach, CA* June 17–20 [7260–71]

Prize money: $7.5 million. Entries: 9,052

1	Graeme McDowell (NIR)	71-68-71-74—284	$1,350,000
2	Grégory Havret (FRA)	73-71-69-72—285	810,000
3	Ernie Els (RSA)	73-68-72-73—286	480,687
4	Phil Mickelson	75-66-73-73—287	303,119
	Tiger Woods	74-72-66-75—287	303,119
6	Matt Kuchar	74-72-74-68—288	228,255
	Davis Love III	75-74-68-71—288	228,255
8	Alex Cejka (GER)	70-72-74-73—289	177,534
	Dustin Johnson	71-70-66-82—289	177,534
	Martin Kaymer (GER)	74-71-72-72—289	177,534
	Brandt Snedeker	75-74-69-71—289	177,534
12	Tim Clark (RSA)	72-72-72-74—290	143,714
	Sean O'Hair	76-71-70-73—290	143,714
14	Ben Curtis	78-70-75-68—291	127,779
	Justin Leonard	72-73-73-73—291	127,779
16	Jim Furyk	72-75-74-71—292	108,458
	Peter Hanson (SWE)	73-76-74-69—292	108,458
	Russell Henley (am)	73-74-72-73—292	
	Scott Langley (am)	75-69-77-71—292	
	Charl Schwartzel (RSA)	74-71-74-73—292	108,458
	Lee Westwood (ENG)	74-71-76-71—292	108,458
22	Angel Cabrera (ARG)	75-72-74-72—293	83,634
	Sergio García (ESP)	73-76-73-71—293	83,634
	Padraig Harrington (IRL)	73-73-74-73—293	83,634
22T	John Malinger	77-72-70-74—293	83,634
	Shaun Micheel	69-77-75-72—293	83,634
27	Ricky Barnes	72-76-74-72—294	67,195
	Robert Karlsson (SWE)	75-72-74-73—294	67,195
29	Robert Allenby (AUS)	74-74-73-74—295	54,871
	Stuart Appleby (AUS)	73-76-76-70—295	54,871
	Henrik Stenson (SWE)	77-70-74-74—295	54,871
	Tom Watson	78-71-70-76—295	54,871
33	Brendon De Jonge (ZIM)	69-73-77-77—296	44,472
	Jason Dufner	72-73-79-72—296	44,472
	Ryo Ishikawa (JPN)	70-71-75-80—296	44,472
	Søren Kjeldsen (DEN)	72-71-75-78—296	44,472
	Ryan Moore	75-73-75-73—296	44,472
	Kenny Perry	72-77-73-74—296	44,472
	David Toms	71-75-76-74—296	44,472
40	Paul Casey (ENG)	69-73-77-78—297	34,722
	Stewart Cink	76-73-71-77—297	34,722
	Bobby Gates	75-74-71-77—297	34,722
	Ross McGowan (ENG)	72-73-78-74—297	34,722
	Noh Seung-yul (KOR)	74-72-76-75—297	34,722
	Vijay Singh (FIJ)	74-72-75-76—297	34,722
	Bo Van Pelt	72-75-82-68—297	34,722

Other players who made the cut: Jason Allred, Rafael Cabrera Bello (ESP), K J Choi (KOR), Luke Donald (ENG), Jason Gore, Jim Herman, Thongchai Jaidee (THA), Edoardo Molinari (ITA), Ian Poulter (ENG), Chris Stroud, Scott Verplank 298; Hiroyuki Fujita (JPN), Lucas Glover, Retief Goosen (RSA), Yuta Ikeda (JPN), Steve Stricker 299; Eric Axley, Jerry Kelly, Steve Marino, Gareth Maybin (NIR), Toru Taniguchi (JPN), Steve Wheatcroft 300; Erick Justesen 301; Matt Bettencourt, David Duval, Fred Funk, Camilo Villegas (COL) 302; Rhys Davies (WAL), Kent Jones 303; Nick Watney 305; Craig Barlow, Zach Johnson, Matthew Richardson (ENG) 306; Ty Tryon, Mike Weir (CAN) 307; Pablo Martin (ESP), Jason Preeo 311

2009 US Open *Bethpage, Farmingdale, NY* June 18–21 [7426–70]

Prize money: $7.5 million. Entries: 9,086

1	Lucas Glover	69-64-70-73—276	$1,350,000
2	Ricky Barnes	67-65-70-76—278	559,830
	David Duval	67-70-70-71—278	559,830
	Phil Mickelson	69-70-69-70—278	559,830
5	Ross Fisher (ENG)	70-68-69-72—279	289,146
6	Søren Hansen (DEN)	70-71-70-69—280	233,350
	Hunter Mahan	72-68-68-72—280	233,350
	Tiger Woods	74-69-68-69—280	233,350
9	Henrik Stenson (SWE)	73-70-70-68—281	194,794
10	Stephen Ames (CAN)	74-66-70-72—282	154,600
	Matt Bettencourt	75-67-71-69—282	154,600
	Sergio García (ESP)	70-70-72-70—282	154,600
	Rory McIlroy (NIR)	72-70-72-68—282	154,600
	Ryan Moore	70-69-72-71—282	154,600
	Mike Weir (CAN)	64-70-74-74—282	154,600
16	Retief Goosen (RSA)	73-68-68-74—283	122,128
	Anthony Kim	71-71-71-70—283	122,128
18	Peter Hanson (SWE)	66-71-73-74—284	100,308
	Graeme McDowell (NIR)	69-72-69-74—284	100,308
	Ian Poulter (ENG)	70-74-73-67—284	100,308
	Michael Sim (AUS)	71-70-71-72—284	100,308
	Bubba Watson	72-70-67-75—284	100,308
23	Sean O'Hair	69-69-71-76—285	76,422
	Steve Stricker	73-66-72-74—285	76,422
	Lee Westwood (ENG)	72-66-74-73—285	76,422
	Oliver Wilson (ENG)	70-70-71-74—285	76,422
27	Stewart Cink	73-69-70-74—286	56,041
	Johan Edfors (SWE)	70-74-68-74—286	56,041
	J B Holmes	73-67-73-73—286	56,041
	Francesco Molinari (ITA)	71-70-74-71—286	56,041
	Vijay Singh (FIJ)	72-72-73-69—286	56,041
	Azuma Yano (JPN)	72-65-77-72—286	56,041
33	Jim Furyk	72-69-74-72—287	47,404
	Kevin Sutherland	71-73-73-70—287	47,404
	Camilo Villegas (COL)	71-71-72-73—287	47,404
36	Todd Hamilton	67-71-71-79—288	42,935
	Carl Pettersson (SWE)	75-68-73-72—288	42,395
	Adam Scott (AUS)	69-71-73-75—288	42,395
	Nick Taylor (am)	73-65-75-75—288	
40	Tim Clark (RSA)	73-71-74-71—289	38,492
	Dustin Johnson	72-69-76-72—289	38,492
	Billy Mayfair	73-70-72-74—289	38,492
	Drew Weaver (am)	69-72-74-74—289	
44	Kenny Perry	71-72-75-72—290	35,536

Other players who made the cut: Thomas Levet (FRA), John Mallinger 291; K J Choi (KOR), Tom Lehman, Rocco Mediate, Geoff Ogilvy (AUS), Andres Romero (ARG), Gary Woodland 292; Kyle Stanley (am) 293; Angel Cabrera (ARG), Jean-François Lucquin (FRA), Andrew McLardy (RSA) 294; Ben Curtis, 296; Jeff Brehaut 297, Trevor Murphy 297; Fred Funk 301

2008 US Open *Torrey Pines, La Jolla, CA* June 12–15 [7643–71]

Prize money: $7.5 million. Entries: 8,390

1	Tiger Woods*	72-68-70-73—283	$1,350,000
2	Rocco Mediate	69-71-72-71—283	810,000
	**Tiger Woods won at the 19th hole of the extra round*		
3	Lee Westwood (ENG)	70-71-70-73—284	491,995
4	Robert Karlsson (SWE)	70-70-75-71—286	307,303
	D J Trahan	72-69-73-72--286	307,303
6	Miguel Angel Jiménez (ESP)	75-66-74-72—287	220,686
	John Merrick	73-72-71-71—287	220,686
	Carl Pettersson (SWE)	71-71-77-68—287	220,686
9	Eric Axley	69-79-71-69—288	160,769
	Geoff Ogilvy (AUS)	69-73-72-74—288	160,769
	Heath Slocum	75-74-74-65—288	160,769
	Brandt Snedeker	76-73-68-71—288	160,769
	Camilo Villegas (COL)	73-71-71-73—288	160,769
14	Stewart Cink	72-73-77-67—289	122,159
	Ernie Els (RSA)	70-72-74-73—289	122,159
	Retief Goosen (RSA)	76-69-77-67—289	122,159
	Rod Pampling (AUS)	74-70-75-70—289	122,159
18	Robert Allenby (AUS)	70-72-73-75—290	87,230
	Chad Campbell	77-72-71-70—290	87,230
	Sergio García (ESP)	76-70-70-74—290	87,230
	Ryuji Imada (JPN)	74-75-70-71—290	87,230
	Brandt Jobe	73-75-69-73—290	87,230
	Hunter Mahan	72-74-69-75—290	87,230
	Phil Mickelson	71-75-76-68—290	87,230
18T	Mike Weir (CAN)	73-74-69-74—290	87,230
26	Anthony Kim	74-75-70-72—291	61,252
	Adam Scott (AUS)	73-73-75-70—291	61,252
	Boo Weekley	73-76-70-72—291	61,252
29	Aaron Baddeley (AUS)	74-73-71-74—292	48,482
	Bart Bryant	75-70-78-69—292	48,482
	Jeff Quinney	79-70-70-73—292	48,482
	Patrick Sheehan	71-74-74-73—292	48,482
	Steve Stricker	73-76-71-72—292	48,482
	Michael Thompson (am)	74-73-73-72—292	
	Scott Verplank	72-72-74-74—292	48,482
36	Stuart Appleby (AUS)	69-70-79-75—293	35,709
	Daniel Chopra (SWE)	73-75-75-70—293	35,709
	Robert Dinwiddie (ENG)	73-71-75-74—293	35,709
	Jim Furyk	74-71-73-75—293	35,709
	Todd Hamilton	74-74-73-72—293	35,709
	Padraig Harrington (IRL)	78-67-77-71—293	35,709
	Justin Leonard	75-72-75-71—293	35,709
	Jonathan Mills	72-75-75-71—293	35,709
	Joe Ogilvie	71-76-73-73—293	35,709
	Pat Perez	75-73-75-70—293	35,709
	Andres Romero (ARG)	71-73-77-72—293	35,709
	Oliver Wilson (ENG)	72-71-74-76—293	35,709

Other players who made the cut: Tim Clark (RSA), Dustin Johnson, Matt Kuchar, Jarrod Lyle (AUS), John Rollins 294; Ben Crane, Søren Hansen (DEN), Martin Kaymer (GER), Davis Love III, Kevin Streelman 295; Stephen Ames (CAN), Rory Sabbatini (RSA) 296; Alastair Forsyth (SCO), Rickie Fowler (am), Brett Quigley, David Toms, Nick Watney 297; Paul Casey (ENG), Trevor Immelman (RSA), John Malinger, Vijay Singh (FIJ) 298; Derek Fathauer (am), D A Points 299; Woody Austin, Andrew Dresser, Andrew Svoboda 300; Justin Hicks, Ian Leggatt (CAN), Jesper Parnevik (SWE) 301; Ross McGowan (ENG) 303; Rich Beem, Chris Kirk 304, Luke Donald (ENG) WD

2007 US Open *Oakmont, PA* June 14–17 [7230–70]

Prize money: $6.8 million. Entries: 8,544

1	Angel Cabrera (ARG)	69-71-76-69—285	$1,260,000
2	Jim Furyk	71-75-70-70—286	611,336
	Tiger Woods	71-74-69-72—286	611,336
4	Niclas Fasth (SWE)	71-71-75-70—287	325,923
5	David Toms	72-72-73-72—289	248,948
	Bubba Watson	70-71-74-74—289	248,948
7	Nick Dougherty (ENG)	68-77-74-71—290	194,245
	Jerry Kelly	74-71-73-72—290	194,245
	Scott Verplank	73-71-74-72—290	194,245
10	Stephen Ames (CAN)	73-69-73-76—291	154,093
	Paul Casey (ENG)	77-66-72-76—291	154,093
	Justin Rose (ENG)	71-71-73-76—291	154,093
13	Aaron Baddeley (AUS)	72-70-70-80—292	124,706
	Lee Janzen	73-73-73-73—292	124,706
	Hunter Mahan	73-74-72-73—292	124,706
	Steve Stricker	75-73-68-76—292	124,706
17	Jeff Brehaut	73-75-70-75—293	102,536
	Jim Clark (RSA)	72-76-71-74—293	102,536
	Carl Pettersson (SWE)	72-72-75-74—293	102,536
20	Anthony Kim	74-73-80-67—294	86,200
	Vijay Singh (FIJ)	71-77-70-76—294	86,200
20T	Mike Weir (CAN)	74-72-73-75—294	86,200
23	Ken Duke	74-75-73-73—295	71,905
	Nick O'Hern (AUS)	76-74-71-74—295	71,905
	Brandt Snedeker	71-73-77-74—295	71,905
26	Stuart Appleby (AUS)	74-72-71-79—296	57,026
	J J Henry	71-78-75-72—296	57,026
	Camilo Villegas (COL)	73-77-75-71—296	57,026
	Boo Weekley	72-75-77-72—296	57,026
30	D J Brigman	74-74-74-75—297	45,313
	Fred Funk	71-78-74-74—297	45,313
	Peter Hanson (SWE)	71-74-78-74—297	45,313
	Pablo Martin (ESP)	71-76-77-73—297	45,313
	Graeme McDowell (NIR)	73-72-75-77—297	45,313
	Charl Schwartzel (RSA)	75-73-73-76—297	45,313
36	Mathew Goggin (AUS)	77-73-74-74—298	37,159
	Shingo Katayama (JPN)	72-74-79-73—298	37,159
	Jeev Milkha Singh (IND)	75-75-73-75—298	37,159
	Tom Pernice	72-72-75-79—298	37,159
	Ian Poulter (ENG)	72-77-72-77—298	37,159
	Lee Westwood (ENG)	72-75-79-72—298	37,159

Other players who made the cut: Kenneth Ferrie (ENG), Geoff Ogilvy (AUS), John Rollins 299; Olin Browne, Ben Curtis, Chris DiMarco, Marcus Fraser (AUS), Zach Johnson, José-María Olazábal (ESP) 300; Ernie Els (RSA), Charles Howell III, Rory Sabbatini (RSA), Dean Wilson 301; Anders Hansen (DEN), Michael Putnam 302; Chad Campbell 303; Michael Campbell (NZL), Bob Estes, Harrison Frazar, Kevin Sutherland 304; Jason Dufner 305; George McNeill 306

2006 US Open *Winged Foot, Mamaroneck, NY* June 15–18 [7264–70]

Prize money: $6.25 million. Entries: 8,584

1	Geoff Ogilvy (AUS)	71-70-72-72—285	$,1225,000
2	Jim Furyk	70-72-74-70—286	501,249
	Phil Mickelson	70-73-69-74—286	501,249
	Colin Montgomerie (SCO)	69-71-75-71—286	501,249
5	Padraig Harrington (IRL)	73-69-74-71—287	255,642
6	Kenneth Ferrie (ENG)	71-70-71-76—288	183,255
	Nick O'Hern (AUS)	75-70-74-69—288	183,255
	Vijay Singh (FIJ)	71-74-70-73—288	183,255
	Jeff Sluman	74-73-72-69—288	183,255
	Steve Stricker	70-69-76-73—288	183,255
	Mike Weir (CAN)	71-74-71-72—288	183,255
12	Luke Donald (ENG)	78-69-70-72—289	131,670
	Ryuji Imada (JPN)	76-73-69-71—289	131,670
	Ian Poulter (ENG)	74-71-70-74—289	131,670
15	Paul Casey (ENG)	77-72-72-69—290	116,735
16	Robert Allenby (AUS)	73-74-72-72—291	99,417
	David Duval	77-68-75-71—291	99,417
	David Howell (ENG)	70-78-74-69—291	99,417
	Miguel Angel Jiménez (ESP)	70-75-74-72—291	99,417
16T	Arron Oberholser	75-68-74-74—291	99,417
21	Peter Hedblom (SWE)	72-74-71-75—292	74,252
	Trevor Immelman (RSA)	76-71-70-75—292	74,252
	José-María Olazábal (ESP)	75-73-73-71—292	74,252
	Tom Pernice Jr	79-70-72-71—292	74,252
	Adam Scott (AUS)	72-76-70-74—292	74,252
26	Craig Barlow	72-75-72-74—293	52,314
	Angel Cabrera (ARG)	74-73-74-72—293	52,314
	Ernie Els (RSA)	74-73-74-72—293	52,314
	Sean O'Hair	76-72-74-71—293	52,314
	Ted Purdy	78-71-71-73—293	52,314
	Henrik Stenson (SWE)	75-71-73-74—293	52,314
32	Woody Austin	72-76-72-74—294	41,912
	Bart Bryant	72-72-73-77—294	41,912
	Scott Hend (AUS)	72-72-75-75—294	41,912
	Steve Jones	74-74-71-75—294	41,912
	Rodney Pampling (AUS)	73-75-75-71—294	41,912
37	Stewart Cink	75-71-77-72—295	36,647
	Jay Haas	75-72-74-74—295	36,647
	Charles Howell III	77-71-73-74—295	36,647

Other players who made the cut: Tommy Armour III, Chad Collins, John Cook, Jason Dufner, Fred Funk, Stephen Gangluff (CAN), Bo Van Pelt, Lee Williams 296; Phillip Archer (ENG), Thomas Bjørn (DEN), Fred Couples, Charley Hoffman, J B Holmes, Kent Jones, Graeme McDowell (NIR), Charl Schwartzel (RSA) 297; Darren Clarke (NIR) 298; Ben Curtis 299; Kenny Perry 301; Skip Kendal, Jeev Milkha Singh (IND), Camilo Villegas (COL) 302; Ben Crane 303; Tim Herron 305

2005 US Open *Pinehurst No.2, NC* June 16–19 [7214–70]

Prize money: $6.25 million. Entries: 9,048

1	Michael Campbell (NZL)	71-69-71-69—280	$1,170,000
2	Tiger Woods	70-71-72-69—282	700,000
3	Tim Clark (RSA)	76-69-70-70—285	320,039
	Sergio García (ESP)	71-69-75-70—285	320,039
	Mark Hensby (AUS)	71-68-72-74—285	320,039
6	Davis Love III	77-70-70-69—286	187,813
	Rocco Mediate	67-74-74-71—286	187,813
	Vijay Singh (FIJ)	70-70-74-72—286	187,813
9	Arron Oberholser	76-67-71-73—287	150,834
	Nick Price (ZIM)	72-71-72-72—287	150,834
11	Bob Estes	70-73-75-70—288	123,857
	Retief Goosen (RSA)	68-70-69-81—288	123,857
	Peter Hedblom (SWE)	77-66-70-75—288	123,857
	Corey Pavin	73-72-70-73—288	123,857
15	K J Choi (KOR)	69-70-74-76—289	88,120
	Stewart Cink	73-74-73-69—289	88.120
	John Cook	71-76-70-72—289	88.120
	Fred Couples	71-74-74-70—289	88.120
	Ernie Els (RSA)	71-76-72-70—289	88.120
	Ryuji Imada (JPN)	77-68-73-71—289	88.120
15T	Peter Jacobsen	72-73-69-75—289	88.120
	David Toms	70-72-70-77—289	88.120
23	Olin Browne	67-71-72-80—290	59.633
	Paul Claxton	72-72-72-74—290	59.633
	Fred Funk	73-71-76-70—290	59.633
	Justin Leonard	76-71-70-73—290	59.633
	Kenny Perry	75-70-71-74—290	59.633
28	Stephen Allan (AUS)	72-69-73-77—291	44.486
	Matt Every (am)	75-73-73-70—291	44.486
	Jim Furyk	71-70-75-75—291	44.486
	Geoff Ogilvy (AUS)	72-74-71-74—291	44.486
	Adam Scott (AUS)	70-71-74-76—291	44.486
33	Angel Cabrera (ARG)	71-73-73-75—292	35.759
	Steve Elkington (AUS)	74-69-79-70—292	35.759
	Tim Herron	74-73-70-75—292	35.759
	Brandt Jobe	68-73-79-72—292	35.759
	Bernhard Langer (GER)	74-73-71-74—292	35.759
	Shigeki Maruyama (JPN)	71-74-72-75—292	35.759
	Phil Mickelson	69-77-72-74—292	35.759
	Ted Purdy	73-71-73-75—292	35.759
	Lee Westwood (ENG)	68-72-73-79—292	35.759

Other players who made the cut: Chad Campbell, Peter Lonard (AUS), Paul McGinley (IRL), Colin Montgomerie (SCO), Tom Pernice, Rob Rashell, Mike Weir (CAN) 293; Jason Gore, J L Lewis, Nick O'Hern (AUS) 294; Thomas Bjørn (DEN), Nick Dougherty (ENG), Richard Green (AUS), Søren Kjeldsen (DEN), Thomas Levet (FRA) 295; Tommy Armour III, Luke Donald (ENG), Keiichiro Fukabori (JPN), J J Henry, Lee Janzen, Steve Jones, Frank Lickliter, Jonathan Lomas (ENG), Ryan Moore (am), Ian Poulter (ENG) 296; Michael Allen, Steve Flesch, Bill Glasson, John Mallinger 297; Stephen Ames (TRI), D J Brigman, J Hayes, Rory Sabbatini (RSA) 298; John Daly, Charles Howell III, Omar Uresti, 299; Jeff Maggert, Bob Tway 300; Graeme McDowell (NIR), Chris Nallen 301; Craig Barlow 303; Jerry Kelly 305

2004 US Open *Shinnecock Hills, Southampton, NY* June 17–20 [6996–70]

Prize money: $6.25 million. Entries: 8,726

1	Retief Goosen (RSA)	70-66-69-71—276	$1,125,000
2	Phil Mickelson	68-66-73-71—278	675,000
3	Jeff Maggert	68-67-74-72—281	424,604
4	Shigeki Maruyama (JPN)	66-68-74-76—284	267,756
	Mike Weir (CAN)	69-70-71-74—284	267,756
6	Fred Funk	70-66-72-77—285	212,444
7	Robert Allenby (AUS)	70-72-74-70—286	183,828
	Steve Flesch	68-74-70-74—286	183,828
9	Stephen Ames (TRI)	74-66-73-74—287	145,282
	Ernie Els (RSA)	70-67-70-80—287	145,282
	Chris DiMarco	71-71-70-75—287	145,282
	Jay Haas	66-74-76-71—287	145,282
13	Tim Clark (RSA)	73-70-66-79—288	119,770
	Tim Herron	75-66-73-74—288	119,770
	Spencer Levin (am)	69-73-71-75—288	
16	Angel Cabrera (ARG)	66-71-77-75—289	109,410
17	Skip Kendall	68-75-74-73—290	98,477
	Corey Pavin	67-71-73-79—290	98,477
	Tiger Woods	72-69-73-76—290	98,477
20	Mark Calcavecchia	71-71-74-75—291	80,644
	Sergio García (ESP)	72-68-71-80—291	80,644
20T	David Toms	73-72-70-76—291	80,644
	Kirk Triplett	71-70-73-77—291	80,644
24	Daniel Chopra (SWE)	73-68-76-75—292	63,328
	Lee Janzen	72-70-71-79—292	63,328
	Tim Petrovic	69-75-72-76—292	63,328
	Nick Price (ZIM)	73-70-72-77—292	63,328
28	Shaun Micheel	71-72-70-80—293	51,774
	Vijay Singh (FIJ)	68-70-77-78—293	51,774
30	Ben Curtis	68-75-72-79—294	46,089
31	K J Choi (KOR)	76-68-76-75—295	41,759
	Padraig Harrington (IRL)	73-71-76-75—295	41,759
	Peter Lonard (AUS)	71-73-77-74—295	41,759
	David Roesch	68-73-74-80—295	41,759
	Bo Van Pelt	69-73-73-80—295	41,759
36	Charles Howell III	75-70-68-83—296	36,813
	Hidemichi Tanaka (JPN)	70-74-73-79—296	36,813
	Lee Westwood (ENG)	73-71-73-79—296	36,813
	Casey Wittenberg (am)	71-71-75-79—296	

Other players who made the cut: Bill Haas (am), Jerry Kelly, Stephen Leaney (AUS), Spike McRoy, Joe Ogilvie, Pat Perez, Geoffrey Sisk, Scott Verplank 297; Kristopher Cox, Jim Furyk, Zachary Johnson, Chris Riley, John Rollins 298; Dudley Hart, Scott Hoch 299; Tom Carter, Trevor Immelman (RSA) 300; Joakim Haeggman (SWE), Tom Kite, Phillip Price (WAL) 302; Alex Cejka (GER), Craig Parry (AUS) 303; Cliff Kresge, Chez Reavie (am) 304; J J Henry 306; Kevin Stadler 307; Billy Mayfair 310

2003 US Open *Olympia Fields CC (North Course), IL* June 12–15 [7190–70]

Prize money: $6 million. Entries: 7,820

1	Jim Furyk	67-66-67-72—272	$108,0000
2	Stephen Leaney (AUS)	67-68-68-72—275	650,000
3	Kenny Perry	72-71-69-67—279	341,367
	Mike Weir (CAN)	73-67-68-71—279	341,367
5	Ernie Els (RSA)	69-70-69-72—280	185,934
	Fredrik Jacobson (SWE)	69-67-73-71—280	185,934
	Nick Price (ZIM)	71-65-69-75—280	185,934
	Justin Rose (ENG)	70-71-70-69—280	185,934
	David Toms	72-67-70-71—280	185,934
10	Padraig Harrington (IRL)	69-72-72-68—281	124,936
	Jonathan Kaye	70-70-72-69—281	124,936
	Cliff Kresge	69-70-72-70—281	124,936
	Billy Mayfair	69-71-67-74—281	124,936
	Scott Verplank	76-67-68-70—281	124,936
15	Jonathan Byrd	69-66-71-76—282	93,359
	Tom Byrum	69-69-71-73—282	93,359
	Tim Petrovic	69-70-70-73—282	93,359
	Eduardo Romero (ARG)	70-66-70-76—282	93,359
	Higemichi Tamaka (JPN)	69-71-71-71—282	93,359
20	Mark Calcavecchia	68-72-67-76—283	64,170
	Robert Damron	69-68-73-73—283	64,170
	Ian Leggatt (RSA)	68-70-68-77—283	64,170
	Justin Leonard	66-70-72-75—283	64,170
	Peter Lonard (AUS)	72-69-74-68—283	64,170
	Vijay Singh (FIJ)	70-63-72-78—283	64,170
	Jay Williamson	72-69-69-73—283	64,170
	Tiger Woods	70-66-75-72—283	64,170
28	Stewart Cink	70-68-72-74—284	41,254
	John Maginnes	72-70-72-70—284	4,1254
	Dicky Pride	71-69-66-78—284	41,254
	Brett Quigley	65-74-71-74—284	41,254
	Kevin Sutherland	71-71-72-70—284	41,254
	Kirk Triplett	71-68-73-72—284	41,254
	Tom Watson	65-72-75-72—284	41,254
35	Angel Cabrera (ARG)	72-68-73-72—285	32,552
	Chad Campbell	70-70-69-76—285	32,552
	Chris DiMarco	72-71-71-71—285	32,552
	Fred Funk	70-73-71-71—285	32,552
	Sergio García (ESP)	69-74-71-71—285	32,552
	Brandt Jobe	70-68-76-71—285	32,552
	Mark O'Meara	72-68-67-78—285	32,552

Other players who made the cut: Darren Clarke (NIR), Retief Goosen (RSA), Bernhard Langer (GER), Steve Lowery, Colin Montgomerie (SCO), Loren Roberts 286; Woody Austin, Marco Dawson, Niclas Fasth (SWE), Dan Forsman, Darron Stiles 287; Charles Howell III, John Rollins 288; Lee Janzen, Phil Mickelson 289; Trip Kuehne (am), Len Mattiace 290; Ricky Barnes (am), Olin Browne 291; Chris Anderson, Alexander Cejka (GER), Brian Davis (ENG) 292; Jay Don Blake, JP Hayes 293; Fred Couples, Brian Henninger 295; Ryan Dillon 301

US Open Championship History

Year	Winner	Runner-up	Venue	Score
1894	W Dunn	W Campbell	St Andrews, NY	2 holes

After 1894 decided by stroke-play. From 1895–1897. 36-holes From 1898 72-holes

Year	Winner	Venue	Score
1895	H J Rawlins	Newport	173
1896	J Foulis	Southampton	152
1897	J Lloyd	Wheaton, IL	162
1898	F Herd	South Hamilton, MA	328
1899	W Smith	Baltimore	315
1900	H Vardon (ENG)	Wheaton, IL	313
1901	W Anderson*	Myopia, MA	315
**After a play-off: Anderson 85, A Smith 86*			
1902	L Auchterlonie	Garden City	305
1903	W Anderson*	Baltusrol	307
**After a play-off: Anderson 82, D Brown 84*			
1904	W Anderson	Glenview	304
1905	W Anderson	Myopia, MA	335
1906	A Smith	Onwentsia	291
1907	A Ross	Chestnut Hill, PA	302
1908	F McLeod*	Myopia, MA	322
**After a play-off: McLeod 77, W Smith 83*			
1909	G Sargent	Englewood, NJ	290
1910	A Smith*	Philadelphia	289
**After a play-off: Smith 71, J McDermott 75, M Smith 77*			
1911	J McDermott*	Wheaton, IL	307
**After a play-off with M Brady and G Simpson: McDermott 80, Brady 82, Simpson 85*			
1912	J McDermott	Buffalo, NY	294
1913	F Ouimet* (am)	Brookline, MA	304
**After a play-off: Ouimet 72, H Vardon 77, T Ray 78*			
1914	W Hagen	Midlothian	297
1915	J Travers (am)	Baltusrol	290
1916	C Evans (am)	Minneapolis	286
1917-18	*No Championship*		
1919	W Hagen*	Braeburn	301
**After a play-off: Hagen 77, M Brady 78*			
1920	E Ray (ENG)	Inverness	295
1921	J Barnes	Washington	289
1922	G Sarazen	Glencoe	288
1923	R Jones Jr* (am)	Inwood, NY	295
**After a play-off: Jones 76, R Cruikshank 78*			
1924	C Walker	Oakland Hills	297
1925	W MacFarlane*	Worcester	291
**After a play-off: MacFarlane 147, R Jones Jr 148*			
1926	R Jones Jr (am)	Scioto	293
1927	T Armour*	Oakmont	301
**After a play-off: Armour 76, H Cooper 79*			
1928	J Farrell*	Olympia Fields	294
**After a play-off: Farrell 143, R Jones Jr (am) 144*			
1929	R Jones Jr* (am)	Winged Foot, NY	294
**After a play-off: Jones 141, A Espinosa 164*			
1930	R Jones Jr (am)	Interlachen	287

US Open Championship History *continued*

Year	Winner	Venue	Score
1931	B Burke*	Inverness	292
**After a play-off: Burke 149-148, G von Elm 149-149*			
1932	G Sarazen	Fresh Meadow	286
1933	J Goodman (am)	North Shore	287
1934	O Dutra	Merion	293
1935	S Parks	Oakmont	299
1936	T Manero	Springfield	282
1937	R Guldahl	Oakland Hills	281
1938	R Guldahl	Cherry Hills	284
1939	B Nelson*	Philadelphia	284
**After a play-off: Nelson 138, C Wood 141, D Shute 76*			
1940	W Lawson Little*	Canterbury, OH	287
**After a play-off: Little 70, G Sarazen 73*			
1941	C Wood	Fort Worth, TX	284
1942–45	*No Championship*		
1946	L Mangrum*	Canterbury	284
**After a play-off: Mangrum 144, B Nelson 145, V Ghezzi 145*			
1947	L Worsham*	St Louis	282
**After a play-off: Worsham 69, S Snead 70*			
1948	B Hogan	Los Angeles	276
1949	Dr C Middlecoff	Medinah, IL	286
1950	B Hogan*	Merion, PA	287
**After a play-off: Hogan 69, L Mangrum 73, D Fazio 75*			
1951	B Hogan	Oakland Hills, MI	287
1952	J Boros	Dallas, TX	281
1953	B Hogan	Oakmont	283
1954	E Furgol	Baltusrol	284
1955	J Fleck*	San Francisco	287
**After a play-off: Fleck 69, B Hogan 72*			
1956	Dr C Middlecoff	Rochester, NY	281
1957	D Mayer*	Inverness	282
**After a play-off: Mayer 72, C Middlecoff 79*			
1958	T Bolt	Tulsa, OK	283
1959	W Casper	Winged Foot, NY	282
1960	A Palmer	Denver, CO	280
1961	G Littler	Birmingham, MI	281
1962	J Nicklaus*	Oakmont	283
**After a play-off: Nicklaus 71, A Palmer 74*			
1963	J Boros*	Brookline, MA	293
**After a play-off: Boros 70, J Cupit 73, A Palmer 76*			
1964	K Venturi	Washington	278
1965	G Player* (RSA)	St Louis, MO	282
**After a play-off: Player 71, K Nagle 74*			
1966	W Casper*	San Francisco	278
**After a play-off: Casper 69, A Palmer 73*			
1967	J Nicklaus	Baltusrol	275
1968	L Trevino	Rochester, NY	275
1969	O Moody	Houston, TX	281
1970	A Jacklin (ENG)	Hazeltine, MN	281
1971	L Trevino*	Merion, PA	280
**After a play-off: Trevino 68, J Nicklaus 71*			

Year	Winner	Venue	Score
1972	J Nicklaus	Pebble Beach	290
1973	J Miller	Oakmont, PA	279
1974	H Irwin	Winged Foot, NY	287
1975	L Graham*	Medinah, IL	287
**After a play-off: Graham 71, J Mahaffey 73*			
1976	J Pate	Atlanta, GA	277
1977	H Green	Southern Hills, Tulsa	278
1978	A North	Cherry Hills	285
1979	H Irwin	Inverness, OH	284
1980	J Nicklaus	Baltusrol	272
1981	D Graham (AUS)	Merion, PA	273
1982	T Watson	Pebble Beach	282
1983	L Nelson	Oakmont, PA	280
1984	F Zoeller*	Winged Foot	276
**After a play-off: Zoeller 67, G Norman 75*			
1985	A North	Oakland Hills, MI	279
1986	R Floyd	Shinnecock Hills, NY	279
1987	S Simpson	Olympic, San Francisco	277
1988	C Strange*	Brookline, MA	278
**After a play-off: Strange 71, N Faldo 75*			
1989	C Strange	Rochester, NY	278
1990	H Irwin*	Medinah	280
**After a play-off: Irwin 74, M Donald 74 (Irwin won sudden death play-off 3 to 4 at first extra hole)*			
1991	P Stewart*	Hazeltine, MN	282
**After a play-off: Stewart 75, S Simpson 77*			
1992	T Kite	Pebble Beach, FL	285
1993	L Janzen	Baltusrol	272
1994	E Els* (RSA)	Oakmont, PA	279
**After a play-off: Els 74, L Roberts 74, C Montgomerie 78 (Els won sudden death playoff: Els 4,4, Roberts 4,5)*			
1995	C Pavin	Shinnecock Hills, NY	280
1996	S Jones	Oakland Hills, MI	278
1997	E Els (RSA)	Congressional, Bethesda, MD	276
1998	L Janzen	Olympic, San Francisco, CA	280
1999	P Stewart	Pinehurst No. 2, NC	279
2000	T Woods	Pebble Beach, CA	272
2001	R Goosen* (RSA)	Southern Hills CC, OK	276
**After a play-off: Goosen 70, M Brooks 72*			
2002	T Woods	Farmingdale, NY	277
2003	J Furyk	Olympia Fields, IL	272
2004	R Goosen (RSA)	Shinnecock Hills, NY	276
2005	M Campbell (NZL)	Pinehurst No.2, NC	280
2006	G Ogilvy (AUS)	Winged Foot, NY	285
2007	A Cabrera (ARG)	Oakmont, PA	285
2008	T Woods*	Torrey Pines, CA	283
**Beat R Mediate at 19th hole of extra round*			
2009	L Glover	Farmingdale, NY	276
2010	G McDowell (NIR)	Pebble Beach, CA	284
2011	R McIlroy (NIR)	Congressional, Bethesda, MD	268
2012	W Simpson	Olympic, San Francisco, CA	281

Month by month in 2012

After surviving the European Tour qualifying school Branden Grace wins back-to-back events in his native South Africa, then in Abu Dhabi England's Robert Rock beats Tiger Woods head-to-head and Rory McIlroy, a shot back in second place, is left to rue a two-stroke penalty for brushing sand away off the green. Brandt Snedeker wins a play-off at Torrey Pines after Kyle Stanley takes a triple bogey eight on the final hole.

The 76th Masters at Augusta

Miracle shot earns Bubba Watson a first coveted Green Jacket

By any stretch of the imagination, this was a seminal staging of The Masters. Not only did Louis Oosthuizen, the runner-up, make the first albatross in the tournament's history on the par 5 second hole before Phil Mickelson, the favourite going into the fourth round, endured meltdown on the par 3 fourth by compiling a triple bogey, but Gerry 'Bubba' Watson also conjured up one of the greatest shots ever struck under pressure in the majors, from deep in the woods on the par 4 tenth, to clinch victory at the second extra hole of a sudden death play-off.

Watson's wonder shot from the trees was both improbable and yet oddly predictable, given that the self-taught left-hander from Florida with such extraordinary hands is a past master at threading the ball through the eye of a needle. After launching a wayward drive into the trees lining the right side of the fairway, Watson found his ball nestling on a bed of pine needles. True, he was fortunate there was an escape route between two towering pines which would allow him to play a relatively straightforward recovery shot back onto the fairway, but it was no place you'd pick to win a sudden death shoot-out.

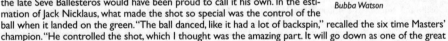

© Phil Sheldon Golf Picture Library

Bubba Watson

As it turned out, Watson swiftly gave short shrift to any idea of a safety shot. Left with 160 yards to the green, he reached for a gap wedge and blasted a massive hook, pulling the ball at least 40 yards from left to right in the air and running the daredevil approach onto the green where it finished 15 feet from the cup. "Had a good lie, had a gap where I had to hook it 40 yards or something – I'm pretty good at hooking it – and somehow it nestled up near the hole," he recalled.

It was a blow of such imagination, adventure and exquisite execution, even the late Seve Ballesteros would have been proud to call it his own. In the estimation of Jack Nicklaus, what made the shot so special was the control of the ball when it landed on the green. "The ball danced, like it had a lot of backspin," recalled the six time Masters' champion. "He controlled the shot, which I thought was the amazing part. It will go down as one of the great shots ever played in the game."

According to Rickie Fowler, the US Ryder Cup player who was watching from the gallery, the extreme nature of the challenge may even have helped his friend, who has a notoriously short attention span, to stay in the moment. "He was probably better off having to play a shot no-one else could play rather than just having to hit it straight," smiled the American.

With Oosthuizen leaving his 5 iron short, failing to get the requisite back spin on a chip which sped past the hole and then missing a twisting ten foot putt for par, Watson was left to take two putts for glory before sobbing on the shoulder of his mother, Molly, who had been waiting for him behind the tenth green. After he'd slipped into a green jacket and pocketed a cheque for $1.44 million, Watson acknowledged the thought of becoming Masters' champion was beyond his wildest imaginings. "I've never had a dream go this far, so I can't say it's a dream come true," he said. "I don't even know what happened on the back nine. I hit a crazy shot that I saw in my head and somehow I'm talking with a Green Jacket on. This is the mecca, an honour and special privilege to put the Green Jacket on."

Like Seve before him, Bubba combines power off the tee with a velvet touch around the greens. Accustomed to talking about himself in the third person, the American quipped: "We always joke about Bubba golf. I just play the game that I love. It's like Seve played. If you watch Phil Mickelson, he also goes for broke. That's why he wins so many times. He's not afraid. I attack. I want to hit the incredible shot. Who doesn't? My favourite club is the driver."

At Augusta, Watson used a pink shafted, pink headed driver and each day wore the same all-white outfit to raise money for charity in memory of his late father, Gerry, who died of cancer two years earlier. If some of the tears he shed were for his Dad, it was also an emotional time for Bubba and his wife, Angie, who had adopted their first child, Caleb, just two weeks previously. "Winning the Masters means everything right now but I know it's not real life," he grinned. "I'm looking forward to enjoying that again. I haven't even changed a nappy yet."

Watson's ten under total of 278 consisted of four rounds below par topped off by a closing 68 which included a brilliant stretch of four consecutive birdies between the 13th and 16th holes. When he dropped a shot at the 12th, few would have tipped the southpaw to overhaul his playing partner, Oosthuizen, and become the fifth left-hander in ten years to win The Masters. becasue the South African had shown the same grace under pressure which helped him win The Open at St Andrews in 2010. Ironically, it was a 7 on the second hole in the second round, his only double bogey of the week, which probably cost the South African his second major title. Not that the South African was complaining, reckoning the golfing gods had more than paid him back on the par 5 with that final day albatross or double eagle as some say.

Although he had to settle for a share of third place – his fourth top three finish in 11 majors – no golfer played better from tee to green throughout the week at the 76th Masters than Lee Westwood, who was only prevented from lapping the field by an indifferent putting stroke. First in the critical category of finding greens in regulation, Westwood took an astonishing 19 putts more than Mickelson, with whom he was eventually tied on eight under par alongside Matt Kuchar and Peter Hanson. On Thursday, though, Westwood's ball striking was so sublime that any concerns about his putting were put to one side as the Englishman set the pace with 67, five under, a score which matched his best effort in 13 trips to Augusta. Hitting 12 of 14 fairways and locating 16 greens in regulation, Westwood purred: "This is a golf course that I love playing. It seems to suit my game."

> "I had a good lie, a gap and I'm good at hooking the ball."
>
> *Bubba Watson on his miracle winning shot*

It seems to have become a feature of major championship golf in recent years that a veteran Champion rolls back the years. In the second round of The Masters, it was Fred Couples' turn to show the young guns the way. Playing at Augusta for the 20th time, the 52-year-old signed for 68 and led the way into the weekend alongside Jason Dufner on the five under total of 139.

Mickelson had predicted Saturday would be the day to make a move at Augusta and was as good as his word with a terrific round of 66, which was particularly memorable for an eagle and four birdies on a back nine of 30. Even more exhilarating was Hanson's 65 which included five birdies over the final seven holes and gave the Scandinavian golfer a one shot lead going into the final round on 207, nine under. With Oosthuizen on 209 and Watson on 210 the stage was set for a thrilling last day. Not that either Tiger Woods or Rory McIlroy, the pre-tournament favourites, were in any position to contend. Both men played poorly, the Ulsterman running up 77 on Saturday after Woods had carded 75 on Friday, letting frustration get the better of him when he kicked a club on the 16th tee after yet another errant swing. These favourites of the galleries eventually finished the tournament locked together – but in 40th place on five over par.

Back at the sharp end of the tournament, play was given a sudden injection of electricity on Sunday when Oosthuizen smoothed a 4 iron from 253 yards on the second hole and watched with pleasure as the ball curved downhill towards the pin and rolled into the cup at the 575 yard hole for the first 2 ever recorded there. The elation of that moment was quickly followed by something akin to disbelief when Mickelson's 4 iron to the fourth green struck a grandstand and disappeared into the woods. The left-hander didn't want to play three off the tee so twice attempted to play right-handed escape shots – barely moving the ball with the first and nearly hitting himself with the second – before eventually finding a greenside bunker and getting up and down for a triple bogey 6.

It was his only mistake of the closing round but a costly one which, in all probability, prevented him collecting a fourth Green Jacket. With Mickelson out of the equation and Hanson labouring, it was left to Watson and Oosthuizen in the penultimate group to grab centre stage. There wasn't a pine straw between them after 72 holes and both men made impressive 4s at the first extra hole, the 18th. The tournament was then decided on the 10th by how the challengers coped with erratic tee shots. The South African came off a 3 wood and followed that mistake with an underhit 5 iron. Watson, on the other hand, made up for a wayward drive with the shot of his life.

Michael Aitken

First Round

–5 Lee Westwood
–4 Louis Oosthuizen
–4 Peter Hanson
–3 Bubba Watson
–3 Ben Crane
–3 Francesco Molinari
–3 Jason Dufner
–3 Paul Lawrie
–3 Miguel Angel Jiménez

Second Round

–5 Fred Couples
–5 Jason Dufner
–4 Louis Oosthuizen
–4 Lee Westwood
–4 Sergio García
–4 Rory McIlroy
–4 Bubba Watson
–3 Paul Lawrie
–3 Matt Kuchar
–3 Miguel Angel Jiménez

Third Round

–9 Peter Hanson
–8 Phil Mickelson
–7 Louis Oosthuizen
–6 Bubba Watson
–5 Matt Kuchar
–4 Padraig Harrington
–4 Hunter Mahan
–4 Henrik Stenson
–4 Lee Westwood
–3 Paul Lawrie

Fourth Round

–10 Bubba Watson
–10 Louis Oosthuizen
–8 Lee Weestwood
–8 Matt Kuchar
–8 Peter Hanson
–8 Phil Mickelson
–5 Ian Poulter
–4 Adam Scott
–4 Justin Rose
–4 Padraig Harrington
Play-off:
Watson 4,4
Oosthuizen 4,5

The 76th Masters Tournament *Augusta National GC, GA* April 5–8 [7435–72]

Prize money: $8m. Final field of 95 players (five amateurs) of whom 62 (including three amateurs) made the final half-way cut on 149 or less.

Players are of American nationality unless stated.

1	Bubba Watson*	69-71-70-68—278	$1,440,000
2	Louis Oosthuizen (RSA)	68-72-69-69—278	864,000
Watson beat Oosthuizen at the second play-off hole – Watson 4,4; Oosthuizen 4,5			
3	Lee Westwood (ENG)	67-73-72-68—280	384,000
	Matt Kuchar	71-70-70-69—280	384,000
	Peter Hanson (SWE)	68-74-65-73—280	384,000
	Phil Mickelson	74-68-66-72—280	384,000
7	Ian Poulter (ENG)	72-72-70-69—283	268,000
8	Adam Scott (AUS)	75-70-73-66—284	232,000
	Justin Rose (ENG)	72-72-72-68—284	232,000
	Padraig Harrington (IRL)	71-73-68-72—284	232,000
11	Jim Furyk	70-73-72-70—285	200,000
12	Kevin Na	71-75-72-68—286	156,000
	Graeme McDowell (NIR)	75-72-71-68—286	156,000
	Sergio García (ESP)	72-68-75-71—286	156,000
	Fred Couples	72-67-75-72—286	156,000
	Hunter Mahan	72-72-68-74—286	156,000
17	Bo Van Pelt	73-75-75-64—287	124,000
	Ben Crane	69-73-72-73—287	124,000
19	Geoff Ogilvy (AUS)	74-72-71-71—288	96,960
	Charles Howell III	72-70-74-72—288	96,960
	Brandt Snedeker	72-75-68-73—288	96,960
	Fredrik Jacobson (SWE)	76-68-70-74—288	96,960
	Francesco Molinari (ITA)	69-75-70-74—288	96,960
24	Anders Hansen (DEN)	76-72-73-68—289	70,400
	Jason Dufner	69-70-75-75—289	70,400
	Paul Lawrie (SCO)	69-72-72-76—289	70,400
27	Keegan Bradley	71-77-73-69—290	56,800
	Rickie Fowler	74-74-72-70—290	56,800
	Vijay Singh (FIJ)	70-72-76-72—290	56,800
	Scott Stallings	70-77-70-73—290	56,800
	Jonathan Byrd	72-71-72-75—290	56,800
32	Luke Donald (ENG)	75-73-75-68—291	45,280
	Angel Cabrera (ARG)	71-78-71-71—291	45,280
	Zach Johnson	70-74-75-72—291	45,280
	Nick Watney	71-71-72-77—291	45,280
	Sean O'Hair	73-70-71-77—291	45,280
37	Thomas Björn (DEN)	73-76-74-69—292	37,600
	Bill Haas	72-74-76-70—292	37,600
	Sang-Moon Bae (KOR)	75-71-69-77—292	37,600
40	Aaron Baddeley (AUS)	71-71-77-74—293	32,000
	Tiger Woods	72-75-72-74—293	32,000
	Rory McIlroy (NIR)	71-69-77-76—293	32,000
	Henrik Stenson (SWE)	71-71-70-81—293	32,000
44	Martin Kaymer (GER)	72-75-75-72—294	26,400
	Kevin Chappell	71-76-71-76—294	26,400
	Webb Simpson	72-74-70-78—294	26,400
47	Patrick Cantlay (am)	71-78-74-72—295	
	Ross Fisher (ENG)	71-77-73-74—295	22,560
	Steve Stricker	71-77-72-75—295	22,560
50	Stewart Cink	71-75-81-69—296	19,960
	Robert Karlsson (SWE)	74-74-77-71—296	19,960
	Charl Schwartzel (RSA)	72-75-75-74—296	19,960
	David Toms	73-73-75-75—296	19,960
54	Scott Verplank	73-75-75-74—297	18,880
	Hideki Matsuyama (JPN) (am)	71-74-72-80—297	

76th Masters Tournament *continued*

56	Miguel Angel Jiménez (ESP)	69-72-76-81—298	18,560
57	Edoardo Molinari (ITA)	75-74-76-74—299	18,240
	Martin Laird (SCO)	76-72-74-77—299	18,240
	Y E Yang (KOR)	73-70-75-81—299	18,240
60	Trevor Immelman (RSA)	78-71-76-76—301	17,920
61	Gonzalo Fernandez-Castano (ESP)	74-75-76-77—302	17,760
62	Kelly Kraft (am)	74-75-77-80—306	

The following players missed the half-way cut. Each professional player received $10,000:

63	Kyung-tae Kim (KOR)	74-76—150
	John Senden (AUS)	74-76—150
65	Paul Casey (ENG)	76-75—151
	Harrison Frazar	73-78—151
	Larry Mize	76-75—151
	José Maria Olazábal (ESP)	75-76—151
	Kyle Stanley	75-76—151
	Tom Watson	77-74—151
	Mike Weir (CAN)	72-79—151
72	Robert Garrigus	77-75—152
	Bernhard Langer (GER)	72-80—152
72T	Ryan Palmer	75-77—152
	Rory Sabbatini (RSA)	72-80—152
76	K J Choi (KOR)	77-76—153
	Ryo Ishikawa (JPN)	76-77—153
	Bryden MacPherson (AUS)	77-76—153
	Chez Reavie	79-74—153
	Johnson Wagner	79-74—153
81	Tim Clark (RSA)	73-81—154
	Darren Clarke (NIR)	73-81—154
	Lucas Glover	75-79—154
	Mark Wilson	76-78—154
	Ian Woosnam (WAL)	77-77—154
86	Simon Dyson (ENG)	78-77—155
	Corbin Mills (am)	74-81—155
	Alvaro Quiros (ESP)	78-77—155
89	Brendan Steele	76-80—156
90	Ben Crenshaw	76-83—159
	Randal Lewis (am)	81-78—159
92	Craig Stadler	81-82—163
93	Sandy Lyle (SCO)	86-78—164
	Gary Woodland	WD
	Jason Day (AUS)	WD

2011 Masters April 7–10 [7435–72]

Prize money: $7.5 million. Field of 93 players (six amateurs) of whom 49 (including one amateur) made the half-way cut.

1	Charl Schwartzel (RSA)	69-71-68-66—274	$1,444,000
2	Jason Day (AUS)	72-64-72-68—276	704,000
	Adam Scott (AUS)	72-70-67-67—276	704,000
4	Luke Donald (ENG)	72-68-69-69—278	330,667
	Geoff Ogilvy (AUS)	69-69-73-67—278	330,667
	Tiger Woods	71-66-74-67—278	330,667
7	Angel Cabrera (ARG)	71-70-67-71—279	268,000
8	K J Choi (KOR)	67-70-71-72—280	240,000
	Bo Van Pelt	73-69-68-70—280	240,000
10	Ryan Palmer	71-72-69-70—282	216,000
11	Edoardo Molinari (ITA)	74-70-69-70—283	176,000
	Justin Rose (ENG)	73-71-71-68—283	176,000
	Steve Stricker	72-70-71-70—283	176,000
	Lee Westwood (ENG)	72-67-74-70—283	176,000
15	Fred Couples	71-68-72-73—284	128,000
	Ross Fisher (ENG)	69-71-71-73—284	128,000
	Trevor Immelman (RSA)	69-73-73-69—284	128,000
	Rory McIlroy (NIR)	65-69-70-80—284	128,000
	Brandt Snedeker	69-71-74-70—284	128,000
20	Ricky Barnes	68-71-75-71—285	93,200
	Ryo Ishikawa (JPN)	71-71-73-70—285	93,200
	Martin Laird (SCO)	74-69-69-73—285	93,200
	Y E Yang (KOR)	67-72-73-73—285	93,200
24	Jim Furyk	72-68-74-72—286	70,400
	David Toms	72-69-73-72—286	70,400
	Gary Woodland	69-73-74-70—286	70,400
27	Charley Hoffman	74-69-72-72—287	54,400
	Miguel Angel Jiménez (ESP)	71-73-70-73—287	54,400
	Robert Karlsson (SWE)	72-70-74-71—287	54,400
	Matt Kuchar	68-75-69-75—287	54,400
	Hideki Matsuyama (JPN) (am)	72-73-68-74—287	
	Phil Mickelson	70-72-71-74—287	54,400
	Ian Poulter (ENG)	74-69-71-73—287	54,400
	Alvaro Quiros (ESP)	65-73-75-74—287	54,400
35	Alex Cejka (GER)	72-71-75-70—288	43,200
	Sergio García (ESP)	69-71-75-73—288	43,200
	Ryan Moore	70-73-72-73—288	43,200
38	Paul Casey (ENG)	70-72-76-71—289	36,600
	Rickie Fowler	70-69-76-74—289	36,600
	Dustin Johnson	74-68-73-74—289	36,600
	Bubba Watson	73-71-67-78—289	36,600
42	Bill Haas	74-70-74-72—290	32,000
	Steve Marino	74-71-72-73—290	32,000
44	Kyung-tae Kim (KOR)	70-75-78-68—291	28,800
	Jeff Overton	73-72-72-74—291	28,800
46	Nick Watney	72-72-75-73—292	26,400
47	Aaron Baddeley (AUS)	75-70-74-74—293	24,000
	Ernie Els (RSA)	75-70-76-72—293	24,000
49	Camilo Villegas (COL)	70-75-73-76—294	21,920

Twenty-nine eagles scored in the 2012 Masters

Golfers competing in the 2012 Masters at Augusta collectively scored 29 eagles – 10 of them at the par 5 13th hole which closes out Amen Corner and nine at the par 5 15th. Four eagles were scored at the par 5 second, two at the par 5 eighth with Luke Donald holing his second shot at the par 4 third and Patrick Cantlay his second at the par 4 seventh. Both Adam Scott and Bo Van Pelt made aces at the short 16th.

2010 Masters April 8–11 [7435–72]

Prize money: $7.5 million. Field of 96 players (six amateurs) of whom 48 (including one amateur) made the half-way cut.

1	Phil Mickelson	67-71-67-67—272	$1,350,000
2	Lee Westwood (ENG)	67-69-68-71—275	810,000
3	Anthony Kim	68-70-73-65—276	510,000
4	K J Choi (KOR)	67-71-70-69—277	330,000
	Tiger Woods	68-70-70-69—277	330,000
6	Fred Couples	66-75-68-70—279	270,000
7	Nick Watney	68-76-71-65—280	251,250
8	Hunter Mahan	71-71-68-71—281	225,000
	Y E Yang (KOR)	67-72-72-70—281	225,000
10	Ricky Barnes	68-70-72-73—283	195,000
	Ian Poulter (ENG)	68-68-74-73—283	195,000
12	Miguel Angel Jiménez (ESP)	72-75-72-66—285	165,000
	Jerry Kelly	72-74-67-72—285	165,000
14	Trevor Immelman (RSA)	69-73-72-72—286	131,250
	Steve Marino	71-73-69-73—286	131,250
	Ryan Moore	72-73-73-68—286	131,250
	David Toms	69-75-71-71—286	131,250
18	Angel Cabrera (ARG)	73-74-69-71—287	94,500
	Ernie Els (RSA)	71-73-75-68—287	94,500
	Adam Scott (AUS)	69-75-72-71—287	94,500
	Heath Slocum	72-73-70-72—287	94,500
	Scott Verplank	73-73-73-68—287	94,500
	Tom Watson	67-74-73-73—287	94,500
24	Ben Crane	71-75-74-68—288	69,000
24T	Matt Kuchar	70-73-74-71—288	69,000
26	Bill Haas)	72-70-71-76—289	57,750
	Geoff Ogilvy (AUS)	74-72-69-74—289	57,750
	Kenny Perry	72-71-72-74—289	57,750
29	Yuta Ikeda (JPN)	70-77-72-71—290	53,250
30	Jason Dufner	75-72-75-69—291	45,563
	Søren Kjeldsen (DEN)	70-71-75-75—291	45,563
	Francesco Molinari (ITA)	70-74-75-72—291	45,563
	Sean O'Hair	72-71-72-76—291	45,563
	Charl Schwartzel (RSA)	69-76-72-74—291	45,563
	Steve Stricker	73-73-74-71—291	45,563
36	Lucas Glover	76-71-71-74—292	38,625
	Matteo Manassero (ITA) (am)	71-76-73-72—292	
38	Steve Flesch	75-71-70-78—294	34,500
	Retief Goosen (RSA)	74-71-76-73—294	34,500
	Dustin Johnson	71-72-76-75—294	34,500
	Camilo Villegas (COL)	74-72-71-77—294	34,500
42	Zach Johnson	70-74-76-75—295	30,750
43	Robert Karlsson (SWE)	71-72-77-76—296	28,500
	Mike Weir (CAN)	71-72-76-77—296	28,500
	Robert Allenby (AUS)	72-75-78-73—298	24,750
	Chad Campbell	79-68-80-71—298	24,750
	Sergio García (ESP)	74-70-76-78—298	24,750
48	Nathan Green (AUS)	72-75-80-75—302	21,750

2009 Masters April 9–12 [7445–72]

Prize money: $7 million. Field of 96 players (five amateurs) of whom 50 (no amateurs) made the half-way cut.

1	Angel Cabrera (ARG)*	68-68-69-71—276	$1,350,000
2	Kenny Perry	68-67-70-71—276	660,000
	Chad Campbell	65-70-72-69—276	660,000

**Cabrera won at the second extra hole – Cabrera 4,4; Campbell 5,–; Perry 4,5*

4	Shingo Katayama (JPN)	67-73-70-68—278	360,000
5	Phil Mickelson	73-68-71-67—279	300,000
6	Steve Flesch	71-74-68-67—280	242,813
	John Merrick	68-74-72-66—280	242,813
	Steve Stricker	72-69-68-71—280	242,813
	Tiger Woods	70-72-70-68—280	242,813
10	Jim Furyk	66-74-68-73—281	187,500
	Hunter Mahan	66-75-71-69—281	187,500
	Sean O'Hair	68-76-68-69—281	187,500
13	Tim Clark (RSA)	68-71-72-71—282	150,000
	Camilo Villegas (COL)	73-69-71-69—282	150,000
15	Todd Hamilton	68-70-72-73—283	131,250
	Geoff Ogilvy (AUS)	71-70-73-69—283	131,250
17	Aaron Baddeley (AUS)	68-74-73-69—284	116,250
	Graeme Mcdowell (NIR)	69-73-73-69—284	116,250
19	Nick Watney	70-71-71-73—285	105,000
20	Stephen Ames (CAN)	73-68-71-74—286	71,400
	Paul Casey (ENG)	72-72-73-69—286	71,400
	Ryuji Imada (JPN)	73-72-72-69—286	71,400
	Trevor Immelman (RSA)	71-74-72-69—286	71,400
	Anthony Kim	75-65-72-74—286	71,400
	Sandy Lyle (SCO)	72-70-73-71—286	71,400
20T	Rory McIlroy (NIR)	72-73-71-70—286	71,400
	Ian Poulter (ENG)	71-73-68-74—286	71,400
	Justin Rose (ENG)	74-70-71-71—286	71,400
	Rory Sabbatini (RSA)	73-67-70-76—286	71,400
30	Stuart Appleby (AUS)	72-73-71-71—287	46,575
	Ross Fisher (ENG)	69-76-73-69—287	46,575
	Dustin Johnson	72-70-72-73—287	46,575
	Larry Mize	67-76-72-72—287	46,575
	Vijay Singh (FIJ)	71-70-72-74—287	46,575
35	Ben Curtis	73-71-74-70—288	38,625
	Ken Duke	71-72-73-72—288	38,625
	Padraig Harrington (IRL)	69-73-73-73—288	38,625
38	Robert Allenby (AUS)	73-72-72-72—289	33,000
	Luke Donald (ENG)	73-71-72-73—289	33,000
	Sergio García (ESP)	73-67-75-74—289	33,000
	Henrik Stenson (SWE)	71-70-75-73—289	33,000
42	Bubba Watson	72-72-73-73—290	29,250
43	Lee Westwood (ENG)	70-72-70-79—291	27,250
44	Dudley Hart	72-72-73-75—292	27,250
45	D J Trahan	72-73-72-76—293	27,250
46	Miguel Angel Jiménez (ESP)	70-73-78-73—294	21,850
	Kevin Sutherland	69-76-77-72—294	21,850
	Mike Weir (CAN)	68-75-79-72—294	21,850
49	Andres Romero (ARG)	69-75-77-76—297	19,200
50	Rocco Mediate	73-70-78-77—298	19,200

2008 Masters April 10–13

[7445–72]

Prize money: $7.4 million. Field of 93 players (three amateurs) of whom 45 (no amateurs) made the half-way cut.

1	Trevor Immelman (RSA)	68-68-69-75—280	$1,350,000
2	Tiger Woods	72-71-68-72—283	810,000
3	Stewart Cink	72-69-71-72—284	435,000
	Brandt Snedeker	69-68-70-77—284	435,000
5	Steve Flesch	72-67-69-78—286	273,750
	Padraig Harrington (IRL)	74-71-69-72—286	273,750
	Phil Mickelson	71-68-75-72—286	273,750
8	Miguel Angel Jiménez (ESP)	77-70-72-68—287	217,500
	Robert Karlsson (SWE)	70-73-71-73—287	217,500
	Andres Romero (ARG)	72-72-70-73—287	217,500
11	Paul Casey (ENG)	71-69-69-79—288	172,500
	Nick Watney	75-70-72-71—288	172,500
	Lee Westwood (ENG)	69-73-73-73—288	172,500
14	Stuart Appleby (AUS)	76-70-72-71—289	135,000
	Sean O'Hair	72-71-71-75—289	135,000
	Vijay Singh (FIJ)	72-71-72-74—289	135,000
17	Retief Goosen (RSA)	71-71-72-76—290	112,500
	Henrik Stenson (SWE)	74-72-72-72—290	112,500
	Mike Weir (CAN)	73-68-75-74—290	112,500
20	Brian Bateman	69-76-72-74—291	84,300
	Zach Johnson	70-76-68-77—291	84,300
	Justin Leonard	72-74-72-73—291	84,300
20T	Bubba Watson	74-71-73-73—291	84,300
	Boo Weekley	72-74-68-77—291	84,300
25	Stephen Ames (CAN)	70-70-77-75—292	54,844
	Angel Cabrera (ARG)	73-72-73-74—292	54,844
	J B Holmes	73-70-73-76—292	54,844
	Arron Oberholser	71-70-74-77—292	54,844
	IanPoulter (ENG)	70-69-75-78—292	54,844
	Adam Scott (AUS)	75-71-70-76—292	54,844
	Jeev Milkha Singh (IND)	71-74-72-75—292	54,844
	Richard Sterne (RSA)	73-72-73-74—292	54,844
33	Nick Dougherty (ENG)	74-69-74-76—293	42,375
	Jim Furyk	70-73-73-77—293	42,375
	Heath Slocum	71-76-77-69—293	42,375
36	Todd Hamilton	74-73-75-73—295	36,875
	Justin Rose (ENG)	68-78-73-76—295	36,875
	Johnson Wagner	72-74-74-75—295	36,875
39	Niclas Fasth (SWE)	75-70-76-75—296	33,000
	Geoff Ogilvy (AUS)	75-71-76-74—296	33,000
41	K J Choi (KOR)	72-75-78-73—298	30,750
42	Robert Allenby (AUS)	72-74-72-81—299	28,500
	David Toms	73-74-72-80—299	28,500
44	Ian Woonam (WAL)	75-71-76-78—300	26,250
45	Sandy Lyle (SCO)	72-75-78-77—302	24,750

2007 Masters April 5–8

[7445–72]

Prize money: $7.4 million. Field of 96 players, of whom 60 (no amateurs) made the half-way cut.

1	Zach Johnson	71-73-76-69—289	$1,305,000
2	Retief Goosen (RSA)	76-76-70-69—291	541,333
	Rory Sabbatini (RSA)	73-76-73-69—291	541,333
	Tiger Woods	73-74-72-72—291	541,333
5	Jerry Kelly	75-69-78-70—292	275,500
	Justin Rose (ENG)	69-75-75-73—292	275,500
7	Stuart Appleby (AUS)	75-70-73-75—293	233,812
	Padraig Harrington (IRL)	77-68-75-73—293	233,812
9	David Toms	70-78-74-72—294	210,250
10	Paul Casey (ENG)	79-68-77-71—295	181,250
	Luke Donald (ENG)	73-74-75-73—295	181,250
	Vaughn Taylor	71-72-77-75—295	181,250
13	Tim Clark (RSA)	71-71-80-74—296	135,937
	Jim Furyk	75-71-76-74—296	135,937
	Ian Poulter (ENG)	75-75-76-70—296	135,937
	Vijay Singh (FIJ)	73-71-79-73—296	135,937
17	Stewart Cink	77-75-75-70—297	108,750
	Tom Pernice Jr	75-72-79-71—297	108,750
	Henrik Stenson (SWE)	72-76-77-72—297	108,750
20	Mark Calcavecchia	76-71-78-73—298	84,462
	Lucas Glover	74-71-79-74—298	84,462
	John Rollins	77-74-76-71—298	84,462
	Mike Weir (CAN)	75-72-80-71—298	84,462
24	Stephen Ames (CAN)	76-74-77-72—299	63,000
	Phil Mickelson	76-73-73-77—299	63,000
	Geoff Ogilvy (AUS)	75-70-81-73—299	63,000
27	K J Choi (KOR)	75-75-74-76—300	53,650
	Davis Love III	72-77-77-74—300	53,650
	Adam Scott (AUS)	74-78-76-72—300	53,650
30	Fred Couples	75-74-78-74—301	43,085
	Charles Howell III	75-77-75-74—301	43,085
30T	Robert Karlsson (SWE)	77-73-79-72—301	43,085
	Scott Verplank	73-77-76-75—301	43,085
	Lee Westwood (ENG)	79-73-72-77—301	43,085
	Dean Wilson	75-72-76-78—301	43,085
	Yong-Eun Yang (KOR)	75-74-78-74—301	43,085
37	Angel Cabrera (ARG)	77-75-79-71—302	31,900
	J J Henry	71-78-77-76—302	31,900
	Tim Herron	72-75-83-72—302	31,900
	Rod Pampling (AUS)	77-75-74-76—302	31,900
	Jeev Milkha Singh (IND)	72-75-76-79—302	31,900
	Brett Wetterich	69-73-83-77—302	31,900
43	Sandy Lyle (SCO)	79-73-80-71—303	26,825
44	Bradley Dredge (WAL)	75-70-76-83—304	22,533
	David Howell (ENG)	70-75-82-77—304	22,533
	Miguel Angel Jiménez (ESP)	79-73-76-76—304	22,533
	Shingo Katayama (JPN)	79-72-80-73—304	22,533
	José-María Olazábal (ESP)	74-75-78-77—304	22,533
49	Jeff Sluman	76-75-79-75—305	18,560
	Craig Stadler	74-73-79-79—305	18,560
51	Brett Quigley	76-76-79-75—306	17,835
52	Aaron Baddeley (AUS)	79-72-76-80—307	17,255
	Carl Pettersson (SWE)	76-76-79-76—307	17,255
54	Rich Beem	71-81-75-81—308	16,820
55	Ben Crenshaw	76-74-84-75—309	16,530
	Niclas Fasth (SWE)	77-75-77-80—309	16,530
	Trevor Immelman (RSA)	74-77-81-77—309	16,530
58	Arron Oberholser	74-76-84-76—310	16,240
59	Billy Mayfair	76-75-83-77—311	16,095
60	Fuzzy Zoeller	74-78-79-82—313	15,950

2006 Masters April 6–9 [7445–72]

Prize money: $7 million. Field of 90 players, of whom 47 (no amateurs) made the half-way cut.

1	Phil Mickelson	70-72-70-69—281	$,1260,000
2	Tim Clark (RSA)	70-72-72-69—283	758,000
3	Chad Campbell	71-67-75-71—284	315,700
	Fred Couples	71-70-72-71—284	315,700
	Retief Goosen (RSA)	70-73-72-69—284	315,700
	José-María Olazábal (ESP)	76-71-71-66—284	315,700
	Tiger Woods	72-71-71-70—284	315,700
8	Angel Cabrera (ARG)	73-74-70-68—285	210,000
	Vijay Singh (FIJ)	67-74-73-71—285	210,000
10	Stewart Cink	72-73-71-70—286	189,000
11	Stephen Ames (CAN)	74-70-70-73—287	161,000
	Miguel Angel Jiménez (ESP)	72-74-69-72—287	161,000
	Mike Weir (CAN)	71-73-73-70—287	161,000
14	Billy Mayfair	71-72-73-72—288	129,500
	Arron Oberholser	69-75-73-71—288	129,500
16	Geoff Ogilvy (AUS)	70-75-73-71—289	112,000
	Rod Pampling (AUS)	72-73-72-72—289	112,000
	Scott Verplank	74-70-74-71—289	112,000
19	Stuart Appleby (AUS)	71-75-73-71—290	91,000
	David Howell (ENG)	71-71-76-72—290	91,000
	Nick O'Hern (AUS)	71-72-76-71—290	91,000
22	Robert Allenby (AUS)	73-73-74-71—291	67,200
	Darren Clarke (NIR)	72-70-72-77—291	67,200
22T	Jim Furyk	73-75-68-75—291	67,200
	Mark Hensby (AUS)	80-67-70-74—291	67,200
	Davis Love III	74-71-74-72—291	67,200
27	Ernie Els (RSA)	71-71-74-76—292	49,700
	Padraig Harrington (IRL)	73-70-75-74—292	49,700
	Shingo Katayama (JPN)	75-70-73-74—292	49,700
	Carl Pettersson (SWE)	72-74-73-73—292	49,700
	Adam Scott (AUS)	72-74-75-71—292	49,700
32	Thomas Bjørn (DEN)	73-75-76-69—293	40,512
	Brandt Jobe	72-76-77-68—293	40,512
	Zach Johnson	74-72-77-70—293	40,512
	Ted Purdy	72-76-74-71—293	40,512
36	Tim Herron	76-71-71-76—294	34,416
	Rocco Mediate	68-73-73-80—294	34,416
	Rory Sabbatini (RSA)	76-70-74-74—294	34,416
39	Jason Bohn	73-71-77-74—295	30,100
	Ben Curtis	71-74-77-73—295	30,100
	Justin Leonard	75-70-79-71—295	30,100
42	Rich Beem	71-73-73-79—296	25,900
	Luke Donald (ENG)	74-72-76-74—296	25,900
	Larry Mize	75-72-77-72—296	25,900
45	Olin Browne	74-69-80-74—297	23,100
46	Sergio García (ESP)	72-74-79-73—298	21,700
47	Ben Crenshaw	71-72-78-79—300	20,300

2005 Masters April 7–10 [7290–72]

Prize money: $7 million. Field of 93 players, of whom 50 (including two amateurs) made the half-way cut.

1	Tiger Woods*	74-66-65-71—276	$1,260,000
2	Chris DiMarco	67-67-74-68—276	756,000
Play-off: Woods 3, DiMarco 4			
3	Luke Donald (ENG)	68-77-69-69—283	406,000
	Retief Goosen (RSA)	71-75-70-67—283	406,000
5	Mark Hensby (AUS)	69-73-70-72—284	237,300
	Trevor Immelman (RSA)	73-73-65-73—284	237,300
	Rodney Pampling (AUS)	73-71-70-70—284	237,300
	Vijay Singh (FIJ)	68-73-71-72—284	237,300
	Mike Weir (CAN)	74-71-68-71—284	237,300
10	Phil Mickelson	70-72-69-74—285	189,000
11	Tim Herron	76-68-70-72—286	168,000
	David Howell (ENG)	72-69-76-69—286	168,000
13	Tom Lehman	74-74-70-69—287	135,333
	Justin Leonard	75-71-70-71—287	135,333
	Thomas Levet (FRA)	71-75-68-73—287	135,333
	Ryan Moore (am)	71-71-75-70—287	
17	Chad Campbell	73-73-67-75—288	112,000
	Darren Clarke (NIR)	72-76-69-71—288	112,000
	Kirk Triplett	75-68-72-73—288	112,000
20	Stewart Cink	72-72-74-71—289	84,840
	Jerry Kelly	75-70-73-71—289	84,840
	Bernhard Langer (GER)	74-74-70-71—289	84,840
	Jeff Maggert	74-74-72-69—289	84,840
	Scott Verplank	72-75-69-73—289	84,840
25	Thomas Bjørn (DEN)	71-67-71-81—290	61,600
25T	Joe Ogilvie	74-73-73-70—290	61,600
	Craig Parry (AUS)	72-75-69-74—290	61,600
28	Jim Furyk	76-67-74-74—291	53,900
29	Steve Flesch	76-70-70-76—292	50,750
	Kenny Perry	76-68-71-77—292	50,750
31	Miguel Angel Jiménez (ESP)	74-74-73-72—293	46,550
	Mark O'Meara	72-74-72-75—293	46,550
33	K J Choi (KOR)	73-72-76-73—294	39,620
	Shingo Katayama (JPN)	72-74-73-75—294	39,620
	Luke List (am)	77-69-78-70—294	
	Ian Poulter (ENG)	72-74-72-76—294	39,620
	Adam Scott (AUS)	71-76-72-75—294	39,620
	Casey Wittenberg	72-72-74-76—294	39,620
39	Tim Clark (RSA)	74-74-72-75—295	32,200
	Fred Couples	75-71-77-72—295	32,200
	Todd Hamilton	77-70-71-77—295	32,200
	Ryan Palmer	70-74-74-77—295	32,200
43	Stuart Appleby (AUS)	69-76-72-79—296	28,000
	Jonathan Kaye	72-74-76-74—296	28,000
45	Stephen Ames (CAN)	73-74-75-75—297	25,200
	Nick O'Hern (AUS)	72-72-76-77—297	25,200
47	Ernie Els (RSA)	75-73-78-72—298	23,100
48	Jay Haas	76-71-76-78—301	21,700
49	Chris Riley	71-77-78-78—304	20,300
50	Craig Stadler	75-73-79-79—306	19,180

2004 Masters April 8–11 [7290–72]

Prize money: $6 million. Field of 93, of whom 44 (including two amateurs) made the half-way cut.

1	Phil Mickelson	72-69-69-69—279	$1,170,000
2	Ernie Els (RSA)	70-72-71-67—280	702,000
3	K J Choi (KOR)	71-70-72-69—282	442,000
4	Sergio García (ESP)	72-72-75-66—285	286,000
	Bernhard Langer (GER)	71-73-69-72—285	286,000
6	Paul Casey (ENG)	75-69-68-74—286	189,893
	Fred Couples	73-69-74-70—286	189,893
	Chris DiMarco	69-73-68-76—286	189,893
	Davis Love III	75-67-74-70—286	189,893
	Nick Price (ZIM)	72-73-71-70—286	189,893
	Vijay Singh (FIJ)	75-73-69-69—286	189,893
	Kirk Triplett	71-74-69-72—286	189,893
13	Retief Goosen (RSA)	75-73-70-70—288	125,667
	Padraig Harrington (IRL)	74-74-68-72—288	125,667
	Charles Howell III	71-71-76-70—288	125,667
	Casey Wittenberg (am)	76-72-71-69—288	
17	Stewart Cink	74-73-69-73—289	97,500
	Steve Flesch	76-67-77-69—289	97,500
	Jay Haas	69-75-72-73—289	97,500
	Fredrik Jacobson (SWE)	74-74-67-74—289	97,500
	Stephen Leaney (AUS)	76-71-73-69—289	97,500
22	Stuart Appleby (AUS)	73-74-73-70—290	70,200
22T	Shaun Micheel	72-76-72-70—290	70,200
	Justin Rose (ENG)	67-71-81-71—290	70,200
	Tiger Woods	75-69-75-71—290	70,200
26	Alex Cejka (GER)	70-70-78-73—291	57,200
27	Mark O'Meara	73-70-75-74—292	51,025
	Bob Tway	75-71-74-72—292	51,025
29	Scott Verplank	74-71-76-72—293	48,100
30	José María Olazábal (ESP)	71-69-79-75—294	46,150
31	Bob Estes	76-72-73-74—295	41,275
	Brad Faxon	72-76-76-71—295	41,275
	Jerry Kelly	74-72-73-76—295	41,275
	Ian Poulter (ENG)	75-73-74-73—295	41,275
35	Justin Leonard	76-72-72-76—296	35,913
	Phillip Price (WAL)	71-76-73-76—296	35,913
37	Paul Lawrie (SCO)	77-70-73-77—297	32,663
	Sandy Lyle (SCO)	72-74-75-76—297	32,663
39	Eduardo Romero (ARG)	74-73-74-77—298	30,550
40	Todd Hamilton	77-71-76-75—299	29,250
41	Tim Petrovic	72-75-75-78—300	27,950
	Brandt Snedeker (am)	73-75-75-77—300	
43	Jeff Sluman	73-70-82-77—302	26,650
44	Chris Riley	70-78-78-78—304	25,350

2003 Masters April 10–13 [7290–72]

Prize money: $6 million. Field of 93, of whom 49 (including three amateurs) made the half-way cut.

1	Mike Weir (CAN)*	70-68-75-68—281	$1,080,000
2	Len Mattiace	73-74-69-65—281	648,000
	Play-off: Weir 4, Mattiace 6		
3	Phil Mickelson	73-70-72-68—283	408,000
4	Jim Furyk	73-72-71-68—284	288,000
5	Jeff Maggert	72-73-66-75—286	240,000
6	Ernie Els (RSA)	79-66-72-70—287	208,500
	Vijay Singh (FIJ)	73-71-70-73—287	208,500
8	Jonathan Byrd	74-71-71-72—288	162,000
	José María Olazábal (ESP)	73-71-71-73—288	162,000
	Mark O'Meara	76-71-70-71—288	162,000
	David Toms	71-73-70-74—288	162,000
	Scott Verplank	76-73-70-69—288	162,000
13	Tim Clark (RSA)	72-75-71-71—289	120,000
	Retief Goosen (RSA)	73-74-72-70—289	120,000
15	Rich Beem	74-72-71-73—290	93,000
	Angel Cabrera (ARG)	76-71-71-72—290	93,000
	K J Choi (KOR)	76-69-72-73—290	93,000
	Paul Lawrie (SCO)	72-72-73-73—290	93,000
	Davis Love III	77-71-71-71—290	93,000
	Tiger Woods	76-73-66-75—290	93,000
21	Ricky Barnes (am)	69-74-75-73—291	
22	Bob Estes	76-71-74-71—292	72,000
23	Brad Faxon	73-71-79-70—293	57,600
	Scott McCarron	77-71-72-73—293	57,600
23T	Nick Price (ZIM)	70-75-72-76—293	57,600
	Chris Riley	76-72-70-75—293	57,600
	Adam Scott (AUS)	77-72-74-70—293	57,600
28	Darren Clarke (NIR)	66-76-78-74—294	43,500
	Fred Couples	73-75-69-77—294	43,500
	Sergio García (ESP)	69-78-74-73—294	43,500
	Charles Howell III	73-72-76-73—294	43,500
	Hunter Mahan (am)	73-72-73-76—294	
33	Nick Faldo (ENG)	74-73-75-73—295	36,375
	Rocco Mediate	73-74-73-75—295	36,375
	Loren Roberts	74-72-76-73—295	36,375
	Kevin Sutherland	77-72-76-70—295	36,375
37	Shingo Katayama (JPN)	74-72-76-74—296	31,650
	Billy Mayfair	75-70-77-74—296	31,650
39	Robert Allenby (AUS)	76-73-74-74—297	27,000
	Craig Parry (AUS)	74-73-75-75—297	27,000
	Kenny Perry	76-72-78-71—297	27,000
	Justin Rose (ENG)	73-76-71-77—297	27,000
	Philip Tataurangi (NZL)	75-70-74-78—297	27,000
44	Jeff Sluman	75-72-76-75—298	23,400
45	Ryan Moore (am)	73-74-75-79—301	
	Pat Perez	74-73-79-75—301	22,200
47	John Rollins	74-71-80-77—302	21,000
48	Jerry Kelly	72-76-77-79—304	19,800
49	Craig Stadler	76-73-79-77—305	18,600

The Masters History (players are American unless stated)

Date	Winner	Score
1934 Mar 22–25	H Smith	284
1935 Apr 4–8	G Sarazen*	282
**After a play-off: Sarazen 144, C Wood 149*		
1936 Apr 2–6	H Smith	285
1937 Apr 1–4	B Nelson	283
1938 Apr 1–4	H Picard	285
1939 Mar 30–Apr 2	R Guldahl	279
1940 Apr 4–7	J Demaret	280
1941 Apr 3–6	C Wood	280
1942 Apr 9–12	B Nelson*	280
**After a play-off: Nelson 69, B Hogan 70*		
1946 Apr 4–7	H Keiser	282
1947 Apr 3–6	J Demaret	281
1948 Apr 8–11	C Harmon	279
1949 Apr 7–10	S Snead	283
1950 Apr 6–9	J Demaret	282
1951 Apr 5–8	B Hogan	280
1952 Apr 3–6	S Snead	286
1953 Apr 9–12	B Hogan	274
1954 Apr 8–12	S Snead*	289
**After a play-off: Snead 69, B Hogan 70*		
1955 Apr 7–10	C Middlecoff	279
1956 Apr 5–8	J Burke	289
1957 Apr 4–7	D Ford	283
1958 Apr 3–6	A Palmer	284
1959 Apr 2–5	A Wall	284
1960 Apr 7–10	A Palmer	282
1961 Apr 6–10	G Player (RSA)	280
1962 Apr 5–9	A Palmer*	280
**After a play-off: Palmer 68, G Player 71, D Finsterwald 77*		
1963 Apr 4–10	J Nicklaus	286
1964 Apr 9–12	A Palmer	276
1965 Apr 8–11	J Nicklaus	271
1966 Apr 7–11	J Nicklaus*	288
**After a play-off: Nicklaus 70, T Jacobs 72, G Brewer Jr 78*		
1967 Apr 6–9	G Brewer	280
1968 Apr 11–14	R Goalby	277
1969 Apr 10–13	G Archer	281
1970 Apr 9–13	W Casper*	279
**After a play-off: Casper 69, G Littler 74*		
1971 Apr 8–11	C Coody	279
1972 Apr 6–9	J Nicklaus	286
1973 Apr 5–9	T Aaron	283
1974 Apr 11–14	G Player (RSA)	278
1975 Apr 10–13	J Nicklaus	276
1976 Apr 8–11	R Floyd	271
1977 Apr 7–10	T Watson	276
1978 Apr 6–9	G Player (RSA)	277
1979 Apr 12–15	F Zoeller*	280
**After a play-off: Zoeller 4,3; T Watson 4,4; E Sneed 4,4*		
1980 Apr 10–13	S Ballesteros (ESP)	275
1981 Apr 9–12	T Watson	280
1982 Apr 8–11	C Stadler*	284
**After a play-off with Dan Pohl: Stadler 4, Pohl 5*		
1983 Apr 7–11	S Ballesteros (ESP)	280
1984 Apr 12–15	B Crenshaw	277
1985 Apr 11–14	B Langer (GER)	282
1986 Apr 10–13	J Nicklaus	279
1987 Apr 9–12	L Mize*	285
**After a play-off ; Mize 4,3, G Norman 4,4, S Ballesteros 5*		
1988 Apr 7–10	A Lyle (SCO)	281
1989 Apr 6–9	N Faldo (ENG)*	283
**After a play-off: Faldo 5,3, S Hoch 5,4*		
1990 Apr 5–8	N Faldo (ENG)*	278
**After a play-off: Faldo 4,4; R Floyd 4,5*		
1991 Apr 11–14	I Woosnam (WAL)	277
1992 Apr 9–12	F Couples	275
1993 Apr 8–11	B Langer (GER)	277
1994 Apr 7–10	JM Olazábal (ESP)	279
1995 Apr 6–9	B Crenshaw	274
1996 Apr 11–14	N Faldo (ENG)	276
1997 Apr 10–13	T Woods	270
1998 Apr 9–12	M O'Meara	279
1999 Apr 8–11	JM Olazábal (ESP)	280
2000 Apr 6–9	V Singh (FIJ)	278
2001 Apr 5–8	T Woods	272
2002 Apr 11–14	T Woods	276
2003 Apr 10–13	M Weir (CAN)*	281
**After a play-off: Weir 4, L Mattiace 6*		
2004 Apr 8–11	P Mickelson	279
2005 Apr 7–10	T Woods*	276
**After a play-off: Woods 3, C DiMarco 4*		
2006 Apr 6–9	P Mickelson	281
2007 Apr 5–8	Z Johnson	289
2008 Apr 10–13	T Immelman (RSA)	280
2009 Apr 9–12	A Cabrera (ARG)	276
**After a play-off with Kenny Perry and Chad Campbell*		
2010 Apr 8–11	P Mickelson	272
2011 Apr 7–10	C Schwartzel (RSA)	274
2012 Apr 5–8	B Watson*	278
**After a play-off: Watson 4,4; Oosthuizen (RSA) 4,5*		

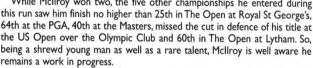

The 94th USPGA at Kiawah Island

Record-breaking McIlroy in total control at Kiawah

After re-writing the record books at Congressional during the summer of 2011when he won the US Open by eight strokes, Rory McIlroy moved into elite company as he clinched the second major of his career, the US PGA Championship on the Ocean Course at Kiawah Island, by a similarly emphatic margin. His eight shot demolition of the field surpassed even Jack Nicklaus' winning mark, set 32 years previously, and established a new record for the PGA since it became a strokeplay event in 1958.

The first British born player to win the PGA since Tommy Armour, the Silver Scot, in 1930, the Northern Ireland golfer also became, at 23 years and three months, the youngest champion to win two major titles since Seve Ballesteros. Four months younger than Tiger Woods when he won his second major, McIlroy is one of only four men in the modern era – Ballesteros, Nicklaus and Woods are the others – to have won a brace of the game's most glittering prizes before the age of 25. (Young Tom Morris, John McDermott and Gene Sarazen were similarly prodigious in earlier eras.)

Rory McIlroy

At this early stage of his career, perhaps Rory could be described as a bulls-eye professional. When he's firing on all cylinders, he's unstoppable, and when he's below his best, he's on the fringes. This dichotomy between hot shower and cold bath is best illustrated by the contrast in his performances in the seven majors staged between the US Open in June of 2011 and the US PGA in August of 2012.

While McIlroy won two, the five other championships he entered during this run saw him finish no higher than 25th in The Open at Royal St George's, 64th at the PGA, 40th at the Masters, missed the cut in defence of his title at the US Open over the Olympic Club and 60th in The Open at Lytham. So, being a shrewd young man as well as a rare talent, McIlroy is well aware he remains a work in progress.

Interestingly, at the start of the week on Kiawah Island, McIlroy began by expressing particular disappointment with his performances in the majors since Congressional. Of course, when those memories of jaw dropping success eventually came flooding back in South Carolina, Rory enjoyed total recall of how imperious a golfer he can be on the game's biggest stage. When level par would have been good enough in the final round to secure victory, Rory instead embraced glory by compiling a thrilling six under par score of 66 to post the winning total of 275, 13 under.

What was most impressive about the Ulsterman's display during the last round was his putting. Having missed three short putts towards the end of his weather delayed third round, McIlroy went on to hole out beautifully when carrying the load of frontrunner in the final group. Knowing the tournament was his to win or lose, McIlroy was unflinching from tee to green and used his putter just 23 times over the closing 18 holes. Dave Stockton, the putting guru, told Rory to play with a smile on his face and the American's advice was as timely as his technical input.

If there was also added steel in his performance, a desire to win as cleanly and clearly as possible, McIlroy admitted he'd been eager to prove the critics wrong. Earlier in the season, when his standards slipped and he performed poorly, missing four cuts out of five, including the European Tour's flagship event at Wentworth, the BMW PGA, the US Open and the Players Championship at Sawgrass, there was speculation his relationship with tennis player Caroline Wozniacki, had taken McIlroy's eye off the ball.

Although Johnny Miller, the US TV analyst and former champion, reckons Kiawah can be the most difficult course in America, the soft conditions were a bonus for McIlroy, who won at Congressional on an even lusher set-up. The 23-year-old was able to take advantage of the Paspalum grass which replaced the Bermuda that made the course such a fast test during the Ryder Cup in 1991. Because of his length and high ball flight, McIlroy was comfortable at Kiawah. He also may have enjoyed an edge over many in the field since he regularly practises on Paspalum at the Bear's Club in Florida.

In the weeks leading up to the 94th staging of the championship, storms had soaked the Ocean Course, rendering fairways wider and greens slower. For McIlroy, the benign conditions on the opening day encouraged him to reach for the driver on ten occasions and still keep a bogey off his card of 67. On a course notable for the severity of the par 3s, Rory struck a wonderful 3 iron within 15 feet of the cup on the 249 yard 14th and duly holed the putt for birdie. And on the 17th, another intimidating short hole, he followed up hitting a spectator on the head at Royal Lytham by watching his tee shot strike a woman on the hip and bounce into a bunker.

A shot off the lead after the first day, Rory trailed Carl Pettersson, the Swedish golfer who won at nearby Hilton Head earlier in the season. Now an American citizen, Pettersson made three birdies in four holes, gave nothing away to par and signed for 66, the first time in 21 attempts at the PGA when he'd bettered 70.

By Friday, the weather had deteriorated and southerly winds gusting up to 30 mph on a demanding lay-out sent scores soaring. There were more rounds in the 90s than the 60s, more than 40 players scored 80 or more and the stroke average of 78.12 was the highest single round average in the history of the championship. The one player who wasn't irked by the conditions was Vijay Singh who signed for 69.

No one in the second round holed more putts than Tiger Woods. After starting smoothly on Thursday, the former world No 1's 71 gave him a share of the lead going into the weekend with Singh and Pettersson, who shot 74. Woods looked like the player of old when he holed putts from 15 feet and 40 feet on his first two holes and thereafter made a number of breathtaking par saves.

> "I had a good feeling ... but never imagined doing this."
>
> *Rory McIlroy*

McIlroy is rarely at his best in strong winds and his 75 didn't include a single birdie until he made 2 on the 14th for the second day running. By Saturday, though, the breeze was lighter yet the Northern Ireland golfer's wish to get off to a fast start very nearly came unstuck up a tree on the fourth hole. After launching his tee shot, McIlroy spent four or five minutes searching for his ball until a TV worker revealed it was stuck in tree bark around seven feet above the ground. Instead of returning to play three off the tee, Rory was able to take a drop under penalty and salvaged par by holing a six foot putt.

It was a turning point in the championship and enabled McIlroy to make five birdies in nine holes before bad weather returned and 26 of the leaders had to complete their rounds on Sunday morning. He looked out of sorts on the greens early on, missing a couple of birdie opportunities before dropping a shot on the 13th. However, Rory fought back with birdies on the 15th and 16th holes, saved par from a bunker on the 17th and finished off with par for 67.

This meant Rory took a three stroke lead over Pettersson into the last round and a five stroke advantage over Woods. For the big Swede, a two stroke penalty for moving a leaf inside the hazard as he took the club back on the first hole put paid to his hopes of victory. And Tiger was again unable to produce his best form, finishing with 72 and failing to break par over the weekend in any of 2012's majors for the first time in his career.

The main threat to McIlroy came from Ian Poulter, who got off to a blistering start by recording six birdies in the first seven holes. Unfortunately, the Englishman, whose ball striking isn't as flawless as his putting, came unstuck after the turn when he was knocked back by three consecutive bogeys. Justin Rose and Keegan Bradley, the defending champion, also posted top five finishes thanks to solid closing rounds.

Easily the most extraordinary accomplishment, though, belonged to David Lynn, the English journeyman who was playing in only his second major at the age of 38 and his first event in America. His weekend rounds of successive 68s were good enough for the runner-up spot, a cheque for nearly £600,000 and a spot in the field for the 2013 Masters.

All of which left McIlroy to decimate the opposition for the second time in 14 months, end the streak of 16 consecutive different major winners and enjoy a loving hug from his father, Gerry, after holing a 20 foot birdie putt on the last which ignited roars of approval from the spectators.

Michael Aitken

First round	Second round	Third round	Fourth round
–6 Carl Pettersson	–4 Tiger Woods	–7 Rory McIlroy	–13 Rory McIlroy
–5 Rory McIlroy	–4 Vijay Singh	–4 Carl Pettersson	–5 David Lynn
–5 Gary Woodland	–4 Carl Pettersson	–3 Bo Van Pelt	–4 Justin Rose
–4 John Daly	–3 Ian Poulter	–3 Trevor Immelman	–4 Ian Poulter
–4 Geoff Ogilvy	–2 Jamie Donaldson	–3 Adam Scott	–4 Carl Pettersson
–4 Joost Luiten	–2 Rory McIlroy	–2 Tiger Woods	–4 Keegan Bradley
–4 Keegan Bradley	–1 Trevor Immelman	–2 Vijay Singh	–3 Steve Stricker
–3 Tiger Woods	–1 Adam Scott	–2 Steve Stricker	–3 Jamie Donaldson
–3 Adam Scott	–1 Aaron Baddeley	–2 Peter Hanson	–3 Peter Hanson
–3 Ryo Ishikawa	–1 Blake Adams	–1 Padraig Harrington	–3 Blake Adams

US PGA Championship (94th) *Kiawah Island Resort (Ocean), Kiawah Island, SC* August 9–12

[7676–72]

Prize money: $8 million. Final field of 156 players, of whom 72 made the half-way cut on 150 or less.

Players are of American nationality unless stated

1	Rory McIlroy (NIR)	67-75-67-66—275	$1,445,000
2	David Lynn (ENG)	73-74-68-68—283	865,000
3	Justin Rose (ENG)	69-79-70-66—284	384,500
	Keegan Bradley	68-77-71-68—284	384,500
	Ian Poulter (ENG)	70-71-74-69—284	384,500
	Carl Pettersson (SWE)	66-74-72-72—284	384,500
7	Blake Adams	71-72-75-67—285	226,000
	Jamie Donaldson (WAL)	69-73-73-70—285	226,000
	Peter Hanson (SWE)	69-75-70-71—285	226,000
	Steve Stricker	74-73-67-71—285	226,000
11	Ben Curtis	69-77-73-67—286	143,285
	Bubba Watson	73-75-70-68—286	143,285
	Tim Clark (RSA)	71-73-73-69—286	143,285
	Geoff Ogilvy (AUS)	68-78-70-70—286	143,285
	Graeme McDowell (NIR)	68-76-71-71—286	143,285
	Tiger Woods	69-71-74-72—286	143,285
	Adam Scott (AUS)	68-75-70-73—286	143,285
18	John Daly	68-77-73-69—287	99,666
	Padraig Harrington (IRL)	70-76-69-72—287	99,666
	Bo Van Pelt	73-73-67-74—287	99,666
21	Joost Luiten (NED)	68-76-75-69—288	72,666
	Louis Oosthuizen (RSA)	70-79-70-69—288	72,666
	Robert Garrigus	74-73-74-67—288	72,666
	Pat Perez	69-76-71-72—288	72,666
	Seung-Yul Noh (KOR)	74-75-74-65—288	72,666
	Jimmy Walker	73-75-67-73—288	72,666
27	Thorbjørn Olesen (DEN)	75-74-71-69—289	51,900
	Miguel Angel Jiménez (ESP)	69-77-72-71—289	51,900
	Jason Dufner	74-76-68-71—289	51,900
	Marc Leishman (AUS)	74-72-71-72—289	51,900
	Trevor Immelman (RSA)	71-72-70-76—289	51,900
32	John Senden (AUS)	73-74-72-71—290	42,625
	Greg Chalmers (AUS)	70-76-72-72—290	42,625
	Bill Haas	75-73-69-73—290	42,625
	Luke Donald (ENG)	74-76-74-66—290	42,625
36	Fredrik Jacobson (SWE)	71-75-73-72—291	34,750
	Rich Beem	72-76-72-71—291	34,750
	Phil Mickelson	73-71-73-74—291	34,750
	Y E Yang (KOR)	73-74-74-70—291	34,750
	Marcel Siem (GER)	72-73-71-75—291	34,750
	Vijay Singh (FIJ)	71-69-74-77—291	34,750
42	J J Henry	72-77-70-73—292	25,750
	Jim Furyk	72-77-70-73—292	25,750
	Aaron Baddeley (AUS)	68-75-74-75—292	25,750
	Gary Woodland	67-79-75-71—292	25,750
	David Toms	72-78-72-70—292	25,750
	Martin Laird (SCO)	71-74-79-68—292	25,750
48	Paul Lawrie (SCO)	73-75-71-74—293	18,625
	Ernie Els (RSA)	72-75-73-73—293	18,625
	Dustin Johnson	71-79-72-71—293	18,625
	Thomas Björn (DEN)	70-79-74-70—293	18,625
	Retief Goosen (RSA)	73-75-75-70—293	18,625
	Scott Piercy	68-78-78-69—293	18,625
54	Francesco Molinari (ITA)	70-75-74-75—294	16,810
	Sang Moon Bae (KOR)	72-78-71-73—294	16,810
	Darren Clarke (NIR)	73-76-72-73—294	16,810

54T	Brendon de Jonge (ZIM)	71-78-72-73—294	16,810
	K J Choi (KOR)	69-77-75-73—294	16,810
59	Charl Schwartzel (RSA)	70-77-74-74—295	16,100
	Ryo Ishikawa (JPN)	69-77-79-70—295	16,100
61	K T Kim (KOR)	69-77-77-73—296	15,900
62	Gonzalo Fernandez-Castano (ESP)	67-78-75-77—297	15,650
	Chez Reavie	74-76-73-74—297	15,650
	Ken Duke	71-78-74-74—297	15,650
	George McNeill	71-76-80-70—297	15,650
66	Alex Noren (SWE)	67-80-73-78—298	15,350
	Marcus Fraser (AUS)	74-75-78-71—298	15,350
68	Toru Taniguchi (JPN)	72-76-78-73—299	15,150
	John Huh	72-78-79-70—299	15,150
70	Zach Johnson	72-73-76-79—300	15,000
71	Matt Every	72-76-74-82—304	14,900
72	Cameron Tringale	69-78-77-82—306	14,800

The following players missed the half-way cut:

73	Thomas Aiken (RSA)	72-79—151
	Robert Allenby (AUS)	75-76—151
	George Coetzee (RSA)	73-78—151
	Nicolas Colsaerts (BEL)	73-78—151
	Hiroyuki Fujita (JPN)	72-79—151
	Sergio Garcia (ESP)	76-75—151
	Anders Hansen (DEN)	72-79—151
	Davis Love III	72-79—151
	Ted Potter Jr	74-77—151
	Webb Simpson	79-72—151
	Johnson Wagner	75-76—151
	Bernd Wiesberger (AUT)	72-79—151
85	Jonathan Byrd	73-79—152
	Rafael Cabrera-Bello (ESP)	71-81—152
	Stewart Cink	74-78—152
	Jason Day (AUS)	72-80—152
	Robert Karlsson (SWE)	74-78—152
	Hunter Mahan	72-80—152
	William McGirt	73-79—152
	Ryan Moore	73-79—152
	Bob Sowards	75-77—152
	Lee Westwood (ENG)	75-77—152
	Mark Wilson	76 76—152
96	Jeff Coston	74-79—153
	Simon Dyson (ENG)	73-80—153
	Branden Grace (RSA)	74-79—153
	Charles Howell III	76-77—153
	Thongchai Jaidee (THA)	73-80—153
96T	Matteo Manassero (ITA)	71-82—153
	Bryce Molder	75-78—153
	Scott Stallings	74-79—153
104	Rickie Fowler	74-80—154
	Brendan Jones (AUS)	76-78—154
	Matt Kuchar	72-82—154
	John Rollins	72-82—154
	Mike Small	76-78—154
	Chris Stroud	73-81—154
	Michael Thompson	73-81—154
111	Bud Cauley	80-75—155
	Lucas Glover	77-78—155
	Darrell Kestner	75-80—155
	Shaun Micheel	72-83—155
	Alan Morin	74-81—155
	Jeff Overton	74-81—155
	Rory Sabbatini (RSA)	73-82—155
	Brandt Snedeker	77-78—155
	Nick Watney	73-82—155
120	Danny Balin	77-79—156
	Angel Cabrera (ARG)	76-80—156
	Roger Chapman (ENG)	78-78—156
	Spencer Levin	78-78—156
124	Charley Hoffman	81-76—157
	Pablo Larrazabal (ESP)	77-80—157
	Kelly Mitchum	76-81—157
	Ryan Palmer	71-86—157
	Rod Perry	75-82—157
	Charlie Wi (KOR)	79-78—157
130	Brian Cairns	75-83—158
	Tommy Gainey	77-81—158
130T	Martin Kaymer (GER)	79-79—158
	Mitch Lowe	79-79—158
	Kyle Stanley	80-78—158
135	Alvaro Quiros (ESP)	76-83—159
	Jeev Milkha Singh (IND)	76-83—159
137	Frank Bensel	84-76—160
	Mark Brooks	78-82—160
	Matt Dobyns	81-79—160
	José María Olazábal (ESP)	74-86—160
	D A Points	73-87—160
142	Brian Gaffney	76-85—161
143	Brian Davis (ENG)	75-87—162
	Marty Jertson	80-82—162
	Robert Rock (ENG)	76-86—162
	Paul Scaletta	75-87—162
147	Corey Prugh	78-85—163
148	Mark Brown	78-86—164
	Paul Casey (ENG)	79-85—164
150	Bill Murchison	82-86—168
151	Michael Frye	79-90—169
152	Doug Wade	83-93—176
	Kevin Na	NC
	Scott Verplank	NC
	Sean O'Hair	NC
	Michael Hoey (NIR)	DQ

A star-studded year for British sport

On the day that witnessed the closing ceremony of the highly-acclaimed 2012 Olympic Games with a record 29 gold medals and third place in the medals table for Team GB, other sportsmen added to Great Britain's golden 2012 success story at the US PGA Championship at wet and windy Kiawah Island.

Northern Ireland's Rory McIlroy followed his success in the 2011 US Open Championship with his second major victory with Englishman David Lynn in second place. Lynn's fellow countrymen, Justin Rose and Ian Poulter, joined last year's victor Keegan Bradley in joint third place while Welshman Jamie Donaldson finished in a creditable joint seventh.

2011 US PGA Championship *Atlanta Athletic Club, Johns Creek, GA* August 12–15 [7467–70]

Prize money: $8 million. Field of 156, of whom 75 made the half-way cut.

1	Keegan Bradley*	71-64-69-68—272	$1,445,000
2	Jason Dufner	70-65-68-69—272	865,000
	**Bradley beat Dufner in three hole play-off*		
3	Anders Hansen (DEN)	68-69-70-66—273	545,000
4	Robert Karlsson (SWE)	70-71-67-67—275	331,000
	David Toms	72-71-65-67—275	331,000
	Scott Verplank	67-69-69-70—275	331,000
7	Adam Scott (AUS)	69-69-70-68—276	259,000
8	Lee Westwood (ENG)	71-68-70-68—277	224,500
	Luke Donald (ENG)	70-71-68-68—277	224,500
10	Kevin Na	72-69-70-67—278	188,000
	D A Points	69-67-71-71—278	188,000
12	Trevor Immelman (RSA)	69-71-71-68—279	132,786
	Gary Woodland	70-70-71-68—279	132,786
	Sergio García (ESP)	72-69-69-69—279	132,786
	Bill Haas	68-73-69-69—279	132,786
	Nick Watney (AUS)	70-71-68-70—279	132,786
	Charl Schwartzel (RSA)	71-71-66-71—279	132,786
	Steve Stricker	63-74-69-73—279	132,786
19	Brian Davis (ENG)	69-73-69-69—280	81,214
	Phil Mickelson	71-70-69-70—280	81,214
	Ryan Palmer	71-70-69-70—280	81,214
	Matt Kuchar	71-71-68-70—280	81,214
	Hunter Mahan	72-72-66-70—280	81,214
	John Senden (AUS)	68-68-72-72—280	81,214
	Brendan Steele	69-68-66-77—280	81,214
26	Charles Howell III	72-68-73-68—281	51,062
	Robert Allenby (AUS)	72-70-71-68—281	51,062
	Jerry Kelly	65-73-74-69—281	51,062
	Bubba Watson	74-68-70-69—281	51,062
	Mark Wilson	69-71-71-70—281	51,062
	Scott Piercy	71-68-71-71—281	51,062
	Brendon de Jonge (RSA)	68-72-69-72—281	51,062
	Spencer Levin	71-70-68-72—281	51,062
34	Chris Kirk	72-72-69-69—282	40,000
	Francesco Molinari (ITA)	72-71-67-72—282	40,000
	Alexander Noren (SWE)	70-72-68-72—282	40,000
37	Matteo Manassero (ITA)	68-74-71-70—283	36,250
	Ben Crane	71-72-66-74—283	36,250
39	Johan Edfors (SWE)	71-70-73-70—284	30,250
	Harrison Frazar	72-69-72-71—284	30,250
	Ian Poulter (ENG)	74-68-70-72—284	30,250
	K J Choi (KOR)	70-73-69-72—284	30,250
	Bill Lunde	71-71-69-73—284	30,250
	Jim Furyk	71-65-73-75—284	30,250

Other players who made the cut: Pablo Larrazabal (ESP), Ross Fisher (ENG), Seung-yul Noh (KOR), Andres Romero (ARG), Yuta Ikeda (JPN), Brandt Jobe 285; Rickie Fowler, John Rollins, Jhonattan Vegas (COL), Johnson Wagner, Simon Dyson (ENG) 286; Ryan Moore, Ricky Barnes, Bryce Molder 287; Michael Bradley, Zach Johnson, K T Kim (KOR) 288; Robert Garrigus, Kevin Streelman 290; Sean O'Hair, Peter Hanson (SWE), Padraig Harrington (IRL), Rory McIlroy (NIR), Miguel Angel Jiménez (ESP) 291; Edoardo Molinari (ITA), Y E Yang (KOR), Mike Small 292; Paul Casey (ENG), Davis Love III 294; Shaun Micheel, Rory Sabbatini (RSA) 295

2010 US PGA Championship *Whistling Straits, Kohler, WI* August 12–15 [7507–72]

Prize money: $7.5 million. Field of 156, of whom 72 made the half-way cut.

1	Martin Kaymer (GER)*	72-68-67-70—277	$1,350,000
2	Bubba Watson	68-71-70-68—277	810,000
	**Kaymer won after a 3-hole play-off: Kaymer 4-2-5; Watson 3-3-6*		
3	Zach Johnson	69-70-69-70—278	435,000
	Rory McIlroy (NIR)	71-68-67-72—278	435,000
5	Dustin Johnson	71-68-67-73—279	206,410
	Jason Dufner	73-66-69-71—279	206,410
	Steve Elkington (AUS)	71-70-67-71—279	206,410
8	Liang Wen-chong (CHN)	72-71-64-73—280	210,000
	Camilo Villegas (COL)	71-71-70-68—280	210,000
10	Jason Day (AUS)	69-72-66-74—281	175,800
	Matt Kuchar	67-69-73-72—281	175,800
12	Paul Casey (ENG)	72-71-70-69—282	138,050
	Simon Dyson (ENG)	71-71-68-72—282	138,050
	Phil Mickelson	73-69-73-67—282	138,050
	Bryce Molder	72-67-70-73—282	138,050
16	Robert Karlsson (SWE)	71-71-71-70—283	110,050
	D A Points	70-72-70-71—283	110,050
18	Stewart Cink	77-68-66-73—284	84,733
	Ernie Els (RSA)	68-74-69-73—284	84,733
	Stephen Gallacher (SCO)	71-69-72-72—284	84,733
	Charl Schwartzel (RSA)	73-69-72-70—284	84,733
	Steve Stricker	72-72-68-72—284	84,733
	Nick Watney	69-68-66-81—284	84,733
24	Jim Furyk	70-68-70-77—285	58,600
	J B Holmes	72-66-77-70—285	58,600
	Simon Khan (ENG)	69-70-71-75—285	58,600
	Carl Pettersson (SWE)	71-70-71-73—285	58,600
28	David Horsey (ENG)	71-70-72-73—286	46,700
	Troy Matteson	72-72-70-72—286	46,700
	Noh Seung-yui (KOR)	68-71-72-75—286	46,700
	Bo Van Pelt	73-67-72-74—286	46,700
	Tiger Woods	71-70-72-73—286	46,700
33	Gonzalo Fernandez-Castaño (ESP)	70-73-73-71—287	37,133
	Edoardo Molinari (ITA)	71-72-70-74—287	37,133
	Francesco Molinari (ITA)	68-73-71-75—287	37,133
	Ryan Palmer	71-68-75-73—287	37,133
	Heath Slocum	73-72-68-74—287	37,133
	David Toms	74-71-67-75—287	37,133
39	K J Choi (KOR)	74-69-71-74—288	25,933
	Tim Clark (RSA)	72-71-70-75—288	25,933
	Ben Crane	73-68-73-74—288	25,933
	Brian Davis (ENG)	71-72-69-76—288	25,933
	Justin Leonard	73-69-73-73—288	25,933
	Hunter Mahan	74-71-68-75—288	25,933
	Adam Scott (AUS)	72-73-71-72—288	25,933
	Vijay Singh (FIJ)	73-66-73-76—288	25,933
	Brandt Snedeker	75-70-67-76—288	25,933

Other players who made the cut: Darren Clarke (NIR), Brendon de Jonge (ZIM), Charles Howell III, Kim Kyung-tae (KOR), Martin Laird (SCO), Marc Leishman (AUS), Shaun Micheel 289; Retief Goosen (RSA), Tom Lehman, Davis Love III 290; Grégory Bourdy (FRA), Rickie Fowler, Peter Hanson (SWE), Kevin Na (KOR) 291; Fredrik Andersson Hed (SWE), Chad Campbell, Rhys Davies (WAL) 292; Brian Gay, Ryan Moore 293; D J Trahan 294; Stuart Appleby (AUS), Rob Labritz 295; Ross McGowan (ENG) 297; Jeff Overton 298; Ian Poulter (ENG) WD

2009 US PGA Championship *Hazeltine, Chaska, MN* August 13–16 [7674–72]

Prize money: $7.5 million. Field of 156, of whom 80 made the half-way cut.

1	Yong-Eun Yang (KOR)	73-70-67-70—280	$1,350,000
2	Tiger Woods	67-70-71-75—283	810,000
3	Rory McIlroy (NIR)	71-73-71-70—285	435,000
	Lee Westwood (ENG)	70-72-73-70—285	435,000
5	Lucas Glover	71-70-71-74—286	300,000
6	Ernie Els (RSA)	75-68-70-74—287	233,125
	Martin Kaymer (GER)	73-70-71-73—287	233,125
	Søren Kjeldsen (DEN)	70-73-70-74—287	233,125
	Henrik Stenson (SWE)	73-71-68-75—287	233,125
10	Padraig Harrington (IRL)	68-73-69-78—288	150,633
	Dustin Johnson	72-73-73-70—288	150,633
	Zach Johnson	74-73-70-71—288	150,633
	Graeme McDowell (NIR)	70-75-71-72—288	150,633
	John Merrick	72-72-74-70—288	150,633
	Francesco Molinari (ITA)	74-73-69-72—288	150,633
16	Tim Clark (RSA)	76-68-71-74—289	106,566
	Hunter Mahan	69-75-74-71—289	106,566
	Vijay Singh (FIJ)	69-72-75-73—289	106,566
19	Michael Allen	74-71-72-73—290	81,760
	Ross Fisher (ENG)	73-68-73-76—290	81,760
	Corey Pavin	73-71-71-75—290	81,760
	Ian Poulter (ENG)	72-70-76-72—290	81,760
	Oliver Wilson (ENG)	74-72-72-72—290	81,760
24	Robert Allenby (AUS)	69-75-75-72—291	53,112
	Stephen Ames (CAN)	74-71-70-76—291	53,112
	K J Choi (KOR)	73-72-73-73—291	53,112
24T	Ben Curtis	73-72-73-73—291	53,112
	Brendan Jones (AUS)	71-70-73-77—291	53,112
	Scott McCarron	75-72-71-73—291	53,112
	Alvaro Quiros (ESP)	69-76-69-77—291	53,112
	John Rollins	73-73-68-77—291	53,112
32	Gonzalo Fernandez-Castaño (ESP)	70-77-73-72—292	40,387
	Steve Flesch	74-73-69-76—292	40,387
	Jeff Overton	72-74-75-71—292	40,387
	Kevin Sutherland	73-72-74-73—292	40,387
36	Woody Austin	73-73-73-74—293	31,735
	Fred Couples	74-74-73-72—293	31,735
	Søren Hansen (DEN)	72-76-74-71—293	31,735
	Thongchai Jaidee (THA)	70-76-73-74—293	31,735
	Miguel Angel Jiménez (ESP)	75-73-71-74—293	31,735
	David Toms	69-75-72-77—293	31,735
	Boo Weekley	74-74-71-74—293	31,735
43	Rich Beem	71-76-75-72—294	21,112
	Chad Campbell	74-73-73-74—294	21,112
	Ben Crane	70-75-72-77—294	21,112
	Luke Donald (ENG)	71-77-73-73—294	21,112
	Kevin Na	73-75-71-75—294	21,112
	Geoff Ogilvy (AUS)	71-73-78-72—294	21,112
	Kenny Perry	74-70-78-72—294	21,112
	Charl Schwartzel (RSA)	76-70-72-76—294	21,112

Other players who made the cut: Retief Goosen (RSA), Anthony Kim, Thomas Levet (FRA), Michael Sim (AUS), Camilo Villegas (COL), 295; Hiroyuki Fujita (JPN), Ryo Ishikawa (JPN), Bob Tway, Charlie Wi (KOR) 296; Richard Green (AUS), Tom Lehman, John Mallinger 297; Angel Cabrera (ARG), Jim Furyk, Nathan Green (AUS), J J Henry 298; Stewart Cink, Paul Goydos, Justin Leonard, Rory Sabbatini (RSA), Jeev Milkha Singh (IND), David Smail (NZL) 299; Phil Mickelson 300; Greg Bisconti 301; Sean O'Hair 302; Bob Estes, Grant Sturgeon, Chris Wood (ENG) 303; Alastair Forsyth (SCO) 305; Richard Sterne (RSA) Rtd

Twelve players made the half-way cut in all four majors

Six Americans, five Europeans and an Australian were the only players to make the half-way cut in all four majors in 2012. Graeme McDowell had the best overall record, finishing in the top 12 in all four events. (T5 at The Open Championship, T2 at the US Open Championship, T12 at the Masters Tournament, and T11 at the US PGA Championship) followed by Adam Scott who finished all events in the top 15 (best result, second place at The Open Championship). Third best placed was Jason Dufner with four finishes in the top 31 (best result, tied fourth at the US Open Championship).

Name	*The Open*	*US Open*	*Masters*	*US PGA*
Keegan Bradley (USA)	T34	T68	T27	T3
Jason Dufner (USA)	T31	T4	T24	T27
Jim Furyk (USA)	T34	T4	11	T42
Padraig Harrington (IRL)	T39	T4	T8	T18
Fredrik Jacobson (SWE)	T54	T15	T19	T36
Zach Johnson (USA)	T9	T41	T32	70
Graeme McDowell (NIR)	T5	T2	T12	T11
Francesco Molinari (ITA)	T39	T29	T19	T54
Ian Poulter (ENG)	T9	T41	T7	T3
Adam Scott (AUS)	2	T15	T8	T11
Steve Stricker (USA)	T23	T15	T47	T7
Tiger Woods (USA)	T3	T21	T40	T11

2008 US PGA Championship *Oakland Hills (South Course), Bloomfield, MI* August 7–10 [7131–70]

Prize money: $7.5 million. Field of 156, of whom 73 made the half-way cut.

1	Padraig Harrington (IRL)	71-74-66-66—277	$1,350,000
2	Ben Curtis	73-67-68-71—279	660.000
	Sergio García (ESP)	69-73-69-68—279	660.000
4	Henrik Stenson (SWE)	71-70-68-72—281	330.000
	Camilo Villegas (COL)	74-72-67-68—281	330.000
6	Steve Flesch	73-70-70-69—282	270.000
7	Phil Mickelson	70-73-71-70—284	231,250
	Andres Romero (ARG)	69-78-65-72—284	231,250
9	Alastair Forsyth (SCO)	73-72-70-70—285	176.725
	Justin Rose (ENG)	73-67-74-71—285	176.725
	Jeev Milkha Singh (IND)	68-74-70-73—285	176.725
	Charlie Wi	70-70-71-74—285	176.725
13	Aaron Baddeley (AUS)	71-71-71-73—286	137,250
	Ken Duke	69-73-73-71—286	137,250
15	Stuart Appleby (AUS)	76-70-69-72—287	107.060
	Paul Casey (ENG)	72-74-72-69—287	107.060
	Graeme McDowell (NIR)	74-72-68-73—287	107.060
	Prayad Marksaeng (THA)	76-70-68-73—287	107.060
	David Toms	72-69-72-74—287	107.060
20	Angel Cabrera (ARG)	70-72-72-74—288	78.900
	Brian Gay	70-74-72-72—288	78.900
	Robert Karlsson (SWE)	68-77-71-72—288	78.900
20T	Boo Weekley	72-71-79-66—288	78.900
24	Mark Brown (NZL)	77-69-74-69—289	57,000
	Retief Goosen (RSA)	72-74-69-74—289	57,000
	Fredrik Jacobson (SWE)	75-71-70-73—289	57,000
	Brandt Snedeker	71-71-74-73—289	57,000
	Nicholas Thompson	71-72-73-73—289	57,000
29	Jim Furyk	71-77-70-72—290	47.550
	J B Holmes	71-68-70-81—290	47.550
31	Robert Allenby (AUS)	76-72-72-71—291	38.825
	Chris DiMarco	75-72-72-72—291	38.825
	Ernie Els (RSA)	71-75-70-75—291	38.825
	Paul Goydos	74-69-73-75—291	38.825
	Geoff Ogilvy (AUS)	73-74-74-70—291	38.825
	Sean O'Hair	69-73-76-73—291	38.825
	Ian Poulter (ENG)	74-71-73-73—291	38.825
	D J Trahan	72-71-76-72—291	38.825
39	Steve Elkington (AUS)	71-73-73-75—292	30.200
	Rory Sabbatini (RSA)	72-73-73-74—292	30.200
	Steve Stricker	71-75-77-69—292	30.200
42	Briny Baird	71-72-73-77—293	24,500
	Michael Campbell (NZL)	73-71-75-74—293	24,500
	Tom Lehman	74-70-75-74—293	24,500
	John Senden (AUS)	76-72-72-73—293	24,500
	Mike Weir (CAN)	73-75-71-74—293	24,500

Other players who made the cut: Michael Allen, Charles Howell III, Billy Mayfair, Carl Petterson (SWE), Dean Wilson 294; Peter Hanson (SWE), John Merrick, Charl Schwartzel (RSA) 295; Tim Clark (RSA), Anthony Kim, James Kingston (RSA) 296; Justin Leonard, Pat Perez 297; John Malinger, Steve Marino, Chez Reavie 298; Paul Azinger, Mark Calcavecchia, Niclas Fasth (SWE), Corey Pavin, Kevin Sutherland 299; Hiroyuki Fujita (JPN), Peter Lonard (AUS) 300; Bubba Watson 301; Richard Green (AUS), 303; Rocco Mediate 304; Louis Oosthuizen (RSA) 306

2007 US PGA Championship *Southern Hills, Tulsa, OK* August 9–12 [7131–70]

Prize money: $7 million. Field of 156, of whom 72 made the half-way cut.

1	Tiger Woods	71-63-69-69—272	$1,260,000
2	Woody Austin	68-70-69-67—274	756,000
3	Ernie Els (RSA)	72-68-69-66—275	476,000
4	Arron Oberholser	68-72-70-69—279	308,000
	John Senden (AUS)	69-70-69-71—279	308,000
6	Simon Dyson (ENG)	73-71-72-64—280	227,500
	Trevor Immelman (RSA)	75-70-66-69—280	227,500
	Geoff Ogilvy (AUS)	69-68-74-69—280	227,500
9	Kevin Sutherland	73-69-68-71—281	170,333
	Scott Verplank	70-66-74-71—281	170,333
	Boo Weekley	76-69-65-71—281	170,333
12	Stephen Ames (CAN)	68-69-69-76—282	119,833
	Stuart Appleby (AUS)	73-68-72-69—282	119,833
	K J Choi (KOR)	71-71-68-72—282	119,833
	Anders Hansen (DEN)	71-71-71-69—282	119,833
	Justin Rose (ENG)	70-73-70-69—282	119,833
	Adam Scott (AUS)	72-68-70-72—282	119,833
18	Ken Duke	73-71-69-71—284	81,600
	Joe Durant	71-73-70-70—284	81,600
	Hunter Mahan	71-73-72-68—284	81,600
	Pat Perez	70-69-77-68—284	81,600
	Brandt Snedeker	74-71-69-70—284	81,600
23	Steve Flesch	72-73-68-72—285	51,000
	Retief Goosen (RSA)	70-71-74-70—285	51,000
	Nathan Green (AUS)	75-68-67-75—285	51,000
23T	Peter Hanson (SWE)	72-71-69-73—285	51,000
	Kenny Perry	72-72-71-70—285	51,000
	Ian Poulter (ENG)	71-73-70-71—285	51,000
	Heath Slocum	72-70-72-71—285	51,000
	Steve Stricker	77-68-69-71—285	51,000
	Camilo Villegas (COL)	69-71-74-71—285	51,000
32	Brad Bryant	74-70-72-70—286	34,750
	Stewart Cink	72-70-72-72—286	34,750
	John Daly	67-73-73-73—286	34,750
	Luke Donald (ENG)	72-71-70-73—286	34,750
	Shaun Micheel	73-71-70-72—286	34,750
	Phil Mickelson	73-69-75-69—286	34,750
	Lee Westwood (ENG)	69-74-75-68—286	34,750
	Brett Wetterich	74-71-70-71—286	34,750
40	Paul Casey (ENG)	72-70-74-71—287	27,350
	Richard Green (AUS)	72-73-70-72—287	27,350
42	Darren Clarke (NIR)	77-66-71-74—288	20,850
	Niclas Fasth (SWE)	71-68-79-70—288	20,850
	Padraig Harrington (IRL)	69-73-72-74—288	20,850
	Charles Howell III	75-70-72-71—288	20,850
	Colin Montgomerie (SCO)	72-73-73-70—288	20,850
	Sean O'Hair	70-72-70-76—288	20,850
	Rod Pampling (AUS)	70-74-72-72—288	20,850
	David Toms	71-74-71-72—288	20,850

Other players who made the cut: Brian Bateman, Lucas Glover, Frank Lickliter II, Shingo Katayama (JPN), Anthony Kim, Nick O'Hern, Bob Tway 289; Chad Campbell, Robert Karlsson (SWE), Will MacKenzie 290; Billy Mayfair, Paul McGinley (IRL) 291; Thomas Bjørn (DEN), Corey Pavin, Brett Quigley, Graeme Storm (ENG) 293; Todd Hamilton, Tim Herron, Troy Matteson 294; Tom Lehman, Mike Small 296; Ryan Benzel 297; Sergio García (ESP) DQ

2006 US PGA Championship *Medinah, Il* August 16–20 [7561–72]

Prize money: $6.5 million. Field of 156, of whom 70 made the half-way cut.

1	Tiger Woods	69-68-65-68—270	$,1224,000
2	Shaun Micheel	69-70-67-69—275	734,400
3	Luke Donald (ENG)	68-68-66-74—276	353,600
	Sergio García (ESP)	69-70-67-70—276	353,600
	Adam Scott (AUS)	71-69-69-67—276	353,600
6	Mike Weir (CAN)	72-67-65-73—277	244,800
7	K J Choi (KOR)	73-67-67-71—278	207,787
	Steve Stricker	72-67-70-69—278	207,787
9	Ryan Moore	71-72-67-69—279	165,000
	Geoff Ogilvy (AUS)	69-68-68-74—279	165,000
	Ian Poulter (ENG)	70-70-68-71—279	165,000
12	Chris DiMarco	71-70-67-72—280	134,500
	Sean O'Hair	72-70-70-68—280	134,500
14	Tim Herron	69-67-72-73—281	115,000
	Henrik Stenson (SWE)	68-68-73-72—281	115,000
16	Woody Austin	71-69-69-73—282	94,000
	Ernie Els (RSA)	71-70-72-69—282	94,000
	Phil Mickelson	69-71-68-74—282	94,000
	David Toms	71-67-71-73—282	94,000
20	Robert Allenby (AUS)	68-74-71-70—283	71,250
	Jonathan Byrd	69-72-74-68—283	71,250
	Harrison Fraser	69-72-69-73—283	71,250
	Fred Funk	69-69-74-71—283	71,250
24	Chad Campbell	71-72-75-66—284	53,100
	Stewart Cink	68-74-73-69—284	53,100
	Tim Clark (RSA)	70-69-75-70—284	53,100
	Steve Flesch	72-71-69-72—284	53,100
	Anders Hansen (DEN)	72-71-70-71—284	53,100
29	Jim Furyk	70-72-69-74—285	41,100
	Robert Karlsson (SWE)	71-73-69-72—285	41,100
	Heath Slocum	73-70-72-70—285	41,100
	Lee Westwood (ENG)	69-72-71-73—285	41,100
	Dean Wilson	74-70-74-67—285	41,100
34	Retief Goosen (RSA)	70-73-68-75—286	34,500
	Trevor Immelman (RSA)	73-71-70-72—286	34,500
	Davis Love III	68-69-73-76—286	34,500
37	Richard Green (AUS)	73-69-73-72—287	29,250
	J B Holmes	71-70-68-78—287	29,250
	Graeme McDowell (NIR)	75-68-72-72—287	29,250
	Billy Mayfair	69-69-73-76—287	29,250
41	Billy Andrade	67-69-78-74—288	23,080
	Daniel Chopra (SWE)	72-67-76-73—288	23,080
	J J Henry	68-73-73-74—288	23,080
	Chris Riley	66-72-73-77—288	23,080
	Justin Rose (ENG)	73-70-70-75—288	23,080

Other players who made the cut: Olin Browne, Lucas Glover 289; Jerry Kelly 290; Rich Beem, Nathan Green (AUS), Ryan Palmer, Corey Pavin, Kenny Perry, Joey Sindelar 291; Stephen Ames (CAN), Stuart Appleby (AUS), Aaron Baddeley (AUS), José-María Olazábal (ESP), Hideto Tanihara (JPN) 292; Ben Curtis, Steve Lowery 293; Jason Gore, Jeff Maggert, Charles Warren 295; Miguel Angel Jiménez (ESP), Bob Tway 296; David Howell (ENG) 297; Jay Haas, Don Yrene 300; Jim Kane 301

2005 US PGA Championship *Baltusrol, NJ* August 11–15 [7392–70]

Prize money: $6.25 million. Field of 156, of whom 79 made the half-way cut.

1	Phil Mickelson	67-65-72-72—276	$1,1700,00
2	Thomas Bjørn (DEN)	71-71-63-72—277	572,000
	Steve Elkington (AUS)	68-70-68-71—277	572,000
4	Davis Love III	68-68-68-74—278	286,000
	Tiger Woods	75-69-66-68—278	286,000
6	Michael Campbell (NZL)	73-68-69-69—279	201,500
	Retief Goosen (RSA)	68-70-69-72—279	201,500
	Geoff Ogilvy (AUS)	69-69-72-69—279	201,500
	Pat Perez	68-71-67-73—279	201,500
10	Steve Flesch	70-71-69-70—280	131,800
	Dudley Hart	70-73-66-71—280	131,800
	Ted Purdy	69-75-70-66—280	131,800
	Vijay Singh (FIJ)	70-67-69-74—280	131,800
	David Toms	71-72-69-68—280	131,800
15	Stuart Appleby (AUS)	67-70-69-75—281	102,500
	Charles Howell III	70-71-68-72—281	102,500
17	Tim Clark (RSA)	71-73-70-68—282	82,500
	Trevor Immelman (RSA)	67-72-72-71—282	82,500
	Jack Johnson	70-70-73-69—282	82,500
	Joe Ogilvie	74-68-69-71—282	82,500
	Bo Van Pelt	70-70-68-74—282	82,500
	Lee Westwood (ENG)	68-68-71-75—282	82,500
23	Sergio García (ESP)	72-70-71-70—283	56,400
23T	Shingo Katayama (JPN)	71-66-74-72—283	56,400
	Paul McGinley (IRL)	72-70-72-69—283	564,00
	Tom Pernice Jr	69-73-69-72—283	56,400
	Kenny Perry	69-70-70-74—283	56,400
28	Chad Campbell	71-71-70-72—284	41,500
	Stewart Cink	71-72-66-75—284	41,500
	Bob Estes	71-72-73-68—284	41,500
	Arron Oberholser	74-68-69-73—284	41,500
	Jesper Parnevik (SWE)	68-69-72-75—284	41,500
	Vaughn Taylor	75-69-71-69—284	41,500
34	Jason Bohn	71-68-68-78—285	31,917
	Ben Curtis	67-73-67-78—285	31,917
	Jim Furyk	72-71-69-73—285	31,917
	Fredrik Jacobson (SWE)	72-69-73-71—285	31,917
	Jerry Kelly	70-65-74-76—285	31,917
	Scott Verplank	71-72-71-71—285	31,917
40	K J Choi (KOR)	71-70-73-72—286	22,300
	Ben Crane	68-76-72-70—286	22,300
	Miguel Angel Jiménez (ESP)	72-72-69-73—286	22,300
	John Rollins	68-71-73-74—286	22,300
	Steve Schneiter (CAN)	72-72-72-70—286	22,300
	Adam Scott (AUS)	74-69-72-71—286	22,300
	Patrick Sheehan	73-71-71-71—286	22,300

Other players who made the cut: Fred Funk, Todd Hamilton, Bernhard Langer (GER), JL Lewis, José María Olazábal (ESP), Greg Owen (ENG), Ryan Palmer, Ian Poulter (ENG), Heath Slocum, Henrik Stenson (SWE). Mike Wier (CAN), Yong-Eun Yang (KOR) 287; Paul Casey (ENG), Carlos Franco (PAR), Peter Hanson (SWE), Mark Hensby (AUS), Scott McCarron, Sean O'Hair, Steve Webster (ENG) 288; Woody Austin, Luke Donald (ENG), Ron Philo Jr, Chris Riley 289; Mark Calcavecchia, Fred Couples 290; Stephen Ames (CAN), Joe Durant 291; John Daly, Rory Sabbatini (RSA) 292; Mike Small 295; Kevin Sutherland 296; Darrell Kestner 299; Hal Sutton 300

2004 US PGA Championship *Whistling Straits, Kohler, WI* August 12–15 [7514–72]

Prize money: $6.25 million. Field of 155, of whom 73 made the half-way cut.

1	Vijay Singh (FIJ)*	67-68-69-76—280	$1,125,000
2	Justin Leonard	66-69-70-75—280	550,000
	Chris DiMarco	68-70-71-71—280	550,000
Three hole play-off: Singh 3-3-4; Leonard 4-3-4; DiMarco 4-3-4			
4	Ernie Els (RSA)	66-70-72-73—281	267,500
	Chris Riley	69-70-69-73—281	267,500
6	K J Choi (KOR)	68-71-73-70—282	196,000
	Paul McGinley (IRL)	69-74-70-69—282	196,000
	Phil Mickelson	69-72-67-74—282	196,000
9	Robert Allenby (AUS)	71-70-72-70—283	152,000
	Stephen Ames (CAN	68-71-69-75—283	152,000
	Ben Crane	70-74-69-70—283	152,000
	Adam Scott (AUS)	71-71-69-72—283	152,000
13	Darren Clarke (NIR)	65-71-72-76—284	110,250
	Brian Davis (ENG)	70-71-69-74—284	110,250
	Brad Faxon	71-71-70-72—284	110,250
	Arron Oberholser	73-71-70-70—284	110,250
17	Stuart Appleby (AUS)	68-75-72-70—285	76,857
	Stewart Cink	73-70-70-72—285	76,857
	Matt Gogel	71-71-69-74—285	76,857
	Fredrik Jacobson (SWE)	72-70-70-73—285	76,857
	Jean-François Remesy (FRA)	72-71-70-72—285	76,857
	Loren Roberts	68-72-70-75—285	76,857
17T	David Toms	72-72-69-72—285	76,857
24	Tom Byrum	72-73-71-70—286	46,714
	Chad Campbell	73-70-71-72—286	46,714
	Luke Donald (ENG)	67-73-71-75—286	46,714
	JL Lewis	73-69-72-72—286	46,714
	Shaun Micheel	77-68-70-71—286	46,714
	Geoff Ogilvy (AUS)	68-73-71-74—286	46,714
	Tiger Woods	75-69-69-73—286	46,714
31	Carlos Daniel Franco (PAR)	69-75-72-71—287	34,250
	Charles Howell III	70-71-72-74—287	34,250
	Miguel Angel Jiménez (ESP)	76-65-75-71—287	34,250
	Nick O'Hern (AUS)	73-71-68-75—287	34,250
	Chip Sullivan	72-71-73-71—287	34,250
	Bo Van Pelt	74-71-70-72—287	34,250
37	Briny Baird	67-69-75-77—288	24,687
	Steve Flesch	73-72-67-76—288	24,687
	Jay Haas	68-72-71-77—288	24,687
	Todd Hamilton	72-73-75-68—288	24,687
	Trevor Immelman (RSA)	75-69-72-72—288	24,687
	Zach Johnson	75-70-69-74—288	24,687
	Ian Poulter (ENG)	73-72-70-73—288	24,687
	Brett Quigley	74-69-73-72—288	24,687

Other players who made the cut: Tommy Armour III, Niclas Fasth (SWE), Padraig Harrington (IRL), David Howell (ENG) 289; Michael Campbell (NZL), Nick Faldo (ENG), Joe Ogilvie, Patrick Sheehan, Duffy Waldorf 290; Carl Pettersson (SWE) 291; Paul Azinger, S K Ho (KOR), Rod Pampling (AUS), Craig Parry (AUS), Eduardo Romero (ARG), Hidemichi Tanaka (JPN), Bob Tway 292; Woody Austin, Shingo Katayama (JPN), Jeff Sluman, Scott Verplank 293; Scott Drummond (SCO), Bernhard Langer (GER) 294; Robert Gamez, Mark Hensby (AUS) 296; Colin Montgomerie (SCO) 297; Roy Biancalana 299; Jeff Coston 301; Skip Kendall 304

2003 US PGA Championship *Oak Hill CC, Rochester, NY* August 14–17 [7134–70]

Prize money: $6 million. Field of 156, of whom 70 made the half-way cut.

1	Shaun Micheel	69-68-69-70—276	$1,080,000
2	Chad Campbell	69-72-65-72—278	648,000
3	Tim Clark (RSA)	72-70-68-69—279	408,000
4	Alex Cejka (GER)	74-69-68-69—280	288,000
5	Ernie Els (RSA)	71-70-70-71—282	214,000
	Jay Haas	70-74-69-69—282	214,000
7	Fred Funk	69-73-70-72—284	175.667
	Loren Roberts	70-73-70-71—284	175.667
	Mike Weir (CAN)	68-71-70-75—284	175.667
10	Billy Andrade	67-72-72-74—285	135,500
	Niclas Fasth (SWE)	76-70-71-68—285	135,500
	Charles Howell III	70-72-70-73—285	135,500
	Kenny Perry	75-72-70-68—285	135,500
14	Robert Gamez	70-73-70-73—286	98,250
	Tim Herron	69-72-74-71—286	98,250
	Scott McCarron	74-70-71-71—286	98,250
	Rod Pampling (AUS)	66-74-73-73—286	98,250
18	Carlos Franco (PAR)	73-73-69-72—287	73,000
	Jim Furyk	72-74-69-72—287	73,000
	Toshimitsu Izawa (JPN)	71-72-71-73—287	73,000
	Rocco Mediate	72-74-71-70—287	73,000
	Kevin Sutherland	69-74-71-73—287	73,000
23	Stuart Appleby (AUS)	74-73-71-70—288	52,000
23T	Luke Donald (ENG)	73-72-71-72—288	52,000
	Phil Mickelson	66-75-72-75—288	52,000
	Adam Scott (AUS)	72-69-72-75—288	52,000
27	Woody Austin	72-73-69-75—289	43,000
	Geoff Ogilvy (AUS)	71-71-77-70—289	43,000
29	Todd Hamilton	70-74-73-73—290	36.600
	Padraig Harrington (IRL)	72-76-69-73—290	36.600
	Frank Lickliter II	71-72-71-76—290	36.600
	Peter Lonard (AUS)	74-74-69-73—290	36.600
	David Toms	75-72-71-72—290	36.600
34	Fred Couples	74-71-72-74—291	29,000
	Lee Janzen	68-74-72-77—291	29,000
	JL Lewis	71-75-71-74—291	29,000
	Jesper Parnevik (SWE)	73-72-72-74—291	29,000
	Vijay Singh (FIJ)	69-73-70-79—291	29,000
39	Robert Allenby (AUS)	70-77-73-72—292	22,000
	Briny Baird	73-71-67-81—292	22,000
	Mark Calcavecchia	73-71-76-72—292	22,000
	Joe Durant	71-76-75-70—292	22,000
	Hal Sutton	75-71-67-79—292	22,000
	Tiger Woods	74-72-73-73—292	22,000

Other players who made the cut: Angel Cabrera (ARG), Tom Pernice Jr, Duffy Waldorf 293; Ben Crane, Trevor Immelman (RSA), Shigeki Maruyama (JPN) 294; José Coceres (ARG), Gary Evans (ENG), Brian Gay, Len Mattiace, José María Olazábal (ESP), 295; Chris DiMarco 296; Aaron Baddeley (AUS), Bob Estes, Scott Hoch, Bernhard Langer (GER) 297; Jonathan Kaye, Billy Mayfair, Ian Poulter (ENG), Eduardo Romero (ARG), Philip Tataurangi (NZL) 298; Paul Casey (ENG) 299; Bob Burns 300; Rory Sabbatini (RSA) 302; Michael Campbell (NZL), K J Choi (KOR) 304

US PGA Championship History

Date	Winner	Runner-up	Venue	By
1916 Oct 8–14	J Barnes	J Hutchison	Siwanoy, NY	1 hole
1919 Sept 15–20	J Barnes	F McLeod	Engineers' Club, NY	6 and 5
1920 Aug 17–21	J Hutchison	D Edgar	Flossmoor, IL	1 hole
1921 Sept 26–Oct 1	W Hagen	J Barnes	Inwood Club, NY	3 and 2
1922 Aug 12–18	G Sarazen	E French	Oakmont, PA	4 and 3
1923 Sept 23–29	G Sarazen	W Hagen	Pelham, NY	38th hole
1924 Sept 15–20	W Hagen	J Barnes	French Lick, IN	2 holes
1925 Sept 21–26	W Hagen	W Mehlhorn	Olympic Fields, IL	6 and 4
1926 Sept 20–25	W Hagen	L Diegel	Salisbury, NY	4 and 3
1927 Oct 31–Nov 5	W Hagen	J Turnesa	Dallas, TX	1 hole
1928 Oct 1–6	L Diegel	A Espinosa	Five Farms, MD	6 and 5
1929 Dec 2–7	L Diegel	J Farrell	Hill Crest, CA	6 and 4
1930 Sept 8–13	T Armour	G Sarazen	Fresh Meadows, NY	1 hole
1931 Sept 7–14	T Creavy	D Shute	Wannamoisett, RI	2 and 1
1932 Aug 31–Sept 4	O Dutra	F Walsh	St Paul, MN	4 and 3
1933 Aug 8–13	G Sarazen	W Goggin	Milwaukee, WI	5 and 4
1934 July 24–29	P Runyan	C Wood	Buffalo, NY	38th hole
1935 Oct 18–23	J Revolta	T Armour	Oklahoma, OK	5 and 4
1936 Nov 17–22	D Shute	J Thomson	Pinehurst, NC	3 and 2
1937 May 26–30	D Shute	H McSpaden	Pittsburgh, PA	37th hole
1938 July 10–16	P Runyan	S Snead	Shawnee, PA	8 and 7
1939 July 9–15	H Picard	B Nelson	Pomonok, NY	37th hole
1940 Aug 26–Sept 2	B Nelson	S Snead	Hershey, PA	1 hole
1941 July 7–13	V Ghezzie	B Nelson	Denver, CO	38th hole
1942 May 23–31	S Snead	J Turnesa	Atlantic City, NJ	2 and 1
1943 *No Championship*				
1944 Aug 14–20	B Hamilton	B Nelson	Spokane, WA	1 hole
1945 July 9–15	B Nelson	S Byrd	Dayton, OH	4 and 3
1946 Aug 19–25	B Hogan	E Oliver	Portland, OR	6 and 4
1947 June 18–24	J Ferrier	C Harbert	Detroit, MI	2 and 1
1948 May 19–25	B Hogan	M Turnesa	Norwood Hills, MO	7 and 6
1949 May 25–31	S Snead	J Palmer	Richmond, VA	3 and 2
1950 June 21–27	C Harper	H Williams	Scioto, OH	4 and 3
1951 June 27–July 3	S Snead	W Burkemo	Oakmont, PA	7 and 6
1952 June 18–25	J Turnesa	C Harbert	Louisville, KY	1 hole
1953 July 1–7	W Burkemo	F Lorza	Birmingham, MI	2 and 1
1954 July 21–27	C Harbert	W Burkemo	St Paul, MN	4 and 3
1955 July 20–26	D Ford	C Middlecoff	Meadowbrook, MI	4 and 3
1956 July 20–24	J Burke	T Kroll	Canton, MA	3 and 2
1957 July 17–21	L Hebert	D Finsterwald	Dayton, OH	3 and 1

Changed to stroke play in 1958

Date	Winner	Venue	Score
1958 July 17–20	D Finsterwald	Llanerch, PA	276
1959 July 30–Aug 2	B Rosburg	Minneapolis, MN	277
1960 July 21–24	J Hebert	Firestone, Akron, OH	281
1961 July 27–31	J Barber*	Olympia Fields, IL	277
**After a play-off: Barber 67, D January 68*			
1962 July 19–22	G Player (RSA)	Aronimink, PA	278
1963 July 18–21	J Nicklaus	Dallas, TX	279
1964 July 16–19	B Nichols	Columbus, OH	271
1965 Aug 12–15	D Marr	Laurel Valley, PA	280
1966 July 21–24	A Geiberger	Firestone, Akron, OH	280
1967 July 20–24	D January*	Columbine, CO	281
**After a play-off: January 69, D Massengale 71*			
1968 July 18–21	J Boros	Pecan Valley, TX	281
1969 Aug 14–17	R Floyd	Dayton, OH	276
1970 Aug 13–16	D Stockton	Southern Hills, OK	279
1971 Feb 25–28	J Nicklaus	PGA national, FL	281
1972 Aug 3–6	G Player (RSA)	Oakland Hills, MI	281
1973 Aug 9–12	J Nicklaus	Canterbury, OH	277
1974 Aug 8–11	L Trevino	Tanglewood, NC	276
1975 Aug 7–10	J Nicklaus	Firestone, Akron, OH	276
1976 Aug 12–16	D Stockton	Congressional, MD	281
1977 Aug 11–14	L Wadkins*	Pebble Beach, CA	287
**After a play-off: Wadkins 4-4-3; G Littler 4-4-4*			
1978 Aug 3–6	J Mahaffey*	Oakmont, PA	276
**After a play-off: Mahaffey 4-3; J Pate 4,4; T Watson 4-4*			
1979 Aug 2–5	D Graham (AUS)*	Oakland Hills, MI	272
**After a play-off: Graham 4-4-2; B Crenshaw 4-4-4*			
1980 Aug 7–10	J Nicklaus	Oak Hill, NY	274
1981 Aug 6–9	L Nelson	Atlanta, GA	273
1982 Aug 5–8	R Floyd	Southern Hills, OK	272
1983 Aug 4–7	H Sutton	Pacific Palisades, CA	274
1984 Aug 16–19	L Trevino	Shoal Creek, AL	273
1985 Aug 8–11	H Green	Cherry Hills, Denver, CO	278
1986 Aug 7–10	R Tway	Inverness, Toledo, OH	276
1987 Aug 6–9	L Nelson*	PGA National, FL	287
**After a play-off: Nelson 4, L Wadkins 5*			
1988 Aug 11–14	J Sluman	Oaktree, OK	272
1989 Aug 10–13	P Stewart	Kemper Lakes, IL	276
1990 Aug 9–12	W Grady (AUS)	Shoal Creek, AL	282
1991 Aug 8–11	J Daly	Crooked Stick, IN	276
1992 Aug 13–16	N Price (ZIM)	Bellerive, MS	278

US PGA Championship History *continued*

Date	Winner	Venue	Score
1993 Aug 12–15	P Azinger*	Inverness, Toledo, OH	272
After a play-off: Azinger 4-4, G Norman 4-5			
1994 Aug 11–14	N Price (ZIM)	Southern Hills, OK	269
1995 Aug 10–13	S Elkington (AUS)*	Riviera, LA	267
After a play-off: Elkington 3, C Montgomerie 4			
1996 Aug 8–11	M Brooks*	Valhalla, Kentucky	277
After a play-off against Kenny Perry: Brooks 4, Perry 5			
1997 Aug 14–17	D Love III	Winged Foot, NY	269
1998 Aug 13–16	V Singh (FIJ)	Sahalee, Seattle, WA	271
1999 Aug 12–15	T Woods	Medinah, IL	277
2000 Aug 17–20	T Woods*	Valhalla, Louisville KY	270
After a play-off: Woods 3,4,5, B May 4,4,5			
2001 Aug 16–19	D Toms	Atlanta Athletic Club, GA	265
2002 Aug 15–18	R Beem	Hazeltine National, MN	278
2003 Aug 14–17	S Micheel	Oak Hill, NY	276
2004 Aug 12–15	V Singh (FIJ)*	Whistling Straits, WI	280
After a play-off: Singh 3,3,4, C DiMarco 4,3,4, J Leonard 4,3,4			
2005 Aug 11–15	P Mickelson	Baltusrol, NJ	276
2006 Aug 16–20	T Woods	Medinah, IL	270
2007 Aug 9–12	T Woods	Southern Hills, OK	272
2008 Aug 7–10	P Harrington	Oakland Hills, MI	277
2009 Aug 14–16	Y E Yang	Hazeltine, Chaska, MN	280
2010 Aug 12–15	M Kaymer*	Whistling Straits, WI	277
After a play-off: Kaymer 4,2,5, B Watson 3,3,6			
2011 Aug 11–14	K Bradley*	Atlanta Athletic Club, GA	272
After a play-off: Bradley 3,3,4, J Dufner 4,4,3			
2012 Aug 9–12	R McIlroy	Kiawah Island, SC	275

How the courses played at the 2012 majors

THE OPEN CHAMPIONSHIP – Royal Lytham & St Annes, Lancashire
Course: 7,086 yards Par 70 – Average score 71.98
Eagles scored during the week 16; Birdies 1,237; Pars 5,451; Bogeys 1,628; Double bogeys or more 272
Toughest Hole: The 6th – 492 yards Par 4 – Average score 4.47*
(*only 15 birdies all week)
Easiest Hole: The 16th – 336 yards Par 4 – Average score 3.84
Winner: Ernie Els (RSA) 273 (–7)

THE US OPEN CHAMPIONSHIP – Olympic Club, San Francisco, CA
Course: 7,170 yards Par 70 – Average score 73.84
Eagles scored during the week 25; Birdies 932; Pars 4,851; Bogeys 2,099; Double bogeys or more 301
Toughest Hole: The 6th – 489 yards Par 4 – Average score 4.54
Easiest Hole: The 17th – 522 yards Par 5 – Average score 4.71
Winner: Webb Simpson (USA) 281 (+1)

THE MASTERS – National Golf Club, Augusta, GA
Course: 7,435 yards Par 72 – Average score 73.5
Eagles scored during the week 29; Birdies 953; Pars 3,370; Bogeys 1.152; Double bogeys or more 155
Toughest Hole: The 1st – 445 yards Par 4 – Average score 4.39*
(*only 11 birdies all week)
Easiest Hole: The 2nd – 575 yards Par 5 – Average score 4.64
Winner: Bubba Watson (USA) 278 (–10)

US PGA CHAMPIONSHIP – Kiawah Island Resort (Ocean), Kiawah Island, SC
Course: 7,676 yards Par 72 – Average score 74.68
Eagles scored during the week 20; Birdies 1,273; Pars 4,817; Bogeys 1,731' Double bogets or more 350
Toughest Hole: The 13th – 497 yards Par 4 – Average score 4.38
Easiest Hole: The 16th – 581 yards Par 5 – Average score 4.78
Winner: Rory McIlroy (NIR) 275 (–13)

Men's Grand Slam Titles

Jack Nicklaus

Tiger Woods

Walter Hagen

The modern Grand Slam comprises four events – the British and US Open Championships, the US PGA Championship and The Masters Tournament at Augusta.

	Open	**US Open**	**Masters**	**US PGA**	***Total Titles***
Jack Nicklaus (USA)	3	4	6	5	18
Tiger Woods (USA)	3	3	4	4	14
Walter Hagen (USA)	4	2	0	5	11
Ben Hogan (USA)	1	4	2	2	9
Gary Player (RSA)	3	1	3	2	9
Tom Watson (USA)	5	1	2	0	8
Arnold Palmer (USA)	2	1	4	0	7
Gene Sarazen (USA)	1	2	1	3	7
Sam Snead (USA)	1	0	3	3	7
Lee Trevino (USA)	2	2	0	2	6
Nick Faldo (ENG)	3	0	3	0	6

The original Grand Slam comprised the British and US Open Championships and the British and US Amateur Championships.

	Open	**US Open**	**Amateur**	**US Amateur**	***Total Titles***
Bobby Jones (USA)	3	4	1	5	13
John Ball (ENG)	1	0	8	0	9
Harold Hilton (ENG)	2	0	4	1	7
Harry Vardon (ENG)	6	1	0	0	7

Note: Tiger Woods won three consecutive US Amateur Championships in 1994, 1995 and 1996. Only Bobby Jones has won all four recognised Grand Slam events in the same year – 1930.

Changes being made to the Old Course for the 2015 Open Championship

The news that changes were being made to nine holes on the Old Course at St Andrews prior to the 2015 Open caused ripples of discontent in some quarters last year but The R&A and the St Andrews Links Trust who agreed the changes are happy that the character of the most famous 18-holes in golf will not be compromised.

Peter Dawson, Secretary of The R&A, says much of the initial adverse comment was ill-informed and called for a more balanced attitude to the plans which had caused several well known players and golfing bodies to suggest changing the Old Course in even a minor way amounts to sacrilege.

Of course, it is wrong to suggest that changes have never been made to the Old Course. Over the years there have been subtle changes and redesigns. The famous Road Hole bunker, for instance, has varied in size and depth several times. A quick glance at old newsreel film confirms that.

Peter Dawson stresses that no two bodies love the Old Course as much as The R&A and the Links Trust do. After all, it is their top priority to preserve what the course is all about.

In a poll of members of the European Institute of Golf Course Architects three out of four of the 112 members contacted in 25 countries thought that changes might be appropriate but only if based on thorough historical research.

Once and for all design

So what is being done to the Old Course in two sections over the next two years and why? Peter Dawson explains:

The 17th hole – "The Road Hole bunker is rebuilt every year and this time we are finalising a design that the greenkeepers can follow every year so that its character always remains faithfully to its former design. It's not being made any harder nor is it being widened."

The 11th Green – "Changes are being made in order to give a pin position on the left-hand side which was always possible in the old days when greens played far slower than they do today. All we are doing is easing off the slope on the left in order that the old variety of pin positions available on that green be restored."

The 7th Fairway – "The hollow in the fairway which can become 'ground under repair' at certain times of the year is being altered. The dip will become a mound which will spread balls around the fairway."

Three bunkers resited

The 2nd hole – "The land to the right of the green is very flat and there is no real neecessity to hit the putting surface with an approach because you can putt just as easily from just off the green So the ground on the right will be made more undulating and the two bunkers currently 25 yards short of the green will be moved closer to it."

The 3rd hole – "The safe line off the tee is up the left but if you do go up the right and avoid the three bunkers there you have a better line into the green. The bunkers may have been sited perfectly for the days when persimmon drivers were being used but are not right for today's equipment. Three bunkers will remain a feature of the hole but what is currently the first one will be removed and a new one built beyond the current second and third bunkers."

The 4th hole – "All that is being done here is to gently undulate the ground on the right beyond the green and move the bunker on the right of the putting surface closer to the green."

The 6th green – "Some gentle undulations are being put in the flat area to the right between the green and the seventh tee."

9th green – "In the old days, if you went for the green it was a much tighter challenge because the heather made the fairway so much narrower. To increase the risk or reward for going for the green now when the fairway is wider there is a proposal to put in a new bunker 25 yards short of the putting surface."

The 15th green – "If you miss the green at the back the ground is reasonably flat so to make the recovery shot more penal this area will be undulated as well."

There always will be, however, two schools of thought on the matter ... those who deplore change of any kind being made to the Old Course, a national treasure, and those who agree that changes now and again are quite acceptable if indeed the character of the game's historic links character is rigorously preserved.

The 37th Women's British Open

Jiyai Shin blows them all away with record win at Hoylake

Asia's dominance of women's golf was never more absolute than in 2012 when Jiyai Shin's runaway victory at Hoylake ensured, for the first time, that all four majors were won by players from South Korea and China. Following in the footsteps of Sun Young Yoo at the Kraft Nabisco, Shanshan Feng at the Wegmans LPGA and Na Yeon Choi at the US Women's Open, Shin eclipsed her compatriot, Inbee Park, by nine strokes to secure the Women's British Open title.

Of all the many virtues displayed by Shin over four days of weather disrupted action at Royal Liverpool – she signed for scores of 71, 64, 71 and 73 in a nine under par total of 279 – perhaps no quality was greater than a reprise of the intense concentration levels which helped the Korean defeat Paula Creamer the previous week in the Kingsmill tournament over the longest play-off, nine holes, in LPGA history.

At Hoylake, following the suspension of the second round because of 60mph winds, Shin, 24, had to play 36 holes on Sunday before adding to the first Women's British Open title she won at Sunningdale in 2008. Her success on the Wirral meant that in the decade between 2003 and 2012, Asian golfers won 17 out of 40 women's majors, compared to 11 for Europeans and nine for Americans. In the three seasons between 2010 and 2012, the win ratio was even more pronounced with nine of the 12 majors won by Asians, including all of the last seven. Stacey Lewis was the last golfer from outside Asia to win a major at the Kraft Nabisco in 2011.

Jiyai Shin

This forest fire of Asian success can likely be traced back to the match lit 14 years previously when Si Re Pak inspired a generation of her compatriots by winning back-to-back majors, the McDonalds LPGA and the US Women's Open, in 1998. "Now there are so many players from Asia on the LPGA Tour," observed Shin, " it makes for a lot of chances to win."

In some of the most brutal conditions any of the players are ever likely to face – after play was cancelled on Friday, there was a further short suspension on Sunday, though this interruption was far harder to justify – Shin was thrilled to win the only women's major held outside America for the second time.

"I can't put into words how happy I feel to win the title for a second time," she said after collecting the winner's cheque for £266,143. "My first win in 2008 changed my life. When I won in 2008, I was not a member of the LPGA, so after that, I got a Tour card on the LPGA, that was the biggest thing. This win, I think it will change it too. I said at the start of the week I wanted to play every round in one under par so to get to nine under in this weather on a course as tough as this is incredible. Now I know I can get a good score on any course, I'm pretty sure of that. But I can't tell you why so many Asian players are winning majors at the moment. Maybe it's down to hard work. Maybe it's luck, or a bit of both."

Shin's nine shot triumph was the widest margin of victory since the Women's British Open was elevated to a major in 2001. (Ayako Okamoto of Japan won by 11 strokes in 1984.) However, given that Shin needed an extra day and nine holes of a play-off to win the Kingsmill the week before the final major of the season, few would have picked out the South Korean as a likely winner at Royal Liverpool. Until Shin won twice in the space of seven days, no golfer with a victory the previous week had ever won the Women's British Open.

Starting steadily with a composed round of 71, Shin was well positioned to keep the leaders in her sights as So Yeon Ryu and Haeji Kang set the first round pace with opening scores of 70, two under par. Even though the wind had dropped on Thursday compared to the gusts which made practice so tricky, only 11 golfers bettered par and the low score was the highest in Women's British Open history.

Had play not been suspended on Friday when the gales returned, heaven knows what the benchmark would have been, though Laura Davies, who started par, birdie, may have been a contender. As it was, even though 36 players recorded some scores in the second round, the Ladies Golf Union, the organisers of the championship, took the decision to halt play and declared the scores recorded by the early groups as "null and void" in accordance with Rule 33-2d. Susan Simpson, the Tournament director, said: "The competitors began their round in extremely adverse weather conditions and conditions subsequently worsened, despite our belief they would remain stable. It would have been unfair to those competitors not to declare null and void and cancel all scores for the round in question."

When the players returned for the second round on Saturday, conditions were much improved, as Shin demonstrated by making an electrifying start. Having begun on the 10th hole, the past champion was five under for her first four holes after starting eagle, birdie, birdie, birdie. Hitting every green in regulation and using her putter just 28 times, she compiled a magnificent 64, eight under, the lowest competitive score ever recorded at Hoylake. The measure of Shin's mark, surely, was that no other player scored lower than 68. It was the best round of her career and meant she led by five strokes going into the last day.

> "Now I know I can get a good score on any course."
>
> *Jiyai Shin on tackling harsh conditions at Royal Liverpool*

In order to facilitate the challenge of finishing on Sunday evening rather than Monday, however, the cut was trimmed on Saturday to the leading 50 and ties rather than the top 65. As it turned out, 57 golfers came back on Sunday morning for 36 holes when Karrie Webb, a seasoned member of the World Golf Hall of Fame and winner of the Women's British at Woburn in 1995, Sunningdale in 1997 and Turnberry in 2002, put Shin under pressure by carding 68 and cutting the South Korean's advantage to just three strokes going into the fourth round.

Bearing in mind that Shin subsequently kicked off her closing round with a triple bogey, the final 18 holes could have been a showdown rather than a procession. However, the return of challenging weather – the average score in the last round was 77.7 – also blew Webb off course as she completed the opening three holes in four over par. By close of play, the Australian's ten over par 82 amounted to 14 shots more than she'd struck in the morning and the path was clear for Shin to coast home.

Adding 73 to the 71 she'd posted on Sunday morning was more than sufficient for Shin to see off the challenges of Park, 76 for 288, and Paula Creamer, 72 for 289.

When she needed to respond, the South Korean was up to the task, firing birdies at the sixth and seventh holes, holing out from 20 feet on both occasions. Only recently recovered from a wrist injury which required surgery, Shin enthused: "I think this course was made for me. I had great confidence here. Always when I come to the British Open I really enjoy myself and that helped my game. The weather was really tough but I kept focused on every single shot."

Meanwhile, the Smyth Salver for low amateur was won by Lydia Ko, the 15-year-old from South Korea who became a citizen of New Zealand. The top ranked amateur in the world and youngest ever player to win a professional event, Ko signed for 297 and tied for a share of 17th at Royal Livepool.

Michael Aitken

First Round	Second Round	Third Round	Fourth Round
–2 Haeji Kang	–9 Jiyai Shin	–10 Jiyai Shin	–9 Jiyai Shin
–2 So Yeon Ryu	–4 Inbee Park	–7 Karrie Webb	+1 Inbee Park
–1 Jiyai Shin	–3 Karrie Webb	–4 Inbee Park	+1 Paula Creamer
–1 Ai Miyazato	–3 Mika Miyazato	–3 Mika Miyazato	+2 Mika Miyazato
–1 Charley Hull	–2 Katie Fucher	–2 Jenny Shin	+3 Karrie Webb
–1 Lydia Hall	–1 Carin Koch	–1 Katie Futcher	+3 So Yeon Ryu
–1 Karrie Webb	–1 Lydia Ko	–1 So Yeon Ryu	+5 Julieta Granada
–1 Stacey Keating	–1 Ai Miyazaro	= Yuki Ichinose	+6 Stacey Lewis
–1 Mika Miyazato	–1 Vicky Hurst	= Ai Miyazato	+6 Katie Futcher
–1 Vicky Hurst	= Yani Tseng	+1 Paula Creamer	+7 Catriona Matthew

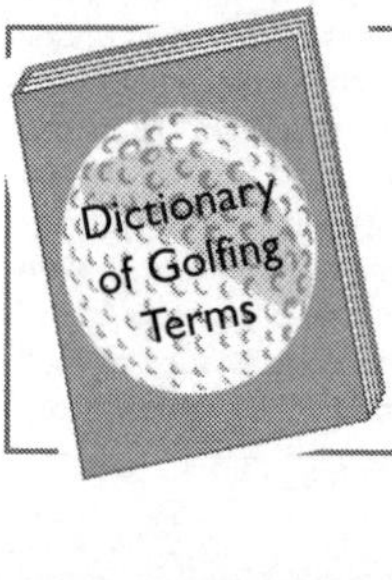

Hack – to strike the ball violently or awkwardly especially in the rough or in a bad lie; make generally ineffective shots; to play poor golf.

Ricoh Women's British Open Championship

Royal Liverpool Sept 13–16 [6660–72]

Prize money: €1,920,130. Final field of 144 (10 amateurs), of whom 56 (4 amateurs) made the half-way cut on 149 or under.

Final Qualifying at Caldy:

69 Amy Hung (TPE)
71 Miriam Nagl (GER)A
72 Aiko Ueno (JPN)
Bronte Law (ENG)
73 Emily Taylor (ENG) (am)
Charley Hull (ENG) (am)
Alexandra Peters (ENG) (am)
73T Rebecca Codd (IRL)
Stephanie Na (AUS)
Danielle Montgomery (ENG)
74 Holly Clyburn (ENG) (am)
Stacy Lee Bregman (RSA)
75 Jing Yan (CHN) (am)
Charlotte Thompson (ENG) (am)
75T Amy Boulden (WAL) (am)
Linda Wessberg (SWE)
Sophie Sandolo (ITA)
Nikki Garrett (AUS)
Tania Elosegui (ESP)
Valentine Derrey (FRA)
Rachel Bailey (AUS)

1	Jiyai Shin (KOR)	71-64-71-73—279	€331,936
2	Inbee Park (KOR)	72-68-72-76—288	208,079
3	Paula Creamer (USA)	73-72-72-72—289	145,655
4	Mika Miyazato (JPN)	71-70-72-77—290	113,948
5	So Yeon Ryu (KOR)	70-74-71-76—291	87,195
	Karrie Webb (AUS)	71-70-68-82—291	87,195
7	Julieta Granada (PAR)	74-71-74-74—293	73,323
8	Stacy Lewis (USA)	74-70-76-74—294	63,415
	Katie Futcher (USA)	71-71-73-79—294	63,415
10	In Kyung Kim (KOR)	75-72-73-75—295	49,873
	Chella Choi (KOR)	72-73-72-78—295	49,873
	Catriona Matthew (SCO)	76-73-71-75—295	49,873
13	Na Yeon Choi (KOR)	73-73-75-75—296	36,785
	Cindy Lacrosse (USA)	73-75-72-76—296	36,785
	Michelle Wie (USA)	75-70-72-79—296	36,785
	Cristie Kerr (USA)	72-73-74-77—296	36,785
17	Carlota Ciganda (ESP)	76-71-77-73—297	28,338
	Lindsey Wright (AUS)	76-72-75-74—297	28,338
	Lexi Thompson (USA)	74-75-76-72—297	28,338
	Jenny Shin (KOR)	75-68-71-83—297	28,338
	Lydia Ko (NZL) (am)	72-71-76-78—297	
	Vicky Hurst (USA)	71-72-79-75—297	28,338
23	Lydia Hall (WAL)	71-75-75-77—298	23,780
	Juli Inkster (USA)	79-69-72-78—298	23,780
	Angela Stanford (USA)	72-72-74-80—298	23,780
26	Hee-Kyung Seo (KOR)	72-73-75-79—299	19,941
	Amy Yang (KOR)	73-72-75-79—299	19,941
	Beatriz Recari (ESP)	72-77-73-77—299	19,941
	Holly Clyburn (ENG) (am)	72-73-74-80—299	
	Yani Tseng (TPE)	72-72-76-79—299	19,941
	Yuki Ichinose (JPN)	72-72-72-83—299	19,941
	Ai Miyazato (JPN)	71-72-73-83—299	19,941
33	Bronte Law (ENG) (am)	75-71-77-77—300	
	Karine Icher (FRA)	75-72-76-77—300	16,596
	Hee Young Park (KOR)	78-71-76-75—300	16,596
	Line Vedel (NOR)	80-69-74-77—300	16,596
	Katherine Hull (AUS)	72-72-77-79—300	16,596
38	Candie Kung (TPE)	73-76-75-77—301	15,358
39	Jane Park (USA)	74-72-78-78—302	14,119
	Hee-Won Han (KOR)	72-75-74-81—302	14,119
	Erina Hara (JPN)	75-73-77-77—302	14,119
	Lee-Anne Pace (RSA)	76-73-77-76—302	14,119
43	Amy Hung (TPE)	72-74-79-78—303	12,137
	Morgan Pressel (USA)	72-73-77-81—303	12,137
	Carin Koch (SWE)	72-71-78-82—303	12,137

Ricoh Women's British Open Championship *continued*

46T	Sarah-Jane Smith (USA)	74-75-77-77—303	12,137
47	Dewi Claire Schreefel (NED)	73-74-79-78—304	9,908
	Becky Morgan (WAL)	72-75-79-78—304	9,908
	Sun Young Yoo (KOR)	74-75-75-80—304	9,908
	Stephanie Na (AUS)	76-73-78-77—304	9,908
	Haeji Kang (TPE)	70-79-77-78—304	9,908
	Jing Yan (CHN) (am)	80-69-77-78—304	
53	Sydnee Michaels (USA)	75-71-82-77—305	8,174
	Eun Hee Ji (TPE)	75-74-75-81—305	8,174
55	Florentyna Parker (ENG)	77-72-76-81—306	7,430
56	Trish Johnson (ENG)	72-77-83-77—309	6,935
57	Mo Martin (USA)	77-72-79-84—312	6,440

The following players missed the cut:

58	Sophie Gustafson (SWE)	80-70—150
	Shanshan Feng (TPE)	77-73—150
	Alison Walshe (USA)	77-73—150
	Amanda Blumenherst (USA)	76-74—150
	Jin Young Pak (KOR)	76-74—150
	Azahara Muñoz (ESP)	76-74—150
	Giulia Sergas (ITA)	76-74—150
	Diana Luna (ITA)	75-75—150
	Pernilla Lindberg (SWE)	74-76—150
	Nikki Garrett (AUS)	74-76—150
	Pornanong Phatlum (THA)	74-76—150
	Belen Mozo (ESP)	74-76—150
	Jacqui Concolino (USA)	74-76—150
	Christine Song (USA)	73-77—150
	Maiko Wakabayashi (JPN)	73-77—150
	Linda Wessberg (SWE)	73-77—150
74	Mi Jung Hur (KOR)	79-72—151
	Gerina Piller (USA)	77-74—151
-	Megumi Kido (JPN)	76-75—151
	Suzann Pettersen (NOR)	76-75—151
	Valentine Derrey (FRA)	76-75—151
	Kris Tamulis (USA)	75-76—151
	Emily Taylor (ENG) (am)	75-76—151
	Marianne Skarpnord (NOR)	75-76—151
	Charley Hull (ENG) (am)	71-80—151
83	Anja Monke (GER)	77-75—152
	Meredith Duncan (USA)	77-75—152
	Kristy McPherson (USA)	77-75—152
	Karen Lunn (AUS)	77-75—152
	Mariajo Uribe (COL)	76-76—152
	Christel Boeljon (NED)	76-76—152
	Veronica Felibert (VEN)	75-77—152
	Anna Nordqvist (SWE)	75-77—152
-	Nicole Castrale (USA)	73-79—152
-	Natalie Gulbis (USA)	73-79—152
93	Momoko Ueda (JPN)	80-73—153
-	Danielle Kang (USA)	79-74—153
-	Karin Sjodin (SWE)	78-75—153
-	Felicity Johnson (ENG)	78-75—153
-	Il Hee Lee (KOR)	76-77—153
-	Caroline Hedwall (SWE)	75-78—153
-	Mina Harigae (USA)	74-79—153
-	Alexandra Peters (ENG) (am)	73-80—153
101	Rachel Bailey (AUS)	79-75—154
101T	Jodi Ewart (ENG)	79-75—154
-	Lorie Kane (CAN)	78-76—154
-	Amy Boulden (WAL) (am)	78-76—154
-	Carly Booth (SCO)	77-77—154
-	Mindy Kim (KOR)	77-77—154
-	Meena Lee (KOR)	77-77—154
-	Rebecca Codd (IRL)	77-77—154
-	Melissa Reid (ENG)	77-77—154
-	Rebecca Hudson (ENG)	76-78—154
-	Maria Hjörth (SWE)	75-79—154
-	Sophie Giquel-Bettan (FRA)	75-79—154
113	Jennifer Rosales (PHI)	81-74—155
-	Rebecca Artis (AIS)	80-75—155
-	Stacy Lee Bregman (RSA)	76-79—155
-	Caroline Masson (GER)	76-79—155
-	Brittany Lincicome (USA)	73-82—155
118	Jessica Korda (USA)	82-74—156
-	Jennifer Song (USA)	81-75—156
-	Beth Allen (USA)	78-78—156
-	Joanna Klatten (FRA)	77-79—156
-	Samantha Richdale (CAN)	77-79—156
-	Danielle Montgomery (ENG)	76-80—156
-	Louise Larsson (SWE)	75-81—156
125	Ursula Wikstrom (FIN)	78-79—157
-	Karen Stupples (ENG)	76-81—157
-	Leona Maguire (IRL) (am)	75-82—157
-	Kaori Ohe (JPN)	74-83—157
129	Charlotte Thompson (ENG) (am)	82-76—158
-	Jennie Lee (USA)	80-78—158
-	Gwladys Nocera (FRA)	79-79—158
132	Jimin Kang (KOR)	83-76—159
-	Sandra Gal (GER)	81-78—159
-	Kathlyn Ekey (USA)	81-78—159
135	Brittany Lang (USA)	82-79—161
-	Tandi Cuningham (RSA)	77-84—161
-	Sophie Sandolo (ITA)	76-85—161
138	Ryann O'Toole (USA)	83-80—163
139	Miriam Nagl (GER)	82-82—164
-	Aiko Ueno (JPN)	82-82—164
141	Anne-Lise Caudal (FRA)	87-81—168
	Laura Davies (ENG)	Retd
	Tania Elosegui (ESP)	DQ
	Stacey Keating (AUS)	DQ

Four Asians win women's majors in 2012

Na Yeon Choi (KOR)	US Open	71-72-65-73—281 (–7)	$585.000
Jiyai Shin (KOR)	Ricoh British	71-64-71-73—279 (–9)	$428.650
Shanshan Feng (CHN)	Wegman's LPGA	72-73-70-67—282 (–6)	$375,000
Young Yoo (KOR)	Kraft Nabisco	69-69-72-69—279 (–9)	$300,000

2011 Ricoh Women's British Open *Carnoustie Links* [6490–72]

Prize money: €1.8 million

1	Yani Tseng (TPE)	71-66-66-69—272	€272,365
2	Brittany Lang (USA)	70-70-69-67—276	170,736
3	Sophie Gustafson (SWE)	68-71-70-68—277	119,515
4	Amy Yang (KOR)	68-70-73-67—278	93,498
5	Catriona Matthew (SCO)	70-69-68-72—279	71,546
	Caroline Masson (GER)	68-65-68-78—279	71,546
7	Sun Young Yoo (KOR)	71-70-69-70—280	52,236
	Anna Nordqvist (SWE)	70-71-69-70—280	52,236
	Na Yeon Choi (KOR)	69-67-72-72—280	52,236
	Inbee Park (KOR)	70-64-73-73—280	52,236
11	Stacy Lewis (USA)	74-68-71-68—281	39,025
	Dewi Claire Schreefel (NED)	70-66-74-71—281	39,025
13	Maria Hjörth (SWE)	72-69-73-68—282	34,147
14	Katie Futcher (USA)	71-74-74-64—283	25,964
	Cristie Kerr (USA)	72-69-74-68—283	25,964
	Candie Kung (TPE)	72-73-69-69—283	25,964
	Song-Hee Kim (KOR)	69-72-71-71—283	25,964
	Sun Ju Ahn (KOR)	71-71-70-71—283	25,964
	Mika Miyazato (JPN)	69-69-72-73—283	25,964
	Se Ri Pak (KOR)	72-64-73-74—283	25,964
21	Jiyai Shin (KOR)	75-66-72-71—284	21,138
22	Karen Stupples (ENG)	74-68-72-71—285	18,394
	Hee-Kyung Seo (KOR)	72-71-71-71—285	18,394
	Karrie Webb (AUS)	70-71-72-72—285	18,394
	Rachel Jennings (ENG)	71-73-69-72—285	18,394
	Momoko Ueda (JPN)	69-71-72-73—285	18,394
	Angela Stanford (USA)	68-72-72-73—285	18,394
28	Michelle Wie (USA)	74-68-72-72—286	15,752
	Vicky Hurst (USA)	70-71-71-74—286	15,752
30	Amy Hung (TPE)	69-72-78-68—287	13,444
	Haeji Kang (KOR)	75-70-73-69—287	13,444
	Beth Allen (USA)	71-70-75-71—287	13,444
	Tiffany Joh (USA)	71-69-75-72—287	13,444
	Caroline Hedwall (SWE)	69-69-76-73—287	13,444
	Brittany Lincicome (USA)	67-71-76-73—287	13,444
	Shanshan Feng (CHN)	70-75-67-75—287	13,444
37	Melissa Reid (ENG)	75-70-73-70—288	10,772
	Eun Hee Ji (KOR)	70-71-75-72—288	10,772
	Suzann Pettersen (NOR)	76-66-73-73—288	10,772
	Meena Lee (KOR)	65-69-80-74—288	10,772
	Linda Wessberg (SWE)	73-66-75-74—288	10,772
	In Kyung Kim (KOR)	71-72-71-74—288	10,772

Other players who made the cut: Hiromi Mogi (JPN), Hee Won Han (KOR), Lorie Kane (CAN), Hee Young Park (KOR), Kristy McPherson (USA), Paula Creamer (USA) 289; Azahara Muñoz Guijarro (ESP), Danielle Kang (USA) (am), Morgan Pressel (USA), Pat Hurst (USA), Cindy LaCrosse (USA) 290; Christel Boeljon (NED), Janice Moodie (SCO), Sandra Gal (GER), Chella Choi (KOR), Amanda Blumenherst (USA) 291; Miki Saiki (JPN), Kylie Walker (SCO), Holly Aitchison (ENG), Julieta Granada (PAR), Sophie Giquel-Bettan (FRA) 292; Virginie Lagoutte-Clement (FRA), Jaclyn Sweeney (USA) 295; Georgina Simpson (ENG) 297; Sophie Popov (GER) (am) 299; Jimin Kang (KOR) RTD

2010 Ricoh Women's British Open *Royal Birkdale* [6463–72]

Prize money: €2.5 million

1	Yani Tseng (TPE)	68-68-68-73—277	€313,530
2	Katherine Hull (AUS)	68-74-66-70—278	196,541
3	Na Yeon Choi (KOR)	74-70-69-68—281	122,604
	In-Kyung Kim (KOR)	70-72-68-71—281	122,604
5	Cristie Kerr (USA)	73-67-72-70—282	77,992
	Hee-Kyung Seo (KOR)	73-69-70-70—282	77,992
	Amy Yang (KOR)	69-71-74-68—282	77,992
8	Morgan Pressel (USA)	77-71-65-71—284	62,707
9	Christina Kim (USA)	74-68-70-74—286	47,544
	Brittany Lincicome (USA)	69-71-71-75—286	47,544
	Ai Miyazato (JPN)	76-70-73-67—286	47,544
	Inbee Park (KOR)	72-71-77-66—286	47,544
	Momoko Ueda (JPN)	72-70-70-74—286	47,544
14	Maria Hernandez (ESP)	73-70-73-71—287	33,224
	Suzann Pettersen (NOR)	73-68-71-75—287	33,224
	Jiyai Shin (KOR)	71-71-72-73—287	33,224
17	Gwladys Nocera (FRA)	71-75-72-70—288	28,779
	Michelle Wie (USA)	70-76-71-71—288	28,779
19	Song-Hee Kim (KOR)	75-73-71-70—289	25,971
	Azahara Muñoz (ESP)	74-71-72-72—289	25,971
21	Chie Arimura (JPN)	77-68-70-75—290	22,032
	Becky Brewerton (WAL)	73-73-71-73—290	22,032
21T	Paula Creamer (USA)	74-74-70-72—290	22,032
	Juli Inkster (USA)	71-70-76-73—290	22,032
	Jeong Jang (KOR)	74-73-74-69—290	22,032
	Lee-Anne Pace (RSA)	74-72-71-73—290	22,032
27	Caroline Hedwall (SWE) (am)	74-75-72-70—291	
	Karine Icher (FRA)	74-72-70-75—291	18,484
	Jimin Kang (KOR)	74-73-74-70—291	18,484
	Mindy Kim (KOR)	72-75-73-71—291	18,484
31	Anne-Lise Caudal (FRA)	69-73-75-75—292	14,292
	Katie Futcher (USA)	74-74-72-72—292	14,292
	M J Hur (KOR)	74-68-75-75—292	14,292
	Vicky Hurst (USA)	77-71-74-70—292	14,292
	Haeji Kang (KOR)	75-74-72-71—292	14,292
	Mi Hyun Kim (KOR)	72-77-73-70—292	14,292
	Stacy Lewis (USA)	71-74-75-72—292	14,292
	Ji Young Oh (KOR)	79-69-75-69—292	14,292
	Melissa Reid (ENG)	77-71-74-70—292	14,292
	Sakura Yokomine (JPN)	74-71-75-72—292	14,292
	Sun Young Yoo (KOR)	69-72-78-73—292	14,292
	Henrietta Zuel (ENG)	74-73-73-72—292	14,292

Other players who made the cut: Sophie Gustafson (SWE), Amy Hung (TPE), Brittany Lang (USA), Meena Lee (KOR), Stacy Prammanasudh (USA), Ashleigh Simon (RSA), Karrie Webb (AUS) 293; Irene Cho (KOR), Moira Dunn (USA), Angela Stanford (USA), Sherri Steinhauer (USA), Kristin Tamulis (USA) 294; Carin Koch (SWE), Janice Moodie (SCO), Hee Young Park (KOR), Florentyna Parker (ENG), Sarah-Jane Smith (AUS), Iben Tinning (DEN), Wendy Ward (USA) 295; Seon Hwa Lee (KOR), Jee Young Lee (KOR) 296; Sarah Lee (KOR), Anja Monke (GER), Alena Sharp (CAN) 297; Stacy Bregman (RSA), Eunjang Yi (KOR) 298; Laura Davies (ENG), Meaghan Francella (USA), Anna Nordqvist (SWE), Mariajo Uribe (COL) 299; Shanshan Feng (CHN), Giulia Sergas (ITA) 300; Jennifer Rosales (PHI) 302

2009 Ricoh Women's British Open *Royal Lytham & St Annes* [6492–72]

Prize money: €1.5 million

1	Catriona Matthew (SCO)	74-67-71-73—285	€235,036
2	Karrie Webb (AUS)	77-71-72-68—288	147,336
3	Paula Creamer (USA)	74-74-70-71—289	76,825
	Hee-Won Han (KOR)	77-73-69-70—289	76,825
	Christina Kim (USA)	73-71-71-74—289	76,825
	Ai Miyazato (JPN)	75-71-70-73—289	76,825
7	Kristy McPherson (USA)	74-74-72-70—290	51,918
8	Na Yeon Choi (KOR)	80-71-70-70—291	42,797
	Cristie Kerr (USA)	76-71-75-69—291	42,797
	Jiyai Shin (KOR)	77-71-68-75—291	42,797
11	Maria Hjörth (SWE)	72-76-73-71—292	28,590
	Song-ee Kim (KOR)	70-73-74-75—292	28,590
	Mika Miyazato (JPN)	76-72-69-75—292	28,590
	Hee Young Park (KOR)	71-75-73-73—292	28,590
	Giulia Sergas (ITA)	74-67-78-73—292	28,590
	Michelle Wie (USA)	73-76-74-69—292	28,590
17	Kyeong Bae (KOR)	73-71-74-75—293	21,048
	Jane Park (USA)	74-72-72-75—293	21,048
	Michelle Redman (USA)	75-75-73-70—293	21,048
20	In-Kyung Kim (KOR)	81-70-70-73—294	17,890
	Se-Ri Pak (KOR)	76-71-73-74—294	17,890
20T	Angela Stanford (USA)	70-76-74-74—294	17,890
	Yani Tseng (TPE)	74-70-78-72—294	17,890
24	Inbee Park (KOR)	76-72-76-71—295	16,137
25	Jeong Jang (KOR)	79-73-72-72—296	15,172
	Shinobu Moromizato (JPN)	74-73-71-78—296	15,172
27	Jade Schaeffer (FRA)	79-71-75-72—297	14,383
28	Katie Futcher (USA)	75-77-70-76—298	12,839
	Vicky Hurst (USA)	74-75-77-72—298	12,839
	Brittany Lincicome (USA)	77-73-79-69—298	12,839
	Teresa Lu (TPE)	75-76-77-70—298	12,839
	Lorena Ochoa (MEX)	75-77-72-74—298	12,839
33	Yuri Fudoh (JPN)	80-73-70-76—299	10,524
	Sandra Gal (GER)	69-80-75-75—299	10,524
	Sophie Gustafson (SWE)	74-71-82-72—299	10,524
	Brittany Lang (USA)	81-70-71-77—299	10,524
	Yuko Mitsuka (JPN)	71-71-79-78—299	10,524
	Becky Morgan (WAL)	80-71-72-76—299	10,524
	Sun-Young Yoo (KOR)	79-73-75-72—299	10,524
40	Allison Hanna (USA)	76-76-73-75—300	8,945
	Katherine Hull (AUS)	75-77-77-71—300	8,945

Other players who made the cut: Martina Eberl (GER), Meena Lee (KOR), Morgan Pressel (USA), Marianne Skarpnord (NOR) 301; Carmen Alonso (ESP), Il Mi Chung (KOR), Laura Davies (ENG), Mi-Jung Hur (JPN), Ursula Wikstrom (FIN) 302; Irene Cho (KOR), Samantha Head (ENG), Sarah Lee (KOR), Anna Nordqvist (SWE) 303; Jin Young Pak (KOR), Louise Stahle (SWE), Momoko Ueda (JPN) 304; Christel Boeljom (NED), Eunjang Yi (KOR) 305; Anne-Lise Caudal (FRA), Young Kim (KOR), Emma Zackrisson (SWE) 306; Lee-Anne Pace (RSA), Reilley Rankin (USA) 307; Kristin Tamulis (USA) 308; Vikki Laing (SCO) 309; Laura Diaz (USA), Shanshan Feng (CHN), Stacy Prammanasudh (USA) 310; Karin Sjodin (SWE) Rtd; Eun Hee Ji (KOR) DQ

2008 Ricoh Women's British Open *Sunningdale* [6408–72]

Prize money: £1.55 million

1	Jiyai Shin (KOR)	66-68-70-66—270	€202,336
2	Ya-Ni Tseng (TPE)	70-69-68-66—273	126.460
3	Eun Hee Ji (KOR)	68-70-69-67—274	79.037
	Yuri Fudoh (JPN)	66-68-69-71—274	79.037
5	Ai Miyazato (JPN)	68-69-68-70—275	56.907
6	Cristie Kerr (USA)	71-65-70-70—276	49.319
7	Lorena Ochoa (MEX)	69-68-71-69—277	42.464
	Momoko Ueda (JPN)	66-72-70-69—277	42.464
9	Paula Creamer (USA)	72-69-70-67—278	30.603
	Natalie Gulbis (USA)	69-68-70-71—278	30.603
	Hee Won Han (KOR)	71-69-71-67—278	30.603
	In-Kyung Kim (KOR)	71-68-72-67—278	30.603
	Karrie Webb (AUS)	72-69-69-68—278	30.603
14	Juli Inkster (USA)	65-70-71-73—279	21.709
	Seon Hwa Lee (KOR)	71-68-70-70—279	21.709
	Hee Young Park (KOR)	69-71-69-70—279	21.709
17	Shi Hyun Ahn (KOR)	68-72-71-69—280	17.625
	Minea Blomqvist (FIN)	68-73-72-67—280	17.625
	Jee Yound Lee (KOR)	71-72-71-66—280	17,625
	Ji Young Oh (KOR)	66-73-71-70—280	17,625
21	Nicole Castrale (USA)	69-72-72-68—281	15,175
	Na Yeon Choi (KOR)	69-71-68-73—281	15,175
21T	Kristy McPherson (USA)	67-75-74-65—281	15,175
24	Meredith Duncan (USA)	71-73-71-67—282	11,786
	Sophie Gustafson (SWE)	69-69-74-70—282	11,786
	Mi Hyun Kim (KOR)	70-70-67-75—282	11,786
	Eun-A Lin (KOR)	74-71-72-65—282	11,786
	Jane Park (USA)	69-70-73-70—282	11,786
	Suzann Pettersen (NOR)	70-70-71-71—282	11,786
	Stacy Prammanasudh (USA)	66-74-72-70—282	11,786
	Annika Sörenstam (SWE)	72-72-70-68—282	11,786
	Karen Stupples (ENG)	67-73-72-70—282	11,786
	Sakura Yokomine (JPN)	71-72-69-70—282	11,786
34	Laura Diaz (USA)	66-72-75-70—283	9,010
	Anja Monke (GER)	73-67-70-73—283	9,010
	Angela Park (BRA)	71-74-71-37—283	9,010
	Bo Bae Song (KOR)	68-68-74-73—283	9,010
38	Ji-Hee Lee (KOR)	68-75-68-73—284	7,745
	Leta Lindley (USA)	71-71-72-70—284	7,745
	Paula Marti (ESP)	68-72-72-72—284	7,745
	Catriona Matthew (SCO)	68-75-72-69—284	7,745

Other players who made the cut: Candie Kung (TPE), Anna Nordqvist (SWE) (am), Reilley Rankin (USA) 285; Lora Fairclough (ENG), Janice Moodie (SCO), Sun Young Yoo (KOR) 286; Hye Jung Choi (KOR), Jin Joo Hong (KOR), Katherine Hull (AUS), Jill McGill (USA), Joanne Mills (AUS), Gloria Park (KOR), Karin Sjodin (SWE), Lotta Wahlin (SWE) 287; Helen Alfredsson (SWE), Il-Mi Chung (KOR), Rebecca Hudson (ENG) 288; Jimin Kang (KOR), Teresa Lu (TPE), Becky Morgan (WAL), Kris Camulis (USA), Wendy Ward (USA) 289; Erica Blasberg (USA), Christina Kim (USA), Gwladys Nocera (FRA), Marianne Skarpnord (NOR), Sherri Steinhauer (USA) 290; Tania Elosegui (ESP), Johanna Head (ENG), Rachel Hetherington (AUS), Maria Hjörth (SWE), Trish Johnson (ENG) 291; Becky Brewerton (WAL) 292; Moira Dunn (USA), Maria Jose Uribe (COL) (am) 294; Laura Davies (ENG) 295; Mhairi McKay (SCO) 296

2007 Ricoh Women's British Open *St Andrews Old Course* [6638–73]

Prize money: £2.5 million

1	Lorena Ochoa (MEX)	67-73-73-74—287	£160.000
2	Maria Hjörth (SWE)	75-73-72-71—291	85,000
	Jee Young Lee (KOR)	72-73-75-71—291	85,000
4	Reilley Rankin (USA)	73-74-74-71—292	55,000
5	Eun Hee Ji (KOR)	73-71-77-72—293	42,000
	Se Ri Pak (KOR)	73-73-75-72—293	42,000
7	Paula Creamer (USA)	73-75-74-72—294	30,500
	Catriona Matthew (SCO)	73-68-80-73—294	30,500
	Miki Saiki (JPN)	76-70-81-67—294	30,500
	Linda Wessberg (SWE)	74-73-72-75—294	30,500
11	Yuri Fudoh (JPN)	74-69-81-71—295	20,300
	Brittany Lincicome (USA)	71-76-75-73—295	20,300
	Mhairi McKay (SCO)	75-74-79-67—295	20,300
	Na On Min (KOR)	72-75-75-73—295	20,300
	Inbee Park (KOR)	69-79-76-71—295	20,300
16	Becky Brewerton (WAL)	74-75-74-73—296	14.041
	Karine Icher (FRA)	72-71-77-76—296	14.041
	Virginie Lagoutte-Clement (FRA)	72-73-78-73—296	14.041
	Gloria Park (KOR)	74-75-76-71—296	14.041
	Stacy Prammanasudh (USA)	74-76-72-74—296	14.041
16T	Melissa Reid (ENG) (am)	73-75-76-72—296	
	Annika Sörenstam (SWE)	72-71-77-76—296	14.041
23	Beth Bader (USA)	73-77-75-72—297	11.060
	Natalia Gulbis (USA)	73-76-76-72—297	11.060
	Alena Sharp (CAN)	77-70-79-71—297	11.060
	Sherri Steinhauer (USA)	72-71-80-74—297	11.060
	Wendy Ward (USA)	71-70-80-76—297	11.060
28	Jimin Kang (KOR)	77-72-75-75—299	9,100
	Sarah Lee (KOR)	72-76-79-72—299	9,100
	Suzann Pettersen (NOR)	74-76-78-71—299	9,100
	Ji-Yai Shin (KOR)	76-74-77-72—299	9,100
	Karrie Webb (AUS)	77-73-74-75—299	9,100
33	Louise Friberg (SWE)	69-76-80-75—300	7,062
	Sophie Gustafson (SWE)	73-72-81-74—300	7,062
	Kim Hall (USA)	74-74-79-73—300	7,062
	Juli Inkster (USA)	79-68-82-71—300	7,062
	Trish Johnson (ENG)	75-75-77-73—300	7,062
	Cristie Kerr (USA)	77-71-79-73—300	7,062
	Candie Kung (TPE)	72-74-79-75—300	7,062
	Meena Lee (KOR)	71-76-79-74—300	7,062
	Gwladys Nocera (FRA)	78-72-75-75—300	7,062

Other players who made the cut: Rebecca Hudson (ENG), In-Kyung Kim (KOR), Michele Redman (USA), Kerry Smith (ENG) (am), Karen Stupples (ENG), Lotta Wahlin (SWE) 301; Hye Yong Choi (KOR) (am), Catrin Nilsmark (SWE) 303; Dina Ammaccapane (USA), Rachel Bell (ENG), Beth Daniel (USA), Grace Park (KOR), Sally Watson (SCO) (am) 304; Rachel Hetherington (AUS), Bélen Mozo (ESP) (am), Momoko Ueda (JPN) 305; Lisa Hall (ENG), Jin Joo Hong (KOR), Christina Kim (USA), Ai Miyazato (JPN), Anna Nordquist (SWE) (am), Iben Tinning (DEN) 306; Joanne Mills (AUS) 308; Diana D'Alessio (USA), Martina Eberl (GER) 309; Nicole Castrale (USA) 310; Meg Mallon (USA) 311; Naomi Edwards (ENG) (am) 312

2006 Weetabix Women's British Open *Royal Lytham & St Annes* [6308–72]

Prize money: £1.05 million

1	Sherri Steinhauer (USA)	73-70-66-72—281	£160,000
2	Sophie Gustafson (SWE)	76-67-69-72—284	85,000
	Cristie Kerr (USA)	71-76-66-71—284	85,000
4	Juli Inkster (USA)	66-72-74-73—285	50,000
	Lorena Ochoa (MEX)	74-73-65-73—285	50,000
6	Beth Daniel (USA)	73-70-71-72—286	37,000
	Lorie Kane (CAN)	73-69-74-70—286	37,000
8	Julieta Granada (PAR)	71-73-70-73—287	32,000
9	Ai Miyazato (JPN)	71-75-75-67—288	29,000
10	Hee Won Han (KOR)	80-71-69-70—290	21,250
	Karine Icher (FRA)	72-73-71-74—290	21,250
	Joo Mi Kim (KOR)	73-73-73-71—290	21,250
	Candie Kung (TPE)	72-70-71-77—290	21,250
	Nina Reis (SWE)	70-76-69-75—290	21,250
	Karen Stupples (ENG)	73-69-70-78—290	21,250
16	Il-Mi Chung (KOR)	72-71-75-73—291	14,041
	Laura Davies (ENG)	72-72-73-74—291	14,041
	Natalie Gulbis (USA)	72-74-67-78—291	14,041
	Gwladys Nocera (FRA)	70-73-71-77—291	14,041
	Sukura Yokomine (JPN)	72-73-75-71—291	14,041
	Heather Young (USA)	72-74-70-75—291	14,041
22	Kyeong Bae (KOR)	73-73-75-71—292	11,500
	Paula Creamer (USA)	72-71-73-76—292	11,500
22T	Jee Young Lee (KOR)	72-77-69-74—292	11,500
25	Shi Hyun Ahn (KOR)	75-73-69-76—293	10,600
26	Jackie Gallagher-Smith (USA)	77-74-71-72—294	9,460
	Tracy Hanson (USA)	74-77-70-73—294	9,460
	Jeong Jang (KOR)	78-73-68-75—294	9,460
	Michelle Wie (USA)	74-74-72-74—294	9,460
	Young-A Yang (KOR)	72-75-68-79—294	9,460
31	Nicole Castrale (USA)	73-75-71-76—295	7,810
	Anja Monke (GER)	75-76-70-74—295	7,810
	Liselotte Neumann (SWE)	76-72-70-77—295	7,810
	Annika Sörenstam (SWE)	72-71-73-79—295	7,810
	Lindsey Wright (USA)	71-71-74-79—295	7,810
36	Becky Brewerton (WAL)	76-73-73-74—296	6,375
	Vicki Goetze-Ackerman (USA)	75-72-71-78—296	6,375
	Young Jo (KOR)	80-70-74-72—296	6,375
	Angela Stanford (USA)	76-69-80-71—296	6,375
	Sun Young Yoo (KOR)	76-74-71-75—296	6,375
	Veronica Zorzi (ITA)	74-76-78-68—296	6,375

Other players who made the cut: Yuri Fudoh (JPN), Nikki Garrett (AUS), Patricia Meunier-Lebouc (FRA) 297; Chieko Amanuma (JPN), Silvia Cavalleri (ITA), Maria Hjörth (SWE), Christina Kim (USA), Sarah Lee (KOR) 298; Marisa Baena (COL), Rita Hakkarainen (FIN), Allison Hanna (USA), Teresa Lu (TPE), Joanne Morley (ENG), Lee Ann Walker-Cooper (USA) 299; Brittany Lincicome (USA), Becky Morgan (WAL), Morgan Pressel (USA), Kris Tamulis (USA) 300; Amy Yang (KOR) (am) 301; Lynnette Brooky (NZL), Seon Hwa Lee (KOR), Elisa Serramia (ESP), Ursula Wikstrom (FIN) 302; Laura Diaz (USA) 303; Marta Prieto (ESP) 304; Helena Alterby (SWE), Wendy Ward (USA) 305; Rachel Hetherington (AUS) 306; Bélen Mozo (ESP) (am) 307; Iben Tinning (DEN) 311

2005 Weetabix Women's British Open *Royal Birkdale, Southport, Lancashire* [6463–72]

Prize money: £1.05 million

1	Jeong Jang (KOR)	68-66-69-69—272	£160.000
2	Sophie Gustafson (SWE)	69-73-67-67—276	100,000
3	Young Kim (KOR)	74-68-67-69—278	70,000
	Michelle Wie (USA) (am)	75-67-67-69—278	
5	Cristie Kerr (USA)	73-66-69-71—279	46,333
	Liselotte Neumann (SWE)	71-70-68-70—279	46,333
	Annika Sörenstam (SWE)	73-69-66-71—279	46,333
8	Natalie Gulbis (USA)	76-70-68-66—280	33,500
	Grace Park (KOR)	77-68-67-68—280	33,500
	Louise Stahle (SWE) (am)	73-65-73-69—280	
11	Ai Miyazato (JPN)	72-73-69-67—281	25,250
	Michele Redman (USA)	75-71-67-68—281	25,250
	Karen Stupples (ENG)	74-71-65-71—281	25,250
	Karrie Webb (AUS)	75-66-69-71—281	25,250
15	Paula Creamer (USA)	75-69-65-73—282	17,300
	Yuri Fudoh (JPN)	75-69-68-70—282	17,300
	Juli Inkster (USA)	74-68-68-72—282	17,300
	Carin Koch (SWE)	76-68-66-72—282	17,300
	Becky Morgan (WAL)	79-66-67-70—282	17,300
20	Pat Hurst (USA)	75-65-70-73—283	14,250
21	Catriona Matthew (SCO)	73-72-72-67—284	13,500
22	Brandie Burton (USA)	74-75-71-65—285	117,67
	Cecilia Ekelundh (SWE)	77-69-71-68—285	11,767
	Candie Kung (TAI)	76-71-67-71—285	11,767
	Nicole Perrot (CHI)	70-72-69-74—285	11,767
	Sophie Sandolo (ITA)	71-73-73-68—285	11,767
	Linda Wessberg (SWE)	72-71-73-69—285	11,767
28	Shi Hyun Ahn (KOR)	78-68-67-73—286	9,283
	Becky Brewerton (WAL)	75-71-65-75—286	9,283
	Laura Davies (ENG)	76-70-66-74—286	9,283
	Christina Kim (USA)	79-70-71-66—286	9,283
	Anja Monke (GER)	73-73-70-70—286	9,283
	Miriam Nagl (GER)	74-75-69-68—286	9,283
34	Heather Bowie (USA)	74-69-72-72—287	7,530
	Marty Hart (USA)	79-70-71-67—287	7,530
	Rebecca Hudson (ENG)	78-70-71-68—287	7,530
	Emilee Klein (USA)	71-73-70-73—287	7,530
	Jill McGill (USA)	76-70-72-69—287	7,530
39	Minea Blomquist (SWE)	78-68-72-70—288	6,500
	Wendy Doolan (AUS)	77-72-67-72—288	6,500
	Sherri Steinhauer (USA)	74-73-70-71—288	6,500

Other players who made the cut: Helen Alfredsson (SWE), Michelle Ellis (AUS), Riikka Hakkarainen (FIN), Rachel Hetherington (AUS), Riko Higashio (JPN), Amanda Moltke-Leth (DEN), Gwladys Nocera (FRA), Kim Saiki (USA), Iben Tinning (DEN), Kris Tschetter (USA) 289; Carlota Ciganda (ESP) (am), Moira Dunn (USA), Kris Lindstrom (USA), Kimberley Williams (USA) 290; Catherine Cartwright (USA), Beth Daniel (USA) 291; Young Jo (KOR), Lorie Kane (CAN), Aree Song (KOR), Bo Bae Song (KOR) 292; Judith Van Hagen (NED), Shani Waugh (AUS) 293; Laura Diaz (USA), Sung Ah Yim (KOR) 294; Amy Hung (TAI), Paula Marti (ESP) 295; Siew-Ai Lim (MAS), Yu Ping Lin (TAI) 296; Karen Lunn (AUS) 301

2004 Weetabix Women's British Open *Sunningdale (Old Course)* [6392–72]

Prize money: £1.05 million

1	Karen Stupples (ENG)	65-70-70-64—269	£160,000
2	Rachel Teske (AUS)	70-69-65-70—274	100,000
3	Heather Bowie (USA)	70-69-65-71—275	70,000
4	Lorena Ochoa (MEX)	69-71-66-70—276	55,000
5	Beth Daniel (USA)	69-69-71-68—277	39,667
	Michele Redman (USA)	70-71-70-66—277	39,667
	Guilia Sergas (ITA)	72-71-67-67—277	39,667
8	Minea Blomqvist (FIN)	68-78-62-70—278	29,000
	Laura Davies (ENG)	70-69-69-70—278	29,000
	Jung Yeon Lee (KOR)	67-72-70-69—278	29,000
11	Pat Hurst (USA)	72-72-66-69—279	23,000
	Cristie Kerr (USA)	69-73-63-74—279	23,000
13	Laura Diaz (USA)	70-69-70-71—280	15,906
	Natalie Gulbis (USA)	68-71-70-71—280	15,906
	Hee Won Han (KOR)	72-68-70-70—280	15,906
	Christina Kim (USA)	73-68-68-71—280	15,906
	Carin Koch (SWE)	70-70-70-70—280	15,906
	Paula Marti (ESP)	73-66-68-73—280	15,906
	Grace Park (KOR)	71-70-69-70—280	15,906
	Annika Sörenstam (SWE)	68-71-70-71—280	15,906
21	Michelle Estill (USA)	70-72-68-71—281	12,250
21T	Se Ri Pak (KOR)	73-70-69-69—281	12,250
23	Jeong Jang (KOR)	70-68-73-71—282	11,250
	Aree Song (KOR)	72-70-70-70—282	11,250
25	Juli Inkster (USA)	71-75-69-68—283	10,200
	Seol-An Jeon (KOR)	69-69-70-75—283	10,200
	Toshimi Kimura (JPN)	70-75-68-70—283	10,200
28	Alison Nicholas (ENG)	75-71-70-69—285	9,450
29	Candie Kung (TPE)	73-69-71-73—286	8,925
	Catriona Matthew (SCO)	68-74-68-76—286	8,925
31	Wendy Doolan (AUS)	71-72-74-70—287	7,950
	Natascha Fink (AUT)	74-70-70-73—287	7,950
	Gloria Park (KOR)	72-73-75-67—287	7,950
	Kirsty Taylor (ENG)	72-74-72-69—287	7,950
35	Soo-Yun Kang (KOR)	71-74-74-69—288	7,000
	Becky Morgan (WAL)	74-72-69-73—288	7,000
	Jennifer Rosales (PHI)	75-70-70-73—288	7,000
38	Denise Killeen (USA)	72-72-70-75—289	6,125
	Jill McGill (USA)	71-72-71-75—289	6,125
	Patricia Meunier-Lebouc (FRA)	70-75-71-73—289	6,125
	Nadina Taylor (AUS)	69-74-72-74—289	6,125

Other players who made the cut: Hiromi Mogi (JPN), Shiho Ohyama (JPN), Ana B Sanchez (ESP), Louise Stahle (SWE) (am), Sherri Steinhauer (USA) 290; Bettina Hauert (GER), Angela Jerman (USA), Pamela Kerrigan 291; Ashli Bunch (USA), Audra Burks (USA), Johanna Head (ENG), Katherine Hull (AUS), Kelli Kuehne (USA), Gwladys Nocera (FRA) 292; Lynnette Brooky (NZL), A J Eathorne (CAN), Wendy Ward (USA) 293; Emilee Klein (USA) 294; Helen Alfredsson (SWE), Hsiao Chuan Lu (CHN), Betsy King (USA), Janice Moodie (SCO) 295; Raquel Carriedo (ESP), Ana Larraneta (ESP) 296; Vicki Goetze-Ackerman (USA), Laurette Maritz (RSA) 297; Samantha Head (ENG) 298; Maria Hjörth (SWE) 305

2003 Weetabix Women's British Open *Royal Lytham and St Annes, Lancashire* [6308–72]

Prize money: £1.05 million

1	Annika Sörenstam (SWE)	68-72-68-70—278	£160,000
2	Se Ri Pak (KOR)	69-69-69-72—279	100,000
3	Grace Park (KOR)	74-65-71-70—280	62,500
	Karrie Webb (AUS)	67-72-70-71—280	62,500
5	Patricia Meunier-Lebouc (FRA)	70-69-67-76—282	45,000
6	Vicki Goetze-Ackerman (USA)	73-71-68-71—283	37,000
	Wendy Ward (USA)	67-71-69-76—283	37,000
8	Sophie Gustafson (SWE)	73-69-71-71—284	32,000
9	Young Kim (KOR)	73-70-72-70—285	29,000
10	Candie Kung (TPE)	73-71-69-73—286	25,000
	Gloria Park (KOR)	70-75-69-72—286	25,000
12	Paula Marti (ESP)	71-70-70-76—287	21,000
	Karen Stupples (ENG)	69-74-70-74—287	21,000
14	Lynnette Brooky (NZL)	70-74-75-69—288	16,150
	Beth Daniel (USA)	74-71-67-76—288	16,150
	Laura Diaz (USA)	73-74-71-70—288	16,150
	Jeong Jang (KOR)	76-69-72-71—288	16,150
	Cristie Kerr (USA)	74-71-71-72—288	16,150
19	Heather Bowie (USA)	70-66-74-79—289	12,500
19T	Laura Davies (ENG)	75-70-70-74—289	12,500
	Hee Won Han (KOR)	75-71-70-73—289	12,500
	Lorie Kane (CAN)	69-75-70-75—289	12,500
	Becky Morgan (WAL)	72-70-71-76—289	12,500
24	Brandie Burton (USA)	76-69-69-76—290	8,996
	Moira Dunn (USA)	70-74-74-72—290	8,996
	Michiko Hattori (JPN)	78-69-71-72—290	8,996
	Pat Hurst (USA)	73-71-74-72—290	8,996
	Soo-Yun Kang (KOR)	70-75-72-73—290	8,996
	Emilee Klein (USA)	72-70-74-74—290	8,996
	Lorena Ochoa (MEX)	74-65-77-74—290	8,996
	Dottie Pepper (USA)	71-75-71-73—290	8,996
	Jennifer Rosales (PHI)	69-72-76-73—290	8,996
	Iben Tinning (DEN)	71-73-73-73—290	8,996
	Hiroko Yamaguchi (JPN)	72-71-75-72—290	8,996
	Young-A Yang (KOR)	71-75-71-73—290	8,996
36	Georgina Simpson (ENG)	69-73-74-75—291	7,000
37	Christine Kuld (DEN)	69-76-75-72—292	6,375
	Meg Mallon (USA)	71-72-71-78—292	6,375
	Michele Redman (USA)	71-69-76-76—292	6,375
	Nadina Taylor (AUS)	71-74-72-75—292	6,375

Other players who made the cut: Elisabeth Esterl (GER), Akiko Fukushima (JPN), Johanna Head (ENG), Juli Inkster (USA), Catrin Nilsmark (SWE) 293; Kelli Kuehne (USA), Elisa Serramia (ESP) (am), Rachel Teske (AUS), Karen Weiss (USA) 294; Kasumi Fujii (JPN), Angela Jerman (USA), Carin Koch (SWE), Kelly Robbins (USA) 295; Cherie Byrnes (AUS), Michelle Ellis (AUS), Woo-Soon Ko (KOR), Shani Waugh (AUS) 296; Heather Daly-Donofrio (USA), Susan Parry (USA), Kirsty Taylor (ENG) 297; Helen Alfredsson (SWE), Alison Nicholas (ENG) 298; Beth Bauer (USA) 299; Silvia Cavalleri (ITA), Sophie Sandolo (ITA), Angela Stanford (USA) 300; Suzanne Strudwick (ENG) 303; Marnie McGuire (NZL) 308

Women's British Open History

Year	Winner	Country	Venue	Score
1976	J Lee Smith	England	Fulford	299
1977	V Saunders	England	Lindrick	306
1978	J Melville	England	Foxhills	310
1979	A Sheard	South Africa	Southport and Ainsdale	301
1980	D Massey	USA	Wentworth (East)	294
1981	D Massey	USA	Northumberland	295
1982	M Figueras-Dotti	Spain	Royal Birkdale	296
1983	*Not played*			
1984	A Okamoto	Japan	Woburn	289
1985	B King	USA	Moor Park	300
1986	L Davies	England	Royal Birkdale	283
1987	A Nicholas	England	St Mellion	296
1988	C Dibnah*	Australia	Lindrick	296
**Won play-off after a tie with S Little*				
1989	J Geddes	USA	Ferndown	274
1990	H Alfredsson*	Sweden	Woburn	288
**Beat J Hill at the fourth exyta hole*				
1991	P Grice-Whittaker	England	Woburn	284
1992	P Sheehan	USA	Woburn	207
Reduced to 54 holes by rain				
1993	K Lunn	Australia	Woburn	275
1994	L Neumann	Sweden	Woburn	280
1995	K Webb	Australia	Woburn	278
1996	E Klein	USA	Woburn	277
1997	K Webb	Australia	Sunningdale	269
1998	S Steinhauer	USA	Royal Lytham & St Annes	292
1999	S Steinhauer	USA	Woburn	283
2000	S Gustafson	Sweden	Royal Birkdale	282

Women's British Open History *continued*

Year	Winner	Country	Venue	Score
2001	S R Pak	Korea	Sunningdale	277
2002	K Webb	Australia	Turnberry	273
2003	A Sörenstam	Sweden	Royal Lytham & St Annes	278
2004	Karen Stupples	England	Sunningdale (Old Course)	269
2005	Jeong Jang	Korea	Royal Birkdale	272
2006	Sherri Steinhauer	USA	Royal Lytham & St Annes	281
2007	Lorena Ochoa	Mexico	St Andrews Old Course	287
2008	Ji-Yai Shin	Korea	Sunningdale	270
2009	Catriona Matthew	Scotland	Royal Lytham & St Annes	285
2010	Yani Tseng	Chinese Tapei	Royal Birkdale	277
2011	Yani Tseng	Chinese Tapei	Carnoustie Links	272
2012	Jiyai Shin	Korea	Royal Liverpool	279

Kingsbarns to host Ricoh Women's British Open Qualifying

Kingsbarns Golf Links, one of the top 100 courses in the world, will hold the final qualifying test for the 2012 Ricoh Women's British Open which is being held for the second time in seven years over the Old Course, St Andrews from August 1–4.

Lorena Ochoa, the Mexican golfer who has now retired from competitive play, was the winner when the Championship was played for the first time at the Home of Golf in 2007.

Shona Malcolm, the CEO of the Ladies Golf Union, said at the time of the announcement: "The Championship committee is very happy to add Kingsbarns to the rotation of prestigious clubs who host final qualifying. It will be a popular choice for players and spectators alike and we look forward to seeing how the golfers will cope with the challenges offered by a magnificent links course."

Thirteen made the cut in all four women's majors

Five Americans,two Europeans, two Australians, two Koreans, a Japanese golfer and a Taiwanese player played all four rounds in the 2012 women's majors but only one was a major winner.

Korean Sun Young Yoo won the Kraft Nabisco, the first major of the season, in Palm Springs. America's Stacy Lewis and Inbee Park from Korea both managed runner-up spots in the Wegman's LPGA Championship and Ricoh Women's British Open respectively and only two other players managed third place finishes – Taiwan's Yani Tseng in the Kraft Nabisco and American Paula Creamer in the British event at Hoylake. In money earned from the four majors, Inbee Park topped the table with $390,407 edging out Sun Young Yoo by over $33,000.

Name	*Kraft*	*LPGA*	*US Open*	*Ricoh*	*Earnings*
Inbee Park (KOR)	26T	9T	9T	2	$390,407
Sun Young Yoo (KOR)	1	15T	32T	47T	$366,729
Paula Creamer (USA)	20T	9T	7T	3	$343,832
Stacy Lewis (USA)	4T	2T	46T	8T	$324,386
Karrie Webb (AUS)	15T	6T	50T	5T	$214,624
So Yeon Ryo (KOR)	56T	25T	14T	5T	$188,264
Cristie Kerr (USA)	22T	12T	9T	13T	$180,277
Yani Tseng (TPE)	3	59T	50T	26T	$173,256
Lexi Thompson (USA)	22T	30T	14T	17T	$127,765
Ai Miyazato (JPN)	56T	6T	28T	26T	$126,424
Katie Futcher (USA)	66T	55T	39T	8T	$103,577
Beatriz Recari (ESP)	26T	45T	35T	26T	$68,801
Katherine Hull (AUS)	20T	51T	57T	33T	$59,572
Dewi Claire Schreefel (NED)	66T	62T	57T	47T	$31,074

The 66th US Women's Open

No Yeon Choi's resilience after her triple bogey won her a first title

Ever since Se Ri Pak secured the most prized title in women's golf at Blackwolf Run in 1998, her compatriots from South Korea have made a habit of emulating Pak's example. When Na Yeon Choi became the latest to followed in Pak's footseteps in Kohler, Wisconsin – she was the sixth Korean to win the US Women's Open – her victory merely served to underline the extraordinary influence exerted by Asian golfers on the women's game.

Along with Birdie Kim in 2005, Inbee Park in 2008, Eun Hee Ji in 2009 and So Yeon Ryu in 2011, Choi was the fifth Korean in eight years to emerge triumphant at America's national championship and the fourth in the last five championships. Like her countrywomen, the 24-year-old acknowledged she would not have dared dream her dreams of glory at the age of nine had Pak not first shown the others the way.

"Before Se Ri won [the US Women's Open] in 1998, my dream was just to be a professional," admitted Choi. "After I watched her succeed, she really inspired me to be an LPGA player. So I really appreciate what Se Ri did before. She is a legend in Korea. I think what she did was significant for all the Korean people. Even some people who didn't play golf. I think we had a bad economy in Korea at that moment, but she won on the LPGA Tour and that was amazing."

© Getty Images

Na Yeon Choi

Fittingly, Pak, the winner of five major titles, was among the first to congratulate Choi, running onto the 18th green at Blackwolf Run with a bottle of champagne to toast the new champion. "She said, 'Hey, Na Yeon, I'm really proud of you. You did a really good job'," Choi recalled.

Choi's winning total of 281, seven under par, was four shots better than runner-up Amy Yang's score and eight strokes clear of Sandra Gal in third place. After a spectacular third round of 65, Choi had threatened to turn the US Women's Open into a one horse canter. However, her seemingly unassailable position at the head of affairs came under threat at the start of the back nine in Sunday's final round when she ran up a triple bogey 8 on the tenth hole. Consequently, it said a lot about the golfer's composure and mental strength that she bounced back with three birdies over the next six holes and signed off with a respectable closing round of 73 to claim the first prize of $585,000.

Choi's resilience had already been evident off the course in 2009 when she took the brave step of asking her parents to return to South Korea and leave her to find her own way in America. Learning to rely on herself, rather than others, was surely one of the factors which helped Choi win her first major. "I told my parents I wanted to be more independent," she said.

Choi, of course, was right. A matter of weeks after sending her parents home, she won her first tournament on the LPGA. By the time she came out on top in Wisconsin, Choi had six victories under her belt and only Yani Tseng stood between her and the coveted world No 1 ranking.

At the start of the week in Kohler, Choi bettered par with a steady opening score of 71, but attracted little media attention as the spotlight fell on three Americans golfers – Cristie Kerr, Brittany Lincicome and Lizette Salas – who claimed a share of the first round lead on 69, three under par. Kerr had made what looked like the most significant move, bearing in mind she'd won the title in 2007 and not finished out of the top 20 at the US Women's Open in the years which followed her success.

In spite of the sweltering heat, the players didn't seem in any particular rush to get round, with many taking more than five hours to play 18 holes. According to Spain's Beatriz Recari, though, it was the severe challenge of the course rather than soaring temperatures which made the day longer. "It's hot out there," she said. "But that doesn't make you much slower. Why it took longer is because of the difficulty of the course, I would say."

Choi maintained a low profile in the second round, matching the par of 72 and staying within six shots of the leader, Suzann Pettersen. The Scandinavian golfer, who overslept by an hour and had to cut short her warm up, was in outstanding form on Friday, shooting 68 on the same day that the joint first round leader, Lincicome, signed for 80. In her tenth appearance at the US Women's Open, the Norwegian player made five birdies and dropped just one stroke to par. "I like the US Open," acknowledged the Solheim

Cup veteran. "It's usually the biggest test of golf throughout the year. I like the way the USGA sets up the courses. They make it tough. They make it fair. And it's by far one of my favourite championships, just because of that. This year there are birdies out there. I probably shouldn't say this, because we come out tomorrow and they'll probably make it impossible. But the course is playable." (Ironically, Pettersen's foresight was more impressive than her golf on Saturday when she took 78, ten shots more than the day before.)

Another player in the groove on Friday was Michelle Wie, who had spent much of the season in 2012 missing cuts rather than contending for titles. Not having finished higher than 33rd at any event, Wie was re-energised by a round of 66, the lowest score of the first two days. Having recently graduated from Stanford, the 22-year-old produced a fine performance on the greens, though she was the first to admit that hitting her approach shots to 15 feet or so rather than 40 greatly enhanced her prospects of holing a few putts.

"Just 26 putts, that was amazing."

Na Yeon Choi after her 65 on the third dayi

After spending the first couple of days at Kohler out of the limelight, Choi commanded centre stage in the third round when she improved Wie's second round score by a shot and signed for 65, the low round of the week at Blackwolf Run. Even though the course offered a substantial test, Choi's 65 was the third lowest score ever recorded in US Women's Open history. Consistency of ball striking and solid putting were the keys to unlocking Blackwolf Run's defences on a breezy day when only five players bettered par. Choi hit a dozen fairways, found 13 greens in regulation and used her putter just 26 times.

The golfer herself reckoned it was a hot putter which made the difference in recording eight birdies and a solitary bogey. "Just 26 putts, that was amazing," she smiled. By way of placing Choi's outstanding performance in the proper perspective, the average score in Kohler on Saturday was 76.9 and no fewer than 19 of the world's leading female players returned cards of 80 or higher.

With a six stroke advantage over her closest rival, Yang, going into the final round, the South Korean had plenty of reasons to feel optimistic about ending her wait for a major title in Wisconsin. Moreover, the 24-year-old had come close in previous major championships by recording seven top ten finishes, most notably a runner up spot at Oakmont in the 2010 US Women's Open. Crossing the winning line for the first time in the events which matter most, however, always brings its own burden.

Any sense of anxiety over the outward half of the final round, mark you, was hard to detect as Choi played sensible championship golf, recovering from a bogey on the first with a birdie at the fourth and reaching the turn in 36 blows on eight under. Just one destructive shot, however, can undo days of good work. When Choi carved her drive into the trees on the tenth hole, she searched for her ball in vain before returning to play three from the tee. Eventually she holed out for 8 and her lead over Yang was trimmed to just two shots.

Keeping her head held high as she walked down the 11th fairway, Choi responded impressively to adversity with a birdie before making a 20 foot par saving putt on the 12th. This was the period in the championship when the winner had to grind to keep herself in front. She had to scramble to make another par on the 13th before the pressure eased considerably on the 14th after Yang dropped a shot and the gap between the leaders was stretched to four strokes.

As Choi closed in on Tseng at the top of the rankings, the world No 1 suffered another weekend of woe as she added a brace of 78s to her opening rounds of 74 and 72. In a confession that would surely have struck a chord with many club golfers, Yani acknowledged: "The harder you try, the worser [sic] you get ..."

Michael Aitlen

First Round	Second Round	Third Round	Fourth Round
–3 Cristie Kerr	–5 Suzann Pettersen	–8 Na Yeon Choi	–7 Na Yeon Choi
–3 Brittany Lincicome	–4 Michelle Wie	–2 Amy Yang	–3 Amy Yang
–3 Lizette Salas	–4 Cristie Kerr	–1 Mika Miyazato	+1 Sandra Gal
–3 Ai Miyazato	–3 Sandra Gal	–1 Lexi Thompson	+2 Giulia Sergas
–2 Lexi Thompson	–3 Vicky Hurst	–1 Sandra Gal	+2 Ihee Lee
–2 Beatriz Recari	–3 Inbee Park	= Vicky Hurst	+2 Shanshan Feng
–2 Jennie Lee	–2 Mika Miyazato	+1 Nicole Castrale	+3 Paula Creamer
–1 Suzann Pettersen	–2 Lizette Salas	+1 Paula Creamer	+3 Mika Miyazato
–1 Vicky Hurst	–1 Nicole Castrale	+1 Suzann Pettersen	+4 Cristie Kerr
–1 Na Yeon Choi	–1 Na Yeon Choi	+1 Cristie Kerr	+4 Suzann Pettersen

US Women's Open Championship (67th) July 5–8

Blackwolf Run, Championship Course, Kohler, WI [6984–72]

Prize Money: $3,250,000. Entries 1,364. Field 156 (28 amateurs) of whom 65 (including three amateurs) made the cut on 149 or less

Players are of American nationality unless stated

1	Na Yeon Choi (KOR)	71-72-65-73—281	$585,000
2	Amy Yang (KOR)	73-72-69-71—285	350,000
3	Sandra Gal (GER)	71-70-74-74—289	218,840
4	Ilhee Lee (KOR	72-71-77-70—290	128,487
4	Shanshan Feng (CHN)	74-74-71-71—290	128,487
	Giulia Sergas (ITA)	74-71-73-72—290	128,487
7	Paula Creamer	73-73-71-74—291	94,736
	Mika Miyazato (JPN)	71-71-73-76—291	94,736
9	Se Ri Pak (KOR)	72-73-76-71—292	72,596
	Nicole Castrale	73-70-74-75—292	72,596
	Inbee Park (KOR)	71-70-76-75—292	72,596
	Cristie Kerr	69-71-77-75—292	72,596
	Suzann Pettersen (NOR)	71-68-78-75—292	72,596
14	Cindy Lacrosse	73-74-74-72—293	55,161
	Danielle Kang	78-70-71-74—293	55,161
	So Yeon Ryu (KOR)	74-71-74-74—293	55,161
	Lexi Thompson	70-73-72-78—293	55,161
18	Hee Kyung Seo (KOR)	72-73-80-69—294	45,263
	Brittany Lincicome	69-80-74-71—294	45,263
	Vicky Hurst	71-70-75-78—294	45,263
21	Yeon-Ju Jung (KOR)	74-72-80-69—295	33,799
	Diana Luna (ITA)	76-72-76-71—295	33,799
	Brittany Lang	73-74-77-71—295	33,799
	Jennie Lee	70-74-79-72—295	33,799
	Numa Gulyanamitta (THA)	73-76-73-73—295	33,799
	Jimin Kang (KOR)	72-72-78-73—295	33,799
	Azahara Muñoz (ESP)	73-73-73-76—295	33,799
28	Anna Nordqvist (SWE)	72-74-79-71—296	23,604
	Mina Harigae	77-71-75-73—296	23,604
	Pornanong Phatlum (THA)	76-69-76-75—296	23,604
	Ai Miyazato (JPN)	70-74-75-77—296	23,604
32	Sun Young Yoo (KOR)	76-72-81-68—297	20,880
	Jin Young Pak (KOR)	73-72-80-72—297	20,880
	Lizette Salas	69-73-75-80—297	20,880
35	Jenny Shin (KOR)	76-71-76-75—298	18,653
	Jennifer Johnson	76-70-76-76—298	18,653
	Beatriz Recari (ESP)	70-75-76-77—298	18,653
	Michelle Wie	74-66-78-80—298	18,653
39	Carlota Ciganda (ESP)	76-72-77-75—300	15,491
	Heather Bowie Young	75-73-77-75—300	15,491
	Lydia Ko (NZL) (am)	74-72-79-75—300	
	Katie Futcher	73-75-74-78—300	15,491
	Jeong Jang (KOR)	73-72-75-80—300	15,491
	Jessica Korda	74-71-75-80—300	15,491
	Sakura Yokomine (JPN)	75-70-75-80—300	15,491
46	Emma Talley (am)	73-75-81-72—301	
	Jennifer Song	72-74-81-74—301	12,651
	Stacy Lewis	77-69-80-75—301	12,651
	Alison Walshe	74-71-75-81—301	12,651
50	Karrie Webb (AUS)	75-72-81-74—302	10,532
	Gerina Piller	73-71-81-77—302	10,532
	Yani Tseng (TPE)	74-72-78-78—302	10,532
	Melissa Reid (ENG)	79-69-75-79—302	10,532
54	Angela Stanford	75-71-81-76—303	9,484
	Meena Lee (KOR)	71-78-76-78—303	9,484

US Women's Open Championship *continued*

56	Sophie Gustafson (SWE)	77-72-84-71—304	9,132
57	Dewi Claire Schreefel (NED)	73-76-82-74—305	8,709
	Angela Oh	75-74-80-76—305	8,709
	Katherine Hull (AUS)	75-73-81-76—305	8,709
60	Ji-Hee Lee (KOR)	79-70-83-74—306	8,267
	Alison Lee (am)	75-74-79-78—306	
	Kristy McPherson	75-71-81-79—306	8,267
63	Lorie Kane (CAN)	76-73-82-76—307	8,055
64	Paige Mackenzie	75-74-83-77—309	7,922
65	Sue Kim (KOR)	75-72-85-81—313	7,789

The following players missed the cut:

66	Christel Boeljon (NED)	75-75—150
	Katie Burnett	72-78—150
	Kyung Kim (am)	77-73—150
	I K Kim (KOR)	74-76—150
	Mindy Kim	72-78—150
	Tessa Teachman	75-75—150
	Wendy Ward	72-78—150
73	Julieta Granada (PAR)	81-70—151
	Hee-Won Han (KOR)	77-74—151
	Mi Jung Hur (KOR)	80-71—151
	Candie Kung (TPE)	74-77—151
	Catriona Matthew (SCO)	75-76—151
	Kris Tamulis	76-75—151
79	Cydney Clanton	79-73—152
	Brianna Do	74-78—152
	Christina Kim	75-77—152
	Seon Hwa Lee (KOR)	78-74—152
	Haru Nomura (JPN)	75-77—152
	Karen Stupples (ENG)	76-76—152
	Momoko Ueda (JPN)	77-75—152
86	Elisabeth Bernabe (am)	74-79—153
	Doris Chen (TPE) (am)	76-77—153
	Jennifer Gleason	73-80—153
	Jaye Marie Green (am)	75-78—153
	Maria Hjörth (SWE)	77-76—153
	Kelly Jacques	77-76—153
	Hee Young Park (KOR)	74-79—153
	Reilley Rankin	80-73—153
	Cheyenne Woods	75-78—153
95	Brittany Altomare (am)	78-76—154
	Hiroko Ayada (JPN)	76-78—154
	Chella Choi (KOR)	81-73—154
	Gabriella Dominguez (am)	80-74—154
	Eun-Hee Ji (KOR)	76-78—154
95T	Tiffany Joh	75-79—154
	Hannah O'Sullivan (am)	76-78—154
	Jisoo Park (KOR) (am)	76-78—154
	Jenny Suh	75-79—154
	Victoria Tanco (ARG)	81-73—154
	Isabelle Beisiegel (CAN)	81-74—155
106	Veronica Felibert (VEN)	79-76—155
	Natalie Gulbis	76-79—155
	Megan Khang (am)	75-80—155
	Mo Martin	78-77—155
	Paola Moreno (COL)	77-78—155
	Mina Nakayama (JPN)	78-77—155
	Brooke Pancake	79-76—155
	Katherine Perry (am)	74-81—155
	Kelly Shon (am)	78-77—155
115	Jamie Hullett	78-78—156
	Belen Mozo (ESP)	76-80—156
	Stacy Prammanasudh	76-80—156
	Haley Wilson	78-78—156
119	Kyeong Bae (KOR)	78-79—157
	Amanda Blumenhurst	75-82—157
	Caroline Hedwall (SWE)	77-80—157
	Moriya Jutanugarn (THA) (am)	80-77—157
	Becky Morgan (WAL)	81-76—157
	Ryann O'Toole	75-82—157
	Hyun-Hwa Sim (KOR)	81-76—157
126	Cathryn Bristow (NZL)	83-75—158
	Jisoo Keel (CAN) (am)	81-77—158
	Birdie Kim (KOR)	81-77—158
126T	Maria Gabriela Lopez (MEX) (am)	80-78—158
130	Soo-Jin Yang (KOR)	77-82—159
131	Mi Hyang Lee (KOR)	74-86—160
	Lindsey Weaver (am)	79-81—160
133	Lili Alvarez (MEX)	84-77—161
	Shannon Aubert (FRA) (am)	82-79—161
	Yukari Baba (JPN)	78-83—161
	Lisa Grimes	83-78—161
	Becca Huffer (am)	79-82—161
	Juli Inkster	79-82—161
	Stephanie Meadow (NIR) (am)	77-84—161
	Aimee Neff	81-80—161
	Lee-Anne Pace (RSA)	78-83—161
142	Ashley Armstrong (am)	80-82—162
	Katy Harris	82-80—162
	Pat Hurst	81-81—162
	Kylene Pulley	81-81—162
146	Amy Hung (KOR)	82-81—163
147	Anya Sarai Alvarez	82-82—164
	Christine Meier (am)	80-84—164
149	Annie Park (am)	81-84—165
	Angel Yin (am)	78-87—165
151	Briana Mao (am)	85-81—166
	Samantha Marks (am)	87-79—166
153	Rinko Mitsunaga (am)	87-81—168
	Jane Rah	80-88—168
155	Gigi Stoll (am)	86-84—170
	Morgan Pressel	74 WD

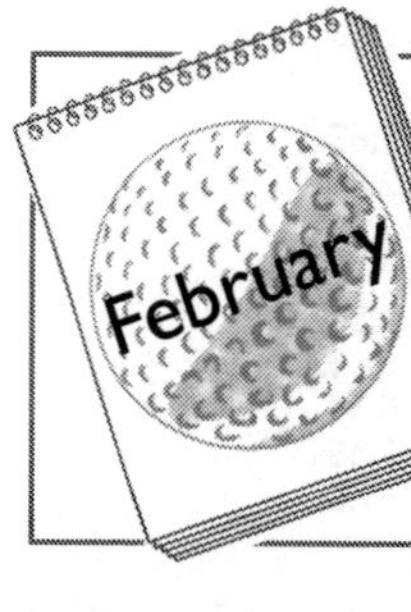

Month by month in 2012

Phil Mickelson shoots 64 from eight behind to win his 40th PGA Tour title at Pebble Beach, thrashing playing partner Tiger Woods by 11 in the process. Hunter Mahan beats Rory McIlroy in the final of the WGC–Accenture Match Play, while 43-year-old Paul Lawrie takes another step towards a Ryder Cup return after 13 years by winning in Qatar – just as he did in 1999 – and Rafa Cabrera Bello springs a surprise in Dubai.

2011 US Women's Open Championship *Colorado Springs, CO* [7047–71]

Prize money: $3.25 million

1	So Yeon Ryu (KOR)*	74-69-69-69—281	$585,000
2	Hee Kyung Seo (KOR)	72-73-68-68—281	350,000
So Yeon Ryu won at the third extra hole			
3	Cristie Kerr	71-72-69-71—283	215,493
4	Angela Stanford	72-70-70-72—284	150,166
5	Mika Miyazato (JPN)	70-67-76-72—285	121,591
6	Karrie Webb (AUS)	70-73-72-71—286	98,128
	Ai Miyazato (JPN)	70-68-76-72—286	98,128
	Inbee Park (KOR)	71-73-70-72—286	98,128
9	Ryann O'Toole	69-72-75-71—287	81,915
10	Jiyai Shin (KOR)	73-72-73-70—288	70,996
	Amy Yang (KOR)	75-69-73-71—288	70,996
	I K Kim (KOR)	70-69-76-73—288	70,996
13	Chella Choi (KOR)	71-76-70-72—289	60,780
	Candie Kung (TPE)	76-69-71-73—289	60,780
15	Karen Stupples (ENG)	72-77-73-68—290	48,658
	Suzann Pettersen (NOR)	71-75-72-72—290	48,658
	Junthima Gulyanamitta (THA)	73-76-68-73—290	48,658
	Yani Tseng (TPE)	73-73-71-73—290	48,658
	Lizette Salas	69-73-73-75—290	48,658
	Paula Creamer	72-70-73-75—290	48,658
21	Catriona Matthew (SCO)	76-70-74-71—291	36,374
21T	Meena Lee (KOR)	75-71-72-73—291	36,374
	Morgan Pressel	75-72-71-73—291	36,374
	Leta Lindley	73-71-72-75—291	36,374
25	Mi-Jeong Jeon (KOR)	72-73-76-71—292	30,122
	Sun Young Yoo (KOR)	74-68-77-73—292	30,122
27	Brittany Lincicome	75-74-74-70—293	24,042
	Sakura Yokomine (JPN)	72-74-77-70—293	24,042
	Beatriz Recari (ESP)	76-72-72-73—293	24,042
	Alison Walshe	74-73-73-73—293	24,042
	Eun-Hee Ji (KOR)	73-69-74-77—293	24,042
32	Natalie Gulbis	73-75-74-72—294	21,189
	Moriya Jutanugarn (THA) (am)	76-69-76-73—294	
34	Shinobu Moromizato (JPN)	76-72-74-73—295	18,370
	Mina Harigae	75-74-72-74—295	18,370
	Sandra Gal (GER)	77-72-72-74—295	18,370
	Maria Hjörth (SWE)	70-78-73-74—295	18,370
	Stacy Lewis	68-73-79-75—295	18,370
	Jessica Korda	73-75-72-75—295	18,370
	Song-Hee Kim (KOR)	73-73-74-75—295	18,370
	Wendy Ward	73-69-74-79—295	18,370

Other players who made the cut: Shanshan Feng (CHN), Karin Sjodin (SWE), Meaghan Francella 296; Vicky Hurst, Hee Young Park (KOR), Azahara Muñoz (ESP), Jennifer Johnson, Se Ri Pak(KOR) 297; Brittany Lang, Jin Young Pak (KOR), Soo-Jin Yang (KOR), Sue Kim (CAN), Lindsey Wright (AUS) 298; Michelle Wie, Danah Bordner, Lee-Anne Pace (RSA), Mariajo Uribe (COL) 299; Yoo Kyeong Kim, Lindy Duncan (am), Victoria Tanco (ARG) (am), Jean Chua (MAS) 300; Amy Anderson (am) 301; Anya Sarai Alvarez, Shin-Ae Ahn (KOR), Haru Nomura (JPN), Becky Morgan (WAL), 302; Danielle Kang (am) 303; Paola Moreno (COL) 304; Sherri Steinhauer 305; Gwladys Nocera (FRA) 307; Bo-Mee Lee (KOR) WD

2010 US Women's Open Championship *Oakmont, PA* [6613–71]

Prize money: $3.25 million

1	Paula Creamer	72-70-70-69—281	$585,000
2	Na Yeon Choi (KOR)	75-72-72-66—285	284,468
	Suzann Pettersn (NOR)	73-71-72-69—285	284,468
4	In-Kyung Kim (KOR)	74-71-73-68—286	152,565
5	Jiyai Shin	76-71-72-68—287	110,481
	Brittany Lang	69-74-75-69—287	110,481
	Amy Yang (KOR)	70-75-71-71—287	110,481
8	Inbee Park (KOR)	70-78-73-68—289	87,202
	Christine Kim	72-72-72-73—289	87,202
10	Alexis Thompson	73-74-70-73—290	72,131
	Saura Yokomine (JPN)	71-71-76-72—290	72,131
	Yani Tseng (TPE)	73-76-73-68—290	72,131
13	Song-Hee Kim (KOR)	72-76-78-65—291	63,524
14	Natalie Gulbis	73-73-72-74—292	56,659
	Stacy Lewis	75-70-75-72—292	56,659
	Wendy Ward	72-73-70-77—292	56,659
17	Cristie Kerr	72-71-75-75—293	49,365
	Karrie Webb (AUS)	74-72-73-74—293	49,365
19	Shi Hyun Ahn (KOR)	72-77-73-72—294	39,285
	Sophie Gustafson (SWE)	72-72-74-76—294	39,285
19T	Jeong Jang (KOR)	73-72-74-75—294	39,285
	Kristy McPherson	72-78-74-70—294	39,285
	Azahara Muñoz (ESP)	75-74-71-74—294	39,285
	Angela Sanford	73-72-74-75—294	39,285
25	Jee Young Lee (KOR)	72-76-76-71—295	29,625
	Brittany Lincicome	73-78-71-73—295	29,625
	So Yeon Ryu (KOR)	74-74-76-71—295	29,625
28	Chie Arimura (JPN)	74-72-76-74—296	24,096
	Maria Hjörth (SWE)	73-72-75-76—296	24,096
	Candie Kung (TPE)	76-72-79-69—296	24,096
31	Ashli Bunch	78-74-75-70—297	21,529
	M J Hur (KOR)	70-81-74-72—297	21,529
	Ai Miyazato (JPN)	73-74-80-70—297	21,529
34	Meaghan Francella	75-72-77-74—298	18,980
	Jeong Eun Lee (KOR)	72-78-73-75—298	18,980
	Mhairi McKay (SCO)	71-78-76-73—298	18,980
	Shinobu Moromizato (JPN)	72-77-77-72—298	18,980
	Morgan Pressel	74-75-75-74—298	18,980

Other players who made the cut: Eun-Hee Ji (KOR). Karen Stupples (ENG) 299; Maria Hernandez (ESP), Katherine Hull (AUS), Vicky Hurst, Jennifer Johnson (am), Hee Young Park (KOR), Jennifer Rosales (PHI), Heather Young 300; Alena Sharp (CAN), Louise Stahle (SWE), Lindsay Wright (AUS) 301; Sandra Gal (GER) 302; Naon Min (KOR), Sherri Steinhauer 303; Allison Fouch 304; Paige Mackenzie, Anna Rawson (AUS), Christine Wong (CAN) (am) 305; Tamie Durdin (AUS), Libby Smith, Jennifer Song 307; Chella Choi (KOR) 308; Lisa McCloskey (am), Heekyung Seo (KOR) 309; Danielle Kang (am) 310; Meredith Duncan, Kelli Shean (RSA) (am) 312; Sarah Kemp (AUS) 313; Tiffany Lim (am) 320

2009 US Women's Open Championship *Interlachen CC, Edina, MN* [6789–73]

Prize money: $3.1 million

1	Eun-Hee Ji (KOR)	71-72-70-71—284	$585,000
2	Candie Kung (TPE)	71-77-68-69—285	350,000
3	Cristie Kerr	69-70-72-75—286	183,568
	In-Kyung Kim (KOR)	72-72-72-70—286	183,568
5	Brittany Lincicome	72-72-73-70—287	122,415
6	Paula Creamer	72-68-79-69—288	99,126
	Ai Miyazato (JPN)	74-74-71-69—288	99,126
	Suzann Pettersen (NOR)	74-71-72-71—288	99,126
9	Kyeong Bae (KOR)	75-73-69-72—289	76,711
	Na Yeon Choi (KOR)	68-74-76-71—289	76,711
	Hee Young Park (KOR)	70-74-72-73—289	76,711
12	Song-Hee Kim (KOR)	74-69-75-72—290	66,769
13	Sun Ju Ahn (KOR)	75-71-72-73—291	59,428
	Morgan Pressel	74-75-69-73—291	59,428
	Jiyai Shin (KOR)	72-75-76-68—291	59,428
	Jennifer Song (am)	72-74-73-72—291	
17	Nicole Castrale	74-71-74-73—292	42,724
	Laura Davies (ENG)	72-75-73-72—292	42,724
	Meaghan Francella	73-72-74-73—292	42,724
17T	Akiko Fukushima (JPN)	76-72-72-72—292	42,724
	Anna Grzebien	73-77-69-73—292	42,724
	Jimin Kang (KOR)	76-71-74-71—292	42,724
	Teresa Lu (TPE)	76-69-70-77—292	42,724
	Jean Reynolds	69-72-74-77—292	42,724
	Lindsey Wright (AUS)	74-70-77-71—292	42,724
26	He Yong Choi (KOR)	77-74-74-68—293	27,420
	Juli Inkster	78-73-72-70—293	27,420
	Jessica Korda (am)	72-77-75-69—293	
	Alison Lee (am)	75-72-76-70—293	
	Anna Nordqvist (SWE)	71-75-75-72—293	27,420
	Lorena Ochoa (MEX)	69-79-73-72—293	27,420
	Inbee Park (KOR)	75-71-77-70—293	27,420
33	Sun Young Yoo (KOR)	72-74-72-76—294	22,603
34	Louise Friberg (SWE)	75-72-73-75—295	20,702
	Maria Hernandez (ESP)	74-72-77-72—295	20,702
	Kristy McPherson	71-74-77-73—295	20,702
	Alexis Thompson (am)	71-73-78-73—295	
	Karrie Webb (AUS)	75-72-74-74—295	20,702
	Amy Yang (KOR)	75-71-75-74—295	20,702

Other players who made the cut: Misun Cho (KOR), Sandra Gal (GER), Young Kim (KOR), Brittany Lang, Azahara Muñoz (ESP) (am), Ji Young Oh (KOR), Michele Redman, Momoko Ueda (JPN) 296; Shanshan Feng (CHN), Stacy Lewis, Hee-Kyung Seo (KOR), Maria Jose Uribe (COL) 297; Amanda Blumenherst, Hye Jung Choi (KOR), Christina Kim, Giulia Sergas (ITA), Karen Stupples (ENG) 298; Yuri Fudoh (JPN), Haeji Kang (KOR), Mika Miyazato (JPN), Stacy Prammanasudh 299; Cindy Lacrosse, Ji Hee Lee (KOR), Meena Lee (KOR), Becky Morgan (WAL) 300; Allison Fouch, Allie White (am) 301; Karine Icher (FRA), Mina Harigae, Jennie Lee 304; Candace Schepperle (am) 306; Carolina Llano (COL) 307; Lisa Ferrero 312

2008 US Women's Open Championship *Interlachen CC, Edina, MN* [6789–73]

Prize money: $3.1 million

1	Inbee Park (KOR)	72-69-71-71—283	$585,000
2	Helen Alfredsson (SWE)	70-71-71-75—287	350,000
3	In-Kyung Kim (KOR)	71-73-69-75—288	162,487
	Stacy Lewis	73-70-67-78—288	162,487
	Angela Park (BRA)	73-67-75-73—288	162,487
6	Nicole Castrale	74-70-74-71—289	94,117
	Paula Creamer	70-72-69-78—289	94,117
	Mi Hyun Kim (KOR)	72-72-70-75—289	94,117
	Giulia Sergas (ITA)	73-74-72-70—289	94,117
10	Teresa Lu (TPE)	71-72-73-74—290	75,734
	Maria Jose Uribe (COL) (am)	69-74-72-75—290	
12	Stacy Prammanasudh	75-72-71-73—291	71,002
13	Cristie Kerr	72-70-75-75—292	60,878
	Jee Young Lee (KOR)	71-75-74-72—292	60,878
	Suzann Pettersen (NOR)	77-71-73-71—292	60,878
	Momoko Ueda (JPN)	72-71-73-76—292	60,878
17	Catriona Matthew (SCO)	70-77-73-73—293	51,380
	Morgan Pressel	74-74-72-73—293	51,380
19	Na Yeon Choi (KOR)	76-71-71-76—294	43,376
	Jeong Jang (KOR)	73-69-74-78—294	43,376
19T	Jessica Korda (CZE) (am)	72-78-75-69—294	
	Candy Kung (TPE)	72-70-79-73—294	43,376
	Jiyai Shin (KOR)	69-74-79-72—294	43,376
24	Pat Hurst	67-78-77-73—295	35,276
	Song-Hee Kim (KOR)	68-76-75-76—295	35,276
	Annika Sörenstam (SWE)	75-70-72-78—295	35,276
27	Minea Blomqvist (FIN)	72-69-76-79—296	28,210
	Laura Diaz	77-70-73-76—296	28,210
	Seon Hwa Lee (KOR)	75-70-73-78—296	28,210
	Ai Miyazato (JPN)	71-72-76-77—296	28,210
31	Sun-Ju Ahn (KOR)	76-71-78-72—297	21,567
	Young Kim (KOR)	74-71-71-81—297	21,567
	Brittany Lang	71-75-74-77—297	21,567
	Lorena Ochoa (MEX)	73-74-76-74—297	21,567
	Ji Young Oh (KOR)	67-76-76-78—297	21,567
	Karen Stupples (ENG)	74-73-75-75—297	21,567
	Alison Walshe (am)	73-74-73-77—297	
38	Amanda Blumenherst (am)	72-78-71-77—298	
	Jennifer Rosales (PHI)	74-72-77-75—298	18,690
	Sherri Steinhauer	75-75-71-77—298	18,690
	Karrie Webb (AUS)	75-75-72-76—298	18,690

Other players who made the cut: Rachel Hetherington (AUS), Katherine Hull (AUS), Eun-Hee Ji (KOR), Ma On Min (KOR), Paola Moreno (COL) (am), Jane Park, Reilley Rankin, Yani Tseng (TPE), Lindsey Wright (AUS) 299; Maria Hjörth (SWE), Sakura Yokamine (JPN) 300; Louise Friberg (SWE), Christina Kim, Leta Lindley, Sherri Turner 301; Linda Wessberg (SWE) 302; Marcy Hart, Brittany Lincicome, Meg Mallon, Karin Sjodin (SWE), Angela Stanford, Whitney Wade 303; Shi Hyun Ahn (KOR), Na Ri Kim (KOR), Sydnee Michaels (am), Janice Moodie (SCO) 304; Jimin Kang (KOR) 305; Kim Hall 306; Michele Redman 307; Il Mi Chung (KOR), Hee-Won Han (KOR), Tiffany Lua (am) 308; Meena Lee (KOR) 311

2007 US Women's Open Championship *Southern Pines, SC* [6664–71]

Prize money: $3.1 million

1	Cristie Kerr	71-72-66-70—279	$560,000
2	Lorena Ochoa (MEX)	71-71-68-71—281	271,022
	Angela Park (BRA)	68-69-74-70—281	271,022
4	Se Ri Pak (KOR)	74-72-68-68—282	130,549
	Inbee Park (KOR)	69-73-71-69—282	130,549
6	Ji-Yai Shin (KOR)	70-69-71-74—284	103,581
7	Jee Young Lee (KOR)	72-71-71-71—285	93,031
8	Jeong Jang (KOR)	72-71-70-73—286	82,464
	Mi Hyun Kim (KOR)	71-75-70-70—286	82,464
10	Kyeong Bae (KOR)	74-71-72-70—287	66,177
	Julieta Granada (PAR)	70-69-75-73—287	66,177
	Ai Miyazato (JPN)	73-73-72-69—287	66,177
	Morgan Pressel	71-70-69-77—287	66,177
14	Joo Mi Kim (KOR)	70-73-70-75—288	55,032
	Brittany Lincicome	71-74-71-72—288	55,032
16	Paula Creamer	72-74-71-72—289	44,219
	Amy Hung (TPE)	70-69-75-75—289	44,219
	Jimin Kang (KOR)	73-73-73-70—289	44,219
	Birdie Kim (KOR)	73-70-71-75—289	44,219
	Catriona Matthew (SCO)	75-67-74-73—289	44,219
	Angela Stanford	72-71-73-73—289	44,219
22	Dina Ammaccapane	75-72-70-73—290	33,878
	Shiho Ohyama (JPN)	69-73-73-75—290	33,878
	Sakura Yokomine (JPN)	72-71-74-73—290	33,878
25	Hye Jung Choi (KOR)	77-68-70-76—291	24,767
25T	Il Mi Chung (KOR)	73-72-74-72—291	24,767
	Katherine Hull (AUS)	72-74-71-74—291	24,767
	Mi-Jeong Jeon (KOR)	76-72-73-70—291	24,767
	Young Kim (KOR)	75-71-72-73—291	24,767
	Seon Hwa Lee (KOR)	72-73-71-75—291	24,767
	Sherri Steinhauer	75-72-72-72—291	24,767
32	Laura Davies (ENG)	72-75-72-73—292	19,754
	Moire Dunn	73-71-74-74—292	19,754
	Annika Sörenstam (SWE)	70-77-72-73—292	19,754
35	Nicole Castrale	75-73-70-75—293	17,648
	Natalie Gulbis	74-72-74-73—293	17,648
	Charlotte Mayorkas	70-73-78-72—293	17,648
	Kris Tamulis	72-71-74-76—293	17,648
39	Shi Hyun Ahn (KOR)	70-72-76-76—294	14,954
	Erica Blasberg	74-69-75-76—294	14,954
	Laura Diaz	74-72-73-75—294	14,954
	Jennie Lee (am)	71-74-75-74—294	
	Janice Moodie (SCO)	71-76-74-73—294	14,954
	Becky Morgan (WAL)	75-72-73-74—294	14,954
	Jennifer Song (KOR) (am)	72-73-73-76—294	
46	Diana D'Alessio	73-70-77-75—295	12,268
	Wendy Doolan (AUS)	73-70-75-77—295	12,268
	Meena Lee (KOR)	71-75-74-75—295	12,268
	Sherri Turner	73-74-73-75—295	12,268

Other players who made the cut: Amanda Blumenherst (am), Jimin Jeong (KOR), Song-Hee Kim (KOR), Su A Kim (KOR), Leta Lindley, Teresa Lu (TPE), Amy Yang (KOR), Sung Ah Yim (KOR) 296; Katie Futcher, Candie Kung (TPE), Jane Park 297; Pat Hurst, In-Kyung Kim (KOR) 298; Allison Fouch, Karin Sjodin (SWE) 300; Aree Song (KOR) 301; Mina Harigae (am), Karine Icher (FRA) 305

2006 US Women's Open Championship *Newport CC, Newport, RI* [6564–71]

Prize money: $3.1 million

1	Annika Sörenstam (SWE)*	69-71-73-71—284	$560,000
2	Pat Hurst	69-71-75-69—284	335,000
Play off: 18 holes: Sörenstam 70, Hurst 74			
3	Se Ri Pak (KOR)	69-74-74-69—286	156,038
	Stacy Prammanasudh	72-71-71-72—286	156,038
	Michelle Wie	70-72-71-73—286	156,038
6	Juli Inkster	73-70-71-73—287	103,575
7	Brittany Lincicome	72-72-69-78—291	93,026
10	Amanda Blumenherst (am)	70-77-73-73—293	
	Sophie Gustafson (SWE)	72-72-71-78—293	66,174
	Young Kim (KOR)	75-69-75-74—293	66,174
	Jee Young Lee (KOR)	71-75-70-77—293	66,174
	Patricia Meunier-Lebouc (FRA)	72-73-73-75—293	66,174
	Jane Park (am)	69-73-75-76—293	
16	Paula Creamer	71-72-76-75—294	53,577
	Natalie Gulbis	76-71-74-73—294	53,577
	Sherri Turner	72-74-76-72—294	53,577
19	Catriona Matthew (SCO)	74-76-72-73—295	48,007
20	Lorena Ochoa (MEX)	71-73-77-75—296	41,654
	Gloria Park (KOR)	70-78-76-72—296	41,654
	Karen Stupples (ENG)	78-72-70-76—296	41,654
20T	Kristina Tucker (SWE)	72-74-74-76—296	41,654
24	Amy Hung (TPE)	76-72-77-72—297	32,873
	Lorie Kane (CAN)	73-72-75-77—297	32,873
	Sherri Steinhauer	72-75-72-78—297	32,873
	Shani Waugh (AUS)	77-72-73-75—297	32,873
28	Tracy Hanson	75-71-78-74—298	22,529
	Jeong Jang (KOR)	72-71-75-80—298	22,529
	Cristie Kerr	73-74-75-76—298	22,529
	Carin Koch (SWE)	74-73-73-78—298	22,529
	Candie Kung (TPE)	74-70-77-77—298	22,529
	Ai Miyazato (JPN)	74-75-70-79—298	22,529
	Becky Morgan (WAL)	70-74-77-77—298	22,529
	Suzann Pettersen (NOR)	73-74-75-76—298	22,529
	Morgan Pressel	76-74-75-73—298	22,529
37	Dawn Coe-Jones (CAN)	74-75-73-77—299	17,647
	Karrie Webb (AUS)	73-76-74-76—299	17,647
	Lindsey Wright (AUS)	74-73-76-76—299	17,647
	Heather Young	76-71-77-75—299	17,647
41	Maria Hjörth (SWE)	74-75-73-78—300	14,954
	Mi Hyun Kim (KOR)	75-72-75-78—300	14,954
	Yu Ping Lin (TPE)	76-74-75-75—300	14,954
	Aree Song (KOR)	77-72-79-72—300	14,954
	Wendy Ward	77-73-77-73—300	14,954

Other players who made the cut: Yuri Fudoh (JPN), Julieta Granada (PAR), Nancy Scranton 301; Dana Dormann, Seon Hwa Lee (KOR), Siew-Ai Lin (MAS), Alena Sharp (CAN), Karin Sjodin (SWE), Angela Stanford 302; Moira Dunn, Karine Icher (FRA) 303; Nicole Castrale, Silvia Cavalleri (ITA), Rosie Jones, Ashley Knoll (am), Diana Luna (MON) 304; Beth Bader 305; Dana Ammaccapane 306; Denise Munzlinger, Sung Ah Yin (KOR) 307; Kimberly Kim (am), Kim Saiki 309; Lynnette Brooky (NZL) 311

2005 US Women's Open Championship *Cherry Hill, CO* [6749–71]

Prize money: $1.5 million

1	Birdie Kim (KOR)	74-72-69-72—287	$560,000
2	Brittany Lang (am)	69-77-72-71—289	
	Morgan Pressel (am)	71-73-70-75—289	
4	Natalie Gulbis	70-75-74-71—290	272,723
	Lorie Kane (CAN)	74-71-76-69—290	272,723
6	Karine Icher (FRA)	69-75-75-72—291	116,310
	Young Jo (KOR)	74-71-70-76—291	116,310
	Candie Kung (TPE)	73-73-71-74—291	116,310
	Lorena Ochoa (MEX)	74-68-77-72—291	116,310
10	Cristie Kerr	74-71-72-75—292	80,523
	Angela Stanford	69-74-73-76—292	80,523
	Karen Stupples (ENG)	75-70-69-78—292	80,523
13	Tina Barrett	73-74-71-75—293	61,402
	Heather Bowie	77-73-69-74—293	61,402
	Jamie Hullett	75-72-70-76—293	61,402
	Soo Yun Kang (KOR)	74-74-74-71—293	61,402
	Paige MacKenzie (am)	75-75-69-74—293	
	Meg Mallon	71-74-75-73—293	61,402
19	Paula Creamer	74-69-72-79—294	47,480
	Rosie Jones	73-72-74-75—294	47,480
	Leta Lindley	73-76-73-72—294	47,480
	Liselotte Neumann (SWE)	70-75-73-76—294	47,480
23	Helen Alfredsson (SWE)	72-73-74-77—296	34,556
	Laura Diaz	75-73-72-76—296	34,556
23T	Sarah Huarte	74-76-73-73—296	34,556
	Gloria Park (KOR)	74-75-74-73—296	34,556
	Nicole Perrot (CHI)	70-70-78-78—296	34,556
	Jennifer Rosales (PHI)	72-76-73-75—296	34,556
	Annika Sörenstam (SWE)	71-75-73-77—296	34,556
	Michelle Wie (am)	69-73-72-82—296	
31	Rachel Hetherington (AUS)	74-69-76-78—297	23,479
	Mi Hyun Kim (KOR)	72-73-76-76—297	23,479
	Brittany Lincicome	74-74-78-71—297	23,479
	Catriona Matthew (SCO)	73-72-75-77—297	23,479
	Karrie Webb (AUS)	76-73-73-75—297	23,479
36	Kim Saiki	74-73-74-77—298	20,386
	Wendy Ward	74-74-75-75—298	20,386
38	Il Mi Chung (KOR)	75-71-76-77—299	17,939
	Johanna Head (ENG)	74-73-75-77—299	17,939
	Juli Inkster	77-71-75-76—299	17,939
	Young Kim (KOR)	73-73-70-83—299	17,939
	Sarah Lee (KOR)	79-70-75-75—299	17,939
	Amanda McCurdy (am)	75-75-71-78—299	17,939
	Aree Song (KOR)	77-70-72-80—299	17,939

Other players who made the cut: Se Ri Pak (KOR), Nancy Scranton 300; Beth Bader, Dorothy Delasin (PHI), Hee Won Han (KOR), 301; Arnie Cochran (am), Jeong Janh (KOR) 302; Katie Allison, Eva Dahllof (SWE), Stephanie Louden, Grace Park (KOR), Suzann Pettersen (NOR), Kris Tschetter 303; Katie Futcher, Sophie Gustafson (SWE), Kaori Higo (JPN), Carri Wood 304; Candy Hannemann (BRA) 307; Jean Bartholomew 309.

2004 US Women's Open Championship *The Orchards, South Hadley, MA* [6473–71]

Prize money: $3.1 million

1	Meg Mallon	73-69-67-65—274	$560,000
2	Annika Sörenstam (SWE)	71-68-70-67—276	335,000
3	Kelly Robbins	74-67-68-69—278	208,863
4	Jennifer Rosales (PHI)	70-67-69-75—281	145,547
5	Candie Kung (TPE)	70-68-74-70—282	111,173
	Michele Redman	70-72-73-67—282	111,173
7	Moira Dunn	73-67-72-71—283	86,744
	Pat Hurst	70-71-71-71—283	86,744
	Jeong Jang (KOR)	72-74-71-66—283	86,744
10	Michelle Ellis (Aus)	70-69-72-73—284	68,813
	Carin Koch (SWE)	72-67-75-70—284	68,813
	Rachel Teske (AUS)	71-69-70-74—284	68,813
13	Paula Creamer (am)	72-69-72-72—285	
	Patricia Meunier-Labouc (FRA)	67-75-74-69—285	60,602
	Michelle Wie (am)	71-70-71-73—285	
16	Mi Hyun Kim (KOR)	76-68-71-71—286	54,052
	Suzann Pettersen (NOR)	74-72-71-69—286	54,052
	Karrie Webb (AUS)	72-71-71-72—286	54,052
19	Catriona Matthew (SCO)	73-71-72-71—287	48,432
20	Dawn Coe-Jones (CAN)	71-73-72-72—288	38,660
20T	Kate Golden	74-71-72-71—288	38,660
	Johanna Head (ENG)	76-69-70-73—288	38,660
	Rosie Jones	74-72-72-70—288	38,660
	Young Kim (KOR)	71-73-76-68—288	38,660
	Kim Saiki	70-68-74-76—288	38,660
	Liselotte Neumann (SWE)	72-72-72-72—288	38,660
27	Beth Daniel	69-74-71-75—289	29,195
	Cristie Kerr	73-71-74-71—289	29,195
29	Shi Hyun Ahn (KOR)	73-71-72-74—290	24,533
	Lorie Kane (CAN)	75-70-72-73—290	24,533
	Deb Richard	71-73-72-74—290	24,533
32	Allison Hanna	71-75-74-71—291	20,539
	Becky Morgan (WAL)	71-74-73-73—291	20,539
	Se Ri Pak (KOR)	70-76-71-74—291	20,539
	Sherri Steinhauer	74-71-73-73—291	20,539
	Karen Stupples (ENG)	71-72-77-71—291	20,539
37	Jenna Daniels	76-71-72-73—292	16,897
	AJ Easthorne (CAN)	73-72-75-72—292	16,897
	Natalie Gulbis	73-71-75-73—292	16,897
	Jamie Hullett	72-74-74-72—292	16,897
	Christina Kim	74-71-76-71—292	16,897
	Jill McGill	71-75-71-75—292	16,897
	Gloria Park (KOR)	76-71-73-72—292	16,897

Other players who made the cut: Donna Andrews, Laura Diaz, Jennifer Greggain, Ji-Hee Lee, Mhairi McKay (SCO), Lorena Ochoa (MEX) 293; Jennie Lee (am) 294; Katherine Hull 295; Tina Barrett, Catherine Cartwright, Hee-Won Han (KOR) 296; Brittany Lincicome (am) 297; Loraine Lambert, Aree Song (KOR) 298; Liz Earley, Allison Finney, Juli Inkster 299; Mee Lee (KOR), Seol-An Jeon (KOR), Courtney Swaim 300; Hilary Lunke, Grace Park (KOR) 301; Li Ying Ye (CHN) 304.

2003 US Women's Open Championship *Pumpkin Ridge GC, North Plains, OR* [6509–71]

Prize money: $3.1 million

1	Hilary Lunke*	71-69-68-75—283	$560,000
2	Kelly Robbins	74-69-71-69—283	272,004
	Angela Stanford	70-70-69-74—283	272,004

Play-off rounds: Hilary Lunke 70, Angela Stanford 71, Kelly Robbins 73

4	Annika Sörenstam (SWE)	72-72-67-73—284	150,994
5	Aree Song (am)	70-73-68-74—285	
6	Jeong Jang (KOR)	73-69-69-75—286	115,333
	Mhairi McKay (SCO)	66-70-75-75—286	115,333
8	Juli Inkster	69-71-74-73—287	97,363
9	Rosie Jones	70-72-73-73—288	90,241
10	Grace Park (KOR)	72-76-73-68—289	79,243
	Suzann Pettersen (NOR)	76-69-69-75—289	79,243
12	Donna Andrews	69-72-72-77—290	71,362
13	Laura Diaz	71-71-74-76—292	56,500
	Natalie Gulbis	73-69-72-78—292	56,500
	Cristie Kerr	72-73-73-74—292	56,500
	Patricia Meunier-Lebouc (FRA)	73-69-74-76—292	56,500
	Lorena Ochoa (MEX)	71-75-72-74—292	56,500
	Jennifer Rosales (PHI)	74-69-76-73—292	56,500
	Rachel Teske (AUS)	71-73-72-76—292	56,500
20	Beth Daniel	73-69-77-74—293	43,491
20T	Yuri Fudoh (JPN)	74-72-75-72—293	43,491
22	Lorie Kane (CAN)	73-75-73-73—294	36,575
	Christina Kim	74-74-72-74—294	36,575
	Leta Lindley	73-69-77-75—294	36,575
	Catriona Matthew (SCO)	74-70-76-74—294	36,575
26	Danielle Ammaccapane	74-74-73-74—295	28,354
	Dorothy Delasin (PHI)	79-70-76-70—295	2,8354
	Kelli Kuehne	72-74-75-74—295	28,354
	Paula Marti (ESP)	71-76-76-72—295	28,354
30	Ashli Bunch	71-73-77-75—296	22,678
	Annette DeLuca	71-73-78-74—296	22,678
	Elizabeth Janangelo (am)	75-73-73-75—296	
	Mi-Hyun Kim (KOR)	73-73-73-77—296	22,678
	Jane Park (am)	76-73-74-73—296	
35	Candy Hannemann (BRA)	75-69-73-80—297	20,360
	Stephanie Louden	71-74-77-75—297	20,360
	Guilia Sergas (ITA)	70-74-79-74—297	20,360
	Kirsty Taylor (ENG)	71-75-73-78—297	20,360
39	Michele Redman	71-74-74-79—298	18,783
	Michelle Wie (am)	73-73-76-76—298	

Other players who made the cut: Heather Bowie, Karen Stupples (ENG) 299; Beth Bauer, Hee-Won Han (KOR), Jamie Hullett, Emilee Klein, Becky Morgan (WAL), Karen Weiss 300; Sherri Turner 301; Se Ri Pak (KOR) 302; Leigh Ann Hardin (am) 303; Morgan Pressel (am) 304; Alison Nicholas (ENG), Suzanne Strudwick (ENG), Michelle Vinieratos 305; Yu Ping Lin (TPE) 306; Mollie Fankhauser (am) 307; Irene Cho (am) 308; Mardi Lunn (AUS) 309

US Women's Open History

Year	Winner	Runner-up	Venue	Score
1946	P Berg	B Jamieson	Spokane	5 and 4

Changed to strokeplay

Year	Winner	Venue	Score
1947	B Jamieson	Greensboro	300
1948	B Zaharias	Atlantic City	300
1949	L Suggs	Maryland	291
1950	B Zaharias	Wichita	291
1951	B Rawls	Atlanta	294
1952	L Suggs	Bala, PA	284
1953	B Rawls*	Rochester, NY	302
After a play-off with J Pung 71-77			
1954	B Zaharias	Peabody, MA	291
1955	F Crocker	Wichita	299
1956	K Cornelius*	Duluth	302
After a play-off with B McIntire (am) 75-82			
1957	B Rawls	Mamaroneck	299
1958	M Wright	Bloomfield Hills, MI	290
1959	M Wright	Pittsburgh, PA	287
1960	B Rawls	Worchester, MA	292
1961	M Wright	Springfield, NJ	293
1962	M Lindstrom	Myrtle Beach	301
1963	M Mills	Kenwood	289
1964	M Wright*	San Diego	290
After a play-off with R Jessen 70-72			

US Women's Open History *continued*

Year	Winner	Venue	Score
1965	C Mann	Northfield, NJ	290
1966	S Spuzich	Hazeltine National, MN	297
1967	C Lacoste (FRA) (am)	Hot Springs, VA	294
1968	S Berning	Moselem Springs, PA	289
1969	D Caponi	Scenic-Hills	294
1970	D Caponi	Muskogee, OK	287
1971	J Gunderson-Carner	Erie, PA	288
1972	S Berning	Mamaroneck, NY	299
1973	S Berning	Rochester, NY	290
1974	S Haynie	La Grange, IL	295
1975	S Palmer	Northfield, NJ	295
1976	J Carner*	Springfield, PA	292
**After a play-off: Carner 76, S Palmer 78*			
1977	H Stacy	Hazeltine, MN	292
1978	H Stacy	Indianapolis	299
1979	J Britz	Brooklawn, CN	284
1980	A Alcott	Richland, TN	280
1981	P Bradley	La Grange, IL	279
1982	J Alex	Del Paso, Sacramento, CA	283
1983	J Stephenson (AUS)	Broken Arrow, OK	290
1984	H Stacy	Salem, MA	290
1985	K Baker	Baltusrol, NJ	280
1986	J Geddes*	NCR	287
**After a play-off with Sally Little*			
1987	L Davies (ENG)*	Plainfield	285
**After a play-off: Davies 71, A Okamoto 73, J Carner 74*			
1988	L Neumann (SWE)	Baltimore	277
1989	B King	Indianwood, MI	278
1990	B King	Atlanta Athletic Club, GA	284
1991	M Mallon	Colonial, TX	283
1992	P Sheehan*	Oakmont, PA	280
**After a play-off: Sheehan 72, J Inkster 74*			
1993	L Merton	Crooked Stick	280
1994	P Sheehan	Indianwood, MI	277
1995	A Sörenstam (SWE)	The Broadmore, CO	278
1996	A Sörenstam (SWE)	Pine Needles Lodge, NC	272
1997	A Nicholas (ENG)	Pumpkin Ridge, OR	274
1998	SR Pak (KOR)*	Blackwolf Run, WI	290
**After a play-off: Pak 5,3; J Chausiriporn (am) 5,4*			
1999	J Inkster	Old Waverley, West Point, MS	272
2000	K Webb (AUS)	Merit Club, Libertyville, IL	282
2001	K Webb (AUS)	Pine Needles Lodge & GC, NC	273
2002	J Inkster	Prairie Dunes, KS	276
2003	H Lunke*	Pumpkin Ridge GC, OR	283
**After a play-off: Lunke 70, A Stanford 71, K Robins 73*			
2004	M Mallon	The Orchards, S Hadley, MA	274
2005	B Kim (KOR)	Cherry Hills CC, CO	287
2006	A Sörenstam (SWE)*	Newport CC, RI	284
**After a play-off: Sörenstam 70, P Hurst 74*			
2007	C Kerr	Southern Pines, NC	279
2008	I Park (KOR)	Interlachen, MN	283
2009	E-H Ji (KOR)	Saucon Valley, PA	284
2010	P Creamer	Oakmont, PA	281
2011	S Y Ryu (KOR)*	The Broadmoor, CO	281
**Beat H K Seo (KOR) at the third extra hole*			
2012	N Y Choi (KOR)	Blackwolf Run, Kohler, WI	281

The 58th LPGA Championship

For China's Shanshan Feng a chapter of golfing history

With a population of 1.3 billion, it was always likely a golfer from China, the world's most populous country, would win a major championship sooner rather than later. The honour duly fell to Shanshan Feng at Locust Hill country club in Rochester, New York, when the 22-year-old produced a thrilling closing round of 67 at the LPGA Championship to post the winning total of 282, six under par, collect the first prize of $375,000 and earn a spot in the record books.

Coached in Florida by Gary Gilchrist, who also teaches women's world No 1 Yani Tseng, Feng had never finished in the top 20 at a major before her success in New York. The daughter of a keen golfer who works for the Chinese Golf Association in Guangzhou, Feng attributed her success at the LPGA to finally delivering a short game on a par with her reliable ball striking. "I think I've always been a good ball striker," she said, "but my short game is usually a little weak. So I focused on practising chipping and putting and I think it worked."

©Getty Images

Shanshan Feng

Previously a winner on the Ladies' European Tour – the World Ladies Championship at Mission Hills in China – as well as on the Japanese LPGA, Feng's first victory in America was partly motivated by her friendship with five time major winner Tseng, who hails from Taiwan. The pair had competed against one another for nearly ten years, ever since their junior days in Asia, and the Chinese woman wanted to emulate her rival. "I've always been chasing her," added Feng. "Maybe now I got a little closer."

As pleased as she was for the sake of her own career and what challenges the future may hold, it wasn't lost on Feng that her victory would also set an example for the next generation of golfers in China. Bearing in mind that the first golf course in China didn't open until 1984 – just five years before Shanshan was born – the LPGA champion is certain others from her country, where estimates of the number of players range from 300,000 to 3 million, will follow in her footsteps.

"I would say, first of all, I was really, really, happy that I won the tournament," she recalled. "I still can't believe it. I think it gave me a lot more confidence. I believe I can win again in the future. And hopefully it's going to help golf in China because I want to be a model for the other juniors to follow in my steps and get on the LPGA.

"There are many good young players in China and we now have our own Chinese Tour, for both ladies and men. They are trying to give exemptions to the juniors and amateurs, trying to let them have more chances to play in big tournaments. We also have the national golf team in China. I think it's going to help. Hopefully my win is going to help a little bit too."

Asked how she reacted to becoming the first Chinese winner of a major, Feng said: "It was amazing. I think I'm just lucky. There are good players from China, young players, right now. I became the first one, but I'm sure there will be a second, a third and then more people winning in the States, winning more majors. My parents told me that Asians are good at controlling small things. I don't know if that's true or not. But I will say if Koreans can do it, the Chinese can do it, and golf in China is really growing up and getting more popular. I believe, in the future, China will be one of the strongest countries in golf."

Known to her friends as Jenny, Feng held off notable challenges to win by two strokes from Stacy Lewis, who narrowly failed to win her third successive stroke-play event on the LPGA Tour, Mika Miyazato, Suzann Pettersen and third-round leader Eun-Hee Ji. Having started the final day three shots off the pace, Feng kept her card bogey free and reeled off five birdies. Her accuracy off the tee helped locate 11 out of 14 fairways and her iron play was good enough to find 16 greens in regulation. True, she was bunkered at the par 5 17th, but an approach shot struck within 12 feet of the cup set up another birdie. Having been left to her own devices for much of the final day, Feng noticed that suddenly around a dozen journalists followed her progress over the closing holes. "OK, I thought, now maybe I have a chance to win ..."

Like Tseng and Se Ri Pak before her, Shanshan's first success on the LPGA came at the LPGA Championship, though she wasn't causing too many ripples on the opening day when she balanced dropped shots at the 13th and 18th with birdies at the second and 16th to match the par of 72. The early pacesetters on a tricky lay-out toughened by thick rough were Spain's Beatriz Recari, Italy's Giulia Sergas and Ryann O'Toole from the USA, who all signed for three-under-par scores of 69. No one on the first page of the leaderboard, however, sparked as much curiosity as Cheyenne Woods, who teed up in her first professional event. The 21-year-old niece of Tiger Woods, reported her uncle had sent her encouraging text messages. "He said to just trust my abilities, have fun and be patient," she said after shooting 75.

There was a more orthodox look about the leaders by the end of Friday's second round – Feng fell back with a round of 73 blighted by four bogeys – when Pak, Paula Creamer and Lewis were among the contenders. Pak was in pole position with a one shot advantage thanks to a 71 for 141 which made light of a shoulder injury. In breezy conditions, the five time major champion coped as well as anyone with the narrow targets from the tee. "You had to use really smart thinking," she said. "If you miss the fairway, the next shot is from the rough."

> "I focused on my chipping and putting and it worked."
>
> *Shanshan Feng on her victory at Locust Hill*

For Creamer, who relished a test where par was a decent score, it also turned out to be an exceptionally emotional tournament. Each time she walked up the 18th, memories of her late grandfather, 'Pops', came flooding back. "I was dreading this week in my mind ever since he passed away," Creamer revealed. "He never missed this event. That's been the hard part for me. Every time I walk up to the 18th green, I get tears in my eyes, because I see him right behind the green." Not that Creamer was the only player in the field wiping away the tears. Grace Park also struggled to contain her emotions after announcing her retirement from competition on the LPGA at the age of 33.

The big move on Saturday was made by Ji, winner of the US Women's Open at Oakmont, who bettered 70 for the second day running. Her score of 69 for 212, three under, was the leading mark after 54 holes. On a day when heavy rain caused a suspension of play for more than two hours, Ji, 26, again showed her liking for a course which provided her first win on the LPGA. "Always when I come back here, I have very good memories," said Ji, who reeled off successive birdies at the 16th and 17th.

As the rain abated and the temperature rose in the afternoon, the test proved easier than during the first two rounds with the average score nearly three strokes lower. Feng, for example, improved on her second round score of 73 with 70, largely thanks to three birdies over the closing four holes. The closest challenger to Ji was Karrie Webb, winner of seven majors, and second only to Annika Sörenstam on the all time money list. She moved into contention with an outstanding round of 68 and promptly rebuked those who questioned her credentials at the age of 37. "Well, when Phil Mickelson was 37 do you think people were asking him that?" she said. "So Tiger Woods is 36 and no one is asking him that? I still have the same drive as those two guys. I don't put the hours in just to be out here to make up the numbers."

Playing in the fourth from last group on Sunday – only 13 players were under par – Feng, who started on one under, was very much an outside bet for the trophy until she reeled off birdies at the second, sixth and eighth holes to reach the turn in just 32 blows. Even at that point, the only Chinese golfer on the LPGA was philosophical about her prospects. "For me, I never thought, 'I must win'," she recalled. "I knew I was three behind, so I knew I had a chance. I was focusing on very shot. If I win, I win. If I don't, I don't. It just worked out."

With a touch of Zen in her locker, Feng made two more birdies at the 12th (which moved her into a tie at the top with Pettersen) and 17th to reach six under. Even then she had work to do on the demanding home hole, splitting the 18th fairway before missing the green. However, she hit an exquisite chip for her third shot inside a couple of feet to make par. Pettersen, meanwhile, drove offline at both the 13th and 14th holes and her hopes disappeared with a brace of bogeys.

In the end, Lewis, who carded a steady 70, Pettersen, 70, Miyazato, 69, and Ji, 72, all had to settle for a share of second place behind China's first major winner. A few days later in San Francisco at the US Open, Andy Zhang, 14, who moved from China to America when he was ten, became the youngest golfer to compete in a men's major since 1865. Within the space of a week, the future of golf had taken on a new shape.

Michael Aitken

First Round	Second Round	Third Round	Fourth Round
–3 Ryann O'Toole	–3 Se Ri Pak	–4 Eun-Hee Ji	–6 Shanshan Feng
–3 Giulia Sergas	–2 Inbee Park	–3 Karrie Webb	–4 Stacy Lewis
–3 Beatriz Recari	–2 Sandra Gal	–2 Giulia Sergas	–4 Mika Miyazato
–2 Paula Creamer	–2 Paula Creamer	–2 Stacy Lewis	–4 Suzann Pettersen
–2 Ai Miyazato	–2 Mika Miyazato	–2 Suzann Pettersen	–4 Eun-Hee Ji
–2 Jeong Jang	–1 Eun-Hee Ji	–2 Inbee Park	–3 Gerina Piller
–2 Mika Miyazato	–1 Mi Jung Hur	–1 Shanshan Feng	–3 Ai Miyazato
–3 Cristie Kerr	–1 So Yeon Ryu	–1 Jennifer Johnson	–3 Karrie Webb
–2 Se Ri Pak	–1 Sydney Michaels	–1 Sun Young Yoo	–2 Paula Creamer
–2 Na Yeon Choi	–1 Suzann Pettersen	–1 Paula Creamer	–2 Giulia Sergas

LPGA Championship *Locust Hill, Pittsford, NY* June 7–10 [6534–72]

Prize Money: $2.5 million. Field of 143 players, of whom 73 made the half-way cut on 151 or less.

Players are of American nationality unless stated

1	Shanshan Feng (CHN)	72-73-70-67—282	$375,000
2	Eun-Hee Ji (KOR)	75-68-69-72—284	158,443
	Suzann Pettersen (NOR)	71-72-71-70—284	158,443
	Stacy Lewis	72-72-70-70—284	158,443
	Mika Miyazato (JPN)	70-72-73-69—284	158,443
6	Karrie Webb (AUS)	74-71-68-72—285	73,285
	Ai Miyazato (JPN)	70-74-73-68—285	73,285
	Gerina Piller	74-71-72-68—285	73,285
9	Paula Creamer	70-72-73-71—286	51,742
	Giulia Sergas (ITA)	69-76-69-72—286	51,742
	Inbee Park (KOR)	72-70-72-72—286	51,742
12	Cristie Kerr	70-76-70-71—287	42,956
	Sandra Gal (GER)	71-71-75-70—287	42,956
14	Hee Young Park (KOR)	77-70-73-68—288	39,028
15	Jeong Jang (KOR)	70-74-71-74—289	33,960
	Karin Sjodin (SWE)	75-69-73-72—289	33,960
	Sun Young Yoo (KOR)	72-72-71-74—289	33,960
	Mina Harigae	74-72-74-69—289	33,960
19	Nicole Castrale	76-74-70-70—290	28,638
	Se Ri Pak (KOR)	70-71-76-73—290	28,638
	Jenny Shin (KOR)	71-75-71-73—290	28,638
	Jennifer Johnson	73-71-71-75—290	28,638
23	Marcy Hart	72-75-73-71—291	25,597
	Christel Boeljon (NED)	74-74-73-70—291	25,597
	Brittany Lincicome	76-73-73-70—292	22,872
25	I K Kim (KOR)	73-73-73-73—292	22,872
	Lizette Salas	74-70-73-75—292	22,872
	So Yeon Ryu (KOR)	73-70-74-75—292	22,872
29	Candie Kung (TPE)	71-77-75-70—293	20,655
30	Sophie Gustafson (SWE)	73-72-74-75—294	18,015
	Mo Martin	71-77-77-69—294	18,015
	Mi Jung Hur (KOR)	74-69-77-74—294	18,015
	Mariajo Uribe (COL)	74-76-71-73—294	18,015
	Sydnee Michaels	72-71-72-79—294	18,015
	Lexi Thompson	74-72-74-74—294	18,015
36	Catriona Matthew (SCO)	75-72-76-72—295	13,263
	Sarah Jane Smith (AUS)	75-72-77-71—295	13,263
	Alison Walshe	73-77-73-72—295	13,263
	Chella Choi (KOR)	75-74-74-72—295	13,263
	Pornanong Phatlum (THA)	75-74-72-74—295	13,263
	Ryann O'Toole	69-76-75-75—295	13,263
	Jodi Ewart (ENG)	75-72-72-76—295	13,263
	Haru Nomura (JPN)	74-77-70-74—295	13,263
	Maude-Aimee Leblanc (CAN)	72-73-75-75—295	13,263
45	Karine Icher (FRA)	75-75-74-72—296	9,820
	Leta Lindley	78-73-72-73—296	9,820
	Morgan Pressel	74-75-69-78—296	9,820
	Ji Young Oh (KOR)	77-72-74-73—296	9,820
	Hee-Won Han (KOR)	74-74-73-75—296	9,820
	Beatriz Recari (ESP)	69-78-75-74—296	9,820
51	Katherine Hull (AUS)	75-76-73-73—297	8,363
	Becky Morgan (WAL)	75-73-77-72—297	8,363
	Haeji Kang (KOR)	77-73-73-74—297	8,363
54	Karen Stupples (ENG)	76-75-74-73—298	7,857
55	Katie Futcher	74-77-76-72—299	7,349
	Amelia Lewis	73-75-77-74—299	7,349
	Jessica Korda	74-74-79-72—299	7,349

LPGA Championship *continued*

58	Anna Nordqvist (SWE)	74-77-72-77—300	6,842
59	Amy Hung (TPE)	76-75-73-77—301	6,379
	Yani Tseng (TPE)	76-75-74-76—301	6,379
	Belen Mozo (ESP)	74-76-75-76—301	6,379
62	Alena Sharp (CAN)	77-71-78-76—302	5,829
	Kris Tamulis	74-74-80-74—302	5,829
	Brittany Lang	72-75-76-79—302	5,829
	Pat Hurst	74-76-75-77—302	5,829
	Dewi Claire Schreefel (NED)	76-74-81-71—302	5,829
67	Jennifer Rosales (PHI)	73-77-78-75—303	5,322
	Ilhee Lee (KOR)	76-75-73-79—303	5,322
	Meaghan Francella	76-74-73-80—303	5,322
70	Taylor Coutu	73-74-77-80—304	5,069
71	Stephanie Louden	73-78-80-74—305	4,974
	Grace Park (KOR)	75-75-76-79—305	4,974
DQ	Na Yeon Choi	70-73-75—218	

The following players missed the cut:

74	Angela Stanford	76-76—152
	Meena Lee (KOR)	73-79—152
	Lorie Kane (CAN)	71-81—152
	Wendy Doolan (AUS)	75-77—152
	Jee Young Lee (KOR)	77-75—152
	Kristy McPherson	75-77—152
	Angela Oh	74-78—152
	Christine Song	72-80—152
	Stephanie Sherlock (CAN)	77-75—152
	Danielle Kang	76-76—152
	Caroline Hedwall (SWE)	77-75—152
85	Christina Kim	76-77—153
	Meredith Duncan	77-76—153
	Seon Hwa Lee (KOR)	80-73—153
	Natalie Gulbis	76-77—153
	Na On Min (KOR)	75-78—153
	Momoko Ueda (JPN)	74-79—153
	Amy Yang (KOR)	76-77—153
	Azahara Muñoz (ESP)	75-78—153
	Maria Hernandez (ESP)	79-74—153
	Amanda Blumenherst	77-76—153
	Kathleen Ekey	77-76—153
85T	Hee Kyung Seo (KOR)	76-77—153
	Rebecca Lee-Bentham (CAN)	77-76—153
98	Reilley Rankin	78-76—154
	Stacy Prammanasudh	78-76—154
	Mindy Kim	77-77—154
	Tiffany Joh	75-79—154
	Dori Carter	73-81—154
	Jacqui Concolino	78-76—154
	Victoria Tanco (ARG)	77-77—154
105	Moira Dunn	76-79—155
	Jimin Kang (KOR)	73-82—155
	Julieta Granada (PAR)	76-79—155
	Irene Cho	75-80—155
	Tanya Dergal (MEX)	75-80—155
	Jennifer Song	76-79—155
111	Beth Bader	78-78—156
	Ashli Bunch	76-80—156
	Heather Bowie-Young	74-82—156
	Laura Davies (ENG)	79-77—156
	Lisa Ferrero	78-78—156
	Sandra Changkija	74-82—156
	Michelle Wie	74-82—156
	Pernilla Lindberg (SWE)	76-80—156
111T	Jane Rah	77-79—156
	Karlin Beck	73-83—156
121	Jennifer Gleason	84-73—157
	Janice Moodie (SCO)	78-79—157
	Jane Park	80-77—157
	Hannah Yun	76-81—157
125	Wendy Ward	79-79—158
	Diana D'Alessio	80-78—158
	Paige Mackenzie	80-78—158
	Jennie Lee	80-78—158
	Cydney Clanton	78-80—158
	Numa Gulyanamitta (THA)	78-80—158
131	Laura Diaz	84-75—159
	Vicky Hurst	79-80—159
	Danah Bordner	79-80—159
134	Maria Hjorth (SWE)	81-79—160
	Veronica Felibert (COL)	77-83—160
	Ayaka Kaneko (JPN)	80-80—160
137	Jin Young Pak (KOR)	78-83—161
	Stephanie Kono	85-76—161
139	Jessica Shepley	82-81—163
	Elisa Serramia	83-80—163
141	Anna Grzebien	83-84—167
142	Song-Hee Kim (KOR)	82-86—168
	Minea Blomqvist (FIN)	84-84 WD

Sörenstam still well clear in LPGA career money

Annika Sörenstam may have retired from competitive golf but she still has a healthy lead in the LPGA Career Money list.

The Swedish player earned $22,573,192 from the 303 events she played on Tour and at the end of 2012 was over $5 million ahead of her nearest rival, Australia's Karrie Webb.

Webb, who has already chalked up appearances in 370 tournaments, has amassed $17,402,217 and is still playing, unlike third place Lorena Ochoa of Mexico whose total prize-money earned from 175 tournaments is $14,863,331.

Top American is Cristie Kerr in fourth place with over $14 million, top Asian Se Ri Pak with close to $12 million and leading British golfer on the list is Laura Davies with $8,843,294 banked.

2011 McDonald's LPGA Championship *Locust Hill, Pitsford, NY* [6534–72]

Prize money: $2.5 million

1	Yani Tseng (TPE)	66-70-67-66—269	$375,000
2	Morgan Pressel	69-69-70-71—279	228,695
3	Suzann Pettersen (NOR)	72-72-69-67—280	132,512
	Paula Creamer	67-72-72-69—280	132,512
	Cristie Kerr	72-72-67-69—280	132,512
6	Meena Lee (KOR)	68-73-70-71—282	77,630
	Stacy Lewis	69-72-70-71—282	77,630
8	Maria Hjörth (SWE)	71-71-70-71—283	53,840
	Pat Hurst	70-67-75-71—283	53,840
	Mika Miyazato (JPN)	72-72-68-71—283	53,840
	Azahara Muñoz (ESP)	70-71-71-71—283	53,840
12	Amy Yang (KOR)	70-69-74-71—284	42,445
	I K Kim (KOR)	73-70-69-72—284	42,445
14	Amy Hung (TPE)	69-73-73-70—285	33,765
	Heather Bowie Young	72-70-73-70—285	33,765
	Inbee Park (KOR)	73-69-71-72—285	33,765
	Katie Futcher	75-68-69-73—285	33,765
	Hee Young Park (KOR)	69-69-72-75—285	33,765
	Cindy LaCrosse	70-69-69-77—285	33,765
20	Brittany Lincicome	74-72-71-69—286	26,795
	Sun Young Yoo (KOR)	73-72-72-69—286	26,795
20T	Paige Mackenzie	72-73-70-71—286	26,795
	Karrie Webb (AUS)	74-69-71-72—286	26,795
	Candie Kung (TPE)	71-71-71-73—286	26,795
25	Hee-Won Han (KOR)	71-72-74-70—287	22,162
	Anna Nordqvist (SWE)	73-70-74-70—287	22,162
	Jimin Kang (KOR)	71-70-73-73—287	22,162
	Pornanong Phatlum (THA)	71-72-71-73—287	22,162
	Tiffany Joh	71-70-72-74—287	22,162
30	Jennifer Song (KOR)	72-72-72-72—288	18,531
	Reilley Rankin	73-68-74-73—288	18,531
	Angela Stanford	68-72-74-74—288	18,531
	Momoko Ueda (JPN)	72-69-71-76—288	18,531
34	Karen Stupples (ENG)	72-74-78-65—289	14,232
	M J Hur (KOR)	70-75-76-68—289	14,232
	Jiyai Shin (KOR)	75-71-73-70—289	14,232
	Se Ri Pak (KOR)	78-68-72-71—289	14,232
	Juli Inkster	74-70-73-72—289	14,232
	Catriona Matthew (SCO)	73-69-75-72—289	14,232
	Michele Redman	73-70-73-73—289	14,232
	Yoo Kyeong Kim (KOR)	72-72-71-74—289	14,232
	Hee Kyung Seo (KOR)	71-73-71-74—289	14,232

Other players who made the cut: Taylor Leon, Eun-Hee Ji (KOR), Mindy Kim (KOR), Mi Hyun Kim (KOR), Na Yeon Choi (KOR), Jennifer Johnson, Karin Sjodin (SWE) 290; Shanshan Feng (CHN), Kristy McPherson, Sarah Jane Smith, Julieta Granada (PAR), Sarah Kemp (AUS), Beatriz Recari (ESP), Danielle Kang (am) 291; Becky Morgan (WAL), Christel Boeljon (NED), Sophie Gustafson (SWE), Ryann O'Toole, Leta Lindley, Dewi Claire Schreefel (NED), Lorie Kane (CAN), Laura Davies (ENG), Jeehae Lee (KOR), Stacy Prammanasudh, Katherine Hull (AUS) 292; Jennie Lee, Jenny Shin (KOR), Natalie Gulbis, Minea Blomqvist (FIN) 293; Kyeong Bae (KOR), Michelle Wie, Haeji Kang (KOR) 294; Sherri Steinhauer, Silvia Cavalleri (ITA) 295; Grace Park (KOR) 296; Diana D'Alessio 301

2010 McDonald's LPGA Championship *Locust Hill, Pitsford, NY* [6506–72]

Prize money: $2.25 million

1	Cristie Kerr	68-66-69-66—269	$337,500
2	Song-Hee Kim (KOR)	72-71-69-69—281	207,790
3	Ai Miyazato (JPN)	76-71-70-66—283	133,672
	Jiyai Shin (KOR)	72-70-70-71—283	133,672
5	In-Kyung Kim (KOR)	72-70-72-70—284	85,323
	Karriev Webb (AUS)	72-72-69-71—284	85,323
7	Meaghann Francella	73-71-70-71—285	54,323
	Jimin Kang (KOR)	74-67-70-74—285	54,323
	Inbee Park (KOR)	69-70-75-71—285	54,323
	Morgan Pressel	72-76-68-69—285	54,323
11	Azahara Muñoz (ESP)	72-69-70-75—286	41,238
	Suzann Pettersen (NOR)	74-72-69-71—286	41,238
13	Mika Miyazato (JPN)	69-70-72-76—287	37,314
14	Stacy Lewis	68-74-73-73—288	31,398
	Brittany Lincicome	71-69-75-73—288	31,398
	Sarah Jane Smith	74-71-69-74—288	31,398
	Lindsey Wright (AUS)	69-74-72-73—288	31,398
	Amy Yang (KOR)	73-67-76-72—288	31,398
19	Meena Lee (KOR)	71-76-74-68—289	24,800
	Seon Hwa Lee (KOR)	68-74-73-74—289	24,800
	Na On Min (KOR)	74-67-74-74—289	24,800
	Karin Sjodin (SWE)	74-73-74-68—289	24,800
	Yani Tseng (TPE)	75-71-70-73—289	24,800
19T	Michelle Wie	72-74-73-70—289	24,800
25	Natalie Gulbis	72-75-71-72—290	18,669
	Sophie Gustafson (SWE)	73-75-72-70—290	18,669
	Jeong Jang (KOR)	71-73-75-71—290	18,669
	Christina Kim	70-76-70-74—290	18,669
	Anna Nordqvist (SWE)	73-72-73-72—290	18,669
	Angela Stanford	74-74-74-68—290	18,669
	Sakura Yokomine (JPN)	71-72-73-74—290	18,669
	Sun Young Yoo (KOR)	72-75-71-72—290	18,669
	Heather Bowie Young	70-77-74-69—290	18,669
34	Shi Hyun Ahn (KOR)	74-71-72-74—291	13,182
	Chie Arimura (JPN)	73-72-73-73—291	13,182
	Katherine Hull (AUS)	74-73-76-68—291	13,182
	Amy Hung (TPE)	72-76-73-70—291	13,182
	M J Hur (KOR)	72-73-73-73—291	13,182
	Haeji Kang (KOR)	73-73-73-72—291	13,182
	Catriona Matthew (SCO)	74-71-69-77—291	13,182
	Jennifer Rosales (PHI)	73-74-72-72—291	13,182
42	Helen Alfredsson (SWE)	75-73-69-75—292	10,079
	Paula Creamer	71-72-74-75—292	10,079
	Mi Hyun Kim (KOR)	75-73-75-69—292	10,079
	Brittany Lang	75-71-71-75—292	10,079
	Michele Redman	74-67-79-72—292	10,079

Other players who made the cut: Chelia Choi (KOR), Laura Davies (ENG), Hee-Won Han (KOR), Yoo Kyeong Kim (KOR), Janice Moodie (SCO), Paola Moreno (COL), Alena Sharp (CAN) 293; Shanshan Feng (CHN), Vicky Hurst, Soo-Yun Kang (KOR), Sherri Steinhauer, Gloria Park (KOR) 294; Irene Cho, Mina Harigae, Teresa Lu (TPE) 295; Silvia Cavalleri (ITA), Juli Inkster 296; Louise Friberg (SWE), Lorie Kane (CAN), Stacy Prammanasudh 297; Louise Stahle (SWE), Mariajo Uribe (COL), Wendy Ward, Leah Wigger 298; Amanda Blumenherst 299; Candie Kung (TPE) 301; Giulia Sergas (ITA) 306

2009 McDonald's LPGA Championship *Bulle Rock, Havre de Grace, MD* [6641–72]

Prize money: $2 million

1	Anna Nordqvist (SWE)	66-70-69-68—273	$300,000
2	Lindsey Wright (AUS)	70-68-69-70—277	182,950
3	Jiyai Shin (KOR)	73-68-69-68—278	132,717
4	Kyeong Bae (KOR)	70-69-72-68—279	102,668
5	Nicole Castrale	65-72-74-69—280	68,947
	Kirsty McPherson	70-70-70-70—280	68,947
	Angela Stanford	70-71-70-69—280	68,947
8	Na Yeon Choi (KOR)	68-71-70-72—281	49,582
9	Song Hee Kim (KOR)	73-72-68-69—282	39,440
	Stacy Lewis	68-72-71-71—282	39,440
	Jin Young Pak	69-71-69-73—282	39,440
	Amy Yang (KOR)	68-74-70-70—282	39,440
13	Brandie Burton	73-71-72-67—283	32,853
14	Irene Cho (KOR)	72-75-65-72—284	29,949
	Inbee Park (KOR)	70-72-73-69—284	29,949
16	Shi Hyun Ahn (KOR)	73-70-72-70—285	25,041
	Paula Creamer	74-70-71-70—285	25,041
	Sophie Gustafsson (SWE)	69-74-70-72—285	25,041
	Katherine Hull (AUS)	69-69-76-71—285	25,041
	In-Kyung Kim (KOR)	72-74-68-71—285	25,041
21	Natalie Gulbis	72-75-69-70—286	21,836
	Hee-Won Han (KOR)	70-69-73-74—286	21,836
23	Allison Hanna-Williams	72-74-69-72—287	18,105
	Maria Hjörth (SWE)	71-75-72-69—287	18,105
23T	Eun-Hee Ji (KOR)	74-69-73-71—287	18,105
	Mindy Kim	74-69-72-72—287	18,105
	Paige Mackenzie	68-77-69-73—287	18,105
	Lorena Ochoa (MEX)	72-69-73-73—287	18,105
	Yani Tseng (TPE)	73-71-69-74—287	18,105
	Michelle Wie	70-74-73-70—287	18,105
31	Beth Bader	73-73-74-68—288	13,146
	Heather Bowie Young	75-70-70-73—288	13,146
	Soo-Yun Kang (KOR)	73-71-72-72—288	13,146
	Cristie Kerr	76-70-70-72—288	13,146
	Na Ri Kim (KOR)	71-73-72-72—288	13,146
	Young Kim (KOR)	72-74-71-71—288	13,146
	Michele Redman	72-73-72-71—288	13,146
	Ashleigh Simon (RSA)	68-74-74-72—288	13,146
39	Brittany Lang	72-72-72-73—289	10,016
	Seon Hwa Lee (KOR)	74-71-76-68—289	10,016
	Mika Miyazato (JPN)	72-74-70-73—289	10,016
	Janice Moodie (SCO)	74-73-70-72—289	10,016
	Ji Young Oh (KOR)	73-74-71-71—289	10,016
44	Minea Blomqvist (FIN)	73-69-70-78—290	8,213
	Anna Grzebien	74-73-69-74—290	8,213
	M J Hur (KOR)	71-72-74-73—290	8,213
	Juli Inkster	73-71-73-73—290	8,213
	Kris Tschetter	70-72-73-75—290	8,213

Other players who made the cut: Sandra Gal (GER), Stacy Prammanasudh, Karrie Webb (AUS), Sun Young Yoo (KOR) 291; Chella Choi (KOR), Moira Dunn, Johanna Mundy (ENG), Eunjung Yi (KOR) 292; Helen Alfredsson (SWE), Il Mi Chung (KOR), Wendy Doolan (AUS), Candie Kung (TPE), Taylor Leon, Karin Sjodin (SWE), Aree Song (KOR), Monoko Ueda (JPN) 293; Marty Hart, Jee Young Lee (KOR), Becky Morgan (WAL), Se Ri Pak (KOR) 294; Katie Futcher, Carin Koch (SWE) 295; Meaghan Francella, Jamie Hullett, Teresa Lu (TPE) 296; Karine Icher (FRA) 297; Julieta Granada (PAR) 298; Marisa Baena (COL) 299; Jackie Gallagher-Smith 303

Multiple winners

Since its inauguration in 1955, there have been 13 multiple winners of the LPGA Championship:

Mickey Wright (USA)	1958, 1960, 1961, 1963
Kathy Whitworth (USA)	1967, 1971, 1975
Nancy Lopez (USA)	1978, 1985, 1989
Patty Sheehan (USA)	1983, 1984, 1993
Annika Sörenstam (SWE)	2003, 2004, 2005
Se Ri Pak (KOR)	1998, 2002, 2006
Betsy Rawls (USA)	1959, 1969
Mary Mills (USA)	1964, 1973
Sandra Haynie (USA)	1965, 1974
Donna Caponi (USA)	1979, 1981
Laura Davies (ENG)	1994, 1996
Juli Inkster (USA)	1999, 2000
Yani Tseng (TPE)	2008, 2011

For the first decade of the championship, players from the USA won every title. They almost achieved a perfect ten for the next decade with only Canadian Sandra Post spoiling their record in 1968. US players maintained their dominance for the next two decades with seven and nine victories with England's Laura Davies spoiling their perfect ten in 1994, the first of her two LPGA victories.

During the following decade (1995–2004), the US victory tally fell to four with Europe coming a close second with Laura Davies' second title in 1996 and Swede Annika Sørenstam's two victories in 2003 and 2004 on her way to a record-breaking three in a row.

Thus far, in the first eight years of the current decade, Asia tops the list with four victories, Europe has three and the US takes the remaining slot.

2008 McDonald's LPGA Championship *Bulle Rock, Havre de Grace, MD* [6596–72]

Prize money: $2 million

1	Yani Tseng (TPE)*	73-70-65-68—276	$300000
2	Maria Hjörth (SWE)	68-72-65-71—276	180180
*Tseng won at the fourth extra hole			
3	Lorena Ochoa (MEX)	69-65-72-71—277	115911
	Annika Sörenstam (SWE)	70-68-68-71—277	115911
5	Laura Diaz	71-68-69-70—278	81,385
6	Shi Hyun Ahn (KOR)	73-69-69-69—280	53,763
	Irene Cho (KOR)	72-68-69-71—280	53,763
	Kelli Kuehne	69-70-71-70—280	53,763
	Morgan Pressel	73-69-70-68—280	53,673
10	Nicole Castrale	68-72-71-70—281	31,938
	Paula Creamer	71-70-71-69—281	31,938
	Jimin Jeong (KOR)	73-68-69-71—281	31,938
	Cristie Kerr	71-70-71-69—281	31,938
	Mi Hyun Kim (KOR)	72-70-71-68—281	31,938
	Candie Kung (TPE)	70-72-70-69—281	31,938
	Seon Hwa Lee (KOR)	73-71-70-67—281	31,938
	Giulia Sergas (ITA)	71-71-69-70—281	31,938
18	Marisa Baena (COL)	68-70-71-73—282	21,929
	Na Yeon Choi (KOR)	75-67-69-71—282	21,929
	Jeong Jang (KOR)	72-72-68-70—282	21,929
	Brittany Lang	70-67-71-74—282	21,929
	Jee Young Lee (KOR)	70-69-65-78—282	21,929
	Jill McGill	72-70-72-68—282	21,929
18T	Lindsey Wright (AUS)	67-68-73-74—282	21,929
25	Jimin Kang (KOR)	72-68-70-73—283	17,806
	Kristy McPherson	73-70-72-68—283	17,806
	Angela Stanford	72-71-67-73—283	17,806
	Momoko Ueda (JPN)	72-67-71-73—283	17,806
29	H J Choi (KOR)	69-74-71-70—284	14,896
	Eun-Hee Ji (KOR)	72-70-72-70—284	14,896
	Liselotte Neumann (SWE)	70-72-71-71—284	14,896
	Ji Young Oh (KOR)	69-68-72-75—284	14,896
	Karrie Webb (AUS)	71-71-69-73—284	14,896
34	Louise Friberg (SWE)	70-73-73-69—285	11,887
	Sophie Gituel (FRA)	70-72-72-71—285	11,887
	Young Kim (KOR)	69-73-69-74—285	11,887
	Brittany Lincicome	75-68-70-72—285	11,887
	Jane Park	72-69-70-74—285	11,887

Other players who made the cut: Kyeong Bae (KOR), Karine Icher (FRA), Rachel Hetherington (AUS), Su A Kim (KOR), Carolina Llano (COL), Se Ri Pak (KOR), Inbee Park (KOR), Stacy Prammanasudh, Jennifer Rosales (PHI), Sherri Steinhauer 287; Wendy Doolan (AUS), Sandra Gal (GER) 288; Silvia Cavelleri (ITA), Shanshan Feng (CHN), Candy Hannemann (BRA), Jin Joo Hong (KOR), Michele Redman, Nancy Scranton, Karen Stupples (ENG) 289; Julieta Granada (PAR), Leta Lindley, Becky Lucidi, Mhairi McKay (SCO), Linda Wessberg (SWE) 290; Angela Park (BRA), 291; Charlotte Mayorkas, Young-A Yang (KOR) 292; Moira Dunn, Tracy Hanson, Soo-Yun Kang (KOR), Alena Sharp (CAN) 293; Meaghan Francella, Sun Young Yoo (KOR) 294; Danielle Downey 295; Jamie Hullett 297; Allison Fouch 299

2007 McDonald's LPGA Championship *Bulle Rock, Havre de Grace, MD* [6596–72]

Prize money: $2 million

1	Suzann Pettersen (NOR)	69-67-71-67—274	$300,000
2	Karrie Webb (AUS)	68-69-71-67—275	179,038
3	Ma On Min (KOR)	71-70-65-70—276	129,880
4	Lindsey Wright (AUS)	71-70-71-66—278	100,473
5	Angela Park (BRA)	67-73-68-71—279	80,869
6	Paula Creamer	71-68-73-68—280	53,422
	Sophie Gustafson (SWE)	70-71-71-68—280	53,422
	Brittany Lincicome	69-69-73-69—280	53,422
	Lorena Ochoa (MEX)	71-71-69-69—280	53,422
10	Nicole Castrale	70-73-68-70—281	35,730
	Jee Young Lee (KOR)	71-72-68-70—281	35,730
	Sarah Lee (KOR)	71-69-72-69—281	35,730
	Catriona Matthew (SCO)	71-69-74-67—281	35,730
14	Morgan Pressel	68-71-70-73—282	30,192
15	Mi Hyun Kim (KOR)	70-73-71-69—283	26,925
	Stacy Prammanasudh	68-74-71-70—283	26,925
	Annika Sörenstam (SWE)	70-69-73-71—283	26,925
18	Cristie Kerr	75-70-73-66—284	23,396
	Siew-Ai Lim (MAS)	72-69-70-73—284	23,396
	Mhairi McKay (SCO)	71-69-74-70—284	23,396
21	Shi Hyun Ahn (KOR)	71-73-71-70—285	20,585
	Meaghan Francella	72-75-68-70—285	20,585
	Juli Inkster	73-73-73-66—285	20,585
21T	In-Kyung Kim (KOR)	73-70-71-71—285	20,585
25	Wendy Doolan (AUS)	76-70-70-70—286	17,350
	Pat Hurst	69-75-76-66—286	17,350
	Jeong Jang (KOR)	73-71-71-71—286	17,350
	Birdie Kim (KOR)	67-71-73-75—286	17,350
	Kim Saiki-Maloney	67-73-70-76—286	17,350
30	Laura Davies (ENG)	68-75-71-73—287	14,801
	Leta Lindley	76-69-72-70—287	14,801
	Teresa Lu (TPE)	70-72-72-73—287	14,801
33	Maria Hjörth (SWE)	69-75-74-70—288	13,069
	Se Ri Pak (KOR)	73-70-74-71—288	13,069
	Angela Stanford	73-71-72-72—288	13,069
36	Kate Golden	74-73-74-68—289	11,096
	Jimin Kang (KOR)	73-72-74-70—289	11,096
	Seon Hwa Lee (KOR)	71-74-71-73—289	11,096
	Nancy Scranton	73-73-74-69—289	11,096
	Giulia Sergas (ITA)	69-74-74-72—289	11,096
41	Irene Cho	72-72-76-70—290	9,037
	Johanna Head (ENG)	75-72-75-68—290	9,037
	Becky Morgan (WAL)	73-72-75-70—290	9,037
	Reilley Rankin	71-71-74-74—290	9,037
	Sherri Turner	71-73-74-72—290	9,037

Other players who made the cut: Kyeong Bae (KOR), Dorothy Delasin, Kimberly Hall, Marcy Hart, Joo Mi Kim (KOR), Mena Lee (KOR), Ji-Young Oh (KOR), Gloria Park (KOR), Michele Redman, Linda Wessberg (SWE) 291; Christina Kim, Charlotte Mayorkas, Sherri Steinhauer 292; Rachel Hetherington (AUS), Karin Sjodin (SWE), Heather Young 293; Silvia Cavalleri (ITA), Katherine Hull (AUS), Lorie Kane (CAN), Yu Ping Lin (TPE), In-Bee Park (KOE), Young-A Yang (KOR) 294; Liselotte Neumann (SWE) 295; Maria Baena (COL), Il Mi Chung (KOR), Moira Dunn, Jackie Gallagher-Smith, Brittany Lang 296; Virada Nirapathpongporn (THA), Jane Park 297; Erica Blasberg, Eva Dahllof (SWE), Karen Davies, Vicki Goetze-Ackerman, Sung Ah Yim (KOR) 298; Laura Diaz 299; Meredith Duncan, Patricia Meunier-Lebouc (FRA) 299; Michelle Wie 309

2006 McDonald's LPGA Championship *Bulle Rock, Havre de Grace, MD* [6596–72]

Prize money: $1.8 million

1	Se Ri Pak (KOR)*	71-69-71-69—280	$270,000
2	Karrie Webb (AUS)	70-70-72-68—280	163,998
Play-off: 1st extra hole: Pak 3, Webb 4			
3	Mi Hyun Kim (KOR)	68-71-71-71—281	105,501
	Ai Miyazato (JPN)	68-72-69-72—281	105,501
5	Shi Hyun Ahn (KOR)	69-70-71-72—282	57,464
9	Young Kim (KOR)	69-72-73-69—283	34,174
	Lorena Ochoa (MEX)	68-72-71-72—283	34,174
	Reilley Rankin	68-73-74-68—283	34,174
	Annika Sörenstam (SWE)	71-69-75-68—283	34,174
	Sung Ah Yim (KOR)	72-68-74-69—283	34,174
14	Jee Young Lee (KOR)	70-71-70-73—284	26,847
	Meena Lee (KOR)	71-72-69-72—284	26,847
16	Silvia Cavalleri (ITA)	69-71-72-73—285	22,896
	Seon Hwa Lee (KOR)	67-74-75-69—285	22,896
	Sherri Steinhauer	70-71-71-73—285	22,896
	Wendy Ward	69-74-70-72—285	22,896
20	Yuri Fudoh (JPN)	69-74-71-72—286	19,215
	Natalie Gulbis	72-73-72-69—286	19,215
	Young Jo (KOR)	72-72-70-72—286	19,215
	Suzann Pettersen (NOR)	70-72-74-70—286	19,215
	Lindsey Wright (AUS)	72-73-68-73—286	19,215
25	Minea Blomqvist (FIN)	71-71-70-75—287	16,207
	Laura Diaz	71-74-72-70—287	16,207
25T	Hee-Won Han (KOR)	68-73-75-71—287	16,207
	Heather Young	71-75-70-71—287	16,207
29	Il-Ne Chung (KOR)	71-72-75-70—288	13,558
	Liselotte Neumann (SWE)	69-74-75-70—288	13,558
	Nancy Scranton	73-73-73-69—288	13,558
	Angela Stanford	70-76-72-70—288	13,558
	Kris Tamulis	73-71-75-69—288	13,558
34	Marisa Baena (COL)	72-72-74-71—289	11,044
	Nicole Castrale	64-75-74-76—289	11,044
	Rachel Hetherington (AUS)	70-72-74-73—289	11,044
	Juli Inkster	70-74-73-72—289	11,044
	Nina Reis (SWE)	70-73-73-73—289	11,044
39	Beth Daniel	71-71-73-75—290	8,979
	Allison Hanna	74-69-78-69—290	8,979
	Maria Hjörth (SWE)	68-77-73-72—290	89,79
	Nicole Perrot (CHI)	70-71-76-73—290	8,979
	Michele Redman	73-72-73-72—290	8,979
44	Julieta Grenada (PAR)	71-73-71-76—291	7,363
	Sophie Gustafson (SWE)	72-72-75-72—291	7,363
	Candie Kung (TPE)	68-78-71-74—291	7,363
	Yu Ping Lin (TPE)	74-72-72-73—291	7,363
	Jessica Reese-Quayle	73-73-72-73—291	7,363

Other players who made the cut: Paula Creamer, Rosie Jones, Carin Koch (SWE), Brittany Lincicome, Kim Saiki 292; Michelle Ellis (AUS), Jill McGill, Miriam Nagl (GER), Mikaela Parmlid (SWE) 293; Jackie Gallagher-Smith, Jeong Jang (KOR), Teresa Lu (TPE) 294; Christina Kim, Siew-Ai Lim (MAS), Gloria Park (KOR), Karin Sjodin (SWE) 295; Laura Davies (ENG), Wendy Doolan (AUS), Birdie Kim (KOR), Sarah Lee (KOR) 296; Ashli Bunch, Dorothy Delasin, Morgan Pressel, Karen Stupples (ENG) 297; Kristi Albers 299; Moira Dunn 300; Jamie Fischer, Becky Iverson 302

2005 McDonald's LPGA Championship *Bulle Rock, Havre de Grace, MD* [6486–72]

Prize money: $1.8 million

1	Annika Sörenstam (SWE)	68-67-69-73—277	$270,000
2	Michelle Wie (am)	69-71-71-69—280	
3	Paula Creamer	68-73-74-67—282	140,517
	Laura Davies (ENG)	67-70-74-71—282	140,517
5	Natalie Gulbis	67-71-73-73—284	82,486
	Lorena Ochoa (MEX)	72-72-68-72—284	82,486
7	Moira Dunn	71-68-72-74—285	43,993
	Pat Hurst	72-73-71-69—285	43,993
	Mi Hyun Kim (KOR)	69-75-74-67—285	43,993
	Young Kim (KOR)	73-68-68-76—285	43,993
	Carin Koch (SWE)	74-70-69-72—285	43,993
	Gloria Park (KOR)	71-71-72-71—285	43,993
13	Juli Inkster	75-71-71-69—286	29,309
	Jeong Jang (KOR)	71-71-69-75—286	29,309
	Candie Kung (TAI)	72-73-73-68—286	29,309
16	Marisa Baena (COL)	70-69-73-75—287	23,899
	Jennifer Rosales (PHI)	71-73-69-74—287	23,899
	Angela Stanford	69-73-73-72—287	23,899
	Lindsey Wright (AUS)	71-72-72-72—287	23,899
20	Beth Bader	72-72-72-72—288	19,797
	Heather Bowie	72-71-71-74—288	19,797
20T	Laura Diaz	67-72-76-73—288	19,797
	Meena Lee (KOR)	70-71-72-75—288	19,797
	Karrie Webb (AUS)	74-75-72-67—288	19,797
25	Shi Hyun Ahn (KOR)	78-71-72-68—289	16,096
	Kirsti Albers	70-72-73-74—289	16,096
	Il Mi Chung (KOR)	71-68-79-71—289	16,096
	Hee-Won Han (KOR)	73-74-72-70—289	16,096
	Leta Lindley	72-72-75-70—289	16,096
	Karen Stupples (ENG)	72-71-71-75—289	16,096
31	Rosie Jones	72-69-74-75—290	13,733
	Liselotte Neumann (SWE)	70-71-74-75—290	13,733
33	Jamie Hullett	70-75-71-75—291	11,225
	Jimin Kang (KOR)	73-74-72-72—291	11,225
	Cristie Kerr	74-72-67-78—291	11,225
	Christina Kim	73-72-78-68—291	11,225
	Brittany Lincicome	72-72-75-72—291	11,225
	Meg Mallon	74-69-76-72—291	11,225
	Janice Moodie (SCO)	73-72-74-72—291	11,225
	Stacy Prammanasudh	72-76-72-71—291	11,225

Other players who made the cut: Birdie Kim (KOR) 292, Rachel Hetherington (AUS), Hilary Lunke, Paula Marti (ESP), Joanne Morley (ENG) 293; Johanna Head (ENG), Lorie Kane (CAN), Aree Song (KOR) 294; Heather Daly-Donofrio, Catriona Matthew (SCO), Suzann Pettersen (NOR), Michele Redman, Kim Saiki 295; Dawn Coe-Jones (CAN), Beth Daniel, Wendy Doolan (AUS), Yu Ping Lin (TAI), Stephanie Louden, Jill McGill, Nicole Perrot (CHI), Nancy Scranton, Sung Ah Yim (KOR) 296; Tina Barrett, Patricia Baxter-Johnson, Tina Fischer (GER), Laurel Kean, Emilee Klein, Bernadette Luse, Sae-Hee Son (KOR), Kris Tschetter 297; Maria Hjörth (SWE) 298; Katie Allison, Catherine Cartwright, A J Eathorne (CAN), Katherine Hull (AUS), Reilley Rankin 299; Laurie Rinker, Nadina Taylor (AUS) 300; Candy Hannemann (BRA) 302; Barb Mucha 305.

2004 McDonald's LPGA Championship *Du Pont CC, DE* [6408–71]

Prize money: $1.6 million

1	Annika Sörenstam (SWE)	68-67-64-72—271	$240,000
2	Shi Hyun Ahn (KOR)	69-70-69-66—274	144,780
3	Grace Park (KOR)	68-70-70-68—276	105,028
4	Gloria Park (KOR)	67-72-68-71—278	73,322
	Angela Stanford	69-71-67-71—278	73,322
6	Juli Inkster	70-66-70-73—279	49,145
	Christina Kim	74-69-64-72—279	49,145
8	Wendy Doolan (AUS)	73-70-65-72—280	35,538
	Soo-Yun Kang	69-68-71-72—280	35,538
	Lorena Ochoa (MEX)	71-67-67-75—280	35,538
11	Carin Koch (SWE)	69-71-68-73—281	28,734
	Reilley Rankin	70-67-71-73—281	28,734
13	Pat Hurst	69-69-75-69—282	24,466
	Mhairi McKay (SCO)	72-69-69-72—282	24,466
	Jennifer Rosales (PHI)	66-70-74-72—282	24,466
16	Meg Mallon	69-73-70-71—283	21,718
17	Kristi Albers	70-74-69-71—284	18,654
	Dawn Coe-Jones (CAN)	72-72-70-70—284	18,654
	Michelle Ellis (AUS)	72-70-69-73—284	18,654
	Cristie Kerr	69-73-71-71—284	18,654
17T	Betsy King	76-70-70-68—284	18,654
	Se Ri Pak (KOR)	69-73-70-72—284	18,654
23	Tina Barrett	75-71-68-71—285	14,596
	Jeong Jang (KOR)	71-71-71-72—285	14,596
	Siew-Ai Lim (MAS)	72-70-71-72—285	14,596
	Stacy Prammanasudh	73-71-69-72—285	14,596
	Kim Saiki	69-72-72-72—285	14,596
	Sherri Steinhauer	69-72-74-70—285	14,596
	Chiharu Yamaguchi (JPN)	67-73-70-75—285	14,596
30	Moira Dunn	68-74-72-72—286	10,631
	Mi-Hyun Kim (KOR)	72-70-74-70—286	10,631
	Young Kim (KOR)	70-73-74-69—286	10,631
	Patricia Meunier-Lebouc (FRA)	71-70-76-69—286	10,631
	Janice Moodie (SCO)	72-71-73-70—286	10,631
	Aree Song (KOR)	71-72-69-74—286	10,631
	Charlotta Sörenstam (SWE)	74-70-70-72—286	10,631
	Karen Stupples (ENG)	67-73-73-73—286	10,631
	Wendy Ward	72-72-71-71—286	10,631

Other players who made the cut: Beth Daniel, Stephanie Louden (AUS), Karrie Webb (AUS) 287; Jean Bartholomew, Ashli Bunch, Laura Davies (ENG), Becky Iverson, Becky Morgan (WAL), Deb Richard, Karen Pearce (AUS) 289; Heather Daly-Donofrio, Hee-Won Han (KOR), Lorie Kane (CAN), Yu Ping Lin (TPE), Kelly Robbins, Giulia Sergas (ITA), Rachel Teske (AUS) 290; Pat Bradley, Diana D'Alessio, Kate Golden, Jamie Hullett, Emilee Klein 291; Helen Alfredsson (SWE), Natalie Gulbis, Catriona Matthew (SCO) 292; Amy Fruhwirth, Tammy Green, Seol-An Jeon (KOR), Angela Jerman, Candie Kung (TPE), Soo Young Moon (KOR) 293; Isabelle Beisiegel (CAN), Vicki Goetz-Ackerman, Jill McGill, Dotty Pepper 294; Jenna Daniels, Sophie Gustafson (SWE), Kim Williams 295; Candy Hannemann (BRA) 296; Jackie Gallagher-Smith 297; Heather Bowie 299.

2003 McDonald's LPGA Championship *Du Pont CC, DE* [6408–71]

Prize money: $1.6 million

1	Annika Sörenstam (SWE)*	70-64-72-72—278	$240,000
2	Grace Park (KOR)	69-72-70-67—278	147,934
3	Beth Daniel	71-71-70-72—284	85718
	Rosie Jones	73-68-72-71—284	85,718
	Rachel Teske (AUS)	69-70-74-71—284	85,718
6	Kate Golden	72-70-68-75—285	41,873
	Young Kim (KOR)	70-73-72-70—285	41,873
	JoAnne Mills (AUS)	68-73-75-69—285	41,873
	Becky Morgan (WAL)	73-70-70-72—285	41,873
	Young-A Yang (KOR)	73-74-69-69—285	41,873
11	Akiko Fukushima (JPN)	72-68-74-72—286	24,037
	Hee-Wan Han (KOR)	67-69-74-76—286	24,037
	Jeong Jang (KOR)	72-73-69-72—286	24,037
	Angela Jerman	73-72-69-72—286	24,037
	Patricia Meunier-Lebouc (FRA)	75-69-72-70—286	24,037
	Suzann Pettersen (NOR)	70-71-75-70—286	24,037
	Michele Redman	74-70-69-73—286	24,037
	Jennifer Rosales (PHI)	74-68-74-70—286	24,037
	Wendy Ward	68-69-75-74—286	24,037
20	Donna Andrews	73-70-70-74—287	16,719
	Tina Barrett	76-69-71-71—287	16,719
	Michelle Ellis (AUS)	73-70-71-73—287	16,719
	Natalie Gulbis	71-69-78-69—287	16,719
	Kelli Kuehne	73-73-65-76—287	16,719
	Lorena Ochoa (MEX)	72-72-71-72—287	16,719
	Karen Stupples (ENG)	73-73-71-70—287	16,719
27	Danielle Ammaccapane	74-72-74-68—288	13,769
	Meg Mallon	74-69-70-75—288	13,769
	Angela Stanford	72-73-71-72—288	13,769
30	Laura Diaz	73-70-75-71—289	11,987
	Tracy Hanson	71-77-70-71—289	11,987
	Mi-Hyun Kim (KOR)	72-72-71-74—289	11,987
	Deb Richard	75-71-74-69—289	11,987
34	Moira Dunn	78-70-72-70—290	10,367
	Lorie Kane (CAN)	72-75-70-73—290	10,367
	Cristie Kerr	74-69-75-72—290	10,367
37	Juli Inkster	71-72-71-77—291	8,970
	Hilary Lunke	72-70-75-74—291	8,970
	Catriona Matthew (SCO)	72-73-75-71—291	8,970
	Jan Stephenson (AUS)	74-72-69-76—291	8,970

**Sörenstam won at the first extra hole*

Other players who made the cut: Jill McGill, Terry-Jo Myers 292; Vicki Goetze-Ackerman, Pat Hurst, Giulia Sergas (ITA) 293; Marisa Baena (COL), Brandie Burton, Jung Yeon Lee (KOR), Se Ri Pak (KOR), Leslie Spalding 294; Yu Ping Lin (TPE), Kathryn Marshall (SCO), Joanne Morley (ENG) 295; Dorothy Delasin (PHI), Kim Saiki 296; Dawn Coe-Jones (CAN), Jane Crafter (AUS), Wendy Doolan (AUS), Jackie Gallagher-Smith, Karrie Webb (AUS) 297; Fiona Pike (AUS) 298; Heather Bowie 299; Marnie McGuire (NZL) 300; Mitzi Edge, Marcy Hart, Michelle McGann 301; Marilyn Lovander, Liselotte Neumann (SWE), Dottie Pepper 304; Kim Williams 306

LPGA Championship History

The Championship was known simply as the LPGA Championship from its inauguration in 1955 until 1987. It was sponsored by Mazda from 1988 until 1993 when the sponsorship was taken over by McDonald's. Only in the first year was it decided by match-play when Beverly Hanson beat Louise Suggs in the final.

1955	B Hanson	Orchard Ridge	4 and 3
1956	M Hagge*	Forest Lake	291
After a play-off with P Berg			
1957	L Suggs	Churchill Valley	285
1958	M Wright	Churchill CC	288
1959	B Rawls	Churchill CC	288
1960	M Wright	French Lick	292
1961	M Wright	Stardust	287
1962	J Kimball	Stardust	282
1963	M Wright	Stardust	294
1964	M Mills	Stardust	278
1965	S Haynie	Stardust	279
1966	G Ehret	Stardust	282
1967	K Whitworth	Pleasant Valley	284
1968	S Post*	Pleasant Valley	294
After a play-off with K Whitworth			
1969	B Rawls	Concord	293
1970	S Englehorn*	Pleasant Valley	285
After a play-off with K Whitworth			
1971	K Whitworth	Pleasant Valley	288
1972	K Ahern	Pleasant Valley	293
1973	M Mills	Pleasant Valley	288
1974	S Haynie	Pleasant Valley	288
1975	K Whitworth	Pine Ridge	288
1976	B Burfeindt	Pine Ridge	287
1977	C Higuchi (JPN)	Bay Tree	279
1978	N Lopez	Kings Island	275
1979	D Caponi	Kings Island	279
1980	S Little (SA)	Kings Island	285
1981	D Caponi	Kings Island	280
1982	J Stephenson (AUS)	Kings Island	279
1983	P Sheehan	Kings Island	279
1984	P Sheehan	Kings Island	272
1985	N Lopez	Kings Island	273
1986	P Bradley	Kings Island	277
1987	J Geddes	Kings Island	275
1988	S Turner	Kings Island	281
1989	N Lopez	Kings Island	274
1990	B Daniel	Bethesda	280
1991	M Mallon	Bethesda	274
1992	B King	Bethesda	267
1993	P Sheehan	Bethesda	275
1994	L Davies (ENG)	Wilmington, Delaware	275
1995	K Robbins	Wilmington, Delaware	274
1996	L Davies (ENG)	Wilmington, Delaware	213
Reduced to 54 holes – bad weather			
1997	C Johnson	Wilmington, Delaware	281
1998	Se Ri Pak (KOR)	Wilmington, Delaware	273
1999	J Inkster	Wilmington, Delaware	268
2000	J Inkster*	Wilmington, Delaware	281
Beat S Croce (ITA) at the second extra hole			
2001	K Webb (AUS)	Wilmington, Delaware	270
2002	Se Ri Pak (KOR)	Wilmington, Delaware	279
2003	A Sörenstam (SWE)*	Wilmington, Delaware	271
Beat G Park (KOR) at the first extra hole			
2004	A Sörenstam (SWE)	Wilmington, Delaware	271
2005	A Sörenstam (SWE)	Bulle Rock, MD	277
2006	Se Ri Pak (KOR)*	Bulle Rock, MD	280
Beat K Webb (AUS) at first extra hole			
2007	S Pettersen (NOR)	Bulle Rock, MD	274
2008	Y Tseng (TPE)*	Bulle Rock, MD	278
Beat M Hjörth (SWE) at the fourth extra hole			
2009	A Nordqvist (SWE)	Bulle Rock, MD	273
2010	C Kerr	Locust Hill, Pitsford, NY	269
2011	Y Tseng (TPE)	Locust Hill, Pitsford, NY	269
2012	S Feng (CHN)	Locust Hill, Pitsford, NY	282

Paula the only golfer under par for all four majors

Taking all four majors together, America's Paul Creamer was the only player to be under par collectively for the 16 rounds she played … and then it was only one under.

Additionally, Creamer was one of only three players who managed three top 10's in the 2012 majors, the others being Player of the Year Stacy Lewis and top money earner Inbee Park.

For the record, these were Creamer's scores in the majors last year:

Kraft Nabisco Championship	69-73-71-72—285 (–3)	T20th	$22,586
Wegman's LPGA Championship	70-72-73-71—286 (–2)	T9th	$51,742
US Women's Open	73-73-71-74—291 (+3)	T7th	$94,736
Ricoh Women's British Open	73-72-72-72—289 (+1)	3rd	$174,768

The 41st Kraft Nabisco Championship

Sun Young Yoo collects when fellow Korean falters at Palm Springs

Even the three foot putt encountered by Doug Sanders in 1970 at St Andrews to win The Open Championship – he duly lost to Jack Nicklaus in a play-off after missing that opportunity on the 18th – was a yawning crevasse by comparison with the mere tap-in from a foot on the final hole at Mission Hills in California which faced I K Kim as she strove to win the Kraft Nabisco Championship.

It was the kind of putt which club golfers routinely concede in match play to their opponents. Of course, there are no concessions in stroke play and, certainly, no 'gimmes' in major championship golf. And if ever there was a cruel reminder that the shortest of putts can sometimes be missed by the most talented of players – just ask Scott Hoch, who twice missed from inside three feet when duelling with Nick Faldo in a play-off for the Masters in 1989 – it surely came when Kim's stroke from 12 inches was pushed to the right side of the cup where it circled the hole before horseshoeing out.

© Getty Images

Sun Young Yoo

It was a stunning error which drew gasps of surprise from the galleries at Rancho Mirage and left Kim stranded in a state somewhere between shock and disbelief. As she bowed her face and raised her hands to hide her eyes, it was immediately clear the 23-year-old from South Korea was in no fit state to bounce back in the play-off. Sun Young Yoo, on the other hand, only felt good vibrations as a door unexpectedly opened into sudden death and she duly holed an 18 foot birdie putt at the first extra hole to win her first major championship.

Just as the 1999 stagings of The Open at Carnoustie and the 1996 Masters are best recalled for the closing round collapses of Jean Van de Velde and Greg Norman, rather than the victories of Paul Lawrie and Nick Faldo, it's likely to be Yoo's fate that she's remembered as the beneficiary of the most glaring miss in major championship history. Not that the golfer seemed troubled by that fate as she looked back on a final round of 69 notable for a steady hand before the turn and three birdies on the back nine.

The first South Korean golfer to win the women's first major of the season since Grace Park in 2004, Yoo seemed almost as surprised as everyone else by the unexpected turn of events on the last hole. "I didn't think about winning because I didn't want to expect too much," she said. "I didn't want to let myself down, but I think I did better than I was hoping, so I'm very happy. I thought I had no chance. I thought I K was going to make that putt, but it didn't happen."

Almost as surprising as Kim's choke and Yoo's success was Yani Tseng's failure to capitalise on a third round lead for the second successive year at Mission Hills. Of course, it's in the nature of golf that even the greatest lose narrowly more often than they win – Jack Nicklaus, for example, can count 28 second or third place finishes in the majors – but few would have bet against the world No 1 when the fourth round began, bearing in mind this was the first time since the Kraft Nabisco in 2011 that Tseng did not win a tournament where she either held or shared the lead going into the final round.

According to Tseng, she fell into the trap at the start of the last day of trying too hard and consequently came up a little short over the early holes. "My attitude was good," she insisted. "I smiled the whole way round, had my chin up and still had a chance on the last hole. I was very happy about that. Last year when I finished I was crying so hard, but this year I was happy. And I think it's because I did my best on every shot."

Tseng knew at the start of the week that she hadn't brought her best golf to the California desert and would need to grind in pursuit of a major title which had slipped through her grasp in the past. While Amy Yang set the early pace in the first round with an impressive 66, Tseng managed to overcome a scruffier than usual command of distance control to post 68. The world No 1 was frank about the lack of gloss in her play. "I didn't hit many good shots and didn't leave myself lots of birdie chances out there," she said. "I always keep telling myself 'you don't have to play perfect, so don't try too hard to be perfect'. That's going to be very hard on me. The last few years I've been learning that even when you don't have your A game, you still can shoot a couple under to put yourself in a good position. That's how I'm learning."

As for Yoo, in spite of dropping a shot at the third – she'd started her round on the tenth – the eventual winner birdied the 17th, 18th, first and second holes to card an opening 69 which kept her within three shots of the lead. Although, unsurprisingly, most of the attention at close of play after the second round focused on the world No 1's rise to the top of the leaderboard, Yoo kept up the good work of the first day by signing for another 69. Even at this stage, the South Korean was optimistic about her chances of success, making the point that she'd been playing well since the RR Donnelley Founders Cup two weeks earlier. "I've been hitting it so good since Phoenix," she said. "I was hoping that I could make some more putts, but I didn't make many. I have two days to go, I have a great feeling and I'm looking forward to it."

> "I did not think about winning because I did not want to expect too much."
>
> *Sun Young Yoo after winning at Palm Springs*

Tseng, meanwhile, had shot another 68 and felt far better about her game on Friday than she'd done on Thursday, reporting that she played with more energy, concentration and eagerness. Her only concern was judging the speed of the greens, which she admitted finding a little perplexing over the opening holes of the second round. By Saturday the desert winds had picked up and the players faced a different challenge. The 20mph winds, gusting up to 30mph, complicated the process, though not for Sweden's Karin Sjodin, who compiled a noteworthy 68 to share the lead with Tseng going into the final day.

Although breezy, conditions were warm and the Scandinavian golfer felt the heat made it easier for her to cope with a rib injury she'd picked up the day before. Tseng again found herself trying too hard and thinking too much, though 71 was hardly calamitous. Yoo could have played herself out of contention with four bogeys but battled away and three birdies in four holes around the turn kept her in sight of the leaders.

On Sunday, the South Korean looked to be out of contention after dropped shots at the third and ninth saw her lose ground on Kim. However, three birdies on the back nine were good enough to match the low total of nine under par after Kim undid the good work of the previous 17 holes – she'd made four birdies and given nothing away to par – before that closing 6. While Yoo acquitted herself well, it was a championship sure to be remembered for Kim's error. A professional facing a one foot putt for glory and then missing the apparently unmissable.

Michael Aitken

First Round	Second Round	Third Round	Fourth Round
–6 Amy Yang	–8 Yani Tseng	–9 Yani Tseng	–9 Sun Young Yoo
–5 Lindsey Wright	–7 Haeji Kang	–9 Karin Sjodin	–9 I K Kim
–4 Yani Tseng	–6 Lindsey Wright	–7 Haeji Kang	–8 Yani Tseng
–3 Paula Creamer	–6 Sun Young Yoo	–6 Na Yeon Choi	–7 Karin Sjodin
–3 Nicole Castrale	–5 Se Ri Pak	–6 Eun-Hee Ji	–7 Amy Yang
–3 Jodi Ewart	–5 Na Yeon Choi	–6 I K Kim	–7 Stacy Lewis
–3 Katherine Hull	–5 Karin Sjodin	–6 Hee Kyung Seo	–7 Hee Kyung Seo
–3 Haeji Kang	–4 Vicky Hurst	–6 Sun Young Yoo	–6 Natalie Gulbis
–3 Hee Kyung Seo	–4 I K Kim	–5 Vicky Hurst	–6 See Ri Pak
–3 Sun Young Yoo	–4 Amy Yang	–5 Katherine Hull	–6 Na Yeon Choi
			Play-off: Sun Young Yoo 4 I K Kim 5

Two new inductees for the Collegiate Hall of Fame

Australian Katherine Hull and American Vicki Goetze-Ackerman were inducted last year into the Collegiate Golf Hall of Fame.

Hull, who attended Pepperdine University and is a former PING National Player of the Year, arrived in America after an impressive junior career in her home state of Queensland.

During her four seasons at Pepperdine she was named WGCA National Player of the year, was a three-time All American, won the Dinah Shore Award in 2003 and holds the top two spots in the University's single season records averaging 72.19 a round in 2001–02 and 72.87 in 2002–03.

Since turning professional she has made over $3 million on the LPGA Tour.

Goetze-Ackerman, the 1989 and 1992 US Women's Amateur champion, attended Georgia University for two years and in 1992 was the University's Female Athlete of the Year.. She was the most successful junior golfer in US history and was three times low amateur in the US Women's Open. After turning professional she retired in 2009.

Kraft Nabisco Championship *Mission Hills CC, Rancho Mirage, CA* March 29–April 1 [6702–72]

Prize money: $2m. Final field of 117 players (including six amateurs), of whom 82 (including four amateurs) made the final half-way cut on 148 or less. *(Players are of American nationality unless stated)*

1	Sun Young Yoo (KOR)	69-69-72-69—279	$300,000
2	I K Kim (KOR)	70-70-70-69—279	182,538
**Yoo won at the first extra hole – Sun Young Yoo 4; I K Kim 5*			
3	Yani Tseng (TPE)	68-68-71-73—280	132,418
4	Karin Sjodin (SWE)	72-67-68-74—281	77,202
	Amy Yang (KOR)	66-74-72-69—281	77,202
	Stacy Lewis	74-71-70-66—281	77,202
	Hee Kyung Seo (KOR)	69-72-69-71—281	77,202
8	Natalie Gulbis	76-71-70-65—282	44,806
	Se Ri Pak (KOR)	70-69-72-71—282	44,806
	Na Yeon Choi (KOR)	72-67-71-72—282	44,806
11	Ha-Neul Kim (KOR)	71-71-70-71—283	34,003
	Angela Stanford	72-71-70-70—283	34,003
	Eun-Hee Ji (KOR)	71-69-70-73—283	34,003
	Vicky Hurst	70-70-71-72—283	34,003
15	Catriona Matthew (SCO)	74-70-70-70—284	26,184
	Suzann Pettersen (NOR)	72-74-66-72—284	26,184
	Karrie Webb (AUS)	71-72-71-70—284	26,184
	Haeji Kang (KOR)	69-68-72-75—284	26,184
	Azahara Muñoz (ESP)	73-72-67-72—284	26,184
20	Paula Creamer	69-73-71-72—285	22,586
	Katherine Hull (AUS)	69-73-69-74—285	22,586
22	Cristie Kerr	71-70-72-73—286	20,587
	Shanshan Feng (CHN)	72-70-73-71—286	20,587
	Ariya Jutanugarn (THA) (am)	71-73-71-71—286	
	Lexi Thompson	72-72-68-74—286	20,587
26	Brittany Lang	74-74-69-70—287	16,401
	Inbee Park (KOR)	71-74-68-74—287	16,401
	Hee Young Park (KOR)	72-71-70-74—287	16,401
	Anna Nordqvist (SWE)	74-74-67-72—287	16,401
	Jiyai Shin (KOR)	72-71-70-74—287	16,401
	Beatriz Recari (ESP)	72-76-70-69—287	16,401
	Cindy LaCrosse	73-71-70-73—287	16,401
	Jodi Ewart ((DEN)ENG)	69-73-73-72—287	16,401
	Jennifer Johnson	72-71-73-71—287	16,401
35	Karine Icher (FRA)	73-73-67-75—288	12,792
	Julieta Granada (PAR)	70-75-73-70—288	12,792
	Mi Jung Hur (KOR)	73-70-75-70—288	12,792
38	Kris Tamulis	72-75-68-74—289	11,068
	Maria Hjörth (SWE)	73-68-75-73—289	11,068
	Sandra Gal (GER)	71-72-72-74—289	11,068
	Mina Harigae	73-71-72-73—289	11,068
	Charley Hull (ENG) (am)	71-77-68-73—289	
43	Heather Bowie Young	74-70-73-73—290	9,594
	Pat Hurst	75-73-71-71—290	9,594
	Lindsey Wright (AUS)	67-71-76-76—290	9,594
46	Morgan Pressel	73-74-73-71—291	8,495
	Lizette Salas	76-70-71-74—291	8,495
	Ji-Hee Lee (KOR)	74-73-69-75—291	8,495
49	Hee-Won Han (KOR)	70-74-73-75—292	7,195
	Candie Kung	70-75-72-75—292	7,195
	Becky Morgan (WAL)	76-72-72-72—292	7,195
	Seon Hwa Lee (KOR)	76-72-68-76—292	7,195
	Chella Choi (KOR)	72-74-75-71—292	7,195
	Caroline Masson (GER)	79-69-70-74—292	7,195
	Austin Ernst (am)	77-70-68-77—292	

Kraft Nabisco Championship *continued*

56	Wendy Ward	71-76-71-75—293	5,608
	Ai Miyazato (JPN)	71-72-74-76—293	5,608
	Pornanong Phatlum (THA)	71-72-73-77—293	5,608
	Jennifer Song	72-71-71-79—293	5,608
	Diana Luna (ITA)	76-68-75-74—293	5,608
	Melissa Reid (ENG)	77-70-71-75—293	5,608
	Caroline Hedwall (SWE)	74-72-71-76—293	5,608
	So Yeon Ryu (KOR)	74-74-73-72—293	5,608
	Christel Boeljon (NED)	74-73-75-71—293	5,608
	Jaye Marie Green (am)	71-77-70-75—293	
66	Katie Futcher	72-72-73-77—294	4,647
	Sarah Kemp (AUS)	71-75-71-77—294	4,647
	Momoko Ueda (JPN)	71-69-80-74—294	4,647
	Dewi Claire Schreefel (NED)	75-72-70-77—294	4,647
70	Reilley Rankin	73-73-70-79—295	4,197
	Mo Martin	74-72-73-76—295	4,197
	Amanda Blumenherst	75-73-72-75—295	4,197
	Cydney Clanton	70-76-75-74—295	4,197
	Yukari Baba (JPN)	75-73-72-75—295	4,197
75	Alena Sharp (CAN)	75-73-73-75—296	3,897
	Christina Kim	74-69-77-76—296	3,897
	Karen Stupples (ENG)	73-72-75-76—296	3,897
78	Leta Lindley	76-70-77-75—298	3,797
79	Nicole Castrale	69-73-81-76—299	3,728
	Lorie Kane (CAN)	74-73-72-80—299	3,728
81	Kyeong Bae (KOR)	74-74-78-75—301	3,657
82	Ji Young Oh (KOR)	74-72-81-76—303	3,611

The following players missed the cut:

83	Jimin Kang (KOR)	72-77—149
	Janice Moodie (SCO)	73-76—149
	Jenny Shin (KOR)	75-74—149
	Jessica Korda	76-73—149
87	Silvia Cavalleri (ITA)	73-77—150
	Amy Hung (KOR)	76-74—150
	Stacy Prammanasudh	74-76—150
	Sherri Steinhauer	73-77—150
	Kristy McPherson	76-74—150
	Lee-Anne Pace (RSA)	75-75—150
	Alison Walshe	75-75—150
	Hyun-Hwa Sim (KOR)	77-73—150
	Michelle Wie	73-77—150-
96	Sophie Gustafson (SWE)	75-76—151
	Jee Young Lee (KOR)	78-73—151
	Mika Miyazato (JPN)	75-76—151
	Maria Hernandez (ESP)	75-76—151
	Moriya Jutanugarn (THA) (am)	77-74—151
101	Meena Lee (KOR)	78-74—152
	Brittany Lincicome	76-76—152
	Paige Mackenzie	77-75—152
	Ryann O'Toole	76-76—152
105	Jeong Jang (KOR)	77-76—153
	Meaghan Francella	77-76—153
	Louise Friberg (SWE)	74-79—153
	Tiffany Joh	76-77—153
109	Grace Park (KOR)	76-78—154
	Na On Min (KOR)	78-76—154
	Belen Mozo (ESP)	83-71—154
112	Laura Davies (ENG)	76-79—155
	Eunjung Yi (KOR)	75-80—155
	Alison Lee (am)	79-76—155
115	Gerina Piller	74-84—158
116	Song-Hee Kim (KOR)	78-81—159
	Mindy Kim (KOR)	77-WD

Multiple winners

Since its classification as a major in 1983, there have been six multiple winners of the Kraft Nabisco Championship:

Amy Alcott (USA)	1983, 1988, 1991
Betsy King (USA)	1987, 1990, 1997
Annika Sörenstam (SWE)	2001, 2002, 2005
Juli Inkster (USA)	1984, 1989
Dottie Pepper (USA)	1992, 1999
Karrie Webb (AUS)	2000, 2006

From 1983 to the present the victory tallies by nationality are: USA 19, Sweden four, Australia and Korea two each and France, Mexico and Taiwan one apiece.

2011 Kraft Nabisco Championship [6238–72]

Prize money: $2 million

1	Stacy Lewis	66-69-71-69—275	$300,000
2	Yani Tseng (TPE)	70-68-66-74—278	184,255
3	Katie Futcher	70-71-74-69—284	106,763
	Angela Stanford	72-72-67-73—284	106,763
	Morgan Pressel	70-69-69-76—284	106,763
6	Michelle Wie	74-67-69-75—285	68,093
7	Julieta Granada (PAR)	72-70-75-69—286	50,608
	Chie Arimura (JPN)	68-73-71-74—286	50,608
	Mika Miyazato (JPN)	67-75-70-74—286	50,608
10	In-Kyung Kim (KOR)	75-67-75-70—287	37,997
	Anna Nordqvist (SWE)	69-74-73-71—287	37,997
	Se Ri Pak (KOR)	73-71-71-72—287	37,997
13	Karrie Webb (AUS)	69-74-74-71—288	32,079
	Brittany Lincicome	66-72-74-76—288	32,079
15	Christel Boeljon (NED)	74-73-71-71—289	27,035
	Juli Inkster	73-73-71-72—289	27,035
	Sandra Gal (GER)	67-74-75-73—289	27,035
	Sophie Gustafson (SWE)	72-68-74-75—289	27,035
19	Stacy Prammanasudh	71-75-73-71—290	21,992
	Suzann Pettersen (NOR)	75-71-72-72—290	21,992
	Paula Creamer	73-74-70-73—290	21,992
19T	Maria Hjorth (SWE)	75-70-72-73—290	21,992
	Amy Yang (KOR)	70-69-76-75—290	21,992
	Jimin Kang (KOR)	72-69-72-77—290	21,992
25	Meaghan Francella	75-71-73-72—291	18,562
	Ariya Jutanugarn (THA) (am)	74-73-71-73—291	
	Alena Sharp (CAN)	71-73-73-74—291	18,562
	Eun-Hee Ji (KOR)	75-71-69-76—291	18,562
29	Inbee Park (KOR)	76-72-71-73—292	16,166
	Jiyai Shin (KOR)	73-72-74-73—292	16,166
	Leta Lindley	72-71-75-74—292	16,166
	Karen Stupples (ENG)	71-72-71-78—292	16,166
33	Song-Hee Kim (KOR)	71-74-76-72—293	12,698
	Ai Miyazato (JPN)	71-75-73-74—293	12,698
	Melissa Reid (ENG)	71-75-73-74—293	12,698
	Hee Kyung Seo (KOR)	76-71-72-74—293	12,698
	Momoko Ueda (JPN)	70-76-73-74—293	12,698
	Becky Morgan (WAL)	72-73-73-75—293	12,698
	Wendy Ward	70-71-77-75—293	12,698
	Mi Hyun Kim (KOR)	70-75-69-79—293	12,698

Other players who made the cut: Karine Icher (FRA), Amanda Blumenherst, Kristy McPherson, So Yeon Ryu (KOR), Vicky Hurst, Jane Park 294; Laura Diaz, Mariajo Uribe (COL), Na Yeon Choi (KOR), Natalie Gulbis, Seon Hwa Lee (KOR) 295; Azahara Muñoz (ESP), Lindsey Wright (AUS), Maria Hernandez (ESP) 296; Shanshan Feng (CHN), Reilley Rankin 297; Shi Hyun Ahn (KOR), Laura Davies (ENG), Paige Mackenzie, Brittany Lang, Gwladys Nocera (FRA) 298; Candie Kung (TPE), Kyeong Bae (KOR), Stephanie Sherlock (CAN), Sun Young Yoo (KOR) 299; Nicole Castrale, Mindy Kim (KOR), Shiho Oyama (JPN) 300; Katherine Hull (AUS) 301; Hee Young Park (KOR), Lee-Anne Pace (RSA) 302; Pornanong Phatlum (THA) 304; Sarah Jane Smith 305; Yukari Baba (JPN) 307; Eunjung Yi (KOR) 309

2010 Kraft Nabisco Championship [6702–72]

Prize money: $2 million

1	Yani Tseng (TPE)	69-71-67-68—275	$300,000
2	Suzann Pettersen (NOR)	67-73-67-69—276	183,814
3	Song-Hee Kim (KOR)	69-68-72-70—279	133,344
4	Lorena Ochoa (MEX)	68-70-71-73—282	103,152
5	Cristie Kerr	71-67-74-72—284	64,408
	Jiyai Shin (KOR)	72-72-69-71—284	64,408
	Karen Stupples (ENG)	69-69-68-78—284	64,408
	Karrie Webb (AUS)	69-70-72-73—284	64,408
9	Chie Arimura (JPN)	73-72-68-72—285	44,784
10	Sophie Gusatafson (SWE)	70-73-70-73—286	35,544
	Brittany Lang	72-71-69-74—286	35,544
	Anna Nordqvist (SWE)	74-72-69-71—286	35,544
	Grace Park (KOR)	71-74-68-73—286	35,544
	Inbee Park (KOR)	73-74-70-69—286	35,544
15	Catriona Matthew (SCO)	73-74-67-73—287	26,971
	Se Ri Pak (KOR)	79-71-67-70—287	26,971
	Hee Young Park (KOR)	73-71-70-73—287	26,971
	Angela Stanford	78-68-69-72—287	26,971
19	Stacy Lewis	71-68-75-74—288	23,549
	Morgan Pressel	71-72-72-73—288	23,549
21	Brittany Lincicome	70-74-72-73—289	21,939
	Hee Kyung Seo (KOR)	72-73-76-68—289	21,939
	Jennifer Song (KOR) (am)	71-71-76-71—289	
24	Katherine Hull (AUS)	72-71-72-75—290	20,329
	Gwladys Nocera (FRA)	75-70-71-74—290	20,329
	Alexis Thompson (am)	74-72-73-71—290	
27	Na Yeon Choi (KOR)	74-73-72-72—291	17,151
	Jimin Kang (KOR)	72-74-72-73—291	17,151
	Na On Min (KOR)	69-75-71-76—291	17,151
	Momoko Ueda (JPN)	72-78-68-73—291	17,151
	Michelle Wie	71-71-71-78—291	17,151
	Amy Yang (KOR)	75-73-72-71—291	17,151
	Sakura Yokomina (JPN)	70-71-72-78—291	17,151
34	Heather Bowie Young	76-74-72-70—292	13,183
	Sandra Gal (GER)	72-70-80-70—292	13,183
	Hee-Won Han (KOR)	71-76-72-73—292	13,183
	Paige Mackenzie	75-74-70-73—292	13,183
	Kirsty McPherson	72-72-78-70—292	13,183
	Melissa Reid (ENG)	73-75-71-73—292	13,183

Other players who made the cut: Mi-Jeong Jeon (KOR), Jee Young Lee (KOR), Mika Miyazato (JPN), Shinobu Moromizato (JPN) 293; Vicky Hurst, In-Kyung Ki, (KOR), Teresa Lu (TPE), Jane Park 294; Laura Davies (ENG), Katie Futcher, Pat Hurst, Jeong Jang (KOR), Haeji Kang (KOR), Sarah Lee (KOR), Stacy Prammanasudh, Michele Redman 295; Shi Hyun Ahn (KOR), Hye Jung Choi (KOR), Karine Icher (FRA), Mi Hyun Kim (KOR), Meena Lee (KOR), Seon Hwa Lee (KOR), Giulia Sergas (ITA), Alena Sharp (CAN) 296; Louise Friberg (SWE), Carin Koch (SWE), So Yeon Ryu (KOR) 297; Jessica Korda (am), Sherri Steinhauer 298; Candie Kung (TPE), Yuko Mitsuka (JPN), Eunjung Yi (KOR) 299; Becky Brewerton (WAL), Allison Fouch, Jennifer Rosales (PHI) 300; Julieta Granada (PAR), Eun-Hee Ji (KOR) 301; Ilmi Chung (KOR), Becky Morgan (WAL) 303; Jennifer Johnson (am) 305

2009 Kraft Nabisco Championship

[6673–72]

Prize money: $2 million

1	Brittany Lincicome	66-74-70-69—279	$300,000
2	Cristie Kerr	71-68-70-71—280	161,853
	Kristy McPherson	68-70-70-72—280	161,853
4	Lindsey Wright (AUS)	70-71-71-70—282	105,281
5	Meaghan Francella	72-73-69-69—283	77,036
	Suzann Pettersen (NOR)	71-72-74-66—283	77,036
7	Christina Kim	69-69-75-72—285	58,034
8	Katherine Hull (AUS)	69-74-71-72—286	44,167
	Pat Hurst	71-71-73-71—286	44,167
	Jimin Kang (KOR)	71-70-71-74—286	44,167
	Karrie Webb (AUS)	73-72-72-69—286	44,167
12	Helen Alfredsson (SWE)	72-70-72-73—287	31,841
	Lorena Ochoa (MEX)	73-73-72-69—287	31,841
	Michele Redman	72-73-72-70—287	31,841
	Angela Stanford	67-75-74-71—287	31,841
	Sun Young Yoo (KOR)	70-78-73-66—287	31,841
17	Paula Creamer	70-72-77-69—288	25,542
	Brittany Lang	67-80-71-70—288	25,542
	Yani Tseng (TPE)	69-75-75-69—288	25,542
20	Jee Young Lee (KOR)	69-80-72-68—289	23,624
21	Tiffany Joh (am)	71-75-73-71—290	
	Song-Hee Kim (KOR)	69-78-72-71—290	22,392
	Jiyai Shin (KOR)	72-76-71-71—290	22,392
	Alexis Thompson (am)	72-72-77-69—290	
25	Nicole Castrale	71-75-73-72—291	20,372
	Allison Fouch	76-73-69-73—291	20,372
	Sakura Yokomine (JPN)	72-73-74-72—291	20,372
28	Hee-Won Han (KOR)	75-73-72-72—292	18,540
	In-Kyung Kim (KOR)	70-73-75-74—292	18,540
30	Young Kim (KOR)	76-71-75-71—293	15,835
	Candie Kung (TPE)	72-73-74-74—293	15,835
	Seon Hwa Lee (KOR)	74-77-69-73—293	15,835
	Janice Moodie (SCO)	75-73-74-71—293	15,835
	Jane Park	74-76-68-75—293	15,835
	Momoko Ueda (JPN)	76-72-75-70—293	15,835
36	Yuri Fudoh (JPN)	71-76-73-74—294	12,891
	Eun-Hee Ji (KOR)	75-72-76-71—294	12,891
	Ji Young Oh (KOR)	67-78-78-71—294	12,891
	Wendy Ward	75-72-74-73—294	12,891

Other players who made the cut: Na Yeon Choi (KOR), Joo Mi Kim (KOR), Azahara Muñoz (ESP) (am), Se Ri Pak (KOR), Morgan Pressel, Alena Sharp (CAN) 295; Hye Jung Choi (KOR), Natalie Gulbis 296; Mi Hyun Kim (KOR), Gwladys Nocera (FRA), Angela Park (BRA), Jennifer Rosales (PHI), Giulia Sergas (ITA) 297; Soo-Yun Kang (KOR), Teresa Lu (TPE), Hee Young Park (KOR) 298; Shi Hyun Ahn (KOR), Moira Dunn, Rachel Hetherington (AUS), Inbee Park (KOR) 299; Laura Diaz, Ji-Hee Lee (KOR), Becky Morgan (WAL) 301; Il Mi Chung (KOR) 302; Sophie Gustafson (SWE), Stacy Lewis, Heather Young 303; Diana D'Alessio, Michelle Wie 304; Ai Miyazato (JPN) 305; Silvia Cavalleri (ITA) 306

2008 Kraft Nabisco Championship

[6673–72]

Prize money: $2 million

1	Lorena Ochoa (MEX)	68-71-71-67—277	$300,000
2	Suzann Pettersen (NOR)	74-75-65-68—282	160,369
	Annika Sörenstam (SWE)	71-70-73-68—282	160,369
4	Maria Hjörth (SWE)	70-70-72-71—283	104,317
5	Seon Hwa Lee (KOR)	73-71-68-72—284	83,963
6	Na Yeon Choi (KOR)	74-72-69-70—285	58,859
	Hee-Won Han (KOR)	72-69-70-74—285	58,859
	Mi Hyun Kim (KOR)	70-70-76-69—285	58,859
9	Inbee Park (KOR)	73-70-70-73—286	45,289
10	Se Ri Pak (KOR)	72-70-73-72—287	39,692
	Heather Young	69-70-74-74—287	39,692
12	Karen Stupples (ENG)	67-75-74-72—288	35,621
13	Natalie Gulbis	69-74-73-73—289	32,364
	Karrie Webb (AUS)	76-70-69-74—289	32,364
15	Diana D'Alessio	74-69-72-75—290	27,275
	Meg Mallon	73-73-72-72—290	27,275
	Liselotte Neumann (SWE)	70-72-71-77—290	27,275
	Angela Stanford	75-73-71-71—290	27,275
19	Janice Moodie (SCO)	73-73-74-71—291	23,815
	Sakura Yokomini (JPN)	76-73-72-70—291	23,815
21	Helen Alfredsson (SWE)	75-72-73-72—292	19,506
21T	Paula Creamer	71-74-73-74—292	19,506
	Cristie Kerr	74-72-66-80—292	19,506
	Candie Kung (TPE)	73-74-75-70—292	19,506
	Brittany Lang	75-70-72-75—292	19,506
	Jee Young Lee (KOR)	73-71-75-73—292	19,506
	Angela Park (BRA)	77-71-73-71—292	19,506
	Michele Redman	71-72-76-73—292	19,506
	Yani Tseng (TPE)	72-71-75-74—292	19,506
30	Amanda Blumenhurst (am)	73-73-73-74—293	
31	Heather Daly-Donofrio	75-71-73-75—294	14,190
	Rachel Hetherington (AUS)	76-69-74-75—294	14,190
	Jeong Jang (KOR)	73-73-74-74—294	14,190
	Ai Miyazato (JPN)	68-74-77-75—294	14,190
	Ji-Young Oh (KOR)	77-72-71-74—294	14,190
	Shiho Oyama (JPN)	72-72-76-74—294	14,190
	Ji-Yai Shin (KOR)	73-71-76-74—294	14,190
38	Katherine Hull (AUS)	76-70-74-75—295	11,271
	Hee Young Park (KOR)	75-72-74-74—295	11,271
	Morgan Pressel	71-74-75-75—295	11,271
	Giulia Sergas ITA)	74-75-77-69—295	11,271

Other players who made the cut: Shi Hyun Ahn (KOR), H J Choi (KOR), Sophie Gustafson (SWE), Mhairi McKay (SCO), Lindsey Wright (AUS), 296; Beth Bader, Marisa Baena (COL), Minea Blomqvist (FIN), Momoko Ueda (JPN), 297; Silvia Cavalleri (ITA), Russy Gulyanamitta (THA), Soo-Yun Kang (KOR), Becky Morgan (WAL), 298; Laura Davies (ENG), Pat Hurst, Reilley Rankin, 299; Il Mi Chung (KOR), Juli Inkster, Teresa Lu (TPE), Maria Jose Uribe (am), Wendy Ward, 300; Moira Dunn, Julieta Granada (PAR), Carin Koch (SWE), Meena Lee (KOR), Sarah Lee (KOR), 301; Mallory Blackwelder (am), Alena Sharp (CAN), 302; Meaghan Francella, 303; Sung Ah Yim (KOR), 312

2007 Kraft Nabisco Championship [6673–72]

Prize money: $1.8 million

1	Morgan Pressel	74-72-70-69—285	$300,000	20	Laura Davies (ENG)	74-73-73-73—293	22,881
2	Brittany Lincicome	72-71-71-72—286	140,945		Cristie Kerr	75-73-72-73—293	22,881
	Catriona Matthew (SCO)	70-73-72-71—286	140,945		Sherri Steinhauer	71-78-70-74—293	22,881
	Suzann Pettersen (NOR)	72-69-71-74—286	140,945	20T	Karrie Webb (AUS)	70-77-73-73—293	22,881
5	Shi Hyun Ahn (KOR)	68-73-74-72—287	69,688	24	Juli Inkster	75-75-72-72—294	20,451
	Meaghan Francella	72-72-69-74—287	69,688		Christina Kim	72-77-71-74—294	20,451
	Stacy Lewis (am)	71-73-73-70—287		26	Jimin Kang (KOR)	76-73-73-73—295	19,337
	Stacy Prammanasudh	76-70-70-71—287	69,688	27	Nicole Castrale	76-71-74-75—296	17,565
9	Maria Hjörth (SWE)	70-73-72-73—288	50,114		Julieta Granada (PAR)	74-77-72-73—296	17,565
10	Lorena Ochoa (MEX)	69-71-77-72—289	41,340		Angela Park (BRA)	73-74-75-74—296	17,565
	Se Ri Pak (KOR)	72-70-70-77—289	41,340		Lindsey Wright (AUS)	74-69-77-76—296	17,565
	Angela Stanford	72-75-73-69—289	41,340	31	Laura Diaz	73-79-71-74—297	14,116
13	Jee Young Lee (KOR)	70-77-71-72—290	34,321		Young Jo (KOR)	74-76-72-75—297	14,116
	Sarah Lee (KOR)	72-74-70-74—290	34,321		Mi Hyun Kim (KOR)	74-72-74-77—297	14,116
15	Paula Creamer	73-67-73-78—291	28,651		Leta Lindley	73-75-73-76—297	14,116
	Brittany Lang	71-73-75-72—291	28,651		Hee-Young Park (KOR)	73-74-77-73—297	14,116
	Ai Miyazato (JPN)	76-73-69-73—291	28,651		Annika Sörenstam (SWE)	75-76-71-75—297	14,116
	Ji-Yai Shin (KOR)	76-72-71-72—291	28,651		Heather Young	74-75-76-72—297	14,116
19	Moira Dunn	76-73-72-71—292	25,108	38	Helen Alfredsson (SWE)	78-69-74-77—298	10,782

Other players who made the cut: Sophie Gustafson (SWE), Kim Saiki-Maloney, Sakura Yokomine (JPN) 299; Wendy Doolan, Shiho Oyama (JPN), Gloria Park (KOR) 300; Tina Barrett, Hee-Won Han (KOR), Young Kim (KOR), Becky Morgan (WAL) 301; Karine Icher (FRA), Jeong Jang (KOR), Reilley Rankin, Veronica Zorzi (ITA) 302; Diana D'Alessio, Soo-Yun Kang (KOR), Aree Song (KOR) 303; Carin Koch (SWE). Candie Kung (TPE), Liselotte Neumann (SWE), Nicole Perrot (CHI) 304; Mi-Jeong Jeon (KOR) 305; Tracy Hanson, Taylor Leon (am), Michele Redman 306; Esther Choe (am); Joo Mi Kim (KOR), Grace Park (KOR) 307; Jin Joo Hong (KOR) 310; Meg Mallon 311

2006 Kraft Nabisco Championship [6569–72]

Prize money: $1.8 million

1	Karrie Webb* (AUS)	70-68-76-65—279	$270,000	19T	Veronica Zorzi (ITA)	74-72-75-71—292	21,221
2	Lorena Ochoa (MEX)	62-71-74-72—279	168,226	24	Paula Creamer	69-71-79-74—293	1,7610
Webb won sudden death play-off:: Webb 5, Ochoa 6					Dorothy Delasin	72-72-74-75—293	17,610
3	Natalie Gulbis	73-71-68-68—280	108,222		Karine Icher (FRA)	73-73-77-70—293	17,610
	Michelle Wie	66-71-73-70—280	108,222		Carin Koch (SWE)	70-72-76-75—293	17,610
5	Juli Inkster	69-73-74-68—284	75,985		Candie King (TAI)	72-75-72-74—293	17,610
6	Hee-Won Han (KOR)	75-72-68-71—286	57,104	29	Young Jo (KOR)	72-73-75-74—294	14,199
	Annika Sörenstam (SWE)	71-72-73-70—286	57,104		Meena Lee (KOR)	72-76-72-74—294	14,199
8	Shi Hyun Ahn (KOR)	70-71-71-75—287	41,293		Patricia Meunier-Lebouc (FRA)	77-67-77-73—294	14,199
	Helen Alfredsson (SWE)	70-72-72-73—287	41,293				
	Brittany Lang	70-74-72-71—287	41,293		Ai Miyazato (JPN)	70-77-72-75—294	14,199
11	Stacy Prammanasudh	67-73-76-72—288	33,388		Becky Morgan (WAL)	76-70-75-73—294	14,199
	Michele Redman	72-72-72-72—288	33,388		Jennifer Rosales (PHI)	72-76-73-73—294	14,199
13	Beth Daniel	72-72-72-73—289	29,289	35	Il Mi Chung (KOR)	72-77-73-73—295	11,329
	Morgan Pressel	69-76-70-74—289	29,289		Cristie Kerr	71-76-75-73—295	11,329
15	Yuri Fudoh (JPN)	75-73-69-73—290	26,710		Grace Park (KOR)	74-72-78-71—295	11,329
	Angela Park (am)	68-73-75-74—290			Sherri Steinhauer	72-77-75-71—295	11,329
17	Pat Hurst	73-73-73-72—291	24,592		Wendy Ward	71-75-76-73—295	11,329
	Karen Stupples (ENG)	69-74-72-76—291	24,592	40	Suzann Pettersen (NOR)	75-72-75-74—296	9,763
19	Tina Barrett	72-75-74-71—292	21,221		Aree Song (KOR)	74-76-72-74—296	9,763
	Jeong Jang (KOR)	71-75-76-70—292	21,221	42	Marisa Baena (COL)	75-72-71-79—297	8,842
	Young Kim (KOR)	74-73-70-75—292	21,221		Mi Hyun Kim (KOR)	75-74-75-73—297	8,842
	Seon Hwa Lee (KOR)	69-69-74-80—292	21,221		Rachel Hetherington (AUS)	74-75-76-72—297	8,842

Other players who made the cut: Kyeong Bae (KOR), Jimin Kang (KOR), Birdie Kim (KOR), Sarah Lee (KOR), Janice Moodie (SCO), Liselotte Neumann (SWE), Se Ri Pak (KOR) 298; Johanna Head (ENG), Christine Kim, Gwladys Nocera (FRA), Kim Saiki 299; Jee Young Lee (KOR), Sung Ah Yim (KOR) 300; Lorie Kane (CAN), Soo Young Moon (KOR), Reilley Rankin 301; Brandie Burton 302; Maru Martinez (am), In-Bee Park (am) 304; Joo Mi Kim (KOR) 305; Nicole Perrot (CHI) 306; Katherine Hull (AUS), Meg Mallon 307; Kate Golden, Sydnee Michaels (am) 308; A J Eathorne (CAN) 314

2005 Kraft Nabisco Championship

[6460–72]

Prize money: $1.8 million

1	Annika Sörenstam (SWE)	70-69-66-68—273	$270,000
2	Rosie Jones	69-70-71-71—281	166,003
3	Laura Diaz	75-69-71-68—283	106,791
	Cristie Kerr	72-70-70-71—283	1067,91
5	Mi Hyun Kim (KOR)	69-71-72-72—284	68,165
	Grace Park (KOR)	73-68-76-67—284	68,165
7	Juli Inkster	70-74-72-69—285	51,350
8	Lorie Kane (CAN)	71-76-69-70—286	44,988
9	Beth Daniel	74-72-69-72—287	34,591
	Dorothy Delasin (PHI)	71-72-73-71—287	34,591
	Wendy Doolan (AUS)	74-69-73-71—287	34,591
	Candie Kung (TPE)	72-73-71-71—287	34,591
	Reilley Rankin	73-68-74-72—287	34,591
14	Brandie Burton	72-71-72-73—288	27,175
	Kim Saiki	74-71-70-73—288	27,175
	Michelle Wie (am)	70-74-73-71—288	
17	Natalie Gulbis	73-71-72-73—289	24,267
	Hee-Won Han (KOR)	76-71-69-73—289	24,267
19	Shi Hyun Ahn (KOR)	77-76-71-66—290	2,1692
	Paula Creamer	74-72-72-72—290	21,692
	Young Kim (KOR)	76-70-70-74—290	21,692
	Morgan Pressel (am)	70-73-72-75—290	
23	Laura Davies (ENG)	73-71-71-77—292	19,086
	Pat Hurst	71-74-74-73—292	19,086
	Sherri Steinhauer	71-72-75-74—292	19,086
	Karen Stupples (ENG)	69-80-70-73—292	19,086
27	Dawn Coe-Jones (CAN)	74-73-74-72—293	16,723
	Jeong Jang (KOR)	77-74-71-71—293	16,723
	Se Ri Pak (KOR)	77-70-70-76—293	16,723
30	Michelle Estill	71-79-71-73—294	14,565
	Julieta Granada (PAR) (am)	75-71-70-78—294	
	Carin Koch (SWE)	70-73-75-76—294	14,565
	Jill McGill	73-72-77-72—294	14,565
	Stacy Prammanasudh	75-74-74-71—294	14,565
35	Helen Alfredsson (SWE)	76-72-74-73—295	12,383
	Leta Lindley	74-77-73-71—295	12,383
	Lorena Ochoa (MEX)	76-75-73-71—295	12,383
	Jennifer Rosales (PHI)	71-79-74-71—295	12,383
39	Tina Barrett	73-77-71-75—296	10,288
	Yuri Fudoh (JPN)	75-75-75-71—296	10,288
	Rachel Hetherington (AUS)	77-73-72-74—296	10,288
	Christina Kim	76-71-73-76—296	10,288
	Janice Moodie (SCO)	74-77-74-71—296	10,288

Other players who made the cut: Joo Mi Kim (KOR), Catriona Matthew (SCO), Ai Miyazato (JPN), Gloria Park (KOR), Charlotta Sörenstam (SWE), Karrie Webb (AUS) 297; Heather Bowie, Tina Fischer (GER), Meg Mallon, Jane Park (am), Wendy Ward 298; Liselotte Neumann (SWE), Giulia Sergas (ITA), Bo Bae Song (KOR) 299; Katherine Hull (AUS), Kelli Kuehne, Michele Redman, Angela Stanford 300; Donna Andrews, Betsy King 301; Trish Johnson (ENG), Aree Song (KOR) 302; Sophie Gustafson (SWE), Emilee Klein 303; Stephanie Arricau (FRA), Hilary Lunke 304; Heather Daly-Donofrio, Candy Hannemann (BRA) 305; Nancy Scranton 306; Catrin Nilsmark (SWE) 310; Jamie Hullett 311; Laurel Kean 316

2004 Nabisco Dinah Shore

[6673–72]

Prize money: $1.6 million

1	Grace Park (KOR)	72-69-67-69—277	$240,000
2	Aree Song (KOR)	66-73-69-70—278	146,826
3	Karrie Webb (AUS)	68-71-71-69—279	106,512
4	Michelle Wie (am)	69-72-69-71—281	
5	Cristie Kerr	71-71-71-69—282	74,358
	Catriona Matthew (SCO)	67-75-70-70—282	74,358
7	Mi-Hyun Kim (KOR)	71-70-71-71—283	54,261
8	Rosie Jones	67-73-71-73—284	36,737
	Christina Kim	72-72-70-70—284	36,737
	Candie Kung (TPE)	69-75-71-69—284	36,737
	Jung Yeon Lee (KOR)	69-69-71-75—284	36,737
	Lorena Ochoa (MEX)	67-76-74-67—284	36,737
13	Hee-Won Han (KOR)	72-71-71-71—285	26,420
	Stacy Prammanasudh	71-71-69-74—285	26,420
	Annika Sörenstam (SWE)	71-76-69-69—285	26,420
16	Laura Davies (ENG)	71-77-70-68—286	20,633
	Wendy Doolan (AUS)	70-69-72-75—286	20,633
	Young Kim (KOR)	74-72-67-73—286	20,633
	Carin Koch (SWE)	70-72-71-73—286	20,633
	Se Ri Pak (KOR)	72-73-72-69—286	20,633
	Karen Stupples (ENG)	70-76-68-72—286	20,633
22	Michele Redman	73-73-70-71—287	17,846
23	Jeong Jang (KOR)	76-71-70-72—289	17,203
24	Brandie Burton	70-76-71-73—290	15,944
	Tammie Green	71-78-71-70—290	15,944
	Jane Park (am)	71-74-73-72—290	
	Dottie Pepper	68-70-74-78—290	15,944
28	Danielle Ammaccapane	75-77-73-66—291	13,682
	Donna Andrews	70-74-73-74—291	13,682
	Tina Barrett	75-70-73-73—291	13,682
	Juli Inkster	74-74-73-70—291	13,682
	Wendy Ward	72-74-70-75—291	13,682
33	Vicki Goetze-Ackerman	73-79-71-69—292	11,897
	Kelly Robbins	69-74-78-71—292	11,897
35	Dorothy Delasin (PHI)	76-71-71-75—293	10,306
	Pat Hurst	72-76-69-76—293	10,306
	Lorie Kane (CAN)	72-74-76-71—293	10,306
	Rachel Teske (AUS)	75-71-71-76—293	10,306
	Iben Tinning (DEN)	70-75-77-71—293	10,306
40	Helen Alfredsson (SWE)	75-72-71-76—294	8,541
	Beth Daniel	72-74-74-74—294	8,541
	Kate Golden	73-78-74-69—294	85,41
	Elizabeth Janangelo (am)	71-78-70-75—294	
	Emilee Klein	71-73-76-74—294	8,541

Other players who made the cut: Beth Bauer, Paula Creamer (am), Jill McGill 295; Sophie Gustafson (SWE), Stephanie Louden, Meg Mallon, Sherri Steinhauer 296; Michelle Ellis (AUS), Laurel Kean, Becky Morgan (WAL) 297; Jackie Gallagher-Smith, Ji-Hee Lee (KOR), Charlotta Sörenstam (SWE) 298; Moira Dunn, Natalie Gulbis, Betsy King, Jennifer Rosales (PHI) 300; Marisa Baena (COL), Heather Bowie, Heather Daly-Donofrio, Soo-Yun Kang (KOR), Miho Koga (JPN), Yu Ping Lin (TPE), Janice Moodie (SCO) 301; Hilary Lunke 302; JoAnne Carner, Dawn Coe-Jones, Joanne Mills (AUS) 303; Mhairi McKay (SCO), Shani Waugh (AUS) 304; Mardi Lunn (AUS) 305; Kelli Kuehne 306; Amy Alcott 308; Nancy Lopez WD

2003 Nabisco Dinah Shore [6520–72]

Prize money: $1.6 million

1	Patricia Meunier Lebouc (FRA)	70-68-70-73—281	$240,000
2	Annika Sörenstam (SWE)	68-72-71-71—282	146,120
3	Lorena Ochoa (MEX)	71-70-74-68—283	106,000
4	Laura Davies (ENG)	70-75-69-70—284	82,,000
5	Beth Daniel	75-74-68-70—287	51,200
	Laura Diaz	76-71-69-71—287	51,200
	Maria Hjörth (SWE)	72-72-73-70—287	51,200
	Catriona Matthew (SCO)	71-74-72-70—287	51,200
9	Jennifer Rosales (PHI)	74-70-72-72—288	35,600
	Michelle Wie (am)	72-74-66-76—288	
11	Juli Inkster	75-74-66-75—290	29,160
	Cristie Kerr	74-71-74-71—290	29,160
	Woo-Soon Ko (KOR)	74-73-70-73—290	29,160
	Rosie Jones	71-75-72-72—290	29,160
15	Dawn Coe-Jones (CAN)	72-74-72-73—291	22,080
	Dorothy Delasin (PHI)	71-71-76-73—291	22,080
	Catrin Nilsmark (SWE)	71-78-73-69—291	22,080
	Se Ri Pak (KOR)	71-72-71-77—291	22,080
	Karen Stupples (ENG)	71-71-76-73—291	22,080
20	Hee-Won Han (KOR)	73-74-75-70—292	19,040
21	Danielle Ammaccapane	75-68-78-72—293	17,440
21T	Jeong Jang (KOR)	75-73-76-69—293	17,440
	Virada Nirapathpongporn (am)	76-72-72-73—293	
	Michele Redman	70-72-76-75—293	17,440
	Aree Song (am)	72-77-73-71—293	
	Karrie Webb (AUS)	70-79-71-73—293	17,440
27	Leta Lindley	76-70-75-73—294	15,840
28	Tammie Green	77-71-73-74—295	14,160
	Christina Kim	72-76-71-76—295	14,160
	Betsy King	75-74-70-76—295	14,160
	Candie Kung (TPE)	74-75-74-72—295	14,160
	Charlotta Sörenstam (SWE)	73-74-71-77—295	14,160
33	Heather Bowie	72-78-72-74—296	11,373
	Heather Daly-Donofrio	74-77-72-73—296	11,373
	Moira Dunn	74-80-73-69—296	11,373
	Amy Fruhwirth	73-75-75-73—296	11,373
	Vicki Goetze-Ackerman	75-74-74-73—296	11,373
	Meg Mallon	72-76-73-75—296	11,373
39	Beth Bauer	74-76-70-77—297	9,440
	Jackie Gallagher-Smith	75-74-74-74—297	9,440
	Lorie Kane (CAN)	72-72-78-75—297	9,440

Other players who made the cut: Brandie Burton, Raquel Carriedo (ESP), Michelle Ellis (AUS), Liselotte Neumann (SWE), Gloria Park (KOR), Kelly Robbins 298; Natalie Gulbis, Rachel Teske (AUS), Wendy Ward 299; Sophie Gustafson (SWE), Pat Hurst, Kelli Kuehne, Barb Mucha, Dottie Pepper, Angela Stanford 300; Nanci Bowen, Akiko Fukushima (JPN), Laurel Kean, Mi-Hyun Kim (KOR), Joanne Morley (ENG), Kim Saiki, Lindsey Wright (AUS) (am) 301; Helen Alfredsson (SWE), Donna Andrews, Emilee Klein, Stephanie Louden, Janice Moodie (SCO), Shani Waugh (AUS) 302; Mhairi McKay (SCO), Patty Sheehan 303; Suzanne Strudwick (ENG) 304; Tina Fischer (GER) 305; Tracy Hanson 306; Kasumi Fujii (JPN), Yu Ping Lin (TPE) 307; Pat Bradley 308; Dale Eggeling 310; Mardi Lunn (AUS) 311

Kraft Nabisco History

This event was inaugurated in 1972 as the Colgate Dinah Shore and continued to be sponsored by Colgate until 1981. Nabisco took over the sponsorship in 1982; and the Nabisco Dinah Shore was designated a Major Championship in 1983. The Championship became the Kraft Nabisco in 2005. Mission Hills CC, Rancho Mirage, California, is the event's permanent venue.

Year	Winner	Score
1972	J Blalock	213
1973	M Wright	284
1974	J Prentice*	289
After a play-off with J Blalock and S Haynie		
1975	S Palmer	283
1976	J Rankin	285
1977	K Whitworth	289
1978	S Post*	283
After a play-off with P Pulz		
1979	S Post*	276
After a play-off with N Lopez		
1980	D Caponi	275
1981	N Lopez	277
1982	S Little	278
1983	A Alcott	282
1984	J Inkster*	280
After a play-off with P Bradley		
1985	A Miller	278
1986	P Bradley	280
1987	B King*	283
After a play-off with P Sheehan		
1988	A Alcott	274
1989	J Inkster	279
1990	B King	283
1991	A Alcott	273
1992	D Mochrie*	279
After a play-off with J Inkster		
1993	H Alfredsson (SWE)	284
1994	D Andrews	276
1995	N Bowen	285
1996	P Sheehan	281
1997	B King	276
1998	P Hurst	281
1999	D Pepper	269
2000	K Webb (AUS)	274
2001	A Sörenstam (SWE)	281
2002	A Sörenstam (SWE)	280
2003	P Meunier-Lebouc (FRA)	281
2004	G Park (KOR)	277
2005	A Sörenstam (SWE)	273
2006	K Webb (AUS)*	279
After a play-off with L Ochoa (MEX)		
2007	M Pressel	285
2008	L Ochoa (MEX)	277
2009	B Lincicombe	279
2010	Y Tseng (TPE)	275
2011	S Lewis	275
2012	S Y Yoo (KOR)*	279
After a play-off with I K Kim (KOR)		

du Maurier Classic History

The du Maurier Classic was inaugurated in 1973 and designated a Major Championship in 1979.
It was discontinued after 2000 and was replaced as a major on the US LPGA schedule by the Weetabix Women's British Open.

Players are of American nationality unless stated

1973	J Bourassa*	Montreal GC, Montreal	214
**After a play-off with S Haynie and J Rankin*			
1974	CJ Callison	Candiac GC, Montreal	208
1975	J Carner*	St George's CC, Toronto	214
**After a play-off with C Mann*			
1976	D Caponi*	Cedar Brae G&CC, Toronto	212
**After a play-off with J Rankin*			
1977	J Rankin	Lachute G&CC, Montreal	214
1978	J Carner	St George's CC, Toronto	278
1979	A Alcott	Richelieu Valley CC, Montreal	285
1980	P Bradley	St George's CC, Toronto	277
1981	J Stephenson (AUS)	Summerlea CC, Dorian, Quebec	278
1982	S Haynie	St George's CC, Toronto	280
1983	H Stacy	Beaconsfield CC, Montreal	277
1984	J Inkster	St George's CC, Toronto	279
1985	P Bradley	Beaconsfield CC, Montreal	278
1986	P Bradley*	Board of Trade CC, Toronto	276
**After a play-off with A Okamoto*			
1987	J Rosenthal	Islesmere GC, Laval, Quebec	272
1988	S Little (RSA)	Vancouver GC, Coquitlam, BC	279
1989	T Green	Beaconsfield GC, Montreal	279
1990	C Johnston	Westmount G&CC, Kitchener, Ontario	276
1991	N Scranton	Vancouver GC, Coquitlam, BC	279
1992	S Steinhauer	St Charles CC, Winnipeg, Manitoba	277
1993	B Burton*	London H&CC, Ontario	277
**After a play-off with B King*			
1994	M Nause	Ottawa Hunt Club, Ontario	279
1995	J Lidback	Beaconsfield CC, Montreal	280
1996	L Davies (ENG)	Edmonton CC, Edmonton, Alberta	277
1997	C Walker	Glen Abbey GC, Toronto	278
1998	B Burton	Essex G&CC, Ontario	270
1999	K Webb (AUS)	Priddis Greens G&CC, Calgary, Alberta	277
2000	M Mallon	Royal Ottawa GC, Aylmer, Quebec	282

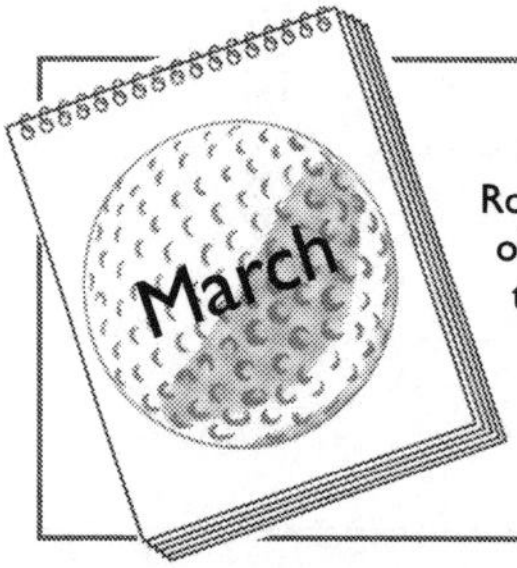

Month by month in 2012

Rory McIlroy, Justin Rose and Luke Donald all win in America. McIlroy holds off Tiger Woods at the Honda Classic to become world number one for the first time. Donald gets top spot back at the Transitions Championship and in between Rose wins his first World Golf Championships title in Miami. Woods hits back by taking the Arnold Palmer Invitational and Yani Tseng continues her domination of the women's game with two more wins.

Women's Grand Slam Titles

Patty Berg

Mickey Wright

Louise Suggs

	British Open[1]	US Open[2]	McDonald's LPGA[3]	Kraft Nabisco[4]	du Maurier[5]	Title-holders[6]	Western[7]	*Total Titles*
Patty Berg (USA)	0	1	0	—	—	7	7	15
Mickey Wright (USA)	0	4	4	—	—	2	3	13
Louise Suggs (USA)	0	2	1	—	—	4	4	11
Annika Sörenstam (SWE)	1	3	3	3	0	—	—	10
'Babe' Zaharias (USA)	0	3	—	—	—	3	4	10
Karrie Webb (AUS)	3	2	1	2	1	—	—	9
Betsy Rawls (USA)	0	4	2	—	—	0	2	8
Juli Inkster (USA)	0	2	2	2	1	—	—	7

[1] The Weetabix Women's British Open was designated a major on the LPGA Tour in 2001
[2] The US Open became an LPGA major in 1950
[3] The McDonald's LPGA Championship was designated a major in 1955
[4] The Kraft Nabisco event was designated a major in 1983
[5] The du Maurier event was designated a major in 1979 but discontinued after 2000
[6] The Titleholders Championship was a major from 1937–1966 and in 1972
[7] The Western event was a major from 1937 to 1967

Super Career Grand Slam: Only Karrie Webb has won five of the qualifying majors – the Women's British Open, the US Open, the LPGA Championship, the Kraft Nabisco and du Maurier. She completed her Super Grand Slam in 2002.

Career Grand Slam: Only Louise Suggs (1957), Mickey Wright (1962), Pat Bradley (1986), Julie Inkster (1999), Karrie Webb (2001) and Annika Sörenstam (2003) have won all the designated majors at the time they were playing.

Grand Slam: Only Babe Zaharias in 1950 (three majors) and Sandra Haynie (USA) in 1964 (two majors) have won all the majors available that season.

Note: Glenna Collett Vare (USA) won six US Amateurs between 1922 and 1935 including three in a row in 1928, 1929 and 1930. Jo Anne Carner (USA) won five US Amateurs between 1957 and 1968. Julie Inkster won three US Amateurs in 1980, 1981 and 1982.

Davis Love III is the 2013 Bob Jones Award winner

The 2012 US Ryder Cup captain Davis Love III has been chosen as the recipient of the 2013 Bob Jones Award.

Presented annually since 1955 the award, the United States Golf Association's highest honour, recognizes an individual who demonstrates the spirit, personal character and respect for the game shown by Jones, winner of nine USGA championships.

"Throughout his impressive career, Davis has distinguished himself with his sense of fair play, integrity and reverence for the game's traditions," said USGA President Glen D Nager. "His passion for the game, as well as the values and principles that guide his everyday life, are emblematic of the characteristics that the Bob Jones Award seeks to identify. Golf and all those who play it are inspired by Davis' example."

Forty-eight-year-old Love won 20 PGA Tour events including the 1997 US PGA Championship at Winged Foot and The Players Championship, in 1992 and 2003.

"Davis epitomizes everything that Bob Jones stood for with his character, integrity, displays of sportsmanship and his spirit of giving back," said PGA Tour Commissioner Tim Finchem. "He truly understands what it means to be a role model and has been a great ambassador for the PGA Tour and golf, both on and off the field of competition. He is a worthy addition to the list of distinguished winners of the USGA's Bob Jones Award."

In 1997, Love earned the USGA International Book Award for *Every Shot I Take*, a tribute to his late father Davis Love Jr, a highly esteemed teaching professional who imparted lessons to his son on golf and life.

Love finished second in the 1995 and 1999 Masters, as well as in the 1996 US Open at Oakland Hills Country Club. His poise, dignity and graciousness in those disappointing outcomes – in addition to the humility, respect and sportsmanship he displayed in his numerous triumphs – were strong factors in his selection for the award.

Off the course he established the Davis Love Foundation in 2005 to assist national and community-based programs that work to build a better future for at-risk children.

In 2008, Love received the PGA Tour's Payne Stewart Award, which is awarded to a player who shares the conduct, respect and philanthropy that were displayed by the 1991 and 1999 US Open champion who died in a plane accident in 1999.

"From the time I was first introduced to Davis by his dad I was impressed," said Tom Kite, the 1992 US Open champion and the 1979 recipient of the Bob Jones Award. "At first it was those booming drives that caught my attention. After I played a few rounds and tournaments with him, I became more in awe of his overall game. Davis had it all, from prodigious drives to a deft putting touch, and there were no limits to the success he was going to have. As he nears his 30th year on the PGA Tour, few have been able to accomplish as much.

"But as much as I have been impressed with his wonderful golf swing and his tournament record, I treasure our friendship so much more. Davis has conducted himself with such style and grace that everyone in the game respects and admires him. And Davis respects and admires those who make our game so rich. The big thing Davis has in common with Bob Jones is that as much as he loves golf, he loves the people in golf more. There can be no more deserving recipient of the Bob Jones Award."

For years, Love has displayed leadership in what is usually an individual game, culminating in his captaincy of the 2012 US Ryder Cup team. Love has represented his country as a player in six Ryder Cups, six Presidents Cups and in the 1985 Walker Cup Match at Pine Valley Golf Club, where he helped lead the USA Team to a narrow 13–11 victory over Great Britain and Ireland by winning two points on the final day.

A longtime resident of Sea Island, Georgia, Love is a fixture in the local community, along with his wife, Robin, daughter, Alexia, and son, Davis IV, as well as his brother, Mark, who is the tournament director of The McGladrey Classic.

PART II

Men's Professional Tournaments

World Golf Rankings 2012

The most notable gains in the 2012 World Rankings top 50 were South African Branden Grace who leapt 224 places to 34th position and the USA's Scott Piercy and Denmark's Thorbjorn Olesen who both improved by 112 places.

Ranking	Name		Country	Points Average	Total Points	No. of Events	2010/2011 Pts Lost	2012 Pts Gained
1	Rory McIlroy	(3)	NIR	13.22	621.31	47	–364.27	+596.99
2	Luke Donald	(1)	ENG	8.62	439.74	51	–447.49	+345.77
3	Tiger Woods	(23)	USA	8.53	341.31	40	–172.24	+369.87
4	Justin Rose	(18)	ENG	6.42	333.73	52	–210.39	+337.66
5	Adam Scott	(5)	AUS	6.21	260.71	42	–212.63	+215.02
6	Louis Oosthuizen	(40)	RSA	6.14	319.27	52	–179.83	+334.85
7	Lee Westwood	(2)	ENG	6.03	313.71	52	–320.61	+271.50
8	Bubba Watson	(21)	USA	5.29	259.43	49	–213.58	+288.71
9	Jason Dufner	(33)	USA	5.29	269.85	51	–158.75	+267.95
10	Brandt Snedeker	(38)	USA	5.23	271.71	52	–162.96	+267.89
11	Webb Simpson	(10)	USA	5.13	256.37	50	–217.61	+202.01
12	Ian Poulter	(16)	ENG	5.00	254.89	51	–171.42	+232.12
13	Keegan Bradley	(31)	USA	5.00	259.85	52	–157.10	+241.47
14	Charl Schwartzel	(9)	RSA	4.90	254.70	52	–222.23	+205.41
15	Graeme McDowell	(13)	NIR	4.81	250.10	52	–245.16	+252.31
16	Sergio García	(17)	ESP	4.73	231.99	49	–148.07	+194.26
17	Phil Mickelson	(14)	USA	4.69	229.87	49	–213.24	+232.79
18	Steve Stricker	(6)	USA	4.65	190.60	41	–204.57	+176.69
19	Peter Hanson	(42)	SWE	4.59	238.89	52	–148.72	+234.55
20	Nick Watney	(12)	USA	4.54	235.98	52	–203.14	+200.84
21	Matt Kuchar	(11)	USA	4.44	226.34	51	–246.10	+218.05
22	Bo Van Pelt	(29)	USA	4.41	229.29	52	–159.96	+206.94
23	Dustin Johnson	(7)	USA	4.36	209.22	48	–230.23	+170.53
24	Ernie Els	(68)	RSA	4.34	225.54	52	–155.40	+252.88
25	Zach Johnson	(37)	USA	4.25	212.34	50	–159.94	+217.60
26	Hunter Mahan	(19)	USA	3.85	200.39	52	–212.04	+209.85
27	Jim Furyk	(50)	USA	3.83	198.95	52	–146.66	+209.36
28	Martin Kaymer	(4)	GER	3.67	190.65	52	–274.42	+131.00
29	Paul Lawrie	(87)	SCO	3.53	176.42	50	–97.44	+187.32
30	Francesco Molinari	(41)	ITA	3.42	177.62	52	–167.98	+181.16
31	Rickie Fowler	(32)	USA	3.37	171.84	51	–161.56	+157.73
32	Carl Pettersson	(110)	SWE	3.34	173.51	52	–103.64	+197.08
33	Gonzalo Fdez-Castano	(49)	ESP	3.31	132.52	40	–82.57	+97.76
34	Branden Grace	(258)	RSA	3.17	164.58	52	–65.55	+197.40
35	Bill Haas	(27)	USA	3.12	162.23	52	–172.45	+149.30
36	Nicolas Colsaerts	(74)	BEL	3.10	161.30	52	–99.57	+169.52
37	Jason Day	(8)	AUS	2.89	127.08	44	–195.35	+79.01
38	John Senden	(43)	AUS	2.85	148.11	52	–128.55	+118.23
39	Robert Garrigus	(108)	USA	2.84	147.57	52	–89.40	+161.44
40	Ryan Moore	(56)	USA	2.76	132.59	48	–106.82	+123.72
41	Scott Piercy	(154)	USA	2.71	141.12	52	–56.69	+141.23
42	David Toms	(26)	USA	2.68	118.09	44	–144.13	+87.21
43	Hiroyuki Fujita	(69)	JPN	2.64	137.44	52	–102.30	+122.29
44	Matteo Manassero	(58)	ITA	2.59	134.77	52	–106.99	+132.29
45	Thomas Bjørn	(35)	DEN	2.52	118.55	47	–134.84	+92.01
46	David Lynn	(94)	ENG	2.42	116.26	48	–71.97	+103.04
47	Jamie Donaldson	(92)	WAL	2.39	112.41	47	–77.86	+103.53
48	K J Choi	(15)	KOR	2.30	119.52	52	–182.66	+69.16
49	George Coetzee	(80)	RSA	2.27	117.84	52	–80.30	+104.60
50	Thorbjorn Olesen	(162)	DEN	2.20	114.27	52	–61.81	+117.78

Ranking in brackets indicates position at end of 2011 season

European Tour Race to Dubai 2012 (at end of 2012 season)

www.europeantour.com

Final Order of Merit (Top 117 keep their cards for the 2013 season)

1	Rory McIlroy (NIR)	€5,519,118	61	Brett Rumford (AUS)	431,687
2	Justin Rose (ENG)	3,768,345	62	David Howell (ENG)	426,781
3	Louis Oosthuizen (RSA)	3,187,364	63	Julien Quesne (FRA)	420,722
4	Peter Hanson (SWE)	3,022,916	64	Jaco Van Zyl (RSA)	420,037
5	Ian Poulter (ENG)	2,581,257	65	Anthony Wall (ENG)	417,294
6	Branden Grace (RSA)	2,502,501	66	Joel Sjöholm (SWE)	412,376
7	Luke Donald (ENG)	2,373,540	67	Martin Laird (SCO)	405,423
8	Francesco Molinari (ITA)	2,215,229	68	Robert Karlsson (SWE)	379,002
9	Graeme McDowell (NIR)	1,945,056	69	Fabrizio Zanotti (PAR)	375,394
10	Paul Lawrie (SCO)	1,910,381	70	Mark Foster (ENG)	373,491
11	Nicolas Colsaerts (BEL)	1,745,744	71	Garth Mulroy (RSA)	373,352
12	Lee Westwood (ENG)	1,671,456	72	Matthew Baldwin (ENG)	372,786
13	Matteo Manassero (ITA)	1,595,093	73	Alvaro Quiros (ESP)	371,186
14	Marcel Siem (GER)	1,368,845	74	Paul Casey (ENG)	368,560
15	Thorbjørn Olesen (DEN)	1,309,271	75	Grégory Bourdy (FRA)	355,331
16	Charl Schwartzel (RSA)	1,224,345	76	Damien McGrane (IRL)	352,205
17	Rafa Cabrera-Bello (ESP)	1,210,858	77	Michael Campbell (NZL)	333,798
18	David Lynn (ENG)	1,208,633	78	Richard Green (AUS)	329,965
19	Jamie Donaldson (WAL)	1,150,624	79	Felipe Aguilar (CHI)	324,195
20	Gonzalo Fernandez-Castaño (ESP)	1,102,696	80	James Morrison (ENG)	322,915
21	George Coetzee (RSA)	1,071,268	81	Jorge Campillo (ESP)	319,348
22	Bernd Wiesberger (AUT)	1,059,691	82	Ricardo Gonzalez (ARG)	312,032
23	Danny Willett (ENG)	1,055,616	83	Paul McGinley (IRL)	300,924
24	Alexander Noren (SWE)	1,045,189	84	Darren Fichardt (RSA)	295,708
25	Marcus Fraser (AUS)	1,016,337	85	John Daly (USA)	285,676
26	Richie Ramsay (SCO)	1,009,417	86	Edoardo Molinari (ITA)	280,976
27	Thongchai Jaidee (THA)	1,009,320	87	Graeme Storm (ENG)	278,448
28	Miguel Angel Jiménez (ESP)	997,737	88	José María Olazábal (ESP)	270,421
29	Shane Lowry (IRL)	996,540	89	Hennie Otto (RSA)	264,522
30	Martin Kaymer (GER)	996,382	90	Ricardo Santos (POR)	264,174
31	Thomas Björn (DEN)	992,086	91	Mikko Ilonen (FIN)	259,176
32	Jeev Milkha Singh (IND)	926,062	92	Keith Horne (RSA)	258,074
33	Robert Rock (ENG)	867,227	93	Magnus A Carlsson (SWE)	255,233
34	Padraig Harrington (IRL)	850,603	94	Emiliano Grillo (ARG)	255,138
35	Stephen Gallacher (SCO)	844,843	95	Oliver Fisher (ENG)	253,418
36	Fredrik Andersson Hed (SWE)	808,131	96	Thomas Levet (FRA)	253,041
37	Pablo Larrazábal (ESP)	796,864	97	S S P Chowrasia (IND)	250,530
38	Ross Fisher (ENG)	793,528	98	Prom Meesawat (THA)	240,110
39	Anders Hansen (DEN)	786,489	99	Steve Webster (ENG)	234,411
40	Henrik Stenson (SWE)	773,620	100	Grégory Havret (FRA)	233,618
41	Raphaël Jacquelin (FRA)	766,859	101	Liang Wenchong (CHN)	233,416
42	Søren Kjeldsen (DEN)	716,555	102	Jean-Baptiste (FRA)	227,642
43	Sergio Garciía (ESP)	699,234	103	Phillip Price (WAL)	224,375
44	Joost Luiten (NED)	687,197	104	Robert Coles (ENG)	223,345
45	Retief Goosen (RSA)	685,815	105	Robert-Jan Derksen (NED)	223,319
46	Chris Wood (ENG)	674,128	106	Lorenzo Gagli (ITA)	217,615
47	Jbe Kruger (RSA)	617,174	107	Ignacio Garrido (ESP)	212,650
48	Peter Lawrie (IRL)	614,629	108	Darren Clarke (NIR)	204,914
49	Richard Sterne (RSA)	598,730	109	Tommy Fleetwood (ENG)	203,699
50	Simon Dyson (ENG)	596,333	110	Peter Whiteford (SCO)	203,365
51	Romain Wattel (FRA)	586,465	111	Gareth Maybin (NIR)	203,296
52	Victor Dubuisson (FRA)	573,249	112	José Manuel (ESP)	202,225
53	Scott Jamieson (SCO)	564,587	113	Johan Edfors (SWE)	199,996
54	Thomas Aiken (RSA)	563,621	114	Maarten Lafeber (NED)	198,152
55	Marc Warren (SCO)	552,905	115	Craig Lee (SCO)	193,334
56	Michael Hoey (NIR)	544,001	116	Simon Khan (ENG)	191,545
57	Alejandro Cañizares (ESP)	508,686	117	Tom Lewis (ENG)	191,516
58	David Drysdale (SCO)	496,672	118	Andrew Dodt (AUS)	185,531
59	Lee Slattery (ENG)	494,398	119	Richard Bland (ENG)	184,018
60	Richard Finch (ENG)	461,863	120	Tjaart Van Der Walt (RSA)	183,325

Career Money List (at end of 2012 season)

Ernie is top again

Ernie Els regained his place at the top of the table pushing Lee Westwwood back to second position. English players occupied 22 places in the top 100 followed by Sweden with 13, Scotland with nine places and South Africa and Spain with seven apiece.

1	Ernie Els (RSA)	€28,300,444
2	Lee Westwood (ENG)	28,018,135
3	Colin Montgomerie (SCO)	24,496,592
4	Padraig Harrington (IRL)	23,336,794
5	Retief Goosen (RSA)	21,795,334
6	Miguel Angel Jiménez (ESP)	19,980,336
7	Darren Clarke (NIR)	19,917,932
8	Ian Poulter (ENG)	18,009,583
9	Sergio García (ESP)	17,153,107
10	Thomas Björn (DEN)	16,366,534
11	Rory McIlroy (NIR)	15,925,946
12	Luke Donald (ENG)	15,511,375
13	Robert Karlsson (SWE)	14,697,179
14	Paul Casey (ENG)	14,657,972
15	Martin Kaymer (GER)	14,359,959
16	Vijay Singh (FIJ)	14,141,701
17	Angel Cabrera (ARG)	13,910,915
18	Graeme McDowell (NIR)	13,879,546
19	Bernhard Langer (GER)	12,681,909
20	José María Olazábal (ESP)	12,067,264
21	Michael Campbell (NZL)	11,829,478
22	Henrik Stenson (SWE)	11,534,747
23	Paul Lawrie (SCO)	11,405,821
24	Justin Rose (ENG)	11,385,126
25	Peter Hanson (SWE)	11,379,131
26	Anders Hansen (DEN)	11,353,445
27	David Howell (ENG)	11,084,460
28	Charl Schwartzel (RSA)	11,057,426
29	Paul Mcginley (IRL)	11,001,010
30	Niclas Fasth (SWE)	10,026,699
31	Francesco Molinari (ITA)	9,955,181
32	Søren Kjeldsen (DEN)	9,626,575
33	Ian Woosnam (WAL)	9,600,129
34	Simon Dyson (ENG)	9,150,693
35	Louis Oosthuizen (RSA)	9,132,219
36	Raphaël Jacquelin (FRA)	8,724,221
37	Soren Hansen (DEN)	8,718,360
38	Richard Green (AUS)	8,702,560
39	Ross Fisher (ENG)	8,286,687
40	Sir Nick Faldo (ENG)	8,001,656
41	Thomas Levet (FRA)	7,739,882
42	David Lynn (ENG)	7,512,837
43	Bradley Dredge (WAL)	7,503,587
44	Trevor Immelman (RSA)	7,346,120
45	Phillip Price (WAL)	7,208,258
46	Anthony Wall (ENG)	6,984,545
47	Barry Lane (ENG)	6,975,306
48	Paul Broadhurst (ENG)	6,840,372
49	Peter O'Malley (AUS)	6,791,754
50	Gonzalo Fernandez-Castaño (ESP)	6,755,631
51	Steve Webster (ENG)	6,608,968
52	Alvaro Quiros (ESP)	6,606,233
53	Ignacio Garrido (ESP)	6,570,441
54	Stephen Gallacher (SCO)	6,461,581
55	Thongchai Jaidee (THA)	6,042,172
56	Nick Dougherty (ENG)	6,039,710
57	Grégory Havret (FRA)	5,912,531
58	Gary Orr (SCO)	5,907,956
59	Oliver Wilson (ENG)	5,816,564
60	Andrew Coltart (SCO)	5,733,959
61	Jeev Milkha Singh (IND)	5,677,455
62	Ricardo Gonzalez (ARG)	5,660,172
63	Sam Torrance (SCO)	5,491,084
64	Mark McNulty (IRL)	5,366,794
65	John Bickerton (ENG)	5,334,989
66	Simon Khan (ENG)	5,259,103
67	Fredrik Jacobson (SWE)	5,216,587
68	Peter Hedblom (SWE)	5,125,446
69	Alastair Forsyth (SCO)	5,078,294
70	Alexander Noren (SWE)	5,074,678
71	Johan Edfors (SWE)	5,004,939
72	Robert-Jan Derksen (NED)	4,889,330
73	Peter Lawrie (IRL)	4,864,356
74	Maarten Lafeber (NED)	4,770,111
75	Graeme Storm (ENG)	4,761,717
76	Brett Rumford (AUS)	4,737,888
77	Jarmo Sandelin (SWE)	4,691,598
78	Marcel Siem (GER)	4,634,390
79	Richard Sterne (RSA)	4,619,631
80	Fredrik Andersson Hed (SWE)	4,601,075
81	José Manuel Lara (ESP)	4,520,046
82	Joakim Haeggman (SWE)	4,487,376
83	Costantino Rocca (ITA)	4,369,211
84	Jean Van de Velde (FRA)	4,354,592
85	Brian Davis (ENG)	4,340,621
86	Pierre Fulke (SWE)	4,310,837
87	Stephen Dodd (WAL)	4,257,874
88	James Kingston (RSA)	4,253,858
89	Marcus Fraser (AUS)	4,175,152
90	Damien McGrane (IRL)	4,166,958
91	Grégory Bourdy (FRA)	4,150,174
92	Y E Yang (KOR)	4,127,795
93	Gordon Brand Jr (SCO)	4,084,502
94	Jamie Donaldson (WAL)	4,055,091
95	Markus Brier (AUT)	4,042,505
96	Robert Rock (ENG)	4,040,112
97	Peter Baker (ENG)	4,030,726
98	Jean-François Remesy (FRA)	3,961,735
99	Mathias Grönberg (SWE)	3,836,116
100	Nicolas Colsaerts (BEL)	3,832,381

Tour Statistics (Genworth Statistics)

Stroke Average

Pos	Name	Total Rounds	Stroke Avg.
1	Louis Oosthuizen (RSA)	57	69.40
2	Justin Rose (ENG)	42	69.55
3	Rory McIlroy (NIR)	50	69.68
4	Prom Meesawat (THA)	26	69.88
5	Luke Donald (ENG)	46	69.89
6	Magnus A Carlsson (SWE)	40	70.03
7	Henrik Stenson (SWE)	49	70.20
8	Ian Poulter (ENG)	52	70.21
9	Peter Hanson (SWE)	71	70.23
10	Nicolas Colsaerts (BEL)	85	70.26

Driving accuracy

Pos	Name	Rounds	%
1	Adilson da Silva (BRA)	22	82.7
2	Adrian Otaegui (ESP)	22	80.2
3	Justin Rose (ENG)	20	76.8
4	David Drysdale (SCO)	87	74.2
5	Wade Ormsby (AUS)	8	74.1
6	Matthew Nixon (ENG)	34	72.0
7	Phillip Price (WAL)	66	71.9

Average putts per round

Pos	Name	Rounds	Putts per Round
1	Marcus Fraser (AUS)	74	27.8
2	Robert Karlsson (SWE)	22	28.5
3	Luke Donald (ENG)	24	28.6
4	Peter Hanson (SWE)	49	28.6
5	Sam Walker (ENG)	28	28.6
6	Brett Rumford (AUS)	69	28.7
7	George Coetzee (RSA)	76	28.9

Driving distance

Pos	Name	Rounds	Avg. yards
1	Nicolas Colsaerts (BEL)	66	318.3
2	Scott Hend (AUS)	30	313.0
3	Alvaro Quiros (ESP)	37	312.5
4	Andreas Hartø (DEN)	9	311.9
5	Lloyd Saltman (SCO)	25	309.1
6	Charles-Edouard Russo (FRA)	18	307.0
7	Gaganjeet Bhullar (IND)	15	305.6

Average one putts per round

Pos	Name	Rounds	One putts Average
1	Luke Donald (ENG)	24	7.63
2	Kristoffer Broberg (SWE)	12	7.17
3	Andrew Parr (CAN)	8	6.88
4	Robert Karlsson (SWE)	22	6.73
5	Roope Kakko (FIN)	26	6.62
6	Thomas Björn (DEN)	50	6.58
7	Charles-Edouard Russo (FRA)	18	6.50

Greens in regulation

Pos	Name	Rounds	%
1	Justin Rose (ENG)	20	80.8
2	Louis Oosthuizen (RSA)	35	80.5
3	Ian Poulter (ENG)	28	79.6
4	Rory McIlroy (NIR)	28	79.2
5	Magnus A Carlsson (SWE)	39	77.9
6	Francesco Molinari (ITA)	65	77.9
7	Sergio García (ESP)	19	77.5

Sand saves

Pos	Name	Rounds	%
1	Gaganjeet Bhullar (IND)	15	100
2	Michiel Bothma (RSA)	10	100
3	Daniel Gaunt (AUS)	19	78.3
4	Luke Donald (ENG)	24	74.4
5	Gonzalo Fdez-Castaño (ESP)	63	71.9
6	Sam Walker (ENG)	28	71.4
7	Jean-Baptiste Gonnet (FRA)	64	71.1

Putts per greens in regulation

Pos	Name	Rounds	Putts per GIR
1	Tyrone Ferreira (RSA)	9	1.646
2	Peter Hanson (SWE)	49	1.698
3	Luke Donald (ENG)	24	1.701
4	Sergio García (ESP)	19	1.706
5	Merrick Bremner (RSA)	10	1.709
6	Marcus Fraser (AUS)	74	1.713
7	Michiel Bothma (RSA)	10	1.720

Scrambles (where player makes par after missing GIR)

Pos	Name	Rounds	%
1	Louis Oosthuizen (RSA)	35	71.5
2	Luke Donald (ENG)	24	68.4
3	Prom Meesawat (THA)	26	66.4
4	Marcus Fraser (AUS)	74	66.0
5	Anders Hansen (DEN)	65	65.1
6	Richard Bland (ENG)	63	64.1
7	Francesco Molinari (ITA)	65	63.6

PGA European Tour statistics 2012

Thirty-seven holes-in-one

Tjaart Van der Walt – Africa Open
Mikael Lundberg – Joburg Open
Richard Finch – Joburg Open
Sergio García – Abu Dhabi HSBC Golf Championship
José Manuel Lara – Abu Dhabi HSBC Golf Championship
Graeme McDowell – Abu Dhabi HSBC Golf Championship
Stephen Gallacher – Omega Dubai Desert Classic
Martin Kaymer – Omega Dubai Desert Classic
Paul Casey – WGC – Cadillac Championship
Thørbjorn Olesen – Open de Andalucía
Bo Van Pelt – Masters Tournament
Adam Scott – Masters Tournament
Ricardo Santos – Volvo China Open
Marcel Siem – BMW PGA Championship
Robert Karlsson – Nordea Masters
John Peterson – US Open Championship
Andrew Marshall – BMW International Open
James Morrison – Irish Open
Jamie Donaldson – Irish Open
Andrew Johnston – Aberdeen Asset Management Scottish Open
Peter Whiteford – Aberdeen Asset Management Scottish Open
Anirban Lahiri – 141st Open Championship
Lloyd Kennedy – Johnnie Walker Championship
Edouard Dubois – Johnnie Walker Championship
Mathias Grönberg – Omega European Masters
Jorge Campillo – BMW Italian
George Murray – BMW Italian Open
Y E Yang – BMW Masters
W U Ashun – BMW Masters
Branden Grace – WGC – HSBC Champions
Edoardo Molinari – Barclays Singapore Open
Juvic Pagunsan – Barclays Singapore Open
Danny Chia – Barclays Singapore Open
Steve Webster – UBS Hong Kong Open
Terrence Boardman – SA Open Championship
Stephen Gallacher – DP World Tour Championship
Joost Luiten – DP World Tour Championship

Thirty-one course records

62 (–11)	Africa Open – Louis Oosthuizen
64 (–9)	Volvo Golf Champions – Nicolas Colsaerts
64 (–8)†	Open de Andalucía Costa del Sol – Matteo Manassero; Julien Quesne
61 (–11)	Trophée Hassan II – Jamie Donaldson
64 (–8)	Sicilian Open – Peter Lawrie; Chris Wood
63 (–9)	Volvo China Open – Alexander Noren
65 (–7)	Ballantine's Championship – Bernd Wiesberger; Kiradech Aphibarnrat; Paul McGinley; Bernd Wiesberger; Adam Scott; Richie Ramsay
65 (–7)†	Irish Open – Jeev Milkha Singh; Grégory Bourdy; Mikael Lundberg
62 (–10)	Aberdeen Asset Management Scottish Open – Francesco Molinari
64 (–6)†	The 141st Open Championship – Adam Scott; Brandt Snedeker
63 (–7)	KLM Open – Graeme Storm
60 (–10)	Alfred Dunhill Links Championship (Kingsbarns) – Branden Grace
62 (–10)†	Alfred Dunhill Links Championship (St Andrews) – Victor Dubuisson; George Coetzee
65 (–7)	ISPS HANDA Perth International – Michael Hendry; Alejandro Canizares
62 (–10)	BMW Masters – Jamie Donaldson
60 (–12)	WGC – HSBC Champions – Brandt Snedeker
63 (–7)	UBS Hong Kong Open – Chris Wood
62 (–10)	SA Open Championship – Hennie Otto
62 (–10)	DP World Tour Championship – Justin Rose

† equals existing record

Six multiple winners

Branden Grace – Joburg Open; Volvo Golf Champions; Volvo China Open; Alfred Dunhill Links Championship
Louis Oosthuizen – Africa Open; Maybank Malaysian Open
Bernd Wiesberger – Ballantine's Championship; Lyoness Open powered by Greenfinity
Paul Lawrie – Commercialbank Qatar Masters presented by Dolphin Energy; Johnnie Walker Championship at Gleneagles
Peter Hanson – KLM Open; BMW Masters
Rory McIlroy – US PGA Championship; DP World Tour Championship

PGA European Tour statistics 2012

Eleven first-time winners

Branden Grace (RSA) – Joburg Open
Jbe Kruger (RSA) – Avantha Masters
Julien Quesne (FRA) – Open de Andalucia
Thorbjørn Olesen (DEN) – Sicilian Open
Bubba Watson (USA) – Masters Tournament
Bernd Wiesberger (AUT) – Ballantine's C/ship
Ricardo Santos (POR) – Madeira Islands Open
Webb Simpson (USA) – US Open C/ship
Danny Willett (ENG) – BMW Int. Open
Jamie Donaldson (WAL) – Irish Open
Bo Van Pelt (USA) – ISPS HANDA Perth Int.

Shane Lowry (IRL) who won the 3 Irish Open in 2009 as an amateur won his first event as a professional in the Portugal Masters

Most top ten finishes

10 Nicolas Colsaerts (BEL)
10 Rory McIlroy (NIR)
9 Francesco Molinari (ITA)
9 Justin Rose (ENG)
9 Paul Lawrie (SCO)
9 Louis Oosthuizen (RSA)
8 Peter Hanson (SWE)
8 Ian Poulter (ENG)
8 Matteo Manassero (ITA)
8 George Coetzee (RSA)
7 Thorbjørn Olesen (DEN)
7 Alexander Noren (SWE)
7 Thomas Björn (DEN)
7 Henrik Stenson (SWE)
6 Rafael Cabrera-Bello (ESPS)
6 Ross Fisher (ENG)
6 Danny Willett (ENG)
6 Lee Westwood (ENG)
6 Marcus Fraser (AUS)
6 Stephen Gallacher (SCO)
6 Matt Kuchar (USA)
6 Pablo Larrazabal (ESP)
6 Martin Kaymer (GER)
6 Branden Grace (RSA)
6 Jamie Donaldson (WAL)

Santos named the Sir Henry Cotton Rookie of the Year

Ricardo Santos is the first Portuguese winner of the Sir Henry Cotton Rookie of the Year Award following a 2012 season in which he won the Madeira Islands Open at Santo da Serra, the course he played many times as a junior.

Santos celebrated the 40th anniversary of the European Tour one week late by becoming only the second Portuguese player to win on the International Schedule – exactly 20 years after Daniel Silva became the first by capturing the Jersey Open.

Born in Faro in 1982, Santos, raised in a home adjacent to the Oceânico Victoria Golf Course in the Algarve, fulfilled his boyhood dream by winning on Portuguese soil with a superb final round of 63, the lowest final round by a winner during the 2012 season.

He was the first rookie winner on the 2012 European Tour and as none of his fellow rookies subsequently won it swung the vote in the 30 year old's favour.

Santos, who dedicated his win to his wife Rita and their daughter Victoria, was naturally thrilled to learn that he had become the 48th recipient of the Sir Henry Cotton Rookie of the Year Award, which was launched in 1960.

He said: "It's an honour to become the first Portuguese player to win the Rookie of the Year award. When you look at some of the players who have won the award in the past, it's a real privilege to see my name next to theirs on the trophy. It's been an amazing season, and to end it be winning the award is more than I could have dreamed of.

"Winning in Madeira has brought me more recognition in Portugal but the award is not just for me – it's also for my coach, Almerindo Sequeira, my fitness coach, David Moura, my sports psychologist, Gonçalo Castanho and for my wife Rita. Our daughter Victoria is probably too young to understand at the moment, but when she grows up I'm sure she'll be proud of her father for winning this award.

"The goal for 2013 is to win again on the European Tour, and to play my first major. This award has given me the confidence to go and achieve my goals."

Sir Nick Faldo, Tony Jacklin, Sandy Lyle, José María Olazábal and Colin Montgomerie and, more recently, Paul Casey, Sergio García, Martin Kaymer, Matteo Manassero and Ian Poulter are all former winners of the award which is judged by representatives from The R&A, the Association of Golf Writers and thge European Tour.

European Tour top 20

MC Missed cut FQ Failed to qualify WD Withdrew

	Africa Open	Joburg Open	Volvo Golf Champions	Abu Dhabi Championship	Qatar Masters	Dubai Desert Clasic	Avantha Masters	5WGC–Accenture C/ship	WGC–Cadillac C/ship	Open de Andalucia	Trophée Hassan II	Sicilian Open	The Masters	Maybank Mal5aysian Open	Volvo China Open
1 Rory McIlroy (NIR)	—	—	—	2	—	T5	—	2	3	—	—	—	T40	—	—
2 Justin Rose (ENG)	—	—	—	—	—	—	—	T33	1	—	—	—		—	—
3 Louis Oosthuizen (RSA)	1	—	T7	—	—	—	T17	T60	—	—	—	2*	1	—	
4 Peter Hanson (SWE)	—	—	—	T35	T2	T51	—	T5	T4	—	—	—	T3	—	T14
5 Ian Poulter (ENG)	—	—	—	—	—	—	—	T33	T60	—	—	—	7	—	T29
6 Branden Grace (RSA)	T14	1	1*	MC	T47	T51	—	—	T35	—	T25	MC	—	T40	1
7 Luke Donald (ENG)	—	—	—	T48	—	—	—	T33	T6	—	—	—	T32	—	—
8 Francesco Molinari (ITA)	—	—	—	T8	T69	T16	—	T17	T13	—	T17	—	T19	—	T6
9 Graeme McDowell (NIR)	—	—	—	T3	T59	—	—	T33	T13	—	—	—	T12	—	—
10 Paul Lawrie (SCO)	—	—	T10	T8	1	T51	—	T9	T60	—	—	—	T24	—	T14
11 Nicolas Colsaerts (BEL)	—	—	4	T24	T9	T9	—	T33	T35	—	—	T3	—	T29	2
12 Lee Westwood (ENG)	—	—	—	T17	T12	T2	—	4	T29	—	—	—	T3	—	—
13 Matteo Manassero (ITA)	—	—	23	T6	MC	T42	—	T17	—	2	T6	MC	—	T7	—
14 Marcel Siem (GER)	—	—	—	T35	T12	4	T2	—	—	T17	T52	—	—	T29	MC
15 Thorbjørn Olesen (DEN)	—	—	—	T8	T59	T42	T6	—	—	MC	35	1	—	—	T52
16 Charl Schwartzel (RSA)	—	MC	5	T17	—	—	—	T17	T4	—	—	—	T50	6	—
17 Rafa Cabrero-Bello (ESP)	—	—	—	T48	T35	1	—	T33	65	T47	—	—	—	T3	T29
18 David Lynn (ENG)	—	—	—	T17	T47	T57	—	—	—	4	MC	T37	—	—	—
19 Jamie Donaldson (WAL)	—	—	—	T30	—	T16	T51	—	—	—	T3	63	—	—	T44
20 Gonzalo Fernandez-Castaño (ESP)	—	—	T26	T17	T12	—	—	T33	T55	T—	—	—	61	—	—

2012 performances at a glance

— Did not play * Involved in play-off

Ballantine's C/ship	Open de España	Madeira Islands Open	Volvo World C/ship	BMW PGA Championship	Handa Wales Open	Nordea Masters	US Open Championship	St Omer Open	BMW International Open	The Iriah Open	Open de France	Scottish Open	141st Open Championship	Lyoness Open	WGC–Bridgestone Inv.	US PGA Championship	Johnnie Walker C/ship	Omega European Masters	KLM Open	Italian Open	Dunhill Links C/ship	Portugal Masters	Perth International	BMW Masters	WGC–HSBC Champions	Barclay's Singapore Open	Hong Kong Open	South African Open	Dubai World Championship
—	—	—	—	MC	—	—	MC	—	—	T10	—	—	T60	—	MC	1	—	—	—	—	—	—	—	2	—	3	MC	—	1
—	—	—	T9	T2	—	—	T21	—	—	—	T9	—	MC	—	T5	T3	—	—	—	—	—	—	—	T6	T24	—	—	—	2
—	—	—	—	—	—	—	MC	—	—	—	—	T24	T19	—	4	T21	—	—	—	—	MC	—	—	T6	T6	2*	—	—	5
—	—	—	T17	MC	—	T3	MC	—	—	T61	—	T23	—	T63	T7	—	T59	1	—	T34	—	—	1	T24	—	—	—	—	T16
T15	—	—	T9	T10	T3	—	—	T41	—	—	T4	—	T9	—	T29	T3	—	—	—	—	—	—	—	4	1	—	—	—	T26
—	—	—	T17	5	—	—	T51	—	—	MC	T17	T68	T77	—	T36	MC	—	T76	—	—	1	—	—	T43	T62	—	—	65	6
—	—	—	—	1	—	—	MC	—	—	—	—	T6	T5	—	T8	T32	—	—	—	—	—	—	—	3	T18	—	—	—	T3
—	1	—	—	T7	T46	—	T29	—	—	T10	2	2*	T39	—	T40	T54	T6	—	—	T46	—	T16	—	T35	T34	T5	—	—	T34
—	—	—	2	MC	—	—	T2	—	—	T16	T17	—	T5	—	T24	T11	—	—	—	—	—	—	—	T11	T42	—	—	—	T52
—	MC	—	T3	T2	T14	—	—	—	T23	T33	—	MC	T34	—	T50	T48	1	T6	—	—	MC	—	—	T35	T36	—	T10	—	T48
—	T7	—	1	MC	—	—	T27	—	—	MC	T11	T36	T7	—	T45	MC	T19	—	T6	T5	—	—	—	T14	T54	—	—	—	T34
—	—	—	—	T33	—	1	T10	—	—	—	T40	—	T45	—	70	MC	—	—	—	—	—	—	—	T14	T6	—	—	—	T48
—	T7	—	—	T43	T28	—	T46	—	—	MC	T17	T6	FQ	—	—	MC	—	T34	T58	T3	MC	T12	—	T46	—	1*	T4	—	T42
—	T12	—	—	T7	T33	—	FQ	—	T6	57	1	T29	MC	—	T60	T36	T19	T14	—	—	MC	T68	—	T51	T11	MC	—	—	T42
MC	T5	—	—	MC	T18	T22	FQ	—	—	T18	MC	T36	T9	5	—	T27	T15	MC	—	T53	2	T16	—	T58	T11	T29	—	5	T21
—	—	—	T17	T18	—	—	T38	—	—	—	—	—	MC	—	T24	T59	—	—	—	—	T66	—	MC	T6	—	—	—	—	T3
—	T27	—	T3	T45	—	T47	MC	—	—	T2	T57	T47	T41	—	T29	MC	T10	—	—	9	MC	T55	—	T35	T46	T50	—	—	T40
—	MC	—	—	MC	T11	T55	—	T12	MC	T4	T36	—	—	—	2	—	T26	T11	T32	—	MC	MC	—	T20	T69	MC	—	—	T54
T15	—	—	—	T53	WD	T26	—	—	—	1	MC	—	T60	—	T36	T7	—	T9	T21	—	MC	T6	—	T6	T42	—	—	—	T9
—	T53	—	—	MC	T2	—	MC	—	T3	MC	T31	—	T54	—	T55	T62	—	T76	T5	1	T29	T12	—	T46	T28	—	—	—	T9

2012 European Tour

(in chronological order)

For past results see earlier editions of *The R&A Golfer's Handbook*

Africa Open *East London, Eastern Cape, RSA* Jan 5–8 [6770–73]

1	Louis Oosthuizen (RSA)	69-62-67-67—265	€158,500
2	Tjaart Van der Valt (RSA)	69-64-65-69—267	115,000
3	Retief Goosen (RSA)	65-68-66-69—268	69,200

Joburg Open *Royal Johannesburg and Kensington, RSA* Jan 12–15 [East 7592–71, West 7237–71]

1	Branden Grace (RSA)	67-66-65-72—270	€206,050
2	Jamie Elson (ENG)	63-75-70-63—271	149,500
3	Michiel Bothma (RSA)	68-66-68-71—273	53,972
	David Drysdale (SCO)	65-72-69-67—273	53,972
	Trevor Fisher Jr (RSA)	68-68-69-68—273	53,972
	Dawie Van der Walt (RSA)	70-66-67-70—273	53,972
	Jaco Van Zyle (RSA)	67-69-69-68—273	53,972
	Marc Warren (SCO)	66-69-70-68—273	53,972

Volvo Golf Champions *The Links at Fancourt, George, RSA* Jan 19–22 [7271–73]

1	Branden Grace (RSA)*	68-66-75-71—280	€350,000
2	Ernie Els (RSA)	71-71-71-67—280	177,500
	Retief Goosen (RSA)	72-68-70-70—280	177,500

**Grace won at the first extra hole*

Abu Dhabi HSBC Golf Championship *Abu Dhabi, UAE* Jan 26–29 [7600–72]

1	Robert Rock (ENG)	69-70-66-70—275	€347,024
2	Rory McIlroy (NIR)	67-72-68-69—276	231,349
3	Thomas Björn (DEN)	73-71-65-68—277	107,577
	Graeme McDowell (NIR)	72-69-68-68—277	107,577
	Tiger Woods (USA)	70-69-66-72—277	107,577

Commercialbank Qatar Masters *Doha* Feb 2–5 [7412–72]

1	Paul Lawrie (SCO)	69-67-65—201	€316,020
2	Jason Day (AUS)	68-72-65—205	164,688
	Peter Hanson (SWE)	69-69-67—205	164,688

Omega Dubai Desert Classic *Emirates, Dubai, UAE* Feb 9–12 [7301–72]

1	Rafael Cabrera-Bello (ESP)	63-69-70-68—270	€315,532
2	Stephen Gallacher (SCO)	69-65-68-69—271	164,434
	Lee Westwood (ENG)	69-65-67-70—271	164,434

Avantha Masters *DLF G&CC, New Delhi, India* Feb 16–19 [7156–72]

1	Jbe Kruger (RSA)	70-69-66-69—274	€300,000
2	Jorge Campillo (ESP)	72-71-66-67—276	156,340
	Marcel Siem (GER)	69-69-68-70—276	156,340

WGC – Accenture Match Play Championship *Ritz-Carlton, Dove Mountain, AZ, USA* Feb 22–26 [7791–72]

Winner:	Hunter Mahan (USA)	€1,060,767
Runner-up:	Rory McIlroy (NIR)	644,037
Third place:	Mark Wilson (USA)	454,614

Full details of this event can be found on page 200

WGC – Cadillac Championship *Doral, Orlando, FL, USA* Mar 8–11 [7334–72]

1	Justin Rose (ENG)	69-64-69-70—272	€1,048,140
2	Bubba Watson (USA)	70-62-67-74—273	632,627
3	Rory McIlroy (NIR)	73-69-65-67—274	386,314

Full details of this event can be found on page 201

Open de Andalucía Costa del Sol *Aloha GC, Andalucia, Spain* Mar 15–18 [6881–72]

1	Julien Quesne (FRA)	68-72-67-64—271	€166,660
2	Matteo Manassero (ITA)	64-73-68-68—273	111,110
3	Eduardo de la Riva (ESP)	67-69-68-70—274	62,600

Trophée Hassan II *Golf du Palais Royal, Agadir, Morocco* Mar 22–25 [6844–72]

1	Michael Hoey (NIR)	74-67-65-65—271	€250,000
2	Damien McGrane (IRL)	65-68-71-70—274	166,660
3	Robert Coles (ENG)	73-70-65-67—275	77,500
	Jamie Donaldson (WAL)	72-68-74-61—275	77,500
	Phillip Price (WAL)	68-66-72-69—275	77,500

Sicilian Open *Verdura Golf & Spa Resort, Sicily, Italy* Mar 29–April 1 [7375–72]

1	Thorbjørn Olesen (DEN)	68-69-67-69—273	€166,660
2	Chris Wood (ENG)	67-71-72-64—274	111,110
3	Nicolas Colsaerts (BEL)	67-71-69-69—276	56,300
	Søren Kjeldsen (DEN)	65-72-71-68—276	56,300

The MASTERS TOURNAMENT *Augusta National, GA, USA* April 5–8 [7435–72]

1	Bubba Watson (USA)*	69-71-70-68—278	€1,086,801
2	Louis Oosthuizen (RSA)	68-72-69-69—278	652,080

**Watson won at the second extra hole*

3	Peter Hanson (SWE)	68-74-65-73—280	289,814
	Matt Kuchar (USA)	71-70-70-69—280	289,814
	Phil Mickelson (USA)	74-68-66-72—280	289,814
	Lee Westwood (ENG)	67-73-72-68—280	289,814

Full details of this event can be found on page 81

Maybank Malaysian Open *Kuala Lumpur, Malaysia* April 12–15 [7000–72]

1	Louis Oosthuizen (RSA)	66-68-69-68—271	€314,700
2	Stephen Gallacher (SCO)	67-68-69-70—274	209,798
3	Rafael Cabrera-Bello (ESP)	67-72-66-71—276	97,559
	David Lipsky (USA)	70-67-69-70—276	97,559
	Danny Willett (ENG)	69-69-67-71—276	97,559

Volvo China Open *Binhai Lake GC, Tianjin, China* April 19–22 [7667–72]

1	Branden Grace (RSA)	67-67-64-69—267	€398,595
2	Nicolas Colsaerts (BEL)	68-67-66-69—270	265,730
3	Richard Finch (ENG)	67-73-65-66—271	149,712

Ballantine's Championship *Blackstone GC, Incheon, South Korea* April 26–29 [7302–72]

1	Bernd Wiesberger (AUT)	72-65-65-68—270	€367,500
2	Richie Ramsay (SCO)	70-72-68-65—275	245,000
3	Victor Dubuisson (FRA)	68-75-68-66—277	124,142
	Marcus Fraser (AUS)	71-67-69-70—277	124,142

Reale Seguros Open de España *Real Club de Golf de Sevilla, Spain* May 3–6 [7134–72]

1	Francesco Molinari (ITA)	70-71-74-65—280	€333,330
2	Alejandro Cañizares (ESP)	74-72-68-69—283	149,140
	Søren Kjeldsen (DEN)	71-70-71-71—283	149,140
	Pablo Larrazánal (ESP)	71-72-69-71—283	149,140

Madeira Islands Open Portugal *Santo da Serra, Madeira, Portugal* May 10–13 [6825–72]

1	Ricardo Santos (POR)	68-67-68-63—266	€112,500
2	Magnus A Carlsson (SWE)	66-66-71-67—270	75,000
3	Andreas Hartø (DEN)	67-71-66-67—271	42,255

Volvo World Match Play Championship *Finca Cortesin, Casares, Andalucía, Spain*
May 17–20 [7290–72]

Quarter Finals:
Graeme McDowell (NIR) beat Sergio García (ESP) at 19th
Paul Lawrie (SCO) beat Retief Goosen (RSA) 6 and 5
Nicolas Colsaerts (BEL) beat Brandt Snedeker (USA) 4 and 3
Rafael Cabrera-Bello (ESP) beat Alvaro Quiros (ESP) 3 and 1

Semi-Finals:
Nicolas Colsaerts beat Paul Lawrie at 20th
Graeme McDowell beat Rafael Cabrera-Bello 2 holes

Final:
Nicolas Colsaerts beat Graeme McDowell 1 hole

Winner: €700,000
Runner-up: €360,000
3rd: €180,000

BMW PGA Championship *Wentworth Club, Surrey, England* May 24–27 [7302–72]

1	Luke Donald (ENG)	68-68-69-68—273	€750,000
2	Paul Lawrie (SCO)	69-71-71-66—277	390,850
	Justin Rose (ENG)	67-71-69-70—277	390,850
4	Peter Lawrie (IRL)	66-71-72-71—280	225,000
5	Branden Grace (RSA)	69-69-73-70—281	190,800
6	Richard Sterne (RSA)	71-68-72-71—282	157,500
7	Ernie Els (RSA)	68-73-70-72—283	116,100
	Francesco Molinari (ITA)	68-70-74-71—283	116,100
	Marcel Siem (GER)	71-67-76-69—283	116,100
10	David Drysdale (SCO)	66-70-78-70—284	78,300
	David Higgins (IRL)	70-70-74-70—284	78,300
	James Morrison (ENG)	68-64-81-71—284	78,300
	Ian Poulter (ENG)	71-73-69-71—284	78,300
	Alvaro Quiros (ESP)	67-70-77-70—284	78,300
15	Rafael Cabrera-Bello (ESP)	68-70-74-73—285	63,450
	S S P Chowrasia (IND)	69-76-71-69—285	63,450
	Martin Kaymer (GER)	71-69-76-69—285	63,450
18	Fredrik Andersson Hed (SWE)	70-68-77-71—286	55,950
	Peter Hedblom (SWE)	68-70-74-74—286	55,950
	Charl Schwartzel (RSA)	69-71-79-67—286	55,950
21	George Coetzee (RSA)	68-77-76-66—287	48,825
	Victor Dubuisson (FRA)	70-71-76-70—287	48,825
	Alexander Noren (SWE)	70-74-73-70—287	48,825
	Julien Quesne (FRA)	74-71-72-70—287	48,825
	Robert Rock (ENG)	68-76-74-69—287	48,825
	Paul Streeter (ENG)	71-74-74-68—287	48,825
27	Federico Colombo (ITA)	69-74-71-74—288	40,725
	Simon Khan (ENG)	71-74-70-73—288	40,725
	Garth Mulroy (RSA)	71-70-76-71—288	40,725
	José María Olazábal (ESP)	70-72-76-70—288	40,725
	Jeev Milkha Singh (IND)	70-74-70-74—288	40,725
	Marc Warren (SCO)	68-76-7-272—288	40,725

33	Niclas Fasth (SWE)	67-73-78-71—289	33,375
	Richard Finch (ENG)	76-67-74-72—289	33,375
	Ricardo Gonzalez (ARG)	71-67-77-74—289	33,375
	Jbe Kruger (RSA)	72-73-74-70—289	33,375
	Paul McGinley (IRL)	73-71-73-72—289	33,375
	Lee Westwood (ENG)	70-75-70-74—289	33,375
39	Andrew Dodt (AUS)	69-73-76-72—290	28,800
	Miguel Angel Jiménez (ESP)	71-70-76-73—290	28,800
	Gareth Maybin (NIR)	70-70-76-74—290	28,800
	Damien McGrane (IRL)	71-72-75-72—290	28,800
43	Thomas Björn (DEN)	74-70-78-69—291	24,300
	Kenneth Ferrie (ENG)	68-74-77-72—291	24,300
	Scott Jamieson (SCO)	68-75-75-73—291	24,300
	Richard S Johnson (SWE)	67-75-75-74—291	24,300
	Matteo Manassero (ITA)	74-69-77-71—291	24,300
	DannyWillett (ENG)	69-71-79-72—291	24,300
49	Alex Cejka (GER)	75-70-76-71—292	19,800
	Tommy Fleetwood (ENG)	72-73-72-75—292	19,800
	Edoardo Molinari (ITA)	69-70-76-77—292	19,800
	Chris Wood (ENG)	73-71-80-68—292	19,800
53	Jamie Donaldson (WAL)	67-73-77-76—293	16,650
	Pablo Martin (ESP)	69-70-76-78—293	16,650
	Bernd Wiesberger (AUT)	68-73-83-69—293	16,650
56	Thongchai Jaidee (THA)	71-72-79-72—294	13,838
	José Manuel Lara (ESP)	72-71-78-73—294	13,838
	Sam Little (ENG)	72-73-76-73—294	13,838
	Christian Nilsson (SWE)	74-70-77-73—294	13,838
60	Bradley Dredge (WAL)	71-72-78-74—295	12,600
61	Robert-Jan Derksen (NED)	71-71-81-73—296	11,475
	Grégory Havret (FRA)	75-67-83-71—296	11,475
	Mikko Illonen (FIN)	74-70-79-73—296	11,475
	Steve Webster (ENG)	69-74-81-72—296	11,475
65	Oscar Floren (SWE)	74-71-80-72—297	9,900
	Richard Green (AUS)	72-73-79-73—297	9,900
	Pablo Larrazábal (ESP)	70-75-77-75—297	9,900
68	Ben Curtis (USA)	70-75-81-72—298	8,775
	Shane Lowry (IRL)	71-74-79-74—298	8,775
70	James Kingston (RSA)	71-74-85-71—301	7,475
	Brett Rumford (AUS)	70-74-79-78—301	7,475
72	Colin Montgomerie (SCO)	69-74-78-81—302	6,747

78 players missed the cut

ISPS Handa Wales Open *Celtic Manor, Newport* May 31–June 3 [7378–71]

1	Thongchai Jaidee (THA)	71-68-67-72—278	€372,720
2	Thomas Börn (DEN)	71-72-68-68—279	148,777
	Gonzalo Fernandez-Castaño (ESP)	69-74-69-67—279	148,777
	Joost Luiten (NED)	74-69-64-72—279	148,777
	Richard Sterne (RSA)	73-69-69-68—279	148,777

Nordea Masters *Bro Hof Slott, Stockholm, Sweden* June 6–9 [7607–72]

1	Lee Westwood (ENG)	68-64-68-69—269	€250,000
2	Ross Fisher (ENG)	70-68-65-71—274	166,660
3	Sergio Garcia (ESP)	69-69-70-67—275	77,500
	Peter Hanson (SWE)	67-68-69-71—275	77,500
	Mikko Ilonen (FIN)	70-69-68-68—275	77,500

112th US OPEN CHAMPIONSHIP *San Francisco, California, USA* June 14–17 [7170–70]

1	Webb Simpson (USA)	72-73-68-68—281	€1,158,115
2	Graeme McDowell (NIR)	69-72-68-73—282	559,688
	Michael Thompson (USA)	66-75-74-67—282	559,688

Full details of this event can be found on page 70

St Omer Open *St Omer, Lumbres, France* June 14–17 [6846–71]

1	Darren Fichardt (RSA)	68-69-69-73—279	€83,330
2	Gary Lockerbie (ENG)	69-75-69-69—282	55,550
3	Simon Wakefield (ENG)	67-72-72-72—283	31,300

BMW International Open *Cologne, Germany* June 21–24 [7228–72]

1	Danny Willett (ENG)*	65-70-69-73—277	€333,330
2	Marcus Fraser (AUS)	64-74-68-71—277	222,220

**Willett won at the fourth extra hole*

3	Gonzalo Fernandez-Castaño (ESP)	71-69-69-69—278	103,333
	Paul McGinley (IRL)	65-70-77-66—278	103,333
	Chris Wood (ENG)	65-70-70-73—278	103,333

The Irish Open *Royal Portrush GC, Co Antrim, Northern Ireland* June 28–July 1 [7143–72]

1	Jamie Donaldson (WAL)	68-67-69-66—270	€333,330
2	Rafael Cabrera-Bello (ESP)	71-67-70-66—274	149,140
	Anthony Wall (ENG)	67-71-67-69—274	149,140
	Fabrizio Zanotti (PAR)	69-71-68-66—274	149,140

Alstom Open de France *Le Golf National, Paris, France* July 5–8 [7347–71]

1	Marcel Siem (GER)	68-68-73-67—276	€525,000
2	Francesco Molinari (ITA	71-68-74-64—277	350,000
3	Raphaël Jacquelin (FRA)	68-71-70-69—278	197,190

Aberdeen Asset Management Scottish Open *Castle Stuart, Inverness, Scotland* July 12–15 [7193–72]

1	Jeev Milkha Singh (IND)*	66-70-68-67—271	€518,046
2	Francesco Molinari (ITA)	62-70-67-72—271	345,360

**Singh won at the fourth extra hole*

3	Alexander Noren (SWE)	66-66-70-70—272	174,999
	Marc Waarren (SCO)	68-69-64-71—272	174,999

The 141st OPEN CHAMPIONSHIP *Royal Lytham & St Annes, Lancashire, England* July 19–22 [7086–70]

1	Ernie Els (RSA)	67-70-68-68—273	€1,136,880
2	Adam Scott (AUS)	64-67-68-75—274	656,684
3	Tiger Woods (USA)	67-67-70-73—277	375,802
	Brandt Snedeker (USA)	66-64-73-74—277	375,802

Full details of this events can be found on page 54

Lyoness Open *Atzenbrugg, Austria* July 25–28 [7386–72]

1	Bernd Wiesberger (AUT)	71-66-67-65—269	€166,660
2	Thomas Levet (FRA)	65-70-69-68—272	86,855
	Shane Lowry (IRL)	70-68-68-66—272	86,855

WGC – Bridgestone Invitational *Firestone CC, Akron, OH, USA* Aug 2–5 [7400–70]

1	Keegan Bradley (USA)	67-69-67-64—267	€972,148
2	Steve Stricker (USA)	68-68-68-64—268	461,770
	Jim Furyk (USA)	63-66-70-69—268	461,770

Full details of this event can be found on page 202

US PGA CHAMPIONSHIP *Kiawah Island, South Carolina, USA* Aug 9–12 [7676–72]

1	Rory McIlroy (NIR)	67-75-67-66—275	€1,190,937
2	David Lynn (ENG)	73-74-68-68—283	712,914
3	Justin Rose (ENG)	69-79-70-66—284	316,896
	Keegan Bradley	68-77-71-68—284	316,896
	Ian Poulter (ENG)	70-71-74-69—284	316,896
	Carl Pettersson (SWE)	66-74-72-72—284	316,896

Full details of this event can be found on page 90

Johnnie Walker Championship *Auchterarder, Perthshire, Scotland* Aug 23–26 [7296–72]

1	Paul Lawrie (SCO)	68-69-67-68—272	€296,119
2	Brett Rumford (AUS)	67-70-71-68—276	197,408
3	Fredrik Andersson Hed (SWE)	73-69-70-65—277	91,798
	Maarten Lafeber (NED)	68-73-67-69—277	91,798
	Romain Wattel (FRA)	74-68-63-72—277	91,798

Omega European Masters *Crans-sur-Sierre, Switzerland since 1939* Aug 30–Sep 2 [6707–70]

1	Richie Ramsay (SCO)	69-68-64-66—267	€350,000
2	Fredrik Andersson Hed (SWE)	65-73-67-66—271	139,708
	Marcus Fraser (AUS)	68-68-69-66—271	139,708
	Romain Wattel (FRA)	67-70-68-66—271	139,708
	Danny Willett (ENG)	67-67-68-69—271	139,708

KLM Open *Hilversum, The Netherlands* Sep 6–9 [6906–70]

1	Peter Hanson (SWE)	66-66-67-67—266	€300,000
2	Pablo Larrazábal (ESP)	69-65-64-70—268	156,340
	Richie Ramsay (SCO)	71-66-64-67—268	156,340

Italian Open *Royal Park I Roveri, Turin, Italy* Sep 13–16 [7282–72]

1	Gonzalo Fernandez-Castaño (ESP)	68-65-67-64—264	€250,000
2	Garth Mulroy (RSA)	66-67-66-67—266	166,660
3	Grégory Bourdy (FRA)	69-64-70-65—268	84,450
3	Matteo Manassero (ITA)	69-69-65-65—268	84,450

The Ryder Cup *Medinah Country Club, Illinois, USA* Sep 28–30 [7668–72]

Europe 14½, USA 13½

Full details of this event can be found on page 206

Alfred Dunhill Links Championship *St Andrews Old course, Kingsbarns and Carnoustie, Scotland*

Oct 4–7 St Andrews [7279–72], Kingbarns [7150–72], Carnoustie [7412–72]

1	Branden Grace (RSA)*	60-67-69-70—266	€617,284
2	Thorbjørn Olesen (DEN)	63-69-68-68—268	411,520
3	Alexander Noren (SWE)	64-72-65-69—270	231,852

Portugal Masters *Oceânico Victoria, Vilamoura, Portugal* Oct 11–14 [7157–71]

1	Shane Lowry (IRL)	67-70-67-66—270	375,000
2	Ross Fisher (ENG)	65-67-69-70—271	250,000
3	Michael Campbell (NZL)	68-69-67-68—272	140,850

IPS HANDA Perth International *Lake Karrinyup CC, Perth, Western Australia* Oct 18–21 [7143–72]

1	Bo Van Pelt (USA)	70-67-67-68—272	€256,585
2	Jason Dufner (USA)	71-67-67-69—274	171,057
3	Alejandro Cañizares (ESP)	65-73-71-68—277	96,374

BMW Masters *Lake Malaren GC, Shanghai, China* Oct 25–28 [7607–72]

1	Peter Hanson (SWE)	66-64-70-67—267	€888,561
2	Rory McIlroy (NIR)	67-65-69-67—268	593,338
3	Luke Donald (ENG)	70-67-68-66—271	333,762

WGC – HSBC Champions *Mission Hills GC, Shenzhen, China* Nov 1–4 [7251–72]

1	Ian Poulter (ENG)	69-68-65-65—267	€921,376
2	Jason Dufner (USA)	68-66-71-64—269	320,562
	Ernie Els (RSA)	70-63-69-67—269	320,562
	Phil Mickelson (USA)	66-69-66-68—269	320,562
	Scott Piercy (USA)	68-68-68-65—269	320,562

Full details of this event can be found on page 204

Barclay's Singapore Open *Sentosa GC* Nov 8–11 [7323–71]

1	Matteo Manassero (ITA)*	70-68-64-69—271	€770,226
2	Louis Oosthuizen (RSA)	70-69-65-67—271	513,479

**Manassero won at the third extra hole*

3	Rory McIlroy (NIR)	70-70-69-65—274	289,297

UBS Hong Kong Open *Hong Kong GC, Fanling* Nov 15–18 [6734–70]

1	Miguel Angel Jiménez (ESP)	65-67-68-65—265	€260,638
2	Fredrik Andersson Hed (SWE)	66-66-70-64—266	173,759
3	Marcus Fraser (AUS)	67-69-68-64—268	97,897

South African Open Championship *Ekurhuleni, South Africa* Nov 15–18 [7761–72]

1	Henrik Stenson (SWE)	66-65-69-71—271	€158,500
2	George Coetzee (RSA)	70-70-63-71—274	115,000
3	Thomas Aiken (RSA)	73-66-69-67—275	59,150
	Martin Kaymer (GER)	70-70-68-67—275	59,150

DP World Tour Championship, Dubai *Jumeirah Golf Estates, Dubai, UAE* Nov 22–25 [7675–72]

1	Rory McIlroy (NIR)	66-67-66-66—265	€1,041,429
2	Justin Rose (ENG)	68-68-69-62—267	694,312
3	Luke Donald (ENG)	65-68-66-71—270	359,302
	Charl Schwartzel (RSA)	68-67-67-68—270	359,302
5	Louis Oosthuizen (RSA)	67-67-68-69—271	249,949
6	Branden Grace (RSA)	69-65-70-68—272	203,240
7	Thongchai Jaidee (THA)	68-69-68-68—273	174,964
	Henrik Stenson (SWE)	68-68-69-68—273	174,964
	Fredrik Andersson Hed (SWE)	67-69-72-66—274	134,973
	Jamie Donaldson (WAL)	68-68-69-69—274	134,973
	Gonzalo Fernandez-Castaño (ESP)	66-72-68-68—274	134,973

9T	Sergio García (ESP)	73-64-73-64—274	134,973
	Padraig Harrington (IRL)	67-71-68-68—274	134,973
14	Scott Jamieson (SCO)	68-69-72-66—275	109,353
	Peter Lawrie (IRL)	68-72-67-68—275	109,353
16	Stephen Gallacher (SCO)	68-70-72-66—276	87,482
	Peter Hanson (SWE)	69-67-70-70—276	87,482
	Raphaël Jacquelin (FRA)	69-67-71-69—276	87,482
	Miguel Angel Jiménez (ESP)	71-71-69-65—276	87,482
	Joost Luiten (NED)	69-68-67-72—276	87,482
21	Anders Hansen (DEN)	69-70-69-69—277	68,736
	Thorbjørn Olesen (DEN)	68-72-68-69—277	68,736
	Robert Rock (ENG)	72-70-69-66—277	68,736
	Jeev Milkha Singh (IND)	71-74-64-68—277	68,736
	Romain Wattel (FRA)	70-68-67-72—277	68,736
26	George Coetzee (RSA)	71-67-67-73—278	56,551
	Martin Kaymer (GER)	67-70-72-69—278	56,551
	Søren Kjeldsen (DEN)	72-69-68-69—278	56,551
	Ian Poulter (ENG)	72-70-67-69—278	56,551
	Richie Ramsay (SCO)	67-68-73-70—278	56,551
	MarcWarren (SCO)	66-67-72-73—278	56,551
	Danny Willett (ENG)	71-65-70-72—278	56,551
	Chris Wood (ENG)	71-69-69-69—278	56,551
34	Nicolas Colsaerts (BEL)	68-68-74-69—279	47,490
	Francesco Molinari (ITA)	72-71-71-65—279	47,490
36	Alejandro Cañizares (ESP)	74-68-71-67—280	44,366
	Victor Dubuisson (FRA)	71-69-71-69—280	44,366
	Pablo Larrazábal (ESP)	70-72-72-66—280	44,366
39	Alexander Noren (SWE)	70-73-71-67—281	41,866
40	Rafa Cabrera-Bello (ESP)	70-70-70-72—282	39,992
	Marcus Fraser (AUS)	69-67-75-71—282	39,992
42	Thomas Aiken (RSA)	70-66-71-76—283	34,993
	Simon Dyson (ENG)	69-69-73-72—283	34,993
	Jbe Kruger (RSA)	72-70-70-71—283	34,993
	Matteo Manassero (ITA)	73-68-73-69—283	34,993
	Marcel Siem (GER)	73-65-75-70—283	34,993
	Bernd Wiesberger (AUT)	72-70-68-73—283	34,993
48	David Drysdale (SCO)	71-74-70-69—284	29,369
	Paul Lawrie (SCO)	71-72-70-71—284	29,369
	Lee Westwood (ENG)	67-74-71-72—284	29,369
51	Richard Sterne (RSA)	74-74-67-71—286	26,870
52	Michael Hoey (NIR)	70-71-71-75—287	24,995
	Graeme McDowell (NIR)	72-73-73-69—287	24,995
54	David Lynn (ENG)	73-77-70-69—289	22,495
	Lee Slattery (ENG)	74-72-75-68—289	22,495
56	Richard Finch (ENG)	76-74-74-71—295	20,621

Injured Jiménez misses first part of the season

As a professional golfer 49-year-old Miguel Angel Jiménez admits he knew the risk he was taking ski-ing in his spare time but he loved it so much he could not give it up.

Sadly, just before Christmas in an accident in Spain's Sierra Nevada mountains in Andalucia, he broke the top of the tibia on his right leg and will be miss the first part of the 2013 season including the big money events in Abu Dhabi, Qatar and Dubai.

The accident happened at a time when he was playing well. At the end of last season he won the Hong Kong Open for the third time and was the Tour's November Golfer of the Month

Jiménez, who hopes he has made no long term damage, is not the first golfer to be injured in a ski-ing accident. Phil Mickelson fractured his left femur in a fall in 1994 and had to have a rod inserted in his leg.

Top money earners on the European Tour 1972–2012

(European Tour members only)

1972	Bob Charles (NZL)	€25,953	
1975	Dale Hayes (RSA)	€28,710	
1980	Greg Norman (AUS)	€104,761	
1985	Sandy Lyle (SCO)	€356,595	
1990	Ian Woosnam (WAL)	€1,033,169	
1995	Colin Montgomerie (SCO)	€1,454,205	
2000	Lee Westwood (ENG)	€3,125,147	
2005	Colin Montgomerie (SCO)	€2,794,223	
2009	Lee Westwood (ENG)	€4,237,762	
2010	Martin Kaymer (GER)	€4,461,011	
2011	Luke Donald (ENG)	€4,216,226	
2012	Rory McIlroy (NIR)	€5,519,118	

Truly international – the PGA European Tour

The European Tour has always had the reputation of being truly international and representatives of no fewer than 35 countries have been winners since it all started in 1972. Here are the countries with the number of players who have been winners and the golfers who have been most successful.

Country	*Winners*	*Wins*	*Most successful*
Argentina	11	30	Eduardo Romero 8
Australia	37	108	Greg Norman 14
Austria	3	5	Markus Brier 2; Bernd Wiesberger 2
Belgium	2	3	Nicolas Colsaerts 2
Brazil	1	1	Jaime Gonzalez 1
Canada	2	3	Mike Weir 2
Chile	1	1	Felipe Aguilar 1
China	2	2	Liang-Wei zhang 1; Liang Wen-chong 1
Denmark	8	26	Thomas Björn 13
England	86	277	Sir Nick Faldo 30
Fiji	1	13	Vijay Singh 13
Finland	1	2	Mikko Ilonen 2
France	11	26	Thomas Levet 6
Germany	6	63	Bernhard Langer 42
Holland	4	5	Robert-Jan Derksen 2
India	3	9	Jeev Milkha Singh 4
Ireland	14	47	Padraig Harrington 47
Italy	8	18	Costantino Rocca 5
Japan	1	1	Isao Aoki 1
New Zealand	7	25	Michael Campbell 8
Northern Ireland	7	46	Darren Clarke 14
Portugal	2	2	Ricardo Santos 1; Daniel Silva 1
Scotland	21	130	Colin Montgomerie 31
Singapore	1	1	Mardan Mamat 1
South Africa	31	110	Ernie Els 27
South Korea	4	6	Y E Yang 4
Spain	28	166	Severiano Ballesteros 50
Sweden	28	94	Robert Karlsson 11
Switzerland	1	1	Andre Bossert 1
Taiwan	2	2	Yeh Wei-tze 1; Lin Wen-tang 1
Thailand	3	7	Thongchai Jaidee 5
Trinidad &Tobago	1	2	Stephen Ames* 2
United States	57	126	Tiger Woods 37
Wales	10	45	Ian Woosnam 29
Zimbabwe	3	29	Mark McNulty** 16

*Stephen Ames now plays out of Canada ** Mark McNulty now plays out of Northern Ireland

European Senior Tour 2012

www.europeantour.com

Final Ranking (Top 30 earn full Tour card for 2013)

1	Roger Chapman (ENG)	€356,751
2	Barry Lane (ENG)	284,636
3	Tim Thelen (USA)	251,772
4	Peter Fowler (AUS)	225,430
5	Paul Wesselingh (ENG)	191,663
6	Chris Williams (RSA)	160,733
7	Gary Wolstenholme (ENG)	154,501
8	Anders Forsbrand (SWE)	152,824
9	Des Smyth (IRL)	150,500
10	Bernhard Langer (GER)	132,108
11	Mark James (ENG)	122,298
12	Carl Mason (ENG)	120,103
13	David J Russell (ENG)	115,919
14	Mark Mouland (WAL)	112,349
15	Andrew Oldcorn (SCO)	97,113
16	Mike Harwood (AUS)	96,981
17	Philip Golding (ENG)	95,302
18	Terry Price (AUS)	91,814
19	Dick Mast (USA)	90,549
20	Marc Farry (FRA)	86,746
21	Ian Woosnam (WAL)	83,357
22	Ross Drummond (SCO)	82,632
23	Andrew Sherborne (ENG)	82,188
24	Boonchu Ruangkit (THA)	71,688
25	Juan Quiros (ESP)	71,392
26	Bill Longmuir (SCO)	65,022
27	Miguel Angel Martin (ESP)	59,001
28	Kevin Spurgeon (ENG)	58,769
29	Angel Franco (PAR)	56,648
30	Mike Cunning (USA)	55,528
31	Bob Cameron (ENG)	51,061
32	Gordon Manson (AUT)	49,808
33	Glenn Ralph (ENG)	47,745
34	Rick Gibson (CAN)	45,848
35	John Harrison (ENG)	44,788
36	Graham Banister (AUS)	42,294
37	George Ryall (ENG)	41,538
38	David Merriman (AUS)	40,587
39	Steve Van Vuuren (RSA)	39,918
40	Gerry Norquist (USA)	39,565
41	John Gould (ENG)	38,898
42	Jerry Bruner (USA)	38,718
43	Steve Cipa (ENG)	35,222
44	Tony Johnstone (ZIM)	33,835
45	Gordon Brand Jr (SCO)	33,469
46	Katsuyoshi Tomori (JPN)	31,672
47	Andrew Murray (ENG)	30,235
48	Sam Torrance (SCO)	29,841
49	Angel Fernandez (CHI)	26,134
50	Stephen Mcallister (SCO)	25,897
51	Mark Belsham (ENG)	i24,977
52	Jeff Hall (ENG)	24,103
53	Peter Mitchell (ENG)	23,903
54	Delroy Cambridge (JAM)	21,646
55	Nick Job (ENG)	21,070
56	Jean Pierre Sallat (FRA)	19,936
57	Tim Elliott (AUS)	19,679
58	Peter A Smith (SCO)	19,200
59	Philip Walton (IRL)	17,277
60	Denis O'Sullivan (IRL)	17,037
61	Domingo Hospital (ESP)	16,801
62	Denis Durnian (ENG)	15,453
63	Noel Ratcliffe (AUS)	14,664
64	Gordon J Brand (ENG)	14,635
65	Jim Rhodes (ENG)	14,500
66	Luis Carbonetti (ARG)	14,459
67	Zeke P Martinez (USA)	12,905
68	Bobby Lincoln (RSA)	11,411
69	Rodger Davis (AUS)	10,542
70	Roger Sabarros (FRA)	9,264
71	Ken Tarling (CAN)	8,226
72	Manuel Piñero (ESP)	7,798
73	Eamonn Darcy (IRL)	7,334
74	Stephen McNally (ENG)	6,697
75	Costantino Rocca (ITA)	6,604
76	José Rivero (ESP)	6,444
77	Steen Tinning (RSA)	6,295
78	Bertus Smit (RSA)	5,647
79	Giuseppe Cali (ITA)	5,507
80	Charlie Bolling (USA)	3,899
81	Terry Burgoyne (SCO)	3,896
82	Peter Dahlberg (SWE)	3,816
83	Mitch Kierstenson (ENG)	3,650
84	Tony Charnley (ENG)	3,541
85	Antonio Garrido (ESP)	3,209
86	Dave Wettlaufer (CAN)	2,535
87	Peter Horrobin (JAM)	2,001
88	Bill Hardwick (CAN)	1,971
89	Maurice Bembridge (ENG)	1,611
90	Barrie Stevens (ENG)	1,505
91	Victor Garcia (ESP)	1,473
92	Roger Roper (ENG)	1,258
93	Stephen Bennett (ENG)	1,149
94	Alan Saddington (SCO)	950
95	Matt Briggs (ENG)	897
96	Glyn Davies (WAL)	730
97	Bradley Smith (ENG)	525
98	Claude Grenier (AUT)	350
99	Mus Deboub (ALG)	317
100	David Thomson (SCO)	300
101	Rinus Van Blankers (NED)	263

Career Money List

1	Carl Mason (ENG)	€2,403,565
2	Tommy Horton (ENG)	1,527,506
3	Nick Job (ENG)	1,498,951
4	Sam Torrance (SCO)	1,496,992
5	Noel Ratcliffe (AUS)	1,371,540
6	Bill Longmuir (SCO)	1,333,475
7	Jerry Bruner (USA)	1,295,584
8	Tom Watson (USA)	1,277,812
9	Denis O'Sullivan (IRL)	1,254,379
10	Jim Rhodes (ENG)	1,209,266
11	Bob Cameron (ENG)	1,143,124
12	John Chillas (SCO)	1,108,551
13	Des Smyth (IRL)	1,068,025
14	Seiji Ebihara (JPN)	1,056,140
15	Delroy Cambridge (JAM)	1,029,204
16	Terry Gale (AUS)	1,026,697
17	Denis Durnian (ENG)	971,429
18	Juan Quiros (ESP)	966,939
19	Gordon J Brand (ENG)	945,995
20	David Good (AUS)	945,648
21	Luis Carbonetti (ARG)	941,378
22	Neil Coles (ENG)	928,968
23	David J Russell (ENG)	899,569
24	Eduardo Romero (ARG)	889,809
25	Giuseppe Cali (ITA)	854,075
26	Ian Woosnam (WAL)	835,378
27	Malcolm Gregson (ENG)	833,972
28	Bernhard Langer (GER)	812,736
29	Maurice Bembridge (ENG)	785,540
30	José Rivero (ESP)	761,367
31	Simon Owen (NZL)	747,697
32	Horacio Carbonetti (ARG)	740,817
33	Loren Roberts (USA)	730,136
34	Bob Charles (NZL)	721,172
35	Roger Chapman (ENG)	711,658
36	Eamonn Darcy (IRL)	694,633
37	Guillermo Encina (CHI)	682,238
38	Ross Drummond (SCO)	679,681
39	John Bland (RSA)	674,808
40	Barry Lane (ENG)	666,703
41	David Creamer (ENG)	664,415
42	Eddie Polland (NIR)	651,591
43	Brian Huggett (WAL)	638,783
44	Angel Franco (PAR)	637,050
45	Peter Fowler (AUS)	619,558
46	Antonio Garrido (ESP)	612,453
47	Tony Johnstone (ZIM)	611,449
48	Ian Stanley (AUS)	607,584
49	Alan Tapie (USA)	590,860
50	Chris Williams (RSA)	583,758
51	Stewart Ginn (AUS)	572,687
52	Costantino Rocca (ITA)	566,258
53	Bobby Lincoln (RSA)	548,545
54	John Grace (USA)	539,694
55	Boonchu Ruangkit (THA)	535,409
56	Mark James (ENG)	534,705
57	Pete Oakley (USA)	528,177
58	Martin Gray (SCO)	528,014
59	Kevin Spurgeon (ENG)	514,562
60	David Merriman (AUS)	513,819
61	David Huish (SCO)	512,325
62	Ray Carrasco (USA)	505,330
63	Jay Haas (USA)	503,353
64	Bobby Verwey (RSA)	496,778
65	Gordon Brand Jr (SCO)	491,520
66	Peter Mitchell (ENG)	490,983
67	Brian Waites (ENG)	482,280
68	Glenn Ralph (ENG)	475,058
69	Alberto Croce (ITA)	469,904
70	Liam Higgins (IRL)	469,088
71	Tom Lehman (USA)	467,894
72	David Frost (RSA)	464,091
73	Bob Lendzion (USA)	462,937
74	Bob Shearer (AUS)	459,657
75	Katsuyoshi Tomori (JPN)	457,337
76	Gary Wolstenholme (ENG)	456,151
77	Mike Miller (SCO)	455,395
78	Andrew Oldcorn (SCO)	449,208
79	Ian Mosey (ENG)	443,469
80	Michael Allen (USA)	431,557
81	Mike Harwood (AUS)	429,362
82	Fred Couples (USA)	426,409
83	Christy O'Connor Jr (IRL)	423,516
84	Bill Hardwick (CAN)	418,276
85	Gery Watine (FRA)	416,791
86	Paul Leonard (NIR)	414,918
87	Tom Kite (USA)	411,637
88	Bertus Smit (RSA)	391,294
89	Bernard Gallacher (SCO)	390,919
90	Peter Senior (AUS)	388,584
91	Priscillo Diniz (BRA)	388,580
92	Gary Player (RSA)	386,948
93	David Jones (NIR)	374,369
94	John Fourie (RSA)	371,197
95	Bruce Heuchan (CAN)	353,380
96	Marc Farry (FRA)	350,823
97	Denis Watson (ZIM)	345,234
98	Mike Cunning (USA)	344,328
99	Angel Fernandez (CHI)	336,460
100	Russ Cochran (USA)	336,054

Did you know?

The first golf club in Continental Europe, Pau Golf Club at Billere in France, was founded in 1856. The first golf played at Pau, however, was by British soldiers who were billeted there for the Battle of Orthez in February 1814.

Tour Results

May 11–13	Mallorca Open Senior	Pula GC, Son Servera	Gary Wolstenholme (ENG)	205 (–8)
May 24–27	**US Senior PGA Championship**	Benton Harbor, Michigan, USA		
	1 Roger Champan (ENG)	68-67-64-72—271		
	2 John Cook (USA)	69-66-69-69—273		
	3 Hale Irwin (USA)	71-66-69-68—274		
June 1–3	Benahavis Sen. Masters	Benahavis, Spain	Gary Wolstenholme (ENG)	200 (–13)
June 7–10	ISPS Handa PGA Seniors Championship	Hexham, England	Paul Wesselingh (ENG)	210 (–6)
June 22–24	Van Lanschot Sen. Open	The Hague, Netherlands	Massy Kuramoto (JPN)	216 (=)
June 29–July 1	Berenberg Bank Masters	Munich, Germany	Tim Thelen (USA)	201 (–15)
July 6–8	Bad Ragaz PGA Sen. Open	Bad Ragaz, Switzerland	Tim Thelen (USA)	198 (–12)
July 12–15	**US Senior Open**	Orion, MI, USA		
	1 Roger Chapman (ENG)	68-68-68-66—270		
	2 Fred Funk (USA)	67-71-67-67—272		
	Tom Lehman (USA)	70-66-68-68—272		
	Corey Pavin (USA)	67-69-68-68—272		
	Bernhard Langer (GER)	66-70-64-72—272		
July 26–29	**The Senior Open**	Turnberry, Ayrshire, Scotland		
	1 Fred Couples (USA)	72-68-64-67—271		
	2 Gary Hallberg (USA)	71-63-73-66—273		
	3 Barry Lane (ENG)	67-74-66-69—276		
	Carl Mason (ENG)	69-74-67-66—276		
	Dick Mast (USA)	66-73-70-67—276		
Aug 17–19	Scottish Senior Open	St. Andrews, Scotland	Anders Forsbrand (SWE)	199 (–17)
Aug 24–26	Wales Senior Open	Conwy, Wales	Barry Lane (ENG)	209 (–7)
Aug 31–Sep 2	Travis Perkins plc Senior Masters	Duke's Course, Woburn GC, Woburn, England	Des Smyth (IRL)	206 (–10)
Sep 7–9	Pon Senior Open	Vorbeck, Germany	Terry Price (AUS)	200 (–16)
Sep 21–23	French Riviera Masters	Provence, France	David J Russell (ENG)*	208 (–8)
	**Beat Tim Thelen (USA) at the third extra hole*			
Nov 9–11	Fubon Senior Open	New Taipei City, Taiwan	Tim Thelen (USA)	202 (–14)
Dec 7–9	MCB Tour Championship	Constance Belle Mare Plage, Mauritius	David Frost (RSA)	205 (–11)

Senior Tour Records 2012

Low 9 holes	29 (–6)	John Gould	Bad Ragaz PGA Seniors Open
Low 18 holes	62 (–9)	Kenny Perry	US Senior PGA Championship
Largest Winning Margin	6 shots	Terry Price	Pon Senior Open Championship
Largest 18 Hole Lead	2 shots	Gordon Brand Jr	Van Lanschot Senior Open
	2 shots	Philip Golding	Speedy Services Wales Senior Open
Largest 36 Hole Lead	3 shots	Tim Thelen	Bad Ragaz PGA Seniors Open
	3 shots	Gary Hallberg	The Senior Open Championship
	3 shots	Anders Forsbrand	SSE Scottish Senior Open
	3 shots	Terry Price	Pon Senior Open
Holes-in-one		Peter Mitchell	Pon Senior Open
Albatrosses		Tim Thelen	Berenberg Bank Masters
Low Finish by a Winner	65 (–7)	David J Russell	French Riviera Masters

Senior Tour Records 2012

First time winners

Roger Chapman	US Senior PGA Championship presented by KitchenAid
Paul Wesselingh	ISPS Handa PGA Seniors Championship
Tim Thelen	Berenberg Bank Masters
Fred Couples	The Senior Open Championship Presented by Rolex
Anders Forsbrand	SSE Scottish Seniors Open
Terry Price	Pon Senior Open

Course records

Kenny Perry	62 (–9)	US Senior PGA Championship
Marc Farry	63 (–8)	Benahavis Senior Masters
Gary Hallberg	63 (–7)*	The Senior Open Championship
Philip Golding	64 (–8)	SSE Scottish Senior Open
Philip Golding	64 (–8)	Speedy Services Wales Senior Open
Chris Williams	65 (–7)	Pon Senior Open

Multiple winners

Gary Wolstenholme — Mallorca Senior Open; Benahavis Senior Masters

Most top 5 finishes

6 Peter Fowler	4 Paul Wesselingh	3 Roger Chapman
5 Barry Lane	3 Chris Williams	3 Des Smyth
4 Anders Forsbrand	3 Mark Mouland	3 Tim Thelen
4 Mark James	3 Gary Wolstenholme	3 Ian Woosnam

*equals existing record

Jiménez joins the oldest winners on the world tours

Spaniard Miguel Angel Jiménez became the oldest winner on the European Tour when he won the Hong Kong Open for a third time last November. His age – 48 years and 318 days which edged out Des Smyth of Ireland who had held the previous record with victory in the Madeira Island Open in 2011 when he was 48 years and 34 days.

Six golfers have won events on the PGA Tour when in their 50's. The late Sam Snead was 52 years 10 months and eight days when he won the 1965 Greater Greensboro Open. Art Wall Jr. Jim Barnes and John Barnum were all in their 52nd year when they won respectively at Milwaukee in 1975, the Long Island Open in 1937 and the 1962 Cajun Classic .

Craig Stadler won the 2003 BC Open in Canada when 50 years 1 month and 18 days and more recently Fred Funk was the winner of the 2007 Mayakoba Classic at aged 50 years 8 months and 12 days.

Choi Sang Ho is the oldest winner on the Asian Tour. He was 50 years and 145 days when he won the 2005 Maekyung Open. In Japan, Masashi "Jumbo" Ozaki is the oldest to have won a title. He was 55 years and 8 months when winning the 2002 ANA Open.

Mark McNulty is the oldest winner on South Africa's Sunshine Tour. He was 49 years and 44 days when he landed the 2003 Vodacom Players Championship while Australia's oldest winner is the much revered Kel Nagle who was 54 when picking up the first prize at the 1975 Clearwater Classic.

In women's golf, Beth Daniel at 46 years and 8 months is the oldest winner on the LPGA Tour following her success in the 2003 Canadian Open while Laura Davies, still as enthusiastic and as competitive as ever wherever she plays in the world, became the oldest winner on the Ladies European Tour when successful in the 2010 Hero Honda Open at the age of 47 years and 1 month.

European Challenge Tour 2012

www.europeantour.com

Final Order of Merit (top 20 earn card for PGA European Tour)

1	Espen Kofstad (NOR)	€131,099
2	Kristoffer Broberg (SWE)	126,508
3	Andreas Hartø (DEN)	121,999
4	Joachim B Hansen (DEN)	120,085
5	Gary Lockerbie (ENG)	117,482
6	Magnus A Carlsson (SWE)	110,487
7	Simon Wakefield (ENG)	108,593
8	Alessandro Tadini (ITA)	101,428
9	Alexandre Kaleka (FRA)	95,944
10	Chris Doak (SCO)	92,730
11	Scott Henry (SCO)	90,688
12	Chris Paisley (ENG)	74,485
13	Eddie Pepperell (ENG)	72,378
14	Maximilian Kieffer (GER)	70,243
15	Justin Walters (RSA)	69,913
16	James Busby (ENG)	67,350
17	Gary Stal (FRA)	66,580
18	Mark Tullo (CHI)	66,436
19	Morten Orum Madsen (DEN)	65,338
20	Seve Benson (ENG)	65,149
21	Daniel Brooks (ENG)	64,776
22	Raymond Russell (SCO)	64,616
23	Eduardo De La Riva (ESP)	64,383
24	Hp Bacher (AUT)	64,339
25	Phillip Archer (ENG)	64,074
26	Peter Uihlein (USA)	61,211
27	Daniel Vancsik (ARG)	60,902
28	Lasse Jensen (DEN)	58,201
29	Mikko Korhonen (FIN)	57,574
30	Alexander Levy (FRA)	57,310
31	Wil Besseling (NED)	56,961
32	Chris Lloyd (ENG)	56,218
33	Marco Crespi (ITA)	53,489
34	Sihwan Kim (KOR)	52,536
35	Bjorn Åkesson (SWE)	49,741
36	Carlos Aguilar (ESP)	48,773
37	John Parry (ENG)	47,196
38	Roope Kakko (FIN)	46,081
39	Nick Dougherty (ENG)	44,683
40	Sam Walker (ENG)	43,991
41	Matteo Delpodio (ITA)	43,698
42	Michael Lorenzo-Vera (FRA)	43,554
43	Brooks Koepka (USA)	42,975
44	Jeppe Huldahl (DEN)	41,282
45	Andrew Mcarthur (SCO)	40,893
46	Steven Tiley (ENG)	36,919
47	Charlie Ford (ENG)	36,349
48	Robert Dinwiddie (ENG)	35,580
49	Andrea Perrino (ITA)	33,476
50	Luke Goddard (ENG)	32,373
51	Pelle Edberg (SWE)	30,212
52	Callum Macaulay (SCO)	30,110
53	Jordi Garcia Pinto (ESP)	30,085
54	Alvaro Velasco (ESP)	28,332
55	Lloyd Saltman (SCO)	27,358
56	José-Filipe Lima (POR)	26,864
57	Rafa Echenique (ARG)	25,879
58	Anthony Snobeck (FRA)	25,587
59	Florian Praegant (AUT)	25,092
60	Agustin Domingo (ESP)	25,027
61	Ben Parker (ENG)	24,940
62	Adam Gee (ENG)	24,531
63	Garry Houston (WAL)	24,310
64	Victor Riu (FRA)	23,335
65	Jens Dantorp (SWE)	23,326
66	Jack Senior (ENG)	23,199
67	Francis McGuirk (ENG)	22,775
68	Steven O'Hara (SCO)	21,714
69	Tyrone Ferreira (RSA)	21,580
70	Klas Eriksson (SWE)	21,392
71	Jamie McLeary (SCO)	21,133
72	Paul Dwyer (ENG)	20,641
73	Christophe Brazillier (FRA)	19,853
74	Julien Guerrier (FRA)	18,434
75	Matt Haines (ENG)	18,412
76	Matthew Nixon (ENG)	18,062
77	Tyrrell Hatton (ENG)	18,015
78	Floris De Vries (NED)	17,914
79	Adrien Bernadet (FRA)	17,900
80	Pedro Oriol (ESP)	17,825
81	Steven Jeppesen (SWE)	17,744
82	Byeong-Hun An (KOR)	17,665
83	Adrian Otaegui (ESP)	17,071
84	Jamie Abbott (ENG)	16,987
85	Peter Baker (ENG)	16,854
86	Matthew Southgate (ENG)	16,604
87	Nicolas Meitinger (GER)	16,472
88	Chris Hanson (ENG)	16,448
89	James Heath (ENG)	16,433
90	Chris Gane (ENG)	16,100
91	Lloyd Kennedy (ENG)	16,086
92	Scott Pinckney (USA)	15,980
93	Daniel Gaunt (AUS)	15,936
94	Benn Barham (ENG)	15,418
95	Matt Ford (ENG)	14,149
96	Luis Claverie (ESP)	13,864
97	Matthew Cryer (ENG)	13,312
98	Cesar Monasterio (ARG)	13,311
99	Roland Steiner (AUT)	13,129
100	Janne Mommo (FIN)	13,042

Results

Jan 26–29	Gujarat Kensville Chall.	Ahmedabad, India	Maximilian Kieffer (GER)*	281 (–7)
	**Beat Rahil Gangjee (IND) at the first extra hole*			
Mar 8–11	Pacific Rubiales Colombia Classic	Barranquilla,Colombia	Phillip Archer (ENG)	280 (–8)
Mar 29–April 1	Barclays Kenya Open	Muthaiga GC, Nairobi, Kenya	Seve Benson (ENG)*	274 (–10)
	**Beat Lasse Jensen (DEN) at the first extra hole*			
May 10–13	ALLIANZ Open Cotes d'Armor – Bretagne	Le Val André, France	Eddie Pepperell (ENG)*	277 (–3)
	**Beat Jeppe Huldahl (DEN) at the first extra hole*			
May 10–13	Madeira Islands Open	Santo da Serra, Portugal	Ricardo Santos (POR)	266 (–22)
May 24–27	Telenet Trophy	Tervuren, Belgium	Marco Crespi (ITA)	270 (–14)
May 31–June 3	Fred Olsen Challenge de España	La Gomera, Canary Is., Spain	Eduardo de la Riva (ESP)	265 (–19)
June 7–10	Kärnten Golf Open	Klagenfurt, Austria	Gary Stal (FRA)	268 (–20)
June 14–17	St Omer Open	St Omer, Lumbres, France	Darren Fichardt (RSA)	279 (–5)
June 21–24	Scottish Hydro Challenge	Aviemore, Scotland	Sam Walker (ENG)*	201 (–12)
	**Beat Simon Wakefield (ENG) at the third extra hole*			
June 27–30	Chall. Provincia di Varese	Luvinate, Italy	Raymond Russell (SCO)	263 (–17)
July 12–15	Credit Suisse Challenge	Lucerne, Switzerland	Gary Stal (FRA)*	273 (–11)
	**Beat Alexandre Kaleka (FRA) at the fourth extra hole*			
July 18–21	Acaya Open	Puglia, Italy	Espen Kofstad (NOR)	271 (–9)
July 26–29	English Challenge	Stoke-by-Nayland, England	Chris Paisley (ENG)	272 (–16)
Aug 2–5	Finnish Challenge	Hyvinkää, Finland	Kristoffer Broberg (SWE)	296 (–15)
Aug 9–12	Norwegian Challenge	Trondheim, Norway	Kristoffer Broberg (SWE)*	266 (–22)
	**Beat Alvaro Velasco (ESP) at the fourth extra hole*			
Aug 15–18	ECCO Tour C/ship	Horsens, Denmark	Alessandro Tadini (ITA)*	276 (–12)
	**Beat James Busby (ENG) at the third extra hole*			
Aug 22–25	Rolex Trophy	Geneva, Switzerland	Kristoffer Broberg (SWE)	261 (–27)
Sep 6–9	M2M Russian Chall. Cup	Moscow, Russia	Alexandre Kaleka (FRA)	281 (–7)
Sep 13–16	Kazakhstan Open	Almaty, Kazakhstan	Henry Scott (SCO)*	269 (–19)
	**Beat H P Bacher (AUT) at the second extra hole*			
Sep 20–23	ALLIANZ Open de Toulouse	Seilh, France	Julien Brun (FRA) (am)	271 (–13)
Sep 27–30	Challenge de Cataluña	Tarragona, Spain	Brooks Koepka (USA)	200 (–16)
Oct 4–7	ALLIANZ Open de Lyon	Monthieux, France	Chris Doak (SCO)*	271 (–13)
	**Beat Tim Sluiter (NED) at the third extra hole*			
Oct 11–14	Czech Challenge Open	Drítec, Czech Republic	Andreas Hartø (DEN)	264 (–24)
Oct 18–21	Crowne Plaza Copenhagen Challenge	Royal GC, Ciopenhagen, Denmark	Kristoffer Broberg (SWE)	270 (–14)
Oct 24–27	Apulia San Domenico Grand Final	Puglia, Italy	Espen Kofstad (NOR)	265 (–19)

Challenge Tour Records 2012

Low 9 holes	27 (–8)	Chris Lloyd (ENG)	Scottish Hydro Challenge
Low 18 holes	61 (–10)	Charlie Ford (ENG)	Challenge de España
Largest winning margin	6 shots	Kristoffer Broberg (SWE)	Finnish Challenge

Multiple winners

Kristoffer Broberg (SWE)	Finnish Challenge Norwegian Challenge Rolex Trophy Crowne Plaza Copenhagen Challenge
Gary Stal (FRA)	Kärnten Golf Open Credit Suisse Challenge

Honorary Membership for double major winner Chapman

Michigan was a happy hunting ground last year for Roger Chapman who won both the US Senior PGA Championship and the US Senior Open in that state. He won the first of those titles at Harbor Shores and the second at Indianwood becoming only the fourth golfer after Gary Player in 1987, Jack Nicklaus in 1991 and Hale Irwin in 1998 to take both titles in the same season.

Chapman, who by finishing top of the European Senior Tour Order of Merit won the John Jacobs Trophy, became the Tour's 45th Honorary Life Member when George O'Grady, the Tour's chief executive, handed over his solid silver member's card.

Taken by surprise, Chapman commented: This is a totally unexpected honour but I am grateful to George and everyone at the Tour for their support and for this recognition.

"What was particularly memorable for me was having my wife Cathy by the 18th green when I won at Indianwood. She has always been my biggest supporter. She told me that she knew I could do it if I just believed in myself. It was so special having her there."

Thongchai Jaidee well ahead in Asian career money

While Thaworn Wirachant may have finished No 1 on the Asian circuit in 2012, he still has some way to go to catch Thongchai Jaidee in the career money list on the Far East Tour.

At the end of last year Jaidee had banked a total of $4.7 million in prize-money – $1 million more than second-placed Wirachant. Jeev Milkha Singh, Jyoti Randhawa and Prayed Marksaeng make up the top five.

	Name	*Played*	*Prize-money*
1	Thongchai Jaidee (THA)	162	US$4,711,077
2	Thaworn Wirachant (THA)	351	3,784,046
3	Jeev Milkha Singh (IND)	136	3,270,471
4	Jyoti Randhawa (IND)	211	2,932,353
5	Prayed Marksaeng (THA)	221	2,802,473

Tom Watson recalled as US Ryder Cup Captain

Five-times Open champion Tom Watson led America to victory in the 1993 Ryder Cup at The Belfry and, having not won again in Europe since then, the Americans have turned the clock back by choosing Watson to captain the team again at Gleneagles next year.

With just two victories in the last nine matches – at Brookline in 1999 and again at Valhalla in 2008 – the PGA of America knew something had to be done to redress the balance. Tom Watson is their ace, their lucky mascot, their match winner – they hope.

"We are just really tired of losing," said PGA of America President Ted Bishop who knows even with Watson at the helm it will not be easy to beat the Europeans. They feel, however, that with Watson in charge they have a better chance of victory to atone for their horror defeat at Medinah last year.

Watson when approached was up for the job. He loves Scotland having won four of his five Opens north of the border at Carnoustie, Turnberry, Troon and Muirfield and at the age of 59 he nearly won again at Turnberry in 2009.

"I so enjoyed being the Cup captain in 1993. The winning feeling I experienced then is why I wanted to come back Winning is what we are all out here for as players but when you do something for your team mates and you win for your country as well that is something extra special. I want to experience it all over again."

Watson, the oldest man ever to captain an American side, may be hugely popular in Scotland but is under no illusion that the home fans will be looking for another European victory. His very presence at Gleneagles, however, gives the match additional status.

US PGA Tour 2012

Players are of US nationality unless stated

www.pgatour.com

Final Ranking

The top 125 on the money list retained their cards for the 2013 season. The top 40 earned a spot at The Masters.

1	Rory McIlroy (NIR)	$8,047,952
2	Tiger Woods	6,133,158
3	Brandt Snedeker	4,989,739
4	Jason Dufner	4,869,304
5	Bubba Watson	4,644,997
6	Zach Johnson	4,504,244
7	Justin Rose (ENG)	4,290,930
8	Phil Mickelson	4,203,821
9	Hunter Mahan	4,019,193
10	Keegan Bradley	3,910,658
11	Matt Kuchar	3,903,065
12	Jim Furyk	3,623,805
13	Carl Pettersson (SWE)	3,538,656
14	Luke Donald (ENG)	3,512,024
15	Louis Oosthuizen (RSA)	3,460,995
16	Ernie Els (RSA)	3,453,118
17	Webb Simpson	3,436,758
18	Steve Stricker	3,420,021
19	Dustin Johnson	3,393,820
20	Robert Garrigus	3,206,530
21	Rickie Fowler	3,066,293
22	Nick Watney	3,044,224
23	Bo Van Pelt	3,043,509
24	Lee Westwood (ENG)	3,016,569
25	Adam Scott AUS)	2,899,557
26	Ryan Moore	2,858,944
27	Scott Piercy	2,699,205
28	John Huh	2,692,113
29	Sergio García (ESP)	2,510,116
30	Ben Curtis	2,494,153
31	Graeme McDowell (NIR)	2,408,279
32	Kyle Stanley	2,351,857
33	Bill Haas	2,349,951
34	Jonas Blixt (SWE)	2,255,695
35	Johnson Wagner	2,225,007
36	Martin Laird (SCO)	2,172,883
37	Mark Wilson	2,144,780
38	Kevin Na	2,029,943
39	Brendon de Jonge (ZIM)	2,015,252
40	Matt Every	1,972,166
41	Marc Leishman	1,933,761
42	John Senden (AUS)	1,916,651
43	Charlie Wi (KOR)	1,845,397
44	Bud Cauley	1,774,479
45	Ian Poulter (ENG)	1,715,271
46	Ben Crane	1,701,365
47	David Toms	1,658,428
48	Jimmy Walker	1,638,419
49	Seung-Yul Noh (KOR)	1,629,751
50	Jonathan Byrd	1,616,789
51	Vijay Singh (FIJ)	1,586,305
52	Jeff Overton	1,563,670
53	Padraig Harrington (IRL)	1,546,272
54	Kevin Stadler	1,546,036
55	Tommy Gainey	1,540,749
56	D A Points	1,533,361
57	Ken Duke	1,511,628
58	Ryan Palmer	1,501,215
59	John Rollins	1,489,155
60	Michael Thompson	1,408,374
61	Tim Clark (RSA)	1,407,028
62	Ted Potter, Jr	1,383,170
63	Charlie Beljan	1,373,528
64	Brian Davis (ENG)	1,318,032
65	J J Henry	1,297,802
66	Scott Stallings	1,293,739
67	Charles Howell III	1,284,578
68	Spencer Levin	1,283,616
69	Charley Hoffman	1,276,663
70	Dicky Pride	1,259,712
71	Geoff Ogilvy (AUS)	1,255,223
72	Tom Gillis	1,238,058
73	Blake Adams	1,234,345
74	William McGirt	1,228,947
75	Cameron Tringale	1,225,737
76	Aaron Baddeley (AUS)	1,215,753
77	Troy Matteson	1,198,953
78	Chris Kirk	1,197,562
79	Harris English	1,186,003
80	J B Holmes	1,179,505
81	Greg Chalmers (AUS)	1,166,627
82	Bryce Molder	1,166,115
83	Sang-Moon Bae (KOR)	1,165,952
84	Sean O'Hair	1,160,981
85	Greg Owen (ENG)	1,151,622
86	John Mallinger	1,146,852
87	Brian Harman	1,146,448
88	Jason Day (AUS)	1,143,233
89	Charl Schwartzel (RSA)	1,138,844
90	Rory Sabbatini (RSA)	1,128,820
91	George McNeill	1,119,535
92	Daniel Summerhays	1,111,522
93	John Merrick	1,084,628
94	Pat Perez	1,064,053
95	Graham DeLaet	1,051,951
96	Martin Flores	1,035,569
97	David Hearn (CAN)	1,012,575
98	Josh Teater	1,011,430
99	Bob Estes	1,009,769
100	Davis Love III	989,753
101	Andres Romero (ARG)	970,919
102	K J Choi (KOR)	969,057
103	Brian Gay	960,658
104	Fredrik Jacobson (SWE)	953,494
105	Chris Stroud	903,570
106	Chad Campbell	895,199
107	Kevin Streelman	893,736
108	Boo Weekley	848,347
109	Colt Knost	848,197
110	Brendan Steele	840,965
111	Robert Allenby (AUS)	808,927
112	Ricky Barnes	805,408
113	Jhonattan Vegas (VEN)	801,803
114	Jason Bohn	795,549
115	Henrik Stenson (SWE)	791,107
116	Troy Kelly	786,832
117	Will Claxton	780,969
118	Roberto Castro	755,095
119	Jason Kokrak	750,221
120	David Mathis	736,765
121	Harrison Frazar	730,203
122	James Driscoll	687,338
123	Jeff Maggert	682,742
124	Tim Herron	660,279
125	Kevin Chappell	647,510
126	Jerry Kelly	645,701
127	Rod Pampling (AUS)	620,893
128	Billy Mayfair	619,961
129	Trevor Immelman (RSA)	617,296
130	Gary Christian	616,457
131	Alexandre Rocha (BRA)	614,658
132	D J Trahan	611,142
133	Bill Lunde	593,598
134	Gary Woodland	592,879
135	Chez Reavie	580,617
136	Retief Goosen (RSA)	571,174
137	Tim Petrovic	558,862
138	Richard H Lee	547,733
139	Vaughn Taylor	547,129
140	Justin Leonard	540,155
141	Bobby Gates	525,293
142	Heath Slocum	518,198
143	Russell Knox	512,584
144	Camilo Villegas (COL)	491,729

Career Money List (at end of 2012 season)

1	Tiger Woods	$100,950,700
2	Phil Mickelson	67,644,698
3	Vijay Singh (FIJ)	67,277,743
4	Jim Furyk	52,719,459
5	Ernie Els (RSA)	44,771,409
6	Davis Love III	42,208,476
7	David Toms	38,865,778
8	Steve Stricker	35,079,561
9	Justin Leonard	31,861,400
10	Kenny Perry	31,797,536
11	Stewart Cink	30,836,995
12	Sergio García (ESP)	30,582,574
13	Luke Donald (ENG)	28,860,433
14	Adam Scott (AUS)	28,306,454
15	Retief Goosen (RSA)	27,525,642
16	Scott Verplank	27,400,942
17	K J Choi (KOR)	27,373,854
18	Mike Weir (CAN)	26,821,949
19	Stuart Appleby (AUS)	26,757,857
20	Robert Allenby (AUS)	26,408,821
21	Zach Johnson	26,277,293
22	Geoff Ogilvy (AUS)	25,738,157
23	Rory Sabbatini (RSA)	25,464,837
24	Mark Calcavecchia	24,147,827
25	Jerry Kelly	23,845,162
26	Charles Howell III	23,748,581
27	Chris DiMarco	22,474,518
28	Fred Couples	22,276,316
29	Hunter Mahan	21,722,893
30	Padraig Harrington (IRL)	21,645,813
31	Tom Lehman	21,475,800
32	Chad Campbell	21,281,217
33	Justin Rose (ENG)	21,131,617
34	Fred Funk	21,097,907
35	Matt Kuchar	20,799,219
36	Bob Estes	20,610,462
37	Nick Price (ZIM)	20,576,104
38	Billy Mayfair	20,088,234
39	Tim Clark (RSA)	19,381,525
40	Stephen Ames (CAN)	19,380,417
41	Carl Pettersson (SWE)	19,140,522
42	David Duval	18,846,173
43	Nick Watney	18,732,275
44	Scott Hoch	18,530,156
45	Tim Herron	18,266,140
46	Jeff Sluman	18,165,266
47	Steve Flesch	18,030,350
48	Jeff Maggert	17,982,079
49	Bo Van Pelt	17,892,037
50	Brad Faxon	17,769,249
51	Ben Crane	16,979,826
52	Bubba Watson	16,959,642
53	Dustin Johnson	16,944,699
54	Rocco Mediate	16,792,617
55	Sean O'Hair	16,704,413
56	John Rollins	16,644,235
57	Jonathan Byrd	16,485,338
58	Brandt Snedeker	16,098,223
59	Corey Pavin	16,021,370
60	Lee Janzen	15,907,711
61	Bob Tway	15,785,815
62	Brian Gay	15,763,981
63	Woody Austin	15,690,734
64	Steve Elkington	15,505,418
65	Kevin Sutherland	15,435,073
66	John Senden (AUS)	15,344,138
67	Aaron Baddeley (AUS)	15,313,911
68	Hal Sutton	15,267,685
69	Jesper Parnevik (SWE)	15,265,141
70	Loren Roberts	15,154,767
71	Heath Slocum	15,124,760
72	Steve Lowery	15,121,961
73	Lucas Glover	14,974,985
74	John Huston	14,967,146
75	Tom Pernice Jr	14,950,594
76	Camilo Villegas (COL)	14,850,148
77	Greg Norman (AUS)	14,484,458
78	Paul Azinger	14,467,496
79	Jay Haas	14,440,317
80	Mark O'Meara	14,169,805
81	Bill Haas	14,099,394
82	Kirk Triplett	14,096,656
83	Ryan Moore	13,977,713
84	Shigeki Maruyama (JPN)	13,809,170
85	Joe Durant	13,780,136
86	Lee Westwood (ENG)	13,644,407
87	Rod Pampling (AUS)	13,600,311
88	Rory McIlroy (NIR)	13,357,560
89	Pat Perez	13,192,774
90	Kevin Na	13,153,736
91	Fredrik Jacobson (SWE)	13,077,103
92	Mark Wilson	12,982,149
93	J J Henry	12,791,915
94	Paul Goydos	12,738,659
95	Ryan Palmer	12,734,921
96	Ben Curtis	12,710,142
97	John Cook	12,685,199
98	Briny Baird	12,634,862
99	Ian Poulter (ENG)	12,620,633
100	Scott McCarron	12,611,793

What is the answer?

Q: Can I hole out if another player's ball is in the hole?

A: You can. There is no penalty for not removing the other player's ball from the hole before you play but this is not recommended practice.

2012 Tour Statistics

Driving accuracy
(Percentage of fairways hit in regulation)

Pos	Name	Rds	%
1	Jerry Kelly	84	73.00
2	Heath Slocum	93	71.69
3	Tim Clark (RSA)	60	71.60
4	Jim Furyk	85	70.71
5	Graeme McDowell (NIR)	55	70.11
6	David Toms	60	69.75
7	Ben Curtis	62	69.70
8	Chris DiMarco	83	69.24
9	Gary Christian (ENG)	91	68.95
10	Richard H Lee	71	68.72

Greens in regulation

Pos	Name	Rds	%
1	Justin Rose (ENG)	69	70.34
2	Bubba Watson	68	69.95
3	Lee Westwood (ENG)	60	69.75
4	Camilo Villegas (COL)	79	69.55
5	Boo Weekley	74	69.53
6	Russell Knox	72	69.36
7	Robert Garrigus	89	69.23
8	Brendon de Jonge (ZIM)	115	69.17
	Jason Dufner	83	69.17
10	John Merrick	83	69.13

Driving distance (Average yards per drive)

Pos	Name	Rds	Yds
1	Bubba Watson	68	315.5
2	Charlie Beljan	61	311.6
3	Robert Garrigus	89	310.3
4	Dustin Johnson	70	310.2
5	Rory McIlroy (NIR)	60	310.1
6	J B Holmes	90	309.7
7	Jason Day (AUS)	57	308.6
8	Kyle Stanley	86	306.9
9	John Daly	50	306.7
10	Adam Scott (AUS)	59	304.6
	Jhonattan Vegas (VEN)	77	304.6

Putting averages (Average per round)

Pos	Name	Rds	Avg
1	Jonas Blixt (SWE)	72	1.718
2	Brandt Snedeker	81	1.725
3	Zach Johnson	95	1.726
4	Greg Chalmers (AUS)	88	1.733
5	Webb Simpson	77	1.735
6	Rory McIlroy (NIR)	60	1.738
	Bo Van Pelt	84	1.738
8	Graeme McDowell (NIR)	55	1.739
9	Ben Crane	73	1.740
	Carl Pettersson (SWE)	92	1.740

Sand saves

Pos	Name	Rds	%
1	Jonas Blixt (SWE)	72	65.44
2	Greg Chalmers (AUS)	88	65.24
3	Jim Furyk	85	65.15
4	Justin Rose (ENG)	69	62.81
5	Brian Gay	91	62.32
6	Bud Cauley	99	60.84
7	Martin Flores	95	60.15
8	Matt Kuchar	86	60.14
9	Chris DiMarco	83	60.13
10	Padraig Harrington (IRL)	67	59.41

Scoring averages

Pos	Name	Rds	Avg
1	Rory McIlroy (NIR)	60	69.63
2	Tiger Woods	69	69.78
3	Jason Dufner	83	69.89
4	Bubba Watson	68	69.98
5	Matt Kuchar	86	70.04
6	Jim Furyk	85	70.10
	Brandt Snedeker	81	70.10
	Steve Stricker	73	70.10
9	Jonas Blixt (SWE)	72	70.14
	Webb Simpson	77	70.14
11	Brendon de Jonge (ZIM)	115	70.17
12	Dustin Johnson	70	70.18
13	Zach Johnson	95	70.20
14	Billy Horschel	63	70.22
	Justin Rose (ENG)	69	70.22
16	Jeff Overton	101	70.23
	Bo Van Pelt	84	70.23
18	Louis Oosthuizen (RSA)	65	70.32
19	Keegan Bradley	90	70.33
	Will Claxton	99	70.33

Tiger Woods topped the $100 million mark in 2012

Tiger Woods may not have added to his tally of 14 majors in 2012 but he did create a prize-money record. When he finished third in the Deutsche Bank event and picked up $544,000 he took his career earnings on the PGA Tour to $100,350,700.

Woods has won 74 events on the PGA Tour which at the end of 2012 was still eight fewer than Sam Snead who holds the record for the most wins but Snead, playing in a far less lucrative period, made only $620,126.

On 38 occasions Woods' first prize has been $1 million or more. For his 293 career starts he averaged $344,541 and 68 cents every time he teed up. Snead's biggest prize was $28,000 and that was for finishing second at Milwaukee in 1968. Of course, in Snead's day the richest events carried a purse of only $100,000. These days most events offer a prize-fund of $1million or more and only a handful offer less than a million.

Heart man Erik Compton regains his PGA Tour card

Erik Compton, the 33-year-old American who has had two heart transplants, is still playing on the PGA Tour this year after winning back at the autumn Qualifying School the card he lost last year.

Compton, who was diagnosed with viral cardiomyopathy when just nine years old, received his first transplant at the age of 12 and his second following a major heart attack in 2008. Four years later he was playing on the 2012 PGA Tour but had not done enough to keep his card automatically.

Compton, who made 16 cuts and had one top-25 finish in 2012 and shot two 67's in the last two rounds of the school to qualify in tied seventh spot, has raised awareness about organ donation.

Now, the United States Sports Academy has honored Compton with the 2012 Mildred "Babe" Didrikson Zaharias Courage Award, presented annually to an individual who demonstrates courageous action in overcoming adversity to excel in sport.

Rory McIlroy is best in both Europe and America

Rory McIlroy, a multiple award winner of trophies and titles in 2012, earned a record $8,047,952 on the PGA Tour and a record €5,519,118 in Europe. The four majors and the four WGC events were included on both the US PGA and European schedules but the 23-year-old from Hollywood in Northern Ireland was still the outstanding star.

Rory finished No 1 on the American money list and took first place in the Race to Dubai. He won the Arnold Palmer and Jack Nicklaus awards, the PGA of America Player of the Year award and was the European Tour's Player of the Year as well.

During the year he had 10 top three finishes – seven on the PGA Tour and three on the European Tour. For these ten events he was 139-under-par shooting 30 scores in the 60's and only twice shooting an over par round. He won another major in record breaking fashion and was disappointed not to be challenging for the title in the other three.

He claims his relationship with Danish tennis star Caroline Wozniaki, a former No 1 herself, has helped his game. "Watching how hard she practised, made me practice harder too," says the likeable Ulsterman. He just wants more of the same in 2013 when he enters a new phase of his professional career with new clubs and ball in a $115 million deal from Nike. These were his ten top three's of the year:

1st	Honda Classic	66-67-66-69—268	(–12)	$1,026,000
1st	US PGA Championship	67-75-67-66—275	(–13)	$1,445,000
1st	Deutsche Bank	65-65-67-67—264	(–20)	$1,440,000
1st	BMW Championship	64-68-69-64—268	(–20)	$1,440,000
1st	Dubai World Tour	66-67-66-66—265	(–23)	$1,333,330
2nd	Accenture Match Play Championship			$850,000
2nd	Wells Fargo	70-68-66-70—274	(–14)	$572,000
2nd	BMW Masters China	67-75-67-66—275	(–13)	$779,000
3rd	Barclays Singapore	70-70-69-65—274	(–10)	$375,600
3rd	WGC – Cadillac	73-69-65-67—274	(–14)	$516,000

US PGA Tour top 20

MC Missed cut — Did not play

Players are of US nationality unless stated otherwise

	Hyundai Tournament	Sony Open	Humana Challenge	Farmers Insurance Open	Phoenix Open	AT&T Pebble Beach	Northern Trust Open	Mayakoba Classic	WGC–Accenture C/ship	The Honda Classic	Puerto Rico Open	WGC–Cadillac C/ship	Transitions Championship	Arnold Palmer Invitational	Shell Houston Open	The Masters	RBC Heritage	Valero Texas Open	Zurich Classic
1 Rory McIlroy (NIR)	—	—	—	—	—	—	—	—	2	1	—	3	—	—	—	T40	—	—	—
2 Tiger Woods	—	—	—	—	—	T15	—	—	T17	T2	—	WD	—	1	—	T40	—	—	—
3 Brandt Snedeker	—	—	T8	1	T50	—	T17	—	T9	—	—	T45	T29	T63	—	T19	T17	—	—
4 Jason Dufner	—	MC	T12	—	T8	—	T52	—	T33	—	—	T29	T10	T15	—	T24	24	—	1*
5 Bubba Watson	T18	—	—	T13	T5	—	T13	—	T17	—	—	2	—	T4	—	1*	—	—	T18
6 Zach Johnson	—	T54	T8	—	—	T29	T17	—	T33	—	—	T17	T46	T11	—	T32	2	—	—
7 Justin Rose (ENG)	—	—	—	T33	—	—	T13	—	T33	T5	—	1	T29	T15	—	T8	—	—	T10
8 Phil Mickelson	—	—	T49	MC	T26	1	T2*	—	—	—	—	T43	—	T24	T4	T3	—	—	—
9 Hunter Mahan	—	—	—	T6	—	T15	T24	—	1	—	—	T24	—	T42	1	T12	—	—	—
10 Keegan Bradley	16	T13	—	T22	T15	—	T2*	—	T17	T12	—	T8	—	—	T4	T27	—	—	MC
11 Matt Kuchar	—	—	T22	—	T33	—	T24	—	5	—	—	T8	T10	—	—	T3	—	T13	—
12 Jim Furyk	—	—	—	—	—	T40	T11	—	T33	MC	—	—	T2*	T11	—	11	T8	—	—
13 Carl Petersson (SWE)	—	T2	T42	—	T33	—	T34	—	—	T36	—	—	MC	MC	2	—	1	—	MC
14 Luke Donald (ENG)	—	—	—	—	—	—	T56	—	T33	—	—	T6	1*	—	—	T32	T37	—	3
15 Louis Oosthuizen (RSA)	—	—	—	—	—	—	—	—	T17	WD	—	T60	T20	—	3	2*	—	—	—
16 Ernie Els (RSA)	—	—	—	T52	—	—	T59	—	T17	T21	—	—	T5	T4	T12	—	MC	—	2*
17 Webb Simpson	T3	T38	—	—	T8	—	—	—	T33	—	—	T35	T10	T36	—	T44	T52	—	T13
18 Steve Stricker	1	T38	—	—	—	—	—	—	T9	—	—	T8	—	—	T36	T47	—	—	6
19 Dustin Johnson	—	—	WD	T43	T61	T5	T4	—	T9	—	—	T35	—	—	—	—	—	—	—
20 Robert Garrigus	—	—	T2	MC	MC	T20	WD	—	—	T30	—	—	T2*	MC	—	MC	T13	—	—

2012 performances at a glance

* Involved in play-off WD Withdrew

Wells Fargo C/ship	The Players C/ship	Byron Nelson C/ship	Crowne Plaza Invitational	Memorial Tournament	Fedex St Jude Classic	US Open Championship	Travelers Championship	AT&T National	Greenbrier Classic	John Deere Classic	True South Classic	The Open Championship	RBC Canadian Open	Reno-Tahoe Open	WGC–CA Bridgestone	US PGA Championship	Wyndham Championship	The Barclays	Deutsche Bank C/ship	BMW Championship	Tour Championship	Justin Timberlake Open	Frys.com Open	The McGladrey Classic	CIMB Classic	WGC–HSBC Champions	Children's Miracle N/work
T2*	MC	—	—	MC	T7	MC	—	—	—	—	—	T60	—	—	T5	1	—	T24	1	1	T10	—	—	—	—	—	—
MC	T40	—	—	1	—	T21	—	1	MC	—	—	T3	—	—	T8	11	—	T38	3	T4	T8	—	—	—	T4	—	—
—	MC	—	—	WD	—	—	—	—	T38	—	—	T3	T34	—	T50	MC	T28	2	6	T37	1	—	—	—	—	T11	—
—	T68	1	2	—	—	T4	—	—	—	—	—	T31	—	—	7	T27	T7	—	T18	T28	T20	—	—	—	T16	22	—
—	—	—	—	MC	—	MC	T2	—	—	—	—	23	—	—	19	11	—	10	MC	12	5	—	—	—	—	33	—
T69	T2	T51	1	—	MC	T41	T64	—	—	1*	—	T9	—	—	T40	70	—	T38	T47	T12	T15	—	—	T49	—	—	—
—	—	—	—	8	—	T21	—	—	—	—	—	MC	—	—	T5	T3	—	T46	MC	T16	2	—	—	—	—	T24	—
T26	T25	T7	—	WD	—	T65	—	—	MC	—	—	MC	—	—	T43	T36	—	T38	T4	T2	T15	—	—	—	—	T2	—
T53	MC	—	T37	T19	—	T38	T11	T8	—	—	—	T34	—	—	1	T3	—	MC	T13	T59	T23	—	—	—	—	23	—
MC	T35	T24	—	MC	—	T68	T29	—	T46	—	—	T34	—	—	1	T3	—	MC	T13	T59	T23	—	—	—	—	23	—
—	1	T15	T26	—	—	T27	T8	—	—	—	—	T9	T34	—	T8	MC	—	T38	T35	T54	T10	—	—	—	—	—	—
T26	—	—	4	T13	—	T4	—	T34	MC	—	—	T34	MC	—	T2	T42	—	MC	T13	9	7	—	—	3	—	—	—
T46	T10	MC	T26	MC	—	MC	—	—	T17	T36	—	T23	—	—	28	T3	T4	T24	T57	69	T20	—	—	—	7	T16	—
—	6	—	—	12	—	MC	—	—	—	—	—	T5	—	—	T8	T32	—	T10	T26	T28	T3	—	—	—	—	T18	—
—	MC	MC	T19	MC	—	MC	T47	—	—	—	—	T19	—	—	4	T21§	—	T5	2	T16	T23	—	—	—	—	T6	—
—	MC	T41	—	T58	—	9	—	—	—	—	—	1	MC	—	T45	T48	—	T54	T26	T28	27	—	T16	—	—	T2	—
4	MC	—	—	MC	—	1	T29	—	T7	—	—	—	—	—	—	MC	T22	MC	T18	T51	T5	—	—	—	—	—	—
—	—	—	—	T50	—	T15	—	—	T22	T5	—	T23	—	—	T2	T7	—	T54	T13	T26	22	—	—	—	—	—	—
—	—	—	—	T19	1	MC	—	T44	T33	—	—	T9	—	—	T19	T48	—	T3	T4	T6	T10	—	—	—	—	T39	—
T15	MC	T9	—	T70	T42	MC	—	T4	—	T25	—	—	T2	—	—	T21	—	T71	T42	T4	T10	T22	—	—	T2	T51	T2

Tour Results 2012 (in chronological order)

Players are of US nationality unless stated

Hyundai Tournament of Champions *Plantation Course, Kapalua, HI* Jan 6–9 [7411–73]

1	Steve Stricker	68-63-69-69—269	$1,120,000
2	Martin Laird (SCO)	68-70-67-67—272	650,000
3	Webb Simpson	68-68-69-68—273	369,000
	Jonathan Byrd	67-71-67-68—273	369,000

Sony Open in Hawaii *Waialae CC, Honolulu, HI* Jan 12–15 [7068–70]

1	Johnson Wagner	68-66-66-67—267	$990,00
2	Carl Pettersson (SWE)	65-67-70-67—269	363,000
	Sean O'Hair	67-67-68-67—269	363,000
	Harrison Frazar	67-68-67-67—269	363,000
	Charles Howell III	67-67-66-69—269	363,000

Humana Challenge *PGA West (Palmer and Nicklaus courses), La Quinta, Jan Bermuda Dunes, CA* Jan 19–22 [6950–72, 7060–72]

1	Mark Wilson	66-62-67-69—264	$1,008,000
2	Johnson Wagner	68-67-66-65—266	418,133
	John Mallinger	67-65-68-66—266	418,133
	Robert Garrigus	73-64-61-68—266	418,133

Farmers Insurance Open *Torrey Pines (South and North courses), La Jolla, CA* Jan 26–29 [7569–72, 6874–72]

1	Brandt Snedeker*	67-64-74-67—272	$1,080,000
2	Kyle Stanley	62-68-68-74—272	648,000

**Snedeker won at the second extra hole*

3	John Rollins	70-65-68-71—274	408,000

Waste Management Phoenix Open *TPC Scottsdale, AZ* Feb 2–5 [7216–71]

1	Kyle Stanley	69-66-69-65—269	$1,098,000
2	Ben Crane	69-67-68-66—270	658,800
3	Spencer Levin	65-63-68-75—271	414,800

AT&T Pebble Beach National Pro-Am *Pebble Beach, CA* Feb 9–12 [6816–72]

1	Phil Mickelson	70-65-70-64—269	$1,152,000
2	Charlie Wi (KOR)	61-69-69-72—271	691,200
3	Ricky Barnes	70-66-70-67—273	435,200

Northern Trust Open *Riviera CC, Pacific Palisades, CA* Feb 16–19 [7298–71]

1	Bill Haas*	72-68-68-69—277	$1,188,000
	Keegan Bradley	71-69-66-71—277	580,800
	Phil Mickelson	66-70-70-71—277	580,800

**Haas won at the second extra hole*

Mayakoba Classic *El Camaleon, Riviera-Cancun Maya, Mexico* Feb 23–26 [6987–71]

1	John Huh*	67-70-71-63—271	$666,000
2	Robert Allenby (AUS)	69-67-70-65—271	399,600

**Huh won at the eighth extra hole*

3	Matt Every	67-71-69-66—273	214,600
	Colt Knost	69-71-67-66—273	214,600

WGC – Accenture Match Play Championship *Ritz-Carlton, Dove Mountain, AZ* Feb 22–26 [7791–72]

Winner:	Hunter Mahan	$1,400,000
Runner-up:	Rory McIlroy (NIR)	850,000
Third place:	Mark Wilson	600,000

Full details of this event can be found on page 200

Honda Classic *Palm Beach Gardens, FL* Mar 1–4 [7158–70]

1	Rory McIlroy (NIR)	66-67-66-69—268	$1,026,000
2	Tom Gillis	68-64-69-69—270	501,600
	Tiger Woods	71-68-69-62—270	501,600

Puerto Rico Open *Rio Grande, Puerto Rico* Mar 8–11 [7569–72]

1	George McNeill	66-70-67-69—272	$630,000
	Ryo Ishikawa (JPN)	70-67-69-68—274	378,000
3	Henrik Stenson (SWE)	70-69-65-71—275	203,000
	Boo Weekley	70-68-71-66—275	203,000

WGC – Cadillac Championship *Doral, Orlando, FL* Mar 8–11 [7334–72]

1	Justin Rose (ENG)	69-64-69-70—272	$1,400,000
2	Bubba Watson	70-62-67-74—273	845,000
3	Rory McIlroy (NIR)	73-69-65-67—274	516,000

Full details of this event can be found on page 201

Transitions Championship *Innisbrook, Copperhead, Palm Harbor, FL* Mar 15–18 [7340-71]

1	Luke Donald (ENG)*	67-68-70-66—271	$990,000
2	Bae Sang-Moon (KOR)	69-66-68-68—271	410,666
	Jim Furyk	66-70-66-69—271	410,666
	Robert Garrigus	67-72-68-64—271	410,666

**Donald won at the first extra hole*

Arnold Palmer Invitational *Bay Hill, Orlando, FL* Mar 22–25 [7381–72]

1	Tiger Woods	69-65-71-70—275	$1,080,000
2	Graeme McDowell (NIR)	72-63-71-74—280	648,000
3	Ian Poulter (ENG)	71-69-68-74—282	408,000

Shell Houston Open *Redstone, Humble, TX* Mar 29–April 1 [7457–72]

1	Hunter Mahan	69-67-65-71—272	$1,080,000
2	Carl Pettersson (SWE)	65-70-67-71—273	648,000
3	Louis Oosthuizen (RSA)	67-66-66-75—274	408,000

THE MASTERS[1] *Augusta National, GA* April 5–8 [7435–72]

1	Bubba Watson	69-71-70-68—278	$1,440,000
2	Louis Oosthuizen (RSA)	68-72-69-69—278	864,000
**Watson won at the second extra hole*			
3	Peter Hanson (SWE)	68-74-65-73—280	384,000
	Matt Kuchar	71-70-70-69—280	384,000
	Phil Mickelson	74-68-66-72—280	384,000
	Lee Westwood (ENG)	67-73-72-68—280	384,000

Full details of this event can be found on page 81

[1]Event not co-sponsored by the PGA Tour

RBC Heritage *Harbour Town, Hilton Head Island, SC* April 12–15 [7101–71]

1	Carl Pettersson (SWE)	70-65-66-69—270	$1,026,000
2	Zach Johnson	71-68-66-70—275	615,600
3	Colt Knost	67-66-69-74—276	387,600

Valero Texas Open *San Antonio, TX* April 19–22 [7522–72]

1	Ben Curtis	67-67-73-72—279	$1,116,000
2	Matt Every	63-74-73-71—281	545,600
	John Huh	77-68-67-69—281	545,600

Zurich Classic of New Orleans *TPC Louisiana, Avondale, LA* April 26–29 [7341–72]

1	Jason Dufner*	67-65-67-70—269	$1,152,000
2	Ernie Els (RSA)	66-68-68-67—269	691,200

**Dufner won at the second extra hole*

3	Luke Donald (ENG)	73-65-66-67—271	435,200

Wells Fargo Championship *Quail Hollow, Charlotte, NC* May 3–6 [7442–72]

1	Rickie Fowler*	66-72-67-69—274	$1,170,000
2	Rory McIlroy (NIR)	70-68-66-70—274	572,000
	D A Points	66-68-69-71—274	572,000

**Fowler won at the first extra hole*

The Players Championship *TPC, Sawgrass, Ponte Vedra Beach, FL* May 10–13 [7215-72]

1	Matt Kuchar	68-68-69-70—275	$1,710,000
2	Martin Laird (SCO)	65-73-72-67—277	627,000
	Zach Johnson	70-66-73-68—277	627,000
	Rickie Fowler	72-69-66-70—277	627,000
	Ben Curtis	68-71-70-68—277	627,000
6	Luke Donald (ENG)	72-69-72-66—279	342,000
7	Bo Van Pelt	71-70-70-69—280	296,083
	Jhonattan Vegas (VEN)	68-74-68-70—280	296,083
	Kevin Na	67-69-68-76—280	296,083
10	David Toms	69-74-73-65—281	247,000
	Carl Pettersson (SWE)	71-72-69-69—281	247,000
12	Geoff Ogilvy (AUS)	70-73-70-69—282	199,500
	Blake Adams	66-73-72-71—282	199,500
	Jonathan Byrd	68-70-72-72—282	199,500
15	Bob Estes	73-69-76-65—283	137,987
	Peter Hanson (SWE)	73-71-71-68—283	137,987
	Spencer Levin	74-68-72-69—283	137,987
	Henrik Stenson (SWE)	71-71-71-70—283	137,987
	Adam Scott (AUS)	68-70-74-71—283	137,987
	Brendon de Jonge (RSA)	69-71-72-71—283	137,987
	Martin Kaymer (GER)	73-69-70-71—283	137,987
	David Mathis	72-71-69-71—283	137,987
23	Chris Couch	72-71-71-70—284	95,000
	John Huh	75-66-72-71—284	95,000
25	Jim Furyk	72-70-72-71—285	66,547
	Pat Perez	69-75-70-71—285	66,547
	Bill Haas	68-71-74-72—285	66,547
	John Rollins	72-72-69-72—285	66,547
	Kevin Stadler	68-71-73-73—285	66,547
	Tim Clark (RSA)	71-70-71-73—285	66,547
	Ian Poulter (ENG)	65-76-71-73—285	66,547
	Phil Mickelson	71-71-70-73—285	66,547
	Charlie Wi (KOR)	71-67-73-74—285	66,547
	Brian Davis (ENG)	68-70-72-75—285	66,547
35	Keegan Bradley	72-70-74-70—286	46,835

35T	Tom Gillis	70-71-73-72—286	46,835
	Jimmy Walker	71-70-71-74—286	46,835
	Jeff Maggert	70-71-71-74—286	46,835
	Johnson Wagner	69-73-69-75—286	46,835
40	J J Henry	71-73-74-69—287	37,050
	Alvaro Quiros (ESP)	72-72-72-71—287	37,050
	Kris Blanks	69-74-72-72—287	37,050
	Tiger Woods	74-68-72-73—287	37,050
	Bryce Molder	72-72-70-73—287	37,050
45	Marc Leishman (AUS)	73-70-73-72—288	31,350
46	Josh Teater	71-71-76-71—289	26,334
	Ryan Moore	69-72-75-73—289	26,334
	Ricky Barnes	74-69-72-74—289	26,334
	Brian Gay	71-72-71-75—289	26,334
	Harrison Frazar	68-76-69-76—289	26,334
51	Justin Rose (ENG)	76-68-75-71—290	22,496
	Brian Harman	73-68-76-73—290	22,496
	Chris Kirk	71-73-72-74—290	22,496
	Michael Thompson	68-71-75-76—290	22,496
	Kevin Streelman	72-68-72-78—290	22,496
56	Rod Pampling (AUS)	71-72-78-70—291	21,280
	Robert Karlsson (SWE)	70-74-76-71—291	21,280
	Nick Watney	71-70-76-74—291	21,280
	Trevor Immelman (RSA)	72-72-72-75—291	21,280
	Sergio García (ESP)	73-71-68-79—291	21,280
61	Robert Allenby (AUS)	72-72-75-73—292	20,520
	Lee Westwood (ENG)	71-70-74-77—292	20,520
	Sung Kang (KOR)	75-68-72-77—292	20,520
64	Stewart Cink	71-72-78-72—293	19,855
	George McNeill	70-73-82-68—293	19,855
	Heath Slocum	73-70-78-72—293	19,855
	Harris English	70-67-79-77—293	19,855
68	David Hearn (CAN)	69-75-77-74—295	19,285
	Jason Dufner	73-71-76-75—295	19,285
70	Graham DeLaet	71-73-76-76—296	18,905
	Justin Leonard	75-68-74-79—296	18,905
72	Cameron Tringale	73-71-77-76—297	18,620
	73 players missed the cut		

HP Byron Nelson Championship *TPC Four Seasons, Irving, TX* May 17–20 [7166–70]

1	Jason Dufner	67-66-69-67—269	$1,170,000
2	Dicky Pride	66-68-69-67—270	702,000
3	Joe Durant	70-71-65-65—271	312,000
	Marc Leishman (AUS)	65-69-71-66—271	312,000
	Jonas Blixt (SWE)	68-70-67-66—271	312,000
	J J Henry	68-68-67-68—271	312,000

Crowne Plaza Invitational *Colonial, Forth Worth, TX* May 24–27 [7204–72]

1	Zach Johnson	64-67-65-72—268	$1,152,000
2	Jason Dufner	65-64-66-74—269	691,200
3	Tommy Gainey	66-67-73-67—273	435,200

Memorial Tournament *Muirfield Village, Dublin, OH* May 31–June 3 [7265–72]

1	Tiger Woods	70-69-73-67—279	$1,116,000
2	Andres Romero (ARG)	69-73-72-67—281	545,600
	Rory Sabbatini (RSA)	69-69-71-72—281	545,600

Fedex St Jude Classic *TPC Southwind, Memphis, TN* June 7–10 [7244–70]

1	Dustin Johnson	70-68-67-66—271	$1,008,000
2	John Merrick	66-69-69-68—272	604,800
3	Ryan Palmer	74-66-67-66—273	268,800
	Chad Campbell	68-67-70-68—273	268,800
	Nick O'Hern (AUS)	70-67-67-69—273	268,800
	Davis Love III	68-68-68-69—273	268,800

112th US OPEN Championship[1] *Olympic Club, San Francisco, CA* June 14–17 [7170–70]

1	Webb Simpson	72-73-68-68—281	$1,440,000
2	Michael Thompson	66-75-74-67—282	695,216
	Graeme McDowell (NIR)	69-72-68-73—282	695,216

Full details of this event can be found on page 70

Travelers Championship *River Highlands, Cromwell, CT* June 21–24 [6844–70]

1	Marc Leishman (AUS)	68-66-70-62—266	$1,080,000
2	Bubba Watson	66-71-65-65—267	528,000
	Charley Hoffman	67-67-67-66—267	528,000

AT&T National *Congressional Country Club, Bethesda, MD* June 28–July 1 [7529–71]

1	Tiger Woods	72-68-67-69—276	$1,170,000
2	Bo Van Pelt	67-73-67-71—278	702,000
3	Adam Scott (AUS)	75-67-70-67—279	442,000

The Greenbrier Classic *White Sulphur Springs, WV* July 5–8 [7274–70]

1	Ted Potter Jr*	69-67-64-64—264	$1,098,000
2	Troy Kelly	69-67-62-66—264	658,800
Potter won at the third extra hole			
3	Charlie Wi (KOR)	67-66-68-65—266	353,800
	Charlie Beljan	70-62-67-67—266	353,800

John Deere Classic *TPC Deere Run, Silvis, IL* July 12–15 [7257–71]

1	Zach Johnson*	68-65-66-65—264	$828,000
2	Troy Matteson	61-68-66-69—264	496,800
Johnson won at the second extra hole			
3	Scott Piercy	65-69-67-65—266	312,800

True South Classic *Annandale GC, Madison, MS* July 19–22 [7199–72]

1	Scott Stallings	68-64-64-68—264	$540,000
2	Jason Bohn	64-67-68-67—266	324,000
3	Billy Horschel	68-63-66-71—268	204,000

141st OPEN CHAMPIONSHIP[1] *Royal Lytham St. Annes, Lancashire, England* July 19–22 [7086–70]

1	Ernie Els (RSA)	67-70-68-68—273	$1,405,890
2	Adam Scott (AUS)	64-67-68-75—274	812,202
3	Tiger Woods	67-67-70-73—277	464,725
	Brandt Snedeker	66-64-73-74—277	464,725

Full details of this event can be found on page 54

RBC Canadian Open *Hamilton G&CC, Ancaster, Ontario, Canada* July 26–29 [6966–70]

1	Scott Piercy	62-67-67-67—263	$936,000
2	Robert Garrigus	64-66-64-70—264	457,600
	William McGirt	63-66-66-69—264	457,600

[1]Event not co-sponsored by the PGA Tour

Reno-Tahoe Open *Montreux G&CC, Reno, NV* Aug 2–5 [7472–72]

Modified Stableford

1	J J Henry	10-12-14-7—43	$540,000
2	Alexandre Rocha (BRA)	8-16-9-9—42	324,000
3	Andres Romero (ARG)	14-7-10-6—37	204,000

WGC – Bridgestone Invitational *Firestone CC, Akron, OH* Aug 2–5 [7400–70]

1	Keegan Bradley	67-69-67-64—267	$1,4000
2	Steve Stricker	68-68-68-64—268	665,000
	Jim Furyk	63-66-70-69—268	665,000

Full details of this event can be found on page 202

US PGA CHAMPIONSHIP[1] *Kiawah Island Resort (Ocean), Kiawah Island, SC* Aug 9–12 [7676–72]

1	Rory McIlroy (NIR)	67-75-67-66—275	$1,445,000
2	David Lynn (ENG)	73-74-68-68—283	865,000
3	Justin Rose (ENG)	69-79-70-66—284	384,500
	Keegan Bradley	68-77-71-68—284	384,500
	Ian Poulter (ENG)	70-71-74-69—284	384,500
	Carl Pettersson (SWE)	66-74-72-72—284	384,500

Full details of this event can be found on page 90

Wyndham Championship *Sedgefield, Greensboro, NC* Aug 16–19 [7130–70]

1	Sergio García (ESP)	67-63-66-66—262	$936,000
2	Tim Clark (RSA)	63-67-67-67—264	561,600
3	Bud Cauley	66-65-66-68—265	353,600

The Barclays *Bethpage State Park, Farmingdale, NY* Aug 23–26 [7468–71]

1	Nick Watney	65-69-71-69—274	$1,440,000
2	Brandt Snedeker	70-69-68-70—277	864,000
3	Dustin Johnson	67-71-72-68—278	464,000
	Sergio García (ESP)	66-68-69-75—278	464,000

Deutsche Bank Championship *TPC Boston, Norton, MA* Aug 31–Sep 3 [7214–71]

1	Rory McIlroy (NIR)	65-65-67-67—264	$1,440,000
2	Louis Oosthuizen (RSA)	66-65-63-71—265	864,000
3	Tiger Woods	64-68-68-66—266	544,000

BMW Championship *Crooked Stick GC, Carmel, IN* Sep 6–9 [7516–72]

1	Rory McIlroy (NIR)	64-68-69-67—268	$1,440,000
2	Lee Westwood (ENG)	68-65-68-69—270	704,000
	Phil Mickelson	69-67-64-70—270	704,000

Tour Championship *East Lake GC, Atlanta, GA* Sep 20–23 [7154–70]

1	Brandt Snedeker	68-70-64-68—270	$1,440,000
2	Justin Rose (ENG)	66-68-68-71—273	864,000
3	Luke Donald (ENG)	71-69-67-67—274	468,000
	Ryan Moore	69-70-65-70—274	468,000

The Ryder Cup[1] *Medinah Country Club, Illinois, USA* Sep 28–30 [7668–72]

Europe 14½, USA 13½

Full details of this event can be found on page 206

[1]Event not co-sponsored by the PGA Tour

JTS Hospitals for Children Open *TPC Summerlin. Las Vegas, NV* Oct 4–7 [7223–71]

1	Ryan Moore	61-68-65-66—260	$810,000
2	Brendon de Jonge (RSA)	62-66-66-67—261	486,000
3	Jonas Blixt (SWE)	64-64-66-70—264	306,000

Frys.com Open *CordeValle GC, San Martin, CA* Oct 11–14 [7368–71]

1	Jonas Blixt (SWE)	66-68-66-68—268	$900,000
2	Tim Petrovic	70-68-67-64—269	440,000
	Jason Kokrak	68-66-67-68—269	440,000

The McGladrey Classic *Sea Island, GA* Oct 18–21 [7055–70]

1	Tommy Gainey	69-67-68-60—264	$720,000
2	David Toms	65-67-70-63—265	432,000
3	Jim Furyk	66-65-66-69—266	272,000

PGA Grand Slam of Golf[1] *Port Royal Golf Course, Bermuda* Oct 22–24 [6845–71]

1	Padraig Harrington (IRL)	66-67—133
2	Webb Simpson	69-65—134
3	Keegan Bradley	72-67—139
	Bubba Watson	68-71—139

CIMB Classic[1] *Mines Resort & GC,Selangor, Malaysia* Oct 25–28 [6966–71]

1	Nick Watney	71-65-65-61—262	$1,300,000
2	Robert Garrigus	64-64-69-66—263	485,000
	Bo Van Pelt	70-65-62-66—263	485,000

WGC – HSBC Champions Tournament *Mission Hills GC, Shenzhen, China* Nov 1–4 [7251-72]

1	Ian Poulter (ENG)	69-68-65-65—267	$1,200,000
2	Jason Dufner (USA)	68-66-71-64—269	419,000
	Ernie Els (RSA)	70-63-69-67—269	419,000
	Phil Mickelson (USA)	66-69-66-68—269	419,000
	Scott Piercy (USA)	68-68-68-65—269	419,000

Full details of this event can be found on page 204

Children's Miracle Network Classic *Magnolia and Palm Courses, Lake Buena Vista, FL* Nov 8–11 [7516–72, 6957–72]

1	Charlie Beljan	68-64-71-69—272	$846,000
2	Matt Every	67-69-70-68—274	413,600
	Robert Garrigus	68-68-70-68—274	413,600

Wendy's 3-Tour Challenge[1] Nov 12–13 *Rio Secco GC, NV* Nov 12–13

See page 244

Tyco Golf Skills Challenge[1] *The Breakers, Palm Beach, FL* Nov 12–14

1	Justin Rose (ENG) and Peter Hanson (SWE)*	$285,000
2	Dustin Johnson and Keegan Bradley	223,000

**Rose and Hanson beat Bradley and Johnson after sudden death chip off*

3	Mark O'Meara and Mark Calcavecchia	158,000
4	Zach Johnson and Kyle Stanley	134,000

[1]Event not co-sponsored by the PGA Tour

World Challenge[1] *Sherwood CC, Thousand Oaks, CA* Nov 29–Dec 2 [7027–72]

1	Graeme McDowall (NIR)	69-66-68-68—271	$1,000,000
2	Keegan Bradley	69-69-67-69—274	500,000
3	Bo Van Pelt (USA)	70-68-70-70—278	300,000

Franklin Templeton Shoot-out[1] *Tiburon GC, Naples, FL* Dec 7–9 [7288–72]

1	Sean O'Hair & Kenny Perry	64-61-60—185	$375,000 each
2	Charles Howell III & Rory Sabbatini	66-63-57—186	$235,000 each
3	Jason Dufner & Vijay Singh	66-63-59—188	$140,000 each

Fathers and Sons Tournament[1] *Ritz-Carlton GC, Orlando, Florida*

1	Davis Love III and Dru Love	60-61—121
2	Larry Nelson and Josh Nelson	62-60—122
3	Vijay DSingh and Qass Singh	62-61—123

[1]Event not co-sponsored by the PGA Tour

Englishman Haigh appointed to top post in America

When it comes to running tournaments there is not much you need to tell Britain's Kerry Haigh who has been promoted to Chief Championship Officer of the PGA of America.

He is an acknowledged expert who is responsible for running the overall operation, administration and course set-up for the US PGA Championship each year, the Ryder Cup every four years, the annual Senior PGA Championship, the PGA Grand Slam of Golf as well as the management of 20 PGA Club Professional, amateur and junior events

A graduate of Leeds University, Kerry worked initially for the PGA organising events in Europe before moving in 1984 to America to work for the LPGA. After working at the US PGA Championship at Kemper Lakes in 1989, he joined the PGA of America on a full time basis and in 2004 was promoted to managing director. He is widely considered one of the foremost experts on the Rules of Golf.

Jason Dufner & Vijay Singh top ten finishes on the 2012 PGA Tour

Top of the list of multiple winners in 2012 was Northern Ireland's Rory McIlroy with four victories (Honda Classic, US PGA Championship, Deutsche Bank Championship, BMW Championship) closely followed by Tiger Woods with three (Arnold Palmer Invitational, Memorial Tournament, AT&A National). Four players achieved double victories. They were: Jason Dufner (Zurich Classic, HP Byron Nelson Championship), Brandt Snedeker (Farmers Insurance Open, Tour Championship), Zach Johnson (Crowne Plaza Invitational, John Deere Classic) and Hunter Mahan (WGC–Accenture Match Play, Shell Houston Open).

Two players achieved top ten finishes in double figures in 2012. They were:

	Top ten	*Events played*
Rory McIlroy (NIR)	10	16
Bo Van Pelt	10	24

US Champions Tour 2012

www.pgatour.com

Final Ranking *Players are of American nationality unless stated*

1	Bernhard Langer (GER)	$2,140,296
2	Tom Lehman	1,982,575
3	Michael Allen	1,686,488
4	Fred Funk	1,427,937
5	Jay Don Blake	1,378,180
6	Mark Calcavecchia	1,361,067
7	Jay Haas	1,234,571
8	Fred Couples	1,229,067
9	David Frost (RSA)	1,189,740
10	John Cook	1,182,008
11	Kenny Perry	1,100,450
12	Peter Senior (AUS)	1,077,781
13	Roger Chapman (ENG)	1,021,985
14	Corey Pavin	1,021,578
15	Willie Wood	1,012,869
16	Bill Glasson	905,365
17	Brad Bryant	876,249
18	Jeff Sluman	869,474
19	Kirk Triplett	833,717
20	Gary Hallberg	795,138
21	Olin Browne	773,896
22	Loren Roberts	721,267
23	Mark Wiebe	711,992
24	Russ Cochran	693,402
25	Dan Forsman	662,281
26	Chien Soon Lu (TPE)	633,547
27	Joe Daley	630,081
28	Mike Goodes	614,521
29	Larry Mize	599,069
30	Mark McNulty (IRL)	543,169
31	Tom Kite	512,338
32	Steve Pate	482,053
33	Joey Sindelar	462,433
34	David Eger	460,776
35	Mark O'Meara	449,480
36	John Huston	441,892
37	Hale Irwin	391,657
38	Dick Mast	388,252
39	Bobby Clampett	366,307
40	Joel Edwards	357,718
41	Brad Faxon	345,209
42	Tommy Armour III	343,954
43	Rod Spittle (CAN)	317,724
44	Bob Tway	299,292
45	Tom Pernice Jr	289,869
46	Andrew Magee	283,247
47	Jeff Hart	278,013
48	Duffy Waldorf	271,883
49	Jim Rutledge (CAN)	270,434
50	Tom Jenkins	263,427

Career Money List

1	Kenny Perry	$33,876,460
2	Hale Irwin	32,553,303
3	Fred Funk	29,172,188
4	Mark Calcavecchia	28,252,595
5	Jay Haas	27,792,310
6	Tom Lehman	27,368,246
7	Loren Roberts	26,965,170
8	Fred Couples	26,893,230
9	Tom Kite	26,436,880
10	Nick Price (ZIM)	26,265,199
11	Gil Morgan	25,482,824
12	Jeff Sluman	24,717,423
13	Tom Watson	24,546,262
14	Scott Hoch	21,722,423
15	John Cook	21,323,608
16	Bernhard Langer (GER)	20,154,049
17	Mark O'Meara	19,710,938
18	Corey Pavin	18,812,724
19	Brad Faxon	18,446,169
20	Craig Stadler	18,118,539
21	Larry Nelson	18,054,311
22	Bob Tway	17,343,833
23	Tom Pernice Jr	17,162,138
24	Hal Sutton	16,788,657
25	Bruce Fleisher	16,512,579
26	John Huston	16,291,868
27	Steve Lowery	15,813,643
28	Jim Thorpe	15,696,527
29	Greg Norman (AUS)	15,182,769
30	Kirk Triplett	15,146,817
31	Joey Sindelar	14,964,230
32	Dana Quigley	14,928,634
33	Raymond Floyd	14,797,084
34	Paul Azinger	14,504,591
35	Bob Gilder	14,111,856
36	Tom Jenkins	14,103,695
37	Bruce Lietzke	13,891,017
38	Allen Doyle	13,639,378
39	Lee Trevino	13,347,942
40	Jim Colbert	13,289,345
41	D A Weibring	12,890,457
42	David Frost (RSA)	12,670,226
43	Dave Stockton	12,514,752
44	Dan Forsman	12,338,601
45	Duffy Waldorf	12,260,466
46	Tom Purtzer	11,965,764
47	Brad Bryant	11,953,599
48	Olin Browne	11,709,702
49	Tommy Armour III	11,554,465
50	Scott Simpson	11,318,643

Tour Results

Jan 20–22	Mitsubishi Electric C/ship	Hualalai, Ka'upulehu-Kona, HI	Dan Forsman	201 (–15)
Feb 10–12	Allianz Championship	Broken Sound, Boca Raton, FL	Corey Pavin*	205 (–11)
	**Beat Peter Senior (AUS) at the first extra hole*			
Feb 17–19	The ACE Group Classic	The Quarry, Naples, FL	Kenny Perry	196 (–20)
Mar 16–18	Toshiba Classic	Newport Beach, CA	Loren Roberts	205 (–8)
Mar 23–25	Mississippi GR Classic	Fallen Oak, Biloxi, MI	Fred Couples	202 (–14)
April 13–15	Encompass Insur. Pro-Am	TPC Tampa Bay, Lutz, FL	Michael Allen	201 (–12)
April 20–22	Liberty Mutual Legends of Golf	Savannah Harbor, GA	Michael Allen and David Frost (RSA)	187 (–29)
	Round Four was cancelled due to bad weather			
May 4–6	Insperity Championship	The Woodlands, TX	Fred Funk	202 (–14)
May 24–27	**US Senior PGA Championship**	Benton Harbor, MI		
	1 Roger Chapman (ENG)	68-67-64-72—271		
	2 John Cook	69-66-69-69—273		
	3 Hale Irwin	71-66-69-68—274		
June 1–3	Principal Charity Classic	Des Moines, IA	Jay Haas	197 (–16)
June 7–10	Regions Tradition	Shoal Creek, AL	Tom Lehman	274 (–14)
June 22–24	Montreal Championship	Sainte-Julie, Quebec, Canada	Marc Calcavecchia	200 (–16)
June 28–July 1	Constellation Senior Players Championship	Pittsburgh, PA	Joe Daley	266 (–14)
July 6–8	Nature Valley First Tee Open	Pebble Beach, CA	Kirk Triplett	206 (–10)
July 12–15	**US Senior Open**	Lake Orion, MI		
	1 Roger Chapman (ENG)	68-68-68-66—270		
	2 Fred Funk	67-71-67-67—272		
	Tom Lehman	70-66-68-68—272		
	Corey Pavin	67-69-68-68—272		
	Bernhard Langer (GER)	66-70-64-72—272		
July 26–29	**The Senior Open**	Turnberry, Ayrshire, Scotland		
	1 Fred Couples	72-68-64-67—271		
	2 Gary Hallberg	71-63-73-66—273		
	3 Barry Lane (ENG)	67-74-66-69—276		
	Carl Mason (ENG)	69-74-67-66—276		
	Dick Mast	66-73-70-67—276		
Aug 3–5	3M Championship	TPC Twin Cities, Blaine, MN	Bernhard Langer (GER)	198 (–18)
Aug 17–19	Dick's Sporting Goods Open	En-Joie GC, Endicott, NY	Willie Wood*	203 (–13)
	**Beat Michael Allen at the first extra hole*			
Aug 24–26	Boeing Classic	Snoqualmie, WA	Jay Don Blake*	206 (–10)
	**Beat Mark O'Meara at the second extra hole*			
Sep 14–16	Pacific Links Hawai'i Championship	Kapolei, HI	Willie Wood	202 (–14)
Oct 5–7	SAS Championship	Prestonwood CC, Cary, NC	Bernhard Langer (GER)	203 (–9)
Oct 12–14	Greater Hickory Classic	Rock Barn, Conover, NC	Fred Funk	201 (–15)
Oct 26–28	AT&T Championship	San Antonio, TX	David Frost (RSA)*	208 (–8)
	**Beat Bernhard Langer (GER) at the second extra hole*			
Nov 1–4	Charles Schwab Cup Championship	Scottsdale, AZ	Tom Lehman	258 (–22)
Nov 14	Wendy's 3-Tour Challenge	*Rio Secco GC, NV*	See page 244	

Tour Statistics

Driving accuracy

Pos	Name	Rounds	%
1	Fred Funk	70	79.86
2	Jeff Hart	57	79.13
3	Corey Pavin	68	78.31
4	Bernhard Langer (GER)	65	77.57
5	Wayne Levi	52	76.79
6	Bob Gilder	72	76.51
7	D A Weibring	46	76.45
8	Mark McNulty (IRL)	71	76.43
9	Tom Lehman	63	75.00
10	Hale Irwin	65	74.86

Driving distance

(Average yards per drive)

Pos	Name	Rounds	Yds
1	Fred Couples	36	298.6
2	John Huston	61	296.8
3	Kenny Perry	57	295.4
4	Steve Lowery	62	288.6
5	Tom Lehman	63	288.1
6	Mark Calcavecchia	75	286.4
7	Brad Bryant	61	284.9
8	Michael Allen	72	283.9
9	Sandy Lyle (SCO)	47	283.8
10	Russ Cochran	60	283.6

Greens in regulation

Pos	Name	Rounds	%
1	Tom Lehman	63	77.68
2	Fred Couples	36	77.20
3	Bernhard Langer (GER)	65	75.77
4	Kenny Perry	57	75.51
5	Mike Goodes	73	72.73
6	Bill Glasson	67	72.57
7	Joel Edwards	55	72.55
8	John Cook	71	72.31
9	David Eger	72	72.14
10	Fred Funk	70	72.13

Sand saves

Pos	Name	Rounds	%
1	David Frost (RSA)	74	58.23
2	Willie Wood	45	57.14
3	Kirk Triplett	59	56.67
4	Gary Hallberg	76	55.93
5	Ted Schulz	57	55.84
6	Bernhard Langer (GER)	65	55.56
7	Jeff Freeman	45	55.17
8	Michael Allen	72	55.00
9	Peter Jacobsen	47	53.85
10	Sandy Lyle (SCO)	47	53.33

Scrambling

(Made par after missing greens in regulation)

Pos	Name	Rounds	%
1	Willie Wood	45	71.67
2	Bernhard Langer (GER)	65	69.96
3	Corey Pavin	68	65.31
4	Kirk Triplett	59	65.25
5	Peter Senior (AUS)	75	64.96
6	Tom Lehman	63	64.44
7	Michael Allen	72	63.38
8	Fred Funk	70	63.29
9	Jay Don Blake	78	62.97
10	Dana Quigley	40	62.59

Putts per round

Pos	Name	Rounds	%
1	Michael Allen	72	28.66
2	David Frost (RSA)	74	28.72
3	Corey Pavin	68	28.77
4	Gary Hallberg	76	28.86
5	Willie Wood	45	28.87
6	Bernhard Langer (GER)	65	29.14
7	Morris Hatalsky	35	29.19
	Steve Jones	39	29.19
9	Jay Don Blake	78	29.20
10	Olin Browne	73	29.23
	Jay Haas	69	29.23

US Champions Tour Records 2012

Multiple winners

Michael Allen	Encompass Insurance Pro-Am; Liberty Mutual Legends of Golf
Fred Couples	Mississippi GR Classic; The Senior Open
David Frost (RSA)	Liberty Mutual Legends of Golf; AT&T Championship
Fred Funk	Insperity Championship; Greater Hickory Classic
Bernhard Langer (GER)	3M Championship; SAS Championship
Tom Lehman	Regions Tradition; Charles Schwab Cup Championship
Willie Wood	Dick's Sporting Goods Open; Pacific Links Hawai'i Championship

Top Ten Finishes

Bernhard Langer (GER)	17	Mark Calcavecchia	11	Peter Senior (AUS)	10
Michael Allen	12	John Cook	10		
Tom Lehman	12	Jay Haas	10		

web.com Tour 2012

formerly the Nationwide Tour

www.pgatour.com

Players are of American nationality unless stated

Final Ranking (Top 25 earned US Tour Card)

1	Casey Wittenberg	$433,453
2	Luke Guthrie	410,593
3	Russell Henley	400,116
4	Luke List	363,206
5	James Hahn	337,530
6	Shawn Stefani	307,371
7	Robert Streb	305,591
8	Ben Kohles	303,977
9	Justin Bolli	300,924
10	David Lingmerth (SWE)	287,148
11	Justin Hicks	277,159
12	Paul Haley II	263,841
13	Cameron Percy (AUS)	256,238
14	Andres Gonzales	235,505
15	Scott Gardiner (AUS)	234,145
16	Lee Williams	223,468
17	Darron Stiles	213,031
18	Brad Fritsch (CAN)	212,168
19	Morgan Hoffmann	207,540
20	Brian Stuard	205,711
21	Andrew Svoboda	203,717
22	Nicholas Thompson	192,751
23	Alistair Presnell (AUS)	190,567
24	Doug LaBelle II	186,320
25	Jim Herman	182,001
26	Camilo Benedetti (COL)	181,061
27	Hudson Swafford	179,278
28	Joseph Bramlett	177,973
29	Michael Putnam	169,023
30	Adam Hadwin (CAN)	168,713
31	Cliff Kresge	165,925
32	Paul Claxton	164,394
33	Alex Aragon	161,544
34	Chris Wilson	157,856
35	Scott Parel	147,301
36	Edward Loar	145,901
37	B J Staten	144,521
38	Skip Kendall	143,045
39	Aaron Watkins	138,668
40	Dawie van der Walt (RSA)	137,683
41	Philip Pettitt, Jr	135,745
42	Rob Oppenheim	132,065
43	Tyrone Van Aswegen	130,916
44	Matt Weibring	130,239
45	Nick Flanagan (AUS)	130,047
46	Aaron Goldberg	129,017
47	Brice Garnett	126,872
48	Tag Ridings	122,410
49	Scott Gutschewski	122,331
50	Sam Saunders	122,149
51	Peter Tomasulo	120,169
52	Kevin Foley	119,202
53	Richard Scott (CAN)	113,619
54	Ben Martin	112,570
55	Fabian Gomez (ARG)	112,212
56	Steve LeBrun	105,646
57	Tim Wilkinson (NZL)	100,862
58	Michael Letzig	99,987
59	Jim Renner	99,500
60	Woody Austin	98,433
61	Duffy Waldorf	94,556
62	Lee Janzen	91,915
63	Aron Price (AUS)	91,155
64	Matt Harmon	88,533
65	Jeff Gove	87,297
66	D J Brigman	82,526
67	Alex Prugh	82,506
68	Derek Fathauer	81,508
69	Scott Harrington	79,373
70	Reid Edstrom	78,730
71	Jason Gore	78,337
72	Matt Hendrix	76,725
73	Will Wilcox	75,660
74	Jin Park (KOR)	75,431
75	Josh Broadaway	74,929
76	Bronson La'Cassie (AUS)	74,152
77	Bio Kim (KOR)	74,067
78	Glen Day	72,856
79	Patrick Cantlay	72,460
80	James Sacheck	71,771
81	Jason Allred	70,367
82	Peter Lonard (AUS)	69,154
83	Brian Smock	69,028
84	Danny Lee (NZL)	66,668
85	Jamie Lovemark	63,758
86	Troy Merritt	63,063
87	Tom Hoge	62,006
88	Billy Horschel	61,175
89	Ron Whittaker	61,062
90	Fernando Mechereffe (BRA)	60,497
91	Andy Winings	60,073
	Wes Roach	60,073
93	Kevin Johnson	59,768
94	Chris Riley	59,733
95	Steve Allan (AUS)	59,235
96	Steve Wheatcroft	58,926
97	Andy Pope	55,309
98	Christopher DeForest	55,141
99	Will MacKenzie	55,108
100	Michael Connell	54,799

Tour Results

Feb 16–19	Pacific Rubiales Colombia Championship	Bogotá	Skip Kendall	274 (–10)
Mar 1–4	Panama Claro C/ship	Panama City	Edward Loar	276 (–4)
Mar 8–11	Chile Classic	Santiago	Paul Haley II	266 (–22)
Mar 22–25	Chitimacha Louisiana Open	Le Triomphe, Broussard, LA	Casey Wittenberg	260 (–24)
April 5–8	Soboba Golf Classic	San Jacinto, CA	Andres Gonzales	276 (–8)
April 12–15	TPC Stonebrae C/ship	Stonebrae, Hayward, CA	Alex Aragon	270 (–10)
April 26–29	South Georgia Classic	Kinderlou Forest, Valdosta, GA	Luke List	272 (–16)
May 3–6	Stadion Classic	Univ. of GA	Hudson Swafford	267 (–17)
May 17–20	BMW Charity Pro-Am	Greer, SC; Mill Greenville, SC; Spartanburg, SC	Nick Flanagan (AUS)*	271 (–15)
	**Beat Cameron Percy (AUS) at the third extra hole*			
May 31–June 1	Rex Hospital Open	Wakefield Plantation, Raleigh, NC	James Hahn*	271 (–13)
	**Beat Scott Parel at the second extra hole*			
June 7–10	Mexico Open	El Bosque Golf Club, Leon, Guanajuato, Mexico	Lee Williams	274 (–14)
June 21–24	Preferred Health Systems Wichita Open	Wichita, KS	Casey Wittenberg	266 (–18)
June 28–July 1	United Leasing Championship	Newburgh, IN	Peter Tomasulo*	277 (–11)
	**Beat David Lingmerth (SWE) at the fourth extra hole*			
July 12–15	Utah Championship	Willow Creek CC, Sandy, UT	Doug LaBelle II	269 (–15)
July 26–29	Nationwide Children's Hospital Invitational	Scarlet, Columbus, OH	Ben Kohles*	272 (–12)
	**Beat Luke Guthrie at the first extra hole*			
Aug 2–5	Cox Classic	Champions Run, Omaha, NE	Ben Kohles	260 (–24)
Aug 9–12	Price Cutter Charity C/ship	Springfield, MO	Chris Wilson*	267 (–5)
	**Beat Scott Harrington at the first extra hole*			
Aug 16–19	Midwest Classic	Overland Park, KS	Shawn Stefani	267 (–17)
Aug 23–26	News Sentinel Open	Knoxville, TN	Darron Stiles	266 (–18)
Aug 30–Sep 2	Mylan Classic	Canonsburg, PA	Robert Streb	266 (–18)
Sep 13–16	Albertsons Boise Open	Boise, ID	Luke Guthrie	262 (–22)
Sep 20–23	WNB Golf Classic	Midland, TX	Luke Guthrie	271 (–17)
Sep 27–30	Chiquita Classic	Weddington, NC	Russell Henley*	266 (–22)
	**Beat Morgan Hoffman and Patrick Cantlay at the first extra hole*			
Oct 4–7	Neediest Kids C/ship	Avenel Farm, Potomac, MD	David Lingmerth (SWE)	272 (–8)
Oct 11–14	Miccosukee Championship	Miami, FL	Shawn Stefani	269 (–15)
Oct 18–21	Winn-Dixie Jacksonville Open	Ponte Vedra, FL	Russell Henley*	270 (–10)
	**Beat B J Staten at the first extra hole*			
Oct 25–28	Web.com Tour C/ship	Craig Ranch, McKinney, TX	Justin Bolli	268 (–16)

web.com Tour records 2012

Multiple winners

Casey Wittenberg – Chitimacha Louisiana Open; Preferred Health Systems Wichita Open

Ben Kohles – Nationwide Children's Hosspital Invitational; Cox Classic

Shawn Stefani – Midwest Classic; Miccosukee Championship

Luke Guthrie – Albertsons Boise Open; WNB Golf Classic

Russell Henley – Chiquita Classic; Winn-Dixie Jacksonville Open

Top 10 finishes (number of events in brackets)

1	Justin Hicks	(25)	10
2	Casey Wittenberg	(25)	8
3	Brad Fritsch	(26)	7
T3	Luke Guthrie	(10)	7
	Russell Henley	(26)	7

Asian Tour 2012

www.asiantour.com

Feb 2–5	Zaykabar Myanmar Open	R Mingalardon G&CC, Yangon	Kieran Pratt (AUS)*	273 (–15)
	**Beat Adam Blyth (AUS) and Kiradech Aphibarnrat (THA) at the second extra hole*			
Feb 9–12	ITCSI Philippine Open	Wack Wack G&CC, Manila	Mardan Mamat (SIN)	280 (–8)
Feb 16–19	Avantha Masters	DLF G&CC, Gurgaon, India	Jbe Kruger (RSA)	274 (–14)
Feb 22–25	SAIL-SBI Open	Delhi GC, New Delhi	Anirban Lahiri (IND)*	274 (–14)
	**Beat Prom Meesawat (THA) at the first extra hole*			
Feb 22–26	WGC – Accenture Match Play Championship	Ritz Carlton GC, AZ	Final: Hunter Mahan (USA) beat Rory McIlroy (NIR) 2 and 1	
Mar 8–11	WGC – Cadillac C/ship	TPC Blue Monster at Doral, FL	Justin Rose (ENG)	272 (–16)
Mar 14–17	Handa Faldo Cambodian Classic	Angkor Golf Resort, Siem Reap	David Lipsky (USA)*	273 (–15)
	**Beat Elmer Salvador (PHI) at the first extra hole*			
Mar 29–April 1	Panasonic Open India	Delhi GC, New Delhi	Digvijay Singh (IND)	277 (–11)
April 5–8	IPS Handa Singapore Classic	Orchid CC, Singapore	Scott Hend (AUS)	199 (–11)
	Round Four was cancelled due to bad weather			
April 5–8	Masters Tournament	Augusta National GC, GA	Bubba Watson (USA)*	278 (–10)
	**Beat Louis Oosthuizen (RSA) at the second extra hole*			
April 12–15	Maybank Malaysian Open	Kuala Lumpur G&CC	Louis Oosthuizen (RSA)	271 (–17)
April 19–22	Indonesian Masters	Royale Jakarta GC	Lee Westwood (ENG)	272 (–16)
April 26–29	Ballantines Championship	Seoul, South Korea	Bernd Weisberger (AUT)	270 (–18)
June 14–17	Queen's Cup	Koh Samul, Thailand	Thaworn Wirichant (THA)	277 (–7)
June 14–17	US Open	San Francisco, California, USA	Webb Simpson (USA)	281 (–2)
June 21–24	Volvik Hildesheim Open	Hildesheim GC, South Korea	Lee in Woo (KOR)	276 (–12)
July 19–22	The Open Championship	Lytham and St Annes GC, Lancashire, England	Ernie Els (RSA)	273 (–7)
Aug 2–5	WGC – Bridgestone Inv.	Akron, Ohio, USA	Keegan Bradley (USA)	267 (–13)
Aug 9–12	US PGA Championship	Kiawah Island, SC, USA	Rory McIlroy (NIR)	275 (–13)
Aug 30–Sep 2	Omega European Masters	Crans-sur-Sierre, Switzerland	Richie Ramsay (SCO)	267 (–16)
Sep 5–8	Worldwide Holdings Selangor Masters	Kota Permai G&CC, Shah Alam, Malaysia	Thaworn Wiratchant (THA)	272 (–16)
Sep 13–16	Yeangder Tournament Players' Championship	Linkou International G&CC, Taipei, Taiwan	Ghaganjeet Bullar (IND)	204 (–12)
	Event reduced to 54 holes because of bad weather			
Sep 20–23	Asia Pacific Panasonic Open	Higashi Hirono GC, Hyogo	Masamori Kobayshi (JPN)	267 (–17)
Sep 27–30	Mercuries Taiwan Masters	Taiwan GC, Taipei, Taiwan	Tsai Chi-huang (TPE)	284 (–4)
Oct 4–7	CJ Invitational	Nine Bridges GC, Korea	K J Choi (KOR)	269 (–15)
Oct 11–1 4	Venetian Macau Open	Macau G&CC	Gaganjeet Bhullar (IND)	268 (–16)
Oct 25–28	CIMB Classic	Kuala Lumpur, Malaysia	Nick Watney (USA)	262 (–22)
Nov 1–4	WGC – HSBC Champions	Mission Hills, China	Ian Poulter (ENG)	267 (–21)
Nov 8–11	Barclays Singapore Open	Sentosa GC, Singapore	Matteo Manassero (ITA)*	271 (–13)
	**Beat Louis Oosthuizen at the third extra hole*			
Nov 15–18	UBS Hong Kong Open	Hong Kong GC, Fanling	Miguel Angel Jiménez (ESP)	265 (–15)
Nov 29–Dec 2	King's Cup	Singha Park Khon Kaen GC, Thailand	Arnond Vongvanij (THA)	266 (–22)
Dec 6–9	Thailand Golf Championship	Amata Spring CC, Bangkok	Charl Schwartzel (RSA)	263 (–25)
Dec 13–16	Iskandar Johor Open	Johor Bahru, Malaysia	Sergio García (ESP)	198 (–18)
	Tournament reduced to 54 holes because of rain			

Final money list (Figures in brackets denote number of events played)

1 Thaworn Wirachant (THA)	(25)	US$738,046	6 Prom Meesawat (THA)	(22)	385,910
2 Marcus Fraser (AUS)	(10)	672,744	7 Jonathan Moore (USA)	(17)	370,927
3 Jbe Kruger (RSA)	(10)	474,988	8 Shiv Kapur (IND)	(14)	358,725
4 Masanori Kobayashi (JPN)	(10)	471,079	9 Chapchai Nirat (THA)	(17)	335,152
5 Gaganjeet Bhullar (IND)	(20)	451,245	10 Anirban Lahiri (IND)	(19)	289,731

PGA Tour of Australasia 2012

Players are of Australian nationality unless stated

www.pgatour.com.au

Jan 5–8	Victorian Open	Spring Valley GC	Scott Arnold	272 (–12)
Jan 16–19	Adroit Insurance Group Victorian PGA C/ship	Forest Resort, Creswick	Gareth Paddison (NZL)	277 (–7)
Jan 23–26	Coca-Cola Queensland PGA	City GC, Toowoomba	Andrew Tschudin	199 (–11)
Mar 29–April 1	NZ PGA Pro-Am C/ship	The Hills GC, Queenstown	Michael Hendry (NZL)	272 (–16)
Sep 26–29	South Pacific Golf Open	Tina GC, New Caledonia	Max Shilton	271 (–13)
Oct 11–14	WA Goldfields PGA Championship	Kalgoorlie GC, Kalgoorlie	Peter Wilson	283 (–5)
Oct 18-21	ISPS Handa Perth International	Lake Karinyup CC, Perth	Bo Van Pelt (USA)	272 (–4)
Oct 25–28	John Hughes Geely/Nexus Risk Services WA Open Championship **Beat Brady Watt (am) in play-off*	Royal Perth GC	Oliver Goss (am)*	272 (–16)
Nov 15–18	Talisker Masters (formerly Australian Masters)	Kingston Heath, Melbourne	Adam Scott	271 (–5)
Nov 22–25	BMW New Zealand Open	Clearwater Resort, Christchurch	Jack Higginbottom (am)	281 (–7)
Dec 6–9	**Emirates Australian Open**	The Lakes GC Sydney	Peter Senior	284 (–4)

1904 Hon Michael Scott (am)
1905 Dan Soutar
1906 Carnegie Clark (am)
1907 Hon Michael Scott (am)
1908 Clyde Pearce (am)
1909 C Felstead (am)
1910 Carnegie Clark (am)
1911 Carnegie Clark (am)
1912 Ivo Whitton (am)
1913 Ivo Whitton (am)
1914–1919 *not played*
1920 Joe Kirkwood
1921 A Le Fevre
1922 C Campbell
1923 T Howard
1924 A Russell (am)
1925 Fred Popplewell
1926 Ivo Whitton (am)
1927 R Stewart
1928 Fred Popplewell
1929 Ivo Whitton (am)
1930 F Eyre
1931 Ivo Whitton (am)
1932 Mick Ryan (am)
1933 M Kelly
1934 Bill Bolger
1935 F McMahon
1936 Gene Sarazen (USA)
1937 George Naismith
1938 Jim Ferrier (am)
1939 Jim Ferrier (am)
1940–1945 *not played*
1946 Ossie Pickworth
1947 Ossie Pickworth
1948 Ossie Pickworth
1949 Eric Cremin
1950 Norman Von Nida
1951 Peter Thomson
1952 Norman Von Nida
1953 Norman Von Nida
1954 Ossie Pickworth
1955 Bobby Locke (RSA)
1956 Bruce Crampton
1957 Frank Phillips
1958 Gary Player (RSA)
1959 Kel Nagle
1960 Bruce Devlin (am)
1961 Frank Phillips
1962 Gary Player (RSA)
1963 Gary Player (RSA)
1964 Jack Nicklaus (USA)
1965 Gary Player (RSA)
1966 Arnold Palmer (USA)
1967 Peter Thomson
1968 Jack Nicklaus (USA)
1969 Gary Player (RSA)
1970 Gary Player (RSA)
1971 Jack Nicklaus (USA)
1972 Peter Thomson
1973 J C Snead (USA)
1974 Gary Player (RSA)
1975 Jack Nicklaus (USA)
1976 Jack Nicklaus (USA)
1977 David Graham
1978 Jack Nicklaus (USA)
1979 Jack Newton
1980 Greg Norman
1981 Bill Rogers (USA)
1982 Bob Shearer
1983 Peter Fowler
1984 Tom Watson (USA)
1985 Greg Norman
1986 Rodger Davis
1987 Greg Norman
1988 Mark Calcavecchia (USA)
1989 Peter Senior
1990 John Morse (USA)
1991 Wayne Riley
1992 Steve Elkington
1993 Brad Faxon (USA)
1994 Robert Allenby
1995 Greg Norman
1996 Greg Norman
1997 Lee Westwood (ENG)
1998 Greg Chalmers
1999 Aaron Baddeley (am)
2000 Aaron Baddeley
2001 Stuart Appleby
2002 Steve Allan
2003 Peter Lonard
2004 Peter Lonard
2005 Robert Allenby
2006 John Senden
2007 Peter Lonard
2008 Tim Clark*
**Beat Matthew Coggin at 1st extra hole*
2009 Adam Scott
2010 Geoff Ogilvy
2011 Greg Chalmers

Dec 13–16	Australian PGA Championship	Palmer Coolum Resort, Sunshine Coast, Queensland	Daniel Popovic	272 (–18)

Final money list (Figures in brackets denote number of events played)

1	Peter Senior	(3)	Aus$268,291
2	Michael Hendry (NZL)	(9)	249,625
3	Daniel Popovic	(13)	238,858
4	Adam Scott	(2)	199,750
5	Mark Brown (NZL)	(7)	144,439
6	Rod Pampling	(2)	132,500
7	Anthony Brown	(12)	128,797
8	Jason Norris	(11)	106,133
9	Peter Wilson	(12)	93,800
10	Gareth Paddison (NZL)	(9)	87,979

Canadian Tour 2012

www.cantour.com

Players are of Canadian nationality unless stated

June 7–10	Times Colonist Island Savings Open	Uplands GC, BC	Andrew Roque (USA)	266 (–14)
June 21–24	ATB Financial Classic	Windermere, Edmonton, AB	Michael Gligic*	270 (–14)
	**Beat Matt Marshall (USA) at the second extra hole*			
June 28–July 1	Syncrude Boreal Open	Fort McMurray GC, AB	Cory Renfrew*	271 (–17)
	**Beat Matt Hill at fourth extra hole*			
July 5–8	Dakota Dunes Casino Open	Dakota Dunes, Saskatoon, SK	Matt Hill*	269 (–19)
	**Beat Will Strickler (USA) at fourth extra hole*			
July 12–15	Canadian Tour Players Championship	Pine Ridge GC, Winnipeg, MA	Chris Kilmer* (USA)	269 (–15)
	**Beat Vince Covello (USA) at fourth extra hole*			
July 26–29	**RBC Canadian Open**	Hamilton G&CC, ON	Scott Piercy (USA)	263 (–17)

1904 J H Oke
1905 G Cumming
1906 C Murray
1907 P Barrett
1908 A Murray
1909 K Keffer
1910 D Kenny
1911 C Murray
1912 G Sargent
1913 A Murray
1914 K Kesser
1915–1918 *not played*
1919 J D Edgar
1920 J D Edgar
1921 W H Trovinger
1922 A Watrous
1923 C W Hackney
1924 L Diegel
1925 L Diegel
1926 M Smith
1927 T Armour
1928 L Diegel
1929 L Diegel
1930 T Armour
1931 W Hagen
1932 H Cooper
1933 J Kirkwood
1934 T Armour
1935 G Kunes
1936 L Little
1937 H Cooper
1938 S Snead (USA)
1939 H McSpaden (USA)
1940 S Snead (USA)
1941 S Snead (USA)
1942 C Wood (USA)
1943–1944 *not played*
1945 B Nelson (USA)
1946 G Fazio (USA)
1947 AD Locke (RSA)
1948 CW Congdon
1949 E J Harrison
1950 J Ferrier
1951 J Ferrier
1952 J Palmer (USA)
1953 D Douglas (USA)
1954 P Fletcher
1955 A Palmer (USA)
1956 D Sanders (am) (USA)
1957 G Bayer (USA)
1958 W Ellis Jr (USA)
1959 D Ford (USA)
1960 A Wall Jr (USA)
1961 J Cupit (USA)
1962 T Kroll (USA)
1963 D Ford (USA)
1964 KDG Nagle (AUS)
1965 G Littler (USA)
1966 D Massengale (USA)
1967 W Casper (USA)
1968 RJ Charles (NZL)
1969 T Aaron (USA)
1970 D Zarley (USA)
1971 L Trevino (USA)
1972 G Brewer Jr (USA)
1973 T Weiskopf (USA)
1974 B Nichols (USA)
1975 T Weiskopf (USA)
1976 J Pate (USA)
1977 L Trevino (USA)
1978 B Lietzke (USA)
1979 L Trevino (USA)
1980 B Gilder (USA)
1981 P Oosterhuis (ENG)
1982 B Lietzke (USA)
1983 J Cook (USA)
1984 G Norman (AUS)
1985 C Strange (USA)
1986 B Murphy (USA)
1987 C Strange (USA)
1988 K Green (USA)
1989 S Jones (USA)
1990 W Levi (USA)
1991 N Price (ZIM)
1992 G Norman (AUS)
1993 D Frost (RSA)
1994 N Price (ZIM)
1995 M O'Meara (USA)
1996 D Hart (USA)
1997 S Jones (USA)
1998 B Andrade (USA)
1999 H Sutton (USA)
2000 T Woods (USA)
2001 S Verplank (USA)
2002 J Rollins (USA)
2003 R Tway (USA)
2004 V Singh (FIJ)
2005 M Calcavecchia (USA)
2006 J Furyk (USA)
2007 J Furyk (USA)
2008 C Reavie (USA)
2009 N Green (AUS)*
**Beat R Goosen (RSA) at the 2nd extra hole*
2010 C Petterssen (SWE)
2011 S O'Hair (USA)*
Beat K Blanks (USA) at the 1st extra hole

Aug 16–19	Windsor Roseland Charity Classic	Roseland GC, Windsor, ON	Alan McLean (SCO)	270 (–10)
Aug 23–26	Canadian Tour C/ship	Scarboro G&CC, Toronto, ON	Eugene Wong	270 (–14)
Sep 6–9	Great Waterway Classic	Gananoque, ON	Eugene Wong	266 (–18)

Final Ranking (Figure in brackets indicates number of tournaments played)

1	Matt Hill	(7)	$48.273	6	Chris Kilmer (USA)	(5)	27,596
2	Michael Gligic	(7)	42.950	7	Matt Marshall (USA)	(7)	27.160
3	Cory Renfrew	(8)	41,436	8	Joe Panzeri (USA)	(8)	27.116
4	Eurgene Wong	(4)	33.936	9	Will Stickler (USA)	(8)	25,612
5	Andrew Roque (USA)	(7)	31,367	10	Roger Sloan	(8)	22,261

From 2013, the Canadian Tour will be known as the PGA Tour Canada and will be run by the PGA Tour in America in similar fashion to the rebranded Latinoamérica Tour which replaced the former Tour de las Americas.

Japan PGA Tour 2012

Players are of Japanese nationality unless stated www.jgto.org/jgto/WG01000000Init.do

April 5–8	Masters Tournament	Augusta National GC	Bubba Watson (USA)*	278 (–10)
	**Beat Louis Oosthuizen (RSA) at the second extra hole*			
April 12–15	Token Homemate Cup	Token Tado CC, Nagoya	Brendan Jones (AUS)	269 (–15)
April 19–22	Tsuruya Open	Yamanohara GC, Hyogo	Hiroyuki Fujita	269 (–15)
April 26–29	The Crowns	Nagoya GC (Wago course), Aichi	I J Yang (KOR)	272 (–8)
May 10–13	PGA Championship Nissin Cupnoodles Cup	Karasuyamajo CC, Tochiga	Toru Taniguchi	284 (–4)
May 24–27	Diamond Cup Golf	The Country Club Japan, Chiba	Hiroyuki, Fujita	274 (–14)
May 31–June 3	Citibank Cup	Shishido Hills	Yoshimori Fujimoto	271 (–17)
June 14–17	112th US Open	The Olympic Club, San Francisco	Webb Simpson (USA)	281 (+1)
June 21–24	Gateway to the Open Mizumo Open	JFE Setonakai GC, Okayama	Brad Kennedy (AUS)	271 (–17)
July 5–8	Nagashime Shigeo Inv. (Sega Sammy Cup)	The North Country GC, Hokkaido	Kyoung-Hoon Lee (KOR)	269 (–10)
July 19–22	The Open	Royal Lytham & St Annes	Ernie Els (RSA)	273 (–7)
July 26–29	Sun Chlorella Classic	Otaru CC, Hokkaido	Brendan Jones (AUS)	273 (–15)
Aug 16–19	Kansai Open	Izumigaoka CC, Osaka	Toshinori Muto	266 (–18)
Aug 23–26	Vana H Cup KBC Augusta	Keya GC, Fukuoka	Hyung-Sung Kim (KOR)	270 (–18)
Aug 30–Sep 2	Fujisankei Classic	Fujizakura CC, Yamanashi	Kyung-tae Kim (KOR)	276 (–8)
Sep 6–9	Toshin Golf Tournament	Ryosen GC, Mie	Wu Ashun (CHN)*	198 (–18)
	**Beat Yuta Ikeda at the fourth extra hole*	*Reduced to 54 holes because of bad weather*		
Sep13–16	ANA Open	Sapporo GC, Hokkaido	Hiroyuki Fujita	272 (–16)
Sep 20–23	Asia-Pacific Panasonic Open	Higashi Hirono GC, Hyogo	Masamori Kobayshi	267 (–17)
Sep 27–30	Coca-Cola Tokai Classic	Miyoshi CC, Hokaido	Hyun-Woo Ryu (KOR)*	282 (–6)
	**Beat Shingo Kayayama at the first extra hole*			
Oct 4–7	Canon Open	Totsuka CC, Kanagawa	Yuta Ikeda	271 (–17)
Oct 11–14	Japan Open	Naha GC, Okinawa	Keanichi Kuboya	292 (+8)
Oct 18–21	Bridgestone Open	Sodegaura CC, Chiba	Toru Taniguchi	272 (–12)
Oct 25–28	Mynavi ABC Championship	ABC GC, Hyogo	Han Lee (USA)	271 (–17)
Nov 8–11	Mitsui Sumitomo VISA Taiheiyo Masters	Taiheiyo Club, Shizuoka	Ryo Ishikawa	273 (–15)
Nov 15–18	Dunlop Phoenix Open	Dunlop Phoenix CC, Miyazaki	Luke Donald (ENG)	268 (–16)
Nov 22–25	Casio World Open	Kochi Kuroshio CC, Kochi	Jung-Gon Hwang (KOR)	269 (–19)
Nov 29–Dec 2	Golf Nippon Series JT Cup	Tokyo Yomiuri CC, Tokyo	Hiroyuki Fujita	262 (–18)

Final money list (Japanese Tour events only)

1	Hiroyuki Fujita	¥175,159,972	6	Jung-Gon Hwang (KOR)	84,348,350
2	Toru Taniguchi	102,686,994	7	Ryo Ishikawa	78,178,145
3	Brendan Jones (AUS)	92,078,892	8	Hyung Sung Kim (KOR)	76,660,630
4	Yuta Ikeda	88,948,069	9	Kyung-Tae Kim (KOR)	76,570,535
5	Yoshinori Fujimoto	88,659,122	10	Kyoung-Hoon Lee (KOR)	73,411,694

Korean PGA Tour 2012

Players are of Korean nationality unless stated

http://eng.kgt.co.kr/main/english.aspx

April 26–29	Ballantines Championship	Blackstone Resort, Seoul, South Korea	Bernd Weisberger (AUT)	270 (–18)
May 10–13	GS Caltex Maekyung Open	NamSeoul G&CC	Kim Bi-o	273 (–15)
May 31–June 3	7th Meritz Solmoro Open	Solmoro CC	Choi Jin-Ho	276 (–8)
June 21–24	Volvik Hildesheim Open	Hildesheim GC, South Korea	Lee in Woo	276 (–12)
Aug 29–31	SBS Happiness KJB 55th KPGA Championship	Happiness CC	Lee-Sang Hee	203 (–13)
Aug 30–Sep 2	SBS Happiness KJB (55th KPGA Championship)	Happiness CC	Lee Sang Hee	203 (–13)
Sep 6–9	The Charity High 1 Open	High 1 CC	Matthew Griffin (AUS)	279 (–9)
Sep 13–16	Dongbu Promi Open	Ostar GR	Kim Dae Sub	273 (–15)
Oct 4–7	CJ Invitational	Haesley Nine Bridges CC	K J Choi	269 (–15)
Oct 11–14	28th Shinhan Donghae Open **Beat Kevin Na (USA) in the play-off*	Jack Nicklaus GC	Kim Meen Whee*	284 (–4)
Oct 18–21	Kolon Korean Open	Woo Jung Hills GC	Cheonan Kim Dae-sub	279 (–5)
Oct 25–28	Windsor Classic	Ildong Lake CC	Baek Joo Yeob	203 (–10)

Final Ranking

1	Kim Bio	₩444,000,000	6	Kim Meen Whee	278,367.874
2	Kim Dae Sub	398,493,137	7	Lee Sang Hee	253,979,813
3	Kang Kyung Nam	332,562,772	8	Choi Ho Sang	180,267,722
4	Park Sang Hyun	308,326,923	9	Choi Jin Ho	178,969,449
5	Kim Dae Hyun	307,189,457	10	Ryu Hyun Woo	173,733,537

Other Tours

Results from the following Tours can be found on the following websites:

Adams Tour	www.adamsgolfprotourseries.com	Gateway Tour	www.gatewaytour.com
Allianz Tour	www.allianzgolftour.fr	Golden State Tour	www.gstour.com
Alps Tour	www.alpstourgolf.com	Hi5 Tour	www.hi5protour.com
Asean Tour	www.aseanpgatour.com	Hooters Tour	www.ngatour.com
Asian Development Tour	www.asiantour.com	Iberian Tour	www.igtour.net
Charles Tour	www.golf.co.nz	Italian Tour	www.italianprotour.com
Dakotas Tour	www.dakotastour.com	Jamega Tour	ww.jamegatour.co.uk
Ecco Tour	www.ecco.com	Japan Challenge Tour	www.jgto.org
e-golf Tour	www.egolf.org.uk	Nordic Tour	www.nordicgolftour.com
EPD Tour	www.epdtour.de	PGTI Feeder Tour	www.pgtofindia.com
Europro Tour	www.europrotour.com	PGA New Zealand	www.pga.org.nz
France Tour	www.franceprogolftour.com	Singha Tour	www.pgtofindia.com
		Suncoast Tour	www.suncoastseries.com
		TPGA Argentina	www.pgargentina.org.ar

Tour de las Americas 2012

www.tourdelasamericas.com

Mar 15–18	Abierto de Golf Los Lirios	Rancagua, Chile	Julián Etulain (ARG)	273 (–15)
Mar 22–25	International Open La Vitalicia	Barquisimeto, Venezuela	Rafael Romero (COL)	270 (–14)
Mar 27–30	Copa La Vitalicia	Caracas, Venezuela	Venezuela 11½, South American Select 4½[1]	
April 12–15	81st Abierto del Centro	Cordoba, Argentina	Cesar A Costilla (ARG)	280 (–4)
May 16–19	Abierto del Nordeste	Chaco GC	Luciano Dodda (ARG)	273 (–15)
May 23–27	Televisa TLA Players C/ship	Acapulco Princess, Mexico	Marco Ruiz (PAR)	193 (–17)
May 31–June 3	Taca Airlines Open	CC La Panicie, Lima, Peru	Marco Ruiz (PAR)	272 (–16)

[1]Not an official money event

Final Order of Merit

1	Marco Ruiz (PAR)	16,884 pts	6	Diego Vanegas (COL)	13,054
2	Rafael Romero (COL)	22,060	7	Jesus Amaya (COL)	12,557
3	Rafael Campos (PUR)	17,788	8	Julio Zapata (ARG)	12,248
4	Julian Etulain (ARG)	16,258	9	Ariel Canete (ARG)	11.095
5	Daniel Barbetti (ARG)	13,574	10	Emilio Dominguez (ARG)	10,908

At the end of season 2011–2012, the Tour de las Americas was wound up to emerge for the 2012–2013 season as the PGA Tour Latinoamérica

PGA Tour Latinoamérica 2012

www.pgatourla.com

Sep 3–8	Mundo Maya Open	Yucatan CC, Mérida, Mexico	Tommy Cocha (ARG)	266 (–22)
Sep 10 16	TransAmerican Power Products Open	La Herradura, GC, Monterrey, Mexico	Ariel Canete (ARG)	270 (–18)
Sep 17–23	65 Arturo Calle Colombian Open	El Rincon de Cajica GC, Bogotá	Matias O Curry (ARG)	279 (–9)
Oct 1–6	Brazil Open	São Paulo, Brazil	Clodomiro Carranza (ARG)*	269 (–15)
	Beat José De Jesus Rodriguez (MEX) at the first extra hole			
Oct 8–14	Roberto De Vicenzo Inv.	Buenos Aires, Argentina	Alan Wagner (ARG)	273 (–15)
Oct 29–Nov 4	Lexus Perú Open	Los Inkas GC, Lima	Sebastiian Salem (CAN)	275 (–13)
Nov 5–11	Dominican Republic Open	Cana Bay GC, Punta Cana	Oscar Fraustro (MEX)	278 (–10)
Nov 12–18	Puerto Rico Classic	San Juan, Puerto Rico	Sebastian Vazquez (MEX)	274 (–14)
Nov 26–Dec 2	Colombian Coffee Classic	Club Campestre de Cali, Colombia	Sebastian Fernandez* (ARG)	275 (–9)
	Beat José Manuel Garrido (COL) at first extra hole			
Dec 6–9	Olivos Golf Classic–Copa Personal	Buenos Aires, Buenos Aires, Argentina	Ariel Canete (ARG)	275 (–9)
Dec 13–16	107th. Visa Open de Argentina	Nordelta GC, Buenos Aries	Angel Cabrera (ARG)	270 (–18)

Final Order of Merit (Figures in brackets indicate number of events played)

1	Ariel Canete (ARG)	(11)	US91,395	6	Andres Echavarria (COL)	(11)	41,041
2	Oscar Fraustro (MEX)	(10)	70,914	7	Sebstian Fernandez (ARG)	(11)	38,859
3	Clodomiro Carranza (ARG)	(11)	63,597	8	Alan Wagner (ARG)	(10)	28,425
4	Matias O Curry (ARG)	(11)	54,285	9	José de Jesus Rodriguez (MEX)	(10)	27,434
5	Tommy Cocha (ARG)	(11)	52,385	10	Armando Favela (MEX)	(11)	26,686

PGTI Tour 2012

www.pgtofindia.com

Players are of Indian nationality unless stated

Jan 17–20	Bangladesh Open	Kurmitola GC, Dhaka	Md Zamal Hossain Mollah (BAN)	277 (–11)
Jan 26–29	Gujarat Kensville Challenge	Kensville G&CC, Ahmedabad	Maximilian Kieffer (GER)*	281 (–7)
	**Beat Rahil Gangjee (IND) at the first extra hole*			
Feb 16–19	Avantha Masters	DLF G&CC, Gurgaon	Jbe Kruger (RSA)	274 (–14)
Feb 22–25	SAIL-SBI Open	Delhi GC, New Delhi	Anirban Lahiri*	274 (–14)
	**Beat Prom Meesawat (THA) at the first extra hole*			
Mar 7–10	Louis Philippe Cup	Karnataka Golf Ass., Bangalore	Anura Rohana (SRI)	133 (–11)
Mar 14–17	19th Surya Nepal Masters	Gokama GR, Kathmandu	Abhijit Singh Chadha	276 (–12)
Mar 21–24	PGTI Players C/ship	Noida Golf Course, Noida	Jyoti Randhawa	286 (–2)
Mar 29–April 1	Panasonic Open	Delhi GC, New Delhi	Digvijay Singh	277 (–11)
April 17–20	PGTI Players C/ship	Poona GC, Pune	Shamim Khan	278 (–6)
April 24–27	PGTI Players C/ship	Oxford G&CC, Pune	Om Prakash Chouhan	275 (–13)
May 29–June 1	PGTI Players' C/ship	Chandigarh GC	Harendra P Gupta	278
June 5–8	PGTI Players C/ship	Golden Greens G&CC, Gurgaon	Kunal Bhasin	277 (–11)
June 6–8	Vodacom Origins of Golf	Zebula CC	Bryce Easton (AUS)	200 (–16)
June 14–17	Indo Zambia Bank Zambia Open	Lusaka		
Aug 7–10	PGTI Players Championship	Prestige Golfshire Club, Bangalore	Anura Rohana (SRI)	281 (–7)
Aug 15–18	Standard Chartered Open	R. Colombo GC, Sri Lanka	Mithun Perera (SRI)	271 (–13)
Aug 22–25	PGTI Players C/ship	Coimbatore GC	Rashid Khan*	282 (–6)
	**Beat Vikrant Chopra at the third extra hole*			
Sep 11–14	PGTI Players C/ship	Golden Greens G&CC	Om Prakash Chouhan	281 (–7)
Sep 26–29	IndianOil XtraPremium Masters	Digboi Golf Links, Assam	Mukesh Kumar	273 (–11)
Oct 3–6	CG Open	Bombay Presidency GC, Mumbai	Harendrap Gupta*	267 (–13)
	**Beat Rachid Khan at the first extra hole*			
Oct 18–21	Hero Indian Open	Karnakata Golf Assn, Bangalore	Thaworn Wirachant (THA)*	270 (–14)
	**Beat Richie Ramsay (SCO) at the first extra hole*			
Oct 23–26	PGTI Feeder Tour Jaipur	Rambagh GC, Jaipur	Rahul Bajaj	204 (–6)
Nov 1–4	DLF Masters	DLF G&CC, Gurgaon	Ajeetesh Sandhu*	282 (–6)
	**Beat Jyoti Randhawa in play-off*			
Nov 7–10	PGTI Players C/ship	Poona Club, Puna	Mukesh Kumar	269 (–15)
Nov 13–16	PGTI Players C/ship	Aamby Valley GC	Vinod Kumar	279 (–9)
Nov 22-25	11th TATA Open	Golmuri GC, Jamshedpur	Mithun Perera (SRI)	274 (–11)
Nov 28–Dec 1	McLeod Russel Tour Championship	Royal Calcutta GC	S S P Chowrasia	279 (–9)

Final money list

1	Shamim Khan	₹5,747,713	6	Ajeetesh Sandhu	2,660,991
2	Rashid Khan	4,881,910	7	Om Prakesh Chouhan	2,477,817
3	Harendrap P Gupta	3,917,285	8	Vinod Kumar	2,417,488
4	Mithun Perera (SRI)	3,907,688	9	Shankar Das	2,147,950
5	Mukesh Kumar	3,487,593	10	Manav Jaini	2,037,513

OneAsia Tour 2012

www.oneasia.asia

Mar 22–25	Enjoy Jakarta Indonesian Open	Emeralda GC	Nick Cullen (AUS)	279 (–9)
April 19–22	Volvo China Open	Binhai Lake GC	Branden Grace (RSA)	267 (–21)
May 10–13	GS Caltex Maekyung Open	Namseoul G&CC	Kim Bi-o (KOR)	273 (–15)
May 17–20	SK Telecom Open	Pinx G&CC	Kim Bi-o (KOR)	270 (–18)
Aug 9–12	Thailand Open	Suwan G&CC	Chris Wood (ENG)	265 (–23)
Sep 6–9	High1 Resort Open	High 1 CC	Matthew Griffin (AUS)	279 (–9)
Oct 11–14	Nanshan China Masters	Nanshan Int. GC	Liang Wenchong (CHN)*	276 (–8)
	**Beat Y E Yang (KOR) at the fifth extra hole*			
Oct 18–21	Kolon Korea Open	Woo Jeong Hills CC	Cheonan Kim Dae-sub (KOR)	279 (–5)
Nov 3–Dec 2	Dongfen Nissan Cup	CTS Tycoon GC, Shenzhen, China	China 10, Asia–Pacific 14	
	Full details can be found on page 224			
Dec 6–9	Emirates Australian Open	The Lakes GC, Sydney	Peter Senior (AUS)	284 (–4)
Dec 13–16	Australian PGA Championship	Palmer Coolum Resort, Queensland	Daniel Popovic (AUS)	272 (–16)

Final money list (Figures in brackets denote number of events played)

1	Kim Bi-o (KOR)	(4)	US$380,745	6	Liang Wenchong (CHN)	(4)	194,458
2	Daniel Popovic (AUS)	(3)	239,461	7	Ryu Hyun-woo (KOR)	(4)	140,523
3	Matthew Griffin (AUS)	(7)	230,856	8	Choi Ho-sung (KOR)	(6)	129,058
4	Park Sang-hyun (KOR)	(7)	216,492	9	Anthony Brown (NZL)	(8)	128,530
5	Nick Cullen (AUS)	(7)	208,638	10	Aaron Townsend (AUS)	(9)	119,049

OneAsia and Japan co-sanction two events

The Thailand Open and the Indonesian PGA Championship, the opening events on the 2013 OneAsia circuit this year, were co-sanctioned with the Japanese Golf Tour.

Welcoming the move Katsuji Ebisawa, chairman of the Japan Tour, said "We have long sought opportunities to establish a presence outside of Japan. By jointly working with other tours and organisations we are able to provide our members with greater playing opportunities."

Sang Y Chun, commissioner and chairman of OneAsia, described the move to co-sanction events with Japan as a significant development.

"Since our launch in 2009 our objective at OneAsia has been to build a circuit that brings together the whole of the Asia-Pacific region."

In 2012 the Enjoy Jakarta Indonesian Open was co-sanctioned between the two Tours.

The Volvo China Open, the third event on the OneAsia Tour's 2013 calendar is co-sanctioned with the European Tour.

Month by month in 2012

The Masters goes to Bubba Watson thanks to a superb recovery from the trees on the first play-off hole against Louis Oosthuizen, who earlier leapt into the lead with an albatross two on the second. Five Europeans are in the top 10, but their last winner remains José Maria Olazábal in 1999. With South Korean Sun Young Yoo capturing the Kraft Nabisco title, Asians hold all four of the women's majors for the first time.

South African Sunshine Tour

Players are of South African nationality unless stated www.sunshinetour.com

Jan 5–8	Africa Open	East London GC	Louis Oosthuizen	265 (–27)
Jan 12–15	Joburg Open	Royal Johannesburg and Kensington GC	Branden Grace	270 (–17)
Feb 16–19	Dimension Data Pro-am	Fancourt, George	Oliver Bekker	276 (–13)
Feb 23–26	Telkom PGA Championship	Country Club, Johannesburg	Keith Horne	269 (–19)
Mar 22–24	Platinum Classic	Mooinooi GC North West	Jake Roos*	202 (–14)
	**Beat Anthony Michael and Chris Swanepoel at the fifth extra hole*			
Apr 19–22	Golden Pilsner Zimbabawe Open	Royal Harare	Chris Swanepoel*	273 (–15)
	**Beat Trevor Fisher Jr at the second extra hole*			
May 2–5	Investec Royal Swazi Open	Royal Swazi Sun CC	Christiaan Basson	50pts
May 9–11	Vodacom Origins of Golf	Simola	Ryan Cairns (ZIM)*	201 (–15)
	**Beat Vaughn Groenewald at the first extra hole*			
May 24–26	Sun City Challenge	Lost City GC	Bryce Easton*	207 (–9)
	**Beat Allan Versfeld, Brandon Pieters and Andrew Georgiou at the first extra hole*			
June 1–3	Lombard Insurance Classic	Royal Swazi Sun CC	Jake Roos*	199 (–17)
	**Beat Justin Harding at the first extra hole*			
July 25–27	Vodacom Origins of Golf	De Zalze GC, Western Cape	Alan Versfeld	198 (–18)
Aug 22–24	Vodacom Origins of Golf	Selborne Hotel, Spa & Golf Estate	Adilson da Silva (BRA)	204 (–12)
Aug 29–31	Wild Waves Golf Challenge	Wild Coast CC	Trevor Fisher Jr*	202 (–14)
	**Beat Christiaan Basson at the first extra hole*			
Sep 26–28	Vodacom Origins of Golf Final	The Links, Fancourt	Branden Grace	209 (–10)
Oct 19–21	BMG Classic	Glendower GC	Teboho Sefatsa	206 (–10)
Oct 25–27	Suncoast Classic	Durban CC	Ruan de Smidt	208 (–8)
Nov 1–4	ISPS Handa Match Play Championship	Zwartkop CC	Final: Daniel Slabbart beat Conrad Stoltz 2 and 1	
Nov 6–8	Nedbank Affinity Cup	Lost City GC, Sun City	Trevor Fisher Jr	207 (–9)
Nov 15–18	**South African Open Championship**	Serengeti Golf and Wildlife Estate, Ekurhuleni	Henrik Stenson (SWE)	271 (–17)

1903 Laurie Waters
1904 Laurie Waters
1905 AG Gray
1906 AG Gray
1907 Laurie Waters
1908 George Fotheringham
1909 John Fotheringham
1910 George Fotheringham
1911 George Fotheringham
1912 George Fotheringham
1913 James Prentice
1914 George Fotheringham
1915–1918 *Not played*
1919 WH Horne
1920 Laurie Waters
1921 Jock Brews
1922 F Jangle
1923 Jock Brews
1924 Bertie Elkin
1925 Sid Brews
1926 Jock Brews
1927 Sid Brews
1928 Jock Brews
1929 Archie Tosh
1930 Sid Brews
1931 Sid Brews
1932 Charles McIlveny
1933 Sid Brews
1934 Sid Brews
1935 Bobby Locke
1936 Clarence Olander
1937 Bobby Locke
1938 Bobby Locke
1939 Bobby Locke
1940 Bobby Locke
1941–1945 *Not played*
1946 Bobby Locke
1947 Ronnie Glennie (am)
1948 Mickey Janks
1949 Sid Brews
1950 Bobby Locke
1951 Bobby Locke
1952 Sid Brews
1953 Jimmy Boyd
1954 Reg Taylor (am)
1955 Bobby Locke
1956 Gary Player
1957 Harold Henning
1958 Arthur Stewart (am)
1959 Denis Hutchinson (am)
1960 Gary Player
1961 Retief Waltman
1962 Harold Henning
1963 Retief Waltman
1963 Allan Henning
1964 *No tournament (two played in 1963)*
1965 Gary Player
1966 Gary Player
1967 Gary Player
1968 Gary Player
1969 Gary Player
1970 Tommy Horton
1971 Simon Hobday
1972 Gary Player
1973 Bob Charles (NZL)
1974 Bobby Cole
1975 Gary Player
1976 Dale Hayes
1976 Gary Player
1977 Gary Player
1978 Hugh Baiocchi
1979 Gary Player
1980 Bobby Cole
1981 Gary Player
1982 *No tournament (two played in 1976)*
1983 Charlie Bolling
1984 Tony Johnstone
1985 Gavin Levenson
1986 David Frost
1987 Mark McNulty (IRL)
1988 Wayne Westner
1989 Fred Wadsworth
1990 Trevor Dodds
1990–91 Wayne Westner
1991–92 Ernie Els
1992–93 Clinton Whitelaw
1993–94 Tony Johnstone
1994–95 Retief Goosen
1995–96 Ernie Els
1996–97 Vijay Singh (FIJ)
1997–98 Ernie Els
1998–99 David Frost
1999–2000 Matthias Grönberg (SWE)
2000–01 Mark McNulty (IRL)
2001–02 Tim Clark
2002–03 Trevor Immelman
2003–04 Trevor Immelman
2004–05 Tim Clark
2005–06 Retief Goosen
2006–07 Ernie Els
2007 James Kingston
2008 Richard Sterne*
**Beat Gareth Maybin (NIR) at 1st extra hole*
2009 Richie Ramsay (SCO)*
**Beat Shiv Kapur (IND) at 1st extra hole*
2010 Ernie Els
2011 Hennie Otto

South African Sunshine Tour *continued*

Nov 23–25	Lion of Africa Cape Town Open	Royal Cape GC	Jake Roos*	279 (–9)
	**Beat Jaco Van Zyle, Tyrone van Aswegen and Mark Williams at the second extra hole*			
Nov 29–Dec 2	Nedbank Golf Challenge	Gary Player CC, Sun City	Martin Kaymer (GER)	280 (–8)
Dec 8–9	Nelson Mandela Championship	Royal Durban GC	Scott Jamieson (SCO)*	123 (–7)
	**Beat Steve Webster (ENG) and Eduardo de la Riva (ESP) at the second extra hole*			
	(Event reduced to 36-holes and course reduced from par 70 to par 65 because of bad weather)			
Dec 13–16	Alfred Dunhill Championship	Leopard Creek GC	Charl Schwartzel	264 (–24)

Final Order of Merit (Figures in brackets indicate number of events played)

*	Charl Schwartzel	(4)	SAR3,203,886	5	Tjaart van der Walt	(6)	1,464,182
1	Brendan Grace	(8)	2,760,319	6	Thomas Aiken	(6)	1,259,881
2	George Coetzee	(6)	1,930,564	7	Darren Fichardt	(12)	1,177,700
*	Louis Oosthuizen	(3)	1,737,955	8	Keith Horne	(10)	1,152,349
3	Jaco Van Zyl	(8)	1,655,984	9	Garth Mulroy	(6)	1,042,704
4	Trevor Fisher Jr	(21)	1,502,092	10	Oliver Bekker	(21)	977,196

*indicates did not play enough events to be included on official Order of Merit

Branden Grace rocketed up the World Rankings in 2012

Things looked bleak for South African Branden Grace when he lost his European Tour card in 2011 but what a difference a year makes. His 2012 was simply stellar.

After winning his European card back at the 2012 Qualifying School, he celebrated with victories in the early season Joburg Open and the élite Volvo Champions event where he went head to head in a play-off with the vastly more experienced Ernie Els and Retief Goosen and won.

Later in the year he proved his competitive qualities with two more European Tour wins at the Volvo China Open and, even more impressively, the Alfred Dunhill Links Championship played over Carnoustie, Kingsbarns and the Old course at St Andrews.

He was a comfortable winner of the Sunshine Circuit's Order of Merit and finished sixth in the European Tour's Race to Dubai. He had started the year in 271st spot on the World Rankings. He finished the year lying 34th. His season was that good.

Jamieson and van Zyl shoot 57 – but its unofficial!

Scotland's Scott Jamieson won his first European Tour title when he beat Steve Webster and Eduardo de la Riva at the second extra hole of the rain shortened Nelson Mandela Championship in Durban.

Jamieson joined England's Webster and Spain's de la Riva on 123 after shooting a 57 – the lowest round ever scored on the European Tour. It is, of course, an unofficial score. The course had been reduced from a 6,733 yards par 70 to a 5,133 yards 65 because of the rain which prevented any play on the first two days. Jamieson's score, and that of Jaco van Zyl who also shot 57 and finished tied 8th, beat the previous unofficial low score of 59 returned at the 1985 German Open by Mark McNulty. On that occasion many of the holes were played as par 3's because of flooding. Alexandre Kaleka from France was another who shot a round under 60 in Durban. His 59 – 10 lower than his opening round – earned him a tie in 32nd spot.

Three Scots to be inducted into World Golf Hall of Fame: Ken Schofield, Colin Montgomerie and Willie Park Jr

Three Scots are included in the Class of 2013 to be inaugurated into the World Golf Hall of Fame in Florida later this year. Joining Fred Couples and Ken Venturi will be Ken Schofield, formerly chief executive of the PGA European Tour, Colin Montgomerie, eight times top money earner on the European Tour and, posthumously, Willie Park Jr whose father has already been honoured.

When Ken Schofield took over from John Jacobs as Chief Executive of the European Tour in 1975 it comprised 17 events and offered total prize-money of just £430,000. When he retired in 2004 the Tour schedule comprised 45 tournaments offering prize-money of over £73 million.

It was Schofield who transformed the Tour into a global organisation arguing that it was the players who consitituted a European Tour event and not the country in which the event was being played.

Today the Tour, which has celebrated its 40th anniversary, criss-crosses the globe staging events in South Africa, the Middle East and in the huge growth area of Asia including China. During his term in office he initiated the setting up of the European Challenge Tour and of the Senior Tour.

Formerly the youngest bank manager in Scotland but with a real passion for all sports, Schofield was the dynamic driving force which enabled the Tour to grow in stature over the years but, typically, he said on hearing of his up-coming inauguration: "I am delighted not just for myself but for all those who have helped the Tour become what it has become today."

While Schofield enters the Hall of Fame in May on the Lifetime Achievement ticket, Colin Montgomerie makes it on the International ballot. Since turning professional in 1987, "Monty" has won 40 events worldwide and been eight times the leading money earner on the European Tour including seven No 1's in a row – a feat unlikely to be matched.

Although a major title has eluded him – he did come close on several occasions to landing a Grand Slam title – he has been a tower of strength for Europe in the Ryder Cup, playing eight times and remaining unbeaten in singles play. He captained the side to victory at Celtic Manor in 2010.

The third Scot elected to the Hall of Fame in the Veterans Category is the 1887 and 1889 Open champion Willie Park Jr. Mungo Park, Willie Park Jr's great nephew, said his great uncle, possibly more than any other, marked the transition from old-school caddie and player to the modern professional golfer and business man. He gave up playing in high stake money matches to concentrate energetically on golf course design. Mungo Park added: "His playing skill was undoubted, particularly with the putter, but it is the courses he designed that provide his most impressive legacy."

Popular Fred Couples, a 15-time winner on the PGA Tour in America including the 1992 Masters at Augusta was chosen on the PGA Tour ballot. A five time Ryder Cup player he is now captain of the US President's Cup team and will lead the side for a third time at Muirfield Village later this year.

Ken Venturi, who makes it into the Hall of Fame like Ken Schofield in the Lifetime Achievement category, won 14 times on the PGA Tour but never more dramatically than in 1964 when, playing in temperatures of over 100 degrees Fahrenheit, he battled dehydration to win the US Open in Washington. When he retired from competitive golf he began a highly respected 35-year television career as lead analyst for CBS.

When told of his award Venturi said "It's a dream of a lifetime. The greatest reward in life is to be remembered and I thank the World Golf hall of Fame for remembering me."

There are now 146 honorees in the World Golf Hall of Fame but among notable absentees is Samuel Ryder who helped maintain the biennial match between the American and originally the British but now the European professionals in the Cup match which bears his name.

World Championship Events

WGC – Accenture Match Play Championship

Ritz-Carlton, Dove Mountain, AZ, USA [7791–72]

First Round:
Ernie Els (RSA) beat Luke Donald (ENG) 5 and 4
Peter Hanson (SWE) beat Jason Dufner (USA) 2 and 1
Kyle Stanley (USA) beat K J Choi (KOR) 2 and 1
Brandt Snedeker (USA) beat Retief Goosen (RSA) at 21st
Robert Rock (ENG) beat Adam Scott (AUS) 1 up
Mark Wilson (USA) beat Bo Van Pelt (USA) 3 and 2
Dustin Johnson (USA) beat Jim Furyk (USA) at 20th
Francesco Molinari (ITA) beat Thomas Björn (DEN) at 20th

Martin Kaymer (GER) beat Greg Chalmers (AUS) 4 and 2
David Toms (USA) beat Rickie Fowler (USA) 1 up
Matt Kuchar (USA) beat Jonathan Byrd (USA) 1 up
Bubba Watson (USA) beat Ben Crane (USA) 3 and 2
Steve Stricker (USA) beat Kevin Na (USA) 2 and 1
Louis Oosthuizen (RSA) beat Aaron Baddeley (AUS) 2 and 1
Y E Yang (KOR) beat Graeme McDowell (NIR) 2 and 1
Hunter Mahan (USA) beat Zack Johnson (USA) at 19th

Rory McIlroy (NIR) beat George Coetze (RSA) 2 up
Anders Hansen (DEN) beat Anthony Kim (USA) 5 and 3
Miguel Angel Jiménez (ESP) beat Sergio García (ESP) 2 and 1
Keegan Bradley (USA) beat Geoff Ogilvy (AUS) 4 and 3
Jason Day (AUS) beat Rafael Cabarera-Bello (ESP) at 19th
John Senden (AUS) beat Simon Dyson (ENG) 4 and 3
Charl Schwartzel (RSA) beat Gary Woodland (USA) 4 and 2
Bae Sang-Moon (KOR) beat Ian Poulter (ENG) 4 and 3

Lee Westwood (ENG) beat Nicolas Colsaerts (BEL) 3 and 1
Robert Karlsson (SWE) beat Fredrik Jacobson (SWE) 6 and 5
Nick Watney (USA) beat Darren Clarke (NIR) 5 and 4
Tiger Woods (USA) beat Gonzalo Fernandez-Castano (ESP) 1 up
Matteo Manassero (ITA) beat Webb Simpson (USA) 3 and 2
Martin Laird (SCO) beat Alvaro Quiros (ESP) 1 up
Ryo Ishikawa (JPN) beat Bill Haas (USA) 1 up
Paul Lawrie (SCO) beat Justin Rose (ENG) 1 up

Second Round:
Hanson beat Els 5 and 4
Snedeker beat Stanley 2 and 1
Wilson beat Rock 3 and 2
Johnson beat Molinari 7 and 5
Kaymer beat Toms 2 up
Kuchar beat Watson 3 and 2
Stricker beat Oosthuizen 1 up
Mahan beat Yang 5 and 3
McIlroy beat Hansen 3 and 2
Jiménez beat Bradley 2 and 1
Senden beat Day 6 and 5
Bae beat Schwartzel 1 up
Westwood beat Karlsson 3 and 2
Watney beat Woods 1 up
Laird beat Manassero 2 and 1
Lawrie beat Ishikawa 1 up

Third Round:
Hanson beat Snedeker 5 and 3
Wilson beat Johnson 4 and 3
McIlroy beat Jiménez 3 and 2
Bae beat Senden 1 up
Kuchar beat Kaymer 4 and 3
Mahan beat Stricker 4 and 3
Westwood beat Watney 3 and 2
Laird beat Lawrie 3 and 1

Quarter-finals:
Wilson beat Hanson 4 and 3
McIlroy beat Bae 3 and 2
Mahan beat Kuchar 6 and 5
Westwood beat Laird 4 and 2

Semi-finals:
Mahan beat Wilson 2 and 1
McIlroy beat Westwood 3 and 1

Final:
Hunter Mahan beat Rory McIlroy 2 and 1

Third Place Match:
Wilson beat Westwood 1 up

Winner:	$1,400,000	€1,027,923	Quarter Finals:	$270,000	€198,242
Runner-up:	$850,000	€624,095	3rd Round:	$140,000	€102,792
3rd Place:	$600,000	€440,538	2nd Round:	$95,000	€69,751
4th Place:	$490,000	€359,772	1st Round:	$45,000	€33,040

2000 Darren Clarke (NIR) beat Tiger Woods (USA) 4 and 3 at La Costa, Carlsbad, CA, USA
2001 Steve Stricker (USA) beat Pierre Fulke (SWE) 4 and 3 at Metropolitan GC, Melbourne, Australia
2002 Kevin Sutherland (USA) beat Scott McCarron (USA) 1 hole at La Costa, Carlsbad, CA, USA
2003 Tiger Woods (USA) beat David Toms (USA) 2 and 1 at La Costa, Carlsbad, CA, USA
2004 Tiger Woods (USA) beat Davis Love III (USA) 3 and 2 at La Costa, Carlsbad, CA, USA
2005 David Toms (USA) beat Chris DiMarco (USA) 6 and 5 at La Costa, Carlsbad, CA, USA
2006 Geoff Ogilvy (AUS) beat Davis Love III (USA) 3 and 2 at La Costa, Carlsbad, CA, USA
2007 Henrik Stenson (SWE) beat Geoff Ogilvy (AUS) 2 and 1 at Gallery, Tucson, AZ, USA
2008 Tiger Woods (USA) beat Stewart Cink (USA) 8 and 7 at Gallery, Tucson, AZ, USA
2009 Geoff Ogilvy (AUS) beat Paul Casey (ENG) 4 and 3 at Dove Mountain, AZ, USA
2010 Ian Poulter (ENG) beat Paul Casey (ENG) 4 and 3 at Dove Mountain, AZ, USA
2011 Luke Donald (ENG) beat Martin Kaymer (GER) 3 and 2 at Dove Mountain, AZ, USA

WGC – Cadillac Championship (formerly WGC – CA Championship)

Doral, Orlando, FL, USA [7334–72]

1	Justin Rose (ENG)	69-64-69-70—272	$1,400,000
2	Bubba Watson (USA)	70-62-67-74—273	845,000
3	Rory McIlroy (NIR)	73-69-65-67—274	516,000
4	Charl Schwartzel (RSA)	68-69-70-68—275	362,500
	Peter Hanson (SWE)	70-65-69-71—275	362,500
6	John Senden (AUS)	76-67-68-65—276	260,000
	Luke Donald (ENG)	70-68-69-69—276	260,000
8	Bo Van Pelt (USA)	73-65-70-69—277	165,000
	Steve Stricker (USA)	69-70-69-69—277	165,000
	Matt Kuchar (USA)	72-67-66-72—277	165,000
	Keegan Bradley (USA)	69-67-66-75—277	165,000
12	Aaron Baddeley (AUS)	69-74-68-67—278	120,000
13	Francesco Molinari (ITA)	75-68-71-65—279	101,000
	Graeme McDowell (NIR)	75-67-67-70—279	101,000
	Adam Scott (AUS)	66-68-74-71—279	101,000
	Johnson Wagner (USA)	70-69-67-73—279	101,000
17	Nick Watney (USA)	71-73-69-67—280	92,000
	Charles Howell III (USA)	70-67-71-72—280	92,000
	Zach Johnson (USA)	70-68-67-75—280	92,000
20	Robert Karlsson (SWE)	75-68-70-68—281	85,000
	Jason Day (AUS)	73-67-70-71—281	85,000
	Greg Chalmers (AUS)	71-70-68-72—281	85,000
	Martin Kaymer (GER)	73-64-70-74—281	85,000
24	Marcus Fraser (AUS)	76-68-69-69—282	76,000
	Robert Rock (ENG)	75-70-68-69—282	76,000
	Thomas Björn (DEN)	68-68-75-71—282	76,000
	Martin Laird (SCO)	72-73-66-71—282	76,000
	Hunter Mahan (USA)	71-72-66-73—282	76,000
29	Bill Haas (USA)	74-70-70-69—283	67,500
	Garth Mulroy (RSA)	73-71-69-70—283	67,500
	Gary Woodland (USA)	71-70-70-72—283	67,500
	Jason Dufner (USA)	66-72-73-72—283	67,500
	Anders Hansen (DEN)	70-72-69-72—283	67,500
	Lee Westwood (ENG)	76-67-68-72—283	67,500
35	Dustin Johnson (USA)	75-68-73-68—284	60,500
	Branden Grace (RSA)	78-72-64-70—284	60,500

WGC – Cadillac Championship *continued*

35T	Nicolas Colsaerts (BEL)	73-70-70-71—284	60,500
	Juvic Pagunsan (PHI)	69-71-72-72—284	60,500
	Chez Reavie (USA)	78-68-67-71—284	60,500
	Jonathan Byrd (USA)	72-70-70-72—284	60,500
	K J Choi (KOR)	74-67-70-73—284	60,500
	Webb Simpson (USA)	75-66-66-77—284	60,500
43	Darren Clarke (NIR)	74-74-68-69—285	55,500
	Phil Mickelson (USA)	72-71-71-71—285	55,500
45	Retief Goosen (RSA)	74-71-71-70—286	52,000
	Rickie Fowler (USA)	74-70-72-70—286	52,000
	Mark Wilson (USA)	72-70-72-72—286	52,000
45	Brandt Snedeker (USA)	75-69-70-72—286	52,000
	Miguel Angel Jiménez (ESP)	69-71-73-73—286	52,000
50	Hennie Otto (RSA)	73-66-71-77—287	49,000
51	Ben Crane (USA)	73-71-73-71—288	46,875
	K T Kim (KOR)	74-72-70-72—288	46,875
	Kyle Stanley (USA)	69-69-76-74—288	46,875
	Paul Casey (ENG)	76-71-68-73—288	46,875
55	Gonzalo Fernandez-Castano (ESP)	74-70-73-72—289	45,250
	Geoff Ogilvy (AUS)	73-73-70-73—289	45,250
57	Jbe' Kruger (RSA)	72-71-73-74—290	44,250
	Alvaro Quiros (ESP)	69-74-71-76—290	44,250
59	Y E Yang (KOR)	72-67-76-76—291	43,500
60	Tadahiro Takayama (JPN)	74-73-75-71—293	42,000
	Ian Poulter (ENG)	76-77-71-69—293	42,000
	Louis Oosthuizen (RSA)	77-70-74-72—293	42,000
	Sergio García (ESP)	75-74-68-76—293	42,000
	Paul Lawrie (SCO)	70-74-72-77—293	42,000
65	Rafael Cabrera Bello (ESP)	75-70-75-74—294	40,500
66	Pablo Larrazabal (ESP)	76-73-71-75—295	39,750
	Vijay Singh (FIJ)	75-73-72-75—295	39,750
68	Fredrik Jacobson (SWE)	72-76-71-77—296	39,000
69	Alexander Noren (SWE)	74-75-72-76—297	38,500
70	Tetsuji Hiratsuka (JPN)	78-73-70-77—298	38,000
71	Sang-Moon Bae (KOR)	79-76-73-71—299	37,750
72	Simon Dyson (ENG)	74-72-73-81—300	37,500
	Tiger Woods (USA)	72-67-68-WD—207	
	David Toms (USA)	72-70-WD—142	

1999	Tiger Woods* (USA)	71-69-70-68—278	at Valderrama GC, Cadiz, Spain

**Woods beat Miguel Angel Jiménez (ESP) at the first extra hole*

2000	Mike Weir (CAN)	68-75-65-69—277	at Valderrama GC, Cadiz, Spain
2001	*Cancelled*		
2002	Tiger Woods (USA)	65-65-67-66—263	at Mount Juliet, Kilkenny, Ireland
2003	Tiger Woods (USA)	67-66-69-72—274	at Capital City, Atlanta, GA
2004	Ernie Els (RSA)	69-64-68-69—270	at Mount Juliet, Kilkenny, Ireland
2005	Tiger Woods* (USA)	67-68-68-67—270	at Harding Park, San Francisco, CA

**Woods beat John Daly at the second extra hole*

2006	Tiger Woods (USA)	63-64-67-67—261	at The Grove, Chandlers Cross, Herts
2007	Tiger Woods (USA)	71-66-68-73—278	at Doral, Orlando, FL, USA
2008	Geoff Ogilvy (AUS)	65-67-68-71—271	at Doral, Orlando, FL, USA
2009	Phil MIckelson (AUS)	65-66-69-69—269	at Doral, Orlando, FL, USA
2010	Ernie Els (RSA)	68-66-70-66—270	at Doral, Orlando, FL, USA
2011	Nick Watney (USA)	67-70-68-67—272	at Doral, Orlando, FL, USA

WGC – Bridgestone Invitational *Firestone CC, Akron, OH* [7400–70]

1	Keegan Bradley (USA)	67-69-67-64—267	$1,400,000
2	Steve Stricker (USA)	68-68-68-64—268	665,000
	Jim Furyk (USA)	63-66-70-69—268	665,000
4	Louis Oosthuizen (RSA)	67-65-68-69—269	365,000
5	Justin Rose (ENG)	70-69-66-67—272	276,500
	Rory McIlroy (NIR)	70-67-67-68—272	276,500

7	Jason Dufner (USA)	67-66-73-68—274	210,000
8	Aaron Baddeley	73-66-71-66—276	128,750
	Tiger Woods (USA)	70-72-68-66—276	128,750
	Matt Kuchar (USA)	70-70-70-66—276	128,750
	K J Choi (KOR)	71-72-67-66—276	128,750
	David Toms (USA)	68-67-73-68—276	128,750
	Lee Slattery (ENG)	65-71-72-68—276	128,750
	Luke Donald (ENG)	66-69-71-70—276	128,750
	Bo Van Pelt (USA)	70-69-66-71—276	128,750
16	Kyle Stanley (USA)	69-73-68-67—277	90,000
	Simon Dyson (ENG)	66-71-70-70—277	90,000
	John Senden (AUS)	66-70-69-72—277	90,000
19	Bubba Watson (USA)	66-73-72-67—278	82,000
	Nick Watney (USA)	69-70-72-67—278	82,000
	Dustin Johnson (USA)	69-68-73-68—278	82,000
	Scott Piercy (USA)	69-70-70-69—278	82,000
	Bill Haas (USA)	67-71-70-70—278	82,000
24	Geoff Ogilvy (AUS)	67-70-72-70—279	74,500
	Charl Schwartzel (RSA)	69-75-72-63—279	74,500
	K T Kim (KOR)	67-67-74-71—279	74,500
	Graeme McDowell (NIR)	70-67-70-72—279	74,500
28	Carl Pettersson (SWE)	67-70-71-72—280	72,000
29	Martin Kaymer (GER)	68-72-72-69—281	68,000
	Retief Goosen (RSA)	67-72-73-69—281	68,000
	Ian Poulter (ENG)	74-69-69-69—281	68,000
	Sergio García (ESP)	67-72-71-71—281	68,000
	Jason Day (AUS)	75-70-70-66—281	68,000
	Rafael Cabrera Bello (ESP)	66-65-77-73—281	68,000
	Martin Laird (SCO)	68-72-68-73—281	68,000
36	Johnson Wagner (USA)	71-74-68-69—282	62,500
	Y E Yang (KOR)	69-71-74-68—282	62,500
	Jamie Donaldson (WAL)	68-73-75-66—282	62,500
	Branden Grace (RSA)	72-70-66-74—282	62,500
40	Francesco Molinari (ITA)	74-70-69-70—283	59,000
	Thomas Björn (DEN)	71-70-74-68—283	59,000
	Zach Johnson (USA)	68-73-68-74—283	59,000
43	Alvaro Quiros (ESP)	70-71-72-71—284	56,500
	Phil Mickelson (USA)	71-69-73-71—284	56,500
45	Marc Leishman (AUS)	70-72-70-73—285	53,000
	Adam Scott (AUS)	71-70-71-73—285	53,000
	Ernie Els (RSA)	73-73-68-71—285	53,000
	Nicolas Colsaerts (BEL)	73-68-74-70—285	53,000
	Mark Wilson (USA)	72-71-73-69—285	53,000
50	Ryo Ishikawa (JPN)	71-72-70-73—286	49,000
	Brandt Snedeker (USA)	71-70-70-75—286	49,000
	Paul Lawrie (SCO)	72-68-74-72—286	49,000
	Fredrik Jacobson (SWE)	71-73-73-69—286	49,000
	Danny Willett (ENG)	72-74-73-67—286	49,000
55	Gonzalo Fernandez-Castano (ESP)	71-73-70-73—287	46,500
	Hunter Mahan (USA)	73-73-69-72—287	46,500
	Jonathan Byrd (USA)	73-73-69-72—287	46,500
	Bernd Wiesberger (AUT)	70-71-74-72—287	46,500
	Greg Chalmers (AUS)	71-75-71-70—287	46,500
60	Marcel Siem (GER)	76-71-70-71—288	44,500
	Yoshinori Fujimoto (JPN)	73-74-71-70—288	44,500
	Rickie Fowler (USA)	70-80-69-69—288	44,500
63	Peter Hanson (SWE)	73-71-71-74—289	43,500
	Kevin Na (USA)	72-76-72-69—289	43,500
	Joost Luiten (NED)	72-71-77-69—289	43,500
66	Sang-Moon Bae (KOR)	72-66-76-76—290	43,000
67	Toshinori Muto (JPN)	73-71-73-74—291	42,625

WGC – Bridgestone Invitational *continued*

67T	Jeev Milkha Singh (IND)	73-74-71-73—291	42,625
69	Robert Allenby (AUS)	73-79-72-68—292	42,250
70	Lee Westwood (ENG)	68-72-81-73—294	42,000
71	Robert Rock (ENG)	76-72-74-73—295	41,625
	Michael Hoey (NIR)	78-75-70-72—295	41,635
73	Ted Potter Jr (USA)	72-72-75-80—299	41,250
74	Tom Lewis (ENG)	78-76-74-73—301	41,000
75	Oliver Bekker (RSA)	77-72-76-77—302	40,750
	Ben Crane (USA)	66-75-WD—141	
	Thongchai Jaidee (THA)	73-WD—73	
	Toru Taniguchi (JPN)	72-78-WD—150	

1999	T Woods (USA)	66-71-62-71—270	at Firestone CC, Akron, OH
2000	T Woods (USA)	64-61-67-67—259	at Firestone CC, Akron, OH
2001	T Woods (USA)	66-67-66-69—268	at Firestone CC, Akron, OH
2002	C Parry (AUS)	72-65-66-65—268	at Sahalee, Redmond, WA
2003	D Clarke (NIR)	65-70-66-67—268	at Firestone CC, Akron, OH
2004	S Cink (USA)	63-68-68-70—269	at Firestone CC, Akron, OH
2005	T Woods (USA)	66-70-67-71—274	at Firestone CC, Akron, OH
2006	T Woods (USA)	67-64-71-68—270	at Firestone CC, Akron, OH
2007	V Singh (FIJ)	67-66-69-68—270	at Firestone CC, Akron, OH
2008	V Singh (FIJ)	67-66-69-68—270	at Firestone CC, Akron, OH
2009	T Woods (USA)	68-70-65-65—268	at Firestone CC, Akron, OH
2010	H Mahan (USA)	71-67-66-64—268	at Firestone CC, Akron, OH
2011	A Scott (AUS)	62-70-66-65—263	at Firestone CC, Akron, OH

WGC – HSBC Champions Tournament *Mission Hills GC, Shenzhen, China* [7251-72]

1	Ian Poulter (ENG)	69-68-65-65—267	€921,376
2	Jason Dufner (USA)	68-66-71-64—269	320,562
	Ernie Els (RSA)	70-63-69-67—269	320,562
	Phil Mickelson (USA)	66-69-66-68—269	320,562
	Scott Piercy (USA)	68-68-68-65—269	320,562
6	Louis Oosthuizen (RSA)	65-63-70-72—270	145,885
	Lee Westwood (ENG)	70-67-61-72—270	145,885
8	Adam Scott (AUS)	65-68-71-67—271	119,011
9	kaymer Martin (GER)	68-69-67-68—272	107,494
10	Bill Haas (USA)	69-67-66-71—273	95,977
11	Hiroyuki Fujita (JPN)	73-67-67-67—274	75,246
	Prom Meesawat (THA)	67-70-69-68—274	75,246
	Thorbjørn Olesen (DEN)	71-65-70-68—274	75,246
	Marcel Siem (GER)	71-70-66-67—274	75,246
	Brandt Snedeker (USA)	72-71-60-71—274	75,246
16	Carl Pettersson (SWE)	70-68-66-71—275	61,809
	Nick Watney (USA)	72-72-69-62—275	61,809
18	Gaganjeet Bhullar (IND)	73-68-63-72—276	57,586
	Luke Donald (ENG)	68-68-69-71—276	57,586
	Marc Leishman (AUS)	73-68-65-70—276	57,586
21	Thomas Björn (DEN)	72-70-68-67—277	53,747
	Thongcha Jaidee (THA)	70-68-69-70—277	53,747
23	Keegan Bradley (USA)	71-68-68-71—278	51,443
24	Peter Hanson (SWE)	66-71-73-69—279	47,796
	Scott Hend (AUS)	70-74-67-68—279	47,796
	Wenchong Liang (CHN)	72-73-66-68—279	47,796
	Justin Rose (ENG)	72-70-67-70—279	47,796
28	Thomas Aiken (RSA)	68-73-69-70—280	44,149
	Gonzalo Fernandez-Castaño (ESP)	71-67-69-73—280	44,149
	John Senden (AUS)	72-70-70-68—280	44,149
	Bernd Wiesberger (AUT)	72-72-68-68—280	44,149
32	Shane Lowry (IRL)	66-68-72-75—281	42,230
	Bubba Watson (USA)	66-72-69-75—282	41,462
34	Ik-Jae Jang (KOR)	68-71-72-72—283	40,310

34T	Tadahiro Takayama (JPN)	73-69-70-71—283	40,310
36	Paul Lawrie (SCO)	69-71-72-72—284	38,391
	Joost Luiten (NED)	72-72-68-72—284	38,391
	shun Wu (CHN)	68-70-71-75—284	38,391
39	Dustin Johnson (USA)	67-68-84-66—285	36,087
	Francesco Molinari (ITA)	74-69-74-68—285	36,087
	Thaworn Wiratchant (THA)	72-70-70-73—285	36,087
42	Jamie Donaldson (WAL)	71-74-71-70—286	33,400
	Marcus Fraser (AUS)	73-72-70-71—286	33,400
	Graeme McDowell (NIR)	71-75-68-72—286	33,400
	Julien Quesne (FRA)	71-71-71-73—286	33,400
	Rafa Cabrera-Bello (ESP)	75-69-76-67—287	30,713
	Greg Chalmers (AUS)	71-71-68-77—287	30,713
	Brendan Jones (AUS)	74-69-70-74—287	30,713
	Jeev Milkha Singh (IND)	72-71-73-71—287	30,713
	Mark Wilson (USA)	73-74-69-71—287	30,713
51	Robert Garrigus (USA)	76-68-69-75—288	29,177
	Brad Kennedy (AUS)	73-77-67-71—288	29,177
	Geoff Ogilvy (AUS)	75-74-72-67—288	29,177
54	Nicolas Colsaerts (BEL)	73-73-71-72—289	28,217
	Han Lee (USA)	73-70-75-71—289	28,217
56	Robert Allenby (AUS)	76-72-69-73—290	26,682
	George Coetzee (RSA)	73-76-68-73—290	26,682
	Hyung-Sung Kim (KOR)	78-70-70-72—290	26,682
	Garth Mulroy (RSA)	70-74-73-73—290	26,682
	Jaco Van Zyl (RSA)	74-75-70-71—290	26,682
	Xin-Jun Zhang (CHN)	75-69-76-70—290	26,682
62	Branden Grace (RSA)	75-76-70-70—291	24,954
	Hennie Otto (RSA)	76-73-71-71—291	24,954
	Danny Willett (ENG)	74-73-71-73—291	24,954
65	Alvaro Quiros (ESP)	72-76-68-76—292	23,802
	Richie Ramsay (SCO)	78-71-72-71—292	23,802
	Kyle Stanley (USA)	79-70-74-69—292	23,802
68	Jbe Kruger (RSA)	83-72-71-67—293	23,034
69	Kenichi Kuboya (JPN)	77-83-66-69—295	22,267
	David Lynn (ENG)	76-69-73-77—295	22,267
	Toshinori Muto (JPN)	74-71-76-74—295	22,267
72	Yuta Ikeda (JPN)	70-70-82-75—297	21,115
	David Lipsky (USA)	78-74-69-76—297	21,115
	Robert Rock (ENG)	78-70-76-73—297	21,115
75	Johnson Wagner (USA)	75-74-73-76—298	20,347
76	Mohd Siddikur (BAN)	77-76-76-72—301	19,963
77	Mu Hu (CHN)	79-74-79-75—307	19,579
78	Masanori Kobayashi (JPN)	72-77-WD—149	

2006 David Howell (ENG)
2007 Yang-Eun Yang (KOR)
2008 Phil Mickelson (USA)*
**Beat Ross Fisher (ENG) at 2nd extra hole*

2008 (2009 season)
Sergio García (ESP)*
**Beat O Wilson (ENG) at 2nd extra hole*
2009 Phil Mickelson (USA)

2010 F Molinari (ITA)
2011 M Kaymer (GER)

DP World Tour Championship, Dubai *Jumeirah Golf Estates, Dubai, UAE*

Full results can be found on page 160

International Team Events 2012

39th Ryder Cup *Medinah, Chicago, Illinois* September 28–30 [7668–72]

The 2012 Ryder Cup played at the Medinah Club in Chicago was one of the closest, most enthralling, dramatic, nail-biting matches of all time with the Europeans, led by Spaniard José Maria Olazábal, staging a last day-fight back that enabled them to keep the Cup. It was Europe's seventh win in the last nine matches but for two days the Americans, led by Davis Love III, were in control and looked unbeatable.

The Americans led 5–3 after the first series of foursomes and four-balls then took the second series of foursomes 3–1 to lead 8–4.

For most of the Saturday afternoon it looked as if the home side might take the second series of four-balls 4–0 and take a stranglehold on the outcome of the match until, late in the afternoon, Sergio García and Luke Donald beat Tiger Woods and Steve Stricker and Ian Poulter and Rory McIlroy beat Jason Dufner and Zach Johnson. Poulter holed birdie putts on the last five greens as the day ended with the Americans still ahead 10–6.

They were still the bookmakers' favourites to bring the Cup home but the Europeans had not lost hope. They were determined to battle on in the way the late Seve Ballesteros used to do in those matches. The two late points the team won on Saturday afternoon were crucial.

Olazábal had hoped to win the first five points in the 12 singles on Sunday and Donald, Poulter, McIlroy, Rose and Lawrie duly obliged. European rookie Nicholas Colsaerts, Graeme McDowell and Peter Hanson lost their games but García beat Furyk, Westwood found his game to beat Kuchar, Kaymer holed the putt on the last against Steve Stricker that ensured a drawn match and retention of the Cup and Francisco Molinari had a last green win over former world No 1 Tiger Woods to give Europe a well-deserved if unexpected victory.

It was the Miracle of Medinah.

For full report see pages 25–28

Non-playing captains: USA: David Love III; Europe: José Maria Olazábal (ESP)

***First day* – Foursomes:**
Jim Furyk & Brandt Snedeker lost to Rory McIlroy & Graeme McDowell 1 up
Phil Mickelson & Keegan Bradley beat Luke Donald & Sergio García lost to 4 and 3
Jason Dufner & Zach Johnson beat Lee Westwood & Francesco Molinari 3 and 2
Tiger Woods & Steve Stricker lost to Ian Poulter & Justin Rose 2 and 1

Fourballs:
Bubba Watson & Webb Simpson beat Paul Lawrie and Peter Hanson 5 and 4
Phil Mickelson & Keegan Bradley beat Rory McIlroy & Graeme McDowell 2 and 1
Tiger Woods & Steve Stricker lost to Lee Westwood & Nicolas Colsaerts 1 up
Dustin Johnson & Matt Kuchar beat Justin Rose & Martin Kaymer 3 and 2

Match position: USA 5, Europe 3

***Second day* – Foursomes:**
Bubba Watson & Webb Simpson lost to Justin Rose & Ian Poulter 1 up
Keegan Bradley & Phil Mickelson beat Lee Westwood & Luke Donald 7 and 6
Jason Dufner & Zach Johnson beat Nicolas Colsaerts & Sergio García 2 and 1
Jim Furyk & Brandt Snedeker beat Rory McIlroy & Graeme McDowell 1 up

Fourballs:
Dustin Johnson & Matt Kuchar beat Nicolas Colsaerts & Paul Lawrie 1 up
Bubba Watson & Webb Simpson beat Justin Rose & Francesco Molinari 5 and 4
Tiger Woods & Steve Stricker lost to Sergio García & Luke Donald 1 up
Jason Dufner & Zach Johnson lost to Rory McIlroy & Ian Poulter 1 up

Match position: USA 10, Europe 6

***Third day* – Singles:**
Bubba Watson lost to Luke Donald (ENG) 2 and 1
Webb Simpson lost to Ian Poulter (ENG) 2 up
Keegan Bradley lost to Rory McIlroy (NIR) 2 and 1
Phil Mickelson lost to Justin Rose (ENG) 1 up
Brandt Snedeker lost to Paul Lawrie (SCO) 5 and 3
Dustin Johnson beat Nicolas Colsaerts (BEL) 3 and 2
Zach Johnson beat Graeme McDowell (NIR) 2 and 1
Jim Furyk lost to Sergio García (ESP) 1 up
Jason Dufner beat Peter Hanson (SWE) 2 up
Matt Kuchar lost to Lee Westwood (ENG) 3 and 2
Steve Stricker lost to Martin Kaymer (GER) 1 up
Tiger Woods halved with Francesco Molinari (ITA)

Result: Europe 14½, USA 13½

Ryder Cup – inaugurated 1927

2010 *Celtic Manor, Wales* Oct 1–4

Result: Europe 14½, USA 13½

Captains: Colin Montgomerie (Eur), Corey Pavin (USA)

Heavy rain delayed play from the first day forcing a departure from the customary format, requiring an extra day to complete all the matches

***First Session* – Fourballs**
Westwood & Kaymer beat Mickelson & Johnson 3 and 2
McIlroy & McDowell halved with Cink & Kuchar
Poulter & Fisher lost to Stricker & Woods 2 holes
Donald & Harrington lost to Watson & Overton 3 and 2

***Second Session* – Foursomes**
E Molinari & F Molinari lost to Johnson & Mahan 2 holes
Westwood & Kaymer halved with Furyk & Fowler
Harrington & Fisher beat Mickelson & Johnson 3 and 2
Jiménez & Hanson lost to Stricker & Woods 4 and 3
Poulter & Donald Bubba Watson & Overton 2 and 1
McIlroy & McDowell lost to Cink & Kuchar 1 hole

***Third Session* – Foursomes**
Donald & Westwood beat Stricker & Woods 6 and 5
McIlroy & McDowell beat Johnson & Mahan 3 and 1

Fourballs
Harrington & Fisher beat Furyk & Johnson 2 and 1
Jiménez & Hanson beat Watson & Overton 2 holes
E Molinari & F Molinari halved with Cink & Kuchar
Poulter & Kaymer beat Mickelson & Fowler 2 and 1

***Fourth Session* – Singles**
Lee Westwood (ENG) lost to Steve Stricker 2 and 1
Rory McIlroy (NIR) halved with Stewart Cink
Luke Donald (ENG) beat Jim Furyk 1 hole
Martin Kaymer (GER) lost to Dustin Johnson 6 and 4
Ian Poulter (ENG) beat Matt Kuchar 5 and 4
Ross Fisher (ENG) lost to Jeff Overton 3 and 2
Miguel Angel Jiménez (ESP) beat Bubba Watson 4 and 3
Francesco Molinari (ITA) lost to Tiger Woods 4 and 3
Edoardo Molinari (ITA) halved with Rikki Fowler
Peter Hanson (SWE) lost to Phil Mickelson 4 and 2
Padraig Harrington (IRL) lost to Zach Johnson 3 and 2
Graeme McDowell (NIR) beat Hunter Mahan 2 and 1

2008 *Valhalla, Louisville, KY* Sept 18–20

Result: USA 16½, Europe 11½

Captains: Paul Azinger (USA), Nick Faldo (Eur)

***First Day, Morning* – Foursomes**
Mickelson & Kim halved with Harrington & Karlsson
Leonard & Mahan beat Stenson & Casey 3 and 2
Cink & Campbell beat Poulter & Rose 1 hole
Perry & Furyk halved with Westwood & García

***Afternoon* – Fourballs**
Mickelson & Kim beat Harrington & McDowell 2 holes
Stricker & Curtis lost to Poulter & Rose 4 and 2
Leonard & Mahan beat García & Jiménez 4 and 3
Holmes & Weekley halved with Westwood & Hansen

***Second Day, Morning* – Foursomes**
Cink & Campbell lost to Poulter & Rose 4 and 3
Leonard & Mahan halved with Jiménez & McDowell
Mickelson & Kim lost to Stenson & Wilson 2 and 1
Perry & Furyk beat Harrington & Karlsson 3 and 1

***Afternoon* – Fourballs**
Holmes & Weekley beat Westwood & Hansen 2 and 1
Stricker & Curtis halved with García & Casey
Perry & Furyk lost to Poulter & McDowell 1 hole
Mickelson & Mahan halved withStenson & Karlsson

***Third Day* – Singles**
Anthony Kim beat Sergio García (ESP) 5 and 4
Hunter Mahan halved with Paul Casey (ENG)
Justin Leonard lost to Robert Karlsson (SWE) 5 and 3
Phil Mickelson lost to Justin Rose (ENG) 3 and 2
Kenny Perry beat Henrik Stenson (SWE) 3 and 2
Boo Weekley beat Oliver Wilson (ENG) 4 and 2
J B Holmes beat Søren Hansen (DEN) 2 and 1
Jim Furyk beat Miguel Angel Jiménez (ESP) 2 and 1
Stewart Cink lost to Graeme McDowell (NIR) 2 and 1
Steve Stricker lost to Ian Poulter (ENG) 3 and 2
Ben Curtis beat Lee Westwood (ENG) 2 and 1
Chad Campbell beat Padraig Harrington (IRL) 2 and 1

2006 *K Club, Straffan, Ireland* Sept 22–24

Result: Europe 18½, USA 9½

Captains: Ian Woosnam (Eur), Tom Lehman (USA)

***First Day, Morning* – Fourballs**
Harrington & Montgomerie lost to Woods & Furyk 1 hole
Casey & Karlsson halved with Cink & Henry
García & Olazábal beat Toms & Wetterich 3 and 2
Clarke & Westwood beat Mickelson & DiMarco 1 hole

***Afternoon* – Foursomes**
Harrington & McGinley halved with Campbell & Johnson
Howell & Stenson halved with Cink & Toms
Westwood & Montgomerie halved with Mickelson & DiMarco
Donald & García beat Woods & Furyk 2 holes

***Second Day, Morning* – Fourballs**
Casey & Karlsson halved with Cink & Henry
García & Olazábal beat Mickelson & DiMarco 3 and 2
Clarke & Westwood beat Woods & Furyk 3 and 2
Stenson & Harrington lost to Verplank & Johnson 2 and 1

2006 *continued*

***Afternoon* – Foursomes**

García & Donald beat Mickelson & Toms 2 and 1
Montgomerie & Westwood halved with Campbell & Taylor
Casey & Howell beat Cink & Johnson 5 and 4
Harrington & McGinley lost to Woods & Furyk 3 and 2

***Third Day* – Singles**

Colin Montgomerie (SCO) beat David Toms 1 hole
Sergio García (ESP) lost to Stewart Cink 4 and 3
Paul Casey (ENG) beat Jim Furyk 2 and 1
Robert Karlsson (SWE) lost to Tiger Woods 3 and 2
Luke Donald (ENG) beat Chad Campbell 2 and 1
Paul McGinley (IRL) halved with JJ Henry
Darren Clarke (NIR) beat Zach Johnson 3 and 2
Henrik Stenson (SWE) beat Vaughn Taylor 4 and 3
David Howell (ENG) beat Brett Wetterich 5 and 4
José María Olazábal (ESP) beat Phil Mickelson 2 and 1
Lee Westwood (ENG) beat Chris DiMarco 2 holes
Padraig Harrington (IRL) lost to Scott Verplank 4 and 3

2004 *Oakland Hills Country Club, Bloomfield, Detroit, MI, USA* Sept 17–19

Result: USA 9½, Europe 18½

Captains: Hal Sutton (USA), Bernhard Langer (Eur)

***First Day*, Morning – Fourball**

Woods & Mickelson lost to Montgomerie & Harrington 2 and 1
Love & Campbell lost to Clarke & Jiménez 5 and 4
Riley & Cink halved with McGinley & Donald
Toms & Furyk lost to García & Westwood 5 and 3

Afternoon – Foursomes

DiMarco & Haas beat Jiménez & Levet 3 and 2
Love & Funk lost to Montgomerie & Harrington 4 and 2
Mickelson & Woods lost to Clarke & Westwood 1 hole
Perry & Cink lost to García & Donald 2 and 1

***Second Day*, Morning – Fourball**

Haas & DiMarco halved with García & Westwood
Woods & Riley beat Clarke & Poulter 4 and 3
Furyk & Campbell lost to Casey & Howell 1 hole
Cink & Love beat Montgomerie & Harrington 3 and 2

Afternoon – Foursomes

DiMarco & Haas lost to Clarke & Westwood 5 and 4
Mickelson & Toms beat Jiménez & Levet 4 and 3
Funk & Furyk lost to Donald & García 1 hole
Love & Woods lost to Harrington & McGinley 4 and 3

***Third Day* – Singles**

Tiger Woods beat Paul Casey (ENG) 3 and 2
Phil Mickelson lost to Sergio García (ESP) 3 and 2
Davis Love III halved with Darren Clarke (NIR)
Jim Furyk beat David Howell (ENG) 6 and 4
Kenny Perry lost to Lee Westwood (ENG) 1 hole
David Toms lost to Colin Montgomerie (SCO) 1 hole
Chad Campbell beat Luke Donald (ENG) 5 and 3
Chris DiMarco beat Miguel Angel Jiménez (ESP) 1 hole
Fred Funk lost to Thomas Levet (FRA) 1 hole
Chris Riley lost to Ian Poulter (ENG) 3 and 2
Jay Haas lost to Padraig Harrington (IRL 1 hole
Stewart Cink lost to Paul McGinley (IRL) 3 and 2

2002 *The Brabazon Course, The De Vere Belfry, Sutton Coldfield, West Midlands, England* Sept

Result: Europe 13½, USA 12½

Captains: Sam Torrance (Eur), Curtis Strange (USA)

First Day, Morning – Fourball

Bjørn & Clarke beat Azinger & Woods 1 hole
García & Westwood beat Duval & Love 4 and 3
Langer & Montgomerie beat Furyk & Hoch 4 and 3
Fasth & Harrington lost to Mickelson & Toms 1 hole

Afternoon – Foursomes

Bjørn & Clarke lost to Sutton & Verplank 2 and 1
García & Westwood beat Calcavecchia & Woods 2 and 1
Langer & Montgomerie halved with Mickelson & Toms
Harrington & McGinley lost to Cink & Furyk 3 and 2

Second Day, Morning – Foursomes

Fulke & Price lost to Mickelson & Toms 2 and 1
García & Westwood beat Cink & Furyk 2 and 1
Langer & Montgomerie beat Hoch & Verplank 1 hole
Bjørn & Clarke lost to Love & Woods 4 and 3

Afternoon – Fourball

Fasth & Parnevik lost to Calcavecchia & Duval 1 hole
García & Westwood lost to Love & Woods 1 hole
Harrington & Montgomerie beat Mickelson & Toms 2 and 1
Clarke & McGinley halved with Furyk & Hoch

Third Day – Singles

Colin Montgomerie (SCO) beat Scott Hoch 5 and 4
Sergio García (ESP) lost to David Toms 1 hole
Darren Clarke (NIR) halved with David Duval
Bernhard Langer (GER) beat Hal Sutton 4 and 3
Padraig Harrington (IRL) beat Mark Calcavecchia 5 and 4
Thomas Bjørn (DEN) beat Stewart Cink 2 and 1
Lee Westwood (ENG) lost to Scott Verplank 2 and 1
Niclas Fasth (Swe) halved with Paul Azinger
Paul McGinley (IRL) halved with Jim Furyk
Pierre Fulke (SWE) halved with Davis Love III
Phillip Price (WAL) beat Phil Mickelson 3 and 2
Jesper Parnevik (SWE) halved with Tiger Woods

1999 *The Country Club, Brookline, MA., USA* Sept 24–26

Result: USA 14½, Europe 13½

Captains: Ben Crenshaw (USA), Mark James (Eur)

First Day: Morning – Foursomes

Duval & Mickelson lost to Montgomerie & Lawrie 3 and 2
Lehman & Woods lost to Parnevik & García 2 and 1
Love & Stewart halved with Jiménez & Harrington
Sutton & Maggert beat Clarke & Westwood 3 and 2

Afternoon – Fourball

Love & Leonard halved with Montgomerie & Lawrie
Mickelson & Furyk lost to Parnevik & García 1 hole
Sutton & Maggert lost to Jiménez & Olazábal 2 and 1
Duval & Woods lost to Clarke & Westwood 1 hole

Second Day: Morning – Foursomes

Sutton & Maggert beat Montgomerie & Lawrie 1 hole
Furyk & O'Meara lost to Clarke & Westwood 3 and 2
Pate & Woods beat Jiménez & Harrington 1 hole
Stewart & Leonard lost to Parnevik & García 3 and 2

Afternoon – Fourball

Mickelson & Lehman beat Clarke & Westwood 2 and 1
Love & Duval halved with Parnevik & García
Leonard & Sutton halved with Jiménez & Olazábal
Pate & Woods lost to Montgomerie & Lawrie 2 and 1

Third Day – Singles

Tom Lehman beat Lee Westwood 3 and 2
Hal Sutton beat Darren Clarke 4 and 2
Phil Mickelson beat Jarmo Sandelin 4 and 3
Davis Love III beat Jean Van de Velde 6 and 5
Tiger Woods beat Andrew Coltart 3 and 2

David Duval beat Jesper Parnevik 5 and 4
Mark O'Meara lost to Padraig Harrington 1 hole
Steve Pate beat Miguel Angel Jiménez 2 and 1
Justin Leonard halved with José Maria Olazábal
Payne Stewart lost to Colin Montgomerie 1 hole
Jim Furyk beat Sergio García 4 and 3
Jeff Maggert lost to Paul Lawrie 4 and 3

1997 *Valderrama Golf Club, Sotogrande, Cadiz, Spain* Sept 26–28

Result: Europe 14½, USA 13½

Captains: Seve Ballesteros (Eur), Tom Kite (USA)

First Day: Morning – Fourball
Olazábal & Rocca beat Love & Mickelson 1 hole
Faldo & Westwood lost to Couples & Faxon 1 hole
Parnevik & Johansson beat Lehman & Furyk 1 hole
Montgomerie & Langer lost to Woods & O'Meara 3 and 2

Afternoon – Foursomes
Rocca & Olazábal lost to Hoch & Janzen 1 hole
Langer & Montgomerie beat O'Meara & Woods 5 and 3
Faldo & Westwood beat Leonard & Maggert 3 and 2
Parnevik & Garrido halved with Lehman & Mickelson

Second Day: Morning – Fourball
Montgomerie & Clarke beat Couples & Love 1 hole
Woosnam & Bjørn beat Leonard & Faxon 2 and 1
Faldo & Westwood beat Woods & O'Meara 2 and 1
Olazábal & Garrido halved with Mickelson & Lehman

Afternoon – Foursomes
Montgomerie & Langer beat Janzen & Furyk 1 hole
Faldo & Westwood lost to Hoch & Maggert 2 and 1
Parnevik & Garrido halved with Leonard & Woods
Olazábal & Rocca beat Love & Couples 5 and 4

Third Day – Singles
Ian Woosnam lost to Fred Couples 8 and 7
Per-Ulrik Johansson beat Davis Love III 3 and 2
Costantino Rocca beat Tiger Woods 4 and 2
Thomas Bjørn halved with Justin Leonard
Darren Clarke lost to Phil Mickelson 2 and 1
Jesper Parnevik lost to Mark O'Meara 5 and 4
José Maria Olazábal lost to Lee Janzen 1 hole
Bernhard Langer beat Brad Faxon 2 and 1
Lee Westwood lost to Jeff Maggert 3 and 2
Colin Montgomerie halved with Scott Hoch
Nick Faldo lost to Jim Furyk 3 and 2
Ignacio Garrido lost to Tom Lehman 7 and 6

1995 *Oak Hill Country Club, Rochester, NY, USA* Sept 22–24

Result: USA 13½, Europe 14½

Captains: Lanny Wadkins (USA), Bernard Gallacher (Eur)

First Day: Morning – Foursomes
Pavin & Lehman beat Faldo & Montgomerie 1 hole
Haas & Couples lost to Torrance & Rocca 3 and 2
Love & Maggert beat Clark & James 4 and 3
Crenshaw & Strange lost to Langer & Johansson 1 hole

Afternoon – Fourball
Faxon & Jacobsen lost to Gilford & Ballesteros 4 and 3
Maggert & Roberts beat Torrance & Rocca 6 and 5
Couples & Love beat Faldo & Montgomerie 3 and 2
Pavin & Mickelson beat Langer & Johansson 6 and 4

Second Day: Morning – Foursomes
Haas & Strange lost to Faldo & Montgomerie 4 and 2
Love & Maggert lost to Torrance & Rocca 6 and 5
Roberts & Jacobsen beat Woosnam & Walton 1 hole
Pavin & Lehman lost to Langer & Gilford 4 and 3

Afternoon – Fourball
Faxon & Couples beat Torrance & Montgomerie 4 and 2
Love & Crenshaw lost to Woosnam & Rocca 3 and 2
Haas & Mickelson beat Ballesteros & Gilford 3 and 2
Pavin & Roberts beat Faldo & Langer 1 hole

Third Day – Singles
Tom Lehman beat Seve Ballesteros 4 and 3
Peter Jacobsen lost to Howard Clark 1 hole
Jeff Maggert lost to Mark James 4 and 3
Fred Couples halved with Ian Woosnam
Davis Love III beat Costantino Rocca 3 and 2
Brad Faxon lost to David Gilford 1 hole
Ben Crenshaw lost to Colin Montgomerie 3 and 1
Nick Faldo beat Curtis Strange 1 hole
Loren Roberts lost to Sam Torrance 2 and 1
Corey Pavin beat Bernhard Langer 3 and 2
Jay Haas lost to Philip Walton 1 hole
Phil Mickelson beat Per-Ulrik Johansson 2 and 1

1993 *The Brabazon Course, The De Vere Belfry, Sutton Coldfield, West Midlands, England* Sept 24–26

Result: Europe 13, USA 15

Captains: Bernard Gallacher (Eur), Tom Watson (USA)

***First Day:* Morning – Foursomes**
Torrance & James lost to Wadkins & Pavin 4 and 3
Woosnam & Langer beat Azinger & Stewart 7 and 5
Ballesteros & Olazábal lost to Kite & Love 2 and 1
Faldo & Montgomerie beat Floyd & Couples 4 and 3

Afternoon – Fourball
Woosnam & Baker beat Gallagher & Janzen 1 hole
Lane & Langer lost to Wadkins & Pavin 4 and 2
Faldo & Montgomerie halved with Azinger & Couples
Ballesteros & Olazábal beat Kite & Love 4 and 3

***Second Day:* Morning – Foursomes**
Faldo & Montgomerie beat Wadkins & Pavin 3 and 2
Langer & Woosnam beat Couples & Azinger 2 and 1
Baker & Lane lost to Floyd & Stewart 3 and 2
Ballesteros & Olazábal beat Kite & Love 2 and 1

Afternoon – Fourball
Faldo & Montgomerie lost to Beck & Cook 2 holes
James & Rocca lost to Pavin & Gallagher 5 and 4
Woosnam & Baker beat Couples & Azinger 6 and 5
Olazábal & Haeggman lost to Floyd & Stewart 2 and 1

***Third Day* – Singles**
Ian Woosnam halved with Fred Couples
Barry Lane lost to Chip Beck 1 hole
Colin Montgomerie beat Lee Janzen 1 hole
Peter Baker beat Corey Pavin 2 holes
Joakim Haeggman beat J Cook 1 hole
Sam Torrance (withdrawn at start of day) halved with Lanny Wadkins (withdrawn at start of day)
Mark James lost to Payne Stewart 3 and 2
Constantino Rocca lost to Davis Love III 1 hole
Seve Ballesteros lost to Jim Gallagher Jr 3 and 2
José Maria Olazábal lost to Ray Floyd 2 holes
Bernhard Langer lost to Tom Kite 5 and 3
Nick Faldo halved with Paul Azinger

1991 *The Ocean Course, Kiawah Island, SC, USA* Sept 26–29

Result: USA 14½, Europe 13½

Captains: Dave Stockton (USA), Bernard Gallacher (Eur)

***First Day:* Morning – Foursomes**
Azinger & Beck lost to Ballesteros & Olazábal 2 and 1
Floyd & Couples beat Langer & James 2 and 1

1991 *continued*

***First Day:* Morning – Foursomes (continued)**
Wadkins & Irwin beat Gilford & Montgomerie 4 and 2
Stewart & Calcavecchia beat Faldo & Woosnam 1 hole

Afternoon – Fourball
Wadkins & O'Meara halved with Torrance & Feherty
Azinger & Beck lost to Ballesteros & Olazábal 2 and 1
Pavin & Calcavecchia lost to Richardson & James 5 and 4
Floyd & Couples beat Faldo & Woosnam 5 and 3

***Second Day:* Morning – Foursomes**
Irwin & Wadkins beat Torrance & Feherty 4 and 2
Calcavecchia & Stewart beat James & Richardson 1 hole
Azinger & O'Meara beat Faldo & Gilford 7 and 6
Couples & Floyd lost to Ballesteros & Olazábal 3 and 2

Afternoon – Fourball
Azinger & Irwin lost to Woosnam & Broadhurst 2 and 1
Pate & Pavin lost to Langer & Montgomerie 2 and 1
Wadkins & Levi lost to James & Richardson 3 and 1
Couples & Stewart halved with Ballesteros & Olazábal

***Third Day* – Singles**
Ray Floyd lost to Nick Faldo 2 holes
Payne Stewart lost to David Feherty 2 and 1
Mark Calcavecchia halved with Colin Montgomerie
Paul Azinger beat José Maria Olazábal 2 holes
Corey Pavin beat Steven Richardson 2 and 1
Wayne Levi lost to Seve Ballesteros 3 and 2
Chip Beck beat Ian Woosnam 3 and 1
Mark O'Meara lost to Paul Broadhurst 3 and 1
Fred Couples beat Sam Torrance 3 and 2
Lanny Wadkins beat Mark James 3 and 2
Hale Irwin halved with Bernhard Langer
Steve Pate (withdrawn – injured) halved with David Gilford (withdrawn)

1989 *The Brabazon Course, The De Vere Belfry, Sutton Coldfield, West Midlands, England* Sept 22–24

Result: Europe 14, USA 14
Captains: Tony Jacklin (Eur), Ray Floyd (USA)

***First Day:* Foursomes – Morning**
Faldo & Woosnam halved with Kite & Strange
Clark & James lost to Stewart & Wadkins 1 hole
Ballesteros & Olazábal halved with Beck & Watson
Langer & Rafferty lost to Calcavecchia & Green 2 and 1

Fourball – Afternoon
Brand & Torrance beat Azinger & Strange 1 hole
Clark & James beat Couples & Wadkins 3 and 2
Faldo & Woosnam beat Calcavecchia & McCumber 1 hole
Ballesteros & Olazábal beat O'Meara & Watson 6 and 5

***Second Day:* Foursomes – Morning**
Faldo & Woosnam beat Stewart & Wadkins 3 and 2
Brand & Torrance lost to Azinger & Beck 4 and 3
O'Connor & Rafferty lost to Calcavecchia & Green 3 and 2
Ballesteros & Olazábal beat Kite & Strange 1 hole

Fourball – Afternoon
Faldo & Woosnam lost to Azinger & Beck 2 and 1
Canizares & Langer lost to Kite & McCumber 2 and 1
Clark & James beat Stewart & Strange 1 hole
Ballesteros & Olazábal beat Calcavecchia & Green 4 and 2

***Third Day:* Singles**
Seve Ballesteros lost to Paul Azinger 1 hole
Bernhard Langer lost to Chip Beck 3 and 1
José Maria Olazábal beat Payne Stewart 1 hole
Ronan Rafferty beat Mark Calvecchia 1 hole
Howard Clark lost to Tom Kite 8 and 7
Mark James beat Mark O'Meara 3 and 2
Christy O'Connor Jr beat Fred Couples 1 hole
José Maria Canizares beat Ken Green 1 hole
Gordon Brand Jr lost to Mark McCumber 1 hole
Sam Torrance lost to Tom Watson 3 and 1
Nick Faldo lost to Lanny Wadkins 1 hole
Ian Woosnam lost to Curtis Strange 1 hole

1987 *Muirfield Village Golf Club, Dublin, OH, USA* Sept 25–27

Result: Europe 15, USA 13
Captains: Jack Nicklaus (USA), Tony Jacklin (Eur)

***First Day:* Foursomes – Morning**
Kite & Strange beat Clark & Torrance 4 and 2
Pohl & Sutton beat Brown & Langer 2 and 1
Mize & Wadkins lost to Faldo & Woosnam 2 holes
Nelson & Stewart lost to Ballesteros & Olazábal 1 hole

Fourball – Afternoon
Crenshaw & Simpson lost to Brand & Rivero 3 and 2
Bean & Calcavecchia lost to Langer & Lyle 1 hole
Pohl & Sutton lost to Faldo & Woosnam 2 and 1
Kite & Strange lost to Ballesteros & Olazábal 2 and 1

***Second Day:* Foursomes – Morning**
Kite & Strange beat Brand & Rivero 3 and 1
Mize & Sutton halved with Faldo & Woosnam
Nelson & Wadkins lost to Langer & Lyle 2 and 1
Crenshaw & Stewart lost to Ballesteros & Olazábal 1 hole

Fourball – Afternoon
Kite & Strange lost to Faldo & Woosnam 5 and 4
Bean & Stewart beat Brand & Darcy 3 and 2
Mize & Sutton beat Ballesteros & Olazábal 2 and 1
Nelson & Wadkins lost to Langer & Lyle 1 hole

***Third Day:* Singles**
Andy Bean beat Ian Woosnam 1 hole
Dan Pohl lost to Howard Clark 1 hole
Larry Mize halved with Sam Torrance
Mark Calcavecchia beat Nick Faldo 1 hole
Payne Stewart beat José Maria Olazábal 2 holes
Scott Simpson beat José Rivero 2 and 1
Tom Kite beat Sandy Lyle 3 and 2
Ben Crenshaw lost to Eamonn Darcy 1 hole
Larry Nelson halved with Bernhard Langer
Curtis Strange lost to Seve Ballesteros 2 and 1
Lanny Wadkins beat Ken Brown 3 and 2
Hal Sutton halved with Gordon Brand Jr

1985 *The Brabazon Course, The De Vere Belfry, Sutton Coldfield, West Midlands, England* Sept 13–15

Result: Europe 16½, USA 11½
Captains: Tony Jacklin (Eur), Lee Trevino (USA)

***First Day:* Foursomes – Morning**
Ballesteros & Pinero beat Strange & O'Meara 2 and 1
Faldo & Langer lost to Kite & Peete 3 and 2
Brown & Lyle lost to Floyd & Wadkins 4 and 3
Clark & Torrance lost to Stadler & Sutton 3 and 2

Fourball – Afternoon
Way & Woosnam beat Green & Zoeller 1 hole
Ballesteros & Pinero beat Jacobsen & North 2 and 1
Canizares & Langer halved with Stadler & Sutton
Clark & Torrance lost to Floyd & Wadkins 1 hole

Second Day: Fourball – Morning
Clark & Torrance beat Kite & North 2 and 1
Way & Woosnam beat Green & Zoeller 4 and 3
Ballesteros & Pinero lost to O'Meara & Wadkins 3 and 2
Langer & Lyle halved with Stadler & Strange

Foursomes – Afternoon
Canizares & Rivero beat Kite & Peete 7 and 5
Ballesteros & Pinero beat Stadler & Sutton 5 and 4
Way & Woosnam lost to Jacobsen & Strange 4 and 3
Brown & Langer beat Floyd & Wadkins 3 and 2

***Third Day:* Singles**
Manuel Pinero beat Lanny Wadkins 3 and 1
Ian Woosnam lost to Craig Stadler 2 and 1
Paul Way beat Ray Floyd 2 holes
Seve Ballesteros halved with Tom Kite
Sandy Lyle beat Peter Jacobsen 3 and 2
Bernhard Langer beat Hal Sutton 5 and 4
Sam Torrance beat Andy North 1 hole
Howard Clark beat Mark O'Meara 1 hole
Nick Faldo lost to Hubert Green 3 and 1
José Rivero lost to Calvin Peete 1 hole
José Maria Canizares beat Fuzzy Zoeller 2 holes
Ken Brown lost to Curtis Strange 4 and 2

1983 *PGA National Golf Club, Palm Beach Gardens, FL, USA* Oct 14–16

Result: USA 14½, Europe 13½
Captains: Jack Nicklaus (USA), Tony Jacklin (Eur)

***First Day:* Foursomes – Morning**
Watson & Crenshaw beat Gallacher & Lyle 5 and 4
Wadkins & Stadler lost to Faldo & Langer 4 and 2
Floyd & Gilder lost to Canizares & Torrance 4 and 3
Kite & Peete beat Ballesteros & Way 2 and 1

Fourball – Afternoon
Morgan & Zoeller lost to Waites & Brown 2 and 1
Watson & Haas beat Faldo & Langer 2 and 1
Floyd & Strange lost to Ballesteros & Way 1 hole
Crenshaw & Peete halved with Torrance & Woosnam

***Second Day:* Foursomes – Morning**
Floyd & Kite lost to Faldo & Langer 3 and 2
Wadkins & Morgan beat Canizares & Torrance 7 and 5
Gilder & Watson lost to Ballesteros & Way 2 and 1
Haas & Strange beat Waites & Brown 3 and 2

Fourball – Afternoon
Wadkins & Stadler beat Waites & Brown 1 hole
Crenshaw & Peete lost to Faldo & Langer 2 and 1
Haas & Morgan halved with Ballesteros & Way
Gilder & Watson beat Torrance & Woosnam 5 and 4

***Third Day:* Singles**
Fuzzy Zoeller halved with Seve Ballesteros
Jay Haas lost to Nick Faldo 2 and 1
Gil Morgan lost to Bernhard Langer 2 holes
Bob Gilder beat Gordon J Brand 2 holes
Ben Crenshaw beat Sandy Lyle 3 and 1
Calvin Peete beat Brian Waites 1 hole
Curtis Strange lost to Paul Way 2 and 1
Tom Kite halved with Sam Torrance
Craig Stadler beat Ian Woosnam 3 and 2
Lanny Wadkins halved with José Maria Canizares
Ray Floyd lost to Ken Brown 4 and 3
Tom Watson beat Bernard Gallacher 2 and 1

1981 *Walton Heath GC, Tadworth, Surrey, England* Sept 18–20

Result: USA 18½, Europe 9½
Captains: John Jacobs (Eur), Dave Marr (USA)

***First Day:* Foursomes – Morning**
Langer & Pinero lost to Trevino & Nelson 1 hole
Lyle & James beat Rogers & Lietzke 2 and 1
Gallacher & Smyth beat Irwin & Floyd 3 and 2
Oosterhuis & Faldo lost to Watson & Nicklaus 4 and 3

Fourball – Afternoon
Torrance & Clark halved with Kite & Miller
Lyle & James beat Crenshaw & Pate 3 and 2
Smyth & Canizares beat Rogers & Lietzke 6 and 5
Gallacher & Darcy lost to Irwin & Floyd 2 and 1

***Second Day:* Fourball – Morning**
Faldo & Torrance lost to Trevino & Pate 7 and 5
Lyle & James lost to Nelson & Kite 1 hole
Langer & Pinero beat Irwin & Floyd 2 and 1
Smyth & Canizares lost to Watson & Nicklaus 3 and 2

Foursomes – Afternoon
Oosterhuis & Torrance lost to Trevino & Pate 2 and 1
Langer & Pinero lost to Watson & Nicklaus 3 and 2
Lyle & James lost to Rogers & Floyd 3 and 2
Gallacher & Smyth lost to Nelson & Kite 3 and 2

***Third Day:* Singles**
Sam Torrance lost to Lee Trevino 5 and 3
Sandy Lyle lost to Tom Kite 3 and 2
Bernard Gallacher halved with Bill Rogers
Mark James lost to Larry Nelson 2 holes
Des Smyth lost to Ben Crenshaw 6 and 4
Bernhard Langer halved with Bruce Lietzke
Manuel Pinero beat Jerry Pate 4 and 2
José Maria Canizares lost to Hale Irwin 1 hole
Nick Faldo beat Johnny Miller 2 and 1
Howard Clark beat Tom Watson 4 and 3
Peter Oosterhuis lost to Ray Floyd 2 holes
Eamonn Darcy lost to Jack Nicklaus 5 and 3

From 1979 GB&I became a European team

1979 *The Greenbrier, White Sulphur Springs, WV, USA* Sept 14–16

Result: USA 17, Europe 11
Captains: Billy Casper (USA), John Jacobs (Eur)

***First Day:* Fourball – Morning**
Wadkins & Nelson beat Garrido & Ballesteros 2 and 1
Trevino & Zoeller beat Brown & James 3 and 2
Bean & Elder beat Oosterhuis & Faldo 2 and 1
Irwin & Mahaffey lost to Gallacher & Barnes 2 and 1

Foursomes – Afternoon
Irwin & Kite beat Brown & Smyth 7 and 6
Zoeller & Green lost to Garrido & Ballesteros 3 and 2
Trevino & Morgan halved with Lyle & Jacklin
Wadkins & Nelson beat Gallacher & Barnes 4 and 3

***Second Day:* Foursomes – Morning**
Elder & Mahaffey lost to Lyle & Jacklin 5 and 4
Bean & Kite lost to Oosterhuis & Faldo 6 and 5
Zoeller & Hayes halved with Gallacher & Barnes
Wadkins & Nelson beat Garrido & Ballesteros 3 and 2

Fourball – Afternoon
Wadkins & Nelson beat Garrido & Ballesteros 5 and 4
Irwin & Kite beat Lyle & Jacklin 1 hole
Trevino & Zoeller lost to Gallacher & Barnes 3 and 2
Elder & Hayes lost to Oosterhuis & Faldo 1 hole

***Third Day:* Singles**
Lanny Wadkins lost to Bernard Gallacher 3 and 2
Larry Nelson beat Seve Ballesteros 3 and 2
Tom Kite beat Tony Jacklin 1 hole
Mark Hayes beat Antonio Garrido 1 hole
Andy Bean beat Michael King 4 and 3
John Mahaffey beat Brian Barnes 1 hole
Lee Elder lost to Nick Faldo 3 and 2
Hale Irwin beat Des Smyth 5 and 3
Hubert Green beat Peter Oosterhuis 2 holes
Fuzzy Zoeller lost to Ken Brown 1 hole
Lee Trevino beat Sandy Lyle 2 and 1
Gil Morgan, Mark James: injury; match a half

1977 *Royal Lytham & St Annes GC, St Annes, Lancs, England* Sept 15–17

Result: USA 12½, GB&I 7½

Captains: Brian Huggett (GB&I), Dow Finsterwald (USA)

***First Day:* Foursomes**

Gallacher & Barnes lost to Wadkins & Irwin 3 and 1
Coles & Dawson lost to Stockton & McGee 1 hole
Faldo & Oosterhuis beat Floyd & Graham 2 and 1
Darcy & Jacklin halved with Sneed & January
Horton & James lost to Nicklaus & Watson 5 and 4

***Second Day:* Fourball**

Barnes & Horton lost to Watson & Green 5 and 4
Coles & Dawson lost to Sneed & Wadkins 5 and 3
Faldo & Oosterhuis beat Nicklaus & Floyd 3 and 1
Darcy & Jacklin lost to Hill & Stockton 5 and 3
James & Brown lost to Irwin & Graham 1 hole

***Third Day:* Singles**

Howard Clark lost to Lanny Wadkins 4 and 3
Neil Coles lost to Lou Graham 5 and 3
Peter Dawson beat Don January 5 and 4
Brian Barnes beat Hale Irwin 1 hole
Tommy Horton lost to Dave Hill 5 and 4
Bernard Gallacher beat Jack Nicklaus 1 hole
Eamonn Darcy lost to Hubert Green 1 hole
Mark James lost to Ray Floyd 2 and 1
Nick Faldo beat Tom Watson 1 hole
Peter Oosterhuis beat Jerry McGee 2 holes

1975 *Laurel Valley Golf Club, Ligonier, PA, USA* Sept 19–21

Result: USA 21, GB&I 11

Captains: Arnold Palmer (USA), Bernard Hunt (GB&I)

***First Day:* Foursomes – Morning**

Nicklaus & Weiskopf beat Barnes & Gallacher 5 and 4
Littler & Irwin beat Wood & Bembridge 4 and 3
Geiberger & Miller beat Jacklin & Oosterhuis 3 and 1
Trevino & Snead beat Horton & O'Leary 2 and 1

Fourball – Afternoon

Casper & Floyd lost to Jacklin & Oosterhuis 2 and 1
Weiskopf & Graham beat Darcy & Christy O'Connor Jr 3 and 2
Nicklaus & Murphy halved with Barnes & Gallacher
Trevino & Irwin beat Horton & O'Leary 2 and 1

***Second Day:* Fourball – Morning**

Casper & Miller halved with Jacklin & Oosterhuis
Nicklaus & Snead beat Horton & Wood 4 and 2
Littler & Graham beat Barnes & Gallacher 5 and 3
Geiberger & Floyd halved with Darcy & Hunt

Foursomes – Afternoon

Trevino & Murphy lost to Jacklin & Barnes 3 and 2
Weiskopf & Miller beat O'Connor & O'Leary 5 and 3
Irwin & Casper beat Oosterhuis & Bembridge 3 and 2
Geiberger & Graham beat Darcy & Hunt 3 and 2

***Third Day:* Singles – Morning**

Bob Murphy beat Tony Jacklin 2 and 1
Johnny Miller lost to Peter Oosterhuis 2 holes
Lee Trevino halved with Bernard Gallacher
Hale Irwin halved with Tommy Horton
Gene Littler beat Brian Huggett 4 and 2
Billy Casper beat Eamonn Darcy 3 and 2
Tom Weiskopf beat Guy Hunt 5 and 3
Jack Nicklaus lost to Brian Barnes 4 and 2

Singles – Afternoon

Ray Floyd beat Jacklin 1 hole
JC Snead lost to Oosterhuis 3 and 2
Al Geiberger halved with Gallacher
Lou Graham lost to Horton 2 and 1
Irwin beat John O'Leary 2 and 1
Murphy beat Maurice Bembridge 2 and 1
Trevino lost to Norman Wood 2 and 1
Nicklaus lost to Barnes 2 and 1

1973 *Honourable Company of Edinburgh Golfers, Muirfield, Gullane, East Lothian, Scotland* Sept 20–22

Result: USA 19, GB&I 13

Captains: Bernard Hunt (GB&I), Jack Burke (USA)

***First Day:* Foursomes – Morning**

Barnes & Gallacher beat Trevino & Casper 1 hole
O'Connor & Coles beat Weiskopf & Snead 3 and 2
Jacklin & Oosterhuis halved with Rodriguez & Graham
Bembridge & Polland lost to Nicklaus & Palmer 6 and 5

Fourball – Afternoon

Barnes & Gallacher beat Aaron & Brewer 5 and 4
Bembridge & Huggett beat Nicklaus & Palmer 3 and 1
Jacklin & Oosterhuis beat Weiskopf & Casper 3 and 1
O'Connor & Coles lost to Trevino & Blancas 2 and 1

***Second Day:* Foursomes – Morning**

Barnes & Butler lost to Nicklaus & Weiskopf 1 hole
Jacklin & Oosterhuis beat Palmer & Hill 2 holes
Bembridge & Huggett beat Rodriguez & Graham 5 and 4
O'Connor & Coles lost to Trevino & Casper 2 and 1

Fourball – Afternoon

Barnes & Butler lost to Snead & Palmer 2 holes
Jacklin & Oosterhuis lost to Brewer & Casper 3 and 2
Clark & Polland lost to Nicklaus & Weiskopf 3 and 2
Bembridge & Huggett halved with Trevino & Blancas

***Third Day:* Singles – Morning**

Brian Barnes lost to Billy Casper 2 and 1
Bernard Gallacher lost to Tom Weiskopf 3 and 1
Peter Butler lost to Homero Blancas 5 and 4
Tony Jacklin beat Tommy Aaron 3 and 1
Neil Coles halved with Gay Brewer
Christy O'Connor lost to JC Snead 1 hole
Maurice Bembridge halved with Jack Nicklaus
Peter Oosterhuis halved with Lee Trevino

Singles – Afternoon

Brian Huggett beat Blancas 4 and 2
Barnes lost to Snead 3 and 1
Gallacher lost to Brewer 6 and 5
Jacklin lost to Casper 2 and 1
Coles lost to Trevino 6 and 5
O'Connor halved with Weiskopf
Bembridge lost to Nicklaus 2 holes
Oosterhuis beat Arnold Palmer 4 and 2

1971 *Old Warson Country Club, St Louis, MO, USA* Sept 16–18

Result: USA 18½, GB&I 13½

Captains: Jay Hebert (USA), Eric Brown (GB&I)

***First Day:* Foursomes – Morning**

Casper & Barber lost to Coles & O'Connor 2 and 1
Palmer & Dickinson beat Townsend & Oosterhuis 2 holes
Nicklaus & Stockton lost to Huggett & Jacklin 3 and 2
Coody & Beard lost to Bembridge & Butler 1 hole

Foursomes – Afternoon

Casper & Barber lost to Bannerman & Gallacher 2 and 1
Palmer & Dickinson beat Townsend & Oosterhuis 1 hole
Trevino & Rudolph halved with Huggett and Jacklin
Nicklaus & Snead beat Bembridge & Butler 5 and 3

***Second Day:* Fourball – Morning**
Trevino & Rudolph beat O'Connor & Barnes 2 and 1
Beard & Snead beat Coles & John Garner 2 and 1
Palmer & Dickinson beat Oosterhuis & Gallacher 5 and 4
Nicklaus & Littler beat Townsend & Bannerman 2 and 1

Fourball – Afternoon
Trevino & Casper lost to Oosterhuis & Gallacher 1 hole
Littler & Snead beat Huggett & Jacklin 2 and 1
Palmer & Nicklaus beat Townsend & Bannerman 1 hole
Coody & Beard halved with Coles & O'Connor

***Third Day:* Singles – Morning**
Lee Trevino beat Tony Jacklin 1 hole
Dave Stockton halved with Bernard Gallacher
Mason Rudolph lost to Brian Barnes 1 hole
Gene Littler lost to Peter Oosterhuis 4 and 3
Jack Nicklaus beat Peter Townsend 3 and 2
Gardner Dickinson beat Christy O'Connor 5 and 4
Arnold Palmer halved with Harry Bannerman
Frank Beard halved with Neil Coles

Singles – Afternoon
Trevino beat Brian Huggett 7 and 6
JC Snead beat Jacklin 1 hole
Miller Barber lost to Barnes 2 and 1
Stockton beat Townsend 1 hole
Charles Coody lost to Gallacher 2 and 1
Nicklaus beat Coles 5 and 3
Palmer lost to Oosterhuis 3 and 2
Dickinson lost to Bannerman 2 and 1

1969 *Royal Birkdale Golf Club, Southport, Lancs, England* Sept 18–20

Result: USA 16, GB&I 16

Captains: Eric Brown (GB&I), Sam Snead (USA)

***First Day:* Foursomes – Morning**
Coles & Huggett beat Barber & Floyd 3 and 2
Gallacher & Bembridge beat Trevino & Still 2 and 1
Jacklin & Townsend beat Hill & Aaron 3 and 1
O'Connor & Alliss halved with Casper & Beard

Foursomes – Afternoon
Coles & Huggett lost to Hill & Aaron 1 hole
Gallacher & Bembridge lost to Trevino & Littler 2 holes
Jacklin & Townsend beat Casper & Beard 1 hole
Hunt & Butler lost to Nicklaus & Sikes

***Second Day:* Fourball – Morning**
O'Connor & Townsend beat Hill & Douglass 1 hole
Huggett & Alex Caygill halved with Floyd & Barber
Barnes & Alliss lost to Trevino & Littler 1 hole
Jacklin & Coles beat Nicklaus & Sikes 1 hole

Fourball – Afternoon
Townsend & Butler lost to Casper & Beard 2 holes
Huggett & Gallacher lost to Hill & Still 2 and 1
Bembridge & Hunt halved with Aaron & Floyd
Jacklin & Coles halved with Trevino & Barber

***Third Day:* Singles – Morning**
Peter Alliss lost to Lee Trevino 2 and 1
Peter Townsend lost to Dave Hill 5 and 4
Neil Coles beat Tommy Aaron 1 hole
Brian Barnes lost to Billy Casper 1 hole
Christy O'Connor beat Frank Beard 5 and 4
Maurice Bembridge beat Ken Still 1 hole
Peter Butler beat Ray Floyd 1 hole
Tony Jacklin beat Jack Nicklaus 4 and 3

Singles – Afternoon
Barnes lost to Hill 4 and 2
Bernard Gallacher beat Trevino 4 and 3
Bembridge lost to Miller Barber 7 and 6
Butler beat Dale Douglass 3 and 2
O'Connor lost to Gene Littler 2 and 1
Brian Huggett halved with Casper
Coles lost to Dan Sikes 4 and 3
Jacklin halved with Nicklaus

1967 *Champions Golf Club, Houston, TX, USA* Oct 20-22

Result: USA 23½, GB&I 8½

Captains: Ben Hogan (USA), Dai Rees (GB&I)

***First Day:* Foursomes – Morning**
Casper & Boros halved with Huggett & Will
Palmer & Dickinson beat Alliss & O'Connor 2 and 1
Sanders & Brewer lost to Jacklin & Thomas 4 and 3
Nichols & Pott beat Hunt & Coles 6 and 5

Foursomes – Afternoon
Boros & Casper beat Huggett & Will 1 hole
Dickinson & Palmer beat Gregson & Boyle 5 and 4
Littler & Geiberger lost to Jacklin & Thomas 3 and 2
Nichols & Pott beat Alliss & O'Connor 2 and 1

***Second Day:* Fourball – Morning**
Casper & Brewer beat Alliss & O'Connor 3 and 2
Nichols & Pott beat Hunt & Coles 1 hole
Littler & Geiberger beat Jacklin & Thomas 1 hole
Dickinson & Sanders beat Huggett & Will 3 and 2

Fourball – Afternoon
Casper & Brewer beat Hunt & Coles 5 and 3
Dickinson & Sanders beat Alliss & Gregson 4 and 3
Palmer & Boros beat Will & Boyle 1 hole
Littler & Geiberger halved with Jacklin & Thomas

***Third Day:* Singles – Morning**
Gay Brewer beat Hugh Boyle 4 and 3
Billy Casper beat Peter Alliss 2 and 1
Arnold Palmer beat Tony Jacklin 3 and 2
Julius Boros lost to Brian Huggett 1 hole
Doug Sanders lost to Neil Coles 2 and 1
Al Geiberger beat Malcolm Gregson 4 and 2
Gene Littler halved with Dave Thomas
Bobby Nichols halved with Bernard Hunt

Singles – Afternoon
Palmer beat Huggett 5 and 3
Brewer lost to Alliss 2 and 1
Gardner Dickinson beat Jacklin 3 and 2
Nichols beat Christy O'Connor 3 and 2
Johnny Pott beat George Will 3 and 1
Geiberger beat Gregson 2 and 1
Boros halved with Hunt
Sanders lost to Coles 2 and 1

1965 *Royal Birkdale Golf Club, Southport, Lancs, England* Oct 7–9

Result: GB&I 12½, USA 19½

Captains: Harry Weetman (GB&I), Byron Nelson (USA)

***First Day:* Foursomes – Morning**
Thomas & Will beat Marr & Palmer 6 and 5
O'Connor & Alliss beat Venturi & January 5 and 4
Platts & Butler lost to Boros & Lema 1 hole
Hunt & Coles lost to Casper & Littler 2 and 1

Foursomes – Afternoon
Thomas & Will lost to Marr & Palmer 6 and 5
Martin & Hitchcock lost to Boros & Lema 5 and 4
O'Connor & Alliss beat Casper & Littler 2 and 1
Hunt & Coles beat Venturi & January 3 and 2

***Second Day:* Fourball – Morning**
Thomas & Will lost to January & Jacobs 1 hole
Platts & Butler halved with Casper & Littler
Alliss & O'Connor lost to Marr & Palmer 5 and 4
Coles & Hunt beat Boros & Lema 1 hole

1965 *continued*

Fourball – Afternoon
Alliss & O'Connor beat Marr & Palmer 1 hole
Thomas & Will lost to January & Jacobs 1 hole
Platts & Butler halved with Casper & Littler
Coles & Hunt lost to Lema & Venturi 1 hole

***Third Day:* Singles – Morning**
Jimmy Hitchcock lost to Arnold Palmer 3 and 2
Lionel Platts lost to Julius Boros 4 and 2
Peter Butler lost to Tony Lema 1 hole
Neil Coles lost to Dave Marr 2 holes
Bernard Hunt beat Gene Littler 2 holes
Peter Alliss beat Billy Casper 1 hole
Dave Thomas lost to Tommy Jacobs 2 and 1
George Will halved with Don January

Singles – Afternoon
Butler lost to Palmer 2 holes
Hitchcock lost to Boros 2 and 1
Christy O'Connor lost to Lema 6 and 4
Alliss beat Ken Venturi 3 and 1
Hunt lost to Marr 1 hole
Coles beat Casper 3 and 2
Will lost to Littler 2 and 1
Platts beat Jacobs 1 hole

1963 *East Lake CC, Atlanta, GA, USA* Oct 11–13

Result: USA 23, GB&I 9

Captains: Arnold Palmer (USA), John Fallon (GB&I)

***First Day:* Foursomes – Morning**
Palmer & Pott lost to Huggett & Will 3 and 2
Casper & Ragan beat Alliss & O'Connor 1 hole
Boros & Lema halved with Coles & B Hunt
Littler & Finsterwald halved with Thomas & Weetman

Foursomes – Afternoon
Maxwell & Goalby beat Thomas & Weetman 4 and 3
Palmer & Casper beat Huggett & Will 5 and 4
Littler & Finsterwald beat Coles & G Hunt 2 and 1
Boros & Lema beat Haliburton & B Hunt 1 hole

***Second Day:* Fourball – Morning**
Palmer & Finsterwald beat Huggett & Thomas 5 and 4
Littler & Boros halved with Alliss & B Hunt
Casper & Maxwell beat Weetman & Will 3 and 2
Goalby & Ragan lost to Coles & O'Connor 1 hole

Fourball – Afternoon
Palmer & Finsterwald beat Coles & O'Connor 3 and 2
Lema & Pott beat Alliss & B Hunt 1 hole
Casper & Maxwell beat Haliburton & G Hunt 2 and 1
Goalby & Ragan halved with Huggett & Thomas

***Third Day:* Singles – Morning**
Tony Lema beat Geoffrey Hunt 5 and 3
Johnny Pott lost to Brian Huggett 3 and 1
Arnold Palmer lost to Peter Alliss 1 hole
Billy Casper halved with Neil Coles
Bob Goalby beat Dave Thomas 3 and 2
Gene Littler lost to Tom Haliburton 6 and 5
Julius Boros lost to Harry Weetman 1 hole
Dow Finsterwald lost to Bernard Hunt 2 holes

Singles – Afternoon
Arnold Palmer beat George Will 3 and 2
Dave Ragan beat Neil Coles 2 and 1
Tony Lema halved with Peter Alliss
Gene Littler beat Tom Haliburton 6 and 5
Julius Boros beat Harry Weetman 2 and 1
Billy Maxwell beat Christy O'Connor 2 and 1
Dow Finsterwald beat Dave Thomas 4 and 3
Bob Goalby beat Bernard Hunt 2 and 1

1961 *Royal Lytham & St Annes GC, St Annes, Lancs, England* Oct 13–14

Result: USA 14½, GB&I 9½

Captains: Jerry Barber (USA), Dai Rees (GB&I)

***First Day:* Foursomes – Morning**
O'Connor & Alliss beat Littler & Ford 4 and 3
Panton & Hunt lost to Wall & Hebert 4 and 3
Rees & Bousfield lost to Casper & Palmer 2 and 1
Haliburton & Coles lost to Souchak & Collins 1 hole

Foursomes – Afternoon
O'Connor & Alliss lost to Wall & Hebert 1 hole
Panton & Hunt lost to Casper & Palmer 5 and 4
Rees & Bousfield beat Souchak & Collins 4 and 2
Haliburton & Coles lost to Barber & Finsterwald 1 hole

***Second Day:* Singles – Morning**
Harry Weetman lost to Doug Ford 1 hole
Ralph Moffitt lost to Mike Souchak 5 and 4
Peter Alliss halved with Arnold Palmer
Ken Bousfield lost to Billy Casper 5 and 3
Dai Rees beat Jay Hebert 2 and 1
Neil Coles halved with Gene Littler
Bernard Hunt beat Jerry Barber 5 and 4
Christy O'Connor lost to Dow Finsterwald 2 and 1

Singles – Afternoon
Weetman lost to Wall 1 hole
Alliss beat Bill Collins 3 and 2
Hunt lost to Souchak 2 and 1
Tom Haliburton lost to Palmer 2 and 1
Rees beat Ford 4 and 3
Bousfield beat Barber 1 hole
Coles beat Finsterwald 1 hole
O'Connor halved with Littler

1959 *Eldorado Country Club, Palm Desert, CA, USA* Nov 6–7

Result: USA 8½, GB&I 3½

Captains: Sam Snead (USA), Dai Rees (GB&I)

Foursomes
Rosburg & Souchak beat Hunt & Brown 5 and 4
Ford & Wall lost to O'Connor & Alliss 3 and 2
Boros & Finsterwald beat Rees & Bousfield 2 holes
Snead & Middlecoff halved with Weetman & Thomas

Singles
Doug Ford halved with Norman Drew
Mike Souchak beat Ken Bousfield 3 and 2
Bob Rosburg beat Harry Weetman 6 and 5
Sam Snead beat Dave Thomas 6 and 5
Dow Finsterwald beat Dai Rees 1 hole
Jay Hebert halved with Peter Alliss
Art Wall Jr beat Christy O'Connor 7 and 6
Cary Middlecoff lost to Eric Brown 4 and 3

1957 *Lindrick Golf Club, Sheffield, Yorks, England* Oct 4–5

Result: GB&I 7½, USA 4½

Captains: Dai Rees (GB&I), Jack Burke (USA)

Foursomes
Alliss & Hunt lost to Ford & Finsterwald 2 and 1
Bousfield & Rees beat Art Wall Jr & Hawkins 3 and 2
Faulkner & Weetman lost to Kroll & Burke 4 and 3
O'Connor & Brown lost to Mayer & Bolt 7 and 5

Singles
Eric Brown beat Tommy Bolt 4 and 3
Peter Mills beat Jack Burke 5 and 3
Peter Alliss lost to Fred Hawkins 2 and 1

Ken Bousfield beat Lionel Hebert 4 and 3
Dai Rees beat Ed Furgol 7 and 6
Bernard Hunt beat Doug Ford 6 and 5
Christy O'Connor beat Dow Finsterwald 7 and 6
Harry Bradshaw halved with Dick Mayer

1955 *Thunderbird G and C Club, Palm Springs, CA, USA* Nov 5–6

Result: USA 8, GB&I 4

Captains: Chick Harbert (USA), Dai Rees (GB&I)

Foursomes

Harper & Barber lost to Fallon & Jacobs 1 hole
Ford & Kroll beat Brown & Scott 5 and 4
Burke & Bolt beat Lees & Weetman 1 hole
Snead & Middlecoff beat Rees & Bradshaw 3 and 2

Singles

Tommy Bolt beat Christy O'Connor 4 and 2
Chick Harbert beat Syd Scott 3 and 2
Cary Middlecoff lost to John Jacobs 1 hole
Sam Snead beat Dai Rees 3 and 1
Marty Furgol lost to Arthur Lees 3 and 1
Jerry Barber lost to Eric Brown 3 and 2
Jack Burke beat Harry Bradshaw 3 and 2
Doug Ford beat Harry Weetman 3 and 2

1953 *West Course, Wentworth GC, Surrey, England* Oct 2–3

Result: USA 6½, GB 5½

Captains: Henry Cotton (GB), Lloyd Mangrum (USA)

Foursomes

Weetman & Alliss lost to Douglas & Oliver 2 and 1
Brown & Panton lost to Mangrum & Snead 8 and 7
Adams & Hunt lost to Kroll & Burke 7 and 5
Daly & Bradshaw beat Burkemo & Middlecoff 1 hole

Singles

Dai Rees lost to Jack Burke 2 and 1
Fred Daly beat Ted Kroll 9 and 7
Eric Brown beat Lloyd Mangrum 2 holes
Harry Weetman beat Sam Snead 1 hole
Max Faulkner lost to Cary Middlecoff 3 and 1
Peter Alliss lost to Jim Turnesa 1 hole
Bernard Hunt halved with Dave Douglas
Harry Bradshaw beat Fred Haas Jr 3 and 2

1951 *Pinehurst No.2, Pinehurst, NC, USA* Nov 2–4

Result: USA 9½, GB 2½

Captains: Sam Snead (USA), Arthur Lacey (GB)

Foursomes

Heafner & Burke beat Faulkner & Rees 5 and 3
Oliver & Henry Ransom lost to Ward & Lees 2 and 1
Mangrum & Snead beat Adams & Panton 5 and 4
Hogan & Demaret beat Daly & Bousfield 5 and 4

Singles

Jack Burke beat Jimmy Adams 4 and 3
Jimmy Demaret beat Dai Rees 2 holes
Clayton Heafner halved with Fred Daly
Lloyd Mangrum beat Harry Weetman 6 and 5
Ed Oliver lost to Arthur Lees 2 and 1
Ben Hogan beat Charlie Ward 3 and 2
Skip Alexander beat John Panton 8 and 7
Sam Snead beat Max Faulkner 4 and 3

1949 *Ganton Golf Club, Scarborough, Yorks, England* Sept 16–17

Result: USA 7, GB 5

Captains: Charles Whitcombe (GB), Ben Hogan (USA)

Foursomes

Faulkner & Adams beat Harrison & Palmer 2 and 1
Daly & Ken Bousfield beat Hamilton & Alexander 4 and 2
Ward & King lost to Demaret & Heafner 4 and 3
Burton & Lees beat Snead & Mangrum 1 hole

Singles

Max Faulkner lost to Dutch Harrison 8 and 7
Jimmy Adams beat Johnny Palmer 2 and 1
Charlie Ward lost to Sam Snead 6 and 5
Dai Rees beat Bob Hamilton 6 and 4
Dick Burton lost to Clayton Heafner 3 and 2
Sam King lost to Chick Harbert 4 and 3
Arthur Lees lost to Jimmy Demaret 7 and 6
Fred Daly lost to Lloyd Mangrum 1 hole

1947 *Portland Golf Club, Portland, OR, USA* Nov 1–2

Result: USA 11, GB 1

Captains: Ben Hogan (USA), Henry Cotton (GB)

Foursomes

Oliver & Worsham beat Cotton & Lees 10 and 9
Snead & Mangrum beat Daly & Ward 6 and 5
Hogan & Demaret beat Adams & Faulkner 2 holes
Nelson & Herman Barron beat Rees & King 2 and 1

Singles

Dutch Harrison beat Fred Daly 5 and 4
Lew Worsham beat Jimmy Adams 3 and 2
Lloyd Mangrum beat Max Faulkner 6 and 5
Ed Oliver beat Charlie Ward 4 and 3
Byron Nelson beat Arthur Lees 2 and 1
Sam Snead beat Henry Cotton 5 and 4
Jimmy Demaret beat Dai Rees 3 and 2
Herman Keiser lost to Sam King 4 and 3

1937 *Southport & Ainsdale GC, Southport, Lancs, England* June 29–30

Result: USA 8, GB 4

Captains: Charles Whitcombe (GB), Walter Hagen (USA)

Foursomes

Padgham & Cotton lost to Dudley & Nelson 4 and 2
Lacey & Bill Cox lost to Guldahl & Manero 2 and 1
Whitcombe & Rees halved with Sarazen & Shute
Alliss & Burton beat Picard & Johnny Revolta 2 and 1

Singles

Alf Padgham lost to Ralph Guldahl 8 and 7
Sam King halved with Densmore Shute
Dai Rees beat Byron Nelson 3 and 1
Henry Cotton beat Tony Manero 5 and 3
Percy Alliss lost to Gene Sarazen 1 hole
Dick Burton lost to Sam Snead 5 and 4
Alf Perry lost to Ed Dudley 2 and 1
Arthur Lacey lost to Henry Picard 2 and 1

1935 *Ridgewood Country Club, Paramus, NJ, USA* Sept 28–29

Result: USA 9, GB 3

Captains: Walter Hagen (USA), Charles Whitcombe (GB)

Foursomes

Sarazen & Hagen beat Perry & Busson 7 and 6
Picard & Revolta beat Padgham & Alliss 6 and 5
Runyan & Smith beat Cox & Jarman 9 and 8
Dutra & Laffoon lost to C Whitcombe & E Whitcombe 1 hole

1935 *continued*

Singles

Gene Sarazen beat Jack Busson 3 and 2
Paul Runyon beat Dick Burton 5 and 3
Johnny Revolta beat Charles Whitcombe 2 and 1
Olin Dutra beat Alf Padgham 4 and 2
Craig Wood lost to Percy Alliss 1 hole
Horton Smith halved with Bill Cox
Henry Picard beat Ernest Whitcombe 3 and 2
Sam Parks halved with Alf Perry

1933 *Southport & Ainsdale GC, Southport, Lancs, England* June 26–27

Result: GB 6½, USA 5½

Captains: JH Taylor (GB), Walter Hagen (USA)

Foursomes

Alliss & Whitcombe halved with Sarazen & Hagen
Mitchell & Havers beat Dutra & Shute 3 and 2
Davies & Easterbrook beat Wood & Runyan 1 hole
Padgham & Perry lost to Dudley & Burke 1 hole

Singles

Alf Padgham lost to Gene Sarazen 6 and 4
Abe Mitchell beat Olin Dutra 9 and 8
Arthur Lacey lost to Walter Hagen 2 and 1
William H Davies lost to Craig Wood 4 and 3
Percy Alliss beat Paul Runyan 2 and 1
Arthur Havers beat Leo Diegel 4 and 3
Syd Easterbrook beat Densmore Shute 1 hole
Charles Whitcombe lost to Horton Smith 2 and 1

1931 *Scioto Country Club, Columbus, OH, USA* June 26–27

Result: USA 9, GB 3

Captains: Walter Hagen (USA), Charles Whitcombe (GB)

Foursomes

Sarazen & Farrell beat Compston & Davies 8 and 7
Hagen & Shute beat Duncan & Havers 10 and 9
Diegel & Espinosa lost to Mitchell & Robson 3 and 1
Burke & Cox beat Easterbrook & E Whitcombe 3 and 2

Singles

Billy Burke beat Archie Compston 7 and 6
Gene Sarazen beat Fred Robson 7 and 6
Johnny Farrell lost to William H Davies 4 and 3
Wilfred Cox beat Abe Mitchell 3 and 1
Walter Hagen beat Charles Whitcombe 4 and 3
Densmore Shute beat Bert Hodson 8 and 6
Al Espinosa beat Ernest Whitcombe 2 and 1
Craig Wood lost to Arthur Havers 4 and 3

1929 *Moortown Golf Club, Leeds, Yorkshire, England* May 26–27

Result: GB 7, USA 5

Captains: George Duncan (GB), Walter Hagen (USA)

Foursomes

C Whitcombe & Compston halved with Farrell & Turnesa
Boomer & Duncan lost to Diegel & Espinosa 7 and 5
Mitchell & Robson beat Sarazen & Dudley 2 and 1
E Whitcombe & Cotton lost to Golden & Hagen 2 holes

Singles

Charles Whitcombe beat Johnny Farrell 8 and 6
George Duncan beat Walter Hagen 10 and 8
Abe Mitchell lost to Leo Diegel 9 and 8
Archie Compston beat Gene Sarazen 6 and 4
Aubrey Boomer beat Joe Turnesa 4 and 3
Fred Robson lost to Horton Smith 4 and 2
Henry Cotton beat Al Watrous 4 and 3
Ernest Whitcombe halved with Al Espinosa

1927 *Worcester Country Club, Worcester, MA, USA* June 3–4

Result: USA 9½, GB 2½

Captains: W Hagen (USA), E Ray (GB)

Foursomes

Hagen & Golden beat Ray & Robson 2 and 1
Farrell & Turnesa beat Duncan & Compston 8 and 6
Sarazen & Watrous beat Havers & Jolly 3 and 2
Diegel & Mehlhorn lost to Boomer & Whitcombe 7 and 5

Singles

Bill Mehlhorn beat Archie Compston 1 hole
Johnny Farrell beat Aubrey Boomer 5 and 4
Johnny Golden beat Herbert Jolly 8 and 7
Leo Diegel beat Ted Ray 7 and 5
Gene Sarazen halved with Charles Whitcombe
Walter Hagen beat Arthur Havers 2 and 1
Al Watrous beat Fred Robson 3 and 2
Joe Turnesa lost to George Duncan 1 hole

Unofficial Ryder Cups

Great Britain v USA

1926 *West Course, Wentworth GC, Surrey, England* June 4–5

Result: GB 13½, USA 1½

Singles

Abe Mitchell beat Jim Barnes 8 and 7
George Duncan beat Walter Hagen 6 and 5

Although no matches were played between 1939 and 1945, Great Britain selected a side in 1939 and the Americans chose sides in 1939 to 1943. No alternative fixture was played in 1939 but the Americans played matches amongst themselves in the other four years. They resulted in:

1940	Cup Team 7, Gene Sarazen's Challengers 5
1941	Cup Team 6½, Bobby Jones' Challengers 8½
1942	Cup Team 10, Walter Hagen's Challengers 5
1943	Cup Team 8½, Walter Hagen's Challengers 3½

Aubrey Boomer beat Tommy Armour 2 and 1
Archie Compston lost to Bill Mehlhorn 1 hole
George Gadd beat Joe Kirkwood 8 and 7
Ted Ray beat Al Watrous 6 and 5
Fred Robson beat Cyril Walker 5 and 4
Arthur Havers beat Fred McLeod 10 and 9
Ernest Whitcombe halved with Emmett French
Herbert Jolly beat Joe Stein 3 and 2

Foursomes
Mitchell & Duncan beat Barnes & Hagen 9 and 8
Boomer & Compston beat Armour & Kirkwood 3 and 2
Gadd & Havers beat Mehlhorn & Watrous 3 and 2
Ray & Robson beat Walker & McLeod 3 and 2
Whitcombe & Jolly beat French & Stein 3 and 2

1921 *King's Course, Gleneagles Hotel, Perthshire, Scotland* June 6

Result: GB 9 USA 3
(no half points were awarded)

Singles
George Duncan beat Jock Hutchison 2 and 1
Abe Mitchell halved with Walter Hagen
Ted Ray lost to Emmet French 2 and 1
JH Taylor lost to Fred McLeod 1 hole
Harry Vardon beat Tom Kerrigan 3 and 1
James Braid beat Charles Hoffner 5 and 4
AG Havers lost to WE Reid 2 and 1
J Ockenden beat G McLean 5 and 4
J Sherlock beat Clarence Hackney 3 and 2
Joshua Taylor beat Bill Melhorn 3&2

Foursomes
George Duncan & Abe Mitchell halved with Jock Hutchison & Walter Hagen
Ted Ray & Harry Vardon beat Emmet French & Tom Kerrigan 5 and 4
James Braid & JH Taylor halved with Charles Hoffner & Fred McLeod
AG Havers & J Ockenden beat WE Reid & G McLean 6 and 5
J Sherlock & Joshua Taylor beat Clarence Hackney & W Melhorn 1 hole

Three matches were halved

INDIVIDUAL RECORDS

Matches were contested as Great Britain *v* USA from 1927 to 1953; as Great Britain & Ireland *v* USA from 1955 to 1977 and as Europe *v* USA from 1979. Non-playing captains are shown in brackets.

GB/GB&I/Europe

Name	Year	Played	Won	Lost	Halved
Jimmy Adams	*1939-47-49-51-53	7	2	5	0
Percy Alliss	1929-33-35-37	6	3	2	1
Peter Alliss	1953-57-59-61-63-65-67-69	30	10	15	5
Laurie Ayton	1949	0	0	0	0
Peter Baker	1993	4	3	1	0
Severiano Ballesteros (ESP)	1979-83-85-87-89-91-93-95-(97)	37	20	12	5
Harry Bannerman	1971	5	2	2	1
Brian Barnes	1969-71-73-75-77-79	25	10	14	1
Maurice Bembridge	1969-71-73-75	16	5	8	3
Thomas Bjørn (DEN)	1997-2002	6	3	2	1
Aubrey Boomer	1927-29	4	2	2	0
Ken Bousfield	1949-51-55-57-59-61	10	5	5	0
Hugh Boyle	1967	3	0	3	0
Harry Bradshaw	1953-55-57	5	2	2	1
Gordon J Brand	1983	1	0	1	0
Gordon Brand Jr	1987-89	7	2	4	1
Paul Broadhurst	1991	2	2	0	0
Eric Brown	1953-55-57-59-(69)-(71)	8	4	4	0
Ken Brown	1977-79-83-85-87	13	4	9	0
Stewart Burns	1929	0	0	0	0
Dick Burton	1935-37-*39-49	5	2	3	0
Jack Busson	1935	2	0	2	0
Peter Butler	1965-69-71-73	14	3	9	2
José Maria Canizares (ESP)	1981-83-85-89	11	5	4	2
Paul Casey	2004-06-08	9	3	2	4
Alex Caygill	1969	1	0	0	1
Clive Clark	1973	1	0	1	0
Howard Clark	1977-81-85-87-89-95	15	10	7	3
Darren Clarke	1997-99–2002-04-06	20	7	7	3
Neil Coles	1961-63-65-67-69-71-73-77	40	12	21	7
Andrew Coltart	1999	1	0	1	0
Archie Compston	1927-29-31	6	1	4	1
Henry Cotton	1929-37-*39-47-(53)	6	2	4	0
Bill Cox	1935-37	3	0	2	1
Allan Dailey	1933	0	0	0	0

** In 1939 a GB team was named but the match was not played because of the Second World War*

Name	Year	Played	Won	Lost	Halved
Fred Daly	1947-49-51-53	8	3	4	1
Eamonn Darcy	1975-77-81-87	11	1	8	2
William Davies	1931-33	4	2	2	0
Peter Dawson	1977	3	1	2	0
Luke Donald	2004-06-10	11	8	2	1
Norman Drew	1959	1	0	0	1
George Duncan	1927-29-31	5	2	3	0
Syd Easterbrook	1931-33	3	2	1	0
Nick Faldo	1977-79-81-83-85-87-89-91-93-95-97-(08)	46	23	19	4
John Fallon	1955-(63)	1	1	0	0
Niclas Fasth (SWE)	2002	3	0	2	1
Max Faulkner	1947-49-51-53-57	8	1	7	0
David Feherty	1991	3	1	1	1
Ross Fisher	2010	4	2	2	0
Pierre Fulke (SWE)	2002	2	0	1	1
George Gadd	1927	0	0	0	0
Bernard Gallacher	1969-71-73-75-77-79-81-83-(91)-(93)-(95)	31	13	13	5
Sergio García (ESP)	1999-2002-04-06-08	24	14	6	4
John Garner	1971-73	1	0	1	0
Antonio Garrido (ESP)	1979	5	1	4	0
Ignacio Garrido (ESP)	1997	4	0	1	3
David Gilford	1991-95	6	3	3	0
Eric Green	1947	0	0	0	0
Malcolm Gregson	1967	4	0	4	0
Joakim Haeggman (SWE)	1993	2	1	1	0
Tom Haliburton	1961-63	6	0	6	0
Søren Hansen (DEN)	2008	3	0	2	1
Peter Hanson (SWE)	2010	3	1	2	0
Jack Hargreaves	1951	0	0	0	0
Padraig Harrington	1999-2002-04-06-08-10	25	9	13	3
Arthur Havers	1927-31-33	6	3	3	0
Jimmy Hitchcock	1965	3	0	3	0
Bert Hodson	1931	1	0	1	0
Reg Horne	1947	0	0	0	0
Tommy Horton	1975-77	8	1	6	1
David Howell	2004-06	5	3	1	1
Brian Huggett	1963-67-69-71-73-75-(77)	25	9	10	6
Bernard Hunt	1953-57-59-61-63-65-67-69-(73)-(75)	28	6	16	6
Geoffrey Hunt	1963	3	0	3	0
Guy Hunt	1975	3	0	2	1
Tony Jacklin	1967-69-71-73-75-77-79-(83)-(85)-(87)-(89)	35	13	14	8
John Jacobs	1955-(79)-(81)	2	2	0	0
Mark James	1977-79-81-89-91-93-95-(99)	24	8	15	1
Edward Jarman	1935	1	0	1	0
Miguel Angel Jiménez (ESP)	1999-2004-08-10	15	4	8	3
Per-Ulrik Johansson (SWE)	1995-97	5	3	2	0
Herbert Jolly	1927	2	0	2	0
Robert Karlsson (SWE)	2006-08	7	1	2	4
Martin Kaymer (GER)	2010	4	2	1	0
Michael King	1979	1	0	1	0
Sam King	1937-*39-47-49	5	1	3	1
Arthur Lacey	1933-37-(51)	3	0	3	0
Barry Lane	1993	3	0	3	0
Bernhard Langer (GER)	1981-83-85-87-89-91-93-95-97-2002-(04)	42	21	15	6
Paul Lawrie	1999	5	3	1	1
Arthur Lees	1947-49-51-55	8	4	4	0
Thomas Levet (FRA)	2004	3	1	2	0
Sandy Lyle	1979-81-83-85-87	18	7	9	2
Graeme McDowell	2008-10	8	4	2	2
Paul McGinley	2002-04-06	9	2	2	5
Rory McIlroy (NIR)	2010	4	1	1	2
Jimmy Martin	1965	1	0	1	0
Peter Mills	1957-59	1	1	0	0
Abe Mitchell	1929-31-33	6	4	2	0
Ralph Moffitt	1961	1	0	1	0
Edoardo Molinari (ITA)	2010	3	0	1	2
Francesco Molinari (ITA)	2010	3	0	2	1
Colin Montgomerie	1991-93-95-97-99-2002-04-06-(10)	36	20	9	7
Christy O'Connor Jr	1975-89	4	1	3	0
Christy O'Connor Sr	1955-57-59-61-63-65-67-69-71-73	36	11	21	4
José María Olazábal (ESP)	1987-89-91-93-97-99-2006	31	18	8	5
John O'Leary	1975	4	0	4	0
Peter Oosterhuis	1971-73-75-77-79-81	28	14	11	3

** In 1939 a GB team was named but the match was not played because of the Second World War*

Name	Year	Played	Won	Lost	Halved
Alf Padgham	1933-35-37-*39	6	0	6	0
John Panton	1951-53-61	5	0	5	0
Jesper Parnevik (SWE)	1997-99-2002	11	4	3	4
Alf Perry	1933-35-37	4	0	3	1
Manuel Pinero (ESP)	1981-85	9	6	3	0
Lionel Platts	1965	5	1	2	2
Eddie Polland	1973	2	0	2	0
Ian Poulter	2004-08-10	11	8	3	0
Phillip Price	2002	2	1	1	0
Ronan Rafferty	1989	3	1	2	0
Ted Ray	1927	2	0	2	0
Dai Rees	1937-*39-47-49-51-53-55-57-59-61-(67)	18	7	10	1
Steven Richardson	1991	4	2	2	0
José Rivero (ESP)	1985-87	5	2	3	0
Fred Robson	1927-29-31	6	2	4	0
Costantino Rocca (ITA)	1993-95-97	11	6	5	0
Justin Rose	2008	4	3	1	0
Jarmo Sandelin (SWE)	1999	1	0	1	0
Syd Scott	1955	2	0	2	0
Des Smyth	1979-81	7	2	5	0
Henrik Stenson (SWE)	2006-08	7	2	3	2
Dave Thomas	1959-63-65-67	18	3	10	5
Sam Torrance	1981-83-85-87-89-91-93-95-(2002)	27	7	15	5
Peter Townsend	1969-71	11	3	8	0
Jean Van de Velde (FRA)	1999	1	0	1	0
Brian Waites	1983	4	1	3	0
Philip Walton	1995	2	1	1	0
Charlie Ward	1947-49-51	6	1	5	0
Paul Way	1983-85	9	6	2	1
Harry Weetman	1951-53-55-57-59-61-63-(65)	15	2	11	2
Norman Wood	1975	3	1	2	0
Ian Woosnam	1983-85-87-89-91-93-95-97-(2006)	31	14	12	5
Lee Westwood	1997-99-2002-04-06-08-10	28	14	8	6
Charles Whitcombe	1927-29-31-33-35-37-*39-(49)	9	3	2	4
Ernest Whitcombe	1929-31-35	6	1	4	1
Reg Whitcombe	1935-*39	1	0	1	0
George Will	1963-65-67	15	2	11	2
Oliver Wilson	2008	2	1	1	0

United States of America

Name	Year	Played	Won	Lost	Halved
Tommy Aaron	1969-73	6	1	4	1
Skip Alexander	1949-51	2	1	1	0
Paul Azinger	1989-91-93-2002-(08)	16	5	8	3
Jerry Barber	1955-61	5	1	4	0
Miller Barber	1969-71	7	1	4	2
Herman Barron	1947	1	1	0	0
Andy Bean	1979-87	6	4	2	0
Frank Beard	1969-71	8	2	3	3
Chip Beck	1989-91-93	9	6	2	1
Homero Blancas	1973	4	2	1	1
Tommy Bolt	1955-57	4	3	1	0
Julius Boros	1959-63-65-67	16	9	3	4
Gay Brewer	1967-73	9	5	3	1
Billy Burke	1931-33	3	3	0	0
Jack Burke	1951-53-55-57-59-(73)	8	7	1	0
Walter Burkemo	1953	1	0	1	0
Mark Calcavecchia	1987-89-91-2002	14	6	7	1
Chad Campbell	2004-06-08	9	3	4	2
Billy Casper	1961-63-65-67-69-71-73-75-(79)	37	20	10	7
Stewart Cink	2002-04-06-08-10	19	5	7	7
Bill Collins	1961	3	1	2	0
Charles Coody	1971	3	0	2	1
John Cook	1993	2	1	1	0
Fred Couples	1989-91-93-95-97	20	7	9	4
Wilfred Cox	1931	2	2	0	0
Ben Crenshaw	1981-83-87-95-(99)	12	3	8	1
Ben Curtis	2008	3	1	1	1
Jimmy Demaret	*1941-47-49-51	6	6	0	0
Gardner Dickinson	1967-71	10	9	1	0
Leo Diegel	1927-29-31-33	6	3	3	0

** In 1939 a GB team was named but the match was not played because of the Second World War*

Name	Year	Played	Won	Lost	Halved
Chris DiMarco	2004-06	8	2	4	2
Dale Douglass	1969	2	0	2	0
Dave Douglas	1953	2	1	0	1
Ed Dudley	1929-33-37	4	3	1	0
Olin Dutra	1933-35	4	1	3	0
David Duval	1999-2002	7	2	3	2
Lee Elder	1979	4	1	3	0
Al Espinosa	1927-29-31	4	2	1	1
Johnny Farrell	1927-29-31	6	3	2	1
Brad Faxon	1995-97	6	2	4	0
Dow Finsterwald	1957-59-61-63-(77)	13	9	3	1
Ray Floyd	1969-75-77-81-83-85-(89)-91-93	31	12	16	3
Doug Ford	1955-57-59-61	9	4	4	1
Rikki Fowler	2010	3	0	1	2
Fred Funk	2004	3	0	3	0
Ed Furgol	1957	1	0	1	0
Marty Furgol	1955	1	0	1	0
Jim Furyk	1997-99-2002-04-06-08-10	27	8	15	4
Jim Gallagher Jr	1993	3	2	1	0
Al Geiberger	1967-75	9	5	1	3
Vic Ghezzi	*1939-*41	0	0	0	0
Bob Gilder	1983	4	2	2	0
Bob Goalby	1963	5	3	1	1
Johnny Golden	1927-29	3	3	0	0
Lou Graham	1973-75-77	9	5	3	1
Hubert Green	1977-79-85	7	4	3	0
Ken Green	1989	4	2	2	0
Ralph Guldahl	1937-*39	2	2	0	0
Fred Haas Jr	1953	1	0	1	0
Jay Haas	1983-95-2004	12	4	6	2
Walter Hagen	1927-29-31-33-35-(37)	9	7	1	1
Bob Hamilton	1949	2	0	2	0
Chick Harbert	1949-55	2	2	0	0
Chandler Harper	1955	1	0	1	0
EJ (Dutch) Harrison	1947-49-51	3	2	1	0
Fred Hawkins	1957	2	1	1	0
Mark Hayes	1979	3	1	2	0
Clayton Heafner	1949-51	4	3	0	1
Jay Hebert	1959-61-(71)	4	2	1	1
Lionel Hebert	1957	1	0	1	0
J J Henry	2006	3	0	0	3
Dave Hill	1969-73-77	9	6	3	0
Jimmy Hines	*1939	0	0	0	0
Scott Hoch	1997-2002	7	2	3	2
Ben Hogan	*1941-47-(49)-51-(67)	3	3	0	0
J B Holmes	2008	3	2	0	1
Hale Irwin	1975-77-79-81-91	20	13	5	2
Tommy Jacobs	1965	4	3	1	0
Peter Jacobsen	1985-95	6	2	4	0
Don January	1965-77	7	2	3	2
Lee Janzen	1993-97	5	2	3	0
Dustin Johnson	2010	4	1	3	0
Zach Johnson	2006–10	7	3	3	1
Herman Keiser	1947	1	0	1	0
Anthony Kim	2008	4	2	1	1
Tom Kite	1979-81-83-85-87-89-93-(97)	28	15	9	4
Ted Kroll	1953-55-57	4	3	1	0
Matt Kuchar	2010	4	1	3	0
Ky Laffoon	1935	1	0	1	0
Tom Lehman	1995-97-99-(2006)	10	5	3	2
Tony Lema	1963-65	11	8	1	2
Justin Leonard	1997-99-08	12	2	4	6
Wayne Levi	1991	2	0	2	0
Bruce Lietzke	1981	3	0	2	1
Gene Littler	1961-63-65-67-69-71-75	27	14	5	8
Davis Love III	1993-95-97-99-2002-04	26	9	12	5
Jeff Maggert	1995-97-99	11	6	5	0
John Mahaffey	1979	3	1	2	0
Hunter Mahan	2008–10	8	3	2	3
Mark McCumber	1989	3	2	1	0
Jerry McGee	1977	2	1	1	0
Harold McSpaden	*1939-*41	0	0	0	0
Tony Manero	1937	2	1	1	0

** US teams were selected in 1939 and 1941, but did not play because of the Second World War*

Name	Year	Played	Won	Lost	Halved
Lloyd Mangrum	*1941-47-49-51-53	8	6	2	0
Dave Marr	1965-(81)	6	4	2	0
Billy Maxwell	1963	4	4	0	0
Dick Mayer	1957	2	1	0	1
Bill Mehlhorn	1927	2	1	1	0
Dick Metz	*1939	0	0	0	0
Phil Mickelson	1995-97-99-2002-04-06-08–10	34	11	17	6
Cary Middlecoff	1953-55-59	6	2	3	1
Johnny Miller	1975-81	6	2	2	2
Larry Mize	1987	4	1	1	2
Gil Morgan	1979-83	6	1	2	3
Bob Murphy	1975	4	2	1	1
Byron Nelson	1937-*39-*41-47-(65)	4	3	1	0
Larry Nelson	1979-81-87	13	9	3	1
Bobby Nichols	1967	5	4	0	1
Jack Nicklaus	1969-71-73-75-77-81-(83)-(87)	28	17	8	3
Andy North	1985	3	0	3	0
Ed Oliver	1947-51-53	5	3	2	0
Mark O'Meara	1985-89-91-97-99	14	4	9	1
Jeff Overton	2010	4	2	2	0
Arnold Palmer	1961-63-65-67-71-73-(75)	32	22	8	2
Johnny Palmer	1949	2	0	2	0
Sam Parks	1935	1	0	0	1
Jerry Pate	1981	4	2	2	0
Steve Pate	1991-99	4	2	2	0
Corey Pavin	1991-93-95–(2010)	8	5	3	0
Calvin Peete	1983-85	7	4	2	1
Kenny Perry	2004-08	6	2	3	1
Henry Picard	1935-37-*39	4	3	1	0
Dan Pohl	1987	3	1	2	0
Johnny Pott	1963-65-67	7	5	2	0
Dave Ragan	1963	4	2	1	1
Henry Ransom	1951	1	0	1	0
Johnny Revolta	1935-37	3	2	1	0
Chris Riley	2004	3	1	1	1
Loren Roberts	1995	4	3	1	0
Chi Chi Rodriguez	1973	2	0	1	1
Bill Rogers	1981	4	1	2	1
Bob Rosburg	1959	2	2	0	0
Mason Rudolph	1971	3	1	1	1
Paul Runyan	1933-35-*39	4	2	2	0
Doug Sanders	1967	5	2	3	0
Gene Sarazen	1927-29-31-33-35-37-*41	12	7	2	3
Densmore Shute	1931-33-37	6	2	2	2
Dan Sikes	1969	3	2	1	0
Scott Simpson	1987	2	1	1	0
Horton Smith	1929-31-33-35-37-*39-*41	4	3	0	1
C Snead	1971-73-75	11	9	2	0
Sam Snead	1937-*39-*41-47-49-51-53-55-59-(69)	13	10	2	1
Ed Sneed	1977	2	1	0	1
Mike Souchak	1959-61	6	5	1	0
Craig Stadler	1983-85	8	4	2	2
Payne Stewart	1987-89-91-93-99	19	7	10	2
Ken Still	1969	3	1	2	0
Dave Stockton	1971-77-(91)	5	3	1	1
Curtis Strange	1983-85-87-89-95-2002	20	6	12	2
Steve Stricker	2008-10	7	3	3	1
Hal Sutton	1985-87-99-2002-(04)	16	7	5	4
Vaughn Taylor	2006	2	0	1	1
David Toms	2002-04-06	12	4	6	2
Lee Trevino	1969-71-73-75-79-81-(85)	30	17	7	6
Jim Turnesa	1953	1	1	0	0
Joe Turnesa	1927-29	4	1	2	1
Ken Venturi	1965	4	1	3	0
Scott Verplank	2002-06	5	4	1	0
Lanny Wadkins	1977-79-83-85-87-89-91-93-(95)	33	20	11	2
Art Wall Jr	1957-59-61	6	4	2	0
Al Watrous	1927-29	3	2	1	0
Bubba Watson	2010	4	1	3	0
Tom Watson	1977-81-83-89-(93)	15	10	4	1
Boo Weekley	2008	3	2	0	1
Tom Weiskopf	1973-75	10	7	2	1
Brett Wetterich	2006	2	0	2	0

** US teams were selected in 1939 and 1941, but did not play because of the Second World War*

Name	Year	Played	Won	Lost	Halved
Craig Wood	1931-33-35-*41	4	1	3	0
Tiger Woods	1997-99-2002-04-06-10	29	13	14	2
Lew Worsham	1947	2	2	0	0
Fuzzy Zoeller	1979-83-85	10	1	8	1

The Vivendi Seve Trophy (inaugurated 2000) Continental Europe *v* GB&I

2000	Sunningdale, England	GB&I 12½, Europe 13½
2002	Druid's Glen, Ireland	Europe 12½, GB&I 14½
2003	El Saler, Spain	Europe 13, GB&I 15
2005	The Wynyard, England	GB&I 16½, Europe, 11½
2007	The Heritage, Ireland	GB&I 16½, Europe 11½
2009	Golf de Saint-Nom-la-Bretèche, France	GB&I 16½, Europe 11½
2011	Golf de Saint-Nom-la-Bretèche, France	GB&I 15½, Europe 12½

PGA Cup (Llandudno Trophy) (Instituted 1973)

Great Britain and Ireland Club Professionals *v* United States Club Professionals

1973	USA	Pinehurst, NC	13–3
1974	USA	Pinehurst, NC	11½–4½
1975	USA	Hillside, Southport, England	9½–6½
1976	USA	Moortown, Leeds, England	9½–6½
1977	Halved	Mission Hills, Palm Springs	8½–8½
1978	GB&I	St Mellion, Cornwall	10½–6½
1979	GB&I	Castletown, Isle of Man	12½–4½
1980	USA	Oak Tree, Edmond, OK	15–6
1981	Halved	Turnberry Isle, Miami, FL	10½–10½
1982	USA	Holston Hills, Knoxville, TN	13–7
1983	GB&I	Muirfield, Scotland	14½–6½
1984	GB&I	Turnberry, Scotland	12½–8½
Played alternate years from 1984			
1986	USA	Knollwood, Lake Fore, IL	16–9
1988	USA	The Belfry, England	15½–10½
1990	USA	Turtle Point, Kiawah Island, SC	19–7
1992	USA	K Club, Ireland	15–11
1994	USA	Palm Beach, Florida	15–11
1996	Halved	Gleneagles, Scotland	13–13
1998	USA	The Broadmoor, Colorado Springs, CO	11½–4½
2000	USA	Celtic Manor, Newport, Wales	13½–12½
2002	*Cancelled*		
2003	USA	Port St Lucie, FL	19–7
2005	GB&I	K Club, Dublin, R.o.I.	15–11
2007	USA	Reynolds Plantation, GA	13½–12½
2009	USA	The Carrick, Loch Lomond, Scotland	17½–8½
2011	USA	CordeValle, San Martin, CA	17½–8½

PGAs of Europe International Team Championship

Lumine Beach and Golf Resort, Costa Dorada, Spain

1	Craig Swingburn (ENG) and Matthew McGuire (ENG)	61-65-67—193
2	Michael Jones (ENG) and Garry Houston (WAL)	66-65-65—196
3	Matthew Dearden (WAL) and Ian Brown (FRA)	66-67-65—198
	Simon Edwards (WAL) and David Shacklady (ENG)	65-67-66—198
	Grant Hamilton (ENG) and David Smith (ENG)	63-67-68—198
	Alessando Napoleoni (ITA) and Emanuelle Canonica (ITA)	66-68-64—198
	Mariano Siz (ESP) and Mikel Galdos (ESP)	66-66-66—198

1990	Scotland
1991	Netherlands
1992	Scotland
1993	Scotland
1994	*Not played*
1995	Spain
1996	Scotland
1997	Scotland
1998	Ireland
1999	England
2000	Wales
2001	Spain
2002	Spain
2003	Spain
2004	England
2005	France
2006	Scotland
2007	Austria*
2008	Ireland
2009	Wales
2010	England
2011	France

**Beat Wales at 2nd extra hole*

At last Sandy makes into the Scottish Hall of Fame

Sandy Lyle, who was honoured in 2011 by being voted into the World Hall Golf Hall of Fame, made it into the Scottish Hall of Fame in 2013.

The 54-year-old former Open and Masters winner, Lyle who also played in five Ryder Cup matches, will join earlier honourees Sam Torrance, Paul Lawrie and Colin Montgomerie at the event which was organised by the Scottish Golf Union, the Scottish Ladies Golf Association and ClubGolf.

The Royal Trophy (Asia *v* Europe) *Empire CC, Brunei*

European names first

***First Day* – Foursomes**

Gonzalo Fernandez-Castano (ESP) and Henrik Stenson (SWE) beat Ryo Ishikawa (JPN) and Bae Sang-moon (KOR) 5 and 4
Edoardo and Francisco Molinari (ITA) beat Wu Ashun (CHN) and Yoshinori Fujimoto (JPN) 2 and 1
Nicolas Colsaerts (BEL) and Marcel Siem (GER) beat Kiradech Aphibarnrat (THA) and Jeev Milkha Sing (IND) 1 hole
Miguel Angel Jiménez and José Maria Olazábal (ESP) halved with Kim Kyung-tae and Yang Young-eun (KOR)

***Second Day* – Fourball**

Olazébal and Jiménez halved with Singh and Aphibarnrat
Fernandez-Castono and Stenson lost to Kim and Yang 2 and 1
Colsaerts and Siem halved with Bae and Wu Ashun
E and F Molinari lost to Ishikawa and Fujimoto 3 and 1

***Third Day* – Singles**

Olazabal (withdrew injured) halved with Aphibarnrat
Jiménez lost to Singh 1 hole
Stenson beat Ishikawa 1 hole
Fernandez-Castano halved with Kim
Siem lost to Fujimoto 1 hole
Colsaerts beat Bae 1 hole
E Molinari halved with Wu Ashun
F Molinari lost to Yang 1 hole

Result: Asia 7, Europe 9

2006 Europe 9, Asia 7 Amata Spring CC, Chonburi, Thailand
2007 Europe 12½, Asia 3½ Amata Spring CC, Chonburi, Thailand
2008 *Cancelled*
2009 Asia 10, Europe 6 Amata Spring CC, Chonburi, Thailand
2010 Europe 8½, Asia 7½ Amata Spring CC, Chonburi, Thailand
2011 Europe 9, Asia 7 Black Mountain CC, Hua Hin, Thailand

Presidents Cup (Instituted 1994) USA *v* International

1994 United States 20 International Team 12
Captains: USA Hale Irwin; International David Graham
Robert Trent Jones GC, Prince William County, Virginia
1996 United States 18½, International 15½
Captains: USA Arnold Palmer; International Peter Thomson
Robert Trent Jones GC, Prince William County, Virginia
1998 Interntational 20½, USA 12½
Captains: USA Jack Nicklaus; Internationals Peter Thomson
Royal Melbourne GC, Victoria , Australia
2000 United States 21½, Interntational 10½
Captains: USA Ken Venturi; International Peter Thomson
Robert Trent Jones GC, Prince William County, Virginia
2003 United States 17, International Team 17
Captains: USA Jack Nicklaus; International Gary Player
The Links at Fancourt Hotel and CC Estate, South Africa
2005 United States 18½, International 15½
Captains: USA Jack Nicklaus; International Gary Player
Robert Trent Jones GC, Prince William County, Virginia
2007 United States 19½, International 14½
Captains: USA Jack Nicklaus; International Gary Player
The Royal Montreal GC, Quebec, Canada
2009 United States 19½, International 14½
Captains: USA Fred Couples; International Greg Norman
Harding Park Golf Course, San Francisco, California
2011 United States 19, International 15
Captains: USA Fred Couples; International Greg Norman
Royal Melbourne GC, Victoria, Australia

2013 Match at Muirfield Village GC, Dublin , Ohio October 1–6

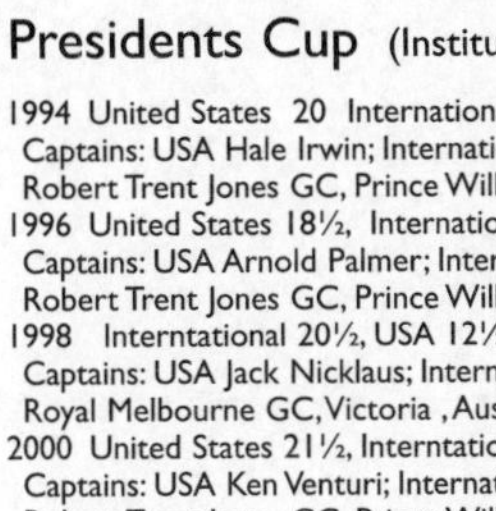

Month by month in 2012

Rory McIlroy is back as world number one despite losing a play-off to Rickie Fowler at Quail Hollow, but Luke Donald knocks him off his perch for a third time after a successful defence of the BMW PGA title at Wentworth. Matt Kuchar lifts the Players Championship, while Nicolas Colsaerts takes a huge step towards becoming the first Belgian in the Ryder Cup by winning the Volvo World Match Play in Spain.

Dongfen Nissan Cup (China v Asia–Pacific) *CTS Tycoon Club, Shenzhen, China*

Captains: China: Wang Jun; Asia–Pacific: Peter Thomson (AUS)

Chinese names first

***Friday* – Fourballs**

Liang Wenchong & Guan Tianlang lost to Andrew Stolz & Scott Laycock 2 and 1
Zhang Xinjun & Wu Kangchun beat Mark Brown & Michael Long 3 and 2
Han Ran & Yuan Tian lost to Yosuke Tsakudaa & Soshi Tajima 1 hole
Wu Weihuang & Zhou Guowu beat Choi Jin-ho & Jason Kang 3 and 2
Ouyang Zhang & Jin Daxing beat Choo Tze Huang & Rory Hie one hole
Zhang Lianwei & Yuan Hao beat Nicholas Fung & Wiaut Artjanawat 2 and 1

Match position: China 4, Asia–Pacific 2

***Saturday* – Foursomes**

Zhang Lianwei & Yuan Hao beat Choo Tze Huang & Rory Hie one hole
Jin Daxing & Ouyang Zhang lost to Nicholas Fung & Wiaut Artjanawat 5 and 3
Yuan Tian & Han Ran lost to Choi Jin-ho & Jason Kang 1 hole
Liang Wenchong & Guan Tianlang beat Soshi Tajima & Yosuke Tsakuda 4 and 2
Wu Weihuang & Zhou Guowu lost to Mark Brown & Scott Laycock 3 and 2
Zhang Xinjun & Wu Kangchun beat Michael Long & Andre Stolz 5 and 3

Match position: China 7, Asia–Pacific 5

***Sunday* – Singles**

Guan Tianlang (am) lost to Mark Brown (NZL) 2 and 1
Liang Wenchiong beat Andre Stolz (AUS) 3 and 1
Ouyang Zhang lost to Rory Hie (INA) 2 and 1
Jin Daxing halved with Choo Tze Huang (SIN)
Zhou Guowu lost to Nicholas Fung (MAS) 1 hole
Yuan Tian lost to Yosuke Tsukada (JPN) 4 and 3
Wu Weihuang lost to Michael Long (NZL) 3 and 2
Wu Kangchun lost to Wiaut Artjanawat (THA) 3 and 2
Han Ran lost to Choi Jin-ho (KOR) 3 and 2
Yuan Hao lost to Jason Kang (KOR) 6 and 5
Zhang Lianwei beat Soshi Tajima (JPN) 7 and 6
Zhang Xinjun halved with Scott Laycock (AUS).

Result: China 10, Asia–Pacific 14

2011 Asia–Pacific 12½, China 11½

World Cup of Golf

(formerly known as the Canada Cup but now run separately by the various world golf tours. In 2010, it was announced that the event would change from annual to biennial, held in odd-numbered years, to accommodate the 2016 inclusion of golf in the Olympics)

1953 1 Argentina (A Cerda and R de Vicenzo); 2 Canada (S Leonard and B Kerr) (Individual: A Cerda, Argentina, 140)	287	Montreal
1954 1 Australia (P Thomson and K Nagle); 2 Argentina (A Cerda and R de Vicenzo) (Individual: S Leonard, Canada, 275)	556	Laval-Sur-Lac
1955 1 United States (C Harbert and E Furgol); 2 Australia (P Thomson and K Nagle) (Individual: E Furgol*, USA (*after a play-off with P Thomson and F van Donck, 279*))	560	Washington
1956 1 United States (B Hogan and S Snead); 2 South Africa (A Locke and G Player) (Individual: B Hogan, USA, 277)	567	Wentworth
1957 1 Japan (T Nakamura and K Ono); 2 United States (S Snead and J Demaret) (Individual: T Nakamura, Japan, 274)	557	Tokyo
1958 1 Ireland (H Bradshaw and C O'Connor); 2 Spain (A Miguel and S Miguel) (Individual: A Miguel*, Spain (*after a play-off with H Bradshaw, 286*))	579	Mexico City
1959 1 Australia (P Thomson and K Nagle); 2 United States (S Snead and C Middlecoff) (Individual: S Leonard*, Canada, 275 (*after a tie with P Thomson, Australia*))	563	Melbourne
1960 1 United States (S Snead and A Palmer); 2 England (H Weetman and B Hunt) (Individual: F van Donck, Belgium, 279)	565	Portmarnock
1961 1 United States (S Snead and J Demaret); 2 Australia (P Thomson and K Nagle) (Individual: S Snead, USA, 272)	560	Puerto Rico
1962 1 United States (S Snead and A Palmer); 2 Argentina (F de Luca and R De Vicenzo) (Individual: R De Vicenzo, Argentina, 276)	557	Buenos Aires

1963	1 United States (A Palmer and J Nicklaus); 2 Spain (S Miguel and R Sota) (Individual: J Nicklaus, USA, 237 – *tournament reduced to 36 holes because of fog*)	482	St Nom-La-Breteche
1964	1 United States (A Palmer and J Nicklaus); 2 Argentina (R De Vicenzo and L Ruiz) (Individual: J Nicklaus, USA, 276)	554	Maui, Hawaii
1965	1 South Africa (G Player and H Henning); 2 Spain (A Miguel and R Sota) (Individual: G Player, South Africa, 281)	571	Madrid
1966	1 United States (J Nicklaus and A Palmer); 2 South Africa (G Player and H Henning) (Individual: G Knudson* Canada, 272 (**after a play-off with H Sugimoto, Japan*))	548	Tokyo
1967	1 United States (J Nicklaus and A Palmer); 2 New Zealand (R Charles and W Godfrey) (Individual: A Palmer, USA, 276)	557	Mexico City
1968	1 Canada (A Balding and G Knudson); 2 United States (J Boros and L Trevino) (Individual: A Balding, Canada, 274)	569	Olgiata, Rome
1969	1 United States (O Moody and L Trevino); 2 Japan (T Kono and H Yasuda) (Individual: L Trevino, USA, 275)	552	Singapore
1970	1 Australia (B Devlin and D Graham); 2 Argentina (R De Vicenzo and V Fernandez) (Individual: R De Vicenzo, Argentina, 269)	545	Buenos Aires
1971	1 United States (J Nicklaus and L Trevino); 2 South Africa (H Henning and G Player) (Individual: J Nicklaus, USA, 271)	555	Palm Beach, Florida
1972	1 Taiwan (H Min-Nan and LL Huan); 2 Japan (T Kono and T Murakami) (Three rounds only – Individual: H Min-Nan, Taiwan, 217)	438	Melbourne
1973	1 United States (J Nicklaus and J Miller); 2 South Africa (G Player and H Baiocchi) (Individual: J Miller, USA, 277)	558	Marbella, Spain
1974	1 South Africa (R Cole and D Hayes); 2 Japan (I Aoki and M Ozaki) (Individual: R Cole, South Africa, 271)	554	Caracas
1975	1 United States (J Miller and L Graham); 2 Taiwan (H Min-Nan and KC Hsiung) (Individual: J Miller, USA, 275)	554	Bangkok
1976	1 Spain (S Ballesteros and M Pinero); 2 United States (J Pate and D Stockton) (Individual: EP Acosta, Mexico, 282)	574	Palm Springs
1977	1 Spain (S Ballesteros and A Garrido); 2 Philippines (R Lavares and B Arda) (Individual: G Player, South Africa, 289)	591	Manilla, Philippines
1978	1 United States (J Mahaffey and A North); 2 Australia (G Norman and W Grady) (Individual: J Mahaffey, USA, 281)	564	Hawaii
1979	1 United States (J Mahaffey and H Irwin); 2 Scotland (A Lyle and K Brown) (Individual: H Irwin, USA, 285)	575	Glyfada, Greece
1980	1 Canada (D Halldorson and J Nelford); 2 Scotland (A Lyle and S Martin) (Individual: A Lyle, Scotland, 282)	572	Bogota
1981	*Not played*		
1982	1 Spain (M Pinero and JM Canizares); 2 United States (B Gilder and B Clampett) (Individual: M Pinero, Spain, 281)	563	Acapulco
1983	1 United States (R Caldwell and J Cook); 2 Canada (D Barr and J Anderson) (Individual: D Barr, Canada, 276)	565	Pondok Inah, Jakarta
1984	1 Spain (JM Canizares and J Rivero); 2 Scotland (S Torrance and G Brand Jr) (Played over 54 holes because of storms – Individual: JM Canizares, Spain, 205)	414	Olgiata, Rome
1985	1 Canada (D Halidorson and D Barr); 2 England (H Clark and P Way) (Individual: H Clark, England, 272)	559	La Quinta, Calif.
1986	*Not played*		
1987	1 Wales* (I Woosnam and D Llewelyn); 2 Scotland (S Torrance and A Lyle) (**Wales won play-off* – Individual: I Woosnam, Wales, 274)	574	Kapalua, Hawaii
1988	1 United States (B Crenshaw and M McCumber); 2 Japan (T Ozaki and M Ozaki) (Individual: B Crenshaw, USA, 275)	560	Royal Melbourne, Australia
1989	1 Australia (P Fowler and W Grady); 2 Spain (JM Olazábal and JM Canizares) (Played over 36 holes because of storms – Individual: P Fowler)	278	Las Brisas, Spain
1990	1 Germany (B Langer and T Giedeon); 2 England (M James and R Boxall) / Ireland (R Rafferty and D Feherty) tied (Individual: P Stewart, USA, 271)	556	Grand Cypress Resort, Orlando, Florida
1991	1 Sweden (A Forsbrand and P-U Johansson); 2 Wales (I Woosnam and P Price) (Individual: I Woosnam, Wales, 273)	563	La Querce, Rome
1992	1 USA (F Couples and D Love III); 2 Sweden (A Forsbrand and P-U Johansson) (Individual: B Ogle*, Australia, 270 (**after a tie with Ian Woosnam, Wales*))	548	La Moraleja II, Madrid, Spain
1993	1 USA (F Couples and D Love III); 2 Zimbabwe (N Price and M McNulty) (Individual: B Langer, Germany, 272)	556	Lake Nona, Orlando, Forida
1994	1 USA(F Couples and D Love III); 2 Zimbabwe (M McNulty and T Johnstone) (Individual: F Couples, USA, 265)	536	Dorado Beach, Puerto Rico
1995	1 USA (F Couples and D Love III); 2 Australia (B Ogle and R Allenby) (Individual: D Love III, USA, 267)	543	Mission Hills, Shenzhen, China
1996	1 South Africa (E Els and W Westner); 2 USA (T Lehman and S Jones) (Individual: E Els, S. Africa, 272)	547	Erinvale, Cape Town South Africa
1997	1 Ireland (P Harrington and P McGinley); 2 Scotland (C Montgomerie and R Russell) (Individual: C Montgomerie, Scotland, 266)	545	Kiawah Island, SC

World Cup of Golf *continued*

1998	1 England (N Faldo and D Carter); 2 Italy (C Rocca and M Florioli) (Individual: Scott Verplank, USA, 279)	568	Auckland, New Zealand
1999	1 USA (T Woods and M O'Meara); 2 Spain (S Luna and MA Martin) (Individual: Tiger Woods, USA, 263)	545	The Mines Resort, K Lumpur, Malaysia
2000	1 USA (T Woods and D Duval); 2 Argentina (A Cabrera & E Romero)	254	Buenos Aires GC Argentina
2001	1 South Africa* (E Els and R Goosen); 2 New Zealand (M Campbell and D Smail) / USA (D Duval and T Woods) / Denmark (T Bjørn and S Hansen) tied	254	The Taiheiyo Club, Japan
	**South Africa won at the second extra hole*		
2002	1 Japan (S Maruyama and T Izawa); 2 USA (P Mickelson and D Toms)	252	Puerto Vallarta, Mexico
2003	1 South Africa (T Immelman and R Sabbatini); 2 England (J Rose and P Casey)	275	Kiawah Island, SC
2004	1 England (L Donald and P Casey); 2 Spain (MA Jiménez and S García) *Reduced to 54 holes because of rain*	257	Real Club de Sevilla, Spain
2005	1 Wales (B Dredge and S Dodd); 2 Sweden (N Fasth and H Stenson) *Reduced to 54 holes because of bad weather*	189	Vilamoura, Portugal
2006	1 Germany* (B Langer and M Siem); 2 Scotland (C Montgomerie and M Warren) **Germany beat Scotland at the first extra hole*	268	Sandy Lane Resort, Barbados
2007	1 Scotland* (C Montgomerie and M Warren); 2 Germany (B Weekley and H Slocum) **Scotland beat USA at the third extra hole*	263	Shenzhen, China
2008	1 Sweden (R Karlsson and H Stenson); 2 Spain (MA Jiménez and P Larrazabal)	261	Shenzhen, China
2009	1 Italy (E Molinari and F Molinari); 2T Ireland (G McDowell and R McIlroy)/ Sweden (R Karlsson and H Stenson)	259	Shenzhen, China
2010	*Not played – this event will now be held bienially in odd-numbered years*		
2011	1 USA (M Kuchar and G Woodland); 2T England (I Poulter and J Rose)/Germany (A Cejka and M Kaymer)	264	Shenzhen, China

European Tour now has 45 Honorary Members

Honorary Membership was conferred on four more players by the European Tour in 2012. Luke Donald, who became the first player to top the money list on both sides of the Atlantic in 2011, was joined by two former Ryder Cup captains, Mark James and Brian Huggett, Roger Chapman, winner of two US Senior major titles in 2012, and 71-year-old Tommy Horton, who was a founder member of the European Senior Tour on which he had 23 successes.

The total of Honorary Members is now 45.

The full list is: John Jacobs OBE, Bernard Hunt MBE, Dai Rees CBE, Peter Butler, Severiano Ballesteros (ESP), Tony Jacklin CBE, Sir Henry Cotton MBE, Fred Daly MBE, Max Faulkner OBE, Bernhard Langer (GER), Sandy Lyle MBE, Sir Nick Faldo MBE, Ian Woosnam OBE, José Maria Olazábal (ESP), Sir Bob Charles (NZL), Arnold Palmer (USA), Gary Player (RSA), Colin Montgomerie OBE, Ernie Els (RSA), Paul Lawrie MBE, Greg Norman (AUS), Vijay Singh (FIJ), Retief Goosen (RSA), Peter Alliss, Bernard Gallacher OBE, Neil Coles MBE, Christy O'Connor (IRL), John Panton, Michael Campbell (NZL), Angel Cabrera (ARG), Padraig Harrington (IRL), Trevor Immelman (RSA), Martin Kaymer (GER), Graeme McDowell MBE, Louis Oosthuizen (RSA), Tom Watson (USA), Darren Clarke OBE, Rory McIlroy MBE, Charl Schwartzel (RSA), Lee Westwood OBE, Luke Donald MBE, Tommy Horton MBE, Brian Huggett MBE, Roger Chapman and Mark James.

Month by month in 2012

Webb Simpson makes it nine first-time major winners in a row when he comes from four back to take the US Open at Olympic Club. Britain and Ireland's women amateurs regain the Curtis Cup at Nairn, placing it alongside the Ryder, Solheim and Walker Cups for the first time. China has its first major champion, Shanshan Feng taking the LPGA Championship, and Northern Ireland's success story goes on with Alan Dunbar becoming Amateur champion.

National Championships 2012

Glenmuir PGA Club Professionals' Championship
De Vere Carden Park (Nicklaus course)

1	Gareth Wright (West Linton)	66-69-71-65—271
2	Craig Shave (Whitstone)	67-67-74-67—275
3	Steve Parry (North-West Golf Academy)	70-67-74-66—277
	Stuart Little (Minchinhampton)	69-66-72-70—277

ISPS Handa PGA Seniors Championship *De Vere Slaley Hall (Hunting course)*

1	Paul Wesselingh (Kedleston Park)	72-71-67—210
2	Andrew Oldcorn (King's Acre)	72-69-70—211
3	Anders Forsbrand (SWE)	70-71-70—211

Senior PGA Professional Championship *Northamptonshire County*

1	Paul Wesselingh (Kedleston Park)	72-65-69—206
2	Garry Harvey (Kinross)	71-66-72—209
3	Alastair Webster (Edzell)	73-67-70—210
	John Hoskison (Newbury)	67-71-72—210
	Mark Stokes (Rayleigh Golf Range)	67-68-75—210

Powerade PGA Assistants' Championship *East Sussex National*

1	Matthew Cort (Rothley Park)	69-71-71—211
2	Kevin Harper (Sidmouth)	67-72-74—213
	Thomas Murray (Didsbury)	71-68-74—213

Southern PGA Championship *The Drift GC*

1	Adam Wootton (Oxford Golf Centre)	71-70-70—211
2	Guy Woodman (East Berkshire)	72-68-72—212
3	William Hodkin (Performance Golf)	72-70-71—213
	Craig Cowper (Horton Park)	67-76-70—213

102nd Irish PGA Championship *Mount Juliet GC, Kilkenny*
(Championship reduced to 54 holes because of heavy rain on first day)

1	David Higgins (Waterville Golf Links)*	70-72-67—209
2	Noel Murray (Massereene GC)	70-70-69—209
	Gary Murphy (Laytown and Bettystown)	70-69-70—209

**Higgins won play off at the third extra hole*

Irish Club Professionals Tournament *Dundalk GC*

1	Michael Allen (Pure Golf Leopardstown)	65
2	Mark O'Sullivan (Ashbourne)	67
	Brendan McGovern (Headfort)	67
	Richard Creamer (Tuam)	67

(Event reduced to 18-holes because of bad weather

Gleneagles Scottish PGA Championship *Gleneagles Golf Resort, (King's course)*

1	Graham Fox (Rowallan Castle)	68-67-65-69—269
2	Greig Hutcheon (Banchory)	68-68-68-67—271
3	Scott Henderson (King's Links)	68-69-66-69—272

Scottish Young Professionals Championship *West Lothian GC*

1	Graeme Brown (Montrose Golf Links)	72-69-70-73—284
2	Michael Patterson (Kilmacolm)	72-71-73-69—285
3	Keir McNicoll (Gullane)	68-72-71-75—286

Paul Lawrie Invitational *Desside GC (Houghton course)*

1	Greg McBain (Gamola Golf)	67-68-68—203
2	Gareth Wright (West Linton)	68-67-69—204
3	Paul Lawrie (The Carnegie Club)	70-68-69—205

Aberdeen Asset Management Northern Open *Meldrum House GC*

1	James Byrne (Banchory)	66-66-66-70—268
2	David Orr (Mearns Castle)	69-66-66-69—273
	David Law (Paul Lawrie Golf Centre)	73-68-63-69—273

Welsh National PGA Championship *Cardiff GC*

1	Stuart Manley (Machynys Peninsula GC)	64-71—135
2	Richard Disndale (Parc Golf Academy)	72-66—138
	Andrew Barnet (North Wales Golf Range)	69-69—138

Farmfoods British Par-3 Championship *Nailcote Hall Hotel*

1	David Russell (Archerfield)	50-50—100
2	Simon Lilly (Wellingborough)	47-56—103
3	Mark Murphy (IRL)	56-59—105
	Gary Wolstenholme (Carus Green)	53-52—105

PGAs of Europe Fourball Championship *Lumine Golf and Beach Club, Spain*

1	Matt Maguire (ENG) and Craig Swinburn (ENG)	61-65-67—193
2	Michael Jones (ENG) and Gary Houston (ENG)	66-65-65—196
3	Matthew Dearden (WAL) and Paul Brown (FRA)	66-67-65—198
	Simon Edwards (WAL) and David Shacklady (ENG)	65-67-66—198
	Grant Hamerton (ENG) and David Smith (ENG)	63-67-68—198
	Alessandro Napoleoni and Emanuele Canonica (ITA)	66-68-64—198
	Mariano Saiz (ESP) and Mikel Galdos (ESP)	66-66-66—198

Unicredit PGAs of Europe Championship *Pravets GR and Spa, Bulgaria*

1	Hugo Santon (POR)	68-70-68-72—278
2	Lee Rooke (WAL)	71-71-67-71—279
	Frederic Cupillard (FRA)	72-70-65-72—279
	Mikel Galdos (ESP)	67-71-66-75—279

Nedbank Golf Challenge *Gary Player CC, Sun City, South Africa*

1	Martin Kaymer (GER)	72-69-70-69—280
2	Charl Schwartzel (RSA)	72-71-70-69—282
3	Bill Haas (USA)	70-73-71-71—285

County, District and other Regional Championships

Bedford & Cambridge PGA: Stuart Brown

Berks, Bucks & Oxon: David Stanton

Channel Islands Challenge: Wayne Stephens

Cheshire & North Wales: William Barnes (S); Matthew Parsley (M)

Cornish Festival: Simon Lilly/Paul Broadbent (tie)

Cumbria Masters: Mark Ridley

Dorset Open: Lee James

East Anglian Open: James Scade

East Region Championship: Alex Woodward (am)

Essex Open: Ben Horton (am)

Essex PGA: Jason Levermore

Hampshire, Isle of Wight and Channel Islands PGA: Andrew Cloke

Hampshire, Isle of Wight and Channel Islands Stroke Play: Nick Redfern

Hampshire, Isle of Wight and Channel Islands Open: James Ablett

Hertfordshire County PGA: Laurence Allen (M); Paul Hetherington (S)

Kent Open: Zane Scotland

Kent PGA: Richard Wallis

Lancashire Open: Adrian Ambler

Leeds Cup: Garry Houston

Midland Open: Lee Clarke

Midland PGA: Jak Hamblett

Midland Masters: Peter Baker

Middlesex PGA: Alistair Bennett

Middlesex Open: Vanslow Phillips

Norfolk PGA: Ian Ellis

Norfolk Open: Ian Ellis

Northamptonshire PGA: Dan Wood (S); Sam Jarman (M)

North East/North West: John Harrison

North Region PGA: Adrian Ambler

Northumberland & Durham Open: Darren Pearce

Shropshire & Hereford Open: Phil Hinton

Southern Open: Adam Wootton

Southern PGA: Ben St John

South Wales Festival: Stuart Manley

Suffolk Open: Lawrence Dodd

Suffolk PGA: Kevin Earp (M); Keith Preston (S)

Surrey Open: Richard Wallis

Surrey PGA: David Callaway

Sussex Open: Russell Buxton

Sussex PGA: Ryan Fenwick

Ulster PGA: Niall Kearney

Welsh National PGA: Stuart Manley

West Region PGA: Matthew Dearden

West Region Championship: Liam Bond

Perfectionist Jaime Ortiz-Patino – the man who brought the Ryder Cup to Continental Europe

Jaime Ortiz-Patino, who has died in Southern Spain in a hospital not far from his beloved Valderrama, was one of the European golf's most ardent supporters. In 2010 he was made an Honorary Life Vice-President of the European Tour in recognition of the work he had done in support of European golf. It was an award richly deserved.

George O'Grady, chief executive of the European Tour said: "Jaime Ortiz-Patino provided many proud moments in European golf and in many ways changed the face of golf in Europe. His foresight and dedication to the game was legendary as was his dedication to excellence in the preparation of a golf course. He raised the bar in that respect."

Tireless in his efforts to improve Valderrama, the golf course he originally bought with some friends so that they could play without being disturbed but of which he later became sole owner, he was rewarded in 1997 when he hosted the Ryder Cup which, under the captaincy of the late Severiano Ballesteros, Europe won.

That match was played in almost monsoon-like conditions which would have caused extensive flooding and made completion of the match on any other course impossible but such was the care Mr Ortiz-Patino, helped by friends from the USGA, had taken to ensure proper drainage the match finished on schedule.

Jimmy, as he was affectionately known to his many friends, was such an enthusiast that he was not averse to getting up in the middle of the night to go and help the greenkeeping staff get the course in the best possible condition. Tirelessly, he transformed Valderrma into one of the top courses in Europe and certainly the best in Spain.

In addition to the Cup match he was the always generous host at 16 Volvo Masters and at two World Golf Championships run jointly by the US PGA and the European Tour. The course, designed and later improved by Robert Trent Jones, was an excellent test especially when the wind blew, not that that prevented Bernhard Langer once shooting a fabulous record 62, arguably the best round of his career.

Valderrama brought out the best in the best with Langer, Sir Nick Faldo, Sandy Lyle, Graeme McDowell, Ian Poulter, Justin Rose, Colin Montgomerie and Tiger Woods among those who won there.

Jimmy, born to Bolivian parents in Paris in 1930, took an interest in golf after he offered to step in as a replacement caddie for Dai Rees in the last round of the 1956 Italian Open. Rees just happened to be the captain of the side that would go on to beat the Americans at Lindrick the following year and instead of paying Ortiz-Patino he gave him two tickets for the match. Jimmy was hooked.

John Hopkins, formerly golf correspondent of *The Times*, summed up Jimmy Patino as "a man with impeccable manners, endless charm, lots of money and a determination to achieve whatever he set his mind to." Whether that be to weed out corruption in bridge when he became chairman of the World Bridge Federation or to learn as much as he could about the many different strains of grass to help him make Valderrama one of the best conditioned courses in the world.

He had a wide range of interests – the buying of impressionist paintings and old golf memorabilia among the most rewarding. He enjoyed watching soccer in Spain and in England initially with Manchester United but, after they were bought out by the Americans, he switched his allegiance to Arsenal.

Nuno de Brito e Cunha, President of the Club de Golf Valderrama, paying his tribute, said: "Don Jaime's work will endure for all time. The historic moments during the tournaments at Valderrama will remain for ever in the memory of golf fans around the world."

It was fortunate in so many different ways that he loved golf so much because it proved so beneficial to us all. With Jaime Ortiz-Patino's death at the age of 82, world golf and European golf in particular has lost a true champion, a worthy and enthusiastic ambassador and a loyal and trusted friend.

PART III

Women's Professional Tournaments

Rolex Women's World Golf Rankings

at the end of the European, American and Japanese Tour seasons

Rank	*Name*	*Country*	*Events*	*Average points*	*Total points*
1	Yani Tseng	TPE	50	11.44	571.82
2	Na Yeon Choi	KOR	55	9.53	524.28
3	Stacy Lewis	USA	53	8.90	471.61
4	Inbee Park	KOR	65	8.39	545.13
5	Shanshan Feng	CHN	60	7.57	454.26
6	Suzann Pettersen	NOR	47	7.43	349.02
7	Jiyai Shin	KOR	52	7.05	366.64
8	So Yeon Ryu	KOR	51	6.98	356.06
9	Ai Miyazato	JPN	49	6.94	340.16
10	Mika Miyazato	JPN	50	6.14	306.92
11	Cristie Kerr	USA	46	5.92	272.53
12	Paula Creamer	USA	47	5.61	263.67
13	Sun Ju Ahn	KOR	49	5.52	270.69
14	Catriona Matthew	SCO	43	5.36	230.59
15	Amy Yang	KOR	46	5.35	245.97
16	Azahara Muñoz	ESP	52	5.24	272.69
17	Karrie Webb	AUS	42	5.21	218.94
18	Brittany Lincicome	USA	46	4.92	226.22
19	Chie Arimura	JPN	53	4.85	256.96
20	Angela Stanford	USA	48	4.85	232.64
21	I K Kim	KOR	43	4.59	197.39
22	Mi-Jeong Jeon	KOR	59	4.57	269.53
23	Sun Young Yoo	KOR	47	4.35	204.66
24	Lexi Thompson	USA	39	4.25	165.93
25	Ji-Hee Lee	KOR	55	4.06	223.42
26	Se-Ri Pak	KOR	35	3.91	137.01
27	Brittany Lang	USA	47	3.74	175.55
28	Anna Nordqvist	SWE	49	3.72	182.06
29	Ha Neul Kim	KOR	43	3.69	158.59
30	Hee Kyung Seo	KOR	52	3.28	170.76
31	Bo-Mee Lee	KOR	56	3.26	182.37
32	Sandra Gal	GER	53	3.24	171.48
33	Karine Icher	FRA	34	3.19	111.57
34	Sakura Yokomine	JPN	63	3.05	192.26
35	Miki Saiki	JPN	62	3.02	187.15
36	Chella Choi	KOR	48	2.95	141.69
37	Hee Young Park	KOR	54	2.79	150.49
38	Morgan Pressel	USA	48	2.76	132.56
39	Yuri Fudoh	JPN	46	2.68	123.18
40	Caroline Hedwall	SWE	48	2.63	126.42
41	Rikako Morita	JPN	65	2.57	167.07
42	Soo-Jin Yang	KOR	40	2.55	101.86
43	Lydia Ko	NZL	12	2.53	88.71
44	Mayu Hattori	JPN	65	2.42	157.59
45	Jenny Shin	KOR	41	2.40	98.38
46	Haeji Kang	KOR	44	2.34	102.78
47	Ritsuko Ryu	JPN	65	2.29	149.06
48	Caroline Masson	GER	36	2.29	82.46
49	Carlota Ciganda	ESP	26	2.21	77.31
50	Char Young Kim	KOR	39	2.13	83.09

Ladies European Tour

www.ladieseuropeantour.com

ISPS Handa Order of Merit

(figures in brackets show number of tournaments played)

1	Carlota Ciganda (ESP)	(19)	€251,289
2	Caroline Masson (GER)	(19)	241,831
3	Shanshan Feng (CHN)	(3)	202,147
4	Julieta Granada (PAR)	(6)	164,042
5	Carly Booth (SCO)	(19)	164,020
6	Stacey Keating (AUS)	(22)	159,782
7	Lee-Anne Pace (RSA)	(19)	159,616
8	Diana Luna (ITA)	(16)	150,477
9	Laura Davies (ENG)	(18)	130,293
10	Trish Johnson (ENG)	(19)	124,438
11	Catriona Matthew (SCO)	(4)	118,183
12	Anne-Lise Caudal (FRA)	(19)	117,402
13	Anna Nordqvist (SWE)	(3)	106,404
14	Christel Boeljon (NED)	(6)	104,884
15	Florentyna Parker (ENG)	(18)	101,237
16	Lydia Hall (WAL)	(14)	100,476
17	Gwladys Nocera (FRA)	(22)	99,744
18	Pernilla Lindberg (SWE)	(14)	99,404
19	Beatriz Recari (ESP)	(3)	96,082
20	Felicity Johnson (ENG)	(21)	93,263
21	Line Vedel (DEN)	(17)	91,853
22	Beth Allen (USA)	(20)	87,278
23	Nontaya Srisawang (THA)	(15)	86,219
24	Dewi Claire Schreefel (NED)	(8)	86,140
25	Joanna Klatten (FRA)	(19)	84,572
26	Giulia Sergas (ITA)	(10)	83,545
27	Rebecca Hudson (ENG)	(17)	82,944
28	Melissa Reid (ENG)	(12)	82,752
29	Caroline Hedwall (SWE)	(6)	80,779
30	Carin Koch (SWE)	(14)	78,895
31	Mikaela Parmlid (SWE)	(12)	77,842
32	Holly Aitchison (ENG)	(17)	76,532
33	Lindsey Wright (AUS)	(7)	76,286
34	Veronica Zorzi (ITA)	(18)	74,979
35	Karen Lunn (AUS)	(21)	73,280
36	Stacy Lee Bregman (RSA)	(18)	71,327
37	Nikki Garrett (AUS)	(20)	70,777
38	Ashleigh Simon (RSA)	(18)	70,020
39	Suzann Pettersen (NOR)	(4)	69,211
40	Karine Icher (FRA)	(4)	68,229
41	Ursula Wikstrom (FIN)	(12)	67,245
42	Cindy Lacrosse (USA)	(6)	67,235
43	Linda Wessberg (SWE)	(22)	65,368
44	Caroline Afonso (FRA)	(18)	63,457
45	Rebecca Artis (AUS)	(22)	63,049
46	Anja Monke (GER)	(14)	62,769
47	Sophie Giquel-Bettan (FRA)	(21)	61,577
48	Azahara Muñoz (ESP)	(4)	60,059
49	Bree Arthur (AUS)	(21)	59,204
50	Tandi Cuningham (RSA)	(14)	58,818
51	Cassandra Kirkland (FRA)	(16)	58,523
52	Becky Brewerton (WAL)	(22)	56,367
53	Julie Greciet (FRA)	(18)	56,169
54	Marianne Skarpnord (NOR)	(19)	56,127
55	Jade Schaeffer (FRA)	(13)	55,415
56	Frances Bondad (AUS)	(17)	50,459
57	Becky Morgan (WAL)	(10)	49,939
58	Lexi Thompson (USA)	(5)	49,637
59	Ai Miyazato (JPN)	(2)	49,582
60	Elizabeth Bennett (ENG)	(19)	48,917
61	Danielle Montgomery (ENG)	(22)	48,381
62	Stefania Croce (ITA)	(16)	47,681
63	Alison Walshe (USA)	(6)	46,907
64	Marjet Van Der Graaff (NED)	(14)	45,130
65	Sarah Kemp (AUS)	(11)	44,914
66	Amy Yang (KOR)	(2)	44,527
67	Stephanie Na (AUS)	(17)	43,790
68	Rebecca Codd (IRL)	(21)	42,562
69	Henni Zuel (ENG)	(12)	41,068
70	Esther Choe (USA)	(11)	40,335
71	Anais Maggetti (SUI)	(17)	37,316
72	Connie Chen (RSA)	(20)	37,122
73	Tania Elosegui (ESP)	(18)	36,816
74	Titiya Plucksataporn (THA)	(19)	33,706
75	Rachel Bailey (AUS)	(15)	32,613
76	Hannah Burke (ENG)	(11)	31,218
77	Sahra Hassan (WAL)	(17)	31,176
78	Hannah Jun (USA)	(6)	30,659
79	Sophie Walker (ENG)	(16)	28,363
80	Lucie Andre (FRA)	(19)	27,843
81	Kylie Walker (SCO)	(20)	26,980
82	Virginie Lagoutte-Clement (FRA)	(20)	26,893
83	Alison Whitaker (AUS)	(14)	25,110
84	Jessica Yadloczky (USA)	(13)	24,689
85	Valentine Derrey (FRA)	(10)	24,350
86	Lisa Holm Sorensen (DEN)	(11)	23,626
87	Margherita Rigon (ITA)	(16)	23,431
88	Sophie Gustafson (SWE)	(6)	22,457
89	Minea Blomqvist (FIN)	(9)	22,448
90	Klara Spilkova (CZE)	(15)	22,306
91	Celine Palomar (FRA)	(15)	21,675
92	Amelia Lewis (USA)	(8)	20,536
93	Miriam Nagl (GER)	(11)	20,527
94	Sophie Sandolo (ITA)	(15)	20,446
95	Louise Larsson (SWE)	(21)	19,711
96	Caroline Westrup (SWE)	(11)	19,229
97	Stefanie Michl (AUT)	(15)	18,820
98	Yu Yang Zhang (CHN)	(13)	17,697
99	Meaghan Francella (USA)	(4)	17,670
100	Malene Jorgensen (DEN)	(17)	17,416

2012 Tour Statistics

Scoring average

		Points			Points
1	Shanshan Feng (CHN)	69.00	6	Azahara Muñoz (ESP)	71.29
2	Carlota Ciganda (ESP)	70.50	7	Julieta Granada (PAR)	71.52
3	Caroline Hedwall (SWE)	70.55	8	Caroline Masson (GER)	71.78
4	Diana Luna (ITA)	71.13		Pernilla Lindberg (SWE)	71.78
5	Nontaya Srisawang (THA)	71.17	10	Veronica Zorzi (ITA)	71.84

Driving distance

		Yards			Yards
1	Carly Booth (SCO)	268.8	6	Carmen Alonso (ESP)	265.8
2	Marjet Van Der Graaff (NED)	267.9	7	Kylie Walker (SCO)	265.0
3	Jade Schaeffer (FRA)	267.8	8	Laura Davies (ENG)	264.8
4	Lisa Holm Sorensen (DEN)	267.3	9	Tania Elosegui (ESP)	264.4
5	Joanna Klatten (FRA)	266.0	10	Melissa Reid (ENG)	264.1

Greens in regulation

		%			%
1	Sophie Sandolo (ITA)	89.68	6	Stefania Croce (ITA)	76.09
2	Carlota Ciganda (ESP)	80.36	7	Barbara Genuini (FRA)	75.76
3	Felicity Johnson (ENG)	79.06	8	Dewi Claire Schreefel (NED)	75.07
4	Rebecca Hudson (ENG)	78.67	9	Linda Wessberg (SWE)	74.76
5	Charlotte Ellis (ENG)	76.78	10	Trish Johnson (ENG)	74.68

Putts per round

		Av.			Av.
1	Melissa Reid (ENG)	28.9	6	Line Vedel (DEN)	29.4
2	Nicole Gergely (AUT)	29.1	7	Stefanie Michl (AUT)	29.4
3	Stacey Keating (AUS)	29.2	8	Dewi Claire Schreefel (NED)	29.6
4	Ashleigh Simon (RSA)	29.2	9	Becky Morgan (WAL)	29.7
5	Minea Blomqvist (FIN)	29.3	10	Lee-Anne Pace (RSA)	29.7

Total eagles

		Total			Total
1	Carly Booth (SCO)	7	7T	Bree Arthur (AUS)	4
	Florentyna Parker (ENG)	7		Rebecca Hudson (ENG)	4
3	Stacey Keating (AUS)	5		Stefania Croce (ITA)	4
	Rebecca Codd (IRL)	5		Stacy Lee Bregman (RSA)	4
	Veronica Zorzi (ITA)	5		Celine Palomar (FRA)	4
	Lee-Anne Pace (RSA)	5		Diana Luna (ITA)	4
7	Gwladys Nocera (FRA)	4		Jade Schaeffer (FRA)	4
	Trish Johnson (ENG)	4			

Total birdies

		Total			Total
1	Carlota Ciganda (ESP)	204	6	Anne-Lise Caudal (FRA)	182
2	Carly Booth (SCO)	192		Gwladys Nocera (FRA)	182
3	Stacey Keating (AUS)	189	8	Joanna Klatten (FRA)	170
4	Trish Johnson (ENG)	186	9	Felicity Johnson (ENG)	168
	Laura Davies (ENG)	186	10	Lee-Anne Pace (RSA)	164

2012 Tour Results (in chronological order)

For past results see earlier editions of *The R&A Golfer's Handbook*

Gold Coast RACV Ladies' Masters *Royal Pines, Gold Coast, Queensland, Australia* Feb 2–5 [5182m–72]

1	Christel Boeljon (NED)	66-65-68-68—267	€63,631
2	Diana Luna (ITA)	71-64-66-67—268	30,967
	So Yeon Ryu (KOR)	66-61-69-72—268	30,967
	Ha-Neul Kim (KOR)	72-65-64-67—268	30,967

ISPS Handa Women's Australian Open *Royal Melbourne, Victoria, Australia* Feb 9–12 [6505–73]

1	Jessica Korda (USA)*	72-70-73-74—289	€122,595
2	Hee-Kyung Seo (KOR)	75-66-75-73—289	47,391
	Stacey Lewis (USA)	69-73-77-70—289	47,391
	Brittany Lincicombe (USA)	70-75-73-71—289	47,391
	Julieta Granada (PAR)	70-72-76-71—289	47,391
	So Yeon Ryu (KOR)	71-69-76-73—289	47,391

**Korda won at the second extra hole*

ISPS Handa New Zealand Women's Open *Pegasus, Christchurch, New Zealand* Feb 17–19 [5631m–72]

1	Lindsey Wright (AUS)	70-68-68—206	€33,333
2	Jessica Speechley (AUS)	69-73-65—207	18,666
	Alison Walshe (USA)	68-70-69—207	18,666

World Ladies Championships *Mission Hills, Hainan, China* Mar 2–4 [7363–72]

Individual

1	Shanshan Feng (CHN)	66-69-71—206	€56,275
2	Pornanong Phatlum (THA)	68-69-70—207	38,080
3	Pernilla Lindberg (SWE)	69-70-69—208	26,262

Team

1	China I		134-136-145—415	€36,000
	Shanshan Feng	66-69-71—206		
	Li Ying Ye	68-67-74—209		
2	Thailand		138-140-139—417	20,000
	Pornanong Phatlum	68-69-70—207		
	Nontaya Srisawang	70-71-69—210		
3	Sweden		138-142-140—420	10,000
	Pernilla Lindberg	69-70-69—208		
	Linda Wessberg	69-72-71—212		

4 Italy; 5 England; 6 Chinese Tapei; 7 France; 8 Norway; 9 Germany, South Africa; 11 Scotland; 12 Philippines, USA; 14 Australia; 15 Spain; 16 Denmark; 17 China II; 18 Netherlands; 19 Korea; 20 Wales

Amateur

1	Jing Yan (CHN)	72-73-71—216
2	Lydia Ko (NZL)	71-71-76—218

Clean sweep for China as Shanshan Feng makes history

Shanshan Feng's one stroke victory in the individual stroke play event for professionals at Mission Hills, Hainan, China, saw her enter the pages of history as the first player from mainland China to win on the Ladies European Tour. Feng's partner in their team event victory, Li Ying Ye, shared fourth place with Italian Diana Luna. It was a clean sweep for Chinese players with Jin Yang winning the amateur individual event.

Lalla Meryem Cup *Golf de l'Ocean, Agadir, Morocco* Mar 22–25 [5747m–71]

1	Karen Lunn (AUS)	72-66-68-66—272	€48,750
2	Tandi Cuningham (RSA)	71-70-67-67—275	27,868
	Marianne Skarpnord (NOR)	70-65-71-69—275	27,868

Aberdeen Asset Management Ladies Scottish Open
Archerfield Links, East Lothian, Scotland May 3–5

1	Carly Booth (SCO)	70-71-71—212	€32,706
2	Frances Bondad (AUS)	71-75-67—213	18,696
	Florentyna Parker (ENG)	72-69-72—213	18,696

Turkish Airlines Ladies Open *National GC, Antalya, Turkey* May 10–13 [6279–72]

1	Christel Boeljon (NED)	70-73-69-73—285	€37,500
2	Ursula Wikstrom (FIN)	73-70-71-74—288	25,375
3	Carin Koch (SWE)	72-77-68-73—290	15,500
	Carlota Ciganda (ESP)	73-76-66-75—290	15,500

UniCredit Ladies German Open *Gut Häusern, Munich* May 24–27 [5832m–72]

1	Anne-Lise Caudal (FRA)*	74-67-67-67—275	€52,500
2	Laura Davies (ENG)	69-71-68-67—275	35,525

**Caudal won at the second extra hole*

3	Rebecca Hudson (ENG)	71-68-67-71—277	24,500

Deloitte Ladies Open *Broekpolder, Rotterdam, Netherlands* June 1–3 [5225m–72]

1	Carlota Ciganda (ESP)	71-67-69—207	€37,500
2	Ursula Wikstrom (FIN)	71-68-70—209	25,375
3	Lee-Anne Pace (RSA)	71-70-71—212	17,500

Allianz Ladies Slovak Open *Tále, Slovakia* June 8–10

1	Line Vedel (DEN)	71-69-69—209	€33,750
2	Caroline Masson (GER)	75-67-69—211	22,837
3	Nontaya Srisawang (THA)	70-73-70—213	13,950
	Veronica Zorzi (ITA)	70-72-71—213	13,950

Deutsche Bank Ladies Swiss Open *Ticino, Switzerland* June 14–17 [6292–72]

1	Carly Booth (SCO)*	70-71-67-68—276	€78,750
2	Anja Monke (GER)	71-72-67-66—276	45,018
	Caroline Masson (GER)	70-69-69-68—276	45,018

**Booth won at the fourth extra hole*

Raiffeisenbank Prague Golf Masters *Prague, Czech Republic* June 22–24 [6246–72]

1	Melissa Reid (ENG)	68-67-72—207	€37,500
2	Diana Luna (ITA)	70-69-69—208	25,375
3	Rachel Bailey (AUS)	70-73-66—209	15,500
	Rebecca Hudson (ENG)	70-68-71—209	15,500

South African Women's Open *KwaZulu-Natal, South Africa* July 13–15 [4794m–72]

1	Caroline Masson (GER)	69-75-71—215	€39,000
2	Lee-Anne Pace (RSA)	75-71-70—216	22,295
	Danielle Montgomery (ENG)	74-70-72—216	22,295

Evian Masters *Evian-Les-Bains, France* July 26–29 [6457–72]

1	Inbee Park (KOR)	71-64-70-66—271	€397,068
2	Karrie Webb (AUS)	70-69-67-67—273	210,392
	Stacy Lewis (USA)	63-69-73-68—273	210,392

Ladies Irish Open *Killeen Castle, Co Meath, R.o.I.* Aug 3–5

1	Catriona Matthew (SCO)	67-71-71—209	€52,500
2	Suzann Pettersen (NOR)	72-69-69—210	35,525
3	Laura Davies (ENG)	74-71-68—213	24,500

ISPS Handa Ladies British Masters *Denham, Buckinghamshire, England* Aug 16–18 [6401–72]

1	Lydia Hall (WAL)	66-71-72—209	€66,960
2	Beth Allen (USA)	68-69-73—210	45,310
3	Trish Johnson (ENG)	69-72-70—211	19,076
	Stacy Lee Bregman (RSA)	67-74-70—211	19,076
	Rebecca Artis (AUS)	71-70-70—211	19,076
	Henrietta Zuel (ENG)	66-75-70—211	19,076
	Mikaela Parmlid (SWE)	71-68-72—211	19,076
	Ashleigh Simon (RSA)	69-66-76—211	19,076

UNIQA Ladies Golf Open *Föhrenwald, Wiener Neustadt, Austria* Sep 7–9 [5078m–72]

1	Caroline Hedwall (SWE)	67-66-70—203	€30,000
2	Mikaela Parmlid (SWE)	68-71-68—207	17,150
	Laura Davies (ENG)	70-69-68—207	17,150

RICOH WOMEN'S BRITISH OPEN *Royal Liverpool GC, England* Sep 13–16 [6660–72]

1	Jiyai Shin (KOR)	71-64-71-73—279	€331,936
2	Inbee Park (KOR)	72-68-72-76—288	208,079
3	Paula Creamer (USA)	73-72-72-72—289	145,655

Full details of this event can be found on page 103

Tenerife Open de España Femenino *Las Americas Golf Course, Tenerife, Spain* Sep 20–23

1	Stacey Keating (AUS)*	70-69-70-70—279	€52,500
2	Caroline Masson (GER)	69-69-70-71—279	35,525

**Keating won at the first extra hole*

3	Trish Johnson (ENG)	67-74-72-67—280	24,500

Lacoste Ladies Open de France *Aquitaine, France* Oct 4–7 [6104–70]

1	Stacey Keating (AUS)	62-71-69-64—266	€37,500
2	Diana Luna (ITA)	67-64-68-68—267	25,375
3	Hannah Jun (USA)	68-68-67-66—269	15,500
	Azahara Muñoz (ESP)	66-71-66-66—269	15,500

China Suzhou Taihu Open *Suzhou, China* Oct 26–28

1	Carlota Ciganda (ESP)	65-70-64—199	€52,500
2	Caroline Masson (GER)	68-69-69—206	35,525
3	Julie Greciet (FRA)	71-70-69—210	21,700
	Florentyna Parker (ENG)	67-74-69—210	21,700

Sanya Ladies Open *Sanya, China* Nov 2–4

1	Cassandra Kirkland (FRA)	73-67-70—210	€37,500
2	Jade Schaeffer (FRA)	71-72-69—212	21,437
	Holly Aitchison (ENG)	72-69-71—212	21,437

Hero Honda Women's Indian Open *New Delhi, India* Nov 30–Dec 2

1	Pornanong Phatlum (THA)	72-65-66—203	€34,704
2	Caroline Hedwall (SWE)	76-62-69—207	23,483
3	Nontaya Srisawang (THA)	71-70-68—209	16,195

Omega Dubai Ladies Masters *Dubai, UAE* Dec 5–8 [6425–72]

1	Shanshan Feng (CHN)	66-65-67-69—267	€75,000
2	Dewi Claire Schreefel (NED)	69-71-63-69—272	50,750
3	Becky Brewerton (WAL)	70-73-68-65—276	31,000
	Caroline Masson (GER)	68-68-69-71—276	31,000

Women's World Cup

Not played

For list of past winners, see page 256

LET Access Series

www.letaccess.com

Mar 14–16	Terre Blanche Ladies Open	Terre Blanche, Nice, France	Marion Ricordeau (FRA)	211 (–8)
April 12–14	Dinard Ladies Open	Dinard Golf, Saint Briac Sur Mer, France	Carly Booth (SCO)*	206 (–1)
	**Beat Marion Ricordeau (FRA) in the play-off*			
April 19–21	Banesto Tour Zaragoza	CG La Peñaza, Zaragoza, Spain	Marjet van der Graaff (NED)	211 (–5)
May 10–12	Kristianstad Åhus Ladies Open	Kristianstad GC Åhus, Sweden	Cecilie Lundgreen (NOR)	222 (–6)
May 16–18	Ljungbyhed Park PGA Ladies Open	Ljungbyhed GC, Ljungbyhed, Sweden	Pamela Pretswell (SCO) (am)	212 (–1)
May 22–24	GolfStream Ladies Open	Kiev GC, Kiev, Ukraine	Anastasia Kostina (RUS)	215 (–1)
July 4–6	Ladies Norwegian Challenge	Losby GC, Oslo, Norway	Marianne Skarpnord (NOR)	212 (–4)
Aug 9–11	Women's Bank Open	Hill Side GC, Helsinki, Finland	Cecilie Lundgreen (NOR)	206 (–7)
Aug 16–18	Samsø Ladies Open	Samsø GC, Samsø, Denmark	Antonella Cvitan (SWE)	213 (–3)
Sep 13–15	Fourqueux Ladies Open	Golf de Fourqueux, Paris, France	Caroline Alfonso (FRA)	212 (–4)
Oct 5–7	Azores Ladies Open	Furnas Golf Course, São Miguel Island, Portugal	Anna Rossi (ITA)	147 (+3)
	The event was reduced to two rounds due to extremely high winds			
Oct 28–30	Crete Ladies Open	Crete GC, Greece	Christine Wolf (AUT)*	67 (–4)
	**Beat Chrisje de Vries (NED) at 1st extra hole – match reduced to 18 holes due to bad weather*			
Nov 8–10	Banesto Tour Valencia	CG Escorpion, Valencia, Spain	Holly Clyburn (ENG)*	213 (–3)
	**Beat Carmen Alonso (ESP) at the first extra hole*			

Final Ranking

1	Pamela Pretswell (SCO)	19,372 Pts	6	Antonella Cvitan (SWE)	10,735
2	Marion Ricordeau (FRA)	18,946	7	Anastasia Kostina (RUS)	10,083
3	Cecilie Lundgreen (NOR)	15,276	8	Viva Schlasberg (SWE)	9,964
4	Katy Mcnicoll (SCO)	15,165	9	Tamara Johns (AUS)	9,790
5	Julie Tvede (DEN)	12,027	10	Pamela Feggans (SCO)	9,580

Ladies European Tour honours Louise Solheim

Her husband, the late Karsten Solheim, founder of the Ping golf manufacturing company, was the innovator but Louise, his wife, who in 2012 was awarded honorary membership of the Ladies European Tour, walked with him every step of the way.

Her mother died just two months after she was born and with her school teacher father unable to care for her she was brought up for a time by an aunt and uncle in Texas. She met 18-year-old Karsten at church when she was just 17 and they married a year later.

Initially, engineer Karsten had little interest in golf but when that changed Louise was right there with him as he developed the Ping putter in his garage. When he was heat-treating the putters on her stove dinner was simply delayed. When the putters were successful she packaged the orders, kept the books and worked tirelessly behind the scenes to make Karsten's dream a reality.

When orders for the putters were flooding in from outside America, Louise attended a seminar on foreign trade at Arizona State University to learn how to process the overseas orders. She prepared the company's early legal contracts and even visited American golf shops to try and sell the putters, impressing her husband by being able to sell a putter to a customer in 10 minutes when it took him an hour to do so.

Together they travelled the world but she surprised Karsten on one occasions when she challenged him to a round of golf. Unbeknown to her surprised husband she had been taking lessons and the look on his face when she hit her opening drive at Flagstaff straight down the middle of the fairway was worth seeing.

Recipients together and individually of golfing awards from various organisations and countries, one of 92-year-old Louise Karsten's most treasured honours was the granting of an Honorary Doctor of Science to her from the Arizona State University. She had enrolled at the University of Washington when 17 but had been unable to attend.

In announcing her honorary membership, the Ladies European Tour have acknowledged Louise Solheim's graciousness and the Christian spirit she instills in all those who are fortunate to know her.

Augusta National Club now has women members

Monday August 20 was the day that history was made at the Augusta National Golf Club where the Masters Tournament is played each year,

For long the club had been solidly all male. Previous chairmen of the exceptionally private club had always indicated it was likely to stay that way, but not any more.

After 79 years the club, which was founded by Bobby Jones and investment banker Clifford Roberts in 1932, has admitted two women to membership.

Dr Condoleeza Rice, former national security adviser and Secretary of State under President George W Bush, and Ms Darla Moore, a South Carolina investment banker, will now be able to slip on their own Green Jackets.

Billy Payne, who has been chairman since 2006, described the move as "a joyous occasion and a significant and positive time in the National Club's history." ormer chairman William C "Hootie" Johnson, Billy Payne's predecessor, added: "This is wonderful news for Augusta National Golf Club. I could not be more pleased."

Referring to the two new members, Billy Payne said: "Both these accomplished women share our passion for the game of golf and both are well known and respected by our membership."

Dr Rice, whose home is in Stanford, California, said: "I have long admired the important role Augusta National has played in the traditions and history of golf. I have immense respect for the Masters Tournament and its commitment to grow the game of golf, particularly with youth, here in the United States and throughout the world. Golf is a wonderful source of enjoyment for me and I feel very fortunate to have this opportunity to grow my love for this great game."

Fifty-eight-year-old Ms Moore is vice-president of Rainwater Inc., an investment bank founded by her billionaire husband. The University of South Carolina's business school is named in her honour.

"I am fortunate to have many friends who are members at Augusta National so to be asked to join them as a member represents a very happy and important occasion in my life," she said. "Above all, Augusta National and the Masters Tournament have always stood for excellence and that is so important to me. I am extremely grateful for this privilege."

LPGA Tour

www.lpga.com

Players are American unless stated

Money List

1	Inbee Park (KOR)	$2,266,638
2	Stacy Lewis	1,863,956
3	Na Yeon Choi (KOR)	1,481,834
4	Yani Tseng (TPE)	1,419,850
5	Ai Miyazato (JPN)	1,286,927
6	Jiyai Shin (KOR)	1,222,366
7	Azahara Muñoz (ESP)	1,202,940
8	So Yeon Ryu (KOR)	1,176,294
9	Suzann Pettersen (NOR)	1,169,202
10	Mika Miyazato (JPN)	1,094,672
11	Shanshan Feng (CHN)	1,073,336
12	Amy Yang (KOR)	832,074
13	Karrie Webb (AUS)	825,275
14	Paula Creamer	809,750
15	Cristie Kerr	809,503
16	Angela Stanford	785,841
17	Sun Young Yoo (KOR)	770,259
18	Catriona Matthew (SCO)	705,819
19	Anna Nordqvist (SWE)	660,892
20	Chella Choi (KOR)	630,836
21	Lexi Thompson	604,294
22	Hee Kyung Seo (KOR)	591,950
23	Brittany Lang	561,605
24	Sandra Gal (GER)	557,841
25	I K Kim (KOR)	547,644
26	Brittany Lincicombe	504,460
27	Karine Icher (FRA)	502,219
28	Candie Kung (TPE)	479,236
29	Haeji Kang (KOR)	451,280
30	Jenny Shin (KOR)	444,586
31	Julieta Granada (PAR)	432,027
32	Se Ri Pak (KOR)	430,338
33	Beatriz Recari (ESP)	428,138
34	Hee Young Park (KOR)	423,203
35	Vicky Hurst	394,730
36	Eun-Hee Ji (KOR)	379,714
37	Katherine Hull (AUS)	367,739
38	Meena Lee (KOR)	367,585
39	Giulia Sergas (ITA)	351,331
40	Ilhee Lee (KOR)	347,327
41	Jessica Korda	336,175
42	Natalie Gulbis	315,648
43	Karin Sjodin (SWE)	306,085
44	Mina Harigae	293,748
45	Morgan Pressel	268,665
46	Hee-Won Han (KOR)	267,354
47	Katie Futcher	262,576
48	Gerina Piller	255,658
49	Lindsey Wright (AUS)	246,743
50	Jennifer Johnson	240,854
51	Nicole Castrale	224,008
52	Danielle Kang	222,702
53	Lizette Salas	221,593
54	Jodi Ewart (ENG)	214,934
55	Pornanong Phatlum (THA)	212,412
56	Momoko Ueda (JPN)	210,197
57	Cindy LaCrosse	205,748
58	Mi Jung Hur (KOR)	199,691
59	Caroline Hedwall (SWE)	195,632
60	Alison Walshe	190,733
61	Mariajo Uribe (COL)	190,536
62	Sydnee Michaels	184,091
63	Mo Martin	168,200
64	Sophie Gustafson (SWE)	158,089
65	Michelle Wie	155,809
66	Dewi Claire Schreefel (NED)	150,341
67	Sarah Jane Smith	148,626
68	Belen Mozo (ESP)	139,658
69	Jimin Kang (KOR)	133,130
70	Pernilla Lindberg (SWE)	127,418
71	Jennifer Song	124,494
72	Karen Stupples (ENG)	116,909
73	Jennie Lee	114,885
74	Becky Morgan (WAL)	111,725
75	Veronica Felibert (VEN)	107,217
76	Amanda Blumenherst	105,668
77	Mindy Kim	103,050
78	Jeong Jang (KOR)	100,946
79	Maria Hjörth (SWE)	96,685
80	Paige Mackenzie	94,045
81	Christel Boeljon (NED)	89,817
82	Kristy McPherson	88,674
83	Jennifer Rosales (PHI)	88,177
84	Taylor Coutu	82,210
85	Carlota Ciganda (ESP)	79,679
86	Kris Tamulis	77,166
87	Numa Gulyanamitta (THA)	71,511
88	Jin Young Pak (KOR)	70,413
89	Lorie Kane (CAN)	70,396
90	Jee Young Lee (KOR)	68,650
91	Moira Dunn	67,755
92	Jane Rah	59,862
93	Amy Hung (TPE)	58,361
94	Jane Park	54,648
95	Ryann O'Toole	53,590
96	Wendy Ward	50,459
97	Jacqui Concolino	50,097
98	Heather Bowie Young	50,027
99	Dori Carter	49,778
100	Juli Inkster	48,815

Asian players on top again

In a continuing theme, Asian golfers once again dominated the list of LPGA Tour event winners. Of the 28 events, 20 were won by non-American players with Asian golfers capturing 16 of these. Top of the list of multiple winners was the USA's Stacy Lewis with four victories with Taipei's Yani Tseng taking three titles. Ai Miyazato (JPN), Inbee Park (KOR), Suzann Pettersen (NOR), Jiyai Shin (KOR) and Na Yeon Choi (KOR) won two apiece.

2012 Tour Results (in chronological order)

ISPS Handa Women's Australian Open *Victoria, Australia* Feb 9–12 [6505–73]

1	Jessica Korda*	72-70-73-74—289	$165,000
2	Brittany Lincicome	70-75-73-71—289	63,784
	Julieta Granada (PHI)	70-72-76-71—289	63,784
	Stacy Lewis	69-73-77-70—289	63,784
	Hee Kyung Seo (KOR)	75-66-75-73—289	63,784
	So Yeon Ryu (KOR)	71-69-76-73—289	63,784

**Korda won at the second extra hole*

Honda LPGA Thailand *Chonburi, Thailand* Feb 16–19 [6477–72]

1	Yani Tseng (TPE)	73-65-65-66—269	$225,000
2	Ai Miyazato (JPN)	67-70-65-68—270	140,688
3	Jiyai Shin (KOR)	70-66-68-67—271	102,059

HSBC Women's Champions *Tanah Merah, Singapore* Feb 22–26 [6547–72]

1	Angela Stanford*	66-70-71-71—278	$210,000
2	Shanshan Feng (CHN)	69-71-69-69—278	102,564
	Na Yeon Choi (KOR)	68-71-71-68—278	102,564
	Jenny Shin (KOR)	69-67-71-71—278	102,564

**Stanford won at the third extra hole*

RR Donnelley LPGA Founders Cup *Phoenix, AZ* Mar 15–18 [6613–72]

1	Yani Tseng (TPE)	65-70-67-68—270	$225,000
2	Ai Miyazato (JPN)	68-68-66-69—271	118,654
	Na Yeon Choi (KOR)	67-69-67-68—271	118,654

KIA Classic *Carlsbad, CA* Mar 22–25 [6490–72]

1	Yani Tseng (TPE)	67-68-69-70—274	$255,000
2	Sun Young Yoo (KOR)	69-73-67-71—280	156,242
3	Shanshan Feng (CHN)	72-71-71-67—281	100,511
	Jiyai Shin (KOR)	68-71-68-74—281	100,511

KRAFT NABISCO CHAMPIONSHIP *Mission Hills CC, Rancho Mirage, CA* Mar 29–April 1 [6738–72]

1	Sun Young Yoo (KOR)*	69-69-72-69—279	$300,000
2	I K Kim (KOR)	70-70-70-69—279	182,538

**Yoo won at the first extra hole*

3	Yani Tseng (TPE)	68-68-71-73—280	132,418

Full details of this event can be found on page 133

LPGA LOTTE Championship *Kapolei, Oahu, HI* April 18–21 [6421–72]

1	Ai Miyazato (JPN)	71-65-70-70—276	$255,000
2	Meena Lee (KOR)	74-65-71-70—280	135,444
	Azahara Muñoz (ESP)	72-64-73-71—280	135,444

Mobile Bay LPGA Classic *Mobile, AL* April 26–29 [6521–72]

1	Stacy Lewis	68-67-67-69—271	$187,500
2	Lexi Thompson	70-71-66-65—272	114,347
3	Karine Icher (FRA)	72-65-68-68—273	82,951

HSBC Brasil Cup *Rio de Janeiro, Brazil* May 5–6 [6285–73]

1	Pornanong Phatlum (THA)	66-67—133	$108,000
2	Amy Hung (TPE)	72-65—137	83,990
3	Paula Creamer	69-69—138	54,031
	Chella Choi (KOR)	71-67—138	54,031

Sybase Match-Play Championship *Hamilton Farm, Gladstone, NJ* May 17–20 [6553–72]

Final: Azahara Muñoz (ESP) ($375,000) beat Candie Kung (TPE) ($225,000) 2 and 1

ShopRite LPGA Classic *Dolce Seaview Resort, Galloway, NJ* June 1–3 [6155–71]

1	Stacy Lewis	65-65-71—201	$225,000
2	Katherine Hull (AUS)	71-66-68—205	134,854
3	Mika Miyazato (JPN)	65-73-68—206	86,752
	Azahara Muñoz (ESP)	69-68-69—206	86,752

Wegmans LPGA Championship *Locust Hill, Pittsford, NY* June 7–10 [6534–72]

1	Shanshan Feng (CHN)	72-73-70-67—282	$375,000
2	Eun-Hee Ji (KOR)	75-68-69-72—284	158,443
	Suzann Pettersen (NOR)	71-72-71-70—284	158,443
	Stacy Lewis	72-72-70-70—284	158,443
	Mika Miyazato (JPN)	70-72-73-69—284	158,443

Full details of this event can be found on page 123

Manulife Financial LPGA Classic *Waterloo, Ontario, Canada* June 21–24 [6354–71]

1	Brittany Lang*	69-65-67-67—268	$195,000
2	Chella Choi (KOR)	69-66-70-63—268	90,231
	Hee Kyung Seo (KOR)	66-68-67-67—268	90,231
	Inbee Park (KOR)	69-64-66-69—268	90,231

**Lang won at the third extra hole*

Walmart NW Arkansas Championship *Rogers, AR* June 29–July 1 [6356–71]

1	Ai Miyazato (JPN)	68-68-65—201	$300,000
2	Mika Miyazato (JPN)	70-65-67—202	159,739
	Azahara Muñoz (ESP)	69-68-65—202	159,739

67th US WOMEN'S OPEN CHAMPIONSHIP *Kohler, WI* July 5–8 [6984–72]

1	Na Yeon Choi (KOR)	71-72-65-73—281	$585,000
2	Amy Yang (KOR)	73-72-69-71—285	350,000
3	Sandra Gal (GER)	71-70-74-74—289	218,840

Full details of this event can be found on page 113

Evian Masters *Evian Masters GC, France* July 26–29 [6457–72]

1	Inbee Park (KOR)	71-64-70-66—271	$487,500
2	Karrie Webb (AUS)	70-69-67-67—273	258,309
	Stacy Lewis	63-69-73-68—273	258,309

Jamie Farr Toledo Classic Classic *Sylvania, OH* Aug 9–12 [6428–71]

1	So Yeon Ryu (KOR)	67-68-67-62—264	$195,000
2	Angela Stanford	66-70-69-66—271	119,765
3	Inbee Park (KOR)	69-65-69-69—272	77,045
	Chella Choi (KOR)	66-67-70-69—272	77,045

Safeway Classic *North Plains, OR* Aug 17–19 [6611–72]

1	Mika Miyazato (JPN)	65-68-70—203	$225,000
2	Brittany Lincicome	67-71-67—205	118,654
	Inbee Park (KOR)	66-70-69—205	118,654

CN Canadian Women's Open *Coquitlam, BC, Canada* Aug 23–26 [6681–72]

1	Lydia Ko (NZL) (am)	68-68-72-67—275	
2	Inbee Park (KOR)	68-71-70-69—278	$300,000
3	Na Yeon Choi (KOR)	67-72-73-68—280	140,103
	Chella Choi (KOR)	72-64-73-71—280	140,103
	Jiyai Shin (KOR)	70-70-69-71—280	140,103

Kingsmill Championship *Williamsburg, VA* Sep 6–9 [6384–71]

1	Jiyai Shin (KOR)*	62-68-69-69—268	$195,000
2	Paula Creamer	65-67-65-71—268	120,655
Jiyai Shin won at the ninth extra hole			
3	Karine Icher (FRA)	70-68-67-65—270	77,618
	Danielle Kang	67-64-70-69—270	77,618

RICOH WOMEN'S BRITISH OPEN *Royal Liverpool GC, England* Sep 13–16 [6660–72]

1	Jiyai Shin (KOR)	71-64-71-73—279	$428,650
2	Inbee Park (KOR)	72-68-72-76—288	249,668
3	Paula Creamer	73-72-72-72—289	174,768

Full details of this event can be found on page 103

Navistar LPGA Classic *Prattville, AL* Sep 20–23 [6607–72]

1	Stacy Lewis	66-70-65-69—270	$195,000
2	Lexi Thompson	63-69-74-66—272	120,962
3	Angela Stanford	67-68-68-70—273	70,089
	Mi Jung Hur (KOR)	68-65-72-68—273	70,089
	Haeji Kang (KOR)	70-68-67-68—273	70,089

Sime Darby LPGA Malaysia *Kuala Lumpur, Malaysia* Oct 11–14 [6246–71]

1	Inbee Park (KOR)	69-68-65-67—269	$285,000
2	Na Yeon Choi (KOR)	65-67-68-71—271	179,747
3	Karrie Webb (AUS)	65-71-68-68—272	130,394

LPGA HanaBank Championship *Incheon, South Korea* Oct 19–21 [6364–72]

1	Suzann Pettersen (NOR)*	63-68-74—205	$270,000
2	Catriona Matthew (SCO)	68-70-67—205	168,366
Pettersen won at the third extra hole			
3	Yani Tseng (TPE)	67-70-69—206	122,138

Sunrise LPGA Taiwan Championship *Yang Mei, Taoyuan, Taiwan* Oct 25–28 [6390–72]

1	Suzann Pettersen (NOR)	69-65-66-69—269	$300,000
2	Inbee Park (KOR)	65-69-64-74—272	185,159
3	Yani Tseng (TPE)	67-69-66-71—273	134,320

Mizuno Classic *Shima-Shi Mie, Japan* Nov 2–4 [6506–72]

1	Stacy Lewis	71-70-64—205	$180,000
2	Bo-Mee Lee (KOR)	70-64-72—206	109,523
3	Ayako Uehara (JPN)	68-72-67—207	79,451

Lorena Ochoa Invitational *Guadalajara CC, Jalisco, Mexico* Nov 8–11 [6626–72]

1	Cristie Kerr	67-69-67-69—272	$200,000
2	Angela Stanford	66-67-72-68—273	88,415
	Inbee Park (KOR)	67-68-66-72—273	88,415

CME Group Titleholders *Naples, FL* Nov 15–18

1	Na Yeon Choi (KOR)	67-68-69-70—274	$500,000
2	So Yeon Ryu (KOR)	66-72-68-70—276	106,379
3	Brittany Lincicombe	68-69-70-70—277	77,171

Wendy's 3-Tour Challenge *Rio Secco GC, Henderson, NV* Nov 14

1	PGA Tour* (Jason Day 65, Davis Love III 73, Nick Watney 65)	19-under-par.	$166,666 each
2	LPGA Tour (Cristie Kerr 65, Natalie Gulbis 67, Stacey Lewis 67)	19-under-par	$90,000 each
3	Champions Tour (Bernhard Langer 68, Tom Lehman 68, Fred Funk 71)	14-under-par	$90,000 each

**After Watney and Kerr parred the play-off hole, Day birdied it to win the first prize. Stacey parred*

To date, the PGA Tour have won on nine occasions, the Champions Tour seven times and the LPGA on five occasions

Symetra Tour 2012 (formerly Futures Tour)

Players are of American nationality unless stated

www.symetratour.com

Mar 23–25	Florida's Natural Charity Classic	Winter Haven, FL	Megan McChrystal	211 (–5)
April 20–22	Sara Bay Classic	Sarasota, FL	Esther Choe	217 (+1)
April 27–29	Riviera Nayarit Classic	Nuevo Vallarta, Nayarit, Mexico	Esther Choe	207 (–12)
June 1–3	My Marsh Golf Classic	Fishers, IN	Sara Brown	211 (–5)
June 8–10	Ladies Titan Tire Challenge **Beat Marissa Steen at the first extra hole*	Marion, IA	Lauren Doughtie*	212 (–4)
June 15–17	Tate & Lyle Players C/ship	Decatur, IL	Kristie Smith (AUS)	203 (–13)
June 29–July 1	Island Resort Championship	Harris, MI	Leah Wigger	209 (–7)
July 20–22	Northeast Delta Dental International **Beat Esther Choe at first the extra hole*	Concord, NH	Jenny Gleason*	211 (–5)
July 27–29	Credit Union Classic	Syracuse, NY	Victoria Elizabeth	210 (–12)
Aug 3–5	The Empire Championship	Albany, NY	Jaclyn Sweeney	203 (–10)
Aug 10–12	Four Winds Invitational	South Bend, IN	Julia Boland (AUS)	212 (–4)
Aug 17–19	Eagle Classic	Richmond, VA	Paola Moreno (COL)	207 (–9)
Aug 24–26	Challenge at Musket Ridge	Myersville, MD	Misun Cho (KOR)	205 (–11)
Sep 14–16	Symetra Classic	Charlotte, NC	Mi Hyang Lee (KOR)	208 (–8)
Sep 21–23	Vidalia Championship	Vidalia, GA	Sydnee Michaels	207 (–9)
Sep 28–30	Daytona Beach Invitational	Daytona Beach, FL	Daniela Iacobelli	205 (–11)

Final Ranking

1	Esther Choe	$55,690	6	Mi Hyang Lee (KOR)	40,882
2	Paola Moreno	50,908	7	Jenny Gleason	38,741
3	Victoria Elizabeth	46,565	8	Julia Boland (AUS)	38,447
4	Thidapa Suwannapura (THA)	42,884	9	Nicole Smith	38,004
5	Daniela Iacobelli	41,049	10	Sara-Maude Juneau (CAN)	37,632

LPGA Tour statistics

Scoring average

	Total Rounds	Average
1 Inbee Park (KOR)	85	70.21
2 So Yeon Ryu (KOR)	86	70.30
3 Jiyai Shin (KOR)	65	70.31
4 Stacy Lewis	93	70.33
5 Na Yeon Choi (KOR)	82	70.49
6 Ai Miyazato (JPN)	78	70.56
7 Suzann Pettersen (NOR)	86	70.74
8 Shanshan Feng (CHN)	69	70.84
9 Azahara Muñoz (ESP)	88	70.90
10 Mika Miyazato (JPN)	66	70.94

Driving average

	Average
1 Brittany Lincicome	276
2 Lexi Thompson	271
3 Gerina Piller	268
4 Michelle Wie	268
5 Yani Tseng (TPE)	266
6 Maria Hjörth (SWE)	266
7 Suzann Pettersen (NOR)	265
8 Karin Sjodin (SWE)	264
9 Cydney Clanton	263
10 Sandra Changkija	263

Driving accuracy

	Fairways	Possible Fairways	%
1 Mika Miyazato, (JPN)	580	684	84.8
2 Mo Martin	671	800	83.9
3 Jiyai Shin (KOR)	530	635	83.5
4 Marcy Hart	382	462	82.7
5 Leta Lindley	413	501	82.4
6 Jane Rah	463	575	80.5
7 Beatriz Recari (ESP)	843	1,052	80.1
8 Meredith Duncan	323	406	79.6
9 Ai Miyazato (JPN)	630	794	79.3
10 Paula Creamer	739	936	79.0

Greens in Regulation

	%
1 Karin Sjodin (SWE)	76.1
2 Sun Young Yoo (KOR)	75.2
3 Stacy Lewis	75.2
4 Azahara Muñoz (ESP)	74.1
5 Jiyai Shin (KOR)	73.7
6 Shanshan Feng (CHN)	73.0
7 Paula Creamer	72.9
8 Suzann Petteresen (NOR)	72.8
9 Na Yeon Choi (KOR)	72.7
10 Beatriz Recari (ESP)	72.5

Top money earners on the LPGA Tour 1950–2012

1950	Babe Zaharias	$14,800
1960	Louise Suggs	$16,892
1970	Kathy Whitworth	$30,235
1980	Beth Daniel	$231,000
1990	Beth Daniel	$863,578
2000	Karrie Webb (AUS)	$1,876,853
2005	Annika Sörenstam (SWE)	$2,588,240
2006	Lorena Ochoa (MEX)	$2,592,872
2007	Lorena Ochoa (MEX)	$4,364,994
2008	Lorena Ochoa (MEX)	$2,763,193
2009	Ji Yai Shin (KOR)	$1,807,334
2010	Na Yeon Choi (KOR)	$1,871,166
2011	Yani Tseng (TPE)	$2,921,713
2012	Inbee Park (KOR)	$2,266,638

LPGA Legends Tour

Players are of American nationality unless stated

Jul 28-30	Cure Classic	Inglewood GC, Kenmore, WA	Nancy Scranton	142 (–2)
Aug 12-13	Wendy's Charity Challenge **Beat Cindy Rarick in play-off*	Country Club of Jackson, MI	Barb Mucha*	140 (–2)
Sep 19	BJ's Charity Pro-am	Pinehills GC, Plymouth, MA	Laurie Rinker 70 (Jones course); Pat Bradley, Val Skinner 70 (Nicklaus course)	
Nov 1–4	ISPS Handa Cup	Reunion Resort, Orlando, FL	Team USA 24, Team World 24 *America retain the trophy*	
Nov 9–11	ISPS Handa Legends Tour Open	Innisbrook, Palm Harbour, FL	Laura Davies (ENG)	141 (–5)

Ladies Asian Golf Tour 2012

www.lagt.org

Dec 3 2011– Jan 2 2012	Royal Open	Hsinchu, Taiwan	Shih Huei Ju (TPE)	209 (–7)
Jan 6–8	Hitachi Classic	Taoyan, Taiwan	Teresa Lu (TPE)	212 (–4)
Feb 8–10	Thailand Ladies Open	Lakewood, Bangkok	Srisawang Nontaya (THA)	207 (–1)
Feb 23–24	Miyazaki Ladies Open	Miyazaki	Mami Fukuda JPN)	139 (–2)
Mar 23–25	Yumeya Dream Cup	Hirao, Nagoya, Japan	Yu Rei Lin (TPE)	217 (E)
Aug 8–10	Technology Cup	Hsinchu G&CC, Taiwan	Tiranan Yoopan (THA)	221 (+5)
Oct 5–7	Taiwan LPGA Fubon Open	Tong Hwa CC, Linkou	Yao Hsuan-Yu (TPE)	205 (–11)
Oct 18–20	Enjoy Jakarta Indonesian Ladies Open	Palm Hill CC, Jakarta, Indonesia	Kongkapan Patcharachuta (THA)	209 (–7)
Oct 26–28	Suzhou Taihu Ladies Open	Suzhou Taihu International GC, Jiangsu, China	Carlota Ciganda (ESP)	199 (–17)
Nov 2–4	Sanya Ladies Open	Yalong Bay GC, Sanya City, Hainan, China	Cassandra Kirkland (FRA)	210 (E)
Nov 8–10	TLPGA Chinatrust Open	Orient GC, Linkou, Taiwan	Numa Gulyanamitta (THA)	205 (–11)
Nov 30– Dec 2	Hero Women's Indian Open	DLF Golf and CC, New Delhi, India	Pornanong Phatlum (THA)	203 (–13).
Dec 14–16	Taifong Ladies' Open	Changhua, Taiwan	Teresa Lu (TPE)	207 (–9)

Final Money List (Figures in brackets denote number of events played)

1	Patcharachuta Kongkapan (THA)	(10)	US$87,966
2	Pornanong Phatlam (THA)	(4)	60,795
3	Numa Gulyanamitta (THA)	(7)	47.766
4	Pei Lin Yu (TPE)	(2)	37,200
5	Nontaya Srisawang (THA)	(5)	36,376
6	Megumi Shimokawa (JPN)	(2)	35,650
7	Tiranan Yoopan (THA)	(12)	35,081
8	Thidapa Suwannapura (THA)	(9)	31,787
9	Danah Bordner (USA)	(2)	23,508
10	Mami Fukuda (JPN)	(2)	22,803

Australian LPG Tour 2011–2012

Players are of Australian nationality unless stated

www.alpg.com.au

Nov 24	Hahn Premium Light and Ko-Nami Pro-am	Port Kembla GC	Stacey Keating	69
Nov 25	Power Ford Pro-am	Castle Hill CC	Bree Arthur	70
Nov 27–28	Mount Broughton GC Pro-am		Stacey Keating	138
Nov 29	Lady Anne Funerals ALPG	Ryde Paramatta GC	Bree Arthur	68
Dec 3–4	Xstrata Coal Golf	Branxton GC	Tamara John	67
Jan 6–8	Women's Victoria Open	Woodlands GC and Spring Valley GC	Joanna Klatton (FRA)	212
Jan 12–13	Moss Vale ALPG Pro-am	Woolongong	Cathryn Bristow (NZL)	133
Jan 20–22	Actew AGL Royal Canberra Ladies Classic	Royal Canberra GC	Karen Lunn	207
Jan 27–29	Bing Lee Samsung New South Wales Open	NSW GC	Lydia Ko (NZL) (am)	202
Feb 3–5	Gold Coast RAVC Australian Ladies Masters	Royal Pines Resort, Queensland	Christel Boeljon (NED)	267
Feb 9–12	ISPS Handa Women's Australian Open	Royal Melbourne GC	Jessica Korda (USA)*	289
	**Beat Julieta Granada (PAR), Stacey Lewis (USA), Brittany Lincicome (USA), So Yeon Ryu (KOR) and Hee Kyung Seo (KOR) at the second extra hole*			
Feb 17–19	ISPS Handa New Zealand Women's Open	Pegasus GC, Christchurch	Lindsey Wright (AUS)	206

Order of Merit 2011–2012 (tournaments played in brackets)

1 Lindsey Wright	(6)	A$70,666	6 Stacy Keating	(11)	23,922
2 Sarah Kemp	(12)	36,479	7 Stephanie Na	(4)	21,356
3 Nikki Campbell	(4)	33,968	8 Bree Arthur	(12)	21,155
4 Jessica Speechley	(7)	28,673	9 Frances Bondad	(11)	20,536
5 Karen Lunn	(6)	28,024	10 Rachel L Bailey	(11)	18,733

Money List 2011–2012

1 Jessica Korda (USA)	A$158,809	6 Julieta Granada (PAR)	63,952
2 So Yeon Ryu (KOR)	95,969	Hee Kyung See (KOR)	63,952
3 Christel Boeljon (NED)	75,000	8 Brittany Lincicome (USA)	59,469
4 Lindsey Wright	70,066	9 Ha Neul Kim (KOR)	46,153
5 Stacy Lewis (USA)	64,986	10 Diana Luna (ITA)	36,500

China LPGA Tour

www.clpga.org

Players are of Chinese nationality unless stated

Mar 2–4	World Ladies Championship	Vintage course, Mission Hills, Haikou, Hainan Island, China	Shanshan Feng	206 (–10)
May 24–26	Beijing Pearl Challenge **Beat Miho Mori (JPN) in play-off*		Yuexia Lu*	214 (–2)
June 7–9	Shanghai Classic		Taoli Yang	209 (–7)
June 26–28	Halun Energy Championship		Taanaporn Kongjiakrai (THA)	210 (–6)
Aug 24–26	Wuhan Orient Masters Chall.		Simin Feng (am)	209 (–7)
Sep 12–15	Tianjin Challenge	Tianjin Binhai Lake GC	Lin Xiyu	209 (–7)
Oct 12–14	Chongqing Challenge	Chongqing Poly GC	Liu Yu (am)	211 (–5)
Oct 26–28	Suzhou Taihu Ladies Open	Suzhou Taihu International GC, Jiansu, China	Carlota Ciganda (ESP)	199 (–17)
Nov 2–4	Sanya Ladies Open	Yalong Bay GC, Sanya City, Hainan, China	Cassandra Kirkland (FRA)	210 (E)
Dec 14–16	Hyundai China Ladies Open	Orient Xiamin GC, Fujian	Kim Hyo-joo (KOR)	205 (–11)

Final Order of Merit (Figures in brackets denote number of events played)

1 Feng Shanshan	(2)	495,017 pts	6 Zhang Na	(7)	203,265
2 Lin Xiyu	(7)	457,221	7 Pan Yanhong	(9)	188,347
3 Tanaporn Konkiakrai (THA)	(7)	296,382	8 Yan Panpan	(10)	165,276
4 Lu Yuexia	(11)	239,263	9 Kongraphan Patcharajutar (THA)	(3)	154,730
5 Tian Hong	(9)	225,832	10 Ye Liying	(1)	151,782

Victory No 82 for big-hitter Laura Davies

England's Laura Davies made her début on the LPGA Legends Tour – for professionals 45 and over – a winning one when she took the 2012 ISPS Handa Legends Tour Open title at Innisbrook in Florida. It was the 82nd win of her career.

The big-hitting 49-year-old shot a 70 and 71 to beat Beth Daniel and Barb Moxness by two. Jane Crafter, Rosie Jones and Michele Redman were tied fourth on 141

Japan LPGA Tour 2012

Players are of Japanese nationality unless stated

http://en.wikipedia.org/wiki/LPGA_of_Japan_Tour

Mar 2–4	Daikin Orchid Ladies	Okinawa	Airi Saitchi*	208 (–10)
	**Beat Yuko Mitsuka and Lee Ji-Hee (KOR) at the second extra hole*			
Mar 9–11	Yokohama Tire PRGR Ladies Cup	Kochi	Lee Bo-Mee (KOR)*	213 (–7)
	**Beat Ahn Sun-ju (KOR) at the second extra hole*			
Mar 16–18	T Point Ladies	Kagoshima	Lee Ji-Hee (KOR)	209 (–7)
Mar 30–April 1	Yamaha Ladies Open *(event reduced to 36 holes because of heavy rain)*	Shizuoka	Ritsuko Ryo	141 (–3)
April 6–8	Studio Alice Open	Hyago	Miki Saiki	209 (–7)
April 13–15	Nishijin Ladies Classic	Kumamoto	Maiko Wakabayashi	209 (–3)
April 20–22	Fujisankei Ladies Classic	Shizuoka	Kaori Ohe	207 (–9)
April 27–29	Cyber Agent Ladies	Chiba	Chie Arimura	201 (–15)
May 3–6	World Ladies Championship (Salonpas Cup)	Ibaraki	Ahn Sun-ju (KOR)*	208 (–8)
*	*Beat Morgan Pressel (USA) and In-Bee Park (KOR) at the first extra hole*			
May 11–13	Fundokin Ladies	Fukuoka	In-Bee Park (KOR)	207 (–9)
May 18–20	Chukyo TV Bridgestone Ladies Open	Chukyo GC (Ishino course), Aichi	Lee Ji-Hee (KOR)	200 (–16)
May 25–27	Yonex Ladies Golf	Niigata	Feng Shan-shan (CHN)*	208 (–8)
	**Beat Yukari Baba at the second extra hole*			
June 1–3	Resort Trust Ladies	Nagano	Jeon Mi-Jeong (KOR)	212 (–14)
June 7–10	Suntory Ladies Open	Kobe	Kim Hyo-joo (KOR) (am)	271 (–17)
June 15–17	Nicherei Ladies Championship	Sodegaura CC Shinsode, Chiba	Hyun-Ju Shin (KOR)	205 (–11)
June 22–24	Earth Mondahamin Cup	Camelia Hills CC, Sodegaura, Chiba	Mayu Hattori	201 (–15)
June 29–July 1	Nichi-Iko Women's Open	Toyama	Jeon Mi-Jeong (KOR)	208 (–8)
July 13–15	Stanley Ladies	Shizuoka	Chie Arimura	103 (–5)
	Event reduced to 27 holes due to bad weather			
July 20–22	Samantha Thavasa Girls' Collection Ladies	Ami GC, Ibaraki	Megumi Kido	202 (–14)
Aug 3–5	Meijii Cup	Kitahiroshima, Hokkaido	Shanshan Feng (CHN)*	209 (–7)
	**Beat Ahn Sun-ju (KOR) and Shinobu Moromizato (JPN) at the fifth extra hole*			
Aug 10–12	NEC Karuizawa 72	Nagano	Yumiko Yoshida*	205 (–11)
	**Beat Jan Eun-bi (KOR) at the sixth extra hole*			
Aug 17–19	CAT Ladies	Kanagawa	Jeon Mi Jeong (KOR)	206 (–3)
Aug 24–26	Nitori Ladies	Katsura GC, Hokkaida	Ahn Sun-ju (KOR)	202 (–14)
Aug 31–Sep 2	Golf 5 Ladies	Gifu	Ahn Sun-ju (KOR)	273 (–15)
Sep 6–9	Japan LPGA Championship (Konica Minolta Cup)	Shiga	Chie Arimura	275 (–13)
Sep 14–16	Munsingwear Ladies Tokai Classic	Aichi CC	Natsu Nagai	204 (–12)
Sep 21–23	Miyagi TV Cup Dunlop Women's Open	Miyagi	Rikaka Morita	202 (–14)
Sep 27–30	48th Japan Women's Open C/ship	Kanagawa	Shanshan Feng (CHN)	288 (0)
Oct 12–14	Fujitsu Ladies	Chiba	Misuzu Narita	207 (–9)
Oct 19–21	Masters GC Ladies	Hyogo	Kim So-Hee (KOR)*	205 (–11)
	**Beat Sakura Yokomine and Yomiko Yoshida in play-off*			
Oct 26–28	Hisako Higuchi Morinaga Wieder Ladies	Chiba	Jeon Mi Jeong (KOR)	204 (–12)
Nov 2–4	Mizuno Classic	Kintetsu Kashikojima CC, Mie	Stacy Lewis (USA)	205 (–11)
Nov 9–11	Ito-en Ladies	Great Island CC, Chiba	Lee Bo-Mee (KOR)	276 (–12)
	**Beat Chie Armura in play-off*			
Nov 16–18	Daio Paper Elleair Ladies Open	Itsuura Feien CC, Fukishima	Miki Saiki	204 (–12)
Nov 22–25	Japan LPGA Tour Championship (Ricoh Cup)	Miyazaki	Lee Bo-mee (KOR)	275 (–13)

Final Money List

1	Mi-Jeong Jeon (KOR)	¥132,380,915	6	Shanshan Feng (CHN)	81,875,053
2	Bo-Mee Lee (KOR)	108,679,454	7	Rikako Morita	76,354,957
3	Chie Arimura	101,889,564	8	Ji-Hee Lee (KOR)	75,293,583
4	Sun-ju Ahn (KOR)	101,206,438	9	Inbee Park (KOR)	72,879,424
5	Miki Saiki	91,972,093	10	Mayu Hattori	71,681,783

Korean LPGA Tour 2012

http://wapedia.mobi/en/LPGA_of_Korea_Tour

Players are of Korean nationality unless stated

Dec 16–18 2011	Hyundai China Ladies Open	Orient Xiamin GC	Kim Hye-youn	210 (–6)
April 12–15	Lotte Mart Ladies Open	Sky Hill, Seogwipo	Kim Hyo-joo (am)	272
April 27–29	eDaily Livart Ladies Open	Yeoju	Lee Ye-jeong	205 (–11)
May 18–20	Woori Ladies Championship	Lakeside CC, Yongin	Kim Ja-young *	204 (+2)
	**Beat Lee Mi-run at the first extra hole*			
May 24–27	Doosan Match Play Challenge	Ladena, Chuncheon	Final: Kim Ja-young beat Yeon Ju Jung	1 hole
June 8–10	Lotte Cantata Ladies Open	Lotte Sky Hill CC, Jeju	Jeong Hye-jin	209 (–7)
June 15–17	S-Oil Champions Invitational	Jeju City	Yang Soo-Jin	205 (–11)
Aug 10–12	SBS Tour Hidden Valley Ladies Open	Jincheon	Kim Ja-young	206 (–10)
Aug 16–19	Nets Masterpiece	Hongcheon	Yang Je-yoon	280 (–8)
Aug 23–26	Kia Motors Korean Women's Open		Lee Mi Rim	381 (–7)
Aug 31–Sep 2	LIG Classic	Ildong Links	Joney Moon*	211 (–5)
	**Beat Ming Young Lee at the third extra hole*			
Sep 6–9	Hanwha Finance Classic		So Yeon Ryu	279 (–9)
Sep 13–16	MetLife Hankyung KLPGA Championship	Ansan	Jung Hee-won	279 (–9)
Sep 21–23	KDB Daewoo Securities Classic	Pyeongchang	Se Ri Pak	200 (–16)
Oct 5–7	Rush and Cash Charity Classic	Jeju City	Kim Ha-Neul	208 (–8)
Oct 11–14	Hite Jinro Championship	Yeoju	Yoon Sul-A	284 (–4)
Oct 19–21	PGA KEB HanaBank Championship	Sky 72 GC (Ocean Course)	Suzann Pettersen (NOR)*	205 (–11)
	**Beat Catriona Matthew (SCO) at third extra hole*			
Oct 25–28	KB Financial Group STAR Championship	Sky 72 GC	Jang Ha-na	211 (–5)
Nov 2–4	Seokyung Ladies Open		Lee Jung-Min	209 (–6)
Nov 9–11	Kim Young Joo Ladies Open	Lake Hills Jeju Resort	Jo Hee Kim*	66
	**Led after first round. Remaining two rounds cancelled – bad weather. Event declared unofficial*			
Nov 16–18	ADT CAPS Championship	Sky Hill, Jeju	Yang Je-yoon	206 (–10)
Dec 1–2	KB Finance Cup (Korea v Japan)	Bayside GC, Busan	Korea 23, Japan 13	
2013 season				
Dec 14–16	Hyundai China Ladies Open	Orient Xiamin GC, Fujian	Kim Hyo Joo	205 (–11)

Final Money List (Figures in brackets denote number of events played)

1	Kim Ha-Neul	(17)	₩458,898,803	6	Lee Jung-Min	(16)	336,763,214
2	Heo Yoon-Kyung	(17)	420,245,833	7	Lee Mi-Rim	(18)	286,794,395
3	Kim Char Young	(17)	417,909,039	8	Jung Hee-Won	(18)	263,560,930
4	Yang Je-yoon	(18)	406,398,333	9	Kim Hye Youn	(19)	262,578,571
5	Yang Soo Jin	(18)	344,267,667	10	Jang Ha-na	(12)	258,763,706

International Team Events

The Solheim Cup

2011 *Killeen Castle, Ireland* Sept 23–25

Result: Europe 15, USA 13

Captains: Alison Nicholas (Europe), Rosie Jones (USA)

***First Day*, Foursomes**

Maria Hjörth (SWE) and Anna Nordqvist (SWE) lost to Michell Wie and Cristie Kerr 2 and 1
Karen Stupples (ENG) and Melissa Reid (ENG) lost to Paula Creamer and Brittany Lincicome 1 hole
Catriona Matthew (SCO) and Azahara Muñoz (ESP) beat Stacey Lewis and Angela Stanford 3 and 2
Suzann Pettersen (NOR) and Sophie Gustafson (SWE) beat Brittany Lang and Julie Inkster 1 up

***First Day*, Fourballs**

Laura Davies (ENG) and Reid lost to Morgan Pressell and Creamer 1 hole
Matthew and Sandra Gal (GER) halved with Christina Kim and Ryanne O'Toole
Gustafson and Caroline Hedwall (SWE) beat Vicky Hurst and Lincicome 5 and 4
Pettersen and Nordqvist beat Kerr and Wie 2 holes

***Second Day*, Foursomes**

Hedwall and Gustafson beat Stanford and Lewis 6 and 5
Stupples and Christel Boeljon (NED) lost to Pressel and O'Toole 3 and 2
Hjörth and Nordqvist beat Lang and Inkster 3 and 2
Matthew and Muñoz halved with Kerr and Creamer

***Second Day*, Fourballs**

Davies and Reid beat Lang and Wie 4 and 3
Pettersen and Hedwall lost to Pressel and Kerr 1 hole
Gal and Boeljon lost to Lewis and O'Toole 2 and 1
Hjörth and Muñoz lost to Creamer and Lincicome 3 and 2

***Third Day* – Singles**

Matthew beat Creamer 6 and 5
Gustafson beat Lewis 2 holes
Norqvist lost to Pressel 2 and 1
Davies halved with Inkster
Reid lost to Hurst 2 holes
Boeljon beat Lincicome 2 holes
Gal lost to Lang 6 and 5
Hjörth lost to Kim 4 and 2
Pettersen beat Wie 1 hole
Hedwall halved with O'Toole
Muñoz beat Stanford 1 hole
Stupples beat Kerr (withdrew, wrist injury)

2009 *Rich Harvest Farms, IL, USA* Aug 17–23

Result: USA 16, Europe 12

Captains: Beth Daniel (USA), Alison Nicholas (Europe)

***First Day* – Fourballs**

Creamer and Kerr beat Pettersen and Gustafson 1 hole
Stanford and Inkster lost to Alfredsson and Elosegui 1 hole
Lang and Lincicome beat Davies and Brewerton 5 and 4
Pressel and Wie halved with Matthew and Hjörth

Foursomes

Kim and Gulbis beat Pettersen and Gustafson 4 and 2
Stanford and Castrale lost to Brewerton and Nocera 3 and 1
McPherson and Lincicome lost to Hjörth and Nordqvist 3 and 2
Creamer and Inkster beat Matthew and Moodie 2 and 1

***Second Day* – Fourballs**

Kim and Wie beat Alfredsson and Elosegui 5 and 4
Lang and Stanford halved with Luna and Matthew
Castrale and Kerr lost to Nordqvist and Pettersen 1 hole
Lincicome and McPherson lost to Hjörth and Nocera 1 hole

Foursomes

Creamer and Inkster lost to Gustafson and Moodie 4 and 3
McPherson and Pressel beat Alfredsson and Pettersen 2 holes
Gulbis and Kim lost to Brewerton and Nocera 5 and 4
Kerr and Wie beat Hjörth and Nordqvist 1 hole

***Third Day* – Singles**

Paula Creamer beat Suzann Pettersen (NOR) 3 and 2
Angela Stanford beat Becky Brewerton (WAL) 5 and 4
Michelle Wie beat Helen Alfredsson (SWE) 1 hole
Brittany Lang halved with Laura Davies (ENG)
Juli Inkster halved with Gwladys Nocera (FRA)
Kristy McPherson lost to Catriona Matthew (SCO) 3 and 2
Brittany Lincicome beat Sophie Gustafson (SWE) 3 and 2
Nicole Castrale lost to Diana Luna (ITA) 3 and 2
Christina Kim beat Tania Elosegui (ESP) 2 holes
Cristie Kerr halved with Maria Hjörth (SWE)
Morgan Pressel beat Anna Nordqvist (SWE) 3 and 2
Natalie Gulbis halved with Janice Moodie (SCO)

2007 *Halmstad, Tylosand, Sweden* Sept 14–16

Result: USA 16, Europe 12

Captains: Helen Alfredsson (Europe), Betsy King (USA)

***First Day* – Foursomes**

Pettersen & Gustafson halved with Hurst & Kerr
Sörenstam & Matthew lost to Steinhauer & Diaz 4 and 2
Davies & Brewerton lost to Inkster & Creamer 2 and 1
Nocera & Hjörth beat Gulbis & Pressel 3 and 2

Fourballs

Matthew & Iben Tinning beat Hurst & Lincicome 4 and 2
Sörenstam & Hjörth halved with Stanford & Prammanasudh
Gustafson & Nocera lost to Castrale & Kerr 3 and 2
Johnson & Davies halved with Creamer & Pressel

***Second Day* – Foursomes**

Hjörth & Nocera halved with Steinhauer & Diaz
Gustafson & Pettersen halved with Inkster & Creamer
Tinning & Hauert lost to Hurst & Stanford 4 and 2
Sörenstam & Matthew beat Castrale & Kerr 1 hole

Fourballs
Wessberg & Hjörth halved with Creamer & Lincicome
Johnson & Tinning halved with Inkster & Prammanasudh
Brewerton & Davies beat Gulbis & Castrale 1 hole
Sörenstam & Pettersen beat Kerr & Pressel 3 and 2

***Third Day* – Singles**
Catriona Matthew (SCO) beat Laura Diaz 3 and 2
Sophie Gustafson (SWE) lost to Pat Hurst 2 and 1
Suzann Pettersen (NOR) lost to Stacy Prammanasudh 2 holes
Iben Tinning (DEN) lost to Juli Inkster 4 and 3
Becky Brewerton (WAL) halved with Sherri Steinhauer
Trish Johnson (ENG) lost to Angela Stanford 3 and 2
Annika Sörenstam (SWE) lost to Morgan Pressel 2 and 1
Laura Davies (ENG) beat Brittany Lincicome 4 and 3
Bettina Hauert (GER) lost to Nicole Castrale 3 and 2
Maria Hjörth (SWE) lost to Paula Creamer 2 and 1
Linda Wessberg (SWE) beat Cristie Kerr 1 hole
Gwladys Nocera (FRA) lost to Natalie Gulbis 4 and 3

2005 *Crooked Stick GC, Carmel, IN, USA* Sept 9–11

Result: USA 15½, Europe 12½

Captains: Nancy Lopez (USA), Catrin Nilsmark (Europe)

***First Day* – Foursomes**
Daniel & Creamer halved with Koch & Matthew
Kerr & Gulbis lost to Davies & Hjörth 2 and 1
Kim & Hurst halved with Gustafson & Johnson
Redman & Diaz lost to Sörenstam & Pettersen 1 hole

Fourballs
Jones & Mallon beat Hjörth & Tinning 3 and 2
Hurst & Ward beat Sörenstam & Matthew 2 and 1
Kerr & Gulbis lost to Gustafson & Stupples 2 and 1
Creamer & Inkster lost to Davies & Pettersen 4 and 3

***Second Day* – Foursomes**
Kim & Gulbis beat Nocera & Kreutz 4 and 2
Creamer & Inkster beat Davies & Hjörth 3 and 2
Diaz & Ward lost to Gustafson & Koch 5 and 3
Redman & Hurst beat Sörenstam & Matthew 2 holes

Fourballs
Hurst & Kim lost to Davies & Sörenstam 4 and 2
Daniel & Inkster halved with Tinning & Johnson
Kerr & Creamer beat Koch & Matthew 1 hole
Jones & Mallon halved with Gustafson & Pettersen

***Third Day* – Singles**
Juli Inkster beat Sophie Gustafson (SWE) 2 and 1
Paula Creamer beat Laura Davies (ENG) 7 and 5
Pat Hurst beat Trish Johnson (ENG) 2 and 1
Laura Diaz beat Iben Tinning (DEN) 6 and 5
Christina Kim beat Ludivine Kreutz (FRA) 5 and 4
Beth Daniel lost to Annika Sörenstam (SWE) 4 and 3
Natalie Gulbis beat Maria Hjörth (SWE) 2 and 1
Wendy Ward lost to Catriona Matthew (SCO) 3 and 2
Michele Redman lost to Carin Koch (SWE) 2 and 1
Cristie Kerr lost to Gwladys Nocera (FRA) 2 and 1
Meg Mallon beat Karen Stupples (ENG) 3 and 1
Rosie Jones halved with Suzann Pettersen (NOR)

2003 *Barsebäck, Sweden* Sept 12–14

Result: Europe 17½, USA 10½

Captains: Catrin Nilsmark (Europe), Patty Sheehan (USA)

***First Day* – Foursomes**
Koch & Davies halved with Daniel & Robbins
Moodie & Matthew beat Inkster & Ward 5 and 3
Sörenstam & Pettersen beat Diaz & Bowie 4 and 3
Gustafson & Esterl beat Mallon & Jones 3 and 2

Fourball
Davies & Matthew lost to Kuehne & Kerr 2 and 1
Sörenstam & Koch lost to Inkster & Daniel 1 hole
Pettersen & Meunier-Labouc beat Stanford & Mallon 3 and 2
Tinning & Gustafson lost to Redman & Jones 2 holes

***Second Day* – Foursomes**
Gustafson & Pettersen beat Kuehne & Kerr 3 and 1
Esterl & Tinning halved with Stanford & Redman
Sörenstam & Koch beat Ward and Bowie 3 and 4
Moodie & Matthew halved with Mallon & Robbins

Fourball
Sanchez & McKay lost to Daniel & Inkster 5 and 4
Gustafson & Davies lost to Kerr & Kuehne 2 and 1
Matthew & Moodie beat Ward & Jones 4 and 3
Sörenstam & Pettersen beat Robbins & Diaz 1 hole

***Third Day* – Singles**
Janice Moodie (SCO) beat Kelli Kuehne 3 and 2
Carin Koch (SWE) lost to Juli Inkster 5 and 4
Sophie Gustafson (SWE) beat Heather Bowie 5 and 4
Iben Tinning (DEN) beat Wendy Ward 2 and 1
Ana Belen Sanchez (ESP) lost to Michele Redman 3 and 1
Catriona Matthew (SCO) beat Rosie Jones 2 and 1
Annika Sörenstam (SWE) beat Angela Stanford 3 and 2
Suzann Pettersen (NOR) lost to Cristie Kerr conceded
Laura Davies (ENG) beat Meg Mallon conceded
Elisabeth Esterl (GER) lost to Laura Diaz 5 and 4
Mhairi McKay (SCO) beat Beth Daniel conceded
Patricia Meunier-Labouc (FRA) beat Kelly Robbins conceded

2002 *Interlachen CC, Madina, MN* Sept 20–22

Result: USA 15½, Europe 12½

Captains: Patty Sheehan (USA), Dale Reid (Europe)

***First Day* – Foursomes**
Inkster & Diaz lost to Davies & Marti 2 holes
Daniel & Ward beat Carriedo & Tinning 1 hole
Hurst & Robbins lost to Alfredsson & Pettersen 4 and 2
Kuehne & Mallon lost to Koch & Sörenstam 3 and 2

Fourball
Jones & Kerr beat Davies & Marti 1 hole
Diaz & Klein beat Gustafson & Icher 4 and 3
Mallon & Redman beat Hjörth & Sörenstam 3 and 1
Inkster & Kuehne lost to Koch & McKay 3 and 2

***Second Day* – Foursomes**
Kerr & Redman lost to Koch & Sörenstam 4 and 3
Klein & Ward beat McKay & Tinning 3 and 2
Inkster & Mallon beat Davies & Marti 2 and 1
Diaz & Robbins beat Alfredsson & Pettersen 3 and 1

Fourball
Daniel & Ward lost to Koch & Sörenstam 4 and 3
Hurst & Kuehne lost to Hjörth & Tinning 1 hole
Jones & Kerr lost to Carriedo & Icher 1 hole
Klein & Robbins lost to Davies & Gustafson 1 hole

***Third Day* – Singles**
Juli Inkster beat Raquel Carriedo (ESP) 4 and 3
Laura Diaz beat Paula Marti (ESP) 5 and 3
Emilee Klein beat Helen Alfredsson (SWE) 2 and 1
Kelli Kuehne lost to Iben Tinning (DEN) 3 and 2
Michele Redman halved with Suzann Pettersen (NOR)
Wendy Ward halved with Annika Sörenstam (SWE)
Kelly Robbins beat Maria Hjörth (SWE) 5 and 3
Cristie Kerr lost to Sophie Gustafson (SWE) 3 and 2
Meg Mallon beat Laura Davies (ENG) 3 and 2
Pat Hurst beat Mhairi McKay (SCO) 4 and 2
Beth Daniel halved with Carin Koch (SWE)
Rosie Jones beat Karine Icher (FRA) 3 and 2

2000 *Loch Lomond* Oct 6–8

Result: Europe 14½, USA 11½

Captains: Dale Reid (Europe), Pat Bradley (USA)

***First Day* – Foursomes**

Davies & Nicholas beat Pepper & Inkster 4 and 3
Johnson & Gustafson beat Robbins & Hurst 3 and 2
Nilsmark & Koch beat Burton & Iverson 2 and 1
Sörenstam & Moodie beat Mallon & Daniel 1 hole

***First Day* – Foursomes**

Davies & Nicholas lost to Iverson & Jones 6 and 5
Johnson & Gustafson halved with Inkster & Steinhauer
Neumann & Alfredsson lost to Robbins & Hurst 2 holes
Moodie & Sörenstam beat Mallon & Daniel 1 hole

***Second Day* – Fourball**

Nilsmark & Koch beat Scranton & Redman 2 and 1
Neumann & Meunier Labouc halved with Pepper & Burton
Davies & Carriedo halved with Mallon & Daniel
Sörenstam & Moodie lost to Hurst & Robbins 2 and 1
Johnson & Gustafson beat Jones & Iverson 3 and 2
Nicholas & Alfredsson beat Inkster & Steinhauer 3 and 2

***Third Day* – Singles**

Annika Sörenstam lost to Juli Inkster 5 and 4
Sophie Gustafson lost to Brandie Burton 4 and 3
Helen Alfredsson beat Beth Daniel 4 and 3
Trish Johnson lost to Dottie Pepper 2 and 1
Laura Davies lost to Kelly Robbins 3 and 2
Liselotte Neumann halved with Pat Hurst
Alison Nicholas halved with Sherri Steinhauer
Patricia Meunier Labouc lost to Meg Mallon 1 hole
Catrin Nilsmark beat Rosie Jones 1 hole
Raquel Carriedo lost to Becky Iverson 3 and 2
Carin Koch beat Michele Redman 2 and 1
Janice Moodie beat Nancy Scranton 1 hole

1998 *Muirfield Village, Dublin, OH* Sept 18–20

Result: USA 16, Europe 12

Captains: Judy Rankin (USA), Pia Nilsson (Europe)

***First Day* – Foursomes**

Pepper & Inkster beat Davies & Johnson 3 and 1
Mallon & Burton beat Alfredsson & Nicholas 3 and 1
Robbins & Hurst beat Hackney & Neumann 1 hole
Andrews & Green beat A Sörenstam & Matthew 3 and 2

Fourball

King & Johnson halved with Davies & C Sörenstam
Hurst & Jones beat Hackney & Gustafson 7 and 5
Robbins & Steinhauer lost to Alfredsson & de Lorenzi 2 and 1
Pepper & Burton beat A Sörenstam & Nilsmark 2 holes

***Second Day* – Foursomes**

Andrews & Steinhauer beat A Sörenstam & Matthew 3 and 2
Mallon & Burton lost to Davies & C Sörenstam 3 and 2
Pepper & Inkster beat Alfredsson & de Lorenzi 1 hole
Robbins & Hurst beat Neumann & Nilsmark 1 hole

Fourball

King & Jones lost to A Sörenstam & Nilsmark 5 and 3
Johnson & Green lost to Davies & Hackney 2 holes
Andrews & Steinhauer beat Alfredsson & de Lorenzi 4 and 3
Mallon & Inkster beat Neumann & C Sörenstam 2 and 1

***Third Day* – Singles**

Pat Hurst lost to Laura Davies 1 hole
Juli Inkster lost to Helen Alfredsson 2 and 1
Donna Andrews lost to Annika Sörenstam 2 and 1
Brandie Burton lost to Liselotte Neumann 1 hole
Dottie Pepper beat Trish Johnson 3 and 2
Kelly Robbins beat Charlotta Sörenstam 2 and 1
Chris Johnson lost to Marie Laure de Lorenzi 1 hole
Rosie Jones beat Catrin Nilsmark 6 and 4
Tammie Green beat Alison Nicholas 1 hole
Sherri Steinhauer beat Catriona Matthew 3 and 2
Betsy King lost to Lisa Hackney 6 and 5
Meg Mallon halved with Sophie Gustafson

1996 *St Pierre, Chepstow* Sept 20–22

Result: USA 17, Europe 11

Captains: Judy Rankin (USA), Mickey Walker (Europe)

***First Day* – Foursomes**

Sörenstam & Nilsmark halved with Robbins & McGann
Davies & Nicholas lost to Sheehan & Jones 1 hole
de Lorenzi & Reid lost to Daniel & Skinner 1 hole
Alfredsson & Neumann lost to Pepper & Burton 2 and 1

Fourball

Davies & Johnson beat Robbins & Bradley 6 and 5
Sörenstam & Marshall beat Skinner & Geddes 1 hole
Neumann & Nilsmark lost to Pepper & King 1 hole
Alfredsson & Nicholas halved with Mallon & Daniel

***Second Day* – Foursomes**

Davies & Johnson beat Daniel & Skinner 4 and 3
Sörenstam & Nilsmark beat Pepper & Burton 1 hole
Neumann & Marshall halved with Mallon & Geddes
de Lorenzi & Alfredsson beat Robbins & McGann 4 and 3

Fourball

Davies & Hackney beat Daniel & Skinner 6 and 5
Sörenstam & Johnson halved with McGann & Mallon
de Lorenzi & Morley lost to Robbins & King 2 and 1
Nilsmark & Neumann beat Sheehan & Geddes 2 and 1

***Third Day* – Singles**

Annika Sörenstam beat Pat Bradley 2 and 1
Kathryn Marshall lost to Val Skinner 2 and 1
Laura Davies lost to Michelle McGann 3 and 2
Liselotte Neumann halved with Beth Daniel
Lisa Hackney lost to Brandie Burton 1 hole
Trish Johnson lost to Dottie Pepper 3 and 2
Alison Nicholas halved with Kelly Robbins
Marie Laure de Lorenzi lost to Betsy King 6 and 4
Joanne Morley lost to Rosie Jones 5 and 4
Dale Reid lost to Jane Geddes 2 holes
Catrin Nilsmark lost to Patty Sheehan 2 and 1
Helen Alfredsson lost to Meg Mallon 4 and 2

1994 *The Greenbrier, WA* Oct 21–23

Result: USA 13, Europe 7

Captains: JoAnne Carner (USA), Mickey Walker (Europe)

***First Day* – Foursomes**

Burton & Mochrie beat Alfredsson & Neuman 3 and 2
Daniel & Mallon lost to Nilsmark & Sörenstam 1 hole
Green & Robbins lost to Fairclough & Reid 2 and 1
Andrews & King lost to Davies & Nicholas 2 holes
Sheehan & Steinhauer beat Johnson & Wright 2 holes

***Second Day* – Fourball**

Burton & Mochrie beat Davies & Nicholas 2 and 1
Daniel & Mallon beat Nilsmark & Sörenstam 6 and 5
Green & Robbins lost to Fairclough & Reid 4 and 3
Andrews & King beat Johnson & Wright 3 and 2
Sheehan & Steinhauer lost to Alfredsson & Neumann 1 hole

***Third Day* – Singles**

Betsy King lost to Helen Alfredsson 2 and 1
Dottie Pepper Mochrie beat Catrin Nilsmark 6 and 5
Beth Daniel beat Trish Johnson 1 hole
Kelly Robbins beat Lora Fairclough 4 and 2

***Third Day* – Singles** *continued*
Meg Mallon beat Pam Wright 1 hole
Patty Sheehan lost to Alison Nicholas 3 and 2
Brandie Burton beat Laura Davies 1 hole
Tammie Green beat Annika Sörenstam 3 and 2
Sherri Steinhauer beat Dale Reid 2 holes
Donna Andrews beat Liselotte Neumann 3 and 2

1992 *Dalmahoy, Edinburgh* Oct 2–4

Result: Europe 11½, USA 6½

Captains: Mickey Walker (Europe), Kathy Whitworth (USA)

***First Day* – Foursomes**
Davies & Nicholas beat King & Daniel 1 hole
Neumann & Alfredsson beat Bradley & Mochrie 2 and 1
Descampe & Johnson lost to Ammaccapane & Mallon 1 hole
Reid & Wright halved with Sheehan & Inkster

***Second Day* – Fourball**
Davies & Nicholas beat Sheehan & Inkster 1 hole
Johnson & Descampe halved with Burton & Richard
Wright & Reid lost to Mallon & King 1 hole
Alfredsson & Neumann halved with Bradley & Mochrie

***Third Day* – Singles**
Laura Davies beat Brandie Burton 4 and 2
Helen Alfredsson beat Danielle Ammaccapane 4 and 3
Trish Johnson beat Patty Sheehan 2 and 1
Alison Nicholas lost to Juli Inkster 3 and 2
Florence Descampe lost to Beth Daniel 2 and 1
Pam Wright beat Pat Bradley 4 and 3
Catrin Nilsmark beat Meg Mallon 3 and 2
Kitrina Douglas lost to Deb Richard 7 and 6
Liselotte Neumann beat Betsy King 2 and 1
Dale Reid beat Dottie Pepper Mochrie 3 and 2

1990 *Lake Nona, FL* Nov 16–18

Result: USA 11½, Europe 4½

Captains: Kathy Whitworth (USA), Mickey Walker (Europe)

***First Day* – Foursomes**
Bradley & Lopez lost to Davies & Nicholas 2 and 1
Gerring & Mochrie beat Wright & Neumann 6 and 5
Sheehan & Jones beat Reid & Alfredsson 6 and 5
Daniel & King beat Johnson & de Lorenzi 5 and 4

***Second Day* – Fourball**
Sheehan & Jones beat Johnson & de Lorenzi 2 and 1
Bradley & Lopez beat Reid & Alfredsson 2 and 1
King & Daniel beat Davies & Nicholas 4 and 3
Gerring & Mochrie lost to Neumann & Wright 4 and 2

***Third Day* – Singles**
Cathy Gerring beat Helen Alfredsson 4 and 3
Rosie Jones lost to Laura Davies 3 and 2
Nancy Lopez beat Alison Nicholas 6 and 4
Betsy King halved with Pam Wright
Beth Daniel beat Liselotte Neumann 7 and 6
Patty Sheehan lost to Dale Reid 2 and 1
Dottie Mochrie beat Marie Laure de Lorenzi 4 and 2
Pat Bradley beat Trish Johnson 8 and 7

Solheim Cup – Individual Records
Brackets indicate non-playing captain

Europe

Name		Year	Played	Won	Lost	Halved
Helen Alfredsson	SWE	1990-92-94-96-98-2000-02-(07)-09	28	11	15	2
Becky Brewerton	WAL	2007-09	7	3	3	1
Christel Boeljon	NED	2011	3	1	2	0
Raquel Carriedo	ESP	2000-02	5	1	3	1
Laura Davies	ENG	1990-92-94-96-98-2000-02-03-05-07-09-11	46	22	18	6
Florence Descampe	BEL	1992	3	0	2	1
Kitrina Douglas	ENG	1992	1	0	1	0
Tania Elosegui	ESP	2009	3	1	2	0
Elisabeth Esterl	GER	2003	3	1	1	1
Lora Fairclough	ENG	1994	3	2	1	0
Sandra Gal	GER	2011	3	0	2	1
Sophie Gustafson	SWE	1998-2000-02-03-05-07-09-11	31	14	11	6
Lisa Hackney	ENG	1996-98	6	3	3	0
Caroline Hedwall	SWE	2011	4	2	1	1
Bettina Hauert	GER	2007	2	0	2	0
Maria Hjörth	SWE	2000-04-05-07-09-11	21	6	7	8
Karine Icher	FRA	2002	3	1	2	0
Trish Johnson	ENG	1990-92-94-96-98-2000-05-07	25	5	13	7
Carin Koch	SWE	2000-02-03-05	16	10	3	3
Ludivine Kreutz	FRA	2005	2	0	2	0
Laure de Lorenzi	FRA	1990-96-98	11	3	8	0
Diana Luna	ITA	2009	2	1	0	1
Mhairi McKay	SCO	2002-03	5	2	3	0
Kathryn Marshall	SCO	1996	3	1	1	1
Paula Marti	ESP	2002	4	1	3	0
Catriona Matthew	SCO	1998-03-05-07-09-11	25	11	8	6
Patricia Meunier Labouc	FRA	2000-03	4	2	1	1
Janice Moodie	SCO	2000-03-09	11	7	2	2
Joanne Morley	ENG	1996	2	0	2	0
Azara Muñoz	ESP	2011	4	2	1	1
Liselotte Neumann	SWE	1990-92-94-96-98-2000	21	6	10	5
Alison Nicholas	ENG	1990-92-94-96-98-2000-(09)-(11)	18	7	8	3

Name		Year	Played	Won	Lost	Halved
Catrin Nilsmark	SWE	1992-94-96-98-2000-(03)-(05)	16	8	7	1
Pia Nilsson	SWE	(1998)	0	0	0	0
Gwladys Nocera	FRA	2005-07-09	10	5	3	2
Anna Nordqvist	SWE	2009-11	8	4	4	0
Suzann Pettersen	NOR	2002-03-05-07-09-11	25	11	8	6
Dale Reid	SCO	1990-92-94-96-(2000-02)	11	4	6	1
Melissa Reid	ENG	2011	4	1	3	0
Ana Belen Sanchez	ESP	2003	2	0	2	0
Annika Sörenstam	SWE	1994-96-98-2000-02-03-05-07	37	21	12	4
Charlotta Sörenstam	SWE	1998	4	1	2	1
Karen Stupples	ENG	2005-11	5	2	3	0
Iben Tinning	DEN	2002-03-05-07	14	4	7	3
Mickey Walker	ENG	(1990)-(92)-(94)-(96)	0	0	0	0
Linda Wessberg	SWE	2007	2	1	0	1
Pam Wright	SCO	1990-92-94	6	1	4	1

United States

Name	Year	Played	Won	Lost	Halved
Danielle Ammaccapane	1992	2	1	1	0
Donna Andrews	1994-98	7	4	3	0
Heather Bowie	2003	3	0	3	0
Pat Bradley	1990-92-96-(2000)	8	2	5	1
Brandie Burton	1992-94-96-98-2000	14	8	4	2
Jo Anne Carner	(1994)	0	0	0	0
Nicole Castrale	2007-09	7	2	5	0
Paula Creamer	2005-07-09-11	19	11	6	2
Beth Daniel	1990-92-94-96-2000-02-03-05-(09)	29	10	9	7
Laura Diaz	2002-03-05-07	13	6	6	1
Jane Geddes	1996	4	1	2	1
Cathy Gerring	1990	3	2	1	0
Tammie Green	1994-98	6	2	4	0
Natalie Gulbis	2005-07-09	10	4	5	1
Pat Hurst	1998-2000-02-05-07	20	11	6	3
Vicky Hurst	2011	2	1	1	0
Juli Inkster	1992-98-2000-02-03-05-07-09-11	34	15	14	5
Becky Iverson	2000	4	2	2	0
Chris Johnson	1998	3	0	2	1
Rosie Jones	1990-96-98-2000-02-03-05-(11)	22	11	9	2
Cristie Kerr	2002-03-05-07-09-11	26	10	13	3
Christina Kim	2005-09-11	10	6	2	2
Betsy King	1990-92-94-96-98-(07)	15	7	6	2
Emilee Klein	2002	4	3	1	0
Kelli Kuehne	2002-03	8	2	6	0
Brittany Lang	2009-11	7	2	3	2
Stacy Lewis	2011	4	1	3	0
Brittany Lincicome	2007-09-11	11	5	6	0
Nancy Lopez	1990-(2005)	3	2	1	0
Michelle McGann	1996	4	1	1	2
Kristy McPherson	2009	4	1	3	0
Meg Mallon	1992-94-96-98-2000-02-03-05	29	13	9	7
Alice Miller	(1992)*	0	0	0	0
Ryanne O'Toole	2011	4	2	0	2
Dottie Pepper	1990-92-94-96-98-2000	20	13	5	2
Stacy Prammanasudh	2007	3	1	1	1
Morgan Pressel	2007-09-11	11	7	2	2
Judy Rankin	(1996)-(98)	0	0	0	0
Michele Redman	2000-02-03-05	11	4	5	2
Deb Richard	1992	2	1	0	1
Kelly Robbins	1994-96-98-2000-02-03	24	10	10	4
Nancy Scranton	2000	2	0	2	0
Patty Sheehan	1990-92-94-96-(2002)-(03)	13	5	7	1
Val Skinner	1996	4	2	2	0
Angela Stanford	2003-07-09-11	10	4	4	2
Sherri Steinhauer	1994-98-2000-07	13	6	5	2
Wendy Ward	2002-03-05	11	3	7	1
Kathy Whitworth	(1990)-(92)*	0	0	0	0
Michelle Wie	2009-11	8	4	3	1

Solheim Cup statistics

Largest margin of victory (individual matches):
In the 1990 Singles, Pat Bradley (USA) beat Trish Johnson by 8 and 7. Also in 1990, Cathy Gerring and Dottie Mochrie (USA) beat Pam Wright and Liselotte Neumann by 6 and 5 and Patty Sheehan and Rosie Jones (USA) beat Dale Reid and Helen Alfredsson by the same margin, both in Foursomes matches.

This margin was repeated in the 2000 Foursomes when Becky Iverson and Rosie Jones (USA) beat Laura Davies and Alison Nicholas.

In the 1998 Fourballs, Pat Hurst and Rosie Jones (USA) beat Lisa Hackney and Sophie Gustafson by 7 and 5.

Largest margin of victory (overall competition):
In 1990, the USA defeated Europe by a score of 11½ to 4½, a margin of seven points. This margin was repeated in 2003 when Europe were the victors with a score of 17½ to 10½.

Most events played (from 12 contests):
12 Laura Davies (EUR); 9 Juli Inkster (USA); 8 Beth Daniel (USA), Trish Johnson (EUR), Meg Mallon (USA); Annika Sörenstam (EUR), Helen Alfredsson (EUR), Sophie Gustafson (EUR); 7 Rosie Jones (USA) 6 Liselotte Neumann (EUR), Alison Nicholas (EUR), Dottie Pepper (USA), Kelly Robbins (USA).

Most matches won:
22 Annika Sörenstam (EUR), Laura Davies (EUR); 15 Juli Inkster (USA).

Most points earned:
25 Laura Davies (EUR); 24 Annika Sörenstam (EUR); 18½ Juli Inkster (USA); 16½ Meg Mallon (USA).

Teams' won and lost record (*denotes a home win):
USA 8–4 (1990*; 1994*; 1996; 1998*; 2002*; 2005*; 2007; 2009*).
Europe 4–8 (1992*; 2000*; 2003*; 2011*).

Most times as captain:
4 Mickey Walker (EUR), 1990, 1992, 1994, 1996.

LPGA Legends Handa Cup (USA *v* Rest of World) *Inglewood GC, Kenmore, Washington, USA*

USA names first

Saturday morning – Four ball:
Johnson and Daniel lost to Stephenson and Crafter
Figg-Currier and Turner beat Alfredsson and Nicholas
Bradley and King beat Dibos and Nilsmark
Scranton and Lopez halved with Graham and Lidback
Steinhauer and Rarick lost to Little and Palli
Sheehan and Jones beat Kane and Coe-Jones

Match position: USA7, World 5

Saturday morning – Foursomes:
Johnson and Daniel lost to Graham and Lidback
Figg-Currier and Turner lost to Dibos and Nilsmark
Bradley and King beat Alfredsson and Nicholas
Scranton and Lopez lost to Kane and Coe-Jones
Steinhauer and Rarick halved with Stephenson and Palli
Sheehan and Jones beat Crafter and Little

Match position: USA 12, World 12

Sunday – Singles:
Patty Sheehan lost to Alison Nicholas (ENG)
Cindy Rarick lost to Jane Crafter (AUS)
Pat Bradley beat Helen Alfredsson (SWE)
Christa Johnson lost to Jenny Lidback (PER)
Betsy King lost to Dawn Coe-Jones (CAN)
Beth Daniel beat Catrin Nilsmark (SWE)
Rosie Jones beat Sally Little (RSA)
Sherri Steinhauer beat Jan Stephenson (AUS)
Cindy Figg-Currier beat Anne Marie Palli (FRA)
Nancy Lopez beat Gail Graham (CAN)
Nancy Scranton lost to Alicia Dibos (PER)
Sherri Turner lost to Lorie Kane (CAN)

Result: USA 24, The World 24 – USA retain the Cup

Lexus Cup (Team Asia v Team International) (inaugurated 2005)

2005	Asia 8, International 16	Tanah Merah GC, Singapore
2006	Asia 12½, International 11½	Tanah Merah GC, Singapore
2007	Asia 15, International 9	The Vines, Perth, Australia
2008	Asia 11½, International 12½	Singapore Island GC
2009	*Not played*	
2010	*Not played*	
2011	*Not played*	
2012	*Not played*	

Women's World Cup

2000	Sweden (K Koch and S Gustafson)	425
2001–2004	*Not played*	
2005	Japan (A Miyazato and R Kitada)	289
2006	Sweden (A Sörenstam and L Neumann)	281
2007	Paraguay (J Granada and C Troche)	279
2008	Philippines (J Rosales and D Deelasin)	198
2009	*Not played*	
2010	*Not played*	
2011	*Not played*	
2012	*Not played*	

National Championships 2012

Glenmuir Women's PGA Professional Championship

De Vere Carden Park (Nicklaus course)

1	Alexandra Keighley (Huddersfield)	75-71—146
2	Maria Tulley (Wellhurst)	76-71—147
	Tracey Loveys (Bigbury)	72-75—147

Spain's Carlota completed a hat trick of awards

Raise a glass to Carlota Ciganda, the 22-year-old Spanish golfer from Pamplona, who completed a clean sweep of awards on the Ladies European Tour in 2012.

Helped by two victories – in China by seven shots in the Suzhou Taihu event and in Holland at the Deloitte tournament – and by ten other top 10 finishes, Carlota ended up the Tour's top money earner on the ISPS Handa Order of Merit with €251,289 edging out Caroline Masson of Germany by less than €10,000. Her prize-money was enough to ensure she was also the Rolex Rookie of the Year – a double that had not been achieved by a Tour player since England's Laura Davies had last managed the feat 27 years earlier. Finishing No 1 also earned Carlota a €20,000 bonus and a ten year exemption on the Ladies European circuit.

Carlota played several times with Laura Davies during the season and admitted: "I learned so much from her because she is so talented. It is a real priviledge to follow her in achieving this double."

Before turning professional, Carlota had done well as an amateur winning the 2007 British Amateur and European titles in 2004 and again in 2008.

Alexandra Armas, the retiring director of the LET, said: "This caps a magnificent year for Carlota. It will go down in the record books as one of the most outstanding achievements by any player in the 34 year history of the Tour."

It was no surprise when the Tour players selected Carlota as their Player of the Year, enabling her to complete the hat-trick of awards available each year on Tour. She will have the opportunity to play both on the European and American Tours in 2013.

PART IV

Men's Amateur Tournaments

World Amateur Golf Ranking

Chris Williams is the 2012 McCormack Medal winner

A Muscovite ended up the winner of the 2012 World Amateur Golf Rankings Mark McCormack medal but he does not play his golf in Russia! Chris Williams comes from a less well known Moscow, the one in Iowa in America.

Williams won an exciting battle to land the prize in the 12-calendar-month points gathering period that began in September 2011 and ended following the US Amateur Championship in August 2012.

In that final event Williams was beaten in the quarter-finals by the eventual winner Steven Fox but the University of Washington Senior still managed to finish ahead of fellow Americans Jordan Spieth, Justin Thomas and Bobby Wyatt, Japanese golfer Hideki Matsuyamma and the Dutchman Daan Huizing.

American Chris Williams from Washington State was the proud winner of the Mark H McCormack Medal in 2012

Williams made a significant move in the rankings when he led the qualifiers at the Western Amateur and then went on to win the title. Among other successes he had during the qualifying period were the NCAA Southwest Regional Championship and the Washington State Amateur. He also played well in the Palmer Cup won by the Americans at Royal County Down in Northern Ireland.

Named as a First Team All-American by the Golf Coaches Association of America, Williams had success in 2011 when taking the Sahalee Amateur Players' Championship and the Pacific Coast Amateur title.

"It's a huge honour to finish No 1," said Williams whose team mate Nick Taylor is a former winner of the medal. "I never dreamed that I would win it. Last year Patrick Cantlay, a friend of mine, was the McCormack winner and I never thought I'd find myself in the same circle as these two guys."

Williams added: "There's tons and tons of good players out there and to be top of the rankings is something I definitely cherish."

Glen D Nager, President of the USGA, praised Williams for his play. "Chris has had two terrific years of golf. His body of work in major events is to be congratulated and the USGA wishes him continued success in his career as an amateur and beyond."

Johnny Cole-Hamilton, the Executive Director of Championships for The R&A, who jointly with the USGA administer the rankings, said: "I would like to congratulate Chris on his outstanding performances. He has shown great consistency."

Williams by finishing No 1 at the end of the counting period earned exemption into both the 2013 US Open being played at the Merion golf course in Pennsylvania and The Open at Muirfield.

The WAGR is becoming an increasingly important means of tracking the performance of amateur golfers around the world on a week-to week basis. Currently the Men's World Amateur Golf Ranking, launched in 2007 (and which enjoys the support of the Rolex company), involves recording the results of 2,500 counting events involving more than 6,600 golfers in 101 countries.

The award is named after Mark H McCormack, the late founder of the sports marketing company IMG. Mark was always an avid supporter of the amateur game. Numerous event organisers now use the rankings as a criterion for automatic inclusion in their fields. The ranking in the 52-week period is updated every Wednesday.

Previous winners of the medal are: 2007 Colt Knost (USA); 2008 Danny Lee (NZL); 2009 Nick Taylor (CAN); 2010 Peter Uihlein (USA) and in 2011 Patrick Cantlay (USA).

A Womens Amateur Golf Ranking run on the same lines as the Men's event was started in 2011. That year, and again this year, Lydia Ko, the New Zealand teenager, ended up in the No 1 spot.

R&A World Amateur Golf Ranking 2011–2012 – Top 100

Players from the USA occupy most places in the Top 100 with 42 entries, six in the top ten. England takes second place with eight entries, none in the top ten. Australian players account for seven entries with Canada and Korea on four and France, Germany and Ireland on three apiece. By region the totals are: Americas 49, Europe 31, Asia 11, Australasia seven and Africa two.

			Divisor	*Points*
1	Chris Williams	USA	70	1481.61
2	Justin Thomas	USA	75	1385.83
3	Jordan Spieth	USA	68	1365.81
4	Daan Huizing	NED	71	1345.77
5	Hideki Matsuyama	JPN	41	1343.29
6	Bobby Wyatt	USA	65	1340.46
7	Patrick Rodgers	USA	60	1256.67
8	Cheng-tsung Pan	TPE	63	1242.26
9	Peter Williamson	USA	58	1241.95
10	Robert Karlsson	SWE	50	1237.00
11	Thomas Pieters	BEL	53	1231.84
12	Julien Brun	FRA	53	1223.58
13	Marcel Schneider	GER	62	1220.97
14	Jake Higginbottom	AUS	55	1201.82
15	T J Vogel	USA	55	1198.18
16	Matthias Schwab	AUT	40	1197.50
17	Julian Suri	USA	41	1187.20
18	Steven Fox	USA	55	1171.59
19	Jon Rahm-Rodriguez	ESP	32	1170.90
20	Adrien Saddier	FRA	64	1166.80
21	Matthew NeSmith	USA	57	1164.04
22	Cory Whitsett	USA	71	1160.39
23	Alan Dunbar	IRL	46	1158.70
24	Matthew Fitzpatrick	ENG	35	1153.33
25	Oliver Goss	AUS	51	1151.96
26	Ricardo Gouveia	POR	47	1149.47
27	Daniel Nisbet	AUS	75	1140.89
28	Brandon Hagy	USA	73	1132.02
29	Beau Hossler	USA	53	1129.25
30	Pedro Figueiredo	POR	55	1129.09
31	Brandon Stone	RSA	73	1126.03
32	Brett Drewitt	AUS	68	1120.96
33	Max Homa	USA	71	1107.39
34	Michael Weaver	USA	43	1102.33
35	Albin Choi	CAN	59	1101.27
36	Robin Kind	NED	65	1100.77
37	Jordan Russell	USA	77	1098.70
38	Moritz Lampert	GER	53	1098.11
39	Haydn Porteous	RSA	90	1093.98
40	Eric Chun	KOR	44	1091.02
41	Cameron Smith	AUS	50	1078.00
42	Sang Yi	KOR	51	1076.47
43	Chase Seiffert	USA	41	1068.90
44	Zac Blair	USA	67	1067.24
45	Sebastian Cappelen	DEN	48	1065.63
46	James Frazer	WAL	45	1065.19
47	Andrew Yun	USA	65	1064.42
48	Kevin Penner	USA	48	1059.29
49	Corey Conners	CAN	53	1058.96
50	Kevin Aylwin	USA	52	1057.69
51	Michael Miller	USA	54	1052.78
52	Kevin Phelan	IRL	57	1046.05
53	Talor Gooch	USA	51	1044.61
54	Edouard Espana	FRA	69	1042.03
55	Gavin Moynihan	IRL	40	1040.00
56	Dominic Bozzelli	USA	57	1034.87
57	Justin Shin	CAN	65	1034.42
58	Michael Kim	USA	68	1032.90
59	Jack Hiluta	ENG	41	1031.71
60	Ben Taylor	ENG	65	1031.54
61	Ricky Kato	AUS	59	1029.37
62	Shun Yat Hak	HKG	29	1029.31
63	Sean Dale	USA	58	1028.66
64	Andy Hyeon Bo Shim	KOR	31	1028.23
65	Matthew Stieger	AUS	87	1027.01
66	Jeffrey Kang	USA	63	1021.83
67	Jim Liu	USA	70	1019.82
68	Derek Ernst	USA	59	1018.22
69	Nadaraja Thangaraja	SRI	69	1018.12
70	Ben Geyer	USA	74	1013.85
71	Soo-min Lee	KOR	31	1013.71
72	Nathan Kimsey	ENG	53	1010.53
73	Taylor Moore	USA	31	1010.08
74	Pontus Widegren	SWE	53	1008.49
75	A J McInerney	USA	28	1008.21
76	Sebastian Vazquez	MEX	40	1007.50
77	Daniel Berger	USA	47	1006.38
78	Scott Harvey	USA	48	1006.25
79	Denny McCarthy	USA	58	1004.31
80	Khalin Joshi	IND	57	1001.75
81	Craig Hinton	ENG	41	1001.22
82	Andrew Presley	USA	41	997.26
83	Jace Long	USA	56	996.88
84	Neil Raymond	ENG	54	996.30
85	Maximilian Rottluff	GER	37	994.59
86	Max Orrin	ENG	51	992.48
87	Juan Cerda	CHI	78	991.99
88	Poom Saksansin	THA	28	989.29
89	James White	USA	52	987.98
90	Julio Vegas	VEN	55	987.27
91	Johannes Veerman	USA	39	987.18
92	Joe David	USA	34	986.76
93	Carlos Pigem	ESP	56	985.27
94	Garrick Porteous	ENG	56	983.93
95	Anton Arboleda	PHI	55	982.73
96	Cameron Peck	USA	39	982.69
97	Jonathan Garrick	USA	32	982.19
98	Jack McDonald	SCO	53	981.37
99	Mackenzie Hughes	CAN	67	980.60
100	Graeme Robertson	SCO	77	979.22

The European Amateur Ranking Top 100 can be found on page 291

World Amateur Golf Ranking 2011–2012

The World Amateur Golf Ranking, compiled by The R&A and the USGA as a service to golf, comprises a men's ranking which was launched in January 2007 and a women's ranking which began in January 2011. The week's rankings are announced every Wednesday at 12.00 noon.

Statistics are compiled each week for over 8,000 players in over 2,000 events around the world. The ranking is based on counting every stroke reported to The R&A in stroke play events and matches won in counting match play events. The men's ranking runs throughout a rolling period of 52 weeks culminating at the end of either the European or US Amateur Championship which ever is later on the calendar. The leading player at the end of the ranking period wins the Mark McCormack Medal. The women's ranking also runs through a rolling period of 52 weeks.

Counting events are divided into seven categories:

The elite events: For men: The Amateur Championship, the US Amateur, the European Amateur and the Asia–Pacific Amateur; and for women: The Ladies British Amateur, the NCAA Championship, the US Women's Amateur and the European Women's Amateur.

Category A: Counting events ranked 1-30 in the World Ranking Event Rating
Category B: Counting events ranked 31-100
Category C: Counting events ranked 101-200
Category D: Counting events ranked 201-300
Category E: Counting events ranked 301-400
Category F: Counting events ranked from 401

Counting events are stroke play competitions over a minimum of three rounds or two rounds if it is a match play qualifying competition.

Full details of how a ranking is earned and information on how the ranking works can be found on The R&A website – www.RandA.org

The rankings are displayed by month and are subdivided into the following regions:

Africa
The Americas (North, South and Central America and the Caribbean)
Asia (incorporating the Middle East)
Australasia (incorporating the Pacific Islands)
Europe

Players are from the country hosting the event unless otherwise stated.

An asterisk indicates a newly ranked player.

A list of country abbreviations can be found on page 51; WWAGR can be found on page 362.

Elite and Category "A" Events

Elite

Week 25 **2012 Amateur Championship** *Royal Troon GC/Glasgow Gailes GC, Scotland*

June 18–23 (RSS Royal Troon: Rd 1 – 74; Rd 2 – 76; Glasgow Gailes: Rd 1 – 74; Rd 2 – 74)

			SP	MP	Pts	Div
1	Alan Dunbar (NIR)	74-70—144	20	180	200	8
2	Mathias Schwab (AUT)	68-75—145	19	140	159	7
3	Paul Ferrier (SCO)	69-73—142	22	104	126	6
	Jack McDonald (SCO)	72-71—142	21	104	125	6

Full details can be found on page 295

Week 32 **2012 International European Amateur Championship**

Carton House, Co Kildare, Ireland (RSS 73-73-73-75)

			SP	Bonus	Pts	Div
1	Rhys Pugh (WAL)	68-71-72-66—277	49	48	97	4
2	James Frazer (WAL)	71-74-62-71—278	48	36	84	4
3	Thomas Sørensen (DEN)	69-67-71-72—279	47	18	65	4

Full details can be found on page 301

For further information, visit www.RandA.org/wagr

Week 33 **2012 US Amateur Championship** *Cherry Hills Village, CO, USA*

(RSS 75-71)

			SP	MP	Pts	Div
Winner	Steven Fox	72-71—143	19	180	199	8
Runner-up	Michael Weaver	73-70—143	20	140	159	7
Semi-finalists	Brandon Hagy	65-72—137	25	104	130.5	6
	Justin Thomas	65-74—139	23	104	127	6

Full details can be found on page 303

Week 44 **2012 Asia–Pacific Amateur Championship** *Amata Spring, Thailand*

(RSS 76-74-74-73)

			SP	Bonus	Pts	Div
1	Tianlang Guan (CHN)	66-64-72-71—273	56	48	104	4
2	Cheng-tsung Pan (TPE)	75-67-67-65—274	55	36	91	4
3	Oliver Goss (AUS)	70-65-69-72—276	53	18	71	4

Full details can be found on page 293

Category "A"

2011

Week 37 **Walker Cup** *Royal Aberdeen, Scotland* Sept 10–11

Rhys Pugh (WAL)	36 pts	Divisor 2
Jordan Spieth (USA)	36 pts	Divisor 2
Patrick Cantlay (USA)	16 pts	Divisor 1
Chris Williams (USA)	16 pts	Divisor 1

Week 42 **The Prestige at PGA West** *La Quinta, California, USA* Oct 9–11 (RSS 72-71-71)

			SP	Bonus	Pts	Div
1	Cheng-tsung Pan (TPE)	69-67-65—201	37	36	73	3
2	Eugene Wong (CAN)	70-64-70—204	34	18	52	3
3	Alex Ching	71-67-68—206	32	12	44	3

Week 44 **US Collegiate Championship** *Alpharetta, Georgia, USA* Oct 23–25

(RSS 74-74-74)

1	Dominic Bozzelli	67-73-70—210	36	36	72	3
2	Thomas Veerman	71-70-69—210	36	36	72	3
3	Blayne Barber	72-70-70—212	34	12	46	3
	Patrick Cantlay	69-71-72—212	34	12	46	3
	Michael Johnson	69-71-72—212	34	12	46	3
	Cheng-Tsung Pan (TPE)	71-68-73—212	34	12	46	3
	Julian Suri	67-74-71—212	34	12	46	3

Week 45 **Gifford Collegiate – Corde-Valle** *San Martin, California, USA* Oct 31–Nov 2

(RSS 73-74-74)

1	Steve Lim	66-67-69—202	43	27	70	3
2	Patrick Cantlay	63-70-70—203	42	13.5	55.5	3
3	Eugene Wong (CAN)	66-68-72—206	39	9	42	3

Week 48 **Western Refining College All American** *El Paso, Texas, USA* Nov 21–23

(RSS 72-72-73)

1	Cory Whitsett	69-69-68—206	35	27	62	3
2	Jace Long	70-67-69—206	35	11.25	46.25	3
	Todd Back	70-69-67—206	35	11.25	46.25	3

Week 53 **Patriot All-America** *Litchfield Park, Arizona, USA* Dec 28–30 (RSS 74-71-73)

			SP	Bonus	Pts	Div
1	Cory Whitsett	69-64-66—199	43	27	70	3
2	Bobby Wyatt	69-66-67—202	40	13.5	53.5	3
3	Austin Cook	70-70-69—209	33	6.75	39.75	3
	Julian Suri	71-68-70—209	33	6.75	39.75	3

2012

Week 5 **Jones Cup Invitational** *Sea Island, Georgia, USA* Feb 3–5 (RSS 79-75-76)

1	Justin Thomas	72-75-69—216	38	27	65	3
2	Manav Shah	71-71-76—218	36	13.5	49.5	3
3	Ben Taylor (ENG)	73-75-71—219	35	9	44	3

Week 5 **The Amer Ari Invitational** *Kohala Coast, Hawaii, USA* Feb 1–3 (RSS 71-73-72)

1	Jeffrey Kang	67-69-69—205	35	27	62	3
2	Jordan Spieth	69-69-67—205	35	13.5	48.5	3
3	Patrick Rodgers	67-69-71—207	33	9	42	3

Week 7 **San Diego Intercollegiate** *Chula Vista, California USA* Feb 13–14 (RSS 75-76-74)

1	Alex Ching	74-68-72—214	35	27	62	3
2	Garrick Porteous	73-73-69—215	34	13.5	47.5	3
3	Steve Lim	72-71-73—216	33	4.125	37.125	3
	Cheng-tsung Pan (TPE)	71-74-71—216	33	4.125	37.125	3
	Martin Trainer	70-77-69—216	33	4.125	37.125	3
	Chris Williams	70-72-74—216	33	4.125	37.125	3

Week 8 **Puerto Rico Classic** *Rio Grande, Puerto Rico* Feb19–21 (RSS 74-73-73)

1	Justin Thomas (USA)	67-71-68—216	38	27	65	3
2	Talor Gooch (USA)	72-69-66—217	37	13.5	50.5	3
3	James White (USA)	70-66-72—218	36	9	45	3

Week 10 **Southern Highlands Collegiate Masters** *Las Vegas, Nevada, USA* Mar 9–11 (RSS 75-75-78)

1	Blake Biddle	71-72-69—212	40	27	67	3
2	Ty Dunlap	68-72-74—214	38	11.25	49.25	3
	Pontus Widegren (swe)	69-71-74—214	38	11.25	49.25	3

Week 13 **Stanford Intercollegiate** *Stanford, California, USA* Mar 30–April 1 (RSS 72-75-73)

1	Daniel Miernicki	66-72-66—204	40	27	67	3
2	Pedro Figueredo (POR)	67-74-68—209	35	9	44	3
	Jay Hwang	70-71-68—209	35	9	44	3
	Sam Smith	70-69-70—209	35	9	44	3

Week 15 **Western Intercollegiate** *Santa Cruz, California, USA* April 14–15 (RSS 74-74-74)

1	Patrick Rodgers	67-71-68—206	40	27	67	3
2	Patrick Cantlay	69-71-68—208	38	11.25	49.25	3
	Justin Shin (CAN)	68-69-71—208	38	11.25	49.25	3

Week 17 **PAC 12 Championship** *Corvallis, Oregon, USA* April 27–29 (RSS 75-74-73-74)

1	Andrew Yun	68-70-69-68—275	53	36	89	4
2	Daniel Miernicki	68-72-66-71—277	51	18	69	4
3	Sam Smith	77-68-67-67—279	49	9	58	4
	Eugene Wong (CAN)	69-68-69-73—279	49	9	58	4

Week 17 Sir Michael Bonallack Trophy (Europe v Asia) *Monte Rei G and CC, Portugal*

April 25–27

	Points	*Divisor*
Rhys Enoch (WAL)	20	1
Jake Higginbottom (AUS)	20	1
Daan Huizing (NED)	20	1
Khalin Joshi (IND)	20	1
Robert Karlsson (SWE)	20	1
Hideki Matsuyama (JPN)	20	1
Jon Rahm-Rodriguez (ESP)	20	1
Ben Taylor (ENG)	20	1
Manuel Trappel (AUT)	20	1
Thomas Detry (BEL)	20	1

Week 20 NCAA Central Regional *Ann Arbor, MI, USA* May 17–19 (RSS 74-72-72)

			SP	*Bonus*	*Pts*	*Div*
1	Albin Choi (CAN)	69-66-68—203	39	27	66	3
2	Ben Kohles	71-65-70—206	36	9	45	3
	Sebastian MacLean (BOL)	68-70-68—206	36	9	45	3
	Daniel Miernicki	71-65-70—206	36	9	45	3

Week 20 NCAA South Central Regional *Bowling Green, KY, USA* May 17–19

(RSS 75-74-74)

1	Stephan Jaeger (GER)	70-67-66—203	44	27	71	3
2	Pedro Figueiredo (POR)	68-69-70—207	40	13.5	53.5	3
3	Ty Dunlap	71-70-70—211	36	4.125	40.125	3
	Jonathan Fly	68-73-70—211	36	4.125	40.125	3
	Steven Fox	76-64-71—211	36	4.125	40.125	3
	Scott Vincent (ZIM)	70-69-72—211	36	4.125	40.125	3

Week 20 NCAA Southwest Regional *Norman OK, USA* May 17–19 (RSS 73-76-76)

1	Chris Williams	73-68-68 - 209	40	27	67	3
2	Thiomas Pieters (BEL)	68-69-73 - 210	39	13.5	52.5	3
3	Daniel Berger	69-69-75 - 213	36	9	45	3

Week 22 NCAA DI Medal Championship *Los Angeles, CA, USA* May 29–31

(RSS 74-75)

1	Thomas Pieters (BEL)	69-68-71—203	39	27	66	3
2	Julien Brun (FRA)	72-72-67—211	36	11.25	47.25	3
	Tyler McCumber	68-71-72—211	36	11.25	47.25	3

Week 22 NCAA Match Play Championship *Los Angeles, CA, USA* June 1-3

	Pts	*Div*
Cody Gribble	72	3
Dylan Frittelli (RSA)	44	2
Toni Hakula (FIN)	44	2
Michael Kim	44	2
Daniel Miernicki	44	2
Jordan Speith	44	2
Scott Strohmeyer	44	2
Julio Vegas (VEN)	44	2
Cory Whitsett	44	2
Eugene Wong (CAN)	44	2

Week 23 **St Andrews Links Trophy** *St Andrews, Scotland* June 8–10 (RSS 75-73-72-72)

			SP	Bonus	Pts	Div
1	Daan Huizing (NED)	65-64-68-67—264	60	36	96	4
2	Alan Dunbar (IRL)	75-68-67-68—278	46	18	64	4
3	Graeme Robertson	70-73-72-64—279	45	12	57	4

Week 24 **Sunnehanna Amateur** *Johnstown, Pennsylvania, USA* June 14–1 (RSS 72-71-72-75)

1	Bobby Wyatt	65-70-68-68—271	49	36	85	4
2	Michael Miller	68-69-66-70—273	47	18	65	4
3	Nicholas Reach	67-71-68-68—274	46	7	53	4
	Justin Thomas	65-69-70-70—274	46	7	53	4
	Sebastian Vazquez (MEX)	67-69-67-71—274	46	7	53	4

Week 25 **Northeast Amateur Championship** *Wannamoisett CC, USA* June 20–23 (RSS 71-71-70-70)

1	Justin Shin (CAN)	68-71-65-65—269	45	36	81	4
2	Jordan Russell	63-66-71-69—269	45	18	63	4
3	Brandon Hagy	68-71-67-67—273	41	9	50	4
	Michael Hebert	72-65-65-71—273	41	9	50	4

Week 26 **Palmer Cup** *Royal County Down, Northern Ireland* June 28–30

		MP	Div
1	Julien Brun (FRA)	44	2
	Daan Huizing (NED)	44	2
	Robert Karlsson (SWE)	44	2

Full results can be found on page 356

Week 28 **Players Amateur** *Bluffton, South Carolina, USA* July 9–15 (RSS 74-74-73)

			SP	Bonus	Pts	Div
1	Daniel Nisbet (AUS)	69-66-70—205	40	27	67	3
2	Bobby Wyatt	66-73-67—206	39	13.5	52.5	3
3	Michel Hebert	73-74-66—203	32	9	41	3

Week 29 **Southern Amateur** *Chenal CC July 18–21* (RSS 74-73-74-74)

1	Peter Williamson	70-69-70-67—276	51	36	87	4
2	Bobby Wyatt	71-68-70-67—276	51	18	69	4
3	Daniel Berger	70-72-68-67—277	50	12	62	4

Week 29 **Porter Cup** *Niagara Falls CC* July 18–21 (RSS 69-70-71-71)

1	Richard Werenski	66-62-67-68—263	50	36	86	4
2	Denny McCarthy	64-69-67-65—265	48	18	66	4
3	Patrick Rodgers	67-65-69-66—267	46	12	58	4

Week 31 **Western Amateur** *Highland Park, Illinois, USA* July 30–Aug 4 (RSS 74-72-70-70)

			SP pts	MP pts	SP Bonus	Pts	Div
1	Chris Williams	72-66-66-67—271	47	120	36	203	8
2	Jordan Russell	69-70-70-70—279	39	84	—	123	7
3	Abraham Ancer	69-68-72-67—277	42	52	7	101	6

How a player makes it onto the World Amateur Golf Rankings is a question often asked. The system is easy to understand if, by necessity, somewhat complex. It is best to look at the criteria in three different ways – by doing well in a Stroke Play event, with a good performance in a Match Play tournament or in an event in which both Stroke and Match Play elements are involved. Just taking part does not necessarily mean a place on the ranking. There are certain criteria to becoming one of now over 3,000 ranked players around the world.

In Stroke Play a player will have to have:
- Made the cut in an Elite event
- Finished in the top 40 and ties in an "A" event
- Finished in the top 32 and ties in a "B" event
- Finished in the top 16 and ties in a "C" event
- Finished in the top 8 and ties in a "D" event
- Finished in the top 4 and ties in an "E" event
- Finished in the top 2 and ties in an "F" event

Or, for male players, participation in The Open, Masters or US Open Championship, an event on the European or US PGA Tours, the Australasian or Japan Tours, the Asian Tour. Nationwide or Sunshine Tours the Canadian, Challenge, Korean or OneAsia Tours or the Tour de las Americas.

Finish in a position to gain bonus points in any other professional event recognised by the committee.

In Match Play a player will make the ranking if they:
- Make the last 32 in a Category "A" event
- Make the last 16 in a Category "B:" event
- Make the last 8 in a Category "C" event
- Make the last 8 in a Category "D" event
- Make the last 4 in a Category "E" event
- Make the last 4 in a Category "F" event
- Win a match against ranked player in an Elite team Match Play event

If the event is a combination of Stroke Play and Match Play what a player needs to become ranked is:
- Qualify for the Match Play stage or finish on the qualifying score in an Elite Stroke Play event
- Finish in the top 32 and ties in a Category "A" Stroke Play event
- Make the last 32 of a Category "A" event
- Finish in the top 16 and ties in the Stroke Play stage of a Category "B" event
- Make the last 16 of a Category "B" event
- Finish in the top 8 and ties in the Stroke Play stage of a Category "C" event
- Make the last 8 in a Category "C" event
- Finish in the top 4 and ties in the Stroke Play stage of a Category "D" event
- Make the last 8 in a Category "D" event.
- Finish in the top 2 and ties in the Stroke Play stage of a Category "E" event
- Make the last 4 in a Category "E" event
- Lead the qualifiers in the Stroke Play section of a Category "F" event
- Make the last 4 of a Category "F" event.

Ranking Scratch Score

The RSS is the calculated standard used to convert a player's Counting Scores to Stroke Play Ranking Points.

The RSS for a Counting Round is calculated by use of the formula (a) / (b), where (a) is the sum total of the gross scores of the leading (X) players in the round, with (X) representing the total number of Ranked Players in the round and (b) is the total number of gross scores in (a) above.

Fractions from the RSS calculation will be rounded to the nearest whole number.

If less than three Ranked Players play a Counting Round, the RSS for that round will be the average of the lowest three scores by amateur golfers.

If fewer than three Amateurs play a Counting Round, the RSS will equate to par.

In any official event from other professional tours, the RSS will equate to par.

August

Americas

F	Show Me Summer Shootout	Chris Reinert*/Julian USA		Taylor (ENG)*	

September

Africa

D	Mpumalanga Open	Middelburg, Mpumalanga	9–11	Hendre Celliers	RSA

Americas

B	Carpet Capital Collegiate	Rocky Face, GA	9–11	Justin Thomas	USA
B	Golfweek Conference Challenge	Burlington, IA	25–27	Stephan Jaeger (GER)	USA
B	OFCC/Fighting Illini Invite		16–18	Patrick Rodgers	USA
B	The Gopher Invitational	Wazata, MN	11–12	Chris Brant	USA
C	Adams Cup of Newport	Newport, RI	19–20	Ricardo Gouveia (POR)	USA
C	California State Fair Amateur	Sacramento, CA	3–5	Matt Hansen	USA
C	Fighting Irish Gridiron Classic	South Bend, IN	26–27	Paul McConnell	USA

Americas (continued)

C	Gene Miranda Falcon Invite	USAF Academy, CO	18–19	Kevin Penner/TJ Carpenter	USA
C	Inverness Intercollegiate	Toledo, OH	26–27	Dugan Murphy*	USA
C	Junior Players Championship	Ponte Vedra Beach, FL	2–4	Gavin Hall	USA
C	Kikkor Husky Invitational	Bremerton, WA	27–27	Chris Williams	USA
C	Mason Rudolph Championship	Franklin, TN	23–25	Hunter Green	USA
C	Northern Intercollegiate	Sugar Grove, IL	9–11	Brad Schneider/Tyler Merkel	USA
C	Saint Mary's Invitational	Seaside, CA	19–20	Chris Russo	USA
C	The Sam Hall Intercollegiate	Hattiesburg, MS	12–13	Blake Kelley/Jason Shufflebotham (WAL)	USA
C	Turning Stone Tiger Intercollegiate	Verona, NY	4–5	Julien Brun (FRA)	USA
C	US Mid-Amateur	Shadow Hawk, TheHoustonian	17–22	Randal Lewis*	USA
C	VCU Shootout	Manakin Sabot, VA	26–27	Scott Fernandez (ESP)	USA
C	Wolverine Intercollegiate	Ann Arbor, MI	12–13	Jace Long	USA
D	Golfweek Program Challenge	Myrtle Beach, SC	10–13	Tomasz Anderson (ENG)	USA
D	Kansas Invitational	Lawrence, KS	19–20	Christoph Weninger (AUT)/ Daily Young/David Smith	USA
D	Mark Simpson Colorado Invite	Boulder, CO	12–13	Alex Ching/Beau Schoolcraft	USA
D	Middle Atlantic Amateur	Lakewood CC	22–25	Jake An	USA
D	The McLaughlin	Farmingdale, NY	15–16	Carlos Rodriguez Jr (COL)	COL

E	Marshall Invitational	Alex Redfield	USA
E	North Carolina Mid-Amateur	Brian Westveer	USA
E	The Carmel Cup (Individual)	Clement Sordet (FRA)	USA
E	UTA/Waterchase Invitational	Rafael Becker (BRA)	USA
E	Wichita Diet Pepsi Shocker Inv. Invitational	Calvin Pearson (RSA)/ Hunter Sparks	USA
F	I Copa Laguna	Juan Carlos Serrano*	MEX
F	Alabama State Mid-Am	Matt Johnson	USA
F	Atlantic Region Invitational	Richie Schembechler	USA
F	Battle at the Tetons	Mason Casper*	USA
F	BSU Dash Thomas Memorial	Jesse Heinly	USA
F	Bucknell Fall Invite	Austin Gray	USA
F	CA State Intercollegiate	Thane Ringler	USA
F	Canadian Int. Junior Challenge	Kristian Johannessen (NOR)	CAN
F	Canadian Mid-Amateur	Rob Couture (USA)	CAN
F	Cardinal Intercollegiate	Nicklaus Benton	USA
F	Carroll College Invitational	Jim Mee*	USA
F	Chaps Fall Invitational	Bradley Sinnett (RSA)	USA
F	Chico City Championship	Lee Gearhart*	USA
F	Colorado Mid-Amateur	Keith Humerickhouse	USA
F	Cornell Invitational	Carter Rufe	USA
F	Dornick Hills Classic	Andrew Green	USA
F	Erv Kaiser Invitational	Trent Olson*	USA
F	Evangel Fall Invitational	Jack Jackson (ENG)*	USA
F	Fairway Club Invitational	Daily Young	USA
F	Flagler Coll. Jennison Memorial	SJeff Evanier*	USA
F	Fort Worth City C/ship	Clarke Kincaid	USA
F	Gordin Classic NCAA D3 Preview	Noah Ratner	USA
F	Grizzly Invitational	Brandon Bingaman	USA
F	Hartford Hawk Invitational	Jeb Buchanan	USA
F	High Country Shootout	Richard Farmer (ENG)*	USA
F	Jim Redgate Invitational	J M O'Toole*	USA
F	John Bohmann Memorial Inv.	Jonathan Allen*	USA
F	John Piper Intercollegiate	Alex Cusumano*	USA
F	Maryland Intercollegiate	Brian Dorfman/ Damon Postal/ Max Marsico/Taylor Dickson*	USA
F	Massachusetts Mid-Amateur	Mike Calef	USA
F	Minnesota Mid-Amateur	Sam Schmitz	USA
F	Missouri Intercollegiate	Julian Taylor (ENG)	USA
F	Nevada State Mid-Amateur	Brady Exber	USA
F	New Hampshire Mid-Am	Phil Pleat	USA
F	New York State Mid-Am	Jimmy Welch*	USA
F	NSIC/RMAC Crossover	Jim Knous	USA
F	NSU Classic	Ethan Adamson	USA
F	Oldfield Labor Day Classic 15-19	Ben Schlottman*	USA
F	Outlaw Cup	Brian Sunker	USA
F	Pacific Am. Classic Scratch	Jin Ahn*	USA
F	Pacific Northwest Mid-Am.	Sandy Harper (CAN)	USA
F	Palouse Collegiate	Jarred Bossio	USA
F	Peaks Classic	Bradley Sinnitt (RSA)	USA
F	Rocky Mountain Invitational	Drew Reinland	USA
F	Rutgers Invitation	Adam Goins	USA
F	Sandestin Collegiate C/ship	Marcelo Rozo (COL)	USA
F	Spring Hill Suites Intercoll.	Matt Broome	USA
F	St. Martin's Invitational	Jamie Hall*	USA
F	The Fossum	Michael Davan	USA
F	The Vandersluis Memorial	Bruce Hegland*	USA
F	UK Bluegrass Invitational	Bosten Miller	USA
F	UNK Invitational	Mike Shukis*	USA
F	USGA Senior Amateur	Louis Lee*	USA
F	Utah Mid Amateur	Dan Horner	USA
F	Wallace State Fall Invite	William Anderson	USA
F	Warner Pacific CCC Invitation	Jesse Heinly	USA
F	Wasioto Winds Fall Kick-off	David Lawrence	USA
F	Webber Intercollegiate	Elrick van Eck (RSA)	USA
F	Woodward Video Junior	John Boehme*	USA
F	Abierto de Golf Farallones	Nicolas Herrera	COL
F	Abierto Del Guayaquil	Rafael Miranda*	ECU
F	Argentinian Mid-Amateur	José Manuel Alvarez Castro*	ARG
F	Campeonato Argentino De Menores	Alejandro Tosti	ARG

F	Campeonato Auspiciador	Jean Pierre Peglau	PER
F	Camp. Juvenil de Venezuela	Manuel Torres	VEN
F	Camp. Nacional de Menores 11 Parada 13–14	Ivan Camilo Ramirez	COL
F	Camp. Nacional de Menores 11 Parada 15–17	Matias Molina Tellez*	COL
F	Campeonato Nacional Infantil	Mauricio Cuartas	COL
F	Maringa Open	Arthur Lang	BRA
F	Torneo Abierto Jockey Club de Rosario	Alejandro Tosti*	ARG

Asia

D	Putra Cup	The Clearwater Bay G&CC	6–9	Tze Huang Choo (SIN)	HKG

E	Hur Chungkoo Cup-Korean Amateur	Gyu Bin Kim	KOR
F	China Amateur Championship	Xiao Jun Zhang*	CHN
F	China Amateur Tour Leg 6	Guan Tianlang	CHN
F	China Futures Tour Leg 6	Zhang Huilin	CHN
F	Faldo Series India	Vashishta Pawar*	IND
F	Hokkaido Mid Amateur	Masaki Sato*	JPN
F	Hokkaido Open	Eiji Mizoguchi*/ Akira Endo*	JPN
F	Ilsong Cup 12-14	Yo seop Seo*	KOR
F	Ilsong Cup 15-17	Si-woo Kim	KOR
F	Kanto Mid Amateur	Masaya Takahashi	JPN
F	Kyushu Open	Mitsunobu Fukunaga*	JPN
F	Lion City Cup	Low Khai Jei (MAS)/ Chanachoke Dejpiratanamongkol (THA)	HKG
F	Malaysian Junior Open	Mohd Azry Asyraf Mohd Azam	MAS
F	National Middle School-Junior	Yung-Hua Liu*	TPE
F	National Middle School-Senior	Day-Wei Shen*	TPE
F	September Grand Prix	Nadaraja Thangaraja	SRI
F	SGA 4th Nat. Ranking Game	Jerome Ng	SIN
F	Taiwan Amateur C/ship	Taihei Sato (JPN)	JPN
F	Terengganu Open	Ahmad Zahir Abd Ghani*	MAS
F	TGA-CAT Junior Ranking # 3	Nanfa Somnuek	THA

Australasia

F	Gary Player Classic 16–17	Jordan McCarthy	AUS
F	Gary Player Classic 18–20	Simon Viitakangas	AUS
F	Gary Player Classic U15	Jack Lane-Weston*	AUS
F	NSW Junior Championship	Peter Stojanovski*	AUS
F	Pacific Games Individual	Adrien Peres (FRA)*	FIJ
F	Queensland Mid-Amateur	Lee Manning*	AUS
F	Samoa Open	Malase Maifea*	SAM
F	South Australian Senior Am.	Stefan Albinski	AUS
F	Wellington Stroke Play	Marc Jennings	NZL

Europe

A	Walker Cup	Royal Aberdeen Golf Club	10–11	Marc Jennings (NZL)	SCO
B	Turkish Amateur Open	Antalya	22–25	Daan Huizing (NED)	TUR
C	French Team Cup Individual	Bondues	9–11	Adrien Saddier	FRA
C	South of England Amateur	Walton Heath Golf Club	1–2	William Shucksmith	ENG
D	D. of York Young Champions Trophy	Royal Liverpool GC, Hoylake	13–15	Harry Casey	ENG
D	German National Championship	GC Gleidingen	8–11	Max Kramer*	GER

E	Faldo Series Grand Final	Gavin Samuels (ENG)	IRL
E	Titleist Tour 7	Andreas Gjesteby	NOR
F	Austrian Mid-Amateur	Johann Quickner*	AUT
F	Austrian Seniors	Herbert Plenk (GER)*	AUT
F	Bulgaria Open	Florian Kolberg (TUR)	BUL
F	Campeonato de Cataluna	Carles Perez Gelma*	ESP
F	Camp. Internacional Junior	Mario Galiano Aguilar	ESP
F	Cancello D'Oro	Gianmaria Mazzetto*	ITA
F	Connacht Mid-Amateur	Alan Condren	IRL
F	Edward Trophy	Graham Robertson	SCO
F	Estonian National Match Play	Martin Unn*	EST
F	European Boys' Chall. Trophy	Simon Zach (CZE)	SVK
F	European Universities C/ship	Graeme Robertson (SCO)	SLO
F	Fiorino D'Oro	Jacopo Jori	ITA
F	Grand Prix de Montpellier Massane	Nicolas Peyrichou	FRA
F	Grand Prix de Saint Germain	Hugo Rouillon	FRA
F	Internat. de France . Mid-Amateur	Thomas Ansersson (SWE)*	FRA
F	Italian Stroke Play	Mattia Miloro	ITA
F	Italian Under 16 Championship	Renato Paratore	ITA
F	Junior Masters Invitational	Mikael Lindberg	SWE
F	Junior National Match Play	Rowin Caron	NED
F	Munster Mid Amateur Open	Gary O'Flaherty	IRL
F	National Match Play	Fernand Osther	NED
F	Polish Amateur Championship	Mateusz Gradecki	POL
F	Skandia Tour Elit #6	Rasmus Olsson*	SWE
F	Stirling Invitational	Jack McDonald	SCO
F	Suisse Romande C/ship	Nicolas Thommen	SUI
F	Titleist Tour 6	Andreas Gjesteby	NOR
F	West of England Open Am.	David Gregory	ENG

October

Africa

C	Ekurhuleni Open	Benoni, Gauteng	1–2	Brandon Stone	RSA
D	African Team Championship	Lake Club Benoni	17–21	Riekus Nortje	RSA
F	Kenya Stroke Play			David Opati*	KEN

Americas

A	The Prestige at PGA WEST	La Quinta, CA	9–11	Cheng-tsung Pan (TPE)	USA
A	U.S. Collegiate Championship	Alpharetta, GA	23–25	Dominic Bozzelli/Johannes Veerman	USA
B	Alister MacKenzie Invitational	Fairfax, CA	17–18	Eugene Wong (CAN)	USA
B	Bank of Tennessee @ Blackthorn	Jonesborough, TN	14–16	Jace Long/Mark McMillen	USA
B	Brickyard Collegiate Championship	Macon, GA	7–9	Brooks Koepka	USA
B	Isleworth Collegiate Invitational	Windermere, FL	23–25	Jordan Spieth	USA
B	Jack Nicklaus Invitational	Dublin, OH	10–11	Thomas Pieters (BEL)	USA
B	Jerry Pate National Intercollegiate	Birmingham, AL	304	Corbin Mills	USA
B	William H Tucker	Albuquerque, NM	S30–O1	Zac Blair	USA
B	Windon Memorial	Skokie, IL	16–17	Matt Thompson	USA
C	AutoTrader.com Collegiate Classic	Duluth, GA	17–18	Harold Varner	USA
C	Bridgestone Collegiate	Greensboro, NC	29–30	Albin Choi (CAN)	USA
C	David Toms Intercollegiate	Shreveport, LA	17–18	Andrew Noto	USA
C	Herb Wimberly Intercollegiate	Las Cruces, NM	24–25	Hunter Sparks	USA
C	Lone Star Invite@ Briggs Ranch	San Antonio, TX	16–18	Jeff Wibawa	USA
C	Ping Invitational	Stillwater, OK	8–10	A J McInerney	USA
C	Rees Jones Invitational	Daufuskie Island, SC	3–4	Nate McCoy	USA
C	Rod Myers Invitational	Durham, NC	1–2	Julian Suri	USA
C	Santa Clara Cabo Collegiate	Cabo	27–29	Sebastian Cappelen (DEN)	MEX
C	Wolfpack Intercollegiate	Raleigh, NC	3–4	Robert Hoadley	USA
D	DA Weibring Intercollegiate	Normal, IL	1–2	Luke Guthrie	USA
D	Firestone Invitational	Akron, OH	10–11	Mac McClung	USA
D	Invitational at Kiawah	Kiawah Island, SC	17–18	Sam Love	USA
D	John Dallio Memorial	Lemont, IL	8–9	Emilio Cuartero (ESP)	USA
D	Old Dominion / OBX collegiate	Powell's Point, NC	23–25	T J Mitchell	USA
D	Otter Invitational	Monterey, CA	24–25	Ben Taylor (ENG)	USA
D	Wolf Pack Classic	Stateline, NV	3–4	Jay Myers	USA

F	Aflac/Cougar Invitational	Craig Gibson (CAN)	USA
F	Ashford Invitational	Michael Fitzgerald*	USA
F	Atlanta Match Play	Fred Rescigno*	USA
F	Bearcat Invitational	Brian Dorfman	USA
F	Bill Cullum Invitational	Spencer Fletcher/ Tyler Torano	USA
F	Bill Ross Intercollegiate	Pep Angles Ros (ESP)	USA
F	Bruce Williams Memorial Inv.	Alex Carpenter	USA
F	Burbank City Championship	Jon Levitt*	USA
F	Butler Fall Invitational	Andrew Wegeng	USA
E	CMS Invitational	Tain Lee	USA
E	Cobra PUMA Invitational	Billy Peel Jr	USA
E	Crump Cup	Stephen Summers	USA
E	Donald Ross Intercollegiate	Kristopher Gray (ENG)*/Matt Sizemore*	USA
F	Firestone Grill Cal Poly Inv.	Pedro Figueiredo (POR)	USA
E	Georgetown Intercollegiate	Vaita Guillaume (FRA)	USA
E	LA Tech Squire Creek Invite	Scott Kelly	USA
E	NSU Shark Invitational	Simon Forsslund (SWE)	USA
F	CCU Fall Golf Invite-RMAC #3	Kyle Grassel*/Michael O'Connor (ENG)*	USA
F	Connecticut Cup	Jeffrey Merrell*	USA
F	Connecticut Mid-Amateur	Raymond Floyd*	USA
F	Corban Invitational	Jesse Heinly	USA
F	Embry Riddle AZ Invitational	Tain Lee	USA
F	F&M Bank APSU Intercoll.	Marco Iten (SUI)	USA
F	Florida Mid-Amateur	Stephen Anderson	USA
F	GLIAC Championship	Chris Cunningham*	USA
F	Golfweek Fall Invitational D3	Noah Ratner	USA
F	Golfweek National C/ship	Jim Aughtry*	USA
F	Grand Canyon Fall Invitational	Kyle Souza	USA
F	Greater Houston City C/ship	James Bartell*	USA
F	Gustavus Twin Cities Classic	Coy Papachek*	USA
F	Harvey Penick Invitational	Patrick Christovich	USA
F	HBU Intercollegiate	Gregory Yates	USA
F	Jim Colbert Intercollegiate	Taeksoo Kim	USA
F	Joe Agee Invitational	Austin Gray	USA
F	John Telich Sr CSU Invite	Andrew Bailey	USA
F	Laker Collegiate Invitational	Jordan Walor	USA
F	Lindsay Olive Wildcat Classic	Kyle Souza	USA
F	Macdonald Cup	Peter Williamson	USA
F	MIAC Championship	Alex Kapraun*/ Justin Volling*	USA
F	Mission Inn Fall Intercollegiate	Sam Ryder	USA

F	Montverde Acad. Junior All-Star Invitational	Sam Burns	USA
F	Murray State Invitational	Patrick Newcomb	USA
F	Nassau Invitational	Joe Saladino	USA
F	NCAA D2 Regional Preview	Casey Nelson	USA
F	NCCAA Championship	Justin Burns	USA
F	NJCAA D2 Preview	Jake Argento*	USA
F	NJCAA DI National Championship Preview	Richard James (WAL)	USA
F	NJCAA District 4 Preview	Dylan Brown	USA
F	Northwood Fall Shootout	Chase Lindsey	USA
F	Odessa College Invite	Richard James (WAL)	USA
F	Rollins College Invitational	Spencer Cole	USA
F	Ryan Palmer Foundation Invite	Alex Carpenter	USA
F	SeeMore Putters NAIA Intercollegiate	Omar Tejeira (PAN)/ Matt Luckett*	USA
F	Service Academy Classic	Kyle Westmoreland	USA
F	SIUE Intercoll. by Doubletree	David Lawrence	USA
F	Skyhawk Classic	Jake Erickson	USA
F	Society of Senior C/ship	Paul Simson	USA
F	South Carolina Mid-Amateur	Josh Branyon*	USA
F	St Augustine Amateur	A J Crouch	USA
F	Stocker Cup	Randy Haag	USA
F	Tennessee Mid-Amateur	Todd Burgan	USA
F	Texas Mid-Amateur	Beau Davis	USA
F	Texoma Championship	Vilhelm Bogstrand (NOR)	USA
			USA
F	TVA Credit Union Invite	Jake Greer	USA
F	UMAC Championships	Dean Goodwin*	USA
F	Virginia State Mid-Am	Nick Biesecker	USA
F	Wildcat Invitational	Cameron Rappleye	USA
F	Will Wilson Tanglewood Intercollegiate	Howard Duffin (ENG)*	USA
F	WVIAC Championship	Sebastian Starud (SWE)*	USA
F	Abierto Barquisimeto	Jose Chagin*	VEN
F	Abierto Cuenca	Andres Felipe Arango	ECU
F	Abierto de Golf Serrezuela	Luis Carlos Pardo	COL
F	Abierto Internac. Copa Claro	Juan Carlos Cortes	CHI
F	Abierto Opita de Golf	Eduardo Quintero*	COL
F	Camp. National Por Golpes	Julien Duxin*	URU
F	Camp. Sudamericano Prejuvenil	Manuel Torres (VEN)	PAR
F	Colombian Mid Amateur	Juan Fernando Mejia	COL
F	Copa Claro	Patricio Alzamora	PER
F	Copa Eduardo Herrera	Juan Camilo Giraldo	COL
F	Copa Enrique Santos	Gustavo Silva (CHI)	ECU

Asia

E	Maharashtra Open	Udayan Mane	IND
F	China Junior C/ship 11-14	Jiang Zhi Jie*	CHN
F	China Junior C/ship 15-17	Shan Chuan ChenZe*	CHN
F	Deccan Open Amateur	Brijesh Yadav*	IND
F	Faldo Series Malaysia	Mohamad Hisyam Abdul Majid	MAS
F	Fangshan Changyang Amateur	Yuan Li	CHN
F	Hong Kong Open and Mid-Am.	Huang Yongle (CHN)	HKG
F	HSBC Nat. Junior C/ship Final	Jin Cheng*	CHN
F	Kedah Amateur Open	Mohd Wafiyuddin*	MAS
F	KSC International Amateur	Richard Han (USA)*	HKG
F	National Sports Festival	Chang-woo Lee	KOR
F	Punjab Amateur	Sardar Murad Khan*	PAK
F	Punjab Open	Khalid Mehmood*	PAK
F	Singapore Senior Am. Open	Lakshman Singh (IND)*	SIN
F	Singha Thailand Open	Netipong Srithong	THA
F	Sri Lanka Amateur	Nadaraja Thangaraja	SRI
F	TGA-CAT Junior C/ship	Tawan Phongphun*	THA

Australasia

B	Four Nations Cup	The Hills Golf Club	13–16	Brett Drewitt (AUS)	NZL

F	Australian Senior Match Play	Stefan Albinski	AUS
F	Fiji Golf Club Open	PC Goundar*	FIJ
F	Lindisfarne Cup	Mark Shulze*	AUS
F	Srixon Int. Junior Classic	Ricky Kato	AUS
F	Stewart Gold Cup	Nick Voke*	NZL
F	Victorian Senior Amateur	Stefan Albinski	AUS
F	Waitomo Classic	Compton Pikari	NZL
F	Wanganui Open	Junior Tatana*	NZL

Europe

C	Trophee des Regions	Saint Cyprien	29–31	Hugo Rouillon	FRA
D	Copa Nacional Puerta de Hierro	CG la Dehesa	13–16	Mario Galiano Aguilar	ESP
D	European Club Trophy Individual	National GC, Antalya	20–22	Adrien Saddier (FRA)	TUR

F	Austrian Match Play	Lukas Nemecz	AUT
F	BUCS Order of Merit # 2	Chris Harkins	SCO
F	Championnat de France Cadet	Robin Sciot-Siegrist	FRA
F	Coppa d'Oro Castelli	Jacopo Guasconi	ITA
F	Grand Prix de la cote D'Opale	Julien De Poyen	FRA
F	Grifo d'Oro	Alessandro Chiorri*	ITA
F	Israel Junior	Asaf Cohen	ISR
F	Israel Masters Gold	Barry Shaked*	ISR
F	Israel Open	Assaf Cohen	ISR
F	Italian Mid-Am	Marcello Grabau	ITA
F	La Quercia d'Oro	Filippo Campigli*	ITA
F	Portuguese Federation Cup	Goncalo Pinto	POR
F	Tournoi Federal Jeunes	Romain Langasque	FRA
F	Trofeo Glauco Lolli Ghetti	Lorenzo Guanti	ITA

November

Africa

C	Central Gauteng Open	Royal Johannesburg & Kensington	18–20	Daniel Hammond	RSA
D	Eastern Province Stroke Play	Port Elizabeth GC	5–6	Ray Taverner	RSA

Africa (continued)

E	Harry Oppenheimer Trophy	Jacquin Hess	RSA
E	International Teams C/ship Ind.	Drikus Bruyns	RSA
F	Egyptian Amateur Open	Amr Abu El Ela/ Ramy Taher*	EGY
F	Orange Classic	Kealeboga Makoko	BOT
F	Tanzania Open	David Opati (KEN)	TAN
F	Uhuru Shield	Frank Matilo*	KEN

Americas

A	Gifford Collegiate-CordeValle	San Martin, CA	O31–N2	Steve Lim	USA
A	Western Refining Col All-Am	El Paso, TX	21–22	Cory Whitsett	USA
B	Royal Oaks Intercollegiate	Dallas, TX	O31–N1	MJ Daffue (RSA)	USA
B	Copa Juan Carlos Tailhade	Los Lagartos	10–13	Daan Huizing (NED)	ARG
C	Argentine Amateur	San Isidro	15–20	Daan Huizing (NED)	ARG
C	Copa Simon Bolivar	Caracas	2–5	Robin Kind (NED)	VEN
C	Amelia Island Intercollegiate	Fernandina Beach	7–8	Sean Dale	USA
C	SCVB Pacific Invitational	Stockton, CA	O31–N2	Kevin Lucas	USA
D	Kauai Collegiate Invite	Lihue, HI	O30–N1	Thomas Kua	USA
D	Kiawah Island Intercollegiate	Kiawah, SC	O30–N1	Andres Pumariega/Vaita Guillaume (FRA)	USA
D	Marjorie Whitney Invitational	TPC Sawgrass	O30–N1	Greg Mergel*	USA
D	Polo Junior Classic	Palm each Gardens, FL	19–25	Matthew Nesmith	USA

E	Abierto Las Palmas	Claudio Correa	CHI
F	Champions Gate (13–15)	Camilo Mexsen (MEX)*	USA
F	Champions Gate (16–18)	Maxime Blandin (FRA)*	USA
F	CSU San Marcos Fall Classic	Jeremy Sanders	USA
F	Dennis Rose Invitational	Jamie Hall	USA
F	IJGT Major at TPC Sawgrass 15–19	Tiger Lee (HKG)*	USA
F	IJGT Major at TPC Sawgrass U 14	Daulet Tuleubayev (KAZ)*	USA
F	Mustang Invitational	Adam Loran*	USA
F	Oklahoma Christian Intercoll.	Alasdair Dalgliesh (ENG)*	USA
F	Omni Tucson National (13–15)	Patrick Murphy*	USA
F	Omni Tucson National (16–18)	Jonah Texeira	USA
F	Sonoma State Invite	Kyle Souza	US
F	Stetson/CFSC Invitational	Sam Ryder	USA
F	Wildcat Invitational	Jordan Carpenter*	USA
F	Guatemala Amateur	Alvaro Ortiz (CRC)	GUA
F	Abierto del Litoral	Santiago Bauni	ARG
F	Abierto Los Leones	Juan Carlos Cortes	CHI
F	Abierto Prince of Wales CC	Andres Jabalquinto	CHI
F	Abierto Sambil	Rodolfo Escalera*	VEN
F	Abierto Valle Escondido	Martin Cancino	CHI
F	Copa Ciudad de Barranquilla	Juan Camilo Giraldo	COL
F	Copa Luis Enrique Rueda Otero	Juan Arias*	COL
F	Federacao de Baiana de Golfe	Pedro Costa Lima	BRA
F	Internacional Infantil y Juvenil Caribe	Nicholas Polo Espinosa*	COL
F	Pan American Maccabi Games	Daniel Charen (USA)	BRA
F	Tercera Parada Nacional Menores	Ivan Camilo Ramirez	COL
F	Torneo Abierto Del Oriente	Daniel Patino	BOL
F	Torneo Nacional La Paz	Rodrigo Soria*	BOL
F	Tourneo Ciudad de Cucuta	Mateo Gomez	COL
F	Tourneo Shalom	Mateo Gomez	COL
F	V Parada Mid-Amateur	David Penalosa Armel*	COL

Asia

E	Western India Amateur	Senapaa Chikkarangappa	IND
F	Abu Dhabi Junior	Daniel Hendry (SCO)	UAE
F	Acer National Fall Ranking Tournament	Teng Kao	TPE
F	Albatross International Junior	Manu Gandas	IND
F	China Am. Tour Match Play	Guan Tianlang	CHN
F	Eastern India Junior	Syed Saqib Ahmed	IND
F	Japan Mid-Amateur	Masayoshi Tanaka	JPN
F	KPK Amateur	Hamza Amin	PAK
F	Melaka Amateur Open	Nicklaus Chiam (SIN)	MAS
F	November Grand Prix	M Arumugam	SRI
F	Penang Amateur Open	Charles Davies (WAL)	MAS
F	Rajasthan Junior	Shubhankar Sharma*	IND
F	Sarawak Chief Minister's Cup	Paul San	MAS
F	SEA Games (Individual)	Ratanon Wannasrichan (THA)	INA
F	Selangor Amateur Open	Jerome Ng (SIN)	MAS
F	SGA 5th Nat. Ranking Game	Joshua Ho	SIN
F	Shaikh Rashid Trophy	Daniel Hendry (SCO)	UAE
F	Sindh Amateur	Mohd Ali Hai	PAK
F	Singha Junior World C/ship	Wei-Hsiang Wong (TPE)*	THA

Australasia

F	Australian Mid-Amateur	Jason Perry	AUS
F	Bream Bay Classic	Kevin Budden	NZL
F	Omanu Classic	James Hamilton	NZL
F	Panasonic Auckland Stroke Play	Fraser Wilkin	NZL

Europe

E	Grand Prix de la Ligue PACA	Clement Batut	FRA

December

Africa

F	JGF Strokeplay	Mohit Mediratta*	KEN
F	Nyali Open	Francis Kimani*	KEN

Americas

A	Patriot All-America	Litchfield Park, AZ	28–30	Cory Whitsett	USA
B	Dixie Amateur	Coral Springs, FL	19–22	Curtis Thompson	USA
B	South Beach International Amateur	Miami, FL	20–23	Kelly Kraft	USA
C	Junior Orange Bowl	Coral Gables, FL	27–30	Juan Eduardo Cerda (CHI)	USA
D	Gate American Junior	Ponte Vedra Beach, FL	19–22	Cody Proveaux	USA
D	Jones Cup Junior Invitational	St Simons Island, GA	18–20	Matthew Nesmith	USA

E	San Diego Junior Boys	Jonah Texeira	USA
E	TPC Craig Ranch Collegiate	Sang Yi (KOR)	USA
E	Abierto Las Brisas de Chicureo	Claudio Correa	CHI
E	Campeonato Abierto Ciudad de Montevideo	Juan Eduardo Cerda (CHI)	URU
F	Barton Creek Collegiate	Paul Otte*	USA
F	CJGA World Junior Challenge 14 & Under	Kyle MacDonald (CAN)*	USA
F	CJGA World Junior Challenge 15–19	Chad Merzbacher*	USA
F	Dixie Senior	Ron Carter	USA
F	Doral Publix Junior Classic 14–15	Pierre Mazier (FRA)	USA
F	Doral Publix Junior Classic 16–18	Nicolas Manifacier (FRA)	USA
F	Florida International Junior	Dominic Foos (GER)	USA
F	Holiday Classic @ Barton Creek	Dillon vanEssen*	USA
F	Ka'anapali Hawaiian Junior	Royce Rosenthal*	USA
F	Senior Tour Championship	Bev Hargraves*	USA
F	SOS Ralph Bogart	Chip Lutz	USA
F	Toyota Junior Tour Cup Series	Jonathan Sanders	USA
F	USA Open Collegiate Players Championship	Andrew Cornella*	USA
F	Costa Rica Nat. Stroke Play	Alvaro Ortiz	CRC
F	Copa Arturo Calle	Ivan Camilo Ramirez	COL
F	Torneo Abierto Nacional BCP	Marcelo Wilde*	BOL
F	Torneo Hyundai	Ricardo A Piiroja*	PER
F	Torneo Nac. Abierto Del Valle	Alejandro Valenzuela	BOL
F	Tourneo Nac. Vuelta Bolivia	George Scanlon	BOL

Asia

D	East India Amateur	RCGC, Kolkata	19–25	Honey Basoya	IND
D	RCGC Cup	Royal Calcutta Golf Club	13–16	Angad Cheema	IND

F	Aaron Baddeley Internat. Junior	Guan Tianlang	CHN
F	All India Junior Championship	Rigel Fernandes	IND
F	Arab Games Individual	Ahmed Almusharekh (UAE)	QAT
F	Bhutan Amateur Open	Jeewan Gurung*	BHU
F	China Amateur Open	Guan Tian-Lang	CHN
F	HSBC Youth Chall. 3rd Leg	Joshua Ho	SIN
F	Jharkhand Open	Vikram Rana	IND
F	Sabah Internat. Junior Masters	Albright Chong*	MAS
F	SICC Junior Invitational	Gregory Foo	SIN
F	TSM Challenge	Low Khai Jei	MAS
F	Western India Junior	Syed Saqib Ahmed	IND

Australasia

D	Dunes Medal	The Dunes GC, VIC	N29–D2	Todd Sinnott	AUS

E	Port Phillip Amateur & Victorian Amateur	Cruze Strange	AUS
F	2XU Champions Trophy	Kevin Yuan*	AUS
F	Asia Pacific Senior C/ship	Peter King	AUS
F	GNJGF Junior Masters	Anthony Murdaca	AUS
F	Queensland Schoolboys	Jack Hulyer	AUS

Europe

F	TGF Ligi 1 Ayak	Hamza Sayin	TUR
F	TGF Ligi 2	Fahrettin Kok	TUR

January

Africa

C	Gauteng North Open	Pretoria, Gauteng	27–29	Toby Tree (ENG)	RSA
D	KwaZulu Natal Open	Durban CC	20–22	Brandon Stone	RSA
D	Prince's Grant Invitational	KwaZulu Natal	16–18	Brandon Stone	RSA

F	Sigona Bowl	Matthew Omondi*	KEN

Americas

B	JU Invitational	Ponte Vedra, FL	30–31	T J Vogel	USA
C	Arizona Intercollegiate	Tucson, AZ	30–31	John Catlin	USA
C	New Year's Invitational	St Petersburg, FL	5–8	Garland Green	USA

E	Crane Cup Mid-Amateur	Robert Funk	USA
E	Puerto Rico Junior Open	Edward Figueroa	PUR
E	Abierto Marbella	Philippe Guidi*	CHI
E	Copa Jose G Artigas Individual	Juan Eduardo Cerda (CHI)	URU
F	Crane Cup Senior	Paul Simson	USA
F	Gateway Senior Invitational	Richard Pfeil*	USA
F	Golfweek Senior C/ship	Richard Pfeil	USA
F	Kingsway Senior Invitational	Mike Occi*	USA
F	Old Corkscrew Senior Inv.	Ron Carter	USA
F	Central American Junior	Jose Mendez Vargas (CRC)	ESA
F	National Junior Stroke Play	Jose Mendez Vargas	CRC
F	Abierto Cachagua	Gustavo Silva	CHI
F	Abierto de Granadilla	Anibal Reinoso	CHI
F	Abierto de Temuco	Thomas Burgemeister	CHI
F	Internacional de Menores Junior	Luis Barco	PER
F	Int. de Menores Pre-Juvenil Junior	Ivan Camilo Ramirez (COL)	PER
F	Torneo I de Menores	Luis Barco*	PER
F	Torneo II de Menores	Eithel McGowen	PER
F	Torneo III de Menores	Miguel Tola	PER

Asia

D	All India Amateur	Chandigarh GC	17–22	Angad Cheema	IND
D	Asian Junior Team Championship	Damai Laut Golf & Country Club	8–12	Kenta Konishi (JPN)	MAS

F	Federal Amateur	Taimur Hassan Amin	PAK
F	Hong Kong Close and Mid Amateur	Steven Lam	HKG
F	HSBC China Junior Open	Marc Ong (SIN)	CHN
F	MGA National Trial	Mohd Afif Mohd Razif	MAS
F	National Junior Master Chall.	Chen Zihao	CHN
F	Pakistan Open	Chen Zihao (CHN)	PAK
F	Philippine Amateur Open	Gregory Foo (SIN)	PHI
F	Philippine International Junior	Nicklaus Chiam (SIN)	PHI
F	Qatar Open Amateur	Yoseph Dance (USA)*	QAT

Australasia

B	Australian Amateur	Woodlands GC, Huntingdale GC	17–22	Marcel Schneider (GER)	AUS
B	Australian Master of the Amateurs	Royal Melbourne Golf Club	10–13	Nathan Holman	AUS
B	Lake Macquarie Amateur	Belmont GC, NSW	26–29	Daniel Nisbet	AUS

F	Auckland Anniversary Tourn.	Tae Koh*	NZL
F	Canterbury Strokeplay	Owen Burgess (WAL)	NZL
F	Danny Lee Springfield Open	Landyn Edwards	NZL
F	Harvey Norman Junior	Ricky Kato	AUS
F	Hastings Open	Harry Bateman	NZL
F	Morcom Cup	Andrew Phillips	AUS
F	North Island U19	Compton Pikari	NZL
F	Otago Stroke Play	Brent McEwan	NZL
F	SA Junior Amateur	Jake McLeod	AUS
F	SA Junior Masters	Anthony Murdaca	AUS
F	Tamar Valley Junior Cup	Viraat Badhwar	AUS
F	Tasmanian Junior Masters	Viraat Badhwar	AUS
F	Tasmanian U24 Championship	Cameron Bell*	AUS
F	Victorian Junior Masters	Teremoana Beaucousin (FRA)	AUS

Europe

F	Andalucia Junior European Open	Samuel Church (ENG)*	ESP
F	TGF League 3rd Leg	Florian Kolberg	TUR
F	Titleist Winter Tourn.–Norway	Vetle Maroy (NOR)	ESP

February

Africa

C	South African Stroke Play	Glendower GC	7–10	Haydn Porteous	RSA
E	Free State & Northern Cape Am.	Harrismith CC	17–19	Muzi Nethunzwi	RSA

F	Muthaiga Open	John Ndichu*	KEN

Americas

A	Jones Cup Invitational	Sea Island, GA	3–5	Justin Thomas	USA
A	San Diego Intercollegiate	Chula Vista, CA	13–14	Alex Ching	USA
A	The Amer Ari Invitational	Kohala Coast, HI	1–3	Jeffrey Kang	USA
A	Puerto Rico Classic	Rio Grande, PR	19–21	Justin Thomas (USA)	PUR
B	Big Ten Match Play	Bradenton, FL	10–11	Jeffrey Kang	USA
B	Del Walker Match Play	Long Beach, CA	27–28	Jeffrey Kang	USA
B	HP Boys At Carlton Woods	The Woodlands, TX	18–20	Shun Yat Hak (HKG)	USA
B	John Burns Intercollegiate	Wahiawa, HI	15–17	Julian Suri	USA
B	John Hayt Collegiate Invitatational	Ponte Vedra, FL	26–28	Julien Brun (FRA)	USA
B	Mobile Bay Intercollegiate	Mobile, AL	20–21	Alex Rowland/Lee Bedford	USA
B	North Ranch Collegiate	Westlake Village, CA	27–28	Matt Hoffenberg	USA
B	SunTrust Gator Invitational	Gainesville, FL	11–12	Dominic Bozzelli	USA
B	Wyoming Desert Intercollegiate	Palm Desert, CA	25–26	Kevin Penner	USA
C	Seahawk Intercollegiate	Wilmington, NC	26–27	Wesley Bryan	USA
C	UTSA / Oak Hills Invitational	San Antonio, TX	13–14	Joakim Mikkelsen (NOR)	USA
D	Charleston Shootout	Charleston, SC	27–28	T J Vogel	USA
D	Rice Intercollegiate	Houston, TX	20–21	Zach Fullerton	USA
D	UNO Mardi Gras Invitational	Avondale, LA	27–28	Carlos Rodriguez Jr (COL)	USA

E	Matlock Collegiate Classic	Case Gard*	USA
E	WSU Snowman Getaway	Mario Clemens	USA
E	Abierto de Golf Santa Augusta	Juan Eduardo Cerda	CHI
E	Abierto La Serena	Juan Eduardo Cerda	CHI
E	Abierto Las Brisas de S. Domingo	Matias Calderon	CHI
F	Armstrong Pirate Invitational	Patrick Garrett	USA
F	Challenge at Fleming Island	Ewen Ferguson (SCO)*	USA
F	Copa Yucatan	Alvaro Ortiz	MEX
F	Coyote Classic	Kyle Souza	USA
F	CSU San Marcos Invitational	Ryan Ellerbrock	USA
F	Folino Invitational	Parker Page/Tyler Torano	USA
F	Gary Freeman BCU Spring Inv.	Clint Wilhelm	USA
F	Gasparilla Invitational	Doug Lacrosse*	USA
F	Jack Brown Memorial Invite	Jim Knous	USA
F	Jim McLean Doral	Jackson Stroup*	USA
F	Moot Thomas Senior Inv.	Bill Leonard*	USA
F	NMMI Invitational	Richard James (WAL)	USA
F	Presidents Boys Cup	Sahith Theegala	USA
F	San Antonio Shoot-Out	Joel Thelen	USA
F	Southeastern Fire Invitational	Tom Gamble (ENG)	USA
F	Spring Cardinal Classic	Derek Oland*	USA
F	Start 2 Finish	Gustaf Hydbom (SWE)	USA
F	Texoma Chevy Dealers Intercollegiate	Josh Buchanan*	USA
F	Titan Winter Invitational	Joe Sakulpolphaisan (THA)	USA
F	Western States Boys Players Cup	Bobby Gojuangco	USA
F	Wexford Plantation Intercoll.	Damon Stephenson (AUS)	USA
F	Abierto Internac. de Menores	Anibal Reinoso	CHI
F	Abierto La Sabana	Sebastian Pinzon	COL
F	Camp. Nacional de Menores	Matias Molina Tellez	COL
F	Camp. Nacional de Menores Boys Match Play	Miguel Tola	PER
F	Camp. Nacional por Golpes	Jorge Fernandez Valdes	ARG
F	Camp. Nacional Prejuvenil y Juvenil	Nicolas Teuten	URU
F	Clasificacion al Sudamericano Juvenil	Gustavo Leon	VEN
F	Clasificatorio I Juvenil	Nicolas Handal	BOL
F	Clasificatorio II Juvenil	Mohamad Mosheni*	BOL
F	Copa Subaru	Sebastian Pinzon	COL
F	Nacional Mid Am. Parada I	Jose Ricaurte Marin	COL
F	Southamerican Am. Qualifier	Eithel McGowen	PER
F	Torneo de Golf Aficionado	Mateo Gomez	COL
F	Torneo Nac. Abierto de Carnaval	Johnny Montano/ Christian Vezjak*	BOL
F	Torneo Nac. de Aficionados	Santiago Tobon	COL
F	Torneo V de Menores	Eithel McGowen	PER
F	Torneo VI de Menores de Verano Jun.	Luis Barco	PER

Asia

E	Bangladesh Amateur	Manav Das (IND)	BAN
F	Emirates Amateur Open	Peter Stojanovski (AUS)	UAE
F	February Grand Prix	Nadaraja Thangaraja	SRI
F	Kuala Lumpur Amateur Open	Abdul Hadi (SIN)*	MAS
F	Mission Hills Junior Tour Grand Final	Tianlang Guan/ Yi Chen Wang*	CHN
F	North Zone Qualifier	Samarth Dwivedi*	IND
F	President's Cup	Ashish Pariyar*	NEP
F	SGA 1st Nat. Ranking Game	Marc Ong	SIN
F	Taiwan Nat. Winter Ranking Tourn.	Fang Yinren	TPE
F	TGA-CAT Junior Ranking 4	Danthai Boonma	THA

Australasia

B	New South Wales Medal & Amateur	Long Reef & Mona Vale Golf Clubs	1–8	Brett Drewitt/Neil Raymond (ENG)	AUS
B	Riversdale Cup	Melbourne, VIC	16–19	Jake Higginbottom	AUS
C	Tasmanian Open	Tasmania	23–26	Ricky Kato	AUS
D	South Island Stroke Play	Christchurch GC	23–26	Compton Pikari	NZL

E	Avondale Amateur Medal	Callan O'Reilly	AUS	F	LawnMaster Classic	Harry Bateman	NZL
E	Grant Clements Memorial	Sam An	NZL	F	Lindisfarne Cup	Andrew Phillips	AUS
F	Dunedin Stroke Play	Matt Tautari	NZL	F	New Zealand Seniors	Rodney Barltrop (AUS)	NZL
F	GNW Championship	Cameron Bell	AUS				
F	Int. Seniors Mid-Winter C/ship	Jerry Hutton (USA)*	NZL	F	Tasmanian Senior Amateur	Michael Leedham*	AUS

Europe

B	Portuguese International Amateur	Golf de Montado	15–18	Moritz Lampert (GER)	POR
D	Copa Baleares	CG Son Antem	2–5	Robin Kind (NED)	ESP

F	Grand Prix de Saint Donat	Clement Berardo	FRA	F	TGF League 4th Leg	Hasan Ceylan/ Guray Yazici	TUR
F	Italian Boys U18 C/ship	Gianmaria Trinchero	ITA				
F	Spanish Int. Senior Amateur	John Ambridge (ENG)	ESP				

March

Africa

C	Northern Amateur Open	Randpark Golf Club	11–16	Paul Shields (SCO)/Aubrey Barnard	RSA
C	South African Amateur	Cape Town	F26–M2	Brian Soutar (SCO)	RSA
D	North West Open	Leopard Park Golf Club	23–25	Zander Lombard	RSA

E	KeNako South African World Juniors	Hannes Ronneblad (SWE)	RSA	F	Northern Cape Open	Desne van den Bergh	RSA
				F	Windsor Classic	Nelson Simwa	KEN
F	EP/Border Strokeplay	Oswin Schlenkrich*	RSA	F	Windsor Junior Open	Abraham Abdullahi	KEN
F	Jwaneng Open	Muller Keabetswe*	BOT				

Americas

A	Southern Highlands Coll. Masters	Las Vegas, NV	9–11	Blake Biddle	USA
B	Bandon Dunes Championship	Bandon, OR	16–18	Chris Williams	USA
B	Barona Collegiate Cup	Lakeside, CA	22–23	JJ Spaun	USA
B	Callaway Match Play Championship	Bradenton, FL	18–20	JJ Spaun	USA
B	Cleveland Palmetto Invite	Aiken, SC	5–6	Ben Kohles	USA
B	Furman Intercollegiate	Greenville, SC	16–18	Sebastian Soderberg (SWE)	USA
B	General Hackler Championship	Pawleys Island	11–12	Sean Dale	USA
B	Hootie @ Bulls Bay Intercollegiate	Awendaw, SC	25–27	Niclas Carlsson (SWE)	USA
B	Linger Longer Invitational	Greensboro, GA	24–25	Cory Whitsett	USA
B	Louisiana Classics	Lafayette, LA	5–6	Andrew Presley	USA
B	Morris Williams Intercollegiate	Austin, TX	16–17	Dylan Frittelli (RSA)/Jordan Spieth/Julio Vegas (VEN)	USA
B	National Invitational Tournament	Tucson, AZ	16–17	J J Spaun	USA
B	Schenkel Invitational	Statesboro, GA	16–18	Ben Kohles	USA
C	Border Olympics	Laredo, TX	16–17	M J Daffue (RSA)	USA
C	Desert Shootout	Goodyear, AZ	22–24	Rafael Becker (BRA)	USA
C	Fresno State Lexus Classic	Fresno, CA	5–6	Alex Ching	USA
C	Seminole Intercollegiate	Tallahassee, FL	9–11	Brooks Koepka	USA
C	The Duck Invitational	Eugene, OR	26–27	Andrew Vijarro	USA
C	The Farms Invitational	Rancho Santa Fe, CA	12–13	JJ Spaun	USA
C	UCF Rio Pinar Invitational	Orlando, FL	19–20	Jack Hernandez	USA
C	USF Invitational	Dade City, FL	4–6	Chris Pledger/Justin Dorward	USA
C	Campeonato Sudamericano Amateur	Los Farallones, Cali	19–25	Jorge Fernandez Valdes (ARG)	COL
D	Argent Financial Classic	Choudrant, LA	11–13	Hunter Green	USA
D	Bobcat Intercollegiate	Eatonton, GA	19–20	Daniel Young (SCO)	USA
D	C&F Bank Intercollegiate	Williamsburg, VA	25–27	Kamito Hirai	USA
D	FAU Spring Break Championship	Lake Worth, FL	23–25	Brooks Koepka	USA
D	Golf Pride Pinehurst Intercollegiate	Pinehurst, NC	10–11	Michael Kania	USA

D	Southeastern Collegiate	Valdosta, GA	12–13	Tyler Chandler	USA
D	St Edward's Invitational	Austin, TX	5–6	Daniel Stapff (BRA)	USA
D	UALR/First Tee Classic	Little Rock, AR	26–27	Will Hogan	USA

E	Bash at the Beach	Sebastian MacLean (BOL)/Vaita Guillaume (FRA)	USA
E	Carter Plantation Intercoll.	Philipp Westermann (GER)	USA
E	NDNU Argonaut Invitational	Kyle Souza	USA
E	San Francisco City C/ship	Cody Blick	USA
F	Annual SEKI	Aaron Watkins	USA
F	Arizona Publinks	Kale Davidson*	USA
F	Battle at Primm	Alasdair Dalgliesh (ENG)	USA
F	Bearcat Classic	Joel Dahlenburg	USA
F	Cavalier Classic	Carson Kallis (CAN)	USA
F	Eagle Invitational	Hunter Fikes*	USA
F	Florida Azalea	Darryl Donovan*	USA
F	George Washington Invite	Max Marsico	USA
F	Goosepond Fling	Dylan Brown	USA
F	Grand Canyon Thunderbird Invite	Eddie DeLashmutt/ Trevor Blair	USA
F	Hawaii State Amateur	John Oda	USA
F	Hawaii State Senior Am. Stroke Play	Shigeru Matsui*	USA
F	Jackrabbit Invitational	Korbin Kuehn	USA
F	Jekyll Island Collegiate Invite	Mike Wesko	USA
F	Jekyll Island Individual Coll.	Teddy Kon*	USA
F	Jones Cup Senior Invitational	Doug Hanzel	USA
F	Lou Hart Invitational	Joe Sakulpolphaisan (THA)	USA
F	Midland CC Spring Invitational	Antonio Morales (MEX)*	USA
F	Mississippi Mid-Amateur	Clay Homan	USA
F	Mustang Intercollegiate	Alex Estrada	USA
F	North Alabama Spring Classic	Ricky Stimets*	USA
F	North Texas Mid-Amateur	Mike Calef	USA
F	Panther Invitational	Ray Badenhorst (ZIM)*	USA
F	Pioneer Shootout	Chris Herzog	USA
F	Point Loma/Smee Builders Invite	Steven Watson*	USA
F	Ronnie Black Collegiate Invite	Richard James (WAL)	USA
F	Salinas City Match Play	Ricky Stockton	USA
F	Samford Intercollegiate	Casey O'Toole	USA
F	Sand Shark Classic	Mark Phillips (BER)*	USA
F	Scratch Players Mid-Amateur	Randy Haag	USA
F	Scratch Players Senior Am.	Jeff Burda*	USA
F	Senior Florida Azalea Amateur	Chip Lutz	USA
F	SoCal Intercollegiate D2	Alex Marry	USA
F	Society of Seniors Spring Classic	Mike Bodney*	USA
F	South Texas Mid-Amateur	David Pocknall	USA
F	TaylorMade Adidas Intercoll.	Noah Ratner	USA
F	The Grover Page Classic	Jake Erickson/ Patrick Newcomb	USA
F	The Magnolia Invitational	Bryn Powers/ Jonathan McCurry/ Jordan Walor	USA
F	Torneo III Nacional Campeon de Campeones Interzonas	Sebastian Vazquez	MEX
F	Triumph at Pauma Valley	Ji Hwan Park	USA
F	Wyndham Spring Invitational	Jared Consoli (AUS)	USA
F	Bermuda Match Play	Jarryd Dillas	BER
F	Caribbean Intercollegiate	Pat Wilson (USA)	PUR
F	Central American Amateur	Herbert Day (ESA)	HON
F	Costa Rica Nat.Match Play	Jose Mendez Vargas	CRC
F	Trinidad & Tobago Open	James Johnson (BAR)	TRI
F	Abierto Club Campestre de Cali	Mateo Gomez	COL
F	Abierto De Arrayanes CC	Gonzalo Leon	ECU
F	Abierto La Posada	Pablo Viterbo	CHI
F	Abierto Las Araucarias	Martin Cancino	CHI
F	Clasificatorio III Juvenil	George Scanlon	BOL
F	Clasificatorio IV Juvenil	George Scanlon	BOL
F	Copa Donovan	Mateo Gomez	COL
F	Master Internacional Infantil y Juvenil	Julian Otero	COL
F	Vuelta Bolivia XXXX	Camilo Avila	BOL

Asia

D	Northern India Amateur	Golden Green Resort, Gurgaon	13–16	Syed Saqib Ahmed	IND
D	Samarvir Sahi Championship	Chandigarh Golf Club	F28–M2	Khalin Joshi	IND

E	Delhi NCR Cup	Nadaraja Thangaraja (SRI)	IND
E	Faldo Series Asia Grand Final	Masamichi Ito (JPN)	CHN
F	All India Mid-Amateur	Vikram Rana	IND
F	All India Seniors	Vijay Kumar*	IND
F	Gulf Cooperation Council Championship	Ahmed Al Musharekh	UAE
F	HSBC Youth Challenge 1st Leg	Thomas Tan Wei Hao/Nicklaus Chiam	SIN
F	Malaysian School Sports	Low Khai Jei	MAS
F	Montecillo Junior C/ship	Angelo Jose Gandionco/ Suwannarut Sarit (THA)*	PHI
F	Perlis Amateur Open	Low Khai Jei	MAS
F	PGI-BNI Series 1	Ian Andrew	INA
F	Pin Fernando Grand Prix	Nadaraja Thangaraja	SRI
F	Royal Palm Team Trophy – Ind.	Mohd Ali Hai	PAK
F	Royal Selangor Junior Open	Adam Shaw (CAN)*	MAS
F	Ryo Ishikawa Cup Junior Championship	Kouhei Kinoshita*	JPN
F	Sindh Amateur	Mohd Ali Hai	PAK
F	TGA-CAT Junior Ranking 5	Danthai Boonma	THA
F	TrueVisions Singha Junior	Sarit Suwannarut	THA
F	WWWExpress-DHL National Amateur	Shin Jin Woo*	PHI

Australasia

D	New Zealand Stroke Play	Hastings GC	22–25	Vaughan McCall	NZL
D	North Island Stroke Play	Lochiel Golf Club, Hamilton	15–18	Daniel Pearce	NZL
D	SBS Invitational – Individual	Invercargill GC, Southland	3–4	Blair Riordan	NZL

E	Western Australia State Am.	Oliver Goss	AUS
F	Boorandara Cup	James Zappelli	AUS
F	NSW Senior Championship	Rodney Dale*	AUS
F	Western Australia State Senior	Stefan Albinski	AUS

Europe

B	European Nations Cup Individual	RCG Sotogrande	21–24	Robin Kind (NED)	ESP
B	Spanish Amateur – Copa S.M El Rey	Alcanada	29–04	Jack Hiluta (ENG)	ESP
D	Grand Prix du Cap d'Agde	Cap D'agde	16–18	Clement Berardo	FRA

F	BUCS Regional Qualifier 3	Jack McDonald	SCO
F	BUCS Stroke Play	David Booth (ENG)	SCO
F	Campeonato de Castellon	Jose Bondia	ESP
F	Catalonian Junior C/ship	Adria Arnaus	ESP
F	Copa Andalucia	Victor Pastor Rufian	ESP
F	Darwin Salver	Nathan Kimsey	ENG
F	Gran Premio Vecchio Monastero	Giacomo Garbin	ITA
F	Italian Amateur Match Play	Paolo Ferraris	ITA

April

Africa

C	Sanlam Cape Province Open	Kimberley Golf Club	M31–A1	Brandon Stone	RSA
D	African Zone VI Championship	Lilongwe Golf Club	24–26	Brandon Stone (RSA)	MAW
D	W. Province Strokeplay & Amateur	Mowbray GC, Cape Metropole	23–28	Justin Turner	RSA

F	Botswana Amateur	Hamadzangu Kamunga	BOT
F	SA U23 Interprovincial B	Hamadzangu Kamunga (BOT)	RSA
F	Sigona Junior Open	Abraham Abdullahi	KEN
F	South African Under 19 C/ship	Tristen Strydom/ Lawrence Thriston*	RSA

Americas

A	Pac 12 Championship	Corvallis, OR	27–29	Andrew Yun	USA
A	Stanford Intercollegiate	Stanford, CA	M30–A1	Daniel Miernicki	USA
A	Western Intercollegiate	Santa Cruz, CA	14–15	Patrick Rodgers	USA
B	ASU Thunderbird Invitational	Tempe, AZ	6–7	Derek Ernst	USA
B	Atlantic Coast Conference C/ship	New London, NC	20–22	Benjamin Rusch (SUI)	USA
B	Big 12 Championship	Trinity, TX	27–29	Joakim Mikkelsen (NOR)	USA
B	Big Ten Championship	French Lick, IN	27–29	Luke Guthrie	USA
B	Boilermaker Invitational	West Lafayette, IN	21–22	Luke Guthrie	USA
B	ECU/UNCW River Landing Intercoll.	Wallace, NC	6–7	Brinson Paolini	USA
B	Gary Koch Invitational	Tampa, FL	7–8	Joey Petronio	USA
B	Insperity ASU Invitational	Augusta, GA	M31–A1	Julien Brun (FRA)	USA
B	Junior Invitational	Sage Valley Golf Club	20–22	Zach Olsen	USA
B	LSU Invitational	Baton Rouge, LA	M31–A1	Austin Gutsgell	USA
B	SEC Championship	Sea Island, GA	20–22	Justin Thomas	USA
B	The Aggie Invitational	Bryan, TX	21–22	Victor Perez (FRA)	USA
B	The Woodlands All-American	Woodlands, TX	9–10	Geoff Shaw	USA
C	Atlantic Sun Championship	Braselton, GA	16–18	Sam Ryder	USA
C	Azalea Invitational	CC of Charleston, SC	M29–A1	Matthew NeSmith	USA
C	BancorpSouth Intercollegiate	Madison, MS	2–3	Jonathan Fly	USA
C	Cougar Classic	Provo, UT	27–28	Zahkai Brown	USA
C	C-USA Championship	Texarkana, TX	22–24	Gregory Eason (ENG)	USA
C	Hawkeye-Great River Entertainment	Iowa City, IA	14–15	Nate McCoy	USA
C	Irish Creek Collegiate	Kannapolis, NC	M31–A1	James Beale (NZL)	USA
C	Robert Kepler Intercollegiate	Columbus, OH	14–15	Max Buckley	USA
C	Terra Cotta Invitational	Naples National GC	13–15	Donald Constable	USA
C	West Coast Conference C/ship	Hollister, CA	16–18	Ben Geyer	USA
C	Wyoming Cowboy Classic	Scottsdale, AZ	9–10	Ben Juffer	USA
D	Alameda Commuters Tournament	Almeda GC, CA	21–29	Michael Weaver	USA
D	Anteater Invitational	Newport Beach, CA	23–24	Kevin Lim (KOR)	USA
D	Big South Championship	Ninety-Six, SC	16–18	Robert Karlsson (SWE)	USA
D	Buccaneer Presented by Carrabbas	Miami Beach, FL	2–3	Oscar Lengden (SWE)	USA

D	Coca-Cola Wofford Invitational	Spartanburg, SC	9–10	Vaita Guillaume (FRA)	USA
D	COG Mizzou Intercollegiate	Columbia, MO	9–10	Ryan Zech	USA
D	Coleman Mid Amateur Invitational	Seminole Golf Club	26–28	Tim Jackson	USA
D	Memphis Intercollegiate	Memphis, TN	9–10	Ben Greene	USA
D	NYX Hoosier Invitational	Bloomington, IN	7–8	Eric Chun (KOR)	USA
D	OGIO UC Santa Barbara Invite	Goleta, CA	2–3	Xander Schauffele	USA
D	Southern Conference Championship	Florence, SC	15–17	Stephan Jaeger (GER)	USA
D	Southland Conference	McKinney, TX	23–25	M J Daffue (RSA)	USA
D	SSC Tournament	Bradenton, FL	16–17	Ben Taylor (ENG)	USA
D	Sun Belt Conference Tournament	Muscle Shoals, AL	23–25	Ty Spinella	USA

E	Argonaut Invitational	Carlos Rodriguez Jr (COL)	USA
E	Atlantic 10 Championship	Raoul Menard (CAN)	USA
E	Carolinas Mid Amateur	Scott Harvey	USA
E	Gulf South Conference	Nate Anderson*	USA
E	Junior at Traditions	Branson Davis	USA
E	Los Angeles City Junior	Alex Angard	USA
E	Winn Grips Heather Farr Classic	Beau Hossler	USA
E	Camp. Int. de Aficionados	Patricio Alzamora	PER
E	Camp. SubAmericano Juvenil	Jose Luis Montano/ Franco Romero (ARG)	BOL
F	AAC Direct Qualifier	Michael Alread	USA
F	ACC Junior Championship	Preyer Fountain*	USA
F	American Sen. (ASGA) MP	Chip Ward*	USA
F	Arizona Stroke Play	C J Kim	USA
F	ASC Championships	Jacob Walsh	USA
F	ASU Red Wolf Intercollegiate	Sawyer Radler*	USA
F	Baker U Spring Invite	Ben Johnson (ENG)*	USA
F	Bash at the Beach	Billy Nisbet*	USA
F	Beu/Mussatto Invitational	Michael McGee*	USA
F	Bobby Krig Invitational	Jimmy Hutchings	USA
F	Braveheart Classic	Ji Hwan Park	USA
F	CAA Conference C/ship	Greg Matthias*	USA
F	Cal Pac Championship	Kyle Schrader*	USA
F	Camp LeJeune Gold	Omar Tejeira (PAN)	USA
F	Camp LeJeune Scarlet Consolation	Brandon Ketron*	USA
F	Camp. Nacional Interzonas LII	Diego Gudino Moros*	MEX
F	CBU Spring Break	Marcus Sanna*	USA
F	CCAA Championship	Alex Sobstad (NOR)	USA
F	Centennial Conference C/ship	Cameron Warner	USA
F	Central Oklahoma Invitational	Scott Wyers/Baer Aneshansley*	USA
F	Coleman Senior Invitational	Brady Exber	USA
F	College of Idaho Invitational	Jesse Heinly	USA
F	Conference Carolina's C/ship	Adam Black*	USA
F	DBU Classic	Brandon Johnson	USA
F	Detroit Titans Invitational	Kurt Slattery	USA
F	Earl Yestingsmeier Invitational	Chris Malec	USA
F	Fireline Towson Invitational	Jay Mulieri	USA
F	Florida State Senior Amateur	A J Kroeger	USA
F	Frontier Conference Tourn.	Dane Jensen	USA
F	Georgia Senior Invitational	Emile Vaughn*	USA
F	GLVC Championship	Corey Richmond*	USA
F	GNAC Championship	Craig Crawford*	USA
F	Golfweek Senior Amateur	Douglas Pool	USA
F	Great American Conf. C/ship	Matt Jennings*	USA
F	Grub Mart Intercollegiate	Tom Robson (ENG)	USA
F	Hanny Stanislaus Invitational	Trevor Blair	USA
F	Heartland Conference C/ship	Matt McKown*	USA
F	Horizon League Championship	Chad Ebert	USA
F	Hotels at Grand Prairie Inv.	Daniel Young*	USA
F	Ivy League Championship	Peter Williamson	USA
F	Jim West Intercollegiate	Mitchell McLeroy	USA
F	Junior All-Star at Chateau Elan	James Clark III*	USA
F	Junior at Innisbrook	James Yoon (PAR)	USA
F	Kelly Cup Invitational	Brad Wilder	USA
F	KIAC Conference Tournament	Jordan Leisinger*	USA
F	KJCCC C/ship Kansas Iowa Clash	Mariano Rossi (ARG)*	USA
F	LeTourneau Spring Classic	Matt Stephens*	USA
F	Lone Star Championships	Alex Carpenter	USA
F	MAAC Championship	Jay Mulieri	USA
F	Manor Intercollegiate	Dylan Jensen	USA
F	MEAC Showcase	Matthew McKnight (IRL)	USA
F	MIAA Championship	Riley Piles*	USA
F	Mid South Conference	Aaron Watkins	USA
F	Midlands Collegiate C/ship	Justin Burns	USA
F	Midwest Conference C/ship	Yousaf Khan (ENG)	USA
F	Mount St Mary's Spring Inv.	Richard Dowling*	USA
F	NAIA All Conference	Carson Kallis (CAN)	USA
F	NAIA SSAC Championship	Nic Ishee	USA
F	NCAC Championship #2	Craig Osterbrock	USA
F	NJCAA DI Region 17 C/ship	Joe Sakulpolphaisan (THA)	USA
F	NJCAA DI Region I C/ship	Joseph Courtney*	USA
F	NJCAA District 2 C/ship	Donavin Sanchez	USA
F	NJCAA District 4 C/ship	Jake Stirling (AUS)	USA
F	NJCAA Region I Div II C/ship	Jimmy Kozikowski	USA
F	OAC Championship	Ben Adams	USA
F	OAC Spring Invitational	Alex DiPalma*	USA
F	ODAC Championship	Brandon Ketron	USA
F	Ohio Valley Conference Championship	Anthony Bradley (ENG)*	USA
F	Pac West Conference C/ship	Steven Watson	USA
F	Patriot League Championship	William Park*	USA
F	Peach Belt Conference C/ship	Joel Dahlenburg	USA
F	Phoenix City Amateur C/ship	Michael Wog	USA
F	Princeton Invitational	Peter Williamson	USA
F	RMAC DQ Wolf Pack Inv..	Jim Knous	USA
F	RMAC Spring Championship	Jim Knous	USA
F	RRAC Championships	Dillon Watkins*	USA
F	Rutherford Intercollegiate	Brad Boyle (CAN)	USA
F	SAC Championship	Matthew Campbell	USA
F	Sacramento Valley Match Play	Blake Abercrombie*	USA
F	San Diego County Match Play	Buddy Duncan	USA
F	SCAC Conference C/ship	Eric Quinn	USA
F	SCGA Mid-Amateur	Tim Hogarth	USA
F	Skyhawk Desert Shootout	Eddie DeLashmutt	USA
F	SLIAC Championship	Kyler Scott*	USA
F	Sooner Athletic Conference	Clark Collier	USA

Americas (continued)

F	SOS Senior Masters	Tom Hyland*	USA
F	Summit League Championship	Michael Davan	USA
F	SWAC Championship	Clay Myers*	USA
F	Texas Junior College C/ships	Mathias Boesmans (BEL)	USA
F	TranSouth Championship	Brett Barry/Joey Bradley	USA
F	TSU Big Blue Intercollegiate	Patrick Newcomb	USA
F	ULM Wallace Jones Invitational	Garrett Driver	USA
F	Under Armour/Hunter Mahan Championship	Ryan Burgess*	USA
F	USA South Athletic Conf.	Scott Novicki*	USA
F	West Region Invitational	Jack Cersosimo*	USA
F	WHAC Championship	Vince Carango*	USA
F	Wildcat Invitational	Matthew Turner (ENG)	USA
F	Winchester Classic	Jarred Bossio	USA
F	Caribbean Junior Open C/ship	Robert Boocock*	BAR
F	PRGA Junior Island C/ship	Sebastian Toro*	PUR
F	Sir Garry Sobers C/ship	James Johnson	BAR
F	WJG Team C/ship Qualifier	Adam Svensson (CAN)	PUR
F	Abierto De Brasilia	Leonardo Conrado	BRA
F	Abierto del Centro	German Tagle	ARG
F	Camp. Nacional Stroke Play	Jose Rodriguez	PER
F	Copa Manuel J de la Rosa	David Torres	COL
F	Hyundai Championship	Diego Romero	PER
F	Nac. Abierto "BCP" Semana Santa	George Scanlon	BOL
F	Nac. Mid Am. Parada II	Jose Ricaurte Marin	COL
F	Torn. VIII Copa Heliodoro Ordonez	Francisco Yesid Medina*	COL

Asia

F	April Grand Prix	Nadaraja Thangaraja	SRI
F	China Am. Futures Tour Leg 1	Li Long*	CHN
F	Faldo Series Philippines	Lawrence Celestino	PHI
F	Haryana Junior Championship	Manu Gandas	IND
F	KPK Open	Waseem Rana/ Ghazanfar Mahmood	PAK
F	North Malaysian Open	Abel Tam	MAS
F	Pakistan Amateur	Nadaraja Thangaraja (SRI)	PAK
F	Philippine Am. Closed MP	John Abdon	PHI
F	Philippine Mid-Am. Closed MP	Raymond Bunquin*	PHI
F	Philippine Sen. Am. Closed MP	Lino Magpanty*	PHI
F	Rajasthan Junior C/ship	Manu Gandas	IND
F	Sabah Amateur Open	Paul San	MAS
F	Sarawak Amateur Open	Lee ka Tung	MAS
F	SGA 2nd Nat. Ranking Game	Thomas Tan Wei Hao	SIN
F	SICC Open Invitation	Marc Ong	SIN
F	TGA-CAT Jun. C/ship (Asia Pacific)	Danthai Boonma	THA
F	TGA-CAT Junior Ranking #6	Ekthumrong Luanganuruk*	THA
F	Thailand National Qualifier	Kasidit Lepkurte*	THA
F	TrueVisions International Junior	Jordan Surya Irawan (INA)	THA
F	TrueVisions Singha Junior	Puwit Anupansuebsai*	THA
F	USHA Delhi Juniors	Manu Gandas	IND
F	West Zone Qualifier	Kailash Dhiwar*	IND

Australasia

C	South Australian Amateur Classic	Glenelg GC	12–15	Chris Brown	AUS
D	Australian Boys Amateur	Bribie Island Golf Club	11–13	Tyler Hodge (NZL)	AUS

E	New Zealand Amateur	Vaughan McCall	NZL
F	BOP Seniors Championship	Owen Kendall*	NZL
F	Northern Territory Open	Jake McLeod	AUS
F	Rotorua Open	Peter Lee	NZL
F	S. Australian Medal & Amateur Championship	Chris Brown/ Jack Williams	AUS
F	South Island U19	Jordan Bakermans	NZL
F	Tasmanian Centenary Am.	Neville Hogan	AUS

Europe

A	Sir Michael Bonallack Trophy	Monte Rei Golf Country Club	25–27	Adam Svensson (CAN)	POR
D	Championnat de France C/ship Flight	Golf de Granville	25–29	Adam Svensson (CAN)	FRA
D	Coupe Frayssineau-Mouchy	Fontainebleau	20–22	Edouard Espana	FRA
D	Hampshire Salver	Blackmoor & North Hants GCs	21–22	Jack Bartlett/Matthew Fitzpatrick	ENG
D	International de France Juniors (Trophée Michel Carlhian)	Fort Mahon Plage	5–9	Vetle Maroy (NOR)	FRA

E	Battle Trophy	Fraser McKenna	SCO
E	BUCS Student Tour Finals	Jack McDonald (SCO)	ENG
E	Camp. de Espana Junior y Boys	Jon Rahm-Rodriguez	ESP
E	Craigmillar Park Open	Graeme Robertson	SCO
E	R&A Found. Scholars Tourn.	David Booth (ENG)	SCO
E	Scottish Ch. of Champions	Fraser McKenna	SCO
E	The Duncan Putter	Ben Westgate/Luke Thomas	WAL
E	West of England Open	Joshua White/ Mathew Daley/ Charlie McLean*	ENG
E	West of Ireland Am. Open	Harry Diamond	IRL
F	Campeonato de Barcelona	Carlos Pigem	ESP
F	Camp. de Espana Universitario	Jose Bondia	ESP
F	Camp. Nacional Absoluto	Goncalo Pinto	POR
F	Championnat de Ligue Am. (Thomas de Kristofy)	Thomas Detry (BEL)	FRA
F	Coppa d'Oro Citta' di Roma	Francesco Laporta	ITA
F	Cyprus Amateur Open	Mathew Daley (ENG)	CYP
F	Czech Amateur Tour 1	Jiri Korda	CZE
F	German Match Play	Dominic Foos	GER
F	Grand Prix D'Albi	Thomas Vayssieres	FRA

F	Grand Prix de Bordeaux	Matthieu Pavon	FRA
F	Grand Prix de Haute Savoie	Nicolas Marin	FRA
F	Grand Prix de la Nivelle	Christophe Mouhica	FRA
F	Grand Prix de Limere	Clement Batut	FRA
F	Grand Prix de Nimes Campagnes	Thomas Grava	FRA
F	Grand Prix du Lys Chantilly	Mathieu Lamote*	FRA
F	Grand Prix GBB (Open Amateur BBCC)	Louis Bilbault	FRA
F	Italian Nat. Am. Team C/ship	Louis Bilbault (FRA)	ITA
F	Italian Team Championship Qualifying – Lecco	Jacopo Fossa Vecchi	ITA
F	Italian Team Championship Qualifying – Punta Ala	Andrea Bolognesi	ITA
F	Italian Team Championship Qualifying – Valtellina	Edoardo Repetti*	ITA
F	IV Nextgolf.net Trophy	Fedderico Ripamonti*	ITA
F	Leinster Youths Am. Open	Colin Fairweather	IRL
F	Leone di San Marco	Filippo Campigli	ITA
F	Open du Bassin d'Arcachon	Leo Lespinasse	FRA
F	Peter McEvoy Trophy	Gavin Moynihan (IRL)	ENG
F	Scottish Boys Championship	Craig Howie*	SCO
F	Scottish Junior Tour Event 1	Anthony Blaney/ Alexander Wilson*	SCO
F	TGF League 5	Hasan Ceylan	TUR
F	Ticino Championship	Edouard Amacher	SUI
F	Trubshaw Cup	Gary Hurley (IRL)	WAL

May

Africa

D	Boland Open Amateur	Worcester GC	A30–M5	Haydn Porteous	RSA
D	KwaZulu Natal Amateur	Port Shepstone	23–27	Haydn Porteous	RSA

E	SA U23 Interprovincial A	Haydn Porteous	RSA
F	Central Open	Leroy Pearmain*	BOT
F	SA Mid Am Stroke Play	Neil Homann	RSA
F	SA Under 15 Stroke Play	J Rebula*	RSA

Americas

A	NCAA Central Regional	Ann Arbor, MI	17–19	Albin Choi (CAN)	USA
A	NCAA DI Medal Championship		29–31	Thomas Pieters (BEL)	USA
A	NCAA South Central Regional	Bowling Green, KY	17–19	Stephan Jaeger (GER)	USA
A	NCAA Southwest Regional	Norman, OK	17–19	Chris Williams	USA
B	Mountain West Championship	Tucson, AZ	4–6	Johan De Beer (RSA)	USA
B	NCAA East Regional	Grandover Resort, Greensboro, NC	17–19	Matt Schovee/Robert Karlsson (SWE)/Vaita Guillaume (FRA)	USA
B	NCAA Southeast Regional	Athens, GA	17–19	Justin Thomas	USA
B	NCAA West Regional	Stanford, CA	17–19	Josh Anderson	USA
C	AJGA Thunderbird Inte. Junior	Scottsdale, AZ	26–28	Max Orrin (ENG)	USA
D	Big West Championship	Mission Viejo, CA	A29–M1	Alex Edfort	USA
D	Horton Smith Invitational	Detroit, MI	10–12	Wes Gates	USA
D	Memorial Amateur	Carmichael, CA	26–28	John Catlin	USA
D	Mid-American Conference C/ship	Sugar Grove, IL	4–6	Corey Conners (CAN)	USA
D	NCAA D2 South – SE Region	Conover, NC	7–9	Matt Atkins	USA
D	NCAA Division II Championship	Simpsonville, KY	15–17	Joshua Creel	USA
D	State Farm MVC Championship	Hutchinson, KS	A30–M1	Hunter Sparks	USA

E	Lupton Invitational	Kris Mikkelsen	USA
E	Texas A&M @ Traditions Coll.	Sang Yi (KOR)	USA
E	WAC Championship	Jay Myers	USA
E	Aberto Sul-Brasileiro	Juan Cerda (CHI)	BRA
E	Abierto del Norte	Matias Lezcano*	ARG
F	Alabama State Senior	Tom Jungkind*	USA
F	America Sky Conf. C/ship	Cameron Rappleye	USA
F	Big East Championship	Max Scodro	USA
F	Camp. Nacional Infantil Juvenil	Juan Carlos Serrano	MEX
F	Carlton Woods Inv. Mid-Am.	Kevin Marsh	USA
F	Carlton Woods Inv. Seniors	Mike Booker	USA
F	Charleston City Amateur	Bert Atkinson	USA
F	Chicago DGA Senior Am. MP	Tom Miler*	USA
F	CN Future Links Ontario	Matt Williams	CAN
F	CN Future Links Pacific	Zach Anderson*	CAN
F	Colorado Mid-Amateur MP	Jon Lindstrom	USA
F	Colorado Senior Match Play	Ray Makloski*	USA
F	FCWT 11-13 National C/ship	Frankie Capan*	USA
F	FCWT 13-15 National C/ship	Luis Garza (MEX)*	USA
F	FCWT 16-19 National C/ship	Corey Pereira*	USA
F	FJT Innisbrook 16–18	Ryan Orr*	USA
F	FJT Orange County 13–15	David Gao*	USA
F	Florida Mid-Amateur SP	Don Bell	USA
F	Fox-Puss Invitational	Buck Brittain	USA
F	Fresno City Championship	Danny Paniccia	USA
F	Georgia Mid-Amateur	David Noll	USA
F	Georgia Senior Match Play	Walter Hope*	USA
F	Havemeyer Invitational	Matthew DeMeo	USA
F	Heart of America Conf. C/ship	Jordan Dickson*	USA
F	IIAC Championship	Sam Herrmann*	USA
F	IJGT Tourn.of Champs	Peter Mathison*	USA
F	IJGT Tourn. of Champions U14	Rij Patel	USA
F	Illinois State Mid-Amateur	Kyle Nathan*	USA
F	Investors Group Jun. Spring Classic	John Boncoddo*	CAN
F	JAGS ASU Mem. Jun. C/ship	Jacob Schulze	USA
F	Jim Rivers Seniors	Robert Shelton Sr*	USA
F	KCAC Conference C/ship	James Tisdale (ENG)	USA
F	Long Beach Senior C/ship	Bob Valerio*	USA
F	MCCAA Championship	Jonny Walraven	USA

Americas (continued)

F	Metropolitan Match Play	Justin Bryant	USA
F	Mid Central Conf. C/ship	Trey Pfund	USA
F	Mississippi Norman Bryant Colonial Invitational	Chris Tharpe*	USA
F	MWC Championship	Bobby Stuebi*	USA
F	NAIA Championships	Carson Kallis (CAN)	USA
F	NAIA Unaffiliated Grouping #1	Morgan Hough*	USA
F	NAIA Unaffiliated Grouping #2	Mitch Card*	USA
F	NCAA D2 Cent. – West Reg.	Jim Knous	USA
F	NCAA D2 East – Atlantic Reg.	Paul Tighe	USA
F	NCAA D2 MW – S. Cent. Reg.	Joshua Creel	USA
F	NCAA Division III C/ship	Anthony Maccaglia	USA
F	NEC Championship	Leo Garcia (PUR)*	USA
F	New Jersey Mid Amateur	Brian Komline	USA
F	NJCAA D1 Reg. XXII C/ship	Zac Love*	USA
F	NJCAA District III Region VI Championship	Ben Ludlam (ENG)*	USA
F	NJCAA Division II C/ship	Ryan Mulvany (AUS)*	USA
F	NJCAA II Region 12 C/ship	Caleb Johnson*	USA
F	NJCAA National C/ship DI	Jake Stirling (AUS)	USA
F	NJCAA Region 24 C/ship	Aaron Bravick*	USA
F	North Carolina Senior Am.	Paul Simson	USA
F	Palm Springs Desert Amateur	KK Limbhasut	USA
F	Pasadena City Championship	Jean Birren*	USA
F	PGA Minority C/ship D1	Cedomir Ilic (SRB)*	USA
F	PGA Minority C/ship D2	Jake Barge*	USA
F	PGA Minority C/ship Ind.	Justin Watkins*	USA
F	Richardson Memorial Inv.	Edward Gibstein*	USA
F	Russell C Palmer Cup	Sam Bernstein	USA
F	Santa Barbara City C/ship	Brian Helton*	USA
F	Scott Robertson Memorial	Davis Womble	USA
F	Signal Mountain Invitational	Chris Schmidt	USA
F	South Carolina Senior C/ship	Rick Cloninger	USA
F	Sun Conference Championshp	Omar Tejeira (PAN)	USA
F	Texas Junior Masters – Junior World	Kyle Francis*	USA
F	The Tower Invitational	Mac McGee*	USA
F	Trans-Mississippi Senior	Patrick Duncan	USA
F	Tucson City Amateur	Grant Cesarek	USA
F	Utah Senior Match Play	Bill Probst*	USA
F	Walter J Travis Invitational	Joe Saladino	USA
F	Walter J Travis Senior Inv.	Gary Daniels*	USA
F	West Virgina Mid Amateur	Pat Carter	USA
F	West Virginia Jun. Match Play	Thadd Obecny	USA
F	Camp. Nacional del Istmo	Miguel A Ordonez*	PAN
F	Camp. Nacional Match Play	Daniel Gurtner	GUA
F	Int. Camp. National Mid Am.	Felipe Harker Delgado (COL)	DOM
F	Abierto Guataparo	Mario Maya	VEN
F	Camp. de Chile Match Play	Gustavo Silva	CHI
F	Campeonato Nacional Juvenil Copa Arturo Calle	Pablo Torres	COL
F	Camp. Nacional Prejuvenil Copa Arturo Calle	Ivan Camilo Ramirez	COL
F	Chilean Senior Championship	Matias Lopez	CHI
F	Copa Ron Abuelo	Gonzalo Leon	ECU
F	Torneo Nacional Mapaizo BCP	Jorge Salvatierra	BOL

Asia

C	Malaysian Amateur Open	Glenmarie Golf & Country Club	24–27	Gavin Kyle Green	MAS
C	Saujana Championship	Saujana Golf & Country Club	28–31	Gavin Kyle Green	MAS
D	Inter State Championship	Oxford G&CC, Pune	1–4	Khalin Joshi	IND

F	Acer National Spring Ranking Tournament	Han-Ting Chiu	TPE
F	Asia Pacific Junior	Danthai Boonma (THA)	MYA
F	China Am. Futures Tour Leg 2	Wu Haochuan	CHN
F	China Amateur Tour Beijing	Zhang Jin*	CHN
F	China Amateur Tour Leg 2	He Chao*	CHN
F	Guam Amateur	Louie Sunga	GUM
F	Jack Nicklaus Junior C/ship	Jin Cheng	CHN
F	Kyushu Amateur	Jinichiro Kozuma	JPN
F	Malaysian Amateur Close	Mohd Afif Mohd Razif	MAS
F	May Grand Prix	Nadaraja Thangaraja	SRI
F	Negeri Sembilan Am. Open	Muhammad Arie Ahmad Fauzi	MAS
F	PGI BNI Am. C/ship Series 11	Sainuddin Bob*	INA
F	Philippine Junior Am. Open	Angelo Jose Gandionco	PHI
F	Rolex Junior Championship	Kento Nakai	JPN
F	TGA-CAT Junior World	Amarin Kraivixien*	THA
F	Usha Karnataka Junior C/ship	Aman Raj	IND

Australasia

B	Australian Interstate	Royal Adelaide Golf Club, Adelaide	1–4	Aman Raj (IND)	AUS

F	Fiji Amateur Championship	Vikrant Chandra	FIJ
F	Waikato Seniors	Dave Izzard*	NZL
F	Wairarapa Open	Jeff Tuoro	NZL

Europe

B	The Lytham Trophy	Royal Lytham & St Annes	4–6	Daan Huizing (NED)	ENG
C	Int. de France (Coupe Murat)	Chantilly GC	25–27	Lionel Weber	FRA
C	Irish Amateur Open	The Royal Dublin Golf Club	11–13	Gavin Moynihan	IRL
C	Welsh Amateur Open Stroke Play	Prestatyn Golf Club	25–27	Craig Hinton (ENG)	WAL

E	Irish Amateur Close	Chris Selfridge	IRL	F	Lagonda Trophy	Michael Saunders	ENG
E	Italian International Match Play	Francesco Testa	ITA	F	Leman Championship	Marc Dobias	SUI
E	Scottish Area Team C/ship	Francesco Testa (ITA)	SCO	F	Middlesex County C/ship	Ross Dickson	ENG
E	South East of England Links	Oliver Carr	ENG	F	Munster Stroke Play	Brian Casey	IRL
F	Amateur Tour Event 2	Simon Zach	CZE	F	Munster Youths Open	Eugene Smith	IRL
F	Basel Championship	Edouard Amacher	SUI	F	National U21 SP C/ship	Rowin Caron	NED
F	Campeonato de Canarias	Carlos Pigem	ESP	F	North Wales Boys Open	Evan Griffith	WAL
F	Camp. de Castilla la Mancha	Sigot Lopez Ferrez*	ESP	F	Palla d'Oro Memorial G Silva	Valerio Pelliccia	ITA
F	Campe. de Catalunya Absoluto	Carlos Pigem	ESP	F	Polish Match Play C/ship	Mateusz Gradecki	POL
F	Camp. de Espana de Cadetes	Burgaz Jorge José Utrilla*	ESP	F	Scottish Youths Open	Ewan Scott	SCO
				F	SGF Senior Tour H35 U1	Fredrik Kampe*	SWE
F	Clwyd Open	Will Jones	WAL	F	SGF Senior Tour H35 U2	Niklas Rosenkvist	SWE
F	Copa Nac. Puerta De Hierro	Mario Galiano Aguilar	ESP	F	SGU Junior Tour Event 2	Jamie Savage	SCO
F	Cornwall Amateur C/ship	Mike Reynard*	ENG	F	Skandia Junior Open	Anti Lassila (FIN)	SWE
F	Coupe Didier Illouz	Mathieu Decottignies-Lafon	FRA	F	Skandia Tour Elite #1 Ystad	Hampus Nilsson	SWE
				F	Skandia Tour Riks #1 Gullbringa	Felix Norderhaug*	SWE
F	Coupe Yves Caillol	Amaury Rosaye	FRA	F	Skandia Tour Riks #1 Halmstad	Max Helgesson*	SWE
F	Czech Int. Mid-Amateur	Marc Mazur (GER)	CZE	F	Skandia Tour Riks #1 Ljungbyheds	Anton Nilsson*	SWE
F	Devon Gold Medal & Amateur	Steve Daniels*	ENG	F	Skandia Tour Riks #2 – Ostergotland	Mans Berglund*	SWE
F	DGU Challenger Tour 1	Frederik Andersen*	DEN	F	Skandia Tour Riks #2 – Smaland	Victor Theandersson*	SWE
F	DGU Elite Tour 1	Jacob Lauridsen	DEN	F	Skandia Tour Riks #2 – Vastergotland	Adam Falk*	SWE
F	DGU Junior Tour 1	Peter Bring-Larsen*	DEN	F	Slovenian Int. Amateur	Matthias Schwab (AUT)	SLO
F	Dorset Amateur C/ship	Sonny Wilkinson*	ENG	F	Staffordshire Stag	Edward Peters*	ENG
F	Eimskipsmotarodin 1	Birgir Leifur Hafthorsson*	ISL	F	Suisse Orientale Championship	Andy-Chris Orsinger	SUI
F	Fairhaven Trophy	Patrick Kelly	ENG	F	Team Rudersdal Open	Niklas Norgaard Moller	DEN
F	Furesopokalen	Mathias Boksa	DEN	F	The Lancashire Links Trophy	John Carroll	ENG
F	Gloucestershire County Championship	Laurie Potter*	ENG	F	Titleist Tour 1	Petter Mikalsen	NOR
F	Gran Premio Monticello	Giorgio de Filipppi	ITA	F	Titleist Tour2	Vetle Maroy	NOR
F	Grand Prix AFG	Thomas Detry	BEL	F	Trofeo Umberto Agnelli	Francesco Laporta	ITA
F	Grand Prix de Bondues	Erwan Vieilledent	FRA	F	Wiltshire County C/ship	Garry Slade*	ENG
F	Grand Prix de Rennes	Gabriel Mocquard	FRA				
F	Hovborg Kro Open	Daniel Hollen Nielsen	DEN				
F	Internat. De France Seniors	Bart Nolte (NED)*	FRA				
F	Italian Senior Amateur	Lorenzo Sartori	ITA				
F	King's Prize	Pierre-Alexis Rolland	BEL				

June

Africa

F	Border Open Stroke Play	Gerlou Roux	RSA	F	South African U17 Stroke Play	Xander Basson/ David Meyers*	RSA
F	Kenya Am. Match Play C/ship	Tony Omuli	KEN				

Americas

A	NCAA Match Play	Los Angeles, CA	1–3	Henry James (ENG)*	USA
A	Northeast Amateur	Wannamoisett CC	20–23	Justin Shin (CAN)	USA
A	Sunnehanna Amateur	Johnstown, PA	14–17	Bobby Wyatt	USA
B	Dogwood Invitational	Atlanta, GA	27–30	Ben Kohles	USA
C	California Amateur Championship	La Cumbre Country Club	25–30	Kevin Marsh	USA
C	FJ Invitational	Greensbobo, NC	12–15	Matthew NeSmith	USA
C	Monroe Invitational	Pittsford, NY	13–16	Thomas Pieters (BEL)	USA
C	Rolex Tournament of Champions	Alpharetta, GA	25–29	Matthew NeSmith	USA
C	Texas Amateur Championship	The Honors Golf Club Dallas	15–17	Thomas Birdsey	USA
C	Washington State Amateur	Eagles Pride	12–15	Chris Williams	USA
D	Campeonato Nacional de Aficionados Banorte	Guadalajara Country Club	7–10	Sebastian Vazquez	MEX
D	Florida Amateur	Jupiter, FL	21–24	Chase Seiffert	USA

Americas (continued)

D	Ike Championship	Bridgehampton, NY	26–27	Cameron Wilson	USA
D	Missouri Amateur	Dalhousie Golf Club	19–24	Nick Wilson	USA
D	Palmetto Amateur	Palmetto Amateur	7–10	Mitchell Gray	USA
D	Rice Planters Amateur	Snee Farm CC	18–23	Thomas Bradshaw	USA
D	Southwestern Amateur	Ritz-Carlton GC, Dove Mountain	12–15	Kevin Dougherty	USA
D	Sun Country Match Play	Twin Warriors Golf Club	7–10	Patrick Beyhan	USA
D	Virginia Amateur Championship	Bayville Golf Club	26–30	Jake Mondy	USA

E	Alabama State Amateur	Andy McRae*	USA
E	Kenridge Invitational	Garland Green	USA
E	North Carolina Amateur	Matthew Crenshaw	USA
E	Oregon Amateur	Nick Chianello	USA
E	Southeastern Amateur	Dykes Harbin	USA
E	Tennessee Match Play	John Tyner*	USA
E	TPC San Antonio – PGA Tour Series Championship	Sang Yi (KOR)	USA
E	Westchester Amateur C/ship	Michael Miller	USA
E	Aberto do Estado do Rio de Janeiro	Daniel Ishii*	BRA
F	54 Hole Mid Season C/ship	Jimmy Stanger	USA
F	AJGA Florida Junior	Ryan Orr	USA
F	AJGA Music City Junior	Ben Reeves*	USA
F	Alberta Mid-Amateur C/ship	David Schultz*	CAN
F	Arborlinks	Rylee Reinertson	USA
F	Arkansas Stroke Play	Wes McNulty*	USA
F	Aspen Junior Golf Classic	Joshua Seiple*	USA
F	Atlanta Collegiate Challenge	Josh Oneal*	USA
F	BilliardFactory.com Jun. C/ship	Benjamin Arnett*	USA
F	Birmingham National Inv.	Patrick Christovich	USA
F	British Columbia Mid Amateur	Kevin Carrigan	CAN
F	Bubba Conlee National Junior	Noah Edmondson*	USA
F	Burgett H Mooney Junior Rome Classic	Justin Connelly	USA
F	Canadian University & College Championship	Garrett Rank	CAN
F	Carroll Amateur	Luke Vermeer*	USA
F	Chicago DGA Amateur	Michael Davan	USA
F	Cleveland Junior Open	Evan Deroche	USA
F	ClubCorp Mission Hills Desert Junior	Derek Castillo*	USA
F	CN Future Links Prairie Championship	Gajan Sivabalasingham*	CAN
F	Colorado Junior Stroke Play	Jimmy Makloski*	USA
F	Colorado Public Links	Eric Parish*	USA
F	Connecticut Amateur C/ship	Matt Smith	USA
F	Cook County Amateur	Jason Miller*	USA
F	CPT- Bear Trace Coll. Open	Justin McMillen*	USA
F	Evitt Foundation RTC Junior All-Star	Braden Thornberry	USA
F	Florida Public Links	T J Shuart*	USA
F	Florida Senior Am. Match Play	Howard Logan*	USA
F	Fort Dodge Amateur	Tanner Kesterson	USA
F	Future Masters	Robby Shelton	USA
F	GAM Senior Match Play	Ray Emsley*	USA
F	George C Thomas – Mid Am.	Brad Shaw*	USA
F	George C Thomas – Senior	Chip Lutz	USA
F	Georgia Junior Championship	Andy Shim	USA
F	Greater San Antonio Amateur	Adam Lowe	USA
F	Greater San Antonio Jun. MP	Levi Valadez*	USA
F	Greystone Invitational	Michael Johnson	USA
F	Hawaii State MP – Manoa Cup	Matthew Ma	USA
F	Heatherwoode Coll. Open	Alex Carpenter	USA
F	Hilton Head Junior Open	Ben Reeves	USA
F	HP Byron Nelson Jun. C/ship	Benjamin Arnett	USA
F	Hudson Junior Invitational	Matthew Gerard	USA
F	Hurricane Coll. Tour – Disney	Landon Michelson	USA
F	Idaho Match Play	Jimmy Burnett*	USA
F	Illinois State Junior Amateur	Raymond Knoll*	USA
F	Indian Valley Collegiate Open	Eric Poplowski*	USA
F	Indiana Amateur	Tyler Merkel	USA
F	International Junior Masters	Joey Savoie (CAN)	USA
F	Iowa Match Play	Michael Wuertz	USA
F	Iowa Senior Match Play	Gene Elliott	USA
F	Junior All-Star at Eagle Ridge	Jake Carter*	USA
F	Junior All-Star at Gainey Ranch	Jacob Solomon*	USA
F	Junior All-Star at Penn State	Varun Chopra*	USA
F	Junior at Quad Cities	Kyle Sterbinsky*	USA
F	Junior at Steelwood	Brendon Jelley*	USA
F	Kansas Junior Amateur	Travis Mays*	USA
F	Kansas Stroke Play (The Railer)	Jack Courington	USA
F	Kearney Hill Golf Links	Tyler McDaniel	USA
F	Kentucky State Amateur	Patrick Newcomb	USA
F	Killington Junior C/ship	Brian Carlson*	USA
F	Las Vegas Junior Open	Charlie Danielson	USA
F	Long Beach Match Play C/ship	Derek Zellmer	USA
F	Long Island Amateur	Tim Rosenhouse	USA
F	Los Angeles City C/ship	Michael Turner*	USA
F	Louisiana Amateur	Patrick Christovich	USA
F	Manitoba Match Play	Aaron Cockerill	CAN
F	Maryland Amateur	Josh Eure	USA
F	Michigan Amateur	Drew Preston	USA
F	Minnesota Mid Championship	Sam Schmitz	USA
F	Minnesota Players' C/ship	Andy Jacobson	USA
F	Mississippi State Amateur	Clay Homan	USA
F	Missouri Junior Match Play	Joey Johnson*	USA
F	National Senior Hall of Fame	Paul Simson	USA
F	Natural Resource Partners Bluegrass Juniors	Jeffrey Meade*	USA
F	Nebraska Junior Match Play	Zach Taylor*	USA
F	Nebraska Match Play	Kevin Stanek	USA
F	New Hampshire Junior C/ship	Chelso Barrett	USA
F	New Jersey Amateur	Ryan McCormick	USA
F	NJCAA Division III C/ship	Shane Dobesh*	USA
F	North Carolina Junior C/ship	Carter Jenkins*	USA
F	North Dakota Stroke Play	Coy Papachek	USA
F	Nova Scotia Mid Amateur	Aaron Nickerson*	CAN
F	Oklahoma State Junior C/ship	Hayden Wood	USA
F	Ontario Match Play	Michael Lancaster*	CAN
F	Ontario Mid Amateur	Drew Symons	CAN
F	Oregon Junior Amateur	Clayton Madey	USA
F	Oregon Junior Stroke Play	Dylan Wu	USA
F	Ottumwa Amateur	Conner Steele*	USA
F	Pacific Northwest Senior Am.	Tom Brandes	USA

F	Philadelphia Amateur	Brian Colbert	USA
F	Philadelphia Junior Boys	Mariano Medico*	USA
F	Ping Phoenix Junior at ASU Karsten	Blake Barens	USA
F	Provincial Mid-Amateur	Dwight Reinhart	CAN
F	R J Sigel Amateur	David (PA) Brown	USA
F	Royal Oaks Invitational	Travis Johnsen	USA
F	Royal Oaks Junior-Senior Inv.	Erik Hanson	USA
F	Santa Clara County C/ship	Carlos Briones	USA
F	South Carolina Junior C/ship	Jeremy Grab*	USA
F	South Carolina Match Play	Matthew Laydon	USA
F	Southern Junior C/ship 13–14	Brett Barron*	USA
F	Southern Junior C/ship 15–18	Ben Crancer	USA
F	State Farm Collegiate Open	Nicolas Paez*	USA
F	Texas Oklahoma Junior	Brooklin Bailey*	USA
F	Texas Public Links	Michael Smith	USA
F	The Links at Kokopelli	Jack Holmgren*	USA
F	Tony Blom Metropolitan Am.	Bill Williamson	USA
F	Troy Invitational	Stephen Quillinan*	USA
F	US Senior Challenge	Sam Till	USA
F	Virginia Junior Match Play	Adam Ball	USA
F	Western Junior Championship	Adam Wood	USA
F	Western Pennsylvania Amateur	Greg Podufal*	USA
F	Wisconsin Match Play	Sam Frank*	USA
F	Woodlands Collegiate Open	Scott Newell*	USA
F	World Golf Village C/ship	Travis Williamson*	USA
F	Wyoming Match Play	Kamrin Allen	USA
F	Bermuda Open Championship	Mitchell Campbell*	BER
F	Segundo Torn.Honor Al Merito	Daniel Gurtner	GUA
F	Aberto do Estado do Parana	Thomas Mantovanini	BRA
F	Abierto Amateur Caracas CC	Juan Carlos Bringas*	VEN
F	Abierto Cafetero De Golf	Federico Arango*	COL
F	Abierto Cafetero de Golf – Torneo 36	Santiago Gomez	COL
F	Ab. de Golf Ciudad de Ibague	Juan Sebastian Munoz	COL
F	Ab. Los Cerros Club de Golf	Juan Miguel Heredia	ECU
F	Abierto Manizales	Esteban Restrepo	COL
F	Abierto Scotiabank	Eithel McGowen	PER
F	Campeonato Nacional MP	Juan Alvarez	URU
F	Camp. Sudam. Pre Juvenil	Leonardo Coll	VEN
F	Copa Escalafon	Gustavo Silva	CHI
F	Torneo Aficionado Cartagena de Indias	Ricardo Jose Celia	COL
F	Torneo Nacional La Paz	Johnny Montano	BOL
F	Vuelta Bolivia La Paz	Alejandro Valenzuela	BOL

Asia

C	Toyota Junior World Cup	Chukyo GC Ishino Course	19–22	Viraat Badhwar (AUS)	JPN
D	Western India Amateur	Bombay Presidency Golf Club	5–8	Khalin Joshi	IND

E	Hosim Cup	Hyo-seok Kim*	KOR
F	Chammaroo Cup – Korean Mid Amateur	Sang-Soo Lee*	KOR
F	China Am. Futures Tour Leg 3	Jin Cheng	CHN
F	Chubu Amateur Championship	Takaya Onoda	JPN
F	Chugoku Am. Championship	Shun Murayama	JPN
F	Enjoy Jakarta World Jun. C/ship	Joshua Wirawan*	INA
F	Hokkaido Amateur	Yoshifumi Sugishita	JPN
F	HSBC Youth Challenge Leg 2	Nicklaus Chiam	SIN
F	Indonesia Junior Open C/ship	Jordan Surya Irawan	INA
F	June Grand Prix	Nadaraja Thangaraja	SRI
F	Junior Asian Masters	Shinichi Mizuno (HKG)	THA
F	Kansai Amateur	Gaburiere Debaruba*	JPN
F	Kanto Amateur Championship	Mikumu Horikawa	JPN
F	Maharashtra Amateur	Samarth Dwivedi	IND
F			MAS
F	Mindanao Regional C/ship	Micah Shin*	PHI
F	Mindanao Regional Mid-Am.	Joel Yamyamin*	PHI
F	Myanmar Amateur Open	Thein Naing Soe*	MYA
F	Philippine Junior Am. Closed	Rupert Zaragosa	PHI
F	Philippine Senior & Mid Am.	Manfred Guangko*	PHI
F	Selangor Int. Junior Open	Low Khai Jei	MAS
F	Seletar Junior Open	Thomas Tan Wei Hao	SIN
F	Shikoku Amateur	Kenta Endo*	JPN
F	Singapore Junior C/ship	Chieh-Po Lee (TPE)	SIN
F	Southern India Junior	Piyush Sangwan*	IND
F	Sutera Harbour Am. Open	Park Young Sik*	MAS
F	TGA-CAT Junior Rankings #1	Thanadol Sangkoranee*	THA
F	Tohoku Amateur	Shinji Tomimura	JPN

Australasia

F	Fiji Open	Anuresh Chandra	FIJ

Europe

A	Palmer Cup	The Royal County Down GCb	28–30	Daniel Gurtner (GUA)	IRL
A	St Andrews Links Trophy	St Andrews (New and Old)	8–10	Daan Huizing (NED)	SCO
A	The Amateur Championship	Royal Troon & Gailes Links	18–23	Alan Dunbar (IRL)	SCO
B	Scottish Open Stroke Play	Kilmarnock (Barassie)	1–3	Paul Barjon (FRA)	SCO
C	Turkish Amateur Open	AGC-Sultan	M29–J3	Maximilian Rottluff (GER)	TUR
D	East of Ireland Open Championship	County Louth	2–4	Chris Selfridge	IRL
D	The Berkshire Trophy	The Berkshire Golf Club	23–24	Joshua White	ENG

E	Tennant Cup	Liam Johnston	SCO
F	Aberconwy Trophy	Luke Jackson	WAL
F	Amateur Tour Event 3	Ondrej Lieser	CZE
F	Austrian Stroke Play	Nikolaus Wimmer*	AUT
F	Bedfordshire County C/ship	Robert Sutton	ENG
F	Cambridgeshire County C/ship	Toby Crisp	ENG
F	Citta di Milano Trofeo Gianni Albertini	Corrado De Stefani	ITA
F	Coupe Cachard	Antoine Le Saux	FRA
F	Coupe Wallaert Devilder	Felix MORY*	FRA

Europe (continued)

F	Czech National Match Play	Ondrej Lieser	CZE
F	DGU Challenger Tour II	Nicolai Sorensen*	DEN
F	DGU Elite Tour Herrer II	Niklas Norgaard Moller	DEN
F	DGU Junior Tour drenge II	Daniel Hollen Nielsen	DEN
F	Eimskipmotarodin (2)	Haraldur Franklin Magnus	ISL
F	English Seniors Championship	Alan Squires*	ENG
F	European Mid Amateur	Morten Findsen Schou (DEN)	EST
F	European Seniors	Adrian Morrow (IRL)*	AUT
F	Faldo Series Czech C/ship	Vitek Novak	CZE
F	Finnish International Junior	Jeremy Freiburghaus (SUI)	FIN
F	German Boys Open	Dominic Foos	GER
F	German Mid-Amateur	Christoph Stadler*	GER
F	Hertfordshire County C/ship	Alex Collman*	ENG
F	Irish Boys Amateur Open	Gareth Lappin*	IRL
F	Isle of Wight & Channel Islands Amateur	Jordan Ainley	ENG
F	Italian Under 16 C/ship	Guido Migliozzi	ITA
F	JSM Slag Boys	Anton Nilsson/ Olle Widegren*	SWE
F	Kent Amateur Championship	Max Orrin	ENG
F	Lancashire Amateur C/ship	Mark Young	ENG
F	Mattone d"Oro	Federico Galli*	ITA
F	Mollea Open	Mathias Boksa	DEN
F	National Match Play C/ship	David van den Dungen	NED
F	Norfolk County Championship	Kit Holmes*	ENG
F	Ostgota Junior Open	Joacim Neumann	SWE
F	Polish Mid Amateur C/ship	David Parkinson*	POL
F	SGF Senior Tour H35 U3	Niklas Rosenkvist	SWE
F	SGU Junior Tour Event 3	Lawrence Allan	SCO
F	Sir Henry Cooper Jun. Masters	Craig Howie (SCO)	ENG
F	Skandia Tour Riks #3 – Blekinge	Jesper Olsson*	SWE
F	Skandia Tour Riks #3 – Bohuslan	Lukas Crisp*	SWE
F	Skandia Tour Riks #3 – Orebro	Oliver Pousette*	SWE
F	Suisse Romande Championship	Adrien Michellod*	SUI
F	Surrey Amateur Championship	Matt Chapman*	ENG
F	Sussex County Amateur	Alasdair Dalgliesh	ENG
F	Swiss National MP C/ship	Marc Dobias	SUI
F	Titleist Tour 3	Daniel Aulin Jansen	NOR
F	Trophée Jean-Louis Jurion	Gregoire Schoeb	FRA
F	Turkish Amateur	Koray Varli	TUR
F	US Kids – European C/ship	Joey Lamb (ENG)*	SCO
F	Valles Region Championship	Ramon Ventura Camp	ESP
F	Vejlematchen	Mathias Gladbjerg*	DEN
F	Welsh Mid Amateur	Nigel Sweet*	WAL
F	Welsh Open Youths C/ship	Nick Marsh (ENG)	ENG
F	Wiibroe Cup	Patrick Rasmussen	DEN
F	Worcestershire County C/ship	Henry James*	ENG

July

Africa

C	Malaysian Amateur Open	Glenmarie Golf & Country Club	24–27	Gavin Kyle Green	MAS
C	Limpopo Open	Warmbaths	6–8	Haydn Porteous	RSA

F	Limuru Open	Joseph Karanja	KEN
F	Nomads National Order of Merit Championship	Thriston Lawrence	RSA

Americas

A	Players Amateur	Bluffton, SC	9–15	Daniel Nisbet (AUS)	USA
A	Porter Cup	Niagara Falls Country Club	18–21	Richard Werenski	USA
A	Southern Amateur	Chenal Country Club	18–21	Peter Williamson	USA
B	Sahalee Players	Sahalee Country Club	4–6	Kevin Penner	USA
B	Trans-Mississippi Championship	Oak Tree National, Edmond, OK	9–12	Tyler Raber	USA
B	US Amateur Public Links	Soldier Hollow Golf Club	9–14	T J Vogel	USA
C	Callaway Junior World C/ship	Torrey Pines Golf Course	10–13	Rico Hoey	USA
C	North & South Amateur	Pinehurst No 8	3–7	Peter Williamson	USA
C	Ontario Amateur	The Summit Golf & Country Club	10–13	Albin Choi	CAN
C	Pacific Coast Amateur	Brandon Dunes Golf Resort	24–27	David Fink	USA
C	U.S. Junior Amateur Championship	Stratham, NH	16–21	Andy Shim (KOR)	USA
C	Wyndham Cup	Arnold Palmer's Bay Hill Club & Lodge	23–26	Andy Shim (KOR)	USA
D	Barton Creek Resort Coll. C/ship	Barton Creek – Crenshaw Cliffside	17–18	Sang Yi (KOR)	USA
D	Carolinas Amateur	Charlotte, NC	12–15	Carson Young	USA
D	Northern Amateur	Sand Creek Country Club	25–27	Trey Mullinax	USA
D	Pacific Northwest Amateur	Wine Valley GC	9–14	Shotaro Ban	USA
D	Spirit of America Championship	Burning Tree GC	5–8	Will McCurdy	USA
D	Utah State Amateur	The Country Club	18–22	Jon Wright*	USA

E	Eastern Amateur	Roger Newsom	USA
E	Monterey City Championship	John Catlin	USA
E	New York State Amateur	Dominic Bozzelli	USA
E	Northern California SP	Ben Geyer	USA
E	Oglethorpe Invitational	Chase Seiffert	USA
E	SCGA Amateur Championship	Bhavik Patel	USA
E	WE Cole Cotton States Inv.	Tyler Klava	USA
F	Aaron's – Bob Estes Abilene Junior	Alex Levy	USA
F	AJGA Junior @ River Landing	Stephen Saleeby*	USA
F	AJGA Junior @ Ruby Hill	Jacob Solomon	USA
F	AJGA Junior Challenge	Harold Calubid*	USA
F	AJGA Junior Open @The Legends	Franklin Huang*	USA
F	AJGA Nebraska Junior @ Quarry Oaks	Luis Gagne	USA
F	Alaska State Amateur C/ship	Greg Sanders	USA
F	Alberta Amateur	Riley Fleming	CAN
F	Alberta Boys	Matt Williams	CAN
F	Arkansas State Junior	Tyler Green*	USA
F	Barbers Point Invitational	Jonathan Ota	USA
F	BC Junior	Matthew Broughton*	CAN
F	British Columbia Amateur	Riley Fleming	CAN
F	British Columbia Senior	Sandy Harper	CAN
F	C R Miller Match Play Inv.	Brent Richard Rodgers*	USA
F	Carolinas Junior Boys	Keenan Huskey*	USA
F	Chick Evans Junior Match Play	Ryan Craig*	USA
F	CN Future Links Atlantic	Brett McKinnon	CAN
F	CN Future Links Quebec	Daniel Knight*	CAN
F	CN Future Links Western	Aaron Crawford	CAN
F	Coca-Cola Junior C/ship	Raymond Knoll	USA
F	Colorado Junior Match Play	Andrew Romano*	USA
F	Colorado Match Play	Brian Dorfman	USA
F	Connecticut Junior Amateur	John Vanderlaan*	USA
F	Delaware Amateur	Paul Tighe	USA
F	Deutsche Bank Jun. Shoot Out	Robert Deng*	USA
F	E Z GO Vaughn Taylor C/ship	Connor Smith*	USA
F	Eddie Burke Sr. Young Houstonian	Chris Causey*	USA
F	FCG Collegiate Championship	Ryann Ree	USA
F	FCG World Championship at PGA West	Derek Castillo	USA
F	Firecracker Open	Dillon Rust	USA
F	Florida Junior Championship	Hank Lebioda	USA
F	Florida Junior MP (16–18)	Jake Kevorkian*	USA
F	Francis Ouimet Mem. Tourn.	Jack Whelan	USA
F	Furman University C/ship	Clement Kurniawan (INA)*	USA INA
F	Future Champions Match Play	Kevin Cline*	USA
F	Genesis Shootout Presented by Valero Texas Open	Matt Gilchrest	USA
F	Georgia Amateur	Lee Knox	USA
F	Golden Isles Invitational	Carter Collins	USA
F	Golf Pride Junior Classic	Max Greyserman*	USA
F	Golf Quebec Junior	Hugo Bernard	CAN
F	Golf Quebec Provincial Am.	Charles Cote	CAN
F	Greater San Antonio Junior	Kevin Pourasef*	USA
F	Greater San Antonio MP	Edward Sanchez	USA
F	Harry Hammond Award	Cole Berman*	USA
F	HGA Junior Match Play	Luke Sheehan*	USA
F	Hogan's Alley Collegiate C/ship	Austen Moix	USA
F	Idaho State Amateur	Taeksoo Kim	USA
F	Indiana Match Play	Matt Spicuzza*	USA
F	Indiana Senior Match Play	Sam Till	USA
F	Indiana State Junior	Mark Whipple*	USA
F	Industry Hills City C/ship	Mark Anguiano	USA
F	Iowa Amateur	Jon Olson	USA
F	Iowa Masters	Michael McCoy	USA
F	Iowa Senior Masters	Tony Maliza*	USA
F	Jack Kramer Memorial	Shinichi Mizuno (HKG)	USA
F	Junior America's Cup	Rico Hoey	USA
F	Junior at Centennial	Kevin Murphy	USA
F	Kansas Amateur	Kyle Smell	USA
F	Kansas City Amateur	Steve Groom	USA
F	Kansas Junior Match Play	Preston Flennor*	USA
F	KPMG Stacy Lewis Jun. Open	Max McGreevy	USA
F	Lake Creek Amateur	Gene Elliott	USA
F	Laurel Springs Coll. Open	Daniel Wood	USA
F	Lessing's Classic	James Park*	USA
F	Lockton Kansas City Junior	Preston Fleenor	USA
F	Long Beach City C/ship	Nicolas Paez	USA
F	Lousiana Junior Amateur	Sam Burns	USA
F	Magnolia Amateur	Myles Lewis	USA
F	Maine Amateur	Seth Sweet*	USA
F	Manitoba Junior	Ryan Sholdice*	CAN
F	Manitoba Mid-Amateur	Garth Collings	CAN
F	Massachusetts Amateur	Mike Calef	USA
F	McArthur Towel & Sports Future Legends	Matthew Weber*	USA
F	Memorial Junior Presented by Border Energy	Joo-Young Lee*	USA
F	Metropolitan Junior C/ship	Scott Kim	USA
F	Midwest Junior Players C/ship	Jakob Garstecki	USA
F	Minnesota Amateur	Frederick van Rooyen (RSA)	USA
F	Mississippi Greenwood Inv.	Joe Sakulpolphaisan (THA)	USA
F	Mississippi Junior	Braden Thornberry	USA
F	Missouri Stroke Play	Brad Nurski	USA
F	Montana State Amateur	Nathan Bailey	USA
F	NB Mid-Amateur	Darren Roach*	CAN
F	Nebraska Amateur	Greg Sohl*	USA
F	Nebraska Junior Amateur	Mitchell Klooz	USA
F	Nevada State Amateur	Roman Mudd*	USA
F	Nevada State Mid Amateur	Craig Erickson	USA
F	New Brunswick Am. C/ship	Mathieu Gingras	CAN
F	New Brunswick Junior C/ship	Justin Shanks*	CAN
F	New Brunswick Senior	Herrick Hansen*	CAN
F	New England Amateur	Christopher Swift*	USA
F	New Hampshire State Am.	Joe Leavitt	USA
F	New Jersey Junior	Ryan Rose*	USA
F	New Mexico–West Texas Am.	Alex Estrada	USA
F	NLGA Amateur	Michael Tibbo*	CAN
F	NLGA Junior Championship	Blair Bursey	CAN
F	North & South Junior	Kendrick Vinar*	USA
F	North Dakota Match Play	Duane Wager III*	USA
F	N. California Jun. Ch/ship	Taylor Bromley*	USA
F	Nova Scotia Amateur	Mathieu Gingras	CAN
F	Nova Scotia Junior	Brett McKinnon	CAN
F	Ohio Amateur	Nathan Kerns	USA
F	Oklahoma State Amateur	Stephen Carney	USA

Americas (continued)

F	Ontario Boys Match Play	Sam Hebert*	CAN
F	Ontario Junior	Gajan Sivabalasingham	CAN CAN
F	Optimist Int. Junior 16–18	Joey Lane*	USA
F	Penn State University	Scott Jaster*	USA
F	Purdue University	Kyle Meihofer*	USA
F	Ravenwood Junior C/ship	Victor Fox*	USA
F	Rhode Island Amateur	Charlie Blanchard	USA
F	Rhode Island Junior Amateur	Will Dickson*	USA
F	Rose Creek Collegiate Open	Casey Fernandez	USA
F	San Diego City Amateur	Steven Kearney	USA
F	San Joaquin Valley Match Play	T J Masters*	USA
F	Santa Maria Collegiate Open	Daniel Wood*	USA
F	Saskatchewan Amateur	Tyler Frank	CAN
F	Saskatchewan Junior	Cory Selander*	CAN
F	Saskatchewan Mid Amateur	Tyler Frank*	CAN
F	Savannah Low Country Am.	Danny Nelson*	USA
F	Shreveport Junior	Eric Ricard	USA
F	South Carolina Junior MP	Carson Young	USA
F	South Dakota Match Play	Ben Irlbeck*	USA
F	Tennessee Junior Amateur	Ben Reeves	USA
F	Texas Mid-Amateur MP	Lucas Boyd	USA
F	Texas State Junior	Wes Artac	USA
F	The Birchmont	Josh Bergrud*	USA
F	The Birchmont Junior	Aaron Leintz	USA
F	Tippecanoe City C/ship	Brent Hofman*	USA
F	Toronto Star Amateur	Brian Churchill-Smith	CAN
F	Toyota Tour Cup – Santa Ana	Barrett Taylor	USA
F	TPC San Antonio – PGA Tour Series Championship	Andrew Winters*	USA
F	Under Armour–Jeff Overton Junior	Blake Messer*	USA
F	US Kids Teen World C/ship	David Mackey*	USA
F	Utah Senior Amateur	Craig Woodward*	USA
F	Veritas World Junior	Tyler Collier*	USA
F	Vermont Amateur	Mike Stackus	USA
F	Vermont Junior Match Play	Jona Scott*	USA
F	Washington State Junior	Ross Kukula*	USA
F	Waterloo Open	Ben Juffer	USA
F	West Texas Amateur	Mike Calef	USA
F	Westbrook Country Club	Michael Bernard	USA
F	William Penn Junior C/ship	Luke Graboyes*	USA
F	Wisconsin State Amateur	Brady Strangstalien	USA
F	Wyoming Amateur	Ryan Graham*	USA
F	Caribbean Junior C/ship	Matthew Marquez (TRI)*	DOM
E	Abierto Int. del eje Cafetero	Matias Molina Tellez	COL
F	Abierto de Golf	Juan Sebastian Munoz	COL
F	Abierto De Golf – Militar	Santiago Mejia	COL
F	Abierto Del Guayaquil Country Club	Jose Pedro Chaparro	ECU
F	Abierto Internacional de Golf – Copa Sura	Juan Carlos Rodriguez	COL
F	Amador do Brasil	Rafael Becker	BRA
F	Brazilian Junior	Cristian Barcelos da Silva	BRA
F	Campeonato Auspiciador	Joaquin Lolas	PER
F	Camp. Nacional de Aficionados	Jose L Rodriguez*	PER
F	Faldo Series Brazil	Juan Alvarez (URU)	BRA

Asia

C	Japan Amateur	Nara	3–7	Hideto Kobukuro	JPN
C	Neighbors Trophy	Ora Country Club	18–20	Chien-Yao Hung (TPE)	KOR

E	July Grand Prix	Nadaraja Thangaraja	SRI
F	Asean Schools Games	Jordan Surya Irawan	INA
F	China Amateur Futures Tour Leg 4	Gao Chong*	CHN
F	China Amateur Tour Leg 3	Wang Xichen	CHN
F	China National Junior C/ship	Bai Zhengkai	CHN
F	CNS Open	Mohd Ali Hai/ Mubariz Ahmed	PAK
F	Hanwha Finance Network Cup	Jeong-woo Ham*	KOR
F	Independence Day Open	Ghazanfar Mahmood	PAK
F	Kelantan Amateur Open	Abel Tam	MAS
F	SGA 3rd Nat. Ranking Games	Kenji Cheung	SIN
F	Sindh Open	Ghazanfar Mahmood	PAK
F	Sukan Malaysia	Albright Chong	MAS
F	Warren-Ford Amateur Open	Jonathan Ke-Jun Woo	SIN

Australasia

F	Bargara Junior Classic	Ryan Gaske*	AUS
F	Darwin Open	Andrew Wilson	AUS
F	Newman and Brooks Junior Championship	Curtis Luck	AUS
F	QLD Schools Championship	Jack Sullivan	AUS
F	Subaru State Age C/ship	Dylan Perry*	AUS
F	Victoria Junior Amateur	Kade McBride	AUS
F	Waikato Winter Stroke Play	Tyler Hodge	NZL

Europe

B	Brabazon Trophy	Walton Heath	Jn28–Jy1	Neil Raymond	ENG
B	European Challenge Trophy	Keilir GC	12–14	Ben Stow (ENG)	ISL
C	Biarritz Cup	Golfe de Biarritz	12–15	Thomas Elissalde	FRA
C	Campeonato De Espana Amateur	RG Pedrena	24–27	Carlos Pigem	ESP
C	European Boys' Team Championship	Lidingo GC	10–14	Carlos Pigem (ESP)	SWE
C	European Boy' Team C/ship – Ind.	Lidingo GC	10–14	Carlos Pigem (ESP)	SWE
C	German International Amateur	Golfenlage Green Eagle	19–22	Moritz Lampert	GER

C	South of England Amateur	Walton Heath Golf Club	24–26	Ryan Evans	ENG
D	Campeonato Absoluto Pais Vasco	Neguri	29–31	Jon Rahm-Rodriguez	ESP
D	Carris Trophy	Royal Cinque Ports	24–27	Patrick Kelly	ENG
D	Luxembourg International Amateur	Grand-Ducal	12–14	Claas-Eric Borges (GER)/ Niklas Koerner (GER)*	LUX
D	Newlands Trophy	Lanark Golf Club	21–22	Matthew Clark	SCO
D	North of Ireland Open	Royal Portrush Golf Club	9–13	Rory McNamara	IRL
D	World University Championship	Ypsilon Golf Resort	3–6	Carlos Pigem (ESP)	CZE

E	Cameron Corbett Vase	Daniel Young	SCO
E	Dutch Junior Open	Joe Dean (IRL)	NED
E	Tillman Trophy	Alasdair Dalgliesh	ENG
E	Tucker Trophy	James Frazer	WAL
F	Austrian Stroke Play U16	Johannes Schwab*	AUT
F	Austrian Stroke Play U18	Robin Goger	AUT
F	Austrian Stroke Play U21	Daniel Moretti*	AUT
F	Balkan Challenge Trophy	Cedomir Ilic (SRB)	BUL
F	Barloseborg Elite Open	Martin Beuchert Sorensen/Sebastian Czyz Bendsen*	DEN
F	Belgian National Match Play	Bertrand Mommaerts	BEL
F	Belgian Stroke Play	Raphael Higuet	BEL
F	Boyd Quaich	Gary Hurley (IRL)/ Steven Smith*/ Freddie Edmunds (ENG)*/Oliver Roberts*	SCO
F	Campeonato de Alicante	Jose Bondia	ESP
F	Campeonato de Madrid Junior	Javier Gallegos	ESP
F	Cheshire Stroke Play	James McCormick	ENG
F	Citta di Mogliano	Lorenzo Magagnin	ITA
F	Classic du Prieure	Louis Cohen Boyer	FRA
F	Connacht U18 Boys Open	James Sugrue	IRL
F	Copa Comunidad Valenciana	Noel Grau	ESP
F	Copa Siero	Hugo Menendez	ESP
F	Czech Int. Junior U18	Simon Zach	CZE
F	Czech Int. Junior U21	Ondrej Lieser	CZE
F	Czech National Youth C/ship	Marek Siakala*	CZE
F	Danish Int. Amateur C/ship	Victor Gebhard Osterby	DEN
F	Danish Int. Youth Ch/ship	Tobias Larsen	DEN
F	Danish Senior Open Amateur	Ian Brotherston (SCO)*	DEN
F	DM Hulspil	Mads Sogaard	DEN
F	DM Mid Amateur	Anders Freund*	DEN
F	East of Scotland Amateur	Allyn Dick	SCO
F	Eimskipsmotarodin 4	Haraldur Franklin Magnus	ISL
F	Essex Amateur Championship	Bobby Keeble	ENG
F	Estonian Amateur Open	Teemu Toivonen (FIN)	EST
F	European Young Masters	Renato Paratore (ITA)	HUN
F	Faldo Series Austria	Keanu Jahns (GER)	AUT
F	Faldo Series Netherlands	Max Albertus	NED
F	Finnish Mid Amateur	Timo Tuunanen	FIN
F	Finnish Stroke Play	Tapio Pulkkanen	FIN
F	Fioranello d'Oro	Philip Geerts	ITA
F	GGL International Junior Open	Richard Broadhurst	ITA
F	Gran Premio Citta di Cervia	Alessandro Caselli*	ITA
F	Gran Premio Padova	Lars Van Meilel (NED)*	ITA
F	Grand Prix d'Apremont	Mathias Boesmans (BEL)	FRA
F	Grand Prix de Chiberta	Mads Sogaard (DEN)	FRA
F	Grand Prix de la Baule	Lambert Cochet*	FRA
F	Grand Prix de la Cote d'Albatre	Antoine Leroy*	FRA
F	Grand Prix de Palmola	Leo Lespinasse	FRA
F	Grand Prix de Saint Laurent	Antoine Le Saux	FRA
F	Grand Prix De Saint Nom La Breteche	Arnaud Abbas	FRA
F	Grand Prix des Landes	Thomas Elissalde	FRA
F	Grand Prix du Golf de Lyon	Bastien Melani	FRA
F	Hillerod Pokalen	Christian Hillersborg Gloet	DEN
F	Icelandic Junior Stroke Play	Ragnar Mar Garoarsson*	ISL
F	ISAGS Summer Championship – St Andrews	Jorge Gaudiano (MEX)*	SCO
F	Italian U14 Championship	Giovanni Magagnin*	ITA
F	Italian U18 Stroke Play	Guido Migliozzi	ITA
F	Kronborg Masters	Tobias Larsen	DEN
F	Latvian Amateur	Roberts Eihmanis	LAT
F	Latvian Match Play	Mikus Gavars	LAT
F	Leinster Boys Open	Alec Myles*	IRL
F	Lithuanian Amateur Open	Kornelijus Baliukonis	LTU
F	Logan Trophy	Tom Burley	ENG
F	McGregor Trophy	Jake Storey*	ENG
F	Message Elitecup	Mads Kristensen	DEN
F	Molleaens Junior	Morten Toft Hansen*	DEN
F	Munster Boys Amateur	Ewen Ferguson (SCO)	IRL
F	National Youths U16	Pedro Guedes Almeida*	POR
F	National Youths U18	Antonio Oliveira Mendes	POR
F	Niitvalja Karikas	Egeti Liiv*	EST
F	Norgesmesterskapet	Kristoffer Ventura	NOR
F	Oceanico World Junior	Tomas Gouveia	POR
F	Rosen Pokalen	John Axelsen*	DEN
F	Russian Amateur	Vladimir Osipov	RUS
F	Scottish Boys Open SP	Greig Marchbank	SCO
F	Scottish Boys U16	Oskar Bergqvist (SWE)	SCO
F	SGF Senior Tour H35 U4	Fredrik Kampe	SWE
F	Slovak Mid-Amateur	Thomas Krieger*	SVK
F	Slovenian Int. Mid Amateur	Miran Zebaljec*	SLO
F	Solvogn Pokalen	Nicklas Munkebo	DEN
F	South Wales Boys C/ship	Greg Tickell*	WAL
F	St David's Gold Cross	David Boote	WAL
F	Sutherland Chalice	James Ross	SCO
F	Swedish Seniors Open H35	Michael Ryden	SWE
F	Swiss Junior Championship	Neal Woernhard	SUI
F	Targa d'Oro	Andrea Vercesi*	ITA
F	The Junior Open	Renato Paratore (ITA)	ENG
F	Tirol International Junior	Clemens Rainer	AUT
F	Titleist Tour 4	Petter Mikalsen	NOR

Europe (continued)

F	Titleist West Coast Jun. Masters	Mads Birk*	DEN
F	TOYA Polish Junior	Adrian Meronk	POL
F	Ukrainian Open Amateur	Dmytro Dutchyn*	UKR
F	Waterford Sen. Scratch Trophy	Des Morgan	IRL
F	Welsh Boys' Championship	Henry James	WAL

August

Africa

D	Southern Cape Open	George GC	10–12	Sipho Bujela	RSA

F	BATA Open	Benjamin Follett-Smith	ZIM
F	Harare Amateur	Scott Vincent	ZIM
F	Kabete Open	Nelson Simwa	KEN
F	Kenya Junior Stroke Play	Daniel Nduva	KEN
F	Limuru Junior Open	Jonathan Chebukati	KEN
F	R&A Trophy	John Mburu	KEN
F	Zimbabwe Amateur	Ray Badenhorst	ZIM

Americas

A	US Amateur	Cherry Hills Village, CO	13–19	Steven Fox	USA
A	Western Amateur	Highland Park, IL	J30–A4	Chris Williams	USA
C	Canadian Amateur	Camelot Golf & CC and Club de golf Outaouais	7–10	Mackenzie Hughes	CAN
C	Junior PGA Championship	Sycamore Hills GC, Ft Wayne, IN	J31–A3	Robby Shelton	USA
D	Cardinal Amateur	Cardinal Golf & Country Club	10–12	Justin Clement*	USA
D	Met Amateur Championship	Hollywood GC, Deal, NJ	1–5	Ryan McCormick	USA
D	Northern California Match Play	Spyglass Hill	13–17	Jake Yount	USA
D	Redstone GC – PGA Tour Series Championship	Humble, TX	7–8	Sang Yi (KOR)	USA
D	Tour C/ship@TPC Craig Ranch	TPC Craig Ranch, TX	13–14	Sang Yi (KOR)	USA

E	Florida Match Play	Chase Seiffert	USA
E	North Carolina Match Play	Matthew Crenshaw	USA
E	Oklahoma Stroke Play	Talor Gooch	USA
E	Oregon Stroke Play	Michael Johansen*	USA
E	South Carolina Am. C/ship	Cody Proveaux	USA
F	Alabama State Junior	Forrest Gamble*	USA
F	Alabama State Match Play	Casey O'Toole	USA
F	Alberta Senior Amateur	Frank Van Dornick	CAN
F	Arizona Amateur	Andy Aduddell	USA
F	Arizona Mid-Amateur	Andy Aduddell	USA
F	Arkansas Match Play	Nick Wilson	USA
F	Austin City Championship	Brian Noonan*	USA
F	Bass Pro Shops – Payne Stewart Junior	Noah Edmondson	USA
F	Canadian Junior Championship	Adam Svensson	CAN
F	Canyon Springs Coll. Open	Stanton Tondre	USA
F	CJGA Mizuno National Junior	Scott Banks*	CAN
F	Collegiate Players Tour – National Championship	Curtis Donahoe	USA
F	Colorado Stroke Play	Steven Kupcho	USA
F	Connecticut Mid-Amateur	Brian Ahern	USA
F	CorseMax-Phadelphia Runner Junior	Davis Womble	USA
F	Dogwood State Junior Boys	Carter Jenkins	USA
F	Florida Mid-Senior	Ken Moody*	USA
F	Genesis Junior Championship	Cheng Jin (CHN)	USA
F	Genesis Junior Open	Matthew Lowe	USA
F	Goodman Networks Junior @ Timarron	Matt Gilchrest	USA
F	Greens & Dreams Junior Inv.	Owen Bates	CAN
F	GST Amateur Match Play	Nico Garcia	USA
F	Harvey Penick Junior	Matt Gilchrest	USA
F	Humboldt County Amateur	Cody Bates*	USA
F	Illinois State Amateur	Quinlan Prchal	USA
F	Iowa Senior Amateur	Bill Watson*	USA
F	Junior @ Fox Hill	Jimmy Makloski	USA
F	Junior All-Star @ Stockton	Jacob Solomon	USA
F	Junior All-Star at Ocala	Ben Albin*	USA
F	Jun. All-Star at Townsend Ridge	Mason Weld*	USA
F	Junior at Robinson Ranch	Thomas Lim	USA
F	Junior at Southwind	Connor Smith	USA
F	Los Angeles City Match Play	Mike Brockington	USA
F	Louisiana Mid-Amateur	Patrick Christovich	USA
F	Louisiana Senior Amateur	Doug Farr*	USA
F	Maine Amateur Match Play	John Hayes	USA
F	Manitoba Seniors C/ship	Ken Mould*	CAN
F	Massachusetts Junior Amateur	Patrick Frodigh*	USA
F	Metropolitan Amateur	Kyle Weldon*	USA
F	MGA MetLife Boys C/ship	Willis Huynh	USA
F	Michigan Junior State Am.	Mike Nagy	USA
F	Michigan Stroke Play	Jared Dalga	USA
F	Montana State Mid Amateur	Spencer Williams*	USA
F	Nebraska Senior Match Play	Larry Sock*	USA
F	Nevada State Match Play	Roman Mudd	USA
F	New England Junior	Brian Carlson	USA
F	New Hampshire Stroke Play	Ryan Kohler	USA
F	North Texas Amateur	Chris Gilbert	USA
F	Northwest Iowa Amateur	Scott Benson	USA
F	Nova Scotia Senior	Gerry MacMillan	CAN
F	Ontario Senior Amateur	Warren Sye*	CAN
F	Ontario Summer Games	Bryce Evon	CAN
F	Pacific Northwest Junior Boys' Amateur	Kevin Vigna*	USA
F	Pacific Northwest Master – 40	Kevin Vigna*	USA
F	Palm Beach County Amateur	Austin Powell	USA
F	Pennsylvania Amateur	Andrew Mason	USA
F	Philadelphia Junior	Theo Humphrey	USA
F	Pine to Palm Championship	Beau Hanson*	USA

F	Pine to Palm Mid Amateur	A J Greff*	USA
F	Quebec Junior Match Play	Etienne Papineau*	CAN
F	Quebec Match Play	Paolo Addona*	CAN
F	Randy Wise Junior Open	Nick Carlson	USA
F	Rhode Island Stroke Play	Jamison Randall	USA
F	SCGA Match Play	Niall Platt	USA
F	SCGA Public Links C/ship	Dan Sullivan	USA
F	SCPGA Junior Match Play	Jin Jen*	USA
F	Silver Cross Award	Brandon Matthews	USA
F	Sooner Junior All-Star	Nathan Jeansonne	USA
F	South Dakota Amateur	Brandon Sigmund	USA
F	South Texas Amateur	Albert Miner	USA
F	Stonehenge Junior Open	J D Lehman	USA
F	Sunriver Junior Open	Nicholas Scrymgeour (CAN)*	USA
F	Tennessee Senior Amateur	Danny Green	USA
F	Tennessee State Amateur	Tim Jackson	USA
F	Texas Senior Amateur	Chuck Palmer*	USA
F	The Peninsula Junior Classic	Ryan Cole	USA
F	Tournament of Champions at TPC San Antonio	Kevin Pourasef	USA
F	Trusted Choice Big I National Championship	Austin Smotherman	USA
F	Under Armour Steve Marino Championship	Clay Brown*	USA
F	US Army Hawaii Amateur Inv.	Matthew Ma	USA
F	Valentine Invitational	Weston Eklund	USA
F	Vermont Mid-Amateur	Garren Poirier	USA
F	Virginia Junior Stroke Play	Adam Ball	USA
F	Virginia Public Links	Jon Hurst	USA
F	Washington Metropolitan Am.	Joseph Rice	USA
F	Webb Simpson Junior	Chris Williams	USA
F	West Virginia Amateur	Pat Carter	USA
F	West Virginia Senior Amateur	Steve Fox*	USA
F	Wisconsin Junior C/ship	Charlie Danielson	USA
F	Wyoming Mid-Amateur	Todd Griffin*	USA
F	Caribbean Amateur C/ship	Paul Michael (ANT)*	SKN
F	Tercer Torn. Honor Al Merito	Rodrigo Olivero/ Alejandro Villavicencio*	GUA
F	Abierto de Lacosta CC	Juan Miguel Heredia	ECU
F	Campeonato Aberto do Estado De Sao Paulo	Pedro Costa Lima	BRA
F	Camp. Internacional Juvenil	Jaime Lopez Rivarola (ARG)	COL
F	Camp. Suramericano Prejuvenil	Ivan Camilo Ramirez	COL
F	Chile Junior Open	Thomas Burgemeister	CHI
F	Copa Coomeva – Amateur	Juan Sebastian Veloza	COL
F	Copa Coomeva – Mid Am.	Alan W Eder*	COL
F	Copa La Prensa	Thomas Baik	ARG
F	National Colombian Mid-Am.	Juan Fernando Mejia	COL
F	Torneo Nacional BCP	Fernando Gonzales	BOL

Asia

C	Japan Collegiate Championship	Sayama GC, Saitama	21–24	Hideki Matsuyama	JPN
D	Putra Cup	Emeralda Golf Club	27–31	Jonathan Ke-Jun Woo (SIN)	INA
D	Singapore Open Amateur	Raffles CC	J31–A4	Joshua Shou	SIN

E	Pin Fernando Grand Prix	Nadaraja Thangaraja	SRI
E	Song Am Cup	Namhun Kim	KOR
F	China Am. Futures Tour Leg 5	Wang Xichen	CHN
F	China Amateur Tour Leg 4	Zhang Jin	CHN
F	Chubu Collegiate	Shinnosuke Fujisawa*	JPN
F	Guam National Tryout	Louie Sunga	GUM
F	HSBC Junior Championship	Zhang Jin	CHN
F	Japan Junior	Kenta Konishi	JPN
F	Kansai Regional Collegiate	Ryo Harada*	JPN
F	Kanto Junior	Daisuke Matsubara	JPN
F	Kanto Regional Collegiate	Mikihito Kuromiya*	JPN
F	Lion City Cup	Danthai Boonma (THA)	INA
F	Ryo Ishikawa World Junior Inv.	Namhun Kim (KOR)*	JPN
F	Singapore National Amateur	Jonathan Ke-Jun Woo	SIN
F	Sunrise National Summer Ranking Tournament	Yin-Jen Fang	TPE
F	TGA-CAT Junior #2	Phanuwich Onchu*	THA

Australasia

F	Bay of Plenty Open	Joshua Munn	NZL
F	Cambridge Classic	Justin Morris	NZL
F	Cobram Barooga Open	Loren Bunting	AUS
F	Jacobs Creek Classic	Lachlan Booth*	AUS
F	Kapi Tareha	Tyler Hodge	NZL
F	Nadi Open	Vikrant Chandra	FIJ
F	North Harbour Stroke Play	Nick Voke	NZL
F	N. Territory Country C/ship	Scott Revie*	AUS
F	Vanuatu Open	Josepho Matuatu	VAN

Europe

B	West of England Open Amateur MP	Burnham & Berrow GC	J30–A2	Rodrigo Olivero (GUA)/ Alejandro Villavicencio (GUA)*	ENG
B	Boys Amateur Championship	Notts GC	14–19	Matthew Fitzpatrick	ENG
B	Home Internationals	Glasgow Gailes	15–17	Matthew Fitzpatrick (ENG)	SCO
B	Zomerwedstrijd – Brabants Open	Eindhovensche GC	2–4	Rowin Caron	NED
C	English Amateur	Seascale & Silloth-on-Solway GC	J30–A4	Harry Ellis	ENG
C	Swiss International Amateur	Schoenenberg GC	3–5	Adrien Saddier (FRA)	SUI
D	Boys Home Internationals	County Louth	7–9	Adrien Saddier (FRA)	IRL
D	Champ. de France Coupe Ganay	Versailles	22–26	Thomas Elissalde	FRA
D	German Team Championship	Sporting Club Berlin	2–5	Thomas Elissalde (FRA)	GER
D	Grand Prix de Savoie	Golf d'Aix les Bains	17–19	Adrien Saddier	FRA
D	Scottish Amateur	Royal Dornoch GC	J30–A4	Grant Forrest	SCO

Europe (continued)

E	Finnish Amateur	Albert Eckhardt	FIN
E	Harder German Junior	Alexander Matlari	GER
E	Norgesmesterskapet Junior (Titleist Tour)	Kristian Johannessen	NOR
E	Welsh Amateur Championship	Jason Shufflebotham	WAL
F	Amateur Tour Event 5	Adam Studeny	CZE
F	Belgian International C/ship	Mathias Eggenberger (SUI)	BEL
F	Berks, Bucks & Oxon Amateur Championship	Max Smith	ENG
F	Campeonato Absoluto del Principado de Asturias	Manuel Elvira Mijares*	ESP
F	Championnat de France Minimes Garcons	Charles Herbert*	FRA
F	Copa Fed. Vasca de Golf	Martin Larrea Puig*	ESP
F	Coppa d'Oro Mario Camicia	Francesco Laporta	ITA
F	Credit Suisse Junior Tour Event – Kuessnacht	Joel Kai Lenz*	SUI
F	Czech International Amateur	Lorenzo Scotto (ITA)	CZE
F	Czech International Senior	Michael Reich (GER)*	CZE
F	DGU Challenger Tour 111	Jannik Hojer Jensen*	DEN
F	DGU Elite Tour Herrer 111	Victor Gebhard Osterby	DEN
F	DGU Junior Tour Drenge 111	Kasper Bossen*	DEN
F	DM Junior	Nicolai Cetti Engstrom	DEN
F	DM Seniorer	Hans Stenderup	DEN
F	Eimskipsmotarodin 5	Olafur Loftsson	ISL
F	Estonian National Matchplay	Kristo Tullus*	EST
F	Estonian National Stroke Play	Egeti Liiv	EST
F	Faldo Series Russia	Vladimir Osipov	RUS
F	Faldo Series Slovakia	Oliver Gabor*	SVK
F	German National Boys C/ship	Dominic Foos	GER
F	Grand Prix de Bretagne	Lambert Cochet	FRA
F	Grand Prix de Valcros	Nivorn Inplad*	FRA
F	Grand Prix du Medoc	Brice Chanfreau	FRA
F	Grand Prix Du Pau	Alexandre Babaud	FRA
F	Grand Prix Valgarde	Sebastien Gandon*	FRA
F	Grand Prix Vichy Val d'Allier	Alban Messageon*	FRA
F	Hertfordshire Bowl	Luke Johnson	ENG
F	Hungarian Amateur Open	Johannes Diedrichs* (GER)	HUN
F	Hungarian Junior Open	Mate Berta*	HUN
F	Icelandic Junior Match Play	Stefan Thor Bogason	ISL
F	International Match Play	Teodoro Soldafi* (ITA)	GER
F	International Slovenian Boys	Enej Sarkanj	SLO
F	Italian U16 Int. C/ship	Guido Migliozzi	ITA
F	Italian U18 Team C/ship	Andrea Saracino	ITA
F	Italian U18 Team Qualifying	Teodoro Soldati	ITA
F	JSM Match	Tobias Eden	SWE
F	Latvian Junior Open	Roberts Eihmanis	LAT
F	Latvian Open	Jani Hietanen (FIN)	LAT
F	Lee Westwood Trophy	Darren Timms	ENG
F	Leinster Mid-Amateur	Tony McClements*	IRL
F	Midland Open	Jack Colegate	ENG
F	Mullingar Scratch Trophy	Brian Casey	IRL
F	National Junior Stroke Play	Bertrand Mommaerts	BEL
F	North East Open	Chris Robb	SCO
F	North of England Open Youths	Jamie Bower	ENG
F	N. of England Under 16 SP	Jonathan Thomson*	ENG
F	North of Ireland Stroke Play	Cormac Sharvin	IRL
F	North of Scotland Amateur	Gordon Stevenson	SCO
F	Polish Amateur	Mateusz Gradecki	POL
F	Reid Trophy	Inigo Lopez-Pizarro* (ESP)	ENG
F	Seniors Open Amateur	Chip Lutz (USA)	WAL
F	SGF Senior Tour H 35 U5	Carl Fjallman	SWE
F	Skandia Tour Elit Pojkar 5	Marcus Gran	SWE
F	Skandia Tour Riks 4 – Gavle	Niklas Kallange-Nilsson	SWE
F	Skandia Tour Riks 4 – Haninge	Jakob Hansson*	SWE
F	Skandia Tour Riks 4 – Jonkopings	Adam Eineving*	SWE
F	Skandia Tour Riks Pojkar 5	Axel Ostensson	SWE
F	Skandia Tour Riks Sala Pojkar 5	William Scheibe*	SWE
F	Skandia Tour Riks Sunne Pojkar 5	Oscar Hertzberg	SWE
F	Slovak Junior Championship	Peter Valasek	SVK
F	Slovak Mid-Am Open	Michael Hjemgard*	SVK
F	Slovak Open	Peter Valasek	SVK
F	SM Reikapeli	Teemu Toivonen	FIN
F	South England Boys	Joe Brooks*	ENG
F	South of Ireland Championship	Pat Murray	IRL
F	Standard Life Am. Gold Medal	Daniel Young	SCO
F	The Solent Salver	Calum Macphail*	ENG
F	Titleist Tour 6	Petter Mikalsen	NOR
F	Ukrainian Open Amateur Team Championship	Dmitriy Olkhovskiy*	UKR
F	Ulster Boys Open	Timothy Jordan*	IRL
F	Ulster Youths Championship	Steffan O'Hara	IRL
F	Yorkshire Amateur C/ship	Daniel Brown	ENG
F	Zurich Championship	Zeno Felder	SUI

Season 2012–2013

The R&A Men's World Amateur Golf Ranking season runs from September until the following August when the Mark McCormack Medal is presented following the US Men's Amateur Championship. Results for the remainder of the calendar year will be included in the following year's edition of *The R&A Golfer's Handbook*.

European Amateur Ranking 2011–2012

English players dominated the European Amateur Ranking in 2011–2012 with 20 entries in the top 100. France was second with 12 places and Ireland third with 11. Sweden had eight players in the top 100 with Scotland and Spain finishing the season with seven apiece. The European Rankings are extracted from WAGR and are finalised at the same time.

			Divisor	Points
1	Daan Huizing	NED	71	1345.77
2	Matthias Schwab	AUT	37	1256.76
3	Robert Karlsson	SWE	50	1237.00
4	Thomas Pieters	BEL	53	1231.84
5	Julien Brun	FRA	53	1223.58
6	Marcel Schneider	GER	62	1220.97
7	Alan Dunbar	IRL	42	1197.62
8	Jon Rahm-Rodriguez	ESP	32	1170.90
9	Adrien Saddier	FRA	61	1168.44
10	Matthew Fitzpatrick	ENG	35	1153.33
11	Ricardo Gouveia	POR	47	1149.47
12	Pedro Figueiredo	POR	55	1129.09
13	Robin Kind	NED	65	1100.77
14	Moritz Lampert	GER	53	1098.11
15	Sebastian Cappelen	DEN	48	1065.62
16	James Frazer	WAL	45	1065.19
17	Kevin Phelan	IRL	57	1046.05
18	Gavin Moynihan	IRL	40	1040.00
19	Jack Hiluta	ENG	41	1031.71
20	Ben Taylor	ENG	65	1031.54
21	Rory McNamara	IRL	29	1024.14
22	Edouard Espana	FRA	65	1021.54
23	Nathan Kimsey	ENG	53	1010.53
24	Pontus Widegren	SWE	53	1008.49
25	Craig Hinton	ENG	41	1001.22
26	Romain Langasque	FRA	66	996.97
27	Neil Raymond	ENG	54	996.30
28	Reeve Whitson	IRL	50	995.00
29	Maximilian Rottluff	GER	37	994.59
30	Richard O'Donovan	IRL	37	992.79
31	Thomas Elissalde	FRA	60	991.25
32	Carlos Pigem	ESP	56	985.27
33	Garrick Porteous	ENG	56	983.93
34	Max Orrin	ENG	47	981.21
35	Toby Tree	ENG	57	978.95
36	Paul Barjon	FRA	54	976.54
37	Graeme Robertson	SCO	75	974.67
38	Jacobo Pastor	ESP	64	973.44
39	Jack McDonald	SCO	55	969.32
40	Ben Stow	ENG	68	967.65
41	Kristoffer Ventura	NOR	48	966.67
42	Thomas Sorensen	DEN	41	964.63
43	Tapio Pulkkanen	FIN	54	963.89
44	Joel Stalter	FRA	53	962.50
45	Clement Sordet	FRA	57	956.29
46	Rhys Pugh	WAL	57	947.37
47	Antoine Schwartz	FRA	69	946.74
48	Paul Ferrier	SCO	56	946.43
49	Mario Galiano Aguilar	ESP	42	944.05
50	Anders Engell	NOR	54	942.92
51	Victor Perez	FRA	58	936.64
52	Patrick Winther	DEN	29	936.21
53	Kenny Subregis	FRA	71	935.21
54	Toni Hakula	FIN	58	931.68
55	Brian Soutar	SCO	60	930.00
56	Thomas Detry	BEL	56	929.46
57	Jamie Rutherford	ENG	53	929.40
58	Daniel Jennevret	SWE	48	929.17
59	Harry Diamond	IRL	34	925.49
60	Paul Shields	SCO	73	925.00
61	Jack Bartlett	ENG	35	924.29
62	Scott Fernandez	ESP	61	922.13
63	Victor Tarnstrom	SWE	30	919.17
64	Gary Hurley	IRL	42	918.45
65	Grant Forrest	SCO	52	918.03
66	Juan Sarasti	ESP	48	915.28
67	Matthew Clark	SCO	50	912.00
68	Renato Paratore	ITA	50	911.00
69	Lionel Weber	FRA	81	906.02
70	Ryan Evans	ENG	49	904.08
71	Petter Mikalsen	NOR	43	900.58
72	Jordan Smith	ENG	41	900.00
73	Philipp Westermann	GER	59	899.58
74	Clement Berardo	FRA	49	899.15
75	Niclas Carlsson	SWE	41	896.34
76	Emilio Cuartero	ESP	57	893.86
77	Nick Marsh	ENG	31	892.47
78	Victor Fasmer Henum	DEN	35	891.43
79	Sebastian Soderberg	SWE	42	890.48
80	Ondrej Lieser	CZE	47	889.36
81	Joshua White	ENG	44	881.82
82	Rowin Caron	NED	38	881.58
83	Dominic Foos	GER	51	878.92
84	Gregory Eason	ENG	39	876.92
85	Maximilian Mehles	GER	37	875.00
86	Brian Casey	IRL	28	875.00
87	Niklas Lindstrom	SWE	32	871.88
88	Goncalo Pinto	POR	35	869.29
89	Jason Shufflebotham	WAL	62	866.13
90	Dermot McElroy	IRL	48	863.89
91	Andreas Gjesteby	NOR	27	861.61
92	Chris Selfridge	IRL	50	859.50
93	Tom Berry	ENG	54	855.90
94	Alfred Kerstis	SWE	32	852.34
95	Lukas Nemecz	AUT	43	852.33
96	Paul Howard	ENG	27	850.00
97	Ben Westgate	WAL	24	850.00
98	Callum Shinkwin	ENG	31	848.39
99	Max Albertus	NED	32	847.27
100	Dylan Boshart	NED	28	846.43

For the full European Amateur Rankings, visit www.ega-golf.ch

Major Amateur Championships 2012

4th Asia–Pacific Amateur Championship (Inaugurated 2009) *Amata Spring CC, Thailand*

Fourteen-year-old Guan Tianlang wins Asia–Pacific Amateur Championship and earns an invitation to The Masters

He only weighs 125 lbs and his longest drive during the tournament was just around the 250 yards mark but the slightly-built Chinese 14-year-old Guan Tianlang is a worthy competitor. In a field of 120 from 60 different countries he outplayed older players and longer-hitters to win the fourth Asia–Pacific Amateur Championship.

Indeed, he led from start to finish. He opened with a 66 at the Amata Spring Country Club in Thailand, putted even better for a second round 64 to lead by five and finished off with rounds of 72 and 71 for a 15-under-par total of 273.

The first Chinese winner of the event finished a single stroke ahead of Pan Cheng-tsung of Taiwan who, after opening with a 75 shot rounds of 67, 67 and 65, edged out Australian Oliver Goss, a quarter-finalist in the 2012 US Amateur Championship, for the runner-up spot. Hideki Matsuyama, who won the past two Championships in Tokyo and Singapore, was fourth on his own on 278.

Guan earned an invitation to play in the 2013 Masters at Augusta and he and Pan are exempt into final international qualifying for The Open being played at Muirfield in 2013.

Guan had made golfing headlines before he teed up in the fourth of amateur golf's major championships. He was already the youngest winner of the China Amateur Open, the youngest golfer ever to compete in a European Tour event when he teed up in the 2012 Volvo China Open and he won the 11–12 category in the Junior World Open Championship at San Diego by 11 shots.

Watched by his parents in Thailand he made an impressive start with 17 birdies in his first two rounds then showed his competitive spirit by holding on under pressure to take the title.

The 2013 Championship will be played on the Danling Garden course at the Nanshan GC in China and the 2014 event will go to Royal Melbourne in Australia, one of the world's best-known and most challenging tests.

Guan has beaten the record set by the previous youngest participant at The Masters – Italy's Matteo Manassero – who was 16 when he earned a place in the 2010 field after winning the Amateur Championship in 2009.

"I am so excited. I am looking forward to going to Augusta. I don't know what is going to happen there but I just want to do well", said the Chinese teenager who has the nickname "Langlang". After holing the five-foot for victory he punched the air and was hugged by his father.

"Pan really did a good job," he added. "I just had to stay focussed and try to make birdies. He had a good front nine but I thought if I managed to make a couple more I'd be the champion."

1	Guan Tianlang (CHN)	66-64-72-71—273
2	Cheng-Tsung Pan (TPE)	75-67-67-65—274
3	Oliver Goss (AUS)	70-65-69-72—276
4	Hideki Matsuyama (JPN)	71-69-70-68—278
5	James McMillan (AUS)	73-69-69-68—279
6	Soo-Min Lee (KOR)	69-70-69-72—280
7	Nattawat Suvajanakorn (THA)	71-72-72-67—282
	Nathan Holman (AUS)	75-64-75-68—282
	Cameron Smith (AUS)	74-66-73-69—282
	Brett Drewitt (AUS)	71-71-71-69—282
	Natipong Srithong (THA)	69-69-73-71—282
12	Chikkarangappa Senapaa (IND)	69-74-71-69—283
13	Mikumu Horikawa (JPN)	71-72-67-74—284
14	Vaughan McCall (NZL)	72-68-76-69—285
	Gyu-Bin Kim (KOR)	71-73-72-69—285

Asian Amateur Championship *continued*

14T	Khalin Joshi (IND)	74-71-69-71—285
	Prin Sirisommai (THA)	70-65-72-78—285
18	Zecheng Dou (CHN)	72-72-76-67—287
	Taihei Sato (JPN)	75-71-73-68—287
	Chang-Woo Lee (KOR)	78-71-68-70—287
	Poom Saksansin (THA)	73-71-73-70—287
	Daniel Pearce (NZL)	68-73-74-72—287
23	Anton Arboleda (PHI)	73-75-70-70—288
	Jonathan Ke-Jun Woo (SIN)	71-70-75-72—288
	Khai Jei Low (MAS)	70-73-71-74—288
	Blair Riordan (NZL)	73-69-71-75—288
27	Kenta Konishi (JPN)	77-71-78-63—289
28	Rico Hoey (PHI)	75-72-70-75—292
29	Peter Lee (NZL)	78-70-73-72—293
30	Angad Cheema (IND)	77-72-72-73—294
	Chieh-Po Lee (TPE)	76-74-75-69—294
32	Abel Tam (MAS)	72-76-73-74—295
33	Udayan Mane (IND)	75-75-70-76—296
	Danthai Boonma (THA)	70-76-74-76—296
	Somprad Rattanasuwan (THA)	79-69-75-73—296
	Rupert Zaragosa (PHI)	74-70-80-72—296
	Shinichi Mizuno (HKG)	75-73-76-72—296
	Manav Das (IND)	79-71-75-71—296
39	Chirat Jirasuwan (THA)	75-75-75-73—298
	Ricky Kato (AUS)	77-75-73-73—298
	Jerome Ng (SIN)	74-76-76-72—298
	Kyo Won Koo (KOR)	78-74-76-70—298
43	Chanachoke Dejpiratanamongkol (THA)	73-73-74-79—299
	Honey Baisoya (IND)	76-72-76-75—299
	Ryutaro Kato (JPN)	73-75-78-73—299
46	Vijitha Bandara (SRI)	74-70-76-80—300
	Teng Kao (TPE)	77-71-75-77—300
	Nadaraja Thangaraja (SRI)	75-71-78-76—300
	Andy Hyeon Bo Shim (KOR)	77-76-72-75—300
50	Vikrant Chandra (FIJ)	75-74-75-77—301
	Tae Wan Lee (KOR)	77-74-77-73—301
	Waseem Rana (PAK)	78-70-80-73—301
53	Md Dulal Hossain (BAN)	73-74-75-80—302
	Ian Andrew (INA)	78-73-78-73—302
55	Maung Maung Oo (MYA)	79-72-74-78—303
	Compton Pikari (NZL)	72-81-77-73—303
57	James Beale (NZL)	76-76-74-78—304
	Wei-Hou Liu (TPE)	74-79-75-76—304
	Olaf Allen (FIJ)	74-78-79-73—304
60	Nanfa Somnuek (THA)	74-72-80-80—306
61	Mohd Afif Mohd Razif (MAS)	79-74-78-79—310

The following players missed the cut:

62	Jordan Surya Irawan (INA)	81-73—154
	Hamad Mubarak (BRN)	79-75—154
	Cheng Jin (CHN)	77-77—154
65	Adiandono Rinaldi (INA)	77-78—155
	Melvin Chew (SIN)	76-79—155
	Wei-Hsiang Wang (TPE)	80-75—155
	Marc Ong (SIN)	81-74—155
	Ghazanfar Mahmood (PAK)	82-73—155
70	Thammasack Bouahom (LAO)	79-77—156
	Muh'd Ahmad Fauzi (MAS)	77-79—156
	M Arumugam (SRI)	79-77—156
73	Llyod Jefferson Go (PHI)	80-77—157
	Doan Van Dinh (VIE)	78-79—157
	Chan Tuck Soon (MAS)	78-79—157
	Thein Naing So (MYA)	79-78—157
77	Nicklaus Chiam (SIN)	78-80—158
	Nirun Sae-Ueng (THA)	77-81—158
	B A Rohana (SRI)	78-80—158
80	Nasser Yacoob (BRN)	81-78—159
	Tshendra Diorji (BHU)	80-79—159
	Hassan Karimian Noshahr (IRI)	82-77—159
83	Sammy Bob (PNG)	78-82—160
	Mohd Ali Hai (PAK)	77-83—160
	Albright Chong (MAS)	81-79—160
83T	Malase Maifea (SAM)	82-78—160
	Abdul Hadi (SIN)	81-79—160
88	Terrence Ng (HKG)	81-80—161
	John Kier Abdon (PHI)	79-82—161
	Saleh Al Kaabi (QAT)	78-83—161
	Han-Ting Chiu (TPE)	83-78—161
92	Sohail al Marzouqi (UAE)	81-81—162
	Seyed Mahmoud Jozi (IRI)	85-77—162
94	Ramzi Khaled (LBA)	82-81—163
	Pulou Faaaliga (SAM)	76-87—163
	Md Sagor (BAN)	79-84—163
	Daryl Poe (GUM)	85-78—163
98	Ziwang Gurung (BHU)	84-80—164

98T	Chak Hou Tang (MAC)	81-83—164
	George Rukabo (SOL)	80-84—164
	Van Seiha Seng (CAM)	87-77—164
	Rachid Akl (LBA)	83-81—164
103	Redge Camacho (GUM)	85-81—166
104	Ta Thuy Vo (VIE)	89-79—168
	Jieyu Xiaao (MAC)	81-87—168
106	Ali Abdulla al Mufleh (QAT)	86-83—169
	Sisira Kumara (SRI)	84-85—169
	Ly Hong (CAM)	88-81—169
106T	Navinda Ranga (SRI)	88-81—169
110	Soti Dinki (PNG)	86-84—170
111	Soulis Chanthalanouvat (LAO)	82-89—171
112	Daniel Joseph Webb (COK)	85-87—172
	William Haimona Browne (COK)	87-85—172
114	Tom Felani (SOL)	89-86—175
	Abdalla al Musharrekh (UAE)	85-90—175
116	Bikash Nogati (NEP)	86-93—179
117	Nurmat Imanaliev (KGZ)	97-97—194
118	Orgil Sodov (MGL)	94-106—200
119	Talgat Sugirbekov (KGZ)	105-108—213
	Ulzii Delger (MGL)	89 WD

2009 Chang-Won Han (KOR)

2010 Hideki Matsuyama (JPN)

2011 Hideki Matsuyama (JPN)

117th British Amateur Championship (Inaugurated 1885) June 18–23

Royal Troon and Glasgow – Gailes Links

Dunbar takes Amateur Trophy back to Ulster

The folks in Northern Ireland are getting used to welcoming home champions – Rory McIlroy, Darren Clarke and Graeme McDowell in the professional ranks and now Alan Dunbar as British Amateur champion.

In one of the tightest finals in some years played in strong wind and rain Dunbar, from the Rathmore Club, edged out 17-year-old Mattias Schwab on the last green. Schwab had been hoping to become the first Austrian to win the title and as a result the first to play in The Masters at Augusta but it was not to be for him. It will be Dunbar who will experience the heady Masters atmosphere for the first time in 2013..

Yet just how close a match it was can be judged from the fact that the two exchanged the lead five times. In the end it was on the greens at Royal Troon that the 23-year-old winner had the edge.

"My putting was great all week," said Dunbar who benefitted from a timely lesson from his coach Seamus Duffy before he left Northern Ireland for the Championship.

It was as well he had his eye in on the greens because he readily admitted he was struggling a bit with the long game. "I had to rely on my putting," said Dunbar who was one down to the teenage Continental after the first 18 holes.

By the fifth in the afternoon, however, it was Dunbar, a former St Andrews Links Trophy winner, who had the advantage. Yet three holes later it was all square again.

The Ulsterman, a member of the winning 2011 Great Britain and Ireland Walker Cup side, found himself one down with six regulation holes to play when his hooked drive cost him the 12th. Dunbar squared at the 15th, and although he lost the 16th he won the last two holes for a one hole victory when his younger opponent failed to make par on both occasions At the last, Schwab missed the four foot putt that would have taken the final into extra holes.

With his win Dunbar matched the feat of two other Northern Irish winners of the title, Garth McGimpsey in 1985 and Michael Hoey in 2001.

Stroke Play Qualifying:

Daniel Jennevret (SWE)	71-65—136
Geoff Drakeford (AUS)	67-71—138
Paul Barjon (FRA)	70-69—139
Richard O'Donovan (Lucan)	73-66—139
Adrien Saddier (FRA)	68-71—139
Edouard Espana (FRA)	71-69—140
Jacobo Pastor (ESP)	70-71—141
Nathan Holman (AUS)	72-69—141
Victor Henum (DEN)	72-69—141
Tim Gornik (SLO)	70-71—141
Federico Zucchetti (ITA)	70-71—141
Antoine Schwartz (FRA)	72-69—141
Kristjan Einarsson (ISL)	71-70—141
Julien Brun (FRA)	70-71—141
Franco Romero (ARG)	70-72—142
Juan F Sarasti (ESP)	73-69—142
Ashley Chgesters (Hawkstone Park)	67-75—142
Joel Stalter (FRA)	73-69—142
Craig Hinton (Oxfordshire)	71-71—142
Daniel Nisbet (AUS)	69-73—142
Stephan Jaeger (GER)	70-72—142
Kevin Phelan (Waterford Castle)	70-72—142
Paul Ferrier (Baberton)	69-73—142
Daniel Young (Craigie Hill)	69-73—142
Jorge Fernandez Valdes (ARG)	71-71—142
Borja Virto (ESP)	69-73—142
Rory McNamara (Headfort)	73-69—142
Nathan Kimsey (Woodhall Spa)	70-73—143
Antoni Ferrer (ESP)	70-73—143
Robert Karlsson (SWE)	71-72—143
Matthew Stieger (AUS)	74-69—143
Thomas Detry (BEL)	73-70—143
Patrick Winther (DEN)	71-72—143
Jack McDonald (Kilmarnock – Barassie)	72-71—143
James White (Lundin)	68-75—143
Daniel Bringolf (AUS)	71-72—143
Daan Huizing (NED)	72-71—143
Jack Bartlett (Worthing)	71-72—143
Mackenzie Hughes (CAN)	72-72—144
Olivier Rozner (FRA)	71-73—144

British Amateur Championship *continued*

Ben Stow (Rushmore)	71-73—144
Peter Valasek (SVK)	74-70—144
Clement Batut (FRA)	74-70—144
Lorenzo Scotto (ITA)	72-72—144
Ricardo Melo Gouveia (POR)	71-73—144
Giulio Castagnara (ITA)	74-70—144
Will McCurdy (USA)	69-75—144
Marcos Pastor (ESP)	72-72—144
Jordan Zunic (AUS)	70-74—144
Brian Soutar (Leven GS)	70-74—144
Carlos Pigem (ESP)	70-74—144
Ben Campbell (NZL)	72-72—144
Kramer Hickok (USA)	73-71—144
Tom Berry (Wentworth)	70-74—144
Clement Sordet (FRA)	73-71—144
Paul Howard (Southport & Ainsdale)	70-74—144
Emilio Cuartero (ESP)	71-73—144
Richard Bentham (St Pierre)	73-71—144
Toby Tree (Worthing)	70-74—144
Alan Dunbar (Rathmore)	74-70—144
Tapio Pulkkanen (FIN)	71-73—144
Tyler Raber (USA)	71-74—145
Rhys Pugh (Vale of Glamorgan)	70-75—145
Joshua White (Chipstead)	73-72—145
Mathias Eggenberger (SUI)	71-74—145
Michael Loppnow (RSA)	71-74—145
Pedro Figueiredo (POR)	69-76—145
Brian Casey (Headfort)	74-71—145
Max Orrin (North Foreland)	68-77—145
James Ross (Royal Burgess)	74-71—145
Florian Loutre (FRA)	70-75—145
Manuel Trappel (AUT)	73-72—145
Jonathan Bale (Royal Porthcawl)	72-73—145
Ciaran Molloy (Ardee)	72-73—145
Daniel Schmeiding (GER)	70-75—145
Matthias Schwab (AUT)	68-77—145
Jason Shufflebotham (Prestatyn)	74-71—145
Todd Sinnott (AUS)	75-70—145
Albin Choi (CAN)	72-74—146
Fraser McKenna (Balmore)	73-73—146
Kristoffer Ventura (NOR)	72-74—146
Paul Dunne (Greystones)	72-74—146
Gavin Samuels (Leighton Buzzard)	72-74—146
Daniel Wasteney (Bondhay)	71-75—146
Marc Dobias (SUI)	75-71—146
Andrew Hogan (Newlands)	74-72—146
Arthur Gabella-Wenne (SUI)	72-74—146
Mateusz Gradecki (POL)	69-77—146
Sebastian Soderberg (SWE)	71-75—146
James White (USA)	72-74—146
Stefano Pitoni (ITA)	73-73—146
James Frazer (Pennard)	71-76—147
Gavin Moynihan (The Island)	71-76—147
David Booth (Rotherham)	76-71—147
Victor Perez (FRA)	74-73—147
Olafur Loftsson (ISL)	74-73—147
Jacob Lauridsen (DEN)	73-74—147
Chikkarangappa Seenappa (IND)	71-76—147
Oskar Arvidsson (SWE)	74-73—147
Haydn Porteous (RSA)	70-77—147
Graham Robertson (Silverknowes)	75-72—147
Matthew Clark (Kilmacolm)	73-74—147
Harry Diamond (Belvoir Park)	72-75—147
Charlie Hughes (CAN)	75-72—147
Charlie Bull (Lake Nona)	74-73—147
Vaughan McCall (NZL)	74-73—147
Jacopo Jori (ITA)	71-76—147
Gert Myburgh (RSA)	72-75—147
Michael Saunders (Dartford)	72-75—147
Pierre Henri Leclerc (FRA)	76-71—147
Reeve Whitson (Mourne)	73-74—147
Graeme Roberetson (Glenbervie)	72-75—147
Greg Eason (Kirby Muxloe)	73-74—147
Victor Gebhard Osterby (DEN)	73-74—147
Khalin Joshi (IND)	73-74—147
Kyle McClung (Wigtownshire County)	74-73—147
Kevin Hesbois (BEL)	70-77—147
Blair Riordan (NZL)	74-74—148
Nicolas Manifacier (FRA)	73-75—148
Niclas Carlsson (SWE)	71-77—148
Xavier Feyaerts (BEL)	69-79—148
Andrea Bolognesi (ITA)	73-75—148
Louis Cohen-Boyer (FRA)	76-72—148
Jimmy Mullen (Royal North Devon)	70-78—148
Paul Kinnear (Formby)	72-76—148
Maximilian Mehles (GER)	70-78—148
Robin Kind (NED)	73-75—148
Eamon Bradley (Mount Ellen)	72-76—148
Callan O'Reilly (AUS)	73-75—148
Valerio Pelliccia (ITA)	77-71—148
Eugene Smith (Ardee)	75-73—148
A J Crouch (USA)	74-74—148
Dominic Foos (GER)	74-74—148
Gary Hurley (West Waterford)	75-73—148
Jamie Rutherford (Knebworth)	73-75—148
Philipp Westermann (GER)	71-78—149
Pierre Mazier (FRA)	74-75—149
Corbin Mills (USA)	72-77—149
Harry Casey (Enfield)	73-76—149
Matthew Fitzspatrick (Hallamshire)	74-75—149
Riccardo Michelini (ITA)	73-76—149
Joshua Loughrey (Wrag Barn)	78-71—149
Cameron Smith (AUS)	70-79—149
Vetle Maroy (NOR)	75-74—149
Adam Dunton (McDonald)	73-76—149
Jake Higginbottom (AUS)	72-77—149
Greig Marchbank (Dumfries & County)	72-77—149
Benjamin Ruscj (SUI)	73-76—149
Maximilian Rottluff (GER)	73-76—149
Aubrey Barnard (RSA)	72-77—149
Dermot McElroy (Ballymena)	75-74—149
Neil Raymond (Corhampton)	77-72—149
Miro Veijalainen (FIN)	75-74—149
Henry Smart (Banstead Downs)	70-79—149
Harrison Greenberry (Exeter)	72-77—149
Luke Humphries (AUS)	76-73—149
John Greene (Portmarnock)	80-69—149
Ricardo Celia (COL)	74-75—149
Sebastian Cappelen (DEN)	73-76—149
Nicholas Grant (Knock	74-75—149
Adrien Monnier (FRA)	74-75—149
Daniel Kay (Dunbar)	74-75—149

Jack Colegate (Roch. & Cobham Park)	76-73—149
Jamie Bower (Meltham)	73-76—149
Ben Loughrey (Wrag Barn)	73-76—149
Patrick Spraggs (Stowmarket)	73-76—149
Joshua Manske (USA)	73-76—149
Hugo Rouillon (FRA)	80-69—149
Scott W Fernandez (ESP)	71-78—149
Clement Berardo (FRA)	78-71—149
Kristian Johannessen (NOR)	74-76—150
Scott Gibson (Southerness)	75-75—150
Rory Bourke (AUS)	74-76—150
Thomas Sorensen (DEN)	76-74—150
Anders Engell (NOR)	74-76—150
Garrick Porteous (Bamburgh Castle)	72-78—150
Darren Renwick (Hill Barn)	74-76—150
Chris Robb (Inchmarlo)	72-78—150
Kevin Turlan (FRA)	75-75—150
Teemu Toivonen (FIN)	75-75—150
Christian Gloeet (DEN)	74-76—150
Ewan Scott (St Andrews)	74-76—150
Jose Maria Joia (POR)	72-78—150
Max Kraemer (GER)	72-78—150
Julien de Poyen (FRA)	77-73—150
Hamza Sayin (TUR)	74-76—150
Kasper Estrup (DEN)	73-77—150
Marco Iten (SUI)	73-77—150
Ben Taylor (Walton Heath)	75-75—150
C J du Plessis (RSA)	76-75—151
Martin Simonsen (DEN)	77-74—151
Daniel Pearce (NZL)	76-75—151
Curtis Griffiths (Wentworth)	73-78—151
Jules Bordonado (FRA)	79-72—151
Jamie Clare (Burnham & Berrow)	76-75—151
Rowin Caron (NED)	75-76—151
Edouard Amacher (SUI)	73-78—151
Jack Hiluta (Chelmsford)	74-77—151
Pep Angles (ESP)	72-79—151
Aaron Kearney (Castlerock)	80-71—151
Craig Hamilton (Omanu)	75-76—151
Matthew Wallace (Moor Park)	74-77—151
Mathieu Fenasse (FRA)	81-70—151
Charlie Wilson (Littlestone)	73-78—151
Matt Pinizzotto (USA)	73-78—151
Francesco Laporta (ITA)	76-75—151
Shaun Smith (RSA)	71-80—151
Alfie Plant (Rochester & Cobham Pk)	76-75—151
Liam Johnston (Dumfries & County)	75-76—151
Edward Richardson (Hemsted Forest)	77-74—151
Callum Shinkwin (Moor Park)	72-80—152
Jean-Paul Strydom (RSA)	71-81—152
Maxwell Buckley (USA)	74-78—152
Robin Sciot-Siegrist (FRA)	76-76—152
Eugenio Rodi (MEX)	75-77—152
Sean Einhaus (GER)	70-82—152
Sam Robertshawe (Army)	79-73—152
Alexander Culverwell (Dunbar)	74-78—152
Jordan Smith (Bowood)	80-72—152
Carl Jonson (USA)	78-74—152
Tom Twilde (Castle Royle)	78-74—152
Romain Langasque (FRA)	77-76—153
Kenneth Svanum (NOR)	75-78—153
Franck Daux (FRA)	77-76—153
Mathias Schjolberg (NOR)	75-78—153
Ross Noon (Craigielaw)	77-76—153
Benjamin Weilguni (AUT)	76-77—153
Grant Forrest (Craigielaw)	77-76—153
Michael Durcan (County Sligo)	75-78—153
Albert Eckhardt (FIN)	76-77—153
Richard Bridges (Stackstown)	77-77—154
Steven Rennie (Drumpellier)	80-74—154
Thomas Elissalde (FRA)	76-78—154
Brad Moules (AUS)	74-80—154
Guray Yazici (TUR)	77-77—154
Andrea Gurini (SUI)	73-81—154
Sam Whitehead (Woburn)	77-77—154
Greg Payne (Chobham)	81-73—154
Garrett Rank (CAN)	73-81—154
Geoff Lenehan (Portmarnock)	80-74—154
Brandon Stone (RSA)	79-75—154
Sam Davis (NZL)	79-75—154
Agustin Tarigo (URU)	76-78—154
Emil Soegaard (DEN)	74-81—155
Pontus Widegren (SWE)	80-75—155
Neil Henderson (Glen)	76-79—155
Paul Shields (Kirkhill)	74-81—155
Stephen Spiers (Kooyonga)	76-79—155
Jan Szmidt (POL)	77-78—155
Juan Jose Salcedo (MEX)	78-77—155
Benedict Staben (GER)	75-80—155
Alexander Sobstad (NOR)	79-76—155
Mikkel Bjerch Andresen (NOR)	80-75—155
Victor Bertran Crous (ESP)	81-74—155
Brett Drewitt (AUS)	82-73—155
Hunter Hawkins (USA)	77-79—156
Nicholas Thommen (SUI)	77-79—156
Rob van Devlin (NED)	80-76—156
Alastair Jones (Radyr)	78-79—157
Matthew Moseley (Carmarthen)	74-83—157
Florian Kolberg (TUR)	79-78—157
Leo Lespinasse (FRA)	76-81—157
Owen Burgess (Russley)	78-80—158
Scott Crichton (Aberdour)	80-78—158
Drikus Bruyns (RSA)	80-78—158
Dylan Boshart (NED)	81-77—158
Finley Ewing IV (USA)	83-75—158
Mikael Lindberg (SWE)	80-78—158
Kenny Subregis (FRA)	78-80—158
James Fox (Portmarnock)	76-83—159
Filippo Bergamaschi (ITA)	74-85—159
Mathew Perry (NZL)	79-80—159
Ville Lagerblom (FIN)	77-82—159
Francesco Testa (ITA)	79-80—159
Fraser Moore (Glenbervie)	81-79—160
Scott Stewart-Cation (The Dukes)	76-84—160
Paul Lockwood (Hessle)	80-80—160
Sebastian Schwind (GER)	83-77—160
Pierre-Alexis Rolland (BEL)	83-78—161
Adrian Meronk (POL)	78-83—161
Julien Marot (FRA)	86-75—161
Jean-Pierre Verselin (FRA)	81-81—162
Mathias Boesmans (BEL)	86-77—163
Christoph Weninger (AUT)	80-85—165
Sam Forgan (Stowmarket)	76-89—165
Xavi Puig (ESP)	78-89—167
John Duff (Newmachar)	81 DQ
Gregoire Schoeb (FRA)	DQ

British Amateur Championship *continued*

Round One:

Daniel Schmieding (GER) beat Peter Valasek (SVK) at 20th
Clement Sordet (FRA) beat Manuel Trappel (AUT) 3 and 1
Matthias Schwab (AUT) beat Ciaran Molloy (Ardee) 4 and 3
Jason Shufflebotham (Prestatyn) beat Brian Casey (Headfort) 2 and 1
Pedro Figueiredo (POR) beat Richard Bentham (St Pierre) 1 hole
Jordan Zunic (AUS) beat Brian Soutar (Leven GS) 2 and 1
Rhys Pugh (Vale of Glamorgan) beat Joshua White (Chipstead) 6 and 4
Toby Tree (Worthing) beat Jonathan Bale (Royal Porthcawl) 3 and 2
Tyler Raber (USA) beat Ben Campbell (NZL) at 20th
Todd Sinnott (AUS) beat Tom Berry (Wentworth) 1 hole
Tapio Pulkkanen (FIN) beat Florian Loutre (FRA) 8 and 7
Max Orrin (North Foreland) beat James Ross (Royal Burgess) 5 and 3
Mathias Eggenberger (SUI) beat Michael Loppnow (RSA) 4 and 3
Will McCurdy (USA) beat Giulio Castagnara (ITA) 3 and 2

Round Two:

Emilio Cuartero (ESP) beat Daniel Jennevret (SWE) 1 hole
Matthew Stieger (AUS) beat Thomas Detry (BEL) 2 and 1
Craig Hinton (Oxfordshire) beat Daan Huizing (NED) at 19th
Daniel Nisbet (AUS) beat Clement Batut (FRA) 2 and 1
Lorenzo Scotto (ITA) beat Nathan Holman (AUS) 2 and 1
Kevin Phelan (Waterford Castle) beat Kramer Hickok (USA) 4 and 3
Victor Henum (DEN) beat Marcos Pastor (ESP) 6 and 5
Paul Ferrier (Baberton) beat Ben Stow (Rushmore) 7 and 6
Nathan Kimsey (Woodhall Spa) beat Richard O'Donovan (Lucan) 2 and 1
Robert Karlsson (SWE) beat Olivier Rozner (FRA) 3 and 1
Ricardo Melo Gouveia (POR) beat Kristjan Einarsson (ISL) 4 and 3
Juan F Sarasti (ESP) beat James White (Lundin) 3 and 2
Paul Barjon (FRA) beat Mackenzie Hughes (CAN) 5 and 3
Jack Bartlett (Worthing) beat Antoni Ferrer (ESP) 4 and 2
Patrick Winther (DEN) beat Federico Zucchetti (ITA) 3 and 1
Alan Dunbar (Rathmore) beat Borja Virto (ESP) 1 hole
Jorge Fernandez Valdes (ARG) beat Carlos Pigem (ESP) at 20th
Jacobo Pastor (ESP) beat Paul Howard (Southport & Ainsdale) 2 and 1
Daniel Schmieding (GER) beat Daniel Young (Craigie Hill) 3 and 2
Edouard Espana (FRA) beat Clement Sordet (FRA) 1 hole
Matthias Schwab (AUT) beat Ashley Chesters (Hawkstone Park) 1 hole
Tim Gornik (SLO) beat Jason Shufflebotham (Prestatyn) 1 hole
Pedro Figueiredo (POR) beat Daniel Bringolf (AUS) at 19th
Jordan Zunic (AUS) beat Adrien Saddier (FRA) 1 hole
Rhys Pugh (Vale of Glamorgan) beat Franco Romero (ARG) 4 and 2
Toby Tree (Worthing) beat Julien Brun (FRA) 2 and 1
Tyler Raber (USA) beat Joel Stalter (FRA) 1 hole
Antoine Schwartz (FRA) beat Todd Sinnott (AUS) 4 and 3
Rory McNamara (Headfort) beat Tapio Pulkkanen (FIN) 2 holes
Stephan Jaeger (GER) beat Max Orrin (North Foreland) 4 and 3
Jack McDonald (Kilmarnock – Barassie) beat Mathias Eggenberger (SUI) 1 hole
Will McCurdy (USA) beat Geoff Drakeford (AUS) 8 and 7

Round Three:

Stieger beat Cuartero 4 and 2
Nisbet beat Hinton 3 and 1
Scotto beat Phelan at 19th
Ferrier beat Henum 4 and 3
Karlsson beat Kimsey 1 hole
Melo Gouveia beat Sarasti 1 hole
Barjon beat Bartlett 4 and 3
Dunbar beat Winther 7 and 6
Pastor beat Fernandez Valdes at 19th
Schmieding beat Espana 2 holes
Schwab beat Gornik 1 hole
Figueiredo beat Zunic 3 and 2
Tree beat Pugh 7 and 6
Raber beat Schwartz 5 and 4
McNamara beat Jaeger 4 and 3
McDonald beat McCurdy at 24th

Round Four:

Stieger beat Nisbet 3 and 2
Ferrier beat Scotto at 19th
Karlsson beat Melo Gouveia 1 hole
Dunbar beat Barjon 2 holes
Pastor beat Schmieding at 20th
Schwab beat Figueiredo 5 and 4

Tree beat Raber 2 and 1
McDonald beat McNamara 1 hole

Quarter Finals:
Ferrier beat Stieger 4 and 3
Dunbar beat Karlsson 3 and 2
Schwab beat Pastor 4 and 3
McDonald beat Tree at 19th

Semi-Finals:
Dunbar beat Ferrier 3 and 2
Schwab beat McDonald 2 holes

Final (36 holes): Alan Dunbar (Rathmore) beat Matthias Schwab (AUT) 1 hole

1885	A MacFie beat H Hutchinson	7 and 6	Hoylake, Royal Liverpool	entrants 44
1886	H Hutchinson beat H Lamb	7 and 6	St Andrews	42
1887	H Hutchinson beat J Ball	1 hole	Hoylake, Royal Liverpool	33
1888	J Ball beat J Laidlay	5 and 4	Prestwick	38
1889	J Laidlay beat L Melville	2 and 1	St Andrews	40
1890	J Ball beat J Laidlay	4 and 3	Hoylake, Royal Liverpool	44
1891	J Laidlay beat H Hilton	at 20th	St Andrews	50
1892	J Ball beat H Hilton	3 and 1	Sandwich, Royal St George's	45
1893	P Anderson beat J Laidlay	1 hole	Prestwick	44
1894	J Ball beat S Fergusson	1 hole	Hoylake, Royal Liverpool	64
1895	L Melville beat J Ball	at 19th	St Andrews	68
From 1896 final played over 36 holes				
1896	F Tait beat H Hilton	8 and 7	Sandwich, Royal St George's	64
1897	A Allan beat J Robb	4 and 2	Muirfield	74
1898	F Tait beat S Fergusson	7 and 5	Hoylake, Royal Liverpool	77
1899	J Ball beat F Tait	at 37th	Prestwick	101
1900	H Hilton beat J Robb	8 and 7	Sandwich, Royal St George's	68
1901	H Hilton beat J Low	1 hole	St Andrews	116
1902	C Hutchings beat S Fry	1 hole	Hoylake, Royal Liverpool	114
1903	R Maxwell beat H Hutchinson	7 and 5	Muirfield	142
1904	W Travis (USA) beat E Blackwell	4 and 3	Sandwich, Royal St George's	104
1905	A Barry beat Hon O Scott	3 and 2	Prestwick	148
1906	J Robb beat C Lingen	4 and 3	Hoylake, Royal Liverpool	166
1907	J Ball beat C Palmer	6 and 4	St Andrews	200
1908	E Lassen beat H Taylor	7 and 6	Sandwich, Royal St George's	197
1909	R Maxwell beat Capt C Hutchison	1 hole	Muirfield	170
1910	J Ball beat C Aylmer	10 and 9	Hoylake, Royal Liverpool	160
1911	H Hilton beat E Lassen	4 and 3	Prestwick	146
1912	J Ball beat A Mitchell	at 38th	Westward Ho!, Royal North Devon	134
1913	H Hilton beat R Harris	6 and 5	St Andrews	198
1914	J Jenkins beat C Hezlet	3 and 2	Sandwich, Royal St George's	232
1915–19	*Not played*			
1920	C Tolley beat R Gardner (USA)	37th hole	Muirfield	165
1921	W Hunter beat A Graham	12 and 11	Hoylake, Royal Liverpool	223
1922	E Holderness beat J Caven	1 hole	Prestwick	252
1923	R Wethered beat R Harris	7 and 6	Deal, Royal Cinque Ports	209
1924	E Holderness beat E Storey	3 and 2	St Andrews	201
1925	R Harris beat K Fradgley	13 and 12	Westward Ho!, Royal North Devon	151
1926	J Sweetser (USA) beat A Simpson	6 and 5	Muirfield	216
1927	Dr W Tweddell beat D Landale	7 and 6	Hoylake, Royal Liverpool	197
1928	T Perkins beat R Wethered	6 and 4	Prestwick	220
1929	C Tolley beat J Smith	4 and 3	Sandwich, Royal St George's	253
1930	R Jones (USA) beat R Wethered	7 and 6	St Andrews	271
1931	E Smith beat J De Forest	1 hole	Westward Ho!, Royal North Devon	171
1932	J De Forest beat E Fiddian	3 and 1	Muirfield	235
1933	Hon M Scott beat T Bourn	4 and 3	Hoylake, Royal Liverpool	269
1934	W Lawson Little (USA) beat J Wallace	14 and 13	Prestwick	225
1935	W Lawson Little (USA) beat Dr W Tweddell	1 hole	Royal Lytham and St Annes	232
1936	H Thomson beat J Ferrier (AUS)	2 holes	St Andrews	283
1937	R Sweeney Jr (USA) beat L Munn	3 and 2	Sandwich, Royal St George's	223
1938	C Yates (USA) beat R Ewing	3 and 2	Troon	241
1939	A Kyle beat A Duncan	2 and 1	Hoylake, Royal Liverpool	167
1940–45	*Not played*			
1946	J Bruen beat R Sweeny (USA)	4 and 3	Birkdale	263
1947	W Turnesa (USA) beat R Chapman (USA)	3 and 2	Carnoustie	200
1948	F Stranahan (USA) beat C Stowe	5 and 4	Sandwich, Royal St George's	168
1949	S McCready beat W Turnesa (USA)	2 and 1	Portmarnock	204
1950	F Stranahan (USA) beat R Chapman (USA)	8 and 6	St Andrews	324
1951	R Chapman (USA) beat C Coe (USA)	5 and 4	Royal Porthcawl	192
1952	E Ward (USA) beat F Stranahan (USA)	6 and 5	Prestwick	286
1953	J Carr beat E Harvie Ward (USA)	2 holes	Hoylake, Royal Liverpool	279
1954	D Bachli (AUS) beat W Campbell (USA)	2 and 1	Muirfield	286

British Amateur Championship *continued*

1955	J Conrad (USA) beat A Slater	3 and 2	Royal Lytham and St Annes	240
1956	J Beharrell beat L Taylor	5 and 4	Troon	200
1957	R Reid Jack beat H Ridgley (USA)	2 and 1	Formby	200
In 1956 and 1957 the Quarter Finals, Semi-Finals and Final were played over 36 holes				
1958	J Carr beat A Thirlwell	3 and 2	St Andrews	488
In 1958, Semi-Finals and Final only were played over 36 holes				
1959	D Beman (USA) beat W Hyndman (USA)	3 and 2	Sandwich, Royal St George's	362
1960	J Carr beat R Cochran (USA)	8 and 7	Royal Portrush	183
1961	MF Bonallack beat J Walker	6 and 4	Turnberry	250
1962	R Davies (USA) beat J Povall	1 hole	Hoylake, Royal Liverpool	256
1963	M Lunt beat J Blackwell	2 and 1	St Andrews	256
1964	G Clark beat M Lunt	at 39th	Ganton	220
1965	MF Bonallack beat C Clark	2 and 1	Royal Porthcawl	176
1966	R Cole (RSA) beat R Shade	3 and 2	Carnoustie (18 holes)	206
Final played over 18 holes because of sea mist				
1967	R Dickson (USA) beat R Cerrudo (USA)	2 and 1	Formby	
1968	MF Bonallack beat J Carr	7 and 6	Royal Troon	249
1969	MF Bonallack beat W Hyndman (USA)	3 and 2	Hoylake, Royal Liverpool	245
1970	MF Bonallack beat W Hyndman (USA)	8 and 7	Newcastle, Royal Co Down	256
1971	S Melnyk (USA) beat J Simons (USA)	3 and 2	Carnoustie	256
1972	T Homer beat A Thirlwell	4 and 3	Sandwich, Royal St George's	253
1973	R Siderowf (USA) beat P Moody	5 and 3	Royal Porthcawl	222
1974	T Homer beat J Gabrielsen (USA)	2 holes	Muirfield	330
1975	M Giles (USA) beat M James	8 and 7	Hoylake, Royal Liverpool	206
1976	R Siderowf (USA) beat J Davies	at 37th	St Andrews	289
1977	P McEvoy beat H Campbell	5 and 4	Ganton	235
1978	P McEvoy beat P McKellar	4 and 3	Royal Troon	353
1979	J Sigel (USA) beat S Hoch (USA)	3 and 2	Hillside	285
1980	D Evans beat D Suddards (RSA)	4 and 3	Royal Porthcawl	265
1981	P Ploujoux (FRA) beat J Hirsch (USA)	4 and 2	St Andrews	256
1982	M Thompson beat A Stubbs	4 and 3	Deal, Royal Cinque Ports	245
Qualifying round introduced				
1983	P Parkin beat J Holtgrieve (USA)	5 and 4	Turnberry	288
1984	JM Olazábal (ESP) beat C Montgomerie	5 and 4	Formby	291
1985	G McGimpsey beat G Homewood	8 and 7	Royal Dornoch	457
1986	D Curry beat G Birtwell	11 and 9	Royal Lytham and St Annes	427
1987	P Mayo beat P McEvoy	3 and 1	Prestwick	373
1988	C Hardin (SWE) beat B Fouchee (RSA)	1 hole	Royal Porthcawl	391
1989	S Dodd beat C Cassells	5 and 3	Royal Birkdale	378
1990	R Muntz (NED) beat A Macara	7 and 6	Muirfield	510
1991	G Wolstenholme beat B May (USA)	8 and 6	Ganton	345
1992	S Dundas beat B Dredge	7 and 6	Carnoustie	364
1993	I Pyman beat P Page	at 37th	Royal Portrush	279
1994	L James beat G Sherry	2 and 1	Nairn	288
1995	G Sherry beat M Reynard	7 and 6	Hoylake, Royal Liverpool	288
1996	W Bladon beat R Beames	1 hole	Turnberry	288
1997	C Watson beat T Immelman (RSA)	3 and 2	Royal St Georges, Royal Cinque Ports	369
1998	S García (ESP) beat C Williams	7 and 6	Muirfield	537
1999	G Storm beat A Wainwright	7 and 6	Royal County Down, Kilkeel	433
2000	M Ilonen (FIN) beat C Reimbold	2 and 1	Royal Liverpool and Wallasey	376
2001	M Hoey beat I Campbell	1 hole	Prestwick & Kilmarnock	288
2002	A Larrazábal (ESP) beat M Sell	1 hole	Royal Porthcawl and Pyle & Kenfig	286
2003	G Wolstenholme beat R De Sousa (SUI)	6 and 5	Royal Troon and Irvine	289
2004	S Wilson beat L Corfield	4 and 3	St Andrews, Old and Jubilee Courses	288
2005	B McElhinney beat J Gallagher	5 and 4	Royal Birkdale and Southport & Ainsdale	406
2006	J Guerrier (FRA) beat A Gee	4 and 3	Royal St George's and Prince's	284
2007	D Weaver (USA) beat T Stewart (AUS)	2 and 1	Royal Lytham & St Annes and St Annes Old Links	284
2008	R Saxton (NED) beat T Fleetwood (ENG)	3 and 2	Turnberry	288
2009	M Manassero (ITA) beat S Hutsby (ENG)	4 and 3	Formby and West Lancashire	284
2010	Jin Jeong (KOR) beat J Byrne (Banchory)	5 and 4	Muirfield and North Berwick	288
2011	B Macpherson (AUS) beat M Stewart (Troon Welbeck)	3 and 2	Hillside and Hesketh	288

The 2013 Amateur Championship is being played from June 17–22 at Royal Cinque Ports and Prince's.

23rd European Amateur Championship (inaugurated 1986)

Carton House, Co Kildare, Ireland

European Victory earns Pugh an invitation to The Open

Welsh golfers finished first and second in the 25th European Amateur Championship played at Carton House Golf Club in Ireland with 18-year-old Rhys Pugh coming from eight shots behind on the final day to beat compatriot James Frazer by a shot on 11-under-par 277. Frazer had moved dramatically into contention on the third day with a 62.

Pugh, from Pontypridd, closed with a title-winning 66 to gain automatic entry into the 142nd Open Championship being played at Muirfield inn 2013. After the biggest win of his career Pugh, unbeaten despite being the youngest member of the successful Great Britain and Ireland Walker Cup side in 2011 at Nairn, told reporters: "It has been my dream to play in The Open since I started to play golf."

Now he has his eye on winning the Silver Medal which goes to the leading amateur in golf's oldest Grand Slam major. In 2011 Tom Lewis, Pugh's Walker Cup team-mate at Nairn, won the medal at Royal St George's. Rhys' winning total comprised rounds of 68, 71, 72 and 66. Denmark's Thomas Sørensen finished third one behind Frazer on 279.

1	Rhys Pugh (WAL)	68-71-72-66—277
2	James Frazer (WAL)	71-74-62-71—278
3	Thomas Sørensen (DEN)	69-67-71-72—279
4	Kevin Phelan (IRL)	73-66-70-71—280
	Pontus Widegren (SWE)	71-67-65-77—280
	Gonçalo Pinto (POR)	68-68-68-76—280
7	Matthias Schwab (AUT)	67-73-72-70—282
8	Axel Boasson (ISL)	71-74-68-70—283
	Ben Stow (ENG)	69-72-70-72—283
	Matthew Clark (SCO)	72-68-71-72—283
	Juan Francisco Sarasti (ESP)	70-70-66-77—283
	Daniel Jennevret (SWE)	64-70-73-76—283
13	Thomas Ellissalde (FRA)	74-70-71-69—284
	Moritz Lampert (GER)	70-74-70-70—284
	Callum Shinkwin (ENG)	74-68-73-69—284
	Graeme Robertson (SCO)	75-65-72-72—284
17	Niklas Lindström (SWE)	68-74-70-73—285
	Thomas Detry (BEL)	72-70-69-74—285
	Clément Sordet (FRA)	73-68-71-73—285
	Robin Kind (NED)	68-72-72-73—285
	Garrick Porteous (ENG)	66-73-74-72—285
22	Victor Perez (FRA)	71-74-72-69—286
	Lorenzo Scotto (ITA)	70-69-71-76—286
	Thomas Pieters (BEL)	66-71-74-75—286
25	Edouard Amacher (SUI)	73-71-73-70—287
	Gregory Eason (ENG)	71-73-73-70—287
	Richard O'Donovan (IRL)	74-69-73-71—287
	Franck Daux (FRA)	72-70-71-74—287
	Maximilian Rottluff (GER)	68-72-74-73—287
	Adrien Saddier (FRA)	69-69-69-80—287
	Jason Shufflebotham (WAL)	68-69-73-77—287
32	Matthias Boesmans (GER)	68-75-72-73—288
	Tim Gornik (SLO)	71-72-71-74—288
	Scott William Fernandez (ESP)	75-67-73-73—288
	Michael Saunders (ENG)	68-72-71-77—288
	Nathan Kimsey (ENG)	71-69-71-77—288
	Philipp Westermann (GER)	69-70-74-75—288
38	Maximilian Röhrig (GER)	69-76-72-72—289
	Carlos Pigem (ESP)	72-73-70-74—289
	Daan Huizing (NED)	70-71-76-72—289
41	Hugo Rouillon (FRA)	70-73-71-76—290
	Alan Dunbar (IRL)	76-64-71-79—290
43	Pep Angles (ESP)	71-75-72-73—291
	Scott Crichton (SCO)	71-74-71-75—291
	Paul Shields (SCO)	74-69-75-73—291

European Amateur Championship *continued*

43T	Antoni Ferrer (ESP)	68-75-73-75—291
47	Paul Dunne (IRL)	73-72-73-74—292
	Brian Soutar (SCO)	74-69-74-75—292
	Paul Barjon (FRA)	69-72-77-74—292
50	Geoff Lenehan (IRL)	70-74-71-78—293
	Filippo Zuchetti (ITA)	70-73-71-79—293
	Kristofer Ventura (NOR)	76-67-68-82—293
	Benjamin Rusch (SUI)	70-72-74-77—293
54	Jamie Rutherford (ENG)	72-74-72-76—294
	Björn Hellgren (SWE)	70-74-72-78—294
	James White (SCO)	71-71-76-76—294
57	Sebastian Söderberg (SWE)	73-72-72-78—295
58	Assaf Cohen (ISR)	76-70-72-79—297
	Emil Søgaard (DEN)	72-74-71-80—297
	Niclas Carlsson (SWE)	71-70-70-86—297
61	Grégore Schoeb (FRA)	75-75-77-81—298
62	Victor Henum (DEN)	73-79-75-84—301

The following players missed the cut after three rounds:

63 (219)
Tapio Pulkkanen (FIN) 77-72-70
Mathieu Decottignies-Lafon (FRA) 75-73-71
Jacobo Pastor (ESP) 74-74-71
Teremoana Beaucousin (FRA) 74-70-75
Lukas Nemecz (AUT) 73-72-74
Harry Casey (ENG) 72-75-72
Filippo Bergamaschi (ITA) 72-72-75
Joel Stalter (FRA) 71-74-74
Clément Berardo (FRA) 71-72-76
Gary Hurley (IRL) 68-77-74
72 (220)
Jack Hume (IRL) 78-70-72
Matt Wallace (ENG) 76-72-72
Marco Iten (SUI) 76-68-76
Borja Virto (ESP) 74-75-71
Marcel Schneider (GER) 74-72-74
Harry Diamond (FRA) 73-72-75
Marc Dobias (SUI) 73-70-77
Jack Hiluta (ENG) 72-73-75
80 (221)
Dermot McElroy (IRL) 77-71-73
Rory McNamara (IRL) 77-70-74
Ben Loughrey (ENG) 76-74-71
Florian Kolberg (TUR) 76-73-72
João Carlotta (POR) 75-73-73
Emilio Cuartero (ESP) 75-71-75
Reeve Whitson (IRL) 73-74-74
Peter Valasek (SLO) 72-76-73
Nick Grant (IRL) 72-72-77
Mathias Schjoelberg (NOR) 71-74-76
91 (222)
Olafur Björn Loftsson (ISL) 77-72-73
KristjanThor Einarsson (ISL) 76-74-72
Luke Thomas (WAL) 75-73-74
94 (223)
Ashley Chesters (ENG) 76-75-72
Lionel Weber (FRA) 75-73-75
Chris Selfridge (IRL) 74-75-74
Aaron Kearney (IRL) 74-73-76
Fraser McKenna (SCO) 73-74-76
Robin Sciot-Siegrist (FRA) 73-73-77
100 (224)
José Maria Joia (POR) 79-67-78
Tom Berry (ENG) 78-70-76
Dominic Foos (GER) 77-72-75
Liam Johnston (SCO) 76-76-72
Joshua White (ENG) 75-71-78
Mateusz Gradecki (POL) 74-75-75
Rowin Caron (NED) 73-75-76
Richard Bridges (IRL) 72-75-77
108 (225)
Miro Veijalainen (FIN) 76-75-74
Kevin Hesbois (BEL) 75-74-76
Antoine Schwartz (BEL) 75-74-76
Javier Sainz (ESP) 74-74-77
Robbie Van West (NED) 72-77-76
Leo Lespinasse (FRA) 71-75-79
114 (226)
Martin Stanic (SLO) 80-72-74
115 (227)
Manuel Trappel (AUT) 79-73-75
Ediz Kemaloglu (TUR) 76-74-77
Niall Gorey (IRL) 76-72-79
118 (228)
Marcos Pastor (ESP) 78-77-73
Mario Galiano (ESP) 77-73-78
Albert Eckhardt (FIN) 77-73-78
Mads Søgaard (DEN) 76-78-74
122 (229)
Tobias Nemecz (ESP) 76-77-76
Francesco Laporta (ITA) 75-77-77
Christoph Weninger (ESP) 75-75-79
Paul Ferrier (SCO) 74-76-79
126 (230)
Mathias Eggenberger (SUI) 82-73-75
James Fox (IRL) 79-74-77
Daniel Kovari (HUN) 77-75-78
Adam Dunton (SCO) 77-74-79
Hamza Sayin (TUR) 76-77-77
Olivier Rozner (FRA) 72-77-81
132 (231)
Vladimir Ozipov (RUS) 77-75-79
Ondrej Lieser (CZE) 76-77-78
134 (232)
Curtis Griffiths (ENG) 79-75-78
Luca Saccarello (ITA) 78-76-78
David Boote (WAL) 77-80-75
137 (233)
Alex Verschaeren (BEL) 87-71-75
138 (234)
Corrado De Stefani (ITA) 78-73-83
Andrea Bolognesi (ITA) 76-77-81
Joel Girrbach (SUI) 74-74-86
141 (235)
Benedict Staben (GER) 78-75-82
W/D
Kenny Subregis (FRA) 72-78
Jack McDonald (SCO) 81

1986	Anders Haglund (SWE)	Eindhoven GC, Netherlands
1988	David Ecob (AUS)	Falkenstein GC, Germany
1990	Klas Erikson (SWE)	Aalborg GC, Denmark
1991	Jim Payne (ENG)	Hillside GC, England
1992	Massimo Scarpa (ITA)	La Querce GC, Italy
1993	Morten Backhausen (DEN)*	Dalmahoy GC, Scotland

**after play-off with Lee Westwood* (ENG)

1994	Stephen Gallacher (SCO)	Aura GC, Finland
1995	Sergio Garcia (ESP)	El Prat GC, Spain
1997	Didier de Voogt (BEL)	Domaine Imperial, Switzerland
1998	Gregory Havret (FRA)	Celtic Manor Resort, Wales
1999	Paddy Gribben (IRL)	Golf du Medoc, France
2000	Carl Pettersen (SWE)	Syrian GC, Austria
2001	Stephen Browne (IRL)	Odense Eventyr GC, Denmark
2002	Ralph Pelicioli (FRA)	Troia GC, Portugal
2003	Brian McElhinney (IRL)	Nairn GC, Scotland
2004	Matthew Richardson (ENG)	Skovde GC, Sweden
2005	Marius Thorp (NOR)	Antwerp International GC, Belgium
2006	Rory McIlroy (NIR)	Biella GC, Italy

2007 Benjamin Hebert (FRA)*	Sporting Club, Berlin, Germany	2009 Victor Dubuisson (FRA)	Golf de Chantilly, France
after play-off with Joel Sjoholm (SWE)		2010 Lucas Bjerregaard (DEN)	Vanajanlinna, Finland
2008 Stephan Gross (GER)	Esberg GC, Denmark	2011 Manuel Trappel (AUT)*	Halmstad, Sweden
		after play-off with Steven Brown (ENG)	

111th United States Amateur Championship *Cherry Hills CC, Colorado* [7500–72]

(US unless stated)

Fox leaves it late to win US Amateur at Cherry Hills

Both finalists in the US Amateur Championship at Cherry Hills Golf Club in Colorado had to survive a 17-man play-off in the stroke-play qualifiying just to make it into the 64-man match-play section of the Championship.

In the end it was 63rd seeded Steven Fox from Tennessee who took the title beating 60th seed Michael Weaver from Fresno in California at the first extra hole – the first time the final had gone beyond the 36th since Nick Flanagan won, also at the 37th, in 2003.

Fox is the first golfer since Italian Edoardo Molinari in 2005 to win the title after having been involved in a play-off. That year Molinari was seeded 55th, Nick Flanagan was also 55th in 2003 and David Gossett was seeded 57th when he won in 1999.

Perhaps the key to the success of University of Tennessee–Chattanooga student Fox was not just the bit of luck he experienced on the final regulation hole but also his decision to replace his tiring father on the bag for the second 18-holes. The man he chose was his University's assistant golf coach Englishman Ben Rickett whom he knew well.

Fox's 53-year-old father Alan who was suffering from blisters after carrying the bag for his son for four stroke-play rounds and 108 match play holes, was only too ready to step aside. When the switch was made Fox was two down after the morning session and Weaver remained favourite to win through the second 18.

Although Fox was more meticulous in the afternoon discussing each shot carefully with his new caddie and making some headway, he still faced defeat when Weaver got back to two up at the 34th with a 12 foot birdie. Fox holed a clutch 10 foot birdie putt to win the 35th.and avoid a 2 and 1 defeat and then he had his slice of luck when Weaver missed a five foot putt to win the title on the 36th.

The pair returned to the par 4 first hole and Weaver's chance of victory disappeared when he hit a crooked tee shot and took three to reach the green. Fox, on in two, grabbed his chance holing an 18-foot downhill birdie putt for a winning 3 and the title.

Twenty-one year-old Fox, who on the way to the final beat World No 1 Chris Williams, said simply: "This is awesome. I just kept fighting. My goal in my first US Amateur Championship appearance was just to make it through to the match-play section." His win earned him exemption into the 2013 US Open, The Open in Britain and almost certainly The Masters.

Stroke Play Qualifying:

Bobby Wyatt (Mobile, AL)	64-68—132
Jeff Osberg (Philadelphia, PA)	69-65—134
Cheng-Tsung Pan (TPE)	69-65—134
Sebastian Vazquez (MEX)	65-70—135
Zac Blair (Ogden, UT)	65-71—136
Brandon Hagy (Westlake Village, CA)	65-72—137
Curtis Thompson (Coral Springs, FL)	70-68—138
Devin Miertschin (El Paso, TX)	68-70—138
Oliver Goss (AUS)	72-66—138
Chris Williams (Moscow, ID)	65-73—138
Richard Lamb (South Bend, IN)	68-70—138
Jordan Spieth (Dallas, TX)	69-69—138
Nicholas Reach (Moscow, PA)	70-69—139
Talor Gooch (Midwest City, OK)	68-71—139
Zack Munroe (Charlotte, NC)	70-69—139
Justin Thomas (Goshen, KY)	65-74—139
Max Homa (Valencia, CA)	65-74—139
Jonathan De Los Reyes (Antioch, CA)	70-69—139
Bryson Dechambeau (Clovis, CA)	67-73—140
Ricardo Gouveia (POR)	69-71—140
Mackenzie Hughes (CAN)	71-69—140
Michael Hebert (Alpharetta, GA)	71-69—140
Adam Stephenson (Greenville, NC)	70-70—140
Brett Drewitt (AUS)	69-71—140
Michael Kim (Del Mar, CA)	72-69—141
Justin Shin (CAN)	72-69—141
Paul Misko (Thousand Oaks, CA)	70-71—141
Patrick Rodgers (Avon, IN)	73-68—141
Adam Schenk (Vincennes, IN)	70-71—141
Gavin Green (MAS)	72-69—141
Douglas Hanzel (Savannah, GA)	73-68—141
Matthew Stieger (AUS)	71-70—141
Jade Scott (Daingerfield, TX)	67-74—141
Andrew Biggadike (Ridgewood, NJ)	68-73—141
Derek Ernst (Clovis, CA)	67-74—141
Oliver Schniederjans (Powder Springs, GA)	74-67—141
Justin Spray (Gold Canyon, AZ)	69-72—141
Kenny Cook (Noblesville, IN)	71-70—141
Brad Valois (Warwick, RI)	71-71—142

US Amateur Championship *continued*

Bobby Leopold (Cranston, RI)	72-70—142
Michael Miller (Brewster, NY)	74-68—142
Carlos Ortiz (MEX)	75-67—142
Todd Sinnott (AUS)	73-69—142
Albin Choi (CAN)	74-68—142
Eric Frazzetta (Long Beach, CA)	74-68—142
Andrew Presley (Fort Worth, TX)	67-75—142
Todd White (Spartanburg, SC)	70-72—142
Corey Conners (CAN)	67-75—142
Barry Dyche (Charlotte, NC)	68-74—142
Michael Schoolcraft (Englewood, CO)	69-73—142
Peter Williamson (Hanover, NH)	76-67—143
T J Mitchell (Albany, GA)	68-75—143
Denny McCarthy (Rockville, MD)	72-71—143
Evan Bowser (Dearborn, MI)	76-67—143
Michael Weaver (Fresno, CA)	73-70—143
Thomas Pieters (BEL)	73-70—143
Steven Fox (Hendersonville, TN)	72-71—143
Taylor Hancock (Clearwater, FL)	77-66—143
Patrick Newcomb (Benton, KY)	74-69—143
Eli Cole (Los Angeles, CA)	71-72—143
Drew Evans (Dallas, TX)	71-72—143
Devon Purser (Clearfield, UT)	69-74—143
Edouard Espana (FRA)	68-75—143
Patrick Duncan Jr (Rancho Santa Fe, CA)	73-70—143

First Round:
Bobby Wyatt beat Taylor Hancock 4 and 2
Matthew Stieger (AUS) beat Jade Scott 7 and 5
Justin Thomas beat Barry Dyche 3 and 1
Max Homa beat Corey Conners (CAN) 5 and 4
Devin Miertschin beat Drew Evans 3 and 2
Bobby Leopold beat Michael Kim at 20th
Oliver Goss (AUS) beat Eli Cole 3 and 1
Michael Miller beat Brett Drewitt (AUS) at 19th
Devon Purser beat Sebastian Vazquez (MEX) 4 and 3
Adam Schenk beat Oliver Schniederjans 2 and 1
Patrick Duncan Jr beat Nicholas Reach 1 up
Ricardo Gouveia (POR) beat Eric Frazzetta 4 and 3
Michael Weaver beat Zac Blair 2 and 1
Patrick Rodgers beat Justin Spray 3 and 2
Thomas Pieters (BEL) beat Jordan Spieth 1 up
Albin Choi (CAN) beat Mackenzie Hughes (CAN) 2 and 1
Steven Fox beat Jeff Osberg 3 and 2
Douglas Hanzel beat Andrew Biggadike 3 and 2
Zack Munroe beat Michael Schoolcraft at 19th
Todd White beat Jonathan De Los Reyes 3 and 1
Edouard Espana (FRA) beat Curtis Thompson 1 up
Justin Shin (CAN) beat Brad Valois 1 up
Chris Williams beat Peter Williamson 3 and 2
Adam Stephenson beat Carlos Ortiz (MEX) 1 up
Cheng-Tsung Pan (TPE) beat Evan Bowser 4 and 3
Gavin Green (MAS) beat Derek Ernst 3 and 1
Talor Gooch beat T J Mitchell 5 and 3
Andrew Presley beat Bryson Dechambeau at 19th
Brandon Hagy beat Denny McCarthy at 19th
Paul Misko beat Kenny Cook at 20th
Patrick Newcomb beat Richard Lamb 2 and 1
Michael Hebert beat Todd Sinnott (AUS) 6 and 4

Second Round:
Bobby Wyatt, beat Matthew Stieger 2 up
Justin Thomas beat Max Homa 2 and 1
Bobby Leopold beat Devin Miertschin 4 and 3
Oliver Goss beat Michael Miller at 20th
Devon Purser beat Adam Schenk at 21st
Ricardo Gouveia beat Patrick Duncan Jr 3 and 2
Michael Weaver beat Patrick Rodgers 2 up
Albin Choi beat Thomas Pieters 4 and 3
Steven Fox beat Douglas Hanzel 1 up
Zack Munroe beat Todd White 2 and 1
Edouard Espana beat Justin Shin 1 up
Chris Williams beat Adam Stephenson 5 and 3
Cheng-Tsung Pan beat Gavin Green 3 and 1
Andrew Presley beat Talor Gooch 1 up
Brandon Hagy beat Paul Misko 5 and 4
Patrick Newcomb beat Michael Hebert at 19th

Third Round:
Justin Thomas beat Bobby Wyatt 1 up
Oliver Goss beat Bobby Leopold 2 and 1
Ricardo Gouveia beat Devon Purser 6 and 4
Michael Weaver beat Albin Choi at 19th
Steven Fox beat Zack Munroe 2 up
Chris Williams beat Edouard Espana 3 and 2
Cheng-Tsung Pan beat Andrew Presley 2 up
Brandon Hagy beat Patrick Newcomb 3 and 2

Quarter Finals:
Justin Thomas beat Oliver Goss 2 up
Michael Weaver beat Ricardo Gouveia 4 and 3
Steven Fox beat Chris Williams 4 and 2
Brandon Hagy beat Cheng-Tsung Pan 4 and 3

Semi-Finals:
Michael Weaver, beat Justin Thomas 3 and 2
Steven Fox beat Brandon Hagy 2 up

Final: Steven Fox (Hendersonville, TN) beat Michael Weaver (Fresno, CA) at 37th

1895	CB Macdonald beat C Sands	12 & 11	Newport GC, RI	*Entrants* 32
1896	HJ Whigham beat JG Thorp	8 & 7	Shinnnecock Hills GC, NY	58
1897	HJ Whigham beat WR Betts	8 & 6	Chicago GC, IL	58
1898	FS Douglas beat WB Smith	5 & 3	Morris County GC, NJ	120
1899	HM Harriman beat FS Douglas	3 & 2	Onwentsia Club, IL	112
1900	WJ Travis beat FS Douglas	2 up	Garden City, GC NY	120
1901	WJ Travis beat WE Egan	5 & 4	CC of Atlantic City, NJ	142
1902	LN James beat EM Byers	4 & 2	Glenview Club, IL	157
1903	WJ Travis beat EM Byers	5 & 4	Nassau CC, NY	140
1904	HC Egan beat F Herreshof	8 & 6	Baltusrol GC, NJ	142

1905	HC Egan beat DE Sawyer	6 & 5	Chicago GC, IL	146
1906	EM Byers beat GS Lyon	2 up	Englewood GC, NJ	141
1907	JD Travers beat A Graham	6 & 5	Euclid Club, OH	118
1908	JD Travers beat MH Behr	8 & 7	Garden City GC, NY	145
1909	RA Gardner beat HC Egan	4 & 3	Chicago GC, IL	120
1910	WC Fownes Jr beat WK Wood	4 & 3	The Country Club, Brookline, MA	217
1911	HH Hilton (ENG) beat F Herreshof	1 up	Apawamis Club, Rye, NY	186
1912	JD Travers beat C Evans Jr	7 & 6	Chicago GC, IL	86
1913	JD Travers beat JG Anderson	5 & 4	Garden City, NY	149
1914	F Ouimet beat JD Travers	6 & 5	Ekwanok CC, VT	115
1915	RA Gardner beat JG Anderson	5 & 4	CC of Detroit, MI	152
1916	C Evans Jr beat RA Gardner	4 & 3	Merion Cricket Club (East), PA	163
1917–18 Not played				
1919	SD Herron beat RT Jones Jr	5 & 4	Oakmont CC, PA	150
1920	C Evans Jr beat F Ouimet	7 & 6	Engineers CC, NY	235
1921	JP Guildford beat RA Gardner	7 & 6	St Louis CC, MO	159
1922	JW Sweetser beat C Evans Jr	3 & 2	The Country Club, Brookline, MA	161
1923	MR Marston beat JW Sweetser	1 up	Flossmoor CC, IL	143
1924	RT Jones Jr beat G Von Elm	9 & 8	Merion Cricket Club (East), PA	142
1925	RT Jones Jr beat W Gunn	8 & 7	Oakmont CC, PA	141
1926	G Von Elm beat RT Jones Jr	2 & 1	Baltusrol CC (Lower), NJ	157
1927	RT Jones Jr beat C Evans Jr	8 & 7	Minikahda Club, MN	174
1928	RT Jones Jr beat TP Perkins	10 & 9	Brae Burn CC, MA	158
1929	HR Johnston beat OF Willing	4 & 3	Del Monte G&CC, CA	162
1930	RT Jones Jr beat EV Homans	8 & 7	Merion Cricket Club (East), PA	175
1931	F Ouimet beat J Westland	6 & 5	Beverly CC, IL	583
1932	CR Somerville beat J Goodman	2 & 1	Five Farms GC (East), MD	600
1933	GT Dunlap Jr beat MR Marston	6 & 5	Kenwood CC, OH	601
1934	W Lawson Little Jr beat D Goldman	8 & 7	The Country Club, Brookline, MA	758
1935	W Lawson Little Jr beat W Emery	4 & 2	The Country Club, Cleveland, OH	945
1936	JW Fischer beat J McLean	37 holes	Garden City GC, NY	1,118
1937	J Goodman beat RE Billows	2 up	Alderwood CC, OR	619
1938	WP Turnesa beat BP Abbott	8 & 7	Oakmont CC, PA	871
1939	MH Ward beat RE Billows	7 & 5	North Shore CC, IL	826
1940	RD Chapman beat WB McCullough	11 & 9	Winged Foot GC (West), NY	755
1941	MH Ward beat BP Abbott	4 & 3	Omaha Field Club, NE	637
1942–45 Not played				
1946	SE Bishop beat S Quick	1 up	Baltusrol CC (Lower), NJ	899
1947	RH Riegel beat JW Dawson	2 & 1	Del Monte G&CC, CA	1,048
1948	WP Turnesa beat RE Billows	2 & 1	Memphis CC, TN	1,220
1949	CR Coe beat R King	11 & 10	Oak Hill CC (East), NY	1,060
1950	S Urzetta beat FR Stranahan	1 up	Minneapolis GC, MN	1,025
1951	WJ Maxwell beat J Gagliardi	4 & 3	Saucon Valley GC (Old), PA	1,416
1952	J Westland beat A Mengert	3 & 2	Seattle GC, WA	1,029
1953	G Littler beat D Morey	1 up	Oklahoma City GC, OK	1,284
1954	A Palmer beat R Sweeney	1 up	CC Of Detroit, MI	1,278
1955	E Harvie Ward beat W Hyndman	9 & 8	CC of Virginia (James River Course), VA	1,493
1956	E Harvie Ward beat C Kocsis	5 & 4	Knollwood Club, IL	1,600
1957	H Robbins beat FM Taylor	5 & 4	The Country Club (Anniversary Course), Brookline, MA	1,578
1958	CR Coe beat TD Aaron	5 & 4	The Olympic Club (Lake Course), CA	1,472
1959	JW Nicklaus beat CR Coe	1 up	Broadmoor GC (East), CO	1,696
1960	DR Beman beat RW Gardner	6 & 4	St Louis CC, MO	1,737
1961	JW Nicklaus beat HD Wysong	8 & 6	Pebble Beach GC, CA	1,995
1962	LE Harris Jr beat D Gray	1 up	Pinehurst CC (No.2 Course), NC	2,044
1963	DR Beman beat RH Sikes	2 & 1	Wakonda Club, IA	1,768
1964	WC Campbell beat EM Tutweiler	1 up	Canterbury GC, OH	1,562

Changed to stroke play

1965	Robert J Murphy Jr	291	Southern Hill CC, OK	1.476
1966	Gary Cowan (CAN)*	285	Merion GC (East), PA	1,902
**Cowan beat Deane Beman 75-76 in 18-hole play-off*				
1967	RB Dickson	285	Broadmoor GC (West), CO	1,784
1968	B Fleisher	284	Scioto GC, OH	2,057
1969	S Melnyk	286	Oakmont CC, PA	2,142
1970	L Wadkins*	279	Waverley GC, OR	1,853
1971	G Cowan (CAN)	280	Wilmington CC (South), DE	2,327
1972	Marvin Giles III	285	Charlotte CC, NC	2,295

Reverted to match play

1973	C Stadler beat D Strawn	6 & 5	Inverness Club OH	2,110
1974	J Pate beat J Grace	2 & 1	Ridgewood CC, NJ	2,420

US Amateur Championship *continued*

1975	F Ridley beat K Fergus	2 up	CC of Virginia (James River Course), VA	2,528
1976	B Sander beat CP Moore	8 & 6	Bel Air CC, CA	2,681
1977	J Fought beat D Fischesser	9 & 8	Aronimink GC, PA	2,950
1978	J Cook beat S Hoch	5 & 4	Plainfield GC, NJ	3,035
1979	M O'Meara beat J Cook	8 & 7	Canterbury GC, OH	3,916
1980	H Sutton beat B Lewis	9 & 8	CC of North Carolina, NC	4,008
1981	N Crosby beat B Lindley	1 up	The Olympic Club (Lake Course), CA	3,525
1982	J Sigel beat D Tolley	8 & 7	The Country Club, Brookline, MA	3,685
1983	J Sigel beat C Perry	8 & 7	North Shore CC, IL	3,553
1984	S Verplank beat S Randolph	4 & 3	Oak Tree GC, OK	3,679
1985	S Randolph beat P Persons	1 up	Montclair GC, NJ	3,816
1986	S Alexander beat C Kite	5 & 3	Shoal Creek GC, AL	4,069
1987	W Mayfair beat E Rebmann	4 & 3	Jupiter Hills Club (Hills Course), FL	4,085
1988	E Meeks beat D Yates	7 & 6	Hot Springs CC (Cascades Course), VA	4,320
1989	C Patton beat D Green	3 & 1	Merion GC (East), PA	4,603
1990	P Mickelson beat M Zerman	5 & 4	Cherry Hills CC, CO	4,763
1991	M Voges beat M Zerman	7 & 6	The Honors Course, TN	4,985
1992	J Leonard beat T Scherrer	8 & 7	Muirfield Village GC, OH	5,758
1993	J Harris beat D Ellis	5 & 3	Champions GC (Cypress Creek Course), TX	5,614
1994	T Woods beat T Kuehne	2 up	TPC at Sawgrass (Stadium Course), FL	5,128
1995	T Woods beat G Marucci	2 up	Newport CC, RI	5,248
1996	T Woods beat S Scott	38 holes	Pumpkin Ridge GC, OR	5,538
1997	M Kuchar beat J Kribel	2 & 1	Cog Hill G&CC (No.4 Course), IL	6,666
1998	H Kuehne beat T McKnight	2 and 1	Oak Hill CC (East), NY	6,627
1999	D Gossett beat Sung Yoon Kim	9 and 8	Pebble Beach GC, CA	7,920
2000	J Quinney beat J Driscoll	39 holes	Baltusrol GC, NJ	7,124
2001	B Dickerson beat R Hamilton	1 up	Eastlake GC, GA	7,762
2002	R Barnes beat H Mahon	2 and 1	Oakland Hills CC (South Course), MI	7,597
2003	N Flanagan (AUS) beat C Wittenberg	37 holes	Oakmont CC, PA	7,541
2004	R Moore beat L List	2 up	Winged Foot GC (West Course), NY	7,356
2005	E Molinari (ITA) beat D Dougherty	4 and 3	Merion GC (East Course), PA	7,320
2006	R Ramsay (SCO) beat J Kelly	4 and 2	Hazeltine National GC, MN	7,182
2007	C Knost beat M Thompson	2 and 1	The Olympic Club (Lake Course), CA	7,398
2008	D Lee (NZL) beat D Kittleson	5 and 4	Pinehurst Resort and CC, NC	7,298
2009	B An (KOR) beat B Martin	7 and 5	Southern Hills CC, Tulsa, OK	9,086
2010	P Uihlein beat D Chung	4 and 3	Chambers Bay, WA	6,485
2011	K Kraft beat P Cantlay	2 holes	Erin Hills CC, WI	6,265

NCAA Championships (Men) *Riviera CC, Pacific Palisades, California*

Texas win after Fratelli's dramatic last green triumph

At every important golf match there is someone at the end of the day on whose shoulders rests the difference between victory and defeat. At the 2012 NCAA Championship played at the Riveria Country Club in Pacific Palisades it was a South African who found himself in that position

With Alabama and Texas having each won two points it was Longhorn Dylan Fratelli who grabbed the moment rolling in a 30 foot winning putt on the final green to give him victory over Cory Whitsett and Texas their first national golf title success since 1972.

Alabama were top seeded going into the match play section of the Championship having edged out UCLA by just two shots and third place Texas by 10 in the stroke play qualifying. In the quarter finals Alabama beat Kent State to book a semi-final date with California whom they beat 3–2. So their final match was against Texas, who had white-washed Washington State 5-0 in the quarter-finals and scored a 3-2 semi-final victory over Oregan, who had surprised UCLA in the previous round.

In the final, Alabama made the early running Bobby Wyatt was one down with two play but eagled the 17th and birdied the last to edge out Texas' Tony Hakula and Hunter Hamrick, six up after nine, easily beat Julio Vegas 6 and 5 but Texas golfer Jordan Spieth beat Justin Thomas 3 and 2 and Cody Gribble, never behind, earned another point for the Longhorns against Scott Strohmeyer. So 2–2 and the result depended on the match between Whitsett and Fratelli.

Whitsett was one down with two to play against his South African opponent, joint winner in 2012 of the Byron Nelson award for excellence not only in the classroom and on the golf course but for outstanding citizenship as well, but birdied the 17th to level matters. The result depended on who could win the last and it was Fratelli who, after his opponent had bogeyed, rolled in the winning putt in dramatic fashion.

Thomas Pieters from Illinois with rounds of 69, 68 and 71 won the individual competition by three shots from Julien Brun (TCU) and Tyler McCumber (Florida) but the week belonged to Texas.

Stroke Play Championship – Team event:

1	Alabama	285-287-287—859
2	UCLA	289-287-285—861
3	Texas	290-295-284—869
4	California	295-289-287—871
	San Diego State	292-295-284—871

6 Washington 872; 7 Oregon 873; 8 Kent State, Florida State 875; 10 Liberty 876; 11 Oklahoma 877; 12 North Florida, Florida 878; 14 Texas A&M 879; 15 Auburn, Southern California 880; 17 Georgia 881; 18 Chattanooga 884; 19 Stanford, UCF 885, 21 Illinois 887; 22 Iowa, Virginia 888; 24 Virginia Tech 890; 25 Lamar 892; 26 East Carolina 895; 27 TCU 897; 28 Memphis 901; 29 UAB 902; 30 Tulsa 918

Winning team: Alabama 859 – Cory Whitsett 73-68-71—212; Justin Thomas 70-70-73—213; Hunter Hamrick 73-73-70—216; Bobby Wyatt 71-77-73—221; Scott Strohmeyer 71-76-75—221

Individual Championship:

1	Thomas Pieters (Illinois)	69-68-71—208
2	Julien Brun (TCU)	72-72-67—211
	Tyler McCumber (Florida)	68-71-72—211
	Patrick Cantlay (UCLA)	74-72-66—212
	Corey Conners (Kent State)	68-75-69—212
	Cory Whitsett (Alabama)	73-68-71—212
7	Blayne Barber (Auburn)	69-74-70—213
	Justin Thomas (Alabama)	70-70-73—213
9	Max Homa (California)	76-70-68—214
	Will Kropp (Oklahoma)	69-75-70—214
	Keith Mitchell (Georgia)	73-72-69—214
	Patrick Rodgers (Stanford)	69-72-73—214
13	Anton Arboleda (UCLA)	67-72-76—215
	Dominic Bozzelli (Auburn)	69-75-71—215
	Greg Eason (UCF)	71-72-72—215
	Pedro Figueiredo (UCLA)	74-72-69—215
	Steve Lim (South California)	74-72-69—215
	J J Spaun (San Diego State)	72-74-69—215
	Joseph Winslow (Iowa)	69-75-71—215
	Eugene Wong (Oregon)	72-74-69—215
21	Abraham Ancer (Oklahoma)	70-72-74—216
	Daniel Berger (Florida State)	75-69-72—216
	Dylan Frittelli (Texas)	72-72-72—216
	Hunter Hamrick (Alabama)	73-73-70—216
	Daniel Miernicki (Oregon)	73-70-73—216
	Kevin Phelan (North Florida)	72-71-73—216
	Julio Vegas (Texas)	72-73-71—216
	Chris Williams (Washington)	75-71-70—216
29	Tom Berry (San Diego State)	73-73-71—217
	M J Daffue (Lamar)	74-71-72—217
	Tyler Dunlap (Texas A&M)	72-74-71—217
	Brooks Koepka (Florida State)	71-72-74—217
	Chase Marinell (Liberty)	71-70-76—217
	Nate McCoy (Iowa State)	72-73-72—217
	Cheng-Tsung Pan (Washington)	73-72-72—217
	Andrew Vijarro (Oregon)	70-75-72—217
37	Josh Anderson (Pepperdine)	72-76-70—218
	Albin Choi (North Carolina State)	71-77-70—218
	Ricardo Gouveia (UCF)	72-73-73—218
37T	Kyle Kmiecik (Kent State)	74-70-74—218
	T J Mitchell (Georgia)	71-74-73—218
	Geoff Shaw (Texas A&M	76-72-70—218
	Trevor Simsby (Washington)	76-70-72—218
	Bruce Woodall (Virginia)	71-75-72—218
45	Kevin Aylwin (North Florida)	74-71-74—219
	Luke Guthrie (Illinois)	73-72-74—219
	Brandon Hagy (California)	71-73-75—219
	Stephan Jaeger (Chattanooga)	76-73-70—219
	Scott Vincent (Virginia Tech)	73-75-71—219
50	Mackenzie Hughes (Kent State)	76-72-72—220
	Alex Kang (San Diego State)	72-73-75—220
	Robert Karlsson (Liberty)	75-72-73—220
	Johannes Veerman (Texas A&M)	74-74-72—220
54	Steven Fox (Chattanooga)	76-75-70—221
	Charlie Hughes (Washington)	72-73-76—221
	Alex Kim (UCLA)	76-71-74—221
	Jordan Spieth (Texas)	73-79-69—221
	Martin Trainer (South California)	73-74-74—221
	Chris Worrell (Tulsa)	74-75-72—221
	Bobby Wyatt (Alabama)	71-77-73—221
61	Zach Edmondson (East Carolina)	75-74-73—222
	Michael Furci (Florida)	72-77-73—222
	Pace Johnson (California)	72-78-72—222
	Michael Kim (California)	76-73-73—222
	Michael Schoolcraft (Oklahoma)	76-70-76—222
	Chase Seiffert (Florida State)	73-73-76—222
	Scott Strohmeyer (Alabama)	71-76-75—222
	T J Vogel (Florida)	72-74-76—222
69	Jonathan Fly (Memphis)	71-71-81—223
	Matt Hoffenberg (San Diego State)	75-77-71—223
	Jeffrey Kang (South California)	75-71-77—223
	Ben Kohles (Virginia)	78-74-71—223
	M J Maguire (North Florida)	71-78-74—223

NCAA Championships *continued*

69T	Chris Robb (Chattanooga	76-72-75—223
	Harold Varner (East Carolina)	71-73-79—223
	Andrew Yun (Stanford)	74-79-70—223
77	Trevor Cone (Virginia Tech)	76-76-72—224
	Paul Dunne (UAB)	75-74-75—224
	Mathieu Fenasse (Liberty)	75-75-74—224
	Xavier Feyaerts (Lamar)	75-78-71—224
	Cody Gribble (Texas)	73-79-72—224
	Vaita Guillaume (Campbell)	75-77-72—224
	Steven Kearney (Stanford)	74-77-73—224
	Barrett Kelpin (Iowa)	75-72-77—224
	Niklas Lindstrom (Liberty)	83-71-70—224
	Denny McCarthy (Virginia)	79-70-75—224
	Sam Smith (South California)	79-69-76—224
	Thomas Sutton (UAB)	79-74-71—224
89	Chris Brant (Iowa)	75-77-73—225
	Bryce Chalkley (Virginia Tech)	73-77-75—225
	Jonathan De Los Reyes (St Mary's CA)	72-76-77—225
	Toni Hakula (Texas)	80-71-74—225
	Taylor Pendrith (Kent State)	75-74-76—225
	Joey Petronio (North Florida)	73-76-76—225
	Nick Reach (Georgia)	74-77-74—225
	Blake Redmond (Virginia Tech)	80-74-71—225
	Joel Stalter (California)	78-73-74—225
	Adam Stephenson (East Carolina)	72-75-78—225
99	Davis Bunn (Chattanooga)	76-75-75—226
	Brian Carter (Georgia)	77-77-72—226
	Wesley Graham (Florida State)	77-76-73—226
	Matt Mabrey (Tulsa)	76-75-75—226
	Will McCurdy (Auburn)	74-76-76—226
	Jordan Russell (Texas A&M)	76-78-72—226
105	Jack Belote (Memphis)	79-76-72—227
	Colin Featherstone (San Diego State)	79-75-73—227
	Joey Garber (Georgia)	77-75-75—227
	Steven Ihm (Iowa)	72-77-78—227
	Luke Jerling (Lamar)	74-80-73—227
	Jose Joia (UCF)	72-78-77—227
	Steve Lee (Memphis)	76-76-75—227
	Sam Love (UAB)	74-75-78—227
	Ian Vandersee (Iowa)	74-75-78—227
114	Eric Banks (Florida)	76-74-78—228
114T	Johan de Beer (TCU)	75-83-70—228
	Liam Johnston (Chattanooga)	71-80-77—228
	Ben Rusch (Virginia)	78-78-72—228
	Brad Schneider (UCF)	75-76-77—228
	Greg Yates (Texas A&M)	79-76-73—228
120	Patrick Grimes (Stanford)	76-76-77—229
	Riley Pumphrey (Oklahoma)	78-75-76—229
	Pontus Widegren (UCLA)	74-78-77—229
123	Brian Campbell (Illinois)	77-73-80—230
	Niclas Carlsson (Auburn)	76-77-77—230
	Sean Dale (North Florida)	77-73-80—230
	Mason Jacobs (Illinois)	76-76-78—230
	Daniel Jennevret (TCU)	77-72-81—230
	Cameron Wilson (Stanford)	79-77-74—230
	Jonathan Woo (Oregon)	76-75-79—230
130	Philip Chian (Long Beach State)	74-77-80—231
	Kevin Hesbois (Lamar)	76-75-80—231
	Michael Johnson (Auburn)	81-74-76—231
	Wilson McDonald (UAB)	73-80-78—231
	J D Tomlinson (Florida)	76-82-73—231
135	Ryan Eibner (East Carolina)	77-82-73—232
	Michael Gellerman (Oklahoma)	74-75-83—232
	Ian McConnell (Liberty)	74-80-78—232
	Will Pearson (Memphis)	79-79-74—232
	Kyle Wilshire (UCF)	80-77-75—232
140	John Young Kim (Tulsa)	78-77-78—233
	Kevin Miller (Kent State)	79-77-77—233
	Anthony Paolucci (Southern California)	76-80-77—233
	Ji Soo Park (Virginia)	81-73-79—233
144	Ty Chambers (Washington)	82-76-76—234
	Hunter Hawkins (UAB)	75-80-79—234
	Ian Phillips (TCU)	75-77-82—234
	Robbie Ziegler (Oregon)	76-84-74—234
148	Tor-Erik Knudson (Lamar)	82-79-74—235
	Grant Milner (Memphis)	73-83-79—235
150	Joaquin Lolas (Florida State)	71-84-81—236
	David Watkins (East Carolina)	82-81-73—236
152	Thomas Mantovanini (TCU)	78-78-81—237
153	Mark Mumford (Tulsa)	78-81-80—239
154	Colton Staggs (Tulsa)	82-80-81—243
155	Alex Burge (Illinois)	81-87-80—248
	Mikey Moyers (Virginia)	77 WW

Match Play Championship:

Quarter-finals: Alabama 3, Kent State 1
California 3, San Diego State 2
Oregon 3, UCLA 2
Texas 4, Washington 0

Semi-finals: Alabama 3, California 2
Texas 3, Oregon 2

Final: Texas 3, Alabama 2

Toni Hakula lost to Bobby Wyatt 1 up
Dylan Frittelli beat Cory Whitsett 1 up
Cody Gribble beat Scott Strohmeyer 2 and 1
Jordan Spieth beat Justin Thomas 3 and 2
Julio Vegas lost to Hunter Hamrick 6 and 5

Callaway Handicapping

It frequently occurs in social competitions such as office or business association outings that many of the competitors do not have official handicaps. In such cases the best solution is to use the Callaway handicapping system, so called after the name of its inventor, as it is simple to use yet has proved equitable.

Competitors complete their round marking in their gross figures at every hole and their handicaps are awarded and deducted at the end of the 18 holes using the following table:

Competitor's Gross Score	*Handicap Deduction*
par or less	none
one over par – 75	½ worst hole
76–80	worst hole
81–85	worst hole plus ½ next worse
86–90	two worst holes
91–95	two worst holes plus ½ next
96–100	three worst holes
101–105	three worst holes plus ½ next
106–110	four worst holes
111–115	four worst holes plus ½ next
116–120	five worst holes
121–125	five worst holes plus ½ next
126–130	six worst holes

Note 1: Worst hole equals highest score at any hole regardless of the par of the hole except that the maximum score allowed for any one hole is twice the par of the hole.

Note 2: The 17th and 18th holes are not allowed to be deducted.

Example: Competitor scores 104. From the table he should deduct as his handicap the total of his three worst (i.e. highest) individual hole scores plus half of his fourth worst hole. If he scored one 9, one 8 and several 7's he would therefore deduct a total of 27½ from his gross score of 104 to give a net score of 76½.

National Championships 2012

For past winners see earlier editions of *The R&A Golfer's Handbook*

Players are from the host nation unless stated

Africa

Egyptian Amateur Open Championship *The Allegria GC*

1	Thomas Faucher	71-67-69—207
2	Soliman El Asser	78-72-75—225
3	Abdelmonen El Shafei	83-74-70—227

Kenya Stroke Play Championship *Karen G&CC*

1	Justus Madoya	73-72-72-73—290
2	Matthew Ormondi	72-74-73-72—291
3	Nelson Simwa	70-73-77-75—295

Sanlam South African Amateur Championship (inaugurated 1892)

Mowbray Feb 26–Mar 2

Semi-finals: Brian Soutar (SCO) beat Shaun Smith at 19th.
Brandon Stone beat Jamie Clare (ENG) at 19th

Final: Brian Soutar (SCO) beat Brendan Stone 2 and 1

South African Amateur Stroke Play Championship (inaugurated 1969)

Glendower Feb 7–10

1	Haydn Porteous	68-71-69-72—280
2	Andrea Bolognesi (ITA)	69-70-68-74—281
3	Drikus Bruyns	72-72-70-68—282
	Filippo Bergamaschi (ITA)	73-69-69-71—282

South African Mid-Amateur Stroke Play Championship *Vaal de Grace*

1	Neil Homann (Randpark)	70-71-70-70—281
2	Graeme Watson (Serengeti)	73-74-66-71—284
3	Tyrol Auret (Ebotse)	74-68-72-71—285

South African Senior Championship *Wingate Park CC and Woodmill CC*

1	Mellette Hendrikse (Akasia CC)	71-70-74—215
2	Lawrence Franklin (Houghton GC)	70-74-75—219
3	Jock N Wellington (Kyaiami GC)	77=70-74—221

Zimbabwe Amateur Championship *Hillside GC*

1	Ray Badenhorst	72-75-74-72—293
2	Barry Painting	71-70-77-79—297
3	Benjamin Follett-Smith	71-76-75-83—305

Americas

Argentine Amateur Championship *Estancias GC*

Semi-finals: Joshua Munn (NZL) beat Garrett Rank (CAN) 2 and 1
Antoni Ferrer Mercant (ESP) beat Drikus Bruyns (RSA) 2 and 1

Final: Antoni Ferrer Mercant beat Joshua Munn 5 and 3

Leading qualifier: Garrett Rank (CAN) 69-69—138

29th United Insurance Barbados Open *Sandy Lane GC*

1	James Johnson	70-69-74—213
2	Judd Crozier	78-76-75—229
3	Marcus Clarke	80-72-79—231

Canadian Amateur Championship (inaugurated 1895) *Camelot G&CC, Cumberland, Ontario*

1	Mackenzie Hughes	72-67-65-72—276
2	Brian Churchill-Smith	67-71-71-68—277
	Chris Hemmerich	69-69-67-72—277

Canadian Men's Senior Championship *Le Griffon des Sources, Mirabel, Quebec*

1	Chip Lutz (USA)	75-71-73-68—287
2	Ian Harris (USA)	72-72-73-75—292
3	Grahame Cooke	78-76-73-68—295

Caribbean Amateur Championship (Hoerman Cup) *Royal St Kitts GC, St Kitts*

1	Paul Michael (OECS*)	73-73-69-75—290
2	George Riley (DOM)	69-72-72-78—291
3	Robert Calvesbert (PUR)	73-70-75-74—292

OECS (Organisation of Eastern Caribbean States) won the team event (Adrian Norford, Omary James, Anand Harridyal, Paul Michael and Raymond Percival)

Colombian Championship *El Rincon*

1	Marcelo Rozo	70-67-73—210
2	Santiago Mejia	74-72-76—222
3	Santiago Tobon	74-74-75—223

Mexican Amateur Championship *Guadalajara CC*

1	Sebastian Vazquez	67-71-70-69—277
2	Adam Svensson (CAN)	73-70-73-65—281
3	Luis Rogelio Medina	70-77-69-68—284
	Marcelo Rozo Rengifo (COL)	74-60-70-70—284

Team competition: 1 Mexico (Sebastian Vazquez and Carlos Ortiz) 419; 2 Canada (Adam Svensson and Riley Fleming) 432

112th North and South Men's Amateur Championship *Pinehurst Resort*

Semi-finals: Peter Williamson beat Matt Ewald 2 and 1
Thomas Bradshaw beat David Erdy 4 and 2

Final: Williamson beat Bradshaw 4 and 3

Medallist: Peter Williamson (beat Albin Choi and Michael Cromie at first extra hole of play-off)

South American Amateur Championship *Faralonnes, Cali, Colombia* Mar 21–25

1	Jorge Fernandez (ARG)	71-65-72-74—282
2	Carlos Ernesto Rodriguez (COL)	69-72-74-70—285
	Augustin Tarigo (URU)	69-72-70-74—285

Americas (continued)

US Amateur Championship *see page 303*

32nd US Mid-Amateur Championship *Conway Farms GC, Lake Forest, Illinois*

Semi-finals: Nathan Smith (Pittsburgh, PA) beat Tim Jackson (Germantown, TN) 3 and 1
Garrett Rank (CAN) beat Todd White (Spartanburg, SC) 1 hole
Final: Nathan Smith beat Garrett Rank 1 hole

US Amateur Seniors Championship *Mountain Ridge GC, West Caldwell, Illinois*

Semi-finals: Paul Simson (Raleigh NC) beat Jim Knoll (Sunnyvale, California) 3 and 2
Curtis Skinner (Lake Bluff, Illinois) beat Douglas Hanzel (Savannah, Georgia) 2 and 1
Final: Paul Simson beat Curtis Skinner 4 and 3

US Amateur Public Links Championship *Soldier Hollow GC, Midway, Utah*

Semi-finals: Kevin Aylwin (New Smyrna Beach, FL) beat Kyle Beversdorf (Plymouth, MN) 2 and 1
T J Vogel (Miami, FL) beat Derek Ernst (Clovis, CA) 4 and 3
Final: T J Vogel beat Kevin Aylwin 12 and 11

Uruguay Stroke Play Championship *Club de Golf del Uruguay*

1	Juan Alvarez	73-71-70—214
2	Augustin Tarigo	68-73-74—215
3	Federico Levinsky	73-70-76—219

Venezuela Amateur Championship *Valle Ariba GC*

1	Gustavo Morantes	71-68—139
2	Gustavo Leon	68-73—141
3	Juan Carlos Bringas	77-68—145

Asia and the Middle East

Asia–Pacific Amateur Championship *see page 293*

Bangaladesh Amateur Championship *Kurmitola GC*

1	Manav Das (IND)	69-68-71-74—282
2	Mohammad Nazim	73-71-69-72—285
3	Mohammed Dulai Hossain	75-73-71-69—288

China National Championship *Nanshan GC*

1	Ziting Wang	70-71-73—214
2	Zhang Xiaojun	73-71-73—217
3	Wu Haochuan	72-78-71—221

Emirates Open Amateur Championship *Emirates GC*

1	Peter Stojanovski (AUS)	74-74-70—218
2	Michael Harradine (SUI)	71-76-71—218
3	Jamie Donaldson (ENG)	75-70-75—220

Hong Kong Close Amateur Championship *Hong Kong GC (New course)*

1	Steven Lam (HKGA)	71-69-75-72—287
2	Wong Chen Kun (HKGC)	79-68-71-70—288
3	Roderick De Lacy Staunton (HKGC)	71-71-75-73—290

Hong Kong Open and Mid-Amateur Championship *Clearwater Bay CC*

1	Edward Richardson (ENG)	73-75-65-68—281
2	Yu-Jui Liu (TPE)	73-73-72-77—295
3	Shinichi Mizuno	73-74-73-76—296

All-India Amateur Championship *Chandigarh* Jan 17–22

Semi-finals: Gagan Verma beat SK Pappu 4 and 2
Angad Cheema beat Syed Saqib Ahmed 1 hole

Final: Anghad Cheema beat Gagan Verma 5 and 4

Medallists: Rashav Bhandari and Honey Baisoya 143

Israel Amateur Open *Caesarea GC*

1	Assaf Cohen	74-76-78-71—299
2	Shiomi Asayag	73-72-78-77—300
3	Yair Thaler	75-81-81-81—318

Israel Amateur Masters *Caesarea GC*

1	Barry Shaleed	70-79-74-83—306
2	Ron Solomon	77-79-75-78—309

Japanese Amateur Championship *Nara International GC, Nara* June 21-25

Semi-finals: Hideto Kobukuro beat Jinichiro Kozuma 3 and 2
Kazuki Higa beat Kenta Konishi at 19th

Final: Hideto Kobukuro beat Kazuki Higa 2 holes

Leading qualifiers: Shinji Tomimura 67-71—138; Kazuya Koura 69-69—138

Korean Amateur Championship (Hur Chung Koo Cup) *Nameseoul GC*

1	Soo-min Lee	68-68-70-69—275
2	Nam-hun Kim	70-71-67-67—275
3	Chang-woo Lee	68-66-68-73—275

110th Malaysian Open Amateur Championship *Glenmarie GC (Valley course)*

1	Gavin Kyle Green (SIN)	72-65-69-68—274
2	Poom Saksansin (THA)	69-71-69-71—280
3	Jordan Irawan (INA)	72-71-71-69—283

46th Malaysian Close Amateur Championship *Templer Park, Rawang*

1	Mohamad Afif	71-75-72—218
2	Low Khai Jei	77-77-71—225
3	Amiral Aizat	68-86-74—228

Myanmar Open Amateur Championship *Yangon GC*

1	Thein Naing Soe	72-68-66-72—278
2	Kasidit Lepurte (THA)	71-73-71-71—286
3	Muhammad Arie Ahmad Fauzi (MAS)	73-72-82-71—288

Pakistan Amateur Championship *Royal Palm G&CC* Mar 29–April 1

1	Nadaraja Thangaraja (SRI)	74-68-73-72—287
2	Dulai Hossain (BAN)	71-71-76-73—291
3	Wasim Rana (PAK)	73-71-73-77—294

Asia and the Middle East (continued)

Philippines Amateur Championship *Canlubang G&CC*

1	Gregory Foo (SIN)	70-69-69-79—287
2	Jobin Carlos	70-69-75-75—289
3	Clyde Mondilla	70-74-70-76—290

13th Singapore National Amateur Championship *Singapore Island GC*

Semi-finals: Jonathan Woo beat Wong Qi Wen 5 and 4
Nicklaus Chiam beat Jerome Ng 5 and 3

Final: Jonathan Woo beat Nicklaus Chiam 6 and 5

Singapore Open Amateur Championship *Raffles CC*

1	Joshua Shou	74-73-70-72—289
2	Christopher John Harrop (AUS)	76-73-67-74—290
	Chang-Hen Lin (TPE)	72-68-72-78—290
	Kevin Marques (AUS)	73-72-72-73—290
	Nadaraja Thangaraja (SRI)	73-74-71-72—290

Sri Lanka Championship *Royal Colombo GC*

Semi-finals: Nadaraja Thangaraja beat Zen Dharmaratne 3 and 2
Dulal Hossain (BAN)) beat M Arumugan 3 and 2

Final: Nadaraja Thangaraja beat Dulal Hossain 3 and 2

International team event: Sri Lanka "B" (M Arumugam and GP Sisira Kumara) 285

Team match: Sri Lanka "A" (N Thangaraja and N Ranga) 287, Pakistan (Md Rehman and Md Waseem Rana) 305

Taiwan Amateur Championship *Sunrise G&CC, Taoyuan, Taipei*

1	Chien Po Lee	62-69-73-75—279
2	Teng Kao	67-72-70-76—285
3	Han Ting Chui	71-72-71-77—291

Thailand Amateur Championship *Panya Indra GC*

1	Itthipat Buranatanyarat	67-67-67-71—272
2	Nadaraja Thangaraja	68-67-71-75—281
3	Samarth Dwivedi	68-74-70-71—283

Australasia

Australian Amateur Championship (inaugurated 1894) *Woodlands and Huntingdale*

Jan 17–22

Semi-finals: Marcel Schneider (GER) beat Ruben Sondaja (NSW) at 21st
Daniel Nisbet (QLD) beat Jordan Zunic (NSW) 5 and 4

Final: Marcel Schneider beat Daniel Nisbet at 37th

Leading qualifier: Cameron Smith (QLD) 73-68—141

Australian Stroke Play Championship (inaugurated 1958) *Woodlands and Huntingdale GCs*

1	Cameron Smith (QLD)*	73-68—141
2	Nathan Holman (VIC)	73-69—142
	Oliver Goss (WA)	72-70—142
	Matthew Wittenberg (NSW)	69-73—142

Australian Men's Mid-Amateur Championship *Moonah Links, Victoria*

1	Andrew Tharle (ACT)	73-74-76—223
2	Daniel Ong (VIC)	77-75-75—227
3	Jasopn Perry (VIC)	74-75-80—229
	James Brownlow (NSW)	75-75-79—229

Australian Men's Senior Amateur Championship *Yarra Yarra GC, Melbourne*

1	Samuel Christie (QLD)	77-74—151
2	Peter King (QLD)	76-77—153
	Graham Blizard (NSW)	78-75—153
	Gregory Welsh (VIC)	80-73—153

Interstate Team event: 1 Victoria 471; 2 New South Wales 473; 3 Western Australia 473; 4 Queensland 478; 5 South Australia 506; 6 Australian Capital Territory 508

Winning team: Alan Bullas, Michael Jackson, Ross Percy amd Barry Tippett

ISPS Handa Senior Australian Open Championship *Royal Perth GC*

1	Peter Fowler	67-70-70—207
2	David Merriman	70-71-72—213
	Mike Harwood	72-70-71—213

Fiji Open Amateur Championship *Fiji GC, Suva*

1	Anuresh Chandra	70-69-69—208
2	Mark Bolton (AUS)	69-75-69—213
3	Olaf Allen	68-77-73—218

New Zealand Amateur Championship (inaugurated 1893) *Mt Maunganui* April 18–22

Semi-finals: Vaughan McCall (Gore) beat Tom Brockelsby (Royal Wellington) 4 and 3
Peter Lee (Rotorua) beat Tae Koh (Manakau) 1 hole

Final: Vaughan McCall (Gore) beat Peter Lee (Rotorua) 6 and 5

Leading qualifier: Ryan McCarthy (Tasmania, Australia) 67-66—131

New Zealand Stroke Play Championship (inaugurated 1969) *Bridge Pa, Hastings* Mar 22–25

1	Vaughan McCall	73-68-65-69—275
2	Fraser Wilkin	70-71-69-70—280
3	Mathew Perry	69-67-73-72—281

Europe

Austrian Stroke Play Championship *Murhof GC*

1	Nikolaus Wimmer	71-72-67-76—276
2	Tobias Nemecz	71-72-70-67—280
	Lukas Nemecz	70-71-67-72—280

Austrian International Men's Championship *GC Linz St Florian*

1	Christopher Carstensen (GER)	72-67-68-69—280
2	Edouard Amacher (SUI)	70-72-69-67—282
3	Matthias Schwab	66-69-69-74—278

Europe (continued)

Belgian International Amateur Championship *Royal Antwerp GC*

1	Mathias Eggenberger (SUI)*	69-70-69-73—281
2	Philip Bootsma (NED)	68-69-72-72—281

**Eggenberger won at the third extra hole*

3	Curtis Griffiths (ENG)	68-72-74-68—282
	Alan de Bondt	70-69-72-71—282

Belgian Stroke Play Championship *Royal Ostend GC*

1	Ralph Higuet	75-70-68-79—292
2	Rens Megens	77-71-70-74—292
3	Patrick Hanauer	74-75-75-71—295

British Amateur Championship *see page 295*

British Seniors Open Amateur Championship (inaugurated 1969) *Machynys Peninsula*

1	Chip Lutz (USA)	73-70-68—211
2	Douglas Pool (USA)	70-74-71—215
	Steve Rogers (USA)	70-73-72—215
	Paul Simson (USA)	73-69-73—215

The 2013 Championship will be played at Royal Aberdeen GC from August 7–9

8th Bulgarian Amateur Open Championship *St Sofia GC and Pravets GS*

1	Vladimir Osipov (RUS)	72-74-70—216
2	Nikita Ponomarev (RUS)	70-73-76—219
3	Vasily Belov (RUS)	78-78-71—227

Women's champion: Ksenia Ishkova

Czech Republic Amateur Open Championship *Kaskada GC*

1	Lorenzo Scotto (ITA)	67-71-71-75—282
2	Ondrej Lieser	69-71-73-73—286
3	Andrea Bolognesi (ITA)	72-71-71-74—288

Danish International Amateur Championship *Silkeborg GC*

1	Victor Gebhard Osterby	72-74-74-76—296
2	Simon Willer Hauskjold Christensen	73-73-77-76—299
3	Jeppe Kristian Andersen	79-74-71-76—300

Dutch National Open Championship *Utrecht GC de Pan*

1	Daan Huizing	71-67-66-73—277
2	Robin Child	67-72-72-67—278
3	Inder de Neerelt	69-73-69-69—280

Dutch National Championship *Noordwyke GC*

1	Robin Child	69-70-73—212
2	Rutger Buschow	72-74-73—219
3	Robbie West	73-70-80—235

High winds caused cancellation of the second round

English Open Amateur Stroke Play Championship (Brabazon Trophy) *Walton Heath* (inaugurated 1947)

1	Neil Raymond (Corhampton)	73-71-71-72—287
2	Kevin Phelan (Waterford Castle)	68-75-74-72—289
3	Jamie Rutherford (Knebworth)	75-72-75-68—290

English Amateur Championship (inaugurated 1925) *Silloth-on-Solway*

Leading Qualifier: Jordan Smith (Bowood) 69-71—140

Semi-Finals: Harry Ellis (Meon Valley) beat Jordan Smith (Bowood) 1 hole
Henry Tomlinson (R. Lytham & St Anne's) beat Nathan Kimsey (Woodhall Spa) at 19th

Final: Harry Ellis beat Henry Tomlinson 2 and 1

English Seniors' Amateur Championship *Aldeburgh and Thorpeness*

1	Alan Squires (Oldham)	75-77-69—221
2	Chris Reynolds (Littlestone)	75-74-75—224
3	Andrew Stracey (Denham)	76-76-73—225
	David Potter (Naunton Downs)	73-74-78—225
	John Baldwin (Sunningdale)	73-73-79—225
	Douglas Cameron (Moor Park)	73-72-80—225

English Open Mid-Amateur Championship (Logan Trophy) *Saunton*

1	Thomas Burley (Burnham & Berrow)*	74-75-67—216
2	Neill Williams (Walton Heath)	67-78-71—216
Burley won at the second extra hole		
3	James Wallis (Burhill)	67-77-73—217
	Ian Crowther (R. Lytham & St Anne's)	71-72-74—217

English County Champions Tournament *Woodhall Spa*

1	Sam Dodds (Warwickshire)*	73-73—146
Dodds won on countback		
2	Mark Young (Lancashire)	72-74—146
	David Gibson (Leicestershire)	71-75—146

Estonian Open Amateur Championship *Saare GC, Kuresaare, Saaremaa*

1	Teemu Toivonen (FIN)*	79-74—153
2	Jani Jietanen (FIN)	80-73—153
Toivonen won at the first extra hole		
3	Marten Palm	77-78—155

Nations Cup: 1 Estonia I (Egeti Livi, Marten Palm, Andri Laine) +27; 2 Finland III +32; 3 Finland II +39

European Amateur Championship see page 295

European Seniors' Championship (inaugurated 1999) *Achensee, Austria*

1	Adrian Morrow (IRL)	70-73-69—212
2	Tomas Persson (SWE)	71-71-71—213
3	Bart Nolte (NED)	73-71-73—217

Super Seniors (over 65): Veit Pagel (GER) 225

European Mid-Amateur Championship (inaugurated 1999) *Estonian G&CC*

1	Morten Findsen Schou (DEN)	75-73-73—221
2	Alexander Keller (GER)	73-75-74—222
	Timo Tuunanen (FIN)	72-76-74—222

Europe (continued)

Finnish Open Amateur Championship (Erkko Trophy) *Helsinki GK*

1	Albert Ekhardt	67-68-68—203
2	David Booth (ENG)	69-68-68—205
3	Keijo Jaakola	70-68-69—207
	Joel Girrbach (SUI)	69-71-67—207

Finnish Stroke Play Championship *Aulangon GK*

1	Tapio Pukkananen	71-65-62-67—265
2	Erik Myllymaki	65-76-65-70—266
3	Laun Ruuska	73-70-69-69—271

French International Amateur Championship *Chantilly GC* May 24–27

1	Lionel Weber	71-70-76-70—287
2	Romain Langasque	72-74-69-73—288
3	Kenny Subregis	72-77-65-75—289

German International Amateur Championship *Golfenlage Green Eagle e.V*

1	Moritz Lampert (St Leon Rot)	69-69-73-71—282
2	Marten Bosch (NED)	72-70-74-77—293
3	Maximilian Rohrig (Frankfurter)	79-71-73-71—294

German National Championship *GR Hardenberg*

1	Sebastian Schwind (St Leon Rot GC)	68-73-69-73—283
2	Alexander Matlari (St Leon Rot GC)	70-73-72-70—285
3	Benedict Gebhardt (Neuhof GC)	74-69-74-74—291
	Jonas Robert Kugel (St Leon Rot GC)	70-72-74-75—291

Hungarian Amateur Open Championship *Pannonia G&CC*

1	Johannes Diedrichs (GER)	74-70-67—211
2	Markus Habeler (AUT)	73-71-68—212
3	Vladimir Osipov (RUS)	70-70-75—215

Irish Open Amateur Championship *Royal Dublin* May 10–13

(inaugurated 1892 but not contested between 1960 and 1994)

1	Gavin Moynihan (The Island)	74-70-76-75—295
2	Robin Kind (NED)	73-71-77-75—296
3	Brian Casey (Headfort)	80-72-74-72—298

Irish Close Amateur Championship (inaugurated 1893) *Royal Portrush*

1	Chris Selfridge (Moyola Park)	66-72-70-75—283
2	Reeve Whitson (Mourne)	72-70-70-73—285
	Gary Hurley (West Waterford)	71-71-73-70—285

Irish Seniors' Amateur Open Championship *Atherny*

1	Adrian Morrow (Portmarnock)	70-73-71—214
2	Ian Brotherston (Dumfries & County)	71-75-71—217
3	Tom Cleary (Cork)	73-74-73—220

Irish Seniors' Amateur Close Championship *Clandeboye*

1	Garth McGimpsey (Bangor)	70-75—145
2	Adrian Morrow (Portmarnock)	72-75—147
3	John Mitchell (Tramore)	74-75—149

Italian Open Amateur Championship *Circolo Golf, Villa d'Este GC*

Final: Francesco Testa beat Joel Girrbach (SUI) 8 and 7

Leading qualifiers: Maximilian Rottluff (GER) 66-69—135; Paul Barjon (FRA) 65-70—135

Nations Trophy – best two rounds to count each day:

1	Italy (F LaPorta 69-73, A Bolegnesi 68-72, F Bergamaschi 65-71)	276
2	France (A Abbas 72-77, P Barjon 65-70, F Daux 73-72)	279
3	Netherlands (A Geers 69-70, M Bosch 70-73, D Boschart 69-69)	280
	Switzerland (R Fueg 71-73, E Amacher 67-73, J Girrbach 67-73)	280

5 Italy 284; 6 Germany I 285; 7 Germany II 304; 8 Russia 306

Italian Stroke Play Championship *Castelconturbia GC*

1	Georgio De Filippi	67-71-67-68—273
2	Andrea Bolognesi	72-72-68-71—283
3	Filippo Campigli	73-72-67-73—285
	Renato Paratore	73-70-71-71—285
	Valerio Pelliccia	76-68-70-71—285

Latvian National Amateur Championship *Ozo GC*

1	Roberts Eihmanis	79-75-80—234
2	Gustavs Fricis Jankovs	80-85-75—240
3	Vilis Kristopans	79-82-81—242

Latvian Open Amateur Championship *Ozo GC*

1	Jani Hietenan (FIN)	75-74-72—221
2	Serkan Akersu	83-74-76—223
3	Evgeny Volkov	80-80-75—225

Lithuanian Amateur Championship *National Golf Resort*

1	Kornelijus Baliokonis	81-74-73—228
2	Juozapas Budrikis	80-80-88—248
3	Mindangas Markevicius	77-93-84—254

Luxembourg International Amateur Championship *Golf Club Grand-Ducal*

1	Niklas Koerner (GER)	69-72—141
2	Class Eric Borges	69-72—141
3	Christopher Wuest (GER)	72-70—142
	Joel Salter (AUT)	70-72—142

Luxembourg Men's Amateur Championship *Grand-Ducal GC*

1	Max Biwar	69-71—140
2	Jeremy Abel	69-73—142
3	Jeremy Moise	72-73—145

Polish Amateur Championship *Rosa Private GC*

1	Mateusz Gradeki	69-72-72—213
2	William Carey (USA)	72-73-73—218
3	Mateusz Jedrzejczyk	70-79-74—223

Europe (continued)

Portuguese Amateur Championship *Montado* Feb 15–18

1	Moritz Lampert (GER)	68-74-65-72—279
2	Marcel Schneider (GER)	77-68-70-66—281
	Adrien Saddler (FRA)	72-70-70-69—281

Russian Amateur Championship *Tsleevo GC*

1	Vladimir Osipov	69-75-70-73—287
2	Alexander Kleszcz (AUT)	70-72-72-77—291
3	Nikita Ponomarev	79-70-72-77—298
	Kevin Reints	76-76-73-73—298

Scottish Amateur Championship (inaugurated 1922) *Royal Dornoch*

Semi-Finals: Richard Docherty (Bearsden) beat Bryan Fotheringham (Inverness) 2 holes
Grant Forrest (Craigielaw) beat Lewis Mutch (Duff House Royal) 4 and 3

Final: Grant Forrest beat Richard Docherty 9 and 7

Scottish Open Amateur Stroke Play Championship (inaugurated 1967)

Kilmarnock (Barassie)

1	Paul Barjon (FRA)	70-71-73-68—282
2	Haydn Porteous (RSA)	65-75-78-68—286
	Rory Bourke (AUS)	69-71-73-73—286

Scottish Seniors Open Amateur Stroke Play Championship *Luffness New*

1	Lindsay Blair (Grangemouth)	74-70-75—219
2	Robert Jack (Liberton)	72-78-70—220
3	John Fraser (Royal Burgess)	75-76-72—223
	John Baldwin (Sunningdale)	70-72-81—223

Scottish Seniors Match Play Championship *West Kilbride*

Semi-Finals: David Gardner (Broomieknowe) beat Derek Murphy (Kinross) at 19th
Richard Gray (Irvine) beat Ian Taylor (Royal Burgess) 2 and 1

Final: David Gardner beat Richard Gray 4 and 3

Scottish Champion of Champions *Leven*

1	Fraser McKenna (Balmore)	68-69-70-68—275
2	Brian Soutar (Leven)	73-70-66-69—278
	Graeme Robertson (Glenbervie)	64-69-73-72—278

Slovak Amateur Championship *Penati Golf Resort*

1	Peter Valasek	71-75-73—219
2	Martin Tovoda	79-74-70—223
3	Juraj Zvarik (CZE)	77-74-73—224

Slovak Open Amateur Championship *Sajdikove Humence*

1	Peter Valsek	71-75-73—219
2	Alexander Kleszcz (AUT)	72-76-74—222
	Jaka Vidmar (SVK)	76-72-74—222

Slovenian International Amateur Championship *Bled GC*

1	Patrick Murray (AUT)	71-68-72-70—281
2	Vitek Novak (CZE)	75-69-73-73—290
3	Enej Sarkanj	72-72-79-73—296

Spanish Amateur Championship *Al Canada* Feb 29–Mar 4

Semi-finals: Jack Hiluta (ENG) beat Daan Huizing (NED) 1 hole
Marcel Schneider (GER) beat Franck Daux (FRA) 5 and 3

Final: Jack Hiluta (ENG) beat Marcel Schneider (GER) 4 and 3

Leading qualifier: Romain Langasque (FRA) 67-74—138

Swiss International Amateur Championship *Schoenenberg GC*

1	Adrien Saddler (FRA)	69-65-69-69—272
2	Luigi Botta	69-71-66-72—278
3	Ugo Coussaud	71-68-71-69—279
	Joel Girrbach	71-69-72-67—279

11th Turkish Amateur Championship *Gloria GC (Old and New)*

1	Maximilian Rottluff (GER)	68-64-71-74—277
2	Marcel Schneider (GER)	76-67-73-64—280
3	Ben Taylor (ENG)	73-67-66-75—281

Welsh Amateur Championship (inaugurated 1895) *Royal St David's*

Semi-finals: Jason Shufflebotham (Prestatyn) beat Geraint Jones (Royal St David's) 2 and 1
Will Jones (Oswestry) beat Richard James (Aberystwyth) 4 and 3

Final: Jason Shufflebotham beat Will Jones 1 hole

Welsh Open Amateur Stroke Play Championship (inaugurated 1967) *Prestatyn*

1	Craig Hinton (The Oxfordshire)	69-75-70-67—281
2	Vaughan McCall (Gore)	72-75-70-71—288
3	Sam Binning (Ranfurly Castle)	74-74-70-71—289

Welsh Seniors' Close Amateur Championship (inaugurated 1975) *always at Aberdovey*

1	Glyn Rees (Fleetwood)*	77-71-81—229
2	Phil Jones (Bromborough)	77-76-76—229

Rees won at the first extra hole

3	Mike Rooke (Llanynymech)	73-80-77—230
	Basil Griffiths (Llanynymech)	75-78-77—230

Welsh Seniors' Open Championship *St Mellons*

1	Andrew Stracey (Denham)	71-70-73—214
2	John E Ambridge (Moor Park)	71-68-76—215
3	Ian Brotherston (Dumfries & County)	71-72-74—217
	Charles Banks (Stanton-on-The-Wolds)	73-70-74—217

Welsh Tournament of Champions *always at Cradoc*

1	Alyn Torrance (Wrexham)	73-69—142
2	Stuart Westley (Newport)	73-73—146
3	Gwyn Jones (Radyr)	76-72—148
	Lee Bannister (Cradoc)	76-72—148
	Zach Galliford (Borth & Ynyslas)	74-74—148

USA State Championships 2012

US nationality unless stated

Alabama	Andy McRae (SP) Casey O'Toole (MP)
Alaska	Greg Sanders
Arizona	Bowen Osborn
Arkansas	Wes McNulty. (SP) Nick Wilson (MP)
California	Kevin Marsh
Colorado	Steven Kupcho (SP) Brian Dorfman (MP)
Connecticut	Matt Smith
Delaware	Paul Tighe
Florida	Chase Sieffert
Georgia	Lee Knox
Hawaii	Matthew Ma (MP)
Idaho	Taeksoo Kim
Illinois	Quinn Prchal
Indiana	Tyler Merkel
Iowa	Jon Olson
Kansas	Kyle Smell
Kentucky	Patrick Newcomb
Louisiana	Pat Christovich
Maine	Charlie Blanchard (SP) John Hayes (MP)
Maryland	Josh Eure
Massachusetts	Mike Calef
Michigan	Jared Dalgo (SP) Drew Preston (MP)
Minnesota	Eric van Rooyan
Mississippi	Clay Homan
Missouri	Brevin Giebler (SP) Nick Wilson (MP)
Montana	Nathan Bailey
Nebraska	Kevin Stanek (MP)
Nevada	Roman Mudd (MP)
New England	Christopher Swift
N. Hampshire	Ryan Kohler
New Jersey	Ryan McCormick
New Mexico	Alex Estrada
New York	Dominic Bozzelli
N. Carolina	Matthew Crenshaw
N. Dakota	Coy Papcheck (SP) Duane Wages III (MP)
Ohio	Nathan Kerns
Oklahoma	Talor Gooch (SP) Stephen Carney (MP)
Oregon	Nick Chianello
Pennsylvania	Andrew Mason
Rhode Island	Jamison Randall
S. Carolina	Cody Proveaux (SP) Matt Laydon (MP)
S. Dakota	Brandon Sigmund (SP) Ben Irlbeck (MP)
Tennessee	Tim Jackson (SP) John Tyner (MP)
Texas	Thomas Birdsey
Utah	Jon Wright
Vermont	Mike Stackus
Virginia	Jake Mondy
Washington	Chris Williams
West Virginia	Pat Carter
Wisconsin	Brady Strangstalien (SP) Sam Frank (MP)
Wyoming	Kamrin Allen (MP)

Metropolitan GA (NY)	Ryan MCormack
Carolinas	Carson Young
110th Western Amateur	Chris Williams
North and South	Peter Williamson

Further details of these and other US amateur events can be found on page 446

Canadian Provincial Championships 2012

Canadian nationality unless stated

Alberta	Riley Fleming	Medicine Hat G&CC
British Columbia	Riley Fleming	Swan-e-set Bay Resort, Pitt Meadows
Manitoba	Joshua Wytinck	Glendale G&CC
New Brunswick	Mathieu Gingras	The Algonquin GC
Newfoundland and Labrador	Michael Tibbo	Blomidon G&CC
Nova Scotia	Mathieu Gingras	Bell Bay GC
Ontario	Albin Choi	The Summit G&CC
Prince Edward Is.	Greg MacAuley	Avondale GC
Quebec	Charles Coté	Summerlea G&CC
Saskatchewan	Tyler Frank	Deer Park Municipal, York

Further details of these and other Canadian amateur events can be found on page 444

Australian State Championships 2012

Australian nationality unless stated

New South Wales	Brett Drewitt (NSW)	Eleanora GC
S. Australia	Jack Williams (SA)	Flagstaff Hill, Mt Osmond and The Grange
Tasmania	Neville Hogan (QLD)	Launceston GC
Victoria	Taylor MacDonald	
W. Australia	Oliver Goss (WA)	Mount Lawley, Perth

Further details of these and other Australian amateur events can be found on page 448

South African Provincial Championships 2012

South African nationality unless stated

Cape Province Open	Brandon Stone	Durban CC
Eastern Province and Border Open	Oswin Schlenkrich	Fish River Sun
Ekurhuleni Open	Dylan Raubenheimer	
Free State & N. Cape Open	Musiwalo Nethunzwi	Harrismith
Gauteng North Open	Toby Tree (ENG)	Pecanwood GC
KwaZulu-Natal Open	Brandon Stone	Durban CC
Limpopo Open	Haydn Porteous	Koro Creek GC
Mpumalanga Open	Callum Mowat	Graceland
N. Cape Open	Desne Van Den Bergh	Kimberley GC
North West Open	Zander Lombard	Leopard Park GC
S. Cape Open	Sipho Bujela	George GC
W. Province Open	Justin Turner	Mowbray GC

Further details of these and other South African amateur events can be found on page 442

New Zealand Provincial Championships 2012

New Zealand nationality unless stated

North Island Stroke Play Championship	Daniel Pearce	Lochiel GC
South Island Stroke Play Championship	Compton Pikari	Christchurch GC

Further details of these and other New Zealand amateur events can be found on page 449

Month by month in 2012

Adam Scott bogeys the final four holes at Royal Lytham and Ernie Els, having birdied the last, suddenly finds himself Open champion again. It comes a week after Marc Warren drops four shots in the last four to lose the Scottish Open by one. Jamie Donaldson is finally a European Tour winner, the Irish Open at Royal Portrush being his 255th event, while Tiger Woods goes past Jack Nicklaus with his 74th PGA Tour victory.

National Orders of Merit 2012

Titleist/Footjoy English Order of Merit

1	Neil Raymond (Corhampton)	609.09	6	Ryan Evans (Wellingborough)	428.81
2	Craig Hinton (The Oxfordshire)	606.19	7	Jamie Rutherford (Knebworth)	375.86
3	Edward Richardson (Hemsted Forest)	547.97	8	Nathan Kimsey (Woodhall Spa)	355.28
4	Joshua White (Chipstead)	463.69	9	Jack Hiluta (Chelmsford)	343.75
5	Darren Timms (Mid-Kent)	450.73	10	Ben Taylor (Walton Heath)	339.81

Willie Gill Irish Order of Merit

1	Alan Dunbar (Rathmore)	777	6	Harry Diamond (Belvoir Park)	328
2	Chris Selfridge (Moyola Park)	475	7	Gavin Moynihan (The Island)	320
3	Rory McNamara (Headfort)	450	8	Eddie McCormack (Galway)	264
4	Richard O'Donovan (Lucan)	410	9	Reeve Whitson (Mourne)	263
5	Kevin Phelan (Waterford Castle)	370	10	Nick Grant (Knock)	250

Scottish Order of Merit

1	Scott Borrowman (Dollar)	285	6	Michael Daily (Erskine)	248
2	Adam Dunton (McDonald)	276	7	Graham Gordon (Newmachar)	245
	Matthew Clark (Kilmalcolm)	276	8	Sam Binning (Ranfurly Castle)	237
4	Ross Bell (Downfield)	268	9	Fraser Moore (Glenbervie)	226
5	Conor O'Neil (Pollok)	257	10	Alexander Culverwell (Dunbar)	217

Pinnacle Welsh Order of Merit

1	Ben Westgate (Trevose)	481.02	6	James Frazer (Pennard)	241.58
2	Jason Shufflebotham (Prestatyn)	345.00	7	Geraint Jones (Royal St Davids)	225.00
3	David Boote (Walton Heath)	305.43	8	Richard Bentham (St Pierre)	216.00
4	Will Jones (Oswestry)	259.50	9	Luke Thomas (Pontypridd)	212.50
5	Rhys Pugh (Vale of Glamorgan)	257.40	10	Richard James (Aberystwyth)	180.83

New Zealand Order of Merit

(events played in brackets)

1	Vaughan McCall	(18)	172.20	6	Blair Riordan	(18)	76.92
2	Benjamin Campbell	(17)	91.73	7	Tyler Hodge	(16)	75.23
3	Sam An	(18)	91.37	8	Fraser Wilkin	(19)	74.58
4	Joshua Munn	(21)	87.26	9	Compton Pikari	(18)	65.53
5	Daniel Pearce	(17)	81.39	10	Peter Lee	(17)	62.36

Australian Order of Merit

(events played in brackets)

1	Daniel Nisbet (QLD)	(13)	115.75	6	Brett Drewitt (NSW)	(10)	86.45
2	Cameron Smith (QLD)	(10)	92.60	7	Nathan Holman (VIC)	(15)	84.70
3	Matt Steiger (NSW)	(12)	92.09	8	Geoff Drakeford (VIC)	(12)	82.11
4	Oliver Goss (WA)	(8)	88.10	9	Brady Watt (WA)	(16)	80.83
5	Jake Higginbotham (NSW)	(10)	87.21	10	Rory Bourke (VIC)	(14)	80.31

Canadian Order of Merit

(events played in brackets)

1	Albin Choi	(10)	4,648.57	6	Adam Svensson	(5)	1,925.00
2	Mackenzie Hughes	(10)	3,925.57	7	Justin Shin	(4)	1,596.52
3	Corey Conners	(10)	3,223.75	8	Chris Hemmerich	(6)	1,522.50
4	Garrett Rank	(6)	2,640.00	9	Taylor Pendrith	(6)	1,452.25
5	Riley Fleming	(4)	1,955.62	10	Brian Churchill-Smith	(3)	1,435.00

German Order of Merit

1	Moritz Lampert	3,763.80	6	Stephan Jäger	1,345.00
2	Marcel Schneider	2,734.10	7	Maximilian Rottluff	1,282.27
3	Sebastian Schwind	1,927.50	8	Maximilian Röhrig	1,191.60
4	Dominic Foos	1,822.50	9	Philipp Westermann	1,116.20
5	Alexander Matlari	1,677.00	10	Maximilian Mehles	1,000.00

South African Order of Merit

1	Haydn Porteous	59.7849	6	Sipho Bujela	28.5526
2	Brandon Stone	44.9999	7	Dylan Raubenheimer	25.6100
3	Zander Lombard	41.7065	8	Louis Taylor	25.4218
4	Drikus Bruyns	37.6952	9	Gert Myburgh	25.0601
5	C J Du Plessis	32.0794	10	Aubrey Barnard	24.7376

Belgian Order of Merit

1	Thomas Pieters	29,915	6	Dewi Merckx	5,988
2	Thomas Detry	20,841	7	Alan de Bondt	5,597
3	Cédric Van Wassenhove	9,192	8	Jamie Donaldson (ENG)	5,083
4	Mathias Boesmans	8,407	9	Stefan Quy	4,942
5	Kevin Hesbois	7,186	10	Bertrand Mommaerts	4,7741

Nathan Smith joined a very exclusive club in 2012

When Nathan Smith beat Canadian Garret Rank by a hole at Conway Farms GC in the final of the US Mid-Amateur Championship last year he probably had no idea that he was joining a very select group of golfers. Total membership just 15.

These are the golfers who have won a USGA Championship more than once and in Smith's case he joined the four wins group which also includes Jack Nicklaus and Ben Hogan. Hogan and Nicklaus won four US Opens but Smith was the first to win four US Mid-Amateur titles.

Topping the list of repeat winners, however, is the legendary Glenna Collett Vare who won the US Women's Amateur titles six times between 1922 and 1935. She stands alone just ahead of Bobby Jones (five US Amateur titles), JoAnne Gunderson Carr (five US Women's Amateur titles and the less well-known Carolyn Cudone who won five US Women's Senior Championships in a row from 1968.

Smith is the 15th golfer to win four or more USGA run Championships. With him in on the four mark in addition to Hogan and Nicklaus are Willie Anderson (US Open), Ellen Port (Women's Mid-Amateur), Dorthy Porter, Carole Semple Thompson and Anne Sander (all Senior Women's Amateur), Jerome D Travers (US Amateur) and Mickey Wright (US Women's Open).

Team Events

For past winners not listed here, please see earlier editions of *The R&A Golfer's Handbook*

International

Walker Cup (Instituted 1922)

Great Britain & Ireland v USA (*home team names first*)

2011 *Royal Aberdeen GC, Scotland* Sept 10–11

Result: GBI 14, USA 12

Captains: Nigel Edwards (GBI), Jim Holtgrieve (USA)

***First Day* – Foursomes**

Tom Lewis & Michael Stewart beat Peter Uihlein & Harris English 2 and 1
Jack Senior & Andy Sullivan beat Russell Henley & Kelly Kraft 2 and 1
Paul Cutler & Alan Dunbar beat Nathan Smith & Blayne Barber 5 and 4
Steven Brown & Stiggy Hodgson lost to Patrick Cantlay & Chris Williams 5 and 4

Singles

Tom Lewis lost to Peter Uihlein 2 and 1
Jack Senior lost to Jordan Spieth 3 and 2
Andy Sullivan lost to Harris English 2 and 1
Rhys Pugh beat Patrick Rodgers 2 and 1
Steven Brown beat Russell Henley 1 hole
James Byrne beat Nathan Smith 2 and 1
Paul Cutler beat Kelly Kraft 2 and 1
Michael Stewart lost to Patrick Cantlay 2 and 1

***Second Day* – Foursomes**

Tom Lewis & Michael Stewart halved with Jordan Spieth & Patrick Rodgers
Jack Senior & Andy Sullivan beat Peter Uihlein & Harris English 3 and 2
Paul Cutler & Alan Dunbar beat Kelly Kraft & Blayne Barber 2 and 1
James Byrne & Rhys Pugh beat Patrick Cantlay & Chris Williams 5 and 3

Singles

Tom Lewis (Welwyn Garden City) lost to Russell Henley (Macon, GA) 4 and 2
Andy Sullivan (Nuneaton) lost to Jordan Speith (Dallas, TX) 3 and 2
Jack Senior (Heysham) halved with Nathan Smith (Pittsburgh, PA)
Michael Stewart (Troon Welbeck) beat Patrick Rodgers (Avon, IN) 3 and 2
Stiggy Hodgson (Sunningdale) lost to Peter Uihlein (Orlando, FL) 2 and 1
Steven Brown (Wentworth) halved with Blayne Barber (Lake City, FL) 1 hole
Rhys Pugh (Vale of Glamorgan) beat Kelly Kraft (Dallas, TX) 2 and 1
Alan Dunbar (Rathmore) lost to Chris Williams (Moscow. ID) 1 hole
James Byrne (Banchory) lost to Harris English (Thomasville, GA) 2 and 1
Paul Cutler (Portstewart) halved with Patrick Cantlay (Los Alamitos, CA)

2009 *Merion GC, Ardmore, PA* Sept 12–13

Result: USA 16½, GB&I 9½

Captains: George Marucci (USA), Colin Dalgleish (GB&I)

***First Day* – Foursomes**

B Harman & M Hoffmann beat W Booth & S Hutsby 2 and 1
P Uihlein & N Smith beat G Dear & M Haines 1 hole
R Fowler & B Cauley beat L Goddard & D Whitnell 6 and 5
C Tringale & A Mitchell lost to S Hodgson & N Kearney 3 and 1

Singles

B Harman halved with G Dear
R Fowler beat S Hutsby 7 and 6
C Tringale halved with W Booth
M Hoffmann halved with M Haines
P Uihlein beat T Fleetwood 2 and 1
D Weaver halved with C Paisley
B Cauley beat N Kearney 2 and 1
B Gielow lost to S Hodgson 2 and 1

***Second Day* – Foursomes**

B Harman & A Mitchell beat G Dear & M Haines 3 and 2
R Fowler & B Caley beat S Hodgson & N Kearney 1 hole
D Weaver & B Gielow lost to W Booth & S Hutsby 3 and 2
N Smith & P Uihlein beat C Paisley & D Whitnell 5 and 4

Singles

Brian Harman lost to Gavin Dear (SCO) 3 and 2
Ricki Fowler beat Matt Haines (ENG) 2 and 1
Peter Uihlein beat Stiggy Hodgson (ENG) 3 and 1
Morgan Hoffmann beat Wallace Booth (SCO) 1 hole
Bud Cauley halved with Chris Paisley (ENG)
Adam Mitchell lost to Sam Hutsby (ENG) 1 hole
Drew Weaver lost to Tommy Fleetwood (ENG) 1 hole
Cameron Tringale beat Luke Goddard (ENG) 8 and 6
Nathan Smith lost to Niall Kearney (IRL) 3 and 2
Brendan Gielow beat Dale Whitnell (ENG) 4 and 3

2007 *Royal County Down GC, Co Down* Sept 8–9

Result: USA 12½, GB&I 11½

Captains: Colin Dalgliesh (GB&I), Buddy Marucci (USA)

***First Day* – Foursomes**

L Saltman & R Davies lost to B Horschel & R Fowler 4 and 3
R McIlroy & J Caldwell halved with C Knost & D Johnson
J Parry & D Horsey beat T Kuehne & K Stanley 2 and 1
J Moul & D Willett halved with W Simpson & J Moore

Singles
R McIlroy lost to B Horschel 1 hole
L Saltman lost to R Fowler 5 and 4
R Davies beat D Johnson 5 and 4
D Willett lost to C Knost 2 holes
L Matthews lost to J Lovemark 5 and 4
N Edwards beat K Stanley 1 hole
J Moul beat C Kirk 1 hole
D Horsey beat W Simpson 1 hole

***Second Day* – Foursomes**
Caldwell & McIlroy lost to Horschel & Fowler 2 and 1
Davies & Edwards lost to Knost & Johnson 1 hole
Moul & Willett lost to Kuehne & Moore 4 and 2
Horsey & Parry lost to Kirk & Lovemark 1 hole

Singles
McIlroy beat Horschel 4 and 2
Davies beat Fowler 3 and 2
Willett halved with Knost
Saltman beat Kuehne 2 and 1
Caldwell beat Stanley 2 holes
Edwards lost to Moore 1 hole
Moul lost to Lovemark 4 and 3
Horsey beat Simpson 1 hole

2005 *Chicago GC, Wheaton, IL* Aug 13–14

Result: USA 12½, GB&I 11½

Captains: Bob Lewis (USA), Garth McGimpsey (GB&I)

***First Day* – Foursomes**
A Kim & B Harman halved with NB Edwards & R Davies
L Williams & M Every beat G Lockerbie & R Dinwiddie 1 hole
J Overton & M Putnam beat O Fisher & M Richardson 2 and 1
K Reifers & B Hurley lost to R Ramsay & L Saltman 4 and 3

Singles
M Every lost to R Davies 4 and 3
A Kim beat G Lockerbie 6 and 5
L Overton beat NB Edwards 5 and 4
M Putnam lost to O Fisher 2 holes
N Thompson lost to M Richardson 5 and 4
B Hurley lost to L Saltman 1 hole
J Holmes beat G Wolstenholme 1 hole
L Williams beat B McElhinney 2 and 1

***Second Day* – Foursomes**
Kim & Harman beat Ramsay & Saltman 4 and 2
Every & Williams lost to Davies & Edwards 2 and 1
Thompson & Holmes beat Fisher & Richardson 2 and 1
Putnam & Overton lost to Lockerbie & Dinwiddie 5 and 3

Singles
Kim lost to Wolstenholme 1 hole
Harman beat Davies 6 and 5
Putnam halved with Fisher
Every halved with Dinwiddie
Holmes lost to Richardson 5 and 4
Reifers lost to Saltman 1 hole
Overton beat Edwards 1 hole
Williams beat Lockerbie 4 and 3

2003 *Ganton GC, North Yorkshire* Sept 6–7

Result: GB&I 12½, USA 11½

Captains: Garth McGimpsey (GB&I), Bob Lewis (USA)

***First Day* – Foursomes**
GP Wolstenholme & M Skelton lost to W Haas & T Kuehne 2 and 1
S Wilson & D Inglis beat L Williams & G Zahringer 2 holes
NB Edwards & S Manley beat C Nallen & R Moore 3 and 2
N Fox & C Moriarty beat A Rubinson & C Wittenberg 4 and 2

Singles
GP Wolstenholme lost to W Haas 1 hole
O Wilson halved with T Kuehne
D Inglis lost to B Mackenzie 3 and 2
S Wilson halved with M Hendrix
NB Edwards beat G Zahringer 3 and 2
C Moriarty lost to C Nallen 1 hole
N Fox lost to A Rubinson 3 and 2
G Gordon lost to C Wittenberg 5 and 4

Second Day – *Foursomes*
GP Wolstenholme & O Wilson beat W Haas & T Kuehne 5 and 4
N Fox & C Moriarty lost to B Mackenzie & M Hendrix 6 and 5
S Wilson & D Inglis halved with C Wittenberg & A Rubinson
NB Edwards & S Manley halved with L Williams & G Zahringer

Singles
O Wilson beat W Haas 1 hole
GP Wolstenholme beat C Wittenberg 3 and 2
M Skelton beat A Rubinson 3 and 2
C Moriarty lost to B Mackenzie 3 and 1
S Wilson lost to M Hendrix 5 and 4
D Inglis beat R Moore 4 and 3
NB Edwards halved with L Williams
S Manley beat T Kuehne 3 and 2

2001 *Ocean Forest, Sea Island, GA* Aug 11–12

Result: GB&I 15, USA 9

Captains: D Yates Jr (USA), P McEvoy (GB&I)

***First Day* – Foursomes**
D Green & DJ Trahan lost to S O'Hara & GP Wolstenholme 5 and 3
N Cassini & L Glover beat L Donald & N Dougherty 4 and 3
D Eger & B Molder halved with J Elson & R McEvoy
J Driscoll & J Quinney lost to G McDowell & M Hoey 3 and 1

Singles
E Compton beat G Wolstenholme 3 and 2
DJ Trahan beat S O'Hara 2 and 1
J Driscoll lost to N Dougherty 2 and 1
N Cassini beat N Edwards 5 and 4
J Harris lost to M Warren 5 and 4
J Quinney lost to L Donald 3 and 2
B Molder beat G McDowell 2 and 1
L Glover beat M Hoey 1 hole

***Second Day* – Foursomes**
E Compton & J Harris lost to L Donald & N Dougherty 3 and 2
N Cassini & L Glover lost to G McDowell & M Hoey 2 and 1
D Eger & B Molder beat S O'Hara & M Warren 7 and 6
D Green & DJ Trahan lost to J Elson & R McEvoy 1 hole

Singles
L Glover lost to L Donald 3 and 2
J Harris lost to S O'Hara 4 and 3
DJ Trahan lost to N Dougherty 1 hole
J Driscoll lost to M Warren 2 and 1
B Molder beat G McDowell 1 hole
D Green lost to M Hoey 1 hole
E Compton halved with J Elson
N Cassini lost to GP Wolstenholme 4 and 3

1999 *Nairn GC, Nairnshire, Scotland* Sept 11–12

Result: GB&I 15, USA 9

Captains: P McEvoy (GB&I), D Yates Jr (USA)

***First Day* – Foursomes**

Rankin & Storm lost to Haas & Miller 1 hole
Casey & Donald beat Byrd & Scott 5 and 3
Gribben & Kelly lost to Gossett & Jackson 3 and 1
Rowe & Wolstenholme beat Kuchar & Molder 1 hole

Singles

G Rankin lost to E Loar 4 and 3
L Donald beat T McKnight 4 and 3
G Storm lost to H Haas 4 and 3
P Casey beat S Scott 4 and 3
D Patrick lost to J Byrd 6 and 5
S Dyson halved with D Gossett
P Gribben halved with B Molder
L Kelly lost to T Jackson 3 and 1

***Second Day* – Foursomes**

Rankin & Storm beat Loar & McKnight 4 and 3
Dyson & Gribben lost to Haas & Miller 1 hole
Casey & Donald beat Gossett & Jackson 1 hole
Rowe & Wolstenholme beat Kuchar & Molder 4 and 3

Singles

Rankin beat Scott 1 hole
Dyson lost to Loar 5 and 4
Casey beat Miller 3 and 2
Storm beat Byrd 1 hole
Donald beat Molder 3 and 2
Rowe beat Kuchar 1 hole
Gribben beat Haas 3 and 2
Wolstenholme beat Gossett 1 hole

1997 *Quaker Ridge GC, NY* Aug 9–10

Result: USA 18, GB&I 6

Captains: AD Gray Jr (USA), C Brown (GB&I)

***First Day* – Foursomes**

Elder & Kribel beat Howard & Young 4 and 3
Courville & Marucci beat Rose & Brooks 5 and 4
Gore & Harris beat Wolstenholme & Nolan 6 and 4
Leen & Wollman beat Coughlan & Park 1 hole

Singles

D Delcher lost to S Young 5 and 4
S Scott lost to C Watson 1 hole
B Elder beat B Howard 5 and 4
J Kribel lost to J Rose 1 hole
R Leen beat K Nolan 3 and 2
J Gore beat G Rankin 3 and 2
C Wollman halved with R Coughlan
J Harris beat GP Wolstenholme 1 hole

***Second Day* – Foursomes**

Harris & Elder beat Young & Watson 3 and 2
Courville & Marucci beat Howard & Rankin 5 and 4
Delcher & Scott beat Coughlan & Park 1 hole
Leen & Wollman lost to Wolstenholme & Rose 2 and 1

Singles

Kribel lost to Young 2 and 1
Gore halved with Watson
J Courville beat Rose 3 and 2
Elder beat Nolan 2 and 1
Harris beat M Brooks 6 and 5
G Marucci beat D Park 4 and 3
D Delcher beat Wolstenholme 2 and 1
Scott beat Coughlan 2 and 1

1995 *Royal Porthcawl GC, Mid Glamorgan, Wales* Sept 9–10

Result: GB&I 14, USA 10

Captains: C Brown (GB&I), AD Gray Jr (USA)

***First Day* – Foursomes**

Sherry & Gallacher lost to Harris & Woods 4 and 3
Foster & Howell halved with Bratton & Riley
Rankin & Howard lost to Begay & Jackson 4 and 3
Harrington & Fanagan beat Cox & Kuehne 5 and 3

Singles

G Sherry beat N Begay 3 and 2
L James lost to K Cox 1 hole
M Foster beat B Marucci 4 and 3
S Gallacher beat T Jackson 4 and 3
P Harrington beat J Courville Jr 2 holes
B Howard halved with A Bratton
G Rankin lost to J Harris 1 hole
GP Wolstenholme beat T Woods 1 hole

***Second Day* – Foursomes**

Sherry & Gallacher lost to Bratton & Riley 4 and 2
Howell & Foster beat Cox & Kuehne 3 and 2
Wolstenholme & James lost to Marucci & Courville 6 and 5
Harrington & Fanagan beat Harris & Woods 2 and 1

Singles

Sherry beat Riley 2 holes
Howell beat Begay 2 and 1
Gallacher beat Kuehne 3 and 2
Fanagan beat Courville 3 and 2
Howard halved with Jackson
Foster halved with Marucci
Harrington lost to Harris 3 and 2
Wolstenholme lost to Woods 4 and 3

1993 *Interlachen GC, Edina, MN* Aug 18–19

Result: USA 19, GB&I 5

Captains: M Giles III (USA), G Macgregor (GB&I)

***First Day* – Foursomes**

Abandoned – rain & flooding

Singles

A Doyle beat I Pyman 1 hole
D Berganio lost to M Stanford 3 and 2
J Sigel lost to D Robertson 3 and 2
K Mitchum halved with S Cage
T Herron beat P Harrington 1 hole
D Yates beat P Page 2 and 1
T Demsey beat R Russell 2 and 1
J Leonard beat R Burns 4 and 3
B Gay lost to V Phillips 2 and 1
J Harris beat B Dredge 4 and 3

***Second Day* – Foursomes**

Doyle & Leonard beat Pyman & Cage 4 and 3
Berganio & Demsey beat Stanford & Harrington 3 and 2
Sigel & Mitchum beat Dredge & Phillips 3 and 2
Harris & Herron beat Russell & Robertson 1 hole

Singles

Doyle beat Robertson 4 and 3
Harris beat Pyman 3 and 2
Yates beat Cage 2 and 1
Gay halved with Harrington
Sigel beat Page 5 and 4
Herron beat Phillips 3 and 2
Mitchum beat Russell 4 and 2
Berganio lost to Burns 1 hole
Demsey beat Dredge 3 and 2
Leonard beat Stanford 5 and 4

1991 *Portmarnock GC, Co Dublin, Ireland* Sept 5–6

Result: USA 14, GB&I 10

Captains: G Macgregor (GB&I), JR Gabrielsen (USA)

***First Day* – Foursomes**

Milligan & Hay lost to Mickelson & May 5 and 3
Payne & Evans lost to Duval & Sposa 1 hole
McGimpsey & Willison lost to Voges & Eger 1 hole
McGinley & Harrington lost to Sigel & Doyle 2 and 1

Singles

A Coltart lost to P Mickelson 4 and 3
J Payne beat F Langham 2 and 1
G Evans beat D Duval 2 and 1
R Willison lost to B May 2 and 1
G McGimpsey beat M Sposa 1 hole
P McGinley lost to A Doyle 6 and 4
G Hay beat T Scherrer 1 hole
L White lost to J Sigel 4 and 3

***Second Day* – Foursomes**

Milligan & McGimpsey beat Voges & Eger 2 and 1
Payne & Willison lost to Duval & Sposa 1 hole
Evans & Coltart beat Langham & Scherrer 4 and 3
White & McGinley beat Mickelson & May 1 hole

Singles

Milligan lost to Mickelson 1 hole
Payne beat Doyle 3 and 1
Evans lost to Langham 4 and 2
Coltart beat Sigel 1 hole
Willison beat Scherrer 3 and 2
Harrington lost to Eger 3 and 2
McGimpsey lost to May 4 and 3
Hay lost to Voges 3 and 1

1989 *Peachtree GC, GA* Aug 16–17

Result: GB&I 12½, USA 11½

Captains: F Ridley (USA), GC Marks (GB&I)

***First Day* – Foursomes**

Gamez & Martin beat Claydon & Prosser 3 and 2
Yates & Mickelson halved with Dodd & McGimpsey
Lesher & Sigel lost to McEvoy & O'Connell 6 and 5
Eger & Johnson lost to Milligan & Hare 2 and 1

Singles

R Gamez beat JW Milligan 7 and 6
D Martin lost to R Claydon 5 and 4
E Meeks halved with SC Dodd
R Howe lost to E O'Connell 5 and 4
D Yates lost to P McEvoy 2 and 1
P Mickelson beat G McGimpsey 4 and 2
G Lesher lost to C Cassells 1 hole
J Sigel halved with RN Roderick

***Second Day* – Foursomes**

Gamez & Martin halved with McEvoy & O'Connell
Sigel & Lesher lost to Claydon & Cassells 3 and 2
Eger & Johnson lost to Milligan & Hare 2 and 1
Mickelson & Yates lost to McGimpsey & Dodd 2 and 1

Singles

Gamez beat Dodd 1 hole
Martin halved with Hare
Lesher beat Claydon 3 and 2
Yates beat McEvoy 4 and 3
Mickelson halved with O'Connell
Eger beat Roderick 4 and 2
Johnson beat Cassells 4 and 2
Sigel halved with Milligan

1987 *Sunningdale GC, Berkshire, England* May 27–28

Result: USA 16½, GB&I 7½

Captains: GC Marks (GB&I), F Ridley (USA)

***First Day* – Foursomes**

Montgomerie & Shaw lost to Alexander & Mayfair 5 and 4
Currey & Mayo lost to Kite & Mattice 2 and 1
Macgregor & Robinson lost to Lewis & Loeffler 2 and 1
McHenry & Girvan lost to Sigel & Andrade 3 and 2

Singles

D Currey beat B Alexander 2 holes
J Robinson lost to B Andrade 7 and 5
CS Montgomerie beat J Sorenson 3 and 2
R Eggo lost to J Sigel 3 and 2
J McHenry lost to B Montgomery 1 hole
P Girvan lost to B Lewis 3 and 2
DG Carrick lost to B Mayfair 2 holes
G Shaw beat C Kite 1 hole

***Second Day* – Foursomes**

Currey & Carrick lost to Lewis & Loeffler 4 and 3
Montgomerie & Shaw lost to Kite & Mattice 5 and 3
Mayo & Macgregor lost to Sorenson & Montgomery 4 and 3
McHenry & Robinson beat Sigel & Andrade 4 and 2

Singles

Currey lost to Alexander 5 and 4
Montgomerie beat Andrade 4 and 2
McHenry beat Loeffler 3 and 2
Shaw halved with Sorenson
Robinson beat Mattice 1 hole
Carrick lost to Lewis 3 and 2
Eggo lost to Mayfair 1 hole
Girvan lost to Sigel 6 and 5

1985 *Pine Valley GC, NJ* Aug 21–22

Result: USA 13, GB&I 11

Captains: J Sigel (USA), CW Green (GB&I)

***First Day* – Foursomes**

Verplank & Sigel beat Montgomerie & Macgregor 1 hole
Waldorf & Randolph lost to Hawksworth & McGimpsey 4 and 3
Sonnier & Haas lost to Baker & McEvoy 6 and 5
Podolak & Love halved with Bloice & Stephen

Singles

S Verplank beat G McGimpsey 2 and 1
S Randolph beat P Mayo 5 and 4
R Sonnier halved with J Hawksworth
J Sigel beat CS Montgomerie 5 and 4
B Lewis lost to P McEvoy 2 and 1
C Burroughs lost to G Macgregor 2 holes
D Waldorf beat D Gilford 4 and 2
J Haas lost to AR Stephen 2 and 1

***Second Day* – Foursomes**

Verplank & Sigel halved with Mayo & Montgomerie
Randolph & Haas beat Hawksworth & McGimpsey 3 and 2
Lewis & Burroughs beat Baker & McEvoy 2 and 1
Podolak & Love beat Bloice & Stephen 3 and 2

Singles

Randolph halved with McGimpsey
Verplank beat Montgomerie 1 hole
Sigel lost to Hawksworth 4 and 3
Love beat McEvoy 5 and 3
Sonnier lost to Baker 5 and 4
Burroughs lost to Macgregor 3 and 2
Lewis beat Bloice 4 and 3
Waldorf lost to Stephen 2 and 1

1983 *Royal Liverpool GC, Merseyside, England* May 25–26

Result: USA 13½, GB&I 10½

Captains: CW Green (GB&I), J Sigel (USA)

***First Day* – Foursomes**

Macgregor & Walton beat Sigel & Fehr 3 and 2
Keppler & Pierse lost to Wood & Faxon 3 and 1
Lewis & Thompson lost to Lewis & Holtgrieve 7 and 6
Mann & Oldcorn beat Hoffer & Tentis 5 and 4

Singles

P Walton beat J Sigel 1 hole
SD Keppler lost to R Fehr 1 hole
G Macgregor halved with W Wood
DG Carrick lost to B Faxon 3 and 1
A Oldcorn beat B Tuten 4 and 3
P Parkin beat N Crosby 5 and 4
AD Pierse lost to B Lewis Jr 3 and 1
LS Mann lost to J Holtgrieve 6 and 5

***Second Day* – Foursomes**

Macgregor & Walton lost to Crosby & Hoffer 2 holes
Parkin & Thompson beat Faxon & Wood 1 hole
Mann & Oldcorn beat Lewis & Holtgrieve 1 hole
Keppler & Pierse halved with Sigel & Fehr

Singles

Walton beat Wood 2 and 1
Parkin lost to Faxon 3 and 2
Macgregor lost to Fehr 2 and 1
Thompson lost to Tuten 3 and 2
Mann halved with Tentis
Keppler lost to Lewis 6 and 5
Oldcorn beat Holtgrieve 3 and 2
Carrick lost to Sigel 3 and 2

1981 *Cypress Point Club, CA* Aug 28–29

Result: USA 15, GB&I 9

Captains: J Gabrielsen (USA), R Foster (GB&I)

***First Day* – Foursomes**

Sutton & Sigel lost to Walton & Rafferty 4 and 2
Holtgrieve & Fuhrer beat Chapman & McEvoy 1 hole
Lewis & von Tacky beat Deeble & Hutcheon 2 and 1
Commans & Pavin beat Evans & Way 5 and 4

Singles

H Sutton beat R Rafferty 3 and 1
J Rassett beat CR Dalgleish 1 hole
R Commans lost to P Walton 1 hole
B Lewis lost to R Chapman 2 and 1
J Mudd beat G Godwin 1 hole
C Pavin beat IC Hutcheon 4 and 3
D von Tacky lost to P Way 3 and 1
J Sigel beat P McEvoy 4 and 2

***Second Day* – Foursomes**

Sutton & Sigel lost to Chapman & Way 1 hole
Holtgrieve & Fuhrer lost to Walton & Rafferty 6 and 4
Lewis & von Tacky lost to Evans & Dalgleish 3 and 2
Rassett & Mudd beat Hutcheon & Godwin 5 and 4

Singles

Sutton lost to Chapman 1 hole
Holtgrieve beat Rafferty 2 and 1
Fuhrer beat Walton 4 and 3
Sigel beat Way 6 and 5
Mudd beat Dalgleish 7 and 5
Commans halved with Godwin
Rassett beat Deeble 4 and 3
Pavin halved with Evans

1979 *Muirfield, East Lothian, Scotland* May 30–31

Result: USA 15½, GB&I 8½

Captains: R Foster (GB&I), RL Siderowf (USA)

***First Day* – Foursomes**

McEvoy & Marchbank lost to Hoch & Sigel 1 hole
Godwin & Hutcheon beat West & Sutton 2 holes
Brand Jr & Kelley lost to Fischesser & Holtgrieve 1 hole
Brodie & Carslaw beat Moody & Gove 2 and 1

Singles

P McEvoy halved with J Sigel
JC Davies lost to D Clarke 8 and 7
J Buckley lost to S Hoch 9 and 7
IC Hutcheon lost to J Holtgrieve 6 and 4
B Marchbank beat M Peck 1 hole
G Godwin beat G Moody 3 and 2
MJ Kelley beat D Fischesser 3 and 2
A Brodie lost to M Gove 3 and 2

***Second Day* – Foursomes**

Godwin & Brand lost to Hoch & Sigel 4 and 3
McEvoy & Marchbank beat Fischesser & Holtgrieve 2 and 1
Kelley & Hutcheon halved with West & Sutton
Carslaw & Brodie halved with Clarke & Peck

Singles

McEvoy lost to Hoch 3 and 1
Brand lost to Clarke 2 and 1
Godwin lost to Gove 3 and 2
Hutcheon lost to Peck 2 and 1
Brodie beat West 3 and 2
Kelley lost to Moody 3 and 2
Marchbank lost to Sutton 3 and 1
Carslaw lost to Sigel 2 and 1

1977 *Shinnecock Hills GC, NY* Aug 26–27

Result: USA 16, GB&I 8

Captains: LW Oehmig(USA), AC Saddler (GB&I)

***First Day* – Foursomes**

Fought & Heafner beat Lyle & McEvoy 4 and 3
Simpson & Miller beat Davies & Kelley 5 and 4
Siderowf & Hallberg lost to Hutcheon & Deeble 1 hole
Sigel & Brannan beat Brodie & Martin 1 hole

Singles

L Miller beat P McEvoy 2 holes
J Fought beat IC Hutcheon 4 and 3
S Simpson beat GH Murray 7 and 6
V Heafner beat JC Davies 4 and 3
B Sander lost to A Brodie 4 and 3
G Hallberg lost to S Martin 3 and 2
F Ridley beat AWB Lyle 2 holes
J Sigel beat P McKellar 5 and 3

***Second Day* – Foursomes**

Fought & Heafner beat Hutcheon & Deeble 4 and 3
Miller & Simpson beat McEvoy & Davies 2 holes
Siderowf & Sander lost to Brodie & Martin 6 and 4
Ridley & Brannan lost to Murray & Kelley 4 and 3

Singles

Miller beat Martin 1 hole
Fought beat Davies 2 and 1
Sander lost to Brodie 2 and 1
Hallberg beat McEvoy 4 and 3
Siderowf lost to Kelley 2 and 1
Brannan lost to Hutcheon 2 holes
Ridley beat Lyle 5 and 3
Sigel beat Deeble 1 hole

1975 *St Andrews, Fife, Scotland* May 28–29

Result: USA 15½, GB&I 8½

Captains: DM Marsh (GB&I), ER Updegraff (USA)

***First Day* – Foursomes**
James & Eyles beat Pate & Siderowf 1 hole
Davies & Poxon lost to Burns & Stadler 5 and 4
Green & Stuart lost to Haas & Strange 2 and 1
Macgregor & Hutcheon lost to Giles & Koch 5 and 4

Singles
M James beat J Pate 2 and 1
JC Davies halved with C Strange
P Mulcare beat RL Siderowf 1 hole
HB Stuart lost to G Koch 3 and 2
MA Poxon lost to J Grace 3 and 1
IC Hutcheon halved with WC Campbell
GRD Eyles lost to J Haas 2 and 1
G Macgregor lost to M Giles III 5 and 4

***Second Day* – Foursomes**
Mulcare & Hutcheon beat Pate & Siderowf 1 hole
Green & Stuart lost to Burns & Stadler 1 hole
James & Eyles beat Campbell & Grace 5 and 3
Hedges & Davies lost to Haas & Strange 3 and 2

Singles
Hutcheon beat Pate 3 and 2
Mulcare lost to Strange 4 and 3
James lost to Koch 5 and 4
Davies beat Burns 2 and 1
Green lost to Grace 2 and 1
Macgregor lost to Stadler 3 and 2
Eyles lost to Campbell 2 and 1
Hedges halved with Giles

1973 *The Country Club, Brookline, MA* Aug 24–25

Result: USA 14, GB&I 10

Captains: JW Sweetser (USA), DM Marsh (GB&I)

***First Day* – Foursomes**
Giles & Koch halved with King & Hedges
Siderowf & Pfeil beat Stuart & Davies 5 and 4
Edwards & Ellis beat Green & Milne 2 and 1
West & Ballenger beat Foster & Homer 2 and 1

Singles
M Giles III beat HB Stuart 5 and 4
RL Siderowf beat MF Bonallack 4 and 2
G Koch lost to JC Davies 1 hole
M West lost to HK Clark 2 and 1
D Edwards beat R Foster 2 holes
M Killian lost to MG King 1 hole
W Rodgers lost to CW Green 1 hole
M Pfeil lost to WT Milne 4 and 3

***Second Day* – Foursomes**
Giles & Koch & Homer & Foster 7 and 5
Siderowf & Pfeil halved with Clark & Davies
Edwards & Ellis beat Hedges & King 2 and 1
Rodgers & Killian beat Stuart & Milne 1 hole

Singles
Ellis lost to Stuart 5 and 4
Siderowf lost to Davies 3 and 2
Edwards beat Homer 2 and 1
Giles halved with Green
West beat King 1 hole
Killian lost to Milne 2 and 1
Koch halved with Hedges
Pfeil beat Clark 1 hole

1971 *St Andrews, Fife, Scotland* May 26–27

Result: GB&I 13, USA 11

Captains: MF Bonallack (GB&I), JM Winters Jr (USA)

***First Day* – Foursomes**
Bonallack & Humphreys beat Wadkins & Simons 1 hole
Green & Carr beat Melnyk & Giles 1 hole
Marsh & Macgregor beat Miller & Farquhar 2 and 1
Macdonald & Foster beat Campbell & Kite 2 and 1

Singles
CW Green lost to L Wadkins 1 hole
MF Bonallack lost to M Giles III 1 hole
GC Marks lost to AL Miller III 1 hole
JS Macdonald lost to S Melnyk 3 and 2
RJ Carr halved with W Hyndman III
W Humphreys lost to JR Gabrielsen 1 hole
HB Stuart beat J Farquhar 3 and 2
R Foster lost to T Kite 3 and 2

***Second Day* – Foursomes**
Marks & Green lost to Melnyk & Giles 1 hole
Stuart & Carr beat Wadkins & Gabrielsen 1 hole
Marsh & Bonallack lost to Miller & Farquhar 5 and 4
Macdonald & Foster halved with Campbell & Kite

Singles
Bonallack lost to Wadkins 3 and 1
Stuart beat Giles 2 and 1
Humphreys beat Melnyk 2 and 1
Green beat Miller 1 hole
Carr beat Simons 2 holes
Macgregor beat Gabrielsen 1 hole
Marsh beat Hyndman 1 hole
Marks lost to Kite 3 and 2

1969 *Milwaukee GC, WI* Aug 22–23

Result: USA 10, GB&I 8†

Captains: WJ Patton (USA), MF Bonallack (GB&I)

***First Day* – Foursomes**
Giles & Melnyk beat Bonallack & Craddock 3 and 2
Fleisher & Miller halved with Benka & Critchley
Wadkins & Siderowf lost to Green & A Brooks
W Hyndman III & Inman Jr beat Foster & Marks 2 and 1

Singles
B Fleisher halved with MF Bonallack
M Giles III beat CW Green 1 hole
AL Miller III beat B Critchley 1 hole
RL Siderowf beat LP Tupling 6 and 5
S Melnyk lost to PJ Benka 3 and 1
L Wadkins lost to GC Marks 1 hole
J Bohmann beat MG King 2 and 1
ER Updegraff beat R Foster 6 and 5

***Second Day* – Foursomes**
Giles & Melnyk halved with Green & Brooks
Fleisher & Miller lost to Benka & Critchley 2 and 1
Siderowf & Wadkins beat Foster & King 6 and 5
Updegraff & Bohmann lost to Bonallack & Tupling 4 and 3

Singles
Fleisher lost to Bonallack 5 and 4
Siderowf halved with Critchley
Miller beat King 1 hole
Giles halved with Craddock
Inman beat Benka 2 and 1
Bohmann lost to Brooks 4 and 3
Hyndman halved with Green
Updegraff lost to Marks 3 and 2

† *No points were given for halved matches between 1922 and 1969. There was a total of 12 points 1922–61 and 24 points 1963–69*

1967 *R. St George's GC, Kent, England* May 19–20
Result: USA 13, GB&I 7†
Captains: JB Carr (GB&I), JW Sweetser (USA)

***First Day* – Foursomes**
Shade & Oosterhuis halved with Murphy & Cerrudo
Foster & Saddler lost to Campbell & Lewis 1 hole
Bonallack & Attenborough lost to Gray & Tutwiler 4 and 2
Carr & Craddock lost to Dickson & Grant 3 and 1

Singles
RDBM Shade lost to WC Campbell 2 and 1
R Foster lost to RJ Murphy Jr 2 and 1
MF Bonallack halved with AD Gray Jr
MF Attenborough lost to RJ Cerrudo 4 and 3
P Oosterhuis lost to RB Dickson 6 and 4
T Craddock lost to JW Lewis Jr 2 and 1
AK Pirie halved with DC Allen
AC Saddler beat MA Fleckman 3 and 2

***Second Day* – Foursomes**
Bonallack & Craddock beat Murphy & Cerrudo 2 holes
Saddler & Pirie lost to Campbell & Lewis 1 hole
Shade & Oosterhuis beat Gray & Tutwiler 3 and 1
Foster & Millensted beat Allen & Fleckman 2 and 1

Singles
Shade lost to Campbell 3 and 2
Bonallack beat Murphy 4 and 2
Saddler beat Gray 3 and 2
Foster halved with Cerrudo
Pirie lost to Dickson 4 and 3
Craddock beat Lewis 5 and 4
Oosterhuis lost to Grant 1 hole
Millensted lost to Tutwiler 3 and 1

1965 *Baltimore GC, MD* Sept 3–4
Result: USA 11, GB&I 11†
Captains: JW Fischer (USA), JB Carr (GB&I)

***First Day* – Foursomes**
Campbell & Gray lost to Lunt & Cosh 1 hole
Beman & Allen halved with Bonallack & Clark
Patton & Tutwiler beat Foster & Clark 5 and 4
Hopkins & Eichelberger lost to Townsend & Shade 2 and 1

Singles
WC Campbell beat MF Bonallack 6 and 5
DR Beman beat R Foster 2 holes
AD Gray Jr lost to RDBM Shade 3 and 1
JM Hopkins lost to CA Clark 5 and 3
WJ Patton lost to P Townsend 3 and 2
D Morey lost to AC Saddler 2 and 1
DC Allen lost to GB Cosh 2 holes
ER Updegraff lost to MSR Lunt 2 and 1

***Second Day* – Foursomes**
Campbell & Gray beat Saddler & Foster 4 and 3
Beman & Eichelberger lost to Townsend & Shade 2 and 1
Tutwiler & Patton beat Cosh & Lunt 2 and 1
Allen & Morey lost to CA Clark & Bonallack 2 and 1

Singles
Campbell beat Foster 3 and 2
Beman beat Saddler 1 hole
Tutwiler beat Shade 5 and 3
Allen lost to Cosh 4 and 3
Gray beat Townsend 1 hole
Hopkins halved with CA Clark
Eichelberger beat Bonallack 5 and 3
Patton beat Lunt 4 and 2

1963 *Turnberry, Ayrshire, Scotland* May 24–25
Result: USA 12, GB&I 8†
Captains: CD Lawrie (GB&I), RS Tufts (USA)

***First Day* – Foursomes**
Bonallack & Murray beat Patton & Sikes 4 and 3
Carr & Green lost to Gray & Harris 2 holes
Lunt & Sheahan lost to Beman & Coe 5 and 3
Madeley & Shade halved with Gardner & Updegraff

Singles
SWT Murray beat DR Beman 3 and 1
MJ Christmas lost to WJ Patton 3 and 2
JB Carr beat RH Sikes 7 and 5
DB Sheahan beat LE Harris 1 hole
MF Bonallack beat RD Davies 1 hole
AC Saddler halved with CR Coe
RDBM Shade beat AD Gray Jr 4 and 3
MSR Lunt halved with CB Smith

***Second Day* – Foursomes**
Bonallack & Murray lost to Patton & Sikes 1 hole
Lunt & Sheahan lost to Gray & Harris 3 and 2
Green & Saddler lost to Gardner & Updegraff 3 and 1
Madeley & Shade lost to Beman & Coe 3 and 2

Singles
Murray lost to Patton 3 and 2
Sheahan beat Davies 1 hole
Carr lost to Updegraff 4 and 3
Bonallack lost to Harris 3 and 2
Lunt lost to Gardner 3 and 2
Saddler halved with Beman
Shade beat Gray 2 and 1
Green lost to Coe 4 and 3

1961 *Seattle GC, WA* Sept 1–2
Result: USA 11, GB&I 1
Captains: J Westland (USA), CD Lawrie (GB&I)

Foursomes
Beman & Nicklaus beat Walker & Chapman 6 and 5
Coe & Cherry beat Blair & Christmas 1 hole
Hyndman & Gardner beat Carr & G Huddy 4 and 3
Cochran & Andrews beat Bonallack & Shade 4 and 3

Singles
DR Beman beat MF Bonallack 3 and 2
CR Coe beat MSR Lunt 5 and 4
FM Taylor Jr beat J Walker 3 and 2
W Hyndman III beat DW Frame 7 and 6
JW Nicklaus beat JB Carr 6 and 4
CB Smith lost to MJ Christmas 3 and 2
RW Gardner beat RDBM Shade 1 hole
DR Cherry beat DA Blair 5 and 4

1959 *Muirfield, East Lothian, Scotland* May 15–16
Result: USA 9, GB&I 3
Captains: GH Micklem (GB&I), CR Coe (USA)

Foursomes
Jack & Sewell lost to Ward & Taylor 1 hole
Carr & Wolstenholme lost to Hyndman & Aaron 1 hole
Bonallack & Perowne lost to Patton & Coe 9 and 8
Lunt & Shepperson lost to Wettlander & Nicklaus 2 and 1

Singles
JB Carr beat CR Coe 3 and 1
GB Wolstenholme lost to EH Ward Jr 9 and 8
RR Jack beat WJ Patton 5 and 3
DN Sewell lost to W Hyndman III 4 and 3
AE Shepperson beat TD Aaron 2 and 1
MF Bonallack lost to DR Beman 2 holes
MSR Lunt lost to HW Wettlander 6 and 5
WD Smith lost to JW Nicklaus 5 and 4

† No points were given for halved matches between 1922 and 1969. There was a total of 12 points 1922–61 and 24 points 1963–69

1957 *The Minikahda Club, MN* Aug 30–31

Result: USA 8, GB&I 3†

Captains: CR Coe (USA), GH Micklem (GB&I)

Foursomes

Baxter & Patton beat Carr & Deighton 2 and 1
Campbell & Taylor beat Bussell & Scrutton 4 and 3
Blum & Kocsis lost to Jack & Sewell 1 hole
Robbins & Rudolph halved with Shepperson & Wolstenholme

Singles

WJ Patton beat RR Jack 1 hole
WC Campbell beat JB Carr 3 and 2
R Baxter Jr beat A Thirlwell 4 and 3
W Hyndman III beat FWG Deighton 7 and 6
JE Campbell lost to AF Bussell 2 and 1
FM Taylor Jr beat D Sewell 1 hole
EM Rudolph beat PF Scrutton 3 and 2
H Robbins Jr lost to GB Wolstenholme 2 and 1

1955 *St Andrews, Fife, Scotland* May 20–21

Result: USA 10, GB&I 2

Captains: GA Hill (GB&I), WC Campbell (USA)

Foursomes

Carr & White lost to Ward & Cherry 1 hole
Micklem & Morgan lost to Patton & Yost 2 and 1
Caldwell & Millward lost to Conrad & Morey 3 and 2
Blair & Cater lost to Cudd & Jackson 5 and 4

Singles

RJ White lost to EH Ward Jr 6 and 5
PF Scrutton lost to WJ Patton 2 and 1
I Caldwell beat D Morey 1 hole
JB Carr lost to DR Cherry 5 and 4
DA Blair beat JW Conrad 1 hole
EB Millward lost to BH Cudd 2 holes
RC Ewing lost to JG Jackson 6 and 4
JL Morgan lost to RL Yost 8 and 7

1953 *The Kittansett, MA* Sept 4–5

Result: USA 9, GB&I 3

Captains: CR Yates (USA), AA Duncan (GB&I)

Foursomes

Urzetta & Venturi beat Carr & White 6 and 4
Ward & Westland beat Langley & AH Perowne 9 and 8
Jackson & Littler beat Wilson & MacGregor 3 and 2
Campbell & Coe lost to Micklem & Morgan 4 and 3

Singles

EH Ward Jr beat JB Carr 4 and 3
RD Chapman lost to RJ White 1 hole
GA Littler beat GH Micklem 5 and 3
J Westland beat RC MacGregor 7 and 5
DR Cherry beat NV Drew 9 and 7
K Venturi beat JC Wilson 9 and 8
CR Coe lost to JL Morgan 3 and 2
S Urzetta beat JDA Langley 3 and 2

1951 *Birkdale GC, Lancashire, England* May 11–12

Result: USA 6, GB&I 3†

Captains: RH Oppenheimer (GB&I), WP Turnesa (USA)

Foursomes

White & Carr halved with Stranahan & Campbell
Ewing & Langley halved with Coe & McHale
Kyle & Caldwell lost to Chapman & Knowles Jr 1 hole
Bruen Jr & Morgan lost to Turnesa & Urzetta 5 and 4

Singles

SM McCready lost to S Urzetta 4 and 3
JB Carr beat FR Stranahan 2 and 1
RJ White beat CR Coe 2 and 1
JDA Langley lost to JB McHale Jr 2 holes
RC Ewing lost to WC Campbell 5 and 4
AT Kyle beat WP Turnesa 2 holes
I Caldwell halved with HD Paddock Jr
JL Morgan lost to RD Chapman 7 and 6

1949 *Winged FootGC. NY* Aug 19–20

Result: USA 10, GB&I 2

Captains: FD Ouimet (USA), PB Lucas (GB&I)

Foursomes

Billows & Turnesa lost to Carr & White 3 and 2
Kocsis & Stranahan beat Bruen & McCready 2 and 1
Bishop & Riegel beat Ewing & Micklem 9 and 7
Dawson & McCormick beat Thom & Perowne 8 and 7

Singles

WP Turnesa lost to RJ White 4 and 3
FR Stranahan beat SM McCready 6 and 5
RH Riegel beat J Bruen Jr 5 and 4
JW Dawson beat JB Carr 5 and 3
CR Coe beat RC Ewing 1 hole
RE Billows beat KG Thom 2 and 1
CR Kocsis beat AH Perowne 4 and 2
JB McHale Jr beat GH Micklem 5 and 4

1947 *St Andrews, Fife, Scotland* May 16–17

Result: USA 8, GB&I 4

Captains: JB Beck (GB&I), FD Ouimet (USA)

Foursomes

Carr & Ewing lost to Bishop & Riegel 3 and 2
Crawley & Lucas beat Ward & Quick 5 and 4
Kyle & Wilson lost to Turnesa & Kammer 5 and 4
White & Stowe beat Stranahan & Chapman 4 and 3

Singles

LG Crawley lost to MH Ward 5 and 3
JB Carr beat SE Bishop 5 and 3
GH Micklem lost to RH Riegel 6 and 5
RC Ewing lost to WP Turnesa 6 and 5
C Stowe lost to FR Stranahan 2 and 1
RJ White beat AF Kammer Jr 4 and 3
JC Wilson lost to SL Quick 8 and 6
PB Lucas lost to RD Chapman 4 and 3

1938 *St Andrews, Fife, Scotland* June 3–4

Result: GB&I 7, USA 4†

Captains: JB Beck (GB&I), FD Ouimet (USA)

Foursomes

Bentley & Bruen halved with Fischer & Kocsis
Peters & Thomson beat Goodman & Ward 4 and 2
Kyle & Stowe lost to Yates & Billows 3 and 2
Pennink & Crawley beat Smith & Haas 3 and 1

Singles

J Bruen Jr lost to CR Yates 2 and 1
H Thomson beat JG Goodman 6 and 4
LG Crawley lost to JW Fischer 3 and 2
C Stowe beat CR Kocsis 2 and 1
JJF Pennink lost to MH Ward 12 and 11
RC Ewing beat RE Billows 1 hole
GB Peters beat R Smith 9 and 8
AT Kyle beat F Haas Jr 5 and 4

† No points were given for halved matches between 1922 and 1969. There was a total of 12 points 1922–61 and 24 points 1963–69

1936 *Pine Valley GC, NJ* Sept 2–3

Result: USA 9, GB&I 0†

Captains: FD Ouimet (USA), W Tweddell (GB&I)

Foursomes

Goodman & Campbell beat Thomson & Bentley 7 and 5
Smith & White beat McLean & Langley 8 and 7
Yates & Emery halved with Peters & Dykes
Givan & Voigt halved with Hill & Ewing

Singles

JG Goodman beat H Thomson 3 and 2
AE Campbell beat J McLean 5 and 4
JW Fischer beat RC Ewing 8 and 7
R Smith beat GA Hill 11 and 9
W Emery beat GB Peters 1 hole
CR Yates beat JM Dykes 8 and 7
GT Dunlap Jr halved with HG Bentley
E White beat JDA Langley 6 and 5

1934 *St Andrews, Fife, Scotland* May 11–12

Result: USA 9, GB&I 2†

Captains: Hon M Scott (GB&I), FD Ouimet (USA)

Foursomes

Wethered & Tolley lost to Goodman & Little 8 and 6
Bentley & Fiddian lost to Moreland & Westland 6 and 5
Scott & McKinlay lost to Egan & Marston 3 and 2
McRuvie & McLean beat Ouimet & Dunlap 4 and 2

Singles

Hon M Scott lost to JG Goodman 7 and 6
CJH Tolley lost to WL Little Jr 6 and 5
LG Crawley lost to FD Ouimet 5 and 4
J McLean lost to GT Dunlap Jr 4 and 3
EW Fiddian lost to JW Fischer 5 and 4
SL McKinlay lost to GT Moreland 3 and 1
EA McRuvie halved with J Westland
TA Torrance beat MR Marston 4 and 3

1932 The Country Club, *Brookline, MA* Sept 1–2

Result: USA 8, GB&I 1†

Captains: FD Ouimet (USA), TA Torrance (GB&I)

Foursomes

Sweetser & Voigt beat Hartley & Hartley 7 and 6
Seaver & Moreland beat Torrance & de Forest 6 and 5
Ouimet & Dunlap beat Stout & Burke 7 and 6
Moe & Howell beat Fiddian & McRuvie 5 and 4

Singles

FD Ouimet halved with TA Torrance
JW Sweetser halved with JA Stout
GT Moreland beat RW Hartley 2 and 1
J Westland halved with J Burke
GJ Voigt lost to LG Crawley 1 hole
MJ McCarthy Jr beat WL Hartley 3 and 2
CH Seaver beat EW Fiddian 7 and 6
GT Dunlap Jr beat EA McRuvie 10 and 9

1930 *Royal St George's GC, Sandwich, Kent* May 15–16

Result: USA 10, GB&I 2

Captains: RH Wethered (GB&I), RT Jones Jr (USA)

Foursomes

Tolley & Wethered beat Von Elm & Voigt 2 holes
Hartley & Torrance lost to Jones & Willing 8 and 7
Holderness & Stout lost to MacKenzie & Moe 2 and 1
Campbell & Smith lost to Johnston & Ouimet 2 and 1

Singles

CJH Tolley lost to HR Johnston 5 and 4
RH Wethered lost to RT Jones Jr 9 and 8
RW Hartley lost to G Von Elm 3 and 2
EWE Holderness lost to GJ Voigt 10 and 8
JN Smith lost to OF Willing 2 and 1
TA Torrance beat FD Ouimet 7 and 6
JA Stout lost to DK Moe 1 hole
W Campbell lost to RR MacKenzie 6 and 5

1928 *Chicago GC, IL* Aug 30–31

Result: USA 11, GB&I 1

Captains: RT Jones Jr (USA), W Tweddell (GB&I)

Foursomes

Sweetser & Von Elm beat Perkins & Tweddell 7 and 6
Jones & Evans beat Hezlet & Hope 5 and 3
Ouimet & Johnston beat Torrance & Storey 4 and 2
Gunn & MacKenzie beat Beck & Martin 7 and 5

Singles

RT Jones Jr beat TP Perkins 13 and 12
G Von Elm beat W Tweddell 3 and 2
FD Ouimet beat CO Hezlet 8 and 7
JW Sweetser beat WL Hope 5 and 4
HR Johnston beat EF Storey 4 and 2
C Evans Jr lost to TA Torrance 1 hole
W Gunn beat RH Hardman 11 and 10
RR MacKenzie beat GNC Martin 2 and 1

1926 *St Andrews, Fife, Scotland* June 2–3

Result: USA 6, GB&I 5†

Captains: R Harris (GB&I), RA Gardner (USA)

Foursomes

Wethered & Holderness beat Ouimet & Guilford 5 and 4
Tolley & Jamieson lost to Jones & Gunn 4 and 3
Harris & Hezlet lost to Von Elm & Sweetser 8 and 7
Storey & Brownlow lost to Gardner & MacKenzie 1 hole

Singles

CJH Tolley lost to RT Jones Jr 12 and 11
EWE Holderness lost to JW Sweetser 4 and 3
RH Wethered beat FD Ouimet 5 and 4
CO Hezlet halved with G Von Elm
R Harris beat JP Guilford 2 and 1
Hon WGE Brownlow lost to W Gunn 9 and 8
EF Storey beat RR MacKenzie 2 and 1
A Jamieson Jr beat RA Gardner 5 and 4

1924 *Garden City GC, NY* Sept 12–13

Result: USA 9, GB&I 3

Captains: RA Gardner (USA), CJH Tolley (GB&I)

Foursomes

Marston & Gardner beat Storey & Murray 3 and 1
Guilford & Ouimet beat Tolley & Hezlet 2 and 1
Jones & Fownes Jr lost to Scott & Scott Jr 1 hole
Sweetser & Johnston beat Torrance & Bristowe 4 and 3

Singles

MR Marston lost to CJH Tolley 1 hole
RT Jones Jr beat CO Hezlet 4 and 3
C Evans Jr beat WA Murray 2 and 1
FD Ouimet beat EF Storey 1 hole
JW Sweetser lost to Hon M Scott 7 and 6
RA Gardner beat WL Hope 3 and 2
JP Guilford beat TA Torrance 2 and 1
OF Willing beat DH Kyle 3 and 2

† *No points were given for halved matches between 1922 and 1969. There was a total of 12 points 1922–61 and 24 points 1963–69*

1923 *St Andrews, Fife, Scotland* May 18–19

Result: USA 6, GB&I 5†

Captains: R Harris (GB&I), RA Gardner (USA)

Foursomes

Tolley & Wethered beat Ouimet & Sweetser 6 and 5
Harris & Hooman lost to Gardner & Marston 7 and 6
Holderness & Hope beat Rotan & Herron 1 hole
Wilson & Murray beat Johnston & Neville 4 and 3

Singles

RH Wethered halved with FD Ouimet
CJH Tolley beat JW Sweetser 4 and 3
R Harris lost to RA Gardner 1 hole
WW Mackenzie lost to GV Rotan 5 and 4
WL Hope lost to MR Marston 6 and 5
EWE Holderness lost to FJ Wright Jr 1 hole
J Wilson beat SD Herron 1 hole
WA Murray lost to OF Willing 2 and 1

1922 *National Golf Links, NY* Aug 28–29

Result: USA 8, GB&I 4

Captains: WC Fownes (USA), R Harris (GB&I)

Foursomes

Guilford & Ouimet beat Tolley & Darwin 8 and 7
Evans & Gardner lost to Wethered & Aylmer 5 and 4
Jones & Sweetser beat Torrance & Hooman 3 and 2
Marston & Fownes beat Caven & Mackenzie 2 and 1

Singles

JP Guilford beat CJH Tolley 2 and 1
RT Jones Jr beat RH Wethered 3 and 2
C Evans Jr beat J Caven 5 and 4
FD Ouimet beat CC Aylmer 8 and 7
RA Gardner beat WB Torrance 7 and 5
MR Marston lost to WW Mackenzie 6 and 5
WC Fownes Jr lost to B Darwin 3 and 1
JW Sweetser lost to CVL Hooman at 37th

Unofficial match

1921 *Hoylake* 21 May

Result: USA 9, GB&I 3

Foursomes

Simpson & Jenkins lost to Evans & Jones 5 and 3
Tolley & Holderness lost to Ouimet & Guilford 3 and 2
de Montmorency & Wethered lost to Hunter & Platt 1 hole
Aylmer & Armour lost to Wright & Fownes 4 and 2

Singles

CJH Tolley beat C Evans Jr 4 and 3
JLC Jenkins lost to FD Ouimet 6 and 5
RH de Montmorency lost to RT Jones Jr 4 and 3
JG Simpson lost to JP Guilford 2 and 1
CC Aylmer beat P Hunter 2 and 1
TD Armour beat JW Platt 2 and 1
EWE Holderness lost to F Wright 2 holes
RH Wethered lost to WC Fownes Jr 3 and 1

Walker Cup – INDIVIDUAL RECORDS

Notes: Bold type indicates captain; in brackets, did not play
† indicates players who have also played in the Ryder Cup

Great Britain and Ireland

Name		Year	Played	Won	Lost	Halved
MF Attenborough	ENG	1967	2	0	2	0
CC Aylmer	ENG	1922	2	1	1	0
†P Baker	ENG	1985	3	2	1	0
JB Beck	ENG	1928-(**38**)-(**47**)	1	0	1	0
PJ Benka	ENG	1969	4	2	1	1
HG Bentley	ENG	1934-36-38	4	0	2	2
DA Blair	SCO	1955-61	4	1	3	0
C Bloice	SCO	1985	3	0	2	1
MF Bonallack	ENG	1957-59-61-63-65-67-**69**-**71**-73	25	8	14	3
JT Bookless	SCO	(1932)	0	0	0	0
W Booth	SCO	2009	4	1	2	1
†G Brand Jr	SCO	1979	3	0	3	0
OC Bristowe	ENG	(1923)-24	1	0	1	0
A Brodie	SCO	1977-79	8	5	2	1
A Brooks	SCO	1969	3	2	0	1
M Brooks	SCO	1997	2	0	2	0
C Brown	WAL	(**1995-97**)	0	0	0	0
S Brown	ENG	2011	3	1	1	1
Hon WGE Brownlow	IRL	1926	2	0	2	0
J Bruen	IRL	1938-49-51	5	0	4	1
JA Buckley	WAL	1979	1	0	1	0
J Burke	IRL	1932	2	0	1	1
R Burns	IRL	1993	2	1	1	0
AF Bussell	SCO	1957	2	1	1	0
J Byrne	SCO	2011	3	2	1	0
S Cage	ENG	1993	3	0	2	1
I Caldwell	ENG	1951-55	4	1	2	1
J Caldwell	IRL	2007	3	1	1	1
W Campbell	SCO	1930	2	0	2	0
JB Carr	IRL	1947-49-51-53-55-57-59-61-63-(**65**)-**67**	20	5	14	1

Name		Year	Played	Won	Lost	Halved
RJ Carr	IRL	1971	4	3	0	1
DG Carrick	SCO	1983-87	5	0	5	0
IA Carslaw	SCO	1979	3	1	1	1
†P Casey	ENG	1999	4	4	0	0
C Cassells	ENG	1989	3	2	1	0
JR Cater	SCO	1955	1	0	1	0
J Caven	SCO	1922-(23)	2	0	2	0
BHG Chapman	ENG	1961	1	0	1	0
R Chapman	ENG	1981	4	3	1	0
MJ Christmas	ENG	1961-63	3	1	2	0
†CA Clark	ENG	1965	4	2	0	2
GJ Clark	ENG	1965	1	0	1	0
†HK Clark	ENG	1973	3	1	1	1
R Claydon	ENG	1989	4	2	2	0
†A Coltart	SCO	1991	3	2	1	0
GB Cosh	SCO	1965	4	3	1	0
R Coughlan	IRL	1997	4	0	3	1
T Craddock	IRL	1967-69	6	2	3	1
LG Crawley	ENG	1932-34-38-47	6	3	3	0
B Critchley	ENG	1969	4	1	1	2
D Curry	ENG	1987	4	1	3	0
P Cutler	IRL	2011	4	3	0	1
CR Dalgleish	SCO	1981-(**07**)-(**09**)	3	1	2	0
B Darwin	ENG	1922	2	1	1	0
JC Davies	ENG	1973-75-77-79	13	3	8	2
R Davies	WAL	2005-07	8	4	3	1
G Dear	SCO	2009	4	1	2	1
P Deeble	ENG	1977-81	5	1	4	0
FWG Deighton	SCO	(1951)-57	2	0	2	0
R Dinwiddie	ENG	2005	3	1	1	3
SC Dodd	WAL	1989	4	1	1	2
†L Donald	ENG	1999-01	8	7	1	0
N Dougherty	ENG	2001	4	3	1	0
B Dredge	WAL	1993	3	0	3	0
†NV Drew	IRL	1953	1	0	1	0
A Dunbar	IRL	2011	3	2	1	0
AA Duncan	WAL	(**1953**)	0	0	0	0
JM Dykes	SCO	1936	2	0	1	1
S Dyson	ENG	1999	3	0	2	1
NB Edwards	WAL	2001-03-05-07-(**2011**)	12	4	5	3
R Eggo	ENG	1987	2	0	2	0
J Elson	ENG	2001	3	1	0	2
D Evans	WAL	1981	3	1	1	1
G Evans	ENG	1991	4	2	2	0
RC Ewing	IRL	1936-38-47-49-51-55	10	1	7	2
GRD Eyles	ENG	1975	4	2	2	0
J Fanagan	IRL	1995	3	3	0	0
EW Fiddian	ENG	1932-34	4	0	4	0
O Fisher	ENG	2005	4	1	2	1
T Fleetwood	ENG	2009	2	1	1	0
J de Forest	ENG	1932	1	0	1	0
M Foster	ENG	1995	4	2	0	2
R Foster	ENG	1965-67-69-71-73-(**79**)-(**81**)	17	2	13	2
N Fox	IRL	2003	3	1	2	0
DW Frame	ENG	1961	1	0	1	0
S Gallacher	SCO	1995	4	2	2	0
†D Gilford	ENG	1985	1	0	1	0
P Girvan	SCO	1987	3	0	3	0
L Goddard	ENG	2009	2	0	2	0
G Godwin	ENG	1979-81	7	2	4	1
G Gordon	SCO	2003	1	0	1	0
CW Green	SCO	1963-69-71-73-75-(**83**)-(**85**)	17	4	10	3
P Gribben	IRL	1999	4	1	2	1
M Haines	ENG	2009	4	1	3	0
RH Hardman	ENG	1928	1	0	1	0
A Hare	ENG	1989	3	2	0	1
†P Harrington	IRL	1991-93-95	9	3	5	1
R Harris	SCO	(**1922**)-**23-26**	4	1	3	0
RW Hartley	ENG	1930-32	4	0	4	0

Name		Year	Played	Won	Lost	Halved
WL Hartley	ENG	1932	2	0	2	0
J Hawksworth	ENG	1985	4	2	1	1
G Hay	SCO	1991	3	1	2	0
P Hedges	ENG	1973-75	5	0	2	3
CO Hezlet	IRL	1924-26-28	6	0	5	1
GA Hill	ENG	1936-(**55**)	2	0	1	1
S Hodgson	ENG	2009-11	6	2	4	0
M Hoey	IRL	2001	4	3	1	0
Sir EWE Holderness	ENG	1923-26-30	6	2	4	0
TWB Homer	ENG	1973	3	0	3	0
‡CVL Hooman	ENG	1922-23	3	†1	2	†0
WL Hope	SCO	1923-24-28	5	1	4	0
D Horsey	ENG	2007	4	3	1	0
DB Howard	SCO	1995-97	6	0	4	2
†D Howell	ENG	1995	3	2	0	1
G Huddy	ENG	1961	1	0	1	0
W Humphreys	ENG	1971	3	2	1	0
IC Hutcheon	SCO	1975-77-79-81	15	5	8	2
S Hutsby	ENG	2009	4	2	2	0
D Inglis	SCO	2003	4	2	1	1
RR Jack	SCO	1957-59	4	2	2	0
L James	ENG	1995	2	0	2	0
†M James	ENG	1975	4	3	1	0
A Jamieson Jr	SCO	1926	2	1	1	0
N Kearney	IRL	2009	4	2	2	0
MJ Kelley	ENG	1977-79	7	3	3	1
L Kelly	SCO	1999	2	0	2	0
SD Keppler	ENG	1983	4	0	3	1
†MG King	ENG	1969-73	7	1	5	1
AT Kyle	SCO	1938-47-51	5	2	3	0
DH Kyle	SCO	1924	1	0	1	0
JA Lang	SCO	(1930)	0	0	0	0
JDA Langley	ENG	1936-51-53	6	0	5	1
CD Lawrie	SCO	(**1961**)-(**63**)	0	0	0	0
ME Lewis	ENG	1983	1	0	1	0
T Lewis	ENG	2011	4	1	2	1
G Lockerbie	ENG	2005	4	1	3	0
PB Lucas	ENG	(1936)-47-(**49**)	2	1	1	0
MSR Lunt	ENG	1959-61-63-65	11	2	8	1
†AWB Lyle	SCO	1977	3	0	3	0
AR McCallum	SCO	1928	1	0	1	0
SM McCready	IRL	1949-51	3	0	3	0
JS Macdonald	SCO	1971	3	1	1	1
†G McDowell	IRL	2001	4	2	2	0
B McElhinney	IRL	2005	1	0	1	0
P McEvoy	ENG	1977-79-81-85-89-(**99**)-(**01**)	18	5	11	2
R McEvoy	ENG	2001	2	1	0	1
G McGimpsey	IRL	1985-89-91-(**03**)-(**05**)	11	4	5	2
†P McGinley	IRL	1991	3	1	2	0
G Macgregor	SCO	1971-75-83-85-87-(**91**)-(**93**)	14	5	8	1
RC MacGregor	SCO	1953	2	0	2	0
J McHenry	IRL	1987	4	2	2	0
†R McIlroy	IRL	2007	4	1	2	1
P McKellar	SCO	1977	1	0	1	0
WW Mackenzie	SCO	1922-23	3	1	2	0
SL McKinlay	SCO	1934	2	0	2	0
J McLean	SCO	1934-36	4	1	3	0
EA McRuvie	SCO	1932-34	4	1	2	1
JFD Madeley	IRL	1963	2	0	1	1
S Manley	WAL	2003	3	2	0	1
LS Mann	SCO	1983	4	2	1	1
B Marchbank	SCO	1979	4	2	2	0
GC Marks	ENG	1969-71-(**87**)-(**89**)	6	2	4	0
DM Marsh	ENG	(1959)-71-(**73**)-(**75**)	3	2	1	0
GNC Martin	IRL	1928	1	0	1	0
S Martin	SCO	1977	4	2	2	0
L Matthews	WAL	2007	1	0	1	0
P Mayo	WAL	1985-87	4	0	3	1
GH Micklem	ENG	1947-49-53-55-(**57**)-(**59**)	6	1	5	0

‡*In 1922 Hooman beat Sweetser at the 37th – on all other occasions halved matches have counted as such.*

Name		Year	Played	Won	Lost	Halved
DJ Millensted	ENG	1967	2	1	1	0
JW Milligan	SCO	1989-91	7	3	3	1
EB Millward	ENG	(1949)-55	2	0	2	0
WTG Milne	SCO	1973	4	2	2	0
†CS Montgomerie	SCO	1985-87	8	2	5	1
JL Morgan	WAL	1951-53-55	6	2	4	0
C Moriarty	IRL	2003	4	1	3	0
J Moul	ENG	2007	4	2	1	1
P Mulcare	IRL	1975	3	2	1	0
GH Murray	SCO	1977	2	1	1	0
SWT Murray	SCO	1963	4	2	2	0
WA Murray	SCO	1923-24-(26)	4	1	3	0
K Nolan	IRL	1997	3	0	3	0
E O'Connell	IRL	1989	4	2	0	2
S O'Hara	SCO	2001	4	2	2	0
A Oldcorn	ENG	1983	4	4	0	0
†PA Oosterhuis	ENG	1967	4	1	2	1
R Oppenheimer	ENG	(**1951**)	0	0	0	0
P Page	ENG	1993	2	0	2	0
C Paisley	ENG	2009	3	0	1	2
D Park	WAL	1997	3	0	3	0
P Parkin	WAL	1983	3	2	1	0
J Parry	ENG	2007	2	1	1	0
D Patrick	SCO	1999	1	0	1	0
J Payne	ENG	1991	4	2	2	0
JJF Pennink	ENG	1938	2	1	1	0
TP Perkins	ENG	1928	2	0	2	0
GB Peters	SCO	1936-38	4	2	1	1
V Phillips	ENG	1993	3	1	2	0
AD Pierse	IRL	1983	3	0	2	1
AH Perowne	ENG	1949-53-59	4	0	4	0
AK Pirie	SCO	1967	3	0	2	1
MA Poxon	ENG	1975	2	0	2	0
D Prosser	ENG	1989	1	0	1	0
R Pugh	WAL	2011	3	3	0	0
I Pyman	ENG	1993	3	0	3	0
†R Rafferty	IRL	1981	4	2	2	0
R Ramsay	SCO	2005	2	1	1	0
G Rankin	SCO	1995-97-99	8	2	6	0
M Richardson	ENG	2005	4	2	2	0
D Robertson	SCO	1993	3	1	2	0
J Robinson	ENG	1987	4	2	2	0
RN Roderick	WAL	1989	2	0	1	1
J Rose	ENG	1997	4	2	2	0
P Rowe	ENG	1999	3	3	0	0
R Russell	SCO	1993	3	0	3	0
AC Saddler	SCO	1963-65-67-(**77**)	10	3	5	2
L Saltman	SCO	2005-07	7	4	3	0
Hon M Scott	ENG	1924-**34**	4	2	2	0
R Scott, Jr	SCO	1924	1	1	0	0
PF Scrutton	ENG	1955-57	3	0	3	0
J Senior	ENG	2011	4	2	1	1
DN Sewell	ENG	1957-59	4	1	3	0
RDBM Shade	SCO	1961-63-65-67	14	6	6	2
G Shaw	SCO	1987	4	1	2	1
DB Sheahan	IRL	1963	4	2	2	0
AE Shepperson	ENG	1957-59	3	1	1	1
G Sherry	SCO	1995	4	2	2	0
AF Simpson	SCO	(1926)	0	0	0	0
M Skelton	ENG	2003	2	1	1	0
JN Smith	SCO	1930	2	0	2	0
WD Smith	SCO	1959	1	0	1	0
M Stanford	ENG	1993	3	1	2	0
AR Stephen	SCO	1985	4	2	1	1
M Stewart	SCO	2011	4	2	1	1
EF Storey	ENG	1924-26-28	6	1	5	0
G Storm	ENG	1999	4	2	2	0
JA Stout	ENG	1930-32	4	0	3	1
C Stowe	ENG	1938-47	4	2	2	0
HB Stuart	SCO	1971-73-75	10	4	6	0

Name		Year	Played	Won	Lost	Halved
A Sullivan	ENG	2011	4	2	2	0
A Thirlwell	ENG	1957	1	0	1	0
KG Thom	ENG	1949	2	0	2	0
MS Thompson	ENG	1983	3	1	2	0
H Thomson	SCO	1936-38	4	2	2	0
CJH Tolley	ENG	1922-23-**24**-26-30-34	12	4	8	0
TA Torrance	SCO	1924-28-30-**32**-34	9	3	5	1
WB Torrance	SCO	1922	2	0	2	0
†PM Townsend	ENG	1965	4	3	1	0
LP Tupling	ENG	1969	2	1	1	0
W Tweddell	ENG	**1928**-(**36**)	2	0	2	0
J Walker	SCO	1961	2	0	2	0
†P Walton	IRL	1981-83	8	6	2	0
M Warren	SCO	2001	3	2	1	0
C Watson	SCO	1997	3	1	1	1
†P Way	ENG	1981	4	2	2	0
RH Wethered	ENG	1922-23-26-**30**-34	9	5	3	1
L White	ENG	1991	2	1	1	0
RJ White	ENG	1947-49-51-53-55	10	6	3	1
D Whitnell	ENG	2009	3	0	3	0
D Willett	ENG	2007	4	0	2	2
R Willison	ENG	1991	4	1	3	0
J Wilson	SCO	1923	2	2	0	0
JC Wilson	SCO	1947-53	4	0	4	0
O Wilson	ENG	2003	3	2	0	1
S Wilson	SCO	2003	4	1	1	2
GB Wolstenholme	ENG	1957-59	4	1	2	1
GP Wolstenholme	ENG	1995-97-99-01-03-05	19	10	9	0
S Young	SCO	1997	4	2	2	0

United States of America

Name	Year	Played	Won	Lost	Halved
†TD Aaron	1959	2	1	1	0
B Alexander	1987	3	2	1	0
DC Allen	1965-67	6	0	4	2
B Andrade	1987	4	2	2	0
ES Andrews	1961	1	1	0	0
D Ballenger	1973	1	1	0	0
B Barber	2011	3	0	2	1
R Baxter, Jr	1957	2	2	0	0
N Begay III	1995	3	1	2	0
DR Beman	1959-61-63-65	11	7	2	2
D Berganio	1993	3	1	2	0
RE Billows	1938-49	4	2	2	0
SE Bishop	1947-49	3	2	1	0
AS Blum	1957	1	0	1	0
J Bohmann	1969	3	1	2	0
M Brannan	1977	3	1	2	0
A Bratton	1995	3	1	0	2
GF Burns III	1975	3	2	1	0
C Burroughs	1985	3	1	2	0
J Byrd	1999	3	1	2	0
AE Campbell	1936	2	2	0	0
JE Campbell	1957	1	0	1	0
WC Campbell	1951-53-(**55**)-57-65-67-71-75	18	11	4	3
P Cantlay	2011	4	2	1	1
N Cassini	2001	4	2	2	0
B Cauley	2009	4	3	0	1
RJ Cerrudo	1967	4	1	1	2
RD Chapman	1947-51-53	5	3	2	0
D Cherry	1953-55-61	5	5	0	0
D Clarke	1979	3	2	0	1
RE Cochran	1961	1	1	0	0
CR Coe	1949-51-53-(**57**)-**59**-61-63	13	7	4	2
R Commans	1981	3	1	1	1
E Compton	2001	3	1	1	1
JW Conrad	1955	2	1	1	0

Name	Year	Played	Won	Lost	Halved
J Courville Jr	1995-97	6	4	2	0
K Cox	1995	3	1	2	0
N Crosby	1983	2	1	1	0
BH Cudd	1955	2	2	0	0
RD Davies	1963	2	0	2	0
JW Dawson	1949	2	2	0	0
D Delcher	1997	3	2	1	0
T Demsey	1993	3	3	0	0
RB Dickson	1967	3	3	0	0
A Doyle	1991-93	6	5	1	0
J Driscoll	2001	3	0	3	0
GT Dunlap Jr	1932-34-36	5	3	1	1
†D Duval	1991	3	2	1	0
D Edwards	1973	4	4	0	0
HC Egan	1934	1	1	0	0
D Eger	1989-91-01	8	4	3	1
D Eichelberger	1965	3	1	2	0
B Elder	1997	4	4	0	0
J Ellis	1973	3	2	1	0
W Emery	1936	2	1	0	1
H English	2011	4	2	2	0
C Evans Jr	1922-24-28	5	3	2	0
M Every	2005	4	1	2	1
J Farquhar	1971	3	1	2	0
†B Faxon	1983	4	3	1	0
R Fehr	1983	4	2	1	1
JW Fischer	1934-36-38-(**65**)	4	3	0	1
D Fischesser	1979	3	1	2	0
MA Fleckman	1967	2	0	2	0
B Fleisher	1969	4	0	2	2
J Fought	1977	4	4	0	0
†R Fowler	2007-09	8	7	1	0
WC Fownes Jr	**1922-24**	3	1	2	0
F Fuhrer III	1981	3	2	1	0
JR Gabrielsen	1977-(**81**)-(**91**)	3	1	2	0
R Gamez	1989	4	3	0	1
RA Gardner	1922-**23-24-26**	8	6	2	0
RW Gardner	1961-63	5	4	0	1
B Gay	1993	2	0	1	1
B Gielow	2009	3	1	2	0
M Giles III	1969-71-73-75-(**93**)	15	8	2	5
HL Givan	1936	1	0	0	1
L Glover	2001	4	2	2	0
JG Goodman	1934-36-38	6	4	2	0
J Gore	1997	3	2	0	1
D Gossett	1999	4	1	2	1
M Gove	1979	3	2	1	0
J Grace	1975	3	2	1	0
JA Grant	1967	2	2	0	0
AD Gray Jr	1963-65-67-(**95**)-(**97**)	12	5	6	1
D Green	2001	3	0	3	0
JP Guilford	1922-24-26	6	4	2	0
W Gunn	1926-28	4	4	0	0
B Haas	2003	4	2	2	0
†F Haas Jr	1938	2	0	2	0
H Haas	1999	4	3	1	0
†JD Haas	1975	3	3	0	0
J Haas	1985	3	1	2	0
G Hallberg	1977	3	1	2	0
GS Hamer Jr	(1947)	0	0	0	0
B Harman	2005-09	7	4	1	2
J Harris	1993-95-97-01	14	10	4	0
LE Harris Jr	1963	4	3	1	0
V Heafner	1977	3	3	0	0
M Hendrix	2003	3	2	0	1
R Henley	2011	3	1	2	0
SD Herron	1923	2	0	2	0
T Herron	1993	3	3	0	0
†S Hoch	1979	4	4	0	0

Name	Year	Played	Won	Lost	Halved
W Hoffer	1983	2	1	1	0
M Hoffmann	2009	3	2	0	1
J Holmes	2005	3	2	1	0
J Holtgrieve	1979-81-83-(**2011**)	10	6	4	0
JM Hopkins	1965	3	0	2	1
B Horschel	2007	4	3	1	0
R Howe	1989	1	0	1	0
W Howell	1932	1	1	0	0
B Hurley	2005	2	0	2	0
W Hyndman III	1957-59-61-69-71	9	6	1	2
J Inman Jr	1969	2	2	0	0
JG Jackson	1953-55	3	3	0	0
T Jackson	1995-99	6	3	2	1
†D Johnson	2007	3	1	1	1
GK Johnson	1989	3	1	2	0
HR Johnston	1923-24-28-30	6	5	1	0
RT Jones Jr	1922-24-26-**28-30**	10	9	1	0
AF Kammer Jr	1947	2	1	1	0
M Killian	1973	3	1	2	0
A Kim	2005	4	2	1	1
C Kirk	2007	2	1	1	0
C Kite	1987	3	2	1	0
†TO Kite Jr	1971	4	2	1	1
RE Knepper	(1922)	0	0	0	0
C Knost	2007	4	2	0	2
RW Knowles Jr	1951	1	1	0	0
G Koch	1973-75	7	4	1	2
CR Kocsis	1938-49-57	5	2	2	1
K Kraft	2011	4	0	4	0
J Kribel	1997	3	1	2	0
†M Kuchar	1999	3	0	3	0
T Kuehne	1995-03-07	10	2	7	1
F Langham	1991	3	1	2	0
R Leen	1997	3	2	1	0
†J Leonard	1993	3	3	0	0
G Lesher	1989	4	1	3	0
B Lewis Jr	1981-83-85-87-(**03**)-(**05**)	14	10	4	0
JW Lewis	1967	4	3	1	0
WL Little Jr	1934	2	2	0	0
†GA Littler	1953	2	2	0	0
E Loar	1999	3	2	1	0
B Loeffler	1987	3	2	1	0
†D Love III	1985	3	2	0	1
J Lovemark	2007	3	2	1	0
B Mackenzie	2003	3	3	0	0
RR Mackenzie	1926-28-30	6	5	1	0
MJ McCarthy Jr	(1928)-32	1	1	0	0
BN McCormick	1949	1	1	0	0
T McKnight	1999	2	0	2	0
JB McHale	1949-51	3	2	0	1
MR Marston	1922-23-24-34	8	5	3	0
D Martin	1989	4	1	1	2
G Marucci	1995-97-(**07**)-(**09**)	6	4	1	1
L Mattiace	1987	3	2	1	0
R May	1991	4	3	1	0
B Mayfair	1987	3	3	0	0
E Meeks	1989	1	0	0	1
SN Melnyk	1969-71	7	3	3	1
†P Mickelson	1989-91	8	4	2	2
AL Miller III	1969-71	8	4	3	1
J Miller	1999	3	2	1	0
L Miller	1977	4	4	0	0
A MItchell	2009	3	1	2	0
K Mitchum	1993	3	2	0	1
DK Moe	1930-32	3	3	0	0
B Molder	1999-01	8	3	3	2
B Montgomery	1987	2	2	0	0
G Moody III	1979	3	1	2	0
J Moore	2007	3	2	0	1
R Moore	2003	2	0	2	0

Name	Year	Played	Won	Lost	Halved
GT Moreland	1932-34	4	4	0	0
D Morey	1955-65	4	1	3	0
J Mudd	1981	3	3	0	0
†RJ Murphy Jr	1967	4	1	2	1
C Nallen	2003	2	1	1	0
JF Neville	1923	1	0	1	0
†JW Nicklaus	1959-61	4	4	0	0
LW Oehmig	(**1977**)	0	0	0	0
FD Ouimet	1922-23-24-26-28-30-**32**-**34**-(**36**)-(**38**)-(**47**)-(**49**)	16	9	5	2
†J Overton	2005	4	3	1	0
HD Paddock Jr	1951	1	0	0	1
†J Pate	1975	4	0	4	0
WJ Patton	1955-57-59-63-65-(**69**)	14	11	3	0
†C Pavin	1981	3	2	0	1
M Pfeil	1973	4	2	1	1
M Podolak	1985	2	1	0	1
M Putnam	2005	4	1	2	1
M Peck	1979	3	1	1	1
SL Quick	1947	2	1	1	0
J Quinney	2001	2	0	2	0
S Randolph	1985	4	2	1	1
J Rassett	1981	3	3	0	0
K Reifers	2005	2	0	2	0
F Ridley	1977-(**87**)-(**89**)	3	2	1	0
RH Riegel	1947-49	4	4	0	0
C Riley	1995	3	1	1	1
H Robbins Jr	1957	2	0	1	1
P Rodgers	2011	3	0	2	1
†W Rogers	1973	2	1	1	0
GV Rotan	1923	2	1	1	0
A Rubinson	2003	4	1	2	1
†EM Rudolph	1957	2	1	0	1
B Sander	1977	3	0	3	0
T Scherrer	1991	3	0	3	0
S Scott	1997-99	6	2	4	0
CH Seaver	1932	2	2	0	0
RL Siderowf	1969-73-75-77-(**79**)	14	4	8	2
J Sigel	1977-79-81-**83**-**85**-87-89-91-93	33	18	10	5
RH Sikes	1963	3	1	2	0
JB Simons	1971	2	0	2	0
†S Simpson	1977	3	3	0	0
W Simpson	2007	3	0	2	1
CB Smith	1961-63	2	0	1	1
N Smith	2009-11	6	2	3	1
R Smith	1936-38	4	2	2	0
R Sonnier	1985	3	0	2	1
J Sorensen	1987	3	1	1	1
J Speith	2011	3	2	0	1
M Sposa	1991	3	2	1	0
†C Stadler	1975	3	3	0	0
K Stanley	2007	3	0	3	0
FR Stranahan	1947-49-51	6	3	2	1
†C Strange	1975	4	3	0	1
†H Sutton	1979-81	7	2	4	1
‡JW Sweetser	1922-23-24-26-28-32-(**67**)-(73)	12	7	†4	1
FM Taylor	1957-59-61	4	4	0	0
D Tentis	1983	2	0	1	1
N Thompson	2005	2	1	1	0
DJ Trahan	2001	4	1	3	0
C Tringale	2009	3	1	1	1
RS Tufts	(**1963**)	0	0	0	0
WP Turnesa	1947-49-**51**	6	3	3	0
B Tuten	1983	2	1	1	0
EM Tutweiler Jr	1965-67	6	5	1	0
ER Updegraff	1963-65-69-(**75**)	7	3	3	1
S Urzetta	1951-53	4	4	0	0
P Uihlein	2009	8	6	2	0
†K Venturi	1953	2	2	0	0
†S Verplank	1985	4	3	0	1

‡In 1922 Hooman beat Sweetser at the 37th – on all other occasions halved matches have counted as such.

Name	Year	Played	Won	Lost	Halved
M Voges	1991	3	2	1	0
GJ Voigt	1930-32-36	5	2	2	1
G Von Elm	1926-28-30	6	4	1	1
D von Tacky	1981	3	1	2	0
†JL Wadkins	1969-71	7	3	4	0
D Waldorf	1985	3	1	2	0
EH Ward Jr	1953-55-59	6	6	0	0
MH Ward	1938-47	4	2	2	0
D Weaver	2009	3	0	2	1
M West III	1973-79	6	2	3	1
J Westland	1932-34-53-(**61**)	5	3	0	2
HW Wettlaufer	1959	2	2	0	0
E White	1936	2	2	0	0
C Williams	2011	3	2	1	0
L Williams	2003-05	7	3	2	2
OF Willing	1923-24-30	4	4	0	0
JM Winters Jr	(**1971**)	0	0	0	0
C Wittenberg	2003	4	1	2	1
C Wollman	1997	3	1	1	1
W Wood	1983	4	1	2	1
†T Woods	1995	4	2	2	0
FJ Wright Jr	1923	1	1	0	0
CR Yates	1936-38-(**53**)	4	3	0	1
D Yates III	1989-93-(**99**)-**01**	6	3	2	1
RL Yost	1955	2	2	0	0
G Zahringer	2003	3	0	2	1

World Amateur Team Championship (Eisenhower Trophy) (inaugurated 1958)

Antalya GC (Sultan course) and Cornelia GC (Faldo course)

Championship reduced to 54 holes because of bad weather

1	United States	131-135-138—404	(Chris Williams, Justin Thomas and Steven Fox)
2	Mexico	135-139-135—409	(Sebastian Vzquez, Carlos Ortiz and Rodolfo Cazaubon)
3	South Korea	134-138-141—413	(Chang-woo Lee, Soo-min Lee and Si-woo Kim)
	Germany	141-135-137—413	(Moritz Lampert, Max Rotluff and Marcel Schneider)
	France	135-140-138—413	(Julien Brun, Edouardo Espana and Paul Barjon)
6	Canada	136-138-143—417	(Albin Choi, Mackenzie Hughes and Corey Connors)
	Norway	140-136-141—417	(Anders Engell, Kristian Johannessen and Kristoffer Venture)
8	England	137-143-138—418	(Garrick Porteous, Craig Hinton and Neil Raymond)
9	Venezuela	138-142-139—419	(Julio Vegas, Gustavo Leon and Jorge A Garcia)
	Japan	141-139-139—419	(Hedeki Matsuyama, Jinichiro Kozuma and Kenta Konishi)
	Spain	137-144-138—419	(Jacobo Pastor, Carlos Pigem and Scott Fernandez)

12 Sweden, Malaysia 420; 14 Italy 422; 15 Australia 423; 16 Colombia 44; 17 Netherlands, Thailand, Wales, Poland, Zimbabwe 425; 22 Austria 426; 23 South Africa 427; 24 India, New Zealand 428; 26 Brazil 429; 17 Denmark, Slovakia, Iceland, Chile, Ireland 430; 32 Portugal, Slovenia 431; 34 Belgium 432; 35 Finland 433; 35 Turkey 434; 37 Singapore 436; 38 China 437; 39 Puerto Rico 438; 40 Czech Republic 439; 41 Guatemala 441; 42 Switzerland 442; 43 Russian Federation 442; 44 Scotland, Hong Kong 444; 46 Argentina 446; 47 Chinese Taipei, Uruguay 452; 49 Bolivia 453; 54 Pakistan 464; 55 Latvia 469; 56 Greece 475; 57 Costa Rica 478; 58 Qatar, Egypt 481; 60 Estonia 484; 61 United Arab Emirates 490; 62 Serbia 491; 63 FYR Macedonia 492; 64 Islamic Republic of Iran 496; 65 Malta 498; 66 Guam 499; 67 Bahrain 514; 68 Bulgaria 524; 69 Oman 528; 70 Ukraine 534; 71 Croatia 551; 71 Kyrgyzstan 642

Individual:

1	Sebastian Vazquez (MEX)	66-67-66—199
2	Chris Williams (USA)	64-67-69—200
3	Moritz Lampert (GER)	70-66-65—201
4	Julien Brun (FRA)	67-72-65—204
	Julio Vegas (VEN)	69-70-65—204
6	James Frazer (WAL)	70-70-66—206

History: From 1958 to 2004, Great Britain & Ireland competed as a team. Now each Home country is represented, hence Scotland's win in 2008.

The 2014 Eisenhower Trophy competition will be played in Japan and Mexico will host the event in 2016

International (continued)

World Amateur Team Championship *continued*

1958	1 Australia* 918; 2 United States 918 **Play-off: Australia 222; United States 224*	Old Course, St Andrews, Fife, Scotland
1960	1 United States 834; 2 Australia 836	Merion GC East, Ardmore, PA, USA
1962	1 United States 854; 2 Canada 862	Fuji GC, Kawana, Japan
1964	1 Great Britain & Ireland 895; 2 Canada 897	Olgiata GC, Rome, Italy
1966	1 Australia 877; 2 United States 879	Club de Golf, Mexico City, Mexico
1968	1 United States 868; 2 Great Britain & Ireland 869	Royal Melbourne GC, Australia
1970	1 United States 854; 2 New Zealand 869	Real Club de Puerta Hierro, Madrid, Spain
1972	1 United States 865; 2 Australia 870	Olivos GC 1980, Buenos Aires, Argentina
1974	1 United States 888; 2 Japan 898	Campo de Golf Cajules, Dominican Republic
1976	1 Great Britain & Ireland 892; 2 Japan 894	Penina GC, Portimão, Algarve, Portugal
1978	1 United States 873; 2 Canada 886	Pacific Harbour GC, Fiji
1980	1 United States 848; 2 South Africa 875	Pinehurst No.2, NC, USA
1982	1 United States 859; 2 Sweden 866	Lausanne GC, Switzerland
1984	1 Japan 870; 2 United States 877	Royal Hong Kong GC, Fanling, Hong Kong
1986	1 Canada 838; 2 United States 841	Lagunita CC, Caracas, Venezuela
1988	1 Great Britain & Ireland 882; 2 United States 887	Ullna GC, Stockholm, Sweden
1990	1 Sweden 879; 2 New Zealand 892	Christchurch GC, New Zealand
1992	1 New Zealand 823; 2 United States 830	Capilano G&CC and Marine Drive GC, Vancouver, BC, Canada
1994	1 United States 838; 2 Great Britain & Ireland 849	La Boulie GC and Le Golf National, Versailles, France
1996	1 Australia 838; 2 Sweden 849	Manila Southwoods (Masters and Legends) GC, Philippines
1998	1 Great Britain and Ireland 852; 2 Australia 856	Club de Golf los Leones and Club de Golf La Dehesa, Santiago, Chile
2000	1 United States 841; 2 Great Britain & Ireland 857	Berlin Sporting Club and Club de Golf Bad Saaron, Germany
2002	1 United States 568; 2 France 571	Sanyana G&CC (Palm and Bunga Raya Courses), Malaysia
2004	1 United States 407; 2 Spain 416	Rio Mar GC (Ocean and River Courses), Puerto Rico
2006	1 Netherlands 554; 2 Canada 556	De Zalse GC and Stellenbosch GC, South Africa
2008	1 Scotland 560; 2 USA 569	The Grange GC (West Course) and Royal Adelaide GC, Australia
2010	1 France 423; 2 Denmark 427	Buenos Aires GC and Olivos GC, Argentina

Europe *v* Asia–Pacific (Sir Michael Bonallack Trophy) (inaugurated 1998)

Monte Rei G&CC, Portugal

Captains: Europe – Andrew Bennett Morgan (WAL), Asia–Pacific – Taimur Hassan Amin (PAK)

Day 1 – Foursomes

Jack Hiluta and Ben Taylor beat Chien-Yao Hung and Natipong Srithong 3 and 2
Daan Huizing and Moritz Lampert beat Cameron Smith and Jake Higginbottom 4 and 2
Thomas Detry and Jon Rahm-Rodriguez lost to Hideki Matsuyama and Seenappa Chikkarangappa 4 and 3
Alan Dunbar and Rhys Enoch beat Mathew Perry and Benjamin Campbell 4 and 3
Marcel Schneider and Robin Kind beat Soo-Min Lee and Khalin Hitesh Joshi 1 hole

Day 1 – Fourball

Daan Huizing and Moritz Lampert lost to Cameron Smith and Mathew Perry 2 and 1
Alan Dunbar and Rhys Enoch beat Benjamin Campbell and Jake Higginbottom 2 holes
Jack Hiluta and Ben Taylor lost to Hideki Matsuyama and Taihei Sato 2 and 1
Manuel Trappel and Robin Kind beat Seenappa Chikkarangappa and Khalin Hitesh Joshi 4 and 3
Thomas Detry and Jon Rahm-Rodriguez lost to Chang-Woo Lee and Soo-Min Lee 4 and 3

Day 2 – Foursomes

Marcel Schneider and Robin Kind beat Hideki Matsuyama and Seenappa Chikkarangappa 3 and 2
Alan Dunbar and Rhys Enoch beat Soo-Min Lee and Khalin Hitesh Joshi 3 and 1
Daan Huizing and Manuel Trappel beat Chien-Yao Hung and Chang-Woo Lee 5 and 4
Jack Hiluta and Ben Taylor beat Jake Higginbottom and Benjamin Campbell 5 and 3
Robert Karlsson and Thomas Detry lost to Mathew Perry and Cameron Smith 1 hole

Day 2 – Fourball
Alan Dunbar and Rhys Enoch beat Seenappa Chikkarangappa and Natipong Srithong 3 and 2
Moritz Lampert and Jon Rahm-Rodriguez beat Hideki Matsuyama and Taihei Sato 1 hole
Jack Hiluta and Ben Taylor lost to Jake Higginbottom and Khalin Hitesh Joshi 7 and 6
Marcel Schneider and Robin Kind beat Soo-Min Lee and Chien-Yao Hung 4 and 3
Daan Huizing and Manuel Trappel halved with Mathew Perry and Cameron Smith

Day 3 – Singles
Manuel Trappel (AUT beat Benjamin Campbell (NZL) 7 and 6
Alan Dunbar (IRL) halved with Seenappa Chikkarangappa (IND)
Rhys Enoch (WAL) beat Cameron Smith (AUS) 2 holes
Robin Kind (NED) lost to Khalin Hitesh Joshi (IND) 4 and 3
Daan Huizing (NED) beat Soo-Min Lee (KOR) 1 hole
Robert Karlsson (SWE) beat Taihei Sato (JPN) 2 and 1
Jack Hiluta (ENG) lost to Hideki Matsuyama (JPN) 3 and 2
Marcel Schneider (GER) lost to Jake Higginbottom (AUS) 3 and 2
Moritz Lampert (GER) halved with Mathew Perry (NZL)
Ben Taylor (ENG) beat Chien-Yao Hung (TPE) 5 and 4
Jon Rahm-Rodriguez (ESP) beat Natipong Srithong (THA) 3 and 1
Thomas Detry (BEL) beat Chang-Woo Lee (KOR) 3 and 2

Result: Europe 21½, Asia-Pacific 10½

St Andrews Trophy (Great Britain & Ireland *v* Continent of Europe)

Match inaugurated 1956, trophy presented 1964 *Portmarnock GC, Dublin, Ireland*

Captains: GBI – Nigel Edwards (WAL); Europe – Alexis Godillot (FRA)

First Day – **Foursomes**
Alan Dunbar (IRL) and Neil Raymond (ENG) lost to Edoardo Espana (FRA) and Moritz Lampert (GER) 2 and 1
Craig Hinton (ENG) and Ben Taylor (ENG) beat Robert Karlsson (SWE) and Thomas Sorensen (DEN) 2 and 1
Rhys Pugh (WAL) and Garrick Porteous (ENG) beat Manuel Trappel (AUT) and Marcel Schneider (GER) 5 and 4
Nathan Kimsey (ENG) and Kevin Phelan (IRL) lost to Carlos Pigem (ESP) and Jacobo Pastor (ESP) 3 and 2

Singles
Pugh lost to Trappel 3 and 2
Hinton beat Pastor 4 and 2
Dunbar lost to Espana 2 holes
Porteous beat Tapio Pulkannen (FIN) 6 and 5
Graeme Robertson (SCO) lost to Pigem 3 and 2
Raymond beat Schneider 3 and 1
Phelan beat Lampert 1 hole
Taylor beat Karlsson 2 holes

Second Day – **Foursomes**
Pugh and Porteous lost to Trappel and Schneider 2 holes
Hinton and Taylor lost to Karlsson and Sorensen 4 and 3
Dunbar and Raymond lost to Espana and Lampert 1 hole
Kimsey and Phelan beat Pigem and Pastore 3 and 2

Singles
Dunbar lost to Karlsson 1 hole
Hinton beat Schneider 1 hole
Porteous beat Pigem 1 hole
Raymond beat Sorensen 2 and 1
Pugh halved with Pastor
Robertson lost to Trappel 3 and 2
Kimsey lost to Espana 3 and 2
Phelan lost to Lampert 2 and 1

Match Result: Continent of Europe 12½, Great Britain and Ireland 11½

History: Since 1956, Great Britain & Ireland have won 24 times, Continent of Europe on five occasions.

Asia–Pacific Amateur Team Championship (Nomura Cup)

This event will next be held in 2013

Africa

African Amateur Team Championship *The Club Benoi*

This event will next be played in 2013

52nd South African Men's Inter-Provincial Championship *Port Elizabeth GC*

Day 1: Central Gauteng 8, Limpopo 4; Western Province 5, Boland 7; Gauteng North 6, Kwa-Zulu Natal 6

Day 2: Boland 5, Gauteng North 7l Limpopo 3, Western Province 9 Kwa-Zulu Natal 3½, Central Gauteng 8½

Day 3: Western Province 7, Gauteng North 5; Limpopo 5½, Kwa-Zulu Natal 6½; Central Gauteng 4½, Boland 7½

Day 4: Central Gauteng 8½, Gauteng North 3½; Boland 7, Limpopo 5; Western Province 8, Kwa-Zulu Natal 4

Day 5: Kwa-Zulu Natal 3, Boland 9; Gauteng North 6, Limpopo 6; Western Province 6½, Central Gauteng 5½

Final table:	*Points*	*Games*
1 Western Province	4	35½
Boland	4	35½
3 Central Gauteng	3	35
4 Gauteng North	2	27
5 Kwa-Zulu Natal	1½	23
6 Limpopo	½	23½

Winning teams: Western Province – Dylan Raubenheimer, Michael Loppnow, Delin Erasmus, Werner Theart, Justin Turner, Le Riche Ehiers, Geriou Roux, Jean Paul Strydom
Boland – Jacquin Hess, Karl Ochse, Anton Oosthuizen. Philip Spies. Armandt Scholtz, Drikus Bruyns, Cedric Rool and Mark Mahoney

South African Mid-Amateur Provincial Tournament *Schoeman Park GC*

Day 1: KwaZulu Natal 9, Eastern Province 3; Central Gauteng 7, Boland 5; Ekurhuleni 9, Western Province 3

Day 2: Boland 5½, Ekurhuleni 6½; Eastern Province 2, Central Gauteng 10; Western Province 7, KwaZulu Natal 5

Day 3: Central Gauteng 6½, Ekurhuleni 5½; Eastern Province 4, Western Province 8; KwaZulu Natal 6½, Boland 5½

Day 4: KwaZulu Natal 7, Ekurhuleni 5; Boland 9½, Eastern Province 2½; Central Gauteng 5, Western Province 7

Day 5: Central Gauteng 10, KwaZulu Natal 2; Western Province 7, Boland 5; Ekurhuleni 9½, Eastern Province 2½

Final table – "A" Section:	*P*	*W*	*D*	*L*	*Pts*	*Games*
1 Central Gauteng	5	4	0	1	8	38½
2 Western Province	5	4	0	1	8	32
3 Ekurhuleni	5	3	0	2	6	35½
4 KwaZulu Natal	5	3	0	2	6	29½
5 Boland	5	1	0	4	2	30½
6 Eastern Province	5	0	0	5	0	14

Winning team: Neil Fusedale, Neil Homann, Stephen Johnston, David Muller, Norman Raad, Kevin Sharp, Steve Williams and Grant Wood

Eastern Province are relegated to "B" Section and will be replaced in 2013 by "B" Section winners North West Province

13th Zone VI African Team Championship *Lilongwe Club, Malawi*

1 South Africa 22½ pts; 2 Namibia 15; 3 Kenya 13½; 4 Malawi, Zimbabwe 13; 6 Uganda 12½; 7 Tanzania 11; 8 Zambia 8½; 9 Mozambique 6½; 10 Mauritius 4½

Winning team: Shaun Smith (Southern Cape), Drikus Bruyns (Boland), J P Strydom (Western Province), C J Du Plessis (Limpopo), Muzi Nethunzi (Central Gauteng), Gert Myburgh (Ekurhuleni), Haydn Porteous (Central Gauteng), Zander Lombard (Gauteng North)

South African Senior Men's Inter-Provincial Championship

Woodhill CC and Wingate Park CC

1	KwaZulu Natal	917
2	Western Province	922
3	Gauteng North	923

4 Eastern Province 941; 5 Border 947; 6 Central Gauteng "B" 951; 7 Central Gauteng 958; 8 Mpumalanga, Gauteng North "B" 967; 10 Erkuhuleni 968; 11 Western Province "B" 978; 12 Boland 981; 13 Southern Cape 1,004; 14 Limpopo 1,007; 15 Free State/Northern Cape 1,011; 16 North-West 1,022; 17 Karoo 1,051.

Winning team: Basil Naido, Lynton Bennett, Richard Nel. Morgan Phillips, Hennie Heyns, Max Magnussen, Dudley Dowling and Graham Van der Veen

Americas

USGA Men's State Team Championship *Galloway NJ*

1	New York	428 (Max Buckley, Michael Miller, Joseph Saladino)
2	Iowa	434 (Dennis Bull, Jon Olson, Gene Elliott)
3	Tennessee	435 (Craig Smith, Todd Burgan, Tim Jackson)

4 Pennsylvania 436; 5 Georgia 437; 6 California 438; 7 Florida 440; 8 Ohio 441; 9 North Carolina 442; 10 Missouri 443; 11 Michigan 444; 12 Louisiana 445; 13 Washington, South Carolina; 15 Vermont 447; 16 Texas 451; 17 Rhode Island, Wisconsin 453; 19 New Hampshire 454; 20 Colorado 456; 21 Indiana, Arizona, Oregon 457; 24, Minnesota, Virginia, Maryland 458; 27 Nebraska, Illinois, Connecticut 459; 30 Alaska, Oklahoma 460; 32 New Jersey 461; 33 Mississippi, Massachusetts 462; 35 Kentucky 463; 36 West Virginia, Utah 464; 38 Delaware, Kansas, Wyoming 466; 41 District of Columbia, Nevada 467; 43 Alabama 468; 44 Montana 469; 45 New Mexico 470; 46 Arkansas 472; 47 North Dakota 477; 48 479; 49 Hawaii, Puerto Rico 503; 51 South Dakota 512; 52 Maine withdrew

Juan Carlos Tailhade Cup *Los Lagartos G&CC, Buenos Aires, Argentina*

1 Australia 564; 2 New Zealand 577; 3 Ireland 579; 4 Argentina, South Africa 580; 6 Mexico 583; 7 Canada 584; 8 Peru 588; 9 Uruguay 591; 10 Spain 593; 11 Netherlands 602; 12 Italy 604; 13 Finalnd, Switzerland 607; 15 Colombia NR.

Winning team: Geoff Drakeford and Jordan Zunic

Individual competition:

1	Geoff Drakeford (AUS)	71-69-66-74—280
2	Juan Alvarez (URU)	67-76-69-70—282
3	Alejandro Tosti (ARG)	72-73-68-70—283
	Joshua Munn (NZL)	67-71-73-72—283

Asia

Etiqa Asean Cup *Royal Selangor GC, Malaysia*

Semi-finals:	Nattawat Suwajanakorn (MAS) beat Jordan Jude Tay Kinjin (MAS) 1 hole
	Low Khai Jei (MAS) beat Puk Praditttan (THA) 1 hole
Final:	Nattawat Suwajanakorn beat Low Khai Jei

Australasia

Australian Men's Interstate Team Championships *Royal Adelaide GC, South Australia*

Round 1 – New South Wales 1, S. Australia 3; Victoria 4, Queensland 3; Tasmania 4, W. Australia 3
Round 2 – Victoria 5, S. Australia 2; New South Wales 4½, Tasmania 2½; Queensland 5½, W. Australia 1½
Round 3 – Tasmania 4, Queensland 3; S. Australia 4½, W. Australia 2½; New South Wales 4, Victoria 3
Round 4 – W. Australia 4, New South Wales 3; Tasmania 4, Victoria 2½; S. Australia 4½, Queensland 2½
Round 5 – Victoria 3½, W. Australia 3½; New South Wales 4½, Queensland 2½; Tasmania 3½, S, Australia 3½

Final table: 1 New South Wales – games won 20, matches won 4; 2 Tasmania 18½–3½; 3 Victoria 18–3½; 4 South Australia 17½–2½; 5 Western Australia 14½–1½; 6 Queensland 16½–1

Final: New South Wales 4½, Tasmania 2½; 3rd place play-off: Victoria 6, South Australia 2; 5th place play-off: Queensland 4½, Western Australia 3½

Winning team: Jake Higginbottom, Brett Drewitt, Daniel Bringolf, Jordan Zunic, Dimi Papadatos, Ricky Kato, Ben Clementson, Callam O'Reilly

Australian Mid-Amateur Team Championship *Moonah Links, Victoria*

1 Victoria	230-222-232—684
2 New South Wales	233-239-246—718
3 Queensland	251-246-243—740
4 Northern Territory	261-248-262—771

Winning team: Jason Perry, Daniel Ong and Sue Wooster.

Europe

113th *Edinburgh Evening News Dispatch* Trophy (inaugurated 1890) *always at Braid Hills*

Semi-finals: Harrison "B" beat BBT 1 hole
Caermount beat British Rugby Club of Paris 2 and 1

Final: Caermount beat Harrison "B" 4 and 3

Winning team: Ian Dickson, Mark Dickson, Martin Hopley and Gary Henshaw

European Men's Challenge Trophy (inaug. 2002) *Keilir GC, Hafnarfjordur, Reykjavik, Iceland*

1 England	352-358-344—1,054
2 Netherlands	355-359-350—1,064
3 Portugal	361-353-362—1,076

4 Iceland 1,087; 5 Belgium 1,102; 6 Slovakia 1,153; 7 Russia 1,159; 8 Serbia 1,222

Winning team: Ben Stow 68-69-67—204; Jack Hiluta 68-74-71—213; Callum Shinkwin 73-74-66—213; Craig Hinton 75-70-70—215; Garrick Porteous 75-72-70—217; Ben Taylor 76-72-74—222

European Amateur Team Championship (inaugurated 1959)

This event will next be held in 2013

European Senior Men's Team Championship (inaugurated 2006) Estoril GC, Portugal

Stroke play qualifying: 1 England 709; 2 Scotland 720; 3 Ireland 724; 4 Germany 728; 5 Spain 736; 6 Italy 744; 7 Sweden 745; 8 Belgium 746; 9 Switzerland 753; 10 Portugal 756; 11 France 764; 12 Finland 778; 13 Czech Republic 781; 14 Denmark 783; 15 Netherlands 789; 16 Norway 791; 17 Austria 792; 18 Israel 821; 19 Slovenia 830; 20 Luxembourg 843

Leading qualifiers England: John Ambridge, Martin Galway, Andrew Stracey, Alan Squires, Tyrone Carter and Chris Reynolds

Individual: 1 John Ambridge (ENG 68-66—134; 2 John Fraser (SCO) 66-73—139; 3 Martin Galway (ENG) 72-69—141, Ian Brotherston (SCO) 71-70—141, Hans-Gunter Reiter (GER) 70-71—141

Match Play

Quarter-finals: Sweden 3, Scotland 2; Italy 3, Ireland 2; Germany 3, Spain 2; England 3, Belgium 2

Semi-finals: Sweden 3, Italy 2; Germany 3, England 2

Final: Sweden 3½, Germany 1½

Winning team: Bob Backstedt, Hans Ivarsson, Mats Anderson, Per Hildebrand, Stefan Lindberg and Tomas Persson

Final ranking: 1 Sweden; 2 Germany; 3 England; 4 Italy; 5 Ireland; 6 Spain; 7 Scotland; 8 Belgium; 9 Switzerland; 10 France; 11 Portugal; 12 Czech Republic; 13 Finland; 14 Netherlands; 15 Denmark; 16 Norway; 17 Austria; 18 Luxembourg; 19 Slovenia; 20 Israel

European Club Cup (Albacom Trophy) (inaugurated 1975) *Corfu, Greece*

1	Basozabal (ESP)	421
2	St Leon-Rot (GER)	425
3	Château de la Tournette (BEL)	431

13 teams took part

Winning team: Ane Urchegui Garcia, Ainhoa Olarra Mujika, Laura Urbistondo Murua

Individual: Katerina Vlasinova (CZW) 70-74-64--208

European Nations Championship (Sotogrande Cup) *Real Club de Golf Sotogrande, Spain*

1	France	215-218-222-217—872
2	Holland	295-209-296-277—877
3	Spain	286-218-146-229—879

4 Portugal 881; 5 Ireland 881; 6 Norway 883; 7 Italy 887; 8 Denmark 888; 9 Austria 890; 10 England 894; 11 Germany 897; 12 Wales 904; 13 Belgium 904; 14 Switzerland 907; 15 Czech Republic 915; 16 Finland 919; 17 Turkey 921

Winning team: Edouard Espana, Mathieu de Cottignes, Adrien Saddler and Kenny Subregis

EGA European Men's Club Trophy *Minthis Hills GC, Cyprus*

1	France	129-131-139—399
2	Germany	132-136-135—403
3	Swtzerland	141-138-138—417

4 Spain 421; 5 Scotland 423; 6 France (Holders), Iceland 424; 8 England 425; 9 Denmark, Austria, Italy, Portugal 427; 13 Netherlands 428; 14 Ireland 430; 15 Belgium 431; 16 Slovkia 438; 17 Czech Republic, Wales 439; 19 Finland 442; 20 Slovenia 450; 21 Luxembourg 451; 22 Greece 464; 23 Estonia 472; 24 Croatia 482; 25 Cyprus 509

Winning team: Adrien Saddler, Lionel Weber and Clement Berardo

Home Internationals (Raymond Trophy) (inaug. 1932) *Gailes Links, Ayrshire, Scotland*

Day One: England 9½, Wales 5½; Ireland 8, Scotland 7
Day Two: Scotland 10½, England 4½; Ireland 11½, Wales 3½
Day Three: Scotland 9½, Wales 5½; England 9½, Ireland 5½

Result: 1 Scotland 2 pts; 2 Ireland 2 pts; 3 England 2 pts, 4 Wales 0 pts. Scotland win the Raymond Trophy having won more games than Ireland or England

Winning team: Scott Borrowman (Dollar), Ross Bell (Downfield), Matthew Clark (Kilmacolm), Paul Ferrier (Baberton), Grant Forrest (Craigielaw), Jack McDonald (Kilmarnock Barassie), Fraser McKenna (Balmore), Graham Robertson (Glenbervie), Paul Shields (Kirkhill), Brian Soutar (Leven Golfing Society) and James White (Lundin). Team captain: Scott Knowles

History: England 36 wins, Scotland 21, Ireland 8, Wales 1. England, Ireland and Scotland have tied on four occasions, Ireland and Scotland once, England and Ireland once and Scotland and England once.

Europe (continued)

Senior Home Internationals (inaugurated 2002) *Southerndown GC, Wales*

Day One: Ireland 7½, Wales 1½; England 6, Scotland 3
Day Two: Ireland 5, Scotland 4; Wales 3, England 6
Day Three: Scotland 4, Wales 5; Ireland 3, England 6

Winning team: England – John Ambridge, Andrew Stracey, Charles Banks, Leslie Bruckner Tyrone Carter, Chris Reynolds and Douglas Cameron

English County Championship (inaugurated 1928) *Beau Desert GC, Cannock*

Day One:
Lancashire 6, Suffolk 3
Wiltshire 7, Worcester 2

Day Two:
Lancashire 6½, Worcester 2½
Wiltshire 6½, Suffolk 2½

Day Three:
Suffolk 6, Worcester 3
Lancashire4½, Wiltshire 4½

Final table	*W*	*D*	*L*	*Pts*
1 Wiltshire	2	1	0	18
2 Lancashire	2	1	0	17
3 Suffolk	1	0	2	11½
4 Worcestershire	0	0	3	7½

Winning team: Alistair James, Jordan Smith, Josh Loughrey, Garry Slade, Robbie Busher and Ben Loughrey

History: Since 1928, the following countries have won: Yorkshire 19 times, Surrey and Lancashire 10, Staffordshire 6, Warwickshire 5, Northumberland 4, Berkshire, Buckinghamshire, Oxfordshire, Middlesex, Worcestershire 3, Gloucestershire, Wiltshire 2, Cheshire, Devon, Dorset, Essex, Hampshire, Hertfordshire, Kent, Lincolnshire 1. In 1985, Hertfordshire and Devon tied.

English Champion Club Tournament (inaugurated 1984) *Stoneham GC*

1	Walsall	216-209—425
2	Farrington	216-212—428
3	Rotherham	217-214—431

4 Coventry 432; 5 Spalding 437; 6 East Sussex National 438; 7 King's Lynn 441; 8 Formby 443; 9 Horsley Lodge 444; 10 Carlisle 445; 11 Dartford 446; 12 South Beds 450; 13 Trevose, Burhill, Wellingborough 452; 16 Woburn, Hintlesham 456; 18 Ferndown 457; 19 Brickhampton Court, Brockenhurst Manor 458; 21 Worksop 459; 22 Longcliffe 462; 23 Rowany 467; 24 Reddish Vale 471; 25 The Northumberland 475; 26 Salisbury and South Wilts, Stover, Ely 480; 29 The Vale 485; 30 Letchworth 488; 31 Wrekin 374

Irish Inter-Provincial Championship *Royal County Down*

Day One: Munster 6½, Connacht 4½
Ulster 9, Leinster 2
Day Two: Munster 6, Leinster 5
Ulster 8½, Connacht 2½
Day Three: Leinster 8, Connacht 3
Munster 7, Ulster 4

Table	*Pld*	*W*	*D*	*L*	*Pts*
1 Munster	3	3	0	0	3
2 Ulster	3	2	0	1	2
3 Leinster	3	1	0	2	1
4 Connacht	3	0	0	3	0

Winning team: Kevin Phelan, Alan Thomas, Gary Hurley, Geoff Lenehan, Pat Murray, Ian O'Rourke. Gary O'Flaherty and Niall Gorey

Scottish Area Team Championship (inaugurated 1990) *Blairgowrie*

Stroke Play Qualifying: Perth & Kinross 712; Fife 713; Renfrewshire 724; Stirlingshire, North East 725; Lanarkshire, South 734; Ayrshire 736; Clackmannanshire 740; Lothians, Dumbartonshire, Glasgow 741; Angus 744; North 747; Argyll & Bute 751; Borders 770

Individual: Glenn Campbell (Perth & Kinross) 68-70—138
James White (Fife) 71-67—138

Match-play – Semi-finals:
Perth & Kinross beat Stirlingshire 3½–1½
Fife beat Renfrewshire 4½–½

Final:
Perth & Kinross beat Fife 3½–1½

Winning team: Stuart McKendrick (Dunkeld & Birnam), Glenn Campbell, George Brass, Bradley Neil, Stuart Graham (all Blairgowrie), Mark Cameron (Alyth), Scott Michie (Kinross)

Belhaven Best Scottish Club Handicap Championship *The Fairmont (Torrance course)*

1	Huntley (Graham Farquharson and Graham Nicol 5)*	68
2	Arbroath Artisan (Keith Ewart and Stewart Cargill 8)	68

*Huntley won on countback

3	Earlsgate (Bryan Coyie and Colin Mclure 10)	69
	Castle Park (William Halliday 9)	69
	Turnhouse (Andrew Young and Steven Armstrong 2)	69

Scottish Men's Club Championship (inaugurated 1985) *Arbroath GC*

1	Blairgowrie	143-142—285
2	Murcar Links	147-145—292
3	Glenbervie	145-151—296
4	Sandhills	152-146—298

5 Girvan 300; 6 Torwoodlee 304; 7 Glencruitten 305; 8 Dumfries and Galloway 307; 9 Dollar 309; 10 Gourock 310; 11 Kirkintilloch 313; 12 Inverness 316; 13 Harburn 317;14 Downfield 318; 15 St Andrews 320; 16 Airdrie 321

Winning team: Stuart Graham, Glenn Campbell and Bradley Neil

Welsh Inter-Counties Championship *Borth & Ynyslas GC*

1	Glamorgan	717	5	Caernarvonshire	749
2	Dyfed	728	6	Brecon and Radner	785
3	Denbighshire	732	7	Flintshire	787
4	Gwent	740	8	Angelsey	803

Winning team: Ian Flower, Richard Hooper, Craig Melding, Brent O'Neill, Chris O'Neill and Luke Thomas

Welsh Team Championship *Newport GC*

Semi-Finals: Newport 3, Neath 2
Radyr 3, Wrexham 2

Final: Newport 3, Radyr 2

11th Turkish Amateur Nations Cup *Gloria GC*

1	Germany	144-131-144—419 (Benedict Staben, Marcel Schneider, Maximilian Rottluff)
2	Denmark	137-140-151—428
3	Turkey	148-139-146—433

Sclaff – the sound produced when a golfer accidentally hits the ground with the clubhead before hitting the ball. Sclaff is thought to resemble thesound of a slap and, indeed, is from the Scottish word *sclaff* meaning 'to slap'.

Other Tournaments 2012

For past results see earlier editions of *The R&A Golfer's Handbook*

Amateur Champion Gold Medal (inaugurated 1870) *always at Leven Links, Fife*

Daniel Young (Craigie Hill) 69-70-67-73—279

Aberconwy Trophy (inaugurated 1976) *always at Conwy and Llandudno (Maesdu), Gwynedd*

Luke Jackson (Lindrick) 78-68-70-74—290

The Antlers (inaugurated 1933) *always at Royal Mid-Surrey*

Not played

The Battle Trophy (inaugurated 2011) *Crail, Craighead*

Fraser McKenna (Balmore) 69-68-72-69—278

Berkhamsted Trophy (inaugurated 1960) *always at Berkhamsted*

Jack Bartlett (Worthing) 68-72–140
Beat John Kemp (Woburn) at the second extra hole

Berkshire Trophy (inaugurated 1946) *always at The Berkshire*

Josh White (Chipstead) 74-67-70-69—280

Burhill Family Foursomes (inaugurated 1937) *always at Burhill, Surrey*

Final: Jane & Harry Bathurst (Hankley Common) beat Andrew & Leonie Baker (Royal Wimbledon) 2 and 1

Cameron Corbett Vase (inaugurated 1897) *always at Haggs Castle, Glasgow*

Daniel Young (Craigie Hill) 68-65—133
Reduced by bad weather

Clwyd Open (inaugurated 1991) *always at Prestatyn and Wrexham*

Will Jones (Oswestry) 67-69-73-73—282

Craigmillar Park Open (inaugurated 1961) *always at Craigmillar Park, Edinburgh*

Graeme Robertson (Glenbervie) 64-70-66-67—267

Duncan Putter (inaugurated 1959) *always at Southerndown, Bridgend, Glamorgan*

Ben Westgate (Trevose [Southerndown]) 71-72-66-71—280

East of Ireland Open Amateur (inaugurated 1989) *Co. Louth*

Chris Selfridge (Moyola Park) 74-73-69-70--286
Beat Nicky Grant (Knock) at the third extra hole

East of Scotland Open Amateur Stroke Play (inaugurated 1989) *Lundin*

Allyn Dick (Kingsknowe) 71-63-71-71—276

Eden Tournament (inaugurated 1919) *always at St Andrews (Eden Course)*

Final: Andrew Day (Broadstone) beat David Henderson-Sowerby (Burford) 1 hole

Edward Trophy (inaugurated 1892) *always at Glasgow GC*

Craig Wilson (Troon Welbeck) 70-70—140
Reduced by bad weather

Fathers and Sons Foursomes *always at West Hill, Surrey*

Final: Nigel and Max O'Hagan (West Hill) beat Charles and John Stapleton (Gerrards Cross/Thetford) 2 holes

Frame Trophy (inaugurated 1986 for players aged 50+) *always at Worplesdon, Surrey*

Douglas Cameron 72-71—143

Golf Illustrated Gold Vase (inaugurated 1909, discontinued 2003)

For results see 2007 edition of The R&A Golfer's Handbook

Hampshire Hog (inaugurated 1957) *always at North Hants*

Callum Shinkwin (Moor Park) 68-68—136

Hampshire Salver (inaugurated 1979) *always at North Hants/Blackmoor*

Jack Bartlett (Worthing) 71-67-65-75—278
Beat Matthew Fitzpatrick (Hallamshire) on countback

Hertfordshire Bowl *Porters Park and Moor Park*

Luke Johnson (King's Lynn) 73-70-72-72—287

John Cross Bowl (inaugurated 1957) *always at Worplesdon, Surrey*

Mark Booker (Royal Wimbledon) 73-68—141
Beat Ben Smith (Sandy Lodge) at the first extra hole

King George V Coronation Cup *always at Porters Park, Herts*

George Morris (Eaton) 70-72—142

Lagonda Trophy *1975–1989 at Camberley and from 1990 at The Gog Magog*

Michael Saunders (Dartford) 69-67-69-70—275

Lake Macquarie Tournament (inaugurated 1958) *always at Belmont GC, NSW, Australia*

(Australian unless stated)
Daniel Nisbet 273

Lytham Trophy (inaugurated 1965) *always at Royal Lytham & St Annes and Fairhaven*

Daan Huizing (NED) 67-67-71-68—273

Midland Open (inaugurated 1976) *St Ives*

Jack Colegate (Rochester & Cobham Park) 67-67-70-72—276

Mullingar Grant Thornton Scratch Trophy *Mullingar*
Paul Casey (Headfort) 68-75-71-70—284

Newlands Trophy *Lanark*
Matthew Clark (Kilmacolm) 66-71-67-72—276

North of Ireland Open Amateur (inaugurated 1989) *always at Royal Portrush*
Final: Rory McNamara (Headford) beat Michael Sinclair (Knock) 1 hole

North of Scotland Open Amateur Stroke Play (David Blair Trophy) *Tain*
Gordon Stevenson (Whitecraigs) 70-70-67-67—274

North-East Scotland Open *Newmachar GC (Hawkshill course)*
Chris Robb (Meldrum House) 67-71-72—210

North-East Scotland Open *Newmachar*
Chris Robb (Meldrum House) 67-71-72—210

Prince of Wales Challenge Cup (inaugurated 1928) *always at Royal Cinque Ports*
This event will next be held in 2013

Rosebery Challenge Cup (inaugurated 1933) *always at Ashridge*
Mark Wharton (John O'Gaunt) 72-70—142
Beat Matt Wallace at the second extra hole

St Andrews Links Trophy (inaugurated 1989) *always at St Andrews (Old and New)*
Daan Huizing (NED) 65-64-68-67—264

St David's Gold Cross (inaugurated 1930) *always at Royal St David's, Gwynedd*
David Boote (Walton Heath)* 66-69-76-76—287
Beat Geraint Jones (Royal St David's) at the first extra hole

Selborne Salver (inaugurated 1976) *always at Blackmoor*
Matthew Fitzpatrick (Hallamshire) 63-70—133

South of England Open Amateur (inaugurated 2005) *Walton Heath*
Ryan Evans (Wellingborough) 74-69-68-70—281

South East England Links Championship (inaugurated 2010)
Royal Cinque Ports and Royal St George's
Oliver Carr (Heswall) 69-69-76-73—287

South of Ireland Open Amateur *Lahinch*
Final: Pat Murray (Limerick) beat Stephen Healy (Claremorris) 2 holes

South-East Scotland District Championship *Longniddry*
Adam Dunton (McDonald) 69-67-72-69--277

Sunningdale Foursomes (inaugurated 1934) *always at Sunningdale*

Final: J Wilcox (Blankney) and G Payne (Chobham) beat J Little (PGAET) and L Bond (PGAET) 3 and 1

Sutherland Chalice (inaugurated 2000) *Dumfries & Galloway*

James Ross (Royal Burgess) 70-68-68-70—276

Tennant Cup (inaugurated 1880) *always at Glasgow GC (Glasgow Gailes and Killermont)*

Liam Johnston (Dumfries & County) 76-75-68-62—281

Tillman Trophy (inaugurated 1980) *Moor Park*

Alasdair Dalgliesh (Hayward's Heath) 66-72-72-65—275

Beat David Boote (Walton Heath) at the fifth extra hole

Trubshaw Cup (inaugurated 1989) *always at Ashburnham and Tenby*

Gary Hurley (West Waterford) 72-72—144

Tucker Trophy (inaugurated 1991) *Whitchurch*

James Frazer (Pennard) 68

Reduced by bad weather

West of England Open Amateur Match Play (inaugurated 1912)

always at Burnham & Berrow

Final David Gregory (Burnham & Berrow) beat James Popham (Enmore Park)

West of England Open Amateur Stroke Play (inaugurated 1968) *Royal North Devon*

Josh White (Chipstead) 71-78-74—223

Reduced to 54 holes due to bad weather

West of Ireland Open Amateur (inaugurated 1989) *Co. Sligo (Rosses Point)*

Final: Harry Diamond (Belvoir Park) beat Stephen Healy (Claremorris) 1 hole

West of Scotland Open Amateur

Not played

Worplesdon Mixed Foursomes (inaugurated 1921) *always at Worplesdon, Surrey*

Final: Trevor & Aileen Greenfield (Pyecombe)beat James Earley (Hankley Common) & Kay Bowman (West Hill) 6 and 5

Month by month in 2012

Winner of his first major title by eight, Rory McIlroy does it again at the USPGA Championship to beat Jack Nicklaus' record win margin in the event and return to world number one. Keegan Bradley wins the WGC–Bridgestone Invitational when Jim Furyk double bogeys the last, Sergio García clinches a Ryder Cup return with his first win in America for four years and wild cards are handed to uncapped Nicolas Colsaerts and Ian Poulter.

University and School Events 2012

For past results see earlier editions of *The R&A Golfer's Handbook*

Palmer Cup (USA university students *v* European university students) *R. Co. Down GC, N. Ireland*

Round One – Fourballs (European names first):
Daan Huizing (NED) and Thomas Pieters (BEL) lost to Chris Williams and Andrew Yun 1 hole
Julien Brun (FRA) and Sebastian Cappelen (DEN) halved with Derek Ernst and Corbin Mills
David Booth (ENG) and Graeme Robertson (SCO) lost to Blayne Barber and James Whyte 6 and 4
Robert Karlsson (SWE) and Pontus Widegren (SWE) lost to Patrick Rodgers and Justin Thomas 2 holes

Round Two – Foursomes:
Huizing and Pieters lost to Ernst and Yun 1 hole
Robertson and Widegren lost to Mills and Williams 6 and 4
Booth and Karlsson beat Barber and White 2 and 1
Brun and Cappelen lost to Rodgers and Thomas 1 hole

Round Three – Singles:
Robertson lost to Williams 3 and 2
Brun beat Barber 2 and 1
Huizing beat Mills 1 up
Booth lost to Yun 4 and 2
Pieters halved with White
Karlsson beat Ernst 4 and 2
Cappelen halved with Thomas
Widegren halved with Rodgers

Round Four – Singles:
Canppelen beat Williams 3 and 2
Huizing beat Thomas 4 and 3
Karlsson beat Rodgers 2 and 1
Pieters halved with Mills
Booth beat White 2 up
Robertson beat Ernst 2 and 1
Brun beat Barber 6 and 5
Widegren beat Yun 3 and 1

Result: Europe 13½, USA 10½

History: The United States of America have won the event eight times, Europe on seven occasions and Great Britain and Ireland once with one match drawn.

1997	USA 19, Great Britain and Ireland 5	Bay Hill GC
1998	USA 12, Great Britain and Ireland 12	Old Course, St Andrews
1999	USA 17½, Great Britain and Ireland 6½	Honors GC Chattanooga
2000	Great Britain and Ireland 12½, USA 11½	Royal Liverpool GC
2001	USA 18, Great Britain and Ireland 6	Baltusrol (Lower) GC
2002	USA 15½, Great Britain and Ireland 8½	Doonbeg GC
2003	Europe 14, USA 10	Cassique GC Kiawah
2004	Europe 14½, USA 9½	Ballybunion GC.
2005	USA 14, Europe 10	Whistling Straits GC
2006	Europe 19½, USA 4½	Prestwick GC
2007	USA 18, Europe 6	Caves Valley GC
2008	Europe 14, USA 10	Glasgow Gailes GC
2008	Europe 14, USA 10	Glasgow Gailes GC
2009	Europe 13, USA 11	Cherry Hills CC, CO
2010	USA 13, Europe 11	Royal Portrush
2011	USA 13, Europe 11	Greenwich, CT

Halford-Hewitt Cup (inaugurated 1924)

always at Royal Cinque Ports, Deal, and Royal St George's

Final: Charterhouse beat Epsom 3–2

Winning team: M S P Benka, T D L Orgill, C A M Ayres, A P Hollingsworth, R I C Caldwell, R F Manning, R J Hill, R G McKinnia, B P Mote, A T H Stanley

The Prince's Plate was won by Loretto, beating Hurstpierpoint 2–1

Senior Halford-Hewitt Competitions (inaugurated 2000)

Bernard Darwin Trophy (Original 16) *always at Woking GC:* Radley beat Uppingham 2–1

GL Mellin Salver (Second 16) *always at West Hill GC* Shrewsbury beat Oundle 2–1

Cyril Gray Trophy (Remaining 32) *always at Worplesdon:* Wrekin beat Canford 2–1

Grafton Morrish Trophy (inaugurated 1963) *Hunstanton GC and Royal West Norfolk GC*

Final: Uppingham beat Haileybury 2–1

Winning team: Damian Pitts (captain), Eddie Allingham, David Dean, Sam Debenham, James Gunton, David Patrick, Ewen Wilson

Solihull Salver: Charterhouse

Committee Bowl: Bedford beat Oakham

123rd Oxford *v* Cambridge University Match (inaugurated 1878) *Hunstanton*

Result: Oxford beat Cambridge by 8 matches to 7

History: Cambridge have won the match on 64 occasions, Oxford on 52. Seven matches were halved

Oxford and Cambridge Golfing Society for the President's Putter

(inaugurated 1920) *Littlestone and Rye*

Final: A P Stracey (Fitzwilliam) beat M S P Benka (Lady Margaret Hall) 2 and 1

64th Boyd Quaich *(always at St Andrews (Old and New)*

1	Oliver Roberts (Stirling)*	73-71-70-70—284
2	Freddie Edmunds (St. Andrews)	72-69-73-70—284
	Gary Hurley (National University Ireland Maynooth)	74-68-69-73—284
	Steven Smith (Western Carolina)	69-70-71-74—284

**Roberts won; all four places were decided on countback*

57th Queen Elizabeth Coronation Schools Trophy (inaugurated 1953)

always at Royal Burgess, Barnton

Final: Glasgow High School FP beat Daniel Stewart's/Melville FP 2–1

Winning Team: N Crilley A Farmer, C Gray, R Hardey, K J Macnair, K Shanks

History: Winning teams: 11 Watsonians, Glasgow HSFP; 6 Merchistonians; 4 Daniel Stewart's FP; 3 Old Lorettonians, George Heriot's FP; 2 Dollar Academicals, Hillhead HSFP, Levinside Academy, Old Carthusians, Perth Academy FP, Breadalbane Academicals; 1 Glasgow Academicals, Fettesians, Morrisonians, Hutcheson GSFP, Old Uppinghamians, Ayr Academy FP, Gordonians, Madras College FP, Lenzie Academicals

British Universities Championship *West Lancashire*

1	Jack McDonald (Stirling)	74-73-70-72—289
2	Darren Timms (Stirling)	75-77-71-67—290
3	Zander Culverwell (Stirling)*	75-72-74-70—291
4	Dewi Merkx (Stirling)	77-76-68-70—291

**Culverwell placed third on countback*

Scottish Universities Championship *Moray GC, Lossiemouth*

Jack Allen Trophy

1	David Booth (Stirling)	69-69-71-69—278
2	Darren Timms (Stirling)	69-66-72-77—284
3	Keith Shanks (Aberdeen)	73-68-73-73—287

Mitchell Trophy (Team Championship – match play)

Final: Stirling 10, St Andrews 5

Canadian University and Colleges Championship *Cordova Bay GC, Victoria, BC*

1	Universitie de Laval	276-291-273-286—1,126
2	University of Waterloo	281-285-290-282—1,138
3	University of British Columbia	290-283-288-295—1,156

Winning team: Julien Prouix, Charles Cote, Sonny Michaud, Ugo Coussaud and Max Gilbert

Individual:

1	Garrett Rank (University of Waterloo)	68-72-70-68—278
2	Max Gilbert (Universitie de Laval)	71-72-65-73—281
3	Ugo Coussaud (Universitie de Laval)	68-72-72-70—282

World Universities Men's Championship *Ypsilon Golf Resort, Czech Republic*

1	Carlos Pigem Xammar (ESP)	69-64-68-69—270
2	Juan Sarasti Bemaras (ESP)	69-64-73-67—273
	David Booth (SCO)	71-67-68-67—273
	Philip Eriksson (SWE)	67-69-64-73—273

Team Championship:

1	Spain	202-197-206-203—808
2	Great Britain	213-206-213-203—835
	Ireland	214-205-209-207—835

4 South Korea 838; 5 Chinese Taipei 840; 6 Sweden 841; 7 France 842; 8 Italy 843; 9 Canada 846; 10 USA 848; 11 Switzerland, Japan 853; 13 Czech Republic 863; 14 Norway 871; 18 South Africa 876; 16 Malaysia 893; 17 Slovenia 900; 18 Slovakia 903; 19 China 989.

Winning team: Scott Fernandez Salmon, Jacobo Pastor Lopez, Carlos Pigem Xammar and Juan Sarasti Bernaras

Switzerland will host the next Championship in 2014

66th Japanese Men's Collegiate Championship *Sayama GC*

1	Hideki Matsuyama	66-68-67-68—269
2	Mikihito Kuromiya	71-67-68-69—275
3	Ryutaro Kato	72-70-72-64—278

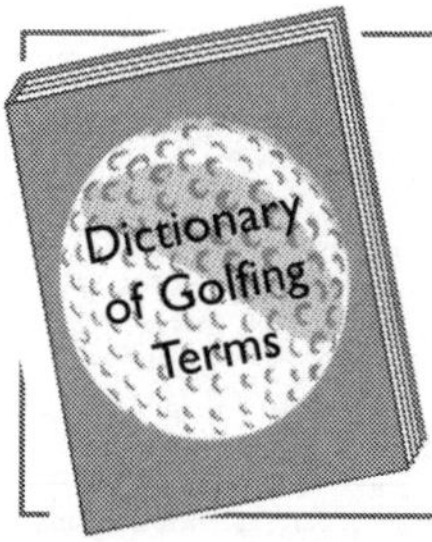

Gutta percha – originating from the Malayan *getah* (sap) and *percha*, the Malay name for the tree that yields the sap, gutta percha is a hard though resilient and easily-moulded substance. Derived from the sap of several trees indigenous to Malaya and of the family *Sapotaceae*, gutta percha golf balls were made from 1848 until the beginning of the 20th century.

County and other Regional Championships 2012

England

Bedfordshire: Robert Sutton

Berks, Bucks & Oxon: Max Smith

Cambridgeshire: Toby Crisp

Cheshire: James McCormick

Cornwall: Mike Reynard

Cumbria: Rob Spence

Derbyshire: Danny Tomlinson

Devon: Steve Daniels

Dorset: Sonny Wilkinson

Durham: Ricky Lee

Essex: Bobby Keeble

Gloucestershire: Laurie Potter

Hampshire, Isle of Wight and Channel Islands: Jordan Ainley

Hertfordshire: Alex Collman

Isle of Man: Paul Lowey

Kent: Max Orrin

Lancashire: Mark Young

Leicestershire and Rutland: David Gibson

Lincolnshire: James Burnett

Middlesex: Ross Dickson

Norfolk: Kit Holmes

Northamptonshire: Miles Mudge

Northumberland: Mathew Webb

Nottinghamshire: Ross Overton

Shropshire and Herefordshire: Will Enefer

Somerset: Tom Small

Suffolk: Sam Forgan

Surrey: Matthew Chapman

Sussex: Alasdair Dalgleish

Warwickshire: Sam Dodds

Wiltshire: Garry Slade

Worcestershire: Josh Carpenter

Yorkshire: Daniel Brown

Ireland

East of Ireland Open: Chris Selfridge

North of Ireland Open: Rory McNamara

South of Ireland Open: Pat Murray

West of Ireland Open: Harry Diamond

Scotland

Angus: William Bremner (M), Connar Cook (S)

Argyll and Bute: Stephen Renfrew (M). Robert MacIntyre (S)

Ayrshire: David Wilson (M+S)

Borders: Callum McNeil (M), Allan Ballantyre (S)

Clackmannanshire: S Moffat (M), A Watson (S)

Dunbartonshire Craig Checkley (M+S)

Fife: Paul Ratcliffe (M), Brian Erskine (S)

Glasgow Stephen Machin (M), Gordon Miller (S)

Lanarkshire: Mark Lutton (M), Betlan Dooney (S)

Lothians: Paul Drake (M), Allyn Dick (S)

North-East: Clark Brechin (M), Chris Rodd (D)

Perth and Kinross: Connor Neil (M), Glenn Campbell (S)

South: Dean Armstrong (M), Kyle McClung (S)

Stirlingshire: Stuart McMehan (M), Stephen Aitken (S)

Wales

Anglesey: D G Parry

Brecon and Radnor: Gareth Jones

Caernarfon and District: Alwyn Thomas

Denbigh: Alyn Torrence

Dyfed: Richard James

Glamorgan: Ian Flower

PART V

Women's Amateur Tournaments

World Amateur Golf Ranking

New Zealand teenager Lydia retains the McCormack Medal

In 2011 Lydia Ko finished in top spot in the Women's Amateur Golf Rankings, administered by The R&A and the USGA, and she kept top spot and collected her second Mark McCormack Medal this year by playing even more impressive golf around the world..

The talented teenager, born in Korea but now a New Zealand citizen, topped the rankings in style at the end of the 12-month qualifying period winning the US Women's Amateur Championship, the last counting event. In the final at The Country Club in Cleveland, Miss Ko beat another teenager, 18-year-old Jaye Marie Green, 3 and 1.

New Zealand teenager Lydia ended the year still holding the No 1 spot in the World Amateur Golf Rankings

"I should like to thank the USGA and The R&A because without them the ranking would not be possible," said Lydia, who gained an automatic entry into the 2013 US Women's Open being played at the Sebonack Golf Club at Southampton in New York State.

Helping her keep the No 1 spot for another year was her victory in the 2012 New South Wales Open on the Australian Ladies Professional Golf Tour when aged just 14. She also won the Australian Women's Amateur Championship and was runner-up in that country's Stroke Play Championship.

She received the leading amateur's silver medal in the 2012 US Women's Open and reached the semi-final of the US Girl's Junior Championship. At the end of the 2011–2012 qualifying period she had held the No 1 spot for 68 weeks and may well be difficult to budge.

Following the conclusion of the McCormack Medal qualifying period she became the youngest winner of an event on the LPGA Tour with her victory over the professionals in the CN Canadian Women's Open at Coquitlam in British Columbia, then she took the top individualm spot in the Women's World Amateur Team Championship in Turkey.

"It's pretty amazing. I became World No 1 on my birthday in 2011 and it is good to continue in that spot. It means I will get more invites to top professional events. It's good to be known as the New Zealand No 1 but World No 1 is totally different because there are so many great players today."

Ko first hit the headlines as a 12-year-old when she finished leading amateur in the Pegasus New Zealand Women's Open, tieing for seventh spot. That week she became the youngest golfer to make the cut on the Ladies European Tour. In 2011 she had become the first golfer to win both the Australian and New Zealand Amateur Stroke Play Championships in the same year.

John Boenhammer, Senior Managing Director Rules, Competitions and Amateur Status at the USGA said: "Lydia is to be congratulated. She has accomplished so much for someone so young. The USGA wishes her continued success."

Johnnie Cole-Hamilton, Executive Director – Championships at The R&A, added: "Lydia deserves a huge amount of credit for performing so well throughout the last two years She is a wonderful player who shows a great level of maturity at such a young age."

The Women's World Amateur Golf Ranking, updated every Wednesday, embraces 2,000 counting events featuring 3,600 golfers in 81 different countries and has become a valuable reference tool highlighting the growing strength in depth of the women's game.

The award is named after Mark H McCormack, the late founder of IMG, the sports marketing company. Mr McCormack always took a keen interest in the amateur game.

R&A World Amateur Golf Ranking 2011–12 – Top 100

Players from the USA occupy most places in the Top 100 with 32 entries. England takes second place with eight entries with Australia following close behind with seven. Players from New Zealand, Spain and South Africa accounted for five places apiece. By region the totals are: Americas 39, Europe 36, Australasia 12, Africa seven and Asia six.

			Divisor	*Points*
1	Lydia Ko	NZL	60	2035.83
2	Ariya Jutanugarn	THA	69	1832.61
3	Hyo Joo Kim	KOR	56	1805.36
4	Jaye Marie Green	USA	46	1759.78
5	Minjee Lee	AUS	44	1694.89
6	Nobuhle Dlamini	SWZ	41	1666.46
7	Breanna Elliott	AUS	73	1596.58
8	Charley Hull	ENG	37	1574.32
9	Lindy Duncan	USA	33	1562.50
10	Georgia Hall	ENG	25(28)	1535.71
11	Kim Williams	RSA	41	1521.34
12	Moriya Jutanugarn	THA	61	1497.13
13	Stephanie Meadow	IRL	50	1494.13
14	Austin Ernst	USA	46	1450.54
15	Celine Boutier	FRA	79	1447.57
16	Alison Lee	USA	36	1430.56
17	Bonita Bredenhann	NAM	47	1410.37
18	Perrine Delacour	FRA	61	1407.38
19	Whitney Hillier	AUS	77	1403.25
20	Nicole Broch Larsen	DEN	52	1402.88
21	Su-Hyun Oh	AUS	62	1395.16
22	Paula Reto	RSA	43	1386.63
23	Amy Boulden	WAL	39	1357.69
24	Leona Maguire	IRL	36	1347.92
25	Lisa McCloskey	COL	41	1340.09
26	Chirapat Jao-Javanil	THA	41	1334.15
27	Amy Anderson	USA	32	1303.13
28	Ashlee Dewhurst	AUS	55	1287.73
29	MacKenzie Brooke Henderson	CAN	34	1286.03
30	Maria Salinas	PER	43	1283.72
31	Wenyung Keh	NZL	43	1276.16
32	Grace Lennon	AUS	68	1272.79
33	Cassy Isagawa	USA	40	1266.63
34	Bronte Law	ENG	26(28)	1264.29
35	Karolin Lampert	GER	47	1246.81
36	Holly Clyburn	ENG	43	1239.53
37	Mun Chin Keh	NZL	51	1235.29
38	Kimberly Kaufman	USA	53	1234.43
39	Jennifer Kirby	CAN	44	1232.67
40	Emily Tubert	USA	42	1228.27
41	Manon Gidali	FRA	46	1227.17
42	Shannon Aubert	FRA	49	1221.68
43	Camilla Hedberg	ESP	50	1221.25
44	Marijosse Navarro	MEX	32	1219.14
45	Dottie Ardina	PHI	60	1217.92
46	Karen Chung	USA	39	1216.67
47	Chloe Williams	WAL	28	1216.07
48	Guilia Molinaro	ITA	47	1214.10
49	Nicole Morales	USA	38	1211.18
50	Manuela Carbajo Re	ARG	40	1207.50
51	Laura Gonzalez-Escallon	BEL	43	1203.49
52	Marta Silva Zamora	ESP	33	1200.76
53	Lauren Stratton	USA	46	1197.83
54	Casey Danielson	USA	28	1196.43
55	Ha Rang Lee	ESP	32	1193.75
56	Charlotte Thomas	ENG	67	1191.79
57	Katerina Ruzickova	CZE	45	1191.67
58	Doris Chen	USA	52	1189.42
59	Erynne Lee	USA	42	1186.61
60	Emily Taylor	ENG	39	1185.90
61	Becky Harries	WAL	27(28)	1182.14
62	Alana Van Greuning	RSA	45	1176.67
63	Daniela Holmqvist	SWE	37	1176.18
64	Emily Perry	NZL	77	1171.27
65	Quirine Eijkenboom	GER	43	1167.44
66	Catherine O'Donnell	USA	29	1162.93
67	Christina Miller	USA	31	1161.29
68	Grace Na	USA	37	1159.12
69	Fanny Cnops	BEL	48	1156.25
70	Meghan Stasi	USA	40	1155.63
71	Brittany Altomare	USA	41	1154.12
72	Alex Stewart	USA	49	1148.98
73	Hayley Davis	ENG	50	1144.50
74	Rachel Rohanna	USA	45	1144.44
75	Rocio Sanchez Lobato	ESP	46	1143.48
76	Tiffany Lua	USA	41	1141.77
77	Ann-Kathrin Lindner	GER	40	1140.00
78	Lee Lopez	USA	45	1138.89
79	Magda Kruger	RSA	39	1136.86
80	Andrea Lee	USA	35	1136.43
81	Julianne Alvarez	NZL	44	1134.09
82	Marta Sanz	ESP	49	1133.67
83	Gabriella Dominguez	USA	46	1131.79
84	Bertine Strauss	RSA	45	1130.56
85	Ashlan Ramsey	USA	46	1129.89
86	Caroline Nistrup	DEN	46	1126.63
87	Kelsey Vines	USA	42	1125.60
88	Ashley Armstrong	USA	37	1125.00
89	Nina Holleder	GER	42	1123.81
90	Hayley Bettencourt	AUS	67	1120.90
91	Linnea Strom	SWE	32	1117.19
92	Caroline Powers	USA	49	1106.12
93	Soo-Bin Kim	CAN	40	1105.00
94	Charlotte Kring Lorentzen	DEN	36	1098.61
95	Kristina Merkle	USA	47	1098.40
96	Emily Talley	USA	48	1097.40
97	Annie Park	USA	50	1096.50
98	Meghan MacLaren	ENG	34	1096.32
99	Princess Mary Superal	PHI	42	1095.83
100	Nanna Madsen	DEN	34	1090.44

World Amateur Golf Ranking 2011–2012

The World Amateur Golf Ranking, compiled by The R&A and the USGA as a service to golf, comprises a men's ranking which was launched in January 2007 and a women's ranking which began in January 2010. The week'srankings are announced every Wednesday at 12.00 noon.

Statistics are compiled each week for over 8,000 players in over 2,000 events around the world. The ranking is based on counting every stroke reported to The R&A in stroke play events and matches won in counting match play events. The women's ranking also runs through a rolling period of 52 weeks.

Counting events are divided into seven categories:

The elite events: For men: The Amateur Championship, the US Amateur, the European Amateur and the Asian Amateur; and for women: The Ladies British Amateur, the NCAA Championship, the US Women's Amateur and the European Ladies Amateur.

Category A: Counting events ranked 1-30 in the World Ranking Event Rating
Category B: Counting events ranked 31-100
Category C: Counting events ranked 101-200
Category D: Counting events ranked 201-300
Category E: Counting events ranked 301-400
Category F: Counting events ranked from 401

Counting events are stroke play competitions over a minimum of three rounds or two rounds if it is a match play qualifying competition.

Full details of how a ranking is earned and information on how the ranking works can be found on The R&A website – www.RandA.org

The rankings are displayed by month and are subdivided into the following regions:

Africa
The Americas (North, South and Central America and the Caribbean)
Asia (incorporating the Middle East)
Australasia (incorporating the Pacific Islands)
Europe

Players are from the country hosting the event unless otherwise stated.

An asterisk indicates a newly ranked player.

A list of country abbreviations can be found on page 51; MWAGR can be found on page 268.

Elite and Category "A" Events

Elite

Week 26 **Ladies British Amateur Championship** *Carnoustie Links, Scotland* (RSS 80-79)

			SP	MP	Pts	Div
1	Stephanie Meadow (NIR)	81-75—156	19	180	199	8
2	Rocio Sanchez Lobato (ESP)	81-76—157	18	140	158	7
3	Perrine Delacour (FRA)	72-77—149	26	104	130	6
	Georgia Hall (ENG)	78-76—154	21	104	125	6

Full details can be found on page 390

Week 30 **European International Amateur Championship** *Ljubljana, Slovenia*
July 24–28 (RSS 73-73-74-73)

			SP	Bonus	Pts	Div
1	Celine Boutier (FRA)	68-66-66-68—268	57	48	105	4
2	Shannon Aubert (FRA)	67-71-68-68—274	51	27	78	4
	Marina Steutz (GER)	68-69-68-69—274	51	27	78	4

Full details can be found on page 393

Week 32 **US Women's Championship** *Cleveland, OH, USA* (RSS 75-75)

			SP	MP	Pts	Div
1	Lydia Ko (NZL)	66-71—137	30	180	228	8
2	Jaye Marie Green	73-73—146	21	140	161	7
3	Ariya Jutanugarn (THA)	71-68—139	28	104	139.5	6
	Nicole Zhang (CAN)	73-71—144	23	104	127	6

Full details can be found on page 395

Category "A"

2011

Week 38 Cougar Classic *Charleston, North Carolina, USA* Sept 11–13 (RSS 75-75-73)

			SP	Bonus	Pts	Div
1	Austin Ernst	67-69-67—203	44	36	80	3
2	Erica Popson	66-69-72—207	40	18	58	3
3	Camilla Hedberg (ESP)	71-67-70—208	39	12	51	3
	Tessa Teachman	67-72-69—208	39	12	51	3

Week 39 Junior Solheim Cup *Knightsbrook, Ireland* Sept 20–21

	Pts	Div
Amy Boulden (WAL)	16	1
Jaye Marie Green (USA)	16	1
Alison Lee (USA)	16	1
Leona Maguire	16	1
Summar Roachell (USA)	16	1
Antonia Scherer (GER)	16	1
Gabriella Then (USA)	16	1
Margaux Vanmol (BEL)	16	1
Lindsay Weaver (USA)	16	1

Week 39 Mason Rudolph Fall Preview *Nashville, Tennessee, USA* Sept 23–25 (RSS 76-75-76)

			SP	Bonus	Pts	Div
1	Lindy Duncan	75-69-68—202	39	36	75	3
2	Jennifer Kirby (CAN)	72-66-74—202	39	18	57	3
3	Brittany Altomare	75-70-69—204	37	12	49	3
	Lauren Stratton	72-71-71—204	37	12	49	3

Week 41 Tar Heel Invitational *Chapel Hill, North Carolina, USA* Oct 7–9 (RSS 74-74-74)

1	Marta Sanz (ESP)	69-70-68—207	39	36	75	3
2	Augusta James	70-69-69—208	38	18	56	3
	Brooke Pancake	69-70-69—208	38	18	56	3
	Caroline Powers	69-68-71—208	38	18	56	3

Week 42 Stanford Intercollegiate *Stanford, California, USA* Oct 14–16 (RSS 72-72-73)

1	Soo-Bin Kim	66-68-66—200	41	36	77	3
2	Stephanie Kono	67-69-66—202	39	18	57	3
3	Cassy Isagawa	67-67-70—204	37	12	49	3

Week 43 Mercedes-Benz SEC/PAC 12 Challenge *Knoxville, Tennessee, USA* Oct 21–23 (RSS 76-75-75)

1	Stephanie Meadow (IRL)	68-71-72—211	39	36	75	3
2	Lauren Stratton	68-72-73—213	37	18	55	3
3	Kaitlyn Rohrback	71-72-71—214	36	12	48	3
	Marta Sanz (ESP)	74-71-69—214	36	12	48	3

2012

Week 1 Dixie Amateur *Coral Springs, Florida, USA* Dec 30 2011 (RSS 75-74-74-74)

1	Paula Reto	69-67-70-69—275	54	36	90	4
2	Moriya Jutanugarn (THA)	68-75-69-68—280	49	18	67	4
3	Jaye Marie Green	71-74-67-69—281	48	12	60	4

Week 1 Harder Hall Invitational *Sebring, Florida, USA* Jan 4–7 (RSS 78-78-77-77)

			SP	Bonus	Pts	Div
1	Charley Hull (ENG)	70-74-69-69—282	60	36	96	4
2	Ariya Jutanugarn (THA)	72-72-67-73—284	58	18	76	4
3	Moriya Jutanugarn (THA)	75-71-68-71—285	57	12	69	4

Week 3 Australian Amateur Championship *Woodlands and Huntingdale, Melbourne* Jan 17–22 (RSS 81-82-79-79)

			SP	MP	Pts	Div
1	Lydia Ko (NZL)	76-71—147	30	156	186	8
2	Breanna Elliott	73-72—145	32	120	152	7
3	Minjee Lee	81-69—150	26	88	114	6
4	Whitney Hillier	80-78—158	19	88	107	6

Week 7 Lady Puerto Rico Classic *San Juan, Puerto Rico* Feb 12–14 (RSS 77-77-78)

			SP	Bonus	Pts	Div
1	Maria Silva Zamorra (ESP)	74-66-73—213	43	27	70	3
2	Emilie Burger (USA)	66-74-75—215	41	9	50	3
	Laura Gonzalez-Escallion (BEL)	75-65-75—215	41	9	50	3
	Emily Tubert (USA)	71-70-74—215	41	9	50	3

Week 7 Northrup Grumman Reg Challenge *Palos Verde, California, USA* Feb 13–15 (RSS 76-78-76)

1	Lindy Duncan	69-71-70—210	44	27	71	3
2	Sophia Popov (GER)	74-73-67—214	40	13.5	53.5	3
3	Erynne Lee	72-69-75—216	38	9	47	3

Week 9 All State Sugar Bowl *New Orleans, Louisiana, USA* Feb 26–28 (RSS 76-75-74)

1	Alex Stewart	71-73-67—211	41	27	68	3
2	Cassy Isagawa	71-65-76—212	40	13.5	53.5	3
3	Lisa McCloskey (COL)	71-71-71—213	39	9	48	3

Week 9 Darius Rucker Inter-Collegiate *Hilton Head, South Carolina, USA* Mar 3–4 (RSS 76-77)

1	Stephanie Meadow (IRL)	67-70—137	32	18	50	2
2	Brooke Pancake	71-69—140	29	9	38	2
3	Katherine Perry	72-69—141	28	6	34	2

Week 10 LSU Classic *Baton Rouge, Louisiana, USA* Mar 9–11 (RSS 78-77-71)

1	Catherine O'Donnell	72-71-71—214	42	20.25	62.25	3
	Erica Popson	75-70-69—214	42	20.25	62.25	3
3	Madelene Sagstrom (SWE)	71-71-74—216	40	9	49	3

Week 11 Sun Trust Gator Invite *Gainesville, Florida, USA* Mar 16–18 (RSS 75-76-75)

1	Maria Salinas (PER)	68-72-66—206	44	27	71	3
2	Camilla Hedberg (ESP)	68-71-69—208	42	11.25	53.25	3
	Christina Miller	68-67-72—208	42	11.25	53.25	3

Week 12 Battle at Rancho Bernardo *Rancho Bernardo, California, USA* Mar 19–20 (RSS 77-77)

1	Sophia Popov (GER)	71-71—142	28	27	55	2
2	Patricia Garcia (PUR)	72-72—144	26	13.5	39.5	2
3	Jennifer Hirano	74-71—145	25	9	34	2

Week 13 **Liz Murphey Collegiate Classic** *Athens, Georgia, USA* Mar 30–April 1 (RSS 75-75-75)

			SP	Bonus	Pts	Div
1	Jennifer Kirby (CAN)	66-72-71—209	40	27	67	3
2	Laura Gonzalez-Escallion (BEL)	75-65-75—210	39	13.5	52.5	3
3	Marta Silva Zamorra (ESP)	70-69-72—211	38	6.75	44.75	3
	Emily Tubert	72-70-69—211	38	6.75	44.75	3

Week 13 **Ping ASU Invitational** *Tempe, Arizona, USA* Mar 31– April 1 (RSS 74-74-77)

1	Ani Gulugian	72-69-71—202	37	20.25	57.25	3
	Demi Runas	70-68-74—202	37	20.25	57.25	3
3	Lee Lopez	72-71-71—204	35	4.125	39.125	3
	Tiffany Lua	68-69-77—204	35	4.125	39.125	3
	Marissa Mar	68-73-73—204	35	4.125	39.125	3
	Rachel Raastad (NOR)	75-71-68—204	35	4.125	39.125	3

Week 14 **Bryan National Collegiate** *Brown Summit, North Carolina, USA* April 6–8 (RSS 76-76-76)

1	Lindy Duncan	71-71-70 - 212	40	27	67	3
2	Fanny Cnops (BEL)	73-70-71 - 214	38	13.5	51.5	3
3	Erica Popson	71-70-75 - 216	36	6.75	42.75	3
	Rachel Rohanna	71-70-75 - 216	36	6.75	42.75	3

Week 16 **SEC Championship** *Fayetteville, Arkansas, USA* April 20–22 (RSS 79-78-81)

1	Patricia Sanz (ESP)	69-73-77—209	43	27	70	3
2	Alex Marina	70-73-77—210	42	13.5	55.5	3
3	Emily Tubert	78-70-73—211	41	9	50	3

Week 17 **Queen Sirikit Cup** *Tanah Merah CC Singapore* April 25–27 (RSS 77-76-75)

1	Hyo Joo Kim (KOR)	69-65-70—204	48	27	75	3
2	Lydia Ko (NZL)	69-73-68—210	42	13.5	55.5	3
3	Kyu-jung Baek (KOR)	73-72-66—211	41	9	50	3

Week 19 **NCAA D1 Central Regional** *Columbus, Ohio, USA* May 10–12 (RSS 79-78-77)

1	Lisa McCloskey (COL)	73-68-72—213	45	20.25	65.25	3
	Maria Salinas (PER)	71-72-70—213	45	20.25	65.25	3
3	Marina Alex	70-73-72—215	43	9	52	3

Week 19 **NCAA D1 West Regional** *Erie, Colorado, USA* May 10–12 (RSS 76-76-75)

1	Catherine O'Donnell	70-69-70—209	42	27	69	3
2	Austin Ernst	71-69-70—210	41	13.5	54.5	3
3	Hayley Davis (ENG)	69-74-69—212	39	9	48	3

Week 19 **NCAA D1 East Regional** *Blue State College, Pennsylvania, USA* May 10–12 (RSS 77-76-75)

1	Katerina Ruzickova (CZE)	67-73-73—203	39	27	66	3
2	Jennifer Kirby (CAN)	71-74-70—205	37	13.5	50.5	3
3	Katie Burnett	72-71-73—206	36	4.125	40.125	3
	Lindy Duncan	73-72-71—206	36	4.125	40.125	3
	Justine Lee (AUS)	74-73-69—206	36	4.125	40.125	3
	Lindsey Solberg	74-75-67—206	36	4.125	40.125	3

Week 21 NCAA Championship *Franklin, Tennessee, USA* May 22–25 (RSS 75-75-76-74)

1	Chirapat Jao-Javanil (THA)	69-73-70-70—282	50	36	86	4
2	Brooke Pancake	68-70-75-73—286	46	18	64	4
3	Laura Gonzalez-Escallon (BEL)	67-76-74-70—287	45	9	54	4
	Tessa Teachman	69-74-70-74—287	45	9	54	4

Week 23 Curtis Cup *Nairn GC, Scotland* June 8–10

	Pts	*Div*
Amy Boulden (WAL)	20	1
Holly Clyburn (ENG)	20	1
Charley Hull (ENG)	20	1
Tiffany Lua (USA)	20	1
Lisa McCloskey (COL)	20	1
Stephanie Meadow (IRL)	20	1
Brooke Pancake (USA)	20	1
Kelly Tidy (ENG)	20	1

Full details can be found on page 414

Week 25 US Amateur Public Links Championship *Neshanic Station New Jersey, USA*

June 18–23 (Qualifying rounds RSS 74-74)

			SP	*Bonus*	*Pts*	*Div*
1	Kyung Kim	73-71—144	20	156	176	8
2	Ashlan Ramsey	71-73—144	20	120	140	7
3	Kimberly Kaufman	72-72—144	20	88	108	6
	Alice Jeong	71-74—145	19	88	107	6

Week 28 European Girls Team Championship *GC St Leon Rot, Heidelberg, Germany*

July 10–14

	Pts	*Div*
Linnea Strom (SWE)	66	3
Mia Landegren (SWE)	40	2
Ha Rang Lee (ESP)	40	2
Ainhoa Olarra (ESP)	40	2

Week 28 European Girls Team Championship Individual

GC St Leon Rot, Heidelberg, Germany July 10–11 (RSS 74–74)

			SP	*Bonus*	*Pts*	*Div*
1	Georgia Hall (ENG)	67-66—133	31	13.5	44.5	2
2	Elizabeth Mallett (ENG)	64-69—133	31	13.5	44.5	2
3	Charley Hull (ENG)	68-66—134	30	6	36	2

Week 29 Women's North and South Amateur Championship

Pinehurst, North Carolina, USA July 16–21 (RSS 77-76-75)

1	Austin Ernst	74-74-72—220	32		152	7
2	Doris Chen	74-71-72—217	35	1.5	120.5	6
3	Ashley Armstrong	72-72-70—214	38	11.25	101.25	5

Week 29 US Girls' Junior Championship *Daly City, Ca;ifornia USA* July 16–21 (RSS 79-77)

			SP	*MP*	*SPBonus*	*Pts*	*Div*
1	Minjee Lee (AUS)	79-71—150	22	156		178	7
2	Alison Lee	78-74—152	20	120		140	6
3	Ariya Jutanugarn (THA)	71-71—142	30	88	18	36	5
	Lydia Ko (NZL)	74-71—145	27	88	9	24	5

For further information, visit www.RandA.org/wagr

Week 30 **Canadian Amateur Championship** *Lethbridge GC, Lethbridge, Alberta* July 24–27 (RSS 77-75-74-75)

			SP	Bonus	Pts	Div
1	Ariya Jutanugarn (THA)	69-67-65-73—274	59	36	95	4
2	Moriya Jutanugarn (THA)	74-68-69-68—279	54	18	72	4
3	Kimberly Kaufman	73-69-70-70—282	51	12	63	4

How a player makes it onto the World Amateur Golf Rankings is a question often asked. The system is easy to understand if, by necessity, somewhat complex. It is best to look at the criteria in three different ways – by doing well in a Stroke Play event, with a good performance in a Match Play tournament or in an event in which both Stroke and Match Play elements are involved. Just taking part does not necessarily mean a place on the ranking. There are certain criteria to becoming one of now over 3,000 ranked players around the world.

In Stroke Play a player will have to have:
Made the cut in an Elite event
Finished in the top 40 and ties in an "A" event
Finished in the top 32 and ties in a "B" event
Finished in the top 16 and ties in a "C" event

Or, for female players, participation in The Ladies British Amateur, the NCAAA Championships, the US Women's Amateur and the European Women's Amateur.

Finish in a position to gain bonus points in any other professional event recognised by the committee.

In Match Play a player will make the ranking if they:
Make the last 32 in a Category "A" event
Make the last 16 in a Category "B:" event
Make the last 8 in a Category "C" event
Win a match against ranked player in an Elite team Match Play event

If the event is a combination of Stroke Play and Match Play what a player needs to become ranked is:
Qualify for the Match Play stage or finish on the qualifying score in an Elite Stroke Play event
Finish in the top 32 and ties in a Category "A" Stroke Play event
Make the last 32 of a Category "A" event
Finish in the top 16 and ties in the Stroke Play stage of a Category "B" event
Make the last 16 of a Category "B" event
Finish in the top 8 and ties in the Stroke Play stage of a Category "C" event
Make the last 8 in a Category "C" event
Finish in the top 4 and ties in the Stroke Play stage of a Category "D" event
Make the last 8 in a Category "D" event.
Finish in the top 2 and ties in the Stroke Play stage of a Category "E" event
Make the last 4 in a Category "E" event
Lead the qualifiers in the Stroke Play section of a Category "F" event
Make the last 4 of a Category "F" event.

Ranking Scratch Score

The RSS is the calculated standard used to convert a player's Counting Scores to Stroke Play Ranking Points.

The RSS for a Counting Round is calculated by use of the formula (a) / (b), where (a) is the sum total of the gross scores of the leading (X) players in the round, with (X) representing the total number of Ranked Players in the round and (b) is the total number of gross scores in (a) above.

Fractions from the RSS calculation will be rounded to the nearest whole number.

If less than three Ranked Players play a Counting Round, the RSS for that round will be the average of the lowest three scores by amateur golfers.

If fewer than three Amateurs play a Counting Round, the RSS will equate to par.

In any official event from other professional tours, the RSS will equate to par.

August

Americas

E	Arizona State Stroke Play	Saki Iida	USA

September

Americas

A	Cougar Classic	Charleston, NC	11–13	Austin Ernst	USA
A	Mason Rudolph Fall Preview	Nashville, TN	23–25	Lindy Duncan	USA
B	Branch Law Firm/Dick McGuire	Albuquerque, NM	25–26	Sofia Hoglund (FIN)*	USA

Americas (continued)

B	Golfweek Conference Challenge	Vail, CO	19–21	Chirapat Jao-Javanil (THA)	USA
B	Ptarmigan Ram Fall Classic	Fort Collins, CO	12–13	Demi Runas	USA
B	Texas A & M Mo'morial	Bryan, TX	11–13	Carlie Yadloczky	USA
C	AJGA Girls Championship	Greenville, SC	3–5	Emma Talley	USA
C	Chip-N Club Invitational	Lincoln, NE	12–13	Felicia Espericueta	USA
C	Dale McNamara Invitational	Owasso, OK	12–14	Guilia Molinaro (ITA)	USA
C	WSU Cougar Cup	Pullman, WA	19–20	Sally Watson (SCO)	USA
C	Abierto Jockey Club de Rosario	Rosario	16–18	Victoria Tanco	ARG
D	Camp. de Menores y Menores de 15	Jockey Club Venado Tuerto	23–25	Manuela Carbajo Re	ARG
D	Campeonato National Infantil 14-15	Baranquilla	A31–S2	Laura Sojo	COL
D	Badger Invitational	Madison, WI	25–26	Felicia Espericueta	USA
D	Chris Banister Gamecock Classic	Huntsville, AL	5–6	Marissa Steen	USA
D	Circling Raven Collegiate Invitational	Worley, IN	12–13	Caitlin McCleary	USA
D	Golfweek Program Challenge	Myrtle Beach, SC	11–13	Christina Miller	USA
D	Marilynn Smith Sunflower Invitational	Manhattan, KS	26–27	Malin Lundberg (SWE)	USA
D	Mary Fossum Invitational	E Lansing, MI	17–18	Caroline Powers	USA

E	Princeton Women's Inv.	Tiffany Lim	USA
E	US Women's Mid-Amateur	Ellen Port	USA
E	Yale Fall Intercollegiate	Seo Hee Moon	USA
F	Bucknell Women's Invitational	Kortnie Maxoutopoulis	USA
F	Carroll College Invitational	Mari Hutsi (EST)*	USA
F	Copa Laguna	Giovana Maymon	MEX
F	Murray State Drake Creek Inv.	Marisa Kamelgarn	USA
F	Redbird Invitational	Bailey Arnold*	USA
F	Rocky Mountain Invitational	Kalli Stanhope	USA
F	Rose City Collegiate	Rochelle Chan	USA
F	South Carolina Stroke Play	Cecilia Fournil*	USA
F	ULM Fred Marx Invitational	Whitney McAteer	USA
F	USGA Senior Women's Am.	Terri Frohnmayer*	USA
F	Warner Pacific Invitational	Trish Gibbens	USA
F	Woodward Video Junior	Lauren Salazar	USA
F	Abierto de Farallones	Anna Bohmer	COL
F	Abierto del Guayaquil	Coralia Arias	ECU
F	Camp. Juvenil de Venezuela	Ana Raga	VEN
F	Camp. Nacional de Menores	Maria Andrea Donado*	COL COL
F	Camp. National Infantil 12–13	Maria Vesga	COL
F	Copa BBVA	Manuela Uribe	COL
F	Torneo Nac. Abierto Del Valle	Raquel Gumucio	BOL

Asia

C	Hong Kong Ladies Open	Hong Kong GC	20–22	Jayvie Agojo (PHI)	HKG
C	Santi Cup	Clearwater Bay	6–9	Pinrath Loomboonruang (THA)	HKG
D	Korea Junior C/ship Women (High)	Lakehills Jeju	6–8	Hyo-Joo Kim	KOR
D	Malaysian Junior Open	Saujana, Subang	13–15	Dottie Ardina (PHI)	MAS

E	National Middle School Senior High	Chi Wang	TPE
F	China Amateur Championship	Xiao Yi	CHN
F	China Amateur Tour – Suzhou Leg	Yang Jiaxin	CHN
F	China Futures Tour Leg 6	Luo Yin*	CHN
F	Faldo Series (Hong Kong) Qualifying	Tiffany Chan/ Kitty Tam	HKG
F	Faldo Series Asia – India	Aditi Ashok	IND
F	Korea Junior C/ship Women (Middle)	Su-Min Park*	KOR
F	Nat. Middle School – Junior High	Ssu-Chia Cheng	TPE
F	National Ranking Game 4	Amelia Yong	SIN
F	Southern India Ladies	Mehar Atwal	IND
F	Taiwan Amateur C/ship	Saki Nagamine (JPN)*	TPE
F	Terengganu Amateur Open	Nur Durriyah Damian	MAS
F	TGA-CAT Junior Ranking 3	Suthavee Chanachai*	THA

Australasia

B	Australia Interstate Teams	Western Australian	13–16	Suthavee Chanachai (THA)*	AUS

E	Carrus Open	Emily Perry	NZL
E	Katherine Hull Classic – Open	Lauren Mason	AUS
E	Victorian Amateur Girls	Rio Watanabe*	AUS
F	Katherine Hull Classic – U15	Jessica Park	AUS
F	Victorian Amateur Girls U16	Sian Zigomanis*	AUS
F	Wellington Stroke Play	Julianne Alvarez	NZL

Europe

A	Junior Solheim Cup	Knightsbrook	20–21	Julianne Alvarez (NZL)	IRL
B	Duke of York Young Champions	Royal Liverpool	13–15	Ha Rang Lee (ESP)	ENG
B	Home Internationals Women	Hillside	7–9	Ha Rang Lee (ESP)	ENG
C	German National Championship	Gleidingen	8–11	Antonia Scherer	GER
C	Turkish Amateur	Gloria, Antalya	22–25	Nicole Broch Larsen (DEN)	TUR

D	European Ladies Club Trophy	Corfu	22–24	Ane Urchegui (ESP)	GRE
D	Stirling Invitational	Gleneagles	12–13	Eilidh Briggs	SCO

E	Faldo Series Grand Final	Brogan Townend (ENG)	IRL
E	Finnish Tour 9	Anne Hakula	FIN
E	Italian National Stroke Play	Bianca Fabrizio	ITA
E	Mandatum Life Final	Noora Tamminen	FIN
E	Netherlands Nat. Match Play	Lianne Jansen	NED
E	Skandia Tour Elit 6	Emma Henrikson	SWE
E	Suisse Romande	Anais Maggetti	SUI
F	Bulgarian Amateur	Damla Bilgic (TUR)	BUL
F	Cancello D'Oro	Tullia Calzavara	ITA
F	Chevrolet Open	Sunna Vidisdottir	ISL
F	European Universities C/ship	Harriet Beasley (ENG)	SLO
F	Finnish Tour Karsinta	Kati Nieminen*	FIN
F	Fiorino D'Oro	Martina Flori*	ITA
F	French Mid-Amateur Women	Jenny Bjerling (SWE)*	FRA
F	Grand Prix de Massane	Claire Ulmann	FRA
F	Junior Masters Invitational	Jenny Haglund	SWE
F	National Match Play U21	Giulia van den Berg	NED
F	Norgescup Finale	Mariell Bruun*	NOR
F	Titleist Tour 6	Marthe Wold	NOR
F	Titleist Tour Finale	Marthe Wold	NOR

October

Africa

B	Boland Championship	Strand Golf Club	9–12	Kim Williams	RSA
B	Gus Ackerman Championship	Westlake Golf Club	15–16	Cara Gorlei	RSA

Americas

A	Mercedes-Benz SEC/PAC 12 Chall.	Knoxville, TN	21–23	Stephanie Meadow (IRL)	USA
A	Stanford Intercollegiate	Stanford, CA	14–16	Soo-Bin Kim (CAN)	USA
A	Tar Heel Invitational	Chapel Hill, NC	7–9	Marta Sanz (ESP)	USA
B	Landfall Tradition	Wilmington, NC	28–30	Paula Reto (RSA)	USA
B	Ping Invitational	Stillwater, OK	8–10	Jaye Marie Green	USA
B	Windy City Collegiate	Golf, IL	3–4	Isabelle Boineau (FRA)/Kelsey Vines	USA
C	Edean Ihlanfeldt Invitational	Sammamish, WA	3–5	Madeleine Sheils	USA
C	Lady Northern Intercollegiate	French Lick, IN	10–11	Meagan Bauer	USA
C	Lady Paladin Invitational	Greenville, SC	28–30	Charlotte Kring Lorentzen (DEN)	USA
C	Lady Pirate Intercollegiate	Greenville, NC	10–11	Samantha Morrell	USA
C	Las Vegas Collegiate Showdown	Boulder City, NV	24–26	Grace Na	USA
C	Price's Give Em Five Intercollegiate	Las Cruces, NM	10–12	Jaclyn Jansen/Kayla Mortellaro	USA
C	Susie Maxwell Berning Classic	Norman, OK	16–18	Anne-Catherine Tanguay (CAN)	USA
C	USGA State Team C/ship Individual	Savannah, GA	4–6	Rachel Dai	USA
D	Bettie Lou Evans Fall Invitational	Lexington, KY	S30–O2	Ashleigh Albrecht	USA
D	Bob Hurley Auto ORU Shootout	Tulsa, OK	3–4	Jessica Schiele (ENG)	USA
D	Hoosier Fall Invitational	Carmel, IN	17–18	Becca Huffer	USA
D	Johnie Imes Invitational	Old Hawthorne, Columbia, MO	3–4	Lejan Lewthwaite (RSA)	USA
D	LPGA Xavier International	Daytona Beach, FL	7–9	Amy Anderson	USA
D	Memphis Invitational	Germantown, TN	24–25	Marissa Steen	USA
D	Nittany Lion Women's Invitational	State College, PA	S30–O1	Ariel Witmer	USA
D	Palmetto Intercollegiate	Kiawah Island, SC	23–24	Fanny Cnops (BEL)	USA
D	UNCG Starmount Fall Classic	Greensboro, NC	2–4	Charlotte Kring Lorentzen (DEN)	USA
D	Copa Eduardo Herrera	Club Los Andes	6–9	Laura Estefenn	COL
D	Sudamericano Pre-Juvenil	Cuidad del Este	S28–O1	Sofia Goicoechea (ARG)	PAR

E	Copa Enrique Santos	Lucia Gutierrez (PER)	ECU
E	Blue Raider Invitational	Karisa Akin	USA
E	FIU Pat Bradley Invitational	Shelby Coyle	USA
E	MSU/Payne Stewart Memorial	Hermine Greyling	USA
E	Spider Invitational	Stephanie Hsieh	USA
E	USF-Waterlefe Invitational	Christina Miller	USA
E	Wyoming Cowgirl Desert Invite	Christine Wong (CAN)	USA
F	CCIW Championship	Katie Klosterman	USA
F	Corban Invitational	Trish Gibbens	USA
F	Embry Riddle AZ Invitational	Lisa Copeland*	USA
F	Firestone Grill College Inv.	Caitlin McCleary	USA
F	IIAC Championship	Sarah Paulson*	USA
F	Lady Red Wolf Classic	Jennifer Loiacano	USA
F	MIAC Championship	Vanessa Kleckner*	USA
F	Midwest Conference C/ship	Angelina Parrinello*	USA
F	Montverde Acad. Junior All-Star Inv.	Sierra Brooks	USA
F	NAC Championships	Muriel Mcintyre (CAN)*	USA
F	Nevada State Stroke Play	Laurie Johnson*	USA
F	WIAC Championships	Mary Welsh	USA
F	Wolf Pack Classic	Alex Buelow	USA
F	Abierto de Golf Serrezuela	Ana Maria Morales*	COL
F	Abierto Internac. Copa Claro	Valentina Haupt	CHI
F	Abierto San Cristobal	Maria Jose Vial	CHI
F	Colombian Mid Amateur	Julie Pauline Saenz Starnes*	COL

Asia

C	National Sports Festival	Dongyeoju Country Club	4–7	Ji-Hee Kim	KOR
C	Singha Thailand Open	Panya Indra Golf Course	4–7	Dottie Ardina (PHI)	THA

E	Fangshan Changyang Amateur	Andrea Unson (PHI)	CHN	F	China Junior C/ship 15-17	Wang Xi Yue*	CHN
E	Pune Open Amateur	Mehar Atwal	IND	F	Faldo Series Malaysia	Aretha Herng Pan	MAS
E	Western India Amateur	Vani Kapoor	IND	F	HSBC Nat. Junior C/ship Final	Guan Ruqing*	CHN
F	China Junior C/ship 11-14	Wu Sha	CHN	F	TGA-CAT Junior C/ship	Jinjuta Thongtan	THA

Australasia

C	Grange Classic	The Grange GC, Auckland	29–30	Cecilia Cho	NZL
C	Srixon International Junior Classic	Maitland GC, NSW	4–7	Minjee Lee	AUS

E	Port Taranaki Open	Emily Perry	NZL	F	Shirley Open	Emily Perry	NZL
F	Australian Senior C/ship	Sylvia Donohoe*	AUS	F	Wanganui Open	Stephanie McKillop*	NZL
F	BOP Classic	Emily Perry	NZL				

Europe

B	Cecile De Rothchild Trophy	Monfontaine Golf Club	7–9	Perrine Delacour	FRA
C	Trophee des Regions	Saint Cyprien	29–31	Manon Gidali	FRA
D	Championnat de France Cadet	St Cyprien	23–26	Manon Gidali	FRA

F	Austrian Match Play	Marina Stuetz	AUT	F	La Quercia D'Oro Girls	Alice Di Piero	ITA
F	Camp. Nazionale Mid-Amateur	Giuliana Colavito*	ITA	F	Taca de FPG	Susana Ribeiro	POR
F	Coppa d'Oro Castelli	Virginia Paglialunga*	ITA	F	Tournoi Federal Jeunes	TMathilde Poirrier*	FRA
F	Grifo d'Oro	Anna Dalessio*	ITA	F	Trofeo Glauco Lolli Ghetti	Elisabetta Bertini	ITA
F	Israel Open	Hadas Libman	ISR				

November

Africa

F	South African Mid-Amateur	Sandra Winter	RSA

Americas

B	Betsy Rawls Longhorn Invite	Austin, TX	O31–N2	Nicole Vandermade (CAN)	USA
B	Polo Junior Classic	Palm Beach Gardens, FL	19–25	Nicole Morales	USA
B	Rainbow Wahine Invitational	Kapolei, HI	1–2	Lee Lopez	USA
C	Alamo Invitational	San Antonio, TX	O30–N1	Fabiola Arriaga (MEX)	USA
C	Challenge at Onion Creek	Austin, TX	7–8	Gabriella Dominguez	USA
D	Fighting Camel Fall Classic	Buies Creek, NC	O31–N1	Amy Anderson	USA
D	Argentine Amateur	San Isidro Golf Club	15–20	Manuela Carbajo Re	ARG

E	Tourneo Shalom	Natalia Forero	COL	F	Copa Ciudad de Barranquilla	Laura Sojo	COL
F	California Amateur	Jenni Jenq	USA	F	Federacao de Baiana de Golfe	Lucia Maria Guilger	BRA
F	Champions Gate (13-18)	Kari Bellville	USA	F	Internacional Infantil y Juvenil Caribe	Laura Estefenn	COL
F	Dennis Rose Invitational	Courtney Soekland	USA				
F	Holiday Inn Express/ Hatter	Alex Buelow	USA	F	Tercera Parada Nac. Menores	Maria Vesga	COL
F	IJGT Major at TPC Sawgrass	Ana Ruiz (MEX)	USA	F	Torneo Abierto del Oriente	Michelle Ledermann	BOL
F	Omni Tucson National 13-18	Haley Moore*	USA	F	Torneo Ciudad de Cucuta	Maria Camila Serrano	COL
F	Guatemala Amateur	Lucia Polo	GUA				
F	Abierto Las Palmas	Macarena Haupt	CHI	F	Torneo Nacional La Paz	Natalia Soria*	BOL
F	Abierto Los Leones	Carla Jane	CHI	F	V Parada Mid-Amateur	Diana Rueda Jaramillo*	COL
F	Abierto Prince of Wales CC	Valentina Haupt	CHI				
F	Abierto Valle Escondido	Florencia Vinagre*	CHI				

Asia

C	Abu Dhabi Junior	Abu Dhabi GC	22–24	Hayley Davis (ENG)	UAE
C	SEA Games (Individual)	Jagorawi Golf & Country Club	15–17	Tatiana W*	INA

E	Acer Nat. Fall Ranking Tourn.	Szu-Han Chen	TPE	F	DGC Open	Gurbani Singh	IND
F	Albatross International Junior	Moyu Sasaki (JPN)*	IND	F	Melaka Amateur Open	Loy Hee Ying	MAS
F	Army Ladies Amateur	Gurbani Singh	IND	F	Northern India Amateur	Vani Kapoor	IND
F	China Am. Tour Match Play	Chen Cuixia	CHN	F	Rajasthan Junior	Millie Saroha	IND

F Sarawak Chief Minister's Cup Aretha Herng Pan MAS
F Selangor Amateur Open Aretha Herng Pan MAS
F SGA 5th Nat. Ranking Game Lim Jia Yi SIN
F Singha Junior World C/ship Pannarat Thanapolboonyaras THA

Australasia

B Tasmanian Stroke Play Lauceston GC, TAS 20–22 Minjee Lee AUS
F Australian Mid-Amateur Katrina Jones AUS
F Bream Bay Classic Samantha Dangen*/ Kylie Jacoby* NZL
F Omanu Classic Emily Perry NZL

Europe

F Champ. de Nouvelle Caledonie Ophelie Rague* FRA

December

Africa

F JGF Stroke Play Naomi Wafula* KEN
F KwaZulu Natal Nomads Cara Gorlei RSA

Americas

B Junior Orange Bowl Coral Gables, FL 27–30 Hyo-Joo Kim (KOR) USA
C Doral Publix Junior Classic 16-18 Miami, FL 21–23 Matilda Castren (FIN) USA
D Gate American Junior Ponte Vedra Beach, FL 19–22 Marina Stuetz (AUT) USA
D Joanne Winter Arizona Silver Belle Whirlwind Golf Crse – Devils Claw 28–30 Briana Mao/Angel Yin USA
D USA Open Collegiate Players C/ship ASU Karsten, AZ 27–29 Lee Lopez USA
E Doral Publix Junior Classic Emily Pedersen (DEN) USA
E Florida International Junior Samantha Fuller (ENG) USA
E Campeonato Abierto Ciudad de Montevideo Paloma Vaccaro (PAR) URU
F Barton Creek Collegiate Minami Levonowich USA
F CJGA World Junior Challenge Mika Liu USA
F Holiday Classic @ Barton Creek Resort Taylor Stockton* USA
F Ka'anapali Hawaiian Junior Lisa Kang USA
F San Diego Junior Girls Bryana Nguyen USA
F Toyota Junior Tour Cup Series Avery French* USA
F TPC Craig Ranch Collegiate Taylor Schmidt (CAN) USA
F Costa Rica Nat. Stroke Play HHilda Von Saalfeld*/ Silvia Perez* CRC
F Copa Arturo Calle Maria Camila Serrano/Ana Maria Rengifo COL
F Tourn. Nacional Vuelta Bolivia Michelle Ledermann* BOL

Asia

C Aaron Baddeley International Junior Lion Lake CC, Guangzhou 1–4 Su-Hyun Oh (AUS) CHN
E All India Championship Aditi Ashok IND
E All India Junior Championship Gurbani Singh IND
E East India Tolly Ladies Aditi Ashok IND
F Arab Games Individual Feriel Chahed (TUN)* QAT
F China Amateur Open Saya Aono (JPN) CHN
F HSBC Youth Chall. 3rd Leg Phoebe Nicole Tan SIN
F Sabah Int. Junior Masters Diana Tham MAS
F SICC Junior Invitational Benyapa Niphatsophon (THA) SIN

Australasia

B Dunes Medal The Dunes GC, VIC O29–N2 Lee Park AUS
B New Zealand Interprovincial Whakatane Golf Club 6–10 Lee Park (AUS) NZL
C Victorian Amateur Melbourne, VIC 8–14 Charlotte Thomas (ENG) AUS
D GNJGF Junior Masters Coolangatta Tweed Heads GC 12–15 Su-Hyun Oh AUS
F 2XU Champions Trophy Shelly Shin (KOR) AUS
F Queensland Schoolgirls Lauren Mason AUS

Europe

F TGF Ligi 1 Ayak Tugce Erden/ Yasemin Sari TUR
F TGF Ligi 2 Sena Ersoy/ Tugce Erden TUR

January

Americas

A	Dixie Amateur	Coral Springs, FL	D30–J2	Paula Reto (RSA)	USA
A	Harder Hall Invitational	Sebring, FL	4–7	Charley Hull (ENG)	USA
B	ANNIKA Invitational	Reunion Resort, FL	14–16	Alison Lee	USA
B	Ione D Jones/Doherty Championship	Coral Ridge Country Club, FL	16–21	Meghan Stasi	USA
B	Sally Championship	Oceanside CC, Ormond Beach, FL	11–14	Moriya Jutanugarn (THA)	USA
C	Torneo Nacional de Aficionadas	Club de Golf Vallescondido	9–12	Marijosse Navarro	MEX

E	Copa de Oro Dr Eugenio Blanco	Delfina Acosta	ARG
E	Copa Rio de la Plata Individual	Milagros Chaves (PAR)	URU
E	Internacional de Menores Junior Girls	Lucia Gutierrez	PER
E	Torneo I I de Menores	Lucia Gutierrez	PER
E	Torneo I I I de Menores	Lucia Gutierrez	PER
F	Dixie Senior Amateur	Diane Lang (JAM)	USA
F	Ione D Jones/Doherty Senior Championship	Andrea Kraus*	USA
F	Central American Junior	Margine Arguello (NCA)*	ESA
F	Abierto Cachagua	Valentina Fontaine	CHI
F	Abierto de Granadilla	Isidora San Martin	CHI
F	Abierto Marbella	Isidora San Martin	CHI
F	Abierto Rocas de S. Domingo	Isidora San Martin	CHI
F	Torneo I De Menores	Lucia Gutierrez	PER

Asia

C	Philippine Amateur Open	Canlubang G&CC	5–8	Lovelyn Guioguio	PHI

F	HSBC China Junior Open	Ji Rong	CHN
F	MGA National Trial	Nur Durriyah Damian	MAS
F	National Junior Girls Master Challenge	Zhang Yushan	CHN
F	Philippine International Junior	Daniela Uy	PHI
F	West Bengal Open	Gurbani Singh	IND

Australasia

A	Australian Amateur	Woodlands & Huntingdale GCs	17–22	Lydia Ko (NZL)	AUS
C	Lake Macquarie Amateur	Belmont GC, NSW	10–13	Whitney Hillier	AUS

E	Danny Lee Springfield Open	Mun Chin Keh	NZL
E	North Island U19	Wenyung Keh	NZL
F	Canterbury Womens S/play	Seon-Woo Bae (KOR)	NZL
F	Harvey Norman Junior	Esther Yoon	AUS
F	Hastings Womens Open	Kate Chadwick	NZL
F	Judy Elphinstone Tournament	Tammy Hall	AUS
F	SA Junior Amateur	Jenny Lee	AUS
F	SA Junior Masters	Jenny Lee	AUS
F	Tamar Valley Junior Girls Cup	Hayley Bettencourt	AUS
F	Tasmanian Junior Girls Masters	Hayley Bettencourt	AUS
F	Victorian Junior Masters	Bianca Ling	AUS

Europe

B	Portuguese International Ladies Am.	Golf Montado	26–29	Roberta Roeller (GER)	POR
C	Spanish International Stroke Play	Alicante Golf	9–11	Ha Rang Lee	ESP

F	Andalucia Junior Girls European Open	Samantha Giles (ENG)	ESP
F	TGF Ladies League 3rd Leg	Tugce Erden	TUR
F	Titleist Winter Tournament–Norway	Marthe Wold (NOR)	ESP

February

Africa

D	Border Ladies Championship	East London GC	26–28	Alana Van Greuning	RSA
D	Eastern Cape Ladies Championship	Port Elizabeth	5–7	Nobuhle Dlamini (SWZ)	RSA

Americas

A	Allstate Sugar Bowl Women's Intercollegiate	New Orleans, LA	26–28	Alex Stewart	USA
A	NorthropGrumman Reg Women's Challenge	Palos Verdes, CA	13–15	Lindy Duncan	USA
A	Lady Puerto Rico Classic	San Juan, PR	12–14	Marta Silva Zamora (ESP)	PUR
B	Arizona Wildcat Women's Inv.	Tucson, AZ	5–7	Manon Gidali (FRA)	USA
B	Central District Women's Inv.	Parrish, FL	20–21	Chirapat Jao-Javanil (THA)	USA

B	UCF Women's Challenge	Sorrento, FL	12–14	Victoria Trapani	USA
C	Kiawah Island Women's Intercoll.	Kiawah, SC	26–28	Fanny Cnops (BEL)	USA
C	Sir Pizza Cards Women's Challenge	Weston, FL	27–28	Brittany Marchand (CAN)	USA
C	UNLV Spring Rebel Women's Inv.	Boulder City, NV	20–21	Isabelle Boineau (FRA)/Manon Gidali (FRA)	USA
C	Westbrook Women's Invitational	Peoria, AZ	26–27	Nora Lucas	USA
D	Claud Jacobs Women's Challenge	Victoria, TX	19–20	Ali Lucas	USA
D	Islander Women's Classic	Crp Christi, TX	27–28	Summer Batiste/Taylor Newlin	USA
D	Camp. Nacional por Golpes Ladies	Olivos Golf Club	10–12	Maria Olivero	ARG

E	Camp. Nac. de Menores Girls MP	Lucia Gutierrez	PER
E	Torneo V de Menores Girls	Lucia Gutierrez	PER
E	Torn. VI de Menores de Verano Girls	Lucia Gutierrez	PER
E	Lady Moc Classic	Elia Folch (ESP)	USA
F	Annual USA Women's Inv.	Lina Lagergren (SWE)	USA
F	Challenge at Fleming Is. Girls	Anna Bohmer (COL)	USA
F	Copa Yucatan Ladies	Gabriela Lopez	MEX
F	Folino Women's Invitational	Tara Green	USA
F	Jim McLean Doral Girls	Kari Bellville	USA
F	JU Women's Courtyard Classic	Lacey Fears	USA
F	Presidents Girls Cup	Yang Yue Hill	USA
F	Western States Girls Players Cup	Pailin Ruttanasupagid (THA)	USA
F	Abierto Int. De Menores Girls	Isidora Morgan	CHI
F	Abierto La Sabana Ladies	Isabella Loza	COL
F	Abierto La Serena Ladies	Sarah Guidi*	CHI
F	Abierto Las Brisas de Santo Domingo Ladies	Isidora Morgan*	CHI
F	Camp. Nac. de Menores Girls	Isabella Cardenas Giron*	COL
F	Camp. Nac. Prejuvenil y Juvenil Girls	Sofia Garcia Austt*	URU
F	Clas. al Sudamericano Juvenil Girls	Dismary Marquez*	VEN
F	Clasificatorio I Juvenil Girls	Natalia Soria	BOL
F	Clasificatorio I I Juvenil Girls	Tamara Paz	BOL
F	Southamerican Amateur Ladies Qualifier	Lucia Gutierrez	PER
F	Torneo de Golf Aficionado Ladies	Maria Alejandra Villalobos	COL
F	Torneo Nac. de Aficionados Ladies	Ana Maria Rengifo	COL

Asia

C	Kuala Lumpur Ladies Amateur Open	KGPA	21–23	Aretha Herng Pan	MAS

E	TGA-CAT Junior Girls Ranking 4	Ornicha Konsunthea	THA
F	Hong Kong Ladies Close	Tiffany Chan	HKG
F	Mission Hills Junior Tour Girls Grand Final	Sha Wu	CHN
F	SGA 1st Nat. Ladies Ranking Game	Koh Sock Hwee	SIN
F	Taiwan Nat. Women's Winter Ranking Tournament	Ssu-Chia Cheng	TPE

Australasia

B	Riversdale Women's Cup	Melbourne, VIC	22–24	Whitney Hillier	AUS
D	LawnMaster Ladies Classic	Manawatu GC, Manawatu	4–5	Carly Beck (AUS)	NZL

E	S. Island Women's Stroke Play	Celyn Khoo	NZL
F	Grant Clements Ladies Mem.	Caryn Khoo	NZL

Europe

F	Grand Prix de Saint Donat Ladies	Ariane Provot	FRA
F	Hacienda del Alamo Ladies Open	Jessica Wilcox (ENG)	ESP
F	Italian Girls U 18 C/ship	Roberta Liti	ITA
F	TGF Ladies League 4th Leg	Tugce Erden	TUR

March

Africa

C	Kwazulu-Natal Championship	Maritzburg GC	25–27	Nobuhle Dlamini (SWZ)	RSA
D	Western Province Championship	Royal Cape Golf Club	18–20	Nicole Loesch	RSA

F	KeNako SA World Juniors	Lara Weinstein	RSA

Americas

A	Battle at Rancho Bernardo	Rancho Bernardo, CA	19–20	Sophia Popov (GER)	USA
A	Darius Rucker Intercollegiate	Hilton Head, SC	3–4	Stephanie Meadow (IRL)	USA
A	LSU Classic	Baton Rouge, LA	9–11	Catherine O'Donnell/Erica Popson	USA
A	SunTrust Gator Invite	Gainesville, FL	16–18	Maria Salinas (PER)	USA
B	Anuenue Spring Break Classic	Kapalua, HI	26–27	Daniela Holmquist (SWE)	USA
B	Bruin Wave Invitational	Tarzana, CA	5–6	Christine Wong (CAN)	USA
B	Clover Cup	Mesa, AZ	16–18	Jessica Wallace (CAN)	USA
C	BYU at Entrada Classic	St George, UT	19–20	Kelsey Vines	USA
C	Dr Donnis Thompson Invitational	Honolulu, HI	13–14	Kayla Mortellaro	USA
C	Hurricane Invitational	Miami, FL	5–6	Charlotte Kring Lorentzen (DEN)	USA
C	Insperity Lady Jaguar Intercollegiate	Augusta, GA	16–18	Paula Reto (RSA)	USA
C	JMU Eagle Landing Invite	Orange Park, FL	9–11	Kaylin Yost	USA
C	John Kirk/Panther Intercollegiate	Stockbridge, GA	26–27	Gabriella Wahl (GER)	USA
C	Juli Inkster Spartan Invite	San Jose, CA	5–6	Joanne Lee	USA
C	Mountain View Collegiate	Tucson, AZ	23–24	Jennifer Brumbaugh	USA
C	Pinehurst Challenge	Pinehurst, NC	19–20	Brittany Marchand (CAN)	USA
C	UALR Classic	Hot Springs, AR	26–27	Karisa Akin	USA
C	Campeonato Sudamericano Amateur	Los Farallones, Cali	19–25	Delfina Acosta (ARG)	COL
D	Anteater Invitational	Dove Canyon, CA	26–27	Mallory Kent	USA
D	Jackrabbit Invitational	Primm, NV	12–13	Monica Jung (AUS)	USA
D	Monterey Bay Invitational	Monterey, CA	18–20	Chiara Citterio (ITA)*	USA
D	Peggy Kirk Bell Invitational	Winter Springs, FL	5–6	Abbey Gittings (ENG)	USA
D	Rio Verde Invitational	Rio Verde, AZ	9–11	Kristen Hill	USA
D	UNCW Seahawk Classic	Wallace, NC	24–25	Nicole Sakamoto	USA
D	University of Cincinnati Spring Invite	Crystal River, FL	23–25	Shelby Coyle	USA
D	Abierto Club Campestre de Cali Ladies	Club Campestre de Cali	2–4	Valentina Romero	COL
D	Gran Premio Tortugas	Tortugas CC	8–10	Manuela Carbajo Re	ARG

E	Copa Donovan	Cynthia Diaz	COL
E	Master Internacional Infantil y Juvenil	Natalia Forero	COL
E	Fresno State Lexus Classic	Madeleine Ziegert (SWE)	USA
E	Spider Intercollegiate	Harin Lee	USA
E	Spider Invitational St James	Katia Joo	USA
F	Bison Invitational in Vegas	Brittany Atterbury/ Crystal Reeves	USA
F	C&F Bank Intercollegiate	Kameron Carter	USA
F	Cavalier Classic	Megan Woodland (CAN)	USA
F	Jekyll Island Collegiate	Jennifer Sullivan*	USA
F	LadyJack Crown Classic	Julie Aime (FRA)	USA
F	MSU Ocala Spring Invitational	Alex Buelow	USA
F	San Francisco City C/ship	Alexandra Wong	USA
F	Bermuda Match Play	Kathy Lloyd-Hines	BER
F	Central American Ladies Am.	Pamela Abreu (GUA)	HON
F	Costa Rica Nat. Match Play	Ximena Montealegre*	CRC
F	Abierto De Arrayanes	Daniela Darquea	ECU
F	Abierto La Posada Ladies	Valentina Haupt	CHI
F	Abierto Las Auracarias	Florencia Vinagre	CHI
F	Clasificatorio III Juvenil	Natalia Soria	BOL
F	Clasificatorio IV Juvenil	Michelle Ledermann	BOL
F	Vuelta Bolivia XXXX	Natalia Perez	BOL

Asia

C	Thailand Ladies Amateur Open	Green Valley CC, Samutprakarn	14–15	Pinrath Loomboonruang	THA
C	WWWExpress-DHL National Am.	Canlubang G&CC	27–30	Dottie Ardina	PHI
D	Faldo Series Asia Grand Final	Mission Hills GC, Shenzhen	14–16	Mai Arai (JPN)	CHN
D	Montecillo Junior Championship	Orchard Golf & Country Club	6–9	Princess Mary Superal	PHI
D	Royal Selangor Junior Open	Kuala Lumpur	13–15	Dottie Ardina (PHI)	MAS

F	HSBC Youth Challenge 1st Leg	Ariel Lee Zhi Zhen*	SIN
F	Mackwoods Stroke Play C/ship	Niloo Jayathilake*	SRI
F	Malaysian Schools Sports	Nur Durriyah Damian	MAS
F	PGI-BNI Series 1	Ika Woro Palupi	INA
F	Ryo Ishikawa Cup Junior Girls Championship	Kana Nagai	JPN
F	TGA-CAT Junior Ranking 5	Thamonpatsorn Siriko	THA
F	Thailand National Qualifier	Kanphanitnan Muangkhumsakul	THA
F	TrueVisions Singha Junior	Benyapa Niphatsophon	THA

Australasia

B	New Zealand Stroke Play	Hastings GC	22–25	Emily Perry	NZL
C	Trans Tasman Cup	Frankston, VIC	8–9	Emily Perry (NZL)	AUS
C	Victorian Women's Stroke Play	Melbourne, VIC	A27–M1	Grace Lennon	AUS
C	Western Australia State Amateur	Mount Lawley GC	14–18	Breanna Elliott	AUS
D	North Island Stroke Play	Lochl Golf Club, Hamilton	15–18	Emily Perry	NZL

Europe

B	European Nations Cup Individual	RCG Sotogrande	21–24	Celine Boutier (FRA)	ESP
B	Spanish Ladies Amateur – Copa S.M. La Reina	El Valle	29–04	Karolin Lampert (GER)	ESP
D	Madrid Ladies Championship	El Encin	23–25	Nuria Iturrios	ESP

E	BUCS Regional Qualifier 3	Eilidh Briggs	SCO
F	BUCS Stroke Play	Eilidh Briggs	SCO
F	Castellon Ladies Amateur	Silvia Banon	ESP
F	Catalonian Junior C/ship	Andrea Jonama	ESP
F	Coupe de France Dames	Mathilda Cappeliez	FRA
F	Gran Premio Vecchio Monastero	Tullia Calzavara	ITA
F	Grand Prix du Cap d'Agde	Lara Plachetka	FRA
F	Italian Amateur Match Play	Stefania Avanzo	ITA
F	TGF League 5	Damla Bilgic	TUR

April

Africa

B	South African Stroke Play	Umhlali CC	14–17	Nobuhle Dlamini (SWZ)	RSA
D	Free State & N. Cape Championship	Bloemfontein GC	21–22	Olivia Le Roux	RSA

F	NOMADS Rose Bowl	Kelly Erasmus	RSA
F	Sigona Junior Open	Naomi Angela Wafula	KEN

Americas

A	Bryan National Collegiate	Brown Summit, NC	6–8	Lindy Duncan	USA
A	Liz Murphey Collegiate Classic	Athens, Georgia	M30–A1	Jennifer Kirby (CAN)	USA
A	PING/ASU Invitational	Tempe, AZ	M31–A1	Ani Gulugian/Demi Runas	USA
A	SEC Championship	Fayetteville, AR	20–22	Patricia Sanz (ESP)	USA
B	ACC Championship	Greensboro, NC	13–15	Lindy Duncan	USA
B	Big 12 Championship	Lawrence, KS	27–29	Mary Michael Maggio	USA
B	Knights & Pirates Invite	Melbourne, FL	9–10	Deborah DeVilla (PHI)	USA
B	Lady Buckeye Spring Invite	Columbus, OH	21–22	Rachel Rohanna	USA
B	PAC-12 Championship	Pullman, WA	27–29	Doris (Yann-Ning) Chen	USA
B	Pacific Coast Intercollegiate	HalfMoon Bay, CA	16–17	Erynne Lee	USA
C	Big Ten Championship	French Licks, IN	27–29	Laura Gonzalez-Escallon (BEL)	USA
C	C-USA Championship	Gulf Shores, AL	23–25	Maribel Lopez (COL)	USA
C	Junior at Innisbrook	Palm Harbor, FL	6–8	Maria Torres (PUR)	USA
C	Rebel Intercollegiate	Oxford, MS	6–8	Jaclyn Jansen	USA
D	Big East Championship	Orlando, FL	22–24	Ashley Armstrong	USA
D	Big West Championships	San Luis Obispo, CA	22–24	Beverley Vatananugulkit	USA
D	CAA Championship	Southport, NC	20–22	Charlotte Kring Lorentzen (DEN)	USA
D	Hoya Invitational	Beallsville, MD	2–3	Elizabeth Haycock (ENG)	USA
D	Indiana Invitational	Bloomington, IN	14–15	Kristtini Cain	USA
D	Junior at Traditions	Bryan, TX	6–8	Sierra Sims	USA
D	Mountain West Conference C/ship	Phoenix, AZ	20–22	Sanna Nuutinen (FIN)	USA
D	Southern Conference Championship	Hilton Head, SC	15–17	Jordan Britt	USA
D	Southland Conference	Blanco, TX	16–18	Shannon Jungman	USA
D	Summit League Championship	Primm, NV	23–24	Amy Anderson	USA
D	Sun Belt Conference	Muscle Shoals, AL	16–18	Rachael Watton (SCO)	USA
D	WAC Championship	Mesa, AZ	23–25	Kayla Mortellaro	USA
D	West Coast Conference C/ship	Hollister, CA	16–18	Victoria Fallgren	USA
D	Winn Grips Heather Farr Classic	Mesa, AZ	6–8	Lindsey Weaver	USA
D	Abierto del Centro	Cordoba Golf Club	4–7	Manuela Carbajo Re	ARG
D	Camp. Sudamericano Juvenil Damas	Country Club Las Palmas, Bolivia	23–29	Laura Sojo (COL)	BOL

E	Abierto De Chile	Maria Serrano*	CHI
E	Atlantic Sun Championship	Gabriella Wahl (GER)	USA
E	Big South Championship	Brittany Henderson (CAN)	USA
E	Houston Baptist Intercoll.	Alyssa Smith/Shelby Hardy	USA
E	Ivy League Championship	Bonnie Hu	USA
E	Los Angeles City Junior	Elisabeth Bernabe	USA

Americas (continued)

E	SSC Championship	Lilliana Camisa (ARG)	USA
E	Wyoming Cowgirl Classic	Brianna Espinoza	USA
E	PRGA Junior Island C/ship	Yudika Rodriguez*	PUR
F	Sir Garry Sobers C/ship	Lyn DeCambra-McLeod*	BAR
F	ACC Junior Championship	Gina Kim*	USA
F	Alabama State Senior	Sue Raines*	USA
F	Big Sky Championship	Carleigh Silvers	USA
F	Camp. Nacional Interzonas LII	Gabriela Lopez	MEX
F	College of Idaho Invitational	Sara Molyneux	USA
F	Conference Carolina's C/ship	Tegan Skirpstas*	USA
F	EKU Lady Colonel Classic	Jenna Hague (CAN)*	USA
F	Frontier Conference Tourn.	Jenteal Jackson	USA
F	GLIAC Championship	Sarah Hoffman	USA
F	Great American Conference Championship	Rebecka Surtevall (SWE)*	USA
F	Great West Conference C/ship	Lynn-Marie Nagel (RSA)	USA
F	Horizon League Championship	Lindsey Lammers*	USA
F	Hotels at Grand Prairie Invite	Brittany Atterbury	USA
F	Junior All-Star at Chateau Elan	Karen Arimoto*	USA
F	Lady Otter Spring Invitational	Courtney Soekland	USA
F	MAAC Championship	Victoria Nguyen*	USA
F	MAC Championship	Jenna Hague (CAN)	USA
F	Marsh Landing Invitational	Alex Buelow	USA
F	Mount St.Mary's Spring Inv.	Ellen Huffman*	USA
F	NEC Championship	Cristina Felip (ESP)	USA
F	Ohio Valley Conference Championship	Marisa Kamelgarn/ Ornella Arrizon (MEX)	USA
F	SAC Championship	Maria Luz Besio (ARG)	USA
F	Samford University Intercoll.	Maria Luz Besio (ARG)	USA
F	SCAC Championship	Emily Bachert	USA
F	State Farm MVC C/ship	Katie Jean	USA
F	Under Armour/Hunter Mahan Championship	Sierra Sims	USA
F	Aberto De Brasilia	Carla Ziliotto	BRA
F	Copa Manuel J de la Rosa	Ana Maria Rengifo	COL
F	Hyundai Championship	Patty Hoyos	PER
F	Nac. Abierto "BCP" Semana Santa	Michelle Ledermann	BOL
F	Nacional Mid Am. Parada 11	Diana Rueda Jaramillo	COL

Asia

A	Queen Sirikit Cup	Tanah Merah Country Club	25–27	Hyo-Joo Kim (KOR)	SIN
C	Philippine Amateur C/ship (Closed)	Sherwood Hills GC	11–15	Dottie Ardina	PHI
C	Sabah Amateur Open	Sabah Golf & Country Club	6–8	Kelly Tan	MAS

E	TrueVisions Int.l Junior	Benyapa Niphatsophon	THA
E	TrueVisions Singha Junior	Kanyalak Preedasuttijij*	THA
E	USHA Delhi Ladies	Aditi Ashok	IND
F	China Am. Futures Tour Leg 1	Zhang Jienalin	CHN
F	China Amateur Tour Beijing	Luo Ying	CHN
F	Faldo Series Philippines	Anne Therese Sabater/Lareina Daniella Gonzales	PHI
F	Sarawak Amateur	Loy Hee Ying	MAS
F	SGA 2nd Nat. Ranking Game	Joey Poh	SIN
F	TGA-CAT Jun. Championship (Asia Pacific)	Parinda Phokan	THA
F	TGA-CAT Junior Ranking # 6	Chayanid Prapassarangkul	THA

Australasia

B	Rene Erichsen Salver	Glenelg GC, Adelaide, SA	12–15	Breanna Elliott	AUS
B	Western Australian Stroke Play	Lake Karrinyup CC, Perth	2–4	Breanna Elliott	AUS
C	Australian Girls Amateur	Carbrook Golf Club	11–13	Su-Hyun Oh	AUS
C	New Zealand Amateur	Mount Maunganui GC, BOP	18–22	Mun Chin Keh	NZL
E	South Australian Amateur	Adelaide, SA	M26–A1	Nadine Smith	AUS
E	Taranaki Ladies Open	Taranki, New Zealand	12–15	Emily Perry	NZL
E	Tasmanian Centenary Amateur	Launceston GC	M29–A1	Ashlee Dewhurst	AUS

F	South Island U19	Jesse Hamilton	NZL

Europe

B	Internationaux De France Juniors (Trophee Esmond)	St Cloud	5–9	Celine Boutier	FRA
B	Scottish Open Stroke Play	Troon Portland/Old Course Troon	27–29	Amy Boulden (WAL)	SCO
C	German Match Play	Frankfurter Golf Club	26–29	Nina Holleder	GER
C	Irish U18 Open Stroke Play	Roganstown	21–22	Leona Maguire	IRL
D	BUCS Student Tour Finals	West Lancashire Golf Club	17–19	Hannah McCook (SCO)/Gemma Bradbury (WAL)	ENG
D	Internationaux De France Juniors (Trophée Claude-Roger Cartier)	Saint Cloud	7–9	Meghan MacLaren (ENG)	FRA
D	R&A Foundation Scholars Tourn.	Eden & Old, St Andrews	9–10	Kelsey MacDonald	SCO

E	Amateur Tour # 1	Karolina Vlckova	CZE
E	Italian Nat. Am. Team Championship	Karolina Vlckova (CZE)	ITA
E	Spanish National Team C/ship	Ainhoa Olarra	ESP
E	Ticino Championship	Fanny Vuignier	SUI
F	Camp. de Espana Universitario	Tatiana Morato	ESP
F	Camp. Nacional Absoluto	Ana Rita Felix*	POR
F	Championnat de Ligue Am. (Thomas de Kristofy)	Agathe Sauzon	FRA
F	Coppa d'Oro Citta di Roma	Laura Lonardi	ITA
F	Grand Prix D'Albi	Alexandra Moisand	FRA
F	Grand Prix de Bordeaux	Charlotte Maguin-Leopold*	FRA
F	Grand Prix de Haute Savoie	Clara Pietri (SUI)	FRA
F	Grand Prix de la Nivelle	Carmen Sainz (ESP)	FRA
F	Grand Prix de Limere	Marion Veysseyre	FRA
F	Grand Prix de Nimes Campagnes Womens	Alice Dubois	FRA
F	Grand Prix du Lys	Carole Danten-Azfi	FRA
F	Grand Prix GBB (Open Am. BBCC)	Alexandra De Lavigne*	FRA
F	Italian Team C/ship Qualifying	Elisabetta Bertini	ITA
F	Leone di San Marco	Katja Pogacar (SLO)	ITA
F	Munster Junior Championship	Zoe Allen*	IRL
F	Munster Women's C/ship	Amy Farrell	IRL
F	Nextgolf.net Trophy	Anna Taboni*	ITA
F	Open du Bassin d'Arcachon	Louise Latorre	FRA
F	TGF League 6	Yasemin Sari	TUR

May

Africa

B	Gauteng Amateur	Glendower GC	6–9	Kim Williams/Nobuhle Dlamini (SWZ)	RSA
B	WGSA 72 Hole Teams C/ship – Individual	Polokwane GC	20–23	Kim Williams	RSA

Americas

A	NCAA Championship	Frankin, TN	22–25	Chirapat Jao-Javanil (THA)	USA
A	NCAA D1 Central Regional	Columbus, OH	10–12	Lisa McCloskey (COL)/Maria Salinas (PER)	USA
A	NCAA D1 East Regional	Blue State College, PA	10–12	Katerina Ruzickova (CZE)	USA
A	NCAA D1 West Regional	Erie, CO	10–12	Catherine O'Donnell	USA
B	AJGA Thunderbird Inte. Junior	Scottsdale, AZ	26–28	Ariya Jutanugarn (THA)	USA
B	Scott Robertson Memorial	Roanoke, VA	18–20	Moriya Jutanugarn (THA)	USA
D	Florida State Amateur Match Play	Weston, FL	7–11	Meghan Stasi	USA

E	CN Future Links Ontario	Anna Younjin Kim	CAN
E	CN Future Links Pacific	Anna Younjin Kim	CAN
E	Jennie K Wilson Invitational	Nicole Sakamoto	USA
E	NCAA D2 Super Region 2	Lilliana Camisa (ARG)	USA
E	NCAA Division II C/ship	Abbey Gittings (ENG)	USA
E	Southern Amateur	Emee Herbert	USA
E	Campeonato de Chile MP	Maria Jose Vial	CHI
E	Copa Ron Abuelo	Daniela Darquea	ECU
F	California Senior Women's Am.	Sandy Woodruff*	USA
F	Camp. Nacional Infantil Juvenil	Maria Fernanda Lira*	MEX
F	FCWT National C/ship	JiaXin Yang (CHN)*	USA
F	FJT Orange County 13–15	Summer Moser*	USA
F	FJT Orange County 16–18	Kristine Odaiyar	USA
F	IJGT Tourn. of Champions	Susana Vik*	USA
F	Investors Group Junior Spring Classic	Grace Chung	CAN
F	JAGS ASU Memorial Junior Championship	Crystal Wang	USA
F	NAIA Championships	Megan Woodland (CAN)	USA
F	NCAA D2 Super Region 1	Amy Thompson	USA
F	NCAA D2 Super Region 3	Faylyn Beyale/ Jennifer Hilts	USA
F	NCAA D2 Super Region 4	Spencer Heller/ Katy Ward*	USA
F	NCAA Division III C/ship	Catherine Wagner	USA
F	NJCAA National C/ship	Sarah Schober (AUT)	USA
F	PGA Minority Championship	Tiana Jones*	USA
F	PGA Minority C/ship–Ind.	Ariel McNair*	USA
F	Texas A&M @ Traditions Collegiate	Phon Angwarawong (THA)*	USA
F	Texas Junior Masters–Junior World	Alexandra White	USA
F	Campeonato Nacional MP	Pilar Echeverria	GUA
F	Int. Camp. National Mid Am.	Julie Pauline Saenz Starnes (COL)	DOM
F	Aberto Sul-Brasileiro	Manuela Barros (URU)	BRA
F	Camp. Nacional Juvenil Copa Arturo Calle	Camila Serrano	COL
F	Camp. Nacional Prejuvenil Copa Arturo Calle	Cynthia Diaz	COL
F	Torneo Nacional Mapaizo BCP	Ana Karen Melgar	BOL

Asia

B	Malaysian Amateur Open	Kuala Lumpur G&CC	29–31	Whitney Hillier (AUS)	MAS

E	Acer Nat. Spring Ranking Tourn.	Yu-Hsin Chang	TPE
E	Asia Pacific Junior	Kanphanitnan Muangkhumsakul (THA)	MYA

Asia (continued)

F	China Am. Futures Tour Leg 2	Sha Wu	CHN
F	China Amateur Tour Leg 2	Min Li*	CHN
F	Guam Ladies Amateur	Nalathai Vongjalorn	GUM
F	Jack Nicklaus Junior C/ship	Yu-Hsin Chang (TPE)	CHN
F	Kansai Amateur	Ayumi Takeuchi	JPN
F	Kanto Championship	Mio Kouno*	JPN
F	Malaysian Amateur Close	Nur Durriyah Damian	MAS
F	Negeri Sembilan Amateur	Amelia Yong (SIN)	MAS
F	PGI BNI Amateur C/ship Series 11	Juriah Juriah	INA
F	Philippine Junior Am. Open	Pamela Mariano*	PHI
F	Rolex Junior Championship	Ere Okayama*	JPN
F	SEM Ventures Ladies Classic	Amelia Yong	SIN
F	TGA-CAT Junior World	Wad Phaewchimplee	THA

Australasia

B	Australian Interstate	West Lakes Golf Club, Adelaide	1–4	Wad Phaewchimplee (THA)	AUS
B	NSW Amateur Championship	Castle Hill Golf Club	14–22	Breanna Elliott/Hayley Bettencourt	AUS
C	South Pacific Masters	Surfers Paradise GC, QLD	28–30	Ali Orchard	AUS
D	Wairarapa Open	Masterton GC, Wellington	5–6	Julianne Alvarez	NZL

E	North Shore Classic	Mun Chin Keh	NZL

Europe

B	German International Amateur	Stuttgarter GC	17–20	Celine Boutier (FRA)	GER
C	Championnat de France C/ship Flight	Golf de Chantilly	2–6	Celine Boutier	FRA
C	English Ladies Close Amateur	Royal Birkdale	15–17	Kelly Tidy	ENG
C	Irish Women's Open Stroke Play	The Island	26–27	Emily Taylor (ENG)	IRL
C	Welsh Close Championship	Cardigan GC	20–22	Amy Boulden	WAL
C	Welsh Open Stroke Play	Ashburnham Golf Club	5–6	Becky Harries	WAL
D	DGU Elite Tour 1	Frederikssund Golfklub	12–13	Nicole Broch Larsen	DEN
D	Furesopokalen	Fureso GC	19–20	Emily Pedersen	DEN
D	Scottish Ladies' Amateur Closed	Tain	15–19	Laura Murray	SCO
D	Skandia Junior Open	Varbergs GK	25–27	Jenny Haglund	SWE
D	Skandia Tour Elit #1 – Flickor	Ystad GK	5–6	Linn Andersson	SWE
D	Team Rudersdal Ladies Open	Fureso Golf Club	26–27	Nicole Broch Larsen	DEN

E	Basel Championship	Fanny Vuignier	SUI
E	Italian International Ladies MP	Laura Lonardi	ITA
E	King's Prize	Chloe Leurquin	BEL
E	Leman Championship	Isabelle Dumont*	SUI
E	National U21 SP C/ship	Charlotte Puts	NED
E	Slovenian International Am.	Bianca Fabrizio (ITA)	SLO
E	Suisse Orientale Championship	Fanny Vuignier	SUI
F	Amateur Tour Event 2	Johanka Steindlerova	CZE
F	Camp. de Catalunya Absoluto	Eva Domingo Graells*	ESP
F	Camp. de Espana Cadete Reale	Marta Martin Garcia	ESP
F	Championnat de France Pool 1	Marta Martin Garcia (ESP)	FRA
F	Championnat de France Pool 2	Marta Martin Garcia (ESP)	FRA
F	Coupe Didier Illouz	Alexandra Vilatte*	FRA
F	Coupe Yves Caillol	Emie Peronnin	FRA
F	Czech International Mid-Am.	Marketa Subrtova	CZE
F	DGU Junior Tour 1	Puk Lyng Thomsen	DEN
F	Eimskipsmotarodin 1	Olafia Kristinsdottir	ISL
F	Fairhaven Trophy	Lida Nikka (FIN)	ENG
F	Golfstream Ladies Am. Open	Zhanna Tarasko (RUS)	UKR
F	Gran Premio Monticello	Catrolina Caminoli*	ITA
F	Grand Prix AFG	Leslie Cloots	BEL
F	Grand Prix de Rennes	Diane Buisson	FRA
F	Italian Ladies Senior C/ship	Silvia Valli*	ITA
F	Palla d'oro Memorial G Silva	Alessandra Braida	ITA
F	Polish Match Play C/ship	Dominika Czudkova (CZE)	POL
F	Skandia Tour Riks #1 – Goteborg	Fanny Johansson*	SWE
F	Skandia Tour Riks #1 – Halland	Sally Fridstrom*	SWE
F	Skandia Tour Riks #1 – Skane	Anna Magnusson	SWE
F	Skandia Tour Riks #2 – Ostergotland	Jessica Ljungberg	SWE
F	Skandia Tour Riks #2 – Smaland	Martina Edberg	SWE
F	Skandia Tour Riks #2 – Vastergotland	Michaela Finn*	SWE
F	Titleist Tour 1	Marthe Wold	NOR
F	Titleist Tour 2	Mariell Bruun	NOR
F	Trofeo Umberto Agnelli	Virginia Elena Carta	ITA

June

Africa

C	Ekurhuleni Open	State Mines Country Club	3–4	Nobuhle Dlamini (SWZ)	RSA
D	South African Girls	Orkney GC	23–26	Michaela Fletcher	RSA

Americas

A	US Amateur Public Links	Neshanic Station, NJ	18–23	Kyung Kim	USA
B	Rolex Girls Junior Championship	Bradenton, FL	12–15	Ariya Jutanugarn (THA)	USA
B	Rolex Tournament of Champions	Alpharetta, GA	25–29	Jaye Marie Green	USA
B	Women's Western Amateur	Monroe Golf & Country Club	18–23	Ariya Jutanugarn (THA)	USA
C	Eastern Women's Amateur	Country Club of York, York, PA	12–14	Isabelle Lendl	USA
D	Tennessee Women's Amateur	Gallatin, TN	4–8	Lauren Stratton	USA

E	Idaho GA Amateur	Madeleine Sheils	USA
E	Junior at Quad Cities	Evelyn Dole	USA
E	Mississippi State Amateur	Ally McDonald	USA
E	North Carolina Amateur	Courtney McKim	USA
E	Oregon Amateur	Amy Simanton	USA
E	Ping Phoenix Junior at ASU Karsten	Lindsey Weaver	USA
F	54 Hole Mid Season C/ship	Yang Jiaxin (CHN)	USA
F	AJGA Florida Junior Girls	Claudia De Antonio (VEN)	USA
F	AJGA Music City Junior Girls	Sophia Schubert	USA
F	Alabama State Junior Girls	Gabi Oubre'	USA
F	Alabama Women's State Am.	Kathy Hartwiger	USA
F	Arborlinks Girls	Cha Cha Willhoite*	USA
F	Arizona Womens' State MP	Stephanie Kim	USA
F	Arkansas Match Play	Summar Roachell	USA
F	Aspen Junior Girls Classic	Naomi Ko (CAN)	USA
F	Atlanta Coll. Women's Chall.	Lauren Dunbar	USA
F	BilliardFactory.com Jun. C/ship	Julia Beck*	USA
F	Bubba Conlee National Junior	Summar Roachell	USA
F	Burgett H Mooney Jr Girls Rome Classic	Madison Lellyo	USA
F	California Girls' Championship	Kathleen Scavo	USA
F	Canadian University & College Championship	Devon Rizzo*	CAN
F	Carolinas Junior Championship	Lucia Polo (GUA)	USA
F	Cleveland Junior Girls Open	Jessica Porvasnik	USA
F	ClubCorp Mission Hills Desert Junior Girls	Amy Lee	USA
F	CN Future Links Girls Prairie Championship	Ally Shin*	CAN
F	Colorado Junior Girls Stroke Play Championship	Calli Ringsby	USA
F	Connecticut Championship	Nicole Yatsenick	USA
F	CPT – Bear Trace Coll. Open	Camry Tardy*	USA
F	Delaware Women's Amateur	Emily Ransone	USA
F	Evitt Foundation RTC Junior All-Star	Jordan Daniel*	USA
F	Georgia Girls' Championship	Rachel Dai	USA
F	Georgia Match Play	Laura Coble	USA
F	Greater Cincinnati Amateur	Erin Michel*	USA
F	Greater San Antonio C/ship	Meghan Musk	USA
F	Greater San Antonio Jun. MP	Morgan Best*	USA
F	Heatherwoode Collegiate Ladies Open	Allison Harper	USA
F	Hilton Head Jun. Girls Open	Taylor Tomlinson	USA
F	Hudson Junior Invitational	Fai Khamborn*	USA
F	Hurricane Coll. Tour – Disney	Maia Schechter	USA
F	Idaho Match Play	Sheryl Scott*	USA
F	Illinois Women's Amateur	Elizabeth Szokol	USA
F	Indiana Girls State C/ship	Morgan Nadaline*	USA
F	Iowa Match Play	Kelly Nelson*	USA
F	IWGA Match Play	Meghan Potee	USA
F	Junior All-Star Girls @Eagle Ridge	Bing Singhsumalee*	USA
F	Junior All-Star Girls at Gainey Ranch	Patricia Wong*	USA
F	Jun. All-Star Girls at Penn State	Lauren Waller*	USA
F	Junior at Steelwood	Aliea Clark	USA
F	Kearney Hill Girls Golf Links	Jordan Lippetz	USA
F	Kentucky Women's State Am.	Karisa Akin	USA
F	Killington Junior Girls C/ship	Mia Landegren	USA
F	Las Vegas Junior Girls	Haley Moore	USA
F	Manitoba Match Play	Bri-ann Tokariwski*	CAN
F	Michigan Junior State Amateur	Aya Johnson*	USA
F	Natural Resource Partners Bluegrass Juniors	Haylee Harford*	USA
F	Nebraska Junior Match Play	Danielle Lemek*	USA
F	Nebraska State Amateur	McKayla Anderson	USA
F	North Carolina Junior C/ship	Isabella Rusher*	USA
F	Northern California SP	Eva Monisteri	USA
F	Ohio Women's State Amateur	Allison Schultz	USA
F	Oklahoma Women's State Am.	Amber Hensley	USA
F	Ontario Women's Match Play	Kaitlin Marrin	CAN
F	Oregon Junior Amateur	Hannah Swanson*	USA
F	Oregon Junior Stroke Play	Haleigh Krause*	USA
F	State Farm Collegiate Open	Monica Villarreal	USA
F	Tennessee Girls Amateur	Sarah Harris	USA
F	Texas Oklahoma Junior	Megan Blonien	USA
F	The Links at Kokopelli	Katherine Hepler	USA
F	Toronto Star Amateur	Robyn Doig	CAN
F	TPC San Antonio – PGA Tour Series Championship	Charter Lawson*	USA
F	Virginias Women's Stroke Play	Amanda Steinhagen	USA
F	Washington State Amateur	Karinn Dickinson	USA
F	West Texas Championship	Marian Barker*	USA
F	Wisconsin Match Play C/ship	Casey Marschall*	USA
F	Woodlands Collegiate Open	Christine Lin	USA
F	World Golf Village C/ship	Emily Tillo*	USA
F	Bermuda Open Championship	Ann Symonds	BER
F	Puerto Rico Golf Association Ladies Championship	Paola Robles	PUR
F	Segundo Torn. Honor Al Merito	Pilar Echeverria	GUA
E	Ab. Los Cerros Club de Golf	Coralia Arias	ECU
E	Copa Escalafon	Florencia Vinagre	CHI
F	Aberto do Estado do Parana	Carla Ziliotto	BRA
F	Aberto do Estado do Rio de Janeiro	Ruriko Nakamura	BRA
F	Abierto Cafetero de Golf	Maria Alejandra Hoyos	COL
F	Abierto de Golf Ciudad de Ibague	Maria Alejandra Villalobosr	COL
F	Abierto Manizales	Maria Alejandra Hoyos	COL
F	Abierto Scotiabank	Kiara Hayashida	PER
F	Andes Cup Ladies Qual.	Natalia Perez	BOL

Americas (continued)

F	Campeonato Nacional MP	Maria Garcia Austt	URU	F	Torneo Aficionado Cartagena de Indias	Jennifer Ayala*	COL
F	Campeonato Sudamericano Pre Juvenil	Gabriela Coello	VEN	F	Vuelta Bolivia La Paz	Melanie Vezjak	BOL

Asia

C	Hosim Cup	Hwasun Country Club	19–22	Hyo Joo Kim	KOR
C	KangMinKoo Cup	Yoosung Country Club	26–28	Hyo Joo Kim	KOR
C	Southern Ladies Tournament	Cebu Country Club	6–8	Princess Mary Superal	PHI
D	Japan Amateur	Aichi CC	19–23	Mamiko Higa	JPN

E	KGNS Amateur Open	Nur Durriyah Damian	MAS	F	HSBC Youth Challenge Leg 2	Asha Lakshme (MAS)	SIN
E	Malaysian Junior Close	Nur Durriyah Damian	MAS	F	Indonesia Junior Open C/ship	Victoria Chandra	INA
E	Seletar Junior Open	Benyapa Niphatsophon (THA)	SIN	F	Mindanao Regional C/ship	Pamela Mariano	PHI
E	Southern India Ladies Amateur	Gurbani Singh	IND	F	Philippine Junior Am. Closed	Mia Legaspi	PHI
E	USHA Army Championship	Aditi Ashok	IND	F	Selangor International Junior Open	Genevieve Ling I-Ryn/Isza Fariza Ismail	MAS
F	China Ladies Amateur Futures Tour Leg 3	Yan Jing	CHN	F	Singapore Junior C/ship	Yu-Hsin Chang (TPE)	SIN
F	Enjoy Jakarta World Jun. C/ship	Yu Okamura (JPN)	INA	F	SLGA Open Championship	Ssu-Chia Cheng (TPE)	SIN
F	Hokkaido Amateur C/ship	Hikari Fujita	JPN	F	Sutera Harbour Am. Open	Aretha Herng Pan	MAS
				F	TGA-CAT Junior Ranking #1	Kanphanitnan Muangkhumsakul	THA

Australasia

C	Northern Territory Amateur	Darwin Golf Club	1–3	Charlotte Thomas (ENG)	AUS
D	North Harbour Provincial MP	Muriwai GC	9–10	Mun Chin Keh	NZL
F	Fiji Open			Sylvia Joe	FIJ

Europe

A	Curtis Cup	Nairn Golf Club	8–10	Pilar Echeverria (GUA)	SCO
B	Turkish Amateur Open	Gloria – New Course	M29–J3	Nicole Broch Larsen (DEN)	TUR
C	DGU Elite Tour Damer II	Sohojlandets	9–10	Nanna Madsen	DEN
C	German Girls Open	GC St Leon-Rot	1–3	Karolin Lampert	GER
C	Irish Women's Close	Co Louth	16–19	Leona Maguire	IRL
C	Spanish National Ladies	El Saler	M31–J3	Camilla Hedberg	ESP
C	St Rule Trophy	New/Old GC, St Andrews	2–3	Laura Murray	SCO
C	Wiibroe Cup	Helsingor GC	16–17	Nicole Broch Larsen	DEN
D	Coupe Cachard	Golf De Saint Cloud	8–10	Amandine Guignard	FRA
D	Finnish Ladies Tour 2	St Lawrence GC	7–9	Krista Bakker	FIN

E	Austrian Ladies Stroke Play	Anja Purgauer	AUT	F	Italian U16 Stroke Play C/ship	Camilla Mortigliengo	ITA
E	Citta di Milano Trofeo Gianni Albertini	Virginia Elena Carta	ITA	F	Italian U18 Stroke Play	Francesca Avanzini	ITA
				F	Mattone d'Oro	Anna Taboni	ITA
E	Czech National Match Play	Lucie Hinnerova	CZE	F	Memorial Olivier Barras Ladies	Clara Pietri	SUI
E	National Match Play C/ship	Myrte Eikenaar	NED	F	Ostgota Junior Open	Charlotte Arklid*	SWE
E	Paltamo Ladies Open	Noora Tamminen	FIN	F	Skandia Tour Riks #3 – Blekinge	Linnea Knutsson	SWE
E	Skandia Tour Elit	Linnea Strom	SWE				
E	Swiss National MP C/ship	Fanny Vuignier	SUI	F	Skandia Tour Riks #3 – Bohuslan	Felicia Leftinger	SWE
E	Vejlematchen	Malene Krolboll	DEN				
F	Amateur Tour Event 3	Barbora Bakova	CZE	F	Skandia Tour Riks #3 – Orebro	Moa Folke*	SWE
F	Connacht Women's C/ship	Sinead Sexton	IRL				
F	DGU Junior Tour Piger II	Puk Lyng Thomsen	DEN	F	Spanish National Mid Amateur	Macarena Campomanes Eguiguren*	ESP
F	Eimskipsmotarodin (2)	Berglind Bjornsdottir*	ISL				
F	European Seniors	Rocio Ruiz de Velasco (ESP)*	AUT	F	Suisse Romande Ladies C/ship	Rachel Rossel	SUI
F	Faldo Series Czech C/ship	Johanka Steindlerova	CZE	F	Titleist Ladies Tour 3	Nicoline Skaug	NOR
F	Finnish International Junior	Sandra Salonen	FIN	F	Trophee Jean-Louis Jurion	Jeanne Metivier	FRA
F	Finnish Ladies Tour Opener	Annika Nykanen	FIN	F	Turkish Amateur	Elcin Ulu	TUR
F	German Mid-Amateur	Chris Utermarck	GER	F	Ulster Under 18 C/ship	Ariana Coyle Diez	IRL

F	US Kids – European C/ship	Teresa Casasus Artiles (ESP)*	SCO
F	Valles Region Championship	Andrea Jonama	ESP

July

Africa

B	Gauteng North Championship	Irene CC	1–4	Bertine Strauss	RSA
B	South African Match Play	Benoni CC	8–11	Bonita Bredenhann (NAM)	RSA
F	Zimbabwe Ladies Open	Claire Lyn Minter	ZIM		

Americas

A	Canadian Amateur	Lethbridge Country Club	24–27	Ariya Jutanugarn (THA)	CAN
A	U.S. Girls Junior Championship	Daly City, CA	16–21	Minjee Lee (AUS)	USA
A	Women's North & South Amateur	Pinehurst, NC	16–21	Austin Ernst	USA
B	Callaway Junior World C/ship	Torrey Pines Golf Course	10–13	Benyapa Niphatsophon (THA)	USA
B	Trans National Amateur	Elgin, SC	23–28	Breanna Elliott (AUS)	USA
B	Wyndham Cup	Arnold Palmer's Bay Hill Club & Lodge	23–26	Breanna Elliott (AUS)	USA
C	Judson Collegiate Invitational	Roswell, GA	15–18	Rachel Rohanna	USA
C	Ontario Women's Amateur	Loyalist Country Club	17–19	Brittany Marchand	CAN
D	AJGA Junior Challenge	Beaumont, CA	24–26	Kaitlin Park	USA
D	AJGA Junior Girls Open @The Legends	Temecula, CA	2–5	Chayanid Prapassarangkul (THA)	USA
D	BC Amateur	Christina Lake Golf Club	3–6	Christine Wong	CAN
D	Hawaii Women's Match Play	Oahu Country Club	17–20	Cassy Isagawa	USA
D	Ontario Junior	Shelburne Golf & Country Club	10–13	MacKenzie Brooke Henderson	CAN
D	Ravenwood Junior Girls C/ship	Victor, NY	2–5	MacKenzie Brooke Henderson (CAN)	USA
D	Campeonato Auspiciador	CC La Planicie	3–8	Maria Salinas	PER
D	Campeonato Nacional de Aficionados	Asia Golf Club	Jn24–Jy1	Lucia Gutierrez	PER

E	AJGA Junior @ River Landing	Bailey Tardy*	USA
E	California State Championship	Emily Talley	USA
E	Carolinas Women's Match Play	Dawn Woodard	USA
E	Florida Stroke Play	Ericka Schneider	USA
E	Golf Pride Junior Classic	Lauren Stephenson*	USA
E	Hogan's Alley Collegiate C/ship	Mary Michael Maggio	USA
E	Lessing's Classic	Taylor Totland	USA
E	Maryland Women's Amateur	Andrea Kraus	USA
E	New England Amateur	Kristen MacDonald	USA
E	Purdue University	Abbey Carlson	USA
E	US Kids Teen World C/ship	Kelly Whaley	USA
E	Virginia Amateur	Lauren Coughlin	USA
F	Aaron's – Bob Estes Abilene Junior	Sarah Moore*	USA
F	AJGA Junior @ Ruby Hill	Ziyi Wang (CHN)	USA
F	AJGA Nebraska Junior @ Quarry Oaks	Ailin Li	USA
F	Alabama State Women's SP	Cammie Gray	USA
F	Alaska State Amateur C/ship	Terri McAngus	USA
F	Alberta Girls	Jennifer Ha	CAN
F	Alberta Ladies Amateur	Jocelyn Alford	CAN
F	Alberta Senior Ladies	Alison Murdoch*	CAN
F	Arkansas State Junior	Kaylee Benton*	USA
F	Arkansas Women's Stroke Play	Julie Oxendine*	USA
F	Barton Creek Resort Women's Collegiate Championship	Phon Angwarawong (THA)	USA
F	BC Junior	Anica Yoo	CAN
F	Chick Evans Junior Match Play	Grace Kil	USA
F	CN Future Links Girls Atlantic Championship	Meghan McDougall	CAN
F	CN Future Links Quebec Girls	Katherine Gravel-Coursol	CAN
F	CN Future Links Western Girls Championship	Jaclyn Lee*	CAN
F	Coca-Cola Junior Girls C/ship	Abbey Carlson	USA
F	Colorado Match Play	Allie Johnston	USA
F	Deutsche Bank Jun. Shoot Out	Samantha Marks	USA
F	E Z GO Vaughn Taylor C/ship	August Kim	USA
F	Eddie Burke Sr. Young Houstonian	Christina Cantu	USA
F	FCG Collegiate Championship	Alleman Zech*	USA
F	FCG World Girls C/ship at PGA West	Kitty Tam (HKG)	USA
F	Florida Girls Match Play	Lauren Riehle*	USA
F	Furman University C/ship	Lily Bartell*	USA
F	Future Champions Match Play	Pitsinee Winyarat (THA)	USA
F	Genesis Shootout Presented by Valero Texas Open	Marijosse Navarro (MEX)	USA
F	Georgia Amateur	Laura Coble	USA
F	Golf Quebec Junior	Valerie Tanguay	CAN
F	Golf Quebec Provincial C/ship	Anne-Catherine Tanguay	CAN
F	Greater San Antonio Junior	Taylor Coleman	USA
F	HGA Junior Match Play	Emma Ballard*	USA
F	Indiana State Amateur	Meghan Potee	USA
F	Iowa Women's Amateur	Kimmy Askelson*	USA
F	Jack Kramer Memorial	Tiffany Chan (HKG)	USA
F	Junior at Centennial	Bethany Wu	USA
F	Kansas Amateur	Audrey Yowell	USA

Americas (continued)

F	KPMG Stacy Lewis Junior Girls Open	Cheyenne Knight	USA
F	Laurel Springs Women's Collegiate Open	Anna Lesher	USA
F	Lockton Kansas City Junior	Alexandra Harkins	USA
F	Maine Women's Amateur	Emily Bouchard	USA
F	Manitoba Amateur	Bri-ann Tokariwski	CAN
F	Manitoba Junior	Jenna Roadley	CAN
F	McArthur Towel & Sports Future Legends	Samantha Stewart*	USA
F	Memorial Junior Presented by Border Energy	Lindsey Weaver	USA
F	Michigan Women's Amateur	Emmie Pietila	USA
F	Midwest Junior Players C/ship	Harley Dubsky	USA
F	Missouri Women's Amateur	Ellen Port	USA
F	Montana State Amateur	Katelyn Frank*	USA
F	Nebraska Match Play	Elizabeth Lydiatt*	USA
F	New Brunswick Junior Girls Championship	Morgan Matchett	CAN
F	New Brunswick Provincial Championship	Margo McLeod	CAN
F	New York State Amateur & Mid-Amateur	Ellen Oswald*	USA
F	NLGA Amateur	Kathleen Jean*	CAN
F	North & South Junior	Catherine Ashworth*	USA
F	Nova Scotia Amateur	Julia Henderson	CAN
F	Nova Scotia Junior	Bernadette Little	CAN
F	Nova Scotia Senior Amateur	Leslie Houde*	CAN
F	Optimist Int. Junior 15-18	Marcella Pranovia*	USA
F	Pacific Northwest Women's Amateur	Chessey Thomas (USA)	CAN
F	Penn State University	Kuriko Tsukiyama	USA
F	Pennsylvania Junior C/ship	Madelein Herr*	USA
F	Philidelphia Junior	Jamie Susanin*	USA
F	Rhode Island Women's Am.	Nicole Scola	USA
F	Rose Creek Collegiate Open	Kendra Mann	USA
F	San Diego City Amateur	Devon Brown	USA
F	Santa Maria Collegiate Open	Kelsey Haynie*	USA
F	Saskatchewan Amateur	Anna Young	CAN
F	Saskatchewan Junior	Brooke Hobson*	CAN
F	Shreveport Junior	Elizabeth Doty	USA
F	South Carolina Junior MP	Morgan Webber*	USA
F	South Dakota Women's MP	Shannon Johnson	USA
F	Texas State Junior	Courtney Dow	USA
F	Texas Women's State Amateur	Emily Collins	USA
F	The Birchmont	Missy Tabery*	USA
F	Toyota Tour Cup – Santa Ana	Megan Kim*	USA
F	TPC San Antonio – PGA Tour Series Championship	Christina Cantu	USA
F	Under Armour – Jeff Overton Junior	Lindsey Weaver	USA
F	Veritas World Junior Girls	Sara Diaz (COL)	USA
F	Washington State Junior	Catherina Li	USA
F	West Virginia Amateur	Brooke Bellomy	USA
F	Westbrook CC Girls	Jessica Porvasnik	USA
F	Western Junior	Chakansim Khamborn (THA)*	USA
F	Western Pennsylvania C/ship	Carol Semple Thompson*	USA
F	Western Philadelphia MP	Alessandra Liu	USA
F	William Penn Junior C/ship	Erica Herr	USA
F	Wisconsin Stroke Play C/ship	Jessica Gerry	USA
F	Wyoming Women's Amateur	Haley Shackelford*	USA
F	Caribbean Junior C/ship	Maria Torres (PUR)	DOM
F	Abierto de Golf	Maria Vesga	COL
F	Abierto de Golf – Militar	Alejandra Alvarez	COL
F	Abierto Del Guayaquil CC	Claudia Orrantia*	ECU
F	Abierto Int. del eje Cafetero	Sara Diaz	COL
F	Amador do Brasil	Nathalie Silva	BRA
F	Brazilian Junior	Vitoria Teixeira	BRA
F	Faldo Series Brazil	Valentina Haupt (CHI)	BRA

Asia

E	Neighbors Trophy	Min-sun Kim/ Kyu-jung Baek	KOR
E	Sukan Malaysia	Aretha Herng Pan	MAS
E	Warren-Ford Amateur Open	Michelle Koh (MAS)	SIN
F	Asean Schools Games	Sherman Santiwiwattanapong (THA)	INA
F	China Am. Futures Tour Leg 4	Jin Man	CHN
F	China Amateur Tour Leg 3	Min Li	CHN
F	China National Junior C/ship	Zhang YunJie	CHN
F	Hanwha Finance Network Cup	Ju-hee Son	KOR
F	KB Financial Group Cup	Jin-Young Ko	KOR
F	SGA 3rd Nat.Ranking Games	Jo Ee Kok/ Koh Sock Hwee/ Melissa Loh	SIN

Australasia

C	Ruth Middleton Classic	Matamata, Waikato	7–8	Mun Chin Keh	NZL
C	Waikato Classic	Ngaruawahia GC	20–22	Wenyung Keh	NZL
D	Newman and Brooks Junior C/ship	Harvey, Bunbury & Sanctuary GCs	18–20	Hannah Green	AUS

E	Subaru State Age C/ship	Shelly Shin (KOR)	AUS
F	Bargara Junior Classic	Anna Stanton	AUS
F	Darwin Open	Vicki Purser*	AUS
F	QLD Schools Girl's C/ship	Dee Dee Russell*	AUS

Europe

A	European Girls Team Championship	GC St Leon Rot	10–14	Maria Torres (PUR)	GER
A	European Girls Team C/ship – Ind.	GC St Leon Rot	10–14	Maria Torres (PUR)	PGER
B	World University Championship	Ypsilon Golf Resort	3–6	Camilla Hedberg (ESP)	CZE
C	Belgian Stroke Play	Royal Ostend GC	Jn29–Jy1	Chloe Leurquin	BEL
C	Danish International Ladies C/ship	Silkeborg Golf Club	20–22	Nicole Broch Larsen	DEN
C	DM Hulspil	Rungsted GC	Jn29–Jy1	Nanna Madsen	DEN
C	English Open Mid Amateur	Wetherby GC	6–7	Emma Carberry	ENG
C	Grand Prix de Chiberta	Golf Anglet Chiberta	5–8	Celia Barquin (ESP)	FRA
C	Luxembourg International Amateur	Grand-Ducal	12–14	Nicole Broch Larsen (DEN)	LUX
C	The Junior Open	Fairhaven	16–18	Asuka Kashiwabara (JPN)	ENG
D	Belgian National Match Play	Royal Latem Golf Club	17–21	Fanny Cnops	BEL
D	Campeonato de Alicante	Las Colinas G&CC	13–15	Silvia Banon	ESP
D	European Young Masters	Balataon Golf & Yacht Club	26–28	Cavadonga Sanjuan (ESP)	HUN
D	Grand Prix des Landes	Hossegor	19–22	Ainhoa Olarra (ESP)	FRA

E	Biarritz Cup	Laure Castelain	FRA
E	Estonian Amateur Open	Leena Makkonen (FIN)	EST
E	Finnish Stroke Play	Noora Tamminen	FIN
E	Latvian Amateur	Krista Puisite	LAT
E	Norgesmesterskapet	Marita Engzelius	NOR
E	North of Scotland C/ship	Sheena Wood	SCO
E	Welsh Girls' Championship	Chloe Williams	WAL
F	Austrian Seniors	Karin Gumpert*	AUT
F	Austrian Stroke Play U16	Francesca Baratta-Dragono*	AUT
F	Austrian Stroke Play U18	Katja Pogacar (SLO)	AUT
F	Austrian Stroke Play U21	Nadine Dreher	AUT
F	Camp. Absoluto Pais Vasco	Irene Rollan	ESP
F	Campeonato de Madrid Junior	Irene Calvo	ESP
F	Citta di Mogliano	Tullia Calzavara	ITA
F	Classic du Prieure	Helene Malvy	FRA
F	Copa Comunidad Valenciana	Marta Perez Sanmartin	ESP
F	Czech Int. Junior U18	Katerina Krasova	CZE
F	Czech Int. Junior U21	Karolina Vlckova	CZE
F	Czech National Youth C/ship	Nikol Chrenkova*	CZE
F	Danish Int. Youth C/ship	Oona Vartiainen (FIN)	DEN
F	Danish Senior Open Amateur	Else Kalstad*	DEN
F	DM Mid Amateur	Stinne Thorsen*	DEN
F	Dutch Junior Open	Lauren Taylor (ENG)	NED
F	Eimskipsmotarodin 4	Valdis Jonsdottir	ISL
F	Faldo Series Austria	Marlies Krenn	AUT
F	Faldo Series Netherlands	Michelle Naafs	NED
F	Finnish Mid Amateur	Minna Kaarnalahti*	FIN
F	Fioranello d'Oro	Anna Dalessio	ITA
F	GGL Int. Junior Open	Rosso Lucrezia Colombotia	ITA
F	Gran Premio Citta di Cervia	Martina Flori	ITA
F	Gran Premio Padova	Anna Giulia Martinis	ITA
F	Grand Prix d'Apremont	Claudia Rocco (GER)	FRA
F	Grand Prix de la Baule	Melodie Jean Dit Berthelot	FRA
F	Grand Prix de la Côte d'Albatre	Helene Poels*	FRA
F	Grand Prix de Palmola	Marion Benzekri	FRA
F	Grand Prix de Saint Laurent	Julia Ravot	FRA
F	Grand Prix De Saint Nom La Breteche	Sophie Pfeiffer	FRA
F	Grand Prix du Golf Club de Lyons	Clothilde Weyrich*	FRA
F	Hillerod Pokalen	Cecilie Bofill	DEN
F	Icelandic Junior 15–16	Ragnhildur Kristinsdottir	ISL
F	Icelandic Junior Stroke Play	Gudrun Bjorgvinsdottir	ISL
F	Irish Girls' Close	Jessica Carty	IRL
F	Italian U14 Championship	Arianna Scaletti	ITA
F	Kronborg Masters	Christine Holm Skylvad	DEN
F	Latvian Match Play	Mara Puisite	LAT
F	Leinster Girls	Jessica Ross	IRL
F	Leinster Women's C/ship	Amy Farrell	IRL
F	Mid Leinster Championship	Shannen Brown	IRL
F	National Youths U16	Beatriz Themudo*	POR
F	National Youths U18	Ana Rita Felix	POR
F	Niitvalja Karikas	Mari Hutsi	EST
F	Omnium Suisse Championship	Tamara Scheidegger*	SUI
F	Rosen Pokalen	Trine Marie Ronholdt Byo	DEN
F	Russian Amateur	Nina Pegova	RUS
F	Scottish Girls' Closed	Lauren Whyte	SCO
F	Scottish Ladies' Junior SP	Nicola Callendar*	SCO
F	Solvogn Pokalen	Camilla Schou	DEN
F	Swiss Junior Championship	Rachel Rossel	SUI
F	Targa d'Oro	Elisabetta Bertini	ITA
F	Tirol International Junior	Anna Fuld	AUT
F	Titleist Tour 4	Sandra Nordaas*	NOR
F	Titleist West Coast Junior Masters	Camilla Bofill	DEN
F	TOYA Polish Junior	Pornvipa Sakdee (THA)	POL
F	Ukrainian Open Amateur	Mariia Pedenko*	UKR
F	Ynglinge Cup	Anna Frandsen	DEN

August

Africa

F	Limuru Junior Open	Naomi Angela Wafula	KEN

Americas

B	Junior PGA Girls Championship	Sycamore Hills, Fort Wayne, IN	J31–A3	Ariya Jutanugarn (THA)	USA
D	Canadian Junior Championship	River Spirit GC	J31–A3	MacKenzie Brooke Henderson	CAN
D	Genesis Junior Championship	El Cajon, CA	J31–A2	Erin Choi	USA
D	Genesis Junior Open	Bedminster, NJ	21–23	Nicole Morales	USA
D	Hawaii State Stroke Play	Mid-Pacific CC	J31–A2	Nicole Sakamoto	USA
D	Pennsylvania Women's State Amateur	Sewickley, PA	14–17	Ellen Ceresko	USA
D	South Dakota Women's Amateur	Brookings CC	10–12	Kimberly Kaufman	USA

E	CorseMax-Phaldelphia Runner Junior	Elisabeth Bernabe	USA
E	Junior At Robinson Ranch	Grace Park	USA
E	The Peninsula Junior Classic	Elisabeth Bernabe	USA
E	Under Armour Steve Marino Championship	Bryana Nguyen	USA
F	Arizona State Stroke Play	Samantha Postillion	USA
F	Bass Pro Shops – Payne Stewart Junior Girls C/ship	Anne Freman	USA
F	Canadian Senior	Terrill Samuel	CAN
F	Canyon Springs Women's Collegiate Open	Stephanie Gibri*	USA
F	CJGA Mizuno National Junior	Grace Chung	CAN
F	Collegiate Players Tour – National Championship	Kelsey Haynie	USA
F	Colorado Junior Match Play	Calli Ringsby	USA
F	Colorado Women's SP	Somin Lee (KOR)	USA
F	Connecticut State Amateur	Mia Landegren	USA
F	Dogwood State Junior Girls	Victoria Allred	USA
F	Golf Quebec Womens Provincial Match Play	Elyse Archambault	CAN
F	Goodman Networks Girls @ Timarron	Alexandra White	USA
F	Harvey Penick Junior Girls	Patricia Wong	USA
F	Junior @ Fox Hill	Catherina Li	USA
F	Junior All-Star @ Stockton	Kathleen Scavo	USA
F	Junior All-Star at Ocala	Bailey Tardy	USA
F	Junior All-Star at Townsend Ridge	Brooke McDougald	USA
F	Junior at Southwind	Emily Kurey*	USA
F	Manitoba Women's Senior	Tammy Gibson*	CAN
F	Massachusetts Women's Am.	Claire Sheldon	USA
F	Minnesota Women's State Am.	Sarah Burnham	USA
F	Minnesota Women's State MP	Jaclyn Shepherd	USA
F	Nebraska Senior C/ship	Susan Marchese	USA
F	New Hampshire Women's Am.	Dana Harrity*	USA
F	New Jersey Women's Amateur	Alexandra Hershberger	USA
F	Ontario Junior Match Play	Meghan Bennett*	CAN
F	Ontario Mid-Am	Jayne Chalmers*	CAN
F	Ontario Senior Women	Mary Ann Hayward	CAN
F	Ontario Summer Games	Samantha Spencer	CAN
F	Pacific Northwest Junior Am.	Jordan Ferreira	USA
F	Pennsylvania Women's Senior State Amateur	Connie Shorb*	USA
F	Philadelphia Junior	Mackenzie Perez*	USA
F	Quebec Junior Match Play	Valerie Tanguay	CAN
F	Randy Wise Junior Open	Muni He (CAN)	USA
F	Redstone GC – PGA Tour Series Championship	Susannah Grunden	USA
F	SCPGA Junior Match Play	Meigi Gao (CHN)*	USA
F	Sooner Junior All-Star	Courtney Dow	USA
F	Stonehenge Junior Open	Madelin Gedeon*	USA
F	Sunriver Junior Open	Marianne Li	USA
F	Tour Championship@TPC Craig Ranch	Mary Michael Maggio	USA
F	Tournament of Champions at TPC San Antonio	Mackenzie Boydston	USA
F	Trusted Choice Big I National Championship	Summar Roachell	USA
F	Utah State Women's Amateur	Kelsey Chugg	USA
F	Vermont State Championship	Holly Reynolds*	USA
F	Virginia Women's Senior Am.	Shelley Savage*	USA
F	Webb Simpson Junior	Kuriko Tsukiyama	USA
F	Wyoming Mid-Amateur	Sarah Bowman	USA
F	Abierto Damas de Lacosta Country Club	Daniela Darquea	ECU
F	Campeonato Aberto do Estado De Sao Paulo	Lucia Maria Guilger	BRA
F	Camp. Internacional Juvenil	Lina Aguillon	COL
F	Camp. Suramericano Prejuvenil	Cynthia Diaz	COL
F	Chile Junior Open	Faustina Peve (ARG)*	CHI
F	National Colombian Mid-Am.	Ana Maria Gonzalez de Llano*	COL
F	Torneo Nacional BCP	Michelle Ledermann	BOL
F	Tercer Torneo Honor Al Merito	Beatriz De Arenas	GUA

Asia

C	Santi Cup	Emeralda Golf Club	28–31	Jayvie Agojo (PHI)/Kelly Tan (MAS)	INA

F	Limuru Junior Open	Naomi Angela Wafula	KEN
F	ANNIKA Invitational 12–15	Jin Man	CHN
F	ANNIKA Invitational 16–18	Xiang Sui*	CHN
F	China Am. Futures Tour Leg 5	Xiang Sui	CHN
F	China Amateur Tour Leg 4	Xiao Jiayi*	CHN
F	Guam National Tryout	Nalathai Vongjalorn	GUM
F	HSBC Junior Championship	Chang Wenhui	CHN

F	Japan Collegiate Championship	Emi Sato	JPN
F	Japan Junior	Sakura Kito	JPN
F	Kansai Regional Collegiate	Miyu Araki	JPN
F	Kanto Junior	Akiho Sato	JPN
F	Kanto Regional Collegiate	Emi Sato	JPN
F	Ryo Ishikawa World Junior Inv.	Su Jin Lee (KOR)*	JPN
F	Singapore National Amateur	Amelia Yong	SIN
F	Song Am Cup	So-Young Lee	KOR
F	Sunrise National Summer Ranking Tournament	Ssu-Chia Cheng/ Yu-Hsin Chang	TPE
F	TGA-CAT Junior #2	Parinda Phokan	THA

Australasia

D	Kapi Tareha Ladies	Napier, Hawkes Bay	4–5	Emma Clayton/Kate Chadwick	NZL

E	Bay of Plenty Ladies Open	Sarah Bradley	NZL
E	Cambridge Womens Classic	Chantelle Cassidy	NZL
F	Jacob's Creek Classic	Ceri Nicholson*	AUS
F	Northern Territory Country Championship	Chantelle Shaw	AUS

Europe

B	English Open Stroke Play	Little Aston GC	7–9	Alexandra Peters	ENG
B	Girls' British Open Amateur	Tenby	13–17	Georgia Hall (ENG)	WAL
C	Czech International Amateur	Kaskada	1–4	Karolina Vlckova	CZE
C	English Girls' Close	Sandiway GC	J31–A2	Emily Taylor	ENG
C	German National Girls C/ship	Castrop-Rauxel Golf Club	24–26	Quirine Eijkenboom	GER
C	German Team Championship	Sporting Club Berlin	2–5	Quirine Eijkenboom	GER
C	Girls Home Internationals	Radyr	7–9	Quirine Eijkenboom (GER)	WAL
C	Harder German Junior Girls	Heddesheim, Germany	7–9	Caroline Nistrup (DEN)	GER
C	Ladies' British Amateur Stroke Play	Shandon Park Golf Club	22–24	Sarah-Jane Boyd (ENG)	IRL
C	Swiss International Amateur	Schoenenberg GC	3–5	Guilia Molinaro (ITA)	SUI
D	Belgian International Championship	Royal Antwerp GC	23–26	Camille Richelle	BEL
D	Champ. de France Coupe Gaveau	Bossey	22–26	Ariane Provot	FRA
D	Finnish Amateur	Helsingin GC	16–18	Julie Finne-Ipsen (DEN)	FIN
D	Zomerwedstrijd – Brabants Open	Eindhovensche GC	2–4	Karlijn Zaanen	NED

E	DGU Elite Tour Damer 111	Emily Pedersen	DEN
E	DM Junior	Anna Frandsen	DEN
E	JSM Match Girls	Linnea Strom	SWE
E	Latvian Open	Margarita Kim (RUS)	LAT
F	Amateur Tour Event 5	Katerina Krasova	CZE
F	Campeonato Absoluto del Principado de Asturias	Alejandra Pasarin	ESP
F	Championnat de France Minimes Filles	Lena Gautier	FRA
F	Connacht Girls	Jessica Ross	IRL
F	Copa Fed. Vasca de Golf	Teresa Diez	ESP
F	Coppa D'Oro Mario Camicia	Giulia Miglietta*	ITA
F	Credit Suisse Junior Tour Event – Kuessnacht	Virginia Birrer	SUI
F	Czech International Senior	Helena Janoudova*	CZE
F	DGU Junior Tour Piger 111	Mathilde Fredensborg*	DEN
F	DM Seniorer	Else Kalstad	DEN
F	Eimskipsmotarodin 5	Olafia Kristinsdottir	ISL
F	Estonian National Stroke Play	Annika Meos	EST
F	Faldo Series Russia	Nina Pegova	RUS
F	Faldo Series Slovakia	Natalia Heckova/ Katarina Chovancova	SVK
F	Grand Prix de Bretagne	Virginie Burrus	FRA
F	Grand Prix de Savoie	Clotilde Chazot	FRA
F	Grand Prix de Valcros	Marion Benzekri	FRA
F	Grand Prix de Vichy Val d'Allier Ladies	Celia Mansour	FRA
F	Grand Prix du Medoc	Lauralie Migneaux	FRA
F	Grand Prix Du Pau	Lauralie Migneaux*	FRA
F	Grand Prix Valgarde	Emilie Alonso	FRA
F	Hungarian Junior Open	Csilla Rozsa	HUN
F	Hungarian Ladies Amateur	Marlies Krenn (AUT)	HUN
F	Icelandic Junior Match Play	Gudrun Bjorgvinsdottir	ISL
F	International Match Play	laura Kowohl	GER
F	Italian U18 Team C/ship	Camilla Mortigliengo	ITA
F	Latvian Junior Open	Anna Diana Svanka	LAT
F	National Junior Stroke Play	Clara Aveling	BEL
F	Norgesmesterskapet Junior (Titleist Tour)	Nicoline Skaug	NOR
F	North of England U-16 SP	Gabriella Cowley	ENG
F	Polish Ladies' Amateur Open	Martyna Mierzwa	POL
F	Skandia Tour Elite Flickor 5	Charlotte Arklid	SWE
F	Skandia Tour Riks 4 – Gavle	Marina Hedlund	SWE
F	Skandia Tour Riks 4 – Haninge	Stephanie Henning*	SWE
F	Skandia Tour Riks 4 – Jonkopings	Filippa Moork	SWE
F	Skandia Tour Riks Flickor 5	Johanna Larsson	SWE
F	Skandia Tour Riks Sala Flickor 5	Mimmi Gullberg	SWE
F	Skandia Tour Riks Sunne Flickor 5	Filippa Moork	SWE
F	Slovak Junior Championship	Natalia Heckova	SVK
F	Slovak Open	Katerina Vlasinova (CZE)	SVK
F	Slovenian Girls	Katja Pogacar	SLO
F	SM Reikapeli	Annika Nykanen	FIN
F	St Andrews Junior Ladies	Nicola Haynes (ENG)	SCO
F	Strathtyrum Tournament	Karen Marshall	SCO
F	Titleist Tour 6	Pernille Sol Langseth Orlien	NOR NOR

Europe (continued)

F	Ukrainian Open Amateur Team Championship	Rachael Maitland* (ENG)	UKR	F	Zurich Championship	Rebecca Suenderhauf	SUI
F	Ulster Women's Championships	Rachael Maitland* (ENG)	IRL ENG				

Season 2012–2013

The R&A Women's World Amateur Golf Ranking season runs from September until the following August when the Mark McCormack Medal is presented following the US Women's Amateur Championship. Results for the remainder of the calendar year will be included in the following year's edition of *The R&A Golfer's Handbook.*

Death of former double champion Liz Pook

Liz Pook (née Chadwick), who won the British Amateur title in 1967 and again the following year, has died aged 69 after a long illness.

She always had the reputation of being a great fighter never more so than in the two Championships she won. Against French star Catherine Lacoste, who won the US Women's Open Championship as an amateur, she birdied all the short holes and then rolled in a 35 footer for victory moving on to beat Vivien Saunders in the final.

The following year she recovered from four down after five holes to beat Linda Bayman and in the final that year beat Mary Everard.

After giving up golf to devote time to her family, she was on the point of returning to the game when an operation on her back went badly wrong. She was paralysed from the waist down but Cheshire County provided her with a lightweight wheelchair and hand controls for her car and, with the members at Bramall Park giving her the computer. she said a whole new world had opened up for her.

Later, she acted as a spokesperson for the Spinal Injuries Assocation. Always positive in her attitude despite her misfortune, Liz Pook swore by Vincent Peale's "Power of Positive Thinking" as did Gary Player whose card she marked during the 1967 Open won by Roberto de Vicenzo at Hoylake.

When she was at her lowest in hospital and aware that she would never play golf again she was sent a little card which sums up her own philosophy to life. It read simply: "Misfortune is an occasion to demonstrate character. "

Month by month in 2012

Europe's stunning comeback from 4–10 retains the Ryder Cup by a point in Chicago, Ian Poulter starring with four wins out of four. Rory McIlroy, who just makes the tee after a mix-up over his start time, had earlier won two FedEx Cup play-off events, but Brandt Snedeker lands £7million Tour Championship jackpot. Jiyai Shin's nine-shot Ricoh British Women's Open win completes unprecedented Asian clean sweep of 2012 women's majors.

European Amateur Ranking 2011–2012

English players dominated the European Amateur Ranking in 2011–2012 with 13 entries in the top 100. Spain was second with 12 places and Germany third with 11. Denmark had nine players in the top 100 with Sweden finishing the season with seven. The European Rankings are extracted from WAGR and are finalised at the same time.

			Divisor	*Points*
1	Georgia Hall	ENG	32	1787.50
2	Charley Hull	ENG	36	1619.44
3	Stephanie Meadow	IRL	50	1494.12
4	Celine Boutier	FRA	79	1447.57
5	Perrine Delacour	FRA	62	1444.35
6	Nicole Broch Larsen	DEN	52	1394.23
7	Amy Boulden	WAL	41	1325.61
8	Bronte Law	ENG	26	1297.62
9	Karolin Lampert	GER	51	1263.73
10	Ha Rang Lee	ESP	34	1255.88
11	Quirine Eijkenboom	GER	48	1252.08
12	Guilia Molinaro	ITA	43	1240.99
13	Leona Maguire	IRL	32	1238.28
14	Holly Clyburn	ENG	42	1238.10
15	Shannon Aubert	FRA	48	1232.55
16	Manon Gidali	FRA	46	1227.17
17	Clara Baena	ESP	33	1226.77
18	Emily Taylor	ENG	39	1222.65
19	Camilla Hedberg	ESP	50	1221.25
20	Chloe Williams	WAL	30	1218.33
21	Charlotte Thomas	ENG	60	1207.50
22	Laura Gonzalez-Escallon	BEL	43	1203.49
23	Marta Silva Zamora	ESP	33	1200.76
24	Becky Harries	WAL	31	1170.97
25	Fanny Cnops	BEL	48	1156.25
26	Daniela Holmqvist	SWE	40	1154.22
27	Hayley Davis	ENG	50	1144.50
28	Rocio Sanchez Lobato	ESP	46	1143.48
29	Ariane Provot	FRA	59	1142.37
30	Marta Sanz	ESP	49	1133.67
31	Katerina Ruzickova	CZE	41	1129.88
32	Linnea Strom	SWE	32	1129.69
33	Ann-Kathrin Lindner	GER	43	1124.42
34	Nina Holleder	GER	45	1121.11
35	Nanna Madsen	DEN	33	1093.18
36	Sophia Popov	GER	45	1083.75
37	Marina Stuetz	AUT	28	1080.36
38	Emily Pedersen	DEN	53	1072.64
39	Sally Watson	SCO	44	1071.59
40	Silvia Banon	ESP	49	1071.43
41	Kelly Tidy	ENG	44	1070.45
42	Ainhoa Olarra	ESP	34	1059.56
43	Caroline Nistrup	DEN	44	1055.68
44	Isabelle Boineau	FRA	54	1055.09
45	Madelene Sagstrom	SWE	36	1054.17
46	Gabriella Wahl	GER	30	1054.17
47	Meghan MacLaren	ENG	30	1052.50
48	Krista Puisite	LAT	50	1051.25
49	Antonia Scherer	GER	29	1044.83
50	Charlotte K.Lorentzen	DEN	38	1040.79
51	Chloe Leurquin	BEL	39	1033.97
52	Karolina Vlckova	CZE	28	1032.14
53	Laura Murray	SCO	25	1029.91
54	Abbey Gittings	ENG	34	1023.53
55	Marita Engzelius	NOR	39	1017.31
56	Sarah Schober	AUT	37	1008.11
57	Ileen D. Nieuwenhuis	NED	43	1006.98
58	Noora Tamminen	FIN	47	1005.72
59	Vicki Troeltsch	GER	29	1003.45
60	Katja Pogacar	SLO	30	1003.33
61	Lauren Taylor	ENG	29	1000.86
62	Laure Castelain	FRA	47	994.68
63	Fanny Vuignier	SUI	29	992.24
64	Nuria Iturrios	ESP	27	991.07
65	Katie Mundy	ENG	30	986.67
66	Laetitia Beck	ISR	42	976.19
67	Leslie Cloots	BEL	52	972.12
68	Camille Richelle	BEL	30	966.67
69	Laura Lonardi	ITA	33	965.91
70	Alessandra Braida	ITA	36	962.50
71	Jane Turner	SCO	40	951.25
72	Elcin Ulu	TUR	30	950.00
73	Gabriella Cowley	ENG	42	947.02
74	Eilidh Briggs	SCO	53	942.92
75	Virginia Elena Carta	ITA	43	941.86
76	Carolin Pinegger	GER	32	939.06
77	Nathalie Mansson	SWE	30	936.67
78	Patricia Sanz	ESP	46	930.43
79	Isabell Gabsa	GER	51	925.49
80	Natalie Wille	SWE	31	922.58
81	Tullia Calzavara	ITA	29	915.52
82	Malene Krolboll	DEN	34	914.71
83	Tonje Daffinrud	NOR	29	906.90
84	Matilda Castren	FIN	42	902.98
85	Linn Andersson	SWE	29	901.72
86	Roberta Roeller	GER	31	896.77
87	Olafia Kristinsdottir	ISL	45	896.67
88	Sara Monberg	DEN	41	894.51
89	Emma Henrikson	SWE	27	884.82
90	Ana Belac	SLO	34	883.82
91	Manon De Roey	BEL	54	883.33
92	Christine H. Skylvad	DEN	29	880.17
93	Julie Finne-Ipsen	DEN	38	878.95
94	Andrea Jonama	ESP	32	878.12
95	Sanna Nuutinen	FIN	50	875.38
96	Julie Aime	FRA	29	875.00
97	Gemma Dryburgh	SCO	34	869.85
98	Rachael Watton	SCO	32	867.19
99	Celia Barquin	ESP	33	866.67
100	Bianca Fabrizio	ITA	57	863.60

For the full European Amateur Rankings, visit www.ega-golf.ch

Major Amateur Championships 2012

Ladies British Open Amateur Championship (inaugurated 1893)

Carnoustie June 26–30 [6563–72]

Stephanie takes the title in double-quick time

Slow play is a constant topic on both the amateur and professional scene these days but it was not a problem at the final of the Ladies British Open Amateur Championship at Carnoustie.

Let's give a round of applause to Stephanie Meadow from Northern Ireland and Spain's Rocio Sanchez Lobato for the not only the quality of the golf but the speed with which they completed the 18-hole final. The match was over in under three hours with 20-year-old Meadow a 4 and 3 winner over her 19-year-old opponent.

Meadow, from Jordanstown, had earlier in the year helped Great Britain and Ireland overwhelm America on the final day to win the Curtis Cup at Nairn. Her excellent summer of golf also included being a member of the University of Alabama golf team – the "Crimson Tide" – who won the coveted NCAA title with a tense one shot victory over Southern California in Franklin, Tennessee. In short, she arrived at Carnoustie very much in form.

Meadow had left Northern Ireland when 14 to attend the Junior International Academy run by Hank Haney and is known for her straight hitting and consistency. In the final she got off to a great start, winning three of the first four holes. Although the Ulster golfer lost the third where she was bunkered, she quickly won the sixth where lobato was out of bounds and the seventh again with a par.

A fine birdie 2 at the eighth enabled the Spaniard to win a hole back so Meadow, whose father was caddying for her, was three up at the turn. She quickly went four up again with her fourth birdie of the round at the 11th.

Not to be outdone Lobato birdied the 12th but immediately Meadow came close to a hole-in-one at the short 13th. to go four up with five to go. Two halves saw Meadow home by 4 and 3 as her wonderful summer continued.

Stroke Play Qualifying (64 go to First Round):

Sally Watson (Elie & Earlsferry Ladies)	72-69—141
Celine Boutier (FRA)	70-71—141
Amy Boulden (Conwy)	73-73—146
Daniela Holmqvist (SWE)	72-74—146
Giulia Molinaro (ITA)	70-76—146
Bronte Law (Bramhall)	73-74—147
Holly Clyburn (Woodhall Spa)	75-73—148
Perrine Delacour (FRA)	72-77—149
Vicki Troeltsch (GER)	79-71—150
Brittany Marchand (CAN)	78-72—150
Isabel Gabsa (GER)	77-73—150
Johanna Tillstrom (SWE)	76-74—150
Gabriella Cowley (West Essex)	78-73—151
Emily Taylor (Hillside)	76-75—151
Charley Hull (Woburn)	76-75—151
Alexandra Peters (Notts)	72-79—151
Meghan Maclaren (Wellingborough)	79-73—152
Josephine Janson (SWE)	78-74—152
Rachael Watton (Mortonhall)	77-75—152
Kyle Roig (PUR)	76-76—152
Brooke Henderson (CAN)	76-76—152
Ariane Provot (FRA)	75-77—152
Sophia Popov (GER)	74-78—152
Jessica Meek (Carnoustie Ladies)	82-71—153
Lauren Taylor (Woburn)	81-72—153
Marita Engzelius (NOR)	79-74—153
Anne Van Dam (NED)	77-76—153
Manon Gidali (FRA)	76-77—153
Hayley Davis (Ferndown)	75-78—153
Marina Stuetz (AUT)	75-78—153
Meghan Stasi (USA)	74-79—153
Ann-Kathrin Lindner (GER)	79-75—154
Augusta James (CAN)	79-75—154
Georgia Hall (Remedy Oak)	78-76—154
Sara Monberg (DEN)	78-76—154
Anna Young (CAN)	77-77—154
Marta Sanz Barrios (ESP)	75-79—154
Laure Castelain (FRA)	75-79—154
Christine Wong (CAN)	75-79—154
Patricia Sanz Barrios (ESP)	73-81—154
Olivia Winning (Rotherham)	81-74—155
Amanda Strang (SWE)	80-75—155
Nina Holleder (GER)	80-75—155
Justine Dreher (FRA)	80-75—155
Noemí Jiménez (ESP)	78-77—155
Nathalie Mansson (SWE)	78-77—155
Rachael Goodall (Heswall)	77-78—155
Laetitia Beck (ISR)	76-79—155
Jisoo Keel (CAN)	76-79—155
Isabelle Boineau (FRA)	75-80—155
Stephanie Meadow (Royal Portrush)	81-75—156
Claudia Chemin (FRA)	80-76—156

Camilla Hedberg (ESP)	79-77—156
Noora Tamminen (FIN)	78-78—156
Emilie Alonso (FRA)	78-78—156
Kelly Tidy (Royal Birkdale)	77-79—156
Kerry Smith (Waterlooville)	74-82—156
Nina Muehl (AUT)	86-71—157
Alyson McKechin (Elderslie)	82-75—157
Rocio Sanchez Lobato (ESP)	81-76—157
Fanny Vuignier (SUI)	81-76—157
Myrte Eikenaar (NED)	79-78—157
Leona Maguire (Slieve Russell)	73-84—157
Emilee Taylor (Holme Hall)	83-75—158
Krista Bakker (FIN)	81-77—158
Jo Ee Kok (SIN)	81-77—158
Karolin Lampert (GER)	80-78—158
Louise Gateau Chovelon (FRA)	80-78—158
Laura Murray (Alford)	79-79—158
Emelie Lundstrom (SWE)	77-81—158
Susan Jackson (Ladybank)	84-75—159
Emily Perry (NZL)	84-75—159
Alexandra Bonetti (FRA)	84-75—159
Whitney Hillier (AUS)	80-79—159
Anna Christina Kindgren (COL)	79-80—159
Teresa Caballer (ESP)	77-82—159
Leigh Whittaker (GER)	82-78—160
Sanna Nuutinen (FIN)	82-78—160
Megan Briggs (Kilmacolm)	81-79—160
Ileen Domela Nieuwenhuis (NED)	81-79—160
Sophia Pauline Zeeb (GER)	81-79—160
Demis Runas (USA)	80-80—160
Amber Ratcliffe (Royal Cromer)	79-81—160
Nicoline Engstr Skaug (NOR)	79-81—160
Natalie Lowe (Styal)	83-78—161
Lisa Maguire (Slieve Russell)	83-78—161
Rosie Davies (USA)	83-78—161
Abbey Gittings (Walmley)	82-79—161
Kelsey Macdonald (Nairn Dunbar)	82-79—161
Silvia Banon Ibanez (ESP)	80-81—161
Emma Goddard (Royal Liverpool)	80-81—161
Antonia Scherer (GER)	79-82—161
Jane Turner (Craigielaw)	79-82—161
Jacqueline Sneddon (Alyth)	79-82—161
Emily Childs (USA)	78-83—161
Karlijn Zaanen (NED)	78-83—161
Natalie Wille (SWE)	78-83—161
Annika Nykänen (FIN)	76-85—161
Claire Smith (Silsden)	82-80—162
Chloe Ryan (Castletroy)	81-81—162
Ellie Robinson (Brass Castle)	81-81—162
Charlotte Thompson (Channels)	78-84—162
Nicola Rossler (GER)	78-84—162
Gemma Clews (Ashton on Mersey)	87-76—163
Madelene Sagstrom (SWE)	85-78—163
Olivia Hullert (NOR)	82-81—163
Ann Ramsay (Kirriemuir)	82-81—163
Jerry Lawrence (Rochester)	81-82—163
Adriana Brent (AUS)	86-78—164
Joi Pentin (USA)	85-79—164
Ashley Cramond (AUS)	84-80—164
Bethany Garton (R. Lytham & St Annes)	82-82—164
Charlotte Wild (The Mere)	79-85—164
Charlotte Puts (NED)	76-88—164
Emma Sheffield (Newark)	84-81—165
Jessica Bradley (Tiverton)	84-81—165
Elin Arvidsson (SWE)	83-82—165
Gemma Bradbury (Cottrell Park)	81-84—165
Tessa De Bruijn (NED)	87-79—166
Andrea Vilarasau (ESP)	85-81—166
Isabella Deilert (SWE)	85-81—166
Ailsa Summers (Carnoustie Ladies)	84-82—166
Molle Manon (FRA)	84-82—166
Morgan Thompson (USA)	87-80—167
Jacquiline Chang (USA)	86-81—167
Nikki Foster (Pleasington)	85-82—167
Alessandra Braida (ITA)	84-83—167
Paula Grant (Lisburn)	83-85—168
Stefania Avanzo (ITA)	83-85—168
Rachel Drummond (Beaconsfield)	88-81—169
Hadas Libman (ISR)	88-82—170
Minna Vuorenpaa (FIN)	85-85—170
Gemma Dryburgh (Beaconsfield)	85-85—170
Eugenia Ferrero (ITA)	89-82—171
Lara Katzy (GER)	83-88—171
Jacqueline Williams (USA)	82-89—171
Jess Wilcox (Blankney)	83-89—172
Anna Christenson (USA)	88-85—173
Camilla Vik (NOR)	83-90—173
Gill Nutter (Formby)	89-86—175
Nicola Rawlinson (Royal Birkdale)	93-84—177
Taylor Kim (CAN)	89-90—179
Kathleen Griffith (AUS)	98-90—188
Roberta Roeller (GER)	97-94—191

First Round:

Sally Watson (Elie & Earlsferry) beat Emilee Taylor (Holme Hall) 2 holes
Augusta James (CAN)) beat Ann-Kathrin Lindner (GER) 3 and 1
Laetitia Beck (ISR) beat Meghan Maclaren (Wellingborough) 3 and 1
Jisoo Keel (CAN) beat Alexandra Peters (Notts) 2 and 1
Kelly Tidy (Royal Birkdale) beat Vicki Troeltsch (GER) 3 and 2
Olivia Winning (Rotherham) beat Jessica Meek (Carnoustie Ladies) 5 and 4
Patricia Sanz Barrios (ESP) beat Lauren Taylor (Woburn) 2 and 1
Perrine Delacour (FRA) beat Kerry Smith (Waterlooville) 6 and 5
Rocio Sanchez Lobato (ESP) beat Giulia Molinaro (ITA) 1 hole
Marta Sanz Barrios (ESP) beat Manon Gidali (FRA) 1 hole
Justine Dreher (FRA) beat Brooke Henderson (CAN) 3 and 2
Camilla Hedberg (ESP) beat Johanna Tillstrom (SWE) 7 and 5
Gabriella Cowley (West Essex) beat Claudia Chemin (FRA) 3 and 1
Noemí Jiménez (ESP) beat Kyle Roig (PUR) 3 and 2
Anna Young (CAN) beat Hayley Davis (Ferndown) at 19th

Ladies British Amateur Championship *continued*

First Round *continued:*
Daniela Holmqvist (SWE) beat Fanny Vuignier (SUI) at 19th
Amy Boulden (Conwy) beat Myrte Eikenaar (NED) at 23rd
Marina Stuetz (AUT) beat Sara Monberg (DEN) 3 and 2
Nathalie Mansson (SWE) beat Rachael Watton (Mortonhall) 1 hole
Stephanie Meadow (Royal Portrush) beat Emily Taylor (Hillside) at 22nd
Isabel Gabsa (GER) beat Noora Tamminen (FIN) 2 and 1
Ariane Provot (FRA) beat Nina Holleder (GER) 2 and 1
Laure Castelain (FRA) beat Anne Van Dam (NED) 4 and 3
Alyson Mckechin (Elderslie) beat Bronte Law (Bramhall) 5 and 3
Nina Muehl (AUT) beat Holly Clyburn (Woodhall Spa) 4 and 3
Christine Wong (CAN) beat Marita Engzelius (NOR) 2 and 1
Amanda Strang (SWE) beat Sophia Popov (GER) 2 holes
Brittany Marchand (CAN) beat Emilie Alonso (FRA) 2 and 1
Isabelle Boineau (FRA) beat Charley Hull (Woburn) 1 hole
Josephine Janson (SWE) beat Rachael Goodall (Heswall) 1 hole
Georgia Hall (Remedy Oak) beat Meghan Stasi (USA) 4 and 3
Celine Boutier (FRA) beat Leona Maguire (Slieve Russell) 5 and 3

Second Round:
James beat Watson 2 up
Beck beat Keel 4 and 3
Tidy beat Winning 7 and 5
Delacour beat P Sanz Barrios 7 and 6
Sanchez Lobato beat M Sanz Barrios 1 up
Hedberg beat Dreher 4 and 3
Jiménez beat Cowley 3 and 2
Holmqvist beat Young 3 and 2
Boulden beat Stuetz 4 and 3
Meadow beatb Mansson 4 and 2
Provot beat Gabsa 2 and 1
Castelain beat McKechin 2 up
Muehl beat Wong 2 and 1
Strang beat Marchand 2 up
Boineau beat Janson 2 and 1
Hall beat Boutier at 19th

Third Round:
Beck beat James 5 and 4
Delacour beat Tidy 4 and 2
Sanchez Lobato beat Hedberg 1 up
Jiménez beat Holmqvist 1 up
Meadow beat Boulden 2 and 1
Provot beat Castelain 2 and 1
Strang beat Muehl 3 and 1
Hall beat Boineau at 19th

Quarter Finals:
Delacour beat Beck 4 and 2
Sanchez Lobato beat Jiménez 1 up
Meadow beat Provot 2 and 1
Hall beat Strang 6 and 4

Semi-Finals:
Sanchez Lobato beat Delacour 2 up
Meadow beat Hall 3 and 2

Final: Stephanie Meadow (Royal Portrush) beat Rocio Sanchez Lobato (ESP) 4 and 3

1893	M Scott beat I Pearson 7 and 5
1894	M Scott beat I Pearson 2 and 2
1895	M Scott beat E Lythgoe 5 and 4
1896	Miss Pascoe beat L Thomson 2 and 2
1897	EC Orr beat Miss Orr 4 and 2
1898	L Thomson beat EC Neville 7 and 5
1899	M Hezlet beat Magill 2 and 1
1900	Adair beat Neville 6 and 5
1901	Graham beat Adair 2 and 1
1902	M Hezlet beat E Neville at 19th
1903	Adair beat F Walker-Leigh 4 and 3
1904	L Dod beat M Hezlet 1 hole
1905	B Thompson beat ME Stuart 2 and 2
1906	Kennon beat B Thompson 4 and 3
1907	M Hezlet beat F Hezlet 2 and 1
1908	M Titterton beat D Campbell at 19th
1909	D Campbell beat F Hezlet 4 and 3
1910	Miss Grant Suttie beat L Moore 6 and 4
1911	D Campbell beat V Hezlet 2 and 2
1912	G Ravenscroft beat S Temple 2 and 2
1913	M Dodd beat Miss Chubb 8 and 6
1914	C Leitch beat G Ravenscroft 2 and 1
1915–18	*Not played*
1919	*Abandoned because of railway strike*
1920	C Leitch beat M Griffiths 7 and 6
1921	C Leitch beat J Wethered 4 and 3
1922	J Wethered beat C Leitch 9 and 7
1923	D Chambers beat A Macbeth 2 holes
1924	J Wethered beat Mrs Cautley 7 and 6
1925	J Wethered beat C Leitch at 37th
1926	C Leitch beat Mrs Garon 8 and 7
1927	T de la Chaume (FRA) beat Miss Pearson 5 and 4
1928	N Le Blan (FRA) beat S Marshall 2 and 2
1929	J Wethered beat G Collett (USA) 2 and 1
1930	D Fishwick beat G Collett (USA) 4 and 3
1931	E Wilson beat W Morgan 7 and 6
1932	E Wilson beat CPR Montgomery 7 and 6
1933	E Wilson beat D Plumpton 5 and 4
1934	AM Holm beat P Barton 6 and 5
1935	W Morgan beat P Barton 2 and 2
1936	P Barton beat B Newell 5 and 3
1937	J Anderson beat D Park 6 and 4
1938	AM Holm beat E Corlett 4 and 3
1939	P Barton beat T Marks 2 and 1

1940–45 *Not played*
1946 GW Hetherington beat P Garvey 1 hole
1947 B Zaharias (USA) beat J Gordon 5 and 4
1948 L Suggs (USA) beat J Donald 1 hole
1949 F Stephens beat V Reddan 5 and 4
1950 Vicomtesse de St Sauveur (FRA) beat J Valentine 3 and 2
1951 PJ MacCann beat F Stephens 4 and 3
1952 M Paterson beat F Stephens at 39th
1953 M Stewart (CAN) beat P Garvey 7 and 6
1954 F Stephens beat E Price 4 and 3
1955 J Valentine beat B Romack (USA) 7 and 6
1956 M Smith (USA) beat M Janssen (USA) 8 and 7
1957 P Garvey beat J Valentine 4 and 3
1958 J Valentine beat E Price 1 hole
1959 E Price beat B McCorkindale at 37th
1960 B McIntyre (USA) beat P Garvey 4 and 2
1961 M Spearman beat DJ Robb 7 and 6
1962 M Spearman beat A Bonallack 1 hole
1963 B Varangot (FRA) beat P Garvey 2 and 1
1964 C Sorenson (USA) beat BAB Jackson at 37th
1965 B Varangot (FRA) beat IC Robertson 4 and 3
1966 E Chadwick beat V Saunders 2 and 2
1967 E Chadwick beat M Everard 1 hole
1968 B Varangot (FRA) beat C Rubin (FRA) at 20th
1969 C Lacoste (FRA) beat A Irvin 1 hole
1970 D Oxley beat IC Robertson 1 hole
1971 M Walker beat B Huke 2 and 1
1972 M Walker beat C Rubin (FRA) 2 holes
1973 A Irvin beat M Walker 2 and 2
1974 C Semple (USA) beat A Bonallack 2 and 1
1975 N Syms (USA) beat S Cadden 2 and 2
1976 C Panton beat A Sheard 1 hole
1977 A Uzielli beat V Marvin 6 and 5
1978 E Kennedy (AUS) beat J Greenhalgh 1 hole
1979 M Madill beat J Lock (AUS) 2 and 1
1980 A Quast (USA) beat L Wollin (SWE) 2 and 1
1981 IC Robertson beat W Aitken at 20th
1982 K Douglas beat G Stewart 4 and 2
1983 J Thornhill beat R Lautens (SUI) 4 and 2
1984 J Rosenthal (USA) beat J Brown 4 and 3
1985 L Beman (IRL) beat C Waite 1 hole
1986 M McGuire (NZL) beat L Briars (AUS) 2 and 1
1987 J Collingham beat S Shapcott at 19th
1988 J Furby beat J Wade 4 and 3
1989 H Dobson beat E Farquharson 6 and 5
1990 J Hall beat H Wadsworth 2 and 2
1991 V Michaud (FRA) beat W Doolan (AUS) 2 and 2
1992 P Pedersen (DEN) beat J Morley 1 hole
1993 C Lambert beat K Speak 2 and 2
1994 E Duggleby beat C Mourgue d'Algue 2 and 1
1995 J Hall beat K Mourgue d'Algue 2 and 2
1996 K Kuehne (USA) beat B Morgan 5 and 3
1997 A Rose beat M McKay 4 and 3
1998 K Rostron beat G Nocera (FRA) 2 and 2
1999 M Monnet (FRA) beat R Hudson 1 hole
2000 R Hudson beat E Duggleby 5 and 4
2001 M Prieto (ESP) beat E Duggleby 4 and 3
2002 R Hudson beat L Wright 5 and 4
2003 E Serramia (ESP) beat P Odefey (GER) 2 holes
2004 L Stahle (SWE) beat A Highgate 4 and 2
2005 L Stahle (SWE) beat C Coughlan 2 and 2
2006 B Mozo (ESP) beat A Nordqvist (SWE) 2 and 1
2007 C Ciganda (ESP) beat A Nordqvist (SWE) 4 and 3
2008 A Nordqvist (SWE) beat C Hedwall (SWE) 3 and 2
2009 A Muñoz (ESP) beat C Ciganda (ESP) 2 and 1
2010 K Tidy beat K MacDonald 2 and 1
2011 L Taylor beat A Bonetti (ITA) 6 and 5

European Ladies Amateur Championship (inaugurated 1986)

Diners, Ljubljana, Slovenia [5432–71]

French golfer Celine Boutier at her best to win the European title

French golfer Celine Boutier swept impressively to victory in the European Ladies International Amateur Championship played over the par 71 Diners Golf and Country Club at Ljubljana in Slovenia.

From Montrouge in France, Celine returned four rounds in the 60's for a 16-under-par total of 268 to win comfortably by six shots. Ahead at the halfway stage on 134 after rounds of 68 and 66, she moved five clear with another 66 and completed an excellent week on the excellently prepared par 71 course with a 68.

During the week the winner, who plans to continue her studies at Duke University in America, made 19 birdies and dropped only three shots – ironically one of them at the last hole of the tournament when victory was assured.

"It was amazing," she said afterwards, "I am delighted I could win in the presence of so many great golfers. I had a great final day, Thank you all. I had a great time in Slovenia."

Another French player, Shannon Aubert, and Austria's Marina Stutz finished tied second on 274. Of the top three players, only Aubert failed to beat par in all four rounds. She had a par-matching 71 on day two.

There must have been considerable sympathy from the Austrian supporters for Stutz who, like the winner, scored four rounds in the 60's which would normally have been good enough to win, but not in a week when Boutier was playing so well.

Stutz made 17 birdies and dropped seven shots over the week – four of them at the last three holes. Aubert, whose birdie tally was 15, had only five bogeys. So collectively the three players made 51 birdies and dropped only 15 shots.

Earlier in the year Celine, who was a member of the winning 2010 and 2011 French European Team Championship side, had lost on the last green in the third round of the US Women's Amateur Championship to eventual winner Lydia Ko from New Zealand.

European Ladies Amateur Championship *continued*

1	Celine Boutier (FRA)	68-66-66-68—268
2	Shannon Aubert (FRA)	67-71-68-68—274
	Marina Stütz (AUT)	68-69-68-69—274
4	Karolin Lampert (GER)	72-67-67-69—275
5	Ann-Kathrin Lindner (GER)	68-68-71-70—277
6	Nina Holleder (GER)	71-69-69-69—278
7	Marta Silva (ESP)	68-71-73-67—279
8	Giulia Molinaro (ITA)	71-70-70-69—280
	Sophia Popov (GER)	69-70-70-71—280
10	Quirine Eijkenboom (GER)	71-69-71-70—281
	Perrine Delacour (FRA)	68-71-70-72—281
12	Rocio Sanchez Lobato (ESP)	73-70-70-70—283
13	Marta Sanz (ESP)	73-68-70-73—284
	Caroline Nistrup (DEN)	71-71-73-69—284
	Isabelle Boineu (FRA)	71-68-73-72—284
	Daniela Holmqvist (SWE)	70-71-71-72—284
	Marion Duvernay (FRA)	70-67-73-74—284
	Silvia Banon (ESP)	69-72-71-72—284
	Katerina Ruzickova (CZE)	66-74-70-74—284
20	Samantha Krug (GER)	73-68-70-74—285
	Johanna Tillström (SWE)	73-67-73-72—285
	Camilla Hedberg (ESP)	72-68-73-72—285
	Nicole Broch Larsen (DEN)	69-74-72-70—285
	Katja Pogačar (SLO)	68-70-73-74—285
25	Sanna Nuutinen (FIN)	76-68-73-69—286
	Manon Gidali (FRA)	73-72-71-70—286
	Karolina Vickova (CZE)	72-68-74-72—286
	Noora Tamminen (FIN)	71-72-73-70—286
	Patricia Sanz (ESP)	70-72-71-73—286
30	Chloe Leurquin (BEL)	76-68-72-71—287
	Noemi Jiménez (ESP)	74-72-70-71—287
	Fanny Cnops (BEL)	74-69-68-76—287
	Laura Gonzales Escallon (BEL)	72-72-73-70—287
	Nanna Koerstz Madsen (DEN)	69-76-70-72—287
	Nastja Banovec (SLO)	68-73-72-74—287
36	Nuria Iturrios (ESP)	76-70-70-72—288
	Vicki Troeltsch (GER)	74-69-72-73—288
	Leslie Cloots (BEL)	73-74-71-70—288
	Ileen D.Nieuwenhuis (NED)	71-71-74-72—288
	Margaux Vanmol (BEL)	69-70-70-79—288
	Manon de Roey (BEL)	68-69-74-77—288
42	Olivia Cowan (GER)	72-69-78-70—289
	Laure Castelain (FRA)	70-76-71-72—289
44	Milena Savik (SRB)	73-71-72-74—290
	Emily Penttilä (FIN)	70-73-73-74—290
	Bianca Maria Fabrizio (ITA)	70-72-77-71—290
	Clotilde Chazot (FRA)	70-70-74-76—290
48	Anna-Lena Krämer (GER)	73-72-70-76—291
	Leigh Whittaker (GER)	73-71-73-74—291
	Roberta Liti (ITA)	71-73-73-74—291
	Sally Watson (SCO)	68-73-75-75—291
	Isabell Gabsa (GER)	68-72-74-77—291
53	Agathe Sauzon (FRA)	70-76-72-74—292
	Hayley Davis (ENG)	70-74-74-74—292
	Krista Bakker (FIN)	69-67-80-76—292
56	Rachel Rossel (SUI)	76-72-71-74—293
	Anna Appert Lund (SWE)	75-71-73-74—293
	Lisa Warrilow (ENG)	71-70-76-76—293
59	Becky Harries (WAL)	73-72-72-77—294
	Camille Chevalier (FRA)	69-73-77-75—294

61	Nicola Wolf (AUT)	73-73-72-78—296
	Andrea Vilarasau Amoros (ESP)	66-73-78-79—296
63	Isabel Gadea (GER)	70-76-73-78—297
64	Johanna Björk (SWE)	66-79-71-83—299
65	Isabella Deilert (SWE)	76-72-71-81—300

The remaining 78 players missed the cut on 219

1986	Martina Koch (GER)	Morfontaine GC, France
1988	Florence Descampe (BEL)*	Pedrena GC, Spain

**after a play-off with Delphine Bourson (FRA)*

1990	Matina Koch (GER)	Zumikon GC, Switzerland
1991	Delphine Bourson (FRA)	Schonborn GC, Austria
1992	Joanne Morton (ENG)	Estoril GC, Portugal
1993	Vibeke Stensrud (NOR)	Torino GC, Italy
1994	Martina Fischer (GER)	Bastadt GC, Sweden
1995	Maria Hjorth (SWE)	Berlin GC, Germany
1996	Silvia Cavalerri (ITA)	Furesoe GC, Denmark
1997	Silvia Cavalerri (ITA)	Formby GC, England
1998	Guilia Sergas (ITA)	Noordwijke GC, Netherlands
1999	Sofia Sandolo (ITA)	Karlovy Vary GC, Czech Rep.
2000	Emma Duggelby (ENG)	Amber Baltic GC, Poland
2001	Martina Eberl (GER)	Biella GC, Italy
2002	Becky Brewerton (WAL)	Kristianstad GC, Sweden
2003	Virginie Beauchet (FRA)	Shannon GC, Ireland
2004	Carlota Ciganda (ESP)	Ulzama GC, Spain
2005	Jade Schaeffer (FRA)	Santo da Serra GC, Madeira
2006	Belen Mozo (ESP)	Falkenstein GC, Germany
2007	Caroline Hedwall (SWE)*	Golf National, France

**after play-off with Carlota Ciganda (ESP)*

2008	Carlota Ciganda (ESP)*	GC Schloss Schonborn, Austria

**after play-off with Maria Hernandez (ESP)*

2009	Caroline Hedwall (SWE)	Falsterbo GC, Sweden
2010	Sophia Popov (GER)	Kunetickà Hora, Czech Rep.
2011	Lisa Maquire (IRL)	Noordwijksee, Netherlands

112th United States Women's Amateur Championship (inaugurated 1895)

Country Club, Cleveland Ohio (Players are of US nationality unless stated) [6512–72]

World No 1 Ko lands US Women's title

Perhaps it was not all that surprising that Lydia Ko, the hugely talented Korean-born 15-year-old who now lives in New Zealand, won the US Amateur Championship at The Country Club at Cleveland.

She had arrived at the Championship having already taken the medal for low amateur at the US Women's Open and having reached the semi-final of the US Girls' Junior Championship.

"I've won three medals at the three USGA events I have played in this summer so that's pretty good," said World No 1 Ko modestly after beating another teenager 18-year-old Jaye Marie Green 3 an 1 in the 36-hole final.

Ko is not the youngest winner of the title. At 15 years three months and 18 days she is four months older than Kimberly Kim who took the title in 2006. The young New Zealander, who is given time off school to play golf around the world but catches up on the lessons she has missed while on the road, ensured she kept the World No 1 spot for the second year running with her victory.

Ko, whose mother Tina caddies for her, was one up after the first 18 holes but in the afternoon opened up a four-hole lead on her American rival from Boca Raton in Florida.

Green won back the 29th hole when Ko three-putted but with five holes to play the New Zealander was comfortably three up. Her American opponent lipped out for birdies at the 31st and 32nd before winning the 34th but when Green could not get down in two from off the green at the 35th it was all over.

In defeat Green praised Ko: "She has a great attitude. She laughs at everything and is great fun to play with. I didn't want the day to end."

The first New Zealand winner of the title does not plan a quick move into the paid ranks. "I want to go to college. Turning professional is not a priority." She told reporters.

Stroke Play Qualifying:

Hyo-Joo Kim (KOR)	68-68—136
Lydia Ko (NZL)	66-71—137
Ariya Jutanugarn (THA)	71-68—139
Alison Lee (Valencia, CA)	68-71—139
Sierra Brooks (Sorrento, FL)	72-68—140
Emily Tubert (Burbank, CA)	72-69—141
Brogan McKinnon (CAN)	73-68—141
Natalie Gleadall (CAN)	70-71—141
Alina Ching (Honolulu, HI)	70-71—141
Paula Reto (RSA)	73-68—141
Minjee Lee (AUS)	72-69—141
Kelly Shon (Port Washington, NY)	70-72—142
Lisa McCloskey (Houston, TX)	72-70—142
Celine Boutier (FRA)	72-71—143
Cyna Rodriguez (PHI)	74-69—143
Breanna Elliott (AUS)	71-72—143
Nicole Zhang (CAN)	73-71—144
Brooke Mackenzie Henderson (CAN)	69-75—144
Ashlee Dewhurst (AUS)	71-73—144
Lauren Diaz-Yi (Thousand Oaks, CA)	72-72—144
Casey Grice (College Station, TX)	75-69—144
Elisabeth Bernabe (Anaheim Hills, CA)	72-72—144
Chirapat Jao-Javanil (THA)	72-72—144
Su-Hyun Oh (AUS)	73-71—144
Jayvie Marie Agojo (PHI)	76-69—145
Yueer Feng (CHN)	73-72—145

US Women's Amateur Championship *continued*

Dottie Ardina (PHI)	72-73—145
Ashlan Ramsey (Milledgeville, GA)	71-74—145
Jenna Hague (CAN)	71-74—145
Bethany Wu (Diamond Bar, CA)	72-73—145
Moriya Jutanugarn (THA)	74-71—145
Isabelle Lendl (Goshen, CT)	73-73—146
Whitney Hillier (AUS)	73-73—146
Amy Anderson (Oxbow, ND)	74-72—146
Samantha Swinehart (Lancaster, OH)	72-74—146
Jaye Marie Green (Boca Raton, FL)	73-73—146
Harin Lee (Bayside, NY)	73-74—147
Austin Ernst (Seneca, SC)	70-77—147
Jessica Vasilic (Anaheim Hills, CA)	73-74—147
Emily Childs (Alameda, CA)	72-75—147
Holly Clyburn (ENG)	75-72—147
Bronte Law (ENG)	75-72—147
Demi Frances Runas (Torrance, CA)	75-72—147
Lee Lopez (Whittier, CA)	73-75—148
Jennifer Kirby (CAN)	73-75—148
Alexandra Papell (Boca Raton, FL)	78-70—148
Karen Chung (Livingston, NJ)	75-73—148
Jaclyn Jansen (Effingham, IL)	75-73—148
Ani Gulugian (Irvine, CA)	78-70—148
Mathilda Poulsen (AUS)	73-75—148
McKenzie Niesen (New Prague, MN)	70-79—149
Maia Schechter (Takoma Park, MD)	73-76—149
Grace Na (Alameda, CA)	75-74—149
Sarah Beth Davis (Victoria, TX)	71-78—149
Madeleine Sheils (Boise, IS)	75-74—149
Andrea Lee (Hermosa Beach, CA)	74-75—149
Haley Millsap (Pace, FL)	75-74—149
Marijosse Navarro (MEX)	74-75—149
Diana Fernandez (PAR)	72-77—149
Jennifer Yang (KOR)	74-75—149
Amy Beth Simanton (Lake Oswego, OR)	79-70—149
Casey Danielson (Osceola, WI)	74-75—149
Megan Khang (Rockland, MA)	76-73—149
Erynne Lee (Silverdale, WA)	72-77—149

First Round:
Hyo-Joo Kim (KOR) beat Megan Khang 7 and 6
Isabelle Lendl beat Whitney Hillier (AUS) 2 and 1
Cyna Rodriguez (PHI) beat Ani Gulugian 1 up
Nicole Zhang (CAN) beat Jaclyn Jansen 6 and 5
Natalie Gleadall (CAN) beat Grace Na 2 and 1
Jayvie Marie Agojo (PHI) beat Emily Childs 1 up
Maia Schechter beat Alina Ching 4 and 3
Su-Hyun Oh (AUS) beat Holly Clyburn (ENG) 4 and 2
Andrea Lee beat Alison Lee 1 up
Jaye Marie Green beat Jenna Hague (CAN) 6 and 4
Lisa McCloskey beat Haley Millsap 2 and 1
Lauren Diaz-Yi beat Jennifer Kirby (CAN) at 22nd
Madeleine Sheils beat Sierra Brooks 3 and 1
Ashlan Ramsey beat Harin Lee 6 and 5
Marijosse Navarro (MEX) beat Kelly Shon 3 and 2
Lee Lopez beat Casey Grice 1 up
Lydia Ko (NZL) beat Amy Beth Simanton 4 and 3
Amy Anderson beat Moriya Jutanugarn (THA) 1 up
Celine Boutier, (FRA) beat Mathilda Poulsen (AUS) 4 and 3
Karen Chung beat Brooke Mackenzie Henderson (CAN) 4 and 3
Diana Fernandez (PHI) beat Brogan McKinnon (CAN) at 19th
Jessica Vasilic beat Yueer Feng (CHN) 4 and 3
Paula Reto (RSA) beat McKenzie Neisen 6 and 5
Bronte Law (ENG) beat Chirapat Jao-Javanil (THA) 3 and 2
Ariya Jutanugarn (THA) beat Jennifer Yang (KOR) 3 and 1
Bethany Wu beat Samantha Swinehart 2 and 1
Breanna Elliott (AUS) beat Casey Danielson 3 and 2
Ashlee Dewhurst (AUS) beat Alexandra Papell 6 and 5
Sarah Beth Davis beat Emily Tubert 3 and 2
Austin Ernst beat Dottie Ardina (PHI) 4 and 3
Erynne Lee beat Minjee Lee (AUS) 5 and 4
Elisabeth Bernabe beat Demi Frances Runas 1 up

Second Round:
Hyo-Joo Kim beat Isabelle Lendl 2 and 1
Nicole Zhang beat Cyna Rodriguez 4 and 3
Jayvie Marie Agojo beat Natalie Gleadall 1 up
Su-Hyun Oh beat Maia Schechter 5 and 4
Jaye Marie Green beat Andrea Lee 2 and 1
Lisa McCloskey beat Lauren Diaz-Yi 4 and 3
Madeleine Sheils beat Ashlan Ramsey 1 up
Marijosse Navarro beat Lee Lopez 1 up
Lydia Ko beat Amy Anderson 3 and 2
Celine Boutier beat Karen Chung 1 up
Jessica Vasilic beat Diana Fernandez 6 and 4, 12
Paula Reto beat Bronte Law 2 and 1
Ariya Jutanugarn beat Bethany Wu 6 and 4
Ashlee Dewhurst, beat Breanna Elliott at 20th
Austin Ernst beat Sarah Beth Davis 3 and 2
Erynne Lee beat Elisabeth Bernabe 3 and 2

Third Round:
Nicole Zhang beat Hyo-Joo Kim 1 up
Su-Hyun Oh beat Jayvie Marie Agojo 4 and 3
Jaye Marie Green beat Lisa McCloskey 2 up, 4
Marijosse Navarro beat Madeleine Sheils 3 and 2
Lydia Ko beat Celine Boutier 1 up
Paula Reto beat Jessica Vasilic 4 and 2
Ariya Jutanugarn beat Ashlee Dewhurst 3 and 2
Erynne Lee beat Austin Ernst 2 and 1

Quarter Finals:
Nicole Zhang beat Su-Hyun Oh 2 and 1
Jaye Marie Green beat Marijosse Navarro 2 and 1
Lydia Ko beat Paula Reto 3 and 1
Ariya Jutanugarn beat Erynne Lee 5 and 4

Semi-Finals:
Jaye Marie Green beat Nicole Zhang 2 up
Lydia Ko beat Ariya Jutanugarn 3 and 1

Final: Lydia Ko (NZL) beat Jaye Marie Green (Boca Raton, FL) 3 and 1

1895	LB Brown (132) beat N Sargent 134	Meadowbrook GC, NY	
Changed to match play			
1896	B Hoyt beat A Tunure 2 and 1	Morris County GC, NJ	*Entrants* 29
1897	B Hoyt beat N Sargent 5 and 4	Essex CC, MA	29
1898	B Hoyt beat M Wetmore 5 and 3	Ardsley Club, NY	61
1899	R Underhill beat M Fox 2 and 1	Philadelphia CC (Bala Course)	78
1900	FC Griscom beat M Curtis 6 and 5	Shinnecock Hills GC, NY	62
1901	G Hecker beat L Herron 5 and 3	Baltusrol GC, NJ	89
1902	G Hecker beat LA Wells 4 and 3	The Country Club, Brookline, MA	96
1903	B Anthony beat JA Carpenter 7 and 6	Chicago GC, IL	64
1904	GM Bishop beat EF Sanford 5 and 3	Merion Cricket Club, PA	86
1905	P Mackay beat M Curtis 1 hole	Morris City GC, NJ	69
1906	HS Curtis beat MB Adams 2 and 1	Brae Burn CC, MA	75
1907	M Curtis beat HS Curtis 7 and 6	Midlothian CC (Blue Island Course), IL	87
1908	KC Harley beat TH Polhemus 6 and 5	Chevy Chase GC, MD	41
1909	D Campbell beat N Barlow 3 and 2	Merion Cricket Club, PA	86
1910	D Campbell beat GM Martin 2 and 1	Homewood CC, IL	57
1911	M Curtis beat LB Hyde 5 and 4	Baltusrol GC, NJ	67
1912	M Curtis beat N Barlow 3 and 2	Essex CC, MA	62
1913	G Ravenscroft beat M Hollins 2 holes	Wilmington CC, DE	88
1914	KC Harley beat EV Rosenthal 1 hole	Nassau CC, NY	93
1915	F Vanderbeck beat M Gavin (ENG) 3 and 2	Onwentsia Club, IL	119
1916	A Stirling beat M Caverly 2 and 1	Belmont Springs CC, MA	63
1917–1918	*Not played*		
1919	A Stirling beat M Gavin (ENG) 6 and 5	Shawnee CC, De	114
1920	A Stirling beat D Campbell Hurd 5 and 4	Mayfield CC, OH	114
1921	M Hollins beat A Stirling 5 and 4	Hollywood GC, NJ	181
1922	G Collett beat M Gavin (ENG) 5 and 4	Glenbrier GC, WV	196
1923	E Cummings beat A Stirling 3 and 2	Westchester GC, NY	196
1924	D Campbell Hurd beat MK Browne 7 and 6	Rhode Island CC, RI	98
1925	G Collett beat A Stirling Fraser 9 and 8	St Louis CC, MO	85
1926	H Stetson beat E Goss 2 and 1	Merion Cricket Club (East), PA	134
1927	MB Horn beat M Orcutt 5 and 4	Cherry Valley Club, NY	150
1928	G Collett beat V Van Wie 13 and 12	Hot Springs CC (Cascades Course), VA	123
1929	G Collett beat L Pressler 4 and 3	Oakland Hills CC (South Course), MI	98
1930	G Collett beat V Van Wie 6 and 5	Los Angeles CC (North Course), CA	102
1931	H Hicks beat G Collett Vare 2 and 1	CC of Buffalo, NY	102
1932	V Van Wie beat G Collett Vare 10 and 8	Salem CC, MA	90
1933	V Van Wie beat H Hicks 4 and 3	Exmoor CC, IL	120
1934	V Van Wie beat D Traung 2 and 1	Whitemarsh Valley CCm PA	157
1935	G Collett Vare beat P Berg 3 and 2	Interlachen CC, MN	94
1936	P Barton (ENG) beat M Orcutt 4 and 3	Canoe Brook CC (South Course), NJ	188
1937	EL Page beat P Berg 7 and 6	Memphis CC, TN	136
1938	P Berg beat EL Page 6 and 5	Westmoreland CC, IL	118
1939	B Jameson beat D Kirby 3 and 2	Wee Burn CC, CT	201
1940	B Jameson beat J Cochran 6 and 5	Del Monte G&CC, CA	163
1941	E Hicks Newell beat H Sigel 5 and 3	The Country Club, Brookline, MA	124
1942–1945	*Not played*		
1946	B Zaharias beat C Sherman 11 and 9	Southern Hills CC, OK	69
1947	L Suggs beat D Kirby 2 holes	Franklin Hills CC, MI	83
1948	G Lenczyk beat H Sigel 4 and 3	Del Monte G&CC, CA	116
1949	D Porter beat D Kielty 3 and 2	Merion Cricket Club (East), PA	171
1950	B Hanson beat M Murray 6 and 4	Atlanta Athletic Club, GA	110
1951	D Kirby beat C Doran 2 and 1	Town and CC, MN	79
1952	J Pung beat S McFedters 2 and 1	Waverley CC, OR	159
1953	ML Faulk beat P Riley 3 and 2	Rhode Island CC, RI	158
1954	B Romack beat M Wright 4 and 2	Allegheny CC, PA	151
1955	P Lesser beat J Nelson 7 and 6	Myers Park CC, NC	112
1956	M Stewart beat J Gunderson 2 and 1	Meridian Hills CC, IN	116
1957	J Gunderson beat AC Johnstone 8 and 6	Del Paso CC, CA	100
1958	A Quast beat B Romack 3 and 2	Wee Burn CC, CT	195
1959	B McIntyre beat J Goodwin 4 and 3	Congressional CC, Washington, DC	128
1960	J Gunderson beat J Ashley 6 and 5	Tulsa CC, OK	109
1961	A Quast beat P Preuss 14 and 13	Tacoma G&CC, WA	107
1962	J Gunderson beat A Baker 9 and 8	CC of Rochester, NY	128
1963	A Quast beat P Conley 2 and 1	Taconic CC, MA	128
1964	B McIntyre beat J Gunderson 3 and 2	Prairie Dunes CC, KS	93
1965	J Ashley beat A Quast 5 and 4	Lakewood CC, CO	88
1966	J Gunderson Carner beat JD Stewart Streit at 41st	Sewickley Heights GC, PA	115
1967	ML Dill beat J Ashley 5 and 4	Annandale GC, CA	119

US Women's Amateur Championship *continued*

1968	J Gunderson Carner beat A Quast 5 and 4	Birmingham CC, MA	110
1969	C Lacoste (FRA) beat S Hamlin 3 and 2	Las Colinas CC, TX	103
1970	M Wilkinson beat C Hill 3 and 2	Wee Burn CC, CT	139
1971	L Baugh beat B Barry 1 hole	Atlanta CC, GA	102
1972	M Budke beat C Hill 5 and 4	St Louis CC, MO	134
1973	C Semple beat A Quast 1 hole	Montclair GC, NJ	142
1974	C Hill beat C Semple 5 and 4	Broadmoor GC, WA	121
1975	B Daniel beat D Horton 3 and 2	Brae Burn CC, MA	154
1976	D Horton beat M Bretton 2 and 1	Del Paso CC, CA	157
1977	B Daniel beat C Sherk 3 and 1	Cincinnati GC, OH	162
1978	C Sherk beat J Oliver 4 and 3	Sunnybrook GC, PA	207
1979	C Hill beat P Sheehan 7 and 6	Memphis CC, TN	273
1980	J Inkster beat P Rizzo 2 holes	Prairie Dunes CC, KS	281
1981	J Inkster beat L Goggin (AUS) 1 hole	Waverley CC, OR	240
1982	J Inkster beat C Hanlon 4 and 3	Broadmoor GC (South Course), CO	262
1983	J Pacillo beat S Quinlan 2 and 1	Canoe Brook CC (North Course), NJ	259
1984	D Richard beat K Williams at 37th	Broadmoor GC, WA	290
1985	M Hattori (JPN) beat C Stacy 5 and 4	Fox Chapel CC, PA	329
1986	K Cockerill beat K McCarthy 9 and 7	Pasatiempo GC, CA	387
1987	K Cockerill beat T Kerdyk 3 and 2	Rhode Island CC, RI	359
1988	P Sinn beat K Noble 6 and 5	Minikahda Club, MN	384
1989	V Goetze beat B Burton 4 and 3	Pinehurst CC (No.2), NC	376
1990	P Hurst beat S Davis at 37th	Canoe Brook CC (North Course), NJ	384
1991	A Fruhwirth beat H Voorhees 5 and 4	Prairie Dunes CC, KS	391
1992	V Goetze beat A Sörenstam (SWE) 1 hole	Kemper Lakes GC, IL	441
1993	J McGill beat S Ingram 1 hole	San Diego CC, CA	442
1994	W Ward beat J McGill 2 and 1	The Homestead (Cascades Course), VA	451
1995	K Kuehne beat A-M Knight 4 and 2	The Country Club, Brookline, MA	452
1996	K Kuehne beat M Baena 2 and 1	Firethorn GC, NE	495
1997	S Cavalleri (ITA) beat R Burke 5 and 4	Brae Burn CC, MA	557
1998	G Park (KOR) beat J Chuasiriporn 7 and 6	Barton Hills CC, MI	620
1999	D Delasin beat J Kang 4 and 3	Biltmore Forest CC, NC	676
2000	N Newton beat L Myerscough 8 and 7	Waverley CC, OR	682
2001	M Duncan beat N Perrot at 37th	Flint Hills National GC, KS	768
2002	B Lucidi beat B Jackson 3 and 2	Sleepy Hollow CC, NY	793
2003	V Nirapathpongporn beat J Park 2 and 1	Philadelphia CC, PA	814
2004	J Park beat A McCurdy 2 holes	The Kahkwa Club, PA	868
2005	M Pressel beat M Martinez 9 and 8	Ansley GC (Settingdown Creek Course)	873
2006	K Kim* beat K Schallenberg	Pumpkin Ridge GC (Witch Hollow Course)	969
*at 14, the youngest-ever winner			
2007	MJ Uribe beat A Blumenherst 1 hole	Crooked Stick GC, IN	935
2008	A Blumenhurst beat A Muñoz (ESP) 2 and 1	Eugene CC, OR	920
2009	J Song beat J Johnson 3 and 1	St Louis, MO	1,278
2010	Danielle Kang beat Jessica Korda 2 and 1	Charlotte CC, NC	1,296
2011	Danielle Kang beat Moriya Jutanugarn (THA)	Rhode Island CC	1,013

1896–1952	18-hole stroke play qualifying before match play
1953–1963	All match play
1964–1972	36-hole stroke play qualifying before match play
1973–1979	18-hole stroke play qualifying before match play
1980–	36-hole stroke play qualifying before match play

NCAA Championships (Women) *Vanderbilt Legends Club, Franklin, Tennessee*

The perfect end for Pancake as Alabama take the title

Brooke Pancake ended her college career by rolling in a four foot putt to give Alabama and their coach Mic Potter a first national golf title. At the end of a tense final day Alabama secured victory by just a single shot over Southern California at the Vanderbilt Legends Club in Franklin, Tennessee.

In truth it was much closer than Alabama expected it to be. After 36-holes they were 11 shots ahead and 14 in front of Southern California whose fight back in the third round reduced the gap between the two Universities to just two shots.

It was looking good for the Californians, however, when they built up a five shot lead with just nine to play but it all went wrong for them as they carded eight bogeys and a double-bogey in the last five holes of the tough back nine.

In a dramatic see-saw match, Alabama had turned that five shot deficit at the turn into a four shot lead when Hannah Collier birdied the 17th and 18th but then the Red Tide's Jennifer Kirby double-bogeyed the last and California's Inah Park birdied. So just one shot in it with Pancake needing a par at the last to win.

In such pressure-packed circumstances even a four-footer demands a player's full attention and the Alabama golfer was equal to the task.

In the end Alabama's 1171 total was one better than Southern California and two better than third-placed LSU. Virginia and South Carolina were fourth and fifth respectively on 1175 and 1176.

Chirapat Jao-Javanil from Oklahoma with a four round total of 282 won the individual competition by four shots from Pancake and five from Laura Gonzalez (Purdue) and Tessa Teachman (LSU). Pancake did have a chance to take the individual honours but in the end her disappointment at not winning the individual crown was quickly forgotten as she and her Alabama colleagues Kirby, Collier, Courtney McKim and Stephanie Meadow collected the Team Championship title for the first time.

Team event

1	Alabama	286-285-306-294—1,171
2	Southern Cal	297-288-294-293—1,172
3	LSU	293-294-297-289—1,173
4	Virginia	288-294-301-292—1,175

5 South Carolina 1,176; 6 Arizona State, Oklahoma 1,179; 8 UCLA 1,181; 9 Purdue 1,182; 10 North Carolina 1,184; 11 Vanderbilt 1,186; 12 Florida 1,190; 13 Texas, North Carolina State 1,191; 15 Duke 1,192; 16 Baylor, Texas A&M 1,193; 18 Colorado 1,196; 19 Tennessee 1,200; 20 Michigan State 1,201; 21 Pepperdine 1,204; 22 Ohio State 1,211; 23 Arkansas 1,214; 24 Stanford 1,216

Winning team: Alabama 1,171 – Brooke Pancake 68-70-75-73—286; Jennifer Kirby 74-71-74-74—293; Hannah Collier 75-71-80-70—296; Stephanie Meadow 69-73-78-77—297; Courtney McKim 82-77-79-78—316

Individual Championship

1	Chirapat Jao-Javanil (Oklahoma)	69-73-70-70—282
2	Brooke Pancake (Alabama)	68-70-75-73—286
3	Laura Gonzalez (Purdue)	67-76-74-70—287
	Tessa Teachman (LSU)	69-74-70-74—287
5	Katie Burnett (South Carolina)	74-67-74-73—288
6	Lindy Duncan (Duke)	70-75-75-70—290
	Brittany Marchand (NC State)	71-70-76-73—290
8	Gabriella Dominguez (Texas Tech)	75-74-73-69—291
	Kimberly Kaufman (Texas Tech)	70-73-76-72—291
	Giulia Molinaro (Arizona State)	69-71-72-79—291
	Katherine Perry (North Carolina)	75-70-73-73—291
	Portland Rosen (Virginia)	66-75-74-76—291
13	Katerina Ruzickova (Texas A&M)	73-72-74-73—292
14	Marina Alex (Vanderbilt)	77-68-76-72—293
	Doris Chen (Southern Cal)	75-69-72-77—293
	Brianna Do (UCLA)	72-71-77-73—293
	Jaclyn Jansen (Baylor)	71-78-74-70—293
	Jennifer Kirby (Alabama)	74-71-74-74—293
	Paula Reto (Purdue)	73-73-77-70—293
	Rachel Rohanna (Ohio State)	72-75-72-74—293
21	Laura Blanco (Arizona State)	73-73-76-72—294
	Alina Ching (Pepperdine)	74-73-73-74—294
	Lisa McCloskey (Southern Cal)	76-72-74-72—294
	Inah Park (Southern Cal)	74-73-73-74—294
21T	Taylor Schmidt (Oklahoma)	74-75-73-72—294
	Lindsey Solberg (Michigan State)	72-76-74-72—294
	Amanda Strang (South Carolina)	75-73-76-70—294
	Anne Tanguay (Oklahoma)	72-73-76-73—294
29	Brittany Altomare (Virginia)	71-73-80-71—295
	Austin Ernst (LSU)	78-75-74-68—295
	Erynne Lee (UCLA)	72-73-76-74—295
	Lauren Stratton (Vanderbilt)	75-70-81-69—295
33	Hannah Collier (Alabama)	75-71-80-70—296
	Camilla Hedberg (Florida)	76-69-74-77—296
	Kendall Martindale (Vanderbilt)	75-72-77-72—296
	Bertine Strauss (Texas)	74-76-74-72—296
	Emily Tubert (Arkansas)	73-74-77-72—296
38	Augusta James (NC State)	75-75-76-71—297
	Briana Mao (Virginia)	77-75-72-73—297
	Stephanie Meadow (Alabama)	69-73-78-77—297
	Sophia Popov (Southern Cal)	75-74-75-73—297
	Emily Talley (Colorado)	71-76-76-74—297
	Mariko Tumangan (Stanford)	71-75-79-72—297
	Nicole Vandermade (Texas)	76-72-78-71—297
45	Jennifer Coleman (Colorado)	76-73-74-75—298
	Noemi Jimenez (Arizona State)	74-74-80-70—298
	Caroline Powers (Michigan State)	75-74-73-76—298

NCAA Championships (Women) *continued*

45T Margarita Ramos (Arizona) 76-72-77-73—298
Alex Stewart (Colorado) 75-73-79-71—298
Chessey Thomas (Tennessee) 76-78-74-70—298
51 Alejandra Cangrejo (Duke) 72-74-77-76—299
Chelsey Cothran (Baylor) 79-75-73-72—299
Aurora Kan (Purdue) 77-74-69-79—299
Stacey Kim (Duke) 72-75-72-80—299
Isabelle Lendl (Florida) 82-78-73-66—299
Lee Lopez (UCLA) 73-73-77-76—299
Natalie Reeves (Texas A&M) 75-75-76-73—299
Madelene Sagstrom (LSU) 70-72-83-74—299
59 Lindsay Gahm (LSU) 76-73-77-74—300
Tiffany Lua (UCLA) 75-73-82-70—300
Catherine O'Donnell (North Carolina) 68-76-80-76—300
Meredith Swanson (South Carolina) 76-71-75-78—300
63 Patricia Garcia (Texas A&M) 76-74-75-76—301
Casey Grice (North Carolina) 77-72-77-75—301
Evan Jensen (Florida) 74-73-74-80—301
Justine Lee (Arizona State) 78-73-76-74—301
Mary Michael Maggio (Texas A&M) 77-77-75-72—301
Erica Popson (Tennessee) 77-76-76-72—301
Sally Watson (Stanford) 78-76-74-73—301
70 Nathalie Mansson (Tennessee) 74-76-78-74—302
71 Anna Leigh Keith (Vanderbilt) 80-74-77-72—303
Emma Lavy (Arkansas) 75-77-78-73—303
Rocio Sanchez Lobato (Georgia) 74-75-75-79—303
Katelyn Sepmoree (Texas) 71-76-80-76—303
Valerie Sternebeck (Baylor) 79-73-76-75—303
Allie White (North Carolina) 75-74-78-76—303
77 Hayley Davis (Baylor) 74-78-79-73—304
Justine Dreher (South Carolina) 77-77-75-75—304
Somin Lee (Pepperdine) 75-73-79-77—304
Rachel Morris (Southern Cal) 73-80-77-74—304
Grace Na (Pepperdine) 80-73-76-75—304
Kishi Sinha (Purdue) 76-72-76-80—304
Haley Stephens (Texas) 76-72-83-73—304
84 Liv Cheng (Pepperdine) 77-76-77-75—305
Courtney Gunter (North Carolina) 72-83-75-75—305
Suzie Lee (South Carolina) 79-70-81-75—305
Claudia Lim (Ohio State) 78-75-77-75—305
Amy Meier (Ohio State) 73-79-81-72—305
Ana Menendez (NC State) 78-74-77-76—305
84T Emily Podzielinski (Arkansas) 78-72-76-79—305
91 Courtney Ellenbogen (Duke) 75-79-78-74—306
Mia Piccio (Florida) 76-74-76-80—306
93 Desiree Dubreuil (Texas) 81-75-81-70—307
Jacqueline Hedwall (LSU) 83-75-76-73—307
Christine Meier (Michigan State) 74-82-74-77—307
Sara Monberg (Tennessee) 75-77-81-74—307
A J Newell (Tennessee) 75-83-79-70—307
98 Amanda Baker (NC State) 75-75-76-82—308
Ani Gulugian (UCLA) 77-77-76-78—308
Daniela Ordonez (Arizona State) 76-74-82-76—308
Andrea Watts (Florida) 76-77-80-75—308
102 Allyssa Ferrell (Michigan State) 76-81-73-79—309
Lauren Greenlief (Virginia) 74-72-82-81—309
Maria Salinas (Florida State) 80-80-79-70—309
Stani Schiavone (Baylor) 75-79-77-78—309
106 Sydney Burlison (Stanford) 81-77-76-76—310
Kaitlin Drolson (Pepperdine) 80-74-78-78—310
Marissa Mar (Stanford) 80-76-79-75—310
Liz Nagel (Michigan State) 75-80-80-75—310
Vivian Tsui (NC State) 78-77-82-73—310
Jessica Wallace (Colorado) 78-76-80-76—310
112 Jacki Marshall (Oklahoma) 79-80-76-76—311
113 Jan Chanpalangsri (Ohio State) 80-81-76-75—312
Kristin Coleman (Colorado) 75-80-76-81—312
Victoria Vela (Arkansas) 77-78-78-79—312
Kelsey Vines (Oklahoma State) 72-83-81-76—312
117 Laetitia Beck (Duke) 78-78-77-81—314
Emily Collins (Oklahoma) 79-78-77-80—314
119 Susana Benavides (Ohio State) 81-78-80-76—315
Hally Leadbetter (Arkansas) 79-80-79-77—315
121 Courtney McKim (Alabama) 82-77-79-78—316
122 Victoria Scherer (Purdue) 79-76-76-86—317
123 Rene Sobolewski (Vanderbilt) 79-76-84-79—318
124 Kristina Wong (Stanford) 80-83-78-78—319
125 Sarah Beth Davis (Texas A&M) 83-82-79-76—320
Elizabeth Brightwell D 74-75-72

National Championships 2012

For past winners see earlier editions of *The R&A Golfer's Handbook*

Players are from the host nation unless stated

Africa

Botswana Ladies Open Amateur Championship *Gaberone GC*

1	Bertine Strauss	77-73—150
2	Kim Williams	79-73—152
	Lejan Lewthwaite	78-74—152

Sanlam South African Amateur Stroke Play Championship *Umhlali* April 14–17

1	Nobuhle Dlamini (Centurion)	70-69-73—212
2	Izel Pieters (Sable River Bungalows)	75-74-73—222
3	Lumien Orton (Schoeman Park)	77-71-76—224
	Lara Weinstein (R J/burg & Kensington)	75-77-72—224

South African Mid-Amateur Championship *Kingswood Golf Estate*

1	Sandra Winter (Kingswood GE)	74-75-70—219
2	Kate Brett-Castle (Kloof CC)	78-75-74—227
3	Soinja Bland (Fancourt CC)	77-80-75—232

Zimbabwe Ladies Championship *Chapman GC*

1	Claire Minter	78-75-77—230
2	Naik Devanish (ZAM)	74-81-79—234
3	Batsirai Tilowakuti	84-75-80—239

Triangular match: 1 Zimbabwe 18 pts; 2 Botswana 14 pts; 3 Zambia 4 pts

Americas

Argentine Women's Amateur Championship *SEstancias GC*

Semi-finals: Delfina Acosta beat Maria Olivero de Artica 1 hole
Maria Victoria Villanueva beat Ayelen Irizar 2 and 1

Final: Maria Victoria Villanueva beat Delfina Acosta 1 hole

Leading qualifier: Delfina Acosta 72-7—144

29th United Insurance Barbados Open *Sandy Lane GC*

1	Muffin Stollmeyer	84-72-79—235
2	Mavi Vergos	83-82-94—259
3	Julia Stephenson	93-85-89—267

Canadian Women's Amateur Championship *Lethbridge Country Club, Lethbridge, Alberta*

1	Ariya Jutanugarn (THA)	69-67-65-73—274
2	Moriya Jutanugarn (THA)	74-68-69-68—279
3	Kimberly Kaufman (USA)	73-69-70-70—282

Americas (continued)

Royale Cup Canadian Women's Senior Championship *Belevedere G&CC*

1	Terrill Samuel (Etobicoke)	74-79-71—224
2	Helene Chartrand (Pincourt)	76-75-74—225
3	Mary Kay Thanos-Zordani (USA)	81-71-75—239

Caribbean Amateur Championship (George Teale Trophy) *Royal St Kitts GC, St Kitts*

1	Maria Torres (PUR)	72-73-69-77—291
2	Monifa Sealy (TRI)	76-69-76-78—299
	Kelsey Lou Hing (TRI)	76-73-74-76—299

110th North and South Women's Championship *Pinehurst Resort*

Semi-Finals: Doris Chen (Bradenton) beat Alejandro Cangrejo (COL) 4 and 2
Austin Ernst (Seneca) beat Ashley Armstrong (Flossmoor) 3 and 2

Final: Austin Ernst beat Doris Chen 2 and 1

Medallist: Jaye Marie Green (Boca Raton) 69-71-72—212

US Women's Mid-Amateur Championship *Briggs Ranch GC, San Antonio, Texas*

Semi-Finals: Liz Waynick (Scottsdale, AZ) beat Stacy Dennis (Huntsville, TX) at 20th
Meghan Stasi (Oakland Park, FL) beat Laura Coble (Augusta, GA) 6 and 5

Final: Meghan Stasi beat Liz Waynick 6 and 5

51st US Amateur Women's Senior Championship *Hershey CC, Hershey, Pennsylvania*

Semi-Finals: Jane Fitzgerald (Kensington, MD) beat Lisa Schlesinger (Laytonsville, MD) 4 and 3
Ellen Port (St Louis, MO) beat Lecia Alexander (Stafford, TX) 6 and 4

Final: Ellen Port beat Jane Fitzgerald 4 and 2

US Amateur Public Links Championship *Neshanic Valley GC, Neshanic Station, New Jersey*

Semi-Finals: Kyung Kim (Chandler. AZ) beat Alice Jeong (Gardena, CA) 4 and 2
Ashlan Ramsey (Milledgeville, GA) beat Kim Kaufman (Clark, SD) 1 hole

Final: Kyung Kim beat Ashlan Ramsey 4 and 2

Leading qualifiers: Lisa McCloskey (Houston, TX) 137, Karen Chung 138, Steffi Neisen 138

US Women's Amateur Championship *see page 395*

Asia and the Middle East

China National Amateur Championship *Nanshan*

1	Shi Yutang	69-68-72—209
2	Chen Cuixia	72-73-70—215
3	Ye Ziqi	75-75-75—225

Hong Kong Ladies Close Amateur Championship *Hong Kong GC (New course)*

1	Tiffany Chan (HKGA)	74-74-71—219
2	Michelle Cheung (HKGA)	70-76-75—221
3	Mimi Ho (DBGC)	74-73-75—222

All-India Women's Amateur Championship *Tollygunge GC, Kolkata*

Final: Gurbani Singh beat Gursima Badwal 10 and 9

Israel Amateur Women's Open *Caesarea GC*

1	Hadas Libman	74-82-79—235
2	Limor Sidi	95-83-90—268
3	Ruth Oren	97-90-93—280

54th Japanese Amateur Championship *Aichi CC, Aichi*

Semi-finals: Mamiko Higa beat Mayu Hosaka 3 and 2
Haruka Morita beat Yumi Matsubara 5 and 4

Final: Mimiko Higa beat Haruka Morita 2 and 1

Third place play-off: Mayu Hosaka beat Yumi Matsubara at 20th

Leading qualifier: Mamika Higa 70-68—138

29th Malaysian Women's Open Amateur Championship

Kuala Lumpur GC (East course)

1	Whitney Hillier (AUS)	68-75-65—208
2	Kelly Tan	68-72-74—209
3	Dottie Ardina (PHI)	68-75-68—211

46th Malaysian Amateur Close Championship *Templer Park, Rawang*

1	Nur Durriyah	74-81-77—232
2	Aretha Pan	74-81-79—234
3	Loy Hee Ying	82-76-80—238

Pakistan Women's Amateur Championship *Royal Palm GC, Lahore*

1	Ghazala Yasmin	85-83-88—256
2	Kashifa Zafar	
3	Nushmiya Sukhera	

Philippines Women's Amateur Championship *Canlubang G&CC*

1	Lovelyn Guioguio	72-70-71—219
2	Andie Unson	75-78-72—225
3	Princess Superal	75-76-75—226

Singapore National Women's Amateur Championship *Singapore Island CC*

Semi-finals: Amelia Yong beat Fariza Izanie 2 and 1
Joey Poh beat Low Si Xuan at 21st

Final: Amelia Yong beat Joey Poh 9 and 7

125th Sri Lanka Women's Championship *Royal Colombo GC*

Semi-finals: Gursimar Badwal (IND) beat Nanaki Chadha 8 and 7
Jackie Dias beat Niloo Jayathilake at 19th

Final: Gursimar Badwal beat Jackie Dias 4 and 3

International team event: India (Gursimar Badwal and Anisha Padukone) 323

Thailand Amateur Open *Panya Indra GC*

1	Benyapa Niphatsophon	72-72-68-72—284
2	Princess Mary Superal	72-68-74-71—285
3	Parinda Phokan	67-70-73-76—286

Australasia

Australian Women's Amateur Championship (inaugurated 1894)

Woodlands and Huntingdale

Semi-finals: Breanna Elliott (VIC) beat Whitney Hillier (WA) 5 and 4
Lydia Ko (NZL) beat Minjee Lee (WA) 6 and 4

Final: Lydia Ko (NZL) beat Breanna Elliott (VIC) 4 and 3

Leading qualifier: Breanna Elliott (VIC) 73-72—145

Australian Women's Mid-Amateur Championship *Moonah Links, Victoria*

1	Sue Wooster (VIC)	79-72-77—228
2	Gemma Dooley (NSW)	77-82-83—242
3	Katrina Jones (QLD)	82-82-79—243

New Zealand Amateur Championship (inaugurated 1893) *Mt Maunganui* April 18–22

Semi-finals: Wenyung Keh (Titarangi) beat Lita Guo (Remuera) 4 and 3
Munchin Keh (Titarangi) beat Joanna Kim (Manakau) 2 and 1

Final: Munchin Keh (Titarangi) beat Wenyung Keh (Titarangi) one hole

Leading qualifier: Julianne Alvarez (Manor Park) 73-72—145

New Zealand Stroke Play Championship (Mellsop Cup) (inaugurated 1911)

Hastings Mar 22–25

1	Emily Perry*	69-75-71-69—284
2	Lydia Ko	71-72-72-69—284

**Perry won at the first extra hole*

3	Chantelle Cassidy	76-70-72-73—291

Europe

Austrian International Women's Championship *GC Linz St Florian*

1	Anne van Dam (NED)	76-68-72—216
2	Karolina Vickova (CZE)	72-72-72—217
3	Charlotte Puts (NED)	71-72-76—219

Belgian International Ladies Championship *Royal Antwerp GC*

1	Camille Richelle	72-68-77-70—287
2	Chloe Leurquin	71-71-71-73—292
	Laura Lonardi (ITA)	69-72-76-75—292

Ladies British Amateur Championship *see page 390*

Ladies' British Open Amateur Stroke Play Championship (inaugurated 1969)

Shandon Park

1	Sarah-Jane Boyd (Truro)	69-73-77-75—294
2	Amy Boulden (Conwy)	70-74-74-78—296
3	Kelly Tidy (Royal Birkdale)	77-78-71-71—297

Senior Ladies' British Open Amateur Championship *Hunstanton GC*

1	Katherine Russell (R. Ashdown Forest)*	79-81-74—234
2	Pat Doran (Donabate)	81-79-74—234
3	Minna Kaamaiahti (FIN)	78-83-74—235

**Russell won at the second extra hole*

Danish International Ladies Championship *Silkeborg GC*

1	Nicole Broch Larsen	74-72-73-68—287
2	Emily Pedersen	82-72-74-78—306
3	Mette Kryger Pedersen	79-75-75-78—307

Dutch National Open Championship *Utrecht GC*

1	Ileen Domela	75-75-74-74—298
2	Elise Boehmer	71-76-71-81—299
3	Karlijn Zaanen	76-75-74-75—300

Dutch National Championship *Noordwyke GC*

1	Myrte Eikenaar	78-75-78—231
2	Dewi Weber	82-73-78—233
3	Desire Blaaun	75-79-81—235

High winds caused cancellation of the second round

English Women's Close Amateur Championship (inaugurated 1912) *Royal Birkdale*

1	Kelly Tidy (Royal Birkdale)*	78-74-71-81—304
2	Georgia Hall (Remedy Oak)	77-74-75-78—304
Tidy won at the first extra hole		
3	Holly Clyburn (Woodhall Spa)	80-76-76-75—307

English Women's Open Amateur Stroke Play Championship (inaugurated 1984)

Little Aston

1	Alexandra Peters (Notts Ladies)	73-72-71-73—289
2	Charlotte Thompson (Channels)	71-71-77-76—295
3	Emily Taylor (Hillside)	73-77-72-74—296

English Women's Open Mid-Amateur Championship (inaugurated 1982) *Wetherby*

1	Emma Carberry (Highwoods)	71-68—139
2	Kirsty Rands (Burhill)	72-70—142
3	Charlotte Thompson (Channels)	72-71—143

Senior Women's English Close Stroke Play Championship *Shifnal*

1	Janet Melville (Sherwood Forest)	76-76-72—224
2	Sue Dye (Delamere Forest)	76-74-77—227
3	Lindsey Shaw (Chevin)	78-74-78—230

Senior Women's English Close Match Play Championship *Tidworth Garrison*

Leading Qualifiers: Amanda Mayne (Saltford), Janet Melville (Sherwood Forest), Lulu Housman (Highgate), Carol Cass (Broadstone) 76 *(reduced to 18 holes due to bad weather)*

Semi-Finals: Roz Adams (Addington Court) beat Linda Hunt (Newbury & Crookham) 4 and 3
Chris Quinn (Hockley} beat Carol Cass (Broadstone) 5 and 3

Final: Chris Quinn beat Roz Adams 2 and 1

Estonia Open Women's Amateur Championship *Saare GC Kuresaare, Saarmaa*

1	Leena Makkonen (FIN)	79-73—152
2	Mara Puisite (LAT)	78-75—153
3	Merlin Palm	82-73—155
	Krista Puisite (LAT)	81-74—155

Nations Cup: 1 Latvia (Mara Puisite, Linda Dobele, Krista Puisite) +30; 2 Finland 1 +32; 3 Estonia 1 +48

Europe (continued)

Ladies European Open Amateur Championship *see page 393*

European Senior Women's Championship (inaugurated 2000) *Achensee, Austria*

1	Rocio Ruiz de Velasco (ESP)	74-73-74—221
2	Chris Utermarck (GER)	77-77-69—223
3	Isabelle Dumont (BEL)	79-73-74—226

Super Seniors (over 65): Mimmi Guglielmone (SUI) 228

European International Women's Amateur Championship

Golf und Landclub. Achensee, Austria June 14-16

1	Rocio Ruiz De Velasco (ESP)	74-73-74—221
2	Chris Utermarck (GER)	77-77-69—223
3	Isabelle Dumont (BEL)	79-73-74—226

Seniors (over 60): Mimmi Guglielmone (SUI) 75-78-75—228

International European Ladies Amateur Championship

Diners G&CC, Ljubljana, Slovenia July 25–28

1	Celine Boutier (FRA)	68-66-66-68—208
2	Shannon Aubert (FRA)	68-69-68-69—274
	Marion Stutz (AUT)	67-71-68-68—274

Finnish Amateur Championship *Heksinki GK*

1	Julie Finne-Ipsen (DEN)	71-73-71—215
2	Nina Pegova (RUS)	73-70-73—216
3	Noora Tamminen	74-71-72—217
	Sanna Nuutinen	73-74-70—217
	Marika Vass	73-72-72—217
	Krista Bakker	70-76-71—217

Finnish Women's Stroke Play Championship *Aulangon GK*

1	Noora Tamminen	70-71-72-72—285
2	Krista Pakker	74-76-70-73—293
3	Marika Voss	73-76-75-75—299

German Women's Championship *GR Hardenberg*

1	Karolin Lampert (St Leon Rot GC)	72-77-73-69—291
2	Ann Kathrin Lindner (St Leon Rot GC)	72-71-75-78—296
3	Nina Holleder (St Leon Rot GC)	72-82-72-74—300

German International Women's Amateur Championship *Stuttgarter GC*

1	Celine Boutier (FRA)	72-70-68-66—276
2	Sylvia Banon (ESP)	67-70-73-76—286
3	Ann-Kathrin Lindner	74-70-71-75—290

Hungarian Ladies Amateur Championship *Pannonia G&CC*

1	Marlies Krenn	78-70-72—220
2	Nina Pegova	71-77-75—223
3	Csilla Rozsa	72-78-74—224

Irish Women's Close Amateur Championship (inaugurated 1894) *Co Louth*

Leading Qualifier: Lisa Maguire (Slieve Russell) 72-72—144

Semi-Finals: Stephanie Meadow (Royal Portrush) beat Lucy Simpson (Massereene) 6 and 5
Leona Maguire (Slieve Russell) beat Carla Reynolds (Seapoint) 3 and 1

Final: Leona Maguire beat Stephanie Meadow 2 holes

Irish Women's Open Amateur Stroke Play Championship (inaugurated 1993)

The Island

1	Emily Taylor (R Lytham & St Anne's)	85-72-76—233
2	Mary Dowling (New Ross)	81-79-76—236
	Gillian O'Leary (Cork)	79-77-80—236

Irish Senior Women's Close Amateur Championship *Bunclody*

Semi-Finals: Helen Jones (Strabane) beat Pat Doran (Donabate) at 21st
Violet McBride (Belvoir Park) beat Suzanne Corcoran (Portumna) at 19th

Final: Helen Jones beat Violet McBride 4 and 2

Irish Women's Senior Championship *Royal Belfast GC*

1	Minna Kaarnalahti (FIN)	83-71-76—238
2	Sheena McElroy (Grange)	82-81-80—243
3	Marilyn Henderson (Royal Belfast)	87-76-83—246

Nations Cup: 1 Ireland "A" 325; 2 Canada "A", Ireland "B" 338; 4 Scotland 355; 5 USA "A" 357; 6 Canada "B" 366; 7 USA "B" 389; 8 Scandinavia 399

Winning team: Helen Jones, Sheena McElroy and Violet McBride

Italian Ladies Stroke Play Championship *Castelconturbia*

1	Elisabetta Bertini	76-72-74-69—291
2	Laura Lonardi	74-74-75-71—294
3	Alessandra Braida	78-71-77-69—295

Latvian International Amateur Championship *Ozo GC*

1	Krista Puisite	74-74-70—218
2	Maria Puisite	70-78-75—223
3	Linda Dobele	81-79-76—236

Luxembourg Women's Amateur Championhip *Golf Club Grand-Ducal*

1	Cyrielle Kern (Christnach)	78-80—138
2	Amandine Kern (Christnach)	80-78—138
3	Marielle Marque (Luxembourg)	81-77—138

82nd Portuguese Women's Championship *Montado Golf Resort, Lisbon*

1	Roberta Roeller (GER)	66-74-70-73—283
2	Leona Maguire (IRL)	72-74-72-68—286
3	Perrine Delacour (FRA)	70-76-72-72—290

Russian Women's Amateur Championship *Tsleevo GC*

1	Nina Pegova	65-76-68-71—280
2	Angelina Monakhova	74-78-69-76—297
3	Margarita Kim	73-75-73-79—300

Europe (continued)

Scottish Ladies' Close Amateur Championship (inaugurated 1903) *Tain*

Leading Qualifier: Jane Turner (Craigielaw) 75-75—150

Semi-Finals: Jane Turner (Craigielaw) beat Eilidh Watson (Muckhart) 7 and 6
Laura Murray (Alford) beat Eilidh Briggs (Kilmacolm) 6 and 4

Final: Laura Murray beat Jane Turner 2 holes

Scottish Ladies' Open Stroke Play Championship (Helen Holm Trophy) (inaugurated 1973) *Troon Portland & Royal Troon*

1	Amy Boulden (Conwy)	70-72-73—215
2	Perrine Delacour (FRA)	70-72-74—216
3	Laura Murray (Alford)	74-72-72—218
	Pamela Pretswell (Bothwell Castle)	71-70-77—218

Scottish Senior Ladies' (Close) Amateur Championship *Kemnay*

Stroke Play

1	Alison Bartlett (Royal Dornoch)*	82-72—154
2	Alex Glennie (Kilmarnock/Barassie)	75-79—154

**Bartlett won at the first extra hole*

3	Mary Smith (Tain)	77-81—158

Match Play

Semi-Finals: Janice Paterson (Drumpeller) beat Linda Urquhart (Banchory) 1 hole
Heather Anderson (Blairgowrie) beat Karen Burns (Bathgate) 5 and 3

Final: Heather Anderson beat Janice Paterson 4 and 3

Scottish Champion of Champions *Glasgow Gailes*

1	Eilidh Briggs (Scottish Universities)	75
2	Alyson McKechin (Renfrewshire)	78
3	Hannah McCook (Northern Counties)	80

Scottish Veteran Ladies Championship *Rosemount GC (Lansdowne course), Blairgowrie*

Semi-Finals: Ruth Brown (East) beat Liz Campbell (Borders) 1 hole
May Hughes (West) beat Ann Ryan (Highlands) 2 and 1

Final: May Hughes beat Ruth Brown 2 and 1

Slovak Women's Amateur Championship *Penati Golf Resort*

1	Katerina Chancova (CZE)	73-77-79—229
2	Aneta Abrahamova	82-81-75—236
3	Karolina Cordieri (CZE)	76-78-83—237

Slovak Women's Open Amateur Championship *Sajdikova Humence GC*

1	Katerina Vlasinova (CZE)	75-75-72—222
2	Barbara Borin (ITA)	76-76-76—228
3	Ana Belac	78-77-74—229
	Katerina Chovancova (SVK)	73-77-79—229

Slovenian Women's International Championship *Igrisce GC*

1	Bianka Fabrizio (ITA)	69-73-73—215
2	Fanny Wolte (AUT)	73-72-72—217
3	Katja Pogacar	69-75-76—220

79th Spanish Women's Championship *Alicante Golf*

1	Ha Rang Lee Jae	67-71-74—212
2	Andrewa Jonama Rovira	69-72-73—214
3	Clara Baena Sanchez	74-70-71—215

Swiss International Women's Amateur Championship *Schoenenberg GC*

1	Guilia Molinaro	67-73-71-66—277
2	Laure Castelain	72-74-69-72—287
	Manon Gidali	73-70-71-73—287

11th Turkish Women's Amateur Championship *Gloria GC (New course) Antalya. Turkey*

1	Nicole Broch Larsen (DEN)	71-72-68-73—284
2	Marion Gidali (FRA)	74-72-73-70—289
3	Leigh Whittaker (GER)	76-67-75-71—290
	Kotone Hori (JPN)	70-70-77-73—290
	Celine Boutier (FRA)	72-77-70-72—290

Ukranian Ladies Amateur Open Championship *Kiev GC*

1	Maria Pedenko	91-74-93—258
2	Yulia Malimon	101-83-99—283
3	Valeria Aapronova	105-83-106—294

Welsh Ladies' Close Amateur Championship (inaugurated 1905) *Cardigan*

Leading Qualifier: Amy Boulden (Conwy) 71-71—142

Semi-Finals: Amy Boulden (Conwy) beat Samantha Birks (Wolstanton) 3 and 2
Becky Harries (Haverfordwest) beat Chloe Williams (Wrexham) 7 and 6

Final: Amy Boulden beat Becky Harries 4 and 2

Welsh Ladies' Open Amateur Stroke Play Championship (inaugurated 1976)

Ashburnham

1	Becky Harries (Haverfordwest)	76-75-69—220
2	Chloe Williams (Wrexham)	74-73-75—222
3	Georgia Hall (Remedy Oak)	80-70-74—224

Welsh Senior Ladies' Championship *Langland Bay GC*

1	Anne Lewis (Royal St David's)	77-74—151
2	Jane Rees (Hendon)	81-77—158
	Vicki Thomas (Carmarthen)	79-79—158

Tegwen Matthews retains Curtis Cup Captaincy

Tegwen Matthews, who captained Great Britain and Ireland to a marvellous come-from-behind victory in the Curtis Cup at Nairn last year, will captain the side again in defence of the trophy at the 38th. playing of the match at the St Louis Country Club in Missouri in June 2014.

The first Welsh player to captain the side which ended a run of defeats stretching back to 1996, Matthews, an inspirational and popular leader, will also captain the Great Britain and Ireland team against the Continent of Europe for the Vagliano Trophy at Chantilly in France this June.

Matthews, who also captained the GB & I side to victory in 2011 in the Astor Trophy Tournament at Fairhaven, said she was "thrilled, honoured and excited" to be given the chance again to captain the Curtis Cup team.

USA State Championships 2012

US nationality unless stated

Alabama	Cammie Gray (SP)
	Kathy Hartwiger (MP)
Alaska	Terri McAngus
Arizona	Samantha Postillion (SP)
	Stephanie Kim (MP)
Arkansas	Julie Oxendine (SP)
	Summar Roachell (MP)
California	Emily Talley
Colorado	Somin Lees (SP)
	Allie Johnston (MP)
Connecticut	Mia Landegren (SP)
	Nicole Yatsenik (MP)
Delaware	Emily Ransone
Florida	Ericka Schneider (SP)
	Meghan Stasi (MP)
Georgia	Laura Coble (MP)
Hawaii	Nicole Sakamoto (SP)
	Cassy Isagawa (MP)
Idaho	Madeleine Sheils
Illinois	Elizabeth Szokol
Iowa	Kimmy Askelson (SP)
	Kelly Nelson (MP)
Indiana	Meghan Potee
Kansas	Audrey Yowell
Kentucky	Karisa Akin
Louisiana	Heather Lott
Maine	Emily Bouchard
Maryland	Andrea Kraus
Massachusetts	Clare Sheldon
Michigan	Gabrielle Yurik
Minnesota	Sarah Burnham
Mississippi	Ally McDonald
Missouri	Ellen Port
Montana	Katelyn Frank
Nebraska	McKayla Anderson (SP)
	Elizabeth Lydiatt (MP)
New England	Kristen MacDonald
N. Hampshire	Dana Harrity
New Jersey	Alexandra Hershberger
New York	Ellen Oswald
N. Carolina	Courtney McKim
Ohio	Allison Schultz
Oklahoma	Amber Hensley
Oregon	Amy Simanton
Pennsylvania	Charlie Blanchard
Rhode Island	Nicole Scola
S. Dakota	Kimberley Kaufman (SP)
	Shannon Johnson (MP)
Tennessee	Lauren Stratton
Texas	Emily Collins
Utah	Kelswy Hugg
Vermont	Holly Reynolds
Virginia	Lauren Coughlin
Washington	Karinn Dickinson
West Virginia	Brooke Bellamy
Wisconsin	Jessica Gerry (SP)
	Casey Marschall (MP)
Wyoming	Haley Shackelford

Virginias	Amanda Steinhagen
North & South	Austin Ernst
Carolinas	Katy Rose Higgins
Metropolitan (NY)	Laura Algiero

Further details of these and other USA amateur events can be found on page 446

Canadian Provincial Championships 2012

Canadian nationality unless stated

Alberta	Jocelyn Alford	Sturgeon Valley GC
Brit. Columbia	Christine Wong	Christina Lake GC
Manitoba	Bri-ann Tokariwski	The Meadows GC
N. Brunswick	Margo McLeod	Fraser Edmunston GC
Newfoundland and Labrador	Kathleen Jean	Blomidon GC
Nova Scotia	Julia Henderson	Bell Bay GC
Ontario	Brittany Marchand (SP)	Loyalist GC
	Kaitlin Marrin (MP)	Hank Ridge G&CC
Quebec	Anne-Catherine Tanguay	Chicoutimi GC
Saskatchewan	Anna Young	The Willows GC

Pacific North West	Megan Haase	Bear Mountain Golf Resort

Further details of these and other Canadian amateur events can be found on page 444

Australian State Championships 2012

Australian nationality unless stated

New S. Wales	Hayley Bettancourt (MP)	Twin Creeks GC
	Breanna Elliott (SP)	Castle Hill GC
N. Territory	Charlotte Thomas (ENG)	Darwin GC
Queensland	Hayley Bettancourt (SP and MP)	Pacific Harbour G&CC
South Australia	Nadine Smith (MP)	Mt Osmond GC, The Grange GC
	Breanna Elliott (SP)	Glenelg GC
Tasmania	Ashlee Dewhurst (MP)	Launceston GC
	Minjee Lee (SP)	Royal Hobart GC
Victoria	Grace Lennon (SP)	Devilbend GC, Flinders GC
	Su Hyun Oh (MP)	Yarra Yarra GC
West Australia	Breanna Elliott (MP)	Lake Karrinyup CC

Further details of these and other Australian amateur events can be found on page 448

South African Provincial Championships 2012

South African nationality unless stated

Boland	Nobuhle Dlamini	Hermanus GC
Border	Lara Weinstein (SP)	
	Alana van Greuning (MP)	East London GC
Eastern Cape	Nobuhle Dlamini (SP and MP)	Port Elizabeth GC
Ekurhuleni	Nobuhle Dlamini	State Mines GC
Free State and North Cape	Olivia Le Roux	Blomfontein GC
Gauteng	Kim Williams (SP)	
	Nobuhle Dlamini (MP)	Glendower GC
Gauteng North	Kim Williams (SP)	
	Bertine Strauss (MP)	Irene CC
KwaZulu Natal	Lara Weinstein (SP)	
	Nobuhle Dlamini (MP)	Maritzburg CC
Limpopo	Lynn-Marie Nagel	Polokwane GC
Mpumalanga	Monja Richards	Nelspruit GC
North West	Nobuhle Dlamini	Potchefstroom GC
Southern Cape	Ji Sun Kang	Mossel Bay GC
Western Province	Se Young Chun (SP)	
	Nicoel Loesch (MP)	Royal Cape GC

Further details of these and other South African amateur events can be found on page 442

New Zealand Provincial Championships 2012

New Zealand nationality unless stated

North Island Stroke Play Championship	Emily Perry	Lochiel GC
South Island Stroke Play Championship	Celyn Khoo	Christchurch GC

Further details of these and other New Zealand amateur events can be found on page 449

National Orders of Merit 2012

Lorrin English Order of Merit

1	Kelly Tidy (Royal Birkdale)	1,463	6	Georgia Hall (Remedy Oaks)	1,169
2	Emily Taylor (Hillside)	1,419	7	Charlotte Thompson (Channels)	1,037
3	Holly Clyburn (Woodhall Spa)	1,401	8	Charley Hull (Woburn)	873
4	Bronte Law (Bramhall)	1,211	9	Sarah Jane Boyd (Truro)	728
5	Alexandra Peters (Notts Ladies)	1,178	10	Kerry Smith (Waterlooville)	557

Irish Order of Merit

1	Leona Maguire (Slieve Russell)	878	6	Maria Dunne (Skerries)	579
2	Stephanie Meadow (Royal Portrush)	698	7	Lisa Maguire (Slieve Russell)	492
3	Gillian O'Leary (Cork)	678	8	Jessica Carty (Hollywood)	491
4	Paula Grant (Llsburn)	623	9	Chloe Ryan (Castletroy)	488
5	Mary Dowling (New Ross)	596	10	Jean O'Driscoll (IMuskerry)	475

Scottish Order of Merit

1	Laura Muncey (Alford)	2,965	6	Jessica Meek (Carnoustie Ladies)	1,205
2	Jane Turner (Craigielaw)	2,398	7	Hannah McCook (Grantown-on-Spey)	1,155
3	Eilidh Briggs (Kilmacolm)	1,925	8	Clara Young (North Berwick)	1,110
4	Kelsey MacDonald (Nairn Dunbar)	1,725	9	Alyson McKechin (Elderslie)	1,095
5	Megan Briggs (Kilmacolm)	1,235	10	Ailsa Summers (Carnoustie Ladies)	940

Ping Welsh Order of Merit

1	Amy Boulden (Conwy)	1,050.00	6	Gemma Bradbury (Cottrell Park)	113.50
2	Becky Harries (Haverfordwest)	1,014.33	7	Sam Birks (Wolstanton)	111.25
3	Katherine O'Connor (Tadmarten Heath)	401.83	8	Jessica Evans (Newport_	89,00
4	Chloe Williams (Wrexham)	352.50	9	Rachel Lewis (Southerndown)	60.00
5	Katie Bradbury (Cottrell Park)	175.50	10	Lucy Gould (Bargoed)	50.00

Australian Order of Merit

(events played in brackets)

1	Breanna Elliott (VIC)	(14)	125.17	6	Minjee Lee (WA)	(7)	88,56
2	Whitney Hillier (WA)	(17)	103.29	7	Ashlee Dewhurst (TAS)	(13)	84.25
3	Grace Lennon (VIC)	(18)	99.31	8	Ellen Davies-Graham (QLD)	(16)	83.61
4	Charlotte Thomas (ENG)	(13)	97.85	9	Lydia Ko (NZL)	(4)	83.39
5	Hayley Bettancourt (WA)	(14)	91.89		Emily Perry (NZL)	(9)	83.39

Month by month in 2012

Branden Grace's fifth win of the year comes at the Dunhill Links Championship before Shane Lowry joins Pablo Martin as the only players to capture European Tour titles as an amateur and professional. Peter Hanson, the only member of Europe's Ryder Cup side not to contribute toward the team total, holds off Rory McIlroy at the BMW Masters in Shanghai. Round of the month is a closing 60 from Tommy Gainey to take the McGladrey Classic.

Canadian Order of Merit

(events played in brackets)

1	Jennifer Kirby	(12)	3,994.10	6	Jisoo Keel	(8)	2,352.92
2	Brooke Henderson	(9)	3,424.65	7	Christine Wong	(10)	2,265.00
3	Augusta James	(10)	2,647.91	8	Natalie Gleadall	(5)	2,254.50
4	Brogan McKinnon	(8)	2,397.50	9	Nicole Zhang	(6)	1,945.38
5	Brittany Marchand	(8)	2,383.38	10	Anne-Catherine Tanguay	(8)	1,653.75

German Order of Merit

1	Karolin Lampert	2,919.38	6	Isabell Gabsa	1,605.00
2	Nina Holleder	2,581.32	7	Roberta Röller	1,453.90
3	Ann-Kathrin Lindner	2,497.40	8	Franziska Friedrich	1,425.00
4	Sophia Popov	2,387.50	9	Vicki Troeltsch	1,122.57
5	Quirine-Louise Eijkenboom	2,261.25	10	Samantha Krug	1,009.42

Belgian Order of Merit

1	Chloé Leurquin	19,696	6	Camile Richelle	11,121
2	Lara Gonzalez-Escallon	16,192	7	Joëlle Van Baarle	8,779
3	Fanny Cnops	15,777	8	Charlotte de Corte	7,875
4	Leslie Cloots	156,36	9	Margaux Vanmol	5,447
5	Manon de Roey	11,333	10	Elodie Van Dievoet	4,3681

The R&A helping golf in Portugal, Thailand and South Africa

During 2012 The R&A spent £4.75 million on golf development around the world. Some of the interesting awards included:

To the Portuguese Golf Federation – £50,000 towards the recently opened national centre and public course in Lisbon. A further £25,000 was awarded to purchase teaching equipment at the country's only public course.

To the Thailand Golf Association – £14,000 paid to Australian agronomist John Neylan to visit and advise on the recovery of 30 courses badly affected by flooding.

To the Ernie Els and Fancourt Foundation in South Africa – £10,000 a year through 2014.

Team Events

For past winners not listed here see earlier editions of *The R&A Golfer's Handbook*

International

The 37th Curtis Cup (Instituted 1932)

Great Britain & Ireland v USA *(home team names first)*

Nairn GC, Scotland June 8–10 [6774–72]

Last day Curtis Cup come-back shocks the Americans

When the 37th Curtis Cup match started at Nairn and the GB and I side lost the first series of foursomes 3–0 it looked as if it would herald a 28th American success ... but the scenario turned out very differently for home captain Tegwen Perkins and her team. After seven successive defeats the GB and I team won for only the seventh time in the history of the match.

They did it with a tremendous last day comeback in the singles which they won 5–3. The GB and I success meant that for the first time the Americans did not have possession of the Curtis Cup, the Walker Cup, the Solheim Cup and, at this moment in time, the Ryder Cup.

"This is the best thing ever in my whole life," said the euphoric captain who had come in as replacement for the late Sue Turner.

Only once in 24 matches had the Americans when leading going into the singles not gone to win but although Austin Ernst and Emily Tubert were quickly up in the first two singles they lost respectively to Kelly Tidy and and Amy Boulden. The momentum had swung dramatically and when Holly Clyburn and 16-year-old Charley Hull won their matches the overall result depended on Ulster golfer Stephanie Meadow beating Amy Anderson. She did by 4 and 2 and the comeback was complete.

Captains: Tegwen Matthews (GBI); Pat Cornett (USA)

First Day – Foursomes:
Kelly Tidy & Amy Boulden lost to Austin Ernst & Brooke Pancake 1 hole
Holly Clyburn & Bronte Law lost to Amy Anderson & Tiffany Lua 2 and 1
Leona Maguire & Stephanie Meadow lost to Lindy Duncan & Lisa McCloskey 5 and 4

First Day – Fourball:
Pamela Pretswell & Charley Hull lost to Amy Anderson & Emily Tubert 4 and 3
Kelly Tidy & Holly Clyburn beat Brooke Pancake & Erica Popson 2 and 1
Bronte Law & Amy Boulden beat Lindy Duncan & Lisa McCloskey 3 and 2

Second Day – Foursomes:
Pamela Pretswell & Charley Hull lost to Amy Anderson & Tiffany Lua 3 and 2
Holly Clyburn & Amy Boulden lost to Austin Ernst & Brooke Pancake 2 holes
Stephanie Meadow & Leona Maguire beat Lindy Duncan & Lisa McCloskey 3 and 1

Second Day – Fourball:
Holly Clyburn & Kelly Tidy beat Emily Tubert & Amy Anderson 1 hole
Leona Maguire & Bronte Law halved with Brooke Pancake & Austin Ernst
Stephanie Meadow & Pamela Pretswell beat Tiffany Lua & Erica Popson 2 holes

Third Day – Singles:
Kelly Tidy beat Austin Ernst 2 and 1
Amy Boulden beat Emily Tubert 3 and 1
Holly Clyburn beat Erica Popson 3 and 2
Pamela Pretswell lost to Lisa McCloskey 4 and 3
Bronte Law lost to Tiffany Lua 2 holes
Charley Hull beat Lindy Duncan 5 and 3
Stephanie Meadow beat Amy Anderson 4 and 2
Leona Maguire lost to Brooke Pancake 6 and 5

Result: Great Britain & Ireland 10½, USA 9½

2010 *Essex CC, Manchester-by-the-Sea, MA* June 11–13

Result: USA 12½, GB&I 7½

Captains: Noreen Mohler (USA), Mary McKenna (GB&I)

First Day – Foursomes:
Jennifer Song & Jennifer Johnson halved with Sally Watson & Rachel Jennings
Alexis Thompson & Jessica Korda halved with Hannah Barwood & Holly Clyburn
Cydnet Clanton & Stephanie Kono halved with Danielle McVeigh & Leona Maguire

First Day – Fourball:
Song & Kimberly Kim lost to McVeigh & Pamela Pretswell 4 and 3
Thompson & Johnson beat Jennings & Leona Maguire 3 and 2
Korda & Tiffany Lua lost to Watson & Lisa Maguire 1 hole

Second Day – Fourball:
Thompson & Korda beat McVeigh & Pretswell 2 and 1
Song & Clanton beat Maguire & Maguire 3 and 2
Kono & Kim beat Watson & Jennings 2 holes

Second Day – Foursomes:
Thompson & Korda beat McVeigh & Leona Maguire 3 and 1
Song & Kono beat Barwood & Clyburn 3 and 1
Lua & Johnson beat Watson & Jennings 3 and 2

Third Day – Singles:
Jennifer Song lost to Danielle McVeigh (IRL) 3 and 2
Alexis Thompson beat Sally Watson (SCO) 6 and 5
Jennifer Johnson beat Rachel Jennings (ENG) 5 and 4
Kimberly Kim lost to Lisa Maguire (IRL) 1 hole
Cydney Clanton beat Hannah Barwood (ENG) 4 and 3
Tiffany Lua lost to Leona Maguire (IRL) 2 and 1
Jessica Korda beat Pamela Pretswell (SCO) 4 and 3
Stephanie Kono lost to Holly Clyburn (ENG) 2 and 1

2008 *Old Course, St Andrews* May 30–June 1

Result: GB&I 7, USA 13

Captains: Mary McKenna (GB&I), Carol Semple Thompson (USA)

First Day – Foursomes
E Bennett & J Ewart lost to S Lewis & A Walshe 3 and 1
S Watson &M Thomson beat M Harigae & J Lee 1 hole
B Loucks & F Parker lost to A Blumenherst & T Joh 1 hole

First Day – Fourballs
C Booth & M Thomson lost to K Kim & M Harigae 3 and 2
S Watson & K Caithness beat T Joh & M Bolger 3 and 2
F Parker & E Bennett lost to A Blumenherst & S Lewis 3 and 1

Second Day – Foursomes
C Booth & B Loucks beat K Kim & J Lee 3 and 2
S Watson & M Thomson lost to A Walshe & S Lewis 5 and 4
E Bennett & J Ewart halved with A Blumenherst & T Joh

Second Day – Fourballs
C Booth & B Loucks lost to K Kim & M Harigae 2 and 1
S Watson & K Caithness beat A Blumenherst & M Bolger 3 and 2
E Bennett & F Parker lost to A Walshe & S Lewis 1 hole

Third Day – Singles
Breanne Loucks (WAL) lost to Kimberly Kim 3 and 1
Jodi Ewart (ENG) lost to Amanda Blumenherst 2 and 1
Elizabeth Bennett (ENG) lost to Stacy Lewis 3 and 2
Carly Booth (SCO) lost to Tiffany Joh 6 and 5
Michele Thomson (SCO) halved with Jennie Lee
Florentyna Parker (ENG) beat Meghan Bolger 6 and 4
Krystle Caithness (SCO) beat Mina Harigae 2 and 1
Sally Watson (SCO) lost to Alison Walshe 1 hole

2006 *Bandon Dunes, OR* July 29–30

Result: USA 11½, GB&I 6½

Captains: Carol Semple Thompson (USA), Ada O'Sullivan (Monkstown) (GB&I)

First Day: Foursomes
P Mackenzie & A Blumenherst beat T Mangan & K Matharu 5 and 4
D Grimes & A McCurdy beat M Gillen & N Edwards 2 holes
J Park & T Leon beat C Coughlan & M Reid 1 hole

Singles
Jenny Suh lost to Kiran Matharu (Cookridge Park) 2 and 1
Jennie Lee beat Martina Gillen (Beaverstown) 4 and 3
Amanda Blumenherst lost to Breanne Loucks (Wrexham) 5 and 4
Paige Mackenzie beat Melissa Reid (Chevin) 5 and 4
Jane Park beat Tara Delaney (Carlow) 3 and 2
Taylor Leon beat Claire Coughlan (Cork) 5 and 4

Second Day: Foursomes
J Park & T Leon halved with T Mangan & T Delaney
J Lee & J Suh lost to M Reid & B Loucks 7 and 5
P Mackenzie & A Blumenherst lost to M Gillen & N Edwards 1 hole

Singles
Virginia Grimes lost to M Gillen 3 and 2
Amanda McCurdy lost to B Loucks 3 and 2
P Mackenzie beat Tricia Mangan (Ennis) 1 hole
T Leon beat Naomi Edwards (Ganton) 5 and 4
J Lee beat M Reid 3 and 2
J Park beat T Delaney 3 and 2

2004 *Formby* June 12–13

Result: GB&I 8, USA 10

Captains: Ada O'Sullivan (Monkstown) (GB&I), Martha Kironac (USA)

First Day: Foursomes
S McKevitt & E Duggleby beat P Creamer & J Park 3 and 2
N Timmins & D Masters beat S Huarte & A Thurman 1 hole
A Laing & C Coughlan beat B Lang & M Wie 1 hole

Singles
Emma Duggleby beat Elizabeth Janangelo 3 and 2
Danielle Masters lost to Erica Blasberg 1 hole
Fame More lost to Paula Creamer 5 and 3
Anna Highgate lost to Michelle Wie 5 and 4
Shelley McKevitt lost to Jane Park 4 and 3
Anne Laing lost to Anne Thurman 4 and 3

Second Day: Foursomes
E Duggleby & S McKevitt beat E Blasberg & Sarah Huarte 2 and 1
A Laing & C Coughlan beat E Janangelo & M Wie 3 and 2
N Timmins & D Masters lost to B Lang & A Thurman 5 and 4

2004 *continued*

Singles

E Duggleby lost to P Creamer 3 and 2
A Laing beat J Park 3 and 1
S McKevitt lost to E Janangelo 1 hole
Nicola Timmins lost to M Wie 6 and 5
Claire Coughlan beat Brittany Lang 2 holes
D Masters lost to A Thurman 1 hole

2002 *Fox Chapel, PA* Aug 3–4

Result: USA 11, GB&I 7

Captains: Mary Budke (USA), Pam Benka (GB&I)

First Day: Foursomes

Duncan & Jerman beat Duggleby & Hudson 4 and 3
Fankhauser & Semple Thompson beat Laing & Stirling 1 hole
Myerscough & Swaim beat Coffey & Smith 3 and 2

Singles

Emily Bastel lost to Rebecca Hudson 2 holes
Leigh Anne Hardin beat Emma Duggleby 2 and 1
Meredith Duncan beat Fame More 5 and 4
Angela Jerman beat Sarah Jones 6 and 5
Courtney Swaim beat Heather Stirling 4 and 2
Mollie Fankhauser lost to Vikki Laing 1 hole

Second Day: Foursomes

Hardin & Bastel lost to Laing & Stirling 3 and 1
Myerscough & Swaim beat Hudson & Smith 4 and 2
Duncan & Jerman lost to Coffey & Dugglesby 4 and 2

Singles

Mollie Fankhauser beat Rebecca Hudson 3 and 1
Carol Semple Thompson Beat Vikki Laing 1 hole
Leigh Anne Hardin lost to Emma Duggleby 4 and 3
Laura Myerscough beat Heather Stirling 2 holes
Meredith Duncan beat Akison Coffey 3 and 1
Courtney Swaim lost to Sarah Jones 5 and 3

2000 *Ganton* June 24–25

Result: USA 10, GB&I 8

Captains: Claire Hourihane Dowling (GB&I), Jane Bastanchury Booth (USA)

First Day: Foursomes

Andrew & Morgan lost to Bauer & Carol Semple Thompson 1 hole
Brewerton & Hudson lost to Keever & Stanford 1 hole
Duggleby & O'Brien halved with Derby Grimes & Homeyer

Singles

Kim Rostron Andrew lost to Beth Bauer 3 and 2
Fiona Brown lost to Robin Weiss 1 hole
Rebecca Hudson lost to Stephanie Keever 4 and 2
Lesley Nicholson halved with Angela Stanford
Suzanne O'Brien beat Leland Beckel 3 and 1
Emma Duggleby lost to Hilary Homeyer 1 hole

Second Day: Foursomes

Brewerton & Hudson beat Bauer & Thompson 2 and 1
Duggleby & O'Brien beat Keever & Stanford 7 and 6
Andrew & Morgan lost to Derby Grimes & Homeyer 3 and 1

Singles

Hudson lost to Bauer 1 hole
O'Brien beat Weiss 3 and 2
Duggleby beat Keever 4 and 2
Becky Brewerton lost to Homeyer 3 and 2
Becky Morgan beat Stanford 5 and 4
Andrew beat Virginia Derby Grimes 6 and 5

1998 *Minikahda, Minneapolis, MN* Aug 1–2

Result: USA 10, GB&I 8

Captains: Barbara McIntire (USA), Ita Burke Butler (GB&I)

First Day: Foursomes

Bauer & Chuasiriporn lost to Ratcliffe & Rostron 1 hole
Booth & Corrie Kuehn beat Brown & Stupples 2 and 1
Burke & Derby Grimes beat Morgan & Rose 3 and 2

Singles

Kellee Booth beat Kim Rostron 2 and 1
Brenda Corrie Kuehn beat Alison Rose 3 and 2
Jenny Chuasiriporn halved with Rebecca Hudson
Beth Bauer beat Hilary Monaghan 5 and 3
Jo Jo Robertson lost to Becky Morgan 2 and 1
Carol Semple Thompson lost to Elaine Ratcliffe 3 and 2

Second Day: Foursomes

Booth & Corrie Kuehn beat Morgan & Rose 6 and 5
Bauer & Chuasiriporn lost to Brown & Hudson 2 holes
Burke & Derby Grimes beat Ratcliffe & Rostron 2 and 1

Singles

Booth beat Rostron 2 and 1
Corrie Kuehn beat Morgan 2 and 1
Thompson lost to Karen Stupples 1 hole
Robin Burke lost to Hudson 2 and 1
Robertson lost to Fiona Brown 1 hole
Virginia Derby Grimes halved with Ratcliffe

1996 *Killarney* June 21–22

Result: GB&I 11½, USA 6½

Captains: Ita Burke Butler (GB&I), Martha Lang (USA)

First Day: Foursomes

Lisa Walton Educate & Wade lost to K Kuehne & Port 2 and 1
Lisa Dermott & Rose beat B Corrie Kuehn & Jemsek 3 and 1
McKay & Moodie halved with Kerr & Thompson

Singles

Julie Wade lost to Sarah LeBrun Ingram 4 and 2
Karen Stupples beat Kellee Booth 3 and 2
Alison Rose beat Brenda Corrie Kuehn 5 and 4
Elaine Ratcliffe halved with Marla Jemsek
Mhairi McKay beat Cristie Kerr 1 hole
Janice Moodie beat Carol Semple Thompson 3 and 1

Second Day: Foursomes

McKay & Moodie beat Booth & Ingram 3 and 2
Dermott & Rose beat B Corrie Kuehn & Jemsek 2 and 1
Educate & Wade lost to K Kuehne & Port 1 hole

Singles

Wade lost to Kerr 1 hole
Ratcliffe beat Ingram 3 and 1
Stupples lost to Booth 3 and 2
Rose beat Ellen Port 6 and 5
McKay halved with Thompson
Moodie beat Kelli Kuehne 2 and 1

1994 *Chattanooga, TN* July 30–31

Result: GB&I 9, USA 9

Captains: Lancy Smith (USA), Elizabeth Boatman (GB&I)

First Day: Foursomes

Sarah LeBrun Ingram & McGill halved with Matthew & Moodie
Klein & Thompson beat McKay & Kirsty Speak 7 and 5
Kaupp & Port lost to Wade & Walton 6 and 5

Singles
Jill McGill halved with Julie Wade
Emilee Klein beat Janice Moodie 3 and 2
Wendy Ward lost to Lisa Walton 1 hole
Carol Semple Thompson beat Myra McKinlay 2 and 1
Ellen Port beat Mhairi McKay 2 and 1
Stephanie Sparks lost to Catriona Lambert Matthew 1 hole

Second Day: Foursomes
Ingram & McGill lost to Wade & Walton 2 and 1
Klein & Thompson beat McKinlay & Eileen Rose Power 4 and 2
Sparks & Ward lost to Matthew & Moodie 3 and 2

Singles
McGill beat Wade 4 and 3
Klein lost to Matthew 2 and 1
Port beat McKay 7 and 5
Wendy Kaupp lost to McKinlay 3 and 2
Ward beat Walton 4 and 3
Thompson lost to Moodie 2 holes

1992 *Hoylake* June 5–6

Result: GB&I 10, USA 8

Captains: Elizabeth Boatman (GB&I), Judy Oliver (USA)

First Day: Foursomes
Hall & Wade halved with Fruhwirth & Goetze
Lambert & Thomas beat Ingram & Shannon 2 and 1
Hourihane & Morley beat Hanson & Thompson 2 and 1

Singles
Joanne Morley halved with Amy Fruhwirth
Julie Wade lost to Vicki Goetze 3 and 2
Elaine Farquharson beat Robin Weiss 2 and 1
Nicola Buxton lost to Martha Lang 2 holes
Catriona Lambert beat Carol Semple Thompson 3 and 2
Caroline Hall beat Leslie Shannon 6 and 5

Second Day: Foursomes
Hall & Wade halved with Fruhwirth & Goetze
Hourihane & Morley halved with Lang & Weiss
Lambert & Thomas lost to Hanson & Thompson 3 and 2

Singles
Morley beat Fruhwirth 2 and 1
Lambert beat Tracy Hanson 6 and 5
Farquharson lost to Sarah LeBrun Ingram 2 and 1
Vicki Thomas lost to Shannon 2 and 1
Claire Hourihane lost to Lang 2 and 1
Hall beat Goetze 1 hole

1990 *Somerset Hills, NJ* July 28–29

Result: USA 14, GB&I 4

Captains: Leslie Shannon (USA), Jill Thornhill (GB&I)

First Day: Foursomes
Goetze & Anne Quast Sander beat Dobson & Lambert 4 and 3
Noble & Margaret Platt lost to Wade & Imrie 2 and 1
Thompson & Weiss beat Farquharson & Helen Wadsworth 3 and 1

Singles
Vicki Goetze lost to Julie Wade 2 and 1
Katie Peterson beat Kathryn Imrie 3 and 2
Brandie Burton beat Linzi Fletcher 3 and 1
Robin Weiss beat Elaine Farquharson 4 and 3
Karen Noble beat Catriona Lambert 1 hole
Carol Semple Thompson lost to Vicki Thomas 1 hole

Second Day: Foursomes
Goetze & Sander beat Wade & Imrie 3 and 1
Noble & Platt lost to Dobson & Lambert 1 hole
Burton & Peterson beat Farquharson & Wadsworth 5 and 4

Singles
Goetze beat Helen Dobson 4 and 3
Burton beat Lambert 4 and 3
Peterson beat Imrie 1 hole
Noble beat Wade 2 holes
Weiss beat Farquharson 2 and 1
Thompson beat Thomas 3 and 1

1988 *Royal St George's* June 10–11

Result: GB&I 11, USA 7

Captains: Diane Robb Bailey (GB&I), Judy Bell (USA)

First Day: Foursomes
Bayman & Wade beat Kerdyk & Scrivner 2 and 1
Davies & Shapcott beat Scholefield & Thompson 5 and 4
Thomas & Thornhill halved with Keggi & Shannon

Singles
Linda Bayman halved with Tracy Kerdyk
Julie Wade beat Cindy Scholefield 2 holes
Susan Shapcott lost to Carol Semple Thompson 1 hole
Karen Davies lost to Pearl Sinn 4 and 3
Shirley Lawson beat Pat Cornett-Iker 1 hole
Jill Thornhill beat Leslie Shannon 3 and 2

Second Day: Foursomes
Bayman & Wade lost to Kerdyk & Scrivner 1 hole
Davies & Shapcott beat Keggi & Shannon 2 holes
Thomas & Thornhill beat Scholefield & Thompson 6 and 5

Singles
Wade lost to Kerdyk 2 and 1
Shapcott beat Caroline Keggi 3 and 2
Lawson lost to Kathleen McCarthy Scrivner 4 and 3
Vicki Thomas beat Cornett-Iker 5 and 3
Bayman beat Sinn 1 hole
Thornhill lost to Thompson 3 and 2

1986 *Prairie Dunes, KS* Aug 1–2

Result: GB&I 13, USA 5

Captains: Judy Bell (USA), Diane Robb Bailey (GB&I)

First Day: Foursomes
Kessler & Schreyer lost to Behan & Thornhill 7 and 6
Ammaccapane & Mochrie lost to Davies & Johnson 2 and 1
Gardner & Scrivner lost to McKenna & Robertson 1 hole

Singles
Leslie Shannon lost to Patricia (Trish) Johnson 1 hole
Kim Williams lost to Jill Thornhill 4 and 3
Danielle Ammaccapane lost to Lillian Behan 4 and 3
Kandi Kessler beat Vicki Thomas 3 and 2
Dottie Pepper Mochrie halved with Karen Davies
Cindy Schreyer beat Claire Hourihane 2 and 1

Second Day: Foursomes
Ammaccapane & Mochrie lost to Davies & Johnson 1 hole
Shannon & Williams lost to Behan & Thornhill 5 and 3
Gardner & Scrivner halved with McKenna & Belle McCorkindale Robertson

Singles
Shannon halved with Thornhill
Kathleen McCarthy Scrivner lost to Trish Johnson 5 and 3
Kim Gardner beat Behan 1 hole
Williams lost to Thomas 4 and 3
Kessler halved with Davies
Schreyer lost to Hourihane 5 and 4

1984 *Muirfield* June 8–9

Result: USA 9½, GB&I 8½

Captains: Diane Robb Bailey (GB&I), Phyllis Preuss (USA)

First Day: Foursomes

New & Waite beat Pacillo & Sander 2 holes
Grice & Thornhill halved with Rosenthal & Smith
Davies & McKenna lost to Farr & Widman 1 hole

Singles

Jill Thornhill halved with Joanne Pacillo
Claire Waite lost to Penny Hammel 4 and 2
Claire Hourihane lost to Jody Rosenthal 3 and 1
Vicki Thomas beat Dana Howe 2 and 1
Penny Grice beat Anne Quast Sander 2 holes
Beverley New lost to Mary Anne Widman 4 and 3

Second Day: Foursomes

New & Waite lost to Rosenthal & Smith 3 and 1
Grice & Thornhill beat Farr & Widman 2 and 1
Hourihane & Thomas halved with Hammel & Howe

Singles

Thornhill lost to Pacillo 3 and 2
Laura Davies beat Sander 1 hole
Waite beat Lancy Smith 5 and 4
Grice lost to Howe 2 holes
New lost to Heather Farr 6 and 5
Hourihane beat Hammel 2 and 1

1982 *Denver, CO* Aug 5–6

Result: USA 14½, GB&I 3½

Captains: Betty Probasco (USA), Maire O'Donnell (GB&I)

First Day: Foursomes

Inkster & Semple beat McKenna & Robertson 5 and 4
Baker & Smith halved with Douglas & Soulsby
Benz & Hanlon beat Connachan & Stewart 2 and 1

Singles

Amy Benz beat Mary McKenna 2 and 1
Cathy Hanlon beat Jane Connachan 5 and 4
Mari McDougall beat Wilma Aitken 2 holes
Kathy Baker beat Belle McCorkindale Robertson 7 and 6
Judy Oliver lost to Janet Soulsby 2 holes
Juli Inkster beat Kitrina Douglas 7 and 6

Second Day: Foursomes

Inkster & Semple beat Aitken & Connachan 3 and 2
Baker & Smith beat Douglas & Soulsby 1 hole
Benz & Hanlon lost to McKenna & Robertson 1 hole

Singles

Inkster beat Douglas 7 and 6
Baker beat Gillian Stewart 4 and 3
Oliver beat Vicki Thomas 5 and 4
McDougall beat Soulsby 2 and 1
Carol Semple beat McKenna 1 hole
Lancy Smith lost to Robertson 5 and 4

1980 *St Pierre, Chepstow* June 6–7

Result: USA 13, GB&I 5

Captains: Carol Comboy (GB&I), Nancy Roth Syms (USA)

First Day: Foursomes

McKenna & Nesbitt halved with Terri Moody & Smith
Stewart & Thomas lost to Castillo & Sheehan 5 and 3
Caldwell & Madill halved with Oliver & Semple

Singles

Mary McKenna lost to Patty Sheehan 3 and 2
Claire Nesbitt halved with Lancy Smith
Jane Connachan lost to Brenda Goldsmith 2 holes
Maureen Madill lost to Carol Semple 4 and 3
Linda Moore halved with Mary Hafeman
Carole Caldwell lost to Judy Oliver 1 hole

Second Day: Foursomes

Caldwell & Madill lost to Castillo & Sheehan 3 and 2
McKenna & Nesbitt lost to Moody & Smith 6 and 5
Moore & Thomas lost to Oliver & Semple 1 hole

Singles

Madill lost to Sheehan 5 and 4
McKenna beat Lori Castillo 5 and 4
Connachan lost to Hafeman 6 and 5
Gillian Stewart beat Smith 5 and 4
Moore beat Goldsmith 1 hole
Tegwen Perkins Thomas lost to Semple 4 and 3

1978 *Apawamis, NY* Aug 4–5

Result: USA 12, GB&I 6

Captains: Helen Wilson (USA), Carol Comboy (GB&I)

First Day: Foursomes

Daniel & Brenda Goldsmith lost to Greenhalgh & Marvin 3 and 2
Cindy Hill & Smith lost to Everard & Thomson 2 and 1
Cornett & Carolyn Hill halved with McKenna & Perkins

Singles

Beth Daniel beat Vanessa Marvin 5 and 4
Noreen Uihlein lost to Mary Everard 7 and 6
Lancy Smith beat Angela Uzielli 4 and 3
Cindy Hill beat Julia Greenhalgh 2 and 1
Carolyn Hill halved with Carole Caldwell
Judy Oliver beat Tegwen Perkins 2 and 1

Second Day: Foursomes

Cindy Hill & Smith beat Everard & Thomson 1 hole
Daniel & Goldsmith beat McKenna & Perkins 1 hole
Oliver & Uihlein beat Greenhalgh & Marvin 4 and 3

Singles

Daniel beat Mary McKenna 2 and 1
Patricia Cornett beat Caldwell 3 and 2
Cindy Hill lost to Muriel Thomson 2 and 1
Lancy Smith beat Perkins 2 holes
Oliver halved with Greenhalgh
Uihlein halved with Everard

1976 *Royal Lytham & St Annes* June 11–12

Result: USA 11½, GB&I 6½

Captains: Belle McCorkindale Robertson (GB&I), Barbara McIntyre (USA)

First Day: Foursomes

Greenhalgh & McKenna lost to Daniel & Hill 3 and 2
Cadden & Henson lost to Horton & Massey 6 and 5
Irvin & Perkins beat Semple & Syms 3 and 2

Singles

Ann Irvin lost to Beth Daniel 4 and 3
Dinah Oxley Henson beat Cindy Hill 1 hole
Suzanne Cadden lost to Nancy Lopez 3 and 1
Mary McKenna lost to Nancy Roth Syms 1 hole
Tegwen Perkins lost to Debbie Massey 1 hole
Julia Greenhalgh halved with Barbara Barrow

Second Day: Foursomes

Cadden & Irvin lost to Daniel & Hill 4 and 3
Henson & Perkins beat Semple & Syms 2 and 1
McKenna & Anne Stant lost to Barrow & Lopez 4 and 3

Singles
Henson lost to Daniel 3 and 2
Greenhalgh beat Syms 2 and 1
Cadden lost to Donna Horton 6 and 5
Jennie Lee-Smith lost to Massey 3 and 2
Perkins beat Hill 1 hole
McKenna beat Carol Semple 1 hole

1974 *San Francisco, CA* Aug 2–3
Result: USA 13, GB&I 5
Captains: Sis Choate (USA), Belle McCorkindale Robertson (GB&I)

First Day: Foursomes
Hill & Semple halved with Greenhalgh & McKenna
Booth & Sander beat Lee-Smith & LeFeuvre 6 and 5
Budke & Lauer lost to Everard & Walker 5 and 4

Singles
Carol Semple lost to Mickey Walker 2 and 1
Jane Bastanchury Booth beat Mary McKenna 5 and 3
Debbie Massey beat Mary Everard 1 hole
Bonnie Lauer beat Jennie Lee-Smith 6 and 5
Beth Barry beat Julia Greenhalgh 1 hole
Cindy Hill halved with Tegwen Perkins

Second Day: Foursomes
Booth & Sander beat McKenna & Walker 5 and 4
Budke & Lauer beat Everard & LeFeuvre 5 and 3
Hill & Semple lost to Greenhalgh & Perkins 3 and 2

Singles
Anne Quast Sander beat Everard 4 and 3
Booth beat Greenhalgh 7 and 5
Massey beat Carol LeFeuvre 6 and 5
Semple beat Walker 2 and 1
Mary Budke beat Perkins 5 and 4
Lauer lost to McKenna 2 and 1

1972 *Western Gailes* June 9–10
Result: USA 10, GB&I 8
Captains: Frances Stephens Smith (GB&I), Jean Ashley Crawford (USA)

First Day: Foursomes
Everard & Beverly Huke lost to Baugh & Kirouac 2 and 1
Frearson & Robertson beat Booth & McIntyre 2 and 1
McKenna & Walker beat Barry & Hollis Stacy 1 hole

Singles
Mickey Walker halved with Laura Baugh
Belle McCorkindale Robertson lost to Jane Bastanchury Booth 3 and 1
Mary Everard lost to Martha Wilkinson Kirouac 4 and 3
Dinah Oxley lost to Barbara McIntire 4 and 3
Kathryn Phillips beat Lancy Smith 2 holes
Mary McKenna lost to Beth Barry 2 and 1

Second Day: Foursomes
McKenna & Walker beat Baugh & Kirouac 3 and 2
Everard & Huke lost to Booth & McIntyre 5 and 4
Frearson & Robertson halved with Barry & Stacy

Singles
Robertson lost to Baugh 6 and 5
Everard beat McIntyre 6 and 5
Walker beat Booth 1 hole
McKenna beat Kirouac 3 and 1
Diane Frearson lost to Smith 3 and 1
Phillips lost to Barry 3 and 1

1970 *Brae Burn, MA* Aug 7–8
Result: USA 11½, GB&I 6½
Captains: Carolyn Cudone (USA), Jeanne Bisgood (GB&I)

First Day: Foursomes
Bastanchury & Hamlin lost to McKenna & Oxley 4 and 3
Preuss & Wilkinson beat Irvin & Robertson 4 and 3
Jane Fassinger & Hill lost to Everard & Greenhalgh 5 and 3

Singles
Jane Bastanchury beat Dinah Oxley 5 and 3
Martha Wilkinson beat Ann Irvin 1 hole
Shelley Hamlin halved with Belle McCorkindale Robertson
Phyllis Preuss lost to Mary McKenna 4 and 2
Nancy Hager beat Margaret Pickard 5 and 4
Alice Dye beat Julia Greenhalgh 1 hole

Second Day: Foursomes
Preuss & Wilkinson beat McKenna & Oxley 6 and 4
Dye & Hill halved with Everard & Greenhalgh
Bastanchury & Hamlin beat Irvin & Robertson 1 hole

Singles
Bastanchury beat Irvin 4 and 3
Hamlin halved with Oxley
Preuss beat Robertson 1 hole
Wilkinson lost to Greenhalgh 6 and 4
Hager lost to Mary Everard 4 and 3
Cindy Hill beat McKenna 2 and 1

1968 *Newcastle, Co Down* June 14–15
Result: USA 10½, GB&I 7½
Captains: Zara Bolton (GB&I), Evelyn Monsted (USA)

First Day: Foursomes
Irvin & Robertson beat Hamlin & Welts 6 and 5
Pickard & Saunders beat Conley & Dill 3 and 2
Howard & Pam Tredinnick lost to Ashley & Preuss 1 hole

Singles
Ann Irvin beat Anne Quast Welts 3 and 2
Vivien Saunders lost to Shelley Hamlin 1 hole
Belle McCorkindale Robertson lost to Roberta Albers 1 hole
Bridget Jackson halved with Peggy Conley
Dinah Oxley halved with Phyllis Preuss
Margaret Pickard beat Jean Ashley 2 holes

Second Day: Foursomes
Oxley & Tredinnick lost to Ashley & Preuss 5 and 4
Irvin & Robertson halved with Conley & Dill
Pickard & Saunders lost to Hamlin & Welts 2 and 1

Singles
Irvin beat Hamlin 3 and 2
Robertson halved with Welts
Saunders halved with Albers
Ann Howard lost to Mary Lou Dill 4 and 2
Pickard lost to Conley 1 hole
Jackson lost to Preuss 2 and 1

1966 *Hot Springs, VA* July 29–30
Result: USA 13, GB&I 5
Captains: Dorothy Germain Porter (USA), Zara Bolton (GB&I)

First Day: Foursomes
Ashley & Preuss beat Armitage & Bonallack 1 hole
Barbara McIntire & Welts halved with Joan Hastings & Robertson
Boddie & Flenniken beat Chadwick & Tredinnick 1 hole

1966 *continued*

Singles
Jean Ashley beat Belle McCorkindale Robertson 1 hole
Anne Quast Welts halved with Susan Armitage
Barbara White Boddie beat Angela Ward Bonallack 3 and 2
Nancy Roth Syms beat Elizabeth Chadwick 2 holes
Helen Wilson lost to Ita Burke 3 and 1
Carol Sorenson Flenniken beat Marjory Fowler 3 and 1

Second Day: Foursomes
Ashley & Preuss beat Armitage & Bonallack 2 and 1
McIntire & Welts lost to Burke & Chadwick 1 hole
Boddie & Flenniken beat Hastings & Robertson 2 and 1

Singles
Ashley lost to Bonallack 2 and 1
Welts halved with Robertson
Boddie beat Armitage 3 and 2
Syms halved with Pam Tredinnick
Phyllis Preuss beat Chadwick 3 and 2
Flenniken beat Burke 2 and 1

1964 *Porthcawl* Sept 11–12

Result: USA 10½, GB&I 1½
Captains: Elsie Corlett (GB&I), Helen Hawes (USA)

First Day: Foursomes
Spearman & Bonallack beat McIntyre & Preuss 2 and 1
Sheila Vaughan & Porter beat Gunderson & Roth 3 and 2
Jackson & Susan Armitage lost to Sorenson & White 8 and 6

Singles
Angela Ward Bonallack lost to JoAnne Gunderson 6 and 5
Marley Spearman halved with Barbara McIntyre
Julia Greenhalgh lost to Barbara White 3 and 2
Bridget Jackson beat Carol Sorenson 4 and 3
Joan Lawrence lost to Peggy Conley 1 hole
Ruth Porter beat Nancy Roth 1 hole

Second Day: Foursomes
Spearman & Bonallack beat McIntyre & Preuss 6 and 5
Armitage & Jackson lost to Gunderson & Roth 2 holes
Porter & Vaughan halved with Sorenson & White

Singles
Spearman halved with Gunderson
Lawrence lost to McIntyre 4 and 2
Greenhalgh beat Phyllis Preuss 5 and 3
Bonallack lost to White 3 and 2
Porter lost to Sorenson 3 and 2
Jackson lost to Conley 1 hole

1962 *Broadmoor, CO* Aug 17–18

Result: USA 8, GB&I 1
Captains: Polly Riley (USA), Frances Stephens Smith (GB&I)

Foursomes
Decker & McIntyre beat Spearman & Bonallack 7 and 5
Jean Ashley & Anna Johnstone beat Ruth Porter & Frearson 8 and 7
Creed & Gunderson beat Vaughan & Ann Irvin 4 and 3

Singles
Judy Bell lost to Diane Frearson 8 and 7
JoAnne Gunderson beat Angela Ward Bonallack 2 and 1
Clifford Ann Creed beat Sally Bonallack 6 and 5
Anne Quast Decker beat Marley Spearman 7 and 5
Phyllis Preuss beat Jean Roberts 1 hole
Barbara McIntyre beat Sheila Vaughan 5 and 4

1960 *Lindrick* May 20–21

Result: USA 6½, GB&I 2½
Captains: Maureen Garrett (GB&I), Mildred Prunaret (USA)

Foursomes
Price & Bonallack beat Gunderson & McIntyre 1 hole
Robertson & McCorkindale lost to Eller & Quast 4 and 2
Frances Smith & Porter lost to Goodwin & Anna Johnstone 3 and 2

Singles
Elizabeth Price halved with Barbara McIntyre
Angela Ward Bonallack lost to JoAnne Gunderson 2 and 1
Janette Robertson lost to Anne Quast 2 holes
Philomena Garvey lost to Judy Eller 4 and 3
Belle McCorkindale lost to Judy Bell 8 and 7
Ruth Porter beat Joanne Goodwin 1 hole

1958 *Brae Burn, MA* Aug 8–9

Result: GB&I 4½, USA 4½
Captains: Virginia Dennehy (USA), Daisy Ferguson (GB&I)

Foursomes
Riley & Romack lost to Bonallack & Price 2 and 1
Gunderson & Quast lost to Robertson & Smith 3 and 2
Johnstone & McIntire beat Jackson & Valentine 6 and 5

Singles
JoAnne Gunderson beat Jessie Anderson Valentine 2 holes
Barbara McIntire halved with Angela Ward Bonallack
Anne Quast beat Elizabeth Price 4 and 2
Anna Johnstone lost to Janette Robertson 3 and 2
Barbara Romack beat Bridget Jackson 3 and 2
Polly Riley lost to Frances Stephens Smith 2 holes

1956 *Prince's, Sandwich* June 8–9

Result: GB&I 5, USA 4
Captains: Zara Davis Bolton (GB&I), Edith Flippin (USA)

Foursomes
Valentine & Garvey lost to Lesser & Smith 2 and 1
Smith & Price beat Riley & Romack 5 and 3
Robertson & Veronica Anstey lost to Downey & Carolyn Cudone 6 and 4

Singles
Jessie Anderson Valentine beat Patricia Lesser 6 and 4
Philomena Garvey lost to Margaret Smith 9 and 8
Frances Stephens Smith beat Polly Riley 1 hole
Janette Robertson lost to Barbara Romack 6 and 4
Angela Ward beat Mary Ann Downey 6 and 4
Elizabeth Price beat Jane Nelson 7 and 6

1954 *Merion, PA* Sept 2–3

Result: USA 6, GB&I 3
Captains: Edith Flippin (USA), Mrs JB Beck (GB&I)

Foursomes
Faulk & Riley beat Stephens & Price 6 and 4
Doran & Patricia Lesser beat Garvey & Valentine 6 and 5
Kirby & Barbara Romack beat Marjorie Peel & Robertson 6 and 5

Singles
Mary Lena Faulk lost to Frances Stephens 1 hole
Claire Doran beat Jeanne Bisgood 4 and 3
Polly Riley beat Elizabeth Price 9 and 8
Dorothy Kirby lost to Philomena Garvey 3 and 1
Grace DeMoss Smith beat Jessie Anderson Valentine 4 and 3
Joyce Ziske lost to Janette Robertson 3 and 1

1952 *Muirfield* June 6–7

Result: GB&I 5, USA 4

Captains: Lady Katherine Cairns (GB&I), Aniela Goldthwaite (USA)

Foursomes

Donald & Price beat Kirby & DeMoss 3 and 2
Stephens & JA Valentine lost to Doran & Lindsay 6 and 4
Paterson & Garvey beat Riley & Patricia O'Sullivan 2 and 1

Singles

Jean Donald lost to Dorothy Kirby 1 hole
Frances Stephens beat Marjorie Lindsay 2 and 1
Moira Paterson lost to Polly Riley 6 and 4
Jeanne Bisgood beat Mae Murray 6 and 5
Philomena Garvey lost to Claire Doran 3 and 2
Elizabeth Price beat Grace DeMoss 3 and 2

1950 *Buffalo, NY* Sept 4–5

Result: USA 7½, GB&I 1½

Captains: Glenna Collett Vare (USA), Diana Fishwick Critchley (GB&I)

Foursomes

Hanson & Porter beat Valentine & Donald 3 and 2
Helen Sigel & Kirk lost to Stephens & Price 1 hole
Dorothy Kirby & Kielty beat Garvey & Bisgood 6 and 5

Singles

Dorothy Porter halved with Frances Stephens
Polly Riley beat Jessie Anderson Valentine 7 and 6
Beverly Hanson beat Jean Donald 6 and 5
Dorothy Kielty beat Philomena Garvey 2 and 1
Peggy Kirk beat Jeanne Bisgood 1 hole
Grace Lenczyk beat Elizabeth Price 5 and 4

1948 *Birkdale* May 21–22

Result: USA 6½, GB&I 2½

Captains: Doris Chambers (GB&I), Glenna Collett Vare (USA)

Foursomes

Donald & Gordon beat Suggs & Lenczyk 3 and 2
Garvey & Bolton lost to Kirby & Vare 4 and 3
Ruttle & Val Reddan lost to Page & Kielty 5 and 4

Singles

Philomena Garvey halved with Louise Suggs
Jean Donald beat Dorothy Kirby 2 holes
Jacqueline Gordon lost to Grace Lenczyk 5 and 3
Helen Holm lost to Estelle Lawson Page 3 and 2
Maureen Ruttle lost to Polly Riley 3 and 2
Zara Bolton lost to Dorothy Kielty 2 and 1

1938 *Essex, MA* Sept 7–8

Result: USA 5½, GB&I 3½

Captains: Frances Stebbins (USA), Mrs RH Wallace-Williamson (GB&I)

Foursomes

Page & Orcutt lost to Holm & Tiernan 2 holes
Vare & Berg lost to Anderson & Corlett 1 hole
Miley & Kathryn Hemphill halved with Walker & Phyllis Wade

Singles

Estelle Lawson Page beat Helen Holm 6 and 5
Patty Berg beat Jessie Anderson 1 hole
Marion Miley beat Elsie Corlett 2 and 1
Glenna Collett Vare beat Charlotte Walker 2 and 1
Maureen Orcutt lost to Clarrie Tiernan 2 and 1
Charlotte Glutting beat Nan Baird 1 hole

1936 *Gleneagles* May 6

Result: USA 4½, GB&I 4½

Captains: Doris Chambers (GB&I), Glenna Collett Vare (USA)

Foursomes

Morgan & Garon halved with Vare & Berg
Barton & Walker lost to Orcutt & Cheney 2 and 1
Anderson & Holm beat Hill & Glutting 3 and 2

Singles

Wanda Morgan lost to Glenna Collett Vare 3 and 2
Helen Holm beat Patty Berg 4 and 3
Pamela Barton lost to Charlotte Glutting 1 hole
Charlotte Walker lost to Maureen Orcutt 1 hole
Jessie Anderson beat Leona Pressley Cheney 1 hole
Marjorie Garon beat Opal Hill 7 and 5

1934 *Chevy Chase, MD* Sept 27–28

Result: USA 6½, GB&I 2½

Captains: Glenna Collett Vare (USA), Doris Chambers (GB&I)

Foursomes

Van Wie & Glutting halved with Gourlay & Barton
Orcutt & Cheney beat Fishwick & Morgan 2 holes
Hill & Lucille Robinson lost to Plumpton & Walker 2 and 1

Singles

Virginia Van Wie beat Diana Fishwick 2 and 1
Maureen Orcutt beat Molly Gourlay 4 and 2
Leona Pressley Cheney beat Pamela Barton 7 and 5
Charlotte Glutting beat Wanda Morgan
Opal Hill beat Diana Plumpton 3 and 2
Aniela Goldthwaite lost to Charlotte Walker 3 and 2

1932 *Wentworth* May 21

Result: USA 5½, GB&I 3½

Captains: J Wethered (GB&I), M Hollins (USA)

Foursomes

Wethered & Morgan lost to Vare & Hill 1 hole
Wilson & JB Watson lost to Van Wie & Hicks 2 and 1
Gourlay & Doris Park lost to Orcutt & Cheney 1 hole

Singles

Joyce Wethered beat Glenna Collett Vare 6 and 4
Enid Wilson beat Helen Hicks 2 and 1
Wanda Morgan lost to Virginia Van Wie 2 and 1
Diana Fishwick beat Maureen Orcutt 4 and 3
Molly Gourlay halved with Opal Hill
Elsie Corlett lost to Leona Pressley Cheney 4 and 3

Mexico to host 2016 World Amateur Team Championships

Mexico has been chosen as the 2016 venue for the 30th Eisenhower Trophy and the 27th Espirito Santo events – the world amateur team championships. El Camaleon GC at the Fairmont Mayakoba and the Grand Coral Riviera Maya Resort will be used for both events. Mexico last held the Championships in 1966 in Mexico City. The 2014 Championships are set for Karuizawa in Japan.

Curtis Cup INDIVIDUAL RECORDS

Bold print: captain; bold print in brackets: non-playing captain
Maiden name in parentheses, former surname in square brackets

Great Britain and Ireland

Name		Year	Played	Won	Lost	Halved
Jean Anderson (Donald)	SCO	1948	6	3	3	0
Kim Andrew (Rostron)	ENG	1998-2000	8	2	6	0
Diane Bailey [Frearson] (Robb)	ENG	1962-72-(**84**)-(**86**)-(**88**)	5	2	2	1
Sally Barber (Bonallack)	ENG	1962	1	0	1	0
Pam Barton	ENG	1934-36	4	0	3	1
Hannah Barwood	ENG	2010	3	0	2	1
Linda Bayman	ENG	1988	4	2	1	1
Baba Beck (Pym)	IRL	(**1954**)	0	0	0	0
Charlotte Beddows [Watson] (Stevenson)	SCO	1932	1	0	1	0
Lilian Behan	IRL	1986	4	3	1	0
Veronica Beharrell (Anstey)	ENG	1956	1	0	1	0
Pam Benka (Tredinnick)	ENG	1966-68 (**2002**)	4	0	3	1
Elizabeth Bennett	ENG	2008	5	0	4	1
Jeanne Bisgood	ENG	1950-52-54-(**70**)	4	1	3	0
Elizabeth Boatman (Collis)	ENG	(**1992**)-(**94**)	0	0	0	0
Zara Bolton (Davis)	ENG	1948-(**56**)-(**66**)-(**68**)	2	0	2	0
Angela Bonallack (Ward)	ENG	1956-58-60-62-64-66	15	6	8	1
Carly Booth	SCO	2008	4	1	3	0
Amy Boulden	WAL	2012	8	4	3	1
Becky Brewerton	WAL	2000	3	1	2	0
Fiona Brown	ENG	1998-2000	4	2	2	0
Ita Butler (Burke)	IRL	1966-(**96**)	3	2	1	0
Lady Katherine Cairns	ENG	(1952)	0	0	0	0
Krystle Caithness	SCO	2008	3	3	0	0
Carole Caldwell (Redford)	ENG	1978-80	5	0	3	2
Doris Chambers	ENG	(**1934**)-(**36**)-(**48**)	0	0	0	0
Holly Clyburn	ENG	2010-12	5	1	1	1
Alison Coffey	IRL	2002	3	1	2	0
Carol Comboy (Grott)	ENG	(**1978**)-(**80**)	0	0	0	0
Jane Connachan	SCO	1980-82	5	0	5	0
Elsie Corlett	ENG	1932-38-(**64**)	3	1	2	0
Claire Coughlan	IRL	2004-06	5	3	2	0
Diana Critchley (Fishwick)	ENG	1932-34-(**50**)	3	1	2	0
Alison Davidson (Rose)	SCO	1996-98	7	4	3	0
Karen Davies	WAL	1986-88	7	4	1	2
Laura Davies	ENG	1984	2	1	1	0
Tara Delanbey	ENG	2006	3	0	2	1
Lisa Dermott	WAL	1996	2	2	0	0
Helen Dobson	ENG	1990	3	1	2	0
Kitrina Douglas	ENG	1982	4	0	3	1
Claire Dowling (Hourihane)	IRL	1984-86-88-90-92-(**2000**)	8	3	3	2
Marjorie Draper [Peel] (Thomas)	SCO	1954	1	0	1	0
Emma Duggleby	ENG	2000-04	8	5	2	1
Lisa Educate (Walton)	ENG	1994-96	6	3	3	0
Naomi Edwards	ENG	2006	3	1	2	0
Mary Everard	ENG	1970-72-74-78	15	6	7	2
Jodi Ewart	ENG	2008	3	0	2	1
Elaine Farquharson	SCO	1990-92	6	1	5	0
Daisy Ferguson	IRL	(**1958**)	0	0	0	0
Marjory Ferguson (Fowler)	SCO	1966	1	0	1	0
Elizabeth Price Fisher (Price)	ENG	1950-52-54-56-58-60	12	7	4	1
Linzi Fletcher	ENG	1990	1	0	1	0
Maureen Garner (Madill)	IRL	1980	4	0	3	1
Marjorie Ross Garon	ENG	1936	2	1	0	1
Maureen Garrett (Ruttle)	ENG	1948-(**60**)	2	0	2	0
Philomena Garvey	IRL	1948-50-52-54-56-60	11	2	8	1
Carol Gibbs (Le Feuvre)	ENG	1974	3	0	3	0
Martine Gillen	IRL	2006	4	2	2	0
Jacqueline Gordon	ENG	1948	2	1	1	0
Molly Gourlay	ENG	1932-34	4	0	2	2
Julia Greenhalgh	ENG	1964-70-74-76-78	17	6	7	4
Penny Grice-Whittaker (Grice)	ENG	1984	4	2	1	1
Caroline Hall	ENG	1992	4	2	0	2

Name		Year	Played	Won	Lost	Halved
Marley Harris [Spearman] (Baker)	ENG	1962-64	6	2	2	2
Dorothea Hastings (Sommerville)	SCO	1958	0	0	0	0
Lady Heathcoat-Amory (Joyce Wethered)	ENG	**1932**	2	1	1	0
Dinah Henson (Oxley)	ENG	1968-70-72-76	11	3	6	2
Anna Highgate	WAL	2004	1	0	1	0
Helen Holm (Gray)	SCO	1936-38-48	5	3	2	0
Ann Howard (Phillips)	ENG	1956-68	2	0	2	0
Rebecca Hudson	ENG	1998-2000-02	11	5	5	1
Shirley Huggan (Lawson)	SCO	1988	2	1	1	0
Beverley Huke	ENG	1972	2	0	2	0
Charley Hull	ENG	2012	3	1	2	0
Ann Irvin	ENG	1962-68-70-76	12	4	7	1
Bridget Jackson	ENG	1958-64-68	8	1	6	1
Rachel Jennings	ENG	2010	5	0	4	1
Patricia Johnson	ENG	1986	4	4	0	0
Sarah Jones	WAL	2002	2	1	1	0
Anne Laing	SCO	2004	4	3	1	0
Vikki Laing	SCO	2002	4	2	2	0
Susan Langridge (Armitage)	ENG	1964-66	6	0	5	1
Bronte Law	ENG	2012	4	1	2	1
Joan Lawrence	SCO	1964	2	0	2	0
Wilma Leburn (Aitken)	SCO	1982	2	0	2	0
Jenny Lee Smith	ENG	1974-76	3	0	3	0
Breanne Loucks	WAL	2006-08	7	4	3	0
Kathryn Lumb (Phillips)	ENG	1970-72	2	1	1	0
Leona Maquire	IRL	2010-12	9	2	5	2
Lisa Maquire	IRL	2010	3	2	1	0
Mhairi McKay	SCO	1994-96	7	2	3	2
Mary McKenna	IRL	1970-72-74-76-78-80-82-84-86-(**2008-10**)	30	10	16	4
Shelley McKevitt	ENG	2004	4	2	2	0
Myra McKinlay	SCO	1994	3	1	2	0
Suzanne McMahon (Cadden)	SCO	1976	4	0	4	0
Danielle McVeigh	IRL	2010	5	2	2	1
Sheila Maher (Vaughan)	ENG	1962-64	4	1	2	1
Tricia Mangan	IRL	2006	3	0	2	1
Kathryn Marshall (Imrie)	SCO	1990	4	1	3	0
Vanessa Marvin	ENG	1978	4	1	3	0
Danielle Masters	ENG	2004	3	1	2	0
Kiran Matharu	ENG	2006	2	1	1	0
Catriona Matthew (Lambert)	SCO	1990-92-94	12	7	4	1
Tegwen Matthews [Thomas] (Perkins)	WAL	1974-76-78-80-(**2012**)	14	4	8	2
Stephanie Meadow	NIR	2012	4	3	1	0
Moira Milton (Paterson)	SCO	1952	2	1	1	0
Hilary Monaghan	SCO	1998	1	0	1	0
Janice Moodie	SCO	1994-96	8	5	1	2
Fame More	ENG	2002-04	2	0	2	0
Becky Morgan	WAL	1998-2000	7	2	5	0
Wanda Morgan	ENG	1932-34-36	6	0	5	1
Joanne Morley	ENG	1992	4	2	0	2
Nicola Murray (Buxton)	ENG	1992	1	0	1	0
Beverley New	ENG	1984	4	1	3	0
Lesley Nicholson	SCO	2000	1	0	0	1
Suzanne O'Brien	IRL	2000	4	3	0	1
Maire O'Donnell	IRL	(**1982**)	0	0	0	0
Ada O'Sullivan	IRL	(**2004-06**)	0	0	0	0
Florentyna Parker	ENG	2008	4	1	3	0
Margaret Pickard (Nichol)	ENG	1968-70	5	2	3	0
Diana Plumpton	ENG	1934	2	1	1	0
Elizabeth Pook (Chadwick)	ENG	1966	4	1	3	0
Doris Porter (Park)	SCO	1932	1	0	1	0
Pamela Pretswell	SCO	2010-12	7	2	5	0
Eileen Rose Power (McDaid)	IRL	1994	1	0	1	0
Elaine Ratcliffe	ENG	1996-98	6	3	1	2
Clarrie Reddan (Tiernan)	IRL	1938-48	3	2	1	0
Joan Rennie (Hastings)	SCO	1966	2	0	1	1
Melissa Reid	ENG	2006	4	1	3	0
Maureen Richmond (Walker)	SCO	1974	4	2	2	0
Jean Roberts	ENG	1962	1	0	1	0

Name		Year	Played	Won	Lost	Halved
Belle Robertson (McCorkindale)	SCO	1960-66-68-70-72-(**74**)-(**76**)-82-86	24	5	12	7
Claire Robinson (Nesbitt)	IRL	1980	3	0	1	2
Vivien Saunders	ENG	1968	4	1	2	1
Susan Shapcott	ENG	1988	4	3	1	0
Linda Simpson (Moore)	ENG	1980	3	1	1	1
Ruth Slark (Porter)	ENG	1960-62-64	7	3	3	1
Anne Smith [Stant] (Willard)	ENG	1976	1	0	1	0
Frances Smith (Stephens)	ENG	1950-52-54-56-58-60-(**62**)-(**72**)	11	7	3	1
Kerry Smith	ENG	2002	2	0	2	0
Janet Soulsby	ENG	1982	4	1	2	1
Kirsty Speak	ENG	1994	1	0	1	0
Gillian Stewart	SCO	1980-82	4	1	3	0
Heather Stirling	SCO	2002	4	1	3	0
Karen Stupples	ENG	1996-98	4	2	2	0
Vicki Thomas (Rawlings)	WAL	1982-84-86-88-90-92	13	6	5	2
Michele Thomson	SCO	2008	4	1	2	1
Muriel Thomson	SCO	1978	3	2	1	0
Jill Thornhill	ENG	1984-86-88	12	6	2	4
Kelly Tidy	ENG	2012	4	3	1	0
Nicola Timmins	ENG	2004	3	1	2	0
Angela Uzielli (Carrick)	ENG	1978	1	0	1	0
Jessie Valentine (Anderson)	SCO	1936-38-50-52-54-56-58	13	4	9	0
Julie Wade	ENG	1988-90-92-94-96	19	6	10	3
Helen Wadsworth	WAL	1990	2	0	2	0
Claire Waite	ENG	1984	4	2	2	0
Mickey Walker	ENG	1972-74	4	3	0	1
Pat Walker	IRL	1934-36-38	6	2	3	1
Verona Wallace-Williamson	SCO	(**1938**)	0	0	0	0
Nan Wardlaw (Baird)	SCO	1938	1	0	1	0
Sally Watson	SCO	2008-10	10	4	5	1
Enid Wilson	ENG	1932	2	1	1	0
Janette Wright (Robertson)	SCO	1954-56-58-60	8	3	5	0
Phyllis Wylie (Wade)	ENG	1938	1	0	0	1

United States of America

Name	Year	Played	Won	Lost	Halved
Roberta Albers	1968	2	1	0	1
Danielle Ammaccapane	1986	3	0	3	0
Amy Anderson	2012	5	3	2	0
Kathy Baker	1982	4	3	0	1
Barbara Barrow	1976	2	1	0	1
Beth Barry	1972-74	5	3	1	1
Emily Bastel	2002	2	0	2	0
Beth Bauer	1998-2000	7	4	3	0
Laura Baugh	1972	4	2	1	1
Leland Beckel	2000	1	0	1	0
Judy Bell	1960-62-(**86**)-(**88**)	2	1	1	0
Peggy Kirk Bell (Kirk)	1950	2	1	1	0
Amy Benz	1982	3	2	1	0
Patty Berg	1936-38	4	1	2	1
Erica Blasberg	2004	2	1	2	1
Amanda Blumenherst	2006-08	8	4	3	1
Barbara Fay Boddie (White)	1964-66	8	7	0	1
Meghan Bolger	2008	3	0	3	0
Jane Booth (Bastanchury)	1970-72-74-(**2000**)	12	9	3	0
Kellee Booth	1996-98	7	5	2	0
Mary Budke	1974-(**2002**)	3	2	1	0
Robin Burke	1998	3	2	1	0
Brandie Burton	1990	3	3	0	0
Jo Anne Carner (Gunderson)	1958-60-62-64	10	6	3	1
Lori Castillo	1980	3	2	1	0
Leona Cheney (Pressler)	1932-34-36	6	5	1	0
Sis Choate	(**1974**)	0	0	0	0
Jenny Chuasiriporn	1998	3	0	2	1
Cydney Clanton	2010	3	2	0	1
Peggy Conley	1964-68	6	3	1	2
Mary Ann Cook (Downey)	1956	2	1	1	0
Patricia Cornett	1978-88-(**2012**)	4	1	2	1
Brenda Corrie Kuehn	1996-98	7	4	3	0

Name	Year	Played	Won	Lost	Halved
ean Crawford (Ashley)	1962-66-68-(**72**)	8	6	2	0
Paula Creamer	2004	3	2	1	0
Clifford Ann Creed	1962	2	2	0	0
Grace Cronin (Lenczyk)	1948-50	3	2	1	0
Carolyn Cudone	1956-(**70**)	1	1	0	0
Beth Daniel	1976-78	8	7	1	0
Virginia Dennehy	(**1958**)	0	0	0	0
Virginia Derby Grimes	1998-2000	6	3	1	2
Mary Lou Dill	1968	3	1	1	1
Lindy Duncan	2012	4	1	3	0
Meredith Duncan	2002	4	3	1	0
Alice Dye	1970	2	1	0	1
Austin Ernst	2012	4	2	1	1
Mollie Fankhauser	2002	3	1	2	0
Heather Farr	1984	3	2	1	0
Jane Fassinger	1970	1	0	1	0
Mary Lena Faulk	1954	2	1	1	0
Carol Sorensen Flenniken (Sorensen)	1964-66	8	6	1	1
Edith Flippin (Quier)	(**1954**)-(**56**)	0	0	0	0
Amy Fruhwirth	1992	4	0	1	3
Kim Gardner	1986	3	1	1	1
Charlotte Glutting	1934-36-38	5	3	1	1
Vicki Goetze	1990-92	8	4	2	2
Brenda Goldsmith	1978-80	4	2	2	0
Aniela Goldthwaite	1934-(**52**)	1	0	1	0
Joanne Goodwin	1960	2	1	1	0
Virginia Grimes	2006	2	1	1	0
Mary Hafeman	1980	2	1	0	1
Shelley Hamkin	1968-70	8	3	3	2
Penny Hammel	1984	3	1	1	1
Nancy Hammer (Hager)	1970	2	1	1	0
Cathy Hanlon	1982	3	2	1	0
Beverley Hanson	1950	2	2	0	0
Tracy Hanson	1992	3	1	2	0
Patricia Harbottle (Lesser)	1954-56	3	2	1	0
Leigh Anne Hardin	2002	3	1	2	0
Mina Harigae	2008	4	2	2	0
Helen Hawes	(**1964**)	0	0	0	0
Kathryn Hemphill	1938	1	0	0	1
Helen Hicks	1932	2	1	1	0
Carolyn Hill	1978	2	0	0	2
Cindy Hill	1970-74-76-78	14	5	6	3
Opel Hill	1932-34-36	6	2	3	1
Marion Hollins	(**1932**)	0	0	0	0
Hilary Homeyer	2000	4	3	0	1
Dana Howe	1984	3	1	1	1
Sarah Huarte	2004	2	0	2	0
Juli Inkster	1982	4	4	0	0
Elizabeth Janangelo	2004	3	1	2	0
Maria Jemsek	1996	3	0	2	1
Angela Jerman	2002	3	2	1	0
Tiffany Joh	2008	4	2	1	1
Jennifer Johnson	2010	4	3	0	1
Ann Casey Johnstone	1958-60-62	4	3	1	0
Mae Murray Jones (Murray)	1952	1	0	1	0
Wendy Kaupp	1994	2	0	2	0
Stephanie Keever	2000	4	2	2	0
Caroline Keggi	1988	3	0	2	1
Tracy Kerdyk	1988	4	2	1	1
Cristie Kerr	1996	3	1	1	1
Kandi Kessler	1986	3	1	1	1
Dorothy Kielty	1948-50	4	4	0	0
Kimberly Kim	2008-10	7	4	3	0
Dorothy Kirby	1948-50-52-54	7	4	3	0
Martha Kirouac (Wilkinson)	1970-72–(**2004**)	8	5	3	0
Emilee Klein	1994	4	3	1	0
Nancy Knight (Lopez)	1976	2	2	0	0
Stephanie Kono	2010	4	2	1	1
Jessica Korda	2010	5	3	1	1
Kelli Kuehne	1996	3	2	1	0

Name	Year	Played	Won	Lost	Halved
Brittany Lang	2004	3	1	2	0
Martha Lang	1992-(**96**)	3	2	0	1
Bonnie Lauer	1974	4	2	2	0
Sarah Le Brun Ingram	1992-94-96	7	2	4	1
Taylor Leon	2006	4	3	0	1
Tiffany Lua	2010	7	3	3	1
Stacy Lewis	2008	5	5	0	0
Marjorie Lindsay	1952	2	1	1	0
Patricia Lucey (O'Sullivan)	1952	1	0	1	0
Paige Mackenzie	2006	4	3	1	0
Lisa McCloskey	2012	4	2	2	0
Amanda McCurdy	2006	2	1	1	0
Mari McDougall	1982	2	2	0	0
Jill McGill	1994	4	1	1	2
Barbara McIntire	1958-60-62-64-66-72-(**76**)	16	6	6	4
Lucile Mann (Robinson)	1934	1	0	1	0
Debbie Massey	1974-76	5	5	0	0
Marion Miley	1938	2	1	0	1
Dottie Mochrie (Pepper)	1986	3	0	2	1
Noreen Mohler (Uihlein)	1978-(**2010**)	3	1	1	1
Evelyn Monsted	(**1968**)	0	0	0	0
Terri Moody	1980	2	1	0	1
Laura Myerscough	2002	3	3	0	0
Karen Noble	1990	4	2	2	0
Judith Oliver	1978-80-82-(**92**)	8	5	1	2
Maureen Orcutt	1932-34-36-38	8	5	3	0
Joanne Pacillo	1984	3	1	1	1
Estelle Page (Lawson)	1938-48	4	3	1	0
Brooke Pancake	2012	5	3	1	1
Jane Park	2004-06	7	4	2	1
Katie Peterson	1990	3	3	0	0
Margaret Platt	1990	2	0	2	0
Frances Pond (Stebbins)	(**1938**)	0	0	0	0
Erica Popson	2012	3	0	3	0
Ellen Port	1994-96	6	4	2	0
Dorothy Germain Porter	1950-(**66**)	2	1	0	1
Phyllis Preuss	1962-64-66-68-70-(**84**)	15	10	4	1
Betty Probasco	(**1982**)	0	0	0	0
Mildred Prunaret	(**1960**)	0	0	0	0
Polly Riley	1948-50-52-54-56-58-(**62**)	10	5	5	0
Jo Jo Robertson	1998	2	0	2	0
Barbara Romack	1954-56-58	5	3	2	0
Jody Rosenthal	1984	3	2	0	1
Anne Sander [Welts] [Decker] (Quast)	1958-60-62-66-68-74-84-90	22	11	7	4
Cindy Scholefield	1988	3	0	3	0
Cindy Schreyer	1986	3	1	2	0
Kathleen McCarthy Scrivner (McCarthy)	1986-88	6	2	3	1
Carol Semple Thompson	1974-76-80-82-90-92-94-96-(**98**)-2000-02-(**06**)-(**08**)	33	16	13	4
Leslie Shannon	1986-88-90-92	9	1	6	2
Patty Sheehan	1980	4	4	0	0
Pearl Sinn	1988	2	1	1	0
Grace De Moss Smith (De Moss)	1952-54	3	1	2	0
Lancy Smith	1972-78-80-82-84-(**94**)	16	7	5	4
Margaret Smith	1956	2	2	0	0
Jennifer Song	2010	5	2	2	1
Stephanie Sparks	1994	2	0	2	0
Hollis Stacy	1972	2	0	1	1
Claire Stancik (Doran)	1952-54	4	4	0	0
Angela Stanford	2000	4	1	2	1
Judy Street (Eller)	1960	2	2	0	0
Louise Suggs	1948	2	0	1	1
Jenny Suh	2006	2	0	2	0
Courtney Swaim	2002	4	3	1	0
Nancy Roth Syms (Roth)	1964-66-76-(**80**)	9	3	5	1
Alexis Thompson	2010	5	4	0	1
Anne Thurman	2004	4	3	1	0
Emily Tubert	2012	3	1	2	0
Virginia Van Wie	1932-34	4	3	0	1
Glenna Collett Vare (Collett)	1932-(**34**)**-36**-38-**48**-(**50**)	7	4	2	1

Name	Year	Played	Won	Lost	Halved
Alison Walshe	2008	4	4	0	0
Wendy Ward	1994	3	1	2	0
Jane Weiss (Nelson)	1956	1	0	1	0
Robin Weiss	1990-92-2000	7	4	2	1
Donna White (Horton)	1976	2	2	0	0
Mary Anne Widman	1984	3	2	1	0
Michelle Wie	2004	4	2	2	0
Kimberley Williams	1986	3	0	3	0
Helen Sigel Wilson (Sigel)	1950-66-(**78**)	2	0	2	0
Joyce Ziske	1954	1	0	1	0

Women's World Amateur Team Championship for the Espirito Santo Trophy

(Inaugurated 1964)

Gloria GC (New and Old courses), Antalya, Turkey [New 5665m–72], [Old 5670m–72]

1	Korea	144-136-141-142—563 (Min-Sun Kim, HyoJoo Kim, Kyu-Jung Baek)
2	Germany	144-141-144-137—566 (Nina Holleder, Sophia Popov, Karolin Lampert)
3	Finland	148-139-143-137—567 (Sanna Nuutinen, Krista Bakker, Noora Tamminen)
	Australia	144-141-142-140—567 (Minjee Lee, Whitney Hillier, Breanna Elliott)

5 Spain, New Zealand 568; 7 Canada 569; 8 United States 570; 9 France 572; 10 Japan 574; 11 Italy 577; 12 Belgium 578; 13 Sweden, England 579; 15 Denmark, Ireland, Czech Republic 580; 18 Mexico 581; 19 Norway 582; 20 Puerto Rico 583; 21 China, Latvia 585; 23 Wales 588; 24 Argentina 589; 25 Malaysia, Hong Kong 590; 27 Thailand 591; 28 – Chinese Taipei, Netherlands 592; 30 Scotland, Slovenia 593; 32 Singapore 595; 33 Colombia 596; 34 India 599; 35 South Africa 604; 36 Iceland, Austria, Turkey, Russian Federation 605; 40 Switzerland 608; 41 Venezuela, Peru 620; 43 Serbia 621; 44 Slovakia, Brazil 626; 46 Poland 630; 47 Portugal 631; 48 Guatemala 644; 49 Estonia 661; 50 Guam 673; 51 Tunisia 678; 52 Bosnia and Herzegovina 717; 53 Ukraine 791

History – The United States of America have won the event on 13 occasions, Korea, France, Australia and Sweden twice and South Africa once.

Individual:

1	Lydia Ko (NZL)	70-69-67-68—274
2	Krista Bakker (FIN)	72-70-69-69—280
	Camilla Hedberg (ESP)	70-72-70-68—280
4	Hyo-Joo Kim (KOR)	72-67-70-72—281
	Lisa McCloskey (USA)	70-71-67-73—281
6	Sophia Popov (GER)	72-70-72-68—282
7	Bianca Fabrizio (ITA)	74-71-72-67—284
8	Kyu-JungBaek (KOR)	73-71-71-70—285
	Breanna Elliott (AUS)	74-70-72-69—285
	Kotone Hori (JPN)	70-70-74-71—285
	Karolin Lampert (GER)	72-71-72-70—285
12	Celine Boutier (FRA)	71-69-72-74—286
	Fanny Cnops (BEL)	71-71-75-69—286
	Perrine Delacour (FRA)	73-74-72-67—286
	Nina Holleder (GER)	73-72-72-69—286
	Augusta James (CAN)	74-71-69-72—286
	Zhang Wei Wei (CHN)	73-71-71-71—286
18	Brooke Henderson (CAN)	71-71-74-71—287
	Min-Sun Kim (KOR)	72-69-72-74—287
	Emily Taylor (ENG)	75-69-72-71—287
	Karolina Vickova (CZE)	72-73-68-74—287

1964	1 France 588; 2 USA 589	St Germain GC, Paris, France
1966	1 USA 580; 2 Canada 589	Mexico City GC, Mexico
1968	1 USA 626; 2 Australia 622	Victoria GC, Melbourne, Australia
1970	1 USA 598; 2 France 599	RSHE Club de Campo, Madrid, Spain
1972	1 USA 583; 2 France 587	The Hindu GC, Argentina
1974	1 USA 620; 2 GB and I, Spain 636	Campo de Golf Cajuiles Dominican Republic
1976	1 USA 605; 2 France 622	Vilamoura GC, Portugal
1978	1 Australia 596; 2 Canada 597	Pacific Harbour GC, Fiji
1980	1 USA 588; 2 Australia 595	Pinehurst No.2, NC, USA
1982	1 USA 579; 2 New Zealand 596	Geneva GC, Switzerland
1984	1 USA 585; 2 France 597	Royal Hong Kong GC
1986	1 Spain 580; 2 France 583	Lagunita CC, Colombia
1988	1 USA 587; 2 Sweden 588	Drottningholm GC, Sweden
1990	1 USA 585; 2 New Zealand 597	Russley GC, Christchurch, New Zealand
1992	1 Spain 588; 2 GB&I 599	Marine Drive GC Vancouver, Canada
1994	1 USA 569; 2 South Korea 573	Golf National, Versailles, France
1996	1 South Korea 438; 2 Italy 440	St Elena GC, Philippines
1998	1 USA 558; 2 Italy, Germany 579	Prince of Wales GC, Santiago, Chile
2000	1 France 580; 2 South Korea 587	Sporting Club, Berlin (Faldo Course) and Bad Sarrow, GC, Germany
2002	1 Australia* 578; 2 Thailand 578	Saujana G&CC (Palm and Bunga Raya Courses), Malaysia

**Australia won play-off*

International (continued)

(Inaugurated 1959)

2004	1 Sweden 567; 2 USA, Canada 570	Rio Mar GC (River and Ocean Courses), Puerto Rico
2006	1 South Africa* 566; 2 Sweden 566	De Zalze GC and Stellenbosch GC South Africa
South Africa won play-off		
2008	1 Sweden 561; 2 Spain 573	The Grange GC (East and West Courses), Adelaide, Australia
2010	1 Korea 546; 2 USA 563	Olivos Golf Club and Buenos Aires GC, Argentina

Astor Trophy (Formerly the Commonwealth Trophy) (Inaugurated 1959)

This event will next be held in 2015

Vagliano Trophy – Great Britain & Ireland *v* Continent of Europe

(Inaugurated 1959)

History: Great Britain & Ireland have won the event 15 times, the Continent of Europe 11 and in 1979 the match was drawn.

1973	Great Britain and Ireland 20, Continent of Europe 10	Eindhoven GC, Netherlands
1975	Great Britain and Ireland 13½, Continent of Europe 10½	Muirfield, Scotland
1977	Great Britain and Ireland 15½, Continent of Europe 8½	Llunghusen GC, Sweden
1979	Great Britain and Ireland 12, Continent of Europe 12	Royal Porthcawl GC, Wales
1981	Continent of Europe 14, Great Britain and Ireland 10	RC de Puerto de Hierro, Madrid, Spain
1983	Great Britain and Ireland 14, Continent of Europe 10	Woodhall Spa GC, England
1985	Great Britain and Ireland 14, Continent of Europe 10	Hamburg GC, Germany
1987	Great Britain and Ireland 15, Continent of Europe 9	The Berkshire GC, England
1989	Great Britain and Ireland 14½, Continent of Europe 9½	Venezia GC, Italy
1991	Great Britain and Ireland 13½, Continent of Europe 10½	Nairn GC, Scotland
1993	Great Britain and Ireland13 ½, Continent of Europe 10½	Morfontaine GC, France
1995	Continent of Europe 14, Great Britain and Ireland 10	Ganton GC, England
1997	Continent of Europe 14, Great Britain and Ireland 10	Halmstad GC, Sweden
1999	Continent of Europe 13, Great Britain and Ireland 11	North Berwick GC, Scotland
2001	Continent of Europe 13 Great Britain and Ireland 11	Circolo GC, Italy
2003	Great Britain and Ireland 12½, Continent of Europe 11½	Co. Louth GC, Ireland
2005	Great Britain and Ireland 13, Continent of Europe 11	Chantilly GC, France
2007	Continent of Europe 15, Great Britain and Ireland 9	Fairmont Hotel, Scotland
2009	Continent of Europe 13, Great Britain and Ireland 11	Hamburg GC, Germany
2011	Continent of Europe 15½, Great Britain and Ireland 8½	Royal Porthcawl GC, Wales

This event will next be held in 2013

34th Asia-Pacific Women's Team Championship: (Queen Sirikit Cup)

(inaugurated 1979) *Tanah Merah, Singapore (Garden course)* April 25–27

1	South Korea	142-135-136—413	(Kim Hyo-Joo, Baek Kyu-Jung, Park Chae-Yoon)
2	New Zealand	146-149-143—438	(Lydia Ko, Chantelle Cassidy, Emily Perry)
3	Australia	145-147-148—440	(Whitney Hillier, Breanna Elliott, Su-Hyun Oh)

Other placings: 4 Philippines 444; 5 Malaysia 445; 6 Thailand, China 446; 8 Indonesia 449; 9 Japan 452; 10 India 457; 11 Chinese Taipei 458; 12 Hong Kong 470; 13 Singapore 476

Individual:

1	Kim Hyo-Joo (KOR)	69-65-70—204
2	Lydia Ko (NZL)	69-73-68—210
3	Baek Kyu-Jung (KOR)	73-72-66—211

History: South Korea have won 13 times, Australia 8, Japan 6, New Zealand 3, Chinese Taipei 2

Africa

All-Africa Challenge (inaugurated 1992) *Phakalane Golf Estate, Botswana*

1	South Africa	146-136-146—428
2	Zambia	156-146-150—452
3	Zimbabwe	157-154-153—464

4 Tanzania 467; 5 Namibia 469; 6 Kenya 473; 7Senegal 476; 8 Botswana, Uganda 487; 10 Gabon 505; 11 Egypt 506; 12 Nigeria 512; 13 Ghana 535; 14 Swaziland 537; 15 Sierre Leone 563; 16 Reunion 600; 17 Malawi 601; 18 Lesotho 644; 19 Rwanda 662; 20 Togo 663; 27 Mauritius 300 (only one player)

Winning team: Lejan Lewthwaite. Alana van Greuning and Kim Williams

Individual:

1	Kim Williams (RSA)	73-66-72—211
2	Alana van Greuning (RSA)	73-73-74—220
3	Claire Minter (ZIM)	77-75-73—225

South African Women's Team Championship (Swiss Team Trophy) *Polokwane GC*

1	Gauteng North A	581	7	Gauteng A	621
2	Ekurhuleni	597	8	Southern Cape A	626
3	Gauteng North B	611	9	Gauteng B	627
4	Western Province	613	10	North West A	632
5	KwaZulu Natal	618	11	Mpumalanga	641
6	Boland A	620	12	KwaZulu Natal B	650

Winning team: Kim Williams, Nobuhle Dlamini and Magda Kruger

Individual:

1	Kim Williams (GN)	68-75-77-70—290
2	Bonita Bredenhann (EK)	75-76-72-71—294
3	Nobuhle Dlamini (GN)	73-72-74-78—297

South African Women's Interprovincial Championships *Country Club, Johannesburg*

Day One – Section One: Gauteng North A 7, Gauteng A 2
Ekurhuleni 2½, Western Province A 6½
Section Two: Southern Cape 2, North West 7
Boland 5½, KwaZulu Natal 3½

Day Two – Section One: Gauteng North A 5, Western Province A 4
Ekurhuleni 3, Gauteng A 6
Section Two: Southern Cape 3, KwaZulu Natal 6
Boland 6½, North West 2½

Day Three – Section One: Gauteng A 8, Ekurhuleni 1
Western Province A 4, Gauteng A 5
Section Two: Southern Cape 4, Boland 5
KwaZulu Natal 5½, North West 3½

Winning team Section One: Gauteng North A – Eugeni Clack, Nobuhle Dlamini, Emma du Bryn, Magda Kruger, Carrie Park and Kim Williams

Winning team Section Two: Boland – Lynne Behagg, Olivia de la Roux, Biana Lohbauer, Maggie Minnie, Bianca Theron and Leanke Vlok

Individual:

1	Benita Bredenhann	68
2	Kim Williams	69
3	Tiffany Avern-Taplin	71
	Nobuhle Dlamini	71

Gilly Feldbutt Trophy: Kim Williams

Americas

US Women's State Team Championship

This event will next be held in 2013

Australasia

Australian Women's Interstate Team Championship

for the Gladys Hay Memorial Cup *West Lakes GC, South Australia*

Round 1 – New South Wales 4½, S. Australia ½; Queensland 3, Victoria 2; W. Australia 3, Tasmania 0
Round 2 – Victoria 5, S. Australia 0; New South Wales 3, Tasmania 2; W. Australia 4, Queensland 1
Round 3 – Tasmania 3, Queensland 2; 0, W. Australia 4½, S. Australia ½; Victoria 3½, New South Wales 1½
Round 4 – W. Australia 2½, New South Wales 2½; Victoria 4, Tasmania 1; Queensland 5, S. Australia 0
Round 5 – Victoria 4½, W. Australia ½; New South Wales 4, Queensland 1; Tasmania 4, S. Australia 1

Final table: 1 Victoria – games won 19, matches won 4; 2 W. Australia 16½–3½; 3 New South Wales 15½–3½; 4 Queensland 12–2; 5 Tasmania 10–2; 6 South Australia 2–0

Final: Western Australia 6, Victoria 0; 3rd place play-off: Queensland 4, New South Wales 2; 5th place play-off: South Australia 4, Tasmania 3

Winning team: Whitney Hillier, Minjee Lee, Hayley Bettencourt, Whitney Harvey, Alyssa Kerr and Hannah Green

Europe

English Ladies County Championship *East Devon GC*

Day 1: Essex 6½, Surrey 2½
Gloucestershire 5, Lincolnshire 4
Lancashire 6, Buckinghamshire 3

Day 2: Lincolnshire 5, Lancashire 4
Essex 4½, Gloucestershire 4½
Buckinghamshire 1, Surrey 8

Day 3: Gloucestershire 8, Buckinghamshire 1
Surrey 4½, Lancashire 4½
Lincolnshire 2½, Essex 6½

Day 4: Surrey 4, Lincolnshire 5
Essex 5½, Buckinghamshire 3½
Lancashire 6, Gloucestershire 3

Day 5: Lancashire 5½, Essex 3½
Buckinghamshire 0, Lincolnshire 9
Gloucestershire 3, Surrey 6

Results table	*Won*	*Halved*	*Lost*	*Points*
1 Essex	24	5	16	26½
2 Lancashire	24	4	17	26
3 Lincolnshire	24	3	18	25½
4 Surrey	23	4	18	25
5 Gloucestershire	23	1	21	23½
6 Buckinghamshire	7	3	35	8½

Winning team: Gabriella Cowley, Paige Kemp, Charlotte Thompson, Daisy Dyer, Ashleigh Greenham, Sophie Madden and Kelly Martin

European Ladies Club Trophy *Corfu GC, Greece*

1	GC Basozabal (ESP)	145-135-141—421
2	GC St Leon-Rot (GER)	145-140-140—425
3	GC Chateau de la Tournette (BEL)	141-142-148—431

4 GC Austerlitz (CZE) 432; 5 Colony Club Gutenhof (AUT), Paris Country Club (FRA), GC Koninklijke Haagshe (NED) 438; 8 GC Lausanne (SUI) 439; 9 GC Nordcenter (FIN) 440; 10 GC Welton (SLO) 461; 11 GC Christnach (LUX) 463; 12 GC Rezkjavic (ISL) 465; 13 GC Glyfada (GRE) 518

Winning team: Ane Urchegui Garcia. Ainhoa Olarra Mujika and Laura Urbistondo Murua

Individual: Katerina Vlasinova (GC Austerlitz) 70-74-64—208

Women's GB&I Internationals

This event will next be held in 2013

European Ladies Team Championship (Inaugurated 1959)

This event will next be held in 2013

European Senior Women's Team Championship *Lugano GC, Switzerland*

Stroke play qualifying: 1 France 764; 2 England 775; 3 Italy, Germany 783; 5 Spain 864; 6 Sweden 793; 7 Ireland 799; 8 Switzerland 803; 9 Belgium 806; 10 Scotland 814; 11 Austria 817; 12 Netherlands 824; 13 Denmark 827; 14 Finland 847; 15 Iceland 901

Leading qualifiers: France – Carine Bourdy, Veronique Ewald, Sophie Pfeiffer, Virginie Burrus, Marie-Ange Michaud and Laurence Rozner

Match Play:

Semi-finals: France 3½, Spain 1½; Italy 3, Ireland 2

Final: Italy 3½, France 1½

Final ranking: 1 Italy; 2 France; 3 Ireland; 4 Spain; 5 Sweden; 6 Germany; 7 England; 8 Switzerland; 9 Belgium; 10 Scotland; 11 Denmark; 12 Finland; 13 Austria; 14 Netherlands; 15 Iceland

Winning team: Giovanna Foglia, Camilla Dettori, Francesca Christillin, Emanuela Gumirato, Guenda Preti Moavero, Silvia Valli and Emanuela Gumirato

Individual Championship:

1	Sophie Pfeiffer (FRA)	73-69—142
2	Maria Orueta (ESP)	71-77—148
3	Christine Quinn (ENG)	73-76—149
	Helene Maxe (SWE)	76-73—149
	Laurette Vanderlinden (BEL)	77-72—149

Jamboree (Ladies Veterans) *The Hirsel GC*

Day One: Scotland 4, North 5; Midland 4½, South 4½
Day Two: North 6, Midland 3; South 6, Scotland 3
Day Three: South 3½, North 5½; Midland 6, Scotland 3

Results table	*P*	*W*	*D*	*L*	*Pts*
1 North	3	3	0	0	3
2 South	3	1	1	1	1½
3 Midland	3	1	1	1	1½
4 Scotland	3	0	0	3	0

Winning team: Barbara Laird, Caroline Berry, Fiona Anderson, Sue Dye, Sandra Paul, Ruth Lindley, Gill Mellor and Karen Lee

12th Ladies Veterans Match (fMary McKenna Trophy) *Hilton Templepatrick GC*

Ireland 9½, Scotland 2½

Winning team: Suzanne Corcoran, Pat Doran, Helen Jones, Maired McNamara, Sheena McElroy, Pauline Walsh and Carol Wickham

Senior Home Internationals (Sue Johnson Cup) *Elie and Earlsferry GC*

Day 1: Scotland 5, Wales 3; England 2, Ireland 6
Day 2: Ireland 5, Wales 3; England 6½, Scotland 1½
Day 3: England 6, Wales 2; Scotland 1, Ireland 7

Result: 1 Ireland 18 pts; 2 England 14½; 3 Wales 8; 4 Scotland 7½

Winning team: Helen Jones, Pat Doran, Sheena McElroy, Carol Wickham, Suzanne Corcoran, Kate Evans and Gertie McMullen

Europe (continued)

Scottish Ladies County Championship (inaugurated 1992) *Montrose GC*

Day 1: Angus 5, Renfrewshire 4
Midlothian 7½, Dumfriesshire 1½
Day 2: Renfrewshire 3, Midlothian 6
Angus 6½, Dumfriesshire 2½
Day 3: Angus 6½, Midlothian 2½
Renfrewshire 6, Dumfriesshire 3

Result: 1 Angus 3 pts, 18 games; 2 Midlothian 2–16; 3 Renfrewshire 1–13; 4 Dumfriesshire 0–5

Winning team: Jackie Brown (Monifieth), Gemma Chalmers (Monifieth), Jessica Meek (Carnoustie Ladies), Heather Munro (Monifeith), Ann Ramsay (Kirriemuir), Ashley Smith (Monifeith), Ailsa Summers (Carnoustie Ladies and Rebecca Wilson (Monifeith). Captain Mary Summers

History: East Lothian have won 5 times, Northern Counties 3, Fife and Midlothian 2, Dunbartonshire & Ayrshire, Stirlingshire & Clackmannanshire, Renfrewshire and Angus 1

Welsh Ladies County Championship *Ashburnham GC*

Southern Division winners: Monmouthshire
Northern Division winners: Mid Wales

Final: Mid Wales 7½, Monmouthshire 1½

Winning team: Sharon Roberts, Judith Davies, Sally Wilkinson, Sara Rees-Evans, Juill Evans, Sherrie Edwards and Jill McAloon. Captain: Sharon Roberts

Welsh Ladies Team Championship (inaugurated 1992) *Portmadog GC*

Semi-Finals: Southerndown 3, Creigiau 2
Royal St David's 4, Newport 1

Final: Southerndown 3½, Royal St David's 1½

Winning team: Amy Rees, Rachel Lewis, Myriam Hassan, Georgia Lewis and Alaitz Zubukarai. Reserves who played in preliminary round – Helen Calvert and Amy Watkins

11th Turkish Amateur Nations Cup *Gloria GC*

1	Germany	142-143-143—428	(Ann Kathrin Lindner, Lara Katzy and Sophia Popov)
2	Denmark	142-143-144—429	
3	France	146-145-144—435	

New role for New Zealand trailblazer Hankins

Patsy Hankins' legacy as a trailblazer in golf administration has continued with her appointment as the Women's Chairman of the International Golf Federation.

Ms. Hankins, who was elected as New Zealand Golf's first President when the men's and women's governing bodies amalgamated in 2005, is the first New Zealander to hold a position of this authority with the IGF.

She was a central figure in the men's and women's games coming together in New Zealand and wants to use that experience on the international stage.

Her appointment is the biggest achievement by a New Zealand golf administrator since Sir Thomas Gault became the first New Zealander to be elected Captain of the Royal and Ancient Golf Club of St Andrews in 2005.

"It is an absolute privilege to be elected the International Golf Federation Women's Chairman," she said.

Ms. Hankins said the strong backing of Asia Pacific countries for a New Zealander played a significant role in the election going her way.

New Zealand Golf Chief Executive Dean Murphy said: "Patsy has been a wonderful ambassador for New Zealand Golf. She is well liked and respected by all members of the golfing community both here in New Zealand and around the world, and for good reason.She has a real passion for the game and I cannot think of anyone better suited for this appointment."

Precision has never been
more spectacular to look at.
Dedicated to the perfect drive. facebook.com/MercedesBenzGolf
Mercedes-Benz
The best or nothing.
A Daimler Brand

PATRON AND OFFICIAL OUTFITTER OF THE OPEN CHAMPIONSHIP
RALPH LAUREN
THE OPEN CHAMPIONSHIP
MEET THE GREATEST GOLFERS IN THE WORLD AND GET EXCLUSIVE VIDEO GOLF TIPS AT
RALPHLAUREN.CO.UK/GOLF

Other Tournaments 2012

For past winners see earlier editions of *The R&A Golfer's Handbook*

Astor Salver (inaugurated 1951) *always at The Berkshire*

Hayley Davis (Ferndown) 71-71—142

Bridget Jackson Bowl (inaugurated 1982) *always at Handsworth*

Becky Harries (Haverfordwest) 67-72—139

Burhill Family Foursomes (inaugurated 1937) *always at Burhill, Surrey*

Final: Jane & Harry Bathurst (Hankley Common) beat Andrew & Leonie Baker (Royal Wimbledon) 2 and 1

Critchley Salver (inaugurated 1982) *always at Sunningdale*

Georgia Hall (Remedy Oak) 72-70—142

Hampshire Rose (inaugurated 1973) *always at North Hants*

Georgia Hall (Remedy Oak) 76-69—145

The Leveret (inaugurated 1986) *always at Formby*

Amy Boulden (Maesdu) 64-70—134

Liphook Scratch Cup (inaugurated 1992) *always at Liphook*

Kerry Smith (Waterlooville) 78-71—149

London Ladies Foursomes *The Berkshire*

Final: Wentworth (Inci Mehmet, Annabel Dimmock) beat Worplesdon 4 and 3

Mackie Bowl (inaugurated 1974) *always at Gullane No 1*

Alyson McKechin (Elderslie) 72-75—147

Mothers and Daughters Foursomes 27-hole event *Royal Mid-Surrey*

Christine and Charlotte Griffith (Walton Heath) 73-41—114

Munross Trophy (inaugurated 1986) *always at Montrose Links*

Jane Turner (Craigielaw) 71-70—141

Peugeot 208 LGU Coronation Foursomes *St Andrews (Eden course)*

Tina Hollyoake and Elaine Cochrane (Manor of Groves)* 33 pts
**Beat Shaw Hill on countback with better inward half*

Pleasington Putter (inaugurated 1995) *always at Pleasington*

Olivia Winning (Rotherham)* 74-74—148
**Beat Becky Harries (Haverfordwest) at the first extra hole*

Riccarton Rose Bowl (inaugurated 1970) *always at Hamilton*

Cancelled

Roehampton Gold Cup (inaugurated 1926) *always at Roehampton*

(This event has included women professionals since 1982 and has been an open event since 1987)

Georgia Hall (Remedy Oak) 72-72—144

Royal Birkdale Scratch Trophy (inaugurated 1984) *always at Royal Birkdale*

Hollie Vizard (Pleasington) 74-70—144

Royal County Down Scratch Salver *always at Royal County Down*

Paula Grant (Lisburn) 76-75—151

St Rule Trophy (inaugurated 1984) *always at St Andrews (Old and New)*

Laura Murray (Alford) 73-74-73—220

The International Trophy was won by Scotland (Laura Murray, Eilidh Briggs, Jane Turner)

Scottish Ladies Foursomes *Muckhart GC (Naemoor-Cowden course)*

Semi-finals: Muckhart beat Erskine 2 and 1
Carnoustie Caledonia beat Williamwood 4 and 2

Final: Muckhart beat Carnoustie Caledonia 4 and 2

Winning team: Laura Walker and Louise Woodburn, Res: Eilidh Watson

Stroke Play winners: Jenny Potter (Cathkin Braes) and Susan Wood (Drumpelier) 81

Champion club: Stirling (Alison Davidson and Patricia Chillas) 83

SLGA Silver and Bronze Medals *Crieff GC*

Silver:

Gael Davidson (Clydebank and District 7) 75

Tenby Ladies Open (inaugurated 1994) *always at Tenby*

Becky Harries (Haverfordwest) 70-71--141

Whittington Trophy *always at Whittington Heath*

Elizabeth Mallett (Sutton Coldfield) 70-67—137

Worplesdon Mixed Foursomes (inaugurated 1921) *always at Worplesdon, Surrey*

Final: Trevor & Aileen Greenfield (Pyecombe)beat James Earley (Hankley Common) & Kay Bowman (West Hill) 6 and 5

Month by month in 2012

Ian Poulter follows up his Ryder Cup heroics with victory in the HSBC Champions, his second World Golf Championships title. Rory McIlroy secures the same European and PGA Tour money list double achieved by Luke Donald in 2011, then celebrates by winning the DP World Tour Championship in Dubai. Two months short of his 49th birthday, Miguel Angel Jiménez becomes the European Tour's oldest-ever winner with a third Hong Kong Open crown.

University and School Events 2012

Canadian University and Colleges Championship *Cordova Bay GC, Victoria, BC*

1	University of British Columbia	235-220-221-220—896
2	University of Victoria	232-226-224-227—909
3	Universitie de Montreal	238-248-226-236—948

Winning team: Kylie Barros, Reagan Witson, Alyssa Human and Stephanie Wong

Individual:

1	Devon Rizzo (University of Waterloo)	74-73-74-71—292
2	Megan Woodland (University of Victoria)	77-73-71-71—292
3	Alyssa Human (University of B. Columbia)	77-71-72-75—295

World Universities Women's Championship *Ypsilon Golf Resort, Czech Republic*

1	Camila Hedberg Bertrand (ESP)	68-72-67-64—271
2	Amy Anderson (USA)	67-69-68-68—272
3	Caroline Powers (USA)	72-69-68-68—277
	Marta Sanz Barrio (ESP)	73-70-64-70—277

Team Championship:

1	Spain*	139-141-131-134—545
2	United States of America	139-134-136-136—545
3	Germany	140-145-134-138—557

**Spain took first place on countback*

4 Sweden 561; 5 Chinese Taipei 567; 6 Japan 580; 7 Great Britain 581; 8 France 582; 9 Czech Republic 583; 19 Canada 587; 11 Ireland 594; 2 Norway 599; 13 South Africa 602; 14 Italy 606; 15 Malaysia 608; 16 China 689

Winning Team:: Camila Hedberg Bertrand, Rocio Sanchez Lobato and Marta Sanz Barrio

Switzerland will host the next Championship in 2014

British Universities Golf Championship *West Lancashire*

1	Hannah McCook (Stirling)*	84-76-75-70—305
2	Gemma Bradbury (St Andrews)	82-76-74-73—305
3	Eilidh Briggs (Stirling)*	78-77-78-73—306
4	Charlotte Austwick (York)	74-77-71-84—306

**McCook placed first and Briggs third on countback*

Scottish Universities Golf Championship *Moray GC, Lossiemouth*

1	Eilidh Briggs (Stirling)	73-68-74-78—293
2	Hannah McCook (Stirling)	75-73-70-76—294
3	Gabrielle MacDonald (St Andrews)	75-75-73-77—300

Team Championship – stroke play: Stirling

49th Japanese Women's Collegiate Championship *Sayama GC*

1	Emi Sato	73-68-71—212
2	Chihiro Sato	72-72-72—216
	Miyo Araki	67-71-78—216

County and other Regional Championships 2012

England

Bedfordshire: Sophie Hillier
Berkshire: Laura Webb
Buckinghamshire: Evie Ing
Cambridgeshire & Huntingdonshire: Miranda Brain
Cheshire: Natalie Lowe
Cornwall: Sarah-Jane Boyd
Cumbria: Rebecca McIntyre
Derbyshire: Debbie Deakin
Devon: Emma Taylor
Dorset: Sophie Keech
Durham: Pauline Dobson
Essex: Charlotte Thompson
Gloucestershire: Shelby Smart
Hampshire: Emma Allen
Hertfordshire: Harriet Key
Kent: Jerri Sewell
Lancashire: Catherine Roberts
Leicestershire & Rutland: Tracy Bourne
Lincolnshire: Helen Hewlett
Middlesex: Tara Watters
Norfolk: Amber Ratcliffe
Northamptonshire: Sarah Carter
Northumberland: Nicola Haynes
Nottinghamshire: Alex Peters
Oxfordshire: Samantha Round
Shropshire: Victoria Bradbeer
Somerset: Catherine Nicholson
Staffordshire: Julie Brown
Suffolk: Vicki Inglis
Surrey: Inci Mehmet
Sussex: Katherine Russell
Warwickshire: Katrine Gani
Wiltshire: Katie Warren
Worcestershire & Herefordshire: Lucy Walton
Yorkshire: Ellie Robinson

Ireland

Connacht: Sinead Sexton
East Leinster: Amy Farrell
Mid Leinster: Shannen Brown
Munster: Amy Farrell
Ulster: Paula Grant

Scotland

Aberdeenshire: Sheena Wood
Angus: Ailsa Summers
Ayrshire: Lesley Hendry
Border Counties: Judith Anderson
Dumfriesshire: Susan Clark
Dunbartonshire and Argyll: Nichola Ferguson
East Lothian: Lesley Nicholson
Eastern Division: Jane Turner
Fife: Susan Jackson
Galloway: Sheila McMurtrie
Lanarkshire: Mary Hughes
Midlothian: Linda Cain
Northern Counties: Hanah McCook
Northern Division: Jemma Chambers
Perth and Kinross: E Muirhead
Renfrewshire: Alyson McKechin (Elderslie)
Southern Division: Rachel Walker
Stirling and Clackmannan: Louise MacGregor
Western Division: Elidh Briggs

Wales

Carmarthen and Pembroke: Vicki Thomas
Denbighshire & Flintshire: Jo Nicolson
Glamorgan County: Katie Bradbury
Mid-Wales: Sharon Roberts
Monmouthshire: Lauren Hillier
Western Wales: Becky Harries

PART VI

Mixed Men's and Women's Amateur Tournaments

For past results see earlier editions of *The R&A Golfer's Handbook*

European Nations Cup (formerly the Sherry Cup) *Sotogrande, Spain*

Men:

1	Robin Kind (NED)	72-77-66-71—286.
	Kristoffer Ventura (NOR)	73-76-69-68—286
	Jon Rahm Rodriguez (ESP)	72-71-71-72—286

Team event:

1 France 872; 2 Netherlands 877; 3 Spain 879; 4 Portugal 881; 5 Ireland 881; 6 Norway 883; 7 Italy 887; 8 Denmark 888; 9 Austria 890; 10 England 894; 11 Germany 897; 12 Wales 904; 13 Belgium 904; 14 Switzerland 907; 15 Czech Republic 915; 16 Finland 919; 17 Turkey 921

Winning Team: Edouard Espana, Mathieu de Cottignies, Adrien Saddier, Kenny Subregis

Women:

1	Celine Boutier (FRA)	73-75-72-71—291
2	Nicole Broch Larsen (DEN)	74-73-76-71—294
3	Nina Holleder (GER)	76-72-69-78—295

Team event:

1 France 581; 2 Germany 595; 3 Norway, Denmark 604; 5 Slovenia 612; 6 Netherlands 614; 7 Spain 615; 8 Switzerland 619, Italy 619; 10 England 620; 11 Belgium 624

Winning Team: Alexandra Bonetti, Celine Boutier, Perrine Delacour

Spirit International

This event will next be held in 2013

Grand Prix de Chiberta *Chiberta, Biarritz* [6690–70]

Men:

1	Mads Sogaard (SUI)	67-71-69-67—274
2	Jordan Smith (ENG)	70-70-70-65—275
	Klaus Ganter (ESP)	66-69-72-68—275

Women:

1	Celia Barquin Arozmena (ESP)	68-75-72-71—286
2	Ariane Provot (FRA)	72-74-71-70—287
3	Noemi Jiménez (ESP)	72-73-72-71—288
	Silvia Banon (ESP)	74-70-71-73—288

Challenge International de la Ville d'Anglet *Golf de Chiberta, Anglet*

Men:

1	Spain 1	133-139—272 (Alberto Fernandez-Lopez, Borja Virto Astudillo, Javier Sanchez)
2	England 2	139-135—274
3	England 1	138-137—275

Women:

1	Spain 2	138-148—286 (Cavagonda Sanjuan, Ane Urechequi, Celia Barquin Arozamena)
2	Spain 1	145-142—287
3	France 1	144-147—291

Copa Los Andes *Lagunita CC, Venezuela*

Men's competition

1 Chile 14 pts; 2 Argentina 14; 3 Venezuela 10; 4 Uruguay 10; 5 Brazil 7; 6 Paraguay 6; 7 Peru 5; 8 Colombia 5; 9 Ecuador 1

Winning team: Matias Dominguez, Claudio Correa, Antonio Costa, Gustavo Silva, Cristobal Del Solar. Captain – Gabril Morgan

Women's competition

1 Argentina 16 pts; 2 Colombia 12; 3 Paraguay 11; 4 Peru 11; 5 Venezuela 9; 6 Brazil 6; 7 Ecuador 5; 8 Bolivia 2; 9 Uruguay 0

Winning team: Delfina Acosta, Maria Oliveros, Manuela Carbajo Re, Maria Villanueva, Liliana Cammisa. Captain – Gonzalo Casa Grande

South-East Asia Amateur Team Championships *Emeralda GC, Desa Tapos Depek, Indonesia*

52nd Putra Cup (men)

1	Thailand	854	5	Hong Kong	901
2	Singapore	867	6	Philippines	909
3	Indonesia	891	7	Brunei Darussalam	976
	Malaysia	891			

Winning team: Srithong Natipong, Buranatanyarat Ithipat, Saksansin Poom, Rattanasuwan Somprad

Indvidual:	1	Jonathan Woo (SIN)	72-69-69-66—276
	2	Srithong Natipong (THA)	74-70-73-68—285
	3	Buranatanyarat Ithipat (THA)	76-68-67-76—287

6th Lion City Cup (boys under 18)

1	Thailand	870	4	Hong Kong	917
2	Malaysia	903	5	Singapore	922
3	Philippines	910	6	Indonesia	924

Winning team: Boonma Danthai, Suvajanakorn Nattawat, Pradittan Puk, Kognta Vee Kwanchai.

Individual:	1	Boonma Danthai (THA)	71-66-73-74—284
	2	Suvajanakorn Nattawat (THA)	75-75-66-71—287
	3	Low Khai Jei (MAS)	76-73-73-73—295

4th Santi Cup (women)

1	Thailand	871	4	Indonesia	894
2	Philippines	876	5	Singapore	913
3	Malaysia	879	6	Hong Kong	927

Winning team: Supamas Sangchan, Budsabakorn Sukapan, Chanya Prathetrat, Ornicha Konsurthea

Individual:	1	Jayvie Marie Agojo (PHI)	75-74-69-71—289
		Kelly Tan (MAS)	74-74-69-72—289
	3	Supamas Sangchan (THA)	73-74-72-71—290

Asian Games

The next staging of this event (the 17th) will be held between September 18 to October 4, 2014 in Incheon, South Korea

Pan Arab Championship

This event will next be held in 2013

Trans Tasman Cup *Peninsula CC, Frankston, Australia*

Australia 34½, New Zealand 13½

Men (Sloan Morpeth Trophy):
Australia 5½, New Zealand 6½

Winning team: Ben Campbell, Vaughn McCall, Mathew Perry and Blair Riordan

Women (Tasman Cup):
Australia 10, New Zealand 2

Winning team: Adriana Brent, Ashlee Dewhurst, Breanna Elliott and Grace Lennon

For Boys' and Girls' events see page 472

Copa de las Americas *Doral Golf Resort and Spa, Florida, USA*

Overall Competition

1 Canada (Corey Conners, Albin Choi, Augusta James and Brooke Mackenzie Henderson) 300-290-293-294—1,177
2 Mexico (Carlos Ortiz, Rodolfo Cazaubon, Fabiola Arriaga and Gabriela Lopez) 298-296-294-290—1,178
3 United States of America (Chris Williams, Steven Fox, Erynee Lee and Lindy Duncan) 295-302-291-291—1,179

4 Colombia, Argentina 1,203; 6 Trinidad and Tobago 1,250

Men's Competition

1	Mexico (Rodolfo Cazaubon amnd Carlos Ortiz)	575
2	Canada (Albin Choi and Corey Conners)	579
3	USA (Steven Fox and Chris Williams)	582

4 Argentina 584; 5 Colombia 589; 6 Venezuela 600; 7 Panama 604; 8 Peru, Puerto Rico 605; 10 Trinidad and Tobago 623; 11 Guatemala WD

Women's Competition

1	USA (Lindy Duncan and Erynne Lee)	597
2	Canada (Brooke Mackenzie Henderson and Augusta James)	598
3	Mexico (Gabriela Lopez and Fabiola Arriaga)	603

4 Colombia 614; 5 Argentina 619; 6 Trinidad and Tobago 627; 7 Venezuela and Guatemala Disqualified

Individual Competition – Men

1	Carlos Ortiz (MEX)	68-74-72-73—287
2	Rodolfo Cazaubon (MEX)	77-70-71-70—288
	Chris Williams (USA)	71-75-70-72—288
	Albin Choi (CAN)	76-68-70-74—288

Individual Competition – Women

1	Erynne Lee (USA)	73-75-71-72—291
2	Gabriela Lopez (MEX)	73-71-75-73—292
3	Brooke Mackenzie Henderson (CAN)	71-77-75-70—293

Whitworth heads multiple winners on the LPGA Tour

Kathy Whitworth may have won her last title 28 years ago but she is unlikely to see her record of 88 wins between 1962 and 1985 being broken for many years yet!

Whitworth, whose winning tally included six majors, heads the LPGA all-time winners record table by six from Mickey Wright who did, however, win 13 majors in her winning span stretching from 1956 to 1973.

Sweden's Annika Sörenstam, who has retired from golf, ended up with 72 victories including 10 majors and is in third spot just ahead of the late Patty Berg (60 wins) and Louise Suggs (58). Berg won 15 majors and Suggs 11.

Betsy Rawls, Nancy Lopez, JoAnne Carner, Sandra Haynie and the late Babe Zaharias make up the top 10. The only non-Americans in the top 25 after Sörenstam are Australia's Karrie Webb, tied 11th with 38 victories, Mexico's Lorena Ochoa, tied 19th with 27 to her name when she retired in 2009, and Se Ri Pak from South Korea lying 23rd with 25 victories.

England's Laura Davies with four major title successes amongst her 20 wins is lying 26th.

PART VII

Amateur Golf Around the World

Amateur Golf Around the World

Results from organisations affiliated to The R&A and the USGA

For results marked [1], [2], [3] or [4], further details can be found on pages 310–321, 401–409, 456–459 and 463–465

Players are from the host nation unless stated

Africa

Botswana

Population: 2m Golf Courses: 10
Men's Champion: Hamadzangu Kamunga
Women's Champion: Bertine Strauss[2]

Egypt

Population: 82m Golf Courses: 14
Egyptian Closed Championship: Ayman Mamoud
Egyptian Men's Open Championship: Thomas Faucher[1]
Mirage Ladies Open; Malia El Senoussi
Junior Champion: Saphir Gohar

Kenya

Population: 42.7m
Men's Stroke Play Champion: Justus Madoya
Men's Match Play Champion: Tony Omuli
Junior Champion (Boys): Daniel Nduva

South Africa

Population: 59.4m
Golfers: 500,000 Golf Courses: 451
Sanlam South African Amateur Championship – Mowbray: Brian Soutar (SCO) beat Brendan Stone 2 and 1[1]
South African Amateur Stroke Play Championship – Glendower: Haydn Porteous 280[1]
Sanlam South African Amateur Stroke Play Championship – Umhlali: Nobuhle Dlamini (Centurion) 212[2]
Women's Match Play: Final – Bonita Brendenhann beat Michaela Fletcher 3 and 2
Volvo South African Men's Mid-Amateur Championship – Vaal de Grace: Neil Homan (Randpark) 281
Men's Senior Championship – WingatePark and Woodmill: Mellette Hendrikse[1]
Mid-Amateur Champion (Women): Sandra Winter[2]
Mid-Amateur Friendship Cup – Roodeport GC: South Africa 17, Namibia 1. Winning team: Josef Fourie (capt), Kevin Sharp, Steven Williams, Neil Homann, Tyrol Auret and Graeme Watson
Kenko South African World Junior Masters – Kingswood: Haines Ronneblad 211; Lara Weinstein 220
Nomads Coastal Stroke Play – Somerset West: Hadyn Porteous 203
Nomads South African Boys Under 15 Stroke Play – Somerset West: Jovan Rebula 296
Nomads South African Boys Under 19 Stroke Play – Katberg Eco Estate: Tristen Strydom (Gauteng North) 282. Match Play – Katberg GC: Thirsten Lawrence beat Darin de Smidt 2 and 1
Junior Champion (Girls): Michaela Fletcher
Prince's Grant Invitational: Brandon Stone 274
Ernie Els Primary Schools Championship – Oubaai Glenwood House "A"
Retief Goosen High Schools Championship – Country Club, Johannesburg: Hoerskool Waterkloof
SA Boys Under-13 Championship: Jayden Schaper. Team prize: Southern Cape
SA Boys Under-17 Championship: Xander Basson/ David Meyers
Triangular Match: Scotland 5, South African Golf Development Board 0; Scotland 3, South Africa Juniors 2; South Africa Juniors 5, South African Golf Development Board 0. Overall winners: Scotland (Greg Paterson, Kris Nicol, David Law, James White, Scott Gibson, Paul Shields, Philip McLean, Jordan Findlay, Ross Kellet and Michael Stewart)
SA Rose Bowl – Pearl Valley Estate: Kelly Nicole Erasmus (Durbanville) 216
The Leopard Trophy – Leopard Creek CC: Scotland 11½, South Africa 9½. Winning team: S Crichton, F McKenna, P Shields, D Kay. J White, B Soutar, C O'Neill
Provincial Championships:
South African Men's Interprovincial Championship – Port Elizabeth GC: 1 Western Province, Boland; 3 Central Gauteng; 4 Gauteng North; 5 Kwa-Zulu Natal; 6 Limpopo. Winning teams: Western Province – Dylan Raubenheimer, Michael Loppnow, Delin Erasmus, Werner Theart, Justin Turner, Le Riche Ehiers, Geriou Roux, Jean Paul Strydom; Boland – Jacquin Hess, Karl Ochse, Anton Oosthuizen. Philip Spies. Armandt Scholtz, Drikus Bruyns, Cedric Rool and Mark Mahoney[1]
South African Women's Interprovincial Championship – Johannesburg: Section One – Gauteng North A (Eugeni Clack, Nobuhle Dlamini. Emma du Bryn, Magda Kruger, Carrie Park and Kim William; Section Two – Boland (Lynne Behagg, Olivia de la Roux, Biana Lohbauer, Maggie Minnie, Bianca Theron and Leanke Vloks)[2]
South African Mid-Amateur Provincial Tournament – Schoeman Park GC: 1 Central Gauteng; 2 Western Province; 3 Ekurhuleni; 4 KwaZulu Natal; 5 Boland; 6 Eastern Province. Winning team: Neil Fusedale, Neil Homann, Stephen Johnston, David Miller, Norman Raad, Kevin Sharp, Steve Williams and Grant Wood
Under 23 Interprovincial Championship – Nelspruit: 1 Central Gauteng 9 pts, 41 games won; 2 Western Province 9–39; 3 Southern Cape 8–36; 4 Limpopo 5–36; 5 Gauteng North 5–36; 6 KwaZulu Natal 3–32.5; 7 North West 3–31. Winning team: Sipho Bujela. Jonathan Dixon, Matthew Kiewitz, Ryan Lane, Victor Lange, Alfred Sutton, Louis Taylor, Johan Theron

South African Junior Inter-Provincial Championship: Gauteng North
Boland Open – Worcester CC: Haydn Porteous 209
Boland Mid-Amateur Championship: Gerlou Roux
Boland Senior Open – Paarl: Jock Wellington 137
Boland Junior Championship – Kuilsriver: Bianca Theron
Border Open – East London: Gerlou Roux
Border Ladies Championshiup – East London: Alana Van Greuning
44th Border Stroke Play – East London: Lara Weinstein 144
44th Border Match Play – East London: Alana van Greuning beat Chevonne Botha 5 and 4
Cape Province Open – George and Kingswood: 1 Brandon Stone 277; 2 Haydn Porteous 280; 3 Leonard Loxton 283
Cape Winelands Senior Amateur Open – De Zalze: Mark Hair 144
Country Districts Championship – Polokwane GC: 1 Free State and Northern Cape 6 match pts, 26½ game points; 2 Mpumalanga 6–26; 3 Ekurhuleni 4–23; 4 KwaZulu Natal 2–22½; 5 Boland 2–21½. Winning team: Pieter Cronje, Roedu de Plessis, Heinrich Erasmus, Stephan Erasmus, Kobus Moolman, Marius Nel, Eddie Taylor, Desne Van den Bergh
Eastern Cape Stroke Play (Women) – Port Elizabeth: Nobuhle Dlamini (SWZ) 140
Eastern Province and Border Open – Fish River Sun: Oswin Schlenkrich
Eastern Province Mid-Amateur – Port Elizabeth GC: *Cancelled: bad weather*
Ekurhuleni Mid Amateur – Benoni: Tyrol Auret 137
Ekurhuleni Open (Men) – State Mines CC: Dylan Raubenheimer
Ekurhuleni Open (Women) – State Mines CC: Nobuhle Dlamini (SWZ)
Free State and Northern Cape Open – Harrismith: 1 Musiwalo Nethunzwi 278; 2 Gert Myburgh 280; 3 Zander Lombard 281
Free State and Northern Cape Championship – Bloemfontein: Olivia le Roux (Boland)* 218 (**Beat Talia Nel (Gauteng) at first extra hole*)
Free State and Northern Cape Mid-Amateur: Clifton Stanley
Free State Senior Open – Vaal de Grace: M Hendrikse 142
Gauteng North Open – Pecanwood: 1 Toby Tree (ENG) 271; 2 Zander Lombard 273; 3 Brandon Stone 275
Gauteng Ladies Championship: Kim Williams
Gauteng Match Play Championship: Monique Smit beat Bertine Strauss 4 and 3
Gauteng 54-hole Stroke Play – Glendower: Kim Williams 225
Gauteng Central Mid Amateur – Reading: Marius Lourens 69 (*beat Jaco Jacobs*)
Gauteng Central Senior Open – Randfontein: Jock Wellington 143
Gauteng North Mid Amateur – Bronkhorstspruit: Graeme Watson 137
Gauteng North Senior Open – Waterkloof: G Van Aswegan 146
Gauteng North Junior Championship – Zwartkops CC: Carrie Park
Highveld Mid Amateur – Middleburg: Graeme Watson 141
Interprovincial Challenge – Cullinan: 1 Central Gauteng 10 match pts, 35 games pts; 2 Gauteng North 8–33; 3 Western Province 4–28; 4 President's Team 3–29½; 5 SA Junior Golf 3–27; 6 USSA 2–27½. Winning team: Terence Boardman, Darrin De Smidt. Andi Dill, Jaco Mouton, Alfred Sutton, Johan Theron, Otto Van Greunen, Graeme Vrugtman
Indwe Senior Inter-Provincial – Durban: Ind. C/ship: Mellette Hendrikse 140. Team C/ship: 1 KwaZulu Natal 917; 2 Western Province 922; 3 Gauteng North 923; 4 Eastern Province 941; 5 Border 947; 6 Central Gauteng B 951; 7 Central Gauteng 958; 8 Mpumalanga, Gauteng North B 967; 10 Ekurheleni 968; 11 Western Province B 976; 12 Boland 981; 13 Southern Cape 1004; 14 Limpopo 1,007; 15 Free State/North Cape 1,011; 16 North West 1,022; Karoo 1,051. Winning team: KwaZulu Natal: Basil Nadoo, Lynton Beckett, Richard Nel, Morgan Phillips, Hennie Heyns, Max Magnussen, Dudley Dowling, Graham Van Der Veen[1]
KwaZulu Natal Open – Durban: 1 Brandon Stone 280; 2 Conway Kunneke 283, Gert Myburgh 283
KwaZulu Natal Stroke Play – Brandon Stone (Durban); Lara Weinstein (Royal J/burg and Kensington) 138
KwaZulu Natal Match Play – Shepstone: Haydn Porteous; Maritzburg – Nobuhle Dlamini (Centurion) beat Monja Richards (Nelspruit) 4 and 2
KwaZulu Natal Senior Open: Moran Phillips 147
Limpopo Open: Haydn Porteous
Lowveld Mid-Amateur Championship: Craig Bell
Mpumalanga Open: Callum Mowat
Northern Amateur Stroke Play – Randpark: 1 Zander Lombard 275; 2 Victor Lange 277; 3 Otto van Greunen 278
Northern Amateur Match Play: *Final between Paul Shields and Aubrey Barnard abandoned because of bad weather*
Northern Cape Open – Kimberley: 1 Desne Van Den Bergh 208; 2 Terence Salo 214, Rian Coetzee 214
North West Mid-Amateur Championship: Steven Williams
North West Open – Leopard Park: 1 Zander Lombard 272; 2 Gert Myburgh 278; 3 C J Du Plessis 279
North West Championship – Pitchefstrom: Nobuhle Dlamini 70 (*reduced to one round because of bad weather*)
Southern Cape Open: Sipho Bujela
Southern Cape Mid Amateur – Fancourt: Dolf Kotze 141
Southern Cape Senior Amateur Championship: Brian Mamples (Western Cape) 145.
Southern Cape Super Seniors Championship: Ivan Palframan (Western Cape) 155
Western Province Open – Mowbray: Justin Turner 272
Western Province Stroke Play Championship – Royal Cape: Se Yung Chun (Milnerton) 150
Western Province Match Play (Men) – Mowbray: Justin Turner beat Jacques De Villiers at 39th
Western Province Match Play (Women) – Royal Cape: Nicole Loesch (Kingswood) beat Alana van Greuning (Walker Park) 3 and 2
Western Province Senior Open – Steenberg: Jan Vorster 146
Western Province Junior Championship – Bellville GC: Lara Weinstein 148
WGSA Teams Championship (Swiss Team Trophy) – Polokwane GC: 1 Gauteng North "A" 581; 2 Ekurhuleni 597; 3 Gauteng North "B" 611. Winning team: Kim Williams, Nobuhle Dlamini and Magda Kruger. Individual winner: Kim Williams (GN) 68-75-77-70—290[2]

Africa (continued)

Zimbabwe
Population: 12.7m
Men's Champion: Ray Badenhorst[1]
Women's Champion: Claire Lyn Minter[2]

Americas

Argentina
Population: 40.1m
Golfers: 100,000 Golf Courses: 310
Argentinian Amateur Championship: Antoni Ferrer Mercant (ESP) beat Joshua Munn (NZL) 5 and 3[1]
Argentinian Women's Championship: Maria Victoria Villanueva beat Delfina Acosta 1 hole[2]
Women's Stroke Play Champion: Maria Olivero

Barbados
Population: 276,000 Golf Courses: 5
Men's Champion: James Johnson[1]
Women's Champion: Muffin Stollmeyer[2]

Bermuda
Population: 64,237
Golfers: 2,960 Golf Courses: 7
Men's Match Play Champion: Jarryd Dillas
Men's Open Stroke Play Champion: Mitchell Campbell
Bermuda Open Championship: Ann Symonds

Brazil
Population: 192.3m
Men's Champion: Leonardo Conrado
Junior Champion (Boys): Cristian Barcelos da Silva
Regional championships:
Parana (Men): Thomas Mantovanini
Rio de Janeiro (Men): Daniel Ishii
São Paulo (Men): Pedro Costa Lima
South: Juan Cerda (CHI)

Canada
Population: 34.7m
Golfers: 5.95m Golf Courses: 2,400
Men's Champion: Mackenzie Hughes[1]
Women's Champion: Ariya Jutanugarn (THA)[2]
Mid-Amateur Champion (Men): Kevin Carrigan
Senior Champion (Men): Chip Lutz (USA)[1]
Senior Champion (Women): Terrill Samuel[2]
Junior Champion (Boys): Adam Svensson 283[3]
Junior Champion (Girls): Brooke Henderson[4]
Canadian Universities/College Championship (Men): Gerrett Rank
Canadian Universities/College Championship (Women): Devon Rizzo
Provincial Championships:
Alberta:
Men – Medicine Hat G&CC: Riley Fleming (Country Hills GC) 283 (–1)
Women) – Sturgeon Valley G&CC, St Albert: Jocelyn Alford (Earl Grey GC) 288 (E)
Mid-Amateur (Men) – Wolf Creek, Ponoka: David Schulz (Country Hills GC) 216 (–3)
Senior Ladies – Highlands GC: Alison Murdoch (Victoria GC) 233 (+14)
Junior (Boys) – Wintergren G&CC, Bragg Creek: Matt Williams (Pinebrook) 271 (–17)
Junior (Girls) – River's Edge GC, Okotoks: Jennifer Ha (Glencoe G&CC) 297 (+13)
British Columbia:
Men – Swan-e-Set Bay Resort: Riley Fleming (Country Hills GC) 280 (–8)
Women) – Christina Lake GC: Christine Wong (Quilchena GC, Richmond) 274 (–14)
Mid-Amateur (Men) – Summerland G&CC: Kevin Carrigan (Royal Colwood CC, Victoria) 212 (–4)
Mid-Amateur (Women) – Christina Lake GC: Kyla Inaba (Gallagher's Canyon GC, Kelowna) 214 (–2)
Senior (Men) – Nanaimo GC: Sandy Harper (Nainamo GC) 210 (–6)
Senior (Women) – Highland Pacific Golf: Jackie Little (Port Alberin) 232 (+16)
Junior (Boys) – Sunshine Coast GC: Matthew Broughton (R.Colwood GC, Victoria) 283 (–5)
Junior (Girls) – Osoyoos G&CC, Park Meadows: Anica Yoo (Swan-e-Set Bay Resort, Port Coquitlam) 277 (–11)
Manitoba:
Men – Glendale G&CC: Joshua Wytinck (Pine Ridge GC) 289 (+1)
Women: Bri-ann Tokariwski
Men's Match-Play Championship – Pine Ridge GC: Aaron Cockerill beat Justin McDonald 1 hole
Senior (Men) – Teulon G&CC: Ken Mould (St Charles CC) 219 (+3)
Senior (Women) – Teulon G&CC: Tammy Gibson (St Boniface GC) 227 (+8)
Junior (Boys) – John Blumberg course, St Charles CC: Ryan Sholdice (Bel Acres G&CC) 287 (–1)
Junior (Girls) – John Blumberg course, St Charles CC: Jenna Roadley (Glendale G&CC) 229 (+12)
Women's City and District Championship – St Boniface G&CC): Faye Zachedniak (Southwood GC) 75 (+1)
New Brunswick:
Men – The Algonquin GC: Mathieu Gingras (Moncton GC) 286 (–2)
Men's Fourball Championship: Mathieu Gingras (Moncton) and Stephane Boudreau (Royal Oaks) 130 (–14)
Women – Fraser Edmunston GC: Margo McLeod (Woodstock G&CC) 230 (+11)
Ladies Rosebowl: Sussex G&CC (Doris Roulston, Judy Juteua and Janet Murray)
Ladies Fourball – Fredericton GC: Allison Chisholm (Riverside CC) and Morgo McLeod (Woodstock G&CC) 69 (–2)
Mid-Amateur (Men) – Moncton G&CC: Darren Roach (The Riverside GC) 206 (–4)
Senior (Men) – Aroostook Valley CC): Herrick Hansen (Aroostook Valley CC) 208 (–8)
Junior Championship – Sussex G&CC: Justin Shanks (Sussex G& CC) 220 (+4)
East Coast Junior – Golf Boutouche Inc: Ryan Nowe (Dayspring Bridgewater) 214 (–2)

Newfoundland and Labrador
Men – Blomidon G&CC: Michael Tibbo (Blomidon) 212
Women – Blomidon G&CC: Kathleen Jean (Harmon Seaside Links) 244
Mid Amateur (Men) – Blomidon G&CC: Jaron Flynn (Bally Haly GC) 227
Mid Amateur (Women) – Blomidon G&CC: Kathleen Jean (Harmon Seaside Links) 244
Men's Mid Masters – Blomidon G&CC: Gary Dunville (Harmon Seaside Links) 232
Senior (Men) – Blomidon G&CC: Allan Masters (Blomidon GC) 228
Senior (Women) – Blomidon G&CC: Judy Gillam (Humber River GC) 259
Men's Super Seniors – Blomidon G&CC: Johnny Williams (Clovelly GC) 244
Women's Super Senior – Blomidon G&CC: Judy Gillam (Humber River GC) 255
Junior (Boys) – Grand Falls GC: Blair Bursey (Gander GC) 229
Junior (Girls) – Grand Falls GC: Deanna Moulton (Gros Morne GC) 269
Juvenile Boys – Grand Falls GC: Blair Bursey (Gander GC) 229
Juvenile Girls: Raylene MacKay (Gledenning GC) 295
Nova Scotia:
Men – Bell Bay GC: Mathieu Gingras (Moncton) 282 (–6)
Women – Mountain G&CC: Julia Henderson 227 (+11)
Women's Senior – Mountain G&CC: Leslie Houde 237 (+27)
Junior Boys – Abercrombie CC: Brett McKinnon (Bell Bay GC) 296 (+12)
Family Classic: David Canfield (Northumberland Links) and Mark Canfield (Truro GC) 144 (E)
Ontario:
Men – The Summit G&CC: Albin Choi (Beacon Hall GC) 276 (–12)
Women – Loyalist CC, Bath: Brittany Marchand (Brampton GC) 209 (–7)
Women's Match Play: Kaitlin Marrin
Men's Mid Amateur – Cobble Beach Golf Links: Drew Symons (Craigowan, Oxford G&CC 214 (–2)
Men's Better-Ball – Oakdale G&CC: Un Cho (Hidden Lake GC) and Sean Carlino (Heron Point GC) 67
Women's Senior – Twenty Valley G&CC, Vineland: Mary Ann Hayward 222 (+3)
Junior Boys – The Mandarin G&CC: Gajan Sivabalasingham (The Mandarin) 282 (–2)
Boys Spring Classic – Wooden Sticks GC: John Boncaddo 216
Girls' Spring Classic – Sleepy Hollow GC: Grace Chung 224 (+8)
Prince Edward Island:
Men – Avondale GC: Greg MacAuley 139
Avondale Open – Avondale GC: Tim Yorke 149
Anderson's Creek Tournament: Tim Yorke 143
Lobster Carnival – Summerside GC: Cody Mackay 144
Potato Blossom Tournament – Mill River GC: Matt Wood 71
Quebec:
Men – Summerlea G&CC: Charles Cole (Royal Quebec) 289 (+1)
Men's Four-ball – Beleoil GC: Mathieu Perron (CC of Montreal) and Jean-Philip Cornelier (Royal Bremont GC) 64 (–7)
Women – Chicoutimi GC – Anne Catherine Tanquay (Royal Quebec) 211 (–5)
Women's Four-ball – Beleoil GC: Louise Hoitte (Rivermead GC) and Lauraince Letarte (Boucherville) 72 (E)
Mid-Amateur (Men) – Whitlock G&CC: Dwight Reinhart (Arnprior GC) 218 (+2)
Mid-Amateur (Women) – Whitlock G&CC: Helene Chartrand (Summerlea G&CC) 150 (+6)
Spring Open – Beaconsfield GC: Jerome Blais (Venise GC) 65 (–6)
Alexander of Tunis Tournament – Rivermead GC: Shawn Langlois (Drummondville GC) 141 (–3)
Duke of Kent Tournament – Royal Quebec GC: Sonny Michaud 137 (–7)
Mixed Tournament – Elm Ridge GC (South course): Marc Cousineau (Mirage GC) and Caroline Aubry (Val-Morin GC) 73 (+1)
Women's Players' Cup – Brockville CC: Josee Doyon (Beauceville GC) 145 (+1)
Debbie Savoy Morel Cup – Mirage GC, Carolina: Josee Doyon (Beauceville GC) 141(+1)
Women's Memphremagog Cup – Josee Doyon (Beauceville GC) 72 (E)
Junior Classic – Milby GC, Sherbrooke: Hugo Bernard (Vallee de Richelieu GC) 145 (+1)
Junior Classic at Le Bic – Le Bic GC: Ian Moffat St-Onge (Sherbrooke GC) 144 (E)
Pee-Wee and Mosquito Championship – Charles-Eric Belanger (Royal Quebec GC) 151 (+7)
Quebec Games – Memorial GC: Jonathan Fortun (Capitale-Nationale) 73 (+2)
Saskatchewan:
Men – Deer Park Municipal, Yorkton: Tyler Frank (Saskatoon) 279 (–9)
Women – The Willows G&CC, Saskatoon: Anna Young (Saskatoon GC) 211 (–5)
Men's Mid Amateur – The Willows GC: Tyler Frank (Saskatoon) 207 (–9)
Senior (Men) – Metfort G&CC: Colin Coben (Delisle GC) 208 (–8)
Senior (Women) – Melfort G&CC: Lorie Boyle (Harbor GC and Resort, Moose Jaw) 238 (+22)
Junior (Boys) – The Legands, Warman: Cory Selander (Cooke Municipal GC, Prince Albert) 234 (+18)
Junior (Girls) – The Legends, Warman: Brooke Hobson (Cooke Municipal, Prince Albert) 259 (+43)
Toronto Star Amateur: Robyn Doig

Chile

Population: 17.4m
Men's Match Play Champion: Gustavo Silva
Women's Stroke Play Champion: Maria Serrano
Women's Match Play Champion: Maria Jose Vial
Men's Senior Champion: Matias Lopez
Junior Champion (Boys): Thomas Burgemeister
Junior Champion (Girls): Isadora Morgan

Colombia

Population: 46.5m
Men's Champion: Marcelo Rozo[1]
Women's Champion: Delfina Acosta (ARG)
Mid-Amateur Champion (Men): Juan Fernando Mejia
Mid-Amateur Champion (Women): Ana Maria Gonzalez de Llano
Junior Champion (Boys): Matias Molina Tellez
Junior Champion (Girls): Isabella Cardenas Giron

Americas (continued

Costa Rica
Population: 4.3m
Golfers: 3,500 Golf Courses: 11
Men's Match Play Champion: Jose Mendez Vargas
Women's Match Play Champion: Ximena Montealegre
Junior Champion (Boys): Jose Mendez Vargas

Mexico
Population: 112.3m Golf Courses: 150+
Men's Champion: Sebastian Vazquez[1]
Junior Champion (Boys): Juan Carlos Serrano
Junior Champion (Girls): Maria Fernanda Lira

Peru
Population: 30.1m
Men's Champion: Jose Rodriguez
Junior Champion (Girls): Lucia Gutierrez

Puerto Rico
Population: 3.7m
Puerto Rico Classic: Justin Thomas (USA)
Lady Puerto Rico Classic: Marta Silva Zamora (ESP)
Junior Champion (Boys): Edward Figueroa
Junior Champion (Girls): Lucia Gutierrez

Trinidad and Tobago
Population: 1.3m
Men's Champion: James Johnson (BAR)

Uruguay
Population: 3.2m
Men's Champion: Juan Alvarez
Women's Champion: Maria Garcia Austt
Boy's Champion: Nicolas Teuten
Girl's Champion: Sofia Garcia Austt

USA
Population: 313.5m
Golfers: 26.2m Golf Courses: 16,547
112th US Amateur Championship: Steven Fox (Hendersonville, TN) beat Michael Weaver (Fresno, CA) at 37th[1]
112th US Women's Amateur Championship: Lydia Ko (NZL) beat Jaye Marie Green (Boca Raton, FL) 3 and 1[2]
North and South Championships (Men): Peter Williamson beat Thomas Bradshaw 4 and 3[1]
North and South Championships (Women): Austin Ernst beat Doris Chen 2 and 1[2]
Mid-Amateur Champion (Men): Nathan Smith beat Garrett Rank 1 hole[1]
Mid-Amateur Champion (Women): Meghan Stasi (Oakland Park, Fklorida) beat Liz Waynick (Scottsdale) 6 and 5[2]
Senior Champion (Men): Paul Simson (Raleigh) beat Curtis Skinner (Lake Bluff) 4 and 3[1]
Senior Champion (Women): Ellen Port beat Jane Fitzgerald 4 and 2[2]
North and South Senior Championship (Men): Rick Cloninger (Fort Mill SC) 68-72-73—213
North and South Senior Championship (Women): Noreen Mohler (Bethlehem PA) 71-75-75—221
Junior Champion (Boys): Andy Hyeon Bo Shim beat Jim Liu 4 and 3[3]
North and South Junior Championships (Boys): Kendrick Vinow Jr (Hillsborough) 71-66-67—204
Junior Champion (Girls): Minjee Lee (AUS) beat Alison Lee 1 hole[4]
North and South Junior Championships (Girls): Catherine Ashworth (Fuquay-Varina, NC) 71-73-73—217
US Amateur Public Links Championship (Men): T J Vogel beat Kevin Aylwin 12 and 11[1]
US Amateur Public Links Championship (Women): Kyung Kim
For US State championships see pages 322 and 410

Venezuela
Population: 27.1m
Venezuela Amateur Championship: Gustavo Morantes[1]
Junior Champion (Girls): Dismary Marquez

Asia and the Middle East

Bangladesh
Population: 142.3m
Men's Champion: Manav Das (IND)[1]

China
Population: 1,347m Golf Courses: 200+
Men's Champion: Ziting Wang[1]
Women's Champion: Shi Yutang[2]
Junior Champion (Boys): Bai Zhengkai
Junior Champion (Girls): Zhang YunJie

Chinese Taipei (Taiwan)
Population: 23.2m
Men's Champion: Chien Po Lee[1]
HSBC China Junior Open (Boys): Marc Ong (SIN)
HSBC China Junior Open (Girls): Ji Rong
National Junior Master Challenge (Boys): Chen Zihao

Hong Kong
Population: 7.1m
Golfers: 200,000 Golf Courses: 6 (18), 4 (9)
Mizuno Hong Kong Men's Close Amateur Championship – Hong Kong GC (New course): Steven Lam (Hong Kong) 287[1]
Mizuno Hong Kong Close Ladies Amateur Championship – Hong Kong GC (New course): Tiffany Chan 219[2]
Mizuno Hong Kong Men's Mid-Amateur Close Championship – Hong Kong GC (New course): Chen Kun Max Wong (Hong Kong) 288
Hong Kong Open and Mid-Amateur Championship – Clearwater Bay CC: Edward Richardson (ENG)[1]
Hong Kong Close Ladies Mid-Amateur Championship – Hong Kong GC (New course): Si Nga Cindy Lee 238
McGregor Hong Kong Seniors Amateur Close Championship – Discovery Bay GC (Ruby and Jade courses): William Chung (Discovery Bay) 239

Hong Kong Boys' Close Championship – Discovery Bay: Fritz Lo (Hong Kong) 143[3]
Hong Kong Girls' Close Championship – Discovery Bay: Mimi Ho (Discovery Bay) 147[4]
Hong Kong Boys' Open Championship – Discovery Bay: Kevin Yuan (AUS) 108[3]
Hong Kong Girls' Open Championship – Discovery Bay: Benyapa Niphatsophon (THA) 109[4]
Hong Kong Inter-Club Championship – First Day: Discovery Bay (Jade and Ruby courses): Clearwater Bay 4, Shek O 2; Hong Kong 3½, Discovery Bay 2½. Second Day: Shek O 0, Discovery Bay 6; Clearwater Bay 1, Hong Kong 5

India
Population: 1,210m
Men's Champion: Anghad Cheema beat Gagan Verma 5 and 4[1]
Women's Champion: Gurbani Singh beat Gursima Badwal 10 and 9
Mid-Amateur Champion (Men): Vikram Raana
11th All India Team Championship – Chandigarh: 1 India B 290 (Honey Baisoya; Angad Cheema); 2; India A 292 (S Chikkaranga; Khalin Joshi); 3 England (Curtis Griffiths; Jack Colegate)
All India Championship (Men): Angad Cheema[1]
All India Championship (Boys): Rigel Fernandes
Senior Championship (Men): Vijay Kumar
Samarvir Sahi Championship: Khalin Joshi
Toyota 7th NRC Cup: N Thangaraja (SRI)
Provincial Championships:
The Delhi NCR Cup: Nadaraja Thangaraja (SRI)
Delhi Juniors: Manu Gandas
Haryana Junior Championship: Manu Gandas
Northern India Amateur (Men): Syed Saqib Ahmed
Karnataka Junior Championship: Aman Raj
Maharashtra Amateur: Samarth Dwivedi
Rajasthan Junior Championship: Manu Gandas
Southern India Ladies: Gurbani Singh
Southern India Junior: Piyush Sangwan
West Bengal Open (Women): Gurbani Singh
Western India Amateur (Men): Khalin Joshi
Inter-State Amateur: Khalin Joshi

Israel
Population: 7.8m
Golfers: 1,300 Golf Courses: 2
Men's Champion: Assaf Cohen[1]
Women's Champion: Hadas Libman[2]

Japan
Population: 127.6m Golf Courses: 2,442
Men's Champion: Hideto Kobukuro[1]
Women's Champion: Mamiko Higa[2]
Japanese Women's Senior Championship – Sagami CC, Kanagawa: Itsuko Miki 149
Junior Golf Championship – Kasumigaseki GC: Boys 15–17: Kenta Konishi 204; 12–14: Issei Tanabe 212 Girls 15–17: Sakura Kito 209; 12–14: Yumi Matsubara 210
66th Men's Collegiate Championship – Sayama GC: Hideki Matsuyama 269
49th Women's Collegiate Championship: Emi Sato 212

Korea
Population: 48.5m
Men's Champion: Soo-min Lee[1]
Mid-Amateur Champion (Men): Sang-Soo Lee

Malaysia
Population: 28.3m
Golfers: 376,000 Golf Courses: 219
KL Amateur Open: Abdul Hladi (SIN) 218
KL Women's Amateur Open: Aretha Pan 215
Malaysian Amateur Open (Men) – Glenmarie G&CC: Gavin Kyle Green (SIN)[1]
Malaysian Amateur Open (Women) – Kuala Lumpur G&CC: Whitney Hillier (AUS)[2]
Malaysian Amateur Close (Men): Mohamad Afif[1]
Malaysian Amateur Close (Women): Nur Durriyah[2]
Malaysian Junior Close: Ervin Chang
Perlis Amateur Open: Low Khai Jei 224
Datuk Robin Loh Trophy – Sabah G and CC: East Malaysia Women 8½, West Malaysian Women 7½
Dato' Thomas Loh Trophy: West Malaysian Men 8½, East Malaysian Men 7½
20th Sabah Amateur Open – Sabah GC: Paul Saqn 221
Sabah Women's Amateur Open: Kelly Tan 213
North Malaysian Amateur Championship – Royal Perak GC: Final: Abel Tam beat Chan Tuck Soon 4 and 3
43rd Sarawak Amateur Open – Miri GC: Lee Ka Tung 226
29th Negen Sembilan Amateur Open Championship – Seramban International GC: Arie Fauzi 211
Sarawak Women's Amateur Championship – Miri GC: Loy Hee Ying 225
21st Negen Sembilan Amateur Championship – Seremban international GC: Amelia Yong (SIN) 226

Pakistan
Population: 179.5m
Golfers: 5,528 Golf Courses: 8 (18), 11 (9)
Men's Champion: Nadaraja Thangaraja (SRI)[1]
Pakistan Open (Men): Chen Zihao (CHN)
Women's Champion: Ghazala Yasmin[2]

Philippines
Population: 92.3m
Men's Champion: Gregory Foo (SIN)[1]
Women's Champion: Lovelyn Guioguio[2]
Junior Champion (Boys): Nicklaus Chiam (SIN)
Junior Champion (Girls): Daniella Uy

Qatar
Population: 1.6m
Men's Champion: Yoseph Dance (USA)

Singapore
Population: 5.1m
Open Amateur Champion: Joshua Shou[1]
International Amateur Champion: Jonathan Woo beat Nicklaus Chiam 6 and 5[1]
Women's Champion: Amelia Yong beat Joey Poh 9 and 7[2]
Junior Champion (Boys): Chieh-Po Lee (TPE)
Junior Champion (Girls): Daniela Uy

Sri Lanka
Population: 20.6m
Pin Fernando Grand Prix: Nadaraja Thangaraja 277
Sri Lanka Championship: Nadaraja Thangaraja beat Dulal Hossain 3 and 2[1]
Women's Champion: Gursimar Badwal beat Jackie Dias 4 and 3[2]

Asia and the Middle East (continued)

United Arab Emirates
Population: 8.2m
Men's Champion: Peter Stojanovski (AUS)

Thailand
Population: 65.4m
Men's Champion: Itthipat Buranatanyarat
Women's Champion: Pinrath Loomboonruang
Thailand Amateur Open (Women): Benyapa Niphatsophon[2]

Australasia

Australia
Population: 22.9m
Golfers: 450,000 Golf Courses: 1,511
Australian Amateur Championship – Woodlands and Huntingdale: Marcel Schneider (GER) beat Daniel Nisbet at 37th[1]
Australian Women's Amateur Championship – Woodland and Huntingdale: Lydia Ko (NZL) beat Breanna Elliott (VIC) 4 and 3[2]
Men's Stroke Play Champion: Cameron Smith[1]
Foursomes – Riversdale, Melbourne: Rory Bourke and Geoff Drakeford 140; Jaimee Dougan and Ashley Ona 145
Australian Master of Amateurs – R. Melbourne: 1 Nathan Holman (Woodlands) 278; 2 Daniel Nisbet (QLD) 283; 3 Ben Campbell (NZL) 285
Riversdale Cup (inst. 1896) – Riversdale, Melbourne: 1 Jake Higginbottom (NSW) 269; 2 Daniel McGraw (QLD) 276; 3 Cameron Smith (QLD) 278. 1 Whitney Hillier (Joondalup) 286; 2 Su-Hyun Oh, Emily Perry (NZL) 290
Men's Mid-Amateur Championship – Moonah Links, Victoria: Andrew Tharle (ACT)[1]
Women's Mid-Amateur Championship – Moonah Links, Victoria: Sue Wooster (VIC)[2]
Mid-Amateur Team Championship: Victoria[1]
Australian Women's Mid-Amateur Team Event – Moonah Links: Victoria
National Seniors Masters – The National, Mornington Peninsula: Graham Blizzard 222
Senior Champion (Men) – Yarra Yarra GC: Sam Christie (QLD)
Senior Match Play Championship " Twin Creeks G&CC: Stefan Albinski (NSW) beat Richard Greville (NSW) 4 and 3
Senior Champion (Women – Gunghalin Lakes GC, Canberra: Jacqui Morgan (NSW) beat Sylvia Donohoe (NSW) 4 and 2
Junior Boys Amateur – Bribie Island: Tyler Hodge (NZL) 283
Junior Champion (Girls) – Carbrook, Brisbane: Su-Hyun Oh (VIC) 280
Lake Macquarie Tournament – Newcastle NSW: 1 Daniel Nisbet (QLD) 273; 2 Cameron Smith (QLD) 275. 1 Whitney Hillier (WA) 290; 2 Breanna Elliott (WA) 297
Ross Herbert National Tournament – Woodlands and Huntingdale: 1 Victoria 588 (Geoff Drakeford, Nathan Holman, Breanna Elliott, Grace Lennon); 2 New South Wales 604 (Jake Higginbottom, Matthew Steiger, Adriana Brent, Cathleen Sentosa); 3 Queensland 609 (Daniel McGraw, Cameron Smith, Ellen Davies-Graham, Ali Orchard); 4 Western Australia 625 (Ryan Peake, Brady Watt, Whitney Hillier, Minjee Lee); 5 South Australia 634 (Brad Moules, Anthony Murdaca, Emma Ash, Caitlin Roberts)
Ross Herbert International Tournament – Woodlands and Huntingdale: 1 New Zealand 596 (Ben Campbell, Vaughn McCall, Lydia Ko, Emily Perry); 2 Australia 598 (Jake Higginbottom, Matt Steiger, Ashlee Dewhurst, Minjee Lee)
Tamar Valley Cup – Greens Beach, Tasmania: Viraat Badhwar (QLD) 210; Hayley Bettencourt 220
Commemoration Cup – Mosman Park, Perth: Ros Fisher (Gosnell) 125
South Pacific Ladies Open Classic – Surfer's Paradise, Queensland: Ali Orchard 230
South Pacific Ladies Senior Masters – Surfer's Paradise, Queensland: Jacqui Morgan 245
Jack Newton International Classic – Maitland GC and Kurri Kurri GC, Newcastle: Boys: Ryan Ruffels (Victoria) 272; Girls: Su Oh (Victoria) 287
Port Philip Amateur Championship (Men): Simon Vitakangas 287
Port Philip Amateur Championship (Women): Su Hyun Oh 289
Greg Norman Juniior Masters – Palmer Colonial GC, Gold Coast GC and Coolum Resor: Boys – Ryan Gaske (QLD) 284; Girls: Anne Choi (QLD) 283
State Championships:
NSW Men's Amateur Championship – Eleanora: Final: Brett Drewitt (Long Reef) beat Michael Lambert (NSW) 1 hole
NSW Women's Amateur Championship – Twin Creeks GC, Sydney: Final: Hayley Bettencourt (WA) beat Ali Orchard (QLD) 4 and 3
NSW Women's Stroke Play Championship – Castle Hill CC, Sydney: Breanna Elliott (WA) 284
NSW Senior Open – Lynwood, Sydney: 1 Peter King (QLD)* 223; 2 Rod Dale 223 (*King won at first extra hole*)
NSW Senior Classic – The Lakes and The Australian, Sydney: Graham Blizzard 153
NSW Senior Amateur (Women) – Coffs Harbour: Final: Sylvia Donohoe (Nrooma) beat Jacquie Morgan (Monash) 4 and 3 (*Donohoe adds a 7th NSW Senior title to her seven Australian Senior titles*)
NSW Men's Medal (*reduced to 36-holes because of bad weather*) – Long Reef and Mona Vale: 1 Neil Raymond (ENG)* 141; 2 Brad Drewitt (Long Reef) 141 (*Raymond won play-off*)
NSW Junior Championship: Lucas Herbert (VIC)
N. Territory Amateur Championship – Alice Springs: Jake McLeod 286 (–2)
N. Territory Women's Amateur Championship – Darwin GC: Charlotte Thomas (ENG) 213
N. Territory Senior Amateur – Alice Springs: Gregory Corben 227
Northern Territory Women's Senior Amateur – Darwin GC: Jacqui Morgan (NSW) 229
N. Territory Boys Amateur – Alice Springs: Jake McLeod 286

N. Territory Girls' Amateur – Darwin GC: Hayley Bettencourt 218
Queensland Amateur Championship (Men): Jake McLeod beat Luke Humphries at fifth extra hole
Queensland Amateur Championship (Women)l: Hayley Bettencourt beat Ali Orchard
Queensland Amateur Stroke-play Championship (Men) – Pacific Harbour GC and Southport GC: Dimitrios Papadopolus (Moore Park GC, NSW) 273
Queensland Amateur Stroke-play Championship (Women) – Pacific Harbour GC: Hayley Bettencourt (Mandurah CC, WA) 294
Queensland Junior Amateur – Indoorpilly GC: Boys – K McBride (NSW) 290; Girls – S Shin (NSW)
SA Amateur Championship (Men) – Flagstaff and Grange: Final; Jack Williams (Grange) beat Brad Moules (Royal Adelaide) at 38th
SA Amateur Classic – Glenelg: Christopher Brown (SA) 283
SA Amateur Championship (Women) – Mt. Osmond, Flagstaff and Grange: Final: Nadine Smith (Royal Perth) beat Cassidy Evreniadis (Grange) 3 and 1
SA 72-hole Stroke Play Championship (Erichsen Salver) – Glenelg, Adelaide: Breanna Elliott (Yarrawonga) 290
16th SA Junior Masters (Boys) – Royal Adelaide: Anthony Murdaca (The Grange) 290
2nd SA Junior Masters (Girls) – Royal Adelaide: Jenny Lee (Glenelg) 312
Tasmanian Open – CC Tasmania, Launceston: 1 Ricky Kato 275; 2 Brett Drewitt (NSW) 277; 3 Geoff Drakeford 278
Tasmanian Women's Stroke Play Championship (Elvie Whiteside Trophy) – Royal Hobart GC: Minjee Lee 71-68-69-65—273 (–19)
Tasmanian Senior Open – Golf Tasmania: 1 Michael Leedham (TAS) 212; 2 Ross Percy (VIC) 219; 3 David Burton (QLD) 221
Centenary Tasmanian Amateur Championship – Launceston: Neville Hogan (QLD) beat Cameron Bell (TAS) 3 and 2; Ashlee Dewhurst (Royal Hobart) beat Sara Johnstone 4 and 3
Tasmanian Junior Masters – Launceston: Viraat Badhwar (QLD) 287; Hayley Bettencourt (WA) 301
52nd Victorian Open (Men) – Spring Valley & Woodlands: 1 Scott Arnold (NSW) 272; leading amateur: Daniel Bringhof (NSW) 282
Victoria Open (Women) – Spring Valley and Woodlands: 1 Joanna Katten (FRA) 212; leading amateur: Su-Hyun Oh 217
Victorian Amateur Championship (Men) – Yarra Yarra GC: Taylor MacDonald beat Anthony Houston 4 and 3
Victorian Women's Stroke-play – Devilbend and Flinders, Mornington Peninsula: Grace Lennon (Kingston Heath) 286
Victorian Women's Match-play – Yarra Yarra GC: Su Hyun Oh beat Minjee Lee 5 and 3
Victorian Veteran Women's Amateur Championship – Bright GC and Myrtle Ford GC: Final: Jill Blenky (Newcastle) beat Brenda Chalmers (Elanora CC) 2 and 1. Leading qualifier: Louise Briers (Commonwealth) 151
Victoria Junior Masters – Waverley, Melbourne: Teremoana Beacousin (French Polynesia) 285; Bianca Ling 308
WA Amateur Championship – Mount Lawley: Oliver Goss (Royal Fremantle) beat Brady Watt (Royal Perth) 1 hole; Breanna Elliott (VIC) beat Grace Lennon (VIC) 4 and 3
WA Open – Royal Perth GC: Oliver Goss 272 (–16) (*beat Brady Watt at fifth extra hole of play-off*)
WA Stroke-play Championship (Women) – Lake Karrinyup, Perth: 1 Breanna Elliott (VIC) 289; 2 Whitney Hillier 292; 3 Charlotte Thomas 295
WA Senior Open – Cottesloe, Perth: 1 Stefan Albinski (NSW) 222; 2 Graham Bowen (WA) 227; 3 Ian MacPherson (WA) 228
Men's Interstate Championship – Royal Adelaide and West Lakes: New South Wales 5½, Tasmania 2½. Final rankings: 1 New South Wales 4 match points, 20 games points; 2 Tasmania 3½–18½; 3 Victoria 2½–18; 4 South Australia 2½–17½; 5 West Australia 1½–14½; 6 Queensland 1–16½. Winning team: Jake Higginbottom, Brett Drewitt, Daniel Bringolf, Jordan Zunic, Dimi Papadatos, Ricky Kato, Ben Clementson, Callan O'Reilly
Women's Interstate Championship – West Lakes, Adelaide: Western Australia 6 Victoria 0. Final rankings: 1 Victoria 4 match points, 19 game points; 2 Western Australia 3½–16½; 3 New South Wales 3½–15½; 4 Queensland 2–12; 5 Tasmania 2–10; 6 South Australia 2–0. Winning team: Bree Elliott, Su Oh, Grace Lennon, Tilly Poulson, Julienne Soo, Jo Charlton)[2]
Senior Men's Interstate Team Championship: 1 Victoria (Alan Bullas, Michael Jackson, Ross Percy and Barry Tippett) 471; 2 New South Wales, Western Australia 473; 4 Queensland 478; 5 South Australia 506; 6 ACT 508
Senior Women's Interstate Team Championship: 1 NSW (Jacqui Morgan, Sylvia Donohoe and Brenda Chalmers) 326; 2 Queensland 330; 3 ACT 347; 4 W. Australia 350; 5 Tasmania 365; 6 Victoria 381
Boys Interstate Team Championship – Pacific Harbour, Bribie Island: 1 SA (Anthony Murdaca, Matthew Lisk, Jack Williams, Kieran Barratt, Jordan Bishop, Lachlan Booth); 2 QLD; 3 VIC; 4 NSW: 5 WA; 6 NT; 7 ACT; 8 TAS
Girls' Interstate Championship (Burtta Cheney Cup) – Carbook, Brisbane: QLD (Lauren Mason, Gennai Goodwin, Nadine White, Tiffany-Claire Lewis, Dee Dee Russell, Victoria Fricot); 2 WA; 3 NSW; 4 VIC; 5 SA

Fiji

Population: 868,000
Men's Champion: Vikrant Chandra[1]
Women's Champion: Sylvia Joe
Open Championship: Anuresh Chandra[1]

New Zealand

Population: 4.4m
Golfers: 482,000 Golf Courses: 400+
New Zealand Amateur Championship (Men) – Mount Maunganui: Vaughan McCall beat Peter Lee 6 and 5[1]
New Zealand Amateur Championship (Women) – Mount Mauganui: Munchin Keh beat Wenyung Keh 1 hole[2]
New Zealand Stroke Play Championship (Men) – Hastings: Vaughan McCall 275[1]
New Zealand Stroke Play Championship (Women) – Hastings: Emily Perry* 284 (**beat Lydia Ko at first extra hole*)[2]
Foursomes – Mount Maunganui: Craig Hamilton (Anau) and Sam Davis (Taranaki) 141
Lawnmaster Classic – Manawatu: Harry Bateman 281; Julianne Alvarez 290

Australasia (continued)

New Zealand Under-19 Championship (Men) – Waipu: Tyler Hodge 213
New Zealand Under-19 Championship (Women) – Mangawhai Te Rongopal Clay 230
Senior Champion (Men) – Waitikiri: Rodney Barltrop 215
New Zealand Golf Mixed Foursomes Championship – Taupo GC: Malcolm Gullery and Alanah Braybrook beat Craig Hamilton and Grace Senior 4 and 3
Danny Lee Open – Springfield: Landyn Edwards 201; Keh Mun Chin 217
Grant Clements Cup – Mt Maunganui: Sam An 275; Caryn Khoo 296
Ruth Middleton Cup: Mun Chin Keh
Provincial Championships:
Auckland Anniversary – Akarana: Tae Koh 209
Cambridge Classic: Justin Morris (Men); Chantelle Cassidy (Women)
Canterbury Stroke Play – Hazelwood: Owen Burgess 292; Bea Sun woo (KOR) 212
Dunedin Stroke Play – St Clair: Mathew John Tautari 271
Hastings Stroke Play – Hastings: Harry Bateman 284
Hastings Womens Open: Kate Chadwick
Kapi Tareha Open: Kate Chadwick, Emma Clayton
Mangawhai Open (Tom Bonnington Cup): Anthony Cope
North Island Stroke Play – Lochiel: Daniel Pearce 275; Emily Perry 280
North Island Under-19 – Hamilton: Compton Pikari 207; Keh Wen Yung 223
North Shore Classic: Mun Chin Keh
Otago Stroke Play – Otago: Brent McEwan
Rotorua Open: Peter Lee
South Island Stroke Play: Jesse Hamilton 229
South Island Under-19 – Timaru: Jordan Bakermans 207; Jesse Hamilton
Waikato Winter Stroke Play: Tyler Hodge (Men); Wenyung Keh (Women)
Wairapara Open – Masterton: Jeffrey Tuoro 282
Wanganui Open: Trent Munn (Men); Imogen Donnelly-Lawrence (Women)
Wellington Stroke Play: Lachie McDonald (Men); Julianne Alvarez (Women)

Europe

Austria
Population: 8.4m
Golfers: 104,490 Golf Courses: 149
Men's Stroke Play Champion: Nikolaus Wimmer[1]
Women's Stroke Play Champion: Anja Purgauer
International Amateur Championship (Men): Christopher Carstensen (GER)[1]
International Amateur Championship (Women): Anne van Dam (NED)[2]
Mid-Amateur Champion (Men): Stuart Duff
Senior Champion (Women): Karin Gumpert
Junior Champion (Boys): Johannes Schwab (U16); Robin Goger (U18); Daniel Moretti (U21)
Junior Champion (Girls): Francesca Baratta-Dragono (U16); Katja Pogacar (SLO) (U18); Nadine Dreher (U21)

Belgium
Population: 10.9m
Golfers: 55,206 Golf Courses: 79
International Men's Champion: Mathias Eggenberger (SUI)[1]
National Stroke Play (Men): Raphael Higuet[1]
National Match Play (Men): Bertrand Mommaerts
Internation Ladies Champion: Camille Richelle[2]
National Stroke Play (Women): Chloe Leurquin
National Match Play (Women): Fanny Cnops
International Juniors (Girls): Camille Richelle
Junior Champion (Boys): Bertrand Mommaerts
Junior Champion (Girls): Clara Aveling

Bulgaria
Population: 7.3m
Golfers: 535 Golf Courses: 6
Men's Champion: Vladimir Osipov (RUS)[1]

Cyprus
Population: 838,897
Golfers: 1,351 Golf Courses: 9
Cyprus Men's Open: Matthew Daley (ENG)
Cyprus Men's Senior Open: Stephen Earnden (ENG)
Cyprus Women's Senior Open: Barbara Woodham (ENG)
CGF Cup (Stableford): Minthis Hills GC 203 pts

Czech Republic
Popkulation: 10.5m
Golfers: 49,849 Golf Courses: 89
Czech Open Amateur Championship: Lorenzo Scotto (ITA)[1]
Czech National Match Play: Ondrej Lieser
Women's Champion: Lucie Hinnerova
Czech International Mid-Amateur (Men): Marc Mazur (GER)
Czech International Mid-Amateur (Women): Marketa Subrtova
Czech International Senior Champion: Michael Reich (GER)
Junior Champion (Boys): Simon Zach (U18); Ondrej Lieser (U21)
Faldo Series Czech Championship: Vitek Novak
National Youth Championship (Boys): Marek Siakala
National Youth C/ship (Girls): Nikol Chrenkova
Junior Champion (Girls): Nikol Chrenkova

Denmark
Population: 5.5m
Golfers: 151,185 Golf Courses: 181
Men's Champion: Victor Genhard Osterby[1]
Women's Champion: Nicole Broch Larsen[2]
Senior Champion (Men): Ian Brotherston (SCO)
Senior Champion (Women): Else Kalstad
Junior Champion (Boys): Tobias Larsen
Danish International Youth Championship: Oona Vartiainen (FIN)

England
Population: 49.13m
Golfers: 688,195 affiliated to the EGU; 115,456 affiliated to the EWGA
Golf Courses: 1,954 affiliated to the EGU; 1,774 affiliated to the EWGA
English Open Amateur Stroke Play Championship (Brabazon Trophy) – Walton Heath: Neil Raymond (Corhampton)[1]
English Amateur Championship – Silloth-on-Solway: Harry Ellis beat Henry Tomlinson 2 and 1[1]
English Ladies Close Amateur Championship – Royal Birkdale: Kelly Tidy (Royal Birkdale)[2]
English Women's Open Amater Stroke Play Championship – Little Aston: Alexandra Peters (Notts Ladies)[2]
English Open Mid-Amateur Championship (Logan Trophy) – Saunton: Thomas Burley (Burnham & Berrow)[1]
English Women's Open Mid-Amateur Championship – Wetherby: Emma Carberry (Highwoods)[2]
English Seniors' Amateur Championship – Aldeburgh and Thorpeness: Alan Squires (Oldham)[1]
Senior Women's English Close Stroke Play C/ship – Shifnal: Janet Melville (Sherwood Forest)[2]
Senior Women's English Close Match Play C/ship – Tidworth Garrison: Chris Quinn (Hockley) beat Roz Adams (Addington Court) 4 and 2[2]
English County Champions Tournament – Woodhall Spa: Sam Dodds[1]
English Ladies County Championship – East Devon GC: Essex
English Boys' Stroke Play Championship (Carris Trophy) – Royal Cinque Ports: Patrick Kelly (Boston West)[3]
English Boys' Under-16 Championship (McGregor Trophy) – Trevose: Jake Storey (Alnmouth)[3]
English Boys County Championships – Cotswold Hills: Yorkshire[3]
English Girls' Close Championship – Sandiway: Emily Taylor (Hillside)[4]

Estonia
Population: 1.3m
Golfers: 2,088 Golf Courses: 8
Men's Champion: Teemu Toivonen (FIN)[1]
Women's Champion: Leena Makkonen (FIN)[2]

Finland
Population: 5.4m
Golfers: 142,184 Golf Courses: 126
Men's Open Champion: Albert Ekhardt[1]
Men's Stroke Play Champion: Tapio Pukkananen[1]
Women's Champion: Julie Finne-Ipsen (DEN)[2]
Mid-Amateur (Men): Timo Tuunanen
Junior Champion (Boys): Jeremy Freiburghaus (SUI)
Junior Champion (Girls): Sandra Salonen

France
Population: 65.3m
Golfers: 407,530 Golf Courses: 578
International Amateur Champion: Lionel Weber[1]
International De France Seniors: Bart Nolte (NED)
Regional Championships:
Grand Prix D'Albi (Men): Thomas Vayssieres
Grand Prix D'Albi (Women): Alexandra Moisand
Grand Prix D'Apremonte (Men): Lambert Cochet
Grand Prix de la Baule (Women): Lambert Cochet
Grand Prix de Bordeaux (Men): Matthieu Pavon
Grand Prix de Bordeaux (Women): Charlotte Maguin-Leopold
Grand Prix De Bondues (Men): Erwan Vieilledent
Grande Prix de Bretagne (Men): Lambert Cochet
Grande Prix de Bretagne (Women): Virginie Burrus
Grand Prix du Cap D'Agde (Men): Clement Berardo
Grand Prix du Cap D'Agde (Women): Lara Plachetka
Grand Prix de Chiberta (Men): Mads Sogaard (DEN)
Grand Prix de Chiberta (Women): Celia Barquin (ESP)
Grand Prix de la Cote d'Albatre: Antoine Leroy
Grand Prix De Haute Savoie (Men): Nicolas Marin
Grand Prix De Haute Savoie (Women): Clara Pietri (SUI)
Grand Prix du Golf de Lyon (Men): Bastien Melan
Grand Prix des Landes-Hossegor (Women): Ainhoa Olarra (ESP)
Grand Prix de Limere (Men): Clement Batut
Grand Prix de Limere (Women): Marion Veysseyre
Grand Prix Du Lys Chantilly (Men): Mathieu Lamote
Grand Prix Du Lys (Women): Carole Danten-Azfi
Grand Prix du Medoc (Men): Brice Chanfreau
Grand Prix de Nîmes Campagnes (Men): Thomas Grava
Grand Prix de Nîmes Campagnes (Women): Alice Dubois
Grand Prix de la Nivelle (Men): Christophe Mouhica
Grand Prix de la Nivelle (Women): Carmen Sainz (ESP)
Grand Prix De Palmola (Men): Leo Lespinasse
Grand Prix du Pau (Men): Alexandre Babaud
Grand Prix de Rennes (Men): Gabriel Mocquard
Grand Prix de Rennes (Women): Diane Buisson
Grand Prix de Savoie (Men): Adrien Saddler
Grand Prix de Savoie (Women): Clotilde Chazot
Grand Prix De Saint Donat (Men): Clement Berardo
Grand Prix de Saint Laurent: Antoine Le Saux
Grand Prix de Saint Nom La Breteche (Men): Arnaud Abbas
Grand Prix de Valcros (Men): Nivorn Inplad
Grand Prix de Valcros (Women): Marion Benzakri
Grand Prix Valgarde (Men): Sebastien Gandon

Germany
Population: 81.8m
Golfers: 610,104 Golf Courses: 708
Men's Champion: Sebasstian Schwind[1]
Women's Champion: Karolin Lampert[2]
International Men's Amateur Championship: Moritz Lampert[1]
International Women's Amateur Championship: Celine Boutier (FRA)[2]
Mid-Amateur Champion (Men): Christoph Stadler
Mid-Amateur Champion (Women): Chris Utermarck
German Girls Open: Karolin Lampert
Junior Champion (Boys): Dominic Foos

Hungary
Population: 9.9m
Golfers: 2,509 Golf Courses: 13
Men's Champion: Johannes Diedrichs[1]
Women's Champion: Marlies Krenn[2]
Junior Champion (Boys): Mate Berta

Iceland
Population: 320,060
Golfers: 15,529 Golf Courses: 66
Junior Stroke Play Champion (Boys): Ragnar Mar Garoarsson
Junior Match Play Champion (Boys): Stefan Thor Bogason

Europe (continued)

Ireland (N. Ireland and Rep. of Ireland)

Population: 6.2m
Golfers: 201,838 Golf Courses: 430
Irish Amateur Open Championship – Royal Dublin: Gavin Moynihan[1]
Irish Amateur Close Championship: Chris Selfridge[1]
Irish Women's Close Amateur Championship – Co Louth: Leona Maguire (Slieve Russell) beat Stephanie Meadow (Royal Portrush) 2 holes[2]
Irish Women's Open Amateur Stroke Play Championship – The Island: Emily Taylor (ENG)[2]
Irish Seniors' Amateur Open Championship – Atherny: Adrian Morrow (Portmarnock)[1]
Irish Seniors' Amateur Close Championship – Clandeboye: Garth McGimpsey (Bangor)[1]
Irish Senior Women's Close Amateur Championship – Bunclody: Helen Jones (Strabane) beat Violet McBride (Belvoir Park) 4 and 2[2]
Irish Senior Women's Open Stroke Play Championship – R. Belfast: Minna Kaamalahti (FIN)[2]
Irish Boys' Close Championship – Enniscorthy: D McElroy[3]
Irish Boys' Open Championship – Hermitage GC: Garth Lappin[3]
Irish Youths Close Championship – Loughreagh: Stuart Grehan[3]
Irish Boys' Under-15 Open Championship – City of Derry GC: K Le Blanc[3]
Irish Boys' Inter-Provincial Championship – Royal Co Down GC: Leinster[3]
Irish U18 Open Stroke Play – Roganstown: Leona Maguire
Irish Girls' Close Championship (Blake Cup) – Waterford: Jessica Carty (Holywood) beat (Royal Co Down) 2 and 1[4]
Irish Girls' 54 Hole Open – Roganstown: Leona Maguire (Slieve Russell)[4]
Irish Girls' Inter-Provincial Championship – Ballinrobe GC: Munster[4]

Italy

Population: 59.4m
Golfers: 100,317 Golf Courses: 269
Italian International Match Play: Francesco Testa beat Joel Girrbach (SUI) 8 and 7[1]
Men's Stroke Play Champion: Georgio De Filippi[1]
Women's Stroke Play Champion: Elisabetta Bertini[2]
Women's Match Play Champion: Stefania Avanzo
Mid-Amateur Championship: Nicolo de Lucis (Men); Giuliana Colavito (Women)
Senior Champion (Men): Lorenzo Sartori
Senior Champion (Women): Silvia Valli
International Amateur Championship: Laura Lonardi
Junior Champion (Boys): Gianmaria Trinchero (U18); Guido Migliozzi (U16); Giovanni Magagnin (U14)
Junior Champion (Girls): Francesca Avanzini (U18); Camilla Mortigliengo (U16)

Latvia

Population: 2m
Golfers: 775 Golf Courses: 3
Men's Stroke Play Champion: Roberts Eihmanis[1]
Men's Match Play Champion: Mikus Gavars
Latvian Open Amateur Championship: Jani Hietenan (FIN)[1]
Women's Champion: Krista Puisite[2]
Junior Champion (Boys): Roberts Eihmanis

Lithuania

Population: 3.1m
Golfers: 430 Golf Courses: 5
Men's Champion: Kornelijus Baliokonis[1]

Luxembourg

Population: 511,800
Golfers: 4,023 Golf Courses: 6
Men's Champion: Mac Biwar[1]
International Men's Champion: Nicklas Koerner (GER)[1]
Women's Champion: Cyrielle Kern[2]

The Netherlands

Population: 16.7m
Golfers: 367,659 Golf Courses: 201
Men's Match Play Champion: David van den Dungen
Women's Champion: Myrte Eikenaar
Junior Champion (Boys): Joe Dean (IRL)
National Match Play (Boys U21): Rowin Caron
Durch Junior Open: Joe Dean (IRL)

Poland

Population: 38.5m
Golfers: 2,750 Golf Courses: 29
Men's Champion: Mateusz Gradecki[1]
Women's Champion: Dominika Czudkova (CZE)
Mid-Amateur Champion (Men): David Parkinson
Junior Champion (Boys): Adrian Meronk

Portugal

Population: 10.5m
Golfers: 14,556 Golf Courses: 88
Portuguese Amateur Championship – Montado: Moritz Lampert (GER) 279[1]
Portuguese International Ladies Amateur – Golf Montado: Roberta Roeller (GER)[2]
Portuguese Federation Cup: Goncalo Pinto
Mid-Amateur Champion (Men) – Aroeira: Ricardo Pessoa* 153 (*Beat Paul Rodriguez at first extra hole)
Mid Amateur Champion (Women) – Club de Golfe, Estoril: Ana Paula Saude 164
Junior Champion (Boys): Antonio Oliveira Mendes (U18); Pedro Guedes Almeida (U16)

Russia

Population: 143m
Golfers: 500 Golf Courses: 17
Men's Champion: Vladimir Osipov[1]
Women's Champion: Nina Pegova[2]

Scotland

Population: 5.16m
Golfers: 183,758 Golf Courses: 541
Scottish Amateur Championship – Royal Dornoch: Grant Forrest (Craigielaw) beat Richard Docherty (Bearsden) 9 and 7[1]
Scottish Open Amateur Stroke Play Championship – Kilmarnock (Barassie): Paul Barjon (FRA)[1]
Scottish Ladies' Close Amateur Championship – Tain: Laura Murray (Alford) beat Jane Turner (Craigielaw) 2 holes[2]

Scottish Ladies' Open Stroke Play Championship (Helen Holm Trophy) – Troon Portland & Royal Troon: Amy Boulden (Conwy)[2]
Scottish Seniors Open Amateur Stroke Play C/ship – Luffness New: Lindsay Blair (Grangemouth)[1]
Scottish Seniors Match Play Championship – West Kilbride: David Gardner (Broomieknowe) beat Richard Gray (Irvine) 4 and 3[1]
Scottish Senior Ladies' (Close) Amateur Championship – Kemnay: Stroke Play: Alison Bartlett (Royal Dornoch) *(beat Alex Glennie (Kilmarnock/Barassie) at the first extra hole)*. Match Play: Heather Anderson (Blairgowrie) beat Janice Paterson (Drumpeller) 4 and 3[2]
Scottish Champion of Champions (Men) – Leven: Fraser McKenna (Balmore)[1]
Scottish Champion of Champions (Women) – Glasgow Gailes: Eilidh Briggs (Scottish Universities)[2]
Scottish Ladies County Championship – Montrose GC: Angus[2]
Scottish Veteran Ladies – Blairgowrie: May Hughes beat Ruth Brown 2 and 1[2]
Scottish Boys Championship – Murcar: Craig Howie (Peebles) beat Ewan Scott (St Andrews) 2 and 1[3]
Scottish Boys' Open Stroke Play Championship – Cardross: Greig Marchbank (Dumfries & County)[3]
Scottish Boys Under-16 Open Stroke Play Championship – Strathaven: Oskar Bergqvist (SWE)[3]
Scottish Youths' Open Amateur Stroke Play Championship – Ladybank: Ewan Scott (St Andrews)3
Scottish Ladies' Junior Open Stroke Play Championship – Blairgowrie Lansdowne: Nicola Callander (Mill Green)[4]
Scottish Boys' Area Team Championship – Cowglen: Lothians[3]
Scottish Girls' Close Championship – Balcomie: Lauren Whyte beat Ailsa Summers 4 and 2[4]
SLGA Under-16 Stroke Play Championship – Strathmore: Gabriella Cowley (ENG)[4]

Slovakia
Population: 5.4m
Golfers: 6,732 Golf Courses: 13
Men's Champion: Peter Valasek[1]
Open Amateur Champion: Peter Valasek[1]
Women's Champion: Katerina Chovancova (CZE)[2]
Mid-Amateur (Men): Thomas Krieger
Junior Champion (Boys): Peter Valasek

Slovenia
Population: 2m
Golfers: 7,900 Golf Courses: 12
Men's Champion: Matthias Schwab (AUT)
Women's Champion: Bianca Fabrizio (ITA)
International Amateur Champion: Patrick Murray (AUT)[1]
Mid-Amateur (Men): Miran Zebaljec
Junior Champion (Boys): Enej Sarkanj

Spain
Population: 46m
Golfers: 338,160 Golf Courses: 345
Spanish Amateur Championship – Al Canada: Jack Hiluta (ENG) beat Marcel Schneider (GER) 4 and 3[1]
Spanish Women's Amateur – Ha Rang Lee Jae2
Spanish International Stroke Play (Women) – Alicante Golf: Ha Rang Lee
Mid-Amateur Champion (Women): Macarena Campomanes Eguiguren
Spanish International Senior Amateur: John Ambridge (ENG)
Junior Champion (Boys): Jon Rahm-Rodriguez

Switzerland
Population: 7.9m
Golfers: 79,843 Golf Courses: 94
Men's Champion: Marc Dobias
Women's Champion: Fanny Vuignier
International Men's Champion: Adrien Saddler (FRA)[1]
International Women's Champion: Guilia Molinaro[2]
Junior Champion (Boys): Neal Woernhard

Turkey
Population: 74.7m
Golfers: 5,538 Golf Courses: 18
Turkish Amateur Open: Maximilian Rottluff (GER)[1]
Turkish Amateur: Koray Varli
Women's Champion: Nicole Broch Larsen (DEN)[2]
11th Turkish Amateur Nations Cup – Gloria GC: Germany[2]

Ukraine
Population: 45.6m
Golfers: 515 Golf Courses: 4
Men's Champion: Dmytro Dutchyn
Women's Champion: Maria Pedenko[2]

Wales
Population: 2.94m
Golfers: 56,69 Golf Courses: 157
Welsh Amateur Championship – Royal St David's: Jason Shufflebotham (Prestatyn) beat Richard James (Aberystwyth) 1 hole[1]
Welsh Open Amateur Stroke Play Championship – Prestatyn GC: Craig Hinton (ENG)[1]
Welsh Ladies' Close Amateur Championship – Cardigan GC: Amy Boulden (Conwy) beat Becky Harries (Haverfordwest) 4 and 2[2]
Welsh Ladies' Open Amateur Stroke Play Championship – Ashburnham: Becky Harries (Haverfordwest)[2]
Welsh Mid Amateur: Nigel Sweet
Welsh Seniors' Close Amateur Championship – Aberdovey: Glyn Rees (Fleetwood)[1]
Welsh Seniors' Open Championship – St Mellons: Andrew Stracey (Denham)[1]
Welsh Senior Ladies' Championship – Langland Bay: Anne Lewis[2]
Welsh Tournament of Champions: Alyn Torrance[1]
Welsh Ladies County Championship – Ashburnham GC: Mid Wales[2]
Welsh Ladies Team Championship – Portmadog GC: Southerndown[2]
Welsh Boys' Championship – Cradoc: Henry James (Kidderminster) beat Evan Griffith (North Wales) 2 holes[3]
Welsh Boys' Under-13 Championship – Abersoch GC Tom Colin James Froom (Nefyn)[3]
Welsh Boys' Under-15 Championship – Abersoch GC: Thomas Wayne Williams (Wrexham)[3]
Welsh Open Youths' Championship – Bull Bay: Nick Marsh (ENG)[3]
Welsh Girls' Championship – Cardiff: Chloe Williams (Wrexham) beat Ella Griffiths (Pyle & Kenfig) at 19th[4]
Welsh Girls' Under-16 – Cardigan: Danielle Jones (Padeswood & Buckley)[4]

PART VIII

Junior Tournaments and Events

Boys' and Youths' Tournaments

For past results see earlier editions of *The R&A Golfer's Handbook*

British Boys' Amateur Championship *Notts and Coxmoor*

Leading Qualifier: Romain Langasque (FRA) 68-70—138

Quarter Finals:

Alasdair McDougall (Elderslie) beat Matthias Schwab (AUT) at 23rd

Matthew Fitzpatrick (Hallamshire) beat Morten Schroetgens (GER) 5 and 4

Pierre Mazier (FRA) beat Nick Marsh (Huddersfield) 1 hole

Henry James (Kidderminster) beat Jamie Savage (Cawder) 1 hole

Semi-Finals:

Fitzpatrick beat McDougall 3 and 1

James beat Mazier 1 hole

Final:

Matthew Fitzpatrick beat Henry James 10 and 8

British Youths Amateur Championship

This championship bridged the gap between the Boys and the Men's tournaments from 1954 until 1994, when it was discontinued because it was no longer needed. The date on the schedule was used to introduce the Mid Amateur Championship for players over 25 but this event was discontinued after 2007.

For results see the R&A website – www.randa.org

English Boys' Stroke Play Championship (Carris Trophy) *Royal Cinque Ports*

1	Patrick Kelly (Boston West)*	71-68-69-73—281
2	Bobby Keeble (Abridge)	69-74-67-71—281

**Kelly won at the fourth extra hole*

3	Max Orrin (North Foreland)	75-71-70-68—284
	Matthew Fitzpatrick (Hallamshire)	73-69-72-70—284

English Boys' Under-16 Championship (McGregor Trophy) *Woodhall Spa (Hotchkin course)*

1	Jake Storey (Alnmouth)	73-72-71-69—285
2	Ewen Ferguson (Bearsden)	72-74-70-73—289
3	Klaus Ganter (ESP)	75-71-73-73—292

England Boys County Champion of Champions *Woodhall Spa (Hotchkin course)*

1	Ashton Turner (Kenwick Park, Lincolnshire)	71-68—139
2	Nicholas Marsh (Huddersfield, Yorkshire)	69-71—140
3	David Langley (Castle Royale, Berkshire)	77-64—141

English Junior County Champion Tournament *Trevose*

1	Jevan Parmar (Leicestershire and Rutland)	75-73—148
	Jack Singh Brar (Hampshire, Isle of Wight and Channel Islands	72-76—148
	Greg Payne (Surrey)	73-75—148
	Matthew Fitzpatick (Yorkshire)	74-74—148

Irish Boys' Close Championship (inaugurated 1983) *Enniscorthy GC*

1	D McElroy (Ballymena)	69-70-75-73—287
2	G Glynn (Carton House)	76-69-76-73—294
	S Graham (Tullamore)	75-68-74-77—294

C Glynn won the Under-17 Trophy and S. Graham the Under-16

Irish Boys' Open Championship (inaugurated 1983) *Hermitage GC*

1	Garth Lappin (Belvoir Park)	69-73-70-75—287
2	Ronan Mullarney (Galway)	77-73-74-71—295
3	Gavin Moynihan (The Island)	73-80-67-77—297
	Alec Myles (Newlands)	74-74-74-75—297
	K Le Blanc (The Island)	70-76-74-77—297

R Mullarney won the Under-17 Trophy and K Le Blanc the Under-16

Irish Boys' Under-15 Open Championship *City of Derry GC*

1	K Le Blanc (The Island)*	75-75—150
2	R Williamson (Holywood)	77-73—150
	C Morris (ENG)	76-74—150
	T Mulligan (Laytown and Bettystown)	76-74—150

**Le Blanc won at the third extra hole*

Irish Youths Amateur Close Championship (inaugurated 1969) *Loughrea*

1	Stuart Grehan (Tullamore)*	74-70-67-72—283
2	Conor Coyne (Youghal)	76-70-67-70—283

**Grehan won in the play-off*

3	Shaun Carter (Stackstown)	69-72-71-73--285

Scottish Boys' Championship *Murcar*

Quarter Finals:
Craig Howie (Peebles) beat Jakwe Scott (Blackpool) at 19th
Connar Cook (Caird Park) beat Lawrence Allen (Alva) 2 and 1
Ewan Scott (St Andrews) beat Bradley Neil (Blairgowrie) 1 hole
Alan Waugh (Cowglen) beat Lewis Bain (Musselburgh) 1 hole

Semi-Finals:
Howie beat Cook 2 and 1
E Scott beat Waugh 2 and 1

Final:
Craig Howie beat Ewan Scott 2 and 1

Scottish Boys' Open Stroke Play Championship (inaugurated 1970) *Cardross*

1	Greig Marchbank (Dumfries & County)	70-67-73-67—277
2	Ewen Ferguson (Bearsden)	70-71-70-70—281
3	Cameron Farrell (Cardross)	74-69-71-68—282
	Ewan Scott (St Andrews)	67-73-73-69—282

Scottish Boys Under-16 Open Stroke Play Championship (inaug. 1990) *Strathaven*

1	Oskar Bergqvist (SWE)	69-71-72-74—286
2	Patrice Schumacher (GER)	77-69-73-68—287
	Robert Macintyre (Glencruitten)	69-72-73-73—287

Scottish Youths' Open Amateur Stroke Play Championship (inaugurated 1979)

Ladybank

1	Ewan Scott (St Andrews)	72-67-75-74—288
2	Bradley Neil (Blairgowrie)	71-72-74-74—291
3	Ryan Walsh (Kirkcaldy)	78-71-72-72—293
	Jack McDonald (Kilmarnock (Barassie))	73-71-72-77—293

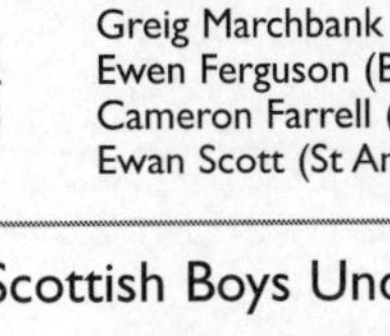

What is the answer?

Q: Can I place a club on the ground to help me with my alignment before playing a stroke?

A: Yes, as long as you remove the club before playing the stroke.

Welsh Boys' Championship (inaugurated 1954) *Cradoc*

Leading Qualifiers: 140 Evan Griffith (North Wales) 72-68; Zach Galliford (Borth & Ynyslas) 67-73

Quarter Finals:
Evan Griffith (North Wales) beat Delon Hau (Vale) 2 and 1
Gareth Roberts (North Wales) beat Daniel King (Newport) 2 holes
Henry James (Kidderminster) beat Joe Du Fue (Celtic Manor) 4 and 2
Zach Galliford (Borth & Ynyslas) beat Jack Davidson (Llanwern) 2 and 1

Semi-Finals:
Griffith beat Roberts 2 and 1
James beat Galliford 3 and 2

Final:
Henry James beat Evan Griffith 2 holes

Welsh Boys Under-13 Championship *Abersoch GC*

1	Tom Colin James Froom (Nefyn)	75
2	Lewis Jones (Monmouthshire)	76
	Luke Harries (South Pembrokeshire)	78

Welsh Boys' Under-15 Championship (inaugurated 1985) *Abersoch GC*

1	Thomas Wayne Williams (Wrexham)	73-69—142
2	Tim Harry (Vale Resort)	70-73—143
3	Daniel Pickering (Pontypridd)	71-74—145
	Thomas davies (Penrhos)	72-73—145

Welsh Open Youths' Championship (inaugurated 1993) *Bull Bay*

1	Nick Marsh (Huddersfield)	67-68-70-82—287
2	Will Jones (Oswestry)	70-67-77-81—295
3	Richard James (Aberystwyth)	76-70-77-73—296

Peter McEvoy Trophy (inaugurated 1988) *always at Copt Heath*

1	Gavin Moynihan (Island)	68-68-69-70—275
2	Nick March (Huddersfield)	72-67-71-70—280
	Max Orrin (North Foreland)	71-66-69-74—280

Midland Boys' Amateur Championship *Oundle GC*

1	Jack Sallis (Notts GC)	70-68—138
2	Isaac Walker (Notts GC)	68-71—139
3	Bradley Moore (Keddleston Park)	73-68—141
	Billy Spooner (Boston)	71-70—141

Midland Youths' Championship *Stoke Rochford GC*

1	Liam Taylor (Sherwood Forest)*	70-69-67—206
2	Craig Young (Ashbourne)	68-69-69—206

**Taylor won at the third extra hole*

3	Ashley Mason (Glen Gorse)	72-68-69—209

Event reduced to 54 holes because of bad weather

Sir Henry Cooper Junior Masters *Nizels GC. Kent*

1	Craig Howie (Peebles)	69-70-65—204
2	Max Orrin (North Foreland)	71-68-70—209
3	Bradley Neil (Blairgowrie)	73-71-68—212
	Josh Hayes (Sussex National)	73-71-68—212

US Junior Amateur Championship *Golf Cub of New England, Stratham, New Hampshire*

Semi-finals: Jim Liu (Smithtown, NY) beat Matthew Scobie (CAN) 3 and 1
Andy Hyeon Bo Shim (Duluth, GA) beat Nicolas Echavarria (COL) 2 and 1

Finals: Andy Hyeon Bo Shim beat Jim Liu 4 and 3

Canadian Junior Boys Championship *Osprey Ridge GC Nova Scotia*

1	Adam Svensson (Surrey, BC)	75-69-75-64—83
2	Kevin Kwon (Pitt Meadows, BC)	70-77-72-66—285
	Luke Moser (Waterloo, ON)	73-75-67-70—285

Inter-Provincial Team Championship:
1 British Columbia* (Matthew Broughton, Kevin Ko and Chrisologo) 299
**Beat Ontario at the first extra hole*

Hong Kong Boys' Close Championship *Discovery Bay GC (Diamond and Jade courses)*

1	Fritz Lo (HKGA)	74-69—143
2	K H Jackie Chan (HKGA)	78-73—151
3	Michael Regan Wong	78-74—152
	Shinya Mizuno (DBGC)	78-74—152

Hong Kong Boys' Open Championship *Discovery Bay GC (Diamond and Jade courses)*

1	Kevin Yuan (AUS)	71-37—108
2	Jackie Chan (HKGA)	74-37—111
3	Natithorn Thippong (THA)	75-37—112

Enjoy Jakarta World Junior Golf Championship

Damai Indah GC (Pantai Indah Kapuk course), Jakarta, Indonesia

Boys "A"	Joshuo Andrew Wirawan (IND)	75-76-67-69—287 (–1)
Boys "B:"	Sarit Suwannarut (THA)	75-73-70-74—290 (+2)
Boys "C"	Puwit Anupansuebsai (THA)	68-68-73—209 (–7)
Boys "D"	Nattabutara Sornkaew (THA)	74-73-70—219 (+3)

Highland Spring Junior Masters *Gleneagles Hotel, (Queen's course)*

1	Cameron McAndrew (Linlithgow 12)	42 points
2	Samuel Yule (Ballater 15)	40
	Michael Baber (Hopeman 13)	40

HSBC Junior Boys Championship *Shanghai*

1	Bai Zhengkai	71-70-71—212
2	Chen Zihao	71-70-75—216
3	Jin Cheng	72-76-74—222

British Boys' champion in junior coaching session

Seventeen-year-old Matthew Fitzpatrick, who won the British Boys' Championship last year with a resounding 10 and 8 triumph over Harry James, took part in a junior coaching session with single-figure youngsters at Fulford in York last year. He talked about his own experiences and helped with the coaching.

The day was organised by former English amateur internationalist Jonathan Plaxton who summed up the success of the day this way: "We really appreciated Matthew spending time with the young players. It is so important for them to have role models and good that Matthew was willing to give something back to the game in this way."

The clinics are held every two weeks.

Team Events

European Boys Team Championship *Lidingo GK, Sweden*

Qualifying:	1 England	338-347—685
	1 Italy	349-363—712
	2 Sweden	362-352—714
	3 Norway	364-360—724
	4 England	362-366—727
	Ireland	362-365—727
	6 Germany	
	7 France	364-366—730
	8 Scotland	363-368—731

9 Spain 732; 10 Finland 735; 11 Austria 736; 12 Denmark. Netherlands 742; 14 Czech Republic 750; 15 Switzerland 760; 16 Switzerland, Wales 760

Leading Match Play qualifiers: Italy (Reneto Paratore 69-73—142; Federico Zucchetti 60-73—142; Luigi Botta 70-72—142; Filippo Campiligli 70-74—144; Guilio Castaghara 71-71—142; Guido Migliozzi 73 – 82—155)

Match Play:

Semi-finals: Sweden 5½, Germany 1½
Italy 4, England 3

Final: Sweden 5, Italy 2
(Swedish names first)
Hannes Ronneblad & Hampus Bergman beat Filippo Campigli & Guido Migliozzi 3 and 2
Marcus Gran & Tobias Eden lost to Renato Paratore & Guilio Castagnara 2 and 1
Hannes Ronneblad beat Federico Zucchetti 3 and 2
Tobias Eden lost to Luigi Botta 3 and 2
Marcus Gran beat Renato Paratore 1 hole
Adam Strom beat Filippo Campigli 4 and 2
Victor Tarnstrom beat Guilio Castagnara 2 and 1

Germany beat England 4–3 to take third place

Great Britain & Ireland *v* Continent of Europe (Jacques Léglise Trophy)

Portmarnock GC, Dublin, Ireland

Captains: Europe: Gerald Strangl (AUT); GB&I: Rhys Pugh (WAL)

Continent of Europe names first:

First Day – **Foursomes**

Kenny Subregis (FRA) and Romain Langasque (FRA) lost to Gavin Moynihan (IRL) and Alex Gleeson (IRL) 5 and 4
Victor Tarnstrom (SWE) and Hannes Ronneblad (SWE) beat Toby Tree (ENG) and Max Orrin (ENG) 1 hole
Mathias Schwab (AUT) and Dominic Foos (GERT) beat Ashton Turner (ENG) and Patrick Kelly (ENG) 3 and 2
Mario Galiano (ESP) and Giulio Castagnara (ITA) halved with Harry Ellis (ENG) and Matthew Fitzpatrick (ENG)

Singles

Schwab halved with Moynihan
Ronneblad beat Bradley Neil (SCO) 4 and 2
Foos beat Gleeson 3 and 1
Renato Paratore (ITA) beat Tree 3 and 2
Galiano lost to Orrin 6 and 5
Subregis lost to Turner 4 and 3
Langasque beat Kelly 1 hole
Tarnstrom lost to Fitzpatrick 4 and 2

Second Day – **Foursomes**

Castagnara and Paratore beat Moynihan and Gleeson 4 and 3
Schwab and Foos beat Tree and Orrin 1 hole
Tarnstrom and Ronneblad beat Turner and Kelly 2 and 1
Langasque and Subregis beat Ellis and Fitzpatrick 2 holes

Singles

Castagnara beat Moynihan 1 hole
Galiano beat Gleeson 2 and 1
Paratore lost to Orrin 2 and 1
Ronneblad lost to Tree 5 and 4
Langasque lost to Fitzpatrick 2 and 1
Schwab lost to Turner 1 hole
Tarnstrom lost to Neil 2 holes
Foos halved with Ellis

Match result: Continent of Europe 13½, Great Britain and Ireland 10½

European Boys Challenge Trophy *St Sofia GC*

1	Switzerland	353-379-363—1,095
2	Denmark	353-384-361—1,097
3	Belgium	352-387-361—1,100
4	Iceland	359-387-356—1,102
5	Poland	363-386-370—1,119
6	Russia	389-403-354—1,146
7	Estonia	375-416-383—1,174
8	Hungary	406-444-403—1,253
9	Bulgaria	459-479-440—1,378.

Individual competition:

1	Jan Szmidt (POL)	68-67-73—208
2	Jeppe Andersen (DEN)	69-75-66—210
3	Bjarki Petursson (ISL)	70-75-67—212

Winning team: Mike Iff, Adrien Michellod, Jeremy Freiburghaus, Neil Woernhard, Louis Bemberg and Philippe Schweizer

Boys' Home Internationals (R&A Trophy) (inaugurated 1985) *County Louth, Ireland*

Day One: England 9½, Ireland 5½; Wales 5½, Scotland 9½
Day Two: England 9½, Wales 5½; Scotland 8½, Ireland 6½
Day Three: Ireland 10, Wales 5; England 10, Scotland 5

Final points: 1 England 3; 2 Scotland 2; 3 Ireland 1; 4 Wales 0

Winning Team: Jack Singh Brar (Bramshaw), Dan Brown (Bedale), Rob Burlison (Oxley Park), Joe Dean (Lindrick), Matt Fitzpatrick (Hallamshire), Bobby Keeble (Abridge), Patrick Kelly (Boston West), Nick Marsh (Huddersfield), Max Orrin (North Foreland), Toby Tree (Worthing), Ashton Turner (Kenwick Park)

English Boys County Championships *Cotswold Hills*

1 Yorkshire
2 Staffordshire
3 Hampshire, Isle of Wight and Channel Islands
4 Devon

Winning Team: Ben Brewster, Joseph Dean, Nicholas Marsh, Daniel Brown, Jonathan Thomson, James Walker and Will Whitlock. Coach: Steve Robinson

Irish Boys' Inter-Provincial Championship *Royal County Down GC*

Day One: Munster 6½, Connaught 3½;Leinster 5½, Ulster 4½
Day Two: Ulster 6½, Munster 3½;Leinster 8, Connaught 2
Day Three: Leinster 6, Munster 4;Ulster 6½, Connaught 3½

Table	*P*	*W*	*D*	*L*
1 Leinster	3	3	0	0
2 Ulster	3	2	0	1
3 Munster	3	1	0	2
4 Connaught	3	0	0	3

Irish Boys' Inter- Provincial Championship *continued*

Winning team: Gavin Moynihan, Evan Farrell, Niall Foley, Jack Walsh, David Foy, Paul McBride and Alec Myles

Scottish Boys Area Team Championship *Cowglen*

1 Lothians 346; 2 Glasgow 351; 3 Dunbartonshire 353; 4 Fife 359; 5 South 361; 6 North 365; 7 Renfrewshire 368; 8 Perth & Kinross 369; 9 Borders, Angus 371, Lanarkshire 371; 12 Stirlingshire 372; 13 Argyll & Bute 373; 14 Clackmannanshire 374; 15 North East 378,; 16 Ayrshire 379

Winning Team: Anthony Blaney, Calum Hill, Murray Naysmith, Alexander Wilson

Individual (Niagara Cup): Bradley Neil (Perth & Kinross) 65

Toyota Junior World Cup *Chukyo GC (Ishino course), Aichi, Japan*

1	Australia	216-202-218-203—839
2	Japan	219-200-216-206—841
	Canada	212-201-215-213—841
4	United States of America	212-210-212-209—843
5	Thailand	219-208-213-207—847
6	Mexico	209-212-217-213—851
	Spain	215-209-215-212—851
8	Argentina	227-212-210-211—860
9	Chinese Taipei	219-217-211-215—862
10	South Africa	222-214-213-218—867
11	Austria	226-213-216-216—871
12	Venezuela	223-217-228-220—888
13	China	228-221-236-236—921

Winning team: Peter Knight, Oliver Goss, Anthony Murdaca, Ri Kudai Kato and Viraat Badwhar

Individual Winner (Maruyama Cup): Viraat Badwhar (AUS) 72-68-65-67—272

All-Africa Junior Golf Challenge *Gaborone GC, Botswana*

1	South Africa	845
2	Zimbabe	876
3	Namibia	888
4	Uganda	932
5	Kenya	939
6	Zambia	947
7	Swaziland	963

Winning team: Christian Bezuidenhout, Dylan Raubenheimer, Zander Lombard and Ian Snyman

Individual competition:

1	Christian Bezuidenhout (RSA)	75-68-65-72—280
2	Dylan Raubenheimer (RSA)	74-69-71-71—285

South African Boys Under 19 Stroke Play Championship *Katberg Eco Golf Estate*

1	Tristen Strydom (Gauteng North)	72-71-69-70—282
2	Philip Kruse (Gauteng North)	75-71-69-68—283
3	Gideon Van Der Vyver (W. Province)	73-71-71-69—284

South African Junior Inter-Provincial Championship *Paarl GC*

		Pld	*W*	*L*	*D*	*Pts*
1	Gauteng North	5	4	0	1	36½
2	Central Gauteng	5	3	1	1	32
3	Eastern Province	5	3	0	2	27½
4	Western Province	5	2	0	3	31
5	Ekurhuleni	5	1	2	2	26
6	KwaZulu Natal	5	0	1	4	27

Girls' and Junior Ladies' Tournaments

For past results see earlier editions of *The R&A Golfer's Handbook*

British Girls' Open Amateur Championship *Tenby*

Leading Qualifier: Perrine Delacour (FRA) 72-71—143

Quarter-Finals:
Georgia Hall (Remedy Oak) beat Karolin Lampert (GER) 5 and 3
Quirine Eijkenboom (GER) beat Celia Barquin (ESP 3 and 2
Olivia Cowan (GER) beat Yasemin Sari (TUR) 4 and 3
Clara Baena (ESP) beat Ha Rang Lee (ESP) 6 and 5

Semi-Finals:
Hall beat Eijkenboom 1 hole
Baena beat Cowan 1 hole

Final: Georgia Hall beat Clara Baena 6 and 5

English Girls' Close Championship *Sandiway*

1	Emily Taylor (Hillside)	73-72-72-66—283
2	Meghan Maclaren (Wellingborough)	75-71-68-73—287
3	Bronte Law (Bramhall)	73-72-71-72—288

Irish Girls' Close Championship (Blake Cup) (inaugurated 1951) *Waterford*

Leading Qualifiers: Jean O'Driscoll (Muskerry) 76-76—152; Chloe Ryan (Castleroy) 74-78—152

Semi-Finals: Olivia Mehaffey (Royal Co Down) beat Niamh Ward (Lurgan) at 19th
Jessica Carty (Holywood) beat Mary Doyle (The Heath) 3 and 2

Final: Jessica Carty beat Olivia Mehaffey 2 and 1

Irish Girls' 54 Hole Open *Roganstown*

1	Leona Maguire (Slieve Russell)	72-69-74—215
2	Manon Molle (FRA)	76-72-75—223
	Mathilda Cappeliez (FRA)	73-73-77—223

Scottish Ladies' Junior Open Stroke Play Championship (inaugurated 1955)

(formerly Scottish Under-21 Girls Open Stroke Play Championship) *Blairgowrie Lansdowne*

1	Nicola Callander (Mill Green)	74-69-78—221
2	Gemma Dryburgh (Beaconsfield)	78-69-75—222
	Gabrielle MacDonald (Craigielaw)	73-71-78—222

Scottish Girls' Close Championship (inaugurated 1960) *Crail Golfing Society, Balcomie (Craighead Links)*

Semi-Finals:
Lauren Whyte (St Regulus) beat Rachel Walker (Dumfries and County) 1 hole
Ailsa Summers (Carnoustie Ladies) beat Tegan Seivwright (Deeside) 1 hole

Final: Lauren Whyte beat Ailsa Summers 4 and 2

SLGA Under-16 Stroke Play Championship *Strathmore*

1	Gabriella Cowley (West Essex)	73-73—146
2	Ludovica Farina (ITA)	74-73—147
3	Nicola Callander (Mill Green)	80-68—148

SLGA Under-16 Stroke Play Championship *continued*

International Team Event:

1	Italy	294 (Ludovica Farina, Camilla Mazzola, Camila Mortigliengo]])
2	Scotland	298
3	England	300

Welsh Girls' Championship (inaugurated 1957) *Cardiff*

Leading Qualifiers: 153: Jessica Evans (Newport) 77-76; Teleri Hughes (Gettysvue) 75-78

Semi-Finals:

Chloe Williams (Wrexham) beat Lottie Turner (Aberdovey) 6 and 4
Ella Griffiths (Pyle & Kenfig) beat Teleri Hughes (Gettysvue) at 19th

Final: Chloe Williams beat Ella Griffiths at 19th

Welsh Girls' Under-16 *Cardigan*

1	Danielle Jones (Padeswood & Buckley)	77
2	Ella Griffiths (Pyle & Kenfig)	78
	Harrie Llewellyn (Vale of Glamorgan)	78

St Andrews Junior Ladies *St Andrews (Strathtyrum, New and Old Courses)*

Golf Monthly Trophy:

Semi-Finals: Nicola Hayes (Gosforth Park Ladies) beat Lucy Eaton (Skipton) 1 hole
Connie Jaffrey (Troon Ladies) beat Tegan Seivwright (Deeside) 2 and 1

Final: Nicola Haynes beat Connie Jaffrey 1 hole

Girls' Open Quaich:

Semi-Finals: Mirren Fraser (Powfoot) beat Kirsty Brodie (Strathmore) 4 and 3
Emily Sutton (Walsall) beat Charlotte Heeps (Thornberry) 4 and 2

Final: Emily Sutton beat Mirren Fraser 6 and 5

US Girls' Junior Amateur Championship *Lake Merced GC, Daly City, California*

Semi-finals: Minjee Lee (AUS) beat Ariya Jutanugarn (THA) 2 and 1
Alison Lee (Valencia, CA) beat Lydia Ko (NZL) 2 and 1

Finals: Minjee Lee beat Alison Lee 1 hole

Royale Cup Canadian Junior Girls Championship *River Spirit GC, Calgary, Alberta*

1	Brooke Henderson (Smith Falls,ON)	68-67-69-71—275
2	Brogan McKinnon (Mississauga, ON)	69-67-74-69—279
	Jisoo Keel (Coquitlam, BC)	72-70-73-74 —289

Hong Kong Girls' Close Championship *Discovery Bay GC*

1	Mimi Ho (HKGA)	72-75—147
2	Kitty Tam (HKGA)	73-74—147
3	Isabella Leung (HKGA)	78-75—153
	Ching Suet Ming Lee (DBGC)	77-76—153

Hong Kong Junior Open Championship *Discovery Bay GC*

1	Benyapa Niphatsophon (THA)	73-36—109
2	Kanyalak Preedasuttijit (THA)	76-36—112
3	Tiana Gwenn Lau (HKGA)	77-38—115

Enjoy Jakarta World Junior Golf Championship

Damai Indah GC (Pantai Indah Kapuk course), Jakarta, Indonesia

Girls "A"	Yu Okamura (JPN)	72-73-70—215 (–1)
Girls "B"	Cheng Ssu Chia (TPE)	70-73-70—213 (–3)
Girls "C"	Papangkorn Tawattanakit (THA)	77-68-68—213 (–3)
Girls "D"	Natasha Andrea Oon (MAS)	80-77-76—233 (+17)

Paul Lawrie Foundation Scottish Girls Close Championship *Craig Craighead*

Leading Qualifiers: 153: Jessica Evans (Newport) 77-76; Teleri Hughes (Gettysvue) 75-78

Semi-Finals:

Lauren Whyte (St Regulas) beat Rachel Walker (Dumfries and County) 1 hole

Ailsa Summers (Carnoustie) beat Tegan Seivwright (Deeside) 1 hole

Final: Lauren Whyte beat Ailsa Summers 4 and 2

HSBC Junior Girls Championship *Shanghai*

1	Wang Meixing	73-78-74—225
2	Meiji Gau	76-75-76—227

Foundation scholars success in Argentina

Eilidh Briggs and Charlotte Austwick, two R&A Foundation scholars had a notable victory in Argentina last year when they won the Freddy Zorraquin Trophy at the Argentine Ladies Open Championship at the Club de Campo Los Pinguinos near Buenos Aries.

Briggs and Austwick led by nine shots after the first two rounds of the scheduled 54-hole event which ws curtailed to 36 holes because of bad weather.

Briggs, the 2011 Scottish Girls champion from Stirling University, and Austwick, a third year student at York University, had previous attended The R&A Foundation Scholars programme which supports more than 100 students in several countries during their studies. This year's R&A Scholars' Tournament is scheduled to be played over the Old and Eden courses at St Andrews.

The R&A support coaching programme in Myanmar

A special programme for coaching the Myanmar national team and developing the country's coaching infrastructure is being supported by The R&A as part of the Working for Golf programme.

Run by Australian professional Mark Holland, the programme will not only help the Myanmar Golf Federation with the coaching of the leading players in the country but also provide invaluable help to the coaches themselves.

Holland, a former playing professional on the Australasian circuit but since then involved as head coach of the much-praised Australian Institute of Sport's golf programme, will make four visits to Myanmar to work with the 70 professionals in the country. The Asian Golf Industry Federation is also helping the programme.

Dominic Wall, The R&A's Director, Asia–Pacific, says: "Mark Holland has a wealth of experience in developing talented young players and will help working out a training regime for the Myanmar National Team for the South-East Asian Games."

Team Events

European Lady Juniors Team Championship

Discontinued – for past results see the 2008 edition of The R&A Golfer's Handbook

European Girls Team Championship *St Leon Rot GC, Heidelberg, Germany*

Qualifying:

1	England	338-347—685
2	Spain	357-349—706
3	Germany	360-360—720
4	Italy	364-358—722
5	Netherlands	366-363—729
6	Denmark	367-363—730
7	France	366-366—732
8	Sweden	371-363—734

9 Finland 735; 10 Belgium 736; 11 Czech Republic 752; 12 Switzerland 752; 13 Ireland 753; 14 Scotland 759; 15 Turkey 760; 16 Norway 772; 17 Austria 774; 18 Icelamnd 776; 19 Wales 782; 20 Slovakia 815

Leading Match Play qualifiers: England (Georgia Hall 67-66—133; Elizabeth Mallett 64-69—133; Charley Hull 68-66—134; Emily Taylor 67-71—138; Bronte Law 72-75—147; Meghan MacLaren 72-78—150)

Match Play:

Semi-finals: Sweden 5½, Italy 1½
Spain 4½, Denmark 2½

Final: Sweden 4 Spain 2

Winning team: Linn Andersson, Linnea Strom, Mia Landegren, Emma Nilsson, Elsa Westin, Isabella Dellert

Denmark beat Italy 5½–1½ to take third place

Girls Home Internationals (Stroyan Cup) *Radyr*

Day 1: Wales 4½, Scotland 4½; Ireland 4½, England 4½
Day 2: England 5½, Scotland 3½; Ireland 4½, Wales 4½
Day 3: Scotland 4, Ireland 5; Wales 4, England 5

Final Table: 1 England 15; 2 Ireland 14; 3rd Wales 13; 4th Scotland 12

Winning team: Non-playing captain: Chris Pascall, Gabriella Cowley (West Essex), Georgia Hall (Remedy Oak), Meghan Maclaren (Wellingborough), Elizabeth Mallett (Sutton Coldfield), Amber Ratcliffe (Royal Cromer), Shelby Smart (Knowle), Brogan Townend (Pleasington), Olivia Winning (Rotherham)

Junior Solheim Cup

2002	USA 17, Europe 7	2005	USA 16, Europe 8	2009	USA 15½, Europe 8½
2003	Europe 12½, USA 11½	2007	Europe 14, USA 10	2011	Europe 7, USA 5

GB&I Under 16 *v* Continent of Europe Under 16

This event will next be held in 2013

Irish Girls' Inter-Provincial Championship *Ballinrobe GC*

Day One: Ulster 3½, Munster 4½; Connacht 1, Leinster 7
Day Two: Leinster 3, Munster 5; Connacht 1½, Ulster 7½
Day Three: Munster 7½, Connacht ½; Ulster 2½, Leinster 5½

Final table	*P*	*W*	*D*	*L*	*Pts*
1 Munster	3	3	0	0	3
2 Leinster	3	2	0	1	2
3 Ulster	3	1	0	2	1
4 Connacht	3	0	0	3	0

Winning team: Gemma McCarthy, Tara Whelan, Ciara Magill, Lisa O'Shea, Aoife Barry, Michelle Tierney, Ciara Leonard and Paula Walsh

SLGA Under-16 Stroke Play Championship *Strathmore*

1	Italy	294 (Ludovica Farina, Camilla Mazzola, Camila Mortigliengo)
2	Scotland	298
3	England	300

The R&A supports junior golf in Cambodia

Through its Working for Golf programme, The R&A provided golf clubs and other equipment including rule books, golf caps, pens, badges, towels and backpacks to juniors involved in golf clinics in Cambodia.

The clinics, the first of their kind in Cambodia, proved popular with children who had never played golf before. Organised by the Cambodian Golf Federation they were managed by former Australian captain Roger Hunt, the Federation's advisor.

Staged last year at the Golf Village Range in Phnom Penh they continued this year when they were open to newcomers. Previous students, however, received more advanced coaching to help develop further their skills and understanding of not just the rules but also the etiquette of the game.

Month by month in 2012

Further wins by European Ryder Cup team members keep on coming. Martin Kaymer triumphs in South Africa on the same day that Graeme McDowell takes a second World Challenge in California, then Sergio García is successful in Indonesia. Player of the month, however, is South African Charl Schwartzel – he follows an 11-stroke win in Thailand with a 12-shot margin at the Alfred Dunhill Championship on home soil. Tom Watson, 63, is named American Ryder Cup captain.

Mixed Boys' and Girls' Events

For past results see earlier editions of *The R&A Golfer's Handbook*

R&A Junior Open Championship *Fairhaven*

1	Asuka Kashiwabara (JPN)	66-69-71—206
2	Renato Paratore (ITA)	75-72-73—220
3	Gabriella Cowley (ENG)	74-72-78—224

European Young Masters *Royal Balaton GC, Hungary* July 26–29

Team competition:

1	Italy	215-215-215—645
2	Spain	222-214-228—664
3	Czech Republic	226-221-219—666

4 Germany, England 668; 6 Sweden 670; 7 Belgium, France 677; 9 Austria 678; 10 Slovenia 682; 11 Netherlands, Norway 684; 13 Ireland 691; 14 Switzerland, Scotland 697; 16 Denmark 698; 17 Wales 700; 18 Turkey 709; 19 Finland 718; 20 Hungary 724; 21 Portugal 728; 22 Iceland 735; 23 Slovakia 747; 24 Latvia 778; 25 Poland 780; 26 Russia 781

Winning team (two best scores out of three to count each day): Italy (Francesca Avanzini 77-75-73; Virginia Elena Carta 83-74-71; Renato Paratore 67-69-73; Guido Migliozzi 71-72-71)

Boys Individual:

1	Renato Paratore (ITA)	67-69-73—209
2	Guido Migliozzi (ITA)	71-72-71—214
3	John Axelsen (DEN)	75-70-70—215

Girls Individual:

1	Covadonga Sanjvan (ESP)	74-73-74—221
2	Ana Belac (SLO)	75-75-74—224
3	Francesca Avanzini (ITA)	77-75-73—225

Faldo Series

Great Britain:

Boys:

Moortown	Jordan Wrisdale (ENG)	71
R Ashdown Forest	Freddie Price (ENG)	72
Trentham	Oliver Farrell (ENG)	143
West Lancs	Louis Tomlinson (ENG)	145
Pyle & Kenfig	David Blick (ENG)	145
Old Fold Manor	Robbie Busher (ENG)	142
Panmure	Ewan Scott (SCO)	139
Hollinwell	Kyson Lloyd (ENG)	142

Girls:

Rochelle Morris (ENG)	74
Samantha Giles (ENG)	73
Gemma Batty (ENG)	153
Hollie Muse (ENG)	158
Elizabeth Swallow (ENG)	152
Gabriella Cowley (ENG)	144
Kimberley Beveridge (SCO)	152
Amber Ratcliffe (ENG)	143

Europe:

Czech Rep.	Vitek Novak (CZE)	208	Telc GC
Russia	Vladimir Osipov (RUS)	213	Agalarov G&CC
Greece	Assaf Cohen (ISR)	150	Glyfada GC
Netherlands	Max Albertus (NED)	203	Goyer G&CC
Germany	Yannick Bludau (GER)	142	Sporting Club Berlin
Slovakia	Oliver Gabor (SVK)	218	Black Stork
Ireland	Rowan Lester (IRL)	141	Lough Erne
Austria	Keanu Jahns (GER)	210	Waldhofen Golf Resort

South America:

Brazil	Juan Alvarez (URU)	216	Brasilia GC
Chile	Claudio Correa (CHI)	141	Club de Golf Sport Francés

2012 16th Faldo European Series Grand Final *Lough Erne*

1	Jack Singh-Brar (ENG)	72-78-72—222
2	Rochelle Morris (ENG)	72-75-77—224
	Ewan Scott (SCO)	72-75-77—224

Asia:

China	Abhijit Chada (IND)	216	Mission Hills

2012–2013 Series:

Philippines	Lawrence Celestino (PHI)	224	Filipinas
Shanghai	Wu haochuan (CHN)	139	Taihu International
China	Wang You Xin (CHN)	138	Mission Hills
Chinese Taipei	Wei-hsiang Wang (TPE)	65	Sunrise G&CC
Vietnam	Bao Nghi Ngo (VIE)	148	Ocean Dunes
India – Boys	Shubhankar Sharma (IND)	292	Chandigarh GC
India – Girls	Gurbani Singh (IND)	212	The Tollygunge Club
Singapore	Edgar Oh (SIN)	209	Warren G&CC
Malaysia	Muhammad Wafiyuddin Abdul Manus (MAS)	218	Royal Sengalor
Nepal	Ziwaing Gurung (BHU)	149	Gokarna Forest Resort, Kathmandu
Hong Kong	Terrence Ng (HKG)	143	Kau Sai Chau (North)
Brunei	Joshua Gibbons (ENG)	143	Empire CC
Cambodia	Kim Dong Hyun (KOR)	139	Angkor Golf Resort

Fairhaven Trophies *Fairhaven*

Nations Cup

England I	288
England II	290
Finland I	293

Germany II 295; England III 296; Scotland III, Finland II, Germany I 307; Scotland II 300; Scotland I 308; Finland III 316 [11 teams played]

Winning team: Gabriella Cowley (West Essex), Max Orrin (North Foreland), Patrick Kelly (Boston West)

Boys Individual:

Patrick Kelly (Boston West)	69-74-71-71—285
Joe Dean (Lindrick)	68-73-71-75—287
Ashton Turner (Kenwick Park)	70-74-71-73—288
Nick Marsh (Huddersfield)	70-71-73-74—288

Girls Individual:

Iida Nikka (FIN)	74-79-72-73—298
Olivia Winning (Rotherham)	70-79-75-75—299
Miia Pulliainen (FIN)	74-73-78-76—301

The Junior Ryder Cup *Olympia Fields CC (South course), Illinois*

Non-Playing Captains: Europe – Stuart Wilson; USA – Roger Warren

European names first

***First Day* – Foursomes:**

Toby Tree & Gavin Moynihan halved with Cameron Champ & Beau Hossler
Bronte Law & Quirine Eijkenboom lost to Casie Cathrea & Samantha Wagner 3 and 2
Matthias Schwab & Dominic Foos beat Scottie Scheffler & Robby Shelton 5 and 4
Harang Lee & Covadonga Sanjuan lost to Casey Danielson & Karen Chung 2 and 1
Victor Tarnstrom & Renato Paratore beat Gavin Hall & Jim Liu 3 and 2
Linnea Strom & Emily Pedersen lost to Esther Lee & Alison Lee 1 hole

Four balls:

Toby Tree & Bronte Law lost to Casie Cathrea & Cameron Champ 1 hole
Gavin Moynihan & Emily Pedersen beat Beau Hossler & Samantha Wagner 2 and 1
Renato Paratore & Harang Lee beat Scottie Scheffler & Casey Danielson 5 and 3
Dominic Foos & Covadonga Sanjuan lost to Robby Shelton & Karen Chung 3 and 2

The Junior Ryder Cup *continued*

Matthias Schwab & Quirine Eijkenboom halved with Gavin Hall & Alison Lee
Victor Tarnstrom & Linnea Strom lost to Jim Liu & Esther Lee 6 and 5

***Second Day* – Singles:**
Emily Pedersen (DEN) lost to Casie Cathrea 2 holes
Toby Tree (ENG) halved with Cameron Champ
Quirine Eijkenboom (SWE) lost to Karen Chung 4 and 2
Renato Paratore (ITA) lost to Robby Shelton 2 and 1
Harang Lee (ESP) lost to Casey Danielson 3 and 2
Dominic Foos (GER) beat Beau Hossler 3 and 1
Covadonga Sanjuan (ESP) beat Samantha Wagner 1 hole
Matthias Schwab (AUT) beat Scottie Scheffler 3 and 2
Linnea Strom (SWE) lost to Alison Lee 6 and 5
Victor Tarnstrom (SWE) lost to Gavin Hall 2 and 1
Bronte Law (ENG) lost to Esther Lee 1 hole
Gavin Moynihan (IRL) beat Jim Liu 4 and 3

Match result: Europe 9½, USA 14½

1995	Exhibition Match won by Europe	1999	Europe	2006	Europe
1997	United States	2002	Europe	2008	USA
		2004	Europe	2010	USA

12th Duke of York Young Champions Trophy *Royal Troon GC*

Field included 53 champions from 31 countries

1	Ragnar Gardarsson (ISL)*	76-77-72—225
2	Max Orrin (ENG)	71-77-77—225
3	Katya Pogacar (SLO)	72-74-79—225

**Gardarsson won at the third extra hole*

The 13th Duke of York Young Champions event will be played at Royal St George's from September 10–12 2013

Paul Lawrie Foundation Junior Open *Deeside GC*

Boys Scratch:

1	Sam Kiloh (Portlethen)	71
2	Ben Murray (Portlethen)	73
3	Jack Harding (Banchory)	73
4	Jamie Pryde (Deeside)	74

Junior Ryder Cuppers met Love and Olazábal at Medinah

Quirine Eijkenboom of Germany and Gavin Moynihan of Ireland teamed up with Americans Alison Lee from California and Robby Wilmer from Atlanta to win the Junior Ryder Cup Friendship Match played two days before the Ryder Cup at Medinah.

The 24 youngsters involved in the Junior Ryder Cup, won by the Americans 14–9 at Olympia Field Country Club in Illinois, split into six teams of four each comprising a boy and a girl from both teams.

Before they played their 10-hole match involving holes on both the back and front nines of the Medinah Ryder Cup course, they met with US Ryder Cup captain Davis Love and the European captain José Maria Olazábal.

The winning mixed four-ball partnership was four-under-par for the 10 holes with Gavin Moynihan making two birdies.

Boys Handicap:

1	Patrick McKenna (Royal Aberdeen 5)	69
2	Sam Locke (Inchmarlo 10)	70
	Ross Kennedy (Stonehaven 25)	70
	Daniel Wilson (Turriff 5)	70
	Andrew George (Royal Aberdeen 25)	70

Girls Scratch:

1	Tegwen Seivwright (Deeside)	77

Girls Handicap:

1	Fiona Sutherland (Deeside 20)	72

Paul Lawrie Foundation Match Play Championship *Newmachar*

Boys under 18:

Semi-finals: Craig Lawrie (Deeside) beat Ben Murray (Portlethen) 5 and 4
Lewis McvWilliam (Aboyne) beat Kerr Baptie (Duff House) 1 hole

Final: Lewis McWilliam beat Craig Lawrie 1 hole

Girls under 18:

Semi-finals: Kimberley Beveridge (Aboyne) beat Tegan Seivwright (Deeside) 5 and 4
Sophie Alexander (Deeside) beat Molly Stewart (Murcar Links) 1 hole

Final: Kimberley Beveridge beat Sophie Alexander 4 and 3

Junior Orange Bowl *Biltmore GC, Florida*

[Boys: 6742–71; Girls: 6089–71]

Boys:

1	Patrick Kelly (ENG)	65-68-66-66—265
2	Jamie Lopez-Rivarola (ARG)	69-67-70-72—278
3	Corey Pereira (USA)	68-66-74-71—279

Girls:

1	Maria Torres (PUR)	75-73-66-74—288
2	Nicole Morales (USA)	72-72-72-73—289
3	Megan Khang (USA)	69-70-74-77—290

Callaway Junior Golf Championship *California, USA*

	Boys:		Girls:	
15–17	Rico Hoey (USA)	286	Benyapa Niphatsophon (THA)	280
13–14	Rhett Rasmussen (USA)	204	Lilia Kha-Tu Vu (USA)	205
11–12	Parathakorn Suyasri (THA)	211	Sifan He (CHN)	217
9–10	Karl Vilips (AUS)	182	Francesca Bernice Olivarez-Ilas (PHI)	167
7–8	Jed Llamado Dy (PHI)	184	Tsubasa Kajitani (JPN)	177
6 and under	Ryusei Sawada (JPN)	163	Pimchompoo Chaisilprungruang (THA)	181

Team event:

15–17 1 USA; 2 Canada; 3 Philippines — 1 USA 2 Australia; 3 Japan

4th World Golf Schools Challenge *St Andrews Beach, Eagle Ridge and Moonah Links, Mornington Peninsula, Victoria, Australia*

Division I Boys	Matt Morris (St Peter's School)	75-76-72-71—294.
Division II Boys	Bailey Watson (Haileybury College)	84-78-77-78—317
Division III Boys	Matt Scott (St Peterís School)	78-87-79-83—327
Division IV Boys	Constantyn TenCate (St Peter's School)	82-94-86-89—351
Girls Division	Lillie Callow (Haileybury College)	79-82-83-87—331

Mixed Teams: 1 St Peter's School (Team 2) 797 (Constantyn TenCate, Kyra Alexander, Ryan Coxon, Tian Chi Song); 2 Haileybury (Team 3) 806 (Lillie Callow, Mason Shephard, Will Garner, Bryanna Armao)

Girls Team: 1442 (Caro Els, Jessica Dreesbeimdieke, Sebrina Schneider and Anja Vermaak)

4th World Golf Schools Challenge *continued*

Boys Team: 1 Whangerei Boys High (Team 1) 921 (Chase McKeown, Luke Brown, Kadin Neho, Sean Master); 2 Haileybury College (Team 1) 932 (Leigh Pritchard, Conor Davis, David Shimmin, Bailey Watson)

The 5th World Schools Challenge will be staged at Hua Hin, Thailand from March 31 to April 5 2013

KeNako South Africa World Juniors Championship *Kingswood Estate*

Boys: Sweden (Hampus Bergman 76-72-72—220; Hannes Ronneblad 70-70-71—211)
Individual: Hannes Ronneblad (SWE) 70-70-71—211.

Girls: South Africa (Bianca Theron 80-72-84—236; Lara Weinstein 78-74-68—220

Trans Tasman Cup *Peninsula CC, Frankston, Australia*

Australia 34½, New Zealand 13½

Boys (Clare Higson Trophy):
Australia 9, New Zealand 3

Winning team: Lucas Herbert, Ruben Sondaja, Anthony Murdaca and Oliver Goss

Girls (Junior Tasman Cup):
Australia 10, New Zealand 2

Winning team: Hannah Green, Lauren Mason, Jaimee Dougan and Su On

For Men's and Women's events see page 439

USA *v* China Youths International *CordeValle GC, San Martin, California*

Day One – Foursomes:
Sebastian Crampton and Patrick Cover beat Li Yuan and Jin Cheng 1 hole
Michael Pisciotta and Thomas Walsh beat Guan Tian Lang and Dou Ze Cheng 1 hole
Hana Ku and Divya Manthena lost to Shi Yu Ting and Wang Zi Yi 5 and 4
Jessica Kittelberger and Calli Ringsby lost to Liu Yu and Ji Rong 6 and 4

Fourballs:
Crampton and Walsh beat Jin Cheng and Dou Ze Cheng 2 and 1
Cover and Pisciotti beat Guan Tian Lang and Li Yuan 4 and 3
Manthena and Ringsby beat Shi Tu Ying and Liu Yu 1 hole
Ku and Kittelberger halved with Ji Rong and Wang Zi Yi

Match position: USA 5½, China 2½

Day Two – Singles:
Pisciotta lost to Li Yuan 3 and 2
Cover lost to Dou Ze Chang 3 and 1
Crampton halved with Guan Yian Lang
Walsh halved with Jin Cheng
Ringsby halved with Wang Zi Yi
Kittelberger lost to Ji Rong 6 and 5
Ku lost to Liu Yu 5 and 3
Manthena lost to Shi Yu Ting 4 and 3

Final Result: USA 7, China 9

China recover to beat USA in Youth Challenge

It is a measure of the growing strength of Chinese golf that in the Ryder Cup style youths match between China and the United States at the CordeValle Resort it was the visitors who triumphed.

The first series of foursomes involving four boys and four girls in competition were halved 2–2 and the USA edged ahead with a solid showing in the fourballs which they won 3½–½ to lead 5½–2½ but the final day belonged to the Chinese.

Li Yuan and Dou Ze Cheng beat Michael Pisciotta and Patrick Cover respectively and the remaining two games were halved. In the top girls singles match Wang Si Yi halved with Calli Ringsby but the other Chinese girls – Shi Tu Ying, Liu Yu and Ji Rong all won comfortably to give the visitors a 6½–1½ victory in the singles and a 9–7 win overall.

PART IX

Tournaments for the Disabled

Tournaments for the Disabled

For past results see earlier editions of *The R&A Golfer's Handbook*

British Blind Open *Cardrona Hotel G&CC, Peebles, Scotland*

Men:

B1: Andrea Calcaterra (ITA) 134-125—259
B2: Pieta Le Roux (ENG) 95-88—183
B3: John Eakin (ENG) 91-86—177

Women:

Chiara Pozzi Giacosa (ITA) B1

British Blind Masters *Tewkesbury Park GC. Gloucestershire*

Stroke Play:

Allan Morgan B3 82-78-74-71—305

Stableford:

Euin Hill 39-82-38-29—128 points

Billy McAllister won the Terry Wallace Trophy for the best four day score by a B1 player

English Match Play Championship (for blind golfers) *Patshull Park GC, Shropshire*

Pieta Le Roux beat John Eakin 6 and 5

English Stroke Play Championship (for blind golfers) *Bankhouse Hotel, Worcestershire*

Pieta Le Roux B2 83-80—163

Scottish Match Play Championship (for blind golfers) *Murrayshall GC, Scone*

Ally Reid beat John Miller 5 and 4

Scottish Stroke Play Championship (for blind golfers) *Drumoig GC*

John Imrie 82-72—154

Scotland v England Blind Golf Competition for the Auld Enemy Cup

Padeswood & Buckley GC, Flintshire

Scotland 13½, England 10½

The Celtic Cup (for blind golfers) Ireland v Scotland *Templepatrick GC, Belfast*

Scotland 5½, Ireland 3½

World Blind Golf Championships *Truro Golf Club, Nova Scotia, Canada*

1	Zohar Sharon (ISR)	118-98—216
2	Andrea Calcaterra (ITA)	114-108—222
3	Gerry Nelson (CAN)	122-116—238

Blind Golf Categories: B1 Totally blind; B2 From the ability to recognise the shape of a hand up to visual acuity of 20/600; B3 From visual acuity above 20/600 up to visual acuity of less than 20/200

75th One-Armed Golf Society World Championships (inaugurated 1932)

St Andrews (Eden, Old, New and Strathtyrum courses)

Match Play Final: Alex Hjallmarson (Haverdals GC, Sweden) beat Robert Paul (Walmer & Kingsdown GC, England) 6 and 4

Stroke Play Champion: Robert Paul 162

Bob Hughes Cup: Robert Paul 42 points (74 gross)

President's Prize: Bill Boyes (McDonald GC, Scotland) 42 points

Disabled British Open (inaugurated 2009) *East Sussex National*

Overall Gross Champion: Alasdair Berry (Ravenspark GC) 76-77—153

Nett Champion Category 1 (Handicap 0–13.4): Alasdair Berry (Ravenspark GC)

Nett Champion Category 2 (Handicap 13.5–20.4): Andrew Sellars (Normanton GC)

Nett Champion Category 3 (Stableford – H/cap 20.5+): Scott Richardson (Stockwood Park GC)

Junior Stableford Winner: Frankie Jones (Welshpool) 45-43—88 points

International Cup (formerly the College Park Cup) *Brickyard Crossing Golf Course, Indianapolis, IN*

USA *v* International (USA names first)

***Morning* – foursomes:**

John Barton & Roe Skidmore *v* George MacDonald (CAN) & Dallas Smith (CAN)
John Novak & Kim Moore *v* Vic McClelland (CAN) & Jennie Frost (RSA)
Brent Bleyenberg & Adam Benza *v* Johannes Grames (CAN) & Yoshio Asano (JPN)
Kellie Valentine & Toby Plasencio *v* Ken Furuta (JPN) & Takuya Akiyama (JPN)
Kenny Bontz & Mike Carver *v* Gwen Davies (CAN) & Ron Versteegen (CAN)
Barry Hill & Chad Pfeifer *v* Woody Walker (AUS) & Josh Williams (CAN)
Lucian Newmann III & Rob Reddick *v* Rod Reimer (CAN) & Juma Hekmati (AFG)
Shawn Brown & Derek Seifert *v* Bernard Ouellet (CAN) & Jesse Florkowski (CAN)

Match position: USA 5½, International 2½

Afternoon – singles:

Skidmore *v* Williams
Hill *v* Ken Nichols (CAN)
Barton *v* Davies
Carver *v* MacDonald
Brown *v* Hekmati
Bontz *v* Florkowski
Newmann *v* Akiyama
Moore *v* Asano
Novak *v* McClelland
Bleyenberg *v* Furuta
Valentine *v* Walker
Plasencio v Frost
Reddick *v* Versteegen
Seifert *v* Grames
Pfeifer *v* Ouellet
Benza *v* Reimer

Result: USA 16, International 8

History: The College Park Cup (formerly the Robinson Cup), a Ryder Cup-style competition for amputee golfers between US and International teams of 16 players apiece, was inaugurated in 1999 by College Park Industries of Fraser, Michigan, USA. Following the 2011 matches, College Park felt they were unable to continue as sole sponsors and the event was taken up by the US National Amputee Golf Association and renamed the International Cup. At the end of the 2011 season, the tally of victories was seven for the USA and six the International team with one match rained off and declared a draw.

The 2nd International Cup will be held at Wilderness Ridge Country Club in Lincoln, Nebraska.

BALASA National Championships *Broome Manor Golf Complex, Swindon*

Gross Champion: Duncan Hamilton-Martin 142

Category 1 Nett (hcps 0–12):

1	Shaun Bakker	141
2	Bill West	148
3	Mark Smith	149

Category 2 Nett (hcps 13–18):

1	Richard Saunders	138
2	Ian Dixon	152
3	Doug Holt	154

Category 3 Stableford: (hcps 19–28):

1	Bill Savage	64 pts
2	David Walker	62 pts
3	Simon Mugglestone	61 pts

3rd Fightmaster Cup *Hilton Indian Lakes Resort, Chicago, IL, USA*

North America *v* Europe (North America names first)

Day One: *Morning* – four balls:
Mike Benning & John Trenchik lost to Alex Hjalmarsson & Stefan Ostling 4 and 3
Vince Biser & Pat Schroeder halved with Robert Paul & Brendan Swan
Laurent Hurtubise & Klaus Schaloske lost to Nick Champness & Michael O'Grady 1 up
Alan Gentry & Steve Day lost to Darren Grey & Cian Arthurs 1 up

***Afternoon* – foursomes:**
Mike Benning & Carson Novins lost to Alex Hjalmarsson & David Schutsander 4 and 3
Vince Biser & Clay Kemper lost to Robert Paul & Doug Jopp 3 and 2
Alan Gentry & Scott Lusk lost to Darren Grey & Stuart Griffin 3 and 2
Laurent Hurtubise & Steve Quevillon lost to Cian Arthurs & David Waterhouse 4 and 3

Day Two: *Morning* – four balls:
Laurent Hurtubise & John Trenchik lost to Alex Hjalmarsson & Stefan Ostling 4 and 3
Vince Biser & Steve Day lost to Robert Paul & Brendan Swan 3 and 2
Mike Benning & Klaus Schaloske halved with Nick Champness & Michael O'Grady
Pat Schroder & Carson Novins lost to Darren Grey & Cian Arthurs 3 and 2

***Afternoon* – foursomes:**
Alan Gentry & Scott Lusk lost to Alex Hjalmarsson & David Schutsander 2 and 1
Robert Paul & Doug Jopp lost to Laurent Hurtubise & Clay Kemper 3 and 2
Mike Benning & Vince Biser lost to Darren Grey & Stuart Griffin 1 up
Steve Quevillon & John Trenchik beat Cian Arthurs & David Waterhouse 5 and 4

Day Three – Singles:
Alan Gentry (USA) halved with Darren Grey (ENG)
Scott Lusk (USA) lost to Cian Arthurs (IRL) 1 up
Steve Day (USA) lost to Stuart Griffin (SCO) 3 and 2
Mike Benning (USA) beat David Schutsander (SWE) 1 up
Laurent Hurtubise (CAN) halved with Stefan Ostling (SWE)
John Trenchik (USA) beat Brendan Swan (IRL) 4 and 3
Pat Schroeder (USA) beat David Waterhouse (ENG) 5 and 4
Klaus Schaloske (CAN) lost to Doug Jopp (SCO) 6 and 5
Carson Novins (USA) lost to Robert Paul (ENG) 6 and 5
Clay Kemper (USA) lost to Nick Champness (ENG) 8 and 7
Vince Biser (USA) halved with Michael O'Grady (IRL)
Steve Quevillion (CAN) lost to Alex Hjalmarsson (SWE) 4 and 3

Result: Europe 20½, North America 7½

SDGP Competitions

St Michaels GC; Bob Drysdale
The Dukes GC: Bob Drysdale
Cluny GC: Bob Drysdale
Swanston GC: Bob Drysdale
Charleton GC: Derek Milne
Morecambe GC: Garry McNulty
Liberton GC: Mike Mayo
Broomiknowe GC: Gary Gardner
Alloa GC: M G-Hansen, J Elliot and J MacLeod
Pumpherston GC: Jim Gales
Bonnyton GC: Jocky Elliot
Scottish Championships, Dullatur GC: Colin Brock
Dalmahoy East: Bob Drysdale
Kinross GC: Adrian Canny (net) and Kevin Harmison (gross)
Lundin GC: Derek Milne
Kittocks GC: Jim Gales
Carricknowe GC: Daniel Harper
Conrad German Open, Schwanhof GC: Jim Gales
Elmwood GC: Derek Milne
Eden GC St Andrews: Stevie Cunningham
Tulliallen GC: Frank Morrison

Scottish Order of Merit Championship final placings:
1 Bob Drysdale
2 Derek Milne
3 Colin Brock
4 Stevie Cunningham
5 Jim Gales

Other Events (winners from host nation unless stated)

Alberta Amputee Open
Jesse Florkowski 146

Australian Amputee Open
Open Champion: Shane Luke; Ladies Champion: Trudy Tassone; Senior Champion: Rod Carroll

Australian Blind Golf Open
Overall Champion: Inchan Cho (KOR)

Australian Stableford Championship
Jeff Ellis (Victoria) B3

Canadian Amputee National Open
Men's Overall Champion: Josh Williams; Senior Champion: Rod Reimer; Super Senior Champion: Dan Hewitt; Super Super Senior Champion: Bill Harding; Ladies' Overall Champion: Jennie Frost

Canadian Blind Golf Open
Zohar Sharon (ISR)

Danish Paragolf Championship
Stefan Mørkholt 221

Nedbank SA Disabled Golf Open
Daniel Slabbert

New South Wales Blind Open
Jenny Abela B2

Swedish Handigolf Open
Cauneau Mathieu (FRA) 157

64th USA National Amputee Championship
National Champion (Men): Josh Williams; (Women): Kimberly Moore

23rd USA National Senior Amputee Championship
National Champion (Men): Jim O'Keane; (Women): Jennie Frost

Victorian Blind Open
David Byth B1

Golf organisations for the disabled

International Blind Golf Association	www.internationalblindgolf.org
English Blind Golf Association	www.blindgolf.co.uk
Scottish Blind Golf Association	www.scottishblindgolf.com
BALASA	01773 715984
British Amputee Golf Association	www.baga.org.uk
The Society of One Armed Golfers	www.onearmgolf.org
European Disabled Golf Association	www.edgagolf.com
Deaf Golf Association	www.deafgolf.com
Disabled British Open	www.disabledbritishopen.org

Donations to special needs groups

The R&A supports several organisations which run golf events for players with special needs. In 2012, £50,000 was set aside for this purpose and a similar amount will be allocated this year. In addition, The R&A does, on occasion, send referees and other representatives to events run for disabled golfers.

PART X

Record Scoring

Record Scoring

In the Major Championships nobody has shot lower than 63. There have been eight 63s in the Open, four 63s in the US Open, two 63s in The Masters and 11 63s in the USPGA Championship. The lowest first 36 holes is 130 by Nick Faldo in the 1992 Open at Muirfield and Brandt Snedeker in the 2012 Open at Royal Lytham and the lowest 72 hole total is 265 by David Toms in the 2001 USPGA Championship at the Atlanta Athletic Club.

The Open Championship

Most times champions
6 Harry Vardon, 1896–98–99–1903–11–14
5 James Braid, 1901–05–06–08–10; JH Taylor, 1894–95–1900–09–13; Peter Thomson, 1954–55–56–58–65; Tom Watson, 1975–77–80–82–83

Most times runner-up
7 Jack Nicklaus, 1964–67–68–72–76–77–79
6 JH Taylor, 1896–1904–05–06–07–14

Oldest winner
Old Tom Morris, 46 years 99 days, 1867
Roberto De Vicenzo, 44 years 93 days, 1967

Youngest winner
Young Tom Morris, 17 years 5 months 8 days, 1868
Willie Auchterlonie, 21 years 24 days, 1893
Severiano Ballesteros, 22 years 3 months 12 days, 1979

Youngest and oldest competitor
Young Tom Morris, 15 years, 4 months, 29 days, 1866
Gene Sarazen, 71 years 4 months 13 days, 1973

Widest margin of victory
13 strokes Old Tom Morris, 1862
12 strokes Young Tom Morris, 1870
8 strokes JH Taylor, 1900 and 1913; James Braid, 1908; Tiger Woods, 2000
7 strokes Louis Oosthuizen, 2010

Lowest winning aggregates
267 Greg Norman, 66-68-69-64, Sandwich, 1993
268 Tom Watson, 68-70-65-65, Turnberry, 1977; Nick Price, 69-66-67-66, Turnberry, 1994
269 Tiger Woods, 67-66-67-69, St Andrews, 2000
270 Nick Faldo, 67-65-67-71, St Andrews, 1990; Tiger Woods 67-65-71-67, Hoylake, 2006

Lowest in relation to par
19 under Tiger Woods, St Andrews, 2000
18 under Nick Faldo, St Andrews, 1990; Tiger Woods, Hoylake, 2006

Lowest aggregate by runner-up
269 (68-70-65-66), Jack Nicklaus, Turnberry, 1977; (69-63-70-67), Nick Faldo, Sandwich, 1993; (68-66-68-67), Jesper Parnevik, Turnberry, 1994

Lowest aggregate by an amateur
281 (68-72-70-71), Iain Pyman, Sandwich, 1993; (75-66-70-70), Tiger Woods, Royal Lytham, 1996

Lowest round
63 Mark Hayes, second round, Turnberry, 1977; Isao Aoki, third round, Muirfield, 1980; Greg Norman, second round, Turnberry, 1986; Paul Broadhurst, third round, St Andrews, 1990; Jodie Mudd, fourth round, Royal Birkdale, 1991; Nick Faldo, second round, Payne Stewart, fourth round, Sandwich, 1993; Rory McIlroy, first round, St Andrews, 2010

Lowest round by an amateur
65 Tom Lewis, first round, Sandwich, 2011

Lowest first round
63 Rory McIlroy, St Andrews, 2010

Lowest second round
63 Mark Hayes, Turnberry, 1977; Greg Norman, Turnberry, 1986; Nick Faldo, Sandwich, 1993

Lowest third round
63 Isao Aoki, Muirfield, 1980; Paul Broadhurst, St Andrews, 1990

Lowest fourth round
63 Jodie Mudd, Royal Birkdale, 1991; Payne Stewart, Sandwich, 1993

Lowest first 36 holes
130 (66-64) Nick Faldo, Muirfield 1992; (66-64) Brandt Snedeker, Royal Lytham 2012
131 (64-67) Adam Scott, Royal Lytham 2012

Lowest second 36 holes
130 (65-65), Tom Watson, Turnberry, 1977; (64-66) Ian Baker-Finch, Royal Birkdale, 1991; (66-64) Anders Forsbrand, Turnberry, 1994

Lowest first 54 holes
198 (67-67-64), Tom Lehman, Royal Lytham, 1996
199 (67-65-67), Nick Faldo, St Andrews, 1990; (66-64-69), Nick Faldo, Muirfield, 1992; (64-67-68), Adam Scott, Royal Lytham 2012

Lowest final 54 holes
199 (66-67-66), Nick Price, Turnberry, 1994
200 (70-65-65), Tom Watson, Turnberry, 1977; (63-70-67), Nick Faldo, Sandwich, 1993; (66-64-70), Fuzzy Zoeller, Turnberry, 1994; (66-70-64), Nick Faldo, Turnberry 1994

Lowest 9 holes
28 Denis Durnian, first 9, Royal Birkdale, 1983

Champions in three decades
Harry Vardon, 1986, 1903, 1911; JH Taylor, 1894, 1900, 1913; Gary Player, 1959, 1968, 1974

Biggest span between first and last victories
19 years – JH Taylor, 1894–1913
18 years – Harry Vardon, 1896–1914
15 years – Willie Park, 1860–75
15 years – Gary Player, 1959–74
14 years – Henry Cotton, 1934–48

Successive victories
4 Young Tom Morris, 1868–72 (no championship 1871)
3 Jamie Anderson, 1877–79; Bob Ferguson, 1880–82, Peter Thomson, 1954–56

2 Old Tom Morris, 1861–62; JH Taylor, 1894–95; Harry Vardon, 1898–99; James Braid, 1905–06; Bobby Jones, 1926–27; Walter Hagen, 1928–29; Bobby Locke, 1949–50; Arnold Palmer, 1961–62; Lee Trevino, 1971–72; Tom Watson, 1982–83; Tiger Woods, 2005–06; Padraig Harrington, 2007–08

Amateur champions

John Ball, 1890, Prestwick; Harold Hilton, 1892, Muirfield and 1897, Royal Liverpool; Bobby Jones, 1926, Royal Lytham; 1927, St Andrews; 1930 Royal Liverpool

Highest number of top five finishes

16 JH Taylor and Jack Nicklaus
15 Harry Vardon and James Braid

Players with four rounds under 70

Ernie Els (68-69-69-68), Sandwich, 1993; Greg Norman (66-68-69-64), Sandwich, 1993; Jesper Parnevik (68-66-68-67), Turnberry, 1994; Nick Price (69-66-67-66), Turnberry, 1994; Tiger Woods (67-66-67-69), St Andrews, 2000; Ernie Els (69-69-68-68), Royal Troon, 2004

Highest number of rounds under 70

39 Ernie Els	**33** Jack Nicklaus
37 Nick Faldo	**29** Tom Watson
36 Ernie Els	**26** Greg Norman

Outright leader after every round (since Championship became 72 holes in 1892)

James Braid, 1908; Ted Ray, 1912; Bobby Jones, 1927; Gene Sarazen, 1932; Henry Cotton, 1934; Tom Weiskopf, 1973; Tiger Woods, 2005

Record leads (since 1892)

After 18 holes: 4 strokes – Bobby Jones, 1927; Henry Cotton, 1934; Christy O'Connor jr, 1985
After 36 holes: 9 strokes – Henry Cotton, 1934
After 54 holes: 10 strokes – Henry Cotton, 1934. 7 strokes – Tony Lema, 1964. 6 strokes – James Braid, 1908; Tom Lehman, 1996; Tiger Woods, 2000

Champions with each round lower than previous one

Jack White, 1904, Sandwich, 80-75-72-69; James Braid, 1906, Muirfield, 77-76-74-73; Ben Hogan, 1953, Carnoustie, 73-71-70-68; Gary Player, 1959, Muirfield, 75-71-70-68

Champion with four rounds the same

Densmore Shute, 1933, St Andrews, 73-73-73-73 (excluding the play-off)

Biggest variation between rounds of a champion

14 strokes – Henry Cotton, 1934, second round 65, fourth round 79. 11 strokes – Jack White, 1904, first round 80, fourth round 69; Greg Norman, 1986, first round 74, second round 63, third round 74

Biggest variation between two rounds

20 strokes: RG French, 1938, second round 71, third round 91; Colin Montgomerie, 2002, second round 64, third round 84. 18 strokes: A Tingey Jr, 1923, first round 94, second 76. 17 strokes – Jack Nicklaus, 1981, first round 83, second round 66; Ian Baker-Finch, 1986, first round 86, second round 69; Rory McIlroy, 2010, first round 63, second round 80

Best comeback by champions

After 18 holes: Harry Vardon, 1896, 11 strokes behind the leader
After 36 holes: George Duncan, 1920, 13 strokes behind leader
After 54 holes: Paul Lawrie, 1999, 10 strokes behind the leader (won four-hole play-off)

Best comeback by non-champions

Of non-champions, Greg Norman, 1989, seven strokes behind the leader and lost in a play-off

Best finishing round by a champion

64 Greg Norman, Sandwich, 1993
65 Tom Watson, Turnberry, 1977; Severiano Ballesteros, Royal Lytham, 1988; Justin Leonard, Royal Troon, 1997

Worst finishing round by a champion since 1920

79 Henry Cotton, Sandwich, 1934
78 Reg Whitcombe, Sandwich, 1938
77 Walter Hagen, Hoylake, 1924

Best opening round by a champion

65 Louis Oosthuizen, St Andrews, 2010

Worst opening round by a champion since 1919

80 George Duncan, Deal, 1920 (he also had a second round of 80)
77 Walter Hagen, Hoylake, 1924

Biggest recovery in 18 holes by a champion

George Duncan, Deal, 1920, was 13 strokes behind the leader, Abe Mitchell, after 36 holes and level after 54

Most consecutive appearances

47 Gary Player, 1955–2001

Championship since 1946 with the fewest rounds under 70

St Andrews, 1946; Hoylake, 1947; Portrush, 1951; Hoylake, 1956; Carnoustie, 1968. All had only two rounds under 70

Longest course

Carnoustie, 2007, 7,421 yards (par 71)

Largest entries

2,499 in 2005, St Andrews

Courses most often used

St Andrews 28; Prestwick 24 (but not since 1925); Muirfield 15; Sandwich 13; Hoylake 11; Royal Lytham and St Annes 11; Royal Birkdale 8; Royal Troon 8; Carnoustie 7; Musselburgh 6; Turnberry 4; Deal 2; Royal Portrush and Prince's 1

Albatrosses

Both Jeff Maggert (6th hole, 2nd round) and Greg Owen (11th hole, 3rd round) made albatrosses during the 2001 Open Championship at Royal Lytham and St Annes. No complete record of albatrosses in the history of the event is available but since 1979 there have been only five others – by Johnny Miller (Muirfield 5th hole) in 1980, Bill Rogers (Royal Birkdale 17th) 1983, Manny Zerman (St Andrews 5th) 2000, Gary Evans (Royal Troon 4th) 2004 and Paul Lawrie (Turnberry 7th) 2009

US Open

Most times champion

4 Willie Anderson, 1901–03–04–05; Bobby Jones, 1923–26–29–30; Ben Hogan, 1948–50–51–53; Jack Nicklaus, 1962–67–72–80

Prize Money

Year	Total	First Prize £	Year	Total	First Prize £	Year	Total	First Prize £
1860	nil	nil	1963	8500	1,500	1991	900,000	90,000
1863	10	nil	1965	10,000	1,750	1992	950,000	95,000
1864	16	6	1966	15,000	2,100	1993	1,000,000	100,000
1876	20	20	1968	20,000	3,000	1994	1,100,000	110,000
1889	22	8	1969	30,000	4,250	1995	1,250,000	125,000
1891	28.50	10	1970	40,000	5,250	1996	1,400,000	200,000
1892	110	(am)	1971	45,000	5,500	1997	1,586,300	250,000
1893	100	30	1972	50,000	5,500	1998	1,774,150	300,000
1910	125	50	1975	75,000	7,500	1999	2,029,950	350,000
1920	225	75	1977	100,000	10,000	2000	2,722,150	500,000
1927	275	100	1978	125,000	12,500	2001	3,229,748	600,000
1930	400	100	1979	155,000	15,500	2002	3,880,998	700,000
1931	500	100	1980	200,000	25,000	2003	3,931,000	700,000
1946	1000	150	1982	250,000	32,000	2004	4,006,950	720,000
1949	1700	300	1983	300,000	40,000	2005	3,854,900	720,000
1953	2450	500	1984	451,000	55,000	2006	3,990,916	720,000
1954	3500	750	1985	530,000	65,000	2007	4,185,400	750,000
1955	3750	1,000	1986	600,000	70,000	2008	4,260,000	750,000
1958	4850	1,000	1987	650,000	75,000	2009	4,206,354	750,000
1959	5000	1,000	1988	700,000	80,000	2010	4,546,305	850,000
1960	7000	1,250	1989	750,000	80,000	2011	5,000,000	900,000
1961	8500	1,400	1990	815,000	85,000	2012	5,000,000	900,000

Most times runner-up
5 Phil Mickelson 1999–2002–04–06–09

Oldest winner
Hale Irwin, 45 years, 15 days, Medinah, 1990

Youngest winner
Johnny McDermott, 19 years, 10 months, 12 days, Chicago, 1911

Youngest competitor
Andy Zhang, 14 years 6 months, Olympic Club 2012

Biggest winning margin
15 strokes Tiger Woods, Pebble Beach, 2000

Lowest winning aggregate
268 Rory McIlroy, Congressional, 2011

Lowest in relation to par
16 under Rory McIlroy, Congressional, 2011

Lowest round
63 Johnny Miller, fourth round, Oakmont, 1973; Jack Nicklaus, first round, Baltusrol, 1980; Tom Weiskopf, first round, Baltusrol, 1980; Vijay Singh, second round, Olympia Fields, 2003

Lowest 9 holes
29 Neal Lancaster, Shinnecock Hills, 1995, and Oakland Hills, 1996

Lowest first 36 holes
131 Rory McIlroy, Congressional, 2011

Lowest final 36 holes
132 Larry Nelson, Oakmont, 1983

Lowest first 54 holes
199 Rory McIlroy, Congressional, 2011

Lowest final 54 holes
203 Rory McIlroy, Congressional, 2011

Most consecutive appearances
44 Jack Nicklaus 1957 to 2000

Successive victories
3 Willie Anderson, 1903–04–05

Players with four rounds under 70
Lee Trevino, 69-68-69-69, Oak Hill, 1968; Lee Janzen, 67-67-69-69, Baltusrol, 1993; Rory McIlroy, 65-66-68-69, Congressional, 2011

Open attendances

Year	Attendance	Year	Attendance	Year	Attendance	Year	Attendance
1962	37,098	1975	85,258	1988	191,334	2001	178,000
1963	24,585	1976	92,021	1989	160,639	2002	161,000
1964	35,954	1977	87,615	1990	207,000	2003	182,585
1965	32,927	1978	125,271	1991	192,154	2004	176,000
1966	40,182	1979	134,501	1992	150,100	2005	223,000
1967	29,880	1980	131,610	1993	140,100	2006	230,000
1968	51,819	1981	111,987	1994	128,000	2007	153,000
1969	46,001	1982	133,299	1995	180,000	2008	201,500
1970	82,593	1983	142,892	1996	170,000	2009	123,000
1971	70,076	1984	193,126	1997	176,797	2010	201,000
1972	84,746	1985	141,619	1998	180,000	2011	180,100
1973	78,810	1986	134,261	1999	158,000	2012	181,300
1974	92,796	1987	139,189	2000	230,000		

Outright leader after every round
Walter Hagen, Midlothian, 1914; Jim Barnes, Columbia, 1921; Ben Hogan, Oakmont, 1953; Tony Jacklin, Hazeltine, 1970; Tiger Woods, Pebble Beach, 2000; Tiger Woods, Bethpage, 2002

Best opening round by a champion
63 Jack Nicklaus, Baltusrol, 1980

Worst opening round by a champion
91 Horace Rawlins, Newport, RI, 1895
***Since World War II:* 76** Ben Hogan, Oakland Hills, 1951; Jack Fleck, Olympic, 1955

Amateur champions
Francis Ouimet, Brookline, 1913; Jerome Travers, Baltusrol, 1915; Chick Evans, Minikahda, 1916; Bobby Jones, Inwood, 1923, Scioto, 1926, Winged Foot, 1929, Interlachen, 1930; Johnny Goodman, North Shore, 1933

The Masters

Most times champion
6 Jack Nicklaus, 1963–65–66–72–75–86
4 Arnold Palmer, 1958–60–62–64; Tiger Woods, 1997–2001–02–05

Most times runner-up
4 Ben Hogan, 1942–46–54–55; Jack Nicklaus, 1964–71–77–81

Oldest winner
Jack Nicklaus, 46 years, 2 months, 23 days, 1986

Youngest winner
Tiger Woods, 21 years, 3 months, 15 days, 1997

Biggest winning margin
12 strokes Tiger Woods, 1997

Lowest winning aggregate
270 Tiger Woods, 1997

Lowest in relation to par
18 under Tiger Woods, Augusta, 1997

Lowest aggregate by an amateur
281 Charles Coe, 1961 (joint second)

Lowest round
63 Nick Price, 1986; Greg Norman, 1996

Lowest 9 holes
29 Mark Calcavecchia, 1992; David Toms, 1998

Lowest first 36 holes
131 Raymond Floyd, 1976

Lowest final 36 holes
131 Johnny Miller, 1975

Lowest first 54 holes
201 Raymond Floyd, 1976; Tiger Woods, 1997

Lowest final 54 holes
200 Tiger Woods, 1997

Most appearances
52 Gary Player 1957–2009
50 Arnold Palmer 1955–2004

Successive victories
2 Jack Nicklaus, 1965–66; Nick Faldo, 1989–90; Tiger Woods, 2001–02

Players with four rounds under 70
None

Outright leader after every round
Craig Wood, 1941; Arnold Palmer, 1960; Jack Nicklaus, 1972; Raymond Floyd, 1976; Rory McIlroy, Congressional, 2011

Best opening round by a champion
65 Raymond Floyd, 1976

Worst opening round by a champion
75 Craig Stadler, 1982

Worst closing round by a champion
75 Trevor Immelman, 2008

Albatrosses
There have been four albatross twos in the Masters at Augusta National: by Gene Sarazen at the 15th, 1935; by Bruce Devlin at the eighth, 1967; by Jeff Maggert at the 13th, 1994 and Louis Oosthuizen at the 2nd in 2012.

USPGA Championship

Most times champion
5 Walter Hagen, 1921–24–25–26–27; Jack Nicklaus 1963–71–73–75–80

Most times runner-up
4 Jack Nicklaus, 1964–65–74–83

Oldest winner
Julius Boros, 48 years 4 months 18 days, Pecan Valley, 1968

Youngest winner
Gene Sarazen, 20 years 5 months 22 days, Oakmont, 1922

Biggest winning margin
8 strokes Rory McIlroy, Kiawah Island, 2012

Lowest winning aggregate
265 –15: David Toms, Atlanta Athletic Club, 2001
267 –17: Steve Elkington and Colin Montgomerie, Riviera, 1995 (beat Colin Montgomerie in sudden death play-off)

Lowest aggregate by runner-up
266 –14: Phil Michelson, Atlanta Athletic Club, 2001
267 –17: Colin Montgomerie, Riviera, 1995 (lost sudden death play-off to Steve Elkington)

Lowest in relation to par
18 under Tiger Woods and Bob May, Valhalla, 2000 (May lost three-hole play-off); Tiger Woods, Medinah, 2006

Lowest round
63 Bruce Crampton, Firestone, 1975; Raymond Floyd, Southern Hills, 1982; Gary Player, Shoal Creek, 1984; Vijay Singh, Inverness, 1993; Michael Bradley and Brad Faxon, Riviera, 1995; José Maria Olazábal, Valhalla, 2000; Mark O'Meara, Atlanta Athletic Club, 2001; Thomas Bjørn, Baltusrol, 2005; Tiger Woods, Southern Hills, 2007; Steve Stricker, Atlanta Athletic Club, 2011

Most successive victories
4 Walter Hagen, 1924–25–26–27

Lowest 9 holes
28 Brad Faxon, Riviera, 1995

Lowest first 36 holes
131 Hal Sutton, Riviera, 1983; Vijay Singh, Inverness, 1993; Ernie Els and Mark O'Meara, Riviera, 1995; Shingo Katayama and David Toms, Atlanta Athletic Club, 2001

Lowest final 36 holes
131 Mark Calcavecchia, Atlanta Athletic Club, 2001
132 Miller Barber, Dayton, 1969; Steve Elkington and Colin Montgomerie, Riviera, 1995; Padraig Harrington, Oakland Hills, 2008

Lowest first 54 holes
196 David Toms, Atlanta Athletic Club, 2001

Lowest final 54 holes
199 Steve Elkington, Colin Montgomerie, Riviera, 1995; Mark Calcavecchia, David Toms, Atlanta Athletic Club, 2001; David Toms, Atlanta Athletic Club, 2011

Most appearances
37 Arnold Palmer; Jack Nicklaus

Outright leader after every round
Bobby Nichols, Columbus, 1964; Jack Nicklaus, PGA National, 1971; Raymond Floyd, Southern Hills, 1982; Hal Sutton, Riviera, 1983

Best opening round by a champion
63 Raymond Floyd, Southern Hills, 1982

Worst opening round by a champion
75 John Mahaffey, Oakmont, 1978

Worst closing round by a champion
76 Vijay Singh, Whistling Straits, 2004 (worst in any major since Reg Whitcombe's 78 in 1938 Open)

Albatrosses
Joey Sindelar had an albatross at the fifth hole at Medinah Country Club during the third round of the 2006 PGA Championship

PGA European Tour

Lowest 72-hole aggregate
258 –14: David Llewellyn, AGF Biarritz Open, 1988. –18: Ian Woosnam, Monte Carlo Open, 1990.
259 –29: Ernie Els, Johnnie Walker Classic, Lake Karrinyup, 2003. –25: Mark McNulty, German Open, Frankfurt, 1987. –21: Tiger Woods, NEC Invitational, 2000 (*Note:* Sergio Garcia scored 257, 27 under par, at the 2011 Castello Masters, but preferred lies were in operation)

Lowest 9 holes
27 –9: José María Canizares, Swiss Open, Crans-sur-Sierre, 1978; Joakim Haeggman, Alfred Dunhill Cup, St Andrews, 1997; Simon Khan, Wales Open, Celtic Manor, 2004; –7: Andrew Coltart, KLM Open, Kennemer, 2007; Robert Lee, Johnnie Walker Monte Carlo Open, Mont Agel, 1985. –6: Robert Lee, Portuguese Open, Estoril, 1987. (*Note:* Rafa Echenique, BMW International Open, 2009, also scored 27 (–9), but preferred lies were in operation)

Lowest 18 holes
60 –12: Jamie Spence, Canon European Masters, Crans-sur-Sierre, 1992; Bernhard Langer, Linde German Masters, Motzener See, 1997; Darren Clarke, Smurfit European Open, K Club, 1999; Fredrik Jacobson, Linde German Masters, Gut Larchenhof, 2003; Ernie Els, Heineken Classic, Royal Melbourne, 2004; Branden Grace, Dunhill Links Championshjp, Kingsbarns, 2012; Brandt Snedeker, WGC–HSBC Champions, 2012. –11: Baldovino Dassu, Swiss Open, Crans-sur-Sierre, 1971; Rafael Cabrera-Bello, Austrian Open, Fontana GC, Vienna, 2009; –10: Paul Curry, Bell's Scottish Open, Gleneagles, 1992; Tobias Dier, TNT Open, Hilversum, 2002; –9: Ian Woosnam, Torras Monte Carlo Open, Mont Agel, 1990; Darren Clarke and Johan Rystrom, Monte Carlo Open, Mont Agel, 1992; Phillip Archer, Celtic Manor Wales Open, Celtic Manor, 2006; –8: David Llewellyn, AGF Biarritz Open, Biarritz GC, 1988 (*Note:* Bradley Dredge, Madeira Island Open, 2003, Colin Montgomerie, Indonesia Open, 2005, Ross McGowan, Madrid Masters, 2009 and Ian Poulter, Hong Kong Open 2010, also scored 60, but preferred lies were in operation)

Lowest 36 holes
124 –18: Colin Montgomerie, Canon European Masters, Crans-sur-Sierre, 1996 (3rd and 4th rounds). –14: Robert Karlsson, Celtic Manor Wales Open, Celtic Manor, 2006 (1st and 2nd rounds). (*Note:* Ian Poulter also scored 124 (–16, 60-64) in the 2nd and 3rd rounds of the 2010 UBS Hong Kong Open, but preferred lies were in operation)

Lowest 54 holes
189 –18 Robert Karlsson, Celtic Manor Wales Open, 2006 (rounds 1-2-3). (*Note:* Sergio García scored 190, 23 under par, in rounds 2-3-4 at the 2011 Castello Masters, butpreferred lies were in operation

Lowest 54 holes under par
192 –24 Anders Forsbrand, Ebel European Masters Swiss Open, Crans-Sur-Sierre, 1987 (rounds 2-3-4). (*Note:* Ross McGowan, Madrid Masters 2009, rounds 1-2-3, and Mikko Ilonen, Madrid Masters 2009, rounds 2-3-4, also scored 192, 24 under par, but preferred lies were in operation)

Lowest round by amateur
62 –10 Shane Lowry, 3 Irish Open, County Louth, 2009; –9 Sven Struver, German Open, Frankfurt GC, 1989; –8 David Palm, SAS Masters, Arlandastad 2008 (*Note:* Adam Scott's 63 at the 2000 Greg Norman Holden International at The Lakes was 10 under par)

Lowest first 36 holes
125 –17: Frankie Minoza, Caltex Singapore Masters, Singapore Island, 2001. –15: Tiger Woods, NEC Invitational World Championship, Firestone, Akron, Ohio, 2000

Largest winning margin
15 strokes Tiger Woods, United States Open, Pebble Beach, 2000. (*Note:* Bernhard Langer's 17-stroke victory in 1979 at Cacharel Under-25's Championship in Nîmes is not considered a full European Tour event)

Highest winning score
306 Peter Butler, Schweppes PGA Close Championship, Royal Birkdale, 1963

Youngest winner
Matteo Manassero, 17 years 188 days, Castello Masters, 2010

Youngest to make cut
Jason Hak (amateur), 14 years 304 days, Hong Kong Open, 2008

Oldest to make cut
Bob Charles 71 years 8 months, 2007 Michael Hill New Zealand Open, The Hills Golf Club, Queenstown

Oldest winner
Des Smyth, 48 years 34 days, Madeira Island Open, 2001

Most wins in one season
7 Norman von Nida, 1947

Amateur winners
Pablo Martin, Estoril Portuguese Open, 2007; Danny Lee, Johnnie Walker Classic, 2009; Shane Lowry, 3 Irish Open, 2009

US PGA Tour

Lowest 72-hole aggregate
254 –26: Tommy Armour III, Valero Texas Open, 2003. (*Note:* Steve Stricker's 255 at the 2009 Bob Hope Classic was a record 33 under par)

Lowest 54 holes
188 –25: Steve Stricker, John Deere Classic, 2010 (rounds 1-3). (*Note:* Tim Herron's 190 at the 2003 Bob Hope Chrysler Classic (rounds 2-4) was a record 26 under par)

Lowest 36 holes
122 –18: Troy Matteson, 2009 Frys.com Open (2nd and 3rd rounds). (*Note*: record under par was 123 (–21) Steve Stricker, 2009 Bob Hope Classic (3rd and 4th rounds)

Lowest first 36 holes
124 –20: Pat Perez, 2009 Bob Hope Classic; –16 David Toms, 2001 Crowne Plaza Invitational at Colonial

Lowest 18 holes
59 –13: Al Geiberger, 2nd round, Memphis Classic Colonial CC, 1977 (preferred lies in operation); Chip Beck, 3rd round, Las Vegas Invitational, Sunrise, 1991; David Duval, final round, Bob Hope Chrysler Classic, PGA West Palmer Course, 1999 (won tournament with last hole eagle); –12: Paul Goydos, 1st round, John Deere Classic, TPC Deere Run, 2010 (preferred lies); –11: Stuart Appleby, final round, Greenbrier Classic, Old White course, The Greenbrier, 2010 (won by one with three closing birdies)

Lowest 9 holes
26 –8: Corey Pavin, US Bank Championship, 2006
27 –9: Billy Mayfair, Buick Open, 2001; Robert Gamez, Bob Hope Chrysler Classic, 2004; Brandt Snedeker, Buick Invitational, 2007. –8: Mike Souchak, Texas Open, 1955. –7: Nick Watney, AT&T National, 2011; Andy North, BC Open, 1975

Lowest round by amateur
60 –10 Patrick Cantlay, Travelers Championship, TPC River Highlands, 2011

Largest winning margin
16 strokes J Douglas Edgar, Canadian Open Championship, 1919; Joe Kirkwood, Corpus Christi Open 1924; Bobby Locke, Chicago Victory National Championship, 1948

Youngest winner
Johnny McDermott, 19 years 10 months, US Open, 1911

Youngest to make cut
Bob Panasik, 15 years 8 months 20 days, Canadian Open, 1957

Oldest winner
Sam Snead, 52 years 10 months, Greater Greensboro Open, 1965

Most wins in one season
18 Byron Nelson, 1945

New course records (2011 season)
60 –10 Patrick Cantlay (amateur), Travelers Championship, TPC River Highlands
61 –11 Scott Piercy, Reno-Tahoe Open, Montreux; –10 Brandt Snedeker, The Barclays, Painfield
62 –9 Will MacKenzie, Frys.com Open, Cordevalle; –8 Jeff Maggert, AT&T Pebble Beach Pro-Am, Monterey Peninsular; Nick Watney, AT&T National, Aronimink
63 –7 Steve Stricker, PGA Championship, Atlanta Athletic Club

Albatrosses (2011 season)
Alex Cejka, AT&T Pebble Beach Pro-Am, Monterey Peninsular; J B Holmes, Wells Fargo Championship, Quail Hollow; Fabian Gomez, Wyndham Championship, Sedgefield

Holes in one (2011 season)
Shaun Micheel, Sony Open; Lee Janzen, Humana Challenge; Jarrod Lyle and Brendan Steele, Waste Management Phoenix Open; Nick O'Hern and Sunghoon Kang, AT&T Pebble Beach National Pro-Am; George McNeill, Mayakoba Classic; Cameron Tringale and Scott Stallings, Transitions Championship; Brandt Jobe, Shell Houston Open; Daniel Summerhays, The Heritage; Jim Furyk, Crowne Plaza Invitational at Colonial; Steve Stricker, Memorial Tournament; D J Brigman, Nate Smith and J B Holmes, Travelers Championship; Robert Allenby, AT&T National; Dustin Johnson and Tom Watson, Open Championship; Jim Furyk, WGC–Bridgestone Invitational; Derek Lamely, Wyndham Championship; Greg Chalmers and Brandt Snedeker, Deutsche Bank Championship

National Opens – excluding Europe and USA

Lowest 72-hole aggregate
255 Peter Tupling, Nigerian Open, Lagos, 1981

Lowest 36-hole aggregate
124 –18: Sandy Lyle, Nigerian Open, Ikoyi GC, Lagos, 1978 (his first year as a professional)

Lowest 18 holes
59 Gary Player, second round, Brazilian Open, Gavea GC (6,185 yards), Rio de Janeiro, 1974

Professional events – excluding Europe and US PGA Tour

Lowest 72-hole aggregate
260 Bob Charles, Spalding Masters at Tauranga, New Zealand, 1969; Jason Bohn, Bayer Classic, Huron Oaks, Canada, 2001; Brian Kontak, Alberta Open, Canada, 1998.

Lowest 18-hole aggregate
58 –13: Jason Bohn, Bayer Classic, Huron Oaks, Canada, 2001; –12: Ryo Ishikawa, The Crowns, Japan, 2010

59 Sam Snead, Greenbrier Open, The Greenbrier 1959; Miguel Angel Martin, South Argentine Open, 1987

Lowest 9-hole aggregate
27 Bill Brask at Tauranga in the New Zealand PGA in 1976

Amateur winners
Charles Evans, 1910 Western Open, Beverly, Illinois; John Dawson, 1942 Bing Crosby, Rancho Santa Fe, California; Gene Littler, 1954 San Diego Open, Rancho Santa Fe, California; Doug Sanders, 1956 Canadian Open, Beaconsfield, Quebec; Scott Verplank 1985 Western Open, Butler National, Illinois; Phil Mickelson 1991 Northern Telecom Open, Tucson, Arizona; Brett Rumford, 1999 ANZ Players Championship, Royal Queensland; Aaron Baddeley, 1999 Australian Open, Royal Sydney

Asian PGA Tour

Lowest 72 holes
256 –32: Chapchai Nirat, 2009 SAIL Open, India
259 –29: Ernie Els, 2003 Johnnie Walker Classic. (*Note:* Thaworn Wiratchant achieved a 25 under par total of 255 in the 2005 Enjoy Jakarta Standard Chartered Indonesian Open, but preferred lies were in use as they were when Ian Poulter scored a 22 under par 258 in the 2010 UBS Hong Kong Open)

Highest winning score
293 +5: Boonchu Ruangkit, 1996 Myanmar Open

Lowest 54 holes
189 –27: Chapchai Nirat, 2009 SAIL Open, India
193 –23: Ernie Els, 2003 Johnnie Walker Classic; David Howell, 2006 TCL Classic. (*Note:* Thaworn Wiratchant achieved an 18 under par total of 192 in the 2005 Enjoy Jakarta Standard Chartered Indonesia Open, but preferred lies were in use)

Lowest 36 holes
124 –20 Chapchai Nirat, 2009 SAIL Open, India; Lee Westwood, 2011 Thailand Championship
125 –17 Frankie Minoza, 2001 Caltex Singapore Masters (*Note:* Peter Karmis has an 18 under par 126 in the 2010 Handa Singapore Classic, but preferred lies were in operation)

Lowest 18 holes
60 60 -12: Liang Wen-chong, 2008 Hero Honda Indian Open; Lee Westwood, 2011 Thailand Championship (Note: Kim Felton had an 11 under par 60 in the 2000 Omega Hong Kong Open, Colin Montgomerie a 10 under par 60 in the 2005 Enjoy Jakarta Standard Chartered Indonesian Open and Ian Poulter a 10 under par 60 in the 2010 UBS Hong Kong Open, but preferred lies were in operation)

Lowest 9 holes
28 –8: Chung Chun-hsing, 2001 Maekyung LG Fashion Open; Liang Wen-chong, 2008 Hero Honda Indian Open. –7: Chinnarat Phadungsil, 2007 Midea China Classic; Henrik Bjornstad, 2001 Omega Hong Kong Open; Maarten Lafeber, 2005 UBS Hong Kong Open; Mardan Mamat, 2009 Singha Thailand Open; Brett Rumford, 2009 Omega European Masters; Masanori Kobayashi, 2012 Asia-Pacific Panasonic Open

Biggest margin of victory
13 strokes Ernie Els, 2005 BMW Asian Open
12 strokes Bradley Hughes, 1996 Players Championship

Youngest winners
Chinarat Phadungsil (am), 17 years 5 days, 2005 Double A International Open; Kim Dae-sub (am), 17 years 83 days, 1998 Korean Open; Noh Seung-yul, 17 years 143 days, 2008 Midea China Classic

Youngest to play in an Asian event
Ye Jian-fe, 13 years and 20 days, 2004 Sanya Open

Oldest winner
Choi Sang-ho, 50 years and 145 days, 2005 Maekyung Open; Boonchu Ruangkit, 47 years and 258 days, 2004 Thailand Open

Amateur winner
Kim Dae-sub, 1998 Korean Open; Eddie Lee, 2002 Maekyung Open, South Korea; Chinnarat Phadungsil, 2005 Double A International, Thailand

Most wins in a season
4 Thaworn Wiratchant, 2005

Most wins on Tour
14 Thongchai Jaidee

First par 6 hole
878-yard fourth, St Andrews Hill, Rayong, Thailand, 2005 Double A International Open

Youngest player to make the cut
Atiwit Janewattananond, 14 years 71 days, 2010 Asian Tour International

Oldest player to make the cut
Hsieh Min-nan, 70 years 53 days, 2010 Mercuries Taiwan Masters

Holes in one at same hole
Chen Chung-cheng, 2004 Thailand Open, fourth hole, days 1 and 3

First woman to make halfway cut
Michelle Wie, 2006 SK Telecom Open, Korea (finished tied 35th)

Japan Golf Tour

Lowest 72 holes
260 –20: Masashi 'Jumbo' Ozaki, 1995 Chunichi Crowns, Nagoya Wago
262 –26: Masashi Ozaki, 1996 Japan Series, Tokyo Yomiuri
263 –17: Tetsuji Hiratsuka, 2009 The Crowns, Nagoya

Lowest 54 holes
192 –18 Shingo Katayama, The Crowns 2004 and 2006

Lowest 36 holes
126 –18: Masahiro Kuramoto, 1987 Maruman Open, Higashi Matsuyama

Lowest 18 holes
58 –12: Ryo Ishikawa, 2010 The Crowns (this is the lowest round on a major tour. He came from six behind to win by five, aged 18 at the time); **59** –12 Masahiro Kuramoto, 2003 Acom International

Lowest 9 holes
28 –8: Yoshinori Kaneko, 1994 Nikkei Cup, Mitsui-kanko Tomakomai; Masayuki Kawamura, 1995 Gene

Sarazen Jun Classic; Tsuyoshi Yoneyama, 1998 Sapporo Tokyu, Sapporo Kokusai; Toshimitsu Izawa, 2000 TPC Iiyama Cup, Horai; Hideto Tanihara 2004; –7 Dinesh Chand 2005; Hideto Tanihara 2008; Ryo Ishikawa 2010; Masanori Kobayashi 2012

Largest winning margin
15 Masashi Ozaki, 1994 Daiwa International Hatoyama (pre-1973 tour formation: 19 Akira Muraki, 1930 Japan PGA Championship, Takarazuka)

Youngest winner
Ryo Ishikawa (amateur), 15 years 8 months, 2007 Munsingwear Open KBS Cup

Oldest winner
Masashi Ozaki, 55 years 8 months, 2002 ANA Open, Sapporo Wattsu

Most wins in a season
8 Tsuneyuki 'Tommy' Nakajima, 1983; Masashi 'Jumbo' Ozaki, 1996

Amateur winners
Masahiro Kuramoto, 1980 Chugoku-Shikoku Open; Ryo Ishikawa, 2007 Munsingwear Open KBS Cup; Hideki Matsuyama, 2011 Taiheiyo Masters

South African Sunshine Tour

Lowest 9-hole score
28 Simon Hobday, 2nd round of the 1987 Royal Swazi Sun Pro Am at Royal Swazi Sun Country Club; Mark McNulty, 2nd round of 1996 Zimbabwe Open at Chapman Golf Club; David Frost, 2nd round of the 1997 Alfred Dunhill PGA Championship at Houghton Golf Club; Tertius Claassens, 1st round of the 1982 SAB Masters at Milnerton; Brenden Pappas, 2nd round of the 1996 Dimension Data Pro-Am at Gary Player Country Club; Murray Urquhart, 2nd round of the 2001 Royal Swazi Sun Open at Royal Swazi Sun CC

Lowest 18-hole score
60 Shane Pringle 30-30, 2002 Botswana Open, Gabarone Golf Club

Lowest first 36 holes
127 Barry Painting 62-65, 2004 FNB Botswana Open, Gabarone Golf Club

Lowest last 36 holes
126 Mark McNulty 64-62, 1987 Royal Swazi Sun Pro-Am, Royal Swazi Sun Country Club

Lowest 54 holes
195 Nick Price 61-69-65, 1994 ICL International; Barry Painting 62-65-68, 2004 FNB Botswana Open, Gaberone GC

Lowest 72-hole score
259 Mark McNulty 68-65-64-62, 1987 Royal Swazi Sun Pro-Am, Royal Swazi Sun Country Club; David Frost 64-67-65-63, 1994 Lexington PGA, Wanderers Golf Club

Largest winning margin
12 strokes Nick Price, 1993 Nedbank Million Dollar, Sun City (non-Order of Merit event)
11 strokes Nico van Rensburg, 2000 Vodacom Series Gauteng, Silver Lakes

Most wins in a season
Seven wins in 11 tournaments by Mark McNulty, 1986-87 season – Southern Suns SA Open, AECI Charity Classic, Royal Swazi Sun Pro-Am, Trust Bank Tournament of Champions, Germiston Centenary Golf Tournament, Safmarine Masters, Helix Wild Coast Sun Classic

Most wins in succession
Four Gary Player, 1979-80 – Lexington PGA, Krönenbrau SA Masters, B.A. / Yellow Pages SA Open, Sun City Classic; Mark McNulty, 1986-87 – Southern Suns SA Open, AECI Charity Classic, Royal Swazi Sun Pro-Am, Trust Bank Tournament of Champions

Most birdies in one round
11 Allan Henning, 1st round of the 1975 Rolux Toro Classic, Glendower Golf Club; John Bland, 1st round of the 1993 SA Open Championship, Durban Country Club; Mark McNulty, 2nd round of the 1996 Zimbabwe Open, Royal Harare Golf Club; Alan McLean, 3rd round of the 2005 Telkom PGA Championship at Woodhill Country Club. (*Note:* Shane Pringle had 10 birdies and an eagle in the 2nd round of the 2002 FNB Botswana Open at Gaborone Golf Club; Marc Cayeux had nine birdies and an eagle in the final round of the 2004 Vodacom Players Championship at Country Club Johannesburg)

Most birdies in a row
9 Alan McLean, from the seventh to the 15th in the 3rd round of the 2005 Telkom PGA Championship at Woodhill Country Club
8 Bobby Lincoln, from the eighth to the 15th in the final round of the AECI Classic, Randpark Golf Club; Mark McNulty, from the ninth to the 16th in the 2nd round of the 1996 Zimbabwe Open, Royal Harare Golf Club

Lowest finish by a winner
62 Gavan Levenson, last round of the 1983 Vaal Reefs Open, Orkney Golf Club; Mark McNulty, 1987 Royal Swazi Sun Pro-Am, Royal Swazi Sun Country Club

Most Order of Merit victories
Eight Mark McNulty, 1981, 82, 85, 86, 87, 93, 98

Youngest winners
Anton Haig, 19 years 4 months, 2005 Seekers Travel Pro-Am, Dainfern; Dale Hayes, 19 years 5 months, Bert Hagerman Invitational, Zwartkops, Dec 1971; Charl Schwartzel, 20 years 3 months, 2004 dunhill championship at Leopard Creek. (*Note:* Dale Hayes was 18 years 6 months when he won the unofficial Newcastle Open at Newcastle Golf Club in 1971); Mark Murless, 20 years 5 months, 1996 Platinum Classic, Mooinooi Golf Club; Adam Scott, 20 years 6 months, 2001 Alfred Dunhill Championship, Houghton Golf Club; Marc Cayeux, 20 years 9 months, 1998 Zambia Open, Lusaka Golf Club; Trevor Immelman, 20 years 11 months, Vodacom Players Championship, Royal Cape Golf Club

Oldest winner
Mark McNulty, 49 years 44 days, 2003 Vodacom Players Championship, Royal Cape Golf Club

Australasian Tour

Most wins
31 Greg Norman

Youngest winner
A Baddeley (19 years), 1999 Australian Open

Oldest winner
Kel Nagle (54 years), 1975 Clearwater Classic (now the New Zealand PGA Championship

Lowest round
60 –12: Paul Gow, 2001 Canon Challenge, Castle Hill; Ernie Els, 2004 Heineken Classic, Royal Melbourne

Canadian Tour

Lowest 72 holes
256 –28: Brian Unk, 2009 Seaforth Country Classic

Lowest 54 holes
192 –21: Brian Unk, 2009 Seaforth Country Classic

Lowest 36 holes
126 –18: Matt Cole, 1988 Windsor Charity Classic. –16: James Hahn, 2009 Seaforth Country Classic

Lowest 18 holes
58 –13: Jason Bohn, 2001 Bayer Championship

Lowest 9 holes
26 –9: Jason Bohn, 2001 Bayer Championship

Most consecutive birdies
8 Jason Bohn, 2002 Texas Challenge

Most birdies in a round
10 Jason Bohn, 2001 Bayer Championship

Largest winning margin
11 Arron Oberholser, 1999 Ontario Open Heritage Classic

Most wins
13 Moe Norman

Most wins in a season
4 Trevor Dodds (1996 Alberta Open, ED TEL Planet Open, Infiniti Championship, Canadian Masters); Moe Norman (1966 Manitoba Open, Canadian PGA Championship, Quebec Open, Alberta Open)

Oldest winner
Moe Norman, 46 years 11 months, 1976 Alberta Open

Youngest winner
James Lepp, 19 years 7 months, 2003 Greater Vancouver Charity Classic

Youngest to play
Michelle Wie, 13 years 10 months, 2003 Bay Mills Championship

Oldest to make cut
Jim Rutledge, 51 years 2 months, 2010 Players Cup

Tour de las Americas

Lowest 72 holes
265 –23: Jamie Donaldson, Telefonica de Guatemala Open, 2007; Felipe Aguilar, Chile Open, 2008

Largest winning margin
11 Felipe Aguilar, Chile Open, 2008

Youngest winner
Luciano Giometti, 18 years 9 months, Open del Sur Personal, Argentina, 2006

Oldest winner
Vicente Fernandez 54 years 7 months, Argentina Open, Jockey Club, Buenos Aires, 2002

Highest winning aggregate
289 +5: Rafael Gomez and Marco Ruiz, Costa Rica Open, 2002 (Gomez won play-off)

Most wins in a season
3 Jesus Amaya 2001-02; Rafael Gomez, 2008

Most wins
8 Rafael Gomez

Lowest round
59 –11: Cipriano Castro, Siemens Venezuela Open, Valle Arribe, Caracas, 2006

Biggest comeback to win
9 strokes Venezuela, Copa de Naciones, El Tigre, Nueva Vallarta, Mexico 2004; Rafael Ponce, Acapulco Fest, Fairmont Princess, Acapulco, Mexico, 2004 LPGA Tour

LPGA Tour

Lowest 72 holes
258 –22: Karen Stupples, Welch's/Fry's Championship, Dell Urich, Arizona, 2004. (*Note:* Annika Sörenstam's 261 at 2001 Standard Register Ping, Moon Valley, Arizona, was a record 27 under par)

Lowest 54 holes
192 –24: Annika Sörenstam, Mizuno Classic, Shiga, Japan, 2003

Lowest 36 holes
124 –20: Annika Sörenstam, Standard Register Ping, Moon Valley, Arizona, 2001. –16: Meg Mallon, Welch's/Fry Championship, Dell Urich, Arizona, 2003

Lowest 18 holes
59 –13: Annika Sörenstam, Standard Register Ping, Moon Valley, Arizona, 2001

Lowest 9 holes
27 –8: Jimin Kang, ShopRite Classic, Seaview, New Jersey, 2005. –7: In-kyung Kim, Jamie Farr Owens Corning Classic, Highland Meadows, Ohio, 2007; Paula Creamer, Jamie Farr Corning Classic, Highland Meadows, Ohio, 2008 (*Note:* the 28s by Mary Beth Zimmerman, Rail Charity Classic, Springfield, Illinois, 1984, Annika Sörenstam, Standard Register Ping, Moon Valley, Arizona, 2001; Candie Kung, Wendy's Championship, Tartan Field, Ohio, 2006; Sarah Lee, Corona Championship, Tres Marias, Mexico, 2007; Sun Young Yoo, State Farm Classic, Panther Creek, Illinois, 2008 and Yani Tseng, Corning Classic, Corning CC, New York, 2009 were also 8 under par, as were the 29s by Nicky Le Roux, Rochester International, Locust Hill, New York, 1990, and Kris Tschetter, Weetabix Women's British Open, Royal Birkdale, England, 2005)

Most birdies in a round
13 Annika Sorenstam, Standard Register Ping, Moon Valley, Arizona, 2004

Most consecutive birdies
9 Beth Daniel, Philips Invitational, Onion Creek, Texas, 1999

Largest winning margin
14 strokes Cindy Mackey, MasterCard International Pro-am, Knollwood, New York, 1986

Youngest winner
Lydia Ko (amateur), 15 years 4 months 2 days, 2012 Canadian Women's Open

Oldest winner
Beth Daniel, 46 years 8 months 29 days, Canadian Open, 2003

Most wins in a season
13 Mickey Wright, 1963

Most wins
88 Kathy Whitworth

Most majors
15 Patty Berg

Most majors won in a season
3 Babe Zaharias (1950 US Women's Open, Titleholders, Western Open); Mickey Wright (1961 LPGA Championship, US Women's Open, Titleholders); Pat Bradley (1986 Nabisco Dinah Shore, LPGA Championship, Du Maurier Classic)

Most consecutive seasons with a victory
17 Kathy Whitworth (1962–78)

Biggest comeback to victory
10 Mickey Wright (1964 Tall City Open); Annika Sörenstam (2001 Office Depot); Louise Friberg (2008 MasterCard Classic)

Youngest major winner
Morgan Pressel, 18 years 10 months 9 days, Kraft Nabisco Championship, 2007

Oldest major winner
Fay Crocker, 45 years 7 months 11 days, Titleholders Championship, 1960

Youngest player
Beverly Klass, 10 years 6 months 3 days, Dallas Civitan Open, 1967

Oldest player
JoAnne Carner, 65 years 11 months 21 days, Kraft Nabisco Championship, 2005

Youngest to make cut
Michelle Wie 13 years 5 months 17 days, Kraft Nabisco Championship, 2003

Oldest to make cut
JoAnne Carner, 64 years 26 days, Chick-fil-A Charity Championship, 2004

Amateur winners
Polly Riley, 1950 Tampa Open; Pat O'Sullivan, 1951 Titleholders Championship; Catherine LaCoste, 1967 US Women's Open; JoAnne Carner, 1969 Burdine's Invitational

Lowest major round
62 –10: Minea Blomqvist, 2004 Weetabix Women's British Open, Sunningdale; –10: Lorena Ochoa, 2006 Kraft Nabisco Championship, Rancho Mirage

Most birdies in a round
13 Annika Sörenstam, Moon Valley Country Club, Phoenix, 2001 Standard Register Ping

Most consecutive birdies
9 Beth Daniel, Onion Creek Club, Austin, 1999 Philips Invitational

Ladies European Tour

Lowest 72 holes
249 –11: Dale Reid and Trish Johnson, 1991 Bloor Homes Eastleigh Classic, Fleming Park

Lowest 72 holes in relation to par
259 –29: Gwladys Nocera, 2008 Goteborg Masters, Lycke, Sweden

Lowest 54 holes
193 –23: Gwladys Nocera, 2008 Goteborg Masters, Lycke, Sweden

Lowest 36 holes
128 –16: Gwladys Nocera, 2008 Goteborg Masters, Lycke, Sweden. (*Note:* Sophie Gustafson's 129 at the 2003 Ladies Irish Open, Killarney, was a record 17 under)

Lowest 18 holes
58 –7: Dale Reid and Trish Johnson, 1991 Bloor Homes Eastleigh Classic, Fleming Park; Jane Connachan, 1991 Bloor Homes Eastleigh Classic, Fleming Park

Lowest 18 holes in relation to par
61 –11: Kirsty Taylor, 2005 Wales Ladies Championship, Machynys Peninsula; Nina Reis, 2008 Goteborg Masters, Lycke, Sweden; Karrie Webb, 2010 ANZ Ladies Masters, Royal Pines; So Yeon Ryu, 2012 Gold Coast RACV Australian Ladies Masters, Royal Pines
62 –11: Trish Johnson, 1996 Ladies French Open, Golf D'Arras; Lisa Holm Sorensen, 2009 SAS Masters, Larvik, Norway

Lowest 9 holes
28 –7: Tamie Durdin, 2010 ANZ Ladies Masters, Royal Pines

Highest winning score
292 +4: Raquel Carriedo, 2002 Tenerife Ladies Open, Golf del Sur; Sherri Steinhauer, 1998 Weetabix Women's British Open, Royal Lytham and St Annes

Largest winning margin
16 strokes Laura Davies, 1995 Guardian Irish Holidays Open, St Margaret's

Youngest winner
Amy Yang (amateur), 16 years 191 days, 2006 ANZ Ladies Masters, Royal Pines

Youngest to play
Leona and Lisa Maguire, 12 years 6 months, 2007 BT Northern Ireland Ladies Open

Youngest to make cut
Ariya Jutanugarn, 12 years 9 months, 2008 Finnair Masters, Helsinki Golf Club

Oldest winner
Laura Davies, 47 years 1 month 8 days, 2010 Hero Honda Women's Indian Open

Most wins
45 Laura Davies

Most wins in a year
7 Marie-Laure de Lorenzi, 1988 (French Open, Volmac Open, Hennessy Cup, Gothenburg Open, Laing Charity Classic, Woolmark Matchplay, Qualitair Spanish Open)

Most birdies in a round
12 Kristie Smith, 2009 ANZ Masters, Royal Pines, Australia

Miscellaneous British

72-hole aggregate

Andrew Brooks recorded a 72-hole aggregate of 259 in winning the Skol (Scotland) tournament at Williamwood in 1974.

Lowest rounds

Playing on the ladies' course (4,020 yards) at Sunningdale on 26th September, 1961, Arthur Lees, the professional there, went round in 52, 10 under par. He went out in 26 (2, 3, 3, 4, 3, 3, 3, 3, 2) and came back in 26 (2, 3, 3, 3, 2, 3, 4, 3, 3).

On 1st January, 1936, AE Smith, Woolacombe Bay professional, recorded a score of 55 in a game there with a club member. The course measured 4,248 yards. Smith went out in 29 and came back in 26 finishing with a hole-in-one at the 18th.

Other low scores recorded in Britain are by CC Aylmer, an English International who went round Ranelagh in 56; George Duncan, Axenfels in 56; Harry Bannerman, Banchory in 56 in 1971; Ian Connelly, Welwyn Garden City in 56 in 1972; James Braid, Hedderwick near Dunbar in 57; H. Hardman, Wirral in 58; Norman Quigley, Windermere in 58 in 1937; Robert Webster, Eaglescliffe in 58, in 1970. Harry Weetman scored 58 in a round at the 6171 yards Croham Hurst on 30th January, 1956.

D Sewell had a round of 60 in an Alliance Meeting at Ferndown, Bournemouth, a full-size course. He scored 30 for each half and had a total of 26 putts. In September 1986, Jeffrey Burn, handicap 1, of Shrewsbury GC, scored 60 in a club competition, made up of 8 birdies, an eagle and 9 pars. He was 30 out and 30 home and no. 5 on his card. Andrew Sherborne, as a 20-year-old amateur, went round Cirencester in 60 strokes. Dennis Gray completed a round at Broome Manor, Swindon (6906 yards, SSS 73) in the summer of 1976 in 60 (28 out, 32 in).

Playing over Aberdour on 13th June, 1936, Hector Thomson, British Amateur champion, 1936, and Jack McLean, former Scottish Amateur champion, each did 61 in the second round of an exhibition. McLean in his first round had a 63, which gave him an aggregate 124 for 36 holes.

Steve Tredinnick in a friendly match against business tycoon Joe Hyman scored a 61 over West Sussex (6211 yards) in 1970. It included a hole-in-one at the 12th (198 yards) and a 2 at the 17th (445 yards).

Another round of 61 on a full-size course was achieved by 18-year-old Michael Jones on his home course, Worthing GC (6274 yards), in the first round of the President's Cup in May, 1974.

In the Second City Pro-Am tournament in 1970, at Handsworth, Simon Fogarty did the second 9 holes in 27 against the par of 36.

Miscellaneous USA

Lowest rounds

The lowest known scores recorded for 18 holes in America are 55 by E F Staugaard in 1935 over the 6419 yards Montebello Park, California, and 55 by Homero Blancas in 1962 over the 5002 yards Premier course in Longview, Texas. Staugaard in his round had 2 eagles, 13 birdies and 3 pars.

In July 2010 Bobby Wyatt had a 14 under par 57 at the 6,628-yard Country Club of Mobile in the Alabama Boys State Junior Championship. He was 17 at the time. The round contained an eagle and 12 birdies and beat the course record by six.

Equally outstanding is a round of 58 (13 under par) achieved by a 13-year-old boy, Douglas Beecher, on 6th July, 1976, at Pitman CC, New Jersey. The course measured 6180 yards from the back tees, and the middle tees, off which Douglas played, were estimated by the club professional to reduce the yardage by under 180 yards.

In 1941 at a 6100 yards course in Portsmouth, Virginia, Chandler Harper scored 58.

Jack Nicklaus in an exhibition match at Breakers Club, Palm Beach, California, in 1973 scored 59 over the 6200-yard course.

The lowest 9-hole score in America is 25, held jointly by Bill Burke over the second half of the 6384 yards Normandie CC, St Louis in May, 1970 at the age of 29; by Daniel Cavin, who had seven 3s and two 2s on the par 36 Bill Brewer Course, Texas, in September, 1959; and by Douglas Beecher over the second half of Pitman CC, New Jersey, on 6th July, 1976, at the amazingly young age of 13. The back 9 holes of the Pitman course measured 3150 yards (par 35) from the back tees, but even though Douglas played off the middle tees, the yardage was still over 3000 yards for the 9 holes. He scored 8 birdies and 1 eagle.

Horton Smith scored 119 for two consecutive rounds in winning the Catalina Open in California in December, 1928. The course, however, measured only 4700 yards.

Miscellaneous – excluding GB and USA

Tony Jacklin won the 1973 Los Lagartos Open with an aggregate of 261, 27 under par.

Henry Cotton in 1950 had a round of 56 at Monte Carlo (29 out, 27 in).

In a Pro-Am tournament prior to the 1973 Nigerian Open, British professional David Jagger went round in 59.

Max Banbury recorded a 9-hole score of 26 at Woodstock, Ontario, playing in a competition in 1952.

Women

The lowest score recorded on a full-size course by a woman is 59 by Sweden's Annika Sörenstam on the 6459 yards, par 72 Moon Valley course in Phoenix, Arizona. It broke by two the previous record of 61 by South Korean Se Ri Pak. Sörenstam had begun the tournament with a 65 and by adding rounds of 69 and 68 she equalled the LPGA record of 261 set by Pak (71-61-63-66) at Highland Meadows in Ohio in 1998. Sörenstam's score represents 27 under par, Pak's 23 under.

The lowest 9-hole score on the US Ladies' PGA circuit is 28, first achieved by Mary Beth Zimmerman in the 1984 Rail Charity Classic and since equalled by Pat Bradley, Muffin Spencer-Devlin, Peggy Kirsch, Renee Heiken, Anika Sörenstam and Danielle Ammaccapane.

The Lowest 36-hole score is the 124 (20 under par) by Sörenstam at Moon Valley and the lowest 54-hole score 193 (23 under par) by Karrie Webb at Walnut Hills, Michigan, in the 2000 Oldsmobile Classic and equalled by Sörenstam at Moon Valley.

Patty Berg holds the record for the most number of women's majors with 15; Kathy Whitworth achieved a record number of tournament wins with 88; Mickey Wright's 13 wins in 1963 was the most in one season and the youngest and oldest winners of LPGA events were Marlene Hagge, 18 years and 14 days when she won the 1952 Sarasota Open and JoAnne Carner, 46 years 5 months 11 days when she won the 1985 Safeco Classic.

The lowest round on the European LPGA is 62 (11 under par) by Trish Johnson in the 1996 French Open. A 62 was also achieved by New Zealand's Janice Arnold at Coventry in 1990 during a Women's Professional Golfers' Association tournament.

The lowest 9-hole score on the European LPGA circuit is 29 by Kitrina Douglas, Regine Lautens, Laura Davies, Anne Jones and Trish Johnson.

In the Women's World Team Championship in Mexico in 1966, Mrs Belle Robertson, playing for the British team, was the only player to break 70. She scored 69 in the third round.

At Westgate-on-Sea GC (measuring 5002 yards), Wanda Morgan scored 60 in an open tournament in 1929.

Since scores cannot properly be taken in matchplay no stroke records can be made in matchplay events. Nevertheless we record here two outstanding examples of low scoring in the finals of national championships. Mrs Catherine Lacoste de Prado is credited with a score of 62 in the first round of the 36-hole final of the 1972 French Ladies' Open Championship at Morfontaine. She went out in 29 and came back in 33 on a course measuring 5933 yards. In the final of the English Ladies' Championship at Woodhall Spa in 1954, Frances Stephens (later Mrs Smith) did the first nine holes against Elizabeth Price (later Mrs Fisher) in 30. It included a hole-in-one at the 5th. The nine holes measured 3280 yards.

Amateurs

National championships

The following examples of low scoring cannot be regarded as genuine stroke play records since they took place in match play. Nevertheless they are recorded here as being worthy of note.

Michael Bonallack in beating David Kelley in the final of the English championship in 1968 at Ganton did the first 18 holes in 61 with only one putt under two feet conceded. He was out in 32 and home in 29. The par of the course was 71.

Charles McFarlane, playing in the fourth round of the Amateur Championship at Sandwich in 1914 against Charles Evans did the first nine holes in 31, winning by 6 and 5.

This score of 31 at Sandwich was equalled on several occasions in later years there. Then, in 1948, Richard Chapman of America went out in 29 in the fourth round eventually beating Hamilton McInally, Scottish Champion in 1937, 1939 and 1947, by 9 and 7.

Francis Ouimet in the first round of the American Amateur Championship in 1932 against George Voigt did the first nine holes in 30. Ouimet won by 6 and 5.

Open competitions

The 1970 South African Dunlop Masters Tournament was won by an amateur, John Fourie, with a score of 266, 14 under par. He led from start to finish with rounds of 65, 68, 65, 68, finally winning by six shots from Gary Player.

Jim Ferrier, Manly, won the New South Wales championship at Sydney in 1935 with 266. His rounds were: 67, 65, 70, 64, giving an aggregate 16 strokes better than that of the runner-up. At the time he did this amazing score Ferrier was 20 years old and an amateur.

Aaron Baddeley became the first amateur to win the Australian Open since Bruce Devlin in 1960 when he took the title at Royal Sydney in 1999. After turning pro he successfully defended the title the following year at Kingston Heath.

On the European Tou,r Spaniard Pablo Martin won the Estoril Open de Portugal as an amateur in 2000 and both Danny Lee (AUS) and Shane Lowry (IRL) were amateur winners in 2009. Lee won the now defunct Johnnie Walker Classic at The Vines in Perth Australia and Lowry the 3 Irish Open at Baltray.

Holes below par

Most holes below par

E.F. Staugaard in a round of 55 over the 6419 yards Montbello Park, California, in 1935, had two eagles, 13 birdies and three pars.

American Jim Clouette scored 14 birdies in a round at Longhills GC, Arkansas, in 1974. The course measured 6257 yards.

Jimmy Martin in his round of 63 in the Swallow-Penfold at Stoneham in 1961 had one eagle and 11 birdies.

In the Ricarton Rose Bowl at Hamilton, Scotland, in August, 1981, Wilma Aitken, a women's amateur internationalist, had 11 birdies in a round of 64, including nine consecutive birdies from the 3rd to the 11th.

Mrs Donna Young scored nine birdies and one eagle in one round in the 1975 Colgate European Women's Open.

Jason Bohn had two eagles and 10 birdies in his closing 58 at the 2001 Bayer Classic on the Canadian Tour at the par 71 Huron Oaks.

Consecutive holes below par

Lionel Platts had ten consecutive birdies from the 8th to 17th holes at Blairgowrie GC during a practice round for the 1973 Sumrie Better-Ball tournament.

Roberto De Vicenzo in the Argentine Centre of the Republic Championship in April, 1974 at the Cordoba GC, Villa Allende, broke par at each of the first nine holes. (By starting his round at the 10th hole they were in fact the second nine holes played by Vicenzo.) He had one eagle (at the 7th hole) and eight birdies. The par for the 3,602 yards half was 37, completed by Vicenzo in 27.

Nine consecutive holes under par have been recorded by Claude Harmon in a friendly match over Winged Foot GC, Mamaroneck, NY, in 1931; by Les Hardie at Eastern GC, Melbourne, in April, 1934; by Jimmy Smith at McCabe GC, Nashville, Tenn, in 1969; by 13-year-old Douglas Beecher, in 1976, at Pitman CC, New Jersey; by Rick Sigda at Greenfield CC, Mass, in 1979; and by Ian Jelley at Brookman Park in 1994.

TW Egan in winning the East of Ireland Championship in 1962 at Baltray had eight consecutive birdies (2nd to 9th) in the third round.

On the United States PGA tour, eight consecutive holes below par have been achieved by six players – Bob Goalby (1961 St Petersburg Open), Fuzzy Zoeller (1976 Quad Cities Open), Dewey Arnette (1987 Buick Open),

Edward Fryatt (2000 Doral-Ryder Open), JP Hayes (2002 Bob Hope Chrysler Classic) and Jerry Kelly (2003 Las Vegas Invitational).

Fred Couples set a PGA European Tour record with 12 birdies in a round of 61 during the 1991 Scandinavian Masters on the 72-par Drottningholm course. This has since been equalled by Ernie Els (1994 Dubai Desert Classic), Russell Claydon (1995 German Masters) and Darren Clarke (1999 European Open). Ian Woosnam, Tony Johnstone, Severiano Ballesteros, John Bickerton, Mark O'Meara, Raymond Russell, Darren Clarke, Marcello Santi, Mårten Olander and Craig Spence share another record with eight successive birdies.

The United States Ladies' PGA record is seven consecutive holes below par achieved by Carol Mann in the Borden Classic at Columbus, Ohio in 1975.

Miss Wilma Aitken recorded nine successive birdies (from the 3rd to the 11th) in the 1981 Ricarton Rose Bowl.

This has since been equalled by Ernie Els (1994 Dubai Desert Classic), Russell Claydon and Fredrik Lindgren (1995 Mercedes German Masters) and Darreb Clarke (1999 Smurfit European Open). Ian Woosnam, Tony Johnstone, Severiano Ballesteros, John Bickerton, Mark O'Meara, Raymond Russell, Darren Clarke and Marcello Santi and Marten Olander share another record with eight successive birdies.

Low scoring rarities

At Standerton GC, South Africa, in May 1937, F F Bennett, playing for Standerton against Witwatersrand University, did the 2nd hole, 110 yards, in three 2s and a 1 Standerton is a 9-hole course, and in the match Bennett had to play four rounds.

In 1957 a fourball comprising HJ Marr, E Stevenson, C Bennett and WS May completed the 2nd hole (160 yards) in the grand total of six strokes. Marr and Stevenson both holed in one while Bennett and May both made 2.

The old Meadow Brook Club of Long Island, USA, had five par 3 holes and George Low in a round there in the 1950s scored two at each of them.

In a friendly match on a course near Chicago in 1971, assistant professional Tom Doty (23 years) had a remarkable low run over four consecutive holes: 4th (500 yards) 2; 5th (360 yards, dogleg) 1; 6th (175 yards) 1; 7th (375 yards) 2.

R W Bishop, playing in the Oxley Park, July medal competition in 1966, scored three consecutive 2s. They occurred at the 12th, 13th and 14th holes which measured 151, 500 and 136 yards respectively.

In the 1959 PGA Close Championship at Ashburnham, Bob Boobyer scored five 2s in one of the rounds. American Art Wall scored three consecutive 2s in the first round of the US Masters in 1974. They were at the 4th, 5th and 6th holes, the par of which was 3, 4 and 3.

Nine consecutive 3s have been recorded by RH Corbett in 1916 in the semi-final of the Tangye Cup; by Dr James Stothers of Ralston GC over the 2056 yards 9-hole course at Carradale, Argyll, during the summer of 1971; by Irish internationalist Brian Kissock in the Homebright Open at Carnalea GC, Bangor, in June, 1975; and by American club professional Ben Toski.

The most consecutive 3s in a British PGA event is seven by Eric Brown in the Dunlop at Gleneagles (Queen's Course) in 1960.

Hubert Green scored eight consecutive 3s in a round in the 1980 US Open.

The greatest number of 3s in one round in a British PGA event is 11 by Brian Barnes in the 1977 Skol Lager tournament at Gleneagles.

Fewest putts

The lowest known number of putts in one round is 14, achieved by Colin Collen-Smith in a round at Betchworth Park, Dorking, in June, 1947. He single-putted 14 greens and chipped into the hole on four occasions.

Professional Richard Stanwood in a round at Riverside GC, Pocatello, Idaho on 17th May, 1976 took 15 putts, chipping into the hole on five occasions.

Several instances of 16 putts in one round have been recorded in friendly games.

For 9 holes, the fewest putts is five by Ron Stutesman for the first 9 holes at Orchard Hills G&CC, Washington, USA in 1978.

Walter Hagen in nine consecutive holes on one occasion took only seven putts. He holed long putts on seven greens and chips at the other two holes.

In competitive stroke rounds in Britain and Ireland, the lowest known number of putts in one round is 18, in a medal round at Portpatrick Dunskey GC, Wilmslow GC professional Fred Taggart is reported to have taken 20 putts in one round of the 1934 Open Championship. Padraigh Hogan (Elm Park), when competing in the Junior Scratch Cup at Carlow in 1976, took only 20 putts in a round of 67.

The fewest putts in a British PGA event is believed to be 22 by Bill Large in a qualifying round over Moor Park High Course for the 1972 Benson and Hedges Match Play.

Overseas, outside the United States of America, the fewest putts is 19 achieved by Robert Wynn in a round in the 1973 Nigerian Open and by Mary Bohen in the final round of the 1977 South Australian Open at Adelaide.

The USPGA record for fewest putts in one round is 18, achieved by Andy North (1990); Kenny Knox (1989); Mike McGee (1987) and Sam Trehan (1979). For 9 holes the record is eight putts by Kenny Knox (1989), Jim Colbert (1987) and Sam Trehan (1979).

The fewest putts recorded for a 72-hole US PGA Tour event is 93 by Kenny Knox in the 1989 Heritage Classic at Harbour Town Golf Links.

The fewest putts recorded by a woman is 17, by Joan Joyce in the Lady Michelob tournament, Georgia, in May, 1982.

PART XI

Fixtures 2013

European Tour Race to Dubai

www.europeantour.com

Dec 6–9	The Nelson Mandela Championship, Royal Durban GC, Durban, South Africa
Dec 13–16	Alfred Dunhill Championship, Leopard Creek CC, Malelane, South Africa
Jan 10–13	Volvo Golf Champions, Durban CC, Durban, South Africa
Jan 17–20	Abu Dhabi HSBC Golf Championship, Abu Dhabi GC, Abu Dhabi ,United Arab Emirates
Jan 23–26	Commercialbank Qatar Masters, Doha GC, Doha, Qatar
Jan 31–Feb 3	Omega Dubai Desert Classic, Emirates GC, Dubai, United Arab Emirates
Feb 7–10	Joburg Open, Royal Johannesburg & Kensington GC, Johannesburg, South Africa
Feb 14–17	Africa Open, East London GC, East London, Eastern Cape, South Africa
Feb 20–24	WGC–Accenture Match Play Championship, Ritz-Carlton GC, Marana, Arizona, USA
Feb 28–Mar 3	Tshwane Open, Copperleaf Golf & Country Estate, Centurion, South Africa
Mar 7–10	WGC–Cadillac Championship, Doral Golf Resort & Spa, Doral, Florida, USA
Mar 14–17	Avantha Masters, India (venue to be announced)
Mar 21–24	Maybank Malaysian Open, Kuala Lumpur G&CC, Kuala Lumpur, Malaysia
Mar 28–31	Trophée Hassan II, Golf du Palais Royal, Agadir, Morocco
Apr 4–7	Event and venue to be announced
Apr 11–14	**Masters Tournament**, Augusta National GC, Augusta, Georgia, USA
Apr 18–21	Reale Seguros Open de España, Spain (venue to be announced)
Apr 25–28	Ballantine's Championship, Blackstone GC, Icheon, Seoul, South Korea
May 2–5	Volvo China Open, Binhai Lake GC, Tianjin, China
May 16–19	Volvo World Match Play Championship, Thracian Cliffs Golf & Beach Resort, Kavarna, Bulgaria
May 23–26	BMW PGA Championship, Wentworth Club, Virginia Water, Surrey, England
May 30–Jun 2	Nordea Masters, Bro Hof Slott GC, Stockholm, Sweden
Jun 6–9	Lyoness Open, Diamond CC, Atzenbrugg, Austria
Jun 13–16	**US Open Championship**, Merion GC, Ardmore, Pennsylvania, USA
Jun 13–16	Open Najeti Hotels and Golf, Aa St Omer GC, St Omer, France
Jun 20–23	BMW International Open, Golfclub München Eichenried, Munich, Germany
Jun 27–30	The Irish Open, Montgomerie Course, Carton House GC, Maynooth, Co. Kildare, R.o.I.
Jul 4–7	Alstom Open de France, Le Golf National, Paris, France
Jul 11–14	Aberdeen Asset Management Scottish Open, Castle Stuart Golf Links, Inverness, Scotland
Jul 18–21	**The 142nd Open Championship**, Muirfield, Gullane, East Lothian, Scotland
Jul 25–28	Russian Masters, Russia (venue to be announced)
Aug 1–4	WGC–Bridgestone Invitational, Firestone CC, Akron, Ohio, USA
Aug 8–Aug 11	**US PGA Championship**, Oak Hill CC, Rochester, New York, USA
Aug 15–18	Event and venue to be announced
Aug 22–25	Johnnie Walker Championship, Gleneagles, Perthshire, Scotland
Aug 29–Sep 1	ISPS Handa Wales Open, The Celtic Manor Resort, City of Newport, Wales
Sep 5–8	Omega European Masters, Crans-sur-Sierre GC, Crans Montana, Switzerland
Sep 12–15	KLM Open, Kennemer G&CC, Zandvoort, The Netherlands
Sep 19–22	Italian Open, Italy (venue to be announced)
Sep 26–29	Alfred Dunhill Links Championship, Old Course St. Andrews, Carnoustie and Kingsbarns, Scotland
Oct 3–6	Vivendi Seve Trophy (venue to be announced)
Oct 10–13	Portugal Masters, venue to be announced, Portugal
Oct 17–20	Perth International, Lake Karrinyup CC, Perth, Western Australia
Oct 24–27	BMW Masters, Lake Malaren GC, Shanghai, China
Oct 31–Nov 3	WGC–HSBC Champions, Sheshan International GC, Shanghai, China
Nov 7–10	Turkish Open, The Montgomerie Maxx Royal, Antalya, Turkey
Nov 14–17	**DP World Tour Championship**, Jumeirah Golf Estates, Dubai, United Arab Emirates
Dec 13–16	South African Open Championship, Serengeti GC, Ekurhuleni, South Africa (date to be confirmed)

Low rounds on the European Tour but no 59 yet

American Ryder Cup golfer Brandt Snedeker was the latest player to come tantalisingly close to breaking 60 on the European Tour when his 20 foot birdie putt on the last green in the third round of the HSBC Champions event being played on the Olazábal course at Mission Hills GC at Guangdon Province in China just slipped past the cup.

Fifteen golfers since 1988 have played themselves into a position to shoot 59 including three Englishmen, two South Africans, two Germans, two Swedes and two Welshmen plus one player from Northern Ireland, the United States and Spain. Only Ulsterman Darren Clarke has scored two rounds of 60 once at Mont Agel, high above Monte Carlo and again at the K Club outside Dublin.

Those who have:

60 (–12)	Jamie Spence (ENG)	Canon European Masters, Crans-sur-Sierre, 1992
60 (–12)	Bernhard Langer (GER)	Linde German Masters, Berliner G&CC, 1997
60 (–12)	Darren Clarke (NIR)	Smurfit European Open, The K Club (Palmer), 1998
60 (–12)	Frederick Jacobsen (SWE)	Linde German Masters, Gut Larchenhof, 2003
60 (–12)	Ernie Els (RSA)	Heineken Classic, Royal Melbourne, 2004
60 (–12)	Branden Grace (RSA)	Alfred Dunhill Links, Kingsbarns GC, 2012
60 (–12)	Brandt Snedeker (USA)	HSBC Champions, Mission Hills GC (Olazábal), 2012
60 (–11)	Rafael Cabrera-Bello (ESP)	Austrian Open, Fontana GC, 2009
60 (–10)	Paul Curry (ENG)	Bell's Scottish Open, Gleneagles Hotel (Kings), 1992
60 (–10)	Tobias Dier (GER)	TNT Dutch Open, Hilversumsche GC, 2002
60 (–10)	Kenneth Ferrie (ENG)	Open de Andalucia, Parador de Golf, Malaga, 2011
60 (–10)	Ian Woosnam (WAL)	Torras Monte Carlo Open, Mont Agel GC. 1990
60 (–10)	Johan Rystrom (SWE)	European Monte Carlo Open Mont Agel GC, 1992
60 (–10)	Darren Clarke (NIR)	European Monte Carlo Open Mont Agel GC, 1992
60 (–10(	Philip Archer (ENG)	Celtic Manor Wales Open, Celtic Manor Resort (Roman), 2006
60 (–8)	David Llewellyn (WAL)	AGF Biarritz Open, Biarritz GC, 1988

US PGA Tour

www.pgatour.com

Dec 31–Jan 7	Hyundai Tournament of Champions, Plantation Course, Kapalua, Hawaii
Jan 7–13	Sony Open in Hawaii, Waialae Country Club, Honolulu, Hawaii
Jan 14–20	Humana Challenge, PGA West, La Quinta CC, La Quinta, California
Jan 21–27	Farmers Insurance Open, Torrey Pines, San Diego, California
Jan 28–Feb 3	Waste Management Phoenix Open, TPC Scottsdale), Scottsdale, Arizona
Feb 4–10	AT&T Pebble Beach National Pro-Am, Pebble Beach, California
Feb 11–17	Northern Trust Open, Riviera Country Club, Pacific Palisades, California
Feb 18–24	WGC–Accenture Match Play Championship, Ritz-Carlton GC, Marana, Arizona
Feb 25–Mar 3	The Honda Classic, PGA National, Palm Beach Gardens, Florida
Mar 4–10	WGC–Cadillac Championship, Doral Golf Resort, Doral, Florida
Mar 4–10	Puerto Rico Open, Trump International Puerto Rico, Rio Grande, Puerto Rico
Mar 11–17	Tampa Bay Championship, Innisbrook Resort & GC, Palm Harbor, Florida
Mar 18–24	Arnold Palmer Invitational, Bay Hill Golf Club and Lodge, Orlando, Florida
Mar 25–31	Shell Houston Open, Redstone GC, Houston, Texas
Apr 1–7	Valero Texas Open, TPC San Antonio, San Antonio, Texas
Apr 8–14	Masters Tournament, Augusta National GC, Augusta, Georgia
Apr 15–21	RBC Heritage, Harbour Town GL, Hilton Head Island, South Carolina
Apr 22–28	Zurich Classic of New Orleans, TPC Louisiana, New Orleans, Louisiana
Apr 29–May 5	Wells Fargo Championship, Quail Hollow Club, Charlotte, North Carolina
May 6–12	THE PLAYERS Championship, TPC Sawgrass, Ponte Vedra Beach, Florida
May 13–19	HP Byron Nelson Championship, Four Seasons Las Colinas, Irving, Texas
May 20–26	Crowne Plaza Invitational at Colonial, Colonial Country Club, Fort Worth, Texas
May 27–Jun 2	The Memorial Tournament, Muirfield Village Golf Club, Dublin, Ohio
Jun 3–9	FedEx St. Jude Classic, TPC Southwind, Memphis, Tennessee
Junn 10–16	US Open, Merion Golf Club, Ardmore, Pennsylvania
Jun 17–23	Travelers Championship, TPC River Highlands, Cromwell, Connecticut

US PGA Tour *continued*

Jun 24–30	AT&T National, Congressional Country Club, Bethesda, Maaryland
July 1–7	The Greenbrier Classic, The Greenbrier, White Sulphur Springs, West Virginia
Jul 8–14	John Deere Classic, TPC Deere Run, Silvis, Illinois
Jul 15–21	British Open, Muirfield, East Lothian, Scotland
Jul 15–21	True South Classic, Annandale Golf Club, Madison, Mississippi
Jul 22–28	RBC Canadian Open, Glen Abbey Golf Club, Oakville, Ontario, Canada
Jul 29–Aug 4	WGC–Bridgestone Invitational, Firestone Country Club, Akron, Ohio
Jul 29–Aug 4	Reno-Tahoe Open, Montreux Golf & CC, Reno, Nevada
Aug 5–11	PGA Championship, Oak Hill Country Club, Rochester, New York
Aug 12–18	Wyndham Championship, Sedgefield Country Club, Greensboro, North Carolina
Aug 19–25	The Barclays, Liberty National Golf Course, Jersey City, New Jersey
Aug 26–Sep 2	Deutsche Bank Championship, TPC Boston, Norton, Massachusetts
Sep 9–15	BMW Championship, Conway Farms Golf Club, Lake Forest, Illinois
Sep 16–22	TOUR Championship, East Lake Golf Club, Atlanta, Goergia
Sep 30–Oct 6	The Presidents Cup, Muirfield Village Golf Club, Dublin Ohio

The 2013 PGA Tour Season officially ends in late September with the TOUR Championship and the 2013–2014 season begins three weeks later with the first Fall Tournament

European Golf Association Championships

www.ega-golf.ch

Jan 24–27	Portuguese International Ladies' Amateur Championship (venue to be announced)
Feb 13–16	Portuguese International Amateur Championship (venue to be announced)
Feb 27–Mar 3	Spanish International Ladies Amateur Championship (Copa S.M. El Rey), Pula GC, Mallorca
Feb 27–Mar 3	Spanish International Amateur Championship (Copa S.M. El Rey), La Manga GC, Murcia
Mar 9–13	Italian International Ladies Match-Play Championship, Castelgandolfo GC, Rome
Mar 28–Apr 1	French International Lady Juniors Championship (Esmond Trophy), Saint Cloud GC
Mar 28–Apr 1	French International Boys Championship (Michel Carlhian Trophy) (venue to be announced)
Apr 18–21	Cyprus Amateur Men's Open, Aphrodite Hills
Apr 26–28	Scottish Ladies' Open Stroke Play Championship (Helen Holm) (venue to be announced)
May 3–5	Lytham Trophy, Royal Lytham & St Annes
May 4–5	Welsh Ladies' Open Stroke Play Championship, Vale of Glamoran (National)
May 10–12	Spanish International Ladies' Stroke Play Championship, Las Colinas, Alicante
May 10–12	Scottish Youths Open Amateur Stroke Play Championship, Lanark GC
May 10–12	Irish Amateur Open Championship. Royal Dublin GC
May 14	English Men's Open Amateur Stroke Play Championship (Southern Pre-qualifier Brabazon Trophy), Enmore Park
May 11–15	Italian International Amateur Match-Play Championship, Villa d'Este GC
May 17–19	Welsh Amateur Open Stroke Play Championship. Royal Porthcawl
May 18–20	French International Senior Men's Championship (venue to be announced)
May 21	English Men's Open Amateur Stroke Play Championship (Northern Pre-qualifier Brabazon Trophy), Pleasington
May 22–25	Slovenian International Ladies Amateur Championship (venue to be announced)
	Slovenian International Amateur Championship (venue to be announced)
May 23–26	German International Ladies Amateur Championship, GC Ulm
May 24–26	French Men's Amateur Stroke Play Championship (Murat Cup), Chantilly GC
May 24–26	Skandia Lady Junior Open (Youth), Lyckorna GC
May 24–26	Skandia Junior Open (Youth), Lyckorna GC
May 24–26	Lithuanian Amateur Open Championship, The Capitals GC
May 25–26	Irish Women's Open Stroke Play Championship, Castle GC
May 30–Jun 2	Turkish Open Amateur Championship (Ladies) (venue to be announced)
May 30–Jun 2	Turkish Open Amateur Championship (Men) (venue to be announced)
May 31–Jun 2	Scottish Open Stroke Play Championship, Southerness
May 31–Jun 2	Danish International Ladies Amateur Championship, Silkeborg GC
May 31–Jun 2	Danish International Amateur Championship, Silkeborg GC

Jun 1–2	Welsh Open Youths Championship, Monmouthshire
Jun 7–9	German Girls Open, GC St. Leon-Rot
Jun 7–9	German Boys Open, GC St. Leon-Rot
Jun 11–15	Ladies' British Open Amateur Championship, Machynys Peninsula, Wales
Jun 17–22	The Amateur Championship, Royal Cinque Ports/Prince's
Jun 19–21	Scottish Seniors (over 55's) Open Stroke Play Championship, Golf House Club, Elie
Jun 26–29	English Men's Open Amateur Stroke Play Championship (Brabazon Trophy), Formby
Jun 26–30	Russian Ladies Amateur Open Championship, GC Agalarov, Moscow
Jun 26–30	Russian Amateur Open Championship, GC Agalarov, Moscow
Jun 28–30	Estonian Open Ladies Amateur Championship, Niitvälja GC
Jun 28–30	Estonian Open Amateur Championship, Niitvälja GC
Jun 28–30	Macedonian Amateur Open Championship, St Sofia GC
Jun 28–30	Swiss Ladies Amateur Championship, Lausanne GC
Jun 28–30	Swiss Amateur Championship, Lausanne GC
Jul 4–6	Balkan Challenge Trophy (venue to be announced)
Jul 5–7	Ukrainian Open Amateur Championship (venue to be announced)
Jul 5–7	Ukrainian Ladies Open Amateur Championship (venue to be announced)
Jul 11–13	Luxembourg Ladies Amateur Championship, Kikuoka CC
Jul 11–13	Luxembourg Men Amateur Championship, Kikuoka CC
Jul 12–14	Polish Ladies Amateur Open Championship, Gradi GC
Jul 16–18	Czech International Girls & Lady Juniors Championship (venue to be announced)
Jul 16–18	Czech International Boys & Juniors Championship (venue to be announced)
Jul 16–18	Danish International Lady Junior Championship, Smørum GC
Jul 16–18	Danish International Youth Championship, Smørum GC
Jul 17–20	Dutch Lady Junior International, Toxandria GC
Jul 17–20	Dutch Junior International, Toxandria GC
Jul 25–28	German International Amateur Championship. GC Neuhof
Jul 23–25	Scottish Boys (under 18's) Open Stroke Play Championship, The Roxburghe
Jul 23–26	English Boys (under 18) Open Amateur Stroke Play Championship (Carris Trophy), West Lancs
Jul 24–26	Scottish Ladies' Junior Open Stroke Play Championship (venue to be announced)
Jul 31–Aug 3	Czech International Ladies Amateur Championship, GC Karlovy Vary
Jul 31–Aug 3	Czech International Amateur Championship, GC Karlovy Vary
Jul 31–Aug 3	Belgian International Ladies Amateur Championship, Royal Antwerp GC
Jul 31–Aug 3	Belgian International Amateur Amateur Championship, Royal Antwerp GC
Aug 2–4	Polish Men's Amateur Open Championship, Postolowo GC
Aug 6–8	English Women's Open Amateur Stroke Play Championship, Mannings Heath
Aug 7–9	British Senior Open Amateur Championship, Royal Aberdeen
Aug 7–9	ANNIKA Invitational (Girls), Landskrona GC
Aug 9–11	Latvian Ladies Amateur Open Championship, Ozo GC
Aug 9–11	Latvian Amateur Open Championship, Ozo GC
Aug 9–11	Hungarian Junior Amateur Open Championship, Pannonia G&CC, Máriavölgy
Aug 12–16	Girls' British Open Amateur Championship, Fairhaven
Aug 13–15	Slovak Ladies Amateur Open Championship (venue to be announced)
Aug 13–15	Slovak Amateur Open Championship (venue to be announced)
Aug 13–18	British Boys Championship, Royal Liverpool/Wallasey
Aug 15–17	Finnish Ladies Amateur Championship, Helsinki GC
Aug 15–17	Finnish Amateur Championship, Helsinki GC
Aug 15–18	English Women's Open Mid Amateur Championship, John O'Gaunt
Aug 21–23	Ladies' British Open Amateur Stroke Play Championship, Prestwick, Scotland
Aug 22–24	Hungarian Open Ladies' Amateur Championship, Royal Balaton G&YC, Balatonudvari
Aug 22–24	Hungarian Open Amateur Championship, Royal Balaton G&YC, Balatonudvari
Aug 26–28	Polish Junior Championship, Toya G&CC, Wroclaw
Aug 27–29	Italian International Individual (Under 16) Championship (venue to be announced)
Aug 28–31	Belgian International Girls (U18) Championship, Royal GC of Belgium, Ravenstein
Aug 28–31	Belgian International Boys (U18) Championship, Royal GC of Belgium, Ravenstein
Aug 30–Sep 1	Brabants Ladies' Open Eindhovensche Golf (venue to be announced)
Aug 30–Sep 1	Brabants Men's Open Eindhovensche Golf (venue to be announced)
Sep 5–7	Austrian International Men's Amateur Championship (venue to be announced)
Sep 5–8	Spanish International Junior Stroke Play Championship, Empordá GC
Sep 5–7	Bulgarian Open Amateur Championship, Pravetz GC & St Sofia

European Golf Association Championships *continued*

Sep 5–7	Bulgarian Open Ladies' Amateur Championship, Pravetz GC & St Sofia
Sep 11–13	Irish Senior Women's Open Stroke Play Championship, Castlerock GC
Sep 13–15	Austrian International Ladies Amateur Championship (venue to be announced)
Sep 14–15	Liechtenstein Open Ladies' Amateur Championship, GC Gams-Werdenberg
Sep 14–15	Liechtenstein Open Amateur Championship, GC Gams-Werdenberg
Sep 17–19	Senior Ladies' British Open Amateur Championship, Royal Portrush, Northern Ireland
Oct 2–4	Israel Ladies Amateur Open Championship (venue to be announced)
Oct 2–4	Israel Juniors Boys and Girls Championship (venue to be announced)
Oct 11–13	French International Ladies' Amateur Stroke Play Championship (Cécile De Rothschild Trophy), Morfontaine GC
Oct 21–24	Israel Amateur Open Championship (venue to be announced)

European Team Championships

Jul 9–13	Ladies, Fulford GC, Yorkshire, England
Jul 9–13	Amateur, Silkeborg GC, Denmark
Jul 9–13	Girls, Linköpings GC, Sweden
Jul 9–13	Boys, Murcar Links GC, Scotland
Sep 3–7	Senior Ladies', Bled GC, Slovenia
Sep 3–7	Senior Men's, Pannonia G&CC, Hungary
Sep 19–21	Boys' Challenge Trophy, Skalica GC, Slovakia

International European Championships

Jun 6–8	Mid-Amateur, Senica GC, Slovakia
Jun 13–15	Seniors, Estonian G&CC, Estonia
Jul 24–27	Ladies, Aura GC (Turku), Finland
Jul 25–27	European Young Masters, Hamburger GC, Germany
Aug 7–10	Men, Real Club de Golf el Prat, Spain
Sep 26–28	European Ladies' Club Trophy, St Sofia Golf & Spa, Bulgaria
Oct 24–26	European Men's Club Trophy, Portugal (venue to be announced)

International Matches

Jun 28–29	Vagliano Trophy, Golf de Chantilly, France
Jun 28–29	Junior Vagliano Trophy, Golf de Chantilly, France
Aug 30–31	Jacques Léglise Trophy, Royal St. David's, Wales

Tournaments recommended by the EGA

Mar 13–16	European Nations Championship (Copa R.G.C. Sotogrande), Sotogrande GC, Spain
Jul 21–22	Evian Masters Junior Cup (Under 14), Evian Masters GC, France

United States Golf Association Championships

www.usga.org

Jun 13–16	US Open, Merion Golf Club, Ardmore, Pennsylvania
Jun 17–22	US Women's Amateur Public Links, Jimmie Austin OU Golf Club, Norman, Oklahoma
Jun 27–30	US Women's Open, Sebonack Golf Club, Southampton, New York
Jul 11–14	US Senior Open, Omaha Country Club, Omaha , Nebraska
Jul 15–20	US Amateur Public Links, Laurel Hill Golf Club, Lorton, Virginia
Jul 22–27	US Girls' Junior, Sycamore Hills Golf Club, Fort Wayne, Indiana
Jul 22–27	US Junior Amateur, Martis Camp, Truckee, California
Aug 5–11	**US Women's Amateur**, Country Club of Charleston, Charleston, South Carolina
Aug 12–18	**US Amateur**, The Country Club, Brookline, Massachusetts
Sep 7–8	**Walker Cup**, National Golf Links of America, Southampton, New York
Sep 17–19	Women's State Team, NCR C.C. (South Course), Kettering, Ohio
Sep 21–26	USGA Senior Women's Amateur, CordeValle, San Martin, California
Sep 21–26	USGA Senior Amateur, Wade Hampton Golf Club, Cashiers, North Carolina
Oct 5–10	US Women's Mid-Amateur, Biltmore Forest CC, Asheville, North Carolina
Oct 5–10	US Mid-Amateur, Country Club of Birmingham, Birmingham, Alabama

Japan PGA Tour

www.jgto.org/jgto/WG01000000Initi.do

Feb 20–24	**WGC–Accenture Match Play Championship**, The GC At Dove Mountain, USA
Mar 7–10	**WGC–Cadillac Championship**, TPC Blue Monster at Doral, Florida, USA
Mar 14–17	Thailand Open (venue to be announced)
Mar 28–31	Indonesia PGA Championship (venue to be announced)
Apr 11–14	**Masters Tournament**, Augusta National GC, Georgia, USA
Apr 18–21	Token Homemate Cup, Token Tado CC, Nagoya
Apr 25–28	Tsuruya Open, Yamanohara GC, Yamanohara Course, Hyogo
May 2–5	The Crowns, Nagoya GC, Wago Course, Aichi
May 16–19	PGA Championship Nissin Cupnoodles Cup, Sobu CC, Sobu Course, Chiba
May 30–Jun 2	Diamond Cup Golf, Oarai GC, Ibaraki
Jun 13–16	**US Open Championship**, Merion GC, Pennsylvania, USA
Jun 20–23	Japan Golf Tour Championship, Shishido Hills CC, West Course, Ibaraki
Jun 27–30	Gate Way To The Open Mizuno Open, JFE Setonaikai GC, Okayama
Jul 4–7	Nagashima Shigeo Invitational Sega Sammy Cup, The North Country GC, Hokkaido
Jul 18–21	**British Open**, Muirfield, East Lothian, Scotland
Aug 1–4	**WGC–Bridgestone Invitational**, Firestone CC, Ohio, USA
Aug 8–11	**US PGA Championship**, Oak Hill CC, New York, USA
Aug 22–25	Kansai Open Golf Championship, Olympic GC, Hyogo
Aug 29– Sep 1	Vana H Cup KBC Augusta, Keya GC, Fukuoka
Sep 5–8	Fujisankei Classic, Fujizakura CC, Yamanashi
Sep 19–22	ANA Open, Sapporo GC, Wattsu Course, Hokkaido
Sep 26–29	Asia-Pacific Panasonic Open, Ibaraki CC, Osaka
Oct 3–6	Coca-Cola Tokai Classic, Miyoshi CC, West Course, Aichi
Oct 10–13	Toshin Golf Tournament (venue to be announced)
Oct 17–20	Japan Open, Ibaraki GC, East Course, Ibaraki
Oct 24–27	Bridgestone Open, Sodegaura CC, Sodegaura Course, Chiba
Oct 31–Nov 3	WGC–HSBC Champions, Sheshan International GC, China
Oct 31–Nov 3	Mynavi ABC Championship, ABC GC, Hyogo
Nov 7–10	Heiwa PGM Dream Cup in Kasumigaura, Miho GC, Ibaraki
Nov 14–.17	Mitsui Sumitomo VISA Taiheiyo Masters, Taiheiyo Club, Gotemba Course, Shizuoka
Nov 21–24	Dunlop Phoenix, Phoenix CC, Miyazaki
Nov 28–Dec 1	Casio World Open, Kochi Kuroshio CC, Kochi
Dec 5–8	Golf Nippon Series JT Cup, Tokyo Yomiuri CC, Tokyo
Dec 15	Hitachi 3tours Championship, Hirakawa CC, Chiba

Ladies European Tour

www.ladieseuropeantour.com

Feb 1–3	Volvik RACV Ladies Masters, RACV Royal Pines Resort, Queensland, Australia
Feb 8–10	ISPS Handa New Zealand Women's Open, Clearwater Golf Club, Christchurch, New Zealand
Feb 14–17	ISPS Handa Women's Australian Open, Royal Canberra Golf Club, Canberra, Australia
Mar 7–10	Mission Hills World Ladies Championship, Mission Hills, Haikou, Hainan, China
Mar 28–31	Lalla Meryem Cup, Golf de l'Ocean, Agadir, Morocco
Apr 19–21	South African Women's Open, Southbroom Golf Club, Hibiscus Coast, South Africa
May 9–12	Turkish Airlines Ladies Open, National Golf Club, Belek, Antalya, Turkey
May 24–26	Deloitte Ladies Open, The International, Amsterdam, Netherlands
May 30–Jun 2	UniCredit Ladies German Open, Golfpark Gut Häusern. Nr. Munich, Germany
Jun 13–16	Open de España Femenino, Span (venue to be announced)
Jun 20–23	Allianz Ladies Slovak Open. Golf Resort Tale. Brezno, Tále, Slovakia
July	United Kingdom (event, date and venue to be announced)
Aug 1–4	**Ricoh Women´s British Open**, St Andrews old course, St Andrews, Scotland
Aug 9–11	Pilsen Golf Masters, Golf Park Plzeň – Dýšina, Prague, Czech Republic
Aug 16–18	**The Solheim Cup**, Colorado Golf Club, Parker, Colorado, USA

Ladies European Tour *continued*

Aug 30–Sep 1	Aberdeen Asset Management Ladies Scottish Open, Archerfield Links, East Lothian, Scotland
Sep 5–8	The Helsinborg Open, Vasatorp Golf Club, Helsingborg, Skane, Sweden
Sep 12–15	**Evian Masters**, Evian Masters Golf Club, Evian-Les-Bains, France
Sep 26–29	Lacoste Ladies Open de France, Chantaco Golf Club, Saint-Jean-de-Luz, Aquitaine, France
October	Date, event and venue to be announced
October	Sanya Ladies Open, Yalong Bay Golf Club, Sanya, China (date to be announced)
November	China Suzhou Taihu Open, Suzhou Taihu International Golf Club, Suzhou, China (date to be announced)
Nov 28–30	Hero Women's Indian Open, DLF Golf and Country Club, New Delhi, India
Dec 4–7	**Omega Dubai Ladies Masters**, Emirates Golf Course, Dubai, United Arab Emirates

Champions Tour

www.pgatour.com

JJan 18–20	Mitsubishi Electric Championship, Hualalai Golf Course, Ka'upulehu-Kona, HI
Feb 8–10	Allianz Championship, The Old Course at Broken Sound, Boca Raton, FL
Feb 15–17	ACE Group Classic, TwinEagles GC (Talon Course), Naples, FL
Mar 15–17	Toshiba Classic, Newport Beach CC, Newport Beach, CA
Mar 22–24	Mississippi Gulf Resort Classic, Fallen Oak, Biloxi, MS
Apr 19–21	Greater Gwinnett Championship, TPC Sugarloaf, Duluth, GA
Apr 26–28	Liberty Mutual Insurance Legends of Golf, Savannah Harbor Golf Resort, Savannah, GA
May 3–5	Insperity Championship, The Woodlands CC, The Woodlands, TX
May 23–26	Senior PGA Championship (venue to be announced)
May 31–Jun 2	Principal Charity Classic (venue to be announced)
Jun 6–9	Regions Tradition, Shoal Creek, Shoal Creek, AL
Jun 21–23	Encompass Championship, North Shore Country Club
Jun 27–30	Constellation Senior Players Championship, Fox Chapel Golf Club, Pittsburgh, PA
Jul 11–14	**US Senior Open Championship** (venue to be announced)
Jul 25–28	**The Senior Open Championship** (venue to be announced)
Aug 2–4	3M Championship, TPC Twin Cities, Blaine, MN
Aug 16–18	Dick's Sporting Goods Open, En-Joie GC, Endicott, NY
Aug 22–23	Boeing Classic, TPC Snoqualmie Ridge, Snoqualmie, WA
Aug 30–Sep 1	Calgary Golf Classic, Canyon Meadows G&CC, Calgary, AB, Canada
Sep 6–8	Montreal Championship, Vallee du Richelieu Vercheres, Sainte-Julie (Quebec), Canada
Sep 20–22	Pacific Links Hawai'i Championship, Kapolei Golf Course, Kapolei, HI
Sep 27–29	Nature Valley First Tee Open, Pebble Beach Golf Links, Monterey Peninsula, CA
Oct 11–13	SAS Championship, Prestonwood CC, Cary, NC
Oct 18–20	Greater Hickory Classic at Rock Barn,Rock Barn G&S, Conover, NC
Oct 25–27	AT&T Championship, TPC San Antonio–ATT Canyons, San Antonio, TX
Oct 31–Nov 3	Charles Schwab Cup Championship (venue to be announced)

Gary Player is top title winner on the Sunshine Circuit

Gary Player may not have won on the South African Sunshine circuit since 1981 but between 1955 and then he recorded no fewer than 73 victories.

A winner of nine majors on the world stage, Player heads Zimbabwe's Mark McNulty by 40 wins on the Sunshine Tour table with the late Bobby Locke lying third with 30.

Sid Brews (26), John Bland (21), and another Zimbabwean Tony Johnstone (17), come in behind McNulty just ahead of seventh placed Ernie Els with 16 wins.

PART XII

Annual Awards

Annual Awards

European

European Tour Player of the Year

1985 Bernhard Langer (GER)
1986 Severiano Ballesteros (ESP)
1987 Ian Woosnam (WAL)
1988 Severiano Ballesteros (ESP)
1989 Nick Faldo (ENG)
1990 Nick Faldo (ENG)
1991 Severiano Ballesteros (ESP)
1992 Nick Faldo (ENG)
1993 Bernhard Langer (GER)
1994 Ernie Els (RSA)
1995 Colin Montgomerie (SCO)
1996 Colin Montgomerie (SCO)
1997 Colin Montgomerie (SCO)
1998 Lee Westwood (ENG)
1999 Colin Montgomerie (SCO)
2000 Lee Westwood (ENG)
2001 Retief Goosen (RSA)
2002 Ernie Els (RSA)
2003 Ernie Els (RSA)
2004 Vijay Singh (FIJ)
2005 Michael Campbell (NZL)
2006 Paul Casey (ENG)
2007 Padraig Harrington (IRL)
2008 Padraig Harrington (IRL)
2009 Lee Westwood (ENG)
2010 Martin Kaymer (GER) and Graeme McDowell (NIR)
2011 Luke Donald (ENG)
2012 Rory McIlroy (NIR)

Association of Golf Writers' Trophy

(Awarded to the man or woman who, in the opinion of golf writers, has done most for European golf during the year)

1951 Max Faulkner (ENG)
1952 Miss Elizabeth Price (ENG)
1953 Joe Carr (IRL)
1954 Mrs Roy Smith (Miss Frances Stephens) (ENG)
1955 LGU's Touring Team (Mrs BR Bostock capt.)
1956 John Beharrell (ENG)
1957 Dai Rees (WAL)
1958 Harry Bradshaw (IRL)
1959 Eric Brown (SCO)
1960 Sir Stuart Goodwin
1961 Commander Charles Roe
1962 Marley Spearman (ENG)
1963 Michael Lunt (ENG)
1964 GB&I Eisenhower Trophy Team (Joe Carr capt.)
1965 Gerald Micklem (ENG)
1966 Ronnie Shade (SCO)
1967 John Panton (SCO)
1968 Michael Bonallack (ENG)
1969 Tony Jacklin (ENG)
1970 Tony Jacklin (ENG)
1971 GB&I Walker Cup Team (Michael Bonallack capt.)
1972 Miss Michelle Walker (ENG)
1973 Peter Oosterhuis (ENG)
1974 Peter Oosterhuis (ENG)
1975 Golf Foundation
1976 GB&I Eisenhower Trophy Team (Sandy Saddler capt.)
1977 Christy O'Connor (IRL)
1978 Peter McEvoy (ENG)
1979 Severiano Ballesteros (ESP)
1980 Sandy Lyle (SCO)
1981 Bernhard Langer (GER)
1982 Gordon Brand Jr (SCO)
1983 Nick Faldo (ENG)
1984 Severiano Ballesteros (ESP)
1985 European Ryder Cup Team (Tony Jacklin capt.)
1986 GB&I Curtis Cup Team (Diane Bailey capt.)
1987 European Ryder Cup Team (Tony Jacklin capt.)
1988 Sandy Lyle (SCO)
1989 GB&I Walker Cup Team (Peter McEvoy capt.)
1990 Nick Faldo (ENG)
1991 Severiano Ballesteros (ESP)
1992 European Solheim Cup Team (Mickey Walker capt.)
1993 Bernhard Langer (GER)
1994 Laura Davies (ENG)
1995 European Ryder Cup Team (Bernard Gallacher capt.)
1996 Colin Montgomerie (SCO)
1997 Alison Nicholas (ENG)
1998 Lee Westwood (ENG)
1999 Sergio García (ESP)
2000 Lee Westwood (ENG)
2001 GB&I WalkerCup Team (Peter McEvoy capt.)
2002 Ernie Els (RSA)
2003 Annika Sörenstam (SWE)
2004 European Ryder Cup team (Bernhard Langer capt.)
2005 Annika Sörenstam (SWE)
2006 European Ryder Cup team (Ian Woosnam capt.)
2007 Padraig Harrington (IRL)
2008 Padraig Harrington (IRL)
2009 Lee Westwood (ENG)
2010 Graeme McDowell (NIR)
2011 Luke Donald (ENG)
2012 Rory McIlroy (NIR)

New CEO for Ladies European Tour

Ivan Khodabakhsh has taken over as Chief Executive Officer of the Ladies European Tour in succession to Alexandra Armas who, having achieved a great deal, decided to leave after eight years at the helm.

Mr Khodabakhsh was formerly CEO of World Series Boxing based in Switzerland and before that he was event director of the European Athletic Association. He was selected from over 100 applicants for the post for his vision and commercial expertise as the Tour looks for further ways to expand playing opportunities for its members.

The 2013 season currently comprises 21 events in 17 countries – China, Morocco, South Africa, Turkey, Holland, Germany, Spain, Slovakia, England, Scotland, the Czech Republic, the United States, Sweden France, Italy, India and Dubai.

European Tour Harry Vardon Trophy

(Awarded to the PGA member heading the Order of Merit at the end of the season)

1937 Charles Whitcombe
1938 Henry Cotton
1939 Roger Whitcombe
1940–45 *In abeyance*
1946 Bobby Locke
1947 Norman Von Nida
1948 Charlie Ward
1949 Charlie Ward
1950 Bobby Locke
1951 John Panton
1952 Harry Weetman
1953 Flory van Donck
1954 Bobby Locke
1955 Dai Rees
1956 Harry Weetman
1957 Eric Brown
1958 Bernard Hunt
1959 Dai Rees
1960 Bernard Hunt
1961 Christy O'Connor
1962 Christy O'Connor
1963 Neil Coles
1964 Peter Alliss
1965 Bernard Hunt
1966 Peter Alliss
1967 Malcolm Gregson
1968 Brian Huggett
1969 Bernard Gallacher
1970 Neil Coles
1971 Peter Oosterhuis
1972 Peter Oosterhuis
1973 Peter Oosterhuis
1974 Peter Oosterhuis
1975 Dale Hayes
1976 Severiano Ballesteros
1977 Severiano Ballesteros
1978 Severiano Ballesteros
1979 Sandy Lyle
1980 Sandy Lyle
1981 Bernhard Langer
1982 Greg Norman
1983 Nick Faldo
1984 Bernhard Langer
1985 Sandy Lyle
1986 Severiano Ballesteros
1987 Ian Woosnam
1988 Severiano Ballesteros
1989 Ronan Rafferty
1990 Ian Woosnam
1991 Severiano Ballesteros
1992 Nick Faldo
1993 Colin Montgomerie
1994 Colin Montgomerie
1995 Colin Montgomerie
1996 Colin Montgomerie
1997 Colin Montgomerie
1998 Colin Montgomerie
1999 Colin Montgomerie
2000 Lee Westwood
2001 Retief Goosen
2002 Retief Goosen
2003 Ernie Els
2004 Ernie Els
2005 Colin Montgomerie
2006 Padraig Harrington
2007 Justin Rose
2008 Robert Karlsson
2009 Lee Westwood
2010 Martin Kaymer
2011 Luke Donald
2012 Rory McIlroy

Sir Henry Cotton European Rookie of the Year

1960 Tommy Goodwin
1961 Alex Caygill (ENG)
1962 *No Award*
1963 Tony Jacklin (ENG)
1964 *No Award*
1966 Robin Liddle (SCO)
1967 *No Award*
1968 Bernard Gallacher (SCO)
1969 Peter Oosterhuis (ENG)
1970 Stuart Brown (ENG)
1971 David Llewellyn (WAL)
1972 Sam Torrance (SCO)
1973 Philip Elson (ENG)
1974 Carl Mason (ENG)
1975 *No Award*
1976 Mark James (ENG)
1977 Nick Faldo (ENG)
1978 Sandy Lyle (SCO)
1979 Mike Miller (SCO)
1980 Paul Hoad (ENG)
1981 Jeremy Bennett (ENG)
1982 Gordon Brand Jr (SCO)
1983 Grant Turner (NZL)
1984 Philip Parkin (WAL)
1985 Paul Thomas (WAL)
1986 José Maria Olazàbal (ESP)
1987 Peter Baker (ENG)
1988 Colin Montgomerie (SCO)
1989 Paul Broadhurst (ENG)
1990 Russell Claydon (ENG)
1991 Per-Ulrik Johansson (SWE)
1992 Jim Payne (ENG)
1993 Gary Orr (SCO)
1994 Jonathan Lomas (ENG)
1995 Jarmo Sandelin (SWE)
1996 Thomas Bjørn (DEN)
1997 Scott Henderson (SCO)
1998 Olivier Edmond (FRA)
1999 Sergio García (ESP)
2000 Ian Poulter (ENG)
2001 Paul Casey (ENG)
2002 Nick Dougherty (ENG)
2003 Peter Lawrie (IRL)
2004 Scott Drummond (SCO)
2005 Gonzolo Fernandez-Castano (ESP)
2006 Marc Warren (SCO)
2007 Martin Kaymer (GER)
2008 Pablo Larrazabal (ESP)
2009 Chris Wood (ENG)
2010 Matteo Manassero (ITA)
2011 Tom Lewis (ENG)
2012 Carlos Santos (POR)

2012 Payne Stewart Award for Steve Stricker

Ryder Cup golfer Steve Stricker is the latest recipient of the Payne Stewart Award given annually to a player who shares the late golfer's respect for the traditions of the game, who works for charitable causes and through dress and conduct presents himself in a professional manner.

Winner of 12 titles on the PGA Tour, 45-year-old Ryder Cup golfer Stricker said he was humbled and honoured at being the recipient of the award. PGA Tour commissioner Tim Finchem said: "Steve has epitomised for years everything that the award represents. From his professionalism on the course to his compassion for others off it, it is hard to think of a more fitting recipient."

Stricker, who follows previous winners including Jack Nicklaus, Arnold Palmer, Ben Crenshaw, Nick Price, Gary Player and Tom Watson among others, said: "Golf obviously means a lot to me. I have tried to conduct myself over the years in such a way as to set an example to others as Payne did."

In 1994 Stricker was a rookie on the PGA Tour when Payne Stewart was going through a difficult time with his game. He told the Associated Press that he remembers watching him rededicate and refocus himself to get everything right,. When I had troubles of my own in the mid-2000 I remembered how he had coped."

Ladies European Tour ISPS Handa Order of Merit

1979 Catherine Panton-Lewis (SCO)
1980 Muriel Thomson (SCO)
1981 Jenny Lee-Smith (ENG)
1982 Jenny Lee-Smith (ENG)
1983 Muriel Thomson (SCO)
1984 Dale Reid (SCO)
1985 Laura Davies (ENG)
1986 Laura Davies (ENG)
1987 Dale Reid (SCO)
1988 Marie-Laure Taud (FRA)
1989 Marie-Laure de Laurenzi (FRA)
1990 Trish Johnson (ENG)
1991 Corinne Dibnah (AUS)
1992 Laura Davies (ENG)
1993 Karen Lunn (AUS)
1994 Liselotte Neumann (SWE)
1995 Annika Sörenstam (SWE)
1996 Laura Davies (ENG)
1997 Alison Nicholas (ENG)
1998 Helen Alfredsson (SWE)
1999 Laura Davies (ENG)
2000 Sophie Gustafson (SWE)
2001 Raquel Carriedo (ESP)
2002 Paula Marti (ESP)
2003 Sophie Gustafson (SWE)
2004 Laura Davies (ENG)
2005 Iben Tinning (DEN)
2006 Laura Davies (ENG)
2007 Sophie Gustafson (SWE)
2008 Gwladys Nocera (FRA)
2009 Sophie Gustafson (SWE)
2010 Lee-Anne Pace (RSA)
2011 Ai Miyazato (JPN)
2012 Carlota Ciganda (ESP)

Ladies European Tour Players' Player of the Year

1995 Annika Sörenstam (SWE)
1996 Laura Davies (ENG)
1997 Alison Nicholas (ENG)
1998 Sophie Gustafson (SWE)
1999 Laura Davies (ENG)
2000 Sophie Gustafson (SWE)
2001 Raquel Carriedo (ESP)
2002 Annika Sörenstam (SWE)
2003 Sophie Gustafson (SWE)
2004 Stephanie Arricau (FRA)
2005 Iben Tinning (DEN)
2006 Gwladys Nocera (FRA)
2007 Sophie Gustafson (SWE)
2008 Gwladys Nocera (FRA)
2009 Catriona Matthew (SCO)
2010 Lee-Anne Pace (RSA)
2011 Caroline Hedwall (SWE)
2012 Carlota Ciganda (ESP)

Ladies European Tour Rolex Rookie of the Year

1984 Katrina Douglas (ENG)
1985 Laura Davies (ENG)
1986 Patricia Gonzales (COL)
1987 Trish Johnson (ENG)
1988 Laurette Maritz (USA)
1989 Helen Alfredsson (SWE)
1990 Pearl Sinn (KOR)
1991 Helen Wadsworth (WAL)
1992 Sandrine Mendiburu (FRA)
1993 Annika Sörenstam (SWE)
1994 Tracy Hansen (USA)
1995 Karrie Webb (AUS)
1996 Anne-Marie Knight (AUS)
1997 Anna Berg (SWE)
1998 Laura Philo (USA)
1999 Elaine Ratcliffe (ENG)
2000 Guila Sergas (ITA)
2001 Suzann Pettersen (NOR)
2002 Kirsty S Taylor (ENG)
2003 Rebecca Stevenson (AUS)
2004 Minea Blomqvist (FIN)
2005 Elisa Serramia (ESP)
2006 Nikki Garrett (AUS)
2007 Louise Stahle (SWE)
2008 Melissa Reid (ENG)
2009 Anna Norqvist (SWE)
2010 Kim In-Kyung (KOR)
2011 Anna Nordqvist (SWE)
2012 Carlota Ciganda (ESP)

Daily Telegraph Amateur Woman Golfer of the Year

1982 Jane Connachan (SCO)
1983 Jill Thornhill (ENG)
1984 Gillian Stewart and Claire Waite (ENG)
1985 Belle Robertson (SCO)
1986 GBI Curtis Cup Team (Diane Bailey capt.)
1987 Linda Bayman (ENG)
1988 GBI Curtis Cup Team
1989 Helen Dobson (ENG)
1990 Angela Uzielli (ENG)
1991 Joanne Morley (ENG)
1992 GBI Curtis Cup Team (Liz Boatman capt.)
1993 Catriona Lambert and Julie Hall
1994 GBI Curtis Cup Team (Liz Boatman capt.)
1995 Julie Hall (ENG)
1996 GBI Curtis Cup Team (Ita Butler capt.)
1997 Alison Rose (ENG)
1998 Kim Andrew
1999 Welsh International Team (Olwen Davies capt.)
2000 Rebecca Hudson (ENG)
2001 Rebecca Hudson (ENG)
2002 Becky Brewerton (WAL)
2003 Becky Brewerton (WAL)
2004 Emma Duggleby (ENG)
2005 Felicity Johnson (ENG)
2006 *Not awarded*
2007 Melissa Reid (ENG)
2008 *Discontinued*

Joyce Wethered Trophy (Awarded to the outstanding amateur under 25)

1994 Janice Moodie (SCO)
1995 Rebecca Hudson (ENG)
1996 Mhairi McKay (SCO)
1997 Rebecca Hudson (ENG)
1998 Liza Walters (ENG)
1999 Becky Brewerton (WAL)
2000 Sophie Walker (ENG)
2001 Clare Queen (ENG)
2002 Sarah Jones (ENG)
2003 Sophie Walker (ENG)
2004 Melissa Reid (ENG)
2005 Becky Harries (ENG)
2006 Sally Little (SCO) and Carly Booth (SCO)
2007 Henrietta Brockway (ENG)
2008 *Discontinued*

American

Winners American unless stated

Arnold Palmer Award (Awarded to the Tour's leading money winner)

1981 Tom Kite
1982 Craig Stadler
1983 Hal Sutton
1984 Tom Watson
1985 Curtis Strange
1986 Greg Norman (AUS)
1987 Paul Azinger
1988 Curtis Strange
1989 Tom Kite
1990 Greg Norman (AUS)
1991 Corey Pavin
1992 Fred Couples
1993 Nick Price (ZIM)
1994 Nick Price (ZIM)
1995 Greg Norman (AUS)
1996 Tom Lehman
1997 Tiger Woods
1998 David Duval
1999 Tiger Woods
2000 Tiger Woods
2001 Tiger Woods
2002 Tiger Woods
2003 Tiger Woods
2004 Vijay Singh (FIJ)
2005 Tiger Woods
2006 Tiger Woods
2007 Tiger Woods
2008 Vijay Singh (FIJ)
2009 Tiger Woods
2010 Matt Kuchar
2011 Luke Donald (ENG)
2012 Rory McIlroy (NIR)

Jack Nicklaus Award (Player of the Year decided by player ballot)

1990 Wayne Levi
1991 Fred Couples
1992 Fred Couples
1993 Nick Price (ZIM)
1994 Nick Price (ZIM)
1995 Greg Norman (AUS)
1996 Tom Lehman
1997 Tiger Woods
1998 Mark O'Meara
1999 Tiger Woods
2000 Tiger Woods
2001 Tiger Woods
2002 Tiger Woods
2003 Tiger Woods
2004 Vijay Singh (FIJ)
2005 Tiger Woods
2006 Tiger Woods
2007 Tiger Woods
2008 Padraig Harrington (IRL)

PGA Tour Rookie of the Year (Decided by player ballot)

1990 Robert Gamez
1991 John Daly
1992 Mark Carnevale
1993 Vijay Singh (FIJ)
1994 Ernie Els (RSA)
1995 Woody Austin
1996 Tiger Woods
1997 Stewart Cink
1998 Steve Flesch
1999 Carlos Franco (PAR)
2000 Michael Clark II
2001 Charles Howell III
2002 Jonathan Byrd
2003 Ben Curtis
2004 Todd Hamilton
2005 Sean O'Hair
2006 Trevor Immelman (RSA)
2007 Brandt Snedeker
2008 Andres Romero (ARG)
2009 Marc Leishman (AUS)
2010 Rickie Fowler
2011 Keegan Bradley
2012 John Huh

PGA of America Player of the Year (Decided on merit points)

1948 Ben Hogan
1949 Sam Snead
1950 Ben Hogan
1951 Ben Hogan
1952 Julius Boros
1953 Ben Hogan
1954 Ed Furgol
1955 Doug Ford
1956 Jack Burke
1957 Dick Mayer
1958 Dow Finsterwald
1959 Art Wall
1960 Arnold Palmer
1961 Jerry Barber
1962 Arnold Palmer
1963 Julius Boros
1964 Ken Venturi
1965 Dave Marr
1966 Billy Casper
1967 Jack Nicklaus
1968 *not awarded*
1969 Orville Moody
1970 Billy Casper
1971 Lee Trevino
1972 Jack Nicklaus
1973 Jack Nicklaus
1974 Johnny Miller
1975 Jack Nicklaus
1976 Jack Nicklaus
1977 Tom Watson
1978 Tom Watson
1979 Tom Watson
1980 Tom Watson
1981 Bill Rogers
1982 Tom Watson
1983 Hal Sutton
1984 Tom Watson
1985 Lanny Wadkins
1986 Bob Tway
1987 Paul Azinger
1988 Curtis Strange
1989 Tom Kite
1990 Nick Faldo (ENG)
1991 Corey Pavin
1992 Fred Couples
1993 Nick Price (ZIM)
1994 Nick Price (ZIM)
1995 Greg Norman (AUS)
1996 Tom Lehman
1997 Tiger Woods
1998 Mark O'Meara
1999 Tiger Woods
2000 Tiger Woods
2001 Tiger Woods
2002 Tiger Woods
2003 Tiger Woods
2004 Vijay Singh (FIJ)
2005 Tiger Woods
2006 Tiger Woods
2007 Tiger Woods
2008 Padraig Harrington (IRL)
2009 Tiger Woods
2010 Jim Furyk
2011 Luke Donald (ENG)
2012 Rory McIlroy (NIR)

Congressional Gold Medal for Arnold Palmer

Arnold Palmer became only the sixth athlete and the second golfer to receive the Congressional Gold Medal at a ceremony in Washington in 2012.

The Congressional Gold Medal and the Presidential Medal of Freedom, which Palmer received in 2004, are America's highest civilian awards. Palmer was honoured by Congress and the House of Representatives for promoting excellence and good sportsmanship in golf.

At the ceremony in the Rotunda of the Capitol Building, Jack Nicklaus said: "Arnold Palmer is the everyday man's hero. From his modest upbringing, Arnold embodies the hard-working strength of America. The game has given so much to Arnold Palmer but he has given back to golf so much more."

PGA of America Vardon Trophy (For lowest scoring average over 60 PGA Tour rounds or more)

1937	Harry Cooper	
1938	Sam Snead	
1939	Byron Nelson	
1940	Ben Hogan	
1941	Ben Hogan	
1942–46	*No Awards*	
1947	Jimmy Demarel	69.90
1948	Ben Hogan	69.30
1949	Sam Snead	69.37
1950	Sam Snead	69.23
1951	Lloyd Mangrum	70.05
1952	Jack Burke	70.54
1953	Lloyd Mangrum	70.22
1954	Ed Harrison	70.41
1955	Sam Snead	69.86
1956	Cary Middlecoff	70.35
1957	Dow Finsterwald	70.30
1958	Bob Rosburg	70.11
1959	Art Wall	70.35
1960	Billy Casper	69.95
1961	Arnold Palmer	69.85
1962	Arnold Palmer	70.27
1963	Billy Casper	70.58
1964	Arnold Palmer	70.01
1965	Billy Casper	70.85
1966	Billy Casper	70.27
1967	Arnold Palmer	70.18
1968	Billy Casper	69.82
1969	Dave Hill	70.34
1970	Lee Trevino	70.64
1971	Lee Trevino	70.27
1972	Lee Trevino	70.89
1973	Bruce Crampton (AUS)	70.57
1974	Lee Trevino	70.53
1975	Bruce Crampton (AUS)	70.51
1976	Don January	70.56
1977	Tom Watson	70.32
1978	Tom Watson	70.16
1979	Tom Watson	70.27
1980	Lee Trevino	69.73
1981	Tom Kite	69.80
1982	Tom Kite	70.21
1983	Ray Floyd	70.61
1984	Calvin Peete	70.56
1985	Don Pooley	70.36
1986	Scott Hoch	70.08
1987	Dan Pohl	70.25
1988	Chip Beck	69.46
1989	Greg Norman (AUS)	69.49
1990	Greg Norman (AUS)	69.10
1991	Fred Couples	69.59
1992	Fred Couples	69.38
1993	Nick Price (ZIM)	69.11
1994	Greg Norman (AUS)	69.81
1995	Steve Elkington (AUS)	69.82
1996	Tom Lehman	69.32
1997	Nick Price (ZIM)	68.98
1998	David Duval	69.13
1999	Tiger Woods	68.43
2000	Tiger Woods	67.79
2001	Tiger Woods	68.81
2002	Tiger Woods	68.56
2003	Tiger Woods	68.41
2004	Vijay Singh (FIJ)	68.84
2005	Tiger Woods	68.66
2006	Jim Furyk	68.66
2007	Tiger Woods	67.79
2008	Phil Mickelson	69.17
2009	Tiger Woods	68.05
2010	Matt Kuchar	69.61
2011	Luke Donald (ENG)	68.86
2012	Rory McIlroy (NIR)	69.02

Payne Stewart Award (Presented for respecting and upholding the traditions of the game)

2000 Byron Nelson, Jack Nicklaus, Arnold Palmer
2001 Ben Crenshaw
2002 Nick Price
2003 Tom Watson
2004 Jay Haas
2005 Brad Faxon
2006 Gary Player (RSA)
2007 Hal Sutton
2008 Davis Love III
2009 Kenny Perry
2010 Tom Lehman
2011 David Toms
2012 Steve Stricker

Bob Jones Award in 2012 went to Annika Sörenstam

Winner of 90 titles in her 15-year career, Sweden's Annika Sörenstam is the 2012 recipient of the prestigious Bob Jones Award which recognises a person who emulates Jones' spirit, his personal qualities and his attitude to the game and its players.

In announcing the 2012 award Jim Hyler, President of the United States Golf Association, said: "Annika has consistently exhibited the specific character trait – distinguished sportsmanship – that this, the highest honour that the USGA can bestow, was established to recognize. She has done this while achieving a record of success that few have equalled. It is not just the number of tournaments and Championships she won but the way she conducted herself – gracious in victory and defeat – and always respectful of her opponents and the game itself."

Since 2008, Annika has acted as an ambassador of the USGA helping to make the game more accessible to players of all skill levels. In 2009 she became a global ambassador for the International Golf Federation and she supported the successful bid to have golf introduced into the 2016 Olympic Games in Rio de Janiero.

She is a keen supporter of junior golf and spends much time with her own ANNIKA Foundation which teaches children the importance of embracing a healthy active lifestyle through fitness and nutrition.

Winner of a record eight Rolex LPGA Player of the Year awards, Annika Sörenstam said: "It is truly an honour to receive this award. Some of the previous recipients are among the some of the greatest names in the history of the game. Although I am no longer competing I appreciate the USGA recognising our hard work and I will continue to try to grow the game through many Foundation initiatives."

PGA of America Distinguished Service Award

1988 Herb Graffis
1989 Bob Hope
1990 *No award*
1991 Gerald Ford
1992 Gene Sarazen
1993 Byron Nelson
1994 Arnold Palmer
1995 Patty Berg
1996 Frank Chirkinian
1997 George Bush
1998 Paul Runyan
1999 Bill Dickey
2000 Jack Nicklaus
2001 Mark McCormack
2002 Tim Finchem
2003 Vince Gill
2004 Pete Dye
2005 Wally Uihlein
2006 Fred Ridley
2007 Jack Burke Jr
2008 Dennis Walters
2009 William J Powell
2010 Billy Casper
2011 Larry Nelson
2012 Dave Stockton

Bob Jones Award (Awarded by USGA for distinguished sportsmanship in golf)

1955 Francis Ouimet
1956 Bill Campbell
1957 Babe Zaharias
1958 Margaret Curtis
1959 Findlay Douglas
1960 Charles Evans Jr
1961 Joe Carr (IRL)
1962 Horton-Smith
1963 Patty Berg
1964 Charles Coe
1965 Mrs Edwin Vare
1966 Gary Player (RSA)
1967 Richard Tufts
1968 Robert Dickson
1969 Gerald Micklem (ENG)
1970 Roberto De Vicenzo (ARG)
1971 Arnold Palmer
1972 Michael Bonallack (ENG)
1973 Gene Littler
1974 Byron Nelson
1975 Jack Nicklaus
1976 Ben Hogan
1977 Joseph C Dey
1978 Bob Hope and Bing Crosby
1979 Tom Kite
1980 Charles Yates
1981 JoAnne Carner
1982 Billy Joe Patton
1983 Maureen Garrett (ENG)
1984 Jay Sigel
1985 Fuzzy Zoeller
1986 Jess W Sweetser
1987 Tom Watson
1988 Isaac B Grainger
1989 Chi-Chi Rodriquez (PUR)
1990 Peggy Kirk Bell
1991 Ben Crenshaw
1992 Gene Sarazen
1993 P J Boatwright Jr
1994 Lewis Oehmig
1995 Herbert Warren Wind
1996 Betsy Rawls
1997 Fred Brand
1998 Nancy Lopez
1999 Ed Updegraff
2000 Barbara McIntyre
2001 Thomas Cousins
2002 Judy Rankin
2003 Carol Semple Thompson
2004 Jackie Burke
2005 Nick Price (ZIM)
2006 Jay Haas
2007 Louise Suggs
2008 George H W Bush
2009 Gordon Brewer
2010 Mickey Wright
2011 Lorena Ochoa (MEX)
2012 Annika Sörenstam (SWE)
2013 Davis Love III

US LPGA Rolex Player of the Year

1966 Kathy Whitworth
1967 Kathy Whitworth
1968 Kathy Whitworth
1969 Kathy Whitworth
1970 Sandra Haynie
1971 Kathy Whitworth
1972 Kathy Whitworth
1973 Kathy Whitworth
1974 JoAnne Carner
1975 Sandra Palmer
1976 Judy Rankin
1977 Judy Rankin
1978 Nancy Lopez
1979 Nancy Lopez
1980 Beth Daniel
1981 Jo Anne Carner
1982 Jo Anne Carner
1983 Patty Sheehan
1984 Betsy King
1985 Nancy Lopez
1986 Pat Bradley
1987 Ayako Okamoto (JPN)
1988 Nancy Lopez
1989 Betsy King
1990 Beth Daniel
1991 Pat Bradley
1992 Dottie Mochrie
1993 Betsy King
1994 Beth Daniel
1995 Annika Sörenstam (SWE)
1996 Laura Davies (ENG)
1997 Annika Sörenstam (SWE)
1998 Annika Sörenstam (SWE)
1999 Karrie Webb (AUS)
2000 Karrie Webb (AUS)
2001 Annika Sörenstam (SWE)
2002 Annika Sörenstam (SWE)
2003 Annika Sörenstam (SWE)
2004 Annika Sörenstam (SWE)
2005 Annika Sörenstam (SWE)
2006 Lorena Ochoa (MEX)
2007 Lorena Ochoa (MEX)
2008 Lorena Ochoa (MEX)
2009 Lorena Ochoa (MEX)
2010 Yani Tseng (TPE)
2011 Yani Tseng (TPE)
2012 Stacy Lewis

Louise Suggs Rolex Rookie of the Year

1962 Mary Mills
1963 Clifford Ann Creed
1964 Susie Berning
1965 Margie Masters
1966 Jan Ferraris
1967 Sharron Moran
1968 Sandra Post
1969 Jane Blalock
1970 JoAnne Carner
1971 Sally Little (RSA)
1972 Jocelyne Bourassa
1973 Laura Baugh
1974 Jan Stephenson
1975 Amy Alcott
1976 Bonnie Lauer
1977 Debbie Massey
1978 Nancy Lopez
1979 Beth Daniel
1980 Myra Van Hoose
1981 Patty Sheehan
1982 Patti Rizzo
1983 Stephanie Farwig
1984 Juli Inkster
1985 Penny Hammel
1986 Jody Rosenthal
1987 Tammi Green
1988 Liselotte Neumann (SWE)
1989 Pamela Wright (SCO)
1990 Hiromi Kobayashi (JPN)
1991 Brandie Burton
1992 Helen Alfredsson (SWE)
1993 Suzanne Strudwick (ENG)
1994 Annika Sörenstam (SWE)
1995 Pat Hurst
1996 Karrie Webb (AUS)
1997 Lisa Hackney (ENG)
1998 Se Ri Pak (KOR)
1999 Mi Hyun Kim (KOR)
2000 Dorothy Delasin (PHI)
2001 Hee Won Han (KOR)
2002 Beth Bauer
2003 Lorena Ochoa (MEX)
2004 Shi Hyun Ahn (KOR)
2005 Paula Creamer
2006 Seon-Hua Lee (KOR)
2007 Angela Park (KOR)
2008 Yani Tseng (KOR)
2009 Ji-Yai Shin (KOR)
2010 Azahara Muños (ESP)
2011 Hee Kyung Seo (KOR)
2012 So Yeon Ryu (KOR)

LPGA Vare Trophy

	Scoring av.
1953 Patty Berg	75.00
1954 Babe Zaharias	75.48
1955 Patty Berg	74.47
1956 Patty Berg	74.57
1957 Louise Suggs	74.64
1958 Beverly Hanson	74.92
1959 Betsy Rawls	74.03
1960 Mickey Wright	73.25
1961 Mickey Wright	73.55
1962 Mickey Wright	73.67
1963 Mickey Wright	72.81
1964 Mickey Wright	72.46
1965 Kathy Whitworth	72.61
1966 Kathy Whitworth	72.60
1967 Kathy Whitworth	72.74
1968 Carol Mann	72.04
1969 Kathy Whitworth	72.38
1970 Kathy Whitworth	72.26
1971 Kathy Whitworth	72.88
1972 Kathy Whitworth	72.38
1973 Judy Rankin	73.08
1974 JoAnne Carner	72.87
1975 JoAnne Carner	72.40
1976 Judy Rankin	72.25
1977 Judy Rankin	72.16
1978 Nancy Lopez	71.76
1979 Nancy Lopez	71.20
1980 Amy Alcott	71.51
1981 Jo Anne Carner	71.75
1982 Jo Anne Carner	71.49
1983 Jo Anne Carner	71.41
1984 Patty Sheehan	71.40
1985 Nancy Lopez	70.73
1986 Pat Bradley	71.10
1987 Betsy King	71.14
1988 Colleen Walker	71.26
1989 Beth Daniel	70.38
1990 Beth Daniel	70.54
1991 Pat Bradley	70.66
1992 Dottie Mochrie	70.80
1993 Nancy Lopez	70.83
1994 Beth Daniel	70.90
1995 Annika Sörenstam (SWE)	71.00
1996 Annika Sörenstam (SWE)	70.47
1997 Karrie Webb (AUS)	70.01
1998 Annika Sörenstam (SWE)	69.99
1999 Karrie Webb (AUS)	69.43
2000 Karrie Webb (AUS)	70.05
2001 Annika Sörenstam (SWE)	69.42
2002 Annika Sörenstam (SWE)	68.70
2003 Se Ri Pak (KOR)	70.03
2004 Grace Park (KOR)	69.99
2005 Annika Sörenstam (SWE)	69.25
2006 Lorena Ochoa (MEX)	69.23
2007 Lorena Ochoa (MEX)	69.68
2008 Lorena Ochoa (MEX)	69.58
2009 Lorena Ochoa (MEX)	70.16
2010 Choi Na Yeon (KOR)	69.96
2011 Yani Tseng (TPE)	69.66
2012 Inbee Park (KOR)	70.21

First Lady of Golf Award

(PGA of America award for women who have made a significant contribution to the game)

From 2009 this award was presented every second year

1998 Barbara Nicklaus
1999 Judy Rankin
2000 *No award given*
2001 Judy Bell
2002 Nancy Lopez
2003 Renee Powell
2004 Alice Dye
2005 Carole Semple-Thompson
2006 Kathy Whitworth
2007 Peggy Kirk Bell
2008 Carol Mann
2009 Donna Caponi-Byrnes
2011 Mary Bea Porter-King

Dave Stockton receives Distinguished Service Award

Dave Stockton, who twice won the US PGA Championship and captained the US Ryder Cup team to victory at Kiawah Island in 1991, has been presented with the PGA of America's Distinguished Service Award.

Alan Wronowski, President of the PGA of America, when presenting Stockton with his trophy said: "Dave Stockton's imprint on golf extends beyond the boundaries of the course where he excelled at the highest level. He has coached many of the world's finest men and women players to success and has selflessly supported charitable efforts that benefit higher education, the under-priviledged and our nation's heroes. He is a champion in so many ways."

Born in San Bernardino, California, the son of golf professional Gail Stockton, he recovered from a broken back in a surfing accident when he was just 15. After earning All-American honours at University he graduated in 1964 with a degree in general management then turned professional.

"I have been fortunate to have many good things happen to me in golf. I believed I had a gift as a motivational speaker and used that to help others gain a better understanding about what golf can do to help them feel better about themselves", says Stockton.

Winner of 10 titles on the PGA Tour and 14 more on the Champions Tour, he was a member of four unbeaten Ryder Cup sides before taking on the captaincy at Kiawah where he led his side to a nail-biting one point victory. His charity work includes hosting the Stater Brothers Charities Dave Stockton Heroes Challenge which, since 2008 has raised over $3 million.

More recently Stockton, with his sons Dave Jr and Ron, both of whom are professionals, has turned to teaching putting and the short game to many of the leading players on Tour.

PART XIII

Who's Who in Golf

Who's Who in Golf – Men

Aaron, T.
Allenby, R.
Alliss, P.
An, B.H.
Aoki, I.
Atwal, A.
Azinger, P.
Baddeley, A.
Baker, P.
Baker-Finch, I.
Barnes, B.
Beem, R.
Bjørn, T.
Bonallack, M.
Bradley, K.
Brooks, M.
Brown, K.
Cabrera, A.
Cabrera Bello, R.
Calcavecchia, M.
Campbell, W.C.
Canizares, A.
Canizares, J.M.
Cantlay, P.
Casey, P.
Casper, B.
Chapman, R.
Charles, Sir Bob
Choi, K.-J.
Cink, S.
Clark, C.
Clark, H.
Clarke, D.
Coles, N.
Coltart, A.
Couples, F.
Crenshaw, B.
Curtis, B.
Daly, J.
Darcy, E.
Davis, R.
Day, J.
De Vincenzo, R.
Dickson, B.
Donald, L.
Drew, N.
Duval, D.
Dyson, S.
Edfors, J.
Edwards, N.
Elkington, S.
Els, E.
Faldo, Sir N.
Fasth, N.
Faxon, B.
Feherty, D.
Fernandez, V.
Fernandez-Castano, G.
Finsterwald, D.
Fisher, O.
Fisher, R.
Floyd, R.
Ford, D.
Frost, D.
Funk, F.
Furyk, J.
Gallacher, B.
García, S.
Garrido, A.
Garrido, I.
Goosen, R.
Grace, B.
Grady, W.
Graham, D.
Green, C,
Green, H.
Haas, B.
Haas, J.
Haeggman, J.
Hamilton, T.
Han, C.W.
Hansen, A.
Hansen, S.
Hanson, P.
Harrington, P.
Hayes, D.
Hoch, S.
Horton, T.
Howell, D.
Huggett, B.
Hunt, B.
Ilonen, M.
Immelman, T.
Irwin, H.
Ishikawa, R.
Jacklin, T.
Jacobs, J.
Jacquelin, R.
Jaidee, T.
James, M.
January, D.
Janzen, L.
Jiminéz, M.A.
Johansson, P.-U.
Johnson, D.
Johnson, Z.
Jones, S.
Karlsson, R.
Kaymer, M.
Kim, K.T.
Kuchar, M.
Kite, T.
Laird, M.
Lane, B.
Langer, B.
Lawrie, P.
Lee, D.
Lehman, T.
Leonard, J.
Levet, T.
Lewis, T.
Liang W.-C.
Littler, G.
Love III, D.
Lowry, S.
Lyle, S.
McDowell, G.
McEvoy, P.
McGimpsey, G.
McGinley, P.
Macgregor, G.
McIlroy, R.
McNulty, M.
Mahan, H.
Mamat, M.
Manassero, M.
Marsh, D.
Marsh, G.
Martin, P.
Mason, C.
Matsuyama, H.
Micheel, S.
Mickelson, P.
Miller, J.
Milligan, J.
Mize, L.
Molinari, E.
Molinari, F.
Montgomerie, C.
Nagle, K.
Nelson, L.
Newton, J.
Nicklaus, J.
Nirat, C.
Nobilo, F.
Noh, S.Y.
Norman, G.
North, A.
O'Connor, C., Sr
O'Connor, C., Jr
Ogilvy, G.
Olazábal, J.M.
O'Leary, J.
O'Meara, M.
Oosterhuis, P.
Oosthuizen, L.
Ozaki, M.
Pagunsan, J.
Palmer, A.
Parnevik, J.
Parry, C.
Pate, J.
Pavin, C.
Perry, K.
Phadungsil, C.
Player, G.
Poulter, I.
Price, N.
Price, P.
Quigley, D.
Quiros, A.
Rafferty, R.
Ramsay, R.
Randhawa, J.
Remesy, J.-F.
Rivero, J.
Roberts, L.
Rocca, C.
Rogers, B.
Romero, E.
Rose, J.
Sandelin, J.
Schwartzel, C.
Scott, A.
Senior, P.
Sigel, J.
Simpson, S.
Simpson, W.
Singh, J.M.
Singh, V.
Smyth, D.
Snedeker, B.
Stadler, C.
Stenson, H.
Stranahan, F.R.
Strange, C.
Stricker, S.
Sutton, H.
Thomas, D.
Thomson, P.
Toms, D.
Torrance, S.
Townsend, P.
Trevino, L.
Van de Velde, J.
Verplank, S.
Wadkins, L.
Walton, P.
Warren, M.
Watney, N.
Watson, B.
Watson, T.
Weekley, B.
Weir, M.
Weiskopf, T.
Westwood, L.
Williams, C.
Wilson, O.
Wirachant, T.
Wolstenholme, G.
Wood, C.
Woods, E.
Woosnam, I.
Yang, Y-e
Yeh, W.-t.
Zhang, L.-W.
Zoeller, F.

Aaron, Tommy (USA)

Born Gainesville, Georgia, 22 February 1937
Turned professional 1961

The 1973 Masters champion who, five years earlier inadvertently marked down a 4 on Roberto de Vicenzo's card for the 17th hole when the Argentinian had taken 3. De Vicenzo signed for the 4 and lost out by one shot on a play-off with Bob Goalby for the Green Jacket.

Allenby, Robert (AUS)

Born Melbourne, 12 July 1971
Turned professional 1992

Pipped by a shot from winning the Australian Open as an amateur in 1991 by Wayne Riley's birdie, birdie, birdie finish at Royal Melbourne, he won the title three years later as a professional and won it again in 1955. After competing on the European Tour and winning four times, he now plays on the US Tour.

Alliss, Peter (ENG)

Born Berlin, 28 February 1931 Turned professional 1946

Following a distinguished career as a tournament golfer in which he won 18 titles between 1954 and 1966 and played eight times in the Ryder Cup between 1953 and 1969, he turned to golf commentating. In Britain he works for the BBC and for the American network ABC at The Open. Twice captain of the PGA in 1962 and 1987 he won the Spanish, Italian and Portuguese Opens in 1958. Author or co-author of several golf books and a novel with a golfing background, he has also designed several courses including the Brabazon course at The Belfry in association with Dave Thomas. In 2003 he was awarded Life Membership of the PGA in honour of his lifelong contribution and commitment to the game. In 2005 he received an honorary degree from St Andrews University and in 2010 a PGA distinguished service award. He was selected through the international ballot to be inducted into the World Golf Hall of Fame in 2012.

An, Byeong-Hun (Ben) (KOR)

Born Korea, 17 September 1991

When just 18 years old he became the youngest winner in the 109-year history of the US Amateur Championship when he beat Ben Martin 7 and 5 in the 2009 final at Southern Hills in Oklahoma. He was the 13th. Korean-born golfer to win a USGA title. An All-American at the University of California he was introduced to the game at the age of seven by his parents both of who were table tennis medallists in the 1988 Olympics in Seoul.

Aoki, Isao (JPN)

Born Abiko, Chiba, 31 August 1942
Turned professional 1964

Successful international performer whose only victory on the PGA Tour came dramatically in Hawaii in 1983 when he holed a 128 yards pitch for an eagle 3 at the last at Waialae to beat Jack Renner. Only Japanese golfer to win on the European Tour taking the European Open in 1983. He also won the World Match Play in 1978 beating Simon Owen and was runner up the following year. He holed in one at Wentworth in that event to win a condominium at Gleneagles. He was top earner five times in his own country and is the Japanese golfer who has come closest to winning a major title finishing runner-up two shots behind Jack Nicklaus in the 1980 US Open at Baltusrol. Inducted into the World Golf Hall of Fame in 2004.

Atwal, Arjun (IND)

Born Asansol, India, 20 March 1973
Turned professional 1995

The first Indian golfer to win on the PGA Tour. In 2010 he triumphed at the Wyndham Championship and in the process became the first Monday qualifier for 24 years to win. When he won the 2002 Caltex Malaysian Open he became only the second Indian to earn a European To The first was Jeev Milkha Singh. He learned the game at Royal Calcutta.

Azinger, Paul (USA)

Born Holyoke, Massachusetts, 6 January 1960
Turned professional 1981

Winner of the 1993 USPGA Championship at the Inverness CC by beating Greg Norman at the second le of a play-off. He had finished joint runner-up with Rodger Davis to Nick Faldo in the 1987 Open at Muirfield. In 1994 he was diagnosed with lymphoma in his right shoulder blade but happily made a good recovery. He played in four Ryder Cup matches between 1989 and 2001 when he holed a bunker shot at the last to halve with Niclas Fasth. He successfully captained the US Ryder Cup side at Valhalla in 2008.

Baddeley, Aaron (AUS)

Born New Hampshire, USA, 17 March 1981
Turned professional 2000

Became the first amateur to win the Australian Open since Bruce Devlin in 1969 and the youngest when he took the title at Royal Sydney in 2000. Then, having turned professional he successfully defended it at Kingston Heath. He had shown considerable promise when at age 15, he qualified for the Victorian Open. Represented Australia in the Eisenhower Trophy and holds both Australian and American passports. He led going into the last round at the US Open at Oakmont in 2007 but finished joint 13th. Now plays on the PGA Tour but returned to Australia to beat Swede Daniel Chopra in a play-off for the 2007 MasterCard Australian Masters at Huntingdale.

Baker, Peter (ENG)

Born Shifnal, Shropshire, 7 October 1967
Turned professional 1986

Rookie of the year in 1987, Peter was hailed as the best young newcomer by Nick Faldo when he beat Faldo in a play-off for the Benson and Hedges International in 1988. Several times a winner since then he played in the 1993 Ryder Cup scoring three points out of four and in the singles beat former US

Open champion Corey Pavin. He was a vice-captain to Ian Woosnam at the 2006 match.

Baker-Finch, Ian (AUS)

Born Namour, Queensland, 24 October 1960
Turned professional 1979

Impressive winner of The Open Championship in 1991 at Royal Birkdale he lost his game completely when teeing up in Tour events and was forced, after an agonising spell, to retire prematurely. He commentated originally for Channel Seven in Australia then for ABC and now for CBS in America.

Barnes, Brian (SCO)

Born Addington, Surrey, 3 June 1945
Turned professional 1964

Extrovert Scottish professional whose father-in-law was the late former Open champion Max Faulkner. He was a ten times winner on the European Tour between 1972 and 1981 and was twice British Seniors champion successfully defending the title in 1996. He played in six Ryder Cup matches most notably at Laurel Valley in 1975 when, having beaten Jack Nicklaus in the morning, he beat him again in the afternoon. Although he retired early because of ill-health caused by rheumatoid arthritis he has started to play and fish again after his rheumatic problem was re-diagnosed as caused by eating meat. He often commentates for Sky Television.

Beem, Rich (USA)

Born Phoenix Arizona, 24 August 1974
Turned professional 1994

Playing in only his fourth major championship he hit the headlines in 2002 when he held off the spirited challenge of Tiger Woods to win the USPGA Championship at Hazeltine preventing Woods from winning three majors in one year for a second time. Rich, a winner of two previous Tour titles, admitted he was "flabbergasted to have won" having arrived with no expectations. On the final day at Hazeltine, Beem hit a fairway wood to to seven feet for an eagle at the at the 587 yards 11th and a holed a 40 foot putt for a birdie at the 16th to hold off Woods who finished with four birdies in a row. Just a year after turning professional Beem had given up the game to sell car stereos and mobile phones. After becoming an assistant club professional he returned once again to tournament play in 1999. In 2012 he took up the last year of an exemption on the European Tour where he competed regularly.

Bjørn, Thomas (DEN)

Born Silkeborg, 18 February 1971
Turned professional 1993

A former Danish Amateur champion in 1990 and 1991, he became the first Dane to play in the Ryder Cup when he made the team in 1997. Four down after four holes against Justin Leonard in the last day singles at Valderrama he fought back to halve the match and gain a valuable half-point in the European victory. He missed out because of injury on the 1999 match but was back in the team in 2002 and 2004 and was a vice-captain at Celtic Manor in 2010. He has come close four times to winning major titles. He was third to runaway winner Tiger Woods at Pebble Beach in the 2000 US Open and second to him at St Andrews in The Open a few weeks later. He looked set to win the 2003 Open at Royal St George's when three clear with four to play but dropped a shot at the 15th. and 17th and two shots after taking three to recover from a bunker at the short 16th. losing out eventually to Ben Curtis. In 2005 at Baltusrol he equalled the low round in a major with a 63 at the US PGA Championship but finished third to Phil Mickelson. In 2007 he became chairman of the European Tour Players' committee and in 2011 rediscovered his best form to win on the European Tour in Qatar, at Gleneagles and in Switzerland.

Bonallack KT, OBE, Sir Michael (ENG)

Born Chigwell, Essex, 31 December 1934

One of only four golfing knights (the others are the late Sir Henry Cotton, Sir Bob Charles and Sir Nick Faldo) he won the Amateur Championship five times between 1961 and 1970 and was five times English champion between 1962 and 1968. He also won the English stroke play Championship (the Brabazon Trophy) four times and was twice leading amateur in The Open in 1968 and 1971. In his hugely impressive career he played in nine Walker Cup matches captaining the side on two occasions. He participated in five Eisenhower Trophy matches and five Commonwealth team competitions. He scored his first national title win in the 1952 British Boys' Championship and took his Essex County title 11 times between 1954 and 1972. After serving as secretary of The R&A from 1983 to 1999 he was elected captain for 1999/2000. Twice winner of the Association of Golf Writers' award in 1968 and 1999, he also received the Bobby Jones award for sportsmanship in 1972, the Donald Ross and Gerald Micklem awards in 1991 and the Ambassador of Golf award in 1995. In 2000 he was inducted into the World Hall Golf of Fame. A former chairman of The R&A selection committee, he served as chairman of the PGA from 1976 to 1981 and is now a non-executive director of the PGA European Tour. He served for a time as chairman of the Golf Foundation and was president of the English Golf Union in 1982. His wife is the former English champion Angela Ward.

Bradley, Keegan (USA)

Born Woodstock, Vermont, 1986
Turned professional 2008

Winner of the US PGA Championship in 2011 after savouring a breakthrough success in the Byron Nelson, Bradley enjoyed a notable rookie season on the PGA Tour, earning $3.8 million in his first year among the elite. A graduate from the Nationwide Tour, he was the first golfer since Shaun Micheel in 2003 to win the PGA in his first appearance as well as the first player since Ben Curtis to win any major at the first attempt. In 2012 he won the Bridgestone

Invitational, a World Golf Championship event, and made an impressive début for the USA in the Ryder Cup, winning three matches in the company of Phil Mickelson. He hails from a golfing family and is the nephew of former LPGA player Pat Bradley.

Brooks, Mark (USA)

Born Fort Worth, Texas, 25 March 1961
Turned professional 1983

Winner of the USPGA Championship title in 1996 after a play-off with Kenny Perry at Valhalla. On that occasion he birdied the 72nd hole and the first extra hole to win but lost b two shots to South African Retief Goosen in the 18-hole play-off for the 2000 US Open at Southern Hills in Tulsa.

Brown, Ken (SCO)

Born Harpenden, Hertfordshire, 9 January 1957
Turned professional 1974

Renowned as a great short game exponent, especially with his hickory-shafted putter, he won four times in Europe between 1978 and 85, and took the Southern Open on the US tour in 1987. He played in five Ryder Cups and was on the winning side in 1985 and 1987. After retiring from professional tournament play he became an accomplished and highly respected television commentator working closely for the BBC (with Peter Alliss) and for The Golf Channel.

Cabrera, Angel (ARG)

Born Córdoba, Argentina, September 12, 1969
Turned professional 1989

Big hitting Argentinian winner of two major titles who learned much from former Open champion Roberto de Vicenzo. He won his first major when he held off a strong challenge from Jim Furyk and Tiger Woods to win the 2007 US Open and two years later won The Masters in a play-off at Augusta with Chad Campbell and Kenny Perry.

Cabrera Bello, Rafael (ESP)

Born Las Palmas, Gran Canaria, Spain, May 25, 1984
Turned professional 2005

Young Spanish golfer who won his first event on the European Tour in 2009 by firing a closing record 12-under-par 60 to win the Austrian Open at the Fontana Club in Vienna. Cabrera Bello, who started the final day eight off the lead, missed his eagle putt on the last for what would have been an historic 59. He was the 14th first-time winner of the season and the 13th person to shoot a 60 on the European Tour. His sister is a professional on the Ladies European Tour.

Calcavecchia, Mark (USA)

Born Laurel, Nebraska, 12 June 1960
Turned professional 1981

Winner of the 1989 Open Championship at Royal Troon after the first four-hole play-off against Australians Greg Norman and Wayne Grady. He was runner-up in the 1987 Masters at Augusta to Sandy Lyle and came second to Jodie Mudd in the 1990 Players' Championship. He played in the 1987, 1989, 1991 and 2002 Ryder Cup sides.

Campbell, Bill (USA)

Born West Virginia, 5 May 1923

One of America's most distinguished amateur players and administrators. He won the US Amateur Championship in 1964 ten years after finishing runner-up in the Amateur Championship at Muirfield to Australian Doug Bachli. One of a select group who have been both President of the United States Golf Association (in 1983) and captain of the Royal and Ancient Golf Club of St Andrews (in 1987/88). He played in eight Walker Cup matches between 1951 and 1975 and was captain in 1955.

Canizares, Alejandro (ESP)

Born Manilva, Malaga, 9 January 1983
Turned professional 2006

A four-time All-American golfer when studying at Arizona State University, he is the son of José Maria Canizares. When he turned professional in July 2006 he won his third event – the Imperial Collection Russian Open in Moscow.

Canizares, José Maria (ESP)

Born Madrid, 18 February 1947
Turned professional 1967

A popular seven-time winner on the European Tour between 1972 and 1992 the popular Spaniard retired after playing on the European Senior and US Champions Tours for a number of years. A former caddie, he played in four Ryder Cup matches in the 1980's winning five and halving two of his 11 games.

Cantlay, Patrick (USA)

Born Long Beach, California, March 17, 1992
Turned professional 2012

Winner of the Mark H McCormack medal for the world's top ranked amateur male golfer at the end of 2011. His first appearance at the US Open in 2011 was auspicious since he finished 21st and during one round at Congressional covered the back nine in just 30 blows. He also signed for 60 in the Travelers Championship on the US PGA Tour, eventually finishing in 24th place. All told, he registered four top 25s in the four professional events he entered. He joined the paid ranks in the summer of 2012, missing out on an exempt amateur spot at The Open to play events on both the PGA and web.com Tours. His best finish was runner-up at the Chiquita Classic.

Casey, Paul (ENG)

Born Cheltenham, 21 July 1977
Turned professional 2001

After successfully defending the English Amateur Championship in 2000, he attended Arizona State University where he was a three time All-American and broke records set by Phil Mickelson and Tiger Woods. In the 1999 Walker Cup match, which Great Britain and Ireland claimed at Nairn, he won all of his

Sir Bob Charles (NZL)

Born Auckland, 14 March 1936 *Turned professional 1960*

The first left-handed golfer to win a major championship, Sir Bob became the only New Zealander so far to lift the Claret Jug in 1963 when, three years after turning professional, he defeated Phil Rodgers in a 36-hole play-off for the title at Royal Lytham. He carded 140 to the American's 148. Until the emergence of Mike Weir and Phil Mickelson, Charles was the game's pre-eminent left-hander – an ironic distinction since he does pretty much everything else right-handed apart from games which require the use of both hands.

While 40 years would elapse before another lefty won a major, Charles himself was a runner-up in The Open to Gary Player in 1968 at Carnoustie and to Tony Jacklin in 1969 at Lytham as well as to Julius Boros, the oldest major winner, at the PGA Championship in 1968 at Pecan Valley. He was also a contender at the US Open in 1964 and 1970 when he finished third both times. One of the reasons for his success was that he putted beautifully. When Charles won The Open, he averaged 30 putts per round over the course of 72 holes and just 26 putts during the first round of the play-off.

Blessed with a sure touch from long range on the greens, he was also nerveless from close range. He rarely missed from inside five feet and also holed the majority of ten footers. During the 1972 season, the former bank worker completed 11 successive rounds without a three-putt. That same season he received the OBE from Her Majesty the Queen before being awarded the CBE in 1992. He was knighted in 1999 for his services to golf.

The winner of more than 60 events around the world, Charles enjoyed a new lease of life after turning 50. He won 23 tournaments on the Champions Tour and posted the low scoring average three times in 1988, 1989 and 1993. He was the first left-hander to be inducted into the Hall of Fame and, at 71, he became the oldest player to make the cut on any of the world's Tours when he shot a second round 68 in the Michael Hill New Zealand Open in 2007.

four games. After turning professional he earned his European Tour card after just five events and became a winner in only his 11th event when taking the Scottish PGA title at Gleneagles. He won the BMW PGA Championship in 2009, rising to No 3 in the world, but struggled with injury over the next three years and slipped outside the top 100.

Casper, Billy (USA)

Born San Diego, California, 24 June 1931
Turned professional 1954

A three-time major title winner he took the US Open in 1959 and 1966 and the US Masters in 1970. In 1966 he came back from seven strokes behind Arnold Palmer with nine to play to force a play-off which he then won. Between 1956 and 1975 he picked up 51 first prize cheques on the US Tour. His European victories were the 1974 Trophée Lancôme and Lancia D'Oro and the 1975 Italian Open. As a senior golfer he won nine times between 1982 and 1989 including the US Senior Open in 1983. Played in eight Ryder Cups and captained the American side in 1979 at The Greenbrier. He and wife Shirley have 11 children several of them adopted. He was named Father of the Year in 1966. Started playing golf aged 5 and rates Ben Hogan, Byron Nelson and Sam Snead as his heroes. Five times Vardon Trophy winner (for low season stroke-average) and twice top money earner he was USPGA Player of the Year in 1966 and 1970. He was inducted into the World Golf Hall of Fame in 1978 and the USPGA Hall of Fame in 1982. Encouraged by his family to play in The Masters for one last time in 2005 he shot 106 but was disqualified for not handing in his card.

Chapman, Roger (ENG)

Born Nakuru, Kenya, 1 May 1959
Turned professional 1981

He became the first English golfer to win the US Senior PGA Championship in August of 2012 at Harbor Shores in Michigan. Remarkably, on a visit to Michigan the month before, he also won the US Senior Open at Indianwood. He is only the fourth golfer after Gary Player, Jack Nicklaus and Hale Irwin to win both these senior majors in the same season. Chapman's astonishing success as a senior came after playing on the European Tour for 18 years without a victory. He lost his card and returned to the qualifying school in 1999. Regaining his playing privileges with a 12th place finish in the six round competition, he made his breakthrough win in his 472nd tournament by beating Padraig Harrington at the second hole of a play-off in the Brazil Rio de Janeiro Five Hundred Years Open. A former English Amateur Champion in 1981 he played in the Walker Cup the same year beating Hal Sutton twice in a day at Cypress Point. In 2010 he earned his card to play the Champions Tour in America where his career would enjoy an Indian summer.

Choi, K-J (KOR)

Born Wando, South Korea, 19 May 1970
Turned professional 1994

When his high school teacher suggested he take up golf, he studied all Jack Nicklaus' videos. Son of a rice farmer he was the first Korean to earn a PGA Tour card and in 2003 became the first Korean to win on the European Tour when he was successful in the

Clarke, Darren OBE (NIR)

Born Dungannon, Northern Ireland, 14 August 1968 Turned professional 1990

Darren became the fourth golfer from Northern Ireland to win a major when he beat Dustin Johnson and Phil Mickelson in the 2011 Open at Royal St George's. The rough weather did not phase Clarke who learned his golf at Royal Portrush. His victory came weeks after another Ulsterman, Rory McIlroy, had been successful at the US Open and a year after Northern Ireland's Graeme McDowell had won the American title at Pebble Beach. The other Ulster winner of a major was Fred Daly who won The Open in 1947. Darren became the first European Tour player to shoot 60 twice when he returned a record equalling low score at the European Open at the K Club in 1999. Seven years earlier he had shot a nine under par 60 at Mont Angel in the Monte Carlo Open. His 60 in Dublin was 12 under. Tied second in the 1997 Open behind Justin Leonard at Royal Troon he was third behind David Duval at the 2001 Open at Royal Lytham and St Annes before winning the title at Sandwich in 2011. Cigar smoking Clarke became the first European to win a World Golf Championship event when he beat Tiger Woods 4 and 3 in the final of the 2000 Accenture Match Play Championship picking up a $1 million first prize.

He took a second World Championship event in 2003 when he was an impressive winner of the NEC Invitational at Firestone. He played in the 1997, 1999, 2002 and 2004 Ryder Cup matches and again in 2006, bravely competing just a few months after his wife Heather lost her battle with cancer. In that match he won twice with good friend Lee Westwood and gained a single point against Zach Johnson. In 2010 he was a vice captain at Celtic Manor but it was in 2011 that he scored his greatest success with victory at Royal St George's. He received the OBE in the 2011 Queen's New Year Honours list.

Linde German Masters. Better known as KJ he finished fifth behind Tiger Woods on the 2007 American money list having earned over $4.5 million but failed to become the first Korean to win a major when YE Yang beat Woods in the 2009 US PGA Championship at Hazeltine.

Cink, Stewart (USA)

Born Huntsville, Alabama, 21 May 1973
Turned professional 1995

In a dramatic play-off at Turnberry in 2009 he won his first major by beating Tom Watson by six shots in their four hole play-off after both had tied at the end of 72-holes. This win by the former PGA Tour Rookie of the Year made up for the two-foot putt he missed which would have earned him a play-off for the 2002 US Open won by Retief Goosen. He has played in every Ryder Cup since 2002. In the 2006 Cup match at the K Club, he beat Sergio García in the singles to prevent the Spaniard winning five points out of five.

Clark, Clive (ENG)

Born Winchester, 27 June 1945
Turned professional 1965

In the 1965 Walker Cup at Five Farms East in Maryland, he holed a 35-foot putt to earn a half point against Mark Hopkins and ensure a first ever drawn match against the Americans on their home soil. After turning professional he played in the 1973 Ryder Cup. Following a career as commentator with the BBC he continued his golf course architecture work in America, and has received awards for his innovative designs.

Clark, Howard (ENG)

Born Leeds, 26 August 1954
Turned professional 1973

A scratch player by the age of 16, he turned professional after playing in the 1973 Walker Cup. An eleven-time winner on the European tour he played in six Ryder Cups and was in the winning team three times – in 1985 at The Belfry, 1987 at Muirfield Village, when the Europeans won for the first time on American soil, and in 1995 when he gained a vital point helped by a hole in one in the last day singles against Peter Jacobsen. In the 1985 World Cup played at La Quinta in Palm Springs he was the individual champion. He played 494 tournaments before giving up full-time competition to concentrate on his job as a highly respected golf analyst for Sky television.

Coles MBE, Neil (ENG)

Born 26 September 1934 Turned professional 1950

An Honorary Life Member of the European Tour he won golf tournaments in six decades. In 2003 he did not win but in the Travis Perkins event over Wentworth's Edinburgh Course (which he helped design) he shot a 64 – outstanding golf by a man who had been a pro at that time for 54 years. He scored his first victory at the Gor-Ray tournament in 1956 when 22 and won the Lawrence Batley Seniors Open at Huddersfield in 2002 when 67 years and 276 days. From 1973 to 1979 he played in 56 events on the main European Tour without missing a half-way cut and became the then oldest winner when he won the Sanyo Open in Barcelona in 1982 at the age of 48 years and 14 days (Des Smyth has since become an even older winner). A member of eight Ryder Cup teams, he has represented his country 19 times since turning professional at the age of 16 with a handicap of 14. He has been chairman of the PGA European Tour's Board of Directors since its inception in 1971 and in 2000 was inducted into the World Golf Hall of Fame. Internationally respected he might well have won more in America but for an aversion to flying caused by a bad experience on an internal flight from Edinburgh to London.

Coltart, Andrew (SCO)

Born Dumfries, 12 May 1970
Turned professional 1991

Twice Australian PGA champion in 1994 and 1997 he was the Australasian circuit's top money earner for the 1997/98 season. He made his Ryder Cup début at Brookline in 1999 as a captain's pick and, having not been used in the foursomes and fourballs he lost in the singles on the final day to Tiger Woods. A former Walker Cup and Eisenhower Trophy player he was a member of the only Scottish team to win the Alfred Dunhill Cup at St Andrews in 1995. His sister Laurae is married to fellow professional Lee Westwood.

Couples, Fred (USA)

Born Seattle, Washington, 3 October 1959
Turned professional 1980

Troubled continually with a back problem he has managed to win only one major – the 1992 US Masters but remains one of the most popular of all American players. He has always been willing to travel and his overseas victories include two Johnnie Walker World Championships, the Johnnie Walker Classic, the Dubai Desert Classic and the Tournoi Perrier de Paris. On the US Tour he won 14 times between 1983 and 1998 and later won the Shell Houston Open. He played in five Ryder Cup matches and has teed up four times for the US in the Presidents Cup in which he acted as captain in 2009 and again in 2011. He will lead the side again in 2011. Couples kept up his winning ways on the Champions Tour in 2010 with a victory in only his second senior start at the Ace Group Classic. He also won the Toshiba Classic and the Cap Cana Championship to become the first 50-year-old to win three of the first four senior events in which he played. In 2011 he captained the US side in the President's Cup at Royal Melbourne.

Crenshaw, Ben (USA)

Born Austin, Texas, 11 January 1952
Turned professional 1973

One of golf's great putters who followed up his victory in the 1984 Masters with an emotional repeat success in 1995 just a short time after the death of his long-time coach and mentor Harvey Pennick. He played in four Ryder Cup matches between 1981 and 1995 before captaining the side in 1999 when the Americans came from four points back to win with a scintillating last day singles performance. Winner of the Byron Nelson award in 1976 he was also named Bobby Jones award winner in 1991. Now combines playing with an equally successful career as a golf course designer and is an acknowledged authority on every aspect of the history of the game. In 2002 he won the Payne Stewart Award which recognises a player's respect for and upholding of the traditions of the game.

Curtis, Ben (USA)

Born Columbus, Ohio, 26 May 1977
Turned professional 2000

Shock 750–1 outsider who played superbly at Royal St George's to get his name engraved with all the other golfing greats on the famous Claret Jug. His victory in the 2003 Open, while well deserved, was one of golf's biggest shocks in years. It was his first major appearance. He only qualified for the Championship with a 14th place finish in the Western Open in Chicago – a designated qualifying event. He had never played in Britain nor had he any experience of links golf but he outplayed Tiger Woods, Thomas Bjørn, David Love III and Vijay Singh to take the title with a score of 283. He learned the game in Ohio at the golf course his grandfather built at Ostrander. In 2008 he chased Padraig Harrington home to finish second behind the Irishman in the USPGA Championship at Oakland Hill. That year he made his début in captain Paul Azinger's Ryder Cup side which won the trophy back at Valhalla.

Daly, John (USA)

Born Sacramento, California, 28 April 1966
Turned professional 1987

Winner of two majors – the 1991 USPGA Championship and the 1995 Open Championship at St Andrews after a play-off with Costantino Rocca, his career has not been without its ups and downs. He admits he has battled alcoholism and, on occasions, has been his own worst enemy when having run-ins with officialdom but he remains popular because of his long hitting. His average drive is over 300 yards. When he won the USPGA Championship at Crooked Stick he got in as ninth alternate, drove through the night to tee it up without a practice round and shot 69, 67, 69, 71 to beat Bruce Lietzke by three. Given invaluable help by Fuzzy Zoeller he writes his own songs and is a mean performer on the guitar. Despite winning two majors he has never played in the Ryder Cup and now no longer holds a PGA Tour card. He had a stomach band inserted in 2009 in a successful bid to lose weight.

Darcy, Eamonn (IRL)

Born Dalgeny, 7 August 1952
Turned professional 1969

One of Ireland's best known players who played more than 600 tournaments on the European Tour despite suffering for many years with back trouble. First played when he was 10 years old and is renowned for his very distinctive swing incorporating a flying right elbow. He played in four Ryder Cups including the memorable one at Muirfield Village in 1987 when Europe won for the first time in America. He scored a vital point in the last day singles holing a tricky left to right downhill seven footer for a valuable point against Ben Crenshaw. Now plays on the European Senior Tour.

Davis, Rodger (AUS)

Born Sydney, 18 May 1951 Turned professional 1974

Experienced Australian who came joint second with Paul Azinger in the 1987 Open Championship behind Nick Faldo at Muirfield. A regular on the European Tour and for a time on the US Champions Tour he has won 27 titles – 19 of them on the Australasian circuit where, in 1988, he picked up an Aus $1 million first prize in the bicentennial event at Royal Melbourne. Usually played in trademark 'plus twos' but has now retired from all but Australian golf.

Day, Jason (AUS)

Born Beaudesert, Queensland, 1987
Turned professional 2006

Already the winner of more than $9million in prize money after just four seasons on the PGA Tour, Day was runner-up in both the Masters and the US Open in 2011. These excellent performances in the majors followed on from a top ten finish at the US PGA in 2010. He also won the Byron Nelson in 2010. A successful amateur when he was growing up in Queensland, he won the 2006 Australian Amateur Stroke-Play Championship as well as the Australian Junior Championship and the World Junior Championship.

De Vicenzo, Roberto (ARG)

Born Buenos Aires, 14 April 1923
Turned professional 1938

Although he won The Open in 1967 at Royal Liverpool the impressive South American gentleman of the game is perhaps best known for the Major title he might have won. In 1968 he finished tied with Bob Goalby at Augusta or he thought he had. He had finished birdie, bogey to do so but sadly signed for the par 4 that had been inadvertently and carelessly put down for the 17th by Tommy Aaron who was marking his card. Although everyone watching on television and at the course saw the Argentinian make 3 the fact that he signed for 4 was indisputable and he had to accept that there would be no play-off. It remains one of the saddest incidents in golf with the emotion heightened by the fact that that Sunday was de Vicenzo's 45th birthday. The gracious manner in which he accepted the disappointment was remarkable. What a contrast to the scenes at Hoylake nine months earlier when, after years of trying, he finally won The Open beating Jack Nicklaus and Clive Clark in the process thanks to a pressure-packed brilliant last round 70. It was well deserved. He had been runner-up in 1950 and had finished third six times. The father of South American golf he was a magnificent driver and won over 200 titles in his extraordinary career including nine Argentinian Opens between 1944 and 1974 plus the 1957 Jamaican, 1950 Belgian, 1950 Dutch, 1950, 1960 and 1964 French, 1964 German Open and 1966 Spanish Open titles. He played 15 times for Argentina in the World Cup and four times for Mexico. Inducted into the World Golf Hall of Fame in 1989 he is an honorary member of the Royal and Ancient Golf Club of St Andrews. Although he was unable to return to Britain for the 2006 Open Championship at Hoylake were he won in 1967 he made it to the 150th. Anniversary celebrations of The Open at St Andrews in 2010. He was pleased when fellow Argentinian Angel Cabrera won the 2007 US Open but even more elated when Cabrera, inspired by him, became the first Argentinian winner of a Masters Green Jacket.

Dickson, Bob (USA)

Born McAlester, Oklahoma, 25 January 1944
Turned professional 1968

Best remembered for being one of only four players to complete a Transatlantic amateur double. In 1967 he won the US Amateur Championship at Broadmoor with a total of 285 (the Championship was played over 72 holes from 1965 to 1972) and the British Amateur title with a 2 and 1 win over fellow American Ron Cerrudo at Formby.

Donald, Luke (ENG)

Born Hemel Hempstead, Herts., 7 December 1977
Turned professional 2001

The game's outstanding golfer in 2011, Donald made history when he became the first ever player to top the money list on both the European and US PGA Tours. He was also named the PGA Tour's player of the year and enjoyed the same honour in Europe, where he was also celebrated by the Association of Golf Writers. Donald won four times in 2011, twice in America where he claimed the Accenture Match Play and the Childrens Miracle Network Hospital Classic; and twice in Europe at the BMW PGA and the Scottish Open. All told, he racked up 20 top ten finishes and missed only two cuts. His short game was second to none and he was the best putter on both sides of the Atlantic. A formidable amateur as well as a successful professional, he was a member of the winning Great Britain and Ireland team against the Americans in the 1999 Walker Cup at Nairnand again in 2001 before joining the paid ranks. In 1999 while attending the North-Western University in Chicago he won the NCAA Championship and was named NCAA Player of the Year. He was twice Big Ten Individual Championship winner and is a former Jack Nicklaus Trophy winner. Prior to 2011, he won three times on the European Tour in Sweden, Switzerland and Spain but went on to play more of his golf in America where he won the rain-shortened Southern Farms Bureau event in 2002 and the Honda tournament in 2006. He was one of five rookies in the winning 2004 European Ryder Cup team in Detroit having been a captain's pick and played again in 2006 and 2010 missing the chance of a place in the 2008 team because of a wrist injury that required surgery. He played an important part in the 2010 European Ryder Cup victory at Celtic Manor and in 2010 finished 15th in the Race to Dubai and 7th on the PGA Tour money list before moving from 28th to 9th in the world rankings. Made history with his consistency in 2011 when he finished the year as World No 1. In 2012 he lost the No 1 spot to Rory

Ernie Els (RSA)

Born Johannesburg, 17 October 1969 Turned professional 1989

Blessed with a powerful, smooth swing which laid the foundation for more than 65 tournament wins around the world, the big South African has lifted four major championships – two US Opens and The Open twice at Muirfield and Royal Lytham – while building a reputation as a formidable matchplay golfer, winning the World Matchplay on a record seven occasions. Although his nickname "the Big Easy" reflected an engaging personality as well as that rhythmic golf swing, it didn't tell the whole story. From his first victory at the Amatola Sun Classic in 1991 to The Open in 2012, Els was able to call upon the ruthless instincts of a serial winner.

As a youngster, he was a budding athlete and won a regional tennis tournament in South Africa at the age of 13. At 14, however, his career path was set after he won the world junior golf championship in California. After joining the professional ranks and following up wins on the Sunshine Tour with victories around the world, he first made his mark in the majors at the 1994 US Open. He came out on top at Oakmont after winning a play-off against Loren Roberts and Colin Montgomerie. The Scot was to regard Els as a nemesis in the majors since he also lost out to the South African in the 1997 US Open at Congressional. Long tipped by his compatriot, Gary Player, to lift the Claret Jug, Els realised his dream of glory in 2002 at The Open by defeating Thomas Levet in a sudden-death play-off. His triumph came at the first extra hole after a four hole play-off had eliminated the Australians Stuart Appleby and Steve Elkington. All four golfers had finished on the six-under-par total of 268. Els executed a brilliant recovery shot from an awkward lie in a greenside trap at the 18th to make the four foot putt for par which earned him his third major title.

His career was disrupted by an anterior cruciate ligament knee injury sustained during a sailing holiday with his family. It took time for Els to recover, though he was back in full cry at Doral and Bay Hill in 2010 when he won the World Golf Championship and the Arnold Palmer Invitational in the space of a couple of weeks. In 2012 he secured his first major since 2002 when he took advantage of Adam Scott's collapse over the closing four holes to win The Open for the second time. He's a Lytham specialist, having finished runner-up there in 1996 and third in 2001.His birdie on the 72nd hole marked only the second time in 20 years the champion had finished with a score below par.

In recent seasons, Els has also broadened his horizons beyond the golf course. He became involved in charity work through the Els for Autism Foundation which helps young people such as his son, Ben, who is autistic. He's active in course design and was involved in the re-design of Wentworth. He's also been in the wine business for ten years..

McIlroy but became only the third golfer to successfully defend the BMW PGA, was part of Europe's winning Ryder Cup team in Chicago and received the MBE for his services to golf.

Drew, Norman (NIR)

Born Belfast, 25 May 1932
Turned professional 1958

Twice Irish Open Amateur champion in 1952 and 1953 he played in the 1953 Walker Cup and six years later represented Great Britain and Ireland in the Ryder Cup.

Duval, David (USA)

Born Jacksonville, Florida, 19 November 1971
Turned professional 1993

A regular winner on the US Tour who wears dark glasses because of an eye stigmatism which is sensitive to light, he won his first major at Royal Lytham and St Annes in 2001 when he became only the second American professional to win The Open over that course. In 1998 and 2001 he was runner-up in The Masters and was third at Augusta in 2003. Although illness and injury affected his career he did finish second to Lucas Glover in the US Open at Bethpage Park black but failed to keep his US Tour card that year. He won the US Tour Championship in 1997 and the Players' Championship in 1999. As an amateur he played in the 1991 Walker Cup and was a member of the winning Ryder Cup side on his début in 1999 but on a losing side in 2002.

Dyson, Simon (ENG)

Born York, 21 December 1977
Turned professional 1999

A three-time winner on the Asian Tour where he was top earner in 2000, he scored his first European Tour success in the joint Asian–European venture in Indonesia in 2006 and later in the season he beat Australian Richard Green in a play-off for the KLM Open at Zandvoort. He won that title again in 2009 and later in that season was successful in the Dunhill Links Championship played over the Old course, St Andrews, Carnoustie and Kingsbarns. In 2007 he shot 64 in the final round of the USPGA Championship to finish in joint sixth place – his best performance in a major. In 2011 he won the KLM Open for the second time and was also successful in the Irish Open. He was a member of the GB&I side in the Vivendi Seve Trophy.

Edfors, Johan (SWE)

Born Varberg, Sweden, 10 October 1975
Turned professional 1997

The number one player on the 2003 Challenge Tour he had a brilliant year on the main Tour in 2006, winning three events – the TCL Classic in China, the Quinn Direct British Masters and the Barclays Scottish Open at Loch Lomond. Since then he has won on the Asian Tour but has not had any more success on the European Tour.

Edwards, Nigel (WAL)

Born Caerphilly, 9 August 1968

Top scoring member of the winning Walker Cup sides in 2001 and again in 2003 at Ganton, he captained the side that won the cup at Royal Aberdeen in 2011. In 2003 he had holed from off the green with the putter at the 17th to ensure a half point with Lee Williams and overall victory for the team. He was again involved in a dramatic finish to the 2005 Walker Cup but one down with one to play and needing to win the last against Jeff Overton his putt narrowly missed. Welshman Edwards also played in the match in 2007, inspired his side to a surprise victory over a talented US side in 2011 reminding his team that although on paper the Americans were the stronger side the game was not played on paper.

Elkington, Steve (AUS)

Born Inverell, 8 December 1962
Turned professional 1985

A former Australian and New Zealand champion he was a regular winner on the PGA Tour despite an allergy to grass. Helped by a closing string of birdies at the Riviera CC in Los Angeles in 1995 he beat Colin Montgomerie in a play-off for the USPGA Championship. He has one of the finest swings in golf and is also an accomplished artist in his spare time. He played four times in the Presidents Cup. In 2002 after pre-qualifying for The Open at Dunbar he played off for the title at Muirfield with Thomas Levet, Stuart Appleby and eventual winner Ernie Els. He nearly won the USPGA Championship in 2005 finishing second with Thomas Bjørn behind Phil Mickelson at Baltusrol and was again in contention in the 2010 Championship at Whistling Straits.

Fasth, Niclas (SWE)

Born Gothenburg, Sweden, 29 April 1972
Turned professional 1989

The studious-looking Swede made the headlines in 2001 when finishing second to David Duval in The Open. He played in the 2002 Ryder Cup and in 2007 he came a creditable fourth in the US Open at Oakmont. In 2008 he split with his long-time coach Graham Crisp who was working with him revamping his swing. The changes took time to settle and he missed out on a Ryder Cup place that year.

Faxon, Brad (USA)

Born Oceanport, New Jersey, 1 August 1961
Turned professional 1983

A former Walker Cup player in 1983 match he has played in two Ryder Cup matches (1995 and 1997). A successful winner on the US Tour he also putted superbly to win the Australian Open at Metropolitan in 1993. In 2005 was named recipient of the Payne Stewart award for respecting and upholding the traditions of the game. He is a member of the PGA Tour Committee.

Feherty, David (NIR)

Born Bangor, Northern Ireland, 13 August 1958
Turned professional 1976

Quick-witted Ulsterman who gave up his competitive golfing career to become a successful commentator for CBS in America where his one-liners are legendary. He had five European title wins and three victories on the South African circuit before switching his golf clubs for a much more lucrative career behind the microphone.

Fernandez, Vicente (ARG)

Born Corrientes, 5 May 1946
Turned professional 1964

After playing on the European Tour where "Chino" won five times between 1975 and 1992 he joined the US Champions Tour competing with considerable success. Born with one leg shorter than the other he is remembered in Europe for the 87 foot putt he holed up three tiers on the final green at The Belfry in 1992 to win the Murphy's English Open.

Fernandez-Castano, Gonzalo (ESP)

Born Madrid, 13 October 1980
Turned professional 2004

Twice Spanish amateur champion he began playing golf as a five-year-old and turned professional in 2004 when he was playing off plus 4. He represented Spain in the 2002 Eisenhower Trophy and played for the Continent of Europe against Great Britain and Ireland in 2004. He played twice in the Palmer Cup leading the European students to success against the Americans at Ballybunion in 2004. He won for the first time when he took the 2005 KLM Dutch Open title at Hilversum and was named Sir Henry Cotton Rookie of the Year. Since then he's won five more events in Europe, including the BMW Italian Open in 2012 for the second time when he shot a closing round of 64. His form last year was consistent enough to move inside the world's top 40.

Finsterwald, Dow (USA)

Born Athens, Ohio, 6 September 1929
Turned professional 1951

Winner of the 1958 USPGA Championship he won 11 other competitions between 1955 and 1963. He played in four Ryder Cup matches in a row from 1957 and captained the side in 1977. He was USPGA Player of the Year in 1958.

Sir Nicholas A. Faldo (ENG)

Born Welwyn Garden City, 18 July 1957 Turned professional 1976

By a wide margin the most successful British golfer of the modern era – he spent 92 weeks in all as the world number one – his achievements were recognised in style when he became the first professional golfer since Sir Henry Cotton to receive a knighthood for his services to the game. Always single minded in his approach to winning tournaments, few would dispute Peter McEvoy's observation that Faldo sets the gold standard against which everyone else of recent vintage in English golf must be measured.

From the moment a careers officer at school warned him that only one in 10,000 made it as a professional – the Englishman insisted if that was the case then he would prove to be that solitary success – the golfer was as dedicated in his pursuit of glory as he was ambitious. At 14 he had never picked up a club, yet by 17 he was a top rank amateur. He won the British Youths and the English Amateur in 1975 before joining the paid ranks a year later. It was a measure of his rapid progress in the sport that by 20 he was playing in the Ryder Cup. He had only decided to take up the game after watching the Masters on his parents' new colour television when he followed the performance of Jack Nicklaus. "I was just absolutely mesmerised," he recalls.

He is Europe's most successful Major title winner having won three Open Championships in 1987 and 1992 at Muirfield and in 1990 at St Andrews along with three Masters titles in 1989, 1990 and 1996. Of contemporary players only Tiger Woods with 14 majors and Tom Watson with eight have won more majors. When he successfully defended the Masters in 1990 he became only the second golfer (after Nicklaus) to win in successive years. One of the most memorable moments of his career came when he staged a dramatic last day revival to win the 1996 Masters having started the last round six strokes behind Greg Norman.

Unkindly dubbed 'Nick Foldo' when he missed out on opportunities to win both The Open and The Masters in the early Eighties, Faldo nevertheless appreciated his swing was not good enough to win majors and completely revamped his action with the help of coach David Leadbetter. His revised swing and remarkable sense of poise under pressure duly helped him win more major titles than any other player between 1987 and 1996.

His 31 European Tour victories include a record three consecutive Irish Open victories. In 1992 he became the first player to win over £1 million in prize-money during a season. He also played with distinction in 11 Ryder Cup matches including the winning European teams in 1985, 1987, 1995 and 1997. He holds the record for most games played in the Cup, 46, and most points won, 25. In 1995 at Oak Hill he came from behind to score a vital last day point against Curtis Strange, the American who had beaten him in a play-off for the US Open title in 1988 at The Country Club in Boston. He also captained the Ryder Cup side at Valhalla in 2008 when Europe were disappointing and missed out on winning four in a row. His assistant, José Maria Olazábal, blamed Faldo's "poor communication" for the team's failure.

He became the first international player to be named USPGA Player of the Year in 1990 and led the official World Golf Rankings for 81 weeks in 1993–1994. After teaming up with Swedish caddie Fanny Sunesson for ten years, they split, only to be reunited as one of golf's most formidable partnerships in 2001 before parting company a second time.

His Faldo Junior Series, designed to encourage the best young players to improve, continues to expand. It organises more than 30 tournaments in 25 countries for boys and girls aged between 12 and 21. His company, Faldo Enterprises, runs a successful international golf course design business.

In 2006, he embarked on a TV commentating career with the Golf Channel and CBS. He signed an $8m eight-year contract with the American broadcaster and covers many PGA Tour events. He is an insightful analyst who sees his role as stimulating the interest of a broad audience. In 2009 he was knighted by Her Majesty the Queen for his services to golf.

Fisher, Oliver (ENG)

Born Chingford, Essex, 19 August 1988
Turned professional 2006

Became the youngest ever Walker Cup player when he made the 2005 Great Britain and Ireland side at the age of 17. In 2006 he played in the Eisenhower and Bonallack Trophy matches and when he turned professional he was playing off plus 4 He won the Czech Open in 2011 but only came up with three top 20 finishes in 2012.

Fisher, Ross (ENG)

Born Ascot, Berkshire, 22 November 1980
Turned professional 2004

Attached to the Wentworh Club, he has been playing since he was three. In 2007 he won his first European

Tour title at the KLM Open. Later in the season he won the European Open at the London Club leading from start to finish and ending up six clear of his nearest rival. He also won the Volvo Match Play Championship beating Anthony Kim at Finca Cortesin in Spain. In 2010, helped by victory in the 3-Irish Open, he made his début in the Ryder Cup at Celtic Manor.In 2012 he missed out on a fifth victory when he was runner-up at both the Nordea Masters and the Portugal Masters.

Floyd, Raymond (USA)

Born Fort Bragg, North Carolina, 4 September 1942
Turned professional 1961

A four time major winner whose failure to win an Open Championship title prevented his completing a Slam of Majors. He won the US Open in 1986, the Masters in 1976 when he matched the then 72-hole record set by Jack Nicklaus to win by eight strokes and took the USPGA title in 1969 and 1982. In addition to coming second and third in The Open he was also runner-up three times in the Masters and in the USPGA once. After scoring 22 victories on the main US Tour he has continued to win as a senior. Inducted into the World Golf Hall of Fame in 1989 he is an avid Chicago Cubs baseball fan. Played in eight Ryder Cup matches between 1969 and 1993 making history with his last appearance by being the oldest player to take part in the match. He was 49. He was non-playing captain in 1989 when the match was drawn at The Belfry and was an assistant to Paul Azinger at the 2008 match at Valhalla.

Ford, Doug (USA)

Born West Haven, Connecticut, 6 August 1922
Turned professional 1949

His 25 wins on the PGA Tour between 1955 and 1963 included the 1975 Masters. USPGA Player of the Year in 1955, he competed in four Ryder Cup matches in succession from 1955.

Frost, David (RSA)

Born Cape Town, 11 September 1959
Turned professional 1981

He has won as many titles overseas as on the US Tour and played regularly on the European Tour until 2009. The 1993 season was his best in America when he made over $1 million and finished fifth on the money list. He has established a vineyard in South Africa growing 100 acres of vines on the 300-acre estate and has very quickly earned a reputation for producing quality wines. He now plays on the Champions Tour in America and on Europe's Senior Tour.

Funk, Fred (USA)

Born Tacoma Park, Missouri, 14 June 1956
Turned professional 1981

One of five rookies in the 2004 US Ryder Cup side, he scored his sixth US Tour success a few weeks later when he won the Southern Farm Bureau Classic. In 2005 he won the Tournament Players' Championship at Sawgrass and now plays on the Champions Tour. In 2009 he and Mark McNulty lost a play-off to Loren Roberts in the Senior Open at Sunningdale and then won the US Senior Open the following week at Crooked Stick.

Furyk, Jim (USA)

Born West Chester, Pennsylvania, 12 May 1970
Turned professional 1992

Once considered one of the best players not to have won a major, Furyk put that right when he won the US Open at Olympia Fields, Chicago. He was one of four first-time major winners in 2003. He clearly enjoys playing in Las Vegas where he has won three Invitational events in 1995, 1999 and 1998. He has teed it up in five Presidents Cups and eight Ryder Cups beating Nick Faldo in the singles at Valderrama in 1997. He has one of the most easily recognisable if idiosyncratic swings in golf. His father Mike has been his only coach. In 2006 he came second to Tiger Woods in the US Tour money list earning $7,213,316 but won the Harry Vardon Trophy for the best average of 68.66 for golfers who played 60 rounds or more. In 2010 he won three times on the PGA Tour, won the Fedex Cup $10 million bonus and was named Player of the Year. He won over $3 million in 2012 without adding to his 16 PGA Tour wins. Furyk was a wild card pick for the USA at the Ryder Cup in Medinah where he bogeyed the last two holes of a lost singles tie against Sergio García.

Gallacher CBE, Bernard (SCO)

Born Bathgate, Scotland, 9 February 1949
Turned professional 1967

For many years he combined tournament golf with the club professional's post at Wentworth where he was honoured in 2000 by being appointed captain. He took up golf at the age of 11 and nine years later was European No 1. He has scored 30 victories world-wide. Gallacher was the youngest Ryder Cup player when he made his début in the 1969 match in which he beat Lee Trevino in the singles. He played in eight Cup matches and captained the side three times losing narrowly in 1991 at Kiawah Island and 1993 at The Belfry before leading the team to success at Oak Hill in 1995. A former member of the European Tour's Board of Directors, he was afforded honorary membership of the European Tour in 2003.

García, Sergio (ESP)

Born Castellon, 9 January 1980
Turned professional 1999

The Spaniard, who was runner-up to Tiger Woods in the 1999 US PGA Championship, lost his best chance of winning a first major when he missed a putt on the final green at Carnoustie in 2007 and was beaten by Ireland's Padraig Harrington in the subsequent four-hole play-off. He had led for most of the four days. He was again pipped by Harrington in the 2008 USPGA Championship at Oakland Hills. Having won the British Boys' Championship in 1997, he took the Spanish and British Amateur titles in 1998 and in both years was the European Amateur Masters champion. Son of a greenkeeper/professional who now plays on the European Senior Tour, Sergio waited until after the 1999 Master before joining the paid ranks at the Spanish Open. Although only just starting to collect Ryder Cup points he easily made the 1999 team and formed an invaluable partnership with Jesper Parnevik at Brookline scoring three and a half points out of four on the first two days. The 1999 Sir Henry Cotton Rookie of the Year in Europe he again formed a useful partnership this time with Lee Westwood in the 2002 Cup match. Together they won three points out of four. They teamed up again in the winning 2004 side at Oakland Hills. He himself was unbeaten, winning 4½ out of five points including victory over Phil Mickelson in the singles. In the 2006 Ryder Cup at the K Club he again played well with José María Olazábal in the fourballs and Luke Donald in the foursomes. He scored four out of five points, losing only his single to Stewart Cink. His form dipped in the 2008 match at Valhalla but that year he did became the first European-born player since 1937 to win the Vardon Trophy on the PGA Tour with a low score average of 69.12. He ended the year as No. 2 in the World Rankings. Loss of confidence saw him take a break from the game and miss out on the 2010 Ryder Cup. By the end of 2010 he had slipped to 78th in the world rankings but improved to 18th in 2011 when he returned to winning ways with victories in successive weeks at his own event – the Castello Masters – and the Andalucia Masters. Last season he won the Wyndham Championship, his first success in America for four years, and returned to Ryder Cup action for Europe at Medinah.

Garrido, Ignacio (ESP)

Born Madrid 2 February 1944
Turned professional 1961

Eldest son of Antonio Garrido who played in the 1979 Ryder Cup, Ignacio emulated his father when he made the team at the 1997 match at Valderrama having earlier that year won the Volvo German Open. A former English Amateur Stroke-play title-holder in 1992 his most impressive win on the European Tour was beating Trevor Immelman in a play-off for the 2003 Volvo PGA Championship at Wentworth. In the 80s used to caddie for his father who has since caddied for him on occasion.

Goosen, Retief (RSA)

Born Pietersburg, 3 February 1969
Turned professional 1990

Introduced to golf at the age of 11 the former South African amateur champion scored his first major professional success when leading from start to finish at the 2001 US Open at Tulsa and then beating Mark Brooks in the 18-hole play-off by two shots. Although he suffered health problems after being hit by lightning as a teenager he has enjoyed a friendly rivalry with fellow South African Ernie Els whom he beat in the 2005 South African Airways Open at Fancourt. In 2004 he again won the US Open, this time at Shinnecock Hills GC on Long Island producing, in the process, not only superb control through the green but inspirational form on the lightning fast putting surfaces to prevent Phil Mickelson winning what would have been his second major of the year. Goosen single-putted 11 of the first 17 holes of his final round of 71. In 2005 after finishing tied third at The Masters, he was leading going into the last round of the US Open at Pinehurst No 2 but shot a closing 81 to miss out on a successful defence of his title. He finished 11th behind Michael Campbell but was fifth at The Open and sixth at the USPGA that same year. When he played again in the Presidents Cup later in the year he beat Tiger Woods in the singles at Lake Mannassas. He continues to play well around the world.

Grace, Branden (RSA)

Born Pretoria, May 20, 1988
Turned professional 2007

The latest in a long line of outstanding South African golfers, Grace won four times on the European Tour in 2012, kicking off the season with victories on home turf at the Joburg Open and the Volvo Golf Champions before adding further triumphs at the Volvo China Open and the Alfred Dunhill Links in St Andrews. A graduate of the Ernie Els and Fancourt Foundation, he enjoyed a fine amateur career before making his mark in the paid ranks. During the Dunhill Links he matched the European Tour's low score with a new course record, 60, at Kingsbarns. He's the first ever player to win his first four events on the European Tour in the same season.

Grady, Wayne (AUS)

Born Brisbane, 26 July 1957
Turned professional 1973 and again in 1978

In 1990 he won the USPGA Championship at Shoal Creek by three shots from Fred Couples. A year earlier he had tied with Greg Norman and eventual winner Mark Calcavecchia for The Open Championship losing out in the first ever four-hole play-off for the title. He is a former chairman of the Australasian Tour and with a reduced schedule on the Champions Tour in America he manages to commentate occasionally for the BBC.

Graham, David (AUS)

Born Windsor, Tasmania, 23 May 1946
Turned professional 1962

Played superbly for a closing 67 round Merion to win the 1981 US Open Championship from George Burns and Bill Rogers. That day he hit every green in regulation. Two years earlier he had beaten Ben Crenshaw at the third extra hole at Oakland Hills to win the USPGA Championship. When he took up the game at age 14 he played with left-handed clubs before making the switch to a right-handed set. Awarded the Order of Australia for his services to golf he is a member of the Cup and Tee committee that sets up Augusta each year for the Masters. A regular winner around the world in the 70s and 80s he won eight times on the US Tour between 1972 and 1983 and has built up a considerable reputation as a course designer.

Green OBE, Charlie (SCO)

Born Dumbarton, 2 August 1932

One of Scotland's most successful amateur golfers who was leading amateur in the 1962 Open Championship. A prolific winner he took the Scottish Amateur title three times in 1970, 1982 and 1983. He played in five and was non-playing captain in two more Walker Cups and was awarded the Frank Moran Trophy for his services to Scottish sport in 1974.

Green, Hubert (USA)

Born Birmingham, Alabama, 18 December 1946
Turned professional 1970

In 1977 he beat Lou Graham at the 1977 US Open at Southern Hills despite being told with four holes to play that he had received a death threat. Three times a Ryder Cup player he also won the 1985 USPGA Championship. Best known for his unorthodox swing and distinctive crouching putting style. he has successfully beaten throat cancer – an illness that has prevented his competing on the US Champions Tour. He was inducted into the World Golf Hall of Fame in 2007.

Haas, Bill (USA)

Born Charlotte, North Carolina, 1982
Turned professional 2004

Winner of three events on the PGA Tour, including the Tour Championship by Coca-Cola in 2011, Haas' victory in Atlanta was sufficient not only to collect the first prize of $1.44 million but also the FedEx Cup jackpot of $10m. The son of Jay Haas, who won nine times on the PGA Tour, Bill received a captain's pick from Fred Couples to play in the Presidents Cup at Royal Melbourne.

Haas, Jay (USA)

Born St Louis, Missouri, 2 December 1953
Turned professional 1976

Winner of nine events on the USPGA Tour, he played in his third Ryder Cup as an invitee of the US captain Hal Sutton. He had played in 1983 and 1995. He has played in three Presidents Cups and was a Walker Cup player in 1975. His uncle is former Masters champion Bob Goalby. In 2004 he was named recipient of the Payne Stewart award for respecting and upholding the traditions of the game and received the Bob Jones award for outstanding sportsmanship in 2005. In 2006 and 2007 he edged out Loren Roberts for the No 1 spot on the US Champions Tour winning five times in 2006 and a further four times in 2007.

Haeggman, Joakim (SWE)

Born Kalmar, 28 August 1969
Turned professional 1989

Became the first Swedish player to play in the Ryder Cup when he made the side which lost to the Americans at The Belfry in 1993. He received one of team captain Bernard Gallacher's 'wild cards' and beat John Cook in his last day singles. Gave up ice hockey after dislocating his shoulder and breaking ribs in 1994. Realised then that ice hockey and golf do not mix but has become an enthusiastic angler when not on the links. Equalled the world record of 27 for the first nine holes in the Alfred Dunhill Cup over the Old course at St Andrews in 1997. Occasionally acts as commentator for Swedish TV and was a member of Sam Torrance's Ryder Cup backroom team at The Belfry in 2002 and Bernhard Langer's vice-captain at Oakland Hills in 2004. Returned to the winner's circle in 2004 at Qatar. It was only his second win on the European Tour and his first since 1993.

Hamilton, Todd (USA)

Born Galesburg, Illinois, 18 October 1965
Turned professional 1997

Winner of the 2004 Open Championship at Royal Troon beating Ernie Els in a four-hole play-off after both had tied on ten-under-par 274. Having learned his craft on the Asian Tour and Japanese circuit where he won four times in 2003, he earned his US Tour card in 2004 and won the Honda Classic. His performance in The Open was flawless as he kept his nerve to win against Els, Phil Mickelson and World No 1 Tiger Woods among others. He was American Rookie of the Year in 2004 but has since lost his card to play there and has been a member of the European Tour.

Han, Chang Won (KOR)

Born Jeju Island

The 17-year-old winner of the first Asian Amateur Championship played at Mission Hills in China, he shot a 12-under par score to earn a place in the 2010 Masters at Augusta joining two other foreign teenagers, US Amateur Champion Byeong-Hu An and British Champion Matteo Manassero there.

Hansen, Anders (DEN)

Born Sonderborg, 16 September 1970
Turned professional 1995

Made up eight shots over the last 36 holes to win the BMW PGA Championship for a second time at Wentworth in 2007. He had also won the event in 2002. He ended top money winner on the South African Sunshine Tour in 2009. He won in 2011.

Hansen, Søren (DEN)

Born Copenhagen, 21 March 1974
Turned professional 1997

Winner of the Murphy's Irish Open in 2002 and the Mercedes-Benz Championship in 2007, he made his début successfully in the 2008 Ryder Cup at Valhalla.

Hanson, Peter (SWE)

Born Svedala, 4 October 1977
Turned professional 1998

In 1998 he won the English Amateur Stroke-play Championship (the Brabazon Trophy) and was also a

Padraig Harrington (IRL)

Born Dublin, Ireland, 31 August 1971 *Turned professional 1995*

The winner of three major championships, Harrington is Ireland's most successful golfer thanks to his triumphs at The Open in 2007 and 2008 and the US PGA in 2007. He became only the second Irishman ever to hoist the Claret Jug when he overcame Sergio García in a four-hole play-off at Carnoustie, 60 years after Belfast's Fred Daly had won the title at Hoylake in 1947.

He savoured the season of his life in 2008 when he became the first European to win both The Open and US PGA titles in the same year and the first European to win the US PGA since Tommy Armour in 1930. At Royal Birkdale he defended the crown by holding off the challenge posed by Ian Poulter and Greg Norman with a closing 66. The highlight of the championship was the 5-wood he struck to two feet on the par 5 17th for a glorious eagle 3 which closed the door on his rivals. It was the first time since James Braid in 1906 that a European had retained the title. At Oakland Hills three weeks later his main challengers were García and Ben Curtis. Again a closing 66 did the trick for the talented Irishman. At the end of his extraordinary year, Harrington was named the European Tour, PGA Tour and PGA of America's Player of the Year. He was only the second European to be given this honour since it was first awarded in 1948.

A qualified accountant, Harrington played three times as an amateur in the Walker Cup before turning professional. He won the Spanish Open in 2006 and has gone on to lift 30 titles, including 14 on the European Tour. His career has been heavily influenced by input from both coach Bob Torrance and sports psychologist Bob Rotella. He won the European Order of Merit in 2006 and has featured on six Ryder Cup teams, four times as a winner. He has gone into the design business with his first course, The Marlbrook, in Co. Tipperary. In 2011, he was named as The R&A's first Working for Golf Ambassador, promoting the work of the game's governing body around the world.

member of the winning Swedish Eisenhower Trophy team. In 2005 he partnered Robert Karlsson for Sweden in the 2007 Mission Hills World Cup of Golf and in 2008 he ended a ten year wait for a home winner when he won the SAS Scandinavian Masters in poor weather at Arlandastat outside Stockholm. He won twice – at Majorca and the Czech Republic – in 2010 which helped him make his début in the Ryder Cup.

Hayes, Dale (RSA)

Born Pretoria, 1 July 1952
Turned professional 1970

Former South African amateur stroke play champion who was a regular winner in South Africa and Europe after turning professional. He was Europe's top money earner in 1975 but retired from competitive golf to move into business. He is now a successful television commentator in South Africa with a weekly programme of his own often working as a double act with veteran Denis Hutchinson.

Hoch, Scott (USA)

Born Raleigh, North Carolina, 24 November 1955
Turned professional 1979

Ryder Cup, Presidents Cup, Walker Cup and Eisenhower Trophy player who was a regular winner on the US Tour soring 10 wins between 1980 and 2001 with six more victories worldwide. In 1989 he donated $100,000 of his Las Vegas Invitational winnings to the Arnold Palmer Children's Hospital in Orlando where his son Cameron had been successfully treated for a rare bone infection in his right knee. Also remembered for missing a short putt at the first extra hole of a play-off that would have won him a Masters Green Jacket and a first major.

Horton MBE, Tommy (ENG)

Born St Helens, Lancashire, 16 June 1941
Turned professional 1957

A former Ryder Cup player who was No 1 earner on the European Seniors Tour in 1993 and for four successive seasons between 1996 and 1999. Awarded an MBE by Her Majesty the Queen for his services to golf, Tommy is a member of the European Tour Board and is chairman of the European Seniors Tour committee. A distinguished coach, broadcaster, author and golf course architect, Tommy retired as club professional at Royal Jersey in 1999 after 25 years in the post. He continues to play occasionally on the Senior Tour.

Howell, David (ENG)

Born Swindon, 23 June 1975 Turned professional 1995

Winner of the 1999 Dubai Desert Classic, he made his Ryder Cup début in 2004 at Oakland Hills where he teamed up with Paul Casey to gain a valuable foursomes point on the second day. He finished seventh in the 2005 European Tour money list making over £1.2 million and a year later despite his schedule being curtailed by injury, he made over £1.5 million and finished third. Although injury has severely restricted his play he remains an enthusiastic competitor and is often used as an expert analyst by Sky television.

Huggett MBE, Brian (WAL)

Born Porthcawl, Wales, 18 November 1936
Turned professional 1951

Brian won the first of his 16 European Tour titles in Holland in 1962 and was still winning in 2000 when he landed the Beko Seniors Classic in Turkey after a play-off. A dogged competitor he played in six Ryder Cup matches before being given the honour of captaining the side in 1977 – the last year the Americans took on players from only Great Britain and Ireland. A respected golf course designer, Huggett was awarded the MBE for his services to golf and in particular Welsh golf.

Hunt MBE, Bernard (ENG)

Born Atherstone, Warwickshire, 2 February 1930
Turned professional 1946

One of Britain's most accomplished professionals he won 22 times between 1953 and 1973. He was third in the 1960 Open at the Old Course behind Kel Nagle and fourth in 1964 when Tony Lema took the title at St Andrews. Among his other victories were successes in Egypt and Brazil. Having made eight appearances in the Ryder Cup he captained the side in 1973 and again in 1975. He was PGA captain in 1966 and won the Harry Vardon Trophy as leading player in the Order of Merit on three occasions.

Ilonen, Mikko (FIN)

Born Lahti, 18 December 1979
Turned professional 2001

Became the first Finnish golfer to win the Amateur Championship when he beat Christian Reimbold from Germany 2 and 1 in the 2000 final at Royal Liverpool. He has won both the Finnish amateur match play and stroke play titles. He represented Finland in the 1998 and 2000 Eisenhower Trophy events. Now plays professionally on the European Tour and in 2007 won the Enjoy Jakarta Astro Indonesian Open, a joint venture with the Asian Tour and the Scandinavian Masters at Arlandastad. In 2008 he won the Indonesian Open title again.

Immelman, Trevor (RSA)

Born Cape Town, South Africa, 16 December 1979
Turned professional 1999

The 2008 Masters champion is son of Johan Immelman, former executive director of the South African Sunshine Tour. A former South African Amateur Match Play and Stroke-play champion and twice South African Open champion Trevor played his early professional golf in Europe before moving to the United States where he scored a first major victory leading from start to finish in the 2008 Masters at Augusta. won his first PGA title when he held off a strong field at the Cialis Western Open at Cog Hill. He has played in two Presidents Cups but his career has been dogged by injury and illness causing him to miss three of the four 2009 majors.

Irwin, Hale (USA)

Born Joplin, Montana, 3 June 1945
Turned professional 1968

A three time winner of the US Open (1974, 1979 and 1990) he has been a prolific winner on the main US Tour and, since turning 50, on the US Champions Tour. He had 20 wins on the main Tour including the 1990 US Open triumph where he holed a 45-foot putt on the final green at Medinah to force a play-off with Mike Donald then after both were still tied following a further 18 holes became the oldest winner of the Championship at 45 when he sank a 10-foot birdie putt at the first extra hole of sudden death. Joint runner-up to Tom Watson in the 1983 Open at Royal Birkdale where he stubbed the ground and missed a tap-in putt on the final day – a slip that cost him the chance of a play-off. Three times top earner on the Champions Tour where, prior to the start of the 2001 season, he had averaged $90,573 per start in 130 events coming in the top three in 63 of those events and finishing over par in only nine of them, he was inducted into the World Golf Hall of Fame in 2008.

Ishikawa, Ryo (JPN)

Born Saitama, 17 September 1991
Turned professional 2008

Already established as one of the most exciting young players in world golf – he's nicknamed the "bashful prince" in Japan – the teenager captured headlines around the globe during 2010 when he carded 58 in the final round to win the Crowns tournament at Nagoya on the Japanese Tour. It was the lowest score ever recorded on a sanctioned Tour and included 12 birdies and six pars. The previous record of 59 was shared on the PGA Tour by the Americans Al Geiberger, Chip Beck, David Duval, Paul Goydos and Stuart Appleby. The Crowns tournament was Ishikawa's seventh victory of his career and followed on from an electrifying start to the final round when he birdied nine of the first 11 holes. He first won on the Japan Tour as an amateur at the 2007 Muningswear Open in Okayama. At just 15 years and 245 days he became the youngest man ever to win a professional event. He then went on to become the youngest player to compete in the US PGA Championship at Hazeltine in 2009 as well as the youngest ever to reach the top 50 of the World Golf Rankings.

Jacobs OBE, John (ENG)

Born Lindrick, Yorkshire, 14 March 1925

The first Executive Director of the independently run PGA European Tour, John Jacobs was awarded the OBE in 2000 for his services to golf as a player, administrator and coach. Known as "Dr Golf" Jacobs has built up an awesome reputation as a teacher around the world and is held in high esteem by the golfing fraternity. Top American coach Butch Harmon summed up John's contribution when he said: "There is not one teacher who does not owe something to John. He wrote the book on coaching." With 75 per cent of the votes he was inducted into the World Golf Teachers' Hall of Fame and was described at that ceremony as 'the English genius'. Last year he was also welcomed into the World Golf Hall of Fame in America. Having played in the 1955 Ryder Cup match he captained the side in 1979 when Continental

Tony Jacklin CBE (ENG)

Born Scunthorpe, 7 July 1944 *Turned professional 1962*

A long and straight driver as well as a formidable ball striker at his peak, Jacklin was a significant force in the game between 1968 and 1974. It could even be argued that there were spells during his ascendancy when the Englishman was as good as anyone in the sport. In 1969 he won The Open Championship at Royal Lytham and St Annes, in the process becoming a national hero as the first British holder of the title since Max Faulkner in 1951. A year later he led from start to finish to win the US Open at Hazeltine by a seven shot margin – again underscoring his national standing as the first British player to win that event since Ted Ray had been successful in 1920. He was also the first Englishman since Harry Vardon to hold The Open and US Open titles simultaneously. He might well have won further Open championships but a thunderstorm thwarted his bid for the title at St Andrews in 1970, he came third in 1971 and in 1972 Lee Trevino chipped in at the 17th at Muirfield to win a title Jacklin had seemed destined to grasp.

The son of a Scunthorpe lorry driver who travelled by bus to play in assistants' events, he was rookie of the year on the European Tour in 1962 and went on to win 14 times on his home circuit. He was a driving force in the Ryder Cup as a player, taking part in seven consecutive matches from 1967. As a four-time captain of Europe, he twice led the Continent to victory including the first ever win on American soil in 1987. He also played an important and often under-rated role in the growth of the PGA European Tour after it became a self-supporting organisation in 1971. Although playing most of his golf in America he was encouraged by John Jacobs, the then executive director of the European Tour, to return to Europe to help build up the circuit.

He is an honorary member of the Royal and Ancient Golf Club of St Andrews having been elected in 2003 along with Lee Trevino. Played in his last Open in 2005. He has built in Florida with Jack Nicklaus a course known as The Concession, so named because of the putt Jack conceded him in the 1969 Ryder Cup to ensure the overall match was halved. He was awarded the OBE in 1970 and a CBE in 1990 in recognition of his influential Ryder Cup captaincy, which helped revive the standing of the match.

players were included for the first time and again in 1981. Ken Schofield who succeeded him as European Tour supremo believes that John changed the face of golf sponsorship. In 2002 he received the Association of Golf Writers' award for outstanding services to golf.

Jacquelin, Rafaël (FRA)

Born Lyons, 8 May 1974
Turned professional 1995

Ten years after turning professional and in his 238th event Rafaël Jacquelin a former French amateur champion, won his first event as a professional – the 2005 Madrid Open at Club de Campo. The Frenchman with a most graceful swing, who originlly wanted to be a soccer player but a knee injury thwarted his plans and he turned instead to tennis and later to golf. In 2007 he led wire-to-wire when winning the BMW Asian Open. He and Gregory Havret finished third behind Scotland and the USA in the 2007 World Cup of Golf at Mission Hills in China. In 2011 he won the Sicilian Open and took over from the injured Alvaro Quiros in the Continental side captained by Jan Van de Velde against Great Britain and Ireland at St Nom la Breteche.

Jaidee, Thongchai (THA)

Born Lop Buri, Thailand, 8 November 1969
Turned professional 1999

The first Thai golfer to win a title on the European Tour when he won the Carlsberg Malaysian Open in 2004. Learned his golf using a bamboo pole with an old 5-iron head and did not play his first nine holes until he was 16. An ex-paratrooper, Jaidee qualified and played all four rounds in the 2001 US Open. An impressive regular on the Asian Tour, he also competes on the European International schedule where in 2009 he won the Ballantines event in Korea and the Indonesian Open in Bali. Finished top money earner on the Asian Tour for the third time in 2009. He is still top career money earner on the Asian Tour with over $2 million.

James, Mark (ENG)

Born Manchester, 28 October 1953
Turned professional 1976

Veteran of over 500 European tournaments he was for a time chairman of the European Tour's Tournament committee. A seven-time Ryder Cup player including the 1995 match at Oak Hill when he scored a vital early last day point against Jeff Maggert, he captained the side at Brookline in 1999. Four times a top five finisher in The Open Championship he has won 18 European Tour events and four elsewhere but caused some raised eyebrows with his comments in his book reviewing the 1999 Ryder Cup entitled *Into the Bear Pit.* Affectionately known as Jesse to his friends. he qualified for the US Champions Tour in 2004 and won one of that Tour's five majors – the Ford Senior Players Championship. Through 2008 continued to play on the US Champions Tour with only infrequent visits back to play in European

Senior events or to join Ken Brown and Peter Alliss on the BBC golf commentating team. In his spare time he is an enthusiastic gardener.

January, Don (USA)

Born Plainview, Texas, 20 November 1929
Turned professional 1955

Winner of the US Open in 1967 he followed up his successful main Tour career in which he had 11 wins between 1956 and 1976 with double that success as a Senior. Much admired for his easy rhythmical style.

Janzen, Lee (USA)

Born Austin, Minnesota, 28 August 1964
Turned professional 1986

Twice a winner of the US Open in 1993 and in 1998 when he staged the best final round comeback since Johnny Miller rallied from six back to win the title 25 years earlier. Five strokes behind the late Payne Stewart after 54 holes at Baltusrol he closed with a 67 to beat Stewart with whom he had also battled for the title in 1993.

Jiménez, Miguel Angel (ESP)

Born Malaga, 4 January 1964
Turned professional 1982

The oldest ever winner of a European Tour event, Jiménez was only five weeks shy of his 49th birthday when he claimed victory at the UBS Hong Kong Open in 2012. One of seven brothers, he did not take up golf until his mid-teens. Miguel loves cars, drives a Ferrari and has been nicknamed 'The Mechanic' by his friends. His best-remembered shot was the 3-wood he hit into the hole for an albatross 2 at the infamous 17th hole at Valderrama in the Volvo Masters. He was also credited with having played the Canon Shot of the Year when he chipped in at the last to win 1998 Trophée Lancôme. In 2000 lost in a play-off at Valderrama in a World Championship event to Tiger Woods. He played in the 2002, 2004, 2008 and 2010 European Ryder Cup sides gaining a vital point in the last day singles at Celtic Manor. He won four times during the 2004 European season, taking the Johnnie Walker Classic title in Bangkok, the Algarve Portuguese Open at Penina, the BMW Asian Open in Shanghai and the BMW German Open in Munich. and was a three time winner during the 2010 season succeeding in Dubai, Paris and at Crans. He was the 2008 BMW PGA champion beating Oliver Wilson in a play-off at Wentworth. He loves his rioja and is often seen smoking a cigar. At Medinah in 2012 he was one of Europe's four vice-captains at the Ryder Cup, a role he previously filled under Seve Ballesteros. His win in Hong Kong was the 19th of his career on the European Tour.

Johansson, Per-Ulrik (SWE)

Born Uppsala, 6 December 1966
Turned professional 1990

A former amateur international at both junior and senior level he became the first Swede to play in two Ryder Cups when he made the 1995 and 1997 teams. In the 1995 match he lost to Phil Mickelson with whom he had studied at Arizona State University. In 1991 he was winner of the Sir Henry Cotton Rookie of the Year award in Europe. For a time, he played in America but returned to Europe, regaining his main Tour card with victory in the Russian Open in Moscow.

Johnson, Dustin (USA)

Born Columbia,South Carolina, 22 June 1984
Turned professional 2007

Winner of the AT&T Pebble Beach Pro-am in both 2009 and 2010, he also led the US Open at Pebble Beach by three strokes after 54 holes but dropped back into a share of eighth place after carding 82 in the final round. Johnson also had a chance to win the US PGA in 2010 after making birdies in the final round at Whistling Straits on the 16th and 17th holes. Standing at 12 under par on the 72nd hole, he hit his tee shot right and landed in a sandy area. Unaware he was in a bunker he grounded his club in the dirt and thought he'd made a bogey to join Martin Kaymer and Bubba Watson in a play-off but he was penalised two strokes for grounding his club and finished in a share of fifth. His victory later in the season over Paul Casey in the BMW Championship, his fourth US PGA Tour win, proved his resilience. He was a member of the 2007 US Walker Cup side and made his début in the Ryder Cup at Celtic Manor in 2010. A year later he was runner-up to Darren Clarke in The Open losing his chance of possible victory by hitting his second shot out of bounds at the par 5 14th at Royal St George's.

Johnson, Zach (USA)

Born Iowa City, 24 February 1976
Turned professional 1998

The winner of the 2004 BellSouth Classic, he made his début in the Ryder Cup at the K Club in 2006 and won The Masters at Augusta in 2007. Later, he won first prize in the AT&T Classic at TPC Sugarloaf and earned a Presidents Cup spot. Surprisingly missed out on Ryder Cup honours in 2008 but made the team in both 2010 and 2012. He made nearly $5 million and won twice on the PGA Tour last season – the John Deere Classic and the Crown Plaza – taking his victories there to nine.

Jones, Steve (USA)

Born Artesia, New Mexico, 27 December 1958
Turned professional 1981

First player since Jerry Pate in 1976 to win the US Open after having had to qualify. His 1996 victory was the result of inspiration he received from reading a Ben Hogan book given to him the week before the Championship at Oakland Hills. Uses a reverse over-lapping grip as a result of injury. Indeed his career was put on hold for three years after injury to his left index finger following a dirt-bike accident. He dominated the 1997 Phoenix Open shooting 62, 64, 65 and 67 for an 11 shot victory over Jesper Parnevik That week his 258 winning total was just one outside the low US Tour record set by Mike Souchak in 1955. Played in the 1999 Ryder Cup.

Karlsson, Robert (SWE)

Born St Malm, Sweden, 3 September 1969
Turned professional 1989

The tall son of a greenkeeper is the most successful Swede on the European Tour having won 11 times by the end of 2010. He was a member of the winning 2006 Ryder Cup side and the losing 2008 team. He played with Peter Hanson in the 2007 Mission Hills World Cup of Golf in Shenzhen and in 2008 teamed up with Henrik Stenson to win the trophy for Sweden for a second time. It was a fitting finale to a year in which he made the cut in all four majors and towards the end of the season won the Mercedez-Benz German Masters and the Alfred Dunhill Links Championship to clinch the No 1 spot on the European Tour's Order of Merit. At one point during the summer of 2008 he was never out of the top four in five consecutive events finishing 3,3,3,2,4. An eye problem caused him to miss many tournaments in 2009. A year later, when back to full fitness he won the Dubai World Championship in 2010 and in 2011 played most of his golf in America.

Kaymer, Martin (GER)

Born Dusseldorf, Germany, 26 December 1984

The 2010 US PGA champion produced an outstanding performance at Whistling Straits to secure his first Major title. Coached by Fanny Sunesson, who is better known as Nick Faldo's former caddie and bag carrier for Henrik Stenson, Kaymer was an out-standing amateur golfer who made an immediate impact as a professional. On a satellite circuit he made a name for himself by carding 59 before winning twice on the Challenge Tour in 2006. When he joined the European Tour the following year he ended up with five top ten finishes and won the Sir Henry Cotton Rookie of the Year award. He also won twice in 2008 at Abu Dhabi and Munich and just failed to make the Ryder Cup side, though he was invited to Valhalla as an observer by Faldo. In 2009 he won back to back titles at the French and Scottish Opens before an ankle injury sustained when go-karting in Arizona sidelined him for a spell. Victory in 2010 at the Abu Dhabi championship propelled Kaymer into the world's top ten. And when he defeated Bubba Watson in a play-off at Whistling Straits, Kaymer became only the second German after Bernhard Langer to become a major champion. He also won his next tournament, the KLM Open, before making his Ryder Cup début at Celtic Manor then adding the Dunhill Links Championship to his list of successes. He went on to win the Race to Dubai and was jointly named European Golfer of the Year with Graeme McDowell. In 2011 he began with a third victory in four years at Abu Dhabi and moved to No 2 in the world but then his form deserted him.He was still out of sorts at the 2012 Ryder Cup but showed a true champion's mettle when he holed a vital putt on the 18th green at Medinah in a singles tie against Steve Stricker which retained the trophy for Europe.

Kim Kyung-Tae (KOR)

Born Seoul, South Korea, 2 September 1986
Turned professional: 2006

It was no surprise that the 24-year-old South Korean topped the Japanese money list in 2010 with total earnings of over 181 million yen. He made it to the top with the help of three victories – the Diamond Cup, the Mynavi ABC Championship and the Japanese Open. His scoring average for the season was 69.41 and he hit more than three greens out of four in regulation during the season. As an amateur he had swept all before him earning a government exemption from National Service for his performance at the 2006 Asian Games where he won the individual honours and helped South Korea to victory in the team event. He won two events on the Korean professional Tour as an amateur and by the end of 2010 had moved from outdo the top 100 in the World Rankings to 30th.

Kite, Tom (USA)

Born Austin, Texas, 9 December 1949
Turned professional 1972

He won the US Open at Pebble Beach in 1992 in difficult conditions when aged 42 to lose the 'best player around never to have won a Major' tag. With 19 wins on the main Tour he was the first to top $6million, $7 million, $8 million and $9 million dollars in prize money. Has been playing since he was 11 and after a lifetime wearing glasses had laser surgery to correct acute near-sightedness. He played in seven Ryder Cups and was captain at Valderrama in 1997. He now plays the US Champions Tour and was inducted into the World Golf Hall of Fame in 2004.

Kuchar, Matt (USA)

Born Winter Park, Florida, 21 June 1978
Turned professional 2000

A member of the US Walker Cup side which lost to GB&I at Nairn in 1999, Kuchar enjoyed a notable amateur career, winning the US Amateur in 1997. In 1998, he finished 14th at the US Open and 21st at the Masters while still at college. Since becoming a professional, the genial Kuchar has won four times on the PGA Tour as well as the Omega Mission Hills World Cup with Gary Woodland in 2011. His most significant victory to date came last year in the Players Championship at Sawgrass. He represented the USA at the Ryder Cup in both 2010 and 2012.

Laird, Martin (SCO)

Born Glasgow, Scotland, 1982
Turned professional 2004

The Arizona based Scot enjoyed his best year so far on the PGA Tour in 20ll, winning the Arnold Palmer Invitational at Bay Hill, the first European golfer ever to do so. He produced six top ten finishes and won $2.7 million. A graduate of the Nationwide Tour, his first PGA Tour win came at the Justin Timberlake Shriners Hospitals for Children Open. Laird's journey from junior captain and champion at Hilton Park in Glasgow to winner on the PGA Tour began in 2003. That was the summer he came from behind to clinch a three stroke victory in the Scottish Youths' Open Amateur Strokeplay Championship. He went to college at Colorado State and hasn't left America since, becoming first Scot in 20 years to play full-time on the PGA Tour.

Lane, Barry (ENG)

Born Hayes, Middlesex, 21 June 1960
Turned professional 1976

After winning his way into the 1993 Ryder Cup he hit the headlines when he won the first prize of $1 million in the Andersen Consulting World Championship beating David Frost in the final at Greyhawk in Arizona. He has played over 500 European events, winning five times between 1988 and 2008. In 2004, aged 44, he won the British Masters at Marriott Forest of Arden.

Lawrie MBE, Paul (SCO)

Born Aberdeen, 1 January 1969
Turned professional 1986

Made golfing history when he came from 10 shots back on the final day to win the 1999 Open Championship at Carnoustie after a play-off against former winner Justin Leonard and Frenchman Jean Van de Velde. With his win he became the first home-based Scot since Willie Auchterlonie in 1893 to take the title. Still based in Aberdeen he hit the opening tee shot in the 1999 Ryder Cup and played well in partnership with Colin Montgomerie in foursomes and four balls and in the singles earned a point against Jeff Maggert. Originally an assistant at Banchory Golf Club on Royal Deeside Lawrie has had a hole named after him at the club. Lawrie was awarded an MBE for his achievements in golf and is a prominent supporter of junior golf in Scotland. In 2011 he won the Andalucian Masters in Malaga, his first victory in nine years. He was also runner-up in the season ending Dubai World Championship. Lawrie continued this run of good form into 2012 where he won twice on the European Tour – the Qatar Masters and the Johnnie Walker at Gleneagles – before moving into the world's top 30. He played in the Ryder Cup at Medinah for the first time since 1999 and demolished Brandt Snedeker by 5 and 3 in the singles.

Lee, Danny (NZL)

Born 24 July 1990

Helped by his victory in the US Amateur Championship in 2008 he moved to the top of the Royal and Ancient Golf Club of St Andrews amateur rankings and won the McCormack Trophy. Although Korean by birth he has been brought up in New Zealand and America. Late in 2008 he became a naturalised New Zealander and led his country in the Eisenhower Trophy competition won by Scotland in Adelaide. He is one of three amateurs to have won titles on the PGA European Tour. Pablo Martin won the Estoril Open de Portugal in 2007 as an a amateur, Lee won the last Johnnie Walker Classic title at The Vines in Perth in 2009 and later that season Irish amateur Shane Lowry won the 3-Irish Open at Baltray.

Lehman, Tom (USA)

Born Austin, Minnesota, 7 March 1959
Turned professional 1982

Winner of The Open Championship at Royal Lytham and St Annes in 1996 he was runner-up in the US Open that year and third in 1997. He was runner-up in the 1994 Masters having come third the previous year. He played in four Ryder Cup matches and led the US team in the 2006 Ryder Cup match at the K Club when the Americans lost 18½–9½ to the Europeans led by Ian Woosnam. In 2011 he was the Champions Tour player of the year, winning three times and earning over $2 milllion on the senior circuit.

Leonard, Justin (USA)

Born Dallas, Texas, 15 June 1972
Turned professional 1994

Winner of the 1997 Open at Royal Troon when he beat Jesper Parnevik and Darren Clarke into second place with a closing 65 and nearly won the title again in 1999 when he lost to Paul Lawfrie in a four-hole play-off with the Scotsman and Jean Van de Velde at Carnoustie. In 1998 came from five back to beat Lee Janzen in the Players Championship and is remembered for his fight back against José Maria Olazábal on the final day of the 1999 Ryder Cup at Brookline. Four down after 11 holes he managed to share a half-point with the Spaniard to help America win the Cup. He was again a member of a winning Ryder Cup side when he played in the 2008 team captained by Paul Azinger at Valhalla but was in the losing side at Celtic Manor in 2010.

Lewis, Tom (ENG)

Born Welwyn Garden City, Hertfordshire, 5 January 1991 Turned professional 2011

After a season in which he led The Open as an amateur and went on to surpass that feat in the paid ranks by winning in only his third start as a professional, it was fitting Lewis should be named as the European Tour's rookie of the year in 2011. It was a 65 in the first round at Royal St George's – the lowest score ever recorded by an amateur at The Open – which first brought the young Englishman, who won the Boys' Championship in 2009, to the attention of the wider golfing public. Just three months later in the final round of the Portugal Masters he uncorked another 65 to pull off the quickest victory by an affiliate member in Tour history. The son of Brian, a former Tour professional,

Bernhard Langer (GER)

Born Anhausen, 27 August 1957 Turned professional 1972

While there have been many notable achievements during his enduring career, including collecting two Masters titles at Augusta, winning 40 titles on the European Tour and proving a mainstay of the European Ryder Cup side as both a player and a captain, the German's remarkable accomplishment in winning senior major titles in successive weeks during the summer of 2010 rivalled anything the veteran had accomplished in his prime. The first senior golfer to win back-to-back majors since Tom Watson in 2003, Langer's triumphs were all the more remarkable bearing in mind that his first success came in The Senior British Open at Carnoustie in Scotland and his second was in The US Senior Open in Seattle, Washington State, venues separated by thousands of miles as well as an eight hour time difference. Langer's success on the Champions' circuit, winning more than $2 million in each of his first three years on Tour, however, came as no surprise to those familiar with the track record of this determined champion.

His success at Carnoustie in The Senior British was particularly rewarding since he had come twice and finished third on three occasions in The Open without lifting the Claret Jug. A prolific winner throughout his career, Langer is the second most prolific champion, after Seve Ballesteros, in European Tour history. His most memorable victories, though, came in America where he won the Masters in 1985 and 1993. The latter triumph is best remembered for the eagle 3 he made at the 13th in the final round to set up a four stroke win over Chip Beck. Perhaps there was an element of irony attached to these triumphs at Augusta since Langer has frequently faced putting problems during his career and the Masters is widely regarded as the most demanding test of putting in championship golf. His most successful year as a pro came in 1985 when he won seven tournaments on five continents and was ranked No 1 in the world. Though far from the longest hitter, the consistency of Langer's game also made him a formidable match play golfer. He played in ten Ryder Cup matches and was an outstanding European captain at Oakland Hills in 2004. A member of the World Golf Hall of Fame, he was awarded an honorary OBE for his services to the game.

Lewis' last act as an amateur was to help Great Britain and Ireland defeat the USA in the Walker Cup match at Royal Aberdeen

Levet, Thomas (FRA)

Born Paris, 9 September 1968
Turned professional 1988

Although he was the first Frenchman to play full time on the US Tour and still has a home in Florida, he lost his card and only regained his European Tour card when he was invited, because of his French national ranking, to play in the 1998 Cannes Open – and won it. Sixth in the 1997 Open at Royal Troon he lost in a play-off to Ernie Els in the 2002 Open at Muirfield. Thomas made his Ryder Cup début at Oakland Hills in 2004, winning his singles game against Fred Funk. He is a gifted linguist speaking seven languages including Japanese. Has also turned his hand very successfully to commentating for French television. In 2011 he won the French Open but injured a food jumping into the lake at the 18th and had to withdraw from The Open at Royal St George's for which he had qualified earlier.

Liang, Wen-Chong (CHN)

Born Zhongshan, China, 2 August 1978
Turned professional 1999

Became the second Chinese winner on the European Tour when he won the Clariden Leu Singapore Open in 2007. His friend and mentor has been Zhang Lian-wei. Introduced to the game while still at school he plays with a most unorthodox swing but it works for him. Finished second to Ian Poulter in the Barclays Singapore Open in 2009 he finished second to Thongchai Jaidee on the Asian Tour's Order of Merit and in 2010 was No 1 on the rival OneAsia Tour's final ranking.

Littler, Gene (USA)

Born San Diego, California, 21 July 1930
Turned professional 1954

Winner of the 1953 US Amateur Championship he had a distinguished professional career scoring 26 victories on the US Tour between 1955 and 1977. He scored his only major triumph at Pebble Beach in 1971 when he beat Bob Goalby and Doug Sanders at Oakland Hills. He had been runner-up in the US Open in 1954 and was runner-up in the 1977 USPGA Championship and the 1970 US Masters. A seven-time Ryder Cup player between 1961 and 1977 he is a former winner of the Ben Hogan, Bobby Jones and Byron Nelson awards. He won the Hogan award after successfully beating cancer.

Love III, Davis (USA)

Born Charlotte, North Carolina, 13 April 1964
Turned professional 1985

Son of one of America's most highly rated teachers who died in a plane crash in 1988, Love has won only one major – the 1997 USPGA Championship at Winged Foot where he beat Justin Leonard by five shots. He has been runner-up in the US Open (1996) and the US Masters (1999). In the World Cup of Golf he won the title in partnership with Fred Couples four years in a row from 1992. He played in five Ryder Cups and was the losing captain of the US team at

Sandy Lyle MBE (SCO)

Born Shrewsbury, 9 February 1958 Turned professional 1977

With his win in the 1985 Open Championship at Royal St George's he became the first British player to take the title since Tony Jacklin in 1969. He was alsothe first British player to win a Green Jacket in the Masters at Augusta in 1988 helped by a majestic 7-iron second shot out of sand at the last for a rare winning birdie 3. Although he represented England as an amateur at boys', youths' and senior level he became Scottish when he turned professional, something he was entitled to do at the time because his late father, the professional at Hawkstone Park, was a Scot. This is no longer allowed. He made his international début at age 14 and, two years later, qualified for and played 54 holes in the 1974 Open at Royal Lytham. A tremendously talented natural golfer who won 17 events on the European Tour, he fell a victim later in his career to becoming over-technical. Now lives in Perthshire and Florida. He was part of captain Ian Woosnam's backroom team for the 2006 Ryder Cup at the K Club in 2006. On the European Senior Tour, Sandy ended a 19 year wait for a tournament victory by winning the inaugural ISPS Handa Senior World Championship presented by Mission Hills China in 2011. He will be inducted into the World Golf Hall of Fame in 2012 after being selected through the international ballot.

Medinah where he admitted to feeling "stunned" by Europe's comeback on the final day.

Lowry, Shane (IRL)

Born Clara, County Offaly, Ireland, 2 April 1987.
Turned professional 2009

The former Irish Amateur Close champion shot a 62 at County Louth GC in the Irish Open in 2009 and led from the second day. In the end in driving rain and a strong wind he held his nerve to beat Robert Rock in a play-off for the title becoming only the third amateur to win on the European Tour. Pablo Martin won as an amateur in 2007 and earlier in 2009 Danny Lee had won the Johnnie Walker Classic. Urged by some to remain amateur until after the Walker Cup he chose to turn professional immediately.

McDowell MBE, Graeme (NIR)

Born Ballymoney, Northern Ireland, 30 July 1979
Turned professional 2002

The first European golfer to win the US Open since Tony Jacklin 40 years earlier, he joined an elite group of golfers which includes Tiger Woods, Tom Watson and Jack Nicklaus who have won America's oldest title at Pebble Beach. McDowell enjoyed the most successful season of his career to date in 2010. Two weeks before his triumph in the US Open he also won the Celtic Manor Wales Open thanks to a thrilling performance over the weekend when he shot 63 and 64. The Ulsterman won the Andalucian Masters before the end of the season and finished the year No. 2 in the Race to Dubai. He was named Golfer of the Year by both the European and American Golf Writers. Late in the year he beat Tiger Woods in a play-off at Woods own tournament in California. A member of the winning Great Britain and Ireland Walker Cup team in 2001, he earned his European Tour card in just his fourth event as a professional. McDowell, who had been signed up to represent the Kungsangen Golf Club in Sweden just two weeks earlier, received a last minute sponsor's invitation to play there in the Volvo Scandinavian Masters … and not only won the event but also broke the course record with an opening round of 64. He beat Trevor Immelman into second place with former USPGA champion Jeff Sluman third. McDowell's winning score of 270 – 14-under-par – earned him a first prize of over £200,000 and a place in the World Golf Championship NEC event at Sahalee in Washington. He was the European Tour's 12th first-time winner of the season and at 23 the youngest winner of the title. In 2008, helped by victories in the Ballantine's Championship in Korea and the Barclays Scottish Open at Loch Lomond, he qualified automatically for the Ryder Cup at Valhalla and was one of the team's most successful performers. He also represented Europe at Celtic Manor in 2010 when on a tense last day he scored the vital winning point with victory over Hunter Mahan. Crucially he holed tricky downhill putt for a winning birdie at the 16th. In his amateur days he attended the University of Alabama where he was rated No 1 Collegiate golfer winning six of 12 starts with a stroke average of 69.6. In 2004, scored his second European success when he won the Telecom Italia Open. At the end of the year he was voted Irish Sport Personality of the Year and was honoured with an MBE for his services to golf in the 2011 New Year's Honours List by Her Majesty the Queen.

McEvoy OBE, Peter (ENG)

Born London, 22 March 1953

The most capped player for England who has had further success as a captain of Great Britain and Ireland's Eisenhower Trophy and Walker Cup sides. The Eisenhower win came in 1998 and the Walker Cup triumphs at Nairn in 1999 and at Ocean Forest, Sea Island, Georgia in 2001. On both occasions his team won 15–9. A regular winner of amateur events McEvoy was amateur champion in 1977 and 1978 and won the English stroke play title in 1980. He reached the final of the English Amateur the same year. In 1978 he played all four rounds in the Masters at Augusta and that year received the Association of Golf Writers' Trophy for his contribution to European golf. He was leading amateur in two Open Championships – 1978 and 1979. In 2003 he was awarded the OBE by Her Majesty the Queen for his services to golf. He received

McIlroy MBE, Rory (NIR)

Born Holywood, May 4 1989 Turned professional 2007

Firmly established by the end of 2012 as the world's leading golfer, McIlroy enjoyed the best season of his fledgeling career last year when he won four times on the PGA Tour and earned over $8 million, thereby becoming the youngest golfer ever to reach $10 million in career earnings. The highlight of his season was a phenomenal eight shot victory in the US PGA Championship at Kiawah Island. It was the most emphatic triumph in the history of the tournament, surpassing even Jack Nicklaus' seven shot success in 1980.

The golfer from Holywood in County Down relished many other notable accomplishments in 2012 as he emulated Luke Donald's feat of winning the money lists in both America and Europe. He was named the PGA Tour's Player of the Year by his peers, won the Association of Golf Writers trophy and ranked as the second most marketable athlete in the world. In an unforgettable year for British sport, he was also shortlisted for the BBC's Sports Personality of the Year award.

The only active player under 40 with two major championship victories on his CV, the 23-year-old had also delivered the most exciting performance of 2011 when he led from the start to finish to win the US Open at Congressional, again by the breathtaking margin of eight strokes. It was the high point of another outstanding season in which he also won the Hong Kong Open by two shots and finished second behind Luke Donald in the Race to Dubai.

In 2010 he caught the attention of the golfing world thanks to a spectacular ten under par closing round of 62 to defeat Phil Mickelson by four shots in the Wells Fargo Championship. His eagle-birdie-par-birdie finish at Quail Hollow was electrifying.

Twice winner of the Irish and European Amateur titles – he was the youngest winner of the Irish event in 2005 – Rory won the silver medal as leading amateur in the 2007 Open at Carnoustie. After turning professional he won his European Tour card by finishing third in the Alfred Dunhill Links Championship, only his second event as a pro. In 2008 he missed a 15 inch putt to lose a play-off to Jean-François Lucquin at the Omega European Masters at Crans-sur-Sierre. In 2009 he won his first title – the Dubai Desert Classic – and finshed joint third in the USPGA Championship behind winner Yong-Eun Yang. He also finished third in the Race to Dubai after a season in which he had 12 top five finishes.

In 2010 he opened with 63 in The Open at St Andrews before carding an 80 on the second day which meant he had to settle for a share of third place. He was also third in the US PGA and made his début in the Ryder Cup at Celtic Manor. He returned to Ryder Cup action at Medinah in 2012, defeating Keegan Bradley in the singles, though only after speeding to the course on Sunday in a police car after a mix-up over his tee time.

Following Medinah, he turned his attention to winning the Race to Dubai, finishing second at the BMW Masters, third at the Barclays Singapore Open and ending the season with a notable victory in Dubai at the DP World Tour Championship thanks to a blistering closing run of five consecutive birdies.

Surprisingly overlooked for the Rookie of the Year award on the PGA Tour in 2010, he received the MBE in the 2011 Queen's New Year Honours List. Introduced to the game by his father, Gerry, Rory is coached by Michael Bannon, the professional at Holywood golf club.

the Association of Golf Writers' Award in 2009 for his outstanding services to the game.

McGimpsey, Garth (IRL)

Born Bangor, 17 July 1955

A long hitter who was Irish long-driving champion in 1977 and UK long-driving title holder two years later. He was amateur champion in 1985 and Irish champion the same year and again in 1988. He played in three Walker Cup matches and competed in the home internationals for Ireland in 1978 and from 1980 to 1998. He captained the winning Great Britain and Ireland Walker Cup side that beat American 12½–11½ at Ganton in 2003 and again two years later in Chicago when the Americans won by a point.

McGinley, Paul (IRL)

Born Dublin, 16 December 1966
Turned professional 1991

Popular Irish golfer who turned to the game after breaking his left kneecap playing Gaelic football. With Padraig Harrington won the 1977 World Cup at Kiawah and made his Ryder Cup début when the postponed 2001 match was played in 2002. In a tense finish to his match with Jim Furyk he holed from nine feet to get the half point the Europeans needed for victory. He made the side again in 2004 and was unbeaten as Europe beat the USA 18½–9½ and was one of three Irishmen who helped Europe win by the same margin in 2006. Europe might have won 19–9 had he not conceded a half to J.J. Henry at the last when a streaker ran over the line of the American's 20 foot downhill putt. In 2005 he finished third behind Colin Montgomerie and Michael Campbell in the European Tour Order of Merit making over £1.5 million. During the year he finished third behind Tiger Woods in the WGC–NEC Invitational at Firestone, lost the HSBC World Match-Play at Wentworth to Michael Campbell but ended the season on a high note with victory in the Volvo Masters of Andalucia. In 2007 he was appointed by Nick Faldo to be one of his vice-captains at the 2008 Ryder Cup but later declined in order to try and play himself into the side. He failed to do so. He was a surprise omission from the Great Britain and Ireland side against the Continent of Europe for the Seve Trophy when it was played in Ireland in 2007 but led the Great Britain and Ireland side to victory at St Nom La Breteche in 2009. In 2010 he accepted a vice-captain's role from Colin Montgomerie at the Ryder Cup at Celtic Manor and reprised that position under Jose Maria Olazabal at Medinah.

Macgregor, George (SCO)

Born Edinburgh, 19 August 1944

After playing in five Walker Cup matches he captained the side in 1991 and later served as chairman of The R&A Selection committee. He won the Scottish Stroke Play title in 1982 after having been runner up three times.

McNulty, Mark (IRL)

Born Zimbabwe, 25 October 1953
Turned professional 1977

Recognised as one of the best putters in golf he was runner-up with the late Payne Stewart to Nick Faldo in the 1990 Open at St Andrews. Although hampered throughout his career by a series of injuries and illness he has scored 16 wins on the European Tour and 33 around the world including 23 on the South African Sunshine circuit. He won the South African Open in 1987 and again in 2001 holing an 18-foot putt on the last green at East London to beat Justin Rose. Qualified in 2004 to join the US Champions Tour and although originally from Zimbabwe he now plays out of Ireland. He lost a play-off at Sunningdale in the 2009 Senior Open to Loren Roberts. Injury prevented his playing much in 2010.

Mahan, Hunter (USA)

Born Orange, California, 17 May 1982
Turned professional 2003

Although born in California, Mahan was raised in Texas where he went on to win the USGA Junior Championship. An outstanding amateur, he attended Oklahoma State and finished 28th on his début in the Masters before joining the professional ranks. In 2007 he finished sixth in the Open and played on the Presidents Cup. A year later he represented the US in the Ryder Cup and was their top scorer with 3½ points. In 2010 he enjoyed his most successful year to date, winning the Phoenix Open before shooting 64 in the final round to win the WGC–Bridgestone Invitational. He was second in the US Ryder Cup standings for Celtic Manor, earning one of the eight automatic qualifying spots but lost a crucial last day singles to Graeme McDowell. Although he won twice in 2012, including the WGC Match Play where he defeated Rory McIlroy in the final, Mahan missed out on the Ryder Cup at Medinah.

Mamat, Mardan (SIN)

Born Singapore, 31 October 1967
Turned professional 1994

Became the first Singaporean to win an Asian/European joint venture in his home country when he took the Osim Singapore Masters in 2006.

Manassero, Matteo (ITA)

Born Verona, 19 April 1993

Made history when he became not only the youngest but the first Italian to win the Amateur Championship with a 3 and 1 victory over Sam Hutsby in the final at Formby in 2009. He was only the third golfer in the 124-year history of the event to win after leading the qualifying. Later in the year earned the Silver Medal as leading amateur in The Open at Turnberry where he finished joint 13th. After playing all four rounds in The Masters he turned professional and made his début in the BMW Italian Open. He quickly secured his Tour card and when he won the Castello Masters he became the youngest title winner in European Tour history. In 2011 he won again in Malaysia and in 2012 was runner-up at the Andalucia Open and third at the Italian Open.

Marsh MBE, Dr David (ENG)

Born Southport, Lancashire, 29 April 1934

Twice winner of the English Amateur Championship in 1964 and 1970, he was captain of The R&A in 1990/1991. He played in the 1971 Walker Cup match at St Andrews and helped the home side win by scoring a vital one hole victory in the singles against Bill Hyndman. He captained the team in 1973 and 1975 and had a distinguished career as a player and then captain for England between 1956 and 1972. He was chairman of The R&A selection committee from 1979 to 1983 and in 1987 was president of the English Golf Union. He was appointed an MBE in the 2011 New Year's Honours List for his voluntary services to amateur golf.

Marsh, Graham (AUS)

Born Kalgoorlie, Western Australia, 14 January 1944
Turned professional 1968

A notable Australian who followed up his international playing career by gaining a reputation for designing fine courses. Although he played in Europe, America and Australasia he spent most of his time on the Japanese circuit where he had 17 wins between 1971 and 1982 . He won 11 times in Europe and scored victories also in the United States, India, Thailand and Malaysia.

Martin, Pablo (ESP)

Born Malaga, 20 April 1986
Turned professional 2007

Became the first amateur to win on the PGA European Tour when he edged out Raphaël Jacquelin of France by a shot in the Estoril Open de Portugal in 2007. A former British Boys' champion in 2001, he played in two Eisenhower Trophy competitions and two Palmer Cups. Winner of the Jack Nicklaus award for top national amateur in 2006 when at Oklahoma State University he gave up his studies to join the professional rank. Curiously another Oklahoma "cowboy", Scott Verplank, has also won as an amateur in his case on the PGA Tour. Martin won the Alfred Dunhill Championship at the start of the 2010 and 2011 European seasons.

Phil Mickelson (USA)

Born San Diego, California, 16 June 1970
Turned professional 1992

The winner of four major championships, Mickelson is the game's most successful left-handed golfer. He has won more than 50 events and has career earnings on the PGA Tour of $60 million. He has been particularly successful at Augusta where he's won the Masters three times in 2004, 2006 and 2010. He also won the PGA Championship in 2005 at Baltusrol. A hugely gifted amateur golfer, the left-hander won his first PGA Tour event when he was still a student at Arizona State University. When he was nine he watched on TV as Seve Ballesteros won the Masters and told his mother he would be a Masters' champion one day too. He was proved right 22 years later when he pulled off his first major success thanks to a run of five birdies over the closing seven holes, including an 18 foot putt on the last to thwart Ernie Els.

Right-handed in everything else, Mickelson played golf left-handed after watching his father swing a club and mirroring the action. The first left-hander to win the US Amateur, he was only the sixth amateur ever to win a PGA Tour event when he came out on top at the Northern Telecom Open in 1991. He turned professional a year later and broke into the world's top ten in 1996 where he has remained ever since.

His brilliant short game helped set up a second major triumph on the final hole at the PGA when he pitched from greenside rough to a couple of feet and finish a stroke in front of Thomas Björn. The following spring he won his second successive major and third in all thanks to another expert performance at Augusta. In 2010, he won the Masters for the third time by carding a final round of 67 to defeat Lee Westwood by three strokes. His total of 16 under par was the lowest score at Augusta since Tiger Woods in 2001. Perhaps the highlight of his fourth major victory came in Saturday's third round when he made back to back eagles on the 13th and 14th holes. Both his wife Amy and mother Mary have been recovering from breast cancer while Phil himself was diagnosed with arthritis.He won at Pebble Beach in 2012 and drew widespread admiration for both his play and sportsmanship in the Ryder Cup at Medinah.

Mason, Carl (ENG)

Born Buxton, Derbyshire, 25 June 1953
Turned professional 1973

Carl won twice on the main European Tour in 1994 but has played his best golf on the European Seniors Tour. He finished second on the money list in his first two years and first for the next three years. In 2004 and again in 2007 he won five events in a season.

Matsuyama, Hideki (JPN)

Born Japan, 25 February 1992

Yet to join the paid ranks at the close of 2011, Matsuyama won his first professional event last year after beating an impressive field which included defending champion Ryo Ishikawa and the Masters champion Charl Schwartzel to win the Taiheiyo Masters in Japan. He was only the third amateur to win on the Japanese Tour and had to eagle the final hole to secure victory. The 19-year-old first caught the eye of the golfing world beyond Japan when he finished 27th on his début at the Masters and earned the accolade of low amateur at Augusta. Ranked fourth in the World Amateur Golf Ranking, he's won the Asian Amateur twice as well as the Japan Collegiate Championship and the World University Games.

Micheel, Shaun (USA)

Born Orlando, Florida, 5 January 1969
Turned professional 1962

Surprise winner of the USPGA Championship at Oak Hill in 2003. He fired rounds of 69, 68, 69 and 70 for a winning total of 276. He completed his victory with one of the most brilliant approach irons from the rough to just one foot of the hole at the last. In 2006 at Medinah, he finished second to Tiger Woods again in the USPGA Championship. Later he beat Woods en route to the final of the HSBC World Match Play at Wentworth but lost in the final to Paul Casey.

Milligan, Jim (SCO)

Born Irvine, Ayrshire, 15 June 1963

The 1988 Scottish Amateur champion had his moment of international glory in the 1989 Walker Cup which was won by the Great Britain and Ireland side for only the third time in the history of the event and for the first time on American soil. With GB&I leading by a point at Peachtree in Atlanta only Milligan and his experienced opponent Jay Sigel were left on the course. The American looked favourite to gain the final point and force a draw when two up with three to play but Milligan hit his approach from 100 yards to a few inches to win the 16th with a birdie then chipped in after both had fluffed chips to square at the 17th. The last was halved leaving the Great Britain and Ireland side historic winners by a point.

Mize, Larry (USA)

Born Augusta, Georgia, 23 September 1958
Turned professional 1980

Only local player ever to win the Masters and he did it in dramatic style holing a 140-foot pitch and run at the

Johnny Miller (USA)

Born San Francisco, California, 29 April 1947 Turned professional 1969

Now perhaps best known as an often insightful and invariably acerbic TV commentator for NBC in America, Miller won two major titles, The Open and the US Open, during the early Seventies when he was one of the leading players in world golf. Like a comet, Miller's game burned brightly for a short period of time. During 1974, when he won five of the first 11 events on the PGA Tour, and 1975 he won 12 tournaments in total and was the most successful player in the game, earning a clothing sponsorship deal worth $1million. He recalls that period of grace as a "sort of golfing Nirvana."

The high point of his career came at Royal Birkdale in 1976 when he followed in the footsteps of Tony Lema, a fellow member of the Olympic Club in San Francisco, and lifted the Claret Jug. He thwarted both Seve Ballesteros and Jack Nicklaus by the judicious use of a 1 iron off the tee which helped the American card a closing round of 66 and win the championship by six shots. He was also second behind Tom Weiskopf at Royal Troon in 1973. That was the season he secured victory in the US Open in spite of trailing the leader by six shots after 54 holes. He started the final round at Oakmont with four consecutive birdies and eventually posted 63 – the lowest closing score ever recorded in America's national championship. He found all 18 greens in regulation and racked up nine birdies after firing ten of his approach shots inside 15 feet.

After his success at Birkdale, however, Miller wouldn't win another tournament until 1980. He lost the burning desire to win which spurs on the greatest players and became a victim of the yips. Putting with his eyes closed for much of the time, Miller was a grandfather when he won his last PGA Tour event, the AT&T Pebble Beach Pro-Am in 1994. All told, he won 32 events as a professional around the world after first making a name for himself as an amateur in the Sixties by winning the US Junior Amateur title. A member of the World Golf Hall of Fame, he owns a golf design company.

second extra hole to edge out Greg Norman and Seve Ballesteros. He had made the play-off by holing a 10-foot birdie on the final green. In 1993 he beat an international field to take the Johnnie Walker World Championship title at Tryall in Jamaica. His middle name is Hogan.

Molinari, Edoardo (ITA)

Born Turin, 11 February 1981
Turned professional 2006

Became the first Italian to win the US Amateur Championship when he beat Dillon Dougherty 4 and 3 in the 2005 final at Merion, Pennsylvania. The 24-year-old, who has earned an engineering degree in his home country, joined his brother Francesco on the European Tour in 2006. He and his brother represented Italy in the 2007 and 2009 World Cup of Golf at Mission Hills in Shenzhen, China and were successful the second time. In 2009 he won three times and topped the Challenge Tour and then, a few weeks later, won the Dunlop Phoenix Tournament in Japan beating Robert Karlsson in a play-off. In 2010 he won twice in Scotland at Loch Lomond and Gleneagles where he finished with three birdies to join his brother in the 2010 Ryder Cup team. He was troubled by a wrist injury last year and slipped from 15th in the rankings in 2010 to a spot outside the top 200 in 2012.

Molinari, Francesco (ITA)

Born Turin, 8 November 1982
Turned professional 2004

Brother of Eduardo Molinari, winner of the US Amateur in 2005, he won his first European Tour title when he took the Italian Open at Castello di Tolcinasco in 2006. Partnering his brother Eduardo he gave Italy a first win in the World Cup of Golf in 2009. A year later he made his Ryder Cup début with his brother at Celtic Manor in 2010 and a few weeks later duelled with and beat the then World No 1 Lee Westwood in the WGC–HSBC Champions event in Shanghai. Played for the Continent in the Vivendi Seve Trophy in 2011 and enjoyed another consistent season last year, winning the Spanish Open as well as posting eight top ten finishes. He earned a half point against Tiger Woods in the final singles match at Medinah in 2012 to ensure Europe won the Ryder Cup.

Montgomerie OBE, Colin (SCO)

Born Glasgow, 23 June 1963
Turned professional 1987

Europe's most consistent golfer who topped the Order of Merit an unprecedented seven years in a row between 1993 and 1999 and again in 2004. He never won a major but came close several times particularly in the US Open He lost a play-off for the US title to Ernie Els in 1994, was pipped by the South African again in 1997 and was joint second behind Geoff Ogilvy in 2006. In 1992 he was third to Tom Kite. He has come close in The Open and the US PGA Championship as well. He was Open runner-up to Tiger Woods in 2005 at St Andrews and in 1995 he was beaten in a play-off for the USPGA Championship at the Riviera CC in Los Angeles by Australian Steve Elkington who birdied the last three holes to force a play-off and the first extra hole to beat him.. He has had 31 victories around the world and has played with distinction in seven Ryder Cups matches. In 2010 he captained the side to victory at Celtic Manor. He has twice won the Association of Golf Writers' Golfer of the Year award and has been three times Golfer of the Year in Europe. He was honoured by Her Majesty the Queen for his record-breaking golfing exploits with an MBE which was later upgraded to OBE. In 2007 he teamed up with Marc Warren to win the World Cup of Golf at Mission Hills in China. It was Scotland's first win in the 54-year history of the event. For one reason or another he has found it difficult to hit his best form in the past two years but, free of his Ryder Cup duties, he is determined to move back up the world rankings after dropping from inside the top 50 to outside the top 400. As an amateur he played in the 1985 and 1987 matches and is a former Scottish amateur champion.

Nagle, Kel (AUS)

Born North Sydney, 21 December 1920
Turned professional 1946

In the dramatic Centenary Open at St Andrews in 1960 he edged out Arnold Palmer, winner already that year of the Masters and US Open, to become champion. It was the finest moment in the illustrious career of a golfer who has been a wonderful ambassador for his country. Along with Peter Thomson he competed nine times in the World Cup winning the event in 1954. He is an honorary member of the Royal and Ancient Golf Club of St Andrews and was inducted into the World Golf Hall of Fame in 2007.

Nelson, Larry (USA)

Born Fort Payne, Alabama, 10 September 1947
Turned professional 1971

Often underrated he learned to play by reading Ben Hogan's The Five Fundamentals of Golf and broke 100 first time out and 70 after just nine months. Active as well these days on course design he has won the Jack Nicklaus award. He has been successful in the US Open (1983 at Oakmont) and two USPGA Championships (in 1981 at the Atlanta Athletic Club and in 1987 after a play-off with Lanny Wadkins at PGA National). Three times a Ryder Cup player he has competed equally successfully as a Senior having won 15 titles. He did not play as a youngster but visited a driving range after completing his military service and was hooked. He was named Senior PGA Tour Player of the Year for finishing top earner and winning six times in 2000. At the end of his third full season on the Senior Tour and after 87 events he had won just short of $10 million.

Newton, Jack (AUS)

Born Sydney, 30 January 1950
Turned professional 1969

Runner-up to Tom Watson after a play-off in the 1975 Open at Carnoustie and runner-up to Seve Ballesteros in the 1980 Masters at Augusta, he was a popular personality on both sides of the Atlantic and in his native Australia only to have his playing career ended prematurely when he walked into the whirling propeller of a plane at Sydney airport. He lost an eye, an arm and had considerable internal injuries but the quick action of a surgeon who happened to be around saved his life. Learned to play one-handed and still competes in pro-ams successfully. Until his retirement in 2000 he was chairman of the Australasian Tour and for many years was Australia's most respected golf commentator in the days when Channel Seven organised the coverage.

Nirat, Chapchai (THA)

Born Pitsanulok. Thailand, 5 June 1983
Turned professional 1998

Scored his first European Tour International circuit victory when he led from start to finish in the the TCL Classic. He was the 13th Asian to win and was the ninth first-time winner of the 2007 season. He covered the first 36 holes in 127 (61, 66).

Nobilo, Frank (NZL)

Born Auckland, 14 May 1960
Turned professional 1979

Injury affected his playing career but he remains one of his country's most popular commentators with the Golf Channel. After winning regularly in Europe he moved to America where in 1997 he won the Greater Greensboro Classic. He has represented New Zealand in nine World Cup matches between 1982 and 1999, played in 11 Alfred Dunhill Cups and three Presidents Cup sides. In 2009 he was deputy captain to Greg Norman for the Rest of the World team.

Noh Seung-Yul (KOR)

Born Seoul 29 May 1991
Turned professional 2007

Korean Junior Amateur and Amateur champion in 2005 Noh won his first professional event in 2008 at the Midea China Classic. He did even better in 2010 when he played a superb pitch at the last to beat KJ Choi in the Maybank Malaysian Masters which qualified him for a European Tour card. In his first season he finished 34th in the Race to Dubai and topped the Asian Tour's Order of Merit.

North, Andy (USA)

Born Thorp, Wisconsin, 9 March 1950
Turned professional 1972

Although this tall American found it difficult to win Tour events he did pick up two US Open titles. His first Championship success came at Cherry Hills in Denver in 1986 when he edged out Dave Stockton and J.C. Snead and the second at Oakland Hills in 1985 when he finished just a shot ahead of Dave Barr, T.C. Chen and Denis Watson who had been penalised a shot during the Championship for waiting longer than the regulation 10 seconds at one hole to see if his ball would drop into the cup. North is now a golf commentator.

Jack Nicklaus (USA)

Born Columbus, Ohio, 21 January 1940
Turned professional 1961

In the course of a phenomenal playing career which spanned five decades and included 18 victories as a professional in the majors as well as 118 tournament wins around the world, the Golden Bear has been hailed as the outstanding golfer of the 20th century and perhaps the greatest player who ever lived. His career in golf was so illustrious that the magazine, *Sports Illustrated*, chose Nicklaus as the outstanding individual male athlete of the previous century in any sport.

As a fair haired bear of a boy with broad shoulders, a crew cut and the seeds of a revolutionary power game, Jack William Nicklaus from Ohio, in his autobiography, remembers his teenage self as junior version of "the ugly American". If that judgement from the elder statesman seems blunt, he developed the habits of an unrelenting serial winner as an amateur which served him well throughout his professional career. He won his first US national title at 17, made the cut in the US Open at 18 and, as a 19-year-old, won the US Amateur, played in a winning US Walker Cup side at Muirfield and reached the quarter-finals of The Amateur at Royal St George's.

Billed by the American media as "the kid who can beat the pros", in 1960 he was 13th at the Masters as well as runner-up to Arnold Palmer in the US Open at Cherry Hills, where he set a record score for an amateur. Before joining the paid ranks, he won the US Amateur again, was part of a winning US Walker Cup side on home turf and recorded another top four finish at the 1961 US Open.

If the success of his amateur career placed an onerous burden on Nicklaus when he joined the paid ranks in 1962, his first season as a pro made light of that load. From the moment he made his first start in the Los Angeles Open, Nicklaus set the bench mark for a rookie season in golf. He finished in the top ten 16 times and won three tournaments – notably the US Open at Oakmont, only his 17th event as a pro – where he defeated Arnold Palmer in a play-off. In a sign of what was to come in the championships which matter most, he also finished 15th at the Masters, 32nd at the Open and third at the US PGA.

By the time he crossed the Swilken Bridge for the last time in his final major appearance in The Open at St Andrews in 2005, he'd completed an astonishing record of achievment. He won The Open in 1966, 1970 and 1978, the last two at St Andrews. He was runner-up in the oldest major seven times and third on two further occasions. He followed up that US Open win in 1962 with more victories in 1967, 1972 and 1980 and came second four times. He won five US PGA titles in 1963, 1971, 1973, 1975 and 1980 and was runner-up four times and third on two further occasions. He won six Masters in 1963, 1965, 1966, 1972, 1975 and 1986 when, at the age of 46, he became the oldest champion to slip into a Green Jacket. In addition he was runner-up four times and twice third at Augusta. In 1966 he became the first player to successfully defend the Masters. When he retired from competition, Nicklaus had become the only golfer in history to win each of the majors at least three times.

Outisde the majors, he won the Players Championship three times, no fewer than six Australian Opens and played in six Ryder Cups, winning on five occasions, captaining two more in 1983 at Palm Beach Gardens when America won narrowly and in 1987 at Muirfield Village where his side were losers for the first time on home soil.

A shrewd thinker about the game, it was his idea Continental golfers should be included alongside British and Irish players in a European side from 1979. The change transformed the Ryder Cup. Ten years earlier, in a memorable act of sportsmanship, he conceded the 18-inch putt that Tony Jacklin needed to hole for a half at the last when the overall result of the match depended on the result of that game. "I don't think you would have missed," he told the Englishman, "but in the circumstances I would never give you the opportunity".

After winning 73 times on the PGA Tour, he won a further ten times on the US Champions Tour between 1990 and 1996. He has garnered every honour in golf including the Byron Nelson, Ben Hogan and Walter Hagen awards. He was the US top money earner in 1964, 1965, 1967, 1971, 1972, 1973, 1975 and 1976 and is an honorary member of the Royal and Ancient Golf Club of St Andrews. Bobby Jones once said of Nicklaus that 'he played a game with which I am not familiar'. With the constant support of his wife Barbara, Nicklaus has been the personification of all that is good about the game. He joined Arnold Palmer as an honorary starter at the Masters in 2010.

Nicklaus is also a renowned golf course architect who was instrumental in forging the signature design business. So far, he's designed 280 courses world-wide and his company, Nicklaus Design, has 350 courses open for play. He's captained the US Presidents Cup side against the Rest of the World on four occasions so far and when the match is held at his beloved Muirfield Village in 2013 it will mark " my last involvement in anything significant in the game of golf."

Greg Norman (AUS)

Born Mount Isa, Queensland, 10 February 1955
Turned professional 1976

Three times the leading money winner on the PGA Tour, the Australian spent 331 weeks as world No 1 during a career in which he won 91 professional tournaments around the globe. The undoubted highlights of a successful career were his triumphs in 1986 and 1993 at The Open. The fact that he finished in the top ten at the four professional majors on no fewer than 29 occasions – more than 38 per cent of the championships he entered – stands as testimony to his consistency of performance.

If there's a debate that he lost majors he should have won, Norman's most noteworthy achievements came at Turnberry, where he carded a remarkable score of 63 as part of a five shot victory, and at Royal St George's, where his closing 64 set a low winning aggregate of 264 and overcame Nick Faldo by two strokes.

Fair and handsome as well as long off the tee, Norman was handed the moniker of "Great White Shark" during a staging of the Masters in 1981. The nickname was apt and today Norman's various business interests are named Great White Shark Enterprises. Perhaps an even more successful entrepreneur than he was a golfer, Norman didn't take up the sport until he was 15. He'd caddied for his mother and asked to borrow her clubs. Two years later he was a scratch player. He won for the first time as a pro in Australia at the West Lakes Classic in 1976, won the Martini in Europe a year later and first made his mark in the US at the Kemper in 1984. All told he won 20 times on the PGA Tour as well as 71 other events around the world.

For all his success, he also gained a reputation for coming up short in the biggest championships. He lost out in three different types of major play-offs – the 1987 Masters to Larry Mize and the 1993 US PGA to Paul Azinger in sudden death, The Open to Mark Calcavecchia at Royal Troon in a four-hole play-off in 1989 and the US Open over 18 holes to Fuzzy Zoeller at Winged Foot in 1984. In 1986 he led going into the final round of all four majors and won once. Perhaps his most painful loss was at the Masters in 1996 when he led by six strokes going into the final round and lost to Faldo by five shots.

Norman turned the clock back in 2008 at Birkdale to finish third behind Padraig Harrington in The Open after leading with nine holes to play. In 2011 and 2009 he captained the Rest of the World against America in the Presidents Cup. Due to business interests and back issues, he now only plays a handful of events each year.

O'Connor Sr, Christy (IRL)

Born Galway, 21 December 1924
Turned professional 1946

Never managed to win The Open but came close on three occasions finishing runner-up to Peter Thomson in 1965 and being third on two other occasions. Played in ten Ryder Cup matches between 1955 and 1973 and scored 24 wins in tournament play between 1955 and 1972. Known affectionately as 'Himself' by Irish golfing fans who have long admired his talent with his clubs. He is a brilliant shot maker. He is an Honorary Member of the PGA European Tour. In 2006 a special dinner was staged in his honour in Dublin by the Irish Food Board on the eve of the Ryder Cup. In 2009 he was inducted into the World Golf Hall of Fame.

O'Connor Jr, Christy (IRL)

Born Galway, 19 August 1948
Turned professional 1965

Nephew of Christy Sr, he finished third in the 1985 Open Championship. A winner on the European and Safari circuits he won the 1999 and 2000 Senior British Open – only the second man to successfully defend. Played in two Ryder Cup matches hitting a career best 2-iron to the last green at The Belfry in 1989 to beat Fred Couples and ensure a drawn match enabling Europe to keep the trophy. His US Champions Tour career was interrupted when he broke a leg in a motorcycle accident.

Ogilvy, Geoff (AUS)

Born Adelaide, South Australia
Turned professional 1998

He became the first Australian to win a major since Steve Elkington's success in the USPGA Championship in 1992 when he won the US Open at Winged Foot beating Colin Montgomerie, Jim Furyk and Phil Mickelson into second place. In 2007 he was beaten by Henrik Stenson in the final of the Accenture Match Play Championship and finished 14th on the US money list. In 2009 he won the Accenture Match-play Championship beating Paul Casey in the final and in 2010 won the Australian Open for the first time.

Olazábal, José María (ESP)

Born Fuenterrabia, 5 February 1966
Turned professional 1985

Twice a winner of the Masters, his second triumph was particularly emotional. He had won in 1994 but had to withdraw from the 1995 Ryder Cup with a foot problem eventually diagnosed as rheumatoid polyarthritis in three joints of the right foot and two of the left. He was out of golf for 18 months but treatment from Munich doctor Hans-Wilhelm Muller-Wohlfahrt helped him back to full fitness after a period when he was house bound and unable to walk. At that point it seemed as if his career was over, but he came back in 1999 to beat Davis Love III by two shots at Augusta. With over 20 victories in Europe and a further seven abroad, the son of a Real Sebastian greenkeeper who took up the game at the age of four has been one of the most popular players in the game. He competed in seven Ryder Cups between 1987 and 2006 frequently forming the most successful Cup partnership with Severiano Ballesteros winning 11 and losing only two of their 15 games together. He was Nick Faldo's backroom assistant at Valhalla in 2008 and will captain the side at some time in the future. Although he was side-lined again through rheumatic injury in 2008 he still believes he can make the side in 2010. He is a former British Boys', Youths' and Amateur champion. His best performances in The Open have been third behind Nick Faldo in the 1992 Championship at Muirfield and behind Tiger Woods in the 2005 event at St Andrews. Olazábal, who played on both sides of the Atlantic in 2005, finished 10th on the European Money list finishing strongly with a 2nd place finish in the Linde German Masters, victory in the Open de Mallorca and a third place behind Paul McGinley in the Volvo Masters of Andalucia. In 2006 he regained his place in the Ryder Cup team and played well with Sergio García in the fourballs, winning twice. He beat Phil Mickelson in the singles. He is now an irregular competitor on the European and PGA Tours as a result of his continuing rheumatic problems. In 2009 Olazabal, one of the most courageous of competitors, was inducted into the World Golf Hall of Fame. He asked close friend Severiano Ballesteros to do the oration. He was captain of the winning European Ryder Cup side at Medinah where he dedicated the victory to the memory of Ballesteros, who passed away in 2011. Olazabal described the experience as "torture".

O'Leary, John (IRL)

Born Dublin, 19 August 1949
Turned professional 1979

After a successful career as a player including victory in the Carrolls Irish Open in 1982 he retired because of injury and now is director of golf at the Buckinghamshire Club. He is a member of the PGA European Tour Board of Directors.

O'Meara, Mark (USA)

Born Goldsboro, North Carolina, 13 January 1957
Turned professional 1980

A former US Amateur Champion in 1979 Mark was 41 when he won his first Major – the US Masters at Augusta. That week in 1998 he did not three putt once on Augusta's glassy greens. Three months later he won The Open at Royal Birkdale battling with, among others, Tiger Woods with whom he has had a particular friendship. He is the oldest player to win two Majors in the same year and was chosen as PGA Player of the Year that season. When he closed birdie, birdie to win the Masters he joined Arnold Palmer and Art Wall as the only players to do that and became only the fifth player in Masters history to win without leading in the first three rounds. He won his Open championship title in a four hole play-off against Brian Watts. O'Meara played in five Ryder Cups between 1985 and 1999.

Oosterhuis, Peter (ENG)

Born London, 3 May 1948 Turned professional 1968

Twice runner up in The Open Championship in 1974 and 1982, he was also the leading British player in 1975 and 1978. He finished third in the US Masters in 1973, had multiple wins on the European Tour and in Africa and won the Canadian Open on the US Tour in 1981. He played in six Ryder Cups partnering Nick Faldo at Royal Lytham and St Annes in 1977 when Faldo made his début. He was top earner in Europe four years in a row from 1971. Following his retirement from top-line golf he turned to commentary work for the Golf Channel CBS and SKY. His contribution to European professional golf is frequently underrated.

Oosthuizen, Louis (RSA)

Born Mossel Bay, 19 October 1982
Turned professional 2003

One of the chosen few who have won The Open at St Andrews – he has Bobby Jones, Jack Nicklaus, Nick Faldo and Tiger Woods for company. His victory in the 150th anniversary staging of the game's oldest championship was as comprehensive as it was unexpected. Oosthuizen won by seven strokes from Lee Westwood in what was only his ninth appearance in a majors. He joined Bobby Locke, Gary Player and Ernie Els in the small band of South Africans who have their names on the Claret Jug. A graduate of the Ernie Els Foundation, Oosthuizen won the Irish Amateur and together with Charl Schwartzel won the World Junior Team Championship for South Africa before turning professional. He once shot 57 over his home course at Mossel Bay and had to persuade his family, who have strong connections with tennis, that he wanted to be a golfer. He enjoyed his breakthrough win on the European Tour in 2010 at the Open de Andalucia.

Ozaki, 'Jumbo' Masashi (JPN)

Born Kaiman Town, Tokushima, 24 January 1947
Turned professional 1980

Along with Isao Aoki is Japan's best known player, but unlike Aoki has maintained his base in Japan where he has scored over 80 victories. His only overseas win was the New Zealand Open early in his career. He is a golfing icon in his native country. His two brothers Joe (Naomichi) and Jet also play professionally. In 2005 he was declared bankrupt. In

2011 he was elected into the World Golf Hall of Fame.

Pagunsan, Juvic (PHI)

Born Manila, 11 May 1978
Turned professional 2006

Winner of the Asian Tour of Merit in 2011, he was the first golfer from the Phillipines to achieve that status. Although he didn't win in 2011, his second place finish after a play-off at the Barclays Singapore Open, where he won $666,660, propelled him to the top spot on the money list. Taught by his father, Juanito, Juvic took up the game at 13 and was a successful amateur, winning the Phillipine, Thailand and Malaysian championships in 2005. He joined the paid ranks a year later and his first win on the Asian Tour was the Pertamina Indonesia President Invitational in 2007.

Parnevik, Jesper (SWE)

Born Danderyd, Stockholm, 7 March 1965
Turned professional 1986

Son of a well-known Swedish entertainer he is one of the most extrovert of golfers best known for his habit of wearing a baseball cap with the brim turned up and brightly coloured drain-pipe style trousers. Winner of events on both sides of the Atlantic he plays most of his golf these days in America. He made history in 1995 when he became the first Swede to win in Sweden when he took the Scandinavian Masters at Barsebäck in Malmo. Has twice finished runner-up in The Open. At Turnberry in 1994 he was two ahead but made a bogey at the last and was passed by Nick Price who finished with an eagle and a birdie in the last three holes. He led by two with a round to go in 1998 but shot 73 and finished tied second with Darren Clarke behind Justin Leonard at Royal Troon. Played in the 1997 and 1999 Ryder Cup teaming up successfully with Sergio García to win three and a half points in 1999. Was also in the 2002 team and halved with Tiger Woods in the singles. He has had two hip operations and at one stage began eating volcanic dust to cleanse his system.

Parry Craig (AUS)

Born Sunshine, Victoria, Australia, 12 January 1966
Turned professional 1985

Australian Parry, winner of 18 titles internationally including the 2002 World Golf Championship NEC Invitational at Sahalee in Washington where he picked up his largest career cheque – $1 million. After 15 years of trying to win in America the chances of him being successful at Salahee seemed slim having missed the four previous cuts. However, the 300–1 long-shot played and putted beautifully covering the last 48 holes without making a bogey to win by four from another Australian Robert Allenby and American Fred Funk. Tiger Woods, trying to win the event for a record fourth-successive year was fourth. Only Gene Sarazen and Walter Hagen have ever won the same four titles in successive years. It was Parry's 236th tournament in the United States and moved him from 118th in the world to 45th. In 2004 he eagled the hardest hole on the US Tour in a play-off with Scott Verplank to win the Ford Championship in Florida.

Pate, Jerry (USA)

Born Macon, Georgia, 16 September 1953
Turned professional 1975

Winner of the 1976 US Open when he hit a 5-iron across water to three feet at the 72nd hole at the Atlanta Athletic Club. He was a member of what is regarded as the strongest ever Ryder Cup side that beat the Europeans at Walton Heath in 1981. Has now retired from golf and commentates occasionally on American television.

Pavin, Corey (USA)

Born Oxnard, California, 26 May 1961
Turned professional 1983

Although not one of golf's longer hitters he battled with powerful Greg Norman to take the 1995 US Open title at Shinnecock Hills. A runner-up in the 1994 USPGA Championship and third in the 1992 US Masters he won 14 times between 1984 and 2006. His only victory in Europe came when he took the German Open title in 1983 while on honeymoon. In 2006, he ended a ten-year winning drought by taking the US Bank Championship in Milwaukee and was one of Tom Lehman's vice-captains at the Ryder Cup at the K Club. He was selected to captain the US Ryder Cup side which lost by a point at Celtic Manor in 2010.

Perry, Kenny (USA)

Born Elizabethtown, Kentucky, 10 August 1960
Turned professional 1982

After winning for times between 1991 and 2001, he had a marvellous 2003 winning the Bank of America Colonial, the Memorial Tournament and the Greater Milwaukee Open between May 25 and July 13. He made his Ryder Cup début at Detroit in 2004 having played in the 1996, 2003 and 2005 Presidents Cups. In 2008 he deliberately by-passed two major Championships in order to ensure he had a place in Paul Azinger's Ryder Cup side for the match against Europe at Valhalla in his home state of Kentucky. He achieved his goal and played with considerable success. He tied with Angel Cabrera and Chad Campbell after 72 holes of the 2009 Masters Tournament but lost the play-off. Campbell went out at the first extra hole and Cabrera won The Green Jacket at the second extra hole.

Phadungsil, Chinarat (THA)

Born Bangkok, Thailand
Turned professional 2005

He became the youngest winner on the Asian Tour when he beat Shiv Kapur at the second hole of their play-off for the Double A International title at the St Andrews Hill (2000) GC in Rayong, Thailand. The reigning World Junior champion, he was only 17 years

Arnold Palmer (USA)

Born Latrobe, Pennsylvania, 10 September 1929 Turned professional 1954

It is a measure of the charismatic appeal of Arnold Palmer that when *GQ* magazine listed the 25 "coolest" athletes of all time in 2011, the golfer from Latrobe should figure in the countdown some 38 years after his last PGA Tour win. For all the considerable success he enjoyed in the late Fifties and early Sixties, winning seven major titles between 1958 and 1964, it was the manner in which Palmer played the game rather than the championships he won which sealed his reputation. A handsome man with a thrillingly aggressive approach to the game, Palmer was hugely popular with the global audience for golf and when his competitive days were behind him he was able to build a lifelong career as a businessman and course designer because he connected so effectively with the public.

Palmer's high profile coincided with the expansion of televised golf. Unlike the more consistent power play produced by his rival and friend Jack Nicklaus, Palmer's risk-taking generated excitement for TV viewers. His flamboyant style duly helped to grow interest in the game as a spectator sport, both in America and around the world. At Augusta, "Arnie's Army" tracked his every move at The Masters while in Britain his decision to play in the oldest major is credited with helping Keith Mackenzie, then the secretary of the Royal and Ancient Golf Club of St Andrews, revive the fortunes of The Open. Palmer is now a distinguished honorary member of The R&A as well as Augusta National.

Born in Pennsylvania, he was taught by his father, Deacon, the professional and greenkeeper at Latrobe, before attending Wake Forest University on a golf scholarship. His amateur career between 1946 and 1954 delivered 26 victories, including the US Amateur title. After the death of his friend Bud Worsham, he spent three years with the US coastguard. Palmer then decided to try his luck as a professional. He recalls the season of 1954 as the turning point in his life, that victory in the US Amateur coinciding with the moment when the golf press first noticed his go-for-broke style, the habit of hitching up his pants as he walked the fairway and the open manner in which he shared his emotions and engaged with spectators. It was the summer when lightning struck.

In the early years of his career as a pro, Palmer was an irresistible force. His most dominant period was between 1960 and 1963 when he won 29 PGA Tour events in four seasons. In 1960 having already won The Masters and US Open he came to St Andrews for the Centenary Open, hoping to become the first golfer since Ben Hogan in 1953 to win three majors in a season. Although he lost out to Kel Nagle, Palmer would return to the British linksland and win consecutive stagings of The Open in 1961 and 1962. It was those victories which turned Palmer into an international sporting icon rather than just an American celebrity.

Along with Nicklaus and Gary Player he was a member of the Big Three – a concept developed by his manager, the late Mark McCormack – who signed Palmer as IMG's first client. It was the Big Three who effectively created the commercial environment which has made golf such a lucrative sport around the world. All told, Palmer won 61 tournaments in America and 92 around the world, including The Masters of 1958, 1960,1962 and 1964; the US Open of 1960 and the brace of Claret Jugs. He was second in the US PGA three times and narrowly missed out on the career Grand Slam. He played in six Ryder Cups and was US captain twice. He also captained the US in the 1996 Presidents Cup. He was the leading money winner on the PGA Tour four times. Palmer retired from competitive golf in October 2006.

At 81, he still features among the highest earners in the game. Palmer helped to launch the now hugely successful Golf Channel in the United States and presents the Palmer Cup for annual competition between the best young college golfers in America and Europe. He is an honorary starter at The Masters. The owner of Latrobe Country Club as well as Bay Hill in Orlando, he is arguably the most successfully marketed sportsman of all time.

and 5 days when he won that title and immediately turned professional.

Poulter, Ian (ENG)

Born Hitchen, England, 10 January 1976
Turned professional 1994

One of golf's most extrovert personalities who insists he wants to be noticed for his golfing talent rather than his hairstyles and colourful clothing. Runner-up to Padraig Harrington in The Open at Royal Birkdale in 2008 he was a captain's pick on Nick Faldo's Ryder Cup side later that year at Valhalla. Europe lost but he was top scorer from either side. He also played in the 2004 and 2010 teams. In 2007 he was successful in Japan winning the Dunlop Phoenix event and in 2010 won for the first time on the PGA Tour in America when he beat Paul Casey in the final of the WGC Accenture Matchplay Championship in Arizona. Now based in Lake Nona, Florida he was in a play-off for the Dubai World Championship in 2010 and incurred a penalty when he inadvertently dropped his ball on

Gary Player (RSA)

Born Johannesburg, 1 November 1935 Turned professional 1953

South Africa's pre-eminent sportsman of the 20th century, he celebrated his 50th anniversary as a professional in 2003 and continues to enjoy international admiration for a glorious career which saw the golfer win 176 titles around the world. The highlights of his playing days came in the majors where he won nine championships between 1959 and 1978 as well as nine senior major titles between 1986 and 1997. As the world's most travelled sportsman, clocking up over 14 million air miles, he won at least one tournament in 27 consecutive seasons.

Tipping 5ft 7ins and weighing 11 stone, he was often said to have done more with less than any other player. As well as introducing a revolutionary fitness programme to increase distance, Player's strength of mind was his most enduring asset. His craving for success was insatiable.

Although his swing was flat, Player was one of the most accomplished bunker players the game has ever seen. This prolific winner claimed the Claret Jug on three occasions, in 1959 at Muirfield, 1968 at Carnoustie and 1974 at Royal Lytham and St Annes. He's the only 20th century golfer who succeeded in winning The Open in three different decades.

He also won The Masters three times in 1961, 1974 and 1978, the US PGA championship in 1962 and 1972, and completed the Grand Slam of major titles when he succeeded at the US Open in 1965. His victory that summer at Bellrive at the age of 29, after a play-off against Kel Nagle, was the first by an international player since Ted Ray in 1920. Tiger Woods, Jack Nicklaus, Ben Hogan and Gene Sarazen are the only other players to win all four professional majors.

After taking up the sport at 14, Player spent much of his time during his teenage years on the golf course where all those diligent hours of practice made him a solid judge of distance and a perceptive reader of greens. Perhaps his greatest gift, though, was his indomitability. Player simply never gave up. When he won his first Open at Muirfield – this was in the era when the competitors played 36 holes on the last day – he started the third round eight strokes behind the leader. "Gary has that thing inside him, as much as anyone I ever saw, that champions have," observed Nicklaus.

Player's knack of winning tournaments from situations which many of his peers would have regarded as hopeless was perhaps best illustrated at The Masters in 1974 when, at 42, he went into the last round trailing Hubert Green by seven strokes. However, the South African came home in 30 and equalled the then record score of 64. He birdied seven of the last ten holes at Augusta to win by a stroke.

He was also once seven down to Tony Lema after 19 holes in the semi-final of the World Match Play in 1965 before securing safe passage into the final, where he defeated Peter Thomson, at the first extra hole. "My opponents knew I was like a bull terrier," he said. "I never gave up." One of the exceptional match-play golfers, Player won the World Match Play five times.

The son of a miner and a mother who died when he was eight, Player became a pro at 18 and won his first title, the Egyptian Match Play, in 1955. He liked to wear all black outfits and was one of the first golfers to rely on an exercise programme and a high fibre diet to improve his physique and hit the ball further. It was a regime which helped him to win the Australian Open seven times, the South African Open 13 times and sign for 59 in the 1974 Brazilian Open.

In 2006, he received the Payne Stewart award for his services to golf and charity work, especially in Africa. He has been a captain of the Rest of the World team in the Presidents Cup on three occasions. One of the game's 'Big Three' in the Sixties along with Nicklaus and Arnold Palmer, Player today has widespread global business interests through his company Black Knight International.

his marker causing it to move.The highlight of his career to date came at Medinah in the 2012 Ryder Cup when he was the match's outstanding player, winning four points out of four and inspiring Europe to an improbable comeback victory.

Price, Nick (ZIM)

Born Durban, South Africa, 28 January 1957
Turned professional 1977

One of the game's most popular players his greatest season was 1994 when he took six titles including The Open at Turnberry when he beat Jesper Parnevik and the USPGA at Southern Hills when Corey Pavin was second. He had scored his first Major triumph two years earlier when he edged out John Cook, Nick Faldo, Jim Gallagher Jr and Gene Sauers at the USPGA at Bellerive, St Louis. Along with Tiger Woods his record of 15 wins in the 90s was the most by any player. One of only eight players to win consecutive Majors, the others being Ben Hogan, Jack Nicklaus, Arnold Palmer, Lee Trevino, Tom Watson, Tiger Woods and Padraig Harrington. Four times a Presidents Cup player he jointly holds the Augusta National record of 63 with Greg Norman. One of only two players in the 90s to win two Majors in a year, the others being Nick Faldo in 1990 and Mark O'Meara in 1998. Born of English parents but brought up in Zimbabwe he played his early golf with Mark McNulty and Tony Johnstone. He was named recipient in 2002 of the Payne Stewart Award which goes to the player who respects the traditions of the game and works to uphold them. In 2003, ten years after being named PGA Tour Player of the Year, he was inducted into the World Golf Hall of Fame.He will captain the International team against the USA at the Presidents Cup in 2013 at Muirfield Village.

Price, Phillip (WAL)

Born Pontypridd, 21 October 1966
Turned professional 1989

He made his Ryder Cup début in 2002 and produced a sterling last day performance when he beat the world No.2 Phil Mickelson 3 and 2 for a vital point. He played on the PGA Tour in 2005 with limited success and, back in Europe, has found it difficult to rediscover his old magic.

Quigley, Dana (USA)

Born Lynnfield Centre, Massachussetts, 14 April 1947
Turned professional 1971

Iron man of the US Champions Tour who played in 278 consecutive events for which he was qualified before missing the 2005 Senior British Open at Royal Aberdeen. He had passed the million dollars mark in prize-money by early June that year and with official money of $2,170,258 he topped the Champions Tour money list at the end of the season.

Quiros, Alvaro (ESP)

Born Cadiz, Spain, 21 January 1983
Turned professional 2004

The Spaniard became the first player in European Tour history to win on his first appearance when he won the 2007 dunhill championship at Leopard Creek in South Africa. He has won five times since then in Portugal, Qatar, Spain and Dubai twice. His victory at the Dubai World Championship in 2011 was the biggest of his career and earned him a cheque for more than €922,000. He has the reputation of being one of Europe's longest hitters averaging over 314 yards.

Rafferty, Ronan (NIR)

Born Newry, Northern Ireland, 13 January 1964
Turned professional 1981

He won the Irish Amateur Championship as a 16 year old in 1980 when he also won the English Amateur Open Stroke Play title, competed in the Eisenhower Trophy and played against Europe in the home internationals. Winner of the British Boys', Irish Youths' and Ulster Youths' titles in 1979, he also played in the senior Irish side against Wales that year. A regular winner on the European tour between 1988 and 1993 he was also victorious in tournaments played in South America, Australia and New Zealand. A wrist injury curtailed his career but he is active on the corporate golf front and has an impressive wine collection.

Ramsay, Richie (SCO)

Born Aberdeen, 15 June 1983
Turned professional 2007

A student at Stirling University he became the first Scot since 1898 and the first British golfer since 1911 to win the US Amateur Championship when he beat John Kelly from St Louis 4 and 2 in the final A member of the 2005 Great Britain and Ireland Walker Cup team, he has played in the Palmer Cup and was the winner of the 2004 Scottish Open Amateur Strokeplay title and the 2005 Irish Open Amateur Strokeplay event. He has shot a 62 at Murcar in Aberdeenshire. Ramsay turned professional after the 2007 Open, missing the chance to play again in the Walker Cup. He failed to survive the first stage of the European Tour School and competed on the 2008 Challenge Tour winning twice and earning his card for the main Tour in 2009 winning the 2010 South African Open at Pearl Valley.

Randhawa, Jyoti (IND)

Born New Delhi, 4 May 1972
Turned professional 1994

First Indian winner on the Japanese Tour when he triumphed in the 2003 Suntory Open. Son of an Indian general, he was top earner on the Asian PGA Tour in 2002 despite missing several events after breaking his collarbone in a motorcycle accident. Practices yoga and now plays on both the European and Asian Tours.

Remesy, Jean-François (FRA)

Born Nimes, 5 June 1964   *Turned professional 1987*

In 2004 he became the first Frenchman since Jean Garaialde in 1969 to win the Open de France then successfully defended the title the following year at Golf National, Versailles beating Jean Van de Velde in a play-off. Now lives in the Seychelles.

Rivero, José (ESP)

Born Madrid, 20 September 1955
Turned professional 1973

One of only eight Spaniards who have played in the Ryder Cup he was a member of the winning 1985 and 1987 sides. Worked as a caddie but received a grant from the Spanish Federation to pursue his golf career. With José Maria Canizares won the World Cup in 1984 at Olgiata in Italy.

Roberts, Loren (USA)

Born San Luis Obispo, California, 24 June 1955
Turned professional 1975

An eight times winner on the PGA Tour, he earned the nickname "Boss of the Moss" because of his exceptional putting. He played in two Presidents Cup matches and the 1995 Ryder Cup before joining the Champions Tour. He had chalked up seven wins by the end of 2007 and for the second year running had the low average score on that Tour – an impressive

69.31. In a play-off for the 2009 Senior Open at Sunningdale he beat Mark McNulty and Fred Funk to win the title for a second time.

Rocca, Costantino (ITA)

Born Bergamo, 4 December 1956
Turned professional 1981

The first and to date only Italian to play in the Ryder Cup. In the 1999 match at Valderrama he beat Tiger Woods 4 and 2 in a vital singles. Left his job in a polystyrene box making factory to become a club professional and graduated to the tournament scene through Europe's Challenge Tour. In 1995 he fluffed a chip at the final hole in The Open at St Andrews only to hole from 60 feet out of the Valley of Sin to force a play-off against John Daly which he then lost. Now plays on the European Senior Tour.

Rogers, Bill (USA)

Born Waco, Texas, 10 September 1951
Turned professional 1974

USPGA Player of the Year in 1981 when he won The Open at Royal St George's and was runner-up in the US Open. That year he also won the Australian Open but retired from top line competitive golf not long after because he did not enjoy all the travelling. A former Walker Cup player in 1973 he only entered The Open in 1981 at the insistence of Ben Crenshaw. Now a successful club professional and sometime television commentator.

Romero, Eduardo (ARG)

Born Cordoba, Argentina, 12 July 1954
Turned professional 1982

Son of the Cordoba club professional he learned much from former Open champion Roberto de Vicenzo and has inherited his grace and elegance as a competitor. A wonderful ambassador for Argentina he briefly held a US Tour card in 1994 but preferred to play his golf on the European Tour where he won seven times including the 1999 Canon European Masters. He improved his concentration after studying Indian yoga techniques. Used his own money to sponsor Angel Cabrera with whom he finished second in the 2000 World Cup in Buenos Aries behind Tiger Woods and David Duval. Joined the Senior ranks in July 2004 but still plays from time to time on the main European Tour. In 2008 he won the US Senior Open on the Champions Tour.

Rose, Justin (ENG)

Born Johannesburg, South Africa, 30 July 1980
Turned professional 1998

Walker Cup player who shot to attention in the 1998 Open Championship at Royal Birkdale when he finished top amateur and third behind winner Mark O'Meara after holing his third shot at the last on the final day for a closing birdie. Immediately after that Open he turned professional and missed his first 21 half-way cuts before finding his feet. In 2002 was a multiple winner in Europe and also won in Japan and South Africa. Delighted his father who watched him win the Victor Chandler British Masters just a few weeks before he died of leukaemia. He has played most of his golf in America in recent years shooting 60 at the Funai Classic at Walt Disney World in 2006. Although he played only the minimum 12 events on the European Tour in 2007, he won the end of season Volvo Masters at Valderrama to finish No 1 on the money list and became the highest ranked British golfer in the world ranking, moving into seventh place. Later in the year he partnered Ian Poulter into fourth place in the Mission Hills World Cup of Golf in China. He made his début in the Ryder Cup in the 2008 match at Valhalla but failed to make the 2010 side despite winning two titles on the PGA Tour including the prestigious Memorial event at Muirfield Village. In 2011 he won the BMW Championship. And in 2012 he returned to Ryder Cup action at Medinah where he pulled off a remarkable comeback in the singles against Phil Mickelson thanks to birdies over the closing two holes. It was Rose's best season to date with a WGC victory in the Cadillac and earnings of over $4 million on the PGA Tour.

Sandelin, Jarmo (SWE)

Born Imatra, Finland, 10 May 1967
Turned professional 1987

Extrovert Swede who made his début in the Ryder Cup at Brookline in 1999 although he did not play until the singles. Has always been a snazzy dresser on course where he is one of the game's longest hitters often using, in the early days, a 54-inch shafted driver. Five time winner on Tour he met his partner Linda when she asked to caddie for him at a Stockholm pro-am.

Schwartzel, Charl (RSA)

Born Johannesburg, 31 August 1984
Turned professional 2002

The first Masters champion ever to birdie all four of the closing holes at Augusta, Schwartzel savoured one of the most thrilling finishes seen at the majors when he posted a closing round of 66 to earn a two stroke victory over Australians Jason Day and Adam Scott. After claiming a Green Jacket, he was also ninth at the US Open, 16th at The Open and 12th at the US PGA in 2011. Since finishing 16th at the US Open in 2010 he's reeled off seven consecutive top 20 placings in the majors. Charl was playing off plus 4 when he turned professional after an amateur career that had seen him represent South Africa in the Eisenhower Trophy. In only his third event as a pro he finished joint third in the South African Airways Open and became a winner in his 56th event when he won the dunhill championship in a play-off at Leopard Creek. He was South African No 1 in season 2004–5 and was again No 1 in the 2005–6 season. In the 2007 European Tour season he won the Spanish Open but was winless in 2008 until he again played well in Spain to take the Madrid Masters title. He won the Joburg Open in 2010 and 2011 as well as the Africa Open in 2010. In 2012 he only posted two top finishes on the PGA Tour and the same number in Europe.

Scott, Adam (AUS)

Born Adelaide, 16 July 1980 Turned professional 2000

Esteemed Australian who was ranked

World No 2 as an amateur before he turned professional in 2000. Coached in the early days by his father Phil, himself a golf professional, Scott also once used Butch Harmon whom he met while attending the University of Las Vegas.. He made headlines as an amateur when he fired a 10-under-par 63 at the Lakes in the Greg Norman Holden International in 2000 but has shot 62 in the US Junior Championship at Los Coyotes CC. Made his European Tour card in just eight starts and secured his first Tour win when beating Justin Rose in the 2001 Alfred Dunhill Championship at Houghton in Johannesburg. In 2002 he won at Qatar and at Gleneagles Hotel when he won the Diageo Scottish PGA Championship by ten shots with a 26 under par total. He was 22 under par that week for the par 5 holes. In 2003 he was an impressive winner of the Scandinavian Masters at Barsebäck in Sweden and the Deutsche Bank Championship on the US Tour. In 2005 when he again played in the Presidents Cup, his victories included the Johnnie Walker Classic on the European and Asian Tours, the Singapore Open on the Asian Tour and the Nissan Open on the US Tour. In 2006, he won the Players Championship and Tour Championship in America moving to third in the World rankings in mid November. He also won the Singapore Open again. He continued to play well throughout 2008 but was less successful in 2009.He switched coaches and started working with Brad Malone, his brother-in-law. In 2010 he won the Valero Texas Open and in 2011, after switching to the belly putter, won the Bridgestone and finished runner-up at the Masters. In 2012 he led The Open by four strokes going into the final round at Royal Lytham only to card four bogeys over the closing holes and lose out to Ernie Els by a stroke.

Senior, Peter (AUS)

Born Singapore, 31 July 1959
Turned professional 1978

One of Australia's most likeable and underrated performers who has been a regular winner over the years on the Australian, Japanese and European circuits. Converted to the broomstick putter by Sam Torrance – a move that saved his playing career. A former winner of the Australian Open, Australian PGA and Australian Masters titles he had considerable success off the course when he bought a share in a pawn-broking business. Senior now plays irregularly outside Australia where he has taken over as chairman of the Autralasian Tour from Wayne Grady. In 2010 he won the Handa Australian Seniors title and Australian PGA title for a third time.

Sigel, Jay (USA)

Born Narbeth, Pennsylvania, 13 November 1943
Turned professional 1993

Winner of the Amateur Championship in 1979 when he beat Scott Hoch 3 and 2 at Hillside, he also won the US Amateur in 1982 and 1983. He was leading amateur in the US Open in 1984 and leading amateur in the US Masters in 1981, 1982 and 1988. He played in nine Walker Cup matches between 1977 and 1993 and has a record 18 points to his credit. Turned professional in order to join the US Senior Tour where he has had several successes.

Simpson, Scott (USA)

Born San Diego, California, 17 September 1955
Turned professional 1977

Winner of the US Open in 1987 at San Francisco's Olympic Club, he was beaten in a play-off for the title four years later at Hazeltine when the late Payne Stewart won the 18-hole play-off.

Simpson, Webb (USA)

Born Raleigh, North Carolina, 1985
Turned professional 2008

Thanks to a pair of 68s compiled on the week-end over an exceptionally tricky set-up at the Olympic golf club in San Francisco, Simpson won the US Open by a stroke from Graeme McDowell after setting the one over par mark of 281. His first major title was the highlight of a consistent year in which he finished in the top ten seven times. The previous year he earned nearly $5.8 million thanks to two wins in the space of just three weeks at the Wyndham and Deutche Bank championships. A talented amateur golfer, he was a member of the American Walker Cup team in 2007 which defeated Great Britain and Ireland at Royal County Down. He made his Ryder Cup début for the USA in 2012, winning two points at Medinah in the defeat from Europe.

Singh, Jeev Milkha (IND)

Born Chandigarh, India, 15 December 1971
Turned professional 1993

Stylish swinger, he won his first European event when he took the Volvo China Open in Beijing in 2006 but he scored an even greater triumph when he picked up the first prize at the Volvo Masters at Valderrama later in the year. He is the son of the former Olympian Milkha Singh who won a medal in the 1980 games. His victory in the 2007 Barclays Singapore Open enabled him to became the first player to make US $1 million in one season on the Asian Tour and helped him top the money list for the second time. His Singapore win also moved him into the top 50 in the world rankings for the second time. In 2012 he won the first prize of £470,000 at the Aberdeen Asset Scottish Open after defeating Francesco Molinari in a play-off.

Singh, Vijay (FIJ)

Born Lautoka, 22 February 1963
Turned professional 1982

An international player who began his career in Australasia, he became the first Fijian to win a major when he won the 1998 USPGA Championship at Sahalee but may well be remembered more for his victory in the 2000 US Masters which effectively prevented Tiger Woods winning all four Majors in a year. Tiger went on to win the US Open, Open and USPGA Championship that year and won the Masters the following year to hold all four Major titles at the one time. Introduced to golf by his father, an aeroplane technician, Vijay modelled his swing on that of Tom Weiskopf. Before making the grade on the European Tour where he won the 1992 Volvo German Open by 11 shots he was a club professional in Borneo. He has won tournaments in South Africa, Malaysia, the Ivory Coast, Nigeria, France, Zimbabwe, Morocco, Spain, England, Germany, Sweden, Taiwan and the United States. He ended Ernie Els' run of victories in the World Match Play Championship when he beat him in the final by one hole in 1997 when the South African was going for a fourth successive title. One of the game's most dedicated practisers. In 2003 he won the Phoenix Open, the EDS Byron Nelson Championship, the John Deere Classic and the Funai Classic. On the PGA Tour in 2003 Singh ended Woods' run as top money earner when he finished with prize-money totalling $7,753,907 – the second largest total in Tour history – but he was not named Player of the Year. Woods was again the players' choice. In 2004 he had his best ever season and by mid-October was approaching $10 million in year-long winnings on the US Tour, having won eight times, matching Johnnie Miller's eight wins in 1974. Although finally edged out by Woods for the No 1 spot he earned his third major and second USPGA Championship title with a play-off victory at Whistling Straits.

Smyth, Des (IRL)

Born Drogheda, Ireland, 12 February 1953
Turned professional 1973

Became the oldest winner on the PGA European Tour when he won the Madeira Island Open in 2001. Smyth was 48 years and 34 days – 20 days older than Neil Coles had been when he won the Sanyo Open in Barcelona in 1982. One of the Tour's most consistent performers – he played 592 events before switching to the European Seniors Tour and qualifying for the US Champions Tour where he has been a winner. Five times Irish National champion he was a member of the winning Irish side in the 1988 Alfred Dunhill Cup. Won twice on US Champions Tour in 2005 and In Abu Dhabi on the European Senior Tour. He was a vice-captain for the European team in the 2006 Ryder Cup.

Snedeker, Brandt (USA)

Born Nashville, Tennessee, 12 August 1980
Turned professional 2004

Winner of the FedEx Cup title in 2012 and a $10 million bonus for his efforts thanks to a three shot victory at PGA Tour Championship, Snedeker earned nearly $15m last year and described his success as " like winning the lottery." He also won the Farmers Insurance in 2012 and was third in The Open Championship. One of the best putters in golf, Snedeker won two points for the USA in the Ryder Cup match at Medinah before losing to Paul Lawrie in singles. Won the US Amateur Public Links in 2003 and finished 41st as an amateur on his Masters debut the following year.

Stadler, Craig (USA)

Born San Diego, California, 2 June 1953
Turned professional 1975

Nicknamed "The Walrus" because of his moustache and stocky build, he won the 1982 Masters at Augusta. Winner of 12 titles on the US Tour between 1980 and 1996 he played in two Ryder Cups (1983 and 1985). As an amateur he played in the 1975 Walker Cup two years after winning the US Amateur. He won his first senior major title when he took the Ford Senior Players' Championship just a few weeks after turning 50 then went back to the main tour the following week and won the BC Open against many players half his age. In 2004 he was top earner on the US Champions Tour with over $2 million. His son Kevin, who is also a professional golfer, won the Johnnie Walker Classic at The Vines in 2006.

Stenson, Henrik (SWE)

Born Gothenburg, 5 April 1976
Turned professional 1998

A member of the Swedish Eisenhower Trophy side in 1998 he made his Ryder Cup début In 2006 helping Europe beat the Americans at The K Club in Ireland. He played for Sweden in the 1998 Eisenhower Trophy and made the 2006 Ryder Cup side helping Europe beat America 18½–9½ at the K Club. In the singles he beat Vaughn Taylor. He again played in the 2008 match at Valhalla. Stenson had played the first part of 2007 in America and was quickly a winner of the Accenture Match-Play Championship after having picked up first prize in the Dubai Desert Classic. Stenson rounded off his 2008 season in style by winning the World Cup at Mission Hills in China with Robert Karlsson. In 2009 he won the Players' Championship at Sawgrass to further underline his international reputation.

Stranahan, Frank R (USA)

Born Toledo, Ohio, 5 August 1922
Turned professional 1954

One of America's most successful amateurs he won the Amateur championship at Royal St George's in 1948 and in 1950 the British and US Amateur titles.

He won the Mexican Amateur in 1946, 1948 and 1951 and the Canadian title in 1947 and 1948. He was also leading amateur in The Open in 1947, 1949, 1950, 1951 and 1953. He played in three Walker Cups in 1947, 1949 and 1951.

Strange, Curtis (USA)

Born Norfolk, Virginia, 20 January 1955
Turned professional 1976

Winner of successive US Opens in 1988 and in 1989 when he beat Nick Faldo in an 18-hole play-off at The Country Club Brookline after getting up and down from a bunker at the last to tie on 278. Winner of 17 US Tour titles he won at least one event for seven successive years from 1983. Having played in five Ryder Cup matches he captained the US side when the 2001 match was played at The Belfry in 2002. In 2007 he was inducted into the World Golf Hall of Fame.

Stricker, Steve (USA)

Born Egerton, Wisconsin, 23 February 1967
Turned professional 1990

Started 2001 by winning the $1 million first prize in the Accenture Match Play Championship, one of the World Golf Championship series. In the final he beat Pierre Fulke. Was a member of the winning American Alfred Dunhill Cup side in 1996. In 2007 he won the Barclays Championship … one of the four end of season Fedex Cup events. In 2008 he was a captain's pick in the US Ryder Cup side at Valhalla. He carded 63 in the first round of the PGA Championship in 2011 but is still without a major victory. He won his 12th title on the PGA Tour in 2012 at the Hyundai Tournament of Champions. Was out of sorts at the 2012 Ryder Cup when he lost all four matches. When he started on Tour his wife Nikki caddied for him until having a daughter, Bobbi Maria, in 1998. Her father Dennis Tiziani was his coach.

Sutton, Hal (USA)

Born Shreveport, Louisiana, 28 April 1958
Turned professional 1981

Winner of the 1983 USPGA Championship at the Riviera CC in Los Angeles beating Jack Nicklaus into second place. Played in the 1985, 1987 ,1999 and 2002 Ryder Cup matches. He captained the American team which lost to the Europeans at Oakland Hills in 2004 and in 2007 was given the Payne Stewart award for respecting and upholding the traditions of the game.

Thomas, Dave (WAL)

Born Newcastle-upon-Tyne, 16 August 1934
Turned professional 1949

Twice runner-up in The Open Championship, Welshman Thomas lost a play-off to Peter Thomson in 1958. And was runner-up to Jack Nicklaus in 1966. He played 11 times in the World Cup for Wales and four times in the Ryder Cup. In all he won 10 tournaments between 1961 and 1969 before retiring to concentrate on golf course design. Along with Peter Alliss he designed the Ryder Cup course at The Belfry and was captain of the Professional Golfers' Association in 2001 – their Centenary year – and 2002.

Toms, David (USA)

Born Monroe, LA, 4 January 1967
Turned professional 1989

Highlight of his career was beating Phil Mickelson into second place in the 2001 USPGA Championship at the Atlanta Athletic Club with rounds of 66, 65, 65 and 69 for 265 a record winning Championship aggregate and the lowest aggregate in any Major. Made his Ryder Cup début in 2002, when he was the American side's top points scorer with 3½ points, and played again in 2004. In 2005 Toms won the WGC Accenture Match-play title beating Chris DiMarco 6 and 5 in the final He's won more than $38 million on the PGA Tour with 13 victories, most recently at Colonial in 2011. His best performance last season was fourth at the US Open.

Torrance OBE, Sam (SCO)

Born Largs, Ayrshire, 24 August 1953
Turned professional 1970

Between 1976 and 1998 he won 21 times on the European Tour in which he has played over 700 events hitting that mark at the Barclays Scottish Open at Loch Lomond in 2010. Captain of the 2002 European Ryder Cup side having previously played in eight matches notably holing the winning putt in 1985 to end a 28-year run of American domination. He was an inspired captain when the 2001 match was played in September 2002. Tied 8 points each, Torrance's men won the singles for only the third time since 1979 to win 15½–12½. His father Bob, who has been his only coach, looks after the swings these days of several others on the European Tour including Paul McGinley who holed the nine foot putt that brought the Ryder Cup back to Europe in 2002. He was awarded the MBE in 1996. European Tour officials worked out that in his first 28 years Torrance walked an estimated 14,000 miles and played 15,000 shots earning at the rate of £22 per stroke. In 2003 he retired from full-time competition on the European Tour to play on the European Senior Tour and in 2005, 2006 and 2009 was top earner. He is often a member of the BBC commentary team working with Peter Alliss and Ken Brown.

Townsend, Peter (ENG)

Born Cambridge, 16 September 1946
Turned professional 1966

An outstanding amateur golfer regarded as one of the best prospects of the post war era who won the British Boys twice, the British Youths, the Lytham Trophy and the English Amateur titles. He was selected to play for GB&I in the 1965 Walker Cup match, partnering Ronnie Shade in foursomes, contributing three points, and emerging as one of the heroes of a drawn match against the USA. He turned professional the following season, initially struggled with swing changes, but went on to win 14 times,

Peter Thomson CBE (AUS)

Born Melbourne, 23 August 1929 *Turned professional 1949*

The first golfer who was ever shown live on television winning The Open – the occasion was his triumph at St Andrews in 1955 – Peter Thomson enjoys a deserved reputation as one of the most astute links golfer to emerge since young Tom Morris won four consecutive Open titles. One of only four champions to capture five Opens – his other triumphs were at Birkdale twice, in 1954 and 1965, Hoylake in 1956 and Lytham in 1958 – Thomson was placed in the spotlight when the BBC used just three cameras for their first live broadcast from the Old Course.

The Australian found the incentive to win three consecutive Open titles lay in financial necessity. Prize money was relatively modest in the Fifties and sponsorship deals were scarce. Luckily, this largely self-taught golfer with a fluent swing and a knack of eliminating mistakes produced the kind of low ball flight which reaps dividends on the linksland. He made his début in the oldest major at Portrush in 1951 and between 1952 and 1958 never finished outside the first two. His run of extraordinary results during that seven year stretch was second, second, first, first, first, second and first. During that spell he also became the only golfer in the modern era to win three consecutive championships on three different links. (Jamie Anderson in the 1870s and Bob Ferguson in the 1880s are the other Open champions with this distinction.)

One of only four players to win five Opens – Harry Vardon, with six, has the most victories – he matched the feats of J.H. Taylor and James Braid while Tom Watson also won five in eight years from 1975. Thomson's fifth victory, arguably his most impressive, came at Royal Birkdale in 1965 when more Americans, including Jack Nicklaus, Arnold Palmer and Tony Lema, were in the field. He says that the reason for his success in The Open was simple – he built his career around the championship. In the American majors, he played only three times in the US Open, finishing fourth in 1956. He played at Augusta in five Masters with fifth his best finish in 1957. He also won three Australian Opens and in Europe savoured 24 victories between 1954 and 1972. His first victory in 1950 was at the New Zealand Open, a tournament he would win nine times. All told, he won over 100 tournaments around the world.

Raised in the Brunswick suburb of Melbourne, Thomson took up golf as a 12-year-old and was club champion at 15. He studied to become an industrial chemist and first worked for Spalding before becoming a professional in 1949. With one of the most fluent and reliable swings, gripping the club lightly, he made the links game look deceptively easy. Perhaps the greatest Australian player, he was instrumental in developing golf throughout Asia. Thomson placed a premium on accuracy rather than power and, like his rival Bobby Locke, often used a 3 wood from the tee.

When Thomson was ready to retire from competitive golf, he thought about pursuing a career in Australian politics but narrowly missed out on a seat in a state election. He turned instead to the US Senior Tour where he won 11 titles, including a remarkable nine victories in 1985, a record matched only by Hale Irwin. Thomson was also president of the Australian PGA between 1962 and 1994.

He was elected to the World Golf Hall of Fame in 1988, the year he won the Seniors British PGA, his last title, and is an honorary member of the Royal and Ancient Golf Club of St Andrews. His fondness for the Auld Toun persuaded the Australian to keep a house in St Andrews as well as a place in his heart for the Old Course. After his retirement from golf he concentrated on journalism and a successful golf course design business which built more than 100 courses. He's captained the Rest of the World side at the Presidents Cup, including a notable win over the US at Royal Melbourne in 1998. A member of Victoria golf club since 1949, the club celebrated his 80th birthday in 2009 by unveiling a bronze statue of him. He continues to regard the values of common sense, planning and clear thinking among the most useful golfing assets.

including the Swiss and Dutch Opens on the European Tour. He also won the Western Australian Open as well as recording numerous victories in South America and Africa. Keen to play around the globe, he qualified for the PGA Tour in America where he finished in the top ten three times. Once regarded as a rival to Tony Jacklin, he finished in the top 20 at The Open four times and played in the Ryder Cup matches of 1969 and 1971. A former captain of the PGA he now lives in Sweden.

Van de Velde, Jean (FRA)

Born Mont de Marsan, 29 May 1966
Turned professional 1987

Who ever remembers who came second? Few do but almost everyone recalls Frenchman Jean Van de Velde finishing runner-up after a play-off with eventual winner Paul Lawrie and American Justin Leonard when The Open returned to a somewhat tricked-up Carnoustie in 1999. Playing the last hole he led by three but refused to play safe and paid a

Lee Trevino, (USA)

Born Dallas, Texas, 1 December 1939 Turned professional 1961

The winner of six major championships and an enduring success over nearly half a century of competition, "Supermex" won as many tournaments on the senior circuit, 29, as he did on the PGA Tour. Using a distinctive swing with an open stance and a strong grip, Trevino was a golfer with a hook who faded the ball. His action was once described as five wrongs which make an immaculate right. If his style of play was unusual, it was his personality which struck a chord with the public. He was a charismatic figure with a sense of humour who played a huge role in the emergence of the Champions Tour. He once quipped that "you can talk to a fade but a hook won't listen."

Born in Texas to a family of Mexican ancestry, he left school at 14 and worked as a caddy. He spent four years with the US Marines before becoming an assistant pro in El Paso. Although he joined the paid ranks in 1960, it wasn't until 1967 that he joined the PGA Tour and was named rookie of the year. The following season he made his name with an outstanding performance in the US Open at Oak Hill. He won by four shots from Jack Nicklaus and his total of 275 – made up of scores of 69, 68, 69 and 69 – was the first in America's national championship to break 70 in each round.

The consistency of Trevino's game was never more evident than in the summer of 1971 when, between May 30 and July 10, he won four events, including The Open and the US Open. At Merion he defeated Nicklaus in a play-off while at Royal Birkdale he thwarted Mr Lu and Tony Jacklin. The following year at Muirfield, Trevino again crossed swords with Jacklin. This time the Englishman and the American were paired together over the closing 36 holes and Trevino's chip-in on the penultimate hole proved decisive. He would enjoy further major success in the PGA Championships of 1974 and 1984. His last major win came at the age of 44 over Shoal Creek in Alabama when once more he shot four rounds below 70.

Trevino never finished higher than tenth in the Masters where he felt a course with so many dog-legs did not suit his game. He was a low fader and believed Augusta required a high draw. He was an outstanding Ryder Cup player, playing six times as well as captaining the US in 1985. He won the Vardon Trophy for low scoring average five times in his career and recovered from being struck by lightning while playing in the Western Open in Chicago. He had to undergo back surgery before returning to competition. He was involved in one of the low scoring matches in the World Match Play Championship with Jacklin in 1972 when again he came out on top. In 2003 he was made an honorary member of the Royal and Ancient Golf Club of St Andrews. Trevino was a blue collar hero with a splash of showmanship who broadened the appeal of the game.

severe penalty. He ran up a triple bogey 7 after seeing his approach ricochet off a stand into the rough and hitting his next into the Barry Burn. He appeared to contemplate playing the half-submerged ball when taking off his shoes and socks and wading in but that was never a possibility. Sadly, he was an absentee at the 2007 Open played at the same venue. Took up the game as a youngster when holidaying with his parents in Biarritz. Has scored only one win in Europe (the Roma Masters in 1993) and has returned to the European Tour after a spell in America. Made his Ryder Cup début at Brookline in 1999. Injury prevented him competing regularly in 2003 and 2004 during which time he was part of the BBC Golf Commentary team with, among others, Peter Alliss, Sam Torrance, Mark James and Ken Brown. Came close to winning his national title but lost out in a play-off to fellow Frenchman Jean-François Remesy at Golf National in 2005. Created headlines later in the year when he said that if it was to be made easier for women to play in The Open he thought it only fair that he should be allowed to enter the British Women's Open but never followed through on his threat. Captained the Continental side which lost to Great Britain and Ireland in the 2011 Vivendi Seve Trophy.

Verplank, Scott (USA)

Born Dallas, Texas, 9 July 1964
Turned professional 1986

When he won the Western Open as an amateur in 1985 he was the first to do so since Doug Sanders took the 1956 Canadian Open. Missed most of the 1991 and 1992 seasons because of an elbow injury and the injury also affected his 1996 season. He has diabetes and wears an insulin pump while playing to regulate his medication. Curtis Strange chose him as one of his two picks for the 2002 US Ryder Cup side. In the singles on the final day he beat Lee Westwood 2 and 1. He was again a captain's pick in Tom Lehman's side in 2006 and again won his singles, this time against Padraig Harrington. Surprisingly he failed to make the 2008 US side.

Wadkins, Lanny (USA)

Born Richmond, Virginia, 5 December 1949
Turned professional 1971

His 21 victories on the US Tour between 1972 and 1992 include the 1977 USPGA Championship, his only Major. He won that after a play-off with Gene Littler at Pebble Beach but lost a play-off for the same title in 1987 to Larry Nelson at Palm Beach Gardens.

Tom Watson (USA)

Born Kansas City, Missouri, 4 September 1949
Turned professional 1971

For all the victories he's savoured during an enduringly brilliant career, it was Tom Watson's narrow loss in The Open at Turnberry in 2009, when he was nearing his 60th birthday, which will be discussed and remembered as long as the game of golf is played. A year after undergoing hip replacement surgery, he came within eight feet of relishing a record-equalling sixth championship success. Remarkably, a quarter of a century had elapsed since he'd won his fifth Open. While he missed the putt for glory on the 72nd hole and lost the subsequent play-off for the Claret Jug to Stewart Cink, Watson's performance on the Ailsa, nevertheless, struck a chord with the public and breathed new life into a career already notable for 39 PGA Tour wins, including no fewer than eight major titles. It also led, indirectly, to his appointment as captain of America's Ryder Cup side at Gleneagles.

Born in Missouri, Watson today remains true to his roots and still lives in the midwest of America on a farm near Kansas City. He was introduced to the game by his father, Ray, a scratch golfer, at the age of six. By the time he was 19, he was the state amateur champion, a feat he repeated on three more occasions. After studying psychology at Stanford University, where he graduated in 1971, Watson joined the PGA Tour and earned his first winner's cheque as a pro in 1974 at the Western Open.

When he came up short and twice failed to win the US Open in 1974 and 1975, he was branded as a choker in America. Whether that reputation was deserved or not is moot. But Watson produced the perfect response later in the summer of 1975 when he travelled to Scotland and won The Open on his début at Carnoustie after a play-off with Jack Newton. It was the beginning of the American's life-long affair with the home of golf in which he matched the success rate of J H Taylor, James Braid and Peter Thomson by winning the oldest major five times. He also missed out on an opportunity to collect a sixth Open title by a whisker at St Andrews in 1984 when he struck his second shot close to the wall through the green at the Road Hole and was thwarted by Seve Ballesteros.

Of all his Open triumphs, surely none was more memorable than the "Duel in the Sun" at Turnberry in 1977. At an event many regarded as the greatest championship of modern times, Watson edged out Jack Nicklaus by shooting closing rounds of 65,65 to Nicklaus' 65,66. His other successes on the linksland came in 1980 at Muirfield where he defeated Lee Trevino; in 1982 at Royal Troon where Peter Oosterhuis and Nick Price came second and in 1983 when Andy Bean and Hale Irwin were runners-up.

If his story at The Open provides the legendary narrative for Watson's career, he also produced a spectacular performance in the 1982 US Open at Pebble Beach. Watson's chip shot for birdie from the rough on the short 17th has been immortalised as the most memorable of his life. As at Turnberry, Nicklaus was the man he defeated. He also secured two green jackets at Augusta in 1977 and 1981 where Nicklaus finished second on both occasions. It was this talent for defeating arguably the game's greatest player in the tournaments which mattered most that separated Watson from his peers.

However, since he was never better than a runner-up at the US PGA Championship, Watson was unable to join Gene Sarazen, Ben Hogan, Gary Player, Nicklaus and Tiger Woods in the élite club of Grand Slam golfers who have won all four professional majors. Perhaps it's the only accolade missing from his career. He became the oldest winner on the PGA Tour when he won the Mastercard Colonial in 1998 almost 24 years after his first win. And he was the PGA Tour's player of the year six times and the leading moneywinner five times.

Watson played in four Ryder Cups in 1977, 1981, 1983 and 1989 before captaining the US side to victory in 1993 at The Belfry. Such is his standing in the game, he will become the oldest captain in the history of the match when he leads the USA at the age of 65 years and 22 days in the 2014 event at Gleneagles. He's also the first man to captain America twice since Jack Nicklaus in 1987.

He was inducted into the World Golf Hall of Fame in 1988 and is an honorary member of the Royal and Ancient Golf Club of St Andrews. He also succeeded Sam Snead as the golf professional emeritus at the Greenbrier.

After turning 50, he joined the Champions Tour. He's won 13 events since 1999 in the company of his senior peers, most recently in Hawaii in 2010. Perhaps his finest moment as a senior came at his beloved Turnberry in 2003 when he lifted the Senior British Open title 26 years after the Duel in the Sun.

As a direct consequence of his performance over the Ailsa in 2009, The R&A changed the entry rules and introduced a five year exemption for former champions who finish in the top ten. When the BBC conducted a poll to identify the greatest ever Open champion, it was entirely fitting that Watson was chosen by the British public as the recipient.

He was second on two other occasions to Ray Floyd in 1982 and to Lee Trevino in 1984. In other Majors his best finish was third three times in the US Masters (1990, 1991 and 1993), tied second in the US Open (1986) and tied fourth in the 1984 Open at St Andrews. One of the fiercest of competitors he played eight Ryder Cups between 1977 and 1993 winning 20 of his 33 games, but was a losing captain at Oak Hill in 1995. In 2009 he was inducted into the World Golf Hall of Fame.

Walton, Philip (IRL)

Born Dublin, 28 March 1962
Turned professional 1983 Turned professional 1983

Twice a Walker Cup player he is best remembered for two-putting the last to beat Jay Haas by one hole and clinch victory in the 1995 Ryder Cup at Oak Hill. He played in five Alfred Dunhill Cup competitions at St Andrews and was in the winning side in 1990.

Warren, Marc (SCO)

Born Rutherglen, near Glasgow, 1 April 1981
Turned professional 2002

Holed the winning putt in Great Britain and Ireland's Walker Cup victory over America in 2001. Enjoyed two play-off victories on the European Challenge Tour in 2005 and finished top money Earner in the Ireland Ryder Cup Challenge and the Rolex Trophy. In 2006 Warren scored his first victory on the main Tour when he beat Robert Karlsson in a play-off for the Eurocard Masters at Barsebäck. At the start of the 2007 season he finished fifth behind winner Yang Yong-eun, Tiger Woods, Michael Campbell and Retief Goosen in the HSBC Champions event in Shanghai. He scored his second win in the Johnnie Walker Championship at Gleneagles Hotel by beating Simon Wakefield in a play-off. He was a wild card pick for the GB&I team in the Seve Trophy match and partnered Colin Montgomerie to a first-ever success for Scotland in the 2007 World Cup of Golf at Mission Hills in China. He lost his Tour card in 2010 but won it back in 2011.In 2012 he threw away a three shot lead and an opportunity to win the Aberdeen Asset Management Scottish Open at Castle Stuart when he ran up a double bogey at the 15th and bogeys at the 16th and 17th holes.

Watney, Nick (USA)

Born Sacramento, California, 1981
Turned professional 2003

Enjoyed the best season of his five year career on the PGA Tour in 2011, winning nearly $5.3 million and relishing victories at the AT&T National and the Cadillac Championship. His record of ten top ten finishes was a model of consistency. Also won the Zurich Classic in 2007 and the Buick Invitational in 2009. Made his Presidents Cup début in 2011.

Watson, Bubba (USA)

Born Bagdad, Florida, 11 May 1978
Turned professional 2003

Winner of four events on the PGA Tour, by far the most significant victory of Watson's career came at Augusta last year when he defeated Louis Oosthuizen in a play-off to clinch the Masters. His winning par on the second extra hole, the 18th, was notable for a miraculous recovery shot from the woods. Along with Mike Weir and Phil Mickelson, who won three titles, Watson's success was the fifth in ten Masters by a southpaw. As well as his short game skills, Watson is renowned for his power, once hitting a drive 422 yards in a Nationwide Tour event. His swing is self-taught and the left-hander has never had a lesson. Won two points for the USA at the 2012 Ryder Cup.

Weekley, Boo (USA)

Born Milton, Florida, 23 July 1973
Turned professional 1997

One of six players who made their débuts in the 2008 Ryder Cup at Valhalla. He played well and enjoyed every minute of the American success. Nicknamed Boo after Yogi Bear's sidekick, he made $500,000 on the Nationwide Tour before joining the main Tour. Studied at the Abraham Baldwin Agricultural College and won the Verizon Open in 2007 and 2008.

Weir, Mike (CAN)

Born Sarnia, Ontario, 12 May 1970
Turned professional 1992

A left-hander, he was the first Canadian to play in the Presidents Cup when he made the side in 2000 and the first from his country to win a World Golf Championship event when he took the American Express Championship at Valderrama in 2000. Wrote to Jack Nicklaus as a 13-year-old to enquire whether or not he should switch from playing golf left-handed to right-handed and was told not to switch. In 1997 he led the averages on the Canadian Tour with a score of 69.29 but his greatest triumph came when he became only the third left-hander to win a major when he played beautifully and putted outstandingly to beat Len Mattiace for a Masters Green Jacket in 2003. He had had to hole from 15 feet at the last to take the tournament into extra holes and won at the first when Mattiace failed to make par. He has now assumed hero status in Canada and has been inducted into the Canadian Golf Hall of Fame.

Weiskopf, Tom (USA)

Born Massillon, Ohio, 9 November 1942
Turned professional 1964

Winner of only one Major – the 1973 Open Championship at Royal Troon, he lived in the shadow of Jack Nicklaus throughout his competitive career. He was runner-up in the 1976 US Open to Jerry Pate and was twice third in 1973 and 1977. His best finish in the USPGA Championship was third in 1975 – the year he had to be content for the fourth time with second place at the US Masters. He had been runner-up for a Green Jacket in 1969, 1972 and 1974 but played perhaps his best golf ever in 1975 only to be pipped at the post by Nicklaus. With 22 wins to his name he now plays the US Senior Tour with a curtailed schedule because of his course design work

Eldrick 'Tiger' Woods (USA)

Born Cypress, California, 30 December 1975 *Turned professional 1996*

By a wide margin the dominant golfer of the early 21st century, Woods has been the player to beat around the world ever since he became a professional in the late summer of 1996. His 95 tournament victories include no fewer than 14 major titles – the 1997, 2001, 2002 and 2005 Masters, 1999, 2000, 2006 and 2007 US PGA Championships, 2000, 2002, and 2008 US Open Championships, and The Open Championships of 2000, 2005 and 2006. When he won the Masters for the second time in 2001, Woods became the first golfer in the game's history to hold all four majors at the same time. If the "Tiger Slam" was the highlight to date of a spectacular career, Woods can reflect on many other significant accomplishments. His haul of 71 victories on the US PGA Tour is surpassed only by Sam Snead with 82 and Jack Nicklaus with 73. His career earnings from prize money in America are in excess of $94 million while his global winnings are more than $113m. According to Forbes magazine, he became the first golfer to earn more than a billion dollars from a combination of prize money, sponsorship, appearance fees and golf course design.

From the moment he appeared as a two-year-old child prodigy on the Mike Douglas Show with Bob Hope, Woods carried a gilded reputation. He aced his first hole-in-one at the age of six and was a scratch golfer by 13. He won the US Junior Amateur three times between the ages of 15 and 17 and the US Amateur in three consecutive stagings between 1994 and 1996, the only golfer ever to record 18 consecutive match play wins at that event.

When he left university at Stanford and joined the professional ranks as a 20-year-old in 1996, Woods won twice at Las Vegas and Disney World as well as reeling off five consecutive top five finishes and rocketing up the World Golf Ranking. In 1997, his first full season as a pro, Woods won five of the first 16 events he entered, including his first appearance as a pro at Augusta. The youngest Masters champion at the age of 21 years, three months and 14 days, he won the tournament by 12 strokes and set a record 72 hole score of 270 thanks to rounds of 70,66,65 and 69.

It was a demolition of Augusta National which took the breath away and eventually led to the lengthening and toughening of the course as well as introducing the concept of "Tiger proofing" to the golfing lexicon. He became world No 1 in just 42 weeks as a pro. While this was a frightening pace to set, Woods had no qualms about continuing to floor the accelerator. In 1999 his scoring average of 68.43 was low enough to win eight times on the PGA Tour and 11 times around the globe. There was no let-up in 2000 when he won nine times, including three majors, thereby matching Ben Hogan's feat in 1953. His 15 stroke victory at Pebble Beach was the greatest margin of victory in US Open history. When Woods won The Open at St Andrews in 2000, he became the youngest to complete the career Grand Slam of professional majors and only the fifth golfer ever to do so.

Today, Woods holds or shares the record for the low score in relation to par in each of the four major championships. His records are 270 in the Masters, 272 in the US Open, 269 in The Open, and he shares the record of 270 with Bob May in the 2000 PGA Championship. The US Open and Masters victories came by record margins, 15 strokes and 12 strokes respectively, and the US Open triumph swept aside the 13-stroke major championship standard which had stood for 138 years, established by Old Tom Morris in the 1862 Open. The record margin for the US Open had been 11 strokes by Willie Smith in 1899. In the Masters, Woods broke the record margin of nine strokes set by Nicklaus in 1965. Tiger also won The Open by eight strokes, the largest margin since J.H. Taylor in 1913. Perhaps his most remarkable win of all came at the 2008 US Open at Torrey Pines when he defeated Rocco Mediate in a play-off in spite of suffering from a knee injury and a double stress fracture of his left tibia. When the championship was over, he underwent surgery on his anterior cruciate ligament and missed the rest of the season. All of those extraordinary accomplishments were the work of the son of the late Earl Woods, a retired lieutenant-colonel in the US Army, and Kultida, a native of Thailand. Woods was nicknamed Tiger after a Vietnamese soldier and friend of his father, Vuong Dang Phong, to whom he had also given that nickname.

When Tiger married Elin and the couple had two children, Sam and Charlie, Woods' life seemed blessed. However, controversy surrounding infidelity in his private life led to a divorce from Elin, as well as the loss of numerous sponsorship deals with Gatorade, AT&T, Accenture, Gillette and Golf Digest. For the first time in 15 years he failed to win during 2010 and was dethroned as world No 1 after a total of 623 weeks by Lee Westwood before falling out of the world's top 5 golfers after an injury-blighted season. In 2011 he split with long time caddie Steve Williams and fell as low as 58th in the world rankings. However, he ended a winless streak of 107 weeks when he captured the Chevron World Challenge and rose to 23rd in the world. In 2012, though another major title eluded him, he won three times on the PGA Tour and rose to second in the world rankings.

for which he and his original partner Jay Morrish have received much praise. One of their designs is Loch Lomond, venue for several years of the revived Scottish Open. Played in just two Ryder Cup matches giving up a place in the team one year in order to go Bighorn sheep hunting in Alaska.

Westwood, Lee (ENG)

Born Worksop, Nottinghamshire, 24 April 1973
Turned professional 1993

The year 2010 was very special for Lee Westwood. The consistent Englishman was the man who finally prised Tiger Woods out of the No 1 spot in the World Rankings he had held for five years. He beat Phil Mickelson and Martin Kaymer to top spot following Tiger Woods dramatic loss of form following an off the course scandal. It was just reward for one of the most consistent of golfers who battled back and made it to the top after having very nearly quit the game a few years earlier. His own loss of form had seen him slump from No,. 4 in the world rankings to a position outside the top 250. He credits David Leadbetter for sorting out his game A former British Youths' champion who missed out on Walker Cup honours, he quickly made the grade in the professional ranks and, in 2000 ended the seven-year reign of Colin Montgomerie by taking the top spot in the Volvo Order of Merit. He was a six-time winner that year in Europe and beat Montgomerie at the second extra hole of the Cisco World Match Play final at Wentworth. He has won titles on every major circuit in the world including three victories at the Taiheiyo Masters in Japan, the Australian Open in 1997 when he beat Greg Norman in a play-off and the Freeport McDermott Classic and the New Orleans and St Jude Fedex titles on the US PGATour. He has been a member of the last eight European Ryder Cup teams including the 2012 match at Medinah where he won his singles tie against Matt Kuchar. His victory at the Nordea Masters last year was his 22nd success on the European Tour.

Williams, Chris (USA)

Born Moscow, Idaho, 21 June 1991

The world's top ranked amateur golfer in 2012, Williams won the Mark H McCormack Award for his achievements. He helped the USA win the Eisenhower Trophy, the World Amateur team Championship, in Turkey last year, after winning the Western Amateur. He also represented the USA in the Walker Cup match against GB&I at Royal Aberdeen. Williams is exempt for this year's US Open at Merion and The Open Championship at Muirfield.

Wilson, Oliver (ENG)

Born Mansfield, 14 September 1980
Turned professional 2003

He played his way into the 2008 Ryder Cup side at Valhalla and impressed as a rookie, Having attended Augusta College he now lives much of the time in America. He was a member of the winning Great Britain and Ireland Walker Cup side in 2003. Like Padraig Harrington who had so many runner-up finishes before becoming a regular winner, Wilson is still awaiting his first victory.

Wirachant, Thawarn (THA)

Born Bangkok, Thailand, 28 December 1966
Turned professional 1987

He earned a full year's exemption on the European Tour when he won the Enjoy Jakarta Standard Chartered Indonesian Open – a joint venture between the Asian and European Tours. It was his sixth win on the Asian Tour which he joined 10 years earlier. Wirachant is best known for his unorthodox swing which works effectively for him. He is a former Thai Amateur champion.

Wolstenholme, Gary (ENG)

Born Egham, Surrey, 21 August 1960
Turned professional 2008

Nobody has played more often for England. Between 1988 and 2008 when he turned professional to prepare for the European Senior Tour – he represented England an incredible 218 times. Although he can remember swinging a club at the age of 4½ he was off 23 when he started playing seriously at the age of 17. Within six years he was scratch and by the age of 23 he had started representing England. During his amateur career he played in seven St Andrews Trophy matches against the Continent of Europe between 1992 and 2004 during which time he amassed a P19 W10 L9 H0 points record. In six Walker Cups between 1995 and 2005 he had the most individual and team wins. Awarded the MBE for his services to golf in the 2007 New Year's honours list and the recipient of an honorary MA degree from Northampton University, he represented Leicestershire and Rutland from 1981 to 2007 and Cumbria in 2008. He was playing off plus 4 when he turned professional but at one point was a plus 5 golfer. He has honorary membership of 13 clubs and Associations. Amateur champion at Ganton in 1991 and Royal Troon in 2003 he has also won titles in China. the UAE, Finland, Luxembourg Australia and Spain. He has had 13 holes in one, five of them in competition. Highlights of his outstanding career were beating Tiger Woods at Porthcawl in the 1995 Walker Cup and, more importantly, helping Luke Donald, Paddy Gribben and Lorn Kelly win the World Amateur Team Championship in Chile in 1998. Since becoming a professional, he's won three times on the European Senior Tour, including victories in 2012 at the Mallorca Senior Open and the Benahavis Senior Masters.

Wood, Chris (ENG)

Born Bristol, 26 November 1987
Turned professional 2008

First made the national newspaper headlines when he finished fifth behind Padraig Harrington at the 2008 Open at Royal Birkdale. He turned professional immediately and earned his Tour card at the 2009 European Qualifying School. In 2009 he went even better in The Open when he finished joint third behind Stewart Cink. A bogey at his final hole prevented his being included in the play-off for the title between Cink and Tom Watson. He ended the season being named the Sir Henry Cotton Rookie of the Year.The tallest player on the European Tour at 6ft 5ins, he was runner-up at the Sicilian Open in 2012 and is still seeking his first Tour victory.

Woosnam MBE, Ian (WAL)

Born Oswestry, Shropshire, 2 March 1958
Turned professional 1976

Highlight of his career was winning the Green Jacket at the Masters in 1991 after a last day battle with Spaniard José Maria Olazábal who went on to win in 1994 and again in 1999. Teamed up very successfully with Nick Faldo in Ryder Cup golf and was in four winning teams in 1985, 1987, 1995 and 1997 and was vice-captain in 2001 to Sam Torrance at The K Club before captaining the side to victory in 2006 at the K Club. He scored 28 European Tour victories and twice won the World Match Play Championship in 1987 when he beat Sandy Lyle, with whom he used to play boys' golf in Shropshire, in 1990 when his opponent was Mark McNulty and in 2001 when he beat Retief Goosen, then US Open Champion, Colin Montgomerie, Lee Westwood and then Padraig Harrington in the final. In 1989 he lost a low-scoring final to Nick Faldo on the last green. His lowest round was a 60 he returned in the 1990 Monte Carlo Open at Mont Agel. Partnered by David Llewellyn he won the World Cup of Golf in 1987 beating Scotland's Sam Torrance and Sandy Lyle in a play-off. Honoured with an MBE from Her Majesty the Queen he now lives with his family in Jersey. Finished joint third in the 2001 Open at Lytham after having been penalised two shots for discovering on the second tee he had 15 clubs (one over the limit) in his bag. He now plays on the European Senior Tour and when he topped the money list in 2008 he became the first player to make it to No 1 on the European Tour and the European Seniors Tour.

Yang, Yong-Eun (KOR)

Born Seoul, Korea, 15 January 1972
Turned professional 1996

Winner of events on his home circuit in Korea and also in Japan, he shot to prominence first when beating Tiger Woods into second place in the 2006 HSBC Champions event in Shanghai – a win that earned him his European Tour card. These days he plays mostly in the United States where he followed up his victory in the 2009 Honda Classic with a first major triumph at Hazeltine in the USPGA Championship. Playing with favourite Tiger Woods on the final day he outscored him and outputted the World No 1 to become the first Asian to win a major. It earned him $1.35 million and he moved from 110th in the world rankings to 34th.

Yeh, Wei-tze (TPE)

Born Taiwan, 20 February 1973
Turned professional 1994

Fisherman's son who became the third Asia golfer after "Mr Lu" and Isao Aoki to win on the European Tour when he won the 2000 Benson and Hedges Malaysian Open. In 2003 he won the ANA Open on the Japanese Tour.

Zhang, Lian-Wei (CHN)

Born Shenzhen, 2 May1965
Turned professional 1994

Leading Chinese player whose victory in the 2003 Caltex Singapore Open when he edged out Ernie Els was the first by a Chinese golfer on Tour. Initially he trained as a javelin thrower before turning to golf. Self-taught he was also the first Asian golfer to win on the Canadian Tour but remains a stalwart on the Asian circuit. In 2009 he was pipped by Ian Poulter for the Barclays Singapore Open and finished the year in second spot on the Asian Tour Order of Merit to Thongchai Jaidee.

Zoeller, Fuzzy (USA)

Born New Albany, Indiana, 11 November 1951
Turned professional 1973

Winner of the US Masters in 1979 after a play-off with Ed Sneed (who had dropped shots at the last three holes in regulation play) and Tom Watson and was victorious US Open in 1984 at Winged Foot after an 18-hole play-off with Greg Norman. A regular winner on the US Tour between 1979 and 1980, he played on three Ryder Cups in 1979, 1983 and 1985. He announced that the 2008 Masters would be his final appearance at the event.

Australia's Fraser topped the Asian 2012 Stroke Averages

Marcus Fraser, who plays mostly on the European Tour these days, competed in 10 events on the Asian Tour and topped that circuit's stroke averages table.

Fraser played 33 round in 10 events, had four top 10's and averaged 69.27 a round beating Thongchai Jaidee into second spot on 70.14 from 35 rounds. Thaworn Wirachant, who averaged 70.19 for the 89 rounds he played in 25 events, was third.

In terms of being under par for the season, Wirachant was a runaway winner being 123-under at the end of the season. Prom Meesawat was second best at 102-under par with Fraser third on 65-under.

Who's Who in Golf – Women

Ahn, Sun-Ju (KOR)

Born South Korea, 31 August 1987
Turned professional 2006

The first Korean golfer to top the Japan LPGA Tour money list and be Japanese Rookie of the Year as well in 2010. Only other non-Japanese golfer to finish No.1 in Japan has been Chinese Taipei's Ai Yu Tu. In 2010, Ahn won four events and earned 145,07 million Yen. She topped the money list that season as well as in 2011. In 2012, she won three more events in Japan, taking her number of professional victories to 18.

Alfredsson, Helen (SWE)

Born Gothenburg, 9 April 1965
Turned professional 1989

After earning Rookie of the Year on the 1989 European Tour she won the 1992 Ladies' British Open. Two years later she was Gatorade Rookie of the Year on the American LPGA Tour. She has competed in seven Solheim Cup matches and captained the 2007 Cup side before becoming the first player in the event's history to qualify as a past captain two year later.She has won titles in Europe, America, Japan and Australia and earned nearly $5.7 million during her career on the LPGA.

Andrew, Kim (*née* Rostron) (ENG)

Born 12 February 1974

After taking the English and Scottish Ladies' stroke play titles in 1997 she won the Ladies' British Open Amateur a year later. She played in the 1998 and 2000 Curtis Cup matches.

Bailey MBE, Mrs Diane (Frearson *née* Robb) (ENG)

Born Wolverhampton, 31 August 1943

After playing in the 1962 and 1972 Curtis Cup matches she captained the side in 1984, 1986 and 1988. In 1984 at Muirfield the Great Britain and Ireland side lost narrowly to the Americans but she led the side to a first ever victory on American soil at Prairie Dunes in Kansas two years later. The result was a convincing 13–5. She was in charge again when the GB&I side held on to the Cup two years later this time by 11–7 at Royal St George's.

Bisgood CBE, Jeanne (ENG)

Born Richmond, Surrey, 11 August 1923

Three times English Ladies champion in 1951, 1953 and 1957. Having played in three Curtis Cups she captained the side in 1970. Between 1952 and 1955 she won the Swedish, Italian, German, Portuguese and Norwegian Ladies titles.

Bonallack, Lady (*née* Angela Ward) (ENG)

Born Birchington, Kent, 7 April 1937

Wife of Sir Michael Bonallack OBE, she played in six Curtis Cup matches. She was leading amateur in the 1975 and 1976 Colgate European Opens, won two English Ladies' titles and had victories, too, in the Swedish, German, Scandinavian and Portuguese Championships.

Bradley, Pat (USA)

Born Westford, Massachusetts, 24 March 1951
Turned professional 1974

Winner of four US LPGA majors – the Nabisco Championship, the US Women's Open, the LPGA Championship and the du Maurier Classic, she won 31 times on the American circuit. An outstanding skier and ski instructor as well, she started playing golf when she was 11. Every time she won her mother would ring a bell on the porch of the family home whatever the time of day. The bell is now in the World Golf Hall of Fame. She played in four Solheim Cup sides and captained the team in 2000 at Loch Lomond. Inducted into the LPGA Hall of Fame in 1991 she was Rolex Player of the Year in 1986 and 1991. In 2011 her nephew Keegan Bradley won the USPGA Championship.

Butler, Ita (*née* Burke) (IRL)

Born Nenagh, County Tipperary

Having played in the Curtis Cup in 1966, she captained the side that beat the Americans by 5 points at Killarney thirty years later.

Caponi, Donna (USA)

Born Detroit, Michigan, 29 January 1945
Turned professional 1965

Twice winner of the US Women's Open in 1969 and 1970 she collected 24 titles on the LPGA Tour between 1969 and 1981. Winner of the 1975 Colgate European Open at Sunningdale, she is now a respected commentator/analyst for The Golf Channel in Orlando.

Carner, Jo Anne (*née* Gunderson) (USA)

Born Kirkland, Washington, 4 April 1939
Turned professional 1970

Had five victories in the US Ladies' Amateur Championship (1957, 1960, 1962, 1966 and 1968) before turning professional and winning the 1971 and 1976 US Women's Open. She remains the last amateur to win on the LPGA Tour after having taken the 1969 Burdine's Invitational. Between 1970 and 1985 scored 42 victories on the LPGA Tour and was Rolex Player of the Year in 1974, 1981 and 1982. She was inducted into the LPGA Hall of Fame in 1982 and the World Golf Hall of Fame in 1985. She won the Bobby Jones award in 1981 and the Mickey Wright award in 1974 and 1982.

Cavalleri, Silvia (ITA)

Born Milan, 10 October 1972
Turned professional 1997

Became the first Italian to win the US Amateur when she beat Robin Burke 5 and 4 at Brae Burn in the 1997 final. She was five times Italian National Junior champion and won the British Girls' title in 1990 with a 5 and 4 success over E. Valera at Penrith.

Choi, Na Yeon (KOR)

Born Seoul, 28 October 1987
Turned professional 2004

Winner of the US Women's Open in 2012, Choi was third in the Rolex world rankings thanks to a consistent season in which recorded seven top ten finishes. Started playing golf at 11 and as an amateur played for the Korean national team. She was pipped by Yani Tseng for rookie of the year on the LPGA in 2008 and won twice the following year. She won the money list and recorded the low stroke average on the LPGA in 2010. Her first major success arrived at Blackwolf Run courtesy of a four shot win over Amy Yang.

Creamer, Paula (USA)

Born Pleasanton, California, 5 August 1986
Turned professional 2005

The youngest and first amateur to win the LPGA qualifying school in 2004. As an amateur she was top ranked American junior in 2003 and 2004 winning 19 national titles. After turning professional she became a winner on the LPGA Tour in her ninth start when she won the Sybase Classic. She began playing golf at the age of 10. Despite being sidelined with a hand injury and undergoing surgery on a thumb in 2010, she won her first major with a victory at the US Women's Open. She has played in four Solheim Cup matches.In 2012 she posted seven top ten finishes on the LPGA and has career earnings of more than $9.5million.

Daniel, Beth (USA)

Born Charleston, South Carolina, 14 October 1956
Turned professional 1978

A member of the LPGA Hall of Fame, she won 32 times between 1979 and 1995 including the 1990 US LPGA Championship. She was Rolex Player of the Year in 1980, 1990 and 1994. Before turning professional she won the US Women's Amateur title in 1975 and 1977 and played in the 1976 and 1978 Curtis Cup teams. She has played in eight Solheim Cup competitions since 1990 and was named as vice-captain to Betsy King at the 2007 match in Sweden. She captained of the US side in 2009 at Rich Harvest Farm in Sugar Grove, Illinois. During her career she has won 33 LPGA events and has won $8.7m in prize money. She works as an analyst on the Golf Channel.

Dibnah, Corinne (AUS)

Born Brisbane, 29 July 1962
Turned professional 1984

A former Australian and New Zealand amateur champion, she joined the European Tour after turning professional and won 13 times between 1986 and 1994. A pupil of Greg Norman's first coach Charlie Earp, she was Europe's top earner in 1991.

Laura Davies CBE (ENG)

Born 10 October 1963 *Turned professional 1985*

Record-breaking performer who has won 77 events worldwide including the US and British Women's Opens. For six days in 1987 she held both titles having won the American event before joining the US Tour. She was a founder member of the Women's Tour in Europe.. She still holds the record for the number of birdies in a round – 11 which she scored in the 1987 Open de France Feminin. Her 16-shot victory, by a margin of five shots, in the 1995 Guardian Irish Holidays Open at St Margaret's remains the biggest in European Tour history. Her 267 totals in the 1988 Biarritz Ladies' Open and the 1995 Guardian Irish Holidays Open are the lowest on Tour and have been matched only by Julie Inkster in the 2002 Evian Masters. Other major victories include the LPGA Championship twice and the du Maurier Championship. In 1999 she became the first European Tour player to pass through the £1 million in prize-money earnings and finished European No. 1 that year for a record fifth time. She was No.1 again in 2004. The 1996 Rolex Player of the Year in America, she has won almost $5.5 million in US prize-money. Originally honoured with an MBE by Her Majesty the Queen in 1988, she became a CBE in 2000. Enjoys all sports including soccer (she supports Liverpool FC). Among other awards she has received during her career have been the Association of Golf Writers' Trophy for her contribution to European golf in 1994 and the American version in 1994 and 1996 for her performances on the US Tour.

In 1994 she became the first golfer to score victories on five different Tours – European, American, Australasian, Japanese and Asian in one calendar year. As an amateur she played for Surrey and was a Curtis Cup player in 1984. She has competed in all 11 Solheim Cup matches. In 2000 was recognised by the LPGA in their top 50 players' and teachers' honours list. Laura proved how strong a competitor she still is when she took the No.1 spot on the women's tour in Europe for a seventh time in 2006. Although she only won once she had six second-place finishes and ended the year with a total of €471,727 from the 11 events she played. By the end of 2006 she had stretched her winning record to 67 titles and in 2007 made it 68 with victory in the Austrian Open a week after missing the cut in the Scottish Open, the first time she had missed in 23 years competing in events organised solely by the Ladies European Tour. She has failed only once – in 2005 – to win an event. When she successfully defended the Uniqua Ladies' Golf Open in 2008 she took her victory tally to 69.

Her 2010 season was better than average because she won five titles in as many different lands – Australia, Germany, Austria, Spain and India –taking her tally of victories to 77. In amongst her haul of titles there are four majors, starting with the US Women's Open of 1987. Since then, she has bagged a couple of US LPGA championships and a du Maurier, while she also captured the British Women's Open in the days before the event was given major status. She is the oldest player on the Ladies European Tour but was still a force in 2012, finishing runner-up at the Ladies German Open and the UNIQA Ladies Open.

Dowling, Clare (*née* Hourihane) (IRL)

Born 18 February 1958

Won three Irish Ladies' Championships in a row – 1983, 1984 and 1985 and won the title again in 1987 and 1991. She won the 1986 British Ladies' Stroke play amateur title. Two years earlier she had made the first of five playing appearances in the Curtis Cup before acting as non-playing captain in 2000.

Duggelby, Emma (ENG)

Born Fulford, York, 5 October 1971

Talented English golfer who won the British Ladies' Open Amateur Championship in 1994 and the English Ladies in 2000 when she made her Curtis Cup début. She also played in the 2004 match winning three points out of four.

Feng, Shanshan (CHN)

Born Guangzhou, 5 August 1989
Turned professional 2007

The first Chinese golfer to become a member of the LPGA, Feng won her first major title in 2012 when she won the LPGA Championship. Ranked fourth in the Rolex world rankings last year after a consistent season in which she won over $1m and recorded seven top ten finishes. She won nine events as an amateur in China before turning pro in 2007 after finishing ninth in qualifying for the LPGA. Now coached by Gary Gilchrist, who also teaches world No 1 Yani Tseng.

Fudoh, Yuri (JPN)

Born Kumamoto, 14 October 1976
Turned professional 1996

A multiple winner on the Japanese Tour who won her first Japanese event in 2003 when she took the Japan LPGA Championship title. She has won 20 events on the Japanese Tour and her winnings in 2000 of ¥120,443,924 was a record. By the end of 2010 she had become a yen billionaire in prize-money.

Gustafson, Sophie (SWE)

Born Saro, 27 December 1973
Turned professional 1992

Winner of the 2000 Weetabix Women's British Open she had studied marketing, economics and law before turning to professional golf. Credits Seve Ballesteros and Laura Davies as the two players most influencing her career. Her first European victory was the 1996 Swiss Open and her first on the LPGA Tour was the Chick-fil-A Charity Cup in 2000. She has played in every Solheim Cup match since 1998. Previously married to administrator Ty Votaw, the couple later divorced.

Haynie, Sandra (USA)

Born Fort Worth, Texas, 4 June 1943
Turned professional 1961

Twice a winner of the US Women's Open (1965 and 1974) she won 42 times between 1962 and 1982 on the US LPGA Tour. She was elected to the LPGA Hall of Fame in 1977.

Higuchi, Hisako "Chako" (JPN)

Born Saitama Prefecture, Japan, 13 October 1945
Turned professional 1967

A charter member and star of the Japan LPGA Tour, she won 72 victories worldwide during her career. In 2003 she was elected to the World Golf Hall of Fame.

Hjörth, Maria (SWE)

Born Falun, 10 October 1973
Turned professional 1996

After an excellent amateur career when she won titles in Finland, Norway and Spain, she attended Stirling University in Scotland on a golf bursary and graduated with a BA honours degree in English before turning professional. She has played in the Solheim Cup, most notably in 2011. In 2008 she was beaten in a play-off for the McDonald's LPGA Championship by Yani Tseng.

Hudson, Rebecca (ENG)

Born Doncaster, Yorkshire, 13 June 1979
Turned professional 2002

A member of the 1998, 2000 and 2002 Curtis Cup teams she won both the British Match Play and Stroke Play titles, the Scottish and English Stroke play Championships and the Spanish Women's Open in 2000. In addition she made the birdie that ensured Great Britain and Ireland won a medal in the World Team Championship for the Espirito Santo Trophy in Berlin in 2000.

Inkster, Juli (USA)

Born Santa Cruz, California, 24 June 1960
Turned professional 1983

Winner of two majors in 1984 (the Nabisco Championship and the du Maurier) she also had a double Major year in 1999 when she won the US Women's Open and the LPGA Championship which she won for a second time in 2000. In 2002 she won the US Women's Open for a second time. In all she has won seven major titles. In her amateur career she became the first player since 1934 to win the US Women's amateur title three years in a row (1980, 81, 82). Only four other women and one man (Tiger Woods) have successfully defended their national titles twice in a row. Coached for a time by the late London-based Leslie King at Harrods Store. She is a regular in the Solheim Cup competition having played nine times between between 1992 and 2011. By 2012her career earnings had surpassed $13.4m and she'd won 45 tournaments.

Irvin, Ann (ENG)

Born 11 April 1943

Winner of the British Ladies' title in 1973, she played in four Curtis Cup matches between 1962 and 1976. She was Daks Woman Golfer of the Year in 1968 and 1969 and has been active in administration at junior and county level.

Jackson, Bridget (ENG)

Born Birmingham, 10 July 1936

A former President of the Ladies' Golf Union she played in three Curtis Cup matches and captained the Vagliano Trophy side twice after having played four times. Although the best she managed in the British Championship was runner-up in 1964 she did win the English, German and Canadian titles.

Jang, Jeong (KOR)

Born Daejeon, Korea, 11 June 1980
Turned professional 1999

She scored her breakthrough win on the LPGA Tour when winning the Weetabix Women's British Open at Royal Birkdale. She led from start to finish. As an amateur she won the Korean Women's Open in 1997 and the following year was Korean Women's Amateur champion. Just 5ft tall, she started playing golf at age 13 and has been influenced throughout her career by her father.

Ji, Eun-Hee (KOR)

Born Gapyeong, South Korea, 13 May 1986
Turned professional 2004

A former Korean and Japanese Ladies Tour member she won her first major in 2009 when she was successful in the US Women's Open. She holed a 20-foot putt for a winning birdie at the last to collect a first prize of $580,000.

Johnson, Trish (ENG)

Born Bristol, 17 January 1966
Turned professional 1987

Another stalwart of the Women's Tour in Europe who learned the game at windy Westward Ho. Regular winner on Tour both in Europe and America, she scored two and a half points out of four in Europe's dramatic Solheim Cup win over the Americans at Loch Lomond in 2000. She has played in eight Solheim Cup matches. She was European No.1 earner in 1990. A loyal supporter of Arsenal FC she regularly attends games at The Emirates Stadium.

Kerr, Cristie (USA)

Born Florida, 1977 Turned professional 1997

She relished the second major success of her career in 2010 when she ran away with the LPGA Championship, defeating Song-Hee Kim by a record breaking margin of 12 shots. The first American to hold the No.1 spot in the world rankings, she finished in the top 20 at all four majors in 2010. Her previous major title victory came in the 2007 US Women's Open at Pine Needles, her favourite course. Kerr's official career earnings on the LPGA Tour amount to nearly $12m. In 2006 she had 19 top 10 finishes. In 1996 she played in the Curtis Cup and was low amateur in the US Women's Open. Since turning professional, she's won 14 events and played six times for the USA in the Solheim Cup. Unfortunately, she had to withdraw from the singles in 2011 because of injury, fofeiting a crucial point in the match won by Europe.

Kim, Birdie (KOR)

Born Ik-San, Korea, 26 August 1981
Turned professional 2000

She became the 14th player in the history of the LPGA Tour to score her first win at the US Women's Open and she did it dramatically holing a bunker shot at the last to beat amateurs Brittany Lang and Morgan Pressel by two shots at Cherry Hills, Colorado. A silver medallist at the 1998 Asian Games she won 19 events as an amateur before joining the US Futures Tour in 2001.

Kim, Christina (USA)

Born California, 1984 Turned professional 2002

One of the LPGA's most flamboyant and popular players, the American has won nearly $4m since becoming a regular Tour player in 2003. She's won twice and was a member of the US Solheim Cup teams on three occasions. In 2010 she recorded top ten finishes at both the US Women's Open and the Women's British Open.

King, Betsy (USA)

Born Reading, Pennsylvania, 13 August 1955
Turned professional 1977

Another stalwart of the LPGA Tour in America she won 34 times between 1984 and 2001. Winner of the British Open in 1985 she has also won the US Women's Open in 1989 and 1990, the Nabisco Championship three times in 1987, 1990 and 1997 and the LPGA Championship in 1990. She never managed to win the du Maurier event although finishing in the top six on nine occasions. Three times Rolex Player of the Year in 1984, 1989 and 1993 she was elected to the LPGA Hall of Fame in 1995.

Klein, Emilee (USA)

Born Santa Monica, California, 11 June 1974
Turned professional 1994

The former Curtis Cup player who played in the 1994 match scored her biggest triumph as a professional when winning the Weetabix British Women's Open at Woburn in 1996.

Ko, Lydia (NZL)

Born Korea, April 24 1997

She became the youngest player in 2012 ever to win on the LPGA when she claimed victory at the CN Canadian Women's Open with a 13 under par total of 275. She was 15 years and four months old, 15 months younger than Lexi Thompson when she won in 2011. As the world's leading amateur, she was ineligible for the prize money of $300,000. She also won the NSW Women's Open on the ALPG Tour when she was still 14. The inaugural recipient in 2011 of the Mark H McCormack medal for the top ranked female amateur golfer, she collected the same honour again in 2012. Among her notable amateur successes last year, she won the US Women's Amateur at the Country Club in Cleveland. The 14-year-old Kiwi (she was born in Korea but is a New Zealand citizen) was the first golfer to win both the Australian and New Zealand women's strokeplay championships in the same year. She won four other amateur tournaments in New Zealand in 2011. She became the youngest player ever to make a cut in a Ladies European Tour event after finishing seventh as a 12-year-old at the NZ Women's Open in 2010. On her debut at the Womens British Open she finished 17th at Hoylake last year.

Koch, Carin (SWE)

Born Kungalv, Sweden, 2 February 1971
Turned professional 1992

She has been playing golf since she was nine and in the 2000 and 2002 Solheim Cup matches was unbeaten. In 2000 she won three points out of three and in 2002 she won 2½ points out of three. She also played in the 2003 and 2005 matches.

Kuehne, Kelli (USA)

Born Dallas, Texas, 11 May 1977
Turned professional 1998

Having won the US Women's Amateur Championship in 1995 she successfully defended the title the following year when she also won the British Women's title – the first player to win both in the same year. She was also the first player to follow up her win in the US Junior Girls' Championship in 1994 with victory in the US Women's event the following year. Her brother Hank is also a professional.

Laing, Anne (SCO)

Born Alexandria, Dunbartonshire, 14 March 1975

Winner of three Scottish Championships in 1996, 2003 and 2004. She made her début in the Curtis Cup in 2004 having played in the Vagliano Trophy in 2003.

Lawrence, Joan (SCO)

Born Kinghorn, Fife, 20 April 1930

After a competitive career in which she three times won the Scottish championship and played in the

Nancy Lopez, (*née* Knight) (USA)

Born Torrance, California, 6 January 1957 Turned professional 1977

One of the game's bubbliest personalities and impressive performers who took her first title – the New Mexico Women's Amateur title at age 12. Between 1978 and 1995 she won 48 times on the LPGA Tour and was Rolex Player of the Year on four occasions (1978, 79, 85 and 88). In 1978, her rookie year, she won nine titles including a record five in a row. That year she also lost two play-offs and remains the only player to have won the Rookie of the Year, Player of the Year and Vare Trophy (scoring average) in the same season. A year later she won eight tournaments. Three times a winner of the LPGA Championship in 1978, 1985 and 1989 she has never managed to win the US Women's Open although she was runner-up in 1975 as an amateur, in 1977, 1989 and most recently 1997 when she lost out to Britain's Alison Nicholas. She retired from competitive golf and in 2002 was awarded the PGA's First Lady in Golf award for the contribution she has made to the game. In 2005 she captained the winning American Solheim Cup side at Crooked Stick. She started playing competitively again on a limited basis in 2007.

1964 Curtis Cup, she has played her part in golf administration. She had two four-year spells as an LGU selector, is treasurer of the Scottish Ladies' Golf Association and has also served on the LGU executive.

Lee-Smith, Jennifer (ENG)

Born Newcastle-upon-Tyne, 2 December 1948
Turned professional 1977

After winning the Ladies' British Open as an amateur in 1976 was named Daks Woman Golfer of the Year. She played twice in the Curtis Cup before turning professional and winning nine times in a six year run from 1979. For a time she ran her own driving range in southern England and is back living in Kent again after having spent time in Florida.

Lewis, Stacy (USA)

Born Toledo, Ohio, 1985 Turned professional 2008

She enjoyed her first LPGA win in the majors by lifting the Kraft Nabisco Championship in 2011. After trailing Yani Tseng by two strokes going into the final round, she rallied behind to overtake the world No 1 and win by three shots. In 2012 she won four times on the LPGA and rose to second in the Rolex world rankings, also becoming the first American since Beth Daniels in 1994 to win the LPGA player of the year award.

A formidable amateur golfer who became the first player in the history of the Curtis Cup to win all five of her matches over the Old Course in St Andrews, Lewis suffered from scoliosis and spent nearly eight years in a back brace before undergoing spinal surgery which left her unsure if she would be able to walk again

Lincicome, Britanny (USA)

Born St Petersburg, Florida, 19 September 1985
Turned professional 2004

She won the first 2009 major in spectaular fashion when eagling the final hole at Mission Hills to edge clear of Cristie Kerr and Kristie McPherson. Later in the year played in the Solheim Cup match. As an amateur she won the American Junior Golf Association Championship twice and first hit the headlines as a professional when she won the HSBC Women's World Match-play Championship beating Michelle Wie and Lorena Ochoa on the way to the final where she triumphed over Juli Inkster. She was a member of the 2007, 2009 and 2011 US Solheim Cup sides.

De Lorenzi, Marie-Laure (FRA)

Born Biarritz, 21 January 1961
Turned professional 1986

The stylish French golfer won 20 titles in Europe between 1987 and 1997 setting a record in 1988 when she won eight times but for family reasons never spent time on the US Tour.

Lunn, Karen (AUS)

Born Sydney, 21 March 1966
Turned professional 1985

A former top amateur she won the British Women's Open in 1993 at Woburn following the success in the European Ladies' Open earlier in the year by her younger sister Mardi.She is a former chairman of the LET.

McIntire, Barbara (USA)

Born Toledo, Ohio, 1935

One of America's best amateurs who finished runner-up in the 1956 US Women's Open to Kathy Cornelius at Northland Duluth. Winner of the US Women's Amateur title in 1959 and 1964 she also won the British Amateur title in 1960. She played in six Curtis Cups between 1958 and 1962.

McKay, Mhairi (SCO)

Born Glasgow, 18 April 1975
Turned professional 1997

Former British Girls' Champion (1992 and 1993) she has played in the Vagliano Trophy and Curtis Cup. She was an All-American when studying at Stanford University, where she was a contemporary of Tiger Woods, and made her first appearance in the Solheim Cup at Barsebäck, Sweden, in 2003.

McKenna, Mary (IRL)

Born Dublin, 29 April 1949

Winner of the British Ladies' Amateur Stroke play title in 1979 and eight times Irish champion between 1969 and 1989. One of Ireland's most successful golfers she played in nine Curtis Cup matches and nine Vagliano Trophy matches between 1969 and 1987. She captained the Vagliano team in 1995 and 2009. Three times a member of the Great Britain and Ireland Espirito Santo Trophy side she went on to captain the team in 1986. She was Daks Woman Golfer of the Year in 1979. She captained the Cutis Cup team beaten by the Americans at St Andrews in 2008 and was re-appointed captain for that event in 2010.

Mallon, Meg (USA)

Born Natwick, Maryland, 14 April 1963
Turned professional 1986

Winner of the 1991 US Women's Open, 1991 Mazda LPGA Championship, the 2000 du Maurier Classic and 11 other events between 1991 and 2002. In 2004 she won the US Women's Open for the second time. She holed the winning putt in the 2005 Solheim Cup.

Mann, Carole (USA)

Born Buffalo, New York, 3 February 1940
Turned professional 1960

Winner of 38 events on the LPGA Tour in her 22 years on Tour. A former president of the LPGA she was a key figure in the founding of the Tour and received the prestigious Babe Zaharias award. In 1964 she won the Western Open, then a Major, and in 1965 the US Women's Open but in 1968 she had a then record 23 rounds in the 60s, won 11 times and won the scoring averages prize with a score of 72.04. Enjoys a hugely successful corporate career within golf. In 2008 she was awarded the prestigious First Lady of Golf award from the PGA of America.

Massey, Debbie (USA)

Born Grosse Pointe, Michigan, 5 November 1950
Turned professional 1977

Best known for winning the British Women's Open in 1980 and 1981.

Matthew, Catriona (SCO)

Born Edinburgh, 25 August 1969
Turned professional 1995

Former Scottish Girls Under-21 and Scottish Amateur champion, Catriona also won the British Amateur in 1993. She played in the 1990, 1992 and 1994 Curtis Cup matches and made her début in the Solheim Cup at Barsebäck in 2003 and had the honour of holing the winning putt. She performed impressively throughout, showing considerable coolness under pressure. She was also a member of the 2005, 2007, 2009 and 2011 European teams. Now plays on both sides of the Atlantic. With Janice Moodie came second to Sweden's Annika Sörenstam and Liselotte Neumann in the 2006 Women's World Cup of Golf. In 2007 made the cut in all four women's majors and finished tied second in the Kraft Nabisco Championship. Sixteen years after she had won the Amateur Championship at Royal Lytham and St Annes she won her first major at that course when she won the Ricoh Women's British Open in 2009. Her victory came just two months after giving birth to her second daughter and a week after escaping with her husband who caddies for her, from a fire in the building they were staying in during the Evian Masters. In 2011 she returned to winning ways in the Aberdeen Scottish Open at Archerfield. The Scot also savoured an end of season victory in 2011 when she won the Lorena Ochoa Invitational in Mexico, her fourth career success on the LPGA Tour. And in 2012 she was pipped in a play-off by Suzann Pettersen for the LPGA Hana Bank Championship.

Meunier-Lebouc, Patricia (FRA)

Born Dijon, 16 November 1972
Turned professional 1993

French amateur champion in 1992, she has been a regular winner in Europe. She played in the 2000 and 2002 Solheim Cup matches and won her first major when she took first prize in the Kraft-Nabisco Championship at Mission Hills in California

Miyazato, Ai (JPN)

Born Okinawa, Japan, 19 June, 1985
Turned professional 2004

Miyazato became the first Japanese golfer ever to top the Order of Merit on the Ladies European Tour when she earned more than 363,000 euros from just two appearances in 2011. She earned all of her money from winning the Evian Masters for the second time. She donated a substantial portion of her earnings to the tsunami relief efforts in Japan. She topped the Rolex world rankings for 11 weeks in 2010 and has won nine times on the LPGA, including two victories in 2012.

Moodie, Janice (SCO)

Born Glasgow, 31 May 1973
Turned professional 1997

The 1992 Scottish Women's Stroke play champion played in two winning Curtis Cup teams and earned All American honours at San José State University where she graduated with a degree in psychology. She has won twice on the LPGA, is married to an American and has a young son, Craig. Started playing at age 11 and was helped considerably by Cawder professional Ken Stevely. In the 2000 Solheim Cup she won three out of four points but was controversially left out of the 2002 team. She was reinstated by captain Catrin Nilsmark for the 2003 match at Barsebäck in Sweden where she teamed up with fellow Scot Catriona Matthew and won her singles. She was a wild card pick for the 2009 Solheim Cup but only had one top ten finish in 2010.

Lorena Ochoa (MEX)

Born Guadalajara, 15 November 1981 *Turned professional 2003*

Announced her retirement from the LPGA as world No 1 in the spring of 2010 and finished sixth in her last event. She was thrillingly consistent throughout her career, finishing in the top ten at 109 of the 173 events she entered in America. Ochoa won her first major when she took the Ricoh British Women's Open when it was held for the first time over the Old Course at St Andrews. She was the fastest player to reach $3million in prize-money on the LPGA Tour in 2006, although she did not win a major that season, losing the Kraft Nabisco to Karrie Webb in a play-off at Palm Springs. However, she topped the money list and was Player of the Year. In 2006 she had six victories, five second place finishes, two thirds, two fourths and a fifth earning more than $2.5million. She fared even better in 2007 when she won eight times and pocketed $4.36 million in prize-money. In 2008 she won another major – the Kraft Nabisco. From the beginning of March to April 20 she won five times and enjoyed two more late season victories by the end of September. In 2009, she edged Ji Yai Shin for the Rolex Player of the Year Award by a single point. All told she won 27 times between 2004 and 2010 and earned nearly $15m. She chose to step down at the tender age of 29 because she had achieved her professional goals and wanted to start a family.

Muñoz, Azahara (ESP)

Born Malaga, 19 November 1987
Turned professional 2009

After winning the British Girls Championship at Lanark in 2004, 21-year-old Muñoz won the British Women's Amateur title with a 2 and 1 victory in an all-Spanish final against Carlota Ciganda. She immediately turned professional and in her rookie year won the Madrid Ladies Masters. Later she qualified to play on the LPGA Tour and ended the 2010 season winning the leading rookie award.

Neumann, Liselotte (SWE)

Born Finspang, 20 May 1966
Turned professional 1985

Having won the US Women's Open in 1988 she won the Weetabix British Women's Open title in 1990 to become one of six players to complete the Transatlantic double. The others are Laura Davies, Alison Nicholas, Jane Geddes, Betsy King and Patty Sheehan. The 1988 Rookie of the Year on the LPGA Tour she played in the first six Solheim Cup matches but was a surprising omission from the team in 2005 when she had one of her best years on the US Tour. With Annika Sörenstam won the 2006 World Cup of Golf in South Africa.

Nicholas MBE, Alison (ENG)

Born Gibraltar, 6 February 1978

In Solheim Cup golf had a successful partnership with Laura Davies. In addition they have both won the British and US Open Championships. Alison's first win on the European Tour came in the 1987 Weetabix British Open and she added the US Open ten years later after battling with Nancy Lopez who was trying to win her national title for the first time. Alison is a former winner of the Association of Golf Writers' Golfer of the Year award and has been honoured with an MBE. She announced her retirement from top-line competition in 2004. She captained the European Solheim Cup side in America in 2009. Europe lost but it was much closer than most people imagined it would be. Two year later, however, she led Europe to a famous victory at Killeen Castle.

Nilsmark, Catrin (SWE)

Born Gothenburg, Sweden, 28 Aug 1967
Turned professional 1987

Holed the winning putt in Europe's Solheim Cup victory in 1992. Her early career was affected by whiplash injury after a car crash. Used to hold a private pilot's licence but now rides Harley Davidson motorcycles. She captained the European team to victory in the 2003 Solheim Cup matches at Barsebäck in Sweden and captained the team again at Crooked Stick when America regained the trophy.

Nordqvist, Anna (SWE)

Born Esilstuna, Sweden, 10 June 1987
Turned professional 2008

Swedish Junior Player of the Year in 2004 and 2005 and Swedish Player of the Year in 2005 she won the British Girls' Championship in 2005 and the British Women's title in 2008 the year she was a member of the winning Swedish side in the World Amateur Team Championship for the Espirito Santo Trophy at Adelaide. After a hugely successful amateur career while attending Arizona State University. she turned professional and in only her fifth event on the LPGA Tour she won her first major – the McDonald's LPGA Championship. She credited Annika Sörenstam for the advice that helped her win a major so quickly in her professional career. She was a member of the 2009 European Solheim Cup side.

Okamoto, Ayako (JPN)

Born Hiroshima, 12 April 1951
Turned professional 1976

Although she won the British Women's Open in 1984 she managed only a runner-up spot in the US Women's Open and US LPGA Championships despite finishing in the top 20 28 times and missing the cut only four times. In the LPGA Championships she finished second or third five times in six years from 1986. She scored 17 victories in the USA between 1982 and 1992, won the 1990 German Open and was Japanese Women's champion in 1993 and 1997. The LPGA Tour's Player of the Year in 1987, she was inducted into the World Golf Hall of Fame in 2005.

Otto, Julie (*née* Wade) (ENG)

Born Ipswich, Suffolk, 10 March 1967

Secretary of the Ladies' Golf Union from 1996 to 2000 she was one of the most successful competitors in both individual and team golf. Among the many titles she won were the English Stroke Play in 1987 and 1993, the British Ladies' Stroke Play in 1993 and the Scottish Stroke Play in 1991 and 1993. She shared Britain's Golfer of the Year award in 1993 and won it again in 1995 on her own. She played in five Curtis Cup matches including the victories at Royal Liverpool in 1992 and Killarney in 1996 and the drawn match in 1994 at Chattanooga.

Pace, Lee-Anne (RSA)

Born 15 February 1981, Mosel Bay, South Africa
Turned professional 2005

Became the first South African to top the Ladies European Tour money list when she earned €339,517 from 25 events in 2010 and was named Players' Player of the Year. She won five times in 2010 in Switzerland, Wales, Finland, China and South Korea. She studied at the University of Tulsa and has a degree in Psychology.

Pak, Se Ri (KOR)

Born Daejeon, 28 September 1977
Turned professional 1996

In 1998 she was awarded the Order of Merit by the South Korean government – the highest honour given to an athlete – for having won two Majors in her rookie year on the US Tour. She won the McDonald's LPGA Championship matching Liselotte Neumann in making a major her first tour success. When she won the US Women's Open later that year after an 18-hole play-off followed by two extra holes of sudden death against amateur Jenny Chuasiriporn, she became the youngest golfer to take that title. By the middle of 2001 she had won 12 events on the US tour including the Weetabix Women's British Open at Sunningdale – an event included on the US Tour as well as the European Circuit for the first time. In 2002 she was again a multiple winner on the US Tour adding to her majors by winning the McDonald's LPGA Championship. As an amateur in Korea she won 30 titles and became the first lady professional to make the cut in a men's professional event for 58 years when she played four rounds in a Korean Tour event. In 2006 she returned to the major winner's circle when she beat Karrie Webb in a play off for the McDonald's LPGA Championship. It was her fifth major victory but her first since 2002. In 2007 she was inducted into the World Golf Hall of Fame, the first player from South Korea to be honoured. She posted five top ten finished on the LPGA in 2012 where she's won 25 times.

Panton-Lewis, Cathy (SCO)

Born Bridge of Allan, Stirlingshire, 14 June 1955
Turned professional 1978

A former Ladies' British Open Amateur Champion in 1976 when she was named Scottish Sportswoman of the year. She notched up 13 victories as a professional on the European tour between 1979 and 1988. Daughter of the late John Panton, MBE, former honorary professional to the Royal and Ancient Golf Club of St Andrews.

Park, Grace (KOR)

Born Seoul, Korea, 6 March 1979
Turned professional 1999

After having lost a sudden-death play-off to Annika Sörenstam at the McDonald's LPGA Championship in 2003 she did win her first major in 2004 when she was successful in the Nabisco Dinah Shore at Mission Hills in Palm Springs. She was a graduate of the Futures Tour where in 1999 she won five of the ten events. Before turning professional she attended Arizona State University and in 1998 became the first player since Patty Berg in 1931 to win the US Amateur, Western Amateur and Trans-Amateur titles in the same year. She won 55 national junior, college and amateur titles and tied eighth as an amateur in the 1999 US Women's Open. After years of back, neck and hip injuries, she announced her retirement from the game last year at the age of 33. All told, she won six events on the LPGA with career earnings of $5.4m.

Park, Inbee (KOR)

Born South Korea, 1988
Turned professional 2006

Started playing golf at the age of 10 and won nine events on the American Junior Golf Association circuit. She earned her LPGA card in 2006 and won her first major – the 2008 US Women's Open at Interlachen by four shots from Sweden's Helen Alfredsson In 2012 she rose to fifth in the world rankings after winning the Evian Masters and the Sime Darby LPGA Malaysia.

Pepper (Mochrie, Scarinzi), Dottie (USA)

Born Saratoga Springs, Florida, 17 August 1965
Turned professional 1987

Winner of 17 events on the LPGA Tour including two majors. She ranks 13th on the all-time money list with earnings of nearly $7 million. A fierce competitor she won the Nabisco Dinah Shore title in 1992 and again in 1999. She played in all the Solheim Cup matches up to 2000. In 2004 she announced her retirement from the US LPGA Tour because of injury. The following year she started work as a TV commentator for NBC and the Golf Channel, notoriously describing the US team at the 2007 Solheim Cup as "choking freaking dogs". While she apologised for her poor choice of words, a reputation for plain speaking has enhanced her broadcasting career.

Pettersen, Suzann (NOR)

Born Oslo, April 7 1981
Turned professional 2000

Five times Norwegian Amateur champion, Suzann was World Amateur champion in 2000. She won the French Open in 2001 and made her Solheim Cup début in the 2002 match at Barsebäck. One of the best performers on the week and was unbeaten going into the singles. She also played in the 2003, 2005, 2007, 2009 and 2011 matches and scored her first major success when she won the McDonald's LPGA Championship in 2007 going on that year to finish second to Lorena Ochoa in the LPGA money list. She won three times in 2011, twice on the LPGA and once on the LET, to finish the season in second place on the Rolex rankings She won the Hanabank Championship in 2012, defeating Catriona Matthew in a play-off. The 14th victory of her career took her earnings past the $9m mark. She has been a Working for Golf Ambassador on behalf of The R&A since 2011.

Prado, Catherine (*née* Lacoste) (FRA)

Born Paris 27 June 1945

The only amateur golfer ever to win the US Women's Open she won the title at Hot Springs, Virginia in 1967. She was also the first non-American to take the title and the youngest. Two years later she won both the US and British Amateur titles. She was a four times winner of her own French Championship in 1967, 1969, 1970 and 1972 and won the Spanish title in 1969, 1972 and 1976. She comes from a well-known French sporting family.

Rawls, Betsy (USA)

Born Spartanburg, South Carolina, 4 May 1928
Turned professional 1951

Winner of the 1951, 1953, 1957 and 1960 US Women's Open and the US LPGA Championship in 1959 and 1969 as well as two Western Opens when the Western Open was a Major. She scored 55 victories on the LPGA Tour between 1951 and 1972. One of the best shot makers in women's golf who was noted for her game around and on the greens.

Reid MBE, Dale (SCO)

Born Ladybank, Fife, 20 March 1959
Turned professional 1979

Scored 21 wins in her professional career between 1980 and 1991 and was so successful in leading Europe's Solheim Cup side to victory against the Americans at Loch Lomond in 2000 that she was again captain in 2002 when the Americans won. She had played in the 1990, 1992, 1994 and 1996 matches Following the team's success in the 2000 Solheim Cup she received an MBE.

Robertson MBE, Belle (SCO)

Born Southend, Argyll, 11 April 1936

One of Scotland's most talented amateur golfers who was Scottish Sportswoman of the Year in 1968, 1971, 1978 and 1981. She was Woman Golfer of the Year in 1971, 1981 and 1985. A former Ladies' British Open Amateur Champion and six times Scottish Ladies' Champion, she competed in nine Curtis Cups acting as non-playing captain in 1974 and 1976.

Sander, Anne (Welts, Decker, *née* Quast) (USA)

Born Marysville, 1938

A three times winner of the US Ladies' title in 1958, 1961 and 1963, she also won the British Ladies' title in 1980. She made eight appearances in the Curtis Cup stretching from 1958 to 1990. Only Carole Semple Thompson has played more often, having played ten times.

Saunders, Vivien (ENG)

Born Sutton, Surrey, 24 November 1946
Turned professional 1969

Founder of the Women's Professional Golfers' Association (European Tour) in 1978 and chairman for the first two years. In 1969 she was the first European golfer to qualify for the LPGA Tour in America. She is keen to become a re-instated amateur again.

Segard, Mme Patrick (de St Saveur, *née* Lally Vagliano) (FRA)

Former chairperson of the Women's Committee of the World Amateur Golf Council holding the post from 1964 to 1972. A four times French champion (1948, 50, 51 and 52) she also won the British (1950), Swiss (1949 and 1965), Luxembourg (1949), Italian (1949 and 1951) and Spanish (1951) amateur titles. She represented France from 1937 to 1939, from 1947 to 1965 and again in 1970.

Semple Thompson, Carol (USA)

Born 1950

Winner of six titles including the US Ladies' in 1973 and the British Ladies in 1974, he has played in 12 Curtis Cups between 1974 and 2002 and holed the 27-foot winning putt in the 2002 match. At 53 she is the oldest US Curtis Cup Player. She captained the side in 1998, 2006 and in 2008 when the match was played over the Old Course at St Andrews for the first time. In 2003 she was named winner of the Bob Jones award for sportsmanship and in 2005 received the PGA of America Lady of the Year trophy.

Sheehan, Patty (USA)

Born Middlebury, Vermont, 27 October 1956
Turned professional 1980

Scored 35 victories between 1981 and 1996 including six Majors – the LPGA Championship in 1983, 1984 and 1994, the US Women's Open in 1993 and 1994

Annika Sörenstam (SWE)

Born Stockholm, 9 October 1970 *Turned professional 1992*

Winner of the US Women's Open in 1995 and 1996 she and Karrie Webb of Australia have battled for the headlines on the LPGA Tour over the past few years. A prolific winner of titles in America. She won four in a row in early summer 2000 as she and Webb battled again for the No. 1 spot in 2001. Sörenstam was the No. 1 earner in 1995, 1997 and 1998, Webb in 1996, 1999 and 2000. At the Standard Register Ping event she became the first golfer to shoot 59 on the LPGA Tour. Her second round score 59 included 13 birdies, 11 of them in her first 12 holes. Her 36-hole total of 124 beat the record set by Webb the previous season by three. Her 54-hole score of 193 matched the record set by Karrie Webb and her 72-hole total of 261 which gave her victory by three shots from Se Ri Pak matched the low total on Tour set by Se Ri Pak in 1998. Sörenstam's 27-under-par winning score was a new record for the Tour beating the 26-under-par score Webb returned in the Australian Ladies' Masters in 1999. Her sister Charlotta also plays on the LPGA and Evian Tours.

Before turning professional she finished runner-up in the 1992 US Women's Championship. Sörenstam continued on her winning way in 2002 when her victories included another major – the Kraft Nabisco Championship. By the end of August she had won six times in the US and once more in Europe. By the beginning of October she had won nine times on the 2002 LPGA Tour and collected her 40th LPGA title. Only four players have won more than 9 events in one LPGA season. By October she had won $2.5 million world wide. In 2003 she was awarded the Golf Writers award in Britain for the golfer who had done most for European golf. In 2004 she quickly passed through the 50 mark in titles won in America. Before the middle of October her tally was 54 she had passed the $2 million mark in American Tour earnings for the year. In 2004 she added another major to her list of achievements winning the McDonald's LPGA Championship. She remains the dominant force in women's professional golf. When Annika won the Mizuno Classic in Japan she became the first player for 34 years to win 10 titles in a season.

In 2003 she took up the challenge of playing on the US Men's Tour teeing up in a blaze of publicity in the Colonial event in Texas but missed the half-way cut. She won her fifth Major when she took the McDonald's LPGA Championship in June and when she won the Weetabix British Women's Open at Royal Lytham and St Annes she completed a Grand Slam of major titles. Her tally is now six Majors. Her win at Lytham was her sixth major success. By the end of August 2003 she had won 46 LPGA tournaments and was inducted into the World Golf Hall of Fame. When she won the Mizuno Classic for the third successive year she was winning her 46th LPGA title and had wrapped up the Player of the Year and top money earner award. In 2004 she quickly passed through the 50 mark in titles won and before the middle of October had passed the $2 million mark in US PGA Tour earnings for a fourth successive year. She added another major to her personal tally when she won the McDonald's LPGA Championship. 2005 was another stellar year for Annika who took her career wins on the LPGA Tour to 66 with 10 more victories from her 20 starts. She easily topped the money list with over $2 million and moved her career earnings on the US Tour to $18,332,764. During the year she also won her own event in Sweden.

Her majors total at the end of 2005 after further Grand Slam victories in the Kraft Nabisco Championship and McDonald's LPGA Championship moved to nine. Although she did not win Player of the Year honours in 2006 – that went to Mexico's Lorena Ochoa – Annika again had an excellent season, winning three times and coming second on a further five occasions. She has now won 69 times and her earnings in America have gone through $20 million. She added a further major win to her list of Grand Slam successes and with Liselotte Neumann won the World Cup of Golf in South Africa early in the year. She also hosted and then won her own event in Sweden and beat Helen Alfredsson and Karrie Webb to the first prize at the Dubai Ladies Masters in November. In 2007 her appearances were curtailed because of injury and she announced her retirement from full-time professional golf in 2008 despite having won the SBS Open in Hawaii, the Stanford International and the Michelob Ultra Open in the United States. In her last season she earned $1,617,411 taking her total on Tour since 1994 to $22,454,692. Now runs her own event in Sweden. Appointed an ambassador in the bid to have golf included in the Olympic Games, she gave birth to her first child in 2009. She announced in 2010 she was expecting her second child.

and the Nabisco Championship in 1996. She also won the British Women's Open at Woburn in 1992 before it was designated a major. As an amateur she won all her four games in the 1980 Curtis Cup. She is a member of the LPGA Hall of Fame. She played in four Solheim Cup games between 1990 and 1996 and captained the side in 2002 and 2003.

Shin, Ji-Yai (KOR)

Born Chonnam, Korea, 28 April 1988
Turned professional 2006

She played 18 events on the Korean LPGA Tour in 2007 and won nine times, winning twice as much as her nearest rival with a then record total of $725,000. She was Korea's Player of the Year – a title she retained in 2008 when she became the first player to win all three events that comprise that circuit's Grand Slam. She had broken almost every record set on the Korean Tour by Se Ri Pak before the start of the 2008 season. In 2008 she won her first major – the Ricoh British Women's Open at Sunningdale – and went on to win two more times on the LPGA Tour taking the Mizuno Classic and the end-of-season ADT Championship in which she beat Karrie Webb by a shot to win US $1 million. She was the first non-member to win three times on that Tour. In addition she had three other top 10 finishes and earned US$1.77 million in prize-money. In 2008 she won 11 times – the three on the LPGA Tour, seven times in Korea and once in Japan. In 2009 she earned LPGA Rookie of the Year honours but was pipped at the post by Lorena Ochoa for the Rolex Player of the Year. By the end of 2010 she had played 60 events on the LPGA Tour and missed just one cut. Without a win in 2011, she relished two victories in the space of six days in 2012, following up her success over Paula Creamer at the ninth extra hole in the Kingsmill Championship with a nine stroke romp in the British Women's Open at Hoylake, the largest margin in the event's history.

Steinhauer, Sherri (USA)

Born Madison, Wisconsin, 27 December 1962
Turned professional 1985

Winner of the Weetabix Women's British Open at Woburn in 1999 and at Royal Lytham and St Annes in 1998 and again there in 2006. Her third victory was her first major success because the British Women's Open had been awarded major status. She has also played in four Solheim Cup matches.

Stephenson, Jan (AUS)

Born Sydney, 22 December 1951
Turned professional 1973

She won three majors on the LPGA Tour – the 1981 du Maurier Classic, the 1982 LPGA Championship and the 1983 US Women's Open. She was twice Australian Ladies champion in 1973 and 1977.

Streit, Marlene Stewart (CAN)

Born Cereal, Alberta, 9 March 1934

One of Canada's most successful amateurs she won her national title ten times between 1951 and 1973. She won the 1953 British Amateur, the US Amateur in 1956 and the Australian Ladies in 1963. She was Canadian Woman Athlete of the Year in 1951, 1953, 1956, 1960 and 1963.

Stupples, Karen (ENG)

Born Dover, England, 24 June 1973

English professional who lives in Orlando but hit the headlines at Sunningdale in the summer of 2004 when she won the Weetabix British Women's Open with a 19 under par total of 269. In the final round she began by making an eagle at the first and holing her second shot for an eagle 2 at the second. She finally clinched victory with the help of three birdies in a row on the back nine. Earlier in the year she had won on the LPGA Tour which she had joined in 1999. She has played golf since she was 11. She made her début in the Solheim Cup in 2005 and in 2011 gained a point for Europe without playing in the singles after Cristie Kerr pulled out through injury.

Suggs, Louise (USA)

Born Atlanta, Georgia, 7 September 1923
Turned professional 1948

Winner of 58 titles on the LPGA Tour after a brilliant amateur career which included victories in the 1947 US Amateur and the 1948 British Amateur Championships. She won 11 Majors including the US Women's Open in 1949 and 1952 and the LPGA Championship in 1957. A founder member of the US Tour she was an inaugural honoree when the LPGA Hall of Fame was instituted in 1967. In 2006 she was awarded the Bob Jones award for outstanding sportsmanship and for being a perfect ambassador for the game. She comes from Atlanta and knew Bobby Jones when she was younger.

Thomas, Vicki (*née* Rawlings) (WAL)

Born Northampton, 27 October 1954

One of Wales' most accomplished players who took part in six Curtis Cup matches between 1982 and 1992. She won the Welsh Championship eight times between 1979 and 1994 as well as the British Ladies' Stroke Play in 1990.

Thompson, Alexis (USA)

Born Florida, 10 February1995
Turned professional 2010

An outstanding amateur who won the US Junior girls in 2008, she was the youngest player at the age of 12 ever to qualify for the US Women's Open. After winning four and halving one of her matches in the Curtis Cup, she turned professional at 15 in the summer of 2010. She finished 10th at the US Women's Open and two weeks later at the Evian Masters was runner-up. After just three professional events she'd won $314,842. The LGU caused a stir when they declined to give the teenager an exemption into qualifying for the 2010 Women's British Open at Birkdale. In 2011 Alexis won the Navistar LPGA Classic in Alabama by five shots to become the youngest ever winner on the LPGA circuit. Better known as Lexi, she then became the second youngest ever winner on the LET when she won the Dubai Ladies Masters by four strokes. Aware of her exceptional talent, the LPGA changed their rules – which did not allow players to compete on Tour until they were 18 – in order that the teenager could play full time on the Tour in 2012.

Varangot, Brigitte (FRA)

Born Biarritz, 1 May 1940

Winner of the French Amateur title five times in six years from 1961 and again in 1973. Her run in the French Championship was impressive from

Yani Tseng (TPE)

Born Taoyuan, near Teipei, Taiwan, 1989 Turned professional 2007

With 11 victories around the world – including seven titles on the LPGA where she won nearly $3 million during 2011 –Tseng became the dominant player in women's golf. At just 22-years-old, she's won five major titles, the youngest golfer, male or female, ever to do so. A top-ranked Taiwanese amateur, she was the Asia-Pacific Junior Champion in 2003 and 2005. In 2004 she won the USGA Women's Amateur Public Links Championship, defeating Michelle Wie in the final. After turning professional, she competed initially on the Asian Golf Tour and in Canada. She joined the LPGA in 2008 and won her first major on the circuit that summer when she outlasted Sweden's Maria Hjörth at the fourth extra hole of a play-off for the McDonald's LPGA Championship. She enjoyed an even more successful season in 2010 when she won two more majors – the Kraft Nabisco and the Ricoh Women's British Open. Her victory at Birkdale meant she became the youngest woman ever to win three major titles.

Living in a house in Florida formerly owned by Annika Sörenstam, she has been mentored by the Swede, effectively succeeding both Sörenstam and Lorena Ochoa, who shared the No 1 spot for a decade, as the game's best player. By any standard, 2011 was an extraordinary season for the Taiwanese golfer. She won all of the first four tournaments she entered around the globe: the Taifong Ladies Open on the LPGA of Taiwan Tour; the ISPS Handa Women's Australian Open and ANZ RACV Ladies Open on the Australian Ladies Professional Golf Tour and the Ladies European Tour (LET) and the Honda LPGA Thailand, the season-opener on the LPGA. Thereafter, she was runner up at the Kraft Nabisco, the first major of the season, before adding to her impressive haul of victories in the most prized events with wins at the Wegmans LPGA and the Women's British Open. At Carnoustie, she was the first champion to mount a successful defence. And on the LPGA, where she posted 14 top tens in 22 events, she was only the 17th golfer since 1950 to win six tournaments or more in a single season.By those lofty standards, 2012 was more of a routine season, though she still won three times on the LPGA and earned more than $1.2m.

1960 when her finishes were 2, 1, 1, 2, 1, 1, 1, 2. She was also a triple winner of the British Championship in 1963, 1965 and 1968. One of France's most successful players she also won the Italian title in 1970.

Walker OBE, Mickey (ENG)

Born Alwoodley, Yorkshire, 17 December 1952
Turned professional 1973

Always a popular and modest competitor she followed up an excellent amateur career by doing well as a professional. Twice a Curtis Cup player she won the Ladies' British Open Amateur in 1971 and 1972, the English Ladies' in 1973 and had victories, too, in Portugal, Spain and America where she won the 1972 Trans-Mississippi title. She won six times as a professional but is perhaps best known for her stirring captaincy of the first four European Solheim Cup sides leading them to a five point success at Dalmahoy. In 1992 she galvanised her side by playing them tapes of the men's Ryder Cup triumphs. Now a club professional she also works regularly as a television commentator for Sky

Whitworth, Kathy (USA)

Born Monahans, Texas, 27 September 1939
Turned professional 1958

Won 88 titles on the LPGA Tour between 1959 and 1991 – more than any one else male or female. Her golden period was in the 1960s when she won eight events in 1965, nine in 1966, eight in 1967 and 10 in 1968. When she finished third in the 1981 US Women's Open she became the first player to top $1 million in prize money on the LPGA Tour. She was the seventh member of the LPGA Tour Hall of Fame when inducted in 1975. Began playing golf at the age of 15 and made golfing history when she teamed up with Mickey Wright to play in the previously all male Legends of Golf event. Winner of six Majors – including three LPGA Championship wins in 1967, 1971 and 1975. In addition she won two Titleholders' Championships (1966 and 1967) and the 1967 Western Open when they were Majors. Enjoyed a winning streak of 17 successive years on the LPGA Tour.

Wie, Michelle (USA)

Born Hawaii, 11 October 1989
Turned professional 2005

As an amateur she finished third in the Weetabix British Women's Open in July 2005 and turned professional in October as a 16-year-old with multi-million contract guarantees. In her first event as a professional in the Samsung Championship she finished fourth behind Annika Sörenstam but then was disqualified for a dropped ball infringement incurred in the third round – and spotted by an American journalist who did not report it until the following day. In 2006 she continued to play in a few men's events including the Omega European Masters at Crans-sur-Sierre but failed to make the cut in any. She did make the cut in all four majors in 2006. She combines her professional career with her school work in Hawaii and it is reported she hopes to go eventually to Stanford University. In 2008 she earned a card on the LPGA Tour at the Qualifying School.

Karrie Webb (AUS)

Born Ayr, Queensland, 21 December 1974 *Turned professional 1994*

Blonde Australian who is rewriting the record books with her performances on the LPGA Tour. Peter Thomson, the five times Open champion considers she is the best golfer male or female there is and Greg Norman, who was her inspiration as a teenager, believes she can play at times better than Tiger Woods although Webb herself hates comparisons. She scored her first Major win in 1995 when she took the Weetabix Women's British Open – a title she won again in 1997. When she joined the LPGA Tour she won the 1999 du Maurier Classic, the 2000 Nabisco Championship and the 2000 and 2001 US Women's Open – five Majors out of eight (by the end of July 2001) – the most impressive run since Mickey Wright won five out of six in the early 1960s. In 2002 she became the first player to complete a career Grand Slam when she won her third Weetabix British Open which had become an official major on the US LPGA Tour. It was her sixth major title in four years. Her winning total at Turnberry was 15 under par 273. Enjoyed a close rivalry with Annika Sörenstam. In 2005 she was inducted into the World Golf Hall of Fame. She added to her majors tally in 2006 when she beat Lorena Ochoa in a play-off for the Kraft Nabisco Championship. Later she lost a play-off to Se Ri Pak for another major – the McDonald's LPGA Championship. She is the only player to have victories in the current four majors and the du Maurier event, now discarded as a major. She added more than $800,000 to her career earnings of $17.3m in 2012 thanks to six top ten finishes on the LPGA.

She was chosen as a wild card and played with distinction in the 2009 Solheim Cup side won by the Americans and later in the year won her first event on the LPGA Tour when she took the Lorena Ochoa Mexico Classic.

Wright, Janette (*née* Robertson) (SCO)

Born Glasgow, 7 January 1935

Another of Scotland's most accomplished amateur players she competed four times in the Curtis Cup and was four times Scottish champion between 1959 and 1973. Formerly married to the late Innes Wright. Her daughter Pamela was Collegiate Golfer of the Year 1988 and LPGA Rookie of the Year in 1989.

Wright, Mickey (USA)

Born San Diego, California, 14 February 1935
Turned professional 1954

Her 82 victories on the LPGA Tour between 1956 and 1973 was bettered only by Kathy Whitworth who has 88 official victories. One of the greatest golfers in the history of the Tour she had a winning streak of 14 successive seasons. Winner of 13 Major titles she is the only player to date to have won three in one season. In 1961 she took the US Women's Open, the LPGA Championship and the Titleholders' Championship. That year she became only the second player to win both the US Women's Open and LPGA Championship in the same year having done so previously in 1958. Scored 79 of her victories between 1956 and 1969 when averaging almost eight wins a season. During this time she enjoyed a tremendous rivalry with Miss Whitworth.

Yang, Amy (KOR)

Born South Korea 28 July 1989
Turned professional 2006

Only 16 when she won the ANZ Ladies Masters on the LET in 2006, Yang took up the game at the age of ten before emigrating to Australia when she was 15. Her family moved to Florida in 2007 when she took up membership of the LPGA. Runner-up at the US Women's Open and fourth at the Kraft Nabisco in 2012, she's won three times on the LET but is still seeking her first success on the LPGA.

Yokomine, Sakura (JPN)

Born Konoya Kagoshima, 13 December 1985
Turned professional 2005

Winner of 17 events on the Japan LPGA Tour. She was top earner in Japan in 2009 but took second spot in 2010 to Korean golfer Ahn Sun-Ju.

Yoo, Sun Young (KOR)

Born Seoul, 13 December 1986
Turned professional 2004

Winner of the Kraft Nabisco in 2012, her first major title, thanks to a sudden death play-off win over I.K. Kim, who had missed a short putt for victory on the 72nd hole. It was only her second victory on the LPGA after the Sybase Match Play in 2010. As an amateur, she reached the quarter-finals of the US Women's Amateur in 2004 before turning professional later that year.

Famous Personalities of the Past

In making the difficult choice of the names to be included, effort has been made to acknowledge the outstanding players and personalities of each successive era from the early pioneers to the stars of recent times.

Alliss, Percy
Anderson, Jamie
Anderson, Willie
Archer, George
Armour, Tommy
Auchterlonie, Willie
Balding, Al
Ballesteros, Severiano
Ball, John
Barnes, Jim
Barton, Pamela
Berg, Patty
Bolt, Tommy
Boros, Julis
Bousfield, Ken
Bradshaw, Harry
Braid, James
Brewer, Gay
Brown, Eric
Bruen, Jimmy
Camicia, Mario
Campbell, Dorothy
Carr, Joe
Coe, Charlie
Compston, Archie
Cotton, Sir Henry
Crawley, Leonard
Curtis, The Sisters
Daly, Fred
Darwin, Bernard
Demeret, Jimmy
Dobereiner, Peter
Duncan, George
Faulkner, Max
Ferguson, Bob
Fernie, Willie
Garrett, Maureen
Garvey, Philomena
Goldschmid, Isa
Hagen, Walter
Harper, Chandler
Henning, Harold
Herd, Sandy
Hilton, Harold
Hogan, Ben
Howard, Barclay
Hutchinson, Horace
Jarman, Ted
Jones, Bob
King, Sam
Kirkaldy, Andrew
Laidlay, John
Leitch, Cecil
Lema, Tony
Little, Lawson
Locke, Bobby
Longhurst, Henry
Lunt, Michael
McCormack, Mark
McDonald, CB
Mackenzie, Alister
Mackenzie, Keith
Massy, Arnaud
Micklem, Gerald
Middlecoff, Cary
Minoprio, Gloria
Mitchell, Abe
Moody, Orville
Morgan, Wanda
Morris, Old Tom
Morris, Young Tom
Nelson, Byron
Norman, Moe
Ortiz-Patino, Jaime
Ouimet, Francis
Panton, John
Park, Mungo
Park, Willie
Park, Willie Jr
Patton, Billy Joe
Philp, Hugh
Picard, Henry
Price-Fisher, Elizabeth
Ray, Ted
Rees, Dai
Robertson, Allan
Rosburg, Bob
Ryder, Samuel
Sarazen, Gene
Sayers, Ben
Sewgolum, Sewunker
Shade, Ronnie
Smith, Frances
Smith, Horton
Smith, Macdonald
Snead, Sam
Solheim, Karsten
Souchak, Mike
Spearman, Marley
Stewart, Payne
Tait, Freddie
Taylor, JH
Tolley, Cyril
Travis, Walter
Tumba, Sven
Valentine, Jessie
Van Donck, Flory
Vardon, Harry
Vare, Glenna
Von Nida, Norman
Walker, George
Ward, Charlie
Ward, Harvie
Wethered, Joyce
Wethered, Roger
Whitcombes, The
White, Ronnie
Will, George
Wilson, Enid
Wind, Herbert Warren
Wood, Craig
Wooldridge, Ian
Yates, Charlie
Zaharias, "Babe"

Alliss, Percy (1897–1975)

Father of Peter Alliss he finished in the top six in The Open Championship seven times, including joint third at Carnoustie in 1931, two strokes behind winner Tommy Armour. Twice winner of the Match Play Championship, five times German Open champion and twice winner of the Italian Open. He was a Ryder Cup player in 1933–35–37, an international honour also gained by his son. Spent six yesrs as professional at the Wansee Club in Berlin before moving back to Britain to work at Beaconsfield, Temple Newsam and for 30 years at Ferndown in Dorset.

Anderson, Jamie (1842–1912)

Winner of three consecutive Open Championships – 1877–78–79. A native St Andrean, he once claimed to have played 90 consecutive holes on the Old Course without a bad or unintended shot. He was noted for his straight hitting and accurate putting.

Anderson, Willie (1878–1910)

Took his typically Scottish flat swing to America where he won the US Open four times in a five year period from 1901. Only Bobby Jones, Ben Hogan and Jack Nicklaus have also won the US Open four times.

Archer, George (1940–2005)

The 6ft 5in tall former cowboy won The Masters in 1969 – one of four golfers who won their first major that year. A superb putter Archer was dogged throughout his career by injury but he won 12 times on the PGA Tour and a further 19 times on the US Senior Tour now the Champions Tour. Elizabeth, one of his two daughters, made headlines when she caddied for her father and became the first woman to do so at Augusta.

Armour, Tommy (1896–1968)

Born in Edinburgh, he played for Britain against America as an amateur and, after emigrating, for America against Britain as a professional in the forerunners of the Walker and Ryder Cup matches. Won the US Open in 1927, the USPGA in 1930 and the 1931 Open at Carnoustie. Became an outstanding coach and wrote several bestselling instruction books. Known as "The Silver Scot".

Auchterlonie, Willie (1872–1963)

Won The Open at Prestwick in 1893 at the age of 21 with a set of seven clubs he had made himself. Founded the famous family club-making business in St Andrews. He believed that golfers should master half, three-quarter and full shots with each club. Appointed Honorary Professional to The R&A in 1935.

Balding, Al (1924–2006)

A lovely swinger of the club, he was the first Canadian to win on the US Tour when he took the Mayfair Inn Open in Florida in 1955. In 1968, in partnership with Stan Leonard, he won the World Cup in Rome and was himself low individual scorer that year.

Ball, John (1861–1940)

Finished fourth in The Open of 1878 at the age of 16 and became the first amateur to win the title in 1890 when The Open was played at Prestwick. He won the Amateur Championship eight times and shares with Bobby Jones the distinction of being the winner of The Open and Amateur in the same year – 1890. He grew up on the edge of the links area which became the Royal Liverpool Golf Club and the birthplace of the Amateur. He was a master at keeping the ball low in the wind, but with the same straight-faced club could cut the ball up for accurate approach shots. His run of success could have been greater but for military service in the South African campaign and the First World War.

Barnes, Jim (1887–1966)

Raised in Cornwall before emigrating to California, where he took US citizenship, the 6ft 4ins golfer enjoyed outstanding success in the professional major championships of the early 20th century. He won The Open at Prestwick in 1925 and enjoyed a consistent record in the oldest major throughout the 1920s. He also made his mark with a string of top ten finishes in the US Open before winning America's national championship in 1921 in Maryland by nine strokes, a record which stood for nearly 80 years. And in the US PGA Championship, which was initially a match-play tournament, he won the first two stagings in 1916 and 1919.

Barton, Pamela (1917–1943)

At the age of 19 she held both the British and American Ladies Championships in 1936. She was French champion at 17, runner-up in the British in both 1934 and '35 and won the title again in 1939. A Curtis Cup team member in 1934 and '36 she was a Flight Officer in the WAAF when she was killed in a plane crash at an RAF airfield in Kent.

Berg, Patty (1915–2006)

The golf pioneer who won an LPGA Tour record 15 major titles and was one of the 13 founding members of the tour in 1950. She was the LPGA Tour's first president from 1950–52 and was the tour's money leader in 1954, '55 and '57 ending her career with 60 victories. She was a member of the LPGA Tour and World Golf Halls of Fame. She was described as a pioneer, an athlete, a mentor, a friend and an entertainer and had a great sense of humour.

Bolt, Tommy (1916–2008)

The 1958 US Open champion and two-time Ryder Cup player who is remembered as much for his short temper as his short game. He had a penchant for throwing clubs insisting it was better to throw them ahead of you in order to avoid having to walk back for them! Known as "Terrible Tommy" he was a founding member of the US Champions Tour. In the 1957 Ryder Cup at Lindrick he lost a bad-tempered game to fiery Scot Eric Brown.

Boros, Julius (1920–1994)

Became the oldest winner of a major championship when he won the USPGA in 1968 at the age of 48. He twice won the US Open, in 1952 and again 11 years later at Brookline when he was 43. In a play-off he beat Jackie Cupit by three shots and Arnold Palmer by six. He played in four Ryder Cup matches between 1959–67, winning nine of his 16 matches and losing only three.

Bousfield, Ken (1919–2000)

Although a short hitter even by the standards of his era, he won five out of 10 matches in six Ryder Cup appearances from 1949–61. He captured the PGA Match Play Championship in 1955, one of eight tournament victories in Britain, and also won six European Opens. He represented England in the World Cup at Wentworth in 1956 and Tokyo in 1957.

Bradshaw, Harry (1913–1950)

One of Ireland's most loved golfers whose swing Bernard Darwin described as "rustic and rugged". With Christy O'Connor he won the Canada Cup (World Cup) for Ireland in Mexico in 1958 but he is also remembered for losing the 1949 Open to Bobby Locke after having hit one shot out of a bottle at the fifth on the second day. That bit of bad luck, it was later considered, cost him £10,000.

Braid, James (1870–1950)

Together with Harry Vardon and J.H. Taylor he formed the Great Triumvirate and dominated the game for 20 years before the 1914–18 war. In a 10-year period from 1901 he became the first player in the history of the event to win The Open five times –

Severiano Ballesteros

1957–2011

Adventurous, exciting to watch and always unpredictable, the qualities which laid the foundation for the success of Severiano Ballesteros as a driven stroke-play champion were, if anything, even more formidable assets when the Spaniard conquered the arena of match-play. As well as his five major titles, the crowning achievement of a charismatic career cut short at the early age of 54, was an example he set for European golf in the Ryder Cup.

Of the many attributes Ballesteros shared with Arnold Palmer, the swashbuckling adventurer to whom he was most often compared, fearlessness was perhaps the most significant trait. His whole career was governed by passion and romanticism. And, just like Palmer in America, his blows of brilliance enlarged the audience for professional golf in Europe through TV exposure.

While the world of golf loved Seve's ebullience, he was held in particularly high esteem in the British Isles. The galleries in the UK were smitten from the moment at Royal Birkdale in 1976 when he executed a devious chip sending it running between the bunkers on the home hole rather than taking the aerial route. It was a shot of such sublime touch and imagination, no one who saw the teenager pull it off would have been surprised when the Spaniard went to have his name inscribed on the Claret Jug three times in 1979, 1984 and 1988. All told he won 52 titles between 1976 and 1999 including two stagings of The Masters at Augusta in 1980 and 1983.

When asked to choose the greatest player he'd ever seen, Lee Trevino selected the Spaniard. "Jack Nicklaus made a plan," he said. "Tiger Woods makes a plan. Seve never made a plan. He just made things happen. He had something we didn't have."

Born in a small village near Santander in the north of Spain, Seve was surrounded by family who played the game and caddied at Pedrena. As a boy, his brother Manuel gave him the gift of a 3 iron and the youngster used the club to perfect a variety of shots on a local beach. He became a professional before celebrating his 17th birthday and two years later made his mark in The Open at Birkdale when he led for three days and finished runner-up alongside Jack Nicklaus to Johnny Miller.

Apart from his triumphs on the British linksland, Ballesteros was more at home at Augusta National than anywhere else. It's worth recalling, before chronic back trouble sapped his power, how long Seve was off the tee. The combination of distance and touch was perfect for the Masters. His performances in Georgia in 1980 and 1983 were as dazzling as anything ever produced at Augusta. The bogeys which punished Seve's wayward tendencies were exceeded by electrifying surges of birdies and eagles. When Seve was around, the game was always human, never robotic. For example, in Friday's second round of the 1980 Masters, Seve struck a hook so far left on the 17th hole that his ball finished on the seventh green. However, after taking a free drop, he launched a blind iron shot onto the correct green and recovered by holing the improbable birdie putt.

When the 23-year-old slipped into a Green Jacket, church bells in his home town of Pedrena rang out in celebration. There was more music in 1983 when he started his final round at Augusta with a devastating flurry of birdie, eagle, par, birdie – four under par for the opening four holes – which the Spaniard regarded as "the best I ever played in my life." The greatest stroke, though, was surely that 15 foot birdie putt on the 18th green at St Andrews which sealed his second Open triumph. Ballesteros calls it "El Momento" and a silhouette of his ensuing celebration is surely the defining image of his career.

In the Ryder Cup, the arrival of Ballesteros and the example he set to others changed everything. There was an intensity about Ballesteros' play which galvanised the European cause. In many respects, the story of the modern Ryder Cup can be told in two distinct phases: before and after Seve. He played eight times in the match, finishing on the winning side four times, and was a winning captain in 1997.

Problems in his lower back caused a deterioration in his game in the Nineties and the last of his 50 European Tour wins came at the Spanish Open in 1995. He was diagnosed with a brain tumour after collapsing with an epileptic fit at Madrid Airport in 2008. Caught up in the most daunting challenge of his life, Ballesteros endured four operations, six subsequent courses of chemotherapy and radio-therapy treatment with the resilience of a champion before passing away in 2010. He may have died tragically early but the passion with which he played the game ensures his memory will live for ever.

and also finished second on three occasions. In that same period he won the Match Play Championship four times and the French Open. He was a tall, powerful player who hit the ball hard but always retained an appearance of outward calm. He was one of the founder members of the Professional Golfers' Association and did much to elevate the status of the professional golfer. He was responsible for the design of many golf courses and served as professional at Walton Heath for 45 years. He was an honorary member of that club for 25 years and became one of its directors. He was also an honorary member of The R&A.

Brewer, Gay (1932–2007)

Winner of the 1967 Masters he was one of the most popular figures on the US Tour and later the Champions Tour. His love of the game, his joviality and his story-telling were all part of the legacy of the man from Lexington, Kentucky, whose loopy swing was one of the most unorthodox.

Brown, Eric (1925–1986)

Twice captained the Ryder Cup side and for many years partnered John Panton for Scotland in the World Cup. A larger-than-life personality, he was one of two Cup captains who came from the Bathgate club. The other was Bernard Gallacher, who played in the 1969 match which Brown captained.

Bruen, Jimmy (1920–1972)

Won the Irish Amateur at the age of 17 and defended the title successfully the following year. At 18 he became the youngest ever Walker Cup player at that time and in practice for the match at St Andrews in 1938 equalled the then amateur course record of 68 set by Bobby Jones.

Camicia, Mario (1941–2011)

Often referred to as Italy's "Mr Golf" Mario was a passionate lover of the game who did much to make Italians more aware of and more interested in the game. For many years he ran the Italian Open, wrote in magazines and newspapers and became the country's first television golf commentator. He was the voice of golf in Italy who enjoyed the success Costantino Rocca, the Molinari brothers and Matteo Manassero had on the international scene. Commenting on his death Franco Chimenti, President of the Italian Federation, said: "The game has lost a good friend."

Campbell, Dorothy Iona (1883–1946)

One of only two golfers to win the British, American and Canadian Ladies titles. In total she won these three major championships seven times.

Carr, Joe (1922–2004)

The first Irishman to captain the Royal and Ancient Golf Club of St Andrews, he was winner of three British Amateur Championship titles in 1953, 1958 and 1960. He played in or captained Walker Cup sides from 1947 to 1963 making a record 11 appearances. He was the first Irishman to play in The Masters at Augusta, made 23 consecutive appearances for Ireland in the Home Internationals and was a regular winner of the West of Ireland and East of Ireland Championships. At one point in an illustrious career he held 18 different course records. An ebullient, fast-talking personality with a somewhat eccentric swing, he was one of Ireland's best known and best loved golfers. In 2007 he was inducted posthumously into the World Golf Hall of Fame in St Augustine, Florida.

Coe, Charlie (1923–2007)

Another fine American amateur golfer who finished runner-up with Arnold Palmer to Gary Player in the 1961 Masters at Augusta. Twice US Amateur champion in 1949 and 1958, he played in six Walker Cup matches and was non-playing captain in 1959. He won seven and halved two of the 13 games he played. Winner of the Bobby Jones award in 1964. Born in Oklahoma City, he never considered turning professional.

Compston, Archie (1893–1962)

Beat Walter Hagen 18 and 17 in a 72-hole challenge match at Moor Park in 1928 and tied for second place in the 1925 Open. Played in the Ryder Cup in 1927–29–31.

Cotton, Sir Henry (1907–1987)

The first player to be knighted for services to golf, he died a few days before the announcement of the award was made. He won The Open Championship three times, which included a round of 65 at Royal St George's in 1934 after which the famous Dunlop golf ball was named. His final 71 at Carnoustie to win the 1937 Championship in torrential rain gave him great satisfaction and he set another record with a 66 at Muirfield on the way to his third triumph in 1948 watched by King George VI. He won the Match Play Championship three times and was runner-up on three occasions. He also won 11 Open titles in Europe, played three times in the Ryder Cup and was non-playing captain in 1953. Sir Henry worked hard to promote the status of professional golf and also championed the cause of young golfers, becoming a founder member of the Golf Foundation. He was a highly successful teacher, author and architect, spending much time at Penina, a course he created in southern Portugal. He was an honorary member of The R&A.

Crawley, Leonard (1903–1981)

Played four times in the Walker Cup in 1932–34–38–47 and won the English Amateur in 1931. He also played first-class cricket for Worcestershire and Essex and toured the West Indies with the MCC in 1936. After the Second World War he was golf correspondent for the *Daily Telegraph* for 30 years.

The Curtis sisters, Harriet (1878–1944) Margaret (1880–1965)

Donors of the Curtis Cup still contested biennially between the USA and GB&I. Harriet won the US Women's Amateur in 1906 and lost in the following year's final to her sister Margaret, who went on to win the championship three times.

Daly, Fred (1911–1990)

Daly won The Open at Royal Liverpool in 1947 and in four of the next five years was never out of the top four in the Championship. At Portrush, where he was born, he finished fourth to Max Faulkner in 1951, the only time The Open has been played in Northern Ireland. He was Ulster champion 11 times and three times captured the prestigious PGA Match Play Championship. He was a member of the Ryder Cup team four times, finishing on a high note at Wentworth in 1953 when he won his foursomes match in partnership with Harry Bradshaw and then beat Ted Kroll 9 and 7 in the singles.

Darwin, Bernard (1876–1961)

One of the most gifted and authoritative writers on golf, he was also an accomplished England international player for more than 20 years. While in America to report the 1922 Walker Cup match for The Times, he was called in to play and captain the side when Robert Harris became ill. A grandson of Charles Darwin, he was Captain of the Royal and Ancient Golf Club of St Andrews in 1934–35. In 1937 he was awarded the CBE for services to literature. He was inducted posthumously into the World Golf Hall of Fame in 2005.

Demaret, Jimmy (1910–1983)

Three times Masters champion, coming from five strokes behind over the final six holes to beat Jim Ferrier by two in 1950, he also won six consecutive tournaments in 1940 while still performing as a night club singer. He won all six games he played in the 1947, 1949 and 1951 Ryder Cup matches.

Dey, Joseph C (Joe) (1907–1991)

A former sportswriter who covered the final leg of Bobby Jones' Grand Slam in 1930 he joined the USGA and srved as executive director from 1934 to 1968. Following his retirement he was appointed the first Commissioner of the PGA Tour – a post he held from 1969 to 1974. Dey also helped to synchronise the rules of golf around the world, instigated the PGA Tour's Players Championship and in 1975 was honorary captain of the Royal and Ancient Golf Club of St Andrews.

Dobereiner, Peter (1925–1996)

A multi-talented journalist in various fields who wrote eloquently, knowledgeably and amusingly on golf in many books, *Golf Digest*, and *Golf World* magazines and in *The Observer* and *Guardian* newspapers for whom he was correspondent for many years. Born of English-Scottish-Danish-Red Indian and German parentage he claimed he stubbornly refused all efforts by King's College, Taunton and Lincoln College, Oxford to impart a rudimentary education so chose journalism as a profession.

Duncan, George (1884–1964)

Won The Open in 1920 by making up 13 shots on the leader over the last two rounds and came close to catching Walter Hagen for the title two years later. Renowned as one of the fastest players, his book was entitled *Golf at the Gallop*.

Faulkner, Max (1916–2005)

One of the game's most extrovert and colourful personalities, who won the 1951 Open Championship at Royal Portrush, the only time the event was played in Northern Ireland. He played in five Ryder Cups and was deservedly if belatedly recognised for his contribution to the game with an honour in 2001 when he was awarded the OBE. His son-in-law is Brian Barnes, another golfing extrovert.

Ferguson, Bob (1848–1915)

The Open Championship winner three times in succession between 1880–82. He then lost a 36-hole play-off for the title by one stroke to Willie Fernie in 1883. He had shown his potential when, at the age of 18, he had won a tournament at Leith Links against the game's leading professionals.

Fernie, Willie (1851–1924)

In 1882 he was second to Bob Ferguson in The Open over his home course at St Andrews. The following year he beat the same player in a 36-hole play-off for the championship over Ferguson's home links at Musselburgh.

Garrett, Maureen (née Ruttle) (1922–2011)

President of the Ladies' Golf Union from 1982 to 1985, she captained the Curtis Cup (1960) and Vagliano Trophy (1961) teams. In 1983 won the Bobby Jones award presented annually by the United States Golf Association to a person who emulates Jones' spirit, personal qualities and attitude to the game and its players.

Garvey, Philomena (1927–2009)

Born in Drogheda she was one of Ireland's most successful competitors winning the Irish Ladies title 15 times between 1946 and 1970. She played six times in the Curtis Cup between 1948 and 1960 and won the British Ladies Amateur title in 1957. In 1964 she turned professional but was later re-instated an amateur.

Goldschmid Isa (née Bevione) (1925–2002)

One of Italy's greatest amateurs, she won her national title 21 times between 1947 and 1974 and was ten times Italian Open champion between 1952 and 1969. Among her other triumphs were victories in the 1952 Spanish Ladies and the 1973 French Ladies.

Hagen, Walter (1892–1969)

A flamboyant character who used a hired Rolls Royce as a changing room because professionals were not allowed in many clubhouses, he once gave his £50 cheque for winning The Open to his caddie. He won four consecutive USPGA Championships from 1924 when it was still decided by matchplay. He was four times a winner of The Open, in 1922–24–28–29 and captured the US Open title in 1914 and 1919. He captained and played in five Ryder Cup encounters between 1927–35, winning seven of his nine matches and losing only once. He was non-playing captain in 1937.

Harper, Chandler (1914–2004)

Born in Portsmouth, VA, he was winner of the 1950 US PGA Championship. He won over ten tournaments and was elected to the US PGA Hall of Fame in 1969. Once shot 58 (29-29) round a 6100 yards course in Portsmouth.

Henning, Harold (1934–2005)

One of three brothers from a well-known South African golf family he was a regular winner of golf events in his home country and Europe and had two wins on the US Tour. Played ten times for South Africa in the World Cup winning the event with Gary Player in Madrid in 1965.

Herd, Alexander 'Sandy' (1868–1944)

When he first played in The Open at the age of 17 he possessed only four clubs. His only Championship success came in the 1902 Open at Hoylake, the first player to capture the title using the new rubber-cored ball. He won the Match Play Championship at the age of 58 and took part in his last Open at St Andrews in 1939 at the age of 71.

Hilton, Harold (1869–1942)

Winner of the Amateur Championship four times between 1900 and 1913, he also became the first player and the only Briton to hold both the British and US Amateur titles in the same year 1911. He won The Open in 1892 at Muirfield, the first time the Championship was extended to 72 holes, and again in 1897 at Hoylake. A small but powerful player he was the first editor of *Golf Monthly*.

Hogan, Ben (1912–1997)

One of only five players to have won all four major championships, his record of capturing three in the same season has been matched by Tiger Woods. He dominated the golfing scene in America after the Second World War and in 1953 won the Masters, US Open and The Open Championship. A clash of dates between The Open and USPGA Championship prevented an attempt on the Grand Slam, but his poor state of health after a near fatal car crash four years earlier would have made the matchplay format of 10 rounds in six days in the USPGA an impossibility. After his car collided with a Greyhound bus in fog, it was feared that Hogan might never walk again. He had won three majors before the accident and he returned to capture six more. His only appearance in The Open was in his tremendous season of 1953 and he recorded rounds of 73-71-70-68 to win by four strokes at Carnoustie. His dramatic life story was made into a Hollywood film entitled *Follow the Sun* starring Glenn Ford as Hogan.

Howard, Barclay (1953 – 2008)

Leading amateur in the 1997 Open at Royal Troon he battled leukemia which had been diagnosed after he played in his second Walker Cup in 1997. When Dean Robertson won the 1999 Italian Open he dedicated his victory to Barclay as tribute to the courage and adversity he showed in attempting to beat the disease.

Hutchinson, Horace (1859–1932)

Runner-up in the first Amateur Championship in 1885, he won the title in the next two years and reached the final again in 1903. Represented England from 1902–07. He was a prolific writer on golf and country life and became the first English Captain of the Royal and Ancient Golf Club of St Andrews in 1908.

Jarman, Ted (1907–2003)

He competed in the 1935 Ryder Cup at Ridgewood, New Jersey, and until his death in 2003 he had been the oldest living Cup golfer. When he was 76 years old and before he had to stop playing because of arthritis he shot a 75.

Jones, Bobby (1902–1971)

Always remembered for his incredible and unrepeatable achievement in 1930 of winning The Open and Amateur Championships of Britain and America in one outstanding season – the original and unchallenged Grand Slam. At the end of that year he retired from competitive golf at the age of 28. His victories included four US Opens, five US Amateur titles, three Opens in Britain and one Amateur Championship. Although his swing was stylish and fluent, he suffered badly from nerves and was often sick and unable to eat during championships. He was also an accomplished scholar, gaining first-class honours degrees in law, English literature and mechanical engineering at three different universities. He subsequently opened a law practice in Atlanta and developed the idea of creating the Augusta National course and staging an annual invitation event which was to become known as The Masters. He was made an honorary member of the Royal and Ancient Golf Club in 1956 and two years later was given the freedom of the Burgh of St Andrews at an emotional ceremony. He died after many years of suffering from a crippling spinal disease. The tenth hole on the Old Course bears his name.

King, Sam (1911–2003)

He played Ryder Cup golf immediately before and after World War II and came third in the 1939 Open behind Dick Burton at St Andrews. In the 1947 Ryder Cup he prevented an American whitewash in the singles by beating Herman Kaiser. He was British Senior Champion in 1961 and 1962 and was often described as "the old master" – a golfer noted for his long, straight drives and superb putting.

Kirkaldy, Andrew (1860–1934)

First honorary professional appointed by The R&A, he lost a play-off for The Open Championship of 1889 to Willie Park at Musselburgh. He was second in the championship three times, a further three times finished third and twice fourth. A powerful player, he was renowned for speaking his mind.

Laidlay, John Ernest (1860–1940)

The man who first employed the overlapping grip which was later credited to Harry Vardon and universally known as the Vardon grip, Laidlay was a finalist in the Amateur Championship six times in seven years from 1888, winning the title twice at a time when John Ball, Horace Hutchinson and Harold Hilton were at their peak. He was runner-up in The Open to Willie Auchterlonie at Prestwick in 1893. Among the 130 medals he won, were the Gold Medal and Silver Cross in R&A competitions.

Leitch, Charlotte Cecilia "Cecil" (1891–1977)

Christened Charlotte Cecilia, but universally known as Cecil, her list of international victories would undoubtedly have been greater but for the blank golfing years of the first world war. She first won the British Ladies Championship in 1908 at the age of 17. In 1914 she took the English, French and British titles and successfully defended all three when competition was resumed after the war. In all she won the French Championship five times, the British four times, the English twice, the Canadian once. Her total of four victories in the British has never been beaten and has been equalled only by her great rival Joyce Wethered. The victory in Canada was by a margin of 17 and 15 in the 36-hole final.

Lema, Tony (1934–1966)

His first visit to Britain, leaving time for only 27 holes of practice around the Old Course at St Andrews, culminated in Open Championship victory in 1964 by five shots over Jack Nicklaus. He had won three tournaments in four starts in America before arriving in Scotland and gave great credit for his Open success to local caddie Tip Anderson and to the putter Arnold Palmer had loaned him for the week. He played in the Ryder Cup in 1963 and 1965 with an outstanding record. He lost only once in 11 matches, halved twice and won eight. Lema and his wife were killed when a private plane in which they were travelling to a tournament crashed in Illinois.

Little, Lawson (1910–1968)

Won the Amateur Championships of Britain and America in 1934 and successfully defended both titles the following year. He then turned his amateur form into a successful professional career, starting in 1936 with victory in the Canadian Open. He won the US Open in 1940 after a play-off against Gene Sarazen.

Locke, Bobby (1917–1987)

The son of Northern Irish emigrants to South Africa, Arthur D'Arcy Locke was playing off plus four by the age of 18 and won the South African Boys, Amateur and Open Championships. On his first visit to Britain in 1936 he was leading amateur in The Open Championship. Realising that his normal fade was leaving him well short of the leading players, he deliberately developed the hook shot to get more run on the ball. It was to become his trade-mark throughout a long career. He was encouraged to try the American tour in 1947 and won five tournaments, one by the record margin of 16 shots. More successes followed and the USPGA framed a rule which banned him from playing in their events, an action described by Gene Sarazen as "the most disgraceful action by any golf organisation". Disillusioned by the American attitude, Locke then played most of his golf in Europe, winning The Open four times. He shared a period of domination with Peter Thomson between 1949–1958 when they won the championship four times each, only Max Faulker in 1951 and Ben Hogan in 1953 breaking the sequence. In his final Open victory at St Andrews in 1957 he failed to replace his ball in the correct spot on the 18th green after moving it from fellow competitor Bruce Crampton's line. The mistake, which could have led to disqualification, was only spotted on television replays. The R&A Championship Committee rightly decided that Locke, who had won by three strokes, had gained no advantage, and allowed the result to stand. Following a career in which he won over 80 events around the world he was made an honorary member of The R&A in 1976.

Longhurst, Henry (1909–1978)

Golf captain of Cambridge University he was winner of the German Amateur title and runner-up in the French and Swiss Championships in 1936. He became the most perceptive and readable golf correspondent of his time and a television commentator who never wasted a single word. His relaxed, chatty style was based on the premise that he was explaining the scene to a friend in his favourite golf club bar. For 25 years his *Sunday Times* column ran without a break and became compulsory reading for golfers and non-golfers alike. He had a brief spell as a member of parliament and was awarded the CBE for services to golf.

Lunt, Michael (1935–2007)

The former Amateur and English Amateur champion who played most of his golf at Walton Heath died during his captaincy of the Royal and Ancient Golf

Club of St Andrews – an honour which was well-deserved for a golfer who was liked and admired as much for his work as an administrator as his prowess on the links. Son of Stanley Lunt, the 1934 English amateur champion, Michael played on four Walker Cup teams including the one that shocked the Americans by drawing at Five Farms in 1965. He was also a member of the winning Great Britain and Ireland side captained by Joe Carr in the World Amateur Team Championship for the Eisenhower Trophy a year earlier at Olgiata in Rome. After working in the family business he moved to the Slazenger company and later was secretary manager at the Royal Mid-Surrey club before he retired. He is survived by his wife Vicki and son and daughter.

McCormack, Mark (1931–2003)

The Cleveland lawyer who created a golf management empire after approaching Arnold Palmer to look after his affairs. A keen golfer himself, he became one of the most influential and powerful men in sport, managing many golfing legends including Tiger Woods. He was responsible for the development of the modern game commercially and started the World Match Play Championship at Wentworth in 1964.

McDonald, C.B. (1855–1939)

Credited with building the first 18-hole golf course in the United States and instrumental in forming the United States Golf Association. He won the first US Amateur Championship in 1895. He was elected posthumously into the World Golf Hall of Fame in 2007.

Mackenzie, Alister (1870–1934)

A family doctor and surgeon, he became involved with Harry S. Colt in the design of the Alwoodley course in Leeds, where he was a founder member and honorary secretary. He eventually abandoned his medical career and worked full time at golf course architecture. There are many outstanding examples of his work in Britain, Australia, New Zealand and America. His most famous creation, in partnership with Bobby Jones, is the Augusta National course in Georgia, home of The Masters.

Mackenzie, Keith (1921–1990)

The commanding secretary of the Royal and Ancient Golf Club of St Andrews from 1967 to 1983 who, along with Arnold Palmer, Jack Nicklaus and Gary Player ensured The Open, the oldest of the four majors, remained a truly international event. In addition to his normal club duties, he travelled extensively as an ambassador for The Open making friends with the professionals and encouraging foreign participation in the Championship.

Massy, Arnaud (1877–1958)

The first non-British player to win The Open Championship. Born in Biarritz, France, he defeated J.H. Taylor by two strokes at Hoylake in 1907. Four years later he tied for the title with Harry Vardon at Royal St George's, but in the play-off conceded at the 35th hole when he was five strokes behind. He won the French Open four times, the Spanish on three occasions and the Belgian title once.

Micklem, Gerald (1911–1988)

A pre-war Oxford Blue, he won the English Amateur Championship in 1947 and 1953 and played in the Walker Cup team four times between 1947 and 1955. He was non-playing captain in 1957 and 1959. In 1976 he set a record of 36 consecutive appearances in the President's Putter, an event that he won in 1953. In addition to his playing success he was a tireless administrator, serving as chairman of The R&A Rules, Selection and Championship Committees. He was president of the English Golf Union and the European Golf Association and Captain of the Royal and Ancient Golf Club of St Andrews. In 1969 he received the Bobby Jones award for distinguished sportsmanship and services to the game. He was elected posthumously into the World Golf Hall of Fame in 2007.

Middlecoff, Cary (1921–1998)

Dentist turned golf professional, he became one of the most prolific winners on the US tour, with 37 victories that included two US Opens and a Masters victory. In the US Open of 1949 he beat Sam Snead and Clayton Heafner at Medinah, and seven years later recaptured the title by one shot ahead of Ben Hogan and Julius Boros at Oak Hill. His Masters success came in 1955 when he established a record seven-shot winning margin over Hogan.

Minoprio, Gloria (1907–1958)

Striking a telling blow for women's liberty on the links, Minopro was the first female golfer to wear trousers when competing in the 1933 English Ladies Close Championship. Her stylish navy outfit, white makeup and scarlet lipstick sparked controversy among the Ladies Golf Union which duly condemned the departure at Westward Ho! from billowing skirts. In a further break with convention, she played with only one club, a cleek, similar to a 3 iron. Her striking ensemble is on display today at the British Golf Museum in St Andrews. Outwith golf, she was a magician who performed for the maharajahs.

Mitchell, Abe (1897–1947)

Said by J.H. Taylor to be the finest player never to win an Open, he finished in the top six five times. He was more successful in the Match Play Championship, with victories in 1919, 1920 and 1929. He taught the game to St Albans seed merchant Samuel Ryder and is the figure depicted on top of the famous golf trophy.

Moody, Orville (1933–2008)

His only victory on the PGA Tour came in the 1969 US Open for which he had had to qualify. A descendent of the native American Choctaw tribe, he is best remembered, however, for popularising the long-shafted (broom handle) putter which he had first seen used by Charlie Owens, another "yips" sufferer. If Owens invented the 50in shafted putter Moody brought it to everyone's attention when he won the 1989 US Senior Open using one. Sam Torrance, Peter Senior and Bernhard Langer all started using it after golf's ruling bodies declared the putter legal.

Morgan, Wanda (1910–1995)

Three-time English Amateur champion, in 1931–36–37, she also captured the British title in 1935 and played three times in the Curtis Cup from 1932–36.

Morris, Old Tom (1821–1908)

Apprenticed as a feathery ball maker to Allan Robertson in St Andrews at the age of 18 he was one of the finest golfers of his day when he took up the position of Keeper of the Green at Prestwick, where he laid out the original 12-hole course. He was 39 when he finished second in the first Open in 1860, but subsequently won the title four times. His success rate might have been much greater if he had been a better putter. His son once said: "He would be a much better player if the hole was a yard closer." A man of fierce conviction, he returned to St Andrews to take up the duties of looking after the Old Course at a salary of £50 per year, paid by The R&A. He came to regard the course as his own property and was once publicly reprimanded for closing it without authority because he considered it needed a rest. A testimonial in 1896 raised £1,240 pounds towards his old age from golfers around the world and when he retired in 1903 The R&A continued to pay his salary. He died after a fall on the stairs of the New Club in 1908, having outlived his wife, his daughter and his three sons.

Morris, Young Tom (1851–1875)

Born in St Andrews, but brought up in Prestwick, where his father had moved to become Keeper of the Green, he won a tournament against leading professionals at the age of 13. He was only 17 when he succeeded his father as Open champion in 1868 and then defended the title successfully in the following two years to claim the winner's belt outright. There was no championship in 1871, but when the present silver trophy – the Claret Jug – became the prize in 1872, Young Tom's was the first name engraved thereon. His prodigious talent was best demonstrated in his third successive Open victory in 1870 when he played 36 holes at Prestwick in 149 strokes, 12 shots ahead of his nearest rival, superb scoring given the equipment and the condition of the course at that time. He married in November 1874 and was playing with his father in a money match at North Berwick the following year when a telegram from St Andrews sent them hurrying back across the Firth of Forth in a private yacht. Young Tom's wife and baby had both died in childbirth. He played golf only twice after that, in matches that had been arranged long in advance, and fell into moods of deep depression. He died on Christmas morning of that same year from a burst artery in the lung. He was 24 years old. A public subscription paid for a memorial which still stands above his grave in the cathedral cemetery.

Nelson, Byron (1912–2006)

John Byron Nelson left a legacy which many will aspire to emulate but which few will achieve. He joined the professional circuit in 1935 after a caddie shack apprenticeship which he shared with Ben Hogan and quickly established himself, winning the New Jersey Open in 1935 and going on to take The Masters title two years later. Between 1935 and 1946 he had 54 wins but although he won The Masters in 1937 and 1942, the US Open in 1939 and the US PGA Championship in 1940 and 1945 he didn't manage to pull off a Grand Slam having never won The Open Championship. The 1939 US Open is probably best remembered as the tournament Sam Snead threw away, history tending to overlook the achievement of Byron Nelson, the man who eventually took the title. After a three-way play-off with Craig Wood and Densmore Shute, Nelson went on to win the decisive 18 holes by three shots from Wood. America's entry into the second world war called a temporary halt to competitive golf for many. Nelson, denied the opportunity to serve his country due to a blood disorder, continued to play throughout 1943 and 1944, re-establishing his prominent position when full competition resumed in 1945, winning 18 times including 11 events in a row between March and August – a record unlikely ever to be broken. He was twice a member of US Ryder Cup teams – in 1937 and 1947 and had been picked for the postponed matches in 1939 and 1941. He returned to that competition in 1965 when he captained the victorious US team. His only win in Europe was the 1955 French Open. He was a father figure in US golf and until he retired in 2001 was one of The Masters honorary starters along with the late Gene Sarazen and Sam Snead. In company with Snead and his old sparring partner Ben Hogan, Byron Nelson was one of the sport's most revered figures and had a particularly close friendship with five times Open champion Tom Watson.

Norman, Moe (1929–2004)

Eccentric Canadian golf star who was renowned for the accuracy of his unusual swing. Twice Canadian Amateur Champion and winner of 13 Canadian Tour titles, he was inducted into the Canadian Golf Hall of Fame in 1995. He played very quickly, seldom slowing to line up a putt. He never had a lesson. He was such a character that Wally Uihlein, president of Titleist and Footjoy, paid him $5,000 a month for the last 10 years of his life for just "being himself".

Ortiz-Patino, Jaime (1930–2013)

Will always be remembered for bringing the Ryder Cup to Europe for the first time when he hosted the

1997 match at Valderrama, his course in Southern Spain which he and architect Robert Trent Jones turned into one of the best in Europe. Respected for his drive and dedication to perfection, Ortiz-Patino was awarded with an Honorary Lifetime Membership of the European Tour for his unfailing support over a long number of years.

Ouimet, Francis (1893–1967)

Regarded as the player who started the American golf boom after beating Harry Vardon and Ted Ray in a play-off for the 1913 US Open as a young amateur. Twice a winner of the US Amateur, he was a member of every Walker Cup team from 1922 to 1934 and non-playing captain from then until 1949. In 1951 he became the first non-British national to be elected Captain of the Royal and Ancient Golf Club of St Andrews and was a committee member of the USPGA for many years.

Panton, John (1926–2009)

Former honorary Professional to the Royal and Ancient Golf Club of St Andrews he was one of Scotland's best known, admired and loved profesionals who spent most of his working life at the Glenbervie Club near Stirling. A renowned iron-player he was leading British player in the 1956 Open and beat Sam Snead for the World Seniors' title in 1967 at Southport. He played in three Ryder Cup matches and was 12 times a contestant in the World Cup with the late Eric Brown as his regular partner. It was a partnership that earned considerable admiration although the two were so different in character – Panton quiet and unassuming, Brown extrovert and noisy! He won the Association of Golf Writers Trophy in 1967 for his contribution to the game and was honoured by The Queen with an MBE for his services to the game. In later years he lived with his daughter, herself a professional player of note, at Sunningdale. The ginger beer and lime drink now available in golf clubhouses was John's normal tipple and now bears his name! Over the years he took his film camera with him and left a unique library of some of the golfing greats in action.

Park, Mungo (1839–1904)

Younger brother to Willie Park, he spent much of his early life at sea, but won The Open Championship in 1874 at the age of 35, beating Young Tom Morris into second place by two shots on his home course at Musselburgh.

Park, Willie (1834–1903)

Winner of the first Open Championship in 1860. He won the title three more times, in 1863, 1866 and 1875, and was runner-up on four occasions. For 20 years he issued a standing challenge to play any man in the world for £100 a side. His reputation was built largely around a successful putting stroke and he always stressed the importance of never leaving putts short.

Park Jr, Willie (1864–1925)

Son of the man who won the first Open Championship, Willie Park Jr captured the title twice – in 1887 and 1889 – and finished second to Harry Vardon in 1898. He was also an accomplished clubmaker who did much to popularise the bulger driver with its convex face. He patented the wry-neck putter in 1891. One of the first and most successful professionals to design golf courses, he was responsible for many layouts in Britain, Europe and America and also wrote two highly successful books on the game.

Patton, Billy Joe (1922–2011)

Educated at Wake Forest, he is best remembered for holing out in one at the sixth hole *en route* to a closing 71 in the 1954 Masters at Augusta and failing by just one shot to play off for the Green Jacket with eventual winner Sam Snead and Ben Hogan. He played in five Walker Cups and captained the US side in 1969. In 1962 he won the USGA Bob Jones award for outstanding sportsmanship.

Philp, Hugh (1782–1856)

One of the master craftsmen in St Andrews in the early days of the 19th century, he was renowned for his skill in creating long-nosed putters. After his death his business was continued by Robert Forgan. Philp's clubs are much prized collector's items.

Picard, Henry (1907–1997)

Winner of The US Masters in 1938 and the 1939 USPGA Championship, where he birdied the final hole to tie with Byron Nelson and birdied the first extra hole for the title. Ill health cut short a career in which he won 27 tournaments.

Price-Fisher, Elizabeth (1923–2008)

Born in London she played in six Curtis Cup matches and, in addition to winning the 1959 British Women's Championship took titles in Denmark and Portugal, She turned professional in 1968 but was later reinstated as an amateur in 1971. For many years she worked as the ladies golf correspondent for the *Daily Telegraph* in London.

Ray, Ted (1877–1943)

Born in Jersey, his early years in golf were in competition with Channel Islands compatriot Harry Vardon and his fellow members of the Great Triumvirate, J.H. Taylor and James Braid. His only victory in The Open came in 1912, but he was runner-up to Taylor the following year and second again, to Jim Barnes of America, in 1925 when he was 48 years of age. He claimed the US Open title in 1920 and remains one of only three British players to win The Open and the US Open on both sides of the Atlantic. The others are Harry Vardon and Tony Jacklin.

Rees, Dai (1913–1983)

One of Britain's outstanding golfers for three decades, he played in nine Ryder Cup matches between 1937 and 1961 and was playing captain of the 1957 team which won the trophy for the first time since 1933. He was non-playing captain in 1967. He was runner-up in The Open three times and won the PGA Match Play title four times. He was made an honorary member of the Royal and Ancient Golf Club in 1976.

Robertson, Allan (1815–1859)

So fearsome was Robertson's reputation as a player that when The R&A staged an annual competition for local professionals, he was not allowed to take part in order to give the others a chance. A famous maker of feather golf balls, he strongly resisted the advance of the more robust gutta percha. Tom Morris senior was his apprentice and they were reputed never to have lost a foursomes match in which they were partners.

Rosburg, Bob (1926–2009)

The 1959 US PGA Championship also made a name for himself as a golf commentator. After his playing days were over he was employed by Roone Arledge, the head of sport for ABC television, as golf's first on-course reporter – a job he did for 30 years. His characteristic "say-it-as-it-is" style means he will always be remembered by his response to the question regularly posed by one of his fellow commentators in the box ... when asked how the ball was lying Rossie's regular reply was "He's got no chance!"

Ryder, Samuel (1858–1936)

The prosperous seed merchant was so impressed with the friendly rivalry between British and American professionals at an unofficial match at Wentworth in 1926 that he donated the famous gold trophy for the first Ryder Cup match the following year. The trophy is still presented today for the contest between America and Europe.

Sarazen, Gene (1902–1999)

Advised to find an outdoor job to improve his health, Sarazen became a caddie and then an assistant professional. At the age of 20 he became the first player to win the US Open and PGA titles in the same year. In claiming seven major titles he added The Open at Prince's in 1932 and when he won the second Masters tournament in 1935 he became the first of only five players to date who have won all four Grand Slam trophies during their careers. He played "the shot heard around the world" on his way to his 1935 Masters victory, holing a four-wood across the lake at the 15th for an albatross (double eagle) two. At the age of 71 he played in The Open at Troon and holed-in-one at the Postage Stamp eighth. The next day be holed from a bunker for a two at the same hole. He acted as an honorary starter at the Masters, hitting his final shot only a month before his death at 97.

Sayers, Ben (1857–1924)

A twinkling, elphin figure, the diminutive Sayers played a leading part in the game for more than four decades. He represented Scotland against England from 1903 to 1913 and played in every Open from 1880 to 1923.

Sewgolum, Sewsunker "Pappa" (1930–1978)

A former caddie he played every shot unconventionally with his left hand on the club beneath his right. He first made headlines when he beat a field of white golfers in the Natal Open at the prestigious Durban Country Club. He won the Dutch Open title three times in 1959, 1960 and 1964. The municipal course in Durban bears his name and in 2003 he received a posthumous achievement award.

Shade, Ronnie D.B.M. (1938–1984)

One of Scotland's greatest golfers whom many considered the world's top amateur in the mid 60s. After losing the 1962 Scottish Amateur Golf Championship final to Stuart Murray, he won that title five years in a row winning 43 consecutive ties before losing in the fourth round to Willie Smeaton at Muirfield in 1968. Taught by his father John, professional at the Duddingston club in Edinburgh, he was often referred to as "Right Down the Bloody Middle" because of his initials and consistent play. Shade won the Scottish and Irish Open Championships as a professional but was re-instated as an amateur before his death from cancer at the age of 47.

Smith, Frances – née Bunty Stephens (1925–1978)

Dominated post-war women's golf, winning the British Ladies Championship in 1949 and 1954, was three times a winner of the English and once the victor in the French Championship. She represented Great Britain & Ireland in six consecutive encounters from 1950, losing only three of her 11 matches, and was non-playing captain of the team in 1962 and 1972. She was awarded the OBE for her services to golf.

Smith, Horton (1908–1963)

In his first winter on the US professional circuit as a 20-year-old in 1928–29 he won eight out of nine tournaments. He was promoted to that year's Ryder Cup team and played again in 1933 and 1935 and remained unbeaten He won the first Masters in 1934 and repeated that success two year's later. He received the Ben Hogan Award for overcoming illness or injury and the Bobby Jones Award for distinguished sportsmanship in golf.

Smith, Macdonald (1890–1949)

Born into a talented Carnoustie golfing family, he was destined to become one of the finest golfers never to win The Open. He was second in 1930 and 1932, was twice third and twice fourth. His best chance came at

Prestwick in 1925 when he led the field by five strokes with one round to play, but the enthusiastic hordes of Scottish supporters destroyed his concentration and he finished with an 82 for fourth place.

Snead, Sam (1912–2002)

Few would argue that "Slammin' Sam Snead" possessed the sweetest swing in the history of the game. 'He just walked up to the ball and poured honey all over it', it was said. Raised during the Depression in Hot Springs, Virginia, he also died there on May 23 2002, four days short of his 90th birthday. His seven major titles comprised three Masters, three USPGA Championships and the 1946 Open at St Andrews, while he was runner-up four times but never won the US Open. But for the Second World War he would surely have added several more. He achieved a record 82 PGA Tour victories in America, the last of them at age 52, and was just as prolific round the world across six decades. He played in seven Ryder Cup matches, captained the 1969 United States team which tied at Royal Birkdale and after his retirement acted as honorary starter at The Masters until his death. Perhaps his greatest achievement came in the 1979 Quad Cities Open when he scored 67 and 66. He was 67 years of age at the time.

Solheim, Karsten (1912–2000)

A golfing revolutionary who discovered the game at the age of 42 and, working in his garage, invented the Ping putter with its unique heel-toe weighting design, later adopted in his irons. A keen supporter of women's golf, he presented the Solheim Cup for a biennial competition between the American and European Ladies' Tours.

Souchak, Mike (1927 – 2008)

He won 15 times on the PGA Tour in the 1950's and 1960's, competed in the 1959 and 1961 Ryder Cups and played for 11 years on the Champions Tour before retiring. Although he never won a major title he finished 11 times in the top 10 in majors coming third twice in the US Open.

Spearman, Marley (1938 – 2011)

Superb ambassador for golf in the 1950s and 1960s whose exuberance and *joie de vivre* is legendary. Three times a Curtis Cup player she won the British Ladies in 1961 and again in 1962. She was English champion in 1964. In 1962 was awarded the Association of Golf Writers' Trophy for her services to golf.

Stewart, Payne (1957–1999)

Four months after winning his second US Open title Payne Stewart was killed in a plane crash. Only a month earlier he had been on the winning United States Ryder Cup team. His first major victory was in the 1989 USPGA Championship and he claimed his first US Open title two years later after a play-off against Scott Simpson. In 1999 he holed an 18-foot winning putt to beat Phil Mickleson for the US title he was never able to defend. In 1985 he finished a stroke behind Sandy Lyle in The Open at Royal St George's and five years later he shared second place when Nick Faldo won the Championship at St Andrews.

Tait, Freddie (1870–1900)

In 1890 Tait set a new record of 77 for the Old Course, lowering that to 72 only four years later. He was three times the leading amateur in The Open Championship and twice won the Amateur Championship, in 1896 and 1898. The following year he lost at the 37th hole of an historic final to John Ball at Prestwick. He was killed while leading a charge of the Black Watch at Koodoosberg Drift in the Boer War.

Taylor, J.H. (1871–1963)

Winner of The Open Championship five times between 1894 and 1913, Taylor was part of the Great Triumvirate with James Braid and Harry Vardon. He tied for the title with Vardon in 1896, but lost in the play-off and was runner-up another five times. He also won the French and German Opens and finished second in the US Open. A self-educated man, he was a thoughtful and compelling speaker and became the founding father of the Professional Golfers' Association. He was made an honorary member of The R&A in 1949.

Tolley, Cyril (1896–1978)

Won the first of his two Amateur Championships in 1920 while still a student at Oxford and played in the unofficial match which preceded the Walker Cup a year later. He played in six Walker Cup encounters and was team captain in 1924. Tolley is the only amateur to have won the French Open, a title he captured in 1924 and 1928. After winning the Amateur for the second time in 1929 he was favourite to retain the title at St Andrews the following summer but was beaten by a stymie at the 19th hole in the fourth round by Bobby Jones in the American's Grand Slam year.

Travis, Walter (1862–1925)

Born in Australia, he won the US Amateur Championship in 1900 at the age of 38, having taken up the game only four years earlier. He won again the following year and in 1903. He became the first overseas player to win the Amateur title in Britain in 1904, using a centre-shafted Schenectady putter he had just acquired. The club was banned a short time later. He was 52 years old when he last reached the semi-finals of the US Amateur in 1914.

Tumba, Sven (1931–2011)

A legendary ice-hockey player who played 245 times for his country and a top class soccer player he turned to golf in 1970 and was responsible for popularising the game in Sweden. Having played in the Eisenhower Trophy and won the Swedish Match Play Championship he founded his own club at Ullna and later opened the first golf course in Moscow. Helped by some of the biggest world stars including Jack Nicklaus he introduced top class professional golf with his Scandinavian Enterprise Open. Later in life he organised the World Golfers' Championship, played in 40 different countries. Always enthusiastic and well-loved, Sven was truly a Swedish sporting legend to whom golf owes much.

Valentine, Jessie (1915–2006)

A winner of titles before and after World War II, she was an impressive competitor and was one of the first ladies to make a career out of professional golf. She won the British Ladies as an amateur in 1937 and again in 1955 and 1958 and was Scottish champion in 1938 and 1939 and four times between 1951 and 1956. But for the war years it is certain she would have had more titles and victories. She played in seven Curtis Cups between 1936 and 1958 and represented Scotland in the Home Internationals on 17 occasions between 1934 and 1958.

Van Donck, Flory (1912–1992)

Although his style was unorthodox he will always be remembered as a great putter. He remains Belgium's most successful player. He won the Belgian title 16 times between 1939 and 1956 and was successful, too, often more than once in the Dutch, Italian, French, German, Swiss and Portuguese Championships. In 1963 he won seven titles in Europe. Twice runner-up in The Open in 1956 to Peter Thomson at Hoylake and in 1959 to Gary Player at Muirfield he represented 19 times in the World Cup including the 1967 competition at the age of 67.

Vardon, Harry (1870–1937)

Still the only player to have won The Open Championship six times, Vardon, who was born in Jersey, won his first title in 1896, in a 36-hole play-off against J.H. Taylor and his last in 1914, this time beating Taylor by three shots. He won the US Open in 1900 and was beaten in a play-off by Francis Ouimet in 1913. He was one of the most popular of the players at the turn of the century and did much to popularise the game in America with his whistle-stop exhibition tours. He popularised the overlapping grip which still bears his name, although it was first used by Johnny Laidlay. He was also the originator of the modern upright swing, moving away from the flat sweeping action of previous eras. After his Open victory of 1903, during which he was so ill he thought he would not be able to finish, he was diagnosed with tuberculosis. His legendary accuracy and low scoring are commemorated with the award of two Vardon Trophies – in America for the player each year with the lowest scoring average and in Europe for the golfer who tops the money list.

Vare, Glenna – née Collett (1903–1989)

Won the first of her six US Ladies Amateur titles at the age of 19 in 1922 and the last in 1935. A natural athlete, she attacked the ball with more power than was normal in the women's game. The British title eluded her, although at St Andrews in 1929 she was three-under par and five up on Joyce Wethered after 11 holes, but lost to a blistering counter-attack. She played in the first Curtis Cup match in 1932 and was a member of the team in 1936, 1938 and 1948 and was captain in 1934 and 1950.

Von Nida, Norman (1914–2007)

Generally considered the father of Australian golf, he won over 80 titles worldwide. The Australian development Tour is named after him. Played extensively in Britain in the 1940s and 1960s. In later life he was registered bind. Generally regarded as the first golfer to make his income on Tour rather than being based at a club. In 1947 he won seven times in Europe.

Walker, George (1874–1953)

The President of the United States Golf Association who donated the trophy for the first match in 1922, at Long Island, New York, and which is still presented to the winning team in the biennial matches between the USA and Great Britain & Ireland. His grandson and great grandson, George Walker Bush and George Bush Jr have both become Presidents of the United States.

Ward, Charles Harold (1911–2001)

Charlie Ward played in three Ryder Cup matches from 1947–1951 and was twice third in The Open, behind Henry Cotton at Muirfield in 1948 and Max Faulkner at Royal Portrush in 1951.

Ward, Harvie (1926–2004)

Born in Tarboro, North Carolina, he was winner of the Amateur Championship in 1952 when he beat Frank Stranahan 6 and 5 at Prestwick, he went on to win the US title in 1955 and 1956 and the Canadian Amateur in 1964. He played in the 1953, 1955 and 1959 Walker Cup matches and won all of his six games.

Wethered, Joyce – Lady Heathcoat-Amory (1901–1997)

Entered her first English Ladies Championship in 1920 at the age of 18 and beat holder Cecil Leitch in the final. She remained unbeaten for four years, winning 33 successive matches. After they had played together at St Andrews, Bobby Jones remarked: "I have never played golf with anyone, man or woman, amateur or professional, who made me feel so utterly outclassed."

Wethered, Roger (1899–1983)

Amateur champion in 1923 and runner-up in 1928 and 1930, he played five times in the Walker Cup, acting as playing captain at Royal St George's in 1930, and represented England against Scotland every year from 1922 to 1930. In The Open Championship at St Andrews in 1921 he tied with Jock Hutchison despite incurring a penalty for treading on his own ball. Due to play in a cricket match in England the following day, he was persuaded to stay in St Andrews for the play-off, but lost by 150–159 over 36 holes.

Whitcombe, Ernest (1890–1971)
Charles (1895–1978)
Reginald (1898–1957)

The remarkable golfing brothers from Burnham, Somerset, were all selected for the Ryder Cup team of 1935. Charlie and Eddie were paired together and won the only point in the foursomes in a heavy 9–3 defeat by the American team. Reg won the gale-lashed Open at Royal St George's in 1938, with a final round of 78 on a day when the exhibition tent was blown into the sea. Ernest finished second to Walter Hagen in 1924 and Charlie was third at Muirfield in 1935.

White, Ronnie (1921–2005)

A five times Walker Cup team member between 1947 and 1953 he was one of the most impressive players in post-war amateur golf. He won six and halved one of the 10 games he played in the Walker Cup. He won the English Amateur Championship in 1949, the English Amateur Stroke-play title the following two years and was silver medallist as leading amateur in The Open Championship in 1961 played at his home club of Royal Birkdale.

Will, George (1937–2010)

George Will from Ladybank in Fife was a three-time Ryder Cup player in 1963–65 and 67. He was for many years the club professional at Sundridge Park where he was longtime coach to former Walker Cup and European Tour player Roger Chapman but was also long-time coach to the Belgian National team. An always stylish player he was a former Scottish Boys, British Youths and Army champion.

Wilson, Enid (1910–1996)

Completed a hat-trick of victories in the Ladies British Amateur Championship from 1931–33. She was twice a semi-finalist in the American Championship, won the British Girls' and English Ladies' titles and played in the inaugural Curtis Cup match, beating Helen Hicks 2 and 1 in the singles. Retiring early from competitive golf, she was never afraid to express strongly held views on the game in her role as women's golf correspondent of the *Daily Telegraph*.

Wind, Herbert Warren (1917–2005)

One of if not the most distinguished writers on golf in America, he authored 14 books on the game he loved with a passion. A long-time contributor to the *New Yorker* magazine, he is still the only writer to have received the United States Golf Association's Bobby Jones award for distinguished sportsmanship – an honour bestowed on him in 1995, the year the Association celebrated its centenary. The award was appropriate because he was a life-long admirer of Jones and was a regular at The Masters each year where he has been given the credit for naming, in 1958, the difficult stretch of holes from the 11th to the 13th as Amen Corner, arguing you said "Amen" if you negotiated them without dropping a shot.

Wood, Craig (1901–1968)

Both Masters and US Open champion in 1941, Wood finally made up for a career of near misses, having lost play-offs for all four major championships between 1933 and 1939. He was three times a member of the American Ryder Cup team.

Wooldridge, Ian (1932–2007)

One of the most respected sports writers who enjoyed nothing more than covering golf. His *Daily Mail* column was required reading for 40 years.

Yates, Charlie (1913–2005)

Great friend of the late Bobby Jones he was top amateur in the US Masters in 1934, 1939 and 1940. In 1938 came to Royal Troon and won the British Amateur title beating R. Ewing 3 and 2. For many years acted as chairman of the press committee at The Masters and staged annual parties for visiting golf writers in the Augusta Clubhouse. He was a long-time Vice President of the Association of Golf Writers.

Zaharias, Mildred "Babe" – née Didrickson (1915–1956)

As a 17-year-old, Babe, as she was universally known, broke three records in the 1932 Los Angeles Olympics – the javelin, 80 metres hurdles and high jump, but her high jump medal was denied her when judges decided her technique was illegal. Turning her attention to golf, she rapidly established herself as the most powerful woman golfer of the time and in 1945 played and made the cut in the LA Open on the men's PGA Tour. She won the final of the US Amateur by 11 and 9 in 1946, became the first American to win the British title the following year, then helped launch the women's professional tour. She won the US Women's Open in 1948, 1950 and 1954 and in 1950 won six of the nine events on the tour. In 1952 she had a major operation for cancer, but when she won her third and final Open two years later it was by the margin of 12 shots. She was voted Woman Athlete of the Year five times between 1932 and 1950 and Greatest Female Athlete of the Half-Century in 1949.

Golden year for Thailand's Thaworn Wirachant

Forty-six year old Thaworn Wirachant became the oldest Asian No 1 when he finished top of the Asian money list for the third time in 2012 helped by three victories in the Queen's Cup in his home country, the Worldwide Holdings Selangor Masters in Malaysia and the Hero Indian Open.

These three victories on an Asian Tour schedule which comprised 27 events with prize money of over $44 million, took his career title tally in Asia to 15. Helped also by his first win on the European Tour at the 2012 ISPSA Handa Wales Open, he moved to his best ever position in the world rankings – 69th. His aim for 2013 is to make it into the World's top 50 which opens so many more competitive doors.

"There are so many new younger players on Tour in Asia that I never thought I could win another Order of Merit at my age," says Wirachant whose practice routine six days a week – he always dovotes Sundays to his family – begins at 5.30 every morning.

He was the Asian Tour's Players' Player of the Year and also received a Life-time Achievement award in 2012.

While his swing may not be classic, Wirachant has a much-envied short game which he demonstrated during the King's Cup competition when over four rounds he required only 91 putts, believed to be a new world record.

Respected American golf teacher Jim Flick has died

One of American's best known and renowned teachers Jim Flick died last year from pancreatic cancer. He was 82.

Inducted into the PGA Golf Professional Hall of Fame in 2011, he taught golf in 23 countries but one of his scariest teaching sessions was 16 years ago on the top of the new Orleans Superdome.

His pupil was fellow professional William Earl Morgan who recalls: "People think we posed for the photograph but I quickly remind them that it was a real 15 minute lesson. Half-way up to the roof I thought "You idiot". In the end I was surprised just how much he covered during the 15 minute session."

Among the many professionals who benefited from his advice was 1996 Open champion Tom Lehman but the number of people he helped with their games over the years – professionals, amateurs and juniors can be counted in their thousands.

For many years Flick also ran the Nicklaus-Flick Golf Schools having struck up a business partnership with Nicklaus following the death of the 18-major title winner's long time coach Jack Grout in 1989.

Nicklaus recalls: "I always knew he was a nice guy. He would come and sit behind Jack Grout and I on the practice ground for hours on end. When Mr Grout passed away I was looking for somebody to help me. During my first event as a senior I noticed Jim had walked the last nine holes with me. So I turned to him and asked him: 'What do you see?' He said: 'I don't see Jack Nicklaus' so we went to the practice tee and worked on a few things."

Nicklaus hadn't been playing too well but Jack Flick, having watched him so many times with Jack Grout, sorted him out and he went on to win the tournament.

Perhaps Martin Hall, the 2008 PGA of America Teacher of the Year, summed the remarkable Jack Flick up best when he said: "Aside from what he accomplished in developing golf schools the most amazing thing about him was that he could make a 36-handicap player feel as important as Jack Nicklaus."

It was a rare talent.

Proposed rules change on use of anchored stroke to come into effect in January 2016 if agreed

The R&A and the USGA have announced a proposal which would come into effect in the next four yearly review of the Rules of Golf in 2016 that would prohibit anchoring the club when making a stroke.

Following an extensive review a proposed new Rule 14-1b, would prohibit strokes made with the club or with a hand gripping the club held directly against the player's body, or with a forearm held against the body to establish an anchor point that indirectly anchors the club.

The proposed new rule would not alter current equipment rules and would allow the continued use of all conforming golf clubs, including belly-length and long putters provided such clubs are not anchored when making a stroke. The proposed rule narrowly targets only a few types of strokes, while preserving a golfer's ability to play a wide variety of strokes in his or her individual style.

Prior to taking a final decision on the proposed rule which would come into effect on January 1 2016, The R&A and the USGA will consider any further comments and suggestions from the golf community.

"We believe we have considered this issue from every angle but given the wide ranging interest in this subject we would like to give stakeholders in the game the opportunity to put forward any new matters for consideration," says Peter Dawson, Chief Executive of The R&A.

The timetable for the introduction of the proposed new rule would also provide an extended period in which golfers may, if necessary, adapt their method of stroke to the new requirements.

For more information about the newly proposed Rule, as well as additional information including videos and images of strokes that would be allowed or prohibited by the proposedchanges to Rule 14-1, visit www.RandA.org/anchoring or www.usga.org/anchoring

In proposing the new rule, The R&A and the USGA have concluded that the long-term interests of the game would be served by confirming a stroke as the swinging of the entire club at the ball.

"Throughout the 600-year history of golf, the essence of playing the game has been to grip the club with the hands and swing it freely at the ball,"ˇ says USGA Executive Director Mike Davis. "The player's challenge is to control the movement of the entire club in striking the ball, and anchoring the club alters the nature of that challenge. Our conclusion is that the Rules of Golf should be amended to preserve the traditional character of the golf swing by eliminating the growing practice of anchoring the club.ˇ

Preserving the fundamentals

This proposal reflects The R&A's and USGA's responsibility to define how the game is to be played. Aspects of how a player must make a stroke have been addressed in past rules changes, such as the century-old rule that the ball must be fairly struck and not be pushed, scraped or spooned or the 1968 rule prohibiting croquet style putting.

"As governing bodies, we monitor and evaluate playing practices and developments in golf, with our primary mandate being to ensure that the Rules of Golf continue to preserve the fundamental characteristics of the game,ˇ adds Davis.

Although anchoring the club is not new, until recently it was uncommon and typically seen as a method of last resort by a small number of players. In the last two years, however, more and more players have adopted the anchored stroke. Golf's governing bodies have observed this upsurge at all levels of the game and noted that more coaches and players are advocating this method. The decision to act now is based on a strong desire to reverse this trend and to preserve the traditional golf stroke.

There has been widespread discussion of the issue by amateur and professional organisations throughout the international golf community. Each organisation is expected to take a final decision on the proposed rule change later this year. To date the professional bodies have always agreed to play by the Rules of Golf as determined by The R&A and the USGA..

PART XIV

Governance of the Game

R&A Rules Limited

With effect from 1st January 2004, the responsibilities and authority of The Royal and Ancient Golf Club of St Andrews in making, interpreting and giving decisions on the Rules of Golf and on the Rules of Amateur Status were transferred to R&A Rules Limited.

Gender

In the Rules of Golf, the gender used in relation to any person is understood to include both genders.

Golfers with Disabilities

The R&A publication entitled "A Modification of the Rules of Golf for Golfers with Disabilities", that contains permissible modifications of the Rules of Golf to accommodate disabled golfers, is available through The R&A.

Handicaps

The Rules of Golf do not legislate for the allocation and adjustment of handicaps. Such matters are within the jurisdiction of the National Union concerned and queries should be directed accordingly.

R&A

RULES OF GOLF

As Approved by
R&A Rules Limited
and the
United States Golf Association

32nd Edition
Effective 1 January 2012

Principle changes introduced in the 2012 Code

Definitions

Addressing the Ball

The Definition is amended so that a player has addressed the ball simply by grounding his club immediately in front of or behind the ball, regardless of whether or not he has taken his stance. Therefore, the Rules generally no longer provide for a player addressing the ball in a hazard. (See also related change to Rule 18-2b)

Rules

Rule 1-2. Exerting Influence on Movement of Ball or Altering Physical Conditions

The Rule is amended to establish more clearly that, if a player intentionally takes an action to influence the movement of a ball or to alter physical conditions affecting the playing of a hole in a way that is not permitted by the Rules, Rule 1-2 applies only when the action is not already covered in another Rule. For example, a player improving the lie of his ball is in breach of Rule 13-2 and therefore that Rule would apply, whereas a player intentionally improving the lie of a fellow-competitor's ball is not a situation covered by Rule 13-2 and, therefore, is governed by Rule 1-2.

Rule 6-3a. Time of Starting

Rule 6-3a is amended to provide that the penalty for starting late, but within five minutes of the starting time, is reduced from disqualification to loss of the first hole in match play or two strokes at the first hole in stroke play. Previously this penalty reduction could be introduced as a condition of competition.

Rule 12-1. Seeing Ball; Searching for Ball

Rule 12-1 is reformatted for clarity. In addition, it is amended to (i) permit a player to search for his ball anywhere on the course when it may be covered by sand and to clarify that there is no penalty if the ball is moved in these circumstances, and (ii) apply a penalty of one stroke under Rule 18-2a if a player moves his ball in a hazard when searching for it when it is believed to be covered by loose impediments.

Rule 13-4. Ball in Hazard; Prohibited Actions

Exception 2 to Rule 13-4 is amended to permit a player to smooth sand or soil in a hazard at any time, including before playing from that hazard, provided it is for the sole purpose of caring for the course and Rule 13-2 is not breached.

Rule 18-2b. Ball Moving After Address

A new Exception is added that exonerates the player from penalty if his ball moves after it has been addressed when it is known or virtually certain that he did not cause the ball to move. For example, if it is a gust of wind that moves the ball after it has been addressed, there is no penalty and the ball is played from its new position.

Rule 19-1. Ball in Motion Deflected or Stopped; By Outside Agency

The note is expanded to prescribe the various outcomes when a ball in motion has been deliberately deflected or stopped by an outside agency.

Rule 20-7c. Playing from Wrong Place; Stroke Play

Note 3 is amended so that if a player is to be penalised for playing from a wrong place, in most cases the penalty will be limited to two strokes, even if another Rule has been breached prior to his making the stroke.

Appendix IV

A new Appendix is added to prescribe general regulations for the design of devices and other equipment, such as tees, gloves and distance measuring devices.

Rules of Amateur Status

Definitions

Amateur Golfer

The Definition is amended to establish more clearly that an "amateur golfer", regardless of whether he plays competitively or recreationally, is one who plays golf for the challenge it presents, not as a profession and not for financial gain.

Golf Skill or Reputation

A time limit of five years is introduced for the retention of "golf reputation" after the player's golf skill has diminished.

Prize Vouchers

The Definition is expanded to allow prize vouchers to be used for the purchase of goods or services from a golf club.

Rules

Rule 1-3 Amateurism; Purpose of the Rules

Rule 1-3 is amended to re-state why there is a distinction between amateur and professional golf and why certain limits and restrictions are needed in the amateur game.

Rule 2-1 Professionalism; General

The existing Rules on professionalism are consolidated and re-formatted into new Rule 2-1.

Rule 2-2 Professionalism; Contracts and Agreements

National Golf Unions or Associations – New Rule 2-2(a) is added to allow an amateur golfer to enter into a contract and/or agreement with his national golf union or association, provided he does not obtain any financial gain, directly or indirectly, while still an amateur golfer.

Professional Agents, Sponsors and Other Third Parties – New Rule 2-2(b) is added to allow an amateur golfer, who is at least 18 years of age, to enter into a contract and/or agreement with a third party solely in relation to the golfer's future as a professional golfer, provided he does not obtain any financial gain, directly or indirectly, while still an amateur golfer.

Rule 3-2b Hole-in-One Prizes

New Rule 3-2b excludes from the general prize limit prizes (including cash prizes) awarded for achieving a hole-in-one while playing a round of golf. This exception is specific to prizes for holes-in-one (not longest drive or nearest the hole) and neither separate events nor multiple-entry events qualify.

Rule 4-3 Subsistence Expenses

New Rule added to allow an amateur golfer to receive subsistence expenses to assist with general living costs, provided the expenses are approved by and paid through the player's national golf union or association.

How to use the rule book

It is understood that not everyone who has a copy of the Rules of Golf will read it from cover to cover. Most golfers only consult the Rule book when they have a Rules issue on the course that needs to be resolved. However, to ensure that you have a basic understanding of the Rules and that you play golf in a reasonable manner, it is recommended that you at least read the Quick Guide to the Rules of Golf and the Etiquette Section contained within this publication.

In terms of ascertaining the correct answer to Rules issues that arise on the course, use of the Rule book's Index should help you to identify the relevant Rule. For example, if a player accidentally moves his ball-marker in the process of lifting his ball on the putting green, identify the key words in the question, such as "ball-marker", "lifting ball" and "putting green" and look in the Index for these headings. The relevant Rule (Rule 20-1) is found under the headings "ball-marker" and "lifted ball" and a reading of this Rule will confirm the correct answer.

In addition to identifying key words and using the Index in the Rules of Golf, the following points will assist you in using the Rule book efficiently and accurately:

Understand the Words

The Rule book is written in a very precise and deliberate fashion. You should be aware of and understand the following differences in word use:

- may = optional
- should = recommendation
- must = instruction (and penalty if not carried out)
- a ball = you may substitute another ball (e.g. Rules 26, 27 and 28)
- the ball = you must not substitute another ball (e.g. Rules 24-2 and 25-1)

Know the Definitions

There are over fifty defined terms (e.g. abnormal ground condition, through the green, etc) and these form the foundation around which the Rules of Play are written. A good knowledge of the defined terms (which are italicised throughout the book) is very important to the correct application of the Rules.

The Facts of the Case

To answer any question on the Rules you must consider the facts of the case in some detail. You should identify:

- The form of play (e.g. match play or stroke play, single, foursome or four-ball)
- Who is involved (e.g. the player, his partner or caddie, an outside agency)
- Where the incident occurred (e.g. on the teeing ground, in a bunker or water hazard, on the putting green)
- What actually happened
- The player's intentions (e.g. what was he doing and what does he want to do)
- The timing of the incident (e.g. has the player now returned his score card, has the competi tion closed)

Refer to the Book

As stated above, reference to the Rule book Index and the relevant Rule should provide the answer to the majority of questions that can arise on the course. If in doubt, play the course as you find it and play the ball as it lies. On returning to the Clubhouse, refer the matter to the Committee and it may be that reference to the "Decisions on the Rules of Golf" will assist in resolving any queries that are not entirely clear from the Rule book itself.

Contents

Section I — Etiquette; Behaviour on the Course

Introduction

This section provides guidelines on the manner in which the game of golf should be played. If they are followed, all players will gain maximum enjoyment from the game. The overriding principle is that consideration should be shown to others on the course at all times.

The Spirit of the Game

Golf is played, for the most part, without the supervision of a referee or umpire. The game relies on the integrity of the individual to show consideration for other players and to abide by the Rules. All players should conduct themselves in a disciplined manner, demonstrating courtesy and sportsmanship at all times, irrespective of how competitive they may be. This is the spirit of the game of golf.

Safety

Players should ensure that no one is standing close by or in a position to be hit by the club, the ball or any stones, pebbles, twigs or the like when they make a stroke or practice swing.

Players should not play until the players in front are out of range.

Players should always alert greenstaff nearby or ahead when they are about to make a stroke that might endanger them.

If a player plays a ball in a direction where there is a danger of hitting someone, he should immediately shout a warning. The traditional word of warning in such situations is "fore".

Consideration for Other Players

No Disturbance or Distraction

Players should always show consideration for other players on the course and should not disturb their play by moving, talking or making unnecessary noise.

Players should ensure that any electronic device taken onto the course does not distract other players.

On the teeing ground, a player should not tee his ball until it is his turn to play.

Players should not stand close to or directly behind the ball, or directly behind the hole, when a player is about to play.

On the Putting Green

On the putting green, players should not stand on another player's line of putt or, when he is making a stroke, cast a shadow over his line of putt.

Players should remain on or close to the putting green until all other players in the group have holed out.

Scoring

In stroke play, a player who is acting as a marker should, if necessary, on the way to the next tee, check the score with the player concerned and record it.

Pace of Play

Play at Good Pace and Keep Up

Players should play at a good pace. The Committee may establish pace of play guidelines that all players should follow.

It is a group's responsibility to keep up with the group in front. If it loses a clear hole and it is delaying the group behind, it should invite the group behind to play through, irrespective of the number of players in that group. Where a group has not lost a clear hole, but it is apparent that the group behind can play faster, it should invite the faster moving group to play through.

Be Ready to Play

Players should be ready to play as soon as it is their turn to play. When playing on or near the putting green, they should leave their bags or carts in such a position as will enable quick movement off the green and towards the next tee. When the play of a hole has been completed, players should immediately leave the putting green.

Lost Ball

If a player believes his ball may be lost outside a water hazard or is out of bounds, to save time, he should play a provisional ball.

Players searching for a ball should signal the players in the group behind them to play through as soon as it becomes apparent that the ball will not easily be found. They should not search for five minutes before doing so. Having allowed the group behind to play through, they should not continue play until that group has passed and is out of range.

Priority on the Course

Unless otherwise determined by the Committee, priority on the course is determined by a group's pace of play. Any group playing a whole round is entitled to pass a group playing a shorter round. The term "group" includes a single player.

Care of the Course

Bunkers

Before leaving a bunker, players should carefully fill up and smooth over all holes and footprints made by them and any nearby made by others. If a rake is within reasonable proximity of the bunker, the rake should be used for this purpose.

Repair of Divots, Ball-Marks and Damage by Shoes

Players should carefully repair any divot holes made by them and any damage to the putting green made by the impact of a ball (whether or not made by the player himself). On completion of the hole by all players in the group, damage to the putting green caused by golf shoes should be repaired.

Preventing Unnecessary Damage

Players should avoid causing damage to the course by removing divots when taking practice swings or by hitting the head of a club into the ground, whether in anger or for any other reason.

Players should ensure that no damage is done to the putting green when putting down bags or the flagstick.

In order to avoid damaging the hole, players and caddies should not stand too close to the hole and should take care during the handling of the flagstick and the removal of a ball from the hole. The head of a club should not be used to remove a ball from the hole.

Players should not lean on their clubs when on the putting green, particularly when removing the ball from the hole.

The flagstick should be properly replaced in the hole before the players leave the putting green.

Local notices regulating the movement of golf carts should be strictly observed.

Conclusion; Penalties for Breach

If players follow the guidelines in this section, it will make the game more enjoyable for everyone.

If a player consistently disregards these guidelines during a round or over a period of time to the detriment of others, it is recommended that the Committee considers taking appropriate disciplinary action against the offending player. Such action may, for example, include prohibiting play for a limited time on the course or in a certain number of competitions. This is considered to be justifiable in terms of protecting the interests of the majority of golfers who wish to play in accordance with these guidelines.

In the case of a serious breach of etiquette, the Committee may disqualify a player under Rule 33-7.

Section II — Definitions

The Definitions are listed alphabetically and, in the Rules themselves, defined terms are in *italics*.

Abnormal Ground Conditions

An *"abnormal ground condition"* is any *casual water, ground under repair* or hole, cast or runway on the *course* made by a *burrowing animal*, a reptile or a bird.

Addressing the Ball

A player has *"addressed the ball"* when he has grounded his club immediately in front of or immediately behind the ball, whether or not he has taken his *stance*.

Advice

"Advice" is any counsel or suggestion that could influence a player in determining his play, the choice of a club or the method of making a *stroke*.

Information on the *Rules*, distance or matters of public information, such as the position of *hazards* or the *flagstick* on the *putting green*, is not *advice*.

Ball Deemed to Move

See *"Move or Moved"*.

Ball Holed

See *"Holed"*.

Ball Lost

See *"Lost Ball"*.

Ball in Play

A ball is *"in play"* as soon as the player has made a *stroke* on the *teeing ground*. It remains *in play* until it is *holed*, except when it is *lost*, *out of bounds* or lifted, or another ball has been *substituted*, whether or not the substitution is permitted; a ball so *substituted* becomes the *ball in play*.

If a ball is played from outside the *teeing ground* when the player is starting play of a hole, or when attempting to correct this mistake, the ball is not *in play* and Rule 11-4 or 11-5 applies. Otherwise, *ball in play* includes a ball played from outside the *teeing ground* when the player elects or is required to play his next *stroke* from the *teeing ground*.

Exception in match play: Ball in play includes a ball played by the player from outside the *teeing ground* when starting play of a hole if the *opponent* does not require the *stroke* to be cancelled in accordance with Rule 11-4a.

Best-Ball

See *"Forms of Match Play"*.

Bunker

A *"bunker"* is a *hazard* consisting of a prepared area of ground, often a hollow, from which turf or soil has been removed and replaced with sand or the like.

Grass-covered ground bordering or within a *bunker*, including a stacked turf face (whether grass-covered or earthen), is not part of the *bunker*. A wall or lip of the *bunker* not covered with grass is part of the *bunker*. The margin of a *bunker* extends vertically downwards, but not upwards.

A ball is in a *bunker* when it lies in or any part of it touches the *bunker*.

Burrowing Animal

A *"burrowing animal"* is an animal (other than a worm, insect or the like) that makes a hole for habitation or shelter, such as a rabbit, mole, groundhog, gopher or salamander.

Note: A hole made by a non-burrowing animal, such as a dog, is not an *abnormal ground condition* unless marked or declared as *ground under repair*.

Caddie

A *"caddie"* is one who assists the player in accordance with the *Rules*, which may include carrying or handling the player's clubs during play.

When one *caddie* is employed by more than one player, he is always deemed to be the *caddie* of the player sharing the *caddie* whose ball (or whose *partner's* ball) is involved, and *equipment* carried by him is deemed to be that player's *equipment*, except when the *caddie* acts upon specific directions of another player (or the *partner* of another player) sharing the *caddie*, in which case he is considered to be that other player's *caddie*.

Casual Water

"Casual water" is any temporary accumulation of water on the *course* that is not in a *water hazard* and is visible before or after the player takes his *stance*. Snow and natural ice, other than frost, are either *casual water* or *loose impediments*, at the option of the player. Manufactured ice is an *obstruction*. Dew and frost are not *casual water*.

A ball is in *casual water* when it lies in or any part of it touches the *casual water*.

Committee

The *"Committee"* is the committee in charge of the competition or, if the matter does not arise in a competition, the committee in charge of the *course*.

Competitor

A *"competitor"* is a player in a stroke play competition. A *"fellow-competitor"* is any person with whom the *competitor* plays. Neither is *partner* of the other.

In stroke play *foursome* and *four-ball* competitions, where the context so admits, the word *"competitor"* or *"fellow-competitor"* includes his *partner*.

Course
The *"course"* is the whole area within any boundaries established by the *Committee* (see Rule 33-2).

Equipment
"Equipment" is anything used, worn or carried by the player or anything carried for the player by his *partner* or either of their *caddies*, except any ball he has played at the hole being played and any small object, such as a coin or a tee, when used to mark the position of a ball or the extent of an area in which a ball is to be dropped. *Equipment* includes a golf cart, whether or not motorised.

Note 1: A ball played at the hole being played is *equipment* when it has been lifted and not put back into play.

Note 2: When a golf cart is shared by two or more players, the cart and everything in it are deemed to be the *equipment* of one of the players sharing the cart.

If the cart is being moved by one of the players (or the *partner* of one of the players) sharing it, the cart and everything in it are deemed to be that player's *equipment*. Otherwise, the cart and everything in it are deemed to be the *equipment* of the player sharing the cart whose ball (or whose *partner's* ball) is involved.

Fellow-Competitor
See *"Competitor"*.

Flagstick
The *"flagstick"* is a movable straight indicator, with or without bunting or other material attached, centred in the *hole* to show its position. It must be circular in cross-section. Padding or shock absorbent material that might unduly influence the movement of the ball is prohibited.

Forecaddie
A *"forecaddie"* is one who is employed by the *Committee* to indicate to players the position of balls during play. He is an *outside agency*.

Forms of Match Play
Single: A match in which one player plays against another player.

Threesome: A match in which one player plays against two other players, and each *side* plays one ball.

Foursome: A match in which two players play against two other players, and each *side* plays one ball.

Three-Ball: Three players play a match against one another, each playing his own ball. Each player is playing two distinct matches.

Best-Ball: A match in which one player plays against the better ball of two other players or the best ball of three other players.

Four-Ball: A match in which two players play their better ball against the better ball of two other players.

Forms of Stroke Play
Individual: A competition in which each *competitor* plays as an individual.

Foursome: A competition in which two *competitors* play as *partners* and play one ball.

Four-Ball: A competition in which two *competitors* play as *partners*, each playing his own ball. The lower score of the *partners* is the score for the hole. If one *partner* fails to complete the play of a hole, there is no penalty.

Note: For bogey, par and Stableford competitions, see Rule 32-1.

Four-Ball
See *"Forms of Match Play"* and *"Forms of Stroke Play"*.

Foursome
See *"Forms of Match Play"* and *"Forms of Stroke Play"*.

Ground Under Repair
"Ground under repair" is any part of the *course* so marked by order of the *Committee* or so declared by its authorised representative. All ground and any grass, bush, tree or other growing thing within the *ground under repair* are part of the *ground under repair*. *Ground under repair* includes material piled for removal and a hole made by a greenkeeper, even if not so marked. Grass cuttings and other material left on the *course* that have been abandoned and are not intended to be removed are not *ground under repair* unless so marked.

When the margin of *ground under repair* is defined by stakes, the stakes are inside the *ground under repair*, and the margin of the *ground under repair* is defined by the nearest outside points of the stakes at ground level. When both stakes and lines are used to indicate *ground under repair*, the stakes identify the *ground under repair* and the lines define the margin of the *ground under repair*. When the margin of *ground under repair* is defined by a line on the ground, the line itself is in the *ground under repair*. The margin of *ground under repair* extends vertically downwards but not upwards.

A ball is in *ground under repair* when it lies in or any part of it touches the *ground under repair*.

Stakes used to define the margin of or identify *ground under repair* are *obstructions*.

Note: The *Committee* may make a Local Rule prohibiting play from *ground under repair* or an environmentally-sensitive area defined as *ground under repair*.

Hazards
A *"hazard"* is any *bunker* or *water hazard*.

Hole
The *"hole"* must be 4¼ inches (108 mm) in diameter and at least 4 inches (101.6 mm) deep. If a lining is used, it must be sunk at least 1 inch (25.4 mm) below the *putting green* surface, unless the nature of the soil makes it impracticable to do so; its outer diameter must not exceed 41/4 inches (108 mm).

Holed
A ball is *"holed"* when it is at rest within the circumference of the *hole* and all of it is below the level of the lip of the *hole*.

Honour
The player who is to play first from the *teeing ground* is said to have the *"honour"*.

Lateral Water Hazard
A *"lateral water hazard"* is a *water hazard* or that part of a *water hazard* so situated that it is not possible, or is deemed by the *Committee* to be impracticable, to drop a ball behind the *water hazard* in accordance with Rule 26-lb. All ground and water within the margin of a *lateral water hazard* are part of the *lateral water hazard*.

When the margin of a *lateral water hazard* is defined by stakes, the stakes are inside the *lateral water hazard*, and the margin of the *hazard* is defined by the nearest outside points of the stakes at ground level. When both stakes and lines are used to indicate a *lateral water hazard*, the stakes identify the *hazard* and the lines define the *hazard* margin. When the margin of a *lateral water hazard* is defined by a line on the ground, the line itself is in the *lateral water hazard*. The margin of a *lateral water hazard* extends vertically upwards and downwards.

A ball is in a *lateral water hazard* when it lies in or any part of it touches the *lateral water hazard*.

Stakes used to define the margin of or identify a *lateral water hazard* are *obstructions*.

Note 1: That part of a *water hazard* to be played as a *lateral water hazard* must be distinctively marked. Stakes or lines used to define the margin of or identify a *lateral water hazard* must be red.

Note 2: The *Committee* may make a Local Rule prohibiting play from an environmentally-sensitive area defined as a *lateral water hazard.*

Note 3: The *Committee* may define a *lateral water hazard* as a *water hazard.*

Line of Play

The *"line of play"* is the direction that the player wishes his ball to take after a *stroke*, plus a reasonable distance on either side of the intended direction. The *line of play* extends vertically upwards from the ground, but does not extend beyond the *hole*.

Line of Putt

The *"line of putt"* is the line that the player wishes his ball to take after a *stroke* on the *putting green*. Except with respect to Rule 16-1e, the *line of putt* includes a reasonable distance on either side of the intended line. The *line of putt* does not extend beyond the *hole*.

Loose Impediments

"Loose impediments" are natural objects, including:

- stones, leaves, twigs, branches and the like,
- dung, and •
- worms, insects and the like, and the casts and heaps made by them,

provided they are not:

- fixed or growing,
- solidly embedded, or
- adhering to the ball.

Sand and loose soil are *loose impediments* on the *putting green*, but not elsewhere.

Snow and natural ice, other than frost, are either *casual water* or *loose impediments*, at the option of the player.

Dew and frost are not *loose impediments*.

Lost Ball

A ball is deemed *"lost"* if:

a. It is not found or identified as his by the player within five minutes after the player's *side* or his or their *caddies* have begun to search for it; or
b. The player has made a *stroke* at a *provisional ball* from the place where the original ball is likely to be or from a point nearer the *hole* than that place (see Rule 27-2b); or
c. The player has put another *ball into play* under penalty of stroke and distance under Rule 26-1a, 27-1 or 28a; or
d. The player has put another *ball into play* because it is known or virtually certain that the ball, which has not been found, has been *moved* by an *outside agency* (see Rule 18-1), is in an *obstruction* (see Rule 24-3), is in an *abnormal ground condition* (see Rule 25-1c) or is in a *water hazard* (see Rule 26-1b or c); or
e. The player has made a *stroke* at a *substituted ball*.

Time spent in playing a *wrong ball* is not counted in the five-minute period allowed for search.

Marker

A *"marker"* is one who is appointed by the *Committee* to record a *competitor's* score in stroke play. He may be a *fellow-competitor*. He is not a *referee*.

Move or Moved

A ball is deemed to have *"moved"* if it leaves its position and comes to rest in any other place.

Nearest Point of Relief

The *"nearest point of relief"* is the reference point for taking relief without penalty from interference by an immovable *obstruction* (Rule 24-2), an *abnormal ground condition* (Rule 25-1) or a *wrong putting green* (Rule 25-3).

It is the point on the *course* nearest to where the ball lies:

(i) that is not nearer the *hole*, and
(ii) where, if the ball were so positioned, no interference by the condition from which relief is sought would exist for the *stroke* the player would have made from the original position if the condition were not there.

Note: In order to determine the *nearest point of relief* accurately, the player should use the club with which he would have made his next *stroke* if the condition were not there to simulate the *address* position, direction of play and swing for such a *stroke*.

Observer

An *"observer"* is one who is appointed by the *Committee* to assist a *referee* to decide questions of fact and to report to him any breach of a *Rule*. An *observer* should not attend the *flagstick*, stand at or mark the position of the *hole*, or lift the ball or mark its position.

Obstructions

An *"obstruction"* is anything artificial, including the artificial surfaces and sides of roads and paths and manufactured ice, except:

a. Objects defining *out of bounds*, such as walls, fences, stakes and railings;
b. Any part of an immovable artificial object that is *out of bounds*; and
c. Any construction declared by the *Committee* to be an integral part of the *course*.

An *obstruction* is a movable *obstruction* if it may be moved without unreasonable effort, without unduly delaying play and without causing damage. Otherwise, it is an immovable *obstruction*.

Note: The *Committee* may make a Local Rule declaring a movable *obstruction* to be an immovable *obstruction*.

Opponent

An *"opponent"* is a member of a *side* against whom the player's *side* is competing in match play.

Out of Bounds

"Out of bounds" is beyond the boundaries of the *course* or any part of the *course* so marked by the *Committee*.

When *out of bounds* is defined by reference to stakes or a fence or as being beyond stakes or a fence, the *out of bounds* line is determined by the nearest inside points at ground level of the stakes or fence posts (excluding angled supports). When both stakes and lines are used to indicate *out of bounds*, the stakes identify *out of bounds* and the lines define *out of bounds*. When *out of bounds* is defined by a line on the ground, the line itself is *out of bounds*. The *out of bounds* line extends vertically upwards and downwards.

A ball is *out of bounds* when all of it lies *out of bounds*. A player may stand *out of bounds* to play a ball lying within bounds.

Objects defining *out of bounds* such as walls, fences, stakes and railings are not *obstructions* and are deemed to be fixed. Stakes identifying *out of bounds* are not *obstructions* and are deemed to be fixed.

Note 1: Stakes or lines used to define *out of bounds* should be white.

Note 2: A *Committee* may make a Local Rule declaring stakes identifying but not defining *out of bounds* to be *obstructions*.

Outside Agency

In match play, an *"outside agency"* is any agency other than either the player's or *opponent's side*, any *caddie* of either *side*, any ball played by either *side* at the hole being played or any *equipment* of either *side*.

In stroke play, an *outside agency* is any agency other than the *competitor's side*, any *caddie* of the *side*, any ball played by the *side* at the hole being played or any *equipment* of the *side*.

An *outside agency* includes a *referee*, a *marker*, an *observer* and a *forecaddie*. Neither wind nor water is an *outside agency*.

Partner

A *"partner"* is a player associated with another player on the same *side*. In *threesome*, *foursome*, *best-ball* or *four-ball* play, where the context so admits, the word "player" includes his *partner* or *partners*.

Penalty Stroke

A *"penalty stroke"* is one added to the score of a player or *side* under certain *Rules*. In a *threesome* or *foursome*, *penalty strokes* do not affect the order of play.

Provisional Ball

A *"provisional ball"* is a ball played under Rule 27-2 for a ball that may be *lost* outside a *water hazard* or may be *out of bounds*.

Putting Green

The *"putting green"* is all ground of the hole being played that is specially prepared for putting or otherwise defined as such by the *Committee*. A ball is on the *putting green* when any part of it touches the *putting green*.

R&A

The *"R&A"* means R&A Rules Limited.

Referee

A *"referee"* is one who is appointed by the *Committee* to decide questions of fact and apply the *Rules*. He must act on any breach of a *Rule* that he observes or is reported to him.

A *referee* should not attend the *flagstick*, stand at or mark the position of the *hole*, or lift the ball or mark its position.

Exception in match play: Unless a *referee* is assigned to accompany the players throughout a match, he has no authority to intervene in a match other than in relation to Rule 1-3, 6-7 or 33-7.

Rub of the Green

A *"rub of the green"* occurs when a ball in motion is accidentally deflected or stopped by any *outside agency* (see Rule 19-1).

Rule or Rules

The term *"Rule"* includes:

a. The Rules of Golf and their interpretations as con tained in "Decisions on the Rules of Golf";
b. Any Conditions of Competition established by the *Committee* under Rule 33-1 and Appendix I;
c. Any Local Rules established by the *Committee* under Rule 33-8a and Appendix I; and
d. The specifications on:
  (i) clubs and the ball in Appendices II and III and their interpretations as contained in "A Guide to the Rules on Clubs and Balls"; and
  (ii) devices and other equipment in Appendix IV.

Side

A *"side"* is a player, or two or more players who are *partners*. In match play, each member of the opposing *side* is an *opponent*. In stroke play, members of all *sides* are *competitors* and members of different *sides* playing together are *fellow-competitors*.

Single

See *"Forms of Match Play"* and *"Forms of Stroke Play"*.

Stance

Taking the *"stance"* consists in a player placing his feet in position for and preparatory to making a *stroke*.

Stipulated Round

The *"stipulated round"* consists of playing the holes of the *course* in their correct sequence, unless otherwise authorised by the *Committee*. The number of holes in a *stipulated round* is 18 unless a smaller number is authorised by the *Committee*. As to extension of *stipulated round* in match play, see Rule 2-3.

Stroke

A *"stroke"* is the forward movement of the club made with the intention of striking at and moving the ball, but if a player checks his downswing voluntarily before the clubhead reaches the ball he has not made a *stroke*.

Substituted Ball

A *"substituted ball"* is a ball put into play for the original ball that was either *in play*, *lost*, *out of bounds* or lifted.

Teeing Ground

The *"teeing ground"* is the starting place for the hole to be played. It is a rectangular area two club-lengths in depth, the front and the sides of which are defined by the outside limits of two tee-markers. A ball is outside the *teeing ground* when all of it lies outside the *teeing ground*.

Three-Ball

See *"Forms of Match Play"*.

Threesome

See *"Forms of Match Play"*.

Through the Green

"Through the green" is the whole area of the *course* except:

a. The *teeing ground* and *putting green* of the hole being played; and
b. All *hazards* on the *course*.

Water Hazard

A *"water hazard"* is any sea, lake, pond, river, ditch, surface drainage ditch or other open water course (whether or not containing water) and anything of a similar nature on the *course*. All ground and water within the margin of a *water hazard* are part of the *water hazard*.

When the margin of a *water hazard* is defined by stakes, the stakes are inside the *water hazard*, and the margin of the *hazard* is defined by the nearest outside points of the stakes at ground level. When both stakes and lines are used to indicate a *water hazard*, the stakes identify the *hazard* and the lines define the *hazard* margin. When the margin of a *water hazard* is defined by a line on the ground, the line itself is in the *water hazard*. The margin of a *water hazard* extends vertically upwards and downwards.

A ball is in a *water hazard* when it lies in or any part of it touches the *water hazard*.

Stakes used to define the margin of or identify a *water hazard* are *obstructions*.

Note 1: Stakes or lines used to define the margin of or identify a *water hazard* must be yellow.

Note 2: The *Committee* may make a Local Rule prohibiting play from an environmentally-sensitive area defined as a *water hazard*.

Wrong Ball

A *"wrong ball"* is any ball other than the player's:

- *ball in play*;
- *provisional ball*; or
- second ball played under Rule 3-3 or Rule 20-7c in stroke play;

and includes:

- another player's ball;
- an abandoned ball; and
- the player's original ball when it is no longer *in play*.

Note: Ball in play includes a ball *substituted* for the *ball in play*, whether or not the substitution is permitted.

Wrong Putting Green

A *"wrong putting green"* is any *putting green* other than that of the hole being played. Unless otherwise prescribed by the *Committee*, this term includes a practice *putting green* or pitching green on the *course*.

Section III — The Rules of Play

The Game

Rule 1 – The Game

Definitions

All defined terms are in *italics* and are listed alphabetically in the Definitions section – see pages 592–595.

1-1. General

The Game of Golf consists of playing a ball with a club from the *teeing ground* into the *hole* by a *stroke* or successive *strokes* in accordance with the *Rules*.

1-2. Exerting Influence on Movement of Ball or Altering Physical Conditions

A player must not (i) take an action with the intent to influence the movement of a *ball in play* or (ii) alter physical conditions with the intent of affecting the playing of a hole.

Exceptions: An action expressly permitted or expressly prohibited by another *Rule* is subject to that other *Rule*, not Rule 1-2.

An action taken for the sole purpose of caring for the *course* is not a breach of Rule 1-2.

*PENALTY FOR BREACH OF RULE 1-2:
Match play – Loss of hole; Stroke play – Two strokes.

*In the case of a serious breach of Rule 1-2, the *Committee* may impose a penalty of disqualification.

Note 1: A player is deemed to have committed a serious breach of Rule 1-2 if the *Committee* considers that the action taken in breach of this Rule has allowed him or another player to gain a significant advantage or has placed another player, other than his *partner*, at a significant disadvantage.

Note 2: In stroke play, except where a serious breach resulting in disqualification is involved, a player in breach of Rule 1-2 in relation to the movement of his own ball must play the ball from where it was stopped, or, if the ball was deflected, from where it came to rest. If the movement of a player's ball has been intentionally influenced by a *fellow-competitor* or other *outside agency*, Rule 1-4 applies to the player (see Note to Rule 19-1).

1-3. Agreement to Waive Rules

Players must not agree to exclude the operation of any *Rule* or to waive any penalty incurred.

PENALTY FOR BREACH OF RULE 1-3:
Match play – Disqualification of both *sides*;
Stroke play – Disqualification of *competitors* concerned.

(Agreeing to play out of turn in stroke play – see Rule 10-2c)

1-4. Points Not Covered by Rules

If any point in dispute is not covered by the *Rules*, the decision should be made in accordance with equity.

Rule 2 – Match Play

Definitions

All defined terms are in *italics* and are listed alphabetically in the Definitions section – see pages 592–595.

2-1. General

A match consists of one *side* playing against another over a *stipulated round* unless otherwise decreed by the *Committee*.

In match play the game is played by holes.

Except as otherwise provided in the *Rules*, a hole is won by the *side* that *holes* its ball in the fewer *strokes*. In a handicap match, the lower net score wins the hole.

The state of the match is expressed by the terms: so many "holes up" or "all square", and so many "to play".

A *side* is "dormie" when it is as many holes up as there are holes remaining to be played.

2-2. Halved Hole

A hole is halved if each *side holes* out in the same number of *strokes*.

When a player has *holed* out and his *opponent* has been left with a *stroke* for the half, if the player subsequently incurs a penalty, the hole is halved.

2-3. Winner of Match

A match is won when one *side* leads by a number of holes greater than the number remaining to be played.

If there is a tie, the *Committee* may extend the *stipulated round* by as many holes as are required for a match to be won.

2-4. Concession of Match, Hole or Next Stroke

A player may concede a match at any time prior to the start or conclusion of that match.

A player may concede a hole at any time prior to the start or conclusion of that hole.

A player may concede his *opponent's* next *stroke* at any time, provided the *opponent's* ball is at rest. The *opponent* is considered to have *holed* out with his next *stroke*, and the ball may be removed by either *side*.

A concession may not be declined or withdrawn.

(Ball overhanging hole – see Rule 16-2)

2-5. Doubt as to Procedure; Disputes and Claims

In match play, if a doubt or dispute arises between the players, a player may make a claim. If no duly authorised representative of the *Committee* is available within a reasonable time, the players must continue the match without delay. The *Committee* may consider a claim only if it has been made in a timely manner and if the player making the claim has notified his *opponent* at the time (i) that he is making a claim or wants a ruling and (ii) of the facts upon which the claim or ruling is to be based. A claim is considered to have been made in a timely manner if, upon discovery of circumstances giving rise to a claim, the player makes his claim (i) before any player in the match plays from the next *teeing ground*, or (ii) in the case of the last hole of the match, before all players in the match leave the *putting green*, or (iii) when the circumstances giving rise to the claim are discovered after all the players in the match have left the *putting green* of the final hole, before the result of the match has been officially announced.

A claim relating to a prior hole in the match may only be considered by the *Committee* if it is based on facts previously unknown to the player making the claim and he had been given wrong information (Rules 6-2a or 9) by an *opponent*. Such a claim must be made in a timely manner.

Once the result of the match has been officially announced, a claim may not be considered by the *Committee*, unless it is satisfied that (i) the claim is based on facts which were previously unknown to the player making the claim at the time the result was officially announced, (ii) the player making the claim had been given wrong information by an *opponent* and (iii) the *opponent* knew he was giving wrong information. There is no time limit on considering such a claim.

Note 1: A player may disregard a breach of the *Rules* by his *opponent* provided there is no agreement by the *sides* to waive a *Rule* (Rule 1-3).

Note 2: In match play, if a player is doubtful of his rights or the correct procedure, he may not complete the play of the hole with two balls.

2-6. General Penalty

The penalty for a breach of a *Rule* in match play is loss of hole except when otherwise provided.

Rule 3 – Stroke Play

Definitions

All defined terms are in *italics* and are listed alphabetically in the Definitions section – see pages 592–595.

3-1. General; Winner

A stroke play competition consists of *competitors* completing each hole of a *stipulated round* or rounds and, for each round, returning a score card on which there is a gross score for each hole. Each *competitor* is playing against every other *competitor* in the competition.

The *competitor* who plays the *stipulated round* or rounds in the fewest *strokes* is the winner.

In a handicap competition, the *competitor* with the lowest net score for the *stipulated round* or rounds is the winner.

3-2. Failure to Hole Out

If a *competitor* fails to hole out at any hole and does not correct his mistake before he makes a *stroke* on the next *teeing ground* or, in the case of the last hole of the round, before he leaves the *putting green*, he is disqualified.

3-3. Doubt as to Procedure

a. Procedure

In stroke play, if a *competitor* is doubtful of his rights or the correct procedure during the play of a hole, he may, without penalty, complete the hole with two balls.

After the doubtful situation has arisen and before taking further action, the *competitor* must announce to his *marker* or *fellow-competitor* that he intends to play two balls and which ball he wishes to count if the *Rules* permit.

The *competitor* must report the facts of the situation to the *Committee* before returning his score card. If he fails to do so, he is disqualified.

Note: If the *competitor* takes further action before dealing with the doubtful situation, Rule 3-3 is not applicable. The score with the original ball counts or, if the original ball is not one of the balls being played, the score with the first ball put into play counts, even if the *Rules* do not allow the procedure adopted for that ball. However, the *competitor* incurs no penalty for having played a second ball, and any *penalty strokes* incurred solely by playing that ball do not count in his score.

b. Determination of Score for Hole

(i) If the ball that the *competitor* selected in advance to count has been played in accordance with the *Rules*, the score with that ball is the *competitor's* score for the hole. Otherwise, the score with the other ball counts if the *Rules* allow the procedure adopted for that ball.

(ii) If the *competitor* fails to announce in advance his deci sion to complete the hole with two balls, or which ball he wishes to count, the score with the original ball counts, provided it has been played in accordance with the *Rules*. If the original ball is not one of the balls being played, the first ball put into play counts, provid ed it has been played in accordance with the *Rules*. Otherwise, the score with the other ball counts if the *Rules* allow the procedure adopted for that ball.

Note 1: If a *competitor* plays a second ball under Rule 3-3, the *strokes* made after this Rule has been invoked with the ball ruled not to count and *penalty strokes* incurred solely by playing that ball are disregarded.

Note 2: A second ball played under Rule 3-3 is not a *provisional ball* under Rule 27-2.

3-4. Refusal to Comply with a Rule

If a *competitor* refuses to comply with a *Rule* affecting the rights of another *competitor*, he is disqualified.

3-5. General Penalty

The penalty for a breach of a *Rule* in stroke play is two strokes except when otherwise provided.

Clubs and the Ball

The *R&A* reserves the right, at any time, to change the *Rules* relating to clubs and balls (see Appendices II and III) and make or change the interpretations relating to these *Rules*.

Rule 4 – Clubs

A player in doubt as to the conformity of a club should consult the *R&A*.

A manufacturer should submit to the *R&A* a sample of a club to be manufactured for a ruling as to whether the club conforms with the *Rules*. The sample becomes the property of the *R&A* for reference purposes. If a manufacturer fails to submit a sample or, having submitted a sample, fails to await a ruling before manufacturing and/or marketing the club, the manufacturer assumes the risk of a ruling that the club does not conform with the *Rules*.

Definitions

All defined terms are in *italics* and are listed alphabetically in the Definitions section – see pages 592–595.

4-1. Form and Make of Clubs

a. General

The player's clubs must conform with this Rule and the provisions, specifications and interpretations set forth in Appendix II.

Note: The *Committee* may require, in the conditions of a competition (Rule 33-1), that any driver the player carries must have a clubhead, identified by model and loft, that is named on the current List of Conforming Driver Heads issued by the *R&A*.

b. Wear and Alteration

A club that conforms with the *Rules* when new is deemed to conform after wear through normal use. Any part of a club that has been purposely altered is regarded as new and must, in its altered state, conform with the *Rules*.

4-2. Playing Characteristics Changed and Foreign Material

a. Playing Characteristics Changed

During a *stipulated round*, the playing characteristics of a club must not be purposely changed by adjustment or by any other means.

b. Foreign Material

Foreign material must not be applied to the club face for the purpose of influencing the movement of the ball.

*PENALTY FOR CARRYING, BUT NOT MAKING STROKE WITH, CLUB OR CLUBS IN BREACH OF RULE 4-1 or 4-2:

Match play – At the conclusion of the hole at which the breach is discovered, the state of the match is adjusted by deducting one hole for each hole at which a breach occurred; maximum deduction per round – Two holes.
Stroke play – Two strokes for each hole at which any breach occurred; maximum penalty per round – Four strokes (two strokes at each of the first two holes at which any breach occurred).

Match play or stroke play – If a breach is discovered between the play of two holes, it is deemed to have been discovered during play of the next hole, and the penalty must be applied accordingly.
Bogey and par competitions – See Note 1 to Rule 32-1a.
Stableford competitions – See Note 1 to Rule 32-1b.

*Any club or clubs carried in breach of Rule 4-1 or 4-2 must be declared out of play by the player to his *opponent* in match play or his *marker* or a *fellow-competitor* in stroke play immediately upon discovery that a breach has occurred. If the player fails to do so, he is disqualified.

PENALTY FOR MAKING STROKE WITH CLUB IN BREACH OF RULE 4-1 or 4-2:
Disqualification.

4-3. Damaged Clubs: Repair and Replacement

a. Damage in Normal Course of Play

If, during a *stipulated round*, a player's club is damaged in the normal course of play, he may:

(i) use the club in its damaged state for the remainder of the *stipulated round*; or
(ii) without unduly delaying play, repair it or have it repaired; or
(iii) as an additional option available only if the club is unfit for play, replace the damaged club with any club. The replacement of a club must not unduly delay play (Rule 6-7) and must not be made by borrowing any club selected for play by any other person playing on the *course* or by assembling components carried by or for the player during the *stipulated round*.

PENALTY FOR BREACH OF RULE 4-3a:
See Penalty Statements for Rule 4-4a or b, and Rule 4-4c.

Note: A club is unfit for play if it is substantially damaged, e.g. the shaft is dented, significantly bent or breaks into pieces; the clubhead becomes loose, detached or significantly deformed; or the grip becomes loose. A club is not unfit for play solely because the club's lie or loft has been altered, or the clubhead is scratched.

b. Damage Other Than in Normal Course of Play

If, during a *stipulated round*, a player's club is damaged other than in the normal course of play rendering it non-conforming or changing its playing characteristics, the club must not subsequently be used or replaced during the round.

PENALTY FOR BREACH OF RULE 4-3b: Disqualification.

c. Damage Prior to Round

A player may use a club damaged prior to a round, provided the club, in its damaged state, conforms with the *Rules*.

Damage to a club that occurred prior to a round may be repaired during the round, provided the playing characteristics are not changed and play is not unduly delayed.

PENALTY FOR BREACH OF RULE 4-3c:
See Penalty Statement for Rule 4-1 or 4-2.

(Undue delay – see Rule 6-7)

4-4. Maximum of Fourteen Clubs

a. Selection and Addition of Clubs

The player must not start a *stipulated round* with more than fourteen clubs. He is limited to the clubs thus selected for that round, except that if he started with fewer than fourteen clubs, he may add any number, provided his total number does not exceed fourteen.

The addition of a club or clubs must not unduly delay play (Rule 6-7) and the player must not add or borrow any club selected for play by any other person playing on the *course* or by assembling components carried by or for the player during the *stipulated round*.

b. Partners May Share Clubs

Partners may share clubs, provided that the total number of clubs carried by the *partners* so sharing does not exceed fourteen.

PENALTY FOR BREACH OF RULE 4-4a or b, REGARDLESS OF NUMBER OF EXCESS CLUBS CARRIED:
Match play – At the conclusion of the hole at which the breach is discovered, the state of the match is adjusted by deducting one hole for each hole at which a breach occurred; maximum deduction per round – Two holes.
Stroke play – Two strokes for each hole at which any breach occurred; maximum penalty per round – Four strokes (two strokes at each of the first two holes at which any breach occurred).
Match play or stroke play – If a breach is discovered between the play of two holes, it is deemed to have been discovered during play of the hole just completed, and the penalty for a breach of Rule 4-4a or b does not apply to the next hole.
Bogey and par competitions – See Note 1 to Rule 32-1a.
Stableford competitions – See Note 1 to Rule 32-1b.

c. Excess Club Declared Out of Play

Any club or clubs carried or used in breach of Rule 4-3a(iii) or Rule 4-4 must be declared out of play by the player to his *opponent* in match play or his *marker* or a *fellow-competitor* in stroke play immediately upon discovery that a breach has occurred. The player must not use the club or clubs for the remainder of the *stipulated round*.

PENALTY FOR BREACH OF RULE 4-4c:
Disqualification.

Rule 5 – The Ball

A player in doubt as to the conformity of a ball should consult the *R&A*.

A manufacturer should submit to the *R&A* samples of a ball to be manufactured for a ruling as to whether the ball conforms with the *Rules*. The samples become the property of the *R&A* for reference purposes. If a manufacturer fails to submit samples or, having submitted samples, fails to await a ruling before manufacturing and/or marketing the ball, the manufacturer assumes the risk of a ruling that the ball does not conform with the *Rules*.

Definitions

All defined terms are in *italics* and are listed alphabetically in the Definitions section – see pages 592–595.

5-1. General

The ball the player plays must conform to the requirements specified in Appendix III.

Note: The *Committee* may require, in the conditions of a competition (Rule 33-1), that the ball the player plays must be named on the current List of Conforming Golf Balls issued by the *R&A*.

5-2. Foreign Material

The ball the player plays must not have foreign material applied to it for the purpose of changing its playing characteristics.

PENALTY FOR BREACH OF RULE 5-1 or 5-2:
Disqualification.

5-3. Ball Unfit for Play

A ball is unfit for play if it is visibly cut, cracked or out of shape. A ball is not unfit for play solely because mud or other materials adhere to it, its surface is scratched or scraped or its paint is damaged or discoloured.

If a player has reason to believe his ball has become unfit for play during play of the hole being played, he may lift the ball, without penalty, to determine whether it is unfit.

Before lifting the ball, the player must announce his intention to his *opponent* in match play or his *marker* or a *fellow-competitor* in stroke play and mark the position of the ball. He may then lift and examine it, provided that he gives his *opponent, marker* or *fellow-competitor* an opportunity to examine the ball and observe the lifting and replacement. The ball must not be cleaned when lifted under Rule 5-3.

If the player fails to comply with all or any part of this procedure, or if he lifts the ball without having reason to believe that it has become unfit for play during play of the hole being played, he incurs a penalty of one stroke.

If it is determined that the ball has become unfit for play during play of the hole being played, the player may *substitute* another ball, placing it on the spot where the original ball lay. Otherwise, the original ball must be replaced. If a player *substitutes* a ball when not permitted and makes a *stroke* at the wrongly *substituted ball*, he incurs the general penalty for a breach of Rule 5-3, but there is no additional penalty under this Rule or Rule 15-2.

If a ball breaks into pieces as a result of a *stroke*, the *stroke* is cancelled and the player must play a ball, without penalty, as nearly as possible at the spot from which the original ball was played (see Rule 20-5).

*PENALTY FOR BREACH OF RULE 5-3:
Match play – Loss of hole; Stroke play – Two strokes.
*If a player incurs the general penalty for a breach of Rule 5-3, there is no additional penalty under this Rule.

Note 1: If the *opponent, marker* or *fellow-competitor* wishes to dispute a claim of unfitness, he must do so before the player plays another ball.

Note 2: If the original lie of a ball to be placed or replaced has been altered, see Rule 20-3b.

(Cleaning ball lifted from putting green or under any other Rule – see Rule 21)

Player's Responsibilities

Rule 6 – The Player

Definitions

All defined terms are in *italics* and are listed alphabetically in the Definitions section – see pages 592–595.

6-1. Rules

The player and his *caddie* are responsible for knowing the *Rules*. During a *stipulated round*, for any breach of a *Rule* by his *caddie*, the player incurs the applicable penalty.

a. Match Play

Before starting a match in a handicap competition, the players should determine from one another their respective handicaps. If a player begins a match having declared a handicap higher than that to which he is entitled and this affects the number of strokes given or received, he is disqualified; otherwise, the player must play off the declared handicap.

b. Stroke Play

In any round of a handicap competition, the *competitor* must ensure that his handicap is recorded on his score card before it is returned to the *Committee*. If no handicap is recorded on his score card before it is returned (Rule 6-6b), or if the recorded handicap is higher than that to which he is entitled and this affects the number of strokes received, he is disqualified from the handicap competition; otherwise, the score stands.

Note: It is the player's responsibility to know the holes at which handicap strokes are to be given or received.

6-3. Time of Starting and Groups

a. Time of Starting

The player must start at the time established by the *Committee*.

PENALTY FOR BREACH OF RULE 6-3a:
If the player arrives at his starting point, ready to play, within five minutes after his starting time, the penalty for failure to start on time is loss of the first hole in match play or two strokes at the first hole in stroke play. Otherwise, the penalty for breach of this Rule is disqualification.
Bogey and par competitions – See Note 2 to Rule 32-1a.
Stableford competitions – See Note 2 to Rule 32-1b.

Exception: Where the *Committee* determines that exceptional circumstances have prevented a player from starting on time, there is no penalty.

b. Groups

In stroke play, the *competitor* must remain throughout the round in the group arranged by the *Committee*, unless the *Committee* authorises or ratifies a change.

PENALTY FOR BREACH OF RULE 6-3b:
Disqualification.
(Best-ball and four-ball play – see Rules 30-3a and 31-2)

6-4. Caddie

The player may be assisted by a *caddie*, but he is limited to only one *caddie* at any one time.

*PENALTY FOR BREACH OF RULE 6-4:
Match play – At the conclusion of the hole at which the breach is discovered, the state of the match is adjusted by deducting one hole for each hole at which a breach occurred; maximum deduction per round – Two holes.
Stroke play – Two strokes for each hole at which any breach occurred; maximum penalty per round – Four strokes (two strokes at each of the first two holes at which any breach occurred).
Match play or stroke play – If a breach is discovered between the play of two holes, it is deemed to have been discovered during play of the next hole, and the penalty must be applied accordingly.
Bogey and par competitions – See Note 1 to Rule 32-1a.
Stableford competitions – See Note 1 to Rule 32-1b.
*A player having more than one *caddie* in breach of this Rule must immediately upon discovery that a breach has occurred ensure that he has no more than one *caddie* at any one time during the remainder of the *stipulated round*. Otherwise, the player is disqualified.

Note: The *Committee* may, in the conditions of a competition (Rule 33-1), prohibit the use of *caddies* or restrict a player in his choice of *caddie*.

6-5. Ball

The responsibility for playing the proper ball rests with the player. Each player should put an identification mark on his ball.

a. Recording Scores

After each hole the *marker* should check the score with the *competitor* and record it. On completion of the round the *marker* must sign the score card and hand it to the *competitor*. If more than one *marker* records the scores, each must sign for the part for which he is responsible.

b. Signing and Returning Score Card

After completion of the round, the *competitor* should check his score for each hole and settle any doubtful points with the *Committee*. He must ensure that the *marker* or *markers* have signed the score card, sign the score card himself and return it to the *Committee* as soon as possible.

PENALTY FOR BREACH OF RULE 6-6b:
Disqualification.

c. Alteration of Score Card
No alteration may be made on a score card after the *competitor* has returned it to the *Committee*.

d. Wrong Score for Hole
The *competitor* is responsible for the correctness of the score recorded for each hole on his score card. If he returns a score for any hole lower than actually taken, he is disqualified. If he returns a score for any hole higher than actually taken, the score as returned stands.

Note 1: The *Committee* is responsible for the addition of scores and application of the handicap recorded on the score card – see Rule 33-5.

Note 2: In *four-ball* stroke play, see also Rules 31-3 and 31-7a.

6-7. Undue Delay; Slow Play
The player must play without undue delay and in accordance with any pace of play guidelines that the *Committee* may establish. Between completion of a hole and playing from the next *teeing ground*, the player must not unduly delay play.

PENALTY FOR BREACH OF RULE 6-7:
Match play – Loss of hole; Stroke play – Two strokes.
Bogey and par competitions – See Note 2 to Rule 32-1a.
Stableford competitions – See Note 2 to Rule 32-1b.
For subsequent offence – Disqualification.

Note 1: If the player unduly delays play between holes, he is delaying the play of the next hole and, except for bogey, par and Stableford competitions (see Rule 32), the penalty applies to that hole.

Note 2: For the purpose of preventing slow play, the *Committee* may, in the conditions of a competition (Rule 33-1), establish pace of play guidelines including maximum periods of time allowed to complete a *stipulated round*, a hole or a *stroke*.

In match play, the *Committee* may, in such a condition, modify the penalty for a breach of this Rule as follows:

First offence – Loss of hole;
Second offence – Loss of hole;
For subsequent offence – Disqualification.

In stroke play, the *Committee* may, in such a condition, modify the penalty for a breach of this Rule as follows:

First offence – One stroke;
Second offence – Two strokes;
For subsequent offence – Disqualification.

6-8. Discontinuance of Play; Resumption of Play

a. When Permitted
The player must not discontinue play unless:
(i) the *Committee* has suspended play;
(ii he believes there is danger from lightning;
(iii) he is seeking a decision from the *Committee* on a doubtful or disputed point (see Rules 2-5 and 34-3); or
(iv) there is some other good reason such as sudden ill ness. Bad weather is not of itself a good reason for discontinuing play.

If the player discontinues play without specific permission from the *Committee*, he must report to the *Committee* as soon as practicable. If he does so and the *Committee* considers his reason satisfactory, there is no penalty. Otherwise, the player is disqualified.

Exception in match play: Players discontinuing match play by agreement are not subject to disqualification, unless by so doing the competition is delayed.

Note: Leaving the *course* does not of itself constitute discontinuance of play.

b. Procedure When Play Suspended by Committee
When play is suspended by the *Committee*, if the players in a match or group are between the play of two holes, they must not resume play until the *Committee* has ordered a resumption of play. If they have started play of a hole, they may discontinue play immediately or continue play of the hole, provided they do so without delay. If the players choose to continue play of the hole, they are permitted to discontinue play before completing it. In any case, play must be discontinued after the hole is completed.

The players must resume play when the *Committee* has ordered a resumption of play.

PENALTY FOR BREACH OF RULE 6-8b:
Disqualification.

Note: The *Committee* may provide, in the conditions of a competition (Rule 33-1), that in potentially dangerous situations play must be discontinued immediately following a suspension of play by the *Committee*. If a player fails to discontinue play immediately, he is disqualified, unless circumstances warrant waiving the penalty as provided in Rule 33-7.

c. Lifting Ball When Play Discontinued
When a player discontinues play of a hole under Rule 6-8a, he may lift his ball, without penalty, only if the *Committee* has suspended play or there is a good reason to lift it. Before lifting the ball the player must mark its position. If the player discontinues play and lifts his ball without specific permission from the *Committee*, he must, when reporting to the *Committee* (Rule 6-8a), report the lifting of the ball.

If the player lifts the ball without a good reason to do so, fails to mark the position of the ball before lifting it or fails to report the lifting of the ball, he incurs a penalty of one stroke.

d. Procedure When Play Resumed
Play must be resumed from where it was discontinued, even if resumption occurs on a subsequent day. The player must, either before or when play is resumed, proceed as follows:
(i) if the player has lifted the ball, he must, provided he was entitled to lift it under Rule 6-8c, place the original ball or a *substituted ball* on the spot from which the original ball was lifted. Otherwise, the original ball must be replaced;
(ii) if the player has not lifted his ball, he may, provided he was entitled to lift it under Rule 6-8c, lift, clean and replace the ball, or substitute a ball, on the spot from which the original ball was lifted. Before lifting the ball he must mark its position; or
(iii) if the player's ball or ball-marker is moved (including by wind or water) while play is discontinued, a ball or ball-marker must be placed on the spot from which the original ball or ball-marker was moved.

Note: If the spot where the ball is to be placed is impossible to determine, it must be estimated and the ball placed on the estimated spot. The provisions of Rule 20-3c do not apply.

*PENALTY FOR BREACH OF RULE 6-8d:
Match play – Loss of hole; Stroke play – Two strokes.

*If a player incurs the general penalty for a breach of Rule 6-8d, there is no additional penalty under Rule 6-8c.

Rule 7 – Practice

Definitions
All defined terms are in *italics* and are listed alphabetically in the Definitions section – see pages 592–595.

7-1. Before or Between Rounds
a. Match Play
On any day of a match play competition, a player may practise on the competition *course* before a round.

b. Stroke Play
Before a round or play-off on any day of a stroke play competition, a *competitor* must not practise on the competition *course* or test the surface of any *putting green* on the *course* by rolling a ball or roughening or scraping the surface.

When two or more rounds of a stroke play competition are to be played over consecutive days, a *competitor* must not practise between those rounds on any competition *course* remaining to be played, or test the surface of any *putting green* on such *course* by rolling a ball or roughening or scraping the surface.

Exception: Practice putting or chipping on or near the first *teeing ground* or any practice area before starting a round or play-off is permitted.

PENALTY FOR BREACH OF RULE 7-1b:
Disqualification.

Note: The *Committee* may, in the conditions of a competition (Rule 33-1), prohibit practice on the competition *course* on any day of a match play competition or permit practice on the competition *course* or part of the *course* (Rule 33-2c) on any day of or between rounds of a stroke play competition.

7-2. During Round
A player must not make a practice *stroke* during play of a hole.

Between the play of two holes a player must not make a practice *stroke*, except that he may practise putting or chipping on or near:
a. the *putting green* of the hole last played,
b. any practice *putting green*, or
c. the *teeing ground* of the next hole to be played in the round, provided a practice *stroke* is not made from a *hazard* and does not unduly delay play (Rule 6-7).

Strokes made in continuing the play of a hole, the result of which has been decided, are not practice *strokes*.

Exception: When play has been suspended by the *Committee*, a player may, prior to resumption of play, practise
(a) as provided in this Rule,
(b) anywhere other than on the competition *course* and
(c) as otherwise permitted by the *Committee*.

PENALTY FOR BREACH OF RULE 7-2:
Match play – Loss of hole; Stroke play – Two strokes.
In the event of a breach between the play of two holes, the penalty applies to the next hole.

Note 1: A practice swing is not a practice *stroke* and may be taken at any place, provided the player does not breach the *Rules*.

Note 2: The *Committee* may, in the conditions of a competition (Rule 33-1), prohibit:
(a) practice on or near the *putting green* of the hole last played, and
(b) rolling a ball on the *putting green* of the hole last played.

Rule 8 – Advice; Indicating Line of Play

Definitions
All defined terms are in *italics* and are listed alphabetically in the Definitions section – see pages 592–595.

8-1. Advice
During a *stipulated round*, a player must not:
a. give *advice* to anyone in the competition playing on the *course* other than his *partner*, or
b. ask for *advice* from anyone other than his *partner* or either of their *caddies*.

8-2. Indicating Line of Play
a. Other Than on Putting Green
Except on the *putting green*, a player may have the *line of play* indicated to him by anyone, but no one may be positioned by the player on or close to the line or an extension of the line beyond the *hole* while the *stroke* is being made. Any mark placed by the player or with his knowledge to indicate the line must be removed before the *stroke* is made.

Exception: Flagstick attended or held up – see Rule 17-1.

b. On the Putting Green
When the player's ball is on the *putting green*, the player, his *partner* or either of their *caddies* may, before but not during the *stroke*, point out a line for putting, but in so doing the *putting green* must not be touched. A mark must not be placed anywhere to indicate a line for putting.

PENALTY FOR BREACH OF RULE:
Match play – Loss of hole; Stroke play – Two strokes.

Note: The *Committee* may, in the conditions of a team competition (Rule 33-1), permit each team to appoint one person who may give *advice* (including pointing out a line for putting) to members of that team. The *Committee* may establish conditions relating to the appointment and permitted conduct of that person, who must be identified to the *Committee* before giving *advice*.

Rule 9 – Information as to Strokes Taken

Definitions
All defined terms are in *italics* and are listed alphabetically in the Definitions section – see pages 592–595.

9-1. General
The number of *strokes* a player has taken includes any *penalty strokes* incurred.

9-2. Match Play
a. Information as to Strokes Taken
An *opponent* is entitled to ascertain from the player, during the play of a hole, the number of *strokes* he has taken and, after play of a hole, the number of *strokes* taken on the hole just completed.

b. Wrong Information
A player must not give wrong information to his *opponent*. If a player gives wrong information, he loses the hole.

A player is deemed to have given wrong information if he:
(i) fails to inform his *opponent* as soon as practicable that he has incurred a penalty, unless (a) he was obviously proceeding under a *Rule* involving a penalty and this was observed by his *opponent*, or (b) he corrects the mistake before his *opponent* makes his next *stroke*; or
(ii) gives incorrect information during play of a hole regarding the number of *strokes* taken and does not correct the mistake before his *opponent* makes his next *stroke*; or
(iii) gives incorrect information regarding the number of *strokes* taken to complete a hole and this affects the *opponent's* understanding of the result of the hole, unless he corrects the mistake before any player makes a *stroke* from the next *teeing ground* or, in the case of the last hole of the match, before all players leave the *putting green*.

A player has given wrong information even if it is due to the failure to include a penalty that he did not know he had incurred. It is the player's responsibility to know the *Rules*.

9-3. Stroke Play
A *competitor* who has incurred a penalty should inform his *marker* as soon as practicable.

Order of Play

Rule 10 – Order of Play

Definitions

All defined terms are in *italics* and are listed alphabetically in the Definitions section – see pages 592–595.

10-1. Match Play

a. When Starting Play of Hole

The *side* that has the *honour* at the first *teeing ground* is determined by the order of the draw. In the absence of a draw, the *honour* should be decided by lot.

The *side* that wins a hole takes the *honour* at the next *teeing ground*. If a hole has been halved, the *side* that had the *honour* at the previous *teeing ground* retains it.

b. During Play of Hole

After both players have started play of the hole, the ball farther from the *hole* is played first. If the balls are equidistant from the *hole* or their positions relative to the *hole* are not determinable, the ball to be played first should be decided by lot.

Exception: Rule 30-3b (*best-ball* and *four-ball* match play).

Note: When it becomes known that the original ball is not to be played as it lies and the player is required to play a ball as nearly as possible at the spot from which the original ball was last played (see Rule 20-5), the order of play is determined by the spot from which the previous *stroke* was made. When a ball may be played from a spot other than where the previous *stroke* was made, the order of play is determined by the position where the original ball came to rest.

c. Playing Out of Turn

If a player plays when his *opponent* should have played, there is no penalty, but the *opponent* may immediately require the player to cancel the *stroke* so made and, in correct order, play a ball as nearly as possible at the spot from which the original ball was last played (see Rule 20-5).

10-2. Stroke Play

a. When Starting Play of Hole

The *competitor* who has the *honour* at the first *teeing ground* is determined by the order of the draw. In the absence of a draw, the *honour* should be decided by lot.

The *competitor* with the lowest score at a hole takes the *honour* at the next *teeing ground*. The *competitor* with the second lowest score plays next and so on. If two or more *competitors* have the same score at a hole, they play from the next *teeing ground* in the same order as at the previous *teeing ground*.

Exception: Rule 32-1 (handicap bogey, par and Stableford competitions).

b. During Play of Hole

After the *competitors* have started play of the hole, the ball farthest from the *hole* is played first. If two or more balls are equidistant from the *hole* or their positions relative to the *hole* are not determinable, the ball to be played first should be decided by lot.

Exceptions: Rules 22 (ball assisting or interfering with play) and 31-4 (*four-ball* stroke play).

Note: When it becomes known that the original ball is not to be played as it lies and the *competitor* is required to play a ball as nearly as possible at the spot from which the original ball was last played (see Rule 20-5), the order of play is determined by the spot from which the previous *stroke* was made. When a ball may be played from a spot other than where the previous *stroke* was made, the order of play is determined by the position where the original ball came to rest.

c. Playing Out of Turn

If a *competitor* plays out of turn, there is no penalty and the ball is played as it lies. If, however, the *Committee* determines that *competitors* have agreed to play out of turn to give one of them an advantage, they are disqualified.

(Making stroke while another ball in motion after stroke from putting green – see Rule 16-1f)

(Incorrect order of play in foursome stroke play – see Rule 29-3)

10-3. Provisional Ball or Another Ball from Teeing Ground

If a player plays a *provisional ball* or another ball from the *teeing ground*, he must do so after his *opponent* or *fellow-competitor* has made his first *stroke*. If more than one player elects to play a *provisional ball* or is required to play another ball from the *teeing ground*, the original order of play must be retained. If a player plays a *provisional ball* or another ball out of turn, Rule 10-1c or 10-2c applies.

Teeing Ground

Rule 11 – Teeing Ground

Definitions

All defined terms are in *italics* and are listed alphabetically in the Definitions section – see pages 592–595.

11-1. Teeing

When a player is putting a ball into play from the *teeing ground*, it must be played from within the *teeing ground* and from the surface of the ground or from a conforming tee (see Appendix IV) in or on the surface of the ground.

For the purposes of this Rule, the surface of the ground includes an irregularity of surface (whether or not created by the player) and sand or other natural substance (whether or not placed by the player).

If a player makes a *stroke* at a ball on a non-conforming tee, or at a ball teed in a manner not permitted by this Rule, he is disqualified.

A player may stand outside the *teeing ground* to play a ball within it.

11-2. Tee-Markers

Before a player makes his first *stroke* with any ball on the *teeing ground* of the hole being played, the tee-markers are deemed to be fixed. In these circumstances, if the player moves or allows to be moved a tee-marker for the purpose of avoiding interference with his *stance*, the area of his intended swing or his *line of play*, he incurs the penalty for a breach of Rule 13-2.

11-3. Ball Falling off Tee

If a ball, when not *in play*, falls off a tee or is knocked off a tee by the player in *addressing* it, it may be re-teed, without penalty. However, if a *stroke* is made at the ball in these circumstances, whether the ball is moving or not, the *stroke* counts, but there is no penalty.

11-4. Playing from Outside Teeing Ground

a. Match Play

If a player, when starting a hole, plays a ball from outside the *teeing ground*, there is no penalty, but the *opponent* may immediately require the player to cancel the *stroke* and play a ball from within the *teeing ground*.

b. Stroke Play

If a *competitor*, when starting a hole, plays a ball from outside the *teeing ground*, he incurs a penalty of two strokes and must then play a ball from within the *teeing ground*.

If the *competitor* makes a *stroke* from the next *teeing ground* without first correcting his mistake or, in the case of the last hole of the round, leaves the *putting green* without first declaring his intention to correct his mistake, he is disqualified.

The *stroke* from outside the *teeing ground* and any subsequent *strokes* by the *competitor* on the hole prior to his correction of the mistake do not count in his score.

11-5. Playing from Wrong Teeing Ground
The provisions of Rule 11-4 apply.

Playing the Ball

Rule 12 – Searching for and Identifying Ball

Definitions
All defined terms are in *italics* and are listed alphabetically in the Definitions section – see pages 592–595.

12-1. Seeing Ball; Searching for Ball
A player is not necessarily entitled to see his ball when making a *stroke*.

In searching for his ball anywhere on the *course*, the player may touch or bend long grass, rushes, bushes, whins, heather or the like, but only to the extent necessary to find or identify the ball, provided that this does not improve the lie of the ball, the area of his intended *stance* or swing or his *line of play*; if the ball is *moved*, Rule 18-2a applies except as provided in clauses a–d of this Rule.

In addition to the methods of searching for and identifying a ball that are otherwise permitted by the *Rules*, the player may also search for and identify a ball under Rule 12-1 as follows:

a. Searching for or Identifying Ball Covered by Sand
If the player's ball lying anywhere on the *course* is believed to be covered by sand, to the extent that he cannot find or identify it, he may, without penalty, touch or move the sand in order to find or identify the ball. If the ball is found, and identified as his, the player must re-create the lie as nearly as possible by replacing the sand. If the ball is *moved* during the touching or moving of sand while searching for or identifying the ball, there is no penalty; the ball must be replaced and the lie re-created.

In re-creating a lie under this Rule, the player is permitted to leave a small part of the ball visible.

b. Searching for or Identifying Ball Covered by Loose Impediments in Hazard
In a *hazard*, if the player's ball is believed to be covered by *loose impediments* to the extent that he cannot find or identify it, he may, without penalty, touch or move *loose impediments* in order to find or identify the ball. If the ball is found or identified as his, the player must replace the *loose impediments*. If the ball is *moved* during the touching or moving of *loose impediments* while searching for or identifying the ball, Rule 18-2a applies; if the ball is *moved* during the replacement of the *loose impediments*, there is no penalty and the ball must be replaced.

If the ball was entirely covered by *loose impediments*, the player must re-cover the ball but is permitted to leave a small part of the ball visible.

c. Searching for Ball in Water in Water Hazard
If a ball is believed to be lying in water in a *water hazard*, the player may, without penalty, probe for it with a club or otherwise. If the ball in water is accidentally *moved* while probing, there is no penalty; the ball must be replaced, unless the player elects to proceed under Rule 26-1. If the *moved* ball was not lying in water or the ball was accidentally *moved* by the player other than while probing, Rule 18-2a applies.

d. Searching for Ball Within Obstruction or Abnormal Ground Condition
If a ball lying in or on an *obstruction* or in an *abnormal ground condition* is accidentally *moved* during search, there is no penalty; the ball must be replaced unless the player elects to proceed under Rule 24-1b, 24-2b or 25-1b as applicable. If the player replaces the ball, he may still proceed under one of those Rules, if applicable.

PENALTY FOR BREACH OF RULE 12-1:
Match Play – Loss of Hole; Stroke Play – Two Strokes.

(Improving lie, area of intended stance or swing, or line of play – see Rule 13-2)

Rule 12-2. Lifting Ball for Identification
The responsibility for playing the proper ball rests with the player. Each player should put an identification mark on his ball.

If a player believes that a ball at rest might be his, but he cannot identify it, the player may lift the ball for identification, without penalty. The right to lift a ball for identification is in addition to the actions permitted under Rule 12-1.

Before lifting the ball, the player must announce his intention to his *opponent* in match play or his *marker* or a *fellow-competitor* in stroke play and mark the position of the ball. He may then lift the ball and identify it, provided that he gives his *opponent, marker* or *fellow-competitor* an opportunity to observe the lifting and replacement. The ball must not be cleaned beyond the extent necessary for identification when lifted under Rule 12-2.

If the ball is the player's ball and he fails to comply with all or any part of this procedure, or he lifts his ball in order to identify it without having good reason to do so, he incurs a penalty of one stroke. If the lifted ball is the player's ball, he must replace it. If he fails to do so, he incurs the general penalty for a breach of Rule 12-2, but there is no additional penalty under this Rule.

Note: If the original lie of a ball to be replaced has been altered, see Rule 20-3b.

*PENALTY FOR BREACH OF RULE 12-2:
Match Play – Loss of hole; Stroke Play – Two strokes.

*If a player incurs the general penalty for a breach of Rule 12-2, there is no additional penalty under this Rule.

Rule 13 – Ball Played as It Lies

Definitions
All defined terms are in *italics* and are listed alphabetically in the Definitions section – see pages 592–595.

13-1. General
The ball must be played as it lies, except as otherwise provided in the *Rules*. (Ball at rest moved – see Rule 18)

13-2. Improving Lie, Area of Intended Stance or Swing, or Line of Play
A player must not improve or allow to be improved:
- the position or lie of his ball,
- the area of his intended *stance* or swing,
- his *line of play* or a reasonable extension of that line beyond the *hole*, or
- the area in which he is to drop or place a ball, by any of the following actions:
- pressing a club on the ground,
- moving, bending or breaking anything growing or fixed (including immovable *obstructions* and objects defining *out of bounds*),
- creating or eliminating irregularities of surface,
- removing or pressing down sand, loose soil, replaced divots or other cut turf placed in position, or
- removing dew, frost or water.

However, the player incurs no penalty if the action occurs:

- in grounding the club lightly when *addressing the ball*,
- in fairly taking his *stance*,
- in making a *stroke* or the backward movement of his club for a *stroke* and the *stroke* is made,
- in creating or eliminating irregularities of surface within the *teeing ground* or in removing dew, frost or water from the *teeing ground*, or
- on the *putting green* in removing sand and loose soil or in repairing damage (Rule 16-1).

Exception: Ball in *hazard* – see Rule 13-4.

13-3. Building Stance

A player is entitled to place his feet firmly in taking his *stance*, but he must not build a *stance*.

13-4. Ball in Hazard; Prohibited Actions

Except as provided in the *Rules*, before making a *stroke* at a ball that is in a *hazard* (whether a *bunker* or a *water hazard*) or that, having been lifted from a *hazard*, may be dropped or placed in the *hazard*, the player must not:

a. Test the condition of the *hazard* or any similar *hazard*;
b. Touch the ground in the *hazard* or water in the *water hazard* with his hand or a club; or
c. Touch or move a *loose impediment* lying in or touching the *hazard*.

Exceptions:

1. Provided nothing is done that constitutes testing the condition of the *hazard* or improves the lie of the ball, there is no penalty if the player (a) touches the ground or *loose impediments* in any *hazard* or water in a *water hazard* as a result of or to prevent falling, in removing an *obstruction*, in measuring or in marking the position of, retrieving, lifting, placing or replacing a ball under any *Rule* or (b) places his clubs in a *hazard*.
2. At any time, the player may smooth sand or soil in a *hazard* provided this is for the sole purpose of caring for the *course* and nothing is done to breach Rule 13-2 with respect to his next *stroke*. If a ball played from a *hazard* is outside the *hazard* after the *stroke*, the player may smooth sand or soil in the *hazard* without restriction.
3. If the player makes a *stroke* from a *hazard* and the ball comes to rest in another *hazard*, Rule 13-4a does not apply to any subsequent actions taken in the *hazard* from which the *stroke* was made.

Note: At any time, including at *address* or in the backward movement for the *stroke*, the player may touch, with a club or otherwise, any *obstruction*, any construction declared by the *Committee* to be an integral part of the *course* or any grass, bush, tree or other growing thing.

PENALTY FOR BREACH OF RULE:
Match play – Loss of hole; Stroke play – Two strokes.

(Searching for ball – see Rule 12-1)
(Relief for ball in water hazard – see Rule 26)

Rule 14 – Striking the Ball

Definitions

All defined terms are in *italics* and are listed alphabetically in the Definitions section – see pages 592–595.

14-1. Ball to be Fairly Struck At

The ball must be fairly struck at with the head of the club and must not be pushed, scraped or spooned.

14-2. Assistance

a. Physical Assistance and Protection from Elements

A player must not make a *stroke* while accepting physical assistance or protection from the elements.

b. Positioning of Caddie or Partner Behind Ball

A player must not make a *stroke* with his *caddie*, his *partner* or his *partner's caddie* positioned on or close to an extension of the *line of play* or *line of putt* behind the ball.

Exception: There is no penalty if the player's *caddie*, his *partner* or his *partner's caddie* is inadvertently located on or close to an extension of the *line of play* or *line of putt* behind the ball.

PENALTY FOR BREACH OF RULE 14-1 or 14-2:
Match play – Loss of hole; Stroke play – Two strokes.

14-3. Artificial Devices, Unusual Equipment and Unusual Use of Equipment

The *R&A* reserves the right, at any time, to change the *Rules* relating to artificial devices, unusual *equipment* and the unusual use of *equipment*, and to make or change the interpretations relating to these *Rules*.

A player in doubt as to whether use of an item would constitute a breach of Rule 14-3 should consult the *R&A*.

A manufacturer should submit to The *R&A* a sample of an item to be manufactured for a ruling as to whether its use during a *stipulated round* would cause a player to be in breach of Rule 14-3. The sample becomes the property of The *R&A* for reference purposes. If a manufacturer fails to submit a sample or, having submitted a sample, fails to await a ruling before manufacturing and/or marketing the item, the manufacturer assumes the risk of a ruling that use of the item would be contrary to the *Rules*.

Except as provided in the *Rules*, during a *stipulated round* the player must not use any artificial device or unusual *equipment* (see Appendix IV for detailed specifications and interpretations), or use any *equipment* in an unusual manner:

a. That might assist him in making a *stroke* or in his play; or
b. For the purpose of gauging or measuring distance or conditions that might affect his play; or
c. That might assist him in gripping the club, except that:
   (i) gloves may be worn provided that they are plain gloves;
   (ii) resin, powder and drying or moisturising agents may be used; and
   (iii) a towel or handkerchief may be wrapped around the grip.

Exceptions:

1. A player is not in breach of this Rule if (a) the *equipment* or device is designed for or has the effect of alleviating a medical condition, (b) the player has a legitimate medical reason to use the *equipment* or device, and (c) the *Committee* is satisfied that its use does not give the player any undue advantage over other players.
2. A player is not in breach of this Rule if he uses *equipment* in a traditionally accepted manner.

PENALTY FOR BREACH OF RULE 14-3:
Disqualification.

Note: The *Committee* may make a Local Rule allowing players to use devices that measure or gauge distance only.

14-4. Striking the Ball More Than Once

If a player's club strikes the ball more than once in the course of a *stroke*, the player must count the *stroke* and add a *penalty stroke*, making two *strokes* in all.

14-5. Playing Moving Ball

A player must not make a *stroke* at his ball while it is moving.

Exceptions:

- Ball falling off tee – Rule 11-3
- Striking the ball more than once – Rule 14-4
- Ball moving in water – Rule 14-6

When the ball begins to *move* only after the player has begun the *stroke* or the backward movement of his club for the *stroke*, he incurs no penalty under this Rule for playing a moving ball, but he is not exempt from any penalty under the following Rules:

- Ball at rest *moved* by player – Rule 18-2a
- Ball at rest moving after *address* – Rule 18-2b

(Ball purposely deflected or stopped by player, partner or caddie – see Rule 1-2)

14-6. Ball Moving in Water

When a ball is moving in water in a *water hazard*, the player may, without penalty, make a *stroke*, but he must not delay making his *stroke* in order to allow the wind or current to improve the position of the ball. A ball moving in water in a *water hazard* may be lifted if the player elects to invoke Rule 26.

PENALTY FOR BREACH OF RULE 14-5 or 14-6:
Match play – Loss of hole; Stroke play – Two strokes.

Rule 15 – Substituted Ball; Wrong Ball

Definitions

All defined terms are in *italics* and are listed alphabetically in the Definitions section – see pages 592–595.

15-1. General

A player must hole out with the ball played from the *teeing ground*, unless the ball is *lost* or *out of bounds* or the player *substitutes* another ball, whether or not substitution is permitted (see Rule 15-2). If a player plays a *wrong ball*, see Rule 15-3.

15-2. Substituted Ball

A player may *substitute* a ball when proceeding under a *Rule* that permits the player to play, drop or place another ball in completing the play of a hole. The *substituted ball* becomes the *ball in play*.

If a player *substitutes* a ball when not permitted to do so under the *Rules*, that *substituted ball* is not a *wrong ball*; it becomes the *ball in play*. If the mistake is not corrected as provided in Rule 20-6 and the player makes a *stroke* at a wrongly *substituted ball*, he loses the hole in match play or incurs a penalty of two strokes in stroke play under the applicable *Rule* and, in stroke play, must play out the hole with the *substituted ball*.

Exception: If a player incurs a penalty for making a *stroke* from a wrong place, there is no additional penalty for substituting a ball when not permitted.

(Playing from wrong place – see Rule 20-7)

15-3. Wrong Ball

a. Match Play

If a player makes a *stroke* at a *wrong ball*, he loses the hole.

If the *wrong ball* belongs to another player, its owner must place a ball on the spot from which the *wrong ball* was first played.

If the player and *opponent* exchange balls during the play of a hole, the first to make a *stroke* at a *wrong ball* loses the hole; when this cannot be determined, the hole must be played out with the balls exchanged.

Exception: There is no penalty if a player makes a *stroke* at a *wrong ball* that is moving in water in a *water hazard*. Any *strokes* made at a *wrong ball* moving in water in a *water hazard* do not count in the player's score. The player must correct his mistake by playing the correct ball or by proceeding under the *Rules*.

(Placing and Replacing – see Rule 20-3)

b. Stroke Play

If a *competitor* makes a *stroke* or *strokes* at a *wrong ball*, he incurs a penalty of two strokes.

The *competitor* must correct his mistake by playing the correct ball or by proceeding under the *Rules*. If he fails to correct his mistake before making a *stroke* on the next *teeing ground* or, in the case of the last hole of the round, fails to declare his intention to correct his mistake before leaving the *putting green*, he is disqualified.

Strokes made by a *competitor* with a *wrong ball* do not count in his score. If the *wrong ball* belongs to another *competitor*, its owner must place a ball on the spot from which the *wrong ball* was first played.

Exception: There is no penalty if a *competitor* makes a *stroke* at a *wrong ball* that is moving in water in a *water hazard*. Any *strokes* made at a *wrong ball* moving in water in a *water hazard* do not count in the *competitor's* score.

(Placing and Replacing – see Rule 20-3)

The Putting Green

Rule 16 – The Putting Green

Definitions

All defined terms are in *italics* and are listed alphabetically in the Definitions section – see pages 592–595.

16-1. General

a. Touching Line of Putt

The *line of putt* must not be touched except:

(i) the player may remove *loose impediments*, provided he does not press anything down;
(ii) the player may place the club in front of the ball when *addressing* it, provided he does not press anything down;
(iii) in measuring – Rule 18-6;
(iv) in lifting or replacing the ball – Rule 16-1b;
(v) in pressing down a ball-marker;
(vi) in repairing old *hole* plugs or ball marks on the *putting green* – Rule 16-1c; and
(vii) in removing movable *obstructions* – Rule 24-1.

(Indicating line for putting on putting green – see Rule 8-2b)

b. Lifting and Cleaning Ball

A ball on the *putting green* may be lifted and, if desired, cleaned. The position of the ball must be marked before it is lifted and the ball must be replaced (see Rule 20-1). When another ball is in motion, a ball that might influence the movement of the ball in motion must not be lifted.

c. Repair of Hole Plugs, Ball Marks and Other Damage

The player may repair an old *hole* plug or damage to the *putting green* caused by the impact of a ball, whether or not the player's ball lies on the *putting green*. If a ball or ball-marker is accidentally *moved* in the process of the repair, the ball or ball-marker must be replaced. There is no penalty, provided the movement of the ball or ball-marker is directly attributable to the specific act of repairing an old *hole* plug or damage to the *putting green* caused by the impact of a ball. Otherwise, Rule 18 applies.

Any other damage to the *putting green* must not be repaired if it might assist the player in his subsequent play of the hole.

d. Testing Surface

During the *stipulated round*, a player must not test the surface of any *putting green* by rolling a ball or roughening or scraping the surface.

Exception: Between the play of two holes, a player may test the surface of any practice *putting green* and the *putting green* of the hole last played, unless the *Committee* has prohibited such action (see Note 2 to Rule 7-2).

e. Standing Astride or on Line of Putt

The player must not make a *stroke* on the *putting green* from a *stance* astride, or with either foot touching, the *line of putt* or an extension of that line behind the ball.

Exception: There is no penalty if the *stance* is inadvertently taken on or astride the *line of putt* (or an extension of that line behind the ball) or is taken to avoid standing on another player's *line of putt* or prospective *line of putt*.

f. Making Stroke While Another Ball in Motion
The player must not make a *stroke* while another ball is in motion after a *stroke* from the *putting green*, except that if a player does so, there is no penalty if it was his turn to play.

(Lifting ball assisting or interfering with play while another ball in motion – see Rule 22)

PENALTY FOR BREACH OF RULE 16-1:
Match play – Loss of hole; Stroke play – Two strokes.

(Position of caddie or partner – see Rule 14-2)
(Wrong putting green – see Rule 25-3)

16-2. Ball Overhanging Hole
When any part of the ball overhangs the lip of the *hole*, the player is allowed enough time to reach the *hole* without unreasonable delay and an additional ten seconds to determine whether the ball is at rest. If by then the ball has not fallen into the *hole*, it is deemed to be at rest. If the ball subsequently falls into the *hole*, the player is deemed to have *holed* out with his last *stroke*, and must add a *penalty stroke* to his score for the hole; otherwise, there is no penalty under this Rule.

(Undue delay – see Rule 6-7)

Rule 17 – The Flagstick

Definitions
All defined terms are in *italics* and are listed alphabetically in the Definitions section – see pages 592–595.

17-1. Flagstick Attended, Removed or Held Up
Before making a *stroke* from anywhere on the *course*, the player may have the *flagstick* attended, removed or held up to indicate the position of the *hole*.

If the *flagstick* is not attended, removed or held up before the player makes a *stroke*, it must not be attended, removed or held up during the *stroke* or while the player's ball is in motion if doing so might influence the movement of the ball.

Note 1: If the *flagstick* is in the *hole* and anyone stands near it while a *stroke* is being made, he is deemed to be attending the *flagstick*.

Note 2: If, prior to the *stroke*, the *flagstick* is attended, removed or held up by anyone with the player's knowledge and he makes no objection, the player is deemed to have authorised it.

Note 3: If anyone attends or holds up the *flagstick* while a *stroke* is being made, he is deemed to be attending the *flagstick* until the ball comes to rest.

(Moving attended, removed or held-up flagstick while ball in motion – see Rule 24-1)

17-2. Unauthorised Attendance
If an *opponent* or his *caddie* in match play or a *fellow-competitor* or his *caddie* in stroke play, without the player's authority or prior knowledge, attends, removes or holds up the *flagstick* during the *stroke* or while the ball is in motion, and the act might influence the movement of the ball, the *opponent* or *fellow-competitor* incurs the applicable penalty.

*PENALTY FOR BREACH OF RULE 17-1 or 17-2:
Match play – Loss of hole; Stroke play – Two strokes.

*In stroke play, if a breach of Rule 17-2 occurs and the *competitor's* ball subsequently strikes the *flagstick*, the person attending or holding it or anything carried by him, the *competitor* incurs no penalty. The ball is played as it lies, except that if the *stroke* was made on the *putting green*, the *stroke* is cancelled and the ball must be replaced and replayed.

17-3. Ball Striking Flagstick or Attendant
The player's ball must not strike:

a. The *flagstick* when it is attended, removed or held up;
b. The person attending or holding up the *flagstick* or anything carried by him; or
c. The *flagstick* in the *hole*, unattended, when the *stroke* has been made on the *putting green*.

Exception: When the *flagstick* is attended, removed or held up without the player's authority – see Rule 17-2.

PENALTY FOR BREACH OF RULE 17-3:
Match play – Loss of hole; Stroke play – Two strokes and the ball must be played as it lies.

17-4. Ball Resting Against Flagstick
When a player's ball rests against the *flagstick* in the *hole* and the ball is not *holed*, the player or another person authorised by him may move or remove the *flagstick*, and if the ball falls into the *hole*, the player is deemed to have *holed* out with his last *stroke*; otherwise, the ball, if *moved*, must be placed on the lip of the *hole*, without penalty.

Ball Moved, Deflected or Stopped

Rule 18 – Ball at Rest Moved

Definitions
All defined terms are in *italics* and are listed alphabetically in the Definitions section – see pages 592–595.

18-1. By Outside Agency
If a ball at rest is *moved* by an *outside agency*, there is no penalty and the ball must be replaced. Note: It is a question of fact whether a ball has been *moved* by an *outside agency*. In order to apply this Rule, it must be known or virtually certain that an *outside agency* has *moved* the ball. In the absence of such knowledge or certainty, the player must play the ball as it lies or, if the ball is not found, proceed under Rule 27-1.

(Player's ball at rest moved by another ball – see Rule 18-5)

18-2. By Player, Partner, Caddie or Equipment
a. General
Except as permitted by the *Rules*, when a player's ball is *in play*, if

(i) the player, his *partner* or either of their *caddies*:
- lifts or *moves* the ball,
- touches it purposely (except with a club in the act of *addressing* the ball), or
- causes the ball to *move*, or

(ii) the *equipment* of the player or his *partner* causes the ball to *move*,

the player incurs a penalty of one stroke.

If the ball is *moved*, it must be replaced, unless the movement of the ball occurs after the player has begun the *stroke* or the backward movement of the club for the *stroke* and the *stroke* is made.

Under the *Rules* there is no penalty if a player accidentally causes his ball to *move* in the following circumstances:

- In searching for a ball covered by sand, in the replacement of *loose impediments* moved in a *hazard* while finding or identifying a ball, in probing for a ball lying in water in a *water hazard* or in searching for a ball in an *obstruction* or an *abnormal ground condition* – Rule 12-1
- In repairing a *hole* plug or ball mark – Rule 16-1c
- In measuring – Rule 18-6
- In lifting a ball under a *Rule* – Rule 20-1
- In placing or replacing a ball under a *Rule* – Rule 20-3a
- In removing a *loose impediment* on the *putting green* – Rule 23-1
- In removing movable *obstructions* – Rule 24-1

b. Ball Moving After Address
If a player's *ball in play moves* after he has *addressed* it (other than as a result of a *stroke*), the player is deemed to have *moved* the ball and incurs a penalty of one stroke.

The ball must be replaced, unless the movement of the ball occurs after the player has begun the *stroke* or the backward movement of the club for the *stroke* and the *stroke* is made.

Exception: If it is known or virtually certain that the player did not cause his ball to *move*, Rule 18-2b does not apply.

18-3. By Opponent, Caddie or Equipment in Match Play

a. During Search

If, during search for a player's ball, an *opponent*, his *caddie* or his *equipment moves* the ball, touches it or causes it to *move*, there is no penalty. If the ball is *moved*, it must be replaced.

b. Other Than During Search

If, other than during search for a player's ball, an *opponent*, his *caddie* or his *equipment moves* the ball, touches it purposely or causes it to *move*, except as otherwise provided in the *Rules*, the opponent incurs a penalty of one stroke. If the ball is *moved*, it must be replaced.

(Playing a wrong ball – see Rule 15-3)

(Ball moved in measuring – see Rule 18-6)

18-4. By Fellow-Competitor, Caddie or Equipment in Stroke Play

If a *fellow-competitor*, his *caddie* or his *equipment moves* the player's ball, touches it or causes it to *move*, there is no penalty. If the ball is *moved*, it must be replaced.

(Playing a wrong ball – see Rule 15-3)

18-5. By Another Ball

If a *ball in play* and at rest is *moved* by another ball in motion after a *stroke*, the *moved* ball must be replaced.

18-6. Ball Moved in Measuring

If a ball or ball-marker is *moved* in measuring while proceeding under or in determining the application of a *Rule*, the ball or ball-marker must be replaced. There is no penalty, provided the movement of the ball or ball-marker is directly attributable to the specific act of measuring. Otherwise, the provisions of Rule 18-2a, 18-3b or 18-4 apply.

*PENALTY FOR BREACH OF RULE:
Match play – Loss of hole; Stroke play – Two strokes.

*If a player who is required to replace a ball fails to do so, or if he makes a *stroke* at a ball *substituted* under Rule 18 when such *substitution* is not permitted, he incurs the general penalty for breach of Rule 18, but there is no additional penalty under this Rule.

Note 1: If a ball to be replaced under this Rule is not immediately recoverable, another ball may be *substituted*.

Note 2: If the original lie of a ball to be placed or replaced has been altered, see Rule 20-3b.

Note 3: If it is impossible to determine the spot on which a ball is to be placed or replaced, see Rule 20-3c.

Rule 19 – Ball in Motion Deflected or Stopped

Definitions

All defined terms are in *italics* and are listed alphabetically in the Definitions section – see pages 592–595.

19-1. By Outside Agency

If a player's ball in motion is accidentally deflected or stopped by any *outside agency*, it is a *rub of the green*, there is no penalty and the ball must be played as it lies, except:

a. If a player's ball in motion after a *stroke* other than on the *putting green* comes to rest in or on any moving or animate *outside agency*, the ball must *through the green* or in a *hazard* be dropped, or on the *putting green* be placed, as near as possible to the spot directly under the place where the ball came to rest in or on the *outside agency*, but not nearer the *hole*, and

b. If a player's ball in motion after a *stroke* on the *putting green* is deflected or stopped by, or comes to rest in or on, any moving or animate *outside agency*, except a worm, insect or the like, the *stroke* is cancelled. The ball must be replaced and replayed.

If the ball is not immediately recoverable, another ball may be *substituted*.

Exception: Ball striking person attending or holding up *flagstick* or anything carried by him – see Rule 17-3b.

Note: If a player's ball in motion has been deliberately deflected or stopped by an *outside agency:*

(a) after a *stroke* from anywhere other than on the *putting green*, the spot where the ball would have come to rest must be estimated. If that spot is:
 (i) *through the green* or in a *hazard*, the ball must be dropped as near as possible to that spot;
 (ii) *out of bounds*, the player must proceed under Rule 27-1; or
 (iii) on the *putting green*, the ball must be placed on that spot.

(b) after a *stroke* on the *putting green*, the *stroke* is cancelled. The ball must be replaced and replayed.

If the *outside agency* is a *fellow-competitor* or his *caddie*, Rule 1-2 applies to the *fellow-competitor*.

(Player's ball deflected or stopped by another ball – see Rule 19-5)

19-2. By Player, Partner, Caddie or Equipment

If a player's ball is accidentally deflected or stopped by himself, his *partner* or either of their *caddies* or *equipment*, the player incurs a penalty of one stroke. The ball must be played as it lies, except when it comes to rest in or on the player's, his *partner's* or either of their *caddies'* clothes or *equipment*, in which case the ball must *through the green* or in a *hazard* be dropped, or on the *putting green* be placed, as near as possible to the spot directly under the place where the ball came to rest in or on the article, but not nearer the *hole*.

Exceptions:

1. Ball striking person attending or holding up *flagstick* or anything carried by him – see Rule 17-3b.
2, Dropped ball – see Rule 20-2a.

(Ball purposely deflected or stopped by player, partner or caddie – see Rule 1-2)

19-3. By Opponent, Caddie or Equipment in Match Play

If a player's ball is accidentally deflected or stopped by an *opponent*, his *caddie* or his *equipment*, there is no penalty. The player may, before another *stroke* is made by either *side*, cancel the *stroke* and play a ball, without penalty, as nearly as possible at the spot from which the original ball was last played (Rule 20-5) or he may play the ball as it lies. However, if the player elects not to cancel the *stroke* and the ball has come to rest in or on the *opponent's* or his *caddie's* clothes or *equipment*, the ball must *through the green* or in a *hazard* be dropped, or on the *putting green* be placed, as near as possible to the spot directly under the place where the ball came to rest in or on the article, but not nearer the *hole*.

Exception: Ball striking person attending or holding up *flagstick* or anything carried by him – see Rule 17-3b.

(Ball purposely deflected or stopped by opponent or caddie – see Rule 1-2)

19-4. By Fellow-Competitor, Caddie or Equipment in Stroke Play

See Rule 19-1 regarding ball deflected by *outside agency*.

Exception: Ball striking person attending or holding up *flagstick* or anything carried by him – see Rule 17-3b.

19-5. By Another Ball

a. At Rest

If a player's ball in motion after a *stroke* is deflected or stopped by a *ball in play* and at rest, the player must play his ball as it lies. In match play, there is no penalty. In stroke play, there is no penalty, unless both balls lay on the *putting green* prior to the *stroke*, in which case the player incurs a penalty of two strokes.

b. In Motion

If a player's ball in motion after a *stroke* other than on the *putting green* is deflected or stopped by another ball in motion after a *stroke*, the player must play his ball as it lies, without penalty.

If a player's ball in motion after a *stroke* on the *putting green* is deflected or stopped by another ball in motion after a *stroke*, the player's *stroke* is cancelled. The ball must be replaced and replayed, without penalty.

Note: Nothing in this Rule overrides the provisions of Rule 10-1 (Order of Play in Match Play) or Rule 16-1f (Making Stroke While Another Ball in Motion).

PENALTY FOR BREACH OF RULE:
Match play – Loss of hole; Stroke play – Two strokes.

Relief Situations and Procedure

Rule 20 – Lifting, Dropping and Placing; Playing from Wrong Place

Definitions

All defined terms are in *italics* and are listed alphabetically in the Definitions section – see pages 592–595.

20-1. Lifting and Marking

A ball to be lifted under the *Rules* may be lifted by the player, his *partner* or another person authorised by the player. In any such case, the player is responsible for any breach of the Rules.

The position of the ball must be marked before it is lifted under a *Rule* that requires it to be replaced. If it is not marked, the player incurs a penalty of one stroke and the ball must be replaced. If it is not replaced, the player incurs the general penalty for breach of this Rule but there is no additional penalty under Rule 20-1.

If a ball or ball-marker is accidentally *moved* in the process of lifting the ball under a *Rule* or marking its position, the ball or ball-marker must be replaced. There is no penalty, provided the movement of the ball or ballmarker is directly attributable to the specific act of marking the position of or lifting the ball. Otherwise, the player incurs a penalty of one stroke under this Rule or Rule 18-2a.

Exception: If a player incurs a penalty for failing to act in accordance with Rule 5-3 or 12-2, there is no additional penalty under Rule 20-1.

Note: The position of a ball to be lifted should be marked by placing a ball-marker, a small coin or other similar object immediately behind the ball.

If the ball-marker interferes with the play, *stance* or *stroke* of another player, it should be placed one or more clubhead-lengths to one side.

20-2. Dropping and Re-Dropping

a. By Whom and How

A ball to be dropped under the Rules must be dropped by the player himself. He must stand erect, hold the ball at shoulder height and arm's length and drop it. If a ball is dropped by any other person or in any other manner and the error is not corrected as provided in Rule 20-6, the player incurs a penalty of one stroke.

If the ball, when dropped, touches any person or the *equipment* of any player before or after it strikes a part of the *course* and before it comes to rest, the ball must be re-dropped, without penalty. There is no limit to the number of times a ball must be re-dropped in these circumstances.

(Taking action to influence position or movement of ball – see Rule 1-2)

b. Where to Drop

When a ball is to be dropped as near as possible to a specific spot, it must be dropped not nearer the *hole* than the specific spot which, if it is not precisely known to the player, must be estimated.

A ball when dropped must first strike a part of the *course* where the applicable *Rule* requires it to be dropped. If it is not so dropped, Rules 20-6 and 20-7 apply.

c. When to Re-Drop

A dropped ball must be re-dropped, without penalty, if it:

(i) rolls into and comes to rest in a *hazard;*
(ii) rolls out of and comes to rest outside a *hazard*;
(iii) rolls onto and comes to rest on a *putting green;*
(iv) rolls and comes to rest *out of bounds;*
(v) rolls to and comes to rest in a position where there is interference by the condition from which relief was taken under Rule 24-2b (immovable obstruction), Rule 25-1 (abnormal ground conditions), Rule 25-3 (wrong putting green) or a Local Rule (Rule 33-8a), or rolls back into the pitch-mark from which it was lifted under Rule 25-2 (embedded ball);
(vi) rolls and comes to rest more than two club-lengths from where it first struck a part of the *course*; or
(vii) rolls and comes to rest nearer the *hole* than:
    (a) its original position or estimated position (see Rule 20-2b) unless otherwise permitted by the *Rules*; or
    (b) the *nearest point of relief* or maximum available relief (Rule 24-2, 25-1 or 25-3); or
    (c) the point where the original ball last crossed the margin of the *water hazard* or *lateral water hazard* (Rule 26-1).

If the ball when re-dropped rolls into any position listed above, it must be placed as near as possible to the spot where it first struck a part of the *course* when re-dropped.

Note 1: If a ball when dropped or re-dropped comes to rest and subsequently *moves*, the ball must be played as it lies, unless the provisions of any other *Rule* apply.

Note 2: If a ball to be re-dropped or placed under this Rule is not immediately recoverable, another ball may be *substituted.*

(Use of dropping zone – see Appendix I; Part B; Section 8)

20-3. Placing and Replacing

a. By Whom and Where

A ball to be placed under the *Rules* must be placed by the player or his *partner*.

A ball to be replaced under the *Rules* must be replaced by any one of the following: (i) the person who lifted or *moved* the ball, (ii) the player, or (iii) the player's *partner*. The ball must be placed on the spot from which it was lifted or *moved*. If the ball is placed or replaced by any other person and the error is not corrected as provided in Rule 20-6, the player incurs a penalty of one stroke. In any such case, the player is responsible for any other breach of the *Rules* that occurs as a result of the placing or replacing of the ball.

If a ball or ball-marker is accidentally *moved* in the process of placing or replacing the ball, the ball or ball-marker must be replaced. There is no penalty, provided the movement of the ball or ball-marker is directly attributable to the specific act of placing or replacing the ball or removing the ball-marker. Otherwise, the player incurs a penalty of one stroke under Rule 18-2a or 20-1.

If a ball to be replaced is placed other than on the spot from which it was lifted or *moved* and the error is not corrected as provided in Rule 20-6, the player incurs the general penalty, loss of hole in match play or two strokes in stroke play, for a breach of the applicable *Rule*.

b. Lie of Ball to be Placed or Replaced Altered

If the original lie of a ball to be placed or replaced has been altered:

(i) except in a *hazard*, the ball must be placed in the nearest lie most similar to the original lie that is not more than one club-length from the original lie, not nearer the *hole* and not in a *hazard*;

(ii) in a *water hazard*, the ball must be placed in accordance with Clause (i) above, except that the ball must be placed in the *water hazard*;

(iii) in a *bunker*, the original lie must be re-created as nearly as possible and the ball must be placed in that lie.

Note: If the original lie of a ball to be placed or replaced has been altered and it is impossible to determine the spot where the ball is to be placed or replaced, Rule 20-3b applies if the original lie is known, and Rule 20-3c applies if the original lie is not known.

Exception: If the player is searching for or identifying a ball covered by sand – see Rule 12-1a.

c. Spot Not Determinable

If it is impossible to determine the spot where the ball is to be placed or replaced:

(i) *through the green*, the ball must be dropped as near as possible to the place where it lay but not in a *hazard* or on a *putting green*;

(ii) in a *hazard*, the ball must be dropped in the *hazard* as near as possible to the place where it lay;

(iii) on the *putting green*, the ball must be placed as near as possible to the place where it lay but not in a *hazard*.

Exception: When resuming play (Rule 6-8d), if the spot where the ball is to be placed is impossible to determine, it must be estimated and the ball placed on the estimated spot.

d. Ball Fails to Come to Rest on Spot

If a ball when placed fails to come to rest on the spot on which it was placed, there is no penalty and the ball must be replaced. If it still fails to come to rest on that spot:

(i) except in a *hazard*, it must be placed at the nearest spot where it can be placed at rest that is not nearer the *hole* and not in a *hazard*;

(ii) in a *hazard*, it must be placed in the *hazard* at the nearest spot where it can be placed at rest that is not nearer the *hole*. If a ball when placed comes to rest on the spot on which it is placed, and it subsequently *moves*, there is no penalty and the ball must be played as it lies, unless the provisions of any other *Rule* apply.

*PENALTY FOR BREACH OF RULE 20-1, 20-2 or 20-3:
Match play – Loss of hole; Stroke play – Two strokes.

*If a player makes a *stroke* at a ball *substituted* under one of these Rules when such *substitution* is not permitted, he incurs the general penalty for breach of that Rule, but there is no additional penalty under that Rule. If a player drops a ball in an improper manner and plays from a wrong place or if the ball has been put into play by a person not permitted by the *Rules* and then played from a wrong place, see Note 3 to Rule 20-7c.

20-4. When Ball Dropped or Placed is in Play

If the player's *ball in play* has been lifted, it is again in play when dropped or placed.

A *substituted ball* becomes the *ball in play* when it has been dropped or placed.

(Ball incorrectly substituted – see Rule 15-2)

(Lifting ball incorrectly substituted, dropped or placed – see Rule 20-6)

20-5. Making Next Stroke from Where Previous Stroke Made

When a player elects or is required to make his next *stroke* from where a previous *stroke* was made, he must proceed as follows:

(a) On the Teeing Ground: The ball to be played must be played from within the *teeing ground*. It may be played from anywhere within the *teeing ground* and may be teed.

(b) Through the Green: The ball to be played must be dropped and when dropped must first strike a part of the *course through the green*.

(c) In a Hazard: The ball to be played must be dropped and when dropped must first strike a part of the *course* in the *hazard*.

(d) On the Putting Green: The ball to be played must be placed on the *putting green*.

PENALTY FOR BREACH OF RULE 20-5:
Match play – Loss of hole; Stroke play – Two strokes.

20-6. Lifting Ball Incorrectly Substituted, Dropped or Placed

A ball incorrectly *substituted*, dropped or placed in a wrong place or otherwise not in accordance with the *Rules* but not played may be lifted, without penalty, and the player must then proceed correctly.

20-7. Playing from Wrong Place

a. General

A player has played from a wrong place if he makes a *stroke* at his *ball in play*:

(i) on a part of the *course* where the *Rules* do not permit a *stroke* to be made or a ball to be dropped or placed; or

(ii) when the *Rules* require a dropped ball to be re-dropped or a *moved* ball to be replaced.

Note: For a ball played from outside the *teeing ground* or from a wrong *teeing ground* – see Rule 11-4.

b. Match Play

If a player makes a *stroke* from a wrong place, he loses the hole.

c. Stroke Play

If a *competitor* makes a *stroke* from a wrong place, he incurs a penalty of two strokes under the applicable *Rule*. He must play out the hole with the ball played from the wrong place, without correcting his error, provided he has not committed a serious breach (see Note 1).

If a *competitor* becomes aware that he has played from a wrong place and believes that he may have committed a serious breach, he must, before making a *stroke* on the next *teeing ground*, play out the hole with a second ball played in accordance with the *Rules*. If the hole being played is the last hole of the round, he must declare, before leaving the *putting green*, that he will play out the hole with a second ball played in accordance with the *Rules*.

If the *competitor* has played a second ball, he must report the facts to the *Committee* before returning his score card; if he fails to do so, he is disqualified. The *Committee* must determine whether the *competitor* has committed a serious breach of the applicable *Rule*. If he has, the score with the second ball counts and the competitor must add two penalty strokes to his score with that ball. If the *competitor* has committed a serious breach and has failed to correct it as outlined above, he is disqualified.

Note 1: A *competitor* is deemed to have committed a serious breach of the applicable *Rule* if the *Committee* considers he has gained a significant advantage as a result of playing from a wrong place.

Note 2: If a *competitor* plays a second ball under Rule 20-7c and it is ruled not to count, *strokes* made with that ball and *penalty strokes* incurred solely by playing that ball are disregarded. If the second ball is ruled to count, the *stroke* made from the wrong place and any *strokes* subsequently taken with the original ball including *penalty strokes* incurred solely by playing that ball are disregarded.

Note 3: If a player incurs a penalty for making a *stroke* from a wrong place, there is no additional penalty for:

(a) *substituting* a ball when not permitted;
(b) dropping a ball when the *Rules* require it to be placed, or placing a ball when the *Rules* require it to be dropped;
(c) dropping a ball in an improper manner; or
(d) a ball being put into play by a person not permitted to do so under the *Rules*.

Rule 21 – Cleaning Ball

Definitions

All defined terms are in *italics* and are listed alphabetically in the Definitions section – see pages 592–595.

A ball on the *putting green* may be cleaned when lifted under Rule 16-1b. Elsewhere, a ball may be cleaned when lifted, except when it has been lifted:

a. To determine if it is unfit for play (Rule 5-3);
b. For identification (Rule 12-2), in which case it may be cleaned only to the extent necessary for identification; or
c. Because it is assisting or interfering with play (Rule 22).

If a player cleans his ball during play of a hole except as provided in this Rule, he incurs a penalty of one stroke and the ball, if lifted, must be replaced. If a player who is required to replace a ball fails to do so, he incurs the general penalty under the applicable *Rule*, but there is no additional penalty under Rule 21.

Exception: If a player incurs a penalty for failing to act in accordance with Rule 5-3, 12-2 or 22, there is no additional penalty under Rule 21.

Rule 22 – Ball Assisting or Interfering with Play

Definitions

All defined terms are in *italics* and are listed alphabetically in the Definitions section – see pages 592–595.

22-1. Ball Assisting Play

Except when a ball is in motion, if a player considers that a ball might assist any other player, he may:

a. Lift the ball if it is his ball; or
b. Have any other ball lifted.

A ball lifted under this Rule must be replaced (see Rule 20-3). The ball must not be cleaned, unless it lies on the *putting green* (see Rule 21).

In stroke play, a player required to lift his ball may play first rather than lift the ball.

In stroke play, if the *Committee* determines that *competitors* have agreed not to lift a ball that might assist any *competitor*, they are disqualified.

Note: When another ball is in motion, a ball that might influence the movement of the ball in motion must not be lifted.

22-2. Ball Interfering with Play

Except when a ball is in motion, if a player considers that another ball might interfere with his play, he may have it lifted.

A ball lifted under this Rule must be replaced (see Rule 20-3). The ball must not be cleaned, unless it lies on the *putting green* (see Rule 21).

In stroke play, a player required to lift his ball may play first rather than lift the ball.

Note 1: Except on the *putting green*, a player may not lift his ball solely because he considers that it might interfere with the play of another player. If a player lifts his ball without being asked to do so, he incurs a penalty of one stroke for a breach of Rule 18-2a, but there is no additional penalty under Rule 22.

Note 2: When another ball is in motion, a ball that might influence the movement of the ball in motion must not be lifted.

PENALTY FOR BREACH OF RULE:
Match play – Loss of hole; Stroke play – Two strokes.

Rule 23 – Loose Impediments

Definitions

All defined terms are in *italics* and are listed alphabetically in the Definitions section – see pages 592–595.

23-1. Relief

Except when both the *loose impediment* and the ball lie in or touch the same *hazard*, any *loose impediment* may be removed without penalty.

If the ball lies anywhere other than on the *putting green* and the removal of a *loose impediment* by the player causes the ball to *move*, Rule 18-2a applies.

On the *putting green*, if the ball or ball-marker is accidentally *moved* in the process of the player removing a *loose impediment*, the ball or ball-marker must be replaced. There is no penalty, provided the movement of the ball or ball-marker is directly attributable to the removal of the *loose impediment*. Otherwise, if the player causes the ball to *move*, he incurs a penalty of one stroke under Rule 18-2a.

When a ball is in motion, a *loose impediment* that might influence the movement of the ball must not be removed.

Note: If the ball lies in a *hazard*, the player must not touch or move any *loose impediment* lying in or touching the same *hazard* – see Rule 13-4c.

PENALTY FOR BREACH OF RULE:
Match play – Loss of hole; Stroke play – Two strokes.

(Searching for ball in hazard – see Rule 12-1)
(Touching line of putt – see Rule 16-1a)

Rule 24 – Obstructions

Definitions

All defined terms are in *italics* and are listed alphabetically in the Definitions section – see pages 592–595.

24-1. Movable Obstruction

A player may take relief, without penalty, from a movable *obstruction* as follows:

a. If the ball does not lie in or on the *obstruction*, the *obstruction* may be removed. If the ball *moves*, it must be replaced, and there is no penalty, provided that the movement of the ball is directly attributable to the removal of the *obstruction*. Otherwise, Rule 18-2a applies.
b. If the ball lies in or on the *obstruction*, the ball may be lifted and the *obstruction* removed. The ball must *through the green* or in a *hazard* be dropped, or on the *putting green* be placed, as near as possible to the spot directly under the place where the ball lay in or on the *obstruction*, but not nearer the *hole*.

The ball may be cleaned when lifted under this Rule.

When a ball is in motion, an *obstruction* that might influence the movement of the ball, other than *equipment* of any player or the *flagstick* when attended, removed or held up, must not be moved.

(Exerting influence on ball – see Rule 1-2)

Note: If a ball to be dropped or placed under this Rule is not immediately recoverable, another ball may be *substituted*.

24-2. Immovable Obstruction

a. Interference

Interference by an immovable *obstruction* occurs when a ball lies in or on the *obstruction*, or when the *obstruction* interferes with the player's *stance* or the area of his intended swing. If the player's ball lies on the *putting green*, interference also occurs if an immovable *obstruction* on the *putting green* intervenes on his *line of putt*. Otherwise, intervention on the *line of play* is not, of itself, interference under this Rule.

b. Relief

Except when the ball is in a *water hazard* or a *lateral water hazard*, a player may take relief from interference by an immovable *obstruction* as follows:

(i) Through the Green: If the ball lies *through the green*, the player must lift the ball and drop it, without penalty, within one club-length of and not nearer the *hole* than the *nearest point of relief*. The *nearest point of relief* must not be in a *hazard* or on a *putting green*. When the ball is dropped within one club-length of the *nearest point of relief*, the ball must first strike a part of the *course* at a spot that avoids interference by the immovable *obstruction* and is not in a *hazard* and not on a *putting green*.

(ii) In a Bunker: If the ball is in a *bunker*, the player must lift the ball and drop it either:
- (a) Without penalty, in accordance with Clause (i) above, except that the *nearest point of relief* must be in the *bunker* and the ball must be dropped in the *bunker*; or
- (b) Under penalty of one stroke, outside the *bunker* keeping the point where the ball lay directly between the *hole* and the spot on which the ball is dropped, with no limit to how far behind the *bunker* the ball may be dropped.

(iii) On the Putting Green: If the ball lies on the *putting green*, the player must lift the ball and place it, without penalty, at the *nearest point of relief* that is not in a *hazard*. The *nearest point of relief* may be off the *putting green*.

(iv) On the Teeing Ground: If the ball lies on the *teeing ground*, the player must lift the ball and drop it, without penalty, in accordance with Clause (i) above.

The ball may be cleaned when lifted under this Rule.

(Ball rolling to a position where there is interference by the condition from which relief was taken – see Rule 20-2c(v))

Exception: A player may not take relief under this Rule if (a) interference by anything other than an immovable *obstruction* makes the *stroke* clearly impracticable or (b) interference by an immovable *obstruction* would occur only through use of a clearly unreasonable *stroke* or an unnecessarily abnormal *stance*, swing or direction of play.

Note 1: If a ball is in a *water hazard* (including a *lateral water hazard*), the player may not take relief from interference by an immovable *obstruction*. The player must play the ball as it lies or proceed under Rule 26-1.

Note 2: If a ball to be dropped or placed under this Rule is not immediately recoverable, another ball may be *substituted*.

Note 3: The *Committee* may make a Local Rule stating that the player must determine the *nearest point of relief* without crossing over, through or under the *obstruction*.

24-3. Ball in Obstruction Not Found

It is a question of fact whether a ball that has not been found after having been struck toward an *obstruction* is in the *obstruction*. In order to apply this Rule, it must be known or virtually certain that the ball is in the *obstruction*. In the absence of such knowledge or certainty, the player must proceed under Rule 27-1.

a. Ball in Movable Obstruction Not Found

If it is known or virtually certain that a ball that has not been found is in a movable *obstruction*, the player may *substitute* another ball and take relief, without penalty, under this Rule. If he elects to do so, he must remove the *obstruction* and *through the green* or in a *hazard* drop a ball, or on the *putting green* place a ball, as near as possible to the spot directly under the place where the ball last crossed the outermost limits of the movable *obstruction*, but not nearer the *hole*.

b. Ball in Immovable Obstruction Not Found

If it is known or virtually certain that a ball that has not been found is in an immovable *obstruction*, the player may take relief under this Rule. If he elects to do so, the spot where the ball last crossed the outermost limits of the *obstruction* must be determined and, for the purpose of applying this Rule, the ball is deemed to lie at this spot and the player must proceed as follows:

(i) Through the Green: If the ball last crossed the outermost limits of the immovable *obstruction* at a spot *through the green*, the player may *substitute* another ball, without penalty, and take relief as prescribed in Rule 24-2b(i).

(ii) In a Bunker: If the ball last crossed the outermost limits of the immovable *obstruction* at a spot in a *bunker*, the player may *substitute* another ball, without penalty, and take relief as prescribed in Rule 24-2b(ii).

(iii) In a Water Hazard (including a Lateral Water Hazard): If the ball last crossed the outermost limits of the immovable *obstruction* at a spot in a *water hazard*, the player is not entitled to relief without penalty. The player must proceed under Rule 26-1.

(iv) On the Putting Green: If the ball last crossed the outermost limits of the immovable *obstruction* at a spot on the *putting green*, the player may *substitute* another ball, without penalty, and take relief as prescribed in Rule 24-2b(iii).

PENALTY FOR BREACH OF RULE:
Match play – Loss of hole; Stroke play – Two strokes.

Rule 25 – Abnormal Ground Conditions, Embedded Ball and Wrong Putting Green

Definitions

All defined terms are in *italics* and are listed alphabetically in the Definitions section – see pages 592–595.

25-1. Abnormal Ground Conditions

a. Interference

Interference by an *abnormal ground condition* occurs when a ball lies in or touches the condition or when the condition interferes with the player's *stance* or the area of his intended swing. If the player's ball lies on the *putting green*, interference also occurs if an *abnormal ground condition* on the *putting green* intervenes on his *line of putt*. Otherwise, intervention on the *line of play* is not, of itself, interference under this Rule.

Note: The *Committee* may make a Local Rule stating that interference by an *abnormal ground condition* with a player's *stance* is deemed not to be, of itself, interference under this Rule.

b. Relief

Except when the ball is in a *water hazard* or a *lateral water hazard*, a player may take relief from interference by an *abnormal ground condition* as follows:

(i) Through the Green: If the ball lies *through the green*, the player must lift the ball and drop it, without penalty, within one club-length of and not nearer the *hole* than the *nearest point of relief*. The *nearest point of relief* must not be in a *hazard* or on a *putting green*. When the ball is dropped within one club-length of the *nearest point of relief*, the ball must first strike a part of the *course* at a spot that avoids interference by the condition and is not in a *hazard* and not on a *putting green*.

(ii) In a Bunker: If the ball is in a *bunker*, the player must lift the ball and drop it either:

(a) Without penalty, in accordance with Clause (i) above, except that the *nearest point of relief* must be in the *bunker* and the ball must be dropped in the *bunker* or, if complete relief is impossible, as near as possible to the spot where the ball lay, but not nearer the *hole*, on a part of the *course* in the *bunker* that affords maximum available relief from the condition; or

(b) Under penalty of one stroke, outside the *bunker* keeping the point where the ball lay directly between the *hole* and the spot on which the ball is dropped, with no limit to how far behind the *bunker* the ball may be dropped.

(iii) On the Putting Green: If the ball lies on the *putting green*, the player must lift the ball and place it, without penalty, at the *nearest point of relief* that is not in a *hazard* or, if complete relief is impossible, at the nearest position to where it lay that affords maximum available relief from the condition, but not nearer the *hole* and not in a *hazard*. The *nearest point of relief* or maximum available relief may be off the *putting green*.

(iv) On the Teeing Ground: If the ball lies on the *teeing ground*, the player must lift the ball and drop it, without penalty, in accordance with Clause (i) above.

The ball may be cleaned when lifted under Rule 25-1b.

(Ball rolling to a position where there is interference by the condition from which relief was taken – see Rule 20-2c(v))

Exception: A player may not take relief under this Rule if (a) interference by anything other than an *abnormal ground condition* makes the *stroke* clearly impracticable or (b) interference by an *abnormal ground condition* would occur only through use of a clearly unreasonable *stroke* or an unnecessarily abnormal *stance*, swing or direction of play.

Note 1: If a ball is in a *water hazard* (including a *lateral water hazard*), the player is not entitled to relief, without penalty, from interference by an *abnormal ground condition*. The player must play the ball as it lies (unless prohibited by Local Rule) or proceed under Rule 26-1.

Note 2: If a ball to be dropped or placed under this Rule is not immediately recoverable, another ball may be *substituted*.

c. Ball in Abnormal Ground Condition Not Found

It is a question of fact whether a ball that has not been found after having been struck toward an *abnormal ground condition* is in such a condition. In order to apply this Rule, it must be known or virtually certain that the ball is in the *abnormal ground condition*. In the absence of such knowledge or certainty, the player must proceed under Rule 27-1.

If it is known or virtually certain that a ball that has not been found is in an *abnormal ground condition*, the player may take relief under this Rule. If he elects to do so, the spot where the ball last crossed the outermost limits of the *abnormal ground condition* must be determined and, for the purpose of applying this Rule, the ball is deemed to lie at this spot and the player must proceed as follows:

(i) Through the Green: If the ball last crossed the outermost limits of the *abnormal ground condition* at a spot *through the green*, the player may *substitute* another ball, without penalty, and take relief as prescribed in Rule 25-1b(i).

(ii) In a Bunker: If the ball last crossed the outermost limits of the *abnormal ground condition* at a spot in a *bunker*, the player may *substitute* another ball, without penalty, and take relief as prescribed in Rule 25-1b(ii).

(iii) In a Water Hazard (including a Lateral Water Hazard): If the ball last crossed the outermost limits of the *abnormal ground condition* at a spot in a *water hazard*, the player is not entitled to relief without penalty. The player must proceed under Rule 26-1.

(iv) On the Putting Green: If the ball last crossed the outermost limits of the *abnormal ground condition* at a spot on the *putting green*, the player may *substitute* another ball, without penalty, and take relief as prescribed in Rule 25-1b(iii).

25-2. Embedded Ball

A ball embedded in its own pitch-mark in the ground in any closely-mown area *through the green* may be lifted, cleaned and dropped, without penalty, as near as possible to the spot where it lay but not nearer the *hole*. The ball when dropped must first strike a part of the *course through the green*. "Closely-mown area" means any area of the *course*, including paths through the rough, cut to fairway height or less.

25-3. Wrong Putting Green

a. Interference

Interference by a *wrong putting green* occurs when a ball is on the *wrong putting green*. Interference to a player's *stance* or the area of his intended swing is not, of itself, interference under this Rule.

b. Relief

If a player's ball lies on a *wrong putting green*, he must not play the ball as it lies. He must take relief, without penalty, as follows: The player must lift the ball and drop it within one club-length of and not nearer the *hole* than the *nearest point of relief*. The *nearest point of relief* must not be in a *hazard* or on a *putting green*. When dropping the ball within one club-length of the *nearest point of relief*, the ball must first strike a part of the *course* at a spot that avoids interference by the *wrong putting green* and is not in a *hazard* and not on a *putting green*. The ball may be cleaned when lifted under this Rule.

PENALTY FOR BREACH OF RULE:
Match play – Loss of hole; Stroke play – Two strokes.

Rule 26 – Water Hazards (Including Lateral Water Hazards)

Definitions

All defined terms are in *italics* and are listed alphabetically in the Definitions section – see pages 592–595.

26-1. Relief for Ball in Water Hazard

It is a question of fact whether a ball that has not been found after having been struck toward a *water hazard* is in the *hazard*. In the absence of knowledge or virtual certainty that a ball struck toward a *water hazard*, but not found, is in the *hazard*, the player must proceed under Rule 27-1.

If a ball is found in a *water hazard* or if it is known or virtually certain that a ball that has not been found is in the *water hazard* (whether the ball lies in water or not), the player may under penalty of one stroke:

a. Proceed under the stroke and distance provision of Rule 27-1 by playing a ball as nearly as possible at the spot from which the original ball was last played (see Rule 20-5); or

b. Drop a ball behind the *water hazard*, keeping the point at which the original ball last crossed the margin of the *water hazard* directly between the *hole* and the spot on which the ball is dropped, with no limit to how far behind the *water hazard* the ball may be dropped; or

c. As additional options available only if the ball last crossed the margin of a *lateral water hazard*, drop a ball outside the *water hazard* within two club-lengths of and not nearer the *hole* than (i) the point where the original ball last crossed the margin of the *water hazard* or (ii) a point on the opposite margin of the *water hazard* equidistant from the *hole*.

When proceeding under this Rule, the player may lift and clean his ball or *substitute* a ball.

(Prohibited actions when ball is in a hazard – see Rule 13-4)

(Ball moving in water in a water hazard – see Rule 14-6)

26-2. Ball Played Within Water Hazard

a. Ball Comes to Rest in Same or Another Water Hazard

If a ball played from within a *water hazard* comes to rest in the same or another *water hazard* after the *stroke*, the player may:

(i) proceed under Rule 26-1a. If, after dropping in the *hazard*, the player elects not to play the dropped ball, he may:
   (a) proceed under Rule 26-1b, or if applicable Rule 26-1c, adding the additional penalty of one stroke prescribed by the Rule and using as the reference point the point where the original ball last crossed the margin of this *hazard* before it came to rest in this *hazard*; or
   (b) add an additional penalty of one stroke and play a ball as nearly as possible at the spot from which the last *stroke* from outside a *water hazard* was made (see Rule 20-5); or

(ii) proceed under Rule 26-1b, or if applicable Rule 26-1c; or

(iii) under penalty of one stroke, play a ball as nearly as possible at the spot from which the last *stroke* from outside a *water hazard* was made (see Rule 20-5).

b. Ball Lost or Unplayable Outside Hazard or Out of Bounds

If a ball played from within a *water hazard* is *lost* or deemed unplayable outside the *hazard* or is *out of bounds*, the player may, after taking a penalty of one stroke under Rule 27-1 or 28a:

(i) play a ball as nearly as possible at the spot in the *hazard* from which the original ball was last played (see Rule 20-5); or

(ii) proceed under Rule 26-1b, or if applicable Rule 26-1c, adding the additional penalty of one stroke prescribed by the Rule and using as the reference point the point where the original ball last crossed the margin of the *hazard* before it came to rest in the *hazard*; or

(iii) add an additional penalty of one stroke and play a ball as nearly as possible at the spot from which the last *stroke* from outside a *water hazard* was made (see Rule 20-5).

Note 1: When proceeding under Rule 26-2b, the player is not required to drop a ball under Rule 27-1 or 28a. If he does drop a ball, he is not required to play it. He may alternatively proceed under Rule 26-2b(ii) or (iii).

Note 2: If a ball played from within a *water hazard* is deemed unplayable outside the *hazard*, nothing in Rule 26-2b precludes the player from proceeding under Rule 28b or c.

PENALTY FOR BREACH OF RULE:
Match play – Loss of hole; Stroke play – Two strokes.

Rule 27 – Ball Lost or Out of Bounds; Provisional Ball

Definitions

All defined terms are in *italics* and are listed alphabetically in the Definitions section – see pages 592–595.

27-1. Stroke and Distance; Ball Out of Bounds; Ball Not Found Within Five Minutes

a. Proceeding Under Stroke and Distance

At any time, a player may, under penalty of one stroke, play a ball as nearly as possible at the spot from which the original ball was last played (see Rule 20-5), i.e. proceed under penalty of stroke and distance.

Except as otherwise provided in the *Rules*, if a player makes a *stroke* at a ball from the spot at which the original ball was last played, he is deemed to have proceeded under penalty of stroke and distance.

b. Ball Out of Bounds

If a ball is *out of bounds*, the player must play a ball, under penalty of one stroke, as nearly as possible at the spot from which the original ball was last played (see Rule 20-5).

c. Ball Not Found Within Five Minutes

If a ball is *lost* as a result of not being found or identified as his by the player within five minutes after the player's *side* or his or their *caddies* have begun to search for it, the player must play a ball, under penalty of one stroke, as nearly as possible at the spot from which the original ball was last played (see Rule 20-5).

Exception: If it is known or virtually certain that the original ball, that has not been found, has been moved by an *outside agency* (Rule 18-1), is in an *obstruction* (Rule 24-3), is in an *abnormal ground condition* (Rule 25-1) or is in a *water hazard* (Rule 26-1), the player may proceed under the applicable *Rule*.

PENALTY FOR BREACH OF RULE 27-1:
Match play – Loss of hole; Stroke play – Two strokes.

27-2. Provisional Ball

a. Procedure

If a ball may be *lost* outside a *water hazard* or may be *out of bounds*, to save time the player may play another ball provisionally in accordance with Rule 27-1. The player must inform his *opponent* in match play or his *marker* or a *fellow-competitor* in stroke play that he intends to play a *provisional ball*, and he must play it before he or his *partner* goes forward to search for the original ball.

If he fails to do so and plays another ball, that ball is not a *provisional ball* and becomes the *ball in play* under penalty of stroke and distance (Rule 27-1); the original ball is *lost*.

(Order of play from teeing ground – see Rule 10-3)

Note: If a *provisional ball* played under Rule 27-2a might be *lost* outside a *water hazard* or *out of bounds*, the player may play another *provisional ball*. If another *provisional ball* is played, it bears the same relationship to the previous *provisional ball* as the first *provisional ball* bears to the original ball.

b. When Provisional Ball Becomes Ball in Play

The player may play a *provisional ball* until he reaches the place where the original ball is likely to be. If he makes a *stroke* with the *provisional ball* from the place where the original ball is likely to be or from a point nearer the *hole* than that place, the original ball is *lost* and the *provisional ball* becomes the *ball in play* under penalty of stroke and distance (Rule 27-1).

If the original ball is *lost* outside a *water hazard* or is *out of bounds*, the *provisional ball* becomes the *ball in play*, under penalty of stroke and distance (Rule 27-1).

Exception: If it is known or virtually certain that the original ball, that has not been found, has been moved by an *outside agency* (Rule 18-1), or is in an *obstruction* (Rule 24-3) or an *abnormal ground condition* (Rule 25-1c), the player may proceed under the applicable *Rule*.

c. When Provisional Ball to be Abandoned

If the original ball is neither *lost* nor *out of bounds*, the player must abandon the *provisional ball* and continue playing the original ball. If it is known or virtually certain that the original ball is in a *water hazard*, the player may proceed in accordance with Rule 26-1. In either situation, if the player makes any further *strokes* at the *provisional ball*, he is playing a *wrong ball* and the provisions of Rule 15-3 apply.

Note: If a player plays a *provisional ball* under Rule 27-2a, the *strokes* made after this Rule has been invoked with a *provisional ball* subsequently abandoned under Rule 27-2c and penalties incurred solely by playing that ball are disregarded.

Rule 28 – Ball Unplayable

Definitions

All defined terms are in *italics* and are listed alphabetically in the Definitions section – see pages 592–595.

The player may deem his ball unplayable at any place on the *course*, except when the ball is in a *water hazard*. The player is the sole judge as to whether his ball is unplayable.

If the player deems his ball to be unplayable, he must, under penalty of one stroke:

a. Proceed under the stroke and distance provision of Rule 27-1 by playing a ball as nearly as possible at the spot from which the original ball was last played (see Rule 20-5); or
b. Drop a ball behind the point where the ball lay, keeping that point directly between the *hole* and the spot on which the ball is dropped, with no limit to how far behind that point the ball may be dropped; or c. Drop a ball within two club-lengths of the spot where the ball lay, but not nearer the *hole*.

If the unplayable ball is in a *bunker*, the player may proceed under Clause a, b or c. If he elects to proceed under Clause b or c, a ball must be dropped in the *bunker*.

When proceeding under this Rule, the player may lift and clean his ball or *substitute* a ball.

PENALTY FOR BREACH OF RULE:
Match play – Loss of hole; Stroke play – Two strokes.

Other Forms of Play

Rule 29 – Threesomes and Foursomes

Definitions

All defined terms are in *italics* and are listed alphabetically in the Definitions section – see pages 592–595.

29-1. General

In a *threesome* or a *foursome*, during any *stipulated round* the *partners* must play alternately from the *teeing grounds* and alternately during the play of each hole. *Penalty strokes* do not affect the order of play.

29-2. Match Play

If a player plays when his *partner* should have played, his *side* loses the hole.

29-3. Stroke Play

If the *partners* make a *stroke* or *strokes* in incorrect order, such *stroke* or *strokes* are cancelled and the *side* incurs a penalty of two strokes. The *side* must correct the error by playing a ball in correct order as nearly as possible at the spot from which it first played in incorrect order (see Rule 20-5). If the *side* makes a *stroke* on the next *teeing ground* without first correcting the error or, in the case of the last hole of the round, leaves the *putting green* without declaring its intention to correct the error, the *side* is disqualified.

Rule 30 – Three-Ball, Best-Ball and Four-Ball Match Play

Definitions

All defined terms are in *italics* and are listed alphabetically in the Definitions section – see pages 592–595.

30-1. General

The Rules of Golf, so far as they are not at variance with the following specific Rules, apply to *three-ball, best-ball* and *four-ball* matches.

30-2. Three-Ball Match Play

a. Ball at Rest Moved or Purposely Touched by an Opponent

If an *opponent* incurs a penalty stroke under Rule 18-3b, that penalty is incurred only in the match with the player whose ball was touched or *moved*. No penalty is incurred in his match with the other player.

b. Ball Deflected or Stopped by an Opponent Accidentally

If a player's ball is accidentally deflected or stopped by an *opponent*, his *caddie* or *equipment*, there is no penalty. In his match with that *opponent* the player may, before another *stroke* is made by either *side*, cancel the *stroke* and play a ball, without penalty, as nearly as possible at the spot from which the original ball was last played (see Rule 20-5) or he may play the ball as it lies. In his match with the other *opponent*, the ball must be played as it lies.

Exception: Ball striking person attending or holding up *flagstick* or anything carried by him – see Rule 17-3b.

(Ball purposely deflected or stopped by *opponent* – see Rule 1-2)

30-3. Best-Ball and Four-Ball Match Play

a. Representation of Side

A *side* may be represented by one *partner* for all or any part of a match; all *partners* need not be present. An absent *partner* may join a match between holes, but not during play of a hole.

b. Order of Play

Balls belonging to the same *side* may be played in the order the *side* considers best.

c. Wrong Ball

If a player incurs the loss of hole penalty under Rule 15-3a for making a *stroke* at a *wrong ball*, he is disqualified for that hole, but his *partner* incurs no penalty even if the *wrong ball* belongs to him. If the *wrong ball* belongs to another player, its owner must place a ball on the spot from which the *wrong ball* was first played.

(Placing and Replacing – see Rule 20-3)

d. Penalty to Side

A *side* is penalised for a breach of any of the following by any *partner*:

- Rule 4 Clubs
- Rule 6-4 Caddie
- Any Local Rule or Condition of Competition for which the penalty is an adjustment to the state of the match.

e. Disqualification of Side

(i) A *side* is disqualified if any *partner* incurs a penalty of disqualification under any of the following:

• Rule 1-3	Agreement to Waive Rules
• Rule 4	Clubs
• Rule 5-1 or 5-2	The Ball
• Rule 6-2a	Handicap
• Rule 6-4	Caddie
• Rule 6-7	Undue Delay; Slow Play
• Rule 11-1	Teeing
• Rule 14-3	Artificial Devices, Unusual Equipment and Unusual Use of Equipment

- Rule 33-7 Disqualification Penalty Imposed by Committee

(ii) A *side* is disqualified if all *partners* incur a penalty of disqualification under any of the following:

- Rule 6-3 Time of Starting and Groups
- Rule 6-8 Discontinuance of Play

(iii) In all other cases where a breach of a *Rule* would result in disqualification, the player is disqualified for that hole only.

f. Effect of Other Penalties

If a player's breach of a *Rule* assists his *partner's* play or adversely affects an *opponent's* play, the *partner* incurs the applicable penalty in addition to any penalty incurred by the player.

In all other cases where a player incurs a penalty for breach of a *Rule*, the penalty does not apply to his *partner*. Where the penalty is stated to be loss of hole, the effect is to disqualify the player for that hole.

Rule 31 – Four-Ball Stroke Play

Definitions

All defined terms are in *italics* and are listed alphabetically in the Definitions section – see pages 592–595.

31-1. General

The Rules of Golf, so far as they are not at variance with the following specific Rules, apply to *four-ball* stroke play.

31-2. Representation of Side

A *side* may be represented by either *partner* for all or any part of a *stipulated round*; both *partners* need not be present. An absent *competitor* may join his *partner* between holes, but not during play of a hole.

31-3. Scoring

The *marker* is required to record for each hole only the gross score of whichever *partner's* score is to count. The gross scores to count must be individually identifiable; otherwise, the *side* is disqualified. Only one of the *partners* need be responsible for complying with Rule 6-6b.

(Wrong score – see Rule 31-7a)

31-4. Order of Play

Balls belonging to the same *side* may be played in the order the *side* considers best.

31-5. Wrong Ball

If a *competitor* is in breach of Rule 15-3b for making a *stroke* at a *wrong ball*, he incurs a penalty of two strokes and must correct his mistake by playing the correct ball or by proceeding under the *Rules*. His *partner* incurs no penalty, even if the *wrong ball* belongs to him.

If the *wrong ball* belongs to another *competitor*, its owner must place a ball on the spot from which the *wrong ball* was first played.

(Placing and Replacing – see Rule 20-3)

31-6 Penalty to Side

A *side* is penalised for a breach of any of the following by any *partner*:

- Rule 4 Clubs
- Rule 6-4 Caddie
- Any Local Rule or Condition of Competition for which there is a maximum penalty per round.

31-7. Disqualification Penalties

a. Breach by One Partner

A *side* is disqualified from the competition if either *partner* incurs a penalty of disqualification under any of the following:

- Rule 1-3 Agreement to Waive Rules
- Rule 3-4 Refusal to Comply with a Rule
- Rule 4 Clubs
- Rule 5-1 or 5-2 The Ball
- Rule 6-2b Handicap
- Rule 6-4 Caddie
- Rule 6-6b Signing and Returning Score Card
- Rule 6-6d Wrong Score for Hole
- Rule 6-7 Undue Delay; Slow Play
- Rule 7-1 Practice Before or Between Rounds
- Rule 10-2c Sides Agree to Play Out of Turn
- Rule 11-1 Teeing
- Rule 14-3 Artificial Devices, Unusual Equipment and Unusual Use of Equipment
- Rule 22-1 Ball Assisting Play
- Rule 31-3 Gross Scores to Count Not Individually Identifiable
- Rule 33-7 Disqualification Penalty Imposed by Committee

b. Breach by Both Partners

A *side* is disqualified from the competition:

(i) if each *partner* incurs a penalty of disqualification for a breach of Rule 6-3 (Time of Starting and Groups) or Rule 6-8 (Discontinuance of Play), or

(ii) if, at the same hole, each *partner* is in breach of a *Rule* the penalty for which is disqualification from the competition or for a hole.

c. For the Hole Only

In all other cases where a breach of a *Rule* would result in disqualification, the *competitor* is disqualified only for the hole at which the breach occurred.

31-8. Effect of Other Penalties

If a *competitor's* breach of a *Rule* assists his *partner's* play, the *partner* incurs the applicable penalty in addition to any penalty incurred by the *competitor*.

In all other cases where a *competitor* incurs a penalty for breach of a *Rule*, the penalty does not apply to his *partner*.

Rule 32 – Bogey, Par and Stableford Competitions

Definitions

All defined terms are in *italics* and are listed alphabetically in the Definitions section – see pages 592–595.

32-1. Conditions

Bogey, par and Stableford competitions are forms of stroke play in which play is against a fixed score at each hole. The *Rules* for stroke play, so far as they are not at variance with the following specific Rules, apply.

In handicap bogey, par and Stableford competitions, the *competitor* with the lowest net score at a hole takes the *honour* at the next *teeing ground*.

a. Bogey and Par Competitions

The scoring for bogey and par competitions is made as in match play.

Any hole for which a *competitor* makes no return is regarded as a loss. The winner is the *competitor* who is most successful in the aggregate of holes.

The *marker* is responsible for marking only the gross number of *strokes* for each hole where the *competitor* makes a net score equal to or less than the fixed score.

Note 1: The *competitor's* score is adjusted by deducting a hole or holes under the applicable *Rule* when a penalty other than disqualification is incurred under any of the following:

- Rule 4 Clubs
- Rule 6-4 Caddie
- Any Local Rule or Condition of Competition for which there is a maximum penalty per round.

The *competitor* is responsible for reporting the facts regarding such a breach to the *Committee* before he returns his score card so that the *Committee* may apply the penalty.

If the *competitor* fails to report his breach to the *Committee*, he is disqualified.

Note 2: If the *competitor* is in breach of Rule 6-3a (Time of Starting) but arrives at his starting point, ready to play, within five minutes after his starting time, or is in breach of Rule 6-7 (Undue Delay; Slow Play), the *Committee* will deduct one hole from the aggregate of holes. For a repeated offence under Rule 6-7, see Rule 32-2a.

b. Stableford Competitions

The scoring in Stableford competitions is made by points awarded in relation to a fixed score at each hole as follows:

Hole Played In	Points
More than one over fixed score or no score returned	0
One over fixed score	1
Fixed score	2
One under fixed score	3
Two under fixed score	4
Three under fixed score	5
Four under fixed score	6

The winner is the *competitor* who scores the highest number of points.

The *marker* is responsible for marking only the gross number of *strokes* at each hole where the *competitor's* net score earns one or more points.

Note 1: If a *competitor* is in breach of a *Rule* for which there is a maximum penalty per round, he must report the facts to the *Committee* before returning his score card; if he fails to do so, he is disqualified. The *Committee* will, from the total points scored for the round, deduct two points for each hole at which any breach occurred, with a maximum deduction per round of four points for each *Rule* breached.

Note 2: If the *competitor* is in breach of Rule 6-3a (Time of Starting) but arrives at his starting point, ready to play, within five minutes after his starting time, or is in breach of Rule 6-7 (Undue Delay; Slow Play), the *Committee* will deduct two points from the total points scored for the round. For a repeated offence under Rule 6-7, see Rule 32-2a.

Note 3: For the purpose of preventing slow play, the *Committee* may, in the conditions of a competition (Rule 33-1), establish pace of play guidelines, including maximum periods of time allowed to complete a *stipulated round*, a hole or a *stroke*.

The *Committee* may, in such a condition, modify the penalty for a breach of this Rule as follows: First offence – Deduction of one point from the total points scored for the round; Second offence – Deduction of a further two points from the total points scored for the round; For subsequent offence – Disqualificatio

32-2. Disqualification Penalties

a. From the Competition

A *competitor* is disqualified from the competition if he incurs a penalty of disqualification under any of the following:

- Rule 1-3 — Agreement to Waive Rules
- Rule 3-4 — Refusal to Comply with a Rule
- Rule 4 — Clubs
- Rule 5-1 or 5-2 — The Ball
- Rule 6-2b — Handicap
- Rule 6-3 — Time of Starting and Groups
- Rule 6-4 — Caddie
- Rule 6-6b — Signing and Returning Score Card
- Rule 6-6d — Wrong Score for Hole, i.e. when the recorded score is lower than actually taken, except that no penalty is incurred when a breach of this Rule does not affect the result of the hole
- Rule 6-7 — Undue Delay; Slow Play
- Rule 6-8 — Discontinuance of Play
- Rule 7-1 — Practice Before or Between Rounds
- Rule 11-1 — Teeing
- Rule 14-3 — Artificial Devices, Unusual Equipment and Unusual Use of Equipment
- Rule 22-1 — Ball Assisting Play
- Rule 33-7 — Disqualification Penalty Imposed by Committee

b. For a Hole

In all other cases where a breach of a *Rule* would result in disqualification, the *competitor* is disqualified only for the hole at which the breach occurred.

Administration

Rule 33 – The Committee

Definitions

All defined terms are in *italics* and are listed alphabetically in the Definitions section – see pages 592–595.

33-1. Conditions; Waiving Rule

The *Committee* must establish the conditions under which a competition is to be played.

The *Committee* has no power to waive a Rule of Golf.

Certain specific *Rules* governing stroke play are so substantially different from those governing match play that combining the two forms of play is not practicable and is not permitted. The result of a match played in these circumstances is null and void and, in the stroke play competition, the *competitors* are disqualified.

In stroke play, the *Committee* may limit a *referee's* duties.

33-2. The Course

a. Defining Bounds and Margins

The *Committee* must define accurately:

(i) the *course* and *out of bounds*,
(ii) the margins of *water hazards* and *lateral water hazards*,
(iii) *ground under repair*, and
(iv) *obstructions* and integral parts of the *course*.

b. New Holes

New *holes* should be made on the day on which a stroke play competition begins and at such other times as the *Committee* considers necessary, provided all *competitors* in a single round play with each *hole* cut in the same position.

Exception: When it is impossible for a damaged *hole* to be repaired so that it conforms with the Definition, the *Committee* may make a new *hole* in a nearby similar position.

Note: Where a single round is to be played on more than one day, the *Committee* may provide, in the conditions of a competition (Rule 33-1), that the *holes* and *teeing grounds* may be differently situated on each day of the competition, provided that, on any one day, all *competitors* play with each *hole* and each *teeing ground* in the same position.

c. Practice Ground

Where there is no practice ground available outside the area of a competition *course*, the *Committee* should establish the area on which players may practise on any day of a competition, if it is practicable to do so. On any day of a stroke play competition, the *Committee* should not normally permit practice on or to a *putting green* or from a *hazard* of the competition *course*.

d. Course Unplayable

If the *Committee* or its authorised representative considers that for any reason the *course* is not in a playable condition or that there are circumstances that render the proper playing of the game impossible, it may, in match play or stroke play, order a temporary suspension of play or, in stroke play, declare play null and void and cancel all scores for the round in question. When a round is cancelled, all penalties incurred in that round are cancelled.

(Procedure in discontinuing and resuming play – see Rule 6-8)

33-3. Times of Starting and Groups

The *Committee* must establish the times of starting and, in stroke play, arrange the groups in which *competitors* must play.

When a match play competition is played over an extended period, the *Committee* establishes the limit of time within which each round must be completed. When players are allowed to arrange the date of their match within these limits, the *Committee* should announce that the match must be played at a stated time on the last day of the period, unless the players agree to a prior date.

33-4. Handicap Stroke Table

The *Committee* must publish a table indicating the order of holes at which handicap strokes are to be given or received.

33-5. Score Card

In stroke play, the *Committee* must provide each *competitor* with a score card containing the date and the *competitor's* name or, in *foursome* or *four-ball* stroke play, the *competitors'* names.

In stroke play, the *Committee* is responsible for the addition of scores and application of the handicap recorded on the score card.

In *four-ball* stroke play, the *Committee* is responsible for recording the better-ball score for each hole and in the process applying the handicaps recorded on the score card, and adding the better-ball scores.

In bogey, par and Stableford competitions, the *Committee* is responsible for applying the handicap recorded on the score card and determining the result of each hole and the overall result or points total.

Note: The *Committee* may request that each *competitor* records the date and his name on his score card.

33-6. Decision of Ties

The *Committee* must announce the manner, day and time for the decision of a halved match or of a tie, whether played on level terms or under handicap.

A halved match must not be decided by stroke play. A tie in stroke play must not be decided by a match.

33-7. Disqualification Penalty; Committee Discretion

A penalty of disqualification may in exceptional individual cases be waived, modified or imposed if the *Committee* considers such action warranted.

Any penalty less than disqualification must not be waived or modified.

If a *Committee* considers that a player is guilty of a serious breach of etiquette, it may impose a penalty of disqualification under this Rule.

33-8. Local Rules

a. Policy

The *Committee* may establish Local Rules for local abnormal conditions if they are consistent with the policy set forth in Appendix I.

b. Waiving or Modifying a Rule

A Rule of Golf must not be waived by a Local Rule. However, if a *Committee* considers that local abnormal conditions interfere with the proper playing of the game to the extent that it is necessary to make a Local Rule that modifies the Rules of Golf, the Local Rule must be authorised by The *R&A*.

Rule 34 – Disputes and Decisions

Definitions

All defined terms are in *italics* and are listed alphabetically in the Definitions section – see pages 592–595.

34-1. Claims and Penalties

a. Match Play

If a claim is lodged with the *Committee* under Rule 2-5, a decision should be given as soon as possible so that the state of the match may, if necessary, be adjusted. If a claim is not made in accordance with Rule 2-5, it must not be considered by the *Committee*.

There is no time limit on applying the disqualification penalty for a breach of Rule 1-3.

b. Stroke Play

In stroke play, a penalty must not be rescinded, modified or imposed after the competition has closed. A competition is closed when the result has been officially announced or, in stroke play qualifying followed by match play, when the player has teed off in his first match.

Exceptions: A penalty of disqualification must be imposed after the competition has closed if a *competitor*:

(i) was in breach of Rule 1-3 (Agreement to Waive Rules); or

(ii) returned a score card on which he had recorded a handicap that, before the competition closed, he knew was higher than that to which he was entitled, and this affected the number of strokes received (Rule 6-2b); or

(iii) returned a score for any hole lower than actually taken (Rule 6-6d) for any reason other than failure to include a penalty that, before the competition closed, he did not know he had incurred; or

(iv) knew, before the competition closed, that he had been in breach of any other *Rule* for which the penalty is disqualification.

34-2. Referee's Decision

If a *referee* has been appointed by the *Committee*, his decision is final.

34-3. Committee's Decision

In the absence of a *referee*, any dispute or doubtful point on the *Rules* must be referred to the *Committee*, whose decision is final.

If the *Committee* cannot come to a decision, it may refer the dispute or doubtful point to the Rules of Golf Committee of the *R&A*, whose decision is final.

If the dispute or doubtful point has not been referred to the Rules of Golf Committee, the player or players may request that an agreed statement be referred through a duly authorised representative of the *Committee* to the Rules of Golf Committee for an opinion as to the correctness of the decision given. The reply will be sent to this authorised representative.

If play is conducted other than in accordance with the Rules of Golf, the Rules of Golf Committee will not give a decision on any question.

Appendix I – Contents

Appendix I – Local Rules; Conditions of the Competition

Definitions

All defined terms are in *italics* and are listed alphabetically in the Definitions section – see pages 592–595.

Part A – Local Rules

As provided in Rule 33-8a, the Committee may make and publish Local Rules for local abnormal conditions if they are consistent with the policy established in this Appendix. In addition, detailed information regarding acceptable and prohibited Local Rules is provided in "Decisions on the Rules of Golf" under Rule 33-8 and in "Guidance on Running a Competition".

If local abnormal conditions interfere with the proper playing of the game and the Committee considers it necessary to modify a Rule of Golf, authorisation from the *R&A* must be obtained.

1. Defining Bounds and Margins

Specifying means used to define out *of bounds, water hazards, lateral water hazards, ground under repair, obstructions* and integral parts of the course (Rule 33-2a).

2. Water Hazards

a. Lateral Water Hazards

Clarifying the status of water hazards that may be *lateral water hazards* (Rule 26).

b. Ball Played Provisionally Under Rule 26-1

Permitting play of a ball provisionally under Rule 26-1 for a ball that may be in a *water hazard* (including a *lateral water hazard*) of such character that, if the original ball is not found, it is known or virtually certain that it is in the *water hazard* and it would be impracticable to determine whether the ball is in the *hazard* or to do so would unduly delay play.

3. Areas of the Course Requiring Preservation; Environmentally-Sensitive Areas

Assisting preservation of the *course* by defining areas, including turf nurseries, young plantations and other parts of the *course* under cultivation, as *ground under repair* from which play is prohibited.

When the *Committee* is required to prohibit play from environmentally-sensitive areas that are on or adjoin the *course*, it should make a Local Rule clarifying the relief procedure.

4. Course Conditions – Mud, Extreme Wetness, Poor Conditions and Protection of Course

a. Lifting an Embedded Ball, Cleaning

Temporary conditions that might interfere with proper playing of the game, including mud and extreme wetness, warranting relief for an embedded ball anywhere *through the green* or permitting lifting, cleaning and replacing a ball anywhere *through the green* or on a closely-mown area *through the green.*

b. "Preferred Lies" and "Winter Rules"

Adverse conditions, including the poor condition of the *course* or the existence of mud, are sometimes so general, particularly during winter months, that the *Committee* may decide to grant relief by temporary Local Rule either to protect the *course* or to promote fair and pleasant play. The Local Rule should be withdrawn as soon as the conditions warrant.

5. Obstructions

a. General

Clarifying status of objects that may be *obstructions* (Rule 24).

Declaring any construction to be an integral part of the *course* and, accordingly, not an *obstruction*, e.g. built-up sides of *teeing grounds, putting greens* and *bunkers* (Rules 24 and 33-2a).

b. Stones in Bunkers

Allowing the removal of stones in *bunkers* by declaring them to be movable *obstructions* (Rule 24-1).

c. Roads and Paths

(i) Declaring artificial surfaces and sides of roads and paths to be integral parts of the course, or

(ii) Providing relief of the type afforded under Rule 24-2b from roads and paths not having artificial surfaces and sides if they could unfairly affect play.

d. Immovable Obstructions Close to Putting Green

Providing relief from intervention by immovable *obstructions* on or within two club-lengths of the putting green when the ball lies within two clublengths of the immovable *obstruction*.

e. Protection of Young Trees

Providing relief for the protection of young trees.

f. Temporary Obstructions

Providing relief from interference by temporary obstructions (e.g. grandstands, television cables and equipment, etc).

6. Dropping Zones

Establishing special areas on which balls may or must be dropped when it is not feasible or practicable to proceed exactly in conformity with Rule 24-2b or 24-3 (Immovable Obstruction), Rule 25-1b or 25-1c (Abnormal Ground Conditions), Rule 25-3 (Wrong Putting Green), Rule 26-1 (Water Hazards and Lateral Water Hazards) or Rule 28 (Ball Unplayable).

Part B Specimen Local Rules

Within the policy established in Part A of this Appendix, the Committee may adopt a Specimen Local Rule by referring, on a score card or notice board, to the examples given below. However, Specimen Local Rules of a temporary nature should not be printed on a score card.

1. Water Hazards; Ball Played Provisionally Under Rule 26-1

If a *water hazard* (including a *lateral water hazard*) is of such size and shape and/or located in such a position that:

(i) it would be impracticable to determine whether the ball is in the *hazard* or to do so would unduly delay play, and

(ii) if the original ball is not found, it is known or virtually certain that it is in the *water hazard*, the *Committee* may introduce a Local Rule permitting the play of a ball provisionally under Rule 26-1. The ball is played provisionally under any of the applicable options under Rule 26-1 or any applicable Local Rule. In such a case, if a ball is played provisionally and the original ball is in a *water hazard*, the player may play the original ball as it lies or continue with the ball played provisionally, but he may not proceed under Rule 26-1 with regard to the original ball.

In these circumstances, the following Local Rule is recommended:

"If there is doubt whether a ball is in or is lost in the water hazard (specify location), the player may play another ball provisionally under any of the applicable options in Rule 26-1.

If the original ball is found outside the water hazard, the player must continue play with it.

I f the original ball is found in the water hazard, the player may either play the original ball as it lies or continue with the ball played provisionally under Rule 26-1.

If the original ball is not found or identified within the five-minute search period, the player must continue with the ball played provisionally.

PENALTY FOR BREACH OF LOCAL RULE:
Match play – Loss of hole; Stroke play – Two strokes."

2. Areas of the Course Requiring Preservation; Environmentally- Sensitive Areas

a. Ground Under Repair; Play Prohibited

If the *Committee* wishes to protect any area of the *course*, it should declare it to be *ground under repair* and prohibit play from within that area. The following Local Rule is recommended:

"The ____________(defined by ____) is ground under repair from which play is prohibited. If a player's ball lies in the area, or if it interferes with the player's stance or the area of his intended swing, the player must take relief under Rule 25-1.

PENALTY FOR BREACH OF LOCAL RULE:
Match play – Loss of hole; Stroke play – Two strokes."

b. Environmentally-Sensitive Areas

If an appropriate authority (i.e. a Government Agency or the like) prohibits entry into and/or play from an area on or adjoining the *course* for environmental reasons, the *Committee* should make a Local Rule clarifying the relief procedure.

The *Committee* has some discretion in terms of whether the area is defined as *ground under repair*, a *water hazard* or *out of bounds*. However, it may not simply define the area to be a *water hazard* if it does not meet the Definition of a "*Water Hazard*" and it should attempt to preserve the character of the hole.

The following Local Rule is recommended:

"I. Definition

An environmentally-sensitive area (ESA) is an area so declared by an appropriate authority, entry into and/or play from which is prohibited for environmental reasons. These areas may be defined as ground under repair, a water hazard, a lateral water hazard or out of bounds at the discretion of the Committee, provided that in the case of an ESA that has been defined as a water hazard or a lateral water hazard, the area is, by definition, a water hazard.

Note: The Committee may not declare an area to be environmentally-sensitive.

II. Ball in Environmentally-Sensitive Area

a. Ground Under Repair

If a ball is in an ESA defined as ground under repair, a ball must be dropped in accordance with Rule 25-1b.

If it is known or virtually certain that a ball that has not been found is in an ESA defined as ground under repair, the player may take relief, without penalty, as prescribed in Rule 25-1c.

b. Water Hazards and Lateral Water Hazards

If the ball is found in or if it is known or virtually certain that a ball that has not been found is in an ESA defined as a water hazard or lateral water hazard, the player must, under penalty of one stroke, proceed under Rule 26-1.

Note: If a ball, dropped in accordance with Rule 26 rolls into a position where the ESA interferes with the player's stance or the area of his intended swing, the player must take relief as provided in Clause III of this Local Rule.

c. Out of Bounds

If a ball is in an ESA defined as out of bounds, the player must play a ball, under penalty of one stroke, as nearly as possible at the spot from which the original ball was last played (see Rule 20-5).

III. Interference with Stance or Area of Intended Swing

Interference by an ESA occurs when the ESA interferes with the player's stance or the area of his intended swing. If interference exists, the player must take relief as follows:

(a) Through the Green: If the ball lies through the green, the point on the course nearest to where the ball lies must be determined that (a) is not nearer the hole, (b) avoids interference by the ESA and (c) is not in a hazard or on a putting green. The player must lift the ball and drop it, without penalty, within one club-length of the point so determined on a part of the course that fulfils (a), (b) and (c) above.

(b) In a Hazard: If the ball is in a hazard, the player must lift the ball and drop it either:
(i) Without penalty, in the hazard, as near as possible to the spot where the ball lay, but not nearer the hole, on a part of the course that provides complete relief from the ESA; or
(ii) Under penalty of one stroke, outside the hazard, keeping the point where the ball lay directly between the hole and the spot on which the ball is dropped, with no limit to how far behind the hazard the ball may be dropped. Additionally, the player may proceed under Rule 26 or 28 if applicable.

(c) On the Putting Green: If the ball lies on the putting green, the player must lift the ball and place it, without penalty, in the nearest position to where it lay that affords complete relief from the ESA, but not nearer the hole or in a hazard.

The ball may be cleaned when lifted under Clause III of this Local Rule.

Exception: A player may not take relief under Clause III of this Local Rule if (a) interference by anything other than an ESA makes the stroke clearly impracticable or (b) interference by an ESA would occur only through use of a clearly unreasonable stroke or an unnecessarily abnormal stance, swing or direction of play.

PENALTY FOR BREACH OF LOCAL RULE:
Match play – Loss of hole; Stroke play – Two strokes.

Note: In the case of a serious breach of this Local Rule, the Committee may impose a penalty of disqualification."

3. Protection of Young Trees

When it is desired to prevent damage to young trees, the following Local Rule is recommended:

"Protection of young trees identified by _______. If such a tree interferes with a player's stance or the area of his intended swing, the ball must be lifted, without penalty, and dropped in accordance with the procedure prescribed in Rule 24-2b (Immovable Obstruction). If the ball lies in a water hazard, the player must lift and drop the ball in accordance with Rule 24-2b(i), except that the nearest point of relief must be in the water hazard and the ball must be dropped in the water hazard or the player may proceed under Rule 26. The ball may be cleaned when lifted under this Local Rule.

Exception: A player may not obtain relief under this Local Rule if (a) interference by anything other than such a tree makes the stroke clearly impracticable or (b) interference by such a tree would occur only through use of a clearly unreasonable stroke or an unnecessarily abnormal stance, swing or direction of play.

PENALTY FOR BREACH OF LOCAL RULE:
Match play – Loss of hole; Stroke play – Two strokes."

4. Course Conditions – Mud, Extreme Wetness, Poor Conditions and Protection of the Course

a. Relief for Embedded Ball

Rule 25-2 provides relief, without penalty, for a ball embedded in its own pitch-mark in any closely-mown area *through the green*. On the *putting green*, a ball may be lifted and damage caused by the impact of a ball may be repaired (Rules 16-1b and c). When permission to take relief for an embedded ball anywhere *through the green* would be warranted, the following Local Rule is recommended:

"Through the green, a ball that is embedded in its own pitch-mark in the ground may be lifted, without penalty, cleaned and dropped as near as possible to where it lay but not nearer the hole. The ball when dropped must first strike a part of the course through the green.

Exceptions:

A player may not take relief under this Local Rule if the ball is embedded in sand in an area that is not closely mown.

A player may not take relief under this Local Rule if interference by anything other than the condition covered by this Local Rule makes the stroke clearly impracticable.

PENALTY FOR BREACH OF LOCAL RULE:
Match play – Loss of hole; Stroke play – Two strokes."

b. Cleaning Ball

Conditions, such as extreme wetness causing significant amounts of mud to adhere to the ball, may be such that permission to lift, clean and replace the ball would be appropriate. In these circumstances, the following Local Rule is recommended:

"(Specify area) a ball may be lifted, cleaned and replaced without penalty.

Note: The position of the ball must be marked before it is lifted under this Local Rule – see Rule 20-1.

PENALTY FOR BREACH OF LOCAL RULE:
Match play – Loss of hole; Stroke play – Two strokes."

c. "Preferred Lies" and "Winter Rules"

Ground under repair is provided for in Rule 25 and occasional local abnormal conditions that might interfere with fair play and are not widespread should be defined as *ground under repair*.

However, adverse conditions, such as heavy snows, spring thaws, prolonged rains or extreme heat can make fairways unsatisfactory and sometimes prevent use of heavy mowing equipment. When such conditions are so general throughout a *course* that the *Committee* believes "preferred lies" or "winter rules" would promote fair play or help protect the *course*, the following Local Rule is recommended:

"A ball lying on a closely-mown area through the green (or specify a more restricted area, e.g. at the 6th hole) may be lifted, without penalty, and cleaned. Before lifting the ball, the player must mark its position. Having lifted the ball, he must place it on a spot within (specify area, e.g. six inches, one club-length, etc.) of and not nearer the hole than where it originally lay, that is not in a hazard and not on a putting green.

A player may place his ball only once, and it is in play when it has been placed (Rule 20-4). If the ball fails to come to rest on the spot on which it is placed, Rule 20-3d applies. If the ball when placed comes to rest on the spot on which it is placed and it subsequently moves, there is no penalty and the ball must be played as it lies, unless the provisions of any other Rule apply.

If the player fails to mark the position of the ball before lifting it or moves the ball in any other manner, such as rolling it with a club, he incurs a penalty of one stroke.

Note: "Closely-mown area" means any area of the course, including paths through the rough, cut to fairway height or less.

*PENALTY FOR BREACH OF LOCAL RULE:
Match play – Loss of hole; Stroke play – Two strokes.

*If a player incurs the general penalty for a breach of this Local Rule, no additional penalty under the Local Rule is applied."

d. Aeration Holes

When a *course* has been aerated, a Local Rule permitting relief, without penalty, from an aeration hole may be warranted. The following Local Rule is recommended:

"Through the green, a ball that comes to rest in or on an aeration hole may be lifted, without penalty, cleaned and dropped, as near as possible to the spot where it lay but not nearer the hole. The ball when dropped must first strike a part of the course through the green.

On the putting green, a ball that comes to rest in or on an aeration hole may be placed at the nearest spot not nearer the hole that avoids the situation.

PENALTY FOR BREACH OF LOCAL RULE:
Match play – Loss of hole; Stroke play – Two strokes."

e. Seams of Cut Turf

If a *Committee* wishes to allow relief from seams of cut turf, but not from the cut turf itself, the following Local Rule is recommended:

"Through the green, seams of cut turf (not the turf itself) are deemed to be ground under repair. However, interference by a seam with the player's stance is deemed not to be, of itself, interference under Rule 25-1. If the ball lies in or touches the seam or the seam interferes with the area of intended swing, relief is available under Rule 25-1. All seams within the cut turf area are considered the same seam.

PENALTY FOR BREACH OF LOCAL RULE:
Match play – Loss of hole; Stroke play – Two strokes."

5. Stones in Bunkers

Stones are, by definition, *loose impediments* and, when a player's ball is in a *hazard*, a stone lying in or touching the *hazard* may not be touched or moved (Rule 13-4). However, stones in *bunkers* may represent a danger to players (a player could be injured by a stone struck by the player's club in an attempt to play the ball) and they may interfere with the proper playing of the game.

When permission to lift a stone in a *bunker* is warranted, the following Local Rule is recommended:

"Stones in bunkers are movable obstructions (Rule 24-1 applies)."

6. Immovable Obstructions Close to Putting Green

Rule 24-2 provides relief, without penalty, from interference by an immovable *obstruction*, but it also provides that, except on the *putting green*, intervention on the *line of play* is not, of itself, interference under this Rule.

However, on some courses, the aprons of the *putting greens* are so closely mown that players may wish to putt from just off the green. In such conditions, immovable *obstructions* on the apron may interfere with the proper playing of the game and the introduction of the following Local Rule providing additional relief, without penalty, from intervention by an immovable *obstruction* would be warranted:

"Relief from interference by an immovable obstruction may be taken under Rule 24-2.

In addition, if a ball lies through the green and an immovable obstruction on or within two club-lengths of the putting green and within two club-lengths of the ball intervenes on the line of play between the ball and the hole, the player may take relief as follows:

The ball must be lifted and dropped at the nearest point to where the ball lay that (a) is not nearer the hole, (b) avoids intervention and (c) is not in a hazard or on a putting green.

If the player's ball lies on the putting green and an immovable obstruction within two club-lengths of the putting green intervenes on his line of putt, the player may take relief as follows:

The ball must be lifted and placed at the nearest point to where the ball lay that (a) is not nearer the hole, (b) avoids intervention and (c) is not in a hazard.

The ball may be cleaned when lifted.

Exception: A player may not take relief under this Local Rule if interference by anything other than the immovable obstruction makes the stroke clearly impracticable.

PENALTY FOR BREACH OF LOCAL RULE:
Match play – Loss of hole; Stroke play – Two strokes."

Note: The *Committee* may restrict this Local Rule to specific holes, to balls lying only in closely-mown areas, to specific *obstructions*, or, in the case of *obstructions* that are not on the *putting green*, to *obstructions* in closely-mown areas if so desired. "Closely-mown area" means any area of the course, including paths through the rough, cut to fairway height or less.

7. Temporary Obstructions

When temporary obstructions are installed on or adjoining the *course*, the *Committee* should define the status of such obstructions as movable, immovable or temporary immovable obstructions.

a. Temporary Immovable Obstructions

If the *Committee* defines such obstructions as temporary immovable obstructions, the following Local Rule is recommended:

"I. Definition

A temporary immovable obstruction (TIO) is a non-permanent artificial object that is often erected in conjunction with a competition and is fixed or not readily movable.

Examples of TIOs include, but are not limited to, tents, scoreboards, grandstands, television towers and lavatories. Supporting guy wires are part of the TIO, unless the Committee declares that they are to be treated as elevated power lines or cables.

II. Interference

Interference by a TIO occurs when (a) the ball lies in front of and so close to the TIO that the TIO interferes with the player's stance or the area of his intended swing, or (b) the ball lies in, on, under or behind the TIO so that any part of the TIO intervenes directly between the player's ball and the hole and is on his line of play; interference also exists if the ball lies within one club-length of a spot equidistant from the hole where such intervention would exist.

Note: A ball is under a TIO when it is below the outermost edges of the TIO, even if these edges do not extend downwards to the ground.

III. Relief

A player may obtain relief from interference by a TIO, including a TIO that is out of bounds, as follows:

(a) Through the Green: If the ball lies through the green, the point on the course nearest to where the ball lies must be determined that (a) is not nearer the hole, (b) avoids interference as defined in Clause II and (c) is not in a hazard or on a putting green. The player must lift the ball and drop it, without penalty, within one club-length of the point so determined on a part of the course that fulfils (a), (b) and (c) above.

(b) In a Hazard: If the ball is in a hazard, the player must lift and drop the ball either:

  (i) Without penalty, in accordance with Clause III(a) above, except that the nearest part of the course affording complete relief must be in the hazard and the ball must be dropped in the hazard or, if complete relief is impossible, on a part of the course within the hazard that affords maximum available relief; or

  (ii) Under penalty of one stroke, outside the hazard as follows: the point on the course nearest to where the ball lies must be determined that (a) is not nearer the hole, (b) avoids interference as defined in Clause II and (c) is not in a hazard. The player must drop the ball within one club-length of the point so determined on a part of the course that fulfils (a), (b) and (c) above.

The ball may be cleaned when lifted under Clause III.

Note 1: If the ball lies in a hazard, nothing in this Local Rule precludes the player from proceeding under Rule 26 or Rule 28, if applicable.

Note 2: If a ball to be dropped under this Local Rule is not immediately recoverable, another ball may be substituted.

Note 3: A Committee may make a Local Rule (a) permitting or requiring a player to use a dropping zone when taking relief from a TIO or (b) permitting a player, as an additional relief option, to drop the ball on the opposite side of the TIO from the point established under Clause III, but otherwise in accordance with Clause III.

Exceptions: If a player's ball lies in front of or behind the TIO (not in, on or under the TIO), he may not obtain relief under Clause III if:

Interference by anything other than the TIO makes it clearly impracticable for him to make a stroke or, in the case of intervention, to make a stroke such that the ball could finish on a direct line to the hole;

Interference by the TIO would occur only through use of a clearly unreasonable *stroke* or an unnecessarily abnormal stance, swing or direction of play; or

In the case of intervention, it would be clearly impracticable to expect the player to be able to strike the ball far enough towards the hole to reach the TIO.

A player who is not entitled to relief due to these exceptions may, if the ball lies through the green or in a bunker, obtain relief as provided in Rule 24-2b, if applicable. If the ball lies in a water hazard, the player may lift and drop the ball in accordance with Rule 24-2b(i), except that the nearest point of relief must be in the water hazard and the ball must be dropped in the water hazard, or the player may proceed under Rule 26-1.

IV. Ball in TIO Not Found

If it is known or virtually certain that a ball that has not been found is in, on or under a TIO, a ball may be dropped under the provisions of Clause III or Clause V, if applicable. For the purpose of applying Clauses III and V, the ball is deemed to lie at the spot where it last crossed the outermost limits of the TIO (Rule 24-3).

V. Dropping Zones

If the player has interference from a TIO, the Committee may permit or require the use of a dropping zone. If the player uses a dropping zone in taking relief, he must drop the ball in the dropping zone nearest to where his ball originally lay or is deemed to lie under Clause IV (even though the nearest dropping zone may be nearer the hole).

Note: A Committee may make a Local Rule prohibiting the use of a dropping zone that is nearer the hole.

PENALTY FOR BREACH OF LOCAL RULE:
Match play – Loss of hole; Stroke play – Two strokes."

b. Temporary Power Lines and Cables

When temporary power lines, cables, or telephone lines are installed on the *course*, the following Local Rule is recommended:

"Temporary power lines, cables, telephone lines and mats covering or stanchions supporting them are obstructions:

1. If they are readily movable, Rule 24-1 applies.

2. If they are fixed or not readily movable, the player may, if the ball lies through the green or in a bunker, obtain relief as provided in Rule 24-2b. If the ball lies in a water hazard, the player may lift and drop the ball in accordance with Rule 24-2b(i), except that the nearest point of relief must be in the water hazard and the ball must be dropped in the water hazard or the player may proceed under Rule 26.

3. If a ball strikes an elevated power line or cable, the stroke is cancelled and the player must play a ball as nearly as possible at the spot from which the original ball was played in accordance with Rule 20-5 (Making Next Stroke from Where Previous Stroke Made).

Note: Guy wires supporting a temporary immovable obstruction are part of the temporary immovable obstruction, unless the Committee, by Local Rule, declares that they are to be treated as elevated power lines or cables.

Exception: A stroke that results in a ball striking an elevated junction section of cable rising from the ground must not be replayed.

4. Grass-covered cable trenches are ground under repair, even if not marked, and Rule 25-1b applies.

PENALTY FOR BREACH OF LOCAL RULE:
Match play – Loss of hole; Stroke play – Two strokes."

8. Dropping Zones

If the *Committee* considers that it is not feasible or practicable to proceed in accordance with a Rule providing relief, it may establish dropping zones in which balls may or must be dropped when taking relief. Generally, such dropping zones should be provided as an additional relief option to those available under the Rule itself, rather than being mandatory.

Using the example of a dropping zone for a *water hazard*, when such a dropping zone is established, the following Local Rule is recommended:

"If a ball is in or it is known or virtually certain that a ball that has not been found is in the water hazard (specify location), the player may:

(i) proceed under Rule 26; or
(ii) as an additional option, drop a ball, under penalty of one stroke, in the dropping zone.

PENALTY FOR BREACH OF LOCAL RULE:
Match play – Loss of hole; Stroke play – Two strokes."

Note: When using a dropping zone the following provisions apply regarding the dropping and re-dropping of the ball:

(a) The player does not have to stand within the dropping zone when dropping the ball.
(b) The dropped ball must first strike a part of the *course* within the dropping zone.
(c) If the dropping zone is defined by a line, the line is within the dropping zone.
(d) The dropped ball does not have to come to rest within the dropping zone.
(e) The dropped ball must be re-dropped if it rolls and comes to rest in a position covered by Rule 20-2c(i-vi).
(f) The dropped ball may roll nearer the *hole* than the spot where it first struck a part of the *course*, provided it comes to rest within two club-lengths of that spot and not into any of the positions covered by (e).
(g) Subject to the provisions of (e) and (f), the dropped ball may roll and come to rest nearer the *hole* than:
  - its original position or estimated position (see Rule 20-2b);
  - the *nearest point of relief* or maximum available relief (Rule 24-2, 25-1 or 25-3); or
  - the point where the original ball last crossed the margin of the *water hazard* or *lateral water hazard* (Rule 26-1).

9. Distance-Measuring Devices

If the *Committee* wishes to act in accordance with the Note under Rule 14-3, the following wording is recommended:

"(Specify as appropriate, e.g. In this competition, or For all play at this course, etc.), a player may obtain distance information by using a device that measures distance only. If, during a stipulated round, a player uses a distance-measuring device that is designed to gauge or measure other conditions that might affect his play (e.g. gradient, wind-speed, temperature, etc.), the player is in breach of Rule 14-3, for which the penalty is disqualification, regardless of whether any such additional function is actually used."

Part C – Conditions of the Competition

Rule 33-1 provides, "The Committee must establish the conditions under which a competition is to be played." The conditions should include many matters such as method of entry, eligibility, number of rounds to be played, etc. which it is not appropriate to deal with in the Rules of Golf or this Appendix. Detailed information regarding these conditions is provided in "Decisions on the Rules of Golf" under Rule 33-1 and in "Guidance on Running a Competition".

However, there are a number of matters that might be covered in the Conditions of the Competition to which the Committee's attention is specifically drawn. These are:

1. Specification of Clubs and the Ball

The following conditions are recommended only for competitions involving expert players:

a. List of Conforming Driver Heads

On its website (www.randa.org) the R&A periodically issues a List of Conforming Driver Heads that lists driving clubheads that have been evaluated and found to conform with the Rules of Golf. If the Committee wishes to limit players to drivers that have a clubhead, identified by model and loft, that is on the List, the List should be made available and the following condition of competition used:

"Any driver the player carries must have a clubhead, identified by model and loft, that is named on the current List of Conforming Driver Heads issued the R&A.

Exception: A driver with a clubhead that was manufactured prior to 1999 nis exempt from this condition.

*PENALTY FOR CARRYING, BUT NOT MAKING STROKE WITH, CLUB OR CLUBS IN BREACH OF CONDITION:

Match play – At the conclusion of the hole at which the breach is discovered, the state of the match is adjusted by deducting one hole for each hole at which a breach occurred; maximum deduction per round – Two holes.

Stroke play – Two strokes for each hole at which any breach occurred; maximum penalty per round – Four strokes (two strokes at each of the first two holes at which any breach occurred).

Match play or stroke play – If a breach is discovered between the play of two holes, it is deemed to have been discovered during play of the next hole, and the penalty must be applied accordingly.

Bogey and par competitions – See Note 1 to Rule 32-1a.

Stableford competitions – See Note 1 to Rule 32-1b.

*Any club or clubs carried in breach of this condition must be declared out of play by the player to his opponent in match play or his marker or a fellow-competitor in stroke play immediately upon discovery that a breach has occurred. If the player fails to do so, he is disqualified.

PENALTY FOR MAKING STROKE WITH CLUB IN BREACH OF CONDITION:
Disqualification."

b. List of Conforming Golf Balls

On its website (www.randa.org) the *R&A* periodically issues a List of Conforming Golf Balls that lists balls that have been tested and found to conform with the Rules of Golf. If the *Committee* wishes to require players to play a model of golf ball on the List, the List should be made available and the following condition of competition used:

"The ball the player plays must be named on the current List of Conforming Golf Balls issued by the R&A.

PENALTY FOR BREACH OF CONDITION:
Disqualification."

c. One Ball Condition

If it is desired to prohibit changing brands and models of golf balls during a *stipulated round*, the following condition is recommended:

"Limitation on Balls Used During Round: (Note to Rule 5-1)

(i) "One Ball" Condition

During a stipulated round, the balls a player plays must be of the same brand and model as detailed by a single entry on the current List of Conforming Golf Balls.

Note: If a ball of a different brand and/or model is dropped or placed it may be lifted, without penalty, and the player must then proceed by dropping or placing a proper ball (Rule 20-6).

PENALTY FOR BREACH OF CONDITION:

Match play – At the conclusion of the hole at which the breach is discovered, the state of the match is adjusted by deducting one hole for each hole at which a breach occurred; maximum deduction per round – Two holes.

Stroke play – Two strokes for each hole at which any breach occurred; maximum penalty per round – Four strokes (two strokes at each of the first two holes at which any breach occurred).

Bogey and Par competitions – See Note 1 to Rule 32-1a.

Stableford competitions – See Note 1 to Rule 32-1b.

(ii) Procedure When Breach Discovered

When a player discovers that he has played a ball in breach of this condition, he must abandon that ball before playing from the next teeing ground and complete the round with a proper ball; otherwise, the player is disqualified. If discovery is made during play of a hole and the player elects to substitute a proper ball before completing that hole, the player must place a proper ball on the spot where the ball played in breach of the condition lay."

2. Caddie (Note to Rule 6-4)

Rule 6-4 permits a player to use a *caddie*, provided he has only one *caddie* at any one time. However, there may be circumstances where a *Committee* may wish to prohibit *caddies* or restrict a player in his choice of *caddie*, e.g. professional golfer, sibling, parent, another player in the competition, etc. In such cases, the following wording is recommended:

Use of Caddie Prohibited

"A player is prohibited from using a caddie during the stipulated round."

Restriction on Who May Serve as Caddie

"A player is prohibited from having ____________ serve as his caddie during the stipulated round.

*PENALTY FOR BREACH OF CONDITION:

Match play – At the conclusion of the hole at which the breach is discovered, the state of the match is adjusted by deducting one hole for each hole at which a breach occurred; maximum deduction per round – Two holes.

Stroke play – Two strokes for each hole at which any breach occurred; maximum penalty per round – Four strokes (two strokes at each of the first two holes at which any breach occurred).

Match play or stroke play – If a breach is discovered between the play of two holes, it is deemed to have been discovered during play of the next hole, and the penalty must be applied accordingly.

Bogey and par competitions – See Note 1 to Rule 32-1a.

Stableford competitions – See Note 1 to Rule 32-1b.

*A player having a caddie in breach of this condition must immediately upon discovery that a breach has occurred ensure that he conforms with this condition for the remainder of the stipulated round. Otherwise, the player is disqualified."

3. Pace of Play (Note 2 to Rule 6-7)

The *Committee* may establish pace of play guidelines to help prevent slow play, in accordance with Note 2 to Rule 6-7.

4. Suspension of Play Due to a Dangerous Situation (Note to Rule 6-8b)

As there have been many deaths and injuries from lightning on golf courses, all clubs and sponsors of golf competitions are urged to take precautions for the protection of persons against lightning. Attention is called to Rules 6-8 and 33-2d. If the *Committee* desires to adopt the condition in the Note under Rule 6-8b, the following wording is recommended:

"When play is suspended by the Committee for a dangerous situation, if the players in a match or group are between the play of two holes, they must not resume play until the Committee has ordered a resumption of play. If they are in the process of playing a hole, they must discontinue play immediately and not resume play until the Committee has ordered a resumption of play. If a player fails to discontinue play immediately, he is disqualified, unless circumstances warrant waiving the penalty as provided in Rule 33-7.

The signal for suspending play due to a dangerous situation will be a prolonged note of the siren."

The following signals are generally used and it is recommended that all *Committees* do similarly:

Discontinue Play Immediately: One prolonged note of siren.

Discontinue Play: Three consecutive notes of siren, repeated.

Resume Play: Two short notes of siren, repeated.

5. Practice

a. General

The *Committee* may make regulations governing practice in accordance with the Note to Rule 7-1, Exception (c) to Rule 7-2, Note 2 to Rule 7 and Rule 33-2c.

b. Practice Between Holes (Note 2 to Rule 7)

If the *Committee* wishes to act in accordance with Note 2 to Rule 7-2, the following wording is recommended:

"Between the play of two holes, a player must not make any practice stroke on or near the putting green of the hole last played and must not test the surface of the putting green of the hole last played by rolling a ball.

PENALTY FOR BREACH OF CONDITION:
Match play – Loss of next hole.
Stroke play – Two strokes at the next hole.
Match play or stroke play – In the case of a breach at the last hole of the stipulated round, the player incurs the penalty at that hole."

6. Advice in Team Competitions (Note to Rule 8)

If the *Committee* wishes to act in accordance with the Note under Rule 8, the following wording is recommended:

"In accordance with the Note to Rule 8 of the Rules of Golf, each team may appoint one person (in addition to the persons from whom advice may be asked under that Rule) who may give advice to members of that team. Such person (if it is desired to insert any restriction on who may be nominated insert such restriction here) must be identified to the Committee before giving advice."

7. New Holes (Note to Rule 33-2b)

The *Committee* may provide, in accordance with the Note to Rule 33-2b, that the *holes* and *teeing grounds* for a single round of a competition being held on more than one day may be differently situated on each day.

8. Transportation

If it is desired to require players to walk in a competition, the following condition is recommended:

"Players must not ride on any form of transportation during a stipulated round unless authorised by the Committee.

*PENALTY FOR BREACH OF CONDITION:
Match play – At the conclusion of the hole at which the breach is discovered, the state of the match is adjusted by deducting one hole for each hole at which a breach occurred; maximum deduction per round – Two holes.
Stroke play – Two strokes for each hole at which any breach occurred; maximum penalty per round – Four strokes (two strokes at each of the first two holes at which any breach occurred).
Match play or stroke play – If a breach is discovered between the play of two holes, it is deemed to have been discovered during play of the next hole, and the penalty must be applied accordingly.
Bogey and par competitions – See Note 1 to Rule 32-1a.
Stableford competitions – See Note 1 to Rule 32-1b.

*Use of any unauthorised form of transportation must be discontinued immediately upon discovery that a breach has occurred. Otherwise, the player is disqualified."

9. Anti-Doping

The *Committee* may require, in the conditions of competition, that players comply with an anti-doping policy.

10. How to Decide Ties

In both match play and stroke play, a tie can be an acceptable result. However, when it is desired to have a sole winner, the *Committee* has the authority, under Rule 33-6, to determine how and when a tie is decided. The decision should be published in advance.

The *R&A* recommends:

Match Play

A match that ends all square should be played off hole by hole until one side wins a hole. The play-off should start on the hole where the match began. In a handicap match, handicap strokes should be allowed as in the stipulated round.

Stroke Play

(a) In the event of a tie in a scratch stroke play competition, a play-off is recommended. The play-off may be over 18 holes or a smaller number of holes as specified by the Committee. If that is not feasible or there is still a tie, a hole-by-hole play-off is recommended.

(b) In the event of a tie in a handicap stroke play competition, a play-off with handicaps is recommended. The play-off may be over 18 holes or a smaller number of holes as specified by the Committee. It is recommended that any such play-off consist of at least three holes.

In competitions where the handicap stroke allocation table is not relevant, if the play-off is less than 18 holes, the percentage of 18 holes played should be applied to the players' handicaps to determine their play-off handicaps. Handicap stroke fractions of one half stroke or more should count as a full stroke and any lesser fraction should be disregarded.

In competitions where the handicap stroke table is relevant, such as four-ball stroke play and bogey, par and Stableford competitions, handicap strokes should be taken as they were assigned for the competition using the players' respective stroke allocation table(s).

(c) If a play-off of any type is not feasible, matching score cards is recommended. The method of matching cards should be announced in advance and should also provide what will happen if this procedure does not produce a winner. An acceptable method of matching cards is to determine the winner on the basis of the best score for the last nine holes. If the tying players have the same score for the last nine, determine the winner on the basis of the last six holes, last three holes and finally the 18th hole. If this method is used in a competition with a multiple tee start, it is recommended that the "last nine holes, last six holes, etc." is considered to be holes 10-18, 13-18, etc.

For competitions where the handicap stroke table is not relevant, such as individual stroke play, if the last nine, last six, last three holes scenario is used, one-half, one-third, one-sixth, etc. of the handicaps should be deducted from the score for those holes. In terms of the use of fractions in such deductions, the Committee should act in accordance with the recommendations of the relevant handicapping authority.

In competitions where the handicap stroke table is relevant, such as four-ball stroke play and bogey, par and Stableford competitions, handicap strokes should be taken as they were assigned for the competition, using the players' respective stroke allocation table(s).

11. Draw for Match Play

Although the draw for match play may be completely blind or certain players may be distributed through different quarters or eighths, the General Numerical Draw is recommended if matches are determined by a qualifying round.

General Numerical Draw

For purposes of determining places in the draw, ties in qualifying rounds other than those for the last qualifying place are decided by the order in which scores are returned, with the first score to be returned receiving the lowest available number, etc. If it is impossible to determine the order in which scores are returned, ties are determined by a blind draw.

UPPER HALF	LOWER HALF
64 QUALIFIERS	
1 vs. 64	2 vs. 63
32 vs. 33	31 vs. 34
16 vs. 49	15 vs. 50
17 vs. 48	18 vs. 47
8 vs. 57	7 vs. 58
25 vs. 40	26 vs. 39
9 vs. 56	10 vs. 55
24 vs. 41	23 vs. 42
4 vs. 61	3 vs. 62
29 vs. 36	30 vs. 35
13 vs. 52	14 vs. 51
20 vs. 45	19 vs. 46
5 vs. 60	6 vs. 59
28 vs. 37	27 vs. 38
12 vs. 53	11 vs. 54
21 vs. 44	22 vs. 43
32 QUALIFIERS	
1 vs. 32	2 vs. 31
16 vs. 17	15 vs. 18
8 vs. 25	7 vs. 26
9 vs. 24	10 vs. 23
4 vs. 29	3 vs. 30
13 vs. 20	14 vs. 19
5 vs. 28	6 vs. 27
12 vs. 21	11 vs. 22
16 QUALIFIERS	
1 vs. 16	2 vs.15
8 vs. 9	7 vs.10
4 vs. 13	3 vs.14
8 QUALIFIERS	
1 vs. 8	2 vs. 7
4 vs. 5	3 vs. 6

Appendices II, III and IV

Definitions

All defined terms are in italics and are listed alphabetically in the Definitions section – see pages 592–595.

The R&A reserves the right, at any time, to change the Rules relating to clubs, balls, devices and other equipment and make or change the interpretations relating to these Rules. For up to date information, please contact the R&A or refer to www.randa.org/equipmentrules.

Any design in a club, ball, device or other equipment that is not covered by the Rules, which is contrary to the purpose and intent of the Rules or that might significantly change the nature of the game, will be ruled on by the R&A.

The dimensions and limits contained in Appendices II, III and IV are given in the units by which conformance is determined. An equivalent imperial/metric conversion is also referenced for information, calculated using a conversion rate of 1 inch = 25.4 mm.

Appendix II – Design of Clubs

A player in doubt as to the conformity of a club should consult the *R&A*.

A manufacturer should submit to the *R&A* a sample of a club to be manufactured for a ruling as to whether the club conforms with the Rules.

The sample becomes the property of the *R&A* for reference purposes. If a manufacturer fails to submit a sample or, having submitted a sample, fails to await a ruling before manufacturing and/or marketing the club, the manufacturer assumes the risk of a ruling that the club does not conform with the Rules.

The following paragraphs prescribe general regulations for the design of clubs, together with specifications and interpretations. Further information relating to these regulations and their proper interpretation is provided in "A Guide to the Rules on Clubs and Balls".

Where a club, or part of a club, is required to meet a specification within the Rules, it must be designed and manufactured with the intention of meeting that specification.

1. Clubs

a. General

A club is an implement designed to be used for striking the ball and generally comes in three forms: woods, irons and putters distinguished by shape and intended use. A putter is a club with a loft not exceeding ten degrees designed primarily for use on the *putting green*.

The club must not be substantially different from the traditional and customary form and make. The club must be composed of a shaft and a head and it may also have material added to the shaft to enable the player to obtain a firm hold (see 3 below). All parts of the club must be fixed so that the club is one unit, and it must have no external attachments. Exceptions may be made for attachments that do not affect the performance of the club.

b. Adjustability

All clubs may incorporate features for weight adjustment. Other forms of adjustability may also be permitted upon evaluation by the *R&A*. The following requirements apply to all permissible methods of adjustment:

(i) the adjustment cannot be readily made;

(ii) all adjustable parts are firmly fixed and there is no reasonable likelihood of them working loose during a round; and

(iii) all configurations of adjustment conform with the *Rules*.

During a *stipulated round*, the playing characteristics of a club must not be purposely changed by adjustment or by any other means (see Rule 4-2a).

c. Length

The overall length of the club must be at least 18 inches (0.457 m) and, except for putters, must not exceed 48 inches (1.219 m).

For woods and irons, the measurement of length is taken when the club is lying on a horizontal plane and the sole is set against a 60 degree plane as shown in Fig. I. The length is defined as the distance from the point of the intersection between the two planes to the top of the grip. For putters, the measurement of length is taken from the top of the grip along the axis of the shaft or a straight line extension of it to the sole of the club.

d. Alignment

When the club is in its normal address position the shaft must be so aligned so that:

(i) the projection of the straight part of the shaft on to the vertical plane through the toe and heel must diverge from the vertical by at least 10 degrees (see Fig. II). If the overall design of the club is such that the player can effectively use the club in a vertical or close-to-vertical position, the shaft may be required to diverge from the vertical in this plane by as much as 25 degrees;

(ii) the projection of the straight part of the shaft on to the vertical plane along the intended *line of play* must not diverge from the vertical by more than 20 degrees forwards or 10 degrees backwards (see Fig. III).

Except for putters, all of the heel portion of the club must lie within 0.625 inches (15.88 mm) of the plane containing the axis of the straight part of the shaft and the intended (horizontal) *line of play* (see Fig. IV).

2. Shaft

a. Straightness

The shaft must be straight from the top of the grip to a point not more than 5 inches (127 mm) above the sole, measured from the point where the shaft ceases to be straight along the axis of the bent part of the shaft and the neck and/or socket (see Fig. V).

b. Bending and Twisting Properties

At any point along its length, the shaft must:

(i) bend in such a way that the deflection is the same regardless of how the shaft is rotated about its longitudinal axis; and

(ii) twist the same amount in both directions.

c. Attachment to Clubhead

The shaft must be attached to the clubhead at the heel either directly or through a single plain neck and/or socket. The length from the top of the neck and/or socket to the sole of the club must not exceed 5 inches (127 mm), measured along the axis of, and following any bend in, the neck and/or socket (see Fig. VI).

Exception for Putters: The shaft or neck or socket of a putter may be fixed at any point in the head.

3. Grip (see Fig. VII)

The grip consists of material added to the shaft to enable the player to obtain a firm hold. The grip must be fixed to the shaft, must be straight and plain in form, must extend to the end of the shaft and must not be moulded for any part of the hands. If no material is added, that portion of the shaft designed to be held by the player must be considered the grip.

(i) For clubs other than putters the grip must Fig. VII be circular in cross-section, except that a Circular cross-section continuous, straight, Non-circular slightly raised rib may be incorporated along the cross-section (putters only) full length of the grip, and a slightly indented spiral is permitted on a wrapped grip or a replica of one.

(ii) A putter grip may have a non-circular cross-section, provided the cross-section has no concavity, is symmetrical and remains generally similar Waist throughout the length of (not permitted) the grip. (See Clause (v) overleaf). Bulge (not permitted)

(iii) The grip may be tapered but must not have any bulge or waist. Its cross-sectional dimensions measured in any direction must not exceed 1.75 inches (44.45 mm).

(iv) For clubs other than putters the axis of the grip must coincide with the axis of the shaft.

(v) A putter may have two grips provided each is circular in cross-section, the axis of each coincides with the axis of the shaft, and they are separated by at least 1.5 inches (38.1 mm).

4. Clubhead

a. Plain in Shape

The clubhead must be generally plain in shape. All parts must be rigid, structural in nature and functional. The clubhead or its parts must not be designed to resemble any other object. It is not practicable to define plain in shape precisely and comprehensively. However, features that are deemed to be in breach of this requirement and are therefore not permitted include, but are not limited to:

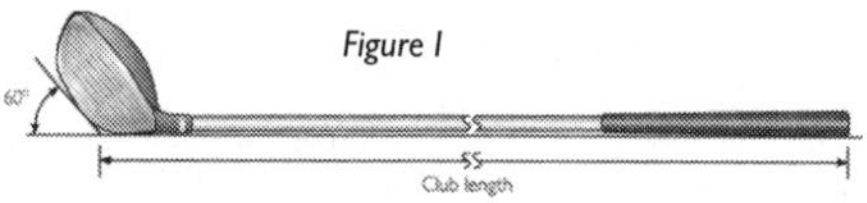

Figure I

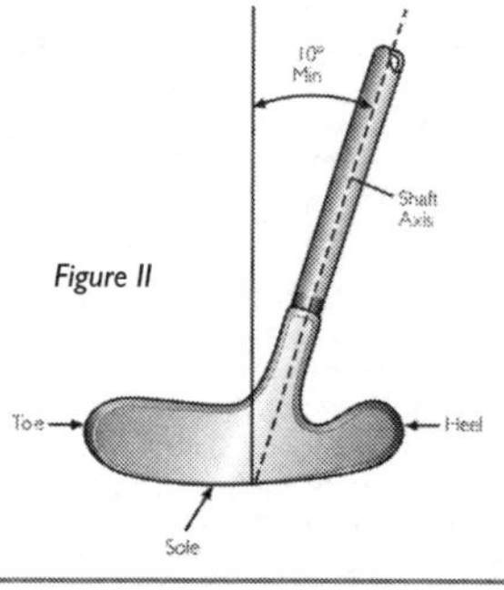

Figure II

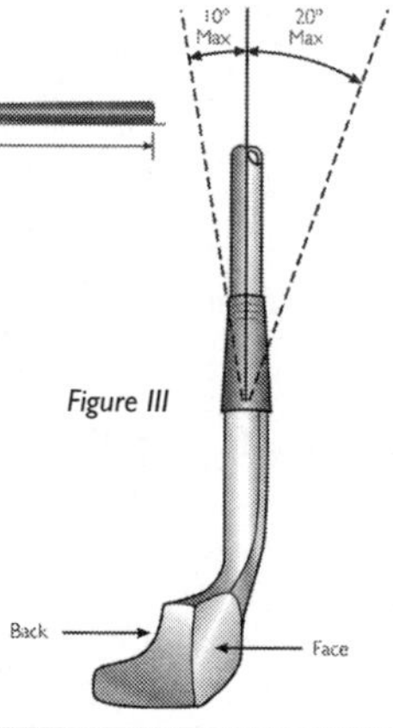

Figure III

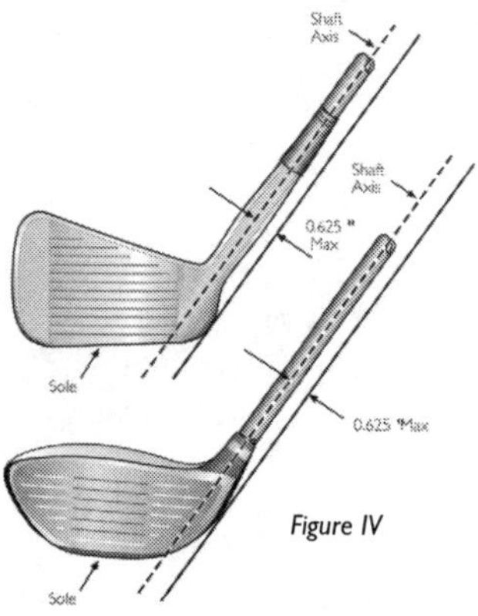

Figure IV

(i) All Clubs

- holes through the ace;
- holes through the head (some exceptions may be made for putters and cavity back irons);
- features that are for the purpose of meeting dimensional specifications;
- features that extend into or ahead of the face;
- features that extend significantly above the top line of the head;
- furrows in or runners on the head that extend into the face (some exceptions may be made for putters); and
- optical or electronic devices.

(ii) Woods and Irons

- all features listed in (i) above;
- cavities in the outline of the heel and/or the toe of the head that can be viewed from above;
- severe or multiple cavities in the outline of the back of the head that can be viewed from above;
- transparent material added to the head with the intention of rendering conforming a feature that is not otherwise permitted; and
- features that extend beyond the outline of the head when viewed from above.

b. Dimensions, Volume and Moment of Inertia

(i) Woods

When the club is in a 60 degree lie angle, the dimensions of the clubhead must be such that:

- the distance from the heel to the toe of the clubhead is greater than the distance from the face to the back;
- the distance from the heel to the toe of the clubhead is not greater than 5 inches (127 mm); and
- the distance from the sole to the crown of the clubhead, including any permitted features, is not greater than 2.8 inches (71.12 mm).

These dimensions are measured on horizontal lines between vertical projections of the outermost points of:

- the heel and the toe; and
- the face and the back (see Fig. VIII, dimension A);

and on vertical lines between the horizontal projections of the outermost points of the sole and the crown (see Fig. VIII, dimension B). If the outermost point of the heel is not clearly defined, it is deemed to be 0.875 inches (22.23 mm) above the horizontal plane on which the club is lying (see Fig. VIII, dimension C).

The volume of the clubhead must not exceed 460 cubic centimetres (28.06 cubic inches), plus a tolerance of 10 cubic centimetres (0.61 cubic inches).

When the club is in a 60 degree lie angle, the moment of inertia component around the vertical axis through the clubhead's centre of gravity must not exceed 5900 g cm^2 (32.259 oz in^2), plus a test tolerance of 100 g cm^2 (0.547 oz in^2).

(ii) Irons

When the clubhead is in its normal address position, the dimensions of the head must be such that the distance from the heel to the toe is greater than the distance from the face to the back.

(iii) Putters (see Fig. IX)

When the clubhead is in its normal address position, the dimensions of the head must be such that:

- the distance from the heel to the toe is greater than the distance from the face to the back;
- the distance from the heel to the toe of the head is less than or equal to 7 inches (177.8 mm);
- the distance from the heel to the toe of the face is greater than or equal to two thirds of the distance from the face to the back of the head;
- the distance from the heel to the toe of the face is greater than or equal to half of the distance from the heel to the toe of the head; and
- the distance from the sole to the top of the head, including any permitted features, is less than or equal to 2.5 inches (63.5 mm).

For traditionally shaped heads, these dimensions will be measured on horizontal lines between vertical projections of the outermost points of:

- the heel and the toe of the head;
- the heel and the toe of the face; and
- the face and the back;

and on vertical lines between the horizontal projections of the outermost points of the sole and the top of the head.

For unusually shaped heads, the toe to heel dimension may be made at the face.

c. Spring Effect and Dynamic Properties

The design, material and/or construction of, or any treatment to, the clubhead (which includes the club face) must not:

(i) have the effect of a spring which exceeds the limit set forth in the Pendulum Test Protocol on file with the *R&A*; or

(ii) incorporate features or technology including, but not limited to, separate springs or spring features, that have the intent of, or the effect of, unduly influencing the clubhead's spring effect; or

(iii) unduly influence the movement of the ball.

Note: (i) above does not apply to putters.

d. Striking Faces

The clubhead must have only one striking face, except that a putter may have two such faces if their characteristics are the same, and they are opposite each other.

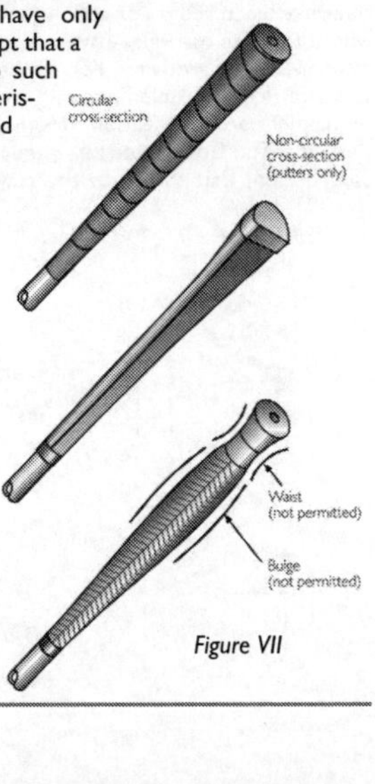

Figure VII

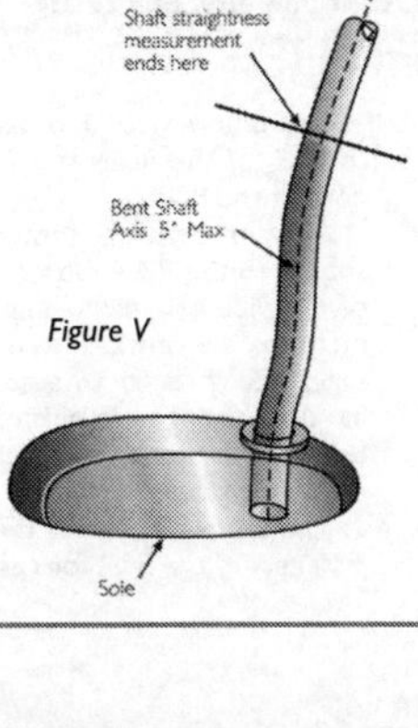

Figure V

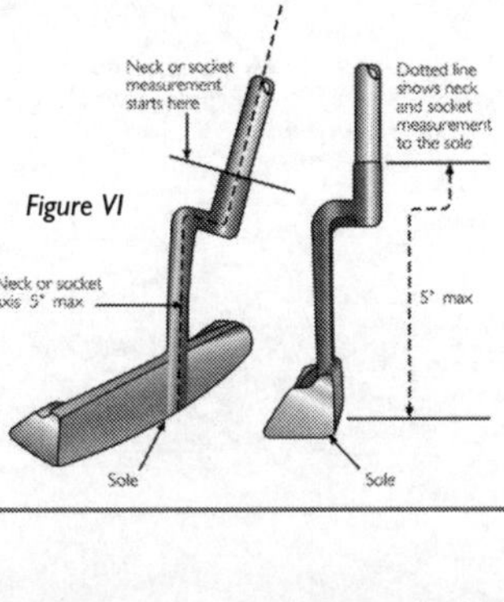

Figure VI

5. Club Face

a. General

The face of the club must be hard and rigid and must not impart significantly more or less spin to the ball than a standard steel face (some exceptions may be made for putters). Except for such markings listed below, the club face must be smooth and must not have any degree of concavity.

b. Impact Area Roughness and Material

Except for markings specified in the following paragraphs, the surface roughness within the area where impact is intended (the "impact area") must not exceed that of decorative sandblasting, Illustrative or of fine milling (see Fig. X).

The whole of the impact area must be of the same material (exceptions may be made for clubheads made of wood).

c. Impact Area Markings

If a club has grooves and/or punch marks in the impact area they must meet the following specifications:

(i) Grooves

- Grooves must be straight and parallel.
- Grooves must have a symmetrical cross-section and have sides which do not converge (see Fig. XI).
- *For clubs that have a loft angle greater than or equal to 25 degrees, grooves must have a plain cross-section.
- The width, spacing and cross-section of the grooves must be consistent throughout the impact area (some exceptions may be made for woods).
- The width (W) of each groove must not exceed 0.035 inches (0.9 mm), using the 30 degree method of measurement on file with the *R&A*.
- The depth of any punch mark must not exceed 0.040 inches (1.02 mm).
- Punch marks must not have sharp edges or raised lips.
- *For clubs that have a loft angle greater than or equal to 25 degrees, punch mark edges must be substantially in the form of a round having an effective radius which is not less than 0.010 inches (0.254 mm) when measured as shown in Figure XIII, and not greater than 0.020 inches (0.508 mm). Deviations in effective radius within 0.001 inches (0.0254 mm) are permissible.

Note 1: The groove and punch mark specifications above indicated by an asterisk (*) apply only to new models of clubs manufactured on or after 1 January 2010 and any club where the face markings have been purposely altered, for example, by re-grooving. For further information on the status of clubs available before 1 January 2010, refer to the "Equipment Search" section of www.randa.org.

Note 2: The Committee may require, in the conditions of competition, that the clubs the player carries must conform to the groove and punch mark specification above indicated by an asterisk (*). This condition is recommended only for competitions involving expert players. For further information, refer to Decision 4-1/1 in "Decisions on the Rules of Golf".

d. Decorative Markings

The centre of the impact area may be indicated by a design within the boundary of a square whose sides are 0.375 inches (9.53 mm) in length. Such a design must not unduly influence the movement of the ball. Decorative markings are permitted outside the impact area.

e. Non-Metallic Club Face Markings

The above specifications do not apply to clubheads made of wood on which the impact area of the face is of a material of hardness less than the hardness of metal and whose loft angle is 24 degrees or less, but markings which could unduly influence the movement of the ball are prohibited.

f. Putter Face Markings

Any markings on the face of a putter must not have sharp edges or raised lips. The specifications with regard to roughness, material and markings in the impact area do not apply.

Appendix III – The Ball

1. General

The ball must not be substantially different from the traditional and customary form and make. The material and construction of the ball must not be contrary to the purpose and intent of the *Rules*.

2. Weight

The weight of the ball must not be greater than 1.620 ounces avoirdupois (45.93 g).

3. Size

The diameter of the ball must not be less than 1.680 inches (42.67mm).

4. Spherical Symmetry

The ball must not be designed, manufactured or intentionally modified to have properties which differ from those of a spherically symmetrical ball.

5. Initial Velocity

The initial velocity of the ball must not exceed the limit specified under the conditions set forth in the Initial Velocity Standard for golf balls on file with the *R&A*.

6. Overall Distance Standard

The combined carry and roll of the ball, when tested on apparatus approved by the *R&A*, must not exceed the distance specified under the conditions set forth in the Overall Distance Standard for golf balls on file with the *R&A*.

Appendix IV – Devices and Other Equipment

A player in doubt as to whether use of a device or other equipment would constitute a breach of the *Rules* should consult the *R&A*.

A manufacturer should submit to the *R&A* a sample of a device or other equipment to be manufactured for a ruling as to whether its use during a *stipulated round* would cause a player to be in breach of Rule 14-3. The sample becomes the property of the *R&A* for ref-

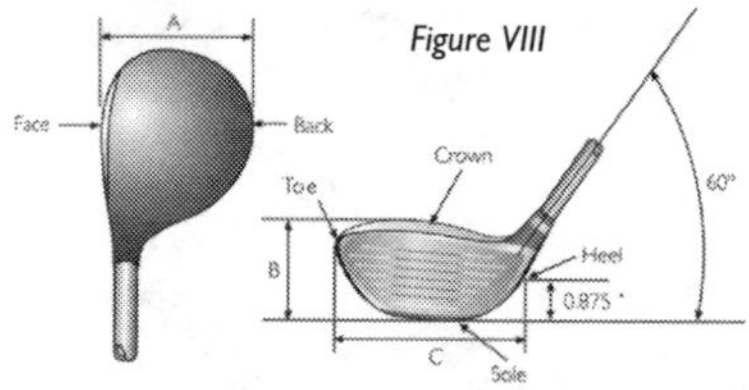

Figure VIII

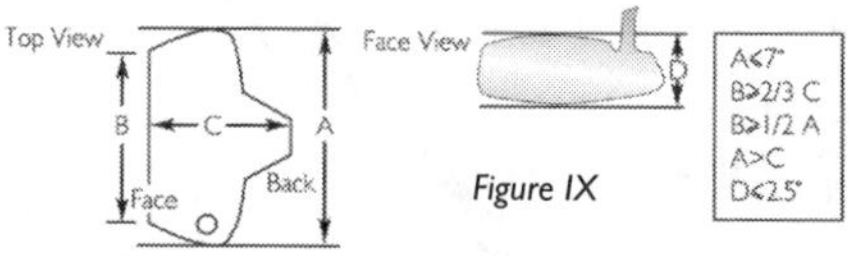

Figure IX

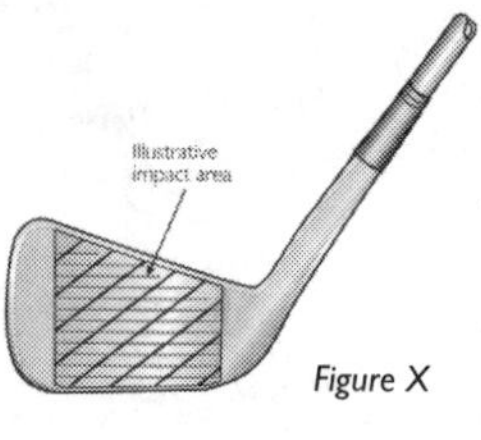

Figure X

erence purposes. If a manufacturer fails to submit a sample or, having submitted a sample, fails to await a ruling before manufacturing and/or marketing the device or other equipment, the manufacturer assumes the risk of a ruling that use of the device or other equipment would be contrary to the *Rules*.

The following paragraphs prescribe general regulations for the design of devices and other equipment, together with specifications and interpretations. They should be read in conjunction with Rule 11-1 (Teeing) and Rule 14-3 (Artificial Devices, Unusual Equipment and Unusual Use of Equipment).

1. Tees (Rule 11)

A tee is a device designed to raise the ball off the ground. A tee must not:

- be longer than 4 inches (101.6 mm);
- be designed or manufactured in such a way that it could indicate *line of play*;
- unduly influence the movement of the ball; or
- otherwise assist the player in making a *stroke* or in his play.

2. Gloves (Rule 14-3)

Gloves may be worn to assist the player in gripping the club, provided they are plain.

A "plain" glove must:

- consist of a fitted covering of the hand with a separate sheath or opening for each digit (fingers and thumb); and
- be made of smooth materials on the full palm and gripping surface of the digits.

A "plain" glove must not incorporate:

- material on the gripping surface or inside of the glove, the primary purpose of which is to provide padding or which has the effect of providing padding. Padding is defined as an area of glove material which is more than 0.025 inches (0.635 mm) thicker than the adjacent areas of the glove without the added material;

Note: Material may be added for wear resistance, moisture absorption or other functional purposes, provided it does not exceed the definition of padding (see above).

- straps to assist in preventing the club from slipping or to attach the hand to the club;
- any means of binding digits together;
- material on the glove that adheres to material on the grip;
- features, other than visual aids, designed to assist the player in placing his hands in a consistent and/or specific position on the grip;
- weight to assist the player in making a *stroke*;
- any feature that might restrict the movement of a joint; or
- any other feature that might assist the player in making a *stroke* or in his play.

3. Shoes (Rule 14-3)

Shoes that assist the player in obtaining a firm *stance* may be worn. Subject to the conditions of competition, features such as spikes on the sole are permitted, but shoes must not incorporate features:

- designed to assist the player in taking his *stance* and/or building a *stance*;
- designed to assist the player with his alignment; or
- that might otherwise assist the player in making a *stroke* or in his play.

4. Clothing (Rule 14-3)

Articles of clothing must not incorporate features:

- designed to assist the player with his alignment; or
- that might otherwise assist the player in making a *stroke* or in his play.

5. Distance-Measuring Devices (Rule 14-3)

During a *stipulated round*, the use of any distance measuring device is not permitted unless the Committee has introduced a Local Rule to that effect (see Note to Rule 14-3 and Appendix I; Part B; Section 9).

Even when the Local Rule is in effect, the device must be limited to measuring distance only. Features that would render use of the device contrary to the Local Rule include, but are not limited to:

- the gauging or measuring of slope;
- the gauging or measuring of other conditions that might affect play (e.g. wind speed or direction, or other climate-based information such as temperature, humidity, etc.);
- recommendations that might assist the player in making a *stroke* or in his play (e.g. club selection, type of shot to be played, green reading or any other advice related matter); or
- calculating the effective distance between two points based on slope or other conditions affecting shot distance.

Such non-conforming features render use of the device contrary to the *Rules*, irrespective of whether or not:

- the features can be switched off or disengaged; and
- the features are switched off or disengaged.

A multi-functional device, such as a smartphone or PDA, may be used as a distance measuring device provided it contains a distance measuring application that meets all of the above limitations (i.e. it must measure distance only). In addition, when the distance measuring application is being used, there must be no other features or applications installed on the device that, if used, would be in breach of the *Rules*, whether or not they are actually used.

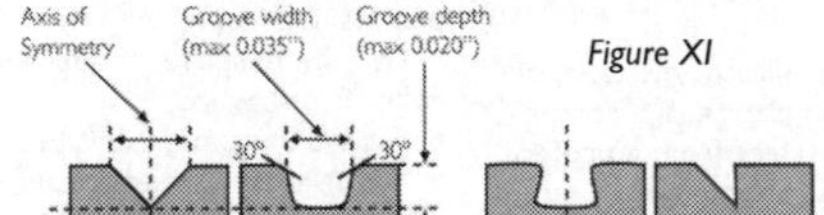

Figure XI

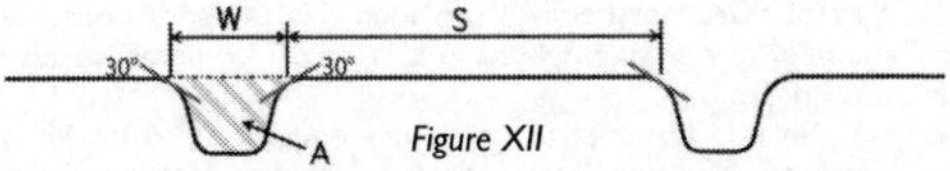

Figure XII

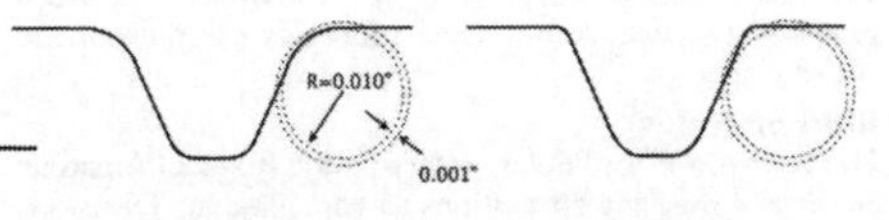

Figure XIII

RULES OF AMATEUR STATUS

As approved by R&A Rules Limited
Effective from 1st January 2012

Preamble

The *R&A* reserves the right to change the Rules of Amateur Status and to make and change the interpretations of the Rules of Amateur Status at any time. For up to date information, please contact the *R&A* or refer to www.randa.org. In the Rules of Amateur Status, the gender used in relation to any person is understood to include both genders.

Definitions

The Definitions are listed alphabetically and, in the *Rules* themselves, defined terms are in *italics*.

Amateur Golfer

An "*amateur golfer*", whether he plays competitively or recreationally, is one who plays golf for the challenge it presents, not as a profession and not for financial gain.

Committee

The "*Committee*" is the appropriate *Committee* of the *Governing Body*.

Golf Skill or Reputation

It is a matter for the *Governing Body* to decide whether a particular *amateur golfer* has *golf skill or reputation*.

Generally, an *amateur golfer* is only considered to have *golf skill* if he:

(a) has had competitive success at regional or national level or has been selected to represent his national, regional, state or county golf union or association; or
(b) competes at an elite level.

Golf reputation can only be gained through *golf skill* and such *reputation* is deemed to continue for five years after that player's *golf skill* has fallen below the standard set by the *Governing Body*.

Governing Body

The "*Governing Body*" for the administration of the Rules of Amateur Status in any country is the national golf union or association of that country.

Note: In Great Britain and Ireland, the *R&A* is the *Governing Body*.

Instruction

"*Instruction*" covers teaching the physical aspects of playing golf, i.e. the actual mechanics of swinging a golf club and hitting a golf ball.

Note: Instruction does not cover teaching the psychological aspects of the game or the etiquette or Rules of Golf.

Junior Golfer

A "*junior golfer*" is an *amateur golfer* who has not reached a specified age as determined by the *Governing Body*.

Prize Voucher

A "*prize voucher*" is a voucher, gift certificate, gift card, or the like approved by the Committee in charge of a competition for the purchase of goods or services from a professional's shop, a golf club or other retail source.

R&A

The "*R&A*" means R&A Rules Limited.

Retail Value

The "*retail value*" of a prize is the price at which the prize is generally available from a retail source at the time of the award.

Rule or Rules

The term "*Rule*" or "*Rules*" refers to the Rules of Amateur Status and their interpretations as contained in "Decisions on the Rules of Amateur Status".

Symbolic Prize

A "*symbolic prize*" is a trophy made of gold, silver, ceramic, glass or the like that is permanently and distinctively engraved.

Testimonial Award

A "*testimonial award*" is an award for notable performances or contributions to golf as distinguished from competition prizes. A *testimonial award* may not be a monetary award.

USGA

The "*USGA*" means the United States Golf Association.

Rule 1 – Amateurism

1-1. General

An amateur golfer must play the game and conduct himself in accordance with the Rules.

1-2. Amateur Status

Amateur Status is a universal condition of eligibility for playing in golf competitions as an *amateur golfer*. A person who acts contrary to the *Rules* may forfeit his amateur status and as a result will be ineligible to play in amateur competitions.

1-3. Purpose of the Rules

The purpose of the *Rules* is to maintain the distinction between amateur and professional golf and to ensure that amateur golf, which is largely self-regulating with regard to the Rules of Golf and handicapping, is free from the pressures that may follow from uncontrolled sponsorship and financial incentive.

Through appropriate limits and restrictions, the *Rules* are also intended to encourage amateur golfers to focus on the game's challenges and inherent rewards, rather than any financial gain.

1-4. Doubt as to Rules

A person who is in doubt as to whether taking a proposed course of action is permitted under the *Rules* should consult the *Governing Body*.

An organiser or sponsor of an amateur golf competition or a competition involving *amateur golfers* who is in doubt as to whether a proposal is in accordance with the *Rules* should consult the *Governing Body*.

Rule 2 – Professionalism

2-1. General

An amateur golfer must not conduct or identify himself as a professional golfer.

For the purpose of applying these *Rules*, a professional golfer is one who:

- plays the game as his profession; or
- works as a professional golfer; or
- enters a golf competition as a professional; or
- holds or retains membership of any Professional Golfers' Association (PGA); or
- holds or retains membership of a Professional Tour limited exclusively to professional golfers.

Exception: An *amateur golfer* may hold or retain a category of PGA membership, provided this category does not confer any playing rights and it is purely for administrative purposes.

Note 1: An *amateur golfer* may enquire as to his likely prospects as a professional golfer, including applying unsuccessfully for the position of a professional golfer, and he may work in a professional's shop and receive payment or compensation, provided he does not infringe the *Rules* in any other way.

Note 2: If an *amateur golfer* must compete in one or more qualifying competitions in order to be eligible for membership of a Professional Tour, he may enter and play in such qualifying competitions without forfeiting his Amateur Status, provided, in advance of play and in writing, he waives his right to any prize money in the competition.

2-2. Contracts and Agreements

(a) National Golf Unions or Associations

An *amateur golfer* may enter into a contract and/or an agreement with his national golf union or association, provided that he does not obtain payment, compensation or any financial gain, directly or indirectly, whilst still an *amateur golfer*, except as otherwise provided in the *Rules*.

(b) Professional Agents, Sponsors and Other Third Parties

An *amateur golfer* may enter into a contract and/or an agreement with a third party (including but not limited to a professional agent or a sponsor), provided:

(i) the golfer is at least 18 years of age,

(ii) the contract or agreement is solely in relation to the golfer's future as a professional golfer and does not stipulate playing in certain amateur or professional events as an *amateur golfer*, and

(iii) except as otherwise provided in the *Rules*, the *amateur golfer* does not obtain payment, compensation or any financial gain, directly or indirectly, whilst still an *amateur golfer*.

Exception: In special individual circumstances, an *amateur golfer* under the age of 18 may apply to the *Governing Body* to be allowed to enter into such a contract, provided it is of no more than 12 months duration and it is non-renewable.

Note 1: An *amateur golfer* is advised to consult the *Governing Body* prior to signing any such third party contract and/or agreement to ensure that it complies with the *Rules*.

Note 2: If an *amateur golfer* is in receipt of an educational golf scholarship (see Rule 6-5), or may apply for such a scholarship in the future, he is advised to contact the national body regulating such scholarships and/or the relevant educational institution to ensure that any third party contracts and/ or agreements are allowable under the applicable scholarship regulations.

Rule 3 – Prizes

3-1. Playing for Prize Money

An *amateur golfer* must not play golf for prize money or its equivalent in a match, competition or exhibition.

However, an *amateur golfer* may participate in a golf match, competition or exhibition where prize money or its equivalent is offered, provided that prior to participation he waives his right to accept prize money in that event.

Exception: Where prize money is offered for a hole-in-one made while playing a round of golf, an *amateur golfer* is not required to waive his right to accept that prize money prior to participation (see Rule 3-2b).

(Conduct contrary to the purpose of the Rules – see Rule 7-2)

(Policy on gambling – see Appendix)

3-2. Prize Limits

a. General

An *amateur golfer* must not accept a prize (other than a *symbolic prize*) or *prize voucher* of *retail value* in excess of £500 or the equivalent, or such a lesser figure as may be decided by the *Governing Body*. This limit applies to the total prizes or *prize vouchers* received by an *amateur golfer* in any one competition or series of competitions.

Exception: Hole-in-one prizes – see Rule 3-2b.

Note 1: The prize limits apply to any form of golf competition, whether on a golf course, driving range or golf simulator, including nearest the hole and longest drive competitions.

Note 2: The responsibility to prove the *retail value* of a particular prize rests with the Committee in charge of the competition.

Note 3: It is recommended that the total value of prizes in a gross competition, or each division of a handicap competition, should not exceed twice the prescribed limit in an 18-hole competition, three times in a 36-hole competition, five times in a 54-hole competition and six times in a 72-hole competition.

b. Hole-in-One Prizes

An *amateur golfer* may accept a prize in excess of the limit in Rule 3-2a, including a cash prize, for a hole-in-one made while playing a round of golf.

Note: The hole-in-one must be made during a round of golf and be incidental to that round. Separate multiple-entry contests, contests conducted other than on a golf course (e.g. on a driving range or golf simulator) and putting contests do not qualify under this provision and are subject to the restrictions and limits in Rules 3-1 and 3-2a.

3-3. Testimonial Awards

a. General

An *amateur golfer* must not accept a *testimonial award* of *retail value* in excess of the limits prescribed in Rule 3-2.

b. Multiple Awards

An *amateur golfer* may accept more than one testimonial award from different donors, even though their total retail value exceeds the prescribed limit, provided they are not presented so as to evade the limit for a single award.

Rule 4 – Expenses

4-1. General

Except as provided in the Rules, an *amateur golfer* must not accept expenses, in money or otherwise, from any source to play in a golf competition or exhibition.

4-2. Receipt of Competition Expenses

An *amateur golfer* may receive reasonable competition expenses, not exceeding the actual expenses incurred, to play in a golf competition or exhibition as prescribed in clauses a-g of this Rule.

If an *amateur golfer* is in receipt of an educational golf scholarship (see Rule 6-5), or may apply for such a scholarship in the future, he is advised to contact the national body regulating such scholarships and/or the relevant educational institution to ensure that any competition expenses are allowable under the applicable scholarship regulations.

a. Family Support

An *amateur golfer* may receive expenses from a member of his family or a legal guardian.

b. Junior Golfers

A *junior golfer* may receive expenses when competing in a competition limited exclusively to *junior golfers*.

Note: If a competition is not limited exclusively to *junior golfers*, a *junior golfer* may receive expenses when competing in that competition, as prescribed in Rule 4-2c.

c. Individual Events

An *amateur golfer* may receive expenses when competing in individual events provided he complies with the following provisions:

(i) Where the competition is to take place in the player's own country the expenses must be approved by and paid through the player's national, regional, state or county golf union or association, or with the approval of such body, may be paid by the player's golf club.

(ii) Where the competition is to take place in another country the expenses must be approved by and paid through the player's national, regional, state or county golf union or association or, subject to the approval of the player's national union or association, paid by the body controlling golf in the territory in which he is competing.

The *Governing Body* may limit the receipt of expenses to a specific number of competitive days in any one calendar year and an *amateur golfer* must not exceed any such limit. In such a case, the expenses are deemed to include reasonable travel time and practice days in connection with the competitive days.

Exception: An *amateur golfer* must not receive expenses, directly or indirectly, from a professional agent (see Rule 2-2) or any other similar source as may be determined by the *Governing Body*.

Note: Except as provided in the *Rules*, an *amateur golfer* of *golf skill or reputation* must not promote or advertise the source of any expenses received (see Rule 6-2).

d. Team Events

An *amateur golfer*, may receive expenses when he is representing:

- his country,
- his regional, state or county golf union or association,
- his golf club,
- his business or industry, or
- a similar body

in a team competition, practice session or training camp.

Note 1: A "similar body" includes a recognised educational institution or military service.

Note 2: Unless otherwise stated, the expenses must be paid by the body that the *amateur golfer* is representing or the body controlling golf in the country in which he is competing.

e. Invitation Unrelated to Golf Skill

An *amateur golfer* who is invited for reasons unrelated to *golf skill* (e.g. a celebrity, a business associate or customer) to take part in a golf event may receive expenses.

f. Exhibitions

An *amateur golfer* who is participating in an exhibition in aid of a recognised charity may receive expenses, provided that the exhibition is not run in connection with another golfing event in which the player is competing.

g. Sponsored Handicap Competitions

An *amateur golfer* may receive expenses when competing in a sponsored handicap competition, provided the competition has been approved as follows:

(i) Where the competition is to take place in the player's own country, the annual approval of the *Governing Body* must first be obtained in advance by the sponsor; and

(ii) Where the competition is to take place in more than one country or involves golfers from another country, the annual approval of each *Governing Body* must first be obtained in advance by the sponsor. The application for this approval should be sent to the *Governing Body* in the country where the competition commences.

4-3. Subsistence Expenses

An *amateur golfer* may receive reasonable subsistence expenses, not exceeding actual expenses incurred, to assist with general living costs, provided the expenses are approved by and paid through the player's national golf union or association.

In determining whether such subsistence expenses are necessary and/ or appropriate, the national golf union or association, which has the sole discretion in the approval of such expenses, should consider, among other factors, applicable socio-economic conditions.

Exception: An *amateur golfer* must not receive subsistence expenses, directly or indirectly, from a professional agent (see Rule 2-2) or any other similar source as may be determined by the *Governing Body*.

Rule 5 – Instruction

5-1. General

Except as provided in the Rules, an *amateur golfer* must not receive payment or compensation, directly or indirectly, for giving golf *instruction*.

5-2. Where Payment Permitted

a. Schools, Colleges, Camps, etc.

An *amateur golfer* who is (i) an employee of an educational institution or system or (ii) a counsellor at a camp or other similar organised programme, may receive payment or compensation for golf instruction to students in the institution, system or camp, provided that the total time devoted to such instruction comprises less than 50 percent of the time spent in the performance of all duties as such an employee or counsellor.

b. Approved Programmes

An *amateur golfer* may receive expenses, payment or compensation for giving golf *instruction* as part of a programme that has been approved in advance by the *Governing Body*.

5-3. Instruction in Writing

An *amateur golfer* may receive payment or compensation for golf *instruction* in writing, provided his ability or reputation as a golfer was not a major factor in his employment or in the commission or sale of his work.

Rule 6 – Use of Golf Skill or Reputation

The following regulations under Rule 6 only apply to *amateur golfers* of *golf skill* or *reputation*.

6-1. General

Except as provided in the *Rules*, an *amateur golfer* of *golf skill* or *reputation* must not use that skill or reputation for any financial gain.

6-2. Promotion, Advertising and Sales

An *amateur golfer* of *golf skill* or *reputation* must not use that skill or reputation to obtain payment, compensation, personal benefit or any financial gain, directly or indirectly, for (i) promoting, advertising or selling anything, or (ii) allowing his name or likeness to be used by a third party for the promotion, advertisement or sale of anything.

Exception: An *amateur golfer* of *golf skill or reputation* may allow his name or likeness to be used to promote:

(a) his national, regional, state or county golf union or association; or

(b) a recognised charity (or similar good cause); or

(c) subject to the permission of his national golf union or association, any golf competition or other event that is considered to be in the best interests of, or would contribute to the development of, the game.

The *amateur golfer* must not obtain any payment, compensation or financial gain, directly or indirectly, for allowing his name or likeness to be used in these ways.

Note 1: An *amateur golfer* of *golf skill or reputation* may accept golf equipment from anyone dealing in such equipment provided no advertising is involved.

Note 2: Limited name and logo recognition is allowed on golf equipment and clothing. Further information relating to this Note and its proper interpretation is provided in "Decisions on the Rules of Amateur Status".

6-3. Personal Appearance

An *amateur golfer* of *golf skill or reputation* must not use that skill or reputation to obtain payment, compensation, personal benefit or any financial gain, directly or indirectly, for a personal appearance.

Exception: An *amateur golfer* of *golf skill or reputation* may receive actual expenses in connection with a personal appearance provided no golf competition or exhibition is involved.

6-4. Broadcasting and Writing

An *amateur golfer* of *golf skill or reputation* may receive payment, compensation, personal benefit or financial gain from broadcasting or writing provided:

(a) the broadcasting or writing is part of his primary occupation or career and golf *instruction* is not included (Rule 5); or

(b) if the broadcasting or writing is on a part-time basis, the player is actually the author of the commentary, articles or books and golf *instruction* is not included.

Note: An *amateur golfer* of *golf skill* or *reputation* must not promote or advertise anything within the commentary, article or books (see Rule 6-2).

6-5. Educational Grants, Scholarships and Bursaries

An *amateur golfer* of *golf skill* or *reputation* may accept the benefits of an educational grant, scholarship or bursary, the terms and conditions of which have been approved by the *Governing Body*.

A *Governing Body* may pre-approve the terms and conditions of educational grants, scholarships and bursaries, such as those that comply with the regulations of the National Collegiate Athletic Association (NCAA) in the United States of America, or other similar organisations governing athletes at educational institutions.

If an *amateur golfer* is in receipt of an educational golf scholarship, or may apply for such a scholarship in the future, he is advised to contact the national body regulating such scholarships and/or the relevant educational institution to ensure that any third party contracts and/or agreements (Rule 2-2b) or competition expenses (Rule 4-2) are allowable under the applicable scholarship regulations.

6-6. Membership

An *amateur golfer* of *golf skill* or *reputation* may accept an offer of membership of a Golf Club or privileges at a golf course, without full payment for the class of membership or privilege, unless such an offer is made as an inducement to play for that Club or course.

Rule 7 – Other Conduct Incompatible with Amateurism

7-1. Conduct Detrimental to Amateurism

An *amateur golfer* must not act in a manner that is detrimental to the best interests of the amateur game.

7-2. Conduct Contrary to the Purpose of the Rules

An *amateur golfer* must not take any action, including actions relating to golf gambling, that is contrary to the purpose of the *Rules*.

(Policy on gambling – see Appendix)

Rule 8 – Procedure for Enforcement of the Rules

8-1. Decision on a Breach

If a possible breach of the *Rules* by a person claiming to be an *amateur golfer* comes to the attention of the *Committee*, it is a matter for the *Committee* to decide whether a breach has occurred. Each case will be investigated to the extent deemed appropriate by the *Committee* and considered on its merits. The decision of the *Committee* is final, subject to an appeal as provided in these *Rules*.

8-2. Enforcement

Upon a decision that a person has breached the *Rules*, the *Committee* may declare the Amateur Status of the person forfeited or require the person to refrain or desist from specified actions as a condition of retaining his Amateur Status.

The *Committee* should notify the person and may notify any interested golf
union or association of any action taken under Rule 8-2.

8-3. Appeals Procedure

Each *Governing Body* should establish a process or procedure through which any decision concerning enforcement of these *Rules* may be appealed by the person affected.

Rule 9 – Reinstatement of Amateur Status

9-1. General

The *Committee* has the sole authority to:

- reinstate to Amateur Status a professional golfer and/or other persons who have infringed the *Rules*,
- prescribe a waiting period necessary for reinstatement, or
- deny reinstatement, subject to an appeal as provided in the *Rules*.

9-2. Applications for Reinstatement

Each application for reinstatement will be considered on its merits, with consideration normally being given to the following principles:

a. Awaiting Reinstatement

Amateur and professional golf are two distinct forms of the game which provide different opportunities and neither benefits if the process of changing status from professional to amateur is too easy. Furthermore, there needs to be a deterrent against all breaches of the *Rules*. Therefore, an applicant for reinstatement to Amateur Status must undergo a period awaiting reinstatement as prescribed by the *Committee*.

The period awaiting reinstatement generally starts from the date of the person's last breach of the *Rules* unless the *Committee* decides that it starts from either (a) the date when the person's last breach became known to the *Committee*, or (b) such other date determined by the *Committee*.

b. Period Awaiting Reinstatement

(i) Professionalism

Generally, the period awaiting reinstatement is related to the period the person was in breach of the *Rules*. However, no applicant is normally eligible for reinstatement until he has conducted himself in accordance with the *Rules* for a period of at least one year.

It is recommended that the following guidelines on periods awaiting reinstatement be applied by the *Committee*:

Period of Breach	Period Awaiting Reinstatement:
under 5 years	1 year
5 years or more	2 years

However, the period may be extended if the applicant has played extensively for prize money, regardless of performance. In all cases, the *Committee* reserves the right to extend or to shorten the period awaiting reinstatement.

(ii) Other Breaches of the Rules

A period awaiting reinstatement of one year will normally be required. However, the period may be extended if the breach is considered serious.

c. Number of Reinstatements

A person is not normally eligible to be reinstated more than twice.

d. Players of National Prominence

A player of national prominence who has been in breach of the *Rules* for more than five years is not normally eligible for reinstatement.

e. Status While Awaiting Reinstatement

An applicant for reinstatement must comply with these *Rules*, as they apply to an *amateur golfer*, during his period awaiting reinstatement.

An applicant for reinstatement is not eligible to enter competitions as an *amateur golfer*. However, he may enter competitions and win a prize solely among members of a Club where he is a member, subject to the approval of the Club. He must not represent such a Club against other Clubs unless with the approval of the Clubs in the competition and/or the organising Committee.

An applicant for reinstatement may enter competitions that are not limited to *amateur golfers*, subject to the conditions of competition, without prejudicing his application, provided he does so as an applicant for reinstatement. He must waive his right to any prize money offered in the competition and must not accept any prize reserved for an *amateur golfer* (Rule 3-1).

9-3. Procedure for Applications

Each application for reinstatement must be submitted to the *Committee*, in accordance with such procedures as may be laid down and including such information as the *Committee* may require.

9-4. Appeals Procedure

Each *Governing Body* should establish a process or procedure through which any decision concerning reinstatement of Amateur Status may be appealed by the person affected.

Rule 10 – Committee Decision

10-1. Committee's Decision

The *Committee's* decision is final, subject to an appeal as provided in Rules 8-3 and 9-4.

10-2. Doubt as to Rules

If the *Committee* of a *Governing Body* considers the case to be doubtful or not covered by the *Rules*, it may, prior to making its decision, consult with the Amateur Status Committee of the R&A.

Appendix – Policy of Gambling

General

An "amateur golfer", whether he plays competitively or recreationally, is one who plays golf for the challenge it presents, not as a profession and not for financial gain.

Excessive financial incentive in amateur golf, which can result from some forms of gambling or wagering, could give rise to abuse of the *Rules* both in play and in manipulation of handicaps to the detriment of the integrity of the game.

There is a distinction between playing for prize money (Rule 3-1), gambling or wagering that is contrary to the purpose of the *Rules* (Rule 7-2), and forms of gambling or wagering that do not, of themselves, breach the *Rules*. An *amateur golfer* or a Committee in charge of a competition where *amateur golfers* are competing should consult with the *Governing Body* if in any doubt as to the application of the *Rules*. In the absence of such guidance, it is recommended that no cash prizes be awarded so as to ensure that the *Rules* are upheld.

Acceptable Forms of Gambling

There is no objection to informal gambling or wagering among individual golfers or teams of golfers when it is incidental to the game. It is not practicable to define informal gambling or wagering precisely, but features that would be consistent with such gambling or wagering include:

- the players in general know each other;
- participation in the gambling or wagering is optional and is limited to the players;
- the sole source of all money won by the players is advanced by the players; and
- the amount of money involved is not generally considered to be excessive.

Therefore, informal gambling or wagering is acceptable provided the primary purpose is the playing of the game for enjoyment, not for financial gain.

Unacceptable Forms of Gambling

Other forms of gambling or wagering where there is a requirement for players to participate (e.g. compulsory sweepstakes) or that have the potential to involve considerable sums of money (e.g. calcuttas and auction sweepstakes – where players or teams are sold by auction) are not approved.

Otherwise, it is difficult to define unacceptable forms of gambling or wagering precisely, but features that would be consistent with such gambling or wagering include:

- participation in the gambling or wagering is open to non-players; and
- the amount of money involved is generally considered to be excessive.

An *amateur golfer's* participation in gambling or wagering that is not approved may be considered contrary to the purpose of the *Rules* (Rule 7-2) and may endanger his Amateur Status.

Furthermore, organised events designed or promoted to create cash prizes are not permitted. Golfers participating in such events without first irrevocably waiving their right to prize money are deemed to be playing for prize money, in breach of Rule 3-1.

Note: The Rules of Amateur Status do not apply to betting or gambling by *amateur golfers* on the results of a competition limited to or specifically organised for professional golfers.

INDEX

The Rules of Golf are here indexed according to the pertinant rule number, definition or appendix that has gone before. Items marked with as asterisk refer to Rules of Amateur Status

The R&A and the modern game

What is The R&A?

The R&A takes its name from The Royal and Ancient Golf Club of St Andrews, which traces its origins back over 250 years. Although the golf club still exists to meet the needs of more than 2,000 international members, The R&A has grown apart to focus on its role as golf's world governance and development body and organiser of The Open Championship.

The R&A is golf's world rules and development body and organiser of The Open Championship. It operates with the consent of 141 national and international amateur and professional organisations from almost 126 countries and on behalf of an estimated 30 million golfers in Europe, Africa, Asia Pacific and the Americas.

The R&A and the United States Golf Association have jointly issued the Rules of Golf since 1952. The USGA is the governing body for the Rules of Golf in the United States and Mexico.

By making The Open Championship one of the world's great sporting events and an outstanding commercial success, The R&A is able to invest a substantial annual surplus for the development of the game through The R&A Foundation. The Foundation is the charitable body that channels money from The Open directly into grassroots development projects around the world.

Particular emphasis is placed on the encouragement of junior golf, on the development of the game in emerging golfing nations, on coaching and the provision of more accessible courses and improved practice facilities.

The R&A also provides best practice guidance on all aspects of golf course management, to help golf grow throughout the world in a commercially and environmentally sustainable way.

Useful links

www.randa.org
www.opengolf.com
www.bestcourseforgolf.org
www.wagr.randa.org
www.theroyalandancientgolfclub.org
www.britishgolfmuseum.co.uk

The future of the game

The R&A is committed to promoting and developing golf both nationally and internationally. Two factors make this possible. One is the annual surplus from The Open Championship and the other is The R&A's position of global influence. Combined, these give scope for the worldwide advancement of golf.

A major priority for The R&A is providing funding for training and the development of the game around the world. In recent years, a determined effort has been directed towards financing development in countries where golf is a relatively new sport. Major contributions are made to women's golf and the Golf Foundation receives substantial help to assist with its work of introducing young people to the game.

The R&A is highly conscious of the need and its obligation to serve the game worldwide. Since 1997 The R&A has provided financial support towards the African VI Tournament. The South American Men's and Women's Amateur Team Championship are also supported as are the equivalent events in the Asia-Pacific region.

The R&A Foundation supports university golf throughout Great Britain and Ireland with the aim of encouraging students to remain competitive while completing their formal education.

The R&A takes a lead in and offers advice on all aspects of golf course management worldwide, with developments in greenkeeping and environmental issues foremost among its concerns. Again, it is particularly concerned with offering assistance in countries where golf is still in its infancy.

Funding the future

Most of The R&A's funding comes from The Open Championship. Worldwide television rights are an important source of income, along with spectator ticket sales, catering, merchandising, corporate hospitality and sponsorship.

The Open Championship is broadcast throughout the world. Television coverage of The Open has a global household reach of 400 million and is delivered by 46 broadcasters in 193 territories. It is the world's largest annual televised sports event alongside Wimbledon.

In recent years The R&A has been at the fore front of modern technology, extending its range of activities to Digital Media rights, whereby income is generated through the internet, and mobile communication devices. These, combined with merchandising, licensing and publishing, increase the ways in which The R&A is able to provide financial assistance for the development of golf throughout the world.

In 2004, Rolex began to sponsor the publication and distribution of the Rules of Golf book, ensuring that golfers worldwide can have a copy of the current Rules of Golf free of charge. Over 4 million copies are distributed and the book is available in over 30 different languages.

Doosan, HSBC, Mercedes, Nikon and Rolex are patrons of the Open Championship. Through their association with The Open, the Patrons provide additional income for the funding of golf development projects worldwide.

The rules of the game

In almost every country where the game is played, the rules followed are those set by The R&A. The exceptions are the USA and Mexico, where the code is set by the United States Golf Association, and Canada, which is self-governing but affiliated to The R&A. There are 141 associations and unions affiliated to The R&A.

The R&A is responsible for the Rules of Golf, the rules affecting equipment standards and the Rules of Amateur Status. The Rules of Golf Committee reviews the Rules of Golf and interprets and makes decisions on the playing Rules. The Equipment Standards Committee interprets and gives decisions on those rules that deal with the form and make of golf clubs and the specifications of the ball. The Amateur Status Committee reviews, interprets and amends the Rules of Amateur Status. All work closely with the equivalent committees of the USGA.

To meet the needs of golfers worldwide the Rules of Golf are published in over 30 languages and in audio CD format. Supplementing these are the biennial decisions on the Rules of Golf. Each volume contains over 1,100 decisions. Together, these help to ensure a consistent interpretation of the Rules throughout the world. The R&A also publish modifications of the Rules for golfers with disabilities.

The Rules Department answers thousands of queries from golf clubs, associations and professional tours on the playing Rules, the equipment Rules and on the Amateur Code.

Rules education is a priority for The R&A. Each year a Referees School is held in St Andrews, and overseas Rules Schools are held on a regular basis. Since the beginning of 2001, countries visited include Argentina, Brazil, the Dominican Republic, Ecuador, Germany, Guatemala, Japan, Luxembourg, New Zealand, Poland, Russia, Singapore, South Africa, South Korea, Thailand and the United Arab Emirates. In 2010, schools were also held in Costa Rica, Columbia and Kenya.

R&A Championships

The R&A promotes, organises and controls a number of championships and matches at both national and international level. Of these events, the biggest and most prestigious is The Open Championship.

In 1920, The Royal and Ancient Golf Club took over the running of the Amateur and Open Championships. The Boys Amateur Championship followed in 1948 and the British Youths Open Championship in 1963. The British Mid-Amateur Championship replaced the Youths event in 1995 but was discontinued in 2007.

In 1969, the Club introduced the Seniors Open Amateur Championship for players aged 55 and over. In 1991, it became involved with and now organises The Senior Open Championship, in conjunction with the PGA European Seniors Tour. The Junior Open Championship, first played in 1994, came under The R&A umbrella in 2000.

The Walker Cup, which is the most famous of the international amateur matches, is played between teams from Great Britain & Ireland and the United States and is run jointly with the United States Golf Association.

The R&A also administers the St Andrews Trophy, inaugurated in 1956, and the Jacques Leglise Trophy, an event for boys. Both are played between teams from Great Britain & Ireland and the Continent of Europe. When these matches are played in Europe, they are organised by the European Golf Association.

The Great Britain and Ireland team selection for the Walker Cup and the St Andrews Trophy is undertaken by The R&A.

In 2004, The Royal and Ancient Golf Club transferred to The R&A the responsibilities and authority of the Club for all aspects of running championships and matches at national and international level.

What is the answer?

Q: Are you allowed to complete a hole if you have only been left with a tap-in?

A: There is no penalty in either stroke play or match play but in match play the opponent is entitled to ask the player who completed the hole to replace the ball and putt again.

Governing Organisations – Professional Golf

The Professional Golfers' Association (PGA)

The PGA was founded in 1901 and is the oldest PGA in the world. It has continued to develop steadily over the years; in the mid seventies major re-structuring of the Association took place with the development of two separate divisions. The administrative operation moved to The Belfry in 1977 to advance and develop the services available to club professionals, and shortly afterwards the Tournament Division established a new base at the Wentworth Club.

In 1984 it was decided that the interests of the members of each division would be best served by forming two separate organisations and on 1st January 1985 The Professional Golfers' Association and the European Tour became independent of each other.

The PGA's activities include training and further education of assistants and members and the organisation of tournaments at national level. National Headquarters is also the administrative base to accounts, marketing, media and the commercial activities of the Association.

There are seven regional headquarters located throughout Great Britain and Ireland and each region organises its own tournaments.

Classes of Membership

Class AA
Only Professionals who have a PGA Qualification; have been qualified for at least three years, and who have engaged in (at least) the minimum amount of proessional development are recognised as class 'AA'.

Class A
A class 'A' status designation is carried by PGA Professionals who have a PGA Qualification and who have either been qualified for less than three years, and/or who have not engaged in sufficient recognised professional devlopment at the time of the annual re-grading of PGA membership status.

Class TP1
Must be a current full member of either the European Tour, Ladies' European Tour, European Seniors' Tour or any tour belonging to the International Federation of PGA Tours subject to the relevant categories as defined by the Association at the time.

Class TP2
Must be a current full member of either the European Tour, Ladies' European Tour or European Seniors' Tour subject to the relevant categories as defined by the Association at the time.

Class TP3
Must be a member of the PGA Europro Tour finishing 1–80 in the immediately preceding year's Order of Merit.

Class TP4
Must be qualified as an active playing Member within PGA Tournaments where Tournament entry criteria so permit and be in the top 100 players in the preceding year home region Order of Merit.

Life Member
Must be a member of the Association who has been recommended by the Board of Directors to Special General Meeting of the Association for appointment as a Life Member and whose recommendation has been approved.

Honorary Member
Must be a member who in the opinion of the Executive Committee through their past or continuing membership and contribution to the Association justifies retaining full privileges of membership as an Honorary Member.

Inactive Member
Shall have been a member for a continuous period of 10 years and no longer engaged in a direct or commercial capacity in the golf industry.

Retired Member
Shall have been a member for a periods of at least 35 years and not be engaged in a direct or commercial capacity in the golf industry.

As well as the class 'A/AA' status, PGA Members are also differentiated through formal recognition of their previous exerience, further education, achievements, accreditation, etc. Once qualified, and with a minimum length of time served in the golf industry, a Member can submit an application to be awarded any one of four additional titles. They rank hierarchically from PGA Advanced Professional up to PGA Master Professional – as below:

Advanced Professional
Qualified members for a minimum of five years. Over a long period of time have demonstrated a strong desire to improve understanding and knowledge. Through attendance at courses, seminars and by taking qualifications related to golf, have

shown commitment and willingness to develop self. Written articles and/or delivered seminars. Recognised by peers as having a high level of skill and knowledge, or qualified through the PGA Advanced Diploma programme.

Fellow Professional
Qualified members for a minimum of eight years. Consistently demonstrated an ability to work at a very high level with contribution to: development of players at different levels and/or a very strong reputation as an ethical business person who has established an extensive business that has benefited the golfing community and/or a strong reputation in equipment technology and/or repairs, which has enhanced the reputations of golf professionals and/or has written articles/books and presented at conferences.

Advanced Fellow Professional
Qualified members for a minimum of ten years. Very strong national – possibly international reputation in one or more areas – coaching, course design, business, retail, equipment technology. Someone who has demonstrated strong leadership and has enhanced the world of golf and may have coached at the highest level or developed a programme method that has enabled ordinary players to play the game and/or designed a number of recognised golf courses and/or developed a strong golf business that has brought benefits to golf and golfers and/or innovative in the retail world with a strong sense of business ethics and/or designed/developed/improved some aspect of equipment (to include training aids or computer software) that has benefited a wide range of people in golf and/or a golf writer whose work has contributed strongly to the understanding and development of golf performance and/or a charity worker whose contribution has helped improve the lot of the disadvantaged through golf or in golf and/or written a number of books, articles and presented at prestigious conferences and seminars.

Master Professional
Qualified member for a minimum of fifteen years. Held in high national or international esteem. Made a significant contribution to the development of golf as a player, coach, administrator or course designer. Someone who has left their mark at conferences and/or through books, articles or videos.

Tel 01675 470333 *Fax* 01675 477888

The Professional Golfers' Associations of Europe

The PGAs of Europe is as an Association of National PGAs (31 European and 7 International) with a collective membership in excess of 21,000 golf professionals whose objective is to represent, promote and advise PGAs on a business-to-business basis. At all times striving to raise standards and opportunities in the education and employment of golf professionals while also representing member countries in dealing with influential bodies and governments regarding the promotion of the game and the interests of PGA professionals.

The PGAs of Europe guides the administration of the professional game throughout the continent and sometimes beyond in order to ensure excellence in the delivery of those services necessary to guarantee highly qualified, highly skilled PGA Professionals equipped to lead the advancement of the game around the world.

It is also a partner in the Ryder Cup with specific responsibility for the management of the Ryder Cup European Development Trust and is widely acknowledged as a lead body in the delivery of golf development expertise on a global basis through its collaboration the The R&A in implementing its Golf Development Programme.

The purpose of the PGAs of Europe is to:

(1) Unify and improve standards of education and qualification;
(2) Advise and assist golf professionals to achieve properly rewarded employment;
(3) Provide relevant playing opportunities;
(4) Be the central point of advice, information and support;
(5) Be a respected link with other golfing bodies throughout Europe and the rest of the world – all for the benefit of its members and the enhancement of the sport.

Tel 01675 477899 *Fax* 01675 4778980

European Tour

The European Tour offers Membership rights and playing opportunities for those players who have earned an Exempt Category on the Tour. To be eligible to become a Full Member of The European Tour for the first time a player must have either graduated from the European Challenge Tour by virtue of his performance in the previous season, gained one of the exemptions available at the annually competed European Tour Qualifying School or won a European Tour/Challenge Tour sanctioned event.

Full details are available from The Wentworth Headquarters:

Tel +44 1344 840400 *Fax* +44 1344 840500

Website www.europeantour.com

Ladies' European Tour

The Ladies European Tour was founded in 1978 to further the development of women's professional golf with a focus in Europe and its membership is open to all nationalities. A qualifying school is held annually and an amateur wishing to participate must have a handicap of 3 or less. Full details can be obtained from the Tour Headquarters at Buckinghamshire Golf Club.

Tel 01895 831028 *Fax* 01895 832301

Website www.ladieseuropeantour.com

Governing Organisations – Amateur Golf

Home Unions

The English Golf Union

The English Golf Union was founded in 1924 and embraces 35 County Unions with 1,949 affiliated clubs. Its objects are:

(1) To further the interests of Amateur Golf in England.

(2) To assist in maintaining a uniform system of handicapping.

(3) To arrange an English Championship; an English Strokeplay Championship; an English County Championship, International and other Matches and Competitions.

(4) To cooperate with The Royal and Ancient Golf Club of St Andrews and the Council of National Golf Unions.

(5) To cooperate with other National Golf Unions and Associations in such manner as may be decided.

Tel 01526 354500 *Fax* 01526 354020

The previously separate English Golf Union and English Women's Golf Association have merged and from January 2012 became one governing body entitled England Golf which will represent all amateur golfers in England. For further information, see pages 702 and 706.

The Scottish Golf Union

The Scottish Golf Union, the governing body for men's golf in Scotland, is dedicated to inspiring people to play golf and to developing and sustaining the game throughout the country. Its over-arching intention is to make golf available to everyone, in an environment that will actively encourage players to fulfil their potential.

Its aims are to:

- **Grow the game** – work with others to develop and grow golf in Scotland by increasing the number of people playing and enjoying golf.
- **Develop talent** – ensure that the pathways to develop young talent are in place to produce excellent golfers at all levels.
- **Support Clubs** – provide core services including handicapping, course rating, membership, marketing and advice on Governance and Legislation to support affiliated clubs.

The organisation is governed by a non executive board of directors who oversee the management of the organisation and an executive council, comprising representatives from 16 area associations, which provides the board with advice on policy matters.

Tel 01334 466477 *Fax* 01334 461361

Golfing Union of Ireland

The Golfing Union of Ireland, founded in 1891, embraces 430 Clubs. Its objects are:

(1) Securing the federation of the various Clubs.

(2) Arranging Amateur Championships, Inter-Provincial and Inter-Club Competitions, and International Matches.

(3) Securing a uniform standard of handicapping.

(4) Providing for advice and assistance, other than financial, to affiliated Clubs in all matters appertaining to Golf, and generally to promote the game in every way, in which this can be better done by the Union than by individual Clubs.

Its functions include the holding of the Open and Close Championships for Amateur Golfers and Tournaments for Team Matches.

Its organisation consists of Provincial Councils in each of the four Provinces elected by the Clubs in the Province – each province electing a limited number of delegates to the Central Council which meets annually.

Tel 00 353 1 505 4000 *Fax* 00 353 1 505 4001

The Golf Union of Wales

The Golf Union of Wales was founded in 2007 following the merger of the Welsh Golfing Union (1895) and the Welsh Ladies Golf Union (1904). The GUW, the first of the Home Unions to merge, has 158 affiliated clubs and its mission statement is:-

To encourage participation and excellence for all golfers at all levels whilst maintaining and preserving the traditions of honesty, integrity and fair play.

The GUW's key goals are:

(1) To develop a network of thriving clubs to "secure the future of Welsh Golf.

(2) To provide competition opportunities for golfers of all ages and standards.

(3) To achieve international success for Wales and its players and produce world class golfers.

The Golf Union of Wales is a limited company with a board of non-executive directors and a Council of 19 members elected by the clubs.

Tel 01633 435040 *Fax* 01633 693568
E-mail office@golfunionwales.org

The Council of National Golf Unions

The British Golf Unions Joint Advisory Committee, later The Council of National Golf Unions (CONGU), came into existence at a conference held in York on 14th February 1924. The conference was convened by the Royal and Ancient Golf Club of St Andrews as a means of enabling the representatives of the Golf Unions of Great Britain and Ireland to formulate a definitive system of calculating Scratch Scores and to arrive at a uniform system of handicapping based on Scratch Scores.

The Consultative Committee was appointed to receive and consider schemes for calculating and allocating the Scratch Scores and adjustments to handicaps throughout Great Britain and Ireland. The Standard Scratch Score and Handicapping Scheme was prepared by the Council in 1925 and has been in operation throughout Great Britain and Ireland since 1st March 1926.

In 2000/2001 discussions began between CONGU and the Ladies Golf Union (LGU), who were reviewing their own system. From these discussions the Unified Handicap System (UHS) emerged. It was passed by CONGU in September 2003 and by the LGU in January 2004. The joint system for men and ladies became effective from 1st February 2004.

The Constitution of CONGU was amended in 2004 to reflect the joint system. This has been further amended in 2007/2008 to recognise the amalgamation of the Welsh Unions and will again be changed to recognise the formation of England Golf following the merger of the English Unions. The CONGU Council now consists of an independent chairperson and sixteen representatives nominated by the six Unions/Associations in Great Britain and Ireland. The six are: England Golf, Golf Union of Wales, Golfing Union of Ireland, Irish Ladies' Golf Union, Scottish Golf Union and Scottish Ladies' Golfing Association. The Royal and Ancient Golf Club of St. Andrews and The Ladies' Golf Union have one representative each on The Council.

March 2012 will see the introduction of the latest updates to the UHS, which is part of the continual process of review and improvement. CONGU have a number of sub-committees, the two most active being the Statistics and Technical Committees. These two Committees continually listen to comments and suggestions, analyse results and data, project the effect any changes would make, and make recommendations for changes to the Board, who must then give approval before they are accepted into the system. This continual process ensures that we have an effective and relevant handicap system. Contact with other handicapping authorities, particularly the EGA, is maintained so that research and technical developments are shared.

Tel 0151 336 3936

Government of the Amateur and Open Golf Championships

In December 1919, on the invitation of the clubs who had hitherto controlled the Amateur and Open Golf Championships, The Royal and Ancient Golf Club took over the government of those events. These two championships are now controlled by a committee appointed by The R&A.

Tel 01334 460000 *Fax* 01334 460001

European Golf Association Association Européenne de Golf

Formed at a meeting held 20 November 1937 in Luxembourg, membership is restricted to European national amateur golf associations or unions. The Association concerns itself solely with matters of an international character. The association is presently composed of 30 member countries and is governed by the following committees:

- Executive Committee
- Championship Committee
- Professional Technical Committee
- EGA Handicapping & Course Rating Committee

Prime objectives are:

(a) To encourage international development of golf, to strengthen bonds of friendship existing between it members.

(b) To encourage the formation of new golf organisations representing the golf activities of European countries.

(c) To co-ordinate the dates of the Open and Amateur championships of its members and to arrange, in conjuction with host Federations, European championships and specific matches of international character.

(d) To ratify and publish the calendar dates of the major Amateur and Professional championships and international matches in Europe.

(e) To create and maintain international relationships in the field of golf and undertake any action useful to the cause of golf on an international level.

The headquarters are situated in Epalinges, Switzerland.

Ladies' Golf Union (LGU)

Founded in 1893, the Ladies' Golf Union (LGU) is the encompassing body for ladies' amateur golf in Great Britain & Ireland. The LGU's administrative base is in St. Andrews, Fife, Scotland, while activities, championships, matches and events take place in Great Britain & Ireland and internationally.

The organisation's strategic objectives have been defined as follows:

To provide ladies and girls with opportunities to participate in the highest standard elite golf competitions;

To achieve international success for Great Britain & Ireland lady and girl golfers and teams;

To increase awareness and raise the profile of ladies' and girls' golf through the Ricoh Women's British Open and other golf events;

To provide a collective strong voice for, and represent the interests of, ladies' and girls' golf in proactive collaboration with the National Organisation and other organisations, both in and outwith the sport;

To actively demonstrate and grow the LGU's key advocacy role as the encompassing body for ladies' golf; and

To build on the present platform of operational and financial sustainability and progress strategically towards financial independence, with reduced reliance on subscription income.

The members of the LGU are the national governing bodies for ladies' golf in the Home Countries – England Golf, the Irish Ladies Golf Union Limited, the Scottish Ladies Golfing Association Limited and the Golf Union of Wales Limited. Clubs affiliated to these bodies pay a small annual subscription for each playing lady member, which is remitted to the LGU as a contribution to its activities.

Brigid McCaw, President of the Ladies' Golf Union

A number of overseas unions, associations and clubs are also affiliated to the LGU.

The LGU's Executive Council is led by a Chairman, whose term of office is three years, and comprises a representative from each of the national governing bodies, two members appointed for reasons of specific skills and contributions, and a non-voting President.

Operational activities are undertaken by a wholly owned subsidiary, LGU Championships Limited (LGUCL), while the LGU holds the assets of the organisation, including property and memorabilia. The members of the Executive Council also serve as members of the Board of LGUCL. Collectively, the LGU and LGUCL are referred to as the LGU Group. The strategic direction and policies of the LGU Group are determined by the Executive Council/ Board members, while responsibility for implementing these policies and strategies is vested in a team of staff, headed by the CEO.

The Annual General Meeting of the LGU is held in February, with the National Organisations being the voting members.

The LGU Group owns and runs the Ricoh Women's British Open, founded by the LGU in 1976 and one of the five Major Tournaments for professional lady golfers. LGUCL also has responsibility for running, on an annual basis:

- the Ladies' British Open Amateur Championship
- the Ladies' British Open Amateur Stroke Play Championship
- the Girls' British Open Amateur Championship
- the Senior Ladies' British Open Amateur Championship
- the three sets of Home International Matches

In addition, international events involving Great Britain & Ireland teams, such as the Curtis Cup (against the USA) and Vagliano and Junior Vagliano Trophies (against the Continent of Europe) are organised and controlled by LGUCL on home soil. Both at home and abroad, the LGU Group selects and prepares the teams, provides uniforms and meets the costs of participation in these matches.

The LGU acts as the co-coordinating body for the Astor Trophy (former Commonwealth Trophy) matches in whichever one of the five participating countries (GB&I, Australia, Canada, South Africa, New Zealand) it is held, four yearly, by rotation.

The LGU also maintains and regulates a number of competitions played under handicap and aimed at supporting participation in the game by club golfers. The Peugeot 208 LGU Coronation Foursomes attracts over 35,000 participants each year, while the

Breakthrough Brooch attracts over 1200 clubs and raises significant funds for the LGU's partner charity. Other handicap competitions – the Australian (Commonwealth) spoons and the Challenge Bowls are delivered with the support of the National Organisations.

A Yearbook is published annually, detailing regulations and venues for forthcoming championships and matches, results of past events and other relevant useful information.

In endeavouring to advance and safeguard ladies' golf, the LGU actively maintains contact with other golfing organisations – The R&A, CONGU, the United States Golf Association, the Professional Golfers Association, the European Golf Association, the Ladies' European Tour, the European Tour and the Ladies' Professional Golf Association. The organisation is also represented on the Rolex Rankings Committee which maintains and publishes the ladies' professional rankings.

Maintaining contact with these organisations keeps the LGU at the forefront of developments and emerging issues and provides an active opportunity to influence and protect the future of the ladies' game.

Tel 01334 475811 *Fax* 01334 472818

United States Golf Association

The USGA is dedicated to promoting and conserving the best interests and true spirit of the game of golf.

Founded on December 22, 1894 by representatives of five American golf clubs, the USGA was originally charged with conducting national championships, implementing a uniform code of rules and maintaining a national system of handicapping.

Today, the USGA comprises more than 9,000 member clubs and courses and its principal functions remain largely unchanged. The USGA annually conducts the U.S. Open, U.S. Women's Open, U.S. Senior Open and 10 national amateur championships. On a biennial basis, it also conducts two state team championships and helps conduct the Walker Cup Match, Curtis Cup Match and World Amateur Team Championships. More than 35,000 players representing more than 80 countries submit entries to play in USGA championships each year.

The USGA and The R&A together govern the game worldwide, including joint administration of the Rules of Golf, Rules of Amateur status and equipment standards. The organizations also work in partnership to administer the World Amateur Golf Rankings, the world's pre-eminent amateur golf ranking system for men and women.

The USGA maintains Handicap and Course Rating and Systems used on six continents in more than 50 countries and also provides handicap computation services to more than 70 national, regional and state golf associations through the Golf Handicap and Information Network.

Additional responsibilities assumed by the association encompass turfgrass and environmental research conducted by the USGA Green Section, a global leader in the development and support of sustainable golf course management practices since 1920; and preservation and promotion of the game's rich history in the USGA Museum and Arnold Palmer Center for Golf History, which houses the world's largest and most complete golf library. Since 1965, the USGA has supported philanthropic activities dedicated to maintaining and improving the opportunities for all individuals to partake fully in the game.

Tel 001 908 234 2300 *Fax* 001 908 234 9687

Glen D Nager of Washington, DC, took over this year as the new President of the United States Golf Association. He served as general counsel to the USGA from 2006 to 2008.

Nager, a partner in the Washington, DC, office of the International law firm Jones Day, is a graduate of the University of Texas and Stanford Law School, where he was president of the Law Review. Among his clerkships was service in 1983 with Justice Sandra Day O'Connor of the US Supreme Court. He lives in the District of Columbia.

As President he will chair the Commercial, Compensation and Rules of Golf Committees and will also serve on the Equipment Standards, Joint Equipment Standards, Management and Joint Rules of Golf Committees.

Major Championship and International Conditions

UK CHAMPIONSHIPS

Men

Amateur Championship

The Championship, until 1982, was decided entirely by match play over 18 holes except for the final which was over 36 holes. Since 1983 the Championship has comprised two stroke play rounds of 18 holes each from which the leading 64 players and ties over the 36 holes qualify for the match play stages. Matches are over 18 holes except for the final which is over 36 holes. Full particulars can be obtained from the Entries Department, R&A, St Andrews, Fife KY16 9JD. Tel: 01334 460000; Fax 01334 460005; e-mail entries@randa.org

Seniors Open Amateur Championship

The Championship consists of 18 holes on each of two days, the leading 60 players and ties over the 36 holes then playing a further 18 holes the following day. Entrants must have attained the age of 55 years prior to the first day of the Championship. Full particulars can be obtained from the Entries Department, R&A, St Andrews, Fife KY16 9JD. Tel 01344 460000; fax 01334 460005; e-mail entries@randa.org

National Championships

The English, Irish, Scottish and Welsh Amateur Championships are played by holes, each match consisting of one round of 18 holes except the final which is contested over 36 holes. Only the English Golf Union hold a 36-hole qualifier for their event. Full particulars of conditions of entry and method of play can be obtained from the secretaries of the respective national Unions.

English Open Amateur Stroke Play Championship (The Brabazon)

The Championship consists of one round of 18 holes on each of two days after which the leading 60 and those tying for 60th place play a further two rounds. The remainder are eliminated.

Conditions for entry include: entrants must have a handicap not exceeding one; the maximum number of entries eligible for qualifying shall be 264 (132 to play at each of the Regional Qualifying courses. Certain players are exempt from qualifying.

Full particulars of conditions of entry and method of play can be obtained from the Secretary, English Golf Union, National Golf Centre, The Broadway, Woodhall Spa, Lincs LN10 6PU. Tel: 01526 354500; Fax: 01526 354020.

Scottish Open Amateur Stroke Play Championship

The Championship consists of one round of 18 holes on each of two days after which the leading 40 and those tying for 40th place play a further two rounds. The remainder are eliminated. Full particulars of conditions of entry and method of play can be obtained from the Events Department of the Scottish Golf Union, The Duke's, St Andrews, Fife KY16 8NX. Tel: 01334 466477; Fax: 01334 461361.

Boys

Boys Amateur Championship

The Championship, until 2009, was decided entirely by match play over 18 holes except for the final which was over 36 holes. Since 2010 the Championship has comprised two stroke play rounds of 18 holes each from which the leading 64 players and ties over the 36 holes qualify for the match play stages. Matches are over 18 holes except for the final which is over 36 holes. Full particulars can be obtained from the Entries Department, R&A, St Andrews, Fife KY16 9JD. Tel: 01334 460000; Fax 01334 460005; e-mail entries@randa.org

Ladies

Ladies' British Open Amateur Championship

The Championship consists of one 18-hole qualifying round on each of two days. The players returning the 64 lowest scores over 36 holes shall qualify for match play. Ties for the last place(s) shall be decided by card countback using the 18 hole second round score.

Ladies' British Open Amateur Stroke Play Championship

The Championship consists of 72 holes stroke play; 18 holes are played on each of two days after which the first 40 and all ties for 40th place qualify for a further 36 holes on the third day. Handicap limit is 6.4. Full details can be obtained from LGU Championships Ltd, The Scores, St Andrews, Fife KY16 9AT.

Ricoh Women's British Open Championship

The Ricoh Women's British Open is a designated major in ladies' professional golf and is the only such major played outside the USA. Owned by LGU Championships Ltd, the championship consists of 72 holes stroke play. 18 holes are played on each of four days, the field being reduced after the first 36 holes. Certain categories of players gain automatic entry to the championship because of past performance in the Ricoh Women's British Open or from current performance in the Rolex Rankings and the LET, LPGA and JLPGA money lists. Those not automatically exempt can gain entry through pre-qualifying and final qualifying competitions.

Full particulars of the above three championships can be obtained from the LTU Championships Ltd, The Scores, St Andrews, Fife KY16 9AT.
Tel: 01334 475811; Fax: 01334 472818.

National Championships

Conditions of entry and method of play for the English, Scottish, Welsh and Irish Ladies' Close Championships can be obtained from the Registered Offices of the respective associations.

Other championships organised by the respective national associations, from whom full particulars can be obtained, include English Ladies', Intermediate, English Ladies' Stroke Play, Scottish Girls' Open Amateur Stroke Play (under 21) and Welsh Ladies' Open Amateur Stroke Play.

Girls

Girls' British Open Amateur Championship

The Championship consists of two 18-hole qualifying rounds, followed by match play. The players returning the 64 lowest scores over 36 holes qualify for the match play. Ties for the last place(s) shall be decided by card countback using the 18 hole second round score.

Entrants must be under 18 years of age on the 1st January in the year of the Championship.

The Championship is open to players of the female gender who are members of a recognised golf club, who have amateur status in accordance with the current rules and who hold a CONGU exact handicap of not more than 8.4 or overseas equivalent at the date of entry.

Full particulars can be obtained from the Administrator, LGU, The Scores, St Andrews, Fife KY16 9AT. Tel: 01334 475811; Fax: 01334 472818.

National Championships

The English, Scottish, Irish and Welsh Girls' Close Championships are open to all girls of relevant nationality and appropriate age which may vary from country to country. A handicap limit may be set by some countries. Full particulars can be obtained via the secretaries of the respective associations.

EUROPEAN CHAMPIONSHIPS

Founded in 1986 by the European Golf Association, the International Amateur and Ladies Amateur Championships are held on an annual basis since 1990. These Championships consist of one round of 18 holes on each of three days after which the leading 70 and those tying for 70th place play one further round.

Full particulars of conditions of entry and method of play can be obtained from the European Golf Association.

Since 1991, the European Golf Association also holds an International Mid-Amateur Championship on an annual basis. The Championship consist of one round of 18 holes on each of two days after which the leading 90 and those tying for 90th place play one further round.

Full particulars of conditions of entry and method of play can be obtained from the European Golf Association.

Since 1996, the European Golf Association holds an International Seniors Championship for ladies and men on an annual basis.

The Championship consists of one round of 18 holes on each of two days after which there is a cut in both ladies and men categories. The competitors who pass the cut play one further round.

Additionally, a nation's cup is played within the tournament on the first two days. Teams are composed of three players. The two best gross scores out of three will count each day. The total aggregate of the four scores over two days will constitute the team's score.

Full particulars of conditions of entry and method of play can be obtained from the European Golf Association, Place de la Croix-Blanche 19, PO Box CH-1066 Epilanges, Switzerland. Tel: +41 21 784 32 32; Fax: +412 1 784 35 91.

TEAM CHAMPIONSHIPS

Men's Amateur

Walker Cup – Great Britain and Ireland *v* United States of America

Mr George Herbert Walker of the United States presented a Cup for international competition to be known as *The United States Golf Association International Challenge Trophy*, popularly described as *The Walker Cup*.

The Cup shall be played for by teams of amateur golfers selected from Clubs under the jurisdiction of the United States Golf Association on the one side and from England, Ireland, Scotland and Wales on the other.

The Walker Cup shall be held every two years in the United States of America and Great Britain and Ireland alternately.

The teams shall consist of not more than ten players and a captain.

The contest consists of four foursomes and eight singles matches over 18 holes on the first day and four foursomes and 10 singles on the final day.

St Andrews Trophy – Great Britain and Ireland *v* Continent of Europe

First staged in 1956, the St Andrews Trophy is a biennial international match played between two selected teams of amateur golfers representing Great Britain and Ireland and the Continent of Europe. Each team consists of nine players and the match is played over two consecutive days with four morning foursomes followed each afternoon by eight singles. Selection of the Great Britain and Ireland team is carried out by the R&A Selection Committee. The European Golf Association select the Continent of Europe team.

Eisenhower Trophy – Men's World Team Championship

Founded in recognition of the need for an official world amateur team championship, the first event was played at St Andrews in 1958 and the Trophy has been played for every second year in different countries around the world.

Each country enters a team of four players who play strokeplay over 72 holes, the total of the three best individual scores to be counted for each round.

European Team Championship

Founded in 1959 by the European Golf Association for competition among member countries of the Association. The Championship has recently been changed to be played on an annual basis and played in rotation round the countries, which are grouped in four geographical zones.

Each team consists of six players who play two qualifying rounds of 18 holes, the five best scores of each round constituting the team aggregate. Flights for match play are then arranged according to qualifying rankings. The match play consists of two foursomes and five singles on each of three days.

A similar championship is held in alternate years for Youths teams, under 21 years of age and every year for Boys teams, under 18 years of age.

Raymond Trophy – Home Internationals

The first official International Match recorded was in 1902 at Hoylake between England and Scotland who won 32 to 25 on a holes up basis.

In 1932 International Week was inaugurated under the auspices of the British Golf Unions' Joint Advisory Council with the full approval of the four National Golf Unions who are now responsible for running the matches. Teams of 11 players from England, Ireland, Scotland and Wales engage in matches consisting of five foursomes and ten singles over 18 holes, the foursomes being in the morning and the singles in the afternoon. Each team plays every other team.

The eligibility of players to play for their country shall be their eligibility to play in the Amateur Championship of their country.

Sir Michael Bonallack Trophy – Europe *v* Asia/Pacific

First staged in 1998, the Sir Michael Bonallack Trophy is a biennial international match played between two selected teams of amateur golfers representing Europe and Asia/Pacific. Each team consists of 12 players and the match is played over three days with five four balls in the morning and five foursomes in the afternoon of the first two days, followed by 12 singles on the last day. Selection of the European team is carried out by the European Golf Association. The Asia/Pacific Golf Confederation selects the Asia/Pacific team.

Men's Professional

The Ryder Cup

This is a biennial match now played between 12-man professional teams from Europe and the United States. The competition started in 1927 between teams from Great Britain and the United States. In 1926 an unofficial match took place at Wentworth Club, Surrey, England, following which Samuel Ryder, a prosperous businessman who owned the Heath and Heather Seed Company, famous for their penny packets of seeds which garden lovers adored, in St Albans, England, famously remarked: "We must do this again." Samuel Ryder donated a trophy – a golden chalice – at a cost of £250. The first official match took place in 1927 at the Worcester Country Club in Worcester, Massachusetts. The United States led 18-3 with one match tied before in 1979 players from the Continent of Europe became eligible. Between 1979 and 2010 Europe has eight victories and the United States seven with one tie. The United States will be seeking their 26th win overall and Europe their 12th when The 2012 Ryder Cup takes place at Medinah Country Club, Illinois, with the format of eight fourballs, eight foursomes and 12 singles which was introduced in 1981

The World Cup of Golf

This is an annual competition founded in 1953 as the Canada Cup – it became The World Cup of Golf in 1967 – by John Jay Hopkins, the noted Canadian industrialist. It has since the start brought together countries each represented by two man teams with the winning team having the lowest aggregate score over 72-holes. Italy became the 16th different country to win The World Cup and in 2011 they defended the 56th edition at the 25th destination to be visited – the Mission Hills Resort, Hainan Island, China – when the format comprised fourballs on the first and third days and foursomes on the second and final day with 28 teams, each one of different nationality, competing at the final stage following a series of World Qualifying Competitions.

Vivendi Seve Trophy

This is a biennial match between ten-man teams from Continental Europe and Great Britain and Ireland. Instigated by the late Seve Ballesteros in 2000 as a team competition to be contested in non-Ryder Cup years, Great Britain and Ireland gained their sixth win in seven editions when they won at Saint-Nom-la-Bretèche, Paris, France, in 2011. The match comprises of two series of five fourball matches; four greensomes; four foursomes; and ten singles on the final day.

Llandudno Trophy (PGA Cup) – Great Britain and Ireland *v* United States of America

The Llandudno International Trophy was first awarded to England in 1939 after winning the first Home Tournament Series against Ireland, Scotland and Wales. With the outbreak of war the series was abolished and the Trophy formed part of Percy Alliss's personal collection. After Percy's death his son Peter donated the Llandudno Trophy to be awarded to the winner of the then annual PGA Cup Match. Now it is a biennial match played since 1973 in Ryder Cup format between Great Britain and Ireland and the United States of America involving top club professionals. No prize money is awarded to the competitors who compete solely for their country. Selection of the Great Britain and Ireland team is determined following completion of the Glenmuir PGA Club Professionals Championship.

Ladies Amateur

Curtis Cup – Great Britain and Ireland *v* United States

For a trophy presented by the late Misses Margaret and Harriot Curtis of Boston, USA, for biennial competition between amateur teams from the United States of America and Great Britain and Ireland. The match is sponsored jointly by the United States Golf Association and the Ladies' Golf Union who may select teams of not more than eight players.

The match, held over three days, consists of three foursomes and three four-ball matches on each of the first two days and eight singles of 18 holes on the final day.

Vagliano Trophy – Great Britain and Ireland *v* Continent of Europe

For a trophy presented to the Comité des Dames de la Fédération Française de Golf and the Ladies' Golf Union by Monsieur AA Vagliano, originally for annual competition between teams of women amateur golfers from France and Great Britain and Ireland but, since 1959, by mutual agreement, for competition between teams from the Continent of Europe and Great Britain and Ireland.

The match is played biennially, alternately in Great Britain and Ireland and on the Continent of Europe, with teams of not more than nine players plus a non-playing captain. The match consists of four foursomes and eight singles of 18 holes on each of two days. The foursomes are played each morning.

Espirito Santo Trophy – Women's World Team Championship

Presented by Mrs Ricardo Santo of Portugal for biennial competition between teams of not more than three women amateur golfers who represent a national association affiliated to the World Amateur Golf Council. First competed for in 1964. The Championship consists of 72 holes strokeplay, 18 holes on each of four days, the two best scores in each round constituting the team aggregate.

Lady Astor Trophy – Five Nations Tournament (formerly Commonwealth Tournament)

For a trophy presented by Nancy, Viscountess Astor CH, and the Ladies' Golf Union for competition once in every four years between teams of women amateur golfers from Commonwealth countries.

The inaugural Commonwealth Tournament was played at St Andrews in 1959 between teams from Australia, Canada, New Zealand, South Africa and Great Britain and was won by the British team. The tournament is played in rotation in the competing countries, Great Britain, Australia, Canada, New Zealand and South Africa, each country being entitled to nominate six players including a playing or non-playing captain. In 2011, a Great Britain and Ireland team will compete for the first time.

Each team plays every other team and each team match consists of two foursomes and four singles over 18 holes. The foursomes are played in the morning.

European Team Championships

Founded in 1959 by the European Golf Association for competition among member countries of the Association. The Championship is held annually and played in rotation round the countries, which are grouped in four geographical zones.

Each team consists of six players who play two qualifying rounds of 18 holes, the five best scores of each round constituting the team aggregate. Flights for matchplay are then arranged according to qualifying rankings. The matchplay consists of two foursomes and five singles on each of three days.

A similar championship is held in alternate years for Lady Juniors teams, under 21 years of age and every year for Girls teams, under 18 years of age.

Home Internationals

Teams from England, Scotland, Ireland and Wales compete annually for a trophy presented to the LGU by the late Mr TH Miller. The qualifications for a player being eligible to play for her country are the same as those laid down by each country for its Close Championship.

Each team, consisting of not more than eight players, plays each other team, a draw taking place to decide the order of play between the teams. The matches consist of three foursomes and six singles, each of 18 holes.

Ladies Professional

Solheim Cup – Europe *v* United States

The Solheim Cup, named after Karsten Solheim who founded the sponsoring Ping company, is the women's equivalent of the Ryder Cup. In 1990 the inaugural competition between the top women professional golfers from Europe and America took place in Florida.

The matches are played biennially in alternate continents. The format is foursomes and fourball matches on the first two days, followed by singles on the third in accordance with the conditions as agreed between the Ladies European Tour and the United States LPGA Tour.

Juniors

R&A Trophy – Boys' Home Internationals

Teams comprising 11 players from England, Scotland, Ireland and Wales compete against one another over three days in a single round robin format. Each fixture comprises five morning foursomes followed by ten afternoon singles.

To be eligible for selection, players must be under the age of 18 at 00.00 hours on 1st January in the year of the matches and have eligibility to play in their national championships.

Jacques Léglise Trophy – Great Britain and Ireland *v* Continent of Europe

The Jacques Léglise Trophy is an annual international match played between two selected teams of amateur boy golfers representing Great Britain and Ireland and the Continent of Europe. Each team consists of nine players and the match is played over two consecutive days with four morning foursomes followed each afternoon by eight singles. Selection of the Great Britain and Ireland team is carried out by the R&A Selection Committee. The European Golf Association selects the Continent of Europe team

To be eligible for selection, players must be under the age of 18 at 00.00 hours on 1st January in the year of the matches.

Junior Ryder Cup

First staged in 1995, the Junior Ryder Cup is a biennial international match played between two selected teams of amateur golfers representing Europe and the USA, prior to the Ryder Cup. Each team consists of four girls and four boys under 16 as well as two girls and two boys under 18. The match is played over two consecutive days with six four balls on the first day and six mixed four balls on the second day.

Selection of the European team is carried out by the European Golf Association. Players and captains are then invited to watch the Ryder Cup.

Girls' Home Internationals

Teams from England, Ireland, Scotland and Wales compete annually for the Stroyan Cup. The qualifications for a player for the Girls' International Matches shall be the same as those laid down by each country for its Girls' Close Championship except that a player shall be under 18 years on the 1st January in the year of the Tournament.

Each team, consisting of not more than eight players, plays each other team, a draw taking place to decide the order of play between the teams. The matches consist of three foursomes and six singles, each of 18 holes.

The Junior Open

Run by The R&A every two years for junior golfers nominated by their various Federations. It is always held during The Open week at a venue close to the course where the Championship is being played.

PART XV

Golf History

R&A Championships and Team Events

In 2004, The Royal and Ancient Golf Club of St Andrews devolved responsibility for the running of The Open Championship and other key golfing events to The R&A. The history of championships and team events organised by The R&A and by The R&A and other golfing bodies are outlined below. Current championship and match conditions are defined elsewhere in the volume.

Championships solely under the administration of The R&A:
The Open Championship
The Amateur Championship
The Seniors Open Amateur Championship
The Boys Amateur Championship
The Junior Open Championship

Team events organised by The R&A:
The Boys Home Internationals

Team events organised by The R&A and other golfing bodies:
The Walker Cup (R&A/USGA)
The World Amateur Team Championships (R&A as part of the International Golf Federation)
The St Andrews Trophy (R&A/EGA)
The Jacques Léglise Trophy (R&A/EGA)
The Senior Open Championship

The Open Championship

The Open Championship began in 1860 at the Prestwick Golf Club and the original trophy was an ornate Challenge Belt, which was subscribed for and presented by the members of Prestwick Golf Club. What is now recognised as the first Open Championship was played on October 17, 1860 at the end of the club's autumn meeting. A total of eight players competed in three rounds of the 12 hole course. No prize money for The Open was awarded until 1863, the winner simply received the Belt for a year. In 1863 it was decided to give money prizes to those finishing second, third and fourth but the winner still only received the Belt. It was not until 1864 that the winner received £6. The average field in the 1860s was only 12 players.

The original rules of the competition stated that the Belt "becomes the property of the winner by being won three years in succession". In 1870 Tom Morris Junior won for the third year in a row and took possession of the Belt. He won £6 for his efforts out of a total prize fund of £12. No Championship was held in 1871 whilst the Prestwick Club entered into discussions with The Royal and Ancient Golf Club and the Honourable Company of Edinburgh Golfers over the future of the event.

One of the key turning points in the history of The Open took place at the Spring Meeting of the Prestwick Club in April 1871. At that meeting it was proposed that "in contemplation of St Andrews, Musselburgh and other clubs joining in the purchase of a Belt to be played for over four or more greens, it is not expedient for the Club to provide a Belt to be played solely for at Prestwick". From that date onwards, The Open ceased to be under the sole control of the Prestwick Golf Club.

The Championship was played again under this new agreement in 1872. A new trophy, the now famous Claret Jug, was purchased for presentation to the winner. Until 1891, the host club remained responsible for all arrangements regarding the Championship, which continued to be played over 36 holes in one day.

In 1892, the Honourable Company of Edinburgh Golfers took four radical steps to transform The Open Championship. It extended play to 72 holes over two days, imposed an entrance charge for all competitors, changed the venue to a new course at Muirfield and increased the total prize fund from £28 10s to £100. These actions were all taken unilaterally by the club. The increased purse to counter a rival tournament held at Musselburgh.

A meeting was held between the three host clubs on June 9, 1893, for the purpose of "placing the competition for The Open Championship on a basis more commensurate with its importance than had hitherto existed". Three resolutions were agreed. Two English clubs, St George's, Sandwich and Royal Liverpool, would be invited to stage the Championship and join the rota, now of five clubs. Four rounds of 18 holes would be played over two days. Each of the five clubs would contribute £15 annually to the cost and the balance would come from an entry fee for all competitors. The prize money would total £100, with £30 for the winner. The date of each year's championship would be set by the host club, which would also bear any additional necessary expenses. The representatives of the five clubs became known as the Delegates of the Associated Clubs.

The increasing number of entrants caused a cut to be introduced after two rounds in 1898 and between 1904 and 1906 the Championship was played over three days. It then reverted to two days in 1907 with the introduction of qualifying rounds. The entire field had to qualify and there were no exemptions.

On January 24, 1920, the Delegates of the Associated Clubs asked The Royal and Ancient Golf Club to take over "the management of the Championship and the custody of the Challenge Cup". The new Cham-pionship Committee was responsible for running both The Open and Amateur Championships and in 1922 it was decided that The Open should only be played over links courses. The venues included in today's circuit are: Carnoustie, Muirfield, Royal Birkdale, Royal Liverpool, Royal Lytham & St Annes, Royal St George's, Royal Troon, the Old Course, St Andrews and Turnberry.

Prestwick, birth place of The Open, played host to the Championship 24 times, the last in 1925. Other courses that have been used in the past are: Musselburgh (1874, 1877, 1880, 1883, 1886, 1889); Royal Cinque Ports, Deal (1909, 1920); Princes, Sandwich (1932) and Royal Portrush (1951).

The Open was played regularly over three days starting in 1926, with a round on each of the first two days and two rounds on the final day, which from 1927 onwards was a Friday. The total prize money had reached £500 by 1939. The prize money was increased to £1000 in 1946 and reached £5000 in 1959.

As The Open went into its second century in the 1960s, it grew tremendously both as a Championship and a spectator event. In 1963, exemptions from pre-qualifying were introduced for the leading players. Play was extended to four days in 1966, with the Championship finishing with a single round on the Saturday. In 1968, a second cut after 54 holes was introduced to further reduce the field on the final day and this remained in effect until 1985. To cope with the increasing spectator numbers, facilities were much improved. Grandstands were first introduced at The Open in 1960 and they became a standard feature from 1963 onwards.

Regional qualifying had been tried as an experiment for one year in 1926, but did not become a regular feature until 1977. Some players were exempt but had to take part in final qualifying, while others were exempt from both regional and final qualifying. In 2004, International Final Qualifying was introduced, enabling players around the world to qualify on five different Continents.

Since 1980, the Championship has been scheduled to end on a Sunday instead of a Saturday. In the event of a tie for first place, play-offs took place over 36 holes up until 1963, when they were reduced to 18 holes. In 1985 a four-hole play-off, followed by sudden death, was introduced.

The Open Championship was first televised live in 1955 and was shown on the BBC. In 1958, the television coverage lasted for a total of three hours, one and a half hours on each of the final two days. In 2011, the total coverage was 3,676 hours worldwide of which 57% was live.

Admission charges to watch The Open were introduced in 1926. Paid admissions went over 50,000 for the first time in 1968 at Carnoustie and over 100,000 for the first time at St Andrews in 1978. The 200,000 attendance figure was reached for the first time at St Andrews in 1990. A new record was set at the Home of Golf in 2000 when 238,787 watched the Millennium Open.

Growth of prize money

Year	*Total Prize Money*	*First Prize*
1861	£0	£0
1871	No Championship	
1881	£21	£8
1891	£28.50	£10
1901	£125	£50
1911	£135	£50
1921	£225	£75
1931	£500	£100
1941	No Championship	
1951	£1,700	£300
1961	£8,500	£1,400
1971	£45,000	£5,500
1981	£200,000	£25,000
1991	£900,000	£90,000
2001	£3,300,000	£600,000
2012	£5,000,000	£900,000

Harry Vardon has scored most victories in The Open Championship. He won it six times between 1896 and 1914. JH Taylor, James Braid, Peter Thomson and Tom Watson have each won The Open five times. Between 1860 and 1889, all of The Open winners were Scottish. John Ball Jr became the first Englishman and the first amateur to claim the title in 1890. Arnaud Massy from France was the first Continental winner in 1907.

Four players have completed a hat trick of Open wins: Tom Morris Jr 1868–1870; Jamie Anderson 1877–1879; Bob Ferguson 1880–1882; Peter Thomson 1954–1956.

The Open Championship has been won by an amateur player six times – John Ball in 1890, Harold Hilton in 1892 and 1897 and Bobby Jones in 1926, 1927 and 1930. Walter Hagen was the first native born American to win The Open when he triumphed in 1922. Jock Hutchison, who had won the previous year, was resident in America at the time of his victory although he was born in St Andrews.

The Amateur Championship

What became recognised as the first Amateur Championship was held at Hoylake in 1885, although earlier national amateur competitions had been played at St Andrews in 1857, 1858 and 1859. The Royal and Ancient Golf Club had considered holding a national amateur tournament in 1876 but decided not to proceed with the idea.

In December 1884, Thomas Owen Potter, the Secretary of Royal Liverpool Golf Club, proposed holding a championship for amateur players. The event was to be open to members of recognised clubs and it was hoped that it would make the game more popular and lead to improved standards of play.

A total of 44 players from 12 clubs entered the first championship. The format was matchplay, with the ruling that if two players tied they would both advance to the following round and play one another again. There were three semi-finalists: John Ball, Horace Hutchinson and Allan Macfie. After a bye to the final, Macfie beat Hutchinson 7 and 6.

Following the success of the first tournament, it was agreed that a championship open to all amateurs should be played at St Andrews, Hoylake and Prestwick in rotation.

Twenty-four golf clubs subscribed for the trophy, which was acquired in 1886. They were:

Alnmouth	Royal Aberdeen
Bruntsfield	Royal Albert (Montrose)
Dalhousie	Royal and Ancient
Formby	Royal Blackheath
Gullane	Royal Burgess
Honourable Company	Royal Liverpool
Innerleven	Royal North Devon
Kilspindie	Royal St George's
King James VI	Royal Wimbledon
North Berwick New	Tantallon
Panmure	Troon
Prestwick	West Lancashire

Representatives, known as Delegates of the Associated Clubs, were elected from these clubs to run the Championship and in 1919 they approached The Royal and Ancient Golf Club to accept future management. The Club agreed and in 1920 the Championship Committee was formed. This committee became responsible for organising the Amateur and Open and for making decisions on the conditions of play. It was not until 1922, however, that the 1885 tournament was officially recognised as the first Amateur Championship and Allan Macfie the first winner.

The venue circuit gradually increased. Sandwich was added in 1892, Muirfield in 1897 and Westward Ho! in 1912. The Championship was first played in Ireland in 1949 (Portmarnock) and Wales in 1951 (Porthcawl).

Prior to 1930, only two non-British players won the Amateur Championship title, Walter Travis, in 1904, and Jesse Sweetser, in 1926. Both hailed from the United States, the former via Australia.

The Americans began to make their presence felt more strongly in the 1930s, with four Americans winning five Amateur Championships. Bobby Jones took the title at St Andrews 1930, the year in which he achieved the Grand Slam. Lawson Little won in 1934 and 1935, Robert Sweeney in 1937 and Charles Yates in 1938.

Following a break during World War II, the Amateur Championship resumed in 1946 at Birkdale when the handicap limit was raised from one to two as an encouragement to those amateurs who had been on war service.

Attempts were made during the 1950s and 1960s to control large numbers of entries. In 1956 the field was limited to 200 so that the quarter-finals, semi-finals and the final could be played over 36 holes. This experiment lasted two years, when it was decided that only the semi-finals and final should be played over two rounds.

Regional qualifying over 36 holes was introduced in 1958 when 14 courses throughout the UK were selected. Using this method, the original entry of 500 was reduced to 200. Any player with a handicap of 5 or better could enter.

In 1961 regional qualifying was scrapped and the quarter-finals and semi-finals were played over 18 holes. Then in 1983 at Turnberry, 36 holes of strokeplay qualifying were introduced during the first two days. This format continues, with the leading 64 players and ties qualifying for the matchplay stages.

The Senior Open Championship

The Senior Open Championship has been part of the European Seniors Tour since 1987, and in 2003 was added to the Champions Tour as one of the five major world events in senior golf. The European Seniors Tour jointly administers the event alongside The R&A. Previous winners include former Open champions Gary Player, Bob Charles and Tom Watson.

The Seniors Open Amateur Championship

The Seniors Open Amateur Championship was the first tournament to be initiated by The Royal and Ancient Golf Club. Prestwick Golf Club had been responsible for starting the Open Championship, while Royal Liverpool Golf Club had introduced the Amateur Championship. Other events, such as the Boys Amateur Championship and Boys Home Internationals were introduced by private individuals and then handed over, by agreement, to The R&A.

The Seniors Open Amateur Championship made its début at Formby in 1969. It started as a means to help choose a Great Britain and Ireland team for the World Senior Amateur Team Championship which had begun in 1967 at Pinehurst, North Carolina, under the auspices of the World Amateur Golf Council.

Initially, the World Senior team event was to be played every two years, alternating with the competition for the Eisenhower Trophy, but it did not survive beyond 1969. The success of the Seniors Open Amateur Championship, however, was evident from the start and it became a popular event in its own right.

It began as a 36-hole strokeplay event, held over two days for players over the age of 55. The handicap limit was 5 and the field was restricted to 100. The winner was Reg Pattinson, who duly played his way onto the World Amateur Senior team in which he was partnered by Alan Cave, AL Bentley and AT Kyle. The short-lived World Senior event was played in 1969 over the Old Course at St Andrews and was won for the second time by the United States. Great Britain and Ireland finished third out of an entry of only 13 teams.

Before the present format was introduced, various alternatives were tried, in order to satisfy increasing entry demands. Two courses were used in 1971, allowing an entry of 250 with the handicap limit being increased to 9. In 1974, a limit of 130 was imposed. Subsidiary competitions were introduced according to age group: 55–59, 60–64 and 65 and over. A fourth age group was added in 1975 for the over 70s and the entry limit was increased to 140. The special categories changed in 1999, to one only for the 65 and over age group.

Today, the Seniors Open Amateur Championship attracts a wide international field, with 144 competitors playing two rounds and the leading 60 players and ties completing a further 18 holes.

The Boys Amateur Championship

The Boys Amateur Championship was introduced in 1921 for the under-16 age group. For the first two years it was played at Royal Ascot under the guidance of DM Mathieson and Colonel Thomas South. In 1948, Colonel South announced his intention to retire from his duties in connection with the event, declaring that "nothing would give him greater pleasure than that The Royal and Ancient Golf Club should take over the conduct of the Championship".

The venue for the first Boys Amateur Championship to be played under the administration of The Royal and Ancient Golf Club was the Old Course, St Andrews. A sub-committee ran the event until 1952 when it was finally handed over to the Championship Committee.

Since that year a prize has been presented to the best performing 16-year-old. This, the Peter Garner Bowl, commemorates the death of a competitor who was killed in a road accident while returning from the 1951 Championship.

Sir Michael Bonallack enjoyed early success in the Boys Amateur Championship. He won in 1952, and went on to win the Amateur Championship in 1961, 1965, 1968, 1969 and 1970.

Professionals who won the title earlier in their careers include Ronan Rafferty (1979), José Maria Olazábal (1983) and more recently Sergio García (1997).

The Junior Open Championship

Inaugurated in 1994, the Junior Open Championship came under The R&A's administrative control in 2000. All national golf unions and federations are invited to send their leading boy and girl under the age of 16 to compete in the three-day event. In previous years, only one player from each union or federation could enter. The biennial event is run on a course close to The Open Championship and in the same week so that all participants can spend time watching the world's finest players in action.

To encourage entries worldwide, there are three categories of competition defined by varying handicap limits. Gold is for those with a handicap of 3 and under, silver 4–9 and bronze 10–18.

TEAM EVENTS

The Walker Cup

The United States Golf Association International Challenge Trophy was originally intended to be presented to the winners of a contest to which all golf playing nations would be invited to compete. However, as The R&A tactfully pointed out to their counterparts in the USGA in 1921, the only two countries capable of entering a team were Great Britain and America.

By this simple process of elimination the trophy presented by USGA President George Herbert Walker became the focal point of a biennial series between the finest amateur players of the two countries. The first unofficial match was played in 1921 on the eve of the Amateur Championship at Hoylake when 19-year-old Bobby Jones helped the American team to a 9–3 victory. For the next three years the event was played annually, but settled into its biennial pattern after 1924.

It was not until 1938 at St Andrews that Great Britain and Ireland recorded a first victory. In 1965 the score was 11–11. There were 2 halved matches.

Only after the first success in America, with a 12½–11½ victory at Peachtree in Georgia in 1989, did the GB&I team finally end American domination of the matches. In the years that followed there were home wins at Porthcawl in 1995 and Nairn in 1999. The GB&I run of victories continued at Ocean Forest in 2001 and Ganton in 2003, before winning most recently at Royal Aberdeen in 2011.

The man after whom the trophy and the matches are named has another claim to a place in world history. His grandson, George Herbert Walker Bush and his great-grandson have both held office as President of the United States of America.

The Eisenhower Trophy

The United States Golf Association approached The Royal and Ancient Golf Club in 1958 with the proposal that the two bodies should sponsor a world-wide amateur golf event. The new competition would take place biennially in non-Walker Cup years, with the first being played at St Andrews in 1958. All golfing bodies that observed the Rules of Golf and Amateur Status as approved by The R&A and the USGA were invited to send one representative to a meeting in Washington at which President Dwight D Eisenhower presented a trophy to be awarded to the winning country. The committee of the event was to be known as the World Amateur Golf Council, which is now the International Golf Federation.

The key objective of the new council was "to foster friendship and sportsmanship among the peoples of the world through the conduct of an Amateur Team Championship for The Eisenhower Trophy". In a meeting with the President in the Rose Garden of the White House, Eisenhower offered his advice to the delegates: "I suggest, aside from the four hotshot golfers you bring, that you take along some high-handicap fellows and let them play at their full handicaps ...

This way golf doesn't become so important". This observation led to the creation of a "Delegates and Duffers Cup" for officials and non-playing captains.

The format decided for the Eisenhower Trophy was strokeplay. Each team consisted of four players who would play four rounds. The team score for each round was the three best individual scores. The first competition was held in St Andrews and attracted teams from 29 countries. After 72 holes of golf, the American and Australian teams were both tied on an aggregate score of 918. A play-off was held and the Australian team won by two strokes. So far this has been the only play-off in the history of the event.

Australia went on to win the trophy twice more, in 1966 and 1996. However, the USA have dominated the event, winning it 13 times in total. The Great Britain and Ireland team have won four times, in 1964, 1976, 1988 and 1998. In 2002 teams were reduced from four to three players with the best two scores counting in each round and for the first time England, Ireland, Scotland and Wales entered separate teams. In 2008, Scotland claimed its first victory in the Eisenhower Trophy at the Royal Adelaide Golf Club, Australia. Fifty years after the Australians won the first Championship at the Old Course in St Andrews, the Scots took the Trophy home from Australia. A parallel event for women, playing for the Espirito Santo Trophy, is held at the same venue prior to the Eisenhower.

The St Andrews Trophy

In November 1955 the Championship Committee of The Royal and Ancient Golf Club put forward a recommendation that "the European Golf Association should be approached with a view to arranging an international match between a Great Britain and Ireland and European side".

The GB&I team, captained by Gerald Micklem, duly triumphed by a score of 12½ to 2½ in the first match played over the West Course at Wentworth in 1956. A resounding success, it was immediately established as a biennial event in non-Walker Cup years and in 1964 the Club donated the St Andrews Trophy to be presented to the winning team.

Although Great Britain and Ireland have dominated the match, winning 23 of the 26 encounters, the Continent of Europe had a convincing victory at Villa d'Este in Italy in 1998 and suffered only a narrow 13–11 defeat at Turnberry in 2000. The Continent of Europe are the current holders of the trophy, winning in 2010 by a score of 14 to 10 at Castelconturbia, near Milan in Italy.

The Jacques Léglise Trophy

The annual boys international match involving GB&I against a team from the Continent of Europe was introduced in 1958. This event was dominated originally by the British and Irish side, which won every match through 1966 prompting the match to be discontinued because it was a one-sided affair.

The match was revived in 1977 when the Continental team won by 7 points to 6. A new trophy, donated by Jean-Louis Dupont on behalf of Golf de Chantilly in memory of Jacques Léglise, a leading French golf administrator, was presented for the first time in 1978 when the Continental team again won. Since then the Continental side has triumphed a further eight times, most recently in 2010. The 2010 match at Castelconturbia resulted in a 15½–8½ victory for the Continent of Europe. The 2008 match at Kingsbarns resulted in a 14–10 victory for GB&I. Great Britain and Ireland won the 2011 match with an impressive 14½–9½ victory over the Continent of Europe. The match was played in conjunction with the Boys Amateur Championship and Home International events until 1995. Since 1996 it has been played concurrently with the St Andrews Trophy, although the Jacques Léglise Trophy remains an annual competition.

The Boys Home Internationals

Introduced at Dunbar in 1923, the Boys Home Internationals started off as a match played between England and Scotland. It was traditionally associated with the Boys Amateur Championship, being played the day before and acting as a prelude to the main event.

The Royal and Ancient Golf Club accepted responsibility for the Boys Amateur Championship in 1949 and with it the running of the England *v* Scotland match. The Championship Committee originally carried out team selection. Today, representatives from the four Home Unions select the teams.

In 1972, a team match between Ireland and Wales was added to the fixture and the current format was established in 1996. The four home countries compete against one another over three consecutive days in a round robin series. Each fixture comprises five morning foursomes, followed by ten afternoon singles.

In 1997, there was a significant break with the past when, for the first time, the venue chosen for the Boys Home Internationals differed to that for the Boys Amateur Championship. This practice has remained, helping to shape the individual identity of the inter-national matches. Since 1985, the R&A Trophy has been awarded to the winning team.

Important dates in the history of St Andrews, The Open Championship and The R&A

1457	Golf is banned by King James II of Scotland; instead, archery is encouraged.
1552	Archbishop John Hamilton grants citizens rights to play games, including golf, on the links.
1744	First set of 13 rules laid out by golfers at Leith.
1754	Twenty-two noblemen and gentlemen of Fife form Society of St Andrews Golfers.
1764	A round at St Andrews changes from 22 to 18 holes and becomes the standard.
1834	King William IV confers his patronage and the Society of St Andrews Golfers becomes The Royal and Ancient Golf Club.
1854	The Royal and Ancient Clubhouse is built.
1860	First Open Championship is held at Prestwick and won by Willie Park Sr.
1870	Tom Morris Jr wins Open Belt for third time and gets to keep it.
1872	The Royal and Ancient Golf Club, Prestwick and Honourable Company of Edinburgh Golfers take over the running of The Open.
1873	First time The Open is played at St Andrews and first time the Claret Jug is presented.
1894	United States Golf Association is formed.
1897	The R&A becomes accepted authority for golf and forms the Rules of Golf Committee.
1904	Lost ball search time reduced from 10 to five minute.
1919	The R&A takes over the running of the Amateur Championship.
1920	The R&A takes responsibility for The Open Championship
1920	First R&A–USGA rules conference
1926	The Open is first played over three days.
1929	USGA legitimises larger ball (1.68in). Smaller ball (1.62in) still used elsewhere.
1929	Steel shafts are legalised.
1951	The R&A and USGA meet to unify rules.
1952	The R&A and USGA standardise rules except for ball size. Stymie is abolished.
1955	First live television coverage of The Open Championship by the BBC.
1956	First four-yearly rules revision.
1960	First grandstands erected at The Open Championship.
1963	Last 36-hole play-off for The Open Championship.
1966	First live coverage of The Open Championship in America.
1966	Open played over four days for first time at Muirfield.
1974	1.68in ball becomes compulsory in The Open Championship for first time.
1980	The Open ends on a Sunday for the first time at Muirfield.
1984	New dropping procedure at arms length from the shoulder.
1985	The R&A change play-off arrangements for The Open to four holes.
1990	The American size 1.68in ball becomes the only legal ball.
2004	The Royal and Ancient Golf Club celebrates its 250th anniversary. Responsibility for external activities, such as running The Open and administering the Rules, is devolved to a newly formed group of companies known as The R&A.
2007	Old Course first used for the Ricoh Women's British Open Championship.
2008	Curtis Cup played over the Old Course for the first time.
2010	The Open celebrates 150 years and is played at the Home of Golf for the 28th time

Interesting Facts and Unusual Incidents

Royal golf clubs

● The right to the designation *Royal* is bestowed by the favour of the Sovereign or a member of the Royal House. In most cases the title is granted along with the bestowal of royal patronage on the club. The Perth Golfing Society was the first to receive the designation *Royal*. That was accorded in June 1833. King William IV bestowed the honour on The Royal and Ancient Club in 1834. The most recent Club to be so designated is Royal Mayfair Golf & Country Club in Edmonton, Canada. The club was granted Royal status in October 2005. The next most recent was Royal Mariánské Lázně in the Czech Republic. In 2003, the club was given the Royal title as a result of its association in the early part of the 20th century with King Edward VII. A full list of Royal clubs can be found on pages 688–689.

Royal and Presidential golfers

● In the long history of the Royal and Ancient game no reigning British monarch has played in an open competition. In 1922 the Duke of Windsor, when Prince of Wales, competed in The Royal and Ancient Autumn Medal at St Andrews. He also took part in competitions at Mid-Surrey, Sunningdale, Royal St George's and in the Parliamentary Handicap. He occasionally competed in American events, sometimes partnered by a professional. On a private visit to London in 1952, he competed in the Autumn competition of Royal St George's at Sandwich, scoring 97. As Prince of Wales he played on courses all over the world and, after his abdication, as Duke of Windsor he continued to enjoy the game for many years.

● King George VI, when still Duke of York, in 1930, and the Duke of Kent, in 1937, also competed in the Autumn Meeting of The Royal and Ancient, when they had formally played themselves into the Captaincy of the Club and each returned his card in the medal round. So too did Prince Andrew, the Duke of York, when he became captain in 2003. He also played in the medal and won the mixed foursomes the following day playing with former British ladies champion Julie Otto.

● King Leopold of Belgium played in the Belgian Amateur Championship at Le Zoute, the only reigning monarch ever to have played in a national championship. The Belgian King played in many competitions subsequent to his abdication. In 1949 he reached the quarter-finals of the French Amateur Championship at St Cloud, playing as Count de Rethy.

● King Baudouin of Belgium in 1958 played in the triangular match Belgium–France–Holland and won his match against a Dutch player. He also took part in the Gleneagles Hotel tournament (playing as Mr B. de Rethy), partnered by Dai Rees in 1959.

● United States President George Bush accepted an invitation in 1990 to become an Honorary Member of The Royal and Ancient Golf Club of St Andrews. The honour recognised his long connection and that of his family with golf and The R&A. Both President Bush's father, Prescott Bush Sr, and his grandfather, George Herbert Walker – who donated the Walker Cup – were presidents of the United States Golf Association. Other Honorary Members of The R&A include Kel Nagle, Jack Nicklaus, Arnold Palmer, Gene Sarazen, Peter Thomson, Roberto de Vicenzo, Gary Player and five-times Open Championship winner Tom Watson, who was made an honorary member in 1999 on his 50th birthday.

● In September 1992, The Royal and Ancient Golf Club of St Andrews announced that His Royal Highness The Duke of York had accepted the Club's invitation of Honorary Membership. The Duke of York is the sixth member of the Royal Family to accept membership along with Their Royal Highnesses The Duke of Edinburgh and The Duke of Kent. He has since become a single handicapper, and has appeared in a number of pro-ams, partnering The Open and Masters champion Mark O'Meara to victory in the Alfred Dunhill Cup pro-am at St Andrews in 1998. His Royal Highness was Captain for 2003–2004, the year in which the Club celebrated its 250th anniversary.

First lady golfer

● Mary Queen of Scots, who was beheaded on 8th February, 1587, was probably the first lady golfer so mentioned by name. As evidence of her indifference to the fate of Darnley, her husband who was murdered at Kirk o' Field, Edinburgh, she was charged at her trial with having played at golf in the fields beside Seton a few days after his death.

Record championship victories

● In the Amateur Championship at Muirfield, 1920, Captain Carter, an Irish golfer, defeated an American entrant by 10 and 8. This is the only known instance where a player has won every hole in an Amateur Championship tie.

● In the final of the Canadian Ladies' Championship at Rivermead, Ottawa, in 1921, Cecil Leitch defeated Mollie McBride by 17 and 15. Miss Leitch lost only 1 hole in the match, the ninth. She was 14 up at the end of the first round, making only 3 holes necessary in the second. She won 18 holes out of 21 played, lost 1, and halved 2.

● In the final of the French Ladies' Open Championship at Le Touquet in 1927, Mlle de la Chaume (St Cloud) defeated Mrs Alex Johnston (Moor Park) by 15 and 14, the largest victory in a European golf championship.

● At Prestwick in 1934, W. Lawson Little of Presidio, San Francisco, defeated James Wallace, Troon Portland, by 14 and 13 in the final of the Amateur Championship, the record victory in the Championship. Wallace failed to win a single hole.

Players who have won two or more majors in the same year

(The first Masters Tournament was played in 1934)

1922 Gene Sarazen – USPGA, US Open
1924 Walter Hagen – USPGA, The Open
1926 Bobby Jones – US Open, The Open
1930 Bobby Jones – US Open, The Open (Bobby Jones also won the US Amateur and British Amateur in this year)
1932 Gene Sarazen – US Open, The Open
1941 Craig Wood – Masters, US Open
1948 Ben Hogan – USPGA, US Open
1949 Sam Snead – USPGA, Masters
1951 Ben Hogan – Masters, US Open
1953 Ben Hogan – Masters, US Open, The Open
1956 Jack Burke – USPGA, Masters
1960 Arnold Palmer – Masters, US Open
1962 Arnold Palmer – Masters, The Open
1963 Jack Nicklaus – USPGA, Masters
1966 Jack Nicklaus – Masters, The Open
1971 Lee Trevino – US Open, The Open
1972 Jack Nicklaus – Masters, The Open
1974 Gary Player – Masters, The Open
1975 Jack Nicklaus – USPGA, Masters
1977 Tom Watson – Masters, The Open
1980 Jack Nicklaus – USPGA, US Open
1982 Tom Watson – US Open, The Open
1990 Nick Faldo – Masters, The Open
1994 Nick Price – The Open, US PGA
1998 Mark O'Meara – Masters, The Open
2000 Tiger Woods* – US Open, The Open, USPGA
2008 Padraig Harrington – The Open, US PGA
2010 Yani Tseng – Women's British Open, Kraft Nabisco
2011 Yani Tseng – Women's British Open, LPGA

*Woods also won the 2001 Masters to become the first player to hold all four Majors at the same time. He was 65-under-par for the four events.

Outstanding records in championships, international matches and on the professional circuit

● The record number of victories in The Open Championship is six, held by Harry Vardon who won in 1896-98-99-1903-11-14.

● Five-time winners of the Championship are J.H. Taylor in 1894-95-1900-09-13; James Braid in 1901-05-06-08-10; Peter Thomson in 1954-55-56-58-65 and Tom Watson in 1975-77-80-82-83. Thomson's 1965 win was achieved when the Championship had become a truly international event. In 1957 he finished second behind Bobby Locke. By winning again in 1958 Thomson was prevented only by Bobby Locke from winning five consecutive Open Championships.

● Four successive victories in The Open by *Young* Tom Morris is a record so far never equalled. He won in 1868-69-70-72. (The Championship was not played in 1871.) Other four-time winners are Bobby Locke in 1949-50-52-57, Walter Hagen in 1922-24-28-29, Willie Park 1860-63-66-75, and *Old* Tom Morris 1861-62-64-67.

● Since the Championship began in 1860, players who have won three times in succession are Jamie Anderson, Bob Ferguson, and Peter Thomson.

● Robert Tyre Jones won The Open three times in 1926-27-30; the Amateur in 1930; the American Open in 1923-26-29-30; and the American Amateur in 1924-25-27-28-30. In winning the four major golf titles of the world in one year (1930) he achieved a feat unlikely ever to be equalled. Jones retired from competitive golf after winning the 1930 American Open, the last of these Championships, at the age of 28.

● Jack Nicklaus has had the most wins (six) in the US Masters Tournament, followed by Arnold Palmer with four.

● In modern times there are four championships generally regarded as standing above all others – The Open, US Open, US Masters, and USPGA. Five players have held all these titles, Gene Sarazen, Ben Hogan, Gary Player, Jack Nicklaus and Tiger Woods in that order. In 1978 Nicklaus became the first player to have held each of them at least three times. His record in these events is: The Open 1966-70-78; US Open 1962-67-72-80; US Masters 1963-65-66-72-75-86; USPGA 1963-71-73-75-80. His total of major championships is now 18. In 1998 at the age of 58, Nicklaus finished joint sixth in the Masters. By not playing in The Open Championship that year, he ended a run of 154 successive major championships for which he was eligible (stretching back to 1957).

In 1953 Ben Hogan won the Masters, US Open and The Open, but did not compete in the USPGA because of a dates clash with The Open.

In 2000 Tiger Woods won the US Open by 15 strokes (a major championship record), The Open by eight strokes, and the USPGA in the play-off. In 2001 he then added the Masters winning by two shots to become the first player to hold all four major titles at the same time. He was 65-under-par for the four events.

● In the 1996 English Amateur Championship at Hollinwell, Ian Richardson (50) and his son, Carl, of Burghley Park, Lincolnshire, both reached the semi-finals. Both lost.

● The record number of victories in the US Open is four, held by Willie Anderson, Bobby Jones, Ben Hogan and Jack Nicklaus.

● Bobby Jones (amateur), Gene Sarazen, Ben Hogan, Lee Trevino, Tom Watson and Tiger Woods are the only players to have won The Open and US Open Championships in the same year. Tony Jacklin won The Open in 1969 and the US Open in 1970 and for a few weeks was the holder of both.

● In winning the Amateur Championship in 1970 Michael Bonallack became the first player to win in three consecutive years.

● The English Amateur record number of victories is held by Michael Bonallack, who won the title five times.

● John Ball holds the record number of victories in the Amateur Championship, which he won eight times. Next comes Michael Bonallack (who was internationally known as *The Duke*) with five wins.

● Cecil Leitch and Joyce Wethered each won the British Ladies' title four times.

● The Scottish Amateur record was held by Ronnie Shade, who won five titles in successive years, 1963 to 1967. His long reign as Champion ended when he was beaten in the fourth round of the 1968 Championship after winning 44 consecutive matches.

● Joyce Wethered established an unbeaten record by winning the English Ladies' in five successive years from 1920 to 1924 inclusive.

● In winning the Amateur Championships of Britain and America in 1934 and 1935 Lawson Little won 31 consecutive matches. Other dual winners of these championships in the same year are R.T. Jones (1930) and Bob Dickson (1967).

● Peter Thomson's victory in the 1971 New Zealand Open Championship was his ninth in that event.

● In a four-week spell in 1971, Lee Trevino won in succession the US Open, the Canadian Open and The Open Championship.

● Michael Bonallack and Bill Hyndman were the Amateur Championship finalists in both 1969 and 1970. This was the first time the same two players reached the final in successive years.

● On the US professional circuit the greatest number of consecutive victories is 11, achieved by Byron Nelson in 1945. Nelson also holds the record for most victories in one calendar year, again in 1945 when he won a total of 18 tournaments.

● Raymond Floyd, by winning the Doral Classic in March 1992, joined Sam Snead as the only winners of US Tour events in four different decades.

● Sam Snead won tournaments in six decades. His first win was the 1936 West Virginia PGA. In 1980 he won the *Golf Digest* Commemorative and in 1982 the Legends of Golf with Don January.

● Neil Coles has won official Tour events in six decades. His first victory was in 1958 and he was a winner on the European Senior Tour in June 2000 when he took the Microlease Jersey Senior Open. Coles still plays well enough to beat his age. Now 67, he shot a closing 64 in the final round of the 2003 Travis Perkins Senior Open over the Edinburgh course he helped design.

● Jack Nicklaus and the late Walter Hagen have had five wins each in the USPGA Championship. All Hagen's wins were at match play; all Nicklaus's at stroke play.

● In 1953 Flory van Donck of Belgium had seven major victories in Europe, including The Open Championships of Switzerland, Italy, Holland, Germany and Belgium.

● Mrs Anne Sander won four major amateur titles each under a different name. She won the US Ladies' in 1958 as Miss Quast, in 1961 as Mrs Decker, in 1963 as Mrs Welts and the British Ladies' in 1980 as Mrs Sander.

● The highest number of appearances in the Ryder Cup matches is held by Nick Faldo who made his eleventh appearance in 1997.

● The greatest number of appearances in the Walker Cup matches is held by Irishman Joe Carr who made his tenth appearance in 1967.

● In the Curtis Cup Mary McKenna made her ninth consecutive appearance in 1986.

● Players who have represented their country in both Walker and Ryder Cup matches are: for the United States, Fred Haas, Ken Venturi, Gene Littler, Jack Nicklaus, Tommy Aaron, Mason Rudolph, Bob Murphy, Lanny Wadkins, Scott Simpson, Tom Kite, Jerry Pate, Craig Stadler, Jay Haas, Bill Rodgers, Hal Sutton, Curtis Strange, Davis Love III, Brad Faxon, Scott Hoch, Phil Mickelson, Corey Pavin, Justin Leonard, Tiger Woods, David Duval, Anthony Kim, Dustin Johnson and Rickie Fowler; and for Great Britain & Ireland, Norman Drew, Peter Townsend, Clive Clark, Peter Oosterhuis, Howard Clark, Mark James, Michael King, Gordon Brand Jr, Paul Way, Ronan Rafferty, Sandy Lyle, Philip Walton, David Gilford, Colin Montgomerie, Peter Baker, Padraig Harrington, Andrew Coltart, Oliver Wilson, Justin Rose, Luke Donald, Paul Casey, Graeme McDowell and Rory McIlroy.

Remarkable recoveries in matchplay

● There have been two remarkable recoveries in the Walker Cup Matches. In 1930 at Sandwich, J.A. Stout, Great Britain, round in 68, was 4 up at the end of the first round against Donald Moe. Stout started in the second round, 3, 3, 3, and was 7 up. He was still 7 up with 13 to play. Moe, who went round in 67, won back the 7 holes to draw level at the 17th green. At the 18th or 36th of the match, Moe, after a long drive placed his iron shot within three feet of the hole and won the match by 1 hole.

● In 1936 at Pine Valley, George Voigt and Harry Girvan for America were 7 up with 11 to play against Alec Hill and Cecil Ewing. The British pair drew level at the 17th hole, or the 35th of the match, and the last hole was halved.

● In the 1965 Piccadilly Match Play Championship Gary Player beat Tony Lema after being 7 down with 17 to play.

● Bobby Cruickshank, the old Edinburgh player, had an extraordinary recovery in a 36-hole match in a USPGA Championship for he defeated Al Watrous after being 11 down with 12 to play.

● In a match at the Army GC, Aldershot, on 5th July, 1974, for the Gradoville Bowl, M.C. Smart was 8 down with 8 to play against Mike Cook. Smart succeeded in winning all the remaining holes and the 19th for victory.

● In the 1982 Suntory World Match Play Championship Sandy Lyle beat Nick Faldo after being 6 down with 18 to play.

● In the 1991 Ryder Cup at Kiawah, Colin Montgomerie, on his début, was five down to Mark Calcavecchia at the turn. The American was still four up with four to play. Although the Scot finished double bogey, par, double bogey, par, he won all the closing holes and squared the match when the American missed the hole from two feet on the last.

Oldest champions

The Open Championship: Belt Tom Morris in 1867 – 46 years 99 days. *Cup* Roberto de Vicenzo, 44 years 93 days, in 1967; Harry Vardon, 44 years 42 days, in 1914; J.H. Taylor, 42 years 97 days, in 1913; Darren Clarke, 42 years 11 months, in 2011.

Amateur Championship Hon. Michael Scot, 54, at Hoylake in 1933.

British Ladies Amateur Mrs Jessie Valentine, 43, at Hunstanton in 1958.

Scottish Amateur J.M. Cannon, 53, at Troon in 1969.

English Amateur Terry Shingler, 41 years 11 months at Walton Heath 1977; Gerald Micklem, 41 years 8 months, at Royal Birkdale 1947.

Welsh Amateur John Jermine, 56, at St David's, in 2000

US Open Hale Irwin, 45, at Medinah, Illinois, in 1990.

US Amateur Jack Westland, 47, at Seattle in 1952 (He had been defeated in the 1931 final, 21 years previously, by Francis Ouimet).

US Masters Jack Nicklaus, 46, in 1986.

European Tour Des Smyth, 48 years, 14 days, Madeira Open 1982; Neil Coles, 48 years 14 days, Sanyo Open 1982

European Senior Tour Neil Coles, 65, in 2000

USPGA Julius Boros, 48, in 1968. Lee Trevino, 44, in 1984.

USPGA Tour Sam Snead, 52, at Greensborough Open in 1965. Sam Snead, 61, equal second in Glen Campbell Open 1974.

Youngest champions

The Open Championship: Belt Tom Morris, Jr, 17 years 5 months, in 1868. *Cup* Willie Auchterlonie, 21 years 24 days, in 1893; Tom Morris, Jr, 21 years 5 months, in 1872; Severiano Ballesteros, 22 years 103 days, in 1979.

US Open Championship: In 2011 Rory McIlroy, at the age of 22, became the youngest player to win the event since Bobby Jones' victory in 1923 at the age of 21.

Amateur Championship J.C. Beharrell, 18 years 1 month, at Troon in 1956; R. Cole (RSA) 18 years 1 month, at Carnoustie in 1966.

British Ladies Amateur May Hezlett, 17, at Newcastle, Co. Down, in 1899; Michelle Walker, 18, at Alwoodley in 1971.

English Amateur Nick Faldo, 18, at Lytham St Annes in 1975; Paul Downes, 18, at Birkdale in 1978; David Gilford, 18, at Woodhall Spa in 1984; Ian Garbutt, 18, at Woodhall Spa in 1990; Mark Foster, 18, at Moortown in 1994.

English Amateur Strokeplay Ronan Rafferty, 16, at Hunstanton in 1980.

British Ladies Open Strokeplay Helen Dobson, 18, at Southerness in 1989.

British Boys Championship Mark Mouland (WAL) 15 years 120 days at Sunningdale in 1976; Pablo Martin (ESP) 15 years 120 days at Ganton 2001.

More records can be found on pages 480–492

Disqualifications

Disqualifications are now numerous, usually for some irregularity over signing a scorecard or for late arrival at the first tee. We therefore show here only incidents in major events involving famous players or players who were in a winning position or incidents which were in themselves unusual.

● J.J. McDermott, the American Open Champion 1911–12, arrived for The Open Championship at Prestwick in 1914 to discover that he had made a mistake of a week in the date the championship began. The American could not play, as the qualifying rounds were completed on the day he arrived.

● In the Amateur Championship at Sandwich in 1937, Brigadier-General Critchley, arriving at Southampton from New York on the *Queen Mary*, which had been delayed by fog, flew by specially chartered aeroplane to Sandwich. He circled over the clubhouse, so the officials knew he was nearly there, but he arrived six minutes late, and his name had been struck out. At the same championship a player, entered from Burma, who had travelled across the Pacific and the American Continent, and was also on the *Queen Mary*, travelled from Southampton by motor car and arrived four hours after his starting time to find after journeying more than halfway round the world he was struck out.

● An unprecedented disqualification was that of A. Murray in the New Zealand Open Championship, 1937. Murray, who was New Zealand Champion in 1935, was playing with J.P. Hornabrook, New Zealand Amateur Champion, and at the 8th hole in the last round, while waiting for his partner to putt, Murray dropped a ball on the edge of the green and made a practice putt along the edge. Murray returned the lowest score in the championship, but he was disqualified for taking the practice putt.

● At The Open Championship at St Andrews in 1946, John Panton, Glenbervie, in the evening practised putting on a green on the New Course, which was one of the qualifying courses. He himself reported his inadvertence to The Royal and Ancient and he was disqualified.

• At The Open Championship, Sandwich, 1949, C. Rotar, an American, qualified by four strokes to compete in the championship but he was disqualified because he had used a putter which did not conform to the accepted form and make of a golf club, the socket being bent over the centre of the club head. This is the only case where a player has been disqualified in The Open Championship for using an illegal club.

• In the 1957 American Women's Open Championship, Mrs Jackie Pung had the lowest score, 298 over four rounds, but lost the championship. The card she signed for the final round read *five* at the 4th hole instead of the correct *six*. Her total of 72 was correct but the error, under rigid rules, resulted in her disqualification. Betty Jameson, who partnered Mrs Pung and also returned a wrong score, was also disqualified.

• Mark Roe and Jesper Parnevik were disqualified in bizarre circumstances in the 2003 Open at Royal St George's, Sandwich. Roe had shot 67 to move into contention but it was discovered after they left the recorder's hut that they had not exchanged cards. Roe's figures were returned on a card with Parnevik's name on it and vice versa. The R&A have since changed the rules to allow the official scorer to erase the wrong name and put the correct one on the card ensuring a Roe–Parnevik incident can never happen again.

• Teenager Michelle Wie will not be allowed to forget her début on the LPGA Tour as a professional in the Samsung World Championship. Although she completed four rounds and finished fourth behind Annika Sörenstam, she was disqualified for taking a drop nearer to the hole in the third round. A reporter, Michael Bamberger from *Sports Illustrated*, saw the incident but did not report it to officials until the next day after he had spoken with his editor. Officials only decided to disqualify the youngster after measuring out distances at the spot where she took the drop with a yard of string.

• Kevin Stadler, son of Ryder Cup and former Masters champion Craig Stadler, was disqualified in the 2005 Funai Classic in Orlando for disclosing he had a bent shaft in his wedge. Lying 163rd in the money list and needing a good finish to keep his card, he was lying joint fifth going into the final round. He discovered the shaft of his wedge was bent on the second hole on the final day and was disqualified for playing with an illegal club – ironically, one that could never have helped him play a decent shot.

Longest match

• W.R. Chamberlain, a retired farmer, and George New, a postmaster at Chilton Foliat, on 1st August, 1922, met at Littlecote, the 9-hole course of Sir Ernest Wills, and agreed to play every Thursday afternoon over the course. This continued until New's sudden death on 13th January, 1938. An accurate record of the match was kept, giving details of each round including wind direction and playing conditions. In the elaborate system nearly two million facts were recorded. They played 814 rounds, and aggregated 86,397 strokes, of which Chamberlain took 44,008 and New 42,371. New, therefore, was 1,637 strokes up. The last round of all was halved, a suitable end to such an unusual contest.

Longest ties

• The longest known ties in 18-hole match play rounds in major events were in an early round of the News of the World Match Play Championship at Turnberry in 1960, when W.S. Collins beat W.J. Branch at the 31st hole, and in the third round of the same tournament at Walton Heath in 1961 when Harold Henning beat Peter Alliss also at the 31st hole.

• In the 1970 Scottish Amateur Championship at Balgownie, Aberdeen, E. Hammond beat J. McIvor at the 29th hole in their second round tie.

• C.A. Palmer beat Lionel Munn at the 28th hole at Sandwich in 1908. This is the record tie of the British Amateur Championship. Munn has also been engaged in two other extended ties in the Amateur Championship. At Muirfield, in 1932, in the semi-final, he was defeated by John de Forest, the ultimate winner, at the 26th hole, and at St Andrews, in 1936, in the second round he was defeated by J.L. Mitchell, again at the 26th hole.

The following examples of long ties are in a different category for they occurred in competitions, either stroke play or match play, where the conditions stipulated that in the event of a tie, a further stated number of holes had to be played – in some cases 36 holes, but mostly 18. With this method a vast number of extra holes was sometimes necessary to settle ties.

• The longest known was between two American women in a tournament at Peterson (New Jersey) when 88 extra holes were required before Mrs Edwin Labaugh emerged as winner.

• In a match on the Queensland course, Australia, in October, 1933, H.B. Bonney and Col H.C.H. Robertson versus B.J. Canniffe and Dr Wallis Hoare required to play a further four 18-hole matches after being level at the end of the original 18 holes. In the fourth replay Hoare and Caniffe won by 3 and 2 which meant that 70 extra holes had been necessary to decide the tie.

• After finishing all square in the final of the Dudley GC's foursomes competition in 1950, F.W. Mannell and A.G. Walker played a further three 18-hole replays against T. Poole and E. Jones, each time finishing all square. A further 9 holes were arranged and Mannell and Walker won by 3 and 2 making a total of 61 extra holes to decide the tie.

• R.A. Whitcombe and Mark Seymour tied for first prize in the Penfold £750 Tournament at St Annes-on-Sea, in 1934. They had to play off over 36 holes and tied again. They were then required to play another 9 holes when Whitcombe won with 34 against 36. The tournament was over 72 holes. The first tie added 36 holes and the extra 9 holes made an aggregate of 117 holes to decide the winner. This is a record in first-class British golf but in no way compares with other long ties as it involved only two replays – one of 36 holes and one of 9.

● In the American Open Championship at Toledo, Ohio, in 1931, G. Von Elm and Billy Burke tied for the title. Each returned aggregates of 292. On the first replay both finished in 149 for 36 holes but on the second replay Burke won with a score of 148 against 149. This is a record tie in a national open championship.

● Cary Middlecoff and Lloyd Mangrum were declared co-winners of the 1949 Motor City Open on the USPGA Tour after halving 11 sudden death holes.

● Australian David Graham beat American Dave Stockton at the tenth extra hole in the 1998 Royal Caribbean Classic, a record on the US Senior Tour.

● Paul Downes was beaten by Robin Davenport at the 9th extra hole in the 4th round of the 1981 English Amateur Championship, a record marathon match for the Championship.

● Severiano Ballesteros was beaten by Johnny Miller at the 9th extra hole of a sudden-death play-off at the 1982 Million Dollar Sun City Challenge.

● José Maria Olazábal beat Ronan Rafferty at the 9th extra hole to win the 1989 Dutch Open on the Kennemer Golf and Country Club course. Roger Chapman had been eliminated at the first extra hole.

Long drives

It is impossible to state with any certainty what is the longest ever drive. Many long drives have never been measured and many others have most likely never been brought to our attention. Then there are several outside factors which can produce freakishly long drives, such as a strong following wind, downhill terrain or bonehard ground. Where all three of these favourable conditions prevail outstandingly long drives can be achieved. Another consideration is that a long drive made during a tournament is a different proposition from one made for length alone, either on the practice ground, a long driving competition or in a game of no consequence. All this should be borne in mind when considering the long drives shown here.

● When professional Carl Hooper hit a wayward drive on the 3rd hole (456 yards) at the Oak Hills Country Club, San Antonio, during the 1992 Texas Open, he wrote himself into the record books but out of the tournament. The ball kept bouncing and rolling on a tarmac cart path until it was stopped by a fence – 787 yards away. It took Hooper two recovery shots with a 4-iron and then an 8-iron to return to the fairway. He eventually holed out for a double bogey six and failed to survive the half-way qualifying cut.

● Tommie Campbell of Portmarnock hit a drive of 392 yards at Dun Laoghaire GC in July 1964.

● Playing in Australia, American George Bayer is reported to have driven to within chipping distance of a 589 yards hole. "It was certainly a drive of over 500 yards", said Bayer acknowledging the strong following wind, sharp downslope where his ball landed and the bone-hard ground.

● In September, 1934, over the East Devon course, T.H.V. Haydon, Wimbledon, drove to the edge of the 9th green which was a hole of 465 yards, giving a drive of not less than 450 yards.

● E.C. Bliss drove 445 yards at Herne Bay in August, 1913. The drive was measured by a government surveyor who also measured the drop in height from tee to resting place of the ball at 57 feet.

Long carries

● At Sitwell Park, Rotherham, in 1935 the home professional, W. Smithson, drove a ball which carried a dyke at 380 yards from the 2nd tee.

● George Bell, of Penrith GC, New South Wales, Australia, using a number 2 wood drove across the Nepean River, a certified carry of 309 yards in a driving contest in 1964.

● After the 1986 Irish Professional Championship at Waterville, Co. Kerry, four long-hitting professionals tried for the longest-carry record over water, across a lake in the Waterville Hotel grounds. Liam Higgins, the local professional, carried 310 yards and Paul Leonard 311, beating the previous record by 2 yards.

● In the 1972 Algarve Open at Penina, Henry Cotton vouched for a carry of 305 yards over a ditch at the 18th hole by long-hitting Spanish professional Francisco Abreu. There was virtually no wind assistance.

● At the Home International matches at Portmarnock in 1949 a driving competition was held in which all the players in all four teams competed. The actual carry was measured and the longest was 280 yards by Jimmy Bruen.

● On 6th April, 1976, Tony Jacklin hit a number of balls into Vancouver harbour, Canada, from the 495-foot high roof of a new building complex. The longest carry was measured at 389 yards.

Long hitting

There have been numerous long hits, not on golf courses, where an outside agency has assisted the length of the shot. Such an example was a "drive" by Liam Higgins in 1986, on the Airport runway at Baldonal, near Dublin, of 632 yards.

● How's this for a long shot? Odd Marthinussen was holidaying in Haparanda in Sweden when he holed in one at the 14th. So what! The curious thing about this ace is that while he teed up in Sweden the green is in Finland which is in a different time zone. Registered as an ace in both countries, the time it took for the ball to go from tee to cup was estimated at 1 hour and 4 seconds ... surely the longest hole ever reported by Simon Pia in his column in *The Scotsman* newspaper.

Longest albatrosses

● The longest-known albatrosses (three under par) recorded at par 5 holes are:

● 647 yards-2nd hole at Guam Navy Club by Chief Petty Officer Kevin Murray of Chicago on 3rd January, 1982.

● 609 yards-15th hole at Mahaka Inn West Course, Hawaii, by John Eakin of California on 12th November, 1972.

● 602 yards-16th hole at Whiting Field Golf Course, Milton, Florida, by 27-year-old Bill Graham with a drive and a 3-wood, aided by a 25 mph tail wind.

● The longest-known albatrosses in open championships are: 580 yards 14th hole at Crans-sur-Sierre, by American Billy Casper in the 1971 Swiss Open; 558 yards 5th hole at Muirfield by American Johnny Miller in the 1972 Open Championship.

● In the 1994 German Amateur Championship at Wittelsbacher GC, Rohrenfield, Graham Rankin, a member of the visiting Scottish national team, had a two at the 592 yard 18th.

Eagles (multiple and consecutive)

● Wilf Jones scored three consecutive eagles at the first three holes at Moor Hall GC when playing in a competition there on August Bank Holiday Monday 1968. He scored 3, 1, 2 at holes measuring 529 yards, 176 yards and 302 yards.

● In a round of the 1980 Jubilee Cup, a mixed foursomes match play event of Colchester GC, Mrs Nora Booth and her son Brendan scored three consecutive gross eagles of 1, 3, 2 at the eighth, ninth and tenth holes.

● Three players in a four-ball match at Kington GC, Herefordshire, on 22nd July, 1948, all had eagle 2s at the 18th hole (272 yards). They were R.N. Bird, R. Morgan and V. Timson.

● Four Americans from Wisconsin on holiday at Gleneagles in 1977 scored three eagles and a birdie at the 300-yard par-4 14th hole on the King's course. The birdie was by Dr Kim Lulloff and the eagles by Dr Gordon Meiklejohn, Richard Johnson and Jack Kubitz.

● In an open competition at Glen Innes GC, Australia on 13th November, 1977, three players in a four-ball scored eagle 3s at the 9th hole (442 metres). They were Terry Marshall, Roy McHarg and Jack Rohleder.

● David McCarthy, a member of Moortown Golf Club, Leeds, had three consecutive eagles (3, 3, 2) on the 4th, 5th and 6th holes during a Pro-Am competition at Lucerne, Switzerland, on 7th August, 1992.

Speed of golf ball and club head and effect of wind and temperature

● In *The Search for the Perfect Swing*, a scientific study of the golf swing, a first class golfer is said to have the club head travelling at 100 mph at impact. This will cause the ball to leave the club at 135 mph. An outstandingly long hitter might manage to have the club head travelling at 130 mph which would produce a ball send-off speed of 175 mph. The resultant shot would carry 280 yards.

● According to Thomas Hardman, Wilson's director of research and development, wind will reduce or increase the flight of a golf ball by approximately 1½ yards for every mile per hour of wind. Every two degrees of temperature will make a yard difference in a ball's flight.

Most northerly course

● Although the most northerly course used to be in Iceland, Björkliden Arctic Golf Club, Sweden, 250 km north of the Arctic Circle, has taken over that role. This may soon change, however, when a course opens in Narvic, Norway, which could be a few metres further north than Björkliden.

Most southerly course

● Golf's most southerly course is Scott Base Country Club, 13° north of the South Pole. The course is run by the New Zealand Antarctic Programme and players must be kitted in full survival gear. The most difficult aspect is finding the orange golf balls which tend to get buried in the snow. Other obstacles include penguins, seals and skuas. If the ball is stolen by a skua then a penalty of one shot is incurred; but if the ball hits a skua it counts as a birdie.

"I'm sure they shouldn't have been allowed on. I don't think they're members"

Highest golf courses

● The highest golf course in the world is thought to be the Tuctu GC in Peru which is 14,335 feet above sea-level. High courses are also found in Bolivia with the La Paz GC being about 13,500 feet. In the Himalayas, near the border with Tibet, a 9-hole course at 12,800 feet has been laid out by keen golfers in the Indian Army.

● The highest course in Europe is at Sestriere in the Italian Alps, 6,500 feet above sea-level.

● The highest courses in Great Britain are West Monmouthshire in Wales at 1,513 feet, Leadhills in Scotland at 1,500 feet and Kington in England at 1,284 feet.

Longest courses

● The longest course in the world is Dub's Dread GC, Piper, Kansas, USA measuring 8,101 yards (par 78).

● The longest course for The Open Championship was 7,361 yards at Carnoustie in 1999.

Longest holes

● The longest hole in the world, as far as is known, is the 6th hole measuring 782 metres (860 yards) at Koolan Island GC, Western Australia. The par of the hole is 7. There are several holes over 700 yards throughout the world.

● The longest hole for The Open Championship is the 577 yards 6th hole at Royal Troon.

Longest tournaments

● The longest tournament held was over 144 holes in the World Open at Pinehurst, N Carolina, USA, first held in 1973. Play was over two weeks with a cut imposed at the halfway mark.

● An annual tournament, played in Germany on the longest day of the year, comprises 100 holes' medal play. Best return, in 1995, was 399 strokes.

Largest entries

● The Open – 2,500, St Andrews, 2010.

● The Amateur – 537, Muirfield, 1998.

● US Open – 9,086, Bethpage Park GC, NY, 2009.

● The largest entry for a PGA European Tour event was 398 for the 1978 Colgate PGA Championship. Since 1985, when the all-exempt ruling was introduced, all PGA tournaments have had 144 competitors, slightly more or less.

● In 1952, Bobby Locke, The Open Champion, played a round at Wentworth against any golfer in Britain. Cards costing 2s. 6d. each (12½p), were taken out by 24,000 golfers. The challenge was to beat the local par by more than Locke could beat the par at Wentworth. 1,641 competitors, including women, succeeded in *beating* the Champion and each received a certificate signed by him. As a result of this challenge the British Golf Foundation benefited to the extent of £3,026, the proceeds from the sale of cards. A similar tournament was held in the US and Canada when 87,094 golfers participated; 14,667 players bettered Ben Hogan's score under handicap. The fund benefited by $80,024.

Largest prize money

● The Machrie Tournament of 1901 was the first tournament with a first prize of £100. It was won by J.H. Taylor, then The Open Champion, who beat James Braid in the final.

● The richest events (at time of writing) are the – US Open and US PGA Championships which carry a prize-fund of $7.5 million. The bonus for victory in the Fedex Cup is $10 million. The biggest first prize is the $1,710,000 which goes to the winner of The Players' Championship on the PGA Tour in America.

Holing-in-one – odds against

● At the Wanderers Club, Johannesburg in January, 1951, forty-nine amateurs and professionals each played three balls at a hole 146 yards long. Of the 147 balls hit, the nearest was by Koos de Beer, professional at Reading Country Club, which finished 10½ inches from the hole. Harry Bradshaw, the Irish professional who was touring with the British team in South Africa, touched the pin with his second shot, but the ball rolled on and stopped 3 feet 2 inches from the cup.

● A competition on similar lines was held in 1951 in New York when 1,409 players who had done a hole-in-one held a competition over several days at short holes on three New York courses. Each player was allowed a total of five shots, giving an aggregate of 7,045 shots. No player holed-in-one, and the nearest ball finished 3½ inches from the hole.

● A further illustration of the element of luck in holing-in-one is derived from an effort by Harry Gonder, an American professional, who in 1940 stood for 16 hours 25 minutes and hit 1,817 balls trying to do a 160 yard hole-in-one. He had two official witnesses and caddies to tee and retrieve the balls and count the strokes. His 1,756th shot struck the hole but stopped an inch from the hole. This was his nearest effort.

● From this and other similar information an estimate of the odds against holing-in-one at any particular hole within the range of one shot was made at somewhere between 1,500 and 2,000 to 1 by a proficient player. Subsequently, however, statistical analysis in America has come up with the following odds: a male professional or top amateur 3,708 to 1; a female professional or top amateur 4,648 to 1; an average golfer 42,952 to 1.

Hole-in-one first recorded

● The earliest recorded hole-in-one was in 1869 at The Open Championship when Tom Morris Jr completed the 145-yard 8th hole at Prestwick in one. This was the first ace in competition for The Open Championship Challenge Belt.

● The first hole-in-one recorded with the 1.66 inch ball was in 1972 by John G. Salvesen, a member of The R&A Championship Committee. At the time this size of ball was only experimental. Salvesen used a 7-iron for his historical feat at the 11th hole on the Old Course, St Andrews.

Holing-in-one in important events

Since the day of the first known hole-in-one by Tom Morris Jr, at the 8th hole (145 yards) at Prestwick in the 1869 Open Championship, holes-in-one, even in championships, have become too numerous for each to be recorded. Only where other unusual or interesting circumstances prevailed are the instances shown here.

● All hole-in-one achievements are remarkable. Many are extraordinary. Among the more amazing was that of 2-handicap Leicestershire golfer Bob Taylor, a member of the Scraptoft Club. During the final practice day for the 1974 Eastern Counties Foursomes Championship on the Hunstanton Links, he holed his tee shot with a one-iron at the 188-yard 16th. The next day, in the first round of the competition, he repeated the feat, the only difference being that because of a change of wind he used a six-iron. When he stepped on to the 16th tee the following day his partner jokingly offered him odds of 1,000,000 to one against holing-in-one for a third successive time. Taylor again used his six-iron – and holed in one!

● 1878 – Jamie Anderson, competing in The Open Championship at Prestwick, holed in one at the 11th. In these days The Open was played over three rounds of 12 holes so his ace, the first hole-in-one in competition for the Claret Jug – came at his penultimate hole in his third round. Although it seemed then that he was winning easily, it turned out afterwards that if he had not taken this hole in one stroke he would very likely have lost. Anderson was just about to make his tee shot when Andy Stuart (winner of the first Irish Open Championship in 1892), who was acting as marker to Anderson, remarked he was standing outside the teeing ground, and that if he played the stroke from there he would be disqualified. Anderson picked up his ball and teed it in a proper place. Then he holed-in-one. He won the Championship by one stroke.

● On a Friday the 13th in 1990, Richard Allen holed-in-one at the 13th at the Barwon Heads Golf Club, Victoria, Australia, and then lost the hole. He was giving a handicap stroke to his opponent, brother-in-law Jason Ennels, who also holed-in-one.

● 1906 – R. Johnston, North Berwick, competing in The Open Championship, did the 14th hole at Muirfield in one. Johnston played with only one club throughout – an adjustable head club.

● 1959 – The first hole-in-one in the US Women's Open Championship was recorded. It was by Patty Berg on the 7th hole (170 yards) at Churchill Valley CC, Pittsburgh.

● 1962 – On 6th April, playing in the second round of the Schweppes Close Championship at Little Aston, H. Middleton of Shandon Park, Belfast, holed his tee shot at the 159-yard 5th hole, winning a prize of £1,000. Ten minutes later, playing two matches ahead of Middleton, R.A. Jowle, son of the professional, Frank Jowle, holed his tee shot at the 179-yard 9th hole. As an amateur he was rewarded by the sponsors with a £30 voucher.

● 1963 – By holing out in one stroke at the 18th hole (156 yards) at Moor Park on the first day of the Esso Golden round-robin tournament, H.R. Henning, South Africa, won the £10,000 prize offered for this feat.

● 1967 – Tony Jacklin in winning the Masters tournament at St George's, Sandwich, did the 16th hole in one. His ace has an exceptional place in the records for it was seen by millions on TV, the ball was in view in its flight till it went into the hole in his final round of 64.

● 1971 – John Hudson, 25-year-old professional at Hendon, achieved a near miracle when he holed two consecutive holes-in-one in the Martini Tournament at Norwich. They were at the 11th and 12th holes (195 yards and 311 yards respectively) in the second round.

● 1971 – In The Open Championship at Birkdale, Lionel Platts holed-in-one at the 212-yard 4th hole in the second round. This was the first instance of an Open Championship hole-in-one being recorded by television. It was incidentally Platts' seventh ace of his career.

● In the 2006 Ryder Cup at the K Club, Ireland, Paul Casey holed his 4-iron shot at the 14th to score the fifth ace in the history of the competition. The following day, at the same hole, Scott Verplank became the first American to score a Ryder Cup hole-in-one. Others who have enjoyed aces in the match include Peter Butler in 1973, Nick Faldo in 1993 and Costantino Rocca and Howard Clark in 1995 at Oak Hill.

● 1973 – In the 1973 Open Championship at Troon, two holes-in-one were recorded, both at the 8th hole, known as the Postage Stamp, in the first round. They were achieved by Gene Sarazen and amateur David Russell, who were by coincidence respectively the oldest and youngest competitors.

● Mrs Argea Tissies, whose husband Hermann took 15 at Royal Troon's Postage Stamp 8th hole in the 1950 Open, scored a hole-in-one at the 2nd hole at Punta Ala in the second round of the Italian Ladies' Senior Open of 1978. Exactly five years later on the same date, at the same time of day, in the same round of the same tournament at the same hole, she did it again with the same club.

● In less than two hours play in the second round of the 1989 US Open at Oak Hill Country Club, Rochester, New York, four competitors – Doug Weaver, Mark Wiebe, Jerry Pate and Nick Price – each holed the 167-yard 6th hole in one. The odds against four professionals achieving such a record in a field of 156 are reckoned at 332,000 to 1.

● On 20th May, 1998, British golf journalist Derek Lawrenson, an eight-handicapper, won a Lamborghini Diablo car, valued at over £180,000, by holing his three-iron tee shot to the 175-yard 15th hole at Mill Ride, Berkshire. He was taking part in a charity day and was partnering England football stars Paul Ince and Steve McManaman.

● David Toms took the lead in the 2001 USPGA Championship at Atlanta Athletic Club with a hole-in-one at the 15th hole in the third round and went on to win. Nick Faldo (4th hole) and Scott Hoch (17th hole) also had holes-in-one during the event.

● In the 2006 Ryder Cup at the K Club, Ireland, Paul Casey holed his 4-iron shot at the 14th to score the fifth ace in the history of the competition. The following day, at the same hole, Scott Verplank became the first American to score a Ryder Cup hole-in-one.

Holing-in-one – longest holes

● Bob Mitera, as a 21-year-old American student, standing 5 feet 6 inches and weighing under 12 stones, claimed the world record for the longest hole-in-one. Playing over the appropriately named Miracle Hill course at Omaha, on 7th October, 1965, Bob holed his drive at the 10th hole, 447 yards long. The ground sloped sharply downhill.

● Two longer holes-in-one have been achieved, but because they were at dog-leg holes they are not generally accepted as being the longest holes-in-one. They were 496 yards (17th hole, Teign Valley) by Shaun Lynch in July 1995 and 480 yards (5th hole, Hope CC, Arkansas) by L. Bruce on 15th November, 1962.

● In March, 1961, Lou Kretlow holed his tee shot at the 427-yard 16th hole at Lake Hefner course, Oklahoma City, USA.

● The longest known hole-in-one in Great Britain was the 393-yard 7th hole at West Lancashire GC, where in 1972 the assistant professional Peter Parkinson holed his tee shot.

● Paul Neilson, a 34-year-old golfer at South Winchester, holed in one at the club's par 4 fifth hole – 391 yards.

● Other long holes-in-one recorded in Great Britain have been 380 yards (5th hole at Tankersley Park) by David Hulley in 1961; 380 yards (12th hole at White Webbs) by Danny Dunne on 30th July, 1976; 370 yards (17th hole at Chilwell Manor, distance from the forward tee) by Ray Newton in 1977; 365 yards (10th hole at Harewood Downs) by K. Saunders in 1965; 365 yards (7th hole at Catterick Garrison GC) by Leslie Bruckner on 18th July, 1980.

● The longest-recorded hole-in-one by a woman was that accomplished in September, 1949 by Marie Robie – the 393-yard hole at Furnace Brook course, Wollaston, Mass, USA.

Holing-in-one – greatest number by one person

59–Amateur Norman Manley of Long Beach, California.

50–Mancil Davis, professional at the Trophy Club, Fort Worth, Texas.

31–British professional C.T. le Chevalier who died in 1973.

22–British amateur, Jim Hay of Kirkintilloch GC.

At One Hole

13–Joe Lucius at 15th hole of Mohawk, Ohio.

5–Left-hander, the late Fred Francis at 7th (now 16th) hole of Cardigan GC.

Holing-in-one – greatest frequency

● The record for the greatest number of holes-in-one in a calendar year is 14, claimed in 2007 by Californian Jacqueline Gagne who hit her fourteenth ace at Mission Hills in front of a television crew who had been sent to check if her claims for the previous 13 were true.

● J.O. Boydstone of California made 11 aces in 1962.

● John Putt of Frilford Heath GC had six holes-in-one in 1970, followed by three in 1971.

● Douglas Porteous, of Ruchill GC, Glasgow, achieved seven holes-in-one in the space of eight months. Four of them were scored in a five-day period from 26th to 30th September, 1974, in three consecutive rounds of golf. The first two were achieved at Ruchill GC in one round, the third there two days later, and the fourth at Clydebank and District GC after another two days. The following May, Porteous had three holes-in-one, the first at Linn Park GC incredibly followed by two more in the one round at Clober GC.

● Mrs Kathleen Hetherington of West Essex has holed-in-one five times, four being at the 15th hole at West Essex. Four of her five aces were within seven months in 1966.

● Mrs Dorothy Hill of Dumfries and Galloway GC holed-in-one three times in 11 days in 1977.

● James C. Reid of Brodick, aged 59 and 8 handicap in 1987, achieved 14 holes-in-one, all but one on Isle of Arran courses. His success was in spite of severe physical handicaps of a stiff left knee, a damaged right ankle, two discs removed from his back and a hip replacement.

● Jean Nield, a member at Chorlton-cum-Hardy and Bramall Park, has had eleven holes-in-one and her husband Brian, who plays at Bramall Park, has had five – a husband and wife total of 16.

● Peter Gibbins holed his tee shot at the 359 yards par 4 13th hole at Hazlemere on November 2 1984 using a 3-wood that was in his bag for the first time. That spectacular ace was his third but he has had nine more since then.

Holing successive holes-in-one

● Successive holes-in-one are rare; successive par 4 holes-in-one may be classed as near miracles. N.L. Manley performed the most incredible feat in September, 1964, at Del Valle Country Club, Saugus, California, USA. The par 4 7th (330 yards) and 8th (290 yards) are both slightly downhill, dog-leg holes. Manley had *aces* at both, en route to a course record of 61 (par 71).

● The first recorded example in Britain of a player holing-in-one stroke at each of two successive holes was achieved on 6th February, 1964, at the Walmer and Kingsdown course, Kent. The young assistant professional at that club, Roger Game (aged 17) holed out with a 4-wood at the 244-yard 7th hole, and repeated the feat at the 256-yard 8th hole, using a 5-iron.

● The first occasion of holing-in-one at consecutive holes in a major professional event occurred when John Hudson, 25-year-old professional at Hendon, holed-in-one at the 11th and 12th holes at Norwich during the second round of the 1971 Martini tournament. Hudson used a 4-iron at the 195-yard 11th and a driver at the 311-yard downhill 12th hole.

● Assistant professional Tom Doty (23 years), playing in a friendly match on a course near Chicago in October, 1971, had a remarkable four-hole score which included two consecutive holes-in-one, sandwiched either side by an albatross and an eagle: 4th hole (500 yards)-2; 5th hole (360 yards dog-leg)-1; 6th hole (175 yards)-1; 7th hole (375 yards)-2. Thus he was 10 under par for four consecutive holes.

● At the Standard Life Loch Lomond tournament on the European Tour in July 2000 Jarmo Sandelin holed-in-one at the 17th with the final shot there in the third round and fellow Swede Mathias Gronberg holed-in-one with the first shot there in the last round. A prize of $100,000 was only on offer in the last round.

Holing-in-one twice (or more) in the same round by the same person

What might be thought to be a very rare feat indeed – that of holing-in-one twice in the same round – has in fact happened on many occasions as the following instances show. It is, nevertheless, compared to the number of golfers in the world, still something of an outstanding achievement. The first known occasion was in 1907 when J. Ireland playing in a three-ball match at Worlington holed the 5th and 18th holes in one stroke and two years later in 1909 H.C. Josecelyne holed the 3rd (175 yards) and the 14th (115 yards) at Acton on 24th November.

- The first mention of two holes-in-one in a round by a woman was followed later by a similar feat by another lady at the same club. On 19th May, 1942, Mrs W. Driver, of Balgowlah Golf Club, New South Wales, holed out in one at the 3rd and 8th holes in the same round, while on 29th July, 1948, Mrs F. Burke at the same club holed out in one at the second and eighth holes.
- The Rev Harold Snider, aged 75, scored his first hole-in-one on 9th June, 1976 at the 8th hole of the Ironwood course, near Phoenix. By the end of his round he had scored three holes-in-one, the other two being at the 13th (110 yards) and 14th (135 yards). Ironwood is a par-3 course, giving more opportunity of scoring holes-in-one, but, nevertheless, three holes-in-one in one round on any type of course is an outstanding achievement.
- When the Hawarden course in North Wales comprised only nine holes, Frank Mills in 1994 had two holes-in-one at the same hole in the same round. Each time, he hit a seven iron to the 134-yard 3rd and 12th.
- The youngest player to achieve two holes-in-one in the same round is thought to be Christopher Anthony Jones on 14 September, 1994. At the age of 14 years and 11 months he holed-in-one at the Sand Moor, Leeds, 137-yard 10th and then at the 156-yard 17th.
- The youngest woman to have performed the feat was a 17-year-old, Marjorie Merchant, playing at the Lomas Athletic GC, Argentina, at the 4th (170 yards) and 8th (130 yards) holes.
- Tony Hannam, left-handed, handicap 16 and age 71, followed a hole-in-one at the 142 yards 4th of the Bude and North Cornwall Golf Club course with another at the 143-yard 10th on Friday, 18th September, 1992.
- Brothers Eric and John Wilkinson were playing together at the Ravensworth Golf Club on Tyneside in 2001 and both holed-in-one at the 148 yards eighth. Eric (46) played first and then John to the hidden green but there is no doubting this unusual double ace. The club's vice-captain Dave Johnstone saw both balls go in! Postman Eric plays off 9. John, a county planner, has a handicap of 20. Next time they played the hole both missed the green.
- Chris Valerro, a 22-handicapper from the Liberty Lake Golf Club, Spokane, Washington, aced the 143 yards 3rd hole at his home club with a 7-iron and then the 140 yards 11th hole with his 8-iron.
- Edinburgh golfer, 25-year-old Chris Tugwell, was representing the Lothianburn club when he aced the 157-yard seventh with a nine iron and then went on to hole-in-one again at the 168-yard 12th with a five iron.
- Eugene O'Brien scored a hole-in-one double on one of Britain's most difficult courses when he aced the 13th and 16th holes at Carnoustie.
- Yusuka Miyazato, a multiple winner on the Japanese circuit, had two holes in one in the same round on the second day at the Montreux Golf Club in 2006.
- Milwaukee resident Sanjay Kuttemperoor scored two aces in 2006 at the Treetops Resort, Michigan, the first on the 150-yard fifth and the second on the 135-yard ninth.
- Some golfers go through their life without ever having a coveted hole-in-one but Alan Domingo had two within an hour in the same round at the Hawick Club in 2011. He aced the 144 yards eighth and then did the same at the 198 yards 13th.
- 75-year-old Peter Wafford, who plays off 13 at Bush Hill Park Golf Club, had a red letter day when playing in a match against Chigwell at Chigwell in 2011. Although only having recently taken up golf he had two holes in one in the same round beating estimated odds of 67 million to one against that happening.

Holes-in-one on the same day

- In July 1987, at the Skerries Club, Co Dublin, Rank Xerox sponsored two tournaments, a men's 18-hole four-ball with 134 pairs competing and a 9-hole mixed foursomes with 33 pairs. During the day each of the four par-3 holes on the course were holed-in-one: the 2nd by Noel Bollard, the 5th by Bart Reynolds, the 12th by Jackie Carr and the 15th by Gerry Ellis.
- Wendy Russell holed-in-one at the consecutive par threes in the first round of the British Senior Ladies' at Wrexham in 1989.
- Clifford Briggs, aged 65, holed-in-one at the 14th at Parkstone GC on the same day as his wife Gwen, 60, aced the 16th.
- In the final round of the 2000 Victor Chandler British Masters at Woburn Alastair Forsyth holed-in-one at the second. Playing partner Roger Chapman then holed-in-one at the eighth.

Two holes-in-one at the same hole in the same game

- *First in World:* George Stewart and Fred Spellmeyer at the 18th hole, Forest Hills, New Jersey, USA in October 1919.
- *First in Great Britain:* Miss G. Clutterbuck and Mrs H.M. Robinson at the 15th hole (120 yards), St Augustine GC, Ramsgate, on 8th May, 1925.

● *First in Denmark:* In a Club match in August 1987 at Himmerland, Steffan Jacobsen of Aalborg and Peter Forsberg of Himmerland halved the 15th hole in one shot, the first known occasion in Denmark.

● *First in Australia:* Dr & Mrs B. Rankine, playing in a mixed "Canadian foursome" event at the Osmond Club near Adelaide, South Australia in April 1987, holed-in-one in consecutive shots at the 2nd hole (162 metres), he from the men's tee with a 3-iron and his wife from the ladies' tee with a 1½ wood.

● Jack Ashton, aged 76, holed-in-one at the 8th hole of the West Kent Golf Club at Downe but only got a half. Opponent Ted Eagle, in receipt of shot, made a 2, net 1.

● Dr Martin Pucci and Trevor Ironside will never forget one round at the Macdonald Club in Ellon last year. Playing in an open competition the two golfers with Jamie Cowthorne making up the three-ball reached the tee at the 169yards short 11th. Dr Pucci, with the honour, hit a 5-iron, Mr Ironside a 6-iron at the hole where only the top of the flag is visible. Both hit good shots but when they reached the green they could spot only one ball and that was Mr Cowthorne's. Then they realised that something amazing might have happened. When they reached the putting surface they discovered that both Dr Pucci's and Mr Ironside's balls were wedged into the hole. Both had made aces. It was Dr Pucci's sixth and Mr Ironside's second.

● Eric and John Wilkinson went out for their usual weekly game at the Ravensworth Golf Club in Wrekenton on Tyneside in 2001 and both holed in one at the 148 yards eighth. Neither Eric, a 46-year-old 9-handicapper who has been playing golf since he was 14, nor John, who has been playing golf for ten years and has a handicap of 20, saw the balls go in because the green is over a hill but club vice-captain Dave Johnston did and described the incident as "amazing". Next time the brothers played the hole both missed the green!

● Richard Evans and Mark Evans may not be related but they have one thing in common – they both holed in one at the same hole when playing in a club competition. The double ace occurred in 2003 at Glynhir Golf Club's third hole which measures 189 yards. Thirty-seven-year-old surveyor Richard, who plays off 7, hit first and made his first hole-in-one in the 15 years he has played the game. His opponent, car worker Mark whose handicap is 12, then followed him in.

● Richard Hall, who plays off 12, and high handicapper Peter McEvoy had never had a hole-in-one until one Saturday night in 2003 at Shandon Park Golf Club in Belfast. Friends since their schooldays they play a lot of golf together so there was much excitement when Hall holed his 5-iron shot for an ace at the 180 yards eighth. Then he challenged McEvoy to match it. And he did!

● Brothers Hanks and Davis Massey were playing a late afternoon practice round at TPC Sawgrass in Florida in 2008 when they came to the par 3 third. Eleven-year-old Hanks was up first and hit a 9-iron 108 yards into the hole. He and his father Scott ran up to the green in wild celebration forgetting that nine-year-old Davis had still to play. When he did he pulled out an 8-iron and also aced.

● Ross Roger and John Downie, two 13-year-olds playing in a foursomes match at the Clober Club in Milngavie near Glasgow, Scotland, made their own little bit of golfing history when they stepped on to the 15th tee and both holed out in one. Ross, teeing up first, watched his ball drop into the hole for his first ace then stepped back and saw John do the same thing.

Three holes-in-one at the same hole in the same game

● During the October monthly medal at Southport & Ainsdale Golf Club on Saturday October 18, 2003, three holes-in-one were achieved at the 153-yard 8th by Stuart Fawcett (5 handicap), Brian Verinder (17 handicap) and junior member Andrew Kent (12 handicap). The players were not playing in the same group.

Holing-in-one – youngest and oldest players

● Elsie McLean, 102, from Chico, California, holed-in-one in April 2007.

● In January 1985 Otto Bucher of Switzerland holed-in-one at the age of 99 on La Manga's 130-yard 12th hole.

● In 2005, Bim Smith, a member of Rochester & Cobham Park Golf Club, Kent, hit a hole-in-one – his fourth – three days before his 91st birthday.

● Bob Hope had a hole-in-one at Palm Springs, California, at the age of 90.

● 76-year-old lady golfer Mrs Felicity Sieghart achieved two holes-in-one when playing in a club Stableford competition at the Aldeburgh club in 2003. Mrs Sieghart aced the 134 yards eighth and the 130 yards 17th – but sadly did not win the competition.

● The youngest player ever to achieve a hole in one is now believed to be Matthew Draper, who was only five when he aced the 122-yard fourth hole at Cherwell Edge, Oxfordshire, in June 1997. He used a wood.

● Six-year-old Tommy Moore aced the 145-yard fourth hole at Woodbrier, West Virginia, in 1968. He had another at the same hole before his seventh birthday.

● Keith Long was just five when he aced on a Mississippi golf course in 1998.
● Five-year-old Eleanor Gamble became one of the youngest to have a hole in one when she made an ace at the Cambridge Lakes club in 2011.
● Alex Evans, aged eight, holed-in-one with a 4-wood at the 136-yard 4th hole at Bromborough, Merseyside, in 1994.
● Nine-year-old Kate Langley from Scotter in Lincolnshire, is believed to have became the youngest girl to score an ace. It is reported that she holed in one at the 134 yards first hole at Forest Pines Beeches in Scunthorpe after having had a lesson from local professional David Edwards. Kate was nine years and 166 days when she hit the ace – 199 days younger than Australian Kathryn Webb who had held the record previously.
● In 2007, 13-year-old Lauren Taylor from Rugby scored two aces and made history at her club. Her first ace was scored on the 145 yard 12th, where she used a seven iron for her shot over the brook whilst playing in a junior medal competition. Her second came during the second round of the 36-hole Junior Championship This time it was achieved on the 100 yard 8th (which plays much harder due to it being all up-hill), using a pitching wedge. From the tee you cannot see what is happening on the green.

Holing-in-one – miscellaneous incidents

● Chemistry student Jason Bohn, aged 19, of State College, Pennsylvania, supported a charity golf event at Tuscaloosa, Alabama, in 1992 when twelve competitors were invited to try to hole-in-one at the 135-yard second hole for a special prize covered by insurance. One attempt only was allowed. Bohn succeeded and was offered US$1m (paid at the rate of $5,000 a month for the next 20 years) at the cost of losing his amateur status. He took the money.
● The late Harry Vardon, who scored the greatest number of victories in The Open Championship, only once did a hole-in-one. That was in 1903 at Mundesley, Norfolk, where Vardon was convalescing from a long illness.
● In a guest day at Rochford Hundred, Essex, in 1994, there were holes-in-one at all the par threes. First Paul Cairns, of Langdon Hills, holed a 4-iron at the 205-yard 15th, next Paul Francis, a member of the home club, sank a 7-iron at the 156-yard seventh and finally Jim Crabb, of Three Rivers, holed a 9-iron at the 136-yard 11th.
● In April 1988, Mary Anderson, a bio-chemistry student at Trinity College, Dublin, holed-in-one at the 290-yard 6th hole at Island GC, Co Dublin.
● In April 1984 Joseph McCaffrey and his son, Gordon, each holed-in-one in the Spring Medal at the 164-yard 12th hole at Vale of Leven Club, Dunbartonshire.
● In 1977, 14-year-old Gillian Field after a series of lessons holed-in-one at the 10th hole at Moor Place GC in her first round of golf.
● When he holed-in-one at the second hole in a match against D. Graham in the 1979 Suntory World Match Play at Wentworth, Japanese professional Isao Aoki won himself a Bovis home at Gleneagles worth, inclusive of furnishings, £55,000. Brian Barnes has aced the short 10th and Thomas Bjørn won a car when he aced the short 14th in 2003.
● On the morning after being elected captain for 1973 of the Norwich GC, J.S. Murray hit his first shot as captain straight into the hole at the 169-yard 1st hole.
● At Nuneaton GC in 1999 the men's captain and the ladies' captain both holed-in-one during their captaincies.
● Using the same club and ball, 11-handicap left-hander Christopher Smyth holed-in-one at the 2nd hole (170 yards) in two consecutive medal competitions at Headfort GC, Co. Meath, in January, 1976.
● Playing over Rickmansworth course at Easter, 1960, Mrs A.E. (Paddy) Martin achieved a remarkable sequence of *aces*. On Good Friday she sank her tee shot at the 3rd hole (125 yards). The next day, using the same ball and the same 8-iron, at the same hole, she scored another *one*. And on the Monday (same ball, same club, same hole) she again holed out from the tee.
● At Barton-on-Sea in February 1989 Mrs Dorothy Huntley-Flindt, aged 91, holed-in-one at the par-3 13th. The following day Mr John Chape, a fellow member in his 80s, holed the par- 3 5th in one.
● In 1995 Roy Marsland of Ratho Park, Edinburgh, had three holes-in-one in nine days: at Prestonfield's 5th, at Ratho Park's 3rd and at Sandilands' 2nd.
● Michael Monk, age 82, a member of Tandridge Golf Club, Surrey, waited until 1992 to record his first hole-in-one. It continued a run of rare successes for his family. In the previous 12 months, Mr Monk's daughter, Elizabeth, 52, daughter-in-law, Celia, 48, and grandson, Jeremy, 16, had all holed-in-one on the same course.
● Lou Holloway, a left-hander, recorded his second hole-in-one at the Mount Derby course in New Zealand 13 years after acing the same hole while playing right-handed.
● Ryan Procop, an American schoolboy, holed-in-one at a 168-yard par 3 at Glen Eagles GC, Ohio, with a putter. He confessed that he was so disgusted with himself after a 12 on the previous hole that he just grabbed his putter and hit from the tee.
● Ernie and Shirley Marsden, of Warwick Golf Club, are believed in 1993 to have equalled the record for holes-in-one by a married couple. Each has had three, as have another English couple, Mr and Mrs B.E. Simmonds.
● Russell Pughe, a 12-handicapper from Nottinghamshire, holed-in-one twice in three days at the 274-yard par-4 18th hole at Sidmouth in Devon in 1998. The hole has a blind tee shot.
● Robert Looney aced the 170 yards 13th at the Thorny Lea Golf Club in Brockton, Massachussetts, 30 years after his father made a hole-in-one at the same hole.
● The odds on the chances of two players having a hole in one when playing together are long but it happened to former club captain Robert Smallwood,

a 58-year-old retired IBM manager, and current captain Mike Wheeler, a 57-year-old retired financial consultant, when they went out for a round at Irvine Golf Club in Ayrshire in 2005. Playing in the rain, Mr Smallwood, using a driver, had his ace at the 289 yards fourth before Mr Wheeler holed in one at the 279 yards fifth.

● Texan blind golfer Charles Adams, sank his tee shot on the 102-yard 14th hole at Stone Creek Golf Club, Oregon City, Oregon, on October 4, 2006, during the US Blind Golf Association National Championship, the first hole-in-one in the 61-year history of the tournament.

● Blind golfer Sheila Drummond, a member of the US Blind Golf Association, is believed to be the only blind woman golfer to have holed-in-one. Sheila's feat was accomplished in August 2007 at the 144-yard par-3 at Mahoning Valley CC in Lehighton, PA.

● Jim Gales, who was awarded the MBE for his services to blind golf, scored a hole in one in 2010 at Wellsgreen, Fife, while practising for the Scottish Pan-Disability Open. Other blind golfers who have scored aces include Jan Dinsdale (NIR), Joel Ludvicek (USA) and Zohar Sharon (ISR).

● Bob Taylor, a Leicestershire County player, achieved what many would consider the impossible when he holed in one at the same hole on three successive days at the Hunstanton Club. Playing in the Eastern Countries Foursomes in 1974 he aced the 188 yards 16th using first a 1-iron and then a 6-iron on the next two occasions.

Challenge matches

One of the first recorded professional challenge matches was in 1843 when Allan Robertson beat Willie Dunn in a 20-round match at St Andrews over 360 holes by 2 rounds and 1 to play. Thereafter until about 1905 many matches are recorded, some for up to £200 a side – a considerable sum for the time. The Morrises, the Dunns and the Parks were the main protagonists until Vardon, Braid and Taylor took over in the 1890s. Often matches were on a home-and-away basis over 72 holes or more, with many spectators; Vardon and Willie Park Jr attracted over 10,000 at North Berwick in 1899.

Between the wars Walter Hagen, Archie Compston, Henry Cotton and Bobby Locke all played several such matches. Compston surprisingly beat Hagen by 18 up and 17 to play at Moor Park in 1928; yet typically Hagen went on to win The Open the following week at Sandwich. Cotton played classic golf at Walton Heath in 1937 when he beat Densmore Shute for £500-a-side at Walton Heath by 6 and 5 over 72 holes.

Curious and large wagers

(See also bets recorded under Cross-Country Matches *and in* Challenge Matches)

● In The Royal and Ancient Golf Club minutes an entry on 3rd November, 1820 was made in the following terms:

Sir David Moncrieffe, Bart, of Moncrieffe, backs his life against the life of John Whyte-Melville, Esq, of Strathkinnes, for a new silver club as a present to the St Andrews Golf Club, the price of the club to be paid by the survivor and the arms of the parties to be engraved on the club, and the present bet inscribed on it. No balls to be attached to it. In testimony of which this bet is subscribed by the parties thereto.

Thirteen years later, Mr Whyte-Melville, in a feeling and appropriate speech, expressed his deep regret at the lamented death of Sir David Moncrieffe, one of the most distinguished and zealous supporters of the club. Whyte-Melville, while lamenting the cause that led to it, had pleasure in fulfilling the duty imposed upon him by the bet, and accordingly delivered to the captain the silver putter. Whyte-Melville in 1883 was elected captain of the club a second time; he died in his eighty-sixth year in July, 1883, before he could take office and the captaincy remained vacant for a year. His portrait hangs in The Royal and Ancient clubhouse and is one of the finest and most distinguished pictures in the smoking room.

● In 1914 Francis Ouimet, who in the previous autumn had won the American Open Championship after a triangular tie with Harry Vardon and Ted Ray, came to Great Britain with Jerome D. Travers, the holder of the American amateur title, to compete in the British Amateur Championship at Sandwich. An American syndicate took a bet of £30,000 to £10,000 that one or other of the two United States champions would be the winner. It only took two rounds to decide the bet against the Americans. Ouimet was beaten by a then quite unknown player, H.S. Tubbs, while Travers was defeated by Charles Palmer, who was 56 years of age at the time.

● In 1907 John Ball for a wager undertook to go round Hoylake during a dense fog in under 90, in not more than two and a quarter hours and without losing a ball. Ball played with a black ball, went round in 81, and also beat the time.

● The late Ben Sayers, for a wager, played the 18 holes of the Burgess Society course scoring a four at every hole. Sayers was about to start against an American, when his opponent asked him what he could do the course in. *Fours* replied Sayers, meaning 72, or an average of 4s for the round. A bet was made, then the American added, *Remember a three or a five is not a four.* There were eight bogey 5s and two 3s on the Burgess course at the time Old Ben achieved his feat.

Feats of endurance

Although golf is not a game where endurance, in the ordinary sense in which the term is employed in sport, is required, there are several instances of feats on the links which demanded great physical exertion.

● Four British golfers, Simon Gard, Nick Harley, Patrick Maxwell and his brother Alastair Maxwell, completed 14 rounds in one day at Iceland's Akureyri Golf Club, the most northern 18-hole course in the world, during June 1991 when there was 24-hour daylight. It was claimed a record and £10,000 was raised for charity.

● In 1971 during a 24-hour period from 6 pm on 27th November until 5.15 pm on 28th November, Ian Colston completed 401 holes over the 6,061 yards Bendigo course, Victoria, Australia. Colston was a top marathon athlete but was not a golfer. However prior to his golfing marathon he took some lessons and became adept with a 6-iron, the only club he used throughout the 401 holes. The only assistance Colston had was a team of harriers to carry his 6-iron and look for his ball, and a band of motorcyclists who provided light during the night. This is, as far as is known, the greatest number of holes played in 24 hours on foot on a full-size course.

● In 1934 Col Bill Farnham played 376 holes in 24 hours 10 minutes at the Guildford Lake Course, Guildford, Connecticut, using only a mashie and a putter.

● To raise funds for extending the Skipton GC course from 12 to 18 holes, the club professional, 24-year-old Graham Webster, played 277 holes in the hours of daylight on Monday 20th June, 1977. Playing with nothing longer than a 5-iron he averaged 81 per 18-hole round. Included in his marathon was a hole-in-one.

● Michael Moore, a 7 handicap 26-year-old member of Okehampton GC, completed on foot 15 rounds 6 holes (276 holes) there on Sunday, 25th June, 1972, in the hours of daylight. He started at 4.15 am and stopped at 9.15 pm. The distance covered was estimated at 56 miles.

● On 21st June, 1976, 5-handicapper Sandy Small played 15 rounds (270 holes) over his home course Cosby GC, length 6,128 yards, to raise money for the Society of Physically Handicapped Children. Using only a 5-iron, 9-iron and putter, Small started at 4.10 am and completed his 270th hole at 10.39 pm with the aid of car headlights. His fastest round was his first (40 minutes) and slowest his last (82 minutes). His best round of 76 was achieved in the second round.

● During the weekend of 20th–21st June, 1970, Peter Chambers of Yorkshire completed over 14 rounds of golf over the Scarborough South Cliff course. In a non-stop marathon lasting just under 24 hours, Chambers played 257 holes in 1,168 strokes, an average of 84.4 strokes per round.

● Bruce Sutherland, on the Craiglockhart Links, Edinburgh, started at 8.15 pm on 21st June, 1927, and played almost continuously until 7.30 pm on 22nd June, 1927. During the night four caddies with acetylene lamps lit the way, and lost balls were reduced to a minimum. He completed fourteen rounds. Mr Sutherland, who was a physical culture teacher, never recovered from the physical strain and died a few years later.

● Sidney Gleave, motorcycle racer, and Ernest Smith, golf professional at Davyhulme Club, Manchester, on 12th June, 1939, played five rounds of golf in five different countries – Scotland, Ireland, Isle of Man, England and Wales. Smith had to play the five rounds under 80 in one day to win the £100 wager. They travelled by plane, and the following was their programme:

Start 3.40a.m. at Prestwick St Nicholas (Scotland), finished 1 hour 35 minutes later on 70.

2nd Course – Bangor, Ireland. Started at 7.15 a.m. and took 1 hour 30 minutes to finish on 76.

3rd Course – Castletown, Isle of Man. Started 10.15 am, scored 76 in 1 hour 40 minutes.

4th Course – Blackpool, Stanley Park, England. Started at 1.30 pm and scored 72 in 1 hour 55 minutes.

5th Course – Hawarden, Wales, started at 6 pm and finished 2 hours 15 minutes later with a score of 72.

● On 19th June, 1995, Ian Botham, the former England cricketer, played four rounds of golf in Ireland, Wales, Scotland and England. His playing companions were Gary Price, the professional at Branston, and Tony Wright, owner of Craythorne, Burton-on-Trent, where the last 18 holes were completed. The other courses were St Margaret's, Anglesey and Dumfries & Galloway. The first round began at 4.30 am and the last was completed at 8.30 pm.

● On Wednesday, 3rd July, 1974, E.S. Wilson, Whitehead, Co. Antrim and Dr G.W. Donaldson, Newry, Co. Down, played a nine-hole match in each of seven countries in the one day. The first 9 holes was at La Moye (Channel Islands) followed by Hawarden (Wales), Chester (England), Turnberry (Scotland), Castletown (Isle of Man), Dundalk (Eire) and Warrenpoint (N Ireland). They started their first round at 4.25 am and their last round at 9.25 pm. Wilson piloted his own plane throughout.

● In June 1986 to raise money for the upkeep of his medieval church, the Rector of Mark with Allerton, Somerset, the Rev Michael Pavey, played a sponsored 18 holes on 18 different courses in the Bath & Wells Diocese. With his partner, the well-known broadcaster on music, Antony Hopkins, they played the 1st at Minehead at 5.55 am and finished playing the 18th at Burnham and Berrow at 6.05 pm. They covered 240 miles in the "round" including the distances to reach the correct tee for the "next" hole on each course. Par for the "round" was 70. Together the pair raised £10,500 for the church.

● To raise funds for the Marlborough Club's centenary year (1988), Laurence Ross, the Club professional, in June 1987, played eight rounds in 12 hours. Against a par of 72, he completed the 576 holes in 3 under par, playing from back tees and walking all the way.

● As part of the 1992 Centenary Celebrations of the Royal Cinque Ports Golf Club at Deal, Kent, and to support charity, a six-handicap member, John Brazell, played all 37 royal courses in Britain and Ireland in 17 days. He won 22 matches, halved three, lost 12; hit 2,834 shots for an average score of 76.6; lost 11 balls and made 62 birdies. The aim was to raise £30,000 for Leukaemia Research and the Spastics Society.

● To raise more than £500 for the Guide Dogs for the Blind charity in the summer of 1992, Mrs Cheryle Power, a member of the Langley Park Golf Club,

Beckenham, Kent, played 100 holes in a day – starting at 5 am and finishing at 8.45 pm.

● David Steele, a former European Tour player, completed 17½ rounds, 315 holes, between 6 am and 9.45 pm in 1993 at the San Roque club near Gibraltar in a total of 1,291 shots. Steele was assisted by a caddie cart and raised £15,000 for charity.

● In 2005 Bernard Wood, a member of Rossendale Golf Club, played all the 18-hole courses in Scotland – 377 in all – to raise money for the Kirsty Appeal which supports the Frances House Children's Hospice in Manchester.

Fastest rounds

● Dick Kimbrough, 41, completed a round on foot on 8th August, 1972, at North Platte CC, Nebraska (6,068 yards) in 30 minutes 10 seconds. He carried only a 3-iron.

● At Mowbray Course, Cape Town, November 1931, Len Richardson, who had represented South Africa in the Olympic Games, played a round which measured 6,248 yards in 31 minutes 22 seconds.

● The women's all-time record for the fastest round played on a course of at least 5,600 yards is held by Sue Ledger, 20, who completed the East Berks course in 38 minutes 8 seconds, beating the previous record by 17 minutes.

● In April, 1934, after attending a wedding in Bournemouth, Hants, Captain Gerald Moxom hurried to his club, West Hill in Surrey, to play in the captain's prize competition. With daylight fading and still dressed in his morning suit, he went round in 65 minutes and won the competition with a net 71 into the bargain.

● On 14th June, 1922, Jock Hutchison and Joe Kirkwood (AUS) played round the Old Course at St Andrews in 1 hour 20 minutes. Hutchison, out in 37, led by three holes at the ninth and won by 4 and 3.

● Fastest rounds can also take another form – the time taken for a ball to be propelled round 18 holes. The fastest known round of this type is 8 minutes 53.8 seconds on 25th August, 1979 by 42 members at Ridgemount CC Rochester, New York, a course measuring 6,161 yards. The Rules of Golf were observed but a ball was available on each tee; to be driven off the instant the ball had been holed at the preceding hole.

● The fastest round with the same ball took place in January 1992 at the Paradise Golf Club, Arizona. It took only 11 minutes 24 seconds; 91 golfers being positioned around the course ready to hit the ball as soon as it came to rest and then throwing the ball from green to tee.

● In 1992 John Daly and Mark Calcavecchia were both fined by the USPGA Tour for playing the final round of the Players' Championship in Florida in 123 minutes. Daly scored 80, Calcavecchia 81.

Curious scoring

● C.W. Allen of Leek Golf Club chipped-in four times in a round in which he was partnered by K. Brint against G. Davies and R. Hollins. The shortest chip was a yard, the longest 20 yards.

● Tony Blackwell, playing off a handicap of four, broke the course record at Bull Bay, Anglesey, by four strokes when he had a gross 60 (net 56) in winning the club's town trophy in 1996. The course measured 6,217 yards.

● In the third round of the 1994 Volvo PGA Championship at Wentworth, Des Smyth, of Ireland, made birdie twos at each of the four short holes, the 2nd, 5th, 10th and 14th. He also had a two at the second hole in the fourth round.

● Also at Wentworth, in the 1994 World Match Play Championship, Seve Ballesteros had seven successive twos at the short holes – and still lost his quarter-final against Ernie Els.

● R.H. Corbett, playing in the semi-final of the Tangye Cup at Mullion in 1916, did a score of 27. The remarkable part of Corbett's score was that it was made up of nine successive 3s, bogey being 5, 3, 4, 4, 5, 3, 4, 4, 3.

● At Little Chalfont in June 1985 Adrian Donkersley played six successive holes in 6, 5, 4, 3, 2, 1 from the 9th to the 14th holes against a par of 4, 4, 3, 4, 3, 3.

● On 2nd September, 1920, playing over Torphin, near Edinburgh, William Ingle did the first five holes in 1, 2, 3, 4, 5.

● In the summer of 1970, Keith McMillan, on holiday at Cullen, had a remarkable series of 1, 2, 3, 4, 5 at the 11th to 15th holes.

● Marc Osborne was only 14 years of age when he equalled the Betchworth Park amateur course record with a 66 in July, 1993. He was playing in the Mortimer Cup, a 36-hole medal competition, and had at the time a handicap of 6.8.

● Playing at Addington Palace, July, 1934, Ronald Jones, a member of Hendon Club, holed five consecutive holes in 5, 4, 3, 2, 1.

● Harry Dunderdale of Lincoln GC scored 5, 4, 3, 2, 1 in five consecutive holes during the first round of his club championship in 1978. The hole-in-one was the 7th, measuring 294 yards.

● At the Open Amateur Tournament of the Royal Ashdown Forest in 1936 Bobby Locke in his morning round had a score of 72, accomplishing every hole in 4.

● George Stewart of Cupar had a four at every hole over the Queen's course at Gleneagles despite forgetting to change into his golf shoes and therefore still wearing his street shoes.

● Nick Faldo scored par figures at all 18 holes in the final round of the 1987 Open Championship at Muirfield to win the title.

● During the Colts Championship at Knowle Golf Club, Bristol, Chris Newman (Cotswold Hills) scored eight consecutive 3s with birdies at four of the holes.

● At the Toft Hotel Golf Club captain's day event L. Heffernan had an ace, D. Patrick a 2, R. Barnett a 3 and D. Heffernan a 4 at the 240 yard par-4 ninth.

● In the European Club Championship played at the Parco de Medici Club in Rome in 1998, Belgian Dimitri van Hauwaert from Royal Antwerp had an albatross 2, Norwegian Marius Bjornstad from Oslo an eagle 3 and Scotsman Andrew Hogg from Turriff a birdie 4 at the 486 metre par-5 eighth hole.

● Henry Cotton told of one of the most extraordinary scoring feats ever. With some other professionals he was at Sestrieres in the 30s for the Italian Open Championship and Joe Ezar, a colourful character in those days on both sides of the Atlantic, accepted a wager from a club official – 1,000 lira for a 66 to break the course record; 2,000 for a 65; and 4,000 for a 64. *I'll do 64*, said Ezar, and proceeded to jot down the hole-by-hole score figures he would do next day for that total. With the exception of the ninth and tenth holes where his predicted score was 3, 4 and the actual score was 4, 3, he accomplished this amazing feat exactly as nominated.

● Earle F. Wilson from Brewerton, Alabama, has had an ace, an albatross and has fired eight birdies in a row.

High scores

● In the qualifying competition at Formby for the 1976 Open Championship, Maurice Flitcroft, a 46-year-old crane driver from Barrow-in-Furness, took 121 strokes for the first round and then withdrew saying, *I have no chance of qualifying*. Flitcroft entered as a professional but had never before played 18 holes. He had taken the game up 18 months previously but, as he was not a member of a club, had been limited to practising on a local beach. His round was made up thus: 7, 5, 6, 6, 6, 6, 12, 6, 7-61; 11, 5, 6, 8, 4, 9, 5, 7, 5-60, total 121. After his round Flitcroft said, "I've made a lot of progress in the last few months and I'm sorry I did not do better. I was trying too hard at the beginning but began to put things together at the end of the round". R&A officials, who were not amused by the bogus professional's efforts, refunded the £30 entry money to Flitcroft's two fellow-competitors. Flitcroft has since tried to qualify for The Open under assumed names: Gerard Hoppy from Switzerland and Beau Jolley (as in the wine)!

● Playing in the qualifying rounds of the 1965 Open Championship at Southport, an American self-styled professional entrant from Milwaukee, Walter Danecki, achieved the inglorious feat of scoring a total of 221 strokes for 36 holes, 81 over par. His first round over the Hillside course was 108, followed by a second round of 113. Walter, who afterwards admitted he felt *a little discouraged and sad*, declared that he entered because he was *after the money*.

● The highest individual scoring ever known in the rounds connected with The Open Championship occurred at Muirfield, 1935, when a Scottish professional started 7, 10, 5, 10, and took 65 to reach the 9th hole. Another 10 came at the 11th and the player decided to retire at the 12th hole. There he was in a bunker, and after playing four shots he had not regained the fairway.

● In 1883 in The Open Championship at Musselburgh, Willie Fernie, the winner, had a 10, the only time double figures appeared on the card of The Open Champion of the year. Fernie won after a tie with Bob Ferguson, and his score for the last hole in the tie was 2. He holed from just off the green to win by one stroke.

● In the French Open at St Cloud, in 1968, Brian Barnes took 15 for the short 8th hole in the second round. After missing putts at which he hurriedly snatched while the ball was moving he penalised himself further by standing astride the line of a putt. The amazing result was that he actually took 12 strokes from about three feet from the hole. The highest scores on the European Tour were also recorded in the French Open. Philippe Porquier had a 20 at La Baule in 1978 and Ian Woosnam a 16 at La Boulie in 1986.

● US professional Dave Hill 6-putted the fifth green at Oakmont in the 1962 US Open Championship.

● Many high scores have been made at the Road Hole at St Andrews. Davie Ayton, on one occasion, was coming in a certain winner of The Open Championship when he got on the road and took 11. In 1921, at The Open Championship, one professional took 13. In 1923, competing for the Autumn Medal of The Royal and Ancient, J.B. Anderson required a five and a four to win the second award, but he took 13 at the Road Hole. Anderson was close to the green in two, was twice in the bunkers in the face of the green, and once on the road. In 1935, R.H. Oppenheimer tied for the Royal Medal (the first award) in the Autumn Meeting of The Royal and Ancient. On the play-off he was one stroke behind Captain Aitken when they stood on the 17th tee. Oppenheimer drove three balls out of bounds and eventually took 11 to the Road Hole.

● In the first Open Championship at Prestwick in 1860 a competitor took 21, the highest score for one hole ever recorded in this event. The record is preserved in the archives of the Prestwick Golf Club, where the championship was founded.

"I wish he'd hurry up and sink this ... I'd like to be home in time for Christmas"

● In the first round of the 1980 US Masters, Tom Weiskopf hit his ball into the water hazard in front of the par-3 12th hole five times and scored 13 for the hole.

● British professional Mark James scored 111 in the second round of the 1978 Italian Open. He played the closing holes with only his right hand due to an injury to his left hand.

● In the 1927 Shawnee Open, Tommy Armour took 23 strokes to the 17th hole. Armour had won the American Open Championship a week earlier. In an effort to play the hole in a particular way, Armour hooked ball after ball out of bounds and finished with a 21 on the card. There was some doubt about the accuracy of this figure and on reaching the clubhouse Armour stated that it should be 23. This is the highest score by a professional in a tournament.

Freak matches

● In 1912, the late Harry Dearth, an eminent vocalist, attired in a complete suit of heavy armour, played a match at Bushey Hall. He was beaten 2 and 1.

● Captain Pennington took part in a match *from the air* against A.J. Young, the professional at Sonning. Captain Pennington, with 80 golf balls in the locker of his machine, had to find the Sonning greens by dropping the balls as he circled over the course. The balls were covered in white cloth to ensure that they did not bounce once they struck the ground. The airman completed the course in 40 minutes, taking 29 *strokes*, while Young occupied two hours for his round of 68. Captain Pennington was eventually killed in an air crash in 1933.

● In 1914, at the start of the First World War, J.N. Farrar, a native of Hoylake, was stationed at Royston, Herts. A bet was made of 10-1 that he would not go round Royston under 100 strokes, equipped in full infantry marching order, water bottle, full field kit and haversack. Farrar went round in 94. At the camp were several golfers, including professionals, who tried the same feat but failed.

"I don't think the greenkeepers will be overjoyed at his choice of buggy"

● In April 1924, at Littlehampton, Harry Rowntree, an amateur golfer, played the better ball of Edward Ray and George Duncan, receiving an allowance of 150 yards to use as he required during the round. Rowntree won by 6 and 5 and had used only 50 yards 2 feet of his handicap. At one hole Duncan had a two – Rowntree, who was 25 yards from the hole, took this distance from his handicap and won the hole in one. Ray (died 1945) afterwards declared that, conceding a handicap of one yard per round, he could win every championship in the world. And he might, when reckoning is taken of the number of times a putt just stops an inch or two or how much difference to a shot three inches will make for the lie of the ball, either in a bunker or on the fairway. Many single matches on the same system have been played. An 18 handicap player opposed to a scratch player should make a close match with an allowance of 50 yards.

● The first known instance of a golf match by telephone occurred in 1957, when the Cotswold Hills Golf Club, Cheltenham, England, won a golf tournament against the Cheltenham Golf Club, Melbourne, Australia, by six strokes. A large crowd assembled at the English club to wait for the 12,000 miles telephone call from Australia. The match had been played at the suggestion of a former member of the Cotswold Hills Club, Harry Davies, and was open to every member of the two clubs. The result of the match was decided on the aggregate of the eight best scores on each side and the English club won by 564 strokes to 570.

Golf matches against other sports

● H.H. Hilton and Percy Ashworth, many times racket champion, contested a driving match, the former driving a golf ball with a driver, and the latter a racket ball with a racket. Best distances: Against breeze – Golfer 182 yards; Racket player 125 yards. Down wind – Golfer 230 yards; Racket player 140 yards. Afterwards Ashworth hit a golf ball with the racket and got a greater distance than with the racket ball, but was still a long way behind the ball driven by Hilton.

● In December, 1913, F.M.A. Webster, of the London Athletic Club, and Dora Roberts, with javelins, played a match with the late Harry Vardon and Mrs Gordon Robertson, who used the regulation clubs and golf balls. The golfers conceded two-thirds in the matter of distance, and they won by 5 up and 4 to play in a contest of 18 holes. The javelin throwers had a mark of two feet square in which to *hole out* while the golfers had to get their ball into the ordinary golf hole. Mr Webster's best throw was one of 160 feet.

● In 1913, at Wellington, Shropshire, a match between a golfer and a fisherman casting a $2^1/_2$ oz weight was played. The golfer, Rupert May, took 87; the fisherman J.J.D. Mackinlay, in difficulty because of his short casts, 102. His longest cast, 105 yards, was within 12 yards of the world record at the time, held by French angler, Decautelle. When within a rod's length of a hole he ran the weight to the rod end and dropped into the hole. Five times he broke his line, and was allowed another shot without penalty.

● In 1954, at the Southbroom Club, South Africa, a match over 9 holes was played between an archer and a fisherman against two golfers. The participants were all champions of their own sphere and consisted of Vernon Adams (archer), Dennis Burd (fisherman), Jeanette Wahl (champion of Southbroom and Port Shepstone), and Ron Burd (professional at

Southbroom). The conditions were that the archer had holed out when his arrows struck a small leather bag placed on the green beside the hole and in the event of his placing his approach shot within a bow's length of the pin he was deemed to have 1-putted. The fisherman, to achieve a 1-putt, had to land his sinker within a rod's length of the pin. The two golfers were ahead for brief spells, but it was the opposition who led at the deciding 9th hole where *Robin Hood* played a perfect approach for a birdie.

● An *Across England* combined match was begun on 11th October, 1965, by four golfers and two archers from Crowborough Beacon Golf Club, Sussex, accompanied by *Penny*, a white Alsatian dog, whose duty it was to find lost balls. They teed off from Carlisle Castle via Hadrian's Wall, the Pennine Way, finally holing out in the 18th hole at Newcastle United GC in 612 teed shots. Casualties included 110 lost golf balls and 19 lost or broken arrows. The match took 5½ days, and the distance travelled was about 60 miles. The golfers were Miss P. Ward, K. Meaney, K. Ashdown and C.A. Macey; the archers were W.H. Hulme and T. Scott. The first arrow was fired from the battlements of Carlisle Castle, a distance of nearly 300 yards, by Cumberland Champion R. Willis, who also fired the second arrow right across the River Eden. R. Clough, president of Newcastle United GC, holed the last two putts. The match was in aid of *Guide Dogs for the Blind* and *Friends of Crowborough Hospital.*

● Several matches have taken place between a golfer on the one side and an archer on the other. The wielder of the bow and arrow has nearly always proved the victor. In 1953 at Kirkhill Golf Course, Lanarkshire, five archers beat six golfers by two games to one. There were two special rules for the match; when an archer's arrow landed six feet from the hole or the golfer's ball three feet from the hole, they were counted as holed. When the arrows landed in bunkers or in the rough, archers lifted their arrow and added a stroke. The sixth archer in this match called off and one archer shot two arrows from each of the 18 tees.

"This doesn't appear to be covered by the Rules"

Cross-country matches

● Taking 1 year, 114 days, Floyd Rood golfed his way from coast to coast across the United States. He took 114,737 shots including 3,511 penalty shots for the 3,397 mile course.

● Two Californian teenagers, Bob Aube (17) and Phil Marrone (18) went on a golfing safari in 1974 from San Francisco to Los Angeles, a trip of over 500 miles lasting 16 days. The first six days they played alongside motorways. Over 1,000 balls were used.

● In 1830, the Gold Medal winner of The Royal and Ancient backed himself for 10 sovereigns to drive from the 1st hole at St Andrews to the toll bar at Cupar, distance nine miles, in 200 teed shots. He won easily.

● In 1848, two Edinburgh golfers played a match from Bruntsfield Links to the top of Arthur's Seat – an eminence overlooking the Scottish capital, 822 feet above sea level.

● On a winter's day in 1898, Freddie Tait backed himself to play a gutta ball in 40 teed shots from Royal St George's Clubhouse, Sandwich, to the Cinque Ports Club, Deal. He was to hole out by hitting any part of the Deal Clubhouse. The distance as the crow flies was three miles. The redoubtable Tait holed out with his 32nd shot, so effectively that the ball went through a window.

● In 1900 three members of the Hackensack (NJ) Club played a game of four-and-a-half hours over an extemporised course six miles long, which stretched from Hackensack to Paterson. Despite rain, cornfields, and wide streams, the three golfers – J.W. Hauleebeek, Dr E.R. Pfaare, and Eugene Crassons – completed the round, the first and the last named taking 305 strokes each, and Dr Pfaare 327 strokes. The players used only two clubs, the mashie and the cleek.

● On 3rd December, 1920, P. Rupert Phillips and W. Raymond Thomas teed up on the first tee of the Radyr Golf Club and played to the last hole at Southerndown. The distance as the crow flies was 15½ miles, but circumventing swamps, woods, and plough, they covered, approximately, 20 miles. The wager was that they would not do the hole in 1,000 strokes, but they holed out at their 608th stroke two days later. They carried large ordnance maps.

● On 12th March, 1921, A. Stanley Turner, Macclesfield, played from his house to the Cat and Fiddle Inn, five miles distance, in 64 strokes. The route was broken and hilly with a rise of nearly 1,000 feet. Turner was allowed to tee up within two club lengths after each shot and the wagering was 6-4 against his doing the distance in 170 strokes.

● In 1919, a golfer drove a ball from Piccadilly Circus and, proceeding via the Strand, Fleet Street and Ludgate Hill, *holed out* at the Royal Exchange, London. The player drove off at 8 am on a Sunday, a time when the usually thronged thoroughfares were deserted.

● On 23rd April, 1939, Richard Sutton, a London stockbroker, played from Tower Bridge, London, to

White's Club, St James's Street, in 142 strokes. The bet was he would not do *the course* in under 200 shots. Sutton used a putter, crossed the Thames at Southwark Bridge, and hit the ball short distances to keep out of trouble.

- Golfers produced the most original event in Ireland's three-week national festival of An Tostal, in 1953 – a cross-country competition with an advertised £1,000,000 for the man who could hole out in one. The 150 golfers drove off from the first tee at Kildare Club to hole out eventually on the 18th green, five miles away, on the nearby Curragh course, a distance of 8,800 yards. The unusual hazards to be negotiated included the main Dublin-Cork railway line and highway, the Curragh Racecourse, hoofprints left by Irish thoroughbred racehorses out exercising on the plains from nearby stables, army tank tracks and about 150 telephone lines. The Golden Ball Trophy, which is played for annually – a standard size golf ball in gold, mounted on a black marble pillar beside the silver figure of a golfer on a green marble base, designed by Captain Maurice Cogan, Army GHQ, Dublin – was for the best gross. And it went to one of the longest hitters in international golf – Amateur Champion, Irish internationalist and British Walker Cup player Joe Carr, with the remarkable score of 52.
- In 1961, as a University Charities Week stunt, four Aberdeen University students set out to golf their way up Ben Nevis (4,406 feet). About half-way up, after losing 63 balls and expending 659 strokes, the quartet conceded victory to Britain's highest mountain.
- Among several cross-country golfing exploits, one of the most arduous was faced by Iain Williamson and Tony Kent, who teed off from Cained Point on the summit of Fairfield in the Lake District. With the hole cut in the lawn of the Bishop of Carlisle's home at Rydal Park, it measured 7,200 yards and passed through the summits of Great Rigg Mann, Heron Pike and Nab Scar, descending altogether 1,900 feet. Eight balls were lost and the two golfers holed out in a combined total of 303 strokes.
- In 2011, Trevor Sandford from Bearsted in Kent played golf on each of the 31 days of August on 31 different courses close to the 31 junctions of the M25 motorway. During Trevor's feat, in which he raised over £8,000 for Cancer Research UK, he walked 210 miles and took 2,789 strokes.

Long-lived golfers

- James Priddy, aged 80, played in the Seniors' Open at his home club, Weston-super-Mare, Avon, on 27th June, 1990, and scored a gross 70 to beat his age by ten shots.
- The oldest golfer who ever lived is believed to have been Arthur Thompson of British Columbia, Canada. He equalled his age when 103 at Uplands GC, a course of over 6,000 yards. He died two years later.
- Nathaniel Vickers celebrated his 103rd birthday on Sunday, 9th October, 1949, and died the following day. He was the oldest member of the United States Senior Golf Association and until 1942 he competed regularly in their events and won many trophies in the various age divisions. When 100 years old, he apologised for being able to play only nine holes a day. Vickers predicted he would live until 103 and he died a few hours after he had celebrated his birthday.
- American George Miller, who died in 1979 aged 102, played regularly when 100 years old.
- In 1999 94-year-old Mr W. Seneviratne, a retired schoolmaster who lived and worked in Malaysia, was still practising every day and regularly competing in medal competitions at the Royal Colombo Golf Club which was founded in 1879.
- Bim Smith, a member of Rochester & Cobham Park Golf Club, Kent, achieved a hole-in-one three days before his 91st birthday.
- Phyllis Tidmarsh, aged 90, won a Stableford competition at Saltford Golf Club, near Bath, when she returned 42 points. Her handicap was cut from 28 to 27.
- George Swanwick, a member of Wallasey, celebrated his 90th birthday with a lunch at the club on 1st April, 1971. He played golf several times a week, carrying his own clubs, and had holed-in-one at the ages of 75 and 85. His ambition was to complete the sequence aged 95 ... but he died in 1973 aged 92.
- The 10th Earl of Wemyss played a round on his 92nd birthday, in 1910, at Craigielaw. At the age of 87 the Earl was partnered by Harry Vardon in a match at Kilspindie, the golf course on his East Lothian estate at Gosford. After playing his ball the venerable earl mounted a pony and rode to the next shot. He died on 30th June, 1914.
- F.L. Callender, aged 78, in September 1932, played nine consecutive rounds in the Jubilee Vase, St Andrews. He was defeated in the ninth, the final round, by 4 and 2. Callender's handicap was 12. This is the best known achievement of a septuagenarian in golf.
- George Evans shot a remarkable one over par 71 at Brockenhurst Manor – remarkable because Mr Evans was 87 at the time. Playing with him that day was Hampshire, Isle of Wight and Channel Islands President John Nettell and former Ferndown pro Doug Sewell. "It's good to shoot a score under your age, but when its 16 shots better that must be a record", said Mr Nettell. Mr Evans qualified for four opens while professional at West Hill, Surrey.
- Bernard Matthews, aged 82, of Banstead Downs Club, handicap 6, holed the course in 72 gross in August 1988. A week later he holed it in 70, twelve shots below his age. He came back in 31, finishing 4, 3, 3, 2, 3, against a par of 5, 4, 3, 3, 4. Mr Matthews's eclectic score at his Club is 37, or one over 2's.

Playing in the dark

On numerous occasions it has been necessary to hold lamps, lighted candles, or torches at holes in order that players might finish a competition. Large entries, slow play, early darkness and an eclipse of the sun have all been causes of playing in darkness.

● Since 1972, the Whitburn Golf Club at South Shields, Tyne and Wear, has held an annual Summer Solstice Competition. All competitors, who draw lots for starting tees, must begin before 4.24 and 13 seconds am, the time the sun rises over the first hole on the longest day of the year.
● At The Open Championship in Musselburgh in November 1889 many players finished when the light had so far gone that the adjacent street lamps were lit. The cards were checked by candlelight. Several players who had no chance of the championship were paid small sums to withdraw in order to permit others who had a chance to finish in daylight. This was the last championship at Musselburgh.
● At the Southern Section of the PGA tournament on 25th September, 1907, at Burnham Beeches, several players concluded the round by the aid of torch lights placed near the holes.
● In the Irish Open Championship at Portmarnock in September, 1907, a tie in the third round between W.C. Pickeman and A. Jeffcott was postponed owing to darkness, at the 22nd hole. The next morning Pickeman won at the 24th.
● The qualifying round of the American Amateur Championship in 1910 could not be finished in one day, and several competitors had to stop their round on account of darkness, and complete it early in the morning of the following day.
● On 10th January, 1926, in the final of the President's Putter, at Rye, E.F. Storey and R.H. Wethered were all square at the 24th hole. It was 5 pm and so dark that, although a fair crowd was present, the balls could not be followed. The tie was abandoned and the Putter held jointly for the year. Each winner of the Putter affixes the ball he played; for 1926 there are two balls, respectively engraved with the names of the finalists.
● In the 1932 Walker Cup contest at Brooklyn, a total eclipse of the sun occurred.
● At Perth, on 14th September, 1932, a competition was in progress under good clear evening light, and a full bright moon. The moon rose at 7.10 and an hour later came under eclipse to the earth's surface. The light then became so bad that on the last three greens competitors holed out by the aid of the light from matches.
● At Carnoustie, 1932, in the competition for the *Craw's Nest Tassie* the large entry necessitated competitors being sent off in 3-ball matches. The late players had to be assisted by electric torches flashed on the greens.
● In February, 1950, Max Faulkner and his partner, R. Dolman, in a Guildford Alliance event finished their round in complete darkness. A photographer's flash bulbs were used at the last hole to direct Faulkner's approach. Several of the other competitors also finished in darkness. At the last hole they had only the light from the clubhouse to aim at and one played his approach so boldly that he put his ball through the hall doorway and almost into the dressing room.
● On the second day of the 1969 Ryder Cup contest, the last 4-ball match ended in near total darkness on the 18th green at Royal Birkdale. With the help of the clubhouse lights the two American players, Lee Trevino and Miller Barber, along with Tony Jacklin for Britain each faced putts of around five feet to win their match. All missed and their game was halved.

The occasions mentioned above all occurred in competitions where it was not intended to play in the dark. There are, however, numerous instances where players set out to play in the dark either for bets or for novelty.

● On 29th November, 1878, R.W. Brown backed himself to go round the Hoylake links in 150 strokes, starting at 11 pm. The conditions of the match were that Mr Brown was only to be penalised *loss of distance* for a lost ball, and that no one was to help him to find it. He went round in 147 strokes, and won his bet by the narrow margin of three strokes.
● In 1876 David Strath backed himself to go round St Andrews under 100, in moonlight. He took 95, and did not lose a ball.
● In September 1928, at St Andrews, the first and last holes were illuminated by lanterns, and at 11 pm four members of The Royal and Ancient set out to play a foursome over the 2 holes. Electric lights, lanterns, and rockets were used to brighten the fairway, and the headlights of motor cars parked on Links Place formed a helpful battery. The 1st hole was won in four, and each side got a five at the 18th. About 1,000 spectators followed the freak match, which was played to celebrate the appointment of Angus Hambro to the captaincy of the club.
● In 1931, Rufus Stewart, professional, Kooyonga Club, South Australia, and former Australian Open Champion, played 18 holes of exhibition golf at night without losing a single ball over the Kooyonga course, and completed the round in 77.
● At Ashley Wood Golf Club, Blandford, Dorset, a night-time golf tournament was arranged annually with up to 180 golfers taking part over four nights. Over £6000 has been raised in four years for the Muscular Dystrophy Charity.
● At Pannal, 3rd July, 1937, R.H. Locke, playing in bright moonlight, holed his tee shot at the 15th hole, distance 220 yards, the only known case of holing-in-one under such conditions.

Fatal and other accidents on the links

The history of golf is, unfortunately, marred by a great number of fatal accidents on or near the course. In the vast majority of such cases they have been caused either by careless swinging of the club or by an uncontrolled shot when the ball has struck a spectator or bystander. In addition to the fatal accidents there is an even larger number on record which have resulted in serious injury or blindness. We do not propose to list these accidents except where they have some unusual feature. We would remind all golfers of the tragic consequences which have so often been caused by momentary carelessness. The fatal accidents which follow have an unusual cause and other accidents given may have their humorous aspect.

● English tournament professional Richard Boxall was three shots off the lead in the third round of the 1991 Open Championship when he fractured his left leg driving from the 9th tee at Royal Birkdale. He was taken from the course to hospital by ambulance and was listed in the official results as "retired" which entitled him to a consolation prize of £3000.

A month later, Russell Weir of Scotland, was competing in the European Teaching Professionals' Championship near Rotterdam when he also fractured his left leg driving from the 7th tee in the first round.

● In July, 1971, Rudolph Roy, aged 43, was killed at a Montreal course; in playing out of woods, the shaft of his club snapped, rebounded off a tree and the jagged edge plunged into his body.

● Harold Wallace, aged 75, playing at Lundin Links with two friends in 1950, was crossing the railway line which separates the fifth green and sixth tee, when a light engine knocked him down and he was killed instantly.

● In the summer of 1963, Harold Kalles, of Toronto, Canada, died six days after his throat had been cut by a golf club shaft, which broke against a tree as he was trying to play out of a bunker.

● At Jacksonville, Florida, on 18th March, 1952, two women golfers were instantly killed when hit simultaneously by the whirling propeller of a navy fighter plane. They were playing together when the plane with a dead engine coming in out of control, hit them from behind.

● In May, 1993, at Ponoka Community GC, Alberta, Canada, Richard McCulough hit a poor tee shot on the 13th hole and promptly smashed his driver angrily against a golf cart. The head of the driver and six inches of shaft flew through the air, piercing McCulough's throat and severing his carotid artery. He died in hospital.

● Britain's first national open event for competitors aged over 80, at Moortown, Leeds in September, 1992, was marred when 81-year-old Frank Hart collapsed on the fourth tee and died. Play continued and Charles Mitchell, aged 80, won the Stableford competition with a gross score of 81 for 39 points.

● Playing in the 1993 Carlesburg-Tetley Cornish Festival at Tehidy Park, Ian Cornwell was struck on the leg by a wayward shot from a player two groups behind. Later, as he was leaving the 16th green, he was hit again, this time below the ear, by the same player, knocking him unconscious. This may be the first time that a player has been hit twice in the same round by the same player.

Lightning on the links

There have been a considerable number of fatal and serious accidents through players and caddies having been struck by lightning on the course. The Royal and Ancient and the USGA have, since 1952, provided for discontinuance of play during lightning storms under the Rules of Golf (Rule 37, 6) and the United States Golf Association has given the following guide for personal safety during thunderstorms:

(a) Do not go out of doors or remain out during thunderstorms unless it is necessary. Stay inside of a building where it is dry, preferably away from fireplaces, stoves, and other metal objects.

(b) If there is any choice of shelter, choose in the following order:
   1. Large metal or metal-frame buildings.
   2. Dwellings or other buildings which are protected against lightning.
   3. Large unprotected buildings.
   4. Small unprotected buildings.

(c) If remaining out of doors is unavoidable, keep away from:
   1. Small sheds and shelters if in an exposed location.
   2. Isolated trees.
   3. Wire fences.
   4. Hilltops and wide open spaces.

(d) Seek shelter in:
   1. A cave.
   2. A depression in the ground.
   3. A deep valley or canyon.
   4. The foot of a steep or overhanging cliff.
   5. Dense woods.
   6. A grove of trees.

Note – Raising golf clubs or umbrellas above the head is dangerous.

● A serious incident with lightning involving well-known golfers was at the 1975 Western Open in Chicago when Lee Trevino, Jerry Heard and Bobby Nichols were all struck and had to be taken to hospital. At the same time Tony Jacklin had a club thrown 15 feet out of his hands.

● Two well-known competitors were struck by lightning in European events in 1977. They were Mark James of Britain in the Swiss Open and Severiano Ballesteros of Spain in the Scandinavian Open. Fortunately neither appeared to be badly injured.

● Two spectators were killed by lightning in 1991: one at the US Open and the other at US PGA Championship.

Spectators interfering with balls

● Deliberate interference by spectators with balls in play during important money matches was not unknown in the old days when there was intense rivalry between the *schools* of Musselburgh, St Andrews, and North Berwick, and disputes arose in stake matches caused by the action of spectators in kicking the ball into either a favourable or an unfavourable position.

● Tom Morris, in his last match with Willie Park at Musselburgh, refused to go on because of interference by the spectators, and in the match on the same course about 40 years later, in 1895, between Willie Park Jr and J.H. Taylor, the barracking of the crowd and interference with play was so bad that when the Park-Vardon match came to be arranged in 1899, Vardon refused to accept Musselburgh as a venue.

● Even in modern times spectators have been known to interfere deliberately with players' balls, though it is usually by children. In the 1972 Penfold Tournament at Queen's Park, Bournemouth, Christy O'Connor Jr had his ball stolen by a young boy, but not being told of this at the time had to take the penalty for a lost ball. O'Connor finished in a tie for first place, but lost the play-off.

● In 1912 in the last round of the final of the Amateur Championship at Westward Ho! between Abe Mitchell and John Ball, the drive of the former to the short 14th hit an open umbrella held by a lady protecting herself from the heavy rain, and instead of landing on the green the ball was diverted into a bunker. Mitchell, who was leading at the time by 2 holes, lost the hole and Ball won the Championship at the 38th hole.

● In the match between the professionals of Great Britain and America at Southport in 1937 a dense crowd collected round the 15th green waiting for the Sarazen-Alliss match. The American's ball landed in the lap of a woman, who picked it up and threw it so close to the hole that Sarazen got a two against Alliss' three.

● In a memorable tie between Bobby Jones and Cyril Tolley in the 1930 Amateur Championship at St Andrews, Jones' approach to the 17th green struck spectators massed at the left end of the green and led to controversy as to whether it would otherwise have gone on to the famous road. Jones himself had deliberately played for that part of the green and had requested stewards to get the crowd back. Had the ball gone on to the road, the historic Jones Quadrilateral of the year – The Open and Amateur Championships of Britain and the United States – might not have gone into the records.

● In the 1983 Suntory World Match Play Championship at Wentworth Nick Faldo hit his second shot over the green at the 16th hole into a group of spectators. To everyone's astonishment and discomfiture the ball reappeared on the green about 30ft from the hole, propelled there by a thoroughly misguided and anonymous spectator. The referee ruled that Faldo should play the ball where it lay on the green. Faldo's opponent, Graham Marsh, understandably upset by the incident, took three putts against Faldo's two, thus losing a hole he might well otherwise have won. Faldo won the match 2 and 1, but lost in the final to Marsh's fellow Australian Greg Norman by 3 and 2.

Golf balls killing animals and fish, and incidents with animals

● An astounding fatality to an animal through being hit by a golf ball occurred at St Margaret's-at-Cliffe Golf Club, Kent on 13th June, 1934, when W.J. Robinson, the professional, killed a cow with his tee shot to the 18th hole. The cow was standing in the fairway about 100 yards from the tee, and the ball struck her on the back of the head. She fell like a log, but staggered to her feet and walked about 50 yards before dropping again. When the players reached her she was dead.

● J.W. Perret, of Ystrad Mynach, playing with Chas R. Halliday, of Ralston, in the qualifying rounds of the Society of One Armed Golfers' Championship over the Darley course, Troon, on 27th August, 1935, killed two gulls at successive holes with his second shots. The *deadly* shots were at the 1st and 2nd holes.

● On the first day of grouse shooting of the 1975 season (12th August), 11-year-old schoolboy Willie Fraser, of Kingussie, beat all the guns when he killed a grouse with his tee shot on the local course.

● On 10th June, 1904, while playing in the Edinburgh High Constables' Competition at Kilspindie, Captain Ferguson sent a long ball into the rough at the Target hole, and on searching for it found that it had struck and killed a young hare.

● Playing in a mixed open tournament at the Waimairi Beach Golf Club in Christchurch, New Zealand, in the summer of 1961, Mrs R.T. Challis found her ball in fairly long spongy grass where a placing rule applied. She picked up, placed the ball and played her stroke. A young hare leaped into the air and fell dead at her feet. She had placed the ball on the leveret without seeing it and without disturbing it.

● In 1906 in the Border Championship at Hawick, a gull and a weasel were killed by balls during the afternoon's play.

● A golfer at Newark, in May, 1907, drove his ball into the river. The ball struck a trout 2lb in weight and killed it.

● On 24th April, 1975, at Scunthorpe GC, Jim Tollan's drive at the 14th hole, called *The Mallard*, struck and killed a female mallard duck in flight. The duck was stuffed and is displayed in the Scunthorpe Clubhouse.

● A. Samuel, Melbourne Club, at Sandringham, was driving with an iron club from the 17th tee, when a kitten, which had been playing in the long grass, sprang suddenly at the ball. Kitten and club arrived at the objective simultaneously, with the result that the kitten took an unexpected flight through the air, landing some 20 yards away.

● As Susan Rowlands was lining up a vital putt in the closing stages of the final of the 1978 Welsh Girls' Championship at Abergele, a tiny mouse scampered up her trouser leg. After holing the putt, the mouse ran down again. Susan, who won the final, admitted that she fortunately had not known it was there.

Interference by birds and animals

● Crows, ravens, hawks and seagulls frequently carry off golf balls, sometimes dropping the ball actually on the green, and it is a common incident for a cow to swallow a golf ball. A plague of crows on the Liverpool course at Hoylake are addicted to golf balls – they stole 26 in one day – selecting only new balls. It was suggested that members should carry shotguns as a 15th club!

● A match was approaching a hole in a rather low-lying course, when one of the players made a crisp chip from about 30 yards from the hole. The ball trickled slowly across the green and eventually disappeared into the hole. After a momentary pause, the ball was suddenly ejected on to the green, and out jumped a large frog.

- A large black crow named Jasper which frequented the Lithgow GC in New South Wales, Australia, stole 30 golf balls in the club's 1972 Easter Tournament.
- As Mrs Molly Whitaker was playing from a bunker at Beachwood course, Natal, South Africa, a large monkey leaped from a bush and clutched her round the neck. A caddie drove it off by clipping it with an iron club.
- In Massachusetts a goose, having been hit rather hard by a golf ball which then came to rest by the side of a water hazard, took revenge by waddling over to the ball and kicking it into the water.
- In the summer of 1963, S.C. King had a good drive to the 10th hole at the Guernsey Club. His partner, R.W. Clark, was in the rough, and King helped him to search. Returning to his ball, he found a cow eating it. Next day, at the same hole, the positions were reversed, and King was in the rough. Clark placed his woollen hat over his ball, remarking, *I'll make sure the cow doesn't eat mine.* On his return he found the cow thoroughly enjoying his hat; nothing was left but the pom-pom.
- On 5 August 2000 in the first round of the Royal Westmoreland Club Championship in Barbados, Kevin Edwards, a five-handicapper, hit a tee shot at the short 15th to a few feet of the hole. A monkey then ran onto the green, picked up the ball, threw it into the air a few times, then placed it in the hole before running off. Mr Edwards had to replace his ball, but was obliged afterwards to buy everyone a drink at the bar by virtue of a newly written rule.

Armless, one-armed, legless and ambidextrous players

- In September, 1933, at Burgess Golfing Society of Edinburgh, the first championship for one-armed golfers was held. There were 43 entries and 37 of the competitors had lost an arm in the 1914–18 war. Play was over two rounds and the championship was won by W.E. Thomson, Eastwood, Glasgow, with a score of 169 (82 and 87) for two rounds. The Burgess course was 6,300 yards long. Thomson drove the last green, 260 yards. The championship and an international match are played annually.
- In the Boys' Amateur Championship 1923, at Dunbar and 1949 at St Andrews, there were competitors each with one arm. The competitor in 1949, R.P. Reid, Cupar, Fife, who lost his arm working a machine in a butcher's shop, got through to the third round.
- There have been cases of persons with no arms playing golf. One, Thomas McAuliffe, who held the club between his right shoulder and cheek, once went round Buffalo CC, USA, in 108.
- Group Captain Bader, who lost both legs in a flying accident prior to the World War 1939–45, took part in golf competitions and reached a single-figure handicap in spite of his disability.
- In 1909, Scott of Silloth, and John Haskins of Hoylake, both one-armed golfers, played a home and away match for £20-a-side. Scott finished five up at Silloth. He was seven up and 14 to play at Hoylake but Haskins played so well that Scott eventually only won by 3 and 1. This was the first match between one-armed golfers. Haskins in 1919 was challenged by Mr Mycock, of Buxton, another one-armed player. The match was 36 holes, home and away. The first half was played over the Buxton and High Peak Links, and the latter half over the Liverpool Links, and resulted in a win for Haskins by 11 and 10. Later in the same year Haskins received another challenge to play against Alexander Smart of Aberdeen. The match was 18 holes over the Balgownie Course, and ended in favour of Haskins.
- In a match, November, 1926, between the Geduld and Sub Nigel Clubs – two golf clubs connected with the South African gold mines of the same names – each club had two players minus an arm. The natural consequence was that the quartet were matched. The players were – A.W.P. Charteris and E. Mitchell, Sub Nigel; and E.P. Coles and J. Kirby, Geduld. This is the first record of four one-armed players in a foursome.
- At Joliet Country Club, USA, a one-armed golfer named D.R. Anderson drove a ball 300 yards.
- Left-handedness, but playing golf right-handed, is prevalent and for a man to throw with his left hand and play golf right-handed is considered an advantage, for Bobby Jones, Jesse Sweetser, Walter Hagen, Jim Barnes, Joe Kirkwood and more recently Johnny Miller were eminent golfers who were left-handed and ambidextrous.
- In a practice round for The Open Championship in July, 1927, at St Andrews, Len Nettlefold and Joe Kirkwood changed sets of clubs at the 9th hole. Nettlefold was a left-handed golfer and Kirkwood right-handed. They played the last nine, Kirkwood with the left-handed clubs and Nettlefold with the right-handed clubs.
- The late Harry Vardon, when he was at Ganton, got tired of giving impossible odds to his members and beating them, so he collected a set of left-handed clubs, and rating himself at scratch, conceded the handicap odds to them. He won with the same monotonous regularity.
- Ernest Jones, who was professional at the Chislehurst Club, was badly wounded in the war in France in 1916 and his right leg had to be amputated below the knee. He persevered with the game, and before the end of the year he went round the Clacton course balanced on his one leg in 72. Jones later settled in the United States where he built fame and fortune as a golf teacher.
- Major Alexander McDonald Fraser of Edinburgh had the distinction of holding two handicaps simultaneously in the same club – one when he played left-handed and the other for his right-handed play. In medal competitions he had to state before teeing up which method he would use.
- Former England test cricketer Brian Close once held a handicap of 2 playing right-handed, but after retiring from cricket in 1977 decided to apply himself as a left-handed player. His left-handed handicap at

the time of his retirement was 7. Close had the distinction of once beating Ted Dexter, another distinguished test cricketer and noted golfer twice in the one day, playing right-handed in the morning and left-handed in the afternoon.

Blind and blindfolded golf

● Major Towse, VC, whose eyes were shot out during the South African War, 1899, was probably the first blind man to play golf. His only stipulations when playing the game were that he should be allowed to touch the ball with his hands to ascertain its position, and that his caddie could ring a small bell to indicate the position of the hole. Major Towse, who played with considerable skill, was also an expert oarsman and bridge player. He died in 1945, aged 81.

● The United States Blind Golfers' Association in 1946 promoted an Invitational Golf Tournament for the blind at Inglewood, California, to be held annually. In 1953 there were 24 competitors, of which 11 completed the two rounds of 36 holes. The winner was Charley Boswell who lost his eyesight leading a tank unit in Germany in 1944.

● In July, 1954, at Lambton Golf and Country Club, Toronto, the first international championship for the blind was held. It resulted in a win for Joe Lazaro, of Waltham, Mass., with a score of 220 for the two rounds. He drove the 215-yard 16th hole and just missed an ace, his ball stopping 18 inches from the hole. Charley Boswell, who won the United States Blind Golfers' Association Tournament in 1953, was second. The same Charles Boswell, of Birmingham, Alabama holed the 141-yard 14th hole at the Vestavia CC in one in October, 1970.

● Another blind person to have holed-in-one was American Ben Thomas while on holiday in South Carolina in 1978.

● Rick Sorenson undertook a bet in which, playing 18 holes blindfolded at Meadowbrook Course, Minneapolis, on 25th May, 1973, he was to pay $10 for every hole over par and receive $100 for every hole in par or better. He went round in 86 losing $70 on the deal.

● Alfred Toogood played blindfolded in a match against Tindal Atkinson at Sunningdale in 1912. Toogood was beaten 8 and 7. Previously, in 1908, I. Millar, Newcastle-upon-Tyne, played a match blindfolded against A.T. Broughton, Birkdale, at Newcastle, County Down.

● Wing-Commander *Laddie* Lucas, DSO, DFC, MP, played over Sandy Lodge golf course in Hertfordshire on 7th August, 1954, completely blindfolded and had a score of 87.

Trick shots

● Joe Kirkwood, Australia, specialised in public exhibitions of trick and fancy shots. He played all kinds of strokes after nominating them, and among his ordinary strokes nothing was more impressive than those hit for low flight. He played a full drive from the face of a wrist watch, and the toe of a spectator's shoe, full strokes at a suspended ball, and played for slice and pull at will, and exhibited his ambidexterity by playing left-handed strokes with right-handed clubs. Holing six balls, stymieing, a full shot at a ball catching it as it descended, and hitting 12 full shots in rapid succession, with his face turned away from the ball, were shots among his repertoire. In playing the last named Kirkwood placed the balls in a row, about six inches apart, and moved quickly along the line. Kirkwood, who was born in Australia lived for many years in America. He died in November, 1970 aged 73.

● On 2nd April, 1894, a 3-ball match was played over Musselburgh course between Messrs Grant, Bowden, and Waggot, the clubmaker, the latter teeing on the face of a watch at each tee. He finished the round in 41 the watch being undamaged in any way.

● In a match at Esher on 23rd November, 1931, George Ashdown, the professional, played his tee shot for each of the 18 holes from a rubber tee strapped to the forehead of Miss Ena Shaw.

● E.A. Forrest, a South African professional in a music hall turn of trick golf shots, played blindfolded shots, one being from the ball teed on the chin of his recumbent partner.

● The late Paul Hahn, an American trick specialist could hit four balls with two clubs. Holding a club in each hand he hit two balls, hooking one and slicing the other with the same swing. Hahn had a repertoire of 30 trick shots. In 1955 he flew round the world, exhibiting in 14 countries and on all five continents.

Balls colliding and touching

● Competing in the 1980 Corfu International Championship, Sharon Peachey drove from one tee and her ball collided in mid-air with one from a competitor playing another hole. Her ball ended in a pond.

● Playing in the Cornish team championship in 1973 at West Cornwall GC Tom Scott-Brown, of West Cornwall GC, and Paddy Bradley, of Tehidy GC, saw their drives from the fourth and eighth tees collide in mid-air.

● During a fourball match at Guernsey Club in June, 1966, near the 13th green from the tee, two of the players, D.G. Hare and S. Machin, chipped up simultaneously; the balls collided in mid-air and Machin's ball hit the green, then the flagstick, and dropped into the hole for a birdie 2.

● In May, 1926, during the meeting of the Army Golfing Society at St Andrews, Colonel Howard and Lieutenant-Colonel Buchanan Dunlop, while playing in the foursomes against J. Rodger and J. Mackie, hit full iron shots for the seconds to the 16th green. Each thought he had to play his ball first, and hidden by a bunker the players struck their balls simultaneously. The balls, going towards the hole about 20 yards from the pin and five feet in the air, met with great force and dropped either side of the hole five yards apart.

● In 1972, before a luncheon celebrating the centenary year of the Ladies' Section of Royal Wimbledon GC, a 12-hole competition was held during which two competitors, Mrs L. Champion and Mrs A. McKendrick, driving from the eighth and ninth tees respectively, saw their balls collide in mid-air.

● In 1928, at Wentworth Falls, Australia, Dr Alcorn and E.A. Avery, of Leura Club, were playing with professional E. Barnes. The tee shots of Avery and Barnes at the 9th hole finished on opposite sides of the fairway. Both players unknowingly hit their seconds (chip shots) at the same time. Dr Alcorn, standing at the pin, suddenly saw two balls approaching the hole from different angles. They met in the air and dropped into the hole.

● At Rugby, 1931, playing in a 4-ball match, H. Fraser pulled his drive from the 10th tee in the direction of the ninth tee. Simultaneously a club member, driving from the ninth tee, pulled his drive. The tees were about 350 yards apart. The two balls collided in mid-air.

● Two golf balls, being played in opposite directions, collided in flight over Longniddry Golf Course on 27th June, 1953. Immediately after Stewart Elder, of Longniddry, had driven from the third tee, another ball, which had been pulled off line from the second fairway, which runs alongside the third, struck his ball about 20 feet above the ground. S.J. Fleming, of Tranent, who was playing with Elder, heard a loud crack and thought Elder's ball had exploded. The balls were found undamaged about 70 yards apart.

Three and two balls dislodged by one shot

● In 1934 on the short 3rd hole (now the 13th) of Olton Course, Warwickshire, J.R. Horden, a scratch golfer of the club, sent his tee shot into long wet grass a few feet over the back of the green. When he played an *explosion* shot three balls dropped on to the putting green, his own and two others.

● A.M. Chevalier, playing at Hale, Cheshire, March, 1935, drove his ball into a grass bunker, and when he reached it there was only part of it showing. He played the shot with a niblick and to his amazement not one but three balls shot into the air. They all dropped back into the bunker and came to rest within a foot of each other. Then came another surprise. One of the *finds* was of the same manufacture and bore the same number as the ball he was playing with.

● Playing to the 9th hole, at Osborne House Club, Isle of Wight, George A. Sherman lost his ball which had sunk out of sight on the sodden fairway. A few weeks later, playing from the same tee, his ball again was plugged, only the top showing. Under a local rule he lifted his ball to place it, and exactly under it lay the ball he had lost previously.

Balls in strange places

● Playing at the John O' Gaunt Club, Sutton, near Biggleswade (Beds), a member drove a ball which did not touch the ground until it reached London – over 40 miles away. The ball landed in a vegetable lorry which was passing the golf course and later fell out of a package of cabbages when they were unloaded at Covent Garden, London.

● In the English Open Amateur Stroke Play at Moortown in 1974, Nigel Denham, a Yorkshire County player, in the first round saw his overhit second shot to the 18th green bounce up some steps into the clubhouse. His ball went through an open door, ricocheted off a wall and came to rest in the men's bar, 20 feet from the windows. As the clubhouse was not out of bounds Denham decided to play the shot back to the green and opened a window 4 feet by 2 feet through which he pitched his ball to 12 feet from the flag. (Several weeks later The R&A declared that Denham should have been penalised two shots for opening the window. The clubhouse was an immovable obstruction and no part of it should have been moved.)

● In The Open Championship at Sandwich, 1949, Harry Bradshaw, Kilcroney, Dublin, at the 5th hole in his second round, drove into the rough and found his ball inside a beer bottle with the neck and shoulder broken off and four sharp points sticking up. Bradshaw, if he had treated the ball as in an unplayable lie might have been involved in a disqualification, so he decided to play it where it lay. With his blaster he smashed the bottle and sent the ball about 30 yards. The hole, a par 4, cost him 6.

● Kevin Sharman of Woodbridge GC hit a low, very straight drive at the club's 8th hole in 1979. After some minutes' searching, his ball was found embedded in a plastic sphere on top of the direction post.

● On the Dublin Course, 16th July, 1936, in the Irish Open Championship, A.D. Locke, the South African, played his tee shot at the 100-yard 12th hole, but the ball could not be found on arrival on the green. The marker removed the pin and it was discovered that the ball had been entangled in the flag. It dropped near the edge of the hole and Locke holed the short putt for a birdie two.

● While playing a round on the Geelong Golf Club Course, Australia, Easter, 1923, Captain Charteris topped his tee shot to the short 2nd hole, which lies over a creek with deep and steep clay banks. His ball came to rest on the near slope of the creek bank. He elected to play the ball as it lay, and took his niblick. After the shot, the ball was nowhere to be seen. It was found later embedded in a mass of gluey clay stuck fast to the face of the niblick. It could not be shaken off. Charteris did what was afterwards approved by The R&A, cleaned the ball and dropped it behind without penalty.

● In October, 1929, at Blackmoor Golf Club, Bordon, Hants, a player driving from the first tee holed out his ball in the chimney of a house some 120 yards distant and some 40 yards out of bounds on the right. The owner and his wife were sitting in front of the fire when they heard a rattle in the chimney and were astonished to see a golf ball drop into the fire.

● A similar incident occurred in an inter-club match between Musselburgh and Lothianburn at Prestongrange in 1938 when a member of the former team hooked his ball at the 2nd hole and gave it up for lost. To his amazement a woman emerged from one of the houses adjacent to this part of the course and handed back the ball which she said had come down the chimney and landed on a pot which was on the fire.

● In July, 1955, J. Lowrie, starter at the Eden Course, St Andrews, witnessed a freak shot. A visitor drove from the first tee just as a north-bound train was passing. He sliced the shot and the ball disappeared through an open window of a passenger compartment. Almost immediately the ball emerged again, having been thrown back on to the fairway by a man in the compartment, who waved a greeting which presumably indicated that no one was hurt.

● At Coombe Wood Golf Club, a player hit a ball towards the 16th green where it landed in the vertical exhaust of a tractor which was mowing the fairway. The greenkeeper was somewhat surprised to find a temporary loss of power in the tractor. When sufficient compression had built up in the exhaust system, the ball was forced out with tremendous velocity, hit the roof of a house nearby, bounced off and landed some three feet from the pin on the green.

● There have been many occasions when misdirected shots have finished in strange places after an unusual line of flight and bounce. At Ashford, Middlesex, John Miller, aged 69, hit his tee shot out of bounds at the 12th hole (237 yards). It struck a parked car, passed through a copse, hit more cars, jumped a canopy, flew through the clubhouse kitchen window, finishing in a cooking stock-pot, without once touching the ground. Mr Miller had previously done the hole in one on four occasions.

"Waiter. There's a golf ball in my soup"

● When carrying out an inspection of the air conditioning system at St John's Hospital, Chelmsford, in 1993, a golf ball was found in the ventilator immediately above the operating theatre. It was probably the result of a hooked drive from the first tee at Chelmsford Golf Club, which is close by, but the ball can only have entered the duct on a rebound through a three-inch gap under a ventilator hood and then descended through a series of sharp bends to its final resting place.

Balls Hit To and From Great Heights

● In 1798 two Edinburgh golfers undertook to drive a ball over the spire of St Giles' Cathedral, Edinburgh, for a wager. Mr Sceales, of Leith, and Mr Smellie, a printer, were each allowed six shots and succeeded in sending the balls well over the weather-cock, a height of more than 160 feet from the ground.

● Some years later Donald McLean, an Edinburgh lawyer, won a substantial bet by driving a ball over the Melville Monument in St Andrew Square, Edinburgh – height, 154 feet.

● Tom Morris in 1860, at the famous bridge of Ballochmyle, stood in the quarry beneath and, from a stick elevated horizontally, attempted to send golf balls over the bridge. He could raise them only to the pathway, 400 feet high, which was in itself a great feat with the gutta ball.

● Captain Ernest Carter, on 28th September, 1922, drove a ball from the roadway at the 1st tee on Harlech Links against the wall of Harlech Castle. The embattlements are 200 feet over the level of the roadway, and the point where the ball struck the embattlements was 180 yards from the point where the ball was teed. Captain Carter, who was laid odds of £100 to £1, used a baffy.

● In 1896 Freddie Tait, then a subaltern in the Black Watch, drove a ball from the Rookery, the highest building on Edinburgh Castle, in a match against a brother officer to hole out in the fountain in Princes Street Gardens 350 feet below and about 300 yards distant.

● Prior to the 1977 Lancôme Tournament in Paris, Arnold Palmer hit three balls from the second stage of the Eiffel Tower, over 300 feet above ground. The longest was measured at 403 yards. One ball was hooked and hit a bus but no serious damage was done as all traffic had been stopped for safety reasons.

● Long drives have been made from mountain peaks, across the gorge at Victoria Falls, from the Pyramids, high buildings in New York, and from many other similar places. As an illustration of such freakish *drives* a member of the New York Rangers' Hockey Team from the top of Mount Edith Cavell, 11,033 feet high, drove a ball which struck the Ghost Glacier 5000 feet below and bounced off the rocky ledge another 1000 feet – a total drop of 2000 yards. Later, in June, 1968, from Pikes Peak, Colorado (14,110 feet), Arthur Lynskey hit a ball which travelled 200 yards horizontally but 2 miles vertically.

Remarkable Shots

● Remarkable shots are as numerous as the grains of sand; around every 19th hole, legends are recalled of astounding shots. One shot is commemorated by a memorial tablet at the 17th hole at the Lytham and St Annes Club. It was made by Bobby Jones in the final round of The Open Championship in 1926. He was partnered by Al Watrous, another American player. They had been running neck and neck and at the end of the third round, Watrous was just leading Jones with 215 against 217. At the 16th Jones drew level then on the 17th he drove into a sandy lie in broken ground. Watrous reached the green with his second. Jones took a mashie-iron (the equivalent to a 4-iron today) and hit a magnificent shot to the green to get his 4. This remarkable recovery unnerved Watrous, who 3-putted, and Jones, getting another 4 at the last hole against 5, won his first Open Championship with 291 against Watrous' 293. The tablet is near the spot where Jones played his second shot.

● Arnold Palmer (USA), playing in the second round of the Australian Wills Masters tournament at Melbourne, in October, 1964, hooked his second shot at the 9th hole high into the fork of a gum tree. Climbing 20 feet up the tree, Palmer, with the head of his 1-iron reversed, played a hammer stroke and knocked the ball some 30 yards forward, followed by a brilliant chip to the green and a putt.

● In the foursome during the Ryder Cup at Moortown in 1929, Joe Turnesa hooked the American side's second shot at the last hole behind the marquee adjoining the clubhouse, Johnny Farrel then pitched the ball over the marquee on to the green only feet away from the pin and Turnesa holed out for a 4.

Miscellaneous Incidents and Strange Golfing Facts

● Gary Player of South Africa was honoured by his country by having his portrait on new postage stamps which were issued on 12th December, 1976. It was the first time a specific golfer had ever been depicted on any country's postage stamps. In 1981 the US Postal Service introduced stamps featuring Bobby Jones and Babe Zaharias. They are the first golfers to be thus honoured by the United States.

● Gary Harris, aged 18, became the first player to make five consecutive appearances for England in the European Boys Team Championship at Vilamoura, Portugal, in 1994.

● In February, 1971, the first ever golf shots on the moon's surface were played by Captain Alan Shepard, commander of the Apollo 14 spacecraft. Captain Shepard hit two balls with an iron head attached to a makeshift shaft. With a one-handed swing he claimed he hit the first ball 200 yards aided by the reduced force of gravity on the moon. Subsequent findings put this distance in doubt. The second was a shank. Acknowledging the occasion The R&A sent Captain Shepard the following telegram: *Warmest congratulations to all of you on your great achievement and safe return. Please refer to Rules of Golf section on etiquette, paragraph 6, quote – before leaving a bunker a player should carefully fill up all holes made by him therein, unquote.* Shepard presented the club to the USGA Museum in 1974.

● Charles (Chick) Evans competed in every US Amateur Championship held between 1907 and 1962 by which time he was 72 years old. This amounted to 50 consecutive occasions discounting the six years of the two World Wars when the championship was not held.

● In winning the 1977 US Open at Southern Hills CC, Tulsa, Oklahoma, Hubert Green had to contend with a death threat. Coming off the 14th green in the final round, he was advised by USGA officials that a phone call had been received saying that he would be killed. Green decided that play should continue and happily he went on to win, unharmed.

● It was discovered at the 1977 USPGA Championship that the clubs with which Tom Watson had won The Open Championship and the US Masters earlier in the year were illegal, having grooves which exceeded the permitted specifications. The set he used in winning the 1975 Open Championship were then flown out to him and they too were found to be illegal. No retrospective action was taken.

● Mrs Fred Daly, wife of the former Open champion, saved the clubhouse of Balmoral GC, Belfast, from destruction when three men entered the professional's shop on 5th August, 1976, and left a bag containing a bomb outside the shop beside the clubhouse when refused money. Mrs Daly carried the bag over to a hedge some distance away where the bomb exploded 15 minutes later. The only damage was broken windows. On the same day several hours afterwards, Dungannon GC in Co. Tyrone suffered extensive damage to the clubhouse from terrorist bombs. Co. Down GC, proposed venue of the 1979 home international matches suffered bomb damage in May that year and through fear for the safety of team members the 1979 matches were cancelled.

● The Army Golfing Society and St Andrews on 21st April, 1934, played a match 200-a-side, the largest golf match ever played. Play was by foursomes. The Army won 58, St Andrews 31 and 11 were halved.

● Jamie Ortiz-Patino, owner of the Valderrama Golf Club at Sotogrande, Spain, paid a record £84,000 (increased to £92,400 with ten per cent buyers premium) for a late seventeenth- or early eighteenth-century rake iron offered at auction in Musselburgh in July, 1992. The iron, which had been kept in a garden shed, was bought to be exhibited in a museum being created in Valderrama.

● In 1986 Alistair Risk and three colleagues on the 17th green at Brora, Sutherland, watched a cow giving birth to twin calves between the markers on the 18th tee, causing them to play their next tee shots from in front of the tee. Their application for a ruling from The R&A brought a Rules Committee reply that while technically a rule had been broken, their action was considered within the spirit of the game and there should be no penalty. The Secretary added that the Rules Committee hoped that mother and twins were doing well.

● In view of the increasing number of people crossing the road (known as Granny Clark's Wynd) which runs across the first and 18th fairways of the Old Course, St Andrews, as a right of way, the St Andrews Links committee decided in 1969 to control the flow by erecting traffic lights, with appropriate green for go, yellow for caution and red for stop. The lights are controlled from the starter's box on the first tee. Golfers on the first tee must wait until the lights turn to green before driving off and a notice has been erected at the Wynd warning pedestrians not to cross at yellow or stop.

● A traffic light for golfers was also installed in 1971 on one of Japan's most congested courses. After putting on the uphill 9th hole of the Fukuoka course in Southern Japan, players have to switch on a go-ahead signal for following golfers waiting to play their shots to the green.

● A 22-year-old professional at Brett Essex GC, Brentwood, David Moore, who was playing in the Mufulira Open in Zambia in 1976, was shot dead it is alleged by the man with whom he was staying for the duration of the tournament. It appeared his host then shot himself.

● Peggy Carrick and her daughter, Angela Uzielli, won the Mothers and Daughters Tournament at Royal Mid-Surrey in 1994 for the 21st time.

● Patricia Shepherd has won the ladies' club championship at Turriff GC Aberdeenshire 30 consecutive times from 1959 to 1988.

● Mrs Jackie Mercer won the South African Ladies' Championship in 1979, 31 years after her first victory in the event as Miss Jacqueline Smith.

● During The Royal and Ancient Golf Club of St Andrews' medal meeting on 25th September, 1907, a member of The Royal and Ancient drove a ball which struck the sharp point of a hatpin in the hat of a lady who was crossing the course. The ball was so firmly impaled that it remained in position. The lady was not hurt.

● John Cook, former English Amateur Champion, narrowly escaped death during an attempted coup against King Hassan of Morocco in July 1971. Cook had been playing in a tournament arranged by King Hassan, a keen golfer, and was at the King's birthday party in Rabat when rebels broke into the party demanding that the King give up his throne. Cook and many others present were taken hostage.

● When playing from the 9th tee at Lossiemouth golf course in June, 1971, Martin Robertson struck a Royal Navy jet aircraft which was coming in to land at the nearby airfield. The plane was not damaged.

● At a court in Inglewood, California, in 1978, Jim Brown was convicted of beating and choking an opponent during a dispute over where a ball should have been placed on the green.

● During the Northern Ireland troubles a home-made hand grenade was found in a bunker at Dungannon GC, Co. Tyrone, on Sunday, 12th September, 1976.

● Tiger Woods, 18, became both the youngest and the first black golfer to win the United States Amateur Championship at Sawgrass in 1994. He went on to win the title three years in a row and then won the first major championship he played as a professional, the 1997 Masters, by a record 12 strokes and with a record low aggregate of 270, 18 under par.

● To mark the centenary of the Jersey Golf Club in 1978, the Jersey Post Office issued a set of four special stamps featuring Jersey's most famous golfer, Harry Vardon. The background of the 13p stamp was a brief biography of Vardon's career reproduced from the *Golfer's Handbook*.

● Forty-one-year-old John Mosley went for a round of golf at Delaware Park GC, Buffalo, New York, in July, 1972. He stepped on to the first tee and was challenged over a green fee by an official guard. A scuffle developed, a shot was fired and Mosley, a bullet in his chest, died on the way to hospital. His wife was awarded $131,250 in an action against the City of Buffalo and the guard. The guard was sentenced to 7½ years for second-degree manslaughter.

● When three competitors in a 1968 Pennsylvania pro-am event were about to drive from the 16th tee, two bandits (one with pistol) suddenly emerged from the bushes, struck one of the players and robbed them of wristwatches and $300.

● In the 1932 Walker Cup match at Brooklyn, Leonard Crawley succeeded in denting the cup. An errant iron shot to the 18th green hit the cup, which was on display outside the clubhouse.

● In Johannesburg, South Africa, three golf officials appeared in court accused of violating a 75-year-old Sunday Observance Law by staging the final round of the South African PGA championship on Sunday, 28th February, 1971. The Championship should have been completed on the Saturday but heavy rain prevented any play.

● In The Open Championship of 1876, at St Andrews, Bob Martin and David Strath tied at 176. A protest was lodged against Strath alleging he played his approach to the 17th green and struck a spectator. The Royal and Ancient ordered the replay, but Strath refused to play off the tie until a decision had been given on the protest. No decision was given and Bob Martin was declared the Champion.

● At Rose Bay, New South Wales, on 11th July, 1931, D.J. Bayly MacArthur, on stepping into a bunker, began to sink. MacArthur, who weighed 14 stone, shouted for help. He was rescued when up to the armpits. He had stepped on a patch of quicksand, aggravated by excess of moisture.

● The late Bobby Cruickshank was the victim of his own jubilation in the 1934 US Open at Merion. In the 4th round while in with a chance of winning he half-topped his second shot at the 11th hole. The ball was heading for a pond in front of the green but instead of ending up in the water it hit a rock and bounced on to the green. In his delight Cruickshank threw his club into the air only to receive a resounding blow on the head as it returned to earth.

● A dog with an infallible nose for finding lost golf balls was, in 1971, given honorary membership of the Waihi GC, Hamilton, New Zealand. The dog, called Chico, was trained to search for lost balls, to be sold back to the members, the money being put into the club funds.

● By 1980 Waddy, an 11-year-old beagle belonging to Bob Inglis, the secretary of Brokenhurst Manor GC, had found over 35,000 golf balls.

● Herbert M. Hepworth, Headingley, Leeds, Lord Mayor of Leeds in 1906, scored one thousand holes in 2, a feat which took him 30 years to accomplish. It was celebrated by a dinner in 1931 at the Leeds club. The first 2 of all was scored on 12th June, 1901, at Cobble Hall Course, Leeds, and the 1,000th in 1931 at Alwoodley, Leeds. Hepworth died in November, 1942.

● Fiona MacDonald was the first female to play in the Oxford and Cambridge University match at Ganton in 1986.

● Mrs Sara Gibbon won the Farnham (Surrey) Club's Grandmother's competition 48 hours after her first grand-child was born.

● At Carnoustie in the first qualifying round for the 1952 Scottish Amateur Championship a competitor drove three balls in succession out of bounds at the 1st hole and thereupon withdrew.

● In 1993, the Clark family from Hagley GC, Worcs, set a record for the county's three major professional events. The Worcestershire Stroke Play Championship was won by Finlay Clark, the eldest son, who beat his father Iain and younger brother Cameron, who tied second. In the Match Play Iain beat his son Finlay by 2 and 1 in the final; Cameron won the play-off for third place. Then in the Worcestershire Annual Pro-Am it was Cameron's turn to win, with his brother Finlay coming second and father Iain third. To add to the achievements of the family, Cameron also won the Midland Professional Match Play Championship.

● During a Captain–Pro foursomes challenge match at Chelmsford in 1993, Club Professional Dennis Bailey, put the ball into a hole only once in all 18 holes – when he holed-in-one at the fourth.

● In 1891, a new kind of matchplay – bogey – was introduced at Great Yarmouth Golf Club where the scratch score of the course was taken and each hole given a value known as the ground score. One of the club's members was described as a "regular bogeyman", a name suggested by a music hall song that was currently popular … and the name stuck.

● Mrs C.C. Gray was Todmorden Golf Club's Ladies Champion 38 out of 42 times between 1951 and 1992, a fact recorded in the *Guinness Book of Records*.

● Llanymynech is a golf club situated in two countries with 15 holes in Wales and three in England. On the fourth tee, players drive from England and putt out in Wales.

● Gary Sutherland, with only his golf bag as his suitcase and using public transport, competed an unusual tribute to his late father by playing 18 rounds on 18 courses on 18 different islands in Scotland. His travels began on the 13-hole course at Port Bannatyne on Bute, took him among other islands to Orkney, Shetland, Harris, South Uist, Arran and ended at Machrie on Islay. Accompanied by his friend golf architect Brian Noble, Sutherland found the trip rekindled his own love of a game his father had enjoyed so much. … and he has recorded his adventures in a new book *The Fairway Isles*.

Strange local rules

● The Duke of Windsor, who played on an extraordinary variety of the world's courses, once took advantage of a local rule at Jinja in Uganda and lifted his ball from a hippo's footprint without penalty.

● At the Glen Canyon course in Arizona a local rule provides that *If your ball lands within a club length of a rattlesnake you are allowed to move the ball.*

● Another local rule in Uganda reads: *If a ball comes to rest in dangerous proximity to a crocodile, another ball may be dropped.*

"I reckon that qualifies as dangerous proximity"

● The 6th hole at Koolan Island GC, Western Australia, also serves as a local air strip and a local rule reads: *Aircraft and vehicular traffic have right of way at all times.*

● A local rule at the RAF Waddington GC reads: *When teeing off from the 2nd, right of way must be given to taxiing aircraft.*

Open Championship Timeline

1860 The first Open Championship is played at Prestwick. There are eight competitors and the trophy, an ornate red leather belt, is won by Willie Park Sr.

1863 Prize money is first awarded, but only to second, third and fourth place finishers. The winner first receives a cash prize of £6 in 1864.

1870 Tommy Morris Jr takes possession of the Challenge Belt after winning The Open for the third consecutive year.

1873 The Claret Jug is first awarded. Played at St Andrews, it is the first time the Championship is held outside Prestwick.

1890 John Ball becomes the first amateur and the first Englishman to win The Open.

1892 Play is extended to two days over 72 holes at Muirfield. Competitors are charged an entrance fee.

1898 The "cut" is introduced after 36 holes.

1907 Arnaud Massy from France is the first continental player to win The Open. Qualifying rounds are first played.

1909 The Golf Exhibition tent makes its first appearance, as a display venue for leading manufacturers.

1922 It is decided that The Open should only be played over links courses.

1925 Prestwick hosts its 24th and final Open Championship.

1926 Admission charges are introduced. Play is extended to three days.

1955 The Open is broadcast live on television by the BBC.

1960 Grandstands are introduced at the Centenary Open played in St Andrews.

1963 Exemptions from pre-qualifying are introduced for the leading players.

1966 America receives its first live Open broadcast. The Championship is played over three days.

1968 The double cut is introduced after 54 holes and remains in effect until 1985.

1970 Jack Nicklaus and Doug Sanders became the first duo to compete in an 18-hole play-off.

1973 The 1.62 inch ball is last used at The Open.

1976 Japan receives its first live Open transmission.

1977 Regional qualifying is introduced as a preliminary to Final Qualifying for most players.

1980 The Championship ends on a Sunday for the first time.

1985 The four-hole play-off, followed by sudden death, is introduced.

2000 A new record is set at the Home of Golf when 238,787 watch the Millennium Open.

2002 History is made when The Open ends for the first time in a four-way tie. In another first, the four-hole play-off results in a tie.

2004 International Final Qualifying is introduced, allowing players to qualify at five international locations.

2006 The 135th Open Championship is broadcast globally for 2,051 hours. Fifty-seven broadcasters across 162 territories show coverage of The Open to a potential household reach of 410 million.

2007 Ireland's Padraig Harrington becomes the first European to win The Open since Paul Lawrie in 1999 and only the second Irishman. Fred Daly preceded him in 1947.

2009 Tom Watson, aged 59 years, 10 months, 15 days, becomes the oldest ever runner-up. Matteo Manassero, aged 16 years and 3 months, becomes the youngest winner of the Silver Medal for the leading amateur.

2010 Golf's oldest Major celebrates its 150th anniversary as The Open is played at the Home of Golf for the 28th time.

Timeline for the Rules of Golf

The earliest known Rules of Golf were drawn up in 1744 by what was to become the Honourable Company of Edinburgh Golfers. For the next 100 years, each club could issue and revise its own code of Rules, and these were mainly based on the codes issued by The Royal and Ancient Golf Club, the Edinburgh Burgess Golfing Society or the Honourable Company. Some of the rules followed by individual clubs were identical to one of these codes, while others were worded with reference to the features of a particular course.

Starting in the second half of the 19th century, more and more clubs based their codes on those issued by The Royal and Ancient Golf Club. In 1897 its governance role was formalised with the creation of the Rules of Golf Committee.

1744 The Honourable company of Edinburgh Golfers produce a written code of rules. Known as the Thirteen Articles, Rule 1 states: "You must tee your ball within a club-length of the hole".

1754 Largely copying from the 1744 Rules, the Society of St Andrews Golfers (later to become The Royal and Ancient Golf Club) record their own Rules in the minutes.

1775 Methods of settling disputes first appear in the Honourable Company's Rules. "Any dispute arising between parties on the green shall be determined by the Captain for the time, if present, or by the latest Captain who may be on the ground".

1812 The R&A's 1754 code is revised and for the first time the Rules of Golf refer to bunkers and the putting green.

1842 The revised R&A code stipulates that "one round of the links, or 18 holes, is reckoned a match" for the first time.

1851 A revised R&A code is issued. In response to the advent of the gutta percha ball, a new rule allows that: "If a ball shall split into two or more pieces, a fresh ball shall be put down in playing for a medal".

1875 Attending the flagstick and dealing with balls resting against the flagstick appear in the Rules for the first time.

1882 The revised R&A code contains an index and a glossary of terms for the first time.

1882 The glossary of terms in the R&A code defines the size of the hole as being four inches in diameter and lined with iron.

1886 The Royal Isle of Wight Golf Club issues a version of the Rules of Golf, which defines the size of the hole as being four inches in diameter and six inches deep.

1888 Local Rules for Playing the Links at St Andrews are separated out from the main Rules of Golf for the first time by The R&A.

1891 The revised R&A code defines the hole as being four and a quarter inches in diameter and at least four inches deep. This remains the definition.

1897 The Royal and Ancient Golf Club is officially recognised as the game's governing body for the Rules of Golf.

1909 Limits on the form and make of clubs are applied for the first time.

1920 The R&A and the USGA agreed that from May 1st, 1921, "the weight of the ball should be no greater than 1.62 ounces and the size not less than 1.62 inches in diameter".

1929 Steel shafts are legalised.

1939 The maximum number of clubs that can be carried is 14.

1952 The R&A and the USGA establish a unified code of Rules.

1960 Distance measuring devices are banned.

1984 The ball is no longer dropped over the player's shoulder, but at arm's length and at shoulder height.

1988 First Joint Decisions on the Rules of Golf book published by The R&A and the USGA.

1990 The 1.68-inch ball becomes the only legal ball, marking the demise of the 1.62-inch British ball.

2002 The R&A announces its decision to limit driver 'spring-like' effect from 2008, with an elite level Condition of Competition effective 1 January 2003.

2004 Entire Rule book redrafted for clarity, adopting a more modern style. Etiquette section amended and expanded. Limits introduced on size and dimensions of wood heads and club length (excluding putters).

2010 New groove specifications introduced, effective immediately at elite level by Condition of Competition. Club level golfers exempt until at least 2024.

Royal Clubs

There are currently 63 clubs with royal titles granted by the British Royal family. In 2009, Auckland Golf Club, New Zealand, was granted Royal status by Her Majesty Queen Elizabeth II as was the Mayfair Golf Club in Edmonton, Canada, in 2005. In 2004, Wellington Golf Club received the title from HRH The Duke of York. Mariánské Lázně Golf Club was honoured in 2003. The club had strong connections with British Royalty in the past; King Edward VII holidayed there, in what is now the Czech Republic. Apart from Mariánské Lázně, the Royal Clubs are in the United Kingdom or the Commonwealth. The oldest club with Royal connections is The Royal and Ancient Golf Club of St Andrews, founded in 1754 and given Royal patronage by King William IV in 1834. Royal Perth Golf Club, which was founded in 1824, received the patronage of King William IV a year earlier, in 1833.

Club	*Year Founded*	*Year of Royal Patronage*	*Royal Patron*
Royal Ancient Golf Club, St Andrews	1754	1834	William IV
Royal Aberdeen	1780	1903	Edward VII (Leopold patron in 1872)
Royal Adelaide	1892	1923	George V
Royal Ascot	1887	1887	Victoria 1887; Elizabeth II 1977
Royal Ashdown Forest	1888	1893	Victoria
Royal Auckland	1894	2009	Elizabeth II
Royal Belfast	1881	1885	Edward, Prince of Wales (later Edward VII)
Royal Birkdale	1889	1951	George VI
Royal Blackheath	1766	1857	*Not known*
Royal Burgess	1773	1929	George V
Royal Calcutta	1829	1912	George V
Royal Canberra	1926	1933	George V
Royal Cape	1885	1910	George V
Royal Cinque Ports	1892	1910	George V
Royal Colombo	1879	1928	George V
Royal Colwood	1913	1931	George V
Royal County Down	1889	1908	Edward VII
Royal Cromer	1888	1887	Edward, Prince of Wales (later Edward VII)
Royal Dornoch	1877	1906	Edward VII
Royal Dublin	1885	1891	Victoria
Duff House Royal	1909	1925	Princess Louise, Dowager Duchess of Fife
Royal Durban	1892	1932	George V
Royal Eastbourne	1887	1887	Victoria
Royal Epping Forest	1888	1888	Victoria
Royal Fremantle	1905	1930	George V
Royal Guernsey	1890	1891	Victoria

Club	Year Founded	Year of Royal Patronage	Royal Patron
Royal Harare	1898	1929	George V
Royal Hobart	1900	1925	George V
The Royal Household	1901	1901	Edward VII
Royal Jersey	1878	1879	Victoria
Royal Johannesburg	1890	1931	George V
Royal Liverpool	1869	1871	Prince Arthur, Duke of Connaught
Royal Lytham	1886	1926	George V
Royal Malta	1888	1888	Prince Alfred, Duke of Edinburgh
Royal Mariánské Lázně	1905	2003	Elizabeth II
Royal Mayfair	1922	2005	Elizabeth II
Royal Melbourne	1891	1895	Victoria
Royal Mid Surrey	1892	1926	George V
Royal Montreal	1873	1884	Victoria
Royal Montrose	1810	1845	Prince Albert
Royal Musselburgh	1774	1876	Prince Arthur, Duke of Connaught
Royal Nairobi	1906	1935	George V
Royal North Devon	1864	1866	Edward, Prince of Wales (later Edward VII)
Royal Norwich	1893	1893	George, Duke of York (later George V)
Royal Ottawa	1891	1912	George V
Royal Perth	1824	1833	William IV
Royal Perth (Australia)	1895	1937	George VI
Royal Port Alfred	1907	1924	George V
Royal Porthcawl	1891	1909	Edward VII
Royal Portrush	1888	1892	George, Duke of York (later George V)
Royal Quebec	1874	1934	George V
Royal Queensland	1920	1921	George V
Royal Regina	1899	1999	Elizabeth II
Royal St Davids	1894	1908	Edward, Prince of Wales (later Edward VII)
Royal St George's	1887	1902	Edward VII
Royal Sydney	1893	1897	Victoria
Royal Tarlair	1926	1926	Princess Louise, Dowager Duchess of Fife
Royal Troon	1878	1978	Elizabeth II
Royal Wellington	1895	2004	Prince Andrew, Duke of York
Royal West Norfolk	1892	1892	Edward, Prince of Wales (later Edward VII)
Royal Wimbledon	1865	1882	Victoria
Royal Winchester	1888	1913	George V
Royal Worlington and Newmarket	1893	1895	Victoria

Websites

The R&A	www.randa.org
United States Golf Association	www.usga.org
English Golf Union	www.englishgolfunion.org
Golf Union of Ireland	www.gui.ie
Scottish Golf Union	www.scottishgolfunion.org
Welsh Golf Union	www.welshgolf.org
European Golf Association	www.ega-golf.ch
Ladies Golf Union (LGU)	www.lgu.org
English Ladies (ELGA)	www.englishladiesgolf.org
Irish Ladies (ILGU)	www.ilgu.ie
European Tour	www.europeantour.com
US PGA Tour	www.pgatour.com
Australasian Tour	www.pgatour.com.au
Asian Tour	www.asiantour.com
Japanese Tour	www.jgto.org
South African Sunshine Tour	www.sunshinetour.com
LPGA Tour	www.lpga.com
Ladies European Tour (LET)	www.ladieseuropeantour.com
Japanese Ladies Tour	www.lpga.or.jp (Japanese only)
Asian Ladies Tour	www.lagt.org
Australian Ladies Tour	www.alpgtour.com
South African Ladies Tour	www.wpga.co.za
Futures Tour	www.duramedfuturestour.com
The Open	www.opengolf.com
US Open	www.usopen.com
The Masters	www.masters.org
US PGA Championship	www.pga.com/pgachampionship/2010
PGA (The Belfry)	www.pga.info
PGAs of Europe	www.pgae.com
PGA of America	www.pga.com

Severiano Ballesteros	www.seveballesteros.com
Angel Cabrera	www.angelcabrera.com
Michael Campbell	www.cambogolf.com
Paul Casey	www.paul-casey.com
Darren Clarke	www.darrenclarke.com
Ernie Els	www.ernieels.com
Nick Faldo	www.nickfaldo.com
Niclas Fasth	www.niclasfasth.com
Sergio García	www.sergiogarcia.com
Retief Goosen	www.retiefgoosen.com
Padraig Harrington	www.padraigharrington.com
David Howell	www.davidhowellgolf.com
Miguel Angel Jiménez	www.mmiworldwide.com
Bernhard Langer	www.bernhardlanger.de
Thomas Levet	www.thomas-levet.com
Paul McGinley	www.paulmcginley.net
Rory McIlroy	www.rorymcilroy,com
Phil Mickelson	www.phil-mickelson.com
Colin Montgomerie	www.colinmontgomerie.com
Jack Nicklaus	www.nicklaus.com
Greg Norman	www.shark.com
Lorena Ochoa	www.lorenaochoa.com
Geoff Ogilvy	www.prosportmanagement.com
José Maria Olazábal	www.gmi.com
Arnold Palmer	www.arnoldpalmer.com
Ian Poulter	www.ianpoulter.co.uk
Eduardo Romero	www.eduardoromero.com
Justin Rose	www.justinrose.com
Adam Scott	www.adamscott.com.au
Jeev Milkha Singh	www.jeevmilkhasingh.net
Annika Sörenstam	www.annikasorenstam.com
Henrik Stenson	www.henrikstenson.com
Lee Westwood	www.westyuk.com
Tiger Woods	www.tigerwoods.com
Ian Woosnam	www.woosie.com

PART XVI

Directory of Golfing Organisations Worldwide

Directory of Golfing Organisations Worldwide

National Associations

The R&A
Ch Exec, Peter Dawson, Beach House, Golf Place, St Andrews, Fife KY16 9JD
Tel (01334) 460000 *Fax* (01334) 460001
E-mail thechiefexecutive@randa.org
Website www.randa.org

CONGU – Council of National Golf Unions
Sec, Melvyn Goddard, 1 Peerswood Court, Little Neston, Neston CH64 0US
Tel (0151) 336 3936 – office
E-mail secretary@congu.com
Website www.congu.com

IGF – International Golf Federation
Exec Dir, Antony Scanlon, Maison Du Sport International, Av De Rhodanie 54, 1007 Lausanne, Switzerland
E-mail igfinfo@igfmail.org
Website www.internationalgolffederation.org

LET – Ladies European Tour
Exec Dir, A Armas, Buckinghamshire GC, Denham Court Drive, Denham UB9 5PG
Tel (01895) 831028 *Fax* (01895) 832301
E-mail mail@ladieseuropeantour.com
Website www.ladieseuropeantour.com

LGU – Ladies' Golf Union
Ch Exec, S Malcolm, The Scores, St Andrews, Fife KY16 9AT
Tel (01334) 475811 *Fax* (01334) 472818
E-mail info@lgu.org
Website www.lgu.org

PGA – The Professional Golfers' Association
Ch Exec, Sandy Jones, Centenary House, The Belfry, Sutton Coldfield B76 9PT
Tel (01675) 470333 *Fax* (01675) 477888
Website www.pga.info

PGA European Tour
Exec Dir, G O'Grady, PGA European Tour, Wentworth Drive, Virginia Water, Surrey GU25 4LX
Tel (01344) 840400 *Fax* (01344) 840500
E-mail info@europeantour.com
Website www.europeantour.com

PGAs of Europe
Ch Exec, I Randell, Centenary House, The Belfry, Sutton Coldfield, B76 9PT
Tel (01675) 477899 *Fax* (01675) 477890
E-mail info@pgae.com
Website www.pgae.com

Artisan Golfers' Association
Hon Sec, K Stevens, 48 The Avenue, Lightwater, Surrey GU18 5RG
Tel (01276) 475103
E-mail kevin@stevens85.freeserve.co.uk
Website www.agagolf.co.uk

Association of Golf Writers
A group of 30 newspapermen attending the Walker Cup match at St Andrews in 1938 founded the Association to protect the interests of golf writers. The principal objective is to maintain a close liaison with all the governing bodies and promoters to ensure good working conditions.

Admin, Andrew Farrell, 1 Pilgrims Bungalow, Mulberry Hill, Chilham, Kent CT4 8AH
Tel/Fax (01227) 732496
E-mail enquiry@agwgolf.org
Website www.agwgolf.org

BAGCC – British Association of Golf Course Constructors
The BAGCC has a small but highly prestigious membership of constructors who have performed work to the highest standard from initial consultation to survey work and design through to the construction of a course and then its regular maintenance. Membership is granted only if the candidates satisfy the demanding criteria of experience, professionalism and workmanship set down by the Association.

Sec, Brian Pierson, 32 New Rd, Ringwood BH24 3AU
Tel (01425) 475584
E-mail brian.pierson@btopenworld,com
Website www.bagcc.org.uk

BALASA – British Amputee & Les Autres Sports Association
Golf Coordinator, Richard Saunders, 25 Kiln Lane, Manningtree, Essex CO11 1HQ
Tel (07967) 169951
E-mail richardsaundersfingers32@btinternet.com

British Golf Collectors' Society
Sec, A Thorpe, 22 Cherry Tree Close, Brinsley, Nottingham NG16 5BA
Tel/Fax (01773) 780420
E-mail anthonythorpe@ntlworld.com
Website www.britgolfcollectors.wyenet.co.uk

BGIA – British Golf Industry Association
Federation House, Stoneleigh Park, Warks CV8 2RF
Tel (024) 7641 4999 (x207) *Fax* (024) 7641 4990
E-mail info@bgia.org.uk
Website www.bgia.org.uk

British Golf Museum
Dir, P N Lewis, Bruce Embankment, St Andrews, Fife KY16 9AB
Tel (01334) 460046 *Fax* (01334) 460064
Website www.britishgolfmuseum.co.uk

BIGGA – British & International Golf Greenkeepers Association
The British & International Golf Greenkeepers Association has over 6,000 members and is dedicated to the continuing professional development of its members and strives, by education and training, for standards of excellence in golf course management. BIGGA organise an annual education conference and Europe's largest indoor turf show.
Ch Exec, J Croxton, BIGGA House, Aldwark, Alne, York YO61 1UF
Tel (01347) 833800 *Fax* (01347) 833801
E-mail info@bigga.co.uk
Website www.bigga.org.uk

BRTMA – British Rootzone & Topdressing Manufacturers Association
Federation House, Stoneleigh Park, Warks CV8 2RF
Tel (024) 7641 4999 *Fax* (024) 7641 4990
E-mail brtma@sportsandplay.com
Website www.brtma.com

BTLIA – British Turf & Landscape Irrigation Association
Sec, M Jones, 41 Pennine Way, Great Eccleston, Preston PR3 0YS
Tel/Fax (01995) 670675
E-mail btlisecretary@btconnect.com
Website www.btlia.org.uk

Club Managers Association of Europe
CEO, Jerry Kilby, Federation House, Stoneleigh Park, Warks CV8 2RF
Tel (024) 7669 2359 *Fax* (024) 7641 4990
E-mail jerry.kilby@cmaeurope.eu
Website www.cmaeurope.org

EDGA – European Disabled Golf Association
Vice Pres, Pieter van Duijn, Wederikhof 8, NL-2215 GJ Voorhout, The Netherlands
Tel +31 252 224161 *E-mail* mail@edgagolf.com
Website www.edgagolf.com

EGIA – European Golf Industry Association
Federation House, Stoneleigh Park, Warks CV8 2RF
Tel (024) 7641 4999 *Fax* (024) 7641 4990
E-mail egia@sportsandplay.com

EIGCA – European Institute of Golf Course Architects
The EIGCA represents the vast majority of qualified and experienced golf course architects throughout Europe. Its goals are to enhance its professional status and to provide educational courses to train future architects.
Exec Off, Mrs Julia Green, Meadow View House, Tannery Lane, Bramley, Surrey GU5 0AJ
Tel/Fax (01483) 891831 *Fax* (01483) 891846
E-mail enquiries@eigca.org *Website* www.eigca.org

Golf Club Managers' Association
Membership of the Association is approximately 2,300, consisting of managers/secretaries and owners of clubs and golfing associations situated mainly in the UK and Europe. The Association offers advice on all aspects of managing a golf club and has an extensive information library available to its members through its website.
Ch Exec, K Lloyd, 7a Beaconsfield Rd, Weston-super-Mare BS23 1YE
Tel (01934) 641166 *Fax* (01934) 644254
E-mail hq@gcma.org.uk
Website www.gcma.org.uk

Golf Club Stewards' Association
The Golf Club Stewards' Association was founded in 1912 to promote the interests of members and to serve as an employment agency for golf club stewards and caterers.
Sec, KG Brothwell, 11 King Charles Court, Sunderland, Tyne & Wear SR5 4PD
Tel (01915) 190137
E-mail k.brothwell@sky.com
Website www.club_noticeboard.co.uk

Golf Consultants Association
Federation House, Stoneleigh Park, Warks CV8 2RF
Tel (024) 7641 4999 *Fax* (024) 7641 4990
E-mail gca@sportsandplay.com
Website www.golfconsultants.org.uk

Golf Foundation
Ch. Exec, Michael Round, The Spinning Wheel, High St, Hoddesdon, Herts EN11 8BP
Tel (01992) 449830 *Fax* (01992) 449840
E-mail info@golf-foundation.org
Website www.golf-foundation.org

Golf Society of Great Britain
Founded in 1955 by the late Sir Aynsley Bridgland of Prince's Golf Club with the object of promoting goodwill and providing funds to further the interest of the game in all its aspects, the Society now has about 850 members and continues its founder's aims of promoting amateur golf through the sponsorship of junior golf tournaments and through donations to the Junior Section of the Society's participating clubs. Five to six meetings are held each year in the UK plus Spring and Autumn Tours abroad.
Sec, Brian Ward, Parkhouse Lodge, Mill Lane, Holmes Chapel, Cheshire CW4 8AU
Tel (07760) 777736
E-mail secretary@golfsocietygb.com
Website www.golfsocietygb.com

Handigolf Foundation
Sec, Ray Lee, 404 Westthorne Ave, Eltham, London SE9 5TL
Tel (0208) 850 7407
E-mail rayndpam@hotmail.com
Website www.handigolf.org

National Association of Public Golf Courses
Affiliated to the English Golf Union, the Association was founded in 1927 by golf course architect FG Hawtree and five times Open champion JH Taylor to provide a relationship between public and proprietory golf clubs, and local councils and course owners.
Hon Sec, E Mitchell, 12 Newton Close, Redditch B98 7YR
Tel (01527) 542106
E-mail secretary@napgc.org.uk
Website www.napgc.org.uk

National Golf Clubs' Advisory Association
Founded in 1922, the Association's aims are to protect the interests of golf clubs in general; to give legal advice and direction, under the opinion of Counsel, on the administrative and legal responsibilities of golf clubs;.and to provide a mediation service to members' clubs within the UK.
Ch Exec, Michael Shaw LLM
Nat Sec, J Howe, The Threshing Barn, Homme Castle Barns, Shelsley Walsh, Worcs WR6 6RR
Tel (01886) 812943 *Fax* (01886) 812935
E-mail jackie.ngaa@idealnet.co.uk
Website www.ngcaa.org.uk

One-Armed Golfers, Society of
Hon Sec, Jerry Woodley, 56 Hillfield Rd, Little Sutton, Ellesmere Port, Cheshire CH66 1JD
Tel (01513) 399 630
E-mail jedro1@sky.com
Website www.onearmgolf.org

Public Schools Old Boys Golf Association
Hon Sec, P de Pinna, Bruins, Wythwood, Haywards Heath, West Sussex RH16 4RD
Tel (01444) 454883
Email fred-.die_@tiscali.co.uk

Public Schools' Golfing Society
Hon Sec, N D Owen, 1 Bruce Grove, Orpington, Kent BR6 0HF
Tel (01689) 810225
E-mail nick.owen@ndowen.com

STRI – Sports Turf Research Institute
STRI is an independent consultancy and research organisation specialising in golf courses. Recognised throughout the world for its expertise in both agronomic and environmental issues relating to golf, STRI is the official adviser to The R&A's Championship Committee for all 'Open' venues. STRI undertakes research into turfgrass and sports surface science, promoting innovative solutions. For golf courses, it provides advisory and architectural services and gives ecological advice. In addition, STRI organises training and produces publications.
Ch Exec, Dr I G McKillop; *Marketing*, Carolyn Beadsmoore, St Ives Estate, Bingley, West Yorks BD16 1AU
Tel (01274) 565131
Fax (01274) 561891
E-mail info@stri.co.uk
Website www.stri.co.uk

Country and Regional Unions and Associations

England

England Golf
Acting CEO, Craig Wagstaff, National Golf Centre, The Broadway, Woodhall Spa, Lincs LN10 6PU
Tel (01526) 354500
Fax (01526) 354020
E-mail info@englandgolf.org
Website www.englandolf.org

Midland Group
Sec, N Harris, 6 Dawson Court, Oakham, Rutland LE15 6SD
Tel (01572) 823036
E-mail secretary@midlandgolfunion.co.uk
Website www.midlandgolfunion.co.uk

Northern Group
Sec, J D Trickett, 8 Derriman Grove, Sheffield S11 9LE
Tel/Fax (0114) 296 2177
E-mail dennistrickett@yahoo.co.uk
Website www.ncgu.co.uk

South Eastern Group
Sec, B J Thompson, 8 Poplar Close, Silsoe, Beds MK45 4EE
Tel (01525) 860010
E-mail secretary@southeastgolfunion.co.uk
Website www.southeastgolfunion.co.uk

South Western Group
Sec, T C Reynolds, The Haven, Velator, Nr Braunton, N Devon EX33 2DX
Tel/Fax (01271) 812228
E-mail trevandjan@onetel.com

English Men's County Unions

Bedfordshire CGU
Sec, S K Goode, 54 Swasedale Rd, Luton LU3 2UD
Tel (01582) 521716
E-mail secretary@bedsgolfunion.org.uk
Website www.bedsgolfunion.org

Berks, Bucks & Oxon UGC
Sec, P M J York, Bridge House, Station Approach, Great Missenden HP16 9AZ
Tel (01494) 867341 *Fax* (01494) 867342
E-mail secretary@bbogolf.com
Website www.bbogolf.com

Cambridgeshire Area GU
Sec, H S Fleming, The Old Chapel, New Path, Fordham CB7 5JX
Tel (01638) 732028
E-mail hamishfleming@fordhamchapel.plus.com
Website www.cagu.co.uk

Cheshire UGC
Sec, S J Foster, County Office Chester GC, Curzon Park North, Chester CH4 8AR

Tel (01244) 346662
E-mail secretary@cheshiregolf.org.uk
Website www.cheshiregolf.org.uk

Cornwall GU
Sec, C Pountney, South Court, South Hill Rd, Callington PL17 7LG
Tel (01579) 384233
E-mail secretary@cornwallgolfunion.org.uk
Website www.cornwallgolfunion.org.uk

Cumbria UGC
Hon Sec, T F Stout, Kingston House, Moresby, Whitehaven CA28 8UW
Tel (01946) 693036
E-mail cumbriaugcsec@yahoo.co.uk
Website www.cumbria-golf-union.org.uk

Derbyshire UGC
Hon Sec, P McGrath, 36 Ilkeston Rd, Stapleford, Notts NG9 8JL
Tel (0115) 922 3603
E-mail secretary@dugc.co.uk
Website www.dugc.co.uk

Devon CGU
Sec, R J Hirst, 20 Plymouth Rd, Tavistock PL19 8AY
Tel (01822) 610640 *Fax* (01822) 610540
E-mail info@devongolfunion.org.uk
Website www.devongolfunion.org.uk

Dorset CGU
Sec, I L Hulse, 5 St James Rd, Ferndown, Dorset BH22 9NY
Tel (01202) 861185
E-mail secretary@dcgu.org.uk
Website www.dcgu.org.uk

Durham CGU
Sec, G P Hope, 7 Merrion Close, Moorside, Sunderland SR3 2QP
Tel/Fax (0191) 522 8605
E-mail graham.p.hope@btinternet.com
Website www.durhamcountygolfunion.co.uk

Essex GU
Sec, A T Lockwood, 2d Maldon Rd, Witham, Essex CM8 2AB
Tel (01376) 500998 *Fax* (01376) 500842
E-mail info@essexgolfunion.org
Website www.essexgolfunion.org

Gloucestershire GU
Sec, I Watkins, The Vyse, Olde Lane, Toddington, Glos GL54 5DQ
Tel/Fax (01242) 621476
E-mail secretary@gloucestershiregolfunion.co.uk
Website www.gloucestershiregolfunion.co.uk

Hampshire, Isle of Wight & Channel Islands GU
Sec, J B Morgan, c/o Liphook GC, Wheatsheaf Enclosure, Liphook, Hants GU30 7EH
Tel/Fax (01428) 725580
E-mail hgu@hampshiregolf.co.uk
Website www.hampshiregolf.org.uk

Hertfordshire GU
Sec, L Matamala, Chesfield Downs GC, Jacks Hill, Graveley, Herts SG4 7EQ
Tel (08081) 682333
E-mail secretary@hertsgolfunion.com
Website www.hertsgolfunion.com

Isle of Man GU
Sec, C Taylor, Inglewhite, Lazayre Pk, Ramsey, Isle of Man IM8 2PU
Tel (01624) 814028
E-mail iomgu.gensec@hotmail.com
Website www.isleofmangolf.im

Kent CGU
Sec, J G Young, Littlestone GC, St Andrew's Rd, Littlestone, New Romney, Kent TN28 8RB
Tel (01797) 367725 *Fax* (01797) 367726
E-mail kcgu@kentgolf.co.uk
Website www.kentgolf.org

Lancashire UGC
Sec, A V Moss, Ashton & Lea GC, TudorAve, Lea, Preston PR4 0XA
Tel (01772) 731330
Fax (01772) 727776
E-mail secretary@lancashiregolf.org
Website www.lancashiregolf.org

Leicestershire & Rutland GU
Hon Sec, B Tuttle, 63 Gwendoline Dr., Countesthorpe, Leicester LE8 5SJ
Tel (0116) 277 1900
E-mail lrgusecretary@gmail.com
Website www.lrgu.net

Lincolnshire UGC
Hon Sec, H Harrison, 27 Orchard Close, Morton, Gainsborough DN21 3BP
Tel (01427) 616904
E-mail secretary@lugc.co.uk
Website www.lugc.co.uk

Middlesex CGU
Sec, R Blower, Northwick Park Golf Centre, Watford Rd, Harrow HA1 3TZ
Tel (0208) 864 4744
Fax (0208) 864 4554
E-mail secretary@mcgu.co.uk
Website www.mcgu.co.uk

Norfolk CGU
Hon Sec, M Devlin, Acacia House, The Street, Tibenham, Norwich NR16 1QA
Tel (01359) 221281
E-mail niblick@btinternet.com
Website www.norfolkcountygolfunion.co.uk

Northamptonshire GU
Hon Sec, J Pearson, 150 Church Green Rd, Bletchley, Milton Keynes MK3 6DD
Tel (01908) 648657
E-mail secretary@northantsgolfunion.co.uk
Website www.northantsgolfunion.co.uk

Northumberland UGC
Hon Sec, W E Procter, Eastfield House, Moor Rd South, Gosforth, Newcastle upon Tyne NE3 1NP
Tel (0191) 285 4981
E-mail elliott@procter.entadsl.com
Website www.nugc.org.uk

Nottinghamshire UGC
Hon Sec, C Bee, Rushcliffe GC, Stocking Lane, East Leake, nr Loughborough LE12 5RL
Tel (01509) 852959
E-mail secretary@nottsgolfunion.co.uk
Website www.nottsgolf.com

Shropshire & Herefordshire UGC
Hon Sec, J R Davies, 23 Poplar Crescent, Bayston Hill, Shrewsbury SY3 0QB
Tel (01743) 872655
E-mail bdavies@shugc.com
Website www.shugc.com

Somerset GU
Acting Sec, G Yates
Tel/Fax (01458) 210228
E-mail secretary@somersetgolfunion.co.uk
Website www.somersetgolfunion.co.uk

Staffordshire UGC
Sec, M A Payne, 20 Kingsbrook Drive, Hillfield, Solihull B91 3UU
Tel (0121) 704 4779 *Fax* (0121) 711 2841
E-mail martin.payne11@btinternet.com
Website www.golfinstaffs.co.uk

Suffolk GU
Hon Sec, C A Wilderspin, 10a Chestnut Avenue, Oulton Broad, Lowestoft, Suffolk, NR32 3JA
Tel (01502) 588028
E-mail charles.wilderspin632@btinternet.com
Website www.suffolkgolfunion.co.uk

Surrey CGU
Sec, J A Davies, Sutton Green GC, New Lane, Sutton Green GU4 7QF
Tel (01483) 755788 *Fax* (01483) 751771
E-mail secretary@surreygolf.org
Website www.surreygolf.org

Sussex CGU
Sec, A Vasant, J.P., Eastbourne Down GC, East Dean Rd, Eastbourne, East Sussex BN20 8ES
Tel (01323) 746677
Fax (01323) 746777
E-mail anupvasant@ sussexgolf.org
Website www.sussexgolf.org

Warwickshire UGC
Sec, M Nixon, PO Box 6184, Stratford upon Avon, Warks CV37 1NG
Tel/Fax (01789) 297198
E-mail matt@nixongolf.com
Website www.warksgolf.co.uk

Wiltshire CGU
Sec, D J Lewis, 39 Ashley Piece, Ramsbury, SN8 2QE
Tel (01672) 520008
E-mail secretary@wcgu.org.uk
Website www.wcgu.org.uk

Worcestershire UGC
Hon Sec, A Boyd, The Bear's Den, Upper St, Defford, Worcester WR8 9BG
Tel (01386) 750657 *Fax* (01386) 750472
E-mail menssecretary@worcestershireamateurgolf.co.uk
Website www.worcestershireamateurgolf.co.uk

Yorkshire UGC
Hon Sec, K H Dowswell, 33 George St, Wakefield WF1 1LX
Tel (01924) 383869 *Fax* (01924) 383634
E-mail yorkshiregolf@lineone.net
Website www.yorkshireunionofgolf.co.uk

English Women's County Associations

Bedfordshire LCGA
Hon Sec, Mrs Paula Foot, 34 Vicarage Road, Silsoe, Bedford MK45 4EF
Tel (01525) 862758
E-mail paula@chilternbrands.com
Website blcga.co.uk

Berkshire CLGA
Hon Sec, Mrs Nicky Luff, 9 Elmwood, Maidenhead Court Park, Maidenhead, Berkshire SL6 8HX
Tel (01628) 674977
E-mail nicky.luff@btinternet.com

Buckinghamshire CLGA
Hon Sec, Mrs Helen Mines, Sobalym, Manor Rd, Princes Risborough, HP27 9DJ
Tel (07538) 306496
E-mail helen_mines@btinternet.com
Website bclga.org.uk

Cambs & Hunts LCGA
Hon Sec, Mrs Jacquie Richardson, Peel House, 11 Doddington Rd, Benwick, Marsh PE15 0UT
Tel (01354) 677856
E-mail j.s.richardson@btinternet.com
Website chlgca.co.uk

Cheshire CLGA
Hon Sec, Mrs A McCormick, Frinton, 22 Buxton Rd West, Disley, Stockport SK12 2LY
Tel (01663) 766807
E-mail ann.mccormick4@ntlworld.com

Cornwall LCGA
Hon Sec, Mrs Pat Crowson, 41 Old Coach Road, Playing Place, Truro TR3 6ET
Tel (01872) 864412
E-mail pat_pmc41@yahoo.co.uk *Website* clga.co.uk

Cumbria LCGA
Hon Sec, Mrs Sandra Stoker, Yew Tree Cottage, Main Rd, Endmoor, Kendal LA8 0EU
Tel (01539) 567826
E-mail stokers1985@btinternet.com

Derbyshire LCGA
Hon Sec, Mrs Tracy Pierrepont, 22 Arnos Grove, Nuthall, Notts NG16 1QA
Tel (01159) 750107
E-mail tracypierrepont@gmail.com

Devon CLGA
Hon Sec, Mrs Rickie Pawsey, 33 Prince of Wales Rd, Crediton EX17 2AG
Tel (01363) 772141
E-mail devonladiessecretary@hotmail.com

Dorset LCGA
Hon Sec, Mrs Zoe Ashley, Honeypot Cottage, 12 Glenwood Rd, West Moor, Ferndown BH22 0EP
Tel (01202) 872277
E-mail zoe.odlcga@yahoo.co.uk

Durham LGA
Hon Sec, Mrs Ann Corbett, 1 Corby Mews, Ashbrooke Rd, Sunderland SR2 7HQ
Tel (0191) 522 9448
E-mail corbettann@hotmail.co.uk
Website durhamladiesgolf.org.uk

Essex LGA
Hon Sec, Mrs Nicola Thomas, 6 Heathgate, Wickham Bishops, Witham CM8 3NZ
Tel (01621) 891592
E-mail ath1343349@aol.com
Website essexladiesgolf.org

Gloucestershire LCGA
Hon Sec, Mrs Gillian Merry, Myles House, Ashmead, Cam, Dursley GL11 5EN
Tel (01453) 542569
E-mail GillianMerry@talktalk.net

Hampshire LCGA
Hon Sec, Mrs Gill Staley, Garth House, 55 Elvetham Rd, Fleet GU51 4QP
Tel (01252) 616442
E-mail gill@staley.org.uk
Website www.hampshireladiesgolf.co.uk

Hertfordshire CLGA
Hon Sec, Mrs Linda Battye, 12 Manor Links, Bishop's Stortford CM23 5RA
Tel (01279) 505393
E-mail lindabattye@gmail.com
Website www.hclga.co.uk

Kent CLGA
Hon Sec, Mrs Sarah Brooks, 10 Hayle Mill, Hayle Mill Rd, Maidstone ME15 6JW
Tel (01622) 761841
E-mail pumplodge@aol.com
Website kentladiesgolf.org.uk

Lancashire LCGA
Hon Sec, Miss Elaine Clark, 3 Derwent Dr, Littleborough, Lancs OL15 0BT
Tel (01706) 376689 *E-mail* lancs2009@live.co.uk

Leicestershire & Rutland LCGA
Hon Sec, Mrs Anita Higginson, The Old Rectory, Main St, Peatling Parva, Leics LE17 5QA
Tel (01162) 478240
E-mail higginsons@talk21.com

Lincolnshire LCGA
Hon Sec, Mrs Beverley Dolman, 10 Caudebec Close, Uppingham, Rutland LE15 9SY
Tel (01572) 821382
E-mail beverleydolman@hotmail.com

Middlesex LCGA
Hon Sec, Mrs Anne Henderson, 5 Ford End, Denham Village, Uxbridge UB9 5AL
Tel (01895) 835154
E-mail anne@eigergroup.co.uk

Norfolk LCGA
Hon Sec, Mrs Yvette Douglas, 204 Norwich Rd, Fakenham NR21 8LX
Tel (01328) 863296
E-mail douglas.yvette@btinternet.com

Northamptonshire LCGA
Hon Sec, Mrs Virginia Jolliffe, 20 Kingsthorpe Grove, Northampton NN2 6NT
Tel (01604) 716023
E-mail ginnyjol@talktalk.net

Northumberland LCGA
Hon Sec, Mrs Helen Woodhouse, Coruisk, Elm Rd, Ponteland, Newcastle upon Tyne NE20 9BS
Tel (01661) 825054
E-mail helenj.woodhouse@gmail.com
Website www.nlcga.co.uk

Nottinghamshire CLGA
Hon Sec, Mrs Bridgett A Patrick, 18 Delville Ave, Keyworth, Nottingham NG12 5JA
Tel (0115) 937 3237
E-mail bapatrick@btinternet.com

Oxfordshire LCGA
Hon Sec, Mrs Iona Smith, Field House, Childrey, Wantage OX12 9UT
Tel (01235) 751250
E-mail nsirsmith@btopenworld.com
Website olcga.org.uk

Shropshire LCGA
Hon Sec, Mrs Vanessa Statham, 24 Abbotts Way, Riverside, Bridgnorth WV16 4JZ
Tel (01746) 768428
E-mail vanessastatham@uwclub.net

Somerset LCGA
Hon Sec, Mrs Sheena Smith, "Findlater" Long Load, Langport, Somerset TA10 9LE
Tel (01458) 241577
E-mail sheena136@btinternet.com

Staffordshire LCGA
Hon Sec, Mrs Pam Siviter, 69 Ward St, Coseley, W Midlands WV14 9LQ
Tel/Fax (01902) 689940
E-mail pam.siviter@blueyonder.co.uk

Suffolk LCGA
Hon Sec, Mrs Jeanette Longman, The Old School House, Chillesford, IP12 3PS
Tel (01394) 450939
E-mail jeanette.longman@gmail.com
Website suffolkladiesgolf.org.uk

Surrey LCGA
Sec, Mrs Penelope Hall, SLGCA, c/o Sutton Green GC, Sutton Green, Guildford GU4 7QF
Tel (01483) 751622 *Fax* (01483) 751771
E-mail secretary@slcga.org
Website www.slcga.org

Sussex CLGA
Hon Sec, Mrs Ann Carnegie, 7 The Wad, West Wittering, West Sussex PO20 8AH
Tel (01243) 511307
E-mail ann@thecarnegies.net
Website sclga.com

Warwickshire LCGA
Hon Sec, Mrs Elizabeth Murdoch, Plestowes House, Hareway Lane, Barford, Warwick CV35 8DD
Tel (01926) 624503
E-mail liz@murdochonline.co.uk
Website warksgolf.co.uk

Wiltshire LCGA
Hon Sec, Mrs Penny Telling, Swanborough Cottage, 46 Mill Lane, Poulshot, Devizes SN10 1SA
Tel (01380) 828370
E-mail pennytelling@aol.com

Worcestershire and Herefordshire LCGA
Hon Sec, Mrs Sue Birch, 159 Hither Green Lane, Abbey Park, Redditch B98 9AZ

Tel (01527) 61958
E-mail SueBirch@btinternet.com

Yorkshire LCGA
Hon Sec, Mrs Dawn Clegg, 10 Usher Park Rd, Haxby, York YO32 3RY
Tel (01904) 761987
E-mail dawnhclegg@hotmail.com
Website www.ylcga.org

English Regional and County PGAs

The PGA in England (East)
Sec, J Smith, Bishop's Stortford GC, Dunmow Road, Bishop's Stortford, Herts CM23 5HP
Tel (01279) 652070 *Fax* (01279) 652732
E-mail john.smith@pga.org.uk

The PGA in England (Midland)
Sec, J Brown, Forward House, 17 High Street, Henley In Arden, Warwickshire B95 5AA
Tel (01564) 330635 *Fax* (01564) 797410
E-mail james.brown@pga.org.uk

The PGA in England & Wales (North)
Sec, G Maly, No 2 Cottage, Bolton GC, Lostock Park, Chorley New Rd, Bolton, Lancs BL6 4AJ
Tel (01204) 496137 *Fax* (01204) 847959
E-mail graham.maly@pga.org.uk

The PGA in England (South)
Sec, S Smith, Clandon Regis GC, Epsom Rd, West Clandon, Guildford, Surrey GU4 7TT
Tel (01483) 224200
E-mail sam.smith@pga.org.uk

The PGA in England & Wales (South West)
Sec, G Ross, The Lodge House, Woodbury Park H&GC, Woodbury Castle, Woodbury, Exeter, EX5 1JJ
Tel (01395) 232288
Fax (01395) 232383
E-mail glenn.ross@ pga.org.uk

Bedfordshire & Cambridgeshire PGA
Sec, B Wake, 6 Gazelle Close, Eaton Socon, St Neots PE19 8QF
Tel (01480) 219760
E-mail brian.wake@btopenworld.com

Berks, Bucks & Oxon PGA
Hon Sec, Martin Morbey, Valderrama, Haywards Road, Drayton, Oxon OX14 4LB
E-mail admin@bbopga.co.uk
Website www.bbopga.co.uk

Cheshire and North Wales PGA
Sec, G Maly, No 2 Cottage, Bolton GC, Lostock Park, Chorley New Road, Bolton BL6 4AJ
Tel (01204) 496137 *Fax* (01204) 847959
E-mail graham.maly@pga.org.uk

Cornwall PGA
Sec, J Greenaway, Bowood Park GC, Camelford PL32 9RF
Tel (01840) 213017 *Fax* (01840) 212622
E-mail golf@bowood-park.co.uk
Website www.bowood-park.co.uk

Derbyshire PGA
Sec, Andrew Smith, Ashbourne GC, Wyaston Rd, Ashbourne DE6 1NB
Tel (01335) 342078
E-mail ashbournegc@tiscali.co.uk
Website www.ashbournegc.co.uk

Devon PGA
Sec, Dan Hendriksen, Churston GC, Churston, Brixham TQ5 0LA
Tel (01803) 843442
E-mail manager@churstongolf.com
Website www.devonpga.co.uk

Dorset PGA
Sec, D Parsons, Bridport & West Dorset GC, Burton Rd, Bridport, Dorset DT6 4PS
Tel (01308) 421491
E-mail bridproshop@tesco.net

Essex PGA
Sec, S Garland-Collins, 27 Willowdene Court, Brentwood, Essex CM14 5ET
Tel/Fax (01277) 223510
E-mail essexpga@googlemail.com
Website www.essexpga.com

Gloucestershire & Somerset PGA
Sec, E Goodwin, Cirencester GC, Cheltenham Rd, Cirencester, GL7 7BH
Tel (01285) 652465

Hampshire PGA
Sec, Paul Brown, HPGA Office, South Winchester GC, Pitt, Winchester SO22 5QX
Mobile 077 159 75258
E-mail secretary@hampshirepga.co.uk
Website www.hampshire-pga.co.uk

Hertfordshire PGA
Sec, M E Plumbley, Stavonga Dell, Pasture Rd, Letchworth SG6 3LP
Tel/Fax (01462) 670774
E-mail meplumbley@hertspga.org
Website www.hertspga.org

Kent PGA
Contact South Region PGA

Lancashire PGA
Sec, Jeff Mathews, No 2 Cottage, Bolton GC, Lostock Park, Chorley New Road, Bolton BL6 4AJ
Tel (01204) 496137 *Fax* (01204) 847959
E-mail graham.maly@pga.org.uk

Leicestershire & Rutland PGA
Sec, Mark Hatton, Golfing Days Ltd, 1 Royal Mews, Station Rd, Ashby de la Zouch LE65 2GJ
Mobile 07920 113 463
E-mail mark@golfingdays.co.uk
Website www.golfingdays.co.uk

Lincolnshire PGA
Sec, D Drake, 23 Manor Rd, Saxilby, Lincoln LN1 2HX
Tel (01522) 703331

Middlesex PGA
Sec, S Rist, 64 Dorchester Avenue, Palmers Green London N13 5DX
Tel (0208) 803 9702
E-mail steve@mdxpga.co.uk
Website www.mdxpga.co.uk

Norfolk PGA
Sec, John Paling, Squirrels Reach, Folgate Lane, Old Costessey, Norwich NR8 5EF

Tel (01603) 741301
E-mail jandjpaling@uwclub.net
Website www.club-noticeboard.co.uk

North East & North West PGA
Hon Sec, T Flowers, 10 Rosedale Rd, Belmont, Durham DH1 2AS
Tel (0191) 383 9385
E-mail tom.flowers@nenwpga.co.uk

Northamptonshire PGA
Sec, R Lobb, 15 Manor Rd, Pitsford, Northampton NN6 9AR
Tel (01604) 881367 *Mobile* (07968) 164151
E-mail richard.lobb@northamptonshiregolf.org.uk
Website www.northamptonshirepga.co.uk

Nottinghamshire PGA
Sec, Louisa Swinburn, 101 Skegby Rd, Kirkby in Ashfield NG17 9FR
E-mail secretary@nottspga.co.uk
Website www.nottspga.co.uk

Shropshire & Hereford PGA
Sec, P Hinton, 29 Stourbridge Rd, Bridgnorth, WV15 5AZ
Tel (01746) 762045
E-mail paulhinton@enta.net
Website www.a1golf.biz

Staffordshire PGA
Sec, R Hill, 80 Old Town Mews, Stratford upon Avon CV37 6GR
Tel (07791) 289 941

Suffolk PGA
Sec, A E D Garnett, 9 Furness Close, Ipswich IP2 9YA
Tel (01473) 685529
E-mail tonygarnett@talktalk.net

Surrey PGA
Contact South Region PGA

Sussex PGU
Sec, C Pluck, 96 Cranston Ave, Bexhill, East Sussex TN39 3NL
Tel/Fax (01424) 221298
E-mail sussexpgu@g.mail.com
Website www.spgu.co.uk

Warwickshire PGA
Sec, N Selwyn-Smith, 18 Cornfield Ave, Stoke Heath, Bromsgrove B60 3QU
Tel (01527) 875 750
E-mail neilss@execgolf.co.uk

Wiltshire PGA
Sec, M Walters, Erlestoke Sands GC, Erlestoke, Devizes SN10 5UB
Tel (01380) 831027

Worcestershire PGA
Sec, K Ball, 136 Alvechurch Rd, West Heath, Birmingham B31 3PW
Tel (0121) 475 7400
E-mail kenball@talktalk.net

Yorkshire PGA
Sec, J Pape, 22 The Locks, Pottery Lane, Woodlesford, Leeds LS26 8PU
Tel (0113) 282 8984

England and Wales Blind Golf
Sec, J T O'Brien, 23 Logan St, Market Harborough LE16 9AW
Tel (01858) 465625
E-mail jim.taggartt@talktalk.net
Website www.blindgolf.co.uk

Ireland

Golfing Union of Ireland
Gen Sec, Pat Finn, National Headquarters, Carton Demesne, Maynooth, Co. Kildare
Tel +353 1 505 4000 *Fax* +353 1 505 4001
E-mail information@gui.ie
Website www.gui.ie

Irish Men's Branches

Connacht Branch: *Gen Sec,* E Lonergan, Breaffy Business Centre, Breaffy, Castlebar, Mayo
E-mail guibc@eircom.net

Leinster Branch: *Exec Off* T Thompson, Carton Demesne, Maynooth, Co.Kildare
Tel +353 1 601 6842 *Fax* +353 1 6016858
E-mail info@leinster.gui.ie

Munster Branch: *Exec Off,* K Walsh, 6 Townview, Mallow, Co Cork
Tel +353 22 21026 *Fax* +353 22 42373
E-mail info@munster.gui.ie

Ulster Branch: *Gen Sec,* K Stevens, Unit 5, Forestgrove Business Park, Newtownbreda Rd, Belfast BT8 6AW
Tel (028) 9049 1891 *Fax* (028) 9049 1615
E-mail info@gui-ulster.co.uk

Irish Ladies' Golf Union
Ch Exec, Sinead Heraty, 103-105 Q House, 76 Furze Rd, Sandyford Ind. Est., Dublin 18
Tel +353 1 293 4833
E-mail sinead@ilgu.ie *Website* www.ilgu.ie

Irish Ladies' Districts

Eastern District: *Hon Sec,* Mrs Lucia Farrell, Bannonstown, Hayes, Navan, Co Meath
Tel +46 902 4707
E-mail easterndistrict@eircom.net

Midland District: *Hon Sec,* Mrs Yvonne Mac-Sweeney, Old Town Lane, Castlebridge, Wexford
Tel +353 83 404 7246
E-mail midlanddistrict@gmail.com

Northern District: *Hon Sec* Mrs Joyce Hughes, 1 Beech Hill Park, Lisburn, Co Antrim BT28 3HP
Tel (028) 70 824 253
E-mail joycehughes16@yahoo.co.uk

Southern District: *Hon Sec,* Mrs Marion Pattenden, Abbeystrewery, Skibbereen. Co Cork
Tel +353 52 89316
E-mail ilgusoutherndistrict@gmail.com

Western District: *Hon Sec,* Mrs Rita Grealish, Glenmore, Carnmore, Oranmore, Co.Galway
Tel +353 83 404 7131
E-mail ilguwest@eircom.net

PGA Irish Region
Sec, M McCumiskey, Dundalk GC, Blackrock, Dundalk, Co Louth, Eire
Tel +353 42 932 1193 *Fax* +353 42 932 1899
E-mail michael.mccumiskey@pga.org.uk

Scotland

Scottish Golf Union
Ch Exec, H Grey, The Duke's, St Andrews KY16 8NX
Tel (01334) 466477 *Fax* (01334) 461361
E-mail sgu@scottishgolf.org
Website www.scottishgolf.org

Scottish Men's Associations/Unions

Angus CGA
Sec, W Miller, 48 Buddon Drive, Monifieth DD5 4TJ
Tel (01382) 533728
E-mail billhmill@blueyonder.co.uk

Argyll & Bute GU
Sec, L. Pirie, 54 Banchory Ave, Inchinnan, Renfrewshire PA4 9PZ
Tel (0141) 561 0535 *E-mail* lrpirie@aol.com
Website www.argyllandbutegolfunion.com

Ayrshire GA
Sec, A J Malcolm, 17 Auchincruive Ave, Prestwick KA9 2DT
Tel (01292) 477657
E-mail ayrshiregolf@fsmail.net
Website www.ayrshiregolf.blogspot.com

Borders GA
Sec, D Little, Greenyard, Drove Rd, Langholm DG13 0JW
Tel (01387) 381308
E-mail dennis.little@btinternet.com
Website www.bordergolf.co.uk

Clackmannanshire CGU
Sec, T Johnson, 75 Dewar Ave, Kincardine on Forth FK10 4RR
Tel 01259) 731520 *Fax* (01259) 769445
E-mail thjohn01@aol.com

Dunbartonshire GU
Sec, A Harris, 11 Millersneuk Dr, Lenzie, Kirkintilloch, Glasgow G66 5JF
Tel (0141) 776 3535
E-mail secretary@dgu.org.uk
Website www.dgu.org.uk

Fife GA
Sec, J Scott, Lauriston, East Links, Leven KY8 4JL
Tel (01333) 423798 *Fax* (01333) 439910
E-mail jscottfga@blueyonder.co.uk
Website www.fifegolf.org

Glasgow GU
Sec, R J G Jamieson, 32 Eglinton St, Beith KA15 1AQ
Tel/Fax (01505) 503000
E-mail r.jamieson-accountants@fsmail.net
Website www.glasgowgolfunion.org

Lanarkshire GA
Sec, T Logan, 41 Woodlands Drive, Coatbridge ML5 1LB
Tel (01236) 428799 *E-mail* tlogan.lga@hotmail.co.uk

Lothians GA
Sec, A G Shaw, 34 Caroline Terrace, Edinburgh EH12 8QX
Tel 0131 334 7291 *Fax* 0131 334 9269
E-mail AllanGShaw@hotmail.com
Website www.lothiansgolfassociation.org.uk

North District GU
Sec, P L Abbott, 21 Manse Rd, Nairn IV12 4RW
Tel (01667) 453625
E-mail p.l.a@btinternet.com
Website www.sgunorth.com

North-East District GA
Sec, G M Young, 24 Shore St, Cairnbulg, Fraserburgh AB43 8YL
Tel (01346) 582324
E-mail georgemyoung24@btinternet.com
Website www.sgunortheast.com

Perth & Kinross CGU
Sec, J J E Simpson, 11 Dunbarney Av, Bridge of Earn, Perth PH2 9BP
Tel (01738) 812588
E-mail auntyeedie@hotmail.com
Website www.perthandkinrosscountygolf.net

Renfrewshire GU
Sec, I Storie, 35 Balmoral Rd, Elderslie PA5 9RA
Tel (01505) 343872
E-mail ian.storie@ntlworld.com
Website www.renfrewshiregolfunion.co.uk

South of Scotland GA
Sec, I Robin, 62 Albert Rd, Dumfries DG2 9DL
Tel (01387) 252004
E-mail iainrobin@tiscali.co.uk

Stirlingshire GU
Sec, J Elliott, 65 Rosebank Ave, Falkirk FK1 5JR
Tel (01324) 634 118
E-mail johnelliott65@blueyonder.co.uk
Website www.stirlingshiregolfunion.co.uk

PGA Scottish Region
Sec, M MacDougall, King's Lodge, Gleneagles, Auchterarder PH3 1NE
Tel (01764) 661840 *Fax* (01764) 661841
E-mail michael.macdougall@pga.org.uk

Scottish Ladies' Golfing Association
Sec, Dr S Hartley, The Den, 2 Dundee Rd, Perth PH2 7DW
Tel (01738) 442357
Fax (01738) 442380
E-mail secretary@slga.co.uk
Website www.slga.co.uk

Scottish Ladies' County Associations

Aberdeen LCGA
Hon Sec, Miss K Stalker, 2 Braemar Court, Fraserburgh AB43 9XE
Tel (01346) 513308
E-mail karen@fairways.eclipse.co.uk
Website www.alcga.co.uk

Angus LCGA
Hon Sec, Aileen Hunter
Tel (07918) 083 951
E-mail aileen@clearoad.co.uk

Ayrshire LCGA
Hon Sec, Fiona Collier, Monkton Hall Lodge, Southwoods, Monkton, Prestwick KA9 1UR
Tel (01292) 315982
E-mail secretary@alcga.com

Border Ladies' CGA
Hon Sec, Julie Birdsall, Highridgehall, Kelso TD5 7QD
Tel (01890) 830605
E-mail highridgehall@btinternet.com
Website www.borderladiesgolf.com

Dumfriesshire LCGA
Hon Sec, Mrs E C Scott, Treweryn, 24 Carlisle Rd, Lockerbie DG11 2DN
Tel (01576) 203507
E-mail malcolmscott228@btinternet.com

Dunbartonshire & Argyll LCGA
Hon Sec, Mrs J Shankland, 25 Thorn Dr., Bearsden, Glasgow G61 4ND
Tel (0141) 942 4696
E-mail je.shankland@btinternet.com
Website www.dalcga.ik.com

East Lothian LCGA
Hon Sec, Gill Ellis-Pow, 85 Laburnum Ave, Port Seton EH32 0UD
Tel (01875) 811527
E-mail agellis-pow@yahoo.co.uk

Fife CLGA
Hon Sec, Mrs Barbara Linton, 5 Abden Ave, Kinghorn KY3 9TQ
Tel (01592) 890140
E-mail pendantiques@btopenworld.com

Galloway CLGA
Hon Sec, Sally Huntly, Tramerry, Wigtown DG8 9JP
Tel (01988) 402309

Lanarkshire LCGA
Capt, Anne Lloyd, 9 Jardine Ter., Gartcosh, Glasgow G69 8AR
Tel (0781) 887 8187
E-mail anne.Lloyd@hotmail.co.uk
Website www.llcga.co.uk

Midlothian CLGA
Hon Sec, Mrs H Anderson, 10 Woodhall Bank, Colinton, Edinburgh EH13 0HY
Tel (0131) 477 1131
E-mail mclga66@hotmail.co.uk
Website www.mclga.co.uk

Northern Counties' LGA
Hon Sec, Mrs J Coulthard, The Larches, Skye of Curr Rd, Dulnain Bridge, Grantown-on-Spey PH26 3PA
Tel (01479) 851361
E-mail jacqui.coulthard@btinternet.com

Perth & Kinross LCGA
Hon Sec, Mrs J Milne, 91 David Douglas Ave., Scone PH2 6QG
Tel (01738) 553352
E-mail jilliancmilne@hotmail.com

Renfrewshire LCGA
Hon Sec, Mrs J Irvine, Wrayburn, Woodside Lane, Brookfield PA5 8UW
Tel (01505) 328411
E-mail jean.Irvine@sky.com
Website rlgca.co.uk

Stirling & Clackmannan CLGA
Hon Sec, Mrs A Hunter, 22 Muirhead Rd, Stenhousemuir, FK5 4JA
Tel (01324) 554515
E-mail annathunter@btinternet.com

Scottish Veteran Ladies' Golfing Association
Hon Sec, Mrs J C Lambert, Balcary, Barcloy Rd, Rockcliffe, Dalbeattie DG5 4QJ
Tel (01556) 630419
E-mail jeanc.lambert@btinternet.com
Website www.svlga.co.uk

Scottish Blind Golf Society
Sec, R Clayden, 5 The Round, Dunfermline, Fife KY12 7YH
Tel (01383) 737717
Website www.scottishblindgolf.com

Scottish Midland Golfing Alliance
Sec, E Sherry, Lundin Tower, Pilmuir Rd, Lundin Links KY8 6BD

Wales

Golf Union of Wales
Ch Exec, Richard Dixon, Catsash, Newport, Gwent NP18 1JQ
Tel (01633) 436040 *Fax* (01633) 693568
E-mail office@golfunionwales.org
Website www.golfunionwales.org

Welsh Men's Unions

Anglesey GU
Hon Sec, GP Jones, 20 Gwelfor Estate, Cemaes Bay, Anglesey LL67 0NL
Tel (01407) 710755
E-mail garethgwelfor@aol.com
Website www.anglestgolfunion.co.uk

Brecon & Radnor GU
Hon Sec, Martyn Hughes, 1 Wool Row, Brecon Rd, Builth Wells LD2 3ED
Tel (01982) 552852
E-mail martynhughes49@googlemail.com

Caernarfonshire & District GU
Hon Sec, EG Angel, 13 Glanrafon Est., Bontnewydd, Caernarfon, Gwynedd LL55 2UW
Tel (01286) 675798
E-mail einionecdgu@talktalk.net

Denbighshire GU
Hon Sec, D Ethelston, Gwylfa, Garth Rd, Garth, Llangollen LL20 7UR
Tel (01978) 820722 *E-mail* ethelgarth@aol.com
Website www.dgugolf.co.uk

Dyfed GU
WD Booth, Rhyd, Croes Y Llan, Llangoedmor, Cardigan SA43 2LH
Tel (01239) 615334
E-mail wdjbooth@btinternet.com
Website www.dyfedgolf.co.uk

Union of Flintshire Golf Clubs
Hon Sec, Mrs G Snead, 1 Cornist Cottages, Flint CH6 5RH
Tel (01352) 733461
E-mail gsnead@hotmail.co.uk

Glamorgan County GU
Hon Sec, P Austerberry, 10 Chestnut Tree Close, Radyr, Cardiff CF15 8RY
Tel (02920) 419823
E-mail p.austerberry@ntlworld.com

Gwent GU
Sec, WG Harris, 4 Rolls Walk, Mount Pleasant, Rogerstone, Gwent NP10 0AE
Tel (01633) 663750
E-mail w.graham.harris@ntlworld.com
Website www.gwentgolf.co.uk

North Wales PGA
See Cheshire & North Wales PGA, page 700

South Wales PGA
See West Region PGA, page 694

Welsh Ladies' County Associations

Caernarvonshire & Anglesey LCGA
Hon Sec, Mrs J Harvey, 10 Craig y Don, Pensarn, Abergele LL22 7RL
Tel (01745) 827239
E-mail alecharvey32@btinternet.com

Carmarthenshire & Pembrokeshire LCGA
Hon Sec, Mrs P Taggart, Neuadd Cothi, Pontargothi, Nantaredig, Carmarthenshire SA16 0HT
Tel (01267) 290174
E-mail pdtaggart@btconnect.com

Denbighshire & Flintshire LCGA
Hon Sec, Mrs K Harcombe, 6 Birch Drive, Gresford, Wrexham LL12 8YZ
Tel (01978) 855933
E-mail kim.harcombe@btinternet.com

Glamorgan LCGA
Hon Sec, Mrs G J Phillips, 17 Martin Close, Heol Gerrig, Merthyr Tydfil CF48 1TY
Tel (01685) 385245
E-mail gloheolg@aol.com
Website www.glamorganladiesgolf.co.uk

Mid Wales LCGA
Hon Sec, Mrs L Price, Coygen, Lower Chapel, Brecon, Powys LD3 9RE
Tel (01874) 690258
E-mail coygen@btclick.com

Monmouthshire LCGA
Hon Sec, Mrs EL Davidson, Jon-Len, Goldcliff, Newport NP18 2AU
Tel (01633) 274477
E-mail lena_mlcga@hotmail.co.uk

Europe

European Golf Association
Gen Sec, Richard Heath, Place de la Croix Blanche 19, Case Postale CH-1066 Epalinges, Switzerland
Tel +41 21 785 7060 *Fax* +41 21 785 7069
E-mail info@ega-golf.ch
Website www.ega-golf.ch

Albanian Golf Federation
Gen Sec, Marin Harxhi, Rr.Suleyman Delvina-Haxhi Kika, P.142/3 Ap.12, AL-Tiranë
Tel +355 68 603 3626
E-mail info@fshgolf.org *Website* www.fshgolf.org

Austrian Golf Association – Őesterreichischer Golf-Verband
Gen Sec, Robert Fiegl, Marxergasse 25, AT-1030 Wien
Tel +43 1 505 3245 *Fax* +43 1 505 4962
E-mail oegv@golf.at *Website* www.golf.at

Royal Belgian Golf Federation
Gen Sec, Christian Moyson, Boulevard Louis Schmidt 87/6, BE-1040 Brussels
Tel +32 2 672 2389 *Fax* +32 2 675 4619
E-mail info@golfbelgium.be
Website www.golfbelgium.be

Bulgarian Golf Association
Gen Sec, Seth Underwood, 19 Oborishte Street, BG-1504 Sofia
Tel +359 2943 0610 *Fax* +359 2946 3740
E-mail s.underwood@golfbg.com
Website www.golfbg.com

Croatian Golf Federation
Chair, Dino Klisovic, Esplanade Hotel, Mihanoviceva 1, HR-10000 Zagreb
Tel +385 1 456 6050
E-mail hrvatskigolfsavez@yahoo.com
Website www.golf.hr

Cyprus Golf Federation
Gen Sec, Nick Rossides, Olympic House, Amfipoleos 21, Office B208, CY-2025 Nicosia
Tel +357 22 449874 *Fax* +357 22 449876
E-mail cgf@cgf.org.cy *Website* www.cgf.org.cy

Czech Golf Federation
Gen Sec, Lubos Klikar, Erpet Golf Centre, Strakonickà 2860, CZ-150 00 Pragha 5-Smichov
Tel +420 296 373111 *Fax* +420 296 373201
E-mail cgf@cgf.cz *Website* www.cgf.cz

Danish Golf Union – Dansk Golf Union
Gen Sec, Morten Backhausen, Idrættens Hus, Brøndby Stadion 20, DK-2605 Brøndby
Tel +45 43 262 700 *Fax* +45 43 262 701
E-mail info@dgu.org *Website* www.dgu.org

Estonian Golf Association
Sec Gen, Rein Raudsepp, Audentese Spordikeskus, Tondi 84, EE-11316 Tallinn
Fax +372 6 314343
E-mail rein.r@golf.ee
Website www.golf.ee

Finnish Golf Union
Gen Sec, Petri Peltoniemi, Radiokatu 20, FI-00093 SLU
Tel +358 9 3481 2520 *Fax* +358 9 147 145
E-mail office@golf.fi *Website* www.golf.fi

French Golf Federation – Federation Française de Golf
Ch Exec, Christophe Muniesa, 68 rue Anatole France, FR-92309 Levallois-Perret Cedex

Tel +33 1 41 497 700 *Fax* +33 1 41 497 701
E-mail ffgolf@ffgolf.org
Website www.ffgolf.org

German Golf Association – Deutscher Golf Verband EV
Pres, Hans Joachim Nothelfer, Postfach 2106, DE-65011 Wiesbaden
Tel +49 611 990 200 *Fax* +49 611 990 20170
E-mail info@dgv.golf.de *Website* www.golf.de

Hellenic Golf Federation
Gen Sec, Constantinos Bakouris, PO Box 70003, GR-166 10 Glyfada, Athens
Tel +30 210 894 1933 *Fax* +30 210 894 5162
E-mail info@hgf.gr *Website* www.hgf.gr

Hungarian Golf Federation
Gen Sec, Ms Lilla Ădám, Istvanmezei út 1-3, HU-1146 Budapest
Tel/Fax +36 1 460 6859
E-mail hungolf@hungolf.hu
Website: www.hungolf.hu

Golf Union of Iceland
Gen Sec, Hordur Thorsteinsson, Sport Center, Laugardal, IS-104 Reykjavik
Tel +354 514 4050 *Fax* +354 514 4051
E-mail gsi@golf.is *Website* www.golf.is

Italian Golf Federation – Federazione Italiana Golf
Sec Gen, Stefano Manca, Viale Tiziano 74, IT-00196 Roma
Tel +39 06 323 1825 *Fax* +39 06 322 0250
E-mail fig@federgolf.it
Website www.federgolf.it

Latvia Golf Federation
Gen Sec, Santa Puce, Milgrãvja Iela 16, LV-1034 Riga
Tel +371 6739 4399 *Fax* +371 6739 4034
E-mail info@golfaskola.lv *Website* www.lgf.lv

Liechtenstein Golf Association – Golfverband Liechtenstein
Pres, Carlo Rampone, Postfach 264, LI-9490 Vaduz
Tel +42 3 232 1991 *Fax* +42 3 232 1992
E-mail info@golf-verband.li
Website www.golf.li

Lithuanian Golf Federation
Pres, Rolandas Dovidaitis, Rotuses a.10, LT-44279 Kaunas
E-mail info@golfofederacija.lt
Website www.golfofederacija.lt

Luxembourg Golf Federation – Federation Luxemburgeoise de Golf
Sec, Roger Weber, Domaine de Belenhaff, LU-6141 Junglinster
Tel +352 26 78 2383 *Fax* +352 26 78 2393
E-mail flgsecretariat@flgolf.lu
Website www.flgolf.lu

Macedonian Golf Federation
Gen Sec, Marijan Pop-Angelov, Tone Tomsic 3A, MK-1000 Skopje
Tel 389 2 2774 071 *Fax* +389 2 2774 072
E-mail mkgolffederation@gmail.com

Malta Golf Association
Pres, William Beck, Aldo Moro St, MT-Marsa LQA 09, Malta
Tel +356 2122 3704 *Fax* +356 2122 7020
E-mail association@maltagolf.org
Website www.maltagolf.org

Netherlands Golf Federation – Nederlandse Golf Federatie
Gen Sec, Jeroen Stevens, PO Box 8585, NL-3503 RN Utrecht
Tel +31 30 242 6370
Fax +31 30 242 6380
E-mail golf@ngf.nl *Website* www.ngf.nl

Norwegian Golf Federation
Gen Sec, Geir Ove Berg, NO-0840 Oslo
Tel +47 21 029 150 *Fax* +47 21 029 151
E-mail post@golfforbundet.no
Website www.golfforbundet.no

Polish Golf Union
Gen Sec, Bartlomiej Chelmecki, Lim Centre, Al.Jerozolimskie 65/79, PL-00-697 Warszawa
Tel +48 22 630 5560 *Fax* +48 22 630 5561
E-mail pzg@pzgolf.pl
Website www.pzgolf.pl

Portuguese Golf Federation – Federacao Portuguesa de Golfe
Gen Sec, Miguel Franco De Sousa, Av das Túlipas No 6, Edifico Miraflores17°, Miraflores, PT-1495-161 Algés
Tel +351 214 123 780
Fax +351 214 107 972
E-mail fpg@fpg.pt *Website* www.fpg.pt

Romanian Golf Federation
Gen Sec, Mircea Asanache, 44 Carierei Str., Breaza, RO-105400 Prahova
Tel +40 244 343 850 *Fax* +40 244 343 525
E-mail gen.secretary@frgolf.ro
Website www.frgolf.ro

Russian Golf Association
Gen Sec, Victor Motchalov, Office 242A, 8 Luzhnetskaya nab, RU – 119992 Moskva
Tel +7 495 363 2385 *Fax* +7 495 725 4719
E-mail russgolf@mail.ru *Website* www.rusgolf.ru

San Marino Golf Federation
Sec Gen, Dr E Casali, Via Rancagalia 30, SM-47899 Serravalle, San Marino
Tel +378 (0549) 885 600
Fax +378 (0549) 885 651
E-mail dzanotti@omniway.sm

Serbia Golf Association
Chair, Vladimir Dukanovic, Ada Ciganlija 2, RS-11000 Belgrad
Tel +381 11 333 2851
Fax +381 11 305 6837
E-mail office@golfas.rs
Website www.golfasocijacijasrbije.rs

Slovak Golf Association
Gen Sec, Juraj Špánik, Kukucínova, Kukucínova 26, SK-831 02 Bratislava, Slovak Republic
Tel/Fax +421 2 4445 0727
E-mail skga@skga.sk *Website* www.skga.sk

Slovenian Golf Association
Sec, Gorazd Kogoj, Dunajska 22, SI-1511 Ljubljana
Tel +386 1 430 3200 *Fax* +386 1 430 3201
E-mail golfzveza@golfzveza-slovenije.si
Website www.golfzveza-slovenije.si

Royal Spanish Golf Federation – Real Federacion Espanola de Golf
Man Dir, Jorge Sagardoy Fidalgo, Arroyo del Monte 5, ES-28035 Madrid
Tel +34 91 555 2682 *Fax* +34 91 556 3290
E-mail rfegolf@rfegolf.es
Website www.rfegolf.es

Swedish Golf Federation – Svenska Golfforbundet
Gen Sec, Gunnar Håkansson, PO Box 84, Kevingestrand, SE-182 11 Danderyd
Tel +46 8 622 1500 *Fax* +46 8 755 8439
E-mail info@sgf.golf.se
Website www.sgf.golf.se

Swiss Golf Association – Association Suisse de Golf
Gen Sec, Christian Bohm, Place de la Croix Blanche 19, CH-1066 Epalinges
Tel +41 21 785 7000 *Fax* +41 21 785 7009
E-mail info@asg.ch *Website* www.asg.ch

Turkish Golf Federation
Pres, Ahmet Agaoglu, GSGM Ulus Is Hani A Blok 2., Kat 205 Ulus 06050, TR-Ankara
Tel +90 312 309 3945 *Fax* +90 312 309 1840
E-mail info@tgf.org.tr
Website www.tgf.org.tr

Ukrainian Golf Federation
Gen Sec, Sergey Kozyrenko, 39 Pushkinskya str. Suite 28, UA-01004 Kyiv
Tel +380 672 345143 *Fax* +380 44 279 3763
E-mail info@ukrgolf.org
Website www.ukrgolf.com

Professional Associations

Austria PGA
Contact: Monika Goss, Grabentrasse 26/1a, AT-8010 Graz
Tel +43 316 890 503 *Fax* +43 316 890 50315
E-mail office@apga.info *Website* www.apga.info

Belgian PGA
Contact: Bernard de Bruyckere, PO Box 1062, BE-8300 Knokke-Heist
Tel +32 467 645414
E-mail info@pga.be *Website* www.pga.be

Bulgarian PGA
Contact: Robin McGarr, Oborishte Street 19. BG-1504 Sofia
Tel /Fax +359 2 943 0610
E-mail info@pga-bulgaria.com
Website www.pga-bulgaria.com

Croatia PGA
Contact: Nikola Smoljenovic, Fancevljec Prilaz 16, HR-100 00 Zagreb
Tel +385 1 667 3308 *Fax* +385 1 660 6798
E-mail pga@pga.hr *Website* www.pga.hr

Czech Republic PGA
Gen Sec, Michael Jon, Villa Golfista, Amerika 782/1C, CZ-353 01 Marianske Lazne
Tel +420 724 050050 *Fax* +420 354 621357
E-mail pga@pga.cz *Website* www.pga.cz

Denmark PGA
Contact: Joan Ejlertsen, Bygaden 20A, DK-9000, Aalborg
Tel +45 20 73 00 41 *Fax* +45 98 662 236
E-mail info@pga.dk *Website* www.pga.dk

Estonia PGA
Gen Sec, Paul Pohi, Kauge Tee 3, Harjumaa, EE-11215 Tallinn
Tel +372 56 492210 *Fax* +372 682 8819
E-mail info@pga.ee *Website* www.pga.ee

Finland PGA
Contact:, Teemu Laakso, Radiokatu 20, FI-00093 SLU
Tel +358 9 3481 2377 *Fax* +358 9 3481 2378
E-mail pgafinland@pga.fi
Website www.pga.fi

France PGA
Contact: Adelaide Vannier, National Golf Club, 2 Avenue du Golf, FR-78 280 Guyancourt
Tel +33 1 3452 0846
Fax +33 1 3452 0548
E-mail a.vannier@pgafrance.org
Website www.pgafrance.org

PGA of Germany
Ch Exec, Rainier Goldrain, Professional Golf AG, Landsbergerstr. 290, DE-80687 München
Tel +49 8917 95880 *Fax* +49 8917 958829
E-mail info@pga.de *Website* www.pga.de

Greece PGA
Gen Sec, Adonis Sotiropoulos, 9 Harilaou Trikoupi str, 2nd Fl, GR-166 75 Glyfada Athens
Tel +30 6938 261 200
Fax +30 2241 052 798
E-mail info@greekpga.com
Website www.greekpga.com

Hungary PGA
Gen Sec, Áron Makszin, Krisztina krt 71, 4/1, HU-1016 Budapest
Tel +36 23 545 440 *Fax* +36 70 454 5663
E-mail pgah@pgah.hu
Website www.pgah.hu

Iceland PGA
Gen Sec, Agnar Már Jonsson, Engjavegur 6, IS-104 Reykjavik
Tel +354 514 4050 *Fax* +354 514 4051
E-mail agnarj@pga.is *Website* www.pga.is

Italy PGA
Contact: Laura Rendina, Via Marangoni 3, IT-20124 Milano
Tel +39 02 670 5670 *Fax* +39 02 669 3600
E-mail pgaitaly@tin.it *Website* www.pga.it

Luxembourg PGA
Contact: Leon Marks, Luxembourg GC Belenhaff, LU-26141 Junglinster
Tel/Fax +352 348394
E-mail leon@golfpro.lu *Website* www.pga.lu

Malta PGA
Contact: Kenneth Cachia, The Royal Malta GC, Aldo Moro St, Marsa LQA 06
Tel +356 212 39302
Fax +356 212 27020
E-mail info@pgamalta.com
Website www.pgamalta.com

Netherlands PGA (Holland PGA)
Contact: Marie Therese Lamers, Postbus 8585, NL-3503 RN Utrecht
Tel +31 651 525 727
E-mail info@pgaholland.nl
Website www.pgaholland.nl

Norway PGA
Contact: Trond Baardseng, PO Box 135, NO-2401 Elverum
Tel +47 913 13912
E-mail trond.bardseng@pganorway.no
Website www.pganorway.no

Poland PGA
Contact: Marek Sokolowski, ul.Kwiatowa 16, PL-81638 Gdynia
Tel +48 58 624 7813 *Fax* +48 58 624 4309
E-mail mareksokolowski@pgapolska.pl
Website www.pgapolska.com

Portugal PGA
Gen Sec, Nelson Cavalheiro, Av Das Túlipas 6-Edif., Miraflores 17°, Miraflores, PT-1495-161 Algés
Tel +351 21 962 6640 *Fax* +351 214 107 972
E-mail nelsoncavalheiro@gmail.com
Website www.pgaportugal.pt

Russia PGA
Contact: Maria Milovidova, Office 242a, Build 8, Luzhnetskaya nab, RU-119992 Moscow
Tel +7 495 363 2385 *Fax* +7 495 725 4719
E-mail maria.milovidova@mail.ru
Website www.rusga.ru

Slovakia PGA
Contact: Martina Svobodova, Dvojkrizna 9, SK-821 07 Bratislava
Tel +421 905 305 246
E-mail info@pga.sk
Website www.pga.sk

Slovenia PGA
Gen Sec, Bogdan Palovšnik, Dunajska cesta 22, SL-1000 Ljubljana
Tel +386 4 148 7280 *Fax* +386 1430 3201
E-mail info@pgaslo.si *Website* www.pgaslo.si

Spain PGA
Contact: Mercedes Santamaria, c/ Capitán Haya 22-5C, ES-28020 Madrid
Tel +34 91 555 1393 *Fax* +34 91 597 0170
E-mail pga@pgaspain.com
Website www.pgaspain.com

Swedish PGA
Contact: Anna Svantesson, Malmovagen 647-36, SE-230 40 Bara
Tel +46 35 320 30 *Fax* +46 4044 7656
E-mail pga@pgasweden.com
Website www.pgasweden.com

Swiss PGA
Gen Sec, Peter Schwager, Zürcherstrasse 20, CH-9014 St Gallen
Tel +41 71 277 1717 *Fax* +41 71 277 7317
E-mail info@swisspga.ch
Website www.swisspga.ch

Turkey PGA
Gen Sec, Andrew McNabola, Doktorlar Sitesi A7 Blok Daire 6, Nato Yolu, Bosna Bulvari, Cengelkoy, Istanbul
Tel +90 533 773 3019
E-mail andrewmmcnabola@gmail.com

North America: Canada and USA

Royal Canadian Golf Association
Exec Dir, Scott Simmons, Suite 1 1333 Dorval Drive, Oakville, Ontario L6M 4X7
Tel +1 905 849 9700 *Fax* +1 905 845 7040
E-mail ssimmons@golfcanada.ca
Website www.rcga.org

Canadian Ladies' Golf Association
See Royal Canadian Golf Association

National Golf Foundation
Ch Exec, Joseph Beditz, 1150 South US Highway One, Jupiter, Florida 33477
Tel +1 561 744 6006
Website www.ngf.org

United States Golf Association
Pres, Walter W Driver jr, Golf House, PO Box 708, Far Hills, NJ 07931-0708
Tel +1 908 234 2300 *Fax* +1 908 234 9687
E-mail usga@usga.org *Website* www.usga.org

Professional Associations

Canadian PGA
Ch Exec, Gary Bernard, 13450 Dublin Line RR#1, Acton, Ontario L7J 2W7
Tel +1 519 853 5450 *Fax* +1 519 853 5449
E-mail cpga@canadianpga.org
Website www.cpga.com

Canadian Tour
Comm, Ian Mansfield, 212 King Street West, Suite 203, Toronto, Ontario M58 1K5
Tel +1 416 204 1564 *Fax* +1 416 204 1368
Website cantour.com

Ladies' Professional Golf Association
Comm, Carolyn Vesper Bivens, 100 International Golf Drive, Daytona Beach, Florida 32124-1092
Tel +1 386 274 6200 *Fax* +1 386 274 1099
Website www.lpga.com

PGA of America
Ch Exec, Joe Steranka, 100 Avenue of the Champions, Palm Beach Gardens, Florida 33418
Tel +1 561 624 8400 *Fax* +1 561 624 8448
Website www.pgaonline.com

PGA Tour
Comm, Tim Finchem, PGA Tour, 112 PGA Tour Boulevard, Ponte Vedra Beach, Florida 32082
Tel +1 904 285 3700

Fax +1 904 285 7913
Website www.pgatour.com

The Caribbean and Central America

Caribbean Golf Association
Sec, David G Bird, PO Box 31329, Grand Cayman, KY1-1206, Cayman Islands
Tel +1 345 947 1903 *Fax* +1 345 947 3439
E-mail bird@candw.ky
Website www.cgagolfnet.com

Bahamas Golf Federation
Sec, Dudley Martinborough, PO Box SS-19092, Nassau, Grand Bahama
Tel +1 242 394 3134
E-mail admin@bgfnet.com
Website www.bgfnet.com

Barbados Golf Association
Sec, Trenton Weeks, PO Box 149W, Worthing, Christ Church, Barbados BB-15000
Tel +1 246 437 2609
Fax +1 246 437 7792
E-mail carib@caribsurf.com
Website www.barbadosgolfassociation.com

Bermuda Golf Association
Sec, Susie Kendell Marshall, Victoria Place Building, 31 Victoria Street, Hamilton, HM 10, Bermuda
Tel +1 441 295 9972 *Fax* +1 441 295 0304
E-mail bdagolf@logic.bm
Website www.bermudagolfasociation.net

Cayman Islands Golf Association
Sec, David G Bird, PO Box 31329, Grand Cayman, KY1-1206
Tel +1 345 947 1903 *Fax* +1 345 947 3439
E-mail bird@candw.ky
Website www.ciga.ky

Costa Rica Golf Federation
Pres, Arnoldo Madrigal, PO Box 10969, San José 1000
Tel +506 296 5772 *Fax* +506 231 1914
E-mail info@anagolf.com
Website www.anagolf.com

Fedogolf (Dominican Republic)
Exec Dir, Carlos Lizarazo, Calle Macao No.7, Urbanizacion Tenis Club, Arroyo Hondo, Santo Domingo, Dominican Republic
Tel +1 809 338 1005 *Fax* +1 809 338 1008
E-mail administracion@fedogolf.org.do
Website www.golfdominicano.com

El Salvador Golf Federation
Pres, Jose Maria Duran Pacheco, Apartado Postal 165, San Salvador, El Salvador
Tel/Fax +1 503 2264 1581
E-mail fesagolf@yahoo.com

National Golf Association of Guatemala
Exec Asst, Nancy Fuentes, 11 Avenida 14-86 zona 10, Guatemala Cuidad 01010
Tel +502 2336 0602 *Fax* +502 2366 7848
E-mail asogolf@asogolfguatemala.org
Website www.asogolfguatemala.org

Hondureña Golf Association
Pres, Henry Kattan, Residential Piñares, Km 6.5 Paseo al Hatillo, PO Box 3555, Tegucigalpa, Honduras
Tel +504 211 9260 *Fax* +504 9992 3489
E-mail Hondurasgolf@gmail.com
Website www.hondurasgolf.org

Jamaica Golf Association
Hon Sec, Orville Marshall, Constant Spring GC, 15–158 Constant Spring Rd, Kingston 8
Tel +1 876 755 3593 *Fax* +1 876 924 7635
E-mail jamgolf2@cwjamaica.com
Website www.jagolfassociation.com

Mexican Golf Federation
Exec Dir, Fernando Erana, Av.Insurgentes Sur 1605 10° Piso Torre Mural, Col. San Jose Insurgentes, C.P. 03900 México, D.F.
Tel +525 1084 2176 *Fax* +525 1084 2179
E-mail direccionfmg@mexgolf.org
Website www.mexgolf.org

Nicaraguan Golf Federation
Exec Sec, J A Narvaez, Nejapa GCC, Managua
Tel +505 8850 5877 *Fax* +505 2278 0333
E-mail procalsa1@hotmail.com

OECS Golf Association
Sec, Cedric Jeffers, c/o PO Box 895, Basseterre, St Kitts
Tel +1 869 662 3036
E-mail golftoddler2009@gmail.com

Panama Golf Association
Exec Dir, Luiz Heley Bárcenas, PO Box 8613, Panama 5
Tel +507 266 7436 *Fax* +507 220 3994
E-mail apagolf@yahoo.es

Puerto Rico Golf Association
Pres, Sidney Wolf, 264 Matadero – Suite 11, San Juan, Puerto Rico 00920
Tel +1 787 793 3444 *Fax* +1 787 723 3138
E-mail swolf00@gmail.com
Website www.prga.org

St Maarten Golf Association
Pres, Steve Mix, PO Box 720, Philipsburg, St Maarten, Netherlands Antilles
Tel +44 599 551 2105 *Fax* +44 599 542 1261
E-mail info@stmaartengolf.com

Trinidad & Tobago Golf Association
Sec, Bill Ramrattan, c/o St Andrews GC, PO Box 3403, Moka, Maraval, T&T, W.I.
Tel +1 868 629 7127
Fax +1 868 629 0411
E-mail TandTGolf@gmail.com
Website www.trinidadandtobagogolfassociation.com

Turks & Caicos Golf Association
Pres, Fraser Dods, PO Box 319, Providenciales, Turks & Caicos Islands
Tel +1 649 946 4417 *Fax* +1 649 946 4437
E-mail physiologic@tciway.tc

Virgin Islands Golf Federation
Pres, Nevin Phillips, PO Box 5187, Kingshill, St Croix, US Virgin Islands 00851
Tel +1 305 281 2670
E-mail NPhillips@MahoganyRunGolf.Com

Professional Association

Jamaica PGA
Chairman, O Marshall, 9 Park Ave., Kingston 5
Tel +1 876 881 4444 *E-mail* pgajamaica@gmail.com

Mexico PGA
Off, D Ross, Nadadores 30, Col.Country Club, Mexico DF, CP 04210
Tel +52 55 5544 6644 *Fax* +52 55 5689 4254
E-mail info@pgamexico.org
Website www.pgamexico.org

South America

South American Golf Federation
Exec Sec, Rafael Enrique Otero Carrera 27 No 156-56 Of 903, Bogotá, Colombia
Tel +57 1 313 0624 *Fax* +57 1 313 0391
E-mail fedesud@cable.net.co
Website www.fedsudgolf.com

Argentine Golf Association
Exec Dir, Mark Lawrie, Av Corrientes 538-Pisos 11y12, 1043 CF, Buenos Aires
Tel +54 11 4325 1113 *Fax* +54 11 4325 8660
E-mail golf@aag.org.ar *Website* www.aag.org.ar

Bolivian Golf Federation
Sec, Gonzalo Viladegut, Calle Cochabamba Esquina Saavedra, Edif Torre Empresarial Piso 2 Of No.4, Santa Cruz
Tel/Fax +591 339 4035
E-mail fbgolf@entelnet.bo
Website www.boliviagolf.com

Brasilian Golf Confederation
Exec Sec, M A Aguiar Giusti, Rua Paez de Araújo 29 conj 42/43, cep 04531-090, São Paulo
Tel/Fax +55 11 3168 4366
E-mail golfe@cbg.com.br *Website* www.cbg.com.br

Chilean Golf Federation
Sec, Mauricio Hederra Pinto, Málaga 655, Las Condes, Santiago
Tel +56 2 690 8700 *Fax* +56 2 690 8720
E-mail secretaria@chilegolf.cl
Website www.chilegolf.cll

Colombian Golf Federation
Sec, Bernardo Mariño González, cra. 7#72-64 Int 26, Bogotá DC
Tel +57 1 310 7664 *Fax* +57 1 235 5091
E-mail fedegolf@federacioncolombianadegolf.com
Website www.federacioncolombianadegolf.com

Ecuador Golf Federation
Sec, Marcelo Roldós Prosser, Av Amazonas N.28-17 y Alemania, Edif.Skorpios Piso 8 of.812, Quito
Tel +593 2 2922 128 *Fax* +593 2 2442 986
E-mail fedecuat@feg.org.ec
Website www.feg.org.ec

Guyana Golf Union
Sec, c/o Demerara Bauxite Co Ltd, Mackenzie, Guyana

Paraguay Golf Association
Sec, Alejandro Rubin, Eduardo Vístor Haedo, No.407 c/ Alberdi, Edif Libra – Planta Baja, Asunción
Tel +595 21 491 217 *Fax* +595 21 447 218
E-mail secretaria@apg.org.py
Website www.apg.org.py

Peru Golf Federation
Exec Dir, Eduardo Ibarra, Calle Conde de la Monclova 315 Of 308, San Isidro, Lima
Tel +51 1 441 1500 *Fax* +51 1 441 1992
E-mail fepegolf@terra.com.pe
Website www.fpg.org.pe

Uruguay Golf Association
Hon Sec, Dr Paul Arrighi, José Ellauri 357 apto.303, Montevideo
Tel/Fax +598 2 711 5285
E-mail augolf@adinet.com.uy
Website www.aug.com.uy

Venezuela Golf Federation
Exec Dir, Julio L Torres, Edifico IASA Mezzanina Of 02, Av. Eugenio Mendoza La Castellana 1060, Municipio Chacao, Caracas 1060
Tel/Fax +58 212 265 2839
E-mail fvg@fvg.org *Website* www.fvg.or

Professional Association

Brazil PGA
Contact, Claci Schneider, Rua Francisco de Paula Brito, 317-Planalto Paulista, cep 04071 050 São Paulo-SP
Tel +55 11 2276 0745 *Fax* +55 11 2276 0789
E-mail pgabrasil@uol.com.br
Website www.pgadobrasil.com.br

Africa

African Golf Confederation
c/o Alfred P Dunn, PO Box 241, Kyalame Estate, Midrand 1684 RSA
Tel +27 823 250 205
E-mail Alfredpd241@gmail.com

Algerian Golf Federation
Pres, Noureddine Djoudi, 28 rue Ahmed, Ouaked, Dely Ibrahim
Tel/Fax +213 35021
E-mail djoudimn@hotmail.com

Arab Golf Federation
Sec Gen, Adel Zarouni, PO Box 31410, Dubai, UAE
Tel +9714 295 2277 *Fax* +9714 95 2288
E-mail info@ugagolf.com
Website www.arabgolf.org

Botswana Golf Union
Exec Sec, Joseph Marudu, PO Box 1033, Gaborone
Tel +267 316 1116 *Fax* +267 391 2262
E-mail bgu@it.bw

Cameroon Golf Federation
Pres, Dr Yves Martin Ahanda Assiga, 295 Rue 1810, Montée Mini prix Bastos-BP 3, 35091 Yaoundé
Tel +237 22 20 4968
E-mail camergreen.golf@yahoo.fr
Website www.federationcamerounaisedegolf.com

D R of Congo Golf Federation
Pres, Alain Nitu, c/o Rainbow Connections, Carrefour des Jeunes, 5151 Avenue Kasa-Vuba, Q/Matonge, Commune Kalamu, Kinshasa
E-mail alainnitu@hotmail.com

Egyptian Golf Federation
Golf Man, Gerard Bent, 6 St. 301, New Maadi, Cairo
Tel +2010 005 0435
E-mail gerardbent@egyptiangolffederation.org
Website www.egyptiangolffederation.org

Gabon Golf Federation
Sec, BP 15159 Libreville
Tel +241 760 378 *Fax* +241 729 079
E-mail golfclublibreville@gmail.com

Ghana Golf Association
Hon Sec, George Lee Mensah, c/o National Sport Council, PO Box 1272, Accra
Tel/Fax +233 21 923434 *Fax* +233 21 220953
E-mail ghanagolfass@yahoo.co.uk

Ghana Ladies Golf Union
Hon Sec, Mrs M Amu, PO Box 70, Accra

Ivory Coast (Côte d'Ivoire) Golf Federation
Sec, Bendey-Diby Valentin, O8 BP 01, Abidjan 08
Tel +225 2243 1076 *Fax* +225 2243 3772
E-mail f.golfci@aviso.ci *Website* www.fgolfci.com

Kenya Golf Union
Hon Sec, Parshu Harini, PO Box 49609, 00100 Nairobi
Tel +254 203 76 3898 *Fax* +254 203 76 5118
E-mail kgu@iconnect.co.ke
Website www.kgu.org.ke

Kenya Ladies' Golf Union
Hon Sec, A Sangar, PO Box 1675-1, Nairobi
Tel +254 2 733 794

KwaZulu-Natal Golf Union
Sec, RT Runge, PO Box 1939, Durban 4000
Tel +27 (0)31 202 7636 *Fax* +27 (0)31 202 1022
E-mail kzngu@kzngolf.co.za

Liberia Golf Association
Pres, Dr C Nelson Oniyama, c/o Monrovia Breweries Inc., Monrovia

Libyan Golf Federation
Gen Sec, Mustafa Ewkaiat, PO Box 3674, Tripoli
Tel +218 21 478 0510
E-mail golf_libya@hotmail.com

Malawi Golf Union
Hon Sec, James Hinde, PO Box 1198, Blantyre 8
Tel +265 1 824 108 *Fax* +265 1 824 027
E-mail medlife@malawi.net

Mauritius Golf Federation
Pres, Raj Ramlackhan, 42 Sir William Newton Street, Port Louis
Tel +230 208 4224 *Fax* +230 483 5163
E-mail mgolffed@intnet.mu

The Royal Moroccan Golf Federation
Sec Gen, Abdelal Latif Benali, Route des Zaers, Rabat, Dar El Salam
Tel +212 3775 5636 *Fax* +212 3775 1026
E-mail abdellatif.benali@manara.ma

Namibia Golf Federation
Treas, Hugh Mortimer, PO Box 2122, Windhoek, Namibia
Tel +264 61 205 5223 *Fax* +264 61 205 5220
E-mail gm@wccgolf.com.na
Website www.wccgolf.com.na

Nigeria Golf Federation
Sec, Patrick Uwagbale, National Stadium Surulere, PO Box 145, Lagos
Tel +234 1 545 6209
Fax +234 1 545 0530
E-mail nigeriagolffederation@yahoo.com

Nigerian Ladies Golf Union
Sec, Mrs K Odukola, c/o Benin GC, Benin City

Senegalese Golf Federation
Dep Gen Sec, Mr Moustaph Baïdy Bâ, BP 24105 Ouakam Dakar, Senegal

Sierra Leone Golf Federation
Sec, Kobi Walker, c/o Captain Freetown GC, PO Box 237, Lumley Beach Rd, Freetown
E-mail kobiwalker@yahoo.co.uk

South African Golf Association
Exec Dir, BA Younge, PO Box 65303, Benmore 2010 RSA
Tel +27 11 476 1713 *Fax* +27 086 503 4653
E-mail admin@saga.co.za *Website* www.saga.co.za

Women's Golf South Africa
Hon Sec, Mrs V Horak, PO Box 209, Randfontein 1760, RSA
Tel/Fax +27 11 416 1263
E-mail salgu@global.co.za *Website* www.salgu.co.za

Swaziland Golf Union
Sec, AP Dunn, PO Box 1739, Mbabane, H100 Swaziland
Tel +268 404 4735 *Fax* +268 404 5401
E-mail adunn2@fnb.co.za

Tanzania Golf Union
Golf Dir, Farayi Chitengwa, c/o Gymkhana Club, PO Box 286, Dar Es Salaam
Tel +255 222 138445 *Fax* +255 222 113583
E-mail info@tgu.or.tz *Website* www.tgu.com

Tunisian Golf Federation
Sec Gen, Mohamed Moncef Gaida, Maison de Fédéracions Sportives, 1004 Cité Olympique, Tunis
Tel +216 71 237 087 *Fax* +216 71 237 299
E-mail ftg@ftg.org.tn
Website www.ftg.org.tn

Uganda Golf Union
Hon Sec, Gadi A Musasizi, Kitante Road, PO Box 2574, Kampala
Tel +256 712 877 036
Fax +256 41 304 832
E-mail gmusasizi@yahoo.com

Uganda Ladies Golf Union
Hon Sec, Mrs R Tumusiime, PO Box 624, Kampala
E-mail ugagolf@africaonline.co.ug

Zaire Golf Federation
Pres, Tshilombo Mwin Tshitol, BP 1648, Lubumbashi

Zambia Golf Union
Hon Sec, A C Mwangata, 37A Twaliilubula Ave, Parklands, PO Box 21602, Kitwe
Tel +260 96 780 095 *Fax* +260 2 226 884
E-mail anthony@coppernet.zm

Zambia Ladies Golf Union
Hon Sec, Mrs H Kapya, PO Box 22151, Kitwe

Zimbabwe Golf Association
Sec, John Nixon, PO Box 3327, Harare
Tel +263 4 746 141 *Fax* +263 4 746 228

Professional Associations

South African PGA
Sec, Anne Du Toit, PO Box 949 Bedfordview 2008, RSA
Tel +27 11 485 1370 *Fax* +27 11 640 4372
E-mail admin@pgasa.com
Website www.pgasa.com

South African Women's PGA
Sec, Mrs V Harrington, PO Box 781547, Sandton 2146
Tel/Fax +27 11 477 8606

South Africa Sunshine Tour
Exec Dir, Louis Martin, 15 Postnet Suite #185, Private Bag X15, Somerset West 7129
Tel +27 21 850 6500 *Fax* +27 21 852 8271

Middle East

Bahrain Golf Committee
Sec Gen, Muneer Ahmed, PO Box 38938, Riffa, Kingdom of Bahrain
Tel +973 1777 7179 *Fax* +973 1776 9484
E-mail bgassoc@gmail.com

Emirates Golf Association
Gen Man, Saeed Al Budoor, PO Box 31410, Dubai, UAE
Tel +971 4 295 6440 *Fax* +971 4 295 6026
E-mail info@ugagolf.com *Website* www.ugagolf.com

Islamic Republic of Iran Golf Federation
Sec Gen, Mohammad Reza Naddafpour, Enghelab Club, Vali-e-asr Avenue, PO Box 15815-1881, Tehran
Tel/Fax +98 21 2201 6617
E-mail info@golfir.com *Website* www.golfir.com

Israel Golf Federation
Sec, Mrs Irit Peleg, PO Box 141, IL-38900 Caesarea
Tel +972 4 610 9600 *Fax* +972 77 870 273
E-mail info@israelgolffed.org
Website www.israelgolffed.org

Jordan Golf Federation
Sec, Ali A Shahin, PO Box 141331, Amman 11814
Tel +962 795 525187 *Fax* +962 658 56913
E-mail ashahin70@yahoo.com

Kuwait Golf Federation
Pres, Saud Al Hajeri, PO Box 1192, Fintas Z-code 51013
Tel +965 390 5287

Lebanese Golf Federation
Tech Comm, Karim S Salaam, c/o GC of Lebanon, PO Box 11-3099, Beirut
Tel 9611 861862 *Fax* +9611 866253
E-mail info@lebanesegolffederation.org

Qatar Golf Association
Pres, Hassan Nasser Al Noaimi, PO Box 13530, Doha
Tel 974 4483 2677 *Fax* +974 4483 2610
E-mail info@qga.com.qa *Website* www.qga.com.qa

Saudi Arabian Golf Federation
Sec, Jun Saporsantos, PO Box 325422, Riyadh 11371, Saudi Arabia
Tel +966 1 4090 004 *Fax* +966 1 4090 002
E-mail saudigolf@yahoo.com
Website www.ksagolf.com

Professional Associations

Israel PGA
Contact, Basil Katz, Sintat Hahoma 3 / 4, Raanana 43331
Tel +972 4 6636 1172 *Fax* +972 4 6636 1173
E-mail basad@013.net
Website www.pgaisrael.com

United Arab Emirates PGA
Off, J Danby, Nad Al Sheba Golf, PO Box 52872, Dubai
Tel +971 4 336 3666 *Fax* +971 4 336 1624
E-mail jdanby@dubaigolf.com

Asia

Asia-Pacific Golf Confederation
Hon Sec, Colin Phillips, Golf Australia, Level 3, 95 Coventry St, South Melbourne, Victoria-3205
Tel +613 9626 5050 *Fax* +613 9626 5095
E-mail apgc@golfaustralia.org.au

Afghanistan Golf Federation
Gen Sec, Azizulah Attaei, Shahr-E-Naw, Charahi Ansari, Shah Bobo Jan St, Kabul
Tel +93 786 024 491
E-mail afgolffederation@yahoo.com
Website www.afghangolf.af

Azerbaijan Golf Federation
Gen Man, Dominik Naughton, 657 Sarabski Str, Baku AZ 1022
Tel +994 12 4998686
E-mail info@agf.az

Bangladesh Golf Federation
Pres, General Moeen U Ahmed ndc, psc, c/o Kurmitola GC, Dhaka Cantonment, Dhaka-1206
Tel/Fax +880 2 988 1615
E-mail kgcdhaka@hotmail.com

Bhutan Golf Confederation
Sec Gen, Tsheringh Namgay, PO Box 939, Thimphu, Bhutan
Tel 975 2 322 138 *Fax* 975 2 323 937
E-mail t_namgay@yahoo.com

Cambodian Golf Association
Sec Gen, Lt Gen Eth Sarath, 295 Eo Street Kampuchea Krom, Sangleat Mittapheap, Khan 7 Makara, Phnom Penh
Tel +855 1243 7888
Fax +855 2388 0045
E-mail ethsarath@hotmail.com
Website www.cambodiangolf-federation.com

China Golf Association
Sec Gen, Zhang Xiaoning, 5 Tiyuguan Rd, Beijing, 100763 China
Tel +86 10 6711 7897

Fax +86 10 6716 2993
E-mail chinagolf@263.net
Website www.golf.org.cn

Chinese Taipei Golf Association
Sec Gen, Hann-Ji Wang, 12 F-1 125 Nanking East Rd, Section 2, Taipei, Taiwan 104, Chinese Taipei
Tel +886 22 516 5611 *Fax* +886 22 516 5904
E-mail garoc.tw@msa.hinet.net
Website www.taiwangolf.org

National Golf Association of Fiji
Gen Sec, Mosese Waqavonovono, PO Box 5363, Raiwaqa, Suva, Fiji
Tel/Fax +679 337 1191
E-mail ngaf@connect.com.fi

Guam National Golf Federation
Pres, Samuel Teker, Suite 2A 130 Aspinall Ave, Agana, Guam 96910
Tel +1 671 653 3100 *Fax* +1 671 472 2601
E-mail st@tttguamlawyers.com

Hong Kong Golf Association Ltd
Ch Exec, F I Valentine, Rm 2003, Olympic House, 1 Stadium Path, So Kon Po, Causeway Bay, Hong Kong
Tel +852 2504 8659 *Fax* +852 2845 1553
E-mail hkgolf@hkga.com *Website* www.hkga.com

Indian Golf Union
Sec-Gen, W/Cdr Satish Aparajit (Retd), First Floor 24, Adchina, New Delhi 110017
Tel +91 11 265 25772 *Fax* +91 11 265 25770
E-mail tigu@vsnl.net *Website* www.tigu.in

Indonesian Golf Association
Sec Gen, Mr Sudrajat, Gedung MEDCO I, Lt.1.JR Ampera Raya no 18-20, Cilandak-Jakarta 12560
Tel +62 21 7884 1214 *Fax* +62 21 7884 1215
E-mail info@pbpgi.org
Website www.pgionline.org

Japan Golf Association
Exec Dir, Takashi Omori, Kyobashi YS Bldg 2nd Floor, 1-12-5 Kyobashi, Chuo-Ku, Tokyo 104-0031
Tel +81 3 3566 0003 *Fax* +81 3 3566 0101
E-mail info@jga.or.jp *Website* www.jga.or.jp

Kazakhstan Golf Federation
Gen Sec, Konstantin Lifanov, c/o Nurtau GC, Alatau Sanatorium, Karasayskiy Region, Kamenka Village, KZ-040918 Almat obl. Kazakhstan
Tel +7 727 295 8823 *Fax* +7 727 295 8830
E-mail golfpro1@yandex.ru

Korean Golf Association
Exec Dir, D W Kim, #513-12, Munbal-ri, Gyoha-eup, Paju-si, Gyeonggi-do 413-832, Korea
Tel +82 31 955 2255 *Fax* +82 31 955 2300
E-mail kga@kgagolf.or.kr *Website* www.kgagolf.or.kr

Kyrgyzstan Golf
Sec, 217 Moskovskaia Street, Leninskiy District, Bishkek City 720010, Kyrgyz Republic
Tel +7 996 905 170 *Fax* +7 996 831 014
E-mail o.larina@skd.kg

Lao National Golf Federation
Sec, Sangkhom Phomphakdy, PO Box 4300, 33 Wat Xiengnhum St, Sethathirat Rd, Vientiane, Lao PDR
Tel/Fax +856 2121 7294
E-mail sangkhom52@hotmail.com

Golf Association of Macau
Sec, Michelle Leong, Rm 15, Estrada Vitoria S/N, Centro Desportivo, Vitoria, Macau
Tel +853 831 555 *Fax* +853 832 555

Malaysian Golf Association
Hon Sec, V Ravindran, 14 Jalan 4/76C, Desa Pandan, 55100 Kuala Lumpur
Tel +60 3 9283 7300 *Fax* +60 3 9282 9300
E-mail mga@tm.net.my
Website www.mgaonline.com.my

Mongolian Golf Association
Sec Gen, Enkh Amgalan.L., MCS Plaza, 4 Seoul St, Ulaanbaatar – 210644, Mongolia
Tel +976 11 323 705 *Fax* +976 11 311 323
E-mail enkh_amgalan@mcs.mn

Golf Federation of the Union of Myanmar
Gen Sec, U Aung Hla Han, no.46 Pyay Rd, Building C 6 1 / 2 miles, Hlaing Township, Yangon
Tel +95 1 537 241 *Fax* +95 1 538 686
E-mail aunghhan@baganmail.net.mm

Nepal Golf Association
Sec, Tashi Ghale, GPO Box 1665 Naya, Baneshwar, Kathmandu
Tel +977 1 447 2836 *Fax* +977 1 478 0191
E-mail hotel@rsingi.wlink.com.np

Pakistan Golf Federation
Pres, Lt Gen Ashfaq Parvez Kayani, Jhelum Road, PO Box 1295, Rawalpindi
Tel +92 51 556 8177 *Fax* +92 51 225 5440
E-mail pakgolffed@yahoo.com

National Golf Association of the Philippines
Sec Gen, Godofredo R Balindez jr, Room 307 Building B, Philsports Complex, Mercalo Av, Pasig City, Metro Manila 1603 Philippines
Tel +632 517 9778 *Fax* +632 706 5926
E-mail ngapgolf@hotmail.com
Website www.ngapgolf.com

Singapore Golf Association
Gen Man, Col (rtd) Peter Teo, Tanglin Post Office, PO Box 457, Singapore 912416
Tel +65 6 256 1318 *Fax* +65 6 256 1917
E-mail sga@pacific.net.sg
Website www.sga.org.sg

Sri Lanka Golf Union
Hon Sec, AG Punchihewa, PO Box 309, 223 Model Farm Rd, Colombo 8, Sri Lanka
Tel +94 11 266 7771 *Fax* +94 11 461 6056
E-mail golfsrilanka@rcgcsl.co

Thailand Golf Association
Sec Gen, Air Mrshl Bureerat Ratanavanich, PO Box 1190, Ramkamhaeng, Bangkok 10241
Tel +66 2 369 3777 *Fax* +66 2 369 3776
E-mail secretary@tga.or.th *Website* www.tga.or.th

Vietnam Golf Association
Sec Gen, Nguyễn Văn Hảo, 125 Nguyễn So'n, Cia Thuy, Long Biên, Hà Nội

Tel +84 4 3872 3194
E-mail info@vga.com.vn
Website www.vga.com.vn

Professional Associations

Asian PGA
Sec, Ramlan Dato Harun, 415-417 Block A Kelana Business Centre, 97 Jalan SS 7/2 Kelana Jaya, Selangor, Malaysia
Tel +603 7492 0099 *Fax* +603 7492 0098
Website www.asianpgatour.com

Asia PGA Tour
Chief Exec, Justin Strachan, 15/F, One Harbourfront, 18 Tak Fung Street, Hunghom, Kowloon, Hong Kong
Tel +852 2330 8227 *Fax* +852 2801 5743
E-mail apgatour@asiaonline.net
Website www.asianpgatour.com

PGA Republic of China
2nd Floor 196 Cheng-Teh Road, Taipei, Taiwan
Tel +886 2 8220318 *Fax* +886 2 8229684
E-mail garoc.tw@msa.hinet.net
Website www.twgolf.org

Hong Kong PGA
Contact, Viola Wong, 70 Ting Kok Rd, Tai Po, N.T. Hong Kong
Tel +852 2761 7455 *Fax* +852 2761 1489
E-mail info@hkpga.com.hk
Website www.hkpga.com.hk

Indian PGA
Sec, P K Bhattacharyya, 109A, 1513 Guman Puri Complex (First Floor), Kotia, Mubarak Pur, New Delhi – 110 003
Tel +91 11 3250 5456
Fax +91 91 11 2461 6331
E-mail pgaofindia@gmail.com

Japan Ladies PGA
7-16-3 Ginza, Nitetsu Kobiki Bldg 8F, Chuo-ku, Tokyo 104-0061
Tel +81 3 3546 7801 *Fax* +81 3 3546 7805

Japan PGA
Int Com, Seien Kobayakawa, Top Hamamatsucho Bldg, 1-5-12 Shiba.Minato-Ku, 8FL, Tokyo 105-0014
Tel +81 3 5419 2614 *Fax* +81 3 5419 2622
E-mail bp@pga.or.jp

PGA of Malaysia
Sec, Brig-Gen Mahendran, 1B Jalan Mamanda 7, Ampang Point, 6800 Selangor Darul Ehsan, Malaysia

Australasia and the Pacific

Golf Australia
Ch Exec, Stephen Pitt, Level 3,95 Coventry St, South Melbourne, Victoria-3205
Tel +613 9626 5050 *Fax* +613 9626 5095
E-mail info@golfaustralia.org.au
Website www.golfaustralia.org.au

Womens Golf Australia
See Golf Australia

Cook Islands Golf Association
Sec, Mrs Tereapii Urlich, Rarotonga GC, PO Box 151, Rarotonga, Cook Islands
Tel +682 20621 *Fax* +682 20631
E-mail toots@oyster.net.ck

National Golf Association of Fiji
Gen Sec, Mosese Waqavonovono, GPO Box 18505, Suva, Fiji
Tel/Fax +679 337 1191
E-mail shamozen@connect.com.fj

Guam National Golf Federation
Pres, Samuel Teker, Suite 2A 130 Aspinall Ave, Agana, Guam 96910
Tel +1 671 653 3100 *Fax* +1 671 472 2601
E-mail st@tttguamlawyers.com

New Zealand Golf Incorporated
Ch Exec, Dean Murphy, PO Box 331768, Takapuna, New Zealand
Tel +64 9 485 3230 *Fax* +64 9 486 6745
E-mail nzgolf@nzgolf.org.nz
Website www.nzgolf.org.nz

Womens' Golf New Zealand Inc
See New Zealand Golf Incorporated

Papua New Guinea Golf Association
Pres, S Walker, PO Box 4632, Boroko, NCD
Tel +675 323 1120 *Fax* +675 323 1300
E-mail swalker@brianbell.com.pg

Papua New Guinea Ladies Golf Association
Hon Sec, Mrs L Illidge, PO Box 348, Lae MP 411

National Golf Association of the Philippines
Sec Gen, Godofredo R Balindez jr, Room 307 Building B, Philsports Complex, Mercalo Av, Pasig City, Metro Manila 1603 Philippines
Tel +632 517 9778
Fax +632 706 5926
E-mail ngapgolf@hotmail.com
Website www.ngaponline.net

Oceana Golf Union
Sec, Mosese Waqavonovono, GPO Box 18505, Suva, Fiji
Tel/Fax +679 337 1191
E-mail shamozen@connect.com.fj

Samoa Golf Incorporated
Sec, Vincent Fepuleai, PO Box 3770, Apia, Samoa
Tel +685 24839 *Mobile* +685 7704767
E-mail golfhut@ipasifika.net

Vanuatu Golf Association
Chairman, Bernie Cain, PO Box 358, Port Vila, Vanuatu, Pacific Ocean
Tel +678 22178 *Fax* +678 25037
E-mail vilare@vanuatu.com.vu

Professional Associations

Australian PGA
Ch Exec, Max Garske, 600 Thompson Rd, Sandhurst, Victoria 3977
Tel +61 2 9439 8111 Fax +61 2 9439 7888
E-mail maxgpga@oze-mail.com.au
Website www.pga.org.au

Australian Ladies Professional Golf
Ch Exec, Warren Savil, PO Box 447, Mudgeeraba, Queensland 4213
Tel +61 7 5592 9343 *Fax* +61 7 5592 9344
E-mail warrens@alpg.com.au
Website www.alpg.com.au

PGA Tour Australasia
Exec Dir, Andrew Georgiou, Suite 302, 77 Berry St, North Sydney, NSW 2060
Tel +61 2 9956 0000 *Fax* +61 2 9956 0099
Website pgatour.com.au

New Zealand PGA
Ch Exec, Duncan Simpson, 1 Papuke Rd, PO Box 33-678, North Shore City 0740
Tel +64 9 488 6616
E-mail duncan.simpson@pga.org.nz
Website www.pga.org.nz

Stymie – defined in the Glossary of Technical Terms in The R&A's 1882 Rules of Golf as being "when your opponent's ball lies in the line of your putt." The word comes from an old Scots word meaning 'obscuring'. Under The R&A's rules, until 1952 the ball would not be lifted in those circumstances unless the balls were within six inches of one another.

PART XVI

Clubs and Courses

Compiled by Paula Taylor

Club Centenaries

1912

Aberlady
Aquarius
Ashton-under-Lyne
Banbridge
Bedford & County
Boldon
Branshaw
Camberley Heath
Childwall
Clontarf
Cooden Beach
Dinas Powis
Dumfries & County
Essex Golf Centres, Hainault Forest
Fishwick Hall
Gatley
Heaton Park Golf Centre
Heworth (Tyne & Wear)
Holyhead
Kinsale Ringenane
Maesteg
Market Rasen & District
Northenden
Port Bannatyne
Ravelston
Reddish Vale
St George's Hill
Saline
Southport Golf Links
Thetford
Upavon
Waterford
Werneth Low
Whalley
Woodcote Park

1913

The Addington
Ashton & Lea
Bargoed
Baxenden & District
Bidston
Blackmoor
Bowring
Bramley
Bull Bay
Castle
Clones
Coxmoor
Davenport
Dore & Totley
Dukinfield
Ellesmere
Ferndown
Garforth
Gathurst
Gay Hill
Hazel Grove
Highcliffe Castle
Letterkenny
Linlithgow
Lytham Green Drive
Milford Haven
Okehampton
Oxley Park
Portumna
Redditch
Royal Automobile Club
St Regulus Ladies'
Sale
Seahouses
Sitwell Park
Stocksfield
Tynemouth
Wheatley

1914

Anglesey
Apsley Guise and Woburn Sands
Balmoral
Blackwood
Buckingham
Burnside
Crosland Heath
Eaglescliffe
Eden Course (St Andrews)
Green Hawarth
Hockley
Nevill
Newtownstewart
Oakdale
Routenburn
Shirley Park
Sonning
Southsea
Sutton Bridge
Thirsk & Northallerton
Whitchurch (Cardiff)

1915

Brokenhurst Manor
Llandudno (Maesdu)
Lowes Park
Spanish Point

Golf Clubs and Courses

How to use this section

Clubs in England, Ireland and Wales are listed in alphabetical order by country and county. Note that some clubs and courses are affiliated to a county different to that in which they are physically located. Clubs in Scotland are grouped under recognised administrative regions. The Great Britain and Ireland county index can be found on page 682.

European clubs and clubs from the rest of the world are listed alphabetically by country and grouped under regional headings. The index for Europe can be found on page 805 and the index for the rest of the world is on page 855. In most European countries, only 18 hole courses are included.

All clubs and courses are listed in the the general index at the back of the book.

With the publication of the 2010 edition, we began introducing a new international look to the *R&A Golfer's Handbook* and to accommodate our global expansion of results and club information, we have modified entries to the Club's Directory as detailed below.

It is apparent that information previously displayed of green fees, membership, personnel, additional features, etc., can be best imparted as current data via the websites that the majority of clubs now operate. Currently, nearly 80 per cent of golf clubs operate websites, a number that is growing by around four per cent per annum.

Club details (see Key to Symbols below)
The date after the name of the club indicates the year it was founded. Courses are private unless otherwise stated. Many public courses play host to members' clubs. Information on these can be obtained from the course concerned.

We are indebted to club secretaries in the British Isles and continental Europe for the information supplied.

Key to Symbols

☎ Telephone	✍ Secretary
Fax	⊕ Additional information in the absence of a website
E-mail	
Website	

European Dialling Codes

Austria +43	Iceland +354	Poland +48
Belgium +32	Republic of Ireland +353	Portugal +351
Cyprus +357	Italy +39	Slovenia +386
Czech Republic +420	Latvia +371	Spain +34
Denmark +45	Luxembourg +352	Sweden +46
Finland +358	Malta +356	Switzerland +41
France +33	Netherlands +31	Turkey +90
Germany +49	Norway +47	
Greece +30		
Hungary +36		

Great Britain and Ireland County Index

England

Ireland

Scotland

Wales

England

Bedfordshire

Aspley Guise & Woburn Sands (1914)
West Hill, Aspley Guise, Milton Keynes MK17 8DX
☎ **(01908) 583596**
(01908) 288140
info@aspleyguisegolfclub.co.uk
Karen Evans (01908) 583596
www.aspleyguisegolfclub.co.uk

Aylesbury Vale (1991)
Proprietary
Wing, Leighton Buzzard LU7 0UJ
☎ **(01525) 240196**
(01525) 240848
info@avgc.co.uk
C Wright (Sec/Mgr)
www.avgc.co.uk

Beadlow Manor Hotel G&CC (1973)
Proprietary
Beadlow, Shefford SG17 5PH
☎ **(01525) 860800**
(01525) 861345
office@beadlowmanor.co.uk
www.beadlowmanor.co.uk

The Bedford (1999)
Proprietary
Carnoustie Drive, Great Denham Golf Village, Biddenham MK40 4FF
☎ **(01234) 320022**
(01234) 320023
geoff@thebedfordgc.com
Geoff Swain
www.thebedfordgc.com

Bedford & County (1912)
Green Lane, Clapham, Bedford MK41 6ET
☎ **(01234) 352617**
(01234) 357195
office@bandcgc.co.uk
R MacDonald (Gen Mgr)
www.bandcgc.co.uk

Bedfordshire (1891)
Spring Lane, Stagsden, Bedford MK43 8SR
☎ **(01234) 822555**
(01234) 825052
office@bedfordshiregolf.com
Geraint Dixon (Gen Mgr)
www.bedfordshiregolf.com

Caddington (1985)
Proprietary
Chaul End Road, Caddington LU1 4AX
☎ **(01582) 415573**
(01582) 415314
info@caddingtongolfclub.co.uk
D Isger
www.caddingtongolfclub.co.uk

Chalgrave Manor (1994)
Proprietary
Dunstable Road, Chalgrave, Toddington LU5 6JN
☎ **(01525) 876556**
(01525) 876556
steve@chalgravegolf.co.uk
S Rumball
www.chalgravegolf.co.uk

Colmworth (1992)
Proprietary
New Road, Colmworth MK44 2NN
☎ **(01234) 378181**
(01234) 376678
julie@colmworthgc.fsnet.co.uk
C Porch (01933) 412398
www.colmworthgolfclub.co.uk

Colworth (1985)
Colworth House, Sharnbrook, Bedford MK44 1LQ
☎ **(01234) 782442**
secretary@colworthgolf.co.uk
Dennis Scott (Sec)
⊕ Visitors can only play as Member's guests
www.colworthgolf.co.uk

Dunstable Downs (1906)
Whipsnade Road, Dunstable LU6 2NB
☎ **(01582) 604472**
(01582) 478700
dunstabledownsgc@btconnect.com
Alan Sigee
www.dunstabledownsgolf.co.uk

Henlow (1985)
RAF Henlow, Henlow SG16 6DN
☎ **(01462) 851515 Ext 7083**
(01462) 816780
www.henlowgolfclub.co.uk

John O'Gaunt (1948)
Sutton Park, Sandy, Biggleswade SG19 2LY
☎ **(01767) 260360**
(01767) 262834
simon@johnogauntgolfclub.co.uk
Simon Davis (Gen Mgr)
www.johnogauntgolfclub.co.uk

Leighton Buzzard (1925)
Plantation Road, Leighton Buzzard LU7 3JF
☎ **(01525) 244800**
(01525) 244801
secretary@leightonbuzzardgolf.net
D Mutton (01525) 244800
www.leightonbuzzardgolf.net

Mentmore G&CC (1992)
Mentmore, Leighton Buzzard LU7 0UA
☎ **(01296) 662020**
(01296) 662592
cmoore@mentmorecountryclub.co.uk
Clint Moore
www.mentmorecountryclub.co.uk

The Millbrook (1980)
Ampthill MK45 2JB
☎ **(01525) 840252**
(01525) 406249
info@themillbrook.com
www.themillbrook.com

Mount Pleasant (1992)
Proprietary
Station Road, Lower Stondon, Henlow SG16 6JL
☎ **(01462) 850999**
(01462) 850257
tarasimkins@mountpleasantgolfclub.co.uk
Tara Simkins (Gen Mgr)
www.mountpleasantgolfclub.co.uk

Mowsbury (1975)
Public
Kimbolton Road, Bedford MK41 8BJ
☎ **(01234) 772700**
TW Gardner (01234) 771041

Pavenham Park (1994)
Proprietary
Pavenham, Bedford MK43 7PE
☎ **(01234) 822202**
(01234) 826602
office@pavenhampark.com
S Pepper
www.pavenhampark.com

South Beds (1892)
Warden Hill Road, Luton LU2 7AE
☎ **(01582) 591500**
(01582) 495381
office@southbedsgolfclub.co.uk
MT Seaton (01582) 591500
www.southbedsgolfclub.co.uk

Stockwood Park (1973)
Public
Stockwood Park, London Rd, Luton LU1 4LX
☎ **(01582) 413704**
(01582) 481001
spgc@hotmail.co.uk
Brian E Clark (Club Admin Officer)
www.activeluton.co.uk

Tilsworth (1972)
Pay and play
Dunstable Rd, Tilsworth, Dunstable LU7 9PU
☎ **(01525) 210721/210722**
(01525) 210465
info@tilsworthgolf.co.uk
N Webb
www.tilsworthgolf.co.uk

Wyboston Lakes (1978)
Public
Wyboston Lakes, Wyboston MK44 3AL
☎ **(01480) 223004**
(01480) 407330
DJ Little (Mgr)
www.wybostonlakes.co.uk

Berkshire

Bearwood Golf Club (1986)
Mole Road, Sindlesham, Berkshire RG11 5DB
☎ **(0118) 976 0060**
(0118) 977 2687
barrytustin@btconnect.com
BFC Tustin (Mgr)
www.bearwoodgolfclub.com

Bearwood Lakes (1996)
Proprietary
Bearwood Road, Sindlesham RG41 4SJ
☎ **(0118) 979 7900**
(0118) 979 2911
info@bearwoodlakes.co.uk
Carl Rutherford (MD)
www.bearwoodlakes.co.uk

The Berkshire (1928)
Swinley Road, Ascot SL5 8AY
☎ **(01344) 621495**
(01344) 623328
admin@theberkshire.co.uk
Lt Col JCF Hunt (01344) 621496
www.theberkshire.co.uk

Billingbear Park (1985)
Pay and play
The Straight Mile, Wokingham RG40 5SJ
☎ **(01344) 869259**
(01344) 869259
info@billingbearpark.com
Mrs JR Blainey
www.billingbearpark.co.uk

Bird Hills Golf Centre (1985)
Public
Drift Road, Hawthorn Hill, Maidenhead SL6 3ST
☎ **(01628) 771030**
(01628) 631023
info@birdhills.co.uk
Hannah Edwards
www.birdhills.co.uk

Blue Mountain Golf Centre (1993)
Pay and play
Wood Lane, Binfield RG42 4EX
☎ **(01344) 300200**
(01344) 360960
bluemountain@crown-golf.co.uk
www.crown-golf.co.uk

Calcot Park (1930)
Bath Road, Calcot, Reading RG31 7RN
☎ **(0118) 942 7124**
(0118) 945 3373
info@calcotpark.com
Kim Brake
www.calcotpark.com

Castle Royle (1994)
Knowl Hill, Reading RG10 9XA
☎ **(01628) 825442**

Caversham Heath (2000)
Proprietary
Chazey Heath, Mapledurham, Reading RG4 7UT
☎ **(0118) 947 8600**
(0118) 947 8700
info@cavershamgolf.co.uk
Michael Palk
www.cavershamgolf.co.uk

Datchet (1890)
Buccleuch Road, Datchet SL3 9BP
☎ **(01753) 543887 (Clubhouse)**
(01753) 541872
secretary@datchetgolfclub.co.uk
KR Smith (01753) 543887
www.datchetgolfclub.co.uk

Deanwood Park (1995)
Pay and play
Stockcross, Newbury RG20 8JP
☎ **(01635) 48772**
(01635) 48772
golf@deanwoodpark.co.uk
John Bowness
www.deanwoodpark.co.uk

Donnington Grove Country Club
Donnington Grove, Grove Road, Donnington RG14 2LA
☎ **(01635) 581000**
(01635) 552259
enquiries@parasampia.com
S Greenacre (Mgr)
www.parasampia.com

Donnington Valley (1985)
Proprietary
Snelsmore House, Snelsmore Common, Newbury RG14 3BG
☎ **(01635) 568142**
(01635) 41889
golf@donningtonvalley.co.uk
Peter Smith (01635) 568144
www.donningtonvalleygolflclub.co.uk

Downshire Golf Complex (1973)
Public
Easthampstead Park, Wokingham RG40 3DH
☎ **(01344) 302030**
(01344) 301020
downshiregc@bracknell-forest.gov.uk
P Stanwick (Golf Mgr)
www.bracknell-forest.gov.uk/downshiregolf

East Berkshire (1903)
Ravenswood Ave, Crowthorne RG45 6BD
☎ **(01344) 772041**
(01344) 777378
thesecretary@eastberkshiregolfclub.com
C Day
www.eastberkshiregolfclub.com

Goring & Streatley (1895)
Rectory Road, Streatley-on-Thames RG8 9QA
☎ **(01491) 873229**
(01491) 875224
secretary@goringgolf.co.uk
M Evans
www.goringgolf.co.uk

Hennerton (1992)
Proprietary
Crazies Hill Road, Wargrave RG10 8LT
☎ **(0118) 940 1000**
(0118) 940 1042
info@hennertongolfclub.co.uk
G Johnson (0118) 940 1000
www.hennertongolfclub.co.uk

Hurst Ladies (1979)
Public
c/o Dinton Pastures Country Park, Davis Street, Hurst, Wokingham RG10 0SU
☎ **(01189) 751693**
Mrs A Haynes
⊕ Mens Club have disbanded – Ladies continues. Course still operating under countryside services.

Lavender Park
Swinley Road, Ascot SL5 8BD
☎ **(01344) 893344**
www.lavenderparkgolf.co.uk

Maidenhead (1896)
Shoppenhangers Road, Maidenhead SL6 2PZ
☎ **(01628) 624693**

The Berkshire Trophy

The Berkshire Trophy, an important 72-hole Tournament in The R&A Calendar for Amateurs with a handicap of +1 or better. Hosted by the Berkshire Golf Club (founded in 1928), the Trophy was first contested in 1946. Its distinquished list of past winners includes Sir Michael Bonallack, Peter Oosterhuis, Nick Faldo, Sandy Lyle and Ross Fisher.

The Club also hosts The Lady Astor Salver for for Amateur Ladies, first contested in 1951.

For key to symbols see page 725

(01628) 780758
manager@maidenheadgolf.co.uk
J Pugh
www.maidenheadgolf.co.uk

Mapledurham (1992)
Mapledurham, Reading RG4 7UD
(0118) 946 3353
(0118) 946 3363
d.reeves@clubhaus.com

Mill Ride (1990)
Mill Ride, Ascot SL5 8LT
(01344) 886777
(01344) 886820
r.greenwood@mill-ride.com
Robin Greenwood (Gen Mgr)
www.mill-ride.com

Newbury & Crookham (1873)
Bury's Bank Road, Greenham Common, Newbury RG19 8BZ
(01635) 40035
ed.richardson@newburygolf.co.uk
E Richardson (01635) 40035
www.newburygolf.co.uk

Newbury Racecourse (1994)
The Racecourse, Newbury RG14 7NZ
(01635) 551464
N Mitchell
www.nrgc.co.uk

Reading (1910)
17 Kidmore End Road, Emmer Green, Reading RG4 8SG
(0118) 947 2909
(0118) 946 4468
secretary@readinggolfclub.com
A Chaundy (0118) 947 2909
www.readinggolfclub.com

Royal Ascot (1887)
Winkfield Road, Ascot SL5 7LJ
(01344) 625175
(01344) 872330
admin@royalascotgolfclub.co.uk
Mrs S Thompson (01344) 625175
www.royalascotgolfclub.co.uk

The Royal Household (1901)
Buckingham Palace, London SW1 1AA
(0207) 930 4832
(0207) 663 4083
rhgc@royal.gsx.gov.uk
Peter Walter (Secretary)
Members and guests only.

Sand Martins (1993)
Proprietary
Finchampstead Road, Wokingham RG40 3RQ
(0118) 979 2711
(0118) 977 0282
info@sandmartins.com
Mr Rob Gumbrell (Mgr) (0118) 9029967
www.sandmartins.com

Sonning (1914)
Proprietary
Duffield Road, Sonning, Reading RG4 6GJ
(0118) 969 3332
(0118) 944 8409
secretary@sonning-golf-club.co.uk
Chris Foley
www.sonning-golf-club.co.uk

Swinley Forest (1909)
Coronation Road, Ascot SL5 9LE
(01344) 620197
(01344) 874733
office@swinleyfgc.co.uk
Stewart Zuill (01344) 295283
18h L6062 Par 69 SSS 70

Temple (1909)
Henley Road, Hurley, Maidenhead SL6 5LH
(01628) 824795
secretary@templegolfclub.co.uk
KGM Adderley (01628) 824795
www.templegolfclub.co.uk

Theale Golf Club (1996)
Proprietary
North Street, Theale, Reading RG7 5EX
(01189) 305331
info@thealegolf.com
M Lowe
www.thealegolf.com

West Berkshire (1975)
Proprietary
Chaddleworth, Newbury RG20 7DU
(01488) 638574
(01488) 638781
info@thewbgc.co.uk
Mrs CM Clayton
www.thewbgc.co.uk

Winter Hill (1976)
Proprietary
Grange Lane, Cookham SL6 9RP
(01628) 527613
(01628) 527479
derek_bond@johnlewis.co.uk
Clare Leech (01628) 536071
www.winterhillgolfclub.net

Wokefield Park (1998)
Proprietary
Goodboys Lane, Mortimer, Reading RG7 3AH
(0118) 933 4072
(0118) 933 4031
wokgolfteam@deverevenues.co.uk
Tim Gilpin (Mgr)
www.deveregolf.co.uk

Buckinghamshire

Aylesbury Golf Centre (1992)
Public
Hulcott Lane, Bierton HP22 5GA
(01296) 393644
kevinpartington@hotmail.co.uk
K Partington (Mgr)
www.aylesburygolfclub.co.uk

Aylesbury Park (1996)
Proprietary
Andrews Way, Oxford Road, Aylesbury HP17 8QQ
(01296) 399196
info@aylesburyparkgolf.com
Damian Brooks
www.aylesburyparkgolf.com

Beaconsfield (1902)
Seer Green, Beaconsfield HP9 2UR
(01494) 676545
(01494) 681148
secretary@beaconsfieldgolfclub.co.uk
D Cliffe
www.beaconsfieldgolfclub.co.uk

Buckingham (1914)
Tingewick Road, Buckingham MK18 4AE
(01280) 815566
admin@buckinghamgolfclub.co.uk
Peter Frost
www.buckinghamgolfclub.co.uk

Buckinghamshire (1992)
Proprietary
Denham Court Mansion, Denham Court Drive, Denham UB9 5PG
(01895) 835777
(01895) 835210
enquiries@buckinghamshiregc.co.uk
D Griffiths (01895) 836803
www.buckinghamshiregc.com

Burnham Beeches (1891)
Green Lane, Burnham, Slough SL1 8EG
(01628) 661448
(01628) 668968
enquiries@bbgc.co.uk
P C Dawson (Mgr)
www.bbgc.co.uk

Chartridge Park (1989)
Chartridge, Chesham HP5 2TF
(01494) 791772
(01494) 786462
info@cpgc.co.uk
www.cpgc.co.uk

Chesham & Ley Hill (1900)
Ley Hill, Chesham HP5 1UZ
(01494) 784541
(01494) 785506
secretary@cheshamgolf.co.uk
www.cheshamgolf.co.uk

Chiltern Forest (1979)
Aston Hill, Halton, Aylesbury HP22 5NQ
(01296) 631267
(01296) 632709
generalmanager@chilternforest.co.uk
Neil Clayton (Gen Mgr)
www.chilternforest.co.uk

Denham (1910)
Tilehouse Lane, Denham UB9 5DE
(01895) 832022
(01895) 835340
www.denhamgolfclub.co.uk

Ellesborough (1906)
Butlers Cross, Aylesbury HP17 0TZ
☎ **(01296) 622114**
(01296) 622114
office@ellesboroughgolf.co.uk
Mr Andy Hayes
www.ellesboroughgolf.co.uk

Farnham Park (1974)
Public
Park Road, Stoke Poges, Slough SL2 4PJ
☎ **(01753) 643332**
(01753) 646617
farnhamparkgolf@southbucks.gov.uk
Nigel Whitton Golf Mgr
www.farnhamparkgolfcourse.co.uk

Flackwell Heath (1904)
Treadaway Road, Flackwell Heath, High Wycombe HP10 9PE
☎ **(01628) 520929**
(01628) 530040
secretary@fhgc.co.uk
P Clarke
www.fhgc.co.uk

Gerrards Cross (1921)
Chalfont Park, Gerrards Cross SL9 0QA
☎ **(01753) 883263**
(01753) 883593
secretary@gxgolf.co.uk
www.gxgolf.co.uk

Harewood Downs (1907)
Cokes Lane, Chalfont St Giles HP8 4TA
☎ **(01494) 762184**
office@hdgc.co.uk
Nigel Daniel
www.hdgc.co.uk

Harleyford (1996)
Harleyford Estate, Henley Road, Marlow SL7 2SP
☎ **(01628) 816161**
(01628) 816160
info@harleyfordgolf.co.uk
Trevor Collingwood 01628 816164
www.harleyfordgolf.co.uk

Hazlemere (1982)
Penn Road, Hazlemere, High Wycombe HP15 7LR
☎ **(01494) 719300**
(01494) 713914
enquiries@hazlemeregolfclub.co.uk
Chris Mahoney
www.hazlemeregolfclub.co.uk

Hedsor (2000)
Pay and play
Broad Lane, Wooburn Common, Bucks HP10 0JW
☎ **(01628) 851285**
info@hedsorgolfcourse.co.uk
Stuart Cannon
www.hedsorgolfcourse.co.uk

Huntswood (1996)
Pay and play
Taplow Common Road, Burnham SL1 8LS
☎ **(01628) 667144**
(01628) 663145
huntswoodgc@btconnect.com
Sue Morris
www.huntswoodgolf.com

Iver (1983)
Hollow Hill Lane, Iver SL0 0JJ
☎ **(01753) 655615**
(01753) 654225
ivergolf@fsmail.net
www.ivergolfcourse.co.uk

Ivinghoe (1967)
Proprietary
Wellcroft, Ivinghoe, Leighton Buzzard LU7 9EF
☎ **(01296) 668696**
(01296) 662755
info@ivinghoegolfclub.co.uk
Mrs E Culley (01296) 668696
www.ivinghoegolfclub.co.uk

Kingfisher CC (1995)
Proprietary
Buckingham Road, Deanshanger, Milton Keynes MK19 6JY
☎ **(01908) 560354**
(01908) 260857
sales.kingfisher@btopenworld.com
www.kingfisher-uk.com

The Lambourne Club (1992)
Proprietary
Dropmore Road, Burnham SL1 8NF
☎ **(01628) 666755**
(01628) 663301
info@lambourneclub.co.uk
D Hart (Gen Mgr)
www.lambourneclub.co.uk

Little Chalfont (1981)
Lodge Lane, Chalfont St Giles HP8 4AJ
☎ **(01494) 764877**

Magnolia Park
Arncott Road, Boarstall HP18 9XX
☎ **(01844) 239700**
(01844) 238991
info@magnoliapark.co.uk
www.magnoliapark.co.uk

Oakland Park (1994)
Proprietary
Three Households, Chalfont St Giles HP8 4LW
☎ **(01494) 871277**
(01494) 874692
info@oaklandparkgolf.co.uk
I Donnelly (Gen Mgr)
www.oaklandparkgolf.co.uk

Princes Risborough (1990)
Lee Road, Saunderton Lee, Princes Risborough HP27 9NX
☎ **(01844) 346989 (Clubhouse)**
(01844) 274938
mlgolfltd@uwclub.net
J Murray (Man Dir)
www.prgc.co.uk

Richings Park (1996)
Proprietary
North Park, Iver SL0 9DL
☎ **(01753) 655352**
(01753) 655409
info@richingspark.co.uk
Steve Coles (01753) 655370
www.richingspark.co.uk

Silverstone (1992)
Proprietary
Silverstone Road, Stowe, Buckingham MK18 5LH
☎ **(01280) 850005**
(01280) 850156
proshop@silverstonegolfclub.co.uk
S Barnes
www.silverstonegolfclub.co.uk

Stoke Park (1908)
Park Road, Stoke Poges SL2 4PG
☎ **(01753) 717171**
(01753) 717181
info@stokepark.com
Mrs Kelly Gorry (01753) 717116
www.stokepark.com

Stowe (1974)
Stowe, Buckingham MK18 5EH
D Procter (01280) 818024

Thorney Park (1992)
Proprietary
Thorney Mill Road, Iver SL0 9AL
☎ **(01895) 422095**
(01895) 431307
sales@thorneypark.com
P Gray
www.thorneypark.com

Three Locks (1992)
Great Brickhill, Milton Keynes MK17 9BH
☎ **(01525) 270050**
(01525) 270470
info@threelocksgolfclub.co.uk
P Critchley
www.threelocksgolfclub.co.uk

Wavendon Golf Centre (1990)
Pay and play
Lower End Road, Wavendon, Milton Keynes MK17 8DA
☎ **(01908) 281811**
(01908) 281257
wavendon@hotmail.co.uk
G Iron
www.jackbarker.com

Weston Turville (1973)
Proprietary
New Road, Weston Turville, Aylesbury HP22 5QT
☎ **(01296) 424084**
(01296) 395376
enquiries@westonturvillegolfclub.co.uk
D Allen
www.westonturvillegolfclub.co.uk

Wexham Park (1977)
Pay and play
Wexham Street, Wexham, Slough SL3 6ND
(01753) 663271
(01753) 663318
info@wexhamparkgolfcourse.co.uk
J Kennedy
www.wexhamparkgolfcourse.co.uk

Whiteleaf (1907)
Whiteleaf, Princes Risborough HP27 0LY
(01844) 343097/274058
info@whiteleafgolfclub.co.uk
M Piercy (01844) 345472
www.whiteleafgolfclub.co.uk

Windmill Hill (1972)
Pay and play
Tattenhoe Lane, Bletchley MK3 7RB
(01908) 631113 (Bookings)
info@thewindmillonline.co.uk
Diana Allen (01908) 647615
www.thewindmillonline.co.uk

Woburn (1976)
Little Brickhill, Milton Keynes MK17 9LJ
(01908) 370756
(01908) 378436
enquiries@woburngolf.com
Jason O'Malley (Gen Mgr)
www.discoverwoburn.co.uk

Wycombe Heights (1991)
Pay and play
Rayners Avenue, Loudwater, High Wycombe HP10 9SZ
(01494) 816686
(01494) 816728
info@wycombeheightsgc.co.uk
www.wycombeheightsgc.co.uk

Cambridgeshire

Abbotsley (1986)
Proprietary
Potton Road, St Neots PE19 6XN
(01480) 474000
(01480) 471018
sales@abbotsley.com
Helen Lavis (01480) 474000
www.abbotsley.com

Bourn (1991)
Proprietary
Toft Road, Bourn, Cambridge CB23 2TT
(01954) 718057
(01954) 718908
info@bourngolfandleisure.co.uk
www.bourngolfand leisure.co.uk

Brampton Park (1991)
Buckden Road, Brampton, Huntingdon PE28 4NF
(01480) 434700
admin@bramptonparkgc.co.uk
Lisa Charlton (Gen Mgr)
www.bramptonparkgc.co.uk

Cambridge (1995)
Station Road, Longstanton, Cambridge CB4 5DS
(01954) 789388
klgcambridgegolf@tiscali.co.uk
K Green

Cambridge Meridian (1944)
Proprietary
Comberton Road, Toft, Cambridge CB23 2RY
(01223) 264700
(01223) 264701
meridian@golfsocieties.com
Steve Creighton
www.golfsocieties.com

Cromwell (1986)
Pay and play
Potton Road, St Neots PE19 6XN
(01480) 408900
(01480) 471018
sales@abbotsley.com
Helen Lavis (01480) 474000
www.abbotsley.com

Elton Furze (1993)
Proprietary
Bullock Road, Haddon, Peterborough PE7 3TT
(01832) 280189
(01832) 280299
helen@efgc.co.uk
Fiona Martin (Sec)
www.efgc.co.uk

Ely City (1961)
107 Cambridge Road, Ely CB7 4HX
(01353) 662751
(01353) 668636
info@elygolf.co.uk
Tom Munt (Mgr) (01353) 662751
www.elygolf.co.uk

Girton (1936)
Dodford Lane, Girton CB3 0QE
(01223) 276169
(01223) 277150
info@girtongolf.co.uk
Miss VM Webb
www.girtongolf.co.uk

The Gog Magog (1901)
Shelford Bottom, Cambridge CB22 3AB
(01223) 247626
(01223) 414990
secretary@gogmagog.co.uk
Mr K Mader
www.gogmagog.co.uk

Hemingford Abbots Golf Club (1991)
Proprietary
New Farm Lodge, Cambridge Road, Hemingford Abbots, Cambs PE18 9HQ
(01480) 495000
(01480) 496000
RD Paton
www.astroman.co.uk

Heydon Grange G&CC (1994)
Heydon, Royston SG8 7NS
(01763) 208988
(01763) 208926
enquiries@heydongrange.co.uk
S Akhtar
www.heydongrange.co.uk

Lakeside Lodge (1992)
Public & Proprietary
Fen Road, Pidley, Huntingdon PE28 3DF
(01487) 740540
(01487) 740852
info@lakeside-lodge.co.uk
Mrs J Hopkins
www.lakeside-lodge.co.uk

March (1922)
Frogs Abbey, Grange Rd, March PE15 0YH
(01354) 652364
secretary@marchgolfclub.co.uk
M Simpson
www.marchgolfclub.co.uk

Menzies Cambridgeshire (1974)
Proprietary
Bar Hill, Cambridge CB23 8EU
(01954) 780098
(01954) 780010
cambridge.golfpro@menzieshotels.co.uk
Tom Turner (Golf Ops Mgr)
www.menzieshotels.co.uk

New Malton (1993)
Proprietary/Members/
Malton Lane, Meldreth, Royston SG8 6PE
(01763) 262200
(01763) 262209
info@newmaltongolf.co.uk
Brian Mudge (Professional)
www.newmaltongolf.co.uk

Old Nene G&CC (1992)
Muchwood Lane, Bodsey, Ramsey PE26 2XQ
(01487) 815622
(01487) 813519
george.stoneman@virgin.net

Orton Meadows (1987)
Public
Ham Lane, Peterborough PE2 5UU
(01733) 237478
omgc@btinternet.com
WL Stocks (01733) 237478
www.omgc.co.uk

Peterborough Milton (1937)
Milton Ferry, Peterborough PE6 7AG
(01733) 380489
(01733) 380489
admin@pmgc.org.uk
Andy Izod (01733) 380489
www.pmgc.org.uk

Ramsey (1964)
4 Abbey Terrace, Ramsey, Huntingdon PE26 1DD
(01487) 812600
(01487) 815746
admin@ramseyclub.co.uk
John Bufton
www.ramseyclub.co.uk

St Ives (1923)
Needingworth Road, St Ives PE27 6NB
☎ **(01480) 499920 Ext 4**
Fax (01480) 301489
✉ manager@stivesgolfclub.co.uk
✍ Mike Kjenstad (01480) 499920 Ext 4
🌐 www.stivesgolfclub.co.uk

St Neots (1890)
Crosshall Road, St Neots PE19 7GE
☎ **(01480) 472363**
Fax (01480) 472363
✉ office@stneots-golfclub.co.uk
✍ M.V.Truswell
🌐 www.stneots-golfclub.co.uk

Stilton Oaks (1997)
Proprietary
High Street, Stilton, Cambridgeshire PE7 3RB
☎ **(01733) 245233**
✍ Mr D Darke (Mgr)

Thorney Golf Centre (1991)
Public
English Drove, Thorney, Peterborough PE6 0TJ
☎ **(01733) 270570**
Fax (01733) 270842
✉ info@thorneygolfcentre.com
✍ Jane Hind
🌐 www.thorneygolfcentre.com

Thorpe Wood (1975)
Pay and play
Nene Parkway, Peterborough PE3 6SE
☎ **(01733) 267701**
Fax (01733) 332774
✉ enquiries@thorpewoodgolfcourse.co.uk
✍ R Palmer
🌐 www.thorpewoodgolfcourse.co.uk

Tydd St Giles Golf & Leisure Estate (1993)
Proprietary
Kirkgate, Tydd St Giles, Cambridgeshire PE13 5NZ
☎ **(01945) 871007**
✉ enquiries@tyddgolf.com
✍ Daniel Newell
🌐 www.pureleisuregroup.com

Waterbeach (1968)
Public
Waterbeach Barracks, Waterbeach, Cambridge CB5 9PA
☎ **(01223) 441199 (Sec)**
Fax (01223) 204636
✉ waterbeach.golfclub@btconnect.com
✍ Maj (Retd) DA Hornby (Hon)
🌐 www.waterbeachgolfclub.co.uk

Channel Islands

Alderney
Route des Carrieres, Alderney GY9 3YD
☎ **(01481) 822835**
Fax (01481) 823609

La Grande Mare (1994)
Proprietary
Vazon Bay, Castel, Guernsey GY5 7LL
☎ **(01481) 253544**
Fax (01481) 255194
✉ golf@lagrandemare.com
✍ N Graham
🌐 www.lagrandemare.com

Les Mielles G&CC (1994)
Public
St Ouens Bay, Jersey JE3 7FQ
☎ **(01534) 482787**
Fax (01534) 485414
✉ golf@lesmielles.co.je
✍ J Le Brun (Golf Dir)
🌐 www.lesmielles.com

La Moye (1902)
La Moye, St Brelade, Jersey JE3 8GQ
☎ **(01534) 743401**
Fax (01534) 747289
✉ secretary@lamoyegolfclub.co.uk
✍ Sue Biard
🌐 www.lamoyegolfclub.co.uk

Les Ormes (1996)
Mont à la Brune, St Brelade, Jersey JE3 8FL
☎ **(01534) 497000**
Fax (01534) 499122
✉ reception@lesormesjersey.co.uk
✍ M Harris (01534) 497015
🌐 www.lesormes.je

Royal Guernsey (1890)
L'Ancresse, Guernsey GY3 5BY
☎ **(01481) 246523**
Fax (01481) 243960
✉ clubmanager@royalguernseygolfclub.com
✍ Roy Bushby
🌐 www.royalguernseygolfclub.com

Royal Jersey (1878)
Grouville, Jersey JE3 9BD
☎ **(01534) 854416**
✉ thesecretary@royaljersey.com
✍ DJ Attwood
🌐 www.royaljersey.com

St Clements (1925)
Public
St Clements, Jersey JE2 6QN
☎ **(01534) 721938**
Fax (01534) 721938
✉ manager@stclementsgolfandsportscentre.co.uk

St Pierre Park (1986)
Rohais, St Peter Port, Guernsey GY1 1FD
☎ **(01481) 727039**
Fax (01481) 712041
✉ golf@stpierrepark.co.uk
✍ James Child
🌐 www.stpierreparkgolf.co.uk

Wheatlands Golf Club (2004)
Off Old Beaumont Hill, St Peter, Jersey JE3 7ED
☎ **(01534) 888877**
Fax (01534) 769880
✉ info@wheatlandsjersey.com
🌐 www.wheatlandsgolf.com

Cheshire

Alder Root (1993)
Proprietary
Alder Root Lane, Winwick, Warrington WA2 8RZ
☎ **(01925) 291919**
Fax (01925) 291961
✉ office@alderrootgolfclub.com
✍ E Lander
🌐 www.alderroot.com

Alderley Edge (1907)
Brook Lane, Alderley Edge SK9 7RU
☎ **(01625) 586200**
✉ office@aegc.co.uk
✍ Club Administrator, 01625 586200 Option 1
🌐 www.aegc.co.uk

Aldersey Green (1993)
Proprietary
Aldersey, Chester CH3 9EH
☎ **(01829) 782157**
✉ bradburygolf@aol.com
🌐 alderseygreengolfclub.co.uk

Altrincham Municipal (1893)
Public
Stockport Road, Timperley, Altrincham WA15 7LP
☎ **(0161) 928 0761**
✍ C J Schofield 0161 861 0201
🌐 www.altrinchamgolfclub.org

Alvaston Hall (1992)
Proprietary
Middlewich Road, Nantwich CW5 6PD
☎ **(01270) 628473**
Fax (01270) 623395

Antrobus (1993)
Proprietary
Foggs Lane, Antrobus, Northwich CW9 6JQ
☎ **(01925) 730890**
✍ Vacant
🌐 www.antrobusgolfclub.co.uk

Ashton-on-Mersey (1897)
Church Lane, Sale M33 5QQ
☎ **(0161) 976 4390 (Clubhouse)**
Fax (0161) 976 4390
✉ golf.aomgc@btconnect.com
✍ R Coppock (0161) 976 4390
🌐 www.aomgc.co.uk

Astbury (1922)
Peel Lane, Astbury, Congleton CW12 4RE
☎ **(01260) 272772**
Fax (01260) 276420
✉ admin@astburygolfclub.com
✍ P Bentley (01260) 272772
🌐 www.astburygolfclub.com

Birchwood (1979)
Kelvin Close, Birchwood, Warrington WA3 7PB
☎ **(01925) 818819, Pro Shop (01925) 225216**
Fax (01925) 822403
✉ enquiries@birchwoodgolfclub.co.uk

For key to symbols see page 725

✍ A Harper (Facilities Mgr)
🖹 www.birchwoodgolfclub.co.uk

Bramall Park (1894)
20 Manor Road, Bramhall, Stockport SK7 3LY
☎ **(0161) 485 3119 (Clubhouse)**
🖷 (0161) 485 7101
✉ secretary@bramallparkgolfclub.co.uk
✍ D E Shardlow (Hon Sec) (0161) 485 7101
🖹 www.bramallparkgolfclub.co.uk

Bramhall (1905)
Ladythorn Road, Bramhall, Stockport SK7 2EY
☎ **(0161) 439 6092**
🖷 (0161) 439 6092
✉ office@bramhallgolfclub.com
✍ D O'Brien (Hon) (0161) 439 6092
🖹 www.bramhallgolfclub.com

Carden Park Hotel Golf Resort & Spa
Chester CH3 9DQ
☎ **(01829) 731534**
🖷 (01829) 731599
✉ reservations.carden@devere-hotels.com
✍ K Proctor (01829) 731000
🖹 www.cardenpark.co.uk

Cheadle (1885)
Shiers Drive, Cheadle Road, Cheadle SK8 1HW
☎ **(0161) 491 4452**
✉ cheadlegolfclub@msn.com
✍ Mrs Vera Moore
🖹 www.cheadlegolfclub.com

Chester (1901)
Curzon Park, Chester CH4 8AR
☎ **(01244) 677760**
✉ secretary@chestergolfclub.co.uk
✍ Mark J Williams (01244) 677760
🖹 www.chestergc.co.uk

Congleton (1898)
Biddulph Road, Congleton CW12 3LZ
☎ **(01260) 273540**
🖷 (01260) 290902
✉ congletongolfclub@btconnect.com
✍ D Lancake
🖹 www.congletongolf.co.uk

Crewe (1911)
Fields Road, Haslington, Crewe CW1 5TB
☎ **(01270) 584227 (Steward)**
🖷 (01270) 256482
✉ secretary@crewegolfclub.co.uk
✍ H Taylor (01270) 584099
🖹 www.crewegolfclub.co.uk

Davenport (1913)
Worth Hall, Middlewood Road, Poynton SK12 1TS
☎ **(01625) 876951**
🖷 (01625) 877489
✉ admin@davenportgolf.co.uk
✍ JC Souter (01625) 876951
🖹 www.davenportgolf.co.uk

Delamere Forest (1910)
Station Road, Delamere, Northwich CW8 2JE
☎ **(01606) 883800**
✉ delamere@btconnect.com
info@delameregolf.co.uk
✍ M Towers (01606) 883800
🖹 www.delameregolf.co.uk

Disley (1889)
Stanley Hall Lane, Disley, Stockport SK12 2JX
☎ **(01663) 764001**
✉ secretary@disleygolfclub.co.uk
✍ Howard Orton
🖹 www.disleygolfclub.co.uk

Dukinfield (1913)
Yew Tree Lane, Dukinfield SK16 5GF
☎ **(0161) 338 2340**
🖷 (0161) 303 0205
✉ secretary@dukinfieldgolfclub.co.uk
✍ K Marsh (0161) 338 2340
🖹 www.dukinfieldgolfclub.co.uk

Dunham Forest G&CC (1961)
Oldfield Lane, Altrincham WA14 4TY
☎ **(0161) 928 2605**
🖷 (0161) 929 8975
✉ enquiries@dunhamforest.com
✍ Mrs A Woolf
🖹 www.dunhamforest.com

Eaton (1965)
Guy Lane, Waverton, Chester CH3 7PH
☎ **(01244) 335885**
🖷 (01244) 335782
✉ office@eatongolfclub.co.uk
✍ K Brown
🖹 www.eatongolfclub.co.uk

Ellesmere Port (1971)
Public
Chester Road, Childer Thornton, South Wirral CH66 1QF
☎ **(0151) 339 7689**

Frodsham (1990)
Simons Lane, Frodsham WA6 6HE
☎ **(01928) 732159**
🖷 (01928) 734070
✉ paulw@frodshamgolf.co.uk
✍ El Roylance
🖹 www.frodshamgolf.co.uk

Gatley (1912)
Waterfall Farm, Styal Road, Heald Green, Cheadle SK8 3TW
☎ **(0161) 437 2091**
✉ secretary@gatleygolfclub.com
✍ Michael J Coffey
🖹 www.gatleygolfclub.com

Gorstyhill Golf Club
Wychwood Village, Weston, Crewe, Cheshire CW2 5TD
☎ **(01270) 829166**
✉ info@gorstyhillgolf.co.uk
🖹 www.gorstyhillgolf.co.uk

Hale (1903)
Rappax Road, Hale, Altrincham WA15 0NU
☎ **(0161) 980 4225**
✉ secretary@halegolfclub.com
✍ C E J Wright (Hon Sec)
🖹 www.halegolfclub.com

Hartford Golf Club (2000)
Burrow Hill, Hartford, Cheshire CW8 3AP
☎ **(01606) 871162**
🖷 (01606) 872182
✉ info@hartfordgolf.co.uk
🖹 www.hartfordgolf.co.uk

Hazel Grove (1913)
Buxton Road, Hazel Grove, Stockport SK7 6LU
☎ **(0161) 483 3978 (Office)**
🖷 (0161) 483 3978
✉ secretary@hazelgrovegolfclub.com
✍ Jane Hill (0161) 483 3978 Opt 4
🖹 www.hazelgrovegolfclub.com

Heaton Moor (1892)
Mauldeth Road, Heaton Mersey, Stockport SK4 3NX
☎ **(0161) 432 2134**
🖷 (0161) 432 2134
✉ heatonmoorgolfclub@yahoo.co.uk
✍ D Linsley
🖹 www.heatonmoorgolfclub.co.uk

Helsby (1901)
Tower's Lane, Helsby WA6 0JB
☎ **(01928) 722021**
🖷 (01928) 726816
✉ secretary@helsbygolfclub.org
✍ C A Stubbs
🖹 www.helsbygolfclub.org

Heyrose (1989)
Proprietary
Budworth Road, Tabley, Knutsford WA16 0HZ
☎ **(01565) 733664**
🖷 (01565) 734578
✉ info@heyrosegolfclub.com
✍ Mrs H Marsh
🖹 www.heyrosegolfclub.com

High Legh Park Golf Club
Pay and play
Warrington Road, High Legh, Knutsford, Cheshire WA16 0WA
☎ **(01565) 830888**
🖷 (01565) 830999
✉ info@highleghpark.com
✍ Martin Cooper (Course Director)
🖹 www.highleghpark.com

Houldsworth (1910)
Houldsworth Park, Houldsworth Street, Reddish, Stockport SK5 6BN
☎ **(0161) 442 1712**
🖷 (0161) 947 9678
✉ houldsworthsecretary@hotmail.co.uk
✍ K Smith (Sec) (0161) 442 1712
🖹 www.houldsworthgolfclub.co.uk

For key to symbols see page 725

Knights Grange (1983)
Public
Grange Lane, Winsford CW7 2PT
☎ **(01606) 552780**
✉ golf@brioleisure.org
✍ Mrs P Littler (Mgr)

Knutsford (1891)
Mereheath Lane, Knutsford WA16 6HS
☎ **(01565) 633355**
✉ secretary@knutsfordgolf.com
✍ Stuart Blake
▤ www.knutsfordgolf.com

Leigh (1906)
Kenyon Hall, Broseley Lane, Culcheth, Warrington WA3 4BG
☎ **(01925) 763130**
🖷 (01925) 765097
✉ golf@leighgolf.fsnet.co.uk
✍ Antony O'Neill (01925) 762943
▤ www.leighgolf.co.uk

Lymm (1907)
Whitbarrow Road, Lymm WA13 9AN
☎ **(01925) 755020**
🖷 (01925) 755020
✉ lymmgolfclub@btconnect.com
✍ A Scully
▤ www.lymm-golf-club.co.uk

Macclesfield (1889)
The Hollins, Macclesfield SK11 7EA
☎ **(01625) 423227**
🖷 (01625) 260061
✉ secretary@maccgolfclub.co.uk
✍ B Littlewood
▤ www.maccgolfclub.co.uk

Malkins Bank Golf Course (1980)
Public
Betchton Road, Malkins Bank, Sandbach CW11 4XN
☎ **(01270) 765931/767878 (Pro shop/Clubhous**
🖷 (01270) 764730
✉ proshop@malkinsbankgolfclub.co.uk
✍ Tony Minshall (Director of Golf)
▤ www.malkinsbankgolfclub.co.uk

Marple (1892)
Barnsfold Road, Hawk Green, Marple, Stockport SK6 7EL
☎ **(0161) 427 2311 Ext 1**
🖷 (0161) 427 2311
✉ secretary@marple-golf-club.co.uk
✍ W Hibbert (0161) 427 2311/427 9525
▤ www.marplegolfclub.co.uk

Mellor & Townscliffe (1894)
Tarden, Gibb Lane, Mellor, Stockport SK6 5NA
☎ **(0161) 427 9700 (Clubhouse)**
🖷 (0161) 427 9700
✍ JV Dixon (0161) 427 2208
▤ www.mellorgolf.co.uk

Mere G&CC (1934)
Chester Road, Mere, Knutsford WA16 6LJ
☎ **(01565) 830155**
🖷 (01565) 830713
✉ sales@meregolf.co.uk
✍ P Whitehead
▤ www.meregolf.co.uk

Mersey Valley (1995)
Proprietary
Warrington Road, Bold Heath, Widnes WA8 3XL
☎ **(0151) 424 6060**
🖷 (0151) 257 9097
✉ chrismgerrard@yahoo.co.uk
✍ RM Bush (Man Dir)
▤ www.merseyvalleygolfclub.co.uk

Mobberley (1996)
Burleyhurst Lane, Mobberley, Knutsford WA16 7JZ
☎ **(01565) 880188**
🖷 (01565) 880178
✉ info@mobgolfclub.co.uk
✍ Gary Donnison (Golf Director)
▤ www.mobgolfclub.co.uk

Mollington Grange (1999)
Townfield Lane, Mollington, Chester CH1 6NJ
☎ **(01244) 851185**
🖷 (01244) 851349
✉ info@mollingtongolfclub.co.uk
✍ Ray Stringer
▤ www.mollingtongolfclub.co.uk

Mottram Hall Hotel (1991)
Proprietary
Wilmslow Road, Mottram St Andrew, Prestbury SK10 4QT
☎ **(01625) 820064**
🖷 (01625) 829284
✉ mhgolf@devere-hotels.com
✍ Tim Hudspith (Head Golf & Leisure)
▤ www.deveregolf.co.uk

Peover (1996)
Proprietary
Plumley Moor Road, Lower Peover WA16 9SE
☎ **(01565) 723337**
🖷 (01565) 723311
✉ mail@peovergolfclub.co.uk
✍ B Pearson (Gen Mgr)
▤ www.peovergolfclub.co.uk

Portal G&CC (1992)
Cobblers Cross Lane, Tarporley CW6 0DJ
☎ **(01829) 733933**
🖷 (01829) 733928
✉ enquiries@portalgolf.co.uk
▤ www.portalgolf.co.uk

Portal Premier (1990)
Forest Road, Tarporley CW6 0JA
☎ **(01829) 733884**
🖷 (01829) 733666
✉ enquiries.premier@portalgolf.co.uk
▤ www.portalgolf.co.uk

Poulton Park (1978)
Dig Lane, Cinnamon Brow, Warrington WA2 0SH
☎ **(01925) 812034/822802**
🖷 (01925) 822802
✉ secretary@poultonparkgolfclub.co.uk
▤ www.poultonparkgolfclub.co.uk

Prestbury (1920)
Macclesfield Road, Prestbury, Macclesfield SK10 4BJ
☎ **(01625) 828241**
🖷 (01625) 828241
✉ office@prestburygolfclub.com
✍ N Young (Gen Mgr)
▤ www.prestburygolfclub.com

Pryors Hayes (1993)
Proprietary
Willington Road, Oscroft, Tarvin CH3 8NL
☎ **(01829) 741250**
🖷 (01829) 749077
✉ info@pryors-hayes.co.uk
✍ JM Quinn
▤ www.pryorshayes.com

Queens Park (1985)
Public
Queens Park Drive, Crewe CW2 7SB
☎ **(01270) 662378**

Reaseheath (1987)
1 Ash Grove, Nantwich, Cheshire CW5 7DQ
☎ **(01270) 625131**
🖷 (01270) 625665
✉ j.soddy@sky.com
✍ John Soddy (01270) 629869
▤ www.reaseheath.ac.uk

Reddish Vale (1912)
Southcliffe Road, Reddish, Stockport SK5 7EE
☎ **(0161) 480 2359**
🖷 (0161) 480 2359
✉ admin@rvgc.co.uk
✍ D J Sanders
▤ www.rvgc.co.uk

Ringway (1909)
Hale Mount, Hale Road, Hale Barns, Altrincham WA15 8SW
☎ **(0161) 980 2630**
🖷 (0161) 980 4414
✉ fiona@ringwaygolfclub.co.uk
✍ Ms F Cornelius
▤ www.ringwaygolfclub.co.uk

Romiley (1897)
Goosehouse Green, Romiley, Stockport SK6 4LJ
☎ **(0161) 430 2392**
✉ office@romileygolfclub.org
✍ C D Haworth
▤ www.romileygolfclub.org

Runcorn (1909)
Clifton Road, Runcorn WA7 4SU
☎ **(01928) 572093 (Members)**
🖷 (01928) 574214
✉ secretary@runcorngolfclub.co.uk

For key to symbols see page 725

G H Mayne (01928) 574214
www.runcorngolfclub.co.uk

Sale (1913)
Sale Lodge, Golf Road, Sale M33 2XU
(0161) 973 1638
(0161) 962 4217
mail@salegolfclub.com
CJ Boyes (Hon Sec)
www.salegolfclub.com

Sandbach (1895)
Middlewich Road, Sandbach, Cheshire CW11 9EA
(01270) 762117
sec@sandbachgolfclub.co.uk
D Ludley
www.sandbachgolfclub.co.uk

Sandiway (1920)
Chester Road, Sandiway CW8 2DJ
(01606) 883247
information@sandiwaygolf.co.uk
Yvonne Bould (01606) 880811
www.sandiwaygolf.co.uk

Stamford (1901)
Oakfield House, Huddersfield Road, Stalybridge SK15 3PY
(01457) 832126
admin@stamfordgolfclub.co.uk
J Kitchen
www.stamfordgolfclub.co.uk

Stockport (1905)
Offerton Road, Offerton, Stockport SK2 5HL
(0161) 427 8369
(0161) 427 8369
info@stockportgolf.co.uk
J O Bolt
www.stockportgolf.co.uk

Styal (1994)
Proprietary
Station Road, Styal SK9 4JN
(01625) 531359 (Bookings)
(01625) 416373
gtraynor@styalgolf.co.uk
G Traynor
www.styalgolf.co.uk

Sutton Hall (1995)
Proprietary
Aston Lane, Sutton Weaver, Runcorn WA7 3ED
(01928) 790747
(01928) 759174
info@suttonhallgolf.co.uk
M Faulkner
www.suttonhallgolf.co.uk

The Tytherington Club (1986)
Macclesfield SK10 2JP
(01625) 506000
(01625) 506040
tytherington.events@theclubcompany.com
James Gathercole
www.theclubcompany.com

Upton-by-Chester (1934)
Upton Lane, Chester CH2 1EE
(01244) 381183
(01244) 376955
admin@uptongc.com
Anne Jennings (01244) 381183
www.uptonbychestergolfclub.co.uk

Vale Royal Abbey (1998)
Proprietary
Whitegate, Northwich CW8 2BA
(01606) 301291
(01606) 301784
secretary@vra.co.uk
Ian Embury
www.vra.co.uk

Vicars Cross (1939)
Tarvin Road, Great Barrow, Chester CH3 7HN
(01244) 335174
(01244) 335686
manager@vicarscrossgolf.co.uk
Mrs K Hunt
www.vicarscrossgolf.co.uk

Walton Hall (1972)
Public
Warrington Road, Higher Walton, Warrington WA4 5LU
(01925) 266775
theclub@waltonhallgolfclub.co.uk
John Diprose
www.waltonhallgolfclub.co.uk

Warrington (1903)
Hill Warren, London Road, Appleton WA4 5HR
(01925) 261775
(01925) 265933
secretary@warringtongolfclub.co.uk
D S Macphee (01925) 261775
www.warringtongolfclub.co.uk

Werneth Low (1912)
Werneth Low Road, Gee Cross, Hyde SK14 3AF
(0161) 368 2503
(0161) 320 0053

Widnes (1924)
Highfield Road, Widnes WA8 7DT
(0151) 424 2995
(0151) 495 2849
office@widnesgolfclub.co.uk
Mrs Nicola Ogburn
www.widnesgolfclub.co.uk

Wilmslow (1889)
Great Warford, Mobberley, Knutsford WA16 7AY
(01565) 872148
(01565) 872172
admin@wilmslowgolfclub.co.uk
Keith Melia (Gen Mgr)
www.wilmslowgolfclub.co.uk

Woodside (1999)
Proprietary
Knutsford Road, Cranage, Holmes Chapel, Cheshire CW4 8HJ
(01477) 532388
(01477) 549207
info@woodsidegolf.co.uk
Marie-Therese Whelan
www.woodsidegolf.co.uk

Cornwall

Bowood Park (1992)
Valley Truckle, Lanteglos, Camelford PL32 9RF
(01840) 213017
(01840) 212622
info@bowood-park.co.uk
Gerald Simmons
www.bowood-park.co.uk

Bude & North Cornwall (1891)
Burn View, Bude EX23 8DA
(01288) 352006
(01288) 356855
secretary@budegolf.co.uk
Mr I V Roddy (Mgr/Sec)
www.budegolf.co.uk

Budock Vean Hotel Golf & Country Club (1932)
Mawnan Smith, Falmouth TR11 5LG
(01326) 252102
(01326) 250892
relax@budockvean.co.uk
Keith Rashleigh (01326) 377091

Cape Cornwall G&CC (1990)
St Just, Penzance TR19 7NL
(01736) 788611
(01736) 788611
golf@capecornwall.com
Ben Ludwell (Mgr)
www.capecornwall.com

Carlyon Bay (1926)
Proprietary
Carlyon Bay, St Austell PL25 3RD
(01726) 814250
(01726) 814250
golf@carlyonbay.com
P Martin
www.carlyongolf.com

China Fleet CC (1991)
Saltash PL12 6LJ
(01752) 848668
(01752) 848456
golf@china-fleet.co.uk
Mrs L Goddard
www.china-fleet.co.uk

Falmouth (1894)
Proprietary
Swanpool Road, Falmouth TR11 5BQ
(01326) 311262/314296
(01326) 211447
clubsec@falmouthgolfclub.com
Steve Burrows (Director)
www.falmouthgolfclub.com

Isles of Scilly (1904)
Carn Morval, St Mary's, Isles of Scilly TR21 0NF
(01720) 422692

✉ iosgcsec@googlemail.com
✍ Peter Leahy (Hon Sec)
🖹 www.islesofscillygolfclub.co.uk

Killiow (1987)
Proprietary
Killiow, Kea, Truro TR3 6AG
☎ **(01872) 270246**
🖷 (01872) 240915
✉ killiowsec@yahoo.co.uk

Lanhydrock Hotel & Golf Club (1991)
Proprietary
Lostwithiel Road, Bodmin PL30 5AQ
☎ **(01208) 262570**
🖷 (01208) 262579
✉ info@lanhydrockhotel.com
✍ G Bond (Dir)
🖹 www.lanhydrockhotel.com

Launceston (1927)
St Stephen, Launceston PL15 8HF
☎ **(01566) 773442**
🖷 (01566) 777506
✉ secretary@launcestongolfclub.co.uk
✍ A Creber
🖹 www.launcestongolfclub.co.uk

Looe (1933)
Bin Down, Looe PL13 1PX
☎ **(01503) 240239**
🖷 (01503) 240864
✉ enquiries@looegolfclub.co.uk
✍ M D Joy (Hon)
🖹 www.looegolfclub.co.uk

Lostwithiel G&CC (1990)
Lower Polscoe, Lostwithiel PL22 0HQ
☎ **(01208) 873550**
🖷 (01208) 873479
✉ reception@golf-hotel.co.uk
✍ D Higman
🖹 www.golf-hotel.co.uk

Merlin (1991)
Proprietary
Mawgan Porth, Newquay TR8 4DN
☎ **(01841) 540222**
🖷 (01841) 541031
✉ play@merlingolfcourse.co.uk
✍ Mr Richard Burrough
🖹 www.merlingolfcourse.co.uk

Mullion (1895)
Cury, Helston TR12 7BP
☎ **(01326) 240276**
🖷 (01326) 241527
✉ secretary@mulliongolfclub.plus.com
✍ R Griffiths (01326) 240685
🖹 www.mulliongolfclub.co.uk

Newquay (1890)
Tower Road, Newquay TR7 1LT
☎ **(01637) 872091/874354 (clubhouse/office)**
🖷 (01637) 874066
✉ newquaygolf@btconnect.com
✍ P F Batty (Sec/Mgr)
🖹 www.newquaygolfclub.co.uk

Perranporth (1927)
Budnic Hill, Perranporth TR6 0AB
☎ **(01872) 572454**
✉ secretary@perranporthgolfclub.co.uk
✍ DC Mugford
🖹 www.perranporthgolfclub.co.uk

Porthpean (1992)
Proprietary
Porthpean, St Austell PL26 6AY
☎ **(01726) 64613**
🖷 (01726) 64613
✉ porthpeangolfclub@hotmail.co.uk
✍ Michelle Baily (Mgr)
🖹 www.porthpeangolfclub.co.uk

Praa Sands Golf and Country Club (1971)
Public
Praa Sands, Penzance TR20 9TQ
☎ **(01736) 763445**
🖷 (01736) 763741
✉ praasands2@haulfryn.co.uk
🖹 www.praa-sands.com

Radnor (1988)
Proprietary
Radnor Road, Treleigh, Redruth, Cornwall TR16 5EL
☎ **(01209) 211059**
✉ jonradnor@btconnect.com
✍ Jon Barber
🖹 www.radnorgolfandleisure.co.uk

Roserrow (1996)
Proprietary
St Minver, Wadebridge PL27 6QT
☎ **(01208) 863000**
🖷 (01208) 863002
✉ info@roserrow.co.uk
✍ Hayley Lane
🖹 www.roserrow.co.uk

St Austell (1911)
Tregongeeves Lane, St Austell PL26 7DS
☎ **(01726) 74756**
🖷 (01726) 71978
✉ office@staustellgolf.co.uk
✍ P Clemo
🖹 www.staustellgolf.co.uk

St Enodoc (1890)
Rock, Wadebridge PL27 6LD
☎ **(01208) 863216**
🖷 (01208) 862976
✉ enquiries@st-enodoc.co.uk
✍ T D Clagett
🖹 www.st-enodoc.co.uk

St Kew (1993)
Proprietary
St Kew Highway, Wadebridge, Bodmin PL30 3EF
☎ **(01208) 841500**
🖷 (01208) 841500
✉ stkewgolf@btconnect.com

Tehidy Park (1922)
Camborne TR14 0HH
☎ **(01209) 842208**
🖷 (01209) 842208
✉ secretary-manager@tehidyparkgolfclub.co.uk
✍ I J Veale (Sec/Mgr)
🖹 www.tehidyparkgolfclub.co.uk

Tregenna Castle Hotel (1982)
St Ives TR26 2DE
☎ **(01736) 795254**
🖷 (01736) 796066
✉ hotel@tregenna-castle.co.uk
🖹 www.tregenna-castle.co.uk

Treloy (1991)
Treloy, Newquay TR8 4JN
☎ **(01637) 878554**
🖹 www.treloygolfclub.co.uk

Trethorne (1991)
Kennards House, Launceston PL15 8QE
☎ **(01566) 86903**
🖷 (01566) 86929
✉ gen@trethornegolfclub.com
🖹 www.trethornegolfclub.com

Trevose (1924)
Constantine Bay, Padstow PL28 8JB
☎ **(01841) 520208**
🖷 (01841) 521057
✉ info@trevose-gc.co.uk
🖹 www.trevose-gc.co.uk

Truro (1937)
Treliske, Truro TR1 3LG
☎ **(01872) 278684**
🖷 (01872) 225972
✉ trurogolfclub@tiscali.co.uk
✍ L Booker (Sec/Mgr)
🖹 www.trurogolf.co.uk

West Cornwall (1889)
Lelant, St Ives TR26 3DZ
☎ **(01736) 753401**
✉ secretary@westcornwallgolfclub.co.uk
✍ GM Evans
🖹 www.westcornwallgolfclub.co.uk

Whitsand Bay Hotel (1906)
Portwrinkle, Torpoint PL11 3BU
☎ **(01503) 230276 (Clubhouse)**
🖷 (01503) 230329
🖹 www.whitsandbayhotel.co.uk

Cumbria

Alston Moor (1906)
The Hermitage, Alston CA9 3DB
☎ **(01434) 381675**
✉ secretary@alstonmoorgolfclub.org.uk
✍ Paul Parkin (01434) 381704
🖹 www.alstonmoorgolfclub.org.uk

Appleby (1903)
Brackenber Moor, Appleby CA16 6LP
☎ **(017683) 51432**
🖷 (017683) 52773
✉ enquiries@applebygolfclub.co.uk
✍ JMF Doig (Hon)
🖹 www.applebygolfclub.co.uk

For key to symbols see page 725

Barrow (1922)
Rakesmoor Lane, Hawcoat, Barrow-in-Furness LA14 4QB
☎ **(01229) 825444**
✉ barrowgolf@supanet.com
✍ S G Warbrick (Hon)
▤ www.barrowgolfclub.co.uk

Brampton (Talkin Tarn) (1909)
Tarn Road, Brampton CA8 1HN
☎ **(0169) 772255**
℻ (0169) 7741487
✉ secretary@bramptongolfclub.com
✍ I J Meldrum (01228) 520982
▤ www.bramptongolfclub.com

Brayton Park (1986)
Pay and play
The Garth, Home Farm, Brayton, Aspatria CA7 3SX
☎ **(01697) 323539**

Carlisle (1908)
Aglionby, Carlisle CA4 8AG
☎ **(01228) 513029**
℻ (01228) 513303
✉ secretary@carlislegolfclub.org
✍ Roger Johnson
▤ www.carlislegolfclub.org

Carus Green (1996)
Proprietary
Burneside Road, Kendal LA9 6EB
☎ **(01539) 721097**
℻ (01539) 721097
✉ info@carusgreen.co.uk
✍ G Curtin or W Dand
▤ www.carusgreen.co.uk

Casterton (1955)
Proprietary
Sedbergh Road, Casterton, Nr Kirkby Lonsdale LA6 2LA
☎ **(015242) 71592**
✉ castertongc@hotmail.com
✍ J & E Makinson (Props)
▤ www.castertongolf.co.uk

Cockermouth (1896)
Embleton, Cockermouth CA13 9SG
☎ **(017687) 76223/76941**
℻ (017687) 76941
✉ secretary@cockermouthgolf.co.uk
✍ RS Wimpress (01900) 825431
▤ www.cockermouthgolf.co.uk

Dalston Hall (1990)
Pay and play
Dalston Hall, Dalston, Carlisle CA5 7JX
☎ **(01228) 710165**
℻ (01228) 710165
✉ info@dalstonholidaypark.com
✍ PS Holder
▤ www.dalstonhallholidaypark.co.uk

The Dunnerholme Golf Club (1905)
Duddon Road, Askam-in-Furness LA16 7AW
☎ **(01229) 462675**
℻ (01229) 462675
✉ dunnerholmegolfclub@btinternet.com
✍ Lynda Preston (Sec)
▤ www.thedunnerholmegolfclub.co.uk

Eden (1992)
Proprietary
Crosby-on-Eden, Carlisle CA6 4RA
☎ **(01228) 573003**
℻ (01228) 818435
▤ www.edengolf.co.uk

Furness (1872)
Central Drive, Walney Island, Barrow-in-Furness LA14 3LN
☎ **(01229) 471232**
℻ (01229) 475100
✉ furnessgolfclub@chessbroadband.co.uk
✍ Mr R S Turner (Secretary)
▤ www.furnessgolfclub.co.uk

Grange Fell (1952)
Fell Road, Grange-over-Sands LA11 6HB
☎ **(015395) 32536**
✉ gfgc@etherway.net
✍ JG Park (015395) 58513

Grange-over-Sands (1919)
Meathop Road, Grange-over-Sands LA11 6QX
☎ **(015395) 33180**
℻ (015395) 33754
✉ office@grangegolfclub.com
✍ G Whitfield (015395) 33180
▤ www.grangegolfclub.co.uk

Haltwhistle (1967)
Wallend Farm, Greenhead, Carlisle CA8 7HN
☎ **(01697) 747367**
✍ Patrick Peace (Hon Sec)
▤ www.haltwhistlegolf.co.uk

Kendal (1891)
The Heights, Kendal LA9 4PQ
☎ **(01539) 723499 (Bookings)**
✉ secretary@kendalgolfclub.co.uk
✍ I Clancy (01539) 733708
▤ www.kendalgolfclub.co.uk

Keswick (1978)
Threlkeld Hall, Threlkeld, Keswick CA12 4SX
☎ **(017687) 79324**
℻ (017687) 79861
✉ secretary@keswickgolfclub.com
✍ May Lloyd (017687) 79324 ext 1
▤ www.keswickgolfclub.com

Kirkby Lonsdale (1906)
Scaleber Lane, Barbon, Kirkby Lonsdale LA6 2LJ
☎ **(015242) 76366**
℻ (015242) 76503
✉ info@kirkbylonsdalegolfclub.com
✍ D Towers (015242) 76365
▤ www.kirkbylonsdalegolfclub.com

Maryport (1905)
Bankend, Maryport CA15 6PA
☎ **(01900) 812605**
℻ (01900) 815626
✉ maryportgolfclub.co.uk
✍ Mrs L Hayton (01900) 815626

Penrith (1890)
Salkeld Road, Penrith CA11 8SG
☎ **(01768) 891919**
℻ (01768) 891919
✉ secretary@penrithgolfclub.co.uk
✍ S D Wright (01768) 891919
▤ www.penrithgolfclub.com

Seascale (1893)
Seascale CA20 1QL
☎ **(019467) 28202/28800**
℻ (019467) 28042
✉ seascalegolfclub@googlemail.com
▤ www.seascalegolfclub.co.uk

Sedbergh (1896)
Proprietary
Dent Road, Sedbergh LA10 5SS
☎ **(015396) 21551**
℻ (015396) 21827
✉ info@sedberghgolfclub.com
✍ Craig or Steve Gardner
▤ www.sedberghgolfclub.com

Silecroft (1903)
Silecroft, Millom LA18 4NX
☎ **(01229) 774250**
✉ sgcsecretary@hotmail.co.uk
✍ K Newton (01229) 770467
▤ www.silecroftgolfclub.co.uk

Silloth-on-Solway (1892)
Silloth, Wigton CA7 4BL
☎ **(016973) 31304**
℻ (016973) 31782
✉ office@sillothgolfclub.co.uk
✍ Alan Oliver
▤ www.sillothgolfclub.co.uk

Silverdale (1906)
Red Bridge Lane, Silverdale, Carnforth LA5 0SP
☎ **(01524) 701300**
℻ (01524) 701986
✉ info@silverdalegolfclub.co.uk
✍ Mr R A Whitaker (Sec) (01524) 702074
▤ www.silverdalegolfclub.co.uk

St Bees (1929)
Peckmill, Beach Road, St Bees CA27 0EJ
☎ **(01946) 820319**
✉ lhinde21@btinternet.com
✍ L Hinde
▤ www.stbeesgolfclub.org.uk

Stony Holme (1974)
Public
St Aidan's Road, Carlisle CA1 1LS
☎ **(01228) 625511**
✍ A McConnell (01228) 625511

Ulverston (1895)
Bardsea Park, Ulverston LA12 9QJ
☎ **(01229) 582824**

℻ (01229) 588910
✉ enquiries@ulverstongolf.co.uk
✍ Mr Charles Dent
🖥 www.ulverstongolf.co.uk

Windermere (1891)
Cleabarrow, Windermere LA23 3NB
☎ **(015394) 43123**
℻ (015394) 46370
✉ office@windermeregolfclub.co.uk
✍ Carol Slater (Sec/Mgr)
🖥 www.windermeregolfclub.co.uk

Workington (1893)
Branthwaite Road, Workington CA14 4SS
☎ **(01900) 603460**
✉ secretary@workingtongolfclub.com
✍ P Hoskin (Sec)
🖥 www.workingtongolfclub.com

Derbyshire

Alfreton (1892)
Oakerthorpe, Alfreton DE55 7LH
☎ **(01773) 832070**
🖥 www.alfretongolfclub.co.uk

Allestree Park (1949)
Public
Allestree Hall, Allestree, Derby DE22 2EU
☎ **(01332) 550616**
✉ mail@allestreeparkgolfclub.co.uk
✍ C Barker
🖥 www.allestreeparkgolfclub.co.uk

Ashbourne (1886)
Wyaston Road, Ashbourne DE6 1NB
☎ **(01335) 342078**
℻ (01335) 347937
✉ ashbournegc@tiscali.co.uk
✍ Andrew Smith
🖥 www.ashbournegolfclub.co.uk

Bakewell (1899)
Station Road, Bakewell DE4 1GB
☎ **(01629) 812307**
✉ administrator@bakewellgolfclub.co.uk
✍ Mr G Holmes
🖥 www.bakewellgolfclub.co.uk

Birch Hall
Sheffield Road, Unstone S18 5DH
☎ **(01246) 291979**

Bondhay (1991)
Bondhay Lane, Whitwell, Worksop S80 3EH
☎ **(01909) 723608**
℻ (01909) 720226
✉ enquiries@bondhaygolfclub.com
✍ M Hardisty (Mgr)
🖥 www.bondhaygolfclub.com

Brailsford (1994)
Proprietary
Pools Head Lane, Brailsford, Ashbourne DE6 3BU
☎ **(01335) 360096**
℻ (01335) 360077
✉ vivian.craig@clowes-developments.com
✍ T Payne (tpayne@talktalk.net)
🖥 www.brailsfordgolfcourse.co.uk

Breadsall Priory Hotel G&CC (1976)
Moor Road, Morley, Derby DE7 6DL
☎ **(01332) 836016**
℻ (01332) 836089
✉ mhrs.emags.golf@marriotthotels.com
✍ I Knox (Dir of Golf)
🖥 www.marriottgolf.co.uk

Broughton Heath (1988)
Proprietary
Bent Lane, Church Broughton DE65 5BA
☎ **(01283) 521235**
✉ info@broughtonheathgc.co.uk
🖥 www.broughtonheathgc.co.uk

Burton-on-Trent (1894)
43 Ashby Road East, Burton-on-Trent DE15 0PS
☎ **(01283) 544551**
✉ clubmanager@burtonontrentgolfclub.co.uk
✍ S A Dixon (01283) 544551
🖥 www.burtonontrentgolfclub.co.uk

Buxton & High Peak (1887)
Townend, Buxton SK17 7EN
☎ **(01298) 26263**
℻ (01298) 26333
✉ sec@bhpgc.co.uk
✍ Garry Bagguley (Sec)
🖥 www.bhpgc.co.uk

Cavendish (1925)
Watford Road, Buxton SK17 6XF
☎ **(01298) 79708**
℻ (01298) 79708
✉ admin@cavendishgolfclub.com
✍ S A Davis
🖥 www.cavendishgolfclub.com

Chapel-en-le-Frith (1905)
The Cockyard, Manchester Road, Chapel-en-le-Frith SK23 9UH
☎ **(01298) 812118**
℻ (01298) 814990
✉ info@chapelgolf.co.uk
✍ Denise Goldfinch (01298) 813943
🖥 www.chapelgolf.co.uk

Chesterfield (1897)
Walton, Chesterfield S42 7LA
☎ **(01246) 279256**
℻ (01246) 276622
✉ secretary@chesterfieldgolfclub.co.uk
✍ T H Glover
🖥 www.chesterfieldgolfclub.co.uk

Chevin (1894)
Duffield, Derby DE56 4EE
☎ **(01332) 841864**
℻ (01332) 844028
✉ secretary@chevingolf.co.uk
✍ M E Riley
🖥 www.chevingolf.co.uk

Derby (1923)
Public
Wilmore Road, Sinfin, Derby DE24 9HD
☎ **(01332) 766323**
✉ secretary@derbygolfclub.co.uk
✍ DP Anderson
🖥 www.derbygolfclub.co.uk

Erewash Valley (1905)
Stanton-by-Dale DE7 4QR
☎ **(0115) 932 3258**
℻ (0115) 944 0061
✉ secretary@erewashvalley.co.uk
✍ Andrew Burrows
🖥 www.erewashvalley.co.uk

Glossop & District (1894)
Sheffield Road, Glossop SK13 7PU
☎ **(01457) 865247 (Clubhouse)**
℻ (01457) 864003
✉ glossopgolfclub@talktalk.net
✍ Steve Mycio
🖥 www.glossopgolfclub.co.uk

Grassmoor Golf Centre (1990)
Proprietary
North Wingfield Road, Grassmoor, Chesterfield S42 5EA
☎ **(01246) 856044**
℻ (01246) 853486
✉ enquiries@grassmoorgolf.co.uk
✍ H Hagues (Club Manager)
🖥 www.grassmoorgolf.co.uk

Horsley Lodge (1990)
Proprietary
Smalley Mill Road, Horsley DE21 5BL
☎ **(01332) 780838**
℻ (01332) 781118
✉ richard@horsleylodge.co.uk
✍ Dennis Wake (07771) 874 882
🖥 www.horsleylodge.co.uk

Kedleston Park (1947)
Kedleston, Quarndon, Derby DE22 5JD
☎ **(01332) 840035**
℻ (01332) 840035
✉ secretary@kedlestonparkgolfclub.co.uk
✍ R Simpson (Gen Mgr)
🖥 www.kedlestonparkgolfclub.co.uk

Lafarge Golf Club (1985)
Lafarge Cement, Hope Works, Hope Valley, Derbyshire S33 6RP
☎ **(01433) 622315**
✍ DS Smith

Matlock (1906)
Chesterfield Road, Matlock Moor, Matlock DE4 5LZ
☎ **(01629) 582191**
℻ (01629) 582135
✉ secretary@matlockgolfclub.co.uk
✍ M Wain (01629) 582191 option 4
🖥 www.matlockgolfclub.co.uk

Maywood (1990)
Proprietary
Rushy Lane, Risley, Derby DE72 3SW
☎ **(0115) 939 2306**

For key to symbols see page 725

maywoodgolfclub@btinternet.com
WJ Cockeram (0115) 932 6772
www.maywoodgolfclub.com

Mickleover (1923)
Uttoxeter Road, Mickleover DE3 9AD
(01332) 516011 (Clubhouse)
(01332) 516011
secretary@mickleovergolfclub.com
www.mickleovergolfclub.com

New Mills (1907)
Shaw Marsh, New Mills, High Peak SK22 4QE
(01663) 743485
Margaret Palmer (01663) 744330 (Sec)
www.newmillsgolfclub.co.uk

Ormonde Fields (1926)
Nottingham Road, Codnor, Ripley DE5 9RG
(01773) 742987
(01773) 744848
info@ormondefieldsgolfclub.co.uk
K Constable
www.ormondefieldsgolfclub.co.uk

Shirland (1977)
Proprietary
Lower Delves, Shirland DE55 6AU
(01773) 834935
geofftowle@hotmail.com

Sickleholme (1898)
Bamford, Sheffield S33 0BH
(01433) 651306
(01433) 659498
sickleholme.gc@btconnect.com
PH Taylor (Mgr)
www.sickleholme.co.uk

Stanedge (1934)
Walton Hay Farm, Chesterfield S45 0LW
(01246) 566156
chrisshaw56@tiscali.co.uk
Mr Chris Shaw 0776 742 6584
www.stanedgegolfclub.co.uk

Devon

Ashbury (1991)
Higher Maddaford, Okehampton EX20 4NL
(01837) 55453
(01837) 55468
www.ashburyhotel.co.uk

Axe Cliff (1894)
Proprietary
Squires Lane, Axmouth, Seaton EX12 4AB
(01297) 21754
(01297) 24371
D.Quinn@axecliff.co.uk
www.axecliff.co.uk

Bigbury (1923)
Bigbury-on-Sea, South Devon TQ7 4BB
(01548) 810557
enquiries@bigburygolfclub.co.uk
Nigel Blenkarne (Director of Golf)
www.bigburygolfclub.com

Bovey Castle (1929)
Proprietary
North Bovey, Devon TQ13 8RE
(01647) 445009
(01647) 440961
richard.lewis@boveycastle.com
R Lewis
www.boveycastle.com

Bovey Tracey Golf Club (2006)
Pay and play
Monks Way, Bovey Tracey, Newton Abbot, Devon TQ13 9NG
(01626) 836464
tonyv.btgc@gmail.com
A Vincent (Sec)
www.boveytraceygolfclub.co.uk

Chulmleigh (1976)
Pay and play
Leigh Road, Chulmleigh EX18 7BL
(01769) 580519
(01769) 580519
chulmleighgolf@aol.com
RW Dow
www.chulmleighgolf.co.uk

Churston (1890)
Churston, Dartmouth Road, Brixham TQ5 0LA
(01803) 842751
(01803) 845738
manager@churstongolf.com
SR Bawden (01803) 842751
www.churstongolf.com

Dainton Park (1993)
Proprietary
Totnes Road, Ipplepen, Newton Abbot TQ12 5TN
(01803) 815000
(01803) 815001
info@daintonparkgolf.co.uk
Mr Daniel Wood
www.daintonparkgolf.co.uk

Dartmouth G&CC (1992)
Blackawton, Nr Dartmouth, Devon TQ9 7DE
(01803) 712686
(01803) 712628
info@dgcc.co.uk
J Waugh (Sec), A Chappell (Assist. Sec)
www.dgcc.co.uk

Dinnaton – McCaulays Health Club, Ivybridge Fitness & Golf (1989)
Ivybridge PL21 9HU
(01752) 892512
(01752) 698334
info@mccaulays.com
P Hendriksen
www.mccaulays.com

Downes Crediton (1976)
Hookway, Crediton EX17 3PT
(01363) 773025
(01363) 775060
golf@downescreditongc.co.uk
Robin Goodey (01363) 773025
www.downescreditongc.co.uk

East Devon (1902)
Links Road, Budleigh Salterton EX9 6DG
(01395) 443370
(01395) 445547
secretary@edgc.co.uk
J Reynolds (01395) 443370
www.edgc.co.uk

Elfordleigh Hotel G&CC (1932)
Proprietary
Colebrook, Plympton, Plymouth PL7 5EB
(01752) 348425
(01752) 344581
reception@elfordleigh.co.uk
Derek Mills (01752) 556205
www.elfordleigh.co.uk

Exeter G&CC (1895)
Countess Wear, Exeter EX2 7AE
(01392) 874139
(01392) 874914
golf@exetergcc.co.uk
Russell Mayne (Golf Manager)
www.exetergcc.com

Fingle Glen (1989)
Proprietary
Tedburn St Mary, Exeter EX6 6AF
(01647) 61817
(01647) 61135
mail@fingleglengolfhotel.co.uk
P Miliffe
www.fingleglengolfhotel.co.uk

Great Torrington (1895)
The Club House, Weare Trees, Torrington EX38 7EZ
(01805) 622229
(01805) 623878
torringtongolfclub@btconnect.com
Mr G S C Green
www.torringtongolfclub.co.uk

Hartland Forest (1980)
Hartland Forest Golf & Leisure Parc, Woolsery, Bideford EX39 5RA
(01237) 431777
hfgadmin@gmail.com
www.hartlandforestgolf.co.uk

Hele Park Golf Centre (1993)
Proprietary
Ashburton Road, Newton Abbot TQ12 6JN
(01626) 336060
(01626) 332661
info@heleparkgolf.co.uk
Wendy Stanbury
www.heleparkgolf.co.uk

Highbullen Hotel G&CC (1961)
Proprietary
Chittlehamholt, Umberleigh EX37 9HD
(01769) 540561
(01769) 540492
info@highbullen.co.uk

For key to symbols see page 725

✍ John Aryes (01769) 540664
🖥 www.highbullen.co.uk

Holsworthy (1937)
Killatree, Holsworthy EX22 6LP
☎ **(01409) 253177**
📠 (01409) 255393
✉ info@holsworthygolfclub.co.uk
✍ Mrs C F Harper
🖥 www.holsworthygolfclub.co.uk

Honiton (1896)
Middlehills, Honiton EX14 9TR
☎ **(01404) 44422**
✉ secretary@honitongolfclub.fsnet.co.uk
✍ Graham Burch (Administrator)
🖥 www.honitongolf club.co.uk

Hurdwick (1990)
Tavistock Hamlets, Tavistock PL19 0LL
☎ **(01822) 612746**
✉ info@hurdwickgolf.com
✍ Mr M J Wood (Mgr)
🖥 www.hurdwickgolf.com

Ilfracombe (1892)
Hele Bay, Ilfracombe EX34 9RT
☎ **(01271) 862176**
✉ ilfracombegolfclub@btinternet.com
✍ Mr D Cook
🖥 www.ilfracombegolfclub.com

Libbaton (1988)
High Bickington, Umberleigh EX37 9BS
☎ **(01769) 560269**
📠 (01769) 560342
✉ gerald.herniman@tesco.net
✍ Gerald Herniman
🖥 www.libbaton-golf-club.com

Mortehoe & Woolacombe (1992)
Easewell, Mortehoe, Ilfracombe EX34 7EH
☎ **(01271) 870566**
✍ M Wilkinson (01271) 870745

Okehampton (1913)
Okehampton EX20 1EF
☎ **(01837) 52113**
✉ secretary@okehamptongolfclub.co.uk
✍ Beverley Lawson
🖥 www.okehamptongolfclub.co.uk

Padbrook Park (1992)
Proprietary
Cullompton EX15 1RU
☎ **(01884) 836100**
📠 (01884) 836101
✉ info@padbrookpark.co.uk
✍ Cary Rawlings (Mgr)
⊕ 40 Bed Hotel, 10 bay Driving Range.
🖥 www.padbrookpark.co.uk

Portmore Golf Park (1993)
Proprietary
Landkey Road, Barnstaple EX32 9LB
☎ **(01271) 378378**
✉ contact@portmoregolf.co.uk
✍ C Webber
🖥 www.portmoregolf.co.uk

Royal North Devon (1864)
Golf Links Road, Westward Ho! EX39 1HD
☎ **(01237) 473817 (Clubhouse)**
📠 (01237) 423456
✉ mark@rndgc.co.uk
✍ M Evans (01237) 473817
🖥 www.royalnorthdevongolfclub.co.uk

Saunton (1897)
Saunton, Braunton EX33 1LG
☎ **(01271) 812436**
📠 (01271) 814241
✉ gm4@sauntongolf.co.uk
✍ P McMullen (Mgr)
🖥 www.sauntongolf.co.uk

Sidmouth (1889)
Cotmaton Road, Sidmouth EX10 8SX
☎ **(01395) 513451**
📠 (01395) 514661
✉ secretary@sidmouthgolfclub.co.uk
✍ JP Lee (Mgr) (01395) 513451
🖥 www.sidmouthgolfclub.co.uk

Sparkwell (1993)
Pay and play
Sparkwell, Plymouth PL7 5DF
☎ **(01752) 837219**
📠 (01752) 837219
✍ G Adamson

Staddon Heights (1904)
Plymstock, Plymouth PL9 9SP
☎ **(01752) 402475**
📠 (01752) 401998
✉ golf@shgc.uk.net
✍ TJH Aggett (01752) 402475
🖥 www.staddonheightsgolf.co.uk

Stover (1930)
Bovey Road, Newton Abbot TQ12 6QQ
☎ **(01626) 352460**
📠 (01626) 330210
✉ info@stovergolfclub.co.uk
✍ W Hendry
🖥 www.stovergolfclub.co.uk

Tavistock (1890)
Down Road, Tavistock PL19 9AQ
☎ **(01822) 612344**
📠 (01822) 612344
✉ info@tavistockgolfclub.org.uk
✍ J Coe
🖥 www.tavistockgolfclub.org.uk

Teign Valley (1995)
Christow, Exeter EX6 7PA
☎ **(01647) 253026**
📠 (01647) 253026
✉ andy@teignvalleygolf.co.uk
🖥 www.teignvalleygolf.co.uk

Teignmouth (1924)
Haldon Moor, Exeter Road, Teignmouth TQ14 9NY
☎ **(01626) 777070**
📠 (01626) 777304
✉ info@teignmouthgolfclub.co.uk
✍ Mark Haskell
🖥 www.teignmouthgolfclub.co.uk

Thurlestone (1897)
Thurlestone, Kingsbridge TQ7 3NZ
☎ **(01548) 560405**
📠 (01548) 562149
✉ info@thurlestonegolfclub.co.uk
🖥 www.thurlestonegolfclub.co.uk

Tiverton (1932)
Post Hill, Tiverton EX16 4NE
☎ **(01884) 252114 (Clubhouse)**
✉ tivertongolfclub@lineone.net
✍ R Jessop (Gen Mgr)
🖥 www.tivertongolfclub.co.uk

Torquay (1909)
Petitor Road, St Marychurch, Torquay TQ1 4QF
☎ **(01803) 327471**
📠 (01803) 316116
✉ info@torquaygolfclub.co.uk
✍ C M Nolan (01803) 314591
🖥 www.torquaygolfclub.co.uk

Warren (1892)
Dawlish Warren EX7 0NF
☎ **(01626) 862255**
✉ assistant@dwgc.co.uk
✍ Cathie Stokes
🖥 www.dwgc.co.uk

Waterbridge (1992)
Pay and play
Down St Mary, Crediton EX17 5LG
☎ **(01363) 85111**
✍ G & A Wren (Props)
🖥 www.waterbridgegc.co.uk

Willingcott Valley (1996)
Willingcott, Woolacombe EX34 7HN
☎ **(01271) 870173**
📠 (01271) 870800
✉ secretary.willingcottgolfclub@virgin.net
🖥 www.willingcott.co.uk

Woodbury Park (1992)
Woodbury Castle, Woodbury EX5 1JJ
☎ **(01395) 233500**
📠 (01395) 233384

Wrangaton (1895)
Golf Links Road, Wrangaton, South Brent TQ10 9HJ
☎ **(01364) 73229**
📠 (01364) 73341
✉ wrangatongolf@btconnect.com
✍ R Clark
🖥 www.wrangatongolfclub.co.uk

Yelverton (1904)
Golf Links Road, Yelverton PL20 6BN
☎ **(01822) 852824**
📠 (01822) 854869
✉ secretary@yelvertongolf.co.uk
✍ Steve West (01822) 852824
🖥 www.yelvertongolf.co.uk

For key to symbols see page 725

Dorset

The Ashley Wood (1896)
Wimborne Road, Blandford Forum DT11 9HN
☎ **(01258) 452253**
(01258) 450590
generalmanager@ashleywoodgolfclub.com
M Batty
www.ashleywoodgolfclub.com

Bridport & West Dorset (1891)
The Clubhouse, Burton Road, Bridport DT6 4PS
☎ **(01308) 421095/422597 (Clubhouse)**
secretary@bridportgolfclub.org.uk
R Wilson (01308) 421095
www.bridportgolfclub.org.uk

Broadstone (Dorset) (1898)
Wentworth Drive, Broadstone BH18 8DQ
☎ **(01202) 692595**
(01202) 642520
office@broadstonegolfclub.com
David Morgan (Gen Mgr) (01202) 642521
www.broadstonegolfclub.com

Bulbury Woods (1989)
Bulbury Lane, Lytchett Minster, Poole BH16 6EP
☎ **(01929) 459574**
(01929) 459000
bulbury-woods@hoburne.com
www.bulbury-woods.co.uk

Came Down (1896)
Higher Came, Dorchester DT2 8NR
☎ **(01305) 813494**
(01305) 815122
manager@camedowngolfclub.co.uk
Matthew Staveley (Gen Mgr)
www.camedowngolfclub.co.uk

Canford Magna (1994)
Proprietary
Knighton Lane, Wimborne BH21 3AS
☎ **(01202) 592552**
(01202) 592550
admin@canfordmagnagc.co.uk
S Hudson (Dir) (01202) 592505
www.canfordmagnagc.co.uk

Canford School (1987)
Canford School, Wimborne BH21 3AD
☎ **(01202) 841254**
(01202) 881009
steve.ronaldson@talk21.com
Steve Ronaldson (Mgr) (01202) 881232
www.canford.com

Charminster (1998)
Proprietary
Wolfedale Golf Course, Charminster, Dorchester DT2 7SG
☎ **(01305) 260186**
(01305) 257074

Chedington Court (1991)
South Perrott, Beaminster DT8 3HU
☎ **(01935) 891413**
info@chedingtoncourtgolfclub.com
M Bowling (Manager)
www.chedingtoncourtgolfclub.com

Christchurch (1977)
Pay and play
Riverside Avenue, Bournemouth BH7 7ES
☎ **(01202) 436436 (Bookings)**
(01202) 436400
ben.chant@playgolfworld.com
Ben Chant
www.playgolfbournemouth.com

Crane Valley (1992)
Proprietary
The Clubhouse, Verwood BH31 7LH
☎ **(01202) 814088**
(01202) 813407
andrew.blackwell@hoburne.com
A Blackwell (Gen Mgr)
www.crane-valley.co.uk

The Dorset G&CC (1978)
Hyde, Bere Regis, Nr. Poole, Wareham BH20 7NT
☎ **(01929) 472244**
(01929) 471294
admin@dorsetgolfresort.com
G Packer (Mgr)
www.dorsetgolfresort.com

Dudmoor Golf Course (1985)
Pay and play
Dudmoor Farm Road, (off Fairmile Road), Christchurch, Dorset BH23 6AQ
☎ **(01202) 473826**
(01202) 480207
peter@dudmoorgolfcourse.co.uk
Peter Hornsby
www.dudmoorfarm.co.uk

Dudsbury (1992)
Proprietary
64 Christchurch Road, Ferndown BH22 8ST
☎ **(01202) 593499**
(01202) 594555
info@dudsburygolfclub.co.uk
Steve Pockneall
www.dudsburygolfclub.co.uk

Ferndown (1913)
119 Golf Links Road, Ferndown BH22 8BU
☎ **(01202) 653950**
(01202) 653960
golf@ferndowngolfclub.co.uk
Ian Walton (Gen Mgr)
www.ferndowngolfclub.co.uk

Ferndown Forest (1993)
Forest Links Road, Ferndown BH22 9PH
☎ **(01202) 876096**
(01202) 894095
golf@ferndownforestgolf.co.uk
www.ferndownforestgolf.co.uk

Folke Golf Club (1995)
Proprietary
c/o Folke Golf Centre, Alweston, Sherborne, Dorset DT9 5HR
☎ **(01963) 23330**
(01963) 23330
info@folkegolfcentre.co.uk
Steve Harris
www.folkegolfcentre.co.uk

Halstock (1988)
Pay and play
Common Lane, Halstock BA22 9SF
☎ **(01935) 891689**
(01935) 891839
halstockgolf@yahoo.com
Paul Flitton
www.halstockgolfclub.co.uk

Highcliffe Castle (1913)
107 Lymington Road, Highcliffe-on-Sea, Christchurch BH23 4LA
☎ **(01425) 272210/272953**
(01425) 272953
secretary@highcliffecastlegolfclub.co.uk
G Fisher (01425) 272210
www.highcliffecastlegolfclub.co.uk

Isle of Purbeck (1892)
Proprietary
Studland BH19 3AB
☎ **(01929) 450361**
(01929) 450501
iop@purbeckgolf.co.uk
Mrs C Robinson
www.purbeckgolf.co.uk

Knighton Heath (1976)
Francis Avenue, Bournemouth BH11 8NX
☎ **(01202) 572633**
(01202) 590774
manager@khgc.co.uk
Reunert Bauser
www.knightonheathgolfclub.co.uk

Lyme Regis (1893)
Timber Hill, Lyme Regis DT7 3HQ
☎ **(01297) 442963**
(01297) 442963
secretary@lymeregisgolfclub.co.uk
www.lymeregisgolfclub.co.uk

Meyrick Park (1890)
Pay and play
Central Drive, Meyrick Park, Bournemouth BH2 6LH
☎ **(01202) 786000**
m.gracehaus.com
www.clubhaus.com

Moors Valley (1988)
Proprietary
Horton Road, Ashley Heath, Ringwood BH24 2ET
☎ **(01425) 479776**
golf@moorsvalleygolf.co.uk
Desmond Meharg (Mgr)
www.moors-valley.co.uk/golf

Parkstone (1909)
49a Links Road, Parkstone, Poole BH14 9QS
☎ **(01202) 707138**
(01202) 706027
admin@parkstonegolfclub.co.uk
Gary Peddie (Gen Mgr)
www.parkstonegolfclub.co.uk

For key to symbols see page 725

Parley Court (1992)
Proprietary
Parley Green Lane, Hurn, Christchurch BH23 6BB
☎ **(01202) 591600**
(01202) 579043
info@parleygolf.co.uk
Mr Adrian Perry
www.parleygolf.co.uk

Queens Park (Bournemouth) (1905)
Public
Queens Park West Drive, Queens Park, Bournemouth BH8 9BY
☎ **(01202) 302611 Secretary**
(01202) 302611
secretary@queensparkgolfclub.co.uk
P Greenwood (01202) 302611
www.queensparkgolfclub.co.uk

Remedy Oak (2006)
Proprietary
Horton Road, Woodlands, Dorset BH21 8ND
☎ **(01202) 812070**
(01202) 812071
info@remedyoak.com
Nigel Tokely
www.remedyoak.com

Sherborne (1894)
Higher Clatcombe, Sherborne DT9 4RN
☎ **(01935) 814431**
(01935) 814218
office@sherbornegolfclub.co.uk
Office Manager
www.sherbornegolfclub.co.uk

Solent Meads Golf Centre (1965)
Public
Rolls Drive, Southbourne, Bournemouth BH6 4NA
☎ **(01202) 420795**
solentmeads@yahoo.co.uk
Matt Steward (01202) 420795
www.solentmeads.com

Sturminster Marshall (1992)
Pay and play
Moor Lane, Sturminster Marshall BH21 4AH
☎ **(01258) 858444**
mike@smgc.eu
Mike Dodd
www.smgc.eu

Wareham (1908)
Sandford Road, Wareham BH20 4DH
☎ **(01929) 554147**
(01929) 557993
secretary@warehamgolfclub.com
Richard Murgatroyd
www.warehamgolfclub.com

Weymouth (1909)
Links Road, Weymouth DT4 0PF
☎ **(01305) 750831**
(01305) 788029
weymouthgolfclub@googlemail.com
John Northover (Sec/Treasurer)
www.weymouthgolfclub.co.uk

Durham

Barnard Castle (1898)
Harmire Road, Barnard Castle DL12 8QN
☎ **(01833) 638355**
(01833) 695551
J A Saunders
www.barnardcastlegolfclub.org

Beamish Park (1906)
Beamish, Stanley DH9 0RH
☎ **(0191) 370 1382**
(0191) 370 2937
beamishgolf@btconnect.com
John Bosanko (Hon Sec) (0191) 370 1382
www.beamishgolfclub.co.uk

Billingham (1967)
Sandy Lane, Billingham TS22 5NA
☎ **(01642) 533816/554494**
(01642) 533816
billinghamgc@btconnect.com
Julie Lapping (Sec/Mgr) (01642) 533816
www.billinghamgolfclub.com

Bishop Auckland (1894)
High Plains, Durham Road, Bishop Auckland DL14 8DL
☎ **(01388) 661618**
(01388) 607005
enquiries@bagc.co.uk
D J Perriss
www.bagc.co.uk

Blackwell Grange (1930)
Briar Close, Blackwell, Darlington DL3 8QX
☎ **(01325) 464458**
secretary@blackwellgrangegolf.com
D C Christie (Hon)
www.blackwellgrangegolf.com

Brancepeth Castle (1924)
The Clubhouse, Brancepeth Village, Durham DH7 8EA
☎ **(0191) 378 0075**
(0191) 378 3835
enquiries@brancepeth-castle-golf.co.uk
Arthur Chadwick
www.brancepeth-castle-golf.co.uk

Castle Eden (1927)
Castle Eden, Hartlepool TS27 4SS
☎ **(01429) 836510**
castleedengolfclub@hotmail.com
S J Watkin (0794) 114 1057
www.castleedengolfclub.co.uk

Chester-Le-Street (1908)
Lumley Park, Chester-Le-Street DH3 4NS
☎ **(0191) 388 3218**
none
clsgcoffice@tiscali.co.uk
Bill Routledge
www.clsgolfclub.co.uk

Consett & District (1911)
Elmfield Road, Consett DH8 5NN
☎ **(01207) 502186 (Clubhouse)**
(01207) 505060
consettgolfclub@btconnect.com
Vincent Kelly (Sec/Treasurer)
www.consettgolfclub.com

Crook (1919)
Low Job's Hill, Crook, Co Durham DL15 9AA
☎ **(01388) 762429**
secretary@crookgolfclub.co.uk
Mr D Hanlon (Sec)
www.crookgolfclub.co.uk

Darlington (1908)
Haughton Grange, Darlington DL1 3JD
☎ **(01325) 355324**
office@darlington-gc.co.uk
M Etherington
www.darlington-gc.co.uk

Dinsdale Spa (1910)
Neasham Road, Middleton, St George, Darlington DL2 1DW
☎ **(01325) 332297**
(01325) 332297
martynstubbings@hotmail.co.uk
A Patterson
www.dinsdalespagolfclub.co.uk

Durham City (1887)
Littleburn, Langley Moor, Durham DH7 8HL
☎ **(0191) 378 0069**
(0191) 378 4265
enquiries@durhamcitygolf.co.uk
David Stainsby (0191) 378 0069
www.durhamcitygolf.co.uk

Eaglescliffe (1914)
Yarm Road, Eaglescliffe, Stockton-on-Tees TS16 0DQ
☎ **(01642) 780238 (Clubhouse)**
(01642) 781128
secretary@eaglescliffegolfclub.co.uk
Alan McNinch (01642) 780238
www.eaglescliffegolfclub.co.uk

Hartlepool (1906)
Hart Warren, Hartlepool TS24 9QF
☎ **(01429) 274398**
(01429) 274129
hartlepoolgolf@btconnect.com
G Laidlaw (Mgr) (01429) 274398
www.hartlepoolgolfclub.co.uk

High Throston (1997)
Proprietary
Hart Lane, Hartlepool TS26 0UG
☎ **(01429) 275325**
Mrs J Sturrock

Knotty Hill Golf Centre (1992)
Pay and play
Sedgefield, Stockton-on-Tees TS21 2BB
☎ **(01740) 620320**
(01740) 622227
knottyhill@btconnect.com

✍ D Craggs (Mgr)
▤ www.knottyhill.com

Mount Oswald (1934)
Pay and play
South Road, Durham City DH1 3TQ
☎ **(0191) 386 7527**
🖷 (0191) 386 0975
✉ info@mountoswald.co.uk
✍ N Galvin
▤ www.mountoswald.co.uk

Norton (1989)
Pay and play
Junction Road, Norton, Stockton-on-Tees TS20 1SU
☎ **(01642) 676385**
🖷 (01642) 608467

Oakleaf Golf Complex (1993)
Pay and play
School Aycliffe Lane, Newton Aycliffe DL5 6QZ
☎ **(01325) 310820**
🖷 (01325) 300873
✉ info@great-aycliffe.gov.uk
✍ A Bailey (Mgr)
▤ www.great-aycliffe.gov.uk

Ramside (1995)
Proprietary
Ramside Hall Hotel, Carrville, Durham DH1 1TD
☎ **(0191) 386 9514**
🖷 (0191) 386 9519
✉ kevin.jackson@ramsidehallhotel.co.uk
✍ Kevin Jackson
▤ www.ramsidehallhotel.co.uk

Roseberry Grange (1987)
Public
Grange Villa, Chester-Le-Street DH2 3NF
☎ **(0191) 370 0660**
🖷 (0191) 370 2047
✉ chrisjones@chester-le-street.gov.uk
✍ R McDermott (Hon)

Royal Hobson (1978)
Hobson, Burnopfield, Newcastle-upon-Tyne NE16 6BZ
☎ **(01207) 271605**
✉ secretary@hobsongolfclub.co.uk
✍ A J Giles (01207) 270941
▤ www.hobsongolfclub.co.uk

Seaham (1908)
Shrewsbury Street, Dawdon, Seaham SR7 7RD
☎ **(0191) 581 2354**
✉ seahamgolfclub@btconnect.com
✍ T Johnson (0191) 581 1268
▤ www.seahamgolfclub.co.uk

Seaton Carew (1874)
Tees Road, Hartlepool TS25 1DE
☎ **(01429) 266249**
✉ secretary@seatoncarewgolfclub.co.uk
✍ Secretary (01429) 266249 Ext 2
▤ www.seatoncarewgolfclub.co.uk

South Moor (1923)
The Middles, Craghead, Stanley DH9 6AG
☎ **(01207) 232848/283525**
🖷 (01207) 284616
✉ secretary@southmoorgc.co.uk
✍ Peter Johnson
▤ www.southmoorgc.co.uk

Stressholme (1976)
Public
Snipe Lane, Darlington DL2 2SA
☎ **(01325) 461002**
🖷 (01325) 461002
✉ stressholme@btconnect.com
✍ R Givens
▤ www.darlington.gov.uk/golf

Woodham G&CC (1983)
Proprietary
Burnhill Way, Newton Aycliffe DL5 4PN
☎ **(01325) 320574**
🖷 (01325) 315254
✉ woodhamproshop@googlemail.com
✍ Ernie Wilson (Mgr)
▤ www.woodhamgolfandcountryclub.co.uk

The Wynyard Club (1996)
Proprietary
Wellington Drive, Wynyard Park, Billingham TS22 5QJ
☎ **(01740) 644399**
🖷 (01740) 644599
✉ chris@wynyardgolfclub.co.uk
✍ C Mounter (Golf Dir)
▤ www.wynyardgolfclub.co.uk

Essex

Abridge G&CC (1964)
Epping Lane, Stapleford Tawney RM4 1ST
☎ **(01708) 688396**
✉ info@abridgegolf.com
▤ www.abridgegolf.com

Ballards Gore G&CC (1980)
Proprietary
Gore Road, Canewdon, Rochford SS4 2DA
☎ **(01702) 258917**
🖷 (01702) 258571
✉ secretary@ballardsgore.com
✍ Susan May (Sec)
▤ www.ballardsgore.com

Basildon (1967)
Pay and play
Clay Hill Lane, Sparrow's Hearne, Basildon, Essex SS16 5HL
☎ **(01268) 533297**
✉ basildongc@onetel.com
✍ G Eaton
▤ www.basildongolfclub.org.uk

Belfairs (1926)
Public
Eastwood Road North, Leigh-on-Sea SS9 4LR
☎ **(01702) 525345 (Starter)**

Belhus Park G&CC (1972)
Pay and play
Belhus Park, South Ockendon RM15 4QR
☎ **(01708) 854260**
✍ D Clifford

Bentley (1972)
Ongar Road, Brentwood CM15 9SS
☎ **(01277) 373179**
🖷 (01277) 375097
✉ info@bentleygolfclub.com
✍ Andy Hall
▤ www.bentleygolfclub.com

Benton Hall Golf & Country Club (1993)
Proprietary
Wickham Hill, Witham CM8 3LH
☎ **(01376) 502454**
🖷 (01376) 521050
✉ bentonhall.retail@theclubcompany.com
✍ Scott Clark
▤ www.theclubcompany.com

Birch Grove (1970)
Layer Road, Colchester CO2 0HS
☎ **(01206) 734276**
✉ maureen@birchgrove.fsbusiness.co.uk
✍ Mrs M Marston
▤ www.birchgrovegolfclub.co.uk

Boyce Hill (1922)
Vicarage Hill, Benfleet SS7 1PD
☎ **(01268) 793625**
🖷 (01268) 750497
✉ secretary@boycehillgolfclub.co.uk
✍ D Kelly
▤ www.boycehillgolfclub.co.uk

Braintree (1891)
Kings Lane, Stisted, Braintree CM77 8DD
☎ **(01376) 346079**
🖷 (01376) 348677
✉ manager@braintreegolfclub.co.uk
✍ Mr N Hawkins
▤ www.braintreegolfclub.co.uk

Braxted Park (1953)
Braxted Park, Witham CM8 3EN
☎ **(01376) 572372**
🖷 (01376) 572372
✉ golf@braxtedpark.com
✍ Mr P Keeble
▤ www.braxtedpark.com

Bunsay Downs Golf Club (1982)
Proprietary
Little Baddow Road, Woodham Walter, Maldon CM9 6RU
☎ **(01245) 222648/222369**
✉ info@bunsaydownsgc.co.uk
✍ J Durham (01245) 223258
▤ www.bunsaydownsgc.co.uk

Burnham-on-Crouch (1923)
Ferry Road, Creeksea, Burnham-on-Crouch CM0 8PQ
☎ **(01621) 782282**
🖷 (01621) 784489

✉ enquiries@burnhamgolfclub.co.uk
✍ S K Golf Ltd
▤ www.burnhamgolfclub.co.uk

The Burstead (1993)
Proprietary
Tye Common Road, Little Burstead, Billericay CM12 9SS
☎ **(01277) 631171**
🖷 (01277) 632766
✉ info@theburssteadgolfclub.com
✍ Stuart Mence (Managing Director)
▤ www.thebursteadgolfclub.com

Canons Brook (1962)
Elizabeth Way, Harlow CM19 5BE
☎ **(01279) 421482**
🖷 (01279) 626393
✉ manager@canonsbrook.com
✍ Mrs SJ Langton
▤ www.canonsbrook.com

Castle Point (1988)
Public
Waterside Farm, Somnes Avenue, Canvey Island SS8 9FG
☎ **(01268) 510830**
✍ Mrs B de Koster

Channels (1974)
Belsteads Farm Lane, Little Waltham, Chelmsford CM3 3PT
☎ **(01245) 440005**
🖷 (01245) 442032
✉ info@channelsgolf.co.uk
✍ Mrs SJ Larner
▤ www.channelsgolf.co.uk

Chelmsford (1893)
Widford Road, Chelmsford CM2 9AP
☎ **(01245) 256483**
🖷 (01245) 256483
✉ office@chelmsfordgc.co.uk
✍ G Winckless (01245) 256483
▤ www.chelmsfordgc.co.uk

Chigwell (1925)
High Road, Chigwell IG7 5BH
☎ **(020) 8500 2059**
🖷 (020) 8501 3410
✉ info@chigwellgolfclub.co.uk
✍ James Fuller (Gen Mgr)
▤ www.chigwellgolfclub.co.uk

Chingford (1923)
158 Station Road, Chingford, London E4 6AN
☎ **(0208) 529 2107**
✍ B W Woods

Clacton-on-Sea (1892)
West Road, Clacton-on-Sea CO15 1AJ
☎ **(01255) 421919**
🖷 (01255) 424602
✉ secretary@clactongolfclub.com
✍ Brian Telford
▤ www.clactongolfclub.com

Colchester GC (1907)
21 Braiswick, Colchester CO4 5AU
☎ **(01206) 853396**
🖷 (01206) 852698
✉ secretary@colchestergolfclub.com
✍ Julie Ruscoe
▤ www.colchestergolfclub.com

Colne Valley (1991)
Station Road, Earls Colne CO6 2LT
☎ **(01787) 224343**
🖷 (01787) 224126
✉ info@colnevalleygolfclub.co.uk
✍ T Smith (01787) 224343
▤ www.colnevalleygolfclub.co.uk

Crondon Park (1994)
Proprietary
Stock Road, Stock CM4 9DP
☎ **(01277) 841115**
🖷 (01277) 841356
✉ info@crondon.com
✍ P Cranwell
▤ www.crondon.com

Crowlands Heath Golf Club (2000)
Pay and play
Wood Lane, Dagenham, Essex RM8 1JX
☎ **(020) 8984 7373**
🖷 (020) 8984 0505
✉ chris@chrisjenkinsgolf.com
✍ Marcus Radmore (Mgr)
▤ www.chrisjenkinsgolf.com

Elsenham Golf and Leisure (1997)
Proprietary
Hall Road, Elsenham, Bishop's Stortford CM22 6DH
☎ **(01279) 812865**
✉ info@elsenhamgolfandleisure.co.uk
✍ Martin McKenna (Gen Mgr)
▤ www.egcltd.co.uk

Epping Golf Club (1996)
Proprietary
Flux Lane, Epping, Essex CM16 7NJ
☎ **(01992) 572282**
🖷 (01992) 575512
✉ info@eppinggolfcourse.org.uk
✍ Mr Neil Sjöberg
⊕ Half mile walk from Epping Central Line Underground Station
▤ www.eppinggolfcourse.org.uk

Essex G&CC (1990)
Earls Colne, Colchester CO6 2NS
☎ **(01787) 224466**
🖷 (01787) 224410
✉ essex.golfops@theclubcompany.com
▤ www.theclubcompany.com

Five Lakes Resort (1995)
Colchester Road, Tolleshunt Knights, Maldon CM9 8HX
☎ **(01621) 868888 (Hotel)**
🖷 (01621) 869696
✉ office@fivelakes.co.uk
▤ www.fivelakes.co.uk

Forrester Park (1975)
Beckingham Road, Great Totham, Maldon CM9 8EA
☎ **(01621) 891406**
🖷 (01621) 891903
✉ housemanager@forresterparkltd.com
✍ T Forrester-Muir
▤ www.forresterparkltd.com

Frinton (1895)
1 The Esplanade, Frinton-on-Sea CO13 9EP
☎ **(01255) 674618**
🖷 (01255) 682450
✉ enquiries@frintongolfclub.com
✍ Deborah Rablin
▤ www.frintongolfclub.com

Garon Park Golf Complex (1993)
Pay and play
Eastern Avenue, Southend-on-Sea, Essex SS2 4FA
☎ **(01702) 601701**
🖷 (01702) 601033
✉ debbie@garonparkgolf.co.uk
✍ Mrs Debbie Wright
▤ www.garonparkgolf.co.uk

Gosfield Lake (1986)
Hall Drive, Gosfield, Halstead CO9 1SE
☎ **(01787) 474747**
🖷 (01787) 476044
✉ gosfieldlakegc@btconnect.com
✍ JA O'Shea (Sec/Mgr)
▤ www.gosfield-lake-golf-club.co.uk

Hainault Golf Club (1912)
Public
Romford Road, Chigwell Row IG7 4QW
☎ **(020) 8500 2131 (Proshop/Reception)**
✍ Gary Ivory (Mgr)
▤ www.hainaultgolfclub.co.uk

Hanover G&CC (1991)
Proprietary
Hullbridge Road, Rayleigh SS6 9QS
☎ **(01702) 232377**
🖷 (01702) 231811
✉ hanovergolf@aol.com

Hartswood (1967)
Pay and play
King George's Playing Fields, Brentwood CM14 5AE
☎ **(01277) 214830 (Bookings)**
🖷 (01277) 218850
✍ D Bonner (01227) 218850

Harwich & Dovercourt (1906)
Station Road, Parkeston, Harwich CO12 4NZ
☎ **(01255) 503616**
🖷 (01255) 503323
✉ secretary@harwichanddovercourtgolfclub.com
✍ K J Feaviour (Hon Sec)
▤ www.harwichanddovercourtgolfclub.com

Ilford (1907)
291 Wanstead Park Road, Ilford IG1 3TR
☎ **(020) 8554 2930**

(020) 8554 0822
secretary@ilfordgolfclub.com
Janice Pinner (Mgr)
www.ilfordgolfclub.com

Langdon Hills (1991)
Proprietary
Lower Dunton Road, Bulphan RM14 3TY
(01268) 548444/544300
(01268) 490084
secretary@golflangdon.co.uk
www.langdonhillsgolfclub.co.uk

Lexden Wood (1993)
Proprietary
Bakers Lane, Colchester CO3 4AU
(01206) 843333
(01206) 854775
secretary@lexdenwood.com
K Hanvey
www.lexdenwood.com

Little Channels (1995)
Pay and play
Pratts Farm Lane West, Little Waltham, Chelmsford CM3 3PR
(01245) 361100 (Golf)
(01245 362210 (General)
info@littlechannelsce.co.uk
D A Wallbank
www.cliffordsestate.co.uk

Lords Golf & CC (Notley) (1995)
The Green, White Notley, Witham, Essex CM8 1RG
(01376) 329328
(01376) 569051
info@lordscountryclub.co.uk
Julia Keenes
www.lordscountryclub.com

Loughton (1981)
Pay and play
Clays Lane, Debden Green, Loughton IG10 2RZ
(020) 8502 2923

Maldon (1891)
Beeleigh Langford, Maldon CM9 4SS
(01621) 853212
(01621) 855232
maldon.golf@virgin.net
Viv Locke
www.maldon-golf.co.uk

Maylands (1936)
Proprietary
Colchester Road, Harold Park, Romford RM3 0AZ
(01708) 341777
(01708) 343777
maylands@maylandsgolf.com
(01708) 341777
www.maylandsgolf.com

North Weald (1996)
Proprietary
Rayley Lane, North Weald, Epping CM16 6AR
(01992) 522118
info@northwealdgolfclub.co.uk
T Lloyd-Skinner
www.northwealdgolfclub.co.uk

Orsett (1899)
Brentwood Road, Orsett RM16 3DS
(01375) 891352
(01375) 892471
suecoleman@orsettgolfclub.co.uk
GH Smith (01375) 893409
www.orsettgolfclub.co.uk

Risebridge (1972)
Pay and play
Risebridge Chase, Lower Bedfords Road, Romford RM1 4DG
(01708) 741429
pa.jennings@btconnect.co.uk
P Jennings

Rivenhall Oaks Golf Centre (1994)
Pay and play
Forest Road, Witham, Essex CM8 2PS
(01376) 510222
(01376) 500316
info@rivenhalloaksgolf.com
B Chapman
www.rivenhalloaksgolf.com

Rochford Hundred Golf Club (1893)
Rochford Hall, Hall Road, Rochford SS4 1NW
(01702) 544302
(01702) 541343
admin@rochfordhundredgolfclub.co.uk
N T Wells
www.rochfordhundredgolfclub.co.uk

Romford (1894)
Heath Drive, Gidea Park, Romford RM2 5QB
(01708) 740007 (Members)
(01708) 752157
info@romfordgolfclub.co.uk
M R J Hall (01708) 740986
www.romfordgolfclub.com

Royal Epping Forest (1888)
Forest Approach, Station Road, Chingford, London E4 7AZ
(020) 8529 2195
office@refgc.co.uk
Mrs D Woodland (0208) 529 2195
www.refgc.co.uk

Saffron Walden (1919)
Windmill Hill, Saffron Walden CB10 1BX
(01799) 522786
(01799) 520313
office@swgc.com
Mrs Stephanie Standen
www.swgc.com

South Essex G&CC
Herongate, Brentwood CM13 3LW
(01277) 811289
(01277) 811304
southessexgolf@crown-golf.co.uk
www.crown-golf.co.uk

St Cleres (1994)
Proprietary
St Cleres Hall, Stanford-le-Hope SS17 0LX
(01375) 361565
(01375) 361565
david.wood@foremostgolf.com
D Wood (01375) 361565

Stapleford Abbotts (1989)
Proprietary
Horseman's Side, Tysea Hill, Stapleford Abbotts RM4 1JU
(01708) 381108
(01708) 386345
staplefordabbotts@crown-golf.co.uk
C Whittaker (Gen Mgr)
www.staplefordabbotts.golf.co.uk

Stock Brook Manor (1992)
Proprietary
Queen's Park Avenue, Stock, Billericay CM12 0SP
(01277) 658181
(01277) 633063
events@stockbrook.com
C Laurence (Golf Dir)
www.stockbrook.com

Theydon Bois (1897)
Theydon Road, Theydon Bois, Epping CM16 4EH
(01992) 813054
(01992) 815602
theydonboisgolf@btconnect.com
D Bowles (01992) 813054
www.theydongolf.co.uk

Thorndon Park (1920)
Ingrave, Brentwood CM13 3RH
(01277) 810345
(01277) 810645
office@thorndonpark.com
Mr G Thomas (mgr)
www.thorndonparkgolfclub.com

Thorpe Hall (1907)
Thorpe Hall Avenue, Thorpe Bay SS1 3AT
(01702) 582205/(01702) 588195 Pro Shop
(01702) 584498
sec@thorpehallgc.co.uk
Ms F Gale
www.thorpehallgc.co.uk

Three Rivers G&CC (1973)
Stow Road, Purleigh, Chelmsford CM3 6RR
(01621) 828631
(01621) 828060
F Teixeria (Gen Mgr)
www.threeriversclub.com

Toot Hill (1991)
Proprietary
School Road, Toot Hill, Ongar CM5 9PU
(01277) 365747
(01277) 364509
office@toothillgolfclub.co.uk
Mrs Cameron
www.toothillgolfclub.co.uk

For key to symbols see page 725

Top Meadow (1986)
Fen Lane, North Ockendon RM14 3PR
☎ **(01708) 852239 (Clubhouse)**
✉ info@topmeadow.co.uk
🌐 www.topmeadow.co.uk

Towerlands Unex Golf Club (1985)
Panfield Road, Braintree CM7 5BJ
☎ **(01376) 326802**
📠 (01376) 552487
✉ info@towerlandspark.com
✍ Colin Cooper
🌐 www.towerlandspark.com

Upminster (1928)
114 Hall Lane, Upminster RM14 1AU
☎ **(01708) 222788**
📠 (01708) 222484
✉ secretary@upminstergolfclub.co.uk
✍ RP Winmill
🌐 www.upminstergolfclub.co.uk

Wanstead (1893)
Overton Drive, Wanstead, London E11 2LW
☎ **(0208) 989 3938**
📠 (020) 8532 9138
✉ wgclub@aol.com
✍ W T Cranston
🌐 www.wansteadgolf.org.uk

Warley Park (1975)
Magpie Lane, Little Warley, Brentwood CM13 3DX
☎ **(01277) 224891**
📠 (01277) 200679
✉ enquiries@warleyparkgc.co.uk
✍ N Hawkins
🌐 www.warleyparkgc.co.uk

The Warren (1932)
Proprietary
Woodham Walter, Maldon CM9 6RW
☎ **(01245) 223258/223198**
📠 (01245) 223989
✉ enquiries@warrengolfclub.co.uk
✍ J Durham (01245) 223258
🌐 www.warrengolfclub.co.uk

Weald Park (1994)
Coxtie Green Road, South Weald, Brentwood CM14 5RJ
☎ **(01277) 375101**
📠 (01277) 374888
🌐 www.wealdparkhotel.co.uk

West Essex (1900)
Bury Road, Sewardstonebury, Chingford, London E4 7QL
☎ **(020) 8529 7558**
📠 (020) 8524 7870
✉ sec@westessexgolfclub.co.uk
✍ Mrs Emma Clifford
🌐 www.westessexgolfclub.co.uk

Woodford (1890)
2, Sunset Avenue, Woodford Green IG8 0ST
☎ **(020) 8504 0553 (Clubhouse)**
📠 (020) 8559 0504
✉ office@woodfordgolf.co.uk
✍ PS Willett (020) 8504 3330
🌐 www.woodfordgolf.co.uk

Woolston Manor (1994)
Woolston Manor, Abridge Road, Chigwell, Essex IP7 6BX
☎ **(020) 8500 2549**
📠 (020) 8501 5452
✉ bradley@woolstonmanor.co.uk
✍ P Spargo
🌐 www.woolstonmanor.co.uk

Gloucestershire

Brickhampton Court Golf Complex (1995)
Proprietary
Cheltenham Road East, Churchdown, Gloucestershire GL2 9QF
☎ **(01452) 859444**
📠 (01452) 859333
✉ info@brickhampton.co.uk
✍ Natalie Dyke
🌐 www.brickhampton.co.uk

Bristol & Clifton (1891)
Beggar Bush Lane, Failand, Clifton, Bristol BS8 3TH
☎ **(01275) 393474/393117**
📠 (01275) 394611
✉ office@bristolgolf.co.uk
✍ J S Macpherson (01275) 393474
🌐 www.bristolgolf.co.uk

Broadway (1895)
Willersey Hill, Broadway, Worcs WR12 7LG
☎ **(01386) 853683**
📠 (01386) 858643
✉ secretary@broadwaygolfclub.co.uk
✍ Mr V Tofts
🌐 www.broadwaygolfclub.co.uk

Canons Court (1982)
Pay and play
Bradley Green, Wotton-under-Edge GL12 7PN
☎ **(01453) 843128**
✍ A Bennett
🌐 www.canonscourtgolf.co.uk

Chipping Sodbury (1905)
Trinity Lane, Chipping Sodbury, Bristol BS37 6PU
☎ **(01454) 319042 (Members)**
📠 (01454) 320052
✉ info@chippingsodburygolfclub.co.uk
✍ Bob Williams
🌐 www.chippingsodburygolfclub.co.uk

Cirencester (1893)
Cheltenham Road, Bagendon, Cirencester GL7 7BH
☎ **(01285) 652465**
📠 (01285) 650665
✉ info@cirencestergolfclub.co.uk
✍ R Collishaw (01285) 652465
🌐 www.cirencestergolfclub.co.uk

Cleeve Hill (1892)
Pay and play
Cleeve Hill, Cheltenham GL52 3PW
☎ **(01242) 672025**
📠 (01242) 678444
✉ hughfitzsimons@btconnect.com
✍ Hugh Fitzsimons (Mgr)
🌐 www.cleevehillgolfclub.co.uk

Cotswold Edge (1980)
Upper Rushmire, Wotton-under-Edge GL12 7PT
☎ **(01453) 844167**
📠 (01453) 845120
✉ cotswoldedge@freenetname.co.uk
✍ NJ Newman
🌐 www.cotswoldedgegolfclub.org.uk

Cotswold Hills (1902)
Ullenwood, Cheltenham GL53 9QT
☎ **(01242) 515264**
📠 (01242) 515317
✉ tania@cotswoldhills-golfclub.com
✍ Mrs A Hale (Club Mgr)
🌐 www.cotswoldhills-golfclub.com

Dymock Grange (1995)
The Old Grange, Leominster Road, Dymock GL18 2AN
☎ **(01531) 890840**
📠 (01531) 890860

Filton (1909)
Golf Course Lane, Bristol BS34 7QS
☎ **(0117) 969 4169**
📠 (0117) 931 4359
✉ thesecretary@filtongolfclub.co.uk
✍ T Atkinson (0117) 969 4169
🌐 www.filtongolfclub.co.uk

Forest Hills (1992)
Proprietary
Mile End Road, Coleford GL16 7BY
☎ **(01594) 810620**
📠 (01594) 810823
🌐 www.fweb.org.uk/forestgolf

Forest of Dean (1973)
Lords Hill, Coleford GL16 8BE
☎ **(01594) 832583**
📠 (01594) 832584
✉ enquiries@bellshotel.co.uk
✍ H Wheeler (Hon Sec)
🌐 www.bellshotel.co.uk

Gloucester Golf & Country Club (1976)
Matson Lane, Gloucester, Gloucestershire GL4 6EA
☎ **(01452) 525653**
✍ K Wood (01452) 411311 (Mgr)

Henbury (1891)
Henbury Road, Westbury-on-Trym, Bristol BS10 7QB
☎ **(0117) 950 0044**
📠 (0117) 959 1928
✉ thesecretary@henburygolfclub.co.uk
✍ Derek Howell (0117) 950 0044
🌐 www.henburygolfclub.co.uk

For key to symbols see page 725

Hilton Puckrup Hall Hotel (1992)
Puckrup, Tewkesbury GL20 6EL
☎ **(01684) 296200/271591**
(01684) 850788
R Lazenby
www.puckrupgolf.co.uk

The Kendleshire (1997)
Proprietary
Henfield Road, Coalpit Heath, Bristol BS36 2TG
☎ **(0117) 956 7007**
(0117) 957 3433
info@kendleshire.com
P Murphy
www.kendleshire.com

Knowle (1905)
Fairway, West Town Lane, Brislington, Bristol BS4 5DF
☎ **(0117) 977 0660**
(0117) 972 0615
admin@knowlegolfclub.co.uk
www.knowlegolfclub.co.uk

Lilley Brook (1922)
Cirencester Road, Charlton Kings, Cheltenham GL53 8EG
☎ **(01242) 526785**
caroline@lilleybrook.co.uk
C Kirby (Sec)
www.lilleybrook.co.uk

Long Ashton (1893)
Clarken Coombe, Long Ashton, Bristol BS41 9DW
☎ **(01275) 392229**
(01275) 394395
secretary@longashtongolfclub.co.uk
Victoria Rose
www.longashtongolfclub.co.uk

Lydney (1909)
Naas Course, Naas Lane, Lydney GL15 5ES
☎ **(01594) 842775**
J Mills (01594) 841186
www.lydneygolfclub.co.uk

Minchinhampton (1889)
Minchinhampton, Stroud GL6 9BE
☎ **(01453) 832642 (Old) 833866 (New)**
(01453) 837360
rob@mgcnew.co.uk
R East (01453) 833866
www.minchinhamptongolfclub.co.uk

Naunton Downs (1993)
Proprietary
Naunton, Cheltenham GL54 3AE
☎ **(01451) 850090**
admin@nauntondowns.co.uk
Jane Ayers
www.nauntondowns.co.uk

Newent (1994)
Pay and play
Coldharbour Lane, Newent GL18 1DJ
☎ **(01531) 820478**
newentgolf@btconnect.com
T Brown
www.newentgolf.co.uk

Painswick (1891)
Golf Course Road, Painswick, Stroud GL6 6TL
☎ **(01452) 812180**
secretary.painswick@virginmedia.com
Mrs Ann Smith
www.painswickgolf.com

Rodway Hill (1991)
Pay and play
Newent Road, Highnam GL2 8DN
☎ **(01452) 384222**
(01452) 313814
info@rodway-hill-golf-course.co.uk
A Price
www.rodway-hill-golf-course.co.uk

Sherdons Golf Centre (1993)
Pay and play
Tredington, Tewkesbury GL20 7BP
☎ **(01684) 274782**
(01684) 275358
info@sherdons.co.uk
R Chatham
www.sherdons.co.uk

Shirehampton Park (1904)
Park Hill, Shirehampton, Bristol BS11 0UL
☎ **(0117) 982 2083**
(0117) 982 5280
info@shirehamptonparkgolfclub.co.uk
Karen Rix (0117) 982 2083
www.shirehamptonparkgolfclub.co.uk

Stinchcombe Hill (1889)
Stinchcombe Hill, Dursley GL11 6AQ
☎ **(01453) 542015**
(01453) 549545
secretary@stinchcombehill.plus.com
Leigh Topping
www.stinchcombehillgolfclub.com

Tewkesbury Park Hotel (1976)
Lincoln Green Lane, Tewkesbury GL20 7DN
☎ **(01684) 295405 (Hotel)**
(01684) 292386
golfsec.tewkesburypark@bespokehotels.com
Club Golf Sec (01684) 272322
www.tewkesburyparkgolfclub.co.uk

Thornbury Golf Centre (1992)
Bristol Road, Thornbury BS35 3XL
☎ **(01454) 281144**
(01454) 281177
info@thornburygc.co.uk
M Drake (Mgr)
www.thornburygc.co.uk

Woodlands G&CC (1989)
Pay and play
Trench Lane, Almondsbury, Bristol BS32 4JZ
☎ **(01454) 619319**
(01454) 619397
golf@woodlands-golf.com
D Knipe
www.woodlands-golf.com

Woodspring G&CC (1994)
Proprietary
Yanley Lane, Long Ashton, Bristol BS41 9LR
☎ **(01275) 394378**
(01275) 394473
info@woodspring-golf.com
D Knipe
www.woodspring-golf.com

Hampshire

Alresford (1890)
Cheriton Road, Tichborne Down, Alresford SO24 0PN
☎ **(01962) 733746**
(01962) 736040
secretary@alresfordgolf.co.uk
D Maskery
www.alresfordgolf.co.uk

Alton (1908)
Old Odiham Road, Alton GU34 4BU
☎ **(01420) 82042**

Ampfield Par Three (1962)
Proprietary
Winchester Road, Ampfield, Romsey SO51 9BQ
☎ **(01794) 368480**
Mark Hazell (MD) 01794 368 480
www.ampfieldgolf.com

Andover (1907)
51 Winchester Road, Andover SP10 2EF
☎ **(01264) 323980**
(01264) 358040
secretary@andovergolfclub.co.uk
www.andovergolfclub.co.uk

Army (1883)
Laffan's Road, Aldershot GU11 2HF
☎ **(01252) 337272**
(01252) 337562
secretary@armygolfclub.com
Jim Galley
www.armygolfclub.com

Barton-on-Sea (1897)
Milford Road, New Milton BH25 5PP
☎ **(01425) 615308**
(01425) 621457
admin@barton-on-sea-golf.co.uk
I Prentice
www.barton-on-sea-golf.co.uk

Basingstoke (1907)
Kempshott Park, Basingstoke RG23 7LL
☎ **(01256) 465990**
(01256) 331793
office@basingstokegolfclub.co.uk
John Hiscock
www.basingstokegolfclub.co.uk

For key to symbols see page 725

Bishopswood (1978)
Proprietary
Bishopswood Lane, Tadley, Basingstoke RG26 4AT
(01189) 408600
kpickett@bishopswoodgc.co.uk
Mrs J Jackson-Smith (0118) 982 0312 (Sec)
www.bishopswoodgc.co.uk

Blackmoor (1913)
Whitehill, Bordon GU35 9EH
(01420) 472775
(01420) 487666
admin@blackmoorgolf.co.uk
Mrs J Dean (Admin Mgr)
www.blackmoorgolf.co.uk

Blacknest (1993)
Blacknest GU34 4QL
(01420) 22888
(01420) 22001
reception@blacknestgolf.co.uk
Tim Russell

Botley Park Hotel G&CC (1989)
Winchester Road, Boorley Green, Botley SO3 2UA
(01489) 780888 Ext 451
(01489) 789242
golf.botley@macdonald-hotels.co.uk
www.macdonald-hotels.co.uk

Bramshaw (1880)
Brook, Lyndhurst SO43 7HE
(023) 8081 3433
(023) 8081 3460
golf@bramshaw.co.uk
Ian Baker
www.bramshaw.co.uk

Brokenhurst Manor (1915)
Sway Road, Brockenhurst SO42 7SG
(01590) 623332
(01590) 624691
secretary@brokenhurst-manor.org.uk
Neil Hallam Jones
www.brokenhurst-manor.org.uk

Burley (1905)
Cott Lane, Burley, Ringwood BH24 4BB
(01425) 402431
(01425) 404168
secretary@burleygolfclub.co.uk
Mrs L J Harfield (01425) 402431
www.burleygolfclub.co.uk

Cams Hall Estate (1993)
Proprietary
Cams Hall Estate, Fareham PO16 8UP
(01329) 827222
(01329) 827111
camshall@crown-golf.co.uk
www.camshallgolf.co.uk

Chilworth (1989)
Main Road, Chilworth, Southampton SO16 7JP
(023) 8074 0544
(023) 8073 3166

Corhampton (1891)
Corhampton, Southampton SO32 3GZ
(01489) 877279
(01489) 877680
secretary@corhamptongc.co.uk
Bob Ashton
www.corhamptongc.co.uk

Dibden Golf Centre (1974)
Public
Main Road, Dibden, Southampton SO45 5TB
(023) 8020 7508 (Bookings)
www.nfdc.gov.uk/golf

Dummer (1992)
Proprietary
Dummer, Basingstoke RG25 2AD
(01256) 397950 (Pro Shop)
(01256) 397889
enquiries@dummergolfclub.com
Steve Wright (Mgr) (01256) 397888
www.dummergolfclub.com

Dunwood Manor (1969)
Danes Road, Awbridge, Romsey SO51 0GF
(01794) 340549
(01794) 341215
admin@dunwood-golf.co.uk
www.dunwoodgolf.co.uk

Fleetlands (1961)
Fareham Road, Gosport PO13 0AW
(023) 9254 4492

Four Marks (1994)
Headmore Lane, Four Marks, Alton GU34 3ES
(01420) 587214
(01420) 587324
General Manager
www.fourmarksgolf.co.uk

Furzeley (1993)
Pay and play
Furzeley Road, Denmead PO7 6TX
(023) 9223 1180
(023) 9223 0921
furzeleygc@btinternet.com

Gosport & Stokes Bay (1885)
Fort Road, Haslar, Gosport PO12 2AT
(023) 925 27941
(023) 925 27941
secretary@gosportandstokesbaygolfclub.co.uk
Clun Manager (023) 925 27941
www.gosportandstokesbaygolfclub.co.uk

The Hampshire (1993)
Pay and play
Winchester Road, Goodworth Clatford, Andover SP11 7TB
(01264) 357555
(01264) 356606
enquiries@thehampshiregolfclub.co.uk
J Miles
www.thehampshiregolfclub.co.uk

Hartley Wintney (1891)
London Road, Hartley Wintney, Hook RG27 8PT
(01252) 844211
(01252) 844211
office@hartleywintneygolfclub.com
P J Gaylor
www.hartleywintneygolfclub.com

Hayling (1883)
Links Lane, Hayling Island PO11 0BX
(023) 9246 4446
members@haylinggolf.co.uk
Ian Walton (023) 9246 4446
www.haylinggolf.co.uk

Hockley (1914)
Twyford, Winchester SO21 1PL
(01962) 713165
admin@hockleygolfclub.com
Mrs A Pfam
www.hockleygolfclub.com

Lee-on-the-Solent (1905)
Brune Lane, Lee-on-the-Solent PO13 9PB
(023) 9255 1170
(023) 9255 4233
enquiries@leegolf.co.uk
Rob Henderson (Mgr) (023) 9255 1170
www.leegolf.co.uk

Liphook (1922)
Liphook GU30 7EH
(01428) 723271/723785
(01428) 724853
secretary@liphookgolfclub.com
John Douglass
www.liphookgolfclub.com

Meon Valley Marriott Hotel & Country Club (1979)
Proprietary
Sandy Lane, Shedfield, Southampton SO32 2HQ
(01329) 833455
(01329) 834411
george.mcmenemy@marriotthotels.com
GF McMenemy (Golf Dir)
www.marriottgolf.co.uk

New Forest (1888)
Southampton Road, Lyndhurst SO43 7BU
(023) 8028 2752
(023) 8028 4030
secretarynfgc@aol.com
Derek Hurlstone/Graham Lloyd
www.newforestgolfclub.co.uk

North Hants (1904)
Minley Road, Fleet GU51 1RF
(01252) 616443
(01252) 811627
secretary@northhantsgolf.co.uk
C J Gotla
www.northhantsgolf.co.uk

Old Thorns (1982)
Longmoor Road, Griggs Green, Liphook GU30 7PE
(01428) 724555

For key to symbols see page 725

(01428) 725036
proshop@oldthorns.com
Greg Knights
www.oldthorns.com

Otterbourne Golf Centre (1995)

Pay and play
Poles Lane, Otterbourne, Winchester SO21 2EL
(01962) 775225
info@chilworthgolfclub.com
www.chilworthgolfclub.com

Park (1995)

Pay and play
Avington, Winchester SO21 1BZ
(01962) 779945 (Clubhouse)
(01962) 779530
office@avingtongolf.co.uk
R Stent (Prop)
www.avingtongolf.co.uk

Paultons Golf Centre (1922)

Pay and play
Old Salisbury Road, Ower, Romsey S O51 6AN
(023) 8081 3992
(023) 8081 3993
www.crown-golf.co.uk

Petersfield (1892)

Tankerdale Lane, Liss GU33 7QY
(01730) 895165
manager@petersfieldgolfclub.co.uk
PD Badger
www.petersfieldgolfclub.co.uk

Petersfield Pay and Play

Pay and play
139 Sussex Road, Petersfield GU31 4LE
(01730) 267732
PD Badger

Portsmouth (1926)

Pay and play
Crookhorn Lane, Widley, Waterlooville PO7 5QL
(023) 9237 2210
portsmouthgc@btconnect.com
Mr Iden Adams (Sec) (023) 9220 1827
www.portsmouthgc.com

Quindell (1997)

Skylark Meadows, Whiteley, Fareham PO15 6RS
(01329) 844441
(01329) 836736
sales@quindell.com
Rob Terry
www.quindell.com

Romsey (1900)

Nursling, Southampton SO16 0XW
(023) 8073 4637
(023) 8074 1036
secretary@romseygolfclub.co.uk
Mike Batty
www.romseygolfclub.com

Rowlands Castle (1902)

Links Lane, Rowlands Castle PO9 6AE
(023) 9241 2784
(023) 9241 3649
manager@rowlandscastlegc.co.uk
KD Fisher (023) 9241 2784
www.rowlandscastlegolfclub.co.uk

Royal Winchester (1888)

Sarum Road, Winchester SO22 5QE
(01962) 852462
(01962) 865048
manager@royalwinchestergolfclub.com
A Buck
www.royalwinchestergolfclub.com

Sandford Springs (1988)

Wolverton, Tadley RG26 5RT
(01635) 296800
(01635) 296801
andreww@sandfordsprings.co.uk
Andrew Wild (01635) 296800
www.sandfordsprings.co.uk

Somerley Park (1995)

Somerley, Ringwood BH24 3PL
(01425) 461496
gordon@somerleyparkgolfclub.co.uk
Gordon Scott
www.somerleyparkgolfclub.co.uk

South Winchester

Pitt, Winchester, Hampshire SO22 5QW
(01962) 877800
(01962) 877900
winchester-sales@crown-golf.co.uk
L Ross (Gen Mgr) (01962) 877800
www.crown-golf.co.uk

Southampton Municipal (1935)

Public
1 Golf Course Road, Bassett, Southampton SO16 7AY
(023) 807 60546
mick.carter7@ntlworld.com
E Hemsley
www.southamptongolfclub.co.uk

Southsea (1914)

Public
The Clubhouse, Burrfields Road, Portsmouth PO3 5JJ
(023) 9266 8667
(023) 9266 8667
southseagolfclub@tiscali.co.uk
R Collinson (02392) 699110
www.southsea-golf.co.uk

Southwick Park (1977)

Pinsley Drive, Southwick PO17 6EL
(023) 9238 0131 Option 1
(0871) 855 6809
jameslever@southwickparkgolfclub.co.uk
J R Lever
www.southwickparkgolfclub.co.uk

Southwood (1977)

Public
Ively Road, Farnborough GU14 0LJ
(01252) 548700
(01252) 549091
ianattoe@ddesure.co.uk
www.southwoodgolfclub.co.uk

Stoneham (1908)

Monks Wood Close, Bassett, Southampton SO16 3TT
(023) 8076 9272
(023) 8076 6320
richard@stonehamgolfclub.org.uk
R Penley-Martin (Mgr)
www.stonehamgolfclub.org.uk

Test Valley (1992)

Micheldever Road, Overton, Basingstoke RG25 3DS
(01256) 771737
(01256) 771285
info@testvalleygolf.com
www.testvalleygolf.com

Tylney Park (1973)

Proprietary
Rotherwick, Hook RG27 9AY
(01256) 762079
(01256) 763079
contact@tylneypark.co.uk
Alasdair Hay (Mgr)
www.tylneypark.co.uk

Waterlooville (1907)

Cherry Tree Ave, Cowplain, Waterlooville PO8 8AP
(023) 9226 3388
(023) 9224 2980
secretary@waterloovillegolfclub.co.uk
J Hay
www.waterloovillegolfclub.co.uk

Wellow (1991)

Proprietary
Ryedown Lane, East Wellow, Romsey SO51 6BD
(01794) 322872
(01794) 323832
Mrs C Gurd
www.wellowgolfclub.co.uk

Weybrook Park (1971)

Rooksdown Lane, Basingstoke RG24 9NT
(01256) 320347
(01256) 812973
info@weybrookpark.co.uk
Mrs S Bowen (Sec)/Mr A Dillon (Mgr)
www.weybrookpark.co.uk

Wickham Park (1991)

Proprietary
Titchfield Lane, Wickham, Fareham PO17 5PJ
(01329) 833342
(01329) 834798
wickhampark@crown-golf.co.uk
Jonathan Tubb
www.crown-golf.co.uk

Worldham (1993)
Proprietary
Cakers Lane, Worldham, Alton GU34 3BF
(01420) 543151/544606
(01420) 544606
manager@worldhamgolfclub.co.uk
Ian Yates (01420) 544606
www.worldhamgolfclub.co.uk

Herefordshire

Belmont Lodge (1983)
Ruckhall Lane, Belmont, Hereford HR2 9SA
(01432) 352666
(01432) 358090
info@belmont-hereford.co.uk
Christopher T Smith (Gen Mgr)
www.belmont-hereford.co.uk

Burghill Valley (1991)
Proprietary
Tillington Road, Burghill, Hereford HR4 7RW
(01432) 760456
(01432) 761654
admin@bvgc.co.uk
Mrs D Harrison (Office Mgr)
www.bvgc.co.uk

Cadmore Lodge (1990)
Pay and play
Berrington Green, Tenbury Wells, Worcester WR15 8TQ
(01584) 810044
(01584) 810044
reception.cadmore@cadmorelodge.com
Mike Miles
www.cadmorelodge.co.uk

Hereford Golf Club (1983)
Public
Hereford Halo Leisure & Golf Club, Holmer Road, Hereford HR4 9UD
(01432) 344376
(01432) 266281

Herefordshire (1896)
Raven's Causeway, Wormsley, Hereford HR4 8LY
(01432) 830219
herfordshire.golf@breathe.com
D Gwynne
www.herefordshiregolfclub.co.uk

Kington (1925)
Bradnor Hill, Kington HR5 3RE
(01544) 230340
info@kingtongolf.co.uk
N P Venables (01544) 388259
www.kingtongolf.co.uk

Leominster (1967)
Ford Bridge, Leominster HR6 0LE
(01568) 610055
(01568) 610055
contact@leominstergolfclub.co.uk
Mr Dilwyn James
leominstergolfclub.co.uk

Ross-on-Wye (1903)
Two Park, Gorsley, Ross-on-Wye HR9 7UT
(01989) 720267
(01989) 720212
admin@therossonwyegolfclub.co.uk
Leighton Walker
www.therossonwyegolfclub.co.uk

Sapey (1991)
Proprietary
Upper Sapey, Worcester WR6 6XT
(01886) 853288
(01886) 853485
anybody@sapeygolf.co.uk
Miss L Stevenson (01886) 853506
www.sapeygolf.co.uk

South Herefordshire (1992)
Twin Lakes, Upton Bishop, Ross-on-Wye HR9 7UA
(01989) 780535
(01989) 740611
info@herefordshiregolf.co.uk
www.herefordshiregolf.co.uk

Summerhill (1994)
Proprietary
Clifford, Nr. Hay-on-Wye, Hereford HR3 5EW
(01497) 820451
competitions@summerhillgolfcourse.co.uk
Michael Tom
www.summerhillgolfcourse.co.uk

Hertfordshire

Aldenham G&CC (1975)
Proprietary
Church Lane, Aldenham, Watford WD25 8NN
(01923) 853929
(01923) 858472
info@aldenhamgolfclub.co.uk
Mrs J Phillips
www.aldenhamgolfclub.co.uk

Aldwickbury Park (1995)
Proprietary
Piggottshill Lane, Wheathampstead Road, Harpenden AL5 1AB
(01582) 760112
(01582) 760113
info@aldwickburyparkgc.co.uk
A Shewbridge
www.aldwickburyparkgolfclub.co.uk

Arkley (1909)
Rowley Green Road, Barnet EN5 3HL
(020) 8449 0394
secretary@arkley.demon.co.uk
A N Welsh
www.arkleygolfclub.co.uk

Ashridge (1932)
Little Gaddesden, Berkhamsted HP4 1LY
(01442) 842244
(01442) 843770
info@ashridgegolfclub.ltd.uk
Secretary
www.ashridgegolfclub.ltd.uk

Barkway Park (1992)
Proprietary
Nuthampstead Road, Barkway, Royston SG8 8EN
(01763) 849070
gc@barkwaypark.fsnet.co.uk
GS Cannon
www.barkwaypark.co.uk

Batchwood Hall (1935)
Pay and play
Batchwood Drive, St Albans AL3 5XA
(01727) 844250
batchwood@leisureconnection.co.uk
Luke Askew
www.leisureconnection.co.uk

Batchworth Park (1996)
London Road, Rickmansworth WD3 1JS
(01923) 711400
(01923) 710200
batchworthpark-sales@crown-golf.co.uk
Rob Davies
www.batchworthparkgolf.co.uk

Berkhamsted (1890)
The Common, Berkhamsted HP4 2QB
(01442) 865832
(01442) 863730
Steve@berkhamstedgc.co.uk
S H Derbyshire
www.berkhamstedgolfclub.co.uk

Bishop's Stortford (1910)
Dunmow Road, Bishop's Stortford CM23 5HP
(01279) 654715
(01279) 655215
office@bsgc.co.uk
Judy Barker
www.bsgc.co.uk

Boxmoor (1890)
18 Box Lane, Hemel Hempstead HP3 0DJ
(01442) 242434 (Clubhouse)
www.boxmoorgolfclub.co.uk

Brickendon Grange (1964)
Pembridge Lane, Brickendon, Hertford SG13 8PD
(01992) 511258
(01992) 511411
play@bggc.org.uk
Jane Coulcher
www.bggc.org.uk

Briggens Park (1988)
Proprietary
Briggens Park, Stanstead Road, Stanstead Abbotts SG12 8LD
(01279) 793867
(01279) 793867
briggensparkgolf@aol.co.uk
Trevor Mitchell
www.briggensparkgolfclub.co.uk

For key to symbols see page 725

Brocket Hall (1992)
Proprietary
Welwyn AL8 7XG
☎ **(01707) 368808**
(01707) 390052
louis.matamala@brocket-hall.co.uk
Louis Matamala (01707) 368740
www.brocket-hall.co.uk

Brookmans Park (1930)
Brookmans Park, Hatfield AL9 7AT
☎ **(01707) 652487**
(01707) 661851
info@bpgc.co.uk
Una Handley
www.bpgc.co.uk

Bushey G&CC (1980)
High Street, Bushey WD23 1TT
☎ **(020) 8950 2283 Pro Shop (020) 8950 2215**
(020) 8386 1181
info@busheycountryclub.com
Mark Young
www.busheycountryclub.com

Bushey Hall (1890)
Proprietary
Bushey Hall Drive, Bushey WD23 2EP
☎ **(01923) 222253**
(01923) 229759
gordon@golfclubuk.co.uk
Gordon Dawson
www.busheyhallgolfclub.co.uk

Chadwell Springs GC (1974)
Pay and play
Hertford Road, Ware SG12 9LE
☎ **(01920) 462075/61447**
chadwell.golfshop@virgin.net
David Smith PGA Pro/Manager
www.chadwellspringsgolfshop.co.uk

Chesfield Downs (1991)
Pay and play
Jack's Hill, Graveley, Stevenage SG4 7EQ
☎ **(08707) 460020**
(08707) 460021

Cheshunt (1976)
Public
Park Lane, Cheshunt EN7 6QD
☎ **(01992) 629777**
accounts.cpgc@btconnect.com
B Furne

Chorleywood (1890)
Common Road, Chorleywood WD3 5LN
☎ **(01923) 282009**
(01923) 286739
secretary@chorleywoodgolfclub.co.uk
RA Botham
www.chorleywoodgolfclub.co.uk

Dyrham Park CC (1963)
Galley Lane, Barnet EN5 4RA
☎ **(020) 8440 3361**
(020) 8441 9836
enquiries@dyrhampark.com
David Adams
www.dyrhampark.com

East Herts (1899)
Hamels Park, Buntingford SG9 9NA
☎ **(01920) 821978**
(01920) 823700
gm@easthertsgolfclub.co.uk
Ms A McDonald
www.easthertsgolfclub.co.uk

Great Hadham (1993)
Proprietary
Great Hadham Road, Bishop's Stortford SG10 6JE
☎ **(01279) 843558**
(01279) 842122
ian@ghgcc.co.uk
I Bailey
www.ghgcc.co.uk

The Grove (2003)
Pay and play
Chandler's Cross, Rickmansworth WD3 4TG
☎ **(01923) 294266**
(01923) 294268
golf@thegrove.co.uk
Anna Darnell (Dir of Golf)
www.thegrove.co.uk

Hadley Wood (1922)
Beech Hill, Hadley Wood, Barnet EN4 0JJ
☎ **(020) 8449 4328**
(020) 8364 8633
gm@hadleywoodgc.com
WM Beckett (Gen Mgr)
www.hadleywoodgc.com

Hanbury Manor G&CC (1990)
Ware SG12 0SD
☎ **(01920) 487722**
(01920) 487692
mhrs.stngs.golfevents@marriotthotels.com
Mike Harrison (Director of Clubs)
www.hanbury-manor.co.uk

Harpenden (1894)
Hammonds End, Redbourn Lane, Harpenden AL5 2AX
☎ **(01582) 712580**
(01582) 712725
office@harpendengolfclub.co.uk
Frank Clapp (Gen Mgr)
www.harpendengolfclub.co.uk

Harpenden Common (1931)
East Common, Harpenden AL5 1BL
☎ **(01582) 711320**
(01582) 711321
admin@hcgc.co.uk
Terry Crump (01582) 711325
www.harpendencommongolfclub.co.uk

Hartsbourne G&CC (1946)
Hartsbourne Avenue, Bushey Heath WD23 1JW
☎ **(020) 8421 7272**
(020) 8950 5357
ian@hartsbournecountryclub.co.uk
I Thomas
www.hartsbournecountryclub.co.uk

Hatfield London CC (1976)
Bedwell Park, Essendon, Hatfield AL9 6HN
☎ **(01707) 260360**
(01707) 278475
info@hatfieldlondon.co.uk
H Takeda
www.hatfieldlondon.co.uk

The Hertfordshire (1995)
Proprietary
Broxbournebury Mansion, White Stubbs Lane, Broxbourne EN10 7PY
☎ **(01992) 466666**
(01992) 470326
hertfordshire-manager@crown-golf.co.uk
J Hetherington

Kingsway Golf Centre (1991)
Proprietary
Cambridge Road, Melbourn, Royston SG8 6EY
☎ **(01763) 262943**
(01763) 263038
kingswaygolf@btconnect.com
Chris Page
www.kingswaygolfcentre.co.uk

Knebworth (1908)
Deards End Lane, Knebworth SG3 6NL
☎ **(01438) 812752 (Clubhouse)**
(01438) 815216
admin@knebworthgolfclub.com
Steve Barrett
www.knebworthgolfclub.com

Lamerwood (1996)
Codicote Road, Wheathampstead AL4 8RH
☎ **(01582) 833013**
(01582) 832604
lamerwood.cc@virgin.net
R Darling (Gen Mgr)
www.lamerwood.humaxuk.com

Letchworth (1905)
Letchworth Lane, Letchworth Garden City SG6 3NQ
☎ **(01462) 683203**
(01462) 484567
secretary@letchworthgolfclub.com
Mrs Niki Hunter
www.letchworthgolfclub.com

Little Hay Golf Complex (1977)
Pay and play
Box Lane, Bovingdon, Hemel Hempstead HP3 0XT
☎ **(01442) 833798**
(01442) 831399
membership@sportspace.co.uk
George Reid (Mgr)
www.sportspace.co.uk

Manor of Groves G&CC (1992)

Proprietary

High Wych, Sawbridgeworth CM21 0JU

- ☎ **(01279) 600777**
- (01279) 603543
- golfsecretary@manorgroves.co.uk
- Bob Walker (01279) 603559
- www.manorgolf.net

Mid Herts (1892)

Gustard Wood, Wheathampstead AL4 8RS

- ☎ **(01582) 832242**
- (01582) 834834
- secretary@mid-hertsgolfclub.co.uk
- Martin Bennet
- www.mid-hertsgolfclub.co.uk

Mill Green (1994)

Proprietary

Gypsy Lane, Mill Green, Welwyn Garden City AL7 4TY

- ☎ **(01707) 276900**
- (01707) 276898
- millgreen@crown-golf.co.uk
- Tim Hudson
- www.millgreengolf.co.uk

Moor Park (1923)

Rickmansworth WD3 1QN

- ☎ **(01923) 773146**
- (01923) 777109
- jon.moore@moorparkgc.co.uk
- JM Moore (01923) 773146
- www.moorparkgc.co.uk

Old Fold Manor (1910)

Old Fold Lane, Hadley Green, Barnet EN5 4QN

- ☎ **(020) 8440 9185**
- (020) 8441 4863
- manager@oldfoldmanor.co.uk
- www.oldfoldmanor.co.uk

Oxhey Park (1991)

Pay and play

Prestwick Road, South Oxhey, Watford WD19 7EX

- ☎ **(01923) 248213/210118**
- oxheyparkgolfclub@live.com
- James Wright (Prop)
- www.oxheyparkgolfclub.co.uk

Panshanger Golf Complex (1976)

Public

Old Herns Lane, Welwyn Garden City AL7 2ED

- ☎ **(01707) 333312/333350 (Bookings)**
- (01707) 390010
- trish.skinner@talk21.com
- Trish Skinner (07982) 259475
- www.finesseleisure.com

Porters Park (1899)

Shenley Hill, Radlett WD7 7AZ

- ☎ **(01923) 854127**
- (01923) 855475
- enquiries@porterspark.com
- P Marshall
- www.porterspark.com

Potters Bar (1923)

Darkes Lane, Potters Bar, Hertfordshire EN6 1DF

- ☎ **(01707) 652020**
- (01707) 655051
- louise@pottersbargolfclub.com
- Louise Alabaster
- www.pottersbargolfclub.com

Radlett Park Golf Club (1984)

Proprietary

Watling Street, Nr. Radlett WD6 3AA

- ☎ **(0208) 953 6115**
- (0208) 207 6390
- info@radlettparkgolfclub.com
- Marc Warwick (Mgr/Pro) (0208) 238694
- www.radlettparkgolfclub.com

Redbourn (1970)

Proprietary

Kinsbourne Green Lane, Redbourn, St Albans AL3 7QA

- ☎ **(01582) 793493**
- (01582) 794362
- info@redbourngc.co.uk
- T Hall (01582) 793493
- www.redbourngolfclub.com

Rickmansworth (1937)

Public

Moor Lane, Rickmansworth WD3 1QL

- ☎ **(01923) 775278**
- (01923) 775278

Royston (1892)

Baldock Road, Royston SG8 5BG

- ☎ **(01763) 243476**
- (01763) 246910
- roystongolf@btconnect.com
- S Clark (Mgr)
- www.roystongolfclub.co.uk

Sandy Lodge (1910)

Sandy Lodge Lane, Northwood, Middx HA6 2JD

- ☎ **(01923) 825429**
- (01923) 824319
- clivebailey@sandylodge.co.uk
- C H Bailey
- www.sandylodge.co.uk

Shendish Manor Hotel & Golf Course (1988)

Pay and play

Shendish Manor, London Road, Apsley HP3 0AA

- ☎ **(01442) 251806**
- (01442) 230683
- golfmanager@shendish-manor.com
- Bronwen Pateman (Membership Co-ordinator)
- www.shendish-manor.com

South Herts (1899)

Links Drive, Totteridge, London N20 8QU

- ☎ **(020) 8445 2035**
- (020) 8445 7569
- secretary@southhertsgolfclub.co.uk
- John Charlton (020) 8445 2035
- www.southhertsgolfclub.co.uk

Stevenage (1980)

Public

Aston Lane, Stevenage SG2 7EL

- ☎ **(01438) 880424**

Verulam (1905)

226 London Road, St Albans AL1 1JG

- ☎ **(01727) 853327**
- (01727) 812201
- gm@verulamgolf.co.uk
- R Farrer
- www.verulamgolf.co.uk

Welwyn Garden City (1922)

Mannicotts, High Oaks Road, Welwyn Garden City AL8 7BP

- ☎ **(01707) 325243**
- (01707) 393213
- secretary@welwyngardencitygolfclub.co.uk
- D Spring (Gen Mgr)
- www.welwyngardencitygolfclub.co.uk

West Herts (1890)

Cassiobury Park, Watford WD3 3GG

- ☎ **(01923) 236484**
- (01923) 222300
- gm@westhertsgolf.demon.co.uk
- R M McCue
- www.westhertsgolfclub.co.uk

Wheathampstead (2001)

Pay and play

Harpenden Road, Wheathampstead, St Albans AL4 8EZ

- ☎ **(01582) 833941**
- (01582) 833941
- nlawrencegolfacademy@hotmail.co.uk
- N Lawrence
- www.wheathampstead.net/golf-course

Whipsnade Park (1974)

Studham Lane, Dagnall HP4 1RH

- ☎ **(01442) 842330**
- (01442) 842090
- secretary@whipsnadeparkgolf.co.uk
- www.whipsnadeparkgolf.co.uk

Whitehill (1990)

Proprietary

Dane End, Ware SG12 0JS

- ☎ **(01920) 438495**
- (01920) 438891
- andrew@whitehillgolf.co.uk
- Mr A Smith (Prop)
- www.whitehillgolf.co.uk

Isle of Man

Castletown Golf Links (1892)

Proprietary

Fort Island, Derbyhaven IM9 1UA

- ☎ **(01624) 822211**
- (01624) 829661
- golfaccounts@manx.net
- www.golfiom.com

Douglas (1891)
Public
Pulrose Road, Douglas IM2 1AE
(01624) 675952 (Clubhouse)
(01624) 616865
douglasgolfclub@manx.net
Mrs J Murley (01624) 616865
www.douglasgolfclub.com

King Edward Bay (1893)
Groudle Road, Onchan IM3 2JR
(01624) 620430/673821
(01624) 676794

Mount Murray G&CC (1994)
Proprietary
Santon IM4 2HT
(01624) 695308
(01624) 611116
sales@mountmurray.com
A Laing (Pro)
www.mountmurray.com

Peel (1895)
Rheast Lane, Peel IM5 1BG
(01624) 843456
peelgc@manx.net
Guy Smith
www.peelgolfclub.com

Port St Mary (1903)
Public
Kallow Road, Port St Mary IM9 5EJ
(01624) 834932
(01624) 837231
N Swimmin (07624) 498848

Ramsey (1891)
Brookfield Avenue, Ramsey IM8 2AH
(01624) 813365/812244
(01624) 815833
ramseygolfclub@manx.net
Mr J M Ferrier (01624) 812244
www.ramseygolfclub.im

Rowany (1895)
Rowany Drive, Port Erin IM9 6LN
(01624) 834108
(01624) 834072
rowany@iommail.net
CA Corrin (Mgr)
www.rowanygolfclub.com

Isle of Wight

Cowes (1909)
Crossfield Avenue, Cowes PO31 8HN
(01983) 280135 (Steward)
(01983) 292303
secretary@cowesgolfclub.co.uk
C lacey (01983) 292303
www.cowesgolfclub.co.uk

Freshwater Bay (1894)
Afton Down, Freshwater, Isle of Wight PO40 9TZ
(01983) 752955
(01983) 756704
secretary@freshwaterbaygolfclub.co.uk
Kevin Garrett (01983) 752955
www.freshwaterbaygolfclub.co.uk

Newport (1896)
St George's Down, Shide, Newport PO30 3BA
(01983) 525076
(01983) 526711
newportgc@btconnect.com
Graham Darke (Pro) (01983) 525076
www.newportgolfclub.co.uk

Osborne (1904)
Osborne House Estate, East Cowes PO32 6JX
(01983) 295421
(01983) 292781
manager@osbornegolfclub.co.uk
AC Waite
www.osbornegolfclub.co.uk

Ryde (1895)
Binstead Road, Ryde PO33 3NF
(01983) 614809
(01983) 567418
ryde.golfclub@btconnect.com
www.rydegolf.co.uk

Shanklin & Sandown (1900)
The Fairway, Lake, Sandown PO36 9PR
(01983) 403217
(01983) 403007
club@ssgolfclub.com
AC Creed
www.ssgolfclub.com

Ventnor (1892)
Steephill Down Road, Ventnor PO38 1BP
(01983) 853326/853388
(01983) 853326
secretary@ventnorgolfclub.co.uk
www.ventnorgolfclub.co.uk

Westridge (1990)
Pay and play
Brading Road, Ryde PO33 1QS
(01983) 613131
(01983) 567017
westgc@aol.com
Simon Hayward
www.westridgegolfcentre.co.uk

Kent

Aquarius (1912)
Marmora Rd, Honor Oak, London SE22 0RY
(020) 8693 1626
secretary@aquariusgolfclub.co.uk
J Halliday
www.aquariusgolfclub.co.uk

Ashford (1903)
Sandyhurst Lane, Ashford TN25 4NT
(01233) 622655
(01233) 627494
info@ashfordgolfclub.co.uk
www.ashfordgolfclub.co.uk

Austin Lodge (1991)
Upper Auston Lodge Road, Eynsford, Swanley DA4 0HU
(01322) 863000
(01322) 862406

Barnehurst (1903)
Public
Mayplace Road East, Bexley Heath DA7 6JU
(01322) 523746
(01322) 523860

Bearsted (1895)
Ware Street, Bearsted, Maidstone ME14 4PQ
(01622) 738198
(01622) 735608
bearstedgolfclub@tiscali.co.uk
Stuart Turner (01622) 738198
www.bearstedgolfclub.co.uk

Beckenham Place Park (1907)
Public
Beckenham Hill Road, Beckenham BR3 2BP
(020) 8650 2292
(020) 8663 1201
beckenhamgolf@glendale-services.co.uk
www.glendale-services.co.uk

Bexleyheath (1909)
Mount Road, Bexleyheath DA6 8JS
(020) 8303 6951
bexleyheathgolf@btconnect.com
Mrs J Smith

Birchwood Park (1990)
Birchwood Road, Wilmington, Dartford DA2 7HJ
(01322) 662038
(01322) 667283
www.birchwoodparkgc.co.uk

Boughton (1993)
Pay and play
Brickfield Lane, Boughton, Faversham ME13 9AJ
(01227) 752277
(01227) 752361
greg@pentlandgolf.co.uk
Sue Coleman
www.pentlandgolf.co.uk

Broke Hill (1993)
Sevenoaks Road, Halstead TN14 7HR
(01959) 533225
(01959) 532680
broke-sales@crows-golf.co.uk
www.brokehillgolf.co.uk

Bromley (1948)
Pay and play
Magpie Hall Lane, Bromley BR2 8JF
(020) 8462 7014
(020) 8462 6916
bromleygolfclub.co.uk
Dave Langford (01959) 573376

Broome Park (1981)
Broome Park Estate, Barham, Canterbury CT4 6QX
(01227) 830728
(01227) 832591
golf@broomepark.co.uk
Mrs D Burtenshaw
www.broomepark.co.uk

Canterbury (1927)
Scotland Hills, Littlebourne Road, Canterbury CT1 1TW
☎ **(01227) 453532**
(01227) 784277
secretary@canterburygolfclub.co.uk
Jonathan Webb (Secretary)
www.canterburygolfclub.co.uk

Chart Hills (1993)
Proprietary
Weeks Lane, Biddenden, Ashford TN27 8JX
☎ **(01580) 292222**
(01580) 292233
info@charthills.co.uk
David Colyer
www.charthills.co.uk

Chelsfield Lakes Golf Centre (1992)
Pay and play
Court Road, Orpington BR6 9BX
☎ **(01689) 896266**
(01689) 824577
manager@chelsfieldlakesgolf.co.uk
Alex Taylor (Mgr)
www.chelsfieldlakesgolf.co.uk

Cherry Lodge (1969)
Jail Lane, Biggin Hill, Westerham TN16 3AX
☎ **(01959) 572250**
info@cherrylodgegc.co.uk
Craig Sutherland
www.cherrylodgegc.co.uk

Chestfield (1925)
103 Chestfield Road, Whitstable CT5 3LU
☎ **(01227) 794411**
(01227) 794454
generalmanager@chestfield-golfclub.co.uk
Alan Briggs
www.chestfield-golfclub.co.uk

Chislehurst (1894)
Camden Place, Camden Park Road, Chislehurst BR7 5HJ
☎ **(020) 8467 6798**
(020) 8295 0874
thesecretary@chislehurstgolfclub.co.uk
M Hickson (020) 8467 2782
www.chislehurstgolfclub.co.uk

Cobtree Manor Park (1984)
Public
Chatham Road, Boxley, Maidstone ME14 3AZ
☎ **(01622) 753276**
cobtree@mytimegolf.co.uk
Steve Miller
www.cobtreemanorparkgolfcourse.co.uk

Darenth Valley (1973)
Pay and play
Station Road, Shoreham, Sevenoaks TN14 7SA
☎ **(01959) 522944 (Clubhouse)**
(01959) 525089
enquiries@dvgc.co.uk
Deborah Terry
www.dvgc.co.uk

Dartford (1897)
The Clubhouse, Heath Lane (Upper), Dartford DA1 2TN
☎ **(01322) 223616**
(01322) 278690
dartfordgolf@hotmail.com
Mrs Amanda Malas (01322) 226455
www.dartfordgolfclub.co.uk

Deangate Ridge Golf & Sports Complex (1972)
Public
Duxcourt Road, Hoo, Rochester ME3 8RZ
☎ **(01634) 254481 (Gen Mgr)**
leisure@medway.gov.uk
Lee Mills (Gen Mgr) (01634) 254481
www.deangateridge.co.uk

Eastwell Manor (2008)
Boughton Lees, Ashford, Kent TN25 4HR
☎ **(01233) 213100**
(01233) 213105
enquiries@eastwellmanor.co.uk
www.eastwellmanor.co.uk

Eltham Warren (1890)
Bexley Road, Eltham, London SE9 2PE
☎ **(0208) 850 4477**
(0208) 850 0522
secretary@elthamwarrengolfclub.co.uk
DJ Mabbott
www.elthamwarrengolfclub.co.uk

Etchinghill (1995)
Pay and play
Canterbury Road, Etchinghill, Folkestone CT18 8FA
☎ **(01303) 863863**
(01303) 863210
deb@pentlandgolf.co.uk
D Francis (01303) 864576
www.pentlandgolf.co.uk

Faversham (1902)
Belmont Park, Faversham ME13 0HB
☎ **(01795) 890561**
(01795) 890561
themanager@favershamgolf.co.uk
Ian Griffiths
www.favershamgolf.co.uk

Fawkham Valley (1987)
Gay Dawn Farm, Fawkham, Dartford DA3 8LZ
☎ **(01474) 707144**
fvgolfcourse@googlemail.com
J Marchant
www.fawkhamvalleygolf.co.uk

Gillingham (1905)
Woodlands Road, Gillingham ME7 2AP
☎ **(01634) 853017/850999**
golf@gillinghamgolf.idps.co.uk
Miss K Snow (01634) 853017
www.gillinghamgolfclub.co.uk

Hawkhurst (1968)
High Street, Hawkhurst TN18 4JS
☎ **(01580) 752396**
(01580) 754074
hawkhurstgolfclub@tiscali.co.uk
HawkhurstGolfClub.org.uk

Hemsted Forest (1969)
Proprietary
Golford Road, Cranbrook TN17 4AL
☎ **(01580) 712833**
(01580) 714274
golf@hemstedforest.co.uk
K Stevenson
www.hemstedforest.co.uk

Herne Bay (1895)
Eddington, Herne Bay CT6 7PG
☎ **(01227) 374097**
sue.brown@hernebaygolfclub.co.uk
www.hernebaygolfclub.co.uk

Hever Castle (1992)
Proprietary
Hever Road, Hever, Edenbridge TN8 7NP
☎ **(01732) 700771**
(01732) 700775
mail@hever.co.uk
Jon Wittenberg
www.hever.co.uk

High Elms (1969)
Public
High Elms Road, Downe, Orpington BR6 7SZ
☎ **(01689) 858175**
(01689) 856326
Mrs P O'Keeffe (Hon)
www.highelmsgolfclub.com

Hilden Golf Centre
Pay and play
Rings Hill, Hildenborough, Tonbridge TN11 8LX
☎ **(01732) 833607**
(01732) 834484
info@hildenpark.co.uk
www.hildenpark.co.uk

Hythe Imperial (1950)
Prince's Parade, Hythe CT21 6AE
☎ **(01303) 233745**
(01303) 267554 (Professional)
h6862-th@accor.com
Clare Gibson (01303) 233724
www.mercure-uk.com

The Kent & Surrey G&CC (1972)
Proprietary
Crouch House Road, Edenbridge TN8 5LQ
☎ **(01732) 867381**
(01732) 867167
info@thekentandsurrey.com
David Taylor/Richard Thorpe
www.thekentandsurrey.com

Kings Hill (1996)
Proprietary
Fortune Way, Kings Hill, West Malling, Kent ME19 4GF
☎ **(01732) 875040/842121 (Bookings)**

(01732) 875019
office@kingshillgolf.co.uk
Margaret Gilbert (Mgr)
www.kingshillgolf.co.uk

Knole Park (1924)
Seal Hollow Road, Sevenoaks TN15 0HJ
(01732) 452150
(01732) 463159
secretary@knoleparkgolfclub.co.uk
N Statham (01732) 452150
www.knoleparkgolfclub.co.uk

Lamberhurst (1890)
Church Road, Lamberhurst TN3 8DT
(01892) 890591
(01892) 891140
secretary@lamberhurstgolfclub.com
Mrs S Deadman (01892) 890591
www.lamberhurstgolfclub.com

Langley Park (1910)
Barnfield Wood Road, Beckenham BR3 6SZ
(020) 8658 6849
(020) 8658 6310
manager@langleyparkgolf.co.uk
S Naylor (Gen Mgr)
www.langleyparkgolf.co.uk

Leeds Castle (1928)
Pay and play
Leeds Castle, Hollingbourne, Maidstone ME17 1PL
(01622) 880467/767828
(01622) 735616
stevepurves@leeds-castle.co.uk
www.leeds-castle.com

Littlestone (1888)
St Andrews Road, Littlestone, New Romney TN28 8RB
(01797) 362310
(01797) 362740
secretary@littlestonegolfclub.org.uk
S Fullager (01797) 363355
www.littlestonegolfclub.org.uk

Littlestone Warren (1993)
Pay and play
St Andrews Road, Littlestone, New Romney TN28 8RB
(01797) 362231
(01797) 362740
secretary@littlestonegolfclub.org.uk
S Fullager 01797 363355
www.romneywarrengolfclub.org.uk

London Beach Golf Club (1998)
Pay and play
Ashford Road, St Michaels, Tenterden TN30 6HX
(01580) 767616
(01580) 763884
enquiries@londonbeach.com
P Edmonds
www.londonbeach.com

London Golf Club (1993)
Stansted Lane, Ash, Nr Brands Hatch, TN15 7EH
(01474) 879899
(01474) 879912
golf@londongolf.co.uk
Austen Gravestock
www.londongolf.co.uk

Lullingstone Park (1967)
Public
Parkgate Road, Chelsfield, Orpington BR6 7PX
(01959) 533793
CJ Pocock (0208) 303 9535
www.lullingstoneparkgolfclub.com

Lydd (1994)
Proprietary
Romney Road, Lydd, Romney Marsh TN29 9LS
(01797) 320808
(01797) 321482
golf@lyddgolfclub.co.uk
Carole Harradine
www.lyddgolfclub.co.uk

Mid Kent (1908)
Singlewell Road, Gravesend DA11 7RB
(01474) 568035
(01474) 564218
pamholden@mkgc.co.uk
Mrs P Holden (01474) 568035
www.mkgc.co.uk

Nizels (1992)
Nizels Lane, Hildenborough, Tonbridge TN11 8NU
(01732) 833833
(01732) 835492
nizels@theclubcompany.com
www.theclubcompany.com

North Foreland (1903)
Convent Road, Broadstairs, Kent CT10 3PU
(01843) 862140
(01843) 862663
office@northforeland.co.uk
AJ Adams (01843) 862140
www.northforeland.co.uk

Oastpark (1992)
Pay and play
Malling Road, Snodland ME6 5LG
(01634) 242661
(01634) 240744
oastparkgolfclub@btconnect.com
Lesley Murrock (01634) 242818

Park Wood (1994)
Proprietary
Chestnut Avenue, Tatsfield, Westerham TN16 2EG
(01959) 577744
(01959) 577765
mail@parkwoodgolf.co.uk
John Hemphrey (Gen Mgr)
www.parkwoodgolf.co.uk

Pedham Place Golf Centre (1996)
Proprietary
London Road, Swanley BR8 8PP
(01322) 867000
(01322) 861646
info@ppgc.co.uk
Tim Milford (Head Pro)
www.ppgc.co.uk

Poult Wood (1974)
Public
Higham Lane, Tonbridge TN11 9QR
(01732) 364039 (Bookings)

Prince's (1906)
Proprietary
Sandwich Bay, Sandwich CT13 9QB
(01304) 611118
(01304) 612000
office@princesgolfclub.co.uk
J T George (Dir) (01304) 626909
www.princesgolfclub.co.uk

Redlibbets (1996)
Proprietary
West Yoke, Ash, Nr Sevenoaks TN15 7HT
(01474) 879190
(01474) 879290
info@redlibbets.com
K Morris
www.redlibbets.co.uk

The Ridge (1993)
Proprietary
Chartway Street, Sutton Valence, Maidstone ME17 3JB
(01622) 844382
info@theridgegolfclub.co.uk
Jemma Stoner (Gen Mngr)
www.theridgegolfclub.co.uk

Rochester & Cobham Park (1891)
Park Pale, by Rochester ME2 3UL
(01474) 823411
(01474) 824446
rcpgc@talk21.com
J S Aughterlony
www.rochesterandcobhamgc.co.uk

Royal Blackheath (1608)
Court Road, Eltham, London SE9 5AF
(020) 8850 1795
(020) 8859 0150
gm@rbgc.com
G Hogg
www.royalblackheath.com

Royal Cinque Ports (1892)
Golf Road, Deal CT14 6RF
(01304) 374007 (Office)
(01304) 379530
Martin.bond@royalcinqueports.com
Martin Bond
www.royalcinqueports.com

Royal St George's (1887)
Sandwich CT13 9PB
(01304) 613090
(01304) 611245

✉ secretary@royalstgeorges.com
✍ Colonel T J Checketts OBE
🖥 www.royalstgeorges.com

Sene Valley (1888)
Sene, Folkestone CT18 8BL
☎ **(01303) 268513**
📠 (01303) 237513
✉ senevalleygolf@btconnect.com
✍ Gordon Syers (Mgr)
🖥 www.senevalleygolfclub.co.uk

Sheerness (1909)
Power Station Road, Sheerness ME12 3AE
☎ **(01795) 662585**
✉ secretary@sheernessgolfclub.co.uk
✍ A Tindall
🖥 www.sheernessgolfclub.co.uk

Shooter's Hill (1903)
Lowood, Eaglesfield Road, London SE18 3DA
☎ **(020) 8854 6368**
📠 (020) 8854 0469
✉ john@shgc.uk.com
✍ J Clement (020) 8854 6368
🖥 www.shgc.uk.com

Shortlands (1894)
Meadow Road, Shortlands, Bromley BR2 0DX
☎ **(020) 8460 2471**
📠 (020) 8460 8828
✉ enquiries@shortlandsgolfclub.co.uk
✍ PS May (020) 8460 8828
🖥 www.shortlandsgolfclub.co.uk

Sidcup (1891)
Hurst Road, Sidcup DA15 9AW
☎ **(020) 8300 2150**
📠 (020) 8300 2150
✉ sidcupgolfclub@googlemail.com
✍ Steve Armstrong (020) 8300 2150
🖥 www.sidcupgolfclub.co.uk

Sittingbourne & Milton Regis (1929)
Wormdale, Newington, Sittingbourne ME9 7PX
☎ **(01795) 842261**
✉ sittingbournegc@btconnect.com
✍ Charles Maxted
🖥 www.sittingbournegolfclub.com

Southern Valley (1999)
Pay and play
Thong Lane, Gravesend, Kent DA12 4LT
☎ **(01474) 568568**
📠 (01474) 360366
✉ info@southernvalley.co.uk
✍ Paul Thornberry (Managing Director)
🖥 www.southernvalley.co.uk

St Augustines (1907)
Cottington Road, Cliffsend, Ramsgate CT12 5JN
☎ **(01843) 590333**
📠 (01843) 590444
✉ sagc@ic24.net
✍ R M Cooper
🖥 www.staugustinesgolfclub.co.uk

Staplehurst Golf Centre
Cradducks Lane, Staplehurst TN12 0DR
☎ **(01580) 893362**
📠 (01580) 893372
🖥 www.staplehurstgolfcentre.co.uk

Sundridge Park (1901)
Garden Road, Bromley BR1 3NE
☎ **(020) 8460 0278**
📠 (020) 8289 3050
✉ luke@spgc.co.uk
✍ Luke Edgcumbe (020) 8460 0278
🖥 www.spgc.co.uk

Sweetwoods Park (1994)
Proprietary
Cowden, Edenbridge TN8 7JN
☎ **(01342) 850729**
📠 (01342) 850866
✉ golf@sweetwoodspark.com
🖥 www.sweetwoodspark.com

Tenterden (1905)
Woodchurch Road, Tenterden TN30 7DR
☎ **(01580) 763987**
📠 (01580) 763430
✉ enquiries@tenterdengolfclub.co.uk
✍ Mrs Teresa Cuff
🖥 www.tenterdengolfclub.co.uk

Thamesview Golf Centre (1991)
Pay and play
Fairway Drive, Summerton Way, Thamesmead, London SE28 8PP
☎ **(020) 8310 7975**
📠 (020) 8312 0546
✉ golf@tvgc.co.uk
✍ Stephen Lee
🖥 www.tvgc.co.uk

Tudor Park (1988)
Proprietary
Ashford Road, Bearsted, Maidstone ME14 4NQ
☎ **(01622) 739412**
📠 (01622) 735360
✉ brad.mclean1@marriotthotels.com
✍ Brad McLean
🖥 www.marriottgolf.com

Tunbridge Wells (1889)
Langton Road, Tunbridge Wells TN4 8XH
☎ **(01892) 523034**
✉ tunbridgewelgolf@btconnect.com
✍ Peter Annington (01892) 536918
🖥 www.tunbridgewellsgolf.com

Upchurch River Valley (1991)
Pay and play
Oak Lane, Upchurch, Sittingbourne ME9 7AY
☎ **(01634) 360626**
📠 (01634) 387784
✉ secretary@urvgc.co.uk
✍ Graham Driscoll (01634) 260594
🖥 www.urvgc.co.uk

Walmer & Kingsdown (1909)
The Leas, Kingsdown, Deal CT14 8EP
☎ **(01304) 373256**
📠 (01304) 382336
✉ info@kingsdowngolf.co.uk
✍ David Nehra
🖥 www.kingsdowngolf.co.uk

Weald of Kent (1992)
Proprietary
Maidstone Road, Headcorn TN27 9PT
☎ **(01622) 890866**
📠 (01622) 890070
✉ proshop@weald-of-kent.co.uk
✍ Matt Pickard (Golf Operations Mgr)
🖥 www.weald-of-kent.co.uk

West Kent (1916)
Milking Lane, Downe, Orpington BR6 7LD
☎ **(01689) 851323**
📠 (01689) 858693
✉ golf@wkgc.co.uk
✍ Sean Trussell
🖥 www.wkgc.co.uk

West Malling (1974)
Addington, Maidstone ME19 5AR
☎ **(01732) 844785**

The Halford-Hewitt Cup

The Halford Hewitt Cup was founded in 1924 as a competition for old boys of 64 English and Scottish public schools.

Described as "the greatest of all truly amateur tournaments", the cup is hosted by the Royal Cinque Ports Golf Club. In 1950, the competition became too large for a single club to host so Royal St George's Golf Club was asked to help. Since then, half the field has played its initial two rounds at Royal St George's.

(01732) 844795
greg@westmallinggolf.com
MR Ellis
www.westmallinggolf.com

Westerham (1997)
Proprietary
Valence Park, Brasted Road, Westerham TN16 1LJ
(01959) 567100
(01959) 567101
info@westerhamgc.co.uk
R Sturgeon (Gen Mgr)
www.westerhamgc.co.uk

Westgate & Birchington (1893)
176 Canterbury Road, Westgate-on-Sea CT8 8LT
(01843) 831115/833905
wandbgc@tiscali.co.uk
TJ Sharp
www.westgate-and-birchington-golfclub.co.uk

Whitstable & Seasalter (1911)
Collingwood Road, Whitstable CT5 1EB
(01227) 272020
(01227) 280822
wandsgolfclub@talktalk.net
MD Moore
www.whitstableandseasaltergolfclub.co.uk

Wildernesse (1890)
Park Lane, Seal, Kent TN15 0JE
(01732) 761199
(01732) 763809
golf@wildernesse.co.uk
Mr A D Lawrence
www.wildernesse.co.uk

Woodlands Manor (1928)
Woodlands, Tinkerpot Lane, Sevenoaks TN15 6AB
(01959) 523806
info@woodlandsmanorgolf.co.uk
CG Robins (01959) 523806
www.woodlandsmanorgolf.co.uk

Wrotham Heath (1906)
Seven Mile Lane, Comp, Sevenoaks TN15 8QZ
(01732) 884800
wrothamheathgolf@btconnect.com
J Hodgson
www.wrothamheathgolfclub.co.uk

Lancashire

Accrington & District (1893)
West End, Oswaldtwistle, Accrington BB5 4LS
(01254) 381614
(01254) 350111
info@accringtongolfclub.com
S Padbury (01254) 350112
www.accringtongolfclub.com

Ashton & Lea (1913)
Tudor Ave, Off Blackpool Rd, Lea, Preston PR4 0XA
(01772) 735282
(01772) 735762
info@ashtonleagolfclub.co.uk
S Plumb (01772) 735282
www.ashtonleagolfclub.co.uk

Ashton-in-Makerfield (1902)
Garswood Park, Liverpool Road, Ashton-in-Makerfield, Wigan WN4 0YT
(01942) 719330
(01942) 719330
secretary@ashton-in-makerfieldgolfclub.co.uk
G S Lacy
www.ashton-in-makerfieldgolfclub.co.uk

Ashton-under-Lyne (1912)
Gorsey Way, Hurst, Ashton-under-Lyne OL6 9HT
(0161) 330 1537
info@ashtongolfclub.co.uk
www.ashtongolfclub.co.uk

Bacup (1910)
Maden Road, Bankside Lane, Bacup OL13 8HN
(01706) 873170
secretary_bgc@btconnect.com
Mrs A Cook (01706) 874372

Baxenden & District (1913)
Top o' th' Meadow, Baxenden, Accrington BB5 2EA
(01254) 234555
baxgolf@hotmail.com
N Turner (01706) 225423
www.baxendengolf.co.uk

Beacon Park G&CC (1982)
Public
Beacon Lane, Dalton, Up Holland WN8 7RU
(01695) 622700
info@beaconparkgolf.com
Mark Prosser
www.beaconparkgolf.com

Blackburn (1894)
Beardwood Brow, Blackburn BB2 7AX
(01254) 51122
(01254) 665578
sec@blackburngolfclub.com
I A McGowan (Hon Sec)
www.blackburngolfclub.com

Blackpool North Shore (1904)
Devonshire Road, Blackpool FY2 0RD
(01253) 352054
(01253) 591240
office@bnsgc.com
Mrs C L Woosnam (01253) 352054 ext 1
www.bnsgc.com

Blackpool Park (1925)
Public
North Park Drive, Blackpool FY3 8LS
(01253) 397916
(01253) 397916
secretary@blackpoolparkgc.co.uk
Don McLeod
www.blackpoolparkgc.co.uk

Bolton (1891)
Lostock Park, Bolton BL6 4AJ
(01204) 843067
(01204) 843067
secretary@boltongolfclub.co.uk
S Higham (01204) 843067
www.boltongolfclub.co.uk

Bolton Old Links (1891)
Chorley Old Road, Montserrat, Bolton BL1 5SU
(01204) 842307
(01204) 497549
mail@boltonoldlinksgolfclub.co.uk
Mrs J Boardman (01204) 842307
www.boltonoldlinksgolfclub.co.uk

Bolton Open Golf Course
Pay and play
Longsight Park, Longsight Lane, Harwood BL2 4JX
(01204) 597659/309778

The St George's Grand Challenge Cup

Inaugurated in 1888, the St George's Grand Challenge Cup is open to amateur golfers from recognised golf clubs and is presented by Royal St George's Golf Club, host to many top amateur and professional tournaments including The Open Championship, the Walker Cup, the Curtis Cup and the PGA Championship.

Sir Michael Bonallack (successful on three occasions), Jack Nicklaus and Lee Westwood are among the competition's prestigious winners.

For key to symbols see page 725

Brackley Municipal (1977)
Public
Bullows Road, Little Hulton, Worsley M38 9TR
☎ **(0161) 790 6076**

Breightmet (1911)
Red Bridge, Ainsworth, Bolton BL2 5PA
☎ **(01204) 527381**
✍ R K Green
🌐 www.breightmetgolfclub.co.uk

Brookdale (1896)
Medlock Road, Woodhouses, Failsworth M35 9WQ
☎ **(0161) 681 4534**
🖷 (0161) 688 6872
✉ brookdalegolf@btconnect.com
✍ P Brownlow
🌐 www.brookdalegolf.co.uk

Burnley (1905)
Glen View, Burnley BB11 3RW
☎ **(01282) 455266**
🖷 (01282) 451281
✉ burnleygolfclub@onthegreen.co.uk
✍ D A Brown
🌐 www.burnleygolfclub.com

Bury (1890)
Unsworth Hall, Blackford Bridge, Bury BL9 9TJ
☎ **(0161) 766 4897**
🖷 (0161) 796 3480
✉ secretary@burygolfclub.com
✍ David Parkinson
🌐 www.burygolfclub.com

Castle Hawk (1975)
Chadwick Lane, Castleton, Rochdale OL11 3BY
☎ **(01706) 640841**
🖷 (01706) 860587
✉ teeoff@castlehawk.co.uk

Chorley (1897)
Hall o' th' Hill, Heath Charnock, Chorley PR6 9HX
☎ **(01257) 480263**
🖷 (01257) 480722
✉ secretary@chorleygolfclub.freeserve.co.uk
✍ Mrs A Green (01257) 480263
🌐 www.chorleygolfclub.co.uk

Clitheroe (1891)
Whalley Road, Clitheroe BB7 1PP
☎ **(01200) 422292**
🖷 (01200) 422292
✉ secretary@clitheroegolfclub.com
✍ Michael Walls
🌐 www.clitheroegolfclub.com

Colne (1901)
Law Farm, Skipton Old Road, Colne BB8 7EB
☎ **(01282) 863391**
🖷 (01282) 870547
✉ colnegolfclub@hotmail.co.uk
✍ A Turpin (Hon)
🌐 www.colnegolfclub.com

Crompton & Royton (1908)
High Barn, Royton, Oldham OL2 6RW
☎ **(0161) 624 0986**
🖷 (0161) 652 4711
✉ secretary@cromptonandroytongolfclub.co.uk
✍ J A Osbaldeston (0161) 624 0986
🌐 www.cromptonandroytongolfclub.co.uk

Darwen (1893)
Winter Hill, Duddon Avenue, Darwen BB3 0LB
☎ **(01254) 701287**
🖷 (01254) 773833
✉ admin@darwengolfclub.com
✍ J Howarth (01254) 704367
🌐 www.darwengolfclub.com

Dean Wood (1922)
Lafford Lane, Up Holland, Skelmersdale WN8 0QZ
☎ **(01695) 622219**
🖷 (01695) 622245
✉ ray.benton@deanwoodgolfclub.co.uk
🌐 www.deanwoodgolfclub.co.uk

Deane (1906)
Broadford Road, Deane, Bolton BL3 4NS
☎ **(01204) 61944**
🖷 (01204) 652047
✉ secretary@deanegolfclub.com
✍ Frank Hodgkiss (01204) 651808
🌐 www.deanegolfclub.co.uk

Dunscar (1908)
Longworth Lane, Bromley Cross, Bolton BL7 9QY
☎ **(01204) 303321**
🖷 (01204) 303321
✉ dunscargolfclub@uk2.net
✍ Mrs A E Jennings (01204) 303321
🌐 www.dunscargolfclub.co.uk

Duxbury Park (1975)
Public
Duxbury Hall Road, Duxbury Park, Chorley PR7 4AS
☎ **(01257) 235095**
🖷 (01257) 241378
✉ fholding2008@hotmail.co.uk
✍ F Holding (01257) 262209

Fairhaven (1895)
Oakwood Avenue, Ansdell, Lytham St Annes FY8 4JU
☎ **(01253) 736741**
🖷 (01253) 736741
✉ secretary@fairhavengolfclub.co.uk
✍ R Thompson
🌐 www.fairhavengolfclub.co.uk

Fishwick Hall (1912)
Glenluce Drive, Farringdon Park, Preston PR1 5TD
☎ **(01772) 798300**
🖷 (01772) 704600
✉ fishwickhallgolfclub@supanet.com
✍ Secretary
🌐 www.fishwickhallgolfclub.co.uk

Fleetwood (1932)
Golf House, Princes Way, Fleetwood FY7 8AF
☎ **(01253) 773573**
✉ secretary@fleetwoodgolf.co.uk
🌐 www.fleetwoodgolf.co.uk

Gathurst (1913)
Miles Lane, Shevington, Wigan WN6 8EW
☎ **(01257) 252861 (Clubhouse)**
🖷 (01257) 255953
✉ secretary@gathurstgolfclub.co.uk
✍ Mrs I Fyffe (01257) 255235
🌐 www.gothurstgolfclub.co.uk

Ghyll (1907)
Ghyll Brow, Skipton Row, Barnoldswick BB18 6JH
☎ **(01282) 842466**
✉ secretary@ghyllgolfclub.co.uk
✍ R Presland (01282) 844359
🌐 www.ghyllgolfclub.co.uk

Great Harwood (1896)
Harwood Bar, Whalley Road, Great Harwood BB6 7TE
☎ **(01254) 884391**
✍ J Spibey
🌐 www.greatharwoodgolfclub.co.uk

Green Haworth (1914)
Green Haworth, Accrington BB5 3SL
☎ **(01254) 237580**
🖷 (01254) 396176
✉ enquiries@greenhaworth.co.uk
🌐 www.greenhaworthgolfclub.co.uk

Greenmount (1920)
Greenmount, Bury BL8 4LH
☎ **(01204) 883712**
✉ secretary@greenmountgolfclub.co.uk
✍ D Beesley
🌐 www.greenmountgolfclub.co.uk

Haigh Hall (1972)
Public
Haigh Hall Country Park, Haigh, Wigan WN2 1PE
☎ **(01942) 833337 (Clubhouse)**
✉ secretary@haighhall-golfclub.co.uk
✍ SG Eyres
🌐 www.haighhall-golfclub.co.uk

Hart Common (1995)
Proprietary
Westhoughton Golf Centre, Wigan Road, Westhoughton BL5 2BX
☎ **(01942) 813195**

Harwood (1926)
Roading Brook Road, Bolton BL2 4JD
☎ **(01204) 522878**
✉ secretary@harwoodgolfclub.com
✍ H Howard
🌐 www.harwoodgolfclub.co.uk

De Vere Herons Reach (1993)
Proprietary
East Park Drive, Blackpool FY3 8LL
☎ **(01253) 766156**

(01253) 798800
richard.bowman@devere-hotels.com
www.deveregolf.co.uk

Heysham (1910)

Trumacar Park, Middleton Road, Heysham, Morecambe LA3 3JH

(01524) 851011
(01524) 853030
secretary@heyshamgolfclub.co.uk
Mrs G E Gardner
www.heyshamgolfclub.co.uk

Hindley Hall (1905)

Hall Lane, Hindley, Wigan WN2 2SQ

(01942) 255131
secretay@hindleyhallgolfclub.co.uk
Ian Rimmer (01942) 255131
www.hindleyhallgolfclub.co.uk

Horwich (1895)

Victoria Road, Horwich BL6 5PH

(01204) 696980
(01942) 205316

Hurlston Hall Golf & Country Club (1994)

Proprietary
Hurlston Lane, Southport Road, Scarisbrick L40 8HB

(01704) 840400
(01704) 841404
info@hurlstonhall.co.uk
Aoife O'Brien (MD)
www.hurlstonhall.co.uk

Ingol (1981)

Proprietary
Tanterton Hall Road, Ingol, Preston PR2 7BY

(01772) 734556
(01772) 729815
ingol@golfers.net
www.ingolgolfclub.co.uk

Knott End (1910)

Wyreside, Knott End-on-Sea, Poulton-le-Fylde FY6 0AA

(01253) 810576
(01253) 813446
louise@knottendgolfclub.com
Louise Freeman (01253) 810576
www.knottendgolfclub.com

Lancaster (1889)

Ashton Hall, Ashton-with-Stodday, Lancaster LA2 0AJ

(01524) 751247 (Secretary)
secretary@lancastergc.co.uk
G Yates (01524) 751247
www.lancastergc.co.uk

Lansil (1947)

Caton Road, Lancaster LA4 3PE

(01524) 39269
M Lynch (01524) 62785
www.lansilgolfclub.org.uk

Leyland (1924)

Wigan Road, Leyland PR25 5UD

(01772) 436457
(01772) 435605
manager@leylandgolfclub.co.uk
S Drinkall
www.leylandgolfclub.co.uk

Lobden (1888)

Whitworth, Rochdale OL12 8XJ

(01706) 343228
(01706) 343228
golf@lobdengolfclub.co.uk
B Harrison (01706) 852752

Longridge (1877)

Fell Barn, Jeffrey Hill, Longridge, Preston PR3 2TU

(01772) 783291
(01772) 783022
secretary@longridgegolfclub.co.uk
D Carling
www.longridgegolfclub.co.uk

Lowes Park (1915)

Hilltop, Lowes Road, Bury BL9 6SU

(0161) 764 1231
lowesparkgc@btconnect.com
Alan Taylor
www.lowesparkgc.co.uk

Lytham Green Drive (1913)

Ballam Road, Lytham St Annes FY8 4LE

(01253) 737390
(01253) 731350
secretary@lythamgreendrive.co.uk
I Stewart (01253) 737390 Opt 4
www.lythamgreendrive.co.uk

Marland (1928)

Public
Springfield Park, Bolton Road, Rochdale OL11 4RE

(01706) 649801
(01706) 523082

Marsden Park (1969)

Public
Townhouse Road, Nelson BB9 8DG

(01282) 661912
(01282) 661384
martin.robinson@pendleleisuretrust.co.uk
www.pendleleisuretrust.co.uk

Morecambe (1905)

Bare, Morecambe LA4 6AJ

(01524) 412841
(01524) 400088
secretary@morecambegolfclub.com
Mrs Judith Atkinson (01524) 412841
www.morecambegolfclub.com

Mossock Hall (1996)

Proprietary
Liverpool Road, Bickerstaffe L39 0EE

(01695) 421717
(01695) 424961
info@mossockhallgolfclub.co.uk
Mel Brooke
www.mossockhallgolfclub.co.uk

Mytton Fold Hotel & Golf Complex (1994)

Proprietary
Whalley Road, Langho BB6 8AB

(01254) 240662 (Hotel)
(01254) 248119
golfshop@myttonfold.co.uk
L Moorhouse
www.myttonfold.co.uk

Nelson (1902)

Kings Causeway, Brierfield, Nelson BB9 0EU

(01282) 611834
(01282) 611834
secretary@nelsongolfclub.com
Richard M Lees
www.nelsongolfclub.com

Oak Royal Golf & Country Club (2008)

Proprietary
Bury Lane, Withnell, Nr Chorley PR6 8SW

01254 830616
enquiries@oakroyalgolf-countryclub.co.uk
Kath Downes
www.oakroyalgolf-countryclub.co.uk

Oldham (1892)

Lees New Road, Oldham OL4 5PN

(0161) 624 4986
(0161) 624 4986
info@oldhamgolfclub.com
J Brooks

Ormskirk (1899)

Cranes Lane, Lathom, Ormskirk L40 5UJ

(01695) 572112
(01695) 572227
mail@ormskirkgolfclub.com
R K Oakes (01695) 572227
www.ormskirkgolfclub.com

Pennington (1977)

Public/Municipal
Pennington Country Park, St Helens Road, Leigh WN7 3PA

(01942) 741873/ (01942) 682852 Shop
penningtongolfclub@blueyonder.co.uk
Mr B W Lythgoe
www.penningtongolfclub.co.uk

Penwortham (1908)

Blundell Lane, Penwortham, Preston PR1 0AX

(01772) 744630
(01772) 740172
admin@penworthamgc.co.uk
N Annandale
www.penworthamgc.co.uk

Pleasington (1891)

Pleasington, Blackburn BB2 5JF

(01254) 202177
secretary-manager@pleasington-golf.co.uk
C J Williams
www.pleasington-golf.co.uk

For key to symbols see page 725

Poulton-le-Fylde (1982)
Public
Myrtle Farm, Breck Road, Poulton-le-Fylde FY6 7HJ
☎ **(01253) 892444**
✉ greenwood-golf@hotmail.co.uk
✍ S Wilkinson
▤ www.poultonlefyldegolfclub.co.uk

Preston (1892)
Fulwood Hall Lane, Fulwood, Preston PR2 8DD
☎ **(01772) 700011**
📠 (01772) 794234
✉ secretary@prestongolfclub.com
▤ www.prestongolfclub.com

Regent Park (Bolton) (1931)
Pay and play
Links Road, Chorley New Road, Bolton BL6 4AF
☎ **(01204) 495421**
✍ N Brazell (Professional) (01204) 495421
⊕ 18 hole Pay and Play. Food Available. Club comps on Saturdays

Rishton (1927)
Eachill Links, Hawthorn Drive, Rishton BB1 4HG
☎ **(01254) 884442**
📠 (01254) 887701
✉ info@rishtongolfclub.co.uk
✍ Mr J Hargreaves MBE (Gen Mgr)
▤ www.rishton-golf-club.co.uk

Rochdale (1888)
Edenfield Road, Bagslate, Rochdale OL11 5YR
☎ **(01706) 643818 (Clubhouse)**
📠 (01706) 861113
✉ admin@rochdalegolfclub.co.uk
✍ P Kershaw (01706) 643818 (opt 2)
▤ www.rochdalegolfclub.co.uk

Rossendale (1903)
Ewood Lane Head, Haslingden, Rossendale BB4 6LH
☎ **(01706) 831339**
📠 (01706) 228669
✉ admin@rossendalegolfclub.net
✍ Mr J Pink
▤ www.rossendalegolfclub.net

Royal Lytham & St Annes (1886)
Links Gate, Lytham St Annes FY8 3LQ
☎ **(01253) 724206**
📠 (01253) 780946
✉ bookings@royallytham.org
✍ RJG Cochrane
▤ www.royallytham.org

Saddleworth (1904)
Mountain Ash, Uppermill, Oldham OL3 6LT
☎ **(01457) 873653**
📠 (01457) 820647
✉ generalmanager@saddleworthgolfclub.org.uk
✍ Alastair Griffiths
▤ www.saddleworthgolfclub.co.uk

Shaw Hill Hotel G&CC (1925)
Proprietary
Preston Road, Whittle-le-Woods, Chorley PR6 7PP
☎ **(01257) 269221**
📠 (01257) 261223
✉ info@shaw-hill.co.uk
✍ Lawrence Bateson (Secretary)
▤ www.shaw-hill.co.uk

St Annes Old Links (1901)
Highbury Road East, Lytham St Annes FY8 2LD
☎ **(01253) 723597**
📠 (01253) 781506
✉ secretary@stannesoldlinks.com
✍ Mrs Jane Donohoe
▤ www.stannesoldlinks.com

Standish Court (1995)
Pay and play
Rectory Lane, Standish, Wigan WN6 0XD
☎ **(01257) 425777**
📠 (01257) 425777
✉ info@standishgolf.co.uk
▤ www.standishgolf.co.uk

Stonyhurst Park (1979)
Stonyhurst, Hurst Green, Clitheroe BB7 9QB
☎ **(01254) 826072 (not manned)**
✉ gmonkspgc@gmail.com
✍ Mr Graham Monk (01200) 423191
▤ www.stonyhurstpark.co.uk

Towneley (1932)
Public
Towneley Park, Todmorden Road, Burnley BB11 3ED
☎ **(01282) 451636**
✉ secretary@towneleygolfclub.co.uk
✍ Peter Witt
▤ www.towneleygolfclub.co.uk

Tunshill (1901)
Kiln Lane, Milnrow, Rochdale OL16 3TS
☎ **(01706) 342095**
✉ secretary@tunshillgolfclub.co.uk
✍ S Reade (01706) 342095
▤ www.tunshillgolfclub.co.uk

Turton (1908)
Wood End Farm, Hospital Road, Bromley Cross, Bolton BL7 9QD
☎ **(01204) 852235**
📠 (01204) 856921
✉ info@turtongolfclub.com
✍ John Drabble
▤ www.turtongolfclub.com

Walmersley (1906)
Garrett's Close, Walmersley, Bury BL9 6TE
☎ **(0161) 764 1429**
📠 (0161) 764 7770
✉ walmersleygc@btconnect.com
✍ V Slater (0161) 764 7770
▤ www.walmersleygolfclub.co.uk

Werneth (1908)
Green Lane, Garden Suburb, Oldham OL8 3AZ
☎ **(0161) 624 1190**
✉ secretary@wernethgolfclub.co.uk
✍ JH Barlow
▤ www.wernethgolfclub.co.uk

Westhoughton (1929)
Long Island, Westhoughton, Bolton BL5 2BR
☎ **(01942) 811085**
✉ honsec.wgc@btconnect.com
✍ Dave Moores (Club Mobile 07760 754933)
▤ www.westhoughtongolfclub.co.uk

Whalley (1912)
Long Leese Barn, Clerkhill Road, Whalley BB7 9DR
☎ **(01254) 822236**
📠 (01254) 824766
✍ P R Benson (01282) 773354
▤ www.whalleygolfclub.co.uk

Whittaker (1906)
Littleborough OL15 0LH
☎ **(01706) 378310**
✍ Paul Jones (07930) 569260
▤ www.secretarywgc.com

Wigan (1898)
Arley Hall, Haigh, Wigan WN1 2UH
☎ **(01257) 421360**
📠 (01257) 426500
✉ info@wigangolfclub.co.uk

The Lytham Trophy

Founded by the Royal Lytham & St Annes Golf Club in 1965, the Lytham Trophy is a 72 hole scratch stroke play competition for amateur golfers and is classified as a Category A event by The R&A's World Amateur Golf Rankings.

Notable past winners include Sir Michael Bonallack, Peter McEvoy, Paul Broadhurst and Lloyd Saltman.

For key to symbols see page 725

✍ A Lawless (Ass Sec)
▤ www.wigangolfclub.co.uk

Wilpshire (1890)
72 Whalley Road, Wilpshire, Blackburn BB1 9LF
☎ **(01254) 248260**
▭ (01254) 246745
✉ admin@wilpshiregolfclub.co.uk
✍ SH Tart
▤ www.wilpshiregolfclub.co.uk

Leicestershire

Beedles Lake (1993)
170 Broome Lane, East Goscote LE7 3WQ
☎ **(0116) 260 6759/7086**
▭ (0116) 269 4127
✉ joncoleman@jelson.co.uk
✍ Jon Coleman (Mgr)
▤ www.beedleslake.co.uk

Birstall (1900)
Station Road, Birstall, Leicester LE4 3BB
☎ **(0116) 267 4450**
✉ sue@birstallgolfclub.co.uk
✍ Mrs SE Chilton (0116) 267 4322
▤ www.birstallgolfclub.co.uk

Breedon Priory Golf Centre (1990)
Green Lane, Wilson, Derby DE73 8LG
☎ **(01332) 863081**
✉ lee@breedonpriory.co.uk
✍ Lee Sheldon (Mgr)

Charnwood Forest (1890)
Breakback Road, Woodhouse Eaves, Loughborough LE12 8TA
☎ **(01509) 890259**
✉ secretary @charnwoodforestgolfclub.com
✍ PK Field
▤ www.charnwoodforestgolfclub.com

Cosby (1895)
Chapel Lane, Broughton Road, Cosby, Leicester LE9 1RG
☎ **(0116) 286 4759**
▭ (0116) 286 4484
✉ secretary@cosbygolfclub.co.uk
✍ Frazer Baxter (0116) 286 4759 Opt 1
▤ www.cosbygolfclub.co.uk

Enderby (1986)
Public
Mill Lane, Enderby, Leicester LE19 4LX
☎ **(0116) 284 9388**
▭ (0116) 284 9388
▤ www.enderbygolfshopandcourse.co.uk

Forest Hill (1991)
Proprietary
Markfield Lane, Botcheston LE9 9FH
☎ **(01455) 824800**
▭ (01455) 828522
✉ admin@foresthillgolfclub.co.uk
✍ Una Handley
▤ www.foresthillgolfclub.co.uk

Glen Gorse (1933)
Glen Road, Oadby, Leicester LE2 4RF
☎ **(0116) 271 4159**
▭ (0116) 271 4159
✉ secretary@gggc.org
✍ Mrs J James (0116) 271 4159
▤ www.gggc.org

Hinckley (1894)
Leicester Road, Hinckley LE10 3DR
☎ **(01455) 615124**
▭ (01455) 890841
✉ proshop@hinckleygolfclub.com
✍ R Mather (Sec), Catherine Merrie (Finance & Admin)
▤ www.hinckleygolfclub.com

Humberstone Heights (1978)
Public
Gipsy Lane, Leicester LE5 0TB
☎ **(0116) 299 5570/1**
✉ hhgc@talktalk.net
✍ Mrs M Weston
▤ www.humberstoneheightsgc.co.uk

Kibworth (1904)
Weir Road, Kibworth Beauchamp, Leicestershire LE8 0LP
☎ **(0116) 279 2301**
▭ (0116) 279 6434
✉ secretary@kibworthgolfclub.freeserve.co.uk
▤ www.kibworthgolfclub.co.uk

Kilworth Springs (1993)
Proprietary
South Kilworth Road, North Kilworth, Lutterworth LE17 6HJ
☎ **(01858) 575082**
▭ (01858) 575078
✉ admin@kilworthsprings.co.uk
✍ Jeremy Wilkinson (Manager)
▤ www.kilworthsprings.co.uk

Kirby Muxloe (1893)
Station Road, Kirby Muxloe, Leicester LE9 2EP
☎ **(0116) 239 3457**
▭ (0116) 238 8891
✉ kirbymuxloegolf@btconnect.com
✍ B N Whipham (Mgr/Professional) (0116) 239 3457
▤ www.kirbymuxloe-golf.co.uk

Lingdale (1967)
Joe Moore's Lane, Woodhouse Eaves, Loughborough LE12 8TF
☎ **(01509) 890703**
▭ (01509) 890703
✉ secretary@lingdalegolfclub.co.uk
✍ T Walker
▤ www.lingdalegolfclub.co.uk

Longcliffe (1906)
Snells Nook Lane, Nanpantan, Loughborough LE11 3YA
☎ **(01509) 239129**
▭ (01509) 231286
✉ secretary@longcliffegolf.co.uk
✍ Mr B Jones
▤ www.longcliffegolf.co.uk

Lutterworth (1904)
Rugby Road, Lutterworth, Leicestershire LE17 4HN
☎ **(01455) 552532**
▭ (01455) 553586
✉ sec@lutterworthgc.co.uk
✍ J Faulks (01455) 552532
▤ www.lutterworthgc.co.uk

Market Harborough (1898)
Great Oxendon Road, Market Harborough LE16 8NF
☎ **(01858) 463684**
▭ (01858) 432906
✉ proshop@mhgolf.co.uk
✍ F J Baxter
▤ www.mhgolf.co.uk

Melton Mowbray (1925)
Waltham Rd, Thorpe Arnold, Melton Mowbray LE14 4SD
☎ **(01664) 562118**
▭ (01664) 562118
✉ meltonmowbraygc@btconnect.com
✍ Sue Millward/Marilyn Connelly
▤ www.mmgc.org

Oadby (1974)
Public
Leicester Road, Oadby, Leicester LE2 4AJ
☎ **(0116) 270 9052/270 0215**
✉ secretaryogc@talktalk.net
✍ RA Primrose (0116) 270 3828
▤ www.oadbygolfclub.co.uk

Park Hill Golf Club (1994)
Proprietary
Park Hill, Seagrave LE12 7NG
☎ **(01509) 815454**
▭ (01509) 816062
✉ mail@parkhillgolf.co.uk
✍ JP Hutson
▤ www.parkhillgolf.co.uk

Rothley Park (1911)
Westfield Lane, Rothley, Leicester LE7 7LH
☎ **(0116) 230 2809**
▭ (0116) 237 4847
✉ clubmanager@rothleypark.co.uk
✍ Danny Spillane (Mgr) (0116) 230 2809
▤ www.rothleypark.com

Scraptoft (1928)
Beeby Road, Scraptoft, Leicester LE7 9SJ
☎ **(0116) 241 9000**
▭ (0116) 241 9000
✉ secretary@scraptoft-golf.co.uk
▤ www.scraptoft-golf.co.uk

Six Hills (1986)
Pay and play
Six Hills, Melton Mowbray LE14 3PR
☎ **(01509) 881225**
▭ (01509) 881846
✍ Mrs J Showler

Stapleford Park (2000)
Stapleford park, Melton Mowbray LE14 2EF
☎ **(01572) 787044**

For key to symbols see page 725

☐ (01572) 787001
✉ clubs@stapleford.co.uk
✍ Richard Alderson
▤ www.staplefordpark.com

The Leicestershire (1890)

Evington Lane, Leicester LE5 6DJ
☎ **(0116) 273 8825**
☐ (0116) 249 8799
✉ secretary @theleicestershiregolfclub.co.uk
✍ AJ Baxter (0116) 273 8825
▤ www.theleicestershiregolfclub .co.uk

Ullesthorpe Court Hotel (1976)

Proprietary
Frolesworth Road, Ullesthorpe, Lutterworth LE17 5BZ
☎ **(01455) 209023**
☐ (01455) 202537
✉ bookings@ullesthorpecourt.co.uk
✍ AP Parr (ext 2446)
▤ www.bw-ullesthorpecourt.co.uk

Western Park (1910)

Public
Scudamore Road, Leicester LE3 1UQ
☎ **(0116) 287 5211**
✍ Paul Williams
▤ www.westerpkgc.co.uk

Whetstone (1965)

Proprietary
Cambridge Road, Cosby, Leicester LE9 1SJ
☎ **(0116) 286 1424**
☐ (0116) 286 1424
✍ N Morris
▤ www.whetstonegolfclub.co.uk

Willesley Park (1921)

Measham Road, Ashby-de-la-Zouch LE65 2PF
☎ **(01530) 414596**
☐ (01530) 564169
✉ info@willesleypark.com
✍ Tina Harlow (01530) 414596
▤ www.willesleypark.com

Lincolnshire

Ashby Decoy (1936)

Ashby Decoy, Burringham Road, Scunthorpe DN17 2AB
☎ **(01724) 866561**
☐ (01724) 271708
✉ info@ashbydecoygolfclub.co.uk
▤ www.ashbydecoy.co.uk

Belton Park (1890)

Belton Lane, Londonthorpe Road, Grantham NG31 9SH
☎ **(01476) 567399**
☐ (01476) 592078
✉ greatgolf@beltonpark.co.uk
✍ S Rowley (01476) 542900
▤ www.beltonpark.co.uk

De Vere Belton Woods Hotel (1991)

Belton, Grantham NG32 2LN
☎ **(01476) 593200**
☐ (01476) 574547
✉ belton.woods@devere-hotels.co.uk
✍ A Cameron (01476) 514364
▤ www.devere.co.uk

Blankney (1904)

Proprietary
Blankney, Lincoln LN4 3AZ
☎ **(01526) 320263**
☐ (01526) 322521
✉ manager@blankneygolfclub.co.uk
✍ G Bradley (01526) 320202
▤ www.blankneygolfclub.co.uk

Boston (1900)

Cowbridge, Horncastle Road, Boston PE22 7EL
☎ **(01205) 350589**
☐ (01205) 367526
✉ steveshaw@bostongc.co.uk
✍ SP Shaw (01205) 350589
▤ www.bostongc.co.uk

Boston West (1995)

Proprietary
Hubbert's Bridge, Boston PE20 3QX
☎ **(01205) 290670**
☐ (01205) 290725
✉ info@bostonwestgolfclub.co.uk
✍ MJ Couture (01205) 290670
▤ www.bostonwestgolfclub.co.uk

Burghley Park (1890)

St Martin's, Stamford PE9 3JX
☎ **(01780) 753789**
✉ secretary@burghleyparkgolfclub .co.uk
✍ S Last (Sec/Mgr)
▤ www.burghleyparkgolfclub.co.uk

Canwick Park (1893)

Canwick Park, Washingborough Road, Lincoln LN4 1EF
☎ **(01522) 542912/522166**
✉ manager@canwickpark.org
✍ N Porteus (01522) 542912
▤ www.canwickpark.org

Carholme (1906)

Carholme Road, Lincoln LN1 1SE
☎ **(01522) 523725**
☐ (01522) 533733
✉ secretary@carholmegolfclub.co.uk
✍ J Lammin
▤ www.carholmegolfclub.co.uk

Cleethorpes (1894)

Kings Road, Cleethorpes DN35 0PN
☎ **(01472) 816110 option 1**
✉ secretary@cleethorpesgolfclub .co.uk
✍ AJ Thompson (01472) 816110 option 3
▤ www.cleethorpesgolfclub.co.uk

Elsham (1900)

Barton Road, Elsham, Brigg DN20 0LS
☎ **(01652) 680291**
☐ (0872) 1113238
✉ office@elshamgolfclub.co.uk
✍ T Hartley (Mgr)
▤ www.elshamgolfclub.co.uk

Forest Pines Hotel & Golf Resort (1996)

Proprietary
Ermine Street, Brigg DN20 0AQ
☎ **(01652) 650756 Golf Shop**
☐ (01652) 650495
✉ forestpines@qhotels.co.uk
✍ Andrew Cook (Director of Golf)
▤ www.qhotels.co.uk

Gainsborough (1894)

Proprietary
Thonock, Gainsborough DN21 1PZ
☎ **(01427) 613088**
✉ info@gainsboroughgc.co.uk
✍ S Keane (Operations Manager)
▤ www.gainsboroughgc.co.uk

Gedney Hill (1991)

Public
West Drove, Gedney End Hill PE12 0NT
☎ **(01406) 330922**
☐ (01945) 581903

Grange Park (1992)

Proprietary
Butterwick Road, Messingham, Scunthorpe DN17 3PP
☎ **(01724) 762945**
✉ info@grangepark.com
✍ I Cannon (Mgr)
▤ www.grangepark.com

Grimsby (1922)

Littlecoates Road, Grimsby DN34 4LU
☎ **(01472) 342630 (Clubhouse) 356981 (Pro-Shop)**
☐ (01472) 342630
✉ secretary@grimsbygc.fsnet.co.uk
✍ D McCully (01472) 342630
▤ www.grimsbygolfclub.com

Holme Hall (1908)

Holme Lane, Bottesford, Scunthorpe DN16 3RF
☎ **(01724) 862078**
☐ (01724) 862081
✉ secretary@holmehallgolf.co.uk
✍ Gerald Pearce
▤ www.holmehallgolf.co.uk

Horncastle (1990)

West Ashby, Horncastle LN9 5PP
☎ **(01507) 526800**
☐ (01507) 517069
✉ info@twinlakescentre.com
▤ www.horncastlegolfclub.com

Humberston Park

Humberston Avenue, Humberston DN36 4SJ
☎ **(01472) 210404**

Immingham (1975)

St Andrews Lane, Off Church Lane, Immingham DN40 2EU
☎ **(01469) 575298**

☐ (01469) 577636
✍ C Todd (Mgr)
▤ www.immgc.com

Kenwick Park (1992)
Kenwick, Louth LN11 8NY
☎ **(01507) 605134**
☐ (01507) 606556
✉ secretary@kenwickparkgolf.co.uk
✍ C James (Gen Mgr)
▤ www.kenwickparkgolf.co.uk

Kirton Holme (1992)
Proprietary
Holme Road, Kirton Holme, Boston PE20 1SY
☎ **(01205) 290669**
✍ Mrs T Welberry
▤ www.kirtonholmegolfcourse.com

Lincoln (1891)
Torksey, Lincoln LN1 2EG
☎ **(01427) 718721**
☐ (01427) 718721
✉ manager@lincolngc.co.uk
✍ Craig Innes
▤ www.lincolngc.co.uk

Louth (1965)
Crowtree Lane, Louth LN11 9LJ
☎ **(01507) 603681**
☐ (01507) 608501
✉ louthgolfclub@btconnect.com
✍ Simon Moody (Gen Mgr)
▤ www.louthgolfclub.com

Manor (Laceby) (1992)
Proprietary
Laceby Manor, Laceby, Grimsby DN37 7LD
☎ **(01472) 873468**
✉ judith@lacebymanorgolfclub.co.uk
✍ Mrs J Mackay
▤ www.lacebymanorgolfclub.co.uk

Market Rasen & District (1912)
Legsby Road, Market Rasen LN8 3DZ
☎ **(01673) 842319**
☐ (01673) 849245
✉ marketrasengolf@onetel.net
▤ www.marketrasengolfclub.co.uk

Market Rasen Racecourse (1990)
Pay and play
Legsby Road, Market Rasen LN8 3EA
☎ **(01673) 843434**
☐ (01673) 844532
✉ marketrasen@jockeyclubracecourses.com
▤ www.marketrasenraces.co.uk

Martin Moor (1993)
Proprietary
Martin Road, Blankney LN4 3BE
☎ **(01526) 378243**
✉ enquiries@martinmoorgolfclub.co.uk
✍ Alan Roberts/Carole Roberts
⊕ 9 hole course with 18 seperate tees. Visitors/Socities/Corporate events welcome

Millfield (1984)
Proprietary
Laughterton, Lincoln LN1 2LB
☎ **(01427) 718473**
✉ millfieldgolfclub@gmail.com
✍ John Thomson (Sec)
▤ www.millfieldgolfclub.co.uk

North Shore (1910)
Proprietary
North Shore Road, Skegness PE25 1DN
☎ **(01754) 763298**
☐ (01754) 761902
✉ info@northshorehotel.co.uk
✍ B Howard (01754) 899030
▤ www.northshorehotel.co.uk

Pottergate (1992)
Moor Lane, Branston, Lincoln
☎ **(01522) 794867**
☐ (01522) 794867
✉ pottergategc@hotmail.co.uk
✍ Lee Tasker
▤ www.pottergategolfclub.co.uk

RAF Coningsby (1972)
RAF Coningsby, Lincoln LN4 4SY
☎ **(01526) 342581 Ext 6828**
✍ N Parsons (01526) 347946

Sandilands (1901)
Proprietary
Sandilands, Sutton-on-Sea LN12 2RJ
☎ **(01507) 441432**
☐ (01507) 441617
✉ sandilandsgolf@googlemail.com
✍ Simon Sherratt (Pro/Mgr)
▤ www.sandilandsgolfclub.co.uk

Seacroft (1895)
Drummond Road, Seacroft, Skegness PE25 3AU
☎ **(01754) 763020**
☐ (01754) 763020
✉ enquiries@seacroft-golfclub.co.uk
✍ R England (Mgr)
▤ www.seacroft-golfclub.co.uk

Sleaford (1905)
Willoughby Road, Greylees, Sleaford, Lincs NG34 8PL
☎ **(01529) 488273**
☐ (0872) 110 7871
✉ manager@sleafordgolfclub.co.uk
✍ Mr N Porteus
▤ www.sleafordgolfclub.co.uk

South Kyme (1990)
Skinners Lane, South Kyme, Lincoln LN4 4AT
☎ **(01526) 861113**
☐ (01526) 861080
✉ southkymegc@hotmail.com
✍ P Chamberlain
▤ www.skgc.co.uk

Spalding (1907)
Surfleet, Spalding PE11 4EA
☎ **(01775) 680386**
☐ (01775) 680988
✉ secretary@spaldinggolfclub.co.uk
✍ Mrs C J Douglas (01775) 680386
▤ www.spaldinggolfclub.co.uk

Stoke Rochford (1924)
Great North Rd, Grantham NG33 5EW
☎ **(01476) 530275**
☐ (01476) 530237
✉ secretary@stokerochfordgolfclub.co.uk
✍ A J Wheeler
▤ www.stokerochfordgolfclub.co.uk

Sudbrook Moor (1991)
Public
Charity Street, Carlton Scroop, Grantham NG32 3AT
☎ **(01400) 250796 all enquiries**
✍ Judith Hutton
▤ www.sudbrookmoor.co.uk

Sutton Bridge (1914)
New Road, Sutton Bridge, Spalding PE12 9RQ
☎ **(01406) 350323 (Clubhouse)**
✉ secretary@sbgolfclub.plus.com
✍ Terry Young (01406) 362959
▤ www.club-noticeboard.co.uk/suttonbridge

Tetney (1993)
Station Road, Tetney, Grimsby DN36 5HY
☎ **(01472) 211644**
☐ (01472) 211644
✍ J Abrams

Toft Hotel (1988)
Proprietary
Toft, Bourne PE10 0JT
☎ **(01778) 590616**
☐ (01778) 590264
▤ www.thetofthotelgolfclub.com

Waltham Windmill (1997)
Proprietary
Cheapside, Waltham, Grimsby DN37 0HT
☎ **(01472) 824109**
☐ (01472) 828391
▤ www.walthamgolf.co.uk

Welton Manor (1995)
Proprietary
Hackthorn Road, Welton LN2 3PA
☎ **(01673) 862827**
☐ (01673) 861888
✉ info@weltonmanorgolfcentre.co.uk
✍ David Ottenell/Hayley Olliver
▤ www.weltonmanorgolfcentre.co.uk

Woodhall Spa (1891)
Proprietary
Woodhall Spa LN10 6PU
☎ **(01526) 352511**
☐ (01526) 351817
✉ booking@englishgolfunion.org
✍ Richard A Latham
▤ www.woodhallspagolf.com

Woodthorpe Hall (1986)
Woodthorpe, Alford LN13 0DD
☎ **(01507) 450000**
☐ (01507) 450000
✉ woodthorpehallgolfclub@live.co.uk
✍ Joan Smith (01507) 450000
▤ www.woodthorpehall.co.uk

London Clubs

Aquarius *Kent*
Bush Hill Park *Middlesex*
Central London Golf Centre *Surrey*
Chingford *Essex*
Dulwich & Sydenham Hill *Surrey*
Eltham Warren *Kent*
Finchley *Middlesex*
Hampstead *Middlesex*
Hendon *Middlesex*
Highgate *Middlesex*
Leaside *Middlesex*
London Scottish *Surrey*
Mill Hill *Middlesex*
Muswell Hill *Middlesex*
North Middlesex *Middlesex*
Richmond Park *Surrey*
Roehampton Club *Surrey*
Royal Blackheath *Kent*
Royal Epping Forest *Essex*
Royal Mid-Surrey *Surrey*
Royal Wimbledon *Surrey*
Shooter's Hill *Kent*
South Herts *Hertfordshire*
Thameside Golf Centre *Kent*
Trent Park *Middlesex*
Wanstead *Essex*
West Essex *Essex*
Wimbledon Common *Surrey*
Wimbledon Park *Surrey*

Manchester

Blackley (1907)
Victoria Avenue East, Manchester M9 7HW
☎ **(0161) 643 2980**
(0161) 653 8300
office@blackleygolfclub.com
B Beddoes (0161) 654 7770
www.blackleygolfclub.com

Boysnope Park (1998)
Proprietary
Liverpool Road, Barton Moss, Eccles M30 7RF
☎ **(0161) 707 6125**
(0161) 707 1888
karensmith63@btconnect.com
Jean Stringer (0161) 707 6125
www.boysnopegolfclub.co.uk

Chorlton-cum-Hardy (1902)
Barlow Hall, Barlow Hall Road, Manchester M21 7JJ
☎ **(0161) 881 3139**
(0161) 881 4532
chorltongolf@hotmail.com
IR Booth (0161) 881 5830
www.chorltoncumhardygolfclub.co.uk

Davyhulme Park (1911)
Gleneagles Road, Davyhulme, Manchester M41 8SA
☎ **(0161) 748 2260**
(0161) 747 4067
davyhulmeparkgolfclub@email.com
www.davyhulmeparkgc.info

Denton (1909)
Manchester Road, Denton, Manchester M34 2GG
☎ **(0161) 336 3218**
(0161) 336 4751
info@dentongolfclub.com
ID McIlvanney
www.dentongolfclub.com

Didsbury (1891)
Ford Lane, Northenden, Manchester M22 4NQ
☎ **(0161) 998 9278**
(0161) 902 3060
golf@didsburygolfclub.com
John K Mort (Mgr)
www.didsburygolfclub.com

Ellesmere (1913)
Old Clough Lane, Worsley, Manchester M28 7HZ
☎ **(0161) 790 2122**
(0161) 790 2122
honsec@ellesmeregolfclub.co.uk
A T Leaver (0161) 790 2122
www.ellesmeregolfclub.co.uk

Fairfield Golf & Sailing Club (1892)
Booth Road, Audenshaw, Manchester M34 5QA
☎ **(0161) 301 4528**
manager@fairfieldgolfclub.co.uk
John Paton (Mgr)
www.fairfieldgolfclub.co.uk

Flixton (1893)
Church Road, Flixton, Urmston, Manchester M41 6EP
☎ **(0161) 748 2116**
(0161) 748 2116
flixtongolfclub@mail.com
A Braithwaite
www.flixtongolfclub.co.uk

Great Lever & Farnworth (1901)
Plodder Lane, Farnworth, Bolton BL4 0LQ
☎ **(01204) 656493**
(01204) 656137
greatlever@btconnect.com

Heaton Park Golf Centre (1912)
Pay and play
Heaton Park, Middleton Road, Prestwich M25 2SW
☎ **(0161) 654 9899**
(0161) 653 2003
hpbookings@macktrading.net
Brian Dique (Gen Mgr)
www.mackgolf.co.uk

The Manchester (1882)
Hopwood Cottage, Rochdale Road, Middleton, Manchester M24 6QP
☎ **(0161) 643 3202**
(0161) 643 3202
secretary@mangc.co.uk
Stephen Armstead
www.mangc.co.uk

New North Manchester (1923)
Rhodes House, Manchester Old Road, Middleton M24 4PE
☎ **(0161) 643 9033**
(0161) 643 7775
tee@nmgc.co.uk
G Heaslip
www.northmanchestergolfclub.co.uk

Northenden (1912)
Palatine Road, Manchester M22 4FR
☎ **(0161) 998 4738**
(0161) 945 5592
manager@northendengolfclub.com
Alison Davidson (Mgr)
(0161) 998 4738
www.northendengolfclub.com

Old Manchester (1818)
Club
☎ **(0161) 766 4157**

Pike Fold (1909)
Hills Lane, Pole Lane, Unsworth, Bury BL9 8QP
☎ **(0161) 766 3561**
(0161) 351 2189
secretary@pikefold.co.uk
Martin Jeffs (Secretary)
www.pikefold.co.uk

Prestwich (1908)
Hilton Lane, Prestwich M25 9XB
☎ **(0161) 772 0700**
(0161) 772 0700
prestwichgolf@btconnect.com
www.prestwichgolf.co.uk

Stand (1904)
The Dales, Ashbourne Grove, Whitefield, Manchester M45 7NL
☎ **(0161) 766 2388**
(0161) 796 3234
secretary@standgolfclub.co.uk
M A Cowsill (0161) 766 3197
www.standgolfclub.co.uk

Swinton Park (1906)
East Lancashire Road, Swinton, Manchester M27 5LX
☎ **(0161) 794 0861**
(0161) 281 0698
info@spgolf.co.uk
www.spgolf.co.uk

Whitefield (1932)
Higher Lane, Whitefield, Manchester M45 7EZ
☎ **(0161) 351 2700**
(0161) 351 2712
enquiries@whitefieldgolfclub.com
Mrs M Rothwell
www.whitefieldgolfclub.co.uk

Withington (1892)
243 Palatine Road, West Didsbury, Manchester M20 2UE
☎ **(0161) 445 9544**
(0161) 445 5210
secretary@withingtongolfclub.co.uk

For key to symbols see page 725

PJ Keane
www.withingtongolfclub.co.uk

Worsley (1894)
Stableford Avenue, Monton Green, Eccles, Manchester M30 8AP
(0161) 789 4202
(0161) 789 3200
office@worsleygolfclub.co.uk
J D Clarke
www.worsleygolfclub.co.uk

Merseyside

Allerton Municipal (1934)
Public
Allerton Road, Liverpool L18 3JT
(0151) 428 1046

Arrowe Park (1931)
Public
Arrowe Park, Woodchurch, Birkenhead CH49 5LW
(0151) 677 1527,
(0151) 678 5285
contact@arroweparkgolfclub.co.uk
P Hickey
www.arroweparkgolfclub.co.uk

Bidston (1913)
Bidston Link Road, Wallasey, Wirral CH44 2HR
(0151) 638 3412
(0151) 638 8685
info@bidstongolf.co.uk
www.bidstongolf.co.uk

Bootle (1934)
Pay and play
Dunnings Bridge Road, Litherland L30 2PP
(0151) 928 1371
(0151) 949 1815
bootlegolfcourse@btconnect.com
G Howarth

Bowring (1913)
Public
Bowring Park, Roby Road, Huyton L36 4HD
(0151) 489 1901
dgwalker36@tiscali.co.uk

Brackenwood (1933)
Public
Bracken Lane, Bebington, Wirral L63 2LY
(0151) 608 3093
secretary@brackenwoodgolf.co.uk
www.brackenwoodgolf.co.uk

Bromborough (1903)
Raby Hall Road, Bromborough CH63 0NW
(0151) 334 2155
(0151) 334 7300
enquiries@bromboroughgolfclub.org.uk
Alisdair Mackay (0151) 334 2155
www.bromboroughgolfclub.org.uk

Caldy (1907)
Links Hey Road, Caldy, Wirral CH48 1NB
(0151) 625 5660
(0151) 625 7394
secretarycaldygc@btconnect.com
Gail M Copple
www.caldygolfclub.co.uk

Childwall (1912)
Naylors Road, Gateacre, Liverpool L27 2YB
(0151) 487 0654
(0151) 487 0654
office@childwallgolfclub.co.uk
Peter Bowen
www.childwallgolfclub.co.uk

Eastham Lodge (1973)
117 Ferry Road, Eastham, Wirral CH62 0AP
(0151) 327 3003 (Clubhouse)
(0151) 327 7574
easthamlodge.g.c@btinternet.com
Mr Nick Sargent (Director of Golf)
www.easthamlodgegolfclub.co.uk

Formby (1884)
Golf Road, Formby, Liverpool L37 1LQ
(01704) 872164
(01704) 833028
info@formbygolfclub.co.uk
M Betteridge (01704) 872164
www.formbygolfclub.co.uk

Formby Hall Golf Resort & Spa (1996)
Proprietary
Southport Old Road, Formby L37 1NN
(01704) 875699
(01704) 832134
golf@formbyhallgolfresort.co.uk
Mark Williams
www.formbyhallgolfresort.co.uk

Formby Ladies' (1896)
Golf Road, Formby, Liverpool L37 1YH
(01704) 873493
(01704) 874127
secretary@formbyladiesgolfclub.co.uk
Mrs CA Bromley (01704) 873493
www.formbyladiesgolfclub.co.uk

Grange Park (1891)
Prescot Road, St Helens WA10 3AD
(01744) 22980 (Members)
(01744) 26318
secretary@grangeparkgolfclub.co.uk
G Brown (01744) 26318
www.grangeparkgolfclub.co.uk

Haydock Park (1877)
Golborne Park, Newton Lane, Newton-le-Willows WA12 0HX
(01925) 228525
(01925) 224984
secretary@haydockparkgc.co.uk
David Hughes
www.haydockparkgc.co.uk

Hesketh (1885)
Cockle Dick's Lane, Cambridge Road, Southport PR9 9QQ
(01704) 536897
(01704) 539250
secretary@heskethgolfclub.co.uk
N P Annandale (Sec)
(01704) 536897 ext 1
www.heskethgolfclub.co.uk

Heswall (1902)
Cottage Lane, Gayton, Heswall CH60 8PB
(0151) 342 1237
(0151) 342 6140
dawn@heswallgolfclub.com
Graham Capewell (Manager)
www.heswallgolfclub.com

Hillside (1911)
Hastings Road, Hillside, Southport PR8 2LU
(01704) 567169
(01704) 563192
secretary@hillside-golfclub.co.uk
SH Newland (01704) 567169
www.hillside-golfclub.co.uk

Houghwood (1996)
Proprietary
Billinge Hill, Crank Road, Crank, St Helens WA11 8RL
(01744) 894754
(01744) 894754
office@houghwoodgolf.co.uk
P Turner (Man Dir)
www.houghwoodgolfclub.co.uk

Hoylake Municipal (1933)
Public
Carr Lane, Hoylake, Wirral CH47 4BG
(0151) 632 2956/4883 (Bookings)
www.hoylakegolfclub.com

Huyton & Prescot (1905)
Hurst Park, Huyton Lane, Huyton L36 1UA
(0151) 489 3948
(0151) 489 0797
secretary@huytonandprescotgolf.co.uk
L Griffin(0151) 489 3948
www.huytonandprescot.myprogolfer.co.uk

Leasowe (1891)
Leasowe Road, Moreton, Wirral CH46 3RD
(0151) 677 5852
(0151) 641 8519
secretary@leasowegolfclub.co.uk
David Knight (0151) 677 5852
www.leasowegolfclub.co.uk

Lee Park (1954)
Childwall Valley Road, Gateacre, Liverpool L27 3YA
(0151) 487 3882 (Clubhouse)
(0151) 498 4666
lee.park@virgin.net
Steve Settle
www.leepark.co.uk

Prenton (1905)
Golf Links Road, Prenton, Birkenhead CH42 8LW
(0151) 609 3426
nigel.brown@prentongolfclub.co.uk
N Brown
www.prentongolfclub.co.uk

RLGC Village Play (1895)
Club
c/o 18 Waverley Road, Hoylake, Wirral CH47 3DD
☎ **(07885) 507263**
🖷 (0151) 632 5156
✉ pdwbritesparks@sky.com
✍ PD Williams (0151) 632 5156

Royal Birkdale (1889)
Waterloo Road, Birkdale, Southport PR8 2LX
☎ **(01704) 552020**
🖷 (01704) 552021
✉ secretary@royalbirkdale.com
✍ Mike Gilyeat (Sec)
🖹 www.royalbirkdale.com

Royal Liverpool (1869)
Meols Drive, Hoylake CH47 4AL
☎ **(0151) 632 3101/3102**
🖷 (0151) 632 6737
✉ secretary@royal-liverpool-golf.com
✍ D R Cromie
🖹 www.royal-liverpool-golf.com

Sherdley Park Municipal (1974)
Public
Eltonhead Road, Sutton, St Helens, Merseyside WA9 5DE
☎ **(01744) 813149**
🖷 (01744) 817967
✉ sherdleyparkgolfcourse@sthelens.gov.uk
✍ Ian Corice (Mgr)
🖹 www.sthelens.gov.uk/goactive

Southport & Ainsdale (1906)
Bradshaws Lane, Ainsdale, Southport PR8 3LG
☎ **(01704) 578000**
🖷 (01704) 570896
✉ secretary@sandagolfclub.co.uk
✍ Ryan O'Connor
🖹 www.sandagolfclub.co.uk

Southport Golf Links (1912)
Public
Park Road West, Southport PR9 0JS
☎ **(01704) 535286**

Southport Old Links (1926)
Moss Lane, Southport PR9 7QS
☎ **(01704) 228207**
🖷 (01704) 505353
✉ secretary@solgc.freeserve.co.uk
✍ BE Kenyon
🖹 www.solgc.freeserve.co.uk

Wallasey (1891)
Bayswater Road, Wallasey CH45 8LA
☎ **(0151) 691 1024**
🖷 (0151) 638 8988
✉ wallaseygc@aol.com
✍ JT Barraclough (0151) 691 1024
🖹 www.wallaseygolfclub.com

Warren (1911)
Public
Grove Road, Wallasey, Wirral CH45 0JA
☎ **(0151) 639 8323 (Clubhouse)**
🖹 www.warrengc.freeserve.co.uk

West Derby (1896)
Yew Tree Lane, Liverpool L12 9HQ
☎ **(0151) 254 1034**
🖷 (0151) 259 0505
✉ secretary@westderbygc.co.uk
✍ Karen Buck
🖹 www.westderbygc.co.uk

West Lancashire (1873)
Hall Road West, Blundellsands, Liverpool L23 8SZ
☎ **(0151) 924 1076**
🖷 (0151) 931 4448
✉ sec@westlancashiregolf.co.uk
✍ S King (0151) 924 1076
🖹 www.westlancashiregolf.co.uk

Wirral Ladies (1894)
93 Bidston Road, Birkenhead, Wirral CH43 6TS
☎ **(0151) 652 1255**
🖷 (0151) 651 3775
✉ wirral.ladies@btconnect.com
✍ Mr P Greville
🖹 www.wirral-ladies-golf-club.co.uk

Woolton (1900)
Doe Park, Speke Road, Woolton, Liverpool L25 7TZ
☎ **(0151) 486 2298**
🖷 (0151) 486 1664
✉ golf@wooltongolf.co.uk
✍ Miss T Rawlinson (0151) 486 2298 opt 4
🖹 www.wooltongolfclub.com

Middlesex

Airlinks (1984)
Public
Southall Lane, Hounslow TW5 9PE
☎ **(020) 8561 1418**
🖷 (020) 8813 6284

Ashford Manor (1898)
Fordbridge Road, Ashford TW15 3RT
☎ **(01784) 424644**
🖷 (01784) 424649
✉ secretary@amgc.co.uk
✍ Peter Dawson (Business Manager)
🖹 www.amgc.co.uk

Brent Valley (1909)
Public
Church Road, Hanwell, London W7 3BE
☎ **(020) 8567 4230 (Clubhouse)**

Bush Hill Park (1895)
Bush Hill, Winchmore Hill, London N21 2BU
☎ **(020) 8360 5738**
🖷 (020) 8360 5583
✉ chris@bhpgc.com
✍ Lee Fickling (Director of Golf)
🖹 www.bhpgc.com

Crews Hill (1916)
Cattlegate Road, Crews Hill, Enfield EN2 8AZ
☎ **(020) 8363 6674**
✉ manager@crewshillgolfclub.com
✍ Brian Cullen
🖹 www.crewshillgolfclub.com

David Lloyd Hampton Golf Club (1977)
Pay and play
Staines Road, Twickenham TW2 5JD
☎ **(0208) 783 1698**
🖷 (0208) 783 9475
✉ golf.hampton@davidlloyd.co.uk
✍ Jamie Skinner
🖹 www.davidlloyd.co.uk

Ealing (1898)
Perivale Lane, Greenford UB6 8TS
☎ **(020) 8997 0937**
🖷 (020) 8998 0756
✉ info@ealinggolfclub.co.uk
✍ David Jones
🖹 www.ealinggolfclub.co.uk

Enfield (1893)
Old Park Road South, Enfield EN2 7DA
☎ **(020) 8363 3970**
🖷 (020) 8342 0381
✉ secretary@enfieldgolfclub.co.uk
✍ Darryl Canthorne
🖹 www.enfieldgolfclub.co.uk

Finchley (1929)
Nether Court, Frith Lane, London NW7 1PU
☎ **(020) 8346 2436**
🖷 (020) 8343 4205
✉ secretary@finchleygolfclub.co.uk
✍ MD Gottlieb
🖹 www.finchleygolfclub.com

Fulwell (1904)
Wellington Road, Hampton Hill TW12 1JY
☎ **(020) 8977 2733**
🖷 (020) 8977 7732
✉ secretary@fulwellgolfclub.co.uk
✍ Sean Whelan
🖹 www.fulwellgolfclub.co.uk

Grim's Dyke (1909)
Oxhey Lane, Hatch End, Pinner HA5 4AL
☎ **(020) 8428 4539**
🖷 (020) 8421 5494
✉ secretary@grimsdyke.co.uk
✍ R Jones (020) 8428 4539
🖹 www.club-noticeboard.co.uk/grimsdyke

Hampstead (1893)
82 Winnington Road, London N2 0TU
☎ **(020) 8455 0203**
🖷 (020) 8731 6194
✉ secretary@hampsteadgolfclub.co.uk
✍ Mark Smith
🖹 www.hampsteadgolfclub.co.uk

For key to symbols see page 725

Harrow Hill Golf Course (1982)
Public
Kenton Road, Harrow, Middx HA1 2BW
☎ **(0208) 8643754**
✉ info@harrowgolf.co.uk
✍ S Bishop
🖳 www.harrowgolf.co.uk

Harrow School (1978)
High Street, Harrow-on-the-Hill HA1 3HP
☎ **(0208) 872 8000**
✉ hsgcsecretary@harrowschool.org.uk
✍ V A Mrowiec (020) 8872 8290
🖳 www.harrowschoolgolfclub.co.uk

Haste Hill (1930)
Public
The Drive, Northwood HA6 1HN
☎ **(01923) 825224**
📠 (01923) 826485
✉ hastehillgc@yahoo.co.uk
✍ S Cella

Heath Park (1975)
Stockley Road, West Drayton
☎ **(01895) 444232**
📠 (01895) 444232
✉ heathparkgolf@yahoo.co.uk
✍ B Sharma (Prop)

Hendon (1903)
Ashley Walk, Devonshire Road, London NW7 1DG
☎ **(020) 8346 6023**
📠 (020) 8343 1974
✉ admin@hendongolf.com
✍ Gabriela Segal (Asst. Sec)
🖳 www.hendongolf.com

Highgate (1904)
Denewood Road, Highgate, London N6 4AH
☎ **(020) 8340 1906**
📠 (020) 8348 9152
✉ admin@highgategc.co.uk
✍ N Sinclair (020) 8340 1906
🖳 www.highgategc.co.uk

Horsenden Hill (1935)
Public
Woodland Rise, Greenford UB6 0RD
☎ **(020) 8902 4555**
✉ hhgchonsec@aol.com
✍ John Leach (0208) 922 3472
🖳 www.horsendenhillgolfclub.co.uk

Hounslow Heath (1979)
Public
Staines Road, Hounslow TW4 5DS
☎ **(020) 8570 5271**
📠 (020) 8570 5205
✉ golf@hhgc.uk.com
✍ J Swanson
🖳 www.hhgc.uk.com

Leaside GC (1974)
Pay and play
Lee Valley Leisure, Picketts Lock Lane, Edmonton, London N9 0AS
☎ **(020) 8803 3611**

Mill Hill (1925)
100 Barnet Way, Mill Hill, London NW7 3AL
☎ **(020) 8959 2339**
📠 (020) 8906 0731
✉ clubOffice@millhillgc.co.uk
✍ David Beal
🖳 www.millhillgc.co.uk

Muswell Hill (1893)
Rhodes Avenue, London N22 7UT
☎ **(020) 8888 1764**
📠 (020) 8889 9380
✉ manager@muswellhillgolfclub.co.uk
✍ A Hobbs (020) 8888 1764
🖳 www.muswellhillgolfclub.co.uk

North Middlesex (1905)
The Manor House, Friern Barnet Lane, Whetstone, London N20 0NL
☎ **(020) 8445 1604**
📠 (020) 8445 5023
✉ manager@northmiddlesexgc.co.uk
✍ Mr Howard Till
🖳 www.northmiddlesexgc.co.uk

Northwood (1891)
Rickmansworth Road, Northwood HA6 2QW
☎ **(01923) 821384**
📠 (01923) 840150
✉ secretary@northwoodgolf.co.uk
✍ S Proudfoot
🖳 www.northwoodgolf.co.uk

Perivale Park (1932)
Public
Stockdove Way, Argyle Road, Greenford UB6 8JT
☎ **(020) 8575 7116**

Pinner Hill (1927)
Southview Road, Pinner Hill HA5 3YA
☎ **(020) 8866 0963**
📠 (020) 8868 4817
✉ phgc@pinnerhillgc.com
✍ Alan Findlater (Gen Mgr)
🖳 www.pinnerhillgc.com

Ruislip (1936)
Public
Ickenham Road, Ruislip HA4 7DQ
☎ **(01895) 638835/623980**
📠 (01895) 635780
✉ ruislipgolf@btconnect.com

Stanmore (1893)
29 Gordon Avenue, Stanmore HA7 2RL
☎ **(020) 8954 2599**
📠 (020) 8954 2599
✉ secretary@stanmoregolfclub.co.uk
✍ Allan Knott (020) 8954 2599
🖳 www.stanmoregolfclub.co.uk

Stockley Park (1993)
Pay and play
The Clubhouse, Stockley Park, Uxbridge UB11 1AQ
☎ **(020) 8813 5700/561 6339 (Bookings)**
📠 (020) 8813 5655
✉ d.peck@stockleypines.com
✍ K Soper
🖳 www.stockleyparkgolf.com

Strawberry Hill (1900)
Wellesley Road, Strawberry Hill, Twickenham TW2 5SD
☎ **(020) 8894 0165**
✉ secretary@shgc.net
✍ Secretary (020) 8894 0165
🖳 www.shgc.net

Sudbury (1920)
Bridgewater Road, Wembley HA0 1AL
☎ **(020) 8902 3713 (office)**
📠 (020) 8902 3713
✉ enquiries@sudburygolfclubltd.co.uk
✍ N Cropley (Gen Mgr)
🖳 www.sudburygolfclubltd.co.uk

Sunbury (1993)
Proprietary
Charlton Lane, Shepperton TW17 8QA
☎ **(01932) 771414**
📠 (01932) 789300
✉ sunbury@crown-golf.co.uk
🖳 www.crown-golf.co.uk

Trent Park (1973)
Pay and play
Bramley Road, Southgate, London N14 4UW
☎ **(020) 8367 4653**
📠 (020) 8366 4581
✉ info@trentparkgolf.co.uk
🖳 www.trentparkgolf.co.uk

Uxbridge (1947)
Public
The Drive, Harefield Place, Uxbridge UB10 8AQ
☎ **(01895) 556750 (Pro Shop)**
📠 (01895) 810262
✉ uxbridgegolfclub@btconnect.com
✍ Mrs A James (01895) 272457
🖳 www.uxbridgegolfclub.co.uk

West Middlesex (1891)
Greenford Road, Southall UB1 3EE
☎ **(020) 8574 3450**
📠 (020) 8574 2383
✉ westmid.gc@virgin.net
✍ Miss R Khanna
🖳 www.westmiddxgolfclub.co.uk

Wyke Green (1928)
Syon Lane, Isleworth, Osterley TW7 5PT
☎ **(020) 8560 8777**
📠 (020) 8569 8392
✉ office@wykegreengolfclub.co.uk
🖳 www.wykegreengolfclub.co.uk

Norfolk

Barnham Broom Hotel (1977)
Honingham Road, Barnham Broom, Norwich NR9 4DD
☎ **(01603) 759393 (Hotel)**
📠 (01603) 758224
✉ golf@barnham-broom.co.uk

✍ M Breen (01603) 757504
🖳 www.barnham-broom.co.uk

Bawburgh (1978)
Glen Lodge, Marlingford Road, Bawburgh, Norwich NR9 3LU
☎ **(01603) 740404**
🖷 (01603) 740403
✉ info@bawburgh.com
✍ I Ladbrooke (Gen Mgr)
🖳 www.bawburgh.com

Caldecott Hall (1993)
Pay and play
Caldecott Hall, Beccles Road, Fritton, Great Yarmouth NR31 9EY
☎ **(01493) 488488**
🖷 (01493) 488561
✉ reception_caldecotthall@hotmail.co.uk
✍ Jill Braybrooke
🖳 www.caldecotthall.co.uk

Costessey Park (1983)
Costessey Park, Costessey, Norwich NR8 5AL
☎ **(01603) 746333**
🖷 (01603) 746185
✉ enquiry@costesseypark.com
✍ GC Stangoe
🖳 www.costesseypark.com

Dereham (1934)
Quebec Road, Dereham NR19 2DS
☎ **(01362) 695900**
🖷 (01362) 695904
✉ office@derehamgolfclub.com
✍ Mr Tim Evans
🖳 www.derehamgolfclub.com

Dunham (1979)
Proprietary
Little Dunham, Swaffham PE32 2DF
☎ **(01328) 701906**
✉ garympotter@hotmail.com
✍ G & S Potter (Props)
🖳 www.dunhamgolfclub.com

De Vere Dunston Hall (1994)
Pay and play
Ipswich Road, Dunston, Norwich NR14 8PQ
☎ **(01508) 470178**
🖷 (01508) 471499

Eagles (1990)
Pay and play
39 School Road, Tilney All Saints, Kings Lynn PE34 4RS
☎ **(01553) 827147**
🖷 (01553) 829777
✉ shop@eagles-golf-tennis.co.uk
✍ D W Horn
🖳 www.eagles-golf-tennis.co.uk

Eaton (1910)
Newmarket Road, Norwich NR4 6SF
☎ **(01603) 451686**
🖷 (01603) 457539
✉ admin@eatongc.co.uk
✍ P Johns
🖳 www.eatongc.co.uk

Fakenham (1973)
The Race Course, Hempton Road, Fakenham NR21 7NY
☎ **(01328) 855678**
🖷 (01328) 855678
✉ fakenhamgolf@tiscali.co.uk
✍ G Cocker (01328) 855678
🖳 www.fakenhamgolfclub.co.uk

Feltwell (1976)
Thor Ave, Wilton Road, Feltwell, Thetford IP26 4AY
☎ **(01842) 827644**
🖷 (01842) 829065
✉ sec.feltwellgc@virgin.net
✍ Jonathan Moore
🖳 www.club-noticeboard.co.uk

Gorleston (1906)
Warren Road, Gorleston, Gt Yarmouth NR31 6JT
☎ **(01493) 661911**
🖷 (01493) 661911
✉ manager@gorlestongolfclub.co.uk
✍ David James (01493) 661911
🖳 www.gorlestongolfclub.co.uk

Great Yarmouth & Caister (1882)
Beach House, Caister-on-Sea, Gt Yarmouth NR30 5TD
☎ **(01493) 728699**
🖷 (01493) 728831
✉ office@caistergolf.co.uk
✍ Brian Lever
🖳 www.caistergolf.co.uk

Hunstanton (1891)
Golf Course Road, Old Hunstanton PE36 6JQ
☎ **(01485) 532811**
🖷 (01485) 532319
✉ secretary@hunstantongolfclub.com
✍ BRB Carrick
🖳 www.hunstantongolfclub.com

King's Lynn (1923)
Castle Rising, King's Lynn PE31 6BD
☎ **(01553) 631654**
🖷 (01553) 631036
✉ secretary@kingslynngc.co.uk
✍ M Bowman
🖳 www.kingslynngc.co.uk

Links Country Park Hotel & Golf Club (1903)
West Runton, Cromer NR27 9QH
☎ **(01263) 838383**
🖷 (01263) 838264
✉ links@mackenziehotels.com
✍ Marc Mackenzie
🖳 www.links-hotel.co.uk

Marriott Sprowston Manor Hotel (1980)
Wroxham Road, Sprowston, Norwich NR7 8RP
☎ **(0870) 400 7229**
🖷 (0870) 400 7329
✉ keith.grant@marriotthotels.com
🖳 www.marriott.co.uk/nwigs

Mattishall (1990)
Proprietary
South Green, Mattishall, Dereham
☎ **(01362) 850464**
✍ B Hall
🖳 www.mattishallgolfclub.co.uk

Middleton Hall (1989)
Proprietary
Middleton, King's Lynn PE32 1RY
☎ **(01553) 841800**
✉ enquiries@middletonhallgolfclub.com
✍ M Johnson
🖳 www.middletonhallgolfclub.com

Mundesley (1901)
Links Road, Mundesley NR11 8ES
☎ **(01263) 720095**
🖷 (01263) 722849
✉ manager@mundesleygolfclub.com
✍ R Pudney
🖳 www.mundesleygolfclub.com

The Norfolk G&CC (1993)
Proprietary
Hingham Road, Reymerston, Norwich NR9 4QQ
☎ **(01362) 850297**
🖷 (01362) 850614
✉ info@thenorfolkgolfclub.co.uk
✍ M de Boltz
🖳 www.club-noticeboard.co.uk/norfolk/

RAF Marham (1974)
RAF Marham, Kings Lynn PE33 9NP
☎ **(01760) 337261 ext 7262**
🖳 www.marhamgolf.co.uk

Richmond Park (1990)
Saham Road, Watton IP25 6EA
☎ **(01953) 881803**
🖷 (01953) 881817
✉ info@richmondpark.co.uk
✍ Simon Jessop
🖳 www.richmondpark.co.uk

Royal Cromer (1888)
Overstrand Road, Cromer NR27 0JH
☎ **(01263) 512884**
🖷 (01263) 512430
✉ general.manager@royal-cromer.com
✍ Gary Richardson
🖳 www.royalcromergolfclub.com

Royal Norwich (1893)
Drayton High Road, Hellesdon, Norwich NR6 5AH
☎ **(01603) 429928**
🖷 (01603) 417945
✉ mail@royalnorwichgolf.co.uk
✍ Phil Grice (Gen Mgr)
🖳 www.royalnorwichgolf.co.uk

Royal West Norfolk (1892)
Brancaster, King's Lynn PE31 8AX
☎ **(01485) 210087**
🖷 (01485) 210087
✉ secretary@rwngc.org
✍ Ian Symington
🖳 www.rwngc.org

Ryston Park (1932)
Ely Road, Denver, Downham Market PE38 0HH
☎ **(01366) 382133**
Fax (01366) 383834
Email rystonparkgc@talktalkbusiness.net
WJ Flogdell
www.club-noticeboard.co.uk

Sheringham (1891)
Sheringham NR26 8HG
☎ **(01263) 823488**
Fax (01263) 826129
Email info@sheringhamgolfclub.co.uk
N R Milton
www.sheringhamgolfclub.co.uk

Swaffham (1922)
Cley Road, Swaffham PE37 8AE
☎ **(01760) 721621**
Fax (01760) 336998
Email manager@swaffhamgc.co.uk
www.club-noticeboard.co.uk

Thetford (1912)
Brandon Road, Thetford IP24 3NE
☎ **(01842) 752258 (Clubhouse)**
Fax (01842) 766212
Email thetfordgolfclub@btconnect.com
Mrs Diane Hopkins (01842) 752169
www.thetfordgolfclub.co.uk

Wensum Valley (1990)
Proprietary
Beech Avenue, Taverham, Norwich NR8 6HP
☎ **(01603) 261012**
Fax (01603) 261664
Email enqs@wensumvalleyhotel.co.uk
Mrs B Hall
www.wensumvalleyhotel.co.uk

Weston Park (1993)
Proprietary
Weston Longville, Norwich NR9 5JW
☎ **(01603) 872998**
Fax (01603) 873040
Email pro@weston-park.co.uk
Michael R Few (PGA Pro)
www.weston-park.co.uk

Northamptonshire

Brampton Heath (1995)
Pay and play
Sandy Lane, Church Brampton NN6 8AX
☎ **(01604) 843939**
Fax (01604) 843885
Email info@bhgc.co.uk
Carl Sainsbury (Head Pro)
www.bhgc.co.uk

Cold Ashby (1974)
Proprietary
Stanford Road, Cold Ashby, Northampton NN6 6EP
☎ **(01604) 740548**
Fax (01604) 743025
Email info@coldashbygolfclub.com
DA Croxton (Prop)
www.coldashbygolfclub.com

Collingtree Park Golf Course (1990)
Proprietary
Windingbrook Lane, Northampton NN4 0XN
☎ **(01604) 700000**
Fax (01604) 702600
Email enquiries@collingtreeparkgolf.com
www.collingtreeparkgolf.com

Daventry & District (1907)
Norton Road, Daventry NN11 2LS
☎ **(01327) 702829**
Email ddgc@hotmail.co.uk
Colin Long
www.daventrygolfclub.co.uk

Delapre (1976)
Pay and play
Eagle Drive, Nene Valley Way, Northampton NN4 7DU
☎ **(01604) 764036**
Fax (01604) 706378
Email delapre@jbgolf.co.uk
Greg Iron (Centre Mgr) John Cuddiny (PGA Pro)
www.delapregolfcentre.co.uk

Farthingstone Hotel (1974)
Farthingstone, Towcester NN12 8HA
☎ **(01327) 361291**
Fax (01327) 361645
Email interest@farthingstone.co.uk
C Donaldson
www.farthingstone.co.uk

Hellidon Lakes Hotel G&CC (1991)
Hellidon, Nr. Daventry, Northamptonshire NN11 6LN
☎ **(01327) 262550**
Fax (01327) 262559
MA Thomas
www.hellidon.co.uk

Kettering (1891)
Headlands, Kettering NN15 6XA
☎ **(01536) 511104**
Fax (01536) 523788
Email secretary@kettering-golf.co.uk
JM Gilding (01536) 511104
www.kettering-golf.co.uk

Kingfisher Hotel (1995)
Proprietary
Buckingham Road, Deanshanger, Milton Keynes MK19 6JY
☎ **(01908) 560354/562332**
Fax (01908) 260857
Email sales.kingfisher@btopenworld.com
www.kingfisher-hotelandgolf.co.uk

Kingsthorpe (1908)
Kingsley Road, Northampton NN2 7BU
☎ **(01604) 711173**
Fax (01604) 710610
Email secretary@kingsthorpe-golf.co.uk
DS Wade (01604) 710610
www.kingsthorpe-golf.co.uk

Northampton (1893)
Harlestone, Northampton NN7 4EF
☎ **(01604) 845155**
Fax (01604) 820262
Email golf@northamptongolfclub.co.uk
B Randall (Director of Golf)
www.northamptongolfclub.co.uk

Northamptonshire County (1909)
Church Brampton, Northampton NN6 8AZ
☎ **(01604) 843025**
Fax (01604) 843463
Email secretary@countygolfclub.org.uk
Peter Walsh (01604) 843025
www.countygolfclub.org.uk

Oundle (1893)
Benefield Road, Oundle PE8 4EZ
☎ **(01832) 273267**
Fax (01832) 273008
Email office@oundlegolfclub.com
L Quantrill (01832) 272267
www.oundlegolfclub.com

Overstone Park (1994)
Proprietary
Overstone Park Ltd, Billing Lane, Northampton NN6 0A5
☎ **(01604) 647666**
Fax (01604) 642635
Email enquiries@overstonepark.com
Nigel Wardle (Gen Mgr)
www.overstonepark.com

Priors Hall (1965)
Public
Stamford Road, Weldon, Corby NN17 3JH
☎ **(01536) 260756**
Fax (01536) 260756
Email p.ackroyd1@btinternet.com
P Ackroyd (01536) 263722

Rushden (1919)
Kimbolton Road, Chelveston, Wellingborough, Northamptonshire NN9 6AN
☎ **(01933) 418511**
Fax (01933) 418511
Email secretary@rushdengolfclub.org
EJ Williams
www.rushdengolfclub.org

Staverton Park (1977)
Staverton Park, Staverton, Daventry NN11 6JT
☎ **(01327) 302000/302118**
Fax (01327) 311428

Stoke Albany (1995)
Proprietary
Ashley Road, Stoke Albany, Market Harborough LE16 8PL
☎ **(01858) 535208**
Email info@stokealbanygolfclub.co.uk
R Want
www.stokealbanygolfclub.com

Wellingborough (1893)
Harrowden Hall, Great Harrowden, Wellingborough NN9 5AD
☎ **(01933) 677234**

(01933) 679379
info@wellingboroughgolfclub.com
David Waite (01933) 677234
www.wellingboroughgolfclub.com

Whittlebury Park G&CC (1992)
Proprietary, Public,
Whittlebury, Towcester NN12 8WP
(01327) 850000
(01327) 850001
enquiries@whittlebury.com
Alison Trubshaw
www.whittlebury.com

Northumberland

Allendale (1906)
High Studdon, Allenheads Road, Allendale, Hexham NE47 9DH
(0700) 580 8246
secretary@allendale-golf.co.uk
Mrs A Woodcock (Hon Sec)
www.allendale-golf.co.uk

Alnmouth (1869)
Foxton Hall, Alnmouth NE66 3BE
(01665) 830231
(01665) 830922
secretary@alnmouthgolfclub.com
P Simpson
www.alnmouthgolfclub.com

Alnmouth Village (1869)
Marine Road, Alnmouth NE66 2RZ
(01665) 830370
bobhill53@live.co.uk
www.alnmouthvillagegolfclub.co.uk

Alnwick Castle (1907)
Proprietary
Swansfield Park, Alnwick NE66 2AB
(01665) 602632
secretary@alnwickgolfclub.co.uk
Club Manager (01665) 602632
www.alnwickcastlegolfclub.co.uk

Arcot Hall (1909)
Dudley, Cramlington NE23 7QP
(0191) 236 2794
(0191) 217 0370
arcothall@tiscali.co.uk
Brian Rumney (0191) 236 2794
www.arcothallgolfclub.com

Bamburgh Castle (1904)
The Club House, 40 The Wynding, Bamburgh NE69 7DE
(01668) 214378
(01668) 214607
sec@bamburghcastlegolfclub.co.uk
MND Robinson (01668) 214321
www.bamburghcastlegolfclub.co.uk

Bedlingtonshire (1972)
Acorn Bank, Hartford Road, Bedlington NE22 6AA
(01670) 822457
(01670) 823048
secretary@bedlingtongolfclub.com
J Laverick (01670) 822457
www.bedlingtongolfclub.com

The Belford (1993)
South Road, Belford NE70 7DP
(01668) 213323
(01668) 213282
www.thebelford.com

Bellingham (1893)
Boggle Hole, Bellingham NE48 2DT
(01434) 220530/220152
admin@bellinghamgolfclub.com
Craig Wright
www.bellinghamgolfclub.com

Berwick-upon-Tweed (Goswick) (1890)
Goswick, Berwick-upon-Tweed TD15 2RW
(01289) 387256
(01289) 387392
goswickgc@btconnect.com
IAM Alsop
www.goswicklinksgc.co.uk

Blyth (1905)
New Delaval, Blyth NE24 4DB
(01670) 540110
(01670) 540134
clubmanager@blythgolf.co.uk
J C Hall
www.blythgolf.co.uk

Burgham Park Golf & Leisure Club (1994)
Proprietary
Felton, Morpeth NE65 9QP
(01670) 787898
(01670) 787164
info@burghampark.co.uk
William Kiely
www.burghampark.co.uk

Close House Hotel & Golf (1968)
Proprietary
Close House, Heddon-on-the-Wall, Newcastle-upon-Tyne NE15 0HT
(01661) 852255
(01661) 853322
events@closehouse.co.uk
John Glendinning
www.closehouse.co.uk

Dunstanburgh Castle (1900)
Embleton NE66 3XQ
(01665) 576562
(01665) 576562
enquiries@dunstanburgh.com
Irene Williams (Mgr)
www.dunstanburgh.com

Hexham (1892)
Spital Park, Hexham NE46 3RZ
(01434) 603072
(01434) 601865
info@hexhamgolf.co.uk
Dawn Wylie (01434) 603072
www.hexhamgolf.co.uk

Linden Hall (1997)
Proprietary
Longhorsley, Morpeth NE65 8XF
(01670) 500011
(01670) 500001
golf@lindenhall.co.uk
Stuart Carnie (Golf Mgr)
www.macdonaldhotels.co.uk/lindenhall

Longhirst Hall Golf Course (1997)
Longhirst Hall, Longhirst NE61 3LL
(01670) 791562 (Clubhouse)
(01670) 791768
enquiries@longhirstgolf.co.uk
Graham Chambers (01670) 791562
www.longhirstgolf.co.uk

Magdalene Fields (1903)
Pay and play
Magdalene Fields, Berwick-upon-Tweed TD15 1NE
(01289) 306130
secretary.magdalenefields@hotmail.co.uk
S Eddington (Sec)
www.magdalene-fields.co.uk

Matfen Hall Hotel (1994)
Proprietary
Matfen, Hexham NE20 0RH
(01661) 886400 (golf)
(01661) 886055
golf@matfenhall.com
Peter Smith
www.matfenhall.com

Morpeth (1906)
The Clubhouse, Morpeth NE61 2BT
(01670) 504942
(01670) 504918
admin@morpethgolf.co.uk
Terry Minett
www.morpethgolf.co.uk

Newbiggin (1884)
Newbiggin-by-the-Sea NE64 6DW
(01670) 817344 (Clubhouse)
info@newbiggingolfclub.co.uk
J Oliphant (Sec)/J Young (Mgr)
www.newbiggingolfclub.co.uk

Percy Wood Golf & Country Retreat (1993)
Coast View, Swarland, Morpeth NE65 9JG
(01670) 787940 (Clubhouse)
enquiries@percywood.com
(01670) 787010
www.percywood.co.uk

Ponteland (1927)
53 Bell Villas, Ponteland, Newcastle-upon-Tyne NE20 9BD
(01661) 822689
(01661) 860077
secretary@thepontelandgolfclub.co.uk
G Waugh
www.thepontelandgolfclub.co.uk

For key to symbols see page 725

Prudhoe (1930)
Eastwood Park, Prudhoe-on-Tyne NE42 5DX
☎ **(01661) 832466 ext 20**
(01661) 830710
secretary@prudhoegolfclub.co.uk
www.prudhoegolfclub.co.uk

Rothbury (1891)
Whitton Bank Road, Rothbury, Morpeth NE65 7RX
☎ **(01669) 621271 Ext 2**
secretary@rothburygolfclub.com
M Arkle (01669) 620487
www.rothburygolfclub.com

Seahouses (1913)
Beadnell Road, Seahouses NE68 7XT
☎ **(01665) 720794**
(01665) 721799
secretary@seahousesgolf.co.uk
Alan Patterson
www.seahousesgolf.co.uk

De Vere Slaley Hall (1988)
Slaley, Hexham NE47 0BX
☎ **(01434) 673154**
(01434) 673350
slaley.hall@devere-hotels.com
www.devere.co.uk

Stocksfield (1913)
New Ridley, Stocksfield NE43 7RE
☎ **(01661) 843041**
(01661) 843046
info@sgcgolf.co.uk
B Garrow (Acting Sec)
www.sgcgolf.co.uk

Warkworth (1891)
The Links, Warkworth, Morpeth, Northumberland NE65 0SW
☎ **(01665) 711596**
David Arkley
www.warkworthgolfclub@btconnect.com

Wooler (1975)
Dod Law, Doddington, Wooler NE71 6AL
☎ **(01668) 282135**
S Lowrey (01668) 281631
www.woolergolf.co.uk

Nottinghamshire

Beeston Fields (1923)
Beeston, Nottingham NG9 3DD
☎ **(0115) 925 7062**
(0115) 925 4280
info@beestonfields.co.uk
J Lewis
www.beestonfields.co.uk

Brierley Forest (1993)
Main Street, Huthwaite, Sutton-in-Ashfield NG17 2LG
☎ **(01623) 550761**
(01623) 550761
D Crafts (01623) 514234

Bulwell Forest (1902)
Hucknall Road, Bulwell, Nottingham NG6 9LQ
☎ **(0115) 976 3172 (secretary)**
secretary@bulwellforestgolfclub.co.uk
R D Savage
www.bulwellforestgolfclub.co.uk

Chilwell Manor (1906)
Meadow Lane, Chilwell, Nottingham NG9 5AE
☎ **(0115) 925 8958**
(0115) 922 0575
info@chilwellmanorgolfclub.co.uk
C Lawrence
www.chilwellmanorgolfclub.co.uk

College Pines (1994)
Proprietary
Worksop College Drive, Sparken Hill, Worksop S80 3AL
☎ **(01909) 501431**
snelljunior@btinternet.com
C Snell (Golf Dir)
www.collegepinesgolfclub.co.uk

Coxmoor (1913)
Coxmoor Road, Sutton-in-Ashfield NG17 5LF
☎ **(01623) 557359**
(01623) 557435
secretary@coxmoorgolfclub.co.uk
Mrs J Chambers
www.coxmoorgolfclub.co.uk

Edwalton (1982)
Pay and play
Wellin Lane, Edwalton, Nottingham NG12 4AS
☎ **(0115) 923 4775**
(0115) 923 1647
edwalton@glendale-services.co.uk
Ms D J Kerrison
www.glendale-golf.com

Kilton Forest (1978)
Public
Blyth Road, Worksop S81 0TL
☎ **(01909) 486563**

Leen Valley Golf Club (1994)
Pay and play
Wigwam Lane, Hucknall NG15 7TA
☎ **(0115) 964 2037**
(0115) 964 2724
leenvalley@live.co.uk
Robert Kerr
www.leenvalleygolfclub.co.uk

Mapperley (1907)
Central Avenue, Plains Road, Mapperley, Nottingham NG3 6RH
☎ **(0115) 955 6672**
(0115) 955 6670
secretary@mapperleygolfclub.org
Michael Mulhern
www.mapperleygolfclub.org

Newark (1901)
Coddington, Newark NG24 2QX
☎ **(01636) 626282**
(01636) 626497
manager@newarkgolfclub.co.uk
DA Collingwood (01636) 626282
www.newarkgolfclub.co.uk

Norwood Park Golf Centre (1999)
Propreitary
Norwood Park, Southwell NG25 0PF
☎ **(01636) 816626**
golf@norwoodpark.co.uk
Paul Thornton
www.norwoodgolf.co.uk

Nottingham City (1910)
Public
Norwich Gardens, Bulwell, Nottingham NG6 8LF
☎ **(0115) 927 2767 (Pro Shop)**
garyandkate1@talktalk.net
GJ Chappell (07740) 288694
www.nottinghamcitygolfclub.co.uk

Notts (1887)
Hollinwell, Kirkby-in-Ashfield NG17 7QR
☎ **(01623) 753225**
(01623) 753655
office@nottsgolfclub.co.uk
S E Lawrence
www.nottsgolfclub.co.uk

Oakmere Park (1974)
Oaks Lane, Oxton NG25 0RH
☎ **(0115) 965 3545**
(0115) 965 5628
enquiries@oakmerepark.co.uk
D St-John Jones
www.oakmerepark.co.uk

Radcliffe-on-Trent (1909)
Dewberry Lane, Cropwell Road, Radcliffe-on-Trent NG12 2JH
☎ **(0115) 933 3000**
(0115) 911 6991
bill.dunn@radcliffeontrentgc.co.uk
B Dunn
www.radcliffeontrentgc.co.uk

Ramsdale Park Golf Centre (1992)
Pay and play
Oxton Road, Calverton NG14 6NU
☎ **(0115) 965 5600**
(0115) 965 4105
info@ramsdaleparkgc.co.uk
N Birch (Mgr)
www.ramsdaleparkgc.co.uk

Retford (1920)
Brecks Road, Ordsall, Retford DN22 7UA
☎ **(01777) 703733/711188**
(01777) 710412
retfordgolfclub@lineone.net
Lesley Redfearn & Diane Moore
www.retfordgolfclub.co.uk

Ruddington Grange (1988)
Wilford Road, Ruddington, Nottingham NG11 6NB
☎ **(0115) 984 6141**
(0115) 940 5165
info@ruddingtongrange.co.uk
P Deacon
www.ruddingtongrange.co.uk

For key to symbols see page 725

Rufford Park G&CC (1990)
Proprietary
Rufford Lane, Rufford, Newark NG22 9DG
☎ **(01623) 825253**
(01623) 825254
enquiries@ruffordpark.co.uk
Club Manager (01623) 825253
www.ruffordpark.co.uk

Rushcliffe (1909)
Stocking Lane, East Leake, Loughborough LE12 5RL
☎ **(01509) 852959**
(01509) 852688
secretary@rushcliffegolfclub.com
www.rushcliffegolfclub.com

Serlby Park (1906)
Serlby, Doncaster DN10 6BA
☎ **(01777) 818268**
serlbysec@talktalkbusiness.net
KJ Crook (01302) 742280

Sherwood Forest (1895)
Eakring Road, Mansfield NG18 3EW
☎ **(01623) 626689/627403**
(01623) 420412
info@sherwoodforestgolfclub.co.uk
Maj Gary J Mason BEM (01623) 626689
www.sherwoodforestgolfclub.co.uk

Southwell (1993)
Proprietary
Southwell Racecourse, Rolleston, Newark NG25 0TS
☎ **(01636) 813706**
(01636) 812271
golf@southwell-racecourse.co.uk
P Salter (Sec) (01636) 819197
www.southwellgolfclub.com

Springwater (1991)
Proprietary
Moor Lane, Calverton, Nottingham NG14 6FZ
☎ **(0115) 965 4946**
(0115) 965 2344
dave.pullan@springwatergolfclub.com
E Brady (0115) 952 3956
www.springwatergolfclub.com

Stanton-on-the-Wolds (1906)
Golf Course Road, Stanton-on-the-Wolds, Nottingham NG12 5BH
☎ **(0115) 937 4885**
(0115) 937 1652
info@stantongc.co.uk
MJ Price (0115) 937 1650
www.stantongolfclub.co.uk

The Nottinghamshire G&CC (1991)
Stragglethorpe, Nr Cotgrave Village, Cotgrave NG12 3HB
☎ **(0115) 933 3344**
(0115) 933 4567
general@thenottinghamshire.com
Nick Lenty
www.thenottinghamshire.com

Trent Lock Golf Centre (1991)
Proprietary
Lock Lane, Sawley, Long Eaton NG10 2FY
☎ **(0115) 946 4398**
(0115) 946 1183
enquiries@trentlockgolf.com
R Prior (F & B Mgr)
www.trentlock.co.uk

Wollaton Park (1927)
Wollaton Park, Nottingham NG8 1BT
☎ **(0115) 978 7574**
secretary@wollatonparkgolfclub.com
Avril J Jamieson
www.wollatonparkgolfclub.com

Worksop (1914)
Windmill Lane, Worksop S80 2SQ
☎ **(01909) 477731**
(01909) 530917
thesecretary@worksopgolfclub.com
Mr A D Mansbridge (01909) 477731
www.worksopgolfclub.com

Oxfordshire

Aspect Park (1988)
Remenham Hill, Henley-on-Thames RG9 3EH
☎ **(01491) 578306**
(01491) 578306

Badgemore Park (1972)
Proprietary
Henley-on-Thames RG9 4NR
☎ **(01491) 637300**
(01491) 576899
info@badgemorepark.com
A Smith (Club Sec) (01491) 637300
www.badgemorepark.com

Banbury Golf Club (1993)
Pay and play
Aynho Road, Adderbury, Banbury OX17 3NT
☎ **(01295) 810419**
(01295) 810056
Mr M Reed
www.banburygolfclub.co.uk

Bicester Hotel Golf and Spa (1973)
Chesterton, Bicester OX26 1TE
☎ **(01869) 241204**
jamie.herbert@bicesterhotelgolfandspa.com
M Odom (01869) 241204
www.bicestergolf.co.uk

Burford (1936)
Burford OX18 4JG
☎ **(01993) 822583**
(01993) 822801
secretary@burfordgolfclub.co.uk
RP Thompson
www.burfordgolfclub.co.uk

Carswell CC (1993)
Carswell, Faringdon SN7 8PU
☎ **(01367) 870422**
(01367) 870592
info@carswellgolfandcountryclub.co.uk
G Lisi (Prop)
www.carswellgolfandcountryclub.co.uk

Cherwell Edge (1980)
Chacombe, Banbury OX17 2EN
☎ **(01295) 711591**
(01295) 713674
enquiries@cherwelledgegolfclub.co.uk
www.cherwelledgegolfclub.co.uk

Chipping Norton (1890)
Southcombe, Chipping Norton OX7 5QH
☎ **(01608) 642383**
(01608) 645422
golfadmin@chippingnortongolfclub.com
Lindsey Dray (Operations Mgr)
www.chippingnortongolfclub.com

Drayton Park (1992)
Pay and play
Steventon Road, Drayton, Abingdon OX14 4lA
☎ **(01235) 550607/528989**
(01235) 525731
draytonpark@btclick.com
Rob Bolton (01235) 528989
www.draytonparkgolfclubabingdon.co.uk

Feldon Valley (1992)
Proprietary
Sutton Lane, Lower Brailes, Banbury OX15 5BB
☎ **(01608) 685633**
info@feldonvalley.co.uk
Neil Simpson (Dir) (01608) 685633
www.feldonvalley.co.uk

Frilford Heath (1908)
Frilford Heath, Abingdon OX13 5NW
☎ **(01865) 390864**
(01865) 390823
generalmanager@frilfordheath.co.uk
A B W James
www.frilfordheath.co.uk

Hadden Hill (1990)
Proprietary
Wallingford Road, Didcot OX11 9BJ
☎ **(01235) 510410**
(01235) 511260
info@haddenhillgolf.co.uk
M V Morley
www.haddenhillgolf.co.uk

Henley (1907)
Harpsden, Henley-on-Thames RG9 4HG
☎ **(01491) 575742**
(01491) 412179

For key to symbols see page 725

info@henleygc.com
Gary Oatham (01491) 635305
www.henleygc.com

Hinksey Heights Golf Club (1995)
Public
South Hinksey, Oxford OX1 5AB
(01865) 327775
sec@oxford-golf.co.uk
Jane Binning
www.oxford-golf.co.uk

Huntercombe (1901)
Nuffield, Henley-on-Thames RG9 5SL
(01491) 641207
(01491) 642060
office@huntercombegolfclub.co.uk
GNV Jenkins
www.huntercombegolfclub.co.uk

Kirtlington (1995)
Proprietary
Kirtlington, Oxon OX5 3JY
(01869) 351133
(01869) 331143
info@kirtlingtongolfclub.com
Miss P Smith (Sec/Mgr)
www.kirtlingtongolfclub.com

North Oxford (1907)
Banbury Road, Oxford OX2 8EZ
(01865) 554415
(01865) 554924
R J Harris (Mgr) (01865) 554924 opt 2
www.nogc.co.uk

Oxford Golf Club (1875)
Hill Top Road, Oxford OX4 1PF
(01865) 242158
(01865) 250023
sgcltd@btopenworld.com
C G Whittle (01865) 242158
www.oxfordgolfclub.net

The Oxfordshire (1993)
Proprietary
Rycote Lane, Milton Common, Thame OX9 2PU
(01844) 278300
(01844) 278003
info@theoxfordshire.com
Mr C Hanks
www.theoxfordshiregolfclub.com

RAF Benson (1975)
Royal Air Force, Benson, Wallingford OX10 6AA
(01491) 837766 Ext 7322
A Molloy (01491) 827017

Rye Hill (1992)
Proprietary
Milcombe, Banbury OX15 4RU
(01295) 721818
(01295) 720089
info@ryehill.co.uk
Tony Pennock
www.ryehill.co.uk

The Springs Hotel & Golf Club (1998)
Proprietary
Wallingford Road, North Stoke, Wallingford OX10 6BE
(01491) 827310
(01491) 827312
proshop@thespringshotel.com
M Ackerman (01491) 827315
www.thespringshotel.com

Studley Wood (1996)
Proprietary
The Straight Mile, Horton-cum-Studley, Oxford OX33 1BF
(01865) 351144
(01865) 351166
admin@swgc.co.uk
www.studleywoodgolfclub.co.uk

Tadmarton Heath (1922)
Wigginton, Banbury OX15 5HL
(01608) 737278
(01608) 730548
secretary@tadmartongolf.com
JR Cox (01608) 737278
www.tadmartongolf.com

Waterstock (1994)
Proprietary
Thame Road, Waterstock, Oxford OX33 1HT
(01844) 338093
(01844) 338036
wgc_oxford@btinternet.com
AJ Wyatt
www.waterstockgolf.co.uk

Witney Lakes (1994)
Downs Road, Witney OX29 0SY
(01993) 893011
(01993) 778866
golf@witney-lakes.co.uk
www.witney-lakes.co.uk

The Wychwood (1992)
Proprietary
Lyneham, Chipping Norton OX7 6QQ
(01993) 831841
(01993) 831775
info@thewychwood.com
Mrs S J Lakin (administrator)
www.thewychwood.com

Rutland

Greetham Valley (1992)
Proprietary
Greetham, Oakham LE15 7SN
(01780) 460444
(01780) 460623
info@greethamvalley.co.uk
RE Hinch
www.greethamvalley.co.uk

Luffenham Heath (1911)
Ketton, Stamford PE9 3UU
(01780) 720205
(01780) 722146
jringleby@theluffenhamheathgc.co.uk
J R Ingleby
www.luffenhamheath.co.uk

RAF Cottesmore (1982)
Oakham, Leicester LE15 7BL
(01572) 812241 Ext 8112
(01572) 812241 ext 7834
ctsdepth-aesffs@cottesmore.raf.mod.uk

Rutland County Golf Club (1991)
Proprietary
Pickworth, Stamford PE9 4AQ
(01780) 460239/460330
(01780) 460437
info@rutlandcountygolf.co.uk
G Lowe (Golf Dir)
www.rutlandcountygolf.co.uk

Shropshire

Aqualate (1995)
Pay and play
Stafford Road, Newport TF10 9DB
(01952) 811699
(01952) 825343
HB Dawes (Mgr) (01952) 811699
www.aqualategolf..co.uk

Arscott (1992)
Proprietary
Arscott, Pontesbury, Shrewsbury SY5 0XP
(01743) 860114
(01743) 860114
golf@arscott.dydirect.net
Sian Hinkins
www.arscottgolfclub.co.uk

Bridgnorth (1889)
Stanley Lane, Bridgnorth WV16 4SF
(01746) 763315
(01746) 763315
secretary@bridgnorthgolfclub.co.uk
A M Jones
www.bridgnorthgolfclub.co.uk

Brow
Proprietary
Welsh Frankton, Ellesmere SY12 9HW
(01691) 622628
browgolf@btinternet.com
www.thebrowgolfclub.com

Chesterton Valley (1993)
Proprietary
Chesterton, Worfield, Bridgnorth WV15 5NX
(01746) 783682
cvgc@hotmail.co.uk
P Hinton
www.a1golf.biz

Church Stretton (1898)
Trevor Hill, Church Stretton SY6 6JH
(01694) 722281
secretary@churchstrettongolfclub.co.uk
J Townsend (Mgr) (07973) 762510
www.churchstrettongolfclub.co.uk

Cleobury Mortimer (1993)
Proprietary
Wyre Common, Cleobury Mortimer DY14 8HQ
☎ **(01299) 271112 (Clubhouse)**
(01299) 271468
pro@cleoburygolfclub.com
G Pain (Gen Mgr)
www.cleoburygolfclub.com

Hawkstone Park Golf Club (1920)
Proprietary
Weston-under-Redcastle, Shrewsbury SY4 5UY
☎ **(01939) 200365**
(01939) 200365
secretary@hpgcgolf.com
T Harrop
www.hpgcgolf.com

Hill Valley G&CC (1975)
Proprietary
Terrick Road, Whitchurch SY13 4JZ
☎ **(01948) 667788**
(01948) 665927
general.hillvalley@mcdonald-hotels.co.uk
www.hillvalleygolfclub.co.uk

Horsehay Village Golf Centre (1999)
Pay and play
Wellington Road, Horsehay, Telford TF4 3BT
☎ **(01952) 632070**
(01952) 632074
horsehayvillagegolfcentre@telford.gov.uk
M Maddison (Mgr)
www.telford.gov.uk/golf

Lilleshall Hall (1937)
Abbey Road, Lilleshall, Newport TF10 9AS
☎ **(01952) 604776**
(01952) 604272
honsec@lhgc.entdsl.com
A Marklew (01952) 604776
www.lilleshallhallgolfclub.co.uk

Llanymynech (1933)
Pant, Oswestry SY10 8LB
☎ **(01691) 830983**
(01691) 183 9184
secretary@llanymynechgolfclub.co.uk
Howard Jones
www.llanymynechgolfclub.co.uk

Ludlow (1889)
Bromfield, Ludlow SY8 2BT
☎ **(01584) 856285**
(01584) 856366
secretary@ludlowgolfclub.com
R Price (01584) 856285
www.ludlowgolfclub.com

Market Drayton (1906)
Sutton, Market Drayton TF9 2HX
☎ **(01630) 652266**
market.draytongc@btconnect.com
CK Stubbs
www.marketdraytongolfclub.co.uk

Mile End (1992)
Proprietary
Mile End, Oswestry SY11 4JF
☎ **(01691) 671246**
(01691) 670580
info@mileendgolfclub.co.uk
R Thompson
www.mileendgolfclub.co.uk

Oswestry (1903)
Aston Park, Queens Head, Oswestry SY11 4JJ
☎ **(01691) 610535**
(01691) 610535
secretary@oswestrygolfclub.co.uk
John Evans (01691) 610535
www.oswestrygolfclub.co.uk

Patshull Park Hotel G&CC (1980)
Pattingham WV6 7HR
☎ **(01902) 700100**
(01902) 700874
John Poole
www.patshull-park.co.uk

Severn Meadows (1990)
Proprietary
Highley, Bridgnorth WV16 6HZ
☎ **(01746) 862212**
noel@severnmeadows.com
Noel Woodman
www.severnmeadows.com

Shifnal (1929)
Decker Hill, Shifnal TF11 8QL
☎ **(01952) 460330**
(01952) 460330
secretary@shifnalgolf.com
Mr J Stewart/Miss L Law
www.shifnalgolf.com

Shrewsbury (1891)
Condover, Shrewsbury SY5 7BL
☎ **(01743) 872977**
(01743) 872977
info@shrewsburygolfclub.co.uk
Anthony Rowe (01743) 872977
www.shrewsburygolfclub.co.uk

The Shropshire (1992)
Muxton, Telford TF2 8PQ
☎ **(01952) 677800**
(01952) 677622
info@theshropshire.co.uk
Stuart Perry (Gen Mgr)
www.theshropshire.co.uk

Telford (1976)
Proprietary
Great Hay Drive, Sutton Heights, Telford TF7 4DT
☎ **(01952) 429977**
(01952) 586602
ibarklem@aol.com
www.telford-golfclub.co.uk

Worfield (1991)
Proprietary
Worfield, Bridgnorth WV15 5HE
☎ **(01746) 716541**
(01746) 716302
enquiries@worfieldgolf.co.uk
W Weaver (Gen Mgr)
www.worfieldgolf.co.uk

Wrekin (1905)
Wellington, Telford TF6 5BX
☎ **(01952) 244032**
(01952) 252906
secretary@wrekingolfclub.co.uk
B P Everitt
www.wrekingolfclub.co.uk

Somerset

Bath (1880)
Sham Castle, North Road, Bath BA2 6JG
☎ **(01225) 463834**
(01225) 331027
enquiries@bathgolfclub.org.uk
www.bathgolfclub.org.uk

Brean (1973)
Coast Road, Brean, Burnham-on-Sea TA8 2QY
☎ **(01278) 752111**
(01278) 752111
proshop@brean.com
D Haines (Director of Golf)
www.breangolfclub.co.uk

Burnham & Berrow (1890)
St Christopher's Way, Burnham-on-Sea TA8 2PE
☎ **(01278) 785760**
(01278) 795440
secretary.bbgc@btconnect.com
MA Blight (01278) 785760
www.burnhamandberrowgolfclub.co.uk

Cannington (1993)
Pay and play
Cannington Centre for Land Based Studies, Bridgwater TA5 2LS
☎ **(01278) 655050**
(01278) 655055
macrowr@bridgwater.ac.uk
R Macrow (Mgr)
www.canningtongolfcentre.co.uk

Clevedon (1891)
Castle Road, Clevedon BS21 7AA
☎ **(01275) 874057**
(01275) 341228
secretary@clevedongolfclub.co.uk
J Cunning (01275) 874057
www.clevedongolfclub.co.uk

Enmore Park (1906)
Enmore, Bridgwater TA5 2AN
☎ **(01278) 672100**
(01278) 672101
manager@enmorepark.co.uk
S.Varcoe (01278) 672100
www.enmorepark.co.uk

For key to symbols see page 725

Entry Hill (1985)
Public
Entry Hill, Bath BA2 5NA
☎ **(01225) 834248**
✉ entryhillgolfcourse.co.uk
✍ J Sercombe

Farrington (1992)
Proprietary
Marsh Lane, Farrington Gurney, Bristol BS39 6TS
☎ **(01761) 451596**
Fax (01761) 451021
✉ info@farringtongolfclub.net
✍ J Cowgill
Web www.farringtongolfclub.net

Fosseway CC (1970)
Charlton Lane, Midsomer Norton, Radstock BA3 4BD
☎ **(01761) 412214**
Fax (01761) 418357
✉ club@centurionhotel.co.uk
✍ Ray D'Arcy
Web www.centurionhotel.co.uk

Frome (1994)
Proprietary
Critchill Manor, Frome BA11 4LJ
☎ **(01373) 453410**
✉ secretary@fromegolfclub.co.uk
✍ Mrs S Austin/Mrs J Vowell
Web www.fromegolfclub.co.uk

Isle of Wedmore (1992)
Proprietary
Lineage, Lascots Hill, Wedmore BS28 4QT
☎ **(01934) 712452**
✉ office@wedmoregolfclub.com
✍ AC Edwards (01934) 712222
Web www.wedmoregolfclub.com

Kingweston (1983)
(Sec) 12 Lowerside Road, Glastonbury, Somerset BA6 9BH
☎ **(01458) 834086**

Lansdown (1894)
Lansdown, Bath BA1 9BT
☎ **(01225) 422138**
Fax (01225) 339252
✉ admin@lansdowngolfclub.co.uk
✍ Mrs E Bacon
Web www.lansdowngolfclub.co.uk

Long Sutton (1991)
Pay and play
Long Load, Langport TA10 9JU
☎ **(01458) 241017**
Fax (01458) 241022
✉ info@longsuttongolf.com
✍ Graham Holloway
Web www.longsuttongolf.com

The Mendip (1908)
Gurney Slade, Radstock BA3 4UT
☎ **(01749) 840570**
✉ secretary@mendipgolfclub.com
✍ J Scott (Managing Secretary)
Web www.mendipgolfclub.com

Mendip Spring (1992)
Proprietary
Honeyhall Lane, Congresbury BS49 5JT
☎ **(01934) 852322**
Fax (01934) 853021
✉ info@mendipspringgolfclub.com
✍ A Melhuish
Web www.mendipspringgolfclub.com

Minehead & West Somerset (1882)
The Warren, Minehead TA24 5SJ
☎ **(01643) 702057**
Fax (01643) 705095
✉ secretary@mineheadgolf.co.uk
Web www.minehead-golf-club.co.uk

Oake Manor (1993)
Oake, Taunton TA4 1BA
☎ **(01823) 461993**
Fax (01823) 461996
✉ golf@oakemanor.com
✍ R Gardner (Golf Mgr)
Web www.oakemanor.com

Orchardleigh Golf Club (1996)
Proprietary
Frome BA11 2PH
☎ **(01373) 454200**
Fax (01373) 454202
✉ info@orchardleighgolf.co.uk
✍ Peter Holloway (Director of Golf)
Web www.orchardleighgolf.co.uk

Saltford (1904)
Golf Club Lane, Saltford, Bristol BS31 3AA
☎ **(01225) 873513**
Fax (01225) 873525
✉ secretary@saltfordgolfclub.co.uk
✍ M Penn (01225) 873513
Web www.saltfordgolfclub.co.uk

Stockwood Vale (1991)
Public
Stockwood Lane, Keynsham, Bristol BS31 2ER
☎ **(0117) 986 6505**
Fax (0117) 986 8974
✉ stockwoodvale@aol.com
✍ M Edenborough
Web www.stockwoodvale.com

Tall Pines (1990)
Proprietary
Cooks Bridle Path, Downside, Backwell, Bristol BS48 3DJ
☎ **(01275) 472076**
Fax (01275) 474869
✍ T Murray
Web www.tallpinesgolf.co.uk

Taunton & Pickeridge (1892)
Corfe, Taunton TA3 7BY
☎ **(01823) 421537**
Fax (01823) 421742
✉ mail@tauntongolf.co.uk
✍ S Stevenson (Golf Professional)
Web www.tauntongolf.co.uk

Taunton Vale (1991)
Proprietary
Creech Heathfield, Taunton TA3 5EY
☎ **(01823) 412220**
Fax (01823) 413583
✉ admin@tauntonvalegolf.co.uk
✍ Reuben Evans
Web www.tauntonvalegolf.co.uk

Tickenham (1994)
Proprietary
Clevedon Road, Tickenham, Bristol BS21 6RY
☎ **(01275) 856626**
✉ info@tickenhamgolf.co.uk
Web www.tickenhamgolf.co.uk

Vivary (1928)
Public
Vivary Park, Taunton TA1 3JW
☎ **(01823) 289274 (Clubhouse)**
Fax 01823 353757
✉ vivarygolfclub@btconnect.com
✍ Bob Stout

Wells (1893)
East Horrington Road, Wells BA5 3DS
☎ **(01749) 675005**
Fax (01749) 683170
✉ secretary@wellsgolfclub.co.uk
✍ Eira Powell (01749) 675005
Web www.wellsgolfclub.co.uk

Weston-super-Mare (1892)
Uphill Road North, Weston-super-Mare BS23 4NQ
☎ **(01934) 626968**
Fax (01934) 621360
✉ wsmgolfclub@eurotelbroadband.com
✍ Mrs K Drake (01934) 626968
Web www.westonsupermaregolfclub.com

Wheathill (1993)
Proprietary
Wheathill, Somerton TA11 7HG
☎ **(01963) 240667**
Fax (01963) 240230
✉ wheathill@wheathill.fsnet.co.uk
✍ A England
Web www.wheathillgc.co.uk

Wincanton Golf Course (1994)
Proprietary
The Racecourse, Wincanton BA9 8BJ
☎ **(01963) 435850**
Fax (01963) 34668
✉ wincanton@thejockeyclub.co.uk
✍ Andrew England
Web wincantonracecourse.co.uk

Windwhistle (1932)
Cricket St Thomas, Chard TA20 4DG
☎ **(01460) 30231**
Fax (01460) 30055
✉ info@windwhistlegolfclub.co.uk
✍ Miss Sarah Wills
Web www.windwhistlegolfclub.co.uk

For key to symbols see page 725

Worlebury (1908)
Monks Hill, Worlebury, Weston-super-Mare BS22 9SX
☎ **(01934) 625789**
(01934) 621935
secretary@worleburygc.co.uk
A S Horsburgh
www.worleburygc.co.uk

Yeovil (1907)
Sherborne Road, Yeovil BA21 5BW
☎ **(01935) 422965**
(01935) 411283
office@yeovilgolfclub.com
S Greatorex (01935) 422965
www.yeovilgolfclub.com

Staffordshire

Alsager G&CC (1992)
Audley Road, Alsager, Stoke-on-Trent ST7 2UR
☎ **(01270) 875700**
(01270) 882207
business@alsagergolfclub.com
M Davenport
www.alsagergolfclub.com

Aston Wood (1994)
Blake Street, Sutton Coldfield B74 4EU
☎ **(0121) 580 7803**
(0121) 353 0354
events@astonwoodgolfclub.co.uk
Simon Smith
www.astonwoodgolfclub.co.uk

Barlaston (1987)
Meaford Road, Stone ST15 8UX
☎ **(01782) 372867 (Admin) 372795 (Pro-Shop)**
(01782) 373648
barlaston.gc@virgin.net
C P Holloway (01782 372867)
www.barlastongolfclub.co.uk

Beau Desert (1911)
Hazel Slade, Cannock WS12 0PJ
☎ **(01543) 422626/422773**
(01543) 451137
enquiries@bdgc.co.uk
Stephen Mainwaring (01543) 422626
www.bdgc.co.uk

Bloxwich (1924)
136 Stafford Road, Bloxwich WS3 3PQ
☎ **(01922) 476593**
(01922) 493449
secretary@bloxwichgolfclub.com
RJ Wormstone
www.bloxwichgolfclub.com

Branston G&CC (1975)
Burton Road, Branston, Burton-on-Trent DE14 3DP
☎ **(01283) 528320**
(01283) 566984
golflodge@branstonclub.co.uk
Richard Odell (Director of Golf)
www.branstonclub.co.uk

Brocton Hall (1894)
Brocton, Stafford ST17 0TH
☎ **(01785) 661901**
(01785) 661591
secretary@broctonhall.com
www.broctonhall.com

Burslem (1907)
Wood Farm, High Lane, Stoke-on-Trent ST6 7JT
☎ **(01782) 837006**
alanbgc@talktalkbusiness.net
A Porter

Calderfields (1983)
Proprietary
Aldridge Road, Walsall WS4 2JS
☎ **(01922) 646888 (Clubhouse)**
(01922) 640540
calderfields@bigfoot.com
www.calderfieldsgolf.com

Cannock Park (1993)
Public
Stafford Road, Cannock WS11 2AL
☎ **(01543) 578850**
(01543) 578850
seccpgc@yahoo.co.uk
www.cpgc.freeserve.co.uk

The Chase (1991)
Proprietary
Pottal Pool Road, Penkridge ST19 5RN
☎ **(01785) 712888**
(01785) 712692
manager@thechasegolf.co.uk
Bryan Davies
www.thechasegolf.co.uk

The Craythorne (1974)
Craythorne Road, Rolleston on Dove, Burton upon Trent DE13 0AZ
☎ **(01283) 564329**
(01283) 511908
admin@craythorne.co.uk
AA Wright (Man Dir/Owner)
www.craythorne.co.uk

Dartmouth (1910)
Vale Street, West Bromwich B71 4DW
☎ **(0121) 588 2131**
(0121) 588 5746
CF Wade (0121) 532 4070
www.dartmouthgolfclub.co.uk

Denstone College (1991)
Denstone, Uttoxeter ST14 5HN
☎ **(01889) 590484**
(01889) 590744
andy.oakes@uwclub.net
Andy Oakes
www.denstonecollege.org

Drayton Park (1897)
Drayton Park, Tamworth B78 3TN
☎ **(01827) 251139**
(01827) 284035
admin@draytonparkgc.com
Jon Northover
www.draytonparkgc.com

Druids Heath (1974)
Stonnall Road, Aldridge WS9 8JZ
☎ **(01922) 455595**
admin@druidsheathgc.co.uk
KI Taylor
www.druidsheathgc.co.uk

Enville (1935)
Highgate Common, Enville, Stourbridge DY7 5BN
☎ **(01384) 872074**
manager@envillegolfclub.co.uk
H L Mulley (Mgr)
www.envillegolfclub.com

Great Barr (1961)
Chapel Lane, Birmingham B43 7BA
☎ **(0121) 358 4376**
(0121) 358 4376
info@greatbarrgolfclub.co.uk
Miss L Pollard (0121) 358 4376
www.greatbarrgolfclub.co.uk

Greenway Hall (1909)
Proprietary
Stockton Brook, Stoke-on-Trent ST9 9LJ
☎ **(01782) 503158**
contact@greenwayhallgolfclub.co.uk
Simon Arnold (Golf Pro)
www.greenwayhallgolfclub.co.uk

Handsworth (1895)
11 Sunningdale Close, Handsworth Wood, Birmingham B20 1NP
☎ **(0121) 554 3387**
(0121) 554 6144
info@handsworthgolfclub.net
PS Hodnett (Hon)
www.handsworthgolfclub.com

Himley Hall (1980)
Pay and play
Himley Hall Park, Dudley DY3 4DF
☎ **(01902) 895207**
(01902) 895207
himleygolf@hotmail.co.uk
B Sparrow (01902) 894973
www.himleyhallgolfclub.com

Ingestre Park (1977)
Ingestre, Stafford ST18 0RE
☎ **(01889) 270845**
(01889) 271434
manager@ingestregolf.co.uk
D Warrilow (Mgr)
www.ingestregolf.com

Izaak Walton (1993)
Cold Norton, Stone ST15 0NS
☎ **(01785) 760900**
(01785) 760900 (opt 4)
secretary@izaakwaltongolfclub.co.uk
Charlie Lightbown
www.izaakwaltongolfclub.co.uk

Keele Golf Centre (1973)
Pay and play
Keele Road, Newcastle-under-Lyme ST5 5AB
☎ **(01782) 627596**

📠 (01782) 714555
✍ L Harris (01782) 751173

Lakeside (1969)

Rugeley Power Station, Rugeley WS15 1PR
☎ **(01889) 575667**
✉ lakeside.golfclub@unicombox.co.uk
✍ TA Yates
🌐 www.lakesidegolf.co.uk

Leek (1892)

Birchall, Leek ST13 5RE
☎ **(01538) 384779**
📠 (01538) 384779
✉ enquiries@leekgolfclub.co.uk
✍ DT Brookhouse
🌐 www.leekgolfclub.co.uk

Lichfield Golf and Country Club (1991)

Proprietary
Elmhurst, Lichfield WS13 8HE
☎ **(01543) 417333**
📠 (01543) 418098
✉ r.gee@theclubcompany.com
✍ Richard Gee
🌐 www.theclubcompany.com

Little Aston (1908)

Roman Road, Streetly, Sutton Coldfield B74 3AN
☎ **(0121) 353 2942**
📠 (0121) 580 8387
✉ manager@littleastongolf.co.uk
✍ Glyn Ridley (Mgr) (0121) 353 2942
🌐 www.littleastongolf.co.uk

Manor (Kingstone) (1991)

Proprietary
Leese Hill, Kingstone, Uttoxeter ST14 8QT
☎ **(01889) 563234**
📠 (01889) 563234
✉ manorgc@btinternet.com
✍ S Foulds
🌐 www.manorgolfclub.net

Newcastle-under-Lyme (1908)

Whitmore Road, Newcastle-under-Lyme ST5 2QB
☎ **(01782) 617006**
📠 (01782) 617531
✉ info@newcastlegolfclub.co.uk
✍ Joe Hyde (Manager)
🌐 www.newcastlegolfclub.co.uk

Onneley (1968)

Onneley, Crewe, Cheshire CW3 9QF
☎ **(01782) 750577**
✉ admin@onneleygolfclub.co.uk
✍ Iain Corville (Mgr) (01782) 721459
🌐 www.onneleygolf.co.uk

Oxley Park (1913)

Stafford Road, Bushbury, Wolverhampton WV10 6DE
☎ **(01902) 773989**
📠 (01902) 773981
✉ office@oxleyparkgolfclub.co.uk
🌐 www.oxleyparkgolfclub.co.uk

Parkhall (1989)

Public
Hulme Road, Weston Coyney, Stoke-on-Trent ST3 5BH
☎ **(01782) 599584**
📠 (01782) 599584
✍ M Robson

Penn (1908)

Penn Common, Wolverhampton WV4 5JN
☎ **(01902) 341142**
📠 (01902) 620504
✉ secretary@penngolfclub.co.uk
✍ D J Tonks
🌐 www.penngolfclub.co.uk

Perton Park (1990)

Proprietary
Wrottesley Park Road, Perton, Wolverhampton WV6 7HL
☎ **(01902) 380073**
📠 (01902) 326219
✉ admin@pertongolfclub.co.uk
✍ Mark Allen (Gen Mgr)
🌐 www.pertongolfclub.co.uk

Sandwell Park (1895)

Birmingham Road, West Bromwich B71 4JJ
☎ **(0121) 553 4637**
📠 (0121) 525 1651
✉ secretary@sandwellparkgolfclub.co.uk
🌐 www.sandwellparkgolfclub.co.uk

Sedgley (1992)

Pay and play
Sandyfields Road, Sedgley, Dudley DY3 3DL
☎ **(01902) 880503**
✉ admin@sedgleygolfcentre.co.uk
✍ David Cox

South Staffordshire (1892)

Danescourt Road, Tettenhall, Wolverhampton WV6 9BQ
☎ **(01902) 751065**
📠 (01902) 751159
✉ suelebeau@southstaffsgc.co.uk
✍ P Baker (Professional)
🌐 www.southstaffsgc.co.uk

St Thomas's Priory (1995)

Armitage Lane, Armitage, Rugeley WS15 1ED
☎ **(01543) 492096**
📠 (01543) 492096
✉ rohanlonpro@acl.com
🌐 www.st-thomass-golfclub.com

Stafford Castle (1906)

Proprietary
Newport Road, Stafford ST16 1BP
☎ **(01785) 223821**
📠 (01785) 223821
✉ sharonscgc@btconnect.com
✍ Mrs S Calvert
🌐 www.staffordcastlegolf.com

Stone (1896)

The Fillybrooks, Stone ST15 0NB
☎ **(01785) 813103**
✍ D M Cole (01785) 817746
🌐 www.stonegolfclub.co.uk

Swindon (1976)

Proprietary
Bridgnorth Road, Swindon, Dudley DY3 4PU
☎ **(01902) 897031**
📠 (01902) 326219
✉ admin@swindongolfclub.co.uk
✍ Mark Allen (Mgr)
🌐 www.swindongolfclub.co.uk

Tamworth (1976)

Public
Eagle Drive, Amington, Tamworth B77 4EG
☎ **(01827) 709303**
📠 (01827) 709304
✍ Elaine Pugh

Three Hammers Golf Complex (1964)

Pay and play
Old Stafford Road, Cross Green, Wolverhampton WV10 7PP
☎ **(01902) 790428**
📠 (01902) 791777
✉ Info@3hammers.co.uk
✍ Mr Julian Chessom
🌐 www.3hammers.co.uk

Trentham (1894)

14 Barlaston Old Road, Trentham, Stoke-on-Trent ST4 8HB
☎ **(01782) 658109**
📠 (01782) 644024
✉ secretary@trenthamgolf.org
✍ Richard Minton (Gen Mgr)
🌐 www.trenthamgolf.org

Trentham Park (1936)

Trentham Park, Stoke-on-Trent ST4 8AE
☎ **(01782) 642245**
📠 (01782) 658800
✉ manager@trenthamparkgolfclub.com
✍ Gordon Martin (01782) 658800
🌐 www.trenthamparkgolfclub.com

Uttoxeter (1970)

Wood Lane, Uttoxeter ST14 8JR
☎ **(01889) 566552**
📠 (01889) 566552
✉ admin@uttoxetergolfclub.com
✍ Mr A McCanaless
🌐 www.uttoxetergolfclub.com

Walsall (1907)

Broadway, Walsall WS1 3EY
☎ **(01922) 613512**
📠 (01922) 616460
✉ secretary@walsallgolfclub.co.uk
✍ P Thompson (01922) 613512
🌐 www.walsallgolfclub.co.uk

Wergs (1990)

Pay and play
Keepers Lane, Tettenhall WV6 8UA
☎ **(01902) 742225**
📠 (01902) 844553
✉ wergs.golfclub@btinternet.com
✍ Tina Bennett (Mgr)
🌐 www.wergs.com

Westwood (1923)
Newcastle Road, Wallbridge, Leek ST13 7AA
(01538) 398385
(01538) 382485
westwoodgolfclubleek@btconnect.com
Mr A J Horton (Hon Sec)
www.westwoodgolfclubleek.co.uk

Whiston Hall (1971)
Whiston, Cheadle ST10 2HZ
(01538) 266260
(01538) 266820
info@whistonhall.co.uk
LC & RM Cliff (Mgr)
www.whistonhall.com

Whittington Heath (1886)
Tamworth Road, Lichfield WS14 9PW
(01543) 432317 (Admin) 432212 (Steward)
(01543) 433962
info@whittingtonheathgc.co.uk
Mrs JA Burton
www.whittingtonheathgc.co.uk

Wolstanton (1904)
Dimsdale Old Hall, Hassam Parade, Wolstanton, Newcastle ST5 9DR
(01782) 622413
(01782) 622413
Mrs VJ Keenan (01782) 622413
www.wolstantongolfclub.com

Suffolk

Aldeburgh (1884)
Saxmunden Road, Aldeburgh IP15 5PE
(01728) 452890
(01728) 452937
info@aldeburghgolfclub.co.uk
Bill Beckett (Sec)
www.aldeburghgolfclub.co.uk

Beccles (1899)
The Common, Beccles NR34 9BX
(01502) 712244
alan@ereira.wanadoo.co.uk
A Ereira (07896) 087297
www.becclesgolfclub.co.uk

Brett Vale (1992)
Proprietary
Noakes Road, Raydon, Ipswich IP7 5LR
(01473) 310718
info@brettvalegolf.co.uk
L Williams
www.brettvale.co.uk

Bungay & Waveney Valley (1889)
Outney Common, Bungay NR35 1DS
(01986) 892337
(01986) 892222
golf@bungaygc.co.uk
A Collison (Director of golf)
www.club-noticeboard.co.uk/bungay

Bury St Edmunds (1924)
Tut Hill, Fornham All Saints, Bury St Edmunds IP28 6LG
(01284) 755979
(01284) 763288
secretary@burygolf.co.uk
M Verhelst
www.burystedmundsgolfclub.co.uk

Cretingham (1984)
Grove Farm, Cretingham, Woodbridge IP13 7BA
(01728) 685275
(01728) 685488
cretinghamgolf@tiscali.co.uk
Mrs K Jackson
www.cretinghamgolfclub.co.uk

Diss (1903)
Stuston Common, Diss IP21 4AA
(01379) 641025
(01379) 644586
sec.dissgolf@virgin.net
Graham Weeks
www.club-noticeboard.co.uk

Felixstowe Ferry (1880)
Ferry Road, Felixstowe IP11 9RY
(01394) 286834
(01394) 273679
secretary@felixstowegolf.co.uk
R Baines (01394) 286834
www.felixstowegolf.co.uk

Flempton (1895)
Flempton, Bury St Edmunds IP28 6EQ
(01284) 728291
secretary@flemptongolfclub.co.uk
MS Clark
www.flemptongolfclub.co.uk

Fynn Valley (1991)
Proprietary
Witnesham, Ipswich IP6 9JA
(01473) 785267
(01473) 785632
enquiries@fynn-valley.co.uk
AR Tyrrell (01473) 785267
www.fynn-valley.co.uk

Halesworth (1990)
Proprietary
Bramfield Road, Halesworth IP19 9XA
(01986) 875567
(01986) 874565
info@halesworthgc.co.uk
Chris Aldred (Mgr)
www.halesworthgc.co.uk

Haverhill (1974)
Coupals Road, Haverhill CB9 7UW
(01440) 761951
(01440) 761951
HAVERHILLGOLF@coupalsroad.eclipse.co.uk
Mrs L Farrant, Mrs K Wilby (Mgr)
www.club-noticeboard.co.uk

Hintlesham (1991)
Proprietary
Hintlesham, Ipswich IP8 3JG
(01473) 652761
(01473) 652750
sales@hintleshamgolfclub.com
Henry Roblin (Owner/Director)
www.hintleshamgolfclub.com

Ipswich Golf Club (Purdis Heath) (1895)
Purdis Heath, Bucklesham Road, Ipswich IP3 8UQ
(01473) 728941
(01473) 715236
neill@ipswichgolfclub.com
NM Ellice (01473) 728941
www.ipswichgolfclub.com

Links (Newmarket) (1902)
Cambridge Road, Newmarket CB8 0TG
(01638) 663000
(01638) 661476
secretary@linksgolfclub.co.uk
ML Hartley
www.linksgolfclub.co.uk

Newton Green (1907)
Newton Green, Sudbury CO10 0QN
(01787) 377217
(01787) 377549
info@newtongreengolfclub.co.uk
Mrs C List
www.newtongreengolfclub.co.uk

Rookery Park (1891)
Beccles Road, Carlton Colville, Lowestoft NR33 8HJ
(01502) 509190
(01502) 509191
office@rookeryparkgolfclub.co.uk
R Pettett
www.rookeryparkgolfclub.co.uk

Royal Worlington & Newmarket (1893)
Golf Links Road, Worlington, Bury St Edmunds IP28 8SD
(01638) 712216 (Clubhouse)
secretary@royalworlington.co.uk
S Ballentine (01638) 717787
www.royalworlington.co.uk

Rushmere (1927)
Rushmere Heath, Ipswich IP4 5QQ
(01473) 725648
(01473) 273852
rushmeregolfclub@btconnect.com
RWG Tawell (01473) 725648
www.club-noticeboard.co.uk/rushmere

Seckford (1991)
Seckford Hall Road, Great Bealings, Woodbridge IP13 6NT
(01394) 388000
(01394) 382818
secretary@seckfordgolf.co.uk
G Cook
www.seckfordgolf.co.uk

Southwold (1884)
The Common, Southwold IP18 6TB
(01502) 723234
mail@southwoldgolfclub.co.uk

For key to symbols see page 725

✍ R Wilshaw (01502) 723248
🌐 www.southwoldgolfclub.co.uk

Stoke-by-Nayland (1972)
Keepers Lane, Leavenheath, Colchester CO6 4PZ
☎ **(01206) 262836**
📠 (01206) 265840
✉ golfsecretary@stokebynayland.com
✍ A Bullock (01206) 265815
🌐 www.stokebynayland.com

Stowmarket (1902)
Lower Road, Onehouse, Stowmarket IP14 3DA
☎ **(01449) 736473**
📠 (01449) 736826
✉ mail@stowmarketgolfclub.co.uk
✍ Alan Feltham (01449) 736473
🌐 www.club-noticeboard.co.uk/stowmarket

The Suffolk Golf & Spa Hotel (1974)
Proprietary
Fornham St Genevieve, Bury St Edmunds IP28 6JQ
☎ **(01284) 706777**
📠 (01284) 706721
✉ proshop.suffolkgolf@ohiml.com
✍ Stephen Hall (Director of Golf)
🌐 www.oxfordhotelsandinns.com

Thorpeness Hotel & Golf Course (1923)
Proprietary
Thorpeness, Leiston IP16 4NH
☎ **(01728) 454926**
📠 (01728) 453868
✉ christopher@thorpeness.co.uk
✍ Christopher Oldrey (01728) 452176
🌐 www.thorpeness.co.uk

Ufford Park Hotel Golf & Spa (1992)
Pay and play
Yarmouth Road, Melton, Woodbridge, Suffolk IP12 1QW
☎ **(01394) 382836**
📠 (01394) 383582
✉ enquiries@uffordpark.co.uk
✍ Michael Halliday
🌐 www.uffordpark.co.uk

Waldringfield (1983)
Newbourne Road, Waldringfield, Woodbridge IP12 4PT
☎ **(01473) 736768**
✉ enquiries@waldringfieldgc.co.uk
✍ Pat Whitham
🌐 www.waldringfieldgc.co.uk

Woodbridge (1893)
Bromeswell Heath, Woodbridge IP12 2PF
☎ **(01394) 382038**
📠 (01394) 382392
✉ info@woodbridgegolfclub.co.uk
✍ AJ Bull
🌐 www.woodbridgegolfclub.co.uk

Surrey

Abbey Moor (1991)
Pay and play
Green Lane, Addlestone KT15 2XU
☎ **(01932) 570741/570765**
📠 (01932) 561313
✍ Richard Payne (01932) 570741

The Addington (1913)
Proprietary
205 Shirley Church Road, Croydon CR0 5AB
☎ **(020) 8777 1055**
📠 (020) 8777 6661
✉ info@addingtongolf.com
✍ Oliver Peel
🌐 www.addingtongolf.com

Addington Court (1932)
Pay and play
Featherbed Lane, Addington, Croydon CR0 9AA
☎ **(020) 8657 0281 (Bookings)**
📠 (020) 8651 0282
✉ addington@crown-golf.co.uk
✍ B Chard (020) 657 0281
🌐 www.addingtoncourt-golfclub.co.uk

Addington Palace (1930)
Addington Park, Gravel Hill, Addington CR0 5BB
☎ **(020) 8654 3061**
📠 (020) 8655 3632
✉ info@addingtonpalacegolf.co.uk
✍ Roger Williams
🌐 www.addingtonpalacegolf.co.uk

Banstead Downs (1890)
Burdon Lane, Belmont, Sutton SM2 7DD
☎ **(020) 8642 2284**
📠 (020) 8642 5252
✉ secretary@bansteaddowns.com
✍ R D Bauser
🌐 www.bansteaddowns.com

Barrow Hills (1970)
Longcross, Chertsey KT16 0DS
☎ **(01344) 635770**
✍ R Hammond (01483) 234807

Betchworth Park (1911)
Reigate Road, Dorking RH4 1NZ
☎ **(01306) 882052**
✉ manager@betchworthparkgc.co.uk
✍ Timothy Lowe (Sec/Mgr)
🌐 www.betchworthparkgc.co.uk

Bletchingley (1993)
Proprietary
Church Lane, Bletchingley RH1 4LP
☎ **(01883) 744666 Functions 744848 Golf**
📠 (01883) 744284
✉ stevec1412@yahoo.co.uk
✍ Steven Cookson (Golf Operations Mgr)
🌐 www.bletchingleygolf.co.uk

Bowenhurst Golf Centre (1994)
Mill Lane, Crondall, Farnham GU10 5RP
☎ **(01252) 851695**
📠 (01252) 852225
✍ GL Corbey (01252) 851695

Bramley (1913)
Bramley, Guildford GU5 0AL
☎ **(01483) 892696**
📠 (01483) 894673
✉ secretary@bramleygolfclub.co.uk
✍ Jeremy Lucas (Club Mgr) (01483) 892696
🌐 www.bramleygolfclub.co.uk

Broadwater Park (1989)
Pay and play
Guildford Road, Farncombe, Godalming GU7 3BU
☎ **(01483) 429955**
✉ info@broadwaterparkgolf.co.uk
✍ Kevin Milton
🌐 www.broadwaterparkgolfclub.co.uk

Burhill (1907)
Burwood Road, Walton-on-Thames KT12 4BL
☎ **(01932) 227345**
📠 (01932) 267159
✉ info@burhillgolf-club.co.uk
✍ D Cook (Gen Mgr)
🌐 www.burhillgolf-club.co.uk

Camberley Heath (1912)
Golf Drive, Camberley GU15 1JG
☎ **(01276) 23258**
📠 (01276) 692505
✉ info@camberleyheathgolfclub.co.uk
✍ Chris Donovan
🌐 www.camberleyheathgolfclub.co.uk

Central London Golf Centre (1992)
Public
Burntwood Lane, Wandsworth, London SW17 0AT
☎ **(020) 8871 2468**
📠 (020) 8874 7447
✉ info@clgc.co.uk
✍ Michael Anscomb (Mgr)
🌐 www.clgc.co.uk

Chessington Golf Centre (1983)
Pay and play
Garrison Lane, Chessington KT9 2LW
☎ **(020) 8391 0948**
📠 (020) 8397 2068
✉ info@chessingtongolf.co.uk
✍ M Bedford
🌐 www.chessingtongolf.co.uk

Chiddingfold (1994)
Petworth Road, Chiddingfold GU8 4SL
☎ **(01428) 685888**
📠 (01428) 685939
✉ enquiries@chiddingfoldgolf.co.uk

Chipstead (1906)
How Lane, Chipstead, Coulsdon CR5 3LN
☎ **(01737) 555781**
(01737) 555404
office@chipsteadgolf.co.uk
Gary Torbett (Director)
www.chipsteadgolf.co.uk

Chobham (1994)
Chobham Road, Knaphill, Woking GU21 2TZ
☎ **(01276) 855584**
(01276) 855663
info@chobhamgolfclub.co.uk
Adrian Wratting
www.chobhamgolfclub.co.uk

Clandon Regis (1994)
Epsom Road, West Clandon GU4 7TT
☎ **(01483) 224888**
(01483) 211781
office@clandonregis-golfclub.co.uk
Paul Napier (Gen Mgr)
www.clandonregis-golfclub.co.uk

Coombe Hill (1911)
Golf Club Drive, Coombe Lane West, Kingston KT2 7DF
☎ **(0208) 336 7600**
(0208) 336 7601
office@chgc.net
Colin Chapman (CEO)
www.coombehillgolfclub.com

Coombe Wood (1904)
George Road, Kingston Hill, Kingston-upon-Thames KT2 7NS
☎ **(0208) 942 0388 (Clubhouse)**
(0208) 942 5665
geoff.seed@coombewoodgolf.com
G Seed (0208) 942 0388
www.coombewoodgolf.com

Coulsdon Manor (1937)
Pay and play
Coulsdon Court Road, Old Coulsdon, Croydon CR5 2LL
☎ **(020) 8660 6083**
(020) 8668 3118
sales.coulsdon@ohiml.com
www.oxfordhotelsandinns.com

The Cranleigh (1985)
Barhatch Lane, Cranleigh GU6 7NG
☎ **(01483) 268855**
(01483) 267251
clubshop@cranleighgolfandleisure.co.uk
www.cranleighgolfandleisure.co.uk

Croham Hurst (1911)
Croham Road, South Croydon CR2 7HJ
☎ **(020) 8657 5581**
(020) 8657 3229
secretary@chgc.co.uk
S Mackinson
www.chgc.co.uk

Cuddington (1929)
Banstead Road, Banstead SM7 1RD
☎ **(020) 8393 0952**
(020) 8786 7025
secretary@cuddingtongc.co.uk
John Robinson
www.cuddingtongc.co.uk

Dorking (1897)
Deepdene Avenue, Chart Park, Dorking RH5 4BX
☎ **(01306) 886917**
(01306) 886917
info@dorkinggolfclub.co.uk
www.dorkinggolfclub.co.uk

Drift (1975)
Proprietary
The Drift, East Horsley KT24 5HD
☎ **(01483) 284641**
(01483) 284642
info@driftgolfclub.com
Ben Beagley (GM)
www.driftgolfclub.com

Dulwich & Sydenham Hill (1894)
Grange Lane, College Road, London SE21 7LH
☎ **(020) 8693 3961**
(020) 8693 2481
info@dulwichgolf.co.uk
MP Hickson
www.dulwichgolf.co.uk

Effingham (1927)
Guildford Road, Effingham KT24 5PZ
☎ **(01372) 452203**
(01372) 459959
secretary@effinghamgolfclub.com
Robin Easton (Business Mgr)
www.effinghamgolfclub.com

Epsom (1889)
Longdown Lane South, Epsom Downs, Surrey KT17 4JR
☎ **(01372) 721666**
(01372) 817183
stuart@epsomgolfclub.co.uk
Stuart Walker (Pro)
www.epsomgolfclub.co.uk

Farnham (1896)
The Sands, Farnham GU10 1PX
☎ **(01252) 782109**
(01252) 781185
farnhamgolfclub@tiscali.co.uk
G Cowlishaw (01252) 782109
www.farnhamgolfclub.co.uk

Farnham Park (1966)
Pay and play
Folly Hill, Farnham GU9 0AU
☎ **(01252) 715216**
farnhamparkgolf@googlemail.com
J Van Der Merwe
⊕ 9 hole par 3 course

Foxhills (1975)
Stonehill Road, Ottershaw KT16 0EL
☎ **(01932) 872050**
(01932) 874762
golf@foxhills.co.uk
R Hyder
www.foxhills.co.uk

Gatton Manor Hotel & Golf Club (1969)
Proprietary
Standon Lane, Ockley, Dorking, Surrey RH5 5PQ
☎ **(01306) 627555**
(01306) 627713
info@gattonmanor.co.uk
Patrick Kiely (owner)
www.gattonmanor.co.uk

Goal Farm Par Three (1978)
Proprietary
Gole Road, Pirbright GU24 0PZ
☎ **(01483) 473183**
(01483) 473205
secretary@goalfarmgolfclub.co.uk
R Little
www.goalfarmgolfclub.co.uk

Guildford (1886)
High Path Road, Merrow, Guildford GU1 2HL
☎ **(01483) 563941**
secretary@guildfordgolfclub.co.uk
Adam Bodimeade (Gen Mgr)
www.guildfordgolfclub.co.uk

Hampton Court Palace (1895)
Hampton Wick, Kingston-upon-Thames KT1 4AD
☎ **(020) 8977 2423**
(020) 8614 4747
hamptoncourtpalace@crown-golf.co.uk

Hankley Common (1896)
Tilford, Farnham GU10 2DD
☎ **(01252) 792493**
(01252) 795699
lynne@hankley.co.uk
IM McColl (01252) 797711
www.hankley.co.uk

Hazelwood Golf Centre (1992)
Pay and play
Croysdale Avenue, Green Street, Sunbury-on-Thames TW16 6QU
☎ **(01932) 770932**
(01932) 770933
hazelwoodgolf@btconnect.com
Roger Ward

Hersham Golf Club (1997)
Proprietary
Assher Road, Hersham, Surrey KT12 4RA
☎ **(01932) 267666**
(01932) 240975
hvgolf@tiscali.co.uk
R Hutton (Golf Dir)
www.hershamgolfclub.co.uk

The Hindhead (1904)
Churt Road, Hindhead GU26 6HX
☎ **(01428) 604614**
(01428) 608508
secretary@the-hindhead-golf-club.co.uk
www.the-hindhead-golf-club.co.uk

Hoebridge Golf Centre (1982)
Public
Old Woking Road, Old Woking GU22 8JH
(01483) 722611
(01483) 740369
info@hoebridgegc.co.uk
M O'Connell (Senior Gen Mgr)
www.hoebridgegc.co.uk

Horne Park (1994)
Proprietary
Croydon Barn Lane, Horne, South Godstone RH9 8JP
(01342) 844443
(01342) 841828
info@hornepark.co.uk
Neil Burke
www.hornepark.co.uk

Horton Park Golf Club (1987)
Pay and play
Hook Road, Epsom KT19 8QG
(020) 8393 8400 (Enquiries)
(020) 8394 3854
info@hortonparkgolf.com
Gillian Nichols
www.hortonparkgolf.com

Hurtmore (1992)
Pay and play
Hurtmore Road, Hurtmore, Surrey GU7 2RN
(01483) 426492
(01483) 426121
hurtmore@hoburne.com
Maxine Burton (01483) 426492
www.hurtmore-golf.co.uk

Kingswood (1928)
Proprietary
Sandy Lane, Kingswood, Tadworth KT20 6NE
(01737) 832188
(01737) 833920
sales@kingswood-golf.co.uk
Mark Stewart (Secretary)
www.kingswood-golf.co.uk

Laleham (1903)
Proprietary
Laleham Reach, Chertsey KT16 8RP
(01932) 564211
info@laleham-golf.co.uk
Managing Director
www.laleham-golf.co.uk

Leatherhead (1903)
Proprietary
Kingston Road, Leatherhead KT22 0EE
(01372) 843966
(01372) 842241
sales@lgc-golf.co.uk
Timothy Lowe
www.lgc-golf.co.uk

Limpsfield Chart (1889)
Westerham Road, Limpsfield RH8 0SL
(01883) 723405/722106
secretary@limpsfieldchartgolf.co.uk
K Johnson
www.limpsfieldchartgolf.co.uk

Lingfield Park (1987)
Racecourse Road, Lingfield RH7 6PQ
(01342) 834602
(01342) 836077
cmorley@lingfieldpark.co.uk

London Scottish (1865)
Windmill Enclosure, Wimbledon Common, London SW19 5NQ
(020) 8788 0135
(020) 8789 7517
secretary.lsgc@btconnect.com
S Barr (020) 8789 1207
⊕ Red upper outer garment must be worn
www.londonscottishgolfclub.co.uk

Malden (1893)
Traps Lane, New Malden KT3 4RS
(020) 8942 0654
(020) 8336 2219
manager@maldengolfclub.com
www.maldengolfclub.com

Merrist Wood (1997)
Coombe Lane, Worplesdon, Guildford GU3 3PE
(01483) 238890
(01483) 238896
Martin Huckleby
www.merristwood-golfclub.co.uk

Milford (1993)
Proprietary
Station Lane, Milford GU8 5HS
(01483) 419200
(01483) 419199
milford-manager@crown-golf.co.uk
Rebecca Prout
www.milfordgolf.co.uk

Mitcham (1924)
Carshalton Road, Mitcham Junction CR4 4HN
(020) 8640 4197
(020) 8648 4197
mitchamgc@hotmail.co.uk
DJ Tilley (020) 8648 4197
www.mitchamgolfclub.co.uk

Moore Place (1926)
Public
Portsmouth Road, Esher KT10 9LN
(01372) 463533
(01372) 463533
www.moore-place.co.uk

New Zealand (1895)
Woodham Lane, Addlestone KT15 3QD
(01932) 345049
roger.marrett@nzgc.org
RA Marrett (01932) 342891

North Downs (1899)
Northdown Road, Woldingham, Caterham CR3 7AA
(01883) 652057
(01883) 652832
secretary@northdownsgolfclub.co.uk
K R Robinson (Sec)
www.northdownsgolfclub.co.uk

Oak Park (1984)
Proprietary
Heath Lane, Crondall, Farnham GU10 5PB
(01252) 850850
(01252) 850851
oakpark@crown-golf.co.uk
S Edwin
www.oakparkgolf.co.uk

Oaks Sports Centre (1973)
Public
Woodmansterne Road, Carshalton SM5 4AN
(020) 8643 8363
(020) 8661 7880
info@theoaksgolf.co.uk
G Edginton
www.theoaksgolf.co.uk

Pachesham Park Golf Centre (1990)
Pay and play
Oaklawn Road, Leatherhead KT22 0BP
(01372) 843453
(01372) 841796
enquiries@pacheshamgolf.co.uk
P Taylor
www.pacheshamgolf.co.uk

Pine Ridge (1992)
Pay and play
Old Bisley Road, Frimley, Camberley GU16 9NX
(01276) 675444
(01276) 678837
pineridge@crown-golf.co.uk
Elaine Jackson (Sec/Mgr)
www.pineridgegolf.co.uk

Purley Downs (1894)
106 Purley Downs Road, South Croydon CR2 0RB
(020) 8657 8347
(020) 8651 5044
info@purleydowns.co.uk
Mr S Graham
www.purleydowns.co.uk

Puttenham (1894)
Puttenham, Guildford GU3 1AL
(01483) 810498
(01483) 810988
enquiries@puttenhamgolfclub.co.uk
G Simmons
www.puttenhamgolfclub.co.uk

Pyrford (1993)
Warren Lane, Pyrford GU22 8XR
(01483) 723555
(01483) 729777
pyrford@crown-golf.co.uk
www.pyrfordgolf.co.uk

Redhill (1993)
Pay and play
Canada Avenue, Redhill RH1 5BF
(01737) 770204
info@redhillgolfcentre.co.uk

For key to symbols see page 725

✍ S Furlonger
▤ www.redhillgolfcentre.co.uk

Redhill & Reigate (1887)
Members Club
Clarence Lodge, Pendleton Road, Redhill RH1 6LB
☎ **(01737) 240777/244433**
🖷 (01737) 242117
✉ mail@rrgc.net
✍ D Simpson (01737) 240777
▤ www.rrgc.net

Reigate Heath (1895)
The Club House, Reigate Heath RH2 8QR
☎ **(01737) 242610**
✉ manager@reigateheathgolfclub.co.uk
✍ Richard Arnold (01737) 242610
▤ www.reigateheathgolfclub.co.uk

Reigate Hill
Proprietary
Gatton Bottom, Reigate RH2 0TU
☎ **(01737) 645577**
🖷 (01737) 642650
✉ proshop@reigatehillgolfclub.co.uk
✍ John Holmes
▤ www.reigatehillgolfclub.co.uk

The Richmond (1891)
Sudbrook Park, Richmond TW10 7AS
☎ **(020) 8940 4351**
🖷 (020) 8332 7914
✉ gm@richmondgolfclub.co.uk
✍ J Maguire (020) 8940 4351
▤ www.therichmondgolfclub.com

Richmond Park (1923)
Public
Roehampton Gate, Richmond Park, London SW15 5JR
☎ **(020) 8876 3205/1795**
🖷 (020) 8878 1354
✉ richmondpark@glendale-services.co.uk
▤ www.richmondparkgolf.co.uk

Roehampton Club (1901)
Roehampton Lane, London SW15 5LR
☎ **(020) 8480 4200**
🖷 (020) 8480 4265
✉ tristan.mcillroy@roehamptonclub.co.uk
✍ Tristan McIllroy
▤ www.roehamptonclub.co.uk

Rokers Golf Course (1993)
Pay and play
Holly Lane, Aldershot Road, Guildford GU3 3PB
☎ **(01483) 236677**
✉ golf@rokers.co.uk
✍ C Tegg
▤ www.rokersgolf.co.uk

Royal Automobile Club (1913)
Woodcote Park, Wilmerhatch Lane, Epsom KT18 7EW
☎ **(01372) 273091**
🖷 (01372) 276117
✉ golf@royalautomobileclub.co.uk
✍ Richard Griffiths (01372) 273091
▤ www.royalautomobileclub.co.uk

Royal Mid-Surrey (1892)
Old Deer Park, Twickenham Road, Richmond TW9 2SB
☎ **(020) 8940 1894**
🖷 (020) 8939 0150
✉ secretary@rmsgc.co.uk
✍ Peter Foord
▤ www.rmsgc.co.uk

Royal Wimbledon (1865)
29 Camp Road, Wimbledon, London SW19 4UW
☎ **(020) 8946 2125**
🖷 (020) 8944 8652
✉ secretary@rwgc.co.uk
✍ R J Brewer
▤ www.rwgc.co.uk

Rusper (1992)
Proprietary
Rusper Road, Newdigate RH5 5BX
☎ **(01293) 871871/871456**
✉ nikki@ruspergolfclub.co.uk
✍ Mr Simon Adby (Mgr)
▤ www.ruspergolfclub.co.uk

Sandown Park Golf Centre (1960)
Public
More Lane, Esher KT10 8AN
☎ **(01372) 469260**
✍ Nick Jones & Craig Morley (Directors)
▤ www.sandownparkgolf.com

Selsdon Park Hotel (1929)
Proprietary
Addington Road, Sanderstead, South Croydon CR2 8YA
☎ **(020) 768 3116**
🖷 (020) 8657 3401
✉ enquiries@principal-hayley.com
✍ Mr C Baron
▤ www.principal-hayley.com

Shirley Park (1914)
194 Addiscombe Road, Croydon CR0 7LB
☎ **(020) 8654 1143**
🖷 (020) 8654 6733
✉ secretary@shirleyparkgolfclub.co.uk
✍ Steve Murphy
▤ www.shirleyparkgolfclub.co.uk

Silvermere (1976)
Pay and play
Redhill Road, Cobham KT11 1EF
☎ **(01932) 584300**
🖷 (01932) 584301
✉ sales@silvermere-golf.co.uk
✍ Mrs P Devereux (01932) 584306
▤ www.silvermere-golf.co.uk

St George's Hill (1912)
Golf Club Road, St George's Hill, Weybridge KT13 0NL
☎ **(01932) 847758**
🖷 (01932) 821564
✉ admin@stgeorgeshillgolfclub.co.uk
✍ B J Hill
▤ www.stgeorgeshillgolfclub.co.uk

Sunningdale (1900)
Ridgemount Road, Sunningdale, Berks SL5 9RR
☎ **(01344) 621681**
🖷 (01344) 624154
✉ info@sunningdalegolfclub.co.uk
✍ S Toon
▤ www.sunningdale-golfclub.co.uk

Sunningdale Ladies (1902)
Cross Road, Sunningdale SL5 9RX
☎ **(01344) 620507**
✉ golf@sunningdaleladies.co.uk
✍ Simon Sheppard
▤ www.sunningdaleladies.co.uk

Surbiton (1895)
Woodstock Lane, Chessington KT9 1UG
☎ **(020) 8398 3101**
🖷 (020) 8339 0992
✉ enqs@surbitongolfclub.com
✍ CJ Cornish
▤ www.surbitongolfclub.com

Surrey Downs (2001)
Proprietary
Outwood Lane, Kingswood KT20 6JS
☎ **(01737) 839090**
🖷 (01737) 839080
✉ booking@surreydownsgc.co.uk
✍ P Townson
▤ www.surreydownsgc.co.uk

Surrey National (1999)
Rook Lane, Chaldon, Caterham CR3 5AA
☎ **(01883) 344555**
✉ caroline@surreynational.co.uk
✍ S Hodsdon (Gen Mgr)
▤ www.surreynational.co.uk

Sutton Green (1994)
New Lane, Sutton Green, Guildford GU4 7QF
☎ **(01483) 747898**
🖷 (01483) 750289
✉ admin@suttongreengc.co.uk
▤ www.suttongreengc.co.uk

The Swallow Farleigh Court (1997)
Proprietary
Old Farleigh Road, Farleigh CR6 9PX
☎ **(01883) 627711**
🖷 (01883) 627722
✉ swallow.farleigh@swallowhotels.com
▤ www.swallowhotels.com

Tandridge (1924)
Oxted RH8 9NQ
☎ **(01883) 712273 (Clubhouse)**
🖷 (01883) 730537
✉ secretary@tandridgegolfclub.com
✍ A J Tanner
▤ www.tandridgegolfclub.com

For key to symbols see page 725

Thames Ditton & Esher (1892)
Portsmouth Road, Esher KT10 9AL
☎ **(020) 8398 1551**

Tyrrells Wood (1924)
The Drive, Tyrrells Wood, Leatherhead KT22 8QP
☎ **(01372) 376025 (2 lines)**
Fax (01372) 360836
✉ office@tyrrellswoodgolfclub.com
Web www.tyrrellswoodgolfclub.com

Walton Heath (1903)
Deans Lane, Walton-on-the-Hill, Tadworth KT20 7TP
☎ **(01737) 812060**
Fax (01737) 814225
✉ secretary@waltonheath.com
✍ Stuart Christie (01737) 812380
Web www.waltonheath.com

Wentworth Club (1924)
Wentworth Drive, Virginia Water GU25 4LS
☎ **(01344) 842201**
Fax (01344) 842804
Web www.wentworthclub.com

West Byfleet (1906)
Sheerwater Road, West Byfleet KT14 6AA
☎ **(01932) 343433**
✉ admin@wbgc.co.uk
✍ I R Attoe (Gen Mgr) (01932) 343433
Web www.wbgc.co.uk

West Hill (1909)
Bagshot Road, Brookwood GU24 0BH
☎ **(01483) 474365**
Fax (01483) 474252
✉ secretary@westhill-golfclub.co.uk
✍ Gina Rivett
Web www.westhill-golfclub.co.uk

West Surrey (1910)
Enton Green, Godalming GU8 5AF
☎ **(01483) 421275**
Fax (01483) 415419
✉ office@wsgc.co.uk
✍ Richard Hall (Sec/Mgr)
Web www.wsgc.co.uk

Wildwood Golf & CC (1992)
Proprietary
Horsham Road, Alfold GU6 8JE
☎ **(01403) 753255**
Fax (01403) 752005
✉ info@wildwoodgolf.co.uk
Web www.wildwoodgolf.co.uk

Wimbledon Common (1908)
19 Camp Road, Wimbledon Common, London SW19 4UW
☎ **(020) 8946 0294 (Pro Shop)**
Fax (020) 8947 8697
✉ office@wcgc.co.uk
✍ Katerina Angliss (Office Mgr) (020) 8946 7571
Web www.wcgc.co.uk

Wimbledon Park (1898)
Home Park Road, London SW19 7HR
☎ **(020) 8946 1250**
Fax (020) 8944 8688
✉ secretary@wpgc.co.uk
✍ P Shanahan
Web www.wpgc.co.uk

Windlemere (1978)
Pay and play
Windlesham Road, West End, Woking GU24 9QL
☎ **(01276) 858727 or (01276) 858271**
Fax (01276) 858271
✉ mikew@windlemeregolf.co.uk
✍ C D Smith/M Walsh

Windlesham (1994)
Proprietary
Grove End, Bagshot GU19 5HY
☎ **(01276) 452220**
Fax (01276) 452290
✉ admin@windleshamgolf.com
✍ Scott Patience
Web www.windleshamgolf.com

The Wisley (1991)
Ripley, Woking GU23 6QU
☎ **(01483) 212110**
Fax (01483) 211662
✉ reception@thewisley.com
✍ Wayne Sheffield
Web www.thewisley.com

Woking (1893)
Pond Road, Hook Heath, Woking GU22 0JZ
☎ **(01483) 760053**
Fax (01483) 772441
✉ info@wokinggolfclub.co.uk
✍ G Ritchie
Web www.wokinggolfclub.co.uk

Woldingham (1996)
proprietary
Halliloo Valley Road, Woldingham CR3 7HA
☎ **(01883) 653501**
Fax (01883) 653502
✉ info@woldingham-golfclub.co.uk
✍ Michael Chubb
Web www.woldingham-golfclub.co.uk

Woodcote Park (1912)
Meadow Hill, Bridle Way, Coulsdon CR5 2QQ
☎ **(0208) 668 2788**
Fax (0208) 660 0918
✉ info@woodcotepgc.com
✍ AP Dawson
Web www.woodcotepgc.com

Worplesdon (1908)
Heath House Road, Woking GU22 0RA
☎ **(01483) 472277**
Fax (01483) 473303
✉ office@worplesdongc.co.uk
✍ CK Symington
Web www.worplesdongc.co.uk

Sussex (East)

Beauport Park Golf Course (1973)
Pay and play
Battle Road, St Leonards-on-Sea, East Sussex TN37 7BP
☎ **(01424) 854245**
Fax (01424) 854245
✉ info@beauportparkgolf.co.uk
✍ C Giddins
Web www.beauportparkgolf.co.uk

Brighton & Hove (1887)
Devils Dyke Road, Brighton BN1 8YJ
☎ **(01273) 556482**
Fax (01273) 554247
✉ phil@brightongolf.co.uk
✍ P Bonsall (Golf Dir)
Web www.brightonandhovegolfclub.co.uk

Cooden Beach (1912)
Cooden Sea Road, Bexhill-on-Sea TN39 4TR
☎ **(01424) 842040**
Fax (01424) 842040
✉ enquiries@coodenbeachgc.com
✍ KP Wiley (01424) 842040
Web www.coodenbeachgc.com

Crowborough Beacon (1895)
Beacon Road, Crowborough TN6 1UJ
☎ **(01892) 661511**
✉ secretary@cbgc.co.uk
✍ John Holmes (Mgr)
Web www.crowboroughbeacongolfclub.co.uk

Dale Hill Hotel & GC (1973)
Ticehurst, Wadhurst TN5 7DQ
☎ **(01580) 200112**
Fax (01580) 201249
✉ golf@dalehill.co.uk
✍ John Tolliday (Dir of Golf)
Web www.dalehill.co.uk

Dewlands Manor (1992)
Cottage Hill, Rotherfield TN6 3JN
☎ **(01892) 852266**
Fax (01892) 853015
✍ T Robins
⊕ 15 minute Tee Times relaxed golf.

Dyke Golf Club (1906)
Devil's Dyke, Devil's Dyke Road, Brighton BN1 8YJ
☎ **(01273) 857296**
Fax (01273) 857078
✉ manager@dykegolfclub.co.uk
✍ Megan Bibby (Gen Mgr)
Web www.dykegolf.com

East Brighton (1893)
Roedean Road, Brighton BN2 5RA
☎ **(01273) 604838**
Fax (01273) 680277
✉ office@ebgc.co.uk
✍ G McKay
Web www.ebgc.co.uk

For key to symbols see page 725

East Sussex National Golf Resort and Spa (1989)
Proprietary
Little Horsted, Uckfield TN22 5ES
☎ **(01825) 880088**
(01825) 880066
reception@eastsussexnational.co.uk
DT Howe
www.eastsussexnational.co.uk

Eastbourne Downs (1908)
East Dean Road, Eastbourne BN20 8ES
☎ **(01323) 720827**
secretary@ebdownsgolf.co.uk
Denise McDowell & Lorna Hardy
www.ebdownsgolf.co.uk

Eastbourne Golfing Park Ltd (1992)
Pay and play
Lottbridge Drove, Eastbourne BN23 6QJ
☎ **(01323) 520400**
(01323) 520400
egpltd@hotmail.co.uk
Maggie Garbutt
www.eastbournegolfingpark.co.uk

Highwoods (1925)
Ellerslie Lane, Bexhill-on-Sea TN39 4LJ
☎ **(01424) 212625**
(01424) 216866
highwoods@btconnect.com
AP Moran
www.highwoodsgolfclub.co.uk

Hollingbury Park (1908)
Public
Ditchling Road, Brighton BN1 7HS
☎ **(01273) 552010**
(01273) 552010
www.hollingburygolfclub.co.uk

Holtye (1893)
Holtye, Cowden, Nr Edenbridge TN8 7ED
☎ **(01342) 850635**
(01342) 851139
secretary@holtye.com
Mrs I O Martin (01342) 850635
www.holtye.com

Horam Park (1985)
Pay and play
Chiddingly Road, Horam TN21 0JJ
☎ **(01435) 813477**
(01435) 813677
angie@horampark.com
Mrs A Briggs
www.horamparkgolfclub.co.uk

Lewes (1896)
Chapel Hill, Lewes BN7 2BB
☎ **(01273) 473245**
(01273) 483474
secretary@lewesgolfclub.co.uk
Mr L C Dorn (01273) 483474
www.lewesgolfclub.co.uk

Mid Sussex (1995)
Proprietary
Spatham Lane, Ditchling BN6 8XJ
☎ **(01273) 846567**
(01273) 847815
admin@midsussexgolfclub.co.uk
www.midsussexgolfclub.co.uk

Nevill (1914)
Benhall Mill Road, Tunbridge Wells TN2 5JW
☎ **(01892) 525818**
(01892) 517861
manager@nevillgolfclub.co.uk
FW Prescott
www.nevillgolfclub.co.uk

Peacehaven (1895)
Proprietary
Brighton Road, Newhaven BN9 9UH
☎ **(01273) 514049**
henry@golfatpeacehaven.co.uk
Henry Hilton (01273) 514049
www.golfatpeacehaven.co.uk

Piltdown (1904)
Piltdown, Uckfield TN22 3XB
☎ **(01825) 722033**
(01825) 724192
secretary@piltdowngolfclub.co.uk
Mike Miller
www.piltdowngolfclub.co.uk

Royal Ashdown Forest (1888)
Chapel Lane, Forest Row, East Sussex RH18 5LR
☎ **(01342) 822018 (Old)**
(01342) 825211
david@royalashdown.co.uk
D S Holmes
www.royalashdown.co.uk

Royal Eastbourne (1887)
Paradise Drive, Eastbourne BN20 8BP
☎ **(01323) 744045**
sec@regc.co.uk
David Lockyer (01323) 744045
www.regc.co.uk

Rye (1894)
New Lydd Road, Camber, Rye TN31 7QS
☎ **(01797) 225241**
(01797) 225460
links@ryegolfclub.co.uk
J H Laidler (Sec)
www.ryegolfclub.co.uk

Seaford (1887)
111 Firle Road, Seaford BN25 2JD
☎ **(01323) 892442**
(01323) 894113
secretary@seafordgolfclub.co.uk
LM Dennis-Smither (Gen Sec)
www.seafordgolfclub.co.uk

Seaford Head (1887)
Public
Southdown Road, Seaford BN25 4JS
☎ **(01323) 890139**
(01323) 890139
seafordheadgolfclub.co.uk
RW Andrews (01323) 894843
www.seaheadgc@tiscali.co.uk

Sedlescombe (1990)
Kent Street, Sedlescombe TN33 0SD
☎ **(01424) 871700**
(01424) 871712
golf@golfschool.co.uk

Wellshurst G&CC (1992)
Proprietary
North Street, Hellingly BN27 4EE
☎ **(01435) 813636**
(01435) 812444
info@wellshurst.com
M Adams (Man Dir)
www.wellshurst.com

West Hove (1910)
Badgers Way, Hangleton, Hove BN3 8EX
☎ **(01273) 413411 (Clubhouse)**
(01273) 439988
info@westhovegolfclub.co.uk
Gary Salt (Mgr) (01273) 419738
www.westhovegolfclub.info

Willingdon (1898)
Southdown Road, Eastbourne BN20 9AA
☎ **(01323) 410981**
(01323) 411510
secretary@willingdongolfclub.co.uk
Mrs J Packham (01323) 410981
www.willingdongolfclub.co.uk

Sussex (West)

Avisford Park (1990)
Pay and play
Yapton Lane, Walberton, Arundel BN18 0LS
☎ **(01243) 554611**
(01243) 554958
avisfordparkgolf@aol.com
Sarah Chitty
www.avisfordparkgolfclub.com

Bognor Regis (1892)
Downview Road, Felpham, Bognor Regis PO22 8JD
☎ **(01243) 821929**
(01243) 860719
sec@bognorgolfclub.co.uk
www.bognorgolfclub.co.uk

Burgess Hill Golf Centre (1995)
Pay and play
Cuckfield Road, Burgess Hill
☎ **(01444) 258585 (shop)**
(01444) 247318
enquiries@burgesshillgolfcentre.co.uk
CJ Collins (Mgr)
www.burgesshillgolfcentre.co.uk

Chartham Park (1993)
Proprietary
Felcourt, East Grinstead RH19 2JT
☎ **(01342) 870340**
(01342) 870719

For key to symbols see page 725

✉ d.hobbs@theclubcompany.com
✍ David Hobbs (PGA Pro)
🖥 www.theclubcompany.com

Chichester (1990)
Proprietary
Hunston Village, Chichester PO20 1AX
☎ **(01243) 533833**
📠 (01243) 538989
✉ info@chichestergolf.com
✍ Helen Howard (01243) 536666
🖥 www.chichestergolf.com

Copthorne (1892)
Borers Arms Road, Copthorne RH10 3LL
☎ **(01342) 712508**
📠 (01342) 717682
✉ info@copthornegolfclub.co.uk
✍ R Moan (01342) 712033
🖥 www.copthornegolfclub.co.uk

Cottesmore (1975)
Proprietary
Buchan Hill, Pease Pottage, Crawley RH11 9AT
☎ **(01293) 528256**
📠 (01293) 522819
✉ cottesmore@crown-golf.co.uk
✍ N Miller
🖥 www.cottesmoregolf.co.uk

Cowdray Park (1904)
Proprietary
Petworth Road, Midhurst GU29 0BB
☎ **(01730) 813599**
📠 (01730) 815900
✉ enquiries@cowdraygolf.co.uk
✍ M Purves
🖥 www.cowdraygolf.co.uk

Effingham Park (1980)
Proprietary
West Park Road, Copthorne RH10 3EU
☎ **(01342) 716528**
📠 (0870) 890 0215
✉ mark.root@mill-cop.com
✍ IWB McRobbie (Hon)
🖥 www.effinghamparkgc.co.uk

Foxbridge (1993)
Foxbridge Lane, Plaistow RH14 0LB
☎ **(01403) 753303 (Bookings)**
📠 (01403) 753303

Golf At Goodwood (1892)
Kennel Hill, Goodwood, Chichester PO18 0PN
☎ **(01243) 755130**
📠 (01243) 755135
✉ golf@goodwood.com
🖥 www.goodwood.com

Ham Manor (1936)
West Drive, Angmering, Littlehampton BN16 4JE
☎ **(01903) 783288**
📠 (01903) 850886
✉ secretary@hammanor.co.uk
✍ Paul Bodle
🖥 www.hammanor.co.uk

Hassocks (1995)
Pay and play
London Road, Hassocks BN6 9NA
☎ **(01273) 846990**
📠 (01273) 846070
✉ admin@hassocksgolfclub.co.uk
✍ Mr Michael Ovett (Gen Mgr)
🖥 www.hassocksgolfclub.co.uk

Haywards Heath (1922)
High Beech Lane, Haywards Heath RH16 1SL
☎ **(01444) 414457**
📠 (01444) 458319
✉ info@haywardsheathgolfclub.co.uk
✍ Graham White
🖥 www.haywardsheathgolfclub.co.uk

Hill Barn (1935)
Public
Hill Barn Lane, Worthing BN14 9QE
☎ **(01903) 237301**
📠 (01903) 217613
✉ info@hillbarn.com
✍ R Haygarth (01903) 237301
🖥 www.hillbarngolf.com

Horsham (1993)
Pay and play
Worthing Road, Horsham RH13 0AX
☎ **(01403) 271525**
📠 (01403) 274528
✉ secretary@horshamgolfandfitness.co.uk
🖥 www.horshamgolfandfitness.co.uk

Ifield (1927)
Rusper Road, Ifield, Crawley RH11 0LN
☎ **(01293) 520222**
📠 (01293) 612973

Lindfield (1990)
Proprietary
East Mascalls Lane, Lindfield RH16 2QN
☎ **(01444) 484467**
📠 (01444) 482709
✉ info@thegolfcollege.com
✍ Paul Lyons
🖥 www.thegolfcollege.com

Littlehampton (1889)
170 Rope Walk, Littlehampton BN17 5DL
☎ **(01903) 717170**
📠 (01903) 726629
✉ lgc@talk21.com
✍ S Graham
🖥 www.littlehamptongolf.co.uk

Mannings Heath (1905)
Proprietary
Fullers, Hammerpond Road, Mannings Heath, Horsham RH13 6PG
☎ **(01403) 210228**
📠 (01403) 270974
✉ enquiries@manningsheath.com
✍ Steve Slinger (01403) 220340
🖥 www.exclusivehotels.co.uk

Pease Pottage Golf Centre (1986)
Horsham Road, Pease Pottage, Crawley RH11 9AP
☎ **(01293) 521706**
📠 (01293) 521706
✍ A Venn (01293) 521766

Petworth Downs Golf Club (1989)
Pay and play
London Road, Petworth GU28 9LX
☎ **(01798) 344097**
✉ petworthdowns@hotmail.co.uk
✍ Annabel Hall (0771) 156 7466
🖥 www.petworthgolf.com

Pyecombe (1894)
Clayton Hill, Pyecombe, Brighton BN45 7FF
☎ **(01273) 845372**
📠 (01273) 843338
✉ info@pyecombegolfclub.com
✍ Alan Davey
🖥 www.pyecombegolfclub.com

Rustington (1992)
Public
Golfers Lane, Angmering BN16 4NB
☎ **(01903) 850790**
📠 (01903) 850982
✉ info@rgcgolf.com
✍ Mr S Langmead
🖥 www.rgcgolf.com

Selsey (1908)
Golf Links Lane, Selsey PO20 9DR
☎ **(01243) 605176 (Members)**
📠 (01243) 607101
✉ secretary@selseygolfclub.co.uk
✍ BE Rogers (01243) 608935
🖥 www.selseygolfclub.co.uk

Shillinglee Park (1980)
Pay and play
Chiddingfold, Godalming GU8 4TA
☎ **(01428) 653237**
📠 (01428) 644391

Singing Hills (1992)
Proprietary
Muddleswood Road, Albourne, Brighton BN6 9EB
☎ **(01273) 835353**
📠 (01273) 835444
✉ golfsecretary@singinghills.co.uk
✍ Jane Covey
🖥 www.singinghills.co.uk

Slinfold Golf & Country Club (1993)
Proprietary
Stane Street, Slinfold, Horsham RH13 0RE
☎ **(01403) 791154 (Clubhouse)**
📠 (01403) 791465
✉ info.slinfold@ccgclubs.com
✍ S Blake (Gen Mgr)
🖥 www.ccgslinford.com

Tilgate Forest (1982)
Public
Titmus Drive, Tilgate, Crawley RH10 5EU
☎ **(01293) 530103**
📠 (01293) 523478

West Chiltington (1988)
Proprietary
Broadford Bridge Road, West Chiltington RH20 2YA
☎ **(01798) 813574**

(01798) 812631
debbie@westchiltgolf.co.uk
D Haines
www.westchiltgolf.co.uk

West Sussex (1931)
Golf Club Lane, Wiggonholt, Pulborough RH20 2EN
(01798) 872563
(01798) 872033
secretary@westsussexgolf.co.uk
A D Stubbs
www.westsussexgolf.co.uk

Worthing (1905)
Links Road, Worthing BN14 9QZ
(01903) 260801
(01903) 694664
enquiries@worthinggolf.com
John Holton
www.worthinggolf.co.uk

Tyne & Wear

Backworth (1937)
The Hall, Backworth, Shiremoor, Newcastle-upon-Tyne NE27 0AH
(0191) 268 1048
backworth.miners@virgin.net
J A Wilkinson
www.backworthgolf.co.uk

Birtley (1922)
Birtley Lane, Birtley DH3 2LR
(0191) 410 2207
(0191) 410 2207
birtleygolfclub@aol.com
K Self
www.birtleyportobellogolfclub.co.uk

Boldon (1912)
Dipe Lane, East Boldon, Tyne & Wear NE36 0PQ
(0191) 536 5360 (Clubhouse)
(0191) 537 2270
info@boldongolfclub.co.uk
Chris Brown (0191) 536 5360
www.boldongolfclub.co.uk

City of Newcastle (1891)
Three Mile Bridge, Gosforth, Newcastle-upon-Tyne NE3 2DR
(0191) 285 1775
(0191) 284 0700
info@cityofnewcastlegolfclub.co.uk
AJ Matthew (Mgr)
www.cityofnewcastlegolfclub.co.uk

Garesfield (1922)
Chopwell NE17 7AP
(01207) 561309
(01207) 561073
garesfieldgc@btconnect.com
Mr Alan Hill (Hon Sec)
www.garesfieldgolfclub.co.uk

Gosforth (1906)
Broadway East, Gosforth, Newcastle upon Tyne NE3 5ER
(0191) 285 0553
gosforth.golf@virgin.net
Grahame Garland
www.gosforthgolfclub.co.uk

Hetton-le-Hill
Pay and play
Elemore Golf Course, Elemore Lane DH5 0QT
(0191) 517 3061
(0191) 517 3054
elemortgolfclub@talktalkbusiness.net
William Allen
www.elemort.co.uk

Heworth (1912)
Gingling Gate, Heworth, Gateshead NE10 8XY
(0191) 469 9832
(0191) 469 9898
secretary@theheworthgolfclub.co.uk
G Peters
www.theheworthgolfclub.co.uk

Houghton-le-Spring (1908)
Copt Hill, Houghton-le-Spring, Tyne & Wear DH5 8LU
(0191) 584 7421 (Pro Shop)
(0191) 584 0048
houghton.golf@virgin.net
Graeme Robinson
www.houghtongolfclub.co.uk

Newcastle United (1892)
Ponteland Road, Cowgate, Newcastle-upon-Tyne NE5 3JW
(0191) 286 9998 (Clubhouse)
(0191) 286 4323
info@newcastleunitedgolfclub.co.uk
P Jobe (Sec/Treasurer)
www.newcastleunitedgolfclub.co.uk

Northumberland (1898)
High Gosforth Park, Newcastle-upon-Tyne NE3 5HT
(0191) 236 2498/2009
(0191) 236 2036
gm@thengc.co.uk
Richard Breakey
www.thengc.co.uk

Parklands (1971)
Proprietary
High Gosforth Park, Newcastle-upon-Tyne NE3 5HQ
(0191) 236 3322
parklands@newcastle-racecourse.co.uk
G Brown (Hon Sec)
www.parklandsgolf.co.uk

Ravensworth (1906)
Angel View, Long Bank, Gateshead NE9 7NE
(0191) 487 6014
secretary@ravensworthgolfclub.co.uk
Marcus Humphrey
www.ravensworthgolfclub.co.uk

Ryton (1891)
Doctor Stanners, Clara Vale, Ryton NE40 3TD
(0191) 413 3253
(0191) 413 1642
secretary@rytongolfclub.co.uk
Mr K McLeod
www.rytongolfclub.co.uk

South Shields (1893)
Cleadon Hills, South Shields NE34 8EG
(0191) 456 0475
thesecretary@south-shields-golf.freeserve.co.uk

Tynemouth (1913)
Spital Dene, Tynemouth, North Shields NE30 2ER
(0191) 257 4578
(0191) 259 5193
secretary@tynemouthgolfclub.com
TJ Scott (0191) 257 3381
www.tynemouthgolfclub.com

Tyneside (1879)
Westfield Lane, Ryton NE40 3QE
(0191) 413 2742
(0191) 413 0199
secretary@tynesidegolfclub.co.uk
Alastair Greenfiled (Club Manager)
www.tynesidegolfclub.co.uk

Wallsend (1973)
Rheydt Avenue, Bigges Main, Wallsend NE28 8SU
(0191) 262 1973

Washington (1979)
Stone Cellar Road, High Usworth, Washington NE37 1PH
(0191) 417 8346
(0191) 415 1166
graeme.amanda@btopenworld.com
www.georgewashington.co.uk

Wearside (1892)
Coxgreen, Sunderland SR4 9JT
(0191) 534 2518
(0191) 534 6186
secretary@wearsidegolf.com
P Hall
www.wearsidegolf.com

Westerhope (1941)
Whorlton Grange, Westerhope, Newcastle-upon-Tyne NE5 1PP
(0191) 286 7636
(0191) 214 6287
wgc@btconnect.com
D Souter (0191) 286 7636
www.westerhopegolfclub.com

Whickham (1911)
Hollinside Park, Fellside Road, Whickham, Newcastle-upon-Tyne NE16 5BA
(0191) 488 1576 (Clubhouse)
(0191) 488 1577
enquiries@whickhamgolfclub.co.uk
Mr M E Pearse
www.whickhamgolfclub.co.uk

For key to symbols see page 725

Whitburn (1931)
Lizard Lane, South Shields NE34 7AF
☎ **(0191) 529 2177**
✉ wgcsec@hotmail.com
✍ Mr R Button (Sec) (0191) 529 2177 option 1
🖹 www.golf-whitburn.co.uk

Whitley Bay (1890)
Claremont Road, Whitley Bay NE26 3UF
☎ **(0191) 252 0180**
🖷 (0191) 297 0030
✉ whtglfclb@aol.com
✍ F Elliott
🖹 www.whitleybaygolfclub.co.uk

Warwickshire

Ansty (1990)
Pay and play
Brinklow Road, Ansty, Coventry CV7 9JL
☎ **(024) 7662 1341/7660 2568**
🖷 (024) 7660 2568
✍ K Smith
🖹 www.anstygolfandconference.co.uk

Atherstone (1894)
The Outwoods, Coleshill Road, Atherstone CV9 2RL
☎ **(01827) 713110**
🖷 (01827) 715686

The Belfry (1977)
Pay and play
Wishaw, Sutton Coldfield B76 9PR
☎ **(01675) 470301**
🖷 (01675) 470178
✉ enquiries@thebelfry.com
✍ Gary Silcock (Dir. of Golf)
🖹 www.thebelfry.com

Boldmere (1936)
Public
Monmouth Drive, Sutton Coldfield, Birmingham BJ3 6JR
☎ **(0121) 354 3379**
🖷 (0121) 353 5576
✉ boldmeregolfclub@hotmail.com
✍ R Leeson
🖹 www.boldmeregolfclub.co.uk

Bramcote Waters (1995)
Pay and play
Bazzard Road, Bramcote, Nuneaton CV11 6QJ
☎ **(01455) 220807**
✉ bwgc@hotmail.co.uk
✍ Sara Britain (01455) 220807
🖹 www.bramcotewatersgolfclub.co.uk

City of Coventry (Brandon Wood) (1977)
Public
Brandon Lane, Coventry CV8 3GQ
☎ **(024) 7654 3141**
🖷 (024) 7654 5108
✉ brandongolf@coventrysports.uk
✍ N Orton (Mgr)
🖹 www.brandonwood.co.uk

Copsewood Grange (1924)
Allard Way, Copsewood, Coventry CV3 1JP
☎ **(024) 76448355**
✍ REC Jones (024) 7645 2973
🖹 www.copsewoodgrange.co.uk

Copt Heath (1907)
1220 Warwick Road, Knowle, Solihull B93 9LN
☎ **(01564) 731620**
🖷 (01564) 731621
✉ golf@copt-heath.co.uk
✍ J A Moon
🖹 www.coptheathgolf.co.uk

Coventry (1887)
St Martins Road, Finham, Coventry CV3 6RJ
☎ **(024) 7641 4152**
🖷 (024) 7669 0131
✉ secretary@coventrygolf.co.uk
✍ A Smith (024) 7641 4152
🖹 www.coventrygolfclub.net

Coventry Hearsall (1894)
Beechwood Avenue, Coventry CV5 6DF
☎ **(024) 7671 3470**
🖷 (024) 7669 1534
✉ secretary@hearsallgolfclub.co.uk
✍ R Meade
🖹 www.hearsallgolfclub.co.uk

Edgbaston (1896)
Church Road, Edgbaston, Birmingham B15 3TB
☎ **(0121) 454 1736**
🖷 (0121) 454 2395
✉ secretary@edgbastongc.co.uk
✍ AD Grint
🖹 www.edgbastongc.co.uk

Harborne (1893)
40 Tennal Road, Harborne, Birmingham B32 2JE
☎ **(0121) 427 3058**
🖷 (0121) 427 4039
✉ adrian@harbornegolfclub.org.uk
✍ Adrian Cooper (0121) 427 3058
🖹 www.harbornegolfclub.com

Harborne Church Farm (1926)
Public
Vicarage Road, Harborne, Birmingham B17 0SN
☎ **(0121) 427 1204**
🖷 (0121) 428 3126
🖹 www.golfbirmingham.co.uk

Hatchford Brook (1969)
Public
Coventry Road, Sheldon, Birmingham B26 3PY
☎ **(0121) 743 9821**
🖷 (0121) 743 3420
✉ idt@hbgc.freeserve.co.uk
✍ ID Thomson (0121) 742 6643
🖹 www.golfpro-direct.co.uk/hbgc

Henley G&CC (1994)
Proprietary
Birmingham Road, Henley-in-Arden B95 5QA
☎ **(01564) 793715**
🖷 (01564) 795754
✉ enquiries@henleygcc.co.uk
✍ G Waller (Director)
🖹 www.henleygcc.co.uk

Hilltop (1979)
Public
Park Lane, Handsworth, Birmingham B21 8LJ
☎ **(0121) 554 4463**
✍ K Highfield (Mgr & Professional)

Ingon Manor (1993)
Ingon Lane, Snitterfield, Stratford-on-Avon CV37 0QE
☎ **(01789) 731857**
✉ golf@ingonmanor.co.uk
✍ Richard James Hampton
🖹 www.ingonmanor.co.uk

Kenilworth (1889)
Crewe Lane, Kenilworth CV8 2EA
☎ **(01926) 854296**
🖷 (01926) 864453
✉ secretary@kenilworthgolfclub.co.uk
✍ Rob Griffiths (01926) 858517
🖹 www.kenilworthgolfclub.co.uk

Ladbrook Park (1908)
Poolhead Lane, Tanworth-in-Arden, Solihull B94 5ED
☎ **(01564) 742264**
✉ secretary@ladbrookparkgolf.co.uk
🖹 www.ladbrookparkgolf.co.uk

Lea Marston Hotel & Leisure Complex (2002)
Proprietary
Haunch Lane, Lea Marston, Warwicks B76 0BY
☎ **(01675) 470707**
🖷 (01675) 470871
✉ golf.shop@leamarstonhotel.co.uk
✍ Darren Lewis (Mgr)
🖹 www.leamarstonhotel.co.uk

Leamington & County (1907)
Golf Lane, Whitnash, Leamington Spa CV31 2QA
☎ **(01926) 425961**
✉ secretary@leamingtongolf.co.uk
✍ David M Beck
🖹 www.leamingtongolf.co.uk

Marriott Forest of Arden Hotel (1970)
Maxstoke Lane, Meriden, Coventry CV7 7HR
☎ **(01676) 526113**
🖷 (01676) 523711
✉ mhrs.cvtgs.golf@marriotthotels.com
✍ I Burns (Golf Dir)
🖹 www.marriott.com/cvtgs

Maxstoke Park (1898)
Castle Lane, Coleshill, Birmingham B46 2RD
☎ **(01675) 466743**
🖷 (01675) 466185
✉ info@maxstokeparkgolfclub.com
🖹 www.maxstokeparkgolfclub.com

For key to symbols see page 725

Menzies Welcombe Hotel, Spa & Golf Club
Warwick Road, Stratford-on-Avon CV37 0NR
☎ **(01789) 413800**
(01789) 262028
Dan Hacker (Director)
www.welcombehotelstratford.co.uk

Moor Hall (1932)
Moor Hall Drive, Four Oaks, Sutton Coldfield B75 6LN
☎ **(0121) 308 6130**
(0121) 308 9560
secretary@moorhallgolfclub.co.uk
DJ Etheridge
www.moorhallgolfclub.co.uk

Newbold Comyn (1973)
Public
Newbold Terrace East, Leamington Spa CV32 4EW
☎ **(01926) 421157**
ian@viscount5.freeserve.co.uk
I Shepherd (07799) 248729

North Warwickshire (1894)
Hampton Lane, Meriden, Coventry CV7 7LL
☎ **(01676) 522464 (Clubhouse)**
(01676) 523004
nwgcltd@btconnect.com
Bob May (Hon) (01676) 522915
www.northwarwickshiregolfclubltd.co.uk

Nuneaton (1905)
Golf Drive, Whitestone, Nuneaton CV11 6QF
☎ **(024) 7634 7810**
(024) 7632 7563
nuneatongolfclub@btconnect.com
Tracey Carpenter
www.nuneatongolfclub.co.uk

Oakridge (1993)
Proprietary
Arley Lane, Ansley Village, Nuneaton CV10 9PH
☎ **(01676) 541389**
(01676) 542709
shane-lovric@golfatoakridge.co.uk
Mrs S Lovric (Admin)
www.oakridgegolfclub.co.uk

Olton (1893)
Mirfield Road, Solihull B91 1JH
☎ **(0121) 704 1936**
(0121) 711 2010
secretary@oltongolfclub.co.uk
R Gay (0121) 704 1936
www.oltongolfclub.co.uk

Purley Chase (1980)
Pipers Lane, Ridge Lane, Nuneaton CV10 0RB
☎ **(024) 7639 3118**
(024) 7639 8015
events@purleychase.com
Linda Jackson

Pype Hayes (1932)
Public
Eachelhurst Road, Walmley, Sutton Coldfield, West Midlands B76 1EP
☎ **(0121) 351 1014**
(0121) 313 0206
C Marson

Robin Hood (1893)
St Bernards Road, Solihull B92 7DJ
☎ **(0121) 706 0061**
(0121) 700 7502
manager@robinhoodgolfclub.co.uk
M J Ward
www.robinhoodgolfclub.co.uk

Rugby (1891)
Clifton Road, Rugby CV21 3RD
☎ **(01788) 544637 (Clubhouse)**
(01788) 542306
rugbygolfclub@tiscali.co.uk
www.rugbygc.co.uk

Shirley (1955)
Stratford Road, Monkspath, Solihull B90 4EW
☎ **(0121) 744 6001 opt 5**
(0121) 746 5645
enquiries@shirleygolfclub.co.uk
Patricia Harris (Mgr)
www.shirleygolfclub.co.uk

Stonebridge (1996)
Proprietary
Somers Road, Meriden CV7 7PL
☎ **(01676) 522442**
(01676) 522447
sales@stonebridgegolf.co.uk
Darren Murphy
www.stonebridgegolf.co.uk

Stoneleigh Deer Park Golf Club (1991)
Proprietary
The Clubhouse, Coventry Road, Stoneleigh CV8 3DR
☎ **(024) 7663 9991**
(024) 7651 1533
info@stoneleighdeerparkgolfclub.com
C Reay
www.stoneleighdeerparkgolfclub.com

Stratford Oaks (1991)
Proprietary
Bearley Road, Snitterfield, Stratford-on-Avon CV37 0EZ
☎ **(01789) 731980**
(01789) 731981
admin@stratfordoaks.co.uk
ND Powell (Golf Dir)
www.stratfordoaks.co.uk

Stratford-on-Avon (1894)
Tiddington Road, Stratford-on-Avon CV37 7BA
☎ **(01789) 205749**
(01789) 414909
sec@stratfordgolf.com
C J Hughes (01789) 205749
www.stratfordgolf.co.uk

Sutton Coldfield (1889)
110 Thornhill Road, Sutton Coldfield B74 3ER
☎ **(0121) 353 9633**
(0121) 353 5503
admin@suttoncoldfieldgc.com
I H Phillips, KM Tempest
www.suttoncoldfieldgc.com

Walmley (1902)
Brooks Road, Wylde Green, Sutton Coldfield B72 1HR
☎ **(0121) 373 0029**
(0121) 377 7272
secretary@walmleygolfclub.co.uk
J C Shakespeare
www.walmleygolfclub.co.uk

Warwick (1971)
Public & Proprietary
Warwick Racecourse, Warwick CV34 6HW
☎ **(01926) 494316**
info@warwickgolfcentre.co.uk
Mrs R Dunkley
www.warwickgolfcentre.co.uk

The Warwickshire (1993)
Proprietary
Leek Wootton, Warwick CV35 7QT
☎ **(01926) 409409**
(01926) 408409

West Midlands (2003)
Marsh House Farm Lane, Barston, Solihull B92 0LB
☎ **(01675) 444890**
(01675) 444891
mark@wmgc.co.uk
Mark Harrhy (01675) 444890
www.wmgc.co.uk

Whitefields Golf Club & Draycote Hotel (1992)
Proprietary
London Road, Thurlaston, Rugby CV23 9LF
☎ **(01788) 815555**
(01788) 521695
mail@draycotehotel.co.uk
B Coleman (01788) 815555
www.draycote-hotel.co.uk

Widney Manor (1993)
Pay and play
Saintbury Drive, Widney Manor, Solihull B91 3SZ
☎ **(0121) 704 0704**
(0121) 704 7999
Tim Atkinson

Windmill Village (1990)
Proprietary
Birmingham Road, Allesley, Coventry CV5 9AL
☎ **(024) 7640 4041**
(024) 7640 4042
leisure@windmillvillagehotel.co.uk
Oliver Thomas (Mgr)
www.windmillvillagehotel.co.uk

Wishaw (1992)
Proprietary
Bulls Lane, Wishaw, Sutton Coldfield B76 9QW
☎ **(0121) 313 2110**
✉ golf@wishawgc.co.uk
✍ PH Burwell
▤ www.wishawgc.co.uk

Wiltshire

Bowood Hotel, Spa and Golf Resort (1992)
Proprietary
Derry Hill, Calne SN11 9PQ
☎ **(01249) 822228**
📠 (01249) 822218
✉ j.hansel@bowood.org
✍ Paul McLean
▤ www.bowood.org

Broome Manor (1976)
Public
Pipers Way, Swindon SN3 1RG
☎ **(01793) 532403**
✉ secretary@bmgc.co.uk
✍ C Beresford 01793 526544
▤ www.bmgc.co.uk

Chippenham (1896)
Malmesbury Road, Chippenham SN15 5LT
☎ **(01249) 652040**
📠 (01249) 446681
✉ chippenhamgolf@btconnect.com
✍ Mr W Williams (General Manager)
▤ www.chippenhamgolfclub.com

Cricklade House (1992)
Pay and play
Common Hill, Cricklade SN6 6HA
☎ **(01793) 750751**
📠 (01793) 751767
✉ reception@crickladehotel.co.uk
✍ C Withers/P Butler
▤ www.crickladehotel.co.uk

Cumberwell Park (1994)
Proprietary
Bradford-on-Avon BA15 2PQ
☎ **(01225) 863322**
📠 (01225) 868160
✉ enquiries@cumberwellpark.com
✍ Alistair James
▤ www.cumberwellpark.com

Defence Academy (1953)
Shrivenham, Swindon SN6 8LA
☎ **(01793) 785725**
✉ golfclub.hq@da.mod.uk
✍ A Willmett (Mgr)
▤ www.dagc.org.uk

Erlestoke (1992)
Proprietary
Erlestoke, Devizes SN10 5UB
☎ **(01380) 831069**
✉ info@erlestokegolfclub.co.uk
✍ R Goboroonsingh
▤ www.erlestokegolfclub.co.uk

Hamptworth G&CC (1994)
Elmtree Farmhouse, Hamptworth Road, Landford SP5 2DU
☎ **(01794) 390155**
📠 (01794) 390022
✉ info@hamptworthgolf.co.uk
✍ Janet Facer
▤ www.hamptworthgolf.co.uk

High Post (1922)
Great Durnford, Salisbury SP4 6AT
☎ **(01722) 782356**
📠 (01722) 782674
✉ manager@highpostgolfclub.co.uk
✍ P Hickling (01722) 782356
▤ www.highpostgolfclub.co.uk

Highworth (1990)
Public
Swindon Road, Highworth SN6 7SJ
☎ **(01793) 766014**
✍ Geoff Marsh

Kingsdown (1880)
Kingsdown, Corsham SN13 8BS
☎ **(01225) 743472**
📠 (01225) 743472
✉ kingsdowngc@btconnect.com
✍ N Newman
▤ www.kingsdowngc@btconnect.com

Manor House (1992)
Proprietary
Castle Combe SN14 7JW
☎ **(01249) 782982**
📠 (01249) 782992
✉ enquiries@manorhousegolf.co.uk
✍ Stephen Browning
▤ www.manorhousegolfclub.co.uk

Marlborough (1888)
The Common, Marlborough SN8 1DU
☎ **(01672) 512147**
📠 (01672) 513164
✉ gm@marlboroughgolfclub.co.uk
✍ L J Trute
▤ www.marlboroughgolfclub.co.uk

Monkton Park Par Three (1965)
Pay and play
Chippenham SN15 3PP
☎ **(01249) 653928**
▤ www.pitchandputtgolf.com

North Wilts (1890)
Bishops' Cannings, Devizes SN10 2LP
☎ **(01380) 860257**
📠 (01380) 860877
✉ secretary@northwiltsgolf.com
✍ Mrs P Stephenson
▤ www.northwiltsgolf.com

Oaksey Park (1991)
Pay and play
Oaksey, Malmesbury SN16 9SB
☎ **(01666) 577995**
📠 (01666) 577174
✉ info@oakseypark.co.uk
▤ www.oakseyparkgolf.co.uk

Ogbourne Downs (1907)
Ogbourne St George, Marlborough SN8 1TB
☎ **(01672) 841327**
✉ office@ogbournedowns.co.uk
✍ Geoff Scott (01672) 841327
▤ www.ogbournedowns.co.uk

Rushmore (1997)
Proprietary
Tollard Royal, Salisbury SP5 5QB
☎ **(01725) 516326**
📠 (01725) 516437
✉ golfmanager@rushmoreuk.com
✍ Declan Healy (Gen Mgr) (01725) 516391
▤ www.rushmoregolfclub.co.uk

Salisbury & South Wilts (1888)
Netherhampton, Salisbury SP2 8PR
☎ **(01722) 742645 ext.1**
📠 (01722) 742676
✉ mail@salisburygolf.co.uk
✍ Alex Taylor (Secretary)
▤ www.salisburygolf.co.uk

Shrivenham Park (1967)
Pay and play
Pennyhooks Lane, Shrivenham, Swindon SN6 8EX
☎ **(01793) 783853**
✉ gplatt@aol.com
✍ G Platt (01793) 783853
▤ www.shrivenhampark.com

Tidworth Garrison (1908)
Bulford Road, Tidworth SP9 7AF
☎ **(01980) 842301 (Clubhouse)**
📠 (01980) 842301
✉ secretary@tidworthgolfclub.co.uk
✍ Geoff Johnson MBE
▤ www.tidworthgolfclub.co.uk

Upavon (1912)
Douglas Avenue, Upavon SN9 6BQ
☎ **(01980) 630281**
✉ richard@richardblake.co.uk
✍ Richard Blake
▤ www.upavongolfclub.co.uk

West Wilts (1891)
Elm Hill, Warminster BA12 0AU
☎ **(01985) 213133**
✉ sec@westwiltsgolfclub.co.uk
✍ GN Morgan
▤ www.westwiltsgolfclub.co.uk

Whitley (1993)
Pay and play
Corsham Road, Whitley, Melksham SN12 8EQ
☎ **(01225) 790099**
✉ info@whitleygolfclub.com
✍ Jack Nicholas
▤ www.whitleygolfclub.com

The Wiltshire (1991)
Proprietary
Vastern, Wootton Bassett, Swindon SN4 7PB
☎ **(01793) 849999**

(01793) 849988
reception@the-wiltshire.co.uk
Jennifer Shah (Gen Mgr)
www.the-wiltshire.co.uk

Wrag Barn G&CC (1990)
Shrivenham Road, Highworth, Swindon SN6 7QQ
(01793) 861327
(01793) 861325
manager@wragbarn.com
T Lee
www.wragbarn.com

Worcestershire

Bank House Hotel G&CC (1992)
Bransford, Worcester WR6 5JD
(01886) 833545
(01886) 833545
bransfordgolfclub@brook-hotels.co.uk
Matt Nixon
www.brook-hotels.co.uk

Blackwell (1893)
Blackwell, Bromsgrove, Worcestershire B60 1PY
(0121) 445 1994
(0121) 445 4911
secretary@blackwellgolfclub.com
Finlay Clark
www.blackwellgolfclub.com

Brandhall (1906)
Public
Heron Road, Oldbury, Warley B68 8AQ
(0121) 552 2195
(0121) 552 1758
john_robinson@sandwell.gov.uk
J Robinson
www.slt@sandwell.gov.uk

Bromsgrove Golf Centre (1992)
Proprietary
Stratford Road, Bromsgrove B60 1LD
(01527) 575886
(01527) 570964
enquiries@bromsgrovegolfcentre.com
P Morris (Director) P Brothwood (Sec)
www.bromsgrovegolfcentre.com

Churchill & Blakedown (1926)
Churchill Lane, Blakedown, Kidderminster DY10 3NB
(01562) 700018
admin@churchillblakedowngolfclub.co.uk
Trevor Hare
www.churchillblakedowngolfclub.co.uk

Cocks Moor Woods (1926)
Public
Alcester Road South, King's Heath, Birmingham, West Midlands B14 6ER
(0121) 464 3584
P J Ellison
www.golfbirmingham.co.uk

Droitwich G&CC (1897)
Ford Lane, Droitwich WR9 0BQ
(01905) 774344
(01905) 796503
CS Thompson
www.droitwichgolfclub.co.uk

Dudley (1893)
Turners Hill, Rowley Regis B65 9DP
(01384) 233877
(01384) 233877
secretary@dudleygolfclub.com
W B Whitcombe
www.dudleygolfclub.com

Evesham (1894)
Craycombe Links, Fladbury, Pershore WR10 2QS
(01386) 860395
eveshamgolf@btopenworld.com
Mr Jerry Cain
www.eveshamgolfclub.co.uk

Fulford Heath (1933)
Tanners Green Lane, Wythall, Birmingham B47 6BH
(01564) 822806 (Clubhouse)
(01564) 822629
secretary@fulfordheathgolfclub.co.uk
Mrs J Morris (01564) 824758
www.fulfordheathgolfclub.co.uk

Gay Hill (1913)
Hollywood Lane, Birmingham B47 5PP
(0121) 430 8544
(0121) 436 7796
secretary@ghgc.org.uk
Mrs D L O'Reilly (0121) 430 8544
www.ghgc.org.uk

Habberley (1924)
Low Habberley, Kidderminster DY11 5RF
(01562) 745756
info@habberleygolfclub.co.uk
DS McDermott
www.habberleygolfclub.co.uk

Hagley (1980)
Proprietary
Wassell Grove, Hagley, Stourbridge DY9 9JW
(01562) 883701
(01562) 887518
enquiries@HagleyGCC.co.uk
GF Yardley (01562) 883701
www.hagleygolfandcountryclub.co.uk

Halesowen (1906)
The Leasowes, Halesowen B62 8QF
(0121) 501 3606
office@halesowengc.co.uk
Mrs N Heath
www.halesowengc.co.uk

Kidderminster (1909)
Russell Road, Kidderminster DY10 3HT
(01562) 822303
(01562) 827866
secretary@thekidderminstergolfclub.com
Malcolm Pritchard (Sec)
www.thekidderminstergolfclub.com

Kings Norton (1892)
Brockhill Lane, Weatheroak, Alvechurch, Birmingham B48 7ED
(01564) 826789
(01564) 826955
info@kingsnortongolfclub.co.uk
T Webb (Mgr)
www.kingsnortongolfclub.co.uk

Little Lakes (1975)
Lye Head, Bewdley, Worcester DY12 2UZ
(01299) 266385
(01299) 266398
info@littlelakes.co.uk
J Dean (01562) 741704
www.littlelakes.co.uk

Moseley (1892)
Springfield Road, Kings Heath, Birmingham B14 7DX
(0121) 444 4957
(0121) 441 4662
secretary@moseleygolfclub.co.uk
Mr M W Wake
www.moseleygolf.co.uk

North Worcestershire (1907)
Frankley Beeches Road, Northfield, Birmingham B31 5LP
(0121) 475 1047
(0121) 476 8681
secretary@nwgolfclub.com
C Overton

Ombersley Golf Club (1991)
Pay and play
Bishopswood Road, Ombersley, Droitwich WR9 0LE
(01905) 620747
(01905) 620047
enquiries@ombersleygolfclub.co.uk
G Glenister (Gen Mgr)
www.ombersleygolfclub.co.uk

Perdiswell Park (1978)
Pay and play
Bilford Road, Worcester WR3 8DX
(01905) 754668
(01905) 756608
perdiswell@leisureconnection.co.uk
B F Hodgetts (01905) 640456
www.harpersfitness.co.uk

Pitcheroak (1973)
Public
Plymouth Road, Redditch B97 4PB
(01527) 541054

Ravenmeadow (1995)
Hindlip Lane, Claines, Worcester WR3 8SA
(01905) 757525

For key to symbols see page 725

Fax (01905) 458876
Contact: James Leaver (Mgr) (01905) 458876
Web: info@ravenmeadowgolf.co.uk

Redditch (1913)
Lower Grinsty, Green Lane, Callow Hill, Redditch B97 5PJ
Tel: **(01527) 543079**
Fax: (01527) 547413
Email: lee@redditchgolfclub.com
Contact: W Kerr
Web: www.redditchgolfclub.com

Rose Hill (1921)
Public
Lickey Hills, Rednal, Birmingham B45 8RR
Tel: **(0121) 453 3159**
Fax: (0121) 457 8779
Email: rosehillgolfclub@hotmail.com
Contact: D C Walker
Web: www.rosehill-golfclub.co.uk

Stourbridge (1892)
Worcester Lane, Pedmore, Stourbridge DY8 2RB
Tel: **(01384) 395566**
Fax: (01384) 444660
Email: secretary@stourbridgegolfclub.co.uk
Contact: Mr M Hughes
Web: www.stourbridgegolfclub.co.uk

Tolladine (1898)
The Fairway, Tolladine Road, Worcester WR4 9BA
Tel: **(01905) 21074 (Clubhouse)**

The Vale (1991)
Proprietary
Hill Furze Road, Bishampton, Pershore WR10 2LZ
Tel: **(01386) 462781 ext 229**
Fax: (01386) 462597
Email: club.manager@thevalegolf.com
Contact: Simon Williams
Web: www.thevalegolf.co.uk

Warley Woods (1921)
Pay and play
Lightwoods Hill, Warley B67 5ED
Tel: **(0121) 429 2440**
Fax: (0121) 420 4430
Email: golfshop@warleywoods.org.uk
Web: www.warleywoods.org.uk

Wharton Park (1992)
Proprietary
Longbank, Bewdley DY12 2QW
Tel: **(01299) 405222 (restaurant)**
Fax: (01299) 405121
Email: enquiries@whartonpark.co.uk
Web: www.whartonpark.co.uk

Worcester G&CC (1898)
Boughton Park, Worcester WR2 4EZ
Tel: **(01905) 422555**
Fax: (01905) 749090
Email: worcestergcc@btconnect.com
Contact: PA Tredwell (01905) 422555
Web: www.worcestergcc.co.uk

Worcestershire (1879)
Wood Farm, Malvern Wells WR14 4PP
Tel: **(01684) 575992**
Fax: (01684) 893334
Email: secretary@worcsgolfclub.co.uk
Contact: Terry Smith (Sec)
Web: www.worcsgolfclub.co.uk

Wyre Forest Golf Centre
Pay and play
Zortech Avenue, Kidderminster DY11 7EX
Tel: **(01299) 822682**
Fax: (01299) 879433
Email: wyreforestgc@hotmail.co.uk
Contact: C Botterill

Yorkshire (East)

Allerthorpe Park (1994)
Proprietary
Allerthorpe, York YO42 4RL
Tel: **(01759) 306686**
Fax: (01759) 305106
Email: enquiries@allerthorpeparkgolfclub.com
Contact: Alex Drinkall/Jan Drinkall
Web: www.allerthorpeparkgolfclub.com

Beverley & East Riding (1889)
The Westwood, Beverley HU17 8RG
Tel: **(01482) 868757**
Fax: (01482) 868757
Email: golf@beverleygolfclub.karoo.co.uk
Contact: A Ashby (01482) 869519
Web: www.beverleygolfclub.co.uk

Boothferry (1982)
Proprietary
Spaldington Lane, Spaldington, Nr Howden DN14 7NG
Tel: **(01430) 430364**
Email: info@boothferrygolfclub.co.uk
Contact: Ben McAllister
Web: www.boothferrygolfclub.co.uk

Bridlington (1905)
Belvedere Road, Bridlington YO15 3NA
Tel: **(01262) 672092/606367**
Email: enquiries@bridlingtongolfclub.co.uk
Web: www.bridlingtongolfclub.co.uk

The Bridlington Links (1993)
Pay and play
Flamborough Road, Marton, Bridlington YO15 1DW
Tel: **(01262) 401584**
Fax: (01262) 401702
Email: bridlingtonlinks@hotmail.co.uk
Contact: Wayne Stephens (Sec)
Web: www.bridlington-links.co.uk

Brough (1893)
Cave Road, Brough HU15 1HB
Tel: **(01482) 667291**
Fax: (01482) 669873
Email: gt@brough-golfclub.co.uk
Contact: G W Townhill (Professional)
Web: www.brough-golfclub.co.uk

Cave Castle (1989)
South Cave, Nr Brough HU15 2EU
Tel: **(01430) 421286**
Fax: (01430) 421118
Email: admin@cavecastlegolf.co.uk
Contact: J Simpson (Admin)
Web: www.cavecastlegolf.co.uk

Cherry Burton (1993)
Proprietary
Leconfield Road, Cherry Burton, Beverley HU17 7RB
Tel: **(01964) 550924**
Email: jonnygraygolf@europe.com
Contact: John Gray 01964 550924
Web: cherryburtongolf.co.uk

Cottingham (1994)
Proprietary
Woodhill Way, Cottingham, Hull HU16 5SW
Tel: **(01482) 846030**
Fax: (01482) 845932
Email: info@cottinghamparks.co.uk
Contact: RJ Wiles (01482) 846030
Web: www.cottinghamparks.co.uk

Driffield (1923)
Sunderlandwick, Driffield YO25 9AD
Tel: **(01377) 253116**
Fax: (01377) 240599
Email: info@driffieldgolfclub.co.uk
Contact: Maxine Moorhouse (Assist. Sec)
Web: www.driffieldgolfclub.co.uk

Flamborough Head (1931)
Lighthouse Road, Flamborough, Bridlington YO15 1AR
Tel: **(01262) 850333**
Email: enquiries@flamboroughheadgolfclub.co.uk
Contact: GS Thornton (Sec)
Web: www.flamboroughheadgolfclub.co.uk

Ganstead Park (1976)
Proprietary
Longdales Lane, Coniston, Hull HU11 4LB
Tel: **(01482) 811280 (Steward)**
Fax: (01482) 817754
Email: secretary@gansteadpark.co.uk
Contact: M Milner (01482) 817754
Web: www.gansteadpark.co.uk

Hainsworth Park (1983)
Brandesburton, Driffield YO25 8RT
Tel: **(01964) 542362**
Fax: (01964) 544666
Email: sec@hainsworthparkgolfclub.co.uk
Contact: A Higgins, BW Atkin (Prop)
Web: www.hainsworthparkgolfclub.co.uk

Hessle (1898)
Westfield Road, Raywell, Cottingham HU16 5ZA
Tel: **(01482) 306840**
Fax: (01482) 652679
Email: secretary@hesslegolfclub.co.uk
Contact: Paul Haddon
Web: www.hesslegolfclub.co.uk

For key to symbols see page 725

Hornsea (1898)
Rolston Road, Hornsea HU18 1XG
(01964) 532020
(01964) 532080
info@hornseagolfclub.co.uk
www.hornseagolfclub.co.uk

Hull (1904)
The Hall, 27 Packman Lane, Kirk Ella, Hull HU10 7TJ
(01482) 660970
(01482) 660978
secretary@hullgolfclub1921.karoo.co.uk
DJ Crossley
www.hullgolfclub.com

KP Club (1995)
Proprietary
Pocklington, York, East Yorkshire YO42 1UF
(01759) 303090
info@kpclub.co.uk
Aaron Pheasant
www.kpclub.co.uk

Springhead Park (1930)
Public
Willerby Road, Hull HU5 5JE
(01482) 656309

Sutton Park (1935)
Public
Salthouse Road, Hull HU8 9HF
(01482) 374242
(01482) 701428
S J Collins

Withernsea (1909)
Egroms Lane, Withernsea HU19 2NA
(01964) 612258 (Clubhouse)
(01964) 612078
info@withernseagolfclub.co.uk
S Dale (Admin)
www.withernseagolfclub.co.uk

Yorkshire (North)

Aldwark Manor (1978)
Aldwark, Alne, York YO61 1UF
(01347) 838353
(01347) 833991
www.Qhotels.co.uk

Ampleforth College (1972)
Castle Drive, Gilling East, York YO62 4HP
(01439) 788274
sec@ampleforthgolf.co.uk
Ian Henley
www.ampleforthgolf.co.uk

Bedale (1894)
Leyburn Road, Bedale DL8 1EZ
(01677) 422451
(01677) 427143
office@bedalegolfclub.com
Mike Mayman (01677) 422451
www.bedalegolfclub.com

Bentham (1922)
Proprietary
Robin Lane, Bentham, Lancaster LA2 7AG
(015242) 62455
golf@benthamgolfclub.co.uk
C Cousins (Pro)
www.benthamgolfclub.co.uk

Catterick (1930)
Leyburn Road, Catterick Garrison DL9 3QE
(01748) 833268
secretary@catterickgolfclub.co.uk
M Young
www.catterickgolfclub.co.uk

Cleveland (1887)
Majuba Road, Redcar TS10 5BJ
(01642) 471798
(01642) 487619
majuba@btconnect.com
www.clevelandgolfclub.co.uk

Crimple Valley (1976)
Pay and play
Hookstone Wood Road, Harrogate HG2 8PN
(01423) 883485
(01423) 881018
Paul Johnson

Drax (1989)
Drax, Selby YO8 8PQ
(01757) 617228
(01757) 617228
draxgolfclub@btinternet.com
Denise Smith
www.draxgolfclub.com

Easingwold (1930)
Stillington Road, Easingwold, York YO61 3ET
(01347) 822474
(01347) 823948
enquiries@easingwoldgolfclub.co.uk
Mrs C Readman
www.easingwoldgolfclub.co.uk

Filey (1897)
West Ave, Filey YO14 9BQ
(01723) 513293
secretary@fileygolfclub.com
Mrs V Gilbank
www.fileygolfclub.com

Forest of Galtres (1993)
Proprietary
Moorlands Road, Skelton, York YO32 2RF
(01904) 766198
(01904) 769400
secretary@forestofgaltres.co.uk
Mrs SJ Procter
www.forestofgaltres.co.uk

Forest Park (1991)
Proprietary
Stockton-on Forest, York YO32 9UW
(01904) 400425
admin@forestparkgolfclub.co.uk
S Crossley (01904) 400688
www.forestparkgolfclub.co.uk

Fulford (York) Golf Club (1906)
Heslington Lane, York YO10 5DY
(01904) 413579
(01904) 416918
info@fulfordgolfclub.co.uk
GS Pearce
www.fulfordgolfclub.co.uk

Ganton (1891)
Station Road, Ganton, Scarborough YO12 4PA
(01944) 710329
(01944) 710922
secretary@gantongolfclub.com
R Penley-Martin
www.gantongolfclub.com

Harrogate (1892)
Forest Lane Head, Harrogate HG2 7TF
(01423) 863158 (Clubhouse)
(01423) 798310
secretary@harrogate-gc.co.uk
Ruth Skaife-Clarke
www.harrogate-gc.co.uk

Heworth (1911)
Muncaster House, Muncastergate, York YO31 9JY
(01904) 424618
(01904) 426156
golf@heworth-gc.fsnet.co.uk
www.heworthgolfclub.co.uk

Hunley Hall (1993)
Brotton, Saltburn TS12 2FT
(01287) 676216
(01287) 678250
enquiries@hhgc.co.uk
G Briffa (01287) 676216
www.hhgc.co.uk

Kirkbymoorside (1951)
Manor Vale, Kirkbymoorside, York YO62 6EG
(01751) 431525
(01751) 433190
enqs@kirkbymoorsidegolf.co.uk
Mrs R Rivis
www.kirkbymoorsidegolf.co.uk

Knaresborough (1920)
Boroughbridge Road, Knaresborough HG5 0QQ
(01423) 862690
(01423) 869345
secretary@kgc.uk.com
M Taylor
www.knaresboroughgolfclub.co.uk

Malton & Norton (1910)
Welham Park, Welham Road, Norton, Malton YO17 9QE
(01653) 697912
(01653) 697844
maltonandnorton@btconnect.com
Mr N J Redman
www.maltonandnortongolfclub.co.uk

Masham (1895)
Burnholme, Swinton Road, Masham, Ripon HG4 4NS
(01765) 688054

✉ info@mashamgolfclub.co.uk
✍ S Blades
🖹 www.mashamgolfclub.co.uk

Middlesbrough (1908)
Brass Castle Lane, Marton, Middlesbrough TS8 9EE
☎ **(01642) 311515**
🖷 (01642) 319607
✉ ian.jackson@middlesbroughgolfclub.co.uk
✍ Ian Jackson (Mgr/Sec)
🖹 www.middlesbroughgolfclub.co.uk

Middlesbrough Municipal (1977)
Public
Ladgate Lane, Middlesbrough TS5 7YZ
☎ **(01642) 315533**
🖷 (01642) 300726
✉ maurice_gormley@middlesbrough.gov.uk
✍ M Gormley (Mgr)
🖹 www.middlesbroughcouncil.gov.uk

Oakdale (1914)
Oakdale, Oakdale Glen, Harrogate HG1 2LN
☎ **(01423) 567162**
🖷 (01423) 536030
✉ manager@oakdalegolfclub.co.uk
✍ MJ Cross
🖹 www.oakdalegolfclub.co.uk

The Oaks (1996)
Proprietary
Aughton Common, Aughton, York YO42 4PW
☎ **(01757) 288001 (Clubhouse)**
🖷 (01757) 288232
✉ sheila@theoaksgolfclub.co.uk
🖹 www.theoaksgolfclub.co.uk

Pannal (1906)
Follifoot Road, Pannal, Harrogate HG3 1ES
☎ **(01423) 872628**
🖷 (01423) 870043
✉ secretary@pannalgolfclub.co.uk
✍ NG Douglas
🖹 www.pannalgolfclub.co.uk

Pike Hills (1904)
Tadcaster Road, Askham Bryan, York YO23 3UW
☎ **(01904) 700797**
🖷 (01904) 700797
✉ secretary@pikehillsgolfclub.co.uk
✍ David Winterburn (Secretary)
🖹 www.pikehillsgolfclub.co.uk

Richmond (1892)
Bend Hagg, Richmond DL10 5EX
☎ **(01748) 825319**
🖷 (01748) 821709
✉ secretary@richmondyorksgolfclub.co.uk
✍ Amy Lancaster (01748) 823231
🖹 www.richmondyorksgolfclub.co.uk

Ripon City Golf Club (1907)
Palace Road, Ripon HG4 3HH
☎ **(01765) 603640**
🖷 (01765) 692880
✉ secretary@riponcitygolfclub.com
✍ MJ Doig MBE
🖹 www.riponcitygolfclub.co.uk

Romanby Golf and Country Club (1993)
Pay and play
Yafforth Road, Northallerton DL7 0PE
☎ **(01609) 778855**
🖷 (01609) 779084
✉ info@romanby.com
🖹 www.romanby.com

Rudding Park (1995)
Pay and play
Rudding Park, Harrogate HG3 1JH
☎ **(01423) 872100**
🖷 (01423) 873011
✉ sales@ruddingpark.com
✍ J King
🖹 www.ruddingpark.com

Saltburn (1894)
Hob Hill, Saltburn-by-the-Sea TS12 1NJ
☎ **(01287) 622812**
✉ secretary@saltburngolf.co.uk
✍ Mrs Julie Annis (Secretary)
🖹 www.saltburngolf.co.uk

Sandburn Hall (2005)
Proprietary
Scotchman Lane, Flaxton, York YO60 7RB
☎ **(01904) 469929**
🖷 (01904) 469923
✉ info@sandburnhall.co.uk
✍ Emma Brown (Clubhouse Manager)
🖹 www.sandburnhall.co.uk

Scarborough North Cliff (1909)
North Cliff Avenue, Burniston Road, Scarborough YO12 6PP
☎ **(01723) 355397**
🖷 (01723) 362134
✉ info@northcliffgolfclub.co.uk
✍ Miss J Duck
🖹 www.northcliffgolfclub.co.uk

Scarborough South Cliff (1902)
Deepdale Avenue, Scarborough YO11 2UE
☎ **(01723) 360522**
🖷 (01723) 360523
✉ clubsecretary@southcliffgolfclub.com
✍ S F Smith
🖹 www.southcliffgolfclub.com

Scarthingwell (1993)
Scarthingwell, Tadcaster LS24 9DG
☎ **(01937) 557878**
🖷 (01937) 557909
✉ ben.burlingham@scarthingwellgolfcourse.co.uk
✍ Ben Burlingham
🖹 www.scarthingwellgolfcourse.co.uk

Selby (1907)
Mill Lane, Brayton, Selby YO8 9LD
☎ **(01757) 228622**
🖷 (01757) 228622
✉ secretary@selbygolfclub.co.uk
✍ Sally Mihale
🖹 www.selbygolfclub.co.uk

Settle (1895)
Giggleswick, Settle BD24 0DH
☎ **(01729) 825288**
✉ drabwright@hotmail.com
✍ Alan Wright (07801) 550 358
🖹 www.settlegolfclub.co.uk

Skipton (1893)
Short Lee Lane, Skipton BD23 3LF
☎ **(01756) 793257 Pro (01756) 795657 Office**
✉ enquiries@skiptongolfclub.co.uk
✍ Beverley Keyworth
🖹 www.skiptongolfclub.co.uk

Teesside (1900)
Acklam Road, Thornaby TS17 7JS
☎ **(01642) 676249**
🖷 (01642) 676252
✉ teessidegolfclub@btconnect.com
✍ M Fleming (01642) 616516
🖹 www.teessidegolfclub.co.uk

Thirsk & Northallerton (1914)
Thornton-le-Street, Thirsk YO7 4AB
☎ **(01845) 525115**
🖷 (01845) 525119
✉ secretary@tngc.co.uk
✍ Secretary (01845) 525115 ext 1
🖹 www.tngc.co.uk

Whitby (1892)
Sandsend Road, Low Straggleton, Whitby YO21 3SR
☎ **(01947) 602719**
🖷 (01947) 600660
✉ office@whitbygolfclub.co.uk
✍ T Mason
🖹 www.whitbygolfclub.co.uk

Wilton (1952)
Wilton, Redcar, Cleveland TS10 4QY
☎ **(01642) 465265**
✉ secretary@wiltongolfclub.co.uk
✍ C Harvey (01642) 465265
🖹 www.wiltongolfclub.co.uk

York (1890)
Lords Moor Lane, Strensall, York YO32 5XF
☎ **(01904) 491840**
🖷 (01904) 491852
✉ secretary@yorkgolfclub.co.uk
✍ MJ Wells
🖹 www.yorkgolfclub.co.uk

Yorkshire (South)

Abbeydale (1895)
Twentywell Rise, Twentywell Lane, Dore, Sheffield S17 4QA
☎ **(0114) 236 0763**

For key to symbols see page 725

(0114) 236 0762
abbeygolf@btconnect.com
Mrs JL Wing (Office Mgr)
www.abbeydalegolfclub.co.uk

Barnsley (1925)
Public
Wakefield Road, Staincross, Barnsley S75 6JZ
(01226) 382856
barnsleygolfclub@btconnect.com
Trevor Jones
www.barnsleygolfclub.co.uk

Bawtry (1974)
Cross Lane, Austerfield, Doncaster DN10 6RF
(01302) 711409
(01302) 711445
enquiries@bawtrygolfclub.co.uk
www.bawtrygolfclub.co.uk

Beauchief (1925)
Public
Abbey Lane, Beauchief, Sheffield S8 0DB
(0114) 236 7274
e-mail@beauchiefgolfclub.co.uk
Mrs B Fryer
www.beauchiefgolfclub.co.uk

Birley Wood (1974)
Public
Birley Lane, Sheffield S12 3BP
(0114) 264 7262
birleysec@hotmail.com
www.birleywood.free-online.co.uk

Concord Park (1952)
Pay and play
Shiregreen Lane, Sheffield S5 6AE
(0114) 257 7378
(0114) 234 7792
concordparkgc@tiscali.co.uk

Crookhill Park (1974)
Public
Carr Lane, Conisborough, Doncaster DN12 2AH
(01709) 862979
secretary@crookhillpark.co.uk
A Goddard (Sec)
www.crookhillpark.co.uk

Doncaster (1894)
Bawtry Road, Bessacarr, Doncaster DN4 7PD
(01302) 865632
(01302) 865994
doncastergolf@aol.com
Malcolm Macphee
www.doncastergolfclub.co.uk

Doncaster Town Moor (1895)
Bawtry Road, Belle Vue, Doncaster DN4 5HU
(01302) 533167
(01302) 533448
dtmgc@btconnect.com
Mike Pears
www.doncastertownmoorgolfclub.co.uk

Dore & Totley (1913)
Bradway Road, Bradway, Sheffield S17 4QR
(0114) 236 0492
(0114) 235 3436
dore.totley@btconnect.com
Mrs SD Haslehurst (0114) 236 9872
www.doreandtotleygolfclub.co.uk

Grange Park (1972)
Pay and play
Upper Wortley Road, Kimberworth, Rotherham S61 2SJ
(01709) 558884

Hallamshire (1897)
Sandygate, Sheffield S10 4LA
(0114) 230 2153
(0114) 230 5413
secretary@hallamshiregolfclub.com
R Hill (0114) 230 2153
www.hallamshiregolfclub.co.uk

Hallowes (1892)
Dronfield, Sheffield S18 1UR
(01246) 413734
(01246) 413753
secretary@hallowesgolfclub.org
N Ogden
www.hallowesgolfclub.org

Hickleton (1909)
Hickleton, Doncaster DN5 7BE
(01709) 896081
info@hickletongolfclub.co.uk
Susan Leach (Sec)
www.hickletongolfclub.co.uk

Hillsborough (1920)
Worrall Road, Sheffield S6 4BE
(0114) 234 9151 (Secretary)
(0114) 229 4105
admin@hillsboroughgolfclub.co.uk
Lewis Horsman (0114) 234 9151
www.hillsboroughgolfclub.co.uk

Lees Hall (1907)
Hemsworth Road, Norton, Sheffield S8 8LL
(0114) 255 4402
(0114) 255 1527
secretary@leeshallgolfclub.co.uk
J Clegg (0114) 255 4402
www.leeshallgolfclub.co.uk

Lindrick (1891)
Lindrick Common, Worksop, Notts S81 8BH
(01909) 475282
(01909) 488685
briannoble@lindrickgolfclub.co.uk
Mr Brian Noble (01909) 475282
www.lindrickgolfclub.co.uk

Owston Hall (the Robin Hood golf course) (1996)
Proprietary
Owston Hall, Owston, Doncaster DN6 9JF
(01302) 722800
(01302) 728885
proshop@owstonhall.com
Gerry Briggs
www.owstonhall.com

Owston Park (1988)
Public
Owston Lane, Owston, Carcroft DN6 8EF
(01302) 330821
michael.parker@foremostgolf.com
MT Parker
www.owstonparkgolfcourse.co.uk

Phoenix (1932)
Pavilion Lane, Brinsworth, Rotherham S60 5PA
(01709) 363788
(01709) 363788
secretary@phoenixgolfclub.co.uk
I Gregory (01709) 363788
www.phoenixgolfclub.co.uk

Renishaw Park (1911)
Golf House, Mill Lane, Renishaw, Sheffield S21 3UZ
(01246) 432044
(01246) 432116
secretary@renishawparkgolf.co.uk
Mark Nelson
www.renishawparkgolf.co.uk

Rother Valley Golf Centre (1997)
Proprietary
Mansfield Road, Wales Bar, Sheffield S26 5PQ
(0114) 247 3000
(0114) 247 6000
info@rothervalleygolfcentre.co.uk
Mr R Hanson
www.rothervalleygolfcentre.co.uk

Rotherham (1902)
Thrybergh Park, Rotherham S65 4NU
(01709) 850466
(01709) 859517
manager@rotherhamgolfclub.com
Mr Chris Allen (Secretary/Chairman)
www.rotherhamgolfclub.com

Roundwood (1976)
Green Lane, Rawmarsh, Rotherham S62 6LA
(01709) 826061
(01709) 523478
golf.secretary@roundwoodgolfclub.co.uk
G Billups (01709) 525208
www.roundwoodgolfclub.co.uk

Sandhill (1993)
Proprietary
Little Houghton, Barnsley S72 0HW
(01226) 753444
(01226) 753444
steven.gavin409@googlemail.com
S Gavin (01226) 780025
www.sandhillgolfclub.co.uk

For key to symbols see page 725

Silkstone (1893)
Field Head, Elmhirst Lane, Silkstone, Barnsley S75 4LD
☎ **(01226) 790328**
📠 (01226) 794902
✉ silkstonegolf@hotmail.co.uk
✍ Alan Cook
🌐 www.silkstone-golf-club.co.uk

Sitwell Park (1913)
Shrogs Wood Road, Rotherham S60 4BY
☎ **(01709) 541046**
📠 (01709) 703637
✉ secretary@sitwellgolf.co.uk
✍ S G Bell
🌐 www.sitwellgolf.co.uk

Stocksbridge & District (1924)
Royd Lane, Deepcar, Sheffield S36 2RZ
☎ **(0114) 288 7479/288 2003**
📠 (0114) 283 1460
✉ stocksbridgegolf@live.co.uk
✍ Mrs A Methley (0114) 288 2003
🌐 www.stocksbridgeanddistrictgolfclub.com

Styrrup Hall (2000)
Proprietary
Main Street, Styrrup, Doncaster DN11 8NB
☎ **(01302) 751112 (Golf) 759933 (Clubhouse)**
📠 (01302) 750622
✉ office@styrrupgolf.co.uk
✍ Dianne Stokoe (Sec/Mgr)
🌐 www.styrrupgolf.co.uk

Tankersley Park (1907)
Park Lane, High Green, Sheffield S35 4LG
☎ **(0114) 246 8247**
📠 (0114) 245 7818
✉ secretary@tpgc.freeserve.co.uk
✍ A Brownhill (0114) 246 8247
🌐 www.tankersleyparkgolfclub.org.uk

Thorne (1980)
Pay and play
Kirton Lane, Thorne, Doncaster DN8 5RJ
☎ **(01405) 815173 (bookings 01405 812084)**
📠 (01405) 741899
✉ carolinehighfield@live.co.uk
✍ E Highfield (Golf Shop)
🌐 www.thornegolf.co.uk

Tinsley Park (1920)
Public
High Hazels Park, Darnall, Sheffield S9 4PE
☎ **(0114) 244 8974**
✍ Wayne Yellott (Professional)
🌐 www.tinsleyparkgolfcourse.co.uk

Wath (1904)
Abdy Rawmarsh, Rotherham S62 7SJ
☎ **(01709) 878609**
📠 (01709) 877097
✉ golf@wathgolfclub.co.uk
✍ M Godfrey (01709) 878609 ext 1
🌐 www.wathgolfclub.co.uk

Wheatley (1914)
Armthorpe Road, Doncaster DN2 5QB
☎ **(01302) 831655**
📠 (01302) 812736
✉ secretary@wheatleygolfclub.co.uk
✍ Ken Gosden
🌐 www.wheatleygolfclub.co.uk

Wortley (1894)
Hermit Hill Lane, Wortley, Sheffield S35 7DF
☎ **(0114) 288 8469**
📠 (0114) 288 8488
✉ wortley.golfclub@btconnect.com
✍ Roy Cooke
🌐 www.wortleygolfclub.co.uk

Yorkshire (West)

The Alwoodley (1907)
Wigton Lane, Alwoodley, Leeds LS17 8SA
☎ **(0113) 268 1680**
✉ alwoodley@btconnect.com
✍ Mrs J Slater
🌐 www.alwoodley.co.uk

Bagden Hall Hotel (1993)
Wakefield Road, Scissett HD8 9LE
☎ **(01484) 865330**
📠 (01484) 861001

Baildon (1896)
Moorgate, Baildon, Shipley BD17 5PP
☎ **(01274) 584266**
✉ secretary@baildongolfclub.com
✍ Paul Weatherill
🌐 www.baildongolfclub.com

Ben Rhydding (1947)
High Wood, Ben Rhydding, Ilkley LS9 8SB
☎ **(01943) 608759**
✉ secretary@benrhyddinggc.freeserve.co.uk
✍ J D B Watts
🌐 www.benrhyddinggolfclub.com

Bingley St Ives (1931)
St Ives Estate, Bingley BD16 1AT
☎ **(01274) 562436**
📠 (01274) 511788
✉ secretary@bingleystivesgc.co.uk
✍ RA Adams
🌐 www.bingleystivesgc.co.uk

Bracken Ghyll (1993)
Skipton Road, Addingham, Ilkley LS29 0SL
☎ **(01943) 831207**
📠 (01943) 839453
✉ office@brackenghyll.co.uk
✍ Peter Knowles
🌐 www.brackenghyll.co.uk

The Bradford Golf Club (1891)
Hawksworth Lane, Guiseley, Leeds LS20 8NP
☎ **(01943) 875570**
✉ secretary@bradfordgolfclub.co.uk
✍ James Washington
🌐 www.bradfordgolfclub.co.uk

Bradford Moor (1906)
Scarr Hall, Pollard Lane, Bradford BD2 4RW
☎ **(01274) 771716**
✉ bfdmoorgc@hotmail.co.uk
✍ C P Bedford (01274) 771693
🌐 www.bradfordmoorgolfclub.co.uk

Bradley Park (1978)
Public
Bradley Road, Huddersfield HD2 1PZ
☎ **(01484) 223772**
📠 (01484) 451613
✉ parnellreilly@pgabroadband.com
✍ Derek M Broadbent
🌐 www.bradleyparkgolfclub.com

Branshaw (1912)
Branshaw Moor, Oakworth, Keighley BD22 7ES
☎ **(01535) 643235**
📠 (01535) 643235
✉ enquiries@branshawgolfclub.co.uk
✍ Simon Jowitt
🌐 www.branshawgolfclub.co.uk

Calverley (1980)
Woodhall Lane, Pudsey LS28 5QY
☎ **(0113) 256 9244**
📠 (0113) 256 4362
✉ calverleygolf@btconnect.com

Castlefields (1903)
Rastrick Common, Brighouse HD6 3HL
✉ secretary@castlefieldsgolfclub.co.uk
✍ David Bartliff
🌐 www.castlefieldsgolfclub.co.uk

City Golf Course (1997)
Pay and play
Red Cote Lane, Kirkstall Road, Leeds LS4 2AW
☎ **(0113) 263 3030**
📠 (0113) 263 3044

City of Wakefield (1936)
Public
Lupset Park, Horbury Road, Wakefield WF2 8QS
☎ **(01924) 367442**

Clayton (1906)
Thornton View Road, Clayton, Bradford BD14 6JX
☎ **(01274) 880047**
✉ secretary@claytongc.plus.com
✍ DA Smith (01274) 572311
🌐 www.claytongolfclub.co.uk

Cleckheaton & District (1900)
483 Bradford Road, Cleckheaton BD19 6BU
☎ **(01274) 851266 (Secretary)**
📠 (01274) 871382
✉ info@cleckheatongolfclub.co.uk
✍ Dick Guiver
🌐 www.cleckheatongolfclub.com

Cookridge Hall (1997)
Proprietary
Cookridge Lane, Cookridge, Leeds LS16 7NL
(0113) 230 0641
(0113) 203 0198
info@cookridgehall.co.uk
Gary Day
www.cookridgehall.co.uk

Crosland Heath (1914)
Felks Stile Road, Crosland Heath, Huddersfield HD4 7AF
(01484) 653216
(01484) 461079
golf@croslandheath.co.uk
Mrs L Salvini
www.croslandheath.co.uk

Crow Nest Park (1995)
Coach Road, Hove Edge, Brighouse HD6 2LN
(01484) 401121
info@crownestgolf.co.uk
L Holmes
www.crownestgolf.co.uk

De Vere Oulton Park Golf Club (1990)
Public
Rothwell Lane, Oulton, Leeds, West Yorkshire LS26 8HN
(0113) 282 3152
(0113) 282 6290
A Cooper (Mgr)

Dewsbury District (1891)
The Pinnacle, Sands Lane, Mirfield WF14 8HJ
(01924) 492399
(01924) 491928
info@dewsburygolf.co.uk
A M Thorpe
www.dewsburygolf.co.uk

East Bierley (1928)
South View Road, Bierley, Bradford BD4 6PP
(01274) 681023
rjwelch@talktalk.net
RJ Welch (01274) 683666

Elland (1910)
Hammerstone Leach Lane, Hullen Edge, Elland HX5 0TA
(01422) 372505
secretary@ellandgolfclub.plus.com
PA Green (01422) 251431
www.ellandgolfclub.plus.com

Fardew (1993)
Pay and play
Nursery Farm, Carr Lane, East Morton, Keighley BD20 5RY
(01274) 561229
davidheaton@btconnect.com
A Stevens
www.fardewgolfclub.co.uk

Ferrybridge (2002)
PO Box 39, Stranglands Lane, Knottingley WF11 8SQ
(01977) 884165
(01977) 884001
Trevor.Ellis@Scottish-southern
TD Ellis

Fulneck (1892)
Fulneck, Pudsey LS28 8NT
(0113) 256 5191
fulneckgolf@aol.com
Mr J McLean (Hon Sec)
www.fulneckgolfclub.co.uk

Garforth (1913)
Long Lane, Garforth, Leeds LS25 2DS
(0113) 286 3308
(0113) 286 3308
garforthgcltd@lineone.net
D R Carlisle
www.garforthgolfclub.co.uk

Gotts Park (1933)
Public
Armley Ridge Road, Armley, Leeds LS12 2QX
(0113) 234 2019

Halifax (1895)
Union Lane, Ogden, Halifax HX2 8XR
(01422) 244171
(01422) 241459
halifax.golfclub@virgin.net
www.halifaxgolfclub.co.uk

Halifax Bradley Hall (1907)
Holywell Green, Halifax HX4 9AN
(01422) 374108
bhgc@gotadsl.co.uk
Mrs J Teale
www.bradleyhallgolf.co.uk

Halifax West End (1906)
Paddock Lane, Highroad Well, Halifax HX2 0NT
(01422) 341878
(01422) 410540
westendgc@btinternet.com
S J Boustead (01422) 341878
www.westendgc.co.uk

Hanging Heaton (1922)
Whitecross Road, Bennett Lane, Dewsbury WF12 7DT
(01924) 461606
(01924) 430100
derek.atkinson@hhgc.org
Derek Atkinson (01924) 430100
www.hangingheatongolfclub.co.uk

Headingley (1892)
Back Church Lane, Adel, Leeds LS16 8DW
(0113) 267 9573 (Clubhouse)
(0113) 281 7334
manager@headingleygolfclub.co.uk
Mr J L Hall
www.headingleygolfclub.co.uk

Headley (1907)
Headley Lane, Thornton, Bradford BD13 3LX
(01274) 833481
(01274) 833481
admin@headleygolfclub.co.uk
D Britton
www.headleygolfclub.co.uk

Hebden Bridge (1930)
Great Mount, Wadsworth, Hebden Bridge HX7 8PH
(01422) 842896
hbgc@btconnect.com
Stepney Calvert (01422) 842896
www.hebdenbridgegolfclub.co.uk

Horsforth (1906)
Layton Rise, Layton Road, Horsforth, Leeds LS18 5EX
(0113) 258 6819
(0113) 258 9336
secretary@horsforthgolfclub.co.uk
Mrs LA Harrison-Elrick
www.horsforthgolfclub.co.uk

Howley Hall (1900)
Scotchman Lane, Morley, Leeds LS27 0NX
(01924) 350100
(01924) 350104
office@howleyhall.co.uk
D Jones (01924) 350100
www.howleyhall.co.uk

Huddersfield (1891)
Fixby Hall, Lightridge Road, Huddersfield HD2 2EP
(01484) 426203
(01484) 424623
secretary@huddersfield-golf.co.uk
S.A.Jones
www.huddersfield-golf.co.uk

Ilkley (1890)
Myddleton, Ilkley LS29 0BE
(01943) 607277
(01943) 816130
honsec@ilkleygolfclub.co.uk
Robert G Lambert (Hon Sec) (01943) 600214
www.ilkleygolfclub.co.uk

Keighley (1904)
Howden Park, Utley, Keighley BD20 6DH
(01535) 604778
(01535) 604778
manager@keighleygolfclub.com
G Cameron Dawson
www.keighleygolfclub.com

Leeds (1896)
Elmete Lane, Roundhay, Leeds LS8 2LJ
(0113) 265 8775
(0113) 232 3369
admin@leedsgolfclub.co.uk
P Mawman (0113) 265 9203
www.leedsgolfclub.co.uk

Leeds Golf Centre (1994)
Proprietary
Wike Ridge Lane, Shadwell, Leeds LS17 9JW
(0113) 288 6000
(0113) 288 6185
info@leedsgolfcentre.com
A Herridge (Director of Golf)
www.leedsgolfcentre.com

Lofthouse Hill
Leeds Road, Lofthouse Hill, Wakefield WF3 3LR
(01924) 823703
(01924) 823703
P Moon
www.lofthousehillgolfclub.co.uk

Longley Park (1910)
Maple Street, Huddersfield HD5 9AX
(01484) 426932
(01484) 515280
longleyparkgolfclub@12freeukisp.co.uk
J Ambler (01484) 431885

Low Laithes (1925)
Park Mill Lane, Flushdyke, Ossett WF5 9AP
(01924) 266067
(01924) 266266
info@lowlaithesgolfclub.co.uk
P Browning (Sec/Mgr)
www.lowlaithesgolfclub.co.uk

The Manor
Proprietary
Bradford Road, Drighlington, Bradford BD11 1AB
(01132) 852644
(01332) 879961
themanorgolfclub@hotmail.co.uk
G Thompson (Sec/Mgr)
www.themanorgolfclub.co.uk

Marriott Hollins Hall Hotel (1999)
Hollins Hill, Baildon, Shipley BD17 7QW
(01274) 534212
(01274) 534220
mhrs.lbags.golf@marriotthotels.com
Stuart Carnie (01274) 534250
www.hollinshallgolf.com

Marsden (1921)
Hemplow, Marsden, Huddersfield HD7 6NN
(01484) 844253
secretary@marsdengolf.co.uk
R O'Brien
www.marsdengolf.co.uk

Meltham (1908)
Thick Hollins Hall, Meltham, Huddersfield HD9 4DQ
(01484) 850227
admin@meltham-golf.co.uk
J R Dixon (Hon)
www.meltham-golf.co.uk

Mid Yorkshire (1993)
Proprietary
Havercroft Lane, Darrington, Pontefract WF8 3BP
(01977) 704522
(01977) 600823
admin@midyorkshiregolfclub.com
Robert Pointon
www.midyorkshiregolfclub.com

Middleton Park (1933)
Public
Ring Road, Beeston Park, Middleton LS10 3TN
(0113) 270 0449
secretary@middletonparkgolfclub.co.uk
www.middletonparkgolfclub.co.uk

Moor Allerton (1923)
Coal Road, Wike, Leeds LS17 9NH
(0113) 266 1154
(0113) 268 0059
info@magc.co.uk
G Pretty (Mgr)
www.magc.co.uk

Moortown (1909)
Harrogate Road, Leeds LS17 7DB
(0113) 268 6521
(0113) 268 0986
secretary@moortown-gc.co.uk
Mr Peter Rishworth
www.moortown-gc.co.uk

Normanton (1903)
Hatfeild Hall, Aberford Road, Stanley, Wakefield WF3 4JP
(01924) 377943
(01924) 200777
office@normantongolf.co.uk
Lynne Pickles
www.normantongolf.co.uk

Northcliffe (1921)
High Bank Lane, Shipley, Bradford BD18 4LJ
(01274) 584085
(01274) 584148
northcliffegc@hotmail.co.uk
C Malloy (01274) 596731
www.northcliffegc.org.uk

Otley (1906)
West Busk Lane, Otley LS21 3NG
(01943) 465329
(01943) 850387
office@otleygolfclub.co.uk
PJ Clarke Ext 1
www.otleygolfclub.co.uk

Outlane (1906)
Slack Lane, off New Hey Road, Outlane, Huddersfield HD3 3FQ
(01422) 374762
(01422) 311789
secretary@outlanegolfclub.ltd.uk
P Turner
www.outlanegolfclub.ltd.uk

Pontefract & District (1904)
Park Lane, Pontefract WF8 4QS
(01977) 792241
(01977) 792241
manager@pdgc.co.uk
J Heald (Mgr) (01977) 792241
www.pdgc.co.uk

Queensbury (1923)
Brighouse Road, Queensbury, Bradford BD13 1QF
(01274) 882155
(01274) 882155
queensburygolf@talktalk.net
MH Heptinstall
www.queensburygc.co.uk

Rawdon (1896)
Buckstone Drive, Micklefield Lane, Rawdon LS19 6BD
(0113) 250 6040
info@rgltc.co.uk
Phil Denison
www.rgltc.co.uk

Riddlesden (1927)
Howden Rough, Riddlesden, Keighley BD20 5QN
(01535) 602148

Roundhay (1923)
Public
Park Lane, Leeds LS8 2EJ
(0113) 266 2695
geoff.hodgson@sky.com
G M Hodgson (Hon Sec)
www.roundhaygc.com

Ryburn (1910)
Norland, Sowerby Bridge, Halifax HX6 3QP
(01422) 831355
secretary@ryburngolfclub.co.uk
Raymond Attiwell (07904) 834320
www.ryburngolfclub.co.uk

Sand Moor (1926)
Alwoodley Lane, Leeds LS17 7DJ
(0113) 268 5180
(0113) 266 1105
info@sandmoorgolf.co.uk
Jackie Hogan (0113) 268 5180
www.sandmoorgolf.co.uk

Scarcroft (1937)
Syke Lane, Scarcroft, Leeds LS14 3BQ
(0113) 289 2311
(0113) 289 3835
secretary@scarcroftgolfclub.co.uk
R A Simpson (Sec/Mgr)
www.scarcroftgolfclub.co.uk

Shipley (1896)
Beckfoot Lane, Cottingley Bridge, Bingley BD16 1LX
(01274) 568652
(01274) 567739
office@shipleygc.co.uk
Mrs MJ Simpson (01274) 568652
www.shipleygolfclub.com

Silsden (1911)
Brunthwaite Lane, Brunthwaite, Silsden BD20 0ND
(01535) 652998
info@silsdengolfclub.co.uk
M Twigg
www.silsdengolfclub.co.uk

South Bradford (1906)
Pearson Road, Odsal, Bradford BD6 1BH
(01274) 679195
secsouthbradford@btconnect.com
B Broadbent (01274) 679195
www.southbradfordgolfclub.co.uk

For key to symbols see page 725

South Leeds (1906)
Gipsy Lane, Ring Road, Beeston, Leeds LS11 5TU
☎ **(0113) 277 1676**
(0113) 277 1676
south-leeds@btconnect.com
B Clayton (0113) 277 1676
www.southleedsgolfclub.co.uk

Temple Newsam (1923)
Public
Temple Newsam Road, Halton, Leeds LS15 0LN
☎ **(0113) 264 5624**
secretary@tngc.co.uk
Mrs Christine P Wood
www.tngolfclub.co.uk

Todmorden (1894)
Rive Rocks, Cross Stone, Todmorden OL14 8RD
☎ **(01706) 812986**
secretarytodgolfclub@msn.com
Peter H Eastwood
www.todmordengolfclub.co.uk

Wakefield (1891)
28 Woodthorpe Lane, Sandal, Wakefield WF2 6JH
☎ **(01924) 258778**
(01924) 242752
wakefieldgolfclub@woodthorpelane.freeserve.co.uk
Elizabeth Newton (01924) 258778
www.wakefieldgolfclub.co.uk

Waterton Park (1995)
The Balk, Walton, Wakefield WF2 6QL
☎ **(01924) 259525**
(01924) 256969
wparkgolfclub@btconnect.com
M Pearson (01924) 255557

West Bradford (1900)
Chellow Grange Road, Haworth Road, Bradford BD9 6NP
☎ **(01274) 542767**
(01274) 482079
secretary@westbradfordgolfclub.co.uk
B K Sutcliffe (Hon Sec) (01274) 542767
www.westbradfordgolfclub.co.uk

Wetherby (1910)
Linton Lane, Linton, Wetherby LS22 4JF
☎ **(01937) 580089**
(01937) 581915
manager@wetherbygolfclub.co.uk
Darren Tear
www.wetherbygolfclub.co.uk

Whitwood (1987)
Public
Altofts Lane, Whitwood, Castleford WF10 5PZ
☎ **(01977) 512835**

Willow Valley Golf (1993)
Pay and play
Clifton, Brighouse HD6 4JB
☎ **(01274) 878624**
sales@wvgc.co.uk
H Newton
www.wvgc.co.uk

Woodhall Hills (1905)
Woodhall Road, Calverley, Pudsey LS28 5UN
☎ **(0113) 256 4771 (Clubhouse)**
(0113) 255 4594
woodhallgolf@btconnect.com
J Hayes (0113) 255 4594
www.woodhallhillsgolfclub.com

Woodsome Hall (1922)
Woodsome Hall, Fenay Bridge, Huddersfield HD8 0LQ
☎ **(01484) 602971**
(01484) 608260
www.woodsomehall.co.uk

Woolley Park (1995)
Proprietary
New Road, Woolley, Wakefield WF4 2JS
☎ **(01226) 380144 (Bookings)**
(01226) 390295
woolleyparkgolf@yahoo.co.uk
RP Stoffel (01226) 382209
www.woolleyparkgolfclub.co.uk

For key to symbols see page 725

R&A help for projects in China, Brazil and India

Among the grants given by The R&A in the past year were the following:

To the HSBC China Golf Association junior programme – £110,000. This is the programme that produced a Chinese boy and girl who played in The R&A's Junior Open at Fairhaven.

To the Japeri project in Rio de Janeiro – £100,000 towards golf course reinstatement following disruption caused by the building of a new highway. This grant also allowed on-going coaching to take place.

For greenkeeper education in India – £26,500 towards an on-going nationwide programme.

Ireland

Co Antrim

Antrim (1997)
Public
Allen Park Golf Centre, 45 Castle Road, Antrim BT41 4NA
(028) 9442 9001
allenpark@antrim.gov.uk
Marie Agnew (Mgr)
www.antrim.gov.uk

Ballycastle (1890)
Cushendall Road, Ballycastle BT64 6QP
(028) 2076 2536
(028) 2076 9909
info@ballycastlegolfclub.com
Mr Robin McHugh (Hon/Sec)
www.ballycastlegolfclub.com

Ballyclare (1923)
25 Springvale Road, Ballyclare BT39 9JW
(028) 9332 2696 (Clubhouse)
(028) 9332 2696
info@ballyclaregolfclub.com
Michael Stone
www.ballyclaregolfclub.com

Ballymena (1903)
128 Raceview Road, Ballymena BT42 4HY
(028) 2586 1207/1487
(028) 2586 1487
admin@ballymenagolfclub.com
Ken Herbison (Hon Sec)

Bentra
Public
Slaughterford Road, Whitehead BT38 9TG
(028) 9335 8000
(028) 9336 6676
greenspace@carrickfergus.org
S Daye (028) 9335 8039
www.bentragolf.co.uk

Burnfield House
10 Cullyburn Road, Newtownabbey BT36 5BN
(028) 9083 8737
michaelhj@ntlworld.com
www.burnfieldhousegolfclub.co.uk

Bushfoot (1890)
50 Bushfoot Road, Portballintrae BT57 8RR
(028) 2073 1317
(028) 2073 1852
bushfootgolfclub@btconnect.com
T McFaull (Hon Sec)
www.bushfootgolfclub.co.uk

Cairndhu (1928)
192 Coast Road, Ballygally, Larne BT40 2QG
(028) 2858 3324
(028) 2858 3324
cairndhugc@btconnect.com
N McKinstry (Sec/Mgr) (028) 2858 3324
www.cairndhugolfclub.co.uk

Carrickfergus (1926)
35 North Road, Carrickfergus BT38 8LP
(028) 9336 3713
(028) 9336 3023
carrickfergusgc@btconnect.com
I McLean (Hon Sec)
www.carrickfergusgolfclub.com

Cushendall (1937)
21 Shore Road, Cushendall BT44 0NG
(028) 2177 1318
(028) 2177 1318
cushendallgc@btconnect.com
S McLaughlin (028) 2175 8366

Down Royal (1990)
Proprietary
6 Dungarton Road, Maze, Lisburn BT27 5RT
(028) 9262 1339
(028) 9262 1339
info@downroyalgolf.com
Bill McCappin (Mgr)
www.downroyalgolf.com

Galgorm Castle (1997)
Proprietary
200 Galgorm Road, Ballymena BT42 1HL
(028) 256 46161
(028) 256 51151
golf@galgormcastle.com
G Henry (Gen Mgr)
www.galgormcastle.com

Gracehill (1995)
Proprietary
141 Ballinlea Road, Stranocum, Ballymoney BT53 8PX
(028) 2075 1209
(028) 2075 1074
info@gracehillgolfclub.co.uk
M McClure (Mgr)
www.gracehillgolfclub.co.uk

Greenacres (1996)
153 Ballyrobert Road, Ballyclare BT39 9RT
(028) 933 54111
(028) 933 44509
www.greenacresgolfclub.co.uk

Greenisland (1894)
156 Upper Road, Greenisland, Carrickfergus BT38 8RW
(028) 9086 2236
greenisland.golf@btconnect.com
FF Trotter (Hon)
www.greenislandgolfclub.co.uk

Hilton Templepatrick (1999)
Proprietary
Castle Upton Estate, Paradise Walk, Templepatrick BT39 0DD
(028) 9443 5542
(028) 9443 5511
eamonn.logue@hilton.com
Eamonn Logue (Golf Ops Mgr)
www.hiltontemplepatrickgolf.com

Larne (1894)
54 Ferris Bay Road, Islandmagee, Larne BT40 3RJ
(028) 9338 2228
(028) 9338 2088
info@larnegolfclub.co.uk
RI Johnston

Lisburn (1891)
68 Eglantine Road, Lisburn BT27 5RQ
(028) 9267 7216
(028) 9260 3608
info@lisburngolfclub.com
John McKeown (Gen Mgr)
www.lisburngolfclub.com

Mallusk (1992)
Antrim Road, Glengormley, Newtownabbey BT36 4RF
(028) 9084 3799

Massereene (1895)
51 Lough Road, Antrim BT41 4DQ
(028) 9442 8096 (office)
(028) 9448 7661
info@massereene.com
www.massereene.com

Rathmore
Bushmills Road, Portrush BT56 8JG
(028) 7082 2996
(028) 7082 2996
rathmoregolfclubvalley@msn.com
W McIntyre (Club Admin.)
www.rathmoregolfclub.com

Royal Portrush (1888)
Dunluce Road, Portrush BT56 8JQ
(028) 7082 2311
(028) 7082 3139
wilma.erskine@royalportrushgolfclub.com
Miss W Erskine
www.royalportrushgolfclub.com

Whitehead (1904)
McCrae's Brae, Whitehead, Carrickfergus BT38 9NZ
(028) 9337 0820
(028) 9337 0825
robin@whiteheadgc.fsnet.co.uk
RA Patrick (Hon)
www.whiteheadgolfclub.com

Co Armagh

Ashfield (1990)
Freeduff, Cullyhanna, Newry BT35 0JJ
(028) 3086 8180

Cloverhill (1999)
Proprietary
Lough Road, Mullaghbawn BT35 9XP
(028) 3088 9374
info@cloverhillgc.com/pilky-03@hotmail.com
Colin Pilkington
www.cloverhillgolfclub.co.uk

County Armagh (1893)
7 Newry Road, Armagh BT60 1EN
(028) 37 525861/(028) 37 525864 (Pro Sh
(028) 3752 8768
lynne@golfarmagh.co.uk
Mrs Lynne Fleming (028) 3752 5861
www.golfarmagh.co.uk

Edenmore G&CC (1992)
Edenmore House, 70 Drumnabreeze Road, Magheralin, Craigavon BT67 0RH
(028) 9261 9241
(028) 9261 3310
info@edenmore.com
K Logan (Sec/Mgr)
www.edenmore.com

Loughgall Country Park & Golf Course
11-14 Main Street, Loughgall
(028) 3889 2900
(028) 3889 2902
g.ferson@btinternet.com
www.armagh.gov.uk

Lurgan (1893)
The Demesne, Windsor Avenue, Lurgan BT67 9BN
(028) 3832 2087 (Clubhouse)
(028) 3831 6166
lurgangolfclub@btconnect.com
Muriel Sharpe
www.lurgangolfclub.com

Portadown (1902)
192 Gilford Road, Portadown BT63 5LF
(028) 383 55356
(028) 383 91394
info@portadowngolfclub.co.uk
Barbara Currie (Sec/Mgr)
www.portadowngolfclub.co.uk

Silverwood (1983)
Turmoyra Lane, Silverwood, Lurgan BT66 6NG
(028) 3832 5380
(028) 3834 7272
silverwoodgolfclub@myrainbow .com
S Ashe
www.silverwoodgolfclub.com

Tandragee (1922)
Markethill Road, Tandragee BT62 2ER
(028) 3884 1272 (Clubhouse)
(028) 3884 0664
office@tandragee.co.uk
A Hewitt (028) 3884 1272
www.tandragee.co.uk

Belfast

Ballyearl Golf Centre
Public
585 Doagh Road, Newtownabbey BT36 5RZ
(028) 9084 8287
(028) 9084 4896
sbartley@newtownabbey.gov.uk
wwwnewtownabbey.gov.uk

Balmoral (1914)
518 Lisburn Road, Belfast BT9 6GX
(028) 9038 1514
(028) 9066 6759
admin@balmoralgolf.com
www.balmoralgolf.com

Belvoir Park (1927)
73 Church Road, Newtownbreda, Belfast BT8 7AN
(028) 9049 1693
(028) 9064 6113
info@belvoirparkgolfclub.com
Ann Vaughan (028) 9049 1693
www.belvoirparkgolfclub.com

Castlereagh Hills Golf Course (2005)
Pay and play
73 Upper Braniel Road, Belfast BT5 7TX
(028) 9044 8477
(028) 9044 9646
golfclub@castlereagh.gov.uk
Lea Booth
www.castlereaghhills.com

Dunmurry (1905)
91 Dunmurry Lane, Dunmurry, Belfast BT17 9JS
(028) 9061 0834
(028) 9060 2540
dunmurrygc@hotmail.com
T Cassidy (Golf Mgr)
www.dunmurrygolfclub.co.uk

Fortwilliam (1891)
8A Downview Avenue, Belfast B15 4EZ
(028) 9037 0770
(028) 9078 1891
administrator@fortwilliam.co.uk
Pat Toal CB (Hon Sec)
www.fortwilliam.co.uk

The Knock Club (1895)
Summerfield, Dundonald, Belfast BT16 2QX
(028) 9048 3251
(028) 9048 7277
knockgolfclub@btconnect.com
Anne Armstrong
www.knockgolfclub.co.uk

Malone (1895)
240 Upper Malone Road, Dunmurry, Belfast BT17 9LB
(028) 9061 2758
(028) 9043 1394
manager@malonegolfclub.co.uk
Peter Kelly (028) 9061 2758
www.malonegolfclub.co.uk

Ormeau (1893)
50 Park Road, Belfast BT7 2FX
(028) 9064 1069 (Members)
(028) 9064 6250

Shandon Park (1926)
73 Shandon Park, Belfast BT5 6NY
(028) 9080 5030
shandonpark@btconnect.com
GA Bailie (Gen Mgr)
www.shandonpark.net

Co Carlow

Borris (1907)
Deerpark, Borris
(059) 977 3310 (office)
(059) 977 3750
borrisgolfclub@eircom.net
Shena Walsh (059) 977 3310

Carlow (1899)
Deer Park, Dublin Road, Carlow
(059) 913 1695
(059) 914 0065
carlowgolfclub@eircom.net
D MacSweeney (Gen Mgr)
www.carlowgolfclub.com

Co Cavan

Belturbet (1950)
Erne Hill, Belturbet
(049) 952 2287

Blacklion (1962)
Toam, Blacklion, via Sligo
(071) 985 3024
(071) 985 3024
www.blackliongolf.eu

Cabra Castle (1978)
Kingscourt
(042) 966 7030
(042) 966 7039
kevcarry@gmail.com
Kevin Carry (087) 655 7538

County Cavan (1894)
Arnmore House, Drumelis, Cavan
(049) 433 1541
(049) 433 1541
info@cavangolf.ie
www.cavangolf.ie

Slieve Russell G&CC (1994)
Ballyconnell
(049) 952 6458
(049) 952 6640
slieve-russell@quinn-hotels.com
(049) 952 5091
www.slieverussell.ie

Virginia (1945)
Park Hotel, Virginia
(049) 854 8066
P Gill (087) 681 3387

Co Clare

Clonlara (1993)
Clonlara
(061) 354141
clonlaragolfclub@eircom.net

Doonbeg (2002)
Doonbeg, Co Clare
(065) 905 5600
(065) 905 5247
reservations@doonbeggolfclub.com
www.doonbeggolfclub.com

Dromoland Castle (1964)
Newmarket-on-Fergus
353 (61) 368444
353 (61) 368498
golf@dromoland.ie
www.dromoland.ie

East Clare (1992)
Bodyke
(061) 921322

Ennis (1907)
Drumbiggle, Ennis
(065) 682 4074
(065) 684 1848
info@ennisgolfclub.com
www.ennisgolfclub.com

Kilkee (1896)
East End, Kilkee
(065) 905 6048
(065) 905 6977
kilkeegolfclub@eircom.net
Jim Leyden (Sec/Mgr)
www.kilkeegolfclub.ie

Kilrush (1934)
Parknamoney, Kilrush
(065) 905 1138
(065) 905 2633
info@kilrushgolfclub.com
www.kilrushgolfclub.com

Lahinch (1892)
Lahinch
(065) 708 1003
(065) 708 1592
info@lahinchgolf.com
Paddy Keane (Gen Mgr)
www.lahinchgolf.com

Shannon (1966)
Shannon
(061) 471849
(061) 471507
info@shannongolfclub.ie
M Corry (061) 471849
www.shannongolfclub.ie

Spanish Point (1915)
Spanish Point, Miltown Malbay
(065) 708 4219
www.spanish-point.com

Woodstock (1993)
Shanaway Road, Ennis
(065) 682 9463
(065) 682 0304
proshopwoodstock@eircom.net
Avril Guerin (Sec/Mgr)
www.woodstockgolfclub.com

Co Cork

Bandon (1909)
Castlebernard, Bandon
(023) 88 41111
(023) 88 20819
enquiries@bandongolfclub.com
Kay Walsh
www.bandongolfclub.com

Bantry Bay (1975)
Donemark, Bantry, West Cork
(027) 50579/53773
(027) 53790
info@bantrygolf.com
Steve Cameron (Mgr) (027) 50579
www.bantrygolf.com

Berehaven (1902)
Millcove, Castletownbere
(027) 70700
(027) 71957
info@berehavengolf.com
B Twomey (Hon)
www.berehavengolf.com

Charleville (1909)
Ardmore, Charleville
353 63 81257
353 63 81274
info@charlevillegolf.com
Patrick Nagle (Sec/Mgr)
www.charlevillegolf.com

Cobh (1987)
Ballywilliam, Cobh
(021) 812399
(021) 812615

Coosheen (1989)
Coosheen, Schull
(028) 28182

Cork (1888)
Little Island, Cork
(021) 435 3451/3037
(021) 435 3410
info@corkgolfclub.ie
M Sands (021) 435 3451
www.corkgolfclub.ie

Doneraile (1927)
Doneraile
(022) 24137
info@donerailegolfclub.com
www.donerailegolfclub.com

Douglas (1909)
Douglas, Cork
(021) 489 1086
(021) 436 7200
admin@douglasgolfclub.ie
Ronan Burke (Mgr)
www.douglasgolfclub.ie

Dunmore Golf Club (1967)
Muckross, Clonakilty
023 8834644
dunmoregolfclub@gmail.com
Liam Santry
www.dunmoregolfclub.ie

East Cork (1971)
Gortacrue, Midleton
(021) 463 1687
(021) 461 3695
eastcorkgolfclub@eircom.net
M Moloney (Sec/Mgr)
www.eastcorkgolfclub.com

Fermoy (1892)
Corrin, Fermoy
(025) 32694
(025) 33072
fermoygolfclub@eircom.net
K Murphy
www.fermoygolfclub.ie

Fernhill (1994)
Carrigaline
(021) 437 2226
(021) 437 1011
fernhill@iol.ie
www.fernhillgolfhotel.com

Fota Island Resort (1993)
Proprietary
Fota Island, Cork
(021) 488 3700
(021) 488 3713
reservations@fotaisland.ie
Jonathon Woods
www.fotaisland.ie

Frankfield (1984)
Frankfield, Douglas
(0214) 363124/3611299
(01214) 366205
frankfieldhouse@gmail.com
James St Leger
www.frankfieldhouse.com

Glengarriff (1935)
Glengarriff
(027) 63150
(027) 63575
glengarriff@gmail.com
N Deasy (Hon)
www.glengarriffgolfclub.com

Harbour Point (1991)
Proprietary
Clash Road, Little Island
(021) 435 3094
(021) 435 4408
hpoint@iol.ie
www.harbourpointgolfclub.com

Kanturk (1971)
Fairyhill, Kanturk
(029) 50534

Kinsale Farrangalway (1993)
Farrangalway, Kinsale
(021) 477 4722
(021) 477 3114
office@kinsalegolf.com
www.kinsalegolf.com

Kinsale Ringenane (1912)
Ringenane, Belgooly, Kinsale
(021) 477 2197

Lee Valley G&CC (1993)
Clashanure, Ovens, Cork
(021) 733 1721
(021) 733 1695
reservations@leevalleygcc.ie
www.leevalleygcc.ie

Macroom (1924)
Lackaduve, Macroom
(026) 41072
(026) 41391
mcroomgc@lol.ie
C O'Sullivan (Mgr)
www.macroomgolfclub.com

Mahon (1980)
Clover Hill, Blackrock, Cork
(021) 429 2543
(021) 429 2604
mahon@golfnet.ie
Martin Groeger (086) 813 5769
www.mahongolfclub.com

Mallow (1948)
Ballyellis, Mallow
(022) 21145
(022) 42501
mallowgolfclubmanager@eircom .net
D Curtin (Sec/Mgr)
www.mallowgolfclub.net

Mitchelstown (1910)
Gurrane, Mitchelstown
(025) 24072
(025) 86631
info@mitchelstown-golf.com
Dan Kelleher
www.mitchelstown-golf.com

Monkstown (1908)
Parkgarriffe, Monkstown
(021) 484 1376
(021) 484 1722
office@monkstowngolfclub.com
H Madden (Sec/Mgr)
www.monkstowngolfclub.com

Muskerry (1907)
Carrigrohane, Co. Cork
(021) 438 5297
(021) 451 6860
muskgc@eircom.net
H Gallagher
www.muskerrygolfclub.ie

Old Head Golf Links (1997)
Kinsale
(021) 477 8444
(021) 477 8022
info@oldhead.com
www.oldhead.com

Raffeen Creek (1989)
Ringaskiddy
(021) 437 8430

Skibbereen (1904)
Licknavar, Skibbereen
(028) 21227
(028) 22994
info@skibbgolf.com
Club Aministrator
www.skibbgolf.com

Youghal (1898)
Knockaverry, Youghal
(024) 92787/92861
(024) 92641
youghalgolfclub@eircom.net
Margaret O'Sullivan
www.youghalgolfclub.ie

Co Donegal

Ballybofey & Stranorlar (1957)
The Glebe, Stranorlar
(074) 913 1093
(074) 913 0158
info@ballybofeyandstranorlar golfclub.com
Cathal Patton (074) 913 1093
www.ballybofeyandstranorlar golfclub.com

Ballyliffin (1947)
Ballyliffin, Inishowen
(07493) 76119
(07493) 76672
info@ballyliffingolfclub.com
John Farren (Gen Mgr)
www.ballyliffingolfclub.com

Buncrana (1951)
Public
Buncrana
(07493) 62279
buncranagc@eircom.net
F McGrory (Hon) (07493) 62279
www.buncranagolfclub.com

Bundoran (1894)
Bundoran
(07198) 41302
(07198) 42014
bundorangolfclub@eircom.net
Noreen Allen (Sec/Mgr)
www.bundorangolfclub.com

Cruit Island (1985)
Kincasslagh, Dunglow
(074) 954 3296
(074) 954 8029
www.homepage.eirecom.net/ ~cruitisland

Donegal (1959)
Murvagh, Laghey
(074) 973 4054
(074) 973 4377
info@donegalgolfclub.ie
Grainne Dorrian
www.donegalgolfclub.ie

Dunfanaghy (1906)
Kill, Dunfanaghy, Letterkenny
(074) 913 6335
(074) 913 6684
dunfanaghygolf@eircom.net
www.dunfanaghygolfclub.com

Greencastle (1892)
Greencastle
(074) 93 81013
(074) 93 81015
b_mc_caul@yahoo.com
Billy McCaul
www.greencastlegc.com

Gweedore (1926)
Pay and play
Magheragallon, Derrybeg, Letterkenny
(07495) 31140
eugenemccafferty@hotmail.com
Eugene McCafferty
www.gweedoregolfclub.com

Letterkenny (1913)
Barnhill, Letterkenny
(+353) 7491 21150
(+353) 7491 21175
info@letterkennygolfclub.com
Cynthia Fuery (Hon Sec) (+353) 7491 21150
www.letterkennygolfclub.com

Narin & Portnoo (1930)
Narin, Portnoo
(074) 954 5107
(074) 945 5994
narinportnoo@eircom.net
Daragh Lyons (PGA Professional)
www.narinportnoogolfclub.ie

North West (1891)
Lisfannon, Buncrana
(074) 936 0127
(074) 936 3284
secretary@northwestgolfclub.com
Eddie Curran (086) 604 7299
www.northwestgolfclub.com

Otway (1893)
Saltpans, Rathmullan, Letterkenny
(074) 915 1665
tolandkevin@eircom.net
Kevin Toland

Portsalon (1891)
Portsalon, Fanad
(074) 915 9459
(074) 915 9919
portsalongolfclub@eircom.net
P Doherty
www.portsalongolfclub.com

Redcastle (1983)
Redcastle, Moville
(074) 938 5555
(074) 938 2214

Rosapenna (1894)
Downings, Rosapenna
(074) 55301
(074) 55128
rosapenna@eircom.net
Frank Casey
www.rosapenna.ie

St Patricks Courses (1994)
Carrigart
(074) 55114
(074) 55250

Co Down

Ardglass (1896)
Castle Place, Ardglass BT30 7PP
(028) 4484 1219
(028) 4484 1841

✉ info@ardglassgolfclub.com
✍ Mrs D Turley
🖹 www.ardglassgolfclub.com

Ardminnan (1995)
Pay and play
15 Ardminnan Road, Portaferry BT22 1QJ
☎ **(028) 4277 1321**
🖷 (028) 4277 1321
✉ lesliejardine104@yahoo.co.uk
✍ L Jardine

Banbridge (1912)
116 Huntly Road, Banbridge BT32 3UR
☎ **(028) 4066 2211 (office)**
🖷 (028) 4066 9400
✉ info@banbridgegolfclub.com
✍ Mrs Sandra Duprey (Club Mgr)
🖹 www.banbridgegolfclub.com

Bangor (1903)
Broadway, Bangor BT20 4RH
☎ **(028) 9127 0922**
✉ office@bangorgolfclubni.co.uk
✍ Mr Stephen Bell
🖹 www.bangorgolfclubni.co.uk

Blackwood (1995)
150 Crawfordsburn Road, Bangor BT19 1GB
☎ **(028) 9185 2706**
🖷 (028) 9185 3785
✉ blackwoodgc@btconnect.com
✍ Chris Widdowson
🖹 www.blackwoodgc@btopenworld.com

Bright Castle (1970)
14 Coniamstown Road, Bright, Downpatrick BT30 8LU
☎ **(028) 4484 1319**

Carnalea (1927)
Station Road, Bangor BT19 1EZ
☎ **(028) 9127 0368**
🖷 (028) 9127 3989
✉ nicola@carnaleagolfclub.com
✍ Nicola Greene (028) 9127 0368
🖹 www.carnaleagolfclub.com

Clandeboye (1933)
Conlig, Newtownards BT23 7PN
☎ **(028) 9127 1767 (office)**
🖷 (028) 9147 3711
✉ info@cgc.ni.com
✍ Gary Steele (Gen Mgr)
🖹 www.cgc-ni.com

Crossgar (1993)
231 Derryboye Road, Crossgar BT30 9DL
☎ **(028) 4483 1523**

Donaghadee (1899)
84 Warren Road, Donaghadee BT21 0PQ
☎ **(028) 9188 3624**
🖷 (028) 9188 8891
✉ office@donaghadeegolfclub.net
✍ Jim Cullen
🖹 www.donaghadeegolfclub.com

Downpatrick (1930)
Saul Road, Downpatrick BT30 6PA
☎ **(028) 4461 5947**
✉ office@downpatrickgolf.org.uk
✍ Elaine Carson (028) 4461 5947
🖹 www.downpatrickgolf.org.uk

Helen's Bay (1896)
Golf Road, Helen's Bay, Bangor BT19 1TL
☎ **(028) 9185 2815 (office)**
🖷 (028) 9185 2660
✉ mail@helensbaygc.com
✍ John McCullough (Sec)
🖹 www.helensbaygc.com

Holywood (1904)
Nuns Walk, Demesne Road, Holywood BT18 9LE
☎ **(028) 9042 2138**
🖷 (028) 9042 5040
✉ mail@holywoodgolfclub.co.uk
✍ Paul Gray (Gen Mgr)
🖹 www.holywoodgolfclub.co.uk

Kilkeel (1948)
Mourne Park, Kilkeel BT34 4LB
☎ **(028) 4176 2296/5095**
🖷 (028) 4176 5579
✉ info@kilkeelgolfclub.org
✍ SC McBride (Hon)
🖹 www.kilkeelgolfclub.org

Kirkistown Castle (1902)
142 Main Road, Cloughey, Newtownards BT22 1JA
☎ **(028) 4277 1233**
🖷 (028) 4277 1699
✉ kirkistown@supanet.com
✍ R Coulter (028) 4277 1233
🖹 www.linksgolfkirkistown.com

Mahee Island (1929)
Comber, 14 Mahee Island, Newtownlands BT23 6ET
☎ **(028) 9754 1234**
🖷 (028) 9754 1234
✉ adrian.ross@ntlworld.com
🖹 www.maheeislandgolfclub.com

Mount Ober G&CC (1985)
Ballymaconaghy Road, Knockbracken, Belfast BT8 6SB
☎ **(028) 9079 2108 (Bookings)**
🖷 (028) 9070 5862
✉ info@mountober.com
✍ E Williams (Sec/Mgr)
🖹 www.mountober.com

Mourne (1946)
Club
36 Golf Links Road, Newcastle BT33 0AN
☎ **(028) 4372 3218/3889**
🖷 (028) 4372 2575
✉ info@mournegolfclub.co.uk
✍ P Keown (Hon)
🖹 www.mournegolfclub.co.uk

Ringdufferin G&CC (1993)
Ringdufferin Road, Toye, Downpatrick BT30 9PH
☎ **(028) 4482 8812**
✉ willismarshall@utvinternet.com

Rockmount (1995)
Proprietary
28 Drumalig Road, Carryduff, Belfast BT8 8EQ
☎ **(028) 9081 2279**
🖷 (028) 9081 5851
✉ d.patterson@btconnect.com
✍ D Patterson (Mgr)
🖹 www.rockmountgolfclub.com

Royal Belfast (1881)
Holywood, Craigavad BT18 0BP
☎ **(028) 9042 8165**
🖷 (028) 9042 1404
✉ royalbelfast@btconnect.com
✍ Mrs SH Morrison
🖹 www.royalbelfast.com

Royal County Down (1889)
Newcastle BT33 0AN
☎ **(028) 4372 3314**
🖷 (028) 4372 6281
✉ wilson@royalcountydown.org
✍ David Wilson
🖹 www.royalcountydown.org

Scrabo (1907)
233 Scrabo Road, Newtownards BT23 4SL
☎ **(028) 9181 2355**
🖷 (028) 9182 2919
✉ admin.scrabogc@btconnect.com
🖹 www.scrabo-golf-club.org

The Spa (1907)
Grove Road, Ballynahinch BT24 8PN
☎ **(028) 9756 2365**
🖷 (028) 9756 4158
✉ spagolfclub@btconnect.com
✍ TG Magee
🖹 www.spagolfclub.net

Temple (1994)
60 Church Road, Boardmills, Lisburn BT27 6UP
☎ **(028) 9263 9213**
🖷 (028) 9263 8637
✉ info@templegolf.com
✍ B McConnell (Mgr)
🖹 www.templegolf.com

Warrenpoint (1893)
Lower Dromore Rd, Warrenpoint BT34 3LN
☎ **(028) 4175 3695**
🖷 (028) 4175 2918
✉ office@warrenpointgolf.com
✍ D Moan
🖹 www.warrenpointgolf.com

Co Dublin

Balbriggan (1945)
Blackhall, Balbriggan
☎ **(01) 841 2229**
🖷 (01) 841 3927
✉ balbriggangolfclub@eircom.net
✍ Brian Finn (Hon Sec)
🖹 www.balbriggangolfclub.com

Balcarrick Golf Club (1972)
Corballis, Donabate
☎ **(01) 843 6957**
📠 (01) 843 6228
✉ balcarr@iol.ie
🗔 www.balcarrickgolfclub.com

Beaverstown (1985)
Beaverstown, Donabate
☎ **(01) 843 6439/6721**
📠 (01) 843 5059
✉ office@beaverstown.com
✍ Gillian Harris (Administrator)
🗔 www.beaverstown.com

Beech Park (1983)
Johnstown, Rathcoole
☎ **(01) 458 0522**
📠 (01) 458 8365
✉ info@beechpark.ie
✍ Mr K M Young (Gen Mgr)
🗔 www.beechpark.ie

Coldwinters (1994)
Newtown House, St Margaret's
☎ **(01) 864 0324**
📠 (01) 834 1400

Corrstown Golf Club (1993)
Corrstown, Killsallaghan
☎ **(01) 864 0533**
📠 (01) 864 0537
✉ info@corrstowngolfclub.com
✍ M Jeanes
🗔 www.corrstowngolfclub.com

Donabate (1925)
Balcarrick, Donabate
☎ **(01) 843 6346**
📠 (01) 843 4488
✉ info@donabategolfclub.com
🗔 www.donabategolfclub.com

Dublin Mountain (1993)
Gortlum, Brittas
☎ **(01) 458 2622**
📠 (01) 458 2048
✉ dmgc.ie
🗔 www.dublinmountaingolf.com

Dun Laoghaire (1910)
Eglinton Park, Tivoli Road, Dun Laoghaire
☎ **(01) 280 3916**
📠 (01) 280 4868
🗔 www.dunlaoghairegolfclub.ie

Forrest Little (1940)
Forrest Little, Cloghran, Swords
☎ **(01) 840 1763**
📠 (01) 840 1000
✉ margaret@forrestlittle.ie
✍ Kevin McIntyre
🗔 www.forrestlittle.com

Glencullen
Glencullen, Co Dublin
☎ **(01) 295 2895**
🗔 www.glencullengc.ie

Hermitage (1905)
Lucan
☎ **(01) 626 5396**
📠 (01) 623 8881
✉ hermitagegolf@eircom.net
✍ Eddie Farrell
🗔 www.hermitagegolf.ie

Citywest (1998)
City West Hotel, Saggert
☎ **(01) 401 0878**
📠 (01) 458 8756
✍ Tony Shine
🗔 www.citywesthotel.com

Hollywood Lakes (1992)
Ballyboughal, Co Dublin
☎ **(01) 843 3406/7**
📠 (01) 843 3002
✉ hollywoodlakesgc@eircom.net
✍ Seamus Kelly (Gen Mgr)
🗔 www.hollywoodlakesgolfclub.com

The Island Golf Club (1890)
Corballis, Donabate
☎ **+353 1843 6205**
📠 +353 1843 6860
✉ info@theislandgolfclub.com
✍ Ronan Smyth
🗔 www.theislandgolfclub.com

Killiney (1903)
Ballinclea Road, Killiney
☎ **(01) 285 2823**
📠 (01) 285 2861
✉ killineygolfclub@eircom.net
✍ MF Walsh CCM
🗔 www.killineygolfclub.ie

Kilternan (1987)
Kilternan
☎ **(01) 295 5559**
📠 (01) 295 5670
✉ kgc@kilternan-hotel.ie

Lucan (1897)
Celbridge Road, Lucan
☎ **(01) 628 0246**
📠 (01) 628 2929
✉ admin@lucangolf.ie
✍ Francis Duffy (Sec/Mgr)
🗔 www.lucangolfclub.ie

Luttrellstown Castle G&CC (1993)
Porterstown Road, Castleknock, Dublin 15
☎ **(353) 1 860 9600**
📠 (353) 1 860 9601
✉ info@luttrellstown.ie
✍ Colm Haunon
🗔 www.luttrellstowncastleresort.com

Malahide (1892)
Beechwood, The Grange, Malahide
☎ **(01) 846 1611**
📠 (01) 846 1270
✉ manager@malahidegolfclub.ie
✍ Mark Gannon (Gen Mgr)
🗔 www.malahidegolfclub.ie

Milltown (1907)
Lower Churchtown Road, Milltown, Dublin 14
☎ **(01) 497 6090**
📠 (01) 497 6008
✉ info@milltowngolfclub.ie
✍ J Burns (Gen Mgr)
🗔 www.milltowngolfclub.ie

Portmarnock (1894)
Portmarnock
☎ **(01) 846 2968 (Clubhouse)**
📠 (01) 846 2601
✍ JJ Quigley (01) 846 2968 (Gen Mgr)
🗔 www.portmarnockgolfclub.ie

Portmarnock Hotel & Golf Links (1995)
Proprietary
Strand Road, Portmarnock
☎ **(01) 846 1800**
📠 (01) 846 2442
✉ golfres@portmarnock.com
✍ Moira Cassidy (Golf Dir)
🗔 www.portmarnock.com

Rush (1943)
Rush
☎ **(01) 843 8177**
📠 (01) 843 8177
✉ info@rushgolfclub.com
✍ Noeline Quirke (Sec/Mgr)
🗔 www.rushgolfclub.com

Silloge Park Golf Club (2010)
Old Ballymun Road, Swords
☎ **(01) 842 9956**
✉ info@sillogeparkgolfclub.com
✍ Damien Connolly
🗔 www.sillogeparkgolfclub.com

Skerries (1905)
Hacketstown, Skerries
☎ **(01) 849 1567 (Clubhouse)**
📠 (01) 849 1591
✉ admin@skerriesgolfclub.ie
✍ I Fraher (01) 849 1567
🗔 www.skerriesgolfclub.ie

Slade Valley (1970)
Lynch Park, Brittas
☎ **(01) 458 2183**
📠 (01) 458 2784
✉ info@sladevalleygolfclub.ie
✍ D Clancy
🗔 www.sladevalleygolfclub.ie

The South County Golf Club (2002)
Lisheen Road, Brittas, Co Dublin
☎ **(01) 458 2965**
📠 (01) 458 2842
✉ info@southcountygolf.ie
✍ Michael Diskin (Gen Mgr)
🗔 www.southcountygolf.com

St Margaret's G&CC (1992)
St Margaret's, Dublin
☎ **(01) 864 0400**
📠 (01) 864 0408
✉ reservations@stmargaretsgolf.com
✍ Gary Kearney (Gen Mgr)
🗔 www.stmargaretsgolf.com

Swords (1996)
Balheary Avenue, Swords
☎ **(01) 840 9819/890 1030**
(01) 840 9819
info@swordsopengolfcourse.com
O McGuinness (Mgr)
www.swordsopengolfcourse.com

Turvey (1994)
Turvey Avenue, Donabate
☎ **(01) 843 5169**
(01) 843 5179
turveygc@eircom.net
Aoife Griffin
www.turveygolfclub.com

Westmanstown (1988)
Clonsilla, Dublin 15
☎ **(01) 820 5817**
(01) 820 5858
info@westmanstowngolfclub.ie
Edward Doyle (Director of Golf)
www.westmanstowngolfclub.ie

Woodbrook (1926)
Dublin Road, Bray
☎ **(01) 282 4799**
(01) 282 1950
golf@woodbrook.ie
www.woodbrook.ie

Dublin City

Carrickmines (1900)
Golf Lane, Carrickmines, Dublin 18
☎ **(01) 295 5972**
(01) 214 9674
carrickminesgolf@eircom.net
B Levis 00353 871682150 (Mobile)

Castle (1913)
Woodside Drive, Rathfarnham, Dublin 14
☎ **(01) 490 4207**
(01) 492 0264
info@castlegc.ie
John McCormack (Gen Mgr)
www.castlegc.ie

Clontarf (1912)
Donnycarney House, Malahide Road, Dublin 3
☎ **(01) 833 1892**
(01) 833 1933
info@clontarfgolfclub.ie
A Cahill (Mgr)
www.clontarfgolfclub.ie

Deer Park (1974)
Deer Park Hotel, Howth
☎ **(01) 832 6039**

Edmondstown (1944)
Rathfarnham, Dublin 16
☎ **(01) 493 2461**
(01) 493 3152
info@edmondstowngolfclub.ie
Mark Lynch (01) 493 1082
www.edmondstowngolfclub.ie

Elm Park (1925)
Nutley House, Donnybrook, Dublin 4
☎ **(01) 269 3438/269 3014**
(01) 269 4505
office@elmparkgolfclub.ie
A McCormack (01) 269 3438
www.elmparkgolfclub.ie

Grange (1910)
Whitechurch Road, Rathfarnham, Dublin 14
☎ **(01) 493 2889**
(01) 493 9490
administration@grangegolfclub.ie
Billy Meehan (Gen Mgr)
www.grangegolfclub.ie

Hazel Grove (1988)
Mount Seskin Road, Jobstown, Dublin 24
☎ **(01) 452 0911**

Howth (1916)
Carrickbrack Road, Sutton, Dublin 13
☎ **(01) 832 3055**
(01) 832 1793
gm@howthgolfclub.ie
Darragh Tighe MPGA
(01) 832 3055
www.howthgolfclub.ie

Kilmashogue (1994)
St Columba's College, Whitechurch, Dublin 16
☎ **(087) 274 9844**

Newlands (1910)
Newlands Cross, Dublin 22
☎ **(01) 459 3157**
(01) 459 3498
info@newlandsgolfclub.com
Gay Nolan (Gen Mgr)
www.newlandsgolf.com

Rathfarnham (1899)
Newtown, Dublin 16
☎ **(01) 493 1201/493 1561**
(01) 493 1561
info@rathfarnhamgolfclub.ie
John Lawler (01) 493 1201
www.rathfarnhamgolfclub.ie

Royal Dublin (1885)
North Bull Island Nature Reserve, Dollymount, Dublin 3
☎ **(01) 833 6346**
(01) 833 6504
info@theroyaldublingolfclub.com
Samual O'Beirne (Hon Sec)
www.theroyaldublingolfclub.com

St Anne's (1921)
North Bull Nature Reserve, Dollymount, Dublin 5
☎ **(01) 833 6471**
(01) 833 4618
info@stanneslinksgolf.com
Ted Power
www.stanneslinksgolf.com

Stackstown (1975)
Kellystown Road, Rathfarnham, Dublin 16
☎ **(01) 494 1993**
(01) 493 3934
info@stackstowngolfclub.ie
Raymond Murphy (Gen Mgr)
www.stackstowngolfclub.com

Sutton (1890)
Cush Point, Sutton, Dublin 13
☎ **(01) 832 3013**
(01) 832 1603
info@suttongolfclub.org
Frank Kennedy (Hon Sec)
www.suttongolfclub.org

Co Fermanagh

Castle Hume (1991)
Belleek Road, Enniskillen BT93 7ED
☎ **(028) 6632 7077**
(028) 6632 7076
info@castlehumegolf.com
Patrick Duffy (Admin)
www.castlehumegolf.com

Enniskillen (1896)
Castlecoole, Enniskillen BT74 6HZ
☎ **(028) 6632 5250**
(028) 6632 5250
enniskillengolfclub@mail.com
Darryl Robinson (Club Steward)
www.enniskillengolfclub.com

Co Galway

Ardacong
Milltown Road, Tuam, Co Galway
☎ **(093) 25525**

Athenry (1902)
Palmerstown, Oranmore
☎ **(091) 794466**
(091) 794971
athenrygc@eircom.net
www.athenrygolfclub.net

Ballinasloe (1894)
Rosgloss, Ballinasloe
☎ **(0905) 42126**
(0905) 42538

Bearna (1996)
Corboley, Bearna
☎ **(091) 592677**
(091) 592674
info@bearnagolfclub.com
Pat Donnellan
www.bearnagolfclub.com

Connemara (1973)
Public
Ballyconneely, Clifden
☎ **(095) 23502/23602**
(095) 23662
info@connemaragolflinks.net
K Burke (Sec/Mgr)
www.connemaragolflinks.com

Connemara Isles
Annaghvane, Lettermore, Connemara
☎ **(091) 572498**
(091) 572498

Curra West (1996)
Curra, Kylebrack, Loughrea
☎ **(091) 45121**

Galway (1895)
Blackrock, Salthill, Galway
☎ **(091) 522033**
🖷 (091) 529783
✉ info@galwaygolf.com
✍ P Fahy
🌐 www.galwaygolf.com

Galway Bay Golf Resort (1993)
Renville, Oranmore
☎ **+353 (91) 790711/2**
🖷 +353 (91) 792510
🌐 www.galwaybaygolfresort.com

Glenlo Abbey
Glenlo Abbey Hotel, Bushy Park, Galway
☎ **(091) 519698**
🖷 (091) 519699
🌐 www.glenlo.com

Gort (1924)
Castlequarter, Gort
☎ **(091) 632244**
🖷 (091) 632387
✉ info@gortgolf.com
🌐 www.gortgolf.com

Loughrea (1924)
Graigue, Loughrea
☎ **(091) 841049**
🖷 (091) 847472
✉ loughreagolfclub@eircom.net

Mountbellew (1929)
Shankill, Mountbellew, Ballinasloe
☎ **(090) 967 9259**
✉ mountbellewgc@eircom.net
✍ Padraic Costello
🌐 www.mountbellewgolfclub.com

Oughterard (1973)
Gortreevagh, Oughterard
☎ **(091) 552131**
🖷 (091) 552733
✉ oughterardgc@eircom.net
✍ Richard McNamarg
🌐 www.oughterardgolfclub.com

Portumna (1913)
Ennis Road, Portumna
☎ **(090) 97 41059**
🖷 (090) 97 41798
✉ portumnagc@eircom.net
✍ Michael Ryan (Secretary)
🌐 www.portumnagolfclub.ie

Tuam (1904)
Barnacurragh, Tuam
☎ **(093) 28993**
🖷 (093) 26003
✉ tuamgolfclub@eircom.net
✍ Mary Burns (Sec/Mgr)
🌐 www.tuamgolfclub.com

Co Kerry

Ardfert (1993)
Sackville, Ardfert, Tralee
☎ **(066) 713 4744**
🖷 (066) 713 4744

Ballybeggan Park
Ballybeggan, Tralee, Co Kerry
☎ **(066) 712 6188**

Ballybunion Golf Club (1893)
Sandhill Road, Ballybunion, Ireland
☎ **+353 (68) 27146**
🖷 +353 (68) 27387
✉ info@ballybuniongolfclub.ie
✍ Vari McGreevy
🌐 www.ballybuniongolfclub.ie

Ballyheigue Castle (1995)
Ballyheigue, Tralee
☎ **(066) 713 3555**
🖷 (066) 713 3934
✍ J Casey (Sec/Mgr)
🌐 www.ballyheiguecastlegolfclub.com

Beaufort (1994)
Churchtown, Beaufort, Killarney
☎ **(064) 44440**
🖷 (064) 44752
✉ beaufortgc@eircom.net
🌐 www.beaufortgolfclub.com

Castlegregory (1989)
Stradbally, Castlegregory
☎ **(066) 713 9444**
🖷 (066) 713 9958
✉ info@castlegregorygolflinks.com
✍ M Keane (Hon Sec)
🌐 www.castlegregorygolfclub.com

Ceann Sibeal (1924)
Ballyferriter
☎ **(066) 915 6255/6408**
🖷 (066) 915 6409
✉ dinglegc@iol.ie
✍ S Fahy (Mgr)
🌐 www.dinglelinks.com

Dooks (1889)
Glenbeigh
☎ **(066) 976 8205**
🖷 (066) 976 8476
✉ office@dooks.com
✍ Brian Hurley
🌐 www.dooks.com

Kenmare (1903)
Kenmare
☎ **(064) 6641291**
🖷 (064) 6642061
✉ info@kenmaregolfclub.com
✍ John Sullivan
🌐 www.kenmaregolfclub.com

Kerries (1995)
Tralee
☎ **(066) 712 2112**

Killarney (1893)
Mahoney's Point, Killarney
☎ **(064) 31034**
🖷 (064) 33065
✉ reservations@killarney-golf.com
🌐 www.killarney-golf.com

Killorglin (1992)
Stealroe, Killorglin
☎ **00353 (66) 9761 979**
🖷 00353 (66) 9761 437
✉ kilgolf@iol.ie
✍ Mike Ashe
🌐 www.killorglingolf.ie

Parknasilla (1974)
Parknasilla, Sneem
☎ **(064) 66 45145**
🖷 (064) 66 45323
✉ parknasillagolfclub@eircom.net
✍ Mr Sean McCarthy (Secretary)
🌐 www.parknasillahotel.ie

Ring of Kerry G&CC (1998)
Proprietary
Templenoe, Killarney
☎ **(064) 66 42000**
🖷 (064) 66 42533
✉ james@ringofkerrygolf.com
✍ James Mitchell (Gen Mgr)
🌐 www.ringofkerrygolf.com

Tralee (1896)
West Barrow, Ardfert, Tralee
☎ **(066) 713 6379**
🖷 (066) 713 6008
✉ info@traleegolfclub.com
✍ A Byrne (Gen Mgr)
🌐 www.traleegolfclub.com

Waterville Golf Links (1889)
Waterville Golf Links, Ring of Kerry, Waterville
☎ **+353-66-947 4102**
🖷 +353-66-947 4482
✉ wvgolf@iol.ie
✍ Noel Cronin (Sec/Mgr)
🌐 www.watervillegolflinks.ie

Co Kildare

Athy (1906)
Geraldine, Athy
☎ **(059) 863 1729**
🖷 (059) 863 4710
✉ info@athygolfclub.com
✍ Kathleen Gray (Sec/Administrator)
🌐 www.athygolfclub.com

Bodenstown (1972)
Bodenstown, Sallins
☎ **(045) 897096**
🖷 (045) 898126
✉ bodenstown@eircom.net
✍ Tom Keightley (0872 264133
🌐 www.bodenstown.com

Carton House (2002)
Carton House, Maynooth
☎ **+353 (0)1 505 2000**
+353 (0)1 651 7703
reservations@cartonhouse.com
Francis Howley (Director of Golf)
www.cartonhouse.com

Castlewarden G&CC (1989)
Straffan
☎ **(01) 458 9254**
(01) 458 8972
info@castlewardengolfclub.ie
Andy Callanan
www.castlewardengolfclub.ie

Celbridge Elm Hall
Elmhall, Celbridge, Co Kildare
☎ **(01) 628 8208**

Cill Dara (1920)
Little Curragh, Kildare Town
☎ **(045) 521295**

Craddockstown (1991)
Blessington Road, Naas
☎ **(045) 897610**
(045) 896968
enquiries@craddockstown.com
Pat Meagher
www.craddockstown.com

The Curragh (1883)
Curragh
☎ **(045) 441238/441714**
(045) 442476
curraghgolf@eircom.net
Ann Culliton (045) 441714
www.curraghgolf-club.com

Highfield Golf & Country Club (1992)
Proprietary
Carbury, Co. Kildare
☎ **(046) 973 1021**
(046) 973 1021
highfieldgolf@eircom.net
Philomena Duggan (Sec/Mgr)
www.highfield-golf.ie

The K Club (1991)
Straffan
☎ **(01) 601 7300**
(01) 601 7399
golf@kclub.ie
B Donald (Golf Dir) (01) 601 7302
www.kclub.ie

Kilkea Castle (1995)
Castledermot
☎ **(059) 914 5555**
(059) 914 5505
kilkeagolfclub@eircom.net
www.kilkeacastlehotelgolf.com

Killeen (1986)
Killeenbeg, Kill
☎ **(045) 866003**
(045) 875881
admin@killeengc.ie
M Kelly
www.killeengolf.com

Knockanally (1985)
Donadea, Naas, North Kildare
☎ **(045) 869322**
golf@knockanally.com
Helen Melady
www.knockanally.com

Naas (1896)
Kerdiffstown, Naas
☎ **(045) 874644**
(045) 896109
info@naasgolfclub.com
Denis Mahon (Mgr)
www.naasgolfclub.com

Newbridge (1997)
Tankardsgarden, Newbridge
☎ **(045) 486110**
(045) 446840

Co Kilkenny

Callan (1929)
Geraldine, Callan
☎ **(056) 7725136**
(056) 7755155
info@callangolfclub.com/manager@callangolfclub.com
Deirdre Power (Sec/Mgr) (056) 77 25136
www.callangolfclub.com

Castlecomer (1935)
Dromgoole, Castlecomer
☎ **(056) 4441139**
(056) 4441139
castlecomergolf@eircom.net
M Dooley (Hon)
www.castlecomergolfclub.com

Kilkenny (1896)
Glendine, Kilkenny
☎ **(056) 776 5400**
(056) 772 3593
enquiries@kilkennygolfclub.com
Sean Boland (056) 776 5400
www.kilkennygolfclub.com

Mount Juliet (1991)
Thomastown
☎ **(056) 777 3071**
(056) 777 3078
info@mountjuliet.com
William Kirby
www.mountjuliet.com

Co Laois

Abbeyleix (1895)
Rathmoyle, Abbeyleix
☎ **(057) 8731450**
info@abbeyleixgolfclub.ie
Gery O'Hara (Hon Sec)
www.abbeyleixgolfclub.ie

The Heath (1930)
The Heath, Portlaoise
☎ **(057) 864 6533**
(057) 864 6735
info@theheathgc.ie
Christy Crawford (Hon)
www.theheathgc.ie

The Heritage Golf & Spa Resort (2004)
Proprietary
The Heritage Golf & Spa Resort, Killenard
☎ **(057) 864 2321**
(057) 864 2392
info@theheritage.com
www.theheritage.com

Mountrath (1929)
Knockanina, Mountrath
☎ **(0502) 32558/32643**
(0502) 56735
mountrathgc@eircom.net
www.mountrathgolfclub.ie

Portarlington (1908)
Garryhinch, Portarlington
☎ **(057) 862 23115**
(057) 862 23044
portarlingtongc@eircom.net
www.portarlingtongolf.com

Rathdowney (1930)
Coulnaboul West, Rathdowney
☎ **(0505) 46170**
(0505) 46065
rathdowneygolf@eircom.net
Martin O'Brian (Hon) (0505) 46338
www.rathdowneygolfclub.com

Co Leitrim

Ballinamore (1941)
Creevy, Ballinamore
☎ **(078) 964 4346**
G Mahon (078) 964 4031,

Co Limerick

Abbeyfeale (1993)
Dromtrasna, Collins Abbeyfeale
☎ **(068) 32033**
(068) 51871
abbeyfealegolf@eircom.net
Conleth Dillon (Hon Sec)
www.abbeyfealegolfclub.com

Adare Manor (1900)
Adare
☎ **(061) 396204**
(061) 396800
info@adaremanorgolfclub.com
Dr Milo Spillane
www.adaremanorgolfclub.com

Castletroy (1937)
Golf Links Road, Castleroy, Co. Limerick
☎ **(061) 335753 (club)**
(061) 335373
golf@castletroygolfclub.ie
Louis Keegan (Gen Mgr)
www.castletroygolfclub.ie

For key to symbols and European dialling codes see page 725

Limerick (1891)
Ballyclough, Limerick
(061) 414083
(061) 319219
information@limerickgolfclub.ie
P Murray (Gen Mgr) (061) 415146
www.limerickgolfclub.ie

Limerick County G&CC (1994)
Ballyneety, Co. Limerick
(061) 351881
(061) 351384
info@limerickcounty.com
www.limerickcounty.com

Newcastle West (1938)
Rathgonan, Ardagh, Co. Limerick
(069) 76500
(069) 76511
info@newcastlewestgolf.com
John Whelan (Sec/Mgr)
www.newcastlewestgolf.com

Rathbane (1998)
Public
Rathbane, Crossagalla, Limerick
(061) 313655
(061) 313655

Co Londonderry

Benone Par Three
53 Benone Avenue, Benone, Limavady BT49 0LQ
(028) 7775 0555

Brown Trout (1984)
209 Agivey Road, Aghadowey, Coleraine BT51 4AD
(028) 7086 8209
(028) 7086 8878
bill@browntroutinn.com
B O'Hara (Sec/Mgr)
www.browntroutinn.com

Castlerock (1901)
65 Circular Road, Castlerock BT51 4TJ
(028) 7084 8314
(028) 7084 9440
info@castlerockgc.co.uk
M Steen (Sec/Mgr)
www.castlerockgc.co.uk

City of Derry (1912)
49 Victoria Road, Londonderry BT47 2PU
(028) 7134 6369
(028) 7131 0008
info@cityofderrygolfclub.com
Andrew A Meenagh
www.cityofderrygolfclub.com

Foyle (1994)
Proprietary
12 Alder Road, Londonderry BT48 8DB
(028) 7135 2222
(028) 7135 3967
mail@foylegolf.club24.co.uk
Rob Gallagher (028) 71 352222
www.foylegolfcentre.co.uk

Kilrea (1919)
47a Lisnagrot Road, Kilrea BT51 5SF
(028) 295 40044
kilreagc@hotmail.co.uk
M R Dean (028) 295 40044
www.kilreagolfclub.co.uk

Moyola Park (1976)
15 Curran Road, Castledawson, Magherafelt BT45 8DG
(028) 7946 8468
(028) 7946 8626
moyolapark@btconnect.com
S McKenna (Hon)
www.moyolapark.com

Portstewart (1894)
117 Strand Road, Portstewart BT55 7PG
(028) 7083 2015
(028) 7083 4097
info@portstewartgc.co.uk
www.portstewartgc.co.uk

Roe Park (1993)
Public/Hotel
Roe Park Golf Club, Radisson Blu Roe Park Resort, Roe Park, Limavady BT49 9LB
(028) 7776 0105
(028) 777 22313
roeparkgolf.limavady@RadissonBlu.com
Terry Kelly (028) 777 60105
www.radissonroepark.com

Traad Ponds
Shore Road, Magherafelt BT45 6LR
(028) 7941 8865

Co Longford

County Longford (1894)
Glack, Dublin Road, Longford
(043) 334 6310
(043) 334 7082
colonggolf@eircom.net
Ms Pauline Corry
www.countylongfordgolfclub.com

Co Louth

Ardee (1911)
Townparks, Ardee
(041) 685 3227
(041) 685 6137
ardeegolfclub@eircom.net
Noel Malone (Sec)
www.ardeegolfclub.com

Carnbeg (1996)
Carnbeg, Dundalk, Co Louth
(042) 933 2518
(042) 939 5731
carnbeggolfcourse@eircom.net
www.dundalk.parkinn.ie

County Louth (1892)
Baltray, Drogheda
(041) 988 1530
(041) 988 1531
reservations@countylouthgolfclub.com
M Delany
www.countylouthgolfclub.com

Dundalk (1904)
Blackrock, Dundalk
(042) 932 1731
(042) 932 2022
manager@dundalkgolfclub.ie
R Woods (Sec/Mgr)
www.dundalkgolfclub.ie

Greenore (1896)
Greenore
(042) 937 3212/3678
(042) 937 3678
greenoregolfclub@eircom.net
Linda Clarke
www.greenoregolfclub.com

Killinbeg (1991)
Killin Park, Dundalk
(042) 933 9303
(042) 932 0848

Seapoint (1993)
Termonfeckin, Drogheda
(041) 982 2333
(041) 982 2331
golflinks@seapoint.ie
www.seapointgolflinks.ie

Townley Hall (1994)
Tullyallen, Drogheda
(041) 984 2229
(041) 984 2229
townleyhall@oceanfree.net

Co Mayo

Achill (1951)
Keel, Achill
(098) 43456
(098) 43456
achillislandgolfclub@gmail.com
Hugo Boyle (087) 798 1225
www.achillgolf.com

Ashford Castle
Cong
(092) 46003

Ballina (1910)
Mossgrove, Shanaghy, Ballina
(096) 21050
(096) 21718
ballinagc@eircom.net
www.ballina-golf.com

Ballinrobe (1895)
Cloonacastle, Ballinrobe, Co Mayo
(094) 954 1118
(094) 954 1889
info@ballinrobegolfclub.com
John G Burke
www.ballinrobegolfclub.com

Ballyhaunis (1929)
Coolnaha, Ballyhaunis
(0907) 30014

Belmullet (1925)
Carne, Belmullet
(00353) 97 82292
pmcintyrecarne@gmail.com
Patrick Mc Intyre (Hon Sec)
www.belmulletgolfclub.ie

Castlebar (1910)
Hawthorn Avenue, Rocklands, Castlebar
(094) 21649
(094) 26088
info@castlebargolfclub.ie
Bernie Murray/Stephanie Ryan
www.castlebargolfclub.ie

Claremorris (1917)
Pay and play
Castlemacgarrett, Claremorris
(094) 937 1527
(094) 937 2919
info@claremorrisgolfclub.com
N McCarthy (Hon)
www.claremorrisgolfclub.com

Mulranny (1968)
Mulranny, Westport
(098) 36262

Swinford (1922)
Brabazon Park, Swinford
(+353) 94 925 1378
(+353) 94 925 1378

Westport (1908)
Carrowholly, Westport
(098) 28262
(098) 24648
info@westportgolfclub.com
Sean Durkan
www.westportgolfclub.com

Co Meath

Ashbourne (1991)
Archerstown, Ashbourne, Co.Meath
(01) 835 2005
(01) 835 9261
info@ashbournegolfclub.ie
Paul Wisniewski
www.ashbournegolfclub.ie

Black Bush (1987)
Thomastown, Dunshaughlin
(01) 825 0021
(01) 825 0400
info@blackbushgolfclub.ie
Kate O'Rourke (Admin)
(01) 825 0021
www.blackbushgolfclub.ie

County Meath (1898)
Newtownmoynagh, Trim
(046) 9431463
(046) 9437554
www.trimgolf.net

Glebe
Kildalkey Road, Trim, Meath
(00353) 4694 31926
(00353) 4694 31926
glebegc@eircom.net
www.glebegolfclub.com

Gormanston College (1961)
Franciscan College, Gormanston
(01) 841 2203
(01) 841 2685
Br Laurence Brady
www.gormanstoncollege.ie

Headfort (1928)
Kells
(046) 924 0146
(046) 924 9282
hgcadmin@eircom.net
www.headfortgolfclub.ie

Kilcock (1985)
Gallow, Kilcock
(01) 628 7592
(01) 628 7283
info@kilcockgolfclub.ie
www.kilcockgolfclub.ie

Laytown & Bettystown (1909)
Bettystown, Co. Meath
(041) 982 7170
(041) 982 8506
links@landb.ie
Helen Finnegan
www.landb.ie

Moor Park (1993)
Moortown, Navan
(046) 27661

Navan (1996)
Public
Proudstown, Navan, Co Meath
(046) 907 2888
(046) 907 6722
info@navangolfclub.ie
Sheila Slattery
www.navangolfclub.ie

Royal Tara (1906)
Bellinter, Navan
(046) 902 5508/902 5584
(046) 902 6684
info@royaltaragolfclub.com
John McGarth (Hon)
www.royaltaragolfclub.com

Summerhill
Agher, Rathmoylan, Co Meath
(046) 955 7857

Co Monaghan

Castleblayney Golf Club, Concrawood (1985)
Onomy, Castleblayney
(042) 974 9485
(042) 975 4576
info@concrawood.ie
Adrian Kelly
www.concrawood.ie

Clones (1913)
Hilton Demesne, Clones
(047) 56017
(047) 56017
clonesgolfclub@eircom.net
Paul Fitzpatrick (087) 766 1778
www.clonesgolfclub.com

Nuremore Hotel & CC (1964)
Nuremore Hotel, Carrickmacross
(042) 966 1438
(042) 966 1853
info@nuremore.com
Maurice Cassidy (Director)
www.nuremore.com

Rossmore (1916)
Rossmore Park, Cootehill Road, Monaghan
(047) 81316
(047) 71227
rossmoregolfclub@eircom.net
www.rossmoregolfclub.com

Co Offaly

Birr (1893)
The Glenns, Birr
(057) 91 20082
(057) 91 22155
birrgolfclub@eircom.net
Tony Hogan (Hon)
www.birrgolfclub.ie

Castle Barna (1992)
Castlebarnagh, Daingean, Offaly
(057) 935 3384
(057) 935 3077
info@castlebarna.ie
E Mangan
www.castlebarna.ie

Edenderry (1910)
Kishawanny, Edenderry
(046) 973 1072
(046) 973 3911
enquiries@edenderrygolfclub.com
www.edenderrygolfclub.com

Esker Hills G&CC (1996)
Proprietary
Tullamore, Co Offaly
(057) 93 55999
(057) 93 55021
info@eskerhillsgolf.com
C Guinan
www.eskerhillsgolf.com

Tullamore (1896)
Brookfield, Tullamore
(057) 93 21439
(057) 83 41806
tullamoregolfclub@eircom.net
Ann Marie Cunniffe (057) 93 21439
www.tullamoregolfclub.ie

Co Roscommon

Athlone (1892)
Hodson Bay, Athlone
(090) 649 2073/649 2235
(090) 649 4080
athlonegolfclub@eircom.net

For key to symbols and European dialling codes see page 725

✍ I Dockery
▤ www.athlonegolfclub.ie

Ballaghaderreen (1936)
Aughalustia, Ballaghaderreen
☎ **(094) 986 0295**
✉ info@ballaghaderreengolfclub.com
✍ Hon Secretary
▤ www.ballaghaderreengolfclub.com

Boyle (1911)
Knockadoo, Brusna, Boyle
☎ **(071) 966 2594**
✍ J Mooney (Hon) (087) 776 0161

Castlerea (1905)
Clonallis, Castlerea
☎ **(0871) 278066**
✉ castlereagolf@oceanfree.net
✍ Cathering O'Loughlin
▤ www.castlereagolfclub.com

Roscommon (1904)
Mote Park, Roscommon
☎ **(09066) 26382**
℻ (09066) 26043
✉ rosgolf@eircom.net

Strokestown (1995)
Strokestown, Co Roscommon
☎ **(07196) 33660**
✉ strokestowngolfclub@gmail.com
✍ L Glover (Hon)
▤ www.strokestowngolfclub.com

Co Sligo

Ballymote (1943)
Ballinascarrow, Ballymote
☎ **(071) 918 3504**
℻ (071) 918 3504
✉ ballymotegolfclub@gmail.ie
✍ J O'Connor
▤ www.ballymotegolfclub.com

County Sligo (1894)
Rosses Point
☎ **(071) 9177134/9177186**
℻ (071) 9177460
✉ teresa@countysligogolfclub.ie
✍ David O'Donovan
▤ www.countysligogolfclub.ie

Enniscrone (1931)
Ballina Road, Enniscrone
☎ **(096) 36297**
℻ (096) 36657
✉ enniscronegolf@eircom.net
✍ Pat Sweeney (Sec/Mgr)
▤ www.enniscronegolf.com

Strandhill (1932)
Strandhill
☎ **(00353) 71 91 68188**
℻ (00353) 71 91 68811
✉ strandhillgc@eircom.net
▤ www.strandhillgc.com

Tubbercurry (1990)
Ballymote Road, Tubbercurry
☎ **(071) 918 5849 (Societies)**
(086) 8306174
✉ contact@tubbercurrygolfclub.com
✍ Billy Kilgannon (071) 918 6124
▤ www.tubbercurrygolfclub.com

Co Tipperary

Ballykisteen Hotel & Golf Resort (1994)
Proprietary
Ballykisteen, Limerick Junction
☎ **(+353) 062 33333 (hotel)**
℻ (+353) 062 31555
✉ golf.ballykisteen@ballykisteenhotel.com
▤ www.ballykisteenhotel.com

Cahir Park (1967)
Kilcommon, Cahir, Co Tipperary
☎ **(052) 7441474**
℻ (052) 7442717
✉ cahirgolfclub@hotmail.com
✍ Paul Adamson (Club Sec)
▤ www.cahirgolfclub.com

Carrick-on-Suir (1939)
Garravoone, Carrick-on-Suir, County Tipperary
☎ **(051) 640047**
℻ (051) 640558
✉ info@carrickgolfclub.com
✍ Michael Kelly (Hon Sec)
▤ www.carrickgolfclub.com

Clonmel (1911)
Lyreanearla, Mountain Road, Clonmel
☎ **(052) 61 24050**
℻ (052) 61 83349
✉ cgc@indigo.ie
✍ A Myles-Keating (052) 6124050 (Ext 20)
▤ www.clonmelgolfclub.com

Dundrum Golf & Leisure Resort (1993)
Dundrum, Cashel
☎ **(062) 71717**
✉ golfshop@dundrumhouse.ie
✍ William Crowe (Mgr) (062) 71717
▤ www.dundrumhousehotel.com

Nenagh (1929)
Beechwood, Nenagh
☎ **(067) 31476**
℻ (067) 34808
✉ nenaghgolfclub@eircom.net
✍ Maeve De Loughry
▤ www.nenaghgolfclub.com

Roscrea (1892)
Derryvale, Roscrea
☎ **00353 (0) 505 21130**
℻ 00353 (0) 505 23410
✉ info@roscreagolfclub.ie
✍ Steve Crofton
▤ www.roscreagolfclub.ie

Slievenamon (1999)
Proprietary
Clonacody, Lisronagh, Co Tipperary
☎ **(052) 61 32213**
℻ (052) 61 30875
✉ info@slievnamongolfclub.com
✍ B Kenny (052) 61 32213
▤ www.slievnamongolfclub.com

Templemore (1970)
Manna South, Templemore
☎ **(0504) 32923/31400**
✉ johnkm@tinet.ie
✍ John Hackett

Thurles (1909)
Turtulla, Thurles
☎ **(0504) 21983**
℻ (0504) 90806
✉ office@thurlesgolfclub.com
✍ Tom Ryan (Hon Sec)
▤ www.thurlesgolfclub.com

Tipperary (1896)
Rathanny, Tipperary
☎ **(062) 51119**
✉ tipperarygolfclub@eircom.net
✍ Michael Tobin (Sec/Mgr)
▤ www.tipperarygolfclub.com

Co Tyrone

Auchnacloy (1995)
Pay and play
99A Tullyvar Road, Auchnacloy BT69 6BL
☎ **(028) 8255 7050**
℻ (028) 8555 7050
✉ Sidney.houston@yahoo.co.uk
✍ Sidney Houston
▤ www.irishgolfcourses.co.uk/auchnacloy

Benburb Valley
Maydown Road, Benburb BT71 7LJ
☎ **(028) 3754 9868**

Dungannon (1890)
34 Springfield Lane, Mullaghmore, Dungannon BT70 1QX
☎ **(028) 8772 2098**
℻ (028) 8772 7338
✉ dungannongolfclub2009@hotmail.co.uk
✍ S T Hughes
▤ www.dungannongolfclub.com

Fintona (1904)
Eccleville Desmesne, 1 Kiln Street, Fintona BT78 2BJ
☎ **(028) 8284 1480**
℻ (028) 8284 1480
✉ fintonagolfclub@btconnect.com

Killymoon (1889)
200 Killymoon Road, Cookstown BT80 8TW
☎ **(028) 8676 3762**
℻ (028) 8676 3762
✉ killymoongolf@btconnect.com
✍ N Weir
▤ www.killymoongolfclub.com

Newtownstewart (1914)
38 Golf Course Road, Newtownstewart BT78 4HU
☎ **(028) 8166 1466**

(028) 8166 2506
newtown.stewart@lineone.net
Lorraine Donnell (Administrator)
www.newtownstewartgolfclub.com

Omagh (1910)
83A Dublin Road, Omagh BT78 1HQ
(028) 8224 3160/1442
(028) 8224 3160

Strabane (1908)
Ballycolman, Strabane BT82 9PH
(028) 7138 2271/2007
(028) 7188 6514
strabanegc@btconnect.com
Claire Keys
www.strabanegolfclub.co.uk

Co Waterford

Dungarvan (1924)
Knocknagranagh, Dungarvan
(058) 43310/41605
(058) 44113
dungarvangc@eircom.net
Irene Lynch (Mgr)
www.dungarvangolfclub.com

Dunmore East (1993)
Proprietary
Dunmore East
(051) 383151
(051) 383151
info@dunmoreeastgolfclub.ie
Alan Skehan
www.dunmoreeastgolfclub.ie

Faithlegg (1993)
Faithlegg House, Faithlegg
(051) 380587/380592
(051) 382010
golf@fhh.ie
Ryan Hunt (051) 380588
www.faithlegg.com

Gold Coast (1993)
Ballinacourty, Dungarvan
(058) 44055
(058) 43378
info@goldcoastgolfclub.com
Mark Lenihan/Brendan O'Brien
www.goldcoastgolfclub.com

Lismore (1965)
Ballyin, Lismore
(058) 54026
(058) 53338
lismoregolfclub@eircom.net
W Henry
www.lismoregolf.org

Tramore (1894)
Newtown, Tramore
(051) 386170/381247
info@tramoregolfclub.com
Owen Kavanagh (Hon Sec)
www.tramoregolfclub.com

Waterford (1912)
Newrath, Waterford
+353 (0) 51 876748
+353 (0) 51 853405
info@waterfordgolfclub.com
Damien Maquire (Sec/Mgr)
www.waterfordgolfclub.com

Waterford Castle (1991)
Proprietary
The Island, Ballinakill, Waterford
(051) 871633
(051) 871634
golf@waterfordcastle.com
www.waterfordcastle.com

West Waterford G&CC (1993)
Dungarvan
(058) 43216/41475
(058) 44343
info@westwaterfordgolf.com
A Spratt (Director)
www.westwaterfordgolf.com

Co Westmeath

Ballinlough Castle
Clonmellon, Co Westmeath
(044) 64544

Delvin Castle (1992)
Clonyn, Delvin
(044) 96 64315
info@delvincastlegolf.com
F Dillon
www.delvincastlegolf.com

Glasson Country House Hotel and Golf Club (1993)
Glasson, Athlone
00353 (0) 90 6485120
00353 (0) 90 6485444
info@glassongolf.ie
Gareth Jones
www.glassoncountryhouse.ie

Moate (1900)
Aghanargit, Moate
(090) 648 1271
(090) 648 2645
moategolfclub@eircom.net
A O'Brien
www.moategolfclub.ie

Mount Temple G&CC (1991)
Proprietary
Mount Temple, Moate
(090) 648 1841
mounttemple@eircom.net
M Dolan
www.mounttemplegolfclub.com

Mullingar (1894)
Belvedere, Mullingar
(0 0353 44) 934 8366
(0 0353 44) 934 1499
mullingargolfclub@hotmail.com
www.mullingargolfclub.com

Co Wexford

Courtown (1936)
Kiltennel, Gorey
(053) 942 5166
(053) 942 5553
info@courtowngolfclub.com
S O'Hara
www.courtowngolfclub.com

Enniscorthy (1906)
Knockmarshall, Enniscorthy
(053) 92 33191
(053) 92 37637
honsec@enniscorthygc.ie
John Cullen
www.enniscorthygc.ie

New Ross (1905)
Tinneranny, New Ross
(051) 421433
(051) 420098
newrossgolf@eircom.net
www.newrossgolfclub.net

Rosslare (1905)
Rosslare Strand, Rosslare
(053) 913 2203 (office)
(053) 913 2263
office@rosslaregolf.com
Frank Codd (Hon Sec)
www.rosslaregolf.com

St Helen's Bay (1993)
Proprietary
St Helen's, Kilrane, Rosslare Harbour
(053) 91 33234
(053) 91 33803
info@sthelensbay.com
www.sthelensbay.com

Tara Glen (1984)
Ballymoney, Gorey, Co Wexford
(053) 942 5413
(053) 942 5612
taraglenplc@eircom.net
Marion Siggins
www.tataglen.ie

Wexford (1960)
Mulgannon, Wexford
(05391) 42238
(05391) 42243
info@wexfordgolfclub.ie
Roy Doyle (Hon Sec)
www.wexfordgolfclub.ie

Co Wicklow

Arklow (1927)
Abbeylands, Arklow
(0402) 32492
(0402) 91604
arklowgolflinks@eircom.net
D Canavan (Hon Sec)/D Roche (Mgr)
www.arklowgolfclublinks.com

Baltinglass (1928)
Baltinglass
☎ **(059) 648 1350**
℻ (059) 648 2842
✉ baltinglassgolfclub@eircom.net
🌐 www.baltinglassgolfclub.ie

Blainroe (1978)
Blainroe
☎ **(0404) 68168**
℻ (0404) 69369
✉ info@blainroe.com
✍ Patrick Bradshaw
🌐 www.blainroe.com

Boystown
Baltyboys, Blessington, Co Wicklow
☎ **(045) 867146**

Bray (1897)
Greystones Road, Bray
☎ **(01) 276 3200**
℻ (01) 276 3262
✉ info@braygolfclub.com
🌐 www.braygolfclub.com

Charlesland (1992)
Greystones
☎ **(01) 287 4350**
℻ (01) 287 0078
✉ teetimes@charlesland.com
✍ Gerry O'Brien (Mgr)
🌐 www.charlesland.com

Delgany (1908)
Delgany
☎ **(01) 287 4536**
℻ (01) 287 3977
✉ delganygolf@eircom.net
✍ Denzil Jones (Hon Sec)
🌐 www.delganygolfclub.com

Djouce (1995)
Roundwood
☎ **(01) 281 8585**
✉ djoucegolfclub@gmail.com
✍ D McGillycuddy (Mgr)
🌐 www.djoucegolfclub.com

Druid's Glen (1995)
Newtownmountkennedy
☎ **(01) 287 3600**
℻ (01) 287 3699
✉ info@druidsglen.ie
✍ D Flinn (Gen Mgr)
🌐 www.druidsglen.ie

Druid's Heath (2003)
Newtownmountkennedy
☎ **(01) 287 3600**
℻ (01) 287 3699
✉ info@druidsglen.ie
✍ D Flinn (Gen Mgr)
🌐 www.druidsglen.ie

The European Club (1989)
Brittas Bay, Wicklow
☎ **(0404) 47415**
℻ (0404) 47449
✉ info@theeuropeanclub.com
🌐 www.theeuropeanclub.com

Glen of the Downs (1998)
Coolnaskeagh, Delgany, Co Wicklow
☎ **(01) 287 6240**
℻ (01) 287 0063
✉ info@glenofthedowns.com
✍ Derek Murphy
🌐 www.glenofthedowns.com

Glenmalure (1991)
Greenane, Rathdrum
☎ **(0404) 46679**
✉ info@glenmaluregolf.ie
✍ Tina O'Shaughnessy (Hon Sec)
🌐 www.glenmaluregolf.com

Greystones (1895)
Greystones
☎ **(01) 287 4136**
℻ (01) 287 3749
✉ secretary@greystonesgc.com
✍ Angus Murray (Mgr)
🌐 www.greystonesgc.com

Kilcoole (1992)
Kilcoole
☎ **(01) 287 2066**
℻ (01) 201 0497
✉ adminkg@eircom.net
🌐 www.kilkoolegolfclub.com

Old Conna (1987)
Ferndale Road, Bray
☎ **(01) 282 6055**
℻ (01) 282 5611
✉ info@oldconna.com
✍ Tom Sheridan (Gen Mgr)
🌐 www.oldconna.com

Powerscourt (East) (1996)
Powerscourt Estate, Enniskerry
☎ **(01) 204 6033**
℻ (01) 276 1303
✍ B Gibbons (Mgr)
🌐 www.powerscourt.ie

Powerscourt (West) (2003)
Powerscourt Estate, Enniskerry
☎ **(01) 204 6033**
℻ (01) 276 1303
✍ B Gibbons (Mgr)
🌐 www.powerscourt.ie

Rathsallagh (1993)
Proprietary
Dunlavin
☎ **(045) 403316**
℻ (045) 403295
✉ info@rathsallagh.com/golf @rathsallagh.com
✍ J O'Flynn (045) 403316
🌐 www.rathsallagh.com

Roundwood (1995)
Ballinahinch, Newtownmountkennedy
☎ **(01) 281 8488**
℻ (01) 284 3642
✉ rwood@indigo.ie
🌐 www.roundwoodgolf.com

Tulfarris (1987)
Blessington Lakes, Blessington
☎ **(045) 867644**
℻ (045) 867601
✉ golf@tulfarris.com

Vartry Lakes (1997)
Proprietary
Roundwood
☎ **(01) 281 7006**
℻ (01) 281 7006
🌐 www.wicklow.ie

Wicklow (1904)
Dunbur Road, Wicklow
☎ **(0404) 67379**
℻ (0404(64756
✉ info@wicklowgolfclub.ie
✍ J Kelly
🌐 www.wicklowgolfclub.ie

Woodenbridge (1884)
Vale of Avoca, Arklow
☎ **(0402) 35202**
℻ (0402) 35754
✉ reception@woodenbridge.ie
✍ Gerry Coloman
🌐 www.woodenbridgegolfclub.com

Scotland

Aberdeenshire

Aboyne (1883)
Formaston Park, Aboyne AB34 5HP
☎ **(013398) 86328**
(013398) 87078
aboynegolfclub@btconnect.com
Mr Allan Taylor (013398) 87078
www.aboynegolfclub.co.uk

Aboyne Loch Golf Centre (2000)
Pay and play
Aboyne Loch, Aboyne AB34 5BR
☎ **(013398) 86444**
(013398) 86488
info@thelodgeontheloch.com
www.thelodgeontheloch.com

Alford (1982)
Montgarrie Road, Alford AB33 8AE
☎ **(019755) 62178**
(019755) 64910
info@alford-golf-club.co.uk
Mrs Julie Alexander
www.alford-golf-club.co.uk

Auchenblae Golf Course (1894)
Pay and play
Auchenblae, Laurencekirk AB30 1TX
☎ **(01561) 320002 (Group Bookings)**
J Thomson (01561) 320245
www.auchenblaegolfcourse.co.uk

Ballater (1892)
Victoria Road, Ballater AB35 5LX
☎ **(013397) 55567**
sec@ballatergolfclub.co.uk
Colin Smith
www.ballatergolfclub.co.uk

Ballindalloch Castle (2003)
Pay and play
Lagmore, Ballindalloch, Banffshire AB37 9AA
☎ **(01807) 500305**
golf@ballindallochcastle.co.uk
www.ballindallochcastle.co.uk

Banchory (1904)
Kinneskie Road, Banchory AB31 5TA
☎ **(01330) 822365**
(01330) 822491
bgc.secretary@btconnect.com
Mrs A Smart
www.banchorygolfclub.co.uk

Braemar (1902)
Cluniebank Road, Braemar AB35 5XX
☎ **(013397) 41618**
info@braemargolfclub.co.uk
C McIntosh (013397) 41618
www.braemargolfclub.co.uk

Craibstone (1999)
Public
Craibstone Estate, Bucksburn, Aberdeen AB29 9YA
☎ **(01224) 716777**
golf@marshall-leisure.co.uk
Iain Buchan

Cruden Bay (1899)
Aulton Road, Cruden Bay, Peterhead AB42 0NN
☎ **(01779) 812285**
(01779) 812945
robbie@crudenbaygolfclub.co.uk
Mr R G Stewart (PGA Dir of Golf)
www.crudenbaygolfclub.co.uk

Cullen (1879)
The Links, Cullen, Buckie AB56 4WB
☎ **(01542) 840685**
cullengolfclub@btinternet.com
Mrs H Bavidge
www.cullengolfclub.co.uk

Duff House Royal Golf Club (1910)
The Barnyards, Banff AB45 3SX
☎ **(01261) 812062**
(01261) 812224
manager@duffhouseroyal.com
www.duffhouseroyal.com

Fraserburgh (1777)
Philorth Links, Fraserburgh AB43 8TL
☎ **(01346) 516616**
secretary@fraserburghgolfclub.org
Lorraine Duncan
www.fraserburghgolfclub.org

Huntly (1892)
Cooper Park, Huntly AB54 4SH
☎ **(01466) 792643**
(01466) 792643
huntlygc@btconnect.com
A Donald/Kathleen Raeburn
www.huntlygc.com

Inchmarlo (1995)
Proprietary
Glassel Road, Banchory AB31 4BQ
☎ **(01330) 826424**
(01330) 826425
secretary@inchmarlo.com
Andrew Shinie (01330) 826427
www.inchmarlogolf.com

Insch (1906)
Golf Terrace, Insch AB52 6JY
☎ **(01464) 820363**
administrator@inschgolfclub.co.uk
Sarah Ellis (Administrator)
www.inschgolfclub.co.uk

Inverallochy
Public
Whitelink, Inverallochy, Fraserburgh AB43 8XY
☎ **(01346) 582000**
(01346) 582000
inverallochygolf@btconnect.com
GM Young
www.inverallochygolfclub.com

Inverurie (1923)
Davah Wood, Inverurie AB51 5JB
☎ **(01467) 624080**
(01467) 672869
administrator@inveruriegc.co.uk
Alan Donald (01467) 624080
www.inveruriegc.co.uk

Keith (1963)
Mar Court, Fife Keith, Keith AB55 5GF
☎ **(01542) 882469**
secretary@keithgolfclub.co.uk
Diane Morrison
www.keithgolfclub.co.uk

Kemnay (1908)
Monymusk Road, Kemnay AB51 5RA
☎ **(01467) 642225**
(01467) 643561
administrator@kemnaygolfclub.co.uk
F Webster (Secretary)
www.kemnaygolfclub.co.uk

Kintore (1911)
Balbithan Road, Kintore AB51 0UR
☎ **(01467) 632631**
(01467) 632995
kintoregolfclub@lineone.net
C Lindsay
www.kintoregolfclub.net

Longside (1973)
West End, Longside, Peterhead AB42 4XJ
☎ **(01779) 821558**
info@longsidegolf.wanadoo.co.uk
J Taylor
www.longsidegolfclub.co.uk

Lumphanan (1924)
Owned privately
Main Road, Lumphanan, Banchory AB31 4PY
☎ **(01339) 883480**
info@lumphanangolfclub.co.uk
Y Taite (Hon Sec) (01339) 883696
www.lumphanangolfclub.co.uk

McDonald (1927)
Hospital Road, Ellon AB41 9AW
☎ **(01358) 720576**
(01358) 720001
mcdonald.golf@virgin.net
G Ironside
www.ellongolfclub.co.uk

Meldrum House (1998)
Meldrum House Estate, Oldmeldrum AB51 0AE
☎ **(01651) 873553**
(01651) 873635
info@meldrumhousegolfclub.co.uk
www.meldrumhousegolfclub.com

Newburgh-on-Ythan (1888)
Beach Road, Newburgh, Aberdeenshire AB41 6BY
☎ **(01358) 789058**
(01358) 788104
secretary@newburghgolfclub.co.uk
Administrator: (01358) 789084
www.newburghgolfclub.co.uk

Newmachar (1989)
Swailend, Newmachar, Aberdeen AB21 7UU
☎ **(01651) 863002**
(01651) 863055
info@newmachargolfclub.co.uk
Alasdair MacGregor
www.newmachargolfclub.co.uk

Oldmeldrum (1885)
Kirk Brae, Oldmeldrum AB51 0DJ
☎ **(01651) 872648**
admin@oldmeldrumgolf.co.uk
Hamish Dingwall (Club Co-ordinator)
www.oldmeldrumgolf.co.uk

Peterhead (1841)
Craigewan Links, Peterhead AB42 1LT
☎ **(01779) 472149/480725**
(01779) 480725
phdgc@freenetname.co.uk
www.peterheadgolfclub.co.uk

Rosehearty (1874)
c/o Mason's Arms Hotel, Rosehearty, Fraserburgh AB43 7JJ
☎ **(01346) 571250 (Capt)**
(01346) 571306
scotthornal@cbtinternet.com

Rothes (1990)
Proprietary
Blackhall, Rothes, Aberlour AB38 7AN
☎ **(01340) 831443**
(01340) 831443
rothesgolfclub@tiscali.co.uk
Kenneth MacPhee (01340) 831676
www.rothesgolfclub.co.uk

Royal Tarlair (1926)
Buchan Street, Macduff AB44 1TA
☎ **(01261) 832897**
(01261) 833455
info@royaltarlair.co.uk
Mrs Muriel McMurray
www.royaltarlair.co.uk

Stonehaven (1888)
Cowie, Stonehaven AB39 3RH
☎ **(01569) 762124**
(01569) 765973
info@stonehavengolfclub.com
Mrs M H Duncan
www.stonehavengolfclub.com

Strathlene (1877)
Portessie, Buckie AB56 4DJ
☎ **(01542) 831798**
strathlenegc@gmail.com
David Lyun
www.strathlenegolfclub.co.uk

Tarland (1908)
Aberdeen Road, Tarland AB34 4TB
☎ **(013398) 81000**
(013398) 81000
secretary@tarlandgolfclub.co.uk
Mrs C Foreman (admin) (019756) 51484
www.tarlandgolfclub.co.uk

Torphins (1896)
Bog Road, Torphins AB31 4JU
☎ **(013398) 82115**
stuartmacgregor5@btinternet.com
S MacGregor (013398) 82402
www.torphinsgolfclub.com

Turriff (1896)
Rosehall, Turriff AB53 4HD
☎ **(01888) 562982 Pro Shop (01888) 563025**
(01888) 568050
secretary@turriffgolf.sol.co.uk
M Smart
www.turriffgolfclub.com

Aberdeen Clubs

Bon Accord (1872)
Club
19 Golf Road, Aberdeen AB24 5QB
☎ **(01224) 633464**

Caledonian (1899)
Club
20 Golf Road, Aberdeen AB2 1QB
☎ **(01224) 632443**

Northern (1897)
Public
22 Golf Road, Aberdeen AB24 5QB
☎ **(01224) 636440**
(01224) 622679
ngcgolf@hotmail.com
D Johnstone
www.northerngolfclub.co.uk

Aberdeen Courses

Auchmill (1975)
Bonnyview Road, West Heatheryfold, Aberdeen AB16 7FQ
☎ **(01224) 715214**
(01224) 715226
auchmill.golf@btconnect.com
Yvonne Sangster (01224) 715214
www.auchmill.co.uk

Balnagask (1955)
Public
St Fitticks Road, Aberdeen
☎ **(01224) 871286**
(01224) 873418
nicebay@btconnect.com
W Gordon

Deeside (1903)
Golf Road, Bieldside, Aberdeen AB15 9DL
☎ **(01224) 869457**
(01224) 861800
admin@deesidegolfclub.com
Ms D Pern (01224) 869457
www.deesidegolfclub.com

Fyvie (2003)
Pay and play
Fyvie, Turriff, Aberdeenshire AB53 8QR
☎ **(01651) 891166**
(01651) 891166
info@fyviegolfcourse.co.uk
Alexander Rankin
www.fyviegolfcourse.co.uk

Murcar Links (1909)
Bridge of Don, Aberdeen AB23 8BD
☎ **(01224) 704354**
(01224) 704354
golf@murcarlinks.com
Carol O'Neill
www.murcarlinks.com

Peterculter (1989)
Proprietary
Oldtown, Burnside Road, Peterculter AB14 0LN
☎ **(01224) 735245**
(01224) 735580
info@peterculterg olfclub.co.uk
D Vannet
www.peterculterg olfclub.co.uk

Portlethen (1983)
Badentoy Road, Portlethen, Aberdeen AB12 4YA
☎ **(01224) 781090**
(01224) 783383
admin@portlethengolfclub.com
www.portlethengolfclub.com

Royal Aberdeen (1780)
Links Road, Bridge of Don, Aberdeen AB23 8AT
☎ **(01224) 702571**
(01224) 826591
ronnie@royalaberdeengolf.com
Ronnie Macaskill (Director of Golf)
www.royalaberdeengolf.com

Westhill (1977)
Westhill Heights, Westhill AB32 6RY
☎ **(01224) 742567**
(01224) 749124
westhillgolf@btconnect.com
George Bruce (Admin)
www.westhillgolfclub.co.uk

Angus

Arbroath Artisan (1903)
Public
Elliot, Arbroath DD11 2PE
☎ **(01241) 872069**
(01241) 875837
captain@arbroathartisangolfclub.co.uk
J R Tollerton
www.arbroathartisangolfclub.co.uk

Ballumbie Castle (2000)
3 Old Quarry Road, Dundee DD4 0SY
☎ **(01382) 770028**
(01382) 730008
ballumbie2000@yahoo.com
www.ballumbiecastlegolfclub.com

For key to symbols see page 725

Brechin (1893)
Trinity, Brechin DD9 7PD
☎ **(01356) 625270 (bookings/pro)**
(01356) 625270
brechingolfclub@tiscali.co.uk
S Rennie (Manager)
www.brechingolfclub.co.uk

Caird Park (1926)
Public
Mains Loan, Caird Park, Dundee DD4 9BX
☎ **(01382) 453606/461460**
(01382) 461460
cp.golf.club@btconnect.com
G Martin (07961) 159636

Camperdown (1960)
Public
Camperdown Park, Dundee DD2 4TF
☎ **(01382) 623398**

Downfield (1932)
Turnberry Ave, Dundee DD2 3QP
☎ **(01382) 825595**
(01382) 813111
downfieldgc@aol.com
Mrs M Campbell
www.downfieldgolf.co.uk

Edzell (1895)
High St, Edzell DD9 7TF
☎ **(01356) 647283**
(01356) 648094
secretary@edzellgolfclub.com
AA Turnbull
www.edzellgolfclub.com

Forfar (1871)
Cunninghill, Arbroath Road, Forfar DD8 2RL
☎ **(01307) 463773/462120**
(01307) 468495
info@forfargolfclub.co.uk
S Wilson
www.forfargolfclub.co.uk

Kirriemuir (1884)
Northmuir, Kirriemuir DD8 4LN
☎ **(01575) 573317**
(01575) 574608
enquiries@kirriemuirgolfclub.co.uk
C Gowrie
www.kirriemuirgolfclub.co.uk

Monifieth Golf Links
Medal Starter's Box, Princes Street, Monifieth DD5 4AW
☎ **(01382) 532767 (Bookings)**
(01382) 535816
secretary@monifiethlinks.com
J Brodie (Managing Sec),
www.monifiethgolf.co.uk

Montrose Golf Links (1562)
Public
Traill Drive, Montrose DD10 8SW
☎ **(01674) 672932**
(01674) 671800
secretary@montroselinks.co.uk
Miss Claire Penman
www.montroselinks.co.uk

Montrose Caledonia (1896)
Club
Dorward Road, Montrose DD10 8SW
☎ **(01674) 672313**

Panmure (1845)
Barry, Carnoustie DD7 7RT
☎ **(01241) 855120**
(01241) 859737
secretary@panmuregolfclub.co.uk
Charles JR Philip
www.panmuregolfclub.co.uk

Royal Montrose (1810)
Club
Traill Drive, Montrose DD10 8SW
☎ **(01674) 672376**
secretary@royalmontrosegolf.com
Michael Cummins (07792) 626931
www.royalmontrosegolf.com

Carnoustie Clubs

Carnoustie Caledonia (1887)
Club
Links Parade, Carnoustie DD7 7JF
☎ **(01241) 852115**
R Reyner
www.carnoustiecaledonia.co.uk

Carnoustie Ladies (1873)
Club
12 Links Parade, Carnoustie DD7 7JF
☎ **(01241) 855252**
Mrs JM Mitchell (01241) 855035

Carnoustie Mercantile (1896)
Club
Links Parade, Carnoustie DD7 7JE
GJA Murray (01241) 854420

The Carnoustie Golf Club (1842)
Club
3 Links Parade, Carnoustie DD7 7JF
☎ **(01241) 852480**
admin@carnoustiegolfclub.com
AJR Mackenzie
www.carnoustiegolfclub.com

Carnoustie Courses

Buddon Links (1981)
Public
20 Links Parade, Carnoustie DD7 7JF
☎ **(01241) 802270**
(01241) 802271
golf@carnoustiegolflinks.co.uk
G Duncan
www.carnoustiegolflinks.co.uk

Burnside (1914)
Public
20 Links Parade, Carnoustie DD7 7JF
☎ **(01241) 802270**
(01241) 802271
golf@carnoustiegolflinks.co.uk
G Duncan
www.carnoustiegolflinks.co.uk

Carnoustie Championship (1842)
Public
20 Links Parade, Carnoustie DD7 7JF
☎ **(01241) 802270**
(01241) 802271
golf@carnoustiegolflinks.co.uk
G Duncan
www.carnoustiegolflinks.co.uk

Argyll & Bute

Blairmore & Strone (1896)
High Road, Strone, Dunoon PA23 8TH
☎ **(01369) 840676**
thompsongg@talk21.com
Graham Thompson (01369) 840208
www.blairmoregc.co.uk

Bute (1888)
32 Marine Place, Ardbeg, Rothesay, Isle of Bute PA20 0LF
☎ **(01700) 503091**
administrator@butegolfclub.com
F Robinson (01700) 503091
www.butegolfclub.com

Carradale (1906)
Carradale, Campbeltown PA28 6RY
☎ **(01583) 431788**
margaretrichardson1977@live.co.uk
Margaret Richardson (Sec)
www.carradalegolf.com

Colonsay
Owned privately
Isle of Colonsay PA61 7YR
☎ **(01951) 200290**
(01951) 200290

Cowal (1891)
Ardenslate Road, Dunoon PA23 8LT
☎ **(01369) 705673**
(01369) 705673
secretary@cowalgolfclub.com
A Douglas (01369) 705673
www.cowalgolfclub.com

Craignure (1895)
Scallastle, Craignure, Isle of Mull PA65 6BA
☎ **(01688) 302517**
pvnbook2@aol.com

Dalmally (1986)
Old Saw Mill, Dalmally PA33 1AE
☎ **(01838) 200619**
dalmallygolfclub@btinternet.com
S Tollan (01631) 710401
www.dalmallygolfclub.co.uk

Dunaverty (1889)
Southend, Campbeltown PA28 6RW
☎ **(01586) 830677**
(01586) 830677
dunavertygc@aol.com
Bill Brannigan
www.dunavertygolfclub.com

Gigha (1992)
Pay and play
Isle of Gigha, Kintyre PA41 7AA
☎ **(01583) 505242**
✉ johngigha@hotmail.co.uk
✍ J Bannatyne
▤ www.gigha.org

Glencruitten (1908)
Glencruitten Road, Oban PA34 4PU
☎ **(01631) 562868**
✉ enquiries@obangolf.com
✍ David Finlayson (01631) 566186
▤ www.obangolf.com

Helensburgh (1893)
25 East Abercromby Street, Helensburgh G84 9HZ
☎ **(01436) 674173**
🖷 (01436) 671170
✉ secretary@helensburghgolfclub.co.uk
✍ Martyn Lawrie (Gen Mgr) (01436) 674173
▤ www.helensburghgolfclub.co.uk

Innellan (1891)
Knockamillie Road, Innellan, Dunoon
☎ **(01369) 830242**
✉ innellangolfclub@btconnect.com
✍ R Milliken (01369) 830415

Inveraray (1893)
North Cromalt, Inveraray, Argyll
☎ **(01499) 600286**
✍ D MacNeill

Islay (1891)
25 Charlotte St, Port Ellen, Isle of Islay PA42 7DF
☎ **(01496) 300094**
▤ www.islay.golf.btinternet.co.uk

Isle of Seil (1996)
Pay and play
Balvicar, Isle of Seil PA34 4TF
☎ **(01852) 300548**
✉ geolladam@yahoo.co.uk
✍ G Adam

Kyles of Bute (1906)
The Moss, Kames, Tighnabruaich PA21 2AB
✍ Dr J Thomson 01700 811 603
▤ www.kylesofbutegolfclub.co.uk

Lochgilphead (1963)
Blarbuie Road, Lochgilphead PA31 8LE
☎ **(01546) 602340**
✍ Bill Dick
▤ www.lochgilphead-golf.com

Lochgoilhead (1994)
Public
Drimsynie Estate, Lochgoilhead PA24 8AD
☎ **(01301) 703247**
🖷 (01301) 703538
✉ info@argyllholidays.com
✍ Colin Park
▤ www.argyllholidays.com

Machrihanish (1876)
Machrihanish, Campbeltown PA28 6PT
☎ **(01586) 810213**
🖷 (01586) 810221
✉ secretary@machgolf.com
✍ Mrs A Anderson
▤ www.machgolf.com

Millport (1888)
Millport, Isle of Cumbrae KA28 0HB
☎ **(01475) 530311**
🖷 (01475) 530306
✉ secretary@millportgolfclub.co.uk
✍ William Reid (01475) 530306
▤ www.millportgolfclub.co.uk

Port Bannatyne (1912)
Bannatyne Mains Road, Port Bannatyne, Isle of Bute PA20 0PH
☎ **(01700) 504544**
✍ R Jardine (01700) 500195
▤ www.portbannatynegolf.co.uk

Rothesay (1892)
Canada Hill, Rothesay, Isle of Bute PA20 9HN
☎ **(01700) 503554**
✉ rothesaygolfclub@btconnect.com
✍ Joan Torrence
▤ www.rothesaygolfclub.com

Tarbert (1910)
Kilberry Road, Tarbert PA29 6XX
☎ **(01880) 820565**
✍ P Cupples (01546) 606896

Taynuilt (1987)
Golf Club House, Taynuilt, Argyll PA35 1JH
☎ **(01866) 822429**
🖷 (01866) 822255 (phone first)
✉ secretary@taynuiltgolfclub.co.uk
✍ J J Church (01631) 770 633
▤ www.taynuiltgolfclub.co.uk

Tobermory (1896)
Erray Road, Tobermory, Isle of Mull PA75 6PS
☎ **(01688) 302387**
🖷 (01688) 302140
✉ secretary@tobermorygolfclub.com
✍ M Campbell (01688) 302743
▤ www.tobermorygolfclub.com

Ayrshire

Annanhill (1957)
Public
Irvine Road, Kilmarnock KA1 2RT
☎ **(01563) 521512 (Starter)**
✉ annanhillgolfclub@btconnect.com
✍ T Denham (01563) 521644/525557
▤ www.annanhillgc.co.uk

Ardeer (1880)
Greenhead Avenue, Stevenston KA20 4LB
☎ **(01294) 464542**
🖷 (01294) 464542
✉ info@ardeergolfclub.co.uk
✍ John Boyle (01294) 464542
▤ www.ardeergolfclub.co.uk

Ballochmyle (1937)
Ballochmyle, Mauchline KA5 6LE
☎ **(01290) 550469**
✉ ballochmylegolf@btconnect.com
✍ J Davidson
▤ www.ballochmylegolfclub.co.uk

Beith (1896)
Threepwood Road, Beith KA15 2JR
☎ **(01505) 503166 (Clubhouse)**
✍ Joe McSorley (Captain)
▤ www.beithgolfclub.co.uk

Brodick (1897)
Brodick, Isle of Arran KA27 8DL
☎ **(01770) 302349**
🖷 (01770) 302349
✉ enquiries@brodickgolf.com
✍ Ann Hart (Sec)
▤ www.brodickgolfclub.com

Brunston Castle (1992)
Golf Course Road, Dailly, Girvan KA26 9GD
☎ **(01465) 811471**
🖷 (01465) 811545
✉ golf@brunstoncastle.co.uk
▤ www.brunstoncastle.co.uk

Caprington (1958)
Public
Ayr Road, Kilmarnock KA1 4UW
☎ **(01563) 53702 (Club)**
✉ caprington.golf@btconnect.com
✍ Michael McDonnell Mob 0791 564 8834

Corrie (1892)
Corrie, Sannox, Isle of Arran KA27 8JD
☎ **(01770) 810223/810606**
✍ George E Welford (01770) 600403
▤ www.corriegolf.com

Dalmilling (1961)
Public
Westwood Avenue, Ayr KA8 0QY
☎ **(01292) 263893**
🖷 (01292) 610543

Doon Valley (1927)
1 Hillside, Patna, Ayr KA6 7JT
☎ **(01292) 531607**
🖷 (01292) 532489

Dundonald Links (2003)
Pay and play
Ayr Road, Gailes, Ayrshire KA11 5BF
☎ **(01294) 314000**
🖷 (01294) 314001
✉ reservations@dundonaldlinks.com
✍ Guy Redford
▤ www.dundonaldlinks.com

Girvan (1860)
Public
Golf Course Road, Girvan KA26 9HW
☎ **(01465) 714272/714346 (Starter)**
🖷 (01465) 714346
✍ WB Tait

Glasgow GC Gailes Links (1892)
Gailes, Irvine KA11 5AE
☎ **(01294) 311258**
(01294) 279366
secretary@glasgowgolfclub.com
AG McMillan (0141) 942 2011
www.gaileslinks.com

Irvine (1887)
Bogside, Irvine KA8 8SN
☎ **(01294) 275979**
(01294) 278209
secretary@theirvinegolfclub.co.uk
W McMahon

Irvine Ravenspark (1907)
Public
Kidsneuk Lane, Irvine KA12 8SR
☎ **(01294) 271293**
secretary@irgc.co.uk
T McFarlane (01294) 213537
www.irgc.co.uk

Kilbirnie Place (1925)
Largs Road, Kilbirnie KA25 7AT
☎ **(01505) 683398**
01505 684444
kilbirnie.golfclub@tiscali.co.uk
Mr J Melvin
www.kilbirnieplacegolfclub.webs.com

Kilmarnock (Barassie) (1887)
29 Hillhouse Road, Barassie, Troon KA10 6SY
☎ **(01292) 313920/311077**
(01292) 318300
golf@kbgc.co.uk
D Wilson (01292) 313920
www.kbgc.co.uk

Lamlash (1889)
Lamlash, Isle of Arran KA27 8JU
☎ **(01770) 600296 (Clubhouse)**
lamlashgolfclub@btconnect.com
D Bilsland
www.lamlashgolfclub.co.uk

Largs (1891)
Irvine Road, Largs KA30 8EU
☎ **(01475) 673594 (Secretary's office)**
(01475) 673594
secretary@largsgolfclub.co.uk
Barry Streets
www.largsgolfclub.co.uk

Lochranza Golf Course (1899)
Pay and play
Lochranza, Isle of Arran KA27 8HL
☎ **(0177083) 0273**
office@lochgolf.demon.co.uk
N Wells
www.lochranzagolf.com

Loudoun Gowf (1909)
Galston KA4 8PA
☎ **(01563) 821993**
(01563) 820011
secy@loudoungowfclub.co.uk
WB Buchanan
www.loudoungowfclub.co.uk

Machrie Bay (1900)
Pay and play
Machrie Bay, Brodick, Isle of Arran KA27 8DZ
☎ **(01770) 840310**
machriebayclubsec@googlemail.com
E Ross
www.machriebay.com

Muirkirk (1991)
Pay and play
c/o 65 Main Street, Muirkirk KA18 3QR
☎ **(01290) 660184 (night)**
R Bradford

New Cumnock (1902)
Lochill, Cumnock Road, New Cumnock KA18 4BQ
☎ **(01290) 332761**
J McGinn

Prestwick (1851)
2 Links Road, Prestwick KA9 1QG
☎ **(01292) 477404**
(01292) 477255
bookings@prestwickgc.co.uk
K W Goodwin
www.prestwickgc.co.uk

Prestwick St Cuthbert (1899)
East Road, Prestwick KA9 2SX
☎ **(01292) 477101**
(01292) 671730
secretary@stcuthbert.co.uk
Jim Jess
www.stcuthbert.co.uk

Prestwick St Nicholas (1851)
Grangemuir Road, Prestwick KA9 1SN
☎ **(01292) 477608**
(01292) 473900
secretary@prestwickstnicholas.com
Eddie Prentice
www.prestwickstnicholas.com

Routenburn (1914)
Routenburn Road, Largs KA30 8QS
☎ **(01475) 686475 – steward/Clubhouse**
R B Connal (01475) 672757

Royal Troon (1878)
Craigend Road, Troon KA10 6EP
☎ **(01292) 311555**
(01292) 318204
secretary@royaltroon.com
D L K Brown (Sec) (01292) 310060
www.royaltroon.com

Seafield (1930)
Public
Belleisle Park, Doonfoot Road, Ayr KA7 4DU
☎ **(01292) 441258**
(01292) 442632
info@ayrseafieldgolfclub.co.uk
Brian Milligan (01292) 445144
www.ayrseafieldgolfclub.co.uk

Shiskine (1896)
Shiskine, Blackwaterfoot, Isle of Arran KA27 8HA
☎ **(01770) 860226**
(01770) 860205

The Edward Trophy

The Edward family, well-known Glasgow jewellers, presented the trophy in 1892 for all amateurs whose handicaps did not exceed three and who were members of any club in membership with the Scottish Golf Union in the counties of Lanark, Ayrshire, Dunbarton. Stirling, Renfrew, Argyll, Bute and Glasgow. The event was, therefore, originally created as a competition for West of Scotland golfers.

Until 1927 it was played over 36 holes at various venues but the Edward family asked Glasgow Golf Club if they would consider playing it annually on the club's course at Gailes in Ayrshire. The club agreed and so the event has been played at Gailes every year since.

William Tulloch's feat of winning the trophy five times in the 1920s and 30s has not been equalled. In 2008, it became an SGU Order of Merit event over 72 holes.

For key to symbols see page 725

✉ info@shiskinegolf.com
✍ Pietre Johnston
▤ www.shiskinegolf.com

Skelmorlie (1891)
Skelmorlie PA17 5ES
☎ **(01475) 520152**
✉ sec@skelmorliegolf.co.uk
✍ Mrs Shelagh Travers (Hon)
▤ www.skelmorliegolf.co.uk

Troon Municipal
Public
Harling Drive, Troon KA10 6NF
☎ **(01292) 312464**
▭ (01292) 312578

Troon Portland (1894)
Club
1 Crosbie Road, Troon KA10
☎ **(01292) 313488**

Troon St Meddans (1909)
Club
Harling Drive, Troon KA10 6NF
✉ secretary@troonstmeddansgolfclub.com
✍ Jim Pennington (01563) 851339

Turnberry Hotel (1906)
Turnberry KA26 9LT
☎ **(01655) 331000**
▭ (01655) 331069
✉ turnberry@luxurycollection.com
✍ Richard Hall (Head golf Proff)
▤ www.westin.com/turnberry

West Kilbride (1893)
33-35 Fullerton Drive, Seamill, West Kilbride KA23 9HT
☎ **(01294) 823911**
▭ (01294) 829573
✉ golf@westkilbridegolfclub.com
✍ Gordon Clark
▤ www.westkilbridegolfclub.com

Western Gailes (1897)
Gailes, Irvine KA11 5AE
☎ **(01294) 311649**
▭ (01294) 312312
✉ enquiries@westerngailes.com
✍ Jerry Kessell
▤ www.westerngailes.com

Whiting Bay (1895)
Golf Course Road, Whiting Bay, Isle of Arran KA27 8QT
☎ **(01770) 700487**
✉ info@whitingbaygolf.com
✍ Mr Richard Fletcher (Hon Sec)
▤ www.whitingbaygolf.com

Borders

Duns (1894)
Hardens Road, Duns TD11 3NR
☎ **(01361) 882194**
✉ secretary@dunsgolfclub.com
✍ G Clark (01361) 883599
▤ www.dunsgolfclub.com

Eyemouth (1894)
Gunsgreen House, Eyemouth TD14 5DX
☎ **(018907) 50551 (Clubhouse)**

Galashiels (1884)
Ladhope Recreation Ground, Galashiels TD1 2NJ
☎ **(01896) 753724**
✉ secretary@galashiels-golfclub.co.uk
▤ www.galashiels-golfclub.co.uk

Hawick (1877)
Vertish Hill, Hawick TD9 0NY
☎ **(01450) 372293**
▭ (01450) 372293
✉ reillyjh@aol.com
✍ J Reilly
▤ www.hawickgolfclub.com

The Hirsel (1948)
Kelso Road, Coldstream TD12 4NJ
☎ **(01890) 882678**
▭ (01890) 882233
✉ info@hirselgc.co.uk
✍ Mr Allan Rodger
▤ www.hirselgc.co.uk

Jedburgh (1892)
Dunion Road, Jedburgh TD8 6TA
☎ **(01835) 863587**
✉ info@jedburghgolfclub.co.uk
✍ R Nagle (01835) 866271
▤ www.jedburghgolfclub.co.uk

Kelso (1887)
Golf Course Road, Kelso TD5 7SL
☎ **(01573) 223009**
▭ (01573) 228490
✉ secretary@kelsogolfclub.com
✍ DR Jack
▤ www.kelsogolfclub.com

Langholm (1892)
Langholm DG13 0JR
☎ **(07724) 875151**
✉ golf@langholmgolfclub.co.uk
✍ Pauline Irving
▤ www.langholmgolfclub.co.uk

Lauder (1896)
Pay and play
Galashiels Road, Lauder TD2 6RS
☎ **(01578) 722526**
▭ (01578) 722526
✉ secretary@laudergolfclub.co.uk
✍ R Towers (01578) 722240
▤ www.laudergolfclub.co.uk

Melrose (1880)
Dingleton Road, Melrose TD6 9HS
☎ **(01896) 822855**
▭ (01896) 822855
✉ info@melrosegolfcourse.co.uk
✍ LM Wallace (01835) 823553
▤ www.melrosegolfcourse.co.uk

Minto (1928)
Denholm, Hawick TD9 8SH
☎ **(01450) 870220**
▭ (01450) 870126
✉ mintogolfclub@btconnect.com
✍ J Simpson
▤ www.mintogolf.co.uk

Newcastleton (1894)
Pay and play
Holm Hill, Newcastleton TD9 0QD
☎ **(013873) 75608**
✍ GA Wilson

Peebles (1892)
Kirkland Street, Peebles EH45 8EU
☎ **(01721) 720197**
✉ secretary@peeblesgolfclub.com
✍ William Baird (Administrator)
▤ www.peeblesgolfclub.com

The Roxburghe Hotel & Golf Course (1997)
Proprietary
Heiton, Kelso TD5 8JZ
☎ **(01573) 450333**
▭ (01573) 450611
✉ golf@roxburghe.net
✍ Craig Montgomerie (Director of Golf)
▤ www.roxburghegolfclub.co.uk

Selkirk (1883)
The Hill, Selkirk TD7 4NW
☎ **(01750) 20621**
✉ secretary@selkirkgolfclub.co.uk
✍ A Robertson (01750) 20519 (pm)
▤ www.selkirkgolfclub.co.uk

St Boswells (1899)
Braeheads, St Boswells, Melrose TD6 0DE
☎ **(01835) 823527**
✉ secretary@stboswellsgolfclub.co.uk
✍ Sue Brooks (Secretary)
▤ www.stboswellsgolfclub.co.uk

Torwoodlee (1895)
Edinburgh Road, Galashiels, Torwoodlee TD1 2NE
☎ **(01896) 752260**
▭ (01896) 752306
✉ torwoodleegolfclub@btconnect.com
✍ L Moffat (Administrator)
▤ www.torwoodleegolfclub.org.uk

West Linton (1890)
Medwyn Road, West Linton EH46 7HN
☎ **(01968) 660970**
▭ (01968) 660622
✉ secretarywlgc@btinternet.com
✍ John Johnson (01968) 661121

Woll Golf Course (1993)
Proprietary
New Woll Estate, Ashkirk, Selkirkshire TD7 4PE
☎ **(01750) 32711**
✉ wollgolf@tiscali.co.uk
✍ Nicholas Brown (01750) 32711
▤ www.wollgolf.co.uk
▤ www.wlgc.co.uk

Clackmannanshire

Alloa (1891)
Schawpark, Sauchie, Alloa FK10 3AX
☎ **(01259) 722745**
▭ (01259) 218796

✉ secretary@alloagolfclub.co.uk
✍ Secretary
🌐 www.alloagolfclub.co.uk

Alva
Beauclerc Street, Alva FK12 5LH
☎ **(01259) 760431**

Braehead (1891)
Cambus, Alloa FK10 2NT
☎ **(01259) 725766**
🖷 (01259) 214070
✉ enquiries@braeheadgolfclub.co.uk
✍ Ronald Murray
🌐 www.braeheadgolfclub.com

Dollar (1890)
Brewlands House, Dollar FK14 7EA
☎ **(01259) 742400**
🖷 (01259) 743497
✉ info@dollargolfclub.com
✍ W D Carln
🌐 www.dollargolfclub.com

Tillicoultry (1899)
Alva Road, Tillicoultry FK13 6BL
☎ **(01259) 750124**
🖷 (01259) 750124
✉ tillygolf@btconnect.com
✍ M Todd
🌐 www.tillygc.co.uk

Tulliallan (1902)
Kincardine, Alloa FK10 4BB
☎ **(01259) 730396**
🖷 (01259) 731395
✉ tulliallangolf@btconnect.com
✍ Amanda Maley
🌐 www.tulliallangolf.co.uk

Dumfries & Galloway

Brighouse Bay (1999)
Pay and play
Borgue, Kirkcudbright DG6 4TS
☎ **(01557) 870509**
🖷 (01557) 870409
✉ enquiries@brighousebay-golfclub.co.uk
✍ E Diamond (01557) 870509
🌐 www.brighousebay-golfclub.co.uk

Castle Douglas (1905)
Abercromby Road, Castle Douglas DG7 1BA
☎ **(01556) 502801**
✉ cdgolfclub@aol.com
✍ J Duguid (01556) 503527
🌐 www.cdgolf.co.uk

Colvend (1905)
Sandyhills, Dalbeattie DG5 4PY
☎ **(01556) 630398**
🖷 (01556) 630495
✉ secretary@colvendgolfclub.co.uk
✍ R N Bailey
⊕ For Tee times and catering email steward@colvendgolfclub.co.uk
🌐 www.colvendgolfclub.co.uk

Crichton Golf Club (1884)
Public/Private
Bankend Road, Dumfries DG1 4TH
☎ **(01387) 264946**
✉ crichtongolf@hotmail.co.uk
✍ Lee Sterritt (Match Sec)
🌐 www.crichtongolfclub.limewebs.com

Dalbeattie (1894)
Maxwell Park, Dalbeattie DG5 4JR
☎ **(01556) 611421**
✉ jbhenderson45@gmail.com
✍ J B Henderson
🌐 www.dalbeattiegc.co.uk

Dumfries & County (1912)
Nunfield, Edinburgh Road, Dumfries DG1 1JX
☎ **(01387) 253585**
🖷 (01387) 253585
✉ admin@thecounty.co.uk
✍ BRM Duguid (01387) 253585
🌐 www.thecounty.org.uk

Dumfries & Galloway (1880)
2 Laurieston Avenue, Maxwelltown, Dumfries DG2 7NY
☎ **(01387) 253582**
🖷 (01387) 263848
✉ info@dandggolfclub.co.uk
✍ Joe Fergusson (Professional) (01387) 256902
🌐 www.dandggolfclub.co.uk

Gatehouse (1921)
Lauriston Road, Gatehouse of Fleet, Castle Douglas DG7 2BE
☎ **(01557) 814766 (Clubhouse – unmanned)**
✉ info@gatehousegolfclub.com
✍ M Ashmore (01559) 814884
🌐 www.gatehousegolfclub.com

Hoddom Castle (1973)
Pay and play
Hoddom Bridge, Ecclefechan DG11 1AS
☎ **(01576) 300251**
🖷 (01576) 300757
✉ hoddomcastle@aol.com
🌐 www.hoddomcastle.co.uk

Kirkcudbright (1893)
Stirling Crescent, Kirkcudbright DG6 4EZ
☎ **(01557) 330314**
🖷 (01557) 330314
✉ kbtgolfclub@lineone.net
✍ N Little (Manager)
🌐 www.kirkcudbrightgolf.co.uk

Lochmaben (1926)
Castlehill Gate, Lochmaben DG11 1NT
☎ **(01387) 810552**
✉ enquiries@lochmabengolf.co.uk
✍ JM Dickie (Sec)
🌐 www.lochmabengolf.co.uk

Lockerbie (1889)
Corrie Road, Lockerbie DG11 2ND
☎ **(01576) 203363**
🖷 (01576) 203363
✉ enquiries@lockerbiegolf.co.uk
✍ Gillian Shanks
🌐 www.lockerbiegolf.co.uk

Moffat (1884)
Coatshill, Moffat DG10 9SB
☎ **(01683) 220020**
✉ bookings@moffatgolfclub.co.uk
✍ Club Manager (01683) 220020
🌐 www.moffatgolfclub.co.uk

New Galloway (1902)
New Galloway, Dumfries DG7 3RN
☎ **(01644) 420737**
✉ brown@nggc.co.uk
✍ Ian Brown
🌐 www.nggc.co.uk

Newton Stewart (1981)
Kirroughtree Avenue, Minnigaff, Newton Stewart DG8 6PF
☎ **(01671) 402172**
✉ newtonstewartgc@btconnect.com
✍ Mrs L Hamilton
🌐 www.newtonstewartgolfclub.com

Dumfriesshire Golf Academy – Pines Golf Centre (1998)
Pay and play
Lockerbie Road, Dumfries DG1 3PF
☎ **(01387) 247444**
🖷 (01387) 249600
✉ info@dumfriesshiregolfcentre.com
🌐 www.dumfriesgolf.com

Portpatrick (1903)
Golf Course Road, Portpatrick DG9 8TB
☎ **(01776) 810273**
🖷 (01776) 810811
✉ enquiries@portpatrickgolfclub.com
✍ Manager
🌐 www.portpatrickgolfclub.com

Powfoot (1903)
Cummertrees, Annan DG12 5QE
☎ **(01461) 204100**
🖷 (01461) 204111
✉ info@powfootgolfclub.com
✍ SR Gardner (Mgr)
🌐 www.powfootgolfclub.com

Sanquhar (1894)
Blackaddie Road, Sanquhar, Dumfries DG4 6JZ
☎ **(01659) 50577**
✉ tich@rossirene.fsnet.co.uk
✍ Ian Macfarlane
🌐 www.scottishgolf.com

Southerness (1947)
Southerness, Dumfries DG2 8AZ
☎ **(01387) 880677**
🖷 (01387) 880471
✉ southernessgc@btconnect.com
✍ P F K Scott
🌐 www.southernessgolfclub.com

St Medan (1904)
Monreith, Newton Stewart DG8 8NJ
☎ **(01988) 700358**
✉ mail@stmedangolfclub.co.uk

✍ William G McKeand (01988) 700804
▤ www.stmedangolfclub.co.uk

Stranraer (1905)
Creachmore, Leswalt, Stranraer DG9 0LF
☎ **(01776) 870245**
🖷 (01776) 870445
✉ stranraergolf@btclick.com
✍ J Burns
▤ www.stranraergolfclub.net

Thornhill (1893)
Blacknest, Thornhill DG3 5DW
☎ **(01848) 330546 (clubhouse)**
✉ info@thornhillgolfclub.co.uk
✍ A Hillier (Co-ordinator)
▤ www.thornhillgolfclub.co.uk

Wigtown & Bladnoch (1960)
Lightlands Terrace, Wigtown DG8 9DY
☎ **(01988) 403354**
✍ I M Thin

Wigtownshire County (1894)
Mains of Park, Glenluce, Newton Stewart DG8 0NN
☎ **(01581) 300420**
🖷 (01581) 300420
✉ enquiries @wigtownshirecountygolfclub.com
✍ Mr Jimmy Caldwell (Steward)
▤ www.wigtownshirecountygolfclub .com

Dunbartonshire

Balmore (1894)
Balmore, Torrance G64 4AW
☎ **(01360) 620284**
🖷 (01360) 622742
✉ balmoregolf@btconnect.com
✍ Karen Dyer (01360) 620284
▤ www.balmoregolfclub.co.uk

Bearsden (1891)
Thorn Road, Bearsden, Glasgow G61 4BP
☎ **(0141) 586 5300**
🖷 (0141) 586 5300
✉ secretary@bearsdengolfclub.com
✍ Alan Harris
▤ www.bearsdengolfclub.com

Cardross (1895)
Main Road, Cardross, Dumbarton G82 5LB
☎ **(01389) 841213 (Clubhouse)**
🖷 (01389) 842162
✉ golf@cardross.com
✍ G A Mill (01389) 841754
▤ www.cardross.com

Clober (1951)
Craigton Road, Milngavie, Glasgow G62 7HP
☎ **(0141) 956 1685**
✉ clobergolfclub@gmail.com
✍ Gary McFarlane
▤ www.clobergolfclub.co.uk

Clydebank & District (1905)
Hardgate, Clydebank G81 5QY
☎ **(01389) 383831**
🖷 (01389) 383831
✉ admin@clydebankanddistrict golfclub.co.uk
✍ Miss M Higgins
▤ www.clydebankanddistrictgolfclub .co.uk

Clydebank Overtoun (1927)
Public
Overtoun Road, Dalmuir, Clydebank G81 3RE
☎ **(0141) 952 2070 (Clubhouse)**

Dougalston (1977)
Strathblane Road, Milngavie, Glasgow G62 8HJ
☎ **(0141) 955 2400**
🖷 (0141) 955 2406
✉ secretary.esportadougalstongc @hotmail.co.uk
✍ Mr S Gilbey
▤ www.esporta.com

Douglas Park (1897)
Hillfoot, Bearsden, Glasgow G61 2TJ
☎ **(0141) 942 2220 (Clubhouse)**
🖷 (0141) 942 0985
✉ secretary@douglasparkgolfclub .co.uk
✍ Christine Scott (0141) 942 0985
▤ www.douglasparkgolfclub.co.uk

Dullatur (1896)
1a Glendouglas Drive, Craigmarloch, Cumbernauld G68 0DW
☎ **(01236) 723230**
🖷 (01236) 727271
✉ secretary@dullaturgolf.com
✍ John Bryceland B.E.M (01236) 723230
▤ www.dullaturgolf.com

Dumbarton (1888)
Broadmeadow, Dumbarton G82 2BQ
☎ **(01389) 765995**
✉ secretary@dumbartongolfclub .co.uk
✍ M Buchanan
▤ www.dumbartongolfclub.co.uk

Hayston (1926)
Campsie Road, Kirkintilloch, Glasgow G66 1RN
☎ **(0141) 775 0723**
🖷 (0141) 776 9030
✉ secretary@haystongolf.com
✍ Jim Smart
▤ www.haystongolf.com

Hilton Park (1927)
Auldmarroch Estate, Stockiemuir Road, Milngavie G62 7HB
☎ **(0141) 956 4657**
🖷 (0141) 956 1215
✉ office@hiltonpark.co.uk
✍ Mr Gordon Simpson
▤ www.hiltonpark.co.uk

Kirkintilloch (1895)
Todhill, Campsie Road, Kirkintilloch G66 1RN
☎ **(0141) 776 1256**
🖷 (0141) 775 2424
✉ secretary@kirkintillochgolfclub .co.uk
✍ T Cummings (0141) 775 2387
▤ www.kirkintillochgolfclub.co.uk

Lenzie (1889)
19 Crosshill Road, Lenzie G66 5DA
☎ **(0141) 776 1535**
🖷 (0141) 777 7748
✉ club-secretary@ntlbusiness.com
✍ Roy McKee (0141) 776 1535
▤ www.lenziegolfclub.co.uk

Loch Lomond (1994)
Rossdhu House, Luss G83 8NT
☎ **(01436) 655555**
🖷 (01436) 655500
✉ info@lochlomond.com
✍ Bill Donald (Gen Mgr)
▤ www.lochlomond.com

Milngavie (1895)
Laighpark, Milngavie, Glasgow G62 8EP
☎ **(0141) 956 1619**
🖷 (0141) 956 4252
✉ secretary@milngaviegolfclub.co.uk
✍ S Woods
▤ www.milngaviegolfclub.com

Palacerigg (1975)
Public
Palacerigg Country Park, Cumbernauld G67 3HU
☎ **(01236) 734969**
🖷 (01236) 721461
✉ palacerigg-golfclub@lineone.net
✍ P O'Hara
▤ www.palacerigg.co.uk

Ross Priory (1978)
Proprietary
Ross Loan, Gartocharn, Alexandria G83 8NL
☎ **(01389) 830398**
🖷 (01389) 830357
✉ ross.priory@strath.ac.uk
▤ www.strath.ac.uk/rosspriory/golf

Vale of Leven (1907)
Northfield Road, Bonhill, Alexandria G83 9ET
☎ **(01389) 752351**
🖷 (01389) 758866
✉ rbarclay@volgc.org
✍ R Barclay
▤ www.volgc.org

Westerwood Hotel G&CC (1989)
Pay and play
St Andrews Drive, Cumbernauld G68 0EW
☎ **(01236) 725281**
🖷 (01236) 738478
✉ westerwoodgolf@qhotels.co.uk
✍ Iain Baird
▤ www.qhotels.co.uk

Windyhill (1908)
Baljaffray Road, Bearsden G61 4QQ
☎ **(0141) 942 2349**
(0141) 942 5874
secretary@windyhill.co.uk
Chris Duffy (PGA Pro)
www.windyhillgolfclub.co.uk

Fife

Aberdour (1896)
Seaside Place, Aberdour KY3 0TX
☎ **(01383) 860080**
(01383) 860050
manager@aberdourgolfclub.co.uk
Jane Cuthill
www.aberdourgolfclub.co.uk

Anstruther (1890)
Marsfield Shore Road, Anstruther KY10 3DZ
☎ **(01333) 310956**
(01333) 310956
secretary@anstruthergolf.co.uk
M MacDonald
www.anstruthergolf.co.uk

Auchterderran (1904)
Public
Woodend Road, Cardenden KY5 0NH
☎ **(01592) 721579**

Balbirnie Park (1983)
Balbirnie Park, Markinch, Fife KY7 6NR
☎ **(01592) 612095**
(01592) 612383
administrator@balbirniegolf.com
J Donnelly (Club Administrator)
www.balbirniegolf.com

Ballingry (1981)
Pay and play
Lochore Meadows Country Park, Crosshill, Lochgelly KY5 8BA
☎ **(01592) 860086**
terryir@hotmail.co.uk
Terry Ironside

Burntisland (1797)
Club
51 Craigkennochie Terrace, Burntisland KY3 9EN
☎ **(01592) 872728**
bgc1797@gmail.com
AD McPherson
www.burntislandgolfclub.co.uk

Burntisland Golf House Club (1898)
Dodhead, Kircaldy Road, Burntisland KY3 9LQ
☎ **(01592) 874093**
info@burntislandgolfhouseclub.co.uk
Administration (01592) 874093 Ext 4
www.burntislandgolfhouseclub.co.uk

Canmore (1897)
Venturefair Avenue, Dunfermline KY12 0PE
☎ **(01383) 724969**
canmoregolfclub@btconnect.com
D Maccallum (Sec)
www.canmoregolfclub.co.uk

Charleton (1994)
Proprietary
Charleton, Colinsburgh KY9 1HG
☎ **(01333) 340505**
(01333) 340583
clubhouse@charleton.co.uk
John Priestley
www.charleton.co.uk

Cowdenbeath (1991)
Public
Seco Place, Cowdenbeath KY4 8PD
☎ **(01383) 511918/(01383) 513079 (Starter)**
mail@cowdenbeath-golfclub.com
Secretary
www.cowdenbeath-golfclub.com

Crail Golfing Society (1786)
Balcomie Clubhouse, Fifeness, Crail KY10 3XN
☎ **(01333) 450686**
(01333) 450416
info@crailgolfingsociety.co.uk
D Roy
www.crailgolfingsociety.co.uk

Cupar (1855)
Hilltarvit, Cupar KY15 5JT
☎ **(01334) 653549**
(01334) 653549
cupargc@fsmail.net
James Elder
www.cupargolfclub.co.uk

Drumoig (1996)
Drumoig Hotel, Drumoig, Leuchars, St Andrews, Fife KY16 0BE
☎ **(01382) 541898**
(01382) 541898
drumoiggolf@btconnect.com
Gordon Taylor
www.drumoigleisure.com

Dunfermline (1887)
Pitfirrane, Crossford, Dunfermline KY12 8QW
☎ **(01383) 723534**
secretary@dunfermlinegolfclub.com
R De Rose
www.dunfermlinegolfclub.com

Dunnikier Park (1963)
Public
Dunnikier Way, Kirkcaldy KY1 3LP
☎ **(01592) 261599**
dunnikierparkgolfclub@btinternet.com
G Macdonald
www.dunnikierparkgolfclub.com

Earlsferry Thistle (1875)
Club
Melon Park, Elie KY9 1AS
J Peters (01333) 424315

Elmwood Golf Course (1997)
Pay and play
Stratheden, Nr Cupar KY15 5RS
☎ **(01334) 658780**
(01334) 658781
clubhouse@elmwood.co.uk/s.sulaiman@elmwood.ac.uk
Sharif Sulaiman (Golf Admin) (01334) 658780
www.elmwoodgc.co.uk

Falkland (1976)
The Myre, Falkland KY15 7AA
☎ **(01337) 857404**
falklandgolfclub@gmail.com
Mrs H Brough
www.falklandgolfclub.com

Glenrothes (1958)
Public
Golf Course Road, Glenrothes KY6 2LA
☎ **(01592) 754561/758686**
(01592) 754561
secretary@glenrothesgolf.org.uk
Miss C Dawson
www.glenrothesgolf.org.uk

Golf House Club (1875)
Elie, Leven KY9 1AS
☎ **(01333) 330301**
(01333) 330895
secretary@golfhouseclub.org
Gordon Fleming
www.golfhouseclub.org

Kinghorn (1887)
Public
Burntisland Road, Kinghorn KY3 9RS
☎ **(01592) 890345**
kgclub@tiscali.co.uk
Mrs Joan Tulloch
www.kinghorngolfclub.co.uk

Kinghorn Ladies (1894)
Club
Golf Clubhouse, Burntisland Road, Kinghorn KY3 9RS
☎ **(01592) 890345**
kgclub@tiscali.co.uk
www.kinghorngolfclub.co.uk

Kingsbarns Golf Links (2000)
Pay and play
Kingsbarns, Fife KY16 8QD
☎ **(01334) 460860**
(01334) 460877
info@kingsbarns.com
Alan Hogg (Chief Executive)
www.kingsbarns.com

Kirkcaldy (1904)
Balwearie Road, Kirkcaldy KY2 5LT
☎ **(01592) 205240**
enquiries@kirkcaldygolfclub.co.uk
M Langstaff
www.kirkcaldygolfclub.co.uk

Ladybank (1879)
Annsmuir, Ladybank, Fife KY15 7RA
☎ **(01337) 830814**

🖷 (01337) 831505
✉ info@ladybankgolf.co.uk
✍ FH McCluskey
🌐 www.ladybankgolf.co.uk

Leslie (1898)
Balsillie Laws, Leslie, Glenrothes KY6 3EZ
☎ **(01592) 620040**
✉ gordon.lewis1@sky.com
✍ G Lewis

Leven Golfing Society (1820)
Club
Links Road, Leven KY8 4HS
☎ **(01333) 426096/424229**
🖷 (01333) 424229
✉ secretary@levengolfingsociety.co.uk
✍ Verne Greger
🌐 www.levengolfingsociety.co.uk

Leven Links (1846)
The Promenade, Leven KY8 4HS
☎ **(01333) 421390 (Starter)**
🖷 (01333) 428859
✉ secretary@leven-links.com
✍ (01333) 428859 (Links Committee)
🌐 www.leven-links.com

Leven Thistle (1867)
Club
Balfour Street, Leven KY8 4JF
☎ **(01333) 426333**
🖷 (01333) 439910
✉ secretary@leventhistlegolf.org.uk
✍ Ian Winn (01333) 426333
🌐 www.leventhistlegolf.org.uk

Lundin (1868)
Golf Road, Lundin Links KY8 6BA
☎ **(01333) 320202**
🖷 (01333) 329743
✉ secretary@lundingolfclub.co.uk
✍ AJ McDonald
🌐 www.lundingolfclub.co.uk

Lundin Ladies (1891)
Woodielea Road, Lundin Links KY8 6AR
☎ **(01333) 320832 (Office)**
✉ llgolfclub@tiscali.co.uk
✍ Lilian Spence (Secretary)
🌐 www.lundinladiesgolfclub.co.uk

Methil (1892)
Club
Links House, Links Road, Leven KY8 4HS
☎ **(01333) 425535**
🖷 (01333) 425187
✉ andrew.traill@btconnect.com
✍ ATJ Traill

Pitreavie (1922)
Queensferry Road, Dunfermline KY11 8PR
☎ **(01383) 722591**
🖷 (01383) 722592
✉ secretary@pitreaviegolfclub.co.uk
✍ Malcom A Brown
🌐 www.pitreaviegolfclub.co.uk

Saline (1912)
Kinneddar Hill, Saline KY12 9LT
☎ **(01383) 852591**
🖷 (01383) 852591
✉ salinegolfclub@btconnect.com
✍ D Hatton
🌐 www.saline-golf-club.co.uk

Scoonie (1951)
Public
North Links, Leven KY8 4SP
☎ **(01333) 307007**
🖷 (01333) 307008
✉ manager@scooniegolfclub.com
✍ Mr J Divers
🌐 www.scooniegolfclub.com

Scotscraig (1817)
Golf Road, Tayport DD6 9DZ
☎ **(01382) 552515**
🖷 (01382) 553130
✉ scotscraig@scotscraiggolfclub.com
✍ BD Liddle
🌐 www.scotscraiggolfclub.com

St Michaels (1903)
Gallow Hill, Leuchars KY16 0DX
☎ **(01334) 839365 (Clubhouse)**
🖷 (01334) 838789
✉ stmichaelsgc@btclick.com
✍ D S Landsburgh (01334) 838666
🌐 www.stmichaelsgolfclub.co.uk

The Standard Life Amateur Champion Gold Medal

It was on July 11th 1870 that the Captain and Council of Innerleven Golf Club, the forerunner to Leven Golfing Society, were notified by their Secretary that the Standard Assurance Company (now Standard Life plc) had presented a Gold Medal for annual competition and Thursday 4th August had been fixed for the event.

The inaugural competition was won by James Elder of Leven Golf Club with a single round score of 85. The competition was, "open to members of Innerleven, Leven and Lundin Golf Clubs and the members of such other clubs as the Captain and Council of Innerleven shall approve, but makers of clubs or balls, or professionals, may not compete".

The competition, hosted annually by Leven Golfing Society and Standard Life plc, continued over 18 holes until 1966 when a 36 holes event was introduced and three years later it moved to the current 72 hole format over two days.

From that historic date, Standard Life has each year presented a gold medallion to the winner and, in more recent times, silver and bronze medallions to the second and third.

Over the decades the tournament, which is played in early August over the classic Leven Links, has grown in stature and is now considered one of the most prestigious competitions in Scottish Golf.

One of the great winners from the past was former Walker Cup player Eric McCruvie who won the medal on no fewer than seven occasions between 1927 and 1950, whilst previous winners who have subsequently gone on to successful professional careers include Pierre Ulrich Johansson, Andrew Coltart and Lee Westwood.

While winning the medal remains a much sought-after prize, each year, every entrant who takes the tee can proudly claim to have played in the world's oldest open amateur stroke-play competition at the eleventh oldest club.

For key to symbols see page 725

Thornton (1921)
Station Road, Thornton KY1 4DW
☎ **(01592) 771173 (Starter)**
(01592) 774955
thorntongolf@btconnect.com
WD Rae (01592) 771111
www.thorntongolfclub.co.uk

St Andrews Clubs

The Royal and Ancient Golf Club of St Andrews (1754)
Club
St Andrews KY16 9JD
☎ **(01334) 460000**
(01334) 460001
thesecretary@randagc.org
P Dawson
www.theroyalandancientgolfclub.org

St Andrews Thistle Golf Club (1817)
Club
c/o Links House, 13 The Links, S Andrews, Fife KY16 9JB
☎ **(01334) 478789**
thistle.secretary@gmail.com
Iain Ross (Secretary)

St Regulus Ladies' (1913)
Club
9 Pilmour Links, St Andrews KY16 9JG
☎ **(01334) 477797**
(01334) 477797
admin@st-regulus-lgc.co.uk
Honorary Secretary
www.st-regulus-lgc.co.uk

The St Rule Club (1898)
Club
12 The Links, St Andrews KY16 9JB
☎ **(01334) 472988**
(01334) 472988
admin@thestruleclub.co.uk
Mr Neil Doctor

The New Golf Club (1902)
3-5 Gibson Place, St Andrews KY16 9JE
☎ **(01334) 473426**
(01334) 477570
admin@newgolfclubstandrews.co.uk
The Secretary
www.newgolfclubstandrews.co.uk

The St Andrews (1843)
Links House, 13 The Links, St Andrews KY16 9JB
☎ **(01334) 479799**
(01334) 479577
sec@thestandrewsgolfclub.co.uk
T Gallacher
www.thestandrewsgolfclub.co.uk

St Andrews Courses

Balgove Course (1993)
Public
St Andrews Links, Pilmour House, St Andrews KY16 9SF
☎ **(01334) 466666**
(01334) 479555
reservations@standrews.org.uk
Euan Loudon (Chief Executive)
Twitter: @thehomeofgolf
www.standrews.org.uk

The Castle Course (2008)
Public
St Andrews Links, Pilmour House, St Andrews KY16 9SF
☎ **(01334) 466666**
(01334) 479555
reservations@standrews.org.uk
Euan Loudon (Chief Executive)
Twitter: @thehomeofgolf
www.standrews.org.uk

Duke's (1995)
Craigtoun, St Andrews KY16 8NX
☎ **(01334) 470214**
(01334) 479456
reservations@oldcoursehotel.co.uk
David Scott (Mgr) (01334) 470214
www.playthedukes.com

Eden Course (1914)
Public
St Andrews Links, Pilmour House, St Andrews KY16 9SF
☎ **(01334) 466666**
(01334) 479555
reservations@standrews.org.uk
Euan Loudon (Chief Executive)
Twitter: @thehomeofgolf
www.standrews.org.uk

Jubilee Course (1897)
Public
St Andrews Links, Pilmour House, St Andrews KY16 9SF
☎ **(01334) 466666**
(01334) 479555
reservations@standrews.org.uk
Euan Loudon (Chief Executive)
Twitter: @thehomeofgolf
www.standrews.org.uk

New Course (1895)
Public
St Andrews Links, Pilmour House, St Andrews KY16 9SF
☎ **(01334) 466666**
(01334) 479555
reservations@standrews.org.uk
Euan Loudon (Chief Executive)
Twitter: @thehomeofgolf
www.standrews.org.uk

Old Course (c140)
Public
St Andrews Links, Pilmour House, St Andrews KY16 9SF
☎ **(01334) 466666**
(01334) 479555
reservations@standrews.org.uk
Euan Loudon (Chief Executive)
Twitter: @thehomeofgolf
www.standrews.org.uk

Strathtyrum Course (1993)
Public
St Andrews Links, Pilmour House, St Andrews KY16 9SF
☎ **(01334) 466666**
(01334) 479555
reservations@standrews.org.uk
Euan Loudon (Chief Executive)
Twitter; @thehomeofgolf
www.standrews.org.uk

The Tennant Cup

The Tennant Cup, presented by Glasgow Golf Club Captain Sir Charles Tennant in 1880, is the oldest golfing trophy in the world for open competition among amateur golfers under medal conditions.

Originally played over two 10-hole rounds at Alexandra Park, it became an 18-hole competition when the course was extended in 1885.

In 1893, the event was transferred to the club's Gailes course and was played there before moving to Killermont in 1906.

In 1927, the competition was extended to two rounds over Killermont and that event was won by William Tulloch of Cathkin Braes, who had been the last player to win in over 18 holes.

In 1976, it was extended to 72 holes with two rounds at Gailes on the Saturday and two at Killermont the following day. That has been the format ever since.

Glasgow

Alexandra Park (1880)
Public
Alexandra Park, Dennistoun, Glasgow G31 8SE
☎ **(0141) 276 0600**
✍ F Derwin

Bishopbriggs (1906)
Brackenbrae Road, Bishopbriggs, Glasgow G64 2DX
☎ **(0141) 772 1810**
⎙ (0141) 762 2532
✉ thesecretarybgc@yahoo.co.uk
≣ www.thebishopbriggsgolfclub.com

Cathcart Castle (1895)
Mearns Road, Clarkston G76 7YL
☎ **(0141) 638 9449**
⎙ (0141) 638 1201
✉ secretary@cathcartcastle.com
≣ www.cathcartcastle.com

Cawder (1933)
Cadder Road, Bishopbriggs, Glasgow G64 3QD
☎ **(0141) 761 1281**
⎙ (0141) 761 1285
✉ secretary@cawdergolfclub.com
✍ Fraser Gemmell (0141) 761 1281
≣ www.cawdergolfclub.com

Cowglen (1906)
301 Barrhead Road, Glasgow G43 1EU
☎ **(0141) 632 7463**
⎙ (0141) 632 7463
✉ secretary@cowglengolfclub.co.uk
✍ Mrs Anne Burnside
≣ www.cowglengolfclub.co.uk

Glasgow (1787)
Killermont, Bearsden, Glasgow G61 2TW
☎ **(0141) 942 1713**
⎙ (0141) 942 0770
✉ secretary@glasgowgolfclub.com
✍ A G McMillan (0141) 942 2011
≣ www.glasgowgolfclub.com

Haggs Castle (1910)
70 Dumbreck Road, Dumbreck, Glasgow G41 4SN
☎ **(0141) 427 0480**
⎙ (0141) 427 1157
✉ secretary@haggscastlegolfclub.com
✍ A Williams (0141) 427 1157
≣ www.haggscastlegolfclub.com

Knightswood (1929)
Public
Knightswood Park, Lincoln Avenue, Glasgow G13 3DN
☎ **(0141) 959 6358**

Lethamhill (1933)
Public
Cumbernauld Road, Glasgow G33 1AH
☎ **(0141) 770 6220**
⎙ (0141) 770 0520

Linn Park (1924)
Public
Simshill Road, Glasgow G44 5TA
☎ **(0141) 633 0377**

Pollok (1892)
90 Barrhead Road, Glasgow G43 1BG
☎ **(0141) 632 1080**
⎙ (0141) 649 1398
✉ secretary@pollokgolf.com
✍ D McKellar (0141) 632 4351
≣ www.pollokgolf.com

Ralston (1904)
Strathmore Avenue, Ralston, Paisley PA1 3DT
☎ **(0141) 882 1349**
⎙ (0141) 883 9837
✉ thesecretary@ralstongolf.co.uk
✍ B W Hanson
≣ www.ralstongolfclub.com

Rouken Glen (1922)
Pay and play
Stewarton Road, Thornliebank, Glasgow G46 7UZ
☎ **(0141) 638 7044**
⎙ (0141) 638 6115
✉ deaconsbank@ngclubs.co.uk
✍ S Armstrong

Sandyhills (1905)
223 Sandyhills Road, Glasgow G32 9NA
☎ **(0141) 778 1179**
✉ admin@sandyhillsgolfclub.co.uk
✍ J Thomson
≣ www.sandyhillsgolfclub.co.uk

Williamwood (1906)
Clarkston Road, Netherlee, Glasgow G44 3YR
☎ **(0141) 637 1783**
⎙ (0141) 571 0166
✉ secretary@williamwoodgc.co.uk
✍ LW Conn (0141) 629 1981
≣ www.williamwoodgc.co.uk

Highland

Caithness & Sutherland

Bonar Bridge/Ardgay (1904)
Migdale Road, Bonar-Bridge, Sutherland IV24 3EJ
☎ **(01863) 766199 (Clubhouse)**
✉ nielsenhunter@btinternet.com
✍ Jeani Hunter (01863) 766 199
⊕ 9 hole scenic course. Catering available May - Sept.
≣ www.bbagc.co.uk

Brora (1891)
Golf Road, Brora KW9 6QS
☎ **(01408) 621417**
⎙ (01408) 622157
✉ secretary@broragolf.co.uk
✍ AJA Gill
≣ www.broragolf.co.uk

The Carnegie Club (1995)
Skibo Castle, Dornoch, Sutherland IV25 3RQ
☎ **(01862) 881 260**
⎙ (01862) 881 260
✉ katy.renwick@carnegieclub.co.uk
✍ Sharon Stewart
≣ www.carnegieclubs.com

Durness (1988)
Pay and play
Balnakeil, Durness IV27 4PN
☎ **(01971) 511364**
⎙ (01971) 511321
✉ lucy@durnessgolfclub.org
✍ Mrs L Mackay (01971) 511364
≣ www.durnessgolfclub.org

Golspie (1889)
Visitors welcome
Ferry Road, Golspie KW10 6ST
☎ **(01408) 633266**
✉ info@golspie-golf-club.co.uk
✍ RI Beaton (Hon) (01408 633927)
≣ www.golspie-golf-club.co.uk

Helmsdale (1895)
Strath Road, Helmsdale KW8 6JL
☎ **(01431) 821063**
✍ R Sutherland
≣ www.helmsdale.org

Lybster (1926)
Main Street, Lybster KW1 6BL
☎ **(01593) 721316**
✍ AG Calder (01593) 721316
≣ www.lybstergolfclub.co.uk

Reay (1893)
Reay, Thurso, Caithness KW14 7RE
☎ **(01847) 811288**
✉ info@reaygolfclub.co.uk
≣ www.reaygolfclub.co.uk

Royal Dornoch (1877)
Golf Road, Dornoch IV25 3LW
☎ **(01862) 810219**
⎙ (01862) 810792
✉ neil@royaldornoch.com
✍ Neil Hampton (Gen Mgr)
≣ www.royaldornoch.com

Thurso (1893)
Pay and play
Newlands of Geise, Thurso KW14 7XD
☎ **(01847) 893807**
⎙ (01847) 892575
✉ thursogolfclub@gmail.com
✍ RM Black
≣ www.thursogolfclub.co.uk

Ullapool (1998)
Pay and play
North Road, Ullapool IV26 2TH
☎ **(01854) 613323**
✉ mail@ullapoolgolfclub.co.uk
✍ A Paterson
≣ www.ullapoolgolfclub.co.uk

Wick (1870)
Reiss, Wick KW1 4RW
☎ **(01955) 602726**

wickgolfclub@hotmail.com
Rognvald Taylor (Secretary)
www.wickgolfclub.org.uk

Inverness

Abernethy (1893)
Nethy Bridge PH25 3EB
(01479) 821305
info@abernethygolfclub.com
Mr M Wright (Captain)
www.abernethygolfclub.com

Aigas (1993)
Proprietary
mains of Aigas, Beauly, Inverness IV4 7AD
(01463) 782942
info@aigas-holidays.co.uk
www.aigas-holidays.co.uk

Alness (1904)
Ardross Rd, Alness, Ross-shire IV17 0QA
(01349) 883877
info@alnessgolfclub.co.uk
Mr Richard Green
www.alnessgolfclub.co.uk

Boat-of-Garten (1898)
Boat-of-Garten, Inverness-shire PH24 3BQ
(01479) 831282
(01479) 831523
office@boatgolf.com
W.N McConachie (clubsec@boatgolf.com)
www.boatgolf.com

Carrbridge (1980)
Inverness Road, Carrbridge PH23 3AU
(01479) 841623 (Clubhouse)
secretary@carrbridgegolf.co.uk
The Secretary
www.carrbridgegolf.co.uk

Fort Augustus (1904)
Pay and play
Markethill, Fort Augustus PH32 4DS
(01320) 366660
fortaugustusgc@aol.com
K Callow
www.fortaugustusgc.webeden.co.uk

Fort William (1974)
North Road, Fort William PH33 6SN
(01397) 704464
fortwilliam01@btconnect.com
Ian Robertson
www.fortwilliamgolf.co.uk

Fortrose & Rosemarkie (1888)
Ness Road East, Fortrose IV10 8SE
(01381) 620529/620733
(01381) 621328
secretary@fortrosegolfclub.co.uk
M MacDonald
www.fortrosegolfclub.co.uk

Grantown-on-Spey (1890)
Golf Course Road, Grantown-on-Spey PH26 3HY
(01479) 872079
(01479) 873725
secretary@grantownonspeygolfclub.co.uk
PR Mackay
www.grantownonspeygolfclub.co.uk

Invergordon (1893)
King George Street, Invergordon IV18 0BD
(01349) 852715
invergordongolf@tiscali.co.uk
David Jamieson
www.invergordongolf.co.uk

Inverness (1883)
Culcabock Road, Inverness IV2 3XQ
(01463) 239882
(01463) 240616
manager@invernessgolfclub.co.uk
E Forbes
www.invernessgolfclub.co.uk

Kingussie (1891)
Pay and play
Gynack Road, Kingussie PH21 1LR
(01540) 661600 (Office)
(01540) 662066
sec@kingussie-golf.co.uk
Ian Chadburn
www.kingussie-golf.co.uk

Loch Ness (1996)
Proprietary
Fairways, Castle Heather, Inverness IV2 6AA
(01463) 713335
(01463) 712695
info@golflochness.com
Secretary (01463) 713335
www.golflochness.com

Muir of Ord (1875)
Great North Road, Muir of Ord IV6 7SX
(01463) 870825
muir.golf@btconnect.com
Mr C Tulloch
www.muirofordgolfclub.co.uk

Nairn (1887)
Seabank Road, Nairn IV12 4HB
(01667) 453208
(01667) 456328
bookings@nairngolfclub.co.uk
Yvonne Forgan (Mgr)
www.nairngolfclub.co.uk

Nairn Dunbar (1899)
Lochloy Road, Nairn IV12 5AE
(01667) 452741
(01667) 456897
secretary@nairndunbar.com
J Gibson
www.nairndunbar.com

Newtonmore (1893)
Owned privately
Golf Course Road, Newtonmore PH20 1AT
(01540) 673878
secretary@newtonmoregolf.com
Heather Bruce (Office Mgr)
www.newtonmoregolf.com

Strathpeffer Spa (1888)
Golf Course Road, Strathpeffer IV14 9AS
(01997) 421219
(01997) 421011
mail@strathpeffergolf.co.uk
Mrs Margaret Spark
www.strathpeffergolf.co.uk

Tain (1890)
Chapel Road, Tain IV19 1JE
(01862) 892314
(01862) 892099
info@tain-golfclub.co.uk
Secretary
www.tain-golfclub.co.uk

Tarbat (1909)
Pay and play
Portmahomack, Tain IV20 1YB
(01862) 871278
(01862) 871598

Torvean (1962)
Public
Glenurquhart Road, Inverness IV3 8JN
(01463) 225651
(01463) 711417
admin@torveangolfclub.co.uk
John Robertson (Administrator)
www.torveangolfclub.co.uk

Orkney & Shetland

Orkney (1889)
Grainbank, Kirkwall, Orkney KW15 1RD
(01856) 872457
(01856) 872457
Gary Farqumar
www.orkneygolfclub.co.uk

Sanday (1977)
Pay and play
Sanday, Orkney KW17 2BW
(01857) 600341
(01857) 600341
nearhouse@triscom.co.uk
R Thorne
⊕ Day Fee £5, Associate Membership (no further fees) £20

Shetland (1891)
Dale, Gott, Shetland ZE2 9SB
(01595) 840369
(01595) 840369
info@shetlandgolfclub.co.uk
S Lamb
www.shetlandgolfclub.co.uk

Stromness (1890)
Stromness, Orkney KW16 3DU
(01856) 850772
www.stromnessgc.co.uk

Whalsay (1976)
Public
Skaw Taing, Whalsay, Shetland ZE2 9AL
(01806) 566450/566481
alan.solvei@lineone.net
HA Sandison, C Hutchison
www.whalsaygolfclub.com

For key to symbols see page 725

West Coast

Askernish (1891)
Pay and play
Lochboisdale, Askernish, South Uist HS81 5ST
(01878) 710312
rthomp4521@btinternet.com
A MacIntyre
www.askernishgolfclub.com

Gairloch (1898)
Gairloch, Ross-Shire IV21 2BE
(01445) 712407
gairlochgolfclub@hotmail.co.uk
J Powell
www.gairlochgolfclub.co.uk

Isle of Harris (1975)
Pay and play
Scarista, Isle of Harris HS3 3HX
(01859) 550226
(01859) 550226
harrisgolf@ic24.net
R A MacDonald
www.harrisgolf.com

Isle of Skye (1964)
Sconser, Isle of Skye IV48 8TD
(01478) 650414

Lochcarron (1908)
Lochcarron, Strathcarron IV54 8YS
(07761) 686261 (mobile)
info@lochcarrongolfclub.co.uk
Bill Roberts
www.lochcarrongolfclub.co.uk

Skeabost (1982)
Skeabost Bridge, Isle of Skye IV51 9NP
(01470) 532202
(01470) 532454

Stornoway (1890)
Lady Lever Park, Stornoway, Isle of Lewis HS2 0XP
(01851) 702240
admin@stornowaygolfclub.co.uk
KW Galloway (01851) 702533
www.stornowaygolfclub.co.uk

Traigh (1947)
Arisaig, Inverness-shire PH39 4NT
(01687) 450337
R Burt (01687) 462 512
www.traighgolf.co.uk

Lanarkshire

Airdrie (1877)
Rochsoles, Airdrie ML6 0PQ
(01236) 762195
(01236) 760584
airdrie.golfclub@btconnect.com
R M Marshall

Bellshill (1905)
Community Road, Orbiston, Bellshill ML4 2RZ
(01698) 745124
(01698) 292576
info@bellshillgolfclub.com
Tony Deerin (Secretary)
www.bellshillgolfclub.com

Biggar (1895)
Public
The Park, Broughton Road, Biggar ML12 6HA
(01899) 220618 (Clubhouse)
frazer@shaungabbit.fsnet.co.uk
F F H Andrews (Sec) (01899) 220624

Blairbeth (1910)
Burnside, Rutherglen, Glasgow G73 4SF
(0141) 634 3355 (Clubhouse)
(0141) 634 3355
secretary@blairbethgolfclub.co.uk
(0141) 634 3325
www.blairbethgolfclub.co.uk

Bothwell Castle (1922)
Uddington Road, Bothwell, Glasgow G71 8TD
(01698) 801971
(01698) 801971
secretary@bcgolf.co.uk
Jim Callaghan CCM (01698) 801971
www.bcgolf.co.uk

Calderbraes (1891)
57 Roundknowe Road, Uddingston G71 7TS
(01698) 813425
calderbraesgolfclub@tiscali.co.uk
S McGuigan (0141) 573 2497
www.calderbraesgolfclub.com

Cambuslang (1892)
30 Westburn Drive, Cambuslang G72 7NA
(0141) 641 3130
(0141) 641 3130
cambuslanggolfclub@tiscali.co.uk
RM Dunlop
www.cambuslandgolf.org

Carluke (1894)
Hallcraig, Mauldslie Road, Carluke ML8 5HG
(01555) 770574/771070
(01555) 770574
carlukegolfsecy@tiscali.co.uk
G White (01555) 770574
www.carlukegolfclub.com

Carnwath (1907)
1 Main Street, Carnwath ML11 8JX
(01555) 840251
(01555) 841070
carnwathgc@hotmail.co.uk
Mrs L Jardine
www.carnwathgc.co.uk

Cathkin Braes (1888)
Cathkin Road, Rutherglen, Glasgow G73 4SE
(0141) 634 6605
secretary@cathkinbraesgolfclub.co.uk
D E Moir
www.cathkinbraesgolfclub.co.uk

Coatbridge Municipal (1971)
Public
Townhead Road, Coatbridge ML52 2HX
(01236) 28975

Colville Park (1923)
Jerviston Estate, Motherwell ML1 4UG
(01698) 263017
(01698) 230418
www.colvillepark.co.uk

Crow Wood (1925)
Cumbernauld Road, Muirhead, Glasgow G69 9JF
(0141) 799 1943
(0141) 779 4873
secretary@crowwoodgolfclub.co.uk
Margaret Laughrey (0141) 779 4954
www.crowwoodgolfclub.co.uk

Dalziel Park (1997)
100 Hagen Drive, Motherwell ML1 5RZ
(01698) 862862
(01698) 862863

Douglas Water (1922)
Rigside, Lanark ML11 9NB
(01555) 880361
(01555) 880361
S Hogg
www.douglaswatergolf.co.uk

Drumpellier (1894)
Drumpellier Ave, Coatbridge ML5 1RX
(01236) 424139
(01236) 428723
administrator@drumpelliergolfclub.com
JM Craig
Visitors; Weekdays only
Round £35.00 / Day £50.00

East Kilbride (1900)
Chapelside Road, Nerston, East Kilbride G74 4PH
(01355) 581804 (Clubhouse)
(01355) 581807
secretary@ekgolfclub.co.uk
Fraser Gow (01355) 581800
www.ekgolfclub.co.uk

Easter Moffat (1922)
Mansion House, Plains, Airdrie ML6 8NP
(01236) 842878
(01236) 842904
secretary@emgc.co.uk

Hamilton Golf Club (1892)
Riccarton, Ferniegair, Hamilton ML3 7UE
(01698) 282872
(01698) 204650
secretary@hamiltongolfclub.co.uk
G B Mackenzie (Mgr)
www.hamiltongolfclub.co.uk

Hollandbush (1954)
Public
Acretophead, Lesmahagow, Coalburn ML11 0JS
(01555) 893484

For key to symbols see page 725

For

mail@hollandbushgolfclub.co.uk
J Hamilton (Secretary)
www.hollandbushgolfclub.co.uk

Kirkhill (1910)
Greenlees Road, Cambuslang, Glasgow G72 8YN
(0141) 641 3083 (Clubhouse)
(0141) 641 8499
secretary@kirkhillgolfclub.org.uk
C Downes (0141) 641 8499
www.kirkhillgolfclub.org.uk

Lanark (1851)
The Moor, Lanark ML11 7RX
(01555) 663219
(01555) 663219
lanarkgolfclub@supanet.com
George H Cuthill
www.lanarkgolfclub.co.uk

Langlands (1985)
Public
Langlands Road, East Kilbride G75 0QQ
(01355) 248173
(01355) 248121

Larkhall (1909)
Public
Burnhead Road, Larkhall, Glasgow
(01698) 881113
M Mallinson

Leadhills (1895)
1 New Row, Wanlockhead, Leadhills, Nr Biggar ML12 6UJ
(01659) 74272
jack@gsx-r750cc.fsnet.co.uk
Jack Arrigoni
See Golf Central

Mount Ellen (1904)
Lochend Road, Gartcosh, Glasgow G69 9EY
(01236) 872277
(01236) 872249
secretary@mountellengolfclub.co.uk
Robert Watt
www.mountellengolfclub.co.uk

Mouse Valley (1993)
East End, Cleghorn, Lanark ML11 8NR
(01555) 870015
(01555) 870022
info@kames-golf-club.com
Helen Howitt
www.kames-golf-club.com

Shotts (1895)
Blairhead, Benhar Road, Shotts ML7 5BJ
(01501) 820431
(01501) 825868
info@shottsgolfclub.co.uk
GT Stoddart (01501) 825868
www.shottsgolfclub.co.uk

Strathaven (1908)
Glasgow Road, Strathaven ML10 6NL
(01357) 520421
(01357) 520539
info@strathavengc.com
IF Neil
www.strathavengc.com

Strathclyde Park (1936)
Public
Mote Hill, Hamilton ML3 6BY
(01698) 429350
K Will
24 bay driving range. Large Practice area. Large Putting Green.

Torrance House (1969)
Public
Strathaven Road, East Kilbride, Glasgow G75 0QZ
(01355) 248638
secretary@torrancehousegc.co.uk
Margaret D McKerlie (01355) 249720

Wishaw (1897)
55 Cleland Road, Wishaw ML2 7PH
(01698) 372869 (Clubhouse)
(01698) 356930
jwdouglas@btconnect.com
JW Douglas (01698) 357480
WD-U until 4.00pm NA-Sat U-Sun

Lothians

East Lothian

Aberlady (1912)
Club
Aberlady EH32 0RB
ithomps3@aol.com

Archerfield Links (2004)
Dirleton, East Lothian EH39 5HU
(01620) 897050
(08700) 515487
mail@archerfieldgolfclub.com
Stuart Bayne (Dir of Golf)
www.archerfieldgolfclub.com

Bass Rock (1873)
Club
43a High Street, North Berwick EH39 4HH
(01620) 895182
bassrockgolfclub@hotmail.com
Tom McGinley

Castle Park (1994)
Pay and play
Gifford, Haddington EH41 4PL
(01620) 810733
castleparkgolf@hotmail.com
JT Wilson (01620) 810733
www.castleparkgolfclub.co.uk

Dirleton Castle (1854)
Club
15 The Pines, Gullane EH31 2DT
(01620) 843591
www.dirletoncastlegolfclub.org.uk

Dunbar (1856)
East Links, Dunbar EH42 1LL
(01368) 862317
(01368) 865202
secretary@dunbargolfclub.com
John I Archibald (Club Mgr)
www.dunbargolfclub.com

Gifford (1904)
Edinburgh Road, Gifford EH41 4JE
(01620) 810591 (Starter)
secretary@giffordgolfclub.com
Robert Stewart (01620) 810267
www.giffordgolfclub.com

Glen (North Berwick) (1906)
East Links, Tantallon Terrace, North Berwick EH39 4LE
(01620) 892726
(01620) 895447
secretary@glengolfclub.co.uk
Rita Wilson (Office Mgr)
www.glengolfclub.co.uk

Gullane (1882)
West Links Road, Gullane, East Lothian EH31 2BB
(01620) 842255
(01620) 842327
secretary@gullanegolfclub.com
S Anthony
www.gullanegolfclub.com

Haddington (1865)
Amisfield Park, Haddington EH41 4PT
(01620) 823627
(01620) 826580
info@haddingtongolf.co.uk
Jane Helmn (Accounts Administrator)
www.haddingtongolf.co.uk

The Honourable Company of Edinburgh Golfers (1744)
Duncur Road, Muirfield, Gullane EH31 2EG
(01620) 842123
(01620) 842977
hceg@muirfield.org.uk
A N G Brown
www.muirfield.org.uk

Kilspindie (1867)
Aberlady EH32 0QD
(01875) 870358
kilspindie@btconnect.com
J R Leslie
www.kilspindlegolfclub.com

Longniddry (1921)
Links Road, Longniddry EH32 0NL
(01875) 852141
(01875) 853371
secretary@longniddrygolfclub.co.uk
RMS Gunning
www.longniddrygolfclub.co.uk

Luffness New (1894)
Aberlady EH32 0QA
(01620) 843114
(01620) 842933
secretary@luffnessnew.com
Gp Capt AG Yeates (01620) 843336
www.luffnessgolf.com

Musselburgh (1938)
Monktonhall, Musselburgh EH21 6SA
(0131) 665 2005

(0131) 665 4435
secretary@themusselburghgolfclub.com
P Millar
www.themusselburghgolfclub.com

Musselburgh Old Course (1982)
Public
10 Balcarres Road, Musselburgh EH21 7SD
(0131) 665 6981
(0131) 653 1770
oldcourseclub@unicombox.com
K Bentley (Sec) (0131) 665 6981
www.mocgc.com

North Berwick (1832)
West Links, Beach Road, North Berwick EH39 4BB
(01620) 895040
(01620) 893274
secretary@northberwickgolfclub.com
Christopher Spencer (01620) 895040
www.northberwickgolfclub.com

Royal Musselburgh (1774)
Prestongrange House, Prestonpans EH32 9RP
(01875) 810276 (advance bookings) opt 3
(01875) 810276
royalmusselburgh@btinternet.com
Colin Ramsay
www.royalmusselburgh.co.uk

Tantallon (1853)
Club
32 Westgate, North Berwick EH39 4AH
(01620) 892114
(01620) 894399
secretary@tantallongolfclub.co.uk
I F Doig
www.north-berwick.co.uk/tantallon

Thorntree Golf Club (1856)
Club
Prestongrange House, Prestonpans EH32 9RP
(0131) 552 3559

Whitekirk (1995)
Pay and play
Whitekirk, North Berwick EH39 5PR
(01620) 870300
(01620) 870330
countryclub@whitekirk.com
D Brodie
www.whitekirk.com

Winterfield (1935)
Public
St Margarets, Back Road, Dunbar EH42 1XE
(01368) 863562
kevinphillips@tiscali.co.uk
Kevin Phillips
www.winterfieldgolfclub.info

Midlothian

Baberton (1893)
55 Baberton Avenue, Juniper Green, Edinburgh EH14 5DU
(0131) 453 4911
(0131) 453 4678
manager@baberton.co.uk
K A Nicholson
www.baberton.co.uk

Braid Hills (1893)
Public
Braid Hills Road, Edinburgh EH10 6JY
(0131) 447 6666 (Starter)

Braids United (1897)
Club
22 Braid Hills Approach, Edinburgh EH10 6JY
(07541) 136133
golf@braids-united.co.uk
WJ Mitchell (0131) 476 2238
www.braids-united.co.uk

Broomieknowe (1905)
36 Golf Course Road, Bonnyrigg EH19 2HZ
(0131) 663 9317
(0131) 663 2152
administrator@broomieknowe.com
R H Beattie
www.broomieknowe.com

Bruntsfield Links Golfing Society (1761)
The Clubhouse, 32 Barnton Avenue, Edinburgh EH4 6JH
(0131) 336 1479
(0131) 336 5538
secretary@bruntsfield.sol.co.uk
Alan Feltham
www.bruntsfieldlinks.co.uk

Carrick Knowe (1930)
Public
Glendevon Park, Edinburgh EH12 5VZ
(0131) 337 1096 (Starter)

Craigmillar Park (1895)
1 Observatory Road, Edinburgh EH9 3HG
(0131) 667 2837
(0131) 662 8091
secretary@craigmillarpark.co.uk
Mrs D Nichol (0131) 667 0047
www.craigmillarpark.co.uk

Duddingston (1895)
Duddingston Road West, Edinburgh EH15 3QD
(0131) 661 7688
(0131) 652 6057
secretary@duddingstongolf.co.uk
Duncan Ireland
www.duddingstongolfclub.co.uk

Glencorse (1890)
Milton Bridge, Penicuik EH26 0RD
(01968) 677177
(01968) 674399
secretary@glencorsegolfclub.com
W Oliver (01968) 677189
www.glencorsegolfclub.com

Gogarburn (1975)
Members and Visitors
Hanley Lodge, Newbridge, Midlothian EH28 8NN
(0131) 333 4718
(0131) 333 2496
secretary@gogarburngc.co.uk
www.gogarburngc.com

Kings Acre (1997)
Proprietary
Lasswade EH18 1AU
(0131) 663 3456
(0131) 663 7076
info@kings-acregolf.com
Alan Murdoch (Dir of Golf)
www.kings-acregolf.com

Kingsknowe (1907)
326 Lanark Road, Edinburgh EH14 2JD
(0131) 441 1144
(0131) 441 2079
clubmanager@kingsknowe.com
Richard J McLuckie (0131) 441 1145
www.kingsknowe.com

Liberton (1920)
Kingston Grange, 297 Gilmerton Road, Edinburgh EH16 5UJ
(0131) 664 3009
info@libertongc.co.uk
John Masterton
www.libertongc.co.uk

Lothianburn (1893)
106a Biggar Road, Edinburgh EH10 7DU
(0131) 445 5067
info@lothianburngc.co.uk
(0131) 445 5067
www.lothianburngc.co.uk

Marriott Dalmahoy Hotel & CC
Dalmahoy, Kirknewton EH27 8EB
(0131) 335 8010
(0131) 335 3577

Melville Golf Centre (1995)
Pay and play
Lasswade, Edinburgh EH18 1AN
(0131) 663 8038 (range, shop, tuition)
(0131) 654 0814
golf@melvillegolf.co.uk
Mr & Mrs MacFarlane (Props)
www.melvillegolf.co.uk

Merchants of Edinburgh (1907)
10 Craighill Gardens, Morningside, Edinburgh EH10 5PY
(0131) 447 1219
(0131) 446 9833
admin@merchantsgolf.com
J W B Harwood
www.merchantsgolf.com

For key to symbols see page 725

Mortonhall (1892)
231 Braid Road, Edinburgh EH10 6PB
☎ **(0131) 447 6974**
(0131) 447 8712
clubhouse@mortonhallgc.co.uk
Ms BM Giefer
www.mortonhallgc.co.uk

Murrayfield (1896)
43 Murrayfield Road, Edinburgh EH12 6EU
☎ **(0131) 337 3478**
(0131) 313 0721
john@murrayfieldgolfclub.co.uk
Mr J A Fraser (0131) 337 3478
www.murrayfieldgolfclub.co.uk

Newbattle (1896)
Abbey Road, Eskbank, Dalkeith EH22 3AD
☎ **(0131) 663 2123**
(0131) 654 1810
mail@newbattlegolfclub.com
HG Stanners (0131) 663 1819
www.newbattlegolfclub.com

Prestonfield (1920)
6 Priestfield Road North, Edinburgh EH16 5HS
☎ **(0131) 667 9665**
(0131) 777 2727
generalmanager@prestonfieldgolf.com
Carol King (Sec)
www.prestonfieldgolf.com

Ratho Park (1928)
Ratho, Edinburgh EH28 8NX
☎ **(0131) 335 0068**
secretary@rathoparkgolfclub.co.uk
D A Scott
www.rathoparkgolfclub.co.uk

Ravelston (1912)
24 Ravelston Dykes Road, Edinburgh EH4 3NZ
☎ **(0131) 315 2486**
(0131) 315 2486
ravelstongc@hotmail.com
Jim Lowrie
www.ravelstongolfclub.com

Royal Burgess Golfing Society of Edinburgh (1735)
181 Whitehouse Road, Barnton, Edinburgh EH4 6BU
☎ **(0131) 339 2075**
graham@royalburgess.co.uk
Graham Callander
www.royalburgess.co.uk

Silverknowes (1947)
Public
Silverknowes Parkway, Edinburgh EH4 5ET
☎ **(0131) 336 3843 (Starter)**

Swanston New Golf Course (1927)
111 Swanston Road, Fairmilehead, Edinburgh EH10 7DS
☎ **(0131) 445 2239**
(0131) 445 5720
golf@swanston.co.uk
Colin McClung
www.swanstongolf.co.uk

Torphin Hill (1895)
37-39 Torphin Road, Edinburgh EH13 0PG
☎ **(0131) 441 1100**
(0131) 441 7166
torphinhillgc@unicombox.com
Secretary
www.torphinhill.com

Turnhouse (1897)
154 Turnhouse Road, Corstorphine, Edinburgh EH12 0AD
☎ **(0131) 339 1014**
(0131) 339 5141
secretary@turnhousegc.com
Lindsay Gordon (Secretary)
www.turnhousegc.com

West Lothian

Bathgate (1892)
Edinburgh Road, Bathgate EH48 1BA
☎ **(01506) 630505**
(01506) 636775
bathgate.golfclub@lineone.net
G Flannigan (01506) 630505
www.bathgategolfclub.com

Bridgend & District (1994)
Willowdean, Bridgend, Linlithgow EH49 6NW
☎ **(01506) 834140**
(01506) 834706
www.bridgendgolfclub.com

Deer Park G&CC (1978)
Golf Course Road, Knightsridge, Livingston EH54 8AB
☎ **(01506) 446699**
(01506) 435608
jdouglas@muir-group.co.uk
John Douglas (Gen Mgr)
www.deer-park.co.uk

Dundas Parks (1957)
South Queensferry EH30 9SS
☎ **(0131)331 4252**
cmkwood@btinternet.com
Mrs C Wood (07747) 854802
www.dundasparks.co.uk

Greenburn (1953)
6 Greenburn Road, Fauldhouse EH47 9HJ
☎ **(01501) 770292**
(01501) 772615
administrator@greenburngolfclub.co.uk
Adrian McGowan
www.greenburngolfclub.co.uk

Harburn (1932)
West Calder EH55 8RS
☎ **(01506) 871131**
(01506) 870286
info@harburngolfclub.co.uk
H Warnock (01506) 871131
www.harburngolfclub.co.uk

Linlithgow (1913)
Braehead, Linlithgow EH49 6QF
☎ **(01506) 842585**
(01506) 842764
linlithgowgolf@talk21.com
TI Adams
www.linlithgowgolf.co.uk

Niddry Castle (1983)
Castle Road, Winchburgh EH52 2RQ
☎ **(01506) 891097**
secretary@niddrycastlegc.co.uk
B Brooks
www.niddrycastlegc.co.uk

Oatridge (2000)
Pay and play
Ecclesmachen, Broxburn, West Lothian EH52 6NH
☎ **(01506) 859636**
info@oatridge.ac.uk
Jim Thomson
www.oatridge.ac.uk

Polkemmet (1981)
Public
Whitburn, Bathgate EH47 0AD
☎ **(01501) 743905**
(01501) 744780
polkemmet@westlothian.gov.uk
Stuart Mungall (01501) 743905
www.beecraigs.com

Pumpherston (1895)
Drumshoreland Road, Pumpherston EH53 0LH
☎ **(01506) 432869/433336**
(01506) 438250
sheena.corner@tiscali.co.uk
James Taylor (01506) 433336
www.pumpherstongolfclub.co.uk

Rutherford Castle (1998)
Proprietary
West Linton EH46 7AS
☎ **(01968) 661233**
(01968) 661233
clubhouse@rutherfordcastle.org.uk
Derek Mitchell (Mgr)
www.rutherfordcastlegc.org.uk

Uphall (1895)
Houston Mains, Uphall EH52 6JT
☎ **(01506) 856404**
(01506) 855358
uphallgolfclub@btconnect.com
Gordon Law (Club Administrator Mgr)
www.uphallgolfclub.com

West Lothian (1892)
Airngath Hill, Bo'ness EH49 7RH
☎ **(01506) 826030**
(01506) 826030
manager@westlothiangc.com
Alan E Gibson (01506) 826030
www.westlothiangc.com

Moray

Buckpool (1933)
Barhill Road, Buckie AB56 1DU
☎ **(01542) 832236**
✉ golf@buckpoolgolf.com
✍ Mrs I Coull
🖹 www.buckpoolgolf.com

Dufftown (1896)
Tomintoul Road, Dufftown AB55 4BS
☎ **(01340) 820325**
🖷 (01340) 820325
✉ admin@dufftowngolfclub.com
✍ IR Montgomery
🖹 www.dufftowngolfclub.com

Elgin (1906)
Hardhillock, Birnie Road, Elgin IV30 8SX
☎ **(01343) 542338**
🖷 (01343) 542341
✉ secretary@elgingolfclub.com
✍ Gary J Abel
🖹 www.elgingolfclub.com

Forres (1889)
Muiryshade, Forres IV36 2RD
☎ **(01309) 672949**
🖷 (01309) 672261
✉ forresgolfclub@tiscali.co.uk
✍ David Mackintosh
🖹 www.forresgolfclub.co.uk

Garmouth & Kingston (1932)
Spey Street, Garmouth, Fochabers IV32 7NJ
☎ **(01343) 870388**
🖷 (01343) 870388
✉ garmouthgolfclub@aol.com
✍ Mrs I Fraser
🖹 www.garmouthkingstongolfclub.com

Hopeman (1909)
Hopeman, Moray IV30 5YA
☎ **(01343) 830578**
🖷 (01343) 830152
✉ hopemangc@aol.com
✍ J Fraser (01343) 835068
🖹 www.hopemangc.co.uk

Moray (1889)
Stotfield Road, Lossiemouth IV31 6QS
☎ **(01343) 812018**
🖷 (01343) 815102
✉ secretary@moraygolf.co.uk
✍ Stevie Grant
🖹 www.moraygolf.co.uk

Spey Bay (1904)
Proprietary
The Links, Spey Bay, Fochabers IV32 7PJ
☎ **(01343) 820424**
✉ info@speybay.co
✍ Mr Iain Ednie
🖹 www.speybay.co

Perth & Kinross

Aberfeldy (1895)
Taybridge Road, Aberfeldy PH15 2BH
☎ **(01887) 820535**
🖷 (01887) 820535
✉ feldyde@tiscali.co.uk
✍ Jim Adams
🖹 www.aberfeldygolfclub.co.uk

Alyth (1894)
Pitcrocknie, Alyth PH11 8HF
☎ **(01828) 632268**
🖷 (01828) 633491
✉ enquiries@alythgolfclub.co.uk
✍ J Docherty
🖹 www.alythgolfclub.co.uk

Auchterarder (1892)
Orchil Road, Auchterarder PH3 1LS
☎ **(01764) 662804**
🖷 (01764) 664423
✉ secretary@auchterardergolf.co.uk
✍ D.D.Smith
🖹 www.auchterardergolf.co.uk

Bishopshire (1903)
Pay and play
Kinnesswood, Woodmarch, Kinross KY13 9HX
✉ ian-davidson@tiscali.co.uk
✍ Ian Davidson (01592) 773224
🖹 www.bishopshiregolfclub.com

Blair Atholl (1896)
Invertilt Road, Blair Atholl PH18 5TG
☎ **(01796) 481407**

Blairgowrie (1889)
Golf Course Road, Rosemount, Blairgowrie PH10 6LG
☎ **(01250) 872622**
🖷 (01250) 875451
✉ office@theblairgowriegolfclub.co.uk
✍ Douglas Cleeton (Managing Secretary)
🖹 www.theblairgowriegolfclub.co.uk

Callander (1890)
Aveland Road, Callander FK17 8EN
☎ **(01877) 330090**
🖷 (01877) 330062
✉ callandergolf@btconnect.com
✍ Miss E Macdonald
🖹 www.callandergolfclub.co.uk

Comrie (1891)
Laggan Braes, Comrie PH6 2LR
☎ **(01764) 670055**
✉ enquiries@comriegolf.co.uk
✍ Manager
🖹 www.comriegolf.co.uk

Craigie Hill (1909)
Cherrybank, Perth PH2 0NE
☎ **(01738) 622644**
🖷 (01738) 620829
✉ admin@craigiehill.co.uk
✍ Administration (01738) 620829
🖹 www.craigiehill.co.uk

Crieff (1891)
Perth Road, Crieff PH7 3LR
☎ **(01764) 652909 (Bookings)**
🖷 (01764) 653803
✉ secretary@crieffgolf.co.uk
✍ A Roy Hunter (01764) 652397
🖹 www.crieffgolf.co.uk

Dalmunzie (1948)
Glenshee, Blairgowrie PH10 7QE
☎ **(01250) 885226**
✉ info@dalmunzieestate.com
✍ Simon Winton
🖹 www.dalmunzieestate.com

Dunkeld & Birnam (1892)
Fungarth, Dunkeld PH8 0ES
☎ **(01350) 727524**
🖷 (01350) 728660
✉ secretary-dunkeld@tiscali.co.uk
✍ Jane Burnett
🖹 www.dunkeldandbirnamgolfclub.co.uk

Dunning (1953)
Rollo Park, Dunning PH2 0QX
☎ **(01764) 684747**
✉ secretary@dunninggolfclub.co.uk
✍ Neil C Morton (01738) 626701
🖹 www.dunninggolfclub.co.uk

Foulford Inn (1995)
Pay and play
Crieff PH7 3LN
☎ **(01764) 652407**
🖷 (01764) 652407
✉ foulford@btconnect.com
✍ M Beaumont
🖹 www.foulfordinn.co.uk

The Gleneagles Hotel (1924)
Auchterarder PH3 1NF
☎ **(01764) 662231**
🖷 (01764) 662134
✉ resort.sales@gleneagles.com
✍ Bernard Murphy (Hotel)
🖹 www.gleneagles.com

Glenisla (1998)
Proprietary
Pitcrocknie Farm, Alyth PH11 8JJ
☎ **(01828) 632445**
🖷 (01828) 633749
🖹 www.golf-glenisla.co.uk

Killin (1911)
Killin FK21 8TX
☎ **(01567) 820312**
🖷 (01567) 820312
✉ info@killingolfclub.co.uk
🖹 www.killingolfclub.co.uk

King James VI (1858)
Moncreiffe Island, Perth PH2 8NR
☎ **(01738) 632460**
✉ mansec@kingjamesvi.com
✍ Mike Brown (Managing Secretary)
🖹 www.kingjamesvi.com

Kinross Golf Courses (1900)
c/o The Green Hotel, 2 The Muirs, Kinross KY13 8AS
☎ **(01577) 863407**

For key to symbols see page 725

(01577) 863180
reception@green-hotel.com
Eileen Gray
www.golfkinross.com

Mains of Taymouth Golf Club (1992)
Pay and play
Mains of Taymouth, Kenmore, Aberfeldy PH15 2HN
(01887) 830226
(01887) 830775
info@taymouth.co.uk
R Menzies (Mgr)
www.kenmoregolfcourse.co.uk

Milnathort (1910)
South Street, Milnathort, Kinross KY13 9XA
(01577) 864069
milnathort.gc@btconnect.com
K Dziennik (Admin. Mgr)

Muckhart (1908)
Drumburn Road, Muckhart, Dollar FK14 7JH
(01259) 781423
enquiries@muckhartgolf.com
A Houston
www.muckhartgolf.com

Murrayshall (1981)
Murrayshall, New Scone, Perth PH2 7PH
(01738) 554804
(01738) 552595
info@murrayshall.co.uk
M Lloyd (Mgr)
www.murrayshall.co.uk

Muthill (1911)
Peat Road, Muthill PH5 2DA
(01764) 681523
(01764) 681557
muthillgolfclub@btconnect.com
Nan Shaw
www.muthillgolfclub.co.uk

North Inch (1892)
Public
c/o Perth & Kinross Council, The Environment Services, Pullar House, 35 Kinnoull St, Perth PH1 5GD
(01738) 636481 (Starter)
(01738) 476410
northinchgolf@pkc.gov.uk
Alison White
www.pkc.gov.uk/northinchgolf

Pitlochry (1909)
Proprietary
Golf Course Road, Pitlochry PH16 5QY
(01796) 472792 (Bookings)
(01796) 473947 (bookings)
pro@pitlochrygolf.co.uk
Mark Pirie (01796) 472792
www.pitlochrygolf.co.uk

Royal Perth Golfing Society (1824)
Club
1/2 Atholl Crescent, Perth PH1 5NG
(01738) 622265
secretary@royal-perth-golfing-society.org.uk
DP McDonald (Gen Sec) (01738) 622265
www.royal-perth-golfing-society.org.uk

St Fillans (1903)
South Loch Earn Rd, St Fillans PH6 2NJ
(01764) 685312
01764 685312
stfillansgc@aol.com
G Hibbert (01764) 685312
www.st-fillans-golf.com

Strathmore Golf Centre (1995)
Proprietary
Leroch, Alyth, Blairgowrie PH11 8NZ
(01828) 633322
(01828) 633533
enquiries@strathmoregolf.com
David Norman
www.strathmoregolf.com

Strathtay (1909)
Donfield, Strathtay, Pitlochry PH9 0PG
(01887) 840493
James Wilson
www.strathtaygolfclub.com

Taymouth Castle (1923)
Kenmore, Aberfeldy PH15 2NT
(01887) 830234
(01887) 830234
secretary@taymouthcastlegolfclub.com
W R McGregor (Sec)
www.taymouthcastlegolfclub.com

Whitemoss (1994)
Whitemoss Road, Dunning, Perth PH2 0QX
(01738) 730300
(01738) 730490
info@whitemossgolf.com
A Nicolson
www.whitemossgolf.com

Renfrewshire

Barshaw (1927)
Public
Barshaw Park, Glasgow Road, Paisley, PA1 3JT
(0141) 889 2908
(0141) 840 2148
jane.mccrindle@renfrewshire.gov.uk
www.renfrewshire.gov.uk

Bonnyton (1957)
Eaglesham, Glasgow G76 0QA
(01355) 303030
(01355) 303151
secretarybgc@btconnect.com
M Crichton
www.bonnytongolfclub.com

Caldwell (1903)
Caldwell, Uplawmoor G78 4AU
(01505) 850329
(01505) 850604
Secretary@caldwellgolfclub.co.uk
Alan Ferguson (01505) 850366
www.caldwellgolfclub.co.uk

Cochrane Castle (1895)
Scott Avenue, Craigston, Johnstone PA5 0HF
(01505) 320146
(01505) 325338
secretary@cochranecastle.com
Mrs PIJ Quin
www.cochranecastle.com

East Renfrewshire (1922)
Pilmuir, Newton Mearns G77 6RT
(01355) 500256
(01355) 500323
secretary@eastrengolfclub.co.uk
G J Tennant (01355) 500256
www.eastrengolfclub.co.uk

Eastwood (1893)
Muirshield, Loganswell, Newton Mearns, Glasgow G77 6RX
(01355) 500285
(01355) 500333
eastwoodgolfclub@btconnect.com
I Brown (01355) 500280
www.eastwoodgolfclub.co.uk

Elderslie (1908)
63 Main Road, Elderslie PA5 9AZ
(01505) 323956
(01505) 340346
eldersliegolfclub@btconnect.com
Mrs A Anderson
www.eldersliegolfclub.com

Erskine (1904)
Golf Road, Bishopton PA7 5PH
(01505) 862302
(01505) 862898
secretary@erskinegolfclub.wanadoo.co.uk
DF McKellar
www.erskinegolfclublimited.co.uk

Fereneze (1904)
Fereneze Avenue, Barrhead G78 1HJ
(0141) 881 1519
(0141) 881 7149
ferenezegc@lineone.net
G McCreadie (0141) 881 7149
www.ferenezegolfclub.co.uk

Gleddoch (1974)
Langbank PA14 6YE
(01475) 540711

Gourock (1896)
Cowal View, Gourock PA19 1HD
(01475) 631001
secretary@gourockgolfclub.com
Margaret Paterson
www.gourockgolfclub.com

Greenock (1890)
Forsyth Street, Greenock PA16 8RE
(01475) 720793
secretary@greenockgolfclub.co.uk
Mrs Heather Sinclair (01475) 791912
www.greenockgolfclub.co.uk

Kilmacolm (1891)
Porterfield Road, Kilmacolm PA13 4PD
☎ **(01505) 872139**
(01505) 874007
secretary@kilmacolmgolfclub.com
VR Weldin
www.kilmacolmgolfclub.com

Lochwinnoch (1897)
Burnfoot Road, Lochwinnoch PA12 4AN
☎ **(01505) 842153**
(01505) 843668
admin@lochwinnochgolf.co.uk
RJG Jamieson
www.lochwinnochgolf.co.uk

Old Course Ranfurly Golf Club (1905)
Ranfurly Place, Bridge of Weir PA11 3DE
☎ **(01505) 613612 (Clubhouse)**
(01505) 613214
secretary@oldranfurly.com
J M R Doyle (01505) 613214
www.oldranfurly.com

Paisley (1895)
Braehead Road, Paisley PA2 8TZ
☎ **(0141) 884 2292 (Clubhouse)**
(0141) 884 3903
paisleygolfclub@btconnect.com
John Devenny (Sec/Mgr)
www.paisleygolfclub.com

Port Glasgow (1895)
Devol Road, Port Glasgow PA14 5XE
☎ **(01475) 704181**
01475 700334
contact@portglasgowgolfclub.co.uk
James Downie
www.portglasgowgolfclub.com

Ranfurly Castle (1889)
Golf Road, Bridge of Weir PA11 3HN
☎ **(01505) 612609**
(01505) 610406
secranfur@aol.com
J King
www.ranfurlycastlegolfclub.co.uk

Renfrew (1894)
Blythswood Estate, Inchinnan Road, Renfrew PA4 9EG
☎ **(0141) 886 6692**
(0141) 886 1808
andy.mclaughlin@renfrewgolfclub.net
Andy McLaughlin
www.renfrewgolfclub.net

Whitecraigs (1905)
72 Ayr Road, Giffnock, Glasgow G46 6SW
☎ **(0141) 639 4530**
(0141) 616 3648
whitecraigsgc@btconnect.com
I M Brown
www.whitecraigsgolfclub.com

Stirlingshire

Aberfoyle (1890)
Braeval, Aberfoyle FK8 3UY
☎ **(01877) 382493**
secretary@aberfoylegolf.co.uk
EJ Barnard (Sec) (01360) 550847
www.aberfoylegolf.com

Balfron (1992)
Kepculloch Road, Balfron G63 0QP
☎ **(0781) 482 7620**
brian.a.davidson23@btinternet.com
Brian Davidson (01360) 550613
www.balfrongolfsociety.org.uk

Bonnybridge (1925)
Larbert Road, Bonnybridge, Falkirk FK4 1NY
☎ **(01324) 812822/812323**
(01324) 812323
bgcl@hotmail.co.uk
Alexander Nolton (01324) 812323

Bridge of Allan (1895)
Sunnylaw, Bridge of Allan, Stirling
☎ **(01786) 832332**
secretary@bofagc.com
David Smeaton
www.bofagc.com

Buchanan Castle (1936)
Proprietary
Drymen G63 0HY
☎ **(01360) 660307**
info@buchanancastlegolfclub.co.uk
Ms JA Dawson
www.buchanancastlegolfclub.com

Campsie (1897)
Crow Road, Lennoxtown, Glasgow G66 7HX
☎ **(01360) 310244**
campsiegolfclub@aol.com
K Stoddart (Administrator)
www.campsiegolfclub.org.uk

Dunblane New (1923)
Perth Road, Dunblane FK15 0LJ
☎ **(01786) 821527**
(01786) 825066
secretary@dngc.co.uk
RD Morrison
www.dngc.co.uk

Falkirk (1922)
Stirling Road, Camelon, Falkirk FK2 7YP
☎ **(01324) 611061/612219**
(01324) 639573
secretary@falkirkgolfclub.co.uk
Aileen Jenkins
www.falkirkgolfclub.co.uk

Falkirk Tryst (1885)
86 Burnhead Road, Larbert FK5 4BD
☎ **(01324) 562415**
(01324) 562054
secretary@falkirktrystgolfclub.com
Mhairi Kemp (01324) 562054
www.falkirktrystgolfclub.com

Glenbervie (1932)
Stirling Road, Larbert FK5 4SJ
☎ **(01324) 562605**
(01324) 551054
secretary@glenberviegolfclub.com
IR Webster CA
www.glenberviegolfclub.com

Grangemouth (1973)
Public
Polmonthill, Polmont FK2 0YA
☎ **(01324) 711500**
greg.mcfarlane@falkirk.gov.uk
Jim McNairney

Kilsyth Lennox (1905)
Tak-Ma-Doon Road, Kilsyth G65 0RS
☎ **(01236) 824115 (Bookings)**
(01236) 823089
admin@kilsythlennox.com
L Reeds (01236) 824115
www.kilsythlennox.com

Polmont (1901)
Manuel Rigg, Maddiston, Falkirk FK2 0LS
☎ **(01324) 711277 (Clubhouse)**
(01324) 712504
polmontgolfclub@btconnect.com
Mrs M Fellows

Stirling (1869)
Queen's Road, Stirling FK8 3AA
☎ **(01786) 464098**
(01786) 460090
enquiries@stirlinggolfclub.tv
AMS Rankin (01786) 464098 Option 2
www.stirlinggolfclub.com

Strathendrick (1901)
Glasgow Road, Drymen G63 0AA
☎ **(01360) 660695**
M Quyn (01360) 660733
www.strathendrickgolfclub.co.uk

Wales

Cardiganshire

Aberystwyth (1911)
Brynymor Road, Aberystwyth SY23 2HY
☎ **(01970) 615104**
✉ aberystwythgolf@talk21.com
✍ Emlyn Thomas
▤ www.aberystwythgolfclub.com

Borth & Ynyslas (1885)
Borth, Ceredigion SY24 5JS
☎ **(01970) 871202**
Fax (01970) 871202
✉ secretary@borthgolf.co.uk
✍ Owen Lawrence
▤ www.borthgolf.co.uk

Cardigan (1895)
Gwbert-on-Sea, Cardigan SA43 1PR
☎ **(01239) 621775**
Fax (01239) 621775
✉ cgc@btconnect.com
✍ Clive Day (Sec) (01239) 621775
▤ www.cardigangolf.co.uk

Cilgwyn (1905)
Llangybi, Lampeter SA48 8NN
☎ **(01570) 493286**
✍ J M Jones
▤ www.cilgwyngolf.co.uk

Penrhos G&CC (1991)
Llanrhystud, Ceredigion SY23 5AY
☎ **(01974) 202999**
Fax (01974) 202100
✉ info@penrhosgolf.co.uk
✍ R Rees-Evans
▤ www.penrhosgolf.co.uk

Carmarthenshire

Ashburnham (1894)
Cliffe Terrace, Burry Port SA16 0HN
☎ **(01554) 832269**
Fax (01554) 836974
✉ golf@ashburnhamgolfclub.co.uk
✍ Mr Huw Morgan
▤ www.ashburnhamgolfclub.co.uk

Carmarthen (1907)
Blaenycoed Road, Carmarthen SA33 6EH
☎ **(01267) 281588**
Fax (01267) 281493
✉ carmarthengolfclub@btinternet.com
✍ Shan Lewis
▤ www.carmarthengolfclub.com

Derllys Court (1993)
Proprietary
Derllys Court, Llysonnen Road, Carmarthen SA33 5DT
☎ **(01267) 211575**
Fax (01267) 211575
✉ derllys@hotmail.com
✍ R Walters
▤ www.derllyscourtgolfclub.com

Garnant Park (1997)
Garnant, Ammanford SA18 1NP
☎ **(01269) 823365**
Fax (01269) 823365
✉ garnantgolf@carmarthenshire.gov.uk
▤ www.parcgarnantgolf.co.uk

Glyn Abbey (1992)
Proprietary
Trimsaran SA17 4LB
☎ **(01554) 810278**
Fax (01554) 810889
✉ info@glynabbey.co.uk
✍ Dafydd Latham (Manager)
▤ www.glynabbey.co.uk

Glynhir (1909)
Glynhir Road, Llandybie, Ammanford SA18 2TF
☎ **(01269) 851365**
Fax (01269) 851365
✉ glynhirgolfclub@tiscali.co.uk
✍ Mr Roburt Edwards
▤ www.glynhirgolfclub.co.uk

Saron Golf Course (1990)
Pay and play
Penwern, Saron, Llandysul SA44 4EL
☎ **(01559) 370705**
Fax (01559) 370705
✍ Mr C Searle
⊕ Answer telephone 24hrs

Conwy

Abergele (1910)
Tan-y-Gopa Road, Abergele LL22 8DS
☎ **(01745) 824034**
Fax (01745) 824772
✉ secretary@abergelegolfclub.co.uk
✍ C P Langdon
▤ www.abergelegolfclub.co.uk

Betws-y-Coed (1977)
Clubhouse, Betws-y-Coed LL24 0AL
☎ **(01690) 710556**
✉ info@golf-betws-y-coed.co.uk
betwsycoedgclub@btinternet.com
✍ Adam Brown
▤ www.golf-betws-y-coed.co.uk

Conwy (Caernarvonshire) (1890)
Beacons Way, Morfa, Conwy LL32 8ER
☎ **(01492) 592423**
Fax (01492) 593363
✉ secretary@conwygolfclub.com
✍ Chris Chance (01492) 592423
▤ www.conwygolfclub.com

Llandudno (Maesdu) (1915)
Hospital Road, Llandudno LL30 1HU
☎ **(01492) 876450**
Fax (01492) 876450
✉ secretary@maesdugolfclub.co.uk
✍ Miss S Thomas
▤ www.maesdugolfclub.co.uk

Llanfairfechan (1971)
Llannerch Road, Llanfairfechan LL33 0EB
☎ **(01248) 680144**
✍ K V Williams

North Wales (Llandudno) (1894)
72 Bryniau Road, West Shore, Llandudno LL30 2DZ
☎ **(01492) 875325**
Fax (01492) 872420
✉ enquiries@northwalesgolfclub.co.uk
✍ Nick Kitchen
▤ www.northwalesgolfclub.co.uk

Old Colwyn (1907)
Woodland Avenue, Old Colwyn LL29 9NL
☎ **(01492) 515581**
✉ colwyngolfclub@tiscali.co.uk
✍ Mike Eccles (07760) 119445
▤ www.oldcolwyngolfclub.co.uk

Penmaenmawr (1910)
Conway Old Road, Penmaenmawr LL34 6RD
☎ **(01492) 623330**
Fax (01492) 622105
✉ clubhouse@pengolf.co.uk
✍ Mrs A H greenwood
▤ www.pengolf.co.uk

Rhos-on-Sea (1899)
Penrhyn Bay, Llandudno LL30 3PU
☎ **(01492) 549641**
Fax (01492) 549100
✉ rhosonseagolfclub@btinternet.com
✍ G Simmonds & I Taylor
▤ www.rhosgolf.co.uk

Denbighshire

Bryn Morfydd Hotel (1982)
Llanrhaeadr, Denbigh LL16 4NP
☎ **(01745) 890280**
Fax (01745) 890488
✉ brynmorfydd@live.co.uk
▤ www.bryn-morfydd.co.uk

Denbigh (1908)
Henllan Road, Denbigh LL16 5AA
☎ **(01745) 816669**
Fax (01745) 814888
✉ denbighgolfclub@aol.com
✍ JR Williams (01745) 816669
▤ www.denbighgolfclub.co.uk

Kinmel Park (1989)
Pay and play
Bodelwyddan LL18 5SR
☎ **(01745) 833548**
✉ info@kinmelgolf.co.uk
✍ Mrs Fetherstonhaugh
▤ www.kinmelgolf.co.uk

Prestatyn (1905)
Marine Road East, Prestatyn LL19 7HS
☎ **(01745) 854320**
🖷 (01745) 834320
✉ enquiries@prestatyngolfclub.co.uk
✍ David Ames (Pro)
🖹 www.prestatyngolfclub.co.uk

Rhuddlan (1930)
Meliden Road, Rhuddlan LL18 6LB
☎ **(01745) 590217**
🖷 (01745) 590472
✉ secretary@rhuddlangolfclub.co.uk
✍ Mr J M Wood
🖹 www.rhuddlangolfclub.co.uk

Rhyl (1890)
Coast Road, Rhyl LL18 3RE
☎ **(01745) 353171**
🖷 (01745) 353171
✉ rhylgolfclub@btconnect.com
✍ Gill Davies
🖹 www.rhylgolfclub.co.uk

Ruthin-Pwllglas (1920)
Pwllglas, Ruthin LL15 2PE
☎ **(01824) 702296**
✉ neillroberts@aol.com
✍ Neil L Roberts 01824 704651
🖹 www.ruthinpwllglasgc.co.uk

St Melyd (1922)
The Paddock, Meliden Road, Prestatyn LL19 8NB
☎ **(01745) 854405**
🖷 (01745) 856908
✉ enquiries@stmelydgolfltd.co.uk
✍ Janette Williams
🖹 www.stmelydgolf.co.uk

Vale of Llangollen (1908)
Holyhead Road, Llangollen LL20 7PR
☎ **(01978) 860906**
🖷 (01978) 869165
✉ secretary@vlgc.co.uk
🖹 www.vlgc.co.uk

Flintshire

Caerwys (1989)
Pay and play
Caerwys, Mold CH7 5AQ
☎ **(01352) 721222**

Hawarden (1911)
Groomsdale Lane, Hawarden, Deeside CH5 3EH
☎ **(01244) 531447**
🖷 (01244) 536901
✉ secretary@hawardengolfclub.co.uk
✍ A Rowland
🖹 www.hawardengolfclub.co.uk

Holywell (1906)
Brynford, Holywell CH8 8LQ
☎ **(01352) 710040 opt 2**
✉ secretary@holywellgc.co.uk
🖹 www.holywellgc.co.uk

Kinsale (1996)
Pay and play
Llanerchymor, Holywell CH8 9DX
☎ **(01745) 561080**
✍ S Leverett
🖹 www.kinsalegolf.wordpress.com

Mold (1909)
Cilcain Road, Pantymwyn, Mold CH7 5EH
☎ **(01352) 740318/741513**
🖷 (01352) 741517
✉ info@moldgolfclub.co.uk
✍ C Mills (01352) 741513
🖹 www.moldgolfclub.co.uk

Northop Country Park (1994)
Northop, Chester CH7 6WA
☎ **(01352) 840440**
🖷 (01352) 840445
✉ john@northoppark.co.uk
✍ John Nolan (01352) 840440 press 1
🖹 www.northoppark.co.uk

Old Padeswood (1978)
Proprietary
Station Road, Padeswood, Mold CH7 4JL
☎ **(01244) 547401 Ext 2 (Clubhouse)**
🖷 (01244) 545082
✉ sec@oldpadeswoodgolfclub.co.uk
✍ Robert Jones (01244) 550414
🖹 www.oldpadeswoodgolfclub.co.uk

Padeswood & Buckley (1933)
The Caia, Station Lane, Padeswood, Mold CH7 4JD
☎ **(01244) 550537**
🖷 (01244) 541600
✉ admin@padeswoodgolf.plus.com
✍ Mrs S A Davies
🖹 www.padeswoodgolfclub.com

Pennant Park (1998)
Proprietary
Whitford, Holywell CH8 9AE
☎ **(01745) 563000**
🖹 www.pennant-park.co.uk

Gwynedd

Aberdovey (1892)
Aberdovey LL35 0RT
☎ **(01654) 767493**
🖷 (01654) 767027
✉ sec@aberdoveygolf.co.uk
✍ Gareth Pritchard (Mgr)
🖹 www.aberdoveygolf.co.uk

Abersoch (1907)
Golf Road, Abersoch LL53 7EY
☎ **(01758) 712636**
🖷 (01758) 712777
✉ admin@abersochgolf.co.uk
🖹 www.abersochgolf.co.uk

Bala (1973)
Penlan, Bala LL23 7YD
☎ **(01678) 520359**
🖷 (01678) 521361
✉ balagolf@btconnect.com
✍ G Rhys Jones
🖹 www.golffbala.co.uk

Clwb Golff Pwllheli (1900)
Golf Road, Pwllheli LL53 5PS
☎ **(01758) 701644**
🖷 (01758) 701644
✉ admin@pwllheligolfclub.co.uk
✍ Dennis Moore (Gen Mgr)
🖹 www.clwbgolffpwllheli.com

Dolgellau (1910)
Proprietary
Hengwrt Estate, Pencefn Road, Dolgellau LL40 2ES
☎ **(01341) 422603**
✉ info@dolgellaugolfclub.com
✍ M White
🖹 www.dolgellaugolfclub.com

Ffestiniog (1893)
Y Cefn, Ffestiniog
☎ **(01766) 762637 (Clubhouse)**
✉ info@ffestinioggolf.org
✍ G Hughes (01766) 590617
🖹 www.ffestinioggolf.org

Nefyn & District (1907)
Lon Golff, Morfa Nefyn, Pwllheli LL53 6DA
☎ **(01758) 720966 (Clubhouse)**
🖷 (01758) 720476
✉ secretary@nefyn-golf-club.com
✍ S Dennis (Sec/Mgr) (01758) 720966 ext 1
🖹 www.nefyn-golf-club.com

Porthmadog (1905)
Morfa Bychan, Porthmadog LL49 9UU
☎ **(01766) 514124**
🖷 (01766) 514124
✉ secretary@porthmadog-golf-club.co.uk
✍ G T Jones (Mgr)
🖹 www.porthmadog-golf-club.co.uk

Royal St David's (1894)
Harlech LL46 2UB
☎ **(01766) 780203**
🖷 (0844) 811 1484
✉ secretary@royalstdavids.co.uk
✍ T Davies (01766) 780361
🖹 www.royalstdavids.co.uk

Royal Town of Caernarfon (1909)
Aberforeshore, LLanfaglan, Caernarfon LL54 5RP
☎ **(01286) 673783**
🖷 (01286) 673783
✉ secretary@caernarfongolfclub.co.uk
✍ EG Angel
🖹 www.caernarfongolfclub.co.uk

St Deniol (1906)
Penybryn, Bangor LL57 1PX
☎ **(01248) 353098**
🖷 (01248) 370792
✉ secretary@st-deiniol.co.uk
✍ R D Thomas MBE (01248) 353098
🖹 www.st-deniol.co.uk

Isle of Anglesey

Anglesey (1914)
Station Road, Rhosneigr LL64 5QX
☎ **(01407) 811127**
✉ info@theangleseygolfclub.com
✍ M Tommis (01407) 811127
▤ www.angleseygolfclub.co.uk

Baron Hill (1895)
Beaumaris LL58 8YW
☎ **(01248) 810231**
Fax (01248) 810231
✉ golf@baronhill.co.uk
▤ www.baronhill.co.uk

Bull Bay (1913)
Bull Bay Road, Amlwch LL68 9RY
☎ **(01407) 830960**
Fax (01407) 832612
✉ info@bullbaygc.co.uk
✍ John Burns
▤ www.bullbaygc.co.uk

Henllys Hall (1996)
Llanfaes, Beaumaris LL58 8HU
☎ **(01248) 811717**
Fax (01248) 811511
✉ hg@hpb.co.uk
✍ Peter Maton
▤ www.henllysgolfclub.co.uk

Holyhead (1912)
Trearddur Bay, Anglesey LL65 2YL
☎ **(01407) 763279/762119**
Fax (01407) 763279
✉ holyheadgolfclub@tiscali.co.uk
▤ www.holyheadgolfclub.co.uk

Llangefni (1983)
Public
Llangefni LL77 8YQ
☎ **(01248) 722193**

RAF Valley
Anglesey LL65 3NY
☎ **(01407) 762241**
Fax (01407) 762241 ext 7705
✉ constables@constables.wanadoo.com
▤ www.rafvalleygolfclub.co.uk

Storws Wen (1996)
Proprietary
Brynteg, Benllech LL78 8JY
☎ **(01248) 852673**
✉ storws.wen.golf@hotmail.co.uk
✍ E Rowlands (Gen Mgr)
▤ www.storwswen.org

Mid Glamorgan

Aberdare (1921)
Proprietary
Abernant, Aberdare CF44 0RY
☎ **(01685) 871188 (Clubhouse)**
Fax (01685) 872797
✉ aberdaregolfclub@hotmail.co.uk
✍ Rhys James (Pro & Club Mgr)
▤ www.aberdaregolfclub.com

Bargoed (1913)
Heolddu, Bargoed CF81 9GF
☎ **(01443) 830143**
Fax (01443) 830608
✍ Mrs Denise Richards (01443) 830608

Bryn Meadows Golf Hotel (1973)
Maes-y-Cwmmer, Ystrad Mynach, Nr Caerphilly CF82 7SN
☎ **(01495) 225590/224103**
Fax (01495) 228272
✉ reception@brynmeadows.co.uk
✍ S Mayo
▤ www.brynmeadows.co.uk

Caerphilly (1905)
Pencapel, Mountain Road, Caerphilly CF83 1HJ
☎ **(029) 2086 3441**
Fax (029) 2086 3441
✉ secretary@caerphillygolfclub.com
✍ Roger Chaffey
▤ www.caerphillygolfclub.com

Coed-y-Mwstwr (1994)
Coychurch, Bridgend CF35 6AF
☎ **(01656) 864934**
Fax (01656) 864934
✉ secretary@coed-y-mwstwr.co.uk
✍ Gareth Summerton
▤ www.coed-y-mwstwr.co.uk

Creigiau (1921)
Creigiau, Cardiff CF15 9NN
☎ **(029) 2089 0263**
Fax (029) 2089 0706
✉ creigiaugolfclub@btconnect.com
✍ Gareth Morgan
▤ www.creigiaugolfclub.co.uk

Grove (1996)
Proprietary
South Cornelly, Bridgend CF33 4RP
☎ **(01656 788771**
Fax (01656) 788414
✉ enquiries@grovegolf.com
✍ M Thomas
▤ www.grovegolf.com

Llantrisant & Pontyclun (1927)
Ely Valley Road, Talbot Green, Llantrisant CF72 8AL
☎ **(01443) 224601**
Fax (01443) 224601
✉ llantrisantgolf@btconnect.com
✍ Andrew Bowen (Professional)
▤ www.llantrisantgolfclub.co.uk

Maesteg (1912)
Mount Pleasant, Neath Road, Maesteg CF34 9PR
☎ **(01656) 734106**
Fax (01656) 731822
✉ manager@maesteg-golf.co.uk
✍ Mr Mark Wilson (Gen Mgr)
▤ www.maesteg-golf.co.uk

Merthyr Tydfil (1909)
Cloth Hall Lane, Cefn Coed, Merthyr Tydfil CF48 2NU
☎ **(01685) 373131**
✍ K Anderson
▤ www.merthyrtydfilgolfclub.co.uk

Mountain Ash (1907)
Cefnpennar, Mountain Ash CF45 4DT
☎ **(01443) 479459 (office)**
Fax (01443) 479628
✉ sec@mountainashgc.co.uk
✍ (01443) 479459 ext 1
▤ www.mountainashgc.co.uk

Mountain Lakes (1988)
Heol Penbryn, Blaengwynlais, Caerphilly CF83 1NG
☎ **(029) 2086 1128**
Fax (029) 2086 3243

Pontypridd (1905)
Ty Gwyn Road, Pontypridd CF37 4DJ
☎ **(01443) 409904**
Fax (01443) 491622
✉ rebekah.craven@pontypriddgolfclub.co.uk
✍ Rebekah Craven (01443) 409904
▤ www.pontypriddgolfclub.co.uk

Pyle & Kenfig (1922)
Waun-y-Mer, Kenfig, Bridgend CF33 4PU
☎ **(01656) 783093**
Fax (01656) 772822
✉ secretary@pandkgolfclub.co.uk
✍ Mr Simon Hopkin (01656) 771613
▤ www.pandkgolfclub.co.uk

Rhondda (1910)
Penrhys, Ferndale, Rhondda CF43 3PW
☎ **(01443) 441384**
Fax (01443) 441384
✉ manager@rhonddagolf.co.uk
✍ Ian Ellis (01443) 441384
▤ www.rhonddagolf.co.uk

Ridgeway (1997)
Proprietary
Caerphilly Mountain, Caerphilly CF83 1LY
☎ **(029) 2088 2255**
✉ petethepro@tiscali.co.uk
✍ Hilary Mears
▤ www.ridgeway-golf.co.uk

Royal Porthcawl (1891)
Rest Bay, Porthcawl CF36 3UW
☎ **(01656) 782251**
Fax (01656) 771687
✉ office@royalporthcawl.com
✍ Mike Perry
▤ www.royalporthcawl.com

Southerndown (1905)
Ogmore-by-Sea, Bridgend CF32 0QP
☎ **(01656) 880476**
Fax (01656) 880317
✉ admin@southerndowngolfclub.com
✍ AJ Hughes (01656) 881111
▤ www.southerndowngolfclub.com

For key to symbols see page 725

Whitehall (1922)
The Pavilion, Nelson, Treharris CF46 6ST
(01443) 740245
m.wilde001@tiscali.co.uk
PM Wilde
www.whitehallgolfclub1922.co.uk

Monmouthshire

Alice Springs (1989)
Proprietary
Kemeys Commander, Usk NP15 1PP
(01873) 880914
(01873) 881381
golf@alicespringsgolfclub.co.uk
www.alicespringsgolfclub.co.uk

Blackwood (1914)
Cwmgelli, Blackwood NP12 1BR
(01495) 223152
blackwoodgolfclub@btconnect.com
Mr John Bills
www.blackwoodgolfclub.org.uk

The Celtic Manor Resort (1995)
Proprietary
Coldra Woods, The Usk Valley, NP18 1HQ
(01633) 413000
(01633) 410309
postbox@celtic-manor.com
Matthew Lewis (Director of Golf)
www.celtic-manor.com

Dewstow (1988)
Proprietary
Caerwent, Monmouthshire NP26 5AH
(01291) 430444
(01291) 425816
info@dewstow.com
D Bradbury
www.dewstow.com

Greenmeadow G&CC (1979)
Treherbert Road, Croesyceiliog, Cwmbran NP44 2BZ
(01633) 869321
(01633) 868430
info@greenmeadowgolf.com
PJ Richardson (01633) 869321
www.greenmeadowgolf.com

Llanwern (1928)
Tennyson Avenue, Llanwern, Newport NP18 2DY
(01633) 412029
(01633) 412260
llanwerngolfclub@btconnect.com
Mrs A Webber
www.llanwerngolfclub.co.uk

Marriott St Pierre Hotel & CC (1962)
St Pierre Park, Chepstow NP16 6YA
(01291) 625261
(01291) 629975
chepstow.golf@btconnect.com

Monmouth (1896)
Leasbrook Lane, Monmouth NP25 3SN
(01600) 712212
(01600) 772399
sec@monmouthgolfclub.co.uk
P Tully (Sec/Mgr)
www.monmouthgolfclub.co.uk

Monmouthshire (1892)
Llanfoist, Abergavenny NP7 9HE
(01873) 852606
(01873) 850470
monmouthshiregc@btconnect.com
C Sobik (Gen Mgr)
www.monmouthshiregolfclub.co.uk

Newport (1903)
Great Oak, Rogerstone, Newport NP10 9FX
(01633) 892643
(01633) 896676
newportgolfclub@btconnect.com
R Thomas (01633) 892643
www.newportgolfclub.org.uk

Oakdale (1990)
Pay and play
Llwynon Lane, Oakdale NP12 0NF
(01495) 220044
M Lewis (Dir)
⊕ 18 bay floodlit golf practice range. PGA Professional Mathew Griffiths

Pontnewydd (1875)
Maesgwyn Farm, Upper Cwmbran, Cwmbran, Torfaen NP44 1AB
(01633) 482170
(01633) 484447
ctphillips@virgin.net
CT Phillips (01633) 484447
www.pontnewyddgolf.uk

Pontypool (1903)
Lasgarn Lane, Trevethin, Pontypool NP4 8TR
(01495) 763655
(01495) 755564
pontypoolgolf@btconnect.com
L Dodd
www.pontypoolgolf.co.uk

Raglan Parc (1994)
Parc Lodge, Raglan NP5 2ER
(01291) 690077
(01291) 69075
info@raglanparc.co.uk
S Dobney
www.raglanparc.co.uk

The Rolls of Monmouth (1982)
The Hendre, Monmouth NP25 5HG
(01600) 715353
(01600) 713115
enquiries@therollsgolfclub.co.uk
Mrs SJ Orton
www.therollsgolfclub.co.uk

Shirenewton (1995)
Shirenewton, Chepstow NP16 6RL
(01291) 641642
(01291) 641472

Tredegar & Rhymney (1921)
Tredegar, Rhymney NP22 5HA
(01685) 840743
tandrgc@googlemail.com
Will Price (07761) 005184
www.tandrgc.co.uk

Tredegar Park (1923)
Parc-y-Brain Road, Rogerstone, Newport NP10 9TG
(01633) 894433
secretary@tredegarparkgolfclub.co.uk
S Salway
www.tredegarparkgolfclub.co.uk

The Duncan Putter

The Duncan Putter was started in 1959 by ex-Walker Cup Captain Tony Duncan in memory of his father, John Duncan – one of the founders of Southerndown Golf Club where the tournament is staged evey April.

A 72-hole scratch competiton, it was originally an invitation event designd to give young Welsh golfers the opportunity to compete against top English amateurs. It is now a Welsh Order of Merit open-entry event which attracts aspiring young golfers from all parts of the UK and occasionally from Europe.

Former winners include Peter McEvoy, Gary Wolstenholme and Nigel Edwards.

Wernddu Golf Centre (1992)
Proprietary
Old Ross Road, Abergavenny NP7 8NG
☎ **(01873) 856223**
(01873) 852177
info@wernddu-golf-club.co.uk
S Cole (Sec)
www.wernddu-golf-club.co.uk

West Monmouthshire (1906)
Golf Road, Pond Road, Nantyglo, Ebbw Vale NP23 4QT
☎ **(01495) 310233**
care@westmongolfclub.co.uk
L B Matthews (01495) 310233
www.westmongolfclub.co.uk

Woodlake Park (1993)
Proprietary
Glascoed, Usk NP4 0TE
☎ **(01291) 673933**
(01291) 673811
golf@woodlake.co.uk
M J Wood
www.woodlake.co.uk

Pembrokeshire

Haverfordwest (1904)
Arnolds Down, Haverfordwest SA61 2XQ
☎ **(01437) 763565**
(01437) 764143
haverfordwestgc@btconnect.com
M Davies (01437) 764523
www.haverfordwestgolfclub.net

Milford Haven (1913)
Clay Lane, Hubberston, Milford Haven SA72 3RX
☎ **(01646) 697822**
milfordgolfclub@aol.com
W S Brown
www.mhgc.co.uk

Newport Links (1925)
Newport SA42 0NR
☎ **(01239) 820244**
(01239) 821338
info@newportlinks.co.uk
Mrs A Payne (Mgr)
www.newportlinks.co.uk

Priskilly Forest (1992)
Castle Morris, Haverfordwest SA62 5EH
☎ **(01348) 840276**
(01348) 840276
jevans@priskilly-forest.co.uk
P Evans
www.priskilly-forest.co.uk

South Pembrokeshire (1970)
Military Road, Pembroke Dock SA72 6SE
☎ **(01646) 621453**
spgc06@tiscali.co.uk
P Fisher (01646) 621453
www.southpembsgolf.co.uk

St Davids City (1903)
Whitesands Bay, St Davids SA62 6PT
☎ **(01437) 721751 (Clubhouse)**
ronaldjgriffiths@btinternet.com
J Griffiths (01437) 721073
www.stdavidscitygolfclub.com

Tenby (1888)
The Burrows, Tenby SA70 7NP
☎ **(01834) 842978**
(01834) 845603
info@tenbygolf.co.uk
DJ Hancock (01834) 842978
www.tenbygolf.co.uk

Trefloyne (1996)
Proprietary
Trefloyne Park, Penally, Tenby SA70 7RG
☎ **(01834) 842165**
(01834) 844288
sarah@trefloyne.com
Sarah Knight
www.trefloyne.com

Powys

Brecon (1902)
Newton Park, Llanfaes, Brecon LD3 8PA
☎ **(01874) 622004**
info@brecongolfclub.co.uk
I Chambers (01874) 611545
www.brecongolfclub.co.uk

Builth Wells (1923)
Golf Links Road, Builth Wells LD2 3NF
☎ **(01982) 553296**
info@builthwellsgolf.co.uk
S Edwards (Professional) (01982) 551155
www.builthwellsgolf.co.uk

Cradoc (1967)
Penoyre Park, Cradoc, Brecon LD3 9LP
☎ **(01874) 623658**
(01874) 611711
secretary@cradoc.co.uk
Robert Southcott (01874) 623658
www.cradoc.co.uk

Knighton (1906)
Ffrydd Wood, Knighton LD7 1DL
☎ **(01547) 528646**
DB Williams (Hon)
www.knightongolfclub.co.uk

Llandrindod Wells (1905)
The Clubhouse, Llandrindod Wells LD1 5NY
☎ **(01597) 823873**
(01597) 828881
secretary@lwgc.co.uk
Mrs Terry Evans (01597) 823873
www.lwgc.co.uk

Machynlleth (1904)
Felingerrig, Machynlleth SY20 8UH
☎ **(01654) 702000**
machgolf2@tiscali.co.uk
John Lewis (Secretary)
www.machynllethgolfclub.com

Mid-Wales Golf Centre (1992)
Maesmawr Golf Club, Caersws, Nr Newtown SY17 5SB
☎ **(01686) 688303**
(01686) 688303

Rhosgoch (1984)
Rhosgoch, Builth Wells LD2 3JY
☎ **(01497) 851251**
rhosgochgolf@yahoo.co.uk
C Dance (Sec) N Lloyd (Mgr)
www.rhosgoch-golf.co.uk

St Giles Newtown (1895)
Pool Road, Newtown SY16 3AJ
☎ **(01686) 625844**
stgilesgolf@gmail.com
Wyn Evans (07739 884198)
www.stgilesgolf.co.uk

St Idloes (1906)
Penrhallt, Llanidloes SY18 6LG
☎ **(01686) 412559**
st.idloesgolfclub@btconnect.com
Mr E Parry (Sec)
www.stidloesgolfclub.co.uk

Welsh Border Golf Complex (1991)
Pay and play
Bulthy Farm, Bulthy, Middletown SY21 8ER
☎ **(01743) 884247**
info@welshbordergolf.com
K Farr (07966) 530042
www.welshbordergolf.com

Welshpool (1907)
Y Golfa, Welshpool, Powys SY21 9AQ
☎ **(01938) 850249**
(01938) 850249
secretary@welshpoolgolfclub.co.uk
Sally Marshall
www.welshpoolgolfclub.co.uk

South Glamorgan

Brynhill (1921)
Port Road, Barry CF62 8PN
☎ **(01446) 720277**
(01446) 740422
louise@brynhillgolfclub.co.uk
Louise Edwards
www.brynhillgolfclub.co.uk

Cardiff (1921)
Sherborne Avenue, Cyncoed, Cardiff CF23 6SJ
☎ **(02920) 754772**
(02920) 680011
cardiff.golfclub@virgin.net
Mrs K Newling (029) 2075 3320
www.cardiffgolfclub.co.uk

Cottrell Park Golf Resort (1996)
Proprietary
St Nicholas, Cardiff CF5 6SJ
☎ **(01446) 781781**
(01446) 781187

For key to symbols see page 725

✉ sales@cottrellpark.com
✍ Mr Derek Smith
▤ www.cottrellpark.com

Dinas Powis (1914)
Old Highwalls, Dinas Powis CF64 4AJ
☎ **(029) 2051 2727**
📠 (029) 2051 2727
✉ dinaspowisgolfclub@yahoo.co.uk
✍ Sally Phelps/Roger Davies
▤ www.dpgc.co.uk

Glamorganshire (1890)
Lavernock Road, Penarth CF64 5UP
☎ **(029) 2070 1185**
📠 (029) 2071 3333
✉ glamgolf@btconnect.com
✍ BM Williams (029) 2070 1185
▤ www.glamorganshiregolfclub.co.uk

Llanishen (1905)
Heol Hir, Cardiff CF14 9UD
☎ **(029) 207 55078**
✉ secretary.llanishengc@virgin.net
✍ Colin Duffield (029) 207 55078
▤ www.llanishengc.co.uk

Peterstone Lakes (1990)
Proprietary
Peterstone, Wentloog, Cardiff CF3 2TN
☎ **(01633) 680009**
📠 (01633) 680563
✉ peterstone_lakes@yahoo.com
✍ P Millar
▤ www.peterstonelakes.com

Radyr (1902)
Drysgol Road, Radyr, Cardiff CF15 8BS
☎ **(029) 2084 2408**
📠 (029) 2084 3914
✉ office@radyrgolf.co.uk
✍ Manager
▤ www.radyrgolf.co.uk

RAF St Athan (1977)
Clive Road, St Athan CF62 4JD
☎ **(01446) 751043**
📠 (01446) 751862
✉ rafstathan@golfclub.fsbusiness.co.uk
✍ A McKinotry (01446) 751043
▤ www.rafstathangc.co.uk

St Andrews Major (1993)
Proprietary
Coldbrook Road East, Cadoxton, Barry CF6 3BB
☎ **(01446) 722227**
📠 (01446) 748953
✉ info@standrewsmajorgolfclub.com
✍ A Edmunds
▤ www.standrewsmajorgolfclub.com

St Mellons (1937)
St Mellons, Cardiff CF3 2XS
☎ **(01633) 680408**
📠 (01633) 681219
✉ stmellons@golf2003.fsnet.co.uk
✍ R Haggerty (01633) 680408
▤ www.stmellonsgolfclub.co.uk

Vale Hotel Golf & Spa Resort (1994)
Hensol Park, Hensol CF7 8JY
☎ **(01443) 665899**
📠 (01443) 222220
✉ golf@vale-hotel.com
▤ www.vale-hotel.com

Wenvoe Castle (1936)
Wenvoe, Cardiff CF5 6BE
☎ **(029) 205 94371**
📠 (029) 205 94371
✉ wenvoe-castlegc@virgin.net

Whitchurch (Cardiff) (1914)
Pantmawr Road, Whitchurch, Cardiff CF14 7TD
☎ **(029) 2062 0985**
📠 (029) 2052 9860
✉ secretary@whitchurchcardiffgolfclub.com
✍ G Perrott
▤ www.whitchurchcardiffgolfclub.com

West Glamorgan

Allt-y-Graban (1993)
Allt-y-Graban Road, Pontlliw, Swansea SA4 1DT
☎ **(01792) 885757**

Clyne (1920)
120 Owls Lodge Lane, Mayals, Swansea SA3 5DP
☎ **(01792) 401989**
📠 (01792) 401078
✉ manager@clynegolfclub.com
✍ N John Hollis (Gen Mgr)
▤ www.clynegolfclub.com

Fairwood Park (1969)
Proprietary
Blackhills Lane, Fairwood, Swansea SA2 7JN
☎ **(01792) 297849**
📠 (01792) 297849
✉ info@fairwoodpark.com
✍ E Golbas (Mgr)
▤ www.fairwoodpark.com

Glynneath (1931)
Penygraig, Pontneathvaughan, Glynneath SA11 5UH
☎ **(01639) 720452**
📠 (01639) 720452
✉ enquiries@glynneathgolfclub.co.uk
✍ Shane McMenamin
▤ www.glynneathgolfclub.co.uk

Gower
Cefn Goleu, Three Crosses, Gowerton, Swansea SA4 3HS
☎ **(01792) 872480**
📠 (01792) 872480
✉ info@gowergolf.com
✍ A Richards (01792) 872480
▤ www.gowergolf.co.uk

Lakeside (1992)
Water Street, Margam, Port Talbot SA13 2PA
☎ **(01639) 899959**
▤ www.lakesidegolf.co.uk

Langland Bay (1904)
Langland Bay Road, Langland, Swansea SA3 4QR
☎ **(01792) 361721**
📠 (01792) 361082
✉ info@langlandbaygolfclub.com
✍ Mr A Minty (Director of Golf)
▤ www.langlandbaygolfclub.com

Morriston (1920)
160 Clasemont Road, Morriston, Swansea SA6 6AJ
☎ **(01792) 796528**
📠 (01792) 796528
✉ morristongolf@btconnect.com
✍ Robert Howells (01792) 796528
▤ www.morristongolfclub.co.uk

Neath (1934)
Cadoxton, Neath SA10 8AH
☎ **(01639) 632759**
📠 (01639) 639955
✉ info@neathgolfclub.co.uk
✍ D M Gee
▤ www.neathgolfclub.co.uk

Palleg & Swansea Valley Golf Course (1930)
Proprietary
Palleg Road, Lower Cwmtwrch, Swansea Valley SA9 2QQ
☎ **(01639) 842193**
📠 (01639) 845661
✉ gc.gcgs@btinternet.com
✍ Graham Coombe (PGA Pro/Director)
▤ www.palleg-golf.com

Pennard (1896)
2 Southgate Road, Southgate, Swansea SA3 2BT
☎ **(01792) 233131**
📠 (01792) 235125
✉ sec@pennardgolfclub.com
✍ Mrs S Crowley (01792) 235120
▤ www.pennardgolfclub.com

Pontardawe (1924)
Cefn Llan, Pontardawe, Swansea SA8 4SH
☎ **(01792) 863118**
📠 (01792) 830041
✉ enquiries@pontardawegolfclub.co.uk
✍ R W Grove (Hon)
▤ www.pontardawegolfclub.co.uk

Swansea Bay (1892)
Proprietary
Jersey Marine, Neath SA10 6JP
☎ **(01792) 812198**
✉ swanseabaygolfclub@hotmail.co.uk
✍ Mrs J Richardson (01792) 812198

Tawe Vale (1965)
Clydach, Swansea SA6 5QR
☎ **(01792) 841257**

secretarytawevalegolfclub@btconnect.com
DE Jones (01792) 842929
www.tawevalegolfclub.co.uk

Wrexham

Chirk (1990)
Proprietary
Chirk, Wrexham LL14 5AD
☎ **(01691) 774407**
enquiries@chirkgolfclub.co.uk
Trudi Maddison (Manager)
www.chirkgolfclub.co.uk

Clays Golf Centre (1992)
Proprietary
Bryn Estyn Road, Wrexham LL13 9UB
☎ **(01978) 661406**
(01978) 661406
sales@claysgolf.co.uk
Steve Williams
www.claysgolf.co.uk

Moss Valley (1990)
Moss Road, Wrexham LL11 6HA
☎ **(01978) 720518**
(01978) 720518
info@mossvalleygolf.co.uk
John Nolan (07588) 104761
www.mossvalleygolf.co.uk

Plassey Oaks Golf Complex (1992)
Eyton, Wrexham LL13 0SP
☎ **(01978) 780020**
(01978) 781397
hjones@plasseygolf.com
www.plasseygolf.com

Wrexham (1906)
Holt Road, Wrexham LL13 9SB
☎ **(01978) 364268**
(01978) 362168
info@wrexhamgolfclub.co.uk
R West (01978) 364268
www.wrexhamgolfclub.co.uk

For key to symbols see page 725

R&A helping the LET, the LGU and the GUW

Among grants distributed in 2012 were the following:

To the Ladies European Tour – £75,000 for 2012 and a further £30,000 for the Tour's Access Series.

To the Golf Union of Wales – £10,000 towards "Golf awareness Month" aimed at enrolling new club members and retaining existing club members.

To the Ladies Golf Union – £170,000 towards the cost of the 2012 Curtis Cup match at Nairn.

Did you know?

The First Open Championship to be staged outside Scotland was held at St George's Golf Club in Kent in 1894. The event was won by J H Taylor with a four round total of 326. Royal status was bestowed on the club by King Edward VII in 1902.

Continent of Europe – Country and Region Index

Austria

St Lorenzen (1990)
8642 St Lorenzen, Gassing 22
(03864) 3961
(03864) 3961-2
gclorenzen@golf.at
Peter Redl
www.gclorenzen.at

Innsbruck & Tirol

Achensee (1934)
Golf und Landclub Achensee, 6213 Pertisau/Tirol
(05243) 5377
(05243) 6202
golfclub-achensee@tirol.com
www.golfclub-achensee.com

Innsbruck-Igls (1935)
Oberdorf 11, 6074 Rinn
(05223) 78177
(05223) 78177-77
office@golfclub-innsbruck-igls.at
www.golfclub-innsbruck-igls.at

Kaiserwinkl GC Kössen (1988)
6345 Kössen, Mühlau 1
(05375) 2122
(05375) 2122-13
club@golf-koessen.at
Stefan Emberger
www.golf-koessen.at

Golfclub Kitzbühel (1955)
Ried Kaps 3, 6370 Kitzbühel
(05356) 63007 Members
(05356) 630077
gckitzbuehel@golf.at
Werner Gandler
www.golfclub-kitzbuehel.at

Kitzbühel-Schwarzsee (1988)
6370 Kitzbühel, Golfweg Schwarzsee 35
(05356) 66660 70
(05356) 66660 71

Seefeld-Wildmoos (1969)
6100 Seefeld, Postfach 22
(0699) 1-606606-0
(0699) 4-606606-3
info@seefeldgolf.com
Mr Werner Seelos
www.seefeldgolf.com

Klagenfurt & South

Bad Kleinkirchheim-Reichenau (1977)
9564 Padergassen, Plass 19
(04275) 594
(04275) 594-4

Golfpark Klopeinersee-Sudkarnten (1988)
9122 St Kanzian, Grabelsdorf 94
(04239) 3800-0
(04239) 3800-18
office@golfklopein.at
www.golfklopein.at

Kärntner GC Dellach (1927)
Golfstrasse 3, 9082 Maria Wörth, Golfstr 3
(04273) 2515
(04273) 2515-20
office@kgcdellach.at
Ronald Krach (Mgr)
www.kgcdellach.at

Golfclub Klagenfurt-Seltenheim (1996)
Seltenheimerstr. 137, A-9061 Wolfnitz
0043 463 40223
0043 463 4022320
office@gcseltenheim.at
www.gcseltenheim.at

Golfclub Millstatter See
Am Golfplatz 1, 9872 Millstatt
+43 (0)4762 82542
+43 (0)4762 82548-10
gcmillstatt@golf.at
www.golf-millstatt.at

Moosburg-Pörtschach (1986)
9062 Moosburg, Golfstr 2
(04272) 83486
(04272) 834 8620
moosburg@golfktn.at
Tanja Starzacher
www.golfmoosburg.at

Wörthersee-Velden (1988)
9231 Köstenberg, Golfweg 41
(04274) 7045
(04274) 7087-15
golf-velden@golfktn.at
Map. Roland Sint (Mgr)
www.golfvelden.at

Linz & North

Amstetten-Ferschnitz (1972)
3325 Ferschnitz, Gut Edla 18
(07473) 8293
(07473) 82934
office@golfclub-amstetten.at
www.golfclub-amstetten.at

Böhmerwald GC Ulrichsberg (1990)
4161 Ulrichsberg, Seitelschlag 50
(07288) 8200
(07288) 82004
office@boehmerwaldgolf.at
www.boehmerwaldgolf.at

Celtic Golf Course – Schärding (1994)
Maad 2, 4775 Taufkirchen/Pram
(0043) 7719 8110
(0043) 7719 811015
office@gcschaerding.at
www.gcschaerding.at

Golfresort Haugschlag (1987)
3874 Haugschlag 160
(02865) 8441
(02865) 8441-522
info@golfresort.at
www.golfresort.at

Herzog Tassilo (1991)
Blankenbergerstr 30, 4540 Bad Hall
(07258) 5480
(07258) 29858
golfherzogtassilo@golf.at
www.golfherzogtassilo.at

Golf Resort Kremstal (1989)
Am Golfplatz 1, 4531 Kematen/Krems
0043 (0)7228 7644
0043 (0)7228 7644 7
info@golfresort-kremstal.at
Günter Obermayr
www.golfresort-kremstal.at
www.golfvillage.at

Linz-St Florian (1960)
4490 St Florian, Tillysburg 28
(07223) 828730
(07223) 828737
gclinz@golf.at
www.gclinz.at

Linzer Golf Club Luftenberg (1990)
4222 Luftenberg, Am Luftenberg 1a
(07237) 3893
(07237) 3893-40
gclinz-luftenberg@golf.at
www.gclinz-luftenberg.at

Maria Theresia (1989)
Letten 5, 4680 Haag am Hausruck
(07732) 3944
(07732) 3944-9
www.members.eunet.at/gcmariatheresia

Ottenstein (1988)
3532 Niedergrünbach 60
(02826) 7476
(02826) 7476-4
info@golfclub-ottenstein.at
www.golfclub-ottenstein.at

St Oswald-Freistadt (1988)
Am Golfplatz 1, 4271 St Oswald
(07945) 7938
(07945) 79384

St Pölten Schloss Goldegg (1989)
3100 St Pölten Schloss Goldegg
(02741) 7360/7060
(02741) 73608

Union Golfclub Schloss Ernegg (1973)
3261 Steinakirchen, Ernegg 4
+43 (0) 7488) 76770
+43 (0) 7488) 71171
gcernegg@golf.at
Kristel Josel (Mgr)
www.ernegg.at

For key to symbols and European dialling codes see page 725

Traunsee Kircham
4656 Kircham, Kampesberg 38
(07619) 2576
(07619) 2576-11

Weitra (1989)
3970 Weitra, Hausschachen
(02856) 2058
(02856) 2058-4
gcweitra@golf.at
www.gcweitra.at

Wels (1981)
4616 Weisskirchen, Golfplatzstrasse 2
(07243) 56038
(07243) 56685
gcwels@golf.at
www.golfclub-wels.at

Salzburg Region

Bad Gastein (1960)
5640 Bad Gastein, Golfstrasse 6
0043 (6434) 2775
0043 (6434) 2775-4
info@golfclub-gastein.com
Verena Kuhlank
www.golfclub-gastein.com

GC Sonnberg (1993)
5241 Höhnart, Strass 1
0043 (7743) 20066
0043 (7743) 20077
golf@gcsonnberg.at
www.gcsonnberg.at

Goldegg
5622 Goldegg, Maierhof 4
(06415) 8585
(06415) 8585-4
info@golfclub-goldegg.com
www.golfclub-goldegg.com

Gut Altentann (1989)
Hof 54, 5302 Henndorf am Wallersee
(06214) 6026-0
(06214) 6105-81
office@gutaltentann.com
Catarina Hofmann
www.gutaltentann.com

Gut Brandlhof G&CC (1983)
5760 Saalfelden am Steinernen Meer, Hohlwegen 4
(06582) 7800-555
(06582) 7800-529

Lungau (1991)
5582 St Michael, Feldnergasse 165
(06477) 7448
(06477) 7448-4
gclungau@golf.at
www.golfclub-lungau.at

Am Mondsee (1986)
St Lorenz 400, 5310 Mondsee
(06232) 3835-0
(06232) 3835-83
gcmondsee@golf.at
Frank Riedel (Senior Golf Mgr) (FH)
www.golfclubmondsee.at

Radstadt Tauerngolf (1991)
Römerstrasse 18, 5550 Radstadt
(06452) 5111
(06452) 5111/15
info@radstadtgolf.at
www.radstadtgolf.at

G&CC Salzburg-Klessheim (1955)
Klessheim 21, 5071 Wals
(0662) 850851
(0662) 857925
office@gccsalzburg.at
www.golfclub-klessheim.com

Salzburg Romantikourse Schloss Fuschl (1865)
5322 Hof/Salzburg
(06229) 2390
(06229) 2390
fuschl@golfclub-salzburg.at
www.golfclub-salzburg.at

Salzkammergut (1933)
Wirling 36, 5360 St. Wolfgang
(06132) 26340
(06132) 26708
office@salzkammergut-golf.at
Cornelia Kogler
www.salzkammergut-golf.at

Urslautal (1991)
Schinking 81, 5760 Saalfelden
(06584) 2000
(06584) 7475-10
info@golf-urslautal.at
www.golf-urslautal.at

Zell am See-Kaprun (1983)
Golfstrasse 25, A-5700 Zell am See
+43 6542 56161
+43 6542 56161-16
golf@zellamsee-kaprun.at
Roland Geringer (Manager)
www.golf-zellamsee.at

Steiermark

Bad Gleichenberg (1984)
Am Hoffeld 3, 8344 Bad Gleichenberg
(03159) 3717
(03159) 3065
gcgleichenberg@golf.at
www.golf-badgleichenberg.at

Dachstein Tauern (1990)
8967 Haus/Ennstal, Oberhaus 59
(03686) 2630
(03686) 2630-15
gccschladming@golf.at
www.schladming-golf.at

Ennstal-Weissenbach G&LC (1977)
Austria 8940 Liezen, Postfach 193
(03612) 24821
(03612) 24821-4
glcennstal@golf.at
Thomas Aigner
www.glcennstal.at

Graz (1989)
8051 Graz-Thal, Windhof 137
(0316) 572867
(0316) 572867-4

Gut Murstätten (1989)
8403 Lebring, Oedt 14
(03182) 3555
(03182) 3688
gcmurstaetten@golf.at
www.gcmurstaetten.at

Maria Lankowitz (1992)
Puchbacher Str 109, 8591 Maria Lankowitz
(03144) 6970
(03144) 6970-4

Murhof (1963)
8130 Frohnleiten, Adriach 53
(03126) 3010-40
(03126) 3000-28
gcmurhof@golf.at
www.murhof.at

Murtal (1995)
Frauenbachstr 51, 8724 Spielberg
(03512) 75213
(03512) 75213
gcmurtal@golf.at
www.gcmurtal.at

Reiting G&CC (1990)
8772 Traboch, Schulweg 7
(0663) 833308/ (03847) 5008
(03847) 5682

St Lorenzen (1990)
8642 St Lorenzen, Gassing 22
(03864) 3961
(03864) 3961-2
gclorenzen@golf.at
www.gclorenzen.at

Schloss Frauenthal (1988)
8530 Deutschlandsberg, Ulrichsberg 7
(03462) 5717
(03462) 5717-5
office@gcfrauenthal.at
www.gcfrauenthal.at

Golf & Country Club Schloss Pichlarn (1972)
8952 Irdning/Ennstal, Zur Linde 1
+43 3682-24440-540
+43 3682-24440-580
golf@pichlarn.at
www.pichlarn.at

TGC Fuerstenfeld (1984)
8282 Loipersdorf, Gillersdorf 50
(03382) 8533
(03382) 8533-33
office@thermergolf.at
www.thermergolf.at

Vienna & East

Adamstal (1994)
Gaupmannsgraben 21, 3172 Ramsal
(02764) 3500
(02764) 3500-15
www.adamstal.at

Bad Tatzmannsdorf Reiters G&CC (1991)
Am Golfplatz 2, 7431 Bad Tatzmannsdorf
☎ **(0043) 3353 8282-0**
🖷 (0043) 3353 8282-1735
✉ golfclub@burgenlandresort.at
🖳 www.reitersburgenlandresort.at

Brunn G&CC (1988)
2345 Brunn/Gebirge, Rennweg 50
☎ **(02236) 33711**
🖷 (02236) 33863
✉ club@gccbrunn.at
🖳 www.gccbrunn.at

Colony Club Gutenhof (1988)
2325 Himberg, Gutenhof
☎ **(02235) 87055-0**
🖷 (02235) 87055-14
✉ club@colonygolf.com
✍ Magira-Xenia Glatz
🖳 www.colonygolf.com

Eldorado Bucklige Welt (1990)
Golfplatz 1, 2871 Zöbern
☎ **(02642) 8451**
🖷 (02642) 8451-52
🖳 www.golf1.at

Enzesfeld (1970)
2551 Enzesfeld
☎ **(02256) 81272**
🖷 (02256) 81272-4
✉ office@gcenzesfeld.at
🖳 www.gcenzesfeld.at

Föhrenwald (1968)
2700 Wiener Neustadt, Postfach 105
☎ **(02622) 29171**
🖷 (02622) 29171-4
✉ office@gcf.at
✍ Zelester Elgar (Mgr)
🖳 www.gcf.at

Fontana (1996)
Fontana Allee 1, 2522 Oberwaltersdorf
☎ **(02253) 6062202**
🖷 (02253) 6062200
✉ gcfontana@fontana.at
✍ Mag. Matthias Wagner
🖳 www.fontana.at

Hainburg/Donau (1977)
2410 Hainburg, Auf der Heide 762
☎ **(02165) 62628**
🖷 (02165) 626283
✉ gchainburg@golf.at
✍ Dietmar Haderer (Mgr)
🖳 www.golfclub-hainburg.at

Lengenfeld (1995)
Am Golfplatz 1, 3552 Lengenfeld
☎ **(02719) 8710**
🖷 (02719) 8738

Neusiedlersee-Donnerskirchen (1988)
7082 Donnerskirchen
☎ **(02683) 8171**
🖷 (02683) 817231

Schloss Ebreichsdorf (1988)
2483 Ebreichsdorf, Schlossallee 1
☎ **(02254)73888**
🖷 (02254) 73888-13
✉ office@gcebreichsdorf.at
🖳 www.gcebreichsdorf.at

Schloss Schönborn (1987)
2013 Schönborn 4
☎ **(02267) 2863/2879**
🖷 (02267) 2879-19
✉ golfclub@gcschoenborn.com
🖳 www.gcschoenborn.com

Schönfeld (1989)
A-2291 Schönfeld, Am Golfplatz 1
☎ **+43 (02213) 2063**
🖷 +43 (02213) 20631
✉ gcschoenfeld@golf.at
🖳 www.golf.at/clubdetail.asp?clubnr=315

Semmering (1926)
2680 Semmering
☎ **(02664) 8154**
🖷 (02664) 2114

Golfclub Spillern (1993)
Wiesenerstrasse 100, A-2104 Spillern
☎ **+43 (0)22 668 1211**
🖷 +43 (0)22 668 121120
✉ gcspillern@golf.at
✍ J Culen
🖳 www.gcspillern.at

Thayatal Drosendorf (1994)
Autendorf 18, 2095 Drosendorf
☎ **(02915) 62625**
🖷 (02915) 62625

Wien (1901)
1020 Wien, Freudenau 65a
☎ **(01) 728 9564 (Clubhouse)**
🖷 (01) 728 9564-20
✉ gcwien@golf.at
🖳 www.gcwien.at

Wien-Süssenbrunn (1995)
Weingartenallee 22, 1220 Wien
☎ **+43 (01) 256 8282**
🖷 +43 (01) 246 8282 -44
✉ golf@sportparkwien.at
✍ Michel Prassé
🖳 www.gcwien-sb.at

Wienerwald (1981)
1130 Wien, Altgasse 27
☎ **(0222) 877 3111 (Sec)**

Vorarlberg

Bludenz-Braz (1996)
Oberradin 60, 6751 Braz bei Bludenz
☎ **(05552) 33503**
🖷 (05552) 33503-3
✉ gcbraz@golf.at
🖳 www.gc-bludenz-braz.at

Bregenzerwald (1997)
Unterlitten 3a, 6943 Riefensberg
☎ **(05513) 8400**
🖷 (05513) 8400-4
✉ office@golf-bregenzerwald.com
🖳 www.golf-bregenzerwald.com

Montafon (1992)
6774 Tschagguns, Zelfenstrasse 110
☎ **(05556) 77011**
🖷 (05556) 77045
✉ info@golfclub-montafon.at
🖳 www.golfclub-montafon.at

Belgium

Antwerp Region

Bossenstein (1989)
Moor 16, Bossenstein Kasteel, 2520 Broechem
☎ **(03) 485 64 46**
🖷 (03) 485 78 41
✉ bossenstein.shop@skynet.be

Cleydael G&CC (1988)
Groenenhoek 7-9, 2630 Aartselaar
☎ **(03) 870 56 80**
🖷 (03) 887 14 75
✉ info@cleydael.be
✍ Maryse Bal (Gen Sec)
🖳 www.cleydael.be

Kempense (1986)
Kiezelweg 78, 2400 Mol-Rauw
☎ **00 32 (0)14 81 46 41 (Clubhouse)**
🖷 00 32 (0)14 81 62 78
✉ kempense@pandora.be
🖳 www.golf.be/kempense

Lilse Golf & Country (1987)
Haarlebeek 3, 2275 Lille
☎ **(014) 55 19 30**
🖷 (014) 55 19 31
✉ info@lilsegolfcountry.be
✍ Vink Nienue
🖳 www.lilsegolfcountry.be

Golf Club Nuclea Mol (1984)
Goorstraat, 2400 Mol
☎ **+32 14 37 0915**
✉ info@golfclubnuclea.be
✍ André Verbruggen
🖳 www.golfclubnucleamol.be

Rinkven G&CC (1980)
Sint Jobsteenweg 120, 2970 Schilde
☎ **(03) 380 12 80**
🖷 (03) 384 29 33
✉ info@rinkven.be
🖳 www.rinkven.be

Royal Antwerp (1888)
Georges Capiaulei 2, 2950 Kapellen
☎ **(03) 666 84 56**
🖷 (03) 666 44 37
✉ info@ragc.be
✍ Jean-Noel Raymakers (Mgr)
🖳 www.ragc.be

Steenhoven (1985)
Steenhoven 89, 2400 Postel-Mol
☎ **(014) 37 36 61**
🖷 (014) 37 36 62
✉ info@steenhoven.be
✍ Luc Hannes (Mgr/Sec)
🖳 www.steenhoven.be

Ternesse G&CC (1976)
Uilenbaan 15, 2160 Wommelgem
☎ **(03) 355 14 30**
🖷 (03) 355 14 35
✉ info@ternessegolf.be
🖹 www.ternessegolf.be

Ardennes & South

Andenne (1988)
Ferme du Moulin 52, Stud, 5300 Andenne
☎ **(085) 84 34 04**
🖷 (085) 84 34 04
✉ jojadin@hotmail.com
✍ Josiane Colson
🖹 www.golfclubandenne.be

Château Royal d'Ardenne
Tour Léopold, Ardenne 6, 5560 Houyet
☎ **(082) 66 62 28**
🖷 (082) 66 74 53

Falnuée (1987)
Rue E Pirson 55, 5032 Mazy
☎ **(081) 63 30 90**
🖷 (081) 63 21 41
✉ info@falnuee.be
✍ Eric Jottrand/Anne Sophie Jottrand
🖹 www.falnuee.be

Five Nations C C (1990)
Ferme du Grand Scley, 5372 Méan (Havelange)
☎ **(086) 32 32 32**
🖷 (086) 32 30 11

Mont Garni Golf Club (1990)
Rue du Mont Garni, 3 7331 Saint Ghislain
☎ **+32 65.52.94.10**
🖷 +32 65 62 34 10
✉ secretariat@golfmontgarni.be
✍ Marie van der Schueren/Jodi De Frenne
🖹 www.golfmontgarni.be

Rougemont (1987)
Chemin du Beau Vallon 45, 5170 Profondeville
☎ **+32 81 41 21 31**
🖷 +32 81 41 21 42
✉ rougemont@skynet.be
✍ Jean-Louis Rousseau (Hon Sec)
🖹 www.golfderougemont.be

Royal GC du Hainaut (1933)
Rue de la Verrerie 2, 7050 Erbisoeul
☎ **(065) 22 96 10 (Clubhouse)**
🖷 (065) 22 02 09
✉ info@golfhainaut.be
🖹 www.golfhainaut.be

Brussels & Brabant

Bercuit (1965)
Les Gottes 3, 1390 Grez-Doiceau
☎ **(010) 84 15 01**
🖷 (010) 84 55 95
✉ info@golfdubercuit.be
🖹 www.golfdubercuit.be

Brabantse Golf (1982)
Steenwagenstraat 11, 1820 Melsbroek
☎ **(02) 751 82 05**
🖷 (02) 751 84 25
✉ secretariaat@brabantsegolf.be
✍ Rob Houben (Mgr/Sec)
🖹 www.brabantsegolf.be

La Bruyère (1988)
Rue Jumerée 1, 1495 Sart-Dames-Avelines
☎ **(071) 87 72 67**
🖷 (071) 87 43 38
✉ info@golflabruyere.be
🖹 www.golflabruyere.be

Golf du Château de la Bawette (1988)
Chaussée du Chateau de la Bawette 5, 1300 Wavre
☎ **(010) 22 33 32**
🖷 (010) 22 90 04
✉ info@labawette.com
🖹 www.golflabawette.com

Château de la Tournette
Chemin de Baudemont 21, 1400 Nivelles
☎ **(067) 89 42 66**
🖷 (067) 21 95 17
✉ info@tournette.com
🖹 www.tournette.com

L'Empereur (1989)
Rue Emile François No.31, 1474 Ways (Genappe)
☎ **(067) 77 15 71**
🖷 (067) 77 18 33
✉ info@golfempereur.com
✍ Capart
🖹 www.golfempereur.com

Hulencourt (1989)
Bruyère d'Hulencourt 15, 1472 Vieux Genappe
☎ **(067) 79 40 40**
🖷 (067) 79 40 48
✉ info@golfhulencourt.be
🖹 www.golfhulencourt.be

Kampenhout (1989)
Wildersedreef 56, 1910 Kampenhout
☎ **(016) 65 12 16**
🖷 (016) 65 16 80
✉ golfclubkampenhout@skynet.be
🖹 www.golfclubkampenhout.be

Keerbergen (1968)
Vlieghavelaan 50, 3140 Keerbergen
☎ **(015) 22 68 78**
🖷 (015) 23 57 37
✉ keerbergen.golfclub@skynet.be
🖹 www.golfkeerbergen.be

Louvain-la-Neuve (1989)
Rue A Hardy 68, 1348 Louvain-la-Neuve
☎ **(010) 45 05 15**
🖷 (010) 45 44 17
✉ info@golflln.com
🖹 www.golflln.com

Overijse (1986)
Gemslaan 55, 3090 Overijse
☎ **(02) 687 50 30**
✉ ogc@golf-overijse.be
🖹 www.overijsegolfclub.be

Pierpont (1992)
1 Grand Pierpont, 6210 Frasnes-lez-Gosselies
☎ **(071) 8808 30**
🖷 (071) 85 15 43
✉ info@pierpont.be
✍ Gary Nisbet
🖹 www.pierpont.be

Rigenée (1981)
Rue de Châtelet 62, 1495 Villers-la-Ville
☎ **(071) 87 77 65**
🖷 (071) 87 77 83
✉ golf@rigenee.be
🖹 www.rigenee.be

Royal Amicale Anderlecht (1987)
Rue Schollestraat 1, 1070 Brussels
☎ **(02) 521 16 87**
🖷 (02) 521 51 56
✉ info@golf-anderlecht.com
🖹 www.golf-anderlecht.com

Royal Golf Club de Belgique (1906)
Château de Ravenstein, 3080 Tervuren
☎ **+32 (0) 2 767 58 01**
🖷 +32 (0) 2 767 28 41
✉ info@rgcb.be
✍ Jos Vankriekelsienne (Dir)
🖹 www.rgcb.be

Royal Waterloo Golf Club (1923)
Vieux Chemin de Wavre 50, 1380 Lasne
☎ **(00) 322 633 1850**
🖷 (00) 322 633 2866
✉ infos@golfwaterloo.be
✍ Henri Bailly
🖹 www.rwgc.be

Sept Fontaines (1987)
1021, Chaussée d'Alsemberg, 1420 Braine L'Alleud
☎ **(02) 353 02 46/353 03 46**
🖷 (02) 354 68 75
✉ info@golf7fontaines.be
✍ Manuel Weymeersch
🖹 www.golf7fontaines.be

Winge G&CC (1988)
Leuvensesteenweg 252, B-3390 Sint Joris Winge
☎ **(016) 63 40 53**
🖷 (016) 63 21 40
✉ info@wingegolf.be
✍ Chris Morton
🖹 www.wingegolf.be

East

Avernas (199)
Route de Grand Hallet 19A, 4280 Hannut
☎ **(019) 51 30 66**
🖷 (019) 51 53 43
✉ info@golfavernas.be
🖹 www.golfavernas.be

Durbuy (1991)
Route d'Oppagne 34, 6940 Barvaux-su-Ourthe
☎ **(086) 21 44 54**

Flanders Nippon Hasselt (1988)
Vissenbroekstraat 15, 3500 Hasselt
☎ **(011) 26 34 82**
(011) 26 34 83
flanders.nippon.golf@pandora.be
www.flandersnippongolf.be

Henri-Chapelle (1988)
Rue du Vivier 3, B-4841 Henri-Chapelle
☎ **(087) 88 19 91**
(087) 88 36 55
info@golfhenrichapelle.be
www.golfhenrichapelle.be

International Gomze Golf Club (1986)
Sur Counachamps 8, 4140 Gomze Andoumont
☎ **(04) 360 92 07/ (04) 278 75 00**
(04) 360 92 06
gomzegolf@skynet.be
Michele Quentainmount
www.gomze.be

Limburg G&CC (1966)
Golfstraat 1, 3530 Houthalen
☎ **(089) 38 35 43**
(089) 84 12 08
limburggolf@telenet.be
Jan Hendrikx
www.lgcc.be

Royal GC du Sart Tilman (1939)
Route du Condroz 541, 4031 Liège
☎ **(041) 336 20 21**
(041) 337 20 26
secretariat|@rgcst.be
www.rgcst.be

Royal Golf des Fagnes (1930)
1 Ave de l'Hippodrome, 4900 Spa
☎ **(087) 79 30 30**
(087) 79 30 39
info@golfdespa.be
www.golfdespa.be

Spiegelven GC Genk (1988)
Wiemesmeerstraat 109, 3600 Genk
☎ **(0032) 893 59616**
(0032) 893 64184
info@spiegelven.be
www.spiegelven.be

West & Oost Vlaanderen

Damme G&CC (1987)
Doornstraat 16, 8340 Damme-Sijsele
☎ **(050) 35 35 72**
(050) 35 89 25
info@dammegolf.be
Chris Morton
www.dammegolf.be

Oudenaarde G&CC (1975)
Kasteel Petegem, Kortrykstraat 52, 9790 Wortegem-Petegem
☎ **(055) 33 41 61**
(055) 31 98 49
oudenaarde@golf.be
www.golfoudenaarde.be

De Palingsbeek (1991)
Eekhofstraat 14, 8902 Hollebeke-Ieper
☎ **(057) 20 04 36**
(057) 21 89 58
golfpalingsbeek@skynet.be
Ian Connerty
www.golfpalingbeek.be

Royal Latem (1909)
9830 St Martens-Latem, Latemstraat 120
☎ **+32 9 282 54 11**
+32 9 282 90 19
secretary@latemgolf.be
Ph Buysse
www.latemgolf.be

Royal Ostend (1903)
Koninklijke Baan 2, 8420 De Haan
☎ **(059) 23 32 83**
(059) 23 37 49
www.golfoostende.be

Royal Zoute (1899)
Caddiespad 14, 8300 Knokke-le-Zoute
☎ **(050) 60 16 17 (Clubhouse)**
(050) 62 30 29
golf@zoute.be
www.zoute.be

Waregem (1988)
Bergstraat 41, 8790 Waregem
☎ **(056) 60 88 08**
(056) 62 18 23
waregem@golf.be
www.golf.be/waregem

Cyprus

Aphrodite Hills GC (2002)
3 Aphrodite Avenue, Aphrodite Hills, Kouklia, 8509 Paphos
☎ **00357 2682 8200**
00357 2695 6706
golfreservations@aphroditehills.com
Nuno T Bastos
www.aphroditehills.com

Minthis Hills GC (1994)
P O Box 62085, 8060 Paphos
☎ **00357 2664 2774/5**
00357 2664 2776
golfers2@cytanet.com.cy
Mr Stelios Patsalides (Manager)
www.minthishills.com

Vikla G&CC (1992)
Vikla Village, Kellaki, Limassol
☎ **00 357 99 674 218**
00 357 25 760 750
viklagolf@cytanet.com.cy
info@vikla-golf.com
www.vikla-golf.com

Paphos (2004)
Box 484 Kamares Club, PO Box 60156, 8101 Paphos
☎ **00357 99394164**
mike_emmett@hotmail.co.uk
Mr Michael Emmett (Secretary)
www.cgf.org.cy

Czech Republic

Karlovy Vary (1904)
Prazska 125, PO Box 67, 360 01 Karlovy Vary
☎ **(017) 333 1001-2**
(017) 333 1101

Lísnice (1928)
252 10 Mnísek pod Brdy
☎ **(0318) 599 151**
(0318) 599 151
www.gkl.cz

Royal Golf Club Mariánské Lázne (1905)
PO Box 47, 353 01 Mariánské Lázne
☎ **+420 354 604300**
+420 354 625195
office@golfml.cz
Cerna Jana/Nechanicky Oldrich
www.golfml.cz

Park Golf Club Mittal Ostrava (1968)
Dolni 412, 747 15 Silherovice
☎ **(+420) 595 054 144**
(+420) 595 054 144
golf@golf-ostrava.cz
Ing. Paval Pniak
www.golf-ostrava.cz

Podebrady (1964)
Na Zalesi 530, 29080 Podebrady
☎ **(0324) 610928**
(0324) 610981
www.golfpodebrady.cz

Semily (1970)
Bavlnarska 521, 513 01 Semily
☎ **(0431) 622443/624428**
(0431) 623000
www.semily.cz

Denmark

Bornholm Island

Bornholm (1972)
Plantagevej 3B, 3700 Rønne
☎ **56 95 68 54**
56 95 68 53
info@bornholmsgolfklub.dk
www.bornholmsgolfklub.dk

For key to symbols and European dialling codes see page 725

Nexø
Dueodde Golfbane, Strandmarksvejen 14, 3730 Nexø
56 48 89 87
56 48 89 69
ngk@dueodde-golf.dk
www.dueodde-golf.dk

Nordbornholm-Rø (1987)
Spellingevej 3, Rø, 3760 Gudhjem
56 48 40 50
56 48 40 52
mail@roegolfbane.dk
www.roegolfbane.dk

Funen

Faaborg (1989)
Dalkildegards Allee 1, 5600 Faaborg
62 61 77 43
62 61 79 34

Lillebaelt (1990)
O.Hougvej 130, 5500 Middelfart
64 41 80 11
64 41 14 11
gkl@post10.tele.dk
www.gkl.dk

Odense (1927)
Hestehaven 200, 5220 Odense SØ
65 95 90 00
sekretariatet@odensegolfklub.dk
Hans Henrik Burkal
www.odensegolfklub.dk

Proark Golf Odense Eventyr (1993)
Falen 227, 5250 Odense SV
7021 1900
6562 2021
pgoe@proarkgolf.dk
Ulla Vahl-Møller (Golf Mgr)
www.proarkgolf.dk

SCT. Knuds Golfklub (1954)
Slipshavnsvej 16, 5800 Nyborg
65 31 12 12
65 30 28 04
mail@sct-knuds.dk
Margit Madsen
www.sct-knuds.dk

Svendborg (1970)
Tordensgaardevej 5, Sørup, 5700 Svendborg
62 22 40 77
62 20 29 77
info@svendborg-golf.dk
www.svendborg-golf.dk

Vestfyns (1974)
Rønnemosegård, Krengerupvej 27, 5620 Glamsbjerg
63 72 19 20
63 72 19 26
vestfyn@golfonline.dk
www.vestfynsgolfklub.dk

Jutland

Aarhus (1931)
Ny Moesgaardvej 50, 8270 Hojbjerg
86 27 63 22
86 27 63 21
aarhusgolf@mail.dk
www.aarhusgolf.dk

Blokhus Golf Klub (1993)
Hunetorpvej 115, Box 37, 9492 Blokhus
98 20 95 00
98 20 95 01
info@blokhusgolfklub.dk
www.blokhusgolf.dk

Breinholtgård (1992)
Koksspangvej 17-19, 6710 Esbjerg V
75 11 57 00
75 11 55 12
bgk@tiscali.dk
www.bggc.dk

Brønderslev Golfklub (1971)
Golfvejen 83, 9700 Brønderslev
98 82 32 81
info@broenderslevgolfklub.dk
Ulla Gade
www.broenderslevgolfklub.dk

Brundtlandbanen (2000)
Brundtland Allé 1-3, 6520 Toftlund
73 83 16 00
73 83 16 19
info@brundtland.dk
www.brundtland.dk

Dejbjerg (1966)
Letagervej 1, Dejbjerg, 6900 Skjern
97 35 00 09
96 80 11 18
kontor@dejbjerggk.dk
Hanne Häggavist
www.dejbjerggk.dk

Ebeltoft (1966)
Galgebakken 14, 8400 Ebeltoft
87 59 6000
post@ebeltoft-golfclub.dk

Esbjerg (1921)
Sønderhedevej 11, Marbaek, 6710 Esbjerg
75 26 92 19
75 26 94 19
kontor@egk.dk
www.egk.dk

Fanø Golf Links (1901)
Golfvejen 5, 6720 Fanø
76 66 00 77
76 66 00 44
golf@fanoe-golf-links.dk
www.fanoe-golf-links.dk

Grenaa (1981)
Vestermarken 1, DK-8500 Grenaa
+45 863 27929
+45 863 09654
info@grenaagolfklub.dk
www.grenaagolfklub.dk

Gyttegård (1974)
Billundvej 43, 7250 Hejnsvig
+45 75 33 63 82
+45 75 33 68 20
info@gyttegaardgolfklub.dk
www.gyttegaardgolfklub.dk

Haderslev (1971)
Viggo Carstensvej 7, 6100 Haderslev
74 52 83 01
74 53 36 01

Han Herreds
Starkaervej 20, 9690 Fjerritslev
98 21 26 66 / 98 21 26 78
98 21 26 77

Henne (1989)
Hennebysvej 30, 6854 Henne
75 25 56 10
post@hennegolfklub.dk
Beverley Elston
www.hennegolfklub.dk

Herning (1964)
Golfvej 2, 7400 Herning
97 21 00 33
97 21 00 34
info@herninggolfklub.dk
www.herninggolfklub.dk

Himmerland G&CC (1979)
Centervej 1, Gatten, 9640 Farsö
96 49 61 00
98 66 14 56
hgcc@himmerlandgolf.dk
www.himmerlandgolf.dk

Hirtshals (1990)
Kjulvej 10, PO Box 51, 9850 Hirtshals
98 94 94 08
98 94 19 35

Hjarbaek Fjord (1992)
Lynderup, 8832 Skals
86 69 62 88
86696268
pghf@proarkgolf.dk
www.proarkgolf.dk

Hjorring (1985)
Vinstrupvej 30, 9800 Hjorring
98 91 18 28
98 90 31 00
info@hjoerringgolf.dk
www.hjoerringgolf.dk

Holmsland Klit
Klevevej 19, Søndervig, 6950 Ringkøbing
97 33 88 00
97 33 86 80
www.holmslandklitgolf.dk

Holstebro Golf Klub (1970)
Brandsbjergvej 4, 7570 Vemb
(+45) 97 48 51 55
post@holstebro-golfklub.dk
Kjeld Rasmussen
www.holstebro-golfklub.dk

Horsens (1972)
Silkeborgvej 44, 8700 Horsens
75 61 51 51
75 61 40 51
www.horsensgolf.dk

For key to symbols and European dialling codes see page 725

Hvide Klit (1972)
Hvideklitvej 28, 9982 Aalbaek
98 48 90 21
98 48 91 12
info@hvideklit.dk
www.hvideklit.dk

Juelsminde (1973)
Bobroholtvej 11a, 7130 Juelsminde
75 69 34 92
75 69 46 11
golf@juelsmindegolf.dk
www.juelsmindegolf.dk

Kaj Lykke (1988)
Kirkebrovej 5, 6740 Bramming
00 45 - 75 10 22 46
00 45 - 75 10 26 68
post@kajlykkegolfklub.dk
Mrs Susanne Noergaard (Sec)
www.kajlykkegolfklub.dk

Kalo (1992)
Aarhusvej 32, 8410 Rønde
86 37 36 00
86 37 36 46

Kolding (1933)
Egtved Alle 10, 6000 Kolding
75 52 37 93
75 52 42 42
kgc@koldinggolfclub.dk
Ronny Kert (Mgr)
www.koldinggolfclub.dk

Lemvig (1986)
Søgårdevejen 6, 7620 Lemvig
97 81 09 20
97 81 09 20
lemviggolfklub@lemviggolfklub.dk
www.lemviggolfklub.dk

Løkken (1990)
Vrenstedvej 226, PO Box 43, 9480 Løkken
98 99 26 57
98 99 26 58
info@loekken-golfklub.dk
www.loekken-golfklub.dk

Nordvestjysk (1971)
Nystrupvej 19, 7700 Thisted
97 97 41 41

Odder (1990)
Akjaervej 200, Postbox 46, 8300 Odder
86 54 54 51
86 54 54 58
oddergolf@oddergolf.dk
Karen Frederiksen
www.oddergolf.dk

Ornehoj Golfklub
Lundegard 70, 9260 Gistrup-Aalborg
98 31 43 44
98 32 39 45
golfklubben@mail.dk
www.ornehojgolfklub.dk

Randers (1958)
Himmelbovej 22, Fladbro, 8900 Randers
86 42 88 69
86 40 88 69
postmaster@randersgolf.dk
www.randersgolf.dk

Ribe (1979)
Rønnehave, Snepsgårdevej 14, 6760 Ribe
30 73 65 18

Rold Skov (1991)
Golfvej 1, 9520 Skørping
96 82 8300
96 82 8309
info@roldskovgolf.dk
www.roldskovgolf.dk

Royal Oak (1992)
Golfvej, Jels, 6630 Rødding
74 55 32 94
74 55 32 95
golf@royal-oak.dk
www.royal-oak.dk

Silkeborg (1966)
Sensommervej 15C, 8600 Silkeborg
86 85 33 99
kontor@silkeborggolf.dk
Mads Rügholm (Mgr)
www.silkeborggolf.dk

Sønderjyllands (1968)
Uge Hedegård, 6360 Tinglev
74 68 75 25
74 68 75 05
sonderjylland@mail.dk
www.sdj-golfklub.dk

Varde (1991)
Gellerupvej 111b, 6800 Varde
+45 75 22 49 44
kontor@vardegolfklub.dk
Lene Godtfredsen
www.vardegolfklub.dk

Vejle (1970)
Faellesslетgard, Ibaekvej, 7100 Vejle
75 85 81 85
75 85 83 01
info@vgc.dk
www.vgc.dk

Viborg (1973)
Spangsbjerg Alle 50, Overlund, 8800 Viborg
86 67 30 10
86 67 34 15
mail@viborggolfklub.dk
www.viborggolfklub.dk

Zealand

Asserbo Golf Club (1946)
Bødkergaardsvej 9, 3300 Frederiksvaerk
47 72 14 90
47 72 14 26
agc@agc.dk
Arne Larsen
www.agc.dk

Copenhagen (1898)
Dyrehaven 2, 2800 Kgs. Lyngby
39 63 04 83
info@kgkgolf.dk
S Pedersen (Mgr)
www.kgkgolf.dk

Dragør Golfklub (1991)
Kalvebodvej 100, 2791 Dragør
32 53 89 75
32 53 88 09
post@dragor-golf.dk
www.dragor-golf.dk

Falster (1994)
Virketvej 44, 4863 Eskilstrup, Falster Island
54 43 81 43
54 43 81 23
info@falster-golfklub.dk
Knud Erik Melgaard
www.falster-golfklub.dk

Frederikssund (1974)
Egelundsgården, Skovnaesvej 9, 3630 Jaegerspris
+45 47 31 08 77
+45 47 31 21 77
fgk@fgkgolf.dk
Jorgen Bundgaard
www.frederikssundgolfklub.dk

Furesø (1974)
Hestkøbgård, Hestkøb Vaenge 4, 3460 Birkerød
+45 45 81 74 44
info@fggolf.dk
Lars Lindegren
www.fggolf.dk

Gilleleje (1970)
Ferlevej 52, 3250 Gilleleje
49 71 80 56
49 71 80 86
info@gillelejegolfklub.dk
www.gillelejegolfklub.dk

Hedeland (1980)
Staerkendevej 232A, 2640 Hedehusene
46 13 61 88
46 13 62 78
klub@hedeland-golf.dk
www.hedeland-golf.dk

Helsingør
GL Hellebaekvej, 3000 Helsingør
49 21 29 70
49 21 09 70

Hillerød (1966)
Nysøgårdsvej 9, Ny Hammersholt, 3400 Hillerød
48 26 50 46/48 25 40 30 (Pro)
48 25 29 87
klubben@hillerodgolf.dk
www.hillerodgolf.dk

Hjortespring Golfklub (1980)
Klausdalsbrovej 602, 2750 Ballerup
44 68 90 09
44 68 90 04
post@hjgk.dk
Jens Åge Dalby
www.hjgk.dk

Holbaek (1964)
Dragerupvej 50, 4300 Holbaek
59 43 45 79
59 43 51 61

info@holbakgolfklub.dk
Jorgen Buur (Mgr)
www.holbakgolfklub.dk

Køge Golf Klub (1970)
Gl.Hastrupvej 12, 4600 Køge
+45 56 65 10 00
+45 56 65 13 45
admin@kogegolf.dk
Helge Caspersen
www.kogegolf.dk

Kokkedal (1971)
Kokkedal Alle 9, 2970 Horsholm
45 76 99 59
45 76 99 03
kg@kokkedalgolf.dk
Ken Lauritsen (Golf Mgr)
www.kokkedalgolf.dk

Korsør Golf Club (1964)
Ornumuey 8, Postbox 53, 4220 Korsør
58 37 18 36
58 37 18 39
golf@korsoergolf.dk
Kevin O'Donoghue
www.korsoergolf.dk

Mølleåens (1970)
Stenbaekgård, Rosenlundvej 3, 3540 Lynge
48 18 86 31/48 18 86 36 (Pro)
48 18 86 43

Odsherred (1967)
Stárupvej 2, 4573 Hojby
59 30 20 76
sek@odsherredgolf.dk
www.odsherredgolf.dk

Roskilde (1973)
Gedevad, Kongemarken 34, 4000 Roskilde
46 37 01 81
46 32 85 79

Rungsted (1937)
Vestre Stationsvej 16, 2960 Rungsted Kyst
45 86 34 44
45 86 57 70
info@rungstedgolfklub.dk
www.rungstedgolfklub.dk

Simon's (1993)
Nybovej 5, 3490 Kvistgaard
+45 49 19 14 78
+45 49 19 14 70
info@simonsgolf.dk
Mrs Helle Kongsted
www.simonsgolf.dk

Skjoldenaesholm (1992)
Skjoldenaesvej 101, 4174 Jystrup
+45 57 53 88 10
pgs@proarkgolf.dk
www.proarkgolf.dk

Søllerød (1972)
Brillerne 9, 2840 Holte
45 80 17 84
info@sollerodgolf.dk
Helle Hessellund
www.sollerodgolf.dk

Sorø (1979)
Suserupvej 7a, 4180 Sorø
57 84 93 95
57 84 85 58
www.soroegolf.dk

Sydsjaellands (1974)
Borupgården, Mogenstrup, 4700 Naestved
(+45) 55 76 15 55
(+45) 55 76 15 88
sydsjaelland@golfonline.dk
www.sydsjaellandsgolfklub.dk

Vaerloese Golfklub (1993)
Christianshoejvej 22, 3500 Vaerloese
(+45) 4447 2124
(+45) 4447 2128
mail@vaerloese-golfklub.dk
Tine Lunding (Sec)
www.vaerloese-golfklub.dk

Finland

Central

Etelä-Pohjanmaan (1986)
P O Box 136, 60101 Seinäjoki
(06) 423 4545
(06) 423 4547
www.ruuhikoskigolf.fi

Karelia Golf (1987)
Vaskiportintie, 80780 Kontioniemi
(013) 732411
(013) 732472

Kokkolan (1957)
P O Box 164, 67101 Kokkola
(06) 823 8600
toimisto@kokkolangolf.fi
www.kokkolangolf.fi

Laukaan Peurunkagolf (1989)
Valkolantie 68, 41530 Laukaa
(014) 3377 300
(014) 3377 305
www.golfpiste.com/lpg

Tarina Golf (1988)
Tarinagolfintie 19, 71800 Siilinjärvi
02 01 87 87 02
toimisto@tarinagolf.fi
www.tarinagolf.fi

Vaasan Golf (1969)
Golfkenttätie 61, 65380 Vaasa
(06) 356 9989
(06) 356 9091
toimisto@vaasangolf.fi
Mr Petri Jolkkonen (Mgr)
www.vaasangolf.fi

Helsinki & South

Aura Golf (1958)
Ruissalon Puistotie 536, 20100 Turku
(02) 258 9201/9221
(02) 258 9121
office@auragolf.fi
www.auragolf.fi

Espoo Ringside Golf (1990)
Nurmikartanontie 5, 02920 Espoo
(09) 849 4940
(09) 853 7132
caddie@ringsidegolf.fi
Ari Vepsä
www.ringsidegolf.fi

Espoon Golfseura (1982)
Mynttiläntie 1, 02780 Espoo
(09) 8190 3444
(09) 8190 3434
www.espoongolfseura.fi

Harjattula G&CC (1989)
Harjattulantie 84, 20960 Turku
(02) 276 2180
(02) 258 7218
www.harjattula.fi

Helsingin Golfklubi (1932)
Talin Kartano, 00350 Helsinki
+358 9 225 23710
+358 9 225 23737
toimisto@helsingingolfklubi.fi
Elkka Ulander
www.helsingingolfklubi.fi

Hyvinkään (1989)
Golftie 63, 05880 Hyvinkää
(019) 456 2400
(019) 456 2410
caddiemaster@hyvigolf.fi
www.hyvigolf.fi

Keimola Golf (1988)
Kirkantie 32, 01750 Vantaa
(09) 276 6650
(09) 896790

Kurk Golf (1985)
02550 Evitskog
(09) 819 0480
(09) 819 04810
kurk@kurkgolf.fi
www.kurkgolf.fi

Master Golf (1988)
Bodomin kuja 7, 02940 Espoo
(09) 849 2300
(09) 849 23011
www.mastergolf.fi

Meri-Teijo (1990)
Mathildedalin Kartano, 25660 Mathildedal
(02) 736 3955
(02) 736 3945

Messilä (1988)
Messiläntie 240, 15980 Messilä
(03) 884040
(03) 884 0440

Nevas Golf (1988)
01150 Söderkulla
(010) 400 6400
ng@nevasgolf.fi
www.nevasgolf.fi

Nordcenter G&CC (1988)
10410 Aminnefors
(019) 2766850
(019) 238871
www.nordcenter.com

Nurmijärven (1990)
Ratasillantie 70, 05100 Röykkä
☎ **(09) 276 6230**
🖷 (09) 276 62330
✉ caddiemaster@nurmijarvi-golf.fi
🖥 www.nurmijarvi-golf.fi

Peuramaa Golf (1991)
Peuramaantie 152, 02400 Kirkkonummi
☎ **(09) 295 588**
🖷 (09) 295 58210
✉ office@peuramaagolf.com
🖥 www.peuramaagolf.com

Pickala Golf (1986)
Golfkuja 5, 02580 Siuntio
☎ **(09) 221 9080**
🖷 (09) 221 90899
✉ toimisto@pickalagolf.fi
🖥 www.pickalagolf.fi

Ruukkigolf (1986)
PL 9, 10420 Skuru
☎ **(019) 245 4485**
🖷 (019) 245 4285
✉ toimisto@ruukkigolf.fi
🖥 www.ruukkigolf.fi

Sarfvik (1984)
P O Box 27, 02321 Espoo
☎ **(09) 221 9000**
🖷 (09) 297 7134
✉ sarfvik@golfsarfvik.fi

Sea Golf Rönnäs (1989)
Kabbölentie 319, 07750 Isnäs
☎ **+358 (0) 19 634 434**
🖷 +358 (0) 19 634 458
✉ toimisto@seagolf.fi
🖥 www.seagolf.fi

St Laurence Golf (1989)
Kaivurinkatu 133, 08200 Lohja
☎ **+358 (0)19 357 821**
🖷 +358 (0)19 386 666
✉ caddie.master@stlaurencegolf.fi
🖥 www.stlaurencegolf.fi

Suur-Helsingin Golf (1965)
Rinnekodintie 29, 02980 Espoo
☎ **+358 9 4399 7110**
🖷 +358 9 437121
✉ toimisto@shg.fi
🖥 www.shg.fi

Golf Talma (1989)
Nygårdintie 115-6, 04240 Talma
☎ **+358 9 274 6540**
🖷 +358 9 274 654 32
✉ golftalma@golftalma.fi
✍ Olli-Pekka Nissinen (Mgr)
🖥 www.golftalma.fi

Tuusula (1983)
Kirkkotie 51, 04301 Tuusula
☎ **(042) 410241**
🖷 (09) 274 60860
🖥 www.golfpiste.com/tgk

Virvik Golf (1981)
Virvik, 06100 Porvoo
☎ **(915) 579292**
🖷 (915) 579292

North

Green Zone Golf (1987)
Näräntie, 95400 Tornio
☎ **(016) 431711**
🖷 (016) 431710

Katinkulta (1990)
88610 Vuokatti
☎ **(08) 669 7488**
✉ golf.katinkulta@sok.fi
🖥 www.katinkultagolf.fi

Oulu (1964)
Sankivaaran Golfkeskus, 90650 Oulu
☎ **(08) 531 5222**
🖷 (08) 531 5129
✉ caddiemaster@oulugolf.fi
🖥 www.oulugolf.fi

South East

Imatran Golf (1986)
Golftie 11, 55800 Imatra
☎ **(05) 473 4954**
🖷 (05) 473 4953

Kartano Golf (1988)
P O Box 60, 79601 Joroinen
☎ **(017) 572257**
🖷 (017) 572263

Kerigolf (1990)
Kerimaantie 65, 58200 Kerimäki
☎ **(015) 252600**
🖷 (015) 252606
✉ clubhouse@kerigolf.fi
🖥 www.kerigolf.fi

Koski Golf (1987)
Eerolanväylä 126, 45700 Kuusankoski
☎ **+358 207 129 820**
🖷 +358 207 129 829
✉ toimisto@koskigolf.fi
🖥 www.koskigolf.fi

Kymen Golf (1964)
Mussalo Golfcourse, 48310 Kotka
☎ **(05) 210 3700**
🖷 (05) 210 3730
🖥 www.kymengolf.fi

Lahden Golf (1959)
Takkulantie, 15230 Lahti
☎ **(03) 784 1311**
🖷 (03) 784 1311

Porrassalmi (1989)
Annila, 50100 Mikkeli
☎ **(015) 335518/335446**
🖷 (015) 335682

Vierumäki Golf (1988)
Kaskelantie 10, 19120 Vierumäki
☎ **+358 (0) 40 837 6149**
🖷 +358 (0) 3 8424 7015
✉ jan.ruoho@vierumaki.fi
✍ Jan Ruoho (Dir)
🖥 www.vierumakigolf.fi

South West

Porin Golfkerho (1939)
P O Box 25, 28601 Pori
☎ **(02) 630 3888**
🖷 (02) 630 38813
✉ toimisto@kalafornia.com
🖥 www.kalafornia.com

River Golf (1988)
Taivalkunta, 37120 Nokia
☎ **(03) 340 0234**
🖷 (03) 340 0235

Salo Golf (1988)
Anistenkatu 1, 24100 Salo
☎ **(02) 721 7300**
🖷 (02) 721 7310
✉ caddiemaster@salogolf.fi
✍ Mr Mika Havulinna
🖥 www.salogolf.fi

Tammer Golf (1965)
Toimelankatu 4, 33560 Tampere
☎ **(03) 261 3316**
🖷 (03) 261 3130

Tawast Golf (1987)
Tawastintie 48, 13270 Hämeenlinna
☎ **(03) 630 610**
🖷 (03) 630 6120
✉ tawast@tawastgolf.fi
🖥 www.tawastgolf.fi

Vammala (1991)
38100 Karkku
☎ **(03) 513 4070**
🖷 (03) 513 90711

Wiurila G&CC (1990)
Viurilantie 126, 24910 Halikko
☎ **+35 8272 78100**
🖷 +35 8272 78107
✉ toimisto@wgcc.fi
🖥 www.wgcc.fi

Yyteri Golf (1988)
Karhuluodontie 85, 28840 Pori
☎ **(02) 638 0380**
🖷 (02) 638 0385
🖥 www.yyterilinks.com

France

Bordeaux & South West

Albret (1986)
Le Pusocq, 47230 Barbaste
☎ **05 53 65 53 69**
🖷 05 53 65 61 19

Arcachon (1955)
Golf International d'Arcachon, 35 Bd d'Arcachon, 33260 La Teste De Buch
☎ **05 56 54 44 00**
🖷 05 56 66 86 32
✉ golfarcachon@free.fr

Arcangues (1991)
64200 Arcangues
05 59 43 10 56
05 59 43 12 60
golf.arcangues@wanadoo.fz
www.golfdarcangues.com

Biarritz (1888)
Ave Edith Cavell, 64200 Biarritz
05 59 03 71 80
05 59 03 26 74
info@golfbiarritz.com
www.golf-biarritz.com

Biscarrosse (1989)
Avenue du Golf, F-40600 Biscarrosse
05 58 09 84 93
05 58 09 84 50
golfdebiscarrosse@wanadoo.fr
www.biscarrossegolf.com

Blue Green-Artiguelouve (1986)
Domaine St Michel, Pau-Artiguelouve, 64230 Artiguelouve
05 59 83 09 29
05 59 83 14 05

Blue Green-Seignosse (1989)
Avenue du Belvédère, 40510 Seignosse
05 58 41 68 30
05 58 41 68 31
golfseignosse@wanadoo.fr
www.golfseignosse.com

Bordeaux-Cameyrac (1972)
33450 St Sulpice-et-Cameyrac
(+33) (0)5 56 72 96 79
(+33) (0)5 56 72 86 56
contact@golf-bordeaux-cameyrac.com
www.golf-bordeaux-cameyrac.com

Bordeaux-Lac (1976)
Public
Avenue de Pernon, 33300 Bordeaux
05 56 50 92 72
05 56 29 01 84
golf.bordeaux@wanadoo.fr
www.golfbordeauxlac.com

Bordelais (1900)
Domaine de Kater, Allee F Arago, 33200 Bordeaux-Caudéran
05 56 28 56 04
05 56 28 59 71
golfbordelais@wanadoo.fr
Franck Koenig
www.golf-bordelais.fr

Casteljaloux (1989)
Route de Mont de Marsan, 47700 Casteljaloux
05 53 93 51 60
05 5320 90 98
golfdecasteljaloux@tiscali.fr
www.golf-casteljaloux.com

Chantaco (1928)
Route d'Ascain, 64500 St Jean-de-Luz
05 59 26 14 22/05 59 26 19 22
05 59 26 48 37
contact@chantaco.com
www.golfdechantaco.com

Château des Vigiers G&CC (1992)
24240 Monestier
05 53 61 50 33
05 53 61 50 31
golf@vigiers.com
Matthew Storm
www.vigiers.com

Chiberta (1926)
Boulevard des Plages, 64600 Anglet
05 59 63 83 20
05 59 63 30 56

Domaine de la Marterie (1987)
St Felix de Reillac, 24260 Le Bugue
05 53 05 61 00
05 53 05 61 01
www.marterie.fr

Graves et Sauternais (1989)
St Pardon de Conques, 33210 Langon
05 56 62 25 43
05 56 76 83 72
golf.langon@laposte.net

Gujan (1990)
Route de Souguinet, 33470 Gujan Mestras
05 57 52 73 73
05 56 66 10 93

Hossegor (1930)
333 Ave du Golf, 40150 Hossegor
05 58 43 56 99
05 58 43 98 52
golf.hossegor@wanadoo.fr
Christophe Raillard
www.golfhossegor.com

Lacanau Golf & Hotel (1980)
Domaine de l'Ardilouse, 33680 Lacanau-Océan
(+33) 556 039292
(+33) 556 263057
info@golf-hotel-lacanau.fr
www.golf-hotel-lacanau.fr

Makila
Route de Cambo, 64200 Bassussarry
05 59 58 42 42
05 59 58 42 48

Médoc
Chemin de Courmateau, Louens, 33290 Le Pian Médoc
05 56 70 11 90
05 56 70 11 99

Moliets (1989)
Public
Rue Mathieu Desbieys, 40660 Moliets
05 58 48 54 65
05 58 48 54 88
resa@golfmoliets.com
www.golfmoliets.com

Pau (1856)
Rue du Golf, 64140 Billère
+33 (05) 5913 1856
+33 (0) 5913 1857
pau.golfclub@wanadoo.fr
www.paugolfclub.com

Pessac (1989)
Rue de la Princesse, 33600 Pessac
05 57 26 03 33
05 56 36 52 89

Stade Montois (1993)
Pessourdat, 40090 Saint Avit
05 58 75 63 05
05 58 06 80 72

Villeneuve sur Lot G&CC (1987)
'La Menuisière', 47290 Castelnaud de Gratecambe
05 53 01 60 19
05 53 01 78 99
info@vsgolf.com
Jenny Lyon
www.vsgolf.com

Brittany

Ajoncs d'Or (1976)
Kergrain Lantic, 22410 Saint-Quay Portrieux
02 96 71 90 74
02 96 71 40 83
golfdesajoncsdor@wanadoo.fr

Baden
Kernic, 56870 Baden
02 97 57 18 96
02 97 57 22 05

Belle Ile en Mer (1987)
Les Poulins, 56360 Belle-Ile-en-Mer
02 97 31 64 65

Brest Les Abers (1990)
Kerhoaden, 29810 Plouarzel
02 98 89 68 33
golf@abersgolf.com
www.abersgolf.com

Brest-Iroise (1976)
Parc de Lann-Rohou, Saint-Urbain, 29800 Landerneau
02 98 85 16 17
02 98 85 19 39
golfhotel@brest-iroise.com
www.brest-iroise.com

Dinard (1887)
53 Boulevard de la Houle, 35800 St-Briac-sur-Mer
02 99 88 32 07
02 99 88 04 53
dinardgolf@dinardgolf.com
Jean-Guillaurne Legros
www.dinardgolf.com

La Freslonnière (1989)
Le Bois Briand, 35650 Le Rheu
02 99 14 84 09
02 99 14 94 98
lafreslo@wanadoo.fr
www.lafreslonniere.com

L'Odet (1986)
Clohars-Fouesnant, 29950 Benodet
02 98 54 87 88

For key to symbols and European dialling codes see page 725

02 98 54 61 40
odet@bluegreen.com
Jean-Luc Leroux
www.bluegreen.com

Les Ormes (1988)
Château des Ormes, Epiniac, 35120 Dol-de-Bretagne
02 99 73 54 44
02 99 73 53 65

Pléneuf-Val André
Rue de la Plage des Vallées, 22370 Pléneuf-Val André
02 96 63 01 12
02 96 63 01 06

Ploemeur Océan Formule Golf (1990)
Kerham Saint-Jude, 56270 Ploemeur
02 97 32 81 82
02 97 32 80 90
www.formule-golf.com

Quimper-Cornouaille (1959)
Manoir du Mesmeur, 29940 La Forêt-Fouesnant
02 98 56 97 09
02 98 56 86 81
golf-de-cornouaille@wanadoo.fr
www.golfdecornouaille.com

Rennes (1957)
Le Temple du Cerisier, 35136 St-Jacques-de-la-Lande
02 99 30 18 18
02 99 30 10 25
directeur.rennes@formulegolf.com

Rhuys-Kerver (1988)
Public
Formule Golf, Domaine de Kerver, 56730 St-Gildas-de-Rhuys
02 97 45 30 09
02 97 45 36 58
golf.rhuys@formule-golf.com
www.formule-golf.com

Les Rochers (1989)
Route d'Argentré du Plessis 3, 35500 Vitré
02 99 96 52 52
02 99 96 79 34

Sables-d'Or-les-Pins (1925)
22240 Fréhel
02 96 41 42 57
02 96 41 51 44

St Laurent (1975)
Ploemel, 56400 Auray
02 97 56 85 18
02 97 56 89 99
golf.stlaurent@formule-golf.com
www.formule-golf.com

St Malo Hotel G&CC (1986)
Le Tronchet, 35540 Miniac-Morvan
02 99 58 96 69
02 99 58 10 39
saintmalogolf@st-malo.com
www.saintmalogolf.com

St Samson (1965)
Route de Kérénoc, 22560 Pleumeur-Bodou
02 96 23 87 34
02 96 23 84 59

St Cast Pen Guen (1926)
22380 Saint-Cast-le-Guildo
02 96 41 91 20
02 96 41 77 62
golf.stcast@wanadoo.fr
Jean Marie Vilpasteur
www.golf-st-cast.com

Val Queven (1990)
Public
Kerruisseau, 56530 Queven
02 97 05 17 96
02 97 05 19 18
www.formule-golf.com

Burgundy & Auvergne

Aubazine (1977)
Public
19190 Aubazine
03 55 27 25 66
03 55 27 29 33

Beaune-Levernois (1990)
21200 Levernois
03 80 24 10 29
03 80 24 03 78
golfdebeaune@wanadoo.fr
www.golfbeaune.free.fr

Chalon-sur-Saône (1976)
Parc de Saint Nicolas, 71380 Chatenoy-en-Bresse
03 85 93 49 65
03 85 93 56 95
contact@golfchalon.com
www.golf_chalon_sur_saone.com

Chambon-sur-Lignon (1986)
Riondet, La Pierre de la Lune, 43400 Le Chambon-sur-Lignon
04 71 59 28 10
04 71 65 87 14
www.golf-chambon.com

Château d'Avoise (1992)
9 Rue de Mâcon, 71210 Montchanin
03 85 78 19 19
03 85 78 15 16

Château de Chailly (1990)
Chailly-sur-Armançon, 21320 Pouilly-en-Auxois
03 80 90 30 40
03 80 90 30 05
reservation@chailly.com
www.chailly.com

Domaine de Roncemay (1989)
89110 Aillant-sur-Tholon
03 86 73 50 50
03 86 73 69 46
info@roncemay.com
Franzoise Couilloud
www.roncemay.com

Jacques Laffite Dijon-Bourgogne (1972)
Bois des Norges, 21490 Norges-la-Ville
03 80 35 71 10
03 80 35 79 27
contacts@golfdijonbourgogne.com
www.golfdijonbourgogne.com

Limoges-St Lazare (1976)
Public
Avenue du Golf, 87000 Limoges
05 55 28 30 02

Mâcon La Salle (1989)
La Salle-Mâcon Nord, 71260 La Salle
03 85 36 09 71
03 85 36 06 70
golf.maconlasalle@wanadoo.fr
www.golfmacon.com

Le Nivernais
Public
Le Bardonnay, 58470 Magny Cours
03 58 18 30
03 58 04 04

La Porcelaine
Célicroux, 87350 Panazol
05 55 31 10 69
05 55 31 10 69
golf@golf.porcelaine.com
www.golf-porcelaine.com

St Junien (1997)
Les Jouberties, 87200 Saint Junien
05 55 02 96 96
05 55 02 32 52
info@golfdesaintjunien.com
www.golfdesaintjunien.com

Sporting Club de Vichy (1907)
Allée Baugnies, 03700 Bellerive/Allier
04 70 32 39 11
04 70 32 00 54

Val de Cher (1975)
03190 Nassigny
04 70 06 71 15
04 70 06 70 00
golfvaldecher@free.fr
http://golfclub.valdecher.free.fr

Les Volcans (1984)
La Bruyère des Moines, 63870 Orcines
04 73 62 15 51
04 73 62 26 52
accueil@golfdesvolcans.com
Gabriel Martin
www.golfdesvolcans.com

Centre

Les Aisses (1992)
RN20 Sud, 45240 La Ferté St Aubin
02 38 64 80 87
02 38 64 80 85
golfdesaisses@wanadoo.fr
www.aissesgolf.com

For key to symbols and European dialling codes see page 725

Ardrée (1988)
37360 St Antoine-du-Rocher
☎ **02 47 56 77 38**
Fax 02 47 56 79 96
✉ tours.ardree@bluegreen.com
www.bluegreen.com/tours
www.golf-ardree.com

Aymerich Golf 'Les Dryades' (1987)
36160 Pouligny-Notre-Dame
☎ **02 54 06 60 67**
Fax 02 54 30 10 24
✉ aymerichgolf.lesdryades@orange.fr

Les Bordes (1987)
41220 Saint Laurent-Nouan
☎ **02 54 87 72 13**
Fax 02 54 87 78 61
✉ reception@lesbordes.com
✍ Mark Vickery (Managing Director)
www.lesbordes.com

Château de Cheverny (1989)
La Rousselière, 41700 Cheverny
☎ **02 54 79 24 70**
Fax 02 54 79 25 52
✉ contact@golf-cheverny.com
✍ Aurélie Rigault
www.golf-cheverny.com

Château de Maintenon (1989)
Route de Gallardon, 28130 Maintenon
☎ **02 37 27 18 09**
Fax 02 37 27 10 12

Château des Sept Tours (1989)
Le Vivier des Landes, 37330 Courcelles de Touraine
☎ **02 47 24 69 75**
Fax 02 47 24 23 74

Cognac (1987)
Saint-Brice, 16100 Cognac
☎ **05 45 32 18 17**
Fax 05 45 35 10 76

Le Connétable (1987)
Parc Thermal, 86270 La Roche Posay
☎ **05 49 86 25 10**
Fax 05 49 19 48 40

Domaine de Vaugouard (1987)
Chemin des Bois, Fontenay-sur-Loing, 45210 Ferrières
☎ **02 38 89 79 00**
Fax 02 38 89 79 01

Haut-Poitou (1987)
86130 Saint-Cyr
☎ **05 49 62 53 62**
Fax 05 49 88 77 14
✉ contact@golfduhautpoitou.com
www.golfduhautpoitou.com

Loudun-Roiffe (1985)
Domaine St Hilaire, 86120 Roiffe
☎ **05 49 98 78 06**
Fax 05 49 98 72 57
www.golf-loudun.com

Marcilly (1986)
Domaine de la Plaine, 45240 Marcilly-en-Villette
☎ **02 38 76 11 73**
Fax 02 38 76 18 73
✉ golf@marcilly.com
✍ Emilie/Sophie
www.marcilly.com

Niort (1984)
Chemin du Grand Ormeau, 79000 Niort Romagne
☎ **05 49 09 01 41**
Fax 05 49 73 41 53
✉ contact@golfclubniort.fr
✍ Eric Fleury
www.golfclubniort.fr

Orléans Donnery
Château de la Touche, 45450 Donnery
☎ **02 38 59 25 15**
Fax 02 38 57 01 98

Golf du Perche (1987)
La Vallée des Aulnes, 28400 Souancé au Perche
☎ **02 37 29 17 33**
Fax 02 37 29 12 88
✉ golfduperche@wanadoo.fr
www.golfduperche.fr

Petit Chêne (1987)
Le Petit Chêne, 79310 Mazières-en-Gâtine
☎ **05 49 63 20 95**
Fax 05 49 63 33 75

La Picardière
Chemin de la Picardière, 18100 Vierzon
☎ **02 48 75 21 43**
Fax 02 48 71 87 61

Poitiers
635 route de Beauvoir, 86550 Mignaloux Beauvoir
☎ **05 49 55 10 50**
Fax 05 49 62 26 70
✉ golf-poitiers@monalisahotels.com

Poitou (1991)
Domaine des Forges, 79340 Menigoute
☎ **0549 69 91 77**
Fax 0549 69 96 84
✉ info@golfdesforges.com
www.golfdesforges.com

La Prée-La Rochelle (1988)
La Richardière, 17137 Marsilly
☎ **05 46 01 24 42**
Fax 05 46 01 25 84
✉ golflarochelle@wanadoo.fr
www.golflarochelle.com

Royan (1977)
Maine-Gaudin, 17420 Saint-Palais
☎ **05 46 23 16 24**
Fax 05 46 23 23 38
✉ golfderoyan@wanadoo.fr
www.golfderoyan.com

Saintonge (1953)
Fontcouverte, 17100 Saintes
☎ **05 46 74 27 61**
Fax 05 46 92 17 92

Sancerrois (1989)
St Thibault, 18300 Sancerre
☎ **02 48 54 11 22**
Fax 02 48 54 28 03
✉ golf.sancerre@wanadoo.fr
✍ D Gaucher
www.golf-sancerre.com

Touraine (1971)
Château de la Touche, 37510 Ballan-Miré
☎ **02 47 53 20 28**
Fax 02 47 53 31 54

Val de l'Indre (1989)
Villedieu-sur-Indre, 36320 Tregonce
☎ **02 54 26 59 44**
Fax 02 54 26 06 37

Channel Coast & North

Abbeville (1989)
Route du Val, 80132 Grand-Laviers
☎ **03 22 24 98 58**
Fax 03 22 24 98 58
✉ abbeville.golfclub@wanadoo.fr
www.golf.abbeville.com

L'Ailette (1985)
02860 Cerny en Laonnais
☎ **03 23 24 83 99**
Fax 03 23 24 84 66
✉ golfdelailette@wanadoo.fr
✍ Philippe Courtin (Dir)
www.ailette.org

Amiens (1925)
80115 Querrieu
☎ **03 22 93 04 26**
Fax 03 22 93 04 61
✉ golfamiens@aol.com
www.golfamiens.fr

Apremont Golf Country Club (1992)
60300 Apremont
☎ **03 44 25 61 11**
Fax 03 44 25 11 72
✉ apremont@club-albatros.com
✍ E Jacob
www.apremont-golf.com

Arras (1989)
Rue Briquet Taillandier, 62223 Anzin-St-Aubin
☎ **03 21 50 24 24**
Fax 03 21 50 29 71
✉ golf@golf-arras.com
www.golf-arras.com

Belle Dune
Promenade de Marquenterre, 80790 Fort-Mahon-Plage
☎ **03 22 23 45 50**
Fax 03 22 23 93 41

Bois de Ruminghem (1991)
1613 Rue St Antoine, 62370 Ruminghem
☎ **03 21 35 31 37**
✉ info@golfdubois.com
✍ Mr Boris Janjic/Mrs Els Verheyen
www.golfdubois.com

Bondues (1968)
Château de la Vigne, 5910 Bondues
☎ **03 20 23 20 62**
Fax 03 20 23 24 11
✉ contact@golfdebondues.com
🖹 www.golfdebondues.com

Champagne (1986)
02130 Villers-Agron
☎ **03 23 71 62 08**
Fax 03 23 71 50 40
✉ golf.de.champagne@wanadoo.fr
🖹 www.golf-de-champagne.com

Chantilly (1909)
Allée de la Ménagerie, 60500 Chantilly
☎ **+33 (0) 3 44 57 04 43**
Fax +33 (0) 3 44 57 26 54
✉ contact@golfdechantilly.com
✍ Remy Dorbeau
🖹 www.golfdechantilly.com

Chaumont-en-Vexin (1968)
Château de Bertichère, 60240 Chaumont-en-Vexin
☎ **03 44 49 00 81**
Fax 03 44 49 32 71
✉ golfdechaumont@golf-paris.net
🖹 www.golf-paris.net

Club du Lys - Chantilly (1929)
Rond-Point du Grand Cerf, 60260 Lamorlaye
☎ **03 44 21 26 00**
Fax 03 44 21 35 52
✉ clubdulys@wanadoo.fr
✍ Christophe Rondelé
🖹 www.club-lys-chantilly.com

Compiègne (1896)
Avenue Royale, 60200 Compiègne
☎ **03 44 38 48 00**
Fax 03 44 40 23 59
✉ directeur-golfcompiegne@orange.fr
✍ Stephane Banteilla (Director)
🖹 www.golf-compiegne.com

Deauville l'Amiraute (1992)
CD 278, Tourgéville, 14800 Deauville
☎ **02 31 14 42 00**
Fax 02 31 88 32 00
🖹 www.amiraute-resort.com

Domaine du Tilleul (1984)
Landouzy-la-Ville, 02140 Vervins
☎ **03 23 98 48 00**
Fax 03 23 98 46 46

Dunkerque (1991)
Public
Fort Vallières, Coudekerque-Village, 59380 Coudekerque
☎ **03 28 61 07 43**
Fax 03 28 60 05 93
✉ golf@golf-dk.com
🖹 www.golf-dk.com

Golf de Raray (1987)
4 Rue Nicolas de Lancy, 60810 Raray
☎ **03 44 54 70 61**
Fax 03 44 54 74 97
✉ golfpari@wanadoo.fr
🖹 www.golfraray.com

Golf Dolce Chantilly (1991)
Route d'Apremont, 60500 Vineuil St-Firmin
☎ **03 44 58 47 74**
Fax 03 44 58 50 28
✉ golf.chantilly@dolce.com
✍ Pierre Jacob (Mgr)
🖹 www.dolce.com

Hardelot Dunes Course (1991)
Ave du Golf, 62152 Hardelot
☎ **03 21 83 73 10**
Fax 03 21 83 24 33
✉ hardelot@opengolfclub.com
✍ Ken Strachan (Mgr)
🖹 www.hardelot-golf.com

Hardelot Pins Course (1931)
Ave du Golf, 62152 Hardelot
☎ **03 21 83 73 10**
Fax 03 21 83 24 33
✉ hardelot@opengolfclub.com
✍ Ken Strachan (Mgr)
🖹 www.hardelot-golf.com

Morfontaine (1913)
60128 Mortefontaine
☎ **03 44 54 68 27**
Fax 03 44 54 60 57
✉ morfontaine@wanadoo.fr
✍ Jean-Maurice Dulout
🖹 www.golfdemorfontaine.fr

Mormal (1991)
Bois St Pierre, 59144 Preux-au-Sart
☎ **03 27 63 07 00**
Fax 03 27 39 93 62
✉ info@golf-mormal.com
🖹 www.golf-mormal.com

Nampont-St-Martin (1978)
Maison Forte, 80120 Nampont-St-Martin
☎ **03 22 29 92 90/ 03 22 29 89 87**
Fax 03 22 29 97 54
✉ golfdenampont@wanadoo.fr
🖹 www.golfdenampont.com

Rebetz (1988)
Route de Noailles, 60240 Chaumont-en-Vexin
☎ **03 44 49 15 54**
Fax 03 44 49 14 26
🖹 www.rebetz.com

Saint-Omer
Chemin des Bois, Acquin-Westbécourt, 62380 Lumbres
☎ **03 21 38 59 90**
Fax 03 21 93 02 47

Le Sart (1910)
5 Rue Jean-Jaurès, 59650 Villeneuve D'Ascq
☎ **03 20 72 02 51**
Fax 03 20 98 73 28
✉ contact@golfdusart.com
🖹 www.golfdusart.com

Thumeries (1935)
Bois Lenglart, 59239 Thumeries
☎ **03 20 86 58 98**
Fax 03 20 86 52 66
✉ golfdethumeries@free.fr
✍ Fransoise Dumoulin
🖹 www.golfdethumeries.com

Le Touquet 'La Forêt' (1904)
Ave du Golf, BP 41, 62520 Le Touquet
☎ **03 21 06 28 00**
Fax 03 21 06 28 01
✉ letouquet@opengolfclub.com
✍ Gilles Grattepanche
🖹 www.opengolfclub.com

Le Touquet 'La Mer' (1931)
Ave du Golf, BP 41, 62520 Le Touquet
☎ **03 21 06 28 00**
Fax 03 21 06 28 01
✉ letouquet@opengolfclub.com
✍ Gilles Grattepanche
🖹 www.opengolfclub.com

Le Touquet 'Le Manoir' (1994)
Ave du Golf, BP 41, 62520 Le Touquet
☎ **03 21 06 28 00**
Fax 03 21 06 28 01
✉ letouquet@opengolfclub.com
✍ Gilles Grattepanche
🖹 www.opengolfclub.com

Val Secret (1984)
Brasles, 02400 Château Thierry
☎ **03 23 83 07 25**
Fax 03 23 83 92 73
✉ accueil@golfvalsecret.com
🖹 www.golfvalsecret.com

Vert Parc (1991)
3 Route d'Ecuelles, 59480 Illies
☎ **03 20 29 37 87**
Fax 03 20 49 76 39
✉ golfduvertparc@sfr.fr
🖹 www.golflevertparc.com

Wimereux (1901)
Avenue F. Mitterrand, 62930 Wimereux
☎ **03 21 32 43 20**
Fax 03 21 33 62 21
✉ accueil@golf-wimereux.com
🖹 www.golf-wimereux.com

Corsica

Sperone (1990)
Domaine de Sperone, 20169 Bonifacio
☎ **04 95 73 17 13**
Fax 04 95 73 17 85
✉ golf@sperone.com
🖹 www.sperone.com

Ile de France

Ableiges (1989)
95450 Ableiges
☎ **01 30 27 97 00**
Fax 01 30 27 97 10
✉ golf@ableigesgolf.com
🖹 www.ableiges-golf.com

Bellefontaine (1987)
95270 Bellefontaine
☎ **01 34 71 05 02**
Fax 01 34 71 90 90

For key to symbols and European dialling codes see page 725

✉ golf-bellefontaine@wanadoo.fr
🖳 www.golfdebellefontaine.com

Bussy-St-Georges (1988)
Promenade des Golfeurs, 77600 Bussy-St-Georges
☎ **01 64 66 00 00**
📠 01 64 66 22 92

Cély (1990)
Le Château, Route de Saint-Germain, 77930 Cély-en-Bière
☎ **01 64 38 03 07**
📠 01 64 38 08 78
🖳 www.celygolf.com

Cergy Pontoise (1988)
2 Allee de l'Obstacle d'Eau, 95490 Vaureal
☎ **01 34 21 03 48**
📠 01 34 21 03 34

Chevannes-Mennecy (1994)
91750 Chevannes
☎ **01 64 99 88 74**
📠 01 64 99 88 67
✉ legolfchevannes@wanadoo.fr

Clement Ader (1990)
Domaine Château Pereire, 77220 Gretz
☎ **01 64 07 34 10**
📠 01 64 07 82 10
✉ golfclementader@voila.fr
🖳 www.golfclementader.com

Coudray (1960)
Ave du Coudray, 91830 Le Coudray-Montceaux
☎ **01 64 93 81 76**
📠 01 64 93 99 95
✉ golf.du.coudray@wanadoo.fr
🖳 www.golfcoudray.org

Courson Monteloup (1991)
91680 Bruyères-le-Chatel
☎ **01 64 58 80 80**
📠 01 64 58 83 06
🖳 www.golf-stadefrancais.com

Crécy-la-Chapelle (1987)
Domaine de la Brie, Route de Guérard, F 77580 Crécy-la-Chapelle
☎ **01 64 75 34 44**
📠 01 64 75 34 45
✉ info@domainedelabrie.com
🖳 www.crecygolfclub.com

Disneyland Golf (1992)
1 Allee de la Mare Houleuse, 77700 Magny-le-Hongre
☎ **01 60 45 68 90**
📠 01 60 45 68 33
✉ dlp.nwy.golf@disney.com
🖳 www.disneylandparis.com

Domaine de Belesbat (1989)
Courdimanche-sur-Essonne, 91820 Boutigny-sur-Essonne
☎ **01 69 23 19 10**
📠 01 69 23 19 01
🖳 www.belesbat.com

Domont-Montmorency
Route de Montmorency, 95330 Domont
☎ **01 39 91 07 50**
📠 01 39 91 25 70

Étiolles Colonial CC (1990)
Vieux Chemin de Paris, 91450 Étiolles
☎ **01 69 89 59 59**
📠 01 69 89 59 62
✉ golf@etiollescolonial.com
🖳 www.etiollescolonial.com

Fontainebleau (1909)
Route d'Orleans, 77300 Fontainebleau
☎ **01 64 22 22 95**
📠 01 64 22 63 76
✉ golf.fontainebleau@orange.fr
✍ Christian Mascher (Mgr)
🖳 www.golfdefontainebleau.org

Fontenailles (1991)
Domaine de Bois Boudran, 77370 Fontenailles
☎ **01 64 60 51 00**
📠 01 60 67 52 12

Forges-les-Bains (1989)
Rue du Général Leclerc, 91470 Forges-les-Bains
☎ **01 64 91 48 18**
📠 01 64 91 40 52
✉ golf.forges-les-bains@wanadoo.fr
🖳 www.golf-forgeslesbains.com

Greenparc (1993)
Route de Villepech, 91280 St Pierre-du-Perray
☎ **01 60 75 40 60**
📠 01 60 75 40 04

L'Isle Adam (1995)
1 Chemin des Vanneaux, 95290 L'Isle Adam
☎ **01 34 08 11 11**
📠 01 34 08 11 19

Marivaux (1992)
Bois de Marivaux, 91640 Janvry
☎ **01 64 90 85 85**
📠 01 64 90 82 22
✉ contact@golfmarivaux.com
🖳 www.golfmarivaux.com

Meaux-Boutigny (1985)
Rue de Barrois, 77470 Boutigny
☎ **01 60 25 63 98**
📠 01 60 25 60 58

Mont Griffon (1990)
RD 909, 95270 Luzarches
☎ **01 34 68 10 10**
📠 01 34 68 04 10
✉ golf@golfmontgriffon.com
🖳 www.golfmontgriffon.com

Montereau La Forteresse (1989)
Domaine de la Forteresse, 77940 Thoury-Ferrottes
☎ **(+33) 01 60 96 95 10**
📠 (+33) 01 60 96 01 41
✉ contact@golf-forteresse.com
✍ Aurelie Maloubier
🖳 www.golf-forteresse.com

Ormesson (1969)
Chemin du Belvedère, 94490 Ormesson-sur-Marne
☎ **01 45 76 20 71**
📠 01 45 94 86 85

Ozoir-la-Ferrière (1926)
Château des Agneaux, 77330 Ozoir-la-Ferrière
☎ **01 60 02 60 79**
📠 01 64 40 28 20

Paris International (1991)
18 Route du Golf, 95560 Baillet-en-France
☎ **01 34 69 90 00**
📠 01 34 69 97 15

St Germain-les-Corbeil
6 Ave du Golf, 91250 St Germain-les-Corbeil
☎ **01 60 75 81 54**
📠 01 60 75 52 89

Seraincourt (1964)
Gaillonnet-Seraincourt, 95450 Vigny
☎ **01 34 75 47 28**
📠 01 34 75 75 47

Villarceaux (1971)
Château du Couvent, 95710 Chaussy
☎ **01 34 67 73 83**
📠 01 34 67 72 66
✉ villarceaux@wanadoo.fr
🖳 www.villarceaux.com

Villeray (1974)
Public
Melun-Sénart, St Pierre du Perray, 91100 Corbeil
☎ **01 60 75 17 47**
📠 01 69 89 00 73

Languedoc-Roussillon

Cap d'Agde (1989)
Public
4 Ave des Alizés, 34300 Cap d'Agde
☎ **04 67 26 54 40**
📠 04 67 26 97 00
✉ golf@ville-agde.fr
🖳 www.ville-agde.fr

Carcassonne (1988)
Route de Ste-Hilaire, 11000 Carcassonne
☎ **06 13 20 85 43**
📠 04 68 72 57 30

Coulondres (1984)
72 Rue des Erables, 34980 Saint-Gely-du-Fesc
☎ **04 67 84 13 75**
📠 04 67 84 06 33
🖳 www.coulondres.com

Domaine de Falgos (1992)
BP 9, 66260 St Laurent-de-Cerdans
☎ **04 68 39 51 42**
📠 04 68 39 52 30
✉ contact@falgos.com
🖳 www.falgos.com

Fontcaude (1991)
Route de Lodève, Domaine de Fontcaude, 34990 Juvignac
☎ **04 67 45 90 10**
📠 04 67 45 90 20
✉ golf@golfhotelmontpellier.com
🖳 www.golfhotelmontpellier.com

For key to symbols and European dialling codes see page 725

La Grande-Motte (1987)
Clubhouse du Golf, 34280 La Grande-Motte
☎ **04 67 56 05 00**
04 67 29 18 84

Montpellier Massane (1988)
Domaine de Massane, 34670 Baillargues
☎ **04 67 87 87 87**
04 67 87 87 90

Nîmes Campagne (1968)
1360 chemin du Mas de Campagne, 30900 Nîmes
☎ **04 66 70 17 37**
04 66 70 03 14
resa@golfnimescampagne.fr
Ruven Estelle
www.golfnimescampagne.fr

Nîmes-Vacquerolles (1990)
1075 chemin du golf, 30900 Nîmes
☎ **04 66 23 33 33**
04 66 23 94 94
vacquerolles.opengolfclub@wanadoo.fr
www.golf-nimes.com

Saint Cyprien Golf Resort (1976)
Le Mas D'Huston, 66750 St Cyprien Plage
☎ **04 68 37 63 63**
04 68 37 64 64
golf@saintcyprien-golfresort.com
www.saintcyprien-golfresort.com

St Thomas (1992)
Route de Bessan, 34500 Béziers
☎ **04 67 39 03 09**
04 67 39 10 65
info@golfsaintthomas.com
www.golfsaintthomas.com

Loire Valley

Avrillé (1988)
Château de la Perrière, 49240 Avrillé
☎ **02 41 69 22 50**
02 41 34 44 60
avrille@bluegreen.com
www.bluegreen.com

Baugé-Pontigné (1994)
Public
Route de Tours, 49150 Baugé
☎ **02 41 89 01 27**
02 41 89 05 50
golf.bauge@wanadoo.fr
www.golf-bauge.fr

La Bretesche (1967)
Domaine de la Bretesche, 44780 Missillac
☎ **02 51 76 86 86**
02 40 88 36 28

Carquefou (1991)
Boulevard de l'Epinay, 44470 Carquefou
☎ **02 40 52 73 74**
02 40 52 73 20

Cholet (1989)
Allée du Chêne Landry, 49300 Cholet
☎ **02 41 71 05 01**
02 41 56 06 94

La Domangère
La Roche-sur-Yon, Route de la Rochelle, 85310 Nesmy
☎ **02 51 07 65 90**
02 51 07 65 95
www.golf-domangere.com

Fontenelles
Public
Saint-Gilles-Croix-de-Vie, 85220 Aiguillon-sur-Vie
☎ **02 51 54 13 94**
02 51 55 45 77

Golf D'Anjou (1990)
Route de Cheffes, 49330 Champigné
☎ **02 41 42 01 01**
02 41 42 04 37
accueil@anjougolf.com
Sean Adamson
www.anjougolf.com

Ile d'Or (1988)
BP 90410, 49270 La Varenne
☎ **02 40 98 58 00**
02 40 98 51 62
nantesiledor@wanadoo.fr

International Barriere-La Baule (1976)
44117 Saint-André-des Eaux
☎ **02 40 60 46 18**
02 40 60 41 41
golfinterlabaule@lucienbarriere.com
Nathalie Primas
www.lucienbarriere.com

Laval-Changé (1972)
La Chabossiere, 53000 Changé-les-Laval
☎ **02 43 53 16 03**
02 43 49 35 15
laval53.golf@sfr.fr
www.laval53-golf.com

Le Mansgolfier (1990)
Rue du Golf, 72190 Sargé les Le Mans
☎ **02 43 76 25 07**
02 43 76 45 25
lemansgolfier@wanadoo.fr

Le Mans Mulsanne (1961)
Route de Tours, 72230 Mulsanne
☎ **02 43 42 00 36**
02 43 42 21 31

Le Mansgolfier Golf Club (1990)
Rue du Golf, 72190 Sarge les Le Mans
☎ **02 43 76 25 07**
02 43 76 45 25
lemansgolfier@wanadoo.fr
www.lemansgolfier.com

Nantes (1967)
44360 Vigneux de Bretagne
☎ **02 40 63 25 82**
02 40 63 64 86
golfclubnantes@aol.com
www.golfclubnantes.com

Nantes Erdre (1990)
Chemin du Bout des Landes, 44300 Nantes
☎ **02 40 59 21 21**
02 40 94 14 32
golf.nanteserdre@nge-nantes.fr
www.nge.fr

Les Olonnes
Gazé, 85340 Olonne-sur-Mer
☎ **02 51 33 16 16**
02 51 33 10 45

Pornic (1912)
49 Boulevard de l'Océan, Sainte-Marie/Mer, 44210 Pornic
☎ **02 40 82 06 69**
02 40 82 80 65

Port Bourgenay (1990)
Avenue de la Mine, Port Bourgenay, 85440 Talmont-St-Hilaire
☎ **02 51 23 35 45**
02 51 23 35 48

Sablé-Solesmes (1991)
Domaine de l'Outinière, Route de Pincé, 72300 Sablé-sur-Sarthe
☎ **02 43 95 28 78**
02 43 92 39 05
golf-sable-solesmes@wanadoo.fr
Yves Pironneau
www.golf-sable-solesmes.com

St Jean-de-Monts (1988)
Ave des Pays de la Loire, 85160 Saint Jean-de-Monts
☎ **02 51 58 82 73**
02 51 59 18 32

Savenay (1990)
44260 Savenay
☎ **02 40 56 88 05**
02 40 56 89 04

Normandy

Bellême-St-Martin (1988)
Les Sablons, 61130 Bellême
☎ **02 33 73 00 07**
02 33 73 00 17

Cabourg-Le Home (1907)
38 Av Président Réné Coty, Le Home Varaville, 14390 Cabourg
☎ **02 31 91 25 56**
02 31 91 18 30
golf-cabourg-le-home@worldonline.fr

Caen (1990)
Le Vallon, 14112 Bieville-Beuville
☎ **02 31 94 72 09**
02 31 47 45 30

Champ de Bataille (1988)
Château du Champ de Bataille, 27110 Le Neubourg
☎ **02 32 35 03 72**
02 32 35 83 10
info@champdebataille.com
www.champdebataille.com

Clécy (1988)
Manoir de Cantelou, 14570 Clécy
☎ **02 31 69 72 72**
02 31 69 70 22
golf-de-clecy@golf-de-clecy.com
www.golf-de-clecy.com

Coutainville (1925)
Ave du Golf, 50230 Agon-Coutainville
☎ **02 33 47 03 31**
02 33 47 38 42

Deauville St Gatien (1987)
14130 St Gatien-des-Bois
☎ **02 31 65 19 99**
02 31 65 11 24
contact@golfdeauville.com
www.golfdeauville.com

Dieppe-Pourville (1897)
51 Route de Pourville, 76200 Dieppe
☎ **02 35 84 25 05**
02 35 84 97 11
golf-de-dieppe@wanadoo.fr
www.golf-dieppe.com

Étretat (1908)
BP No 7, Route du Havre, 76790 Étretat
☎ **02 35 27 04 89**

Forêt Verte
Bosc Guerard, 76710 Montville
☎ **02 35 33 62 94**

Golf barrière de Deauville (1929)
14 Saint Arnoult, 14800 Deauville
☎ **02 31 14 24 24**
02 31 14 24 25
golfdeauville@lucienbarriere.com
www.lucienbarriere.com

Golf de Jumièges (1991)
Jumièges, 76480 Duclair
☎ **02 35 05 32 97**
02 35 37 99 97
jumieges.golf@ucpa.asso.fr

Granville (1912)
Bréville, 50290 Bréhal
☎ **02 33 50 23 06**
02 33 61 91 87
contact@golfdegranville.com
www.golfdegranville.com

Le Havre (1933)
Hameau Saint-Supplix, 76930 Octeville-sur-Mer
☎ **02 35 46 36 50**
02 35 46 32 66
contact@golfduhavre.com
Christian Coty (President)
www.golfduhavre.com

Houlgate (1981)
Route de Gonneville, 14510 Houlgate
☎ **02 31 24 80 49**
02 31 28 04 48

Omaha Beach (1986)
Ferme St Sauveur, 14520 Port-en-Bessin
☎ **02 31 22 12 12**
02 31 22 12 13
omaha.beach@wanadoo.fr
www.omahabeachgolfclub.com

Rouen-Mont St Aignan (1911)
Rue Francis Poulenc, 76130 Mont St Aignan
☎ **02 35 76 38 65**
02 35 75 13 86

Golf-hotel St Saëns (1987)
Domaine du Vaudichon, 76680 St Saëns
☎ **02 35 34 25 24**
02 35 34 43 33
golf@golfdesaintsaens.com
www.golfdesaintsaens.com

Golf barrière de St Julien (1987)
St Julien-sur-Calonne, 14130 Pont-l'Évêque
☎ **02 31 64 30 30**
02 31 64 12 43
golfsaintjulien@lucienbarriere.com
www.lucienbarriere.com

Le Vaudreuil (1962)
27100 Le Vaudreuil
☎ **02 32 59 02 60**
02 32 59 43 88

North East

Ammerschwihr (1990)
Allée du golf, 68770 Ammerschwihr
☎ **+33 3 89 47 17 30**
+33 3 89 47 17 77
golf-mail@golf-ammerschwihr.com
www.golf-ammerschwihr.com

Bâle G&CC (1926)
Rue de Wentzwiller, 68220 Hagenthal-le-Bas
☎ **+33 (0)3 89 68 50 91**
+33 (0)3 89 68 55 66
info@gccbasel.ch
www.gccbasel.ch

Besançon (1968)
La Chevillote, 25620 Mamirolle
☎ **03 81 55 73 54**
03 81 55 88 64
www.golfbesancon.com

Bitche (1988)
Rue des Prés, 57230 Bitche
☎ **03 87 96 15 30**
03 87 96 08 04

Château de Bournel (1990)
25680 Cubry
☎ **03 81 86 00 10**
03 81 86 01 06
info@bournel.com
www.bournel.com

Combles-en-Barrois (1948)
14 Rue Basse, 55000 Combles-en-Barrois
☎ **03 29 45 16 03**
03 29 45 16 06

Épinal (1985)
Public
Rue du Merle-Blanc, 88001 Épinal
☎ **03 29 34 65 97**

Golf de Faulquemont-Pontpierre (1993)
Avenue Jean Monnett, 57380 Faulquemont
☎ **03 87 81 30 52**
03 87 81 30 62
golf.faulquemont@wanadoo.fr
www.golf-faulquemont.com

Golf Hotel Club de la Forêt d'Orient (1990)
Route de Geraudot, 10220 Rouilly Sacey
☎ **03 25 43 80 80**
03 25 41 57 58
contact@hotel-foret-orient.com
www.hotel-foret-orient.com

Gardengolf Metz
3 Rue Félix Savart, 57070 Metz Technopole 2000
☎ **03 87 78 71 04**
03 87 78 68 98
contact@gardengolfmetz.com
www.gardengolfmetz.com

Grande Romanie (1988)
La Grande Romanie, 51460 Courtisols
☎ **03 26 66 65 97**
03 26 66 65 97
contact@par72.net
wwwpar72.net

La Grange aux Ormes (1990)
La Grange aux Ormes, 57155 Marly
☎ **03 87 63 10 62**
03 87 55 01 77
info@grange-aux-ormes.com
Pierre Bogenez
www.grange-aux-ormes.com

Kempferhof (1988)
Golf-Hôtel-Restaurant, 67115 Plobsheim
☎ **0033 (0) 3 88 98 72 72**
0033 (0) 3 88 98 74 76
info@golf-kempferhof.com
www.golf-kempferhof.com

La Largue G&CC (1988)
25 Rue du Golf, 68580 Mooslargue
☎ **03 89 07 67 67**
03 89 25 62 83
lalargue@golf-lalargue.com
www.golf-lalargue.com

Les Rousses (1986)
1305 Route du Noirmont, 39220 Les Rousses
☎ **03 84 60 06 25**
03 84 60 01 73

Metz-Cherisey (1963)
Château de Cherisey, 57420 Cherisey
☎ **03 87 52 70 18**
03 87 52 42 44

Nancy-Aingeray (1962)
Aingeray, 54460 Liverdun
☎ **03 83 24 53 87**

For key to symbols and European dialling codes see page 725

Nancy-Pulnoy (1993)
10 Rue du Golf, 54425 Pulnoy
☎ **03 83 18 10 18**
Fax 03 83 18 10 19

Reims-Champagne (1928)
Château des Dames de France, 51390 Gueux
☎ **03 26 05 46 10**
Fax 03 26 05 46 19

Golf du Rhin (1969)
Ile du Rhin, F-68490 Chalampé
☎ **+33 3 89 83 28 32**
Fax +33 3 89 83 28 42
✉ golfdurhin@wanadoo.fr
✍ Mr Michel Zimmerlin
🌐 www.golfdurhin.com

Rougemont-le-Château (1990)
Route de Masevaux, 90110 Rougemont-le-Château
☎ **03 84 23 74 74**
Fax 03 84 23 03 15
✉ golf.rougemont@wanadoo.fr
✍ Lionel Burnet
🌐 www.golf.rougemont.com

Strasbourg (1934)
Route du Rhin, 67400 Illkirch
☎ **03 88 66 17 22**
Fax 03 88 65 05 67
✉ golf.strasbourg@wanadoo.fr
🌐 www.golf-strasbourg.com

Domaine du Val de Sorne (1989)
Domaine de Val de Sorne, 39570 Vernantois
☎ **03 84 43 04 80**
Fax 03 84 47 31 21
✉ info@valdesorne.com
🌐 www.valdesorne.com

La Wantzenau (1991)
C D 302, 67610 La Wantzenau
☎ **03 88 96 37 73**
Fax 03 88 96 34 71

Paris Region

Béthemont-Chisan CC (1989)
12 Rue du Parc de Béthemont, 78300 Poissy
☎ **01 39 75 51 13**
Fax 01 39 75 49 90

La Boulie
La Boulie, 78000 Versailles
☎ **01 39 50 59 41**

Feucherolles (1992)
78810 Feucherolles
☎ **01 30 54 94 94**
Fax 01 30 54 92 37
✉ cchateaugolf@aol.com
🌐 www.golf-de-feucherolles.com

Fourqueux (1963)
Rue Saint Nom 36, 78112 Fourqueux
☎ **01 34 51 41 47**
Fax 01 39 21 00 70

Golf National (1990)
2 Avenue du Golf, 78280 Guyancourt
☎ **00 33 1 30 43 36 00**
Fax 0 33 1 30 43 85 58
✉ gn@golf-national.com
✍ Olivier Roche (Gen Mgr)
🌐 www.golf-national.com

Isabella (1969)
RN12, Sainte-Appoline, 78370 Plaisir
☎ **01 30 54 10 62**
Fax 01 30 54 67 58
✉ info@golfisabella.com
🌐 www.golfisabella.com

Joyenval (1992)
Chemin de la Tuilerie, 78240 Chambourcy
☎ **01 39 22 27 50**
Fax 01 39 79 12 90
✉ joyenval@golfdejoyenval.com
🌐 www.joyenval.fr

Rochefort (1964)
78730 Rochefort-en-Yvelines
☎ **01 30 41 31 81**
Fax 01 30 41 94 01

St Cloud (1911)
60 Rue du 19 Janvier, Garches 92380
☎ **01 47 01 01 85**
Fax 01 47 01 19 57

St Germain (1922)
Route de Poissy, 78100 St Germain-en-Laye
☎ **01 39 10 30 30**
Fax 01 39 10 30 31
✉ info@golfsaintgermain.org
🌐 www.golfsaintgermain.org

St Quentin-en-Yvelines
Public
RD 912, 78190 Trappes
☎ **01 30 50 86 40**

St Nom-La-Bretêche (1959)
Hameau Tuilerie-Bignon, 78860 St Nom-La-Bretèche
☎ **01 30 80 04 40**
Fax 01 34 62 60 44

La Vaucouleurs (1987)
Rue de l'Eglise, 78910 Civry-la-Forêt
☎ **01 34 87 62 29**
Fax 01 34 87 70 09
✉ vaucouleurs@vaucouleurs.fr
✍ J Pelard
🌐 www.vaucouleurs.fr

Les Yvelines (1989)
Château de la Couharde, 78940 La-Queue-les-Yvelines
☎ **01 34 86 48 89**
Fax 01 34 86 50 31
✉ lesyvelines@opengolfclub.com
🌐 www.opengolfclub.com

Provence & Côte d'Azur

Aix Marseille (1935)
13290 Les Milles, Domaine Riquetti, 13290 Les Milles
☎ **04 42 24 40 41/**
04 42 24 23 01
Fax 04 42 39 97 48
✉ golfaixmarseille@aol.com
✍ Mme Roseline Maillet
🌐 www.golfaixmarseille.com

Barbaroux (1989)
Route de Cabasse, 83170 Brignoles
☎ **04 94 69 63 63**
Fax 04 94 59 00 93
✉ contact@barbaroux.com
🌐 www.barbaroux.com

Les Baux de Provence (1989)
Domaine de Manville, 13520 Les Baux-de-Provence
☎ **04 90 54 40 20**
Fax 04 90 54 40 93
✉ golfbauxdeprovence@wanadoo.fr
🌐 www.golfbauxdeprovence.com

Beauvallon-Grimaud
Boulevard des Collines, 83120 Sainte-Maxime
☎ **04 94 96 16 98**

Biot (1930)
La Bastide du Roy, 06410 Biot
☎ **04 93 65 08 48**
Fax 04 93 65 05 63

Cannes Mandelieu (1891)
Route de Golf, 06210 Mandelieu
☎ **04 92 97 32 00**
Fax 04 93 49 92 90

Cannes Mandelieu Riviera (1990)
Avenue des Amazones, 06210 Mandelieu
☎ **04 92 97 49 49**
Fax 04 92 97 49 42

Cannes Mougins (1923)
175 Avenue du Golf, 06250 Mougins
☎ **04 93 75 79 13**
Fax 04 93 75 27 60
✉ golf-cannes-mougins@wanadoo.fr
✍ Monsieur Bernard Biard
🌐 www.golf-cannes-mougins.com

Châteaublanc
Les Plans, 84310 Morières-les-Avignon
☎ **04 90 33 39 08**
Fax 04 90 33 43 24
✉ info@golfchateaublanc.com
🌐 www.golfchateaublanc.com

Digne-les-Bains (1990)
Public
57 Route du Chaffaut, 0400 Digne-les-Bains
☎ **04 92 30 58 00**
Fax 04 92 30 58 13

✉ contact@golfdignelalavande.com
🌐 www.golfdignelalavande.com

Estérel Latitudes (1989)
Ave du Golf, 83700 St Raphaël
☎ **04 94 52 68 30**
📠 04 94 52 68 31

Frégate (1992)
Dolce Frégate Provence, RD 559, 83270 St Cyr-sur-Mer
☎ **04 94 29 38 00**
📠 04 94 29 96 94
✉ golf-fregate@dolce.com
🌐 www.golfdolcefregate.com

Gap-Bayard (1988)
Centre d'Oxygénation, 05000 Gap
☎ **04 92 50 16 83**
📠 04 92 50 17 05
✉ gap-bayard@wanadoo.fr
✍ Rostaing
🌐 www.gap-bayard.com

Golf Claux-Amic (1992)
1 Route des Trois Ponts, 06130 Grasse
☎ **04 93 60 55 44**
📠 04 93 60 55 19
✉ info@claux-amic.com
🌐 www.chateau-taulane.com

Golf de Roquebrune (1989)
Golf de Roquebrune, CD7, 83520 Roquebrune-sur-Argens
☎ **04 94 19 60 35**
✉ contact@golfderoquebrune.com
✍ Mathieu Sevestre (Mgr)
🌐 www.golfderoquebrune.com

Grand Avignon (1989)
Les Chênes Verts, 84270 Vedene - Avignon
☎ **04 90 31 49 94**
📠 04 90 31 01 21
✉ info@golfgrandavignon.com
🌐 www.golfgrandavignon.com

La Grande Bastide (1990)
Chemin des Picholines 761, 06740 Châteauneuf de Grasse
☎ **04 93 77 70 08**
📠 04 93 77 72 36
✉ grandebastide@opengolfclub.com
✍ Alexis Davet (Mgr)
🌐 www.opengolfclub.com

Luberon (1986)
La Grande Gardette, 04860 Pierrevert
☎ **04 92 72 17 19**
📠 04 92 72 59 12
✉ info@golf-du-luberon.com
✍ Philippe Berrut
🌐 www.golf-du-luberon.com

Marseille La Salette (1988)
65 Impasse des Vaudrans, 13011 La Valentine Marseille
☎ **04 91 27 12 16**
📠 04 91 27 21 33
✉ lasalette@opengolfclub.com
🌐 www.opengolfclub.com

Miramas (1993)
Mas de Combe, 13140 Miramas
☎ **04 90 58 56 55**
📠 04 90 17 38 73

Monte Carlo (1910)
Route du Mont-Agel, 06320 La Turbie
☎ **04 92 41 50 70**
📠 04 93 41 09 55
✉ monte-carlo-golf-club@wanadoo.fr

Opio-Valbonne (1966)
Route de Roquefort-les-Pins, 06650 Opio
☎ **04 93 12 00 08**
📠 04 93 12 26 00
🌐 www.opengolfclub.com

Pont Royal (1992)
Pont Royal, 13370 Mallemort
☎ **04 90 57 40 79**
📠 04 90 57 50 19

Royal Mougins (1993)
424 Avenue du Roi, 06250 Mougins
☎ **04 92 92 49 69 (reception)**
📠 04 92 92 49 70
✉ contact@royalmougins.fr
🌐 www.royalmougins.fr

Saint Donat G&CC (1993)
270 Route de Cannes, 06130 Grasse
☎ **+33 493 097660**
📠 +33 493 097663
✉ info@golfsaintdonat.com
✍ Gaelle Secretary
🌐 www.golfsaintdonat.com

Les Domaines de Saint Endréol Golf & Spa Resort (1992)
Route de Bagnols-en-Fôret, 83 920 La Motte-en-Provence
☎ **04 94 51 89 89**
📠 04 94 51 89 90
✉ accueil.golf@st-endreol.com
🌐 www.st-endreol.com

Sainte Victoire (1985)
Domaine de Château L'Arc, 13710 Fuveau
☎ **0442 298343**
📠 0442 534268
✉ saintevictoiregolfclub@wanadoo.fr
🌐 www.saintevictoiregolfclub.com

La Sainte-Baume (1988)
Golf Hotel, Domaine de Châteauneuf, 83860 Nans-les-Pins
☎ **04 94 78 60 12**
📠 04 94 78 63 52
✉ saintebaume@opengolfclub.com
✍ Marie-Pierre Picard
🌐 www.opengolfclub.com

Sainte-Maxime
Route de Débarquement, 83120 Sainte-Maxime
☎ **04 94 55 02 02**
📠 04 94 55 02 03

Servanes (1989)
Domaine de Servanes, 13890 Mouriès
☎ **04 90 47 59 95**
📠 04 90 47 52 58
✉ servanes@opengolfclub.com
🌐 www.opengolfclub.com

Taulane
Domaine du Château de Taulane, RN 85, 83840 La Martre
☎ **04 93 60 31 30**
📠 04 93 60 33 23
✉ resagolf@chateau-taulane.com
🌐 www.chateau-de-taulane.com

Valcros (1964)
Domaine de Valcros, 83250 La Londe-les-Maures
☎ **04 94 66 81 02**
📠 04 94 66 90 48
✉ golfdevalcros@wanadoo.fr

Valescure (1895)
BP 451, 83704 St-Raphaël Cedex
☎ **04 94 82 40 46**
📠 04 94 82 41 42

Rhone-Alps

Aix-les-Bains (1904)
Avenue du Golf, 73100 Aix-les-Bains
☎ **04 79 61 23 35**
📠 04 79 34 06 01
✉ info@golf-aixlesbains.com
✍ Gerard Bourge
🌐 www.golf-aixlesbains.com

Albon (1989)
Domaine de Senaud, Albon, 26140 St Rambert d'Albon
☎ **04 75 03 03 90**
📠 04 75 03 11 01
✉ golf.albon@wanadoo.fr
🌐 www.golf-albon.com

Annecy (1953)
Echarvines, 74290 Talloires
☎ **(0033)4 50 60 12 89**
📠 (0033)4 50 60 08 80
✉ accucil@golf-lacannecy.com
✍ Emmanuelle Kipper (Mgr)
🌐 www.golf-lacannecy.com

Annonay-Gourdan (1988)
Domaine de Gourdan, 07430 Saint Clair
☎ **04 75 67 03 84**
📠 04 75 67 79 50

Les Arcs
B P 18, 73706 Les Arcs Cedex
☎ **04 79 07 43 95**
📠 04 79 07 47 65

Bossey G&CC (1985)
Château de Crevin, 74160 Bossey
☎ **04 50 43 95 50**
📠 04 50 95 32 57
✉ accueilgolf@golfbossey.com
🌐 www.golfbossey.com

La Bresse
Domaine de Mary, 01400 Condessiat
☎ **04 74 51 42 09**
📠 04 74 51 40 09

Chamonix (1934)
35 Route du Golf, 74400 Chamonix
☎ **+33 4 50 53 06 28**
📠 +33 4 50 53 38 69

✉ info@golfdechamonix.com
✍ David Richalot (Manager)
🖹 www.golfdechamonix.com

Le Clou (1985)
01330 Villars-les-Dombes
☎ **04 74 98 19 65**
🖷 04 74 98 15 15
✉ golfduclou.fr@freesbee.fr
🖹 www.golfduclou.fr

Divonne (1931)
Ave des Thermes, 01220 Divonne-les-Bains
☎ **04 50 40 34 11**
🖷 04 50 40 34 25
✉ golf@domaine-de-divonne.com
🖹 www.domaine-de-divonne.com

Esery (1990)
Esery, 74930 Reignier
☎ **00334 50 36 58 70**
🖷 00334 50 36 57 62
✉ info@golf-club-esery.com
✍ Emmanuel Ballongue
🖹 www.golf-club-esery.com

Evian Masters (1904)
Rive Sud du lac de Genève, 74500 Évian
☎ **04 50 26 85 00**
🖷 04 50 75 65 54
✉ golf@evianroyalresort.com
🖹 www.evianroyalresort.com

Giez (1991)
Lac d'Annecy, 74210 Giez
☎ **04 50 44 48 41**
🖷 04 50 32 55 93
✉ as.golfdegiez@wanadoo.fr
🖹 www.golfdegiez.fr

Le Gouverneur
Château du Breuil, 01390 Monthieux
☎ **04 72 26 40 34**
🖷 04 72 26 41 61
✉ golfgouverneur@worldonline.fr
🖹 www.golfgouverneur.fr

Grenoble-Bresson (1990)
Route de Montavie, 38320 Eybens
☎ **04 76 73 65 00**
🖷 04 76 73 65 51

Grenoble-Charmeil (1988)
38210 St Quentin-sur-Isère
☎ **04 76 93 67 28**
🖷 04 76 93 62 04
✉ info@golfhotelgrenoble.com
🖹 www.golfhotelgrenoble.com

Grenoble-Uriage (1921)
Les Alberges, 38410 Uriage
☎ **04 76 89 03 47**
🖷 04 76 73 15 80
✉ golfuriage@wanadoo.fr
🖹 www.golfuriage.com

Golf Club de Lyon (1921)
38280 Villette-d'Anthon
☎ **04 78 31 11 33**
🖷 04 72 02 48 27
✉ info@golfclubdelyon.com
✍ F Barba
🖹 www.golfclubdelyon.com

Lyon-Verger (1977)
69360 Saint-Symphorien D'Ozon
☎ **04 78 02 84 20**
🖷 04 78 02 08 12

Maison Blanche G&CC (1991)
01170 Echenevex
☎ **04 50 42 44 42**
🖷 04 50 42 44 43

Méribel (1966)
BP 54, 73550 Méribel
☎ **04 79 00 52 67**
🖷 04 79 00 38 85
✉ info@golf-meribel.com
🖹 www.golf-meribel.com

Mionnay La Dombes (1986)
Chemin de Beau-Logis, 01390 Mionnay
☎ **04 78 91 84 84**
🖷 04 78 91 02 73

Mont-d'Arbois (1964)
74120 Megève
☎ **04 50 21 29 79**
🖷 04 50 93 02 63

Pierre Carée (1984)
74300 Flaine
☎ **04 50 90 85 44**
🖷 04 50 90 88 21

St Etienne (1989)
62 Rue St Simon, 42000 St Etienne
☎ **04 77 32 14 63**
🖷 04 77 33 61 23

Salvagny (1987)
100 Rue des Granges, 69890 La Tour de Salvagny
☎ **04 78 48 83 60**
🖷 04 78 48 00 16
✉ accueil@golf-salvagny.com
🖹 www.golf-salvagny.com

La Sorelle (1991)
Domaine de Gravagnieux, 01320 Villette-sur-Ain
☎ **04 74 35 47 27**
🖷 04 74 35 44 51

Tignes (1968)
Val Claret, 73320 Tignes
☎ **04 79 06 37 42 (Summer)**
🖷 04 79 00 53 17
✉ golf.tignes@compagniedesalpes.fr
✍ Fred Sciuller (Mgr)
🖹 www.tignes.net

Valdaine (1989)
Domaine de la Valdaine, Montboucher/Jabron, 26740 Montelimar-Montboucher
☎ **04 75 00 71 33**
🖷 04 75 01 24 49
🖹 www.domainedelavaldaine.com

Valence St Didier (1983)
26300 St Didier de Charpey
☎ **04 75 59 67 01**
🖷 04 75 59 68 19

Toulouse & Pyrenees

Albi Lasbordes (1989)
Château de Lasbordes, 81000 Albi
☎ **05 63 54 98 07**
🖷 05 63 54 98 06
✉ contact@golfalbi.com
🖹 www.golfalbi.com

Ariège (1986)
Unjat, 09240 La Bastide-de-Serou
☎ **05 61 64 56 78**
🖷 05 61 64 57 99

Auch Embats (1970)
Route de Montesquiou, 32000 Auch
☎ **05 62 61 10 11/ 06 81 18 41 43**
🖷 05 62 611057
🖹 www.golf-auch-embats.com

Golf County Club de Bigorre (1992)
65200 Pouzac, Bagnères de Bigorre
☎ **(33) (0) 5 62 91 06 20**
🖷 (33) (0) 5 62 91 38 00
✉ contact@golf-bigorre.fr
🖹 www.golf-bigorre.fr

Étangs de Fiac (1987)
Brazis, 81500 Fiac
☎ **05 63 70 64 70**
🖷 05 63 75 32 91
✉ golf.fiac-sw@wanadoo.fr
🖹 www.etangsdefiac.com

Florentin-Gaillac (1990)
Le Bosc, Florentin, 81150 Marssac-sur-Tarn
☎ **05 63 55 20 50**
🖷 05 63 53 26 41

Golf de tarbes (1987)
1 Rue du Bois, 65310 Laloubère
☎ **05 62 45 14 50**
🖷 05 62 45 11 78
✉ golf.des.tumulus@wanadoo.fr
🖹 www.perso.wanadoo.fr/tumulus

Guinlet (1986)
32800 Eauze
☎ **05 62 09 80 84**
🖷 05 62 09 84 50
🖹 www.guinlet.fr

Lannemezan (1962)
250 Rue uu Dr Vererschlag, 65300 Lannemezan
☎ **0562 98 01 01**
🖷 0562 98 52 32
✉ golflannemezan@wanadoo.fr
✍ Valerie Lasserre (Assistant Mgr)
🖹 www.golflannemezan.com

Lourdes (1988)
Chemin du Lac, 65100 Lourdes
☎ **05 62 42 02 06**
🖷 05 62 42 02 06
✉ golf.lourdes@wanadoo.fr

Mazamet-La Barouge (1956)
81660 Pont de l'Arn
☎ **05 63 61 08 00/05 63 67 06 72**

05 63 61 13 03
golf.labarouge@wanadoo.fr
www.golf-mazamet.net

Toulouse (1951)
31320 Vieille-Toulouse
05 61 73 45 48
05 62 19 04 67

Toulouse-Palmola (1974)
Route d'Albi, 31660 Buzet-sur-Tarn
05 61 84 20 50
05 61 84 48 92
golf.palmola@wanadoo.fr

Toulouse-Teoula (1991)
71 Avenue des Landes, 31830 Plaisance du Touch
05 61 91 98 80
05 61 91 49 66
contact@golftoulouseteoula.com
www.golftoulouseteoula.com

Germany

Berlin & East

Balmer See (1995)
Drewinscher Weg 1, 17429 Benz/Otbalm
(038379) 28199
(038379) 28200
info@golfhotel-usedom.de
www.golfhotel-usedom.de

Golf- und Land-Club Berlin-Wannsee e.V. (1895)
Golfweg 22, 14109 Berlin
+49 (030) 806 7060
+49 (030) 806 706-10
info@wannsee.de
www.wannsee.de

Berliner G&CC Motzener See (1991)
Am Golfplatz 5, 15749 Mittenwalde OT Motzen
(033769) 50130
(033769) 50134
info@golfclubmotzen.de
www.golfclubmotzen.de

GC Dresden Elbflorenz (1992)
Ferdinand von Schillstr 4a, 01728 Possendorf
(035206) 2430
(035206) 24317
info@golfclub-dresden.de
Alfred Hagh
www.golfclub-dresden.de

Potsdamer GC (1990)
Zachower Strasse, 14669 Ketzin OT Tremmen
(033233) 7050
(033233) 70519
clubsekretariat@potsdamergolfclub.de
www.pgc.de

Schloss Meisdorf (1996)
Petersberger Trift 33, 06463 Meisdorf
(034743) 98450
(034743) 98499

Golfclub Schloss Wilkendorf (1991)
Am Weiher 1, 15345 Altlandsberg-Wilkendorf
(0049) 3341 330960
(0049) 3341 330961
service@golfclub-schloss-wilkendorf.de
www.golfclub-schloss-wilkendorf.de

Golf-und Country Club Seddiner See (1994)
Zum Weiher 44, 14552 Michendorf
(033205) 7320
(036) 308140
info@gccseddinersee.de
Mr Horst Schubert (Mgr)
www.gccseddinersee.de

Seddiner See (1993)
Zum Weiher 44, 14552 Wildenbruch
(033205) 7320
(033205) 73229
info@gccseddiner-see.de
www.gccseddiner-see.de

Golfresort Semlin am See (1992)
Ferchesarerstrasse 8b, 14712 Semlin
(03385) 554410
(03385) 554400
golf@golfresort-semlin.de
www.golfresort-semlin.de

Sporting Club Berlin Schwantzelsee e.V (1992)
Parkallee 3, 15526 Bad Sarrow
(033631) 63300
(033631) 63310
info@sporting-club-berlin.de
www.sporting-club-berlin.com

Bremen & North West

Bremer Schweiz e.v. (1991)
Wölpscherstr 4, 28779 Bremen
(0421) 609 5331
(0421) 609 5333
info@golfclub-bremerschweiz.de
www.golfclub-bremerschweiz.de

Herzogstadt Celle (1985)
Beukenbusch 1, D 29229 Celle
(05086) 395
(05086) 8288
golfclub-celle@t-online.de
Godlind Reif/Michael Olville
English Speaking
www.golf-celle.de

Küsten GC Hohe Klint (1978)
Hohe Klint, 27478 Cuxhaven
(04723) 2737
(04723) 5022
www.golf-cuxhaven.de

Münster-Wilkinghege (1963)
Steinfurter Str 448, 48159 Münster
(0251) 214090
(0251) 214 0940
kontakt@golfclub-wilkinghege.de
www.golfclub-wilkinghege.de

Oldenburgischer (1964)
Wemkenstr. 13, 26180 Rastede
(04402) 7240
(04402) 70417
info@oldenburgischer-golfclub.de
www.oldenburgischer-golfclub.de

Ostfriesland (1980)
Fliederstrasse 5, 26639 Wiesmoor
(04944) 6440
(04944) 6441
golf@golfclubostfriesland.de
Stephan Hueller
www.golfclub-ostfriesland.de

Soltau (1982)
Hof Loh, 29614 Soltau
(05191) 967 63 33
(05191) 967 63 34
info@golf-soltau.de
Bernd Ingendahl
www.golf-soltau.de

Tietlingen (1979)
29683 Fallingbostel
(05162) 3889
(05162) 7564
info@golfclub-tietlingen.de
www.golfclub-tietlingen.de

Verden (1988)
Holtumer Str 24, 27283 Verden
(04230) 1470
(04230) 1550

Worpswede (1974)
Giehlermühlen, 27729 Vollersode
(04763) 7313
(04763) 6193

Club Zur Vahr (1905)
Bgm-Spitta-Allee 34, 28329 Bremen
Bremen (0421) 204480
(0421) 244 9248
info@club-zur-vahr-bremen.de
www.club-zur-vahr-bremen.de

Central North

Dillenburg
Auf dem Altscheid, 35687 Dillenburg
(02771) 5001
(02771) 5002
info@gc-dillenburg.de
www.gc-dillenburg.de

Hofgut Praforst (1992)
Dr-Detlev-Rudelsdorff-Allee 3, 36088 Hünfeld
(06652) 9970
(06652) 99755
info@praforst.de
www.praforst.de

Kassel-Wilhelmshöhe (1958)
Ehlenerstr 21, 34131 Kassel
☎ **(0561) 33509**
(0561) 37729
mail@golfclub-kassel.de
www.golfclub-kassel.de

Kurhessischer GC Oberaula (1987)
Am Golfplatz, 36278 Oberaula
☎ **(06628) 91540**
(06628) 915424
info@golfclub-oberaula.de
www.golf-oberaula.de

Licher Golf Club (1992)
35423 Lich, Golfplatz Kolnhausen
☎ **(06404) 91071**
(06404) 91072
info@licher-golf-club.de
www.licher-golf-club.de

Fulda Rhoen (1971)
Am Golfplatz, 36145 Hofbieber
☎ **(06657) 1334**
(06657) 914809
info@golfclub-fulda.de
Nick Staples
www.golfclub-fulda.de

Schloss Braunfels (1970)
Homburger Hof, 35619 Braunfels
☎ **(06442) 4530**
(06442) 6683
info@golfclub-braunfels.de
Gregor Sommer
www.golfclub-braunfels.de

Schloss Sickendorf (1990)
Schloss Sickendorf, 36341 Lauterbach
☎ **(06641) 96130**
(06641) 961335
info@gc-lauterbach.de
www.gc-lauterbach.de

Winnerod (1999)
Parkstr 22, 35447 Reiskirchen
☎ **(06408) 9513-0**
(06408) 9513-13
info@golfpark.de
Michael Sonnenstatter (Mgr)
www.golfpark.de

Zierenberg Gut Escheberg (1995)
Gut Escheberg, 34289 Zierenberg
☎ **(05606) 2608**
(05606) 2609
www.golfclub-escheberg.de

Central South

Bad Kissingen (1910)
Euerdorferstr 11, 97688 Bad Kissingen
☎ **(0971) 3608**
(0971) 60140

Bad Vilbeler Golfclub Lindenhof e.V. (1994)
61118 Bad Vilbel-Dortelweil
☎ **+49 (0)6101 5245200**
+49 (0)6101 5245202
info@bvgc.de
www.bvgc.de

Golfclub Eschenrod e.V. (1996)
Postfach 1227, Lindenstr. 46, 63679 Schotten
☎ **(06044) 8401**
(06044) 951159
br.golf@t-online.de
www.eschenrod.de

Frankfurter Golf Club (1913)
Golfstrasse 41, 60528 Frankfurt/Main
☎ **(069) 666 2318 0**
(069) 666 2318 20
info@fgc.de
Mrs Sanja Bradley
www.fgc.de

Hanau-Wilhelmsbad (1958)
Franz-Ludwig-von-Cancrin-Weg 1a, 63454 Hanau
☎ **(06181) 1 80 19 0**
(06181) 1 80 19 10

Hof Trages
Hofgut Trages, 63579 Freigericht
☎ **(06055) 91380**
(06055) 913838
www.hoftrages.de

Homburger (1899)
Saalburgchaussee 2, 61350 Bad Homburg
☎ **(06172) 306808**
(06172) 32648

Idstein (2001)
Am Nassen Berg, 65510 Idstein
☎ **(06126) 9322-13**
(06126) 9322-33
www.golfpark-idstein.de

Idstein-Wörsdorf (1989)
Gut Henriettenthal, 65510 Idstein
☎ **(06126) 9322-0**
(06126) 9322-22
www.golfpark-idstein.de

Kitzingen (1980)
Zufahrt über Steigweg, 97318 Kitzingen
☎ **(09321) 4956**
(09321) 21936
golfkitzingen@aol.com
www.golfclub-kitzingen.de

Kronberg G&LC (1954)
Schloss Friedrichshof, Hainstr 25, 61476 Kronberg/Taunus
☎ **(06173) 1426**
(06173) 5953
www.gc-kronberg.de

Main-Spessart (1990)
Postfach 1204, 97821 Marktheidenfeld-Eichenfürst
☎ **(09391) 8435**
(09391) 8816
info@main-spessart-golf.de
www.main-spessart-golf.de

Main-Taunus (1979)
Lange Seegewann 2, 65205 Wiesbaden
☎ **(06122) 588680 (Sec)**
(06122) 936099
clubinfo@golf-club-maintaunus.de
Markus Erdmann
www.golfclub-maintaunus.de

Mannheim-Viernheim (1930)
Alte Mannheimer Str 3, 68519 Viernheim
☎ **(06204) 6070-0**
(06204) 607044
info@gcmv.de
www.gcmv.de

Maria Bildhausen (1992)
Rindhof 1, 97702 Münnerstadt
☎ **(09766) 1601**
(09766) 1602
info@maria-bildhausen.de
www.maria-bildhausen.de

Neuhof
Hofgut Neuhof, 63303 Dreieich
☎ **(06102) 327927/327010**
(06102) 327012
info@golfclubneuhof.de
www.golfclubneuhof.de

Rhein Main (1977)
Steubenstrasse 9, 65189 Wiesbaden
☎ **(0611) 373014**

Rheinblick
Weisser Weg, 65201 Wiesbaden-Frauenstein
☎ **(0611) 420675**
(0611) 941 0434

Rheintal (1971)
An der Bundesstrr 291, 68723 Oftersheim
☎ **(06202) 56390**

St. Leon-Rot (1996)
Opelstrasse 30, 68789 St. Leon-Rot
☎ **+49 62 27 86 08- 0**
+49 62 27 86 08-88
info@gc-slr.de
www.gc-slr.de

Spessart (1972)
Golfplatz Alsberg, 63628 Bad Soden-Salmünster
☎ **(06056) 91580**
(06056) 915820
www.gc-spessart.com

Taunus Weilrod (1979)
Merzhäuser Strasse, 61276 Weilrod-Altweilnau
☎ **(06083) 95050**
(06083) 950515
golfclub@taunus-weilrod.de
www.golfclub@taunus-weilrod.de

Wiesbadener Golf Club e.v. (1893)
Chausseehaus 17, 65199 Wiesbaden
☎ **(0611) 460238**
(0611) 463251
info@wiesbadener-golfclub.de
www.wiesbadener-golfclub.de

For key to symbols and European dialling codes see page 725

Golf- und Landclub Wiesloch (1983)
Hohenhardter Hof, 69168 Wiesloch-Baiertal
☎ **(06222) 78811-0**
(06222) 78811-11
info@golfclub-wiesloch.de
www.golfclub-wiesloch.de

Hamburg & North

Altenhof (1971)
Eckernförde, 24340 Altenhof
☎ **(04351) 41227**
(04351) 751304

An der Pinnau e.V. (1982)
Pinneberger strasse 81a, 25451 Quickborn-Renzel
☎ **(04106) 81800**
(04106) 82003
info@pinnau.de
Christoph Lampe
www.pinnau.de

Behinderten Golf Club Deutschland e.V. (1994)
Hauptstrausse 3 c, 37434 Bodensee
☎ **+49 (0) 55079799108**
+49 (0) 5507 979144
rollydrive@aol.com
www.bgc-golf.de

Brodauer Mühle (1986)
Baumallee 14, 23730 Gut Beusloe
☎ **(04561) 8140**
(04561) 407397
gc-brodauermuehle@t-online.de
www.gc-brodauermuehle.de

Buchholz-Nordheide (1982)
An der Rehm 25, 21244 Bucholz
☎ **(04181) 36200**
(04181) 97294
gc-buchholz@t-online.de
www.golfclub-buchholz.de

Buxtehude (1982)
Zum Lehmfeld 1, 21614 Buxtehude
☎ **(04161) 81333**
(04161) 87268
post@golfclubbuxtehude.de
www.golfclubbuxtehude.de

Deinster Mühle (1994)
Im Mühlenfeld 30, 21717 Deinste
☎ **(04149) 925112**
(04149) 925111
golfpark@allesistgdn.de
www.allesistgdn.de

Föhr (1925)
25938 Nieblum
☎ **(04681) 580455**
(04681) 580456
info@golfclubfohr.de
www.golfclubfohr.de

Gut Apeldör (1996)
Apeldör 2, 25779 Hennstedt
☎ **(04836) 9960-0**
(04836) 9960-33
info@apeldoer.de
Karsten Voss
www.apeldoer.de

Gut Grambek (1981)
Schlosstr 21, 23883 Grambek
☎ **(04542) 841474**
(04542) 841476
info@gcgrambek.de
www.gcgrambek.de

Gut Kaden (1984)
Kadenerstrasse 9, 25486 Alveslohe
☎ **(04193) 9929-0**
(04193) 992919

Gut Uhlenhorst (1989)
24229 Daenischenhagen, Mühlenstrasse 37
☎ **(04349) 91700**
(04349) 919400
E-mail:golf@gut-uhlenhorst.de
www.gut-uhlenhorst.de

Gut Waldhof (1969)
Am Waldhof, 24629 Kisdorferwohld
☎ **(04194) 99740**
(04194) 997425
www.gut-waldhof.de

Gut Waldshagen (1996)
24306 Gut Waldshagen
☎ **(04522) 766766**
(04522) 766767
info@gut-golf.de
www.gut-golf.de

Hamburger Golf-Club Falkenstein (1906)
In de Bargen 59, 22587 Hamburg
☎ **(040) 812177**
(040) 817315
info@golfclub-falkenstein.de
Berthold Apel
www.golfclub-falkenstein.de

Hamburg Ahrensburg (1964)
Am Haidschlag 39-45, 22926 Ahrensburg
☎ **(04102) 51309**
(04102) 81410

Hamburg Hittfeld (1957)
Am Golfplatz 24, 21218 Seevetal
☎ **(04105) 2331**
(04105) 52571

Hamburg Holm (1993)
Haverkamp 1, 25488 Holm
☎ **(04103) 91330**
(04103) 913313
info@hchh.de
www.gchh.de

Hamburg Walddörfer (1960)
Schevenbarg, 22949 Ammersbek
☎ **(040) 605 1337**
(040) 605 4879
info@gchw.de
www.gchw.de

Golfclub Hohen Wieschendorf e.V. (1992)
Am Golfplatz 1, 23968 Hohen Wieschendorf
☎ **(0049) 384 28660**
(0049) 384 286666
info@howido.de
www.howido.de

Hoisdorf (1977)
Hof Bornbek/Hoisdorf, 22952 Lütjensee
☎ **(04107) 7831**
(04107) 9934
info@gc-hoisdorf.com
www.gc-hoisdorf.com

Jersbek (1986)
GolfClub Jersbek e.V., Oberteicher Weg, 22941 Jersbek
☎ **(04532) 20950**
(04532) 24779
mail@golfclub-jersbek.de
www.golfclub-jersbek.de

Kieler GC Havighorst (1988)
Havighorster Weg 20, 24211 Havighorst
☎ **(04302) 965980**
(04302) 965981
golfclub.havighorst@t-online.de

Lübeck-Travemünder Golf Klub e.V (1921)
Kowitzberg 41, 23570 Lübeck-Travemünde
☎ **(04502) 74018**
(04502) 72184
info@ltgk.de
www.ltgk.de

Mittelholsteinischer Aukrug (1969)
Zum Glasberg 9, 24613 Aukrug-Bargfeld
☎ **(04873) 595**
(04873) 1698

Peiner Hof
Peiner Hag, 25497 Prisdorf
☎ **(04101) 73790**
(04101) 76640
www.peinerhof.de

Am Sachsenwald (1985)
Am Riesenbett, 21521 Dassendorf
☎ **(04104) 6120**
(04104) 6551
gc-sachsenwald@t-online.de
www.gc-sachsenwald.de

Golf Club Schloss Breitenburg e.v
25524 Breitenburg
☎ **(04828) 8188**
(04828) 8100
golfclubschlossbreitenburg@t-online.de
Elke Gräfin zu Rantzau
www.golfclubschlossbreitenberg.de

Schloss Lüdersburg (1985)
Lüdersburger Strasse 21, 21379 Lüdersburg
☎ **(04139) 6970-0**
(04139) 6970 70
info@luedersburg.de
www.luedersburg.de

St Dionys (1972)
Widukindweg, 21357 St Dionys
☎ **(04133) 213311**

For key to symbols and European dialling codes see page 725

(04133) 213313
info@golfclub-st-dionys.de
www.golfclub-st-dionys.de

GC Sylt e.V. (1982)
Norderrung 5, 25996 Wenningstedt
(04651) 99598-0
(04651) 99598-19
info@gcsylt.de
www.golfclubsylt.de

Golfanlage Seeschlösschen Timmendorfer Strand (1973)
Am Golfplatz 3, 23669 Timmendorfer Strand
(04503) 704400
(04503) 704400-14
info@gc-timmendorf.de
Mrs Birgit Krause (Club Mgr)
www.gc-timmendorf.de

G&CC Treudelberg (1990)
Lemsahler Landstr 45, 22397 Hamburg
(040) 608 228877
(040) 608 228879
golf@treudelberg.com
www.treudelberg.com

Wentorf-Reinbeker Golf-Club e.V. (1901)
Golfstrasse 2, 21465 Wentorf
(040) 72 97 80 68
(040) 72 97 80 67
sekretariat@wrgc.de
www.wrgc.de

Hanover & Weserbergland

Bad Salzuflen G&LC (1956)
Schwaghof 4, 32108 Bad Salzuflen
(05222) 10773
(05222) 13954

British Army Golf Club (Sennelager) (1963)
Bad Lippspringe, BFPO 16
(05252) 53794
(05252) 53811
manager@sennelagergolfclub.de
www.sennelagergolfclub.de

Burgdorf (1969)
Waldstr 27, 31303 Burgdorf-Ehlershausen
(05085) 7628
(05085) 6617
info@burgdorfergolfclub.de
www.burgdorfergolfclub.de

Gifhorn (1982)
Wilscher Weg 69, 38518 Gifhorn
(05371) 16737
(05371) 51092

Gütersloh Garrison (1963)
Princess Royal Barracks, BFPO 47
(05241) 236938
(01241) 236838
timothyholt14@hotmail.com

Hamelner Golfclub e.V. (1985)
Schwöbber 8, 31855 Aerzen
(05154) 987 0
(05154) 987 111
info@hamelner-golfclub.de
www.hamelner-golfclub.de

Hannover (1923)
Am Blauen See 120, 30823 Garbsen
(05137) 73068
(05137) 75851
info@golfclub-hannover.de
www.golfclub-hannover.de

Hardenberg (1969)
Gut Levershausen, 37154 Northeim
(05551) 908380
(05551) 9083820
info@gchardenberg.de
Norbert Hoffmann (Manager)
www.gchardenberg.de

Isernhagen (1983)
Auf Gut Lohne 22, 30916 Isernhagen
(05139) 893185
(05139) 27033
www.golfclub-isernhagen.de

GC Langenhagen e.v. (1989)
Hainhaus 22, D-30855 Langenhagen
(0511) 736832
(0511) 726 1990
golfclub-langenhagen@t-online.de
www.golfclub-langenhagen.de

Lippischer Golfclub e.V. (1980)
Huxoll 14, 32825 Blomberg-Cappel
(05236) 459
(05236) 8102
sekretariat@lippischergolfclub.de
www.lippischergolfclub.de

Marienfeld (1986)
Remse 27, 33428 Marienfeld
(05247) 8880
(05247) 80386
info@gc-marienfeld.de
John Pollitt (Mgr)
www.gc-marienfeld.de

Paderborner Land (1983)
Wilseder Weg 25, 33102 Paderborn
(05251) 4377

Ravensberger Land
Sudstrasse 96, 32130 Enger-Pödinghausen
(09224) 79751
(09224) 699446
golfclub-ravensberger-land@teleos-web.de
www.golfclub-ravensberger-land.de

Senne GC Gut Welschof (1992)
Augustdorferstr 72, 33758 Schloss Holte-Stukenbrock
(05207) 920936
(05207) 88788
info@senne_golfclub.de
www.senne_golfclub.de

Sieben-Berge Rheden (1965)
Schloss Str 1a, 31039 Rheden
(05182) 52336
(05182) 923350
info@gc7berge.de
www.gc7berge.de

Weserbergland (1982)
Weissenfelder Mühle, 37647 Polle
(05535) 8842
(05535) 1225

Westfälischer Gütersloh
Gütersloher Str 127, 33397 Rietberg
(05244) 2340/10528
(05244) 1388
golf-club@golf-gt.de
www.golf-gt.de

Widukind-Land (1985)
Auf dem Stickdorn 63, 32584 Löhne
(05228) 7050
(05228) 1039

Munich & South Bavaria

Allgäuer G&LC (1984)
Hofgut Boschach, 87724 Ottobeuren
(08332) 9251-0
(08332) 5161
info@aglc.de
www.aglc.de

Altötting-Burghausen (1986)
Piesing 4, 84533 Haiming
(08678) 986903
(08678) 986905
office@gc-altoetting-burghausen.de
Johann Brehm (President)
www.gc-altoetting-burghausen.de

Augsburg (1959)
Engelshofer Str 2, 86399 Bobingen-Burgwalden
(08234) 5621
(08234) 7855
www.golfclub-augsburg.de

Bad Tölz (1973)
83646 Wackersberg
(08041) 9994
(08041) 2116

Beuerberg (1982)
Gut Sterz, 82547 Beuerberg
(08179) 671 or 782
(08179) 5234
beurberg@golf.de
www.gc-beurberg.de

Chieming (1982)
Kötzing 1, D-83339 Chieming
(08669) 87330
(08669) 873333
info@golfchieming.de
www.golfchieming.de

Donauwörth (1995)
Lederstatt 1, 86609 Donauwörth
(0906) 4044
(0906) 999 8164
info@gc-donauwoerth.de

For key to symbols and European dialling codes see page 725

✍ Claudia Slimpfie-Taslican
▤ www.gc-donauwoerth.de

Ebersberg (1988)
Postfach 1351, 85554 Ebersberg
☎ **(08094) 8106**
🖷 (08094) 8386
✉ info@gc-ebersberg.de
✍ Stefan Schreyer (Mgr)
▤ www.gc-ebersberg.de

Erding-Grünbach (1973)
Am Kellerberg, 85461 Grünbach
☎ **(08122) 49650**
🖷 (08122) 49684

Eschenried (1983)
Kurfürstenweg 10, 85232 Eschenried
☎ **(08131) 56740**
🖷 (08131) 567418
✉ info@golf-eschenried.de
▤ www.gc-eschenried.de

Feldafing (1926)
Tutzinger Str 15, 82340 Feldafing
☎ **(08157) 9334-0**
🖷 (08157) 9334-99
✉ info@golfclub-Feldafing.de
▤ www.golfclub-Feldafing.de

Garmisch-Partenkirchen (1928)
Gut Buchwies, 82496 Oberau
☎ **(08824) 8344**
🖷 (08824) 944198
✉ golfclubGAP@onlinehome.de
▤ www.golfclub-garmisch-partenkirchen.de

Golfclub Wörthsee e.V. (1982)
Gut Schluifeld, 82237 Wörthsee
☎ **(08153) 93477-0**
🖷 (08153) 93477-40
✉ info@golfclub-woerthsee.de
✍ Andrè Mosig (Manager)
▤ www.golfclub-woerthsee.de

Gut Ludwigsberg (1989)
Augsburgerstr 51, 86842 Turkheim
☎ **(08245) 3322**
🖷 (08245) 3789

Hohenpähl (1988)
82396 Pähl
☎ **(08808) 9202-0**
🖷 (08808) 9202-22
✉ info@gchp.de
✍ Claus Ammer
▤ www.gchp.de

Holledau
Weihern 3, 84104 Rudelzhausen
☎ **(08756) 96010**
🖷 (08756) 815

Höslwang im Chiemgau (1975)
Kronberg 3, 83129 Höslwang
☎ **(08075) 714**
🖷 (08075) 8134
✉ info@golfclub-hoeslwang.de
▤ www.golfclub-hoeslwang.de

Iffeldorf (1989)
Gut Rettenberg, 82393 Iffeldorf
☎ **0049 (8856) 92550**
🖷 0049 (8856) 925559
✉ sekretariat@golf-iffeldorf.de
✍ Uwe Hinz
▤ www.golf-iffeldorf.de

Landshut (1989)
Oberlippach 2, 84095 Furth-Landshut
☎ **(08704) 8378**
🖷 (08704) 8379
✉ gc.landshut@t-online.de
▤ www.golf-landshut.de

Mangfalltal G&LC
Oed 1, 83620 Feldkirchen-Westerham
☎ **(08063) 6300**
🖷 (08063) 6958
▤ www.glcm.de

Margarethenhof (1982)
Gut Steinberg, 83666 Waakirchen/Marienstein
☎ **(08022) 7506-0**
🖷 (08022) 74818
✉ info@margarethenhof.com
▤ www.margarethenhof.com

Memmingen Gut Westerhart (1994)
Westerhart 1b, 87740 Buxheim
☎ **(08331) 71016**
🖷 (08331) 71018
✉ gc-memmingen@t-online.de
▤ www.golfclub-memmingen.de

Golfclub München Eichenried (1989)
Münchner Strasse 57, 85452 Eichenried
☎ **(08123) 93080**
🖷 (08123) 930893
✉ info@gc-eichenried.de
▤ www.gc-eichenried.de

München West-Odelzhausen (1988)
Gut Todtenried, 85235 Odelzhausen
☎ **(08134) 1618**
🖷 (08134) 7623

München-Riedhof e.V. (1991)
82544 Egling-Riedhof, Riedhof 16
☎ **(08171) 21950**
🖷 (08171) 219511
✉ info@riedhof.de
▤ www.riedhof.de

Münchener (1910)
Tölzerstrasse 95, 82064 Strasslach
☎ **(08170) 450**
🖷 (08170) 611

Olching (1980)
Feursstrasse 89, 82140 Olching
☎ **(08142) 48290**
🖷 (08142) 482914
✉ sportbuero@golfclub-olching.de
▤ www.golfclub-olching.de

Pfaffing Wasserburger
Golfclub Pfaffing München-Ost e.V, wsw Golf AG, Köckmühle 132, 83539 Pfaffing
☎ **(08076) 91650**
🖷 (08076) 916514
✉ info@golfclub-pfaffing.de
▤ www.golfclub-pfaffing.de

Reit im Winkl-Kössen (1986)
Postfach 1101, 83237 Reit im Winkl
☎ **(08640) 798250**
🖷 (08640) 798252

Rottaler G&CC (1972)
Am Fischgartl 2, 84332 Hebertsfelden
☎ **(08561) 5969**
🖷 (08561) 2646
✉ info@rottaler-gc.de
▤ www.rottaler-gc.de

Rottbach (1997)
Weiherhaus 5, 82216 Rottbach
☎ **(08135) 93290**
🖷 (08135) 932911
✉ info@rottbach.de
▤ www.golfanlage-rottbach.de

Schloss Maxlrain
Freiung 14, 83104 Maxlrain-Tuntenhausen
☎ **(08061) 1403**
🖷 (08061) 30146
✉ info@golfclub-maxlrain.de
▤ www.golfclub-maxlrain.de

Sonnenalp Oberallgäu (1976)
Hotel Sonnenalp, 87527 Ofterschwang
☎ **(08321) 272181/(08326) 3859410**
🖷 (08326) 3859412
✉ info@golfresort-sonnenalp.de
▤ www.golfresort-sonnenalp.de

Starnberg (1986)
Uneringerstr, 82319 Starnberg
☎ **(08151) 12157**
🖷 (08151) 29115
✉ club@gcstarnberg.de
▤ www.gcstarnberg.de

Tegernseer GC Bad Wiessee (1958)
Rohbognerhof, 83707 Bad Wiessee
☎ **(08022) 271130**
🖷 (08022) 2711333
✉ info@tegernseer-golf-club.de
✍ Eva Meisinger
▤ www.tegernseer-golf-club.de

Tutzing (1983)
82327 Tutzing-Deixlfurt
☎ **(08158) 3600**
🖷 (08158) 7234

Waldegg-Wiggensbach (1988)
Hof Waldegg, 87487 Wiggensbach
☎ **(08370) 93073**
🖷 (08370) 93074
✉ info@golf-wiggensbach.com
▤ www.golf-wiggensbach.com

Wittelsbacher GC Rohrenfeld-Neuburg (1988)
Rohrenfeld, 86633 Neuburg/Donau
☎ **(08431) 90859-0**
(08431) 90859-99
info@wbgc.de
Frank Thonig (Gen Mgr)
www.wbgc.de

Nuremberg & North Bavaria

Abenberg (1988)
Am Golfplatz 19, 91183 Abenberg
☎ **(09178) 98960**
(09178) 989696

Bad Windsheim (1992)
Otmar-Schaller-Alleen, 91438 Bad Windsheim
☎ **(09841) 5027**
(09841) 3448
gcbadwindsheim@t-online.de
www.golf-bw.de

Bamberg (1973)
Postfach 1525, 96006 Bamberg
☎ **(09547) 7109**
(09547) 7817
leimershof@golfclubbamberg.de
www.golfclubbamberg.de

Donau GC Passau-Rassbach (1986)
Rassbach 8, 94136 Thyrnau-Passau
☎ **(08501) 91313**
(08501) 91314
info@golf-passau.de
Anetseder Leonhard
www.golf-passau.de

Fränkische Schweiz (1974)
Kanndorf 8, 91316 Ebermannstadt
☎ **(09194) 4827**
(09194) 5410
fraenkischeschweiz@t-online.de
www.gc-fs.de

Golf Club Fürth e.V. (1951)
Am Golfplatz 10, 90768 Fürth
☎ **(0911) 757522**
(0911) 973 2989
info@golfclub-fuerth.de
www.golfclub-fuerth.de

Gäuboden (1992)
Gut Fruhstorf, 94330 Aiterhofen
☎ **(09421) 72804**
(09421) 72804

Golf Resort Bad Griesbach (1989)
Holzhäuser 8, 94086 Bad Griesbach
☎ **(08532) 790-0**
(08532) 790-45
golfresort@hartl.de
www.hartl.de

Hof (1985)
Postfach 1324, 95012 Hof
☎ **(09281) 470155**
(09821) 470157

Lauterhofen (1987)
Ruppertslohe 18, 92283 Lauterhofen
☎ **(09186) 1574**
(09186) 1527

Lichtenau-Weickershof (1980)
Weickershof 1, 91586 Lichtenau
☎ **(09827) 92040**
(09827) 9204-44

Oberfranken Thurnau (1965)
Postfach 1349, 95304 Kulmbach
☎ **(09228) 319**
(09228) 7219

Oberpfälzer Wald G&LC (1977)
Ödengrub, 92431 Kemnath bei Fuhrn
☎ **(09439) 466**
(09439) 1247

Oberzwieselau (1990)
94227 Lindberg
☎ **(01049) 9922/2367**
(01049) 9922/2924
www.golfpark-oberzwieselau.de

Regensburg (1966)
93093 Jagdschloss Thiergarten
☎ **(09403) 505**
(09403) 4391
sekretariat@golfclub-regensburg.de
Christian Früh
www.golfclub-regensburg.de

Am Reichswald (1960)
Schiestlstr 100, 90427 Nürnberg
☎ **(0911) 305730**
(0911) 301200
info@golfclub-nuernberg.de
Kornelia Knoblich/Petra Ketzmer
www.golfclub-nurnburg.de

Sagmühle (1984)
Golfplatz Sagmühle 1, 94086 Bad Griesbach
☎ **(08532) 2038**
(08532) 3165

Schloss Fahrenbach (1993)
95709 Tröstau
☎ **(09232) 882-256**
(09232) 882-345
www.golfhotel-fahrenbach.de

Schloss Reichmannsdorf (1991)
Schlosshof 4, 96132 Schlüsselfeld
☎ **(09546) 9215-10**
(09546) 9215-20
info@golfanlage-reichmannsdorf.de
Franz von Schrottenberg
www.golfanlage-reichmannsdorf.de

Schlossberg (1985)
Grünbach 8, 94419 Reisbach
☎ **(08734) 7035**
(08734) 7795

Schwanhof (1994)
Klaus Conrad Allee 1, 92706 Luhe-Wildenau
☎ **(09607) 92020**
(09607) 920248

Die Wutzschleife (1997)
Hillstett 40, 92444 Rötz
☎ **(09976) 184460**
(09976) 18180
info@golfanlage-wutzschleife.de
www.golfanlage-wutzschleife.de

Rhineland North

Golf und Landclub Ahaus (1987)
Schmäinghook 36, 48683 Ahaus-Alstätte
☎ **(02567) 405**
(02567) 3524
info@glc-ahaus.de
www.glc-ahaus.de

Alten Fliess (1995)
Am Alten Fliess 66, 50129 Bergheim
☎ **(02238) 94410**
(02238) 944119

Artland (1988)
Westerholte 23, 49577 Ankum
☎ **(05466) 301**
(05466) 91081
info@artlandgolf.de
www.artlandgolf.de

Bergisch-Land (1928)
Siebeneickerst 386, 42111 Wuppertal
☎ **(02053) 7177**
(02053) 7303
info@golfclub-bergischland.de
Philipp Pfannkuche
www.golfclub-bergischland.de

Bochum (1982)
Im Mailand 127, 44797 Bochum
☎ **(0234) 799832**
(0234) 795775

Dortmund (1956)
Reichmarkstr 12, 44265 Dortmund
☎ **(0231) 774133/774609**
(0231) 774403

Düsseldorfer GC (1961)
Rommeljansweg 12, D-40882 Ratingen
☎ **0049 (0) 2102 81092**
0049 (0) 2102 81782
info@duesseldorfer-golf-club.de
Henrike Kleyoldt
www.duesseldorfer-golf-club.de

Elfrather Mühle (1991)
An der Elfrather Mühle 145, 47802 Krefeld
☎ **(02151) 4969-0**
(02151) 477459
info@gcem.de
www.gcem.de

Erftaue (1991)
Zur Mühlenerft 1, 41517 Grevenbroich
☎ **(02181) 280637**
(02181) 280639
gc.erftaue@t-online.de
www.golf-erftaue.de

Essener Golfclub Haus Oefte (1959)
Laupendahler Landstr, 45219 Essen-Kettwig
☎ **(02054) 83911**
(02054) 83850
info@golfclub-oefte.de
Heidrùn Vodnik (Sec)
www.golfclub-oefte.de

Euregio Bad Bentheim (1987)
Postbox 1205, Am Hauptelick 8, 48443 Bad Bentheim
☎ **(05922) 7776-0**
(05922) 7776-18
www.golfclub-euregio.de

Grevenmühle Ratingen (1988)
Grevenmühle, 40882 Ratingen-Homberg
☎ **(02102) 9595-0**
(02102) 959515

Haus Bey (1992)
An Haus Bey 16, 41334 Nettetal
☎ **(02153) 9197-0**
(02153) 919750
golf@hausbey.de
Elmar Claus
www.hausbey.de

Haus Kambach (1989)
Kambachstrasse 9-13, 52249 Eschweiler-Kinzweiler
☎ **(02403) 50890**
(02403) 21270
info@golf-kambach.de
www.golf-kambach.de

Hubbelrath (1961)
Bergische Landstr 700, 40629 Düsseldorf
☎ **(02104) 72178**
(02104) 75685
info@gc-hubbelrath.de
www.gc-hubbelrath.de

Hummelbachaue Neuss (1987)
Norfer Kirchstrasse, 41469 Neuss
☎ **(02137) 91910**
(02137) 4016

Issum-Niederrhein (1973)
Pauenweg 68, 47661 Issum 1
☎ **(02835) 92310**
(02835) 9231-20
www.gc-issum.de

Golf- and Land-Club Köln e.V. (1906)
Golfplatz 2, 51429 Bergisch Gladbach
☎ **0049 (0) 2204-9276-0**
0049 (0) 2204-9276-15
info@glckoeln.de
Achim Lehmstardt (Gen Mgr)
www.glckoeln.de

Kosaido International (1989)
Am Schmidtberg 11, 40629 Düsseldorf
☎ **(02104) 77060**
(02104) 770611
info@kosaido.de
www.kosaido.de

Krefeld (1930)
Eltweg 2, 47809 Krefeld
☎ **(02151) 156030**
(02151) 15603 222
kgc@krefelder-gc.de
Ula Weinforth
www.krefelder-gc.de

Mühlenhof G&CC (1990)
Greilack 29, 47546 Kalkar
☎ **0049 (2824) 924092**
0049 (2824) 924093
awilmsen@muehlenhof.net
Annette Wilmsen
www.muehlenhof.net

Nordkirchen (1974)
Am Golfplatz 6, 59394 Nordkirchen
☎ **(02596) 9191**
(02596) 9195
www.glc-nordkirchen.de

Op de Niep (1995)
Bergschenweg 71, 47506 Neukirchen-Vluyn
☎ **(02845) 28051**
(02845) 28052

Osnabrück (1955)
Am Golfplatz 3, 49143 Bissendorf
☎ **(05402) 5636**
(05402) 5257
info@ogc.de
www.ogc.de

Rheine/Mesum (1998)
Wörstr 201, 48432 Rheine
☎ **(05975) 9490**
(05975) 9491
info@golfclub-rheine.de
www.golfclub-rheine.de

Rittergut Birkhof (1996)
Rittergut Birkhof, 41352 Korschenbroich
☎ **(02131) 510660**
(02131) 510616

St Barbara's Royal Dortmund (1969)
Hesslingweg, 44309 Dortmund
☎ **(0231) 202551**
(0231) 259183

Schloss Georghausen (1962)
Georghausen 8, 51789 Lindlar-Hommerich
☎ **(02207) 4938**
(02207) 81230
gc@schlossgeorghausengolf.de
www.golfclub-schloss-georghausen.de

Schloss Haag (1996)
Bartelter Weg 8, 47608 Geldern
☎ **(02831) 94777**
(02831) 94778

Schloss Myllendonk (1965)
Myllendonkerstr 113, 41352 Korschenbroich 1
☎ **(02161) 641049**
(02161) 648806
info@gcsm.de
Peter Géronne
www.gcsm.de

Golfclub Schloss Westerholt e.V. (1993)
Schloss Strasse 1, 45701 Herten-Westerholt
☎ **(0209) 165840**
(0209) 1658415
info@gc-westerholt.de
www.gc-westerholt.de

Golf- und Landclub Schmitzhof (1975)
Arsbeckerstr 160, 41844 Wegberg
☎ **(02436) 39090**
(02436) 390915
info@golfclubschmitzhof.de
www.golfclubschmitzhof.de

Siegen-Olpe (1966)
Am Golfplatz, 57482 Wenden
☎ **(02762) 9762-0**
(02762) 9762-12
info@gcso.de
Stefan Eisenschmitt
www.gcso.de

Golfclub Siegerland e.V. (1993)
Berghäuser Weg, 57223 Kreuztal-Mittelhees
☎ **(02732) 59470**
(02732) 594724
info@golfclub-siegerland.de
Ursula Kaidel
www.golfclub-siegerland.de

Teutoburger Wald (1990)
Postfach 1250, 33777 Halle/Westfalen
☎ **+49 5201 6279**
+49 5201 6222
info@gctw-halle.de
www.gctw.de

Unna-Fröndenberg (1985)
Schwarzer Weg 1, 58730 Fröndenberg
☎ **(02373) 70068**
(02373) 70069
info@gcuf.de
Mariya Mikli
www.gcuf.de

Vechta-Welpe (1989)
Welpe 2, 49377 Vechta
☎ **(04441) 5539/82168**
(04441) 852480
info@golfclub-vechta.de
Maria Kortenbusch
www.golfclub-vechta.de

Velbert – Gut Kuhlendahl
Kuhlendahler Str 283, 42553 Velbert
☎ **(02053) 923290**
(02053) 923291
golfclub-velbert@t-online.de

For key to symbols and European dialling codes see page 725

✍ Michael Ogger (Director)
🌐 www.golfclub-velbert.de

Golf & Country Club Velderhof (1997)
Velderhof, 50259 Pulheim
☎ **(02238) 923940**
℻ (02238) 9239440
✉ info@velderhof.de
✍ Eva Harzheim
🌐 www.velderhof.de

Vestischer GC Recklinghausen (1974)
Bockholterstr 475, 45659 Recklinghausen
☎ **(02361) 93420**
℻ (02361) 934240
✉ vest.golfclub@t-online.de
🌐 www.gc-recklinghausen.de

Wasserburg Anholt (1972)
Schloss 3, 46419 Isselburg Anholt
☎ **(02874) 915120**
℻ (02874) 915128
✉ sekretariat@golfclub-anholt.de
🌐 www.golfclub-anholt.de

Golfclub Weselerwald (1988)
Steenbecksweg 12, 46514 Schermbeck
☎ **(02856) 91370**
℻ (02856) 913715
✉ info@gcww.de
✍ John Emery
🌐 www.gcww.de

West Rhine (1956)
Javelin Barracks, BFPO 35
☎ **+49 2163 974463**
℻ +49 2163 80049
✉ secretary@westrhinegc.co.uk
✍ David W Hampson
🌐 www.westrhinegc.co.uk

Westerwald (1979)
Steinebacherstr, 57629 Dreifelden
☎ **(02666) 8220**
℻ (02666) 8493
✉ gcwesterwald@t-online.de
🌐 ww.gc-westerwald.de

Rhineland South

Bad Neuenahr G&LC (1979)
Remagener Weg, 53474 Bad Neuenahr-Ahrweiler
☎ **(02641) 950950**
℻ (02641) 950 9595

Golf-Resort Bitburger Land (1995)
Zur Weilersheck 1, 54636 Wissmannsdorf
☎ **(06527) 9272-0**
℻ (06527) 9272-30
✉ info@bitgolf.de
🌐 www.bitgolf.de

Bonn-Godesberg in Wachtberg (1960)
Landgrabenweg, 53343 Wachtberg-Niederbachen
☎ **(0228) 344003**
℻ (0228) 340820

Burg Overbach (1984)
Postfach 1213, 53799 Much
☎ **(02245) 5550**
℻ (02245) 8247
✉ widl@golfclub-burg-overbach.de
✍ Günter Widl
🌐 www.golfclub-burg-overbach.de

Burg Zievel (1994)
Burg Zievel, 53894 Mechernich
☎ **(02256) 1651**
℻ (02256) 3479

Eifel (1977)
Kölner Str, 54576 Hillesheim
☎ **(06593) 1241**
℻ (06593) 9421

Gut Heckenhof (1993)
53783 Eitorf
☎ **(02243) 9232-0**
℻ (02243) 923299
✉ info@gut-heckenhof.de
🌐 www.gut-heckenhof.de

Internationaler GC Bonn (1992)
Gut Grossenbusch, 53757 St Augustin
☎ **(02241) 39880**
℻ (02241) 398888
✉ info@gcbonn.de
🌐 www.golf-course-bonn.de

Jakobsberg (1990)
Im Tal der Loreley, 56154 Boppard
☎ **(06742) 808491**
℻ (06742) 808493
✉ golf@jakobsberg.de
🌐 www.jakobsberg.de

Kyllburger Waldeifel
Lietzenhof, 54597 Burbach
☎ **(06553) 961039**
℻ (06553) 3282
🌐 www.golf-lietzenhof.de

Mittelrheinischer Bad Ems (1938)
Denzerheide, 56130 Bad Ems
☎ **(02603) 6541**
℻ (02603) 13995
✉ info@mgcbadems.de
🌐 ww3w.mgcbadems.de

Nahetal (1971)
Drei Buchen, 55583 Bad Münster am Stein
☎ **(06708) 2145**
℻ (06708) 1731
🌐 www.golfclub-nahetal.de

Stromberg-Schindeldorf (1987)
Park Village Golfanlagen, Buchenring 6, 55442 Stromberg
☎ **(06724) 93080**
℻ (06724) 930818

Trier (1977)
54340 Ensch-Birkenheck
☎ **(06507) 993255**
℻ (06507) 993257
✉ info@golf-club-trier.de
🌐 www.golf-club-trier.de

Waldbrunnen (1983)
Brunnenstr 11, 53578 Windhagen
☎ **(02645) 8041**
℻ (02645) 8042
✉ info@golfclub-waldbrunnen.de
✍ Mrs B Thomas
🌐 www.golfclub-waldbrunnen.de

Wiesensee (1992)
Am Wiesensee, 56459 Westerburg-Stahlhofen
☎ **(02663) 991192**
℻ (02663) 991193
✉ golfclub.wiesensee@lindner.de
🌐 www.golfclub-wiesensee.de

Saar-Pfalz

Pfalz Neustadt (1971)
Im Lochbusch, 67435 Neustadt-Geinsheim
☎ **(06327) 97420**
℻ (06327) 974218
✉ gc-pfalz@t-online.de
🌐 www.gc-pfalz.de

Saarbrücken (1961)
Oberlimbergerweg, 66798 Wallerfangen-Gisingen
☎ **(06837) 91800/1584**
℻ (06837) 91801
🌐 www.golfclub-saarbruecken.de

Websweiler Hof (1991)
Websweiler Hof, 66424 Homburg/Saar
☎ **(06841) 7777-60**
℻ (06841) 7777-666
🌐 www.golf-saar.de

Westpfalz Schwarzbachtal (1988)
66509 Rieschweiler
☎ **(06336) 6442**
℻ (06336) 6408
✉ egw@golf.de
🌐 www.gcwestpfalz.de

Woodlawn Golf Course
6792 Ramstein Flugplatz
☎ **(06371) 476240**
℻ (06371) 42158
✍ R Nichols (Gen Mgr)
🌐 www.ramsteingolf.com

Stuttgart & South West

Bad Liebenzell
Golfplatz 1-9, 75378 Bad Liebenzell
☎ **(07052) 9325-0**
℻ (07052) 9325-25
✉ info@gcbl.de
🌐 www.gcbl.de

Bad Rappenau (1989)
Ehrenbergstrasse 25a, 74906 Bad Rappenau
☎ **(07264) 3666**
℻ (07264) 3838

Bad Salgau (1995)
Koppelweg 103, 88348 Bad Salgau
☎ **(07581) 527459**

(07581) 527487
info@gc-bs.de
www.gc-bs.de

Baden Hills Golf & Curling Club e.v. (1982)
Cabot Trail G208, 77836 Rheinmünster
(07229) 185100
(07229) 1851011
baden-hills@t-online.de
www.baden-hills.de

Baden-Baden (1901)
Fremersbergstr 127, 76530 Baden-Baden
(07221) 23579
(07221) 3025659
info@golfclub-baden-baden.de
Gerhard Kaufmann (Mgr)
www.golfclub-baden-baden.de

GC Bodensee Weissenberg eV (1986)
Lampertsweiler 51, D-88138 Weissensberg
+41 (8389) 89190
+41 (8389) 923907
info@gcbw.de
www.gcbw.de

Freiburg (1970)
Krüttweg 1, 79199 Kirchzarten
(07661) 9847-0
(07661) 984747
fgc@freiburger-golfclub.de
Andrea Bührer
www.freiburger-golfclub.de

Fürstlicher Golfclub Waldsee (1998)
Hopfenweiler, 88339 Bad Waldsee
(07524) 4017 200
(07524) 4017 100
club@waldsee-golf.de
www.waldsee-golf.de

Hechingen Hohenzollern (1955)
Postfach 1124, 72379 Hechingen
(07471) 6478
(07471) 14776
info@golfclub-hechingen.de
www.golfclub-hechingen.de

Heidelberg-Lobenfeld (1968)
Biddersbacherhof, 74931 Lobbach-Lobenfeld
(06226) 952110
(06226) 952111
golf@gchl.de
www.gchl.de

Heilbronn-Hohenlohe (1964)
Hofgasse, 74639 Zweiflingen-Friedrichsruhe
(07941) 920810
(07941) 920819
www.friedrichsruhe.de

Hetzenhof
Hetzenhof 7, 73547 Lorch
(07172) 9180-0
(07172) 9180-30
info@golfclub-hetzenhof.de
www.golfclub-hetzenhof.de

Hohenstaufen (1959)
Unter den Ramsberg, 73072 Donzdorf-Reichenbach
(07162) 27171
(07162) 25744
gc-hohenstaufen@online.de
www.gc-hohenstaufen.de

Kaiserhöhe (1995)
Im Laber 4a, 74747 Ravenstein
(06297) 399
(06297) 599
info@golfclub-kaiserhoehe.de
Martin Arzberger
www.gc-kaiserhoehe.de

Golf-Club Konstanz e.V. (1965)
Hofgut Kargegg 1, D-78476 Allensbach-Langenrain
+49 (0) 75 33 93 03 - 0
+49 (o) 75 33 93 03 - 30
info@golfclubkonstanz.de
www.golfclublkonstanz.de

Lindau-Bad Schachen (1954)
Am Schönbühl 5, 88131 Lindau
(08382) 96170
(08382) 961750
info@golflindau.de
www.gc-lindau-bad-schachen.de

Markgräflerland Kandern (1984)
Feuerbacher Str 35, 79400 Kandern
(07626) 97799-0
(07626) 97799-22
info@gc-mk.com
Graham Currie
www.gc-mk.com

Neckartal (1974)
Aldinger Str. 975, 70806 Kornwestheim
(07141) 871319
(07141) 81716
info@gc-neckartal.de
www.gc-neckartal.de

Nippenburg (1993)
Nippenburg 21, 71701 Schwieberdingen
(07150) 39530
(07150) 353518

Obere Alp (1989)
Am Golfplatz 1-3, 79780 Stühlingen
(07703) 9203-0
(07703) 9203-18
secretariat@golf-oberealp.de
www.golf-oberealp.de

Oberschwaben-Bad Waldsee (1968)
Hopfenweiler 2d, 88339 Bad Waldsee
(07524) 5900
(07524) 6106

Oeschberghof L & GC (1976)
Golfplatz 1, 78166 Donaueschingen
(0771) 84525
(0771) 84540

Land-und Golfclub Oschberghof (1976)
Golfplatz 1, 78166 Donaueschingen
(0771) 84525
(0771) 84540
golf@oeschberghof.com
www.oeschberghof.com

Owingen-Überlingen e.V – Hofgut Lugenhof (1989)
Alte Owinger Str 93, 88696 Owingen
(07551) 83040
(07551) 830422
welcome@golfclub-owingen.de
www.golfclub-owingen.de

Pforzheim Karlshäuser Hof (1987)
Karlshäuser Weg, 75248 Ölbronn-Dürrn
(07237) 9100
(07237) 5161
info@gc-pf.de
Andreas List (CM)
www.gc-pf.de

Reischenhof (1987)
Industriestrasse 12, 88489 Wain
(07353) 1732
(07373) 3824
www.golf.de/gc-reischenhof

Reutlingen-Sonnenbühl (1987)
Im Zerg, 72820 Sonnenbühl
(07128) 92660
(07128) 926692

Rhein Badenweiler (1971)
79401 Badenweiler
(07632) 7970
(07632) 797150

Rickenbach (1979)
Hennematt 20, 79736 Rickenbach
(07765) 777
(07765) 544
info@golfclub-rickenbach.de
www.golfclub-rickenbach.de

Schloss Klingenburg e.v. (1978)
Schloss Klingenburg, 89343 Jettingen-Scheppach
(08225) 3030
(08225) 30350
info@golf-klingenburg.de
www.golf-klingenburg.de

Schloss Langenstein (1991)
Schloss Langenstein, 78359 Orsingen-Nenzingen
(07774) 50651
(07774) 50699
golf-sekretariat@schloss-langenstein.com
www.schloss-langenstein.com

Schloss Liebenstein (1982)
Postfach 27, 74380 Neckarwestheim
(07133) 9878-0
(07133) 9878-18

✉ info@gc-sl.de
✍ Rüdiger Schmid
🖹 www.golfclubliebenstein.de

Schloss Weitenburg (1984)
Sommerhalde 11, 72181 Starzach-Sulzau
☎ **(07472) 15050**
🖷 (07472) 15051
✉ info@gcsw.de
🖹 www.gcsw.de

Sinsheim-Buchenauerhof (1993)
Buchenauerhof 4, 74889 Sinsheim
☎ **(07265) 7258**
🖷 (07265) 7379
✉ mail@golfclubsinsheim.de
✍ Marion Bonn
🖹 www.golfclubsinsheim.de

Steisslingen (1991)
Brunnenstr 4b, 78256 Steisslingen-Wiechs
☎ **(07738) 7196**
🖷 (07738) 923297
✉ info@golfclub-steisslingen.de
✍ Peter Ridley
🖹 www.golfclub-steisslingen.de

Stuttgarter Golf-Club Solitude e.V. (1927)
Schlossfeld/Golfplatz 71297, Mönsheim
☎ **(07044) 911 0410**
🖷 (07044) 911 0420
✉ info@golfclub-stuttgart.com
✍ Birgit Geise
🖹 www.golfclub-stuttgart.com

Ulm e.V. (1963)
Wochenauer Hof 2, 89186 Illerrieden
☎ **(07306) 929500**
🖷 (07306) 9295025
✉ GolfClubUlm@t-online.de
🖹 www.GolfClubUlm.de

Greece

Afandou (1973)
Afandou, Rhodes
☎ **(0241) 51255**

Corfu (1972)
PO Box 71, Ropa Valley, 49100 Corfu
☎ **(26610) 94220**
🖷 (26610) 94221
✉ cfugolf@hol.gr
🖹 www.corfugolfclub.com

Glyfada Golf Club of Athens (1966)
PO Box 70116, 166-10 Glyfada, Athens
☎ **+30 210 894 6459**
🖷 +30 210 894 6834
✉ info@ggca.gr
✍ Nicole Cavadia
🖹 www.ggca.gr

Hungary

Birdland G&CC (1991)
Thermal krt.10, 9740 Bükfürdö
☎ **(+36) 94 358060**
🖷 (+36) 94 359000
✉ info@birdland.hu
🖹 www.birdland.hu

Budapest G&CC
Golf u.1, 2024 Kisoroszi
☎ **(1) 36 26 392 465**
🖷 (1) 36 26 392 465

European Lakes G&CC (1994)
Kossuth u.3, 7232 Hencse
☎ **(82) 481245**
🖷 (82) 481248
✉ info@europeanlakes.com
✍ Medea Zag
⊕ Soft spikes only - No metal spikes
🖹 www.europeanlakes.com

Old Lake (1998)
PO Box 127, 2890 Tata-Remeteségpuszta
☎ **(34) 587620**
🖷 (34) 587623
✉ club@oldlakegolf.com
✍ Dr Ba'bos Réka (Club Director)
🖹 www.oldlakegolf.com

Pannonia G&CC (1996)
Alcsútdoboz, 8087 Mariavölgy
☎ **0036 (22) 594200**
🖷 0036 (22) 594205
✉ info@golfclub.hu
🖹 www.golfclub.hu

St Lorence G&CC
Pellérdi ut 55, 7634 Pécs
☎ **(72) 252844/252142**
🖷 (72) 252844/252173

Iceland

Akureyri (1935)
PO Box 317, 602 Akureyri
☎ **+354 4622974**
✉ gagolf@gagolf.is
✍ Halla Sif Svavarsdóttir
🖹 www.gagolf.is

Borgarness (1973)
Hamar, 310 Borgarnes
☎ **(345) 437 1663**
✉ hamar@gbborgarnes.net
🖹 www.golf.is/gb
www.gbborgarnes.net

Golfklubbur Sudurnesja (1964)
PO Box 112, 232 Keflavik
☎ **(421) 4100**
✉ gs@gs.is
✍ Gunnar Johannsson
🖹 www.gs.is

Húsavík (1967)
PO Box 23, Kötlum, 640 Húsavík
☎ **(464) 1000**
🖷 (464) 1678
✉ palmi.palmason@tmd.is

Isafjardar (1978)
PO Box 367, 400 Isafjördur
☎ **(456) 5081**
🖷 (456) 4547
✉ gi@snerpa.is

Keilir (1967)
Box 148, 222 Hafnarfjördur
☎ **(565) 3360**
🖷 (565) 2560
✉ keilir@ishoff.is
🖹 www.keilir.is

Kopavogs og Gardabaejar (1994)
Postholf 214, 212 Gardabaer
☎ **(+354) 565 7373**
🖷 (+354) 565 9190
✉ gkg@gkg.is
✍ Agnar Mar Jonsson (Manager)
🖹 www.gkg.is

Leynir (1965)
PO Box 9, Akranes
☎ **(00354) 431 2771**
🖷 (00354) 431 3711
✉ leynir@simnet.is
🖹 www.golf.is/gl www.leynir.is

Ness-Nesklúbburinn (1964)
PO Box 66, 172 Seltjarnarnes
☎ **(561) 1930**
🖷 (561) 1966
✉ nk@centrum.is
🖹 www.golf.is/nk

Oddafellowa (1990)
Urridavatnsdölum, 210 Gardabaer
☎ **(565) 9094**
🖷 (565) 9074
🖹 www.oddur.is

Olafsfjardar (1968)
Skeggjabrekku, 625 Olafsfjördur
☎ **(466) 2611**
🖷 (466) 2611

Reykjavíkur (1934)
Grafarholt, 112 Reykjavík
☎ **+354 (585) 0200/0210**
🖷 +354 (585) 0201
✉ gr@grgolf.is
🖹 www.grgolf.is

Saudárkróks (1970)
Hlidarendi, Postholf 56, 550 Saudárkrókur
☎ **(453) 5075**

Vestmannaeyja (1938)
Postholf 168, 902 Vestmannaeyar
☎ **(481) 2363**
🖷 (481) 2362

For key to symbols and European dialling codes see page 725

Italy

Como/Milan/Bergamo

Ambrosiano (1994)
Cascina Bertacca, 20080 Bubbiano-Milan
(0290) 840820
(0290) 849365
info@golfclubambrosiano.com
www.golfclubambrosiano.com

Barlassina CC (1956)
Via Privata Golf 42, 20030 Birago di Camnago (MI)
(0362) 560621/2
(0362) 560934
bccgolf@libero.it

Bergamo L'Albenza (1961)
Via Longoni 12, 24030 Almenno S. Bartolomeo (BG)
(035) 640028
(035) 643066
secreteria@golfbergamo.it
Achille Ridamouti (Sec)
www.golfbergamo.it

Bogogno (1996)
Via Sant'Isidoro 1, 28010 Bogogno
(0322) 863794
(0322) 863798
info@circologolfbogogno.com
www.circolo9golfbogogno.com

Golf Brianza Country Club (1996)
Cascina Cazzu, 4, 20040 Usmate Velate (Mi)
(039) 682 9089/079
(039) 682 9059
brianzagolf@tin.it
Francesco Alajmo (Mgr)
www.brianzagolf.it

Carimate (1962)
Via Airoldi 2, 22060 Carimate (CO)
(031) 790226
(031) 791927
info@golfcarimate.it
Giuseppe Nava
www.golfcarimate.it

Castelconturbia (1984)
Via Suno, 28010 Agrate Conturbia
(0322) 832093
(0322) 832428
castelconturbia@tin.it
www.golfclubcastelconturbia.it

Castello di Tolcinasco (1993)
20090 Pieve Emanuele (MI)
(02) 9042 8035
(02) 9078 9051
golf@golftolcinasco.it
www.golftolcinasco.it

Franciacorta (1986)
Via Provinciale 34b, 25040 Nigoline di Corte Franca, (Brescia)
(030) 984167
(030) 984393
franciacortagolfclub@libero.it

Menaggio & Cadenabbia (1907)
Via Golf 12, 22010 Grandola E Uniti
(0344) 32103
(0344) 30780
segretaria@golfclubmenaggio.it
www.menaggio.it

Milano (1928)
20.900 Parco di Monza (MI)
(039) 303081/2/3
(039) 304427
info@golfclubmilano.com
Arnaldo Cocuzza (Mgr)
www.golfclubmilano.it

Molinetto CC (1982)
SS Padana Superiore 11, 20063 Cernusco S/N (MI)
(02) 9210 5128/9210 5983
(02) 9210 6635

Monticello (1975)
Via Volta 63, 22070 Cassina Rizzardi (Como)
(031) 928055
(031) 880207
monticello@tin.it
www.golfmonticello.it

La Pinetina Golf Club (1971)
Via al Golf 4, 22070 Appiano Gentile (CO)
(031) 933202
(031) 890342
info@golfpinetina.it
Simone Laureti (Club Mgr)
www.golfpinetina.it

Le Robinie (1992)
Via per Busto Arsizio 9, 21058 Solbiate Olona (VA)
(039) 331 329260
(039) 331 329266
info@lerobinie.com
www.lerobinie.com

La Rossera (1970)
Via Montebello 4, 24060 Chiuduno
(035) 838600
(035) 442 7047
golfrossera@libero.it

Le Rovedine (1978)
Via Karl Marx, 20090 Noverasco di Opera (Mi)
(02) 5760 6420
(02) 5760 6405
info@rovedine.com
www.rovedone.com

Varese (1934)
Via Vittorio Veneto 59, 21020 Luvinate (VA)
(0332) 229302/821293
(0332) 811293
info@golfclubvarese.it
Carlo Giraldi
www.golfclubvarese.it

Vigevano (1974)
Via Chitola 49, 27029 Vigevano (PV)
(0381) 346628/346077
(0381) 346091
golfvigevano@yahoo.it

Villa D'Este (1926)
Via Cantù 13, 22030 Montorfano (CO)
(031) 200200
(031) 200786
info@golfvilladeste.com
Andrea Contigiani
www.golfvilladeste.com

Zoate
20067 Zoate di Tribiano (MI)
(02) 9063 2183/9063 1861
(02) 9063 1861

Elba

Acquabona (1971)
57037 Portoferraio, Isola di Elba (LI)
(0565) 940066
(0565) 933410

Emilia Romagna

Adriatic GC Cervia (1985)
Via Jelenia Gora No 6, 48016 Cervia-Milano Marittima
(0544) 992786
(0544) 993410

Bologna (1959)
Via Sabattini 69, 40050 Monte San Pietro (BO)
(051) 969100
(051) 672 0017

Croara Country Club (1976)
Loc. Croara Nuova 23010 Gazzola (PC)
(0523) 977105
(0523) 977100
info@croaracountryclub.com
www.croaracountryclub.com

Matilde di Canossa (1987)
Via Casinazzo 1, 42100 San Bartolomeo, Reggio Emilia
(0522) 371295
(0522) 371204
golfcanossa@libero.it
www.tiscali.it/golfcanossa

Modena G&CC (1987)
Via Castelnuovo Rangone 4, 41050 Colombaro di Formigine (MO)
(059) 553482
(059) 553696
segretaria@modenagolf.it
Davide Colombarini
www.modenagolf.it

Riolo Golf La Torre (1992)
Via Limisano 10, Riolo Terme (RA)
(0546) 74035
(0546) 74076
info@golflatorre.it
Lamberto Di Giacinto
www.golflatorre.it

La Rocca (1985)
Via Campi 8, 43038 Sala Baganza (PR)
(0521) 834037

(0521) 834575
www.officeitalia.it/golflarocca

Gulf of Genoa

Garlenda (1965)
Via Golf 7, 17033 Garlenda
(0182) 580012
(0182) 580561
info@garlendagolf.it
Claudio Rota
www.garlendagolf.it

Marigola (1975)
Via Biaggini 5, 19032 Lerici (SP)
(0187) 970193
(0187) 970193
info@golfmarigola.it
www.golfmarigola.it

Pineta di Arenzano (1959)
Piazza del Golf 3, 16011 Arenzano (GE)
(010) 911 1817
(010) 911 1270

Rapallo (1930)
Via Mameli 377, 16035 Rapallo (GE)
(0185) 261777
(0185) 261779

Sanremo-Circolo Golf degli Ulivi (1932)
Via Campo Golf 59, 18038 Sanremo
(0184) 557093
(0184) 557388
info@golfsanremo.com
www.golfsanremo.com

Versilia (1990)
Via Sipe 100, 55045 Pietrasanta (LU)
(0584) 88 15 74
(0584) 75 22 72

Lake Garda & Dolomites

Asiago (1967)
Via Meltar 2, 36012 Asiago (VI)
(0424) 462721
(0424) 465133
www.golfasiago.it

Bogliaco (1912)
Via Golf 21, 25088 Toscolano-Maderno
(0365) 643006
(0365) 643006
golfbogliaco@tin.it
www.bogliaco.com

Ca' degli Ulivi (1988)
Via Ghiandare 2, 37010 Marciaga di Costermano (VR)
(045) 627 9030
(045) 627 9039
info@golfcadegliulivi.it
www.golfcadegliulivi.it

Campo Carlo Magno (1922)
Golf Hotel, 38084 Madonna di Campiglio (TN)
(0465) 440622
(0465) 440298

Folgaria (1987)
Loc Costa di Folgaria, 38064 Folgaria (TN)
(0464) 720480
(0464) 720480

Gardagolf CC (1985)
Via Angelo Omodeo 2, 25080 Soiano Del Lago (BS)
(0365) 674707 (Sec)
(0365) 674788
info@gardagolf.it
www.gardagolf.it

Karersee-Carezza
Loc Carezza 171, 39056 Welschofen-Nova Levante
(0471) 612200
(0471) 612200

Petersberg (1987)
Unterwinkel 5, 39050 Petersberg (BZ)
+39 0471 615122
+39 0471 615229
info@golfclubpetersberg.it
Hans-Peter Thaler
www.golfclubpetersberg.it

Ponte di Legno (1980)
Corso Milano 36, 25056 Ponte di Legno (BS)
(0364) 900306
(0364) 900555

Verona (1963)
Ca' del Sale 15, 37066 Sommacampagna
(045) 510060
(045) 510242
golfverona@libero.it
www.golfclubverona.com

Naples & South

Riva Dei Tessali (1971)
74011 Castellaneta
(099) 843 9251
(099) 843 9255

San Michele
Loc Bosco 8/9, 87022 Cetraro (CS)
(0982) 91012
(0982) 91430
sanmichele@sanmichele.it
www.sanmichele.it

Rome & Centre

Country Club Castelgandolfo (1987)
Via Santo Spirito 13, 00040 Castelgandolfo
(06) 931 2301
(06) 931 2244
info@golfclubcastelgandolfo.it
www.countryclubcastelgandolfo.it

Fioranello
CP 96, 00134 Roma (RM)
(06) 713 8080 - 213
(06) 713 8212
info@fioranellogolf.it
www.fioranellogolf.com

Marco Simone (1989)
Via di Marco Simone, 00012 Guidonia (RM)
(0774) 366469
(0774) 366476

Marediroma
Via Enna 30, 00040 Ardea (RM)
(06) 913 3250
(06) 913 3592
info@golfmarediroma.it
www.golfmarediroma.it

Nettuno
Via della Campana 18, 00048 Nettuno (RM)
(06) 981 9419
(06) 989 88142

Oasi Golf Club (1988)
Via Cogna 5, 04011 Aprilia (Roma)
0039-06-92746252/9268120
0039-06-9268502
info@oasigolf.it
Marina Lanza (President)
www.oasigolf.it

Olgiata (1961)
Largo Olgiata 15, 00123 Roma
(06) 308 89141
(06) 308 89968
secretaria@olgiatagolfclub.it
www.olgiatagolfclub.it

Parco de' Medici (1989)
Viale Salvatore Rebecchini, 00148 Roma
(06) 655 3477
(06) 655 3344
info@sheratongolf.it
www.sheraton.com/golfrome
www.golfclubparcodemedici.com

Pescara (1992)
Contrado Cerreto 58, 66010 Miglianico (CH)
(0871) 959566
(0871) 950363

Le Querce
San Martino, 01015 Sutri (VT)
(0761) 600789
(0761) 600142
info@golfclublequerce.it
www.golfclublequerce.it

Roma (1903)
Via Appia Nuova 716A, 00178 Roma
(06) 780 3407
(06) 783 46219

Tarquinia
Loc Pian di Spille, Via degli Alina 271, 01016 Marina Velca/Tarquinia (VT)
(0766) 812109

Sardinia

Is Molas (1975)
CP 49, 09010 Pula
(070) 924 1013/4
(070) 924 2121
ismolasgolf@ismolas.it
www.ismolas.it

Pevero GC Costa Smeralda (1972)
Cala di Volpe, 07021 Porto Cervo (SS)
☎ **+39 0789 958000**
🖷 +39 0789 96572
✉ pevero@starwoodhotels.cpm
🗐 www.golfclubpevero.com

Sicily

Il Pìcciolo (1988)
Strada Statale 120 km 200, 95012 Castiglione di Sicilia, (CT)-ITALIA
☎ **+39 (0942) 986252**
🖷 +39 (0942) 986138
✉ segreteria@ilpicciologolf.com
✍ Alfredo Petralia
🗐 www.ilpicciologolf.com

Turin & Piemonte

Alpino Di Stresa (1924)
Viale Golf Panorama 48, 28839 Vezzo (VB)
☎ **(0323) 20642**
🖷 (0323) 208900
✉ info@golfalpino.it
✍ Alessandro Aina
🗐 www.golfalpino.it

Biella Le Betulle (1958)
Regione Valcarozza, 13887 Magnano (BI)
☎ **(015) 679151**
🖷 (015) 679276
✉ info@golfclubbiella.it
✍ Riccardo Valzorio (Sec)
🗐 www.golfclubbiella.it

Golf Club del Cervino (1955)
11021 Breuil- Cervinia (AO)
☎ **+39 0166 949131**
🖷 +39 0166 940700
✉ info@golfcervino.com
🗐 www.golfcervino.com

Cherasco CC (1982)
Via Fraschetta 8, 12062 Cherasco (CN)
☎ **(0172) 489772/488489**
🖷 (0172) 488320
✉ info@golfcherasco.com
✍ Corrado Graglia (Dir)
🗐 www.golfcherasco.com

Cuneo (1990)
Via degli Angeli 3, 12012 Mellana-Bóves (CN)
☎ **(0171) 387041**
🖷 (0171) 390763

Le Fronde (1973)
Via Sant-Agostino 68, 10051 Avigliana (TO)
☎ **(011) 932 8053/0540**
🖷 (011) 932 0928

I Girasoli (1991)
Via Pralormo 315, 10022 Carmagnola (TO)
☎ **(011) 979 5088**
🖷 (011) 979 5228
✉ info@girasoligolf.it
✍ Renzo Dutto
🗐 www.girasoligolf.it

Iles Borromees (1987)
Loc Motta Rossa, 28833 Brovello Carpugnino (VB)
☎ **(0323) 929285**
🖷 (0323) 929190
✉ info@golfdesiles.it
✍ Marco Garbaccio
🗐 www.golfdesiles.it

Golf dei Laghi (1993)
Via Trevisani 6, 21028 Travedona Monate (VA)
☎ **(0332) 978101**
🖷 (0332) 977532

Margara (1975)
Via Tenuta Margara 7, 15043 Fubine (AL)
☎ **(0131) 778555**
🖷 (0131) 778772
✉ margara@golfmargara.com
✍ Gian Marco Griffi
🗐 www.golfmargara.it

La Margherita
Strada Pralormo 29, Carmagnola (TO)
☎ **(011) 979 5113**
🖷 (011) 979 5204
✉ golf.lamargherita@libero.it
🗐 www.golfclubmargherita.com

La Serra (1970)
Via Astigliano 42, 15048 Valenza (AL)
☎ **(0131) 954778**
🖷 (0131) 928294
✉ golfclublaserra@tin.it

Sestrieres (1932)
Piazza Agnelli 4, 10058 Sestrieres (TO)
☎ **(0122) 755170/76243**
🖷 (0122) 76294

Stupinigi (1972)
Corso Unione Sovietica 506, 10135 Torino
☎ **(011) 347 2640**
🖷 (011) 397 8038

Torino (1924)
Via Agnelli 40, 10070 Fiano Torinese
☎ **+39 (011) 923 5440/923 5670**
🖷 +39 (011) 923 5886
✉ info@circologolftorino.it
✍ Mr Mauro Stroppiana
🗐 www.circologolftorino.it

Vinovo (1986)
Via Stupinigi 182, 10048 Vinovo (TO)
☎ **(011) 965 3880**
🖷 (011) 962 3748

Tuscany & Umbria

Casentino (1985)
6 Via Fronzola, 52014 Poppi (Arezzo)
☎ **(0575) 529810**
🖷 (0575) 520167
✉ info@golfclubcasentino.it
🗐 www.golfclubcasentino.it

Circolo Golf Ugolino (1933)
Strada Chiantigiana 3, 50015 Grassina
☎ **(055) 230 1009/1085**
🖷 (055) 230 1141
✉ info@golfugolino.it

Conero GC Sirolo (1987)
Via Betellico 6, 60020 Sirolo (AN)
☎ **(071) 736 0613**
🖷 (071) 736 0380

Cosmopolitan G&CC (1992)
Viale Pisorno 60, 56018 Tirrenia
☎ **(050) 33633**
🖷 (050) 384707
✉ info@cosmopolitangolf.it
🗐 www.cosmopolitangolf.it

Lamborghini-Panicale (1992)
Loc Soderi 1, 06064 Panicale (PG)
☎ **(075) 837582**
🖷 (075) 837582
✉ info@lamborghini.191.it
✍ Zeke Martinez
🗐 www.lamborghinionline.it

Montecatini (1985)
Via Dei Brogi 1652, Loc Pievaccia, 51015 Monsummano Terme (Pistoia)
☎ **(0572) 62218**
🖷 (0572) 617435
✉ golf_montecatini@virgiuo.it
✍ Giannini Maria Stella
🗐 www.montecatinigolf.com

Le Pavoniere (1986)
Via Traversa Il Crocifisso, 59100 Prato
☎ **(0574) 620855**
🖷 (0574) 624558

Golf Club Perugia (1959)
Loc S.Sabina, 06132 - Perugia (PG)
☎ **(075) 517 2204**
🖷 (075) 517 2370
✉ info@golfclubperugia.it
✍ Matteo Bragone (Mgr)
🗐 www.golfclubperugia.it

Poggio dei Medici (1995)
Via San Gavino, 27 - Loc. Cignano, I-50038 Scarperia, (Florence)
☎ **(+39) 055 84350**
🖷 (+39) 055 843439
✉ info@golfpoggiodeimedici.com
✍ Cristiano Bevilacqua (Mgr)
🗐 www.golfpoggiodeimedici.com

Punta Ala (1964)
Via del Golf 1, 58040 Punta Ala (GR)
☎ **(0564) 922121/922719**
🖷 (0564) 920182
🗐 www.puntaAla.net/golf

Tirrenia (1968)
Viale San Guido, 56018 Tirrenia (PI)
☎ **(050) 37518**
🖷 (050) 33286

Venice & North East

Albarella Golf Club
Isola di Albarella, 45010 Rosolina (RO)
☎ **(0426) 330124**
🖷 (0426) 330830
✍ Gabriele Marangon

For key to symbols and European dialling codes see page 725

Cansiglio (1956)
CP 152, 31029 Vittorio Veneto
☎ **(0438) 585398**
(0438) 585398
golfcansiglio@tin.it
www.golfclubcansiglio.it

Colli Berici (1986)
Strada Monti Comunali, 36040 Brendola (VI)
☎ **(0444) 601780**
(0444) 400777

Frassanelle (1990)
Via Rialto, 5/A - 35030 Rovolon (PD)
☎ **(049) 991 0722**
(049) 991 0691
info@golffrassanelle.it
www.golffrassanelle.it

Lignano
Via Bonifica 3, 33054 Lignano Sabbiadoro (UD)
☎ **(0431) 428025**
(0431) 423230
www.golflignano.it

La Montecchia (1989)
Via Montecchia 12, 35030 Selvazzano (PD)
☎ **(049) 805 5550**
(049) 805 5737
info@golfmontecchia.it
www.golfmontecchia.it

Padova (1964)
35050 Valsanzibio di Galzigano Terme (PD)
☎ **(049) 913 0078**
(049) 913 1193
info@golfpadova.it
www.golfpadova.it

San Floriano-Gorizia (1987)
Castello di San Floriano, 34070 San Floriano del Collio (GO)
☎ **(0481) 884252/884234**
(0481) 884252/884052

Trieste (1954)
Via Padriciano 80, 34012 Trieste
☎ **(040) 226159/226270**
(040) 226159

Udine (1971)
Via dei Faggi 1, Località Villaverde, 33034 Fagagna (UD)
☎ **(0432) 800418**
(0432) 801312
info@golfudine.com
www.golfudine.com

Venezia (1928)
Strada Vecchia 1, 30126 Alberoni (Venezia)
☎ **(041) 731333**
(041) 731339
info@circologolfvenezia.it
www.circologolfvenezia.it

Villa Condulmer (1960)
Via della Croce 3, 31020 Zerman di Mogliano Veneto - Tv
☎ **(041) 457062**
(041) 457202
info@golfvillacondulmer.com
www.golfvillacondulmer.com

Latvia

Ozo Golf Club (2002)
Milgravju iela 16, Riga, LV-1034
☎ **+371 6739 4399**
+371 6739 4034
ozogolf@apollo.lv
www.ozogolf.lv

Saliena (2006)
Egluciems, Babites pagasts, Rigas rajons LV-2107
☎ **+371 6716 0300**
+371 6714 6322
golf@saliena.com
www.saliena.com

Viesturi Golf Club (1998)
Viesturi-1, Jaunmärupe, Märupes pagasts, LV-2166
☎ **+371 2921 9699**
+371 6747 0030
sandra@golfsviesturi.lv
www.golfsviesturi.lv

Luxembourg

Christnach (1993)
Am Lahr, 7641 Christnach
☎ **87 83 83**
87 95 64
gcc@gns.lu
Claus Uwe Leske (Mgr)
www.golfclubchristnach.lu

Clervaux (1992)
Mecherwee, 9748 Eselborn
☎ **92 93 95**
92 94 51
gcclerv@pt.lu
www.golfclervaux.lu

Gaichel
Rue de Eischen, 8469 Gaichel
☎ **39 71 08**
39 00 75
infogolf@golfgaichel.com
www.golfgaichel.com

Golf de Luxembourg (1993)
Domaine de Belenhaff, L-6141 Junglinster
☎ **(00252) 78 00 68-1**
(00352) 78 71 28
info@golfdeluxembourg.lu
www.golfdeluxembourg.lu

Grand-Ducal de Luxembourg (1936)
1 Route de Trèves, 2633 Senningerberg
☎ **34 00 90-1**
34 83 91
gcgd@pt.lu
Mr Philippe Dewolf
www.gcgd.lu

Kikuoka Country Club (1991)
Scheierhaff, L-5412 Canach
☎ **+352 35 61 35**
+352 35 74 50
playgolf@kikuoka.lu
Patrick Platz (Gen Mgr)
www.kikuoka.lu

Malta

Royal Malta (1888)
Aldo Moro Street, Marsa MRS 9064
☎ **(356) 21 22 70 19**
(356) 21 22 70 20
sales@royalmaltagolfclub.com
www.royalmaltagolfclub.com

Netherlands

Amsterdam & Noord Holland

Amsterdam Old Course (1990)
Zwarte Laantje 4, 1099 CE Amsterdam
☎ **(020) 663 1766**
(020) 663 4621
info@amsterdamoldcourse.nl
Mr B Flik
www.amsterdamoldcourse.nl

Amsterdamse (1934)
Bauduinlaan 35, 1047 HK Amsterdam
☎ **(020) 497 7866**
(020) 497 5966
agc1934@wxs.nl
www.amsterdamsegolfclub.nl

BurgGolf Purmerend (1989)
Westerweg 60, 1445 AD Purmerend
☎ **(+31) 299 689160**
(+31) 299 647081
purmerend@burggolf.nl
www.burggolf.nl

Haarlemmermeersche Golf Club (1986)
Spieringweg 745, 2142 ED Cruquius
☎ **(023) 558 9000**
(023) 558 9009
info@haarlemmermeersche golfclub.nl
www.haarlemmermeerschegolfclub .nl

Heemskerkse (1998)
Communicatieweg 18, 1967 PR Heemskerk
☎ **(0251) 250088**
(0251) 241627
manager@heemskerksegolfclub.nl
Pien van Nass (Manager)
www.heemskerksegolfclub.nl

Kennemer G&CC (1910)
Kennemerweg 78, 2042 XT Zandvoort
☎ **+31 (0)23 571 2836/8456**
+31 (0)23 571 9520

For key to symbols and European dialling codes see page 725

info@kennemergolf.nl
Mr J Gelderman
www.kennemergolf.nl

De Noordhollandse (1982)
Sluispolderweg 6, 1817 BM Alkmaar
(072) 515 6807
(072) 520 9918
secretariaat @denoordhollandsegolfclub.nl
Anita Von Schie (Club Mgr)
www.denoordhollandsegolfclub.nl

Olympus (1976)
Abcouderstraatweg 46, 1105 AA Amsterdam Zuid-Oost
(0294) 281241
(0294) 286347
www.olympusgolf.nl

Spaarnwoude (1977)
Het Hoge Land 5, 1981 LT Velsen-Zuid
(023) 538 2708 (club)
(023) 538 7274
www.gcspaarnwoude.nl

Waterlandse (1990)
Buikslotermeerdijk 141, 1027 AC Amsterdam
(020) 636 1040
(020) 634 3506
info@golfbaanamsterdam.nl
www.golfbaanamsterdam.nl

Zaanse (1988)
Zuiderweg 68, 1456 NH Wijdewormer
(0299) 438199
(0299) 474416
secretariaat@zaansegolfclub.com
www.zaansegolfclub.com

Breda & South West

Brugse Vaart (1993)
Brugse Vaart 10, 4501 NE Oostburg
(0117) 453410
(0117) 455511
info@golfoostburg.com
www.golfoostburg.com

Domburgsche (1914)
Schelpweg 26, 4357 BP Domburg
(0118) 586106
(0118) 586109
secretariaat@domburgschegolfclub.nl
www.domburgschegolfclub.nl

Efteling Golf Park (1995)
Postbus 18, 5170 AA Kaatsheuvel, Holland
+31 (0) 416 288 499
golfpark@efteling.com
www.efteling.nl

Grevelingenhout (1988)
Oudendijk 3, 4311 NA Bruinisse
(0111) 482650
(0111) 481566

Oosterhoutse (1985)
Dukaatstraat 21, 4903 RN Oosterhout
(0162) 458759
(0162) 433285

info@ogcgolf.nl
www.ogcgolf.nl

Princenbosch (1991)
Bavelseweg 153, 5126 PX Molenschot
(0161) 431811
(0161) 434254
golfclub@princenbosch.nl
Mr R C J Beenackers
www.princenbosch.nl

Toxandria (1928)
Veenstraat 89, 5124 NC Molenschot
(0161) 411200
(0161) 411715
secretariaat@toxandria.nl
Mw E Nollen
www.toxandria.nl

De Woeste Kop (1986)
Justaasweg 4, 4571 NB Axel
(0115) 564467
dewoestekop@planet.nl
www.dewoestekop.nl

Wouwse Plantage (1981)
Zoomvlietweg 66, 4624 RP Bergen op Zoom
(0165) 377100
(0165) 377101
secretariaat@golfwouwseplantage.nl
R W Van de Pol
www.golfwouwseplantage.nl

East Central

Breuninkhof
Bussloselaan 6, 7383 RP Bussloo
(0571) 261955
(0571) 262089
carla@unigolf.ni

Edese (1978)
Papendallaan 22, 6816 VD Arnhem
(026) 482 1985
(026) 482 1348
info@edesegolf.nl
www.edesegolf.nl

De Graafschap (1987)
Sluitdijk 4, 7241 RR Lochem
(0573) 254323
(0573) 258450
info@lochemsegolfclub.nl
P Grootoonk
www.lochemsegolfclub.nl

Hattemse G&CC (1930)
Veenwal 11, 8051 AS Hattem
(038) 444 1909
secretariaat@golfclub-hattem.nl
www.golfclub-hattem.nl

Keppelse (1926)
Oude Zutphenseweg 15, 6997 CH Hoog-Keppel
(0314) 301416
dekeppelse@planet.nl
www.keppelse.com

De Koepel (1983)
Postbox 88, 7640 AB Wierden
(0546) 576150/574070
(0546) 578109
info@golfclubdekoepel.nl
www.golfclubdekoepel.nl

Golfbaan Het Rijk van Nunspeet (1987)
Public
Plesmanlaan 30, 8072 PT Nunspeet
(0341) 255255
(0341) 255285
info@golfbaanhetrijkvannunspeet.nl
www.golfenophetrijk.nl

Rosendaelsche (1895)
Apeldoornseweg 450, 6816 SN Arnhem
+31 26 442 1438
info@rosendaelsche.nl
F J M König (Secretary)
www.rosendaelsche.nl

Sallandsche De Hoek (1934)
Golfweg 2, 7431 PR Diepenveen
(0570) 593269
(0570) 590102
secretariaat@sallandsche.nl
Mrs J Visschers
www.sallandsche.nl

Golfbaan Het Rijk van Sybrook (1992)
Veendijk 100, 7525 PZ Enschede
(0541) 530331
(0541) 531690
info@golfbaanhetrijkvansybrook.nl
www.golfengohetrijk.nl

Twentsche (1926)
Almelosestraat 17, 7495 TG Ambt Delden
(074) 384 1167
(074) 384 1067
info@twentschegolfclub.nl
Ed Davids (Executive Sec)
www.twentschegolfclub.nl

Veluwse (1957)
Nr 57, 7346 AC Hoog Soeren
(055) 519 1275
(055) 519 1126
secretariaat@veluwsegolfclub.nl
www.veluwsegolfclub.nl

Welderen (1994)
POB 114, 6660AC Elst
(0481) 376591
(0481) 377055
golfclub@welderen.nl
E Kleyngeld (Sec)
www.golfclubwelderen.nl

Eindhoven & South East

Best G&CC (1988)
Golflaan 1, 5683 RZ Best
(0499) 391443
(0499) 393221
vereniging@bestgolf.nl
www.bestgolf.nl

BurgGolf Gendersteyn Veldhoven (1994)
Locht 140, 5504 RP Veldhoven
☎ **(040) 253 4444**
(040) 254 9747
gendersteyn@burggolf.nl
www.burggolf.nl

Golfclub BurgGolf Wijchen (1985)
Public
Weg Door de Berendonck 40, 6603 LP Wijchen
☎ **(024) 642 0039**
(024) 641 1254
wijchen@burggolf.nl
www.burggolf.nl

Crossmoor G&CC (1986)
Laurabosweg 8, 6006 VR Weert
☎ **(0495) 518438**
(0495) 518709
crossmoor@planel.nl
www.crossmoor.nl

De Dommel (1928)
Zegenwerp 12, 5271 NC St Michielsgestel
☎ **(073) 551 9168**
(073) 551 9441
info@gcdedommel.nl
www.gcdedommel.nl

Eindhovensche Golf (1930)
Eindhovenseweg 300, 5553 VB Valkenswaard
☎ **(040) 201 4816**
(040) 207 6177
egolf@iae.nl
www.eindhovenschegolf.nl

Geijsteren G&CC (1974)
Het Spekt 2, 5862 AZ Geijsteren
☎ **(0478) 531809/532592**
(0478) 532963
gc.geijsteren@planet.nl
www.golfclubgeijsteren.nl

Havelte (1986)
Kolonieweg 2, 7970 AA Havelte
☎ **(0521) 342200**
(0521) 343152
info@golfclubhavelte.nl
www.golfclubhavelte.nl

Haviksoord (1976)
Maarheezerweg Nrd 11, 5595 XG Leende (NB)
☎ **(040) 206 1818**
(040) 206 2761
info@haviksoord.nl
A W (Tony) Jackson (Manager)
www.haviksoord.nl

Herkenbosch (1991)
Stationsweg 100, 6075 CD Herkenbosch
☎ **(0475) 529529**
(0475) 533580
herkenbosch@burggolf.nl
www.gccherkenbosch.nl

Het Rijk van Nijmegen (1985)
Postweg 17, 6561 KJ Groesbeek
☎ **(024) 397 6644**
(024) 397 6942
info@golfbaanhetrijkvannijmegen.nl
www.golfenophetrijk.nl

De Peelse Golf (1991)
Maasduinenweg 1, 5977 NP Evertsoord-Sevenum
☎ **(077) 467 8030**
(077) 467 8031
info@depeelsegolf.nl
www.depeelsegolf.nl

De Schoot (1973)
Schootsedijk 18, 5491 TD Sint Oedenrode
☎ **(04134) 73011**
(04134) 71358
info@golfbaandeschoot.nl
www.golfbaandeschoot.nl

Tongelreep G&CC (1984)
Charles Roelslaan 15, 5644 HX Eindhoven
☎ **(040) 252 0962**
(040) 293 2238
gcc@golfdetongelreep.nl
H C Smits (Sec)
www.golfdetongelreep.nl

Welschap (1993)
Welschapsedijk 164, 5657 BB Eindhoven
☎ **(040) 251 5797**
(040) 252 9297
secretariaat@golfclubwelschap.nl
www.golfclubwelschap.nl

Limburg Province

Brunssummerheide (1985)
Rimburgerweg 50, Brunssum
☎ **(045) 527 0968**
(045) 527 3939
secr@golfbrunssummerheide.nl
www.golfbrunssummerheide.nl

Hoenshuis G&CC (1987)
Hoensweg 17, 6367 GN Voerendaal
☎ **+31 (0) 45 575 33 00**
+31 (0) 45 575 09 00
info@hoenshuis.nl
www.hoenshuisgolf.nl

De Zuid Limburgse G&CC (1956)
Aubelsweg 1, 6281 NC Gulpen-Wittem, (GPS: Landsrade 1, 6271 NZ Gulpen-Wittem)
☎ **(043) 455 1397/1254**
(043) 455 1576
secretariaat@zlgolf.nl
www.zlgolf.nl

North

BurgGolf St Nicobasga (1990)
Legemeersterweg 16-18, 8527 DS Legemeer
☎ **(0513) 499466**
(0513) 499777
st.nicobasga@burggolf.nl
www.burggolf.nl

Gelpenberg (1970)
Gebbeveenweg 1, 7854 TD Aalden
☎ **(0591) 371929**
(0591) 372422
info@dgcgelpenberg.nl
www.dgcdegelpenberg.nl

Holthuizen (1985)
Oosteinde 7a, 9301 ZP Roden
☎ **(050) 501 5103**
golfclub.holthuizen@planet.nl
www.gc-holthuizen.nl

Lauswolt G&CC (1964)
Van Harinxmaweg 8A, PO Box 36, 9244 ZN Beetsterzwaag
☎ **(0512) 383590**
(0512) 383739
algemeen@golfclublauswolt.nl
www.golfclublauswolt.nl

Noord-Nederlandse G&CC (1950)
Pollselaan 5, 9756 CJ Glimmen
☎ **(050) 406 2004**
(050) 406 1922
secretariaat@nngcc.nl
The Secretary
www.nngcc.nl

De Semslanden (1986)
Nieuwe Dijk 1, 9514 BX Gasselternijveen
☎ **(0599) 564661/565531**
(0599) 565594
semslanden@planet.nl
www.golfclubdesemslanden.nl

Rotterdam & The Hague

Broekpolder (1981)
Watersportweg 100, 3138 HD Vlaardingen
☎ **(010) 249 5566**
(010) 249 5579
secretariaat@golfclubbroekpolder.nl
www.golfclubbroekpolder.nl

Golf & Country Club Capelle a/d IJssel (1977)
Gravenweg 311, 2905 LB Capelle a/d IJssel
☎ **(010) 442 2485**
(010) 284 0606
info@golfclubcapelle.nl
www.golfclubcapelle.nl

Cromstrijen (1989)
Veerweg 26, 3281 LX Numansdorp
☎ **(0186) 654455**
(0186) 654681
info@golfclubcromstrijen.nl
www.golfclubcromstrijen.nl

De Hooge Bergsche (1989)
Rottebandreef 40, 2661 JK Bergschenhoek
☎ **(010) 522 0052/522 0703**
(08) 422 32305
secretariaat@hoogebergsche.nl
www.hoogebergsche.nl

Koninklijke Haagsche G&CC (1893)
Groot Haesebroekeseweg 22, 2243 EC Wassenaar
☎ **(070) 517 9607**
(070) 514 0171
secretariaat@khgcc.nl
H P Wirth (Mgr)
www.khgcc.nl

Kralingen
Kralingseweg 200, 3062 CG Rotterdam
☎ **(010) 452 2283**
secretaris@gckralingen.nl
www.gckralingen.nl

Leidschendamse Leeuwenbergh (1988)
Elzenlaan 31, 2495 AZ Den Haag
☎ **(070) 395 4556**
(070) 399 8615
secretariaat@leeuwenbergh.nl
www.leeuwenbergh.nl

De Merwelanden (1985)
Public
Golfbaan Crayestein, Baanhoekweg 50, 3313 LP Dordrecht
☎ **(078) 621 1221**
(078) 616 1036

Noordwijkse Golf Club (1915)
Randweg 25, PO Box 70, 2200 AB Noordwijk
☎ **(0252) 373761**
(0252) 370044
info@noordwijksegolfclub.nl
N H Smittenaar
www.noordwijksegolfclub.nl

Oude Maas (1975)
(Rhoon Golfcenter), Veerweg 2a, 3161 EX Rhoon
☎ **(010) 501 5135**
(010) 501 5604
golfcluboudemaas@kebelfoon.nl
www.golfcluboudemaas.nl

Rijswijkse (1987)
Delftweg 59, 2289 AL Rijswijk
☎ **(070) 395 4864**
(070) 399 5040
secretariaat@rijswijksegolf.nl
www.rijswijksegolf.nl

Wassenaarse Golfclub Rozenstein (1984)
Dr Mansveltkade 15, 2242 TZ Wassenaar
☎ **+31 (070) 511 7846**
secretariaat@rozenstein.nl
Miss IP Slikker (Office Mgr)
www.rozenstein.nl

Westerpark Zoetermeer (1985)
Heuvelweg 3, 2716 DZ Zoetermeer, Ogoo-Burg Golf
☎ **(0900) 28744653**
(079) 3203132
zoetermeer@burggolf.nl
Mr V Slooten
www.burggolf.nl

Zeegersloot (1984)
Kromme Aarweg 5, PO Box 190, 2400 AD Alphen a/d Rijn
☎ **(0172) 474567**
(0172) 494660
secretariaat@zeegersloot.nl
www.zeegersloot.nl

Utrecht & Hilversum

Almeerderhout (1986)
Watersnipweg 19-21, 1341 AA Almere
☎ **(036) 521 9160**
(036) 521 9131
secretariaat@almeerderhout.nl
www.almeerderhout.nl

Anderstein (1986)
Woudenbergseweg 13a, 3953 ME Maarsbergen
☎ **(0343) 431330**
(0343) 432062
info@golfclubanderstein.nl
www.golfclubanderstein.nl

De Batouwe (1990)
Oost Kanaalweg 1, 4011 LA Zoelen
☎ **(0344) 624370**
(0344) 613096
secretariaat@debatouwe.nl
Mrs ER de Regt-uan Dijk
www.debatouwe.nl

Flevoland (1979)
Parlaan 2A, 8241 BG Lelystad
☎ **(0320) 230077**
(0320) 230932
info@golfflevo.nl
www.golfflevo.nl

De Haar (1974)
PO Box 104, Parkweg 5, 3450 AC Vleuten
☎ **(030) 677 2860**
(030) 677 3903
gcdehaar@xs4all.nl
www.gcdehaar.nl

Hilversumsche Golf Club (1910)
Soestdijkerstraatweg 172, 1213 XJ Hilversum
☎ **(035) 685 70 60 choose 2**
clubmanager @hilversumschegolfclub.nl
Mrs M G van den Hengel-Smink
www.hilversumschegolfclub.nl

De Hoge Kleij (1985)
Loes van Overeemlaan 16, 3832 RZ Leusden
☎ **(033) 461 6944**
(033) 465 2921
secretariaat@hogekleij.nl
www.hogekleij.nl

Nieuwegeinse (1985)
Postbus 486, 3437 AL Nieuwegein
☎ **(030) 604 2192**
(030) 636 9410

Utrechtse Golf Club 'De Pan' (1894)
Amersfoortseweg 1, 3735 LJ Bosch en Duin
☎ **(030) 696 9120**
(030) 696 3769
secretariaat@ugcdepan.nl
Secretary
www.ugcdepan.nl

Zeewolde (1984)
Golflaan 1, 3896 LL Zeewolde
☎ **(036) 522 2103**
(036) 522 4100
secretariaat@golfclub-zeewolde.nl
B Beekmans (Mgr)
www.golfclub-zeewolde.nl

Norway

Arendal og Omegn (1986)
Nes Verk, 4900 Tvedestrand
☎ **37 19 90 30**
37 16 02 11
post@arendalgk.no
www.arendalgk.no

Baerum GK (1972)
Hellerudveien 26, 1350 Lommedalen
☎ **67 87 67 00**
67 87 67 20
bmgk@bmgk.no
Brede Kristoffersen
www.bmgk.no

Bergen Golf Clubb (1937)
Ervikveien 120, 5106 Øvre Ervik
☎ **55 19 91 80**
55 19 91 81
info@bgk.no
www.bgk.no

Borre (1991)
Semb Hovedgaard, 3186 Horten
☎ **416 27000**
33 07 15 16
borregb@online.no
Thomas Pedersen
www.borregolf.no

Borregaard (1927)
PO Box 348, 1702 Sarpsborg
☎ **69 12 15 00**
69 15 74 11
borregaardgk@golf.no
www.borregaardgk.no

Drøbak (1988)
Belsjøveien 50, 1440 Drøbak
☎ **+47 64 98 96 50**
dgko@drobakgolf.no
www.drobakgolf.no

Elverum (1980)
PO Box 71, 2401 Elverum
☎ **62 41 35 88**
62 41 55 13
post@elverumgolf.no
www.elverumgolf.no

Grenland (1976)
Luksefjellvn 578, 3721 Skien
☎ **35 50 62 70**
35 59 06 10
post@grenlandgolf.no
www.grenlandgolf.no

Groruddalen (1988)
Postboks 37, Stovner, 0913 Oslo
☎ **22 79 05 60**
22 79 05 79
post@grorudgk.no
www.grorudgk.no

Hemsedal (1994)
3560 Hemsedal
☎ **32 06 23 77**
32 06 00 84

Kjekstad (1976)
PO Box 201, 3440 Royken
☎ **31 29 79 90**
31 29 79 99

Kristiansand (2003)
PO Box 6090 Søm, 4691 Kristiansand
☎ **38 14 85 60**
38 04 34 15
post@kristiansandgk.no
www.kristiansandgk.no

Larvik (1989)
Fritzøe Gård, 3267 Larvik
☎ **33 140 140**
33 14 01 49
klubben@larvikgolf.no
Horten Ertsas
www.larvikgolf.no

Narvik (1992)
8523 Elvegard
☎ **76 95 12 01**
76 95 12 06
post@narvikgolf.no
www.narvikgolf.no

Nes (1988)
Rommen Golfpark, 2160 Vormsund
☎ **63 91 20 30**
63 91 20 31
bente@nesgolfklubb.no
www.nesgolfklubb.no

Onsøy (1987)
Golfveien, 1626 Manstad
☎ **+47 69 33 91 50**
+47 69 33 91 51

Oppegård (1985)
Kongeveien 198, 1415 Oppegård
☎ **66 81 59 90**
66 81 59 91
leder@opgk.no
www.opgk.no

Oslo (1924)
Bogstad, 0757 Oslo
☎ **22 51 05 60**
22 51 05 61
post@oslogk.no
Niels Vik
www.oslogk.no

Ostmarka (1989)
Postboks 63, 1914 Ytre Enebakk
☎ **64 92 38 40**
64 92 47 55

Oustoen CC (1965)
PO Box 100, 1330 Fornebu
☎ **67 83 23 80/22 56 33 54**
67 53 95 44/22 59 91 83
occ@occ.no
www.occ.no

Sorknes (1990)
PB 100, 2451 Rena
☎ **45 20 86 00**
post@sorknesgk.no
Mr Ken Baareng/Mr Lasse Bendixen
www.sorknesgk.no

Stavanger (1956)
Longebakke 45, 4042 Hafrsfjord
☎ **519 39100**
519 39110
steinar@sgk.no
Steinar Fløisvik
www.sgk.no

Trondheim (1950)
PO Box 169, 7401 Trondheim
☎ **73 53 18 85**
73 52 75 05
www.golfklubben.no

Tyrifjord (1982)
Sturoya, 3531 Krokleiva
☎ **32 16 13 60**
32 16 13 40
www.tyrifjord-golfklubb.no

Vestfold (1958)
PO Box 64, 3108 Vear
☎ **33 36 25 00**
33 36 25 01
vgk@vestfoldgolfklubb.no
Knut Gran
www.vgk.no

Poland

Amber Baltic (1993)
Baltycka Street 13, 72-514 Kolczewo
☎ **(091) 32 65 110/120**
(091) 32 65 333
abgc@abgc.pol.pl
www.abgc.pl

Portugal

Algarve

Clube de Golfe de Vale do Lobo (1968)
Vale Do Lobo, 8135-864 Vale do Lobo
☎ **+351 289 353 465**
+351 289 353 003
golf@vdl.pt
www.valedolobo.com

Floresta Parque (1987)
Vale do Poço, Budens, 8650 Vila do Bispo
☎ **(282) 690 054**
(282) 695 157
alan.hodsongolf@vigiasa.com
Alan Hodson

Oceânico Pinhal (1976)
Apartado 970, 8126-912 Vilamoura, Algarve
☎ **(0289) 310390**
(0289) 310393
bookings@oceanicogolf.com
www.oceanicogolf.com

Oceânico Academy Course (2008)
Apartado 970, 8126-912 Vilamoura, Algarve
☎ **00 351 282 320 800**
00 351 282 313 760
bookings@oceanicogolf.com
www.oceanicogolf.com

Oceânico Faldo Course (2008)
Apartado 970, 8126-912 Vilamoura, Algarve
☎ **00 351 282 320 800**
00 351 282 313 760
bookings@oceanicogolf.com
www.oceanicogolf.com

Oceânico Laguna (1990)
Apartado 970, 8126-912 Vilamoura, Algarve
☎ **(0289) 310180**
(0289) 310183
bookings@oceanicogolf.com
www.oceanicogolf.com

Oceanico Millennium (2000)
Apartado 970, 8126-912 Vilamoura, Algarve
☎ **(0289) 310188**
(0289) 310183
bookings@oceanicogolf.com
www.oceanicogolf.com

Oceânico O'Connor Jnr (2008)
Apartado 970, 8126-912 Vilamoura, Algarve
☎ **00 351 282 320 800**
00 351 282 313 760
bookings@odeanicogolf.com
www.oceanicogolf.com

Oceânico Old Course (1969)
Apartado 970, 8126-912 Vilamoura, Algarve
☎ **(289) 310341**
(289) 310321
bookings@oceanicogolf.com
www.oceanicogolf.com

Oceânico Victoria (2004)
Apartado 970, 8126-912 Vilamoura, Algarve
☎ **00 351 289 320 100**
00 351 289 320 104
bookings@oceanicogolf.com

For key to symbols and European dialling codes see page 725

✍ Romeu Mendes Gonçalves
www.oceanicogolf.com

Palmares (1975)
Apartado 74, Meia Praia, 8601 901 Lagos
☎ **+351 282 790500**
+351 282 290509
golf@palmaresgolf.com
www.palmaresgolf.com

Penina (1966)
PO Box 146, Penina, 8501-952 Portimào
☎ **(351) 282 420223**
(351) 282 420252
golf.penina@lemeridien.com
www.lemeridien.com/peninagolf

Pestana (1991)
Apartado 1011, 8400-908 Carvoeiro Lga
☎ **(0282) 340900**
(0282) 340901
info@pestanagolf.com
www.pestanagolf.com

Pestana Alto Golf (1991)
Quinta do Alto do Poço, 8501 906 Alvor
☎ **(00351) 282 460870**
(00351) 282 460879
info@pestanagolf.com
www.pestanagolf.com

Pine Cliffs G&CC (1991)
Praia da Falesia, PO Box 644, 8200-909 Albufeira
☎ **(+351) 289 500100**
(+351) 289 501950
sheraton.algarve@starwoodhotels.com

Pinheiros Altos (1992)
Quinta do Lago, 8135 Almancil
☎ **(0289) 359910**
(0289) 394392
golf@pinheirosaltos.pt
✍ Christophe Rindlisbacher
www.pinheirosaltos.pt

Quinta do Lago (1974)
Quinta Do Lago, 8135-024 Almancil
☎ **(+351) 289 390 700**
(+351) 289 394 013
geral@quintadolagogolf.com
✍ Patrick Murphy
www.quintadolagogolf.com

Salgados
Apartado 2362, Vale do Rabelho, 8200 917 Albufeira
☎ **(0289) 583030**
(0289) 591112

San Lorenzo (1888)
Quinta do Lago, 8135 Almancil
☎ **+351 289 396 522**
+351 289 396 908
sanlorenzo@jjwhotels.com
✍ António Rosa Santos (Mgr)
www.sanlorenzogolfcourse.com

Vale de Milho (1990)
Apartado 1273, Praia do Carvoeiro, 8401-911 Carvoeiro Lga
☎ **(282) 358502**
(282) 358497
reservas@valedemilhogolf.com
✍ M Stilwell (President)
www.valedemilhogolf.com

Clube de Golfe de Vale do Lobo (1968)
Vale Do Lobo, 8135-864 Vale do Lobo
☎ **+351 289 353 465**
+351 289 353 003
golf@vdl.pt
✍ Hernani Estevão (Golf Mgr)
www.valedolobo.com

Vila Sol Spa & Golf Resort (1991)
Alto do Semino, Morgadinhos, Vilamoura, 8125-307-Quarteira
☎ **(+351) 289 300505**
(+351) 289 316499
golfreservation@vilasol.pt
www.vilasol.pt

Azores

Batalha Golf Course (1996)
Rua do Bom Jesus, Aflitos, 9545-234 Fenais da Luz (Açores)
☎ **+351 296 498 599/560**
+351 296 498 612
info@azoresgolfislands.com
✍ Pilar Melo Antunes
www.azoresgolfislands.com

Furnas Golf Course (1936)
Achada das Furnas, 9675 Furnas
☎ **(+351) 296 498 559/560**
(+351) 296 498 612
info@azoresgolfislands.com
✍ Pilar Melo Antunes
www.azoresgolfislands.com

Terceira Island (1954)
Caixa Postal 15, 9760 909 Praia da Victória (Açores)
☎ **(0295) 902444**
(0295) 902445

Lisbon & Central Portugal

Aroeira (1972)
Herdade da Aroeira, 2820-567 Charneca da Caparica
☎ **+351 (212) 979 110/1**
+351 (212) 971 238
golf.reservas@aroeira.com
www.aroeira.com

Belas Clube de Campo (1998)
Alameda do Aqueduto, Escritórios Belas Clube de Campo, 2605-193 Belas
☎ **(00351) 21 962 6640**
(00351) 21 962 6641
golfe@planbelas.pt
✍ Salvador Leite de Castro (Sec)
www.belasclubedecampo.pt

Estoril (1936)
Avenida da República, 2765-273 Estoril
☎ **(351) 21466 0367**
(351) 21468 2796
reserva@golfestoril.com
www.palacioestorilhotel.com

Estoril-Sol Golf Academy (1976)
Quinta do Outeira, Linhó, 2710 Sintra
☎ **(01) 923 2461**
(01) 923 2461

Lisbon Sports Club (1922)
Casal da Carregueira, 2605-213 Belas
☎ **(21) 431 0077**
(21) 431 2482
geral@lisbonclub.com
www.lisbonclub.com

Marvão (1998)
Quinta do Prado, São Salvador da Aramenha, 7330-328 Marvão
☎ **(245) 993 755**
(245) 993 805

Golf do Montado (1992)
Urbanização do Golf Montando, Lte no.1 - Algeruz, 2950-051 Palmela
☎ **(265) 708150**
(265) 708159
geral@golfdomontando.com.pt
www.golfmontando.com.pt

Penha Longa (1992)
Estrada da Lagoa Azul, Linhó, 2714-511 Sintra
☎ **(021) 924 9011**
(021) 924 9024
reservas.golf@penhalonga.com
www.penhalonga.com

Quinta da Beloura (1994)
Estrada de Albarraque, 2710 692 Sintra
☎ **(021) 910 6350**
(021) 910 6359
beloura.golfe@pestana.com
www.pestanagolf.com

Quinta da Marinha Oitavos Golfe (2001)
Quinta da Marinha, Casa da Quinta No25, 2750-715 Cascais
☎ **351 21 486 06 00**
351 21 486 06 09
oitavosgolfe@quinta-da-marinha.pt
www.quintadamarinha-oitavosgolfe.pt

Quinta do Perú Golf & Country Club (1994)
Alameda da Serra 2, 2975-666 Quinta do Conde
☎ **(021) 213 4320**
(021) 213 4321
pedro@golfquintadoperu.com
✍ Pedro De Mello Breyner (Club Mgr)
www.golfquintadoperu.com

Tróia Golf Championship Course (1980)
Tróia, 7570-789 Carvalhal
(+351) 265 494 112
(+351) 265) 494 315
troiagolf@sonae.pt
www.troiagolf.com

Vimeiro
Praia do Porto Novo, Vimeiro, 2560 Torres Vedras
(061) 984157
(061) 984621

Madeira

Madeira (1991)
Sto Antonio da Serra, 9200 Machico, Madeira
(091) 552345/552356
(091) 552367

Palheiro (1993)
Rua do Balancal No.29, 9060-414 Funchal, Madeira
(00351) 291 790 120
(00351) 291 792 456
reservations.golf@palheiroestate .com
www.palheiroestate.com

North

Amarante (1997)
Quinta da Deveza, Fregim, 4600-593 Amarante
+351 255 44 60 60
+351 255 44 62 02
sgagolfeamarante@oninet.pt
www.amarantegolfclube.com

Golden Eagle (1994)
E.N. 1, Km 63/64, Asseicera, 2040-481 Rio Maior
+351 243 940040
+351 243 940049
reservations@goldeneagle.pt
David Ashington
www.goldeneagle.pt

Miramar (1932)
Av Sacadura Cabral, Miramar, 4405-013 Arcozelo V.N.Gaia
(022) 762 2067
(022) 762 7859
cgm@cgm.pt
President Alvaro Teles De Meneses
www.cgm.pt

Montebelo
Farminhão, 3510 Viseu
(032) 856464
(032) 856401

Oporto Golf Club (1890)
Sisto-Paramos, 4500 Espinho
(022) 734 2008
(022) 734 6895
oportogolfclub@oninet.pt
www.oportogolfclub.com

Ponte de Lima
Quinta de Pias, Fornelos, 4490 Ponte de Lima
(058) 43414
(058) 743424

Praia d'el Rey G&CC (1997)
Vale de Janelas, Apartado 2, 2510 Obidos
(+351) 262 905005
(+351) 262 905009
golf@praia-del-rey.com
www.praia-del-rey.com

Golfe Quinta da Barca (1997)
Barca do Lago, 4740-476 Esposende
(+351) 2539 66723
(+351) 2539 969068
lcatarino@quintabarca.com
www.quintabarca.com

Vidago Palace Golf Course (1936)
Parque de Vidago, Apartado 16, 5425-307 Vidago
00351 276 990 980
00351 276 990 912
golf@vidagopalace.com
Santiago Villar (Asst Mgr)
www.vidagopalace.com

Slovenia

Bled G&CC (1937)
Public
Kidriceva 10 c, 4260 Bled
+386 (0)4 537 77711
+386 (0)4 537 77722
info@golf.bled.si
www.golf.bled.si

Castle Mokrice (1992)
Terme Catez, Topliska Cesta 35, 8250 Brezice
(00386) 7 457 4260
(00386) 7 495 7007
golf@terme-catez.si
Aleš Stopar
www.terme-catez.si

Lipica (1989)
Lipica 5, 66210 Sezana
+386 (0)5 734 6373
+386 (0)5 739 1725
golf@lipica.org
www.lipica.org

Spain

Alicante & Murcia

Alicante (1998)
Av. Locutor Vicente Hipolito 37, Playa San Juan, 03540 Alicante
(96) 515 37 94/515 20 43
(96) 516 37 07
clubgolf@alicantegolf.com
Angel LLopes Molina (Mgr)
www.alicantegolf.org

Altorreal (1994)
Urb Altorreal, 30500 Molina de Segura (Murcia)
(968) 64 81 44
(986) 64 82 48

Bonalba (1993)
Partida de Bonalba, 03110 Mutxamiel (Alicante)
(96) 595 5955
(96) 595 5985
golfbonalba@golfbonalba.com
www.golfbonalba.com

Don Cayo (1974)
Apartado 341, 03599 Altea La Vieja (Alicante)
(96) 584 80 46
(96) 584 65 19
info@golfdoncayo.com
Alexis Garca-Valdes (Mgr)
www.golfdoncayo.com

Ifach (1974)
Crta Moraira-Calpe Km 3, Apdo 28, 03720 Benisa (Alicante)
(96) 649 71 14
(96) 649 9908
golfifach@gmail.com
Gonzalo Gonzalez
9 holes, 3 Par 4's - Par 60

Jávea (1981)
Apartado 148, 03730 Jávea, (Alicante)
(96) 579 25 84
(96) 646 05 54

La Manga (1971)
Los Belones, 30385 Cartagena (Murcia)
(968) 175000 ext 1360
(968) 175058
golf@lamangaclub.es
www.lamangaclub.com

La Marquesa (1989)
Ciudad Quesada II, 03170 Rojales, (Alicante)
(+34) 96 671 42 58
(+34) 96 671 42 67
info@lamarquesagolf.es
www.lamarquesagolf.es

Las Ramblas (1991)
Crta Alicante-Cartagena Km48, 03189 Urb Villamartin, Orihuela (Alicante)
(96) 677 4728
(96) 677 4733
golflasramblas@grupoquara.com
www.grupoquara.com

Real Campoamor (1989)
Crta Cartagena-Alicante Km48, Apdo 17, 03189 Orihuela-Costa (Alicante)
(96) 532 13 66
(96) 532 05 06
golf@lomasdecampoamor.es
Elena Gonzalez
www.lomasdecampoamor.com

La Sella Golf (1991)
Ctra La Xara-Jesús Pobre, 03749 Jesús Pobre (Alicante)
(96) 645 42 52/645 41 10

(96) 645 42 01
info@lasellagolf.com
www.lasellagolfresort.com

Villamartin (1972)
Avenida Las Brisas No 8, Urb. Villamartin, 03189 Orihuela-Costa
(96) 676 51 70/
(96) 676 51 04
(96) 676 51 70
golfvillamartin@grupoquara.com
Juan Miguel Buendia (Manager)
www.grupoquara.com

Almería

Almerimar (1976)
Urb Almerimar, 04700 El Ejido (Almería)
(950) 48 02 34
(950) 49 72 33

El Cortijo Grande Golf Resort (1976)
Apdo 2, Cortijo Grande, 04639 Turre (Almería)
(950) 479176
golf@cortijogrande.net
www.cortijogrande.net

La Envia (1993)
Apdo 51, 04720 Aguadulce (Almería)
(950) 55 96 41

Playa Serena (1979)
Paseo del golf No.8, 04740 Roquetas de Mar (Almería)
+34 (950) 33 30 55
+34 (950) 33 30 55
info@golfplayaserena.com
www.golfplayaserena.com

Badajoz & West

Guadiana (1992)
Crta Madrid-Lisboa Km 393, Apdo 171, 06080 Badajoz
(924) 44 81 88

Norba (1988)
Apdo 880, 10080 Cáceres
(927) 23 14 41
(927) 23 14 80

Salamanca (1988)
Monte de Zarapicos, 37170 Zarapicos (Salamanca)
(923) 32 91 00
(923) 32 91 05
club@salamancagolf.com
www.salamancagolf.com

Balearic Islands

Canyamel
Urb Canyamel, Crta de Cuevas, 07580 Capdepera, (Mallorca)
(971) 56 44 57
(971) 56 53 80

Capdepera (1989)
Apdo 6, 07580 Capdepera, Mallorca
(971) 56 58 75/56 58 57
(971) 56 58 74

Ibiza (1990)
Apdo 1270, 07840 Santa Eulalia, (Ibiza)
(971) 19 61 18
(971) 19 60 51

Mallorca Marriott Golf Son Antem (1993)
Carretera Ma 19, Salida 20-07620 Llucmajor, Mallorca
(+34) 971 12 92 00
(+34) 971 12 92 01
mallorca.golfclub@vacationclub.com
Yago Gonzalez (Director)
www.sonantemgolf.com

Pollensa (1986)
Ctra Palma-Pollensa Km 49.3, 07460 Pollensa, (Mallorca)
(0034) 971 533216
(0034) 971 533265
rec@golfpollensa.com
Cesar Riera
www.golfpollensa.com

Poniente (1978)
Costa de Calvia, 07181 Calvia (Mallorca)
(971) 13 01 48
(971) 13 01 76
golf@ponientegolf.com
Mr Jose Jimenez (Mgr)
www.ponientegolf.com

Pula Golf (1995)
Ctra. Son Servera-Capdepera, E-07550 Son Servera-Mallorca
(971) 81 70 34
(971) 81 70 35
reservas@pulagolf.com
Rahel Wanke
www.pulagolf.com

Real Golf Bendinat (1986)
C. Campoamor, 07181 Calviá, (Mallorca)
(971) 40 52 00
(971) 70 07 86
golfbendinat@terra.es
Alison Bradshaw
www.realgolfbendinat.com

Santa Ponsa (1976)
Santa Ponsa, 07180 Calvia (Mallorca)
(971) 69 02 11
(971) 69 33 64
golf1@habitatgolf.es
www.habitatgolf.es

Golf Son Parc Menorca (1977)
Urb. Son Parc s/n, ES Mercadal-Menorca, Baleares
+34 (971)-188875/ 359059
+34 (971)-359591
info@golfsonparc.com
www.golfsonparc.com

Son Servera (1967)
Costa de Los Pinos, 07759 Son Servera, (Mallorca)
(971) 84 00 96
(971) 84 01 60

Son Vida (1964)
Urb Son Vida, 07013 Palma (Mallorca)
(971) 79 12 10
(971) 79 11 27

Vall d'Or Golf (1985)
Apdo 23, 07660 Cala D'Or, (Mallorca)
(971) 83 70 68/83 70 01
(971) 83 72 99
valldorgolf@valldorgolf.com
Julia Jana Litten (Sec)/Israel Rodrigues Rojas (Mgr)
www.valldorgolf.com

Barcelona & Cataluña

Aro-Mas Nou (1990)
Apdo 429, 17250 Playa de Aro
(972) 82 69 00
(972) 82 69 06

Bonmont Terres Noves (1990)
Urb Terres Noves, 43300 Montroig (Tarragona)
(977) 81 81 40
(977) 81 81 46
www.bonmont.com

Club de Golf Costa Dorada Tarragona (1983)
Apartado 600, 43080 Tarragona
(977) 65 3361/(977) 65 3605
(977) 65 3028
club@golfcostadoradatarragona.com
www.golfcostadoradatarragona.com

Costa Brava (1962)
La Masia, 17246 Sta Cristina d'Aro (Girona), Catalunya
(972) 83 71 50
(972) 83 72 72
info@golfcostabrava.com
Ma Victoria Figueras Garcia
www.golfcostabrava.com

Empordà Golf Resort (1990)
Crta Torroella de Montgri, 17257 Gualta (Gerona)
(972) 76 04 50/76 01 36
(972) 75 71 00
info@empordagolf.com
Anna Gurana
www.empordagolf.com

Fontanals de Cerdanya (1994)
Fontanals de Cerdanya, 17538 Soriguerola (Girona)
(972) 14 43 74

Golf Girona (1992)
Urbanització Golf Girona s/n, 17481 Sant Julia de Ramis, (Girona)
(972) 17 16 41

(972) 17 16 82
golfgirona@golfgirona.com
www.golfgirona.com

Llavaneras (1945)
Cami del Golf 45-51, 08392 San Andreu de Llavaneras, (Barcelona)
(93) 792 60 50
(93) 795 25 58
lucas.bueno@golfllavaneras.com
Mr Lucas Bueno (Gen Mgr)
www.golfllavaneras.com

Masia Bach (1990)
Ctra Martorell-Capellades, 08635 Sant Esteve Sesrovires
(93) 772 8800
(93) 772 8810

Osona Montanya (1988)
Masia L'Estanyol, 08553 El Brull (Barcelona)
(93) 884 01 70
(93) 884 04 07

Peralada Golf (1993)
La Garriga, 17491 Peralada, Girona
+34 972 538 287
+34 972 538 236
casa.club@golfperalada.com
Nuria Bech Diumenge (Mgr)
www.golfperalada.com

Golf Platja de Pals (1966)
Pay and play
Ctra. Golf, Num. 64, Pals - Girona 17256
(+34) 972 66 77 39
(+34) 972 63 67 99
recep@golfplatjadepals.com
www.golfplatjadepals.com

Reus Aigüesverds (1989)
Crta de Cambrils, Mas Guardià, E-43206 Reus-Tarragona
(977) 75 27 25
(977) 12 03 91
info@golfreusaiguesverds.com
J Mourges (Mgr)
www.golfreusaiguesverds.com

Terramar (1922)
Apdo 6, 08870 Sitges
(93) 894 05 80/894 20 43
(93) 894 70 51
reservas@golfterramar.com
www.golfterramar.com

Torremirona (1994)
Ctra N-260 Km 46, 17744 Navata (Girona)
(+34) 972 55 37 37
(+34) 972 55 37 16
golf@torremirona.com
www.torremirona.com

Burgos & North

Castillo de Gorraiz (1993)
Urb Castillo de Gorraiz, 31620 Valle de Egues (Navarra)
(948) 33 70 73
(948) 33 73 15
administracion@golfgorraiz.com
www.golfgorraiz.com

Izki Golf (1992)
C/Arriba, S/N, 01119 Urturi (Alava)
(945) 378262
(945) 378266
izkigolf@izkigolf.com
(945) 378262
www.izkigolf.com

Larrabea (1989)
Crta de Landa, 01170 Legutiano, (Alava)
(945) 46 58 44/46 58 41
(945) 46 57 25

Lerma (1991)
Ctra Madrid-Burgos Km195, 09340 Lerma (Burgos)
(947) 17 12 14/17 12 16
(947) 17 12 16
golflerma@csa.es

La Llorea (1994)
Crta Nacional 632, Km 62, 33394 Gijòn/Xixòn
(985) 10 30
(985) 36 47 26
administraciongolf.pdm@gijon.es
www.golfllallorea.com

Real Golf Castiello (1958)
Apdo Correos 161, 33200 Gijón
(985) 36 63 13
(985) 13 18 00
administracion@castiello.com
www.castiello.com

Real Golf Pedreña (1928)
Apartado 233, Santander
(942) 50 00 01/50 02 66
(942) 50 04 21

Real San Sebastián (1910)
Chalet Borda Gain Jaizubia, 20280, Hondarribia, (Guipúzcoa)
0034 (943) 61 68 45
0034 (943) 61 14 91
rgcss@golfsansebastian.com
Bertol Oria
www.golfsansebastian.com

Real Golf Club De Zarauz (1916)
Lauaxeta, 7, Zarauz, (Guipúzcoa)
(943) 83 01 45
(943) 13 15 68
info@golfzarauz.com
Beatriz Aseguinolaza
www.golfzarauz.com

Ulzama (1965)
31779 Guerendiain (Navarra)
(948) 30 51 62
(948) 30 54 71

Canary Islands

Amarilla (1988)
Urb Amarilla Golf, San Miguel de Abona, 38630 Santa Cruz de Tenerife
(922) 73 03 19
(922) 73 00 85

Costa Teguise (1978)
Avenida del Golf s/n, 35508 Costa Teguise
(928) 59 05 12
(928) 59 23 37
info@lanzarote-golf.com/info@lanzarote-golf.e
www.lanzarote-golf.com

Maspalomas (1968)
Av de Neckerman, Maspalomas, 35100 Gran Canaria
(928) 76 25 81/76 73 43
(928) 76 82 45
www.maspalomasgolf.net

Real Club de Golf de Tenerife (1932)
Campo de Golf No.1 38350, Tacoronte, Tenerife
(922) 63 66 07
(922) 63 64 80
info@rcgt.es
Vidal Carralero Ceva (Mgr)
www.rcgt.es

Real Golf Las Palmas (1891)
PO Box 93, 35380 Santa Brigida, Gran Canaria
(928) 35 10 50/35 01 04
(928) 35 01 10
rcglp@realclubdegolfdelaspalmas.com
www.realclubdegolfdelaspalmas.com

Golf del Sur (1987)
San Miguel de Abona, 38620 Tenerife (Canarias)
(922) 73 81 70
(922) 78 82 72
golfdelsur@aymesichgolf.com
www.golfdelsur.es

Córdoba

Club de Campo de Córdoba (1976)
Apartado 436, 14080 Córdoba
(957) 35 02 08
administracion@golfcordoba.com
www.golfcordoba.com

Pozoblanco (1984)
Ctra. La Canaleja Km. 3,, 14400 Pozoblanco, Córdoba
(957) 33 91 71
(957) 34 48 46
pozoblancogolf@gmail.com

Galicia

Aero Club de Santiago (1976)
General Pardiñas 34, Santiago de Compostela (La Coruña)
(981) 59 24 00
(981) 50 95 03
reception@aerosantiago.es
www.aerosantiago.es

La Toja (1970)
Isla de La Toja, El Grove, Pontevedra
☎ **(986) 73 01 58/73 08 18**
(986) 73 31 22

Ria de Vigo (1993)
San Lorenzo-Domaio, 36957 Moaña (Pontevedra)
☎ **(986) 32 70 51**
(986) 32 70 53
info@riadevigogolf.com
www.riadevigogolf.com

Madrid Region

La Dehesa (1991)
Avda. de la Universidad, 10, 28691 Villanueva La Cañada
☎ **(91) 815 70 22**
(91) 815 54 68
dehesa-direccion @infonegocio.com

Herreria (1966)
PO Box 28200, San Lorenzo del Escorial, (Madrid)
☎ **(91) 890 51 11**
(91) 890 26 13
lsveiro@golflaherreria.com
www.golflaherreria.com

Jarama R.A.C.E. (1967)
Urb Ciudalcampo, 28707 San Sebastian de los Reyes, (Madrid)
☎ **(91) 657 00 11**
(91) 657 04 62
golf@race.es
www.race.es

Lomas-Bosque (1973)
Urb El Bosque, 28670 Villaviciosa de Odón, (Madrid)
☎ **(91) 616 75 00**
(91) 616 73 93

La Moraleja (1976)
La Moraleja, Alcobendas (Madrid)
☎ **(91) 650 07 00**
(91) 650 43 31
info@golflamoraleja.com
www.golflamoraleja.com

Puerta de Hierro (1895)
Avda de Miraflores, Ciudad Puerta de Hierro, 28035 Madrid
☎ **(91) 316 1745**
(91) 373 8111
lmalonso@rcphierro.com

Los Retamares (1991)
Crta Algete-Alalpardo Km 2300, 28130 Valdeolmos (Madrid)
☎ **(91) 620 25 40**

Somosaguas (1971)
Avda de la Cabaña, 28223 Pozuelo de Alarcón, (Madrid)
☎ **(91) 352 16 47**
(91) 352 00 30

Valdeláguila (1975)
Apdo 9, Alcalá de Henares, (Madrid)
☎ **(91) 885 96 59**
(91) 885 96 59

Villa de Madrid CC (1932)
Crta Castilla, 28040 Madrid
☎ **(0034) 91 550 2010**
(0034) 91 550 2023
deportes@clubvillademadrid.com
www.clubvillademadrid.com

Malaga Region

Alhaurín (1994)
Crta A-387 Km 3.4, Alhaurín el Grande-Mijas
☎ **+34 95 25 95 970**
+34 95 25 94 586
reservasgolf@alhauringolf.com
www.alhauringolf.com

Añoreta (1989)
Avenida del Golf, 29730 Rincón de la Victoria, (Málaga)
☎ **(952) 40 40 00**
(952) 40 40 50

La Cala Resort (1991)
La Cala de Mijas, 29649 Mijas-Costa (Málaga)
☎ **(952) 66 90 00**
(952) 66 90 34
golf@lacala.com
www.lacala.com

Guadalhorce (1988)
Crtra de Cártama Km7, Apartado 48, 29590 Campanillas (Málaga)
☎ **(952) 17 93 78**
(952) 17 93 72

Lauro (1992)
Los Caracolillos, 29130 Alhaurín de la Torre, (Málaga)
☎ **(95) 241 2767/296 3091**
(95) 241 4757
info@laurogolf.com
www.laurogolf.com

Málaga Club de Campo (1925)
Parador de Golf, Apdo 324, 29080 Málaga
☎ **(952) 38 12 55**
(952) 38 21 41

Mijas Golf International (1976)
Apartado 145, Fuengirola, Málaga
☎ **(952) 47 68 43**
(952) 46 79 43
info@mijasgolf.org
www.mijasgolf.org

Miraflores (1989)
Urb Riviera del Sol, 29647 Mijas-Costa
☎ **+34 (952) 93 19 60**
+34 (952) 93 19 42

Torrequebrada (1976)
Public
Apdo 120, Crta de Cadiz Km 220, 29630 Benalmadena
☎ **(95) 244 27 42**
(95) 256 11 29
bookings@golftorrequebrada.com
www.golftorrequebrada.com

Marbella & Estepona

Alcaidesa Links (1992)
CN-340 Km124.6, 11315 La Linea (Cádiz)
☎ **(956) 79 10 40**
(956) 79 10 41

Aloha (1975)
Nueva Andalucía, 29660 Marbella
☎ **(952) 81 37 50/90 70 85/86**
(952) 81 23 89
office@clubdegolfaloha.com
www.clubdegolfaloha.com

Los Arqueros Golf & Country Club SA (1991)
Crta de Ronda Km44.5, 29679 Benahavis (Málaga)
☎ **+34 952 784712**
+34 952 786707
admin.losarquerosgolf @es.taylorwimpey.com
Lidia Martin
www.losarquerosgolf.com

Atalaya G&CC (1968)
Crta Benahavis 7, 29688 Málaga
☎ **(952) 88 28 12**
(952) 88 78 97

Las Brisas (1968)
Apdo 147, 29660 Nueva Andalucía, (Málaga)
☎ **(952) 81 08 75/81 30 21**
(952) 81 55 18
info@lasbrisasgolf.com
www.lasbrisasgolf.com

La Cañada (1982)
Ctra Guadiaro Km 1, 11311 Guadiaro (Cádiz)
☎ **(956) 79 41 00**
(956) 79 42 41

Estepona (1989)
Arroyo Vaquero, Apartado 532, 29680 Estepona (Málaga)
☎ **(+34) 95 293 7605**
(+34) 95 293 7600
information@esteponagolf.com
www.esteponagolf.com

Guadalmina (1959)
Guadalmina Alta, San Pedro de Alcántara, 29678 Marbella (Málaga)
☎ **(952) 88 65 22**
(952) 88 34 83

Marbella (1994)
CN 340 Km 188, 29600 Marbella (Málaga)
☎ **(952) 83 05 00**

Monte Mayor (1989)
PO Box 962, 29679 Benahavis (Málaga)
☎ **(+34) 95 293 7111**
(+34) 95 293 7112
reservations@montemayorgolf.com
www.montemayorgolf.com

Los Naranjos (1977)
Apdo 64, 29660 Nueva Andalucía, Marbella
(952) 81 52 06/81 24 28
(952) 81 14 28

El Paraiso (1973)
Ctra Cádiz-Màlaga Km 167, 29680 Estepona (Málaga)
(95) 288 38 35
(95) 288 58 27
info@elparaisogolfclub.com
www.elparaisogolfclub.com

La Quinta G&CC (1989)
Urb. La Quinta, Nueva Andalucía 29660, (Marbella-Málaga)
+34 (952) 76 23 90
+34 (952) 76 23 99
reservas@laquintagolf.com
www.laquintagolf.com

Santa María G&CC (1991)
Urb. Elviria, Crta N340 Km 192, 29604 Marbella (Málaga)
(952) 83 10 36
(952) 83 47 97
caddymaster@santamariagolfclub.com
Rosa Olmo
www.santamariagolfclub.com

Sotogrande (1964)
Paseo del Parque, s/n, 11310 Sotogrande, Cádiz
+34 956 785014
+34 956 795029
info@golfsotogrande.com
www.golfsotogrande.com

The San Roque Club (1990)
CN 340 Km 127, San Roque, 11360 Cádiz
(956) 61 30 30
(956) 61 30 12
info@sanroqueclub.com
Guillermo Navarro
www.sanroqueclub.com

Valderrama (1985)
Avenida de los Cortjos S/N, 11310 Sotogrande (Cadiz)
(956) 79 12 00
(956) 79 60 28
greenfees@valderrama.com
Derek Brown
www.valderrama.com

Seville & Gulf of Cádiz

Isla Canela (1993)
Crta de la Playa, 21400 Ayamonte (Huelva)
(959) 47 72 63
(959) 47 72 71
golf@islacanela.es
www.islacanela.es

Islantilla (1993)
Paseo Barranco Del Moro, S/N, 21410 Isla Cristina (Huelva)
(959) 48 60 39/48 60 49
(959) 48 61 04
reservasgolf@islantillagolfresort.com
www.istantillagolfresort.com

Montecastillo (1992)
Carretera de Arcos, 11406 Jérez
(956) 15 12 00
(956) 15 12 09
commercial@montecastillo.com
www.montecastillo.com

Montenmedio G&CC (1996)
N-340 KM 42,5, 11150 Vejer-Barbate (Cádiz)
(956) 45 50 04
(956) 45 12 95
info@montenmedio.es
Migual Marin (Mgr)
www.monteenmedio.es

Novo Sancti Petri (1990)
Urb. Novo Sancti Petri, Playa de la Barrosa, 11139 Chiclana de la Frontera
0034 (956) 49 40 05
0034 (956) 49 43 50
sales@golf-novosancti.es
Mrs Claudia Kühleitner (Sales & Marketing Mgr)
www.golf-novosancti.es

Real Sevilla (1992)
Autovía Sevilla-Utrera, 41089 Montequinto (Sevilla)
(954) 12 43 01
(954) 12 42 29
www.sevillagolf.com

Zaudin
Crta Tomares-Mairena, 41940 Tomares (Sevilla)
(954) 15 41 59
(954) 15 33 44

Valencia & Castellón

Escorpión (1975)
Apartado Correos 1, Betera (Valencia)
(96) 160 12 11
(96) 169 01 87
escorpion@clubescorpion.com
www.clubescorpion.com

Real Club De Golf Manises (1954)
C/ Maestrat, 1, 46940 Manises (Valencia)
+34 96 153 40 69
+34 96 152 38 04
info@clubgolfmanises.es
D. Juan Jose Penalba Belda (Mgr)
www.realclubgolfmanises.es

Mediterraneo CC (1978)
Urb La Coma, 12190 Borriol, (Castellón)
(964) 32 1653 (bookings)
(964) 65 77 34
club@ccmediterraneo.com
www.ccmediterraneo.com

Oliva Nova (1995)
46780 Oliva (Valencia)
(096) 285 76 66
(096) 285 76 67
golf@chg.es
www.olivanovagolf.com

El Saler (1968)
Avd. de los pinares 151, 46012 El Saler (Valencia)
(96) 161 0384
(96) 162 7366
saler.golf@parador.es
www.parador.es

Valladolid

Entrepinos (1990)
Avda del Golf 2, Urb Entrepinos, 47130 Simancas (Valladolid)
(983) 59 05 11/59 05 61
(983) 59 07 65
golfentrepinos@golfentrepinos.com
Angel Santiago Calleja (Mgr)
www.golfentrepinos.com

Zaragoza

Club de Golf La Penaza (1973)
Apartado 3039, Zaragoza
(976) 34 28 00/34 22 48
(976) 34 28 00
administracion@golflapenaza.com
Pablo Menendez
www.golflapenaza.com

Sweden

East Central

Ängsö (1979)
Box 1007, 72126 Västerås
(0171) 441012
(0171) 441049
kansli@angsogolf.org
www.angsogolf.org

Arboga
PO Box 263, 732 25 Arboga
(0589) 70100
(0589) 701 90
arbogagk@arbogagk.nu
www.arbogagk.nu

Askersund (1980)
Kärravägen 30, 696 75 Ammeberg
(0583) 34943
(0583) 34945
info@askersundsgk.golf.se
www.golf.se/askersundsgk

Burvik (1990)
Burvik, 740 12 Knutby
(0174) 43060
(0174) 43062
info@burvik.se
www.burvik.se

Edenhof (1991)
740 22 Bälinge
(018) 334185
(018) 334186
info@edenhof.se

Enköping (1970)
Box 2006, 745 02 Enköping
(0171) 20830
(0171) 20823
info@enkopinggolf.se
www.enkopinggolf.se

Eskilstuna (1951)
Strängnäsvägen, 633 49 Eskilstuna
(016) 142629
(016) 148729
info@eskilstunagk.se
www.eskilstunagk.se

Fagersta (1970)
Box 2051, 737 02 Fagersta
(0223) 54060
(0223) 54000

Frösåker Golf & Country (1989)
Frösåker Gård, Box 17015, 720 17 Västerås
(021) 25401
(021) 25485
fgcc@telia.com
www.fgcc.se

Fullerö (1988)
Jotsberga, 725 91 Västerås
(021) 50262
(021) 50431
info@fullerogk.se
www.fullerogk.se

Gripsholm (1991)
Box 133, 647 23 Mariefred
(0159) 350050
(0159) 350059
www.golf.se/gripsholmsgk

Grönlund (1989)
PO Box 38, 740 10 Almunge
(0174) 20670
(0174) 20455
info@gronlundgk.se
www.gronlundgk.se

Gustavsvik (1988)
Box 22033, 702 02 Örebro
(019) 244486
(019) 246490
info@gvgk.se
www.gvgk.se

Katrineholm (1959)
Jättorp, 641 93 Katrineholm
(0150) 39270
(0150) 39011
info@katrineholmsgk.golf.se
Olof Pettersson (Mgr)
www.katrineholmsgolf.nu

Köping (1963)
Box 278, 731 26 Köping
(0221) 81090
(0221) 81277
info@kopingsgk.golf.sc
www.kopingsgk.nu

Kumla (1987)
Box 46, 692 21 Kumla
(019) 577370
(019) 577373

Linde (1984)
Dalkarlshyttan, 711 31 Lindesberg
(0581) 87050
(0581) 87059
info@lindegk.com
www.lindegk.com

Mosjö (1989)
Mosjö Gård, 705 94 Örebrö
(019) 225780
(019) 225045

Nora (1988)
Box 108, 713 23 Nora
(0587) 311660
(0587) 15548

Nyköpings (1951)
ÅRILLA, 611 92 Nyköping
(0155) 216617
(0155) 97185
info@nykopingsgk.se
Gary Cosford
www.nykopingsgk.se

Örebro (1939)
Lanna, 719 93 Vintrosa
(019) 164070
(019) 164075
www.golf.se/golfklubbar/orebrogk

Roslagen
Box 110, 761 22 Norrtälje
(0176) 237194
(0176) 237103

Sala (1970)
Norby Fallet 100, 733 92 Sala
(0224) 53077/53055/53064
(0224) 53143
info@salagk.nu
Hans Eljansbo
www.salagk.nu

Sigtunabygden (1961)
Box 89, 193 22 Sigtuna
(08) 592 54012
(08) 592 54167
info@sigtunagk.com
www.sigtunagk.com

Skepptuna
Skepptuna, 195 93 Märsta
(08) 512 93069
(08) 512 93163
www.skepptunagk.nu

Södertälje (1952)
Box 9074, 151 09 Södertälje
(08) 550 91995
(08) 550 62549

Strängnäs (1968)
Kilenlundavägen 3, 645 47 Strängnäs
(0152) 14731
(0152) 14716
info@strangnasgk.se
www.strangnasgk.se

Torshälla (1960)
Box 128, 64422 Torshälla
(016) 358722
(016) 357491
kansli@torshallagk.se
www.torshallagk.com

Tortuna
Nicktuna, Tortuna, 725 96 Västerås
(021) 65300
(021) 65302
kansli@tortunagk.com

Trosa (1972)
Box 80, 619 22 Trosa
(0156) 22458
(0156) 22454

Upsala (1937)
Håmö Gård, Läby, 755 92 Uppsala
(018) 460120
(018) 461205
info@upsalagk.se
www.upsalagk.se

Vassunda (1989)
Smedby Gård, 741 91 Knivsta
+46 (0) 185 72040
(018) 381416
info@vassundagk.se
www.vassundagk.se

Västerås (1931)
Bjärby, 724 81 Västerås
(021) 357543
(021) 357573
info@vasterasgk.se
www.vasterasgk.se

Far North

Boden (1946)
Tallkronsvägen 2, 961 51 Boden
(0921) 69140
(0921) 72047

Funäsdalsfjällen (1972)
Golfbanevägen 8, 840 96 Ljusnedal
(0684) 668241
(0684) 21142
kansli@ffjgk.nu
www.ffjgk.nu

Gällivare-Malmberget (1973)
Box 35, 983 21 Malmberget
(0970) 20770
(0970) 20776
gmgk@telia.com
www.gmgk.se

Haparanda (1989)
Mattila 140, 953 35 Haparanda
(0922) 10660
(0922) 15040

Härnösand (1957)
Box 52, 871 22 Härnösand
(0611) 67000
(0611) 66165
www.harnosand.gk.just.nu

Kalix (1990)
Nyborgsvägen 175, 95251 Kalix
(0923) 15945/15935
(0923) 77735
info@kalixgolfklubb.se
www.kalixgolfklubb.se

Luleå (1955)
Golfbaneväg 80, 975 96 Luleå
(0920) 256300
(0920) 256362
kansli@luleagolf.se
www.luleagolf.se

Norrmjöle (1992)
905 82 Umeå
(090) 81581
(090) 81565
kansli@norrmjole-golf.se
www.norrmjole-golf.se

Örnsköldsviks GK Puttom (1967)
Ovansjö 232, 891 95 Arnäsvall
(0660) 254001
(0660) 254040
kansli@puttom.se
www.puttom.se

Östersund-Frösö (1947)
Kungsgården 205, 832 96 Frösön
(063) 576030
(063) 43765
www.ofg.nu

Piteå (1960)
Nötöv 119, 941 41 Piteå
(0911) 14990
(0911) 14960

Skellefteå (1967)
Rönnbäcken, 931 92 Skellefteå
(0910) 779333
(0910) 779777
info@skelleftegolf.nu
www.skelleftegolf.nu

Sollefteå (1970)
Box 213, 881 25 Sollefteå
(0620) 21477/12670
(0620) 21477/12670

Sundsvall (1952)
Golfvägen 5, 86234 Kvissleby
+46 60 515175
+46 60 515170
info@sundsvallgk.golf.se
www.sundsvallgk.com

Timrå
Golfbanevägen 2, 860 32 Fagervik
(060) 570153
(060) 578136
info@timragk.golf.se
www.timragk.se

Umeå (1954)
Enkan Ramborgs väg 10, 913 35 Holmsund
(090) 58580/58585
(090) 58589
info@umgk.se
Lena D Lindstrom (Club Manager)
www.umgk.se

Gothenburg

Albatross (1973)
Lillhagsvägen, 422 50 Hisings-Backa
(031) 551901/550500
(031) 555900

Chalmers
Härrydavägen 50, 438 91 Landvetter
+46 (0) 31 91 84 30
+46 (0) 31 91 63 38
info@chgk.se
www.chgk.se

Delsjö (1962)
Kallebäck, 412 76 Göteborg
(031) 406959
(031) 703 0431
www.degk.se

Forsgårdens (1982)
Gamla Forsv 1, 434 47 Kungsbacka
(0300) 566350
(0300) 566351
kansli@forsgarden.se
www.forsgarden.se

Göteborg (1902)
Box 2056, 436 02 Hovås
(031) 282444
(031) 685333

Gullbringa G&CC (1968)
Kulperödsvägen 6, 442 95 Hålta
(0303) 227161
(0303) 227778
kansli@gullbringagolf.se
A Joelsson-Soetting
www.gullbringagolf.se

Kungälv-Kode GK (1990)
Ö Knaverstad 140, 442 97 Kode
+46 303 513 00
+46 303 502 05
info@kkgk.se
Pär Svensson
www.kkgk.se

Kungsbacka (1971)
Hamravägen 15, 429 44 Särö
(031) 938180
(031) 938170
info@kungsbackagk.se
Andri Reumert
www.kungsbackagk.se

Lysegården (1966)
Box 532, 442 15 Kungälv
(0303) 223426
(0303) 223075
info@lysegarden.sgk.golf.se
www.lysegarden.sgk.se

Mölndals (1979)
Hällesåkersvägen 14, 437 91 Lindome
(031) 993030
(031) 994901
molndalsgk@telia.com
Lars-Erik Hagbert
www.molndalsgk.se

Öijared (1958)
Pl 1082, 448 92 Floda
(0302) 37300
(0302) 37306
reception@oigk.se
Pia Orrgren (Man Dir)
www.oigk.se

Partille (1986)
Golfrundan 5, 433 51 Öjersjö
+46 31 987043
+46 31 987757
info@partillegk.se
Patrik Skoog
www.partillegk.se

Sjögärde
43963 Frillesås
+46 (0) 340 657865
+46 (0) 340 657861
info@sjogarde.se
www.sjogarde.se

Stenungsund (1993)
Lundby Pl 7480, 444 93 Spekeröd
(0303) 778470
(0303) 778350
www.stenungsundgk.se

Stora Lundby (1983)
Valters Väg 2, 443 71 Grabo
(0302) 44200
(0302) 44125
www.storalundbygk.o.se

Malmö & South Coast

Abbekas (1989)
Kroppsmarksvagen, 274 56 Abbekas
(0411) 533233
info@abbekasgk.golf.se
www.abbekasgk.se

Barsebäck G&CC (1969)
246 55 Löddeköpinge
(046) 776230
(046) 772630
bgcc@barseback-golf.se
www.barsebackresort.se

Bokskogen (1963)
Torupsvägen 408-140, 230 40 Bara
(040) 406900
(040) 406929

Falsterbo (1909)
Fyrvägen 34, 239 40 Falsterbo
+46 (0)40 470078/ 475078
+46 (0)40 472722
info@falsterbogk.se
www.falsterbogk.com

Flommens (1935)
239 40 Falsterbo
(040) 475016
(040) 473157
info@flommensgk.se
www.flommensgk.se

Kävlinge (1989)
Box 138, 244 22 Kävlinge
(046) 736270
(046) 728486
info@kavlingegk.golf.se
www.kavlingegk.com

Ljunghusen (1932)
Kinellsvag, Ljunghusen, 236 42 Höllviken
(040) 458000
(040) 454265
info@ljgk.se
Stig Persson
www.ljgk.se

Lunds Akademiska (1936)
Kungsmarken, 225 92 Lund
(046) 99005
(046) 99146
info@lagk.se
www.lagk.se

Malmö Burlöv (1981)
Segesvängen, 212 27 Malmö
(040) 292535/292536
(040) 292228
malmoburlovgk@telia.com
www.malmoburlovgk.com

Örestads GK (1986)
Golfvägen, Habo Ljung, 234 22 Lomma
(040) 410580
(040) 416320
info@orestadsgk.com
Niklas Karlsson
www.orestadsgk.com

Österlen (1945)
Djupadal, 272 95 Simrishamn
(0414) 412550
(0414) 412551
info@osterlensgk.com
Stefan Minell
www.osterlensgk.com

Romeleåsen (1969)
Kvarnbrodda 1191, 247 96 Veberöd
+46 46 820 12
+46 46 821 13
info@ragk.se
Stellan Ragnar
www.ragk.se

Söderslätts (1993)
Ellaboda, Grevievägen 260-10, 235 94 Vellinge
(040) 429680
(040) 429684
info@soderslattsgK.golf.se
www.4.golf.se/soderslattsgk

Tegelberga (1988)
Alstad Pl 140, 231 96 Trelleborg
(040) 485690
(040) 485691
www.golf.se/tegelbergagk

Tomelilla (1987)
Ullstorp, 273 94 Tomelilla
(0417) 19430
(0417) 13657
info@tomelillagolfklub.com
www.tomelillagolfklubb.com

Trelleborg Golf Club (1963)
Maglarp, Pl 431, 231 93 Trelleborg
(0410) 330460
(0410) 330281
kansli@trelleborgsgk.se
Helen Nilsson
www.trelleborgsgk.se

Vellinge (1991)
Toftadals Gård, 235 41 Vellinge
(040) 443255
(040) 443179
info@vellingegk.golf.se
www.vellingegk.se

Ystad (1930)
Långrevsvägen, 270 22 Köpingebro
(0411) 550350
(0411) 550392
info@ystadgk.com
www.ystadgk.se

North

Alvkarleby
Västanåvägen 5, 814 94 Alvkarleby
(026) 72757
(026) 82307
info@alvkarlebygk.se
www.alvkarlebygk.com

Avesta (1963)
Friluftsvägen 10, 774 61 Avesta
(0226) 55913/10866/12766
(0226) 12578
info@avestagk.se
www.avestagk.se

Bollnäs (1963)
Norrfly 1634, 823 91 Kilafors
(0278) 650540
(0278) 651220
info@bollnasgk.com
www.bollnasgk.com

Dalsjö (1989)
Dalsjö 3, 781 94 Borlänge
(0243) 220080
(0243) 220140
info@dalsjogolf.se
www.dalsjogolf.se

Falun-Borlänge (1956)
Storgarden 10, 791 93 Falun
(023) 31015
(023) 31072
www.fbgu.se

Gävle (1949)
Bönavägen 23, 805 95 Gävle
(026) 120333/120338
(026) 516468

Hagge (1963)
Hagge, 771 90 Ludvika
(0240) 28087/28513
(0240) 28515

Hofors (1965)
Box 117, 813 22 Hofors
(0290) 85125
(0290) 85101

Högbo (1962)
Daniel Tilas Väg 4, 811 92 Sandviken
(026) 215015
(026) 215322
info@hogbogk.golf.se
www.golf.se/hogbogk/

Hudiksvall (1964)
Tjuvskär, 824 01 Hudiksvall
+46 (0) 650 542080
+46 (0) 650 542089

Leksand (1977)
Box 25, 793 21 Leksand
(0247) 14640
(0247) 14157

Ljusdal (1973)
Svinhammarsv.2, 82735 Ljusdal
(0651) 16883
(0651) 16883
kansli@golfiljusdal.nu
www.golfiljusdal.nu

Mora (1980)
Box 264, 792 24 Mora
(0250) 592990
(0250) 592995
info@moragk.se
www.moragk.se

Rättvik (1954)
Box 29, 795 21 Rättvik
(0248) 51030
(0248) 12081

Sälenfjallens (1991)
Box 20, 780 67 Sälen
(0280) 20670
(0280) 20671
info@salenfjallensgk.se
Ingemar Simonsson (Secretary)
www.salenfjallensgk.se

Säter (1984)
Box 89, 783 22 Säter
(0225) 50030
(0225) 51424

Snöå Golfklubb (1990)
Snöå Bruk, S-780 51 Dala-Järna
+46 281 24072
+46 281 24009
snoa.gk@telia.com
Kjell Redhe
www.snoagk.se

Söderhamns GK (1961)
835 Sofieholm, 826 91 Söderhamn
+46 270 281 300
+46 270 281 003
info@soderhamnsgk.com
Hans Wirtavuori
www.soderhamnsgk.com

Sollerö (1991)
Levsnäs, 79290 Sollerön
☎ **(0250) 22236**
(0250) 22854

Skane & South

Allerum (1992)
Turskköpsvägen 154, 260 35 Ödåkra
☎ **(042) 93051**
(042) 93045
info@allerumgk.nu
www.allerum.nu

Ängelholm (1973)
Box 1117, 262 22 Ängelholm
☎ **(0431) 430260/431460**
(0431) 431568
www.golf.se/golfklubbar/angelholmsgk

Araslöv
Starvägen 1, 291 75 Färlöv
☎ **(044) 71600**
(044) 71575

Båstad (1929)
Box 1037, 269 21 Båstad
☎ **(0431) 78370**
(0431) 73331
info@bgk.se
www.bgk.se

Bedinge (1931)
Golfbanevägen, 231 76 Beddingestrand
☎ **(0410) 25514**
(0410) 25411

Bjäre
Salomonhög 3086, 269 93 Båstad
☎ **(0431) 361053**
(0431) 361764

Bosjökloster (1974)
243 95 Höör
☎ **(0413) 25858**
(0413) 25895

Carlskrona (1949)
PO Almö, 370 24 Nättraby
☎ **(0457) 35123**
(0457) 35090
www.carlskronagk.com

Degeberga-Widtsköfle
Segholmsu.126, Box 71, 297 21 Degeberga
☎ **(044) 355035**
(044) 355075
dwgk@telia.com
www.dwgolfklubb.com

Eslöv (1966)
Box 150, 241 22 Eslöv
☎ **(0413) 18610**
(0413) 18613
info@eslovsgk.golf.se
www.eslovsgk.se

Hässleholm (1978)
Skyrup, 282 95 Tyringe
☎ **(0451) 53111**
(0451) 53138

Helsingborg (1924)
260 40 Viken
☎ **(042) 236147**
office@helsingborgsgk.com
www.helsingborgsgk.com

Karlshamn (1962)
Box 188, 374 23 Karlshamn
☎ **(0454) 50085**
(0454) 50160
info@karlshamnsgk.com
Eva Tigerman
www.karlshamnsgk.com

Kristianstad GK (1924)
Box 41, 296 21 Åhus
☎ **(044) 247656**
(044) 247635
info@kristianstadsgk.com
Mats Welff
www.kristianstadsgk.com

Landskrona (1960)
Erikstorp, 261 61 Landskrona
☎ **(0418) 446260**
(0418) 446262
info@landskronagk.se
www.landskronagk.se

Mölle (1943)
263 77 Mölle, Italienska Vägen 215
☎ **(042) 347520**
(042) 347523
info@mollegk.se
Peter Tublén (Manager)
www.mollegk.se

Örkelljunga (1989)
Rya 472, 286 91 Örkelljunga
☎ **(0435) 53690/53640**
(0435) 53670
info@orkelljungagk.com
www.orkelljungagk.com

Östra Göinge (1981)
Riksvägen 12, 289 21 Knislinge
☎ **(044) 60060**
(044) 67862
info@ostragoinge.golf.se
www.golf.se/ostragoingegk

Perstorp (1963)
Gustavsborg 501, 284 91 Perstorp
☎ **+46 (0) 435 35411**
+46 (0) 435 35959
kansli@ppgk.nu
www.ppgk.nu

Ronneby (1963)
Box 26, 372 21 Ronneby
☎ **(0457) 10315**
(0457) 10412
www.golf.se/ronnebygk

Rya (1934)
PL 5500, 255 92 Helsingborg
☎ **(042) 220182**
(042) 220394
kansli@rya.nu
www.rya.nu

St Arild (1987)
Golfvagen 48, 260 41 Nyhamnsläge
☎ **(042) 346860**
(042) 346042
kansliet@starild.se
www.starild.se

Skepparslov (1984)
Sätesvägen 14, 291 92 Kristianstad
☎ **(044) 229508**
(044) 229503
kansli@skepparslovgk.se
www.skepparslovsgk.se

Söderåsen (1966)
Box 41, 260 50 Billesholm
☎ **(042) 73337**
(042) 73963
info@soderasensgk.golf.se
www.soderasensgk.se

Sölvesborg
Box 204, 294 25 Sölvesborg
☎ **(0456) 70650**
(0456) 70650
info@solvesborggk.se
www.solvesborggk.se

Svalöv (1989)
Månstorp Pl 1365, 268 90 Svalöv
☎ **(0418) 662462**
(0418) 663284
svagk@telia.com
www.svagk.se

Torekov (1924)
Råledsv 31, 260 93 Torekov
☎ **(0431) 449840**
(0431) 364916
info@togk.se
www.togk.se

Trummenas (1989)
373 02 Ramdala
☎ **+46 (0) 455 360507**
+46 (0) 455 360571
trummenas.gk@telia.com
www.trummenasgk.se

Vasatorp (1973)
P O Box 130 35, S-250 13 Helsingborg
☎ **+46 42 23 50 58**
+46 42 23 51 35
info@vasatorpsgk.se
Joakim Soderstrom (Club Mgr)
www.vasatorpsgk.se

South East

Älmhult (1975)
Pl 1215, 343 90 Älmhult
☎ **(0476) 14135**
(0476) 16565

Åtvidaberg (1954)
Västantorp, 597 41 Åtvidaberg
☎ **(0120) 35425**
(0120) 13502

Ekerum Golf Resort (1990)
387 92 Borgholm, Öland
☎ **(0485) 80000**

(0485) 80010
info@ekerum.com
www.ekerum.com

Eksjö (1938)
Skedhult, 575 96 Eksjö
(0381) 13525
kansli@eksjogk.se
Peter Börjesson
www.eksjogk.se

Emmaboda (1976)
Kyrkogatan, 360 60 Vissefjärda
(0471) 20505/20540
(0471) 20440
info@emmabodagk.golf.se
www.golf.se/golfklubbar/emmabodagk

Finspångs (1965)
Viberga Gård, 612 92 Finspång
(0122) 13940
(0122) 18888
info@finspangsgk.golf.se
www.finspangsgk.se

Gotska (1986)
Annelund, 62141 Visby, Gotland
(0498) 215545
(0498) 256332
info@gotskagk.golf.se
www.gotskagk.se

Grönhögen (1996)
PL 1270, 380 65 Öland
(0485) 665995
(0485) 665999
www.gronhogen.se

Gumbalde
Box 35, 620 13 Ståga, Gotland
(0498) 482880
(0498) 482884

Hooks
560 13 Hok
(0393) 21420
(0393) 21379
www.hooksgk.com

Jönköpings GK (1936)
Kättilstorp, 556 27 Jönköping
(036) 76567
(036) 76511
info@jonkopingsgk.se
www.jonkopingsgk.se

Kalmar (1947)
Box 278, 391 23 Kalmar
(0480) 472111
(0480) 472314
reception@kalmar-gk.se
Jimmy Grön
www.kalmargk.se

Lagan (1966)
Box 63, 340 14 Lagan
(0372) 30450/35460
(0372) 35307
info@lagansgk.se
www.lagansgk.se

Landeryds GK (1987)
Bogestad Gård, 585 93 Linköping
(+46) 133 62200
(+46) 133 62208
bjorn.sturehed@landerydsgolf.se
Björn Sturehed
www.landerydsgolf.se

Lidhems (1988)
360 14 Väckelsång
(0470) 33660
(0470) 33761
www.golf.se/lidhemsgk

Linköping (1945)
Universitets vägen 8, 583 30 Linköping
(013) 262990
(013) 140769
lggolf@telia.com
Kent Andersson
www.linkopingsgk.se

Mjölby (1986)
Blixberg, Miskarp, 595 92 Mjölby
(0142) 12570
kansli@mjolbygk.se
Viktoria Schedin
www.mjolbygk.se

Motala (1956)
PO Box 264, 591 23 Motala
(0141) 50840
(0141) 208990
info@motalagk.golf.se
www.motalagk.se

Nässjö (1988)
Box 5, 571 21 Nässjö
(0380) 10022
(0380) 12082

Norrköping (1928)
Alsatersvagen 40, 605 97 Norrköping
(011) 158240
(011) 158249
info@ngk.nu
Morgan Allard
www.ngk.nu

Oskarshamn (1972)
Box 148, 572 23 Oskarshamn
(0491) 94033
(0491) 94038

Skinnarebo (1990)
Skinnarebo, 555 93 Jönköping
(036) 69075
(036) 362975
info@skinnarebogcc.golf.se
www.skinnarebo.se

Söderköping (1983)
Hylinge, 605 96 Norrköping
(011) 70579

Tobo (1971)
Fredensborg 133, 598 91 Vimmerby
(0492) 30346
(0492) 30871
info@tobogk.com
www.tobogk.com

Tranås (1952)
Norrc byvagen 8, Norrabyvagen 8, 57343 Tranas
(0140) 311661
(0140) 16161
info@tranasgk.se
www.tranasgk.se

Vadstena (1957)
Hagalund, Box 122, 592 23 Vadstena
(0143) 12440
(0143) 12709
kansli@vadstenagk.nu
www.vadstenagk.nu

Värnamo (1962)
Näsbyholm 5, 331 96 VÄRNAMO
(0370) 23991
(0370) 23992
info@varnamogk.se
Pia Berglund
www.varnamogk.se

Västervik (1959)
Box 62, Ekhagen, 593 22 Västervik
(0490) 32420
(0490) 32421

Växjö (1959)
Box 227, 351 05 Växjö
(0470) 21515
(0470) 21557
www.vaxjogk.com

Vetlanda (1983)
Box 249, 574 23 Vetlanda
(0383) 18310
(0383) 19278

Visby Golf Club (1958)
Västergarn Kronholmen 415, 622 30 Gotlands Tofta
+46 498 200930
+46 498 200932
info@visbygk.com
Matz Bengtsson (Gen Mgr)
www.visbygk.com

Vreta Kloster
Box 144, 590 70 Ljungsbro
(013) 169700
(013) 169707
info@vkgk.se
www.vkgk.se

South West

Alingsås (1985)
Hjälmared 4050, 441 95 Alingsås
(0322) 52421

Bäckavattnet (1977)
Marbäck, 305 94 Halmstad
(035) 162040
(035) 162049
www.backavattnetsgk.com

Billingens GK (1949)
St Kulhult, 540 17 Lerdala
+46 511 80291
info@billingensgk.se
Anders Karlsson
www.billingensgk.se

Borås (1933)
Östra Vik, Kråkered, 504 95 Borås
☎ **(033) 250250**
(033) 250176

Ekarnas (1970)
Balders Väg 12, 467 31 Grästorp
☎ **(0514) 12061**
(0514) 12062
info@ekarnasgk.golf.se
www.golf.se//ekarnasgk

Falkenberg (1949)
Golfvägen, 311 72 Falkenberg
☎ **(0346) 50287**
(0346) 50997
info@falkenberggk.golf.se
Lars Andersson (Sec)
www.falkenbergsgolfklubb.se

Falköping (1965)
Box 99, 521 02 Falköping
☎ **(0515) 31270**
(0515) 31389
info@falkopingsgk.com
Peter Fritzson
www.falkopingsgk.com

Halmstad (1930)
302 73 Halmstad
☎ **+46 35 176800/176801**
+46 35 176820
info@hgk.se
www.hgk.se

Haverdals (1988)
Slingervägen 35, 30570 Haverdal
☎ **(035) 144990**
(035) 53890
info@haverdalsgk.golf.se
Ann Jacobsson
www.haverdalsgk.com

Hökensås (1962)
PO Box 116, 544 22 Hjo
☎ **(0503) 16059**
(0503) 16156

Holms (1990)
Nannarp, 305 92 Halmstad
☎ **(035) 38189**
(035) 38488
info@holmsgk.golf.se
www.holmsgk.com

Hulta (1972)
Box 54, 517 22 Bollebygd
☎ **(033) 204340**
(033) 204345
info@hultagk.se
David Kirkham
www.hultagk.se

Knistad G&CC
541 92 Skövde
☎ **(0500) 463170**
(0500) 463075

Laholm (1964)
Vallen 15, 31298 Vaxtorp
☎ **+46 430 30601**
+46 430 30891
info@laholmgk.com
www.laholmgk.com

Lidköping (1967)
Box 2029, 531 02 Lidköping
☎ **(0510) 546144**
(0510) 546495
www.lidkopingsgk.se

Mariestads Golf Course (1975)
Gummerstadsvägen 45, 542 94 Mariestad
☎ **(0501) 17383**
info@mariestadsgk.se
www.mariestadsgk.se

Marks (1962)
Brättingstorpsvägen 28, 511 58 Kinna
☎ **(0320) 14220**
(0320) 12516
info@marksgk.se
www.marksgk.se

Onsjö (1974)
Box 6331 A, 462 42 Vänersborg
☎ **(0521) 68870**
(0521) 17106
www.onsjogk.com

Ringenäs (1987)
Strandlida, 305 91 Halmstad
☎ **(035) 161590**
(035) 161599
ringenas.golf@telia.com
www.ringenasgolfbana.com

Skogaby (1988)
312 93 Laholm
☎ **(0430) 60190**
(0430) 60225
skogaby.gk@telia.com
www.skogabygk.se

Sotenas Golfklubb (1988)
Pl Onna, 450 46 Hunnebostrand
☎ **(0523) 52302**
(0523) 52390
www.sotenasgolf.com

Töreboda (1965)
Box 18, 545 21 Töreboda
☎ **(0506) 12305**
(0506) 12305

Trollhättan (1963)
Stora Ekeskogen, 466 91 Sollebrunn
☎ **(0520) 441000**
(0520) 441049

Ulricehamn (1947)
523 33 Ulricehamn
☎ **(0321) 27950**
(0321) 27959
info@ulricehamngk.golf.se
www.golf.se/ulricehamngk

Vara-Bjertorp (1987)
Bjertorp, 535 91 Kvänum
☎ **+46 (512) 20261**
+46 (512) 20259
info@vara-bjertorpgk.se
Mr Christian Tiden
www.vara-bjertorpgk.se

Varberg (1950)
432 77 Tvååker
☎ **+46 340 480380**
+46 340 44135
info@varbergsgk.se
www.varbergsgk.se

Vinberg (1992)
Sannagård, 311 95 Falkenberg
☎ **(0346) 19020**
(0346) 19042
info@vinbergsgolfklubb.se
www.vinhergsgolfklubb.se

Stockholm

Ågesta (1958)
123 52 Farsta
☎ **(08) 447 3330**
(08) 447 3337

Botkyrka
Malmbro Gård, 147 91 Grödinge
☎ **(08) 530 29650**
(08) 530 29409
info@botkyrkagk.golf.se
www.golf.se/botkyrkagk

Bro-Bålsta (1978)
Jurstagarosvagen 2, 197 91 Bro
☎ **(08) 582 41310**
(08) 582 40006
info@bbgk.telia.com
www.brobalstagk.se

Djursholm (1931)
Hagbardsvägen 1, 182 63 Djursholm
☎ **(08) 5449 6451**
(08) 5449 6456
info@dgk.nu
www.dgk.nu (Swedish only)

Fågelbro G&CC (1991)
Fågelbro Säteri, Fågelbrovägen 11-15, 139 60 Värmdö
☎ **+46 (08) 571 41800**
+46 (08) 571 40671
kansli@fagelbrogolf.se
Anders Green (Manager)
www.fagelbrogolf.se

Haninge (1983)
Årsta Slott, 136 91 Haninge
☎ **(08) 500 32850**
(08) 500 32851
info@haninggk.golf.se
www.haningegk.se

Huvudstadens
Lindö Park, 186 92 Vallentuna
☎ **(08) 511 70055 (Bookings)**
(08) 511 70613
info@huvudstadensgolf.se
www.huvudstadensgolf.se

Ingarö (1962)
Fågelviksvägen 1, 134 64 Ingarö
☎ **(08) 556 50200**
(08) 546 50299
info@igk.se
www.igk.se

Kungsängen (1992)
Box 133, 196 21 Kungsängen
☎ **(08) 584 50730**
🖷 (08) 581 71002
✉ info@kungsangengc.se
🌐 www.kungsangengc.se

Lidingö (1933)
Box 1035, 181 21 Lidingö
☎ **(08) 731 7900**
🖷 (08) 731 7900
✉ kansli@lidingogk.se
🌐 www.lidingogk.se

Lindö (1978)
186 92 Vallentuna
☎ **(08) 514 30990**
🖷 (08) 511 74122

Nya Johannesberg G&CC (1990)
762 95 Rimbo
☎ **(08) 514 50000**
🖷 (08) 512 92390
🌐 www.golf.se/golfklubbar/johannesberggcc

Nynäshamn (1977)
Korunda 40, 148 91 Ösmo
☎ **(08) 524 30590/524 30599**
🖷 (08) 524 30598
✉ kansli@nynashamnsgk.se
🌐 www.nynashamnsgk.a.se

Österakers
Hagby 1, 184 92 Akersberga
☎ **(08) 540 85165**
🖷 (08) 540 66832
✉ kansli@ostgk.se
🌐 www.ostgk.se www.hagbygolf.se

Österhaninge (1992)
Husby V.11, 136 91 Haninge
☎ **(08) 500 32285**
✉ info@osterhaningegk.golf.se
🌐 www.osterhaningegk.se

Royal Drottningholm Golf Club (1958)
Lovö Kyrkallé 1, 178 93 Drottningholm
☎ **(08) 759 0085**
🖷 (08) 759 0851
✉ info@kdrgk.se
✍ Stefan Andorff
🌐 www.kdrgk.se

Saltsjöbaden (1929)
Box 51, 133 21 Saltsjöbaden
☎ **+46 (0)8 717 0125**
🖷 +46 (0)8 717 9713
✉ klubb@saltsjobadengk.se
🌐 www.saltsjobadengk.se

Sollentuna (1967)
Skillingegården, 192 77 Sollentuna
☎ **(08) 594 70995**
🖷 (08) 594 70999
✉ intendent@sollentunagk.se
🌐 www.sollentunagk.se

Stockholm (1904)
Kevingestrand 20, 182 57 Danderyd
☎ **(08) 544 90710**
🖷 (08) 544 90712

Täby (1968)
Skålhamra Gård, 187 70 Täby
☎ **(08) 510 23261**
🖷 (08) 510 23441

Ullna (1981)
Roslagsvagen 36, 184 94 Åkersberga
☎ **(08) 514 41230**
🖷 (08) 510 26068
✉ ullna@ullnagolf.se
🌐 www.ullnagolf.se

Ulriksdal (1965)
Box 8088, 170 08 Solna
☎ **(08) 855393**
✉ info@ulriksdalsgk.se
🌐 www.ulriksdalsgk.se

Vallentuna (1989)
Box 266, 186 24 Vallentuna
☎ **(08) 514 30560/1**
🖷 (08) 514 30569
🌐 www.vallentunagk.nu

Viksjö (1969)
Fjällens Gård, 175 45 Järfälla
☎ **(08) 580 31300/31310**
🖷 (08) 580 31340
🌐 www.golf.se/viksjogk

Wäsby
Box 2017, 194 02 Upplands Väsby
☎ **(08) 514 103 50**
🖷 (08) 514 103 55

Wermdö G&CC (1966)
Torpa, 139 40 Värmdö
☎ **(08) 574 60700**
🖷 (08) 574 60729
✉ wgcc@telia.com
🌐 www.wgcc.se

West Central

Arvika (1974)
Box 197, 671 25 Arvika
☎ **(0570) 54133**
🖷 (0570) 54233
🌐 www.arvikagk.nu

Billerud (1961)
Valnäs, 660 40 Segmon
☎ **(0555) 91313**
🖷 (0555) 91306
✉ kansli@billerudsgk.se
🌐 www.billerudsgk.se

Eda (1992)
Noresund, 670 40 Åmotfors
☎ **(0571) 34101**
🖷 (0571) 34191
🌐 www.edagk.com

Färgelanda (1987)
Box 23, Dagsholm 1, 458 21 Färgelanda
☎ **(0528) 20385**
🖷 (0528) 20045
✉ info@fargelandagk.golf.se
🌐 www.fargelandagk.se

Fjällbacka (1965)
450 71 Fjällbacka
☎ **(0525) 31150**
🖷 (0525) 32122

Forsbacka (1969)
Box 137, 662 23 Åmål
☎ **(0532) 61690**
🖷 (0532) 61699
✉ info@forsbackagk.golf.se
🌐 www.golf.se/golfklubbar/forsbackagk/

Hammarö (1991)
Barrstigen 103, 663 91 Hammarö
☎ **(054) 522650**
🖷 (054) 521863
✉ info@hammarogk.se
🌐 www.hammarogk.se

Karlskoga (1975)
Bricketorp 647, 691 94 Karlskoga
☎ **(0586) 728190**
🖷 (0586) 728417

Karlstad (1957)
Höja 510, 655 92 Karlstad
☎ **(054) 866353**
🖷 (054) 866478
✉ info@karlstadgk.se
🌐 www.karlstadgk.se

Kristinehamn (1974)
Box 337, 681 26 Kristinehamn
☎ **(0550) 82310**
🖷 (0550) 19535
✉ kristinehamnsgk@telia.com
🌐 www.golf.se/golfklubbar/kristinehamnsgk

Lyckorna (1967)
Box 66, 459 22 Ljungskile
☎ **(0522) 20176**
🖷 (0522) 22304

Orust (1981)
Morlanda 135, 474 93 Ellös
☎ **+46 304 53170**
🖷 +46 304 53174
✉ orustgk@telia.com
🌐 www.orustgk.se

Saxå (1964)
Saxån, 682 92 Filipstad
☎ **(0590) 24070**
🖷 (0590) 24101

Skaftö (1963)
Stockeviksvägen 2, 450 34 Fiskebäckskil
☎ **+0046 (523) 23211**
🖷 +0046 (0523) 23215
✉ kansliet@skaftogk.se
🌐 www.skaftogk.se

Strömstad (1967)
Golfbanevägen, 452 90 Strömstad 1
☎ **(0526) 61788**
🖷 (0526) 14766
🌐 www.golf.se/stromstadgk

Sunne (1970)
Box 108, 686 23 Sunne
☎ **(0565) 14100/14210**

For key to symbols and European dialling codes see page 725

📠 (0565) 14855
✉ info@sunnegk.se
🖳 www.sunnegk.se

Torreby (1961)
Torreby Slott, 455 93 Munkedal
☎ **(0524) 21365/21109**
📠 (0524) 21351

Uddeholm (1965)
Risäter 20, 683 93 Råda
☎ **(0563) 60564**
📠 (0563) 60017
✉ uddeholmsgk@telia.com
🖳 www.uddeholmsgk.com

Switzerland

Bern

Golf & Country Club Blumisberg (1959)
3184 Wünnewil
☎ **(026) 496 34 38**
📠 (026) 496 35 23
✉ secretariat@blumisberg.ch
✍ Heinz Reber (Club Mgr)
🖳 www.blumisberg.ch

Les Bois (1988)
Case Postale 26, 2336 Les Bois
☎ **(032) 961 10 03**
📠 (032) 961 10 17

Neuchâtel (1925)
Hameau de Voëns, 2072 Saint-Blaise, Hameau de Voëns 13
☎ **(032) 753 55 50**
📠 (032) 753 29 40
✉ secretariat@golfdeneuchatel.ch
✍ Sabine Daverat Hasler
🖳 www.golfdeneuchatel.ch

Payerne (1996)
Public
Domaine des Invuardes, 1530 Payerne
☎ **(026) 662 4220**
📠 (026) 662 4221
✉ golf.payerne@vtx.ch
🖳 www.golfpayerne.ch

Wallenried (1994)
Chemin du Golf 18, 1784 Wallenried
☎ **(026) 684 84 80**
📠 (026) 684 84 90
✉ info@golf-wallenried.ch
✍ Mario Roltaris
🖳 www.golf-wallenried.ch

Wylihof (1994)
4542 Luterbach
☎ **(032) 682 28 28**
📠 (032 682 65 17
✉ wylihof@golfclub.ch
🖳 www.golfclub.ch

Bernese Oberland

Interlaken-Unterseen (1964)
Postfach 110, 3800 Interlaken
☎ **(033) 823 60 16**
📠 (033) 823 42 03
✉ info@interlakengolf.ch
✍ Mr Martin Gadient
🖳 www.interlakengolf.ch

Riederalp (1987)
3987 Riederalp
☎ **+41 (0) 27 927 29 32**
📠 +41 (0) 27 927 29 23
✉ info@golfclub-riederalp.ch
✍ Willy Kummer
🖳 www.golfclub-riederalp.ch

Lake Geneva & South West

Bonmont (1983)
Château de Bonmont, 1275 Chéserex
☎ **(022) 369 99 00**
📠 (022) 369 99 09
✉ golfhotel@bonmont.com
🖳 www.bonmont.com

Les Coullaux (1989)
1846 Chessel
☎ **(024) 481 22 46**
📠 (024) 481 66 46
✉ d.berruex@bluewiu.ch

Crans-sur-Sierre (1906)
Rue du Prado 20, 3963 Crans-Montana
☎ **(027) 485 97 97**
📠 (026) 485 97 97
✉ info@golfcrans.ch
🖳 www.golfcrans.ch

Domaine Impérial (1987)
Villa Prangins, 1196 Gland
☎ **+41 22 999 06 00**
📠 +41 22 999 06 06
✉ info@golfdomaineimperial.com
🖳 www.golfdomaineimperial.com

Geneva (1921)
70 Route de la Capite, 1223 Cologny
☎ **(+41) 22 707 48 00**
📠 (+41) 22 707 48 20
✉ secretariat@golfgeneve.ch
✍ François Lautens

Lausanne (1921)
Route du Golf 3, 1000 Lausanne 25
☎ **(021) 784 84 84**
📠 (021) 784 84 80
✉ info@golflausanne.ch
✍ Pierre Rindlisbacher
🖳 www.golfsuisse.ch

Montreux (1900)
54 Route d'Evian, 1860 Aigle
☎ **(024) 466 46 16**
📠 (024) 466 60 47
✉ secretariat@gcmontreux.ch
🖳 www.swissgolfnetwork.ch

Sion (2002)
Rte Vissigen 150, 1950 Sion
☎ **(+41) (0) 027 203 79 00**
📠 (+41) (0) 027 203 79 01
✉ info@golfclubsion.ch
🖳 www.golfclubsion.ch

Verbier (1970)
1936 Verbier
☎ **(027) 771 53 14**
📠 (027) 771 60 93
✉ golf.club@verbier.ch
🖳 www.verbiergolf.com

Villars (1922)
CP 118, 1884 Villars
☎ **(024) 495 42 14**
📠 (024) 495 42 18
✉ info@golf-villars.ch
🖳 www.golf-villars.ch

Lugano & Ticino

Lugano (1923)
6983 Magliaso
☎ **(091) 606 15 57**
📠 (091) 606 65 58
✉ info@golflugano.ch
✍ Massimo Casartelli (Mgr)
🖳 www.golflugano.ch

Patriziale Ascona (1928)
Via al Lido 81, 6612 Ascona
☎ **(+41) 091 785 1177**
📠 (+41) 091 785 1179
✉ info@golfascona.ch
✍ Celeste Taiana (Mgr)
🖳 www.golfascona.ch

St Moritz & Engadine

Golf Club Arosa (1944)
Postfach 95, 7050 Arosa
☎ **(081) 377 42 42**
📠 (081) 377 46 77
✉ info@golfarosa.ch
✍ Christian Danuser
🖳 www.golfarosa.ch

Bad Ragaz (1957)
Hans Albrecht Strasse, 7310 Bad Ragaz
☎ **(081) 303 37 17**
📠 (081) 303 37 27
✉ golfclub@resortragaz.ch
🖳 www.resortragaz.ch

Davos (1929)
Postfach, 7260 Davos Dorf
☎ **(081) 46 56 34**
📠 (081) 46 25 55
✉ info@golfdavos.cl
🖳 www.golfdavos.cl

Engadin (1893)
7503 Samedan
☎ **(081) 851 04 66**
📠 (081) 851 04 67
✉ samedan@engadin-golf.ch
🖳 www.engadin-golf.ch

Lenzerheide (1950)
7078 Lenzerheide
☎ **(081) 385 13 13**
(081) 385 13 19
info@golf-lenzerheide.ch
www.golf-lenzerheide.ch

Vulpera (1923)
7552 Vulpera Spa
☎ **(081) 864 96 88**
(081) 864 96 89
info@vulperagolf.ch
Markus Vesti
www.swissgolfnetwork.ch-9holes-vulpera

Zürich & North

Breitenloo (1964)
Golfstrasse 16, 8309 Oberwil b. Nürensdorf
☎ **+41 (0) 44 836 40 80**
+41 (0) 44 837 10 85
sekretariat@golfbreitenloo.ch

Bürgenstock Golf Club (1928)
6363 Obοürgen
☎ **(041) 610 2434**
(041) 612 9901
info@golfclub-buergenstock.ch
www.buergenstock.ch

Dolder (1907)
Kurhausstrasse 66, 8032 Zürich
☎ **(01) 261 50 45**
(01) 261 53 02

Entfelden (1988)
Muhenstrasse 52, 5036 Oberentfelden
☎ **(062) 723 89 84**
(062) 723 84 36

Erlen (1994)
Schlossgut Eppishausen, Schlossstr 7, 8586 Erlen
☎ **(071) 648 29 30**
(071) 648 29 40
info@erlengolf.ch
Christian Heller
www.erlengolf.ch

Hittnau-Zürich G&CC (1964)
8335 Hittnau
☎ **(+41) 950 24 42**
(+41) 951 01 66
info@gcch.ch
www.gcch.ch

Küssnacht (1994)
Sekretariat/Grossarni, 6403 Küssnacht am Rigi
☎ **(041) 854 4020**
(041) 854 4027
gck@golfkuessnacht.ch
www.golfkuessnacht.ch

Golf Kyburg (2004)
CH-8310 Kemptthal, Zürich
☎ **+41 52 355 06 06**
+41 52 355 06 16
info@golf-kyburg.ch
www.golf-kyburg.ch

Lucerne (1903)
Dietschiberg, 6006 Luzern
☎ **(041) 420 97 87**
(041) 420 82 48
info@golfclubluzern.ch
www.golfclublucerne.ch

Ostschweizerischer Golf Club (1948)
Club
9246 Niederbüren, Golfstrasse 106
☎ **(071) 422 18 56**
(071) 422 18 25
osgc@bluewin.ch
Daniel Schweizer
www.osgc.ch

Schinznach-Bad (1929)
5116 Schinznach-Bad
☎ **(056) 443 12 26**
(056) 443 34 83
golfclub.schinznach@bluewin.ch
www.swissgolfnetwork.ch

Schönenberg G&CC (1967)
8824 Schönenberg
☎ **(044) 788 90 40**
(044) 788 90 45
info@golf-schoenenberg.ch
Peter Aeschbach
www.golf-schoenenberg.ch

Golf Sempachersee (1996)
CH-6024 Hildisrieden, Lucerne
☎ **+41 41 462 71 71**
+41 41 462 71 72
info@golf-sempachersee.ch
www.golf-sempachersee.ch

Zürich-Zumikon (1929)
Weid 9, 8126 Zumikon
☎ **(0041) 43 288 1088**
(0041) 43 288 1078
gccz.zumikon@ggaweb.ch
C R Vane Percy
www.golfsuisse.ch

Turkey

Gloria Golf
Acisu Mevkii PK27 Belek, Serik, Antalya
☎ **(242) 715 15 20**
(242) 715 15 25

Kemer G&CC
Goturk Koyu Mevkii Kemerburgaz, Eyup, Istanbul
☎ **(212) 239 70 10**
(212) 239 73 76

Klassis G&CC
Silivri, Istanbul
☎ **(212) 748 46 00**
(212) 748 46 43

National Golf Club, Antalya (1994)
Belek Turizm Merkezi, 07500 Serik, Antalya
☎ **(242) 725 46 20**
(242) 725 46 23
info@nationalturkey.com
www.nationalturkey.com

Robinson Golf Club Nobilis (1998)
Acisu Mevkii, Belek, 07500 Serik/Antalya, Antalya
☎ **(+90) 242 7100362**
(+90) 242 7100391
golf.nobilis@robinson.de
www.robinson.de

Tat Golf International
Belek International Golf, Kum Tepesi Belek, 07500 Serik, Antalya
☎ **(242) 725 53 03**
(242) 725 52 99

Rest of the World – Region and Country Index

Golf is a global game and more and more golfers are travelling further and further on holiday and often to countries less well known as golfing destinations so, from the 2009 edition *The R&A Golfer's Handbook* has added as an additional service information on clubs from around the world to its existing directory of clubs in Great Britain, Ireland and Continental Europe. The selection is by no means comprehensive but the intention to continue to improve this section continues with many new entries including seven new countries. Those clubs listed have been chosen at random from various sources.

A truly world-wide sport

If anyone remains in any doubt that golf is truly a world-wide sport they should consider the following, proof that the human spirit and a passion for the game will prevail under the most daunting of conditions.

Highest golf course – La Paz Golf Club in Bolivia stands at 10,650 feet above sea level at its highest point. One of the greatest hazards is oxygen deficiency with the compensation that a ball will fly further and faster in the thin mountain air.

Most remote golf course – Royal Thimpu Golf Club in Bhutan, a county so remote that is has only recently seen the arrival of television and the motor vehicle, lies in the heart of the Himalayas surrounded by some of the world's highest mountains.

Most southerly golf course – Ushuaia Golf Club in Argentina sits at the southern tip of the South American continent close to windy Cape Horn.

Most northerly golf course – North Cape Golf Club in Norway lies within the Arctic Circle offering a 24-hour golfing day for several months of the year.

North America

Canada

Alberta

Banff Springs
www.banffspringsgolfclub.com

Jasper Park Lodge (1925)
www.fairmontgolf.com

Kananaskis (1983)
www.kananaskisgolf.com

Stewart Creek (2001)
www.tsmv.ca

Wolf Creek (1984)
www.wolfcreekgolf.com

Atlantic Canada

Crowbush Cove (2000)
www.golflinkspei.com

Dundarave (1999)
www.golflinkspei.com

Fox Harb'r Resort (2001)
www.foxharbr.com

Highlands Links (1939)
www.highlandslinksgolf.com

Humber Valley (2006)
www.humbervalley.com

British Columbia

Bear Mountain (2005)
www.bearmountain.ca

Chateau Whistler (1993)
www.fairmont.com/whistler

Grey Wolf (1999)
www.greywolfgolf.com

Predator Ridge
predatorridge.com

Tobiano (2007)
www.tobianogolf.com

Ontario

Deerhurst Highlands (1990)
www.deerhurstresort.com

Eagles Nest (2004)
www.eaglesnestgolf.com

Muskoka Bay
www.muskokabayclub.com

Rocky Crest (2000)
www.clublink.ca

Taboo Resort (2002)
www.tabooresort.com

Saskatchewan and Manitoba

Cooke Municipal (1909)
www.cookegolf.com

Dakota Dunes (2004)
www.dakotadunes.ca

Falcon Lake
www.falconlakegolfcourse.com

Granite Hills
www.granitehills.ca

Waskesiu
www.golfsask.com/waskesiu.htm

Quebec

Le Château Montebello
chateaumontebello@fairmont.com

Le Diable (1998)
www.golflediamant.com

Le Geant at Mont Tremblant (1995)
www.tremblant.ca

Le Maitre de Mont-Tremblant (2001)
www.clublink.ca

Le Manoir Richelieu
www.fairmont.com/richelieu/Recreation/Golf

USA

Alabama

Kiva Dunes
www.kivadunes.com

Arizona

The Boulders Resort
www.theboulders.com

Camelback Inn
www.camelbackinn.com

Fairmont Scottsdale
www.fairmont.com

Four Seasons Scottsdale
www.fourseasons.com

Loews Ventana Canyon Resort
www.loewshotels.com

The Phonician
www.thephoenician.com

The Lodge at Ventana Canyon
www.thelodgeatventanacanyon.com

Stone Canyon
www.stonecanyon.com

Westin Kierland Resort & Spa
www.kierlandresort.com

California

The Breakers
www.thebreakers.com

Cordevalle
www.cordevalle.com

Four Seasons Aviara
www.fourseasons.com

Pebble Beach
www.pebblebeach.com

Las Quinta Resort
www.laquintaresort.com

The Resort at Pelican Hill
www.pelicanhill.com

The Ritz-Carlton, Half Moon Bay
www.ritzcarlton.com

Torrey Pines
www.lodgetorreypines.com

Westin Mission Hills
www.westin.com

Colorado

The Broadmoor
www.broadmoor.com

The Lodge & Spa at Cordillera
www.cordilleralodge.com

Florida

Bay Hill Club & Lodge
www.bayhill.com

Boca Raton
www.bocaresort.com

Grand Cypress Resort
www.grandcypress.com

Grande Lakes Orlando
www.grandelakes.com

PGA Village
www.pgavillage.com

For key to symbols see page 725

The Ritz-Carlton, Naples
www.ritzcarlton.com

Sandestin Resort
www.sandestin.com

Sawgrass Marriott
www.sawgrassmarriott.com

Walt Disney World Resort
www.disneyworld.com

Georgia

The Ritz-Carlton Lodge
www.ritzcarltonlodge.com

Sea Island
www.seaisland.com

Hawaii

The Fairmont Orchid
www.fairmont.com

Four Seasons (Hualalai, Lanai and Maui)
www.fourseasons.com

Grand Hyatt Kauai
www.grandhyattkauai.com

Grand Wailea
www.grandwailea.com

Kauai Marriott
www.kauaimarriott.com

Mauna Kea Beach Hotel
www.princeresortshawaii.com

Mauna Lani Bay Hotel
www.maunalani.com

The Ritz-Carlton, Kapalua
www.ritzcarlton.com

Turtle Bay
www.turtlebayresort.com

Idaho

Coeur d'Alene
www.cdaresort.com

Sun Valley
www.sunvalley.com

Indiana

French Lick Resort
www.frenchlick.com

Michigan

The Inn at Bay Harbor
www.innatbayharbor.com

Grand Traverse Resort
www.grandtraverseresort.com

Minnesota

Giant's Ridge
www.giantsridge.com

Grand View Lodge
www.grandviewlodge.com

Nevada

Wynn Las Vegas
www.wynnlasvegas.com

New York State

Turning Stone
www.turningstone.com

North Carolina

Pinehurst
www.pinehurst.com

Pine Needles and Mid Pines
www.pineneedles-midpines.com

Oregon

Bandon Dunes
www.bandondunesgolf.com

Sunriver Resort
www.sunriver-resort.com

Pennsylvania

Hershey Resorts
www.hersheypa.com

Nemacolin Woodlands Resort
www.nemacolin.com

South Carolina

Kiawah Island
www.kiawahresort.com

Sea Pines Resort
www.seapines.com

Texas

Barton Creek
www.bartoncreek.com

Weston La Cantera Resort
www.westinlacantera.com

The Woodlands Resort
www.woodlandsresort.com

Vermont

The Equinox
www.equinoxresort.com

Virginia

The Homestead
www.thehomestead.com

Kingsmill Resort
www.kingsmill.com

Williamsburg Inn
www.colonialwilliamsburgresort.com

Washington

Resort Seniahmoo
www.semiahmoo.com

West Virginia

The Greenbrier
www.greenbrier.com

Wisconsin

The American Club
www.destinationkohler.com

All aboard for the 14th hole

The Coeur d'Alene Resort in Idaho, USA, has an unusual feature – the course's 14th hole is located on a floating and movable island which can only be reached by boat.

For key to symbols see page 725

The Caribbean and Central America

Antigua

Cedar Valley GC
PO Box 198, Cedar Valley, St. John's, Antigua
☎ +1 268 462 0161
✉ cedarvalleyg@candw.ag
www.cedarvalleygolf.ag

Jolly Harbour GC
PO Box 1793, St. John's, Antigua
☎ +1 268 462 7771
✉ golf@jollyharbourantigua.com
www.jollyharbourantigua.com/golf.html

Aruba

Aruba GC
Golfweg z/n, PO Box 2280 San Nicolas, Aruba
☎ +1 297 842 006
✉ arubagolfclub@yahoo.com
www.golfclubaruba.com

Tierra del Sol Resort, Spa & CC
PO Box 1257, Malmokweg z/n, Aruba
☎ +1 297 60 978
✉ tdsteetime@setarnet.aw
www.tierradelsol.com

Bahamas

One & Only Atlantis
☎ +1242 888 877 7525
www.oneandonlyresorts.com

Treasure Cay
www.treasurecay.com

Barbados

Barbados GC
Barbados Golf Club
☎ +1 246 428 8463
✉ teetime@barbadosgolfclub.com
www.barbadosgolfclub.com

Sandy Lane GC
Sandy Lane Hotel, St. James
☎ +1 246 432 2829
✉ mail@sandylane.com
www.sandylane.com/golf

Bermuda

Belmont Hills G&CC
97 Middle Road, Warwick Parish, WK 09
☎ +1 441 236 6400
✉ golf@belmonthills.com
www.belmonthills.com

St George's GC
1 Park Road, St George's Parish, GE 03
☎ +1 441 234 8067
✉ sggc@bermudagolf.bm
www.stgeorgesgolf.bm

Cayman Islands

Hyatt Britannia Golf Course
PO Box 1588 George Town, Grand Cayman
☎ +1 345 949 8020
grandcayman.hyatt.com

The Links at SafeHaven
PO Box 1311 George Town, Grand Cayman
☎ +1 345 949 5988
www.safehaven.ky/links.htm

Cuba

El Varadero GC
Villa Xanadú, Dupont de Nemours, Cuba
☎ +53 45 668482
✉ info@varaderogolfclub.com
www.varaderogolfclub.com

Dominican Republic

Casa de Campo: Teeth of the Dog; The Links and Dye Fore
La Romana Province, PO Box 140, La Romana
☎ +1809 523 3333
✉ reserva@ccampo.com.do
www.casadecampo.com.do

Playa Grande Golf Course
Km 9 Carretera Rio San Juan-Cabrera, Maria Trinidad Sanchez Province, North Coast
☎ +1809 582 0860
✉ info@playagrande.com
www.playagrande.com

Grenada

Grenada G&CC
St. George, Grenada
☎ +1 473 444 4128
✉ grenadagolfclub@spiceisle.com
www.grenadagolfclub.com

Jamaica

Ironshore G&CC
www.superclubs.com

Caymanas G&CC
Caymanas Golf & Country Club
☎ +1 876 922 3388
✉ play@caymanasgolfclub.com
www.caymanasgolfclub.com

Martinique

Golf de la Martinique
97229 Les Trois-Ilets
☎ +33 5 96 68 32 81
✉ info@golfmartinique.com
www.golfmartinique.com

Mexico

Baja California

Bajamar GC
4364 Bonita Road #299 Bonita, CA 91902-1421 Ensenada, Baja California
✉ www.bajamar.com
info@bajamar.com

Centre

Club Campestre de Aguascalientes
A.C.Vista Hermosa s/n, Fracc. Campestre 20100, Aguascalientes, Ags.
☎ +52 449 914 1001
www.campestreags.com

Central Pacific Coast

Tamarindo Golf Course
k.m. 7.5 Carretera Barra de Navidad, Puerto Vallarta, Cihuatlan, Jalisco MX 48970
☎ +52 315 351 5032
www.ycwtamarindo.com

North

El Cid G&CC
Av. Camaron Sabalo s/n, P.0. Box 813, Mazatlan, Sinaloa, Mexico 82110
☎ +52 669 913 3333
✉ reserve@elcid.com.mx
www.elcid.com

South

Club de Golf Acapulco
Av. Costera Miguel Aleman s/n Fracc. Club Deportivo, Acapulco
☎ +52 744 484
✉ gclubgolf@prodigy.net.mx

Puerto Rico

Dorado Beach Resort & Club
100 Dorado Beach Drive, Suite 1, Dorado, Puerto Rico 00646
☎ +1 787 796 1234
✉ jcolon@kempersports.com
www.doradobeachclubs.com

Palmas del Mar CC
PO Box 2020 , Humacao, Puerto Rico 00792
☎ +1 787 285 2221
www.palmascountryclub.com

St Kitts and Nevis

Royal St Kitts GC
PO Box 858 Basseterre, St. Kitts, WI
☎ +1 869 466 2700
✉ info@royalstkittsgolfclub.com
www.royalstkittsgolfclub.com

St Lucia

St Lucia G&CC
Cap Estates, PO Box 328, Gros Islet,WI
☎ +1 758 450 8522
✉ golf@candw.lc
www.stluciagolf.com

St Maarten

Mullet Bay Resort
☎ +1 599 545 3069

St Vincent

Trump International GC
Charles Town, Canouan Island, St. Vincent & The Grenadines, WI
☎ +1 784 458 8000
✉ canouan@raffles.com

Trinidad and Tobago

Mount Irvine Bay Hotel and GC
PO Box 222 Scarborough, Tobago, WI
☎ +54 11 4468 1737
✉ mtirvine@tstt.net.tt
www.mtirvine.com/golf/golf.asp

Turks and Caicos

The Provo G&CC
PO Box 662, Providenciales, Turks & Caicos Islands, WI
☎ +1 649 946 5991
✉ provogolf@tciway.tc
www.provogolfclub.com

US Virgin Islands

Buccaneer Hotel Golf Course
The Buccaneer, St Croix, US Virgin Islands
☎ +1 340 712 2144
www.thebuccaneer.com/golf.htm

South America

Argentina

Buenos Aires

Buenos Aires GC
Mayor Irusta 3777, (1661) Bella Vista, Buenos Aires
☎ +54 11 4468 1737
✉ info@bagolf.com.ar
www.bagolf.com.ar

The Jockey Club
Av. Marquez 1702, San Isidro, Buenos Aires
☎ +54 4743 1001
✉ adm.golf@jockeyclub.org.ar

Marayuí CC
Chapadmalal, Buenos Aires Province, Costa Atlantica
☎ +54 0223 460 5163
www.marayui.com

Olivos GC
Ruta Panamericana Ramal Pilar Km 32, Ing. Pablo.Nogués, CP 1613, Buenos Aires
☎ +54 11 4463 1076
✉ secretaria@olivosgolf.com.ar

Sierra de la Ventana GC
Avda. del Golf 300 - Bo. Parque Golf , C.C. N° 33 (8168) - Sierra de la Ventana
☎ +54 0291 491 5113
✉ golfsventana@infovia.com.ar

Córdoba

Ascochinga GC
Sierras Chicas, Córdoba
☎ +54 3525 492015
www.ascochingagolf.com.ar

La Cumbre GC
Belgrano 1095, 5178 La Cumbre, Córdoba, Sierras
☎ +54 03548 452283
✉ lacumbregolf@arnet.com.ar
www.lacumbregolf.com.ar

Jockey Club de Córdoba
Ave. Valparaiso Km. 3 1/2, Córdoba
☎ +54 03543 464 2283
✉ golf@jockeyclubcordoba.com.ar
www.jockeyclubcordoba.com.ar

Mendoza Club de Campo
Elpidio González y Tuyutí s/n 5503 Guaymallén, Mendoza
☎ +54 0261 431 5967
✉ ccampomza@nysnet.com.ar
www.clubdecampomendoza.net.ar

El Potrerillo de Larreta Resort & CC
Road to Los Paredones Km 3 -CC195-(5186), Alta Gracia, Córdoba
☎ +54 03547 423804 425987
✉ golf@potrerillodelarreta.com
www.potrerillodelarreta.com

Cuyo

La Rioja GC
Buenos Aires 148, La Rioja, Cuyo
☎ +54 43822 426142

Amancay GC
Av. Roque Saenz Peña 8116 (Este), Alto de Sierra, San Juan
☎ +54 0264 425 3313
www.jockeyclubvt.com.ar

San Luis GC
C.C.280, 5700 San Luis
☎ +54 02652 490013

Norte

La Esperanza GC
Salta 140, 4500 San Pedro, Jujuy
☎ +54 03884 420000

Salta Polo Club
Av. Bolivia 2800, 4400 Salta, Prov. de Salta
☎ +54 0387 439 2001
www.saltagolfclub.com.ar

Santiago del Estero GC
Nuñez del Prado s/n (C.C. 162), 4200 Santiago del Estero
☎ +54 0385 434 0186

Jockey Club de Tucumán
Av.Solano Vera, Km.2 , CP 4107 Yerba Buena, Tucumán
☎ +54 0381 425 1038
golfalpasumaj@jockeyclubtucuman.com
www.jockeyclubtucuman.com

Parques Nacionales

Golf Club Corrientes
Camino a Santa Ana KM. 1500, 3400 Corrientes, Litoral
☎ +54 03783 424372

Tacurú Social Club
Ruta 12 km 7,5. Posadas, Misiones
☎ +54 03752 480524

Jockey Club de Venado Tuerto
Castelli 657 Golf: Ruta 8 Km 372 , 2600 Venado Tuerto, Santa Fe
☎ +54 03462 421043
www.jockeyclubvt.com.ar

Rosario GC
Morrison 9900, 2000 Rosario, Santa Fe Province, Litoral
☎ +54 0341 451 3438
www.rosariogolfclub.com

Patagonia

Chapelco Golf and Resort
Route 234, Loma Atravesada de Taylor, San Martín de los Andes, Neuquén, Patagonia
☎ +54 2972 421785
reservasgolf@chapelcogolf.com
www.chapelcogolf.com

Ruca Kuyen Golf & Resort
Cruz del Sur 203, B° Las Balsas, Ruca Kuyen, Neuquén
☎ +54 2944 495099
info@rucakuyen.com.ar
www.rucakuyen.com.ar

Llao-Llao Hotel and Resort
Av. Ezequiel Bustillo km. 25, Bariloche, Río Negro Province, Patagonia
☎ +54 02944 448530
www.llaollao.com

Ushuaia GC
Ruta 3 Camino a Lapataia, Tierra del Fuego, Patagonia
☎ +54 2901 432946

Brazil

Rio de Janiero

Búzios Golf Club & Resort
buziosgolf@mar.com.br

Gavea Golf & Country Club
www.gaveagolf.com.br

Hotel do Frade and Golf Resort
www.hoteldofrade.com.br

Itanhangá Golf Club
www.itanhanga.com.br

São Paulo

Damha Golf Club
www.damha.com.br

Guarapiranga G&CC
www.guarapirangagolfe.com.br

Lago Azul GC
www.lagc.com.br

Quinta da Baroneza Golfe Clube
www.qbgc.com.br

São Fernando Golf Club
www.saofernando.com.br

Terras da São José – Itú
www.tsjgolfeclube.com.br

Vista Verde GC
www.vvgc.com.br

Paraná (Curitiba City)

Alphaville Graciosa Clube
www.clubealphaville.com.br

Rio Grande do Sul

Porto Alegre Country Club
www.pacc.com.br

Bahia

Commandatuba Ocean Course
www.transamerica.com.br

Costa de Sauipe Golf Links
www.costadosauipe.com.br

Iberostar Praia do Forte Golf Club
www.praiadofortegolfclub.com.br

Terravista Golf Course
www.terravistagolf.com.br

Chile

Club de Golf Los Leones
Pte. Riesco 3700, Las Condes, Santiago
☎ +56 562 719 3200
clubgolf@entelchile.net
www.golflosleones.cl

Costa Rica

La Iguana Golf Course
Playa Herradura, Puntalenas, Costa Rica
☎ +506 2630 9028
maria.cano@marriott.com
www.golflaiguana.com

Ecuador

Quito Tenis y Golf Club
Urb. El Condado Av. A N73-154 y calle B (Entrada de Socios), Quito 17012411
☎ +593 0224 91420
golf@qtgc.com
www.qtgc.com

French Guyana

Golf de l'Anse
Centre de Loisirs du Centre Spatial, 97310 Guyane
☎ +33 5 94 32 63 02
golf-anse@wanadoo.fr

Paraquay

Carlos Franco Country GC
Arroyos y Esteros
☎ +595 16 252123
✉ secretaria@carlosfrancogolf.com
▤ www.carlosfrancogolf.com

Paraná CC
Supercarretera a Itaipu, Hernandarias
☎ +595 61 570181
✉ secretaria@carlosfrancogolf.com
▤ www.carlosfrancogolf.com

Hotel Resort & Casino Yacht y Golf Club Paraguay
Av. del Yacht 11, Lambaré
☎ +595 21 906 121
▤ www.hotelyacht.com.py

Peru

Amazon Golf Course
#185 Malecon Maldonado, City of Iquitos, North East Peru
☎ +51 965 943267
✉ michaelcollis@amazongolfcourse.com
▤ www.amazongolfcourse.com

Lima GC
Av. Camino Real 770, San Isidro, Lima 27
☎ +51 442 6006
✉ gerencia@limagolfclub.org.pe
▤ www.limagolfclub.org.pe

Los Andes GC
Carretera Central Km. 23, Hacienda Huampani, Chosica District, Lima
☎ +51 497 1066
✉ administracion@losandesgolfclub.org
▤ www.losandesgolfclub.org

Los Inkas GC
Av. El Golf Los Inkas s/n, Monterrico, Surco District, City of Lima
☎ +51 317 7770
✉ email@golflosinkas.com
▤ www.losinkasgolfclub.com

Uruguay

Club del Lago Golf
Ruta 93 Km 116.500, (Departamento de Maldonado), Punta del Este
☎ +598 42 578423
✉ info@lagogolf.com
▤ www.lagogolf.com

Fray Bentos GC
Barrio Anglo, Fray Bentos , Ciudad de Fray Bentos, Rio Negro
☎ +598 56 22427

Sheraton Colonia Golf & Spa Resort
Continuación de la Rambla de Las Américas S/N,Colonia Del Sacramento 70000
☎ +598 52 29000
✉ colonia.golf@arnet.com.ar

Venezuela

Cardon GC
Av. 1, Urb. Zarabón, Comunida Cardon, Punto Fijo, Edo. Falcón
☎ +58 0269 2483739
✉ cardongolfclub@hotmail.com

La Cumaca GC
Sector La Cumaca, Carretera vía Pozo, Urb. Villas San Diego, Country Clu, San Diego, Edo. Carabobo
☎ +58 241 8910077
✉ info@golfclublacumaca.com
▤ www.golfclublacumaca.com

Junko GC
Urbanización Junko Country Club, Calle El Empalme, Kilómetro 19 Carretera El Junquito, Estado Vargas
☎ +58 212 412 1254
✉ junkogc@cantv.net
▤ www.junkogolf.com

San Luis CC
Carretera vieja Tocuyito, antes de la Hacienda San Luis, Valencia, Edo. Carabobo
☎ +58 0241 824 7878
✉ info@sanluiscc.com
▤ www.sanluiscc.com

Africa

Algeria

Algiers GC
Rue Ahmed Ouaked Dely-Ibrahim 16000
☎ +213 757 90

Botswana

Phakalane Golf Estate
Golf Drive, Phakalane, Gaborone
☎ +267 360 4000
▤ http://golfestate.phakalane.com

Cameroon

Likomba GC
Tiko, South West Province Cameroon
☎ +237 3335 1173
▤ www.golflikomba.com

Egypt

Cairo

Dreamland Golf and Tennis Resort
6th of October City Road, Dreamland City, Cairo
☎ +20 11 400 577
✉ pyramidsgolf@hilton.com

The Pyramids G&CC
Soleimania Golf Resort, Kilo 55 Cairo-Alexandria Desert Road 600955
☎ +20 49 600 953
✉ amers@gega.net

Alexandria

Sporting Club Golf Course Alexandria
☎ +20 3543 3627

Hurghada

Cascades Golf Resort & CC
48 km Safaga Road, Soma Bay, Red Sea
☎ +20 65 354 2333
✉ major@thecascades.com
▤ www.residencedescascades.com

The Links at Stella di Mare
Km 46, Suez–Hurgada Road, Ain Al Sokhna
☎ +20 212 4586
✉ golf@stelladimare.com
▤ www.stelladimare.com

Sharm el Sheikh

Jolie Ville Golf & Resort
Um Marikha Bay 46619, Sharm el Sheikh, South Sinai
+20 2 269 01465
monika.elbadramany@jolieville-hotels.com
www.jolieville-golf.com

Luxor

Royal Valley Golf Course
29, El Rahala El Boghdady St., Golf Area, Heliopolis, Cairo
+20 2 418 5234
marketing@royalvalley.com

Sinai Peninsular

Taba Heights Golf Resort
+20 69 358 0073
info@tabaheights.com
www.tabaheights.com

Ghana

Achimota GC
PO Box AH8, Achimota. Accra
+233 21 400220
www.achimotagolf.com

Kenya

Great Rift Valley Lodge & Golf Resort
North Lake Road, Rift Valley
+254 27 123129
www.heritage-eastafrica.com

Karen CC
Karen Rd, Nairobi, Kenya, PO Box 24817, Karen
+254 2 882801
golf@leisurelodgeresort.com
www.westerncapehotelandspa.co.za

Kitale GC
PO Box 30, Kitale
+254 32 531338

Leisure Lodge Beach & Golf Resort
PO Box 84383, Mombasa
+254 40 320 3624
dippd@wchs.co.za
www.leisurelodgeresort.com

Limuru CC
PO Box 10, Limuru
+254 667 3189

Mombasa GC
PO Box 90164, Mombasa
+254 1 22853

Muthaiga GC
PO Box 41651, Nairobi,
+254 2 762414
www.muthaigagolfclub.com

Nakuru GC
PO Box 652, Nakuru
+254 37 40391

Nyali G&CC
Mombasa North Coast, PO Box 95678, Mombasa
+254 11 47 1589

Royal Nairobi GC
P O Box 40221, Nairobi
+254 2 725769
www.royalnairobigc.co.ke

Sigona GC
PO Box 40221, Kikuya
+254 154 32144
www.sigonagolf.com

Windsor G&CC
Ridgeways Road, PO Box 45587, Nairobi
+254 020 862300
reservations@windsor.co.ke
www.windsorgolfresort.com

Madagascar

Golf Club d'Antsirabe
Ivohitra Golf Course , BP 142 Antsirabe
+261 020 44 94 387
contact@golfantsirabe.com
www.golfantsirabe.com

Mauritius

Belle Mare Plage GC (The Legend, Lemuria Championship Golf Course and The Links)
Poste de Flacq
+230 402 2735
info@bellemareplagehotel.com
www.bellemareplagehotel.com/golf

Paradis Hotel & GC
Le Morne Peninsula
+230 401 5050
www.paradis-hotel.com

Tamarina Golf Estate and Beach Club
Tamarin Bay
+230 401 300
www.tamarina.mu

Le Touessrok
Trou d'Eau
+230 402 7400
www.letouessrokresort.com

Morocco

Agadir

Agadir Royal GC
Km12, Route Ait Melloul, Agadir
+212 4824 8551
royalgolfagadir@multimania.com

Golf Club Med les Dunes
Chemin Oued Souss, Agadir
+212 4883 4690

Benslimane

Ben Slimane Royal Golf
Avenue des F.A.R. BP 83 Ben Slimane, Morocco
+212 332 8793

Casablanca

Anfa Royal GC
Hippodrome d'Anfa, Casablanca
+212 0522 351026

Settat University Royal GC
Km 2, Route de Casablanca, BP 575 Settat, Morocco
+212 2340 0755

Don't get your feet wet

Le Touessrok Golf Course is located on the island of Ile Aux Cerfs, just off the East coast of Mauritius and can only be reached via a 10-minute boat ride from the mainland resort.

For key to symbols see page 725

El Jadida

El Jadida Royal Golf & Spa
Route de Casablanca km7, B.P 116 24000 El Jadida
☎ +212 523 37910
✉ H2960@accor.com
🖃 www.accorhotels.com

Fez

Fez Royal GC
Km 15, Route d'Imouzzer, Fez
☎ +212 5566 5210

Meknès

Meknès Royal GC
Jnan Al Bahraouia, Ville Ancienne, Meknès
☎ +212 5553 0753
✉ rgm@royalgolfmeknes.com
🖃 www.royalgolfmeknes.com

Rabat

Dar Es-Salam Royal Golf
KM 9, avenue Mohammed VI / route des Zaers Souissi, Rabat
☎ +212 3775 5864
✉ golfdaressalam@menara.ma
🖃 www.royalgolfdaressalam.com

Namibia

Windhoek G&CC
Western Bypass, Windhoek
☎ +264 61 205 5223
🖃 www.wccgolf.com.na

Nigeria

Ikoyi Club
6 Ikoyi Club 1938 Road, Ikoyi. PO Box 239, Lagos
☎ +234 269 5133
✉ info@ikoyiclub-1938.org
🖃 www.ikoyiclub-1938.org

Le Méridien Ibom Hotel & Golf Resort
Nwaniba Road, PMB 1200, Uyo, Akwa Ibom State
☎ +234 808 052 7411
✉ reservations.ibom@lemeridien.com
🖃 www.lemeridienibom.com

MicCom Golf Hotels and Resort
Ibokun Road, Ada, Osun Estate
☎ +234 1497 5445
🖃 www.gmiccomgolfhotels.com

Réunion

Golf du Bassin Bleu
75 rue Mahatma Gandhi-Villéle, 97435 Saint Gilles les Hauts
☎ +33 262 70 30 00
🖃 www.bassinbleu.fr

Senegal

Le Golf du Méridien-Président
Les Almadies, BP 8181 Dakar
☎ +221 33 869 69 69
✉ resa.meridien@orange.sn

Golf de Saly
BP 145, Nagaparou
☎ +221 33957 2488
🖃 www.golfsaly.com

Seychelles

Lemuria Resort Golf Course
Anse Kerlan, Ile de Praslin
☎ +248 281 281
✉ golf@lemuriaresort.com
🖃 www.lemuriaresort.com

South Africa

Eastern Cape

East London
22 Gleneagles Road, Bunkers Hill, East London
☎ +27 43 735 1356
🖃 www.elgc.co.za

Humewood GC
Marine Drive, Summerstrand, Port Elizabeth 6013
☎ +27 41 583 2137
✉ info@humewoodgolf.co.za
🖃 www.humewoodgolf.co.za

St Francis Bay GC
Lyme Road South, PO Box 3, St Francis Bay 6312
☎ +27 42 294 0467
✉ info@stfrancisclub.co.za
🖃 www.stfrancisgolf.co.za

Gauteng

Blair Atholl
Centurion, Gauteng 2068
☎ +27 11 996 6300
🖃 www.blairatholl.co.za

Blue Valley
54 Buely Avenue, Centurion
☎ +27 11 318 3410
🖃 www.bluevalley.co.za

Bryanston
63 Bryanston Drive, Byranston 2021
☎ +27 11 706 1361
🖃 www.bryanstoncc.co.za

Centurion
Centurion Drive, John Vorster Avenue, Centurion
☎ +27 12 665 0279
🖃 www.centurioncountryclub.co.za

Dainfern
633 Gateside Avenue, Fourways 2021
☎ +27 11 875 0421
🖃 www.dainfern.co.za

Glendower GC
Marais Road, Edenvale, Johannesburg 1610
☎ +27 11 453 1013
✉ glengolf@mweb.co.za
🖃 www.lglendower.co.za

Hodderfontein
Golf Course Drive, Hodderfontein, Johannesburg
☎ +27 11 608 2033
🖃 www.mgclub.co.za

Houghton GC
2nd Ave, PO Box 87240, Houghton 2041
☎ +27 11 728 7337
✉ hgcm@houghton.co.za
🖃 www.houghton.co.za

Johannesberg (Woodmead)
Lincoln Street, Woodmead, Johannesberg 2128
☎ +27 11 202 1600
🖃 www.ccj.co.za

Kyalami CC
Maple Road, Sunninghill 2157
☎ +27 11 702 1610
🖃 www.kyalamicountryclub.co.za

Maccauvlei
Old Sasolburg Road, Vereeniging
☎ +27 16 421 3196

Parkview
Emmarentia Avenue, Parkview 2122
☎ +27 11 646 5725
🖃 www.parkviewgolf.co.za

Pretoria
241 Sydney Avenue, Waterkloof 0181
☎ +27 12 400 6241
🖃 www.ptacc.co.za

Randpark (Randpark & Windsor Park)
Setperk Street, Randpark, Randburg 2194, Johannesberg
☎ +27 11 476 1691
🖃 www.randpark.co.za

Roodepoort
Hole In One Avenue, Ruimsig, Roodeport
☎ +27 11 958 1905
www.roodepoortcc.co.za

Royal Johannesberg (East & West)
1 Fairway Avenue, Linksfield North, Johannesberg 2119
☎ +27 11 640 3021
www.royaljk.za.com

Silver Lakes
263 La Quinta Street, Silver Lakes, Pretoria
☎ +27 12 809 2110
www.silverlakes.co.za

Wanderers
PO Box 55005, Northlands, Johannesburg 2116
☎ +27 11 447 3311
www.wanderersgolfclub.com

KwaZulu-Natal

Champagne Sports
Winterton 3340
☎ +27 36 468 8000
www.champagnesportsresort.com

Durban CC
PO Box 1504, Durban, 4000
☎ +27 31 313 1777
mail@dcclub.co.za
www.dcclub.co.za

Mount Edgecombe CC
PO Box 1800, Mount Edgecombe 4300
☎ +27 31 595330
reception@mountecc.co.za
www.mountedgecombe.com

Prince's Grant Golf Estate
Babu Bodasingh Ave, PO Box 4038, KwaDukuza/Stanger 4450
☎ +27 32 482 0041
pglodge@saol.com

San Lameer
Main Road, Lower South Coast, Southbroom 4277
☎ +27 39 315 5141
www.sanlameer.co.za

Selborne CC
Old Main Road, PO Box 2, Pennington 4185
☎ +27 39 688 1891
golfbookings@selborne.com
www.selborne.com

Southbroom GC
301 Captain Smith Rd, PO Box 24, Southbroom 4277
☎ +27 39 316 6051
info@southbroomgolfclub.co.za
www.southbroomgolfclub.co.za

Umdoni Park
Minerva Road, Pennington 4184
☎ +27 39 975 1615
www.umdonipark.com

Zimbali
Umhali 4390
☎ +27 32 538 1041
www.zimbali.co.za

Mpumalanga

Leopard Creek CC
PO Box 385, Malelane 1320
☎ +27 13 790 3322
www.leopardcreek.co.za

Limpopo

Elements
5 Autumn Street, Rivonia 2128
☎ +27 14 736 6910
www.elementspgr.co.za

Hans Merensky Estate
PO Box 4, Phalaborwa 1390
☎ +27 15 781 5309
gitw@hansmerensky.com

Legend
Entabeni Safari Conservatory, Sterkrivier
☎ +27 32 538 1205
www.legend-resort.com

Zebula
Bela Bela 0840
☎ +27 14 734 7702
www.zebula.co.za

North West

Gary Player CC
PO Box 6, Sun City 0316
☎ +27 14 557 1245/6
kpayet@sunint.co.za
www.sun-international.com

Lost City GC
PO Box 5, Sun City 0316
☎ +27 14 557 3700
kpayet@sunint.co.za
www.sun-international.com

Pecanwood CC
PO Box 638, Broederstroom 0240
☎ +27 21 7821118
craig@pecanwood.biz

Northern Cape

Sishen
Kathu 8446, Northern Cape
☎ +27 53 723 1501
www.sishengolfclub.co.za

Western Cape

Arabella GC
PO Box 788, Kleinmond, 7195
☎ +27 28 284 9383
dippd@wchs.co.za
www.westerncapehotelandspa.co.za

Atlantic Beach
1 Fairway Drive, Melkbossstrand 7441
☎ +27 21 553 2223
www.atlanticbeachgolfclub.co.za

Clovelly CC
PO Box 22119, Fish Hoek 7974
☎ +27 21 782 1118
bookings@clovelly.co.za
www.clovelly.co.za

Devondale Golf Estate
Bottelary Road, Koelenhof, Stellenbosch 7605
☎ +21 865 2080
info@devonvale.co.za
www.devondale.co.za

Durbanville GC
Sportsway, Durbanville 7550
☎ +27 21 975 4834
manager@durbanvillegc.co.za
www.durbanvillegolfclub.co.za

Erinvale Golf & Country Club Estate
Lourensford Road, PO Box 6188, Somerset West 7129
☎ +27 21 847 1906
pro-shop@erinvale.com
www.erinvalegolfclub.com

Fancourt (The Links, Montagu and Outeniqua)
Montagu Street, Blanco, PO Box 2266, George 6530
☎ +27 44 804 0030
golf@fancourt.co.za
www.fancourt.co.za

George GC
PO Box 81, George, 6530
☎ +27 44 873 6116
info@georgegolfclub.co.za
www.georgegolfclub.co.za

Goose Valley GC
PO Box 1320 Plettenberg Bay 6600
☎ +27 44 533 5082
bookings@goosevalleygolfclub.com
www.goosevalleygolfclub.com

Got a head for heights?

The 19th hole at the Legend Golf & Safari Resort in Limpopo, South Africa lays claim, at 400 metres, to be the highest par three hole in the world. The tee can only be reached via a helicopter up Hanglip Mountain where it overlooks a green the shape of Africa.

Hermanus GC
Main Road, PO Box 313, Hermanus 7200
☎ +27 28 312 1954
✉ bookings@hgc.co.za
▤ www.hgc.co.za

Metropolitan GC
Fritz Sonnenberg Rd, Mouille Point, Cape Town 8001
☎ +27 21 434 9582
✉ golfmix@mweb.co.za

Mossel Bay
17th Avenue, Mossel Bay 6500
☎ +27 44 691 2379
▤ www.mosselbaygolfclub.co.za

Mowbray GC
Raapenberg Rd, Mowbray, Cape Town 7450
☎ +27 21 685 3018
✉ info@mowbraygolfclub.co.za
▤ www.mowbraygolfclub.co.za

Oubaii
Herold's Bay, Western Cape
☎ +27 44 851 0131
▤ www.oubaai.co.za

Paarl GC
Wemmershoek Rd, Paarl 7646
☎ +27 21 863 1140
✉ bookings@paarlgolfclub.co.za
▤ www.paarlgolfclub.co.za

Pearl Valley Golf Estate
PO Box 1, Paarl 7646
☎ +27 867 8000
✉ golf@pearlvalley.co.za
▤ www.pearlvalleygolfestates.com

Pezula
Lagoonview Drive, East Head, Knysna 6570
☎ +27 44 302 5332
▤ www.pezula.com

Pinnacle Point
1 Pinnacle Point Road, Mossel Bay 6506
☎ +27 44 693 3438
▤ www.pinnaclepoint.co.za

Plettenberg Bay
Plesang Valley Road, Plettenberg Bay 6600
☎ +27 44 533 2132
▤ www.plettgolf.co.za

Rondebosch GC
3 Klipfontein Road, PO Box 495, Rondebosch, Cape Town 7700
☎ +27 21 689 4176
✉ info@rgc.co.za

Royal Cape GC
174 Ottery Road, PO Box 186, Ottery 7808, Wynberg, 7800
☎ +27 21 797 5246
✉ manager@royalcapegolf.co.za
▤ www.royalcapegolf.co.za

Simola
1 Old Cape Road, Knysna 6570
☎ +267 360 4000
▤ www.simolaestate.co.za

Steenberg
Tokal Road, Tokal 7495
☎ +27 21 713 2233
▤ www.steenberggolfclub.co.za

Stellenbosch GC
PO Box 1, Paarl 7646
☎ +27 21 867 8000
✉ golf@pearlvalley.co.za
▤ www.pearlvalleygolfestates.com

Westlake GC
Westlake Ave, Lakeside 7945
☎ +27 21 788 2530
✉ info@westlakegolfclub.co.za
▤ www.westlakegolfclub.co.za

De Zalze Winelands Golf Estate
PO Box 12706, Die Boord, Stellenbosch 7613
☎ +27 21 880 7300
✉ info@dezalzegolf.com
▤ www.dezalzegolf.com

Swaziland

Royal Swazi Spa CC
Main Road, Mbabane
☎ +268 416 5000
▤ www.suninternation.com/Destinations/Resorts/Golf/Pages/Golf.aspx

Tunisia

Djerba

Djerba GC
Zone Touristique BP360, 4116 Midoun
☎ +216 75 745 055
✉ contact@djerbagolf.com
▤ www.djerbagolf.com

Hammamet

Golf Citrus (Le Fôret and Les Oliviers)
Hammamet BP 132, 8050 Hammamet
☎ +216 72 226 500
✉ golf.citrus@planet.tn
▤ www.golfcitrus.com

Yasmine Golf Course
BP 61, 8050 Hammamet
☎ +216 72 227 001
✉ info@golfyasmine.com
▤ www.golfyasmine.com

Monastir

Flamingo Golf Course
Route de Ouardanine, BP 40, Monastir Gare, 5079 Monastir
☎ +216 73 500 283
✉ booking@golfflamingo.com
▤ www.golfflamingo.com

Palm Links Golf Course
B.P: 216 Monastir République, 5060 Tunisie
☎ +216 73 521 910
✉ info@golf-palmlinks.com
▤ www.golf-palmlinks.com

Port el Kantaoui

El Kantaoui Golf (Sea and Panorama)
Station Touristique, 4089 El Kantaoui BP 32 Port el Kantaoui
☎ +216 73 348 756
▤ www.kantaouigolfcourse.com.tn

The Résidence Golf Course
Boite Postale 697, 2070 La Marsa, Les Côtes de Carthage
☎ +216 71910 101
✉ info@theresidence.com
▤ www.theresidence.com

Tabarka

Tabarka Golf Course
Rte Touristique El Morjènel, 8110 Tabarka
☎ +216 78 670 028
✉ info@tabarkagolf.com
▤ www.tabarkagolf.com

Tozeur

Oasis Golf Tozeur
Société Golf Oasis BP 48, Poste Elchorfa, 2243 Tozeur
☎ +216 76 471 194
✉ reservation.golf@tozeuroasisgolf.com
▤ www.tozeuroasisgolf.com

Tunis/Carthage

Golf de Carthage
Choutrana II, 2036 Soukra
☎ +216 71 765 700
✉ reservationgc@planet.tn
▤ www.golfcarthage.com

Uganda

Entebbe Golf Club
P.O.Box 107, Entebbe
☎ +261 020 44 94 387

Uganda GC
Kitante Road. Kampala, Uganda
☎ +261 236848

Zambia

Chainama Hills
P.O Box 31385 Lusaka
☎ +260 211 250916
✉ dngambi@yahoo.com

Livingstone GC
Victoria Falls, Southern Province
☎ +260 321 323052
✉ info@livingstonegolf.com
🌐 www.livingstonegolf.com

Mufulira GC
PO Box 40141 / 40700, Mufulira, Copperbelt Province
☎ +260 212 411131
✉ mufuliraclub@ovation.co.za
🌐 www.mufulira.co.za

Ndola GC
PO Box 71564, Ndola
☎ +26 005 588 6678
🌐 www.ndolagolfclub.com

Zimbabwe

Chapman GC
Samora Machel, Avenue East, Harare
☎ +263 4 747 328
🌐 www.chapmangolfclub.co.zw

Middle East

Bahrain

Awali GC
PO Box 25413, Awali, Kingdom of Bahrain
☎ +973 1775 6770
✉ secretary@awaligolfclub.com
🌐 www.awaligolfclub.com
⊕ 18 hole sand course

Bahrain GC
✉ salem_1956@hotmail.com
⊕ 18 hole sand course

The Royal GC
PO Box 39117, Riffa, Kingdom of Bahrain
☎ +973 1775 0777
✉ info@theroyalgolfclub.com
🌐 www.theroyalgolfclub.com

Israel

Caesarea G&CC
PO Box 4858, Caesarea 30889
☎ +972 463 61173

Gaash CC
🌐 www.gaashgolfclub.co.il

Kuwait

Sahara G&CC
PO Box 29930 Safat 13160
☎ +965 4769408
✉ info@saharakuwait.com
🌐 www.saharakuwait.com
⊕ Fully illuminated for night time golf

Oman

Muscat G&CC
PO Box 3358, CPO, Postal Code 111, Sultanate of Oman
☎ +968 24 510065
✉ info@muscatgolf.com
🌐 www.muscatgolf.com

The Wave GC
Madinat Al Sultan Qaboos, PO Box 87, PC 118, Sultanate of Oman
☎ +968 245 34444
✉ customerservice@thewavemuscat.com
🌐 thewavemuscat.com

Qatar

Doha GC
PO Box 13530, Doha, State of Qatar
✉ info@dohagolfclub.com

Mesaieed GC
Umm Said, Mesaieed, State of Qatar
☎ +974 476 0874
✉ mgc_golf@yahoo.co.uk

Dukhan GC
PO Box 49776, Dubai, State of Qatar
✉ qatargasgolfopen@qatargas.com.qa

Saudi Arabia

Arizona Golf Resort
PO Box 8080, Riyadh 11482
☎ +966 1 248 4444
✉ management@agr.com.sa
🌐 www.agr.com.sa

United Arab Emirates

Abu Dhabi Golf & Equestrian Club
PO Box 33303
☎ +971 244 59600

Abu Dhabi GC
PO Box 51234
🌐 www.adgolfclub.com

Al Badia GC
PO Box 49776, Dubai
☎ +971 460 10101

Al Ghazal GC
PO Box 3167
☎ +971 257 58040
⊕ Sand course

Al Hamra GC
PO Box 6617, Ras Al Khaimah
🌐 www.alhamragolf.com

Arabian Ranches GC
PO Box 36700, Dubai
🌐 www.arabianranchesgolfdubai.com

Dubai Creek Golf & Yacht Club
PO Box 6302, Dubai
🌐 www.dubaigolf.com

Emirates GC
PO Box 24040, Dubai
🌐 www.dubaigolf.com

Jebel Ali Golf Resort & Spa
PO Box 9255, Dubai
🌐 www.jebelalo-international.com

Jumeirah Golf Estates
PO Box 262080, Dubai
🌐 www.jumeirahgolfestates.com

Palm Sports Resort
PO Box 1671, Al Ain
🌐 www.palmsportsresort.com

Sharjah Golf & Shooting Club
PO Box 6, Sharjah
🌐 www.golfandshootingshj.com

Sharjah Wanderers GC
PO Box 1767, Sharjah
🌐 www.sharjahgolf.com
⊕ 9 holes sand, 9 holes grass

The Els Club
PO Box 111123, Dubai
🌐 www.elsclubdubai.com

The Montgomerie Dubai
PO Box 36700, Dubai
🌐 www.themontgomerie.com

Tower Links GC
PO Box 30888, Ras Al Khaimah
☎ +971 722 79939

Asia

Bangladesh

Army GC
Dhaka Cantonment
☎ 0181 921 2211 (mobile)

Bhatiary G&CC
C/o 24 Infantry Division, Chittagong Cantonment
☎ +880 031 278 7423
✉ bhatiarygolf@yahoo.com

BOF GC
Bangladesh Ordnance Factories, Gazipur Cantonment, Gazipur
☎ +880 920 4613

Bogra GC
C/o 11 Infantry Division, Bogra Cantonment
☎ +880 051 82080

Dhaka Club Limited
Ramna, Dhaka-100
☎ +880 861 9180
✉ dcl@bdonline.com

Jessore G&CC
C/o Headquarters 55 Infantry Division (Ordnance Br), Jessore Cantonment, Jessore
☎ +880 0421 68675
✉ +880 0421 67450

Kurmitola GC
Dhaka Cantonment, Dhaka 1206
☎ +880 875 2520
✉ kgcdhaka@hotmail.com

Mainamati G&CC
C/o 33 Infantry Division, Comilla Cantonment, Comilla
☎ +880 081 76381
✉ mgcc18@yahoo.com

Rangpur GC
C/o66 Infantry Division, Rangpur Cantonment
☎ +880 673000

Savar GC
9 Infantry Division, Savar Cantonment, Savar 01714171790 (XO)
☎ +880 779 1839

Shaheen G&CC
BAF Base Zahurul Haque, Patanga, Chattigong
☎ +880 031-250 2033
✉ sgccpbaf@gmail.com

Bhutan

Royal Bhutan GC
Chhopel Lam, Thimphu
☎ +925 232 5429

Brunei

Pantai Mentiri GC
Km 15½ Jalan Kota Batu, Brunei Darussalam
☎ +673-279102
✉ infodesk@pantaimentirigolfclub.com
🌐 www.pantaimentirigolfclub.com

Royal Brunei G&CC
Jerudong Park, Jerudong BG3122, Brunei Darussalam
☎ +673 261 1582

China

Anhui

Huangshan Pine G&CC
No. 78, Longjing, Jichang Da Av., Tunxi District, Huangshan City, Anhui
☎ +86 559 256 8399
✉ pine@chinahsgolf.com
🌐 www.chinahsgolf.com

Beijing

Beijing CBD International
No.99, Gaobeidian RD, Chaoyang District, Beijing 100023
☎ +86 10 673 84801
✉ hongshuasale@h-cgolf.com
🌐 www.h-cgolf.com

Beijing Taiwei GC
Xiangtang New Culture Town, Cuicun County, Chanping District, Beijing 102212
☎ +86 10 6072 5599
🌐 www.taiweigolf.com

Chongqing

Chongqing International GC
Huaxi Town, Banan District, Chongqing 400055
☎ +86 23 6255 4816
✉ chongqinggolf@sina.com.cn

Fujian

Orient (Xiamen) G&CC
Haicang Investment & Development Zone Xiamen, Fujian Province 528234
☎ +86 592 653 1317
✉ xiamen@orientgolf.com

Quanzhou GC
Zimao Town, Jinjiang, Fujian Province 362213
☎ +86 595 595 1988
✉ golf@pub1.qz.fj.cn
🌐 www.qzgolf.com

Trans Strait GC
New Village, Wenwusha Town, Changle, Fuzhou, Fujian Province, China 350207
☎ +86 591 2878 9567
✉ tsgolfc@pub6.fz.fj.cn

Guangdong

Dongguan Hill View GC
Ying Bin Da Dao, Dong Cheng District, Dongguan, Guangdong
☎ +86 769 222 09980
✉ hillview@tom.com
🌐 www.hillview-golf.com

Nanhai Peach Garden GC
Peach Garden, Songgang, Nanhai District, Foshan City, Guangdong Province 528234
☎ +86 757 852 31888
🌐 www.peachgardengolf.com

Zhuhai Golden Gulf GC
Jinwan Road, Golden Coast, Jinwan District, Zhuhai, Guangdong 519041
☎ +86 756 761 4000
✉ goldengolf@zhggg.com
🌐 www.zhggg.com

Guangxi

Gentle Uptown GC
Nanwu Road, Naning, Guangxi Province 530024
☎ +86 771 580 5501
✉ shichangbu@gentlegolf.com
🌐 www.gentlegolf.com

Li River G&CC
Foreign Marina, Overseas Chinese Tourism District, Guilin, Guangxi Province 541008
☎ +86 773 390 9080
✉ golf@chin-taiwan.com
🌐 www.royal.fide.com

Guizhou

Guiyang GC
Sanyuan, Zha Zuo Town Guiyang, Guizhou Province 550201
☎ +86 851 235 1888
✉ gygolfclub@163.com
🌐 www.guiyanggolf.com

Heilongjiang

Heilongjiang Harbin Baiyun GC
Harbin, Heilongjiang Province
☎ +86 451 600 5242

Hainan

Haikou Meishi Mayflower International GC
88 West Binhai Road, Haikou City, Hainan Province 570311
☎ +86 898 6871 8888
✉ websitesales@meishigolf.com
▤ www.meishigolf.com

Kangle Garden Spa & GC
Xinglong Town, Wanning, Hainan Province 571533
☎ +86 898 6256 8888
✉ golfclub@kangleresort.com
▤ www.kangleresort.com

Yalong Bay GC
No.168 Qiong Dong Road, Dongshan Town, Qiongshan, Hainan Province 572016
☎ +86 898 8856 5888
✉ welcome@yalongbaygolfclub.com
▤ www.yalongbaygolfclub.com

Hebei

Grandeur South G&CC
No.1 Yongle Road, ZhuoZhou, Hebei Province 072750
☎ +86 10 8120 2880
✉ members@gsgcc.com
▤ www.gsgcc.com

Xin'ao Group Elephant Hotel
Jinyuan Road, Economic & Technological Development Zone, Langfang City, Hebei Province 065001
☎ +86 316 606 1188
✉ pyn-golf@163.com

Henan

Synear International GC
No.86, South Bank of The Yellow River, Zhengzhou City, Henan Province 450004
☎ +86 371 636 26699
▤ www.syneargolf.com

Hubei

Orient (Wuhan) Golf Country Club
Xingxing, Jiangti Hanyang District Wuhan, Hubei Province 430051
☎ +86 27 8461 2270
✉ wuhan@orientgolf.com
▤ www.orientgolf.com

Hunan

Changsha Qingzhuhu International GC
Qingzhuhu, Kaifu District, Changsha City, Hunan Province 410152
☎ +86 731 678 3999
✉ golf@hunangolf.com.cn
▤ www.hunangolf.com.cn

Hunan Dragon Lake International GC
Guan Yin Yan Reservoir, Wangcheng District, Changsha, Hunan Province 410217
☎ +86 731 838 8277
✉ longhu.hn@2118.com.cn
▤ www.dragonlakegolf.com

Jiangsu

Gingko Lake International GC
No.1, Gingko Lake, GuLi Town, Jiangning District, Nanjing, Jiangsu Province 211164
☎ +86 25 8613 9988
✉ gingkolake@gingkolake.com
▤ www.gingkolake.com

Nanjing Harvard GC
No. 176 Zhen Zhu Road, Pukhou District, Nanjing City, Jiangsu Province 210031
☎ +86 25 5885 3333
✉ welcome@harvardgolf.com
▤ www.harvardgolf.com

Shanghai West Country GC
128 Huanzhen W. Road, Zhouzhuang, Kunshan, Jiangsu 215325
☎ +86 512 5720 3888
✉ golf@shanghaiwest.com
▤ www.shanghaiwest.com

Jiangxi

Nanchang Mingya G&CC
No. 601, South Lushan Dadao, Nanchang City, Jiangxi.Province 330013
☎ +86 791 382 1600
✉ info@mingya.cn
▤ www.mingya.cn/golf

Jilin

Changchun Jingyetan GC
Ingyuetan National Forest Park, Changchun, Jilin Province 130117
☎ +86 431 528 3815
✉ jingyuetangolf@163.com

Liaoning

Dalian Golden Pebble Beach GC
Dalian Jinshi Tan State Tourist & Vacational Zone, Liaoning 116650
☎ +86 411 8791 2343
✉ jinqiu@dalianjinshigolf.com
▤ www.dalianjinshigolf.com

Dandong Wulong International GC
Lishugou Village, Loufang Town, Zhen An District, Dandong, Liaoning 118000
☎ +86 415 417 1857
✉ golf@wl-golf.com
▤ www.wl-golf.com

Shanghai

Grand Shanghai International G&CC
Yang-Cheng Lake Tour & Holiday Zone, Ba Cheng Town, Kunshan Jiangsu Province 215347
☎ +86 512 5789 1999
✉ uugsighr@public1.sz.js.cn
▤ www.grandshanghaigolfresort.com

Orient (Shanghai) G&CC
High-Technology Garden, Songjiang District, Shanghai 201600
☎ +86 21 5785 4698
✉ shanghai@orientgolf.com

Shanghai Links GC
No. 1600 Ling Bai Road, Pu Dong New District, Shanghai 201201
☎ +86 21 5897 5899
▤ www.thelinks.com.cn

Shandong

Guoke International GC
Economic Development Area in Qihe, Shandong Province 528234
☎ +86 534 8550 0299
▤ www.gk-golf.com

Nanshan International GC
Nanshan Tourist Zone, Dongjiang Town, Longkou, Shandong Province 265718
☎ +86 535 861 6818
✉ service@nanshangolf.com
▤ www.nanshangolf.com

Shaanxi

Xi'an Yajian International GC
Cao-Tang Tourist & Holiday Resort, Hu County, Xi'an, Shaanxi 710304
☎ +86 29 8495 1236
✉ rivergolf@163.com

Shenzhen

Shenzhen Airport Golf Resort
Near to Bao An Airport, Shenzhen 518128
☎ +86 755 2777 9991
✉ airportgolf@sohu.com

Shenzhen GC
Shen Nan Road, Fu Tian Qu, Shenzen, Guangdong 518034
☎ +86 755 330 8888

Shenzhen Tycoon GC
Jiu Wei, Xi Xiang Town, Boan District, Shenzhen, Guangdong 518126
☎ +86 755 2748 3999
✉ member@hkcts.com
▤ www.tycoongolf.com

Sichuan

Sichuan International GC
Mu Ma Shan Development Zone, Shuangliu Country, Chengdu, Sichuan 610026
☎ +86 28 8578 5010
✉ sigc@sigc.com
▤ www.sigc.com

Tianjin

Tianjin Fortune Lake GC
Tuanbo Town, Jinghai County, Tianjin 300193
☎ +86 22 6850 5299
✉ tj_golf@eyou.com

Tianjin Warner International GC
N° 1 Nanhai Road, Teda, Tianjin 300457
☎ +86 22 2532 6009
✉ warner@warner-golf.com
▤ www.warnergolfclub.com

Xinjiang

Xinjiang Urumqi Xuelianshan GC
West Hot Spring Road, Shui Mo Gou District, Urumqi, Xinjiang Province 830017
☎ +86 991 487 3888
▤ www.j-golf.com

Yunnan

Kunming Country GC
14km Anshi Highway, Kunming, Yunnan Province 650601
☎ +86 871 742 6666
✉ fhy@public.km.yn.cn

Lijiang Ancient Town International GC
Huangshan Town, Yulong, Lijiang City, Yunnan Province 674100
☎ +86 888 662 2700
✉ Lg3102331@vip.km169.net

Zhejiang

Huangzhou West Lake International CC
No.200 Zhijiang Road, Zhejiang Province 310024
☎ +86 571 8732 1700
✉ golf@westlakegolf.com
▤ www.westlakegolf.com

Orient (Wenzhou) Golf CC
Yangyi West Suburbia Forest Park, Lucheng District, Wenzhou, Zhejiang Province 325000
☎ +86 577 8881 7718
✉ wenzhou@orientgolf.com
▤ www.orientgolf.com

Chinese Taipei

Chang Hua GC
101 Lane 2, Ta Pu Road, Changhua City, Taiwan
☎ +886 4 7135799

Lily G&CC
55 Hu Tu Tuan, Kuan Hsi, Hsinchu County, Taiwan
☎ +886 3 5875111

National Garden GC
1-1 Shihjhen Village, Yuanli Township, Miaoli County, Taiwan
☎ +886 37 741166

North Bay G&CC
5 Tsau Pu Wei, Tsau-Li Village, Shimen Township, Taipei County, Taiwan
☎ +886 2 26382930

Sunrise G&CC
256 Yang Sheng Road, Yang Mei, Taoyuan County, Taiwan
☎ +886 3 4780099

Taichung G&CC
46 Tungshan Road, Hengshan Village, Taya, Taichung County, Taiwan
☎ +886 4 25665130~2

Taipei GC
34-1, Chihtuchi, Kengtsu-Tsun, Luchu-Hsiang, Taoyuan County, Taiwan
☎ +886 3 3241311-5

Ta Shee G&CC
168 Jih Hsin Road, Ta Hsi Township, Taoyuan County, Taiwan
☎ +886 3 3875699

Wu Fong G&CC
668 Feng-Ku Road, Feng-ku Village, Wu Feng, Taichung County, Taiwan
☎ +886 4 23301199

Hong Kong

Clear Water Bay G&CC
☎ +852 2719 1595

Discovery Bay GC
☎ +852 2987 7273

Hong Kong GC, Deep Water Bay
☎ +852 2812 7070

Hong Kong GC, Fanling
☎ +852 2670 1211

The Jockey Club
☎ +852 2791 3388

Shek O CC
☎ +852 2809 4458

Sky City Eagles GC
☎ +852 3760 6688

India

Agra GC
Tay Road, Agra 282001 UP
☎ +91 5622 226015

Bangalore GC
2 Stanley Road, High Grounds, Bangalore 560001
☎ +91 80 228 1876
✉ bgc1876@bgl.vsnl.net.in

Bombay Presidency GC
Dr Choitram Gidwani Road, Chembur, Mumbai 400074
☎ +91 22 550 5874

Chandigarh GC
Sector 6, Chandigarh
☎ +91 17 274 0350
✉ cgc@chai91.net

Cosmopolitan GC
18 Golf Club Road, Tollygunge, Calcutta 700033 West Bengal
☎ +91 33 473 1352

Delhi GC
Dr Zakhir Hussain Marg, New Delhi 10003
☎ +91 11 243 6278
✉ delhigolf@aibn.on.ca

DLF Club
DLF City, Gurgaon, Haryana
✉ karan@dlfmail.com

Eagleton GC
30th KM Bangalore-Mysore Highway, Bangalore
✉ eagleton@bgol.vsnl.net.in

Gaekwad Baroda GC
Lukshimi Villas Estate Baroda, Gujarat 390001
☎ +91 26 524 33599

Madras Gymkhana GC
Golf Annexe 334 Mount Road, Nandanam, Chennai 600035
☎ +91 44 56881

Motacamuna Gymkhana CC
Finger Post PO, The Nilgirls, Tamilnadu 643006
☎ +91 42 324 42254

Poona GC
Airport Road, Yerawada Pune 411006
☎ +91 20 266 94131

Royal Calcutta
18 Golf Club Road, Tollygunge, Calcutta 700033 West Bengal
☎ +91 33 473 1352
www.royalcalcuttagolfclub.com

Tollegunge GC
120 Deshapran Sasmal Road, Calcutta
☎ +91 33 473 4539

Indonesia

Bukit Darmo Golf
Blok G-2, Jl Bukit Darmo, Surabaya 60226
☎ +62-31-7325555
www.bukitdarmogolf.com

Nirwana Bali GC
Jl. Raya Tanah Lot Kediri, Tabanan 82171, Bali
☎ +62 361 815 960
www.nirwanabaligolf.com

Satelindo Padang Golf
Bukit Sentul, Bogor 16810, West Java
☎ +62 21 879 60266
✉ marketing@golfsatelindo.com
www.golfsatelindo.co.id

Japan

Abiko CC
1110 Okahotto, Abiko-shi, Chiba Pref. 270-1137
☎ +81 (0) 4 7182 0111
www.abikogc.com

Aichi CC
20-1 Yamanonaka, Itaka-cho, Takabari, Meito-ku, Nagoya-shi, Aichi Pref. 465-0067
☎ +81 (0) 52 701 1161
www.aichicc.jp/top.htm

Hirono GC
7-3 Hirono Shijimi-cho, Miki-Shi, Hyogo Pref. 673-0541
☎ +81 (0) 794 85 0123

Hodogaya CC
1324 Kamikawaicho, Asahi-ku, Yokohama-shi, Kanagawa Pref. 241-0802
☎ +81(0) 45 921 0115
www.hodogaya-country-club.jp/

Ibaraki CC
25 Nakahozumi, Ibaraki-shi, Osaka Pref. 567-0034
☎ +81 (0) 72 625 1661
www.ibarakicc.or.jp/

Kasumigaseki CC
3398 Kasahata, Kawagoe-shi, Saitama Pref. 350-1175
☎ +81 (0) 49 231 2181
www.kasumigasekicc.or.jp/

Kawana (Fuji)
1459 Kawana, Ito City, Shizuoka, Chubu, Honshu
☎ +81 557 45 1111
www.princehotels.co.jp/kawana/

Kobe GC
Ichigaya Rokkosancho, Nadaku Kobe-shi, Hyogo Pref. 657-0101
☎ +81 (0) 78 891 0364

Koga GC
1310-1 Shishi-bu, Koga-shi, Fukuoka Pref. 811-3105
☎ +81 (0) 92 943 2261
www.kogagc.co.jp/english/index.html

Nagoya GC
35-1 Dondoro, Wago, Togo-cho, Aichi-gun, Aichi Pref. 470-0153
☎ +81 (0) 52 801 1111
www.nagoyagolfclub-wago.gr.jp/

Naruo GC
1-4 Kanagadani Nishiuneno, Kawanishi-shi, Hyogo Pref. 666-0155
☎ +81 (0) 72 794 1011
www.naruogc.or.jp/

Sagami CC
4018 Shimotsuruma, Yamato-shi, Kanagawa Pref. 242-0001
☎ +81 (0) 46 274 3130
www.h3.dion.ne.jp/~sagamicc/

Takanodai CC
1501 Yokodo-cho, Hanamigawa-ku, Chiba-shi, Chiba Pref. 262-0001
☎ +81 (0) 47 484 3151
www.takanodaicc.or.jp/

Tokyo GC
1984 Kashiwabara, Sayama-shi, Saitama Pref. 350-1335
☎ +81 (0) 4 2953 9111

Korea

Chungcheong

Cheonan Sangnok Resort Golf Course
669-1 Jangsan-ri, Susin-myeon, Cheonan-si, Chungcheongnam-do
☎ +82 41 529 9075

Gangwong

Alps Golf Course
107 Heul-ri, Ganseong-eup, Goseong-gun, Gangwon-do
☎ +82 33 681 5030
www.alpsresort.co.kr

Gyeonggi

Sky 72 GC
2029-1 Woonseo-Dong, Joong-Gu, Incheon
☎ +82 32 743 9108
www.sky72.com/en/index.jsp

Songchoo CC
San 23-1, BeeAhm-Lee, KwangJuk-Myon, YangJu-si, Gyeonggi-Do
☎ +82 31 871 9410
www.songchoo.co.kr/e-htm

Taeyoung CC
San38 Jukrung-ri Wonsam-myun Yong-in-shi, Kyuongki-do
☎ +82 31 334 5051
www.ty-cc.com/english/introd.jsp

Gyeongsang

Bomun CC
180-7 Mulcheon-ri, Cheonbuk-myeon, Gyeongju-si, Gyeongsangbuk-do
☎ +82 54 745 1680 2

Gageun GC
111-1 Ma-dong, Gyeongju-si, Gyeongsangbuk-do
☎ +82 54 740 5161

Mauna Ocean Golf
Shindaeri San 140-1 Yangnammyon Gyeongjusi, Gyeongsangbuk-do
☎ +82 54 77 0900

Jeju

Chungmun Beach GC
3125-1, Saekal-dong, Sogwipo, Cheju-Do
☎ +82 64 735 7241

Nine Bridge Golf Course
Kwangpyong-ri, Anduk-myon, South Jeju-gun, Jeju Island
☎ +82 64 793 9999
www.ninebridge.co.kr

Jeolla

Club 900
San 15-1, Ssangok-ri, Dogok-myeon, Hwasun-gun, Jeollanam-do
☎ +82 61 371 0900

Pusan

Dong Nae CC
San 128, Son-dong, Dongnae-gu, Pusan
☎ +82 51 513 0101

Seoul

Namsungdae GC
419 Jangji-dong, Songpa-gu, Seoul
☎ +82 02 403 0071

Laos

Santisuk Lang Xang GC
Km14 Thadeua Road, Ban Nahai, Vientiane, Laos
☎ +856 21 812 071

Macao

Macau G&CC
☎ +853 871188

Malaysia

Labuan

Labuan GC
PO Box 276, 87008 Labuan, Labuan
☎ +60 87 412 810

Sabah

Borneo G&CC
Km 69, Papar-Beaufort Highway, 89700 Bongawan, Sabah
☎ +60 87 861 888
✉ reservation.bgcc@vhmis.com

Karambunai Resorts GC
PO Box 270, Menggatal, 88450 Kota Kinabalu, Sabah
☎ +60 88 411 215
✉ salesmgrkrgc@borneo-resort.com
▤ www.borneo-resort.com

Shan-Shui Golf & Country Resort
PO Box 973, Mile 9, Jalan Apas,Tawau, 91008 Tawau, Sabah
☎ +60 89 916 888
✉ ssgolfcc@tm.net.my

Sutera Harbour G&CC
1 Sutera Harbour Boulevard, 88100 Kota Kinabalu, Sabah
☎ +60 88 318 888
✉ sutera@suteraharbour.com.my
▤ www.suteraharbour.com.my

Sarawak

Damai G&CC
Jalan Santubong, PO Box 203, 93862 Kuching, Sarawak
☎ +60 82 846 088
✉ dgcc@po.jaring.my
▤ www.damaigolf.com

Hornbill Golf & Jungle Club
Jalan Borneo Heights, Borneo Highlands Resort, 94200 Padawan, Sarawak
☎ +60 82 790 800
✉ enquiry@hornbillgolf.com
▤ www.hornbillgolf.com

Johor

Bukit Banang G&CC
No. 1, Persiaran Gemilang, Bandar Banang Jaya, 83000 Batu Pahat, Johor
☎ +60 7 428 6001
✉ bbgcc@po.jaring.my
▤ www.berjayaclubs.com/banang /index.cfm

Daiman 18 Johor Bahru
No.18 Jalan Pesona, Taman Johor Jaya, 81100 Johor Bahru, Joho
☎ +60 7 353 3100
✉ daiman18@daiman.com.my
▤ www.daiman.com.my

Desaru G&CC
PO Box 26, Bandar Penawa, 81900 Kota Tinggi, Johor
☎ +60 7 8222 333
✉ golf@desaruresort.com
▤ www.desaruresort.com

Palm Resort G&CC
Jalan Persiaran Golf, Off Jalan Jumbo, 81250 Senai, Johor
☎ +60 7 5996 222
✉ marcomm@palmresort.com
▤ www.palm-resort.com

Palm Villa Golf & Country Resort
PTD 44500, Jalan Pindah Utama, Bandar Putra, PO Box 69, 81000 Kulai, Johor
☎ +60 7 599 9099
✉ Honorius@IOI.po.my

Ponderosa G&CC
10-C Jalan Bumi Hijau 3, Taman Molek, 81100 Johor Bahru, Johor
☎ +60 7 354 9999
✉ pgcc@tm.net.my
▤ www.ponderosagolf.com

Royal Johor CC
3211 Jalan Larkin, 80200 Johor Bharu, Johor
☎ +60 7 2224 2098
✉ rjcc@tm.net.my
▤ www.royaljohorcountryclub.com

Sebana Cove
LB 505 Kota Tinggi PO, 81900 Kota Tinggi, Johor
☎ +60 7 826 6688
✉ sebanacove@pacific.net.sg
▤ www.sebanacove.com

Starhill G&CC
6.5 Km Jalan Maju Jaya, Kempas Lama, Skudai, 81300 Johor Baru, Johor
☎ +60 7 5566 325
▤ www.starhillgolf.com.my

Tanjong Puteri G&CC
Ptd 101446, Mukim Plentong, 81700 Pasir Gudang, Johor
☎ +60 7 2711 888
✉ tpgolf@tm.net.my

Kedah

Black Forest G&CC
Zon Bebas Cukai, 06050 Bukit Kayu Hitam, Kedah
☎ +60 4 9222 790
✉ blackforest@sriwani.com.my
▤ www.blackforest.com.my

Cinta Sayang G&CC
Jalan Persiaran Cinta Sayang, 0800 Sungai Petani, Kedah
☎ +60 4 4414 666
✉ cintasayang@cinta-sayang.com.my
▤ www.cintasayangresort.com/ cs_golf.html

Datai Bay GC
Jalan Teluk Datai, PO Box 6, Kuah, 07000 Pulau Langkawi, Kedah
☎ +60 4 9592 700
▤ www.dataigolf.com

Gunung Raya Golf Resort
alan Air Hangat, Kisap, Kuah, 07000 Pulau Langkawi, Kedah
☎ +60 4 9668 148
✉ reservation@golfgr.com.my
▤ www.golfgr.com.my

Sungai Petani Club
23-C Jalan Sungai Layar, 08000 Sungai Petani, Kedah
☎ +60 4 422 4894
✉ info@slgcc.com.my
▤ www.slgcc.com.my/intro.php

Kelantan

Kelantan G&CC
5488 Jalan Hospital, 15200 Kota Bahru, Kelantan
☎ +60 9 7482 102

Kuala Lumpur

Bukit Jalil Golf & Country Resort
Jalan 3/155B, 57000 Bukit Jalil, Kuala Lumpur
☎ +60 3 8994 1600
✉ bgrb@bukitjalil.com.my
▤ www.berjayaclubs.com/jalil

Golf Club Perkhidmatan Awam
Bukit Kiara, Off Jalan Damansara, 60000 Kuala Lumpur
☎ +60 3 7957 1958
✉ gmkgpa@kgpagolf.com
▤ www.kgpagolf.com

Kuala Lumpur G&CC
10, Jalan 1/70D, Off Jalan Bukit Kiara, 60000 Kuala Lumpur
☎ +60 3 2093 1111
✉ klgcc@simedarby.com
▤ www.klgcc.com

Melaka

A'Famosa Golf Resort
Jalan Kemus, Simpang 4
78000 Alor Gajah, Melaka
☎ +60 6 5520 888
✉ enquiries@afamosa.com
▤ www.afamosa.com

Pandanusa GC
PT.30, Pulau Besar, Mukim Pernu,Melaka Tengah Melaka
☎ +60 6 281 5015
▤ www.members.tripodasia .com.my/pulaubesar

Negeri Sembilan

Nilai Springs G&CC
PT 4770, Bandar Baru Nilai, PO Box 50, 71801 Nilai, Negeri Sembilan
☎ +60 6 8508 888
✉ nsgcc@pd.jaring.my
www.nilaispringsgcc.com.my/golfing

Port Dickson G&CC
Batu 5 1/2, Jalan Pantai, 71050 Port Dickson, Negeri Sembilan
☎ +60 6 647 3586
✉ pdgcc@po.jaring.my
www.pdgolf.com.my

Royal Palm Springs GC
Bt.13 Km.21 Jalan Pantai, Mukim Pasir Panjang, Negeri Sembilan
☎ +60 6 661 9599
✉ palmspringsresortcity @tancoresorts.com
www.palmspringsresortcity.com /rpsgc/index

Pahang

Astana G&CC
Sungai Lembing, Bandar Indera Mahkota, 25200 Kuantan, Pahang
☎ +60 9 5735 135
✉ astana@tm.net.my
www.astanagolf@150m.com

Pantai Lagenda G&CC
Lot 877, Kampung Kuala Pahang, 26660 Pekan, Pahang
☎ +60 9 4251 658
✉ pigolf@tm.net.my

Penang

Bukit Jambul G&CC
No.2 Jalan Bukit Jambul, 11900 Bayan Lepas
☎ +60 4 644 2255
✉ bcc@po.jaring.my
www.bjcc.com.my

Bukit Jawi Golf Resort
No.691 Main Road, Sg. Bakap, S.P.S., 14200 Penang
☎ +60 4 5820 759
www.bukitjawi.com.my

Penang Golf Resort
Lot 1687 Jalan Bertam, Seberang Perai, Utara
13200 Kepala Batas, Penang
☎ +60 4 5782 022
www.penanggolfresort.com.my

Perak

Clearwater Sanctuary Golf Resort
Lot 6019 Jalan Changkat Larang, 31000 Batu Gajah, Perak
☎ +60 5 3667 433
✉ cesgolf@po.jaring.my
www.cwsgolf.com.my

Damai Laut G&CC
Hala Damai 2, Jalan Damai Laut , Off Jalan Teluk Senanging
32200 Lumut, Perak
☎ +60 5 6183 333
✉ resvns_dlgcc@swissgarden.com
www.swissgarden.com/hotels/sgrdl

Meru Valley G&CC
Jalan Bukit Meru, Off Jalan Jelapang, 30020 Ipoh, Perak
☎ +60 5 5293 300
✉ info@meruvalley.com.my
www.meruvalley.com.my

Selangor

Bangi Golf Resort
No.1 Persiaran Bandar, Bandar Baru Bangi 43650 Selangor
☎ +60 3 8925 3728
✉ bgr@po.jaring.my

Golf Club Sultan Abdul Aziz Shah
No.1 Rumah Kelab 13/6, 40100 Shah Alam, Selangor
☎ +60 3 5519 1512
✉ cecy@kgsaas.com.my
www.kgaas.com.my

Kelab Golf Seri Selangor
Persiaran Damansara Indah, Off Prsn Tropicana, Kota Damansara, 47410 Petaling Jaya, Selango
☎ +60 3 7806 1111
✉ mktg@seriselangor.com
seriselangor.com.my

Kota Permai G&CC
No.1 Jalan 31/100A, Kota Kemuning Section 31, 40460 Shah Alam, Selangor Darul Ehsan
☎ +60 3 5122 3700
✉ kpgcc@kotapermai.com.my
www.kotapermai.com.my

Palm Garden GC
IOI Resort, 62502 Putrajaya, Selangor
☎ +60 3 8948 7160
✉ pggc@tm.net.my
www.palmgarden.net.my

Rahman Putra GC
Jalan BRP 2/1, Bukit Rahman Putra, 47000 Sungai Buloh, Selangor
☎ +60 3 6156 6870
✉ krpm@streamyx.com
www.krpm.com.my

Terengganu

Awana Kijal Golf, Beach & Spa Resort
Km.28, Jalan Kemaman-Dungun, 24100 Kijal, Kemaman Terengganu
☎ +60 9 8641 188
✉ awanakij@tm.net.my
www.awana.com.my

Tasik Kenyir Golf Resort
Kg. Sg., Gawi, Mukim Telemong, 2300 Hulu Teregganu Terengganu
☎ +60 9 666 8888
✉ resort@lakekenyir.com
www.lakekenyir.com

Maldives

Kuredu Island Resort
Faadhipolhu,, Lhaviyani Atoll
☎ +960 230337
✉ info@kuredu.com
www.kuredu.com

Myanmar

Aye Thar Yar Golf Course
Aye Thar Yar,Taunggyi, Shanstate
☎ +95 81 24245
✉ ayetharyargolfresort@mptmail .net.mm
www.ayetharyargolfresort.com

Bagan Golf Course
Nyaung Oo Township, Mandalay Division
☎ +95 2 67247
✉ bagangolfresort@mptmail.net.mm

Nepal

Le Méridien Gokarna Forest Golf Resort & Spa
Rajnikunj Gokarna, Thali, PO Box 20498, Kathhmandu
☎ +977 1 445 1212
✉ golf@lemeridien-kathmandu.com
www.gokarna.com

Royal Nepal GC
Tilganga, Kathmandu
☎ +977 1 449 4247
✉ rngc@mail.com.np

Pakistan

Arabian Sea CC
Bin Qasim, Karachi
☎ +92 21 475 0408
✉ info@ascl.com
www.ascl.com

Royal Palm G&CC
www.royalpalm.com

Philippines

Fairways and Bluewater Resort
Newcoast, Balabag, Boracay Island, Province of Aklan
☎ +63 36 288 5587
info@fairwaysbluewater.com
www.FairwaysBluewater.com

Eagle Ridge G&CC
Barangay Javalera, Gen. Trias, Cavite
☎ +63 46 419 2841
www.eagle-ridge.com.ph

Singapore

Raffles GC
Raffles Country Club, 450 Jalan Ahmad Ibrahim, Singapore 639932
☎ +65 6861 7649
jacqueline@rcc.org.sg
www.rcc.org.sg

Singapore Island CC
Thomson Road, PO Box 50, Singapore 915702
☎ +65 645 92222
enquiry@sicc.org.sg
www.sicc.org.sg

Sri Lanka

Victoria Golf & Country Resort
PO Box 7, Rajawela
☎ +94 812 376 376
enquiries@victoriagolf.lk
www.srilankagolf.com

Waters Edge GC
316 Ethul Kotte Road, Battaramulla
☎ +94 112 863863
we@watersedge.lk
www.watersedge.lk

Thailand

Central Region

Green Valley CC
92 Moo 3, Bang Na-Trat Road Km.15, Bang Chalong, Bang Phli, Samut Prakan 10540
☎ +66 2312 5883
info@greenvalleybangkok.com
www.greenvalleybangkok.com

Lam Luk Ka CC
29 Moo 7 Lamsai Lam Luk Ka Khlong 11, Patum Thani 12150
☎ +66 2995 2300
info@lamlukkagolf.net
www.lamlukkagolf.net

Royal Bangkok Sport Club
1 Henri Dunant Street, Bangkok 10330
☎ +66 66 2255 1420
www.rbsc.org

Eastern Region

Eastern Star Country Club & Resort
241/5 Moo 3, Pala Ban Chang District, Rayong 21130
☎ +66 3863 0410
info@easternstargolf.net
www.easternstargolf.net

Laem Chabang International CC
106/8 Moo 4, Ban Bung, Sri Racha, Chon Buri 20230
☎ +66 3837 2273
reservation@laemchabanggolf.com
www.laemchabanggolf.com

Soi Dao Highland Golf Club & Resort
153/1 Moo 2, Thap Sai, Pong Nam Ron District, Chanthaburi 22140
☎ +66 3932 0174
booking@soidaohighland.com
www.soidaohighland.com

Northern Region

Chiangmai Green Valley CC
183/2 Chotana Road, Mae Sa, Mae Rim, Chiang Mai 50180
☎ +66 5329 8249
info@cm_golf.com
www.cm_golf.com

Gassan Khuntan Golf & Resort
222 Moo3 Thapladuk, Mae Tha, Lamphun, Thailand 51140
☎ +66 53 507006
info@gassangolf.com
www.gassangolf.com

Santiburi CC
12 Moo 3, Hua Doi-Sob Pau Road, Wiang Chai District, Chiang Rai 57210
☎ +66 5366 2821
cr_golfreservation@santiburi.com
santiburi.com/SantiburiGolfChiangRai

North Eastern Region

Forest Hills CC
195 Moo 3, Mittraphap Road, Muak Lek District, Saraburi 18180
☎ +66 3634 1911
mail@sirjamesresort.com
www.sirjamesresort.com

Mission Hills Golf Club Khao Yai
151 Moo 5,Thumbol Mhoosee, Pakchong, Nakornratchasima 30130
☎ +66 4429 7258
missionhills_khaoyai@yahoo.com
www.golfmissionhills.com/miskao.html

Suwan G&CC
15/3 Moo 2, Sisatong, A. Nakornchaisri, Nakornpathom 73120
☎ +66 343 39333
reservation@suwangolf.com
www.suwangolf.com

Southern Region

Loch Palm GC
38 Moo 5 Vichit Songkram Road, Kathu, Phuket 83120
☎ +66 7632 1929
info@lochpalm.com
www.lochpalm.com

Phuket CC
80/1 Vichit Songkram Road, Katu, Phuket 83120
☎ +66 7632 1038
info@phuketcountryclub.com
www.phuketcountryclub.com

Santiburi Samui CC
12/15 Moo 4, Bandonsai, Tambol Maenam, Amphur Ko Samui, Surat Thani 84330
☎ +66 7742 5031
infosb@santiburi.com
www.santiburi.com

Western Region

Best Ocean GC
4/5 Moo 7 Rama2 Road, Khokkham, Samutsakorn 74000
☎ +66 34 451143
www.bestoceangolf.com

Mission Hills GC
27/7 Moo 7, Pang Thru, Tha Muang, Kanchanaburi 71110Tengah Melaka
☎ +66 3464 4147
hills@ksc.th.com
golfmissionhills.com/miskan.html

Sawang Resort GC
99 Moo 2, Sapang, Khao Yoi District, Petchaburi 76140
☎ +66 3256 2555
info@sawangresortgolf.com
www.sawangresortgolf.com

Vietnam

King's Island GC
Dong Mo, Son Tay Town, Ha Tay Province
☎ +84 34 686555
kings_island@fpt.vn
www.kingsislandgolf.com

For key to symbols see page 725

Ocean Dunes GC
1 Ton Duc Thang, Phan Thiet
☎ +84 62 823366
✉ odgc@vietnamgolfresorts.com
www.vietnamgolfresorts.com/index.php?id=7

Tam Dao Golf & Resort
Hop Chau Commune, Tam Dao District, Vinh Phuc Province
☎ +84 211 896554
✉ marketing@tamdaogolf.com
www.tamdaogolf.com

Australasia and the Pacific

Australia

Australian Capital Territory

Royal Canberra
Bentham St, Yarralumla, ACT 2600
☎ +61 (02) 6282 7000
✉ admin@royalcanberra.com.au
www.royalcanberra.com.au

Yowani Country Club
Northbourne Ave, Lyneham, ACT 2602
☎ +61 (02)6241 2303
✉ golf@yowani.com.au

New South Wales

The Australian
53 Bannerman Crescent, Rosebery, NSW 2018
☎ +61 (02) 9663 2273

Barham
Moulamein Road, Barham, NSW 2732
☎ +61 (03) 5453 2971
✉ Barham.services.club@clubarham.com.au

Howlong
Golf Club Drive, Howlong, NSW 2643
☎ +61 (02) 6026 5822
✉ enquiries@howlonggolf.com.au

Kooindah Waters
Kooindah Boulevard, Wyong, NSW 2259
☎ +61 (02) 4351 0700
✉ info@kooindahwatersgolf.com.au

The Lakes
Corner King St. & Vernon Ave, Eastlakes, NSW 2018
☎ +61 (02) 9669 1311

New South Wales
Henry Head, Botany Bay National Park, La Perouse
☎ + 61 (02) 9661 4455
✉ admin@nswgolfclub.com.au

Royal Sydney
Kent Road, Rose Bay, NSW 2029
☎ +61 (02) 8362 7000
✉ reception@rsgc.com.au
www.rsgc.com.au

Twin Creeks
Twin Creeks Drive, Luddenham, NSW 2745
☎ +61 (02) 9670 8877
✉ karinad@twincreeks.com.au

The Vintage
Vintage Drive, Rothbury, NSW 2320
☎ +61 (02) 4998 6789
✉ golf@thevintage.com.au

Yarrawonga
Gulai Road, Mulwala, NSW 2647
☎ +61 (03) 5744 3983
✉ stayandplay@yarragolf.com.au

Northern Territory

Alice Springs
Cromwell Drive, Alice Springs, NT 870
☎ +61 (08) 8952 1921
✉ admin@asgc.com.au

Darwin
Links Road, North Lakes, NT 812
☎ +61 (08) 8927 1322

Palmerston
Dwyer Circuit & University Avenue, Driver, NT 831
☎ +61 (08) 8932 1324

Queensland

Brisbane
Tennyson Memorial Avenue, Yeerongpilly, QLD 4105
☎ +61 (07) 3848 1008
✉ mail@brisbanegolfclub.com.au

Brookwater
1 Tournament Drive, Brookwater, QLD 4300
☎ +61 (07) 3814 5500
✉ golfshop@brookwatergolf.com

The Colonial
Paradise Springs Avenue, Robina, QLD 4226
☎ +61 (07) 5553 7008
✉ info@playmoregolf.com.au

Glades
Glades Drive, Robina, QLD 4226
☎ +61 (07) 5569 1900
✉ enquiries@theglades.com.au

Indooroopilly
Meiers Road, Indooroopilly, QLD 4068
☎ + 61 (07) 3721 2122
✉ admin@indooroopillygolf.com.au

Links Hope Island
Hope Island Road, Hope Island, QLD 4212
☎ + 61 (07) 5530 9030
✉ golf@linkshopeisland.com.au

Noosa Springs
Links Drive, Noosa Heads, QLD 4567
☎ + 61 (07) 5440 3333
✉ info@noosasprings.com.au

Robina Woods
Ron Penhaligon Way, Robina, QLD 4226
☎ + 61 (07) 5553 7520
✉ info@playmoregolf.com.au

Royal Queensland
Curtin Avenue West, Eagle Farm, Brisbane, QLD 4009
☎ +61 (07) 3268 1127
✉ info@rqgolf.com.au
www.rqgolf.com.au

South Australia

Echunga
Cnr Hahndorf and Dolman Road, Echunga, SA 5153
☎ +61 (08) 8388 8038
✉ info@echungagolf.com.au

Grange
White Sands Drive Seaton, South Australia
☎ +61 (08) 8355 7100
✉ info@grangegolf.com.au

Kooyonga
May Terrace, Lockleys, South Australia
☎ +61 (08) 8352 5444
✉ administrator@kooyongagolf.com.au

Mount Lofty
35 Golf Links Road, Stirling, SA 5152
☎ +61 (08) 8339 1805
✉ admin@mountloftygolfclub.com.au

Royal Adelaide
328 Tapleys Hill Road, Seaton, SA 5023
☎ +61 (08) 8356 5511
✉ ragc@royaladelaidegolf.com.au
www.royaladelaidegolf.com.au

Tea Tree Gully
Hamilton Road, Fairview Park, SA 5126
☎ +61 (08) 8251 1465
✉ ttggc@internode.net.au

Tasmania

Barnbougle Dunes
426 Waterhouse Road, Bridport, Tasmania 7262
☎ +61 (03) 363 560 094
www.barnbougledunes.com

Royal Hobart
81 Seven Mile Beach Road, Seven Mile Beach, Hobart, Tasmania 7170
☎ +61 (03) 6248 6161
admin@rhgc.com.au
www.rhgc.com.au

Victoria

Barwon Heads
Golf Links Road, Barwon Heads, VIC 3227
☎ +61 (03) 5255 6275
golf@bhgc.com.au

Clifton Springs
92-94 Clearwater Drive, Clifton Springs, VIC 3222
☎ +61 (03) 5253 1488
csclubhouse@iprimus.com.au

The Dunes
335 Browns Road, Rye, VIC 3941
☎ +61 (03) 5985 1334
golf@thedunes.com.au

Growling Frog
1910 Donnybrook Road, Yan Yean, VIC 3755
☎ +61 (03) 9716 3477
info@growlingfroggolfcourse.com.au

Huntingdale
Windsor Avenue, South Oakleigh, VIC 3167
☎ +61 (03) 9579 4622
manager@huntingdalegolf.com.au

Kingston Heath
Kingston Rd, Heatherton, Melbourne, VIC 3202
☎ +61 (03) 8558 2700
info@kingstonheath.com.au

Ocean Grove
Guthridge Street, Ocean Grove, VIC 3226
☎ +61 (03) 5256 2795
info@oceangrovegc.com.au

Metropolitan
Golf Road, Oakleigh South, VIC 3167
☎ +61 (03) 9579 3122
admin@metropolitangolf.com.au

Mornington
Tallis Drive, Mornington, VIC 3931
☎ +61 (03) 5975 2784
manager@ morningtongolf.com.au

Royal Melbourne
Cheltenham Road, Black Rock, VIC 3193
☎ +61 (03) 9598 6755
rmgc@royalmelbourne.com.au
www.royalmelbourne.com.au

Settlers Run
1 Settlers Run, Cranbourne South, VIC 3977
☎ +61 (03) 9785 6072
info@settlersrun.com.au

Victoria
Park Road, Cheltenham, VIC 3192
☎ +61 (03) 9584 1733
info@victoriagolf.com.au

Yarra Yarra
567 Warrigal Road East, Bentleigh East, VIC 3165
☎ +61 (03) 9575 0595
reception@yarrayarra.com.au

Western Australia

Joondalup
Country Club Bouvelard, Connolly, WA 6027
☎ +61 (08) 9400 8811
proshop@joondalupresort.com.au

Kennedy Bay
Port Kennedy Drive, Port Kennedy, WA 6172
☎ +61 (08) 9524 5991
info@kennedybay.com.au

Lake Karrinyup
North Beach Road, Karrinyup WA 6018
☎ +61 (08) 9422 8222
info@lkcc.com.au

Mount Lawley
Walter Road, Inglewood, WA 6052
☎ +61 (08) 9271 9622
admin@mlgc.org

The Vines Resort and Country Club
Verdellho Drive, The Vines, Perth, WA 6069
☎ +61 (08) 9297 3000
www.vines.com.au

Cook Islands

Rarotonga Golf Club
Rarotonga, Cook Islands
☎ +682 20621

Fiji

Fiji Golf Club
Suva Area, Viti Levu
☎ +679 382872

Pacific Harbour
Suva Area, Viti Levu
+679 450262

Guam

Guam International CC
495 Battulo Street, Dededo, Guam 96912
☎ +1 671 632 4422
gicclub@netpci.com
www.giccguam.com

New Zealand

Cape Kidnappers
☎ +64 (06) 875 1900
www.capekidnappers.com

Gisborne
☎ +64 (06) 867 9849
www.gisborne.nzgolf.net

Gulf Harbour
☎ +64 (09) 424 0971
www.gulfharbour.nzgolf.net

The Hills
www.thehills.co.nz

Jack's Point
www.jackspoint.com

Kauri Cliffs
www.kauricliffs.com

Lake View
☎ +64 (07) 357 2343
www.lakeview.nzgolf.net

Lakes Resort Pauanui
☎ +64 (07) 864 9999
www.lakesresort.com

North Otoga
☎ +64 (03) 434 6169
www.northotago.nzgolf.net

Palmerston North
☎ +64 (06) 351 0700
www.pngolf.co.nz

Queens Park
☎ +64 (03) 218 8371
www.queenspark.nzgolf.net

Sherwood Park
☎ +64 (09) 434 6900
www.sherwoodpark.nzgolf.net

Waitangi
☎ +64 (09) 402 7713
waitangigolf@xtra.co.nz

Papua New Guinea

Port Moresby GC
PO Box 17 Port Moresby
☎ +675 325 5367

Samoa

Penina Golf Course
77 Faleolo Strip, Mulifanua
✉ golfpenina@samoa.ws
www.peninaresortandgolfclub.com

Tonga

Tonga GC
PO Box 2568, Nuku'alofa
☎ +676 24949

Vanuatu

Port Vila G&CC
Mele, Vanuatu, South Pacific
☎ +678 22564
✉ pvgcc@vanuatu.com.vu

White Sands
PO Box 906, Port Vila, Vanuatu, South Pacific
☎ +678 22090
✉ whitesan@vanuatu.com.vu

7For key to symbols see page 725

Babe Didrickson Zaharias truly was "Wonder Girl"

Don Van Natta Jr is the latest recipient of the Herbert Warren Wind Award for his new book on the life and times of Babe Zaharias. Talking about the book, entitled *Wonder Girl – The Magnificent Sporting Life of Babe Didrickson Zaharias*, Robert Williams, Director of the USGA Museum at Far Hills, New Jersey said: "Van Natta's book is a deeply compelling account of her athleticism, courage and invincibility as she triumphed on the track and on the golf course enduring cancer to achieve a remarkable come-back victory in the 1954 US Women's Open."

Beautifully written, the book chronicles the story of an heroic athlete who captured a nation's heart. She overcame the biases of the time against women athletes to excel in golf, basktball, track and field, baseball, softball, tennis and bowling. She was an All-American in basketball and won two gold medals in track and field at the 1932 Olympics in Los Angeles.

In golf she won 10 major Championships, was a founder member of the LPGA and in 1938 was the first woman to play in a PGA Tour event.

At the height of her fame, however, she was diagnosed with cancer and was told she would never play again but fifteen months after surgery she came-back bravely to win her third US Women's Open by 12 shots!

"There are so many wonderful lessons that can be learned from Babe Zaharias' life and career," says author Van Natta. "She ovrcame so many obstacles through persistence, perseverance and tremendous courage to become the greatest all sport athlete in history"

Mr Van Natta, who works for ESPN and has been a member of three Pulitzer Prize-winning teams when working with the *New York Times* and *Miami Herald*, was scheduled to receive his award during the Masters tournament.

Index

A

B

D

E

F

G

H

I

J

K

M

S

T

W